AMERICAN NATIONAL BIOGRAPHY

AMERICAN
NATIONAL BIOGRAPHY

Published under the auspices of the
AMERICAN COUNCIL OF LEARNED SOCIETIES

General Editors

John A. Garraty

Mark C. Carnes

VOLUME 11

OXFORD UNIVERSITY PRESS
New York   1999   Oxford

OXFORD UNIVERSITY PRESS

Oxford New York
Athens Auckland Bangkok Bogotá
Buenos Aires Calcutta Cape Town Chennai
Dar es Salaam Delhi Florence Hong Kong Istanbul
Karachi Kuala Lumpur Madrid Melbourne Mexico City
Mumbai Nairobi Paris São Paulo Singapore
Taipei Tokyo Toronto Warsaw
and associated companies in
Berlin Ibadan

Published by Oxford University Press, Inc.,
198 Madison Avenue, New York, New York 10016
http://www.oup-usa.org

Oxford is a registered trademark of Oxford University Press

Funding for this publication was provided in part by
the Andrew W. Mellon Foundation, the Rockefeller Foundation,
and the National Endowment for the Humanities,
a federal agency.

Library of Congress Cataloging-in-Publication Data

American national biography / general editors, John A. Garraty, Mark C. Carnes
        p.   cm.
"Published under the auspices of the American Council of Learned Societies."
Includes bibliographical references and index.
1. United States—Biography—Dictionaries. I. Garraty, John Arthur,
1920– . II. Carnes, Mark C. (Mark Christopher), 1950–   .
III. American Council of Learned Societies.
CT213.A68   1998   98-20826   920.073—dc21   CIP
ISBN 0-19-520635-5 (set)
ISBN 0-19-512790-0 (vol. 11)

Printing (last digit): 9 8 7 6 5 4 3 2 1

Printed in the United States of America
on acid-free paper

CONTINUED

HOFSTADTER, Richard (6 Aug. 1916–24 Oct. 1970), historian, writer, and critic, was born in Buffalo, New York, the son of Emil A Hofstadter, a furrier, and Katherine Hill. His father, born in Cracow, Poland, was Jewish, and his mother, whose family had emigrated from Germany in the aftermath of 1848, was an Episcopalian. Although his mother died when he was ten, Richard was raised a Protestant. As an adult he came to identify with his father's secular Jewish heritage, especially after his move to New York City, where he became involved with the city's predominately Jewish, politically left intellectual groups.

Hofstadter entered the University of Buffalo in 1933, majoring in philosophy and history. His logical mind and early enthusiasm for deductive reasoning made him a good student of philosophy, but he "took up American history under the inspiration that came from Charles and Mary Beard's *The Rise of American Civilization*" (Hofstadter, *Progressive Historians*, p. xiv). He was particularly influenced as an undergraduate by Julius Pratt, who supervised his tutorial thesis, "The Tariff and Homestead Issues in the Republican Campaign of 1860." In it Hofstadter examined the Beardian claim that the Civil War represented the triumph of northern capitalism, and he found that the Beards had erred in presuming a unified capitalist class supporting the Republican party. Further refined, this project became Hofstadter's first professional publication, an article in the *American Historical Review* in 1938 when he was a graduate student.

While an undergraduate, Hofstadter had become close to Felice Swados, two years older and a fellow campus radical. While Hofstadter continued at Buffalo, she went to Smith College with a fellowship. In the fall of 1936, when Hofstadter completed his studies at Buffalo (though his B.A. would not be conferred until early 1937), the two moved to New York and married. They had one child. In the evening Hofstadter studied law at New York School of Law, working during the day as a clerk in the law office of Irving R. Kauffmann, a friend of his uncle, New York Supreme Court judge Samuel Hofstadter. The study of law was imposed on Hofstadter by his family (and perhaps also by his wife's), but he found it uninteresting and performed poorly.

Withdrawing from law school after one term, he entered Columbia's graduate program in history as a night student in February 1937. He also began attending meetings of the graduate school's Communist unit, but by early 1939, well before the Hitler-Stalin Pact, he had withdrawn and begun his "deconversion" from Marxism. Merle Curti, whom he met in 1938 and who later supervised his dissertation, was an important example for Hofstadter as he worked his way out of the Marxist eddies of his youth to a conception of himself as a mainstream historian bringing Marxist categories and a left political commitment into a broader historiographical outlook.

Like many New York intellectuals of his generation, Hofstadter rebelled against what he called the "mental attitude" of the "average party member" (Baker, p. 141). He identified himself as "an American liberal" but in a conditional way (Hofstadter papers, box 36). Like the critic Lionel Trilling, later a close friend and colleague, Hofstadter believed that he could be liberal only if liberalism were made deep enough to accommodate the circumstances of modern political and cultural life. He was something of a disenchanted liberal, assuming a critical stance within the liberal tradition he hoped to enrich. The spirit of his embrace of liberalism is evident in a letter he wrote to novelist Harvey Swados, his brother-in-law, in October 1939, two months after the Nazi-Soviet Non-Aggression Pact:

I hate capitalism and everything that goes with it. But I also hate the simpering dogmatic religious-minded Janizaries that make up the CP. I hate their regimented thinking. I rather doubt I wd be permitted to live under any system they cd set up, and I am quite sure if I were I wdnt enjoy it. People like us grow up to believe in a certain set of values—freedom of individual intellectual inquiry, scientific attitude of mind, respect for facts, a certain cultural latitude—which the Stalins, Browders Cannons, and Schactmans dislike and will, if given the chance, stamp out. . . . We are not the beneficiaries of capitalism, but we will not be the beneficiaries of the socialism of the 20th century—if any—any more than Kamenenv & Zinoviev & Rykov & Bucharin were. . . . We are the people with no place to go. (Baker, p. 151)

That sense of political homelessness motivated his quest for a better liberalism. "All of my books," he later recalled, "have been affected by this impulse to reevaluate American liberalism" (Hofstadter papers, box 36).

Hofstadter completed his doctoral study at Columbia in 1942. His dissertation, *Social Darwinism in American Thought, 1860–1915*, won the American Historical Association's Beveridge Prize. During his last two years of graduate study, Hofstadter had taught part time at Brooklyn College and then City College of New York, but in the summer of 1942 he obtained his first regular job at the University of Maryland as assistant professor. Not long afterward Felice Hofstadter became ill with cancer; she died in 1945. Hofstadter had won an Alfred A. Knopf fellowship in 1945, and it enabled him to take the year off to care for his wife and child, working in odd moments on the studies that would be published in 1948 as *The American Political Tradition and the Men Who Made It*. In 1946 he was called back to Columbia, where he remained until his death, with various visiting appointments along the way at Berkeley, Harvard, Cambridge, and Princeton. In 1947 he married Beatrice Kevitt, also of Buffalo; they had one child.

Those who knew him well understood that he had suffered the tragic losses of his mother and his wife, both much too young. They detected an inner pessimism, a melancholy leavened with a remarkable sense of humor and a feel for the comic. Most striking of all, however, was a sense of firmness, emotional as well as moral, and an aura of serenity. A man of passion and commitment, he was also a man of proportion, resisting the quest for certainty in scholarship and perfection in politics. Characteristically, Hofstadter offered in his books neither proof nor theses, but possible interpretations intended to prompt new scholarship and enrich contemporary political discourse.

Hofstadter aspired to a career as a writer, and few historians in this century have been so conscious about literary expression. His prose was marked by a relaxed luminosity, and it had a quality of mobility that carried the ideas and the reader along. Reading his books one is impressed by the richness and breadth of his historical imagination. He readily acknowledged that he devoted more time and energy to "expression" than to research. He repeatedly gave credit to his second wife for her "editorial talent," as in the revised (1955) edition of *Social Darwinism in American Thought*, which clearly shows her capacity to enrich his gifts as a writer.

Probably no historian of Hofstadter's generation ranged more widely in his or her work. His broad scope came no doubt from his willingness and capacity to ground his work on published sources and wide reading in the historical literature rather than archives. He chose topics on the basis of his contemporary concerns, attending at the same time to the possibility of a readership beyond the clan of professional historians. After *The American Political Tradition*, he worked briefly on a cultural history of the 1890s, only to set it aside in favor of a more engaged book, *The Age of Reform, from Bryan to F.D.R.* (1955), for which he won a Pulitzer Prize. Prompted mainly by the threats to academic freedom in the 1950s, he also turned his attention to the history of higher education, publishing with DeWitt Hardy *The Development and Scope of Higher Education in the United States* (1952); with Walter Metzger, *The Development of Academic Freedom in the United States* (1955); and, with Wilson Smith, a documentary history, *American Higher Education* (2 vols., 1961). *Anti-Intellectualism in American Life* (1963), for which he won a second Pulitzer Prize, connected the story of trained intellect to his analysis of American politics. His major works of the 1960s were *The Progressive Historians: Turner, Beard, and Parrington* (1968) and *The Idea of a Party System: The Rise of Legitimate Opposition in the United States, 1780–1840* (1969). He also published an influential collection of essays, *The Paranoid Style in American Politics and Other Essays* (1965). With Michael Wallace, he published *American Violence: A Documentary History* (1970). At the time of his death, he was at work on a three-volume synthetic history of the United States; the partially completed first volume, *America at 1750: A Social Portrait*, was published posthumously in 1971.

Hofstadter's mind, as he often indicated, was formed by the experience of the Great Depression and the political issues of that era. But his intellectual style, with his cosmopolitan, modern, and secular sensibilities, was nourished by the culture of New York City, the metropolitan complexity of which sustained his commitment to cultural and epistemological pluralism. It also encouraged his inclination to sift through the multiple layers of American politics and culture. Like others of his generation, Hofstadter found in the culture and politics of the city the means of reconceiving liberalism, going beyond the stark dualisms of Progressive social thought. His generation of New York intellectuals defined a postwar liberalism marked by an appreciation of complexity and irony.

His strongest intellectual commitment was to the independence of mind itself. The work of the intellectual was for him serious play. He was fascinated with the operation of the human mind in political society, and over the course of his career he searched out a wide variety of American minds, ranging from Thomas Jefferson to William H. "Coin" Harvey to Barry Goldwater. He once characterized his work as a sort of "literary anthropology" of "groups and classes." He was drawn to the unexpected and the overlooked, "the important and unfamiliar," in American politics and culture (Hofstadter papers, box 3). His predilection and great strength as a historian (and he recognized the costs involved) was his commitment, amounting almost to an obsession, to originality. He was impatient with the conventional; orthodoxy bored him. Although his mind was too restless to construct routine histories, he avidly read them. He was driven by temperament as much as by commitment to propose novel ways of thinking about historical issues. This delight in originality and his penchant for extending the terrain of history enabled him to recast the image of the American past and restock the armamentarium of a generation of historians.

Interpretation interested Hofstadter more than did fact. He sometimes bemoaned the profession's "habit of overvaluing facts for facts' sake. I believe that a conjecture, an insight, even if it proves wrong, is worth a thousand facts, and that a conjecture (or insight) that happens to be right is worth ten thousand facts" (Hofstadter papers, box 36). Accordingly, as Arthur M. Schlesinger, Jr., noticed, Hofstadter needed the stimulus of interpretation to become interested in fact; he "reacted more keenly to historians than to history" (Schlesinger, p. 280).

The lodestar of Hofstadter's career was Charles A. Beard. It was Beard's work that drew him from philosophy to American history; it was Beard who gave historiographical expression to the liberalism Hofstadter sought to transform; and it was Beard who provided the most impressive model of the historian as intellectual. Hofstadter at once strove to emulate and destroy Beard, something he recognized when he referred to *The Progressive Historians* as "a reprise of that perennial battle we wage with our elders, particularly with our adopted intellectual fathers" (*Progressive Historians*, p. xiv).

Hofstadter greatly enriched the language of liberalism and historiography by offering a more complex account of political motivation. He understood historical action within a matrix that included history (tradition, myth, ideology, often corrupted into nostalgia), interest (status as well as economic), and personal psychology. His renovation and enlargement of the house of history left the ground floor of material interests, of Beardian realism, more intact than many realized. While he could imaginatively reach and understand a variety of political motivations, Hofstadter was always reluctant to confer legitimacy on any but reasonably bounded material interests. He also extended the historiographical landscape through a remarkable interdisciplinary voracity. Beginning with philosophy, he reached out also to literary criticism, sociology, and psychology. Beyond historians, he accounted himself influenced by Edmund Wilson, Van Wyck Brooks, F. O. Matthiessen, Roberto Michels, Karl Mannheim, Thorstein Veblen, Harold Lasswell, Thurman Arnold, Karl Marx, Sigmund Freud, John Dewey, William James, and, for the satirical tone, H. L. Mencken. As the list suggests, he went to other disciplines not for methods, but rather to expand his historiographical vocabulary. Other disciplines served him by multiplying the ways of configuring his narrative, as prompts to notice more and as means of expanding his language of description and interpretation.

His reading of Karl Mannheim in the 1940s was particularly significant, both for his passage from Marxism to liberalism and for his specification of his historiographical quarry. Though he has been designated both an intellectual and a political historian, Hofstadter considered himself to be neither. From Mannheim he learned to focus not on systematic ideas nor on formal political institutions, but rather on cultural configurations and political styles. He called this the history of political culture, and that is how he identified his work as a historian.

With *The American Political Tradition*, published in the year of Beard's death, Hofstadter established himself as Beard's successor. It is a series of biographical essays, ranging from the Founding Fathers to Franklin Delano Roosevelt. The self-assured critical stance and the literary self-confidence displayed in these essays is striking; Hofstadter here emerges as a mature historian and a major critic. There are no heroes in the book, save perhaps for Wendell Phillips. In a remarkable understatement, he informed the reader that "these portraits are not painted in roseate colors" (*American Political Tradition*, p. x). They are in fact terribly corrosive but neither mean spirited nor cynical. If anything, the sensibility of the book is comic.

The book was enormously successful, selling more than a million copies. It undermined the Whiggism of liberal or Progressive historiography of reform, and, as did *The Age of Reform*, rendered problematic the cycle of reform in America. Motives are rarely pure; results are often ambiguous, sometimes worse. The difference between reform and reaction cannot at times be determined.

But what made *The American Political Tradition* important and controversial was the six-page introduction Hofstadter wrote at the behest of his publisher, who sought something that might tie the several biographies together. As he reread the essays, Hofstadter was struck by the degree to which "the major political traditions," even if often "at odds on specific issues," in fact "shared a belief in the rights of property, the philosophy of economic individualism, the value of competition." He concluded that "they have accepted the economic virtues of capitalist culture as necessary qualities of man" (*American Political Tradition*, p. viii). This comment would later be taken to represent the first statement of so-called consensus history, which radically de-emphasized conflict and devalued ideology. Insofar as some consensus historians, most notably Daniel Boorstin, affirmed these qualities, Hofstadter does not belong in their company. His commentary was description, not prescription. And even as description, it was phrased from a position well to the left of the political culture he described. Nor did he ever deny the reality and drama of conflict in American history. He did, however, deny that conflict was based on a fixed social division, whether Marxian or Beardian in definition. He pluralized conflict. In time he concluded that even descriptively, conflict had been pushed too far to the margins. Writing to Arthur Schlesinger, Jr., in 1968, he acknowledged that "we have to go back to conflict at the center of our story" (Hofstadter papers, catalogued letters). Hofstadter returned to this theme in the conclusion of *The Progressive Historians* and again in *American Violence*.

The Age of Reform was framed by a theme that ran through all of Hofstadter's work: the heavy weight of the past distorted as myth that disabled appropriate modern responses to new conditions. In this book the reference was to agrarian nostalgia and Victorian morality; both crippled rational response to the modernity of urban and industrial society after 1890. In *The Age of Reform* and *The Idea of a Party System*, Hofstadter criticized those trapped by old ideas and ideologies and supported pragmatic political innovators such as Franklin Roosevelt and Martin Van Buren.

His fascination with the pragmatic and practical American politician occasionally conflicted with his commitment to mind. In his political studies he portrayed trained intellect, almost always associated with WASP culture, as rigid, ill adapted to practical needs, and too often moralistic when realism was wanted. But in the histories of higher education and in *Anti-Intellectualism in American Life*, he was essentially uncritical of intellect, seeing its progress as inherently and unambiguously good. He never theorized the relation of trained intellect's quest for coherence to the give-and-take truths of democratic political practice. *Anti-Intellectualism in American Life* was his least well realized book, a one-sided polemic against American suspicion of intellect. Gone is the complexity and the fascination with other cultures characteristic of the literary anthropologist. Writing in the aftermath of Adlai E. Stevenson II's unsuccessful quests for the presidency in 1952 and 1956 and in the wake of McCarthyism, Hofstadter understood the threat to intellect to be external. He aimed to defend the cosmopolitan intellect from the narrow parochialism that threatened it. Only later, in 1968, did he have to confront the possibility of complexity within the realm of academic intellect, of intellect divided against itself.

Perhaps he never theorized the articulation of mind to power because he was himself immune to the lure of power and influence. He asked only for the freedom to think and write about the world around him. This he found in the modern university and in the institution of academic freedom. The university, he explained in the commencement address he delivered at Columbia after the 1968 student uprising (he was the only faculty member ever to address a Columbia graduation), was a peculiar institution—"a collectivity that serves as a citadel of intellectual individualism." The intellectual independence cultivated in the university would supply society with "an intellectual and spiritual balance wheel" (Hofstadter papers, box 23). As he became increasingly discouraged by the direction of American society—in a *Newsweek* interview (6 July 1970) he characterized his own time as "The Age of Rubbish"—he found comfort in the enclave that the university provided. He hoped that here, if not in society generally, ideas would be respected and enough cultural space would be preserved to allow the playfulness inherent in the life of the mind properly lived.

At the time of Hofstadter's premature death of leukemia in a New York City hospital, most historians would have concurred with the judgment of John Higham that Hofstadter was "the finest and also the most humane historical intelligence of our generation" (quoted in Elkins and McKitrick, p. 324n). One ought also to note that his was a distinctly urban voice in American historiography. Until Hofstadter's generation, American historiography, wherever written, had a rural inflection, identifying the meaning of America very much with its origins. Hofstadter, however, established the city—in the phrase of J. R. Pole—as his "base of observation" (Pole, p. 216). The image of the observer well captures Hofstadter's critical style, but the point about the city is equally apt, for Hofstadter participated in a reconfiguration of the American sense of the past that gave a larger place to cities, their people, and their modern, secular, and cosmopolitan values.

• Richard Hofstadter's papers are at Columbia University, but for information on his early political interests they are usefully supplemented by his letters in the Harvey Swados Papers at the University of Massachusetts, Amherst. The best biographical analyses of Hofstadter and his work are those by Arthur M. Schlesinger, Jr., "Richard Hofstadter," in *Pastmasters*, ed. Marcus Cunliffe and Robin Winks (1969), pp. 278–315, and Stanley Elkins and Eric McKitrick, "Richard Hofstadter and Eric McKitrick, "Richard Hofstadter: A Progress," in *The Hofstadter Aegis*, ed. Elkins and McKitrick (1973), pp. 300–367. This volume also contains Paula Fass's full bibliography of Hofstadter's work. For Hofstadter's early politics and their relation to his formation as a historian, see Susan Stout Baker, *Radical Beginnings: Richard Hofstadter and the 1930s* (1985); for a broader appraisal, see Daniel Joseph Singal, "Beyond Consensus: Richard Hofstadter and American Historiography," *American Historical Review* 89 (1984): 976–1004. Essays written by close friends after his death include Alfred Kazin, "Richard Hofstadter, 1916–1970," *American Scholar* 40 (1970–1971): 397–403; C. Vann Woodward, "Richard Hofstadter," *American Historical Review* 76 (1971): 957–59; J. R. Pole, "Richard Hofstadter, 1916–1970," *American Studies* 4 (1971): 215–16; Christopher Lash, "On Richard Hofstadter," *New York Review of Books*, 8 Mar. 1973, pp. 7–13; and Peter Gay, "Richard Hofstadter," *International Encyclopedia of the Social Sciences*, vol. 18 (1979), pp. 310–12. David Hawke, "Interview: Richard Hofstadter," *History* 3 (Sept. 1960; a serial published in New York by Meridian Books): 135–41, is quite informative. The obituary in the *New York Times*, 25 Oct. 1970, was considered by many who knew him to be a serious misrepresentation of the man. See Lionel Trilling's letter to the editor, *New York Times*, 5 Nov. 1970.

THOMAS BENDER

HOFSTADTER, Robert (5 Feb. 1915–17 Nov. 1990), physicist, was born in New York City, the son of Louis Hofstadter, a salesman, and Henrietta Koenigsberg. Hofstadter attended public schools in New York City and later entered the City College (now the City University) of New York with the intention of studying philosophy. At college, however, one of his physics professors convinced him to turn to physics after commenting that the laws of physics could be tested, while those of philosophy could not. Hofstadter received a B.S. in physics magna cum laude in 1935. He then did graduate work at Princeton University on a Coffin Fellowship from the General Electric Company, which stipulated that the holder begin research during his first year of study. Filling a vacancy in the infared laboratory, Hofstadter embarked on his specialization in experimental physics. In 1938 he received an M.A. and a Ph.D.; his doctoral dissertation, "Infrared Absorption by Light and Heavy Formic and Acetic Acids," dealt with the formic acid now known as the hydrogen bond.

Hofstadter remained at Princeton as a Procter Fellow during 1938–1939 before moving to the University of Pennsylvania as a Harrison Research Fellow (1939–1940) and an instructor in physics (1940–1941). There he was involved in the construction of a large Van de Graaff generator. He served as an instructor in physics at the City College of New York in 1941–1942 before becoming engaged in wartime research. In 1942–1943 he was a physicist at the National Bureau of Standards, where he worked with James Van Allen in helping develop proximity fuses; he then joined the Norden Laboratories in New York, where from 1943 to 1946 he worked on servo systems, automatic pilots for aircraft, and altimeter devices. In 1942 he married Nancy Givan; they had a son and two daughters.

Hofstadter returned to Princeton as an assistant professor in 1946, and in 1950 he became an associate professor at Stanford University. He remained at Stanford for the rest of his career as a professor (1954–1971), and served as director of the High Energy Physics Laboratory from 1967 to 1974 and Max H. Stein Professor of Physics from 1971 to his retirement in 1985. He was a Guggenheim Fellow at the European Center for Nuclear Research (CERN) in Geneva, Switzerland, in 1958–1959 and 1974–1975; a National Science Foundation Fellow in 1965–1966; and a Humboldt Fellow in 1981. He was an associate editor of the *Physical Review* (1951–1953), the *Review of Scientific Instruments* (1954–1956), and the *Reviews of Modern Physics* (1959–1962); and was a member of the board of governors of the Weizmann Institute of Science in Israel (1967–1990) and the Israel Institute of Technology (1977–1990).

Hofstadter was much honored in his lifetime. He was elected a member of the National Academy of Sciences in 1958 and shared the 1961 Nobel Prize in physics with Rudolf Mössbauer. In addition, he received the Townsend Harris Medal of the City College of New York (1962); the Roentgen Medal (1985); the Cultural Foundation Medal of Italy (1986); and the National Medal of Science (1986).

Hofstadter worked primarily in experimental physics, and he was one of the first to recognize the possibility of using high-energy accelerators to probe the internal structure of the atomic nucleus. His first task was to devise accurate detection devices for the scattered accelerated electron beams, and in 1948 he made the discovery that the thallium-activated sodium iodide, NaI(Tl), made an excellent scintillation counter. Together with John A. McIntyre in 1950, he showed how NaI(Tl) could be used in a spectrometer for measuring gamma-ray energies. This device, despite the expense and difficulty of working with it, has since been in almost universal use and has led to important results in nuclear physics, high-energy physics, and astrophysics, as well as in nuclear medicine. In his later years, Hofstadter came to regard this—on the basis of its widespread use—as his most important contribution to science.

Hofstadter's 1950 move to Stanford was prompted not only by his friendship with Felix Bloch and Leonard I. Schiff, but also by the fact that a large high-energy accelerator was being built there. By the mid-1950s, Hofstadter and his graduate students Robert W. McAllister and Mason R. Yearin were able to show that the nucleons (a collective term for protons and neutrons), possessed a structure of considerable complexity and were not pointlike particles as had previously been assumed. This involved the measurement of the electromagnetic form factors of the nucleons, which essentially characterize how they interact with other particles and fields. This discovery not only led to a determination of the shape and size of these nucleons, but the behavior of the form factors presented an apparent anomaly, which in 1957 stimulated Japanese theoretician Yoichiro Nambu to propose that the existence of heavy meson might be responsible for the rapid falloff of the magnetic form factors. This observation led to discovery by other researchers of the rho and omega mesons, and the structure originally suggested by Hofstadter was later explained by the quark models of Murray Gell-Mann (1964). For these studies on nuclear structure, Hofstadter was awarded the Nobel Prize for physics in 1961.

In 1968, together with E. Barrie Hughes, Hofstadter devised a new form of detector for high-energy physics, popularly known as the "Crystal Ball," which consisted of a spherical array of more than 900 sodium iodide detectors pointed at the region of collision of the particle beams. This detector was responsible for numerous discoveries in meson physics, including new mesons containing the so-called charmed and bottom quarks. In 1970 Hofstadter proposed putting a large high-energy gamma-ray detector on a satellite in orbit around the Earth to do gamma-ray astronomy. He helped design, build, and test the Energetic Gamma Ray Experiment Telescope (EGRET), which was placed on NASA's Compton Gamma Ray Observatory. The telescope was successfully launched in 1991, a few months after his death, and has continued in operation, with the expectation that it will provide valuable insight into the physics of rotating compact stellar objects (e.g., white dwarfs, neutron stars, and black holes).

In person, Hofstadter was a friendly, unassuming, modest man whose students found him caring and unfailingly helpful. As was the custom at Stanford, he often taught introductory physics courses, and these were marked by a clarity and style that won him high praise from his students. To his graduate students, he was known as simply "Bob," and they came to think of him not merely as a mentor, but as a friend. Two of his postdoctoral students, Jerome I. Friedman and Henry W. Kendall, subsequently became Nobel laureates in physics in 1990. Hofstadter's special talent lay in his ability to conceive an experimental program and then to gather the people, resources, and organization to carry it out. He worked easily with people and displayed exceptional patience in perfecting and refining his measurements. His enthusiasm and leadership made significant contributions to the excellence of the physics program at Stanford and the establishment of the Stanford group as one of the world centers of high-energy accelerator research. Hofstadter died in his home at Stanford.

• Hofstadter's collected papers are in the Stanford University Archives. He contributed an autobiographical sketch to the volume *McGraw-Hill Scientists and Engineers*, vol. 2 (1980), ed. Cybil P. Parker. Of particular interest is his Nobel Prize lecture, "The Electron-Scattering Method and Its Application to the Structure of Nuclei and Nucleons," *Nobel Lectures in Physics, 1942–1962* (1964), which gives a technical overview of his Nobel prize–winning research and contains an extensive set of references dealing with his research. His article, "The Atomic Nucleus," in *Scientific American* 195 (July 1956): 55–68, offers an engaging popular account of his research on nuclear structure. Together with Robert C. Herman, he published *High Energy Electron Scattering Tables* (1960); and he edited the reprint volume, *Electron Scattering and Nuclear and Nucleon Scattering* (1963), and, with L. I. Schiff, *Proceedings of the International Conference on Nucleon Structure at Stanford University* (1964). Obituaries are in *Physics Today* 45 (May 1992): 73–74; and the *New York Times*, 19 Nov. 1990.

JOSEPH D. ZUND

HOGAN, Frank Smithwick (17 Jan. 1902–2 Apr. 1974), attorney, was born in Waterbury, Connecticut, the son of Michael F. Hogan, a watch polisher, and Anne Smithwick, a grocer. During high school, Hogan held a variety of jobs, including working with his father in the watch factory and as an apprentice carpenter. Intent on becoming a journalist, he entered Columbia College; while there he supported himself by selling books and working as a Pullman conductor. He also found time to play on the varsity football team and to serve as president of the senior class and of the fraternity Beta Theta Pi. After graduating with a B.A. in 1924, he worked for a Russian baron, Eugene Ferson, founder of the International Order of Light Bearers. For a fee, Hogan's employer would teach his clients to reconnect themselves to the universal life energy through "star exercises." He then worked for ten months in Guatemala as an accountant for the Guatemala Gold Dredging Company. Returning to the United States, he entered Columbia Law School. He was only an average student, graduating in the middle of his class but failing the course in criminal law. After graduating in 1928, Hogan went to work for the firm of Gleason, McLanahan, Merritt, and Ingraham but left after a short time to begin his own practice with Anthony J. Liebler. The two specialized in insurance and real estate law.

After several years of struggling to establish himself as a case lawyer, Hogan gave up his practice in 1935 and began working for Thomas E. Dewey, the newly appointed special prosecutor in the trials of Charles "Lucky" Luciano for compulsory prostitution and of Democratic leader James J. Hines for conspiracy to conduct a lottery. The prosecution won both cases. Hogan married Mary Egan in 1936; they had no children. When Dewey became New York County district attorney in 1937, Hogan followed him as his assistant. Dewey resigned the office in 1941 to pursue a political career, and Hogan succeeded him, with the support of the Republican, Democratic, and Labor parties.

As district attorney heading the largest criminal law office in the world, Hogan showed himself to be both highly capable and hardworking. In 1942 he set six records for prosecution, including maintaining a conviction rate of 97.4 percent. He was responsible, in 1943, for convicting Joseph S. Fay, "Mr. Labor in the East," for corrupt union practices. Hogan again re-

ceived multiparty support for his reelection in 1945. When Democratic incumbent William O'Dwyer announced in 1949 that he would not seek reelection as New York City mayor, Hogan decided to seek the party's nomination. He had garnered enough support to be assured of this when O'Dwyer suddenly changed his mind and decided to run, dashing Hogan's hopes. Instead, Hogan was reelected to the district attorney's office.

Hogan spent almost a decade investigating Frank Costello, the head of a major crime network and a key figure in the Tammany Hall corruption scandal. Suspected of buying and selling nominations for positions of magistrate, Costello had accumulated most of his wealth through gambling and bootlegging operations and through owning New York's famous nightclub, the Copacabana. Conviction was difficult, because Costello ran much of his business out of New Orleans, outside of Hogan's jurisdiction. However, Hogan provided most of the material used in the 1951 televised Senate committee investigations of crime, chaired by Senator Estes Kefauver. Although the evidence was insufficient to convict Costello on any major counts, he was sentenced to a fourteen-month sentence for contempt of the Senate for refusing to answer questions.

Hogan also secured the 1951 conviction on gambling charges of Joe Adonis, the gangster and bootlegger operating in New Jersey and Brooklyn. In 1953 Hogan's office convicted Frank Erickson, formerly the number one bookmaker in the country, on charges of racketeering. Hogan also investigated corruption in government departments, including bribery involved in the issuance of licenses and illegal political donations made with money from the Firemen's Association.

Although Hogan was one of New York's most effective district attorneys, supported by all parties except the Communists for nine terms from 1941 to 1973, some of his actions in later years evoked criticism as overzealous. Two incidents were especially controversial: his 1964 prosecution of entertainer Lenny Bruce on obscenity charges and his prosecution of hundreds of Columbia University students who took part in the 1968 riots, prosecutions that continued even after the university withdrew charges. In the Lenny Bruce case, an original conviction was overturned on appeal when the appelate judge ruled that "It was error to hold that the performances were without social merit." Hogan's later convictions included Eugene L. Sugarman, the former deputy city controller, who was found guilty of bribery in 1971.

• For further information on Hogan, see articles in *Collier's*, 7 July 1951; the *New York Times*, 31 Aug. 1941 and 9 June 1953; and the *New Yorker*, 14 Apr. 1951. An obituary is in the *New York Times*, 3 Apr. 1974.

ELIZABETH ZOE VICARY

HOGAN, Jim (31 Oct. 1877–20 Mar. 1910), college football player, was born James Joseph Hogan in Glenbane, County Tipperary, Ireland, the son of John J.

Hogan, a stonemason, and Bridget Meehan. The family emigrated when Hogan was five and settled in Torrington, Connecticut. After graduating from high school in Torrington, he worked for Union Hardware Company until he entered Phillips Exeter Academy in 1897, where he captained the 1900 football team.

During four years at Yale College, Hogan played right tackle on the varsity and was captain his senior year. One of the Elis' greatest all-time players, Hogan was among the select group of twelve players chosen three or more times by Walter Camp for his first-team All-America football squad (1902–1904). Named Helms Athletic Foundation 1902 Player of the Year, Hogan was also designated an All-Time All-America by J. C. Kofoed of the *Philadelphia Record* (1911) and by Walter W. Liggett in *Sportlife* (1925). In 1954 Hogan was elected to the National Football Foundation College Football Hall of Fame.

The "barrel chested" 5'10", 210-pound Hogan was "the strongest tackle I ever saw," according to Princeton guard John R. DeWitt; he had "overpowering strength in his legs," which made him "almost irresistible" when he ran the ball. From 1901 through 1904, Yale won 43 games and lost 3 (to Harvard in 1901, Princeton in 1903, and Army in 1904); Yale also tied Army twice. Hogan was a member of the 1902 "Irish Line," which boasted five of Yale's seven first-team All-Americas. Besides winning eleven games, Yale scored 286 points to its opponents' 22. The Elis won the Big Three championship that season by downing Princeton 12–5 and then shutting out Harvard 23–0, with Hogan scoring on both a five-yard and a four-yard tackle-back drive. In 1903, Yale outscored opponents 312 to 26, shutting out the opposition nine times in eleven victories. The Elis bowed only to a strong Princeton team in a game in which Hogan scored on a fifty-yard drive. He scored two touchdowns in Yale's 16–0 defeat of Harvard in the Crimson's new 40,000-seat stadium. In 1904, captain Hogan chose as his field coach the 1903 captain, Charles "Rif" Rafferty; he asked Walter Camp to serve as his major adviser in what proved to be Camp's last year as the dominating force in the Yale system of graduate coaching. The Elis won ten games and outscored opponents by 220 points to 20; Yale was defeated only by Army. Two of Yale's nine shutouts were 12–0 wins over Princeton and Harvard, making Yale the 1904 Big Three champion. In his games against the Crimson and the Tigers, Hogan contributed five touchdowns, two retrieved fumbles, and a blocked punt—feats that earned him the nickname "Yale."

Hogan also was a shot putter on the track team, belonged to the Linonia and Wranglers debating societies, and was manager of the Yale Dramatic Association. Applying himself to his studies with determination, he generally maintained an honor standard; he was awarded the John Benneto Scholarship his junior and senior years. Campus jobs and the football program concession helped pay some of his expenses. A member of Delta Kappa Epsilon Fraternity, he was also tapped by Skull and Bones, one of Yale's elite senior societies. Almost twenty-eight when he earned his B.A. in 1905 ("Hogan's class," as Yale president Arthur Twining Hadley described it), he was appointed class agent for the alumni fund.

During his two years at Columbia University Law School, from which he graduated in 1908, Hogan was on the *Law Review* staff and reported on football for the *New York World*. He worked for the U.S. district attorney's office before joining the New York City law firm of Hatch and Clute. On 1 January 1909, he became New York City's deputy street cleaning commissioner. He won the respect of the department by hard work and fair treatment, curbing graft among foremen and snow removal contractors by hiring substitutes.

Hogan resigned his city post in January 1910, intending to join the New York law firm of Simpson, Thatcher & Bartlett. But having suffered from Bright's disease for a year, he succumbed to an acute attack of uremia worsened by the grippe. At his parents' home in Torrington, he was examined by a New York specialist. His former Yale roommate, Stuyvesant Fish, Jr., provided a train to transport him to New Haven's Elm City Hospital, where Hogan died the next day.

In his memory, Delta Kappa Epsilon funded the James J. Hogan Scholarship at Yale (1911). To many in his day, Hogan's all-round career at Yale exemplified the success being achieved by Irish Americans at the nation's elite universities.

• Manuscripts and Archives, Yale University Library, has rich resources of articles and clippings about Hogan: reel 16 of Arnold Guyot Dana, "Yale Old and New"; and a scrapbook about Yale football, c. 1902–1915, compiled by William Charles Wurtenberg. For Hogan's football career, one of the best secondary sources is Tim Cohane, *The Yale Football Story* (1951). Details of his athletic feats can be found in L. H. Baker, *Football: Facts and Figures* (1945); Thomas Bergin, *The Game: The Harvard-Yale Football Rivalry, 1875–1983* (1984); Cohane, *Gridiron Grenadiers: The Story of West Point Football* (1948); and Allison Danzig, *The History of American Football: Its Great Teams, Players, and Coaches* (1956). A useful reference is Albert Beecher Crawford, ed., *Football Y Men—Men of Yale Series*, vol. 1, *1872–1919* (1962). For additional personal details, see a biographical sketch in *History of the Class of 1905, Yale College* (1905) and an obituary in the *New York Times*, 21 Mar. 1910.

MARCIA G. SYNNOTT

HOGAN, John Vincent Lawless (14 Feb. 1890–29 Dec. 1960), electronics engineer, was born in Philadelphia, Pennsylvania, the son of John Lawless Hogan, a salesman, and Louise Eleanor Shimer, a writer/musician. Hogan graduated from the Horace Mann School in New York and the University School in New Haven, Connecticut. He attended the Sheffield Scientific School at Yale, where he took honors in physics and mathematics. During this period he worked briefly with Dr. Lee de Forest, the inventor of the triode vacuum tube. In 1910, while a junior at Yale, Hogan joined Professor R. A. Fessenden at the National Electric Signaling Co. in Brant Rock, Massachusetts. Although intending to return to the Sheffield School for a doctorate, he remained in professional electronics as an engineer thereafter. With Fessenden, Hogan worked at pioneering wireless transmission not only from the large station in Brant Rock but also for the government at the wireless station in Arlington, Virginia.

In 1912 Hogan helped found the Institute of Radio Engineers. Active in the management of IRE Proceedings, he served, in 1920, as president of the organization, which eventually merged with the American Institute of Electrical Engineers to form the Institute of Electrical and Electronics Engineers (IEEE). Also in 1912 he supervised the erection of the Bush Terminal station, which had the call letters WNY. That same year Hogan was awarded a patent (no. 1,014,002) that became basic to radio tuning when two or more stages needed to be tuned simultaneously. This patent earned him important royalties, especially from manufacturers of broadcast radio receivers during 1925–1928. The research that led to this patent was started while he was still a student. When the United States entered World War I, Hogan and the International Signal Co. manufactured gear for warships and aircraft. In 1917 he married Edith McLennan Schrader, with whom he would have one child. In 1918 Hogan became the manager of the International Radio Telegraph Co. (successor to NES Co.) as well as chairman of the Radio Engineers Committee on National Defense. In 1921 he left International Radio Telegraph when it was absorbed by RCA. He then started his own business as a consulting engineer and was adviser to the Federal Radio Commission during its first years. His experimental station W2XR broadcast the sound for experimental video (TV) transmissions in 1928.

Hogan published widely in technical journals and in popular radio magazines current during the explosive growth of the electronic engineering industry in the 1920s and 1930s. One article, "How to Be a Good Radio Neighbor" (*Radio Broadcast*, July 1925), provides a bit of nostalgia to the reader who operated period-primitive broadcast receivers that, improperly used, would give off their own signal—becoming a small radio transmitter, howling and squealing in neighbors' radio sets. Hogan's *The Outline of Radio* was a popular source for fundamentals in radio. The 1925 edition was published by Little, Brown & Co. Hogan was co-author, with R. M. Wilmotte, of "A Report on the Cost of Providing Auditory Aids by Broadcasting, by Wire Lines, and by Records" (Aug. 1938), which was prepared for the Committee on Scientific Aids to Learning and published under the title *Auditory Aids in the Classroom*.

In 1936, with Elliott M. Sanger, Hogan formed the Interstate Broadcasting Co. to operate broadcast station WQXR in New York City. Widely known as the "good music" station because of its classical music programming, it continued this tradition even after it was purchased by the *New York Times* in 1944. Hogan resigned as president of WQXR in 1949.

During World War II Hogan consulted with the National Defense Research Committee, the Army Signal Corps, and the Army Air Force, also serving as special assistant to Dr. Vannever Bush, director of the Office of Scientific Research and Development. Hogan worked during this period on radar, guided missiles, and the proximity fuse. He was also known for his research into high-speed radio facsimile transmission—in 1948 his instrument produced a four-column newspaper with illustrations at the rate of 500 words per minute. Hogan died at his home in Forest Hills, Queens, New York.

Although Hogan's contributions to early wireless and radio are not as spectacular as those of the well-known inventors, they are basic to the art. Radio receivers continue to utilize his contributions to single-dial tuning.

• For additional information on Hogan, see the *Senior Class Newsletter*, Yale University (1911). For a more detailed look at his contributions to the field of electronics, see Arthur P. Harrison, Jr., "Single-Control Tuning: An Analysis of an Innovation," *Technology and Culture* 20, no. 2 (Apr. 1979): 296–321, and Harrison, "The World versus R.C.A.: Circumventing the Superhet," *IEEE Spectrum* (Feb. 1983). An obituary is in the *New York Times*, 30 Dec. 1960.

ARTHUR P. HARRISON, JR.

HOGAN, William (?1791–3 Jan. 1848), schismatic Catholic priest and lawyer, was born in Limerick, Ireland. Little is known of Hogan's parents, education, life, and clerical ministry in Ireland. Some of his published letters from the 1820s give his birthplace as Limerick, but no known Irish records of his parents' names and occupations exist. Records at St. Patrick's College in Maynooth, Ireland, indicate that Hogan was enrolled in the school studying humanities in 1811, preparing himself for a theological education and the priesthood.

Two personal testimonials, neither of which could be substantiated from authentic public documents, help to piece together something of his education and ministry in Ireland. One of Hogan's fellow students at Maynooth claimed in an 1822 letter to Bishop John England of Charleston, South Carolina, that Hogan was expelled from Maynooth in 1814 during his second year of theology, because he had violated a seminary rule against drinking in his room. Hogan himself asserted in his *Popery As It Was and As It Is* (1855) and other published works of the 1820s and 1830s that he spent four years studying theology at Maynooth (probably from 1810 to 1814), that he was ordained (probably in 1814) for the diocese of Limerick "two years under the canonical age" of twenty-five, and that, "after five years of service in Limerick," he came to the United States (in Nov. 1819). If these dates are correct and he was twenty-three years of age in 1814, he would have been born in 1791 and not in 1788 as most biographical sketches claim.

Hogan's clerical and lay enemies in Philadelphia charged in the 1820s that he had departed from the diocese of Limerick without his bishop's permission and in a cloud of suspicion. Hogan, however, asserted that Bishop Charles Tuohy of Limerick had given him a dimissory letter (written 25 Aug. 1819), testifying to his good services in Ireland. The letter, whose authenticity could not be verified, declared that Hogan had been a curate in the bishop's "mensal parish" in the diocese of Limerick "for some time" and that he had "conducted himself in an exemplary manner."

In November 1819 Hogan arrived in New York, where he found pastoral work in the Catholic missions in the upper Hudson Valley near Albany, Lansingburg, and Schenectady. By 22 April 1820 he was serving as an assistant to the pastor of St. Mary's Parish in Philadelphia, perhaps the wealthiest and most prominent Catholic parish in the country at the time. Hogan earned the respect of many of the prominent lay trustees of the parish between April and November 1820, but he soon became the source of much contention in the parish and created a bitter temporary schism in the church.

Philadelphia had been without a bishop since the death of Bishop Michael Egan in 1814. At the end of November a new bishop, the 75-year-old Henry Conwell, arrived from Ireland to take up the episcopal reins in Philadelphia. Almost immediately Hogan and the bishop clashed over their roles and authority in the church, dividing the parish and the lay trustees into two quarreling camps. Hogan insulted Conwell from the pulpit and later made it clear to the parish that the democratically elected lay trustees, according to U.S. custom and law, had authority over the parish's temporal concerns and even the power to select a pastor. Conwell charged that Hogan's assertions and the American practice of trusteeism were contrary to the Catholic understanding of the church, and on 12 December 1820 he deprived Hogan of his priestly faculties to serve in the diocese of Philadelphia. The majority of the lay trustees, siding with Hogan, opposed the bishop, hired Hogan as their pastor, and entered into a nationally notorious and protracted debate on the relative rights and duties of the laity in the American Catholic church.

The lay trustees, with Hogan's encouragement, contended for the next four years that they had the right to hire and fire pastors and to control the finances of the parish. On 27 May 1821 Rome publicly excommunicated Hogan, because he had disobeyed his bishop's order to withdraw from the parish. In defiance of Roman and episcopal authority, however, Hogan remained as schismatic pastor of St. Mary's until November 1823, creating the so-called heresy of lay trusteeism (or Hoganism, as it was known in Philadelphia). Hoganism was the code word for an assertion of lay and clerical rights within the church and an attempt to reform the structures of the church according to democratic principles.

Though Hogan was brash, impetuous, and haughty, he was also a popular preacher and an effective organizer. The young cleric's popularity threatened the new bishop's position in the community, but the bishop's quick and ill-tempered suspension of Hogan made the bishop himself not only unpopular but also a threat to good order and compassionate leadership in the church.

Hogan published numerous verbal attacks on Bishop Conwell and supported volatile lay opposition to episcopal authority. He also asserted in the Philadelphia newspapers that his fellow Irish immigrants were priest-ridden, ignorant of the Bible, and committed to the elimination of Protestant heretics, charges that had traditionally been made by Protestants and that eventually made him a persona non grata in Philadelphia Catholicism. At the end of 1823 he left Philadelphia and the Catholic church, going to Wilmington, North Carolina, where he studied law, preached in some Protestant churches, and married Henrietta McKay in 1824. On 26 March 1826, after the death of his wife, he was admitted to the practice of law in Georgia. He married Lydia Gibbs Gardener in 1828. Thereafter his career is difficult to follow. He lectured periodically here and there throughout the United States, attacking as un-American Catholic structures of authority and various Catholic religious practices, like confession, which he asserted made the Catholic laity excessively subservient to their priests. He also published some of these popular anti-Catholic lectures, which were frequently republished between 1845 and the 1870s.

In 1843 he was appointed an American consul at Nuevitas, Cuba. He then moved to Nashua, New Hampshire, where he continued to practice law and lecture against Catholicism. He died in Nashua.

• Many of Hogan's published pamphlets on trusteeism in Philadelphia are listed in Wilfred Parson, *Early Catholic Americana* (1939), including *An Address to the Congregation of St. Mary's Church, Philadelphia* (1820), *A Reply to the Sundry Letters of the Right Rev. Dr. England* (1822), and *Strictures on a Pamphlet Written by William Vincent Harold* (1822). He also published a number of anti-Catholic lectures, among which are *Auricular Confession and Popish Nunneries* (1845; numerous repr. until 1878), *A Synopsis of Popery, as It Was and Is* (1845; repr. under various other titles until 1878), and *High and Low Mass in the Roman Catholic Church* (1846). Partial studies of Hogan's life and work are Francis E. Tourscher, *The Hogan Schism and Trustee Troubles in St. Mary's Church, Philadelphia, 1820–29* (1930); and Patrick W. Carey, *People, Priests, and Prelates: Ecclesiastical Democracy and the Tensions of Trusteeism* (1987).

PATRICK W. CAREY

HOGE, Jane Currie Blaikie (31 July 1811–26 Aug. 1890), Civil War relief leader and welfare laborer, was born in Philadelphia, Pennsylvania, the daughter of George D. Blaikie, a wealthy merchant, and Mary Monroe. Jane attended the Young Ladies' College, a classical school in Philadelphia, and graduated first in her class. A talented musician, she continued to play all of her life. In June 1831 she married Alexander Holmes Hoge, a comfortable Pittsburgh merchant. They had thirteen children, eight of whom reached maturity. During their fourteen-year stay in Pittsburgh, Jane Hoge served as secretary of the Pittsburgh Orphan Asylum. In 1848 the couple moved to Chicago, Illinois, where she continued in her charitable activities, establishing and managing the Home for the Friendless, a refuge for women and children. The Hoges were also active in the Old School Presbyterian Church, where Alexander Hoge was a ruling elder.

At the onset of the Civil War, two of Hoge's sons enlisted in the Union army. Like many women in both the North and South, she volunteered to help soldiers and the war effort through supply work. This benevolent reform united women in the war. In 1861, while nursing soldiers at Camp Douglas in Chicago, Hoge and Mary Livermore, a friend, organized and served as cochairmen of the Northwestern Branch of the U.S. Sanitary Commission in Chicago. They were responsible for coordinating aid offered by local relief agencies and societies and for recruiting nurses. Hoge was helpful in any capacity deemed appropriate. Livermore, who had tremendous respect for Hoge and her limitless abilities, later wrote of their relationship that Hoge was a forceful character, assiduous worker, compelling public speaker, and extremely good organizer. In 1862 Hoge and Livermore were appointed Sanitary Commission agents and prepared to visit Mississippi River military hospitals.

In March 1862 Hoge traveled to army hospitals in St. Louis, Missouri; Cairo, Illinois; Mound City, Illinois; and Paducah, Kentucky, on the first of three trips to the Army of the Southwest. She visited an estimated 100,000 men, offering comfort, aid, and supplies. First stopping at Mound City, Hoge wrote "I took my slow and solemn walk through this congregation of suffering humanity, furnished with dainty sheets, and pillows . . . from the Sanitary Commission" (quoted in *Women's Work in the Civil War*). As part of her work for the Sanitary Commission, Hoge inspected military hospitals, reporting on their conditions, and suggesting reforms.

In November 1862 Hoge and Livermore traveled to Washington, D.C., representing the Chicago Branch at the Women's Council, and met with President Abraham Lincoln to discuss their work. On the recommendation of Mark Skinner, president of the Chicago Branch of the Sanitary Commission, Hoge and Livermore were named associate directors in December 1862. Hoge welcomed the challenge of an overwhelming amount of work. She wrote compelling circulars seeking special supplies and lobbied for aid from societies throughout the Northwest, encouraging women to donate money, clothes, food, and medicines. In addition to issuing emotional appeals and providing management and distribution of supplies, Hoge performed nursing and continued her inspection of hospitals. She was unswerving in her devotion to the soldiers, often braving inclement weather and risking disease to help relieve the suffering.

In June 1863 she was invited to Vicksburg, where one of her sons, a colonel in the 113th Regiment Illinois Volunteers, had been wounded. Aware of nutritional deficiencies, she acted as a liaison between the army and homefront, securing a thousand bushels of vegetables to combat scurvy. Hoge talked to soldiers,

sang hymns with them, and promised to deliver messages to their families.

Perhaps Hoge's most significant accomplishment was the staging of the Northwestern Sanitary Fair in Chicago. Planning with Livermore, Eliza Porter, and other civil relief leaders, Hoge hoped through the fair to secure donations to establish a soldiers' home in Chicago. Beginning 27 October 1863, the two-week fair, featuring parades, exhibits, food, entertainment, and merchandise, raised almost $100,000 for war work and a soldiers' home and inspired women in other regions to hold similar fundraising fairs to promote patriotism and unite communities.

Hoge continued to travel with Livermore, and their names became household words. She attended the January 1864 council of women in Washington, D.C., at which she recounted her experiences with aid societies. As the war waned, Hoge continued speaking. In 1867 she published her memoir, *The Boys in Blue; or Heroes of the 'Rank & File'*, one of the first accounts to be written by a woman relief worker and to be focused on soldiers, not officers. Hoge's emotional rhetoric and patriotic imagery biased her information, although historians consider her account of the war in the West to be valuable. She claimed that she wrote the book because "justice to the soldier, and historical accuracy, compel me to represent affairs as they were, thus placing the honor and the shame where they justly belong." Hoge also lauded the "self-denying liberality, labor and zeal of thousands of our countrywomen" who assisted soldiers and wanted to "offer an example, calculated to stimulate and encourage women in all time to come."

After the war, Hoge received numerous public tributes. She continued her charity and social work. In 1869 she and a group of women opened the Chicago Home for the Friendless to provide shelter and aid for impoverished women and children, especially foundlings, wards of the court, and the elderly. Hoge organized an 1871 fundraiser to establish the Evanston College for Ladies. From 1872 to 1885 Hoge served as director of the Women's Presbyterian Board of Foreign Missions in the Northwest, urging women who had nursed during the war to pursue missionary work. Hoge died in Chicago.

Hoge, a religious woman, saw it as her duty to help relieve the suffering of the northern soldiers. Having an unflagging energy and devotion to the cause, Hoge was instrumental in giving significant aid to soldiers all over the North. She often battled weather and disease to provide a reprieve for the sick and dying. She secured supplies and food when it was desperately needed. She also dedicated tremendous enthusiasm to fundraisers, exceeding even her own expectations and facilitating the establishment of a soldiers' home, a homeless shelter, and a women's college. A powerful humanitarian, Hoge made great strides to relieve suffering during the Civil War and is remembered as a "patient, persistent" worker.

• Scant biographical material is in the Northwestern Soldiers' Fair Records at the Chicago Historical Society, and in Chicago Home for the Friendless and Northwestern Sanitary Fair Records at the University of Illinois at Chicago's Circle Library. An excellent source of biographical information is L. P. Brockett and Mary C. Vaughan, *Woman's Work in the Civil War: A Record of Heroism, Patriotism and Patience* (1867). An insightful source on the Sanitary Commission is Sarah E. Henshaw, *Our Branch and Its Tributaries: Being a History of the Work of the Northwestern Sanitary Commission and Its Auxiliaries during the War of the Rebellion* (1868). A valuable record of Hoge's fundraiser is in *History of the Northwestern Soldiers' Fair Held in Chicago* (1864). Hoge's own book, *The Boys in Blue; or, Heroes of the 'Rank & File'* (1867), provides a favorable history of the auxiliary work given by women and other nonofficers. Robert A. Kantor and Marjorie S. Kantor, *Sanitary Fairs: A Philatelic and Historical Study of Civil War Benevolence* (1992), offers another worthy description of beneficent works during the war. Hoge's close friend Mary A. Livermore wrote *My Story of the War* (1889), giving an excellent accounting of her and Hoge's efforts to relieve suffering.

MICHELLE E. OSBORN
ELIZABETH D. SCHAFER

HOGE, Moses (15 Feb. 1752–5 July 1820), Presbyterian clergyman, theologian, and educator, was born in Cedar Grove, Frederick County, Virginia, the son of James Hoge and Nancy Griffiths, farmers. Hoge studied in a classical school in Culpeper, Virginia, under the Reverend Adam Goodlet, then under the Reverend William Graham at Liberty Hall Academy (later Washington and Lee University), from 1778 to 1780. He interrupted his studies for a year to serve during the revolutionary war. Later Hoge prepared for ordination in the Presbyterian Church in the United States of America under James Waddel, a colleague of George Whitefield and Samuel Davies, celebrated evangelists of the First Great Awakening. Hoge was ordained to the ministry on 13 December 1782. He served as a Presbyterian pastor of the Concrete (1782–1787) and the Shepherdstown (1787–1807) congregations in present-day West Virginia. He defended Calvinism in *Strictures upon a Pamphlet by the Rev. Jeremiah Walker, Entitled the Fourfold Foundation of Calvinism Examined and Shaken* (1793). During the Whiskey Rebellion of 1794, when the Synod of Virginia was meeting in Harrisonburg, Virginia, he took the unpopular stand of urging the insurrectionists to obey the laws of the land. He barely escaped being tarred and feathered.

In 1783 Hoge married Elizabeth Poage, the mother of his four sons who grew to manhood. Following her death in 1802, he married Susan Watkins Hunt in 1803. The second marriage was childless.

The Hanover Presbytery voted in 1806 to establish at Hampden-Sydney College a theological library to assist students as they prepared for divinity and to hire Hoge as president of the college with the agreement that he would teach theology as well as attend to the administration of the school. Hoge was inaugurated as president in October 1807. As professor of moral philosophy at Hampden-Sydney, Hoge had the responsibility of teaching apologetics at a time when the faith of his students had been threatened through exposure to Deism and French freethinking. To bring students out of a sea of doubt, he used his own work *The Sophist Unmasked* (1797), written under the pseudonym "Philobiblius," to refute the skepticism found in Thomas Paine's *Age of Reason*. Hoge often found that personal interviews with students turned to discussions about the intellectual objections to Christianity. Some had become skeptics after reading Enlightenment authors. According to William S. Reid, Hoge "had an admirable facility at clearing up difficulties, and illustrating the harmony of the Christian system" so students could be led from doubt to faith (Sprague, vol. 3, pp. 429–30).

Besides defending the faith at the college, Hoge developed a Pietist approach to education "on the principle of mutual improvement in science and piety" modeled after the German August Hermann Francke of the University of Halle (Foote, p. 563). While he was president of Hampden-Sydney College (1807–1820), the Presbyterian Synod of Virginia established on this campus in 1812 another institution, eventually called Union Theological Seminary in Virginia, entirely separate from and independent of the college. Serving as its first professor, Hoge persuaded thirty students to become ministers. Until his death Hoge held the positions of college president and professor of divinity.

As a spiritual guide of students, "he seemed habitually to retain on his mind a sense of the divine presence and was ever ready to engage in the most spiritual conversation" ("Memoir of Graham," p. 137). He was as concerned about his students' spiritual development as he was about their academic progress. Hoge was a revival leader during the Second Great Awakening in Virginia (1785–1820) and favored the use of Pietist conventicles or small groups for prayer and study, which became instrumental in the conversion of college students. The Hampden-Sydney College revival of 1814–1815 began in praying societies at his residence.

Hoge carried on a ministry of spiritual direction beyond the college through correspondence with former parishioners and friends. He provided counsel on trials, death, religious affections, worldliness, and prayer. For example, Hoge provided such guidance to the Congressman John Randolph of Roanoke, who would frequently visit Hoge when he was not in Washington, D.C.

As a Pietist, Hoge instructed others in holiness. His contemporaries noted his "godliness." He guided students to flee fashionable amusements. When a theater in Richmond, Virginia, caught fire in 1811, seventy-two perished. Hoge preached that the fire was a "salutary chastisement" from God upon theatergoing. These performances, he argued, were designed "not to improve but to corrupt the heart." His posthumously published *Sermons* (1821) reflect the preaching of this awakening and his commitment to self-denial.

Hoge was concerned not only for the families of the victims of the Richmond fire but also for poor slaves in his neighborhood. Some of Hoge's students provided slaves with spiritual counsel. In December 1812 they formed a praying society to meet every Sunday afternoon for the benefit of these slaves. During communion seasons, he welcomed African-American communicants to his house for spiritual advice.

Hoge provided his students with an example of his antislavery convictions. When he inherited slaves, he resisted the temptation of enjoying an easy existence through slave labor. Convinced that slaves were part of God's family, Hoge emancipated his slaves. His stepson Thomas P. Hunt also emancipated the slaves he had inherited. Two of Hoge's sons, James Hoge and Samuel Davies Hoge, moved to Ohio to be outside of the slave states for their field of ministry because of their objections to slavery. During a fast day in 1814, Hoge prayed to God to forgive whatever sins America had committed to bring about the trial of the War of 1812. In his fast-day sermon, "The Day of Adversity," Hoge blamed the Lord's "controversy with America" on its "atheism" and its "instances of injustice, violence, and oppression." The last sins seem to be references to slavery (Hoge, *Sermons*, pp. 400–5). He favored the Liberian colonization scheme of the American Colonization Society by which manumitted slaves were given the option of commencing their freedom in this new African colony.

He died in Philadelphia at the General Assembly of the Presbyterian Church and was buried in the Third (Pine Street) Presbyterian Church in Philadelphia. His tombstone summed up his life: "A man of genius, profound erudition & ardent piety." His enduring contributions include his pioneering work as a Protestant "director of souls" based upon German Pietist principles, his Pietist and revivalist scheme for college and seminary education, his defense of the moderate type of evangelical Calvinism that has distinguished Virginia Presbyterianism, his reasoned apologies for the Christian faith during the Enlightenment, and his early antislavery teaching and practice. A former student, W. S. Reid, summed up the driving force of Hoge's scheme for the spiritual guidance of ministerial students. Hoge was not concerned just to impart to his students "a knowledge of the truths of the Gospel" but to "cultivate an ardent piety" and to enable them "to appreciate the responsibilities of the work to which they were devoted" (Sprague, vol. 3, pp. 429–30). Hoge succeeded in making the college and seminary a "nursery of piety and vital religion" (Bradshaw, pp. 133–34).

• Hoge's papers may be found in the Hoge Family Papers (1804–1939), in the Hannah Family Papers (1760–1967), the Hugh Blair Grigsby Papers (1754–1944), and the William Hill Papers (microfilm) at the Virginia Historical Society in Richmond; the Moses Hoge Papers at Union Theological Seminary in Virginia; and the Hoge Family Papers, Department of History, Presbyterian Church U.S.A., Montreat, N.C., and the Moses Hoge Papers at the Library of Congress. His published works include *Sermons Selected from the Manuscripts of the Late Moses Hoge, D.D.* (1821) and the editorship of *Christian Panoply*. The standard early biographies are found in John Blair Hoge, *Sketch of the Life & Character of the Rev. Moses Hoge, D.D.* (1964), transcribed from an early manuscript; William Henry Foote, *Sketches of Virginia Historical and Biographical*, 1st ser. (1850); Peyton Harrison Hoge, *Moses Drury Hoge* (1899); William B. Sprague, *Annals of the American Pulpit* (9 vols., 1857–1869); and "Memoir of the Rev. William Graham," unpublished ms., 137, Princeton Theological Seminary Library. The most complete modern assessments are Arthur Dicken Thomas, Jr., "Moses Hoge: Reformed Pietism and Spiritual Guidance," *American Presbyterians* 71 (Summer 1993): 95–109, and Thomas, "The second Great Awakening in Virginia and Slavery Reform, 1785–1837" (Ph.D. diss., Union Theological Seminary in Virginia, 1981). Other important interpretations include E. T. Thompson, "Moses Hoge: First Professor of Theology at Union Theological Seminary," *Union Seminary Review* 49 (Oct. 1937): 21–34; and Morton H. Smith, *Studies in Southern Presbyterian Theology* (1962). For institutional histories, see Herbert C. Bradshaw, *History of Hampden-Sydney* (1976), and Ernest Trice Thompson, *Presbyterians in the South* (1963–1973). For entries on Moses Hoge, his wife Susan Watkins Hoge, and his son Samuel Davies Hoge, see Donald Lewis, ed., *A Dictionary of Evangelical Biography* (1995). For a Hoge genealogy, see George Norbury MacKenzie, *Colonial Families of the United States of America* (1966).

ARTHUR DICKEN THOMAS, JR.

HOGE, Moses Drury (17 Sept. 1819–6 Jan. 1899), Presbyterian minister, was born in Hampden-Sydney, Virginia, the son of Samuel Davies Hoge, a minister and educator, and Elizabeth Rice Lacy. The family moved to Ohio when Hoge was an infant, and his father died when he was only seven. At the age of sixteen he went to live with an uncle in New Bern, North Carolina. A few years later he returned to Virginia and enrolled at Hampden-Sydney College where two of his grandfathers had been president. He graduated as valedictorian in 1839 and remained as a tutor to collegians while taking theology courses at Union Theological Seminary in Richmond. In 1843 he graduated from that institution and was licensed to preach by the West Hanover Presbytery, located in Lynchburg. Several churches in North Carolina and Alabama invited Hoge to join them, but he declined, preferring to serve as assistant minister at Richmond's First Presbyterian Church. In 1844 he married Susan Morton Wood; the couple had eight children.

Hoge was ordained in 1845 and became the first pastor of Second Presbyterian Church in Richmond, a newly formed congregation that emerged largely as a result of his recruiting zeal. He occupied that position for the rest of his life and quickly built his church into the largest in the Virginia Synod. From its eminence Hoge proved himself to be a compelling orator. His manner of speaking had literary grace to it, and each message contained both sound reasoning and apt illustrations. His cogent thought and urgent sincerity brought Hoge recognition as a master of the pulpit. In 1855 he became part owner and coeditor of a religious journal, changing its name from *Watchman* to the *Central Presbyterian*. The following year Hampden-Sydney College asked him to be its next president, as did Dickinson College in 1860. He accepted neither offer because he was so firmly entrenched in his church and in his city.

While secession from the Union was still being debated, Hoge opposed such rash action. But in April 1861 when Lincoln called for troops to suppress southern defiance, he finally backed his state and championed the Confederacy. As more and more troops arrived in Richmond, Hoge volunteered to minister to them while they were stationed around the city. He did not serve as chaplain to any single regiment but rather toured all the training camps on a regular basis. In addition to providing spiritual guidance to thousands of young men away from home for the first time he also served at times as chaplain to the Confederate Congress. In 1862 Hoge set sail for England, running the Union's naval blockade on passage out of Wilmington, North Carolina. Obtaining help from the British and Foreign Bible Society, he successfully brought back crates of religious books for use among Confederate soldiers. Among the works he smuggled in were 10,000 Bibles, 50,000 New Testaments, and 250,000 pamphlets that contained popular biblical quotations. Work with those materials continued at local military installations throughout the war.

During the Reconstruction era Hoge assisted his region's recovery from devastation while helping his denomination cope with survival. He raised funds for many causes, one of which was the publication committee that produced a hymnbook, or Directory of Worship, for use among southern Presbyterians. He also solicited contributions for improving the state university, for launching a literary magazine, and for erecting a monument to Robert E. Lee. He became a fixture at civic events such as burials and memorial services where his oratory emphasized the good qualities of defeated southern leaders. In 1875, for instance, the state legislature chose him to speak at the unveiling of the Stonewall Jackson statue. That year he was also elected moderator of his church's General Assembly by unanimous vote when it convened in St. Louis, Missouri.

Hoge's vision extended far beyond local affairs, however, and in the last decades of his life he did much to reconcile southern Presbyterians with their northern counterparts. In 1873 he traveled to New York City as a delegate to the pan-Protestant Evangelical Alliance. There his address, "The Mission Field of the South," drew wide and sympathetic attention. As one active in denominational reunion and interdenominational cooperation, he attended further sessions of the Evangelical Alliance: Copenhagen in 1884 and Boston in 1889. He demonstrated additional interest in broader issues as a delegate to the Alliance of Reformed Churches that met at Edinburgh in 1877. He attended similar gatherings in London (1888) and Glasgow (1896), but by then he was beginning to curtail such travels. On the forty-fifth anniversary of his pastorate Hoge was proclaimed the first citizen of Richmond. Another decade elapsed before he died there, faithful to duties that spanned more than half a century.

• A collection of Hoge's public addresses appeared posthumously as *The Perfection of Beauty, and Other Sermons* (1904). Information about him is found in Peyton H. Hoge, *Moses Drury Hoge: Life and Letters* (1899). An obituary is in the *Richmond Times-Dispatch*, 6 Jan. 1899.

HENRY WARNER BOWDEN

HOGG, Ima (10 July 1882–19 Aug. 1975), civic leader, collector, and philanthropist, was born in Mineola, Texas, the daughter of James Stephen Hogg and Sarah Ann "Sallie" Stinson. Her father was governor of Texas in the 1890s and later a wealthy oilman. He named Ima after a character in a poem by his late brother Thomas.

As a girl Hogg studied piano, attended the University of Texas in Austin for two years, and in 1901 went to New York City to study at the National Conservatory of Music. Her father, who had moved to Houston, was busy enlarging his oil holdings. When he fell ill in 1905, Hogg cared for him until his death the next year. Shortly later she went to Germany to resume her musical studies. She returned to Houston in 1909 and lived there the rest of her life but traveled extensively. In 1913 she helped create the Houston Symphony Orchestra. Until her death, she took a major role in helping finance it and in choosing its conductors. She was its president for many years. She also funded scholarships in the fine arts.

The discovery of oil at West Columbia, Texas, in 1918, enlarged the family fortune enormously. About 1920, with the encouragement of her brother Will, she began to travel throughout the eastern United States to purchase American antique furniture and other household goods. In 1927–1928 she and her unmarried brothers Will and Michael built "Bayou Bend," a mansion in newly created River Oaks, an elite subdivision of Houston. Over the years she continued to fill the house with American rarities. Hogg collected many hundreds of examples of antique eighteenth- and nineteenth-century American furniture, paintings, silver, china, and other kinds of fine and decorative art in a variety of styles. Each room at Bayou Bend was authentically furnished after a specific period or style.

After Will died in 1930, most of his estate went to the University of Texas in Austin, which Will loved and had long supported. To honor his memory, Ima Hogg and her surviving brothers Michael and Thomas had the university use the money to create the Hogg Foundation for Mental Health. Planning for the new educational foundation took place in the late 1930s, and it opened in 1940. When Ima Hogg died, most of her estate also went to the foundation. In the late 1940s she served on the Houston Independent School District Board. In 1943 she donated Will's fifty-three Frederick Remington paintings to the Houston Museum of Fine Arts.

During the 1950s and 1960s Hogg worked with a number of civic groups, including the League of Women Voters, the Texas State Historical Survey Commission, and the Harris County Heritage and Conservation Society. She also became interested in funding historic preservation. Her first restoration was the Varner plantation, which was built in the 1830s and which James Hogg had purchased in 1901. She gave it to the state of Texas, and it was renamed the Varner-Hogg State Park. She also funded the restoration of two antebellum sites, the Winedale Inn complex at Winedale, Texas, and the MacGregor house near Roundtop, Texas.

Hogg's greatest contribution to the future was the conversion of Bayou Bend into one of the finest museums of American antiquities in the nation. She gave the house, its contents, and an endowment of $750,000 to the Houston Museum of Fine Arts in 1958. The house opened as a museum in 1966. Hogg, who never married, continued to be active in her old age, traveling and collecting. While in London, she fell in the street and died five days later.

Ima Hogg used her fortune for the encouragement of American culture and the conservation of cultural history and artifacts. She was also concerned with furthering education for mental health. She believed that the wealthy have a moral obligation to help other people. She was a true philanthropist.

• The Hogg Family Papers are located at the Barker Texas History Center at the University of Texas in Austin. There are also some papers at Bayou Bend. An oral interview with Hogg is at the Houston Metropolitan Research Center. Published sources of biographical information include Louise Kosches Iscoe, *Ima Hogg: First Lady of Texas* (1976); Virginia Bernhard, *Ima Hogg: The Governor's Daughter* (1984); and Robert C. Cotner, *James Stephen Hogg: A Biography* (1959). David B. Warren, *Bayou Bend: American Furniture. Paintings and Silver from the Bayou Bend Collection* (1975), contains additional information. An obituary is in the *New York Times*, 21 Aug. 1975.

WALTER A. SUTTON

HOGG, James Stephen (24 Mar. 1851–3 Mar. 1906), governor of Texas, was born at "Mountain Home," his family's estate near Rusk, Cherokee County, Texas, the son of Joseph Lewis Hogg, a planter and delegate to the 1845 Texas Constitutional Convention, and Lucanda McMath. Although his father, who became a brigadier general in the Confederate army, died when Hogg was eleven and his mother died the following year, his older siblings maintained the family home and sent him to school. When a classmate stole his speech and aped his mannerisms in an oratorical contest, Hogg spoke extemporaneously and became aware of his talent, which later made him a magnificent campaigner.

Shortly before he was sixteen, Hogg became a printer's devil for the *Texas Observer* in Rusk, where he slept in the print shop and boarded with the editor. While mastering the printing trade, he learned about politics by typesetting political speeches and editorials. By the end of a year he occasionally got the newspaper out by himself, and when work was slack he set type for newspapers in neighboring towns. In nearby Palestine he met John H. Reagan, former postmaster

general of the Confederacy, who encouraged Hogg to fulfill his dream of becoming a lawyer.

First Hogg tried farming, with disastrous results. After being cheated out of most of his sharecrop earnings in 1869, he persuaded his brother John to join him in farming a rented tract in Wood County. There a ruffian, whom Hogg had earlier helped a sheriff arrest, shot him in retaliation. With a bullet lodged near his spine, Hogg returned to his family home, where his sister nursed him back to partial health and he concluded that heavy farm work was out of the question.

In the summer of 1870 Hogg began work on the *Democratic Reporter* in Tyler, where he studied law seriously, quickly made friends, and joined the Debating Society. Among his new acquaintances was Horace Chilton, who worked for a rival newspaper. Chilton became his lifelong friend, and Hogg, as governor, would appoint him to the U.S. Senate. By the end of 1871 Hogg, at the age of twenty, edited his own newspaper in Longview, but he soon moved it to Quitman, where he helped antirailroad people defeat a $100,000 county bond subsidy for the Texas and Pacific Railroad.

In 1873 Hogg was elected justice of the peace in the First Precinct of Wood County, where he strictly enforced laws and greatly improved the area's finances. That same year he married Sarah Ann "Sallie" Stinson; they had four children. He was admitted to the bar in 1875 and the next year lost his only election, failing by less than a hundred votes to be elected to the state legislature. When running for county attorney, a position he held from 1879 to 1881, Hogg adopted "Enforce the Law" as his slogan, and while district attorney for the Seventh Judicial District, 1881 to 1885, he earned a reputation for fairness among both blacks and whites. Seeking black votes for the Democratic party, he told his cohorts that blacks were in the country to stay and that what they wanted was economic and political justice. Called the "finest prosecuting officer in Texas," Hogg won convictions in twenty-five of the twenty-six cases he prosecuted. One day between cases, when the pain in the small of his back flared up, he insisted that a doctor remove the old bullet, even though he had no anesthetic.

In 1886 Hogg was elected state attorney general and served two terms, from 1887 to 1891. Although he was personally temperate, he opposed prohibition, because under it liquor inevitably would be sold illegally without the safeguards surrounding its legal sale. A master of clear, vigorous expression, he exclaimed in his opposition, "Men cannot be . . . forced into temperance or whipped into religion" (Cotner, *James Stephen Hogg: A Biography*, p. 131). Taking office as a reformer when the Farmers' Alliance and the Knights of Labor were demanding government ownership of railroads, Hogg used the climate they had created to free Texas from the grip of corporations, but he refused to adopt their radical measures.

Determined to protect both the public and those corporations adhering to their charters, Hogg filed suits against forty fraudulent insurance companies and moved to prevent railroads from acquiring, on dubious grounds, state public lands. To encourage construction, Texas offered railroads an average of 10,240 acres of land for each mile of track built (more than a fifth of the giant state). Rushing to collect their generous grants, many railroads in Texas opened "in a green and unfinished condition," with poor roadbeds and bridges and inadequate rolling stock and stations, and failed to live up to the safety and service requirements of their charters. "Fair but firm" and "with a minimum of legal expense to the state," Hogg forced them either to forfeit their land grants or obey their charters and greatly improved railroad service (Cotner, *James Stephen Hogg*, pp. 127, 140). Not only did he dissolve the Texas Traffic Association, in which nine railroads had combined to fix rates, but he also required a railroad that had suspended its operation to rebuild its line and resume service, forced a franchise-abusing road into receivership, kept other roads in line by threatening to take away their charters, and insisted that they all maintain general offices in the state.

When Hogg ran for governor in 1890, a huge hog on a silk banner waved over the Democratic convention hall and fewer than two dozen delegates opposed his nomination, which was tantamount to election. Voters also approved an amendment to the state constitution permitting the establishment of a commission to regulate railroad rates and services. Hogg pushed a commission bill through the legislature in April 1891 and persuaded his early mentor Reagan to resign from the U.S. Senate to head the new railroad commission. A principal author of the federal Interstate Commerce Act (1887), Reagan said that Texas had passed "the best commission law I ever saw." Insisting that the commission must have a good technical staff, Hogg worked to obtain an adequate appropriation. In 1894, when the Supreme Court declared the commission constitutional, "Hoggism"—his Democratic opponents' name for his dynamic leadership and progressive regulatory program—was institutionalized.

During his first gubernatorial term, Hogg also increased the public school year from less than four to six months, demanded more support for the state university and higher education, and worked for stricter law enforcement. Loathing lynching and ashamed that "murderers were less punished in Texas than thieves," Hogg, according to Colonel Edward M. House, a member of his staff and later an intimate adviser of President Woodrow Wilson, "did more than any executive in Texas to break up [the] habit of public killing" (Cotner, *James Stephen Hogg*, pp. 434, 435).

In his 1892 campaign for the Democratic gubernatorial nomination, Hogg was attacked simultaneously by Thomas L. Nugent, a formidable foe on the left who, as a Populist, was "for government ownership of the railroads," and by George Clark, a formidable foe on the right who was "for turning them loose." "I want neither," Hogg said, "but advocate their just control and regulation through the Commission" (Cotner, *James Stephen Hogg*, p. 310). Hogg won, as expected, and Colonel House later said, "It was the first firm

stand the people of any American State had taken against the privileged classes, and it attracted attention throughout the Union" (Cotner, *James Stephen Hogg*, pp. 318–19). Indeed, Hogg was a precursor of the Progressive movement. During his second term he worked to break up large corporate land holdings, "which tended to create islands of sparsely settled areas to the great benefit of the few rather than the many," and to collect "just dues" from those "escaping taxation" (Cotner, *James Stephen Hogg*, pp. 341, 345).

Not yet forty-four and, at 300 pounds, as gargantuan as the state of Texas, Hogg left the governor's seat in January 1895. Early the next year William J. Bryan told him, "You have all the qualifications necessary for president." Later in 1896 Hogg addressed the Democratic National Convention that nominated Bryan for the presidency, but Hogg's "cup of ambition" was "full." He was in debt, and his prime desire was to leave his children well situated in life. He formed a partnership in Austin with Judge James H. Robertson, and from the start their business boomed. Soon rumors were flying that the "people's idol" was doing business for the railroads, but in his dealings with railroads, Hogg neither appeared against the state or the railroad commission nor lobbied for legislation.

In January 1901, when an oil well gushed at Spindletop, near Beaumont, Hogg and his friend James Swayne formed a syndicate and bought land in the area, which they subdivided. Requiring capital, Hogg in late 1901 and early 1902 went to New York and then to England to secure investors. The Hogg-Swayne interests became part of the Texas Company (Texaco), with a pipeline connecting the oil fields to a $150,000 refinery in Port Arthur, which became the world's greatest oil port.

Caught up in buying and selling oil land, Hogg in May 1901 purchased 4,100 acres originally granted to Martin Varner in 1824 by Stephen F. Austin, the father of Texas. Close at hand was West Columbia, the 1836 capital of the Republic of Texas. Glorying in the history around him, Hogg called his new purchase "Varner Plantation" and in early 1905 moved his law practice to Houston to be nearer this land, which he made his country home. His faith that part of it would be a productive oil field was fulfilled during World War I. On Hogg's birthday in 1958, his daughter Ima Hogg, a patron of the arts and education, gave Varner Plantation to the state as a museum and state park.

After Hogg's neck was injured in a train wreck in late January 1905, he developed an abscess in his throat and his health steadily declined. Although he returned to Varner Plantation early the next year, he was not well. He was persuaded to seek treatment in Battle Creek, Michigan, but died en route during a stopover in Houston. Before his death the *Galveston-Dallas News*, which in 1892 had called him the "most perfect specimen of the demagogue that the nineteenth and all other centuries have produced," spoke of the "heroic ex-Governor" and conceded that "few men of this age have accomplished more" (Gambrell, p. 340).

• Hogg's extensive papers are at the University of Texas. For a full biography, see Robert C. Cotner, *James Stephen Hogg: A Biography* (1959), and for a short biography and Hogg's speeches and papers, see Cotner's edition of the *Addresses and State Papers of James Stephen Hogg* (1951). See also Herbert Gambrell, "James Stephen Hogg: Statesman or Demagogue?" *Southwest Review* 13 (1928): 338–66; and James R. Norvell, "The Railroad Commission of Texas: Its Origin and History," *Southwestern Historical Quarterly* 68 (1965): 465–80. Hogg is also mentioned in articles on his daughter and in her biography by Virginia Bernhard, *Ima Hogg, the Governor's Daughter* (1984). An obituary is in the *New York Times*, 4 Mar. 1906.

OLIVE HOOGENBOOM

HOGNESS, Thorfin Rusten (9 Dec. 1894–14 Feb. 1976), chemist and educator, was born in Minneapolis, Minnesota, the son of Peter Gunerius Hogness and Amanda Rusten. He was educated at the University of Minnesota, where he received a B.S. in chemistry in 1918 and a Chem.E. in 1919, and the University of California at Berkeley, at which he earned a Ph.D. in physical chemistry in 1921, working under the noted chemist Joel Hildebrand. During his undergraduate years, in 1918, he served in the U.S. Army. After completing his doctorate he became an instructor at Berkeley, and an assistant professor in 1925. In 1926 and 1927 he was a research fellow at the University of Göttingen, Germany, and in 1928 he was promoted to associate professor at Berkeley.

In 1930 Hogness moved at that rank to the University of Chicago, where he would spend the rest of his academic career. He became a full professor in 1938, director of physical science development in 1947–1948, director of the Institute of Radiobiology and Biophysics from 1948 to 1951, director of the Chicago Midway Laboratories from 1951–1963, and director of the Laboratories of Applied Sciences in 1962–1963. In 1963 he retired from the University of Chicago, becoming an emeritus professor. Hogness had married in 1920 Phoebe Dorothy Swenson; they had two children.

Hogness's research and professional output during his productive years was remarkable for its breadth and depth. His early work, conducted mostly during the 1920s, was strictly physical-chemical: surface tension of molten metals, ionization potentials of elements and small compounds, X-ray analyses, isotope distributions, and gas diffusion in solids. In the 1930s he moved into biochemistry, initially by developing spectrophotometric apparatus and using it in analysis of biochemical materials, but later in the synthesis and characterization of enzymes, steroids, and energy-transfer molecules.

Hogness is also known as the authoritative producer, with Warren C. Johnson, of four texts on what was once a major component of undergraduate chemistry, qualitative analysis: *Qualitative Analysis and Chemical Equilibrium* (1937), which underwent two reprints and one revision; *Elementary Principles of Qualitative Analysis* (1938); *Ionic Equilibrium as Applied to Qualitative Analysis* (1941), which had one reprint and one revi-

sion; and *An Introduction to Qualitative Analysis* (1957, 1958). Half a generation of chemistry majors learned "qual" from Hogness and Johnson.

As the Second World War approached, Hogness became caught up in government service, and his research output fell away to nothing by 1942. In 1941 he was named a member of the Office of Scientific Research and Development (OSRD), and in 1942–1943 he served in London as a scientific liaison officer to the U.S. Embassy. He acted as director of medical research to the Office of Strategic Services in 1943; in the same year he became director of plutonium research, centered at the University of Chicago, and was one of the scientists instrumental in the development of the atomic bomb. He held this position until 1946, also serving as a consultant to the War Department and OSRD, with responsibility for the European Theater of Operations at the end of World War II, and as atomic liaison officer to Europe for the Manhattan Engineering District, which produced the atomic bomb.

After the war, Hogness became more and more involved in the politics of science and scientific administration. He became chairman of the executive committee of the Atomic Scientists of Chicago and was an adviser for the Vandenberg amendments to the Senate's McMahon bill that established the Atomic Energy Commission in early 1946. These amendments clearly defined the commission's civilian control in developing peaceful applications of atomic technology, as opposed to the tight and secret operation desired by the military. In November of the same year the Emergency Committee of Atomic Scientists was formed, with Albert Einstein at its head and Hogness and seven other major scientists as members. Its purpose was to inform the American public of the facts that atomic bombs were relatively cheap and easy to make, that the necessary technical information for their assembly was already part of the open scientific literature, and that it was only a matter of time before the United States' monopoly on their production would be broken by another nation, notably the Soviet Union. The committee's conclusion was that only by worldwide sharing of atomic information and a ban on nuclear warfare could the future of the world be assured.

At the same time that Hogness joined his fellow scientists in concern about atomic weaponry, he was promoting peaceful industrial use of nuclear energy. As director of physical science development at Chicago, he was able in 1948 to engage the university's Institute of Nuclear Studies, Institute for the Study of Metals, and Institute of Radiobiology and Biophysics in an information-sharing consortium with a number of major industries. For the cost of membership in the consortium the firms could receive advance notice of findings from the university's atomic research facilities.

Also in 1948, Hogness and seven other atomic scientists accused the House Un-American Activities Committee and its chairman J. Parnell Thomas of driving the best scientists out of government through its "objectionable smear tactics" that labeled researchers as security risks with little or no supporting evidence. In this concern they were supported by President Harry Truman, but the committee's activities appear to have gone on unchecked "in spite of" the president's position (*New York Times*, 18 Sept. 1948). In 1949 the Soviet Union detonated its first atomic bomb, to cries of atomic spying from the committee and a renewed call for openness from Hogness, Dr. Harold C. Urey, and other atomic scientists from Chicago.

Hogness continued to promote peaceful use of nuclear energy in manufacturing, with a success that is not well known except by those with a knowledge of industry. (To cite only one widespread example: continuous thickness gauging of film and sheet materials was later accomplished, more often than not, by measuring absorption of radiation from synthetic radioactive elements.) He engaged in political confrontation with decreasing frequency as he approached retirement and moved to a retirement home in San Jose, California, in his last years.

Hogness's career as a chemist and teacher was important on three fronts: in routine but valuable research, particularly in his development of analytical spectroscopy; in actual teaching and textbook publication; and in service both in and out of government that was conducted fairly, openly, and without fear. In 1950 he received the Outstanding Achievement Award of the University of Minnesota. Hogness died in San Jose, California.

• *Poggendorff's biographisch-literarisches Handwoerterbuch der exacten Naturwissenschaften*, vol. 6, no. 2, p. 1143, and vol. 7(b), pt. 4, pp. 2047–48, covers Hogness's scientific career reasonably well up to 1963. Details of Hogness's concern with civilian control of the AEC, industrial use of nuclear energy, and anti–House Un-American Activities Committee activity are covered in articles in the *New York Times* between 1946 and 1951. An obituary in the *New York Times*, 17 Feb. 1976, gives a fair sketch of his government and political years.

ROBERT M. HAWTHORNE JR.

HOGUE, Wilson Thomas (6 Mar. 1852–13 Feb. 1920), Free Methodist bishop, was born in Lyndon, near Franklinville, New York, the son of Thomas P. Hogg, a Scottish immigrant farmer (who changed the spelling to Hogue), and Sarah Ann Carpenter, a native of England. At the age of nineteen Hogue was licensed to preach in the Free Methodist church, of which his family were members. In 1873 he joined the Genesee Conference, taking pastorates within its bounds until 1892. In 1874, while pastor at Jamestown, New York, he married Emma Luella Jones; they would have three daughters.

Benjamin T. Roberts, an excommunicated Methodist Episcopal minister who had founded the perfectionist Methodist sect in 1860, ordained Hogue deacon in 1875; he was ordained elder in 1877. Having both the confidence of Roberts and a reputation as a fine preacher, Hogue rapidly gained prominence in the conference and served as district elder on the Genesee and Buffalo districts. In 1892, much to his surprise, he was invited to be president of the newly founded

Greenville College in Greenville, Illinois (not named as such until 1895), the first college of the Free Methodist church, and in 1893 he was elected editor of the *Free Methodist*, the official journal of the denomination. He held these two offices simultaneously until resigning in 1904, having been elected as a general superintendent of the church the previous year.

Although Hogue had campaigned for the founding of the Free Methodist college, he had not sought the presidency. Indeed, he later recorded, somewhat wryly, that there were times during his twelve-year tenure that he would have liked to have been able to extricate himself from the responsibilities of being president. Hogue had received no formal college education, only the four-year conference course. Consequently, despite his commitments, he matriculated through a nonresident program at Illinois Wesleyan University, earning a Ph.B. in 1897, an A.M. in 1899, and a Ph.D. in 1902. As Greenville's first president, he was held in high esteem; his standards and competence put the college on a firm foundation despite its lack of resources.

During Hogue's editorship of the *Free Methodist*, few periodicals of the denomination were not directed by him in some capacity. He, and at various times his wife, edited the Sunday school journals purchased by the Free Methodist Publishing House. He also edited the *Earnest Christian*, previously owned by Roberts. In support of the missionary board, in 1896 he founded and edited a missionary supplement to the *Free Methodist*, which in 1898 became *Missionary Tidings*. Hogue also promoted the development of the Free Methodist Publishing House, finally securing, in 1907, the agreement of the General Conference to purchase a new site in Chicago. With his colleague Mendal B. Miller, Hogue was asked to commission architectural plans, obtain their approval, and execute a financial plan, but he suffered a cerebral hemorrhage in September 1908, followed by paralysis on his right side in July 1909, and thus was unable to continue to work on the project.

Alongside his educational and publishing activities, Hogue was constantly engaged as an officer of the church. In April 1893, after the death of Roberts, he was elected interim general superintendent, fulfilling the duties of this role until the General Conference in 1895. Previously Roberts had made the unprecedented move of appointing Hogue, rather than an elder from his own conference, as acting president of the Canadian Conference. Although this action was challenged, the Discipline was later revised in support of the move. Also, in 1898, at the end of the Spanish-American War, the General Conference placed Hogue on the Committee of Seven formed to draft and present to President William McKinley a statement regarding the treaty negotiations. The committee proposed that, as a condition of the settlement, the Philippines should be ceded to the United States; this was the first time that a national religious body had taken an official position on the terms of a peace settlement.

In June 1903 Hogue was elected general superintendent, a title that the General Conference changed to bishop in 1907. He held that office until 1919, when physical collapse prevented him from continuing. In 1907 Hogue was placed on the Committee of Five appointed to liaise with the Wesleyan Methodist church, but his stroke limited his contribution to that effort as well. He did continue to preside at conferences, organizing, for example, the newly formed Southern Oregon Conference in 1912. Regarded as an outstanding preacher, he gave the commemorative sermon for the semi-centennial anniversary of the Free Methodist church in June 1911.

In the years following his illness, Hogue wrote the two-volume *History of the Free Methodist Church of North America* (1915), the first comprehensive history of the denomination. Having known many of the founding members, Hogue was concerned that the history be transmitted accurately and that its documentary material be preserved. His other publications included the *Handbook of Homiletics and Pastoral Theology* (1887), a guide for pastors that became a popular teaching aid; a biography of the missionary G. Harry Agnew (1904); and *Hymns That Are Immortal* (1906), a compilation and history.

Within the Free Methodist church, Hogue was regarded as the natural successor to B. T. Roberts and as one of the denomination's major figures. As an officer of the church, as a director of its publishing activities, and as president of Greenville College he had a significant impact on the denomination's development in its formative years. Hogue died at his daughter's home in Michigan City, Indiana.

• A list of Hogue's publications is in Frederick DeLand Leete, *Methodist Bishops* (1948). Richard R. Blews, *Master Workmen* (1939), contains a biography of Hogue that is based in part on the author's personal knowledge of the subject. Much detail about Hogue's denominational work can be found in vol. 2 of his *History of the Free Methodist Church of North America* (1915), which also mentions all of his addresses and sermons published in pamphlet form. Further references can be found in Leslie R. Marston, *From Age to Age: A Living Witness* (1960), a history of the denomination. The *Free Methodist*, 23 Mar. 1920, is a memorial issue.

JOANNA HAWKE

HOGUN, James (?–4 Jan. 1781), revolutionary war general, was born in Ireland, but nothing is known about his parents or the date of his birth. He migrated to Halifax County, North Carolina, where he married Ruth Norfleet on 3 October 1751. The Hoguns had one son, Lemuel. Not active in public office until the Revolution, Hogun was appointed in 1774 to the Halifax County Committee of Safety, which replaced the county court when royal authority disintegrated. Elected to three successive provincial congresses in 1775 and 1776, Hogun served on military affairs committees. In April 1776 he was named major of the Halifax County militia. His committee work in the November 1776 North Carolina congress included organizing the militia and serving on the crucial committee to write the state constitution, but Hogun's civil career ended on 26 November when he received his commission as colonel of the Seventh North Carolina Continental Regiment.

During his early months in command, Hogun enlisted and trained his regiment, which he led north in July 1777 to join George Washington's army in time to participate in the battles of Brandywine and Germantown. He was later cited by Thomas Burke, (c. 1747–1783), a North Carolina representative in the Continental Congress, as having served at Germantown with "distinguished intrepidity." When troop losses led to the consolidation of the continental units, Hogun was transferred to the command of the Third North Carolina Continental Regiment. Considered very effective in organization and recruitment, Hogun was dispatched in the spring of 1778 from Valley Forge to North Carolina to raise reinforcements. By September 1778 he brought the newly recruited Seventh Regiment to the Continental army in New York, where they were detailed to improve and extend the key fortifications at West Point. When General Benedict Arnold requested a detachment for the Philadelphia garrison, Hogun and his North Carolinians were dispatched, arriving in January 1779. The need for general officers from North Carolina was finally addressed that month by the Continental Congress when Hogun became one of the state's two brigadier generals. Although the state legislature had recommended the acting brigade commander Colonel Thomas Clark instead, Hogun was selected because of his seniority and his meritorious service at Germantown. In March 1779, Hogun replaced Arnold as commandant of the Philadelphia garrison and served in that capacity for six months.

In November the North Carolina brigade was ordered south to reinforce General Benjamin Lincoln's (1733–1810) army at Charles Town, South Carolina, which was threatened by a British invasion. After a harrowing winter trek, Hogun's brigade arrived in Charles Town in March 1780, lifting the morale of the garrison and bolstering the defense. The besieged city fell two months later, however, and the continental troops were confined in fever-ridden prison ships, while the officers were imprisoned at Haddrell's Point on Sullivan's Island. Offered a parole, Hogun refused, choosing instead to share the privations and hardships of his fellow officers. His health declined in prison, and he died at Haddrell's Point, where he was buried in an unmarked grave.

One of only five general officers of the continental line from North Carolina, Hogun has been characterized by historian Hugh F. Rankin as "competent and reliable, although not a spectacular officer." Possessing a strong sense of duty, Hogun successfully completed the many tasks delegated to him throughout the war. He was also a skilled administrator and an effective field and combat commander. His final sacrifice exhibited moral courage and devotion to the revolutionary cause.

• None of Hogun's personal papers have survived, but his official correspondence and related documents are in William L. Saunders, ed., *The Colonial Records of North Carolina*, vols. 9 and 10 (1890), and Walter J. Clark, ed., *The State Records of North Carolina*, vols. 11–22 (1896–1907). An earlier sketch by Clark is in *The Biographical History of North Carolina*, ed. Samuel A. Ashe, vol. 4 (1906), pp. 196–202, but a more complete sketch is by Hugh F. Rankin in *Dictionary of North Carolina Biography*, ed. William S. Powell, vol. 3 (1988), pp. 163–64. Also useful for Hogun's revolutionary activities is Hugh F. Rankin, *The North Carolina Continentals* (1971).

LINDLEY S. BUTLER

HOHFELD, Wesley Newcomb (8 Aug. 1879–21 Oct. 1918), law professor, was born in Oakland, California, the son of Edward Hohfeld, a piano teacher and German immigrant, and Rosalie Hillebrand. He studied at the University of California, from which he graduated in 1901 with a gold medal for the achievement of the highest possible grade in every course. He entered Harvard Law School in 1901 and received an LL.B. cum laude in 1904. For a short period he assisted John Chipman Gray, law professor and legal philosopher, from whom he may have acquired his respect for the theory of American legal realism, before he was admitted to the bar of California in 1904 and began practice in the San Francisco law offices of Morrison, Cope and Brobeck. Choosing the academic life, he joined the law faculty of Stanford University as an instructor in 1905 and resigned as a full professor in 1914. During that period he also taught law and jurisprudence in the summer sessions of such distinguished universities as California, Chicago, Columbia, and Michigan. In 1914 he moved to the Yale Law School, where he held the position of Southmayd Professor of Law at the time of his death.

Hohfeld was an exceptional teacher of law, especially effective with the best students but often disliked by the mediocre ones. Although he insisted that his students master his conceptual framework, he did not lecture to them or make any attempt to explain to them in simple terms or graceful sentences his own understanding of the law. Instead he asked question after question, demanding that they identify and resolve the most difficult of legal issues posed by actual and hypothetical cases. Relentlessly, he led them to a deeper and more complex interpretation of the law. Although some students were immediately inspired by his teaching, several of those who resented his rigor and rigidity wrote to him years later to confess that they had found his conceptual analysis and intellectual discipline invaluable in their legal practices.

The breadth of Hohfeld's legal scholarship was remarkable. Between 1909 and 1917 he published thoroughly researched and incisive articles on corporate law, the conflict of laws, the law of trusts, and the relation between law and equity. At the time of his premature death at the age of thirty-nine, he was preparing to publish casebooks on trusts, the conflict of laws, and evidence. His intense energy, persistent industry, and immense memory undoubtedly contributed to this output.

As Hohfeld investigated various branches of the law, he detected confusing and misleading ambiguities in legal terminology. He declared that

one of the greatest hindrances to the clear understanding, the incisive statement, and the true solution of legal problems frequently arises from the express or tacit assumption that all legal relations may be reduced to "rights" and "duties," and that these latter categories are therefore adequate for the purpose of analyzing even the most complex legal interests, such as trusts, options, escrows, "future" interests, corporate interests, etc.

This conviction elicited his deep interest in analytical jurisprudence and led to his greatest contribution to legal theory, the two-part article "Fundamental Legal Conceptions as Applied in Judicial Reasoning" (*Yale Law Journal* [1913 and 1917]). This title reveals how thoroughly for Hohfeld the most abstract theory was related to the most practical applications in the pleading of lawyers and the decisions of judges.

Hohfeld showed by the meticulous examination of the language of lawyers, judges, and jurists how the expression "a right" was used indiscriminately to refer to a claim, a privilege, a power, and an immunity. Because each of these refers to a distinct legal relationship between two persons, each can just as well be viewed from the position of the second party. Hence, they logically imply the correlative legal positions of a duty, a no-right, a liability, and a disability, respectively. Together these eight fundamental legal conceptions constituted legal atoms through which all more complex legal situations could be analyzed. Such fundamental conceptions could not, according to Hohfeld, be defined. What he did do was to distinguish one from another, illustrate each with examples from the law, and reveal their relationships as logical correlatives or opposites. Although his initial purpose was to distinguish between very different legal relations that were often confused with one another, he also thought of these simple legal relations as lowest common denominators that would reveal fundamental similarities in apparently diverse legal situations and would permit illuminating generalizations about the legal system.

Hohfeld died of endocarditis brought on by a severe attack of the grippe in the home of his sister at Alameda, California. He never married, and although he enjoyed walking, music, and art, he lived almost entirely for his teaching, scholarship, and jurisprudence. Walter Wheeler Cook, who collected and edited Hohfeld's few articles for posthumous publication as books, wrote that Hohfeld's greatest message to the legal profession was "that an adequate analytical jurisprudence is an absolutely indispensable tool in the equipment of the properly trained lawyer or judge—indispensable, that is, for the highest efficiency in the discharge of the daily duties of his profession."

Gradually, practicing lawyers and legal scholars became acquainted with Hohfeld's terminology, and the

American Law Institute adopted his conceptual scheme for its restatements of several branches of the law. In jurisprudence, Karl Llewellyn's version of American legal realism and Albert Kocourek's theory of jural relations both owe much to Hohfeld. Herbert Hart, one of the most influential philosophers of law of the twentieth century, integrated Hohfeld's conceptions of claims, privileges, powers, and immunities into a general theory of legal rights. More recently Carl Wellman and Judith Jarvis Thomson have used Hohfeld's conceptions in formulating their theories of moral rights. As far away as Sweden, Stig Kanger and Lars Lindahl have developed highly complex formal logics of the law along Hohfeldian lines. Even the anthropologist E. Adamson Hoebel and the economist John R. Commons have employed his terminology in their work. Though Hohfeld died long before he could complete his contributions to legal scholarship and jurisprudence, his influence has had a lasting impact.

• Although no collected papers are available, the Yale University Law Library has notes of Hohfeld's lectures on partnership and suretyship. His articles are collected in *Fundamental Legal Conceptions and Other Legal Essays* (1923). For information about his life and work consult the editorial notes in the *California Law Review* 7 (Nov. 1918): 58–59, and the *Yale Law Journal* 28 (Dec. 1918 and June 1919): 166–68 and 795–98. There is also a useful entry in the *International Encyclopedia of the Social Sciences* (1932 ed.). His influence is most evident in Karl Llewellyn, *The Bramble Bush* (1930); Albert Kocourek, *Jural Relations* (1927); H. L. A. Hart, "Bentham on Legal Rights," in *Oxford Essays in Jurisprudence*, 2d series (1973); Carl Wellman, *A Theory of Rights* (1985); Judith Jarvis Thomson, *The Realm of Rights* (1990); Lars Lindahl, *Position and Change* (1977); E. Adamson Hoebel, *The Law of Primitive Man* (1954); and John R. Commons, *Legal Foundations of Capitalism*, (1924). An obituary is in the *San Francisco Chronicle*, 22 Oct. 1918.

CARL WELLMAN

HOKE, Robert Frederick (27 May 1837–3 July 1912), Confederate soldier, was born in Lincolnton, North Carolina, the son of Michael Hoke, a lawyer and politician, and Frances Burton. His father's early death prompted Robert, at seventeen, to curtail his studies at the Kentucky Military Institute and take over his family's manufacturing interests, which included a cotton mill and an iron foundry. His military training, however brief, stood him in good stead when his state reluctantly left the Union in May 1861. Hoke entered Confederate service as second lieutenant of Company K, First North Carolina Infantry. Soon after his regiment was dispatched to Virginia, he fought as a captain at Big Bethel, 10 June, where Colonel (later lieutenant general) D. H. Hill cited his "coolness, judgment, and efficiency."

Hoke returned to his home state early in 1862 as lieutenant colonel of the Thirty-third North Carolina, which he led in the fighting around New Bern, 14 March. Observing Hoke's outfit as it turned back a Yankee advance, its division leader marveled that "it moved into action with as much promptness and steadiness as I ever saw in its ranks on dress parade and its fire was terrific." After shuttling back to Robert E. Lee's Army of Northern Virginia, Hoke displayed his customary aggressiveness in the Seven Days battles, especially at Glendale (30 June), where the Thirty-third North Carolina charged across open ground to silence a bank of artillery and scatter its infantry support. Two months later, at Second Manassas, Hoke again led his Tar Heels in a headlong charge that "drove the enemy back in disorder." In his final battle in regimental command, Sharpsburg (Antietam, 17 Sept.), he helped the division of Major General A. P. Hill save Lee's right flank by repulsing Federals trying to cross Antietam Creek.

For his repeated heroics, Hoke received the three stars of a colonel and command of the Twenty-first North Carolina Infantry in Brigadier General Isaac R. Trimble's brigade of Major General Jubal Early's division. Entrusted with the entire brigade at Fredericksburg, on that field Hoke turned in perhaps his finest performance at any level of command. Counterattacking across the railroad to Richmond on the morning of 13 December, he helped relieve the pressure being exerted on Lee's right flank. Not content with this achievement, Hoke defiantly held an advanced position for an extended period. By the time he fell back, his men had killed or wounded 200 Yankees and captured another 300 while suffering lightly in return. On 19 January 1863 Lee rewarded Hoke by naming him a brigadier general and permanent successor to the wounded and recently promoted Trimble.

Two months later Hoke once again was sent home, this time to curb the disaffection spreading through outlying parts of North Carolina. Large, lawless bands—mostly deserters from the Confederate army and fugitives from conscription—were terrorizing secessionist and unionist citizens alike. Hoke dispersed some of these groups, executed a few deserters, returned others to the army, and confiscated or destroyed the property of still other criminals. He then rejoined Early's division in time for the Chancellorsville campaign. On 3 May 1863, during the second battle of Marye's Heights, Hoke admirably protected the Confederate right center. The following day, at Salem Church, Early's command helped shove a large part of the Army of the Potomac back across the Rappahannock River. During the final Confederate advance, however, part of Hoke's brigade became entangled with the troops of Brigadier General Harry T. Hays, a mistake blamed on Hays. Trying to restore the marching alignment, Hoke exposed himself to enemy fire and received a painful wound in the arm.

Hoke's recuperation combined with War Department priorities to deny Lee the services of his hard-driving subordinate for over a year. Sent to Lincolnton on convalescent leave, Hoke recovered sufficiently to take command of a detachment from his brigade that Secretary of War James A. Seddon sent to him. At its head, Hoke helped local commanders neutralize threats to the state's western defenses. Afterward, he recruited for his brigade while trying unsuccessfully to rid central North Carolina of the same disaffected elements he had opposed the year before.

In January 1864 Hoke, joined now by the rest of his command, reported to Major General George E. Pickett at Petersburg, Virginia. Under Pickett's orders he advanced against the Union garrison at New Bern, but the operation failed through a lack of cooperation by troops sent to support him. Ten weeks later, however, Hoke was given a free hand to operate against the equally strategic garrison at Plymouth, North Carolina, on the south bank of the Roanoke River. Backed by two other brigades and the ironclad ram *Albemarle*, Hoke on 21 April forced the surrender of Brigadier General Henry W. Wessells and his 2,800 men. For this dramatic triumph, he received wide acclaim, the thanks of the Confederate Congress, and a major generalship.

Early in May Hoke advanced yet again on New Bern, but he was recalled to Petersburg before he was able to launch an all-out assault. From Petersburg he was dispatched on 10 May to Drewry's Bluff, south of Richmond, to block a major Union effort against the capital. On the sixteenth Hoke's troops and other forces under the overall command of General Pierre G. T. Beauregard mounted a two-pronged assault against the larger but less formidable Army of the James. Though Hoke failed to strike with his usual vigor, he pressed the Federals' left flank and center hard enough to force them to retreat to Bermuda Hundred, six miles to the southeast.

The threat to Richmond countered, Hoke was sent to join Lee's army for the first time since Chancellorsville. The reunion marked the onset of a trying time for the North Carolinian. On 1 June, the first day at Cold Harbor, he failed to provide timely support to the corps of Lieutenant General Richard H. Anderson; the result was a Confederate setback. He redeemed himself after returning to Petersburg to stymie a 15 June attack by the Armies of the Potomac and James. Thereafter, however, Hoke's troubles resumed. On 24 June his division botched an attack against the far Union left at Petersburg. Following the loss of Fort Harrison, below Richmond, 29 September, Hoke's command failed in three attempts to retake the work, the third time breaking for cover in unseemly haste. On 7 October Hoke unaccountably disregarded orders to advance against a captured sector of Richmond's outer defenses.

Late in December Hoke returned to North Carolina yet again, this time at the head of 6,000 troops. By Christmas Day his division was positioned to threaten the ability of a Union expedition to capture Fort Fisher, guardian of the strategic port of Wilmington. The potential that Hoke's force represented was wasted when his indecisive superior, Braxton Bragg, twice countermanded orders to strike the rear of the enemy line.

A frustrated Hoke completed his war career by trying to stop William T. Sherman's march through his state. After a last-ditch effort failed at Bentonville, 19–21 March 1865, Hoke disbanded his command, advising his veterans to cherish "the love of liberty which led you into the contest [and which] burns as brightly in your hearts as ever." In civilian life he endured the trials of Reconstruction, including initial postwar poverty and the perceived oppression of carpetbagger politicians and federal occupation troops. He also managed two iron mines and served as director of the North Carolina Railroad. In 1869 he married Lydia Van Wyck; they had six children. He died in Raleigh, North Carolina.

For the first three years of the war, Hoke was one of the most consistent field commanders in the Confederate army in the East. Whether fighting in Virginia or in his native state, he displayed courage, poise, self-confidence, and what Douglas Southall Freeman calls "a certain ferocious quality of leadership." Virtually all of his superiors considered him a tremendous asset; one local historian even claimed that Hoke was Lee's choice to succeed him as commander of the Army of Northern Virginia.

Hoke's succession of inadequate performances in 1864 lowers somewhat his standing in the Confederate pantheon. While he excelled in subordinate command as regimental and brigade leader, and although he performed brilliantly in an independent capacity at Plymouth, he appeared unsuited to the middle level of command, a position he held at Cold Harbor, Petersburg, and Richmond. Freeman suggests that Hoke's deficiencies on this level stemmed from an innate inability to cooperate with other middle-echelon commanders. There may be another reason for his poor showing in 1864. The downturn in Hoke's fortunes coincided with his return to Lee after a second, losing effort at curbing dissent and disloyalty back home. After that painful experience, Hoke's ability to command may have been undermined by his growing perception that the Confederacy was being destroyed from within as well as from without, that its overthrow by one force or the other was a question of time.

• The Robert F. Hoke Papers in the Southern Historical Collection at the University of North Carolina consist of eighty-some items relating to Hoke's postwar business career. Some of his wartime correspondence can be found in the Robert E. Lee Papers at the Virginia Historical Society; the Braxton Bragg Papers, Western Reserve Historical Society; and the Lawrence O'Brian Branch Papers, North Carolina State Department of Archives and History. Douglas Southall Freeman devotes considerable coverage to Hoke's career in the first two volumes of his trilogy, *Lee's Lieutenants: A Study in Command* (1942–1944), while a detailed biography can be found in Clement A. Evans, ed., *Confederate Military History*, vol. 4 (1899). For information on the two regiments Hoke commanded, see Walter Clark, *Histories of the Several Regiments and Battalions from North Carolina in the Great War, 1861–'65* (1901). Campaigns in which Hoke figured prominently are covered in John G. Barrett, *The Civil War in North Carolina* (1963); Richard J. Sommers, *Richmond Redeemed: The Siege at Petersburg* (1981); William Glenn Robertson, *Back Door to Richmond: The Bermuda Hundred Campaign, April–June 1864* (1987); and Rod Gragg, *Confederate Goliath: The Battle of Fort Fisher* (1991). For miscellany relating to

Hoke, see W. Buck Yearns and Barrett, eds., *North Carolina Civil War Documentary* (1980). An obituary is in the *New York Times*, 4 July 1912.

EDWARD G. LONGACRE

HOKINSON, Helen (29 June 1893–1 Nov. 1949), cartoonist, was born Helen Elna Hokinson in Mendota, Illinois, the daughter of Adolph Hokinson (original Swedish spelling, Haakonson), a farm machinery salesman, and Mary Wilcox. Helen attended the public schools in Mendota, and a year after graduating high school in 1913, she enrolled in a two-year course at the Chicago Academy of Fine Arts, studying fashion illustration and design. After completing her studies, she shared a studio with another artist, Alice Harvey, and secured assignments with art service agencies and department stores in Chicago. In 1920 Hokinson moved to New York to pursue a career as a fashion illustrator.

Harvey joined Hokinson in New York in 1921, and they took rooms together at the Smith College Club. Hokinson did work for such Manhattan establishments as Lord and Taylor, B. Altman and Company, and John Wanamaker; Harvey did cartoons for the humor magazine *Life*. The two also did a short-lived comic strip called "Sylvia in the Big City" for the *New York Daily Mirror*. In 1924 they took a course at the School of Fine and Applied Arts (Parson School), where Hokinson learned the Jay Hambidge theory of dynamic symmetry under Howard Giles. Giles recognized Hokinson's talent for depicting realistically and humorously the ordinary people she saw around her, and he encouraged her to concentrate on this kind of artwork. Urged by her fellow students, Hokinson submitted a drawing to a new magazine that had been launched in February 1925. When the *New Yorker* published it in the issue dated 4 July 1925, Hokinson's lifelong association with the magazine began. Thereafter, nearly every issue of the *New Yorker* until 1950 carried at least one of Hokinson's pictures.

At first, Hokinson's drawings appeared as humorous illustrations without captions. She was frequently sent as a visual reporter to cover such events as circuses, flower shows, first nights at the opera, and the like. Eventually, her editors began to caption her drawings, and they also suggested situations for her to draw. Then, in 1931, she met a *New Yorker* writer named James Reid Parker, with whom she collaborated for the next eighteen years, Parker devising situations and supplying captions for most of her drawings. For several years, they met every Friday afternoon and evening to discuss ideas; when Parker began traveling extensively in 1938, they communicated by daily postcard but resumed the Friday sessions when Parker was in the city. After he married, his wife joined them for dinner every Friday. About their partnership, critic John Mason Brown wrote, "Theirs was the happiest of collaborations. Without any of the frictions of the lords of the Savoy, they found themselves as perfectly matched as Gilbert and Sullivan. If Miss Hokinson's was the seeing eye, Mr. Parker's was the hearing ear."

Parker persuaded Hokinson to concentrate their efforts on depicting the preoccupations and enthusiasms of the somewhat matronly suburban women of the upper middle class. Working with the gray tones of a wash and a simple line, Hokinson drew dumpling-plump ladies with double chins (or no chins), perky noses, and tiny feet dressed in modified Queen Mary fashions. The artist became famous for the "Hokinson women" who filled their otherwise apparently idle hours with club meetings, community theatricals, gardening, shopping in bookstores, and visits to the beauty salon and flower and pet shows. As she and Parker portrayed them, these women were determinedly young at heart, eager to keep abreast of trends in thought and fashion, anxious enough about their weight to diet occasionally but not enough to give up desserts, and just a little puzzled by modern life.

The comedy with such characters arises from the juxtaposition of their perpetual (though not at all fanatic) concern for status and propriety with their naïveté. In a liquor store, one of Hokinson's women says, "What would you suggest for a small group of ladies who meet every Tuesday to do needlepoint?" She knows that a wine should be appropriate to the occasion but doesn't realize what constitutes an occasion worthy of wine. Another such woman reveals, as she shops for her husband, that her comprehension of deer hunting is limited mostly to appearances when she says to the salesclerk, "I want to surprise my husband with one of those little red caps that lure deer." As club women—women of dedication and purpose—Hokinson's ladies display the same charming innocence of practicality. One of them arises at a meeting to announce, "I'm sorry, Madam President, there won't be any treasurer's report this month because we have a deficit."

Although her women appeared slightly befuddled, Hokinson never ridiculed her creations for their inability to grasp the utilitarian world. She loved women of the sort she portrayed and even (she said) agreed with much that they represented. Her compassionate identification with them is displayed in cartoons like the one in which a package-laden lady shopper pauses at a beauty salon to inquire, "Have you a treatment that includes lying down?"

Hokinson's humor was gentle and affectionate; portraiture, not satire, was her objective. And the picture that she (and Parker) painted of her women showed them to be very human. In John Mason Brown's view, "They were worldlings whom neither time nor exposure could make worldly. Foolish and self-indulgent as they were, pretense was never one of their follies, [and] they were never guilty of meanness. They were a friendly breed. This explains why they made so many friends. Miss Hokinson's fondness for them was transparent and contagious. Hers was the rarest of gifts. She had no contempt for human failings. She approached foibles with affection."

Hokinson, who never married, maintained an apartment in New York City and a house in Connecticut (first in Silvermine, then in Wilton), where she spent the summers, sharing both initially with an eld-erly Canadian woman named Henderson (first name unknown). Although she was quite shy and self-effac-ing, in later years she undertook a public-appearance crusade to explain her work because she was afraid people were laughing at her "girls" rather than with them. She was en route to one such appearance in Washington, D.C., when the airliner in which she was traveling collided with another aircraft and crashed, killing all fifty-five of its passengers.

• Hokinson's cartoons have been collected in six volumes, *So You're Going to Buy a Book!* (1931), *My Best Girls* (1941), *When Were You Built?* (1948), *The Ladies, God Bless 'Em!* (1950), *There Are Ladies Present* (1952), and *The Hokinson Festival* (1956), which mined the previous volumes for its contents. For *Who's Who in America*, Helen Hokinson sup-plied just the street address of her Manhattan apartment. The details of her life are published only in two affectionate essays written by John Reid Parker, one for the *Dictionary of Ameri-can Biography*, the other as the introduction to the 1950 col-lection of her cartoons. An appreciation of her work by John Mason Brown appears in the *Saturday Review of Literature*, 10 Dec. 1949; another, by Dale Kramer, in the *Saturday Eve-ning Post*, 7 Apr. 1951, rehearses her life story.

ROBERT C. HARVEY

HOLABIRD, William (11 Sept. 1854–19 July 1923), ar-chitect, was born in Amenia Union, New York, the son of Samuel Beckley Holabird, an officer in the U.S. Army, and Mary Theodosia Grant. Because of his fa-ther's military profession, Holabird spent his child-hood years in a variety of United States cities. He grad-uated from high school in St. Paul, Minnesota, in 1871. Intending to embark on a career in the military himself, he entered the U.S. Military Academy at West Point in 1873. He resigned in 1875, however, following an incident in which he was accused of a breach of camp regulations when he aided a sick friend. That year he moved to Chicago, where his fa-ther was then quartermaster colonel. Shortly after his move Holabird married Maria Ford Augur; they had six children.

Once settled in Chicago, Holabird began working for the Quartermaster Corps. Soon afterward, howev-er, he obtained a job as a draftsman for William Le Baron Jenney. Jenney headed an influential architec-tural firm that pioneered iron and steel frame con-struction and fireproofing techniques for commercial buildings in the decades following the great Chicago fire in 1871. Holabird was one of the many young, am-bitious architects Jenney employed; others were Louis Sullivan, Martin Roche, and Daniel Burnham. In Jen-ney's firm Holabird received invaluable practical training and acquired a pragmatic approach to design. During his first few years in Chicago, Holabird also worked briefly as a draftsman for the architectural firm of Burnham and Root.

In 1880 Holabird started his own architectural firm with Ossian Cole Simonds, a landscape gardener he knew from Jenney's office. One year later Roche, also a former colleague from Jenney's office, joined the firm, which became known as Holabird, Simonds and Roche. The fledgling firm received few commissions in its early years, the most notable involving the design of small buildings for Graceland Cemetery (c. 1881–1883). In 1883 Simonds left the firm to pursue a career in landscape architecture, and the partnership became officially known as Holabird and Roche—the name it retained until 1927. The final partnership proved a well-suited match; Holabird's background in engi-neering melded well with Roche's predilection for ar-tistic design and decoration. John A. Holabird, Jr., (William's grandson), contrasted their two sensibili-ties: whereas Holabird was the "engineer-manager-bon vivant," Roche was the "caring artist, designer, thoughtful one" (Blaser, p. 180).

Most of the early commissions Holabird and Roche received were for houses and small apartment build-ings. Their breakthrough commission came in 1886, when they were chosen to design the twelve-story Ta-coma Building (1886–1889, demolished 1929). Struc-turally the Tacoma was one of the most advanced buildings of its day because it utilized a fully riveted iron and steel frame for support. Equally as innova-tive, the Tacoma's street elevations clearly expressed the building's underlying skeleton structure. At the time the building established Holabird and Roche as two of the most prominent architects of commercial buildings in the Midwest. Later, architectural histori-ans claimed the Tacoma, with its emphasis on struc-ture and economy, as an important precedent for mod-ern architecture.

From 1890 until 1900 Holabird and Roche received numerous commissions for tall commercial buildings in the central business district of Chicago. Although both partners supervised all aspects of architectural commissions, as the firm grew larger, each took on distinct areas of responsibility. With his commanding physical presence and amiable personality, Holabird became the firm's "contact" man, who usually secured the commissions and oversaw the most important ele-ments of the buildings' conception and construction. Some of the buildings designed by Holabird and Roche during this period were the Pontiac Building (1884–1891), the Venetian Building (1891), the Mo-nadnock Building addition (1891–1893), the Old Col-ony (1893–1894), and the Ayer-McClurg Building (1898–1899). The most celebrated skyscraper Hola-bird and Roche designed in this period was the Mar-quette Building (1891–1895).

Around 1900 Holabird and Roche began to design different types and styles of buildings. Rather than the tall office buildings that had brought them acclaim, many of their later commissions were for public build-ings, department stores, universities, and hotels. The period from 1900 to 1920 is sometimes regarded as a less daring period for Holabird and Roche, since many of their buildings conveyed a somewhat eclectic inter-est in classical, Gothic, and beaux-arts architectural styles. However, these years were probably their most prolific and lucrative, and their commissions for large architectural projects proved Holabird and Roche capable of design on a grand scale. The firm was responsible for innovations in multi-level basement construction first used in their design for the Chicago Tribune Building (1901–1902). During this time they designed some of the most opulent hotels in the Midwest, including Chicago's Congress Hotel (1901–1902) and Hotel LaSalle (1907–1909, no longer standing). One of the most important commissions that Holabird supervised is undoubtedly the Cook County Court House-City of Chicago Building (1904–1910). The monumental structure, with its six-story Corinthian columns, occupies one full city block in downtown Chicago and successfully combines practical planning and architectural grandeur.

By 1918 John Wellborn Root, Jr., and Holabird's son John Augur Holabird, the next generation of architects to lead the firm, were playing a larger role in its operations. In the last years of his life Holabird decreased his participation in the firm because of poor health. He died in Evanston, Illinois.

Holabird was an important practitioner of post–Civil War American architecture. He is regarded as a key figure in the "Chicago school," a term used to describe architects who designed buildings that emphasized functionality. As a founding partner of the firm Holabird and Roche, he participated in one of the most successful and enduring collaborations in the history of Chicago architecture. From 1883 to 1923 Holabird and Roche were responsible for more than seventy buildings in the central area of Chicago and therefore shaped the city's landscape as few other architectural firms could.

• The Chicago Historical Society has the business correspondence, drawings, and other documents from the firm Holabird and Roche-Holabird and Root (1880–1940). For detailed information about specific commissions see Robert Bruegmann, *Holabird and Roche, Holabird and Root: An Illustrated Catalog of Works* (2 vols., 1991); and Bruegmann, *The Architects and the City: Holafield and Roche of Chicago, 1880–1918* (1997). See Werner Blaser, *Chicago Architecture: Holabird and Root: 1880–1992* (1992); and Carl Condit, *The Chicago School of Architecture: A History of Commercial and Public Building in the Chicago Area, 1875–1925* (1964) for information about the Holabird and Roche firm within the context of Chicago architecture. For further bibliographical references see William Rudd, "Holabird and Roche: Chicago Architects," American Association of Architectural Bibliographers *Papers* 2 (1966): 53–80. Obituaries are in the *Chicago Daily Tribune* and the *Chicago Daily News*, 20 July 1923.

KAREN L. CARTER

HOLBORN, Hajo Ludwig Rudolph (18 May 1902–20 June 1969), historian and government adviser, was born in Berlin, the son of Ludwig Rudolph Holborn, a physicist and director of an imperial research institute, and Helene Bussmann. Enjoying a rapid rise in the academic world, he earned his doctorate in 1924 under Friedrich Meinecke in Berlin, began lecturing at the University of Heidelberg in 1926, and in 1931 received the first permanent appointment to the Carnegie Chair

for History and International Relations at the Deutsche Hochschule für Politik in Berlin, where he also lectured at the university.

Holborn established his reputation early with two articles on Bismarck's relations with Russia published in 1924, which he enlarged as a book with appended documents in 1925 (*Bismarcks europäische Politik zu Beginn der siebziger Jahre und die Mission Radowitz*), and with a short book, published in 1926, on Germany's relationship with Turkey (*Deutschland und die Türkei 1878–1890*). His next book, on Ulrich von Hutten (1929), demonstrated the breadth of his learning; in it he analyzed the distinction between the legacies of humanism and the Reformation. In 1926 he married fellow student Annemarie Bettmann; they had two children. In 1933 they collaborated in editing selected works by Erasmus. While still in Germany, Holborn also published articles on the Weimar constitution (a project for which he was commissioned), reparations, the covenant of the League of Nations, and the German historical profession, of whose insularity he was sharply critical. At the same time he became known as an active supporter—unusual among professional historians—of Germany's democratic republic and as an outspoken critic of Nazism.

Emigrating soon after Hitler's accession, Holborn spent six months in London before he moved in February 1934 to the United States, where his wife and children joined him late in the same year. In the fall of 1934 he began a visiting appointment as assistant professor at Yale, which became his permanent professional home. He was made associate professor in 1938 and full professor in 1940; from 1936 to 1942 he taught concurrently at Yale and at the Fletcher School of Law and Diplomacy. He became a U.S. citizen early in 1940.

During World War II Holborn took leave of absence from Yale to serve in the Research and Analysis Branch of the Office of Strategic Services (1943–1945), where he helped plan the postwar administration of Germany. During these years he also sat on the board of editors of the *Journal of Modern History*. After his return to Yale he advised the State Department on German and European affairs from 1946 to 1948, and in 1947 he published *American Military Government: Its Organization and Policies*. Thus, as consultant and scholar he fulfilled an earlier commitment to himself to become involved politically in behalf of democratic values and simultaneously served the land of his birth.

Despite persistent urging, most notably by his former mentor and friend Meinecke, Holborn firmly declined invitations to university positions in postwar Germany. Having adapted well to life in America and at Yale, he became Townsend Professor in 1946 and Sterling Professor in 1959, and eventually supervised fifty-five doctoral dissertations. Over the years he held visiting appointments at Harvard, Stanford, and Columbia, and twice held semester-long Fulbright grants for teaching in Europe (Vienna in 1954; Bonn and Cologne in 1966). He also gave numerous lectures in various settings in Germany and sought through scholarly avenues and institutional connections "to bring Germany and the Western nations together, not for the purposes of a cold war but in the interests of a common and all-inclusive *humanitas*," which was inspired by his studies of the Enlightenment and of "cosmopolitan classicism" (Hans Kohn's review, p. 146).

Soon after the war he became a member of the international advisory committee charged with editing for publication the captured German documents, which began appearing in 1949 as *Documents on German Foreign Policy, 1918–1945*; in 1963 he assumed the American editorship of the project. In 1960, after having served as unofficial mediator between Bonn and Washington for many years, he became director of the American Council on Germany. The following year he organized a colloquium in Munich that brought together scholars in the social sciences from Yale and German universities for discussions that were intended to strengthen understanding of and support for democracy in Germany. He was also a member of the Council on Foreign Relations from 1947 until his death.

Holborn's steady stream of publications contributed to transatlantic understanding as well as to historical scholarship. In 1951 he published *The Political Collapse of Europe*, which was translated into most European languages and became a standard interpretation. His magnum opus, the balanced and sober, three-volume *History of Modern Germany* (1959, 1964, 1969), stands out as a monument to wisdom and breadth of learning. Lamenting, among other things, the triumph of aggressive nationalism and selfish conservatism under Bismarck, Holborn demonstrated that Nazism had organic roots in German history, without, however, contending that Hitler's tyranny was inevitable. Holborn also published articles and reviews in such journals as the *American Historical Review*, the *Journal of the History of Ideas*, and the *Political Science Quarterly*.

Honors filled the last years of Holborn's life. In 1960 he received the Federal Republic of Germany's Commander's Cross of the Order of Merit. In 1967 twenty-four eminent scholars—friends and former students—presented him with the festschrift *The Responsibility of Power: Historical Essays in Honor of Hajo Holborn* (ed. Leonard Krieger and Fritz Stern). Also during 1967 he served as president of the American Historical Association, one of few scholars born and trained abroad ever to hold the post. He devoted his presidential address to a commentary on the history of ideas, the concluding paragraph of which might be seen as representative of his thought:

It is the task of history to recognize man in time. Only through history are we able to transcend the limitations of our own station in time and space and become aware of our full potentialities. But this requires placing man in the midst of his total social environment, from which we shall learn about his civilizing strength and weakness. Aiming at the highest historical truth we shall for-

tify our courage to be free. (*American Historical Review* 73 [Feb. 1968]: 695)

On 19 June 1969, in a moving ceremony at Bad Godesberg, the ill Holborn became the first recipient of the German Inter Nationes Prize, "bestowed . . . in grateful recognition of his services towards international understanding." A few hours after the presentation, at which he stated that the "question of the relation between law and power has occupied me throughout my career," he died peacefully in his sleep.

Noteworthy for the wide scope and depth of his learning and for his dedication to reconciliation between his adopted America and the Federal Republic, Holborn was one of the most highly acclaimed of the historians who left Germany during the 1930s. Those who knew him best emphasized the universal humanism and the underlying integrity that marked his many contributions to the understanding of history. His academic legacy lived on, not only in his students and publications, but also in his progeny: his daughter, historian Hanna H. Gray, became president of the University of Chicago in 1978.

• The Holborn Papers are in the Sterling Memorial Library at Yale. Two collections of previously published material appeared posthumously: *Germany and Europe: Historical Essays* (1970) and *History and the Humanities*, ed. Leonard Krieger (1972). His *Republic to Reich: The Making of the Nazi Revolution*, trans. Ralph Manheim (1972), is a collection of articles published by German scholars between 1953 and 1964 that Holborn had prepared for publication and for which he wrote an introduction. *Hajo Holborn: Inter Nationes Prize 1969* (1969) contains a biographical outline, a selected list of his writings, several previously published articles, and many encomiums. *Central European History* 3, nos. 1–2 (1970), is a double issue devoted to his memory; it contains "A Memoir" by Felix Gilbert, "Reminiscences" by Dietrich Gerhard, John L. Snell's commemoration of Holborn as teacher and colleague, and Hans Kohn's commentary on the three-volume *History of Modern Germany*. See also Otto Pflanze, "The Americanization of Hajo Holborn," in *An Interrupted Past: German-Speaking Refugee Historians in the United States after 1933*, ed. Hartmut Lehmann and James J. Sheehan (1991), pp. 170–79, and Lewis Coser, *Refugee Scholars in America* (1984). An obituary and encomium by Leonard Krieger is in *American Historical Review*, 73, no. 1 (1969): 333–36.

C. EARL EDMONDSON

HOLBROOK, James (1812–28 Apr. 1864), postal official and journalist, was born in Boston, Massachusetts, the son of unknown parents. Holbrook grew up in Boston, where he was apprenticed to a printer. In 1833, he moved to Connecticut, where he worked as a newspaper editor and in that year married Mary Baker Tyler. He and Tyler had four children. He edited the *Windham County Advertiser* between 1833 and 1835 and between 1835 and 1838, the *Norwich Aurora*. In 1840 he established the *Hartford State Eagle*, which was renamed the *Patriot and Eagle* in 1841.

Holbrook's editorial work landed him clerkships in the general land office and the Boston Custom House, presumably because of his gift for partisan invective. After the victory of James K. Polk in the presidential election of 1844, he won a coveted special agency in the Post Office Department, then the largest organization in the country. Holbrook remained a special agent from 1845 until his death.

Holbrook's appointment was probably a reward for work in Polk's presidential campaign. Holbrook was a Democrat, and special agencies were political plums. Once in office, however, Holbrook cultivated a reputation for nonpartisanship, opposed politically motivated dismissals, and quickly emerged as a leading student of postal procedure. His specialty was the detection of postal officials who had stolen money from the mail. His services were much in demand, since, in this period, merchants routinely enclosed banknotes worth thousands of dollars in ordinary letters. For some postal officials, the temptation to steal these banknotes proved irresistible. To apprehend the guilty parties, Holbrook relied on various techniques, including the mailing of special "decoy letters" containing marked bills. This technique proved so effective, Holbrook boasted, the postal officials soon came to regard *every* oversized envelope as a "sort of Trojan Horse, filled with elements of destruction, ready to overwhelm the explorer of its treacherous recesses" (*Ten Years*, p. 410).

Holbrook described some of his most celebrated official exploits in *Ten Years among the Mail Bags*, a highly melodramatic yet basically factual memoir that he published in 1855. *Ten Years* combined humor and anecdote with didacticism, social criticism, and a keen appreciation of the literary potential of his theme. The mailbag, Holbrook declared in his introduction, is an "epitome of human life," while "the same may be said of the Post-Office system at large, interwoven as it is with the whole social life of civilized man" (*Ten Years*, pp. 3, 5). According to a leading historian of public administration, *Ten Years* deserves to be remembered as the first autobiographical account of a mid-level public officer to have been published in the United States (White, p. 277). It was almost certainly influenced by *Two Years before the Mast* (1840), by Richard Henry Dana, Jr., for it furnished the inspiration for Holbrook's title and was one of the few earlier American works to dignify such a seemingly prosaic occupation with a literary gloss.

Though Holbrook insisted that special agents were more than "mere 'detective officers'" his memoir had much in common with the detective story, which was emerging as a distinct genre at about the same time (*Ten Years*, p. 411). Indeed, Holbrook's literary personae—secretive, observant, and skillful in exploiting the foibles of human nature—plainly anticipated such well-known twentieth-century stock figures as the private eye.

Holbrook's preoccupation with theft stemmed from his distinctive understanding of American law. A principled champion of individual rights, Holbrook considered the unauthorized opening of letters to be unconstitutional even if no theft were involved. The American government, Holbrook maintained, had an obligation to protect not only an individual's life and "material property" but also the "privacy of his thoughts." After all, Holbrook added, in one of his most memorable passages, "Silence is as great a privilege as speech" (*Ten Years*, p. 6).

Holbrook returned to popular journalism in October 1860 with the launching of the *United States Mail and Post-Office Assistant*, a semiofficial monthly magazine for postal officers that combined official announcements and practical advice with short stories, anecdotes, and postal trivia. The *United States Mail* has the distinction of being the second journal to have been published in the United States that was devoted exclusively to contemporary problems in public administration. (The first was the *United States Postal Guide and Official Advertiser*, which ran from 1850 to 1852.) "The basis of social life is the interchange of thought"—Holbrook declared, in explaining its rationale—"and whatever concerns its free and ready transmission is of vital importance to the well being of the nation as well as the individual. We have inherited the privilege of free speech, but have reached only by a gradual process that degree of perfection in the transmission of intelligence which is secured by our present Postal System" (*United States Mail*, Oct. 1860).

Holbrook died in Brooklyn, Connecticut, after a long illness. Postmaster General Montgomery Blair eulogized him as "a noble example of a public officer whose zeal for the service did not abate by the length of his term, and who made the public interests his primary object" (*United States Mail*, June 1864).

• No collection of Holbrook's papers is known to exist. His *Ten Years among the Mail Bags; or, Notes from the Diary of a Special Agent of the Post-Office Department* (1855) was frequently reprinted in Holbrook's lifetime; one edition was published as late as 1888. All quotations are from the 1874 edition. The *United States Mail and Post-Office Assistant* began publication in October 1860 and continued until at least May 1876. In 1985 the first twelve volumes were reprinted by Michael Laurence. On Holbrook's work as a special agent, see Richard R. John, *Spreading the News: The American Postal System from Franklin to Morse* (1995). See also Leonard D. White, *The Jacksonians: A Study in Administrative History, 1829–1861* (1954). Obituaries are in the *United States Mail* 4 (May–June 1864) and the *New York Times*, 30 Apr. 1864.

RICHARD R. JOHN

HOLBROOK, John Edwards (30 Dec. 1794–8 Sept. 1871), physician and naturalist, was born in Beaufort, South Carolina, the son of Silas Holbrook, a teacher, and Mary Edwards. Although he lived in South Carolina for at least the first two years of his life, Holbrook grew up in North Wrentham (later incorporated into Norfolk), Massachusetts, the original home of his father, who died in 1800, and his uncle and, later, stepfather, Daniel Holbrook. After receiving his preparatory education locally at Day's Academy and from a tutor in a neighboring town, he enrolled in Brown University, from which he received his baccalaureate in 1815. Holbrook then studied briefly with a physician in Boston and later entered the medical program of the University of Pennsylvania. Upon receiving his

M.D. in 1818 he went abroad and traveled extensively in Ireland and Great Britain, collecting botanical and mineral specimens, visiting hospitals, and, at the University of Edinburgh, attending lectures in medicine and natural history. He ended his tour in London in December 1819 and then went to the Continent to travel about Italy, Germany, and France. Holbrook spent considerable time at the Jardin des Plantes in Paris and became well-acquainted with a number of prominent naturalists, including Achille Valenciennes.

In 1822 Holbrook returned to the United States and soon settled in Charleston, South Carolina, to practice medicine. Two years later he accepted appointment as professor of anatomy at the newly established Medical College of South Carolina, where he readily earned a reputation for his excellence as a lecturer. Also continuing to practice medicine privately, he gained esteem for his gracious manner with patients. Despite his interest in anatomy, however, he shunned surgery. When a dispute arose in 1833 between the faculty of the Medical College and the controlling body, the Medical Society of South Carolina, over the issue of faculty governance, Holbrook apparently took no active role in the argument. He obviously disagreed with the Medical Society, however, for he joined the faculty of the new Medical College of the State of South Carolina when it opened in 1834. When he married Harriott Pinckney Rutledge in 1827, he assumed joint ownership of her numerous slaves and acquired a plantation located a few miles north of Charleston. He and his wife had no children.

Comparative anatomy especially fascinated Holbrook, and by the early 1820s he had developed a keen interest in fishes, reptiles, and amphibians. Within a few years he built a sizable collection of snakes, turtles, frogs, and salamanders, and he set about to produce a comprehensive work on the reptiles and amphibians east of the Mississippi River, which he titled *North American Herpetology*. Published in four volumes between 1836 and 1840, and in five volumes of a second edition in 1842, this work not only constituted the first comprehensive synthesis of American herpetology, but also contained original illustrations, the latter executed mostly from live specimens by skilled artists. Including twenty-five currently recognized new taxa, *North American Herpetology* gained notice in the United States and Europe, and in 1850 the able American naturalist Charles Girard declared that Holbrook was "the father of American herpetology." In his eulogy to Holbrook in 1871 the distinguished scientist Louis Agassiz said that Holbrook's "elaborate history of American herpetology was far above any previous work on the same subject." Even before the last volume of *North American Herpetology* appeared in print, Holbrook had begun a study of the fishes of southern coasts and rivers. In 1847 he published the first part of his *Southern Ichthyology; or, A Description of the Fishes Inhabiting the Waters of South Carolina, Georgia and Florida*, and during the next year he issued a second part. As he continued his work, however, he decided to restrict the scope of his study and changed the title to *Ichthyology of South Carolina*. In 1855–1857 several copies of the ten parts of that work were published in a complete volume, but, as a fire had destroyed the plates in 1855, before the publisher had pulled enough illustrations for additional copies of the volume, Holbrook had new, and in many cases more accurate, plates done, which appeared in the edition of 1860. In a review of that edition in the *American Journal of Science and Arts* in May 1864, Theodore Gill, a leading American ichthyologist, praised Holbrook for "his great zeal . . . and pains-taking endeavors to perfect his work," and he expressed the hope that Holbrook would be able to complete his study of South Carolina fishes in another volume. Meanwhile, Holbrook had published three other papers on fishes. Altogether, he established two new genera and eight new species of fishes.

A slave owner and a southern sympathizer, Holbrook deplored the work of the abolitionists and supported the decision of the southern states to secede from the Union in 1861. Although he spoke little on the subject of slavery, he shared the belief of his contemporaries that blacks were mentally inferior to whites, and he subscribed to the views of his good friend Agassiz and the Philadelphia craniologist Samuel George Morton that blacks represented a separate creation by God. But even during a highly publicized controversy over the subject of racial origins (1849–1855), Holbrook spoke about his views only among a circle of friends. Although he accepted the common view of his colleagues that natural phenomena were the work of the Divine Creator, he held unorthodox religious views, which he told zoologist John McCrady, he did not wish to discuss with anyone. Supportive of both charitable and cultural institutions, Holbrook was a patron of the Female Orphan Asylum and a founder of the South Carolina Historical Society.

Although he retired from the faculty of the Medical College in 1860, Holbrook served on a South Carolina board to examine surgeons during the Civil War. Widowed in 1863, Holbrook spent much of his time with relatives in Massachusetts after the war. For safekeeping, he had sent his personal library to Pendleton, South Carolina, late in the war, and he apparently never got all of it back. Holbrook was thus scientifically inactive after the Civil War, but he maintained his contact with prominent scientists, especially with Agassiz. In 1868 the National Academy of Sciences elected him to membership. He died at the home of a half sister in Norfolk, Massachusetts. In addition to the association of his name with the genera and species he established, Holbrook holds the honor of having his name attached to several taxa of amphibians, fishes, and reptiles described by other naturalists.

• The private papers of Holbrook are not abundant, but several of his letters can be found in the American Philosophical Society Library; the Library of the Academy of Natural Sciences of Philadelphia; the Houghton Library and the Museum of Comparative Zoology, Harvard University; the Smithsonian Institution Archives; the Boston Museum of Science; and, especially for his later years, the Harriott Horry Rutledge Ravenel Papers, South Carolina Historical Society. Holbrook's manuscript journal of travels in Ireland and Great Britain, 1818–1819, is in the South Caroliniana Library, University of South Carolina. Professor Kraig Adler of Cornell University holds an original Holbrook letter, and the private collections of Claire Holbrook Cowell and Bertram Holbrook Holland, collateral descendents of Holbrook, contain several Holbrook letters. Another important contribution by Holbrook is his "An Account of Several Species of Fishes Observed in Florida, Georgia, etc.," *Journal of the Academy of Natural Sciences of Philadelphia*, 3d ser., 1 (1855): 47–58. The diaries of John McCrady, 1869–1881, presently in possession of a McCrady descendent, contain a number of references to Holbrook. Louis Agassiz, "Dr. John E. Holbrook of Charleston, S.C.," *Proceedings of the Boston Society of Natural History* 14 (1872): 347–51, gives an indication of Holbrook's stature as a naturalist. Useful but not always reliable is the biographical sketch by Holbrook's former student Thomas Louis Ogier, *A Memoir of Dr. John Edwards Holbrook* (1871). A lengthier sketch is in Theodore Gill, "Biographical Memoir of John Edwards Holbrook, 1794–1871," *National Academy of Sciences: Biographical Memoirs* 5 (1905): 47–77. Especially valuable are the biographical and evaluative sketches by Kraig Adler: "Holbrook, John Edwards (1794–1871)," in *Contributions to the History of Herpetology*, vol. 5, ed. Kraig Adler (1989), and "New Genera and New Species Described in Holbrook's 'North American Herpetology'," in *North American Herpetology* (repr. 1976). Also useful in the same reprint edition is Richard D. Worthington and Patricia H. Worthington, "John Edwards Holbrook, Father of American Herpetology." Among the obituaries that typify Holbrook's standing are those in *Harper's Weekly Journal of Civilization*, 28 Oct. 1871, and the *Spectator*, 7 Oct. 1871.

LESTER D. STEPHENS

HOLBROOK, Stewart Hall (22 Aug. 1893–3 Sept. 1964), journalist and historian, was born in Newport, Vermont, the son of Jessie Holbrook, an itinerant businessman, and Kate Stewart. As a result of his father's frequent relocations, Stewart's childhood education was incomplete. He attended Colebrook Academy in New Hampshire but left without graduating when his family moved to Winnipeg, Manitoba, in 1911. Shortly thereafter, his father died, leaving Holbrook to find his own means of support. Pursuing latent interests in writing, he worked as a reporter for the Winnipeg *Daily Telegram*. To supplement his income Holbrook played semiprofessional baseball, performed plays with the Henry St. Clair Stock Company, and traveled throughout western Canada and Minnesota with Boris Karloff, another member of the company. In 1914 Holbrook returned to New England and worked in timber camps as a clerk and log scaler. During the First World War, he served in France as a first sergeant in the 303d Field Artillery.

By 1919 Holbrook was back in the logging camps. The following year, intrigued by stories of vast stands of timber in the Far West, he "bought a fine derby hat" and a round-trip ticket to Vancouver, British Columbia. Once there, Holbrook decided to remain in the Pacific Northwest. He worked at various timber jobs

on the Frazier River and began to write of life in the camps. In 1923, after selling a number of small pieces to regional newspapers and magazines, he broke into the national press with an article for *The Century*. Deciding to give up logging for writing, Holbrook "nailed his derby to a tree" and moved to Portland, Oregon. Between 1923 and 1934 he was a reporter, writer, and editor for the *Lumber News*, a Portland-based publication of the Loyal Legion of Loggers and Lumbermen. This position put him again in close contact with the working men and women of the forest as he traveled throughout Oregon and Washington gathering news and material for feature articles. On his own time, Holbrook continued to write for national publications such as *The Century*, *Saturday Evening Post*, and H. L. Mencken's *American Mercury*. In 1924 he married Katherine Stanton Gill; they had no children.

In 1934 Holbrook left the *Lumber News* and, with a small stipend from a regular column for the Portland *Oregonian*, determined to make it as a freelance writer. In 1935 he was commissioned by the federal Works Progress Administration to edit Oregon's *WPA Guide*. That same year he began writing his first book, published in 1938 as *Holy Old Mackinaw*. Conceived as a history of timber work in the United States, *Mackinaw* avoided business management and government policy issues and focused instead on loggers themselves and on their work methods, culture, and folklore. Holbrook consciously rejected the style and apparatus of scholarly writing and wrote instead for the common man, who, more often than not, was also his subject. Much of *Holy Old Mackinaw* was derived from his own forest experiences and those of loggers he had known. "Some of that tribe," he wrote, "were killed physically by civilization; as for others, civilization has mowed them down spiritually—removing the high, wild color from their lives, ironing flat their personalities, and reducing them to the status of proletarians" (p. 1). Issued during the Great Depression, *Holy Old Mackinaw* was a great success. It spent over five months on national bestseller lists and established Holbrook as a prominent literary figure. Concluding that the place for such a figure was not Portland, he took up residence in July 1938 in Cambridge, Massachusetts.

Over the next five years Holbrook produced another six books, all in the popular genre he proudly called "low-brow history." In 1943 he returned to Portland, where he would live and work for the rest of his life. There, he continued to produce a major work every two years on average, often on a Pacific Northwest subject. Published in 1950, *The Yankee Exodus* examined the role New Englanders had played in the settlement of the West and the Northwest. *The Far Corner* (1952) was Holbrook's personal account of the region. *The Columbia* (1956) was perhaps his best-known work on a regional subject. As always, whether dealing with regional or national subjects, Holbrook preferred to write about ordinary people. In *Lost Men of History* (1946) he pointedly ignored mainstream figures and wrote instead on "mavericks, malcontents, [and] unorthodox thinkers." In *Age of the Moguls* (1953), though, Holbrook retold the story of the great industrialists who "plundered and wasted" but nevertheless did much good. Far from being an apologist for ruthless robber barons, in *Dreamers of the American Dream* (1957) he included such anti-establishment radicals as the feminist Abigail Scott Duniway and socialist labor organizers as heirs to and examples of that dream. In spite of his "low-brow" pretensions, Holbrook's version of America was complex and multifaceted.

In 1947 Holbrook's wife died, and the following year he married Sibyl Walker, a Portland native, with whom he adopted two daughters. By this time Holbrook had emerged as one of the best-known figures in the Pacific Northwest. Combining his theater experiences as a young man with his story-telling instincts, he became known as an entertaining public speaker and master of ceremonies. His Portland home became a literary focal point for the region, attracting such visitors as novelist William Faulkner, poet Robert Frost, and publisher Alfred A. Knopf. Adding to both his regional notoriety and his national reputation were his "primitive-moderne" paintings, all signed with the pseudonym "Mr. Otis."

Before failing health forced him to give up writing in 1963, Holbrook had published twenty-five books and hundreds of articles, reviews, and pieces of ephemera. As a writer Holbrook partook of a mid-twentieth-century impulse that sought to recover the nineteenth-century connection between history and literature. In this regard, he could readily be compared with Winston Churchill, Bernard DeVoto, and Wallace Stegner. Recognizing this connection, in 1950 the Boston *Herald* counted Holbrook as one of the eight greatest historians to come from New England. The others included George Bancroft and Francis Parkman, both of whom were nonacademic historians known in the nineteenth century for their literary accomplishments. Holbrook died in Portland, Oregon.

• The bulk of Holbrook's papers are at the University of Washington Library in Seattle. Important books by Holbrook not discussed above are *Ethan Allen* (1940); *Murder Out Yonder: An Informal Study of Certain Crimes in Back-Country America* (1941); *Burning an Empire: The Study of American Forest Fires* (1943); *The Story of American Railroads* (1947); *Machines of Plenty: Pioneering in American Agriculture* (1955); *The Golden Age of Quackery* (1959); and *The Old Post Road: The Story of the Boston Post Road* (1962). More complete listings of Holbrook's publications as well as more detailed biographical accounts can be found in Robert E. Ficken's chapter on Holbrook in *Historians of the American Frontier: A Bio-Bibliographical Source*, ed. John R. Wunder (1988); and in Brian Booth's introduction to *Wildmen, Wobblies, and Whistle Punks: Stewart Holbrook's Lowbrow Northwest* (1992), a collection of short pieces by Holbrook. An autobiographical sketch appears in *Twentieth Century Authors*, First suppl. (1955), pp. 453–54. Obituaries are in the *Oregonian* and the *New York Times*, 4 Sept. 1964.

TODD FORSYTH CARNEY

HOLCOMB, Roscoe (1913–25 Feb. 1981), singer and banjo player, was born in Daisy, Kentucky, near the town of Hazard, the son of a coal miner. (His parents' names are unknown.) Holcomb remembered hearing music from the time of his birth and was particularly impressed by a neighbor who played the harmonica (which he called a "mouth harp"). He received his first banjo at the age of ten and began accompanying a local fiddler at dances. Holcomb worked as a farm assistant as a teenager and then as a coal miner; he was employed as a miner for several decades. During slow times, he would work laying ties for the railroad.

After his marriage, Holcomb's wife discouraged him from music making, feeling that it was sinful and dangerous to play for dancing. He subsequently laid down his banjo for a period but was again playing sporadically by the 1940s. He gave up mining in the 1950s, working as a laborer helping to build the new superhighways through the Appalachian Mountains. Discovered by folklorist-musician John Cohen in 1959, Holcomb was recorded for an anthology record on the Folkways label, *Mountain Music from Kentucky*. His performance was so strong that he was soon recording on his own. Cohen made a documentary film, *The High Lonesome Sound* (1962), which helped to introduce Holcomb to a wider audience. (The phrase "High Lonesome," originally used to describe Holcomb's vocal style, has been since applied to old-time and bluegrass music in general.) He subsequently performed at many folk festivals, including the Newport Folk Festival and the University of Chicago Festival, as well as at small clubs in major cities and on college campuses across the United States. He participated in a European tour of American folk musicians in 1965–1966.

Holcomb's intense singing style, emphasizing a strained, upper-register, almost breathless voice, was unusual in mountain music. He tended to prefer blues-flavored material and played both banjo and guitar in a similar manner, using quickly executed, repeated patterns to accompany his vocals. Even upbeat banjo tunes like "Roll on Buddy" or "Blackeyed Susie" were given a distinctly lonesome flavor. He also sang unaccompanied the old Baptist hymns he had heard and performed as a child, often giving them a chilling resonance, as well as religious-tinged songs that emphasized a tragic outlook on life, such as "The Village Churchyard" and "Motherless Children." Although recognizably in the old-time mountain style, Holcomb was a unique artist whose sound was so intensely personal and emotional that he was known to be moved to tears during a performance. Although he did not seek a musical career, he became an expert performer and storyteller.

Holcomb continued to tour extensively through the mid-1970s, when his health began to deteriorate. He recorded a final album, *Close to Home*, in 1972 (issued in 1975), consisting half of banjo songs, and the other half of guitar pieces. He was also featured in a second Cohen documentary, *Musical Holdouts*, with interviews and performances from this later period. Holcomb curtailed his performing in the second half of the decade and died near Daisy after suffering from emphysema, black lung, asthma, and a broken back.

• John Cohen wrote extensively about Holcomb, both in the liner notes to the albums that he recorded and produced and also in various articles. A particularly good article appeared in *Sing Out!*, Apr./May 1966. The complete recordings for *Mountain Music from Kentucky* have been reissued on a two-CD set by Smithsonian/Folkways; Holcomb's other Folkways recordings are available on special order cassette from the Smithsonian Institution. An obituary is in *Sing Out!*, Jan./Feb. 1981.

RICHARD CARLIN

HOLCOMB, Thomas (5 Aug. 1879–24 May 1965), commandant of the U.S. Marine Corps and diplomat, was born in New Castle, Delaware, the son of Thomas Holcomb, an attorney, state legislator, and civil servant, and Elizabeth Hindman Barney. The family moved to Washington in 1893 when his father joined the Treasury Department. Holcomb graduated from high school in 1897 and three years later was commissioned as a second lieutenant in the U.S. Marine Corps. After completing the marines' School of Application, Holcomb served from September 1902 to April 1903 with a seagoing battalion attached to the North Atlantic Fleet. In 1903 he was promoted to first lieutenant and stationed in the Philippines in 1904 and 1905 and at the U.S. legation in Peking (Beijing) from 1905 through 1906. He returned to China in 1908 as a naval attaché. Holcomb, by that time a captain, oversaw the training of the legation's marine detachment, placing particular emphasis—as he would throughout his career—on rifle marksmanship. An expert marksman himself, he had served as a member of the U.S. Marine Corps Rifle Team in 1901, 1902, 1903, 1907, and 1908, and would do so again in 1911. Holcomb returned to the United States in 1914 and became inspector of target practice at corps headquarters. He married Beatrice Miller Clover in 1916; the couple had one son.

Holcomb was promoted to major in 1916. The following year he received command of the newly organized Second Battalion, Sixth Regiment, then preparing for overseas service in the First World War. He again emphasized marksmanship training, a factor that contributed to his unit's success in subsequent combat operations. Arriving in France in November 1917, the Second Battalion was among the American forces called upon to counter the German offensive the next spring. Holcomb's battalion fought tenaciously at Belleau Wood in June, holding on to the ground gained after a series of bloody assaults on German machine gun positions. Appointed executive officer of the Sixth Marine Regiment in August 1918, Holcomb saw action at Château-Thierry, Soissons, Marbache, St. Mihiel, Champagne, and the Argonne Forest. Among the honors Holcomb received for this service were the Navy Cross, the Silver Star with three Oak Leaf Clusters, a Meritorious Service Citation from General John

Pershing, and, from the French government, the Cross of the Legion of Honor and the Croix de Guerre.

After serving with the Army of Occupation of the Rhine, Holcomb commanded the Marine Barracks, Guantánamo, Cuba, between 1922 and 1924. He attended the U.S. Army's Command and General Staff College at Fort Leavenworth, Kansas, completing the course with distinction in 1925. After a tour of duty at Headquarters Marine Corps in the Division of Operations and Training, Holcomb returned to Peking in 1927 as commanding officer of the marine detachment at the American legation. Promoted to colonel in 1928, he remained in China until 1930. He next enjoyed the unusual opportunity to study successively at the Naval War College and the Army War College, completing the course at the former in 1931 and at the latter in 1932. He was then assigned to the Office of Naval Operations. Promoted to brigadier general in February 1935, he became commandant of Marine Corps Schools, Quantico, Virginia. In November 1936 President Franklin Roosevelt appointed Holcomb major general commandant of the U.S. Marine Corps, advancing him in grade over more senior officers.

Despite a lack of adequate funds, men, and equipment, Holcomb in his first tour as commandant oversaw the continuing refinement of the amphibious warfare mission laid out by his predecessors, John A. Lejeune and John H. Russell. Amphibious operations would prove one of the most significant and innovative components of American war-making in the Pacific, and under Holcomb's leadership the marine corps began experimenting with new kinds of landing craft: EUREKA, the predecessor to the navy's Landing Craft Vehicle Personnel (LCVP); the fifty-foot lighter or Landing Craft Mechanized (LCM); and the Roebling ALLIGATOR, a tracked, lightly armored assault vehicle (LVT). As world war again loomed, Holcomb superintended the expansion of the marine corps from 16,000 officers and men in 1936 to over 50,000 by mid-1941, and to more than 300,000 by the end of his tenure. He ensured that these marines went to battle well trained and well equipped. Roosevelt, who had reappointed him commandant in December 1940, elevated him to lieutenant general in February 1942.

The most vexing problems Holcomb faced involved control of marines in the field. Because the corps was an arm of the navy, the extent of various commanders' authority had to be clearly defined. Matters came to a head during the Guadalcanal campaign (1942–43). Holcomb regarded Admiral Kelly Turner's wish to reorganize all marine forces into raider units as intrusive meddling and insisted that any such plan be approved by the senior marine commander in the field, General Alexander Vandegrift. Turner's efforts to assert his authority over the disposition of Vandegrift's landing force once it had deployed on Guadalcanal inspired Holcomb to more definitively resolve the question of who commanded what and when during a joint amphibious operation. He persuaded Admiral Chester Nimitz and Chief of Naval Operations Admiral Ernest J. King to establish clear lines of authority during all subsequent operations. Thereafter the marine landing force commander would not be subordinate to the navy amphibious task force commander in either the planning or the execution of individual operations, but would instead enjoy equal authority. Any disputes between the two would be resolved by a superior officer, typically the navy theater commander. This result not only settled a question that had been lingering since early amphibious exercises in the 1920s, but also recognized the marines' central role in the Pacific war effort.

Although Holcomb reached the mandatory retirement age in August 1943, Roosevelt retained him as commandant for another five months, advanced him to full general (making Holcomb the first marine ever to hold that rank) and awarded him the Distinguished Service Medal. In March 1944, Roosevelt appointed Holcomb U.S. minister to the Union of South Africa. Though Holcomb had resisted racial integration of the marine corps when commandant, he was disturbed by the rising tide of Afrikaner nationalism and the harsh repression of the black majority. Given the imperatives of the Cold War, Holcomb believed the United States should maintain close ties to the white government, but he wished that South Africa would steer a middle course between what he termed "the two absurd extremes of complete segregation and complete equality" (Borstelmann, p. 89).

Returning home in 1948, Holcomb resided successively in St. Marys City, Maryland; Chevy Chase, Maryland; and Washington, D.C., before returning to his hometown, Newcastle, Delaware, where he died.

• Official papers and correspondence of Holcomb's military career are at the U.S. Marine Historical Center in Washington, D.C. Diplomatic correspondence has been reproduced in the microform set *Confidential U.S. State Department Central Files, South Africa: Internal Affairs and Foreign Affairs, 1945–1949* (1985). Officially published material includes Frank O. Hough, et al., *Pearl Harbor to Guadalcanal: History of U.S. Marine Corps Operations in World War II*, vol. 1 (1958), and Henry Shaw, *Opening Moves: Marines Gear Up for War* (1991). Karl Schuon, *Home of the Commandants* (1974), and Schuon, *U.S. Marine Corps Biographical Dictionary* (1963), briefly outline his career in the corps. On his World War One service, see Lieutenant General William K. Jones, *A Brief History of the 6th Marines* (1987). His tenure as commandant is covered in John Gordon, "General Thomas Holcomb and 'The Golden Age of Amphibious Warfare'" *Delaware History* 21 (1985): 256–270, as well as in two excellent histories of the marine corps: Robert D. Heinl, Jr., *Soldiers of the Sea: The U.S. Marine Corps, 1775–1962* (1964), and Allan R. Millet, *"Semper Fidelis": The History of the United States Marine Corps* (1980). Holcomb's service as minister to South Africa is briefly discussed in Thomas Borstelmann, *Apartheid's Reluctant Uncle: The United States and Southern Africa in the Early Cold War* (1993).

LEO J. DAUGHERTY

HOLCOMBE, Chester (16 Oct. 1844–25 Apr. 1912), missionary and diplomat to China, was born in Winfield, New York, the son of the Reverend Chester Holcombe, a Presbyterian minister, and Lucy Thomp-

kins. Holcombe's mother, who had intended to be a missionary herself prior to Chester's birth, passed on that intention to her son. Following graduation from Union College in 1861, Holcombe entered the teaching profession. He taught for a number of years at both the high school level and the normal school level in Troy, New York; Hartford and Norwich, Connecticut; and Brooklyn, New York. During the 1860s he also began to study theology and in 1867 was licensed by the Presbytery of Lyons, New York, to begin preaching. In 1868, the same year he was ordained, he began work in Georgia as a missionary for the American Sunday School Union. This first experience as a missionary turned out to be of short duration, for in 1869 Holcombe, accompanied by his wife, Olive Kate Sage, and his brother Gilbert Holcombe, departed for China as a missionary of the American Board of Commissioners for Foreign Missions.

Holcombe's arrival in Peking (Beijing) in the spring of 1869 came on the heels of the 1868 Burlingame Treaty between China and the United States, a treaty that led to even greater U.S. commercial and missionary activity in China. Holcombe quickly understood that effectiveness as a missionary was tied to language skills, and he threw himself into the study of Chinese. While helping to run a missionary school for boys in Peking, Holcombe developed sufficent language abilities to begin producing works in Chinese, including an account of the life of Christ published in 1875. Yet, like other missionaries serving in East Asia during the second half of the nineteenth century—such as Samuel Wells Williams and Edward Thomas Williams in China and Horace N. Allen in Korea—Holcombe found himself being drawn into the world of diplomacy. As early as 1871 he had begun serving as an interpreter for the American legation in Peking. Five years later, when Samuel Wells Williams, who had been something of a mentor to Holcombe, stepped down as secretary of the U.S. legation, Holcombe tendered his resignation with the American Board of Commissioners for Foreign Missions and took over as Williams's replacement. He held the position of secretary of the legation for the next nine years.

Holcombe exercised considerable influence at the legation, perhaps partly because of his own language skills but also because of the frequent turnover in personnel. From 1867 to 1882 there were eleven different U.S. ministers or chargés d'affaires in China, and Holcombe himself served as chargé d'affaires on three separate occasions. Working under Ministers George F. Seward (1876–1880), James B. Angell (1880–1881), and John Russell Young (1882–1885), Holcombe had the opportunity to participate in events that helped to shape the course of late nineteenth-century American–East Asian relations.

The 1868 Burlingame Treaty, among other things, had legalized Chinese immigration to the United States. As the influx of Chinese immigrants began to swell in the 1870s, an American backlash, especially within the western states and territories, began to arise. By 1880 the U.S. government was under considerable pressure to limit Chinese immigration to the United States. That same year a three-member commission led by Angell entered into talks with Chinese representatives to adjust the terms of the Burlingame Treaty. Holcombe assisted in producing a compromise draft that became the basis for the 1880 Sino-American Treaty. While this treaty did not completely prohibit Chinese immigration to the United States, it did give the American government the exclusive right to limit the immigration of Chinese laborers and thus set the stage for the harsher and more controversial exclusion acts that were soon to follow. Holcombe, like Angell, was a moderate on the immigration issue and in the 1890s became an outspoken critic of efforts to prohibit all Chinese immigration to the United States.

As the controversy over immigration began to strain Sino-American relations, another important issue demanded Holcombe's attention—the opening of Korea. The United States had first attempted to sign a commercial treaty with Korea in 1871, but that expedition had ended in complete failure and considerable loss of life for the Koreans. By 1880 the United States was ready to try again and dispatched Commodore Robert W. Shufeldt to East Asia. Upon receiving the news that China might be willing to offer its good offices on behalf of the Korean government, Shufeldt traveled to Tientsin and entered into negotiations with the powerful Chinese official, Li Hung-chang. Holcombe not only served as a translator for these talks but also played a key role in resolving the most difficult aspect of the treaty—Korea's sovereignty. Li, who hoped to use the treaty as a way of blocking growing Japanese influence in the peninsula, insisted that the treaty include a clause stating that Korea was a dependent state of the Chinese empire. Shufeldt, on the other hand, refused to consider the inclusion of such a clause. The diplomatic deadlock was finally broken when both parties agreed that a separate letter declaring Korea's dependence on China would be written by the king of Korea and sent to the president of the United States. Negotiations were then quickly completed in the spring of 1882, and the treaty was officially signed in Korea on 22 May of that year. Although Holcombe served as Shufeldt's chief assistant during these talks and thus deserves much of the credit for their success, the issue of Korean independence continued to haunt Sino-American relations for the next two decades.

With the 1884 election of Grover Cleveland to the presidency of the United States, the Democratic party took control of the Department of State for the first time in twenty-four years. Democrat Charles Denby replaced Republican Young as minister to China, and Holcombe stepped down as secretary of the legation. Holcombe himself had hoped one day to become the U.S. minister to China and, in fact, was selected for the position in 1889, only to have his nomination rejected because of his missionary background by the Chinese government at the suggestion of Li. Holcombe spent the remainder of his years as an occasional adviser on Chinese affairs, as a dealer in Chinese curios, and as a lecturer on Chinese society and culture.

In the mid-1890s he attempted to negotiate a large international loan on behalf of the Chinese government, but his plans fell through. He wrote a number of popular, if relatively unimportant, books on China, including *The Practical Effect of Confucianism upon the Chinese Nation* (1882), *The Real Chinaman* (1895), and *The Real Chinese Question* (1899), later revised as *China's Past and Future* (1904). Holcombe's first wife died during their years in China; in 1906 he married Alice Reeves. By the time of his own death, the missionary turned diplomat that Holcombe typified was increasingly being replaced by trained specialists within the American Foreign Service. Holcombe, who had no children, died in Rochester, New York.

• Important primary materials for Holcombe are in the archives of the American Board of Commissioners for Foreign Missions, Houghton Library, Harvard University; and in the U.S. State Department's Diplomatic Instructions and Dispatches for Both Consuls and Ministers in China, National Archives, Washington, D.C. See also Michael H. Hunt, *The Making of a Special Relationship: The United States and China to 1914* (1983); Shih-shan Henry Tsai, *China and the Overseas Chinese in the United States, 1868–1911* (1983); Frederick C. Drake, *The Empire of the Seas: A Biography of Rear Admiral Robert Wilson Shufeldt, USN* (1984); and Jongsuk Chay, *Diplomacy of Asymmetry: Korean-American Relations to 1910* (1990). An obituary is in the Rochester (N.Y.) *Democrat and Chronicle*, 26 Apr. 1912.

ROBERT R. SWARTOUT, JR.

HOLCOMBE, Henry (22 Sept. 1762–22 May 1824), Baptist minister, was born in Prince Edward County, Virginia, the son of Grimes Holcombe and Elizabeth Buzbee (or Busby), farmers. The family moved to South Carolina when he was a child. His formal education was limited, completed by the time he was eleven years of age. As a young man, he joined the revolutionary army and was made an officer. While in the army he made the decision to relinquish his earlier Presbyterian affiliation and join the Baptists, the religious communion in which he would invest his life's work. Shortly after that, he was granted a license to preach in Baptist churches.

Holcombe's pulpit skills were soon recognized, and he was called to be pastor of a Baptist church at Pike Creek, South Carolina, receiving ordination on 11 September 1785. He was married to Frances Tanner of North Carolina in 1786, and she soon received immersion baptism into the fellowship of the Baptists. The Holcombes had ten children, three of whom died in infancy. His abilities as a preacher enhanced his reputation, and in 1788 Holcombe was appointed to the South Carolina Convention, which ratified the U.S. Constitution. In 1791 he became pastor of the Baptist congregation in Euhaw, South Carolina. Four years later he moved to a pastorate in Beaufort, South Carolina, where he remained until 1799, when he moved to Savannah, Georgia, to serve a congregation composed of Baptists and Presbyterians. That early "ecumenical" endeavor ended in 1800 when the Baptists constituted a church, which became the First

Baptist Church in Savannah, with Holcombe as the pastor.

In Savannah, Holcombe was active in numerous community enterprises, including the establishment of the Savannah Female Asylum, an organization for the support and education of female orphans. He also published a journal of religion and literature entitled the *Georgia Analytical Repository* (1802–1803). He was a founder of the Mount Enon Academy (later Mercer University) in Mount Enon, Georgia (1804), a school supported by Georgia Baptists. His concern about the severity of Georgia criminal law led him to address a memorial to the Georgia legislature in 1802 calling for more humane treatment of offenders. His efforts influenced the establishment of the state penal system, 1803–1804. Concerned for the promotion of public religion and morality, Holcombe frequently criticized Deists, theaters, marital infidelity, and other threats to Baptist morality. In 1810 poor health forced him to relinquish his duties in Savannah and seek rest in Mount Enon. In 1811 he accepted the invitation to become pastor of the First Baptist Church in Philadelphia, and he served that congregation until his death there.

Holcombe was the author of numerous books, including *A Sermon Occasioned by the Death of Lieutenant General George Washington* (1800), a eulogy to the former president; *The First Fruits* (1812), a reflection on the basic issues of the Christian life; and *The Whole Truth Relative to the Controversy betwixt the American Baptists* (1820), a forceful defense of the missionary enterprise against antimission Baptists. *The Whole Truth* was written shortly after the Triennial Convention (1814) urged Baptists to send missionaries throughout the world.

Holcombe's theology was that of a modified or evangelical Calvinist and reflects his conviction that through the preaching of the gospel God would awaken the hearts of the elect. Missionaries were essential to the fulfillment of the church's evangelical calling. Holcombe was widely known for his prowess in the pulpit and his support of the missionary enterprise. His strong opposition to war placed him in a minority among most colonial Baptists. He encouraged Baptists to respond to issues of social and educational reform through the establishment of schools and benevolent institutions.

• J. H. Campbell, *Georgia Baptists: Historical and Biographical* (1874), contains a lengthy essay, highly laudatory, on Holcombe's life and work. W. J. Northen, *Men of Mark in Georgia*, vol. 1 (1907), presents a good summary of the major events of his life. W. B. Sprague, *Annals of the American Pulpit*, vol. 6 (1860), discusses his life in the context of his role as a preacher.

BILL J. LEONARD

HOLCOMBE, James Philemon (20 Sept. 1820–22 Aug. 1873), educator and Confederate official, was born in Powhatan County, Virginia, the son of William James Holcombe, a doctor, and Ann Eliza Clopton. After studying with a private tutor, James enrolled at Yale and later attended the University of Virginia but did not graduate from either school. After studies at the Staunton Law School, he began practicing law in Fincastle, Virginia. In 1844 he left Virginia to join a law firm in Cincinnati, Ohio. While in Cincinnati, he produced an extensive list of publications on legal matters, including *An Introduction to Equity Jurisprudence, on the Basis of Story's Commentaries* (1846), *A Selection of Leading Cases upon Commercial Law* (1847), *A Digest of the Decisions of the Supreme Court of the United States from Its Organization to the Present Time* (1848), and *The Merchants' Book of Reference for Debtor and Creditor, in the United States and Canada* (1848). He also coedited an edition of John William Smith's *Compendium of Mercantile Law* (1850). In 1841 he married Anne Selden Watts, with whom he had six children.

In 1851 Holcombe decided to devote himself fulltime to legal scholarship and moved to Alexandria, Virginia, so he could have better access to the Library of Congress. It was a short stay. During the late 1840s the law school at the University of Virginia had experienced a dramatic increase in the number of new students. To assist John Barbee Minor, the school's only law professor, the board of visitors hired Holcombe as an adjunct professor in October 1851. He was promoted to full professor in 1854. Two years later the school was divided into two departments, with Holcombe responsible for instruction in international law, equity, civil law, mercantile and maritime law, natural and constitutional law, and evidence. During his tenure at the University of Virginia he collaborated with Minor in the design and implementation of a new three-course structure for the law school.

Unlike his father, who had emancipated all of his own slaves in the 1840s, Holcombe embraced the southern plantation ideal. In addition to his teaching duties, Holcombe acquired eleven slaves during the 1850s with an eye on becoming a planter. He also began to take interest in the growing sectional conflict. A great admirer of John C. Calhoun, he employed both his pen and skills as an orator to denounce northern abolitionism and to champion states' rights. Several of his public addresses were circulated in pamphlet form, including *On the Right of the State to Institute Slavery* (1858) and *The Election of a Black Republican President an Overt Act of Aggression on the Right of Property in Slaves* (1860).

When Virginia called a convention to consider secession, Holcombe resigned his professorship to stand for election as a delegate and was elected. At the convention he was one of the most active and eloquent delegates urging secession. His speech to the convention on 20–21 March 1861 was hailed by many as the most effective presentation of the immediate secessionist position. After the convention voted for secession, Holcombe served on the Committee on Military Affairs that offered Robert E. Lee command of the state's armed forces and was one of the six signers of the convention between Virginia and the Confederacy.

In November 1861 Holcombe won election to the Confederate House of Representatives. During his service there, from February 1862 to February 1864, he continued to express strong states' rights sentiments but refused to let them get in the way of what he felt was right for the Confederacy. He backed higher taxes to finance the government, supported laws giving the Jefferson Davis administration power over the economy, and eventually abandoned his constitutional objections to conscription to support extension of the draft. He also worked to ensure the protection of private property, the equalization of tax laws, and the establishment of a court to investigate the activities of the Confederate government.

In February 1864 Holcombe was sent to Canada to represent the interests of the Confederate government in the case of the *Chesapeake*, a northern vessel seized and taken to Halifax by privateers whose leader claimed membership in the southern navy but lacked a legal letter of marque. Upon his arrival in Nova Scotia, Holcombe quickly recognized the weakness of the Confederate case and turned instead to the task of arranging for the repatriation of southern soldiers believed to be in Canada. In July 1864 he helped Clement Claiborne Clay carry out a correspondence with Horace Greeley, who was acting as an unofficial representative of the Union government, with an eye on discussing terms for a possible peace conference at Niagara Falls. The talks went nowhere, however, and it appears clear that Clay and Holcombe's objective was to encourage antiwar sentiment in the North rather than seek an understanding with Greeley. Upon his return to Richmond in November 1864 Holcombe urged Confederate secretary of state Judah P. Benjamin to vigorously support efforts to promote anarchy in the North and to encourage northwestern states to secede from the Union.

After the war Holcombe established Bellevue High School for Boys on a 600-acre tract in Bedford County, Virginia. While building the school, he resumed his literary efforts, editing and publishing *Literature in Letters*, a collection of letters by famous Americans, in 1866. The high point of his postwar career came in January 1871, when he delivered a speech in Lexington, Virginia, on the occasion of the first memorial celebration of Lee's birthday. This was his last public act. Soon afterward, in an effort to revive his failing health, he moved to Capon Springs, West Virginia, where he died.

• No single collection of Holcombe's personal papers exists. Brief sketches of his life and career are in Ezra J. Warner and W. Buck Yearns, *Biographical Register of the Confederate Congress* (1975), Richard N. Current, ed., *Encyclopedia of the Confederacy*, vol. 2 (1993), and Hannah E. W. McPherson, *The Holcombes, Nation Builders* (1947). Information on Holcombe's legal career and tenure at the University of Virginia is in William H. Bryson, ed., *Legal Education in Virginia, 1779–1979* (1982), and Phillip A. Bruce, *History of the University of Virginia* (1921). The best source on the Virginia convention of 1861 is George Reese, ed., *Proceedings of the Virginia State Convention of 1861* (1965); Holcombe's speech to

the convention on 20–21 Mar. 1861, is in vol. 2, pp. 74–111. See also Thomas Webster Richey, "The Virginia State Convention of 1861 and Virginia Secession" (Ph.D. diss., Univ. of Georgia, 1990), for information on the convention and Holcombe's role. J. W. Headley, *Confederate Operations in Canada and New York* (1906), and "Official Correspondence of Confederate State Department," *Southern Historical Society Papers* 7 (1879): 99–106, 132–39, 293–94, 333–43, are good sources on Holcombe's operations in Canada. James P. C. Southall, *Memoirs of the Abbots of Old Bellevue* (1955), is informative on Holcombe's postwar activities.

ETHAN S. RAFUSE

HOLDEN, Edward Singleton (5 Nov. 1846–16 Mar. 1914), astronomer and librarian, was born in St. Louis, Missouri, the son of Edward Holden and Sarah Frances Singleton. His mother died when he was three years old, and he was sent to live with his aunt, the wife of a Boston attorney, in Cambridge, Massachusetts. This family (and his own) were related to William C. Bond and George P. Bond, successively the directors of Harvard College Observatory from 1840 until 1865, and through them Holden was introduced to astronomy at an early age. He returned to St. Louis, where his father still lived, to enter Washington University in 1862. There he studied mathematics and astronomy under William Chauvenet and received his B.S. in 1866. Then he entered the U.S. Military Academy at West Point as a cadet, graduating third in his class in 1870 as a new second lieutenant.

After one year in the field as an artillery officer, Holden returned to West Point as an instructor for two years and then resigned his commission in 1873 to accept another in the navy, as a professor of mathematics at the Naval Observatory in Washington. When the observatory's 26-inch refracting telescope was completed later that year, Holden was assigned to work with it as Simon Newcomb's assistant, and then later as Asaph Hall's. Holden greatly impressed Newcomb, an outstanding theoretician of planetary motions who in 1874 became the chief astronomical adviser for the James Lick Trust, charged with building a telescope "superior to and more powerful than any telescope ever yet made" for the University of California. Already at this very early stage, when Holden was only twenty-seven years old and had not done any significant astronomical research, Newcomb recommended him to Darius O. Mills, the head of the trust, as a future director of Lick Observatory.

Legal complications and then the difficulty of producing the required large glass disks for the lens of what became the Lick 36-inch refractor delayed the project for years. Newcomb had little time to spend on it, and Holden filled the gap, traveling on the Lick Trust's behalf and preparing long, detailed plans and memoranda that at first ingratiated him to its new president, Richard S. Floyd.

In 1881 Holden left the Naval Observatory to become professor of astronomy at the University of Wisconsin and director of its new Washburn Observatory, equipped with a 15.6-inch refracting telescope, on the campus in Madison. None of his research at the Naval

Observatory or at Wisconsin had much of an outcome, but some of his papers, more like reviews than research reports, were quite imaginative and forward-looking. He had married Mary Chauvenet, his teacher's daughter, in 1871; they had three children. The couple separated in 1886, when he went to California, and were later divorced. This was highly unusual for a university professor in the 1880s, and it hurt Holden's reputation for the rest of his life.

In 1886, with the Lick Observatory telescope nearing completion, Holden was offered the presidency of the University of California. He accepted the post on the condition that he could give it up to become director of the observatory when the Lick Trust handed it over to the university. By this time friction had arisen between Floyd and Holden, and the director-to-be had little voice in the final decisions on the research equipment for which he would soon become responsible. In June 1888 the Lick Trust reported the observatory as ready for operation, and Holden moved up to Mount Hamilton as its director. The initial staff he selected was excellent; three of the first four faculty members, S. W. Burnham, James E. Keeler, and Edward E. Barnard, were or became outstanding research astronomers. Although he was not much of an observer himself, Holden was a brilliant organizer. He had begun collecting astronomical books and publications for the observatory library years before; it became one of the most complete libraries of its type in America. In 1889 he founded the Astronomical Society of the Pacific, a combined amateur-professional society that by the 1990s boasted more than five thousand members.

However, Holden's personality repelled most of his staff members. He was a brilliant conversationalist, so sure of his opinions that he always insisted on being right. In addition, he tried to apply the tactics of a commanding officer to a scientific institution, giving orders to staff members who knew they were his superiors in research ability and taking credit for himself for their discoveries (that in fact he had helped make possible). Holden's own research program, direct photography of the moon, was a failure because he did not have the time, skills, and experience to obtain the best possible images with the giant 36-inch refractor. Burnham and Barnard, both experts in photography, were soon openly critical of the director. Keeler was the first to leave Lick Observatory, quietly, in 1891, followed the next year by Burnham, with a bitter public blasting, and then Henry Crew, a young staff member who had come as a replacement for Keeler but who lasted only one year. Then in 1895 Barnard resigned, making no secret of his distaste for Holden.

Also in 1895 the director had his great triumph, persuading the English amateur astronomer Edward Crossley to give his 36-inch reflecting telescope to Lick Observatory. However, a new staff member, William J. Hussey, whom Holden assigned to get it into shape and use it for research, refused to do so, precipitating a staff revolt. Holden was by now unpopular and pilloried in the public press, and he was forced to resign in

September 1897. Most of his ideas were right, but he could not present them effectively to independent scientists who thought that he was treating them like privates in an infantry company. In particular, Keeler, who returned to Lick as its second director in 1898, took over the Crossley reflector himself, soon had it working, and produced outstanding research results with it.

Holden by now was a pariah in American science. He hoped for appointment as president of the Massachusetts Institute of Technology, as head of the U.S. Coast and Geodetic Survey, or as head of the Harvard College Library; but no organization wanted a failed director who could not get along with his underlings. Holden moved to New York City and supported himself by grinding out magazine articles and books, many of them on astronomy, but others on subjects as diverse as poetry, heraldry, deportment, and travel. He published many of these under various pseudonyms, most frequently Edward or Adam Singleton. Holden was supporting his three children and had to write at a frantic pace to make ends meet. In 1901 his West Point background saved him. His former fellow cadet Samuel E. Tillman, a long-time instructor at the military academy, succeeded in getting Holden appointed head of its library. This position suited his talents and interests exactly, and he lived out his life there, known as "Colonel" Holden, the friend of all the officers who were instructors, and the kindly librarian who could always help the cadets find the references they needed to complete their reports. He underwent a serious operation in 1912, from which he never fully recovered, but he continued to work in the library until just a few weeks before his death at West Point.

• A very large collection of Holden's letters is in the Mary Lea Shane Archives of the Lick Observatory, in the University of California at Santa Cruz library. Two published memorial biographies are by Samuel E. Tillman, "Edward S. Holden," *Annual Report of the Association of Graduates of the U.S. Military Academy* (1915), pp. 52–74, and W. Wallace Campbell, "Edward Singleton Holden," National Academy of Sciences, *Biographical Memoirs* 8 (1919): 347–72. Campbell's work contains a complete bibliography of Holden's published scientific papers as well as many of the articles, reviews, and books of all types that he wrote, including some under the various pseudonyms. One of Holden's most creative research papers, which also demonstrates his shortcomings as an observer, is "Monograph on the Central Parts of the Nebula of Orion," *Astronomical and Meteorological Observations, 1878, U.S. Naval Observatory* (1882), appendix 1, pp. 1–230. A popular article that shows Holden's brilliant powers of assimilation of a new subject, astrophysics, is "Photography: The Servant of Astronomy," *Overland Monthly* 8 (1886): 459–67. An admiring article by William C. Winlock, "Sketch of Professor Edward S. Holden," *Popular Science Monthly*, Nov. 1886, pp. 114–19, gives a more complete account of his youth and early life in Cambridge. Another biographical article is Donald E. Osterbrock, "The Rise and Fall of Edward S. Holden," *Journal for the History of Astronomy* 15 (1984): 81–127, 151–76; see also Osterbrock et al., *Eye on the Sky: Lick Observatory's First Century* (1988). An obituary is in the *New York Times*, 17 Mar. 1914.

DONALD E. OSTERBROCK

HOLDEN, William (17 Apr. 1918–12 Nov. 1981), motion picture actor, was born William Franklin Beedle, Jr., in O'Fallon, Illinois, the son of William Franklin Beedle, a chemist, and Mary Ball. Following the family's move to California in 1922, he attended school in Monrovia and South Pasadena. In 1936 he enrolled at Pasadena Junior College, where he took a course in radio drama, acted in several plays on a local station, and pursued his interests in gymnastics and boxing. In 1938 he appeared as the eighty-year-old father-in-law of Marie Curie in *Manya* at the Playbox Theatre, a workshop venue at the Pasadena Playhouse. Milt Lewis, a talent scout for Paramount Pictures, saw the play and was impressed by Holden's performance, in particular by his resonant voice. Lewis arranged for a screen test, and the twenty-year-old was signed as a contract player under the name William Holden.

After giving Holden minor parts in *Prison Farm* (1939) and *Million Dollar Legs* (1939), Paramount allowed Columbia Pictures to cast him as the lead in *Golden Boy* (1939), based on the Clifford Odets play, the story of a young Italian immigrant torn between a career as a boxer and his love for the violin. The film, in which Holden starred with the more experienced actors Barbara Stanwyck and Adolphe Menjou, was only a modest success, and Holden's performance received mixed reviews, but his portrayal of the earnest, clean-cut hero led to a series of films in which he was repeatedly typecast as a wholesome, charming boy-next-door, a character he would later refer to disparagingly as "Smiling Jim." His all-American good looks and likeable manner were perhaps the chief attractions of Paramount and Columbia films like *Invisible Stripes* (1940), *I Wanted Wings* (1941), *The Remarkable Andrew* (1942), and *Meet the Stewarts* (1942). Holden enjoyed taking risks and typically performed his own stunts. At the same time, however, he was the victim of paralyzing stage fright and early in his career turned to alcohol as a way of relaxing his nerves.

In July 1941 Holden married the actress Brenda Marshall (née Ardis Ankerson) and settled in Toluca Lake, California; they had two sons, in addition to Marshall's daughter from a previous marriage. Holden joined the army in 1942 and served for three and a half years, first as a private and later as a second lieutenant, but never left the United States. His first postwar role was as a barnstormer in *Blaze of Noon* (1947), followed by the highly successful comedy *Dear Ruth* (1948). In *The Dark Past* (1948) he faced his first real acting challenge, playing a cold-blooded killer, and won appreciative reviews. Yet he quickly returned to more conventional roles in westerns and romantic comedies.

Holden's career breakthrough came with *Sunset Boulevard* (1950), in which he played the struggling young screenwriter Joe Gillis. Although the role had some superficial resemblances to the handsome young men he had played before, he managed to project behind his ready smile a sense of cynicism and wariness. The romantic relationship between Gillis and Norma Desmond, the aging, faded movie star played by Glo-

ria Swanson, disturbed some audiences, but the film was a great critical success, and Holden was nominated for an Academy Award for best actor. A reviewer for the *New York Times* said that "Holden is doing the finest acting of his career. His range and control of emotions never falters and he engenders a full measure of compassion for a character who is somewhat less than admirable" (11 Aug. 1950).

Sunset Boulevard was also important for Holden in that it established his working relationship with the director Billy Wilder, for whom he was to give some of his best performances. After Holden's success in *Born Yesterday* (also 1950), a romantic comedy directed by George Cukor and starring Judy Holliday, and a few more roles as upstanding citizens in minor films, he worked under Wilder again on *Stalag 17* (1953), the story of a group of American prisoners-of-war in a German camp. As Sefton, the tough, cynical antihero, Holden again impressed audiences with his range. The critic Otis L. Guernsey, Jr., wrote that "Holden acts in quick, hard punches of character, playing a realist who likes his own comforts and is willing to be an outcast or a hero to get them. He forms a kind of bridge between the humor and the drama in a solid performance" (*New York Herald Tribune*, 2 July 1953). This time he won the Academy Award for best actor.

Holden's next film, *The Moon Is Blue* (1953), a risqué comedy for its time, was his first big financial success, earning him $600,000. He followed it with four of his most memorable roles: *Executive Suite* (1954), costarring Barbara Stanwyck; *Sabrina* (1954), with Audrey Hepburn and Humphrey Bogart; and two films in which he starred with Grace Kelly, *The Country Girl* (1954) and *The Bridges at Toko-Ri* (1955). He continued his string of box-office hits with *Love Is a Many-Splendored Thing* (1955), in which he played the American lover of a Eurasian doctor, and *Picnic* (1956), based on the William Inge play about a handsome drifter who mesmerizes the women of a midwestern town. From another high-grossing production, *The Bridge on the River Kwai* (1957), directed by David Lean, Holden earned more than $3 million. As each film confirmed his status in the highest echelon of Hollywood stars, his screen persona began to evolve, and a new, hardbitten character type replaced the former "Smiling Jim" as Holden's signature role.

In 1959 Holden moved his family to Switzerland to escape the high income tax in the United States. Although he was only one of many American film actors to do so, his public image as a model citizen made his choice to leave the country particularly unpopular with his fans, and his career suffered a decline during the 1960s, with such poorly received films as *The World of Suzie Wong* (1960), *Satan Never Sleeps* (1962), and *Paris When It Sizzles* (1964). At the same time his drinking problem was becoming worse, requiring his hospitalization in Lausanne in 1963. In July 1966 Holden was speeding down the autostrada near Florence, Italy, when his Ferrari struck another car, killing the driver. He was tried and convicted of manslaughter, but his eight-month jail sentence was suspended.

Holden had become interested in African culture and wildlife in the late 1950s while on a safari vacation, and he subsequently traveled there as often as possible. In 1968 he made his television debut in an adventure program about Kenya, "William Holden: Unconquered Worlds." In 1969 he experienced a brief return to notoriety when he played Pike Bishop, the leader of the outlaw gang in director Sam Peckinpah's *The Wild Bunch*. While some critics deplored the film's graphic violence, others, including Vincent Canby of the *New York Times*, praised its innovation in the established genre of the western and applauded Holden's skillful portrayal of a complex, multidimensional character. After *The Wild Bunch*, Holden returned to more conventional roles in such films as the western *Wild Rovers* (1971) and the romance *Breezy* (1973). Yet even in these undistinguished films he continued to give quality performances, and his later career was marked by a few notable successes. In 1973 he appeared on television again as an aging policeman obsessed with a dangerous case in "The Blue Knight" (1973), the first example of what would come to be known as the "miniseries," for which he received an Emmy Award. In 1976 he starred in the film *Network* as the nostalgic veteran news executive Max Shumacher. *Network* was Holden's most critically acclaimed film since *Stalag 17*, earning him a third Academy Award nomination. His last film was the black comedy *S.O.B.* (1981), a satire of Hollywood politics directed by Blake Edwards.

In 1973 Holden and his wife had divorced. His drinking problem steadily worsened over the years, despite the efforts of friends to help him overcome his addiction, and his health deteriorated. He died in his Santa Monica apartment after injuring his head in a fall, apparently too intoxicated to realize that he needed medical help. In his 42-year screen career, Holden appeared in more than seventy motion pictures. He always thought of himself as a craftsman rather than an artist, once saying of acting, "It's just a job" (Thomas, p. 179). Although his films varied in quality, his solid, sometimes brilliant acting kept him a highly respected screen presence among critics as well as popular audiences.

• Biographical material regarding William Holden can be found in Alvin H. Marill, "William Holden," *Films in Review* 24, no. 8 (Oct. 1973): 449–69; James Robert Parish and Don E. Stanke, *All-Americans* (1977), pp. 138–95; Bernard Drew, "Where Has Everybody Gone?" *American Film* 2, no. 4 (Feb. 1977): 53–56; Marill, "William Holden," *Films in Review* 33, no. 2 (Feb. 1982): 98–101; Bob Thomas, *Golden Boy: The Untold Story of William Holden* (1983); and Lawrence J. Quirk, *The Complete Films of William Holden* (1986). The two articles by Marill also provide a complete, detailed Holden filmography. Obituaries appear in the *New York Times*, 17 Nov. 1981; *Newsweek*, 30 Nov. 1981; and *Time*, 30 Nov. 1981.

L. MOODY SIMMS, JR.
SARAH WALL

HOLDEN, William Woods (24 Nov. 1818–2 Mar. 1892), editor and political leader, was born near Hillsboro, North Carolina, the illegitimate son of Thomas Holden, a relatively prosperous mill owner, and Priscilla Woods. When he was two or three years old, he went to live with his father. He briefly attended a local "field school," and at age nine or ten he became a printer's apprentice in the office of the *Hillsboro Recorder*. At seventeen he became a typesetter on the *Raleigh Star*, a Whig newspaper. Holden married Ann Young in 1841. They had four children. Only nominally a Whig, Holden in 1843 joined the Democratic party after he became the editor and proprietor of the *North Carolina Standard*, the organ of the state party, in Raleigh.

Holden quickly developed the *Standard* into a powerful statewide newspaper, and his political influence grew in the same proportion. His editorials were written in the hard-hitting style of antebellum journalism and included merciless attacks on the political opposition.

By 1848 Holden had assumed directorship of the state Democratic party, and in 1850 his party won control of the state government. His first wife having died in 1852, Holden married Louisa Virginia Harrison in 1854; they had four children. As the Democratic party consolidated its power in North Carolina during the 1850s, Holden remained its dominant figure. In 1858 he sought his party's nomination for governor but was foiled by John W. Ellis and his supporters, who had chafed at Holden's domination of the party. The split in the party widened during the sectional crisis of 1860–1861 when Holden encouraged moderation toward the North. After Abraham Lincoln's election to the presidency Holden, who during the 1850s had been a strong advocate of states' rights, urged a watch-and-wait policy toward the new president.

Abandoning the Ellis-controlled Democratic party, which supported secession, Holden organized the Constitutional Union party in the state that in February 1861 defeated the secessionist effort to call a convention that could take the state out of the Union. In the brief campaign Holden warned that secession "would end in civil war, in military despotism, and in the destruction of slave property. *Let us give the Northern people time*. . . . The Constitution will be restored, and Mr. Lincoln and his party will be hurled from power in 1864." The fighting at Fort Sumter and Lincoln's call for troops to suppress the rebellion in April, however, caused Holden to reverse his position and call on North Carolinians to resist Lincoln's "gross usurpation" of power. As a delegate to the state convention in May, he voted for the ordinance that took North Carolina out of the Union and into the Confederacy.

Hardly had the war begun when Holden began to criticize state authorities and the Jefferson Davis administration for discriminating against old Union party men in their military appointments and for suppressing North Carolina liberties. The fall of a large area of coastal North Carolina to federal forces and the adoption of conscription by the Richmond government in early 1862 gave Holden additional ammunition to use against Confederate authorities. He soon organized the Conservative party, secured the nomination of young Zebulon B. Vance for governor, and through the columns of the *Standard* led the new party to victory at the polls. Holden continued to criticize Confederate policies, and he threatened to lead North Carolina out of the Confederacy if the Davis administration did not abandon its bias against the state and respect the rights of the people. His stance alarmed staunch Confederates not only in the state but also elsewhere in the South. They repeatedly charged that Holden was giving aid and comfort to the enemy and encouraging desertions from the army, charges that he denied.

When the carnage of the war reached a new high in mid-1863, Holden, though holding no office, called for negotiations to end the conflict. He proposed a peace that would "preserve the rights to the sovereign states and the institutions of the South [slavery]." In response to this call, "peace meetings" were held throughout North Carolina, bitterly dividing the state and raising the possibility of intervention from Richmond. As the crisis deepened in September, Holden called off the meetings a few days before Confederate troops, passing through Raleigh, sacked the office of his newspaper.

In early 1864 Holden proposed that a state convention meet to seek peace in cooperation with other southern states. When the Davis administration suspended the writ of habeas corpus, mainly in reaction to the dissent in North Carolina, Holden announced his candidacy for governor against Vance, who opposed the peace movement. The election, occurring in August, came at a time when Confederate hopes had been revived by widespread war-weariness in the North and the expectation that Lincoln would lose the presidential election. Rejecting Holden's defeatist platform, North Carolina voters resoundingly defeated him at the polls.

After the war President Andrew Johnson appointed Holden provisional governor of North Carolina, with the task of restoring civil government in the state. Holden, having reorganized the state under Johnson's Reconstruction plan, ran for governor in the fall of 1865. He suffered another defeat at the hands of his old political enemies. Disappointed by Johnson's failure to sustain him and disturbed by the course of Presidential Reconstruction, Holden cast his lot with congressional Republicans. When the Military Reconstruction Acts were passed in early 1867, he announced his support for black political rights and led the organizing of the state Republican party. Through the columns of the *Standard*, Holden became the main voice for Republicans in the state. In 1868 he was elected governor by a coalition of black and dissident white voters.

Holden's tenure as governor was turbulent. Most of the white citizens never accepted the legitimacy of the new biracial political order. Furthermore, railroad scandals involving North Carolina Republicans provided grist for the opposition mills, though Holden was not directly implicated. In 1869–1870 the Ku Klux Klan, using terrorist tactics, attempted to overthrow local Republican rule. When President Ulysses S. Grant refused to intervene, Holden dispatched a state military force under Colonel George W. Kirk into Alamance and Caswell counties to suppress the Klan. The so-called Kirk-Holden War in 1870 led to the arrest of more than one hundred Klansmen, but the reaction against Holden for his military action helped defeat the Republicans in the August 1870 election for control of the legislature. In early 1871 Holden, charged with raising an illegal military force and wrongfully directing it to arrest suspected Klansmen, was impeached and removed from office, the first governor in American history to suffer this indignity.

After a brief period of "exile" in Washington, Holden returned to Raleigh in 1872. He was appointed the town's postmaster by President Grant in 1873. His support of Grant for the Republican nomination in 1880 led to his removal from office in 1881 when James A. Garfield became president. Although he ultimately made peace with many of his old political foes, including Vance, Holden spent much of his post-Reconstruction years attempting in vain to obtain a reversal of the impeachment verdict. He died in Raleigh.

• The main collection of Holden papers is in the Manuscript Department, William R. Perkins Library, Duke University. The voluminous Governors' Papers, North Carolina Division of Archives and History, Raleigh, are indispensable for a study of Holden's Reconstruction career. William C. Harris, *William Woods Holden: Firebrand of North Carolina Politics* (1987), is the standard account of his life. For the North Carolina context of Holden's career, see Marc W. Kruman, *Parties and Politics in North Carolina, 1836–1865* (1983), and for the postwar period see Otto H. Olsen, ed., *Reconstruction and Redemption in the South* (1980).

WILLIAM C. HARRIS

HOLDER, Charles Frederick (5 Aug. 1851–10 Oct. 1915), naturalist and sportsman, was born in Lynn, Massachusetts, the son of Joseph Bassett Holder and Emily Augusta Gove. He entered but did not graduate from the U.S. Naval Academy. Influenced by his father's interest in natural sciences, Holder became an assistant curator of zoology at the American Museum of Natural History, where he worked from 1871 to 1875.

Holder left New York in 1885, moving to Pasadena, California, for health reasons. He received an appointment as professor of zoology at the Throop Institute (now the California Institute of Technology). His main source of income and his reputation, however, came from his dozen books and scores of magazine articles describing the animal world. Although he was not an environmentalist—he had a passion for hunting—his descriptions of the mountains, rivers, and wildlife of southern California attracted a large audience and popularized the subject with readers of all ages. His books included *Marvels of Animal Life* (1885), *Living Lights* (1887), *A Strange Company* (1888), *Charles Darwin* (1891), *Antiquities of California* (1891), *Louis Agassiz* (1893), *Big Game Fishes of the U.S.* (1903), *Life in the Open* (1906), and *The Channel Islands of California* (1910). Holder's articles and stories appeared in *Scientific American*, *McClure's*, *Century*, *Outing*, Saint Nicholas, and *Youth's Companion*.

Holder adapted wholeheartedly to life in southern California, finding the region ideally suited to his sportsman's interests. He took horseback trips up the Arroyo Seco Canyon and into the San Gabriel Mountain Range, where he fished in mountain streams and hunted big horn sheep, deer, and mountain lions. Back in Pasadena, he founded the aristocratic Valley Hunt Club, whose members in full uniform chased after foxes. On New Year's Day the club sponsored a large outdoor picnic followed by a ball in the evening. In 1890 the club held its first Tournament of Roses, featuring riding contests. By the early 1900s, encouraged by Holder, the tournament's appeal was broadened to include a floral parade, chariot races, and a ball. Holder helped found the Tournament of Roses Association to run the annual event as it evolved into a civic celebration attracting thousands of parade watchers.

Holder also helped establish the connection between Pasadena and Catalina Island, promoting the island as a resort attraction. He founded the Tuna Club in Avalon in 1898 and was the first person to go deep sea fishing for these fish with rod and reel off the southern California coast, creating a new field of recreation, sport fishing. As with his other natural history interests, Holder popularized the sport through books, such as *Big Game at Sea* (1908), and articles. He also reported on the growth of the abalone handicraft industry whereby abalone shells were sent from Catalina to Vienna, Austria, to be made into trinkets for sale to Catalina tourists.

Holder married Sarah Elizabeth Ufford in 1879. The Holders became a part of Pasadena society, enjoying the resort at Avalon on Catalina Island. When the palatial Raymond Hotel was opened in Pasadena in 1886, Holder was hired to lead tourists on expeditions to examine the local flora and fauna. A Quaker, Holder became interested in the early religious and political history of the Society of Friends, producing *The Quakers in Great Britain and America* (1913). He also completed a family history begun by his father (*The Holders of Holderness* [1902]).

Holder was, by turns and at the same time, an author, lecturer, sportsman, and naturalist. A contemporary Californian observer noted that "with his gift for popularizing, probably no other scientific writer has contributed more to make known, both in America and abroad, this attractive portion of our great State" (Newmark, pp. 557–58).

• Many of Holder's books include personal experiences and biographical information. Brief descriptions of Holder's contributions can be found in John W. Robinson, *The San Ga-*briels II* (1983), pp. 211–12; Kevin Starr, *Inventing the Dream: California through the Progressive Era* (1985), pp. 100–103; and Harris Newmark, *Sixty Years in Southern California, 1853–1913*, 3d ed. (1970), pp. 557–58. An obituary is in the *Los Angeles Times*, 11 Oct. 1915.

ABRAHAM HOFFMAN

HOLE IN THE DAY (1828?–27 June 1868), Ojibwe (or Chippewa) political leader, was born, probably at the Ojibwe village of Sandy Lake, in present-day Minnesota, the son of Hole-in-the-Day, the Elder, a Sandy Lake political leader, and Josephine(?) (no Ojibwe name known), a daughter of Broken Tooth, another Sandy Lake leader. Hole-in-the-Day was born as the United States was becoming a presence in Minnesota, and the Ojibwe, having enjoyed amicable relations with the British and French, sought to establish friendly ties with the Americans. The tribe's past connections with Europeans had been based on the fur trade; thoughtful Ojibwe realized that relations with the Americans would involve a very different economic system.

Hole-in-the-Day, the Elder, grooming his son to succeed him, immersed the youth in the Ojibwe political world. Besides standard male training as hunter and warrior, young Hole-in-the-Day attended both intratribal and Ojibwe-American councils. At the latter, Ojibwe leaders were impressed with the American proposals of economic assistance and religious instruction, although they did not share the Americans' goal that the Ojibwe would forsake their hunter/gatherer life and adopt market-oriented agrarianism and an idealized variant of American culture. Hole-in-the-Day's father was particularly struck by the economic security agriculture promised.

Hole-in-the-Day emerged as a leader following his father's death in 1847. He pursued the same policy of selective adaptation, establishing a farm and encouraging other Ojibwe to do likewise. He briefly explored Christianity in 1860 when his infant son, William, died and the child's grieving mother (name unknown) committed suicide. But Hole-in-the-Day was not prepared to submit unquestioningly to American policy interests. He closely observed Ojibwe-American relations and vigorously challenged American attempts to deny Ojibwe sovereignty. In 1848, for instance, he protested American-made changes in the treaty of 1847. "Why make a treaty with us if our Great Father can alter it without our consent?" he demanded. Skillfully combining highly visible, public appeals to American officials with strong hints that the Ojibwe would resort to force if their grievances were ignored, Hole-in-the-Day repeatedly countered American efforts to undermine Ojibwe sovereignty.

Hole-in-the-Day recognized that continued Ojibwe autonomy must rest on a firm economic foundation. American Indian policy, he felt, was not designed to ensure Indian self-sufficiency. At the treaty of 1855 he argued that cash annuities spread over several years were inadequate to restructure the Ojibwe economy. When divided per capita, the munificent-sounding sum amounted to about $4 per person, hardly enough to launch an agricultural transformation. In ways the Americans did not, Hole-in-the-Day understood an enormous gap existed between the Ojibwe's hunter/gatherer economy and the market-oriented agrarian economy of the United States. Providing the Ojibwe with land was not enough: they needed knowledge of agricultural technology and animal husbandry and an elaborate infrastructure of houses, barns, fenced fields, and farming equipment. The American negotiators remained uncomprehending and unswayed, and the Ojibwe ceded their lands, comprising the bulk of Minnesota, for about fourteen cents an acre.

Ojibwe life deteriorated rapidly after 1855. American emigration and forestry operations drove away the game and furbearing animals on which the Ojibwe depended. The leadership's adaptation policy came under increasing attack, especially by young warriors. Pushed to a more militant stance by the warriors, concerned by continuing American efforts to subjugate the Ojibwe, Hole-in-the-Day developed a new strategy. In the late 1850s and early 1860s he built a power base among the warriors. Simultaneously he cultivated relations with two groups with political influence in the new state of Minnesota: the old fur traders and the bicultural, bilingual mixed-blood population.

On 18 August 1862, spurred by Ojibwe complaints against the Indian Bureau, but also tapping deep-seated resentment over tribal decline, Hole-in-the-Day launched a war against the Americans. Strategically deploying his warriors to destroy property but avoid bloodshed, while utilizing the fur traders and mixed-bloods to intercede politically with American officials, Hole-in-the-Day won a new treaty in 1864 designed to correct existing abuses and place the Ojibwe on sound economic footing at a new large reservation in western Minnesota. His success catapulted him to a position of enormous power and prestige. But his ascendancy won him the enmity of some of the more western Ojibwe villages, who were understandably anxious about a leader of his stature and abilities moving into their territory.

Hole-in-the-Day was assassinated on 27 June 1868 by warriors from Leech Lake. Although the names of the assassins were well known at the time, they were never prosecuted, evidently because no existing American law applied to Indian-Indian crimes and because Hole-in-the-Day's relatives and friends feared their efforts to exact retribution would escalate into a serious blood feud the hard-pressed Ojibwe could ill afford. Controversy has continued to surround Hole-in-the-Day's death. Decades later, allegations surfaced that several traders and mixed-bloods had hired the murderers to eliminate a man they could not control.

Like many Ojibwe leaders, Hole-in-the-Day married polygynously, the matches designed to cement alliances with other important families. Americans salaciously attributed him with up to seven wives; four appears more accurate. Marriage dates are unknown. Besides William's mother he wed Jun-du-je-way-be-quay, or Mary Isabelle (?), with whom he had four children, and O-dun-ew, or Nancy, with whom he had three children. Both women appear to have outlived him. In 1867, while in Washington, D.C., Hole-in-the-Day met Ellen McCarty, a chambermaid at his hotel. She followed him home, claiming they were married by a priest in Chicago. Certainly Hole-in-the-Day and the Ojibwe regarded the union as legitimate. It seems probable that Hole-in-the-Day further understood the marriage as an effort to reestablish ties to the Americans. McCarty also survived her husband. They had one son.

Hole-in-the-Day was a difficult man for Americans to comprehend. Accustomed to thinking of Native leaders as either friendly (pro-American) or hostile (anti-American), they could see no motive in the Ojibwe leader's seemingly contradictory actions. Understood on his own terms, however, Hole-in-the-Day emerges as committed to his own goals of insuring Ojibwe political and social autonomy through a secure economic base. His means and tactics shifted as he saw the need; his end did not.

• Several manuscript collections at the Minnesota Historical Society, Saint Paul, contain information on Hole-in-the-Day. Among the most significant are the Augustus Aspinwall Reminiscence, the Abby Abbe Fuller Papers, the Julia Warren Spears Papers, and the Henry B. Whipple Papers. Letters sent by Hole-in-the-Day to American officials, although written and translated into English for him by others, can be found in the rolls of Letters Received by the Office of Indian Affairs, National Archives Manuscripts.

Little published material exists regarding Hole-in-the-Day's life. Mark Diedrich's short narrative, *The Chiefs Hole-in-the-Day of the Mississippi Chippewa* (1986), is the only biography. Several short articles in the Wisconsin State Historical Society *Collections*, vol. 5 (1907), contain biographical details and relate incidents in Hole-in-the-Day's life.

Not surprisingly, a greater body of documentation exists for the events surrounding the 1862 war. George W. Sweet, "Incidents of the Threatened Outbreak of Hole-in-the-Day," in the Minnesota Historical Society *Collections*, vol. 6 (1894), is an account by a participant. Two articles, Edward A. Bromley's "Hole-in-the-Day, the Chippewa Chief: Why He Failed in 1862 to Capture Minneapolis and Saint Paul," originally published in 1897 and reprinted in *Minnesota Archaeologist* 39 (1980): 138–49, and Stephen P. Hall's "The Hole-in-the-Day Encounter," *Minnesota Archaeologist* 36 (1977): 77–96, base their narratives around extended eyewitness accounts by Anglo-American participants. A recent reassessment of the 1862 war, focusing on U.S. government corruption as a cause, is Mark Diedrich, "Chief Hole-in-the-Day and the 1862 Chippewa Disturbance: A Reappraisal," *Minnesota History* 50 (Spring 1989): 193–203.

REBECCA KUGEL

HOLIDAY, Billie (7 Apr. 1915–17 July 1959), singer, was born Eleanora Fagan in Philadelphia, Pennsylvania, the daughter of Clarence Holiday, a musician, and Sadie Fagan. Her parents probably never married, and shortly after Holiday's birth her father left to pursue his career as a jazz guitarist and her mother moved back to Baltimore, where Holiday spent the early years of her childhood. When her mother moved north in search of work, Holiday remained behind, cared for by relatives. She later wrote of the beatings and unhappiness she endured during these years and of being raped as a ten year old, but some scholars question the reliability of her account. She was certainly strong-willed, playing hooky from school so often (completing only the fifth grade) that in 1925 she was ordered by the juvenile court to spend a year in the Baltimore House of the Good Shepherd for Colored Girls.

After her release, Holiday began to hang out with the hustlers and pimps who populated Baltimore's music scene in the twenties and thirties. Although only twelve, she looked much older and began to work as a prostitute at Alice Dunn's bordello; she also sang for the customers there and elsewhere and listened to recordings by her two primary influences, Bessie Smith and Louis Armstrong. In 1927 she moved to New York City to be with her mother, working as a maid, a prostitute, and a waitress.

Intent on pursuing a music career, Holiday sang at jam sessions throughout the city from 1930 until 1932 and performed regularly at Pod and Jerry's speakeasy. Only fifteen, she was already earning $50 or more a night. John Hammond (1910–1987) first heard her sing in a small after-hours club in Harlem called Monette's, and he convinced Benny Goodman to record with her. Her first effort, a late 1933 recording of "Your Mother's Son-in-Law," was marred by her own nervousness and a stodgy rhythm section. Three weeks later, she recorded "Riffin' the Scotch" with much better results, already showing a highly individual style. From 1933 until 1935 she sang regularly at several clubs, performed at the Apollo Theater for two weeks in April 1935, and sang a blues segment in a short film of Duke Ellington's *Symphony in Black: A Rhapsody of Negro Life.* Her career came into its own on 2 July 1935, when she recorded a session with the pianist Teddy Wilson and a small group. She recorded extensively with Wilson in a variety of settings over the next few years; in 1937 alone they made classics like "They Can't Take That Away From Me," "Easy Living," and "This Year's Kisses."

Holiday had a small voice with a range of only about an octave, but she created a sense of intimacy with her audience. She could transform a song, inflecting words and pitches to give them her own meaning and emotional content. One of her favorite songs, "A Fine Romance" (1936), became a light satire, while she transformed the buoyant "Let's Call the Whole Thing Off" (1937) into a cry of pain and despair; George and Ira Gershwin's "Summertime" (1936) became ominous rather than peaceful and nostalgic. She had a relaxed sense of swing; she stretched rhythms and sang around, behind, and ahead of the beat. She considered herself a musician collaborating with other musicians, and she phrased and improvised like a horn player. Her voice had a reedy timbre, but she could make it brighter or darker, vulnerable or tough, all to suit the needs of the song. She could rescue a piece of fluff and make it a joyful romp—hear her recording of "What a Little Moonlight Can Do," which shows her sheer pleasure in singing.

In 1937 Holiday joined the Count Basie Orchestra, which had a rhythm section famed for its flawless sense of time. Holiday loved singing with the band, and its members appreciated her impeccable musicianship. But she was eventually fired, for reasons that remain unclear. She was also fired from an engagement at the Grand Terrace Cafe in Chicago; the management accused her of singing too slowly. She joined the Artie Shaw Orchestra as one of the first black vocalists to be featured with an all-white band, and she suffered from discrimination and racial slurs as the group toured the country. Again, it remains unclear why she left. She took umbrage at being forced to enter the Lincoln Hotel through the kitchen, while Shaw's management did not like her, claiming her style was not sufficiently commercial.

Holiday was a star by 1939, enjoying the personal freedom and artistic success she had been seeking since her early teens, but her personal life was in a state of constant flux. She had brief affairs with Goodman and Shaw and with Basie's guitarist, Freddie Green, and a relationship with the tenor saxophonist Ben Webster left her with a black eye. Perhaps the most important male relationship she enjoyed during these years, though, was her platonic friendship with the tenor saxophonist Lester Young. It was Young who dubbed her "Lady Day," and the two became inseparable both during and after their days together in Basie's band. Musically, they formed a perfect partnership of voice and instrument; their performances on songs like "I'll Get By" and "Mean to Me" remain classics.

The second stage of Holiday's career began in 1939 with her engagement at the Café Society, a Greenwich Village hangout frequented by an interracial audience of liberal intellectuals, bohemians, and Park Avenue and show business jazz fans. It was here that she first sang "Strange Fruit." Written and set to music by Lewis Allen, the song was a stark, metaphorical portrayal of southern lynchings of blacks, sung by Holiday at a dramatic, funereal tempo. Columbia declined to record it, but Milt Gabler, who had begun his own small Commodore label, readily agreed to issue a studio version. Some critics have argued that this was the beginning of the end of Holiday's great period. But others hold her rendition of "Strange Fruit" (1939) to be one of the most powerful, understated commentaries on prejudice committed to music. At the same session she recorded an exceptional version of "Fine and Mellow," an anguished tune of abandonment and lost love.

Holiday had smoked marijuana regularly since her teenage years, and she now began to use both heroin and opium. In August 1941 she married Jimmy Monroe, a nightclub manager. She traveled to the West Coast, where she drew the admiration of stars like Bob Hope and dated Orson Welles. In the spring of 1945 she divorced Monroe and married jazz trumpeter Joe Guy. The two formed an orchestra and toured, with minimal success. That same year her mother died. It was a devastating blow; despite the rocky early years, the two had become exceptionally close.

Holiday recorded extensively for Decca Records from 1946 until 1950, accompanied by strings and a variety of jazz groups. Her voice seems fuller and stronger than ever during these sessions, her interpretive skills undiminished; she delivers inspired readings of songs like "Them There Eyes" and "Lover Man." Other aspects of her life, though, were less satisfying. She appeared in the movie *New Orleans* (1947) cast as a maid, an unhappy experience. Her drug problem worsened. In the spring of 1947 she entered a clinic to kick her heroin habit, but federal agents arrested her on narcotics charges soon thereafter. She spent almost a year in a federal reformatory, and she was back on heroin shortly after her release. Because she had been convicted of a felony, she was denied the cabaret card necessary to work in New York City nightclubs. In 1947 she met John Levy, a club manager and another in the roster of men who exploited and physically abused her. The two were arrested after a 1948 New Year's Eve nightclub brawl and charged with opium possession. This time, though, Holiday had a good lawyer and escaped a jail sentence. Although she married Levy in January 1949, she eventually left him and began a relationship with Louis McKay, invariably characterized as a "tough guy," whom she married in 1956.

Holiday now entered the final phase of her career. Ravaged by drug abuse, her voice coarsened, but it also took on a dark, sensuous beauty. From 1952 to 1957 she recorded for Verve Records. Even now her off nights were rare, and her best performances reveal an undiminished sense of timing, phrasing, and tonal control. Her 1952 recording of "These Foolish Things," for instance, is considered far superior to her 1936 version, and her rendition of "Fine and Mellow" with Young in rehearsal for "The Sound of Jazz" television show is profoundly moving.

In February 1956 Holiday was arrested again on narcotics charges. Although she successfully overcame the habit in a clinic, her drinking became heavier, and her voice steadily deteriorated. On occasion, she could still sing beautifully, as she did in a February 1959 BBC television performance, but this time there would be no comeback. She gave her last performance on 25 May 1959 at the Phoenix Theater in New York City. She and McKay had separated, and she was living alone in an apartment near Central Park, with only one of her much-loved dogs for companionship.

Holiday collapsed on Memorial Day 1959 and fell into a coma, her body ravaged by liver problems and cardiac failure. She recovered briefly, only to be subject to one final humiliation. The New York police raided her hospital room on 12 June and found a small packet of heroin. They confiscated her radio, record player, flowers, comic books, chocolates, and even a copy of a gossip magazine, and they took mug shots and fingerprints as she lay in her sickbed. She died there.

Many fans and critics have constructed a romantic myth around Holiday's life, portraying her as a naturally gifted artist who struggled against and was ultimately killed by a racist, repressive society. The film *Lady Sings the Blues* (1972) has popularized this version of her life. She was indeed a fragile, vulnerable person who often suffered from the world's cruelties. But she was also a successful and great artist because she worked at it and proved strong enough to overcome many obstacles. She was happy most of her life, particularly when she was with friends and performing music; she sang many more joyful songs (and rarely the blues) than sad ones. Singing gave her a sense of power and control as well as emotional fulfillment. As a vocalist, she was unique. She was a minimalist, singing only the notes that counted and infusing songs with new and deeper meanings. The critic and composer Ned Rorem said of her artistry: "She's so involved . . . her eyes closed, her head back. It's pure theater. It's not real life. . . . It's a concentration of life" (O'Meally, p. 43).

• Holiday's life and work have been the subject of controversy. Her autobiography, *Lady Sings the Blues* (with William Dufty, 1965), must be used cautiously, particularly in its account of her early years; it remains invaluable, however, for her version of many events of her adult life. Critics and scholars have also consistently undervalued her work after 1940. Robert O'Meally, *Lady Day: The Many Faces of Billie Holiday* (1991), builds on the extensive research of the late Linda Kuehl to set the record straight on Holiday's personal life, and he offers the most perceptive and thorough analysis of her career and music. Other useful biographies include John Chilton, *Billie's Blues: Billie Holiday's Story, 1933–1959* (1975), John White, *Billie Holiday* (1987), Donald Clarke, *Wishing on the Moon: The Life and Times of Billie Holiday* (1994), and Stuart Nicholson, *Billie Holiday* (1995). The best succinct musical analysis of her singing is in Gunther Schuller's *The Swing Era: The Development of Jazz, 1930–1945* (1989), pp. 527–47. Of many fine, brief discussions of Holiday's life and work, the best include Melvin Maddocks, *Billie Holiday* (1979), in the Time-Life "Giants of Jazz" series; Will Friedwald, *Jazz Singing: America's Great Voices from Bessie Smith to Bebop and Beyond* (1990); Leonard Feather, *From Satchmo to Miles* (1972), pp. 67–86; Martin Williams, *The Jazz Tradition* (1983), pp. 83–91; James Lincoln Collier, *The Making of Jazz: A Comprehensive History* (1978), pp. 304–12; Nat Hentoff, *Jazz Is* (1976), pp. 43–59; Akira Yamato, "Billie Holiday on Verve," booklet with *Billie Holiday on Verve: 1946–1959* (1985); and Linda Dahl, *Stormy Weather: The Music and Lives of a Century of Jazzwomen* (1984).

RONALD P. DUFOUR

HOLKER, John (1745–1822), agent for the French during the American Revolution and influential merchant, also known as Jean Holker, was born at the time of the last Jacobite Rebellion (exact date and place unknown), the son of John Holker, an English soldier from the Manchester area who had sided with the Pretender. (His mother's name is not known.) John Sr. fled with his family to France when the rebellion collapsed. In exile he turned to pioneering the introduction of new manufacturing techniques from England. He became a prosperous textile merchant-industrialist based in Rouen, and in 1755, thanks to the patronage of a powerful minister at court, Trudaine de Montigny, was appointed inspector general of manufactures. In 1775 he acquired the additional title of chevalier. In 1777 he acted as principal in a large contract for military clothing and uniforms placed by the American commissioners at Versailles on Congress's behalf.

His son followed in his footsteps, visiting England to stay abreast of the latest technology in textiles. Both father and son saw in the American Revolution a unique opportunity for France to take Britain's place in promoting the development of North America. Even before the Franco-American alliance was formalized in 1778, the younger Holker was recruited by the French government and a group of highly placed entrepreneurs to go to the United States as an agent. He finally arrived on the continent in May 1778, in the company of France's first fully accredited diplomatic representative, Conrad Alexandre Gérard. By that time Holker had acquired a third mission, to act as agent for the French navy in North America.

Holker and Gérard traveled from Boston to Philadelphia during the course of the summer and presented themselves to Congress. Gérard received a warm official welcome, but Congress questioned Holker's credentials and insisted they be validated. Gérard responded by appointing Holker consul general of France for the Middle Atlantic states.

After returning to Boston to help Charles Hector Théodat, comte d'Estaing, refit his fleet in the autumn of 1778, Holker took up permanent residence in Philadelphia, where he attended his official duties. The seat of the Continental government was the best place from which to manage a large speculative venture in loan office certificates, a congressional financial instrument resembling a war bond, backed by a syndicate of prominent French investors, in which he had a share. Holker was also in a good position to coordinate the activities throughout the continent of other French consuls and agents in the service of the navy and private adventurers. But his actions brought him into a sequence of bruising confrontations, first with local authorities trying to enforce price regulations during the autumn of 1779, then with the French Court for which he served as representative, and eventually with many of his business partners, both French and American.

In 1779 a popular committee in Wilmington, Delaware, seized a parcel of flour that had been purchased by Jonathan Rumford in violation of local price regulations. Rumford claimed authority from Holker. The Wilmington committee responded by referring the matter to a similar committee in Philadelphia. Gérard intervened in Holker's behalf, going so far as to request Congress to prosecute the *Pennsylvania Packet,* which had published an account of the dispute. Gérard quickly withdrew his demand for a prosecution, and Congress arranged an amiable resolution of the affair with Pennsylvania's authorities. But Holker was wounded by the disclosure of his willingness to violate local market regulations in order to provide for the French fleet in the West Indies and to some extent was held accountable for the acute flour shortages that plagued the Continental army in the winter of 1779–1780. At the same time, the failure of the speculation in American loan office certificates, the difficulties French merchants and his fellow consuls experienced in America, and the enormous discount at which French bills sold in America led to growing criticism of him in France. Finally his reputation among many American merchants became tarnished when bills he had drawn on France, known as "Holker bills," began to be protested because he had exceeded the instructions of his principals in France.

The French Court reacted to complaints against Holker by forcing him to choose between his public duties and his private affairs. Holker responded by resigning his official responsibilities in October 1781. Although Holker's activities had eroded the popularity of the Franco-American alliance in the United States, he had been a reasonably diligent agent for the French navy. He was less successful in assisting French merchants in conducting a wartime trade with the United States. But he played a significant role in partnership with American entrepreneurs such as William Duer (1747–1799), Daniel Parker, Matthew Ridley, William Pringle, and Robert Morris (1734–1806) in sponsoring the resumption of a direct commerce with Europe during the war, and Morris continued to rely on Holker as a principal supplier of imported clothing for the Continental army after Holker had resigned his official commissions. Holker was also a silent partner in two of the contracts let by Morris to merchant syndicates that undertook to provision the army in 1782, the Northern Department Contract and the Moving Army Contract.

Holker and his American partners had high expectations for the continued development of the commercial connection between France and the United States after the war. They also hoped to open new trade, particularly with China, and to speculate in western lands. But the postwar liquidity crisis of 1784–1786 brought Holker into conflict with many of his former associates; he became involved in lengthy controversies, particularly with Morris and Parker, the latter persisting into the next century. Holker's fortunes suffered an additional reversal in 1786 when his father died, effectively severing him from sources of French influence and capital, assets that had hitherto made him attractive to American entrepreneurs. The French Revolution did little to help him repair the damage.

Holker's later career was unspectacular. Throughout the 1790s he remained in the United States, principally in Philadelphia, trying to wind up his wartime partnerships. During these years he became involved in one new venture to establish an iron and salt works in the Pittsburgh area in partnership with wartime associates William Turnbull and Peter Marmie. He returned to France for an extended visit from 1800 and 1804, apparently hoping to use the French courts in his struggle to obtain justice from his former partner

Daniel Parker. Though he had left a wife and young son behind in France when he first came to America in 1778, Holker maintained a distance from his family during his stay in France. He returned to the United States in 1804 to continue the struggle to settle the affairs of his wartime partnerships. Little is known about his last years except that by 1807 he had moved to a farm in Frederick County, Virginia, where it is presumed he died, having outlived most of his revolutionary associates.

Though the younger Holker responded to the upheaval of the revolutionary war more as an aggressive entrepreneur than as a representative of France, his foreign connections were crucial to his initial success. In this respect his career followed the pattern established by his father after he was forced into exile during the Jacobite Rebellion. The son, however, proved notably less successful than the father. While France was eager to keep pace with Britain's new industrial techniques throughout the elder Holker's life, it drew away from the United States in the years after the peace of 1783. The younger Holker's slow descent into obscurity mirrors the declining significance of the Franco-American relationship in the post–revolutionary war period.

• There is a large collection of Holker papers at the Library of Congress and smaller collections at the William L. Clements Library at the University of Michigan, at the Beinecke Library at Yale University, and at the Historical Society of Western Pennsylvania in Pittsburgh. Additional Holker material can be found in the Archives Nationales, Affaires Etrangères, Série BI and Archives des Affaires Etrangères, Correspondance Politique, États-Unis, Paris, and in the papers of the Continental Congress and the papers of most prominent members of Congress for the period. See in particular Paul H. Smith, ed., *Letters of the Delegates to Congress, 1774–1789* (1976–); E. James Ferguson et al., eds. *The Papers of Robert Morris, 1781–1784* (1973–); and John J. Meng, ed., *Despatches and Instructions of Conrad Alexandre Gérard, 1778–1780* (1941). He has not figured prominently in the secondary literature about the period, except in Kathryn Sullivan, *Maryland and France 1774–1789* (1936), though Robert A. East, *Business Enterprise in the American Revolutionary Era* (1938), does mention him occasionally, and Abraham P. Nasatir and Gary Elwyn Monell, eds., *French Consuls in the United States: A Calendar of Their Correspondence in the Archives Nationales* (1967), contains a brief sketch of him. His involvement with Morris's network of investors in the China trade after the war is covered in P. C. F. Smith, *The Empress of China* (1984). His father was the subject of a biography by André Remond, *John Holker, manufacturier et grand fonctionnaire en France au XVIIIème siècle, 1719–1786* (1946), which contains some family information. E. Earl Moore, "An Introduction to the Holker Papers," *Western Pennsylvania Historical Magazine* 42 (1959): 225–39, remains the best source on his later years.

RICHARD BUEL, JR.

HOLLADAY, Ben (14 Oct. 1819–8 July 1887), transportation magnate, was born in Nicholas County, Kentucky, the son of William Holladay and Margaret Hughes, farmers. At age seventeen, with little education or experience beyond that gained as the son of poor farmers on the Kentucky frontier, Holladay left home, sensing opportunity lying to the west. He moved to Weston, on the Missouri-Kansas border, where he began working as a courier for militia fighting against the Mormons in the town of Far West, Missouri. In this role of ferrying messages back and forth between the Mormons and the militia, Holladay was able to gain the Mormons' trust. After this experience, in 1838 Holladay decided to settle in Weston and made a series of entrepreneurial investments, first as a saloonkeeper and then as a druggist and dry-goods merchant. Eventually he opened a hotel and was appointed local postmaster. With his profits, he purchased his first set of freight wagons, fitting them with the extra-wide tires that would become his trademark. In 1840 Holladay met and married Notley Ann Calvert, daughter of a well-to-do Weston family; they had seven children, one of whom died in infancy.

Holladay's first major freighting contract was with the U.S. Army, which in 1846 hired him to carry goods and supplies during the Mexican War. The war not only unlocked a vast frontier to the West, but also netted Holladay a handsome profit with which to further his freighting enterprise. One of his next major undertakings was the establishment of a monopoly of trade with his friends, the Mormons, in Salt Lake City. Soon his wagon freight lines extended from Atchison, near Weston, to Salt Lake City and even to California; these were supplemented with riverboats on the Sacramento River and eventually with steamships sailing from California to Australia and Hawaii.

Holladay's next major coup was the acquisition of U.S. postal contracts to transport the mails across a central route between the East and the West, after the Butterfield Southern Overland Mail Company was forced to abandon its southern route during the Civil War. Between 1862 and 1867 Holladay was in control of the country's major stagecoach lines to the west of the Mississippi River; his Holladay Overland Mail and Express Company was the largest stage and freight company in the world. Customers paid $75 for a trip from Atchison to Denver and fifty cents to ship a pound of mail the same distance. It was a lucrative business but not without great risk: bad weather, poor roads, and frequent Indian raids disrupted the regularity of Holladay's service and marred his reputation. Customers, competitors, and politicians seemed to resent his monopolistic control of the central routes. The *Sacramento Daily Union* blamed his "grasping and speculative spirit" for the irregularity.

Ever seeking to increase his wealth and take advantage of any promising opportunity, Holladay sold his stagecoach business in 1866 in time to begin making investments in the burgeoning railroad industry taking root on the West Coast. In 1866 he had already purchased controlling interest in the Oregon Central Railroad Company in East Portland, Oregon. This company was competing with another railroad of the same name that was located on the west side of the Willamette River. Both the East Siders and West Siders, as they were known, competed with each other to lay the first twenty miles of railroad track in Oregon and become the winners of a substantial federal land grant. Holladay's East Siders won the race, giving Oregon its first operating railroad on Christmas Day 1869. The line ran from Portland to Parrott Creek, six miles south of Oregon City. With investment capital from England and Germany, Holladay eventually took over the property of the West Siders, organizing the Oregon & California Railroad Company. By 1872 he was in control of 245.5 miles of railroad, much of it running the nearly 200-mile stretch from Portland south to Roseburg.

Also in 1872 Holladay gave Portland its first horse-drawn streetcar line, operating along two miles of track on the west side of the Willamette River. He also made major real estate investments on both sides of the river, including sixty-one blocks of property on the east side. He established a park and constructed two hotels—one on each side of the river. He also founded the Oregon Transfer Company, organized the Pacific Warehouse and Dock Company, erected docks on both sides of the river, and incorporated the Willamette Transportation Company through which he monopolized steam traffic up and down the Willamette River. His reach extended to the seaside town of Astoria, where he built an extravagant resort villa on 700 acres of land.

Holladay's success began to take a turn, however, when the entire country's railroading industry became threatened with the collapse of the investment house of Jay Cooke & Company and the panic of 1873. Holladay's wife died on the same day—18 September 1873—that Jay Cooke & Company announced its failure. Holladay himself defaulted on his bonds shortly thereafter. By 1874 his Oregon & California Railroad had defaulted twice more. German bondholders sent Henry Villard, a Bavarian-born, German-educated journalist and future "railroad genius" to investigate Holladay's handling of events. Villard was impressed with the transportation opportunities in Oregon but not with Holladay, whom he described as having "enthroned himself as the absolute ruler of all the lines of transportation on land and by river and sea in western Oregon" (Villard, p. 32). Holladay, Villard reported, "had a fine presence and was dressed in the latest fashion. He appeared a gentleman, at first sight. . . . [but] a short intercourse with him sufficed to disclose his illiteracy, coarseness, presumption, mendacity, and unscrupulousness" (Villard, p. 40). Within two years Villard bought out Holladay, eventually displacing him "as the dominant figure in the development of the Northwest's transportation network" (Buss, pp. 93–94). Once dethroned, Holladay moved east to Washington, D.C., with his second wife Lydia Esther Campbell, whom he had married in 1874; they had two children. When Holladay's health began to fail around 1879 he made one last trip west, back to Portland, where he died within a decade.

Holladay's contributions to transportation history have been given scant attention, partly because many records were destroyed in the San Francisco earthquake and fire of 1906 and partly because of his gruffness, which alienated many with whom he came into contact. Despite his many contributions to Portland's transportation and commerce, Holladay remained an outsider in that city, unable to ingratiate himself with Portland's leading political and business leaders. There was even a "Stop Holladay" movement when he tried to enter the race for U.S. senator in 1872. Holladay's role in the development of transportation in Oregon ranks among the most important factors in the territory's early growth. Equally important is the role he played in opening up and maintaining transportation and communication lines between the eastern and western United States in the years following the Civil War.

• An important group of historical records regarding Ben Holladay was lost when the files of the Holladay Overland Mail and Express Company—kept in the Wells, Fargo & Company Building in San Francisco—were destroyed in the 1906 fire and earthquake. Otherwise, primary records are fairly scattered. The best sources are the historical societies and special archives in Oregon, Oklahoma, California, Colorado, Nebraska, Kansas, Nevada, Wyoming, New York, and Montana. Some attention is devoted to Holladay in general histories of the cities and states where he had the greatest impact, as in Joseph Gaston, *Portland, Oregon* (1911) and *Centennial History of Oregon* (1912). Because Gaston was an archenemy of Holladay's his works must be read with caution. Holladay's enterprises also receive some coverage in works dealing with stagecoach and general transportation history; see, for example, LeRoy R. Hafen, *The Overland Mail* (1926); George Estes, *The Stagecoach* (1931); Oswald Garrison Villard, ed., *Early History of Transportation in Oregon* (1944); and Dietrich G. Buss, *Henry Villard: A Study of Transatlantic Investments and Interests, 1870–1895* (1978). Three works that offer some biographical information are William Harland Boyd, *The Holladay-Villard Transportation Empire in the Pacific Northwest, 1868–1893* (1946); James Vincent Frederick, *Ben Holladay, the Stagecoach King: A Chapter in the Development of Transcontinental Transportation* (1989; repr. of 1968 and 1940 editions); and Ellis Lucia, *The Saga of Ben Holladay, Giant of the Old West* (1959). The Frederick and Lucia books concentrate on his career in stagecoaching through 1867; Lucia also devotes a fair amount of attention to Holladay's career in the Northwest. An obituary is in the *Morning Oregonian*, 9 July 1887.

MARTHA J. BIANCO

HOLLAND, Annie Welthy Daughtry (c. 1871–6 Jan. 1934), educator and promoter of public education for blacks, was born in Isle of Wight County, Virginia, on land adjacent to the Welthy (also spelled Wealthy) plantation, the daughter of Sarah Daughtry and J. W. Barnes. (Her parentage, incorrectly reported in some earlier sources, has been confirmed by her death certificate; see Littlefield, pp. 569–70.) Her grandfather Friday Daughtry had been born and raised a slave but during the 1860s was freed by the Welthy family. Annie had been named after Annie Welthy of the Welthy plantation. Sometime between 1872 and 1879 her mother divorced her father. Her mother later remarried, and the family moved to Southhampton County, Virginia. In 1880 Friday Daughtry brought Annie back to Isle of Wight, where she lived with her grandmother, Lucinda, and worked on the farm while studying at the county school. In 1883, at the age of eleven, she enrolled as an eighth-grade student at Hampton Institute, an agricultural and industrial school for blacks founded in 1868 at nearby Hampton, Virginia. To help pay for her second year of study she spent the summer of 1884 in New York working for a wealthy white family. She had to leave school before the end of the following summer, however, owing to a bout with malaria, which made her unable to work, as well as her grandfather's financial troubles; failing health had made it difficult for him to continue to pay her tuition. She then returned to Isle of Wight where for two years after taking the teachers examination and receiving a second-grade certificate, she taught in the county elementary school. In 1888 she left her teaching post and went to work in New York but soon returned because of the illness of her grandmother. Just before her grandmother died in 1888, she married Willis B. Holland, a Hampton graduate and educator; they would have at least one child, a daughter.

In 1897 the Hollands moved to Franklin, Virginia, where he served as principal of Franklin Public School and she as his assistant, a position she held until early 1899. Later that same year she asked to be transferred to the countryside, both for reasons of health and because she believed that education for blacks was particularly lacking in rural areas. After completing the teacher training course at the Normal Institute in Petersburg in 1903, Holland passed the examination for a five-year teaching certificate. She then taught in the rural schools until 1905, when she succeeded her husband as principal of the Franklin school after he went into insurance and real estate.

In 1911 Holland moved to Gates County, North Carolina, to become county supervisor of rural schools. From her base at the Gates Institute in Sunbury, she supervised industrial classes in twenty-two schools. In 1912 she moved up the road to Corapeake, near the Virginia border. In 1914 she returned to Hampton Institute, where she attended a ten-day summer normal course in agriculture. The following year she was named state home demonstration agent for North Carolina, a post that carried the dual role of state supervisor of the Anna T. Jeanes Fund. The Jeanes Fund, which sent hundreds of teachers around the South beginning in 1907, was a private trust designed to promote the development of public education for rural blacks.

Now in charge of roughly four dozen county supervisors, Holland traveled throughout the state, organizing meetings and fund drives and teaching demonstration classes. Her 1916 schedule required her to visit ten eastern North Carolina counties extending from Virginia to South Carolina. In 1917 she concentrated her efforts on the Piedmont counties, where she taught vegetable canning, nutrition, sewing, and gardening, as well as reading and writing, and also encouraged the homemakers clubs to raise and sell poultry and livestock. Between 1916 and 1917, under Holland's supervision, Jeanes Fund teachers reportedly made more than three thousand visits to more than a thousand schools in thirty-five counties. They worked to improve the physical appearance and structure of many schools, some of which extended their school term from four to five months. Holland's position was jointly funded by the Jeanes Fund and the North Carolina Colored Teachers' Association until 1921, the year the North Carolina General Assembly established the Negro Division of Education, whereupon the post was incorporated into the state educational organization. Holland's title was changed to state supervisor of Negro elementary schools, and from then on the position was paid, in part, with state funds. She continued to travel around the state, organizing reading circles and clubs designed to assist in the education of black students.

In 1923–1924, from out of the Community Leagues that Jeanes teachers had helped to develop, Holland began to organize parent-teacher associations. In 1927 she founded the North Carolina Congress of Colored Parents and Teachers. The National Congress of Colored Parents and Teachers, conceived by black Americans and founded in 1926, was a national parent-teacher association concerned with child welfare, improving the quality of life of black families, and developing effective communication between parents and teachers. The North Carolina congress held its first annual meeting at Shaw University in Raleigh, North Carolina, on 14 April 1928. During its first year (1928), the state PTA established 784 local associations comprising 15,770 members, and within two years the group had raised more than $115,000. Jeanes teachers and the PTA, under Holland's supervision, installed libraries, erected new buildings, and extended school curricula to include dental hygiene and health.

Holland died at a doctor's office in Louisburg, North Carolina, soon after collapsing while addressing a group of black teachers. More than 800 persons attended a memorial for her in Raleigh. She was buried in Franklin, Virginia. In 1938, the tenth anniversary of the North Carolina Congress of Colored Parents and Teachers, a tree was planted in her memory at Shaw University. A women's residence hall at North Carolina Agricultural and Technical State University in Greensboro is named in her honor.

Holland is reported to have been a kind as well as devoted worker in the cause of educating rural blacks in North Carolina. Her organizational abilities and happy disposition helped to unite white and black interests, parents, and professionals in working toward the goal of quality education for all children; and, through her activism and commitment, she forced the issue of funding to the state and national levels. The success of education for North Carolina's rural blacks can be explained, in part, by the cooperative impulse of Annie Holland, an able educator who devoted her life to teaching teachers.

• Holland's student record is in the Hampton University Archives. Papers related to her tenure as state supervisor can be found at the North Carolina Department of Archives, Raleigh. The issue of her parentage is discussed in Valinda Rogers Littlefield's entry on Holland in *Black Women in America: An Historical Encyclopedia*, ed. Darlene Clark Hine (1993). Correspondence between Nathan Newbold, director of the Negro Division of Education, and Holland is included in Nathan C. Newbold, ed., *Five North Carolina Negro Educators* (1939). For more on the PTA in North Carolina and the significance of Holland in it, see Hugh Victor Brown, *A History of the Education of Negroes in North Carolina* (1961). A historiographical overview of black education in North Carolina is presented in Raymond Gavins, "A Sin of Omission," in *Black Americans in North Carolina and the South*, ed. Jeffrey J. Crow and Flora J. Hatley (1984).

DEBI HAMLIN

HOLLAND, Edwin Clifford (1794?–11 Sept. 1824), author and newspaper editor, was born in Charleston, South Carolina, the son of John Holland, formerly of Wilmington, North Carolina, and his wife Jane, the widow of Abraham Marshall of East Florida. Nothing is known concerning Holland's education, but to become a lawyer he probably studied in the office of a practicing attorney. His broad interest in literature and journalism may have come from his association with the youthful circle of cultured residents of Charleston who were later called "fledgling bards," among them William Crafts and Isaac Harby.

In 1812, when he was only about eighteen, Holland submitted several of his poems in a competition sponsored by *Port Folio*, a journal published in Philadelphia, offering two $100 prizes for naval songs. Entries arrived from all over the country, and the editors considered many of them to be "of considerable merit . . . both as odes & as convivial songs." Holland's "Pillar of Glory" was the first winner while another of his poems, "Rise, Columbia, Brave and Free," was "deemed too valuable to be overlooked." Both were published in the November 1813 issue, together with music composed especially for them by Jacob Eckhard, Sr., organist of St. Michael's Church, Charleston. Thoroughly patriotic, they reflected pride in America's victories in the War of 1812 and the expectation that the nation would attain a position of leadership in the world. Typical of their form and sentiment are these lines:

> When Freedom first the triumph sung,
> That crush'd the pomp of Freedom's foes,
> The Harps of Heav'n responsive rung,
> As thus the choral numbers rose:
> Rise, Columbia! brave and free!
> Thy thunder, when in battle hurl'd,
> Shall rule the billows of the sea,
> And bid defiance to the world.

In addition to appearing in *Port Folio*, both of these songs were included in Holland's *Odes, Naval Songs, and Other Occasional Poems (Never before Published)* (1813), which was printed for him by J. Hoff in Charleston in a forty-page booklet. It was dedicated to his highly regarded late stepbrother, James Marshall, of Savannah, Georgia. The seventeen poems contained in it are said to have marked the beginning of romantic poetry in South Carolina. Holland also composed music for one of these songs.

Dramatic presentations had long flourished in Charleston, where plays of varying distinction were presented at the Charleston Theatre, either by hometown troupes or by touring companies. Holland and his friends were among the local writers and actors inspired by these plays to try their own hand at theater. Like many southerners, Holland admired the contemporary English Romantic poet Lord Byron, so, in turning to the theater, he developed a dramatic version of that poet's "The Corsair." In a small format of fifty-three pages, printed in Charleston by A. E. Miller, it appeared in 1818 as *The Corsair, a Melo-Drama in Four Acts, Collected and Arranged for the Stage from Lord Byron's Poem*. It was produced in the same year with local actors and was later appraised by a critic as having "some merit in its unity and compactness of structure." Stage directions called for music that was "soft and plaintive" during the prologue but elsewhere "descriptive of sudden joy." The prologue was written in rhyming couplets, but the remainder was in blank verse that very ingeniously incorporated some of Byron's rhyming lines.

Among Charleston's literary lights in the early nineteenth century was the second principal of the College of Charleston, Thomas Bee, Jr., who in 1821 established a periodical called *Omnium Gatherum*. When Bee published unflattering comments about some of the young poets and writers of the city in this periodical, the latter retaliated by publishing *Omnium Botherum*, to which Holland was a contributor.

In the 1820s, Holland, like many Americans, became concerned with the issue of slavery. In 1822, in the wake of a Charleston slave uprising led by free black Denmark Vesey, Holland, at that time editor of the *Charleston Times*, secured a copyright on an eighty-six-page publication entitled *A Refutation of the Calumnies Circulated against the Southern and Western States, Respecting the Institution and Existence of Slavery among Them*. Although copyrighted by Holland, the work bore only the pseudonym "A South-Carolinian"; it was printed by A. E. Miller, who had also printed *The Corsair* for Holland. Significant information on the history of blacks in South Carolina appeared for the first time in this work.

The author informed his readers that he did "not pretend to anything very novel in his manner of treating the subject" but that he would consider "questions of the most profound and vital importance, affecting every one in all the different relations of life." Although Holland himself favored slavery, he recognized the existence of doubts among southerners as to the usefulness of the institution and noted that they "had uniformly exhibited a disposition to restrict the extension of the evil—and have always manifested as cordial a disposition to ameliorate it as those of the Northern and Eastern divisions of our Empire." He advocated the colonization of free blacks, a class of people that he regarded as "the greatest and most deplorable evil with which we are unhappily afflicted." One modern scholar has characterized this work as "the first autonomous proslavery treatise written and published by a native southerner."

In 1823, using the same pseudonym and the same publisher, Holland authored a thirty-eight page pamphlet, *Practical Considerations Founded on the Scriptures, Relative to the Slave Population of South Carolina.*

On 15 May 1815, Holland was married in the Independent Congregational Church of Charleston to twenty-year-old Selina Parker, daughter of the late Dr. William Parker. He died nine years later in Charleston during one of the epidemics of yellow fever that frequently struck coastal regions of the South.

• Holland's own publications contain a little biographical information. Since only a limited number of issues of the *Charleston Times* survive, it is not possible to determine the period of his editorship. Facts about his life are to be found in scattered sources such as the *South Carolina Historical and Genealogical Magazine* 33 (Jan. 1932) and 40 (July 1939), which contain notices of Holland's marriage. "Memoirs of Frederick Adolphus Porcher," in the same magazine, vol. 47 (Jan. 1946), offers an account of the periodical *Omnium Gatherum.* Arthur H. Quinn, *History of American Drama from the Beginning to the Civil War* (1923), recognizes the place of *The Corsair* in the history of the theater. Volume 251 of the *National Union Catalog* contains bibliographical information as well as locations for Holland's published writings, including two pseudonymous works. Craig A. Newton, "Three Patterns of Local History: South Carolina Historians, 1779–1830," *South Carolina Historical Magazine* 65 (July 1964), cites Holland's *Refutation* for its information on black history, and Larry E. Tise, *Proslavery: A History of the Defense of Slavery in America, 1701–1840* (1987), notes Holland's place among advocates of black slavery. A notice of his death is in the *Charleston Courier,* 14 Sept. 1824.

WILLIAM S. POWELL

HOLLAND, George (6 Dec. 1791–20 Dec. 1870), actor, was born in Lambeth Parish, London, the son of Henry Holland, a teacher of dance (his mother's name cannot be ascertained). The family's prosperity enabled George to attend a boarding school in Hertfordshire, where he distinguished himself as an athlete. After completing his education he worked as a clerk, first in a silk warehouse, then in a broker's office, and finally in a printer's office. Abandoning his business career, he debuted as an actor in 1816 at London's Olympic Theatre. During the next eight years he established himself as a low comedian—the member of an acting company entrusted with broadly comic roles that rely on slapstick, ethnic character types, and regional accents for their comic appeal. Holland's abilities included uncanny mimicry, ventriloquism, and deftness at broad physical farce. Yet he failed to attain a position as principal low comedian at either of the two major London theaters, Drury Lane and Covent Garden. Undaunted, he emigrated to the United States in 1827 and debuted at the Bowery Theatre in September of

that year in a farcical afterpiece in which he played five different outrageous characters. Achieving rapid popularity, Holland toured the major cities on the Eastern Seaboard from 1828 through 1829. He earned enough to retire from the stage and convert his residence in rural Harlem to an inn. His career as a hotelier failed, however, and he went back to work in the theater in 1832.

For the next ten years Holland worked in the southern United States, first as comanager of a theater in Mobile, Alabama, with Sol Smith, who was later to partner with Noah Ludlow managing important theaters in St. Louis, New Orleans, and other cities in the Mississippi Valley. Holland then was secretary-treasurer of James Caldwell's New Orleans Gas Company. His first wife (name unknown), whom he had brought with him from England, died in 1834, leaving him a widower with five dependent children. The stability of Caldwell's employ enabled Holland to remain with his family and provide for them. When Caldwell built and opened the St. Charles Theatre in New Orleans in 1835, Holland became secretary-treasurer of the enterprise and appeared occasionally as principal low comedian. He earned a reputation for being scrupulously honest in his business dealings, and Caldwell entrusted him with the fiscal management of the theater. Caldwell relinquished his managerial position in 1842. Consequently, Holland returned to New York in 1843 as a member of William Mitchell's stock company at the Olympic Theatre. He soon reestablished himself as a favorite of New York audiences, primarily in broad farcical roles such as Jerry in *A Day after the Fair* and as the Specimen Boy in an adaptation of the "Savage and the Maiden" section of Dickens's *Nicholas Nickleby.* Holland became a legendary practical joker. On the evening each year when the box office proceeds were distributed among the actors as their annual bonus, he would sell out his benefits by engaging in extraordinary ruses. One time he feigned drowning after falling off the wharf at the Fulton Street Market; on another occasion, he convincingly threw a faked fit in front of a drugstore on a crowded street.

Holland spent the next twenty-seven years as a member of New York stock companies, going from Mitchell's to William E. Burton's (1848), to James W. Wallack's (1852), and finally as a member of Augustin Daly's company during Daly's inaugural season at the Fifth Avenue Theatre (1869). Each of the companies was lauded as the finest stock company in the country while Holland was a member of it, and the only factor—and a principal source of attraction—common to each company during its period of unrivaled excellence was his presence.

Holland made his last appearance on 12 January 1870 at the Fifth Avenue Theatre as Mr. Jenkins in Olive Logan's *Surf,* thus completing a career of forty-three years in the American theater. Daly tendered Holland a grand complimentary benefit on 15 May 1870. Holland's advanced age had rendered him too debilitated to perform, but he was rolled out onto the stage in a wheelchair, from which he thanked everyone in attendance. For the event, according to the anonymous *Holland Memorial*, "the box office receipts were the largest ever taken in one night" (p. 52) during Daly's first season as manager. Although Holland was thereafter unable to perform, Daly continued to pay his salary until Holland's death in New York. Surviving him were his second wife, Catherine DeLuce Holland, whom he had married in the early 1840s, and his five children, all by his first wife, three of whom became well-known actors—George, Jr., Kate, and E. M.

Most descriptions of Holland's acting style concur with William Knight Northall's 1851 assessment: "It was so rarely that we could detect in George Holland anything like a bit of legitimate acting, that we always attributed such an exhibition, when it did occur, to accident rather than thought or design" (Northall, pp. 85–86). Yet such evaluations do not take into account the skill with which Holland portrayed characters from works by Goldsmith and Sheridan in Wallack's revivals of eighteenth-century comedy during the mid-fifties and the nonfarcical roles from the contemporary dramas of Tom Taylor and T. W. Robertson that he performed in the late fifties and sixties. Although he had been an excellent farceur for over twenty-five years, Holland became equally adept at playing the more realistic characters of the mid-century drama.

Holland's death received more attention than did his life. The refusal of the Reverend Dr. Sabine to conduct Holland's funeral from the Church of the Ascension and the subsequent obsequies at the Church of the Transfiguration, which as a result became known as New York City's Actors Church ("the little church around the corner"), caused a major public outcry against the moral stigma conferred upon theatrical professionals after the close of the Civil War. Whether Sabine's refusal was due to Holland's profession or whether it was because the Church of the Ascension was already decorated for a wedding scheduled for the next day is a point of controversy. In either event, it was not Sabine's statement against Holland's profession but rather the implications about his character that caused the public outcry. Many of Holland's highly visible colleagues had indeed acted in such a way as to deserve their reputations as dissolute and immoral members of the theatrical profession. Actor J. B. Booth's eccentricities, for example, had frequently offended the public, and his son had assassinated Lincoln; Edwin Forrest's divorce from Katherine Sinclair had likewise prompted a titillating scandal. But Holland, by contrast, was a sympathetic figure to the public because of his long service to the cause of what Daly described as "innocent and hearty merriment" and because of his responsible and virtuous personal life. The *New York Times* (22 Dec. 1870) praised Holland as "a sterling actor, a generous man, and a respectable member of society." Thus in death he became a rallying point for a successful frontal assault on the antitheatrical prejudices of some clergymen and morally conservative members of the community. An excellent comedian whose impeccable personal life and lengthy career earned him the respect of his colleagues and the affection of theatergoers, Holland served his profession well.

• Archival materials, including letters and press clippings, are in the Harvard Theatre Collection, the Harry Ransome Humanities Research Center of the University of Texas at Austin, and the performance collection of the New York City Public Library at Lincoln Center. Further biographical details and a survey of Holland's career is in David L. Rinear, "'Innocent and Hearty Merriment': The Life and Work of George Holland," *Theatre History Studies* 12 (1992): 157–71. Useful and entertaining works that feature Holland include Joseph Jefferson, *The Autobiography of Joseph Jefferson* (1899); William L. Keese, *A Group of Comedians* (1901); John S. Kendall, *Golden Age of the New Orleans Theatre* (1952); and William Knight Northall, *Before and Behind the Curtain; or, Fifteen Years' Observations among the Theatres of New York* (1851). The controversy surrounding Holland's funeral is well covered in the anonymous *Holland Memorial: Sketch of the Life of George Holland, the Veteran Comedian, with Dramatic Reminiscences, Anecdotes, etc.* (1871).

DAVID L. RINEAR

HOLLAND, John Philip (24 Feb. 1841–12 Aug. 1914), inventor, was born in Liscannor, County Clare, Ireland, the son of John Holland, a coast guard officer, and Mary Scanlon. The Hollands lived in a small coast guard cottage, and though they had greater economic security than many residents of the village, the poverty, famine, and disease that surrounded them and that led to the death of John's younger brother Robert and two of his uncles had a profound impact on him, initiating a strong anti-British sentiment that influenced much of his life. In 1853 Holland's father died and the family moved to Limerick, where Holland entered the monastery school. He was very committed to his studies and rapidly excelled in the physical sciences. The hardship caused by his father's death, along with Holland's strong interest in education, prompted his entrance into the teaching order of the Irish Christian Brothers in 1858. He was sent to the North Monastery School in Cork for further training and apprentice teaching. Over the next fifteen years Holland moved to various teaching posts throughout Ireland and taught a variety of subjects ranging from the physical sciences to music. However, his poor health forced him to take periodic breaks from his teaching duties and, along with his interest in designing submarines, influenced his decision to move to the United States in 1873 to join his mother and two brothers, who had moved to Boston several years earlier.

Within a year Holland had accepted a teaching position in the boys' division of St. John's Parochial School in Paterson, New Jersey. Holland's interest in submarine design dated back to his reading accounts of the Civil War encounter between the Union *Monitor* and Confederate *Merrimack* in 1862. He believed that the clash between these two ironclad vessels was indicative of a future in which submersible boats would provide a weapon against which there would be no defense. Thus, while still a teacher in Ireland he had begun to draw designs of submarines. In February 1875 he submitted sketches of his submarine designs to the U.S. Navy Department, but naval officials thought the designs were impractical because of what they perceived to be inadequate navigational capabilities. Holland refused to give up and through his younger brother Michael made a connection with the Irish Republican Brotherhood (often referred to as the Fenians), a group that had formed in the United States in the 1860s to support Ireland's independence from Great Britain. Holland convinced this revolutionary organization that his submarines might be a crucial element in combating the strong British navy, and between 1875 and 1883 they gave Holland approximately $60,000 to finance construction of his first three submarines. In 1876, upon receiving funding from the Fenians, Holland ended his eighteen-year teaching career and became a full-time inventor.

His first submarine, the *Holland I*, a one-person, cigar-shaped vessel, fourteen and a half feet long and two and a half feet in diameter, was completed in the spring of 1878. The *Holland I* made use of the new two-cylinder engine that had been patented by George Brayton four years earlier. In addition to the submarine's two main water tanks, it had two small tanks, one at the bow, the other at the stern, that provided a small reserve of positive buoyancy, a characteristic that Holland thought was critical and one that, along with a fixed center of gravity, was incorporated into all of the inventor's submarines. These innovations gave Holland submarines more stability and control than those designed by other inventors.

Holland's construction of his first submarine for the Fenians was conducted secretly. Although the press reported that he was building a submarine, they knew nothing of the internal elements of the vessel nor did they know who was financing Holland. This changed with the second submarine, which Blakely Hall, a reporter for the *New York Sun*, named the *Fenian Ram*, terminology that he thought reflected both the financial origin and primary method of combat of the vessel. The name stuck, and though Holland had been discouraging and unhelpful to reporters in the past, he was grateful to Hall for the publicity. The *Fenian Ram*, though similar in shape, was much larger than his first submarine and measured thirty-one feet in length and six feet in diameter. Its body was constructed of eleven-sixteenths-inch thick iron and was powered by a Brayton engine that enabled it to achieve an underwater speed of approximately nine miles per hour. Thus, its ramming capabilities were believed to be great enough to smash the bottom of most single-hulled ships. The *Fenian Ram* was built for a crew of three: an operator, an engineer, and a gunner. Although the *Fenian Ram* brought Holland considerable publicity, had very successful test runs, and was an early representation of what was to become the model of twentieth-century American submarines, many people in the Fenian Brotherhood felt that their hard-earned money was not furthering the revolutionary cause, and thus Holland was financially cut off.

His third submarine was almost an exact replica of the *Fenian Ram*, only half its size. After completing this boat in 1883, Holland was out of money. Through an associate and fellow inventor who had helped him on his third boat, he became friends with U.S. Navy lieutenant William W. Kimball. Kimball was very supportive but, despite persistent efforts, was unable to secure a government contract for Holland. Another military contact, Edmund L. G. Zalinski, obtained private money from friends and associates for Holland to build his fourth boat, the *Zalinski*. However, there was little commercial interest, and shortly after construction this boat was dismantled and sold for parts.

Although the *Fenian Ram* had given Holland a degree of fame, after the *Zalinski* he was without a source of income. In January 1887 Holland married Margaret Foley of Paterson, New Jersey; they had five children. Over the next five years he was forced to take various engineering positions not directly related to submarine design. During this time Holland was trying to secure a navy contract. In 1893, when it looked as if the U.S. Congress was committed to the idea of financing submarine construction, E. B. Frost, a lawyer associated with the Morris and Cummings Dredging Company where Holland was then working, provided the initial money for the incorporation of the John P. Holland Torpedo Boat Company. In 1895 this company received a $150,000 contract with the navy to construct a submarine, the *Plunger*. However, naval engineers largely controlled the design of the vessel, and Holland, although made manager, was excluded from many design decisions. Unlike Holland's other submarines, the *Plunger* had poor maneuverability, and thus the project was soon terminated by the navy.

Holland, backed by his company and no longer subject to the whims of naval engineers, then began construction of his sixth submarine, the *Holland*, which became the model for U.S. Navy submarines for decades. The *Holland* was built for a crew of six, including a commander, assistant commander, electrician, engineer, gunner, and machinist. The boat was 53.3 feet long with a diameter of 10.3 feet. It had five tanks along the bottom of the vessel including a 1,000-gallon fuel tank and was capable of remaining submerged continuously for forty hours. It ran on a 45 HP Otto gas engine that powered either the propeller or the dynamotor to charge the batteries. The vessel was fitted with a torpedo launcher and could carry two reserve torpedoes in addition to the one loaded in its Whitehead torpedo tube. Above this launcher was the Holland Pneumatic Dynamite Gun, which could fire a 222-pound projectile 1,000 yards in the air or thirty yards in water. While this was by far Holland's most impressive submarine, its success was due largely to elements present in his earlier submarines, including its positive reserve buoyancy, fixed center of gravity, rapid diving capability, and automatic compensation for displacement of torpedoes.

The *Holland* was successfully launched on 17 May 1897 out of Lewis Nixon's Crescent Shipyard in Elizabethport, New Jersey. The John P. Holland Torpedo

Boat Company was prepared to sell it to the highest bidder on the world market. On 11 April 1900 the U.S. Navy purchased the submarine for $150,000. The navy went on to construct other Holland vessels, but the inventor still had little control over the company he managed, and on 28 March 1904 he resigned. He spent the last ten years of his life designing a much faster submarine but was unsuccessful in his efforts to fund the endeavor. Although Holland's designs had become the model for the U.S. Navy and variations on his submarines were used by naval powers throughout the world, he had signed away rights to his designs and never earned more than $90 a week. John Philip Holland died at his home in Newark, New Jersey.

• John Holland's papers, including notes, letters, drawings, and diagrams, are located at the Paterson Museum in Paterson, N.J. This museum also has the hulls of Holland's first two submarines, the *Holland I* and the *Fenian Ram*, on permanent display. The Submarine Library at the U.S. Naval Submarine Base in New London, Conn., has papers of several important associates of Holland, including Charles A. Morris and Frank T. Cable. This library also has the John P. Holland Torpedo Boat Company Letters as well as the papers of Holland's daughter, Marguerite Holland. John P. Holland published two articles, "Submarine Navigation," *Cassier's Magazine* (1897), pp. 541–60, and "The Submarine Boat and Its Future," *North American Review*, July–Dec. 1900, pp. 894–903. Another important source is Richard K. Morris's full-length biography, *John P. Holland: Inventor of the Modern Submarine* (1966).

JEFFREY R. YOST

HOLLAND, Spessard Lindsey (10 July 1892–6 Nov. 1971), lawyer and politician, was born in Bartow, Florida, the son of Benjamin Franklin Holland, an owner of a citrus grove and general farm, and Fannie Virginia Spessard, a teacher in the Summerlin Institute, Bartow. His paternal grandfather, Lindsay Holland, served in the Georgia legislature, and his maternal grandfather, Nat Spessard, served in the Virginia legislature. Holland attended Emory College, Oxford, Georgia, from the fall of 1909 until June 1912, graduating magna cum laude while earning letters in track and football. He then taught high school in Warrenton, Georgia, for two years before enrolling at the University of Florida Law School in Gainesville, Florida, in 1914. Holland served as president of the student body and graduated with an LL.B. in 1916, finishing second in his class. He earned letters in basketball and baseball. Connie Mack, the manager of the Philadelphia Athletics, offered Holland a professional contract after Holland struck out five Athletics in an exhibition baseball game.

Admitted to the Florida bar in 1916, Holland went into partnership with R. B. Huffaker in Bartow. He then volunteered for service in World War I and was commissioned a second lieutenant in August 1917, initially with the Coastal Brigade. Assigned to France, Holland was with the Thirty-first Heavy Artillery Brigade Headquarters and later with the Twenty-fourth Squadron Air Corps as an air observer. He won a Dis-

tinguished Service Cross and retired from service as a captain on 16 July 1919. He married Mary Agnes Groover in February 1919. They had four children.

Holland began his political career as a Democrat when he was appointed as the prosecuting attorney for Polk County, Florida, in 1919. He was elected a county judge the next year and held that office until he retired in 1928. Holland was elected in 1932 to the Florida State Senate, where he remained until 1939, when he ran for governor. In the state senate he helped end the state's poll tax because he thought it led to unsavory machine control and denied poor whites and blacks a voice in their government. Holland became governor in 1940, when he defeated Francis P. Whitehair in a runoff by 66,000 votes. As wartime governor of Florida he set up the state civil defense, helped develop the Everglades National Park and the State Parole Commission, and supported a large expansion of the road-building program in Florida. In 1946 sitting U.S. senator Charles O. Andrews chose not to run for reelection because of ill health. Holland, by now a seasoned and well-known politician, won the Democratic nomination on 7 May 1946 with 60.7 percent of the votes and defeated the Republican candidate in November. When Senator Andrews died in office, Governor Millard Caldwell appointed Holland, on 25 September 1946, to fill out Andrews's unexpired term. Holland began serving his full six-year term on 3 January 1947. He easily won reelection to the Senate every six years until he decided to retire on 3 January 1971 because of ill health.

In the Senate Holland initially served on the Rules Committee and the District of Columbia Committee, but he spent most of his time on the Appropriations, Judiciary, Public Works, Agriculture (twenty-two years), and Space (ten years) committees. Senator Holland strongly supported President Harry Truman's Cold War policies, voting in favor of the Truman Doctrine, the Marshall Plan, and the North Atlantic Treaty Organization, and he favored sending troops to Korea. He voted for statehood for Alaska and Hawaii, the space program (of great economic benefit to Fla.), and the St. Lawrence Seaway, and he actively participated in the enactment of the Taft-Hartley Act. He helped develop the original interstate highway program, opposed the vote for eighteen year olds, and worked hard for the completion of the Inter-American Highway to link the United States culturally and economically with Latin American countries. Holland believed strongly in states' rights and helping individual initiative through the free enterprise system. He characterized himself as a moderate conservative and expressed his political philosophy in his 1941 inaugural address as governor, "Government must be honest, liberal, efficient, economical, wholly non-sectional, and soundly democratic." Holland opposed civil rights legislation, school integration, and the Voting Rights Act of 1965. He also voted against antipoverty bills, Medicare, and federal aid to schools. However, he differed from many of his southern colleagues on the issue of the poll tax. In every congressional session beginning in 1949 he introduced a constitutional amendment to outlaw the poll tax nationwide. Finally, in February 1964, despite vigorous opposition from southern conservatives, three-fourths of the states ratified the Holland Bill, making it the Twenty-Fourth Amendment to the Constitution. Senator Holland took pride in his sponsorship of the Tidelands Bill, in which the federal government returned to individual states (including Fla.) their property rights in the submerged coastal belts.

Lyndon Johnson called Holland one of the five most powerful men in the Senate. Senator Robert Byrd, in the congressional tribute to Holland, said, "I never met a more fair-minded individual, one more dedicated or more conscientious in serving the people." The *Tampa Tribune*, on 7 November 1971, concluded that Holland left the stamp of good government on every office he held and was particularly adept at serving his constituents. His last months were spent as a partner in the firm of Holland and Knight in Bartow. He died in Bartow.

As a conservative southern Democrat, Holland consistently voted for states' rights, and with a few exceptions, such as the space program, the federal poll tax (perhaps his greatest achievement), and federal highway development, he opposed federal intrusion into state activities through such bills as the Civil Rights Act of 1964. His paternalistic view toward blacks and immigrants, while popular in the South, demonstrated a provincial mind-set. He was a nationalist and fervent anti-Communist who seldom left the United States and concentrated on domestic rather than foreign policy. An excellent wartime governor and a capable politician always attentive to the needs of his constituents, Holland was one of the most respected and popular political figures in Florida during the twentieth century. He served on the boards of trustees at Florida Presbyterian College, Florida Southern College, and Emory University. He was a member of the Methodist church, American Legion, Veterans of Foreign Wars, Phi Beta Kappa, Kiwanis Club, and Elks Club. The law school at the University of Florida is named after him.

• Holland's complete papers, including the draft of an unfinished autobiography, are in the P. K. Yonge Library of Florida History at the University of Florida, Gainesville, Fla. These papers also include his gubernatorial and Senate papers, election materials, newspaper clippings, and personal files. Holland put out a weekly newsletter for constituents called the *Washington Report* from 9 Feb. 1947 through 2 Jan. 1971. He wrote an article, "Coming Soon—An Engineer's Dream," *American Engineer*, June 1953, pp. 9–13, about the Inter-American Highway. Holland is mentioned frequently in history books about the state of Fla. and in Numan V. Bartley and Hugh D. Graham, *Southern Politics and the Second Reconstruction* (1975). Other sources include the official program of his inauguration as governor on 7 Jan. 1941, which is included in his papers; "The Spessard Holland Story," telecast on station WFLA-TV, Tampa, Fla., 7 Jan. 1965; an interview by Bill Henry, "The Holland Years," WFLA-TV, Tampa, Fla., 24 June 1971; Charles Stafford, "Senator Spessard Holland: Statesman and Southerner," *St. Peters-*

burg Times, 11 Oct. 1970; *Tampa Tribune*, 7 Nov. 1971; and the *Polk County Record* in Bartow throughout his life. In addition to the *Congressional Record*, 26 Sept. 1946–3 Jan. 1971, see *Tributes to the Honorable Spessard Lindsey Holland of Florida in the Senate of the United States Commemorating Twenty Years of Service as a Senator* (1966) and *Memorial Addresses and Other Tributes in the Congress of the United States on the Life and Contributions of Spessard Holland* (1972). Obituaries are in the *Tampa Tribune* and the *New York Times*, 7 Nov. 1971.

JULIAN M. PLEASANTS

HOLLAND, William Jacob (16 Aug. 1848–13 Dec. 1932), zoologist and paleontologist, was born in Jamaica, West Indies, the son of Francis Raymond Holland, a minister, and Augusta Eliza Wolle. After living in Ohio and North Carolina, the family settled in Bethlehem, Pennsylvania, in 1863. There Holland attended the Moravian College and Theological Seminary; after graduating he attended Amherst College, receiving his A.B. degree in 1869. After serving for a year as principal of Amherst High School and for another year as principal of Westborough High School, both in Massachusetts, Holland entered the Princeton Theological Seminary, completing his course in 1874. While studying at Princeton he was ordained in the Moravian Church. In 1874 Holland became a Presbyterian and moved to Pittsburgh, Pennsylvania, to take a position as pastor of the Bellefield Presbyterian Church. He married Carrie T. Moorhead in 1879; they had two children.

While serving as pastor for the Bellefield Presbyterian Church, Holland was also a trustee of the Pennsylvania College for Women (now Chatham College); he simultaneously held the position of professor of ancient languages there. In addition, he maintained an active presence in the sciences, serving as naturalist for the United States Eclipse Expedition, which was sent to Japan in 1887 by the National Academy of Sciences and the U.S. Navy.

In 1891 Holland became chancellor of the Western University of Pennsylvania (later the University of Pittsburgh), where he taught anatomy and zoology. He remained there until 1901, when his friend Andrew Carnegie invited him to direct the Carnegie Museum in Pittsburgh. Holland directed the museum until 1922 and remained active in its affairs until his death.

Holland attributed his lifelong interest in natural history to his parents: his father collected shells, plants, and insects, and his mother taught young William to draw and paint them. He continued his interest in illustration throughout his career; he drew many of the figures in his *Moth Book* (1903), and late in his life he mourned the fact that his schedule allowed little time for art.

As director of the Carnegie Museum, Holland gave his interest in animals of all kinds free rein for the first time, and under him the museum acquired many of its most important collections. In addition to making use of his connections to European collectors to purchase important insect collections, Holland arranged for the museum to fund fossil-collecting expeditions in Montana, North Dakota, Wyoming, and Utah. The most famous result of these expeditions was the 1911 discovery of the dinosaur *Diplodocus carnegiei*, named by Holland after his friend and benefactor, Andrew Carnegie, who also financed the installation of replicas of the original specimen in the British Museum, and in the national museums of France, Russia, Germany, Italy, Austria, Argentina, and Spain. Holland remained close to Carnegie throughout his career and complained that he was often asked to intercede with Carnegie on behalf of the pet projects of colleagues and acquaintances.

Holland is perhaps best known as an entomologist. He was especially interested in the *Rhopalocera* and *Heterocera* of West Africa, but he also wrote on the Lepidoptera of the Congo, Sierra Leone, the Bahamas, the Seychelles, and North America. His most noted works on North American insects are *The Butterfly Book* (1898) and *The Moth Book* (1903). Both books were intended for both popular and professional audiences and went through several editions and numerous printings. Holland was a prominent figure in turn-of-the-century debates over insect classification.

Throughout his tenure as director of the Carnegie Museum Holland remained active in both public and scientific affairs. He served as president (1904–1922) of the Carnegie Hero Fund, which honors individuals for acts of heroism; he was a founder of the American Association of Museums in 1907 and its president (1907–1909), and he was first president of the Academy of Science and Art of Pittsburgh. He was a fellow of the Royal Society of Edinburgh, the Entomological and Zoological societies of London, the American Association for the Advancement of Science, and the Geological Society of America. He was also a member of the Academy of Natural Sciences, and numerous entomological societies. As chancellor emeritus of the Western University of Pennsylvania and president of the Madame Curie Radium Fund of Pittsburgh, Holland was instrumental in arranging for Curie to tour Pittsburgh in 1921. Holland was especially proud of his work on the city filtration commission, formed in Pittsburgh to combat typhoid; in addition to serving as chairman of the water analysis subcommittee, he authored the *Report of the Filtration Commission* published by the city in 1899. He died in Pittsburgh.

Holland was one of a number of turn-of-the-century museum curators who combined nineteenth-century breadth of interest with increasingly rigorous standards for practice. He is thus symbolic of museums' progress toward professionalism in the early twentieth century. Holland was part of a network of scientists, curators, and dedicated amateurs who relied on personal good will as well as scientific expertise to arrange for publications, specimen exchanges, and the funding of expeditions. Strong-willed, colorful, and vocal, Holland—like his contemporary Roy Chapman Andrews of the American Museum—was the subject of a store of anecdotes that remains an absorbing part of the history of science.

• Collections of Holland's papers are at the Academy of Natural Sciences in Philadelphia and at the Historical Society of Western Pennsylvania in Pittsburgh. At the Academy of Natural Sciences, manuscripts relating to Holland consist of correspondence in various collections; the greatest number are housed in the records of the American Entomological Society. The Historical Society of Western Pennsylvania holds the largest collection of Holland's papers, including Holland's personal and professional papers and manuscripts related to his family. In addition to his books on butterflies and moths, Holland published extensively on lepidoptera of Africa and elsewhere in journals such as *Entomological News*, and the *Annals* and *Memoirs* of the Carnegie Museum. He also authored a travel narrative describing his trip to South America, *To the River Plate and Back* (1913).

The most useful published account of Holland's career appears in Arnold Mallis, *American Entomologists* (1971). Biographical accounts published during Holland's lifetime include John W. Jordan, *Encyclopedia of Pennsylvania Biography*, vol. 11 (1914); and Frank C. Harper, *Pittsburgh of Today: Its Resources and People*, vol. 5 (1932). Obituaries include Andrey Avinoff, "Obituary of William J. Holland," *Annals of the Carnegie Museum* 21 (1931–1933): i–iv. Henry Leighton's memoir in the *Bulletin of the Geological Society of America* 44 (1933), includes a bibliography of Holland's works.

MONIQUE BOURQUE

HOLLANDER, Jacob Harry (23 July 1871–9 July 1940), economist and government consultant, was born in Baltimore, Maryland, the son of Rosa Mayer and Myer Hollander. Hollander's father, a native of Bavaria, Germany, was a successful Baltimore paint manufacturer, and the son was expected to enter the family business. Hollander attended primary schools in Baltimore and spent one year at the Pennsylvania Military Academy, where he developed a taste for strict upright posture, fastidious dress, and conservative attitudes, which he retained all of his adult life. He graduated from Johns Hopkins University in 1891 with a B.A. degree but remained at the institution on scholarship and rapidly earned his Ph.D. in economics in 1894. His thesis, "The Cincinnati Southern Railway," demonstrated his early interest in transportation economics and the problems of regional development. Johns Hopkins appointed Hollander an instructor of economics (and finance), and there he received successive early promotions culminating in a full professorship in economics in 1904.

Hollander's career was filled with interesting committee assignments and important government field-work that he managed to complete while retaining his professorship at Johns Hopkins. In 1897 President William McKinley appointed Hollander secretary of the American Bimetallic Commission, charged with the task of meeting delegates from other nations to hammer out an agreement that would make both gold and silver official international currencies. President McKinley was so impressed with Hollander's performance that in 1900 he asked Hollander to go to

Puerto Rico and help reorganize its desperate fiscal situation. Hollander did this and was named treasurer of Puerto Rico island. Wielding enormous political power, he made the necessary changes within a year, and on 25 July 1901 the region was declared "fiscally self-supporting." This status enabled Puerto Rico to participate fully in a free trade zone with the United States. The legislation that aided Puerto Rico memorializes Hollander's considerable accomplishment in the Caribbean and was nicknamed the Hollander bill.

In 1905 President McKinley sent Hollander to the Dominican Republic to help straighten out its national debt problems. This experience resulted in a special treaty with the United States and a monograph on regional development in Santo Domingo that made use of his doctoral research, titled *Dominican Republic: Railroad and Commercial Development Projected by Virtue of a Treaty with the United States* (1907).

Hollander's lifelong interest in monetary theory and policy was doubly marked, first, by his academic publications and second, by his participation on national committees having to do with monetary issues. In addition to his service on the bimetallism commission, later in 1919 Hollander was appointed to a committee of the America's Banker's Association to evaluate Irving Fisher's plan for a "compensated dollar." Hollander and the other committee members thought that Fisher's proposal to continually alter the gold content of the dollar as a means of stabilizing the currency's purchasing power was unrealistic and unworkable. Again, in 1924, Hollander was appointed by Benjamin Strong of the Federal Reserve Bank of New York to serve on a committee that reviewed the existing composition of the nation's currency and recommended replacing the greenbacks and other government issues held over from earlier war financing with ordinary Federal Reserve notes.

Hollander was a strong supporter of banking reform. In his National Monetary Commission report submitted to the Sixty-first Congress, *Bank Loans and Stock Exchange Speculation* (1911), Hollander explained that the United States was out of step with the other industrial countries. In America the banking system did not provide enough liquidity to the business world in the form of a discount market for commercial paper. The strains on U.S. financial markets were mainly due to the misallocation of bank credit. Rather than purchase the commercial paper issued by business manufacturers, the commercial banks used their cash reserves to purchase stock-exchange securities from the various stock promoters. Alternatively, they accepted the new securities as collateral for cash loans made to stock promoters. These efforts diverted loanable funds to New York City (the home of the New York Stock Exchange) and therefore deprived the rest of the nation of the benefits of a well-functioning open-discount market. According to Hollander, this was the main cause of financial crises and a glaring defect of the American banking system. The inelastic supply of bank credit meant that loans to stock pro-

moters crowded out loans to manufacturers and others.

Hollander's ideas about commercial banking and reform were repeated in a series of journal articles that he wrote. One, "Certificates of Indebtedness" (*Journal of Political Economy* 26 [Nov. 1918]: 901–8), explained how the Liberty Bonds sold to help finance U.S. military operations during World War I were used to help retire large amounts of short-term certificates of indebtedness incurred by the Treasury to mobilize funds for the war effort.

By the start of World War I, Hollander was one of the few who gave shape to the field known as the history of economic thought. As evidenced in his classic article "The Development of the Theory of Money from Adam Smith to David Ricardo" (*Quarterly Journal of Economics* 25 [May 1911]: 429–70), Hollander had mastered the pre-Ricardian pamphlet literature. He cogently summarized the British pamphlet literature between 1776 and 1810, demonstrating that the ideas that David Ricardo made famous actually had their origins in the writings of a talented group of English and Irish writers who dissented from Adam Smith's teachings on money and banking. In subsequent books and articles, including *David Ricardo: A Centenary Estimate* (1910); "The Founder of a School" (in *Adam Smith, 1776–1926*, ed. J. M. Clark et. al. [1928]); *Letters of David Ricardo to Hutches Trower and Others, 1811–1823* (1899); *Letters of David Ricardo to John Ramsey McCulloch, 1816–1823* (1895); *Notes on Malthus's Principles of Political Economy* (1928); and *Minor Papers on the Currency Question, 1809–1823* (1932), Hollander distinguished himself as one of America's leading historians of economics.

In 1931 Hollander served as chair of the Tax Survey of Maryland. One year later Hollander's committee published its report, *Maryland Tax Survey Commission Report of the Tax Survey of Maryland*. Tax theory and policy was a topic in which Hollander had previously demonstrated a strong research interest, in his 1899 work, *The Financial History of Baltimore*, and in 1900 in his *Studies in State Taxation with Particular Reference to the Southern States [of the United States]*. Hollander's firsthand experiences in Baltimore, Puerto Rico, and Santo Domingo with restructuring tax collections also contributed to his reputation as a man of practical affairs—a tax expert—able to bridge the chasm between theory and practice.

As early as 1891, shortly after graduating from college, Hollander traveled to England and began a lifelong search of bookstores, both in London and elsewhere, for early pamphlets and books on economic theory and practice. He sought items that would document the development of economics as a body of thought that is quite separate from political and legal thought. At the end of his life he had successfully amassed a comprehensive set of works of seventeenth- and eighteenth-century writers.

Hollander's personal views on public policy toward business were presented in a series of works including, in addition to the works already cited, *Economic Liber-*

alism (1925) and *Want and Plenty* (1932). It is clear that Hollander repudiated laissez-faire and favored government regulation of many aspects of economic life. Most significantly, Hollander did not embrace socialism. In his presidential address before the American Economic Association in 1932, Hollander predicted that occupational changes and technological change would make existing adversarial labor unions less and less useful to economic life. Instead, he favored moderate regulation, especially about matters involving the ethics of competition and the basic institutions of money and banking. During the 1930s Hollander opposed the New Deal and joined the Liberty League to underscore his displeasure with Franklin Roosevelt's interventionist prolabor policies.

In 1906 Hollander married Theresa G. Hutzler, the sister of Albert D. Hutzler, president of Hutzler Brothers, a prominent upscale Baltimore department store. She died in 1916, prompting the Hutzler family to endow a chair of economics at Johns Hopkins University in 1925, which Jacob Hollander occupied until his death in Baltimore. Hollander was survived by his two daughters.

• Elsie A. Marsh, comp., *Economic Library of Jacob H. Hollander* (1937), is a shelf list of Hollander's collection of works by seventeenth- and eighteenth-century writers. This collection consists of more than 4,400 items and was sold by his heirs in 1958 to the University of Illinois library at Urbana-Champaign. The earliest item in the collection is dated 1574 and the most recent item, 1937. The collection, along with many other letters and materials from Hollander's collections, is in the University of Illinois library's Rare Book and Special Collections Library. Additional information about Hollander's life and work is in Joseph Dorfman, *The Economic Mind in American Civilization*, vols. 1–3 (1949; repr. 1969) and vols. 4–5 (1959; repr. 1969); and Jean A. Major, *Collections Acquired by the University of Illinois Library at Urbana-Champaign, 1897–1974* (1976). An obituary is in the *New York Times*, 10 July 1940.

LAURENCE S. MOSS

HOLLERITH, Herman (29 Feb. 1860–17 Nov. 1929), engineer, was born in Buffalo, New York, the son of Johann George Hollerith and Franciska Brunn. In Germany Johann Hollerith had been a professor of ancient languages in the Gymnasium at Speyer; after immigrating he acquired several farms in states west of New York but lived in Buffalo, where his wife's brothers had a carriage factory. Herman received his secondary schooling largely by being tutored by a Lutheran minister because he hated spelling so much that he once jumped out a second-floor school window to avoid spelling class. He graduated with distinction from Columbia College (now University) School of Mines in 1879. As a special agent in the U.S. Census Office (1879–1881) he worked on statistics of manufacturers; as an outside activity he computed life tables for John Shaw Billings, director of vital statistics at the Census Bureau.

Writing to a friend nearly forty years later, Hollerith described the origin of his most famous invention.

"One evening at Dr. B's [Billings] tea table he said to me, 'There ought to be a machine for doing the purely mechanical work of tabulating population and similar statistics.'" Hollerith considered the problem posed by Billings and decided that it could be solved.

In 1882 Hollerith became an instructor in mechanical engineering at Massachusetts Institute of Technology, where he began work on Billings's challenge, but he found that he disliked teaching. He moved a year later to St. Louis, where he experimented with electromagnetically operated brakes for railroads, including air brakes, and obtained five patents on his inventions. Westinghouse Air Brake Company sixty years later patented a brake almost identical to Hollerith's that became universally used.

From 1884 to 1885 Hollerith was employed as an examiner in the Patent Office in Washington, D.C. Resigning after less than twelve months, he established a consulting office in patent applications; he devoted his spare time to perfecting his electric-mechanical method for tabulating statistical data in time for the 1890 census. Hollerith married Lucia Beverly Talcott in 1890; they had six children, including three sons who followed their father in becoming engineers and obtaining patents.

The machine Hollerith invented (patent no. 395,781, filed 24 Sept. 1884, granted 8 Jan. 1889) relied on a system of nonconducting paper passing between electrically charged pins and a conducting metal drum or plate. Electricity could flow only through the holes punched in the nonconducting material. Holes, representing coded information, were recorded as an electrical circuit to activate an electromagnetic counter, thereby accomplishing rapid tabulation of data. The holes were hand punched along the edges with a conductor's punch. Originally Hollerith used paper tape, but he soon settled on cards the size of dollar bills. This modification resulted from his recognition that searching tapes for single items was less efficient than searching cards, which could be sorted; the identical problem and solution arose seventy years later when IBM invented random-accessible electronic data retrieval using cards rather than magnetic tape.

Hollerith's system was demonstrated in tabulating mortality statistics in Baltimore (1887), and subsequently in New Jersey and New York City. His first machine was leased to the U.S. Army for tabulating medical records. Hollerith's data-processing system was selected by the Census Bureau for tabulating 1890 census data only after competitive trials with two alternative methods of tabulation. Hollerith's machine was three to four times faster than its closer competitor; a census commission estimated that its use would reduce labor in the approaching census by at least 67 percent. His invention subsequently was estimated to have saved the census $5 million and 7.5 years of work by tallying, in just three months, 62,622,250 people then living in the United States. Moreover, it performed the first complete analysis, in less than 2.5 years, of census data done anywhere.

In 1890 the Franklin Institute of Philadelphia designated Hollerith's tabulating machine the outstanding invention of the year and awarded him its highest honor, the gold Elliot Cression Medal. He also received the Medaille d'Or at the Exposition Universelle in 1889 and the Bronze Medal at the World's Columbian Exposition in 1892.

Hollerith's machines were used for tabulating census returns in Canada, Norway, and Austria in 1891. Later Puerto Rico and Cuba conducted censuses under Hollerith's personal supervision. Other achievements included the first census taken since 1854 by the imperial Russian government, requiring about 100 million cards; a French census of about 16 million returns; and the National Registration Act census of 1915 in Great Britain. Recognition of Hollerith's accomplishment was widespread in Europe, although American scholars largely ignored it. Technical papers noting the significance of the invention were published in Austria, England, France, Germany, and Italy. Hollerith was invited to speak before the Royal Statistical Society of London in 1894 and the International Institute of Statistics of Bern in 1895; at the latter he was called "the first statistical engineer." In 1895 the Berlin Customs House began using his machine for import-export statistics.

Between 1890 and 1900 Hollerith improved his invention by adding a mechanical feed device and adapting the machine to add as well as count. A desk-top punch replaced the hand-operated conductor's punch and significantly increased the quantity of data by utilizing the interior portions of cards as well as the margins. Thereafter his machines began to be used for railroad freight statistics and agricultural census data.

In 1896 Hollerith formed the Tabulating Machine Company, incorporated in New York, to manufacture his machines and sell the cards used in them. With a controlling stock interest, he was general manager, but he selected friends to serve as business officers and to manage sales, finances, and inventory. Hollerith began promoting his tabulating machines for cost accounting, management control, industrial accounting, and sales analysis. Manufacturers, factories, large corporations, and major retailers quickly recognized their benefits. Frederick W. Taylor, a pioneering efficiency engineer who studied workers and their tasks with a stopwatch, immediately appreciated the potential of Hollerith's device for his work and urged his clients to use these machines. Already Hollerith's machines had the three basic components inherent in modern machine accounting—data entry (punching), sorting, and tabulating.

Whereas early machines were leased to clients so that Hollerith could ensure proper maintenance, by 1896 he was giving his machines to clients under a contract that required them to buy all their cards from his company. Hollerith made major improvements in 1905 by integrating in a single, space-saving vertical machine counters, sorters, adding machines, and a plugboard that allowed reprogramming easily and quickly. Brushes to sense cards replaced pins, and a continuous feed mechanism allowed 180 to 200 cards to be read per minute.

After the twelfth census in 1901, Hollerith purchased Taft-Peirce Manufacturing Company of Woonsocket, Rhode Island, because of its excellent engineering skills and emphasis on interchangeable parts. Three years later British Tabulation Machine Limited was formed as a subsidiary company, and Deutsche Hollerith Maschinen Gesellschaft (Dehomag) was established in Berlin in 1910.

In 1911 Charles R. Flint, who accrued wealth by buying small companies in similar industries to form larger companies, bought Hollerith's Tabulating Machine Company. He merged it with Computing Scale Company of America (Dayton), International Time Recording Company of New York, and Bundy Manufacturing Co. (Endicott, N.Y.) to form Computing-Tabulating-Recording Company (C-T-R). Major owners and founders of these four companies were retained by Flint as managers of their respective divisions and as a board of directors. Thomas J. Watson, Sr., was hired in 1914 as general manager of C-T-R. Hollerith remained a consulting engineer to C-T-R at 80 percent of Watson's salary until 1921, when he resigned to return to private business as an inventor. In 1924 C-T-R was renamed International Business Machines Corporation (IBM).

Patents, sales of tabulating machines and cards, and the sale of his company made Hollerith a millionaire by 1911. Although he became a gentleman farmer, he never could divorce himself from his work as an engineer. One of his last patents was exceptionally important because it allowed automatic control of his machines, replacing the earlier stop cards. Watson immediately recognized its importance to IBM; it contributed significantly until after World War II to the company's continued growth.

Hollerith's last patent was granted in March 1919. At the time of his death he held thirty-one U.S. patents on his electric tabulating machines, as well as patents from Austria, Belgium, Canada, France, Germany, Great Britain, Italy, and Russia. Ironically, Hollerith's punch cards with clipped corners were never patented because he did not consider them his original idea.

Although his tabulating machine and cards were used widely in businesses for sixty years throughout the world, their best known use began after World War II, when early computers required Hollerith machines and cards for rapid data input. Later most functions of data processing came to be performed electronically and digitally, but more than a century after their invention Hollerith's machines and cards continued to be employed worldwide in voting.

Hollerith died in his home in Washington, D.C. He was remembered as a nonconformist throughout his life; a modest man, but not meek; one who gave credit to others rather than accept it himself; an engineer dedicated to technical excellence and not personal fame; and a doting parent. In retrospect Hollerith was dubbed the "Father of Data Processing." His genius has been called equal to that of Henry Ford, Thomas A. Edison, and Alexander Graham Bell. All were pioneers, and each left a legacy that had a pronounced effect on the modern world.

• A collection of Hollerith's personal papers is in the Manuscripts Division, Library of Congress. The most important biographical source is Geoffrey D. Austrian, *Herman Hollerith: Forgotten Giant of Information Processing* (1982). See also George E. Biles et al., "Herman Hollerith: Inventor, Manager, Entrepreneur—a Centennial Remembrance," *Journal of Management* 15, no. 4 (1989): 603–15; Virginia Hollerith, "Biographical Sketch of Herman Hollerith," *ISIS* 62 (1971): 69–78; Frederick J. Rex, Jr., "Herman Hollerith: The First 'Statistical Engineer,'" *Computers and Automation* 10, no. 8 (1961): 10–13. An obituary is in the *New York Times*, 19 Nov. 1929.

C. JOHN MANN

HOLLEY, Alexander Lyman (20 July 1832–29 Jan. 1882), technical writer and consulting metallurgical engineer, was born in Lakeville, Connecticut, the son of Alexander Hamilton Holley, a manufacturer of cutlery and, later, governor of the state, and Jane Lyman. Holley's mother died within two months of his birth, and three years later his father married Maria Coffing. Holley's parents created a family environment that stressed hard work and religious piety. At a very early age, Holley displayed a distinct talent for things mechanical and for technical drawing. By eleven he was suggesting useful improvements for his father's cutlery machines and before entering college had published an essay on cutlery manufacturing in Henry Varnum Poor's *American Railroad Journal*. Concentrating on mathematics and science, mixed with frequent hands-on work in local area machine shops, Holley graduated from Brown University in 1853 having written a senior thesis on steam locomotives, his particular passion.

Following his graduation, Holley remained in Providence, Rhode Island, finding employment with Corliss, Nightingale & Company as a mechanical draftsman. Pursuing his enthusiasm for steam locomotives, in September 1855 he was hired by the New York Locomotive Works in Jersey City. Shortly thereafter he met Mary Slade, with whom, although she was only sixteen, Holley eloped the following June. Mary Holley provided frequent assistance to her husband throughout the remainder of his career. Together they had four children, of whom two died in childhood.

While working for his new employer, Holley continued to develop his drafting skills, including a special watercolor shading technique. It was at this time that his work came to the attention of the brilliant yet erratic editor of the *Railroad Advocate*, Zerah Colburn. Holley began publishing technical articles in the *Advocate*, and when Colburn decided to go west in 1856, Holley, along with friend Samuel Cozzens, purchased this early venture in technical journalism, renaming it *Holley's Railroad Advocate*. Despite their efforts, the *Railroad Advocate* constantly struggled to stay afloat financially amid the general economic crisis of 1857 and a limited base of circulation. Publication of the journal ceased in July. In partnership with Colburn, Holley next brought out the more broadly focused *American Engineer*, but this venture also quickly collapsed. Although these financial disasters occurred at a time when the young engineer could ill afford them, the editorial experience stood Holley in good stead, and he continued to write and publish widely throughout the remainder of his career.

In the fall of 1857 seven American railroads commissioned Holley and Colburn to survey European railway practices in the hope of improving American performance. The resulting book, *The Permanent Way and Coal-burning Locomotive Boilers of European Railways; with a Comparison of the Working Economy of European and American Lines, and the Principles upon Which Improvement Must Proceed*, published in 1858, clearly highlighted the operating and maintenance cost advantages of British practices. Reviews were mixed: the British were delighted while the American technical press took great umbrage and sought to rationalize American procedures. *The Permanent Way* was another economic disaster, leaving the finances of the ever-strained Holley depleted.

At this time Holley also began to write articles for the *New York Times* on scientific and engineering developments. He contributed several hundred essays over the course of his lifetime, including an 1858–1859 series on the British steamship, the *Great Eastern*. At the same time, Holley was researching a second volume on railroads, *American and European Railway Practice*. Published in 1860, this book further established Holley's credentials as a technical writer, already enhanced by his editorship of the mechanical department of the *American Railway Review*, which he had assumed in January of that year. Despite his talents as an editor and writer, Holley yearned for more practical engineering work and in early 1861 went to work for Edwin Stevens of the Camden and Amboy Railroad. Soon after the famous 1862 battle of the armored ships *Monitor* and *Merrimack*, Stevens, who with his brother Robert had designed an ironclad warship, the *Battery*, sent Holley abroad to study European armament and ordnance. Stevens hoped to complete construction of his ship and convince the navy of its worth. This trip resulted in the publication of *A Treatise on Ordnance and Armor* (1865), not only a landmark record and guide to 1860s artillery and gun manufacture, but also a source book for contemporary iron- and steel-making practices.

On the 1862 fact-finding tour, Holley made a side trip to the Sheffield, England, steel works of Henry Bessemer, an event that affected the final two decades of his career. Holley became convinced of steel's durability over iron and in particular of the advantages of the Bessemer process, which, when combined with the metallurgist Robert Mushet's patented technique of introducing a controlled amount of a manganese pig iron, in turn precisely regulating the carbon content, allowed for the rapid production of large quantities of molten steel suitable for forming directly into various shapes, rather than forging later when cold. Upon his return from England, Holley sought out a company that might be interested in acquiring the American rights to the Bessemer process. He convinced John A. Griswold and John F. Winslow, two Troy, New York, area iron producers, of the value of the process, and they sent Holley back to England to negotiate for them. In late 1863 he returned with a license for Griswold and Winslow to use Bessemer's patents on a royalty basis and a three-year option to acquire permanently the American rights.

Holley's role for Griswold and Winslow was to build and operate a successful pilot plant; this he initially accomplished in February 1865. Following subsequent refinements to the process, Griswold and Winslow formally acquired the American Bessemer patent rights in August and announced that the company was willing to produce Bessemer steel on order and would consider issuing licenses to interested parties. At approximately the same time a second experimental plant using competing and overlapping patents was successfully completed by a Wyandotte, Michigan, group of iron makers led by Eber Ward, Zoheth Durfee, and William Durfee. Determined to avoid a possibly lengthy and costly patent controversy, the two groups joined forces, pooling their patents in 1866 as the Pneumatic Steel Association. This company was later reorganized as the Bessemer Steel Company in 1877 and the Steel Patents Company in 1890. The company issued licenses and plans for the construction of Bessemer process plants for an initial fee plus a tonnage charge on the steel subsequently produced. Of the twelve Bessemer plants eventually constructed, Holley either directly designed and built or indirectly provided the plans for eleven. He was thus the central technical figure in the emergence and growth of the Bessemer-based steel industry in the United States.

Holley contributed numerous technical improvements to the steel industry and all told received sixteen patents, most of them for improvements in the Bessemer process and plants. By 1875 Holley's improved converter vessel bottom, which was his single most important patent and technical improvement to the basic Bessemer process, had been almost universally adopted in both American and European plants. This alteration made it possible to change the bottom of the converter without cooling it, thereby saving both time and money. Holley also received patents for developments related to the casting of ingots and, more important, for the invention of a removable converter shell (1880). Holley also lectured widely on steel making, at the same time absorbing from steel producers in America and abroad the latest in technical developments.

Throughout the last two decades of his life, Holley operated as an independent consulting engineer, working primarily for the Bessemer organization and its associate members. He served as chief engineer for several in succession: Griswold & Winslow (1863–1866, 1868–1872), Pennsylvania Steel Co. (1866–1868), Cambria Iron Works (1870–1872), and Edgar Thompson Steel Works (1872–1875). Of all the plants Holley designed, Andrew Carnegie's Edgar Thompson Steel Works in Pittsburgh probably was the most advanced and well-designed for the time. This plant was ideally located with respect to transportation facilities, bordered as it was by the Monongahela River on the south and the Pennsylvania Railroad on the north; it also had access to the Baltimore and Ohio Railroad. Because Holley was able to create a completely new steel plant rather than convert an older iron-making concern, he was able to take advantage of these existing transportation facilities and the vast acreage of the site to focus his design on enhancing the continuous flow of the production process.

By 1876 steel prices had declined because of excess capacity and a depressed economy, leading Holley to worry about his consulting and financial position within the Pneumatic Steel Association. Following an 1876 trip to Europe, he began to champion the newly developed open-hearth process of steel making in the hopes of expanding his consulting business, which was now faltering in the face of the association's decision not to build any additional Bessemer plants. Holley was able to convince several of his clients, most notably the Cambria Company, of the value of the new process. However, he was not to live long enough to play the same role in the development of the open-hearth process that he had in that of the Bessemer process. Returning exhausted from one of his extensive and fast-paced European fact-finding trips, he died in New York from complications associated with an obstructed gall duct. Despite his extensive contributions to the development of the steel industry, Holley seldom profited personally, and his financial affairs were often in disarray. At the time of his death his business account contained only $1,000. However, three months after his death the Bessemer Steel Company did appropriate $50,000 for the purchase of Holley's last patent for the removable converter shell.

During his consulting years Holley published frequently and widely; his extensive series of forty-one articles on the American iron and steel industry appeared in the leading British technical journal *Engineering* (1877–1880). He was also particularly interested in education, both formal academic training and the continuing exchange and accumulation of knowledge among practical steel men. He served for many years as a trustee of the Rensselaer Polytechnic Institute. Holley was one of the early members of the American Institute of Mining Engineers, serving as its president in 1875. He was also chairman of the committee in charge of arranging the metallurgical engineering section for the 1876 Philadelphia Centennial Exhibition and a founding member of the American Society of Mechanical Engineers, organized in 1880. He was a member of the American Society of Civil Engineers, serving as vice president in 1875, and in 1877 was elected a member of the British Institution of Civil Engineers.

An affable man of great personal integrity, Holley was widely recognized for the extensive contributions he made to the emerging steel industry. In 1882 Holley was posthumously awarded the British Iron and Steel Institute's prestigious Bessemer Medal, and in 1883 the engineering societies to which Holley had belonged placed a memorial bust in his honor in Washington Square, New York City. In part, the plaque's inscription read, "In honor of Alexander Lyman Holley foremost among those whose genius and energy established in America . . . the manufacture of Bessemer steel."

• Manuscripts related to Holley can be found at the Connecticut Historical Society, the Engineering Societies Library in New York City, the New-York Historical Society, the New York Public Library, and the American Iron and Steel Institute. His biography is Jeanne McHugh, *Alexander Holley and the Makers of Steel* (1980), which contains an accessible bibliography of Holley's works; but see also Allida Black's useful biographical essay in *Iron and Steel in the Nineteenth Century*, ed. Paul F. Paskoff (1989) in the Encyclopedia of American Business History and Biography series. Also helpful are William T. Hogan, *History of the Iron and Steel Industry in the United States*, vol. 1 (1971); Peter Temin, *Iron and Steel in Nineteenth-century America: An Economic Inquiry* (1964); and Elting Morison, *Men, Machines, and Modern Times* (1966).

STEPHEN H. CUTCLIFFE

HOLLEY, Horace (13 Feb. 1781–31 July 1827), Unitarian minister and educator, was born in Salisbury, Connecticut, the son of Luther Holley, a merchant, and Sarah Dakin, daughter of a Baptist minister. At the age of three he was sent to elementary school, completing all courses available to him. He then turned to employment in the family store. In 1797 emerging academic interests brought him to enter the Academy of Williams College, a preparatory institution. Two years later Holley entered Yale University, graduating in 1803. During his senior year he came under the influence of a religious revival underway in New Haven. After graduation, he left for New York City to begin the study of law. Holley quickly found law uncongenial and returned to New Haven to study divinity under the Reverend Timothy Dwight. While in New Haven he married Mary Austin in 1805 (the couple had two children) and completed his study for the ministry.

In September 1805 Holley became the pastor at Greenfield Hill, Fairfield County, Connecticut. While at Greenfield Hill, Holley's theological perspective of austere Calvinism changed, and he became a leading exponent of Unitarianism. Remaining there three years, he accepted the ministry of the Unitarian South End Church on Hollis Street, Boston. While he was pastor, church membership doubled, requiring new construction. Furthermore, his considerable oratorical talents gained him a national reputation. While in Boston, Holley participated in community life through membership on the Boston School Committee and Harvard University Board of Overseers.

In 1818, after nine years at the South End Church, he began to receive offers for a number of prominent positions nationwide, including the pulpit of the Independent Church of Baltimore and preaching to the U.S. House of Representatives. Near the same time an offer came from the Board of Trustees of Transylvania University in Lexington, Kentucky. As early as the winter of 1815–1816, University trustees and local Lexington leaders like Henry Clay had touted Holley's candidacy for president. In May 1818 Holley traveled to Kentucky to gauge public opinion toward his potential appointment to the presidency. Received warmly, he accepted the call on 25 June 1818 to the presidency of Transylvania University. Upon assumption of the office in November 1818, he also became a professor of mental and moral philosophy. Holley launched into transforming the institution through an emphasis on the medical and law departments. Among the more prominent scholars and teachers joining the faculty under his tenure were Dr. Daniel Drake, Dr. Charles Caldwell, and Constantine S. Rafinesque. At Holley's ascendancy to the presidency, the university enrolled 110 students. Within two years enrollment increased to 273, comparing favorably with Yale, Harvard, Dartmouth, and Princeton. During the years of his presidency, enrollment rose in later years from 387 in 1821–1822 to a peak of 418 in 1825–1826. Instrumental in achieving the improved numbers was the strong reputation gained by the medical department. At its peak, Transylvania University ranked second nationally to the Medical College of Pennsylvania in the number of physicians trained, and the student body expanded to include scholars from twenty-one states and two foreign countries.

Despite his academic success, Holley came under scrutiny for his liberal religious views, which regarded God not as a merciless tyrant but a kind and indulgent father, worshiped through a mild and benevolent devotion rather than fanatical excess. Holley believed his fellow citizens' religious sentiments inclined toward the liberal, catholic, and Unitarian sentiment. Opposition to him rose to the fore in 1823 after the death of Colonel James Morrison, chairman of the Board of Trustees. In his eulogy of Morrison, Holley defended the liberalism exhibited by the deceased. Such opinions provoked numbers of the Presbyterian clergy who began a newspaper and pamphlet campaign against Holley's theological views. Accusations were made about fiscal mismanagement, yet investigative committees of the Kentucky General Assembly could find no evidence to confirm the allegations. Meanwhile, the general financial climate in Kentucky witnessed difficult times, providing fodder for the lower socioeconomic classes to challenge the financial assistance provided to the university by the state. A salary cut of $1,000 in 1826 combined with the attacks against his administration of the university finally resulted in his resignation in March 1827. Leaving Lexington two weeks later, Holley received an offer to revive the defunct College of New Orleans. After accepting the post, he sought to revitalize his energies before the college's opening by taking a sea voyage to New York. While at sea, he contracted yellow fever, died, and was buried at sea.

Horace Holley's tenure at Transylvania University, although marked by controversy, witnessed an academic revival for the institution in enrollment, faculty appointments, and national reputation. The university moved from academic obscurity to a role of prominence rivaling that of the most renowned New England institutions. His oratorical abilities placed him near the top ranks of early nineteenth-century American pastors.

• The Transylvania University Library retains Horace Holley's papers as well as published catalogs, circulars, and sermon outlines during his tenure at the school. A complete biographical account of Holley is Charles Caldwell, *A Discourse on the Genius and Character of the Rev. Horace Holley* (1828). His educational contributions are highlighted in Walter Wilson Jenning, *Transylvania: Pioneer University of the West* (1955), and Niels Henry Sonne, *Liberal Kentucky, 1780–1828* (1939).

FRANK R. LEVSTIK

HOLLEY, Major Quincy, Jr. (10 July 1924–25 October 1990), bassist, was born in Detroit, Michigan, the son of Major Quincy Holley, a minister and bass singer. The name of his mother, a pianist, is unknown. Holley first studied violin around the age of six with a German teacher named Mr. Hilken, and at first his parents only allowed him to listen to classical music. At age thirteen, he heard on the radio the sound that would eventually draw him to play the string bass—Slam Stewart's bowed bass solo on "Champagne Lullaby."

Holley attended Cass Technical High School in Detroit from 1938, where he studied the tuba. Among his classmates were vibraphonist Milt Jackson, tenor saxophonist Lucky Thompson, trumpeters Donald Byrd and Howard McGhee, and bassist Paul Chambers. His first professional work was in 1937–1938, on violin, for Leroy Smith's group the Ink Spots.

Holley joined the navy in 1942 as a seaman. He trained at the Great Lakes Naval Training Station in Chicago, joining several other outstanding musicians. After a year, he was accepted into the "A" band, where he played sousaphone and learned to double on bass. His bunkmate was Willie Smith, swing alto saxophonist and arranger for the Jimmie Lunceford band. He also met trumpeter Clark Terry, who became a longtime friend and colleague. Terry originally dubbed Holley the "pack mule" because of all the instruments he carried, and the nickname "Mule" stuck. Later, Holley was transferred to San Diego, where he met Charles Mingus. He attended informal bass classes taught by Mingus out of his home and also met bassist Oscar Pettiford and tenor saxophonist Illinois Jacquet.

While in the navy, Holley gravitated toward the bass as his primary instrument, although he continued to double on tuba. Canadian Bobby Rudd was instrumental in strengthening his bass technique. Bill Doggett, the pianist in Lucky Millinder's band, taught him bass line technique based on chord progressions. Between 1943 and 1945 Holley also became familiar with a new instrument, the electric Fender bass.

After his discharge at the end of World War II, Holley embarked on a freelance career. He played at Birdland and the Alvin Hotel in New York City and made his first recordings in 1950 as part of a duo with pianist Oscar Peterson. He performed with such figures as Charlie Parker, Coleman Hawkins, Al Haig, Art Tatum, and Earl Bostic. He landed steady work with tenor saxophonists Wardell Gray and Dexter Gordon, as well as a stint on baritone saxophone for rhythm-and-blues guitarist and singer T-Bone Walker.

In 1951 Holley traveled to England, where he worked for five years as a freelance bassist and studio musician. His first work in England was with pianist Lennie Felix at the Astor Colony restaurant and with tenor saxophonist Ronnie Scott. He also performed with Tubby Hayes, Jimmy Deuchar, Joe Harriot, Vic Ash, and Ray Ellington and on the British television show "Son of Fred" with Reggie Owen. While in England, Holley married for the first time. (Although little information is available about his wives, Holley mentioned in an interview with Bob Rusch that he had several unsuccessful marriages.) He returned to the United States in January 1956, although he traveled back to England to perform on several occasions.

For a while Holley concentrated on freelancing in New York City as a studio and club musician. In 1957 he worked with a group led by Illinois Jacquet, and in 1958 he recorded on tuba with Michel LeGrand alongside legendary tenor saxophonist Ben Webster. He went to Detroit briefly during this time, where he performed with Coleman Hawkins and Ella Fitzgerald. In 1958 and 1959 he performed and recorded in Brazil with Woody Herman's orchestra. Following his return to the United States, he played with a group headed by saxophonists Al Cohn and Zoot Sims (former Herman band members) from 1959 to 1960.

The 1960s brought continued success to Holley. He maintained an active studio career, worked with pianists Bill Evans and Teddy Wilson during 1961–1962, and played with Duke Ellington's band for eight months in 1964. Holley also performed with legendary multireed instrumentalist Rashaan Roland Kirk in 1965, which resulted in the album *Here Comes the Whistleman* (1967). While with Ellington Holley began drinking heavily. Personal problems exacerbated the situation; Holley lost his wife and house as well as other material possessions. He ultimately sought treatment and later became a volunteer for several drug and alcohol rehabilitation programs in New York City. As part of his efforts, he created Piano Playhouse, an open performance forum at Jacques' on Sunday afternoons in Greenwich Village.

By 1966 electric bass had begun to play a greater role in Holley's career. Holley taught electric bass at the Berklee College of Music from 1967 to 1970. In New York he appeared regularly with Jaki Byard at Bradley's. He also performed with singer Aretha Franklin and introduced her to Columbia Records.

But Holley still maintained an active double bass career, working with notable musicians such as the Count Basie Band, Benny Goodman, Roy Eldridge,

Lee Konitz, Roland Hanna, Frank Sinatra, Quincy Jones, and Buddy DeFranco. Holley was the house bassist at Jimmy Ryan's in New York City in the 1970s. Throughout the 1980s he appeared as a sideman at numerous international jazz festivals. He toured Europe with singer Helen Humes and with a group called the Kings of Jazz and returned to Sao Paulo to lead his own group for a short time in the late 1980s. One of his last performances was in the summer of 1990 at the North Sea Festival, where he played with Dorothy Donegan and Ellis Marsalis. He died in Maplewood, New Jersey.

Holley was a dependable sideman on cello, electric bass, baritone saxophone, and tuba in addition to the double bass. When soloing on double bass, he often hummed or sang wordlessly along in unison, a technique employed earlier by Slam Stewart. His 1986 album with Stewart, *Shut Yo' Mouth*, exemplified this style. Throughout his career he played with musicians associated with traditional jazz, swing, bop, cool jazz, modal jazz, avant-garde jazz, rock, soul, and rhythm and blues. Versed in these varied styles of music as well as in multiple instruments, he was able to remain an active freelance musician in a rapidly changing international musical environment. His willingness to help others was displayed by his affiliations with rehabilitation programs and the National Association for Jazz Education.

• Two periodical interviews offer accurate accounts of Holley's life and activities. His interview with Martin Richards at the 1986 Nice Jazz Festival, *Jazz Journal International* 40, no. 4 (1987): 6–8, outlines his career in and out of the United States; the interview with Bob Rusch in *Cadence* 15, no. 7 (1989): 5–12, provides information regarding significant freelance dates. Samuel A. Floyd, Jr.'s article "The Great Lakes Experience; 1942–45," *Black Perspective in Music* 3, no. 1 (Spring 1975): 17–24, discusses Holley in the context of black musicians in the navy during World War II. See also Gérald Arnaud and Jacques Chesnel, *Masters of Jazz* (1992), for Holley's affiliation with Aretha Franklin. An obituary is in the *New York Times*, 27 Oct. 1990.

DAVID E. SPIES

HOLLEY, Marietta (16 July 1836–1 Mar. 1926), writer, was born in Jefferson County, New York, near the villages of Adams and Pierrepont Manor, the daughter of John Milton Holley and Mary Taber, farmers. Her education in the rural district school ended when she was fourteen, but thereafter she read and studied informally. When her brothers left the farm to seek their fortunes in the West after their father's death in the 1860s, Holley supported the family by selling handicrafts and giving music lessons.

At an early age she began composing verses with accompanying illustrations, but she maintained secrecy about her writing until 1857 when her poetry appeared in the *Jefferson County Journal* under various pseudonyms. Soon her fiction, some in dialect, was being published in popular magazines. In 1872 she sent a few sketches to Mark Twain's publisher, Elisha Bliss at American Publishing, who immediately commis-

sioned her to write a novel in the mode of vernacular humorists. The following year, the first of her Samantha novels, *My Opinions and Betsey Bobbet's*, was published under Holley's newest pseudonym, Josiah Allen's Wife. The novel established the characters of Samantha Smith Allen, her husband Josiah Allen, and the spinster Betsey Bobbet, spokeswoman for gentility and antifeminism.

Although she was called "the female Mark Twain," Holley actually melded three American literary traditions as no other writer had: most of her stories combined the attention to regional detail of the local colorists with the sentimental conventions of the domestic novelists and the vernacular comedy developed by earlier humorists.

Her primary contribution was the creation of the first comic female protagonist in American literature. In her books, Holley addressed most of the reforms promoted by women's groups. She used humor to make the ideals of the temperance and suffrage movements accessible and palatable. Her conversion to the Baptist faith during adolescence led to a lifelong concern with piety and spirituality that, with her feminism, informed her writing. Her work was enormously popular with women readers in general as well as reformers advocating women's rights and temperance. Susan B. Anthony and Frances Willard, for example, sought her support and enjoined her to appear with and write for them. However, Holley consistently refused such invitations, even declining to appear before Congress to advance women's issues, especially the vote, because of her shyness and a slight speech impediment.

Over forty-one years, Holley completed twenty-four Samantha books, including the bestseller of 1887, *Samantha at Saratoga*. Seven of her novels were commissioned books about places or events as they might be viewed through Samantha's spectacles, such as the centennial of the Constitution (1887), the Chicago World's Fair (1893), the world seen on the grand tour (1895), the St. Louis Exposition (1904), and Coney Island and the Thousand Islands (1911). Although she was known for her travel writing, Holley rarely traveled. She barely left the precincts of her farm home until she was forty-five. She wrote most of the travel books entirely from maps and guidebooks, occasionally visiting sites after publication of the work.

Although Holley never married, she adopted a young girl and surrounded herself with faithful friends and servants. She retreated from the publicity and glamor of literary circles and built a mansion on her father's farm, where she lived out her circumscribed life until her death.

• Most of Holley's papers are in the collection of Harold B. Johnson, *Watertown Daily Times*; the Flower Memorial Library; and the Jefferson County Historical Society, all in Watertown, N.Y. Her autobiography, "The Story of My Life," was published in the *Watertown Daily Times*, 5 Feb. to 9 Apr. 1931. Katherine Gillette Blyley's doctoral dissertation, "Marietta Holley" (Univ. of Pittsburgh, 1936), is a useful record of impressions and elusive facts. Kate H. Winter's critical biography, *Marietta Holley: Life with "Josiah Allen's Wife"* (1984), connects Holley's life and work with important literary traditions.

KATE H. WINTER

HOLLEY, Myron (29 Apr. 1779–4 Mar. 1841), abolitionist, was born in Salisbury, Connecticut, the son of Luther Holley and Sarah Dakin, farmers. Holley graduated from Williams College in Williamstown, Massachusetts, in 1799 and then studied for the bar under Chancellor James Kent, in Cooperstown, New York. He began the practice of law in Salisbury, Connecticut, in 1802. The following year, having discovered that he disliked the legal profession, Holley became a bookseller in Canandaigua, New York. In 1804 he married Sally House in Canandaigua; they had twelve children. His daughter Sallie Holley later won fame as an abolitionist and then as an educator of freed slaves.

After serving as county clerk (1810–1814), Holley was elected to the New York General Assembly in 1816. He became a strong proponent of the construction of the Erie Canal and served on the board of commissioners overseeing the project (1816–1824). As treasurer of the board, Holley administered over $2.5 million in expenditures but resigned in 1824 after disclosure of a $30,000 deficiency in his accounts. Although later exonerated of any criminal misappropriation, Holley reimbursed the state from his personal finances. After his resignation, he retired from politics to operate a farm near Lyons, New York.

In the late 1820s, Holley became a leader of the state's anti-Masonic movement, authoring the address of the party's only national convention in Philadelphia in 1830. He edited two newspapers opposing Freemasonry: the Lyons *Countryman* (1831–1834) and the Hartford, Connecticut, *Free Elector* (1834–1835). After resettling on a farm in Carthage, near Rochester, New York, Holley publicly entered the abolitionist movement in 1838 as a traveling lecturer. The following year, he sold his farm to finance the founding of the Rochester *Freeman*, in which he attacked both the Whig and the Democratic parties for their toleration of slavery.

Holley led the movement championing the formation of an antislavery third party. His first proposal that abolitionists nominate their own slate of candidates was rejected at a special convention called by the American Anti-Slavery Society at Cleveland in 1839. Despite the opposition of many abolitionists, including the followers of William Lloyd Garrison, Holley became the foremost promoter of abolitionist political action. In the winter of 1840 he argued that "in our judgment, the anti-slavery electors of the United States are bound, by all their regard to civil and religious rights of the great American people, forthwith to form themselves into an independent political party."

In April 1840 Holley helped convene at Albany, New York, a national abolitionist gathering, which ratified his motion to found the Liberty party and nominated James G. Birney for president. Holley continued to edit the *Freeman* and make speeches on behalf of the Liberty party until his death at Rochester. When Garrison learned of the passing of his abolitionist adversary, he praised Holley: "As a writer, he had few superiors in any country; and he always conducted his controversies with dignity and candor."

• Letters from Holley are in the New-York Historical Society. The only published biography of Holley is Elizur Wright, Jr., *Myron Holley; and What He Did for Liberty and True Religion* (1882). See also Richard H. Sewell, *Ballots for Freedom: Antislavery Politics in the United States, 1837–1860* (1976), pp. 54–59, 69–71, and Orlo J. Price, "The Significance of the Early Religious History of Rochester," *Rochester Historical Society Publications* 3 (1924): 180. An obituary is in the Boston *Liberator*, 12 Mar. 1841.

JOHN R. McKIVIGAN

HOLLEY, Sallie (17 Feb. 1818–12 Jan. 1893), abolitionist and educator, was born in Canandaigua, New York, the daughter of Myron Holley, treasurer of the Erie Canal Commission and subsequently an anti-Masonic and Liberty party activist and editor, and Sally House. When Holley was three, the family moved to nearby Lyons, where she spent her childhood and adolescence helping care for her younger siblings, attending briefly a local academy, and absorbing her father's reform zeal. The stimulation that his college education and liberal Unitarian faith provided far overshadowed the influence of her mother's piety in shaping Holley's future.

After her father's death in 1841, Sallie Holley was thrown upon her own emotional and intellectual resources. It was then that she rejected her mother's Methodism to join the Unitarian church and began to teach school in Rochester, New York. Propelled by a need for a clearer purpose in her life as well as the desire for an extended education, she entered Oberlin College in 1847, choosing the simplified classical curriculum of the Ladies Course rather than the more rigorous curriculum leading to the bachelor of arts, which was by then offered to both men and women.

At Oberlin she encountered the major influences that shaped her subsequent career. The college's pervasive antislavery activism had a profound effect on Holley. Not only was the student body coeducational, it was biracial. Moreover, since its chartering in 1834, and especially after 1835, when Theodore Dwight Weld and his fellow transfer students from Lane Theological Seminary brought their abolitionist campaign to Oberlin, the school had attracted reform-minded lecturers. Among them was Abby Kelley, a fiery campaigner and organizer, who became a major influence on Holley. Acting as mentor, Kelley propelled Holley toward radical Garrisonianism, coaching her as an antislavery lecturer and agent. At Oberlin, Holley also met her lifelong companion, Caroline Putnam, a fellow student eight years her junior. Forming an intense personal bond, these women supported each other for the next forty-six years as they pursued their common goals, sometimes living and working together, sometimes separately.

Even before she graduated from Oberlin in 1851, Holley had begun to campaign against slavery. Until the Civil War broke out, she lectured throughout the northern states, concentrating her efforts in western New York and Massachusetts but also traveling as far as Maine, Michigan, Vermont, and Delaware. Wherever she spoke she gained a reputation as an effective and moving orator. Never fully confident of her talents for public speaking, however, she generally opted for small meetings in familiar settings, most often in village or country churches. She consciously avoided the competitive tensions engendered when antislavery leaders argued over strategy and ideology at state and national conventions. Because she rarely attended these gatherings, she never achieved high visibility or a compelling influence in the movement.

Until 1864, when she endorsed the Republican party as the best vehicle for emancipation, Holley had accepted fully the perfectionism and anarchism that made Garrisonian abolitionists oppose all political action. Her closest colleagues included *Liberator* editor William Lloyd Garrison; Samuel J. May, Jr., general agent for the Garrisonians in the 1850s; Maria Weston Chapman, by Holley's time primarily a fundraiser; and Abby Kelley and her husband, Stephen Symonds Foster. Like them, she embraced other reforms encompassed by their shared utopian vision, most notably women's rights. Nevertheless, she maintained ties with the politically oriented abolitionists of western New York, chief among them Gerrit Smith, her longtime friend and adviser. Furthermore, Holley shunned Garrisonian anticlericalism, adopting an evangelical lecturing style appropriate to church settings. By the late 1850s, while maintaining American Anti-Slavery Society sponsorship, she worked independently of the society's direction.

During the Civil War Holley continued to lecture on antislavery and temperance platforms and gathered relief supplies for the freedmen. From 1865 to 1870 she was the principal agent of the American Anti-Slavery Society's *National Anti-Slavery Standard* and lectured in support of full civil rights for black Americans. In 1870 she rejoined Caroline Putnam to teach in the school for former slaves that Putnam had established in 1868 in Lottsburg, a small coastal town in northeastern Virginia. The school was modeled on the Oberlin tradition of missionary uplift and was independent of Virginia's new public school system and northern charitable societies. Supported by voluntary contributions from friends and well-wishers, the two women provided an elementary education to all comers, worked with the Republican party to the extent that women were permitted, and attempted to guide the freedmen and women of their community in all phases of their new lives. But the strains of isolation amid a hostile white community contributed to a sharp break in their intimate friendship, and by 1885 Holley had moved out of their shared home. Before that time, Holley had spent ever longer periods of time in the North and had traveled extensively in England in 1878 and Germany in 1882. Therefore, despite a partial reconciliation, responsibility for the school increasingly devolved on Putnam, who eventually continued it on her own until her death in 1917.

As she grew older, Holley's initial lack of self-confidence gave way to persistent assertiveness that grated on her friends. After 1874 her commitment to reform grew more conservative. Though she supported the enfranchisement of women, she took no part in suffrage organizations. Her crusading liberalism had peaked in the 1850s, and despite her self-identification as a religious and social radical as late as 1865, her subsequent course belied the claim. After a severe bout with pneumonia, she died in New York City and was buried beside her father in Mt. Hope Cemetery, Rochester. Despite Holley's preference for the obscure periphery, she has a secure place among the second rank of those who worked effectively to end slavery and, less visibly, to improve the lot of former slaves.

• There is no substantial collection of Sallie Holley's papers. The Abby Kelley Foster Papers at the American Antiquarian Society in Worcester, Mass., the Gerrit Smith Miller Papers at Syracuse University, the antislavery collection of the Boston Public Library, and the Caroline Dall and Samuel May, Jr., Papers at the Massachusetts Historical Society contain many letters by Holley and substantial references to her. John White Chadwick excerpted many of her letters in his *A Life for Liberty: Anti-Slavery and Other Letters of Sallie Holley* (1899), a sympathetic treatment of her career. The only modern biography is Katherine Lydigsen Herbig, "Friends for Freedom: The Lives and Careers of Sallie Holley and Caroline Putnam" (Ph.D. diss., Claremont Graduate School, 1977), which contains a full bibliography of relevant primary and secondary material.

WILLIAM H. PEASE
JANE H. PEASE

HOLLIDAY, Doc (14 Aug. 1851–8 Nov. 1887), outlaw, was born John Henry Holliday in Griffin, Georgia, the son of Confederate major Henry Burroughs Holliday and Alice Jane McKey, a woman of old Georgia stock. He moved with his family to Valdosta, Lowndes County, where his father was elected mayor in 1863. When Holliday was fifteen, his mother died of tuberculosis and passed the disease to her son. Holliday's sorrow turned to bitterness when in 1866 his father married a 23-year-old war widow. Sent the same year to Philadelphia to live with his mother's relatives, Holliday enrolled at the Pennsylvania College of Dental Surgery in September 1870. He associated with Dr. Arthur C. Ford in Atlanta and practiced resident dentistry in Valdosta, filling and extracting teeth through October 1871. Holliday graduated with twenty-four others in March 1872 with a thesis titled "Diseases of the Teeth."

In 1873, according to Bat Masterson, Holliday fired his pistol at former slaves swimming in an uncle's pond. Threatened by Reconstruction Bureau officials, Holliday headed for Lamar, Missouri, where he inquired after his father's friend, Nicholas Porter Earp. In the fall of 1874 in Dallas, Texas, he established a dental surgery with John A. Seegar. The *Dallas Herald* reported on 1 January 1875 that Holliday exchanged pistol shots with Dallas saloonkeeper Charles W. Austin. Both were arrested and put in jail. Holliday paid his bail, abandoned his practice, and rode west to Jacksboro, Texas. A few weeks later he dealt faro in Fort Griffin's notorious "hidetown" near the Brazos Clear Fork. On 12 June 1875 a grand jury indicted "Dock" Holliday and Mike Lynch for "playing together & with each other at a game with cards in a house in which spirituous liquors were sold." "Long Kate" was named in another indictment. Archivist Joan Farmer of Albany, Texas, claims the latter was "Big Nose Kate," Katherine Elder, Holliday's companion; researchers have discovered that Elder and Holliday had married in 1870, although they kept their marriage hidden. Sheriff John C. Jacobs chained Holliday to an eye bolt in a hotel room floor. According to Farmer, Kate Elder started a haystack fire at the rear of the hotel, cut Holliday's chains, and they escaped after knifing a guard named Bailey. Surviving records indicate that on 30 June 1875 Sheriff Jacobs sent a message to Tom Green County warning that Holliday escaped with a woman named Kate. Holliday, using the name Tom McKey, and Elder arrived in Denver about September, then fleeced mining camps in Colorado until their welcome wore thin. Masterson claims that Holliday stabbed a miner named Bud Ryan, but no newspaper of the time printed a corroborating story. The pair headed for Kansas in late 1876. Holliday and Elder probably went to Wichita and should have met the Earp brothers there, though Earp insisted he met Holliday at Fort Griffin. Stuart N. Lake said Holliday was in a Fort Griffin saloon, possibly the Bee Hive, when he met Wyatt Earp in 1878. Elder was charged with prostitution, and the two returned to Kansas.

In Dodge City on 8 June 1878, Holliday advertised his dental office in Room 24, Dodge House. Six months later Masterson hired Holliday as part of his army in the bloodless "Royal Gorge War." After Masterson lost his popularity, Holliday headed to East Las Vegas, New Mexico, where on 4 July 1879 he purchased interest in a saloon with John Joshua Webb, a former lawman from Dodge City. Holliday and the justice of the peace, Hyman G. "Hoodoo Brown" Neill gave East Las Vegas a reputation as a wide open town. Holliday killed a drunken former army scout named Mike Gordon who was unhappy about his mistress working in Holliday's saloon. Six months later, after wounding Charlie White, Holliday sold his interest in the saloon and left for Prescott, Arizona Territory, where he was counted on the 1880 census living in the household of Secretary of State John J. Gosper, then the acting governor. In September Holliday joined Wyatt Earp in Tombstone, where they and two others purchased the Oriental Saloon. Partly because of Doc's reputation and actions, tension rose against the Earps and Holliday from a local gang called the "Cow Boys." Joining the three Earp brothers, Holliday met the five of the rival faction near the O.K. Corral in October 1881. Doc killed Tom McLaury with a shotgun blast and was slightly wounded. Three months later

assassins crippled Virgil Earp and murdered his brother Morgan. In retaliation, Holliday and Wyatt Earp hunted down and killed Frank Stilwell, Florentino Cruz, and Curly Bill Brocius. Sheriff Johnnie Behan arrested Holliday and Earp twice for the O.K. Corral episode.

In May 1882 Holliday and Earp went to Trinidad, Colorado, where Masterson had a saloon. Behan telegraphed a warrant for their arrest. A bounty hunter named Perry M. Mallon captured Holliday in a Denver saloon and locked him in jail. Governor Frederick W. Pitkin intervened, and Holliday was released from jail but then rearrested on a phony bunco charge. The judge continued the trial "indefinitely," rendering the Arizona warrant harmless. Holliday's fortunes declined rapidly, and in Leadville, Colorado, in 1883 he was tried but released after he severely wounded a bartender over a personal debt. Sinking into poverty, Holliday's chronic pulmonary tuberculosis and alcoholism consumed him; he now became merely a drunken curiosity. In 1886 Silverton's newspaper reported that teenage boys had taunted and harassed the emaciated and pathetic figure as he walked unsteadily along the main street. A year later, Holliday traveled to Glenwood Springs, Colorado, for its mineral waters and checked into the Hotel Glenwood on 5 November. He would never leave his room. Drinking to the end, he died alone three days later and was buried in a pauper's grave. In the mid-twentieth century, town fathers, recognizing his tourist draw, placed a substantial granite marker for Holliday at a mountainside cemetery above the town. The grave is empty, however, his body lost when an especially large flood on the Colorado River destroyed the lower cemetery years before. Holliday, who was raised to be a southern gentleman and was trained as a professional dentist, proved instead to be a clever gambler and alcoholic killer. In confrontations, Holliday compensated for his sickly build and tubercular condition by springing suddenly on his opponents and killing them without mercy.

• For Holliday's activities at Fort Griffin, Texas, see Joan Farmer, Nail Archives, Albany, Shackleford County, Tex. The standard work on Holliday, found in most libraries and bookstores is John Myers Myers, *Doc Holliday* (1955). Serious readers of history are warned that it is full of errors and unfounded claims, and Myers's dates are blurry and usually incorrect. Worth reading are E. Richard Churchill, *Doc Holliday, Bat Masterson and Wyatt Earp: Their Colorado Career* (1974); G. G. Boyer, *Illustrated Life of Doc Holliday* (1966); Albert S. Pendleton, Jr., and Susan McKey Thomas, "Doc Holliday's Georgia Background," *Journal of Arizona History* 14 (Autumn 1973): 185–204; Pat Jahns, *The Frontier World of Doc Holliday* (1957); and Pendleton and Thomas, *In Search of the Hollidays* (1973). Masterson's views must be taken with a grain of salt in W. B. (Bat) Masterson, *Famous Gunfighters of the Western Frontier*, ed. Jack DeMattos (1982). For Holliday's activities in Arizona, see Richard E. Erwin, *The Truth about Wyatt Earp* (1993); and Paula Mitchell Marks, *And Die in the West* (1989).

VERNON R. MADDUX

HOLLIDAY, Judy (21 June 1921–7 June 1965), actress, was born Judith Tuvim in New York City, the daughter of Abe Tuvim, a fundraiser and organizer for Jewish affairs, and Helen Gollomb, a piano teacher. A bright student, Holliday graduated at age fifteen, first in her class, from Julia Richman High School, an all-girls New York public school. Rejected by the Yale School of Drama because of her youth, Holliday took a job as a switchboard operator at Orson Welles's Mercury Theatre. At a summer resort Holliday became friends with Adolph Green, a young actor who was playing in the resort's production of *The Pirates of Penzance*. Soon Green teamed with Betty Comden and two others to form the Revuers, a comedy group. The Revuers' brand of good-natured satire proved popular, and they quickly moved beyond Greenwich Village coffeehouses to high-profile venues such as Radio City Music Hall and the Rainbow Room at Rockefeller Center. Although Holliday (who was still using her original surname, Tuvim) was an insecure and somewhat shy person who was primarily interested in being a writer rather than a performer, onstage she emerged as the Revuers' most charismatic member.

Holliday was offered a movie contract by Twentieth Century–Fox in 1943 and signed with the studio on the condition that her fellow Revuers were also signed. Twentieth Century–Fox agreed but dropped the other Revuers after one film, *Greenwich Village* (1944), from which their scenes, as well as Holliday's, were cut in the final edit. Comden and Green returned to New York and commenced their successful partnership as Broadway lyricists. Holliday lingered in California for another year. Twentieth Century–Fox requested that Judy Tuvim change her name, and before the studio could give her a new one, the actress herself came up with Holliday (a variation of the Hebrew meaning of Tuvim). Holliday was assigned to small parts in two more films—*Winged Victory* (1944) and *Something for the Boys* (1944)—before her contract with Twentieth Century–Fox was voided by the studio.

Returning to New York, Holliday landed a secondary role in the play *Kiss Them for Me*. It was the nightclub and film performer's first effort in the legitimate theater as well her Broadway debut. *Kiss Them for Me*, a comedy about servicemen on leave in San Francisco, was a modest success, running for 110 performances in the spring of 1945, and earned Holliday the Clarence Derwent Award for best supporting actress. Later in 1945, when established star Jean Arthur withdrew from Garson Kanin's comedy *Born Yesterday* before its Broadway opening, Holliday was called in as a last-minute replacement in the role of Billie Dawn, a crooked businessman's clueless moll who wises up once she receives a civics lesson from an idealistic young journalist. *Born Yesterday* opened in New York in January 1946 and ran for 1,641 performances. Though a great deal of the rather thin comedy's success was credited to Holliday's portrayal of Billie Dawn, Columbia Pictures did not want the actress for the film version. Outraged, Garson Kanin wrote a small but flashy part for Holliday in *Adam's Rib*, the

Metro-Goldwyn-Mayer film he was scripting, which would show off her talents as a screen performer. The ploy worked, and Columbia signed Holliday to a seven-picture contract.

The film version of *Born Yesterday*, costarring William Holden and Broderick Crawford, opened in December 1950 to good reviews with most of the kudos going to Holliday. The following spring she won the Academy Award for best actress, despite stiff competition from Bette Davis in *All about Eve* and Gloria Swanson in *Sunset Boulevard*. Since Holliday's contract with Columbia stipulated that she had to make only one film per year over a seven-year period, she returned to New York and starred in a revival of Elmer Rice's *Dream Girl* at the City Center. Married in 1948 to classical clarinetist and recording executive David Oppenheim, Holliday always kept New York as her home base and stayed in Hollywood only as long as her movie work dictated. The couple had one child.

In 1952 Holliday was called to testify before the U.S. Senate's McCarran Committee. It was hoped that the politically liberal New York actress would "name names" of Communist associates; but Holliday's testimony was perfunctory, and the committee lost interest in her. "Communist sympathizer" allegations did only minor damage to Holliday's career (Columbia studios stood behind its star and even paid for her legal counsel in the matter). The inability to find suitable vehicles for Holliday accounts to a far greater degree than politics for the failure of the studio to capitalize on her Oscar-winning debut as a star. Contradictory elements in Holliday's personality and appearance made the actress hard to categorize and difficult to effectively cast. Though a specialist in scatterbrained characters, Holliday's intelligence and natural reticence were often apparent. A tall, heavily built woman (whose weight was a problem even by the generous standards of the 1950s), Holliday possessed no remarkable physical attributes except a pleasantly cherubic, dimpled face and flashy blond hair (dyed from her natural light brown), yet sex appeal was part of her image.

Holliday's second picture for Columbia, *The Marrying Kind*, a comedy/drama about a young working-class couple, was released in the spring of 1952, a career-stalling year and a half after the release of *Born Yesterday*. It was followed by *It Should Happen to You* (1954) and *Phfft!* (1955), both pairing her with newcomer Jack Lemmon; *The Solid Gold Cadillac* (1956), with Paul Douglas; and *Full of Life* (1957), with Richard Conte. All were relatively low-cost black-and-white comedies that suited Holliday's stage-nurtured, subtly nuanced style of acting. In the mid-1950s, however, Columbia moved toward big-budget, widescreen, color ventures, and Holliday did not fit into the studio's plans. A seventh picture for Columbia, called for in her contract, was never made.

In November 1956 Holliday opened on Broadway in the musical *Bells Are Ringing*, written by her old friends Adolph Green and Betty Comden with music by Jule Styne. After her mostly lackluster movie career, Holliday's highly successful return to Broadway in *Bells Are Ringing*, a weakly plotted if pleasingly tuneful vehicle, suggests that her talents were used to better advantage on stage than on film. The show ran for 924 performances, and Holliday won a Tony Award for best actress in a musical. Holliday's final screen appearance was in Metro-Goldwyn-Mayer's film version of *Bells Are Ringing* in 1960. In the same year she was diagnosed with breast cancer and underwent a mastectomy. Holliday recovered sufficiently to star in a second Broadway musical, *Hot Spot*, in 1963, an unsuccessful spoof about the newly formed Peace Corps, but cancer recurred and finally took the actress's life in New York City. Divorced from David Oppenheim in 1957, in the last years of her life Holliday was involved with jazz saxophonist Gerry Mulligan.

• Will Holtzman, *Judy Holliday: A Biography* (1982), and Gary Carey, *Judy Holliday: An Intimate Life Story* (1982), are full-length biographies. An informative essay on Holliday can be found in *Notable Women in the American Theatre: A Biographical Dictionary* (1989), and Bernard F. Dick, ed., *Columbia Pictures: Portrait of a Studio* (1992), offers the chapter "Judy Holliday: The Star and the Studio," a detailed examination of Holliday's film career by Ruth Prigozy. See also Leslie Janet Taubman, "Judy Holliday: A Critical Study of a Star" (Ph.D. diss., Univ. of Southern California, 1980). An obituary is in the *New York Times*, 8 June 1965.

MARY C. KALFATOVIC

HOLLINGWORTH, Harry Levi (26 May 1880–17 Sept. 1956), psychologist, was born in DeWitt, Nebraska, the son of Thomas Hollingworth, a carpenter, and Libbie J. Andrews. From the age of eleven, Hollingworth worked as a carpenter with his father. In his later teens he mailordered volumes by Emerson, Carlyle, Plato, Darwin, and others, the study of which changed the course of his life. At the age of twenty-three he entered the University of Nebraska, from which he received a bachelor's degree in philosophy and psychology in 1906. He then served as principal of Fremont (Nebraska) High School until the following year, when he accepted a graduate assistantship with psychologist James McKeen Cattell at Columbia University. In 1908 he married a classmate from Nebraska, Leta Anna Stetter, who would become a prominent psychologist under the name Leta Stetter Hollingworth; they had no children.

Hollingworth finished his doctorate in psychology at Columbia in 1909, having studied with Cattell, Edward L. Thorndike, and Robert S. Woodworth. After graduation he joined the faculty of Columbia's Barnard College, where he remained until his retirement in 1946. In 1910 he taught a course on applied psychology in the evening college of Columbia University, which was attended by many individuals from New York City's business community. Interaction with these individuals led to an interest in the psychology of advertising and subsequently to a lecture series that Hollingworth offered in 1910–1911 to the Advertising Men's League of New York City.

The most important applied investigation in Hollingworth's career was one of the first studies he undertook after receiving his doctorate. It was a study, begun in 1911, on the effects of caffeine on mental processes and behavior in humans. The research was underwritten by the Coca-Cola Company in preparation for the legal defense of its soft drink in a suit initiated by the federal government. Hollingworth's research showed that caffeine is a mild stimulant whose effect on motor performance is rapid and transient, whereas the effect on cognitive performance appears more slowly but is more persistent. He concluded that there was no evidence in his studies that caffeine produced any deleterious effects in mental or motor performance. When published, Hollingworth's report drew an enthusiastic response from his fellow professional researchers. Arguably, no behavioral studies of such comprehensiveness and scientific control had ever been conducted. The report was praised not only for the valuable findings on caffeine but also for the sophistication of the experimental design. Considered a model of good research, it was frequently cited in the pharmacological literature and remained a reference in the scientific literature more than eighty years later.

The success of this investigation showed Hollingworth that he could apply the scientific methods of psychology to research studies of practical importance, and that such research would be funded by those businesses most likely to benefit from the research. In 1912 he published a book on advertising and selling, which he followed with textbooks on vocational psychology, educational psychology, and applied psychology.

During World War I, Hollingworth was assigned to an army hospital in Plattsburgh, New York, where he worked primarily with veterans suffering from "shell shock." From this experience he wrote *The Functional Psychology of Neuroses* (1922), explaining the shell shock symptoms in terms of "redintegration." According to Hollingworth, shell shock occurs in individuals with a "specific intellectual weakness (lack of scope or sagacity); a past distressing episode; and the present effectiveness of partial features of the old episode in reinstating the similar picture of distress and incapacity." Although Hollingworth did not originate this concept of past states of mind being triggered by the apparent recurrence of distinctive experience, he used it to explain a number of behavioral effects, such as the relief of tension that individuals experience from chewing gum. In a series of studies undertaken in the 1930s for the Beech-Nut Company, he concluded that relaxation was gained from chewing gum because the chewing evoked the relaxation associated with chewing at mealtime.

The Coca-Cola and Beech-Nut studies were but two of scores of investigations that Hollingworth conducted at the request of business and industry. His success in applied research, supported directly by the business community, forged new opportunities for psychologists outside of the university. Thirty years after publishing the caffeine studies he wrote, "I have always been glad that we took on this project, which in the beginning appeared to all concerned to be a somewhat dubious undertaking. . . . The investigation, and its report, did I believe its bit to break down some of the taboos then prevalent and to encourage cooperative investigation in which science provides the insight and technique and industry offers the problems and the means." Later scholars acknowledged that Hollingworth's research significantly enhanced the acceptability of such applied work.

Hollingworth's many honors included the Nicholas Murray Butler Medal from Columbia University in 1921, the presidency of the American Psychological Association in 1927, and the naming of the psychology laboratories at Barnard College for him in 1954.

Hollingworth's first wife died of cancer in 1939. In her memory he wrote the biography *Leta Stetter Hollingworth* (1943). In 1946, the same year that he retired from Barnard, he married Josephine Weischer. He died at his home in Montrose, New York.

• Hollingworth's papers are at the Archives of the History of American Psychology, Akron, Ohio. They contain correspondence, research notes and reports, and an unpublished 600-page autobiography that he wrote in 1940. Hollingworth was the author of more than twenty books and nearly 100 scientific and theoretical articles, including "The Influence of Caffein on Mental and Motor Efficiency," *Archives of Psychology* (Apr. 1912), *Advertising and Selling: Principles of Appeal and Response* (1913), *Applied Psychology*, with A. T. Poffenberger (1917), *The Psychology of Functional Neuroses* (1920), and *Psychology: Its Facts and Principles* (1928). The caffeine studies and the Coca-Cola trial are described in Ludy T. Benjamin, Jr., et al., "Coca-Cola, Caffeine, and Mental Deficiency: Harry Hollingworth and the Chattanooga Trial of 1911," *Journal of the History of the Behavioral Sciences* 27 (1991): 42–55. For a description of Hollingworth's work in the psychology of advertising, see David P. Kuna, "The Psychology of Advertising, 1896–1916" (Ph.D. diss., Univ. of New Hampshire, 1976). Obituaries are in the *New York Times*, 18 Sept. 1956, and the *American Journal of Psychology* 70 (1957): 136–40.

LUDY T. BENJAMIN, JR.

HOLLINGWORTH, Leta Anna Stetter (25 May 1886–27 Nov. 1939), psychologist and feminist, was born in a dugout near Chadron, Nebraska, the daughter of John G. Stetter and Margaret Elinor Danley. Her father, a fun-loving but irresponsible Virginian of German descent, worked as a peddler, entertainer, and itinerant cowboy. Her mother, the well-educated daughter of a neighboring Scotch-Irish farm family, died in 1890, leaving three girls to be reared by their maternal grandparents. At twelve Leta and her sisters moved to Valentine, Nebraska, to live with their father and his new wife, a troubled woman who made life a "fiery furnace."

Despite childhood hardship, Leta Stetter flourished at school, and in 1906 she graduated from the University of Nebraska. She then taught high school for two years before marrying her former college classmate Harry Levi Hollingworth in December 1908 and moving to New York City, where he was completing a Ph.D. in psychology at Columbia University.

Eager to continue working, Leta Hollingworth applied for a teaching position only to find that the New York City Board of Education barred the hiring of married women. She turned to writing short stories, but they did not sell. She applied for fellowships to attend graduate school but found few open to women. Only when her husband completed his Ph.D. and began teaching at Barnard College was the couple's income adequate for her to pursue graduate study. She earned a Ph.D. in educational psychology at Teachers College in 1916 and then joined the faculty there.

Hollingworth entered psychology at the height of the woman's movement. Newly militant suffragists were winning state victories throughout the country. Tens of thousands of women workers were striking for higher wages. Women students, once barred from higher education, now outnumbered men in many of the country's liberal arts colleges. And everywhere women were challenging conventional views about their alleged inferiority to men. Hollingworth, a lone woman in a male profession, quickly joined the assault. Devising an experiment to test the widespread belief that menstruation impaired women's mental functions for a significant part of each month, she addressed one of the chief arguments then used to bar women from high-paying positions. Her doctoral dissertation, *Functional Periodicity* (1914), published as a book even before she had completed course work for her doctorate, tested the mental and motor abilities of a group of women and men over many weeks and found no evidence of a feminine cycle of disability. In addition, Hollingworth devised studies to test the prevailing view, derived from the work of Charles Darwin, that women were inherently less variable than men and were therefore less likely to be either mentally defective or especially talented. Studying admissions patterns at the Clearing House for Mental Defectives, where she worked while still a student giving intelligence tests, Hollingworth found that, as the variability hypothesis predicted, men outnumbered women. She noted, however, that this gender imbalance was a result of the disproportionate number of boys under the age of sixteen. The reason, she suggested, was that girls with low intelligence tended to be kept at home, caring for younger children and doing housework, while boys were given the freedom of the streets, where they often came in conflict with the police. Women came to the Clearing House only after they lost their dependent status ("Variability as Related to Sex Differences in Achievement," *American Journal of Sociology* 19 [1914]). Hollingworth used similar sociological reasoning in explaining the relatively lower numbers of women who had achieved intellectual eminence. Given the widespread pressure on women to bear and rear children, it was hardly surprising, she argued, that they had less success than men in realizing their intellectual potential. By the 1920s Hollingworth had established herself as a prominent figure in psychology, and her work formed part of an increasingly successful assault on the biological determinism that had dominated psychological thinking in the early twentieth century.

Hollingworth's findings made her a popular figure among early feminists fighting for equal opportunity for women. She belonged to Heterodoxy, a group of prominent feminist intellectuals who met regularly to debate issues ranging from civil rights to birth control, and both she and her husband marched in suffrage parades. She believed, however, that fundamental progress for women depended less on public than on private change. Modern women, she believed, must learn to balance domestic lives with careers through "the living of many experimental lives" ("The New Woman in the Making," *Current History*, Oct. 1927). Hollingworth apparently believed that such balancing ought, ideally, to include children, but she remained childless herself and never explained how such a balancing was to be achieved.

In the 1920s and 1930s Hollingworth shifted the focus of her research from women to children. Interested both in children who were mentally deficient and those gifted with special ability, she persuaded the New York City Board of Education in 1936 to establish the Speyer School, an experimental school for "exceptional children." Through her research at the school, Hollingworth became a pioneer in the study of learning disabilities and one of the country's leading advocates of gifted children. Among other projects, she organized a separate public school in New York City, Public School 165, where highly intelligent children from a wide variety of backgrounds could be challenged in a way then uncommon in most classrooms.

Hollingworth continued her enormously productive career at Teachers College until her premature death in New York City from cancer at age fifty-three, but she received little recognition in her lifetime. Psychologist Lewis Terman, writing after her death, attributed this slight to the gender bias Hollingworth had fought so hard to diminish. "Comparable productivity of a man," Terman noted, "would probably have been rewarded by election to the presidency of the American Psychological Association or even to membership in the National Academy of Science" (Carl Degler, *In Search of Human Nature* [1991], p. 129).

• Other books by Leta Hollingworth include *The Psychology of Subnormal Children* (1920); *Gifted Children* (1926); *The Psychology of the Adolescent* (1928); a posthumous collection of poems, *Prairie Years* (1940); and a posthumous publication on gifted children, *Children Above 180 I.Q.* (1942). The best available biography is Harry Levi Hollingworth, *Leta Stetter Hollingworth: A Biography* (1943).

ROSALIND ROSENBERG

HOLLOWAY, Stanley Augustus (1 Oct. 1890–30 Jan. 1982), actor, was born in London, England, the son of George Holloway, a lawyer's clerk, and Florrie, whose maiden name cannot be ascertained. Known in the choir of his Worshipful School of Carpenters as an outstanding boy soprano, Holloway worked in a bootpolish factory and fish market before beginning a show business career that lasted nearly seventy years.

In 1910 Holloway joined a concert party—a troupe, he later wrote, of performers who could hold the stage on their own for at least fifteen minutes, combining in pairs, trios, and ensembles in song, dance, and sketch. Usually garbed as Pierrots (i.e., in the manner of French pantomimes), concert parties throve in British seaside resorts.

In 1913 Holloway married Alice Mary Foran, with whom he had four children. Studying voice in Italy when war broke out in 1914, he spent World War I in an Irish regiment. Holloway's London stage debut came in 1919; in 1920 he scored his first success in *A Night Out*, the musical comedy version of Georges Feydeau's *Hotel Paradiso* with incidental music by Cole Porter.

Holloway began his film career in *The Rotters* (1921). In the same year he joined a number of *A Night Out* compatriots in forming *The Co-Optimists*, a London revue that ran until 1928, with a brief revival in 1931. Holloway's talents emerged: a strong, romantic bass voice in a tall, athletic body; an expressive and open, hawk-nosed face; an ability with dialects; and an irresistible heartiness. By 1928 he was an outstanding monologist in British variety.

Before his first visit to the United States in 1933, Holloway had costarred as a robust sailor in the London production of Vincent Youmans's musical *Hit the Deck* (1927). His New York sojourn led to the lead role in the Jerome Kern–Oscar Hammerstein II London original *Three Sisters* (1934), a musical play whose failure ended Kern's British career.

By the mid-1930s Holloway's monologues increasingly featured the character of Sam Small, a self-respecting and heavily mustached little man who first appeared, balking at arrogant authority, during the battle of Waterloo until asked politely by the Duke of Wellington himself. Holloway starred in several films about Sam Small. The Small monologues and several dealing with Albert Ramsbottom, the unruly Northern English lad unfortunately eaten by a zoo lion, brought Holloway his first American fame in the 1938–1939 radio shows of British expatriate Alec Templeton. Holloway sang lugubriously in Cockney English of the ghost of Anne Boleyn, who "walked the Bloody Tower . . . wiv' er' 'ead tucked underneath 'er arm."

Holloway returned to Britain at the start of World War II. His wife, Alice, had died in 1937; back home in 1939 he married Violet Marion Lane. They had one child, who eventually became a performer re-creating his father's roles. As part of the effort to mobilize and sustain the nation's spirits, Holloway appeared in stalwartly English films such as *Salute John Citizen* (1942), *The Way Ahead* (1944), *This Happy Breed* (1944 or 1947), and *Brief Encounter* (1945 or 1946). After the war he appeared in distinctively English movies of a different sort, classic comedies made at London's Ealing Studios, including *Passport to Pimlico* (1949),

The Lavender Hill Mob (1951), and *The Titfield Thunderbolt* (1952 or 1953). Those films invariably asserted ordinary people's right to subvert bureaucracy and thumb their nose at hollow tradition.

Although his greatest fame, as just such an independent ordinary bloke, lay ahead of him, Holloway indirectly prepared for it by surprisingly taking on a Shakespearean role, the First Grave Digger in Laurence Olivier's *Hamlet* (1948). The role returned him to New York in 1948, and after further British work, Holloway was back on Broadway in 1954 as Bottom in Shakespeare's *A Midsummer Night's Dream*.

For the next twenty years Holloway led a transatlantic life of increasing renown. His most significant theatrical creation came in an American musical. At age sixty-six he originated the role of dustman Alfred Doolittle, "original moral philosopher" and father of the to-be-transformed ugly duckling Eliza in *My Fair Lady*, the long-running Alan Jay Lerner–Frederick Loewe adaptation (2717 performances on Broadway) of George Bernard Shaw's *Pygmalion*. Holloway's rumbustious comic versions of Lerner and Frederick Loewe's "Wiv' a Little Bit o' Luck" and "Get Me to the Church on Time" became classics of the musical stage. Holloway played Doolittle on Broadway from the time it opened in 1956 until he originated the role in London (1958), re-creating it once again when *My Fair Lady* became an Academy Award–Winning film (1964), for which Holloway, then seventy-four was also nominated as a supporting actor.

Over several decades Holloway came to embody for Americans the humor of a hardy, resourceful British working class, just as Noël Coward was Americans' image of blasé urban Britain. Nevertheless, it was American television and recordings which allowed Holloway to widen his range. In 1960 he played Pooh-Bah in a television version of Gilbert and Sullivan's *The Mikado*, starring Groucho Marx. In the same year came recordings of Gilbert, Edwin Lear, and Shakespeare and a one-man Broadway music hall, *Laughs and Other Events*. Back in England, Holloway received the Order of the British Empire in 1960.

Holloway became an American television regular, starring in 1962–1963 as a resolute Scottish gentleman's gentleman in *Our Man Higgins*. When the series ended, Holloway played the Old Actor in a television adaptation of the off-Broadway musical *The Fantasticks* (1964). In 1964 he starred in a musical comedy, *Cool Off*, which played briefly in Philadelphia. After a return to British television, in 1970 Holloway began to make regular appearances at Shaw festivals in Canada. He returned to the British stage in 1971; in 1973 he appeared in Robert Louis Stevenson's *Dr. Jekyll and Mr. Hyde* on American television. Although he made few American appearances after that, in 1977, aged eighty-seven, Holloway toured the light comedy *The Pleasure of His Company* in Australia. In 1990 his life story was broadcast in six episodes by BBC Radio. Holloway died in Littlehampton, England.

In his later years a vigorous, living source of show business history, Holloway succeeded in virtually all his era's entertainment fields and made it look easy. In his *Sunday Times* (London) obituary, Harold Hobson gave one reason: Holloway could "sweep away huge audiences on a gale of laughter and comedy so that for a few moments they forgot all their worries and the problems of humanity in a maelstrom of uncomplicated happiness."

• Stanley Holloway's autobiography (as told to Dick Richards) is *Wiv a Little Bit o' Luck* (1967). His monologues and songs have been collected in two volumes introduced and edited by Michael Marshall (1977 and 1980). Alan Jay Lerner, *The Street Where I Live* (1978), tells the story of *My Fair Lady's* creation. Reviews and other clippings are on file at the Theatre Museum, London, and in the Billy Rose Theatre Collection at the New York Public Library for the Performing Arts, Lincoln Center. Obituaries are in the *Sunday Times* (London), 31 Jan. 1982, and in the *Guardian*, 1 Feb. 1982.

JAMES ROSS MOORE

HOLLOW HORN BEAR (1851–15 Mar. 1913), Lakota chief and diplomat whose Christian name was Daniel, was born in Nebraska Territory, the son of Iron Shell, Sr. (Maza Pankeska), a Lakota chief, and Wants Everything (Wisica Wacin Win). His Lakota name was Mato Hehlogece. Hollow Horn Bear was born in the year the Lakota people (also known as the Teton or Western Sioux) signed a treaty of peace with the United States at Fort Laramie. His family lived among the Sicangu (Brule or Burnt Thigh) division of the Lakota, and his father was the chief of an important family group (*tiospaye*).

During Hollow Horn Bear's childhood, his people were still pursuing an indigenous way of life, depending on hunting buffalo and other game and collecting plant foods. But the Lakota were increasingly affected by larger historical forces, including the fur trade, diminishing buffalo herds, more settlers passing through Lakota country bound for the Far West, increasing pressure to open the Great Plains for development, and a war with the United States over the Powder River country in what is now Wyoming between 1866 and 1868. In 1868 another treaty was signed with the United States, which, from the government's point of view, ended hostilities and concentrated the Lakota on a large reservation in present-day South Dakota, with additional hunting territory beyond. From the Lakota standpoint, the Fort Laramie Treaty of 1868 was a peace treaty that recognized the Lakota as a sovereign nation and guaranteed a perpetual land base that could not be reduced except by cession approved by three-fourths of the adult males of the Lakota nation.

In 1874 Hollow Horn Bear married Good Bed (Ohe Waste Win), daughter of Conquering Bear, the "head chief" of the Lakota recognized by the United States in 1851. Hollow Horn Bear remained married to Good Bed for the rest of his life and had seven children with her. Also in 1874, Hollow Horn Bear went to work for the U.S. Army as a scout, assisting as a guide through Lakota country. The army was attempting to prevent the entry of American settlers into the Black Hills on the Great Sioux Reservation in violation of the 1868 treaty, but the lure of gold discovered there made it impossible to keep the flood of fortune seekers out of these sacred lands of the Lakota people. By 1876 Deadwood, Rapid City, and Custer had been founded, and thousands of miners and boomers were settled in the Black Hills. A Lakota military response to this illegal invasion was not possible, and the government sought to legitimate it by orchestrating an "agreement" by which the Black Hills were ceded in 1876; this agreement was signed by only a handful of Lakota, not the required three-fourths.

By 1880 the buffalo had been all but exterminated, and the Lakota people had been confined to the reservation and brought under the supervision of the Bureau of Indian Affairs. Thus began a period when the Lakota people had daily contact with government agents, who were intent on "civilizing" the Lakota and assimilating Lakota individuals into the body politic, as the Lakota nation withered away. This was the time when Hollow Horn Bear grew into maturity and acted as a leader and diplomat for his people, helping ensure that their point of view was understood by and carried weight with the government agents.

Hollow Horn Bear went to work as a policeman in the Indian Police Force organized by the Bureau of Indian Affairs. Lakota men who served in this force understood themselves to be serving the people the way the "buffalo police" or "soldier societies" (akicita) had protected the people before reservation times. In 1883 Iron Shell died, and Hollow Horn Bear became the leader of his tiospaye. He made at least one trip to Washington, D.C., in the 1880s to discuss reservation problems with government officials.

In 1889 a U.S. commission came to the Great Sioux Reservation to negotiate the sale of Lakota lands in order to open a corridor between eastern Dakota and the Black Hills. The proposal entailed carving up the Great Sioux into six smaller reservations, ceding eleven million acres to the United States, and dividing remaining tribal lands into individual allotments. Hollow Horn Bear was a key spokesperson for the Lakota in these controversial and momentous negotiations over the future of Lakota lands, and he came to see the wisdom of Lakota people taking land allotments. He believed that tribal lands held in common would always be open to unilateral annexation by Congress, but that Indian land held in individual title would be protected by constitutional guarantees of private property. During the unrest on the Lakota reservations in South Dakota after the Ghost Dance and the Wounded Knee massacre in December 1890, when white settlers and the government became convinced that Lakota people meant to revolt against the reservation system, Hollow Horn Bear selected allotments for himself and his children in order to demonstrate to the government that the Lakota wanted to live in peace with the white people.

Although Hollow Horn Bear recognized the necessity of adapting to the new way of life on the reservations and of living in peace with the U.S. government,

he was a strong advocate of Lakota interests. At negotiations regarding remaining tribal lands in the 1890s and the early 1900s, for example, Hollow Horn Bear was repeatedly delegated to speak for his tiospaye and others, to insist that the government could not force land cessions upon the Lakota but must obtain the consent of three-fourths of the men as required by the 1868 treaty. Although he was not able to prevent the government from violating the 1868 treaty because a U.S. Supreme Court decision in 1904 legitimated treaty abrogation, Hollow Horn Bear's presence at the negotiations clearly pushed the agreements in the direction of Lakota interests. Without his presence, things would have been much worse for the Lakota people.

Hollow Horn Bear was not only a diplomat between the Lakota people and the Americans. In 1893 he traveled to the Crow reservation in Montana. The Crow people had been enemies of the Lakota before the reservations were established, and Hollow Horn Bear's visit was for the purpose of making peace. It was on the Crow reservation that one of Hollow Horn Bear's daughters was born, Crow Woman (Psa Win). Hollow Horn Bear also visited the Southern Cheyenne people in Oklahoma. Intertribal visiting by leaders was important in the early reservation period in helping to lay the groundwork for later pan-Indian movements in the twentieth century, when people from different native nations forged alliances to serve the interests of all Native Americans.

In 1907 Hollow Horn Bear took his daughter Crow Woman, who was then ten years old, to be baptized a Catholic by the Jesuits at St. Francis Mission on Rosebud Reservation. The baptism was attended by many friends and relatives, and after the girl was baptized Emelie Hollow Horn Bear, tiospaye members also came forward to be baptized. Hollow Horn Bear was baptized Daniel, and his wife was baptized Susie. Many Lakota people during this period came to see Christianity as not inconsistent with Lakota spirituality and to see Christian mission schools as offering formal education that would better help the people adapt to the new way of life and yet remain Lakota. Hollow Horn Bear remained a Catholic for the rest of his life.

Hollow Horn Bear became a fairly frequent visitor to Washington, D.C., at least by Lakota standards. He attended the inauguration of President Theodore Roosevelt and visited with Presidents William Howard Taft and Benjamin Harrison. In 1913, while ill, he attended the inauguration of President Woodrow Wilson. Hollow Horn Bear died in Washington shortly after the inauguration. He was buried in the cemetery at the St. Francis Mission. He was memorialized by the U.S. Postal Service in 1922 when it issued a stamp with his image.

Hollow Horn Bear was a strong and perceptive leader among the Lakota people during the most traumatic period in their history—the transition from an independent native society to an indigenous nation struggling for survival within an encompassing industrial state. Hollow Horn Bear's skill and wisdom helped the U.S. government to see the point of view of the Lakota people and the Lakota people to see that some of the new ways could help them survive as Lakota.

• There is essentially no secondary literature dealing with the life of Hollow Horn Bear; this description is derived partly from Bureau of Indian Affairs documents and oral sources. Transcripts of government negotiations at which Hollow Horn Bear spoke are available in several sources in the Congressional Serials Set: Senate Exec. Doc. 51, 51st Cong., 1st sess., 1890; Senate Report 1275, 52d Cong., 2d sess., 1893; House Doc. 447, 55th Cong., 2d sess., 1898. Additional transcripts are available in the Major James McLaughlin Papers (Assumption Abbey Archives, Richardton, N.D.), microfilm, rolls 26, 27, 29. Secondary references on Lakota history of this period are Robert M. Utley, *The Last Days of the Sioux Nation* (1963); Julia B. McGillycuddy, *McGillycuddy, Agent: A Biography of Dr. Valentine T. McGillycuddy* (1941); James McLaughlin, *My Friend the Indian* (1989); Luther Standing Bear, *My People the Sioux* (1975); Thomas Biolsi, *Organizing the Lakota*, chaps. 1 and 2 (1992); George E. Hyde, *A Sioux Chronicle* (1956); Raymond J. DeMallie, *The Sixth Grandfather*, pt. 1 (1984); and George E. Hyde, *Spotted Tail's Folk* (1974). Sources on Lakota culture are John G. Neihardt, *Black Elk Speaks* (1961); James R. Walker, *Lakota Belief and Ritual* (1980) and *Lakota Society* (1980); Luther Standing Bear, *Land of the Spotted Eagle* (1978); William K. Powers, *Oglala Religion* (1977); Marla N. Powers, *Oglala Women* (1986); Joseph Epes Brown, *The Sacred Pipe* (1971); Royal B. Hassrick, *The Sioux* (1964); Raymond J. DeMallie and Douglas R. Parks, eds., *Sioux Indian Religion* (1987); and Ella Deloria, *Speaking of Indians* (1944).

ALBERT WHITE HAT
DUANE HOLLOW HORN BEAR
THOMAS BIOLSI

HOLLY, Buddy (7 Sept. 1936–3 Feb. 1959), songwriter, singer, and guitarist, was born Charles Hardin Holley in Lubbock, Texas, the son of Hardin O. Holley, a bricklayer, and Ella Pauline Drake. At age five Holly (who removed the *e* from his last name in 1956) won a $5 prize at a local talent show singing "Down the River of Memories." His Protestant parents thought he would become a minister and had no idea his natural aptitude to compose and play music with a fiddle, piano, and guitar would lead to his international recognition as a rock and roll pioneer.

In 1949 Holly and his junior high school chum Bob Montgomery formed the duo Buddy and Bob after playing bluegrass, rockabilly, and country tunes in Holly's garage. With Larry Welborn joining them on bass, the group's "Buddy and Bob Show" aired every Saturday afternoon on Lubbock's country radio station K-DAV from 1953 to 1954. The group's demos and tapes were released in 1965 on the album *Holly in the Hills*.

By 1953 Holly was energetically performing at local clubs, combining country and western with rhythm and blues. The tie-wearing, nearsighted, bespectacled Holly became well known for singing original, memorable lyrics using a sliding falsetto voice punctuated with hiccups and accompanied by a riveting electric guitar.

On 26 January 1956 Holly and two players recorded as Holly and the Two Tunes for Decca in Nashville, Tennessee. Dissatisfied with the desire of Decca producers for him to sound more hillbilly, Holly left their studio and went back to Texas. In September, at Norman Petty's studio in Clovis, New Mexico, Holly, drummer Jerry Allison, and bassist Larry Welborn recorded for Coral (a Decca associate) the rocking "That'll Be the Day." Guitarist Sonny Curtis joined the band (now renamed Buddy Holly and the Three Tunes), and Petty managed them.

When Elvis Presley convinced Holly to concentrate on blues and rock rather than country music after Holly opened for Presley on 15 October 1956 at Lubbock's Cotton Club, Holly gained confidence. He later admitted, "We owe it all to Elvis."

In February 1957 Holly, Allison, bassist Joe B. Mauldin, and rhythm guitarist Niki Sullivan formed the Crickets (the members of which frequently changed). They recorded for Decca's associate company Brunswick Records a hit version of "That'll Be the Day," which was released in May. Other hits recorded under Holly's name (not the Crickets) included "Oh, Boy" and "Peggy Sue" (at first named "Cindy Lou" and changed to honor Allison's girlfriend). Because promoters thought their rhythm and blues came from a black band, in July they became the first white group to rock Harlem's Apollo Theater, after which came eighty one-night performances with the Biggest Show of Stars of '57, which included Fats Domino, Chuck Berry, and the Drifters.

Their new album, *The Chirping Crickets*, was recorded and released by Coral in November 1957, and the group gained national attention after they performed on the "Ed Sullivan Show" on 1 December 1957 and 26 January 1958. In 1958 Holly (playing a Fender Stratocaster), Allison, and Mauldin toured Europe and Australia as the Crickets. Their song "Rave On" sold more records in the United Kingdom than in the United States, and they appeared on "Sunday Night at the London Palladium." While on tour in Australia with Jerry Lee Lewis and Paul Anka, Holly and the Crickets' "Peggy Sue" sold a million records and reached number 3 on the *Billboard* charts. When they toured the United Kingdom in March, Eric Clapton and Paul McCartney were in the audience. The group returned triumphant to the United States to join Alan Freed's Big Beat Show from 26 March to 9 May 1958.

On 4 August 1958 Holly married Maria Elena Santiago at his parents' home in Lubbock. They had no children. In late 1958, after leaving manager Norman Petty and the Crickets, Buddy and Maria moved to New York City's Greenwich Village, where Buddy focused on songwriting. In December a breakthrough in rock and roll occurred when he recorded with the Dick Jacobs Orchestra.

Because Holly's bank accounts were frozen in litigation after he left Petty, to earn extra money he joined the Winter Dance Party tour of the Midwest in January 1959, with guitarist Tommy Allsup, bassist Waylon Jennings, and drummer Carl Bunch. Other performers in the exhausting tour included Frankie

Sardo, Dion and the Belmonts, Ritchie Valens, and the Big Bopper (Jiles Perry Richardson).

After performing at the Surf Ballroom in Clear Lake, Iowa, on 3 February, the fatigued Holly, the Big Bopper, and Valens hired pilot Roger Peterson to fly them to their next concert in Moorhead, Minnesota. Minutes after the aircraft lifted in bad weather, it crashed near Mason City, Iowa, killing everyone on board.

More than 1,100 people attended Holly's funeral in Lubbock. Coral released the memorial album *The Buddy Holly Story* (1959) and the Crickets regrouped and performed until 1965. Ironically, "It Doesn't Matter Anymore," which reached number 1 in the United States in April 1959, was Holly's last recording.

The resourceful, creative Holly popularized in Europe and the United States the two guitar/bass/drum lineup. He was one of the first rock and roll musicians to record with a full orchestra, and he used innovative techniques such as double-tracking vocals and overdubbing. A prolific songwriter, Holly and his hot, clean, fast, rockabilly blues sound influenced hundreds of musicians, including Bob Dylan, the Beatles, and the Beach Boys.

After Holly's death, his unrecorded original songs and licks left on demo tapes were released in the nine-record set *The Complete Buddy Holly Story*. Paul McCartney of the Beatles bought the rights to Holly's roster of classic songs, and Columbia Pictures' 1978 movie *The Buddy Holly Story* renewed interest in the musician. Dave Marsh, in *The Heart of Rock and Soul* (1989), wrote, "If Buddy Holly had lived . . . he would have been heralded as the Father of the Singer/Songwriters. . . . [The] Beatles . . . professed a love for Buddy Holly so great that they named themselves in mock-homage to the Crickets" (pp. 435–36). Holly has remained a rock and roll legend whose music is still played by European and American bands.

• The most comprehensive source for Holly's life and career is Ellis Amburn, *Buddy Holly: A Biography* (1995). Other biographies include David Laing, *Buddy Holly* (1971); Bradley Denton, *Buddy Holly Is Alive and Well on Ganymede* (1991); John Goldrosen, *The Buddy Holly Story* (1979); and Philip Norman, *Rave On: The Biography of Buddy Holly* (1996). Numerous documentaries, including *Buddy Holly: Reminiscing* (1979), draw on private footage, newsreels, and interviews with Maria Elena Holly. Innumerable articles about Holly's life and music appear in music and social science periodicals.

PATRICIA JOBE PIERCE

HOLLY, James Theodore (30 Oct. 1829–13 Mar. 1911), black emigrationist, missionary, and bishop, was born free in Washington, D.C., the son of James Overton Holly, a bootmaker, and Jane (maiden name unknown). At fourteen he and his family moved to Brooklyn, where he worked with his father. By 1848, while clerking for Lewis Tappan, an abolitionist, Holly became interested in the antislavery movement. In 1850 he and his brother Joseph set up as "fashionable bootmakers" in Burlington, Vermont, where both became involved with the growing debate over black

emigration. James supported the American Colonization Society and Liberia, while Joseph believed that freed slaves should not have to leave the United States.

In 1851 Holly married Charlotte Ann Gordon (with whom he was to have five children) and moved to Windsor, Canada West (now Ontario), to coedit Henry Bibb's newspaper *Voice of the Fugitive*. During his three years in the Windsor-Detroit area, Holly worked for the unsuccessful Refugee Home Society, ran the Amherstburg Emancipation Convention in 1851, and used the *Voice* to argue that emigration was the only solution for the problems of African Americans. He abandoned Roman Catholicism for the Protestant Episcopal church, becoming a deacon in 1855 and a priest in 1856. Holly's new occupation, together with his devotion to the creation of a black nationality, set the course for his adult life.

While teaching grade school in Buffalo, New York, Holly was a delegate to the first National Emigration Convention in 1854 in Cleveland, Ohio. The next year, while representing both the National Emigration Board and the Board of Missions of the Protestant Episcopal Church, he visited Haiti to negotiate an emigration treaty and to locate a possible site for an Episcopal mission. Unsuccessful in both ventures, Holly settled in New Haven, Connecticut, where he taught school and served as priest of St. Luke's Church from 1856 to 1861. After participating in the 1856 National Emigration Convention, Holly traveled extensively to advocate African-American emigration to Haiti. His lecture *Vindication of the Capacity of the Negro Race for Self Government and Civilized Progress*, published in 1857, proclaimed black pride and urged emigration to Haiti, a place of "far more security for the personal liberty and general welfare of the governed . . . than exists in this bastard democracy [the United States]." He also cofounded the Convocation of the Protestant Episcopal Society for Promoting the Extension of the Work among Colored People, a group whose goals included encouraging blacks to join the church and the emigration movement.

Convinced that free blacks needed white allies to support mass departure for Haiti, Holly corresponded in 1859 with Congressman Francis P. Blair, Jr., about U.S. government aid for emigration. He also petitioned, unsuccessfully, the Board of Missions of the Episcopal Church to underwrite him as a missionary to Haiti. In 1860 Holly worked for the Scottish journalist and abolitionist James Redpath, the official Haitian commissioner of emigration. As an agent for the Haitian government, Holly lectured frequently in New England, New Jersey, and Pennsylvania and organized the "New Haven Pioneer Company of Haytian Emigrants." In 1861 Holly and 101 recruits moved to Haiti. As one colonist wrote home, "I am a man in Hayti where I feel as I never felt before, entirely free."

The initial year in Haiti proved to be disastrous for Holly's settlement. The rainy season brought fevers, fatalities, and then desertions. Among those who died were Holly's mother, his wife, two of their children, and thirty-nine others. Only Holly and a few followers remained on the island. In 1862, by then a Haitian citizen dedicated to the "regeneration and purification" of the Black Republic through the establishment of the Episcopal church in Haiti, Holly returned to the United States. He hoped this trip would secure financial support from the General Convention of the Protestant Episcopal Church to establish a Haitian mission station. His request failed, but the American Church Missionary Society did agree to pay his salary in Haiti. In 1865 the Board of Missions of the Protestant Episcopal Church began minimal sponsorship of Holly's mission in Haiti, an arrangement that continued until 1911.

Holly hoped to replace Haiti's dominant Roman Catholicism with a national Episcopal church. In 1874 he became bishop of the Orthodox Apostolic Church of Haiti and was consecrated missionary bishop of Haiti at Grace Church, New York City. As the first black bishop of the Episcopal church and as head of the Haitian Episcopal church, he attended the Lambeth Conference in London in 1878. Recognizing education and good health to be important concerns of the church, Holly worked zealously to establish schools and medical institutions in Haiti. But fires and political upheaval hampered his efforts, and his overall church membership never exceeded a few thousand.

Although an infrequent visitor to the United States after 1861 (he made only seven trips in fifty years), Holly never lost interest in African Americans. He and his second wife, Sarah Henley, whom he married in 1862, sent nine sons to the United States for schooling. Holly also corresponded extensively with American blacks and published frequently on religious, political, and social issues in the *A.M.E. Church Review*.

While other emigration advocates of the mid-1800s spoke of leaving the United States but stayed, Holly spoke of leaving and actually left. Until his death in Port au Prince, Haiti, Holly never abandoned his belief that emigration was the only way for African Americans to improve their lives.

• Holly's papers are in the Archives and Historical Collections of the Episcopal Church in Austin, Tex. Holly's *Vindication of the Capacity of the Negro Race for Self Government and Civilized Progress* is found in Howard Brotz, ed., *Negro Social and Political Thought, 1859–1920: Representative Texts* (1966). For a detailed biography, see David M. Dean, *Defender of the Race: James Theodore Holly, Black Nationalist and Bishop* (1979). Holly's role in the emigration movement of the 1850s is evaluated in Floyd J. Miller, *The Search for a Black Nationality* (1975).

DAVID M. DEAN

HOLM, Hanya (3 Mar. 1893–3 Nov. 1992), choreographer and educator, was born Johanna Eckert in Worms-am-Rhein, Germany, the daughter of Valentin Eckert, a wine merchant, and Marie Moerschel, an inventor with several patented discoveries. Holm received her first twelve years of education at the Konvent der englischen Fraulein, selected by her mother for its excellent reputation and small class size. She began private piano lessons at age ten, and by age sixteen

she was commuting several times each week to the Hoch Conservatory in Frankfurt for expanded music studies. In 1915 she began four years of study at the Dalcroze Institute of Applied Rhythm that included music improvisation, theory, analysis, and composition. The methods of Émile Jaques-Dalcroze were admired for translating sounds into movement, and this "music visualization" influenced a generation of European dancers in ballet and modern companies.

While teaching the Dalcroze methods, Holm saw a dance performance by Mary Wigman in Dresden and decided to join her company in 1921. For ten years she toured Europe as a principal dancer with Wigman's company and became chief instructor at the Central Institute in Dresden. In that role she became an essential part of the development of German Expressionist dance, which sought to associate the art form with deep emotional expression and universal human drama.

In 1923 she changed her name to Hanya Holm. The Wigman School attracted a large number of students from all over Europe who had difficulty pronouncing the name Johanna. Hanya was easier for the tongue and appealed because the related Hebrew meaning for Hannah is grace. She selected Holm as her surname for its alliterative sound and its implication of strength and security.

In 1930–1931 impresario Sol Hurok brought the Wigman company to the United States for a transcontinental tour. Its success led him to offer to finance a Wigman school in New York. Holm, nervous about the political undercurrents of Hitler's rise, volunteered to relocate and direct this American school. Hurok arranged everything: her travel, the studio, and her housing. She arrived on 25 September 1931 and began teaching on 26 September. Hurok, a businessman and producer, expected her to produce a national touring company within a year. Holm insisted it would take five years to create a company. He was not interested, so in 1932 he turned the school over to her. By 1936 she did have a trained company and changed the name from the Wigman to the Hanya Holm School of Dance.

Holm accepted other teaching positions during the summers: at Mills College, California, in 1932 and at Perry-Mansfield, Colorado, in 1933. Finding that Wigman's mysticism and Germanic themes had little to do with American temperament, environment, or rhythms, she developed her own theories and created a modern style that encouraged freedom and a flowing quality for the torso, yet was firmly based on universal principles of motion and the laws of physics. Her natural sense of humor blossomed. While her choreography was still concerned with visionary messages about humanity's relation to the universe, the dancing was widely admired for its lyrical, witty, and accessible style.

From 1934 to 1941 Holm taught at the famous Bennington Summer School of the Dance, the forerunner of the American Dance Festival, and was recognized as one of the famous "four pioneers" of American modern dance along with Martha Graham, Doris Humphrey, and Charles Weidman. In 1941 she founded the influential summer program at Colorado College, Colorado Springs, where she taught for forty-three years.

The Hanya Holm New York school and her summer programs became meccas for dancers of all disciplines. It was widely accepted that any professional dancer, whether East Indian, tap, ballet, or any other style, could improve rapidly under Holm's guidance because her theories could be applied to all forms of dance. Her three-year program offered technique, anatomy, theory, dance history, pedagogy, composition, improvisation, and Labanotation. A few of Holm's famous students include Alwin Nikolais, Valerie Bettis, Glen Tetley, Mary Anthony, Louise Kloepper, Nancy Hauser, Elisabeth Waters, Don Redlich, Anabelle Lyon, Bambi Lynn, and Murray Louis.

Holm's masterwork, *Trend*, commissioned by the Bennington Festival in 1937, had the survival of society as its central theme. Stunning for its architectural form, symphonic development, and emotional intensity, *Trend* received the *New York Times* Award for best dance. *New York Times* critic John Martin wrote that *Trend* was "one of the most important works of the period for it advances the dance significantly along the road it has so rightly chosen." In 1939 *Dance Magazine* awarded Holm's *Tragic Exodus* Best Group Choreography. Also in 1939, *Metropolitan Daily* was selected by the National Broadcasting Company for the first live telecast of modern dance. Viewers within a fifty-mile radius of New York City were treated to Holm's witty, satiric view of newspapers. This same year Holm became a citizen of the United States.

The Holm company remained active until 1947 and was admired for its kinesthetic accessibility. Critic Walter Terry commented in February 1941 that Hanya Holm's company was the most lyric of the moderns and "inevitably danced with feminine grace and charm."

Holm gained distinction as a choreographer and director for opera, theater, and Broadway. In 1948 she created *Ballet Ballads*, a suite of dances to music composed by Jerome Moross with lyrics by John Latouche. After its success, she was invited to choreograph a new Cole Porter musical. *Kiss Me Kate* (1948) was unanimously greeted as a milestone in the development of the American musical, and Holm was recognized with a New York Drama Critics Award as best choreographer that year. At Holm's request, the Labanotation score was registered with the Library of Congress in 1952, the first complete choreography to be so copyrighted.

Holm choreographed thirteen musicals throughout the 1950s and 1960s, earning special accolades for *The Golden Apple* (1954) and great acclaim for *My Fair Lady* (1956). For her work on this smash hit, she was nominated for a Tony Award. In his *New York Times* review John Martin summed up her influence: "Hanya Holm should get some sort of specially designed gold medal for what she has done with *My Fair Lady*, and Moss Hart deserves at least a silver one for grasping the necessity of having her do it. . . . Choreographic phrasing emerges time and time again through the dramatic action. . . . It is just about as ideal a fusion of the literary-dramatic element of the theatre with the choreo-musical element as has been seen in our time."

Other Broadway musicals included *My Darlin' Aida* (1952), *Camelot* (1960), and *Anya* (1965), and among her film and television creations were *The Vagabond King* (Paramount, 1956), *The Dance and the Drama* (Canadian Broadcasting Company, 1957), and *Dinner with the President* (CBS, 1963).

During the 1970s and 1980s the Don Redlich Dance Company became the chief repository for Holm's concert dances. For its 1985 New York season the company presented *Ratatat* (1982), *Jocose* (1983), and *Capers* (1985). These dances revealed that the Holm wry sense of humor, kinetic wit, poignancy, and keen intelligence were as sharp and vital as during the pioneering decade.

Among her numerous prestigious awards were Dance Magazine (1989), Capezio (1958), Samuel H. Scripps/American Dance Festival (1984), and the Theater Hall of Fame (1992). Her teaching at Juilliard, the Nikolais-Louis studio, and Colorado College extended until she was well past age ninety.

Holm remained essentially unimpressed with her greatness as an artist and ever committed to generously sharing all she knew. As an honored guest at the American Film Institute, Kennedy Center, Washington, D.C., for the 1985 Women in Film and Video Festival, she repeated one of her famous remarks: "You will find out that one life is not enough. You will want to have several lives in which to discover what there is to be discovered."

Holm died in New York City. She had been married for a short time during the 1920s in Germany and had one child. Her son, Klaus Holm, and her three granddaughters, Karen Trautlein, Angela Holm, and Jessica Werbin, survived her along with countless students and dancers who were inspired by her remarkable teaching and choreography. On 3 March 1993 many colleagues, students, family, and other admirers celebrated her hundredth birthday at St. Mark's Church in New York City.

Today Hanya Holm is regarded as one of the twentieth century's major choreographers of American modern dance and Broadway musicals. She is credited with introducing improvisation, Labanotation, and theories of spatial dynamics to the American dance scene, areas of study that comprise the core curriculum in university dance programs throughout the United States. Most importantly, she taught much more than movement technique; she imparted the essence and spirit of dance. Holm developed a complex pedagogy that insisted the dancer continually explore the universe of body and mind. Her prime objective, however, was the shaping of the dancer's soul.

• Hanya Holm scrapbooks and other significant resources are available for viewing and research at the Dance Collection of the New York Public Library for the Performing Arts, Lincoln Center. Writings by Holm include "Pioneer of the New Dance," *American Dancer*, Los Angeles, Apr. 1933; "Mary Wigman," *Dance Observer*, Nov. 1935; "Who Is Mary Wigman?" *Dance Magazine*, Nov. 1956; "Mary Wigman Celebrates Eighty Years This Month," *Dance News*, Nov. 1966; and "To Be With It," *Focus on Dance* (1977). An important book about Holm is Walter Sorell, *Hanya Holm: The Biography of an Artist* (1969). Significant articles about Holm and her work include Marcia B. Siegel, "A Conversation with Hanya Holm," *Ballet Review* 9, no. 1 (Spring 1981), and Marilyn Cristofori, "Spotlight on Hanya Holm: Portrait of a Pioneer," *Dance Teacher Now* 12, no. 4 (May 1990). An excellent bibliography of print and video materials is "Hanya Holm: The Life and Legacy," *Journal for Stage Directors and Choreographers* 7, no. 1 (Spring 1993). A one-hour video, *Hanya: Portait of a Pioneer*, produced by Marilyn Cristofori, is available from Dance Horizons Video, POB 57, Pennington, N.J. 08534. The original source tapes for this production are available at the Stanford University libraries. An obituary is in the *New York Times*, 4 Nov. 1992.

MARILYN CRISTOFORI

HOLMAN, Jesse Lynch (24 Oct. 1784–28 Mar. 1842), lawyer, judge, and Baptist preacher, was born near Danville, Kentucky, the son of Henry Holeman and Jane Gordon, farmers. In 1789 Holman's father was killed by Indians, which left his large family poverty-stricken. Holman managed nevertheless to attain a common school education and in his late teens read law in the office of Henry Clay in Lexington, Kentucky. He was admitted to the bar in 1805 and for several years practiced law in small towns in northern Kentucky. In 1810 he married Elizabeth Masterson, daughter of Judge Richard M. Masterson of Kentucky; the couple had six children. In 1811 he moved with his family across the Ohio River to Indiana Territory, settling in Dearborn County.

In the same year Holman (he apparently liked the shortened spelling) was appointed prosecuting attorney for the county by Governor William Henry Harrison. In 1814 the young attorney was elected to fill a vacancy as member of the territorial legislature for Dearborn County. At the next regular election he represented the county in the legislative council (upper house) and was chosen president of that body. In September 1814 Holman was appointed presiding judge of the second judicial circuit. Two years later he was appointed judge of the third judicial circuit.

With Indiana's admission to statehood in 1816, Holman's legislative roles ended. In that year he served as one of three presidential electors for the state and was appointed one of Indiana's first three supreme court judges by Governor Jonathan Jennings. Holman served two consecutive seven-year terms on the highest state bench, only stepping down in 1830 when Governor James Brown Ray refused to reappoint him.

In 1831 the state legislature considered Holman as a U.S. Senate candidate, but the former judge lost by one vote. His retirement from government service was brief. In 1835 President Andrew Jackson granted Holman a recess appointment as federal district judge in Indiana. The president wished to make the appointment permanent, but Holman was not popular with Indiana's two U.S. senators, who favored Stephen C. Stevens for the post, or with much of Indiana's delegation in the House. Congressman Ratliff Boon claimed that Holman was "a fanatic on the subject of slavery . . . and religion." Before submitting the nomination to the Senate, Jackson asked Holman to come to Washington for an interview.

In his 1836 interview with Jackson, Holman shared his views on slavery. His attitude centered on the belief that blacks could never be assimilated in American society. Although he had freed his wife's slaves when he moved into Indiana Territory in 1811, his action was less the result of humanitarian sentiment than respect for the Northwest Ordinance. An active member of the American Colonization Society, Holman felt that blacks were "so shiftless and consequently so illiterate and immoral" that they would have a "pernitious effect upon the whole community" and should be returned to Africa. According to Holman "Interest therefore requir[es] their removal for our own benefit, and benevolence requires it for their's."

In his discussion with Jackson, Holman also pointed to his first federal decision, which gave a certificate for the removal of a fugitive slave to Kentucky and concluded with an endorsement of the constitutionality of the Fugitive Slave Act. Jackson forwarded Holman's nomination to the Senate, which unanimously confirmed the appointment on 29 March. Holman remained on the federal district bench until his death.

Throughout his political and judicial career in both state and federal service, Holman maintained equally strong commitments to public education and religious instruction. In his youth he had written a sentimental novel, *The Prisoners of Niagara; or, Errors of Education* (1810), which stressed love of freedom and hatred of all forms of immorality. Later he supported the local public library and seminary and in 1832 was elected superintendent of the Dearborn County schools. He helped to organize the Indiana Baptist State Convention and served as pastor to his own church after his ordination in 1834. He was active in missionary, Sunday school, and Bible societies in Indiana and was vice president of the American Sabbath School Union and president of the Western Baptist Publication and Sabbath School Society. He was a founder of the Baptist college at Franklin, Indiana, and an early member of the board of visitors of Indiana College (later Indiana University). Holman died at his home, "Veraestau," in Dearborn County, Indiana.

Holman is usually identified as one of Indiana's "pioneer" politicians but is remembered neither as an important political partisan nor as a great judicial craftsman. Holman's recognition as an early leader in Indiana owes as much to his activism in religious and educational affairs as to his positions in government.

• A collection of letters regarding Holman's appointment to the federal district court is "Seeking a Federal Judgeship under Jackson," *Indiana Magazine of History* 35 (1939): 311–25. Israel George Blake, *The Holmans of Veraestau* (1943), provides great detail on Holman's personal life, family associations, and educational and religious activities. Two biographical directories from the late nineteenth century, Charles W. Taylor, *Biographical Sketches and Review of the Bench and Bar of Indiana* (1895), and *Biographical History of Eminent and Self-Made Men of the State of Indiana* (1880), contain moderate-length entries on Holman. An interpretive treatment of his appointment in the context of other Jacksonian judicial choices is provided in Kermit L. Hall, *The Politics of Justice: Lower Federal Judicial Selection and the Second Party System, 1829–1861* (1979). R. E. Banta includes an interesting assessment of Holman as novelist in *Indiana Authors and Their Books, 1816–1916* (1949).

ELIZABETH BRAND MONROE

HOLMAN, Libby (23 May 1906–18 June 1971), actress and singer, was born Elizabeth Holtzman in Cincinnati, Ohio, the daughter of well-to-do lawyer Alfred Holtzman and Rachel Workum. After receiving a B.A. from the University of Cincinnati, Holman made her stage debut in a touring production of the drama *The Fool* in 1924. It was as a singer, however, that she made her mark. She played minor roles in Broadway musicals such as Rodgers and Hart's *Garrick Gaieties* (1925) before becoming a featured performer in *Greenwich Village Follies* (1926), *Merry-Go-Round* (1927), and especially in Vincent Youman's *Rainbow* (1928), in which she scored a major success singing "I Want a Man."

Holman is remembered as the quintessential torch singer of the early 1930s and the logical successor to Helen Morgan. The careers of both were cut short because of tumultuous personal lives. Holman's success was due in part to her deep, smoky voice and frankly emotive style; some critics referred to her as exuding the image of a "dangerous woman." Her voice was frequently referred to as a "contralto baritone." Aside from her obvious talents, her success was due in large measure to the fact that leading composers supplied her with some of the most memorable popular songs of the era. Holman introduced two outstanding songs in *The Little Show* (1929), costarring Clifton Webb and Fred Allen. When the revue's producer realized that Holman needed a torch song, pit pianist Ralph Rainger told them he had a melody that might be right. With lyrics added by Howard Dietz, "Moanin' Low" turned out to be the hit of the show. Holman's other song, "Can't We Be Friends," was contributed by composer Kay Swift and lyricist Paul James (pseudonym for James Warburg).

Some of Holman's other memorable moments included her performances of "Body and Soul" (music by John Green and lyrics by Edward Heyman, Robert Sour, and Frank Eyton) and "Something to Remember You By" (music by Arthur Schwartz and lyrics by Howard Dietz) in *Three's a Crowd* (1930), also costarring Webb and Allen, and "You and the Night and the Music" in Cole Porter's musical *You Never Know* (1938). Holman's 1929 recording of "Am I Blue?" (music by Harry Akst and lyrics by Grant Clarke),

which had been introduced by Ethel Waters, made the top ten on the charts in the United States. Critics uniformly praised her "dark, throaty, insinuating voice."

A dark-haired and sultry beauty, Holman's songs and tempestuous stage personality reflected her tragic offstage life. Her skyrocketing career was seriously damaged following the shooting death of her young husband, North Carolina tobacco heir Zachary Smith Reynolds, only a few months after their marriage in 1932. Following a wild party in their lavish home, Reynolds was found dead with a bullet in his head. Holman and Reynolds's best friend, Alfred Walker, were charged with his murder. Holman was ultimately cleared, largely through the manipulations of her lawyer father and because her husband's family learned she was pregnant, but the damage to her career had been done. Sadly, Holman endured two other significant tragedies in her life. Her son, Christopher, born seven months after Reynolds's death, died at the age of seventeen in a mountain-climbing accident in California, and her second husband, Ralph Holmes, whom she married in 1960, was found dead beside a bottle of sleeping pills shortly after he and Holman had separated. Later in life, she married artist Louis Shanker, who survived her.

Holman made several halfhearted attempts to restart her career. During the 1940s she became interested in what she termed "Americana," traditional American folk songs. To perform in this vein, she teamed with African-American singer Josh White, causing a controversy in an era when black and white performers did not typically appear together in concerts. In 1954 Holman toured in a concert act called "Blues, Ballads and Sin Songs," but another controversy arose resulting from publicity given to her close relationship with troubled film actor Montgomery Clift. It was alleged that she and the much younger Clift, who was believed to be bisexual, were lovers and that Holman, a lifelong drug user, was supplying Clift with drugs. Rumors also persisted that Holman was bisexual. Such information in comparatively innocent times contrived to keep Holman out of the top ranks of show business, but she continued to perform in summer stock roles and cabarets, although she never regained the prominence she had attained with such seeming ease in the 1930s. She gave folksong concerts for charities in her later years, and in 1966 she appeared in two concerts for the United Nations Children's Fund. In 1968, in one of her last public performances, Holman closed her show with the songs that she had made famous at the beginning of her career. The audience gave her a loud and long ovation in tribute, as Brooks Atkinson had written in the *New York Times* in 1929, to "the dark purple menace of Libby Holman in the blues."

Aside from the aforementioned appearances, Holman rarely performed in her last years, although she generously opened her Connecticut mansion to various charity events in the local area. She died in Stamford, Connecticut. Her death was attributed to carbon monoxide poisoning in what may have been a suicide.

Despite the tragedies of her life and her sad end, Holman's recordings have continued to appeal to fans of American popular music. In 1979 two compilations of her early recordings, *The Legendary Libby Holman* and *Something to Remember Her By*, successfully introduced her to new generations of admirers.

• For information on Holman, see Jon Bradshaw, *Dreams That Money Can Buy: The Tragic Life of Libby Holman* (1985); Peter Gammond, *Oxford Companion to Popular Music* (1991); Richard Lamparski, *Whatever Became of . . . ?* (1966); Colin Larkin, *Guinness Encyclopedia of Popular Music* (1992); Milt Machlin, *Libby* (1980); and Hamilton Darby Perry, *Libby Holman: Body and Soul* (1983). The Bradshaw volume gives the most complete account of her personal life, and the Gammond and Larkin books provide reliable accountings of Holman's most important performance credits. An obituary and related tribute is in the *New York Times*, 22 June 1971.

JAMES FISHER

HOLMAN, William Steele (6 Sept. 1822–22 Apr. 1897), congressman, was born in the pioneer district of Veraestau (now Aurora), Dearborn County, Indiana, the son of Jesse Lynch Holman and Elizabeth Masterson, farmers. Holman attended Franklin College but had to leave after two years because of the death of his father. In 1842 he married Abigail Knapp, with whom he had four children. He taught school, studied law, and was admitted to the bar in 1843. While still in his early twenties, he was appointed probate judge, serving from 1843 to 1846, and then was prosecuting attorney from 1847 to 1849. He was a member of the Indiana constitutional convention in 1850 and was elected to the state legislature for one term (1851–1852), where he was the chairman of the Judiciary Committee. He then served as judge of the court of common pleas, completing his term in 1856.

Two years later Holman was elected as a Democratic congressman and served in Washington for over forty years, a total of sixteen terms in Congress. He was in office during the years 1859–1865, 1867–1877, 1881–1895, and 1897.

Holman vigorously opposed secession and supported President Abraham Lincoln's war measures. During the Civil War he made his reputation as a War Democrat and was respected as an able debater. His careful scrutiny of appropriations bills earned him both praise and criticism. His colleagues called him "the Great Objector" because of his habit of blocking any legislation that included appropriations. He was, however, a staunch supporter of Civil War expenditures and voted for any measures that increased pay and improved conditions for soldiers. Even after the war, he continued to be famous for his concern for Union veterans. Holman's opponents denounced him as a demagogue and accused him of "hay-seed statesmanship," perhaps partially because of his inattention to matters of dress and his fondness for simple speech, homely anecdotes, and chewing tobacco.

Holman held a firm and lifelong commitment to his Jeffersonian principles. He believed that a strong government would benefit only the wealthy, that the common people were overtaxed, and that government expenditures would inevitably burden yeoman farmers. He therefore maintained a longstanding opposition to internal improvements. In a speech against the expansion of the navy in 1890, Holman denounced a government based on "physical power" whose schemes were financed by a "vast and dishonoring surplus in the Treasury." This surplus, Holman claimed, was accumulated by unfair taxation of farmers.

Holman served on many committees during his long career, among them the Committees on Claims, Public Lands, and Government Contracts. He chaired the Committee on Appropriations from 1875 to 1877. During the Fifty-third Congress (1893–1895), he chaired the Committee on Indian Affairs and gained a reputation as an authority on Indian agencies. He thwarted speculation on Indian lands and other schemes of corrupt Indian agents.

One of Holman's less successful efforts at curbing government expenditures was the much-criticized Holman Resolution. This amendment to the House rules, adopted in 1876, provided that an appropriation bill could change existing law, "provided it . . . retrenches expenses." In practice, however, this amendment facilitated logrolling legislation and ultimately defeated Holman's original intention.

Holman gave meticulous attention to all possibilities of curtailing government expenditures. He shared with Elihu Washburne the nickname "Watchdog of the Treasury." In fact, he once forced a congressional committee to make one of its inspection tours in an army ambulance to save transportation expenses. However, his zeal for saving money also produced some highly unpopular measures. For example, while serving on the Committee on Public Buildings and Grounds, he drastically reduced funding for the Library of Congress, and he opposed expenditures on internal improvements for Washington, D.C.

Holman supported the 1862 Homestead Law as well as land bounties for Union soldiers. But he remained inimical to any sort of government subsidies, whether for farming or industry. He also successfully removed a series of oppressive taxes on Ohio River commerce that had been imposed by the Louisville and Portland Canals.

By the time of Holman's death, which occurred in Washington while he was still in office, he had served in Congress for forty-four years. He was considered a delightful companion, of a "genial and approachable disposition," and because of his fondness for humorous anecdotes was often compared with Lincoln. Thomas A. Hendricks said that he had been worth "twenty-five millions of dollars a year to the people as long as he was in Congress." James G. Blaine said of him, "Though he may have sometimes been unreasonable . . . the country owes him a debt of gratitude for the integrity, intelligence, and simplicity with which he was illustrated a most honorable career as representative of the people."

• Holman's papers are collected in the Indiana State Library. The best sources of information about his congressional career are the *Congressional Globe* and Israel George Blake, *The Holmans of Veraestau* (1943). See also James G. Blaine, *Twenty Years of Congress* (1884); *A Biographical History of Eminent and Self-Made Men of the State of Indiana* (1880); and Charles C. Carlton's biographical essay in *Twenty Years in the Press Gallery*, ed. O. O. Stealey (1906). His obituary is in the *New York Times*, 23 Apr. 1897.

SILVANA SIDDALI

HOLMES, Bayard Taylor (29 July 1852–1 Apr. 1924), physician, scientist, and teacher, was born in North Hero, Vermont, the son of Hector Adams Holmes, a farmer and inventor, and Olive A. Williamson. During his youth, primarily in New York and Minnesota, Bayard worked on his father's farm but also earned money with his own small plots, raising and selling potatoes and eggs; he used the money to buy books, chemicals, and other educational tools. In 1867 Bayard entered the preparatory department of Carleton College in Northfield, Minnesota, in its first class. He graduated in 1870 and that fall entered the college itself (in its first class) but left after completing his first year. The following year he transferred to the Paw Paw Institute, west of Aurora, Illinois, where he obtained a B.S. in 1874. During his college studies Holmes concentrated on chemistry and anatomy both in formal classes and on his own. For eleven years he taught at schools in De Kalb and La Salle counties, Illinois. In 1878 he married Agnes Anna George; the couple had two children.

Holmes's father, by this time financially comfortable from his agricultural inventions, offered to finance Holmes's education as either a lawyer or a doctor. After completing in 1881 a preceptorship with Dr. E. A. Boardman of Elmira, Illinois, Holmes applied to Harvard University for his formal medical training. When Harvard accepted him but refused credit for his anatomical studies, the elder Holmes advised his son against taking their offer. Holmes returned to Chicago in the fall of 1881 and eventually chose the Homeopathic Medical College, the only school that had a good chemical laboratory. There the professor of chemistry, Clifford Mitchell, hired him as an assistant.

Because Cook County Hospital, where the homeopathic students took part of their training, did not have a laboratory, Holmes created one in a little-used bathroom. He also studied hospital construction and management. During the summer of 1882 Holmes was introduced to the new field of bacteriology by William T. Belfield, who brought back to Chicago news of Robert Koch's discovery of the tubercle bacillus. Holmes attended Belfield's lecture and demonstration at Cook County Hospital, the first time the bacillus had been seen in that city and, possibly, in the United States. Receiving an M.D. in 1884, Holmes won one of three eighteen-month internships at Cook County Hospital.

While an intern, Holmes first became aware of the conflict between homeopathy and regular medicine. Although homeopathy was popular in the United States at that time because of its gentle treatments, regular medicine, or allopathy, remained the strongest school, and Holmes realized the value of a regular degree to succeed both in practice and in teaching. In 1885 he entered the College of Physicians and Surgeons in Chicago and became friendly with the great surgeon Nicholas Senn. On visits to the surgeon's home in Milwaukee, Wisconsin, Holmes became acquainted with Senn's magnificent medical library.

Holmes left the college in 1887 after the college president reneged on an agreement for granting him course credits. Fortunately, Christian Fenger, the pioneering surgeon and pathologist, took him on as an unpaid assistant at the College of Physicians and Surgeons in Chicago. Holmes wrote a major article with Fenger, "Antisepsis in Abdominal Operations: Synopsis of a Series of Bacteriological Studies" (*Journal of the American Medical Association* 9 [1 Oct. 1887]: 444; [8 Oct. 1887]: 470–72), in which his experiments contradicted the prevailing theory that airborne infection was more dangerous than contact infection in surgical operations. This article was later translated into German. Holmes eventually wrote some 300 articles, most dealing with surgery, infectious diseases, medical education, and the importance of the medical literature and medical libraries, and three books.

After demonstrating some of his bacteriological work at a meeting of the Chicago Gynecological Society, Holmes met William W. Jaggard, a faculty member at the Chicago Medical College, who made it possible for Holmes to enroll there and earn his regular degree in 1888. The next year Holmes became director of the bacteriological laboratory at the college and for two years gave lectures and demonstrations to small groups of students.

In 1889 Holmes became attending surgeon at Cook County Hospital and professor of surgery at the Post-Graduate Medical School of Chicago. In 1891, through Frank Waxham, another faculty member at the College of Physicians and Surgeons in Chicago, Holmes was appointed professor of surgical pathology and bacteriology, a position that emphasized surgery's growing reliance on the laboratory. He also was named secretary of the faculty.

By this time Holmes had a broad view of the various types of medical education currently being offered, most of which used the lecture as the primary teaching method, and realized the need for radical changes. A major part of his agreement with the college involved the introduction of laboratory work. He also proposed the freeing of teachers from the requirement of purchasing stock in the college. The teachers Holmes brought in for the laboratories were not required to buy stock. This made it possible to acquire young and enthusiastic (though relatively poor) individuals for these vital positions.

Holmes had complete charge of the laboratory work, hiring his own staff and designing the related courses. This recognition of the importance of laboratory work marked a major change in medical education in the United States. Holmes also improved the curriculum, eventually extending it to four years. The six-story laboratory building Holmes designed for the college was the first in the country at a private medical school.

Realizing the importance of a medical library for both students and faculty, Holmes in 1889 had become founder and secretary of the Medical Library Association of Chicago. The funds the association collected for a library building ultimately went to support the medical department at the new Newberry Library in Chicago. Holmes also established a practical and current library at the college.

Holmes's life experiences, especially those associated with Hull-House, where he lectured several times in the 1890s to its Social Sciences Club, had given him a strong social conscience. He wrote about health and living conditions in Chicago's tenements and clothing sweatshops. The country-bred Holmes learned much from visitors to Hull-House and from his patients. Of a scholarly Russian Jew who had escaped from a Russian penal settlement, Holmes wrote, "While I cured him of malaria he taught me the philosophy of Karl Marx and made economic success and complacency a foregone impossibility for me" ("The Origin of the Economic Conscience," p. 260). Because of his social and economic views, the Populist party nominated Holmes to be its candidate for mayor of Chicago in the 1895 election. In the campaign, Holmes was supported by both Clarence Darrow, a lawyer in social and political cases, and Eugene Debs, a labor activist and, later, frequent Socialist candidate for U.S. president. Holmes came in third with nearly 13,000 votes.

One of the Holmes's sons, Bayard, also became a physician. When the other, Ralph, was struck down by dementia praecox (schizophrenia), Holmes retired in 1908 to care for him. Holmes read and learned as much as possible about the disease and devoted his efforts both to social and research work and to writing articles in the lay and medical literature. Ralph died in 1915.

After suffering from heart disease for several years Holmes died at his winter home in Fairhope, Alabama. Holmes came late to medicine, but his intellectual curiosity and youthful self-reliant labors had prepared him to make substantial and innovative contributions to medical education and practice. His deep social interest helped to better the lives of those trapped in miserable urban dwellings and poorly paid and unhealthy employment.

• No major collection of Holmes's personal papers exists, but the University of Chicago Library, Special Collections, has some material, including reprints, manuscripts on dementia praecox and laboratory conditions at Cook County hospitals, and a scrapbook on the 1895 election for mayor. Among Holmes's most important papers are his pioneering article "Secondary Mixed Infection in Typhoid Fever," *Chicago Medical Journal and Examiner* 57 (1888): 65–74, and "The Sweat-Shops and Smallpox in Chicago," *Journal of the American Medical Association* 23 (1894): 419–22. His major books are *The Surgery of the Abdomen, Pt. I., Appendicitis and Other Diseases about the Appendix* (1904), *The Friends of the Insane, the Soul of Medical Education, and Other Essays* (1911), and *The Insanity of Youth and Other Essays* (1915). The two books of essays (reprinted journal articles) are primarily devoted to Holmes's arguments for research on the "insanity of youth" (dementia praecox), for specially trained physicians and nurses, and for better treatment of such patients in institutions. A bibliography of his work appeared in *Medical Life* 37 (Aug. 1930): 441–54.

Holmes's autobiographical papers include "The Origin of the Economic Conscience: A Country-Bred Boy's Education in Economics," *Medical Life* 31 (July 1924): 256–72, and a six-part series on medical education in Chicago, beginning in 1882, that describes much of Holmes's own philosophy and work, in *Medical Life* 28 (1921): 8–12, 57–62, 160–65, 402–10, 569–74, and 29 (1922): 30–41. Also of interest is William K. Beatty, "Bayard Taylor Holmes—A Forgotten Man," *Proceedings of the Institute of Medicine of Chicago* 34 (1981): 120–23.

WILLIAM K. BEATTY

HOLMES, David (10 Mar. 1770–20 Aug. 1832), first governor of the state of Mississippi, was born in Mary Ann Furnace near Hanover, York County, Pennsylvania. His father, Colonel Joseph Holmes, a native of Ireland, was a successful merchant; his mother, Rebecca Hunter, was the daughter of Colonel David Hunter, a prominent Berkeley County, Virginia, planter. When David, the second of nine children, was an infant, the family moved to Winchester, Virginia. There he and his older brother Hugh, who became a distinguished lawyer, judge, and Speaker of the Virginia House of Delegates, were educated at Winchester Academy. At age fifteen David went to work in his father's mercantile establishment as a clerk and accountant. In 1790, about the time his father was elected to the legislature, David went to Williamsburg to study law. After being admitted to the bar in 1791 he moved to Harrisonburg, where from 1793 to 1797 he was commonwealth's attorney for Rockingham County.

Holmes used the practice of law as a steppingstone to a political career. After holding a few minor political offices on the local level, the Shenandoah Valley district elected him to Congress. Reelected five times, he served from 1797 to 1809. His strong opposition to the Federalist policies of the Adams administration and his warm espousal of Jeffersonian Republicanism did not go unnoticed by Republican party leaders. In one of his first acts as president, James Madison (1751–1836) appointed Holmes on 6 March 1809 to the governorship of the Mississippi Territory.

In June 1809, accompanied only by a few slaves he had inherited from his mother's estate, Holmes arrived in the territorial capital of Washington, near Natchez. A host of problems awaited him. The territorial population of some 30,000 was divided politically between Federalists and Republicans, and bitter factionalism prevailed. Though based in part on rival economic and class interests, this factionalism was primarily a legacy of the unpopular administration of

Nathan Sargent, Mississippi's first territorial governor, a partisan Federalist whose autocratic administrative style and partiality for the influential Natchez merchants alienated the territory's Jeffersonian agrarians. With a political adroitness that owed much to a rare combination of affability, tactfulness, and personal integrity, Holmes quickly established peace among the rival factions, redirecting their attention to important problems relating to the public lands, Indian affairs, banking, internal improvements, and relations with the Spanish in Florida.

The first territorial assembly to meet under Holmes's leadership chartered the first bank in Mississippi and took other steps to give the territory stability. He launched several important internal improvement projects, organized new counties, and reorganized and improved the militia. Holmes was instrumental in expediting the sale of public lands, settling disputed land claims arising from Spanish, French, and British grants, and obtaining support for newly chartered Jefferson College.

After 1810 most of Holmes's attention was given to problems relating to the Creek, Choctaw, and Chickasaw Indians who lived in the territory. The Creeks, allied with the Spanish in Florida, were especially troublesome. Fueling Creek hostility was the seemingly insatiable appetite of white settlers for Indian lands. Holmes's problems were compounded by the restlessness of Americans living under Spanish rule in West Florida and the growing resentment of Mississippians whose free passage to the Gulf of Mexico was blocked by the Spanish presence in East and West Florida. Holmes struggled to restrain territorial citizens from engaging in hostile actions against Indians or foreign powers with whom the United States was at peace. In the summer of 1812, he moved decisively to assist Governor William Charles Cole Claiborne of the Orleans Territory in occupying the District of Baton Rouge and annexing the District of Mobile. These territorial acquisitions gave the United States control of the Gulf Coast from the Mississippi River east to Perdido River.

Following the War of 1812, which ended the Indian problem in the territory with the defeat of the hostile Creek "Red Sticks" and their allies, a great migration of settlers into the region gave momentum to the movement for statehood. In 1817 the western part of the territory was admitted to the Union as the state of Mississippi. The politically popular Holmes, who had worked hard to prepare the territory for statehood and had presided over the constitutional convention, was elected governor without opposition.

During his governorship Holmes organized the new state government and promoted internal improvements essential to economic development, such as making the state's interior rivers navigable and building a turnpike to link Mississippi and New Orleans. He did not stand for reelection in 1819 and left office in January 1820. In November he was elected to the U.S. Senate where he served ably until September 1825. He returned to Mississippi and was elected to a second term as governor, only to be forced by poor health to resign in mid-1826. Hoping to regain his health, Holmes returned to his home in Winchester, where he suffered a stroke that left him paralyzed until his death five years later. He never married.

• The David Holmes Personal Papers (1796–1825) are in the Mississippi Department of Archives and History, along with his executive journals and letterbooks (1810–1820, 1825–1826), and his correspondence and official papers (1809–1826). Additional items can be found in the David Holmes Correspondence in the Mississippi Territory Manuscripts on deposit at the U.S. Department of State in Washington, D.C. His public career is detailed in Elizabeth Melton, "The Public Career of David Holmes, 1809–1820" (M.A. thesis, Emory Univ., 1966), and in William Boyd Horton, "The Life of David Holmes" (M.A. thesis, Univ. of Colo., 1935). Politics in Mississippi during Holmes's governorship are treated by Robert V. Haynes, "A Political History of the Mississippi Territory" (Ph.D. diss., Rice Univ., 1958). A character sketch of Holmes written by his nephew, David Holmes Conrad, can be found in "David Holmes: First Governor of Mississippi," *Publications of the Mississippi Historical Society*, Centenary Ser., 4 (1921): 234–57.

CHARLES D. LOWERY

HOLMES, Ernest Shurtleff (21 Jan. 1887–7 Apr. 1960), founder of Religious Science (a New Thought religious movement), was born in Lincoln, Maine, the son of William Nelson Holmes, a farmer and laborer, and Anna Heath. The family was relatively poor and moved frequently during Holmes's youth, but family members remained close. Raised a Congregationalist, Holmes received little formal schooling after his early teens and was largely self-educated. From ages fifteen to eighteen he worked in and around Lincoln before moving to Boston, where he lived for the next seven years and was briefly involved with a Baptist church congregation.

Holmes's reading of Ralph Waldo Emerson's *Essays* in 1907 marked the turning point in his life. He accepted "Self-Reliance" as his guide. At the same time, his painful, long-term throat ailment healed. The next year he studied public speaking at the Powers School to prepare for a career on the Chautauqua circuits. He also began attending the Christian Science "Mother Church" in Boston and performed his first mental healings. Holmes's system, by placing greatest emphasis on the concept of Mind as the operative healing agency, was a modification of the more theistic Christian Science approach.

In 1912 Holmes joined his mother and his brother Fenwicke in Venice, California. Shortly after arriving he abandoned his career as a public speaker and began assisting in his brother's Congregationalist church while he worked as the city's playground director for schools and purchasing manager. In 1914 he encountered the work of the English New Thought pioneer Thomas Troward and the American mental healer Thomas J. Hudson. That same year the brothers took a correspondence course offered by the New Thought author and lecturer Christian D. Larson.

In 1915 Holmes gave his first lecture on mental healing, and a year later he and Fenwicke started a mental healing periodical, *Uplift*. Holmes immediately attracted clients. Unlike some other mental healing practitioners, he never hesitated to charge for his treatments—at first requesting payment in gold pieces. In 1917 he was ordained a Divine Science minister in Seattle by Agnes J. Galer, who had established the first legally chartered Divine Science church in Washington, D.C. In the same year Fenwicke resigned from his church, and together the brothers opened a mental healing sanitarium in Long Beach and in Los Angeles the Southern California and Metaphysical Institute.

In 1917 the brothers began Sunday morning lectures at the Strand Theater in Los Angeles. The work blossomed until the institute soon was attracting students and clients from around the country. In 1919 the brothers turned to publishing, each writing an important New Thought text, *Creative Mind* by Ernest and *The Law of Mind in Action* by Fenwicke. In the early 1920s they went on successful lecture tours of East Coast cities; Although lectures were free, courses sometimes cost as much as $25. Yet some courses had as many as 1,000 attendants. In 1925, on friendly terms, the brothers ended their professional relationship. Fenwicke went east and enjoyed great success as a lecturer and writer, while Ernest settled in Los Angeles where two years earlier he had begun lecturing at the Philharmonic Theater.

During 1924 Holmes had traveled to New York City to study with Emma Curtis Hopkins, founder of the New Thought movement. Although his studies lasted for less than a year, Hopkins's impact on the development of his religious work was significant. His mature thought and the mental healing system he developed were based on his study of New Thought authors, especially Troward, Hudson, Larson, and Ralph Waldo Trine. Holmes's great work, *The Science of Mind*, was published in 1926, and the following year he launched what would become the Religious Science movement when he founded the Institute of Religious Science and School of Philosophy. His study with Hopkins likely inspired the establishment of the institute, which would later become the Church of Religious Science. Holmes married Hazel Gillen in 1927.

After founding the institute, Holmes reportedly struggled against increasing pressure to develop an actual religion around his teachings and the institute's work. He was unsuccessful. In 1939 the ordination of Religious Science ministers began, and by the mid-1940s Religious Science churches were established. At the time of his death in Los Angeles, Religious Science had become the second (only to Unity) largest denomination in the New Thought movement.

Holmes's most significant contribution to the development of New Thought was his massive *Science of Mind* textbook and his establishment of the Religious Science movement. Not only is *Science of Mind* the standard text for both Religious Science denominations (United Church of Religious Science and Church of Religious Science International), but it is widely read in other New Thought sects, and it has been taken as the name for many independent Science of Mind churches. Although the birth of the Religious Science movement occurred largely because of Holmes's dynamism, the movement's growth and development were the result of such leaders as Carmelita Trowbridge, Robert H. Bitzer, and William Hornaday, who took the institute in an ecclesiastical direction. Holmes's approach, and the approach of the movement he founded, differed from others in the New Thought tradition in at least three ways: (1) it emphasized the nonsectarian (non-Christian) character of its teachings; (2) it deemphasized the theistic elements in its theology; and (3) it accorded great importance to the role of the Practitioner.

• Holmes wrote many books and pamphlets, many of which offer significant insight into the Religious Science sect and New Thought as a whole. Among them are *Creative Mind* (1919), *The Basic Ideas of Science of Mind* (1957), *This Thing Called Life* (1943), *New Thought Terms and Their Meaning* (1942), *The Ebell Lectures on Spiritual Science* (1934), and *Ernest Holmes Seminar Lectures* (1955). A noncritical biography by Fenwicke L. Holmes, *Ernest Holmes: His Life and Times* (1970), supplies a good sketch of his life. Brief biographical data can be found in the chapters on Divine Science in Charles Braden, *Spirits in Rebellion* (1963), and Martin A. Larson, *New Thought, Or, A Modern Religious Approach* (1985).

DELL DECHANT

HOLMES, John (?14 Mar. 1773–7 July 1843), senator, congressman, and lawyer, was born in Kingston, Massachusetts, the son of Malachiah Holmes, an iron works owner, and Elizabeth Bradford. John left the family business to enter Rhode Island College (now Brown University) in 1793 with sophomore standing; he graduated in 1796. After reading law with Benjamin Whitman of Hanover, Massachusetts, he was admitted to the bar in 1799, and that September he moved to Alfred in the District of Maine. Holmes quickly applied his legal skills to the tangle of land claims in the region, using wit, ridicule, and anecdotes to defend proprietor claims against the squatters. In September 1800 he married Sally Brooks, and the couple had two sons and two daughters.

Holmes's legal work quickly made him an important figure in the local Federalist party, and he was elected to represent Alfred in the Massachusetts legislature, serving in 1802 and 1803. The ascendance of the Democratic Republican party in his adopted region interrupted his political career, but in 1811 Holmes switched his political allegiance, a change many critics attributed to opportunism and ambition. One year after changing parties, Holmes was elected to the General Court, and in 1813 he became a member of the state senate. His staunch support of the Madison administration's war efforts and his outspoken criticism of the Hartford Convention were rewarded when the president named him one of the commissioners to adjust the Maine–New Brunswick boundary in Passamaquoddy Bay, in accordance with the fourth article of the Treaty of Ghent.

In 1816, and again in 1818, Holmes was elected to the U.S. House of Representatives. By this time, Holmes joined with like-minded politicians William King, William Pitt Preble, Albion Keith Parris, Ashur Ware, and John Chandler to become one of the leaders of the Maine statehood movement. While Massachusetts's neglect of its eastern frontier during the War of 1812 influenced Holmes's support for an independent Maine, his primary motivation seemed rooted in his belief that Republican control of an independent Maine would provide him with greater political opportunity. Holmes, who played a prominent role at the unsuccessful Brunswick convention in 1816, chaired the committee that wrote Maine's constitution at the constitutional convention in 1819. His decision to support Missouri's admission as a slave state as a condition for Maine's entry into the union in 1820 eased the way toward compromise but brought him considerable public criticism in his adopted state.

Holmes was a member of the "Junto" that dominated the effort to separate from Massachusetts, and Maine statehood provided immediate impetus to his political career. In 1820 the first state legislature selected him to serve in the U.S. Senate, a position he held until 1827. His controversial support of states' rights presidential hopeful William Crawford against New Englander John Quincy Adams in 1824 was a harbinger of greater political divisions among Maine Republicans. The legislature denied Holmes a second term in the U.S. Senate, but when Albion K. Parris resigned his seat in 1828, Holmes replaced him and served until 1833. During his second Senate term, Holmes became a political ally of Henry Clay and the National Republicans. After his term ended he returned to his law practice in Maine but reentered politics in 1836 and 1837 as a Whig representative to the state legislature. Holmes's verbal abuse of political foes undermined his status as one of the grand old men of Maine politics; indeed, a young Hannibal Hamlin responded to one such attack by questioning the senior representative's chronic insobriety.

In 1841 President William Henry Harrison appointed Holmes as the U.S. Attorney for the Maine District, a position he held until his death. In addition to a long political career, Holmes left his mark on the legal profession. He and Attorney General William Wirt had unsuccessfully argued against Daniel Webster and Daniel Hopkinson in the *Dartmouth College v. Woodward* case in 1818–1819. Holmes's reliance on wit and personality rather than on legal expertise and logic left Webster unimpressed. In 1840 Holmes published *The Statesman*, a digest of law. Holmes's wife died in December 1835, and on 31 July 1837 he married Caroline F. Knox Swan, a widow and daughter of former secretary of war Henry Knox. He died in Portland, Maine.

Holmes was a controversial individual whose ambition and reputation for unscrupulousness alienated many of his contemporaries. Despite this, his contributions to Maine were noteworthy. As a leader in the statehood movement, he played a key role in bringing about Maine's separation from Massachusetts. Perhaps more important was his stance on the Missouri compromise; although he was roundly criticized within his own state, Holmes supported Missouri's acceptance as a slave state in order to achieve his more important goal of Maine statehood. Holmes managed to survive the growing factionalism that characterized Maine politics in the 1820s, but the increasingly democratic Maine electorate found him an unsuitable choice in the ensuing decade.

• A collection of Holmes's correspondence can be found in the John Holmes Papers, Maine Historical Society, Portland. A scattering of additional papers can be found under the same name at the New York Public Library. The papers of important contemporaries such as William King, Albion Keith Parris, John Chandler, and Francis O. J. Smith, all at the Maine Historical Society, provide additional background. The best treatments of Holmes's career are in William Willis, "The Honorable John Holmes," *The Law Reporter*, Aug. 1843, pp. 145–55, and William Willis, *The Law, the Courts, and the Lawyers of Maine* (1863). Ronald F. Banks, *Maine Becomes a State: The Movement to Separate Maine from Massachusetts, 1785–1820* (1975), provides the best discussion of prestatehood Maine politics and offers key insights into Holmes's role in the process. Thomas L. Gaffney, "Maine's Mr. Smith: A Study of the Career of Francis O. J. Smith, Politician and Entrepreneur" (Ph.D. diss., Univ. of Maine, 1979), ably fills out the poststatehood political landscape.

J. CHRIS ARNDT

HOLMES, John Haynes (29 Nov. 1879–3 Apr. 1964), Unitarian and later independent minister and a leading advocate of pacifism, was born in Philadelphia, Pennsylvania, the son of Marcus M. Holmes, a businessman, and Alice Haynes. Holmes was educated at Harvard College (A.B. 1902) and Harvard Divinity School (S.T.B. 1904) and entered the Unitarian ministry, holding early pastorates at Danvers (1902–1904) and Dorchester (1904–1907), Massachusetts, before moving in 1907 to the Church of the Messiah in New York City, where his influence as a minister dedicated to social reform began to be felt. In 1904 he married Madeleine Baker, with whom he had two children.

In 1919, after the destruction of the Church of the Messiah by fire, Holmes undertook both a physical and philosophical reconstruction of the church, renaming it the Community Church and breaking his relationship with the American Unitarian Association. He left the Unitarian denomination, he said, "not because of any hostility to that great body of free minds, but rather as a personal sign and pledge of my primary allegiance to the religion of mankind." Other steps, such as the elimination of pew rentals and a process of "democratizing its organization," brought the church more in line with Holmes's aspirations for a modernized religion. "The parish church, the institutional church, the union church, these have come and now are gone," he commented in 1959. "In its place comes, or will come, the community church—not the church but the community itself, here functioning spiritually as elsewhere it is functioning politically, culturally, and socially."

Holmes's long ministry in New York was marked by his advocacy of progressive social and political causes and of the church's central role in them. From the outset of his ministry he took an interest in what was termed "the social question," the place of religion and of the church in the movement for social equality and progressive politics. He felt that his ministry was informed by "a prophetic passion for righteousness" and noted the influence of Ralph Waldo Emerson, Henry David Thoreau, and especially "Theodore Parker and his militant interpretation of Christianity" in forming his orientation toward social religion. During his ministry in Dorchester, he had also read Henry George's (1839–1897) *Progress and Poverty* at the suggestion of a parishioner. "More than any other single influence, Henry George disclosed to me the social aspects of religion," Holmes later recalled. After he accepted the call to the Church of the Messiah in New York, Holmes said that "the social question gained permanent place in my preaching—later on chief place." His 1912 exposition of *The Revolutionary Function of the Modern Church* argued that religious attention must no longer be focused exclusively on "the individual," but on "the social organism," and that the church must take on "the new task of redeeming the social order." This task, as Holmes noted, greatly expanded the scope of religion. "Every question becomes thus at bottom a religious question and all work for human betterment religious work."

Such a commitment manifested itself in Holmes's political activities, including his advocacy of socialism, commitment to racial equality and to civil liberties, and espousal of pacifism. His active advocacy of these causes dominated his ministerial career in the period between the wars. Holmes participated in the founding of the National Association for the Advancement of Colored People (NAACP) in 1909 and the American Civil Liberties Union (ACLU) in 1920, serving as chairman of the board of the ACLU from 1939 to 1949. He described his brand of socialism as "spiritual in thought and not materialistic." "I walked in company with men like Upton Sinclair, John Spargo, and later Norman Thomas."

In the 1920s and 1930s Holmes participated in a wide variety of political and social reform activities. In the arena of electoral politics, he found an effective national leader in Robert M. La Follette (1855–1925) of the Progressive party, whose 1924 presidential campaign he supported. Holmes wrote that he found his own "liberal, even radical" ideas in the Progressive party platform and was also drawn to the "rigorous idealism and fidelity to principle" of La Follette. "I believed in Bob La Follette as in no other man in public life," he declared.

Holmes raised vehement opposition to the controversial trial and execution of Nicola Sacco and Bartolomeo Vanzetti in 1927, and a vigil service was held at his Community Church on the night of their execution. He was also active in New York City politics, chairing the City Affairs Committee in 1929 and working closely with Rabbi Stephen Wise, vice chairman of the committee, to combat the corruption of the administration of Mayor Jimmy Walker.

In 1935–1936 the political drama *If This Be Treason*, which Holmes coauthored with Reginald Lawrence, was produced by the Theatre Guild and ran for six weeks in New York. The play was based on Holmes's intellectual commitment to the principle of nonviolence, which was perhaps his most passionately held, and hotly controversial, conviction. The play attempts to translate Gandhian principles of nonviolence into the arena of American political and foreign policy. The play anticipated, in some respects, the Japanese surprise attack on Pearl Harbor that initiated the entry of the United States into the Second World War, since the catalyst of the play's action is a Japanese attack on an American naval base in Manila. Holmes and Lawrence posit as the key character an American president, John Gordon, who remains committed to principles of nonviolence, even in the face of the attack. Gordon goes to Japan to seek peace, an act that alludes to Gandhi's 1931 visit to London in search of peace with Great Britain.

The pacifist theme of the play was consistent with Holmes's long advocacy of such principles in foreign policy, most notably his opposition, on pacifist grounds, to America's entry into both World War I and World War II. "War is never justifiable at any time or under any circumstances," he wrote in 1916, on the eve of America's entry into World War I. His church, despite its disagreement with his position, supported him in his right to voice his dissent from the pulpit, an act that was, for Holmes, an expression of profound importance for the freedom of the pulpit. Although Holmes had arrived at his pacifist principles before he discovered the example of Gandhi in 1918, he found important support in Gandhi's career and teachings. He became one of the leading American disciples of Gandhi, calling him, in a 1921 sermon, "the greatest man in the world." In 1953 he published *My Gandhi*, an exposition of Gandhi's life and philosophy and of his impact on Holmes.

Holmes retired from his New York ministry in 1949, and even though he was afflicted with Parkinson's disease, he continued to preach monthly at the Community Church until 1959. He resumed his connection with the Unitarian denomination in 1960. After his death in New York, the *New York Times* termed him a "crusading cleric," and at his funeral his successor at the Community Church, Donald S. Harrington, called him "perhaps the greatest leader of the liberal movement in religion." He left an important legacy of political involvement for American liberal religion, and though officially independent from denominational concerns during much of his active ministry, he augmented the trend toward liberal political involvement that has characterized twentieth-century American Unitarianism. His contributions to key institutions of American liberal politics, the ACLU and the

NAACP, were important avenues of his larger influence on American public life.

• Holmes's papers, including correspondence and unpublished writings, are held in the Manuscript Division of the Library of Congress. A collection of letters to Alfred C. Cole is held by the Andover Harvard Theological Library, Harvard Divinity School. Among his publications not mentioned in the text are *New Wars for Old* (1916), a detailed exposition of his pacifism, and his extended critique of patriotism and nationalism, *Patriotism Is Not Enough* (1925). *I Speak for Myself: The Autobiography of John Haynes Holmes* (1959) is the chief source of biographical information. One should also consult Ralph E. Luker's essay on Holmes in the *Dictionary of American Biography*, supp. 7. Carl Hermann Voss discusses Holmes's relationship with Stephen S. Wise in *Rabbi and Minister: The Friendship of Stephen S. Wise and John Haynes Holmes* (1924). Holmes's interest in Gandhi is discussed in Spencer Lavan, *Unitarians and India: A Study of Encounter and Response* (1977). His career is considered in the context of American Unitarian history in David Robinson, *The Unitarians and the Universalists* (1985). A sense of his public prominence can be gleaned from obituaries in the *New York Times*, 4 and 6 Apr. 1964.

DAVID M. ROBINSON

HOLMES, Mary Jane Hawes (5 Apr. 1825–6 Oct. 1907), author, was born in Brookline, Massachusetts, the daughter of Preston Hawes and Fanny Olds. Very little is known about her immediate family, but the death of her father when she was twelve may have produced economic difficulties that led to her beginning a teaching career at age thirteen.

In 1849 Mary Jane Hawes married Daniel Holmes, who had graduated from Yale the year before. Immediately after the wedding, the couple went to Versailles, Kentucky, where Daniel Holmes had been teaching school. Both taught in Versailles for a year, after which they moved to a larger school in Glen's Creek, Kentucky, for two years. Daniel Holmes then left teaching to become a lawyer, and the couple moved to Brockport, New York, which remained their home for the rest of their lives.

Although she had published articles and short stories since 1840, Mary Jane Holmes did not find shorter forms appealing; Fred Lewis Pattee quotes her as saying she tried to avoid them because she found it "hard to bite them off" (*The Development of the American Short Story* [1923], p. 150). Her first novel was not published until 1854, when Appleton's issued *Tempest and Sunshine*, which rapidly became one of the century's most popular novels. Appleton's published more than fourteen editions of the book, and it was also published by at least nine other firms, often in multiple editions, staying in print throughout her lifetime.

This novel introduced themes that Holmes continued to explore through a career spanning more than fifty years, ending with *Connie's Mistake* in 1905. Her novels focus on the home, women's interactions with one another, and daily life; but her tone is generally comic, and her emphasis on education for women and a primarily secular world view sets her books apart from many other women's bestsellers. Nevertheless,

from her first reviews to her obituary, critics praised her writing as "pure in tone and free from the sensational element" (*New York Times*, 8 Oct. 1907). Although libraries found it difficult to keep her books on the shelves (the *Boston Daily Evening Transcript* claimed some found it necessary to have twenty or more sets of her works even as late as 1907), some critics suggested that her writing was so undistinguished that she should not be allowed in the public libraries. Much of her sales were through cheap editions, including those sold to travelers on steamboats and trains, and despite her popularity she received few reviews in the middle-class press.

Although claims vary, and the paucity of publishers' records combined with the number of pirated editions makes it difficult to determine how many copies of Holmes's novels were sold, even the most conservative estimates suggest her books' total sales were in excess of a million copies, and she undoubtedly had many more readers. Some of her novels were serialized in Street and Smith's *New York Weekly* before publication, and many were reissued year after year. In all she wrote more than three dozen novels, and several short-story collections were also published. Holmes and her husband (copyrights for her novels are sometimes in her name, sometimes in his) dealt wisely with her publishers, and she was able to earn $10,000 to $15,000 per year.

One of Holmes's most popular novels was *'Lena Rivers* (1856), which stayed in print well into the twentieth century and was so well known that as late as 1936 Wilbur Braun adapted the story into a one-set play for use by small theater companies. The novel was the basis for several silent films as well as a "talking picture." Like several of her most popular novels, *'Lena Rivers* is set on a southern plantation and tells a Cinderella tale of a poor young relation tormented by a richer but less admirable female cousin, solaced by an older woman, and rewarded with marriage to a handsome and rich "prince." Holmes was not an apologist for slavery, but her novels set in the South can be read as accepting slavery. *Meadow Brook* (reprinted many times between 1857 and 1900), for instance, tells the story of a New England girl who arrives to work as a governess, "becomes converted to the plantation viewpoint, and marries a plantation Bayard" (Gaines, p. 52). Perhaps because the focus of her novels was never the slavery question but rather the life experiences of the heroines, there were few objections to her works from abolitionists.

One contemporary profile noted that Holmes "has no hobbies," except for her frequent foreign travel. She had no children but taught Sunday school and was active in the civic life of Brockport. She died unexpectedly, after both she and her husband were taken ill as they returned to Brockport from their summer home in Oak Bluffs, Massachusetts.

• Most accounts of Holmes's life depend on the little information available in obituaries (the *Buffalo Express*, 7 Oct. 1907; the *New York Times*, 8 Oct. 1907; the *Boston Daily Eve-*

ning Transcript, 7 Oct. 1907; and the *New York Tribune*, 8 Oct. 1907) and a few contemporary sketches (John S. Hart, *A Manual of American Literature* [1873]; Frances E. Willard and Mary A. Livermore, eds., *A Woman of the Century* [1893]; and Laura C. Holloway, *The Woman's Story* [1889]). Evaluations of her work appeared in the *Literary World*, 3 June 1882, and *The Nation*, 10 Oct. 1907. Although she lived most of her life in the Northeast, much of Holmes's fiction uses southern locales, and some attention has been paid to this aspect of her work, as in Francis P. Gaines, *The Southern Plantation: A Study in the Development and the Accuracy of a Tradition* (1924); Jay B. Hubbell, *The South in American Literature* (1954); and John Townsend, *Kentucky in American Letters* (1913). Joyce Appleby, "Reconciliation and the Northern Novelist, 1865–1880," *Civil War History* 10, no. 2 (1964): 117–29, discusses *Rose Mather* and other works by Holmes in arguing that fiction by northern authors after the Civil War was highly conciliatory. Discussions of Holmes in the context of women's fiction of the 1850s has been extensive, ranging from Herbert Brown, *The Sentimental Novel in America, 1789–1860* (1940), and Alexander Cowie, *The Rise of the American Novel* (1948), through Nina Baym, *Woman's Fiction* (1993), and Mary Kelley, *Private Woman, Public Stage: Literary Domesticity in Nineteenth Century America* (1984). The 1993 edition of *Woman's Fiction* includes an extensive and helpful bibliography. Madeleine Sterne's various essays and other publications on nineteenth-century publishers of popular fiction are often illuminating in regard to Holmes.

JoANN E. CASTAGNA

HOLMES, Oliver Wendell (29 Aug. 1809–7 Oct. 1894), physician, teacher of anatomy, and writer, was born in Cambridge, Massachusetts, the son of the Reverend Abiel Holmes and Sarah Wendell, Abiel's second wife. A quintessential Boston Brahmin, Oliver was descended on his mother's side from the old Boston families of Jackson and Quincy and from early Dutch settlers; Anne Bradstreet was a distant relative. Although Abiel served as the orthodox Calvinist minister of the First Congregational Church in Cambridge for thirty-eight years, he was magnanimous toward Christians of other persuasions. Oliver was born and raised in Cambridge in a house dating from 1707, known as the "Old Gambrel-Roofed House," which had a library of some 2,000 volumes. At age fifteen he entered Phillips Andover Academy, where he distinguished himself by translating Virgil's *Aeneid* into English verse. He entered Harvard College in 1825 and was elected to both the Hasty Pudding Club and Phi Beta Kappa. The Unitarian spirit that pervaded Harvard in Holmes's day doubtless contributed to his lifelong rebellion against the puritanical Calvinism inculcated at home and school in his youth.

After graduating from Harvard in 1829, Holmes enrolled in the Dane Law School. Within a year, however, he became disenchanted with his studies, having, as he later wrote, "first tasted the intoxicating pleasure of authorship" with the publication of his poems in the Harvard *Collegian* and also in the *Amateur* and the *New England Galaxy*, both short-lived literary periodicals. Holmes won fame at age twenty-one with his hastily written "Old Ironsides," printed first in the Boston *Daily Advertiser* in 1830. A passionate plea

against the planned scrapping of the frigate *Constitution*, famous from its service in the War of 1812, the poem was reprinted nationwide—even scattered about the capital in handbill form, like an Elizabethan broadside—and saved the antique warship from demolition. Notable also among Holmes's early writings are two essays printed in 1831 and 1832 in *New England Magazine*, both with the title "The Autocrat at the Breakfast Table," which Holmes would reuse twenty-five years later.

Holmes abandoned law for medicine in 1831, entering Boston Medical College, where he studied under James Jackson. After additional study at Harvard Medical School, Holmes traveled to Paris, then regarded as the world center for medical training. In "Some of My Early Teachers," Holmes wrote about some of his Parisian professors, such as one M. Lisfranc, who was given to "phlebotomizing fits," and especially Pierre Louis, who opposed wholesale reliance on therapeutic bleeding and whom Holmes credited with introducing quantitative methods to medical practice. While living in Paris, Holmes journeyed widely in western Europe, recording witty observations that would later appear in the *Life and Letters of Oliver Wendell Holmes*. He finally received his medical degree from Harvard in 1836 and entered private practice in Boston.

Although Holmes worked as a doctor for ten years, he became much more important as a medical writer and teacher than as a practicing physician. He won Harvard's Boylston Prize in 1836 for an essay on auscultation and percussion and again in 1837 for essays on the treatment of malaria and neuralgia. Holmes cofounded the Tremont Medical School, where he taught pathology and physiology and later also surgical anatomy. In 1838 he was appointed professor of anatomy at Dartmouth College, a post he held until his marriage to Amelia Lee Jackson in 1840. Amelia, daughter of Massachusetts supreme court justice Charles Jackson, was Holmes's second cousin, and the niece of his mentor James Jackson; the couple would have three children.

Meanwhile, Holmes's first book, *Poems*, had been published in 1836, and in 1838, at the recommendation of Ralph Waldo Emerson, he had begun to appear on the Boston Lyceum's popular lecture circuit. Although he was limited by his severe asthma from extensive travel, Holmes delivered entertaining and erudite lectures on science and literature that remained in high demand for decades and contributed substantially to both his celebrity and his income.

Holmes made his greatest contribution to medicine in 1843, with the publication of "The Contagiousness of Puerperal Fever" in the *New England Quarterly Journal of Medicine and Surgery*; the paper was originally delivered as a lecture before the Boston Society for Medical Improvement and was quickly reprinted in pamphlet form. Puerperal (or "childbed") fever was a feared, seemingly unpredictable, and often fatal complication of childbirth. Holmes compiled a "long catalogue of melancholy histories" as anecdotal evi-

dence of the disease's infectiousness and supplemented this with a survey of the medical literature of
France, England, and the United States. His case
studies provide a vivid picture of the state of mid-nineteenth-century medical care before the advent of modern bacteriology. He denounced as typical, for example, one Dr. Campbell, who infected a newborn girl
when he arrived at her mother's bedside directly from
the dissection table, where he had conducted a postmortem on another victim of the fever, with the dead
child's "pelvic viscera" in his pocket.

Holmes is generally credited with discovering the
contagious nature of puerperal fever, though he cited
other doctors who understood it as early as 1795.
Holmes, however, decisively confronted American
members of his own profession with their role in transmitting the illness. His work was corroborated in 1846
by a Hungarian doctor, Ignaz Semmelweiss, who was
dismissed from his hospital for challenging established
medical practices. Holmes was likewise vilified in
pamphlets by two leading Philadelphia obstetricians,
Hugh L. Hodge and Charles D. Meigs (published in
1851 and 1853, respectively), in response to which he
reprinted his pamphlet with a new introduction in
1855. Eventually Holmes and Semmelweiss would be
vindicated by the research of Joseph Lister and Louis
Pasteur. Holmes's other medical publications include
Homeopathy and Its Kindred Delusions (1842) and *Medical Essays, 1842–1882* (1883).

In 1847 Holmes was appointed Parkman Professor
of Anatomy and Physiology and dean of Harvard
Medical School. His deanship was once marked by
controversy, when he supported the admission of a
woman and three African Americans to the school,
only to accede to the threats and demands of the remainder of their class, thus barring the four students
from further study. Although this incident suggests
that Holmes held progressive views, albeit none too
firmly, he was a lifelong conservative and a strident
anti-abolitionist, who changed his opinion only with
the outbreak of the Civil War and his elder son's enlistment in the Union army.

Holmes's tenure as dean ended in 1853. In 1871 the
school reduced his responsibilities, reappointing him
Parkman Professor of Anatomy, a post he held until
1882, at which point he became a professor emeritus,
continuing as such until the end of his life. The sound
training he had received in his Paris years and his extraordinary gifts as a lecturer sustained Holmes
through thirty-five years of teaching. So skilled was
Holmes that he was habitually assigned the school's
last of five morning lecture slots, when the students
were notoriously at their most restless. Salting his descriptive analysis with anecdote, imagery, and humorous wordplay, Holmes charmed his exhausted audience, never failing to earn, in the words of one of his
students, "a mighty shout and stamp of applause" (*Life
and Letters*, vol. 1, p. 176).

Not surprisingly, Holmes was also a renowned conversationalist, if somewhat vain, fond of flattery, and
given to monopolizing the flow of talk. Along with

such friends and fellow luminaries as the naturalist
Louis Agassiz and the poet James Russell Lowell,
Holmes reigned at the Saturday Club. Holmes's talents for talk at table and at the podium converged in a
midlife renewal of his literary career that fulfilled the
promise of his youthful efforts and propelled him to
sudden success as a popular writer. Lowell made it a
condition of accepting the editorship of the *Atlantic
Monthly* in 1857 that Holmes should be secured as a
founding contributor. The new magazine, which
Holmes also christened, proved to be the ideal forum
for his wit.

Although Holmes never allowed the original 1830s
pieces called "The Autocrat at the Breakfast Table" to
be reprinted in his lifetime, he revived the title for a
popular series of conversational essays, collected in
book form in 1858. Here for the first time Holmes the
writer borrowed a favorite device from Holmes the orator, often concluding his display of anecdote, epigram, and chat with an original poem; some of his best
verses, including "The Chambered Nautilus," appeared first in this manner. The more austere and contentious "The Professor at the Breakfast Table" series
followed in 1859 (collected in 1860), and was in turn
followed by "The Poet at the Breakfast Table" (collected in 1872). "Over the Teacups" (collected in 1891) finally concluded the sequence. Most critics have noted
a steady decline in quality over the years; *The Autocrat
at the Breakfast Table* remains the best of the collections, and contains Holmes's most characteristic
prose.

Holmes's three "medicated" novels—the term was
applied by a friend to the first of them—have worn less
well (and moreover were not well received in their
day). All three are case studies of abnormal psychic or
physiological states for which the protagonists are not
essentially responsible, and as such the novels can be
read as allegorical critiques of the Calvinist doctrine of
predestination, one of Holmes's favorite essayistic targets. (Holmes's free-thinking religious opinions,
though highly controversial in their day, seemed
harmless enough only a few decades later.) The first
novel, *Elsie Venner* (1861), which was originally published as a serial in the *Atlantic Monthly* in 1859, traces
the fate of a girl whose behavior is strangely influenced
by a snake bite that her mother suffers prior to her
birth. Despite Holmes's stated intent to "test the doctrine of original sin" and "inherited moral responsibility," the book is best remembered for a clear-eyed portrait of the New England aristocracy in its opening
chapter, "The Brahmin Caste of New England." *The
Guardian Angel* (1867), which also first appeared as a
serial (in 1866), examines its heroine's ancestral psychological inheritance, while *A Moral Antipathy* (1885)
concerns a man who is cured of a mysterious case of
"gynophobia" by his encounter with a dominant female.

Holmes's many other prose works include two
books of essays, *Soundings from the Atlantic* (1864) and
Pages from an Old Volume of Life (1883), both mainly
comprising pieces from the *Atlantic Monthly*; and two

biographies, *John Lothrop Motley: A Memoir* (1879)—a portrait of a dear friend—and *Ralph Waldo Emerson* (1885), commissioned for the American Men of Letters series. His travel book, *Our Hundred Days in Europe* (1887), recounts a happy summer Holmes spent in Europe with his daughter, during which he received honorary doctorates at Oxford and Cambridge and revisited places he had known as a student a half century before. In "My Hunt after the Captain," first published in the *Atlantic Monthly* in 1862, Holmes recounts his quest for his namesake son, who was wounded at the battle of Antietam. Holmes Jr. evidently felt that his father had exploited his ordeal for literary effect, a misunderstanding that contributed to the animosity that colored their relationship. One of Holmes's more idiosyncratic works is *The Physiology of Versification* (1883), a theoretical treatment of the connection between the laws of prosody and the laws of respiration and pulse.

Holmes's volumes of poetry, other than successively expanded editions of his 1836 *Poems*, include *Songs in Many Keys* (1862), *Songs of Many Seasons* (1875), *The Iron Gate, and Other Poems* (1880), and *Before the Curfew, and Other Poems* (1888). Editions of *The Complete Poetical Works of Oliver Wendell Holmes* appeared during his lifetime in 1887 and 1890. His best-known serious poems include "The Living Temple" (1858) and "The Last Leaf" (1833); his enduring light verse includes "The Height of the Ridiculous" (1830) and "Dorothy Q." "The Deacon's Masterpiece, or 'The Wonderful One-Hoss Shay'" (1858) is a humorous poem on a serious subject, in which the eponymous vehicle collapses all at once—a parable of the breakdown of Calvinism. For many years Boston's unofficial poet laureate, Holmes was also something of a professional Harvardian. A quarter of his 400-odd poems relate to his alma mater, many composed as light after-dinner *vers d'occasion*.

In his energetic and self-confidant pursuit of multiple careers, Holmes is a representative figure of the nineteenth century—even though Oliver Wendell Holmes, Jr., seems to have considered his father a dilettante. The effortless social fluency that allowed Holmes so to dominate his peers ultimately confined him, too. His inherent parochialism has limited his intellectual influence and denied much of his published work the grace of transcending its time and place. Holmes finished editing the Riverside edition of his collected works in 1891. He died at his house in Boston three years later.

• *The Writings of Oliver Wendell Holmes*, Riverside Edition (13 vols., 1891–1892), which contains all the works discussed above, remains standard. The edition of *The Complete Poetical Works of Oliver Wendell Holmes* edited by Horace E. Scudder (1908) omits "Urania," a controversial poem with anti-abolitionist overtones. John T. Moore, *Life and Letters of Oliver Wendell Holmes* (2 vols., 1896), is a biography incorporating a large amount of Holmes correspondence. Edwin Palmer Hoyt, *Improper Bostonian: Dr. Oliver Wendell Holmes* (1979), is a sympathetic portrait. Liva Baker offers an interesting account of Holmes's ancestry and suggestive speculation about

his influence on his son, Supreme Court Justice Oliver Wendell Holmes Jr., in her *Justice from Beacon Hill: The Life and Times of Oliver Wendell Holmes* (1991). Miriam Rossiter Small's *Oliver Wendell Holmes* (1962), in Twayne's Famous American Authors series, suffers from frequent biographical inaccuracies. Clarence P. Oberndorf proposes that Holmes's novels anticipated modern psychology but takes the thesis to often comic extremes in his *The Psychiatric Novels of Oliver Wendell Holmes* (1903). Also worth consulting are Samuel McChord Crothers, *Oliver Wendell Holmes: The Autocrat and His Fellow Boarders* (1909), and Mark Anthony DeWolfe Howe, *Holmes of the Breakfast Table* (1939).

THE EDITORS

HOLMES, Oliver Wendell (8 Mar. 1841–6 Mar. 1935), Supreme Court justice and scholar, was born in Boston, Massachusetts, the son of Oliver Wendell Holmes, a physician and man of letters, and Amelia Lee Jackson, a leader of Boston society and charitable organizations. The elder Holmes, for whom the future justice was named, was one of the founders of the *Atlantic Monthly* and the author of a celebrated series of essays and poems, *The Autocrat of the Breakfast Table* (1858). The son, known as Wendell Holmes, was tall—somewhat over six feet in height—and painfully thin. He resembled his mother more than his short, round-faced father and was deeply affected by her insistence on duty as a governing principle. Holmes attended private schools and Harvard College (1857–1861), but the principal influences on his intellectual development were outside the classroom. He acquired early, as an article of faith, a belief in evolution, a doctrine compounded of Thomas Robert Malthus and the German Romanticism that was in the Boston air. In later life Holmes said that the great figures of his youth other than his father were John Ruskin, Thomas Carlyle, and Ralph Waldo Emerson, all of whom in different ways espoused an evolutionary idealism. Holmes probably absorbed their ideas as much from conversation in his father's house, where Emerson and other literary figures were occasional callers, as from his reading. Holmes later said that Emerson had passed on to him the "ferment" of philosophical inquiry, partly by encouraging his combative independence of mind.

In undergraduate essays, Holmes announced the need for a "rational" explanation of duty, a sort of scientific substitute for religion that he sought in an evolutionary account of both history and philosophy. Duty, he came to believe, was a moral instinct that was the highest expression of human evolution.

The other great influence on Holmes's youth was a revival of chivalry then sweeping over the United States and Great Britain, partly inspired by the writings of Alfred, Lord Tennyson and Sir Walter Scott. Like many of his contemporaries and with his mother's encouragement, Holmes absorbed courtly ideals and conduct. Chivalry was the code of duty for which he sought, and ultimately believed he had found, scientific justification.

After the outbreak of the Civil War in the spring of 1861, Holmes enlisted in the Massachusetts militia, eventually obtaining a commission as a lieutenant. He served for two years in the Twentieth Massachusetts Volunteer Infantry and fought at Ball's Bluff, the Peninsula campaign, and Antietam. In those first two years he was promoted to captain, was wounded three times, twice nearly fatally, and suffered from dysentery. Exhausted, he completed the third and final year of his enlistment, in the winter of 1863–1864, as aide to General Horatio G. Wright and then to General John Sedgwick of the Sixth Corps. In the relative leisure of winter quarters, Holmes turned to philosophical writing, developing from his combat experience a purely materialist evolutionism. History was shaped by the perpetual conflict of rival nations and races, he believed. Laws were written and governments established by the victors.

Holmes attended Harvard Law School (1864–1866) and, after receiving his degree in the summer of 1866, traveled to Great Britain and the Continent. He made a number of lasting friendships in Great Britain. One of the most important to him was with Leslie Stephen, who reinforced Holmes's commitment to an evolutionist philosophy, which they both believed would provide a scientific, materialist basis for the code of duty. Holmes returned to London whenever he could and kept up an energetic and extensive correspondence with British friends between visits. Many of these letters, published after his death, have become classics, helping to make Holmes a major figure in the history of American letters and thought.

On his return to Boston, Holmes entered a law clerkship and was admitted to the bar in 1867. He then briefly gave up practice and attempted a career as an independent scholar and man of letters, editing the twelfth edition of Chancellor (of New York Courts) James Kent's *Commentaries on American Law* (1873) and writing dozens of brief articles and reviews for the newly formed *American Law Review* and occasional poetry for newspapers.

In 1872 Holmes married a childhood friend, Fanny Dixwell; they had no children. Unable to maintain a separate household on his meager earnings as a scholar, he abandoned scholarly pursuits and joined a Boston law firm that became Shattuck, Holmes, and Munroe with a busy commercial and admiralty practice. Fanny Holmes became seriously ill with rheumatic fever shortly after their marriage, and Wendell Holmes devoted himself to her and to his law practice for several years.

Holmes gradually returned to scholarly work in his spare hours, and in 1877, with "Primitive Notions in Modern Law" (*American Law Review*), he began a series of essays in which he attempted a systematic analysis of the whole of the common law—the judge-made law of Great Britain that in American courts still generally governed disputes between individuals. He completed the series somewhat hastily, gave them as the Lowell Lectures in November–December 1880, and published them as a book, *The Common Law*, in 1881, a few days before his fortieth birthday.

The Common Law, although hastily written and sometimes careless in its scholarship, is filled with novel insights and vivid imagery. Holmes's break with the a priori reasoning of the past is announced in the famous opening sentence: "The life of the law has not been logic, but experience." Despite its flaws, *The Common Law* has been called the greatest work of American legal scholarship. The central insight is that rules of behavior are not the fundamental data of law. Rather, law must be understood as a set of choices, often for unstated reasons, between possible outcomes.

In his earlier work, Holmes had labored unsuccessfully, like his predecessors, to untangle the dense mass of rules established by courts and legislature. In his first scholarly writings he had not been able to make a persuasive case for order or logic in this tangle of rules. In 1880, however, he had hit upon a new organizing principle. In cases of private law—suits for damages—judges decided which of the two parties would bear the burden of an injury. Holmes saw that the judge often found it easier to decide between the parties than to give a clear explanation or rule. The judge's written opinion, purportedly applying a rule, was often no more than a rationalization to explain the decision arrived at on other, sometimes unconscious, grounds. Instead of searching for preexisting principles of natural right or duty, therefore, Holmes turned his attention to the decisions of judges in particular circumstances. He argued that one could generalize from past decisions to predict the future behavior of judges. These empirical generalizations from the data of judicial behavior could be stated as rules or principles of law: "a legal duty so called is nothing but a prediction that if a man does or omits certain things he will be made to suffer in this or that way by judgment of the Court. . . . A man who cares nothing for an ethical rule . . . is likely nevertheless to care a good deal to avoid being made to pay money, and will want to keep out of jail if he can" ("The Path of the Law"). Holmes believed that, even when they contradicted a judge's self-justifying explanation, generalizations based on judges' behavior were the true principles of law and the basis on which the study of law could be made a science. Applying his new method, Holmes thought he had discovered a general organizing principle: modern judges would impose liability on a defendant when his or her conduct resulted in harm that an ordinary person would have foreseen. The injury and not the breach of a rule of conduct was the judge's central motive. Judges usually imposed liability on the blameworthy party, who in the modern world was the one who had caused foreseeable harm without adequate justification and who accordingly was felt to be responsible for the damage.

In *The Common Law*, Holmes traces the evolution of this principle of liability through the history of the law. Law, he argues, began as a substitute for private vengeance, as a means of controlling blood feuds. It then evolved into the instrument of a more highly civilized and complex moral system, in which punishment was imposed for moral culpability. As law continued to evolve in the nineteenth century, it was tending toward reliance on a single "external standard" that restricted personal liberty only to the extent necessary to prevent foreseeable harms. This evolution was driven by Malthusian forces. Only decisions that had contributed to the survival of the race would be preserved. It followed that law concerned itself solely with material aims and that law would continue to evolve until it was a fully self-conscious instrument of social purpose. The principles of a liberal, utilitarian policy of individual liberty and economic efficiency that Holmes found to be the often unstated motive of judicial opinions presumably had been favored by natural selection. Holmes's book itself, he plainly believed, was an important step in the evolution of the law toward self-awareness.

Although this theory of evolution through race and class struggle in which Holmes believed is now discredited, his turn toward the motives and actions of judges and away from formalistic rules of law marked an epoch that continues. Holmes's new methodology had a profound influence. He was considered one of the founders of sociological jurisprudence in Great Britain and the United States, of the school of legal realism that succeeded it, and still more recently of studies of law employing the tools of economics and rational choice analysis.

After *The Common Law* appeared, Holmes gave up his commercial practice and in the fall of 1882 taught for a few months at Harvard Law School. In December of that year he accepted appointment to the Supreme Judicial Court of Massachusetts and promptly resigned his professorship. He served on the state's highest court for twenty years, becoming chief justice in 1899.

Holmes wrote more than 1,400 opinions for the Massachusetts court, and in them he relentlessly worked through the thesis of *The Common Law*, thereby writing his theory into the law of Massachusetts. An incompetent doctor and an abortionist could each be tried for murder, he wrote for the court, because a person of ordinary foresight performing medical services would have known that the treatments provided, even if well intentioned, were likely to kill. Holmes's opinions, despite their harsh tone, influenced courts throughout the English-speaking world.

In the early years of his service on the Massachusetts court Holmes tried to avoid writing opinions in constitutional cases, with which he had had little experience as lawyer or scholar. When obliged to state a view, except when a statute had stripped away a person's right to a fair hearing, he usually expressed deference to the legislature. He based this deference on the English constitutional principle that the legislature was omnipotent, a principle he thought had been modified in the United States only to the extent that written constitutions contained clear limitations on legislative authority. This was the reasoning of Thomas Cooley's famous treatise *Constitutional Limitations* (1868), but it would have been a natural enough conclusion from Holmes's own approach to jurisprudence.

In 1894 Holmes made a major addition to his system of ideas with an article, "Privilege, Malice, and Intent," published in the *Harvard Law Review*. Here the focus is on libel and slander cases that had come before Holmes, in which liability was based, at least in part, on the defendant's state of mind—actual malice—rather than an objective or "external" standard of foreseeable harm. In these cases, which seemed to contradict his central thesis, Holmes argued that the rule of law was still based on prudent social policy. In certain cases a defendant might be privileged to do even foreseeable harm, however. Such a "privilege," like that accorded to a person for truthful speech, Holmes argued, afforded foreseeable benefits that would outweigh the foreseeable harm that it caused. Judges accordingly did not impose liability for harms caused by expressions of honest opinion. But a privilege would be withdrawn when used for the very purpose of causing harm, malicious motives presumably tilting the balance and making harms more likely than benefits. In 1896 he applied his revised theory in a dissenting opinion in *Vegehlan v. Guntner*, in which he argued that a privilege should be extended to trade unions to organize and picket peacefully, so long as these activities were carried on without malice, even though injury to their employer could be expected. (Somewhat confusingly, however, he justified the workers' privilege to picket on grounds of fairness, a similar privilege having been extended to employers; Holmes said that, on economic policy grounds, trade unions in themselves were not desirable.) Holmes's views on labor disputes were gradually adopted by his Massachusetts court and the U.S. Supreme Court, and they eventually were written into statute law in both the United States and Great Britain. His views on privilege generally proved to be more controversial but influenced the development of constitutional law, as we shall see.

In his early years as a judge, Holmes began to deliver public addresses modeled on Emerson's, in which he presented in carefully chiseled images his personal philosophy. Collected into a slim volume (*Speeches*, 1891–1913), these have become classics of the art and are frequently quoted. They provided Holmes the chance to answer the question of his youth: the sense of duty that had led him and so many others to risk their lives and thus seemed contrary to the instinct for survival was itself founded on an instinct, one of individual self-sacrifice in the interest of group survival, and hence was a part of the evolving natural order. The instinct at the root of duty defined the gentleman and was most strongly expressed in a relatively small number of men, officers in the endless war for control of scarce natural resources, men whose self-sacrificing determination would decide the survival of a race, class, or nation. These views were expressed most forcefully in his Memorial Day addresses, commemorating the Civil War, in 1884 and 1895. In later addresses he made the point that judges were expected to be gentlemen, scientist-scholars, like Holmes himself, trying to gauge how the conflicts of social forces would turn out, securing the future growth of civilization even at the expense of their own class interests.

In Holmes's earlier writings he had seemed to say that judges for the most part served as unconscious creatures of the dominant group from which they were drawn and their decisions would survive only to the extent they served the survival interests of the class from which they were drawn. Now a judge himself, Holmes said that judges were called upon by duty to sacrifice even their own class when this was required by a fair decision between contending parties. Their duty was to the human race itself. Having undergone a profound shift, Holmes's philosophy now seemed to be based more on a faith in the ultimate purposes of cosmic evolution than on the data of history; many commentators have remarked on the apparent contradiction between his early theories and his later work as a judge.

On 11 August 1902 President Theodore Roosevelt nominated Holmes to the U.S. Supreme Court. Roosevelt was impressed by Holmes's loyalty to the Progressive wing of the Republican party and by his imperialist views: the fate of the possessions acquired in the Spanish-American War were then the most important issue before the Court. Holmes served under four chief justices, a span of almost thirty years, and wrote 873 opinions for the Court, more than any other justice who has ever served to date. He wrote proportionately fewer dissents than many justices, but as his dissenting opinions were particularly forceful and well written, they were his best known. In the majority of cases in which Holmes dissented, the subsequent development of the law favored Holmes's position, a phenomenon that lent increasing prestige to his opinions. Many of his dissents, especially in constitutional cases, came to be cited as precedent.

During Holmes's tenure on the Supreme Court, a majority of the other justices believed that the Court had the power to base its decisions on general principles of common law, sometimes reversing state courts' decisions on this ground. Although he had done more to elucidate such general principles than anyone else, Holmes doubted whether they had an independent existence, whether they were a "brooding omnipresence in the sky" that the Supreme Court could draw upon. He insisted that these principles of common law were simply generalizations that various writers had drawn from the decisions of particular courts. From his point of view, the U.S. Supreme Court, limited in jurisdiction and with a limited body of precedents of its own, should defer to the laws of the several states except in those few areas where the Constitution expressly gave it law-making power; he concluded that the Court's creation of a national common law was not authorized by the Constitution and therefore was a "usurpation of power." His views gradually gained ground and prepared the way for a decision after his death in *Erie Railroad v. Tompkins* (1937), a historic surrender of power, in which the Court held that it must defer to state courts in matters of general common law.

When construing federal statutes, the Court did not yet consult "legislative history," and Holmes's readings of federal statutes were carefully laid within the four corners of the statutes themselves. Thus, in a famous line of dissents, Holmes insisted that the antitrust laws be narrowly construed. He said bluntly that the majority of the Court were reading into such statutes their own unstated economic views. He was at pains to expose these "inarticulate premises," and in the process he gave his own views of economics in compressed form. These views were highly influential, and scholars in the "law and economics" and "rational choice" movements in later years invoked Holmes's views to support their own.

The basis of Holmes's own views was his often-expressed conviction that the "stream of products," by which he meant what later came to be called the gross national product, was fixed at any one time, and any increase would be quickly absorbed by the consequent growth of population. He believed further that the share of the national product withdrawn by the capitalist class for its own consumption was minuscule in comparison to the total. If essentially all the wealth in society were consumed by the large mass of its citizens, it seemed to follow by an iron logic that workers competed with each other, not with capitalists, for a larger share of the national product and that prices were primarily determined not by costs or competition among producers but by the share of the whole national income that consumers were willing to give to any one commodity. Proposals for the redistribution of wealth or the breakup of large corporations to encourage competition he viewed as equally wrong. He sneered at socialism and even at private charity and insisted that the only hope for improved living conditions lay in eugenics and population control—"taking life in hand"—a view very bluntly expressed in his opinion for the Court in *Buck v. Bell* (1927), upholding Virginia's law allowing the compulsory sterilization of a supposedly mentally defective woman.

Holmes's most important opinions concerned constitutional law. The general terms of the Constitution—freedom of speech, due process of law—he understood to have been intended to embody principles of English common law. As the common law was changing, so too were the meanings of constitutional terms evolving—"the provisions of the Constitution are not mathematical formulas . . . they are organic living institutions transplanted from English soil. Their significance is vital, not formal; it is to be gathered not simply by taking the words and a dictionary, but by considering their origin and the line of their growth" (*Gompers v. United States* [1914]). Fundamental principles were to be viewed from the perspective of centuries, a perspective from which universal suffrage was a recent innovation and in which property rights were by no means fixed or eternal.

To Holmes, the fundamental guarantees of the Constitution were those affording every person the right to a fair trial before being deprived of life, liberty, or property by the government. He objected to unrestrained investigations by the Interstate Commerce Commission that seemed to him to invade the privacy of those being investigated. He refused to accept a procedure of empty forms when African-American and Jewish defendants were tried in lynch-mob settings in the South. He dissented on behalf of anarchist and socialist defendants whom he thought had been prosecuted and sentenced more for their ideas than for their behavior. He insisted on the right of the federal courts to intervene in state proceedings by writ of habeas corpus, and he wrote opinions limiting the power of state and federal courts to punish contempt summarily, without trial. In all of these cases, in which individual rights were pitted against the power of the state, the central question for Holmes was the fairness of the proceeding. He would allow any substantial civil right to be subordinated to the state's paramount interest in its own collective survival but only if proper procedures—"due process of law"—were observed.

The most difficult question for the Court in Holmes's day was the extent to which the so-called Civil War amendments to the Constitution (the Thirteenth, Fourteenth, and Fifteenth amendments) applied federal principles of due process of law to the states, putting limits not only on state court proceedings but also on the power of states to enact statutes. Business corporations and criminal defendants who had been subjected to penalties by state governments had begun to argue that the statutes under which they had been penalized were fundamentally unfair or irrational and so violated the substance of the due process of law guaranteed by the Fourteenth Amendment. In his first opinion for the Court, *Otis v. Parker* (1903), Holmes embraced the doctrine that due process of law set limits on state legislation as well as court proceedings, but he gave it a narrow scope. The due process guaranteed by the Fourteenth Amendment ensured more than a fair hearing in court; legislation must also meet minimum standards of fairness and rationality. The limits on legislation were the fundamental liberties of individuals that had evolved in the common law, the "relatively fundamental principles of right" of the "English-speaking peoples." Holmes seems to have believed that these principles, like the principles of liability in private lawsuits, were generalizations from the decisions of judges in the courts of English-speaking nations.

Holmes did not take an expansive view of the rights of individuals; to him they pertained essentially to procedural questions. He had grown up in a world in which the right to vote was still limited to men of property, and his views of the power of government were formed in the Civil War. Although he had almost lost his life in the abolitionist cause and was as nearly free of racial prejudice as anyone of his time in public life, he repeatedly avoided any defense of the right of African Americans to vote. In the "peonage cases" he dissented from the Court's decision that labor statutes in the southern states, making it a crime for tenant farmworkers to break their contracts, enforced a form of slavery. He did not believe that wiretaps were unrea-

sonable searches and seizures forbidden by the Fourth Amendment, and he expressly rejected the view advanced by Justice Louis D. Brandeis that a general right of privacy existed in the penumbra of the more specific provisions of the Bill of Rights.

Holmes's approach to rights of property was similarly restrained. He believed that property rights were created by the legislatures and could be undone pretty much at will by a political majority. So long as a statute was not irrational or purely for the benefit of a private interest it could withstand legal challenge, the only question usually being whether compensation was owed when the government destroyed a form of property. His opinion in *Pennsylvania Coal Company v. Mahon* (1922) gives the modern formulation of when such compensation is due.

Dissenting in *Lochner v. New York* (1905), perhaps his most famous opinion, Holmes argued for the right of New York's legislature to enact a statute limiting the labor of bakery workers to ten hours per day. A majority of the Court held this to be a violation of the liberty of contract, which accordingly was elevated to the status of a constitutional right. The majority of the Court, Holmes said, had based their opinion on an economic theory that was plainly not an expression of a fundamental principle of right. "The Fourteenth Amendment does not enact Mr. Herbert Spencer's *Social Statics*," Holmes remarked. In a series of opinions beginning in the 1930s, the Court reversed itself, and Holmes's dissenting opinion is now cited to define the role a court should play in constitutional adjudication.

Of all Holmes's opinions, the most important and most controversial were on the First Amendment's guarantee of freedom of speech. During the First World War the federal government had prosecuted thousands of men and women who opposed or resisted mobilization. When appeals from these convictions reached the Court in 1918, Holmes began to dissent vigorously in cases in which he thought prosecutions had been aimed at dissenting political opinion rather than real obstructions of the war effort. Holmes's first dissent, in *Baltzer v. United States* (1918), which he circulated within the Court before the majority had announced their decision, was so forceful that the case was withdrawn, and no opinions were ever published.

The first of the free speech cases to be openly decided by the Court, *Schenck v. United States* (1919), concerned leaflets mailed to men awaiting induction that the government claimed were intended to obstruct the draft and that might have done so in a small way in violation of the Espionage Act. Writing now for a unanimous Court, Holmes said that Congress had the power to forbid speeches and publications that threatened to interfere with the draft. Freedom of speech was not absolute: a person might be punished for falsely crying fire in a theater and causing a panic. As Congress could make it a crime to obstruct the draft, so it might also punish speech that posed a "clear and present danger" of having this forbidden result. Holmes, again writing for the Court, applied this standard to affirm a series of convictions in other cases of obstructing the draft, including the conviction of Eugene Debs, the Socialist candidate for president, for a speech critical of the war and implicitly urging defiance.

Holmes's opinions in *Schenck* and *Debs* (1919) were generally approved at the time, but for many years the Court rarely cited the "clear and present danger" formula except to uphold convictions, and the doctrine gradually came to be identified with the prosecutor's view. Holmes himself, however, strenuously objected to this one-sided use of his doctrine, and in a second group of cases decided in 1919 he dissented. It appeared to Holmes that in this second group of cases, as in the *Baltzer* case, the federal government had broadened its campaign of prosecutions to include political dissidents as well as draft resisters: defendants were being convicted and sentenced to terms of up to twenty years imprisonment for their socialist and anarchist ideas, not for any acts intended or likely to harm the war effort. In *Abrams v. United States* (1919), the first and most powerful of these dissents, Holmes restated the clear and present danger test in terms drawn from his 1894 article, "Privilege, Malice, and Intent." By throwing certain leaflets from a garment factory window, the defendants did not create, and did not intend to create, a clear and present danger to the war effort; by not acting on a motive that would have put the mobilization for war at risk, they could not constitutionally be punished.

Holmes went on to give his statement of the policy that he believed underlay the privilege afforded by the Constitution to honest expressions of opinion, which in turn was based on the principles of the common law that he had described in 1894: "the best test of truth is the power of the thought to get itself accepted in the competition of the market, and that truth is the only ground upon which our wishes safely can be carried out [in law]." Only when speech is uttered with the conscious purpose of doing harm and poses a clear and present danger of succeeding can it be punished. According to Holmes, honest expressions of opinion are to be given near absolute immunity from prosecution. Here again the Court later reversed itself, and Holmes's dissenting view has been adopted.

The task of the judge, Holmes continued to believe, is to choose fairly between contending parties and not to find or formulate rules of behavior. As the administrative state grew up in the First World War and the years following, Holmes increasingly dissented on behalf of individual rights against the operations of the government. However, the rights that Holmes championed are far from absolute. They remain essentially procedural: an individual has the right to join in peaceful debate and to have his or her interests weighed fairly, but when the state's or nation's survival is at issue, individual rights, even lives, can be sacrificed, so long as fair procedures are observed. Yet the inconsistency between Holmes's idea of the law as an instrument of group survival on the one hand and the judge's role as a neutral arbiter, basing decisions not on survival values but on principles of fairness, on the other became more marked as he grew older.

Holmes's self-denying sense of duty, his loyalty to the future of humanity rather than to its present order, was founded on faith in the ultimate purposes of evolution, and he half-jokingly called himself a "mystical materialist." His skepticism about the ability of governments to shape rational legislation grew, and his sense of duty came to predominate, so that his later opinions seemed to speak with the impersonal voice of duty itself. His striking turns of phrase entered not just legal literature but the fabric of our language. The phrase "clear and present danger" is used in thousands of judicial opinions and has become commonplace in ordinary speech. Holmes's metaphors—the marketplace of ideas, "no limit but the sky," and "shouting 'fire!' in a theater"—are almost equally pervasive.

Holmes's literary talents were evident in his opinions, but their impact did not depend entirely on his style. He conceived of an opinion not as a printed document but as a talk delivered from the bench. He paid careful attention both to the writing and to his manner of delivery. As he wrote to a friend, his model was the English judge, a gentleman rather than a professional: "I think that to state the case shortly and the ground of decision as concisely and delicately as you can is the real way. That is the English fashion and I think it is civilized." Holmes's opinions accordingly were brief and well enough written to be read aloud, and they were written so quickly and with so little revision as to seem, like the opinions of English judges, to have been extemporized from the bench. They were conscious works of art, fundamentally dramatic, and they had an impact far out of proportion to the logical force of Holmes's arguments.

Toward the end of his long tenure, Holmes became an admired public figure, an almost mythic embodiment of Olympic detachment, in large part because of his dramatic opinions on behalf of political dissent. Despite his theory formulated early in his career, that judges act on motives of social policy, Holmes was a conservative judge, closely hewing to what he conceived to be the principles established by past decisions of his court. He regularly chastised his colleagues for relying on their own economic or political views when principles of law might have been allowed to govern. It is difficult to point to any case in which dry precedent and legal principles did not supply Holmes's rule of decision. The only clear examples of innovations were his Massachusetts opinions on behalf of union rights to picket peacefully, which he justified on grounds of fairness, and *Olmstead v. United States* (1927), in which he voted to reverse criminal convictions based on illegal wiretaps, resting his decision on the principle that the government should not behave ignobly.

Fanny Holmes died in 1929, and the justice's work began to falter. His own health failed in the summer of 1931, and on 12 January 1932 he resigned from the Court. He died at his home in Washington, D.C., attended by servants and his law clerk.

• The Oliver Wendell Holmes, Jr., Papers are at the Harvard Law School Library and are available in a microfilm edition. His articles, books, speeches, and an extensive selection of his judicial opinions are published as Sheldon M. Novick, ed., *The Collected Works of Justice Holmes* (1995–). Mark De-Wolfe Howe edited Holmes's Civil War diaries and letters, *Touched with Fire* (1946), and his letters to Frederick Pollock, *Holmes-Pollock Letters: The Correspondence of Mr. Justice Holmes and Sir Frederick Pollock, 1874–1932* (2 vols., 1941), and Harold Laski, *Holmes-Laski Letters: The Correspondence of Mr. Justice Holmes and Harold J. Laski, 1916–1935* (2 vols., 1953). Portraits of Holmes and the principal events of his life are in Novick, *Honorable Justice: The Life of Oliver Wendell Holmes* (1989), and Liva Baker, *The Justice from Beacon Hill* (1991). An influential contemporary portrait is "Oliver Wendell Holmes: Justice Touched with Fire" in Elizabeth Shepley Sergeant, *Fire under the Andes* (1927). See also Edward White, *Justice Oliver Wendell Holmes: Law and the Inner Self* (1993), and Howe, *Justice Oliver Wendell Holmes* (2 vols., 1957).

SHELDON M. NOVICK

HOLMES, Theophilus Hunter (13 Nov. 1804–21 June 1880), soldier, was born in Sampson County, North Carolina, the son of Gabriel H. Holmes, a politician who was governor of North Carolina (1821–1824), and Mary Hunter. Holmes graduated from the U.S. Military Academy in 1829, forty-fourth among forty-six cadets in his class. Commissioned a second lieutenant in the Seventh U.S. Infantry, he served during the 1830s and 1840s on the southwestern frontier, in the Second Seminole War, in Northwest Arkansas, Indian Territory, and Texas, and in the Mexican War. Cited for gallantry at Monterrey, as he had been in the Seminole campaign, Holmes was promoted to brevet major in the Eighth U.S. Infantry in 1846. He married Laura Wetmore in 1841; they had six children.

During the 1850s Holmes served on garrison duty at Jefferson Barracks (St. Louis) and a series of frontier forts, including Washita, Arbuckle, and Bliss. He was promoted to full major in 1855, and from 1859 to 1861 he commanded the recruiting station on Governor's Island, New York. He left the U.S. Army on 22 April 1861, one of just fifteen field grade officers who resigned their commissions to join the Confederacy. He would become the ranking Confederate general from North Carolina.

On 5 June 1861 Holmes received a commission as brigadier general from West Point classmate Jefferson Davis, who, as president of the Confederate States, served as Holmes's patron for much of the war. Davis instructed Holmes to organize the military forces in North Carolina but soon afterward made him commander of the Department of Fredericksburg in Virginia. Holmes led a brigade of Arkansas and Tennessee troops at First Manassas, but only his artillery saw action. He was popular among his men in Virginia. When severe outbreaks of measles and diarrhea afflicted them, he established a large hospital for their care. Promoted to major general on 7 October 1861, he took command of the Aquia District, Department of Northern Virginia.

Holmes's early success and popularity soon evaporated. In March 1862 he returned to North Carolina to reorganize coastal defenses in that state, but in June 1862 he went back to Virginia with three brigades of mostly inexperienced troops to participate in the Seven Days' campaign (June–July). From this point on he would earn a reputation among his peers and subordinates for lethargic action and lack of initiative. Finding himself in the thick of the action at Malvern Hill, Holmes missed an opportunity to advance against the Federal lines. He claimed at the time that it would have been "perfect madness" to have attacked the strong Union position, yet his error had been in not moving rapidly enough before the enemy had concentrated its forces.

In July 1862, after Robert E. Lee had made it clear he could do without Holmes, Davis gave his friend command of the Trans-Mississippi Department, to be based in Arkansas. Promotion to lieutenant general followed in October. There is a poignancy about Holmes in the West, for despite his military training and experience, he proved inadequate to the task of high command. He faced formidable problems. Superior numbers of the enemy opposed him, and he suffered severe shortages of weapons and supplies. The Confederacy's American Indian allies to the west had grown despondent and could no longer be depended upon for assistance. Most of his troops were "new and undisciplined," most of his general officers untrained. He lacked cash to purchase provisions and equipment locally, and few entrepreneurs trusted the credit of the Confederate government. He dealt with these problems as well as could be expected, and he understood the military realities of his theater better than some of his younger and more aggressive subordinates.

On the other hand, Holmes lacked the mental and physical stamina to command, the flexibility of mind necessary to wage war. He too often ran his department by the book. He was a strict disciplinarian, and he refused to move an army unless he believed he held the advantage in men and opportunity. Moreover, Holmes lacked administrative skills for such a large task and could not control or get along with impatient or outspoken subordinates. In truth, Holmes himself could wield a sharp tongue and be brusque with even well-meaning associates. Yet one sympathetic officer believed Holmes "had not . . . enough of the 'mustang' in him to deal with Wild Western men" (Skinner, p. 327). His apparent deafness and rigidity of mind and body (he may have suffered from arteriosclerosis) led to his troops calling him "Granny." He was the oldest field commander in the Confederacy.

Perhaps Holmes's most critical weakness was his lack of self-confidence. He shrank with sincere modesty from nearly every promotion in rank or responsibility he received during the war. In the spring of 1862 he told Lee, "I am oppressed with the responsibility on me." A few weeks later he elaborated, "I know my deficiencies." Upon being given command of the Trans-Mississippi, he admitted to the secretary of war his "utter inexperience in a command of such diversified interest." Upon promotion to major general, he told President Davis that he lacked "many of the elements necessary to a high command" (Holmes Papers).

Holmes was devoted to saving Arkansas, even refusing the president's request to send a portion of his troops to reinforce Vicksburg. He praised Arkansans as "true and loyal" and his troops as "noble men," but civilians and soldiers alike lost confidence in him. The Federals advanced steadily into the state and laid waste to northern Arkansas. Holmes admitted that he was unequal to his task as early as October 1862. Davis finally responded to public pressure by replacing him as department commander with General Edmund Kirby Smith in March 1863 and reassigning Holmes to command the District of Arkansas, which also included Indian Territory and Missouri. In this post, too, Holmes proved unsuccessful, most tragically when his outnumbered army failed to take strongly held Federal positions at Helena in July 1863. When Kirby Smith and several leading Arkansas politicians petitioned to have Holmes removed from Arkansas altogether, Holmes resigned in March 1864. In April Davis reassigned Holmes to command reserve troops in his native North Carolina. He served in this largely administrative post until April 1865.

After the war Holmes settled on a farm near Fayetteville, Cumberland County, North Carolina. He lived out his remaining years in obscurity, dying on his farm.

• Two small collections of Holmes papers are to be found in National Archives Record Group 109, although much of this correspondence is printed in *The War of the Rebellion: A Compilation of the Official Records of the Union and Confederate Armies* (128 vols., 1880–1901). There is no biography of Holmes, but a good sketch is Albert Castel, "Theophilus Holmes: Pallbearer of the Confederacy," *Civil War Times Illustrated* 16 (July 1977): 10–17. Among the most important contemporary commentators are Daniel Harvey Hill, *Bethel to Sharpsburg* (2 vols., 1926); James L. Skinner III, ed., *The Autobiography of Henry Merrell: Industrial Missionary to the South* (1991); Daniel E. Sutherland, ed., *Reminiscences of a Private: William E. Bevens of the First Arkansas Infantry, C.S.A.* (1992); and J. H. Wheeler, *Reminiscences and Memoirs of North Carolina and Eminent North Carolinians* (1884). Useful historical perspectives on Holmes are provided in Anne J. Bailey, *Between the Enemy and Texas: Parsons' Texas Cavalry in the Civil War* (1989); Robert L. Kerby, *Kirby Smith's Confederacy: The Trans-Mississippi South, 1863–1865* (1972); Stephen W. Sears, *To the Gates of Richmond: The Peninsula Campaign* (1992); Craig L. Symonds, *Joseph E. Johnston: A Civil War Biography* (1992); and Steven E. Woodworth, *Jefferson Davis and His Generals: The Failure of Confederate Command in the West* (1990). An obituary may be found in the Fayetteville *Examiner*, 22 June 1880.

DANIEL E. SUTHERLAND

HOLSEY, Lucius Henry (3 July 1842–3 Aug. 1920), minister and denominational leader, was born near Columbus, Georgia, the son of James Holsey, a plantation owner, and Louisa, a slave. When his father died in 1848, Holsey was sold to his white cousin, T. L. Wynn, who lived in Hancock County, Georgia.

After Wynn's death in 1857, he became the slave of Richard Johnston, a professor at Franklin College (now the University of Georgia) in Athens. He was spared the rigors of labor in the fields by working as a house servant and carriage driver, and while he received no formal education, he was able to teach himself to read and write. With the outbreak of the Civil War, Johnston left Athens and took Holsey back to Hancock County. In November 1863 Holsey married Harriet Anne Turner, a slave who once belonged to George Foster Pierce, a bishop of the Methodist Episcopal church, South (MECS). Holsey and Turner had nine children.

Following emancipation in 1865, Holsey managed a farm near Sparta, Georgia. During that period he was instructed in theology by Pierce, who wished Holsey to become an evangelist among freed African Americans. Licensed by Pierce as a Methodist preacher in February 1868, Holsey served briefly in the Hancock County circuit. In 1869 he moved to Savannah, Georgia, where he took charge of the Andrew Chapel. He later served as the minister of Trinity Church, Augusta, Georgia, from 1871 until 1873. His principal contributions to his church, however, were as an organizer rather than as a pastor. He was a delegate to the first General Conference of the Colored Methodist Episcopal church (CMEC), which convened in Jackson, Tennessee, in December 1870. (The CMEC, which became the Christian Methodist Episcopal church, had been established by the MECS to provide a separate, autonomous denomination for the approximately 20,000 African Americans who remained affiliated with white Southern Methodism after the Civil War.) When the second General Conference of the CMEC met at Holsey's church in Augusta in March 1873, the gathering elected him the fourth bishop of the fledgling denomination.

Holsey, then barely in his thirties, proved to be a dynamic leader who strengthened the institutional structures of the CMEC during the next four decades. He recognized that education was one of the chief needs of the former slaves who comprised the membership of the CMEC. Since he knew that most white southerners had little desire to lift African Americans out of their traditionally subordinate social position, he sought funds from white Methodists, not to educate the general black population, he said, but to provide training for black clergy and teachers to shape the moral values of their people. Persistent in this effort, he raised sufficient money to open the Paine Institute (later renamed Paine College) in Augusta, Georgia, in 1884. Although overall control of Paine remained solidly in white hands throughout Holsey's lifetime, the school provided an arena in which black and white Methodists were able to interact on an approximately equal plane. Holsey was influential as well in the founding of several other church-related institutions: Lane College in Jackson, Tennessee; the Holsey Normal and Industrial Academy, a secondary school in Cordele, Georgia; and the Helena B. Cobb Institute for Girls in Barnesville, Georgia.

Holsey held a number of prominent honorary positions within the CMEC over the course of his lengthy career. He represented the denomination at the first two Ecumenical Methodist Conferences (in London in 1881 and in Washington, D.C., in 1891), and he served as secretary of the College of Bishops of the CMEC for twenty-five years. He was also instrumental in the establishment of the CME Publishing House and helped launch a denominational newspaper, the *Gospel Trumpet*, in 1896. In addition, he edited *The Hymn Book of the Colored M.E. Church in America* (commonly known as the "Holsey Hymnal") in 1891 and *A Manual of the Discipline of the Colored Methodist Episcopal Church in America* in 1894. He was the senior bishop of the CMEC at the time of his death in Atlanta.

Holsey was the principal spokesperson of his denomination during its formative years. His social philosophy was at first conservative, for his commitment to education and racial uplift enabled him to take advantage of white paternalism in the aftermath of the Civil War. However, toward the end of his life, the dramatic increase of racism in the South led him to advocate the value of racial separatism. Between the Civil War and World War I he played a key role in the successful growth and development of the CMEC and was recognized as one of the most prominent African-American religious figures of the late nineteenth century.

• Material about Holsey's life is scanty. A good primary source is his own *Autobiography, Sermons, Addresses, and Essays* (1898). A brief autobiographical sketch (with an introduction by George E. Clary, Jr.) has been republished as *The Autobiography of Bishop L. H. Holsey* (1988). John Brother Cade, *Holsey—The Incomparable* (1964), is a full, sympathetic biography based on manuscripts that have since been destroyed by fire. Glenn T. Eskew, "Black Elitism and the Failure of Paternalism in Postbellum Georgia: The Case of Bishop Lucius Henry Holsey," *Journal of Southern History* 58 (Nov. 1992): 637–66, provides an excellent scholarly analysis of Holsey's social and educational outlook. See also Reginald F. Hildebrand, *The Times Were Strange and Stirring: Methodist Preachers and the Crisis of Emancipation* (1995).

GARDINER H. SHATTUCK, JR.

HOLT, Claire (23 Aug. 1901–29 May 1970), Indonesian specialist and journalist, was born Claire Bagg in Riga, Latvia, the daughter of Boris Bagg, a successful leather dealer and manufacturer, and Cecile Hodes. In 1914 the family moved to Moscow, where Claire attended Gymnasiums from 1914 to 1918. In 1920 she married Bernard Hopfenberg, and in 1921 the couple emigrated to the United States. They settled in New York, and Claire gave birth to a son in 1927. Her husband died in 1928.

From 1921 to 1924 she studied sculpture with Alexander Archipenko at Cooper Union for the Advancement of Science and Art. She also attended Brooklyn Law School in 1922–1923 and the Columbia University School of Journalism in 1928. From 1928 to 1930 she wrote for the *New York World*, taking the pen name of Claire Holt; she later made this her legal name. Besides doing feature stories and regular reporting, she became the paper's dance critic under the name of Barbara Holveg. She reviewed the early creations of Martha Graham, Doris Humphrey, and other pioneers of modern dance, as well as classical ballet performances. Her involvement with dance was to have great influence on her later in Java, where she studied traditional Javanese dance forms and wrote about their relation to culture and society.

In 1930 Holt embarked on a trip around the world. When she reached the Dutch East Indies, what was intended as a brief visit turned into an extended stay and a lifelong involvement with Indonesia. She spent the greater part of the decade there and published numerous articles on Indonesian art, culture, and life.

Most significant during this period was her association with the archaeologist Willem (or Wilheim) Stutterheim, who became her mentor. While working as his assistant she became part of a glorious circle of scholars and artists living in Java and Bali in the 1930s, including Walter Spies, Margaret Mead, and Jaap Kunst. She also developed close relationships with Javanese nobility. She learned classical Central Javanese dance from the court dance master of the Yogyakarta palace, Prince Aria Tedjakusuma (she was the only westerner he ever undertook to teach). Also crucial to her understanding of Javanese culture was her friendship with Prince Mangkunagara VII, an authority on Javanese art, whose treatise on *wayang kulit* (shadow puppetry) she translated.

Another significant alliance forged during this time was with the Swedish dance archivist and patron Rolf de Mare. In 1938 Holt accompanied de Mare on a sweeping tour through Java, Bali, Sulawesi (Celebes), Sumatra, and Nias, documenting, filming, and photographing different traditional dances for Les Archives Internationales de la Danse in Paris, which had been founded by de Mare. Along with several catalogs and articles that she wrote for that archive, Holt published her first book, *Dance Quest in Celebes* (1939), based on this fieldwork. During the decade she accumulated a sizable portfolio of photographs of classical architecture, sculpture, and dance of Java, Bali, and other islands of the archipelago.

In 1939 she returned to New York, and from 1940 to 1942 she was an assistant to Margaret Mead at the American Museum of Natural History. In 1942 she taught at the Navy School of Military Government at Columbia University, conducting seminars in Indonesian language and culture to prepare military personnel for overseas duty. In 1944 she worked for the Office of Strategic Services in Washington, D.C., as section chief of the Far East Division of Research and Analysis. She was transferred to the State Department's Office of Intelligence Research in 1945 as a foreign affairs specialist in the Far East Division.

She was deeply committed to developing ways of training government personnel to relate to and understand other peoples and to be aware of their own cultural assumptions. She gave lectures on the sociology of the Far East to intelligence officers and trained technical personnel for overseas work in the Point Four Program, which provided technical assistance to industrially underdeveloped countries. In 1953 she resigned in protest over tightening security regulations, an early sign of encroaching McCarthyism. A close colleague and friend from this period was the anthropologist Cora Du Bois, who also left the State Department around the same time and subsequently became chair of the Department of Anthropology at Harvard. The two would remain in close touch throughout their lives.

In 1955 Holt returned to Indonesia, where she resumed her earlier research in preparation for a book on the evolving state of Indonesian art and culture. In 1957 she became a senior research associate at Cornell University in Ithaca, New York, where she continued her research and taught courses in Indonesian language and culture until her death. George Kahin, founder of the Modern Indonesia Project at Cornell, credits her with bringing a "cultural dimension to academic study," a rarity at the time. Her firsthand knowledge of Indonesian art forms inspired many of her students to include the arts as serious components in their research. Among the many she influenced greatly was Benedict Anderson, who studied with her as a graduate student.

Her book *Art in Indonesia: Continuities and Change* was published in 1967. It was a landmark work of its time, incorporating history, politics, sculpture, dance, and traditional and modern painting into a holistic view of a society in flux. It remains a significant and valuable contribution to the field of Indonesian studies and is unique in the scope of its multidisciplinary approach.

Her last years were marked by increasingly poor health, and she died in Ithaca. Compilations of her unpublished notes on Batak, Minangkabau, and Nias dances were published posthumously in the journal *Indonesia* (1971–1972). In a memorial to her published in the October 1970 issue of *Indonesia*, Anderson pointed out that of all the Western scholars who enjoyed their heyday in the colonial Dutch East Indies, Holt was the only one to return to postrevolutionary Indonesia and continue writing about it. Her fascination with the many aspects of growth and change in Indonesia was perhaps mirrored by her own life, her many diverse interests, her state of always evolving from one career to the next, and her essentially multidisciplinary and cross-cultural spirit.

• The major portion of Holt's papers and photographs are in the Claire Holt Collection at the Dance Collection of the New York Public Library for the Performing Arts. The collection consists of sixteen boxes of notes, correspondence, daily calendars, her newspaper articles, manuscripts for her two books, and an unpublished book-length manuscript, "Dancers and Danced Stories of Java." There are also about 9,000 photographic prints, 3,500 photographic negatives, and copies of the films Holt worked on with Rolf de Mare in 1938, which include footage of dance from Bali, Sulawesi, Java, and Sumatra. See Nancy Shawcross, "The Claire Holt Col-

lection," *Dance Research Journal* 19, no. 1 (Summer 1987): 25–35. A *Guide to Claire Holt's Collection* (197?), which itemizes her slides and photographic prints, was published by the Southeast Asia Program of Cornell University. A small amount of material, including some notebooks and a slide collection, remains at the Carl A. Kroch Library at Cornell University. Several boxes of notes and correspondence are also at the Modern Indonesia Project at Cornell University.

Her numerous published articles can also be found in the collection. Notable among these are "Two Dance Worlds—A Contemplation," *Impulse: Annual of Contemporary Dance Theories and Viewpoints* (1958), a comparative study between the Martha Graham Dance Group and traditional Central Javanese dance, and "Form and Function of the Dance in Bali," coauthored with Gregory Bateson and published in Franz Boas, *The Function of Dance in Human Society* (1972). Her work on dance in Sumatra and Nias was published posthumously in a three-part series in *Indonesia*. These are: "Dances of Sumatra and Nias: Notes by Claire Holt" with preface by Arlene Lev, *Indonesia*, no. 11 (Apr. 1971); "Batak Dances: Notes by Claire Holt" *Indonesia*, no. 12 (Oct. 1971); and "Dances of Minangkabau: Notes by Claire Holt," ed. Elizabeth Graves, *Indonesia*, no. 14 (Oct. 1972). Also published posthumously was the book she edited with the assistance of Benedict R. O'G. Anderson and James Siegel, *Culture and Politics in Indonesia* (1972).

DEENA BURTON

HOLT, Edwin Bissell (21 Aug. 1873–25 Jan. 1946), psychologist and philosopher, was born in Winchester, Massachusetts, the son of Stephen Abbott Holt, a Congregational minister, and Nancy Wyman Cutter. A precocious youth, Holt was encouraged in his interests in plant and animal life by his devoted but domineering mother. He graduated from Harvard in 1896 and studied medicine the next year at the University of Freiburg in Germany. He then began graduate work at Harvard before serving briefly in the army during the Spanish-American War. In 1900 he took a master's degree at Columbia University under the psychologists James McKeen Cattell. A year later he received his doctorate in philosophy at Harvard, where he studied under William James and Hugo Münsterberg.

Although his early experimental research on the psychology of vision was performed in Münsterberg's laboratory, Holt drew his inspiration chiefly from James. Like James, Holt was an erudite and original thinker who had little patience with the trappings and posturing of academic life. Along with Ralph Barton Perry, he was among James's favorite students and was a frequent guest in the James household. In 1901 he became an instructor in Münsterberg's laboratory, where he earned a reputation as a meticulous but supportive supervisor of student research on a wide range of topics. Promoted to assistant professor in 1905, Holt turned to more philosophical interests and entered his most productive period.

In a seminal 1904 essay, James had denied the existence of consciousness as a mental substance and reinterpreted it as a set of functional relations between a person's nervous system and the objects of which the person is aware. In *The Concept of Consciousness* (1914), Holt drew on this conception to criticize the subjective view of mind implicit in idealism and dualism. In an act of cognition, he said, the mind neither constitutes the object known (as held by idealists) nor copies it in the form of a private mental representation (as held by dualists). Rather than being a subjective or private affair, cognition is an observable process of adjustment to an object whereby one's behavior has "objective reference" to the thing known. In this motor theory of consciousness, mind does not reside in the nervous system—"the house of the brain is not haunted"—rather it inheres in the outward behavioral relations of objective reference.

By construing mind in terms of publicly observable relations, Holt anticipated the operationism that swept through American psychology in subsequent decades and helped prepare the way for John B. Watson's proclamation of behaviorism in 1913. Against Watson's narrow reflexological view, however, Holt showed that meaningful behavior occurs in integrated wholes rather than as discrete responses to punctate stimuli. This insight was further developed by Holt's Harvard student Edward C. Tolman, whose "molar" cognitive behaviorism later became widely influential and contributed to the resurgence of cognitive psychology during the 1960s.

Despite his protobehaviorism, Holt remained true to the spirit of James's radical empiricism and pluralist ontology by refusing to deny the reality of mental life. He acknowledged that the objects of consciousness encompass a diverse range of entities—prime numbers and subjectively experienced qualities (for example, pains or sensations of redness) no less than houses and trees. Because all such entities could be responded to and thus enter into relations of objective reference, Holt accepted all of them as real. Being neither physical nor mental, they shared equal ontological status as subsistents in the "neutral mosaic" of experience. With this eclectic realism, Holt hoped to give a naturalistic account of the mind without committing the materialist's error of denying the facts of consciousness. In 1912 he, Perry, and four other realists published *The New Realism*, a work that brought Holt recognition as a leader of the American neorealist movement.

Like James, Holt became interested in the dynamics of mind and phenomena of abnormal psychology. Greatly impressed with the work of Freud, whom he encountered at the famous Clark University Conference of 1909, Holt began work on *The Freudian Wish and Its Place in Ethics* (1915). Connecting Freudian drives with his own conception of consciousness as object-response relations, Holt noted that wishes (or drives, desires, impulses) are revealed in the tendency of an organism to approach or avoid objects of cognition according to its needs. He consequently defined the Freudian wish as "*a course of action* which some mechanism of the body is *set* to carry out, whether it actually does so or does not" (pp. 3–4). The conflict of behavioral tendencies, incipient or actual, thus accounted for such phenomena as slips of the tongue and repression. In Holt's naturalistic Freudian ethics,

moral conduct was construed as the realization of multiple, potentially conflicting wishes through integrated adaptations to a complex social and physical environment.

Popular in both America and England, *Freudian Wish* anticipated later efforts to synthesize Freudian and behaviorist psychologies. At the same time, Holt's use of examples in which thinly disguised Harvard personages unwittingly revealed their genuine motives created a stir in the Cambridge community, from which Holt became increasingly alienated. After his mother's death in 1918, he submitted a testy letter of resignation and retired on the inheritance from his mother's estate.

Recruited back to academia in 1926 by his friend Herbert Langfeld, Holt resumed teaching at Princeton. In 1931 he published *Animal Drive and the Learning Process*, which was originally conceived as a revision of James's *Principles of Psychology*. Replacing his earlier neutral monism with an emergent materialism grounded in physiological psychology, Holt traced the development of complex behavior from the primitive "reflex circle" to the higher manifestations of social conduct. Among his students at Princeton was James J. Gibson, whose important research on the role of the perceiver's activity in perception was inspired by Holt's response theory of cognition and whose influential "ecological psychology" embodied strains of Holt's philosophical realism. In 1936 Holt, who never married, retired to the Maine coast with his friend George Bernier and died in Rockland a decade later.

Although Holt was popular with his students, his eccentricity, caustic wit, and neglect of academic proprieties cost him collegial favor and professional esteem. As the prominent psychologist E. G. Boring commented, he was "a thinker who had more influence than prestige, being more often followed than quoted." Nonetheless, Holt helped guide American psychology's transition from a branch of philosophy to a laboratory-based discipline. As a contributor to both philosophical and scientific psychology, he formulated philosophically sophisticated versions of behaviorism and operationism at a time when his more narrowly positivistic contemporaries shunned their philosophical roots. He also played an important role in transmitting the Jamesian legacy to younger generations of psychologists, keeping it alive in the form of an eclectic cognitive behaviorism in learning theory and an ecological realism in perception theory.

• There is no known repository of Holt papers. A bibliography of many of his writings is in the *Psychological Register*, vol. 3 (1932). For biographical information see E. G. Boring's entry in the *International Encyclopedia of the Social Sciences* (1968). Holt's philosophical psychology is treated in Charles W. Morris, *Six Theories of Mind* (1932); his relation to James and Münsterberg, in Bruce Kuklick, *The Rise of American Philosophy* (1977). See also Nathan G. Hale, Jr., *Freud and the Americans* (1971), on his role in popularizing Freudian theory; Laurence D. Smith, *Behaviorism and Logical Positivism* (1986), on his behaviorism and early operationism; and Edward S. Reed, *James J. Gibson and the Psychology of Perception* (1988), on his contributions to theory and research on perception. Obituaries are Herbert S. Langfeld, *Psychological Review* 53 (1946): 251–58; Leonard Carmichael, *American Journal of Psychology* 59 (1946): 478–80; and Daniel Katz, *Science* 103 (1946): 612.

LAURENCE D. SMITH

HOLT, Hamilton Bowen (19 Aug. 1872–26 Apr. 1951), editor, reformer, and college president, was born in Brooklyn, New York, the son of George Chandler Holt, an attorney and judge, and Mary Louisa Bowen. Holt grew up in Spuyten Duyvil, New York, attending several private schools and graduating from Columbia Grammar School in 1890. After receiving his A.B. from Yale in 1894, he studied sociology and economics for three years at Columbia University. In 1899 he married Alexina Crawford Smith; they had four children. In his prime Holt was a large, broad-shouldered man who possessed a warm personality and great energy.

While a graduate student Holt began work on the *Independent*, which was founded by his maternal grandfather, Henry Chandler Bowen, and one of the nation's leading weekly magazines. In 1897 he became managing editor. In 1912 he bought the journal from Bowen, becoming editor in chief as well. He transformed the *Independent*, originally a Congregationalist publication, into a general reformist journal that was not only in the vanguard of the Progressive movement but the leading internationalist journal in the United States. The journal was prosperous enough to purchase several other periodicals, including the *Chautauquan*, *Harper's Weekly*, and the *Countryside Magazine*.

By 1917, however, the *Independent* was losing money, as advertising was failing to keep up with circulation. Furthermore, Holt's many outside involvements pulled him away from editorial responsibilities. In 1914 he was involved in 139 different organizations. Within six years Holt felt forced to enlist articles from government officials and to accept tobacco advertising and paid notices designed as articles, and in 1921 he merged his journal with the *Weekly Review*, a far more conservative enterprise. Holt relinquished the editorship, while remaining as consulting editor until May 1922.

Holt was deeply involved in contemporary reform movements. While a student at Columbia, he had worked in its University Settlement. He was president of the Maxwell House Settlement in Brooklyn. In 1909 he signed the original call for the meeting that founded the National Association for the Advancement of Colored People. He sat on the executive committee of the National Civic Federation and on the council of the American Association for Labor Legislation. From 1910 to 1916 he was a judge of the Board of Arbitration under the Protocol of Peace of the ladies' garment industry, serving alongside Louis D. Brandeis, A. Lincoln Filene, and Morris Hillquit. In an effort to fight machine politics, in 1907 he became president of the New York State Initiative and Referendum League.

Other Holt causes included the direct primary, woman suffrage, and public ownership of natural monopolies, including the railroads, the telegraph, and cable lines.

From 1903 on, Holt was the quintessential internationalist, and until 1925 few Americans worked harder to advance some form of union among the world's nations. Originally a strong nationalist, he was converted by Hayne Davis, a young lawyer, to the idea of a world federation modeled on the U.S. Constitution. He was a perennial at the Lake Mohonk Conference on International Arbitration. In 1907 he attended the Second Hague Peace Conference as an observer for the *Independent*. Two years later he was elected president of the World Federation League, a group that gained passage of a congressional resolution calling for a feasibility study centering on combining the world's navies into an international police force. Theodore Roosevelt's speech accepting the Nobel Peace Prize in 1910 was heavily based upon a Holt editorial. In 1911, as a director of the Peace Society of the City of New York, Holt led in its advocacy of world federation. That same year his presidential address to the Third American Peace Congress in Baltimore was a landmark in internationalist thought, stressing a world court and assembly. Holt was instrumental in the establishment of the Carnegie Endowment for International Peace in 1910. He served as director of the World Peace Foundation from 1911 to 1914 and trustee of the Church Peace Union from 1914 to 1951. Believing that the Allies were fighting in a righteous cause, he chaired the National Committee on the Churches and the Moral Aims of the War in 1918. He was also a founder of the Italy America Society, the Friends of Belgium, and the Netherlands America Foundation and president of the American Scandinavian Foundation (1921) and the Greek America Society (1921–1924).

When World War I broke out, Holt had first favored mediation by neutral powers. To advance this cause, he assumed the presidency of the National Peace Federation and the permanent chairmanship of the American Neutral Conference Committee. He resigned from such groups, however, in 1916 to give his uncompromising support to the League to Enforce Peace (LEP), a group that called for an international body possessing coercive power. Vice chairman of its executive committee, he lectured continually on its behalf. The LEP itself was prompted by a Holt editorial published in the *Independent* on 24 September 1914. In 1919 he represented the LEP at the Paris Peace Conference, and upon his return he threw himself into U.S. ratification of the League Covenant.

In the election of 1920 Holt headed a group of 118 eminent Republicans who endorsed the Democratic presidential nominee, James M. Cox, on the League issue. A year later Holt directed the campaign to establish the Woodrow Wilson Foundation, which centered on awarding a peace prize, and he became its first executive director. In 1922 Holt chaired the organizing team for the League of Nations Non-Partisan Committee (later the League of Nations Association). Serving on both its council and executive committee, he devoted nearly all his time to the society. In a special election held in December 1924, he ran unsuccessfully on the Connecticut Democratic ticket for the U.S. Senate.

From 1925 to 1941 Holt was president of Rollins College in Winter Park, Florida. A radical educational innovator with a flair for publicity, he ended grades, lectures, recitations, and required courses while pushing two-hour conferences, self-directed study, and comprehensive examinations. His innovations had mixed success, and by 1942 many of his plans were abandoned. Although he raised several million dollars and built a stately campus, limited funds hindered the fulfillment of his vision. In 1940 he chaired the Florida Committee to Defend America by Aiding the Allies. Upon retirement he returned to his summer home in Woodstock, Connecticut. He died in Pomfret, Connecticut.

• The Holt papers are at Rollins College. Holt wrote two books: *Commercialism and Journalism* (1909) and *The Life Stories of Undistinguished Americans, as Told by Themselves* (1906). Warren F. Kuehl wrote the definitive biography, *Hamilton Holt: Journalist, Internationalist, Educator* (1960). For focus on Holt's leadership in internationalism, see David L. Hitchins, "Peace, World Organization and the Editorial Philosophy of Hamilton Holt and *The Independent Magazine, 1899–1921*" (Ph.D. diss., Univ. of Georgia, 1968), and Sondra Herman, *Eleven Against War: Studies in American Internationalist Thought, 1898–1921* (1969). For a wider context to Holt's activities, see Ruhl J. Bartlett, *The League to Enforce Peace* (1944); Warren F. Kuehl, "The World Federation League: A Neglected Chapter in the History of a Movement," *World Affairs Quarterly* 30 (1960): 349–64; Kuehl, *Seeking World Order: The United States and International Organization to 1920* (1969); C. Roland Marchand, *The American Peace Movement and Social Reform, 1898–1918* (1972); and David S. Patterson, *Towards a Warless World: The Travail of the American Peace Movement, 1887–1914* (1976). Kuehl also contributed "A Bibliography of the Writings of Hamilton Holt," Rollins College, *Bulletin* (Sept. 1959). An obituary is in the *New York Times*, 27 Apr. 1951.

JUSTUS D. DOENECKE

HOLT, Henry (3 Jan. 1840–13 Feb. 1926), book publisher, was born in Baltimore, Maryland, the son of Daniel Holt, an oyster dealer, and Ann Eve Siebold. Henry was able to read at the age of three and attended a dame school at the age of four. He began his education at General Prosser's school in New Haven at the age of six. At eight he was studying Latin and at eleven took a prize in Greek. He remained at General Prosser's school, with short intervals at home in Baltimore, until he entered Yale with the class of 1861. At Yale Holt objected to the Puritan atmosphere and compulsory chapel attendance. During his freshman year, he was one of a half-dozen students not converted in a religious revival. He and a classmate, the future poet Edward Rowland Sill, "despised and hated the dogmas around us, and were sadly put to find faith in

anything." His intellectual unrest and lack of application to his studies resulted in his having to repeat the sophomore year.

Holt married Mary Florence West in 1863 and discovered that his "patrimony was not equal to matrimony"; they had six children. He wanted to devote himself to literature, but fearing the precarious life of a writer, he enrolled in the Columbia University School of Law, graduating in 1864. He began to think of publishing worthwhile books as a suitable profession. The year before law school graduation, Holt, with George Palmer Putnam, issued a sumptuous edition of Washington Irving's *The Sketch Book* and *The Rebellion Record*. While waiting in his law office for clients who never came, he translated Edmond About's *L'Homme à l'oreille cassée* ("The man with the broken ear") from the French. He called in Frederick Leypoldt, a minor publisher of good reputation, to publish his book. Leypoldt demurred but offered Holt an assistantship in his firm. Eventually Holt invested $6,000 of his own money, inherited from his father, and became a partner in the new publishing firm of Leypoldt and Holt, which opened in 1866.

Leypoldt and Holt was the first American firm to concentrate on publishing exclusively, leaving the printing and retailing to others. Leypoldt, born in Germany, had been a clerk in a Philadelphia bookstore until he opened his own store. He specialized in French and German importations and became the American agent for the Tauchnitz edition of British authors. The firm of Leypoldt and Holt published translations of the works of such European authors as George Sand, Ivan Turgenev, and Heinrich Heine as well as uniform editions of Thackeray and Kingsley.

In 1870 the firm bought out a publisher of French, German, and Italian dictionaries. Leypoldt and Holt then added grammar texts in foreign languages to its list of books. These were widely used and adopted by Harvard, Yale, and other colleges. After Leypoldt's retirement and that of another partner in 1873, the firm became Henry Holt and Company and continued as a major publisher of school and college texts. Hippolyte Taine's *History of English Literature* became Holt's first important business success; 7,000 sets sold in three years, and it continued to be in print in various editions, until the end of the century.

Holt's major interest, however, was in the publication of "trade" books. He was indefatigable in soliciting authors, personally editing their works and supervising production and sales. Among the leading authors he published were Henry Adams, John Buchan, John Dewey, John Fiske (1842–1901), Paul Leicester Ford, Thomas Hardy, William James, Jerome K. Jerome, Fanny Kemble, John Stuart Mill, Lewis H. Morgan, Simon Newcomb, John Addington Symonds, and H. G. Wells. New authors added after 1890 were William Rose Benét, Dorothy Canfield, Benedetto Croce, Robert Frost, A. E. Houseman, Harold Laski, Walter Lippmann, Romain Rolland, Preserved Smith, St. John Ervine, Leon Trotsky, and Louis Untermeyer. Although the publication of some of these authors was not profitable, their works contributed to Holt's reputation.

Before the passage of the International Copyright Law of 1891, many publishers rushed to publish the works of foreign authors, especially English writers, in cheap editions without paying royalties. Holt always paid. He maintained that publishing was a profession. He valiantly fought, sometimes in vain, to have a "courtesy of the trade" principle whereby the publisher who first announced the publication of a foreign book had priority in it.

In his efforts to enlarge the reading public for books he deemed worthy, in 1872 Holt launched his Leisure Hour series, which consisted largely of novels; attractive in appearance, they cost $1 each. The series continued to be successful even after the price was raised to $1.25. By 1889 the series had over 100 titles and, by 1880, over 200. Thomas Hardy's *Far From the Madding Crowd* reached sales of over 7,000 copies. The *New York Tribune* on 3 March 1877 called the series "one of the most popular series in the higher class of cheap literature." Holt published seven volumes of plays by Shakespeare and the novels of Robert Louis Stevenson as well as translations of French, German, Russian, and Scandinavian novels.

In an effort to compete with "pirates," who published books for as little as ten cents a copy, Holt issued a Leisure Moment series that included many of the titles of the Leisure Hour series at 20 to 35 cents a copy. Some 100 titles were available by 1888. The Leisure Season series, launched in 1886, was less successful; the series' few books had flexible bindings and sold for 50 cents a copy. English novels were less readily available after the 1891 copyright law passed, and both the Leisure Hour and Leisure Moment series were abandoned. Nevertheless, by publishing inexpensive editions of books of quality, Holt greatly expanded the reading public and its exposure to, and acceptance of, fine literature.

One of Holt's most innovative ideas was the creation of the American Science series. Comprising fourteen volumes, it presented the writings of leading American scientists, including *Psychology* by William James. Because *Psychology* was too expensive and bulky for class use, James prepared the *Briefer Course*, which sold over 47,000 copies in its first ten years in print.

Although he continued to make all major decisions in the firm, Holt began to devote part of his time, beginning in the 1880s, to his own writing. In the March 1888 issue of *The Forum* he denounced literary piracy. In 1901 he wrote a book entitled *Talks on Civics*. In 1892 Macmillan published his lengthy novel of over 700 pages, *Calmire*, anonymously; it was followed in 1905 by *Sturmsee: Man and Man*, which incorporated his philosophical ideas. In 1919 he brought out a two-volume work entitled *The Cosmic Relations and Immortality*. His last volume, published in 1923, *Garrulities of an Octogenarian*, contained autobiographical material.

Holt's first wife died in 1879. He married Florence Taber in 1886. Holt died in his home in New York City. He left an estate of over $1 million and bequeathed his library on psychic research to the Authors Club with a fund for its maintenance.

• Holt's papers, including business correspondence, are in the Princeton University Library; company records are deposited in the offices of Holt, Rinehart and Winston in New York City. An important source is Charles A. Madison, *The Owl among Colophons: Henry Holt as Publisher and Editor* (1966). See also David S. Edelstein, "Henry Holt and Company," in *Publishers for Mass Entertainment in Nineteenth Century America*, ed. Madeleine B. Stern (1980). Also of interest are "The Publishing Reminiscences of Mr. Henry Holt," *Publisher's Weekly*, 10 Feb. 1910, and "The Bookmakers: Reminiscences and Contemporary Sketches of American Publishers," *New York Evening Post*, 23 Dec. 1875. An obituary and related articles are in the *New York Times*, 14–16 and 24 Feb. 1926.

DAVID S. EDELSTEIN

HOLT, John (1721?–30 Jan. 1784), printer and journalist, was born in Williamsburg, Virginia (parents unknown). After receiving a good education, he became a respectable merchant. In 1749 he married Elizabeth Hunter. In December 1752 he was elected mayor of Williamsburg. Holt's mercantile enterprises faltered, and his wife's brother, William Hunter, printer and deputy postmaster general, taught Holt the rudiments of the printing trade. Hunter recommended him to James Parker (1714–1770) and helped secure an additional recommendation from Benjamin Franklin (1706–1790), and Parker agreed to help Holt learn the printing business. Holt relocated from Virginia to Parker's Woodbridge, New Jersey, printing office. Soon, Parker offered the management of his New Haven printing house to Holt, who declined the position. Once Parker got the *Connecticut Gazette* underway in April 1755, however, Holt recognized that the place would be profitable and convinced Parker to take him on as junior partner. On 13 December 1755 Holt became the *Connecticut Gazette*'s editor while Parker ran a New York press. Holt also sold books and served as New Haven postmaster from 1755 to 1760. He enthusiastically edited the newspaper but took a lackadaisical attitude toward his duties as postmaster and bookseller. Holt mismanaged the business and quickly fell into debt to Parker, the post office, and several British booksellers.

In early 1760 Parker asked Holt to relocate to New York and run his printing operation there. Holt agreed and began editing *Parker's New-York Gazette, or Weekly Post-Boy* on 31 July 1760. When Parker became disgruntled with Holt's shoddy bookkeeping and his chronic inability to pay his bills, Holt insisted on a simplified financial arrangement. He would lease Parker's New York printing materials for four years at a flat rate. Parker agreed, and on 6 May 1762 Holt took over the *New-York Gazette* on his own. Starting in 1765, Holt's opposition to the Stamp Act and his staunch support of the colonial cause ingratiated him with members of the proindependence group, the Sons of Liberty. Because of his southern connections and because the Virginia authorities controlled the 1765 *Virginia Gazette*, Holt printed the Virginia radicals' reactions to the Stamp Act, including Patrick Henry's Stamp Act resolves of July 1765. When Holt's lease expired in 1766, Parker came to New York to reclaim his printing outfit and found that "In the present unhappy Times, when the Sons of Liberty carry all before them, Mr. Holt has gained very great Popularity, and being back'd by them, seems to have a Run of Business" (Parker to Franklin, 6 May 1766). When Holt's numerous debts brought him close to arrest, the Sons of Liberty subsidized his business to keep him out of jail.

Under the impression that Parker was going to resume publication of the *New-York Gazette* himself, Holt gave up the *Gazette* title and began calling his paper the *New-York Journal, or General Advertiser*. In the first issue (29 May 1766), Holt announced that he would continue to support the cause of liberty. When Parker did not immediately resume the *Gazette*, Holt reclaimed the title on 5 June 1766. With the 16 October 1766 issue, Parker himself began publishing the *New-York Gazette*. Holt returned to using the title *New-York Journal, or General Advertiser*. Holt extended his influence in 1775 by establishing a press in Norfolk, Virginia, under the management of his son, John Hunter Holt, who began publishing the *Virginia Gazette, or The Norfolk Intelligencer*. With his father's Whiggish tendencies, however, young Holt was soon put out of business, and his press was seized by the British.

Holt's newspaper as well as his separate publications continued to foment controversy. His first political publication was a reprint of Daniel Dulany's (1722–1797) treatise denying Parliament's right to tax the colonists, *Considerations of the Propriety of Imposing Taxes in the British Colonies* (1765). Holt also printed many broadsides from the Sons of Liberty. Other important publications include William Hicks's *Nature and Extent of Parliamentary Power* (1768); Stephen Sayre's *Englishman Deceived* (1768); John Dickinson's (1732–1808) *Letters from a Farmer in Pennsylvania* (1768); a reprint of the seminal document concerning the freedom of the press, *A Brief Narrative of the Case and Trial of John Peter Zenger* (1770); Granville Sharp's *Declaration of the People's Natural Right to a Share in the Legislature* (1774); and Robert Ross's *Sermon, in Which the Union of the Colonies Is Considered and Recommended* (1776). Based on his total number of publications and the number of his pamphlets that were reprinted throughout the colonies, Holt ranks among the most important colonial American printers before the revolutionary war.

On 29 August 1776 British occupation forced Holt to discontinue his *New-York Journal*. During the summer of 1777 New York's Provincial Congress awarded Holt the Newark press of Loyalist printer Hugh Gaine and made Holt the official New York printer, replacing Samuel Loudon. Holt established a printing operation at Kingston and from 7 July to 13 October 1777 published the *New-York Journal* there.

When the British forces, as Holt would write, "needlessly and maliciously burnt and destroyed that little defenseless town," Holt escaped, saving only the Gaine types, his paper stock, and his account books. Holt removed to Poughkeepsie and on 11 May 1778 issued the first number of the Poughkeepsie *New-York Journal*. Paper shortages and lack of financial support sometimes forced him to suspend the newspaper. By late 1783 Holt had returned to New York City, and on 22 November 1783 he established the *Independent New-York Gazette*. After Holt's death (in New York), his wife ably continued the newspaper and the printing business until her death four years later.

Men who had business associations with Holt held him in contempt for slipshod bookkeeping and blatant disregard of financial responsibilities, but after his death such pecuniary concerns were quickly forgotten. Instead, Holt is remembered for his articulate remarks within the pages of the *New-York Journal* and his unwavering support of the colonial cause. An obituary in the *New-York Gazetteer, and Country Journal* noted that Holt's "indefatigable endeavours to serve the Whig interest . . . justly entitled him to the veneration and esteem of every virtuous son of Columbia."

• Some of Holt's letters survive at the New York Public Library and the New-York Historical Society. Layton Barnes Murphy, "John Holt, Patriot Printer and Publisher" (Ph.D. diss., Univ. of Michigan, 1965), includes a bibliography of Holt's imprints. Additional imprint information can be found in R. W. G. Vail, "A Patriotic Pair of Peripatetic Printers: The Up-State Imprints of John Holt and Samuel Loudon 1776–1783," in *Essays Honoring Lawrence C. Wroth* (1951), and Roger P. Bristol, *Supplement to Charles Evans' American Bibliography* (1970). Holt's newspapers are discussed in Clarence S. Brigham, *History and Bibliography of American Newspapers 1690–1820* (1947). The vicissitudes of Holt's early career can be traced in James Parker's numerous letters in *The Papers of Benjamin Franklin* (1959–). Other sources include Isaiah Thomas, *The History of Printing in America*, ed. Marcus A. McCorison (1970); Victor Hugo Paltsits, "John Holt—Printer and Postmaster: Some Facts and Documents Relating to His Career," *Bulletin of the New York Public Library* 24 (1920): 483–99; Beverly McAnear, "James Parker versus John Holt," *New Jersey Historical Society Proceedings* 59 (1941); Arthur M. Schlesinger, *Prelude to Independence: The Newspaper War on Britain 1764–1776* (1958); and G. Thomas Tanselle, "Some Statistics on American Printing, 1764–1783," in *The Press and the American Revolution*, ed. Bernard Bailyn and John B. Hench (1980).

KEVIN J. HAYES

HOLT, Joseph (6 Jan. 1807–1 Aug. 1894), jurist, secretary of war, and postmaster general, was born near Hardinsburg, Kentucky, the son of John Holt, an attorney, and Eleanor Stephens. Educated at St. Joseph's College in Bardstown and Centre College in Danville, Holt subsequently read law in Lexington. In 1828 he established a practice in Elizabethtown, Kentucky, where he was briefly in partnership with Congressman Ben Hardin. In 1832 Holt moved to Louisville, serving for a short time as assistant editor of the Louisville *Advertiser* and as commonwealth's attorney between 1833 and 1835. He became active in Democratic politics, and his skills as an orator drew particular attention at the party's national convention in 1835.

At about this time Holt moved to Port Gibson, Mississippi. He subsequently relocated to Vicksburg, where he developed a lucrative legal practice. In 1842 he returned to Louisville, having contracted tuberculosis, which had killed his wife, Mary Harrison. He later married Margaret Wickliffe, who died in 1860. Wealthy enough to retire from the law, he traveled in Europe, Africa, and the Middle East between 1848 and 1851.

Holt continued, however, to put in time as a Democratic orator. His work in the party's presidential campaigns of 1852 and 1856 earned him a claim to preferment. He moved to Washington, D.C., shortly after the inauguration of James Buchanan and in September 1857 was named commissioner of patents. He served in this capacity for a year and a half before being elevated to postmaster general. A cabinet colleague (who was later a bitter foe) claimed to have recommended Holt for this post after Buchanan expressed his desire for "a strong, resolute man, with none of the milk of human kindness in his veins" (Auchampaugh, p. 80). Trying to cut the post office's ballooning expenses, he trimmed service, discontinued routes, and scrapped overgenerous contracts with private carriers, but to little avail. Postmaster Holt supported states in their banning of abolitionist material from the mail. In other ways as well there was little at this point that would distinguish Holt from many other southern Democrats. He endorsed the *Dred Scott* decision, chided northern states for passing personal liberty laws, discountenanced any forcible federal attempt to keep southern states in the Union, and supported John Breckinridge's presidential bid in 1860.

Holt's unionism, however, grew considerably more ardent in the wake of Abraham Lincoln's presidential victory. As secession became reality, Holt became, along with Jeremiah Black and Edwin Stanton, one of the stalwart Union men in the lame-duck administration, pressing Buchanan to be resolute, even as other cabinet members equivocated or cast their lot with the South. In December 1860 Secretary of War John Floyd decamped, and Holt was appointed in his stead. Determined to keep hold of what the federal government had retained of its property in the South while avoiding outright provocation, Holt made plain to Robert Anderson, Fort Sumter's commander, that reinforcements would be sent, but only upon Anderson's request. Holt even prepared a force to deliver the men and supplies, but Anderson made no such demand of him. Holt also removed P. G. T. Beauregard, whose secessionist leanings were unmistakable, from his position as superintendent of West Point and bolstered Washington's defenses. After briefing the incoming Lincoln administration, Holt once again took to the stump, denouncing secession in speeches around the nation, most notably in Kentucky, where in July he lambasted his home state's pretensions to neutrality. If something of a late bloomer in his enthusiasm for "coercion," he came to embrace not only a war for the Union but one for freedom. He later endorsed the Emancipation Proclamation and the enlistment of black troops.

Holt's efforts for the Union and his closeness to Stanton, who became secretary of war in 1862, recommended him again for official position. After serving on commissions to examine war contracts, he in September 1862 was named judge advocate general of the army, charged with superintending the Union's system of military justice. A formal Bureau of Military Justice, with Holt at its head, came into being in June 1864. He oversaw proceedings against soldiers, such as the court-martial of Fitz-John Porter, and the work of military tribunals in occupied portions of the Confederacy and areas where martial law had been declared. He did much to ensure that the procedures and decisions of such courts were uniform and to guarantee opportunities to appeal their verdicts. Holt's role in the trial of northern and Border State civilians suspected of disloyal activities (including interfering with enlistment) proved more controversial. He allowed military commissions to try citizens not liable to court-martial, rather than necessarily leaving the proceedings to civil courts. In the case of Clement Vallandigham, the best known of the midwestern "Copperheads" tried by military court, the Supreme Court in 1864 embraced the argument Holt had made in the government's brief that it did not possess the authority to review decisions of the military courts. Two years later, however, the Court overturned another prominent example of these commissions' work, ruling in *Ex Parte Milligan* that the military had no business trying civilians outside war zones or where the civil courts were open. Holt's contemporaries and subsequent scholars have criticized as overdrawn his much publicized 1864 report on secret Copperhead societies, in which he asserted that hundreds of thousands of traitors in the northern and Border States had organized underground military bodies that took their orders from Richmond but were tied also to prominent northern Democrats. However sincere the judge advocate general may have been in his outsized claims, his report was, at the very least, conveniently timed, providing fodder for the Republican press immediately preceding hard-fought state and national elections.

The work of the military commissions did not end with Appomattox, and it is in their postwar operation that Holt's zeal most clearly got the better of his judgment. He oversaw the military trial of Henry Wirz, the commandant of the Confederate prison at Andersonville; headed the investigation of Lincoln's assassination, and prosecuted those charged in the assassination before a commission. Convinced that the Confederate leadership, especially Jefferson Davis, was responsible for the murder, Holt went to unwholesome lengths to prove it, soliciting testimony from witnesses whose credibility his own subordinates questioned. Enemies even charged him with buying the testimony he desired. Holt refused to introduce into evidence John Wilkes Booth's diary, admitting later that it contained no evidence of a broader assassination conspiracy. But while Holt never made a convincing case against Confederate leaders, he did secure the conviction not only of several men clearly involved in Booth's murder plot but also a number of people whose roles were considerably more tangential and less clear-cut. The most enduring controversy in this regard involved the execution of Mary Surratt. Holt claimed that President Andrew Johnson had seen and disregarded a petition from members of the military commission asking that Surratt's life be spared. Johnson and his supporters denied this, and some claimed Holt actually withheld the petition from the president. Despite Holt's tendency to belabor controversies in print, he stayed on as judge advocate general until 1875. He spent his last years in Washington, D.C., and died there, having gone blind.

• Collections of Holt's papers are at the Library of Congress, Washington, D.C., and the Henry E. Huntington Library, San Marino, Calif. Official correspondence is at the National Archives in the Records of the Office of the Postmaster General (RG 28), Records of the Office of the Secretary of War (RG 107), and Records of the Office of the Judge Advocate General (Army) (RG 153). Some of this correspondence is reprinted in *The War of the Rebellion: A Compilation of the Official Records of the Union and Confederate Armies* (128 vols., 1880–1901). Holt's report on secret societies is in *The War of the Rebellion*, ser. 2, vol. 7, pp. 930–53. See also *Digest of the Opinions of the Judge Advocate General of the Army* (1865). Holt's publications include *The Fallacy of Neutrality: An Address by the Hon. Joseph Holt, to the People of Kentucky, Delivered at Louisville, July 13th, 1861* (1861) and *Vindication of Judge Advocate General Holt from the Foul Slanders of Traitors, Confessed Perjurers and Suborners, Acting in the Interest of Jefferson Davis* (1866). Published biographical material is scarce, but consult Mary B. Allen, "Joseph Holt, Judge Advocate General, 1862–1875" (Ph.D. diss., Univ. of Chicago, 1927). On various aspects of Holt's career, see James Bennett, "Joseph Holt: Retrenchment and Reform in the Post Office Department, 1859–1860," *Filson Club Historical Quarterly* 49 (1975): 309–22; Philip Auchampaugh, *James Buchanan and His Cabinet on the Eve of Secession* (1926); Harold Hyman, *A More Perfect Union: The Impact of the Civil War and Reconstruction on the Constitution* (1973); Frank Klement, *Dark Lanterns: Secret Political Societies, Conspiracies, and Treason Trials in the Civil War* (1984); and William Hanchett, *The Lincoln Murder Conspiracies* (1983).

PATRICK G. WILLIAMS

HOLT, Luther Emmett (4 Mar. 1855–14 Jan. 1924), pediatrician and medical educator, was born in Webster, New York, near Rochester, the son of Horace Holt and Sabrah Amelia Curtice, farmers. Educated at Webster Academy and Marion Academy, he entered the University of Rochester, then a small Baptist university, at the age of sixteen and graduated in 1875 seventh in his class. Following graduation Holt taught for a year at the Riverside Institute in Wellsville, New York. During this time he read independently in anatomy and physiology and decided to pursue a career in medicine. His earnings from teaching and contributions from his parents allowed him to enter the University of Buffalo Medical College in 1876. Within a

year he began a student internship at the newly established Hospital for the Relief of the Ruptured and Crippled in New York City, under the noted physician and orthopedic surgeon Virgil Pendleton Gibney. During his internship he also continued his medical education at the College of Physicians and Surgeons. In 1880 he received his M.D. among the top ten of his class; he was awarded his choice of an internship at one of four leading hospitals. He chose Bellevue Hospital, where he worked for eighteen months in the bacteriology laboratory of William Henry Welch. From his internships, Holt acquired two basic building blocks for a highly successful career: under Gibney, his work with children inspired him to later specialize in pediatrics; and under Welch, he learned the value of scientific research in medical advances. In 1881, with physician Charles M. Cauldwell, Holt opened a general practice that he would later devote exclusively to the care of children. Shortly after opening his practice, in a Sunday school class he taught at the Fifth Avenue Baptist Church, he met Linda F. Mairs. They married in 1886 and later had five children.

During the 1880s and 1890s Holt established his reputation as a leader in pediatrics through his private practice and many associations with institutions devoted to the care of children. He was on the staff of the Northwestern Dispensary; an attending physician to the Infants' Hospital on Randall Island; a visiting physician to both the Foundling Hospital and the Nursery and Child's Hospital (1895–1899); and consulting physician to the Hospital for the Ruptured and Crippled, the New York Orthopedic Hospital, and the Lying-In Hospital. Two appointments were particularly influential both in his career and in the birth of pediatrics as a medical specialty: as physician at the county branch of the New York Infant Asylum at Mount Vernon (1885–1892) and as physician in chief at the Babies' Hospital (1888–1924), the first hospital in the United States devoted solely to the care of infants under age three. At both institutions Holt worked with many children suffering from diseases that he carefully documented and researched, leading to a series of publications on the diseases of children. Holt's studies received wide acclaim for their basis in sound clinical and pathological observations. When John M. Keating organized the first attempt at an American pediatrics text, *The Cyclopedia of Diseases of Children* (1890), one of its best articles was Holt's on diarrheal diseases of children.

A year after founding the Babies' Hospital, physicians Sarah J. McNutt and Julia G. McNutt asked Holt to become physician in chief and to help restore the hospital's financial stability. He accepted, and in this capacity he built the struggling hospital into one of the largest and most important American institutions for the care of infants. He obtained secure funding by organizing a prestigious board of directors and began traditions of clinical research and training for children's nurses. To assist in the nurses' training, in 1893 Holt authored a short booklet on the care of children that he expanded the following year under the title *The*

Care and Feeding of Children: A Catechism for the Use of Mothers and Children's Nurses. His book became the most widely used child care manual for educated mothers in the first half of the twentieth century, superseded only by Benjamin Spock's manual in the 1960s. During Holt's lifetime the book went through seventy-five printings, twelve revisions, and several translations. He also authored *The Diseases of Infancy and Childhood* (1897), based on his extensive clinical studies at the Babies' Hospital; it was the authoritative pediatric textbook for several decades.

While engaged in clinical work, Holt held various teaching positions. In 1891 he succeeded his former teacher Gibney as professor of diseases of infants and children at the New York Hospital and Polyclinic. He retired from this post in 1901 to accept the chair of Carpentier Professor of the Diseases of Children at the College of Physicians and Surgeons, Columbia University, a post that he held for twenty years. In the final years of his life he was visiting Lane Lecturer at Stanford University. He expanded his lecture series into his third major work, *Food, Health, and Growth: A Discussion of the Nutrition of Children* (1922).

By the 1890s John D. Rockefeller, also a member of the Fifth Street Baptist Church, wished to fund research in science and medicine, and Holt played a role in realizing this dream. During a conversation on a train ride, Holt inspired Rockefeller's son, John, Jr., to open a facility for medical research. Holt sat on the founding committee, and in 1906 the Rockefeller Institute opened, quickly emerging as a preeminent American medical research institution. Holt sat on the board of directors, served as secretary, and influenced the selection of the institute's research programs.

In addition to his teaching and research activities, Holt played instrumental roles in public health education and reform. In 1909 he was a prime mover in organizing the Association for the Prevention of Infant Mortality (later renamed the American Child Hygiene Association). The association served as a clearinghouse for public information on prenatal and infant child care. He also helped to establish regulations for improvement in the quality of New York City's milk supply: he steered the Rockefeller Institute to study the state of milk contamination in the city's tenements, and he helped to secure the city's first certified milk dairy and infant-formula laboratory, a branch of the Walker-Gordon Laboratory in Boston. Holt also served on the board of directors of the Henry Street Settlement, working closely with Lillian D. Wald, who organized a nurse's service there.

During World War I concern grew over the number of draftees who failed physical examinations, and a survey conducted by the Association for the Improvement of Conditions of the Poor in New York City focused this concern on child health. In response, seven physicians, including Holt, formed the Committee of Wartime Problems in Childhood of the New York Academy of Medicine. In February 1918, at a conference in Atlantic City, U.S. Secretary of the Interior Franklin K. Lane suggested that the committee be de-veloped into a national organization and that Holt be its chair. With Holt's acceptance and Sally Lucas-Jean's appointment as director, the Child Health Organization (CHO) was established in March 1918. The organization worked to educate the public in child health, tailoring its materials to appeal directly to children. On a limited budget, the CHO sent posters to schools and hired a clown, known as Cho-Cho, to spread the message of good hygiene habits. The CHO also addressed the public at large through articles authored by scientific experts (including Holt) that appeared in newspapers and magazines. The CHO and its chair quickly gained international recognition. As a result, in 1919 the Red Cross invited Holt to be a delegate to its international conference at Cannes; during the conference, the delegates formed the League of Red Cross Societies and adopted Holt's proposals for an international child welfare program, the Junior Red Cross. This program had as its aims the health education of school children and fundraising for needy children throughout the world. By 1923, pressured financially and with Holt facilitating negotiations, the CHO merged with the American Child Hygiene Association, becoming the American Child Health Association, with Herbert Hoover as president and Holt as vice president.

At the time of Holt's entry into medicine, pediatrics had just begun to emerge as its own medical specialty. Holt was one of the first U.S. physicians to devote his practice entirely to the care of children, and he helped establish several American pediatric professional organs. He was a founding editor of the first two U.S. journals devoted to pediatrics, *Archives of Pediatrics* (founded in 1884) and *American Journal of Diseases of Children* (founded in 1911). He was also among the founding members of the American Society of Pediatrics when it first met in 1888. He later served twice as president of the society, in 1896 and 1923. He was a member of the Association of American Physicians, the Clinical Society, the New York County Medical Society, and the Pathological Society, and he was a trustee of the New York Academy of Medicine and the University of Rochester.

In professional meetings and in his clinics, lectures, and writings, Holt taught a scientific approach both in the practice of pediatric medicine and in motherhood. As both professional pediatrician and public-health reformer, Holt actively worked to educate both mothers and school-aged children in child care, making it as much a public concern as it was a medical specialty. In his public roles as educator, author, and public-health reformer, he became the single most visible American authority on child health.

Away from his professional duties, Holt played golf and hosted dinner parties. But he devoted the greatest part of his life to his profession, to the very end. In 1923 he traveled to Union College in Peking, China, as a visiting lecturer and medical consultant under the Rockefeller Institute's auspices. He had just completed his lecture series when he suffered a heart attack and died.

• Correspondence by Holt is contained in several archives: Special Collections of the College of Physicians and Surgeons; the Rockefeller Foundation Archives, Rockefeller Family Archives, and Laura Spelman Rockefeller Memorial Archives at the Rockefeller Archive Center, North Tarrytown, N.Y.; the Rockefeller University Archives, New York City; the William H. Welch Papers, Welch Medical Library, Johns Hopkins University; the School of Medicine at the University of Buffalo; and a private collection in possession of Holt's grandson Arnold Holt. Holt's numerous research publications are partially listed in John Shrady, *The College of Physicians and Surgeons, New York, and Its Founders, Officers, Instructors, Benefactors, and Alumni: A History*, vol. 2 (1907), pp. 20–24; remaining publications are indexed in *Index Medicus*. The most important biographies are L. Emmett Holt, Jr., and R. L. Duffus, *L. Emmett Holt: Pioneer of a Children's Century* (1940); and Edwards A. Park and Howard H. Mason, "Luther Emmett Holt," in *Pediatric Profiles*, ed. Borden S. Veeder (1957). George W. Corner, *History of the Rockefeller Institute, 1901–1953: Origins and Growth* (1964), discusses Holt's involvement in the founding of the institute and his influence in its early medical research. Kathleen W. Jones discusses Holt's influence as adviser to mothers in "Sentiment and Science: The Late Nineteenth Century Pediatrician as Mother's Advisor," *Journal of Social History* 17 (1983): 79–96. Obituaries are in *Archives of Pediatrics* 41 (1924): 1–4; *Journal of the American Medical Association* 82, no. 4 (1924): 320; the *New York Times*, 15 Jan. 1924; and *American Journal of Diseases of Children* 27 (1924): 195–96.

DONALD L. OPITZ

HOLT, Rush Dew (19 June 1905–8 Feb. 1955), politician and journalist, was born in Weston, West Virginia, the son of Mathew S. Holt, a physician and politician, and Chilela Dew. He grew up in comfortable circumstances in a politically active and nonconformist family. His mother was the first woman graduate of Salem College in Salem, West Virginia. His father, an outspoken socialist, pacifist, and atheist, was twice elected mayor of Weston. A precocious child, Rush read at age three and completed high school at fourteen. He attended West Virginia University and graduated from Salem College with a bachelor's degree in 1924.

Between 1924 and 1930 he taught history and government at Salem and Glenville State colleges, coached secondary school athletics, and was a part-time sports writer and athletic league administrator. Elected to the West Virginia House of Delegates in 1930, he caused a stir by criticizing state officials' high salaries. After being reelected in 1932, he led dissident "progressive" or "liberal" Democrats against Governor Herman G. Kump's statehouse faction. He eventually achieved popularity by representing small business and local elites against outside interests, by attacking the "invisible government" of private utilities, and by investigating corporate political influence.

In 1934 Holt's youthful brass and opposition to the Kump faction gained him the support of U.S. senator Matthew M. Neely and the United Mine Workers of America. Due to their support and Democratic infighting, the 29-year-old Holt became the party's Senate nominee and, running as a prolabor liberal, defeat-ed the anti–New Deal Republican incumbent, Henry D. Hatfield, in the fall. His election was disputed on constitutional grounds because to satisfy the minimum age requirement for the Senate, Holt could not take his seat until June, over five months into his term. Once seated, however, he soon declared political independence, refusing to act as a freshman protégé to Neely. Like Senator Huey P. Long, whom he admired, Holt was not a party loyalist. A month after taking office he publicly criticized Neely's position on a Senate bill. In 1936, miffed over the distribution of Works Progress Administration patronage in West Virginia, he turned against those who had supported his election: Neely and the UMWA. He charged that "political parasites, political leeches, and political bloodsuckers" controlled the WPA, and he campaigned against Neely's reelection. His successful filibuster against passage of the 1936 Guffey-Vinson coal bill that was favored by the union led to his estrangement from the UMWA and industrial unionism. Refusing to endorse Franklin D. Roosevelt for reelection, in August 1936, just before a well-publicized meeting between Holt and GOP presidential candidate Alfred M. Landon, Holt gave the keynote address at the Cleveland convention of Father Charles E. Coughlin's fanatically anti–New Deal National Union for Social Justice.

After Roosevelt and Neely won by landslides, Democrats in the Senate repaid Holt's apostasy with the "silent treatment," denying him patronage and characterizing him as an immature ingrate and upstart. Their opposition soon rendered him ineffective in the Senate. But even though he suspected that his office had been burglarized, his mail opened, and his phone tapped, he continued to denounce the Democratic leadership.

In 1937 Holt completed his political conversion into a conservative New Deal foe. He spoke loudly against Roosevelt's court-packing plan in 1937 and Harry Hopkins's confirmation as secretary of commerce in 1938. He sought alliances with the dissident Progressive Miners of America and the conservative American Federation of Labor against the UMWA. Thus it was no surprise in 1940 when West Virginia big labor dumped Holt and backed little-known Harley M. Kilgore to replace him in the Senate. Kilgore won the Democratic primary, but in the election West Virginia's other Senate seat became vacant when Neely was elected governor. In a bizarre plot twist, outgoing governor Homer A. Holt appointed Rush Holt (his cousin) to take over Neely's unexpired term. The Senate, however, chose incoming governor Neely's appointee, Joseph Rosier, over Holt to fill the seat.

In 1941 Holt left the Senate, but not controversy, behind. Lecturing and writing were now his principal occupations. His support for isolationism and pacifism came naturally to him. He remembered vividly the abuse his family had suffered when his pacifist father opposed American involvement in World War I. Believing no foreign interests could be worth a war, Holt resisted each step on the United States' path toward World War II: conscription, military preparedness, aid to the Allies, and "neutrality patrol." In 1940 and 1941 on the stump and over the radio he promoted isolationism, sponsored by the America First Committee. Concurrently, he compiled volumes of his antiwar speeches, including one entitled "Who's Who among War Mongers," although they were never published. Holt anticipated conservative Republican, McCarthyera rhetoric when he warned against a conspiracy of the internationalists—"New Dealers, communists, anglophiles, international bankers, and all those individuals they can control." Holt flirted with far right political groups. Although he refused to address the white-supremacist Knights of the White Camellia, he did not reject their support. He also did not condemn the Nazis or distance himself from their American supporters.

In 1941 Holt married Helen Louise Froelich; they had two children and adopted a third. After Pearl Harbor ended his peace crusade, he returned to his native Weston. Thereafter he introduced an anti–big government newsletter, "The West Virginia Taxpayer," and wrote for newspapers and magazines. Beginning in 1942 Lewis County voters sent him to four consecutive terms in the state legislature, but he was never able to win higher office. Defeated in the 1948 Democratic Senate primary, Holt joined the Republicans in 1950 and was soon feuding with GOP leaders. As a Republican candidate, he lost bids for the House of Representatives (1950) and for state governor (1952). In 1954 he was again elected to the state legislature. He died of cancer in Bethesda, Maryland, while in office.

A rebel against the party system and the welfare state, Holt had a national career that was brief and filled with frustration. But, as he explained, "I believe in the things I say. I must say them . . . over and over again, or I could not live with myself " (*Charleston Gazette*, 9 Feb. 1955). His single Senate term and long state legislative career left no enduring legacy. His contribution was to democratic discourse; to publicly stand against the establishment and public opinion for his beliefs.

• Holt's papers are at West Virginia University. For a guide to his papers, see Thomas H. Coode and Agnes M. Riggs, "The Private Papers of West Virginia's 'Boy Senator,' Rush Dew Holt," *West Virginia History* 35 (July 1974): 296–318. The principal assessment of Holt is William E. Coffey, "Rush Dew Holt: The Boy Senator, 1905–1942" (Ph.D. diss., West Virginia Univ., 1970). Coffey's "Matthew S. Holt: A West Virginia Individualist," *West Virginia History* 39 (Jan.–Apr. 1978): 200–209, demonstrates the profound influence on Holt of his father. George Creel, "Youngest and Loudest," *Collier's*, 19 Dec. 1936, describes Holt's banishment from Democratic good graces. Paul F. Lutz, "The West Virginia Gubernatorial Election of 1952," *West Virginia History* 39 (Jan.–Apr. 1978): 210–35, contains much material on Holt. Obituaries are in the *Charleston Gazette*, 9 Feb. 1955, the *Weston Democrat*, 11 Feb. 1955, and the *New York Times*, 9 Feb. 1955.

CHARLES HOWARD MCCORMICK

HOLTEN, Samuel (9 June 1738–2 Jan. 1816), physician and public official, was born in Salem Village (now Danvers), Massachusetts, the son of Samuel Holten

and Hannah Gardner, farmers. Several sources claim that his parents intended to send the youth to college. According to these accounts, as he was tutored for entrance exams his health declined and his parents decided to fit him for a career that would not require collegiate education. Subsequently, at about seventeen years of age, he served an apprenticeship of about a year's duration with physician Jonathan Prince. By 1756 he seems to have started practicing medicine in Gloucester, where he married Mary Warner in March 1758; the couple had three children. Sometime in 1758 they moved to Danvers, where he may have entered a joint practice with his brother-in-law, Jonathan Prince, Jr. With the death of his partner in 1759, Holten became the town's only resident physician, yet his business was modest. Unfortunately, the records are rather ambiguous on whether or not he encountered stiff competition from already established practitioners in the area, or merely inclined toward another calling, politics. Nothing for certain is known about his medical practice, which may have ended entirely by 1775.

Following his initial election as selectman in 1761, and with increasing colonial opposition to British policies and their American administrators, Holten's political fortunes soared in Danvers, in Essex County, and throughout Massachusetts. In 1768 he was again reelected selectman, became moderator and clerk of the town meeting, and began the first of many terms as the Danvers representative to the General Assembly. That same year he joined the Sons of Liberty. He proved to be a very able politician during the Revolution.

In 1774, while holding several town offices, Holten began serving on committees of correspondence, in the Essex County Convention, and in the Provincial Congress. The following year he was appointed to the Committee of Safety and in 1778 became a Massachusetts delegate to the Continental Congress for two years. He served as a delegate to the state constitutional convention in 1780. He favored the Articles of Confederation and remained in its Congress for several years. He opposed revision of the Articles, as he opposed the Constitution at the state ratification convention in 1788. Holten's antifederalist position did not deny him future office. All along, Danvers voters had endorsed him. He served as town moderator from 1789 to 1790 and from 1796 to 1812; as town treasurer from 1789 to 1812; as judge of the Court of Common Pleas of Essex County from 1776 to 1808; as state senator in 1780–1782, 1784, 1786, 1789–1790; and as judge of probate for Essex County from 1796 to 1815. His last national office was as a Massachusetts representative to the Third Congress from 1793 to 1795.

While Holten was not the typical citizen, his medical practice reflects the experience of the average doctor of colonial and early national America. As an apprentice-trained doctor he was among the minority of Massachusetts doctors to have received even that much formal training. However, there are no records of him practicing medicine for most of his adult life;

medicine was a part-time occupation for many would-be doctors, who competed with amateurs and midwives. In his will, probated in 1816, Holten styled himself both as "physician" and "Esquire," and elsewhere "Doctor" and "Deacon." The inventory of his estate reveals that late in life he still possessed the equipment and drugs to make his own prescriptions, as well as a small medical library. Rather than a physician's skills, it was Holten's political power and demonstrable commitment to the republic that won for him in 1781 a founding membership in the Massachusetts Medical Society. Until his death in Danvers, he continued to support medical, agricultural, and humane societies, as well as the temperance movement.

• An accessible collection of correspondence is the Holten manuscripts at the Danvers Historical Society. His diary can be found in the *Historical Collections of the Danvers Historical Society*, vol. 3 (1915), vol. 7–8 (1919–1920), and vol. 10 (1922). Useful accounts placing him in historical context include Eric H. Christianson, "Medicine in New England," in *Medicine in the New World: New Spain, New France, and New England*, ed. Ronald L. Numbers (1987), and Philip Cash et al., eds., *Medicine in Colonial Massachusetts, 1620–1820* (1980).

ERIC HOWARD CHRISTIANSON

HOLTZ, Lou (11 Apr. 1893–22 Sept. 1980), vaudevillian and ethnic comedian, was born in San Francisco, California, the son of Asher Holtz and Olga Levine. He began his theatrical career in his early teens singing in roadhouses in the San Francisco area. As he later recalled it, "That town had the greatest entertainers I've ever seen." Holtz played on a few Orpheum vaudeville bills with George Jessel in 1912. Legendary vaudevillian Elsie Janis saw Holtz perform, and the team of Boland, Holtz, and Harris formed an act called the Elsie Janis Trio. Holtz married Rita Boland, a member of the act, but they subsequently divorced.

For several years Holtz developed his own act, which alternated broad ethnic jokes and comic songs. Producer Max Gordon of the B. F. Keith circuit recommended that he try appearing in blackface. Successful at it, he was viewed for a time as a substantial rival of Al Jolson (Holtz had earlier understudied Jolson), Eddie Cantor, Al Herman, and Harry Jolson, all of whom specialized in the minstrel tradition. Holtz grew in experience and popularity, and in April 1919 he headlined a bill that included Van and Schenck and Jack Norworth at the legendary Palace Theatre. *Variety* reported on Holtz's original material and his natural, if not wholly individual, style, noting that "his gestures and delivery resembled that of Frank Fay and Al Jolson, respectively," and proclaimed the act a "genuine hit." Later recalling his early years on the stage, Holtz described vaudeville as "a good business. A guy would work all over the United States—be away for maybe four years perfecting his act."

To broaden his ethnic appeal, Holtz created a Jewish stage character, Sam Lapidus, who "wore size eight shoes, but size nine felt so comfortable, he always bought size ten." Holtz appeared in the Sigmund Romberg musical comedy *A World of Pleasure* in 1915 but scored his first great successes on Broadway in the revue form, most particularly in the first edition of George White's *Scandals* at the Liberty Theatre in 1919, a job he got only because comedian Lester Allen became ill and had to drop out. Holtz was a success and also appeared in the 1920 and 1921 editions of the *Scandals*. One of his stock lines was to ask of a young lady looking to break into show business, "Would you like to be glorified by Ziegfeld or scandalized by White?" Holtz also appeared in three Winter Garden revues. Buddy DeSylva teamed with George and Ira Gershwin to write the sketches and songs for *Tell Me More* (1925) starring Holtz, who later was featured in two run-of-the-mill musical comedies, *Manhattan Mary* (1927) and *You Said It* (1931). In addition to his revue appearances, he developed into one of the finest vaudeville masters of ceremonies of the day, both at the Palace Theatre and, for a time, at the competing Hollywood Theatre. However, despite his reputation as the preeminent dialect comedian of the 1920s, Holtz's act did not play well outside of New York City.

Holtz's only feature film appearance was in the early talkie *Follow the Leader* (1930), starring Ed Wynn; in it Holtz played "Sam Platz," a character suggested by his Lapidus bits from vaudeville. Many vaudevillians and theatrical performers sought by Hollywood in the early sound film days mistrusted the screen because, like Holtz, they were afraid it would quickly use up material they had spent years carefully honing on stage. Holtz was also distressed to discover that several of his key scenes were cut from the released print of *Follow the Leader*, apparently at Wynn's bidding. Holtz appeared frequently on radio, however, spending six months as a comic on Rudy Vallee's popular show.

In 1934 Holtz appeared in the revue *Calling All Stars*. This was followed in September 1935 by his appearance at Loew's State Theatre. Headlining with Block and Sully and Belle Baker, Holtz was held over—an unprecedented move for that theater. The following year Holtz appeared in two successful London revues, *Transatlantic Rhythm*, with Ruth Etting, Lupe Velez, and Buck and Bubbles, and *Laughter over London*. In 1937 Holtz married Phyllis Gilman, but their union ended in divorce in 1946. During his second marriage, he appeared in the Broadway revues *Priorities of 1942* and *Star Time* (1944). Holtz received respectful reviews for his one-man show at Carnegie Hall, but in the later days of his stage career, critics found his humor to be increasingly risqué and of questionable taste.

In the early 1940s, as vaudeville died and ethnic comedy declined in popularity, Holtz retired to Los Angeles. In 1951 he produced and appeared in an unsuccessful revue, *Patsy*, at the Belmont Theatre in Los Angeles. He also made occasional appearances on television variety shows, but especially on Jack Paar's late-night show, on which he was a guest no less than eighteen times.

Holtz remarried in 1961 and with his wife, Gloria Warfield, had two sons. Having made a considerable fortune through shrewd stock market investments, Holtz was content not to work. He died in Century City, California.

• For more information on Holtz see, in addition to entries in the standard biographical reference works, Douglas Gilbert, *American Vaudeville: Its Life and Times* (1940, 1968). An obituary is in *Variety*, 1 Oct. 1980.

JAMES FISHER

HOLYOKE, Edward Augustus (1 Aug. 1728–31 Mar. 1829), physician, was born in Marblehead, Massachusetts, the son of Edward Holyoke, later president of Harvard College, and Margaret Appleton. Holyoke graduated from Harvard College in 1746, taught school for a year or two, and then read medicine under Thomas Berry of Ipswich, Massachusetts. In 1749 he opened a practice in Salem, Massachusetts, where he lived for the remainder of his long life. It was said of him that eventually there was not a house in Salem to which he had not been called as a physician. As his reputation spread, he was consulted even by older physicians, including his preceptor. Between 1762 and 1817 he was himself the preceptor of thirty-five pupils, including James Jackson, John Collins Warren, and Nathaniel Walker Appleton. In 1755 Holyoke married Judith Pickman, who died the next year of complications following the birth of their child, who also died. In 1759 he married Mary Viall; they had twelve children, of whom eight died in infancy, and she died in 1802.

As a practitioner, Holyoke was informed and progressive. Even in old age he was eager to try new treatments. "The most distinguishing intellectual trait of his whole character," a younger colleague asserted, "was that he was always ready to receive information,—that he kept his mind open, so to speak, and never allowed prejudice, or the conceit of great acquirements, to prevent his examining and adopting any thing which claimed to be a novelty or improvement" (Peirson, p. 31). He was one of the first to adopt vaccination after Benjamin Waterhouse demonstrated its value in 1800; and, always fair-minded, he argued that Elisha Perkins's "metallic tractors" (made up of two small pieces of metal, one brass, one steel, pointed at one end, which, when drawn over the affected parts of a patient, were supposed to effect a cure) should at least be tested before being rejected. So determined was he to understand diseases that he performed autopsies on the bodies of his own children. At the same time, he was cautious in his treatments. He relied principally on mercury, antimony, opium, and Peruvian bark but also prescribed cold baths. In obstetrical cases he was reluctant to use forceps.

The records of his practice show that for more than seventy-five years Holyoke averaged eleven calls a day. In 1777 he opened a smallpox hospital, where he inoculated 600 persons and lost only two. During a measles epidemic in 1787 he is said to have made over 100 professional calls on each of several days. His fees were low, and he never pressed for payment. Younger colleagues did not approve of this attitude, and Holyoke in turn scorned them as "medical bucks" who were overly aware of their dignity. Although committed to high standards, he did not believe that a college diploma should be required of a student of medicine and held that only a moderate acquaintance with Latin and Greek was necessary.

Throughout his life Holyoke was interested in scientific phenomena, especially in astronomy. While still a college student he had observed the aurora borealis and begun to keep a daily record of the weather. As a practicing physician, he endeavored to correlate weather with prevailing diseases. Dissatisfied with existing instruments for that purpose, he invented an "American thermometer" that was based on the freezing points of mercury and water.

Although Holyoke regarded American independence as inevitable, he doubted the people's capacity for self-government and shrank from revolutionary turmoil and violence. In 1774 he signed a public farewell address to Governor Thomas Hutchinson, which the patriots forced him the next year to recant. Otherwise he took no part in the war and remained, undisturbed, in Salem. In the political rivalries of the 1790s he supported the Federalists.

Holyoke was a leader in many Salem institutions. At his death he was president of the Essex Historical Society, the Salem Library, the Salem Athenaeum, and the Salem Dispensary. He was a founder of the Salem Institution for Savings. He gave books to Harvard College to replace its library after it was destroyed by fire in 1764, and in 1769 he gave the college a telescope for its philosophical cabinet.

Holyoke was elected to the American Philosophical Society of Philadelphia in 1768 and was a corresponding member of the Imperiale e Reale Accademia Economico-Agraria of Florence. He was an incorporator of the Massachusetts Medical Society in 1781, its first president from 1782 to 1784, and its president again in 1786–1787. One of the first members of the American Academy of Arts and Science, founded in 1780, he served as the academy's president from 1814 to 1820. He was author of a number of papers on medicine and science, which were printed in the *Memoirs* of the academy and various medical journals. His publications, as well as his official positions, brought him into correspondence with English clergyman and chemist Joseph Priestley, English minister and writer Richard Price, and physician Sir Charles Blagden.

In about 1814 Holyoke compiled a guide and catechism to ethical conduct, which was published in 1830 as *An Ethical Essay; or, An Attempt to Enumerate the Several Duties Which We Owe to God, Our Saviour, Our Neighbour and Ourselves*. Although the work was firmly grounded in Christian teachings, its sentiments were nevertheless universal. It listed virtues that should be cultivated (e.g., love, gratitude, obedience) and the contrasting vices that should be avoided (among them, ill will, hatred, ingratitude, willfulness), and it catalogued the author's duties to God, to his neighbors, and "to every Being with whom I had any Contact," including animals. In an appendix Holyoke offered reasons for belief in the unity of the deity (as opposed to a triune god) and rational arguments for rejecting the widespread popular notion that the world would end any time soon. "May no Prejudices or preconceived Opinions," one of his prayers read, "have any undue Influence over me, or obstruct my Attention to any proper Evidence."

In old age Holyoke found himself something of an oracle and an institution. In 1820 he became Harvard's oldest living alumnus, his appearance at commencements greeted with congratulations and expressions of respect. When asked for the secret of his longevity, he replied, moderation: he avoided pork, ate all fruits in their season, and drank—not more than a pint a day—a mixture of two parts "good West India rum," three parts cider, and nine or ten parts water. On the day of his hundredth birthday his fellow citizens gave a large public dinner in his honor. A few weeks later he attended the celebration of Salem's bicentennial, where he proposed the toast to the founders.

When his health began to fail in the winter of 1828–1829, Holyoke, with characteristic curiosity and detachment, recorded his symptoms and, reaching his own conclusions, disputed his physician's diagnosis. He died at Salem at the age of 100 years and eight months. In accordance with his instructions, his colleagues performed a complete post-mortem and found that the patient's diagnosis of his own illness had been correct.

• Holyoke manuscripts, including his medical diaries, are in the Essex Institute, Salem, Mass. Miscellaneous letters used in this sketch are in the Curwen papers in the American Antiquarian Society and the collections of the Historical Society of Pennsylvania. Extracts from Holyoke's diary are in George F. Dow, ed., *The Holyoke Diaries, 1709–1856* (1911), pp. 31–43. References to Holyoke and the Salem of his time are in William Bentley's *Diary* (4 vols., 1905–1914). The principal biographical accounts are [A. L. Peirson], *Memoir of Edward A. Holyoke, M.D., LL.D.* (1829), prepared for the Essex District Medical Society and printed also in Massachusetts Medical Society, *Medical Dissertations*, vol. 4 (1829), pp. 185–260; John Brazer, *A Discourse . . . at the Interment of Edward Augustus Holyoke* (1829); and Clifford K. Shipton's sketch in *Sibley's Harvard Graduates*, vol. 12 (1962), pp. 30–41, which includes Holyoke's bibliography. For a protégé's delineation of Holyoke's character and manner see James Jackson's *Letters to a Young Physician*, 4th ed. (1856), pp. 19–22.

WHITFIELD J. BELL, JR.

HOLYOKE, Samuel Adams (15 Oct. 1762–7 Feb. 1820), music educator, tune book compiler, and composer, was born in Boxford, Massachusetts, the son of Elizur Holyoke, a minister, and Hannah Peabody. Samuel came from a distinguished Massachusetts family. His father was the Congregationalist minister in Boxford, where he served for some forty-seven years, and the nephew of Harvard College president Edward

Holyoke. Samuel was educated at Phillips Academy in Andover, Massachusetts, and at Harvard College, from which he received a B.A. in 1789.

Little is known of Holyoke's musical education, but it was probably in a singing school. By his Harvard years he was proficient enough to organize a group of students to sing and play at commencement exercises. Following his graduation from Harvard, Holyoke began a series of publications that brought him notoriety, if not great popularity. His first published works were four songs that appeared in Isaiah Thomas's *Massachusetts Magazine* (Aug. 1789, Sept. 1789, May 1790, and Sept. 1790). At about the same time he advertised for subscriptions to his tune book *Harmonia Americana* (1791), which contained only his own compositions. The tune book was initially successful and brought Holyoke the reputation of being in the vanguard of the reform movement in American sacred music.

Holyoke received an M.A. from Harvard in 1792. He then taught school in Groton, Massachusetts (1793), and engaged briefly with his brother Oliver in a mercantile enterprise in Charlestown, Massachusetts. However, neither of these vocations suited his temperament. He returned to music and devoted himself to teaching in singing schools throughout northeastern Massachusetts and southern New Hampshire.

In 1795 Holyoke joined two Boston musicians, Hans Gram and Oliver Holden, in the compilation of *The Massachusetts Compiler*, an important reform-advocating tune book with an extensive theoretical introduction. In 1798 he helped found the Essex Musical Association in Salem, Massachusetts, comprised of the leading singers from the area and devoted to the improvement of church music. Holyoke served as the association's director.

Beginning in 1798 Holyoke produced a series of publications designed to carry out the aims of reform, assist him in his teaching activities, and give him a secure income. For a few years he was successful, and his publications were numerous and in demand. However, following his father's death in 1806, his fortunes declined, and he spent the last decade of his life eking out a living as an itinerant singing-school teacher. He died in East Concord, New Hampshire, but was buried in his hometown of Boxford, Massachusetts.

Holyoke was a prolific composer and compiler of musical publications. His works include *EXETER, for Thanksgiving* (1798); *Hark! From the Tombs and Beneath the Honors* (c. 1800); *The Instrumental Assistant*, vol. 1 (1800), vol. 2 (1807); *A Dedication Service* (1801); *Occasional Music* (1802); *The Columbian Repository* (1803); *Masonic Music* (1803); *The Christian Harmonist* (1804); *A Dedication Service* (1804); *Two Anthems* (c. 1804); *Hymn for the New Year* (c. 1805); *The Occasional Companion* (6 vols., 1806–1809); and *The Vocal Companion* (1807). Many of these are compositions by Holyoke himself, often unattributed. Several other publications were proposed by Holyoke but were not produced.

Holyoke is thought to have composed more than 600 compositions. Many of these are psalm-tunes, published in his various tune books. However, some may be instrumental pieces published anonymously in his two-volume *Instrumental Assistant*. He also composed anthems, several with orchestral accompaniment—a rare occurrence in American sacred music at the time. Holyoke was a fervent advocate of the use of instruments in performing church music and contributed much to fostering performing skills among both singers and instrumentalists. In his music Holyoke followed closely the harmonic precepts of European art music, while adapting the melodic and textural characteristics of American psalmodists. While he had some success as a music teacher and tune book compiler, few of his own compositions were popular among his contemporaries. Following his death his music was largely forgotten. His importance to early American music was aptly summarized by the historian George Hood: "There was no man of his day that did more for the cause of music than Samuel Holyoke."

• Yale University has three manuscript collections of Holyoke's music. For a selection of his music, see Karl Kroeger and Harry Eskew, eds., *Samuel Holyoke and Jacob Kimball: Selected Works*, Music of the New American Nation, vol. 12 (1998). For further information on Holyoke, see George Hood, "Sketches of American Musical Biography and History: Samuel Holyoke, A.M.," *Musical Herald*, 3, no. 12 (Dec. 1882): 318; Barry Kolman, "The Origins of American Wind Music and General Instrumental Tutors" (Ph.D. diss., Northern Colorado Univ., 1985); Kolman, "Early American Wind Music in General Instrumental Tutors," *Journal of Band Research* 23, no. 1 (Fall 1987): 61–77; Frank Metcalf, *American Writers and Compilers of Sacred Music* (1925; repr. 1966); and John Morehen, "Masonic Instrumental Music of the Eighteenth Century: A Survey," *Music Review* 42, nos. 3–4 (Aug.–Nov. 1981): 215–24. Other useful sources include David Music, "The First American Baptist Tunebook," *Foundations* 23 (July–Sept. 1980): 267–73; Relford Patterson, "Three American Primitives: A Study of the Musical Style of Hans Gram, Oliver Holden, and Samuel Holyoke" (Ph.D. diss., Washington Univ., 1963); J. Laurence Willhide, "Samuel Holyoke: American Music Educator" (Ph.D. diss., Univ. of Southern California, 1954); and Richardson Wright, "Our Singing Craft," *Transactions of the American Lodge of Research* 5, no. 1 (Dec. 1947–May 1949): 39–51.

KARL KROEGER

HOMANS, George Caspar (11 Aug. 1910–29 May 1989), sociologist, historian, and poet, was born in Boston, Massachusetts, the son of Robert Homans, an attorney, and Abigail Adams, a homemaker, civic activist, and author. Homans was surely the most blue-blooded American sociologist of the century. All the male ancestors on his father's side had attended Harvard since 1768 and were very successful merchants, lawyers, and physicians in the Boston area. His mother's male ancestors had been at Harvard even longer. Through his mother (author of *Education by Uncles* [1966]), Homans was directly descended from Presidents John Adams and John Quincy Adams, with other significant family members—John Quincy Adams

II, Charles Francis Adams, Brooks Adams, and Henry Adams—adding to this lustrous family tree. "Homans never went out of his way to call attention to his ancestors nor did he shy away from discoursing about them if asked," Ezra Vogel wrote of Homans at his death. Yet it was undeniably the case, well documented both in Homans's professional writing as well as in his spritely autobiography, *Coming to My Senses* (1984), that his secure place in the hierarchy of New England culture and politics strongly affected his view of the world, and the sociology he created to explain it.

Homans entered Harvard in 1928 and spent several additional years beyond his B.A., beginning in 1932, as a junior member of the newly formed Society of Fellows. His peers in this group included William F. Whyte, Arthur Schlesinger, Jr., and B. F. Skinner. It was Homans's lifelong friendship with "Fred" Skinner that helped shape the particular form of social theory he was to compose during the 1950s and 1960s, with its emphasis on the extent to which humans are likely to select one course of action over another depending on anticipated rewards or costs. Another pivotal influence on Homans's intellectual development was Harvard physiologist L. J. Henderson, who introduced Homans to the ideas of Vilfredo Pareto and an astonishing seminar that included, as Homans recalled, economist Joseph Schumpeter, historian Crane Brinton, psychologist Elton Mayo, scientific instrument designer T. North Whitehead (son of Alfred), critic and historian Bernard DeVoto, historian Hans Zinsser, sociologist Robert K. Merton, sociologist and educator Talcott Parsons, and briefly, polymathic sociologist Pitirim Sorokin.

DeVoto's article on Pareto in *Harper's* (Oct. 1933) for a time in the 1930s gave the Italian economist and sociologist widespread recognition. Literate Americans' fascination with Pareto was evident, for instance, in the 25 May 1935 issue of the *Saturday Review of Literature*, which featured four articles about the theorist, all of them admiring and celebrative of this great "genius." Working with a close family friend, the attorney Charles P. Curtis, Homans at twenty-four wrote the first primer on Pareto in English, which DeVoto persuaded Alfred Knopf to publish in 1934 as *An Introduction to Pareto*.

Homans had already published his first book, *Massachusetts on the Sea*, in 1930, with the titular coauthorship of Harvard historian Samuel Eliot Morison, the research for which took Homans to the Customs House of Boston for expert-level inquiry into sailing vessels of the latter nineteenth century. Homans's unique development as an American sociologist continued when he traveled to London in 1934 to do research using the oldest available medieval village and manorial records, having already exhausted Harvard's substantial holdings. From this he published *English Villagers of the Thirteenth Century* in 1941, after joining the U.S. Navy. Homans thereafter enjoyed what he called "inverted snobbery" from the fact that, in keeping with the early rules of the Society of Fellows, he never submitted this estimable work as a dissertation and so did not receive a doctorate. Thus, at a young age he had published three books in three areas of scholarship with only a baccalaureate degree.

In 1941 Homans married Nancy Parshall Cooper, with whom he would have three children. Following active duty in the navy as a commander of small ships during World War II, Homans wrote several scholarly articles exploring the sociological problems facing officers on such vessels. In 1946 he joined the Harvard faculty as a tenured associate professor and soon produced his major sociological work, *The Human Group* (1950). In this important volume, Homans applied his nascent theoretical viewpoint to five famous works in ethnography, in both premodern and industrial settings. Homans's method of clearly laying out a series of testable hypotheses (in this case revolving around sentiment, activity, and interaction) served as a sharp-edged counterbalance to the theoretical nebulousness being promulgated by his senior colleague Talcott Parsons. It was partly the polar opposition represented by Homans and Parsons, who had no use for each other's intellectual work, that gave Harvard sociology its peculiarly interesting complexion during the 1950s but that, in the end, helped doom Parsons's attempt to unite several social sciences within one department of social relations. In 1970 Homans became the first chairman of the reconstituted sociology department over the lonely, but vigorous, opposition of Parsons.

Homans's other major work in social theory, *Social Behavior: Its Elementary Forms* (1961; rev. ed., 1974), summarizes his theory of social life as a forum in which individuals, not aggregates or collectivities, pursue their individual goals for essentially rational reasons; as such, it helped give rise to later versions of similar premises under the names of "social exchange theory" (so called because it is based on the theory that all social relationships revolve around exchanges of goods or services between parties such that each one will try to maximize his or her own benefit at the expense of those with whom they are interacting) and "rational choice theory." The distinction between Homans and theorists working within the latter two camps, however, was that by and large their goal was to imitate physics and their backgrounds were stronger in the sciences and math than in the humanities. Homans's attempt to create a more or less neo-Paretian social theory owes much more to his everyday observations, to the work of top-notch ethnographers, and to history and literature than to the so-called hard sciences—despite his claimed allegiance to a rigorous "covering law" philosophy of science. And it is this interesting amalgam of viewpoints that probably will continue to give Homans's theory a certain readership over time, particularly because it is expressed in lively and straightforward prose.

Homans officially retired from Harvard in 1975 and was celebrated in the festschrift *Behavioral Theory in Sociology* (1976), to which many of his longtime associates contributed. He published a book of collected poems—poetry having been his first and longest love—called *The Witch Hazel* the year before his death.

• Homans's papers (c. 1940–1989) are in the Harvard Archives. In addition to the books mentioned above, he published *The Nature of Social Science* (1967), *Sentiments and Activities* (1962), and *Certainties and Doubts: Collected Papers 1962–1985* (1987), which contains his most famous essay, "Bringing Men Back In," his presidential address to the American Sociological Association in 1964. Another important essay, "A Life of Synthesis," is in *Sociological Self-Images*, ed. I. L. Horowitz (1969). In addition to the festschrift mentioned above, see *Institutions and Social Exchange: The Sociologies of Talcott Parsons and George C. Homans*, ed. Herman Turk and Richard Simpson (1971); Peter Ekeh, *Social Exchange Theory* (1974); and Karen S. Cook, "Exchange Theory: A Blueprint for Structure and Process," in *Frontiers of Social Theory: The New Syntheses*, ed. George Ritzer (1990). Useful obituaries include those by Ezra Vogel in *Footnotes* (American Sociological Association newsletter), Dec. 1990, p. 14; Daniel Bell, *Proceedings of the American Philosophical Society* 136 (1992): 587–93; Charles Tilly, "George Caspar Homans and the Rest of Us," *Theory and Society* 19 (June 1990): 261–68; and the *New York Times*, 31 May 1989.

ALAN SICA

HOME, Archibald (1705?–Apr. 1744), secretary of the colony of New Jersey and poet, was born in Berwick, Scotland, the son of Sir John Home, the baronet of Berwick. His mother's name is not known. Privately educated in Scotland, Home briefly resided in Glasgow before seeking his fortune in New York in 1733. He quickly established himself as the premier wit of the New York City taverns. In hopes of gaining a place in the local government, he plied his pen for Governor William Cosby and the court party, then in the midst of a political contest with the river party. Governor Cosby's exercise of prerogative rights, according to James Sterling, Lewis Morris, and other contributors to John Peter Zenger's *New York Weekly Journal*, invaded the privileges of the legislature and the citizenry. Home's "Memoirs of a Handspike," a mock criminal autobiography of a piece of wood that eventually becomes the pull bar on Zenger's press, was the wittiest and most effective literary counter to the Zenger campaign. Indeed, its quality was so great that Lewis Morris, an opponent and a political poet of no little ability, sought Home out and made him a protégé. When Morris ascended to the governorship of New Jersey in 1737, he appointed Home deputy secretary of the province. Thereafter Morris sponsored in quick succession Home's appointment as secretary of the Provincial Council, member of His Majesty's Council of New Jersey, and finally in 1741, secretary of the province.

While residing in Trenton, the capital of New Jersey, Home organized a literary circle that became the most influential academy of politeness in the province. Its membership was cosmopolitan, including Louis Rowe, the minister of the Huguenot Church in New York City; Abigail Street Coxe, whom Benjamin Rush deemed the most accomplished woman in the American colonies; Attorney General Joseph Worrel; Trenton's sheriff David Martin; Chief Justice Robert Hunter Morris; Moses Franks, British America's first

Jewish belletrist; and his sister, Richa Franks, an accomplished musician and painter. Home improved and corrected the poems composed by his friends, serving as both instructor and literary arbiter.

Home's thwarted courtship of Richa Franks inspired much of the poetry he composed during the 1740s. Forbidden to marry Home by parents whose other daughter and a son had already married gentiles, Richa accepted, but did not encourage, Home's many verses addressed "to Flavia." In these poems Home attempted to create a neoclassical haven where "Florio" and "Flavia" might find mutual joy, unhampered by the divisions between Jew and Christian. Home's early death left the courtship unresolved, and Richa Franks chose never to marry. The members of the Trenton circle collected Home's manuscripts and had a scrivener prepare manuscript books of "Poems on Several Occasions by Archibald Home. Esqr. Late Secretary, and One of His Majestie's Council for the Province of New Jersey: North America." In the elegies prefacing the collection Home was proclaimed "Of Our New World, the Wonder Joy and Fame." Manuscripts of the collection circulated on both sides of the Atlantic. In New Jersey he remained a touchstone of poetic accomplishment for a generation, his work being esteemed by William Livingston and Annis Boudinot Stockton.

Home's thirty-five surviving literary texts included ribald tavern songs, a mock elegy in Scots dialect, four long classical imitations from Ovid and Horace, two fables, four riddles, a Freemasonic psalm, a prologue intended for the reopening of the New York theater in 1739, and a host of epigrams and odes addressed to Flavia. His love poetry employed the courtly style of Edmund Waller. His tavern verse resembled that of his contemporary Allan Ramsay. The classical imitations were among the most correct and polished composed in British America. His writings on natural history subjects do not survive but were reputable enough to win him election as one of the earliest members of the American Philosophical Society.

Abigail Streete Coxe assumed leadership of the Trenton circle after Home's death and oversaw preparation of the posthumous collection of his works.

• A manuscript of "Poems on Several Occasions by Archibald Home" survives as Laing Manuscripts III, 452, University of Edinburgh. Lewis Morris's actions on Home's behalf are chronicled in his official correspondence, collected in *The Papers of Lewis Morris, Governor of the Province of New Jersey, from 1738 to 1746*, ed. William A. Whitehead (1852). For Home's literary work, see David S. Shields, "Cosmopolitanism and the Anglo-Jewish Elite in British America," in *A Mixed Race: Ethnicity in Early America*, ed. Frank Shuffelton (1993).

DAVID S. SHIELDS

HOMER, Louise (30 Apr. 1871–6 May 1947), opera singer, was born Louise Dilworth Beatty in Shadyside, near Pittsburgh, Pennsylvania, the daughter of William Trimble Beatty, a Presbyterian minister, and Sarah Fulton. Her family was close-knit and musical,

and she and her brothers and sisters sang in the church choir. After her father's death in 1882 the family moved to West Chester, Pennsylvania, where Louise continued to sing in choirs. After high school she took a 3-month secretarial course and worked for a lawyer to earn money for voice lessons; she also got a paying job in a church choir.

Homer moved to Philadelphia for a higher-paying job and studied voice with Abbie Whinnery and then Anna Groff. She had a big, beautiful contralto voice, but neither teacher successfully taught her how to control it. In 1893 she moved to Boston to live with her sister Bessie and to look for a solution to her vocal problems. She began harmony studies with Sidney Homer, joined George Chadwick's choir (the best in the city), sang with the Cecilia Society under Benjamin Lang, and studied voice with William L. Whitney. On 9 January 1895 she married Homer, a part-time music teacher and composer who was the son of two deaf parents and a cousin of the painter Winslow Homer. The couple was to have six children.

In 1896 Louise Homer and her husband borrowed enough money to go to Paris for serious music study, he to compose and she to sing. After a year with two highly regarded teachers who nearly ruined her voice, Homer agreed to work with vocal coach Fidèle Koenig. To her initial horror, Koenig extended her range upward, enabling her to sing the mezzo-soprano roles in such operas as Meyerbeer's *Le Prophète*. Her range eventually extended from a low F to a high C, an extraordinary accomplishment. Koenig's work made possible for Homer a career in opera, to which she had been introduced by her husband (her family's religious scruples had barred exposure to both opera and the stage). Homer was engaged for the 1898 summer season by the Vichy Opera Company. She was the first beginner the organization ever took on, and she made her debut in June 1898 as Leonora in Donizetti's *La Favorite*. The following winter she sang with a small company in Angers, and the next summer she was engaged by Maurice Grau to sing at London's Covent Garden. During the 1899–1900 winter season she sang with the acclaimed Théâtre de la Monnaie company in Brussels, where she made her debut as Amneris in Verdi's *Aida*, a role for which she became famous. In 1900 she spent another summer in London, giving a command performance for Queen Victoria on 25 July.

In the fall of 1900 Homer returned to the United States, with a three-year contract from New York's Metropolitan Opera. The season began with a cross-country tour, and Homer made her American debut in San Francisco on 14 November as Amneris, a performance she repeated for her Metropolitan debut on 22 December. During the next three years she sang Ortrud in Wagner's *Lohengrin*, Venus in Wagner's *Tannhäuser*, Siebel in Gounod's *Faust*, Brangäne in Wagner's *Tristan und Isolde*, Emilia in Verdi's *Otello*, and Azucena in Verdi's *Il Trovatore*, the last another of her outstanding roles. In 1903 she signed a contract with the Victor Talking Machine Company and made some of the first Red Seal recordings ever released. In that same year she sang Maddalena in a production of Verdi's *Rigoletto* that was also Enrico Caruso's Metropolitan debut; thereafter she often sang with the great tenor.

At the Metropolitan, Homer sang all the chief contralto roles. Conductors valued her fine musicianship as well as her beautiful voice and unpretentious demeanor. She always knew her part thoroughly and was a remarkably quick study. For example, when singer Olive Fremstad was suddenly taken ill in 1903, Homer learned her role, Fricka in Wagner's *Das Rheingold*, in a single day. Homer was on tour in San Francisco with the company when the 1906 earthquake struck. As a result, Homer, whose third child was expected in August, suffered a miscarriage and became quite ill. She was unable to perform for many months. The following season she sang Suzuki in the American premiere of Puccini's *Madama Butterfly*; the composer supervised the production, staged by David Belasco, and the cast included Caruso as Pinkerton and Geraldine Farrar as Cio-Cio San. In 1908 she sang in *Aida* in Arturo Toscanini's debut performance at the Metropolitan, and in 1909 she opened the new Boston Opera House in a performance of Ponchielli's *La Gioconda*. Later that year, at Toscanini's insistence, she learned the role that would be her greatest triumph, Orfeo in Gluck's *Orfeo ed Euridice*. A portrait of Homer in her Orfeo costume still hangs at the Metropolitan Opera House.

These years were also filled with months of travel, both with the opera company and on concert tours. Homer's separations from her family became increasingly burdensome, as her husband was often in ill health and unable to travel with her or supervise the care of their six children. In 1919 she decided to leave the Metropolitan. Solo concert tours and recordings paid much more than did opera and were easier to arrange. She performed a number of recitals in duet with her daughter Louise, a soprano, and made a number of guest appearances with other opera companies (Chicago, San Francisco, Los Angeles). In 1926 she also began to perform radio concerts. That same year her daughter Katharine, then just nineteen, became Homer's accompanist. Her recitals always included some of her husband's songs, as they had from the start of her career. Her last performance at the Metropolitan was a guest appearance as Azucena in 1929, with four generations of Homers in the audience (including her granddaughter Louise).

This 1929 performance marked Homer's official retirement. Her vocal abilities were unimpaired, but her husband's poor health required a warm winter climate. Their later years were divided between "Homeland," a beautiful house they built on Lake George in upstate New York, and Florida, at first Palm Beach and later Winter Park. At Homeland, they were often visited by other musicians, including their nephew Samuel Barber. In both New York and Florida, Homer taught privately. She received honorary degrees from Tufts, Smith, Middlebury, Russell, Sage, and Miami (Ohio) University. She died in Winter Park.

• Programs, photographs, reviews, and other memorabilia concerning Homer are held by various family members, mainly her daughter Katharine Homer Fryer (New York, N.Y.) and her granddaughter Louise Homer Stires Curtis (Lexington, Mass.). The fullest, most accurate account of Homer's life and career is her daughter Anne Homer's book *Louise Homer and the Golden Age of Opera* (1974). Sidney Homer, *My Wife and I* (1939), is also useful. A compact disc, *Louise Homer*, with some of her most famous renditions, originally recorded between 1903 and 1927, was issued in 1992 by Pavilion Records, Ltd. GEMM CD 9950. An obituary is in the *New York Times*, 7 May 1947.

CHRISTINE AMMER

HOMER, Winslow (24 Feb. 1836–29 Sept. 1910), artist, was born in Boston, Massachusetts, the son of Charles Savage Homer and Henrietta Benson. Both parents came from comfortable, middle-class families with deep New England roots. The family moved from Boston to Cambridge, Massachusetts, when Homer was six years old. Consequently, he passed most of his childhood and all of his youth in a country village as Cambridge then was. Homer's father has been described (on no known documentary basis) as being a well-to-do importer of hardware; however, he seems never to have sustained any productive employment or profession after his return in 1851 from an unsuccessful venture in California. It is likely that Homer's family was at least partially dependent upon his financially successful uncles until his elder brother, Charles Savage Homer, Jr., assumed support of their parents. Homer's mother was a dedicated amateur watercolorist. His first lessons in art are assumed to have come from her. His formal education ended with high school, and he immediately went to work.

Homer probably was doing occasional jobs for Boston's principal lithography firm, John H. Bufford, as early as 1853, with his formal apprenticeship beginning in 1854. According to George W. Sheldon, who profiled Homer in 1878, he found the years at Bufford's "a grindstone [that] unfitted him for further bondage" and taught him to keep free of structured employment ever after. The hated apprenticeship expired on his twenty-first birthday in 1857, leaving him well skilled in the basic principles of drawing; personally disciplined in a strong work ethic; and as free to exercise his creative impulses as a need to earn a living would allow. This conditioning is reflected in much of the behavioral patterns and art of Homer's adulthood.

Immediately on completing his time with Bufford, Homer set up a studio in the same Boston building that housed the offices of *Ballou's Pictorial Drawing Room Companion*. That popular journal published his first original illustration on 13 June 1857. Before the end of that summer he had placed illustrations with the New York pictorial magazine *Harper's Weekly*. Over the two and a half years he remained in Boston, Homer's images of everyday scenes of country and urban life appeared in fifty-five issues of *Ballou's* and *Harper's*; he also contributed illustrations to fourteen story books, among them a charming edition of the *Eventful History of Three Little Mice and How They Be-*

came Blind. All these illustrations were published in the medium of wood engraving: Homer rendered his drawings onto specially prepared wooden blocks that were then carved into relief by technicians. The pictures seen on printed pages were the result of the collaboration of artist and engraver. He had advanced quickly from commercial lithography to the more-respected field of illustration.

Homer's ambition to attain the height of his profession was formed early. One of the reminiscences gathered by his biographer William Howe Downes recalls Homer, with several other Bufford apprentices, visiting "Dobson's picture gallery, where they were looking at a painting of a kitchen interior with figures by Edouard Frère" (an admired French painter of the period). "After a little, Homer said: 'I am going to paint.' Wight asked him what particular line of work he was intending to take up. He pointed to Frère's genre painting, and said: 'Something like that, only a ——sight better'" (Downes, p. 29). Whether the incident happened exactly as Downes retold it is open to question; that from the very beginning Homer planned and shaped his professional career so as to bring himself distinction is apparent from his actions.

Despite Downes's reference to a "picture gallery," opportunities to see contemporary art were rare in Boston at the time, and for art schooling, they were nonexistent. In the autumn of 1859, having established a fledgling reputation as an illustrator, and a solid connection with *Harper's*, Homer moved to New York. Selling his drawings to periodical and book publishers was Homer's basic source of income. New York no doubt offered a wider range of buyers, but the lure that occasioned such a major relocation was more likely the School of the National Academy of Design, one of the very few places in America where art study at a professional level was available.

Homer registered at the academy school for the season of 1859–1860 and was allowed the unusual privilege of entering the life drawing class directly, without first spending at least a half-year drawing from plaster casts of classical sculptures. Sometime within that same season he established his studio in the University Building on Washington Square, where a number of recognized artists made their quarters. Homer was again registered in the academy's life class for the 1860–1861 and 1863–1864 seasons. Probably in the winter of 1861 he had some private instruction in the use of paints from Frederic Rondel, a French émigré painter who had passed some time in Boston. Sheldon reported that these lessons took up the Saturdays of one month. This was the full extent of formal training Homer received, or felt he needed.

While pursuing his study in the fine arts Homer sustained a successful career as a freelance illustrator. His work was to be seen in a number of popular periodicals, but *Harper's* was his principal employer, and it was as a *Harper's* artist-reporter that he made his first contact with the Civil War in the autumn of 1861. He went to Washington, D.C., where General George B. McClellan's Army of the Potomac was encamped all around the city; the entire trip lasted no more than ten days, and only two illustrations reflect this brief visit. However, by the spring of 1862, when McClellan finally took the field, Homer was ready to launch his career as a painter and was looking for a subject. This time it was on his own initiative that Homer traveled to Washington. He then embarked with troops from the port of Alexandria, Virginia, and spent five weeks with the army on its campaign to reach Richmond from the York peninsula. He would again visit the Civil War front in the spring of 1864, but the 1862 tour was his most sustained experience of military life, and it provided the raw material for his first serious work in oil.

Homer made his debut as a painter in the National Academy of Design's annual exhibition of 1863, showing two Civil War subjects; he showed another two scenes related to the war in the academy annual of 1864; and two of his three works in the annual of 1865 were army camp subjects. From the first Homer attracted critical notice (no mean feat in exhibitions that presented five to seven hundred works), and generally his military genre scenes—vignettes of routine camp life far from the drama of battle—found favor. The subject of his major contribution to the annual of 1866 was also drawn from his experience of the Civil War, but the work was of quite different character and would elevate his standing as a painter from promising newcomer to serious professional. *Prisoners from the Front* (Metropolitan Museum of Art, New York) in subject matter referred to an important Confederate surrender at the battle of Spotsylvania Court House in May 1864, but on its introduction a year after the end of the war it was immediately recognized by press and public as an eloquent expression of the fundamental differences in character and conditioning between the North and South and the inevitable outcome of their conflict. In one way the success of *Prisoners* was a curse; it would be nearly twenty years before another of Homer's paintings would be admired enough to overcome its hold on popular and critical memory.

Besides critical approval, Homer received unusually prompt approbation from the professional establishment: he had been elected an associate of the National Academy in 1864 and elevated to full academician the next year; also in 1865 he was elected to membership in the Century Association, the prestigious private club where New York's foremost artists and writers mixed socially with the city's foremost business and professional men—and where artist-members mounted an exhibition each month. In just three years Homer had made a solid start on the career he sought in the high art of figure painting. He then left the country.

No compelling reason is known for Homer's departure for Paris in December 1866. However, it is easy to surmise that, at age thirty, having worked to pay his way, and to make his name respected, since he was seventeen, he felt it was time to explore and enjoy the world. He shared a Paris studio with fellow Bostonian Albert W. Kelsey and traveled in the French countryside with another Bostonian, landscape painter J. Fox-worth Cole. While in France Cole was also an agent for a Boston gallery in acquiring paintings by the Barbizon artists. It is not surprising that to the limited extent Homer's work from this year shows any exposure to contemporary European art it is of the Barbizon School's subject preference for the French peasant.

Homer returned to New York in mid-October 1867. Only gradually over the next five years would he reestablish a place among the leading artists of the city. He renewed the common artists' pattern of spending summers in the country, gathering material for paintings to be executed in the studio over the succeeding winter. Homer's summer itinerary was more peripatetic than that of most of his colleagues, as he visited the fashionable vacation resorts, such as Long Branch, New Jersey, Manchester, Massachusetts, or Mount Washington in New Hampshire, for subject matter of value to *Harper's*. Illustration was again a mainstay in these years but diminished as sales of paintings improved and was given up entirely in 1875; beginning in 1870, Homer reserved at least part of each summer for painting.

Homer made his first visit to the Adirondacks in northern New York State in September 1870; however, the area would not become a favorite vacation site, and source of his art, until many years later. In the decade of the 1870s he preferred the tamer landscape and residents of New York's Catskill Mountains. The village of Hurley was a favorite destination. Two of his most admired paintings of this period were Hurley scenes, and they exemplify his principle figure themes, comely young women and country children: *The Country School* (1871, Saint Louis Art Museum) and *Snap the Whip* (1872, Butler Institute of American Art, Youngstown, Ohio). Later in the decade Homer enjoyed the welcome of a patron, Lawson Valentine, to make short visits to his Houghton Farm in Mountainville, New York, where the Valentine daughters and neighborhood children were the source of a quantity of pictures.

In 1873 Homer made a significant departure from his summer habits. With characteristic deliberateness of purpose he settled in Gloucester, Massachusetts, from June well into August, working exclusively in watercolor, rapidly learning and perfecting his skill in the newly respected medium. Homer's watercolors, first shown in 1874, met the same ambivalent response as did his oils in this period. The majority of critics favored his work, but few could wholeheartedly approve it. He was admired for the economy and truth of his reportage of the American scene, but his rough technique and raw coloring were regularly faulted. Henry James, in the July 1875 issue of *The Galaxy*, gave the most entertaining expression of complaints:

Mr. Homer goes in, as the phrase is, for perfect realism, and cares not a jot for such fantastic hairsplitting as the distinction between beauty and ugliness. He is a genuine painter; that is, to see, and to reproduce what he sees, is his only care; to think, to imagine, to select, to refine, to compose, to drop into any of the intellectual tricks with which other people sometimes try to eke out the dull pictorial vision—all this Mr. Homer triumphantly avoids.

The more serious critics chided his failure to follow up on the promise of *Prisoners* with paintings of deeper meaning than was conveyed by his wholesome farm lads and idle women. There are indications that Homer began to seek more profound subjects. A trip to the Adirondacks in 1877 was the source of *Two Guides* (Sterling and Francine Clark Art Institute, Williamstown, Mass.) and *Camp Fire* (Metropolitan Museum of Art), both 1877 (though the latter is inscribed 1880). The rugged scenes and characters depicted in these two works were uncharacteristic of Homer at this time, yet the paintings were still primarily about visual surfaces. The paintings that show Homer's perceptions reaching below surfaces are four that resulted from trips he made to the South in 1876 and 1877 and that treat the recently freed slaves: *The Cotton Pickers* (Los Angeles County Museum of Art) and *The Visit from the Old Mistress* (National Museum of American Art, Smithsonian Institution, Washington, D.C.), both 1876, and *Dressing for the Carnival* (Metropolitan Museum of Art) and *Sunday Morning in Virginia* (Cincinnati Art Museum), both 1877. Although most of these canvases attracted attention, their departure from his commonplace rural genre subjects was not clearly recognized. Whether for that reason or because they did not satisfy him creatively, these paintings remained isolated experiments.

There were other indications that Homer, though professionally well established, was personally unsatisfied—and planning something meant to cure his malaise. Whereas in the earlier years of the 1870s he had been active on the New York art scene, toward the close of the decade he began to distance himself from his colleagues. Early in 1880 he gave up the studio he had occupied since 1872 in New York's premier artists' residence, the Tenth Street Studio Building. That Homer was already acquiring a reputation for having a prickly personality was noted by a writer in the 22 December 1880 number of *Art Interchange*:

Of Mr. Homer . . . it is hard to know what not to say. Ranking, as he does, among the foremost and most original of American painters, he commands the admiration of all critics. . . . He is *posé* in the extreme, and affects eccentricities of manner that border upon gross rudeness. To visit him in his studio, is literally bearding a lion in his den; for Mr. Homer's strength as an artist is only equalled by his roughness when he does not happen to be just in the humor of being approached.

A series of auctions, each of seventy to eighty watercolors and drawings, suggests a slow gathering in of funds: Boston in May 1878; Chicago, December 1879; and New York, March 1880. Also in 1880 Homer again spent the summer working in Gloucester, completing more than a hundred watercolors and drawings, which just before Christmas 1880 formed a one-man exhibition at Doll & Richards, the Boston dealers. Sales were brisk; Homer could add $1,400 to the account he was accumulating.

His goal seems to have been reached in the spring of 1881; Homer again left New York, this time for the dour fishing village of Cullercoats on the northeast coast of England, just a few miles from Tynemouth. Homer was now forty-five, and his purpose in traveling abroad was wholly focused. The most convincing of a number of explanations proposed for his choice of an obscure village for a stay of twenty months is that a summer colony of English painters had already demonstrated the subject opportunities in the simple, hard-working fishermen and their families. Another would be the world-famous dangers of this treacherous coast—and the equally famous Tynemouth lifesaving station. In his illustrations Homer had occasionally touched on the terrors of the sea. In choosing Cullercoats he seems to have fixed on this theme as the medium for deepening the expressive range of his art.

In Cullercoats Homer used watercolor and charcoal almost exclusively, producing scores of scenes of the local men, women, and children working and waiting on the shore—especially waiting: the women, for the men to bring in the catch at dawn; the men of the lifesaving brigades, for the possible disaster that would call them to dangerous rescue. The physical bulk and strength of the fisherfolk were matched by new expansiveness and strength in Homer's style and technique. His figures became monumental, his compositions simplified, but more significantly, the content of his paintings was transformed from the transitory moments of day-to-day life to the eternal tension between man and the elements, especially the dominating power of the sea over those who lived in close dependency on it.

A few of Homer's English watercolors had been shown in Boston and New York while he was still in England and were immediately recognized as something considerably finer than anything yet produced by his hand. This time on his return from an extended absence abroad, Homer brought with him considerable material for exhibition and immediately set about producing major exhibition pieces in his new impressive manner—but on American subjects. In the summer of 1883 he made a trip to Atlantic City, New Jersey, to observe its naval rescue station's life-saving apparatus. While there he witnessed a dramatic rescue of swimmers. The visit provided the research for one major painting and suggested the subject of another.

During his stay in England, Homer's brothers, Arthur and Charles, began buying land in Prout's Neck, Maine, planning to develop the community into a summer resort. One parcel included a substantial house, which Charles had finished for their parents, also providing a large studio for Homer. In May 1883 Homer bought four Prout's Neck lots from Charles, thus becoming a partner in the project. Excepting the excursion to Atlantic City, he passed the entire summer at Prout's Neck. Probably before the end of the season he had arranged to turn a smaller building on

his brother's property into a live-in studio, ensuring that in the future he could live separately from his vacationing family.

The two subject ideas developed in Atlantic City occupied Homer on his return to his New York studio for the winter of 1883–1884. *Undertow* (Sterling and Francine Clark Art Institute), the dramatic rescue of two women swimmers, which Homer certainly began that winter, was three years in process. But *The Life Line* (Philadelphia Museum of Art), depicting the rescue of a shipwrecked woman by the breeches buoy device, was completed in time to be shown at the National Academy spring exhibition of 1884. The painting proved to be the work that would eclipse *Prisoners from the Front* as the measure of Homer's genius. Besides being generally greeted as the most important work in the exhibition, its purchase during the preview reception by the prominent collector Catherine Lorillard Wolfe for the extraordinary sum of $2,500 added to the painting's—and the artist's—fame.

Just three weeks after this triumph Homer's mother died. His parents had lived in New York since the early 1870s. His widowed father elected to spend winters in Boston. Homer's place in the New York art world was secure, and with no family responsibilities to keep him there, he was free to satisfy what was apparently a deeply felt need for privacy and isolation. That summer the transfer to Prout's Neck, the kind of rugged seacoast for which he had found such affinity, would be permanent.

The remaining quarter century of his life Homer passed in a fairly settled routine that was structured to serve his art, as it provided ample opportunity for travel and especially for his favorite pastime, fly fishing. Homer produced few major oils in these years—the number was limited in order not to swamp the market, he said. In truth he was focusing his energy on a few ideas and painting in intense bursts. Oils would often result from several years of thought and observation. The late autumn, after the distracting summer residents had left Prout's, was when he would concentrate on them, finishing up one or two major pieces in time to send them to New York or Boston for exhibition at the height of the season—and to leave Maine before the worst of the winter had set in.

January into February was Homer's usual time to seek a warm climate. Taking his father to the Bahamas in December 1884 for a stay of four months (he went alone to Cuba for part of the time) was the first of these excursions. However, Florida and its bass fishing was his favorite winter destination. Initially Homer went along the St. Johns River below Jacksonville, but once comfortable rail transit had been extended to the state's Gulf Coast, Homosassa was preferred. The exception to these migrations south were the winters of 1891 through 1898, which Homer passed in Prout's Neck, within easy reach of Boston and his octogenarian father, who died in August 1898. Homer made his second and last visit to the Bahamas that winter and his sole visit to Bermuda in the winter of 1899–1900.

As Homer made his way back northward in March or April he would stop in New York, surely taking in the current exhibitions as well as visiting with his older brother and going to symphony concerts. By spring he would be home in Prout's Neck. Almost every year from 1889 onward Homer spent some weeks of late spring into early summer at the North Woods Club in the Adirondacks; occasionally he returned in the autumn for another stay of as much as a month. Visits to the Tourilli Fish and Game Club, near the Saguenay River in Quebec, where Homer and his brother Charles shared ownership of a cabin, was an occasional alternative to a stay in the Adirondacks. Homer did hunt deer, but his chief pleasure in these luxuriously provisioned excursions into wilderness was the trout and salmon fishing.

These sites and experiences away from Prout's were the principal sources of Homer's work in watercolor. Suites of paintings resulted from many of these trips and formed one-man exhibitions in New York and Boston: Bahamas and Cuba subjects in 1885; the Adirondacks, 1890; and Quebec scenes, 1898. He opted to be represented at the Pan-American Exposition held in Buffalo in 1901 by a group of twenty-one watercolors, all tropical scenes.

Homer's mastery of, and technical innovation in, the watercolor medium was widely admired in his own time, but it was as a painter in oils that his contemporaries truly judged him. *The Life Line* was followed by an informal series of large, dramatic narrative paintings depicting the American commercial fisherman's hard work and high risk at the Grand Banks: *The Herring Net* (Art Institute of Chicago), *The Fog Warning* (Museum of Fine Arts, Boston), *Lost on the Grand Banks* (private collection), all 1885. These three and *Undertow* (finished and first shown in 1886) represented Homer in the major exhibitions of the next several years, during which he took a sabbatical from painting to master the etching medium. By 1890 he was back at work at an easel. Four paintings finished within that year were introduced as an exhibition unto themselves at Homer's New York dealer, Gustav Reichard, in February 1891. These paintings and that occasion began the rapid evolution of Homer's standing from prominent painter to American Master.

At the time admiring critics had no way of recognizing that the four canvases signaled Homer's move beyond the conventions of his art. *The Signal of Distress* (Fundacion Coleccion Thyssen-Bornemisza, Madrid) was a straightforward narrative involving a number of figures rushing about on deck in the tense moments before a ship-to-ship rescue. *A Summer Night* (Musée D'Orsay, Paris), though concerned with mood more than moment, still relied on the image of the central figures to make its point. With *Winter Coast* (Philadelphia Museum of Art) and *Sunlight on the Coast* (Toledo Museum of Art), Homer's first pure seascape, his attention shifted from figures representing man in some relatively specific relationship with nature to the ruthless power and beauty of nature itself. Over the next fifteen years Homer worked out this culminating artistic theme primarily in images of the sea near and on the Prout's Neck shore.

A selection of the formal awards and honors conveyed upon Homer are symptomatic of the level of success he had attained: Pennsylvania Academy of the Fine Arts Gold Medal of Honor, 1895; First prize ($5,000), Carnegie Institute, Pittsburgh, *First Annual Exhibition*, 1897; Gold Medal, Paris, Exposition of 1900, and purchase by the French government of *Summer Night*; Pennsylvania Academy of the Fine Arts Temple Gold Medal, 1902; election to the American Academy of Arts and Letters, as the first occupant of chair 21, 1905.

A stroke in May 1908 temporarily disordered Homer's vision and coordination, but he was off on a fishing trip by the end of June, and by late autumn he was painting his penultimate canvas, the enigmatic *Right and Left* (National Gallery of Art). His last painting, *Driftwood* (Museum of Fine Arts, Boston), was finished in time to be introduced at the Century Association in December 1909. Homer's health then began precipitously to decline; he died in his studio home at Prout's Neck.

Winslow Homer's mature work attained a subtlety and sophistication in formal design and profundity of content beyond that of any American artist of his time, and perhaps any since. His was that rarest of all artistic achievements: evolution and refinement of aesthetic and idea over the whole course of a lifetime, yielding at last timeless, universally potent images. In his own time he earned the admiration of serious critics and collectors but more significantly, the respect of his fellow artists, especially immediately younger generations. Yet he had no real followers or imitators; it was as if artists could best recognize that Homer had a genius beyond possibility of emulation. For all the awe in which his work was, and is, held, it has always been accessible to a popular audience. That combination made him, by the end of the nineteenth century, arguably the best-known and most highly respected artist in America, and as an American, his international rank was exceeded only by the expatriates John Singer Sargent and James M. Whistler. That combination has since sustained his work in the first rank of world art.

• Homer's silence on his life and work as an artist is legendary. Two articles by George W. Sheldon, "American Painters: Winslow Homer and F. A. Bridgman," *The Art Journal* (New York) 4 (Aug. 1878): 225–27 (variant published in the London *Art Journal* [1879]), and "Sketches and Studies, II: The Portfolios of A. H. Thayer, William M. Chase, Winslow Homer, and Peter Moran," *The Art Journal* (New York) 6 (Apr. 1880): 105–9, constitute the only significant evidence of Homer having given a journalist constructive cooperation. The meager biographical sketch provided by the first of these articles is the basis of all the accounts of his early life. In Homer's last years, by which time he was perhaps America's preeminent painter-celebrity, he stymied the efforts of William Howe Downes, critic of the *Boston Evening Transcript*, to bring out a biography. Downes introduced himself, and his hopes, to Homer's brothers and nephews at his funeral and immediately secured their cooperation; his *Winslow Homer* (1911), though flawed, is accepted as an indispensable source. From 1884 on Homer's brothers and nephews preserved his letters, newspaper clippings, and other memorabilia, which they made available to Downes and all interested researchers thereafter. This family archive was given to the Bowdoin College Museum of Art, Brunswick, Maine, by Mrs. Charles Lowell Homer, widow of the younger nephew; it is also available in microfilm from the Archives of American Art, Smithsonian Institution, Washington, D.C. Lloyd Goodrich's definitive monograph, *Winslow Homer* (1944), while making use of Downes and the family archive, expanded knowledge of the artist through extensive original research. Philip C. Beam, *Winslow Homer at Prout's Neck* (1966), concentrates on the last three decades of Homer's life and work and reflects Beam's close personal association with Charles Lowell Homer. *Winslow Homer* (1995), by Nicolai Cikovsky, Jr., and Franklin Kelly, is a major study and presents extensive advances in information and interpretation of the artist's works made by the generation of scholars following Goodrich and Beam. Beam's *Winslow Homer's Magazine Engravings* (1979) and David Tatham's *Winslow Homer in Boston: 1854–1859* (1970) and *Winslow Homer and the Illustrated Book* (1992) are the principal sources on Homer's work as an illustrator. *Winslow Homer Watercolors* (1986) by Helen A. Cooper is the most extensive study of his work in that medium.

ABIGAIL BOOTH GERDTS

HOMES, Henry Augustus (10 Mar. 1812–3 Nov. 1887), missionary and librarian, was born in Boston, Massachusetts, the son of Henry Homes, a wealthy merchant, and Dorcas Freeman. He entered Amherst College in 1826, graduating at age eighteen. Classmates found him introverted, absentminded, and inflexible in his opinions, but friends remembered a dry and sometimes droll wit, all characteristics noted by later acquaintances.

Homes then studied at Andover Theological Seminary, 1830–1832, and Yale College, 1832–1834, including in his studies at Yale medicine, theology and oriental languages, and earned the degree of master of arts at Amherst in 1834. He spent the next year in Paris studying Arabic and other oriental languages and in 1835 was ordained in the French Reformed church. The following year he offered his services to the American Board of Commissioners for Foreign Missions and was sent to the Constantinople mission, where he preached, wrote, practiced medicine, taught English to Turks and Arabs, and served as business manager of the mission.

Also traveling extensively in the Turkish Empire, Homes spent several months in 1837 in Damascus studying Arabic and visited Beirut and Jerusalem. In 1839 he joined physician Asahel Grant on an expedition to Mesopotamia and Kurdistan, where Grant planned to establish a station among the Nestorian Christians. However, Kurdistan was in rebellion against Turkey, and mobs attacked foreigners indiscriminately, forcing the two missionaries to find sanctuary at a Syrian monastery. After two months in almost constant peril, Homes returned to Constantinople.

Over the next several years, Homes wrote and translated religious books, tracts, and papers, which he published and distributed himself. He also frequently contributed articles to the *Missionary Herald* on the culture, religion, history, and geography of the Near East.

In 1841 Homes married Anna Whiting Heath, daughter of John Heath of Brookline, Massachusetts; they had two children. He continued his work at the mission until 1851, when he entered the service of the American legation at Constantinople as an interpreter. After a brief stint as acting consul, he was appointed chargé d'affaires, a position he held until 1853, when he decided to return to Boston.

In 1854 Homes became an assistant librarian at the New York State Library in Albany, a change of career brought about by circumstances unknown even to his friends at the time. There he spent over a year preparing a catalog of the library's collections, published in 1856 in three volumes, and administering a general collection of 30,011 books and a law collection of 13,623 books, in addition to manuscripts, maps, engravings, medals, and coins.

In 1862 Homes was appointed librarian of the state library's General Library, which he developed from a miscellaneous collection into what was considered one of the country's great research libraries for the use of government officials, scientists, and historians, with major collections in political science, American and European history, biography, genealogy, and scientific patents. Homes built the collection over the next twenty-five years to 94,000 volumes and increased the law collection to 39,000 books. During his tenure, the library acquired the state's colonial archives and the draft copies of George Washington's Farewell Address and Abraham Lincoln's Emancipation Proclamation.

Homes accomplished his ends with very limited funds, largely by making good use of a developing network among domestic and foreign libraries, by exchanging copies of historical and scientific publications of the New York State government for similar publications of other agencies, and by seeking gifts of collections and finding donors to make purchases for the library. He himself donated a large number of books.

As a librarian, Homes was noted for his industry. He indexed and calendared many major manuscript collections, and it was said that he had personally handled every book in the library during his tenure. Although he was thought to be a man with no hobbies, entirely content with the labors of his office, he was a founding member of the Albany Institute (now the Albany Institute of History and Art). Members of the institute found him charming and entertaining, exceptionally well informed on a great variety of topics, and fond of a friendly chat.

Homes's annual reports, and his special report *The Future Development of the New York State Library* (1879), show his wide knowledge of the developing field of professional librarianship. In the latter work, he delineated the differences in purpose and clientele between public and research libraries. A strong believer in bringing books to people, he saw a need for locally supported free libraries and interlibrary loan systems. Many of his ideas on the ways in which architecture can reduce heating costs while protecting the condition of books are still valid. He was also a founder of the American Library Association in 1876 and one of its first vice presidents.

In recognition of Homes's work, Columbia College in 1873 granted him the degree of doctor of laws, which Homes considered his greatest honor. The State Board of Regents called him one of the chief librarians of the world. His career was effectively ended in June 1886, when illness caused him to take a leave of absence that continued until his death in Albany, New York. A man who had pursued two very different careers with equal dedication, Homes will be remembered in this country as a great librarian.

• No collection of Homes's personal papers is known to exist, and his official papers at the New York State Library did not survive the capitol fire of 1911. Homes's writings include *Observations on the Design and Import of Medals* (1863), *California and the North-west Coast One Hundred Years Since* (1870), *The Palatine Emigration to England in 1709* (1871), *The Water Supply of Constantinople* (1872), *The Pompey (New York) Stone, with an Inscription and Date of A.D. 1520* (1881), *Description and Analysis of the Remarkable Collection of Unpublished Manuscripts of Robert Morris* (1876), and *The Correct Arms of the State of New York* (1880). His published translations include *The Alchemy of Happiness, by Mohammed Ghazzali* (1873) from Turkish. His experiences in Kurdistan are discussed by his colleague, Asahel Grant, in *The Nestorians; or, The Lost Tribes* (1841), and in Thomas Laurie, *Dr. Grant and the Mountain Nestorians* (1853). His work as a librarian is examined in Cecil R. Roseberry, *For the Government and People of This State: A History of the New York State Library* (1970). Noteworthy obituaries are in the New-England Historic Genealogical Society *Proceedings* 42 (1888): 318; *New York Genealogical and Biographical Record* 19 (1888): 38; and *Albany Evening Journal*, 3 Nov. 1887. Eulogies by George W. Kirchwey, Horace E. Smith, and David Murray are in *Transactions of the Albany Institute* 12 (1893): 1–8, 8–10, and 10–13.

PETER R. CHRISTOPH

HOMMANN, Charles (25 July 1803–?), musician, teacher, and composer, was born in Philadelphia, Pennsylvania, the son of John C. Hommann, a musician, and Constantia (maiden name unknown). Hommann grew up in a home in which string music and German chamber music flourished. His father was a violinist, and his elder brother John C. Hommann, Jr., played the violin and cello. Hommann's elder sister Constantia married Charles Hupfeld, a prominent violinist and conductor. Hommann learned music from his father and Hupfeld, who had both studied in their native Germany.

Hommann's father performed chamber music in the public Quartette Parties, which led to the establishment of the Musical Fund Society in 1820. The society, inspired by its London predecessor, financially benefited aged "decayed musicians" and their families. Hommann was one of the leading violinists in the orchestra at its first benefit concert in May 1821. After the Musical Academy of the Musical Fund Society was opened in 1825, Hommann taught violin there until it closed in 1831. One of his later pupils, Michael Hurley Cross, became a prominent Philadelphia musician and conductor.

Hommann was active in Philadelphia concerts. In February 1826 he played a Boccherini quintet with Hupfeld as the other violinist; George Schetky and another Hommann (probably his elder brother John) were the two cellists. On 16 May 1826 Hommann played in a concert given by Schetky at Musical Fund Hall.

Hommann served as the organist at St. James Church in Philadelphia. The position inspired him to write *Te Deum Laudamus, Hymn for Four Voices with an Accompaniment for the Organ, Composed for the Use of Choirs in the Episcopal Church*, which was published in Philadelphia by C. F. Hupfeld & Son in 1848. The Library of Congress holds compositions for piano composed by Hommann, including *Rondo for Piano Forte Composed for and Dedicated to Miss Harriet H. Graupner of Boston* (date unknown), a dramatic and flamboyant virtuosic composition, published for Hommann by G. E. Blake in Philadelphia. *Oh Come to Me Beloved One, A Canzonetta* (date unknown) was composed for and dedicated to Miss Helen Stanley. Published by Klem and Brother, the words suggest Hommann's love for Helen. He apparently never married. Also at the Library of Congress are *Three Fugues for the Piano Forte, Composed and Dedicated to his Friend, Abraham Ritter Esqr.* (no date), published in Philadelphia by Fiot, Meignen & Co., and *Juvenile Gallopade, Composed for the Piano Forte* (1844), published in Philadelphia by George Willig. The fugues all display a good knowledge of counterpoint, and the *Juvenile Gallopade* is short and lively with repeated chords and melodic passages contrasted in a vivace tempo.

The chamber music written by Hommann suggests his excellent string technique. There are florid passages in high registers, and all parts are melodic and interesting. Although the music was never published, Hommann's quartets are of comparable size and musical inventiveness to the best chamber music of contemporary European composers. The Music Department of the Free Library in Philadelphia holds a well copied score of Hommann's Quintetto in F-sharp Minor (no date), for two violins, two violas, and violoncello. Also at the library are manuscript parts of Hommann's three string quartets, in D Minor, F Major, and G Major (no date). Hommann's Quartet in G Major was performed at the Historical Society of Pennsylvania in 1976, and the Mann Quartet performed his Quartet in F Major in Philadelphia in 1992; it was received with extreme enthusiasm.

One of Hommann's quartets has a hand-written note on the manuscript, probably written by Michael Cross, dated 1897, stating that Hommann "lived almost altogether at Mr. C. F. Hupfeld's in Filbert St., when in Philada. whose house he went away in 1857 and no one knows where and was never heard from again!" Hommann was listed only once in the Philadelphia directories, at his father's address; after 1857 he may have gone to live with his sister Constantia and her husband. There is no information concerning when and where Hommann died.

The Fleisher collection at the Free Library in Philadelphia holds the score and parts for performance of Hommann's Overture in D Major (no date), for which he received a prize from the Musical Fund Society; it has been performed by orchestras throughout the United States. The collection also contains the score and parts of Hommann's four-movement Symphony in E-flat Major (no date), which he dedicated to the Philharmonic Society of Bethlehem, Pennsylvania.

Hommann possibly created the best music composed in the first half of the nineteenth century in Philadelphia and perhaps in the entire United States. In the New York *Musical Review*, Hommann is described as "a teacher of the Violin, and Piano Forte, and a clever organist; quiet and unassuming in his deportment" (1 Sept. 1835). Hommann was a very capable composer of music with a blend of the classical and romantic traditions of European music. The immigrant musicians in Philadelphia taught this native American to write creditable music of which Americans can be proud.

• There is no central repository of Hommann's papers. His music is located at the Free Library of Philadelphia and the Library of Congress. He should not be confused with a Christopher Hommann, a music master who lived in Philadelphia in 1796. Biographical information for Hommann and his contemporaries in Philadelphia is in Louis C. Madeira, *Annals of Music in Philadelphia and History of the Musical Fund Society from Its Organization in 1820 to the year 1858* (1896), and Myrl D. Hermann, "Chamber Music by Philadelphia Composers, 1750–1850" (Ph.D. diss., Bryn Mawr College, 1977).

MYRL DUNCAN HERMANN

HOMOLKA, Oscar (12 Aug. 1898–27 Jan. 1978), motion picture actor, was born Oskar Homolka in Vienna, the son of a fencing equipment manufacturer, who disowned him when he became an actor; his parents' names are not known. Homolka was trained at the Royal Dramatic Academy in Vienna. Following service in the Austrian army during World War I and after performing in minor stage roles, he had a breakthrough in 1924 when he played the title role in the first German production of Eugene O'Neill's *The Emperor Jones*. He then joined Max Reinhardt's renowned Berlin stage company. As a member of that company for ten years, he played major roles in productions ranging from Shakespeare to the Kurt Weill–Bertolt Brecht experimental opera, *The Rise and Fall of the City of Mahagonny*; he also directed *Pygmalion* in 1932.

At the same time, Homolka began his screen career. His German-language films included *The Tragedy of the Street* (1927), *The Trial of Donald Westhof* (1928), *Dreyfus* (1930), and *1914: The Last Days before the War* (1931).

With the rise of Adolf Hitler to German chancellor, Homolka fled to Vienna in 1933, then to Paris, and still that same year to England, where he learned English and spent three years acting in London. His new career included plays and such films as *Rhodes of Africa* (1936), in which he played opposite Walter Huston, and Alfred Hitchcock's *Sabotage* (1936).

During 1936 Homolka was invited to the United States, where he entered the most extensive part of his career. Playing roles as a European or a European immigrant, the husky, urbane, bushy-eyebrowed, thick-accented Homolka soon became typecast as a villain, particularly in spy movies and films of international intrigue. "In Europe I played Othello, but in American pictures . . . I am just the mean fellow who leers at the little heroine and dies hideously in the end," he said. However, he also demonstrated a knack for comedy, as in the Howard Hawks–directed classic *Ball of Fire* (1941), and for portraying sympathetic characters, earning an Academy Award nomination for his delightful performance in *I Remember Mama* (1948) as the loud and threatening but ultimately kindly Uncle Chris, a role he reprised from the stage.

For more than three decades Homolka appeared in a wide variety of American and, occasionally, British and German films. Some of his better-known films were *Comrade X* (1940); *Mission to Moscow* (1943); *The Seven Year Itch* (1955); *War and Peace* (1956), in which he played General Kutuzov; *A Farewell to Arms* (1957); *The Key* (1958); and *The Wonderful World of the Brothers Grimm* (1962). In addition, he appeared in more than a hundred television dramas, with major roles in *Darkness at Noon*, *Rashomon*, *In the Presence of Mine Enemies*, and *The Plot to Kill Stalin*, in which he played Nikita Khrushchev.

During the mid-1960s Homolka returned to England with the intention of retiring. Instead, he remained active in movies there. Of these films, his most memorable part came in the Cold War thrillers *Funeral in Berlin* (1966) and *Billion Dollar Brain* (1967), in which he played Colonel Stok, a menacing Soviet intelligence officer.

Homolka is reported to have been married five times, but the names of only four of his wives are known: Grete Mosheim (dates of marriage and divorce not available); Vally Hatvany, who married Homolka in 1937 and died in 1938; Florence Meyer, the daughter of *Washington Post* publisher Eugene Meyer, with whom Homolka had two children (dates of marriage and divorce not available); and the actress Joan Tetzel, who married Homolka in 1949 and died in 1977. Homolka died in Sussex, England.

• A personal profile of Homolka was published in the *New Yorker*, 2 Dec. 1944. There is no full-length biography. A *New York Times* obituary appeared on 29 Jan. 1978.

CARLOS E. CORTÉS
NARORN KEO

HONE, Philip (25 Oct. 1780–5 May 1851), diarist and socialite, was born in New York City, the son of a German-born joiner. Of humble origins, Hone determined to raise himself socially to the point where he would be able to mingle with the affluent on equal terms. Although the young Hone had little formal education, at the age of sixteen he began working at his elder brother John's auction house. Three years later he became a partner. A hard worker, Hone helped make his brother's business one of the most successful auction firms in the city. Over a period of nearly twenty years Hone amassed over half a million dollars and, in May 1821, at the age of forty, retired from business, toured Europe, and began collecting books and pictures. When he returned to New York, he and his wife, Catharine Dunscomb, whom he had married in 1801, and their six children settled in his home at 235 Broadway.

Hone's cultivation, affable personality, and sense of civic duty helped make him one of New York's most prominent citizens. He believed that a leader of society must not be snobbish but fully aware of the noble nature of serving one's city and nation. Hone strove to lead by example and, taking advantage of a split in New York's Democratic party, was elected in 1825 to a one-year term as mayor of New York. A conservative (he later became one of the leading proponents of the Whig movement) who managed to thrive despite his opposition to the political credos of the Jacksonians, Hone welcomed Lafayette to New York and represented his growing city at the opening of the Erie Canal. After serving as mayor he did not again run for elected office until 1839, when he tried unsuccessfully to win a seat in the state senate. He was then content to serve as a political counselor to some of the nation's prominent Whig leaders. A close friend of Henry Clay, Daniel Webster, and John Quincy Adams (1767–1848), Hone was always eager to help the Whigs by making speeches or raising funds. Hone's famous diary reveals that many of his political friends frequently summoned him to Washington, D.C., to ask his advice on various issues. Quick to support any worthy civic or charitable cause, Hone was also readily welcomed into some of New York's finest homes.

Hone is best known for the personal diary he kept between 1828 and 1851. This work provides historians with an in-depth view of life in mid-nineteenth-century New York. Virtually all of Hone's important activities are chronicled in his diary, but it remains the reflections of the diarist himself that most delight readers. Hone comments on plays, operas, art exhibitions, crime, schools, and many other aspects of New York society. Written in a beautifully clear handwriting, the diary reveals all of Hone's virtues and prejudices. Strongly patriotic and devoted to making New Yorkers more aware of social causes and the arts, Hone also feared that radicals, bad manners, and the Irish might one day ruin the country. His attitude toward women was typical of the nineteenth century: he felt that men must be gallant to women but did not advocate treating them as equals. One of his dinner groups, the Hone Club, required the women to repair upstairs while the men enjoyed gourmet feasts. Hone's diary records the many political, social, and literary person-

alities who attended his famous dinners and also describes the many trips Hone made to Boston, Saratoga, and Washington. In 1836 Hone again visited Europe, but he always found more enjoyment in New York, where he could confer with writers and artists such as Washington Irving, James Fenimore Cooper, Henry Brevoort, and John P. Kennedy.

Not everything Hone touched turned to gold. His attempt to help finance an Italian opera house failed when the theater closed, and he likewise failed in an effort to build a seaside hotel in Rockaway, New York. Eager to help his two eldest sons become successful businessmen, he generously loaned them large sums of money, but during the panic of 1837 their dry goods business went bankrupt, and Hone lost a great deal of his personal fortune. Unable to secure the New York postmastership from President John Tyler (1790–1862), Hone headed an insurance company that soon failed. Fortunately for Hone, President Zachary Taylor granted him a federal position in the port of New York. An 1847 trip left Hone in poor health, and he died a few years later in New York. His diary leaves us with the reflections of a man dedicated to the political, cultural, and social health of his nation.

• Hone's original diary is in the New-York Historical Society. See also Bayard Tuckerman, ed., *The Diary of Philip Hone, 1828–1851* (1889); Allan Nevins, ed., *The Diary of Philip Hone, 1828–1851* (1927); J. W. Francis, *Old New York; or Reminiscences of the Past Sixty Years* (1858); and Louis Auchincloss, ed., *The Hone and Strong Diaries of Old Manhattan* (1989). An obituary is in the *New York Daily Tribune*, 6 May 1851.

MICHAEL L. BURDUCK

HONYMAN, James (1675–2 July 1750), clergyman, was born in Kinneff, Kincardinshire, Scotland, the son of James Honyman, a minister, and Mary Leask. His uncle Andrew Honyman was bishop of the Orkneys and his father was the pastor of Kinneff from 1663 to 1693. Young James probably received his education at a Scottish university and briefly served as a chaplain in the Royal Navy. In his early career he was a missionary for the Society of the Propagation of the Gospel in Foreign Parts (SPG), based in London, and was sent to Jamaica, Long Island, in the Province of New York as a missionary preacher prior to 1704. Honyman left for Newport, Rhode Island, in 1704 after experiencing resistance to the Church of England from Quakers and other dissenting sects. He married Elizabeth Carr circa 1705; they had seven children. After her death in 1737, he married Elizabeth Cranston Brown; they had no children.

Honyman's arrival in Newport as a successor to the Reverend John Lockyer was a welcome event for the parish of Trinity Church, which had been founded by Sir Francis Nicholson, Gabriel Bernon, and fifteen other citizens following the introduction of the Church of England to Boston in 1686. In September 1699 Trinity parishoners appealed to Richard, earl of Bellomont, for a "pious and learned Minister, to settle and abide amongst us." Reminiscent of his Long Island experience, Honyman arrived in a town that was predominantly antiestablishment. Newport's inhabitants were members of Quaker, Baptist, Jewish, Presbyterian (Congregationalist), and other sects who benefited from the religious tolerance offered by Roger Williams and his followers. While all of the diverse religions coexisted in relative harmony, they all held the Church of England in suspicion. Honyman had the difficult task of promoting the Church of England without offending the indigenous population.

After a brief return to Scotland to tend to "his own private affairs," Honyman embarked on his mission to unite the young and struggling Anglican congregations in Rhode Island. In 1709 he petitioned the SPG for a bishop, citing that "these infant settlements would become beautiful nurseries which now seem to languish for want of a father to oversee and bless them." The SPG responded by sending a significant library of seventy-five volumes of the best available theological works. Queen Anne also supported the parish by sending a bell. In 1713 Honyman and the wardens repeated again their appeal for a bishop, without any response. In light of these rejections, Honyman developed, on his own initiative, a program of visiting other parishes throughout the colony. In 1715, for example, he delivered lectures to the Narragansett congregation following the death of their pastor Dudley Bradstreet. Under the guidance of the SPG, Honyman established regularly scheduled visits to congregations in nearby Tiverton and Freetown, and in 1720 he spent time in Providence, helping with efforts there to erect a church building.

Throughout the early 1720s, the congregation in Newport grew considerably as a result of the arrival of new members from other areas, intermarriage, natural growth among the parish, and the conversion of French Huguenots and wealthy Quaker merchants—who did not mind that the Church of England represented the royal establishment and did not discourage displays of conspicuous wealth. In 1724 Honyman reported to the SPG that the original church building of 1702 was no longer suitable to accomodate the growing parish and a new church was needed. In 1725 Trinity employed the architectural and building talents of Richard Munday in the erection of a new facade. Inspiration for Trinity's elaborate, baroque design was derived from the newly completed Christ Church (later Old North Church) in Boston, as well as features from Sir Christopher Wren's London churches, such as St. James's (Piccadilly), St. Anne's (Blackfriars), and St. Andrew's (Holburn). Completed in 1726, Trinity Church was a masterpiece of colonial craftsmanship, measuring seventy feet by forty-six feet and featuring two tiers of windows, box pews, and galleries. It was acknowledged by the people of the day "to be the most beautiful timber structure in America," according to noted architectural historian Norman Isham.

Following the completion of the new church, Honyman continued his regular schedule of parish visits and published a number of sermons and commentaries on the Angliean church, touching upon the errors of dissenting sects of the time. The literary life of Honyman and Newport was enhanced greatly in 1729 when he hosted the arrival of George Berkeley, the dean of Derry, a well–known philosopher, and later the bishop of Cloyne. Berkeley intended to establish a school in Bermuda but could not afford to go there until the institution was adequately financed. So he waited in Newport, where he purchased a 96-acre farm next door to Honyman's estate. Berkeley left Newport in 1731 and returned to England. Two years later Berkeley expressed his appreciation to Honyman and the parish by sending Trinity a gift of an organ and a library of important works.

The 1740s continued to be a period of growth for the parish and the Anglican church throughout the colony. Honyman reported to the SPG that he had a congregation of eighty regular communicants and had baptized 115 parishoners in 1742–1743. With rapid growth and a high turnover of parish schoolmasters, Honyman and the wardens wrote to the SPG requesting an "Episcopally ordained" schoolmaster. He would be paid out of funds provided under the will of Nathaniel Kay, a former customs collector and a dedicated benefactor of the church. In 1748 the SPG chose the Reverend Jeremiah Leaming of New Haven as the schoolmaster and assistant to Honyman. At Trinity's expense, Leaming was educated in England and ordained as a deacon and then as a priest in preparation for his Newport calling. He would eventually succeed Honyman as Trinity's rector and become a candidate for the first Episcopal bishop of the United States.

Honyman's 46-year service to the SPG and the parish of Trinity Church ushered in the establishment of the Anglican church in Rhode Island. With tact and great discretion, he applied his missionary training to the visitation, encouragement, and eventual unification of Rhode Island's small Anglican congregations in the midst of the larger and more influential dissenting sects, which he managed never to offend. By the end of his life, he had baptised 1,579 people and made Trinity Church a center for religious and literary advancement in colonial America. Honyman died in Newport and was buried alongside his first wife near the front door of the church he built.

• Honyman's writings include *A Sermon Preached at the King's Chapel in Boston, N.E., at a Convention of Episcopal Ministers in the year 1726* (1726); *Faults on All Sides: The Case of Religion Consider'd, Showing the Substance of True Godliness; Presented to the Inhabitants (Especially of the Colony of Rhode Island)* (1728); and *Falses on All Sides: Sundrey Errors, Maxims and Corruptions of Men and Sects of This Present Age* (1728). Genealogical and biographical information on the early family is found in A. Van Doren Honeyman, *The Honeyman Family in Scotland and America* (1909). The evolution of the Anglican church in Newport, from the original records on deposit at the Newport Historical Society, is discussed at length by George Champlin Mason, *Annals of Trinity Church, 1698–1821* (1890), and Daniel Goodwin, *A History of the Episcopal Church in Narragansett, Rhode Island* (1907). Architectural highlights of Trinity Church and comparisons of it to other structures in England and America is covered in Norman M. Isham, *Trinity Church in Newport, Rhode Island* (1936).

BERTRAM LIPPINCOTT III

HOOD, Darla Jean (4 Nov. 1931–13 June 1979), actress, was born Dorla Hood in Leedey, Oklahoma, the daughter of J. Claude Hood, a banker, and Elisabeth Danner. When Hood was three, her mother, who had invented the name "Dorla," took her to Oklahoma City for singing and dancing lessons. In 1935 her teacher took her to New York City, where, while pretending to lead the Edison Hotel's orchestra, she was spotted by Joe Rivkin, a casting director for film producer Hal Roach. Hood soon was bound by a seven-year contract as leading "lady" for *Our Gang*, Roach's series of short films; her name became "Darla" when it was misspelled on her contract.

Hood moved to West Hollywood with her mother—her father came along later—where her first appearance, as Darla "Cookie" Hood in *The Our Gang Follies of 1936* (1935) prefigured her career as a tiny soubrette, a miniature sweetheart, or femme fatale. Until her last appearance for *Our Gang* in 1941, Hood was educated in studio schools. She subsequently graduated from Bancroft Junior High School and Fairfax High School (1948) in Los Angeles.

Leonard Maltin claims that *Our Gang*, with 221 titles, was the most successful series in Hollywood history. Beginning as *The Hal Roach Rascals* in 1922, it was quickly renamed for its first, highly successful episode. "Kiddie" series had been a Hollywood fixture since 1915, often featuring guest appearances by stars such as Harold Lloyd, Charley Chase, Stan Laurel, and Oliver Hardy and gradually focusing on new child stars such as Mickey Rooney and Shirley Temple. Before Hood, *Our Gang* had also featured or introduced Jackie Cooper, Edith Fellows, Scotty Beckett, Dickie Moore, and Tommy "Butch" Bond.

What proved the definitive "gang" began to form in 1931 when the croaking George "Spanky" McFarland joined. Billy "Buckwheat" Thomas was added in 1934 to replace another African American (the series was unique among American children's films by being interracial), followed by the freckled country boy Carl "Alfalfa" Switzer and Hood.

Kiddie series often served some of the functions of theatrical revue, satirizing or parodying contemporary fads and productions. *The Our Gang Follies of 1936* was a direct response to Metro-Goldwyn-Mayer's *The Broadway Melody of 1936*. One of a cast of 100, Hood, as "The Billboard Girl," sang "I'll Never Say 'Never Again' Again." Dimpled and talented, with curly brown hair, deep brown eyes, and a baby face, Hood was at her best in musicals.

The 1936 Roach feature version of *The Bohemian Girl* found Hood in the title role, a foundling brought up by Laurel and Hardy. Hood later commented, "I didn't realize who Laurel and Hardy were. I wasn't even aware I was making movies. I didn't know what the camera was." Laurel praised her "radiant inno-

cence." Hood was third-billed in *The Neighborhood House* (1936), a Roach-Metro-Goldwyn-Mayer feature film with longtime silents star Charley Chase in one of his farewell performances. Although she appeared in the feature-length 1939 *Ice Follies*, Hood's career remained focused on *Our Gang*, whose *Bored of Education* won the 1936 Academy Award for best short subject.

Being an *Our Gang* regular dominated the children's lives. They were called on for frequent stage appearances. Hood later wrote of the "jealousy and status-seeking conflicts" among the kids' families but insisted that "the back lot there at Roach was the greatest playground any kid could ever have," asserting, "Our films were based on the kinds of activities kids would normally be involved in anyway. . . . I had a very happy childhood."

Hearts Are Thumps (1936) introduced Hood's winking flirtatiousness. She continued an on-again, off-again sweetheart relationship with Switzer in *The Pigskin Palooka* (1936), which echoed the Judy Garland-Johnny Downs *Pigskin Parade*. In other films she was a demure, cookie-passing young lady. The *Our Gang Follies of 1938* presented Hood and the others singing "The Love Bug Will Bite You If You Don't Look Out."

After 1938 *Our Gang* passed, along with other Hal Roach ventures, into the hands of MGM, which produced its weakest editions. Soon the increasing prevalence of double features doomed short subjects. Although future stars such as Robert Blake joined, the gang gradually broke up and continuity broke down. Hood appeared in only half the *Our Gang* films made during the last year of her contract, ending in her fiftieth comedy, *Wedding Worries* (1941).

Although she appeared briefly in the features *Born to Sing* (1942) and *Happy Land* (1943), Hood, like other gang members, experienced difficulty in adjusting to life outside the studios. "I had to go to public school and I hated it," she said, "I had never been around so many kids before." In her later high school years she formed a vocal group called Darla Hood and the Enchanters. She dubbed Linda Darnell's songs in *A Letter to Three Wives* (1948) and with her group joined *Ken Murray's Blackouts*, a long-running Los Angeles stage revue with burlesque overtones, traveling with it to New York and a three-year run. Hood's group provided the music for Murray's *Bill and Coo*, an Academy Award–winning short film featuring birds. Although official documentation is lacking, Hood may have married Bob Decker at age seventeen, and they may have had one child. They were most likely divorced in 1956.

In 1952 Hood returned to Los Angeles and began a career as a nightclub singer. She was a restaurant hostess, wrote song lyrics, and frequently recorded "cover" versions of others' songs, including "I Just Wanna Be Free" and "Something Cool," but she never had a hit.

Beginning in 1955 the *Our Gang* comedies, renamed *The Little Rascals* because of copyright complications, won a new audience on television, and a flock of Darla Hood impostors sprang up. Once again, in the words of Bob Garner, Hood's screen image "won the hearts of young boys, the envy of young girls and the affection of parents." For a time "Darla" became a popular name for newborn girls. In 1957 Hood married Jose Granson, a music publisher and agent; they had two children. She appeared in small roles in the 1957 films *Calypso Heat Wave* and *The Helen Morgan Story* and in 1959 as a secretary in *The Bat*, a Vincent Price horror film.

In 1961 Hood began to use her three-octave voice in voice-overs for television cartoons and commercials, as well as providing the voice for a bestselling doll. For a time she was a radio regular. On several Jack Benny television programs Hood joined Benny (as Alfalfa), announcer Don Wilson (as Spanky), Eddie Anderson (as Buckwheat), and others in parodies of *Our Gang*. In 1970 she dubbed *Airport* and in 1974 *The Towering Inferno*.

In 1973 the surviving gang was reunited on national television. She told a 1977 interviewer, "It's been tough for me to continue my career. Some people resent child stars. . . . Some are interested in learning all about my life, but not hiring me." She claimed to have been writing a history of the *Our Gang* regulars. Hood died in a Canoga Park, California, hospital of hepatitis. In 1994 a feature remake of *The Little Rascals*, which did not employ any of the surviving originals, was said to retain "Darla's feminine mystique."

• Darla Hood is often mentioned in books about child film stars and discussions of short films. Leonard Maltin, *Our Gang* (1979), gives the history of the series and detailed discussions of some of its episodes; a new edition, coauthored by Richard Bann and titled *The Little Rascals: The Life and Times of Our Gang*, appeared in 1992. Bob Garner's interview with Hood appeared in the *Los Angeles Times*, 25 Dec. 1977. See also Leonard Maltin, *Selected Short Subjects: From Spanky to the Three Stooges*, also known as *Great Movie Shorts* (1972). The *New York Times* obituary, 16 June 1979, is somewhat helpful.

JAMES ROSS MOORE

HOOD, John Bell (29 June 1831–30 Aug. 1879), soldier, was born in Owingsville, Bath County, Kentucky, the son of John W. Hood, a physician, and Theodosia French. Hood grew up near Mount Sterling in Montgomery County, attending local schools and taught by private tutors. In 1849 he was appointed to the U.S. Military Academy at West Point; he had an undistinguished record there, graduating forty-fourth in a class of fifty-two in 1853. He received a commission as brevet second lieutenant in the Fourth U.S. Infantry and was stationed in California. Two years later Hood transferred to the Second U.S. Cavalry and accompanied that regiment to Texas. After serving well in an engagement with Indians, he was promoted to first lieutenant. Hood resigned his commission on 16 April 1861, after the secession of Texas, a state with which he had come to identify strongly. Because his native

Kentucky did not leave the Union, Hood offered his services to the newly formed Confederate government as a Texan.

Commissioned a first lieutenant of cavalry in the Confederate army on 20 April, Hood soon received orders to report to Major General Robert E. Lee in Richmond, Virginia. Hood's performance in a minor action near Yorktown led President Jefferson Davis to promote him to the rank of colonel and assign him to command the newly organized Fourth Texas Infantry Regiment on 1 October. Hood and his men joined the brigade of Brigadier General Louis T. Wigfall and spent the winter of 1861–1862 in camp near Dumfries, Virginia. Wigfall resigned in February 1862 to take a seat in the Confederate Senate, and President Davis appointed Hood a brigadier general on 6 March to rank from 3 March to replace Wigfall. The following month, the brigade marched as a part of Major General William Henry Chase Whiting's division to Yorktown in response to the threat posed by Major General George B. McClellan's Union army.

General Joseph Eggleston Johnston ordered an evacuation of the Yorktown defenses on 3 May before the Union forces could attack. Hood's brigade formed the army's rear guard during the retreat past Williamsburg. On 7 May Hood led his men in their first action, an attack on a Union force that had come ashore from boats on the Pamunkey River at Eltham's Landing. The brigade drove the enemy back to the protection of their gunboats, and Hood received praise from Davis and Johnston. In the battle of Gaines' Mill on 27 June, Hood's heroic leadership in attacking the Union position broke the enemy line and won the engagement for the Confederate army. He and his troops were not engaged again during the Seven Days' Battles. Whiting went on medical furlough in late July, and Hood took command of the division.

Hood led his division during the Second Manassas campaign and won more accolades when he led it in the attack on Major General John Pope's Union army's flank on 30 August. The division marched with General Lee's Army of Northern Virginia in Maryland. Late on 14 September they arrived in time to prevent a union attack from breaking the Confederate line at South Mountain. Hood's men were in reserve when the battle of Sharpsburg began on 17 September. Major General Joseph Hooker's Union corps threatened to break the left flank of the Confederate army, but Hood led his two brigades in a counterattack that knocked Hooker's troops out of the battle and saved the army from certain defeat. Hood's conduct impressed Lee and Major General Stonewall Jackson, who recommended the Texan's promotion. On 10 October Hood became the youngest major general in the army. His division received two additional brigades and assignment to Lieutenant General James Longstreet's First Corps.

During the battle of Fredericksburg on 13 December 1862, Hood's division held a position near the army's center and had no real part in the fighting. A Union threat to Confederate supply lines in southeastern Virginia led Lee to order Hood's division to the Richmond area in February 1863. Soon Longstreet took Hood's and other troops on an abortive campaign against the federal garrison at Suffolk. The Confederates accomplished little. Longstreet and his detachment returned to Lee after the battle of Chancellorsville. As the Army of Northern Virginia marched in Pennsylvania in June, Longstreet's corps was in the rear. Hood and his division reached the battlefield at Gettysburg early on the morning of 2 July. That afternoon Hood received orders to lead his men in an assault on the Union left flank near Little Round Top. Shortly after the division began its attack, Hood was struck in the left arm with shell fragments and had to leave the field; his wounds rendered his left hand permanently useless.

Lee ordered Longstreet with Hood's and Major General Lafayette McLaws's divisions to Georgia in September 1863. During the battle of Chickamauga on 20 September, Hood was again wounded while leading his troops: a Union rifle bullet hit him in the right leg, necessitating amputation of the limb at the thigh. President Davis submitted his name to the Confederate Senate for promotion to the rank of lieutenant general, confirmed on 11 February 1864, with his date of rank made 20 September 1863. General Johnston had recently replaced Bragg as commander of the Army of Tennessee, and Davis appointed Hood commander of one of Johnston's corps.

Hood's performance during the early phases of the Atlanta campaign brought him no great acclaim, though Johnston frequently assigned Hood's corps to the most threatened part of his line. As the army continued to retreat toward Atlanta, Davis despaired of Johnston's ability to prevent the capture of that vital city. On 17 July he removed Johnston from command and named Hood as his successor, with the temporary rank of full general. The new commander quickly went on the offensive. His troops attacked the armies of Major General William Tecumseh Sherman in the battles of Peachtree Creek (20 July), Atlanta (22 July), and Ezra Church (28 July). All three engagements ended in defeats for the Confederates. Sherman cut Hood's supply line south of the city in the battle of Jonesboro (31 Aug.–1 Sept.), forcing an evacuation of Atlanta. Most historians have criticized Hood's aggressiveness in this stage of the campaign, but Stephen Davis cogently argued that Hood "pursued the only plan that had a possibility for success" in preventing the fall of the city and that Johnston's strategy of retreat might have led to the loss of Atlanta earlier (Davis, p. 95).

Now Hood embarked on a campaign that he hoped would force Sherman's armies to abandon Atlanta. He moved his army into northern Georgia, with the idea of cutting the railroads supplying the Federals. This strategy failed, and Hood began looking for some other means of inducing Sherman to give up Atlanta. Eventually he decided to invade Tennessee, hoping to capture Nashville and march toward the Ohio River, where his men would threaten Cincinnati. The army crossed into Tennessee in late November. When his forces failed to trap a portion of the Union forces near Spring Hill on 29 November, Hood became frustrated and ordered an attack on the strongly fortified town of Franklin the next day. A series of assaults failed to accomplish anything except adding to casualty totals. The Federals withdrew during the night to Nashville, and Hood's army took up siege positions south of the city. On 15 and 16 December the Union army, commanded by Major General George Henry Thomas, attacked the Confederates and almost destroyed the Army of Tennessee. On 23 January 1865, Davis relieved Hood of command. After spending some time in Richmond, Hood attempted to travel to the Trans-Mississippi Department. He surrendered to Union troops on 31 May in Natchez, Mississippi.

Settling in New Orleans, Louisiana, Hood worked as a commission merchant and cotton factor and then became president of a life insurance company. He married Anna Marie Hennen on 13 April 1868; the couple had eleven children. Hood died in New Orleans of yellow fever.

Hood was one of the most outstanding brigade and division commanders of the Civil War, but he seemed unfitted for the demands of higher command. Perhaps his physical infirmities contributed to his lack of success, but he never used them as an excuse. He was aggressive but rash in combat. The historian Richard McMurry wrote, "As a fighter, Hood's luck never failed. As a general, he was one of the most unfortunate men ever to head an army" (McMurry, p. 24).

• Some important letters to and from Hood are in the Stephen D. Lee Papers in the Southern Historical Collection at the University of North Carolina and in the Louis T. Wigfall Papers in the Library of Congress. Record Group 109 in the National Archives contains some of Hood's official correspondence. Hood's memoirs, *Advance and Retreat: Personal Experiences in the United States and Confederate States Armies* (1880), were published after his death. The best biography is Richard M. McMurry, *John Bell Hood and the War for Southern Independence* (1982). Two earlier biographies are Richard O'Connor, *Hood, Cavalier General* (1949), and John Percy Dyer, *The Gallant Hood* (1950). A favorable evaluation of Hood's performance as army commander is Stephen Davis, "A Reappraisal of the Generalship of John Bell Hood in the Battles for Atlanta," in *The Campaign for Atlanta and Sherman's March to the Sea: Essays on the American Civil War in Georgia*, ed. Theodore P. Savas and David A. Woodbury (1994). An obituary is in the *New Orleans Democrat*, 31 Aug. 1879.

ARTHUR W. BERGERON, JR.

HOOK, Sidney (20 Dec. 1902–12 July 1989), political philosopher, was born in Brooklyn, New York, the son of Isaac Hook, a garment worker, and Jennie Halpern. Raised in the Jewish immigrant neighborhood of Williamsburg, he graduated from Boys High School in Brooklyn in 1919 and from City College of New York in 1923. His most influential teacher at City College was the legendary practitioner of the Socratic method, Morris R. Cohen. Although he was later to express reservations about Cohen's method, Hook went on to become a skilled polemicist and highly respected public debater. He completed his studies at Columbia University under John Dewey and earned a Ph.D. in philosophy in 1927.

Hook combined the life of social activism with the life of the mind. His activism was in the Enlightenment tradition; that is, he believed the human predicament could be best understood and managed from the perspective of science. He identified his position as secular humanism, which he defined as "the view that morals are autonomous of religious belief, that they are relevant to truths about nature and human nature, truths that rest on scientific evidence" (Paul Kurtz, "An Interview with Sidney Hook at Eighty," *Free Inquiry* 2 [Fall 1982]: 4–10).

As a philosopher he sought to make sense of the relation between thought and action. John Dewey was the greatest philosophical influence on Hook. Dewey's pragmatism held that action is fundamental to thought. Thought emerges from action and is a reflection on action designed to extract norms from previous practice in order to apply and modify those norms in novel contexts. Dewey construed thought as an organic process, not a mechanical one. Hook adopted this general perspective and always remained a pragmatist in his fundamental philosophical orientation.

Hook's doctoral dissertation, *The Metaphysics of Pragmatism*, written under Dewey and published in 1927, was his first attempt to provide a formal and coherent philosophical account of pragmatism. Hook underscored Dewey's insistence that theory must be grounded in prior practice. What this means is that science is a more refined version of the self-corrective dimension of common sense and that common sense contains implicit norms on which science ultimately depends.

Having already published in 1927 a translation of the works of Lenin, Hook gave to Dewey's sense of the social and historical dimension a Marxist bent. In order to accomplish this, Hook reinterpreted Marx's notion of dialectic in pragmatic terms. The point of any theoretical construct or scientific theory is to serve as a recipe for action so that the consequences of employing a construct confirm or discredit it. In *The Meaning of Marx* (1934) Hooks argued, "The implicit prediction that certain consequences will follow upon certain actions, and its truth or falsity is established by the set of actions that realizes or fails to realize the predicted consequences." Each successful action transforms the social world so that further reflection and further modifications of practice become necessary. What Hook objected to in Marxism was the conception of this process as a mechanical one. In combining Dewey and Marx in this fashion, Hook was returning to the Hegelian roots of both Marx and Dewey.

Hook's philosophy was a significant elaboration of American pragmatism. It recognized the presence of norms more basic than scientific practice; it subordinated thought to action; it provided a social and historical dimension for action; and it drew an analogy between the need for self-criticism within science and parliamentary political debate.

Hook began teaching philosophy at New York University in 1927, became chair of the department in 1934, and served until his retirement in 1969. His early students included William Phillips and Delmore Schwartz. His colleagues included James Burnham, Irving Kristol, and William Barrett, who, like Hook, were to move away from Marxism and become critics of it. Hook was a tireless professional in his writing, in organizing conferences, and in presiding over graduate studies. He was a frequent contributor to the *New York Times Magazine* and the *New York Times Book Review* as well as to the periodical *Encounter*, edited by Melvin J. Lasky. He served as president of the Eastern Division of the American Philosophical Association (1959). His closest personal and philosophical friend was Ernest Nagel of Columbia University.

In 1932 Hook supported William Z. Foster, the Communist candidate for president, organizing intellectuals such as Lewis Feuer and Edmund Wilson to sign a manifesto, "Culture and the Crisis," endorsing the Communist cause. In 1933, appalled at Communist party practices, Hook broke with the party and helped to organize the American Workers party with the support of labor unions.

At this time, Hook still considered himself a follower of Karl Marx. He was the first person to have introduced the study of Marx to the American classroom. To distinguish himself from others whom he insisted had misunderstood Marx, he wrote *Towards the Understanding of Karl Marx* (1933). Significantly, Hook was among the first to distinguish Marx from Marxism (i.e., the orthodox communism of the Soviet Union). In a 1934 essay, "On Workers' Democracy," he denounced the Soviet Union for being a dictatorship of the party over the workers. Thereafter, Hook became the leading American anti-Communist and critic of Joseph Stalin. Closely allied with Hook's anti-Stalinism was Sol Levitas, editor of the *New Leader*.

Open discussion had always been important to Hook's understanding of science, of dialectic, and of democratic politics. He was unsparing in his criticism of those who engaged in oppression and violated the spirit of science. Thus, Hook criticized Soviet science and Stalin's great purge and organized a commission, headed by John Dewey in Mexico City in 1938, to investigate Stalin's accusations against Leon Trotsky. It was Hook who at the same time could write an intellectual critique of Trotsky's account of the Bolshevik revolution in *Reason, Social Myths, and Democracy* (1940) and condemn Stalin's persecution of Trotsky.

By 1939 Hook had began to draw a parallel between Nazism and Stalinism as forms of totalitarianism. That year he organized the Committee for Cultural Freedom (along with Dewey, Norman Thomas, John Dos Passos, Sherwood Anderson, and William Carlos Williams) and published a manifesto in the *Nation*. This was the first major organized protest by U.S. intellectuals against Stalin's Soviet Union. A counter group of 400 radicals and liberals led by the *Nation*'s editor,

Freda Kirchwey, denounced Hook's manifesto in a letter and an editorial of the same issue. This was the beginning of a major split in the American liberal Left that has persisted.

By this time Hook was engaged in a deeper critique of Marx and Marxism. He maintained that, understood from the Enlightenment's secular and scientific viewpoint, Marxism was a more consistent development of both liberalism and socialism. Yet he criticized historical materialism and social determinism, stressing the important role of individual initiative and personal responsibility. He articulated this theme in *The Hero in History* (1943). In *Marxism and Beyond* (1983), Hook argued that history is not all class struggle and that there are other contending forces, such as nationalism. He held that Marx's theory of economics was wrong about the issue of surplus value and about the future evolution of capitalism, not foreseeing the welfare state; still, he agreed with Marx's notion that the working class could be a meaningful bearer of humanistic values. Hook continued to oppose what he took to be the misrepresentation of Marxism by Jean-Paul Sartre and Maurice Merleau-Ponty, who had equated it with alienation, and he criticized Herbert Marcuse for denying the capacity of the working class to fight for freedom. In 1947 he dropped the epithet Marxist: "It would appear that if I were justified in my interpretation of Marx's meaning, I would be perhaps the only true Marxist left in the world. This is too much for my sense of humor, and so I have decided to abandon the term as a descriptive epithet of my position" (*Out of Step*, p. 140).

As the Cold War evolved, Hook came to identify himself politically as a social democrat and a "Cold War liberal." He saw the West, flaws and all, as the last bastion of freedom and reasoned self-criticism. Consequently, he opposed both Albert Einstein and Bertrand Russell on the issue of unilateral nuclear disarmament. In 1950 he founded the Congress for Cultural Freedom (along with American intellectuals such as James T. Farrell and European counterparts such as Raymond Aron, Arthur Koestler, and Michael Polanyi). He aimed to counteract that part of the intellectual and cultural Left that was either sympathetic to or covertly sponsored by the Soviet Union. Hook knew Whittaker Chambers and supported his allegations against Alger Hiss on the danger of Soviet subversive penetration of U.S. government agencies.

By 1951 Hook despaired of those intellectuals who had opposed fascism but who refused to resist communism: "In 1935 I could rouse the academic community to Hitler's latest decree. . . . In 1948 when I sought to organize a protest against the cold-blooded execution of Czech students after the Communist coup d'etat, I could hardly raise a corporal's guard."

The debate about the role of American intellectuals in the Cold War reached a new stage with the publication of Hook's *Heresy, Yes, Conspiracy, No* (1952). He argued against the right of Communists to teach because they did not subscribe to the principles of free and open debate and because they engaged in a conspiracy, directed by an enemy power, to undermine academic freedom. Hook distinguished his position from the blacklisting of Communists in Hollywood, something he opposed. In a series of articles written in the *New York Times Magazine*, he deliberately distanced himself from Senator Joseph R. McCarthy. He believed in academic freedom as witnessed by his support of Bertrand Russell's right to teach in the United States, a right that was challenged by others who disliked Russell's social and political views. But Hook did not believe in academic freedom for those who both refused to endorse academic freedom and who tried to undermine it.

During the great debate over the Vietnam conflict, Hook supported the withdrawal of U.S. forces from Vietnam if the North Vietnamese forces also withdrew, although it was then widely maintained that the Vietnam War was a civil war within South Vietnam. In 1972 Hook opposed the presidential campaign of Senator George McGovern, whom he viewed as representing those American intellectuals who refused to denounce communism. At the same time, a new public policy issue, affirmative action, had come to the fore. Hook saw affirmative action, understood as the distribution of positions on the basis of a quota for designated groups, as both inconsistent with academic freedom and as a pretext for introducing what has since become identified as "political correctness" in higher education: the politicization of higher education, especially the use of colleges and universities to promote a particular political agenda as opposed to the reasoned examination of conflicting viewpoints. To oppose it he, along with Milton Friedman, Nathan Glazer, Oscar Handlin, Jeane Kirkpatrick, Paul Kurtz, Daniel Moynihan, and many others, founded University Centers for Rational Alternatives.

In 1973 Hook became a senior research fellow at the Hoover Institution on War, Revolution, and Peace at Stanford University, where he remained until his death in Stanford, California. He was awarded the Presidential Medal of Freedom in 1985. Hook was married twice, in 1924 to Carrie Katz, with whom he had one child, and in 1935 to Ann Zinken, with whom he had two children.

Hook always remained a social democrat, a political activist, and a secularist who rejected the label of "neo-conservative." As a philosopher, he came more and more to dwell on those elusive values that undergird the exercise of reason. He summed up his own life as follows: "I have always been somewhat premature in relation to dominant currents of public opinion. I was prematurely antiwar in 1917–1921, prematurely antifascist, prematurely a Communist fellow-traveler, prematurely an anticommunist [and] a supporter of the war against Hitler, prematurely a cold warrior against Stalin's efforts, . . . prematurely against the policy of detente and appeasement, prematurely for a national civil rights program and against all forms of invidious discrimination, including reverse discrimination" (*Out of Step*, pp. 604–5).

In a remarkable career that spanned most of the century, Hook managed to exercise a profound personal and intellectual influence on academics, labor leaders, educators, public figures, and journalists. He was a principal participant in the major intellectual and political debates in American life in the twentieth century. The evolution of his thinking marked the major transitions in Marxist and leftist debate. He was an academic philosopher who made notable contributions to debate in the larger public context.

• Hook's papers are at the Hoover Institution, Stanford, Calif. Hook's autobiography is *Out of Step: An Unquiet Life in the Twentieth Century* (1987). In addition to Hook's publications mentioned in the text, his most important discussions of philosophical issues are in *The Quest for Being* (1961) and *Pragmatism and the Tragic Sense of Life* (1974). His works related to Dewey include *The Metaphysics of Pragmatism* (1927) and *John Dewey, an Intellectual Portrait* (1939). His other major discussions of Marx and Marxism are in *From Hegel to Marx* (1936) and *Marx and the Marxists: The Ambiguous Legacy* (1955). Hook's general political philosophy and his views on public policy issues are in *Common Sense and the Fifth Amendment* (1957), *Political Power and Personal Freedom* (1959), *The Paradoxes of Freedom* (1962), *The Place of Religion in a Free Society* (1968), and *Revolution, Reform and Social Justice* (1975). He discusses educational issues in *Education for Modern Man* (1946), *Academic Freedom and Academic Anarchy* (1970), and *Education and the Taming of Power* (1973). Two collections of essays about Hook, both edited by Paul Kurtz, are especially noteworthy, *Sidney Hook and the Contemporary World* (1968) and *Sidney Hook, Philosopher of Democracy and Humanism* (1983). An obituary is in the *New York Times*, 14 July 1989.

NICHOLAS CAPALDI

HOOKER, Donald Russell (7 Sept. 1876–1 Aug. 1946), physiologist, was born in New Britain, Connecticut, the youngest child of Frank Henry Hooker, founder and owner of the Henry Hooker Carriage Manufacturing Company of New Haven, and Grace Russell. As a child Donald suffered from polio and was left with a limp. He graduated from Yale University in 1899, stayed to earn an M.A. in 1901, and then entered Johns Hopkins Medical School. As a medical student he demonstrated a talent for research by collaborating with Joseph Erlanger on a study of Hooker's own malady, orthostatic albuminuria. The result, which showed that the output of albumin depended primarily on changes in pulse pressure rather than blood pressure, were published in 1904 as a monograph in the *Johns Hopkins Hospital Reports* (vol. 12).

Receiving an M.D. in 1905, Hooker that same year married Edith Houghton, one of the first women to be admitted as a student at Johns Hopkins School of Medicine. They had five children. From 1905 to 1908 the couple traveled in Europe, making observations of the laboratory methods of famous physiologists. Upon returning to Baltimore, Hooker became an instructor at Johns Hopkins and in 1910 was made an associate professor in recognition of his numerous published contributions to the field of physiology and experimental biology.

As late as 1917 Hooker was one of only four faculty members in Johns Hopkins's Department of Physiology, which was in its infancy, and only ninety students attended the entire medical school. Hooker lectured on the circulation and in the laboratory was engaged with studies on vasomotor control and the capillary and renal circulations. He gave up teaching in 1914 to devote his time exclusively to research and the editing of scientific journals in his field. In 1921 he resigned from Johns Hopkins.

In the 1920s electric utility companies started funding research on the growing incidence of death by electric shock among linemen. Working with Professor William H. Howell, head of Johns Hopkins's School of Hygiene and Public Health, Hooker began to study the problem and was successful in defibrillating a dog's heart but was unable to start it beating again. Continuing his experiments, he finally achieved international attention in 1934 when he revived a small black and white dog that had been clinically dead for eleven minutes. The dog suffered no impairment, was renamed "Knowsy," and became a family pet. Hooker's experiments on ventricular fibrillation ultimately led, in other hands, to the successful development of current methods for electrical shock in restoring the normal rhythms of the heart in cardiac arrest and/or acute arrhythmias.

Hooker's reputation as a national authority on physiology was enhanced by his activities as a writer and editor. In 1914 he became managing editor of the *American Journal of Physiology* and in 1921 a founder and editor of *Physiological Reviews*, which he continued to edit until his death. Commenting on his contributions, the *Journal* in 1947 called Hooker "a truly great editor" over a period of thirty-two years:

The *American Journal* and *Physiological Reviews* were placed and maintained in the front rank of scientific publications. Doctor Hooker's calmness, his sympathy, his good judgment, his fairness, and his sense of social as well as scientific values, were all reflected in his career. . . . No one of his generation has had a greater influence on American physiology.

Hooker was also a founding member of the Federation of American Societies for Experimental Biology and became its first permanent secretary in 1935.

Hooker and his wife were especially interested in helping unmarried mothers, combatting social diseases, and promoting recreation for underprivileged children. Realizing the distressing plight of unmarried mothers who left Johns Hopkins with no resources, they established St. George's Home near the hospital. In 1911 Hooker presented a paper titled "The Social Evil," which contended that Baltimore had nearly 300 disorderly houses; it resulted in a movement to end such vice. He and his wife founded the Roosevelt Park Recreation Center and a Planned Parenthood Clinic in Baltimore. For many years Hooker was a director and chief financial supporter of the Heny Watson Children's Aid Society. He was also chairman of a mayor's committee to survey the city's recreational facilities and bring about their coordination. He died in Baltimore.

• A record of Hooker's publications is in the Alan Mason Chesney Medical Archives at Johns Hopkins. The best account of Hooker's work is in the *American Journal of Physiology* 148 (1947). He is also cited in Harvey A. McGehee, *Adventures in Medical Research* (1976), pp. 277 and 286, which covers a century of discovery at Johns Hopkins. Other information about his life is in the *Johns Hopkins Alumni Magazine* (Nov. 1946). His involvement in social hygiene is described in Diana Long, "Physiological Identity of American Sex Researchers between the Two World Wars" in *Physiology in the American Context, 1850–1940*, ed. Gerald Geison (1987), pp. 264–65. Obituaries are in the *Baltimore Sun*, 3 Aug. 1946, and the *Journal of the American Medical Association*, 17 Aug. 1946.

ELLSWORTH S. GRANT

HOOKER, Earl (15 Jan. 1930–21 Apr. 1970), blues guitarist, was born Earl Zebedee Hooker, Jr., in Clarksdale, Mississippi, the son of Earl Hooker, Sr., and Mary Blare, Delta farmers. Because Earl, Sr., played several instruments, including the guitar, and Mary had once worked as a vocalist with a touring variety show, Earl, Jr., and his twin sister were exposed to music at an early age. Earl, Jr., taught himself to play guitar by age ten, and a year later, after a move to Chicago, he began taking formal lessons at the Lyon and Healy music school, learning not only guitar, but banjo, mandolin, piano, and drums. His primary mentor was an older Arkansas-born guitarist, Robert Nighthawk, an established blues professional who taught Hooker to play electric bottleneck style.

In his teens Hooker performed on the streets, at times with another Mississippi transplant, Ellas McDaniel, later known as Bo Diddley. By 1947 he was working with Nighthawk, touring the South and doing radio shows on KFFA in Helena, Arkansas, WDIA in Memphis, and other stations. In 1949 Hooker relocated to Memphis, where he eventually teamed up with pianist Ike Turner—also a Clarksdale native—and toured the South with Turner's band. In the late 1940s and early 1950s he also worked with harmonica virtuoso Sonny Boy Williamson on the popular "King Biscuit Time" show broadcast on station KFFA.

Working in Florida with his own band in 1952, Hooker recorded several blues tunes, including "Sweet Angel" and "On the Hook," issued on the Rockin' label, and "Race Track" and "Blue Guitar Blues," issued on King. In 1953 he teamed up in Memphis with pianist Pinetop Perkins and guitarist Boyd Gilmore to do some session work for the Memphis Recording Service, but nothing was issued at the time. By the mid-1950s Hooker was touring the Midwest with Chicago-based guitarist and singer Otis Rush. As Rush later recalled, "Earl Hooker . . . stayed with me for six months, longer than anybody in the world that I ever heard of him playing with." Hooker by then had developed a marked preference for working with his own band.

Through the 1950s and early 1960s Hooker worked mainly around Chicago, recording a series of singles for various small-time Chicago labels: Argo, C. J., B+B, Chief, Age, Checker, and Mil-Lon. The best of these were for Mel London's Chief and Age labels, which included collaborations with harmonica player and vocalist Junior Wells and vocalists Lillian Offitt and Ricky Allen. Hooker himself never became a confident blues vocalist, perhaps because of his long battle against tuberculosis. He concentrated instead on playing guitar, eventually mastering not only blues but other styles—jazz, rock, even country and western. Stranded once in Waterloo, Iowa, he played guitar with an all white "hillbilly band" for six months, discovering in the process that his comparatively thin singing voice adapted comfortably to songs by such country stars as Hank Williams and Ernest Tubb.

During the early 1960s Hooker was hospitalized several times as his tuberculosis worsened, but he never quit playing entirely, even if it meant doing hospital benefit concerts. By the mid-1960s he was back on the Chicago and midwestern club circuits, working with various artists—including blues singer Herman "Little Junior" Parker—and recording an instrumental album in Wisconsin. In 1965 he formed a band to back his cousin, singer Joe Hinton, and toured with the band in Europe, where he appeared on a London television show with the British rock group the Beatles. Returning to Chicago, he continued to work clubs with his own band through 1969, also playing at Theresa's, a landmark South Side blues club, with the Junior Wells band. The albums he recorded for Bluesway, Arhoolie, and Blue Thumb during this period brought him newfound recognition, and in 1969 he recorded a blues-rock collaboration with Steve Miller in California, raising the possibility of additional crossover work. That same year, after Hooker returned from a European tour with the American Folk Blues Festival, he put together yet another group, the rock-influenced Electric Dust Band. Although he appeared to be on the brink of crossover success, his chronic illness forced him to enter a municipal tuberculosis sanatorium in Chicago, where he died. He was survived by his wife, Bertha Nixon.

During his 25-year career Hooker played with most of the major blues artists of his era, including B. B. King, Muddy Waters, Bobby Bland, and Jimmy Witherspoon. He also led several exotically named bands of his own: the Roadmasters, the Soul Twisters, the Invaders, and his final group, the Electric Dust Band. Known mainly as a guitarist rather than a singer, Hooker recorded with a long lineup of blues vocalists: Lillian Offitt, Harold Tidwell, Junior Wells, A. C. Reed, and Andrew Odum, among others.

While Hooker's guitar work was influenced by blues, jazz, and country players ranging from slide specialist Robert Nighthawk to country pickers Merle Travis and Joe Maphis, he distilled his many sources into his own easily recognizable sound. Known to his peers as "Zeb," from his middle name, he was the undisputed master of the slide, ultimately surpassing the skill of his mentor Nighthawk. Hooker was also one of the first blues guitarists to master the wah-wah peddle and the double-necked guitar. He influenced many other blues guitarists, as well as crossover rockers such as Ike Turner, Jimi Hendrix, Elvin Bishop, and George Thorogood.

Despite his chronic illness, Hooker had terrific drive when on stage, dazzling audiences with both his technical skill and his showmanship—playing the guitar with his teeth, for example, or behind his back. At the time of his death, Hooker was considered by many other musicians to be the best guitarist in Chicago. But his death cut short the events that might have extended his fame beyond the inner circle of musicians who constituted his most enthusiastic legion of fans.

• For more information, see Sheldon Harris, *Blues Who's Who: A Biographical Dictionary of Blues Singers* (1979; repr. 1989). For a discography, see Mike Leadbitter and Neil Slaven, *Blues Records 1943–1966: A Selective Discography*, vol. 1: *A–K*, rev. ed. (1987). An obituary is in *Living Blues* 1, no. 2 (Summer 1970): 9.

BARRY LEE PEARSON
BILL McCULLOCH

HOOKER, Elon Huntington (23 Nov. 1869–10 May 1938), founder of Hooker Electrochemical Company, was born in Rochester, New York, the son of Susan Pamelia Huntington and Horace B. Hooker. Hooker's parents were descended from old New England families with high social standing. Hooker's father was an engineer in his youth but at the close of the Civil War left engineering for the nursery business and inventing. These activities left family fortunes precarious.

After receiving his early education in Rochester schools, Hooker enrolled in 1887 at the University of Rochester, where, more interested in social affairs and sports than in study, he was not a particularly good student but graduated in 1891 with an A.B. While attending college, Hooker worked summers on water and sewer projects with Emil Kuichling, Rochester's city engineer, to supplement family funds. The experience sparked an interest in engineering. He spent the year after graduation working with Kuichling and then enrolled at Cornell in 1892 to study civil engineering. Finishing his studies in two years, he graduated in 1894 with a B.S. and highest honors, which earned him a graduate fellowship that permitted study abroad. He spent most of 1895 in Europe, studying hydraulic engineering at Zürich Polytechnic and the École des Ponts et Chaussées, and returned to Cornell to finish his Ph.D. by June 1896, with a dissertation on river hydraulics.

From 1896 to 1899 Hooker worked as a hydraulic engineer for Washburn & Washburn. He supervised improvements to Boston's water supply system and Cornell's Hydraulic Laboratory and served on a committee examining the Nicaragua canal route.

In 1899 Theodore Roosevelt, then governor of New York, appointed Hooker deputy superintendent of public works. Roosevelt left office in 1900, but Hooker remained in office under Roosevelt's successor.

Hooker, meanwhile, continued to court the eldest daughter of Detroit "seed baron" Dexter Ferry, Blanche Ferry, whom he had met in Europe in 1895. The two were married in 1901 and had four children.

By now Hooker had superb business and social contacts. In July 1901 a Ferry family friend offered him a vice presidency in the Development Company of America, a venture capital firm. For the next year and a half, Hooker researched investment opportunities for the firm, primarily in timber, mining, and railroad enterprises in the Southwest.

In January 1903 Hooker launched his own venture firm, the Development and Funding Company. After considering more than 250 projects, he decided to commercialize the newly invented Townsend process, an electrochemical means of extracting caustic soda and chlorine, used for making cleaning products and paper, from brine that had been invented by Clinton Townsend, a chemist and patent attorney, and Elmer Sperry, a well-known electrical and mechanical inventor.

After testing the process at an experimental plant in Brooklyn, Hooker purchased the Townsend-Sperry patents in December 1904 and raised funds to build a commercial plant at Niagara Falls, which he selected largely because it had the prime requirement for electrochemical production—cheap electricity. His plant went into production in January 1906 and for the first two years yielded no profits. Rightly convinced that the problem was scale, Hooker began increasing the capacity of the plant, quadrupling it by 1910 to twenty tons of caustic soda and forty-four tons of bleaching powder per day.

In November 1909, with commercial success on the horizon, Hooker organized the Hooker Electrochemical Company as a subsidiary of the Development and Funding Company, with himself as president. Although Hooker Electrochemical was intended as only the first of several subsidiaries, it so absorbed Hooker's energies and capital that it remained the only one, and in 1918 the parent company was dissolved.

In May 1910 a fire destroyed much of Hooker's plant, but by 1911 it was back in operation and turning a profit. Hooker was now able to shift some of his energies elsewhere. In 1912 he served as national treasurer of Roosevelt's Progressive party and was named one of Roosevelt's New York electors. In 1917, after the United States entered World War I, Roosevelt asked Hooker to head the gas warfare section of the abortive Roosevelt division. Hooker also submitted a plan for organizing America's chemical war effort to the Woodrow Wilson administration, but the administration chose not to act on it.

Hooker's company, however, took advantage of the elimination of German chemical competition by the war and rising demand for chemicals to expand its product line from two chemicals in 1914 to seventeen by 1918. In 1915 Hooker built the first American plant to produce monochlorobenzene, a chemical used to produce dyes and explosives. By 1918 this plant was the largest of its kind in the world, producing one and a half million pounds of the chemical per month.

In the postwar era, Hooker again entered politics. Beginning in 1912 he had headed the American Defense Society, an organization dedicated to foiling bolshevism in the United States, and continued in that position into the 1920s. In 1920 he attracted national attention by charging the Wilson administration with mismanagement of the poison gas program during the war for spending millions of dollars on production but failing to get the supply to the American forces. That same year he unsuccessfully sought the Republican nomination for governor of New York on a platform he claimed would, by virtue of his business experience, reduce both the cost of living and the cost of government.

In 1923 and 1924 Hooker became involved in the debate over control of Muscle Shoals, an uncompleted government-constructed complex on the Tennessee River intended to extract nitrogen, a key component of explosives, from the atmosphere. In early 1923 businessman Henry Ford had offered to purchase the complex, setting off a national debate over public versus private ownership of the waterpowers of the Tennessee River. Late in 1923 Hooker and several associates entered a bid on the complex. Although Muscle Shoals remained in government hands, Hooker's proposal derailed Ford's plans. In 1924 and 1925 Hooker served as vice president of the National Republican Club, and in 1928 he used his business ties to lobby American exporters to support the Herbert Hoover presidential campaign.

Remaining professionally active, Hooker served as president of the Research Corporation from 1915 to 1922 and the Manufacturing Chemists' Association from 1923 to 1925. He was on the executive boards of the National Civic Federation, the National Industrial Conference Board, and the National Association of Manufacturers, and he was a trustee of the University of Rochester (1916–1938).

Hooker's appearance and personality enabled him to function effectively in both public and corporate worlds. He was an attractive man—tall, athletic, charming, and meticulously neat. He remained active in sports, especially golf and tennis, for most of his life. He was a dynamic and effective public speaker. As a manager, he was decisive and well organized. He engendered loyalty among his managerial employees by delegating well and by promoting from within. His relations with labor were also good. Although his attitude was paternalistic, he frequently met with his employees and supported and sponsored company sports programs, a company-sponsored "union" (representation plan), and safety programs. As a result, Hooker's plants were virtually free of strikes.

Hooker's company flourished in the 1920s, and in 1929, expanding beyond Niagara Falls, it opened a chlor-alkali plant in Tacoma, Washington, the first such plant in the Pacific Northwest, which produced chlorine and bleaching powder for the paper industry

and alkali for the California oil industry to help purify petroleum products. Although further expansion was blocked by the Great Depression and the ensuing competition in the chemical industry, Hooker's well-engineered and efficiently managed plants recovered quickly. The company expanded its product line in the 1930s from about thirty to nearly seventy chemicals.

In the 1930s Hooker began to devote more time to leisure and travel. In the spring of 1938 on a long vacation to California with his wife and a daughter he caught bronchial pneumonia, which led to a fatal heart attack. He died in Pasadena.

• The Hooker Family Papers and the Huntington-Hooker Family Papers at the University of Rochester contain scattered materials relating to Hooker. The primary published sources for biographical information are *Elon Huntington Hooker: A Tribute to Our Founder* (1938) and Robert E. Thomas's history of the Hooker Electrochemical Company, *Salt and Water, Power and People: A Short History of Hooker Electrochemical Company* (1955). Neither of these accounts is critical or complete. Shorter biographical sketches can be found in Edward Hooker, *The Descendants of Rev. Thomas Hooker* (1909), and Wyndham D. Miles, ed., *American Chemists and Chemical Engineers* (1976). For a brief but good account of the role of Hooker's company in the development of the American electrochemical industry, see James J. Leddy, "Industrial Electrochemistry," in *Electrochemistry, Past and Present*, ed. John T. Stock and Mary Virginia Orna (1989), pp. 499–501. Obituaries are in the *Niagara Falls Gazette* and the *New York Times*, both 11 May 1938.

TERRY S. REYNOLDS

HOOKER, Isabella Beecher (22 Feb. 1822–25 Jan. 1907), suffragist, writer, and women's rights advocate, was born in Litchfield, Connecticut, the daughter of Lyman Beecher, a Presbyterian minister and evangelist, and his second wife, Harriet Porter. At age ten Isabella moved with her family to Cincinnati, Ohio, where Lyman became the first president of Lane Theological Seminary. After her mother's death three years later, Isabella returned to Connecticut to study at the Hartford Female Seminary, founded by her half sisters Catharine Beecher and Harriet Beecher. She divided her education between Hartford and another of Catharine's schools, the Western Female Institute in Cincinnati. Isabella's interest in women's rights originated and matured within her domestic experience, beginning with her resentment of this desultory girlhood education.

By the time of her engagement to John Hooker in 1839, Isabella had begun to connect women's public and private disabilities. She had met Hooker, a law clerk for her brother-in-law Thomas Perkins, in Hartford in 1837. Before their marriage, Isabella wrote to John urging that they avoid the "radical defect" she had observed in the marriages of her brothers and sisters. Gently but firmly, she argued that the legal inequality of nineteenth-century spouses produced much marital unhappiness. She delicately implied that the loving partnership she envisioned for herself and John would entail sexual restraint, to limit the number of children born and thereby preserve to the wife both strength and leisure for self-improvement and usefulness.

Lyman and Catharine Beecher strongly urged John to forsake the law to follow all the Beecher sons into the ordained ministry. Isabella added a somewhat equivocal endorsement to the idea, but John Hooker remained a lawyer, and the couple married in 1841. In future struggles against Beecher opinion, John and Isabella were allies, as her analyses of domesticity drew her further away from the Beecher example.

Isabella's relation to the other Beechers, briefly but decisively shaken in the crisis of her engagement, preoccupied and frustrated her during the early years of her married life. The increasing fame of her sisters and her brother Henry Ward Beecher and the erudite circle of friends settled around "Nook Farm," the Hookers' Hartford home, lent Isabella a certain borrowed distinction. Her own time and energy, however, were consumed by four pregnancies, three surviving children, and the duties incident to being a lawyer's wife. She keenly regretted her public inactivity and to John she both complained of and apologized for her insignificance.

Isabella Hooker's early ability to analyze women's rights within the private sphere, though, led her to pour her intelligence and reform instincts into the contemplation of child rearing and wifehood. Shrewd analyses of her children, a belief in gentle discipline, and flashes of rueful maternal humor give a distinctly modern cast to her musings, which contrasts sharply with the romantic maternalism of her sister Catharine.

In 1868, with her two daughters married and her youngest child nearing majority, Hooker returned to public life with the publication of "A Mother's Letters to a Daughter on Woman's Suffrage" in *Putnam's Magazine*. Over the next forty years, until her death in Hartford, Hooker refined her arguments for and deepened her commitment to the cause of women's rights. From the tentative and unpublished essay "Shall Women Vote? A Matrimonial Dialogue" (1860) through her influential treatise called *Womanhood: Its Sanctities and Fidelities* (1873) to her last published tract, *An Argument on United States Citizenship* (1902), Hooker imagined and argued for a democratic society that made public use of the knowledge and virtue gained by women in their domestic struggles. Women, she maintained, should be judges and juries because they learned to adjudicate at home, equitably settling passionate disputes among their children. Women learned to legislate at home as well, quietly persuading others and spending patient years urging projects forward to completion. Hooker argued that wife- and motherhood provided the best possible training for government service, a view that, for her, made woman suffrage all the more urgent.

Convinced that domestic inequality was the indispensable prop for women's public disfranchisement, Hooker supported Elizabeth Cady Stanton and Susan B. Anthony in the 1860s when they combined suffra-gism with calls for broadening women's legal rights. Hooker's New England friends and her Beecher relations forcefully urged her to ally with the American Woman Suffrage Association, which rejected as immoral and distracting Stanton's call for the reform of marriage and divorce laws. Hooker, however, joined the National Woman Suffrage Association (NWSA), founded a Connecticut branch, and lobbied Congress on behalf of Stanton and Anthony's national woman suffrage amendment.

Hooker's politics of domesticity finally precipitated the great principled confrontation of her life. In the fall of 1872 Victoria Woodhull, a generous contributor to and speaker for the NWSA, publicly accused Henry Ward Beecher of adultery with Elizabeth Tilton, who, with her abolitionist husband, Theodore Tilton, was a pillar of Beecher's Brooklyn congregation. Though the Beecher clan "circled the wagons," Hooker pointedly refused to join them, instead openly doubting her brother's innocence and denouncing the double standard under which both Woodhull and Elizabeth Tilton were savagely attacked. Ostracized by her sons-in-law and her siblings, some of whom questioned her mental stability, she and John, himself worn out from publicly defending both her virtue and her sanity, took a two-year trip to Europe. The Hookers also explored spiritualism during these years, seeking both comfort and vindication. In 1877 Connecticut passed the married women's property act, which John and Isabella had drafted, and though never fully reconciled with the Beechers, the Hookers continued to work for suffrage and women's rights reforms.

Though they were raised in Lyman Beecher's Protestant patriarchate, none of the Beecher sisters fully conformed to it. Isabella Hooker, the "Last Beecher," refined and tested her critique of Beecher family life within her own domestic arrangements. She was the only Beecher to embrace publicly and fervently both the domestic and the political empowerment of American womanhood.

• Hooker's papers have been collected and published, along with a superb guide, as *The Isabella Beecher Hooker Project: A Microfiche Edition of Her Papers and Suffrage-Related Correspondence Owned by the Stowe-Day Foundation* (1979). See *Connecticut Magazine* 9, no. 2 (1905): 287–98 for an autobiographical sketch, "The Last of the Beechers: Memories on My Eighty-third Birthday." Jeanne Boydston, Mary Kelley, and Anne Margolis, in *The Limits of Sisterhood* (1988), compare Hooker with Catharine Beecher and Harriet Beecher. Hooker also figures materially in Elizabeth Cady Stanton and Susan B. Anthony, *History of Woman Suffrage*, vols. 2 (1881) and 3 (1886), and in biographies of her famous relatives. For Hooker's impact on her grandniece Charlotte Perkins Gilman, see Mary A. Hill, *Charlotte Perkins Gilman: The Making of a Radical Feminist, 1860–1896* (1980). For a standard biography of the Beecher clan, including the family's Welsh ancestry, to which Henry Ward credited his "fervid imagination," see Milton Allan Rugoff, *The Beechers: An American Family in the Nineteenth Century* (1981). An obituary of Hooker is in the *Hartford Courant*, 25 Jan. 1907.

SHARON ANN HOLT

HOOKER, Joseph (13 Nov. 1814–31 Oct. 1879), soldier, was born in Hadley, Massachusetts, the son of Joseph Hooker, a businessman, and Mary Seymour. He received his basic education at Hopkins Academy in Hadley and in 1833 was appointed to the U.S. Military Academy at West Point, from which he graduated four years later. Commissioned a second lieutenant in the artillery, during the next nine years he served in Florida, at various posts in the Northeast, and as adjutant at West Point, rising to the rank of first lieutenant. During the Mexican War (1846–1848) he performed so superbly both as a staff and combat officer that he received three brevet promotions, the final one to lieutenant colonel. No other northern commander of the coming Civil War emerged from the Mexican conflict with a better record or higher reputation than Hooker.

In 1849 Hooker, whose regular rank now was captain, assumed the post of adjutant general of the Pacific Division, headquartered in Sonoma, California. Finding his duties dull, prices pushed up by the gold rush, and his salary inadequate, he began gambling for big stakes, evidently with small success, and drinking heavily. In 1851 he applied for and received a two-year leave of absence, and then in 1853 he resigned from the army. For the next seven years Hooker engaged in ranching and various business enterprises along the West Coast, dabbled in California politics, and frequently borrowed money but paid his debts less frequently.

In the late spring of 1861, following the outbreak of the Civil War, Hooker traveled by steamer to the East to seek a military command. Thanks to the backing of Oregon senator Edward D. Baker and following an interview with President Abraham Lincoln, he obtained on 31 July 1861 a brigadier general's commission in the volunteer service with an assignment to head a brigade in the army being assembled at Washington, D.C., by Major General George B. McClellan. Hooker thus began his climb up the ladder of command, one that he confidently predicted would end with his reaching the highest rung.

Throughout the rest of 1861 and well into 1862 Hooker had no opportunity to advance his ambitions, as all was "quiet along the Potomac." Finally, in April 1862, McClellan began his Peninsular campaign—a slow, cautious movement from Fortress Monroe toward the Confederate capital at Richmond, Virginia. At Williamsburg on 5 May, Hooker, now leading a division, made a rash attack that produced severe losses and provoked a Confederate counterthrust that nearly drove his division from the field. Nevertheless northern newspapers hailed the engagement as a victory and began calling Hooker "Fighting Joe." During the remainder of the Peninsular campaign, which ended with the Seven Days' battles (25 June–1 July) and McClellan's retreat, Hooker did much better, notably at White Oak Swamp and Malvern Hill, and won promotion to major general of volunteers. Transferred along with most of McClellan's army to the command of Major General John Pope in northern Virginia, Hooker again performed well at Bristoe Station (27 Aug.) and

at Second Manassas (Second Bull Run, 29–30 Aug.), earning the corps command to which he was assigned on 5 September. Twelve days later, once more serving under McClellan, Hooker opened the battle of Antietam with a ferocious assault by his corps upon the Confederate left that almost surely would have led to the defeat of Robert E. Lee's army had it been supported by other Federal units. Hooker, who was wounded in the foot, received more public acclaim and a brigadier general's commission in the regular army.

Early in November 1862 Lincoln, exasperated by McClellan's "slows," replaced him as commander of the Army of the Potomac with Major General Ambrose Burnside, but not until after he had considered Hooker for the post. Burnside organized the army into three Grand Divisions of two corps each, one of which, the Center Grand Division, he assigned to Hooker. At Fredericksburg, Virginia, on 13 December 1862, Hooker participated in Burnside's blundering and bloody assault on the impregnable Confederate position, losing (in his caustic words) "as many men as my orders required me to lose" (Hebert, p. 159). The Fredericksburg debacle, which was followed by the fiasco of the "Mud March," resulted in Lincoln on 25 January 1863 relieving Burnside and appointing Hooker in his stead. Although Lincoln had some misgivings about Hooker, arising from loose talk at his headquarters about the need for a "dictator," he was the logical choice: no other general in the East of appropriate rank had a comparable combat record.

Hooker spent the next three months reorganizing, rebuilding, and restoring the morale of the Army of the Potomac. Then late in April he launched a campaign designed to smash Lee's Army of Northern Virginia. Taking advantage of his great superiority in numbers—he had 135,000 troops opposed to Lee's 60,000—he used part of his army to pin down the Confederates at Fredericksburg while he led the main portion around Lee's left flank with the object of getting into his rear, which he did on 30 April when his advance reached Chancellorsville. The following day, however, he encountered unexpected resistance from an enemy force of unknown size, whereupon he halted and went over to the defensive. Hooker thus surrendered the initiative to Lee, who on 2 May sent Lieutenant General Thomas J. "Stonewall" Jackson with 28,000 men to strike the exposed Union right flank, a mission that Jackson accomplished with devastating success. Even so, the Federals still heavily outnumbered the Confederates, held a strong position, and could have continued the battle with excellent prospects of victory, something several of Hooker's generals urged him to do. Instead he retreated; although his army had not been defeated, he had been. As he later admitted, "For once I lost confidence in Hooker" (Hebert, p. 199).

Lincoln also lost confidence in Hooker, or at least in his ability to cope with an antagonist such as Lee. Consequently Hooker met with so much interference from Washington in his efforts to counter Lee's invasion of

Pennsylvania that on 27 June 1863 he resigned as commander of the Army of the Potomac. Lincoln, however, still believed that Hooker was a capable combat leader and therefore, following the defeat of Major General William S. Rosecrans's army at Chickamauga, Georgia (19–20 Sept. 1863), he placed Hooker in command of two corps (XI and XII) from the Army of the Potomac that were sent to reinforce Rosecrans at Chattanooga, Tennessee. On 24–25 November Hooker, now serving under Ulysses S. Grant, who had taken command of all Union troops at Chattanooga, captured Lookout Mountain and then moved against the Confederate left on Missionary Ridge, an advance that contributed significantly to the Union victory. Although Grant unfairly disparaged Hooker's role in the battle of Chattanooga, Hooker regained some of the prestige he lost at Chancellorsville and hoped to win more laurels and perhaps restoration to a high command in the forthcoming campaign against Atlanta.

It was not to be. William T. Sherman, commander of the Union forces in the Atlanta campaign (May–Sept. 1864), detested Hooker, who made no attempt to conceal his contempt for Sherman. Therefore, despite the fact that Hooker's corps (the XX, formed by a consolidation of the XI and XII corps) both suffered and inflicted more casualties than any other corps in Sherman's army, Sherman consistently ignored Hooker's successes and constantly criticized him for alleged failures. The final straw, insofar as Hooker was concerned, fell on 26 July 1864 when Sherman named Major General Oliver Otis Howard to replace Major General James B. McPherson, killed four days before, as permanent commander of the Army of the Tennessee. Not only was Howard far junior to Hooker in age and rank, but Hooker also blamed him, not without just cause, for the routing of the Union left flank, which Howard had commanded, at Chancellorsville. At once Hooker asked to be relieved from duty with "an army in which rank and service are ignored." Sherman gladly accepted his request.

Hooker spent the remaining months of the war as head of the Northern Department (Mich., Ohio, Ind., Ill.) and then with the coming of peace commanded the Department of the East, headquartered in New York City. In 1865 he married Olivia Groesbeck, a member of a wealthy Cincinnati family, but soon suffered a stroke that left him partially paralyzed. They had no children. In 1868 his wife died, leaving him financially independent, whereupon he resigned from the army, having achieved the regular rank of major general, and moved to Garden City, New York. During the final decade of his life he traveled extensively, attended veterans reunions, and occasionally lashed out at old enemies; to the end he remained "Fighting Joe." He died in Garden City.

Hooker was tall, well proportioned, and strikingly handsome. Beneath his imposing physical presence, however, were serious flaws of character. His chief flaws were conceit, lack of tact and discretion, and an overweening and not altogether scrupulous ambition. According to one oft-quoted source, Hooker's head-quarters while he commanded the Army of the Potomac "was a combination of bar-room and brothel" (Hebert, p. 180), but although he was fond of the bottle there is no firm evidence that drinking impaired his performance in the field. While it is extremely unlikely that he remained celibate until his marriage at the age of fifty, there is no truth in the allegation that his sexual activities led to the term "hooker" becoming a synonym for prostitute.

As to Hooker's military abilities, two conclusions would seem to be justified. First, he had few equals and perhaps no superior among Union generals as commander of a corps or any force he could personally supervise and inspire. Second, he was deficient, as revealed at Chancellorsville, in those qualities of mind and temperament needed to lead a large army in a successful offensive campaign against a foe as redoubtable as Lee and his Army of Northern Virginia. But, then, the only northern general who ever did so was Grant, and it took him a year and 100,000 casualties to do it. Thus it is quite possible that if Hooker had gone against any Confederate army commander other than Lee, he would have garnered the glory he sought. His failure at Chancellorsville basically was his own fault, but it also can be said that he was unfortunate in his opponent.

• Manuscript letters of a personal nature by and to Hooker are few and mostly in private collections. His military reports and correspondence are readily available in the appropriate volumes of *The War of the Rebellion: A Compilation of the Official Records of the Union and Confederate Armies* (128 vols., 1880–1901), and his testimony concerning various campaigns and battles in the East is in the *Reports* of the Joint Committee on the Conduct of the War (37th and 38th Cong., 1863–1865). Unfortunately he did not file a report on the Atlanta campaign nor did he write his memoirs; what he might have said about Sherman and certain other high-ranking Union generals would have made for lively reading. Walter H. Hebert, *Fighting Joe Hooker* (1944) is a full-fledged biography; its bibliography and notes provide a good guide to primary sources pertaining to Hooker's career. The amount of historical literature dealing with the Chancellorsville campaign, the decisive event in that career, is enormous, with the best studies being John Bigelow, Jr., *Chancellorsville* (1910), and Ernest B. Furguson, *Chancellorsville 1863* (1992). The best accounts of Hooker's role in the other eastern campaigns of 1861–1863 are in Kenneth P. Williams, *Lincoln Finds a General* (5 vols., 1949–1959), and Bruce Catton, *Mr. Lincoln's Army* (1951) and *Glory Road* (1952). For Hooker's part in the battle of Chattanooga and the Atlanta campaign, see, respectively, Wiley Sword, *Mountains Touched with Fire: Chattanooga Besieged, 1863* (1995), and Albert Castel, *Decision in the West: The Atlanta Campaign of 1864* (1992). Castel exposes the slanderous treatment of Hooker in Sherman's *Memoirs* (1886) in "Prevaricating through Georgia: Sherman's *Memoirs* as a Source on the Atlanta Campaign," *Civil War History* 40 (1994): 48–71.

ALBERT CASTEL

HOOKER, Philip (28 Oct. 1766–31 Jan. 1836), architect, was born in the town of Rutland, Worcester County, Massachusetts, the son of Samuel Hooker, a carpenter and builder, and Rachel Hinds. The family moved to

Albany, New York, probably in the 1770s near the outbreak of the American Revolution. Hooker, therefore, spent his formative years amid the wartime bustle of the busy Hudson River port about 150 miles north of New York City. Nothing is known of his early education or possible apprenticeship, but it seems likely that his practical construction skills were developed by working with his father. At least one of Hooker's siblings, John, also entered the building trade, indicating a family enterprise underway by the 1790s.

Knowledge of Hooker's life and career preceding 1797 is conjectural. He is quite possibly the Philip Hooker listed as a "house-carpenter" in the New York City directories for 1792 and 1793, but by the mid-1790s he was back in Albany, where he remained to become the region's most renowned architect of the early nineteenth century. Late in 1796 he submitted the winning proposal for the North Dutch Reformed Church in Albany. This late Georgian design, with twin towers unique in Albany, recalled Charles Bulfinch's Hollis Street Church in Boston (1788). The quality of design and draftsmanship of this, Hooker's earliest authenticated design, indicated a practiced talent well developed at age thirty.

Over the next forty years Hooker designed numerous other churches, civic, commercial, and educational buildings, as well as city and country houses and miscellaneous outbuildings, fences, and garden pavilions. He drew on a variety of sources for inspiration. For example, his design for the New York State Bank in Albany (built in 1803) reflected Robert and James Adam's design for the Society for the Encouragement of Arts, Manufactures and Commerce in London, published in 1778. In plan, and to a lesser extent in elevation, Hooker's design for the New York State Capitol (built 1806–1809; razed 1883) owed much to plate 39 in Robert Morris's *Select Architecture* (1757). One of Hooker's more famous productions, the Albany Academy (1815–1816), apparently was a redraft of a design by Thomas C. Taylor. As built, the academy reflected the influence of the Continental stylishness of New York's City Hall, designed a decade earlier by French émigré Joseph Mangin and John McComb, Jr.

Two residential designs produced for wealthy English immigrant George Clarke indicate a more than passing acquaintance with the eighteenth-century neoclassicism of Claude Nicolas Ledoux and the French Enlightenment, albeit filtered through English regency aesthetic tenets. The Albany dwelling designed for Clarke about 1816 remained unbuilt, but Hyde Hall, Clarke's country villa built in stages between 1818 and 1835 at the head of Otsego Lake about sixty miles west of Albany, became Hooker's most famous production. The austere neoclassical "great house" of coursed ashlar was created to dominate an assemblage of subordinate wings massed around a courtyard. Significantly, its plan resembled a villa, plate XXIII, in John Plaw's *Rural Architecture* (1785). Left unfinished at Clarke's death, only months before Hooker's own demise, Hyde Hall remained Hooker's crowning achievement

and a Clarke residence for several generations. (It now is owned by New York State as a historic site.)

In 1829 an aging Philip Hooker submitted the winning design for a city hall for Albany. This three-story marble block displayed an Ionic portico and a gold-leafed dome, which subsequently provided a focal point on the city's skyline until 1880, when the building was razed following a fire. Hooker's competitors in designing the Albany city hall included Boston's Isaiah Rogers and Edward Shaw as well as New York City's Minard Lafever and partners Ithiel Town and Alexander Jackson Davis. Significantly, Hooker, a virtual local institution by 1829, submitted a design more conservative and less innovative than, for example, the monumental mausoleum effect created by Davis. For decades Hooker had served well a basically conservative regional clientele. With the exception of a few designs, like those for the cosmopolitan Clarke, Hooker's Anglocentric designs were far from the cutting edge. That he was able to produce effectively for the likes of Clarke indicates an artistic potential that by choice or circumstance was never fully realized.

Hooker was active in the civic life of Albany. In 1801 he had been an organizer of the city's Mechanics' Society and in 1814 was elected to membership in the Society for the Promotion of Useful Arts in the State of New-York, serving on the society's Committee of Fine Arts. In 1819 he was appointed city surveyor, a pursuit that furnished him a significant second career in mapping. At different times he served as an alderman, a city superintendent, and a fourth ward assessor. Committee memberships included those for the academy, the Lancaster School, lands, the ferry, flagging and paving, and the engine. In these pursuits he was able to make contacts and secure commissions.

Although his career centered on the Albany-Troy area, Hooker designed significant structures elsewhere, particularly west of Albany in the Mohawk Valley. In 1797 Samuel and John Hooker left Albany for the fledgling settlement of Utica to work for the Holland Land Company. The family remained and became active in the city's development. Philip Hooker subsequently secured commissions, apparently by contacts through his father and brother and the Holland Land Company. Other than Hyde Hall, his most notable upstate New York design was the Hamilton College Chapel (1825–1827; extant) at Clinton, with its distinctive stonework and parapet facade. By 1820 he had designed churches for Episcopal and Presbyterian congregations in Utica, Sherrill, and Cazenovia. He designed at least one bank in Utica and a distinctive twelve-sided academy in Lowville. Hooker also produced sophisticated regency-influenced residential designs for Judge Morris Miller of Utica and for William Alexander of Little Falls. Designs for "country seats" included those for Englishman George W. Featherstonhaugh near Mariaville and for entrepreneur Elkanah Watson at Port Kent on Lake Champlain. (All were built, but only the Miller and Watson houses are extant.)

Hooker was childless through his two marriages. His first wife, Mary (surname unknown), died in 1812, and he married Sarah Monk of Albany in 1814. At his death Philip and Sarah Hooker were living in a modest brick row house at 130 Green Street in Albany, one of a half-dozen matching two-story structures designed about 1829 by the architect for his landlord William James as speculative middle-class housing.

Evidently conservative and unpretentious to the end, Philip Hooker joined at death a pantheon of minor masters of American architecture, those near-greats whose regional influence was indelible in its time and resonant for decades. Hooker's works changed the aura of Albany from colonial to classical and introduced an academic classicism into a burgeoning postrevolutionary-period New York frontier. A few, like Hyde Hall, the Albany Academy, and the Hamilton College Chapel, gained national and international stature as architecturally ambitious, particularly successful undertakings in their respective categories of residential, educational, and religious buildings.

• Two works published more than six decades apart form the nexus of information about Philip Hooker. Edward W. Root, *Philip Hooker: A Contribution to the Study of the Renaissance in America* (1929), and Douglas G. Bucher and W. Richard Wheeler, *A Neat Plain Modern Stile: Philip Hooker and His Contemporaries, 1796–1836* (1993), form complementary analyses of Hooker's life and works. Bucher and Wheeler update the earlier work and provide a comprehensive catalog raisonné of known works and attributions as well as a thorough overview of the numerous manuscript collections wherein Hooker-related materials reside.

RONALD J. BURCH

HOOKER, Samuel Cox (19 Apr. 1864–12 Oct. 1935), chemist, was born in Brenchley, England, the son of John Marshall Hooker, an architect, and Ellen Cox. A teenage interest in photography led Hooker into chemistry. In 1881 he enrolled in the Royal School of Science in London, graduating with highest honors and a prize in chemistry in 1884. An exceptionally talented experimentalist, he received a Ph.D. in organic chemistry from the University of Munich in only one year, during which he also published four papers based on his doctoral dissertation.

In 1885 Hooker emigrated directly from Munich to the United States, hoping to continue his research in an academic institution. Unable to find such a position, he became chief chemist for the Franklin Sugar Refining Company in Philadelphia. In 1887 he married Mary Elizabeth Owens, a graduate of the University of Cincinnati in chemistry and an American classmate of Hooker in London. They had four children.

Hooker had no publications in sugar chemistry, a result of a policy of secrecy among the sugar refining companies. However, Franklin Sugar allowed him to conduct private research in its laboratory in his spare time. Between 1887 and 1896 he published articles on a variety of topics in organic chemistry, the most important being eleven articles on the yellow pigment lapachol. An inquiry by a Philadelphia importer about a yellow substance in the pores of a rare South American wood used in making fishing rods prompted Hooker to develop methods for its isolation. He then explored the reactions of lapachol, established its structure as a naphthoquinone, and converted it into different colored derivatives by altering the side chain of the molecule. During this research he discovered the "Hooker Oxidation," a reaction that stripped one carbon atom from the side chain. He proved it to be a general reaction for shortening side chains in many types of compounds. Although there was more to discover about lapachol, he had to abandon his research for new duties in the sugar business.

The American Sugar Refining Company purchased Franklin Sugar in 1892. Its president, Henry Osborne Havemeyer, had an expansionist policy and gained controlling interest in the new beet sugar industry west of the Mississippi River. In 1896 Havemeyer assigned to Hooker the colossal task of organizing all of the western factories. Hooker planned all of the technical operations, overcame the bottlenecks and inefficiencies in the infant industry, and brought beet sugar refining to a high level of efficiency. This was his most important contribution to American sugar technology. He was also a key figure in organizing the Great Western Sugar Company as the beet sugar division of the Havemeyer enterprise and from 1909 was a member of the board of directors of both American Sugar and Great Western.

In 1909 Hooker made Brooklyn, New York, his home. Retiring in 1915 in order to resume his lapachol research, he established a well-equipped laboratory in a converted stable on his property. He uncovered new reaction sequences and prepared many beautifully colored new derivatives. Yet he did not publish anything for twenty years, being a perfectionist and unwilling to see his work in print until every possible detail had been investigated. After 1926 his health deteriorated, and in 1933, fearing that he would not finish any project, he hired a chemist assistant, Al Steyermark, to carry out the research on the basis of a daily bedside conference.

Hooker's discoveries were revealed to the public only through the intervention of Louis Fieser, a Harvard professor of chemistry and an authority on quinones. In 1926 Fieser was exploring naphthoquinones that have side chains and learned that Hooker had made such substances from lapachol. He wrote to Hooker and received an invitation to come to Brooklyn. Hooker showed him his colored derivatives and demonstrated his methods. Fieser could not persuade Hooker to prepare his work for publication, and only in 1933 did Hooker express a desire to do so. Gratified by Fieser's promise to see that his research would be published, he began writing up his research. After Hooker's death, Fieser completed the task from the notes of Hooker and Steyermark and had the research published in eleven articles in 1936. Fieser then prepared a memorial volume containing both the earlier and later papers on lapachol with a short biography,

The Constitution and Properties of Lapachol, Lomatiol, and Other Hydroxynaphthoquinone Derivatives (1936). After forty years of silence, the 1936 publications came as a complete surprise to chemists, an unexpected contribution to quinone chemistry complete with methods, syntheses, and structure determinations.

Hooker pursued two additional interests in retirement. He accumulated one of the world's most complete chemical libraries. When it was offered for sale after his death and several chemical companies responded, his heirs and private investors purchased it in order to fulfill Hooker's wish for an academic home for his collection. With the aid of a large grant from the Kresge Foundation, it became the Kresge-Hooker Scientific Library at Wayne State University in Detroit. Hooker also resumed his teenage hobby of magic. He became so highly proficient in developing new illusions that some professional magicians regarded him as the greatest living magician. He never performed in public, but gave exhibitions to professionals, baffling them with his technique. In 1934 he revealed his secrets to other magicians, rehearsing with them until they mastered the illusions.

Hooker died in his Brooklyn home. Although he never took a vacation, he always left the business behind when at home in order to devote himself to his family. From 1918 he had a farm in New Jersey, which became a place for large family gatherings in the summer. His long hours of private research revealed the remarkable transformations among the lapachol series of naphthoquinones, an outstanding contribution to the chemistry of natural products.

• The July–Oct. 1946 issue of the *Record of Chemical Progress* (vol. 7) is devoted to Hooker and his chemical library with especially valuable articles by Louis Fieser, "Hooker's Researches on Lapachol," pp. 26–45, and Al Steyermark, "My Association with Samuel Cox Hooker," pp. 46–52. Charles A. Browne provided a good, concise biography, "Samuel Cox Hooker," *Journal of the Chemical Society* 139 (1936): 550–53. See also Sidney J. Osborn, "Samuel Cox Hooker," *Industrial and Engineering Chemistry* 25 (1933): 827–28. For Hooker's contribution to the sugar industry, see Charles A. Browne, "Early Philadelphia Sugar Refiners and Technologists," *Journal of Chemical Education* 20 (1943): 522–30. For Hooker as a magician, see the *New York Times*, 5 Aug. 1936, and for his library see Neil E. Gordon, "Kresge-Hooker Scientific Library," *Chemical and Engineering News* 22 (10 June 1944): 946, 978. An obituary is in the *New York Times*, 14 Oct. 1935.

ALBERT B. COSTA

HOOKER, Thomas (7? July 1586–7 July 1647), Puritan minister, an architect of the New England Way, and a founder of Hartford, Connecticut, was born in Marfield, a village in Leicestershire, England, the son of Thomas Hooker, a steward for the Digby family, and his wife, whose name is unknown. He probably attended the grammar school that had been endowed by Sir Wolstan Dixie in nearby Market Bosworth, since at Cambridge he held a Dixie Fellowship, restricted to relatives of Sir Wolstan or graduates of his school. Before going to Cambridge, he may have taught school briefly in Birstall, Leicestershire. He matriculated at Queens College, Cambridge, in 1604, although he soon transferred to Emmanuel College, which had already acquired a reputation for the Puritan sympathies of its members. He received his B.A. in 1608 and his M.A. in 1611. He subsequently served as lecturer and catechist at Emmanuel College until 1618. As a fellow at Emmanuel he experienced a spiritual rebirth that validated his career as a Puritan minister and provided the substance for many of his popular sermons that were collected and published during his lifetime. He apparently preached at Emmanuel a series of sermons on the nature of the conversion experience.

In 1618 he became the rector of St. George's in Esher, Surrey. Appointed to the living by Francis Drake, Hooker's principal task was to attend to the donor's wife, Joanna, who had despaired of her spiritual state and even attempted to do away with herself. His work with Joanna Drake established his reputation for the care of souls and strengthened his interest in the spiritual difficulties of those undergoing conversion. In Esher he also met Joanna Drake's maid, Susanna Garbrand, and married her in Amersham, Buckinghamshire, in 1621. They had at least six children, four of whom survived him.

After Joanna Drake's death in 1625, Hooker left Esher for Chelmsford, Essex, where he lectured in the Church of St. Mary and began a school. Essex entertained a thriving community of ministers with Puritan sentiments, and, preceded by his reputation, Hooker soon became a respected leader and adviser within it. Cotton Mather, Hooker's first biographer, wrote that through his preaching "there was a great reformation wrought, not only in the town but in the adjacent country, . . . and some of great quality among the rest, would often resort from afar to his assembly." The most important of his sermons took up again the concerns of his preaching in Cambridge a decade before, what he referred to as "the application of redemption." Hooker subscribed to what has been called preparationist theology, believing that the usual course of spiritual rebirth happened not in a moment of blinding insight but over a period of time in which distinct stages of spiritual development could be observed. The substance of the Chelmsford sermons was later published in a series of works with titles indicative of these stages, *The Soules Preparation for Christ* (1632), *The Soules Humiliation* (1637), *The Soules Vocation* (1638), *The Soules Exaltation* (1638), and *The Soules Possession of Christ* (1638). His preaching in other contexts also took on a more social and political edge in sermons like *Spiritual Munition* (1638), *The Danger of Desertion* (1640), and *The Faithful Covenanter* (1644), warning his listeners of the consequences to whole nations of God's displeasure at his people's "unthankfulnesse and carelesnesse." In 1629 he was called before Bishop William Laud to answer for his preaching and nonconformity; released under bond, he was recalled in July 1630 to appear before Laud's Court of High Commission. He defied Laud's summons, went into hiding with the aid of the earl of Warwick, and fled to Holland in 1631.

Hooker left England in response to an invitation from members of the English church in Amsterdam to become an assistant to John Paget, their minister. This invitation did not have the approval of Paget, however, and Hooker stayed in Rotterdam with Hugh Peter, Puritan minister of a church there, as he tried to resolve his differences with Paget. Failing this, he accepted a call to assist John Forbes in the merchant adventurer's church in Delft, but in early 1633 he left the Netherlands for New England, stopping off in England to collect his family, which had not accompanied him in 1631.

Before his flight from England Hooker had already begun talking with the organizers of the Massachusetts Bay Colony, and a group from Essex arriving there in 1632 to take up residence in Newtown (now Cambridge) were already identified as "Mr. Hooker's company." On 4 September 1633 Hooker arrived in Boston on the *Griffin* along with John Cotton and Samuel Stone, his future assistant in the churches in Newtown and Hartford. Hooker and Stone proceeded directly to Newtown, where in the following month they led the foundation of a church on congregational principles.

Hooker's reputation as a mediator and for dealing with cases of conscience involved him in several local controversies. He worked to reconcile differences between John Winthrop (1588–1649), the colony's governor, and Thomas Dudley and John Haynes (1594?–1654), the most important civil leaders in Newtown, and in late 1634 the magistrates asked him for advice on John Endicott's mutilation of the English flag. Endicott had cut the cross out of the flag, maintaining that it was idolatrous and a relic of papist superstition. Hooker's thirteen-page manuscript, "Touching the Cross in the Banners," dealt with Endicott's scruples and resolved that the cross was a civil use only, a mere sign and not a sacred object. More important was the crisis precipitated by the antinomian teachings of Anne Hutchinson and John Wheelwright. Hooker, along with Peter Bulkeley of Concord, presided at the synod convened on 30 August 1637 to deal with the outbreak of antinomianism, which supposedly had received the support of John Cotton. After Hooker and the other ministers extricated Cotton from the antinomian implications of some of his expressions, the synod condemned eighty-two errors and nine "unsavoury speeches," providing the basis for eventual civil action against Hutchinson and Wheelwright. The synod of 1637 also established the preparationist theology of Hooker and his colleagues as the orthodox view of the New England churches.

Members of Hooker's Newtown congregation complained for several years about insufficient land for farming, and in 1635 they arranged to sell their holdings to a new group of immigrants preparatory to relocating on the Connecticut River. In May 1636 Hooker accompanied his congregation to their new settlement, named Hartford in honor of Samuel Stone's birthplace. Concurrent with the settlement of Hartford,

people from Watertown and Dorchester also left Massachusetts in order to settle at Wethersfield and Windsor. These new settlements on the river were outside of the Massachusetts charter, but the river towns did not form a government of their own until 1638, delayed in part by the 1637 war with the Pequot Indians. When a general court met on 31 May 1638 to draw up the Fundamental Orders for a new government, Hooker addressed it with a sermon reminding the court that the choice of public magistrates belongs to the people and that those who have the power to appoint magistrates can also limit the power of the magistrates over them.

The Fundamental Orders has sometimes been called the first American written constitution, and Hooker has been hailed as a pioneer of democracy. More careful historians have limited both of these claims; Perry Miller has noted in the case of Hooker that he was not broaching new doctrine to the magistrates but simply reminding them of conventional truths of political theory they already knew. Nevertheless, Connecticut, unlike Massachusetts, did not make church membership a requirement for voting, and Hooker seems to have set more charitable standards for church membership than many of the Massachusetts ministers did.

In Connecticut Hooker preached once more on his favorite subject, the process of conversion, and these sermons were posthumously published as *The Application of Redemption* (2 vols., 1656). In addition to attending to the needs of his congregation, Hooker became a spiritual leader for New England. Invited back to Massachusetts to preside over the antinomian synod of 1637, he returned again with Connecticut governor John Haynes in 1639, when he met with various New England leaders, and he came to Boston once more in 1643 in order to take part in an assembly of ministers concerned with the presbyterian challenge of the Westminster Assembly of that year. The political and religious upheavals in England during the early 1640s threatened the established order in those colonies, including Connecticut and Massachusetts, who had allied themselves in 1643 as the New England Confederation. Called to meet in Westminster Abbey by the Long Parliament in order to reconsider English church doctrine and discipline, the Calvinist Westminster Assembly included proponents of episcopal, Erastian, independent, and presbyterian forms of church government but was dominated by the latter. Hooker, Cotton, and John Davenport of New Haven had been invited to attend, but Hooker, a defender of the independent way of local, congregational church government, was disinclined to travel so far merely to be an isolated voice in the presence of a presbyterian majority. The meeting at Cambridge (formerly Newtown) discussed possible ways to defend the church polity of New England and requested Hooker to answer the presbyterian arguments. He responded with *A Survey of the Summe of Church-Discipline*, aimed at Samuel Rutherford's *Due Right of Presbyteries* and supporting the New England scheme of independent congregational churches. Approved in 1645 by the

New England ministers, the manuscript was sent off for publication in London but was lost at sea; a second draft was finally published in 1648. During these same years he wrote *The Covenant of Grace Opened* (1649), a defense of infant baptism against anabaptist challenges, and three other titles apparently intended to influence the Westminster Assembly's choice of a standard catechism, *A Briefe Exposition of the Lords Prayer, Heavens Treasury Opened . . .*, and *An Exposition of the Principles of Religion*, all published in 1645.

Hooker was invited to the synod that met in Cambridge in 1646 and 1647 in order to draw up an explicit plan of church order, but he declined on account of poor health. When his colleague, Samuel Stone, returned to Hartford from the 1647 synod, he found Hooker on his deathbed. Hooker's intellectual and spiritual leadership of New England's congregational churches was his main contribution. His preaching and publishing on the course of spiritual rebirth offered important guidelines for ministers called upon to judge applicants for church membership, and his *Survey of the Summe of Church-Discipline* (1648) was a major contribution to the discussion of congregational church government that led up to the Cambridge Platform of 1648.

• Hooker's only surviving manuscripts, a collection of sermon notes, are in the Beinecke Library at Yale University; the Connecticut Historical Society, Hartford, owns several manuscripts by Deacon Matthew Grant and others who recorded sermons by Hooker. *Thomas Hooker: Writings in England and Holland, 1626–1633*, ed. George H. Williams, Norman Pettit, Winfried Herget, and Sargent Bush, Jr. (1975), contains useful essays by each of the editors, early texts by Hooker, and Bush's authoritative bibliography of Hooker's writings. Frank Shuffelton, *Thomas Hooker, 1586–1647* (1977), offers a full-length biographical study of Hooker in the context of the doctrinal and political controversies around him. Bush, *The Writings of Thomas Hooker: Spiritual Adventurer in Two Worlds* (1980), provides an excellent analysis of Hooker's literary craft and theological arguments. John H. Ball III, *Chronicling the Soul's Windings: Thomas Hooker and His Morphology of Conversion* (1992), focuses on Hooker's sermons on spiritual regeneration. Cotton Mather's biography of Hooker is most easily located in his *Magnalia Christi Americana* (1702) under the title "The Light of the Western Churches; or, The Life of Mr. Thomas Hooker."

FRANK SHUFFELTON

HOOKER, Worthington (3 Mar. 1806–6 Nov. 1867), physician and professor, was born in Springfield, Massachusetts, the son of Judge John Hooker and Sarah Dwight, who according to some sources was a granddaughter of Jonathan Edwards (1703-1758). Hooker received a bachelor's degree from Yale in 1825 and a medical degree from Harvard in 1829. In 1830 he married Mary Ingersoll of Springfield and moved to Norwich, Connecticut; they had four children, but only one, a son, survived to maturity.

During more than two decades of general practice in Norwich, Hooker became distressed about the public's lack of respect for the medical profession. The public was skeptical of the varying therapeutic claims

of medical professionals because none could definitely prove that their remedies worked best. Orthodox doctors, such as Hooker, became especially defensive toward homeopathic practitioners who chose to discard the practices of bloodletting and purging in favor of milder, but unproven medicines. During this era of rampant sectarianism in medicine, doctors frequently became dishonest or abusive as they competed for patients.

To deal with this situation, the American Medical Association (AMA) adopted a code of professional ethics in 1847. Hooker then wrote a book-length commentary on this code, *Physician and Patient; or a Practical View of the Mutual Duties, Relations, and Interests of the Medical Profession and the Community*. Published in 1849, this book was the only comprehensive monograph about medical ethics written by an American physician during the nineteenth century. Astonished that an American general practitioner could analyze the ethics of the medical profession in such a thorough fashion, reviewers praised *Physician and Patient* for its balanced analysis of the ethical responsibilities of both physicians and patients.

In 1852 Hooker's wife died, and he moved to New Haven to become a professor of medicine at Yale. In 1855 he married Henrietta Edwards, daughter of a former governor; they had two children, but one died soon after birth. Hooker became an attending physician at the New Haven Hospital and a member of its board of directors, serving on various committees. The hospital's Board of Visitors Committee, including Henrietta, evaluated conditions at the hospital during monthly visits. Esteemed by colleagues in local and national organizations, Hooker became a vice president of the AMA in 1864.

While teaching medical students, Hooker became concerned about their poor educational preparation. To help correct these deficiencies, he wrote several science texts that could be used in elementary and secondary schools as well as in colleges. Some of these texts were reprinted as late as 1888. Hooker aggressively advocated improvements in the teaching of science throughout all stages of formal education. Between 1857 and 1860, he served as a member of the Board of Education of the New Haven City School District. The public school on Canner Street, constructed in 1900, was named for Hooker.

Opposed to Darwin's claims about evolution, Hooker served as a deacon in the Church of the United Society from 1858 until his death and wrote articles for religious and literary newspapers and magazines, such as the *Congregationalist* and *Harper's Weekly*.

A man of medium stature and somewhat portly, Hooker evinced a kind and gentle temper and displayed extraordinary devotion to medical, educational, and religious institutions. He died from typhoid fever in New Haven.

• There are a few letters in the Yale University Library. Other books by Hooker include *Lessons from the History of Medical Delusions* (1850) and *Homeopathy: An Examination of Its*

Doctrines and Evidences (1851). Examples of his science texts are *Human Physiology* (1854), *First Book in Physiology* (1855), *The Child's Book of Nature* (1857), and *First Book in Chemistry* (1862). For more biographical details, see Henry Bronson, "Memoir of Prof. Worthington Hooker, M.D., of New Haven," *Proceedings and Medical Communications of the Connecticut Medical Society* 3 (1871): 397–402; Francis Bacon, "The Practice of Medicine and Surgery," in *History of the City of New Haven to the Present Time*, ed. Edward E. Atwater (1887), p. 280; and Chester R. Burns, "Worthington Hooker (1806–67): Physician, Teacher, Reformer," *Yale Medicine* 2 (1967): 17–18. For an overview of the teaching of medical ethics, see Chester R. Burns, "Medical Ethics and Jurisprudence," in *The Education of American Physicians*, ed. Ronald L. Numbers (1980), pp. 273–89.

CHESTER R. BURNS

HOOPER, Ellen Sturgis (17 Feb. 1812–3 Nov. 1848), poet, was born in Boston, Massachusetts, the daughter of William Sturgis, a prosperous ship owner, and Elizabeth Marston Davis, daughter of U.S. District Court judge John Davis (1761–1847). At the time of her birth, Ellen's father had returned to Boston, after an increasingly successful career as a seaman, navigator, captain, and ship owner, to establish the trading company of Bryant & Sturgis, which soon controlled more than half the shipping trade between the Pacific Coast and China. Thus, Ellen Sturgis was born into one of the wealthiest families in Boston at that time.

Raised in a family that favored the Unitarian strain of Congregationalism, Ellen Sturgis and her sisters attended a private school in Hingham, Massachusetts. There she studied, among other subjects, penmanship, Latin, French, chemistry, astronomy, and Greek history. She did not go to college, as higher education for women was not available during her lifetime. (Her daughter, Ellen Hooper Gurney, was later instrumental in organizing Radcliffe College for women.)

In 1832 Anne Sturgis, Ellen's sister, married Samuel Hooper, of a prominent Massachusetts banking family. In 1833 a younger brother, Robert William Hooper, graduated from Harvard Medical School and began a two-year medical training program in Paris. Soon after his return to Boston in 1835, he began to court Ellen Sturgis. Hooper received his medical degree in 1836, and they were married in 1837 by Unitarian minister Ephraim Peabody, former editor of the *Western Messenger*, a liberal Unitarian newspaper based in Ohio. Despite suffering from poor health since childhood and being diagnosed as consumptive, Ellen Hooper bore three children before her early death, one of whom, "Clover" (Marian Hooper Adams) married Henry B. Adams.

After her marriage, and at the urging of her friends and sister Caroline Sturgis, Hooper became more closely associated with the Transcendentalists, a loosely knit group of young intellectuals, who, inspired by Romantic literature of England and Germany, opposed the negativism of Calvinism and promoted an American culture based on individualism, intuitive knowledge, and an optimistic view of human potential. Ralph Waldo Emerson was the chief spokesman of the movement, and the publication of his book *Nature* in 1836 marks the birth of Transcendentalism.

"Self Culture," or self-education, was an important aspect of Transcendentalism; therefore various methods of individual and group education were practiced. In the early 1840s, Hooper and her sister Caroline visited at the Emerson home and joined the intellectual discussions held there. They also attended "Reading Parties" in Boston; participated in "Conversations," educational dialogues, presented by Margaret Fuller at sundry homes and frequently at Elizabeth Peabody's West Street bookstore; and continued their own individual programs of reading, writing letters, and drawing.

The Transcendentalists also began a literary journal designed as a vehicle of expression for their views. In 1839 plans were completed for the publication of the *Dial* with Fuller as editor. The first volume appeared in July 1840 and included Hooper's most famous poem, subsequently titled "Beauty and Duty," which contains the often quoted lines, "I slept, and dreamed that life was Beauty; / I woke and found that life was Duty." Nine more of her poems were published in various issues of the *Dial*: "The Poor Rich Man," "The Wood-Fire," "The Poet," and "Wayfarers" (vol. 1, no. 2 [Oct. 1840]); "To the Ideal" (vol. 1, no. 3 [Jan. 1841]); "The Out-Bid" and "Farewell" (vol. 1, no. 4 [Apr. 1841]); "The Hour of Reckoning" (vol. 2, no. 3 [Jan. 1842]); and "Sweep Ho!," also called "The Chimney-Sweep" (vol. 4, no. 2 [Oct. 1843]).

James Freeman Clarke was a figure of Transcendentalism who greatly influenced Hooper. Clarke, a poet, contributor to the *Dial*, and Unitarian minister, became Hooper's religious adviser and social conscience. In 1841, after being disappointed by the conservatism of his first parish in Louisville, Kentucky, Clarke returned to his native Boston and formed the Church of the Disciples. Clarke chose as parishioners people who shared his liberal ideas. The congregation was composed of forty-six of Clarke's closest friends, including Ellen Hooper. The intimate nature of the church allowed Clarke to introduce various innovations, such as services formed as conferences, where each member was given the opportunity to ask questions and respond to the sermon. Clarke also encouraged parishioners, such as Hooper, to participate in responsive readings, attend Bible study groups, discuss religious and ethical themes, and even give sermons from the pulpit. Clarke and his congregation were also identified with many of the reforms of the period, including abolitionism, temperance, the peace movement, and woman suffrage. Ten of Hooper's poems were included in *The Disciples' Hymn Book*, which Clarke compiled in 1855.

The demands of her family and her own ill health are probably responsible for Hooper's infrequent publication during her lifetime. Although she continued to write poetry until her death, she shared it only with her friends and family. Some of the poems, for example, "To R. W. E."; "Mr. R. W. Emerson's little boy," a memorial to Waldo Emerson, who died in 1842; and "To S. A. C.," probably artist Sarah Clarke, sister of James Freeman Clarke, are written to and about her associates in Transcendentalism. Some are concerned with places in Massachusetts, such as Lenox, Watertown, and Woburn. However, most of Hooper's poems express her private thoughts on life and death: "Patience—thou art the precious talisman," "Wilt thou bring up the child, Oh Mother dear?," "Stand I condemned for trifling with grave things," "My better self, I know I leave thee here," "My thoughts are bound within a cell of care," "I give thee all my darling, darling child," "My lot is cast with toil and tiresome needs," and "Air, give me air." The only publication of most of these poems was a private printing in 1872 paid for by her son, Edward, and distributed to her family and friends.

Although Hooper's poems are more Transcendental by association than by theme, she is often included with the Transcendentalists. Emerson and Fuller encouraged her writing. Henry David Thoreau included her poem "The Wood-Fire" in his "House-Warming" chapter of *Walden*. Emerson selected four of her poems, "Wayfarers," "The Chimney-Sweep," "The Wood-Fire," and "The Nobly Born," for *Parnassus* as part of a compilation of his favorite poetry in 1874. As Perry Miller remarked, Ellen Sturgis Hooper's early death may have "enshrined her in the memories of her associates as a Transcendental angel."

• A notebook of handwritten poems by Ellen Sturgis Hooper, and a satirical, rhymed description of Brook Farm, the experimental, Transcendental commune, written by Ellen Hooper and her sister Susan Sturgis Bigelow, rests in the Schlesinger Library at Radcliffe. Much material on the Sturgis-Hooper families is held privately by descendents. However, at least two authors have been able to use these collections and have quoted from them extensively in their books. Both books are biographies of Clover Adams, Hooper's daughter: Otto Friedrich, *Clover* (1979), and Eugenia Kaledin, *The Education of Mrs. Henry Adams* (1981). Genealogical information on the Sturgis family can be found in Roger Faxton Sturgis, *Edward Sturgis of Yarmouth, Massachusetts, 1613–1695, and Descendents* (1914), and Charles G. Loring, *Memoir of the Hon. William Sturgis* (1864). Most of the early work on Hooper's poetry was done by George Willis Cooke and appears in *An Historical and Biographical Introduction to Accompany* The Dial (1902) and *The Poets of Transcendentalism* (1903). Perry Miller included five Hooper poems in *The American Transcendentalists: Their Prose and Poetry* (1957). More recent information on the contributors to the *Dial* and its history and context can be found in Joel Myerson, *The New England Transcendentalists and the* Dial (1980).

BARBARA D. WOJTUSIK

HOOPER, Harry Bartholomew (24 Aug. 1887–18 Dec. 1974), baseball player, manager, and coach, was born at Elephant Head Homestead, California, the son of Joseph Hooper, a farmer, and Kathleen Keller. His parents were German immigrants who had settled as sharecroppers in the Santa Clara Valley. From 1889 to 1897 his family farmed at Garrison Ranch in the San Joaquin Valley, but economic hardship compelled the

Hoopers to return to sharecropping in the Santa Clara Valley. After performing well academically at Volta Elementary School and Mendezable District Grammar School, he was given the opportunity to pursue further education. He excelled at St. Mary's High School in Oakland, California; in 1907, at St. Mary's College in the same city, he earned a bachelor's degree in civil engineering. At St. Mary's, Hooper starred for the baseball team and participated in several other sports. Before graduation, the 5′10″, 168-pounder briefly played outfield for Alameda of the California State League, which did business outside baseball's national agreement. Hooper spent the remainder of the 1907 season and all of 1908 with Sacramento of the same league, earning $85 a month for playing baseball and $75 a month working as a surveyor for the Western Pacific Railroad. He considered himself primarily an engineer who played baseball for fun.

Boston Red Sox owner John I. Taylor personally scouted Hooper in August 1908 and signed the speedy outfielder to a $2,800 contract for 1909. Hooper resigned his surveying job, intending to play only a few seasons of baseball. He played with the Red Sox from 1909 to 1920, performing in a legendary outfield with center fielder Tris Speaker and left fielder Duffy Lewis. They composed perhaps baseball's best defensive outfield ever, exhibiting extraordinary quickness and strong throwing arms. Hooper not only covered a great deal of ground but he often made spectacular catches. Since Speaker played unusually shallow, Hooper often covered deep right center field. From its inception in 1912, Hooper mastered Fenway Park's difficult sun field and invented the "rump slide," skidding on one hip with feet forward and knees bent to catch or trap fly balls. He frequently threw out runners trying to advance from first base to third on balls hit to deep right field. Hooper made 344 career assists, setting a major league record for that position.

Among the most intelligent, observant, aggressive, and dedicated of players, Hooper was an effective leadoff hitter for Boston, twice batting over .300. Although a natural right-hander, he batted left-handed to get a stride closer to first base. Hooper also averaged 22 stolen bases a season and set club records for most stolen bases (300) and triples (130). He played on four world championship teams (1912, 1915, 1916, 1918) and distinguished himself in postseason play. His spectacular bare-handed catch in the final game of the 1912 World Series denied victory to the New York Giants. In 1915 Hooper became the first player to hit two home runs in a single World Series game. Altogether, he batted .293 with 27 hits in Series competition.

Hooper convinced Boston manager Ed Barrow in 1919 to start using star left-handed pitcher Babe Ruth in the outfield. Ruth soon became a full-time outfielder, drawing enormous crowds with his spectacular hitting. Meanwhile, owner Harry Frazee decimated the Red Sox by selling or trading several star players in order to cover his expenses as a New York theater producer. In March 1921 Frazee traded the disgruntled Hooper, who had held out for a $15,000 contract, to the Chicago White Sox for two players and cash. Chicago owner Charles A. Comiskey figured Hooper would help the struggling team recover from the devastating 1919 "Black Sox" scandal and signed him to a three-year contract for $13,250 per season. Hooper performed with Chicago from 1921 through 1925, enjoying his best seasons offensively. He hit .327 in 1921, .304 in 1922, and a career-high .328 in 1924. A disagreement with Comiskey over a contract following the 1925 season caused the right fielder to retire. During 17 seasons Hooper batted .281 with 389 doubles, 160 triples, and 75 home runs in 2,309 games. Including 1,136 walks, he reached base 3,602 times, stole 375 bases, and batted in 817 runs.

Hooper sold real estate in Santa Cruz, California, was player-manager of the San Francisco Missions of the Pacific Coast League in 1927, and coached the Princeton University baseball team in 1931 and 1932. From 1937 to 1952 he served as U.S. postmaster of Capitola, California. In 1971 the Veterans Committee elected him to the National Baseball Hall of Fame.

Hooper married Esther Hency on 26 November 1912; the couple had three children. Hooper demonstrated leadership as Boston team captain and ranked among the first college-educated players to achieve major stardom. He died in Santa Cruz.

• The Harry Hooper Diaries are located at St. Mary's College, Moraga, California. The definitive biography is Paul J. Zingg, *Harry Hooper: An American Baseball Life* (1993). The Ellery Clark, Jr., Red Sox Analytical Letter Collection, Annapolis, Maryland, has some of Hooper's correspondence and that of his teammate Duffy Lewis. The National Baseball Library in Cooperstown, N.Y., houses material on Hooper's life. Lawrence Ritter, *The Glory of Their Times* (1966), contains Hooper's reflections on his career. His statistical accomplishments are detailed in *The Baseball Encyclopedia*, 9th ed. (1993), and John Thorn and Pete Palmer, eds., *Total Baseball*, 3d ed. (1993). For Hooper's role with Boston, see Frederick G. Lieb, *The Boston Red Sox* (1947), and Ellery H. Clark, Jr., *Boston Red Sox: 75th Anniversary History* (1975). An obituary appears in the *New York Times*, 19 Dec. 1974.

DAVID L. PORTER

HOOPER, Jessie Annette Jack (8 Nov. 1865–8 May 1935), peace activist, was born on a farm in Winnesheik County, Iowa, the daughter of David Jack, a refrigerator manufacturer and businessman, and Mary Elizabeth Nelings. Her frail health as a child and young woman required her to be educated by a governess until she eventually was able to attend art school, first in Des Moines, Iowa, and later in Chicago, Illinois. On a visit to her older sister in Oshkosh, Wisconsin, she met a young attorney and wholesale grocer, Ben Hooper, whom she married in 1888. They had two children.

While living in Oshkosh, Hooper and her husband were both active supporters of woman suffrage. Before the state legally allowed women to vote, they shared the family ballot. Ben would go to the polls voting Jessie's way one year, his own the next, even if they disagreed on candidates. At the 1893 World's Columbian

Exhibition in Chicago, Jessie heard Susan B. Anthony give a suffrage speech. Afterward she became more devoted to suffrage work in Oshkosh, where she encouraged women to participate in school board elections, the one form of suffrage Wisconsin allowed women. After the 1916 congressional election, Hooper broadened her efforts from voting in Oshkosh to suffrage at the state level, and eventually she became part of the National American Woman Suffrage Association's (NAWSA) lobby in Washington, D.C. Her husband's successful business and law practice in Wisconsin allowed her the freedom to move to Washington and join suffragists lobbying for congressional passage of the Nineteenth Amendment. Hooper was present in the summer of 1919 when the amendment passed both the House and the Senate. She toured western states with fellow suffragist Minnie Fisher Cunningham, asking voters to call special sessions of their legislatures in order to ratify the amendment in time for women to vote in the 1920 presidential election. As part of the effort to encourage political participation among newly enfranchised women, Hooper helped to create the Wisconsin chapter of the League of Women Voters. She served as the league's first president from 1920 until 1922. She maintained the group's strict nonpartisan position and encouraged Wisconsin women to become registered voters.

Like many other women of the postsuffrage generation, Hooper was very interested in world peace. She had faith in the political power of women because they secured franchisement even without the vote. In a letter to her suffrage colleague and former NAWSA president Carrie Chapman Catt, Hooper expressed her desire to work for peace because she believed "there is nothing else that is worthwhile unless we can put an end to war." With organizational tactics learned from the suffrage campaign, she began a statewide and eventually a national lobbying effort on behalf of international disarmament. As president of the Wisconsin League of Women Voters she spoke before a number of groups, hoping to spread her vision of world peace. She insisted men acknowledge responsibility for the murder of the victims of war if they persisted in glorifying the military, and she appealed to women to use their new voting power to encourage lawmakers to settle disputes in other ways besides the killing of "our children." She also encouraged women to become active through exclusively female organizations because of their marginal positions in men's groups.

In 1922 the Wisconsin Democratic party unanimously nominated her to run against U.S. senator Robert La Follette, the Progressive party incumbent. Hooper was reluctant to get involved in partisan politics but felt she had to accept because she did not want to shirk her political responsibility. She knew there was little chance of being elected because of La Follette's enormous popularity. She also believed that the Democratic party had nominated her solely as an attempt to gain the women's vote. Despite her pessimism about the election, Hooper felt that as a senator she could vote directly on issues of international disarmament and military budget reductions. She resigned her presidency of the Wisconsin League of Women Voters in order to keep that organization nonpartisan and ran as a Democrat on a platform of temperance and peace. As she had surmised, La Follete won handily.

After her defeat, Hooper continued her peace activism, encouraging support for the Kellogg-Briand multilateral peace treaty, U.S. entry into the League of Nations, and the establishment of a world court to mediate international disputes. She traveled extensively throughout Wisconsin, the United States, and the Panama Canal Zone, promoting peace efforts of U.S. and South and Central American women. Along with a number of women activists, Hooper helped to organize the annual Conference on the Cause and Cure of War, first held in Washington, D.C., in 1925. The conference consisted of women's organizations devoted to peace. Members elected Hooper chair of the International Relations Department of the General Federation of Women's Clubs (GFWC) in January 1928, a position she held until her resignation in 1932. At the high point of her career as a peace activist, Hooper led a committee of delegates to the first International Disarmament Conference (IDC), scheduled in Geneva for 1932. The members of the Conference on the Cause and Cure of War presented IDC with a petition signed by nearly 1 million American women calling for world peace.

After returning from Geneva and resigning her GFWC position, Hooper continued her lobbying efforts in less formal ways. She continued public speaking and political influence and always encouraged women to keep up a constant public pressure for peace. Her work symbolized the efforts of women who, newly franchised, were struggling for a voice in American politics, and who saw women, in the wake of the tragedy of World War I, as having a special mission to advance the cause of world peace. After battling illnesses that kept her in and out of hospitals for the rest of her life, Hooper died in Oshkosh, Wisconsin.

• Jessie Jack Hooper's papers are located in the Wisconsin State Historical Society Archives in Madison. The twenty-five boxes include her autobiographical manuscript and a shorter biographical manuscript. Also included is an extensive collection of correspondence regarding her activities in the suffrage and peace movements and additional correspondence about her 1922 U.S. senatorial campaign. Lawrence Graves provides an early and brief sketch of Hooper's activities in "Two Noteworthy Wisconsin Women: Mrs. Ben Hooper and Ada James," *Wisconsin Magazine of History* 41, no. 3 (Spring 1958): 174–80. A more complete overview of Hooper's early suffrage activities is outlined in Genevieve G. McBride, *On Wisconsin Women: Working for Their Rights from Settlement to Suffrage* (1993). For a better understanding of women and feminism and their connections to political organizations and the peace movement, see Nancy F. Cott, *The Grounding of Modern Feminism* (1987). Obituaries are in the *Oshkosh Daily Northwestern*, 8 May 1935, *Milwaukee Journal*, 8, 9 May 1935, and *New York Times*, 9 May 1935.

DAWN RAE FLOOD

HOOPER, Johnson Jones (9 June 1815–7 June 1862), author and lawyer, was born in Wilmington, North Carolina, the son of Archibald Maclaine Hooper, a lawyer and newspaper editor, and Charlotte DeBerniere. The elder Hooper's financial distress cut short the formal education of his youngest son, who from ages eleven to seventeen worked as printer's devil in the newspaper his father edited, the *Wilmington Cape Fear Recorder*. In 1835 Hooper emigrated to La Fayette, Alabama, where he apprenticed himself in reading law to his brother George, who had preceded him in settling in the newly opened lands. During the following seven years he was admitted to the bar and practiced law in Dadeville in Tallapoosa County, where he was also appointed census taker, until he returned to La Fayette to become a partner in his brother's law firm. In 1842 Hooper married Mary Mildred Brantley, the daughter of a prominent Whig planter and politician; they had three children.

After 1843 Hooper began to concentrate less on law and more on journalism and Whig politics and on writing political and humorous sketches for the *La Fayette East Alabamian*, which he also edited. His first humorous piece, "Taking the Census in Alabama" (1843), recounted the resistance among backwoods residents to what they saw as governmental intrusion for purposes of levying taxes. The sketch was promptly reprinted in the New York *Spirit of the Times*, whose enterprising editor, William T. Porter, became a friend and influential promoter of Hooper's writings for the next decade. The most famous of these humorous sketches concerned Simon Suggs, a petty confidence man whose motto—"It is good to be shifty in a new country"—came to be popularly associated with the fluid values and opportunism of the entire Southwest, with its unstable economy and heterogeneous population.

Hooper's first Suggs pieces appeared in the *East Alabamian* in late 1844 and was reprinted in *Spirit of the Times* in January 1845. Twelve loosely sequential sketches, comprising a mock "campaign biography" of the illiterate and crafty candidate for sheriff, were gathered in book form and published in 1845 by Carey and Hart of Philadelphia as *Some Adventures of Captain Simon Suggs, Late of the Tallapoosa Volunteers*. Amoral, witty, and shrewd, Simon Suggs became one of the most memorable characters of antebellum American literature. Though the unscrupulous captain was based on the habits and reputation of an early resident of Tallapoosa County, he became so identified with his creator that Hooper came to blame his popular fictional rogue for his electoral defeats for Alabama state representative (1849) and for a second term as state solicitor (1853).

After a brief stint as editor of the *Wetumpka Whig*, engrossing clerk for the state house of representatives, and site commissioner for the new capitol in Montgomery, in 1846 Hooper moved to Montgomery as associate editor of the *Alabama Journal*. Although in 1849 he resigned this position with the state's most influential organ to resume his law practice in La Fayette, he continued his association by writing a weekly humorous column for the *Journal*. Within a year he had become editor and part owner of the *Chambers County Tribune*, and within the next few years contributed humorous sketches to the *New Orleans Daily Delta* and sporting essays to *Spirit of the Times*. In late 1849 a Tuscaloosa publisher issued a second collection of twenty humorous sketches by Hooper, *A Ride with Old Kit Kunker*, which was reprinted two years later by A. Hart of Philadelphia, supplemented with four more pieces, as *The Widow Rugby's Husband, A Night at the Ugly Man's and Other Tales of Alabama*.

From 1849 to 1855 Hooper became more active politically; he ran for public office, sometimes successfully, and founded the *Montgomery Mail* in 1854, nominally as an independent newspaper but partly supportive, first of the Know Nothing party and, later, as secessionist politics intensified in Alabama, of doctrinaire states' rights advocates. Hooper continued his association with the *Montgomery Mail* until 1861. During this period of intense activity, he traveled extensively, usually for political reasons, and continued to write, as well as edit works by others: *Read and Circulate* (1855), a satiric pamphlet aimed at Alabama Democrats; *Dog and Gun* (1856), an anthology of sporting essays by various hands; and *Woodward's Reminiscences* (1859), his edition of essays by Thomas S. Woodward, an old Indian fighter in frontier Alabama.

With the onset of civil war, Hooper dedicated his energies to the secessionist cause, serving as secretary of the provisional Confederate congress in Montgomery in February 1861 and later that year moving with the Confederate government to Richmond, Virginia, as secretary and librarian. Defeated in his bid to be secretary of the permanent congress in 1862, Hooper undertook to edit the records of the provisional congress. He died in Richmond, probably of tuberculosis, before completing that task.

Like many of his waggish newspaper contemporaries of the Old Southwest, Hooper relied on the practical joke as the chief vehicle of his humor, but in the hands of Simon Suggs the joke has little to do with high-spirited fun or even with the humiliation of others. Whether absconding with the collection from a camp meeting or leaving behind the bill for a champagne-and-oyster supper, the captain's goal is modest but material benefit to himself. Although his special targets—a proudly ignorant father, graft-minded office seekers, expedient young bloods, gullible evangelists—are often deserving of his scam because of their own hypocrisy and pretension, Simon Suggs is indiscriminate in his victims. In the ruthless climate of antebellum Alabama, innocents and relatively honest settlers must guard their trusting instincts against the wily captain.

The literary reputations of the antebellum newspaper humorists, in eclipse for a half century, began rising in the 1930s, when the nonromantic tradition of southern writing was once again appreciated. Among those in the top rank of these robust writers, which include A. B. Longstreet, Thomas Bangs Thorpe, George Washington Harris, and Joseph Glover Baldwin, Hooper's place is secure. Although his comic sketches generally are uneven in narrative pace and emphasis, Hooper is second only to Harris in the art of distinctive and memorable characterization. Harris's Sut Lovingood and Hooper's Simon Suggs are portraits of cynical, practical men-on-the-make far removed from the figures of idealized patricians made familiar by conventional fiction from the South from just after the Civil War to the early decades of the twentieth century. The fictional world that Hooper helped to populate—one that he created as well as observed—is ruled not by honor, loyalty, and love but by appetite, competition, and egoistic individualism.

• The Hooper family papers are in the Southern Historical Collection of the University of North Carolina, Chapel Hill. The standard biographical work is W. Stanley Hoole, *Alias Simon Suggs: The Life and Times of Johnson Jones Hooper* (1952); the larger cultural contexts of Hooper's career are covered in Kenneth S. Lynn, *Mark Twain and Southwestern Humor* (1959), and Norris W. Yates, *William T. Porter and the "Spirit of the Times": A Study of the Big Bear School of Humor* (1969). Manly W. Wellman is the editor of one reprint of *Adventures of Captain Simon Suggs* (1969), and Johanna Nichol Shields of another (1993). Howard Winston Smith, *An Annotated Edition of Hooper's "Some Adventures of Captain Simon Suggs"* (Ph.D. diss., Vanderbilt University, 1965), is helpful for dialectal problems and regionalisms.

JAMES H. JUSTUS

HOOPER, Samuel (3 Feb. 1808–14 Feb. 1875), merchant and legislator, was born in Marblehead, Massachusetts, the son of John Hooper and Eunice Hooper. Through both his mother and his father, Samuel was descended from the early and influential settlers of Marblehead, and he carried on the family tradition in trade and shipping. As a boy he learned the business firsthand, sailing on his father's ships to Europe, Russia, and the West Indies. In the counting room of the Marblehead Bank, of which his father was president, Hooper received his first lessons in finance. Although the family lived in a mansion, called the "Hooper House," Hooper attended Marblehead common schools.

In 1832 Hooper settled in Boston and married Anne Sturgis. They had two daughters and one son. Soon he became a junior partner in his father-in-law's firm Bryant, Sturgis and Company. This company sent its ships to the California coast for hides, then a major export from the cattle-grazing region, to the Northwest coast for furs, and then to China for tea and silk. Ten years later Hooper joined William Appleton and Company, importers engaged primarily in the China trade, and in 1862 the firm became Samuel Hooper and Company. Expanding his business pursuits, Hooper invested in railroads and became one of the directors of the Merchant's Bank of Boston. He was particularly interested in the manufacture of iron, holding shares in iron mines and furnaces near Lake Champlain at Port Henry, New York, and in the Bay State rolling mills of South Boston. Hooper also began to study the relation of the iron business to political economy and to formulate the ideas on currency that he articulated later in his public life.

Hooper's political career started in the Massachusetts House of Representatives, where he served three terms, 1851–1854. Still primarily a businessman, he declined reelection for a fourth term. He did return to the state legislature in 1858 as a senator but refused a second term. As a state legislator, Hooper was a prominent participant in matters relating to banking and finance, and he introduced measures to strengthen the state banking system.

Hooper published *Currency or Money: Its Nature and Uses and the Effects of the Circulation of Bank-notes for Currency* (1855) and *An Examination of the Theory and the Effect of Laws Regulating the Amount of Specie in Banks* (1860). These pamphlets were recognized as authoritative studies, based on the author's experiences in finance and foreign trade.

In the preface to *Currency or Money*, Hooper noted that the subject had been unnecessarily considered "abstruse and complicated" and, most unfortunately, "connected with party politics." Acknowledging the "genius" that established a system of paper currency after the Revolution, Hooper stressed that the changed condition of the United States in the 1850s enabled the country to better "possess a sound currency of real money." In fact, he argued later in the text, "It is absurd to suppose, that the prosperity of the United States is the result of the use of paper money. . . . The country has prospered in spite of such money." Hooper concluded this pamphlet with the hope that it would contribute to the eventual establishment of an overall and rational banking system. A few years later, in his second pamphlet, Hooper wrote of the importance of banks holding a sufficient amount of specie in proportion to their liabilities. He stressed his conviction that practices and opinions connected with the prevailing banking and currency methods in the United States were disadvantageous to both the banks and the country.

Hooper soon put his expertise in commercial affairs to use in the Congress of the United States. His business partner William Appleton resigned from the Thirty-seventh Congress in 1861, leaving a vacancy in the Massachusetts delegation. Hooper was chosen as the Republican congressman from Massachusetts to fill out the unexpired term. He turned his attention to public affairs and was reelected six times. With his experience, he was a natural for the several committees on which he served: Ways and Means; Banking and Currency; Coinage, Weights, and Measures; and War Debts of the Loyal States. During the Forty-first Congress, he was chairman of Ways and Means. Not a good debater, he spoke rarely and briefly on the floor, but he worked arduously on his committee assignments. In general, Hooper supported the financial program of the Abraham Lincoln administration, and "at the Treasury Department, his advice was fully appreciated and frequently sought after" (*Congressional Record*, p. 1542). Hooper was influential in negotiating the national loan of April 1861, he supported the issue of legal-tender notes by the Congress, and he was specifically credited with the passage of the National Banking Act of February 1863, which established the overall banking system he advocated in his 1855 pamphlet. Chief Justice Salmon P. Chase, who had been treasury secretary, stated in an 1869 letter that the success of the banking legislation was due to the "good judgment, persevering exertions, and disinterested patriotism of Mr. Hooper" (*National Cyclopaedia of American Biography*, vol. 4, p. 499).

When the Civil War was over, Hooper continued to advocate sound money policies, urging a steady contraction of the greenbacks to establish their parity with gold and working on the Currency Act of 1873. Although he was a consistent Republican, he was not an extreme partisan. In 1866 he was a delegate to the Philadelphia "Loyalists" convention, when southerners who had opposed secession and the Confederacy met with Border State and northern congressmen to promote the role of Congress in reconstructing the Union. This same year Hooper published *Defence of the Merchants of Boston against Aspersions of the Hon. John Z. Goodrich, Ex-Collector of Customs*.

In 1865 Hooper contributed $50,000 for a Sturgis-Hooper Professorship of Geology in the school of mines at Harvard, as memorial to his son Sturgis, who died in the Civil War. He was a faithful supporter of the Boston Public Library. His wealth enabled him to have a home in Washington, where the congressman shared refinement and unostentatious hospitality with the prominent people of the Capital City. "Here learned men, statesmen, jurists and diplomats were . . . brought together . . . in conversations often brilliant. . . . And the host . . . set the example of a good listener" (*Congressional Record*, p. 1543). Hooper's father-in-law provided for a public library in Barnstable, Massachusetts (the town where he was born), and designated Hooper as the "managing editor." The Sturgis Library opened in 1867, and today the Hooper Room, named for Congressman Samuel Hooper and housing the red leather chair he used in Congress, contains a collection of genealogy and local history. In 1874 Hooper declined to be a candidate for renomination. He wished to return to private life, but before he could do so he died in Washington.

• For details on Hooper's business and political careers, it is necessary to use the standard biographical sources, such as the *National Cyclopaedia of American Biography*, vol. 4 (1891; repr. 1967). The *Congressional Record*, 20 Feb. 1875, contains memorials offered to the House of Representatives that provide details on Hooper's life and career and indicate the esteem of his peers. A lengthy obituary in the *New York Times*, 14 Feb. 1875, gives much biographical material.

SYLVIA B. LARSON

HOOPER, William (17 June 1742–14 Oct. 1790), signer of the Declaration of Independence, was born in Boston, Massachusetts, the son of William Hooper, an Episcopal clergyman, and Mary Dennie. At age fifteen Hooper entered Harvard as a member of the sophomore class and graduated in 1760. Though his father wished for Hooper to follow him into the ministry, he instead read law with James Otis at a time when the latter was becoming a leader of resistance to British imperial policy. Finding Boston overcrowded with lawyers, Hooper moved to Wilmington, North Carolina, in 1764 to establish a practice. In 1767 he married Anne Clark; the couple had three children.

Though frequently ill, Hooper established himself among the tidewater elite of the lower Cape Fear River. In 1766 the talented young lawyer was elected borough recorder, and in 1769 he was named deputy attorney general for the Salisbury District. As such, Hooper became a target of backcountry "Regulators" in their attacks on an officialdom they deemed responsible for excessive taxation and legal fees, corruption, and maldistribution of representation. Being roughed up by a crowd in Hillsborough in 1770, Hooper supported stern measures against the malcontents. In the following years Hooper established a small plantation—dubbed "Finian"—on Masonboro Sound near Wilmington and afterward acquired additional plantation and slave property.

Little in Hooper's history to this point—except, perhaps, his association with Otis—suggested an especially militant spirit. Yet after being elected to the colonial assembly in early 1773 as a representative of Campbellton (he was reelected later in the year from New Hanover County), Hooper became one of North Carolina's most prominent Whigs. He was a leader in the assembly's struggles with the royal governor and council over an important court bill that would forbid the attachment locally of colonial property belonging to debtors who resided in England. Hooper believed that such legislation intruded on American rights. The resulting stalemate led to courts being closed and Hooper being prevented from practicing. In December 1773 the assembly named him to a committee of correspondence, and the next year, following the imposition of the Coercive Acts, Hooper raised money and supplies for the relief of his native Boston. During the ensuing crisis Hooper took an important role in the process by which sovereignty in the colony was transferred from royal institutions to extralegal bodies. After the royal governor refused to assemble the legislature, Hooper chaired a meeting that on its own authority called a provincial congress. This body in turn elected Hooper and two others to the new intercolonial congress that was to meet in Philadelphia. Hooper served, as well, in a provincial congress that the next year established a new government for North Carolina.

Arriving in Philadelphia in September 1774, Hooper quickly distinguished himself as the most active of North Carolina's delegates to the Continental Congress. He was counted by John Adams among the body's leading orators. Even before the first Congress met, Hooper had clearly seen independence as the likely consequence of British oppression, but he by no means welcomed the prospect. The goal of the resistance that he had helped orchestrate seemed to be the restoration of the imperial status quo that had prevailed before 1763. Like many others, as adamantly as Hooper resisted Britain's colonial policy, he admired its political institutions and looked askance at the prospect of a rawer sort of democracy being established in an independent America. Through 1774 and 1775 Hooper continued to cherish the prospect of reconciliation and resisted initiatives that seemed to sanction permanent separation. (The instructions he had received from the provincial congresses prevented him, in any case, from doing otherwise.) Still, Thomas Jefferson's assertion late in life that "we had not a greater Tory in Congress than Hooper" seems rather unfair. Hooper urged North Carolinians to support armed resistance and helped procure the supplies that would allow them to do so. He called on Americans to refrain from either importing English products or exporting their own goods.

Only several months into 1776 did Hooper appear to give himself over to American nationhood. The burning by British raiders of a home he was building near Wilmington probably only underscored for him the fading prospects of reconciliation. Returning to North Carolina in April to attend the fourth provincial congress, Hooper found that the body had lately endorsed independence. Reconciling himself to separation, he counseled North Carolina's remaining representative in Philadelphia that "one had better Swim on the democratick [sic] flood than[,] vainly attempting to check it[,] be buried in it" (Morgan and Schmidt, p. 230). Hooper did not return to Philadelphia until late July, and so could not participate in the voting on independence, but he signed Jefferson's Declaration on 2 August. He remained in the Continental Congress until February 1777, serving on committees governing America's military efforts and foreign affairs, including the War Board, Treasury Board, Marine Board, and Committee of Secret Correspondence. After being felled by yellow fever, he returned to Wilmington, formally resigning from Congress in April 1777.

If yielding to the "democratick flood," Hooper nevertheless hoped to see it contained within certain channels. Persuasively, it seems, he pressed those framing North Carolina's constitution to ensure mixed government by establishing a bicameral legislature in which a democratic lower house would be balanced by one governed by men "selected for their Wisdom, remarkable Integrity, or that Weight which arises from property and gives Independence and Impartiality to the human mind" (Saunders, vol. 10, p. 867). He also urged an appointed judiciary rather than an elected one. Hooper served in the new state's general assembly from 1777 to 1781, but his political career would prove more checkered than it had been previously. In 1782, having been forced to flee British forces operating around Wilmington, Hooper established his residence in the backcountry of Hillsborough, North Carolina. The following year he was defeated for an assembly seat by a tavernkeeper. Returned to the assembly in 1784 and 1786, Hooper, one of a conservative faction of lawyers, opposed legislation protecting debtors, supported the restitution of confiscated property to erstwhile Loyalists (among whom he counted several family members), and helped to block further confiscation. He backed the efforts to build a more powerful federal government that eventually yielded the U.S. Constitution but failed in his bid to be elected to the state convention called to consider its ratification. Hooper suffered a relapse of malaria in 1789, his ill health probably exacerbated by heavy drinking. He died in Hillsborough.

• Many of Hooper's papers were destroyed in a fire, but scattered material is held at the New-York Historical Society and in the Southern Historical Collection at the University of North Carolina, Chapel Hill. Important Hooper correspondence has been published in William Saunders, ed., *Colonial Records of North Carolina* (1886–1890); Griffith McRee, ed., *The Life and Correspondence of James Iredell* (1857–1858); and Edmund Burnett, ed., *Letters of Members of the Continental Congress* (1921–1936). Biographical accounts include Robert C. Kneip, "William Hooper, 1742–1790, Misunderstood Patriot" (Ph.D. diss., Tulane Univ., 1980), and Edwin A. Alderman, *Address on the Life of William Hooper, "The Prophet of American Independence"* (1894). Considerable information is more conveniently available in William Powell, ed., *The Dictionary of North Carolina Biography*, vol. 3 (1988). On Hooper and American independence, see David Morgan and William Schmidt, "From Economic Sanctions to Political Separation: The North Carolina Delegation to the Continental Congress, 1774–1776," *North Carolina Historical Review* 52 (1975): 215–34. Hooper's political career in the 1780s is briefly discussed in Norman Risjord, *Chesapeake Politics, 1781–1800* (1978).

PATRICK G. WILLIAMS

HOOTON, Earnest Albert (20 Nov. 1887–3 May 1954), anthropologist, was born in Clemansville, Wisconsin, the son of William Hooton, a Methodist minister, and Margaret Elizabeth Newton, a former schoolteacher. His father had emigrated from Nottinghamshire, England, to Canada, where he married and then moved to eastern Wisconsin. Pastoral assignments were changed every three to five years, so during his childhood Hooton sampled several small-town public schools in preparation for entry into Lawrence University in Appleton, Wisconsin, in 1903. While in college he worked part time for two years at a state penitentiary in nearby Waupun; this experience later sparked his massive, ill-fated study of the physical traits of criminals. He also developed his talent for cartoon sketches working on the *Ariel*, Lawrence's student yearbook; he continued to use this skill throughout his life to illustrate humorously his often cynical views.

Hooton entered graduate school in classics at the University of Wisconsin, Madison, after receiving his B.A. from Lawrence in 1907. He completed his Ph.D. with the dissertation "The Evolution of Literary Art in Pre-Hellenic Rome" in 1911, a year after he entered University College, Oxford, as a Rhodes scholar. At Oxford, however, he was encouraged in his pursuit of anthropology by the classicist-turned-anthropologist R. R. Marett, editor of a book, *Anthropology and the Classics* (1908), that had influenced Hooton at Wiscon-

sin. He began, as one of his classmates said, to spend "much time in dissecting rooms and among medicos" as he earned a diploma in anthropology in 1912.

Hooton was informally tutored in the interpretation of the human skeleton at the Museum of the Royal College of Surgeons in London by the anatomist and human paleontologist Sir Arthur Keith, who became a lifelong friend and confidant. He applied his new skills to the examination of remains from archaeological excavations and even supervised the disinterment of a Saxon graveyard. While returning to England in 1912 for his final year, he met Mary Beidler Camp of Chicago, whom he married three years later. Their three children were born between 1918 and 1924. As adults his two sons continued to be dependent on the family and were well-known to generations of students at the Peabody Museum, even after his death, as occasional laboratory assistants.

Both Harvard University and the University of California at Berkeley offered Hooton appointments as an instructor in anthropology on the completion of his B.Litt. in 1913. He chose Harvard, spent the summer at the University of Wisconsin taking a course in human anatomy, and in the fall began a teaching and research career at Harvard's Peabody Museum that would last forty-one years.

In the summer of 1915 Hooton spent two months in Tenerife in the Canary Islands with the intention of excavating and examining skeletal remains of the early inhabitants, the Guanches. He obtained a large number of measurements, and the Peabody Museum acquired a large collection of Guanche skeletons. Hooton's analysis of this research, *The Ancient Inhabitants of the Canary Islands* (1925), and his similar but more statistically sophisticated research on Native Americans, *The Indians of Pecos Pueblo* (1930), established his reputation as a leading American physical (or biological) anthropologist.

In 1916 Hooton attended the Second Business Men's Military Training Camp at Plattsburg, New York, but he was discharged as severely nearsighted. He spent the war years teaching, but after the Armistice in the summer of 1919 he supervised the measuring of 8,500 soldiers to establish clothing sizes for the Quartermaster Corps.

Hooton's research in the 1930s moved away from osteology and the determination of racial origin and mixture from cranial characteristics and focused on anthropometric variation in living populations. His increasing prestige aided in his acquisition of funds to allow him to conduct two massive studies. He believed that different suites of physical characteristics were found in persons convicted of different crimes and that criminals differed physically from other people. He set out to prove this with measurements taken on about 13,000 prisoners and a control sample of 3,200 civilians in ten states. At about the same time he organized an anthropological survey of Ireland and had one of his students collect measurements and observations on more than 10,000 Irish males. In both projects the costs of analyses and publication thwarted Hooton's original goals. His Irish study, *The Physical Anthropology of Ireland*, with C. W. Dupertuis, was published posthumously in 1955. Hooton wrote a popular book, *Crime and the Man* (1939), outlining his conclusions and illustrated with his own cartoons. Its success was supposed to finance the printing of three research volumes, but only one, *The American Criminal* (1939), on native-born, white males, was published. The academic reaction to his criminal study was largely negative, and he came to believe that he had convinced no one but himself of the relation between the physical man and his crime.

Beginning in the 1930s Hooton developed a persona that eventually made him well known to the public. To some extent he cultivated this by writing for popular magazines, such as *Collier's*, *Ladies' Home Journal*, and *Good Housekeeping*, on topics controversial—a woman for president—and mundane—why he liked to read mysteries. He became a minor celebrity: Walt Disney visited him to discuss an anti-Nazi film; the stripper Ann Corio had tea at his home; and he measured a popular acromegalic French wrestler, the Angel (characteristically, he also quietly arranged for extensive medical evaluation). Actress and author Ilka Chase in *Past Imperfect* (1941), described him as "tall, shaggy, a little stooped, [holding] forth on mankind with penetrating insight and malice." He routinely provided pungent quotes for inquiring reporters, and the media in turn gave him prominence unusual for an anthropologist. His support for a doctor accused of euthanasia in 1950 garnered him an eight-column, front-page headline in the Boston *Traveler*. In the week of his death he was asked to be a television talk-show host, and he prepared several articles for a potential New York newspaper column.

Hooton used his access to the public to put forth a pessimistic view of the future, which he saw as increasingly dismal unless steps were taken to promote human biological well-being. He was both witty and given to harsh pronouncements intended to shock: "There can be little doubt of the increase during the past fifty years of mental defectives, psychopaths, criminals, economic incompetents and the chronically diseased. We owe this to the intervention of charity, 'welfare' and medical science, and to the reckless breeding of the unfit" (*Redbook*, Jan. 1950). Nonetheless, he never went beyond suggesting an array of new government departments to educate the public in needed change.

A resolution filed in 1943 in the Massachusetts General Assembly condemning Hooton for alleged anti-American and anti-religious statements exemplifies the outrage his sentiments provoked in some segments of the public, but he was not a fascist, racist, or anti-Semite. In 1942 he wrote an article, "Science Debunks That Pure Race Myth of the Nazis," for the *American Weekly*, the Hearst newspapers' Sunday supplement. "Individual Quality as the Basis of a Better Society" was written in response to a request to contribute to Boston's *Jewish Advocate*. The National Association for the Advancement of Colored People asked him to present its 1944 Spingarn Award to Charles R. Drew, M.D.; he did so with a biting denunciation of racial prejudice before an audience of 20,000 in Chicago's Washington Park.

In 1940 William H. Sheldon, in *Varieties of Human Physique*, proposed his concept of somatotype, which classified the human body form as varying combinations of endomorphy (roundness), mesomorphy (muscularity), and ectomorphy (linearity), which was determined by examining a set of nude photographs. Hooton became an important advocate of somatotyping, using it as the foundation of what he called constitutional anthropology, or anthropology of the individual. He believed that somatotyping would prove to be a better means than anthropometric measurements for relating variation in the human body form to function and disease. Sheldon's personal eccentricities and his unwillingness to modify or test his system soon led Hooton to distance himself from Sheldon and to simplify the somatotyping technique. Harvard's Grant study involved somatotyping by one of Hooton's students as part of its multidisciplinary examination of 268 Harvard students to determine what constituted the normal, defined as a balanced, harmonious blending of functions producing good integration. Hooton publicized the study in "*Young Man, You Are Normal*" (1945).

Early in 1941 Hooton was asked by the Army Air Forces Aero Medical Research Unit to help correct dangerously inappropriate sizing standards for the design of cockpits and gun turrets. He devised an anthropometric survey of cadet pilots and gunners, carried out the following year, to use in screening aviation candidates and modifying equipment. The success of this effort led to the establishment of an applied anthropological unit that persisted well after World War II at Wright-Patterson Air Force Base near Dayton, Ohio.

In 1944, in what may have been the first collaboration between physical anthropology and private enterprise, the Heywood-Wakefield Company contracted with Hooton to aid in developing new seating for railway cars. With his customary flair for publicity, he set up a measuring chair in Boston's North Station and Chicago's Northwestern Station; this allowed his assistants to measure 3,800 members of the traveling public to determine the most appropriate dimensions for the new design, which was used for many years.

Immediately following World War II Hooton received several contracts from the U.S. Army to establish the range of body build in the army and to relate this to performance of military activities. The enormous task, ultimately requiring the examination of almost 50,000 men, occupied much of his research time until his death.

Although Hooton was continuously active in a diverse range of research projects, his greatest satisfaction at Harvard was the opportunity it provided him to teach (he only took two sabbatical semesters in forty-one years) and to train professional physical anthropologists. He became a full professor in 1930 and was chair of the Department of Anthropology for most of the remainder of his tenure. He still held that position at the time of his death in Cambridge, Massachusetts, after his last class of the semester.

Hooton concurrently held the position of curator of somatology in the Peabody Museum and in that role significantly increased the museum's human skeletal resources and established a statistical laboratory. In the 1930s he was able to persuade IBM to provide him with keypunch and card-sorting equipment that allowed him to develop a data-analysis capacity unique among anthropology programs before the 1960s.

Hooton was an exceptionally popular lecturer to undergraduates, Harvard alumni groups, and others who could persuade him to leave Cambridge. He wrote comic verse in the style of Ogden Nash, some of which he included in his books, such as *Up from the Ape* (1931, 1946), a comprehensive text on physical anthropology that became his best-known work. He was a regular if poor golfer but otherwise rather sedentary and reluctant to travel. The Hootons held teas every afternoon where students, faculty, and noted visitors could mingle informally.

Hooton's research initially sought to understand the history of human population variation in terms of archaic racial categories; he then moved toward demonstrating a causal relationship, however imperfect, between human physical configurations and adaptation to cultural and medical norms. His work earned him many accolades, including election to the National Academy of Sciences. More lasting was his effort to advance and popularize physical anthropology as a scientific discipline in books that were both sound and popular. These works did not all relate to his own research; for example, he advocated the study of nonhuman primate behavior in *Man's Poor Relations* (1942).

Hooton was most influential, however, in mentoring almost thirty doctoral students, of whom seven have been elected to the National Academy of Sciences. For many years he was the foremost teacher of physical anthropology in the United States. The growth of physical anthropology in American universities has largely been the outcome of the success of his students and those they trained. Misanthropic in public pronouncements but kindly and supportive in personal relationships, Hooton encouraged his many graduate students in the pursuit of their own research interests, influencing the broad scope of physical anthropology well into the late twentieth century.

• Hooton's papers are in the archives of the Peabody Museum, Harvard University. An autobiographical sketch is in M. Block, ed., *Current Biography* (1940), pp. 397–400. An early influential article is "The Asymmetrical Character of Human Evolution," *American Journal of Physical Anthropology* 8 (1925): 125–41. A number of his lectures and papers are collected in *Apes, Men, and Morons* (1937), *Twilight of Man* (1939), and *Why Men Behave Like Apes and Vice Versa* (1940). *A Survey in Seating* (1945) provides the results of his railroad coach seat design project. "Body Build in a Sample of the United States Army" (Environmental Protection Research Division Technical Report EP-102, U.S. Army Quartermaster Research and Engineering Center, Natick, Mass., 1959 [AD 214 177]), is the only accessible record of his postwar research. Hooton's public persona is displayed in articles by Walter Stockly, *Life*, 7 Aug. 1939, pp. 60–66, and by Jack Stenbuck, *Esquire*, Oct. 1946, pp. 72, 150–55. An account of Hooton in the Canary Islands is Ronald Ley, "From the Caves of Tenerife to the Stores of the Peabody Museum," *Anthropological Quarterly* 52 (1979): 159–64. Obituaries are in the *New York Times*, 4 May 1954; *The Times* (London), 5 May 1954; *Science* 119 (1954): 861–62; American Philosophical Society, *Year Book 1954*: 418–22; and *American Journal of Physical Anthropology* 12 (1954): 445–53, which provides a bibliography of his scientific publications.

EUGENE GILES

HOOVER, Calvin Bryce (14 Apr. 1897–23 June 1974), economist and educator, was born in the village of Berwick, Illinois, the son of John Calvin Hoover, a railroad worker and part-time farmer, and Margaret Delilah Roadcap. Hoover grew up poor. His father was a railroad section gang foreman, and he himself worked as a "gandy dancer" in his father's gang during summer vacations, weekends, and holidays. He also helped his father farm the rented land that he was sharecropping. He never forgot what it was like to be poor. In his memoirs, he tells of going down to the railroad station to watch the trains come in wearing old clothes and carrying a rifle with a broken stock held together by twine and having a passenger shout at him, "Shades of Daniel Boone!"

From his observations of the differences in people's wealth and status in Berwick, Hoover became what he called a "primitive socialist." He avidly read a socialist periodical called the *Appeal to Reason*, to which his father subscribed. His parents were determined that he get a good education, and he was sent to Monmouth College in Monmouth, Illinois.

In 1917, when the United States entered the war against Germany, Hoover left Monmouth in his third year to enlist in the U.S. Army. As a private in the infantry and then a sergeant in the field artillery, he saw action in the battles of St.-Mihiel and Meuse-Argonne; he was not wounded, but two of his classmates from Monmouth who had enlisted with him were killed. After the war ended, he stayed on in the American Army of Occupation in Germany, suffering severe bouts of influenza and dysentery.

But Hoover felt that military service had done him a lot of good—had toughened him up and rid him of any tendency to romanticize "the common man." "My army experience," he later wrote, "cured me of being a socialist. It did not cure me of being an egalitarian to the extent equality of income could be attained without intolerable sacrifice of either individual liberty or social productivity."

On being discharged from the army in May 1919, he decided that he wanted to get away from the "swarms" of other people and to be a farmer. Also that year he married Faith Sprole, of Garner, Iowa, who had been his friend in college and his fiancée throughout his military service; they had two daughters.

In 1920 Hoover rented a 120-acre farm near Gold-field, Iowa, from his father-in-law, an Iowa banker. But his farming experience turned into a disaster. The farm was too big for him to handle, though he worked from dawn till late at night. In 1921 farm prices collapsed and hog cholera killed most of his hogs. Hoover left the farm, raising what money he could by selling his farm implements, and decided to go back to college. He completed his studies at Monmouth and earned an A.B. in 1922. He went to the University of Wisconsin in Madison in 1922 to do graduate work in economics and quickly was recognized as an outstanding and committed student. His most important professor was John R. Commons, the leading historian of the American labor movement and a pioneer of social legislation. In 1923 Hoover got a job at the School of Business of the University of Minnesota and while teaching there completed work for his doctorate at the University of Wisconsin. In 1925 he left Minnesota to become assistant professor of economics at Duke University.

Two years later Hoover was awarded a grant by the Social Science Research Council to go to Moscow to study the Soviet banking system and the problems of a managed currency. But his interests were broader, and he undertook a study of the entire Soviet system. In his first book, *The Economic Life of Soviet Russia* (1931), he concluded that, despite its dictatorial political system and cruelty toward individuals, the Soviet economy was capable of achieving continuous growth and building the basis for a powerful state. In his pioneering Soviet studies, Hoover had the support of John Maynard Keynes, the distinguished British economist and editor of the *Economic Journal*. Keynes solicited and published Hoover's first articles on the Soviet Union and helped him to get his book, which grew out of the articles, published. Hoover later said of Keynes that "his was the most powerful and creative mind and the most dynamic personality which I was ever to encounter."

Hoover spent 1932 and 1933 in Germany, where he had a close up view of Hitler's rise to power. His book, *Germany Enters the Third Reich* (1933), demonstrated that Hitler was using his rearmament program to restore full employment and raise living standards; this contradicted the left-wing cant of the day, which held that Hitler was rearming by depressing wages and sweating capital out of the working class. Based on his own theory of macroeconomics, Hoover showed that heavy public expenditure on arms, far from impoverishing the working class, enabled a depressed economy to produce both more guns and more butter—and without unleashing inflation—as unemployed workers and factories were drawn back into production. The same lesson was learned in the United States when the country entered the war. His early studies in the Soviet Union and Germany laid the foundation of his life's work on economic systems; he taught the first course on the subject in the United States.

Soon after his return to Duke University in 1933, Hoover was summoned to Washington by Rexford Guy Tugwell, assistant secretary of agriculture, to become an economic consultant to the Agriculture Adjustment Administration (AAA), whose goal was to raise farm prices by reducing acreage and cutting farm output. In February 1935 Hoover was named consumers' counsel of the AAA and was supposed to defend the interests of consumers and to resolve conflicts between landowners and sharecroppers. A report he wrote on "Human Problems in Acreage Reduction in the South" for Secretary of Agriculture, later Vice President, Henry A. Wallace, was softened to the point of ineffectuality, and in September 1935 Hoover resigned to return to his academic post at Duke. In 1937 he became dean of the Graduate School at Duke, and he held this position until 1947.

When the United States entered World War II, Hoover, known for his German and Soviet studies, was called to Washington by Colonel William J. "Wild Bill" Donovan, who was setting up a new intelligence operation under the name COI (Donovan was called coordinator of information.) COI later changed its name to OSS—the Office of Strategic Services.

Hoover played various roles in OSS and eventually became head of Northern European operations, headquartered in Stockholm, Sweden. His intelligence network pinpointed the location of German synthetic oil plants, and, by knocking them out, Allied bombers effectively grounded the Luftwaffe during the Normandy invasion. For this and other wartime achievements, Hoover was awarded the Medal of Freedom by President Truman in 1946.

The war over, Hoover went to Berlin in 1945 to design a basic plan for reconstructing the devastated German economy. Working rapidly under Generals Lucius Clay and William Draper, Hoover designed a plan that called for restoring German steel capacity to 7.8 million tons a year and other industries to a level that would allow Germany to support itself. The report produced a political storm in the United States and the Soviet Union, especially among those who urged that Germany should be reduced to a weak, rural economy to prevent it from ever waging war again. Though a powerful anti-Nazi himself, Hoover believed that peace would be more likely to be preserved by economic health and growth than by wrecking the German economy; the Versailles treaty and Allied efforts after World War I to cripple Germany had actually fed the rise of Hitler and bred World War II. Hoover's plan for rebuilding German industry prevailed; a recurrence of the revanchism after World War I was avoided, and the economic recovery of Germany furthered the unity of Western Europe and the Western defense against the Soviet Union in the Cold War.

After his return to Duke University in late 1945, Hoover was named James B. Duke Professor of Economics. He was elected president of the American Economic Association in 1953. While he continued to advise government whenever asked, he remained at Duke for the rest of his life. He died in Durham, North Carolina.

• Hoover's papers are in the Duke University Archives. His other publications include *Dictators and Democracies* (1937); *International Trade and Domestic Employment* (1944); *Economic Resources and Policies of the South* (1950); *The Economy, Liberty, and the State* (1959); *Memoirs of Capitalism, Communism, and Nazism* (1965), and many journal articles. An obituary is in the *New York Times*, 12 July 1974.

LEONARD SILK

HOOVER, Herbert Clark (10 Aug. 1874–20 Oct. 1964), engineer, philanthropist, and thirty-first president of the United States, was born in West Branch, Iowa, the son of Jesse Clark Hoover and Hulda[h] Minthorn, farmers. Orphaned at the age of nine, he lived with a variety of relatives in Iowa and finally spent his teenage years in Newberg and Salem, Oregon. Although his parents belonged to a "progressive" branch of Quakers who permitted some organ music and gospel hymns at their meeting house, Hoover's religious training was quite rigorous under the tutelage of his mother, an ordained Quaker minister.

Except for his conservative style of dress, Hoover retained few outward signs of his boyhood faith. Not only was his personal and professional aggressiveness as an engineer inconsistent with the Quaker idea of moderation, but Hoover also could swear with the roughest of the miners he directed after graduating with an A.B. in geology from Stanford University's first class in 1895. Moreover, he was a habitual smoker, enjoyed alcoholic drinks, and often fished on Sundays, albeit wearing a high collar and necktie. During his early engineering career he was aided and accompanied to all parts of the world by the equally independent-minded Stanford geology graduate, Lou Henry. Although born into a Quaker family less than 100 miles from West Branch, Henry moved with her parents to California in 1884, where they became Episcopalians. Consequently, Henry and Hoover did not meet until college. Married in 1889, they had two sons.

Hoover had phenomenal success as a mining engineer, becoming a millionaire between 1895 and the outbreak of the First World War in 1914, when he was forty. The years between 1890 and World War I represented the "golden age" of American foreign mining exploits as well as the time when some engineers became involved reformers in the search for a new corporatist economic order in the United States. Hoover specifically endorsed the brand of progressivism that stressed cooperative economic organization, self-regulation by business, and voluntary activity through American society.

Hoover's philanthropic and government work during the First World War confirmed his progressive beliefs and brought him wide public notice at home and abroad. Serving as head of the Commission for the Relief in Belgium, as President Woodrow Wilson's U.S. Food Administrator (1917–1919) in charge of voluntary rationing, and director general of the American Relief Administration in Europe (1919–1920) made him such a popular figure that both parties courted him as a presidential nominee in 1920. Refusing to run for the presidency, Hoover served as secretary of commerce in the administrations of Presidents Warren G. Harding and Calvin Coolidge, transforming that department between 1921 and 1928 into one of the most important and well-publicized federal departments. As commerce secretary he encouraged and helped to develop some of the most advanced economic theories about business cycles and industrial standardization, promoted government regulation of the nascent radio and aviation industries, and supported federal supervision of foreign loans.

Thus in 1927, when President Coolidge enigmatically announced that he "did not choose to run" again, Hoover decided to try for the first elective office of his career against the seasoned New York politician and Democratic governor Alfred E. Smith. Probably no Democrat could have rivaled the popularity that Hoover had established with the press and public by 1928 as a postwar superman. Smith, an Irish Catholic, had the extra disadvantage of being a "wet" from an ethnic New York City neighborhood. Moreover, the prevailing sense of prosperity that most areas of the country were enjoying further helped the Republicans prevail in this classic 1928 contest between two self-made men, neither of whom used the radio successfully as a new campaign tool. In the long run Hoover's victory proved less impressive than Smith's defeat, because the Democratic vote indicated a new partisan and demographic realignment was in the making.

Immediately after his inauguration, Hoover took up the "uncompleted tasks in government" that remained from his cabinet days. Convinced that it was only a matter of time before he could achieve his progressive dream for the United States, he promoted labor legislation that resulted in the 1932 Norris–La Guardia Anti-Injunction Act; set limits on oil drilling; ordered that all large government rebates on income, estate, and gift taxes be made public; reformed downward the graduated income tax; took action against corrupt patronage practices; tentatively reached out to African Americans with the first Republican "southern strategy"; refused to give any government backing to proposed "red hunts" against communists; improved the civil and economic rights of Native Americans through appointments and by acting on advisory committee reports; and pursued conservation by appointing Horace Albright commissioner of the National Park Service and creating the Commission on the Conservation and Administration of the Public Domain.

Unfortunately, Hoover's progressive dream also called a special session of Congress to consider chronic agricultural problems of the 1920s. Although as secretary of commerce he had opposed subsidized agricultural production (known as McNary-Hauganism), Congress passed his Agricultural Marketing Act during the special session on 15 June 1929, and Hoover had to fight to prevent the farm bloc from attaching an export debenture (payback subsidy) to it. Ultimately the Federal Farm Board created by this act lost approximately $345 million, trying to support falling farm prices between 1929 and 1931 with loans to cooperatives and stabilization corporations for the purchase of basic crops. This loss, due largely to the depression that began less than six months after the act was passed, was nonetheless a bitter disappointment for Hoover. It meant the failure of an "almost perfect illustration" of his faith in cooperative associations to regulate the economy.

His other emergency session objective—a revision of the 1922 tariff to benefit farmers—met a similarly dismal fate. It took fourteen months to obtain passage, on 17 June 1931, of the protectionist Hawley-Smoot Tariff, which pleased no one, including the president. While this tariff did not cause the Great Depression, which was already well under way when it passed, it has been widely criticized for contributing further to contracting world trade.

What began as a "dazzling" eight months in foreign as well as domestic affairs ended almost before it began with the stock market crash in October 1929, dashing Hoover's hopes for a progressive transformation of the United States. His methods remained essentially what they had been throughout the previous decade of prosperity: reliance on persuasion to raise private funds voluntarily, educational conferences, and fact-finding commissions. Hoover expanded his cooperative programs to obtain decentralized voluntary cooperation among businesspeople during the crucial depression years of 1930–1931 and the early months of 1932. He attempted to revitalize trade through the Emergency Committee for Employment; encouraged the Cotton Textile Institute's attempts to end destructive competition and thus keep prices up; and appointed a privately financed Timber Conservation Board and the Federal Oil Conservation Board. He created many other agencies to facilitate decentralized, cooperative action without resorting to government coercion or business cartels, including the Federal Drought Relief Committee, the President's Organization on Unemployment Relief, the National Credit Corporation, the Citizens' Reconstruction Organization, the Federal Employment Stabilization Board, the Federal Power Commission, and a new network of business and industrial committees. Far from losing faith in voluntarism and associationalism, Hoover tried to expand both in the face of economic adversity.

Against this background Hoover entered his first or "offensive" phase as a depression president. He began by playing an extremely independent, active role, calling conferences of industrial and labor leaders and obtaining from them voluntary pledges to avoid strikes and to maintain current employment, wage, and production levels. At the same time, he asked the states and cities to speed up their public works in order to maintain employment and increase construction activity. Although Hoover had intended to expand public works when he entered the White House, he did not ask for additional funds for this purpose in his 1929 budget message, because he never thought of his $3 billion reserve fund as an emergency measure.

In very guarded language Hoover's State of the Union address on 4 December 1929 only briefly referred to the six-week-old stock market crash. By the end of 1929 he still thought the economic situation was merely an American recession (refusing yet to use the term depression) caused by "overspeculation in securities." Believing the crash to be domestic in origin and scope, Hoover reasoned that the solution should also be indigenous. Therefore, his initial decision to urge voluntary state and local expenditures over federal ones is understandable: the national government played a relatively small role in the economy in the 1920s and was not the source of expansion that it has since become. Hoover did, however, request from Congress in April 1930 an additional appropriation of $150 million for public buildings. In fact, through Hoover's encouragement of state and local spending, federal increases for public works, and congressional authorization (over the president's veto) of payment up to 50 percent on veterans' certificates, the total fiscal stimulation at all levels of government—federal, state, and local—was larger in that year than for the remainder of the decade. Despite increased federal, state, and local expenditures on public works, private construction fell off drastically in 1930, and so did government revenue at all levels.

By the fall of 1930 the president was publicly admitting there was a worldwide depression, not simply an American recession. Partly to counter congressional Democrats, partly because of foreign developments, but primarily because of his lifelong inability to admit to failure or mistakes, Hoover changed his mind about the origins of the Great Depression. Rather than confess publicly or privately that his cooperative policies were not effective, he became convinced that the worldwide crisis had foreign origins, making European recovery a prerequisite for permanent American recovery. When the European credit structure collapsed in the summer of 1931 and England abandoned the gold standard later that fall, Hoover turned to Congress for approval of several international agreements, including a one-year moratorium on Allied debts and German reparations and a London "standstill" agreement stabilizing short-term German credit. Both were necessary, he said, for world recovery from the depression. At the same time he took steps to try to ensure that the United States would remain on the gold standard, obtaining an increase in the discount rate of the Federal Reserve Board and raising taxes to balance the budget.

While both Democrats and Republicans in Congress passed all his major pieces of remedial legislation, the major bone of contention between the president and legislators became direct relief to the unemployed. Direct relief to Hoover meant the dole, while indirect relief meant public works projects. As president he never changed his mind on this question, even though unemployment figures soared from over seven million in 1931 to over eleven million in 1933, when he left office. Hoover's insistence that locally financed self-help programs were more worthy of

Americans than going on the dole through direct federal aid eventually antagonized many voters.

The simple fact was that, as state and local funds disappeared, the people wanted federal relief, and Congress responded for political as well as humanitarian reasons. Most of the relief proposals from the Seventy-second Congress were in the form of public works bills, which Hoover rejected throughout 1931. From June 1930 through June 1933, however, his administration approved $3.5 billion for various forms of public works. He also reluctantly supported the Federal Employment Stabilization Bill of 1931, which technically created a board with the power to control job fluctuation through public construction projects.

The Emergency and Relief Construction Act, signed on 21 July 1932, appropriated $2 billion for public works and $300 million for direct loans to the states "to be used in furnishing relief and work relief to needy and distressed people." Though Hoover claimed it conformed to his requirements, its passage and signing were tacit admission that private and public works programs at the state and local levels had failed, that emergency rather than long-term public works programs had to be started, and that some direct federal relief was necessary.

The Emergency and Relief Construction Act pushed Hoover's principles on direct and indirect relief to their limits and pushed him into a defensive posture. That he would have been forced to approve direct relief projects, such as those later endorsed by Franklin D. Roosevelt's Works Progress Administration (WPA), remains highly doubtful, given all the restrictions Hoover placed on the implementation of this 1932 relief act. However, the widespread support in congressional and business circles for more federal action to rationalize the depressed economy did prompt Hoover to propose several other defensive pieces of legislation in the spring of 1932. For example, the Federal Farm Board, created during the special session of the Seventy-first Congress, began emergency operations when it launched a large wheat price stabilization effort through the purchase of surpluses. After it became evident during the summer of 1931 that the board was losing money on such purchases without achieving price stabilization, the project was abandoned. Instead, farmers were asked voluntarily to destroy a portion of their staple crops.

On 4 October 1931 Hoover persuaded reluctant bankers and insurance executives to form the National Credit Corporation (NCC) with a capital of $500 million, representing his last attempt to save the country's credit structure through purely voluntary means. Cautiousness on the part of the bankers involved resulted in the NCC's failure as an effective credit pool by the end of November. The president was forced to fall back on the World War I model of the War Finance Corporation (WFC) by recommending the creation of the Reconstruction Finance Corporation (RFC) with Eugene Meyer, who had also headed the WFC, as its chairman. Thus, the ill-fated Hoover administration became the first in American history to use the power of the federal government to intervene directly in the economy in time of peace. Voluntarism had failed. Simultaneously and for the same reason, he pressed for passage of the Glass-Steagall Act of 27 February 1932, which made about $750 million of government gold available for industrial and business purposes.

RFC legislation became effective on 22 January 1932 with a $2 million appropriation from Congress earmarked for endangered financial institutions. Hoover hoped the RFC would increase confidence, stimulate employment, and aid foreign trade. Nonetheless, he looked upon it, as he had on the WFC during the First World War, as a temporary and emergency agency whose functions would end with the economic crisis and whose purpose was to liquefy the nation's frozen assets by loaning only to large businesses and financial institutions rather than to average citizens. Not only did his personal philosophy and experiences with the WFC during World War I prevent him from allowing the RFC to make massive loans for direct relief of unemployment, but in creating the RFC he also indicated that his first concern remained the national credit structure.

Historians and economists now agree that it made more economic (albeit not political) sense to save the country's credit apparatus from further paralysis by extending RFC loans exclusively to leading financial institutions than it did to use such loans to tackle the growing unemployment problem, which was never resolved by New Deal work programs—only U.S. entrance into the Second World War did that. Together the RFC and the Glass-Steagall Act "helped the country get through 1932 without collapse," according to the latest economic evaluations. With the signing of these two acts, the expansion of capital for Federal Land Banks, and the Creation of Home Loan Banks, all economic indices temporarily shot up in the late summer of 1932, and Hoover precipitantly declared that the depression was under control.

To make matters worse, Hoover mishandled the Bonus Expeditionary Force—10,000 ex-servicemen who marched on Washington demanding full and immediate redemption of their 1924 veteran certificates, which Hoover considered the equivalent of a dole. Even the Senate refused to grant this request, and all but 2,000 of the veterans accepted an offer of free railroad tickets home. The remaining ex-servicemen, some with their families, continued to camp in Bonus City in the Anacostia flats outside of Washington, D.C. General Douglas MacArthur routed these veterans and burned their camps on 28 July 1932 in violation of Hoover's specific orders. The president took full public responsibility for MacArthur's insubordination, and by the fall presidential election rumors were rampant that Hoover had authorized "murdering veterans," when no one had been killed by federal troops. Hoover left office in disgrace, falsely blamed for both the depression and the Bonus March fiasco.

Ironically, some of Hoover's ideas for combating the depression, such as the Reconstruction Finance Corporation, aid to agriculture, and long-term public works and relief appropriations, were popularized by his successor, Roosevelt, who also capitalized on the public relations practices that Hoover had set in motion in the 1920s. "We didn't admit it at the time," Roosevelt's aide Rexford Tugwell finally revealed in a 1974 interview, "but practically the whole New Deal was extrapolated from programs that Hoover started."

Drawing on his early Quaker training, Hoover dealt with U.S. foreign relations by relying on the power of negotiation rather than use of force, especially in Central America and the Caribbean, and by his support of arms limitation, international arbitration, and moral suasion. Even before becoming president he had exhibited an enlightened internationalist attitude on foreign affairs, recommending cancellation of the Allied debts resulting from World War I (and later debt reductions), U.S. entrance into both the World Court and League of Nations, and disarmament agreements in the 1920s. As president-elect Hoover had toured Latin America and had begun to use the term "good neighbor," emphasizing reciprocal cultural and economic interests over the previous policy of U.S. military interventionism and arbitrary supervision of elections. Hoover's approval of the 1929 Pan American Treaty of Arbitration, the League of Nations investigation of a dispute between Peru and Colombia in 1933, and his plans for removing the marines from Haiti and Nicaragua laid the foundations for what became the Good Neighbor policy toward Latin America under Roosevelt.

Hoover also refused to sanction the use of force in crisis situations, not only in Russia during its civil war after World War I and in Latin America but also in the Far East, when Japan invaded Manchuria in 1931–1932. The Manchurian crisis resulted in the Stimson Doctrine (named after his secretary of state Henry L. Stimson), stating that the United States would not recognize the fruits of aggression. However, at no time did Hoover support the use of force, economic boycotts, or even his secretary of state's bellicose language to implement the Stimson Doctrine.

Noncoerciveness characterized Hoover's approach to U.S. foreign relations from the time he was elected president until his death. Throughout the 1930s, World War II, and in the 1940s and 1950s he supported various ways to avoid military conflict or to disengage the United States from wars without becoming either an isolationist or anticommunist Cold Warrior. His belief in the superiority of American capitalism made him impervious to ideological fears posed by either fascism or communism. His first major attempt to influence foreign policy as an ex-president came in May 1945, when he sent President Harry Truman two confidential memoranda, recommending ways to end the war against Japan (by abandoning unconditional surrender as a condition for peace) and to improve relations with the Soviet Union (by accepting its military dominance in Eastern Europe). Truman and his advisers ignored these common sense suggestions, but the president and Secretary of War Stimson did consult with Hoover about food relief policy in 1940–1941 and

again in 1948. As the Cold War emerged in the late 1940s, Hoover moved into open opposition to the establishment of the North Atlantic Treaty Organization (NATO) and to the Korean War, maintaining, as he had since the 1920s, that ideologies could be successfully combated not with force but by example. For Hoover the decision to drop the atomic bombs on Nagasaki and Hiroshima was unconscionable. "It revolts my soul, he confided to John Callan O'Laughlin, editor of the *Army-Navy Journal*. "The only difference between this and the use of poison gas is the fear of retaliation. We alone have the bomb."

As a result, the ex-president stressed the desirability of national economic self-sufficiency and a hemisphere "Gibraltar" concept of military defense based largely on air power. In a famous address on 20 December 1950, he launched what has been called the "Great Debate" over the early Cold War policies of the Truman and Eisenhower administrations—a debate he and all other anti–Cold Warriors would lose until its resurrection in the 1960s by those opposing the war in Vietnam. Originally referred to as Hoover's Doctrine, this speech was misunderstood and greatly criticized at the time. What most people did not perceive, according to diplomatic historian William Appleman Williams, was that Hoover was trying "to make foreign policy a means rather than an end. He was struggling to define America primarily in terms of America rather than in terms of an American world." Hoover also refused to endorse the rampant anticommunism that accompanied the emerging Cold War by not participating in the initial session in March 1947 of the House Un-American Activities Committee (HUAC)—the committee that gave rise to McCarthyism—and by turning down an offer to become chair of Truman's bipartisan commission "to report on the question of the infiltration of communists in the Government."

Hoover lived thirty-one years as an ex-president, criticizing the New Deal and the early foreign policy of the Cold War. Personal animosity between Hoover and Roosevelt meant that Hoover was ignored not only by his own party but also by the Democratic party until President Truman and later Republican president Dwight Eisenhower decided to use his organizational skills as head of the Commissions on Organization of the Executive Branch of Government, known now as the Hoover Commissions. They also spawned similar reorganization attempts at the state level, known as "little" Hoover Commissions. The need to reorganize the executive branch arose out of expansions that had taken place during the Second World War and the Korean War. Truman instituted more of Hoover's 1949 report than Eisenhower did of the 1955 one, largely because the former did not make as many policy recommendations. Before, during, and after his presidency, Hoover was a transitional figure: a self-made, ruthless engineer who turned into a philanthropist and progressive reformer; a chief executive who practiced certain features of the modern presidency later associated with Roosevelt; and finally, a private citizen whose criticisms of both the New Deal and the

Cold War would be resurrected in the 1960s among the "New Left" and again in the 1990s among the "New Right." Hoover died in New York City and was buried in West Branch, Iowa.

• Hoover's papers, those of many individuals associated with his career before and after he became president, as well as those of his wife are housed in his presidential library at West Branch, Iowa. In addition to his own books and memoirs, the best sources about his life and ideas are William J. Barber, *From New Era to New Deal: Herbert Hoover, the Economists and American Economic Policy, 1921–1933* (1985); Gary Dean Best, *The Politics of American Individualism: Herbert Hoover in Transition* (1975); Ellis Hawley, *The Great War and the Search for a Modern Order: A History of the American People and Their Institutions*, 2d ed. (1992); David Burner, *Herbert Hoover: A Public Life* (1979); Martin L. Fausold, *The Presidency of Herbert C. Hoover* (1985); David E. Hamilton, *From New Day to New Deal: American Farm Policy from Hoover to Roosevelt, 1928–1933* (1992); Donald Lisio, *Hoover, Blacks, and Lily-Whites: A Study of Southern Strategies* (1985); James S. Olson, *Herbert Hoover and the Reconstruction Finance Corporation* (1931–1933); Jordan A. Schwarz, *Interregnum of Despair: Hoover, Congress, and the Depression* (1970); Joan Hoff Wilson, *Herbert Hoover: Forgotten Progressive* (1975). Also of value are the following collections of essays: Marint L. Fausold and George T. Mazuzan, eds., *The Hoover Presidency: A Reappraisal* (1974); John N. Schacht, *Three Progressives from Iowa* (1980); Hawley, ed., *Herbert Hoover as Secretary of Commerce, 1921–1928: Studies in New Era Thought and Practice* (1981); Mark O. Hatfield, ed., *Herbert Hoover Reassessed* (1980); and Lee Nash, *Understanding Herbert Hoover* (1987). An obituary is in the *New York Times*, 21 Oct. 1964.

JOAN HOFF

HOOVER, Herbert Clark, Jr. (4 Aug. 1903–9 July 1969), undersecretary of state and businessman, was born in London, England, the son of Herbert Clark Hoover, the thirty-first president of the United States, and Lou Henry. The fact that Hoover's father was president remained the dominant fact of his life. Hoover followed in his father's footsteps, graduating from Stanford University in 1925 with a degree in petroleum geology. That same year he married Margaret Watson, with whom he would have three children. He received his M.B.A. from the Harvard Business School three years later and remained at Harvard for the next two years as an instructor and researcher. In 1928 the Guggenheim Foundation awarded him a grant to survey West Coast air routes.

Again like his progenitor, Hoover proved to be a very successful businessman. In 1935 he founded the United Geophysical Company, which utilized radio and electronic technology for oil exploration. The following year Hoover became the president of a second engineering concern, Consolidated Engineering Corporation of California. After the United States entered the Second World War, Hoover's corporation became an important defense contractor. During the second half of the forties, Hoover not only continued to head his own companies, but his prominence in the oil industry was such that he became a consultant to the governments of Venezuela, Brazil, Chile, and Peru. Indeed, Hoover helped devise a path-breaking settlement between Venezuela and various oil companies. The resulting agreement spawned the so-called 50/50 arrangement whereby the companies and the Venezuelan government agreed to divide equally net profits generated in Venezuela. This success led to one of Hoover's greatest tasks: attempting to forge a settlement of the Iran oil imbroglio.

The dispute began in May 1951 when Iranian prime minister Mohammad Mosaddeq nationalized the properties of the British government–owned Anglo-Iranian Oil Company (AIOC; later British Petroleum). Mosaddeq's action proved popular in Iran, where many had long resented the colonial attitudes of AIOC. In response the British government instituted a commercial blockade against Iran. A sixteen-month stalemate ended when the American and British governments jointly initiated a coup that removed Mosaddeq and reinstated the shah of Iran to power in August 1953. After the new government expressed a desire to negotiate over the oil impasse, the State Department selected Hoover as its special representative and charged him with the task of piecing together a settlement.

Multilayered and complex problems awaited Hoover. Various oil companies had both similar and competing interests, as did the American and British governments. The views of various other oil-producing states had to be taken into account without offending the crucially important Iranian government. A settlement was reached in the summer of 1954 and signed by the shah in October, owing much to Hoover's skill and oil company expertise. Under its terms the National Oil Company of Iran, owned by the Iranian government, would now own the oil reserves. However, a multinational consortium of oil companies, as agent, had the right to manage production, determine production quotas, and sell all oil produced as it saw fit. That American companies, formerly shut out of the Iran market, now controlled 40 percent of production occasioned little comment.

Hoover's success brought him a presidential Medal of Freedom and an invitation to become undersecretary of state, the number two position in the department. For Dwight D. Eisenhower, Hoover's appointment had the benefit of providing the president with extra links to the right wing of the Republican party, which had long revered Herbert Hoover, Sr., and still resented Eisenhower. Once in office, Hoover's tenure proved less than successful—he conspicuously lacked the necessary qualities for his position. Hoover impressed foreign dignitaries as knowing little about foreign affairs except as international questions related to oil production. He had apparently inherited both his father's lack of sympathy with foreigners and lack of tact. That Hoover had succeeded the enormously popular Walter Bedell "Beetle" Smith served only to highlight further the former's inadequacies. Finally, Hoover's increasing deafness left some visitors (apparently unfairly) in doubt as to how much of a given conversation he had heard.

These difficulties became particularly apparent during the Suez crisis of 1956, which pitted the United States against Britain, France, and Israel. This crisis grew out of Egyptian president Gamal Abdel Nasser's decision to nationalize the Suez Canal on 26 July 1956. Both the British and French governments saw military action as the only possible response, the British because of the challenge from Nasser, the French because of Nasser's support for the Algerian rebellion. The Eisenhower administration, initially uncertain about what course to follow, decided at the end of August that military action was an unacceptable option. The British and French governments ignored the clearly expressed American sentiments and decided to invade Egypt in cooperation with Israel, which feared the effect of Egypt's acquisition of Soviet arms. The president and his officials responded with swift and unyielding public and private condemnation.

During November 1956, at the height of the serious breach between Britain and the United States, the illness of Secretary of State John Foster Dulles put Hoover temporarily in charge of the department. In company with the president and all senior officials, Hoover believed that both moral imperatives and practical politics dictated that the United States would neither prop up the faltering British pound nor provide oil to Western Europe until the British and French governments agreed to withdraw their forces from Egypt. It fell to Hoover to explain the administration's stance to America's erstwhile closest ally. His brusque manner and obvious lack of sympathy inflamed British diplomats and did little to aid in the settlement of the crisis. On 3 December, however, the British government finally satisfied Washington that British and French forces would speedily depart from Egypt. Thereafter American aid flowed generously.

Hoover retired from the State Department in 1957 and returned to private industry, his departure clearly unmourned by Washington's diplomatic corps. He lived in Pasadena, California, until his death there. The 50/50 oil profits arrangement, which had become the industry standard and covered agreements between oil companies and oil-producing states around the globe, lasted over two decades, only unraveling at the end of the 1960s.

• No specific collection of Hoover's personal papers exists. However, State Department files in the U.S. National Archives contain copies of Hoover's official papers. The best source for general information on Hoover's life is his entry in *Current Biography (Who's News and Why) 1954* (1954). Hoover's role in the Venezuela and Iran oil settlements is detailed in Daniel Yergin, *The Prize: The Epic Quest for Oil, Money and Power* (1991), while his role in the Suez crisis is covered in Diane B. Kunz, *The Economic Diplomacy of the Suez Crisis* (1991).

DIANE B. KUNZ

HOOVER, Herbert William (30 Oct. 1877–11 Sept. 1954), industrialist, was born in New Berlin (now North Canton), Ohio, the son of William Henry Hoover, a saddle maker, and Susan Troxel. Hoover, who liked to be called "H. W.," graduated from high school in 1895 and entered Hiram College, which he left in 1897. In 1898 he joined the his father's successful saddlery business, W. H. Hoover Company, making saddles, harnesses, and other leather goods. In 1903, when the firm was incorporated, Hoover's father became president and Hoover served as vice president, focusing his attention on the new line of leather products for automobiles. In 1905 he married Grace Louise Steele, the daughter of a New Berlin doctor; they had four children.

In 1907 an invention appeared in Canton, Ohio, that changed Hoover's life. James Murray Spangler, a 71-year-old janitor who worked at Zollinger's Dry Goods Store in Canton, realized that the dust he agitated during his cleaning aggravated his asthma. Seeking a solution, he constructed the world's first vacuum cleaner, a crude device that used makeshift components such as a sewing machine motor, a Bissell carpet sweeper brush, and a pillow case for a bag. Together with a partner, Spangler created a new enterprise, the Electric Suction Sweeper Company, to market the device, but the firm foundered. Spangler met with Hoover and his father; the elder Hoover—who foresaw an imminent end to the leather saddlery business because of the automobile—was convinced that vacuum cleaner manufacturing had a promising future.

In August 1908 the Hoovers took over the Electric Suction Sweeper Company, moving its operations to a corner of their saddlery factory. Spangler accepted a generous royalty and was kept on payroll as an official. Hoover's father, president of the new concern, put H. W. in charge of making a profitable business with the vacuum cleaners, naming him vice president, general manager, and sales manager of the company. H. W. provided leadership for the growing venture, since other Hoover family members were still involved in leather goods manufacturing. He moved with dispatch, and by December 1908 his company was producing its first vacuum cleaner, the Model O. The company's first national advertisement, which Hoover wrote, appeared in *The Saturday Evening Post*, asking consumers to try the electric suction sweeper for ten days, free of charge. The company, which favored home demonstrations of the product, developed an extensive network of salesmen to demonstrate and sell the sweeper, rather than relying on retail outlets. The advertisement produced a deluge of inquiries from consumers who were attracted to the new product because it represented an improvement over brooms, carpet beaters, carpet sweepers, and feather dusters. As home electricity became more available, the popularity and success of vacuum cleaners soared. The company's sales multiplied during its early years, with 372 cleaners sold during its first year, 4,000 during 1912, and 9,000 by 1914.

During World War I the company suspended cleaner production in order to manufacture leather goods such as saddles and tool cases for the European Allied forces and tarpaulins and water buckets for the U. S. Army. (During World War I the town of New Berlin changed its name to North Canton as an expression of patriotism.) In 1919, after it had completed its wartime contracts, the company abandoned its leather goods business in order to concentrate on vacuum cleaner manufacturing. That year the company adopted the highly successful advertising slogan, "It Beats As It Sweeps As It Cleans," to promote its vacuum cleaners and also opened a manufacturing plant in England. In 1922 the company dropped the name "Electric Suction Sweeper Company" and became simply the Hoover Company, with H. W. Hoover as president, a position he held for the next twenty-six years. The following year the company reached a milestone when its one-millionth vacuum cleaner rolled off its assembly lines.

Beginning in 1921 Hoover also began to hold international Hoover sales conventions at Hoover Park in Canton. The park was transformed into an enormous tent city, complete with a hospital, post office, and other amenities. Hundreds of Hoover salesmen converged at the site, meeting for several days. The conferences helped to stimulate business and unify policies within the company.

During the Great Depression Hoover spearheaded Canton's drive for relief funds. Vacuum cleaner sales declined, but rather than laying off his employees, Hoover instead cut their working hours. He was deeply committed to maintaining close personal contact with his employees, and as president he visited the assembly lines almost daily to talk to workers, addressing many by their first names. During World War II the Hoover Company virtually halted vacuum cleaner production and switched to wartime manufacturing of radio and radar equipment, parachutes for fragmentation bombs, plastic products, such as helmet liners, and proximity fuses, which were regarded as an invention critical to winning the war. In 1940 Hoover arranged for the evacuation of eighty-four children of employees of his company's British operations. The children were brought to Canton and North Canton homes for the duration of the war. Hoover housed one ten-year-old girl at his own home, and every Thanksgiving he held a party to which he invited all the relocated British children, who affectionately called him "Uncle Hoover."

Hoover presided over the successful postwar conversion of his company; the first year that vacuum cleaner manufacturing resumed yielded a record profit of almost $22 million. In 1948 Hoover retired as president of the Hoover Company, leaving a legacy of successful company leadership that transformed a leather goods business into the world's largest manufacturer of vacuum cleaners. Hoover was succeeded as president by his younger brother, Frank, who had been serving as vice president. Hoover became chairman of the board of directors until 1954, when he became honorary board chairman. In that same year Hoover's son, H. W. Hoover, Jr., assumed the presidency of the company. One of the last and most successful vacuum cleaner innovations that Hoover saw his company introduce was a 1953 model with a disposable paper bag.

By introducing and successfully marketing the vacuum cleaner, Hoover helped to bring fundamental changes to the American home. As the vacuum cleaner represented a considerable expenditure, it enhanced the housewife's role as a consumer, giving her more authority as a discretionary spender. The device quickly became central to domestic cleaning, bringing higher standards of cleanliness to the home and making housework less laborious. The vacuum cleaner also made carpeted homes not only possible but practical. It was a critical part of a movement during the twentieth century that saw the home become more mechanized, clean, and comfortable.

Hoover was actively involved in the civic affairs of both North Canton and Canton. One of his greatest interests was the Young Men's Christian Association (YMCA). He helped to underwrite the cost of a new North Canton YMCA building, which opened in 1923. He served as a trustee of the Canton YMCA for almost a quarter century and was its president from 1924 to 1946. He also directed a YMCA fundraising campaign that raised over $300,000. Hoover's other notable civic achievements included his support of a new library in North Canton and his drive to create Witwer Park, a popular recreational site in North Canton. In 1946, in recognition of his years of civic service, Hoover received the Canton Chamber of Commerce's first annual Award of Merit.

During the last twenty-five years of his life, Hoover spent winters at a Miami Beach, Florida, home that he purchased in 1938. He wife accompanied him on these trips until her death in 1949. Hoover also continued to work daily until 1953, when ill health forced him to curtail his activities. During the last months of his life he suffered a number of health setbacks, including two severe heart seizures and one cerebral attack. He died in Canton.

• The Hoover Historical Center in North Canton, Ohio, contains the most complete collection of exhibits, articles, and corporate biographies pertaining to Herbert William Hoover and the Hoover Company. The Historical Center also houses a research library. Two books yield information on Hoover: Edward Heald, *The Stark County Story*, vol. 3 (1952), a publication of the Stark County (Ohio) Historical Society, and Frank Garfield Hoover, *Fabulous Dustpan: The Story of the Hoover* (1955), a history written by Hoover's younger brother, his successor as company president. Obituaries are in *Time* and *Newsweek*, both on 27 Sept. 1954; and in the *Canton Repository*, the *Cleveland Plain Dealer*, and the *New York Times*, all 17 Sept. 1954.

YANEK MIECZKOWSKI

HOOVER, J. Edgar (1 Jan. 1895–2 May 1972), director of the Federal Bureau of Investigation (FBI), was born John Edgar Hoover in Washington, D.C., the son of Dickerson Naylor Hoover, a printer for the U.S. Coast and Geodetic Survey, and Annie Marie Scheitlin. Born in a secure middle-class enclave of civil servants just behind the Library of Congress on Capitol Hill,

Hoover attended the city's elite public high school, taught Sunday school in the historic First Presbyterian Church on Judiciary Square, and worked his way through the National University Law School (later merged with George Washington University) as a clerk at the Library of Congress, receiving his law degree in 1916. A lifelong bachelor, Hoover's closest relationships were with his mother, with whom he lived on Capitol Hill until her death in 1938, and with FBI subordinates at the bureau, particularly Associate Director Clyde Tolson. Tolson was Hoover's inseparable companion from 1928 until Hoover's death, a relationship that was emotionally, and possibly physically, homosexual.

In 1917 Hoover was hired by the Department of Justice's Alien Enemy Bureau, where he processed German and Austro-Hungarian nationals subject to wartime internment. It was this wartime experience that brought Hoover to the attention of Attorney General A. Mitchell Palmer when Palmer ordered a campaign against alien radicals after the 2 June bombing of the attorney general's house in Washington. The 24-year-old Hoover was put in charge of a new Radical Division in the Justice Department. In this capacity Hoover planned, coordinated, directed, and defended the raids in November 1919 and January 1920 known as the Palmer raids, which included the deportation of the well-known anarchists Emma Goldman and Alexander Berkman. Hoover's firsthand investigations of native and foreign communism during those years of international upheavals sparked by the 1917 Russian Communist revolution and the organization of the Third International (Comintern) in 1919—together with the domestic intelligence files he began to gather that year—made him the government's first expert on domestic communism, a role he jealously guarded for the rest of his life.

Hoover's antiradical campaign collapsed in the spring of 1920 amidst charges of Justice Department abuses of civil liberties. Hoover's bureaucratic skills, however, had made him indispensable to the Justice Department, and in 1921 he was named assistant director of the Bureau of Investigation (it was not called the FBI until 1935). After the Teapot Dome scandals forced a reorganization of the bureau in 1924, Attorney General Harlan Stone named Hoover director and ordered him to limit the bureau's activities to investigations of federal crimes. For the most part, Hoover complied with Stone's directive for the next decade, working to enhance the bureau's reputation as a leader in scientific law enforcement by building a world-renowned fingerprint identification unit, a pioneering crime laboratory, and a system for gathering and analyzing national crime statistics.

The New Deal administration brought a new political style to Washington in 1933. Hoover quickly adapted and, at the behest of Attorney General Homer Cummings, threw the bureau into battle against celebrity criminals like George "Machine Gun" Kelly, "Pretty Boy" Floyd, "Baby Face" Nelson, and John Dillinger (killed by FBI agents on 24 July 1934).

These cases turned FBI agents into national heroes and Hoover into a national celebrity. Popular entertainment featured the FBI in radio adventure dramas, comic strips, pulp magazines, and a wave of FBI movies, most notably James Cagney's *G-Men* (1935).

Meanwhile, President Franklin D. Roosevelt, alarmed by the rise of Adolf Hitler and the activities of American communists and fascists, secretly ordered Hoover back into political surveillance. When the public was swept into a panic over Nazi spies after the 1938 Munich crisis, Roosevelt was able to put the leadership of the American Nazi movement on trial, based on Hoover's undercover investigations. In September 1939, during the public alarm over Hitler's invasion of Poland, Roosevelt reassured the nation by placing Hoover in charge of all domestic counterintelligence.

During World War II Hoover's mere presence at the head of the FBI was enough to persuade the public that the home front, "the FBI front" as the newsreels had it, was in safe hands. He burnished his reputation as a master detective with adroit public relations campaigns that included cooperation with authors of such books as *The FBI in Peace and War* (1943) and with Hollywood producers of such newsreels as "The FBI Front" (1942) and such movies as *The House on 92nd Street* (1945). He also solved dramatic spy cases, such as the capture of the German saboteurs who landed on Long Island from a U-Boat in 1942. Hoover enlisted civic groups like the American Legion into an FBI-supervised network to gather and investigate reports of espionage, thus preventing the civilian hysteria that had disrupted the home front during World War I.

Hoover had been hated and feared by the American Left ever since the Palmer raids. With the end of World War II and the beginning of the Cold War, he emerged as the preeminent symbol of militant domestic anticommunism, venerated on the Right, loathed and feared on the Left. Hoover had been collecting reports of Communist infiltration of the government and of Soviet spy networks for years, but during the wartime alliance between the United States and the Soviet Union these had been of little interest to the Roosevelt administration, which was preoccupied with preserving a friendly relationship with Joseph Stalin.

With the breakdown of relations between the United States and the Soviet Union after the war, however, the Harry Truman administration was forced to pay attention to Hoover's findings, particularly when the Republicans made the issue of communists in government its principal campaign theme in 1946. When Hoover decided that Truman's Loyalty Program of March 1947 was too little, too late, he broke with the president and allied himself with the Republican-dominated House Un-American Activities Committee (HUAC). Hoover envisioned a partnership between the two in which the FBI provided the committee with information that would help them expose the activities of communists and fellow travelers in educational and cultural institutions and in labor unions, while the FBI devoted itself to preparing legal cases against communists and Soviet agents. But in the most notable communist case of the Cold War, Hoover was chagrined to find that HUAC's energetic young member, Richard Nixon, consistently outraced the FBI in gathering the evidence that led to the conviction of former State Department official Alger Hiss on charges of having lied about being a Soviet spy. Hoover prepared evidence for the government's Smith Act prosecution of the leaders of the American Communist party in 1948, and in 1950 he uncovered the Klaus Fuchs atom spy ring (the "Crime of the Century," to Hoover) that resulted in the conviction (in 1951) and execution (in 1953) of Julius and Ethel Rosenberg. Hoover placed the resources of the FBI at the disposal of anticommunist groups inside and outside the government, but he was also willing to cut his losses when anticommunist allies—like his close friend Senator Joseph McCarthy—became liabilities. He spoke and wrote tirelessly for the anticommunist cause, most notably in his book *Masters of Deceit* (1958), and had the bureau's public relations unit, the Crime Records Division, work with the entertainment industry to produce movies, radio shows, and television programs featuring the FBI. Productions included the James Stewart film *The FBI Story* (1959), based on Don Whitehead's 1956 bestseller of the same name, and the long-running television series *The FBI* (1965–1974), starring Efrem Zimbalist, Jr.

During the early years of the Cold War, Hoover's bureau used public relations, cooperation with anticommunist groups, and legal prosecution in its war against domestic communism, all directed toward prosecuting top communists under the Smith Act and preparing for the arrest of communists and their sympathizers in the event of war with the Soviet Union. In 1956, however, the Supreme Court so drastically narrowed the applicability of the Smith Act as to render future prosecutions of the party unfeasible. Hoover's response was to develop a "Counter Intelligence Program" (COINTELPRO), which adapted wartime counterespionage "dirty tricks" to disrupt the Communist party. The Communist Party COINTELPRO was so successful that, with the explicit approval of the John F. Kennedy Justice Department, Hoover expanded it to target the Ku Klux Klan. Later, Hoover developed a "Black Hate Group" COINTELPRO against organizations like the Black Panthers and another against New Left student groups. It was in connection with the "Black Hate" COINTELPRO that Hoover embarked on his notorious campaign to destroy the career of Dr. Martin Luther King, Jr. Hoover's investigation of King developed out of suspicions about the communist backgrounds of some of the civil rights leader's associates, but it escalated into a virulent smear operation motivated by racism, Puritanism, and resentment over King's criticism of the FBI's performance in civil rights cases. Hoover's vendetta against King culminated in his subordinates' mailing King tape recordings dealing with his sexual activities and threatening to make them public, a bizarre and vicious plot that may have been intended to drive King to suicide.

Long after the demise of the American communist movement, and after new law enforcement concerns had moved to the top of the national agenda, Hoover kept repeating his increasingly irrelevant warnings against the communist menace. During his last years Hoover—the defender of old-fashioned patriotism and middle-class values, the bulldog face of government authority cracking down on rebellion and dissent—came to represent everything that the antiwar and civil rights movement feared and hated. As part of the nation's convulsive effort to exorcise the nightmares of Vietnam and Watergate, Hoover's career was exhaustively investigated by Senator Frank Church's Select Committee to Study Governmental Operations with Respect to Intelligence Activities (1975–1976). The committee's conclusion, which to date represents the historical consensus, was that Hoover's career was a horrible example of governmental abuse of authority, that in his harassment of domestic dissidents, COINTELPRO in particular, Hoover had "conducted a sophisticated vigilante operation aimed squarely at preventing the exercise of First Amendment rights of speech and associations." That indictment has remained Hoover's epitaph, while the mass veneration that sustained Hoover's power (far more than the specter of secret files), based on Hoover's uncanny rapport with the values, hopes, and fears of masses of ordinary Americans, has died with the man and the times.

A seemingly endless series of popular exposés of Hoover's secret files and secret life has falsely made him a key plotter in nearly every conspiratorial theory of American history, from Mafia skullduggery to the assassination of the Kennedys to celebrity murders, all straining to gain spurious plausibility from the juicy contradictions between Hoover's public image as a rock-ribbed symbol of middle-class morality and law and order and his undercover illegalities and apparent homosexuality. A fairer evaluation would have to weigh his contributions to national stability and security during the profound international and domestic emergencies of the Bolshevik Revolution, the Nazi threat, and the Cold War against his undeniable abuses of authority and his disregard for civil liberties and fair play. Hoover also deserves to be ranked among the great bureaucratic entrepreneurs and organizers in the history of American government, among such figures as Hyman Rickover of the nuclear submarine program, Robert Moses of New York State's public works programs, and Floyd Dominy of the dam-building Bureau of Reclamation. But even when Hoover's actions are placed in their contemporary context and proper weight is given to his rationales for them, history's final verdict is unlikely to restore the reputation Hoover worked so hard to maintain during his long and incredible career. Cato the Roman observed that it is hard to live in one age and be judged by another. It has been especially hard on J. Edgar Hoover. He died at home in Northeast Washington, D.C.

• Hoover's personal files were destroyed after his death by his secretary Helen Gandy and by Associate Director Tolson. The most important documents relating to Hoover are the FBI files on important investigations, which contain many memos to and from Hoover and copious marginal notations. Files already released can be read at the FOIPA Reading Room at FBI Headquarters, Washington, D.C., and many have been microfilmed. Biographies include Richard Gid Powers, *Secrecy and Power: The Life of J. Edgar Hoover* (1987); and Athan Theoharis and John Cox, *The Boss: J. Edgar Hoover and the American Inquisition* (1988). An obituary is in the *New York Times*, 2 May 1972.

RICHARD GID POWERS

HOOVER, Lou Henry (29 Mar. 1874–7 Jan. 1944), First Lady and national Girl Scout leader, was born in Waterloo, Iowa, the daughter of Charles Delano Henry, a banker, and Florence Weed. Because her mother suffered from asthma, the family, seeking a more favorable climate, moved to Whittier, California, in 1887. Schoolgirl essays reveal her maturity and a growing curiosity about the world. Classmates remembered her leadership and her firm insistence on the inclusion of two African-American boys in her circle of friends. Her interests included writing, drawing, and camping and hiking in the Sierra Nevadas with her father. Later, as president of the Girl Scouts, she fondly recalled being a girl scout long before the organization existed.

Although Lou Henry had studied at what is now California State University at San Jose in preparation for a teaching career and taught briefly, she soon discovered a more interesting calling during a lecture given by Stanford geologist John C. Branner in 1894. Realizing that geologists worked in the outdoors she enjoyed so much, she decided to become a geologist and enrolled at Stanford University. There she was introduced to Branner's laboratory assistant, a shy senior named Herbert Hoover who was studying to be a mine engineer. The future president later remarked that he was attracted by her outgoing personality and obvious enjoyment of the outdoors.

After graduating in 1898 with an A.B. in geology, Henry returned to her parents' home in Monterey, where she was promptly recruited to sew bandages for the Spanish American War and was elected treasurer of the local Red Cross chapter. It was her first public service position and a prophetic one, for she would spend much of her life in service to others. Herbert Hoover, meanwhile, had gone to western Australia to oversee the mining operations of a large British firm. Promoted to a junior partnership in 1897, Hoover was reassigned the following year to develop company holdings in China and to act as a consultant to the Chinese government. He quickly dashed off a cable to Lou proposing marriage, which she answered with a single word.

The Hoovers were married in her parents' home in Monterey on 10 February 1899 and departed for China the next day. Soon after their arrival, they began to record their observations in hopes of having them published in a magazine. Thereafter, Lou accompanied her husband into the field whenever possible,

even following him down into the mines—an unprecedented event that dismayed most of the superstitious Chinese miners.

The Boxer Rebellion, a wave of anti-Western protest during the spring of 1900, prompted Henry Hoover to recall his American engineers from the field. In June the Hoovers found themselves, and about 800 Americans and Europeans, trapped in Tientsin by a force of more than 30,000 Boxers. After the siege was lifted Lou was amused to read her own obituary in American newspapers. She evidently found the experience exhilarating, for she wrote to a friend that "you missed one of the opportunities of your life by not coming to China in the summer of 1900." For the next twelve years, she would accompany her husband to such exotic locations as Siberia, Australia, Burma, and Japan. The couple's two children were taken along as soon as they were old enough to travel.

Between 1902 and 1914 the Hoovers lived in London but were considering plans for a home in California when World War I intervened. During the early weeks of the war the Hoovers' organizing skills were put to use in assisting thousands of American tourists stranded on the Continent. As the winter of 1914–1915 approached it became clear that the entire nation of Belgium, caught in the middle of the fighting, might starve. When her husband became director of the Commission for Relief in Belgium (CRB) in October 1914, Hoover expanded her work as president of the London-based American Women's War Relief Fund. Eventually, the AWWRF operated several small woolen mills in London that produced vests, scarves, socks, and other items for Allied soldiers and maintained a number of dressing stations and hospitals in France and Britain.

The Hoovers returned to America in 1917 after the United States entered the war and President Wilson asked Herbert Hoover to head the new U.S. Food Administration. Hoover's success as chief wartime relief administrator made him an international celebrity and led to his appointment as secretary of commerce in 1921. Meanwhile, Lou Hoover was much in demand as a speaker at bond rallies and CRB and Food Administration events. In 1917 she became a Girl Scout troop leader at the personal invitation of founder Juliette Low and became a national Girl Scout commissioner that same year. In 1921 she was elected vice president of the Girl Scouts and moved up to the presidency the following year. Thus began an unbroken record of service on the Girl Scout national board that stretched from 1917 until her death.

As the wife of an international figure and cabinet member, Hoover received a fair amount of attention from the press, but she remained a private person and made no effort to exploit her popularity. Nevertheless, she attracted an enthusiastic national following among Girl Scouts and their leaders as a result of her terms as vice president (1921; 1925–1929) and president (1922-1925) of the organization. She seldom gave press conferences, did not give interviews, reluctantly gave a few formal speeches, had no political ambitions, and shunned the role of political activist. Even during the presidential campaign of 1928 she made only a few token appearances. Her support and encouragement were undoubtedly important factors in Herbert Hoover's decision to seek the presidency in 1928, but there is no solid evidence that she attempted to influence her husband's political views.

Hoover did become the subject of controversy in 1929 when she entertained the wife of Oscar De Priest, a black Chicago congressman, at a tea for congressional wives. She was denounced by racists in several southern state legislatures but received widespread support from the rest of the country. Her husband defied the critics by immediately inviting Robert Moton, the president of Tuskegee Institute and the nation's leading black educator, to lunch. The Hoovers subsequently invited the Hampton and Tuskegee choirs to perform at White House musicales, partly in defiance of racists, but more likely as just another opportunity to encourage American artists.

Passionately devoted to the enjoyment of all forms of outdoor activity and the cultivation of the potential within every girl, Hoover served as president of the Women's Division of the National Amateur Athletic Federation from 1923 to 1941 and again as Girl Scout president from 1935 to 1937. Under her wise leadership, both organizations expanded their programs and membership. The most dramatic changes occurred in the Girl Scout program after she personally secured more than $575,000 between 1925 and 1929. These grants enabled the Girl Scouts to provide leadership training and to enlarge the scope of their publications and programs. Membership soared from 167,925 in 1927 to more than 1,035,000 girls at the time of her death.

During the campaign of 1928, and later as First Lady, Lou Hoover received a great deal of mail. She referred appeals for help to her wide network of friends across the country for further investigation and assistance. After the stock market crash in 1929 these appeals became much more numerous and more serious, forcing her to hire another secretary to coordinate an informal relief program that brought these situations to the attention of local welfare agencies. When local sources of help were not available she often provided aid and assistance anonymously from her own personal resources. During the Bonus March on Washington in 1932, she quietly arranged to have food, blankets, and clothing sent to the Bonus Marchers' camp.

Despite her efforts to maintain a low profile, one of her projects captured the nation's attention. Seeking relief from hot Washington summers, the Hoovers had built a retreat in the nearby Blue Ridge Mountains. When they discovered that children in the nearby hollows had no school, the Hoovers decided to build one. After consulting some of the leading educators in the nation, Lou Hoover found a teacher familiar with the special needs of mountain families. The comfortable and well-equipped school opened in February 1930 to wide attention and admiration from the media.

Hoover's White House musicales were distinguished for their richness and variety as well as her policy of encouraging emerging American artists such as Rosa Ponselle, Lawrence Tibbett, Lewis Richards, and Mildred Dilling. Her wide cultural interests also included literature, painting and sculpture, dance, theater, and historic preservation. Dismayed to discover that no one had bothered to record the social history of the White House, she and her secretary, Dare Stark McMullin, produced an extensively researched history of the great house and its furnishings. Learning that descendants of President James Monroe had preserved several exquisite pieces from that early period, she donated copies that are still part of the White House collection.

Cultural events remained one of the main focuses of Hoover's post-presidential activities, but she also remained active as a Girl Scout leader throughout the 1930s and 1940s. Only weeks before her seventieth birthday, she attended a concert in New York, where the Hoovers spent much time after leaving the White House. After walking most of the way back to her apartment at the Waldorf Astoria, she lay down to rest and suffered a fatal heart attack.

• Lou Hoover's personal papers (182 linear feet) in the Herbert Hoover Presidential Library, West Branch, Iowa, provide complete coverage of the various periods of her life and public service. The first full-length biography, by her friend Helen B. Pryor, *Lou Henry Hoover: Gallant First Lady* (1969), is based on interviews with members of the Hoover family and with many of their acquaintances. Articles that draw on research in her personal papers include Rebecca Christian, "In Her Own Words: The Remarkable Life of Lou Henry Hoover," *Iowan* 35, no. 1 (Fall 1986): 14–20, 56–66; Dale C. Mayer, "An Uncommon Woman: The Quiet Leadership Style of Lou Henry Hoover," *Presidential Studies Quarterly* 20, no. 4 (Fall 1990): 685–98; and Mayer's earlier article, "Not One to Stay at Home: The Papers of Lou Henry Hoover," *Prologue* 19, no. 2 (Summer 1987): 85–93. Hoover's cultural leadership and musical interests are featured in Elise Kirk, *Music at the White House* (1986). See also Dale C. Mayer, ed., *Lou Henry Hoover: Essays on a Busy Life* (1994), which draws on the latest scholarship and covers her entire life. An obituary in the *New York Times*, 8 Jan. 1944, provides a good summary of her life.

DALE C. MAYER

HOPE, Elmo (27 June 1923–19 May 1967), jazz pianist and composer, was born St. Elmo Sylvester Hope in New York City. His parents (whose names are unknown) were from the West Indies. He studied the European piano tradition and often practiced with his boyhood friend Bud Powell. Hope was giving recitals at the age of fifteen, but the two teenagers recognized that there were impossible barriers to the idea of African Americans pursuing concert careers in classical music, and they turned to jazz. By the mid-1940s Powell was widely acclaimed as the greatest pianist in the bop style. Hope would remain a permanently obscure figure for diverse reasons, of which probably the most important was an incapacitating addiction to heroin. His uncompromising personality and complex musical style also seem to have been factors in limiting his achievements.

Early in his career Hope often performed in unknown bands at low-class venues, and his most stable affiliation was with trumpeter Joe Morris's rhythm-and-blues band from 1948 to 1951. Over the next five years notable activities were restricted to his occasional appearances in the studio. In June 1953 he recorded with trumpeter Clifford Brown, who used two of Hope's compositions at this session: "Carving the Rock" and "De-Dah." That same month he recorded as the leader of a trio that included bassist Percy Heath and drummer Philly Joe Jones, both of whom had also worked with Morris. Further sessions as a leader came in 1954 and 1956, the latter date including tenor saxophonists Hank Mobley and John Coltrane. With tenor saxophonist Frank Foster, he co-led a session released under Foster's name as *Wail, Frank, Wail* (1955), and he recorded as a sideman with alto saxophonists Lou Donaldson (1954) and Jackie McLean (1956).

At some point—probably in 1956—Hope spent several months in jail on Riker's Island in New York, presumably for a narcotics conviction. In 1957, having lost his New York City cabaret card and the consequent right to perform in local nightclubs, he accepted an invitation to tour with trumpeter Chet Baker to Los Angeles. The job offered potential venues for work and also the possibility that the not yet excessively smoggy climate would ease the effects of Hope's emphysema.

Hope had been married at some earlier point, and a son had died; no other details are known. In 1957 he met his future second wife, Bertha (maiden name unknown), a pianist, while he was accompanying Sonny Rollins at the Hillcrest in Los Angeles. In October he recorded as the leader of a quintet that included tenor saxophonist Harold Land. In March 1958 Hope joined bassist Curtis Counce's group and recorded with Counce the following month.

In 1959 Hope worked briefly with vibraphonist Lionel Hampton in Hollywood. Together with bassist Scott LaFaro and drummer Lennie McBrowne, he accompanied Rollins at the Jazz Workshop in San Francisco. Land then took over from Rollins, leading the group for two weeks at the Cellar in Vancouver. In August 1959, as a member of a quintet under Land's leadership, Hope recorded one of his two finest albums, *The Fox*, presenting four of his own compositions: "Mirror-Mind Rose," "One Second, Please," "Sims-a-Plenty," and "One Down." Hope married Bertha in 1960; they had three children. Early that year, with bassist Jimmy Bond and drummer Frank Butler, he recorded his second great album, *Elmo Hope Trio*, including a representative sampling of his compositions: "B's A-Plenty," "Barfly," "Eejah," "Boa," "Something for Kenny," "Minor Bertha," and "Tranquility."

Having found no more than the occasional opportunity to work on the West Coast, Hope returned to New York City, even though he was still without a cabaret card. In the 1960s, as Hope's health declined, he led further recording sessions that resulted in seven albums, all offering additional examples of his talents as a composer and an interpreter of bop. None of these is up to the high standard of the earlier albums, but the quirky brilliance of Hope's playing shines through—for example, in his rendering of Dizzy Gillespie's "A Night in Tunesia" from one of his last sessions in 1966. That same year Hope last performed in public in a concert at New York City's Judson Hall. In May 1967 he was hospitalized for pneumonia and within a few weeks died suddenly in New York City of a heart attack.

Hope was one of the most esoteric of bop musicians. His piano style was too personalized to have served as a model for other players, and his roughly seventy-five bop themes have yet to enter the repertoire of jazz standards, both because of their difficulty and because Hope evidently discarded notated versions once the music had been learned. These compositions range in character from a tortuous nervousness to an introspective, semilyrical romanticism. Some are extraordinarily creative. "Minor Bertha," for example, is notable not merely for the use of a 35-bar theme, with phrases of nine plus nine plus eight plus nine measures, in place of the conventional thirty-two bars (8+8+8+8), but much more importantly for the quality of the repeated nine-bar-long segment, in which Hope elides together uncommon rhythms and purposefully weak harmonic relationships to confuse and to soften transitions from one phrase to the next. "One Down" offers another excellent example of his manner of restlessly spinning out ideas, while pieces like "Barfly" and the drumless but not entirely tranquil "Tranquility" transfer this approach into a ballad setting.

In a description cast negatively though nonetheless accurately, Alan Groves writes: "Hope's scores are complex, original, with typically involved chord sequences, all personally idiosyncratic. . . . Such music . . . is not direct, does not swing violently, and Hope is withdrawn, oblique, and almost ignores the rhythm section at times. Listened to casually, it makes no impression." Hope constantly challenges his audience, but rewards are there if one wishes to make the effort to listen carefully.

• For more information on Hope, see John Tynan, "Bitter Hope," *Down Beat,* 5 Jan. 1961, p. 16; Lawrence Kart, "Harold Land: The Fox," *Down Beat,* 22 Jan. 1970), pp. 21–22; Leonard Feather, liner notes to the album *Elmo Hope Trio* (1970); and Alan Groves, "The Forgotten Ones: Elmo Hope," *Jazz Journal International* 36 (June 1983): 10–11. For an interview with his wife, see Larry Hollis, "Bertha Hope," *Cadence* 14 (Nov. 1988): 18–23. An obituary is in *Jazz Journal* 20 (July 1967): 7.

BARRY KERNFELD

HOPE, James Barron (23 Mar. 1829–15 Sept. 1887), poet, was born at his grandfather's house at the Gosport Navy Yard in Norfolk, Virginia, the son of Wilton Hope, a landed proprietor, and Jane A. Barron.

His mother was the daughter of Commodore James Barron, who was commander of the ill-fated American frigate *Chesapeake* when it was fired upon by the British frigate *Leopard* during an impressment dispute in 1807. Young Hope received his early education in Hampton, Virginia, and Germantown, Pennsylvania, and then studied law at the College of William and Mary, where he graduated in 1847. The following year he practiced law in Williamsburg. However, he interrupted his legal career for three years to become secretary to his uncle, Commodore Samuel Barron. While holding this position, he fought a duel with pistols that was almost fatal to both parties. After recuperating, Hope accompanied Barron on a long cruise in the West Indies. He then returned to his home in Hampton and again began to practice law. In 1856 he was elected commonwealth's attorney, and the following year he married Anne Beverly Whiting of Hampton.

Hope had long exhibited a facility for poetry. Under the pseudonym of "Henry Ellen" he had contributed to the *Southern Literary Messenger* and to other periodicals. His first volume of poetry, *Leoni di Monota and Other Poems*, was published in Philadelphia in 1857. The collection was favorably received by both American and British critics, and "The Charge at Balaklava" led many to compare Hope's work favorably with that of Tennyson. The year 1857 also found Hope acting as the official poet at the 250th anniversary of the settlement of Jamestown. The ode he read on this occasion, which contains a tribute to Pocahontas, is a solemn elegy to a vanished "race of kings," written in heroic couplets.

On 22 February 1858 Hope recited a memorial ode at the unveiling of Thomas Crawford's equestrian statue of George Washington in the Capitol Square at Richmond. Couching his tribute to Washington in lofty, patriotic terms, the poet touched on contemporary problems and prayed "That God will banish those portentous clouds/ Suggesting perils in their warlike shape." A year later, Hope published his second volume, *A Collection of Poems*, in which he gathered his official odes and a few other verses. With the outbreak of the Civil War he immediately joined the Confederate army. Then in his early thirties, Hope was described by contemporaries as being a tall, slender, graceful man with rather light hair, a pale face, and a thin, full beard. Rising to the rank of major in the Confederate quartermaster corps, he did not leave the army until he surrendered with General Joseph E. Johnston's forces near Durham, North Carolina, late in April 1865. When he returned to Hampton he found his home in ashes.

In 1866 Hope was reported to be working on a "History of Southern Authors," a project that seems never to have been completed. His only significant literary output of that year was an "Elegiac Ode Read on the Completion of a Monument to Annie Carter Lee." Having given up the practice of law, Hope moved to Norfolk soon after the war and plunged into the active arena of journalism. He engaged in newspaper work first with the *Norfolk Day Book*, and later with the *Vir-ginian*. In 1873 he founded his own *Norfolk Landmark*, which he edited until his death and which several contemporary sources describe as one of the best papers in the state.

Meanwhile, Hope continued to pursue his own literary interests. The martial vein in his nature responded sympathetically to the wartime experiences of the southern soldier, and in the hours that he could spare for himself he prepared numerous memorial odes and addresses for meetings of different camps of Confederate veterans. He also put into verse scenes that he had witnessed in camp or on the march or, as in "Under One Blanket," on the battlefield. In 1874 he published his *Little Stories for Little People*; and in 1878 he published a prose story of France, *Under the Empire*, which according to the author was based on a play that he had written but had not published or produced.

Recognized as a prominent speaker, Hope was increasingly called upon for renditions at public anniversaries. In 1881 he was chosen by Congress to be the poet of the Yorktown centennial. On that occasion he delivered a long "metrical address" called *Arms and the Man*. Perhaps representing his highest poetic achievement, these verses deal with important events in America's colonial history and the striking events of the battle of Yorktown. Following the centennial celebration, Hope recited *Arms and the Man* in several large cities, and in 1882 the address was published.

In 1885 Hope became superintendent of the Norfolk schools, though he continued his newspaper work. Two years later he was called upon to deliver a poem in Richmond at the laying of the cornerstone of the monument to General Robert E. Lee. In composing his tribute to Lee, Hope compared Lee's greatness with that of George Washington:

> Those two shall ride immortal
> And shall ride abreast of Time,
> Shall light up stately history
> And blaze in Epic Rhyme—
> Both patriots, both Virginians true,
> Both "rebels," both sublime.

Hope completed "The Lee Memorial Ode" but was not destined to read it. The day after the poem was finished he died of a heart attack in Norfolk.

A volume of selections of Hope's poetry, entitled *A Wreath of Virginia Bay Leaves*, was published in 1895 by his daughter, Janey Hope Marr. Though these verses are characterized by dramatic effect and swift observation, they also reveal that the poet's interests rarely included subjects beyond the boundary of his own state. Hope may have devoted too much of his creative energy to occasional pieces, but these poetic efforts won him contemporary recognition as "Virginia's laureate."

• Biographical information dealing with James Barron Hope can be found in William Peterfield Trent, *Southern Writers* (1905); F. V. N. Painter, *Poets of Virginia* (1907); E. A. Alderman and Joel C. Harris, eds., *Library of Southern Literature*, vol. 6 (1908); Armistead C. Gordon, Jr., ed., *Virginia Writers of Fugitive Verse* (1923); Jay B. Hubbell, *The South in*

American Literature, 1607–1900 (1954); and L. Moody Simms, Jr., "James Barron Hope: Virginia's Laureate," *Virginia Cavalcade* 19 (Winter 1970): 22–29.

L. MOODY SIMMS, JR.

HOPE, Lugenia D. Burns (19 Feb. 1871–14 Aug. 1947), community organizer and educator, was born in St. Louis, Missouri, the daughter of Ferdinand Burns, a well-to-do carpenter, and Louisa M. Bertha. Lugenia was raised in a Grace Presbyterian, middle-class family. Her father's sudden death forced her mother to move the family to Chicago to maintain their class standing and provide Lugenia, or "Genie" as she was called, with educational opportunities lacking in St. Louis. From 1890 to 1893, while her older siblings worked to support the family, Lugenia attended high school and special classes, the Chicago School of Design, the Chicago Business College, and the Chicago Art Institute.

Lugenia quit school abruptly to help support the family as a bookkeeper and dressmaker. After several years she became the first African-American secretary to the board of directors of King's Daughters, a charitable organization serving teenage working girls, the sick, and the poor. She also worked as the personal secretary to the director of the Silver Cross Club, which ran cafeterias for Chicago businessmen and women, and she was the person in charge of workers for the Warne Addressing Establishment.

Lugenia's interest in charity and reform work paralleled Chicago's reform movement of the 1880s and 1890s. Her work as a clubwoman with King's Daughters and the Silver Cross Club introduced her to intellectuals from the University of Chicago, African-American intellectuals like Paul Laurence Dunbar, and social worker Jane Addams. These mentors helped her to see how to use community organizations to fight crime and poverty and establish her identity as a social reform worker.

In Chicago Lugenia met Georgia-born John Hope, a theology student from Brown University. They were married on 29 December 1897 and moved to Nashville, Tennessee, where he became an instructor at Roger Williams University and she taught classes in arts and crafts and women's physical education. In 1898 Hope moved into the Deep South when her husband joined the faculty at Atlanta Baptist College (later Morehouse College). He became its first African-American president in 1906. The Hopes lived and worked in Atlanta, Georgia, for forty-nine years and had two sons.

In Atlanta Hope soon joined a group of women working to establish day-care centers in the West Fair community. The Neighborhood Union, the first female social welfare agency for African Americans in Atlanta, was born in 1908. During the twenty-five years that Hope headed the Neighborhood Union, African-American women of the community developed employment and probation services, health and recreation campaigns, clean-up campaigns, fresh-air work, lecture courses, classes, clubs, and reading rooms. They used scientific reform techniques to conduct investigations of schools, sanitation, and vice in order to improve community life and encourage community responsibility.

Together with the sociology department at Morehouse College, Hope helped improve the quality of African-American social work. The techniques developed through Atlanta's Neighborhood Union were used by other communities to help shape their social programs. As an affiliate of the National Urban League, the Neighborhood Union became the model for urban reform recommended by the league. In 1916 Hope also helped found the Atlanta branch of the National Association of Colored Women's Clubs.

During World War I the Young Men's Christian Association's Atlanta War Work Council for African-American soldiers was directed by the Neighborhood Union, which asked for greater access to the city's public facilities, more recreational centers, and increased police protection. Success resulted in Hope's appointment in 1917 as director of the hostess house program for black soldiers at Camp Upton, New York, sponsored by the Young Women's Christian Association (YWCA). Hope thought that African-American service during World War I would lead to improved racial conditions in postwar America. When, in fact, discrimination and segregation worsened, she organized African-American women to pressure the YWCA into pursuing more interracial policies and leadership.

From 1920 to 1940 Hope served as an assistant to Mary McLeod Bethune, director of the Negro Affairs Division of the National Youth Administration (NYA), helping to implement NYA programs in African-American communities. In 1927 she served on Herbert Hoover's Colored Advisory Commission, established to investigate catastrophic flooding in Mississippi. Hope lectured on the national level for the National Council of Negro Women and helped organize the National Association of Colored Graduate Nurses. In 1932 she became the first vice president of the Atlanta chapter of the National Association for the Advancement of Colored People (NAACP).

Hope demonstrated her remarkable organizational skills through implementation of Atlanta's Neighborhood Union of which, from 1908 to 1935, she was founder, president, and chair of the board of managers. By dividing the city into zones, the zones into neighborhoods, and the neighborhoods into districts, her organizational plan called for direct community involvement. She worked tirelessly to provide health care for children and adults in African-American communities and to improve the level of public school education (she was coordinator of the Gate City Free Kindergarten Association in 1908 and chair of the Women's Civic and Social Improvement Committee for better black schools in 1913). She informed and educated African Americans about government and citizenship using the citizenship schools of the NAACP, provided adequate and safe recreational facilities for children, and persuaded the YWCA to organize African-American branches in the South on the basis of equality. She capitalized on her middle-class status, prestige, and influence to muster the support needed to help African Americans in Atlanta move progressively into the twentieth century. Lugenia Hope died of heart failure in Nashville, Tennessee.

• An important biography of Hope is Jacqueline A. Rouse, *Lugenia Burns Hope: Black Southern Reformer* (1989), which documents Hope's reform career. See also Rouse, "The Legacy of Community Organizing: Lugenia Burns Hope and the Neighborhood Union," *Journal of Negro History* 69 (1984): 114–33. Rouse also wrote the entry for Hope in the *Dictionary of Georgia Biography*, vol. 1 (1983). Fred Ridgely Torrence, *The Story of John Hope* (1948), provides much information on the beginnings of Lugenia Hope's career as a reformer and activist as well as insight into the personal and working relationship between Lugenia and John Hope. Obituaries are in the *Pittsburgh Courier* and the *Chicago Defender*, 30 Aug. 1947.

THEA GALLO BECKER

HOPEKIRK, Helen (20 May 1856–19 Nov. 1945), pianist and composer, was born in Edinburgh, Scotland, the daughter of Adam Hopekirk, the owner of a music business, and Helen Croall. She showed musical promise early, began piano lessons at age nine with George Lichtenstein, and studied harmony and composition with Sir Alexander C. MacKenzie. Beginning at age eleven she played at local concerts, and reviewers predicted a brilliant career. In 1876 she realized her father's dying wish by enrolling in the Leipzig Conservatory, where she remained for two years, studying with Louis Maas, Carl Reinecke, Salomon Jadassohn, and Ernst Friedrich Richter. At her graduation recital on 28 November 1878 she played Frédéric Chopin's Piano Concerto no. 2 in F Minor with the Leipzig Gewandhaus Orchestra.

On her return to the British Isles she made her London debut at the Crystal Palace on 15 March 1879, where she premiered Saint-Saëns's Piano Concerto no. 2 in G Minor with an orchestra conducted by August Manns. A London reviewer declared her performance "a complete success." Thereafter she played frequently in both England and Scotland. While in London she met Clara Schumann, who coached her on the interpretation of Robert Schumann's works. On 4 August 1882 she married William A. Wilson of Edinburgh, a businessman and music critic, who soon became her concert manager.

Hopekirk and her husband began a tour of the United States with her American debut in Boston on 7 December 1883, where she played Saint-Saëns's second Piano Concerto with the Boston Symphony Orchestra conducted by Georg Henschel. Bostonians gave her a warm welcome, and a critic called her "an artist of the first rank." Hopekirk's American tour lasted three years, during which time she appeared with leading orchestras in New York, Boston, Philadelphia, and Cincinnati and played sixty-eight chamber and solo recitals in a dozen cities. The critic of the Cincinnati *Commercial Gazette* (19 Mar. 1891) found her playing

"heroic" and characterized by breadth and clarity. In 1891–1892 Hopekirk again toured the United States; otherwise she played in Europe until 1897. She had command of a large repertoire, was an early champion of the works of Edward MacDowell, and introduced American audiences to music of French and Belgian composers such as Camille Saint-Saëns, Vincent D'Indy, César Franck, Gabriel Fauré, and Claude Debussy. Reviewers compared her playing favorably to that of the two greatest pianists of the time, Anton Rubinstein and Hans von Bülow.

Hopekirk twice interrupted her busy performing schedule to study. She spent from 1887 to 1889 in Vienna studying piano with Theodor Leschetizky, who considered her "the finest woman musician I have ever known" (Annette Hullah, *Theodor Leschetizky*, [1906]). While there she also studied composition with Karl Navrátil. As Hopekirk's interest in composition grew, she again retired from the concert stage (1892–1894), this time to study composition and orchestration with Richard Mandl in Paris. Meanwhile, she supported herself by teaching piano. When she began performing again, Hopekirk included some of her own works in her programs, beginning in Dundee, Scotland, on 21 November 1894 with her Concertstück in D Minor for piano and orchestra, the Scottish Orchestra conducted by Henschel. Violinist Gerald Walenn introduced Hopekirk's Sonata for Violin and Piano in E Minor at a recital in London on 22 May 1896.

An accident that resulted in her husband's partial disability ended her life as a touring artist, and the need for a steady income led her to accept an offer of a position from George Whitefield Chadwick, director of the New England Conservatory of Music in Boston and former fellow student of Hopekirk's in Leipzig. She joined the piano faculty of the New England Conservatory in 1897 and taught there for four years. Thereafter she taught privately, playing occasional solo recitals, chamber music concerts, and concertos in the Boston area. Later she became adviser to the music faculty at Wellesley College and taught the advanced piano students. At her last recital, which took place at Steinert Hall, Boston, on 10 April 1939, Hopekirk played her own works exclusively. With the exception of one year in Scotland and summer vacations in Europe, Hopekirk spent the latter part of her life in the United States, becoming a citizen in 1918. She died in Cambridge, Massachusetts.

Hopekirk published about fifty songs, more than thirty works for piano, and three chamber works. An approximately equal number of compositions remain in manuscript, among them six works for orchestra and two for piano and orchestra. The critic of the *Chicago Tribune* (21 Apr. 1892) found Hopekirk's Serenade in F-sharp Major for piano "melodious yet passionate and at times almost *dramatic* in character, skillfully written and revealing no mean creative ability." Her style, while conservative, includes some use of dissonance and shows the influence of contemporary French music. Many of her compositions display the modal and melodic characteristics of Scottish folk music, including her very successful *Five Songs* (1903) to texts by Fiona Macleod. Her most popular publication, *Seventy Scottish Songs* (1905), a set of folk songs she collected, edited, and arranged, reflects her commitment to the Scottish nationalist movement in music. A former student, George R. MacManus, described Hopekirk as "a very gifted composer, but for some reason she never seemed to apply the same exacting criticism to her compositions that she gave her own playing" (Hall and Tetlow, p. 21). While clearly a pianist of the first rank, her compositions, which are attractive and well crafted, do not come up to the level of her pianism.

• The Hopekirk collection at the Library of Congress has most of her manuscripts, including scores of seven of her eight works for orchestra, printed music, a sketchbook, five scrapbooks, photographs, and other memorabilia. The most complete biography is Constance Hall and Helen I. Tetlow, *Helen Hopekirk 1856–1945* (1954). See also Christine Ammer, *Unsung: A History of Women in American Music* (1980), pp. 91–93. An obituary is in the *New York Times*, 20 Nov. 1945.

ADRIENNE FRIED BLOCK

HOPKINS, Arthur Melancthon (4 Oct. 1878–22 Mar. 1950), theater producer and director, was born in Cleveland, Ohio, the youngest son of David John Hopkins, a wire mill foreman, and Mary Jefferies. His mother, a Presbyterian minister's daughter, insisted that the young Hopkins be tutored in elocution, and the bombastic vocal style spawned Hopkins's lifelong aversion to "ham acting." His last formal education was at the boys' preparatory school, Western Reserve Academy, in Hudson, Ohio.

Hopkins worked odd jobs at Cleveland's steel mills and a city hospital. Although he failed as an advertising solicitor for the *St. Paul (Minn.) Daily News*, he was successful as a reporter. It was on the police beat for the *St. Paul Globe* that Hopkins learned the elements of a good story. After a year he returned home and worked for the *Cleveland Press* but was not given a regular assignment until his investigation of President William McKinley's assassination in 1901 "scooped" the identity of the President's assassin. This investigative coup won him the honor of being one of three reporters permitted to attend Theodore Roosevelt's inauguration.

After a 1903 article on variety acts in Cleveland's amusement parks, Hopkins was hired as a press agent for a Cleveland variety theater and later as a booking agent for an amusement park syndicate in New York. He then joined the booking department of the Orpheum Circuit, which controlled vaudeville in the West. During this period he wrote a one-act sketch, *Thunder God*, and its success led to his producing vaudeville acts with sketches that were often written by himself.

Although Hopkins claimed that "It was not a long step from vaudeville production to the production of plays," his transition to the legitimate theater began inauspiciously in 1912 with productions of a three-act

play he wrote, *The Fatted Calf*, and a play he produced, John T. McIntyre's *Steve*; neither was well received. Not until his next production, *Poor Little Rich Girl* in 1913 did he claim success.

In 1913 Hopkins also traveled to Europe to experience firsthand the theater in England, France, and Germany. He was "deeply impressed" by the simplicity of Max Reinhardt's productions and the influences of Gordon Craig. The new theatrical styles confirmed Hopkins's belief that most American theater was "archaic," and he immediately produced and directed a dramatization of Longfellow's *Evangeline* (1913) that experimented with European methods and ideas.

Despite the fact that *Evangeline* was a critical failure, lasting only seventeen performances, it established the trademarks that were to distinguish Arthur Hopkins's productions for the next thirty years. In an age of rampant theatrical commercialism, Hopkins strove for artistic integrity. He produced plays not for their monetary potential but for their artistic merit and because he personally liked and believed in them. Unlike the majority of Broadway producers of the era, especially David Belasco, who reveled in detailed realism, Hopkins believed that "The whole realistic movement was founded on selfishness." Scenically, Hopkins stripped the stage of unnecessary clutter and insisted that the design of a production serve only the needs and themes of a play; rather than draw attention to itself, the design must function as one element in an organic whole.

Hopkins also refused to condescend to the theater audience in his efforts to fill seats. He praised the German audiences who attended Max Reinhardt's Deutsches Theatre and was convinced that the Deutsches attracted an "audience of brains" because it gave "brain plays." Hopkins subsequently operated on the premise that "there is a Deutsches audience in New York and in every large American city, but it is not to be found in the theatre. . . . This is the audience for which the producer of the future must bait his trap." In the eighty-five productions that Arthur Hopkins produced, coproduced and/or directed between *Evangeline* in 1913 and the revival of *Burlesque* in 1946, he was continually baiting his trap.

Hopkins's successful 1914 production of Elmer Rice's *On Trial* launched the young law clerk's playwriting career. The next year Hopkins took enough time out from his producing and directing to marry the Australian actress Eva O'Brien, who had performed under the stage name of Eva McDonald. But it was not long before he was mounting his next production, Edith Ellis's *The Devil's Garden* (1915). While the script was found wanting, the production was most notable for teaming Hopkins with the young scene designer Robert Edmond Jones, the leading American artist of the New Stagecraft. Over the next three decades Hopkins and Jones collaborated on over forty productions that sought to concretize many of Hopkins's theatrical ideals.

Hopkins articulated his ideals in three books. The first, a pithy volume titled *How's Your Second Act?* was published in 1918. The touchstone of his philosophy was his belief that "art is not intended for the intellect any more than sunsets." He felt that theater must appeal to the unconscious, and the stimulation of both the artist's and audience's unconscious guided his choices and techniques in play selection, casting, and directing.

In 1918 Hopkins also began his various attempts to establish a classical presence on the commercial stage. He produced three Ibsen plays, *The Wild Duck, Hedda Gabler*, and *A Doll's House*, for the actress Alla Nazimova, and he also began his association with the Barrymore family, producing the successful *Redemption* by Tolstoy with John Barrymore. That was followed by Sem Benelli's *The Jest* (1919), which teamed brothers Lionel and John Barrymore together. John followed in *Richard III* (1920) and his famous interpretation of *Hamlet* (1922), while Lionel played the title role in the Hopkins production of *Macbeth* (1921). Not to be left out, Ethel was featured in the 1922 production of *Romeo and Juliet* and other Hopkins productions, including Gerhart Hauptmann's *Rose Bernd* (1922), Zoë Akin's *A Royal Fandango* (1923), and Arthur Wing Pinero's *The Second Mrs. Tanqueray* (1924).

Eugene O'Neill's *Anna Christie* (1921) reached new heights of gritty realism as did the 1924 production of Maxwell Anderson's and Laurence Stallings's vivid, deglorification of war, *What Price Glory?* Philip Barry's playwriting career was propelled by the 1925 production of *In a Garden* and was firmly established with the successful *Paris Bound*, which played in 1927 for 197 performances, and *Holiday* (1928), which reached 229 performances.

Hopkins's period of greatest activity and success spanned the 1920s, but his theatrical output over the next decade was considerably diminished and less successful, with Donald Ogden Stewart's *Rebound* (1930) and Robert E. Sherwood's *The Petrified Forest* (1935) as the only two productions to survive over 100 performances. As an alternative to theater, Hopkins tried his hand at fiction with the allegorical novel *The Road to Glory* in 1935 and an autobiography, *To A Lonely Boy* (1937), which contained anecdotal accounts of his years in vaudeville and the theater.

Eva Hopkins died in 1938, and after his wife's death Hopkins produced or directed five more productions. Of those five shows only the 1946 productions of *The Magnificent Yankee* and Jean Dalrymple's revival of *Burlesque* under Hopkins's direction were successful.

Like many theater artists of the time, Hopkins was lured, on occasion, to film; however, he was primarily a man of the stage and his screen dalliances were brief. During the silent era, he directed *The Eternal Magdalene* (1917) in New Jersey, but he went to Hollywood to produce the film version of Barry's *Paris Bound* (1929). He shared directing and writing credits for *His Double Life* (1933) starring Lillian Gish, and in 1937 he collaborated in the adaptation of his successful stage comedy *Burlesque* under the title of *Swing High, Swing Low*. In 1944 Hopkins's artistic energies were transferred to radio where, under the auspices of

NBC, he presented a series of thirty-nine one-hour versions of successful stage plays. Always "baiting the trap," Hopkins was not afraid to utilize the medium of radio to attract an audience who would appreciate artistic theater.

In 1948 Hopkins published a series of lectures under the collective title *Reference Point* in which he reiterated his ideals and summarized his hopes for the theater. Hopkins died in New York City.

A notoriously taciturn man, Hopkins preferred his productions to speak for him. Both his successes and his distinguished failures (and there were many "failures," among them the 1928 production of Sophie Treadwell's *Machinal*) contributed to his being one of the most respected American directors in the early twentieth century. On his death, the *New York Times* acknowledged his contribution: "For more than thirty years the words 'Arthur Hopkins Presents' meant almost invariably, that something new, something exciting, something great was to be shown on the New York stage." In addition to nurturing emerging playwrights (including Rice, Anderson and Stallings, and Barry), introducing young, inexperienced actors (Pauline Lord, Katherine Hepburn, Barbara Stanwyck, and Humphrey Bogart, among others), and collaborating with the vanguard of the new scene design (primarily Robert Edmond Jones), Hopkins tirelessly worked to raise the theater above a level of crass commercialism. As early as 1918 Hopkins said "the theater can . . . ultimately reach a place where it helps mankind to a better human understanding, to a deeper social pity and to a wider tolerance of all that is life." He spent the next three decades trying to reach that place.

• The three books that Hopkins wrote pertaining to the theater, *How's Your Second Act?* (1918), *To a Lonely Boy* (1937), and *Reference Point* (1948), provide the most illuminating insight into the producer's theatrical ideas, techniques, and biography. Hopkins's ideas about the audience are found in his article "Brain Plays in Germany," *Harper's Weekly* 58, 13 Sept. 1913, p. 25. The biographical essay in Samuel L. Leiter's *The Great Stage Directors* (1994) is the most concise summary available of Hopkins's career, ideas, and contributions. Numerous articles about Hopkins are scattered throughout the theatrical and popular publications of the period, but the most informative are Walter Prichard Eaton's "American Producers II: Arthur Hopkins," *Theatre Arts* 5 (July 1921): 230–36, and Brock Pemberton's "Arthur Hopkins, Producer: A Portrait Study of a Man, a Temperament and a Method," *Theatre Guild* 6 (Apr. 1929): 23ff. An obituary is in the *New York Times*, 23 Mar. 1950.

JANE T. PETERSON

HOPKINS, Claude (24 Aug. 1903–19 Feb. 1984), jazz bandleader and pianist, was born Claude Driskett Hopkins in Alexandria, Virginia, the son of Albert W. Hopkins and Gertrude D. (maiden name unknown), supervisors of a school for orphaned boys in Blue Plains, Virginia. Around 1913 the family moved to Washington, D.C., where his father became postmaster at Howard University and his mother became matron of a Howard dormitory. After public schooling,

Hopkins enrolled at Howard, where he excelled in athletics and scholarship. Concentrating on music theory and classical piano while beginning preparations for medical study, he earned a B.A. in music. Despite his parents' preference he chose to become a musician, having already worked casually in nightclubs and theaters during his college years.

Hopkins had heard the Harlem stride piano style on piano rolls by James P. Johnson and Fats Waller, and like other distinguished jazzmen, including Waller himself, Hopkins learned Johnson's test piece, "Carolina Shout," by playing the roll slowly and imitating the fingering. In New York City he worked for a few months with clarinetist Wilber Sweatman. Banjoist Elmer Snowden reported that Hopkins was in his big band, replacing Bill (later Count) Basie as Snowden's pianist at New York's Bamville Club in 1925.

In the summer of 1925 Hopkins led a band in Atlantic City. When the job ended, he brought his five-piece band to the Smile Awhile Café in Asbury Park, New Jersey, where they won a job by outplaying Basie's group at an audition. In turn, their performance at the café of a novelty version of "St. Louis Blues," featuring trumpeter Henry Goodwin as a "preacher" and the other two wind players as the "sisters" of the congregation, secured the band a place in the *Revue Négre*. The revue traveled to Europe with Josephine Baker as its star and reed player Sidney Bechet added to Hopkins's instrumentalists. Hopkins had recently married Mabel (maiden name unknown), and she was taught to dance in the chorus, so that she could join the tour. Hopkins, an inveterate womanizer, had an undisguised affair with Baker while in transit to France. The *Revue Négre* debuted in Paris in October 1925 and toured to Belgium and Germany, finishing in Berlin in March 1926. Baker left for the Folies Bergères in Paris, and most of Hopkins's sidemen took other jobs. Struggling to fulfill commitments and to keep a band together, he spent the next year performing in Europe. He and his wife returned to the United States in March 1927; they had one child.

In Washington Hopkins formed a seven-piece band including trombonist Sandy Williams, saxophonists Hilton Jefferson and Elmer Williams, and guitarist Bernard Addison. The band returned to the Smile Awhile Café and tried to break into the New York scene, but failed. Hopkins then worked on his own. He wrote for and led a band in another musical revue, *The Ginger Snaps of 1928*, which toured the T.O.B.A. (Theater Owners' Booking Circuit), a circuit of theaters presenting African-American performers. He returned to Washington after the show failed.

Hopkins led a band at the Fulton Gardens in Brooklyn for the balance of 1928 and into 1929, and he recorded two titles with Clarence Williams's Blue Five on 20 September 1928. He then replaced pianist Charlie Skeets at a dime-a-dance hall in Manhattan; the band included clarinetist Edmond Hall. After taking over its leadership from Skeets, Hopkins secured a job in January 1930 at the Savoy Ballroom, where his understated approach to big-band jazz gave him a musical identity distinct from the typically extroverted bands that played at this venue. After the first night, Savoy manager Charlie Buchanan suggested a more hard-hitting approach; but Hopkins persisted, and, as it turns out, the Savoy dancers loved his style. The band stayed there for most of 1930 and then moved to the more prestigious Roseland Ballroom.

Hopkins held residencies at Roseland from 1931 to April 1934 and broadcast nationally from the ballroom on the CBS radio network. In the spring of 1932 Hopkins began to take leaves from Roseland for extensive touring and for performances at Harlem theaters, including the Apollo. His band performed in the movies *Dance Team* (1931) and *Wayward* (1932). Hopkins wrote the band's theme song, "I Would Do Anything for You," featuring the trumpet playing and smooth-toned singing of Ovie Alston; this was their first recording, made on 24 May 1932. The same session featured arranger Jimmy Mundy's "Mush Mouth." By 1933 Hopkins had hired a "freak" attraction, singer Orlando Robeson, whose falsetto ballad singing was featured on "Trees," heard in the band's film short *Barber Shop Blues* (1933) and on record in 1935.

Hopkins's touring and Harlem theater engagements continued for a year after the band left Roseland, during which time he recorded "Three Little Words" and "Chasing All the Blues Away" (1934). In a move away from its focus on dance music, the band played for shows at the Cotton Club from March through December 1935 while also appearing in the movie short *Broadway Highlights*, filmed at the Cotton Club. Hopkins's last movie short, *By Request*, dates from late that same year.

When club residencies in New York ended, Hopkins took his band on North American tours from 1936 to 1940. His sidemen during this period included trumpeter Jabbo Smith (1936–1937) and trombonist Vic Dickenson (1936–1939). Finally the band seems to have grown stale, and opportunities for work diminished. Hopkins disbanded in 1940 and declared bankruptcy in 1941.

Hopkins had already written for other bands; Andy Kirk's big band recorded his arrangement of "A Wednesday Night Hop" in 1937. In 1941 Hopkins's former arranger and trombonist, Fred Norman, procured some assignments for Hopkins as a commercial arranger, but he disliked this job and went to work at the Eastern Aircraft defense plant in New Jersey in 1942. In 1944 he formed a big band at the new Club Zanzibar in New York; he stayed there, directing and arranging, until 1947. He toured until 1949 as the leader of a small group, and he participated in USO tours, playing at veterans' hospitals in 1949 and 1950. He formed his own touring variety show, but this venue was unsuccessful.

After a period in Sheraton hotel lounge bands, Hopkins worked alongside trumpeter Doc Cheatham and trombonist Vic Dickenson in pianist and promoter George Wein's band at Mahogany Hall in Boston (1951–1953). He worked with trumpeter Henry "Red" Allen at the Metropole Cafe in New York until 1960.

He spent the next six years working at the Nevele, a Catskill resort in Ellenville, New York, with trumpeter Shorty Baker, a drummer, and a singer. Back in New York City he joined the Jazz Giants, a six-piece group featuring cornetist Wild Bill Davison; they toured for three years and recorded an album in Toronto in 1968. In the 1970s he mainly led his own groups or performed as a soloist, but early in the decade he also worked with trumpeter Roy Eldridge at Jimmy Ryan's Club in New York. In 1972 he recorded the unaccompanied stride piano albums *Crazy Fingers* and *Soliloquy*. From 1974 he made annual tours of European festivals. Hopkins's health started to fail while he was in Europe in 1979. He died in a nursing home in the Riverdale section of New York City.

Studio recordings by Hopkins's big band are routinely criticized as undistinguished, unoriginal, and unmemorable. The solo albums of 1972 are offered as his finest recorded legacy, presenting in high fidelity the prewar Harlem stride piano style. Without arguing with this general assessment, one might make an exception for "Three Little Words" from the session of 6 April 1934. Hopkins's rollicking stride piano solo, underpinned by soft saxophone chords, gives way to his heavily percussive accompaniment to the saxophones' smooth statement of the melody; from there the band moves into tight ensemble work. With these segments glued together by a wonderfully bouncy rhythm section, one can begin to understand why Hopkins's somewhat unusual blend of stride and swing and soft pop was such a favorite of the Savoy and Roseland dancers.

• Warren W. Vaché, *Crazy Fingers: Claude Hopkins' Life in Jazz* (1992), incorporates Hopkins's diary. Interviews of Hopkins and Norman are in Stanley Dance, *The World of Swing* (1974), pp. 31–45, 232–40. Reports and advertisements of Hopkins's big band from the African-American and musical press are detailed in Manfred Selchow, *Profoundly Blue: A Bio-Discographical Scrapbook on Edmond Hall* (1988), pp. 34–67. See also Gene Fernett, *Swing Out: Great Negro Jazz Bands* (1970), pp. 109–10. For lukewarm assessments of Hopkins's big-band recordings, see Albert McCarthy, *Big Band Jazz* (1974), pp. 286–89, and Gunther Schuller, *The Swing Era: The Development of Jazz, 1930–1945* (1989), pp. 317–22. The Club Zanzibar band is recalled in Clyde E. B. Bernhardt, as told to Sheldon Harris, *I Remember: Eighty Years of Black Entertainment, Big Bands, and the Blues* (1986), pp. 168–70. An obituary is in the *New York Times*, 23 Feb. 1984.

BARRY KERNFELD

HOPKINS, Edward (1600–Mar. 1657), the second governor of the Connecticut colony, was born in Shrewsbury, England, the son of Edward or Edmund Hopkins and Katherine Lello. Little is known of his youth. After graduating from the Royal Free Grammar School, he moved to London, made a fortune as a merchant with extensive overseas connections, and inherited or purchased a substantial estate. A devout Puritan of the gentry class, Hopkins was a member of St. Stephen's Parish and counted John Davenport, the minister, and Theophilus Eaton, a wealthy merchant and parishioner, as lifelong friends. His wife, Ann Yale, was the daughter of Eaton's second wife; apparently they had no children.

Throughout his life, Hopkins was esteemed for his fervent piety and charity. Increasingly uneasy after Charles I ascended the throne, he decided to migrate to the Puritan colony of Massachusetts Bay. Along with Davenport and Eaton, he and Ann arrived in Boston on 26 June 1637. Despite pleas that he remain in Boston, Hopkins settled in Hartford, a Connecticut River town established a year earlier by the followers of the Reverend Thomas Hooker, where he had already reserved a house lot. In Connecticut he erected a "mansion," a barn and a warehouse, probably on the 120 acres allotted to him as a Hartford proprietor, and pursued a series of mercantile and other entrepreneurial activities.

From the time of his arrival in Hartford, Hopkins was called on for public service. During its first year, Hartford, along with Windsor and Wethersfield, was governed by commissioners appointed by Massachusetts. A movement for self-government arose quickly. In 1637 and 1638, he represented south Hartford in a general court that emerged to keep order in the newly settled river towns. He also served as secretary of the body and was one of a three-man delegation that successfully negotiated a treaty ending the bloody Pequot War. Hopkins was a member of the committee that drafted the Fundamental Orders of Connecticut in 1639, which established a government composed of four elected officials and a bicameral general court. He served as secretary and assistant in the new government headed by Governor John Haynes. In 1640 he was elected governor and Haynes, deputy-governor. Since the Orders prohibited a governor from succeeding himself, Haynes and Hopkins alternated in the two chief positions from 1643 to 1654. Hopkins was chosen governor in the even years and deputy governor in the odd.

Hopkins proved to be particularly adept at defusing controversies and building coalitions. The status of Fort Saybrook and the land around the Connecticut River mouth posed a major problem for the colony. In London a coterie of Puritan lords and gentlemen asserted that they had acquired the patent for the area in 1632 from Robert Rich, the Earl of Warwick, who, in turn, claimed that he had secured it from the Council for New England. Neither deed has ever been found. Hopkins, who may have been an associate grantee and London manager, insisted that he possessed an accurate and valid copy of the original patent. As governor he chaired a special committee that negotiated for two months with George Fenwick, the only patentee to emigrate. In 1644 Fenwick agreed to cede the fort and all territorial claims to Connecticut in return for the right to collect duties on commodities and livestock that passed from the Connecticut River into Long Island Sound. The cession of the claims removed an obstacle that might have seriously hampered the development of Connecticut.

Hopkins was a prime mover as well in persuading Massachusetts, Plymouth, Connecticut, and New Haven to unite to confront such issues as war and peace with the Indians, Dutch expansion, and colonial boundary disputes. To that end he participated in formulating the Articles of Confederation and establishing the United Colonies of New England in 1643. The Connecticut legislature appointed him as one of its two delegates every year until his return to England, and he served as president of the Confederation.

All his adult life Hopkins was burdened with serious health problems, tuberculosis among them. In the late 1640s, his wife, Ann, suffered a mental breakdown from which she never recovered. Perhaps these concerns lay behind Hopkins's decision to move back to England either in 1651 or 1652. Soon after his return he was again thrust into Puritan politics. Oliver Cromwell appointed him a navy commissioner in December 1652 and an admiralty commissioner three years later. In December 1654, on the death of his older brother, Henry, he inherited the posts of warden of the fleet and keeper of the palace of Westminster. (He was also chosen governor of Connecticut that year but did not serve.) In 1656 he was elected a member of Parliament for Dartmouth in Devonshire.

That Hopkins remained attached to his former home and old friends is evident in the terms of his will. When he died in London, Parish of St. Olave, he left many bequests to friends and institutions in New England, including sums for Harvard College and several grammar schools. With its legacy, Harvard bought a township from friendly Christian Indians and called it "Hopkinton." One of the grammar schools receiving money from the estate, the Hopkins School of New Haven, has survived and is regarded as a distinguished preparatory academy.

• There is neither a collection of Hopkins papers nor a formal biography. Two collections of documents contain numerous reference to Hopkins: J. Hammond Trumbull, ed., *The Public Records of the Colony of Connecticut*, vol. 1 (1850) and *The Acts of the Commissioners of the United Colonies of New England*, vols. 1–2, in David Pulsifer, ed., *The Records of the Colony of New Plymouth in New England*, vols. 9–10 (1859). Citations can also be found in Charles J. Hoadley, ed., *Records of the Colony and Plantation of New Haven*, vols. 1–2 (1857–1858). The most extensive treatment of Hopkins's role in Connecticut appears in Benjamin Trumbull, *A Complete History of Connecticut Civil and Ecclesiastical*, vol. 1 (1797). Hopkins's experience in New England is also discussed in Charles M. Andrews, *The Colonial Period of American History*, vol. 2 (1936); Mary Jeanne Anderson Jones, *Congregational Commonwealth: Connecticut 1636–1662* (1968); and William De-Loss Love, *The Colonial History of Hartford* (1935). For shorter sketches, see Cotton Mather, *Magnalia, Christi Americana*, vol. 1 (1702); James Savage, *A Genealogical Dictionary of the First Settlers of New England*, vol. 2 (1860–1862); Frederick Calvin Norton, *The Governors of Connecticut* (1905); and Albert E. Van Dusen, *Connecticut* (1961).

ESTELLE F. FEINSTEIN

HOPKINS, Emma Curtis (2 Sept. 1849–8 Apr. 1925), founder of the New Thought religious movement, was born in Killingly, Connecticut, the daughter of Rufus Curtis, a real estate agent, and Lydia Phillips. Hopkins, the oldest child in a large and prosperous family, received a good education. She attended Killingly High School. (Recent research reveals that reports of her attendance and teaching at Woodstock, Connecticut, Academy are in error.) In 1874 she married George Irving Hopkins, a high school English teacher; they had one child. The family resided in Nantucket, Massachusetts, until the early 1880s. In 1900, after a separation of several years, her husband divorced Hopkins for abandonment. Her son died in 1905.

By 1883 the family had moved to Manchester, New Hampshire, where Hopkins attended a lecture on Christian Science offered by Mary Baker Eddy. By February 1884 the *Christian Science Journal* listed her as a practitioner. Hopkins quickly ascended to a position of leadership within Eddy's organization; in September 1884 she became editor of the *Journal*, a position she held until she was fired in October 1885. The reasons for her dismissal are unclear, although it appears likely that Hopkins's religious independence was not acceptable in the context of Eddy's dogmatic leadership.

In 1886 Hopkins and another Christian Science dissident, Mary Plunkett, began an independent Christian Science ministry and school in Chicago. Although they recognized their work to be in the Christian Science tradition, their teachings were not based on Eddy's writings. From the beginning, Hopkins's teachings—and those of the New Thought movement that she inspired—rejected Eddy's authority, advanced a more eclectic theology, and allowed greater freedom of institutional religious practice.

Like Christian Science, New Thought was a popular religious expression of Idealism, a theological and philosophical tradition dating back to Plato, which affirmed that Mind (that is, consciousness or thought) was the ultimate reality, and material phenomena were consequences of mental causes. Unlike Christian Science, New Thought groups (1) did not deny the reality of the material world, (2) were nondogmatic, and (3) were relatively open in organization.

In 1887 Hopkins formed the Hopkins Metaphysical Association and traveled to San Francisco and New York to teach classes. She was active in progressive movements of the day, with the new association supporting the Women's Alliance (a group seeking compulsory education), the Woman's Federal Labor Union, and the Labor League. In 1888 in Chicago, Hopkins opened the Christian Science Theological Seminary whose first graduates were ordained in 1889, marking the first time in U.S. history that a woman had ordained women. By 1893 Hopkins had ordained 111 ministers—women and men—and the seminary's enrollment was 350 students.

As a result of her educational endeavors and ordinations, Hopkins was known within the New Thought movement as the "teacher of teachers." She or her protégés taught virtually all of the incipient movement's early leaders: Charles Fillmore and Myrtle Fillmore (cofounders of Unity); Katie Bingham, the teacher of

Nona Brooks (a founder of Divine Science); and Malinda Cramer (another founder of Divine Science). After her retirement from public teaching and administrative work, Hopkins tutored Ernest S. Holmes, who founded the Church of Religious Science.

In 1895 Hopkins closed the Chicago seminary and moved to New York City where she continued to give occasional lectures and regularly met with individual students and clients. During the last two decades of her life, she traveled widely, visiting Australia, Europe, and various U.S. cities. Although often described as reclusive and mystical by nature, she was an active participant in New York's cultural and intellectual life. She became a friend of Mabel Dodge Luhan, was familiar with many in Luhan's social circle, and was called the "court metaphysician" to New York's cultural elite. Although she retired in 1895, Hopkins remained active as mental healer and teacher until the end of her life. She died in Killingly, Connecticut.

Hopkins's importance to the emergence of the American New Thought movement has been ignored or trivialized in the few serious studies of the movement. She established the organizational model, theological parameters, and the religious style that came to be characterized as New Thought. Among her major contributions, she (1) established a seminary and ordained ministers; (2) she created a nondogmatic doctrine; (3) she emphasized Christianity; (4) she separated from Eddy's movement; and (5) she developed a loose organization. Through their founders, the three largest New Thought groups (Unity, Religious Science, and Divine Science) can be directly traced to Hopkins and her work. Her ordination of women stands as her greatest contribution to American religious and cultural history.

• Biographical data on Hopkins are remarkably inconsistent. Otherwise reliable sources offer conflicting dates for most of the significant events in her life. Thus, the information presented here is based on the author's best judgment. Among Hopkins's most notable books are *Bible Interpretation Series* (1974), *High Mysticism* (1920–1922), *Résumé* (1974), and *Scientific Mental Practice* (n.d.). No full-length biography has been published, but a biographical sketch can be found in Charles S. Braden, *Spirits in Rebellion* (1963), which also offers information on New Thought, its institutions, and its relationship with Christian Science. A Ph.D. dissertation by Gail Harley (Florida State Univ.) should help resolve some of the issues and dates in Hopkins's life. In the present essay Harley's dissertation has been used, as has Harley's paper, "The Last Years of Emma Curtis Hopkins" (1990), and J. Gordon Melton's "The Hidden History of Emma Curtis Hopkins" (1987), both papers presented at meetings of the American Academy of Religion.

DELL deCHANT

HOPKINS, Esek (26 Apr. 1718–26 Feb. 1802), naval officer, was born in Providence (present-day Scituate), Rhode Island, the son of William Hopkins and Ruth Wilkinson, farmers. The Hopkins family was large and well respected in Rhode Island. When William Hopkins died in 1738, leaving a widow and nine children, Esek went to sea. Like many Providence seafarers, Hopkins sailed primarily to the West Indies. He did well, proving to be both an astute businessman and a skillful seaman, and within a few years rose to command. He married Desire Burroughs in 1741 and moved with her to Newport, remaining there until 1748, when they returned to Providence. They had ten children.

Esek Hopkins was typical of many New England captains. During wartime when normal trade was disrupted, he turned his attention to privateering. During the French and Indian War (1754–1763) he commanded a Rhode Island privateer that managed to take a number of French prizes. With the profits from his captures he bought a large farm in North Providence but continued to go to sea after the war, making several voyages to Africa and the West Indies. By 1772 he seems to have retired ashore.

As royal authority collapsed in Rhode Island in the spring of 1775, the General Assembly made plans to defend the colony against British attack. The members were particularly concerned about the colony's vulnerability to attack from the sea. On 14 June 1775 the assembly authorized the equipping of two small vessels to patrol the Rhode Island coast. On 26 August they instructed their representatives in the Continental Congress, Stephen Hopkins—Esek Hopkins's elder brother and business associate—and Samuel Ward (1725–1776), to call for the creation of a Continental fleet. After some debate the Congress agreed and appointed a committee to prepare a report. First known as the Naval Committee and later the Marine Committee, this body was dominated by New Englanders, among them Stephen Hopkins. The committee appointed Esek Hopkins commander in chief of the embryo navy with the title of commodore.

Through the fall and winter of 1775–1776 Hopkins and the committee worked to assemble ships and men at Philadelphia. By early January 1776 eight vessels were present and ready to sail. On 5 January Hopkins was ordered to sail into the Chesapeake and there attack and destroy the ships of Lord Dunmore, which were harassing the shores of Maryland and Virginia. He was then to cruise along the southern coast, ridding it of the enemy. After completing those missions, he was to lay a course for Rhode Island and clear those waters as well.

On 17 February 1776 Hopkins, with his squadron of eight vessels, set sail from the Delaware. Believing that British forces in the Chesapeake and along the southern coasts were too strong for his squadron, Hopkins, relying on the discretion granted in his instructions, decided not to follow his congressional orders but rather to set a course for Nassau in the Bahamas. On 3 March he landed a force of 270 men. With little difficulty they captured Forts Nassau and Montagu, taking a large number of cannon and munitions. Hopkins loaded these supplies aboard his vessels and headed for Rhode Island.

Off Block Island the American squadron encountered the British frigate *Glasgow*. In the ensuing battle the superior American force did little to distinguish itself. Neither Hopkins nor his captains had any experience fighting as a unit. The *Glasgow*'s commander, on the other hand, Captain Tyringham Howe, was a Royal Navy veteran, who deftly maneuvered his vessel among the Americans, taking them on one at a time and then managing to flee to the nearby safety of Newport.

Hopkins's failure to follow the orders of Congress and the embarrassing engagement with the *Glasgow* caused many both in and out of Congress to demand answers. Hopkins was summoned to Philadelphia. The debate over his conduct lasted two days. Southern delegates were annoyed because Hopkins had failed to come to their assistance. Hopkins's strongest defenders came from New England. Chief among them were William Ellery of Rhode Island and John Adams (1735–1826) of Massachusetts. Nonetheless, on 16 August 1776 Congress voted to censure him.

Hopkins, angry and humiliated, but still commander in chief, returned to Providence to prepare his vessels for sea. Here he encountered even more problems. When he tried to recruit seamen and purchase supplies, he found local privateersmen outbidding him at every turn. Hopkins's prickly personality also served him ill. In defending his own conduct he was inclined to lay a good deal of blame on his officers, and he tended to personalize differences between himself and others. After the *Glasgow* affair, for example, he accused some of his officers of being incompetent cowards. He had bitter words for nearly everyone. Congress, increasingly unhappy with the general performance of the navy and with Hopkins in particular, was ready to take further action against him. Their opportunity appeared early in 1777 when a letter arrived, signed by every officer aboard Hopkins's flagship, complaining about the commander in chief. One of the complaints accused him of publicly ridiculing Congress. Hopkins was suspended from command. He was left in this uncertain state until January 1778, when the Congress peremptorily voted that he be "dismissed from the service of the United States."

Hopkins never went to sea again. He was convinced, as were many others, including Adams, that he had fallen victim to an anti–New England feeling in the Congress. While sectionalism may well have influenced the anti-Hopkins faction, it is also true that Hopkins's career as a naval officer was hardly stellar. His mediocre record of command, added to his political ineptness, made dismissal inevitable. Embittered, he remained in Rhode Island for the rest of his life. He continued to engage in politics and was elected to the General Assembly (1777–1786). He also served as collector of imposts for Rhode Island (1783) and as a trustee of Rhode Island College (1782–1802). He died in North Providence.

• Materials related to Hopkins may be found in the papers of the Continental Congress at the National Archives. The only biography is Edward Field, *Esek Hopkins: Commander-in-Chief of the Continental Navy* (1898). The following works focusing on the navy during the Revolution contain considerable material concerning Hopkins: Gardner W. Allen, *A Naval History of the American Revolution* (2 vols., 1913); William J. Morgan, *Captains to the Northward: The New England Captains in the Continental Navy* (1959); and William Fowler, *Rebels under Sail: The American Navy during the Revolution* (1976).

WILLIAM M. FOWLER, JR.

HOPKINS, Harry Lloyd (17 Aug. 1890–29 Jan. 1946), New Deal administrator and presidential adviser, was born in Sioux City, Iowa, the son of David Aldona Hopkins, a salesman and merchant, and Anna Picket. Hopkins grew up in modest circumstances. The family moved frequently during his youth and in 1901 settled in Grinnell, Iowa. He attended Grinnell College, where he was instilled with social ideals and Progressive political values of honest government, public service by experts, and aid to the "deserving" poor. After graduating in 1912 he entered social work in New York City. The next year he married Ethel Gross, a social worker. They had three sons. A daughter died in infancy.

Supported by Dr. John A. Kingsbury of New York's Association for Improving the Conditions of the Poor, Hopkins rapidly rose as an administrator. He experimented with work relief and served as executive secretary of New York's first Board of Child Welfare. During World War I he organized civilian relief for the families of servicemen in the Gulf States Division of the Red Cross, later becoming division manager. He centralized administration, established clear channels of communication, and inspired volunteers with confidence and optimism. In 1922 Hopkins returned to New York; the next year he became president of the American Association of Social Workers and the following year director of the New York Tuberculosis Association. Although he remained a Progressive, he now moved toward decentralization, allowing neighborhoods and agencies to retain their individuality under an umbrella organization. By the end of the decade, Hopkins's inability to manage money had strained his marriage, and he had fallen in love with Barbara Duncan, a secretary at the Tuberculosis Association. He and his wife divorced in May 1931, and in June he married Duncan.

The unemployment crisis of the Great Depression transformed Hopkins's career. In 1931 he became director of Governor Franklin D. Roosevelt's Temporary Emergency Relief Administration, which provided jobs for New York's unemployed. When Roosevelt became president in 1933, Hopkins was one of many strong advocates for a federal relief program, which he believed necessary to save the country from chaos. Congress approved the program, and Roosevelt chose Hopkins to head the Federal Emergency Relief Administration (FERA), with $500 million to allocate to states for direct relief, and Hopkins made headlines by rapidly distributing money. An unemployment crisis loomed for the winter of 1933–1934, and Hopkins persuaded President Roosevelt to propose the Civil

Works Administration (CWA) to provide work relief for all able-bodied unemployed workers. Abandoning casework methods, the CWA hired persons simply because they were unemployed without investigating whether they otherwise qualified for relief. Beginning in early November, CWA employed more than four million workers in two and a half months and undertook hundreds of projects, varying from constructing airports to cataloguing museums and decorating post offices. The success of the program convinced Hopkins that employment should be a right of citizenship, and he became an advocate of government spending to combat the depression.

After the CWA ended in the spring of 1934, Hopkins continued to urge the president to expand work relief. After the fall elections, Roosevelt won congressional approval for a $4 billion program, which he then saddled with a complex administrative structure in which Secretary of the Interior Harold Ickes headed an allotments committee that recommended work projects to the president and Hopkins headed the Works Progress Administration (WPA), which was to provide the largest amount of relief labor for the projects. This structure produced a contest for power between Ickes, who favored heavy construction projects with high outlays for materials and close supervision from Washington, and Hopkins, who favored light projects that emphasized high employment and left much to local initiative. After several months' struggle Roosevelt decided to emphasize Hopkins's approach and to make the WPA the principal agency for work relief. Construction projects dominated the WPA's activities, but the agency also funded local art and music programs.

The WPA addressed social issues that no industrial society has resolved. Although most Americans favored helping the unemployed and the destitute, many, including Roosevelt and Hopkins, worried that prolonged relief, even work relief, would foster dependency. Further, although work relief maintained the morale and skills of the labor force, it was more costly than the dole, and WPA spending did little to stimulate employment in basic industries. Still, the suffering created by the depression was so great and the political need to meet it so immediate that the value of the WPA cannot be dismissed.

Hopkins's achievements put him in the inner circles of the New Deal. Roosevelt's secretary Louis Howe championed his programs, as did Eleanor Roosevelt, herself a former social worker. During 1934 Roosevelt occasionally called upon him to advocate government programs to aid individuals instead of institutional reforms. As the importance of the WPA increased, Hopkins moved closer to Roosevelt. After the president's reelection in 1936, Roosevelt thought seriously of Hopkins as a successor.

Then tragedy struck. In the fall of 1937 Hopkins's wife Barbara died of cancer, leaving him responsible for raising their young daughter. Soon thereafter Hopkins himself underwent surgery for stomach cancer. Although he survived, the operation left him unable to take sufficient nourishment. He nearly died in 1939, and his poor health doomed his presidential chances and his tenure as secretary of commerce (1938–1940). After managing Roosevelt's renomination at the 1940 Democratic National Convention, he resigned from the administration.

By this time World War II had erupted. With France overrun and Britain facing a German invasion, Roosevelt asked Congress for Lend-Lease legislation to supply Britain's defense needs, and in early 1941 he dispatched Hopkins to London. Impressed by Prime Minister Winston Churchill's energy, courage, and intellect, Hopkins took up the British cause. Now less a hard-driving administrator than a sympathetic representative, he became the friend and confidant of Churchill and other British leaders. Soon after he returned to Washington, Roosevelt assigned him to organize Lend-Lease. Hopkins also urged the president to take a more aggressive stance against the Nazis. In July 1941 Hopkins flew to London to prepare for Roosevelt and Churchill's Atlantic Conference. Germany had invaded the Soviet Union and, encouraged by Churchill, Hopkins obtained the president's permission to fly to Moscow to offer aid. The dramatic trip, made under punishing conditions that threatened Hopkins's fragile health, opened direct relations with Marshal Joseph Stalin and prepared the way for a British-American supply mission to Moscow that fall.

After the United States entered the war in December 1941, Hopkins played an important role in the mobilization effort. At the Arcadia Conference in Washington, D.C., he designed a system of allocating American materiel among the Allies through the British-American Munitions Assignments Board, which he headed. By placing the board under the military chiefs instead of the civilian authorities, Hopkins won the support of Army Chief of Staff George C. Marshall, who thereafter relied on Hopkins as his channel to the president. Meanwhile, he had built an informal network of Lend-Lease administrators, later known as "the Hopkins Shop": Edward Stettinius (1900–1949), head of Lend-Lease; Major General James H. Burns, head of the Army Ordnance Department; W. Averell Harriman, Lend-Lease representative in London; and Oscar Cox of the Treasury Department. In early 1942 Lewis W. Douglas, head of the newly formed War Shipping Administration (WSA), joined the group.

Hopkins used the Hopkins Shop to convey presidential authority to agencies and businesses and to strengthen the wartime alliance. In 1942, he emerged as a central figure in foreign policy in his own right. He strongly supported Marshall's plan for an Allied invasion of France in 1942 or 1943, but that idea ran aground as the British and Americans wrangled over strategy. Although disappointed, he resisted American opposition to the remaining alternative, the invasion of North Africa. The following year, Hopkins attended the major summit conferences, where he continued to work for Allied cooperation. He pressed for maximum efforts to deliver Lend-Lease supplies and supported Soviet territorial claims to the Baltic states, Byelorussia, and parts of Poland. Although he had once considered himself a socialist, he never sympathized with communism; his efforts were shaped by the strategic importance of the eastern front and the likelihood that the Soviet Union would emerge as the major postwar power in Europe. Since the spring of 1940 Hopkins had been living in the White House with his teenage daughter, Diana, and when he married Louise Macy in the summer of 1942, the three of them continued to live there. Relations between Louise and Eleanor Roosevelt grew strained, however, and the family moved to Georgetown at the end of 1943.

Throughout this time Hopkins's health remained precarious, and his appetite for alcohol and rich foods strained his inadequate digestive system. He was hospitalized for weeks at a time and at other times received transfusions. He had maintained contact with his three sons, all of whom were in the armed forces. In February 1944 the youngest, Stephen, was killed on Namur, one of the Marshall Islands. By this time Hopkins had become hardened to the sacrifices of war. Although shaken by his son's death, he refused George Marshall's offer to remove his son Robert from combat zones, saying that the war was "for keeps" and that he wanted his sons to be "where the going is rough." That spring he underwent surgery at the Mayo Clinic. He returned to work in such a weakened state that Roosevelt turned to others for advice about wartime policies, especially Secretary of the Treasury Henry Morgenthau. But Roosevelt soon lost confidence in Morgenthau, largely because of the controversy surrounding the so-called Morgenthau Plan for the deindustrialization of postwar Germany, and Hopkins was back in favor.

Hopkins extended the influence of the Hopkins Shop. Stettinius became secretary of state, Charles Bohlen became liaison between State and the White House, and Harriman became ambassador to the Soviet Union. Hopkins hoped that these moves would provide the president with expert advice and systematic preparation for summit diplomacy; after Roosevelt's victory in the 1944 election, he sought to increase the State Department's role in policy decisions. These efforts paid dividends at the Yalta Conference in February 1945. On the American side this was the best prepared and best staffed of the wartime summit conferences. The United States arrived with an agenda focused on establishing a postwar United Nations and establishing a balance of power between Britain, the Soviet Union, and Nationalist China. Hopkins played an important role in winning approval for the United Nations, and on other issues he alternately supported the British and the Soviets, indicating an American desire to become a postwar broker between its major allies. Hoping to establish negotiation procedures to realize his objective, he frequently suggested that the plenary sessions refer issues of detail to the foreign ministers.

During the conference, Hopkins developed pneumonia and returned home to enter the Mayo Clinic. There on the afternoon of 12 April, he learned of Roosevelt's death. At once he returned to Washington to confer with President Harry Truman. Eager to serve but fearful that his poor health and the new president's desire to choose his own advisers would deny him the opportunity, he quickly accepted Truman's request to fly to Moscow to settle issues that had stalled the United Nations conference in San Francisco. In several meetings with Stalin, Hopkins won important Soviet concessions.

The Moscow mission was Hopkins's last significant public service. In July he resigned from the government and moved to New York City, where he mediated labor disputes in the garment industry. He returned to Washington once to receive the Distinguished Service Medal, the nation's highest civilian honor. He had planned to write his memoirs but had scarcely begun when his health again failed. Worn to a skeletal appearance, he entered a New York hospital in November 1945. He died several months later.

To many people Harry Hopkins seemed a man of puzzling contrasts. Friends and coworkers found him honest, steadfast, and courageous; detractors found him evasive and given to half-truths and ad hominem arguments. Although personally motivated by high ideals of public service and self-sacrifice, he often declared that nations are motivated only by self-interest. Although he professed a desire for order, he was at his best responding to unforeseen situations and taking responsibility for problems that resulted from previous decisions. Hopkins shaped these traits into those of a great public administrator and an expert negotiator. He had a capacity for understanding opposing positions, a gift for winning the confidence of others, a keen intellect, and the ability to reduce complex issues to their essential elements. These abilities enabled him to understand Roosevelt's goals and methods and to pursue them with originality, skill, and courage in times of crisis.

• The major collection of Harry Hopkins's papers is in the Franklin D. Roosevelt Library, Hyde Park, New York. Other archival sources are cited in George McJimsey, *Harry Hopkins: Ally of the Poor and Defender of Democracy* (1987), the most recent complete biography. Another major biography, which includes many documents, is Robert E. Sherwood, *Roosevelt and Hopkins, an Intimate History* (1948; rev. ed., 1950). Henry H. Adams, *Harry Hopkins: A Biography* (1977), follows Sherwood's treatment. Searle F. Charles, *Minister of Relief: Harry Hopkins and the Depression* (1963), is an excellent analysis. Dwight William Tuttle, *Harry L. Hopkins and Anglo-American-Soviet Relations, 1941–1945* (1983), briefly discusses that aspect of Hopkins's wartime diplomatic service. An obituary appears in the *New York Times*, 30 Jan. 1946.

GEORGE MCJIMSEY

HOPKINS, Isaac Stiles (20 June 1841–3 Feb. 1914), clergyman and educator, was born in Augusta, Georgia, the son of Thomas Hopkins and Rebecca Lambert. Hopkins entered Emory College at Oxford, Georgia, in 1856 and received his A.B. in 1859. He then enrolled in the Medical College of Georgia in Augusta, where he received an M.D. in 1861. He never practiced medicine but, feeling a spiritual call, entered the ministry. In 1861 he joined the Georgia Conference of the Methodist Episcopal Church, South, and served as pastor of a succession of churches. In 1861 he married Emily Gibson. After Emily's death, he married Mary Hunter in 1874. He had a total of five children.

In 1869 Hopkins was called to the chair of natural science at Emory, his alma mater, and was also assigned to the pastorate of the Methodist church in Oxford, Georgia. In 1875 he left Emory to serve as professor of physics at Southern University in Greensboro, Alabama, but he returned to the Emory faculty in 1877, serving first as professor of Latin and then, beginning in 1882, as professor of English.

Hopkins had an avocational interest in wood- and machine-shop work, and he built a small shop in Oxford. Students' desires to share his "recreation" coupled with his own interest in industrial education led Hopkins to advocate a technological department at Emory. His address to alumni in 1883 was a thoughtful summary of the current state of technical education—focusing on the shop system involving active exploration of skills then in vogue at Worcester Free Institute in Massachusetts and the Manual Training School of Washington University in St. Louis—followed by a plea for such a program at Emory. Hands-on experience with machinery, he argued, offered both the first level of training required by modern manufacturing and a healthy convergence of classical studies and practical pursuits.

In 1884, despite objections from some trustees and professors that he was wasting the school's money to build a "blacksmith's shop," Hopkins won approval to establish a school of toolcraft and design. Later in 1884 he became the ninth president of Emory and was thus in a position to carry out his plan. Although in his 1883 speech he had warned that the practice of selling student-made products to support the enterprise "would invite failure at the outset," when he launched the new technological program he proclaimed that it would pay for itself through the sale of products made by students in the shop. Unfortunately, his original assessment proved true. By 1887 the entire college was in financial difficulty, and Hopkins was looking for a position elsewhere.

Hopkins's advocacy of technical education appealed to business and educational leaders in Georgia, and when the state chartered a school of technology, he was widely mentioned as a possible president. The trustees first turned their attention to selecting a site (Atlanta) and a model for the curriculum (Worcester) and finally turned to the selection of a president and faculty. In April 1888 Hopkins was elected president of the new Georgia School of Technology and was appointed to the chair in physics.

Although it may seem unlikely for the founding president of Georgia Tech to have come from the ranks of the clergy, Hopkins had already demonstrated his support for the school's educational philosophy of hands-on exploration. The board of trustees hired Worcester's superintendent of shops, Milton P. Higgins, to come to Atlanta and establish a curriculum. In 1888–1889 Higgins and Hopkins worked together to put the new program in operation. Georgia Tech students in those years spent their mornings in the classrooms and their afternoons in the shops, where they worked under the supervision of Higgins and his staff of foremen.

President Hopkins was remembered by the first chemistry professor as a "dignified and kindly man of broad sympathy and understanding." He presided over the new school and its faculty with firmness but without creating resentment. He also conducted chapel services for the students and faculty. He faced the unenviable task of persuading the legislature, which had barely passed the bill creating the school, to increase its meager funding during an era of economic distress. In addition, he presided over a curriculum that was being overtaken by changes in the field of engineering.

At Georgia Tech, as at Emory, students turned out products of high quality in the shops, but at both institutions, unlike at Worcester, the shop did not pay for itself or help finance the school. Furthermore, rapid advances in science-based engineering education were rendering the shop-based curriculum obsolete. By 1895 Hopkins faced growing opposition to the original curriculum within his own faculty, and he had failed repeatedly to win increases for the school's state appropriation.

In May 1895 Hopkins offered his resignation, only to withdraw it two months later. During that year he helped alter the original curriculum to put greater emphasis on laboratory and classroom work, but the legislature still refused to increase the appropriation. Amid continuing disagreements over the school's finances, Hopkins again tendered his resignation in January 1896, and the trustees immediately accepted it. Hopkins explained that he had been appointed to the pastorate of the First Methodist Church in Atlanta and that he could not do justice to both positions.

After leaving Georgia Tech, Hopkins served Methodist churches in Atlanta, St. Louis, Chattanooga, and elsewhere before retiring in 1908. He died in Atlanta and was buried near the workshop he had built two decades before. His tombstone bears this inscription: "The Father of Technological Training in the South."

• While no central collection of Hopkins's papers exists, manuscript material from and about him is in the James Osgood Andrew Clark Papers and the Warren Candler Papers, Special Collections, Woodruff Library, Emory University; and in the records of the Georgia School of Technology (including faculty minutes) for 1888–1896, Archives Department, Price Gilbert Library, Georgia Institute of Technology. Reminiscences about Hopkins's presidency of Georgia Tech as well as an informal talk by him about his days at Emory and Georgia Tech are published in *Commencement and Quarter-Centennial Celebration of the Georgia School of Technology* (1913). Statements of Hopkins's educational philosophy are in Isaac Stiles Hopkins, *Industrial Education: A Statement and a Plea* (1883), and James E. Brittain and Robert C. McMath, Jr., *A Documentary History of Georgia Tech's Beginnings* (1977). The histories of the two institutions of higher learning that he served as president contain accounts of his administrations, Henry Morton Bullock, *A History of Emory University* (1936), and McMath et al., *Engineering the New South: Georgia Tech, 1885–1985* (1985).

ROBERT MCMATH

HOPKINS, John Henry (30 Jan. 1792–9 Jan. 1868), Protestant Episcopal bishop and controversialist, was born in Dublin, Ireland, the son of Thomas Hopkins, a bookkeeper, and Elizabeth Fitzakerly, a teacher. He came to America with his parents in 1800 and with them resided in different locations in western New Jersey and eastern Pennsylvania. Hopkins's parents eventually separated, and his mother was involved in a number of private schools to support her son. In these and other private schools Hopkins was educated. Always a polymath, he showed an early interest in art and contributed illustrations for Alexander Wilson's *American Ornithology* (1808). Art continued to be a lifelong interest, and in addition to painting and composing music in 1836 he wrote *Essay on Gothic Architecture*, the first American book on the subject. He had previously designed and had built Trinity Episcopal Church, Pittsburgh (1825), one of the early Gothic-style churches in America.

In 1816 he married Melusina Müller, and they had thirteen children. After a failed attempt at iron manufacturing, he moved to Pittsburgh where he studied law and, in a short time, became a very successful lawyer. In 1823, while still a layman, he was elected rector of Trinity Episcopal Church, Pittsburgh. Accepting the call, he abandoned his legal practice and was ordained as a deacon in 1823 and as a priest in 1824. After a successful ministry in western Pennsylvania, he was called as assistant minister of Trinity Church, Boston, and was involved in a failed attempt to found a theological school in Cambridge. In 1832 Hopkins was elected first bishop of the diocese of Vermont. He served in this office until his death and from 1865 to 1868 was also presiding bishop of the entire Episcopal church.

His episcopate, though hampered by a number of financial setbacks, saw the Episcopal church in Vermont more than double in size due to his efforts. In addition to his pastoral responsibilities, Hopkins was a prolific writer of over fifty books and pamphlets and was involved in a great variety of controversies. For Hopkins, religious truth could only be derived from scripture as interpreted through the church of the early centuries; all else was error. Thus, in *The Primitive Church* (1835), he criticized popular aspects of Protestant evangelicalism (such as revivalism and temperance reform), while in *The Church of Rome* (1837) and in a tract controversy with the Roman Catholic Francis P. Kenrick, he attacked modern Roman Catholicism

as a departure from the original faith of the early church. His suspicion of any intellectual movement that smacked of "innovation" made him critical of the Oxford Movement's attempt to restore catholic theology to Anglicanism, since this seemed to entail a moving away from the faith of the early church, and during the 1840s he was also a leading opponent of the movement.

During the 1850s Hopkins was increasingly drawn into the debate over slavery. His basic position, set forth in *Slavery: Its Religious Sanction, Its Political Dangers, and the Best Mode of Doing It Away* (1851), was that of gradual abolition and colonization, but his ire was chiefly directed against the abolitionists, who he believed transformed a political question into a religious question by substituting nineteenth-century moralism for traditional Christianity. The impending national crisis of secession led him to publish his most controversial work, *The Bible View of Slavery* (1861), which was even more sharply critical of the abolitionist argument that slavery was antiscriptural and sinful. This work was republished in 1863 at the behest of a group of Pennsylvania Episcopalians. It became an issue in the 1864 gubernatorial election and was publicly condemned by Alonzo Potter, Episcopal bishop of Pennsylvania, and 162 clergy members. During the war Hopkins unsuccessfully attempted (for example, at the General Convention of 1862) to moderate northern Episcopal support for the war effort. Through his sympathy for the position of southern Episcopalians, however, he was successful in helping bring about a reunion of northern and southern Episcopalians after the war.

In 1866 Hopkins published *The Law of Ritualism*, which defended the use of more elaborate catholic rituals and ceremonies in the church, claiming that these practices did not violate the doctrinal teachings of the church. This too provoked great controversy. He died in Rock Point, Vermont.

• Major works by Hopkins not mentioned in the text include *Christianity Vindicated* (1833); *The Primitive Creed* (1834); *Novelties Which Disturb Our Peace* (1844); *Sixteen Lectures on the . . . British Reformation* (1844); *The History of the Confessional* (1850); *The American Citizen* (1857); *A Scriptural, Ecclesiastical, and Historical View of Slavery* (1864); and *A Candid Examination of the Question Whether the Pope of Rome Is the Great Antichrist of Scripture* (1868). Letters from Hopkins can be found in the Bishops Collection of the General Theological Seminary library in New York. He wrote an informal *Autobiography in Verse* (1866). The best account of his life is still John Henry Hopkins, Jr., *The Life of the late Right Reverend John Henry Hopkins, First Bishop of Vermont and Seventh Presiding Bishop . . . by One of His Sons* (1873). His religious ideas are discussed in R. B. Mullin, *Episcopal Vision/American Reality: High Church Theology and Social Thought in Evangelical America* (1986).

ROBERT BRUCE MULLIN

HOPKINS, Johns (19 May 1795–24 Dec. 1873), merchant and financier, was born on a tobacco plantation in Anne Arundel County (south of Baltimore), Maryland, the son of Samuel Hopkins and Hannah Janney, farmers. The plantation was prosperous through Johns's early years, and the family lived well. In 1807, following the direction of the Society of Friends (Quakers), Samuel freed the family's slaves. As a result, Johns, the second of eleven children, had to leave school to help maintain the farm. Although Johns never received any further formal schooling, he had a hunger for knowledge and worked to educate himself in his spare moments. His distinctive and often misspelled first name came from his great-great-grandfather Richard Johns.

When Hopkins was seventeen, his uncle Gerard Hopkins asked the young man to come to Baltimore and learn the trade of a merchant in his store. Hopkins's mother urged him to accept the offer with the prophetic statement, "Thee has business ability." Within two years, Hopkins proved his mother correct. His uncle left Hopkins in charge of the store for several months while he traveled to Ohio, and Hopkins not only maintained the business but increased its profits significantly.

While living in his uncle's house, Hopkins fell in love with his cousin Elizabeth Hopkins. Although he proposed marriage and she accepted, Gerard opposed the union, citing the Society of Friends' disapproval of the marriage of first cousins. Unable to overcome this opposition, Johns and Elizabeth vowed to marry no one else, and neither ever did marry.

By 1819 Hopkins was ready to strike out on his own. His decision was influenced by a disagreement with his uncle over the ethics of accepting whiskey instead of cash in payment for goods. Gerard opposed this, declaring that he would not "sell souls into perdition." The parting was amicable, however, as Gerard backed his nephew's fledgling enterprise with $10,000.

Hopkins's first business partner was a Quaker named Benjamin Moore. Their wholesale company dissolved after three years, with Moore commenting, "Johns is the only man I know who wants to make money more than I do." Soon after, Hopkins went into business with three of his brothers, forming a wholesale house known as Hopkins Brothers around 1820. Initially, most of their business was in Maryland, Virginia, and North Carolina, but the growing population west of the Appalachians could not be ignored. Using Conestoga wagons, goods were shipped across the mountains, with payment in the form of barrels of whiskey. This whiskey then was bottled and sold under the name Hopkins' Best.

Despite Hopkins's disagreement with the Quakers over their views on marriage, he remained a devoted member of his church. In response to Hopkins's selling whiskey, however, he was expelled briefly from the Society of Friends. While expressing no regret at the time (he was soon reinstated), in his later years he said that he should not have sold liquor.

In 1838 Hopkins purchased a mansion, "Clifton," then located outside the city boundaries, where he lived during the summer months. On the 500-acre grounds he laid out gardens, giving explicit instructions for their maintenance to his gardener and checking progress on his daily walks. He expanded the house, adding an observation tower from which he could observe, through a telescope, ships entering Baltimore's harbor.

While spending little on his own physical comforts, Hopkins entertained lavishly at Clifton, with fine food and champagne always at hand. Disliking pretenses of superiority, he once rebuked a nephew who covered his wine glass as a servant was about to fill it. "Take thy hand off thy glass, Joe. Let the wine stand if thee does not want it, but don't publish thy temperance resolves."

At the age of fifty, after the early deaths of his three younger brothers, Hopkins retired from his family business a wealthy man. He turned from the wholesale merchandise business to that of venture capitalist, using his skills to become a leading financier of his time. An excellent judge of character, Hopkins saw potential in individuals and lent money at generous interest rates, even after they had been turned down by banks. He was seldom disappointed and enjoyed watching young entrepreneurs repay their loans and vindicate his judgment.

Hopkins understood that the prosperity of Baltimore was dependent on transportation, through its Chesapeake Bay port as well as the emerging railroads. He began buying acres of decaying warehouses along the waterfront, erecting new warehouses and office buildings and expanding the port area to ease the movement of goods from ship to shore. Replacing the Conestoga wagons, railroads linked the East Coast to cities, farms, and industries to the west, with trains transporting goods at less cost and in greater volume than before. Many conservative investors refused to back railroads in the 1840s, but Hopkins, perhaps because of his experience with horse-drawn wagons, was quick to recognize their potential. He became the largest stockholder in the Baltimore and Ohio (B&O) Railroad and was named a director in 1847. He became chairman of the finance committee in 1855 and held this position until his death. Twice, in 1857 and 1873, he pledged his private fortune to keep the railroad operating during financial panics.

During the Civil War, Hopkins was a staunch Unionist. Along with B&O president John Work Garrett, he placed the railroad at the disposal of the U.S. government. Despite Confederate sabotage attempts, the railroad remained a valuable asset to the North, transporting troops and supplies westward.

While generous with deserving friends and family, who could count on him for financial backing if he was convinced of their ability to use the money wisely, Hopkins was not known as a philanthropist until late in his life. George Peabody, a contemporary already known for his benefactions, may have convinced Hopkins to bestow his wealth for the benefit of the larger community. With no wife or direct descendants to provide for, he was free to dispose of his wealth. His own lack of formal schooling may have influenced his decision to found a university, and his recognition of the poor state of medical care in Baltimore likely prompted him to found a hospital. Whatever his reasons, in 1867 he incorporated The Johns Hopkins University and The Johns Hopkins Hospital and named trustees for each corporation.

Hopkins left specific instructions regarding the location, mission, and operation of the hospital, and he set aside real estate to ensure that it would be located within the city. He admonished hospital administrators to serve the public without regard to race or financial status. It was his intent that the medical school, which would be part of the university, should cooperate closely with the hospital in all matters concerning medical training. The hospital was thus to be a "teaching hospital," where medical students could learn by observing and questioning practicing physicians as well as by receiving rigorous classroom and laboratory instruction.

In contrast, Hopkins left no instructions regarding the establishment of a university. None of the trustees was an educator, so they were left to decide for themselves what should constitute a university. Through their diligent efforts, in consultation with presidents of established universities, they decided that The Johns Hopkins University would follow the German example of teaching students by requiring that they perform original research and then evaluating the fruits of their research.

In December 1873 Hopkins contracted a cold that developed into pneumonia after he insisted on walking to his office without an overcoat on a bitterly cold day. This gave rise to a popular story that he was too penurious to buy himself a proper coat. Reporting his death in Baltimore, the *Baltimore Sun* added this tribute: "This city owes no small share of its prosperity to his enlightened and energetic efforts." Of his $8 million fortune, $7 million was divided equally between the university and the hospital, with the remainder distributed among family members and servants.

Hopkins was a bundle of contradictions throughout his life. He belonged to a religious sect that preached abstinence from alcohol, yet he sold whiskey under his own name. He received little formal education, yet he became an astute businessman and loved fine literature. He owned several houses and entertained lavishly, yet he was reluctant to replace his own threadbare clothes or furnishings. He had no children of his own, yet he enjoyed the frequent visits of his nieces and nephews. He shunned publicity during his lifetime, yet his name is known worldwide from the hospital and university he founded.

In all of his dealings, Hopkins followed his own conscience and took considerable risk when the objective was worthy. To all, his word was his bond, and his understanding of complex business matters was recognized by associates and competitors alike. Hopkins is remembered as an astute businessman who gave his fortune back to the community.

• Hopkins left little in the way of personal papers. A very small collection is in the Milton S. Eisenhower Library at The Johns Hopkins University, consisting of a few letters, some published tributes, and the Hopkins family Bible. A book-length biography is Helen Hopkins Thom, *Johns Hopkins: A Silhouette* (1929). Written by a great-niece, the book is comprised of anecdotes collected by the author from her frequent childhood visits with Hopkins. John C. French, *A History of the University Founded by Johns Hopkins* (1946), contains a useful biographical sketch on pp. 10–17. The best assessment is Kathryn A. Jacob, "Mr. Johns Hopkins," *Johns Hopkins Magazine* 25 (Jan. 1974): 12–17. Other sources include Gerry O. Myers, "The Legacy of Johns Hopkins," *Maryland Magazine* 15 (Spring 1983): 26–29; and Caroline Jones Franz, "Johns Hopkins," *American Heritage* 27 (Feb. 1976): 31–33, 98–101. Franz focuses primarily on the development of The Johns Hopkins Hospital. Franklin Parker, "Influences on the Founder of The Johns Hopkins University and The Johns Hopkins Hospital," *Bulletin of the History of Medicine* 34 (Mar.–Apr. 1960): 148–53, discusses Peabody's influence in persuading Hopkins to found his institutions. A lengthy obituary is on the front page of the *Baltimore Sun*, 25 Dec. 1873.

JAMES STIMPERT

HOPKINS, Juliet Ann Opie (7 May 1818–9 Mar. 1890), Civil War nurse and hospital administrator, was born on a plantation, "Woodburn," in Jefferson County, Virginia, the daughter of Hierome Lindsay Opie, a planter and U.S. senator, and Margaret Muse. English tutors prepared her for Miss Ritchie's private school in Richmond. She returned home at age sixteen, after her mother's death, to manage her father's vast estate, including two thousand slaves.

In 1837 she married U.S. Navy lieutenant Alexander George Gordon; she was widowed in 1849. Five years later she married Arthur Francis Hopkins, a wealthy planter, lawyer, and former senator and chief justice of the Alabama Supreme Court. The Hopkinses lived in Mobile, Alabama, where he was president of the Mobile and Ohio Railroad and she enjoyed a comfortable life revolving around civic and social concerns. She was childless but considered an adopted niece, also named Juliet Opie, to be her daughter.

After Alabama seceded on 11 January 1861 and war seemed imminent, Hopkins and her husband, like other wealthy southerners seeking leadership, security, and power, offered their services to the state's Confederate government to help organize, finance, and manage hospitals for Alabama soldiers in Virginia. At that time, no medical service had been organized, and private groups arranged for soldiers' care. Initially, southerners believed the war would quickly end and did not plan for long-term medical facilities and personnel.

Only a decade before, Florence Nightingale had been a pioneer in developing military nursing during the Crimean War. By the Civil War, nursing was still not professionalized; nuns were the first Civil War nurses because few women, northern or southern, had been trained in nursing techniques. Nursing was considered an improper task for most white southern women, and any woman's pursuit of medical or nursing education was discouraged and even vilified. Nonetheless, before the war ended many women pursued nursing duties not only for duty, patriotism, and service, but also as an accessible means to achieve some personal autonomy.

The historians Drew Gilpin Faust, Catherine Clinton, and Anne Firor Scott have analyzed how Civil War nursing promoted early feminist thought and work among middle- and upper-class women by enabling them to leave their private domestic spheres and make personal contributions by pursuing public service such as nursing or relief fundraising. Although the war in some ways stopped antebellum feminist activity, it also offered new opportunities for women; traditional attitudes were altered during the political crisis, and women workers were considered necessary because of labor shortages. Nursing was suddenly deemed patriotic and respectable, and southern women eagerly assisted the military effort both to avoid social ostracism and to promote regional success.

Acting primarily as an administrator, Hopkins lacked any nursing training or experience. Already enjoying high social status and financial security, she was more interested in aiding the Confederacy toward victory and assuring perpetuation of a southern culture comfortable to her than in achieving personal power or independence from her husband—although her work did ensure that she received individual attention and recognition apart from being a judge's wife.

The first financial support from Alabama for Virginia hospitals came during the summer of 1861. Hopkins arrived in Richmond before the battle of Bull Run and was in charge of the Alabama section of the Chimborazo Hospital. In November 1861 the state legislature provided funds for a medical depot and designated Judge Hopkins as state hospital agent; although he held this title, he did not work in the hospitals, and his wife acted as superintendent of hospitals, managing both field and base hospitals without salary. Her duties included staffing and supplying the medical centers and maintaining correspondence with the Alabama government, responding to telegrams, letters, and orders, and traveling to Montgomery when necessary. She resourcefully provided good health care despite the deprivations caused by war.

During the first year of the war in 1861, Hopkins founded, funded, and administered three facilities in Richmond known as the First, Second, and Third Alabama hospitals. Devoted to the Confederate cause, Hopkins sold property in Alabama, Virginia, and New York, donating at least $200,000 (some sources estimate she gave half a million dollars) to the Confederacy. Her wealth assured continuation of her lofty administrative position, from which she encouraged her social peers also to contribute generously. The Alabama hospitals were privately funded by family, friends, and citizens. According to James E. Saunders (1899), Hopkins "by her intelligence, her sympathizing, and personal attention to the sick and wounded, gained an enviable reputation," inspiring Alabamians to give money. With increased private and state support, she founded field hospitals at Bristow Station, Monterey, Culpepper Court House, and Yorktown, near troop encampments.

In addition to being a benefactor and administrator, Hopkins aided medical professionals and inexperienced volunteers. Third Alabama Hospital matron Fannie Beers (1889) noted, "If she found any duty neglected by nurse or surgeon or hospital steward, her reprimand was certain and very severe." Hopkins was considered an efficient and devoted hospital matron. Contemporaries called her work patriotic and unselfish. Beers recounted how Hopkins energetically "kept up a voluminous correspondence, made in person every purchase for her charges, received and accounted for hundreds of boxes send from Alabama . . . and visited the wards of the hospitals every day."

Hopkins wrote letters for patients, procured reading materials, and maintained a death list, among other activities. She clipped and mailed deceased soldiers' hair to send to next of kin in Alabama. Such personal attention impressed grateful soldiers in the Fourth Alabama Regiment, who declared that her name was "upon every tongue and prayers . . . daily offered for the friend and benefactor of the sick and wounded solders." Congressman Jabez L. M. Curry admired Hopkins's "sleepless diligence," "faithful zeal," and "tender solicitude."

Hopkins was wounded twice in her hip at the Battle of Seven Pines on 31 May 1862 while helping to remove casualties from the battlefield. After surgery removing bone from her left leg, she returned to her work. She suffered a limp for the rest of her life.

In 1862 the Confederate Congress assumed jurisdiction over the state hospitals in Virginia. They were liquidated and patients transferred to Winder and Chimborazo hospitals in Richmond by 1863. Hopkins, who had almost exhausted her fortune, returned to Alabama, where she briefly directed the hospital at Camp Watts in Notasulga in 1864. By January 1865 she was overseeing a Montgomery hospital and was well known and respected throughout the state. The state legislature passed a vote of thanks, honoring her "untiring and self-sacrificing" service, and her image was printed on Alabama Confederate currency.

In April 1865 Hopkins and her husband fled to Newnan, Georgia, to escape raiding federal forces. After General Robert E. Lee surrendered, the Hopkinses returned to their Mobile home, now emptied of valuables, where Arthur Hopkins died within the year. The Mobile Rifles gave Juliet Hopkins a silver service in gratitude, and Lee praised her, declaring that she had "done more for the South than all the women of the Confederacy."

Soon after Judge Hopkins's death, Juliet Hopkins moved to New York City, where her second husband had owned property. She often visited Washington, D.C., where her adopted niece, Juliet Opie, and son-in-law, General Romeyn Ayres, lived. Little is known about the last twenty-five years of her life, although she probably participated in social and charitable activities considered appropriate for women of her status.

Hopkins died in Washington, D.C., and was buried in Arlington National Cemetery with full military honors. General Joseph E. Johnston and other prominent Confederate leaders attended her funeral. Johnston wrote to Juliet Opie Ayres, stating that Hopkins's hospital service "was more useful to my army than a new brigade." He called her "the Angel of the South," and other contemporaries have dubbed her the "Florence Nightingale of the South," a title granted to several other Civil War nurses.

• Juliet Opie Hopkins's papers are held by the Alabama Department of Archives and History and the Alabama Civil War Centennial Commission Collection at the University of Alabama Library. H. E. Sterkx's books *Partners in Rebellion: Alabama Women in the Civil War* (1970) and *Some Notable Alabama Women during the Civil War* (1962), and Lucille Griffith, "Mrs. Juliet Opie Hopkins and Alabama Military Hospitals," *Alabama Review* 6 (Apr. 1953): 99–120, provide biographical information. Valuable secondary sources include H. H. Cunningham, *Doctors in Gray: The Confederate Medical Service* (1958); Catherine Clinton, *The Other Civil War: American Women in the Nineteenth Century* (1984); Drew Gilpin Faust, *Mothers of Invention: Women of the Slaveholding South in the American Civil War* (1996); and Anne Firor Scott, *The Southern Lady: From Pedestal to Politics, 1830–1930* (1970). Primary accounts include Fannie A. Beers, *Memories: A Record of Personal Experience and Adventure during Four Years of War* (1889); Thomas Cooper DeLeon, *Belles, Beaux, and Brains of the 60's* (1909); and James E. Saunders, *Early Settlers of Alabama* (1899).

ELIZABETH D. SCHAFER

HOPKINS, Lemuel (19 June 1750–14 Apr. 1801), physician and poet, was born in Waterbury, Connecticut, the son of Stephen Hopkins and Dorothy Talmadge, prosperous farmers. Hopkins studied medicine, first with Jared Potter of Wallingford, then with Dr. Seth Bird of Litchfield. His own Litchfield practice, begun in 1776, was interrupted by his brief service with the American army during the revolutionary war. In 1784 he received an honorary master of arts degree from Yale and moved to Hartford, where he maintained his medical practice until his death there. He never married and had no children.

Hopkins's eminence as a physician was acknowledged by his contemporaries. He was a founder of the Connecticut Medical Society in 1792 and was enrolled as an honorary member of the Massachusetts Medical Society. He was admired and frequently consulted as a diagnostician. Particularly devoted to the study of chronic diseases, he composed treatises on colds and consumption; his expertise in the treatment of tuberculosis has been compared to that of Benjamin Rush. Ironically, however, Hopkins's death by pneumonia may have been hastened by the bleeding, reduced diet, and "repeated doses of neutral salts" with which he treated himself.

Hopkins occupies a middle position in the constellation of writers known as the "Connecticut Wits" (or "Hartford Wits"), a shifting association of Connecticut lawyers, educators, and doctors who published a number of influential satires (1775–1815) generally defending the American Revolution but urging caution against what they saw as democratic excesses. Hopkins's literary ambitions were lower than those of the major Wits (Joel Barlow, Timothy Dwight, David Humphreys, and John Trumbull), but his contributions exceeded in importance those of the minor Wits (Richard Alsop, Mason Fitch Cogswell, Theodore Dwight, and Elihu Hubbard Smith). He published no major work under his own name but participated in the major collaborative satires that gave the Wits their identity. Although specific attributions have proven difficult, Hopkins has been credited as the prime mover behind the first and most important of these collaborations, the mock-epic usually called *The Anarchiad*, published in the *New-Haven Gazette, and the Connecticut Magazine* in twelve installments, October 1786–September 1787, and frequently reprinted in other journals; Barlow, Humphreys, and Trumbull were the principal collaborators. Hopkins certainly contributed to another major collaborative satire, *The Echo* and its related poems (1791–1805). He has been given sole credit for *Echo XVIII* (separately published as *The Democratiad* in 1795), *The Guillotina* (1796), and a major part in *The Political Green-House for the Year 1798* (1799, with Alsop and Dwight).

James Thacher's 1828 biography reports that although Hopkins once admired "Voltaire, Rousseau, Volney, and D'Alembert, and other infidel philosophers," he returned to the Bible and dedicated his muse to the conservative service of Christianity and federalism. *The Anarchiad*, the most influential literary contribution to the constitutional debate, appeared in newspapers as the Wits' response to such signs of postrevolutionary social disorder as Shays's Rebellion and the Rhode Island paper money crisis. Hopkins and his collaborators attacked democratic politicians (especially local Antifederalists such as Judge William Williams) and urged the establishment of a stronger central government. Hopkins was probably most responsible for the satire's caustic lampoons of specific individuals such as the Connecticut political leaders Judge William Williams ("William Wimble") and Joseph Hopkins ("Copper"). He made similar contributions to the less urgent satire, *The Echo*. Three interesting short poems are attributed to Hopkins: "Epitaph on a Patient Killed by a Cancer Quack" (1785), a short fable attacking medical charlatans; "On General Ethan Allen" (1786), a denunciation of the deistic arguments in Ethan Allen's *Reason the Only Oracle of Man* (1784); and "The Hypocrite's Hope" (1793), a warning against faith unsupported by good works.

Hopkins's belligerent directness distinguishes his work from that of the other Wits. His personal appearance was evidently remarkable: "ugly and uncouth" (Thacher, p. 301); "tall, lean, stooping, and long-limbed, with large features and light eyes . . . added to a great eccentricity of manner, rendered him at first sight a very striking spectacle" (Kettell, p. 273). Anecdotes relating to his medical practice also suggest his willful eccentricity: he occasionally completed his house calls—diagnosis and treatment—without uttering a word. Hopkins was intolerant of folly and knavery, whether practiced by medical quacks or political democrats, and he exercised his sharp wit to expose them.

• Hopkins's poetry appears in Vernon Louis Parrington, ed., *The Connecticut Wits* (1926); David Humphreys et al., *The Anarchiad*, a facsimile of the Luther G. Riggs edition of 1861, with an introduction by W. K. Bottorff (1967); and Benjamin Franklin V, ed., *The Poetry of the Minor Connecticut Wits* (1970). Secondary sources are reviewed in Franklin's "The Published Commentary on the Minor Connecticut Wits," *Resources for American Literary Study* 8 (1978): 157–67. See also James Thacher, *American Medical Biography* (1828; repr. 1967), pp. 298–304; Samuel Kettell, *Specimens of American Poetry*, vol. 1 (1829), pp. 272–74; W. R. Steiner, "Dr. Lemuel Hopkins," *Johns Hopkins Hospital Bulletin* 21 (1910): 16–27; Leon Howard, *The Connecticut Wits* (1943); and J. K. Van Dover, "The Design of Anarchy: *The Anarchiad*, 1786–87," *Early American Literature* 25 (1990): 237–47.

J. K. VAN DOVER

HOPKINS, Lightnin' (15 Mar. 1912–30 Jan. 1982), blues singer and guitarist, was born Samuel Hopkins in Centerville, Texas, the son of Abe H. Hopkins, a musician, and Frances Sims. His father died when Hopkins was an infant, leaving the family to survive in the stark farmlands of the East Texas "Piney Woods." Hopkins's sister and four brothers were all musicians. He learned to play the organ at church at his mother's urging, but he was drawn to the guitar through the playing of his older brother John Henry. He was forbidden to touch John Henry's guitar, however, so he built his own out of a plank of wood, a cigar box, and chicken wire. He continually pestered John Henry to allow him to play the real guitar and often borrowed it on the sly. After discovering Hopkins skillfully playing the instrument, an impressed John Henry gave it to him. The eight-year-old quit school and took to the road, working odd jobs and playing music wherever he could. In the summer of 1920 he traveled to Buffalo, Texas, and attended a performance by blues legend Blind Lemon Jefferson at a church picnic. Jefferson allowed the green but undaunted Hopkins to accompany him on guitar during his set, which included "I Walk from Dallas" and "You Ain't Got No Mama Now (Black Snake Moan)."

Hopkins's greatest vocal influence was his cousin Alger "Texas" Alexander, a singer and harmonica player with whom he often performed in the streets and bars of Houston and other Texas towns. During a long, arduous itinerancy from the 1920s to the early 1940s, Hopkins traveled throughout the South, accumulating a large repertoire of traditional and original blues songs while also earning money through farm labor and gambling. As he later described, he spent time in prison, as well: "One time I had to cut a man that kept fooling with me, and that put me in the county farm up at Houston County. Several times I had them chains around my legs for stuff I'd got into" (McCormack, p. 315).

Hopkins's original music sprang from his experiences of survival as a black man in a chronically poor region. He was the embodiment of the country blues, the music of hard labor and raw hands, of plaintive voices rising from field workers singing to ease the burn of the sun. The everyday tragedies of a downtrodden life—empty pockets, straying women, fraternal violence, death—were the subjects of his songs, and his deep, unpolished singing voice perfectly suited their evocation.

A brilliant storyteller, Hopkins became known for the nuances he added to a song each time he sang it. His dramatic, often extemporized delivery recalled the African "good talkers" who rambled West African towns, fusing autobiography, folk tale, and social commentary for rapt audiences. The arpeggio wail of his acoustic guitar between verses enhanced the emotional power of his music; his playing style, as described by music writer Wolfgang Saxon, was an alternation of "ominous single-note runs on the high strings with a hard-driving bass in irregular rhythms that matched his spontaneous, conversational lyrics" (*New York Times*, 1 Feb. 1982).

Hopkins was called into the army during World War II, but the night before he was scheduled to report he was stabbed by a disgruntled gambling partner. After recovering, he returned to occasional farm work and his music, once again performing with Alexander in Houston. In 1942 he married Antoinette Charles, who is believed to have been his third wife. He had four children, but some or all of these may have been from his previous marriages.

In 1946 Hopkins was discovered by a talent scout on Houston's Dowling Street. The woman had been sent in search of an "authentic" country-blues musician by Aladdin Records as part of an ongoing trend of transporting Texas artists to Los Angeles in the hope of creating a new, popular blues form "designed by sound engineers for the thump and screech of a juke box" (McCormack, p. 316). Hopkins was at the time playing with Wilson "Thunder" Smith, a barrelhouse pianist; the two, along with pianist Amos Milburn, were taken to Hollywood to record at the RKO studios. Hopkins's free spirit and his penchant for altering his songs, however, did not suit the hit-making aspirations of Aladdin's producers. He made a handful of recordings and accepted the nickname "Lightnin'"—placed on him for his association with Thunder Smith as well as for the often frantic speed of his guitar playing—but he was unhappy in Hollywood and unwilling to change for the sake of wider success. He returned to Houston in 1947 and resumed his life in its familiar black wards.

Bill Quinn of Houston-based Gold Star Records approached Hopkins soon after the musician returned from California, and he subsequently recorded several singles for the label. The classic "Short-Haired Woman" (written after Hopkins saw a woman stumble and lose her wig on a bus) backed by "Big Mama Jump"

(1947) sold more than 40,000 copies. Later that year came "Baby Please Don't Go," which reached sales of 80,000 copies, and "Tim Moore's Farm," a protest song based on Hopkins's experience working for a brutal white farmer. These early efforts exemplify his emotive guitar playing and the boogie-woogie style of many of his songs.

In 1949 Gold Star dropped Hopkins after he made some recordings for another label while in New York City. (Hopkins was not trustful of contracts; after a record company made money by releasing versions of his songs without his knowledge, he insisted on being paid in cash each time he recorded.) Throughout the 1950s he issued hundreds of records, taping as many as three albums in a week. Among his best works during this period are "Coffee Blues" (1950, Jax); "Policy Game" (1953, Decca); "Lonesome in Your Heart" (1954, Herald); and "Penitentiary Blues"/"Bad Luck and Trouble" (1959, FW). He recorded on many labels, including Time, RPM, Ace, Kent, Mercury, TNT, and Harlem. There was surprisingly little repetition within this musical output because of Hopkins's endless improvisations. At times his flowing style was also altered by producers who attempted to impose structure on his songs by adding bass and drums.

While Hopkins's records often sold well, his lifestyle was not conducive to holding onto money, and he constantly found himself in financial need. In 1959 music researcher Sam Charters "rediscovered" Hopkins and introduced him to a national audience through the release of *The Roots of Lightnin' Hopkins* on Folkways Records. Hopkins immediately became a presence on the folk-music circuit, playing at the 1959 University of California Folk Festival in Berkeley and at Carnegie Hall and the Village Gate in New York City the following year. Other aficionados of the blues recorded Hopkins, including Chris Strachwitz, whose Arhoolie Records helped make classic blues performers such as Hopkins popular among white college students. (On Arhoolie, Hopkins recorded "California Showers" in 1961.) He recorded with his guitar-playing brothers John Henry and Joel, as well as with Brownie McGhee, Big Joe Williams, and Sonny Terry, on *Wimmin from Coast to Coast* (1960, World Pacific). He appeared on radio and television programs and was featured in two short Les Blank films, *The Sun's Gonna Shine* (1967) and *The Blues According to Lightnin' Hopkins* (1968).

Throughout the 1960s, Hopkins recorded and toured, although he remained apprehensive toward new situations and preferred not to be away from Houston for long periods. In 1970 he suffered a neck injury in an auto accident that temporarily limited his travels. He eventually resumed his wide-ranging performances, however, which included sets at jazz festivals in Germany and the Netherlands in 1977 and a return to Carnegie Hall in 1979. Just months after undergoing surgery for cancer of the esophagus, he made his last public appearance at the nightclub Tramps in New York City. He died in Houston.

Hopkins is remembered for his rich contribution to the country-blues idiom. His unique lyrical style made him hard to imitate, a fact that may have lessened his influence on rock-and-roll musicians when compared to that of bluesmen such as Muddy Waters and John Lee Hooker. But the immense volume of his work—no blues artist was recorded more in his era—and the honesty of his poetic vision have afforded generations of listeners a window into the vibrant, often tragic world of the twentieth-century rural South.

• A few of the many compilations of Hopkins's songs released on compact disc are *The Complete Prestige/Bluesville Recordings* (1992), *The Complete Aladdin Recordings* (1992), *It's a Sin to Be Rich* (1993, Verve), and *Coffee House Blues* (1993, Charly Blues Master Works). An essay exploring Hopkins's role as a "modern communal bard" is Mack McCormack, "Lightnin' Hopkins: Blues," in *Jazz Panorama*, ed. Martin T. Williams. See also Sam Charters, *The Country Blues* (1959), and Kurt Loder, "Lightnin' Hopkins, 1912–1982: A Classic Blues Life," *Rolling Stone*, 18 Mar. 1982, pp. 17–18. An obituary is in the *New York Times*, 1 Feb. 1982.

GRAHAM RUSSELL HODGES
JAY MAZZOCCHI

HOPKINS, Mark (4 Feb. 1802–17 June 1887), moral philosopher and president of Williams College, was born in Stockbridge, Massachusetts, the son of Archibald Hopkins and Mary Curtis, farmers. He studied at a number of academies and taught school before enrolling in 1821 at Williams College, from which he graduated in 1824. The following six years he taught school, served as tutor at Williams, and studied at Berkshire Medical College in Pittsfield, Massachusetts, receiving an M.D. in 1829. After practicing medicine in Binghamton, New York, and New York City, he was appointed in 1830 professor of moral philosophy and rhetoric at Williams. Though never formally trained in theology, he was licensed to preach in 1833 by the Berkshire Association of Congregational Ministers. In December 1832 he married Mary Hubbell of Williamstown; they had ten children. In 1836 he was named President of Williams College, serving for thirty-six years.

At Williams, as at most colleges in the first half of the nineteenth century, the capstone of a liberal arts education was a course in moral philosophy, taken by all students in their senior year and taught by the president of the college. It was intended to be not an introduction to rigorous philosophy, but a spiritual, intellectual, and practical guide to the conduct of life. Hopkins's course made an enormous impression on generations of students at Williams. He taught with an authority that derived not from a display of scholarship—Hopkins, in fact, never read widely—but from the thoroughness and honesty with which he had thought matters out for himself. Furthermore, he was manifestly interested in what each student thought, convinced as he was that responsible discussion would lead to intellectually sound and socially constructive opinions. He was generously indifferent to questions of grading and apparently did not mind if students missed class. In 1868 while Hopkins was away, the faculty attempted to penalize students who missed classes. Most of the students promptly went on strike, returning only after Hopkins returned, readily convincing themselves that the new rules would be benignly interpreted by Hopkins.

Over the many years of his presidency a growing number of Williams alumni supplemented their warm memories of Hopkins with the full confidence that his students would be a credit not just to the college but to the country. In 1871 James A. Garfield, a former student of Hopkins and later president of the United States, was quoted as declaring that the ideal college consisted of Mark Hopkins on one end of a log, and a student on the other.

From the outset of his presidency, Hopkins was committed to keeping Williams a "safe" college. To him, as to many educators at the time, it was uniquely the responsibility of moral philosophy to allay all doubts about public and private duty engendered by Enlightenment thinkers and by the American and French Revolutions. Like Francis Wayland at Brown University and James McCosh at Princeton, Hopkins found within the Scottish "common-sense" philosophical tradition the basis for triumphant refutations of every skepticism about the existence of God, the truth of revelation, and the authority of natural law. Hopkins rejected the widely used college text, *Principles of Moral and Political Philosophy*, by the English moral philosopher William Paley, as dangerously utilitarian. Against the reckless intuitionism of an Emerson, which Hopkins believed invited moral anarchy, he urged submission to an "instructed conscience."

Hopkins's "ethic" was welcomed by more than college seniors. On four occasions he was invited to give the Lowell lectures in Boston. The presupposition of the first series, published in 1846 as *Lectures on the Evidences of Christianity*, was that a "fair presentation"—devoid of sectarianism—of several kinds of evidence would produce in his audience a "settled and rational conviction of the truth of Christianity," which, he believed, was the only true foundation for the "practice of every social and civic virtue." He emphasized that, properly understood, there was a perfect congruence of revealed Christianity with Nature and with mankind's noblest needs and inclinations. Subsequently he published Lowell lectures on *Moral Science* (1862), *The Law of Love and Love as Law* (1869), and *An Outline Study of Man* (1873).

Hopkins did not have the scholarly tools, or the inclination, to engage in either research or sustained intellectual controversy. His attempts to systematize moral philosophy under three rubrics—the law of ends, the law of the conditional and the conditioned, and the law of limitation—were neither rigorous nor usefully suggestive, despite his attempts to develop pedagogically illuminating graphs and other visual aids.

He seems to have been largely oblivious to the Higher Criticism of the Bible. He rejected Darwinism out-of-hand. He did not preach the Social Gospel that preoccupied his onetime student and longtime admirer, Washington Gladden. Much the most affecting of Hopkins's books are the collections of his occasional addresses such as *Teachings and Counsels* (1884), in which the sense of his personal rectitude and personal concern outweighs the slightness of his philosophical or theological argument.

Very early in the nineteenth century, Williams College students and faculty had been pioneers in supporting foreign missions. For Hopkins, such support was always the most important duty of those fortunate enough to have been born Christians. In 1857 he succeeded Theodore Frelinghuysen as president of the American Board of Commissioners for Foreign Missions. He held that post until his death, winning the admiration of William E. Dodge, a wealthy New York businessman, who subsequently endowed Hopkins's salary at Williams. Hopkins worked hard to prevent the board, which by midcentury drew its support almost exclusively from the Congregational churches, from succumbing to a narrow denominational spirit. In his last published letter he urged the board not to insist that would-be missionaries subscribe to every theological nicety. In the mission fields, as at Williams College, reverence for the Bible and an "instructed conscience" were all that God required. Hopkins died in Williamstown, Massachusetts.

• Hopkins's papers are at Williams College, Williamstown, Mass. Three faculty colleagues wrote illuminating reminiscences: Leverett Spring, *Mark Hopkins, Teacher* (1888); Franklin Carter, *Mark Hopkins* (1891); and Arthur L. Perry, *Williamstown and Williams College* (1899). See also Frederick Rudolph, *Mark Hopkins and the Log: Williams College, 1836–1872* (1956), and D. H. Meyer, *The Instructed Conscience: The Shaping of the American National Ethic* (1972). An obituary is in the *New York Times*, 18 June 1887.

ROBERT D. CROSS

HOPKINS, Pauline Elizabeth (1859–13 Aug. 1930), editor and author, was born in Portland, Maine, the daughter of Northrup Hopkins and Sarah Allen. During her childhood, Hopkins moved with her family to Boston, a city whose rich abolitionist history would provide her fictive milieu. She attended and graduated from Girls High School. A grandniece of poet James Whitfield, she displayed literary talent as a fifteen year old, winning first prize in an essay contest titled "Evils of Intemperance and Their Remedies." The contest's sponsor, abolitionist and author William Wells Brown, would subsequently influence Hopkins's works.

Hopkins's first artistic endeavors were two musical dramas, *Colored Aristocracy* (1877) and *Peculiar Sam; or, The Underground Railroad* (1879). Eventually, Hopkins trimmed *Peculiar Sam* to three acts, and it opened as *Slaves' Escape; or, The Underground Railroad* in July 1880. Presented at the Oakland Garden in Boston by the Hopkins Colored Troubadours, the play included Hopkins's mother and Hopkins herself singing the lead role. Economic exigency required her to become a stenographer, and she worked on the

Massachusetts Decennial Census of 1895. During this time, she also lectured on black history and figures such as Toussaint L'Ouverture. Hopkins remained single throughout her life and supported herself.

Hopkins's career as a novelist began in 1900 with the founding of the *Colored American Magazine* and the Colored Co-operative Publishing Company in Boston by Walter Wallace, Jesse W. Watkins, Harper S. Fortune, and Walter Alexander Johnson. The first issue of the magazine featured Hopkins's story "The Mystery within Us," and she served as editor from 1902 to 1904. Not only did the periodical promote her most important novel, *Contending Forces: A Romance Illustrative of Negro Life North and South* (1900), but it serialized three other novels and featured her nonfiction. The magazine flourished. Abby Arthur Johnson and Ronald Maberry Johnson assert that "more and better fiction and poetry were published by the *Colored American* during the years Pauline Hopkins was editor than at any other time in its history" (*Propaganda and Aesthetics*, p. 6). Indeed, during Hopkins's tenure as editor, the *Colored American* became a vital organ in the black community, celebrating not only the literary achievements of African Americans, but also their social, political, and historical contributions to the United States and to the world.

Though *Contending Forces* clearly fits into the sentimental romance genre of the nineteenth century, the text goes beyond the limitations of that genre in its content. In the book's preface Hopkins posits a literary aesthetic that anticipates Harlem Renaissance luminary Langston Hughes's vow to capture the "heritage of rhythm and warmth" of ordinary blacks:

Fiction is of great value to any people as a preserver of manners and customs—religious, political and social. It is a record of growth and development from generation to generation. *No one will do this for us; we must ourselves develop the men and women who will faithfully portray the inmost thoughts and feelings of the Negro with all the fire and romance which lie dormant in our history,* and, as yet, unrecognized by writers of the Anglo-Saxon race. (pp. 13–14, author's emphasis)

The labyrinthine *Contending Forces* contains multiple plot lines and episodes. We first meet Charles Montfort, a West Indian slaveowner, his wife, Grace, and their sons, Charles and Jesse. Following their relocation to New Bern, North Carolina, Anson Pollock befriends the family, though secretly he plots to control Montfort's land and his wife, who is suspected of having a "black streak." After Grace spurns Pollock's advances, he has her husband killed and seizes the Montfort empire. The archetypal tragic mulatta, Grace cannot bear losing her husband and her privileged status; thus, she commits suicide. Young Charles is purchased by a mineralogist who frees him and takes him to England. Meanwhile, Jesse remains Pollock's servant, though eventually he escapes to Exeter, New Hampshire. The remainder of the novel focuses on his descendants—a daughter, "Ma" Smith, and her children, Will and Dora. The narrative shifts spatially and temporally to Ma Smith's boardinghouse in Boston.

This complex novel draws from myriad traditions, including the slave narrative and the historical romance. Though the text is sometimes melodramatic, Hopkins's provocative narrative strategies infuse it with unequivocal social criticism. The author refutes white hegemonic arguments justifying lynching, rape, and black inferiority; she provides a view of the black woman's experience, which differs from that of the tragic white heroine's; and she demythologizes miscegenation by uniting white and black descendants. Thus Hopkins's narrative disrupts and critiques the discourse surrounding race and sexuality while subverting the expectations of standard romance novels.

Hopkins published other serialized novels that continued and often expanded her treatment of issues raised in *Contending Forces*. The magazine novels also demonstrated Hopkins's command of popular fictive devices such as intrigue, melodrama, identity confusion, and disguise and concealment. *Hagar's Daughter: A Story of Southern Caste Prejudice* (1901–1902) explores the moral turpitude of powerful white southerners and northerners. Prefaced by an introductory plot set in South Carolina, the main action occurs twenty years later in Washington, D.C., during 1880. Hopkins critiques how class, race, and gender inequalities foster the mulatta's victimization: the three "white" female protagonists in reality contain "mixed blood." *Winona: A Tale of Negro Life in the South and Southwest* (1902) incorporates African-American history— John Brown's rebellion and the Fugitive Slave Act of 1850. Reminiscent of the conclusion of *Contending Forces*, *Winona* ends as the ancestry of the mixed-blood hero, Judah, is traced to Britain, while the mulatta, Winona, falls in love with her English rescuer. The denouement invites multiple readings: one can view it as Hopkins's attempt to collapse hierarchies separating Anglo and African cultures, or one could argue that the conclusion exposes her flawed racial logic in suggesting that "whiteness" redeems her black protagonists. Perhaps the most radical of the three magazine novels, *Of One Blood; or, The Hidden Self* (1902–1903) represents an early foray into Afrocentrism and mysticism, as black medical student Reuel Briggs journeys from America to Ethiopia and uncovers a vibrant culture and history. The revelations of incest, coupled with the emergence of a rich African civilization that spawned both black and white life, elucidate the title's rhetorical significance: "one blood" connotes both physiological and historical bonds between cultures often considered diametrically opposite.

Hopkins also wrote nonfiction for the *Colored American*. Her series on famous women and men of the "Negro race" featured sketches on Harriet Tubman and Booker T. Washington. The writer's diasporan interests led her to publish *A Primer of Facts Pertaining to the Greatness of Africa* (1905) herself. Hopkins asserted her revolutionary voice in her prose: "In denying the intellectual capacity of the Negro woman, our fair-skinned sisters have forgotten that they themselves have but just gained intellectual equality in the great world of endeavor." Such statements reflect an early feminist and nationalist voice that presages contemporary black women's writings.

Hopkins's unwillingness to mute her voice may have caused her to lose the editorship in 1904 "soon after the magazine came under the control of persons sympathetic to Booker T. Washington," a financial backer (Johnson and Johnson, p. 8). Though she would go on to publish in the magazines *Voice of the Negro* and *New Era*, she had reached the apex of her career. Forced to resume work as a stenographer, Hopkins died in Cambridge, Massachusetts, at the Cambridge Relief Hospital, from burns suffered after her clothing caught fire. She was buried on 17 August 1930 at the Garden Cemetery in Chelsea, Massachusetts.

Projects such as the groundbreaking Schomburg Library of Nineteenth-Century Black Women Writers in the 1980s have had a major impact on our knowledge of writers such as Hopkins. The Schomburg series reprinted all of her novels; each volume includes a trenchant scholarly introduction. Pauline Hopkins will be remembered as both a counterpart to male color-line writers such as Charles Waddell Chesnutt and Paul Laurence Dunbar and a foremother of contemporary activist-authors such as Lorraine Hansberry and Alice Walker. Her journalistic and fictional contributions to American arts and letters assure her a prominent place in our literary history.

• Hopkins's papers are in the Fisk University Library in Nashville, Tenn. The introductions to the Schomburg editions provide historical information and critical analysis: see Hazel V. Carby's "Introduction" to *The Magazine Novels of Pauline Hopkins* (1988) and Richard Yarborough's "Introduction" to *Contending Forces* (1988). See also Carby's *Reconstructing Womanhood: The Emergence of the Afro-American Woman Novelist* (1987). Key biocritical essays include Ann Allen Shockley, "Pauline Elizabeth Hopkins: A Biographical Excursion into Obscurity," *Phylon* 33 (1972): 22–26 and Claudia Tate, "Pauline Hopkins: Our Literary Foremother," in Marjorie Pryse and Hortense Spillers, eds., *Conjuring: Black Women, Fiction, and Literary Tradition* (1985). Abby Arthur Johnson and Ronald Maberry Johnson, *Propaganda and Aesthetics: The Literary Politics of Afro-American Magazines in the Twentieth Century* (1979), contains valuable information on Hopkins's tenure at the *Colored American*. The first study devoted solely to Hopkins, *The Unruly Voice: Rediscovering Pauline Elizabeth Hopkins* (1996), ed. John Cullen Gruesser, is a seminal volume that contains critical and theoretical interpretations of Hopkins's life and writings.

KEITH CLARK

HOPKINS, Samuel (17 Sept. 1721–20 Dec. 1803), theologian and reformer, was born in Waterbury, Connecticut, the son of Timothy Hopkins, a successful farmer and community leader in Waterbury, and Mary Judd. Timothy Hopkins served the town as a selectman, justice of the peace, and deputy to the Connecticut General Court. He also possessed the financial means to send Samuel to Yale College, from which he graduated in 1741.

During his senior year at Yale, Hopkins became caught up in the religious revivalism that has come to be known as the Great Awakening, and he later claimed to have experienced a spiritual conversion before leaving Yale. While praying in his dormitory room, Hopkins described being overcome by an intense awareness of God's presence, which eased weeks of spiritual agonizing that had been provoked by revivalists. He was also impressed by the commencement address of Jonathan Edwards, the well-known leader of the Great Awakening. In December 1741 Hopkins moved to Northampton, Massachusetts, to prepare for the ministry under Edwards's tutelage. Hopkins was licensed as a Congregational minister in April 1742, and for the next several months he held temporary preaching assignments while continuing his theological studies under Edwards. He did not accept a permanent position until December 1743, when he was ordained as the pastor of the Congregational church in Housatonic (now Great Barrington), Massachusetts, beginning a 26-year ministry on the New England frontier.

In 1748 Hopkins married Joanna Ingersoll; they had eight children. During the 1750s and 1760s Hopkins published major theological works and came to be identified as the leader of a new hyper-Calvinist movement within New England Congregationalism that was referred to as the New Divinity, Consistent Calvinism, or simply Hopkinsianism. Hopkins's doctrinal positions provoked theological controversy throughout New England. For example, in *Sin, thro' Divine Interposition, an Advantage to the Universe* (1759), Hopkins stressed divine sovereignty over creation, arguing that God does not merely permit sin in the world, He wills it into existence for good ends. Hopkins also developed a controversial doctrine of immediate conversion that seemed to diminish the importance of the means of grace—prayer, Bible reading, church attendance. In *An Inquiry into the Promises of the Gospel* (1765), he dismissed a gradual approach to regeneration and depreciated the moral efficacy of the means of grace and of preparation for salvation. Indeed, Hopkins argued, the awakened sinner who attended to the means of grace but remained unconverted became more guilty in God's sight. Such a morally and spiritually aware sinner possessed what Jonathan Edwards described as the "natural ability" to repent but continued to resist the promise of salvation.

These works aroused critics to charge that Hopkins preached a new divinity. Hopkins's uncompromising views helped attract clerical followers to the emerging New Divinity movement but aroused opposition in his congregation. In addition, Hopkins, a studious, learned minister, was neither a skilled or inspiring preacher nor an effective revivalist. Growing opposition and indifference to Hopkins led to his dismissal from Great Barrington in 1769.

In 1770 Hopkins was installed as the pastor of the First Congregational Church in Newport, Rhode Island, where he remained for the rest of his life. He continued to write controversial works that developed the New Divinity. In 1773 he published *An Inquiry into the Nature of True Holiness*, a work that explained his influential doctrine of disinterested benevolence. He defined true holiness as radical selflessness; ultimately, he argued, a truly virtuous person ought to be willing to be damned, if necessary, for the glory of God and the good of humankind. He also began to see the connection between disinterested benevolence and the antislavery cause, and in 1776 he published *A Dialogue Concerning the Slavery of the Africans*. Hopkins described slavery as a sin, claimed that British attacks on American liberty were providential punishment for the oppression of blacks, and insisted that the revolutionary cause would not prosper until freedom was extended to slaves. Thus, in the *Dialogue* and other works Hopkins linked the Revolution and slavery in a providential framework that was one of the central religious elements in the first major antislavery movement in America. A major antislavery work, the *Dialogue* expressed the utopian hope that the American Revolution would lead to a broad social regeneration that would establish a truly Christian society held together by the principle of disinterested benevolence.

Hopkins persisted in his opposition to slavery and the slave trade during the 1780s and the 1790s. He also extended earlier efforts to send former slaves back to Africa as Christian missionaries to begin the conversion of that continent. Continuing his theological writing, in 1793 he published *System of Doctrines Contained in Divine Revelation, Explained and Defended*, a comprehensive two-volume work that attempted to define the New Divinity. In it Hopkins drew on his own writings, on the work of other Consistent Calvinists, and on the ideas of Edwards to explain the distinctive theology of the New Divinity. In *Freedom of the Will* (1754) Edwards had laid the foundation for a Calvinist reconciliation of divine sovereignty with free will and moral accountability. Hopkins's contributions was to extend Edwards's insights into a more systematic and complete body of divinity. Hopkins's *System of Doctrines*, in particular, played a major role in the transmission of the theology of Edwards and the New Divinity's founders to the next generation of Consistent Calvinist theologians, revivalists, and reformers. As the *System of Doctrines* makes clear, the New Divinity evolved out of Edwards's theology and became the first indigenously American school of Calvinism.

In 1793, the same year the *System of Doctrines* was published, Hopkins's first wife died. A year later, at the age of seventy-three, he married Elizabeth West. Hopkins continued to preach and write in Newport during the late 1790s. In 1799, however, he suffered a stroke that partially paralyzed the right side of his body. He died in Newport.

Hopkins was among the most original theologians America has produced. In the years after the publication of his monumental *System of Doctrines*, the New Divinity became increasingly identified as Hopkinsianism. The movement won many clerical followers and came to dominate New England Congregationalism during the first two decades of the nineteenth century. Hopkins's legacy also influenced nineteenth-century reformers. For instance, his doctrine of disinterested benevolence helped inspire the foreign missionary movement in the United States, and his antislavery writings were republished and read by nineteenth-century New England abolitionists.

• The correspondence and private papers of Hopkins are in the Edwards A. Park Family Papers at Yale University, the Simon B. Gratz Collection at the Historical Society of Pennsylvania in Philadelphia, and in the Hopkins papers at Andover-Newton Theology School Library, Newton Center, Mass. His major publications include *An Inquiry Concerning the Promises of the Gospel* (1765); *The Life and Character of the Late Rev. Jonathan Edwards* (1765); *The True State and Character of the Unregenerate* (1769); *A Treatise on the Millennium* (1793); and *Sketches of the Life of Samuel Hopkins, Written by Himself* (1805). For a biographical study see Joseph A. Conforti, *Samuel Hopkins and the New Divinity* (1981). See also Bruce Kuklick, *Churchmen and Philosophers: From Jonathan Edwards to John Dewey* (1985), and Allen C. Guelzo, *Edwards on the Will: A Century of American Theological Debate* (1989).

JOSEPH CONFORTI

HOPKINS, Samuel (9 Apr. 1753–16 Sept. 1819), soldier and politician, was born in Albemarle County, Virginia, the son of Samuel Hopkins, a physician, and Isabella Taylor. He grew up in affluent circumstances and was educated by private tutors. When the American Revolution commenced, he favored the American cause; on 26 February 1776 he was commissioned as a captain of the Sixth Virginia Infantry Regiment. In his first few months of military service, he gained the respect and confidence of his fellow Virginian General George Washington by his willingness to remain on duty while others scrabbled for furloughs and by his ardor for fighting. He participated in the battle of Trenton on 26 December 1776; the battle of Princeton on 3 January 1777; the battle of Brandywine Creek on 11 September 1777; and the battle of Germantown on 4 October 1777. In the latter battle he was severely wounded while commanding a battalion of light infantry that was almost wiped out by the enemy. On 29 November 1777 he was promoted to major of the Sixth Virginia Infantry, and on 28 June 1778 he fought in the battle of Monmouth. A day later he transferred to the Fourteenth Virginia Infantry as a lieutenant colonel, retaining his rank when the regiment was denominated the Tenth Virginia on 14 September 1778.

In the spring of 1780 Hopkins was ordered to South Carolina. On 12 May he was taken prisoner when Major General Benjamin Lincoln surrendered the city of Charleston to the British. While he and his fellow captives were being conveyed to Virginia in a British transport, he threatened a mutiny because they were being starved and abused. Hopkins's protests secured better treatment. Finally, freed in a prisoner exchange, Hopkins transferred on 2 February 1781 to the First Virginia Infantry, where he served until the end of the war.

Hopkins married Elizabeth Branch Bugg on 18 January 1783; they had seven children. In 1797 he was hired by the Transylvania Company as an agent to survey and map a tract of 200,000 acres in western Kentucky, called the Virginia Grant, and to lay out the town of Henderson, Kentucky. He worked on the project from 30 March to 6 April 1797 and then settled with his family on his country estate, "Spring Garden," near Henderson. Taking up the profession of law, he was admitted to the Kentucky bar and began a legal practice.

Hopkins was an ardent Jeffersonian Republican in the political battles of the Federalist era, praising the Virginia and Kentucky resolutions of 1798 and railing against what he called the "Congressional Tyranny" of the Alien and Sedition Acts of that year. He supported Kentucky state constitutional reform in 1799 but urged that it be "cautious," lest the commonwealth lose its reputation among easterners as the "ultimate refuge" for those opposing the "Oppression & Tyranny . . . of Federal Measures" (quoted in Connelly and Coulter, p. 399). He was appointed a chief justice of the first court in Henderson County in 1799, serving until 1801. Also in 1799 he was appointed to survey a road from the town of Henderson to a ferry on the Green River. A responsible citizen, he supported public education in Henderson County, although his own children were taught by private tutors. In 1800 he ran afoul of moral reformers in Henderson; arrested for "profane swearing," he meekly paid his fine and apologized. That same year he was elected as a representative in the Kentucky state legislature, serving four terms (1800–1801 and 1803–1806). When prominent Federalists tried to prosecute Aaron Burr in 1806, Hopkins supported Burr by appearing publicly with him on the courthouse steps in Frankfort, Kentucky. In 1809 Hopkins was a presidential elector, casting his ballot for James Madison. From 1809 to 1813 he was a member of the state senate.

When the War of 1812 broke out, Hopkins was appointed the commander in chief of the western frontier with the rank of major general. On 16 August, barely two months after war was declared, Detroit fell; Kentucky Governor Isaac Shelby, hoping to ameliorate the enemy threat to America's northwest frontier, ordered Hopkins to organize and lead 2,000 mounted Kentucky volunteers against hostile Indian villages in Illinois before winter set in. With little time to prepare his expedition, Hopkins marched into the wilderness of the Indiana Territory toward Fort Harrison on the Wabash River in early October. By the time he reached that post on 14 October, many of his volunteers had saddle sores and were sullen; others had abandoned the expedition and returned home. Nevertheless, he provisioned his remaining men, hired two guides to lead him into Indian country, and on 15 October marched toward the Indian villages. After riding four days and covering 120 miles without finding any Indians, he and his men realized that the guides were lost. Morale among the Kentuckians began to erode and was completely destroyed on 20 October when a prairie fire almost destroyed their camp.

Although Hopkins and his officers pleaded with the Kentucky volunteers to continue their mission, on the morning of 21 October they voted to retreat. As they marched home, Hopkins angrily rode at the rear of his army to express his disgust with his fellow citizens. Writing to Shelby on 26 October, he expressed disappointment in his men but praised his officers as "old Kentucky veterans" who were entitled "to every confidence and praise their country can bestow." Later, both Shelby and a board of inquiry exonerated Hopkins and his officers of any responsibility for the failure of the expedition. In an attempt to repair his military reputation, Hopkins organized another little band of mounted volunteers in November, leading his men up the Wabash River and destroying a few deserted Indian villages. Some of his men were ambushed and killed, and he was forced by the severe cold to withdraw.

Although Hopkins subsequently retired from active military service, he resumed public service when in 1813 he was elected to Congress as a Republican. In Washington he favored strong war measures while the War of 1812 continued and strong peacetime defenses once it ended in 1815. Choosing not to seek a second term in Congress, Hopkins retired to Spring Garden, where he died.

Hopkins was a good junior officer during the American Revolution but a less competent one as a major general during the War of 1812. His most important contribution was as an early settler in Kentucky, where he made a secure reputation for himself as one of the state's early citizens.

• Hopkins's correspondence with John Breckinridge is in the Breckinridge Family Papers at the Library of Congress. Gaius Marcus Brumbaugh, *Revolutionary War Records, vol. 1: Virginia* (1936), and Francis B. Heitman, *Historical Register of Officers of the Continental Army During the War of the Revolution, April, 1775, to December, 1783* (1914), contain materials on Hopkins's role in that war. A useful, if incomplete and sometimes inaccurate, sketch of his life is in Lewis Collins and Richard H. Collins, *History of Kentucky*, vol. 2 (1874). William E. Connelley and E. Merton Coulter, *History of Kentucky*, vol. 1 (1922), provides information on his association with the Breckinridges. Background on his family is in Walter Lee Hopkins, *Hopkins of Virginia and Related Families* (1931), and *Genealogies of Virginia Families: From the Virginia Magazine of History and Biography*, vol. 3 (1982). His careers as lawyer and judge are discussed in H. Levin, *Lawyers and Lawmakers of Kentucky* (1897). Information on his life in Henderson County is in Edmund Lyne Starling, *History of Henderson County, Kentucky* (1887), and Maralea Arnett, *The Annals and Scandals of Henderson County, Kentucky, 1775–1975* (1976). James W. Hammack, *Kentucky and the Second American Revolution: The War of 1812* (1976), delineates Hopkins's part in that war. Obituaries are in the *Daily National Intelligencer*, 27 Oct. 1819, and the *Niles' Weekly Register*, 6 Nov. 1819.

PAUL DAVID NELSON

HOPKINS, Stephen (7 Mar. 1707–13 July 1785), signer of the Declaration of Independence, was born in Cranston (then part of Providence), Rhode Island, the son of William Hopkins and Ruth Wilkinson, farmers. Beyond learning to read and write, Hopkins had no formal education, and the early years of his life were spent farming and surveying. He married Sarah Scott in 1726, and they had seven children. In 1731 he became active in the public affairs of Scituate, a suburb of Providence, at times holding as many as four positions simultaneously. From 1732 to 1741 he served as town clerk, from 1732 to 1738 and from 1741 to 1742 he represented Scituate in the general assembly, from 1735 to 1741 he was president of the town council, and from 1736 to 1739 he served as justice of the court of common pleas for Providence County.

In 1740 Hopkins joined his brother Esek as a shipbuilder and shipowner. Two years later he moved to Providence to further his business interests, which by now included a partnership in smelting iron with four members of the influential Brown family. From 1744 to 1754 he represented Providence in the general assembly and also served as that body's Speaker. Because the colonial charter of Rhode Island concentrated executive and judicial as well as legislative authority in the general assembly, Hopkins, while Speaker, was able to serve as assistant justice of the superior court from 1747 to 1749 and chief justice in 1751. His wife died in 1753, and he married Anne Smith, a widow, two years later. They had no children.

Hopkins represented the colony in 1754 at the Albany Congress and supported Benjamin Franklin's plan of union for the thirteen colonies. In 1755 he was elected to the first of nine one-year terms as governor; his final term ended in 1768. Despite being little more than a ceremonial position, this office was bitterly contested by factions representing Rhode Island's commercial rivals. The Providence faction was led by Hopkins, while the Newport faction was led by Samuel Ward, governor in the years when Hopkins was not between 1757 and 1767.

Hopkins achieved a measure of intercolonial fame in 1764, when he published two important pro-patriot pamphlets. The first, *An Essay on the Trade of the Northern Colonies*, described the intricacies of New England's commerce with the West Indies and considered how the Sugar Act of 1764 might affect that trade. The second, *Rights of the Colonies Examined*, took one of the first steps toward denying Parliament's right to tax the colonials without their consent. Hopkins did not deny the colonies' duty to contribute toward the "necessary burdens of government"; he simply posited that raising revenue in America might be done more properly by the colonial assemblies. He also suggested that Parliament's "supreme and overruling authority" was confined to general matters of empire such as the regulation of money and paper credit and did not extend into the internal affairs of the colonies. The essay, which was reprinted in colonial newspapers throughout America, provoked a vituperative pamphlet war. Martin Howard, Jr., a Rhode Island judge and member of the Newport faction, responded to Hopkins by ably defending the supremacy of Parliament in *Halifax Letter*. James Otis, a Boston lawyer to whom is attributed the phrase "taxation without representation is tyranny," then penned *A Vindication of the British Colonies* in opposition to Howard and in support of Hopkins.

From 1771 to 1776 Hopkins again represented Providence in the general assembly and also served as chief justice. In this latter capacity, he publicly refused to sign any court order allowing the apprehension or extradition of those who had burned the Royal Navy revenue cutter *Gaspee*, among them his nephew and an uncle by marriage, and he stalled the Crown commissioners investigating the incident until they gave up and went home.

Hopkins returned to the intercolonial stage as a delegate to the First Continental Congress in 1774 and the Second Continental Congress the following year. As chair of the naval committee, he played a major role in the creation of the Continental navy; then, as chair of the marine committee, he supervised the civilian administration of that navy. He also represented Rhode Island on the thirteen-member committee that drafted the Articles of Confederation. Poor health forced him to retire from the national arena in September 1776. He represented Providence in the general assembly from 1777 to 1779, then retired from public life.

In addition to his involvement in political affairs, Hopkins was also active in the community affairs of Providence. He helped establish the town's first public library in 1754, and he was one of the founders of the *Providence Gazette and Country Journal*, a patriot newspaper, in 1762. In 1764 he became the first chancellor of Rhode Island College (now Brown University). He was an amateur scientist and was one of the few out-of-town members of the Philosophical Society of Newport.

Hopkins was a man of unusual intelligence, and he overcame his lack of formal education by reading voraciously as well as through his association with the Philosophical Society. John Adams, his colleague on the naval and marine committees, called him a man of "wit, humour, anecdotes, science and learning." He also possessed a hot temper and was not above using his political clout to benefit himself or members of his family. When Howard called him a "ragged country fellow," he responded in rather crude language. He ridiculed his political opponents, particularly Ward, in a biblical parody, *The Fall of Samuel the Squomicutite, and the Overthrow of the Sons of Gideon*. As governor, he once kept for himself the king's portion of a captured cargo of smuggled sugar (for which he was fined a considerable sum), and he secured choice appointments in the Continental navy for three of his relatives. In 1779 he retired to his home in Providence, where he died.

Hopkins contributed significantly to the cause of American independence in several ways. As a pamphleteer, he was one of the first colonials to question the unrestrained right of Parliament to legislate for the

American colonies. As a delegate, he supported colonial unity, at first within the British Empire but later as an independent entity. As a judge, he supported activities that interfered with Britain's dominion over the colonies. As a member of the Continental Congresses, he played an important role in developing the military and constitutional means by which the United States achieved nationhood.

• Hopkins's papers were destroyed in a storm in 1815; however, copies of a few of his letters exist in the Brown University Library. His political career is documented in David S. Lovejoy, *Rhode Island Politics and the American Revolution, 1760–1776* (1958), and Sydney V. James, *Colonial Rhode Island: A History* (1975). His importance as a patriot pamphleteer is assessed in Bernard Bailyn, *The Ideological Origins of the American Revolution* (1967). His contributions to the creation of the Continental navy are discussed in Nathan Miller, *Sea of Glory: The Continental Navy Fights for Independence, 1775–1783* (1974).

CHARLES W. CAREY, JR.

HOPKINSON, Charles Sydney (27 July 1869–16 Oct. 1962), artist, was born in Cambridge, Massachusetts, the son of John Prentiss Hopkinson, a founder and headmaster of the Hopkinson School in Boston, and Mary Elizabeth Watson. Hopkinson recalled that he began drawing when he was ten, a favorite subject being the cows that grazed near his home on Craigie Street. He attended Harvard University, where he drew cartoons for the *Harvard Lampoon*, and enrolled at the Art Students League in New York City in 1891. He studied with noted landscapist John Henry Twachtman and married a fellow student, Angelica Rathbone, in 1893; they had no children. The newlyweds moved to Paris, where they studied at the Académie Julian, but Hopkinson later said that he learned more about painting by copying the old masters in the Louvre. The marriage was not a success; he and Angelica separated in 1896 and divorced three years later.

Hopkinson returned to Europe in 1901, where he studied the works of Frans Hals in Holland and copied paintings by Velázquez at the Prado in Madrid. He subsequently returned to Europe each year for several years to spend his winters in the village of Roscoff in Brittany. There he lived with a local family and painted brooding depictions of Breton fishermen at work.

Hopkinson is known primarily as a portraitist. He began his professional career in 1896 when he was commissioned to paint portraits of a prominent Boston couple, Mr. and Mrs. Edward Cummings, and their two-year-old son Edward Estlin, who grew up to become the poet e. e. cummings (all Massachusetts Historical Society, Boston). That same year he was invited to participate in the annual exhibition of the Carnegie Institute in Pittsburgh; he was included in this show for the next fifty years. He also served several times as a juror, and the exhibition helped to spread his reputation beyond the confines of Boston.

In 1903 Hopkinson married Elinor Curtis, a member of an old, established Boston family and a relative by marriage of Henry Wadsworth Longfellow. They had five daughters. The couple settled in Boston but spent their summers in Manchester, Massachusetts, where Elinor's family owned property. There they had a good view of the harbor, which Hopkinson painted many times.

By 1904 Hopkinson had set up his studio at the Fenway Studios, at 30 Ipswich Street in Boston. Most of his early commissions came from family members and friends, but word of the talented young painter quickly spread. His career and reputation were greatly enhanced by his participation in the important Armory Show held in New York City in 1913. He exhibited a 1911 oil of his daughters, *Three Little Girls*—singled out for praise by noted art critic Frank Jewett Mather—and four watercolors. In 1919 he was one of eight American artists selected by the National Art Committee to paint the leading Allied representatives to the Versailles Peace Conference. Hopkinson was assigned to paint Premier Ionel Brătianu of Romania, Premier Nicola Pašić of Serbia, and Prince Saionji Kimmochi of Japan (all 1920, National Museum of American Art, Washington, D.C.).

These subjects suited Hopkinson well, as their colorful appearances and exotic backgrounds presented an interesting challenge. He depicted the Japanese delegate wearing Western clothing; his expression is somber. Hopkinson emphasized Saionji's Oriental heritage by placing him in a teak chair against a flat brown-and-tan background with no accessories, and by having the sitter write his name in Japanese characters at the upper left of the portrait. He succeeded in capturing not only Saionji's ascetic personality but his culture as well. As the artist's biographer Leah Lipton wrote, "Prince Saionji's portrait has the delicacy, tonality, and subtle geometry of Japanese art" (p. 12). Brătianu, in contrast, is shown in plush surroundings, seated in an ornate gold chair against gold and blue-green drapery. The portrait of Pašić is the most unusual. The 75-year-old Serb is seated at one end of a large sofa; the other end is occupied by a crumpled map of Europe. Pašić's features and square-cut beard are strongly lit from the viewer's left, and the bright orange-red background is half lit, half in shadow. Before he began the portrait, Hopkinson took the unusual step of cutting the canvas into varied shapes and gluing them to a wood panel. This reinforces the disparate elements of the painting. The figure of Pašić, the map on the sofa, and the lit portion of the background look as if they had been lifted from three different paintings.

When the twenty-two paintings commissioned by the National Art Committee were exhibited in 1921, the overall critical reception was decidedly mixed, but Hopkinson's paintings received much praise. W. G. Dooley of the *Boston Globe* called them "the real outstanding artistic successes of the collection." The success of his Versailles portraits boosted Hopkinson's reputation and brought him commissions from outside the Boston area. His sitters included British poet (and Hopkinson's friend) John Masefield (1919, Harvard University); Secretary of State (and later Chief Justice)

Charles Evans Hughes (1923, Brown University); historian Samuel Eliot Morison (1929, private collection); and art historian and future director of the National Gallery of Art John Walker (1930). In 1927 he did a portrait of John D. Rockefeller, Jr., and he subsequently painted two portraits of Abby Aldrich Rockefeller, in 1928 and 1931.

Perhaps Hopkinson's best-known portrait is that of Calvin Coolidge, painted in 1932 for the White House. The artist spent ten days as a guest in Coolidge's home in Northampton, Massachusetts, where the painting was done, and the result is impressive. The former president is shown seated in a Windsor chair against a plain green background, lost in thought, alone. Coolidge often confessed to friends that he felt alienated from current events, and Hopkinson captured well this sense of isolation.

The artist himself felt that his most important sitter was Oliver Wendell Holmes, Jr. Hopkinson painted the portrait of the distinquished legal scholar and associate justice of the U.S. Supreme Court in 1930 on commission from the Harvard law school. A full-length depiction of the old jurist standing and looking directly at the viewer, the canvas is almost exactly the same size as that of a portrait of John Marshall by Chester Harding that Harvard had acquired in the 1840s. Hopkinson's portrait of Holmes was, wrote Holmes, "hung as the pendant to [the] one of Marshall, which of course was the handsomest compliment that they could pay" (qtd. in Voss, p. 130). The portrait thus was not only an excellent likeness of Holmes but also an iconographic representation of his place in American history. Hopkinson painted a second full-length of Holmes the following year (U.S. Supreme Court, Washington, D.C.) in which the justice is shown seated rather than standing.

Hopkinson painted many portraits for Harvard of its distinguished faculty and alumni, including Charles William Eliot (1921), president of the university for forty years and also Hopkinson's uncle, and legendary professor of English literature George Lyman Kittredge (1926). What in other, less capable hands might have been dull, "boardroom portraits" Hopkinson made into unexpectedly lively portrayals. Hopkinson preferred to paint his subjects in action— reading, writing, or even half-rising as if to greet a friend—rather than sitting and posing.

Color, generally an important consideration for any artist, was especially so for Hopkinson. He learned much about color from his fellow artist and Cambridge neighbor Denman W. Ross, who had devised a theory based on an elaborate arrangement of predetermined colors and tones. Hopkinson experimented with color throughout his life. He felt strongly that a portrait's color scheme needed to be worked out well before sittings actually commenced and that the portrait should first and foremost be conceived of as a work of art: "It should not resemble a reflection in a mirror; its shapes and outlines should as much as possible . . . be in a geometric pattern in harmony with the dimensions of the canvas on which it is painted."

He added, "The artist who paints merely to hit off a likeness or, what's worst, to please the sitter, is lost" (quoted in Watson, p. 72).

Hopkinson enjoyed being an artist, even sketching when he relaxed. He set himself a disciplined schedule whereby he painted at fixed times each day. He did a number of genre scenes of his daughters at play, but although he often exhibited these works, he never offered them for sale. He painted nearly seventy self-portraits, the earliest when he was barely into his teens and the last when he was about ninety-two. These seem to have been done as a record of his appearance and, perhaps more importantly, as a way of solving problems relating to color, light, shadow, and the handling of the paintbrush. Hopkinson painted watercolors for pleasure, and as with the paintings of his daughters, he enjoyed exhibiting them but preferred not to sell them.

Hopkinson was popular both with the public and with his peers. He was a member of the National Academy of Design, the American Academy of Arts and Letters, the American Academy of Arts and Sciences, the American Water Color Society, the Philadelphia Water Color Club, and the Guild of Boston Artists. He helped found the Boston Society of Independent Artists. in 1927, an organization designed to give younger artists the opportunity to exhibit their work. He continued to paint until the end of his life; he died in Beverly, Massachusetts.

Critic Lincoln Kirstein described Hopkinson as a painter "of great distinction . . . whose portraits . . . were in the grand line of Copley and Sargent." Except for his early divorce, his personal and professional lives were remarkably happy; he had a loving family and enjoyed a long and successful career, economic security, and social position. His realistic but unconventional portraits and bold, innovative watercolors mark him as one of the best artists of his generation.

• Most of Hopkinson's papers still belong to his family, but a number are available on microfilm at the Archives of American Art. Four of his self-portraits are owned by the National Portrait Gallery, Washington, D.C.; these were painted, respectively, c. 1900, c. 1910, c. 1918, and c. 1959. A self-portrait of 1927 belongs to the National Academy of Design in New York. Leah Lipton, *Charles Hopkinson: Pictures from a New England Past* (1988), is the catalog of an exhibition held at the Danforth Museum of Art in Framingham, Mass., and contains a good biographical sketch. Hopkinson wrote "The Portrait Painter and His Subject," *Atlantic Monthly,* Oct. 1955, pp. 72–75, and he was the subject of Ernest Watson, "Charles Hopkinson and a Half-Century of Portrait Painting," *American Artist* 21, no. 7: 30–35. His work is also discussed in Frederick Platt, "The War Portraits," *Antiques,* July 1984, pp. 146–47; Frederick Voss, *Portraits of the American Law* (1989), a catalog of an exhibition at the National Portrait Gallery; and Trevor J. Fairbrother, *The Bostonians: Painters of an Elegant Age, 1870–1930* (1986), a catalog of an exhibition at the Museum of Fine Arts, Boston.

DAVID MESCHUTT

HOPKINSON, Francis (2 Oct. 1737–9 May 1791), author, composer, and judge, was born in Philadelphia, the son of Thomas Hopkinson, a lawyer and Pennsylvania councillor, and Mary Johnson. Hopkinson's father emigrated from England in 1731. Hopkinson matriculated in the first class of the College of Philadelphia (later the University of Pennsylvania) in 1751; he graduated in 1757 and, with other members of his class, received an M.A. degree three years later.

Besides musical and literary endeavors, Hopkinson had a diversified career before the revolutionary war. He studied law in Philadelphia with Benjamin Chew, the attorney general for Pennsylvania, and he was admitted to the bar in 1761. Specializing as a conveyancer, Hopkinson had little success as a practicing attorney in Philadelphia. His first public service occurred as secretary to the Pennsylvanian Indian commission of 1761, which concluded a treaty with the Delaware and several Iroquois tribes. Appointed customs collector for Salem, New Jersey, in 1763, Hopkinson farmed out the actual duties to a deputy. He visited England from May 1766 to August 1767, in anticipation of being named a commissioner of customs for North America. Although he failed in this quest, he developed close contacts in England with Lord North; John Penn (the proprietor of Pennsylvania); his cousin, the Bishop of Worcester; and Benjamin West, from whom he probably received lessons in painting. Upon his return to Philadelphia, Hopkinson gave much attention to his dry goods business on Front Street. On 1 September 1768 Hopkinson married Ann Borden of Bordentown, New Jersey; one of their five children, Joseph Hopkinson, became a congressman and wrote the lyrics for the patriotic song "Hail Columbia."

On 1 May 1772 Hopkinson assumed the office of customs collector for New Castle, Delaware. In search of greater political opportunity, and because his retail business had started to decline, Hopkinson moved to Bordentown in late 1773 or early 1774. He was admitted to the New Jersey bar on 8 May 1775 and returned to practicing law, this time with much success. Because of his friendship with Lord North, Hopkinson was named to the royal council of New Jersey in 1774. Elected an associate justice of the New Jersey Supreme Court in 1776, he declined the position. That year, having become an avowed Whig and patriot, Hopkinson resigned all his offices held under Crown authority. Hopkinson was also a member of the American Philosophical Society and the Library Company, serving the latter organization as secretary (1759–1769), librarian (1764–1765), and director (1771–1773). An active Anglican layman his entire life, Hopkinson was a vestryman (1769–1773) and a warden (1770–1771) for both Christ Church and St. Peter's Church.

Hopkinson achieved a significant reputation as an author and musician before the Revolution. He published forty poems, mostly relating to public occasions, as well as a number of essays, which included topics on science and education. He turned to satirical essays just before the war, beginning with *A Pretty Story*, a prose allegory relating to events making for a separation from Great Britain (three editions, 1774).

A masterful performer at the harpsichord and organ, Hopkinson had begun studying the harpsichord at age seventeen, probably as a pupil of James Bremner. He taught children psalmody at Christ and St. Peter's Churches and wrote anthems and hymns. In 1759 he collected two hundred pieces, six of them written by himself, including "My Days Have Been So Wondrous Free," set to the words of Thomas Parnell's "Love and Innocence," the first extant secular song by a native American composer. Hopkinson is also the probable compiler of *A Collection of Plain Tunes with a few Anthems and Hymns*, published in Philadelphia in 1763. Hopkinson also played in concert and local chamber music groups and arranged subscription concerts in Philadelphia. From 1770 to 1774 he substituted for the absent James Bremner as organist for Christ Church.

As a delegate to the Continental Congress from New Jersey from 22 June to 30 November 1776, Hopkinson served on the committee for drafting the Articles of Confederation, and he supported and signed the Declaration of Independence. Earlier in the year he had published *A Prophecy*, which predicted independence. On 12 July 1776 Hopkinson was appointed to the congressional Marine Committee and, on 18 November 1776, one of the three members of the new Navy Board. He resigned in July 1778 to accept a congressional post as treasurer of loans, in charge of the Continental Loan Office. In this position Hopkinson became involved in bitter disputes with the Board of Treasury, and Congress grew dissatisfied with his "fancy-work"; as a result, he resigned this position in July 1781. From 1779 to 1789 Hopkinson was judge of the Admiralty Court for Pennsylvania. Impeached for corruption in that office in December 1780, chiefly for receiving small bribes and illegal fees, he won acquittal. In April 1786 Hopkinson was one of the commissioners from Pennsylvania, Delaware, and Maryland who sought improvements for navigation on the Susquehanna River.

Hopkinson allied himself with the Republican party in Pennsylvania, which favored ratification of the U.S. Constitution. He published essays in the newspapers on behalf of the Federalists and also the allegorical poem, "The New Roof," which ridiculed the Antifederalists. Hopkinson also directed the "Grand Federal Procession," a parade of "eighty-seven divisions," on 4 July 1788 in Philadelphia, celebrating the adoption of the Constitution. President George Washington appointed Hopkinson judge of the U.S. District Court for eastern Pennsylvania, a position he held until his death.

Hopkinson continued to participate in community affairs. From 5 January 1781 to 12 January 1791 he was treasurer of the American Philosophical Society, where he occasionally presented learned papers. He was named a trustee of the Episcopal Academy, founded in 1785, and he served as a vestryman. In addition, he was a lay deputy to the general convention that established the Protestant Episcopal church in 1789. In December 1790 he received the American Philosophical Society's Magellanic Prize Medal for his invention of a spring-block to assist in navigation.

During the Revolution Hopkinson wrote a number of ballads and essays poking fun at the British cause and the Loyalists. "The Birds, the Beasts, and the Bat," in Hudibrastic verse, served to ridicule those persons who tried to take both sides during the Revolution. Certain of his ballads were set to music, namely the "Camp Ballad," "The Toast," and "The Battle of the Kegs"; the latter was one of the most popular songs of the Revolution and was regularly sung by the soldiery. On 11 December 1781 Hopkinson's "The Temple of Minerva" was produced in Philadelphia, with George Washington, Nathanael Greene, and their spouses in attendance. This oratorio, or "dramatic allegorical cantata," celebrated the French Alliance and had as its theme the eventual American triumph of arms; its music was a mix of compositions by Hopkinson and by European composers.

During the last years of his life Hopkinson channeled his creativity mainly to the writing of essays and orations to be delivered by students at the college commencements. These writings covered a wide range of topics, including "A Plan for the Improvement of the Art of Paper War" (regarding newspaper disputes), "Some Thoughts on Diseases of the Mind," "Modern Learning Exemplified," "On the Learned Languages," and "On Peace, Liberty, and Independence." In 1788 Hopkinson published *Seven Songs for the Harpsichord or Forte Piano*; actually consisting of eight songs, it was the first public collection of American art songs.

A skilled draftsman, Hopkinson produced heraldic emblems and pastel portraits and designed coins, paper money, and the seals of the new cabinet departments of the federal government, the American Philosophical Society, the state of New Jersey, and the University of Pennsylvania. Hopkinson also claimed to have originated the "Stars and Stripes" design of the American flag; Congress, however, refused to give Hopkinson sole credit, stating in a resolution of 23 August 1781 that many persons had been involved in the flag's design. As an inventor, Hopkinson showed ingenuity but came up with not too important creations, such as floating lamps and a shaded candlestick.

Arguably the most versatile American of the revolutionary generation, Hopkinson struck an unusual figure. "[Hopkinson] is one of your pretty little, curious, ingenius men. His head is not bigger than a large apple," wrote John Adams to his wife. "I have not met with anything in natural history more amusing and entertaining than his personal appearance; yet he is genteel and well-bred, and is very social" (quoted in Hastings, p. 266).

Hopkinson died of apoplexy at his home in Philadelphia. While he may be regarded as a dilettante, and while his prose, poetry, and music were highly derivative of European styles, he made important contributions to American literature and music. Possessing great knowledge, he wrote with clarity and humor. Hopkinson ably served the cause of patriotism and awakened Americans of the revolutionary period to a greater appreciation of the arts.

• A collection of Hopkinson's correspondence for the years 1765–1789 is in the Hopkinson Family Papers, Historical Society of Pennsylvania. Manuscript writings, exclusive of letters, are found at the Massachusetts Historical Society; the Library of Congress; the American Philosophical Society; and the Henry E. Huntington Library, San Marino, Calif. Documents and letters are also in the published papers of Benjamin Franklin and Thomas Jefferson and the manuscript collection of the Papers of the Continental Congress, Library of Congress. Essays, orations for commencement, poems, and judgments of the Admiralty Court of Pennsylvania appear in *The Miscellaneous Essays and Occasional Writings of Francis Hopkinson* (3 vols., 1792). George E. Hastings, *The Life and Works of Francis Hopkinson* (1926), is a comprehensive biography that lists all known writings and their locations; also see this work for verification of Hopkinson's date of death. For Hopkinson as a musician, see Oscar G. T. Sonneck, *Francis Hopkinson, the First American Poet Composer . . .* (1905), and Gilbert Chase, *America's Music* (1966), pp. 97–105. Moses C. Tyler, *The Literary History of the American Revolution, 1763–1783* (2 vols., 1897), and Kenneth Silverman, *A Cultural History of the American Revolution* (1976), offer literary analysis. Articles on particular topics include Dixon Wecter "Francis Hopkinson and Benjamin Franklin," *American Literature* 12 (1940–1941): 200–217; George E. Hastings, "Francis Hopkinson and the Anti-Federalists," *American Literature* 1 (1929–1930): 405–18; and Lewis Leary, "Francis Hopkinson, Jonathan Odell, and 'The Temple of Cloacina': 1782," *American Literature* 15 (1943–1944): 183–91.

HARRY M. WARD

HOPKINSON, Joseph (12 Nov. 1770–15 Jan. 1842), congressman and jurist, was born in Philadelphia, Pennsylvania, the son of Francis Hopkinson, a jurist and signer of the Declaration of Independence, and Ann Borden. He graduated with a B.A. degree from the University of Pennsylvania in 1786, read law with the erudite Philadelphia attorneys William Rawle and James Wilson (1742–1798), and was admitted to the bar in 1791. After practicing briefly in Easton, he returned to Philadelphia and soon established his reputation as a brilliant courtroom advocate in some of the most celebrated trials of the time. In 1795 he defended the "whiskey rebels" against charges of treason stemming from their short-lived insurrection against a federal whiskey tax; in 1799 he represented Dr. Benjamin Rush in a successful libel suit against the vitriolic journalist William Cobbett; and in 1804 he successfully defended Samuel Chase, associate justice of the Marshall Court, in his impeachment trial before the U.S. Senate. Contemporaries attributed much of his success with juries to his skillful use of "decorations"—literary allusions and puns—to enliven his legal arguments.

A legal conservative by temperament and training, Hopkinson strongly opposed Republican demands for democratic law reform and the replacement of judge-made common law with legislative codes. His influential pamphlet, *Considerations on the Abolition of the Common Law in the United States* (1809), provided a cogent and comprehensive defense of the existing legal establishment. Addressed to a lay audience, it helped to ensure the defeat of the codification movement in Pennsylvania. Politically, Hopkinson was a staunch Federalist whose wife, Emily Mifflin, was the daughter of Pennsylvania's first post-revolutionary governor. They were married in 1794 and had nine children. In 1814 he ran for Congress on the Federalist ticket and served two terms in the House of Representatives, from 1815 to 1819. By that time the Federalist party was in decline, and his efforts to promote conservative national policies met with little success. In 1819 he abandoned politics and resumed his law practice, first in Bordentown, New Jersey, from 1820 to 1822, and then in Philadelphia.

During the later stages of his professional career Hopkinson argued several landmark constitutional cases before the U.S. Supreme Court. In *Dartmouth College v. Woodward* (1819) and *Sturges v. Crowninshield* (1819) he successfully urged an expansive reading of the contract clause, a Constitutional prohibition on state laws impairing contract obligations, in order to safeguard the property rights of private corporations and creditors. In *McCulloch v. Maryland* (1819) he argued vigorously, but unsuccessfully, that Congress had no implied power to charter a national bank—a position he had taken several years earlier in congressional debate. His growing friendship with Associate Justice Joseph Story led to his appointment by John Quincy Adams (1767–1848) as federal district judge for the Eastern District of Pennsylvania in 1828. He retained this post, which his father had once held, until his death.

As a judge Hopkinson wrote opinions noted for their clarity and learning. Although he adhered to established rules and seldom innovated, several of his admiralty decisions set important precedents. His most notable opinion, in *Wheaton v. Peters* (1833), established the foundations of modern American copyright law. Sitting alone as circuit judge, Hopkinson ruled that no federal common law of copyright existed in the United States and that all copyright protection depended exclusively upon statutory grants. Since copyright statutes conferred monopolistic privileges upon writers and inventors, moreover, their terms had to be strictly complied with, to protect the public interest. On appeal the following year, a majority of the Marshall Court adopted Hopkinson's views, which tended in this instance to promote competition and democratic access to knowledge above the rigorous enforcement of property rights.

The rise of Jacksonian Democracy, which threatened to bring the courts under popular control, alarmed Hopkinson and impelled him to take a public stand in defense of judicial independence. Elected as a delegate to the Pennsylvania constitutional convention of 1837, he argued eloquently that the existing system of life tenure for judicial appointees should be preserved. A majority of the convention, however, voted to make state judges more responsive to public opinion by limiting their officeholding to a specified term of years.

Witty and urbane, Hopkinson found an outlet for his wide-ranging intellectual and cultural interests through service on the boards of municipal institutions. He was president of the Academy of Fine Arts, vice president of the American Philosophical Society, a founder of the Pennsylvania Horticultural Society in 1827, and a trustee of the University of Pennsylvania. His popular fame rested on a dramatic incident from his early career: In 1798, at the request of Gilbert Fox, a young actor and former classmate, Hopkinson composed the lyrics for a patriotic song to be sung to the tune of "The President's March." The result—the rousing "Hail Columbia"—celebrated national unity at a time of bitter political partisanship and remained a favorite with American audiences for many years. Hopkinson died in Philadelphia.

• Letters from Hopkinson are in the Joseph Hopkinson papers at the Historical Society of Pennsylvania (Philadelphia) and in the Joseph Story papers in the Harry Ransom Humanities Research Center at the University of Texas at Austin. Burton A. Konkle has written the only biography, *Joseph Hopkinson, 1770–1842* (1931). For a contemporary assessment of Hopkinson's career, see "The Late Judge Hopkinson," *Pennsylvania Law Journal* 7 (Jan. 1848): 101–14. On his role in the Pennsylvania codification controversy, see Charles M. Cook, *The American Codification Movement* (1981). The circumstances surrounding the writing of "Hail Columbia" may be traced in John Tasker Howard, *Our American Music: Three Hundred Years of It* (1931). Hopkinson's judicial opinions are reported in Henry Dilworth Gilpin, *Reports of Cases Adjudged in the District Court of the United States for the Eastern District of Pennsylvania, 1828–36* (1837), and in William Henry Crabbe, *United States District Court Reports, 1836–46* (1853).

MAXWELL BLOOMFIELD

HOPPE, Willie (11 Oct. 1887–1 Feb. 1959), billiards champion, was born William Frederick Hoppe in Cornwall-on-Hudson, New York, the son of Frank Hoppe and Frances Hoffman. Hoppe's father had been an itinerant barber and successful professional billiards player before purchasing the Commercial Hotel in the Hudson River town near West Point. Willie and his brother Frank spent far more time practicing billiards under the demanding and sometimes harsh regimen of their father than they did in school. Willie dropped out of school after the fourth grade and spent eight-hour days around the billiard table. By 1899 he was hailed a "boy wonder" as he stood on a wooden crate making brilliant shots, his peculiar sidearm strokes sending the ivory balls rolling smoothly over the green baize. For the rest of his life Hoppe's world was bounded by the four corners of a billiard table. His father sold the hotel and took the two boys on barnstorming tours of upstate New York, earning betting monies along the way. "Father was one tough taskmaster," Willie later recalled. "He trained my older brother and me so we could trim all the visiting drummers, though I had to stand on a box to do it."

At the invitation of the world's champion, Jacob Schaefer, Sr., in 1902 the fifteen-year-old Hoppe traveled to Paris, where he perfected his skills and won the Young Masters Championship. Hoppe gained early sporting immortality in Paris on 15 January 1906, when the eighteen-year-old defeated the world champion, the venerable "Old Lion," Maurice Vignaux. The audience inside the glittering ballroom of the Grand Hotel was both stunned and appreciative as Willie, his hair plastered and parted down the middle "as straight as one of his cue shots," took the measure of the white-haired Frenchman.

For the next fifteen years the young Hoppe was unbeatable at straight-rail billiards, 14.1, 18.1, 18.2, three-cushion competitions, and balkline billiards. *Newsweek* reported that "Wonderful Willie" was nearly unbeatable for two generations. "His only weakness, the masse shot," was done with the cue stick, striking the ball from directly above—a vertical shot. A 4,000-word biography by Robert Lewis Taylor, published in the 16 November 1940 issue of the *New Yorker*, called Hoppe's skill innate and also the result of thousands of hours of scientific practice around the table. He could make billiard balls "roll in circles, hop up in the air, go forward and back up, hit one another on any part of the table, and, what's more, he can do it right-handed or left-handed."

In 1910 Hoppe married Alice Walsh of New York City. They had two children. Hoppe and his wife were divorced in 1924, and soon afterward he married Broadway dancer Dorothy Dowsey, a union that ended in divorce in 1926. Hoppe's string of billiard championships ended during the 1920s, the "Golden Age" of American sport. Jake Schaefer, Jr., won the 18.2 championships in 1921, and it seemed a new era was dawning. Welker Cochran, Jay Bozeman, Johnny Layton, Joe Chamaco, and young Willy Mosconi were superb players. However, Hoppe continued adding championship titles all through the 1920s and 1930s, an eventual total of fifty-one world titles in forty years. In April 1940, at age fifty-two, he won the world's three-cushion championship in Chicago from formidable opponents. It came as the conclusion of thirty-six out of thirty-seven tournament victories. John Lardner's 24 February 1941 essay in *Newsweek* called Hoppe an athletic and psychological genius and "one of the world's greatest competitors in any sport or profession." He repeated the three-cushion title in 1941.

Hoppe moved to Miami, Florida, where he lived until his death there. No athlete had ever come close to dominating a sport for so long a period as had Hoppe. As he said in a *New York Times* magazine article on 19 May 1940: "Natural ability, immense hard work, absolute controlled enthusiasm are secrets of my success. I think that I can play championship billiards at least until I'm 60."

• Hoppe wrote two autobiographies: *Thirty Years of Billiards* (1925) and *Billiards as It Should Be Played* (1941). See also Frank G. Menke, *The Encyclopedia of Sports* (1977), p. 214; *New York Times*, 19 Jan. 1906; 29 Mar. 1906; and 12 May 1906; "Willie Hoppe Is Still a Standout," *Newsweek*, 1 Apr. 1940; "Clean Sweep," *Time*, 15 Apr. 1940, pp. 65–66; *New York Times Magazine*, 19 May 1940, pp. 9, 25; and John Lardner, "The Perpetual Wizard," *Newsweek*, 24 Feb. 1941, p. 56. *Life* magazine, 21 Apr. 1941, pp. 57–60, is revealing in both word and high-speed photography in the unattributed article "At 53 Willie Hoppe Is Still Master of the Trickiest Shots in Billiards." Obituaries are in *Sports Illustrated*, 16 Feb. 1959, and the *New York Times*, 2 Feb. 1959.

JOHN LUCAS

HOPPER, DeWolf (30 Mar. 1858–23 Sept. 1935), actor and singer, was born William D'Wolf Hopper in New York City, the son of John Hopper, a lawyer, and Rosalie D'Wolf. The family lived on East Third Street right off the Bowery and later moved to West Forty-third Street. His paternal grandfather, John Tatum Hopper, was a Quaker and a conductor of the Underground Railroad in Philadelphia, Pennsylvania, who was disciplined by the Quaker Meeting for his participation in the Civil War. Hopper was six when his father died, leaving him and his mother comfortably well off. He studied at J. H. Morse's School. Early on he showed a propensity for the theatrical. As a school boy he mastered the "Senator Dilworthy" monologue, and when he was fifteen he played in a Sunday school production of *Ralph Roister Doister* at Octavius Brooks Frothingham's Unitarian Church in New York.

Hopper read law briefly with his godfather, Joseph H. Choate, who soon gently advised Mrs. Hopper that her son's enthusiasm and histrionics, though perhaps of some use in the courtroom, nonetheless prevented his mastering the fundamentals of law. Thus, with his mother's blessing, Hopper took up acting, playing in *Conscience* at Daniel Frohman's Fourteenth Street Theatre. About this time he dropped his first name. He later mused, "I thought D'Wolf [later spelled De-Wolf], my middle name, *distingué*." With an advance on his inheritance, he then organized the Criterion Comedy Company with Jacob Gosche as manager and F. F. Mackay as director. On 4 November 1878 he opened as Arthur Middlewick in *Our Boys* in New Haven, Connecticut. Later he played in *Caste* and *Freaks*.

In 1879, Hopper, now twenty-one years old, received his full inheritance from his father's estate. He used the money to continue to finance the company, whose name became Gosche-Hopper. He produced *One Hundred Lives*, starring Georgiana Drew Barrymore, the mother of Ethel, Lionel, and Jack Barrymore. The play toured the country before coming to Broadway. By 1881 Hopper had married the first of his six wives, Helen Gardner, his cousin on his mother's side; they had no children.

With his inheritance exhausted by 1882, Hopper dissolved his company and joined the Harrigan & Hart Company, playing in *The Blackbird*. He then went on the road as Pittacus Green in *Hazel Kirke*, with a cast that included Cecile Rush, Charles Wheatley, and Harry Davenport. While performing in Leadville, Colorado, he sang in a saloon "Rocked in the Cradle

Deep," bringing to tears the assembled miners and gamblers.

Hopper had a fine basso voice, and for a time he seriously considered a career in grand opera. He took a year off to study singing with Luigi Meola at the New York College of Music; he often sang at New York's Grace Church. However, at the end of the year he returned to the stage; thereafter in singing roles he usually gagged arias, taking the role of a clown. In the fall of 1885 on the recommendation of Madame Cottrelly, he joined the McCaull Opera Company and was chief comedian for the next five years, playing in *The Black Hussar*, *The Beggar Student*, *Don Caesar*, *Boccaccio*, *Die Fledermaus*, and *The Lady or the Tiger*.

Hopper divorced his first wife and married Ida Mosher, an actress (date of marriage unknown); they had one son. On 14 August 1888 Hopper gave what was to become his most repeated and remembered performance. An avid baseball fan, he had been hired along with others to perform at a benefit at Wallack's Theatre honoring the Chicago White Stockings and the New York Giants. The manager of the theater, right before the show was to begin, handed Hopper a poem, "Casey at the Bat," which he memorized in only twenty minutes. The tragic ballad, written by Ernest L. Thayer and published the previous May in the *San Francisco Daily Examiner*, became Hopper's signature and one of America's best-loved poems. Over the next forty-five years Hopper performed it thousands of times. In it he recognized universal qualities: ambition, hope, hubris, failure. He later commented: "There is no day in the playing season that this same supreme tragedy, as stark as Aristophanes for the moment, does not befall on some field."

The following year in 1889 Hopper played Lord Middleditch in *The May Queen* and Casimir in *Clover*. In May 1890 he starred as Filacondre in *Castles in the Air* at the Broadway Theatre. The next year he appeared in the comic opera *Wang*, playing Wang, the regent of Siam; it was to become one of his most famous roles.

Having divorced his wife Ida, Hopper married Edna Wallace, an actress, in 1893; they had no children. That year he played Pedro in *Panjandrum*. Although by this time he was immensely popular with the public, he did not receive praise from every corner. The number three issue of the *Gallery of Players* (1894) dismissed him as a "gawky, shambling buffoon, utterly wanting in artistic discretion and woefully lacking in artistic taste," predicting that the public would weary of him. Undeterred, Hopper played Dr. Syntax in 1894 in the comic opera of the same name. Two years later he appeared as Don Errico Medigna in *El Capitan*. He divorced his wife Edna and in 1899 married Nella Reardon Bergen, a singer, who became his prima donna. In July he went to England, where he made his London debut, playing in *El Capitan* at the Lyric Theatre.

Upon his return to America he played with Joe Weber and Lew Fields in *Fiddle-dee-dee* and *Hoity Toity*. Then beginning in 1899 he toured in *Happy Land*. In December 1908 he starred in *The Pied Piper* at the Majestic Theatre. The following summer he traveled as Medford Griffin in *A Matinee Idol*. In May 1911 Hopper began one of the major periods of his career when he performed in a revival of W. S. Gilbert and Arthur Sullivan's *H.M.S. Pinafore*. From then on he played in productions of nearly all of their comic operas, including *Patience*, *The Pirates of Penzance*, *The Mikado*, *Iolanthe*, and *The Yeomen of the Guard*, in which he applied his gift of combining laughter and tears. Thereafter he was associated with the names of Gilbert and Sullivan and credited with bringing their work to the lasting attention of the American public.

Hopper continued also to take straight comic roles, playing Falstaff in *The Merry Wives of Windsor* and as David in *The Rivals*, which also starred Joseph Jefferson, Nat Goodwin, and William H. Crane. In 1913 his wife Nella divorced him, and within a month he married Eda Furry, an actress, later known as Hedda Hopper, the legendary Hollywood gossip columnist; they had one son. In 1915 Hopper went to Hollywood, where he had a brief and unsuccessful stint in the new medium of film. He had a part in *Don Quixote*, a production of the Triangle Film Corporation of D. W. Griffith, Thomas Ince, and Mack Sennett. Hopper recalled, "I sank majestically beneath the oily waves of the cinema sea and never was heard of again."

One of Hopper's favorite roles was Old Bill in *The Better Ole*, which he played in 1918–1919. "It was so human, I just reveled in it," he said. In 1922 his wife Eda divorced him and received custody of their son, William DeWolf. In 1925 he married his sixth and last wife Lillian Glaser; they had six children. That year and for the next three years he toured in Sigmund Romberg's *The Student Prince*.

In October 1928 Hopper celebrated the fiftieth anniversary of his stage career at a party at the Savoy Plaza in New York. He explained what had motivated him to choose the roles he played: "It is the contrast, the change from laughter to tears that makes comedy beautiful to do." In 1930–1931 Hopper went on a lecture and concert tour; in 1933 he played in *Uncle Tom's Cabin*. Then in September 1925 he was in Kansas City, Missouri, to narrate a Sunday afternoon radio broadcast of the Kansas City Rhythm Symphony. The day of the broadcast he took sick but insisted that the "show must go on." After the broadcast he was taken to a local hospital, where he died the following day.

Hopper's life was the theater; throughout most of his career he was an active member in the Lamb's Club. He stood six feet, two inches tall and had unusually long arms and legs. He was a master of classic comedy that at its best was exquisitely human and sensitive. He wrote, "The secret of fine acting, the secret of all art, is suggestion, the inflaming of the spectator's imagination, and the amount of suggestion is studied repression."

• See Hopper's reminiscence, written with Wesley W. Stout, *Once a Clown, Always a Clown* (1927), and G. C. D. Odell, *Annals of the N.Y. Stage*, vols. 10–12 (1938–1940). There are two very good studies of the poem he made famous; see Jim Moore and Natalie Vermilyea, *Ernest Thayer's "Casey at the Bat"* (1994), and Eugene C. Murdock, *Mighty Casey, All American* (1984). An obituary is in the *New York Times*, 24 Sept. 1935.

GEOFFREY GNEUHS

HOPPER, Edna Wallace (17 Jan. 1864?–14 Dec. 1959), actress, entrepreneur, and financier, was born and raised in San Francisco, California, the daughter of Walter Wallace. (Her mother's identity is unknown.) Little is verifiable about her early years, except that she was educated at the Van Ness Seminary, as public records were destroyed in the San Francisco earthquake of 1906. She began her stage career on a whim when, at a reception, she met and charmed comedian Roland Reed into issuing her an invitation to join his company. In August 1891 she made her debut as Mabel Douglas in the musical comedy *The Club Friend*, first at the Boston Museum, then two weeks later at the Star Palace in New York City. That November she played a supporting role to Reed in *Lend Me Your Wife*. Delicately beautiful, petite—standing less than five feet tall, she was renowned for never weighing more than eighty-five pounds—and very vivacious, she caught the eye of producer Charles Frohman, who soon made her a member of his own famous stock company.

Frohman was so impressed with Hopper's portrayals of soubrettes in his shows *Jane*, *Chums*, and *Men and Women* that he convinced distinguished playwright-producer David Belasco to create a comedic vehicle especially for her. Beginning on 25 January 1893 she gained both critical and popular success in *The Girl I Left Behind Me*, which Belasco staged for the inauguration of his opulent Empire Theater. In June of that year, having been courted by many rich and famous bachelors, she pleased both Belasco and Frohman by marrying established musical comedy star De-Wolf Hopper. After the couple divorced in 1898, she retained, for professional reasons, the name of Hopper and used it throughout her life.

Beloved by theater goers for her wit, vitality, and alluringly merry style (all of which helped to make up for her lack of vocal talent), Hopper began to divide her time between several stock companies, specializing in roles in light, momentarily memorable diversions, such as *Panjandrum*, *Wang*, *El Capitan*, and *Yankee Doodle Dandy*. Though her parts varied, she basically played herself. One contemporary recorded, "Her dramatic instinct is chiefly concerned in presenting to the best advantage an attractive personality and sparkling temperament backed up by a pretty face and a pleasing figure. . . . Edna Wallace Hopper's Paquita in 'Panjandrum,' for example, was none other than her Estrelda in 'El Capitan.' The environment was different . . . but the character was the same" (Strang, pp. 106–7). The high point of her professional stage life came in 1900–1902, when she starred as Lady Holyrood in *Floradora*. Ironically, the fame she achieved in the role was later overshadowed when the musical

became notable chiefly for introducing the chorus line to the Broadway stage. (According to theater lore, all six of the original Floradora Sextette married millionaires, thus generating the gold-digger myth.)

In 1902 Hopper created the role of Wrenne in *The Silver Slipper* at the Broadway Theater and also appeared for the first time in vaudeville. She subsequently performed in a number of plays, including *The White Chrysanthemums* and Belasco's restaging of *The Heart of Maryland*. She joined the Lew Field company in 1906 and two years later married Albert O. Brown, a stockbroker who subsequently turned to theatrical management; they separated in 1913. By that time her career was clearly on the wane. Although she continued to perform sporadically, including touring with the Richard Carle company, she was becoming too old to play the standard ingenue roles. She was in financial ruin by 1919, and her acting career abruptly ended in 1920 with the failure of her final show. She and Brown got back together in 1927, but the reconciliation was short-lived. Both marriages were childless.

Despite her many setbacks, Hopper did not give up public life. She parlayed her still deceptively youthful looks into a new vaudeville career, embarking in the 1920s on numerous tours to promote her own line of beauty products. These cosmetics, reportedly created from her mother's formulas, were manufactured by the Edna Wallace Hopper Corp., of which she was vice president. Her Strawberry Cream Mask, as she later maintained on the radio, not only enhanced beauty, it also could be used as a dessert topping. In 1927 Hopper took her concept of lifelong youthfulness one step further when she underwent the first of three face lifts, had the operation filmed, and booked personal appearances at local movie houses. Telling audiences that her doctors had "rejuvenated" her to the mental and physical equivalent of a teenager, she lectured on staying young and regaining lost energy and beauty. In case her public needed further convincing of her own vitality, she also performed acrobatic dancing. Always coyly refusing to tell her own age, until the end of her life she dressed in girlish hats and frills.

Hopper was a success on the circuit, but after losing her money on the stock market in the mid-1930s, she left the stage and her public in order to devote all her time to managing her finances. Shifting smoothly from the predominantly female domain of charm and beauty to the traditionally male world of high finance, she proved to be so talented in this her final career that in 1938 the brokerage firm of L. F. Rothschild offered her a desk in their New York office—the only woman among thirty-five men. Within fifteen years Hopper had earned four times her initial investment.

At the invitation of the American National Theater and Academy, in 1953 Hopper appeared in a review honoring the Empire Theater, which was about to be torn down. Hopper, by now in her eighties, surprised the audience by skipping onto the stage just as she had done sixty years before in the same role in *The Girl I Left Behind Me*. She attributed her energy to leading a full but sensible life, eating healthy foods, abstaining from alcohol and tobacco, and getting enough rest as well as exercise. Called the "woman who never grew old," she once told an interviewer, "I feel as if life were only beginning. I can't imagine a time in the future when I shall not be working. I shall retire when I die." Her statement proved prophetic. To the end she continued to ride the subway to the office, where she worked six hours at her desk. She was at work on 11 December 1959, a Friday, caught pneumonia that Saturday, and died two days later at her home in New York City.

• The Billy Rose Theatre Collection at the New York Public Library for the Performing Arts, Lincoln Center, possesses archival material on Hopper, including scrapbooks, clippings, and photographs. For descriptions of Hopper's acting see Lewis C. Strang, *Prima Donnas and Soubrettes of the Light Opera and Musical Comedy in America* (1900). A short feature article with photos appeared in *Life*, 8 June 1953. An obituary is in the *New York Times*, 15 Dec. 1959.

NOLA SMITH

HOPPER, Edward (22 July 1882–15 May 1967), artist, was born in Nyack, New York, the son of Garrett Henry Hopper, the owner of a dry goods store, and Elizabeth Griffiths Smith. After graduating from Nyack High School in 1899, Hopper entered art school in New York City, where he studied commercial illustration for two years. Then he studied painting at the New York School of Art, where his teachers included William Merritt Chase, Kenneth Hayes Miller, and Robert Henri, who was his favorite. Hopper remained in art school through the spring of 1906.

In the autumn of 1906 Hopper went to Paris. He depicted the French in a series of caricatures produced soon after his arrival. Hopper painted his first Parisian oils outdoors, depicting his surroundings and reflecting his awareness of Impressionists such as Camille Pissarro and Claude Monet. By the time he left Paris to tour London, Amsterdam, Haarlem, Berlin, and Brussels in June 1907, he had lightened his palette radically, occasionally working in high-key pastels applied with short, choppy strokes.

After his European tour Hopper returned to New York, where he worked as a commercial illustrator. He first exhibited his work in 1908 in a group show organized by several former classmates. During the spring of 1909 he returned to Paris, which he called "a most paintable city." Working outdoors for nearly five months, he abandoned the pastel colors and broken brushstrokes of 1907 and produced pictures that suggest the structural solidity that would characterize his mature style. After showing one of his French scenes in the Exhibition of Independent Artists in New York, Hopper made his last trip abroad in 1910. Besides Paris, Hopper visited Madrid and Toledo and attended a bullfight, a theme that would later appear in his graphic work.

Despite these trips to Europe, Hopper remained aloof from the avant-garde. Claiming that he met nobody, he later admitted that he had known about Gertrude Stein but insisted, "I don't remember having heard of Picasso at all." Although he had not yet found his mature realist style, Hopper was already resistant to the experiments with abstraction then taking place. Instead, he focused on depicting architectural forms as they appeared in the sunlight.

Hopper struggled to find recognition during the 1910s. Reluctantly, he continued to support himself as an illustrator, contributing to magazines such as *System*, *Farmer's Wife*, and *Adventure*. He maintained that he hated to draw people "gesturing and grimacing." Hopper still managed to find time to paint, particularly during the summers, which he usually spent on the New England coast.

Hopper exhibited one canvas, *Sailing*, in the 1913 Armory Show; it sold for $250. This was the first painting he ever sold and the last for a decade. Later that same year he moved into a studio on the top floor of 3 Washington Square North, where he lived and worked until his death. Although he continued to paint during the 1910s and to exhibit in group shows, primarily at the MacDowell Club of New York, Hopper was discouraged by having to produce illustrations to earn even a meager living.

In 1915 Hopper finally captured the attention of the critics. His small *New York Corner* was praised as "a perfect visualization of New York atmosphere"; however, his much larger and more ambitious scene of figures in a Paris cafe, *Soir Bleu*, was dismissed. The critics reflected the cultural climate that was becoming increasingly nationalistic. Only his former classmate at art school, Guy Pène du Bois, himself of French descent, supported Hopper's interest in French subject matter. Hopper never showed *Soir Bleu* again and gave up painting French subjects.

French subjects do continue, however, in some of Hopper's etchings, a medium that he first tried in 1915. Within a few years he was able to show and sell his prints, benefiting from a print revival then taking place in the United States. By showing in the many print salons around the country, Hopper found more exhibition opportunities than he could find for his paintings and discovered a new arena for recognition.

Hopper's thrift was such that his meager earnings as an illustrator permitted him to take modest summer vacations painting in Maine. In 1914 and 1915 he went to Ogunquit. For the summer of 1916 he visited Monhegan Island, where his former teacher Henri and fellow classmates Rockwell Kent and George Bellows also had painted. The island's remarkable rugged rocky coastline with its high bluffs and turbulent waves became the subject of Hopper's Monhegan pictures, which were mainly painted out of doors on small wood panels. Hopper enjoyed the experience so much that he returned there for the next few summers. Years later, however, he was reluctant to show these paintings with their abstract qualities to Alfred H. Barr, Jr., who, in organizing Hopper's first retrospective, concluded that during these years he devoted "most of his time to pot boiling illustration."

In October 1918 Hopper won a national award in a wartime poster competition conducted by the U.S.

Shipping Board. In a contest of over 1,400 entries, Hopper won the first prize of $300. His winning design for a four-color poster was entitled *Smash the Hun*. This award brought Hopper more fame than he had ever known.

In January 1920 the Whitney Studio Club in Greenwich Village gave Hopper his first one-man show of paintings. Guy Pène du Bois arranged the show, which featured sixteen oil paintings, eleven produced in Paris. None of the paintings was sold by the club, a nonprofit organization for artists founded by sculptor and socialite Gertrude Vanderbilt Whitney.

In the meantime, Hopper developed his skills as an etcher and earned increasing recognition. His 1922 etching *East Side Interior* won awards at both the Art Institute of Chicago and the Los Angeles County Museum when it was shown the following year. The experience of working on his etching in his studio prompted Hopper to improvise in both his choice of subject and composition. This practice contrasted with his habit of painting on location, causing him to rethink his creative process. He later remarked that after he took up etching, his "painting seemed to crystalize."

The Whitney Studio Club held another exhibition of Hopper's work in October 1922, featuring ten of the watercolor caricatures he had produced in Paris. As a member of the Whitney Studio Club, Hopper participated in evening sketch classes held there in 1923. He made numerous life drawings, perhaps underlining for him a need for a regular model.

In the summer of 1923 Hopper returned to Gloucester, Massachusetts, where in 1911 he had painted oils. There he ran into Josephine Nivison, an artist whom he had known since art school. A romance began, and as the two went on sketching excursions together Nivison encouraged Hopper to experiment with watercolor. Although Hopper had painted in watercolor as a boy, he had relegated the medium to illustration since his art school days. Nivison, however, had been exhibiting her watercolors.

That fall, when the Brooklyn Museum invited Nivison to exhibit six watercolors in a group show, she suggested they also include Hopper's work. The museum found his watercolors so appealing that they purchased a view of a Victorian house called *The Mansard Roof*, the first painting Hopper had sold since the Armory Show. Critics, most of whom ignored Nivison's work, also seized upon Hopper's watercolors to proclaim his talent. In all the excitement, Hopper abandoned his usual caution and gloom and married Nivison on 9 July 1924 in the Église Evangélique in Greenwich Village. He was nearly forty-two, and she was just a year younger.

After a honeymoon painting in Gloucester, Hopper took his watercolors to the Frank K. M. Rehn Gallery in New York, which gave him a one-man show that November. He sold all eleven pictures in the show and five more, creating enormous enthusiasm in his dealer, the critics, and his first patrons. He remained with this gallery for the rest of his life. Former classmate George Bellows, to whom success had come easier and

sooner, purchased two of the watercolors. The triumph of this exhibition allowed Hopper to abandon etching and to cease working as an illustrator.

In 1925 the Pennsylvania Academy of Fine Arts in Philadelphia purchased his 1923 canvas, *Apartment Houses*, becoming the first museum to acquire an oil painting by Hopper. The view into an urban interior was a motif that he used again and again. Newly prosperous, the Hoppers made a trip to Santa Fe, New Mexico, in 1925. Although he painted a number of watercolors there, he did not like the picturesque southwestern surroundings and the intense light. For relief, he turned to depicting his wife seated before a mirror in their bedroom. About this time Hopper began to use his wife as an artist's model. A former actress, "Jo" posed for all of the female and many of the male figures in his paintings for the rest of their lives.

Hopper purchased his first automobile in 1927. Driving made travel much easier, and he once remarked: "To me the most important thing is the sense of going on. You know how beautiful things are when you're traveling." Often blocked and unable to paint, Hopper turned to travel in search of inspiration. In fact, the images of travel—hotels, motels, cafeterias, gas stations, highways, trains, and railroad tracks—became themes in his pictures. His car served as a mobile studio with his wife painting in the passenger seat and Hopper stretching out his long legs across the back seat.

Hopper drove to Charleston, South Carolina, where he painted watercolors for more than a month in the spring of 1929. For the summer, however, he returned to the Maine coast, which he recorded in both oil and watercolor. Working out of doors, Hopper developed a particular fascination with lighthouses and coast guard stations, which he depicted dramatized by light and shadow.

By this time, Hopper's mature style had evolved; his paintings are characterized by a spare realism, emphasizing the contrast of light and shadow. His work, like his life, would remain divided between city and country. His boyhood love of nautical life on the Hudson River in Nyack would manifest itself in the attraction that the sea held for him. Thus bridges and rivers figure importantly among his urban scenes. The journey through the country on the way from city to city also became an important theme for Hopper, as in his *House by the Railroad* of 1925.

In 1930 Hopper first visited Cape Cod, where he rented a cottage in South Truro for the summer. He produced a number of oils and watercolors that depict local sites. He liked Truro so much that he and his wife returned for the next three summers, finally purchasing land on a hillside overlooking the bay. Hopper designed the small house that they had built there in 1934.

Hopper liked to remain on Cape Cod through October, after the crowds of summer vacationers departed. It was in autumn when the grass turned a beautiful golden brown that he painted many of his oils such as *Cape Cod Evening* of 1939 or *October on Cape Cod* of

1946. It was not only the rich tonality of autumn that appealed to Hopper, but also the melancholy of the season, with its implicit intimation of death.

In 1930, just after Hopper's inclusion in the exhibition "Nineteen Living Americans" at the Museum of Modern Art in New York, Stephen C. Clark, an important collector and an early patron of Hopper's work, gave *House by the Railroad* to the museum. This painting was the first by any artist to be acquired for the new museum's permanent collection. Hopper's *Early Sunday Morning* of 1930 was purchased that year by the newly established Whitney Museum of American Art. The Metropolitan Museum of Art purchased another of Hopper's major canvases, *Tables for Ladies*, in 1931.

Growing acceptance of Hopper's work prompted the National Academy of Design to elect him an associate member in 1932. He declined to accept the honor because the institution's exhibition juries had repeatedly rejected his paintings. The next year Barr organized Hopper's first retrospective exhibition for the Museum of Modern Art. For the catalog, Hopper wrote a rare statement of his aim in painting, which he described as "the most exact transcription possible of my most intimate impressions of nature." He explained that he viewed great painters as attempting to create "a record of their emotions."

Hopper became restless with the subject matter that he came to know so well on Cape Cod. As a result, from 1935 to 1938 he made annual automobile excursions to Vermont, where he painted watercolors. He no longer painted his canvases on location but produced working drawings that he later synthesized in the studio. Many of his seemingly realistic scenes are actually combinations of several places filtered through his imagination. For example, for *New York Movie* of 1939, Hopper made sketches in several theaters and had his wife pose for the usherette at home.

During the 1940s the Hoppers made several long trips, visiting the West Coast and Mexico. The fresh stimuli these wanderings provided resulted in watercolors. The Art Institute of Chicago gave him awards in 1942 for his painting *Nighthawks* and again in 1945. That same year, the National Institute of Arts and Letters elected him a member.

By the time Lloyd Goodrich organized Hopper's retrospective at the Whitney Museum of American Art in 1950, however, abstract expressionism had begun to make its mark on American art. Several critics contended that Hopper's realist style was too close to illustration. As a result of these attacks, and of his disapproval of the amount of attention American museums paid to abstract art, Hopper joined a number of representational painters in 1953 to publish the short-lived *Reality: A Journal of Artists' Opinion*.

Despite the consideration given to abstract expressionists, Hopper's reputation continued to grow during the 1950s. His work was featured in many exhibitions, and he received numerous awards, including a Gold Medal for Painting from the National Institute of Arts and Letters in 1955. In December 1956 he was featured on the cover of *Time* magazine.

What stuck in Hopper's mind, however, were the negative comments, and he anticipated more knocks on the occasion of another retrospective exhibition at the Whitney Museum of American Art in 1964. Instead, the cynical Hopper, who claimed of all artists, "ninety percent of them are forgotten ten minutes after they're dead," was surprised by the tremendous acclaim he received. His realist style and ordinary subjects prompted critics to hail him as the father of the contemporary movement of Pop Art.

Since Hopper's death, in New York City, his reputation has grown not only in the United States, but across Europe, in Australia, and in Japan. In Germany, Hopper's popularity approaches that of a cult figure. His place in art history seems secure, for his work appears not only to have captured the mood of the America that he knew, but also to embody the very pulse of twentieth-century life. Hopper's understated scenes, with their empty spaces, solitary figures, or several generalized figures, have often suggested loneliness and alienation to observers, allowing each viewer to imagine a different scenario.

• The most comprehensive collection of Edward Hopper's work is in the Whitney Museum of American Art in New York City. The Hopper collection, bequeathed by the artist's widow, also includes the artist's record books (1924–1957) in which works were listed by his wife (and frequently sketched by the artist) as they left the studio for exhibition. The most complete assessment is Gail Levin, *Edward Hopper: A Catalogue Raisonné* (1994), a multivolume complete catalog of the artist's oils, watercolors, and illustrations accompanied by a biographical sketch, a comprehensive bibliography, and an exhibition history. For Hopper's etchings, see Levin, *Edward Hopper: The Complete Prints* (1979), and Carl Zigrosser, "The Etchings of Edward Hopper," in *Prints*, ed. Zigrosser (1962). See also Levin, *Hopper's Places* (1985), for photographs of the exact sites painted and a study of the artist's working methods. A front-page obituary is in the *New York Times*, 17 May 1967.

GAIL LEVIN

HOPPER, Grace Brewster Murray (9 Dec. 1906–1 Jan. 1992), naval officer and pioneer developer of computer languages, was born in New York City, the daughter of Walter Fletcher Murray and Mary Campbell Van Horne. Her grandfathers were important in shaping her future—one was a navy admiral, and the other an engineer with New York City. After attending Hardridge School in Plainfield, New Jersey, she graduated in 1928 with election to Phi Beta Kappa from Vassar College, with a degree in mathematics and physics. She completed a mathematics M.A. in 1930 at Yale and earned a Ph.D. in mathematics and mathematical physics, also from Yale, in 1934.

Grace married Vincent Foster Hopper in 1930; they had no children and were divorced in 1945. She taught at Vassar from 1931 to 1941, rising from instructor to associate professor. After a Vassar faculty fellowship at the Courant Institute of New York University in 1942, and teaching at Barnard College in 1943, she joined the war effort by signing up with the U.S. Naval Reserve in December 1943.

Commissioned as a lieutenant (junior grade) in June 1944, Hopper was assigned to a Harvard University project creating mathematical tables for the navy's Bureau of Ordnance. Her duties included working with Howard Aiken's electro-mechanical Mark I computer project, funded jointly by IBM and the navy. She edited the 500-page *Manual of Operation* for this first American programmable computer, which could develop mathematical tables far faster than human computers.

Fully engaged in her computer research, Hopper declined Vassar's postwar offer to return as a mathematics professor. When the navy turned down her 1946 request for a regular commission (at forty, she was two years too old), she reverted to inactive reserve status. Becoming a research fellow in engineering sciences and applied physics at Harvard, she helped to complete the larger and faster Mark II and Mark III computers, supported by continuing navy contracts with the university. She is often credited with creating the term "computer bug" around this time: in mid-1947 she and others found a dead moth causing a relay to malfunction in the Mark II computer and recorded the event in their log of experiments. Hopper became interested in potential business applications of the computer and helped Prudential Insurance use the Mark I to refine its actuarial tables.

During the late 1940s Hopper also taught mathematics at Harvard part-time, but she did not stay beyond three years because Harvard limited tenured positions to full-time faculty. After entertaining several offers of employment, she sought to further her research interest in computer programming. In 1949 she became a senior mathematician with the Eckert-Mauchly Computer Corporation in Philadelphia, newly formed by the creators of the all-electronic ENIAC computer, which had been developed under army contracts during the war. She stayed on as a senior computer programmer when the company was taken over by Remington Rand a year later.

Hopper served as head programmer for Remington Rand's pioneering UNIVAC I (Universal Automatic Computer) series of computers, forty-six of which were sold between 1951 and 1957. She became director of programming for what became the UNIVAC division of Sperry-Rand after 1955. At UNIVAC Hopper managed a programming team that produced the first computer language "compiler" in 1952. Dubbed the A-0 (later the A-2), it allowed translation of computer programming language into machine-readable binary code instructions. This led in turn to later machine-readable programming languages, including Math-Matic and B-0 or Flow-Matic (1957), which was described as the first computer language in English, using words rather than symbols and numbers. Flow-Matic, in turn, strongly influenced the development (by others) in the late 1950s of Common Business-Oriented Language (COBOL), a word-based computer

language developed in response to the scientific community's more complex, mathematical FORTRAN computer language. Hopper was instrumental in developing compilers for COBOL in the early 1960s. For another two decades, COBOL was the most widely used programming language in the United States, in part because of its relative ease of learning and use.

Throughout this period Hopper had remained in the navy reserve, becoming a lieutenant commander in 1946 and commander in 1952, and reluctantly retiring at the latter rank in 1966 because of age. Just seven months later, the navy recalled her to active service—she was then sixty—to work on standardizing their myriad computer programming languages. She remained for nineteen more years, dubbed "Amazing Grace" by her subordinates, and worked diligently to promote standardized computer program languages in both government and business. Thanks to annual extensions voted by Congress, Hopper became a captain in 1973, commodore in 1983 (in a White House ceremony), and finally retired in August 1986 as a rear admiral at age seventy-nine, the oldest serving officer. She loved to recall the airport agent who, on seeing her in officer's uniform, remarked, "You must be the oldest one they've got."

In September 1986 Hopper reported to Digital Equipment Corporation to work in their public relations department as a senior consultant. She worked actively until a year and a half before her death in Arlington, Virginia. She was buried with full military honors at Arlington National Cemetery.

An accomplished public speaker who gave two hundred or more talks a year, Hopper encouraged young people to enter the expanding computer field. She always told them to experiment—it was far easier to apologize later than to obtain advance permission to try something innovative. She kept a ship's clock in her office that read time backward, to suggest that tradition was not a sufficient reason to do things the same way. Her straightforward, often outspoken approach, her willingness to poke fun at herself as well as others, and her dedication to the quest for computer program standardization in business and government made her an important spokesperson for more widespread application of computers. In the 1950s she predicted that computer software costs would eventually exceed those of hardware and that computers would shrink from room size to desktop units; she lived to see both predictions become fact.

• Hopper described aspects of her life in "The Education of a Computer," in *Proceedings of the Association for Computing Machinery Conference* (May 1952): 271–81; she also authored many technical papers. A book-length biography, written for young people, is Charlene W. Billings, *Grace Hopper: Navy Admiral and Computer Pioneer* (1989). See also "Grace Murray Hopper: Bugs, Compilers and COBOL," in Robert Slater, *Portraits in Silicon* (1987), pp. 219–29; "Grace Brewster Murray Hopper," in J. A. N. Lee, *Computer Pioneers* (1995), pp. 380–87, which includes a full list of Hopper's many awards and honors; Cheryl Wetzstein and Linda Forrestal, "Grace Murray Hopper," *The World & I* (Aug. 1987): 198–

205; and Henry S. Tropp, "Grace Hopper: The Youthful Teacher of Us All," *Abacus* 2, no. 1 (1984): 7–18. An obituary is in the *New York Times*, 3 Jan. 1992.

CHRISTOPHER H. STERLING

HOPPER, Hedda (2 May 1885–1 Feb. 1966), actress and gossip columnist, was born Elda Furry in Hollidays-burg, Pennsylvania, the daughter of David E. Furry, a butcher, and Margaret Miller. The fifth of nine children, Hopper attended school until the eighth grade, after which she stayed home to help her mother with the household. She had an early driving desire to be on the stage, spurred by seeing Ethel Barrymore on screen. Hopper's theatrical aspirations coincided with the purchase of the first of her trademark hats. Pleased by the admiration it inspired in men and the envy it provoked from women, she resolved then that "if a hat can get the attention of this many people, I'll never go bareheaded again" (*From under My Hat*, p. 31). Throughout her career Hopper would be known for her stylish and sometimes outlandish hats and would receive them as gifts from friends and admiring fans.

Hopper attended the Carter Conservatory of Music in Pittsburgh in 1903, and by 1908, without her parents' knowledge, she had moved to New York and gotten a job on a chorus line. While appearing in the chorus of the *Pied Piper*, she met William DeWolf "Wolfie" Hopper, twenty-seven years her senior, who was a popular musical comedy performer. She secretly married him in 1913, becoming his fifth wife, and changed her name to Hedda soon after. The Hoppers lived at the Algonquin Hotel in New York City, where their only son was born in 1915.

Later in 1915 Hopper moved to Hollywood with a number of other prominent theater stars so that her husband could pursue a film career. His screen work proved to be limited, but Hedda, who had given up her career when the couple married, was offered stage and screen roles. After a year in Hollywood, the Hoppers returned to New York, where Hopper hoped to raise her son on Long Island.

In 1922 Hopper divorced her husband on the grounds of adultery and soon after returned to Hollywood, this time as a 38-year-old single mother. She continued her career as a popular character actress, accepting and relishing roles as a "bad" woman. Hopper said of her roles in this era: "I wasn't a star, only a featured player in support of the big shots. I was the mean woman who made the stars look good. I've slapped more children, tumbled down more houses of cards, kicked over more building blocks, and rapped more innocent knuckles than any female fiend in an old-time orphanage" (*From under My Hat*, p. 229). Hopper was under contract with MGM for a number of years, but after the roles offered her began to diminish in the early 1930s and the contract was not renewed, she explored other career options. She tried the agency business; she worked in real estate briefly; and she then returned to New York, where she appeared again on stage. She also joined Elizabeth Arden in the cosmetic business for a few months but left disil-

lusioned. In 1935 she returned again to Hollywood, the town she would consider her home for the rest of her life. By this point, however, Hopper's days as a film actor were for the most part over; she was offered various roles until her death, but most of these were cameo performances, as in *The Women* (1939), in which she had a small part as a gossip columnist.

It was, in fact, as a Hollywood gossip columnist that Hopper achieved her greatest fame. She first attempted to enter the business with the help of Dema Harshbarger, then head of the artists' bureau of NBC. Hopper landed a spot as host of a fifteen-minute radio gossip program hosted by Maro-Oil shampoo, but the show lasted only three months. In 1938 her writing career began when she was approached by Esquire Features to write a syndicated Hollywood column. After an initially shaky start, the column took off. Hopper's style was breezy and colloquial; she was never a strong writer and dictated most of her columns to her staff. The powerful *Los Angeles Times* soon subscribed to her column, and as a result "Hedda Hopper's Hollywood" became important—the column eventually reached 35 million readers, and its popularity led to her hosting a television and radio show as well.

Hopper's accomplishments challenged the reigning queen of gossip, Hearst columnist Louella Parsons. Hopper and Parsons had been friends in the early days, and Parsons even had promoted Hopper as a young actress, but with Hopper's success they launched into an on-again, off-again feud that fueled newspaper sales for more than ten years.

Hopper's columns reflected a love of the "old" Hollywood where glamour, fashion, and excitement prevailed; she protested violently against what she saw as "message movies," instead supporting players, writers, and filmmakers who kept the illusion of a glittering Hollywood alive. Also a staunch political conservative, Hopper took an active part in the fight against communism in the film industry, serving as second vice president for the Motion Picture Alliance for the Preservation of American Ideals. Ultimately, she saw herself as one who would maintain the old glamour that she loved, both in her columns and in her personal life; her trademark hats, for which she was world famous, were a fitting symbol of the glamorous Hollywood she wished to preserve and represent.

Hopper died in Hollywood. Her ashes were returned to her Pennsylvania birthplace.

• Hopper's papers, correspondence, and scrapbooks are at the Margaret Herrick Library of the Academy of Motion Picture Arts and Sciences in Beverly Hills, Calif. Hopper wrote two informal autobiographies, *From under My Hat* (1952), which the *Herald Tribune* called "the longest of all possible gossip columns," and, with J. Brough, *The Whole Truth and Nothing But* (1963), which is more sentimental and nostalgic in tone. Both books are nonlinear, anecdotal accounts of Hopper's life and include gossip about stars both in and out of favor; neither book includes many dates, and Hopper does not adhere scrupulously to fact. The most thorough source of information on Hopper can be found in George Eells, *Hedda and Louella* (1972), which offers biographical information on both women and a history of their ongoing feud. *Time* ran a cover story on Hopper in its 23 July 1947 issue. An obituary is in the *New York Times*, 2 Feb. 1966.

DEBORAH M. EVANS

HOPPER, Isaac Tatem (3 Dec. 1771–7 May 1852), Quaker abolitionist and reformer, was born in Deptford township, near Woodbury, New Jersey, the son of Levi Hopper and Rachel Tatem, farmers. Educated in local schools, Isaac Hopper went to Philadelphia at sixteen to learn tailoring from an uncle, with whom he lived. He made his living there as a tailor and soon came to own his own shop.

At age twenty-two, Hopper joined the Society of Friends, not only because he had become convinced of its principles but also because the young woman he fancied, his distant cousin and childhood sweetheart Sarah Tatum was a Quaker whose father did not want her to marry out of meeting; the couple was wed in 1795. He also became active in the Pennsylvania Abolition Society and as an overseer for an African-American school founded by Anthony Benezet; he taught two or three nights a week at a school for black adults.

By the turn of the century Hopper had won a reputation as a friend of escaped slaves by his ingenuity in outwitting slave-catchers and by serving as escapees' unofficial advocate in legal proceedings. He could not excuse the injustice of one person enslaving another. Quick-witted and sharp-tongued, he often used sarcasm to his opponents' faces. In a case involving a slave named Prince Hopkins, whose owner and lawyer dismissed as "that nigger," Hopper retorted, "I would rather trust 'that nigger,' as you call him, than either of you." Not above using a bit of subterfuge for a good cause, he once negotiated a low price for a slave whose master mistakenly believed was dying. Hopper also helped organize a Free Produce Society to encourage abstinence from goods produced by slave labor.

Hopper's wife Sarah, mother of the couple's ten children and recognized in 1814 as a Quaker minister, died in 1822 at age forty-seven. Two years later he married the much younger Hannah Attmore, with whom he had four more children. In the disputes among Friends in the 1820s, disagreements rooted in attempts by well-to-do urban elders to impose their evangelical definitions of Quakerism on Philadelphia Yearly Meeting, Hopper took an active role on the side of the rural dissidents. Having himself experienced the heavy-handed treatment meted out by the elders, he lined up with the less sophisticated opposition, labeled "Hicksites," and was disowned by his Orthodox meeting in Philadelphia.

In 1829, his tailoring business weakened by the withdrawal of Orthodox patronage, Hopper moved to New York City, where he managed an antislavery bookshop and published some Hicksite works. He carried on his usual activities against slavery, assisted by his daughter Abigail and her husband James Sloan Gibbons. In 1841 he became associated with the American Anti-Slavery Society and its new newspaper, the *National Anti-Slavery Standard*, whose editor, Lydia Maria Child, resided in his home.

Hopper's mingling with the "world's people" in these efforts soon led to trouble with fellow believers. An antiabolitionist Quaker minister, George White, who opposed reformers of every stripe, particularly those with whom Quakers associated, spoke for many New York Friends when he denigrated antislavery groups as "abominations in the sight of God." The Hester Street Hicksite meeting disowned Hopper and Gibbons in 1842 after the *Standard* ran a sarcastic attack on White. They had associated with a publication, their alarmed critics judged, "calculated to excite discord and disunity among Friends." New York Yearly Meeting ultimately upheld this decision, but the old man never changed his habit of attending meeting and wearing outdated Quaker garb. Until 1845 he filled the part-time posts of treasurer and book agent and served on the board of the Anti-Slavery Society; William Lloyd Garrison, founder of the society, usually stayed at his home when he visited New York City.

Parallel to his antislavery activities, if not so notorious, was Hopper's involvement in prison reform. As an inspector of prisons while still in Philadelphia, he became a kind of nineteenth-century social worker, shrewdly seeking inmates who might be amenable to reformation and lending them and their families moral and sometimes financial support. He continued this work after his move, as well as lobbying during two legislative sessions for incorporation of the private Prison Association of New York in 1845 and then becoming its agent in its principal task of assisting freed convicts. He always opposed capital punishment.

After resigning his position as agent after seven years, Hopper had gained renown in Albany as one of the state's leading authorities on prisons. He took a continuing personal interest in discharged inmates, as with escaped slaves. Even after passage of the federal Fugitive Slave Law in 1850, when he was in his seventy-ninth year, he was actively involved with giving succor to runaways. He died in New York City. His children rejected an offer from the now-conciliatory Hester Street Meeting to allow their father to be buried in its graveyard, so he was interred in Greenwood Cemetery, with eulogies offered by fellow Hicksite and abolitionist Friends Lucretia Mott and Thomas McClintock.

Hopper was in many ways a traditional Quaker, determinedly bearing his testimony by carriage, clothing, and conviction against conventional practices. Never rich, sometimes nearly impoverished, he spent himself in a public life of faithfulness to his leadings. He consistently refused to pay the militia tax and had to stand by while the authorities seized his goods. Still, his quickness and consistency—as when he publicly maintained after the 1851 Christiana riots that former slaves who defended themselves against "negro-hunters" were not murderers—inevitably brought him into conflict with more cautious fellow believers. One admirer thought that his life's motto should have read,

"The rich and the poor meet together, and the Lord is the Father of them all."

• There are no collections of Hopper's papers, although a scattering of letters can be found in the papers of Benjamin Ferris and some other contemporaries in the Friends Historical Library at Swarthmore College. On Quakers and slavery, see Thomas E. Drake, *Quakers and Slavery in America* (1950). The only biography, L. Maria Child, *Isaac T. Hopper: A True Life* (1853; repr. 1969), was written soon after Hopper's death. For his disownment by his Hicksite meeting, see *Narrative of the Proceedings of the Monthly Meeting of New York . . . in the Case of Isaac T. Hopper* (1843). There is also some information in issues of the *National Anti-Slavery Standard.*

H. LARRY INGLE

HOPWOOD, Avery (28 May 1882–1 July 1928), playwright, was born James Avery Hopwood in Cleveland, Ohio, the son of James Hopwood and Jule Pendergast, dealers in wholesale and retail provisions. A Phi Beta Kappa graduate of the University of Michigan (1905), Hopwood was interested in writing from an early age. He wrote short fiction for the university literary magazine, served as cub reporter on the *Cleveland Leader*, and wrote his first play, *Clothes*, during his senior year after reading "The Call for the Playwright," an article by drama critic Louis Vincent DeFoe that described the vast fortune in royalties to be earned from writing a few good plays.

Upon graduation, Hopwood moved to New York City, where seasoned playwright Channing Pollock collaborated with him on *Clothes* (1906) and made it a successful vehicle for actress Grace George. Hopwood's next two solo efforts, *The Powers That Be* (1907) and *This Woman and This Man* (1909), were social thesis dramas that met with little success. He achieved his first major Broadway hit with *Seven Days* (1909), a preposterous farce, when popular mystery writer Mary Roberts Rinehart asked him to collaborate on dramatizing her novel of the same name. The financial success of *Seven Days* turned Hopwood away from serious drama, and he devoted the remainder of his career primarily to writing comedies and farces, particularly of the bedroom variety. *Nobody's Widow* (1910), a romantic farce commissioned by David Belasco for Blanche Bates, and *Judy Forgot* (1910), written for comedienne Marie Cahill, followed, as did disastrous attempts at an operetta with Gustav Luders, *Somewhere Else* (1913), and a second piece for Grace George, *Miss Jenny O'Jones* (1913). After threatening to give up playwriting, Hopwood returned to Broadway in 1915 with two smart bedroom comedies, *Sadie Love*, starring Marjorie Rambeau, and the highly popular *Fair and Warmer*, starring Madge Kennedy. So successful was *Fair and Warmer* that at one time there were six road companies touring the country. Hopwood had become the king of bedroom farce. In 1916, after seeing Hopwood's risqué *Our Little Wife*, critic George Jean Nathan praised him for having "a quick eye to the crazy-quilt of sex humours and a keen vision to the foibles of the cosmopolite."

The height of Hopwood's career came in 1920 when he achieved the distinction of having four plays running concurrently on Broadway: *The Gold Diggers* (1919, starring Ina Claire and Bruce McRae), which gave birth to the spectacular gold-digger movie musicals of the 1930s; *Ladies' Night (In a Turkish Bath)* (1920, written with Charlton Andrews, featuring Doris Kenyon and Charles Ruggles); *Spanish Love* (1920, written with Mary Roberts Rinehart, featuring William Powell); and the still-popular mystery-thriller, *The Bat* (1920, also written with Rinehart). After 1920 Hopwood became increasingly dissatisfied with his career in the theater and mainly doctored plays—for example, *Getting Gertie's Garter* (1921, written with Wilson Collison, starring Hazel Dawn); *The Best People* (1924, written with David Gray)—or adapted popular foreign hits, such as *The Demi-Virgin* (1921, starring Hazel Dawn); *The Alarm Clock* (1923, starring Bruce McRae); *Little Miss Bluebeard* (1923, starring Irene Bordoni); *The Harem* (1924, starring Lenore Ulrich);/: and *Naughty Cinderella* (1925, starring Irene Bordoni). Hopwood's other plays include *Double Exposure* (1918); *The Girl in the Limousine* (1919, written with Wilson Collison, featuring Charles Ruggles); *Why Men Leave Home* (1922); and *The Garden of Eden* (1927, starring Miriam Hopkins).

Between 1915 and 1925 Hopwood's farces ran an average of 168 performances each, compared to the average run of ninety-one performances for all other farces during the same period. When combined, all of Hopwood's plays ran a total of 4,932 performances in New York, or, an average of 206 performances each—this at a time when 100 performances still ensured a profitable hit. In addition, his plays were performed around the world and in countless stock companies across the United States. At least twenty of his scripts were made into motion pictures. Hopwood amassed a fortune on the theory that the drama was a "democratic art" and that the playwright was not the "monarch, but the servant of the public." He admitted that he wrote for Broadway, "to please Broadway." As a result, his plays turned greater profits than did any other playwright's of the day. Hopwood was a master at giving theatergoers what they wanted: cleverly built plays that presented characters whose breezy dialogue typified the attitudes of the time. He came to realize, however, that his axiom, "the voice of the public should be considered the voice of the gods," was destroying him. Lacking sufficient versatility to free himself from the formulae that had made him a success, Hopwood allowed his life to deteriorate into a self-indulgent masquerade characteristic of the cynical gaiety of the times. At age forty-six, cocaine and alcohol abuse induced a heart attack while he was swimming at the beach of Juan-les-Pin on the French Riviera. Rumors about Hopwood committing suicide cannot be substantiated. According to eyewitness accounts, he gave one piercing shriek and sank into shoulder-deep water, dying almost instantly. Hopwood left an estate worth well over $1 million and is buried in Riverside Cemetery, Cleveland. He never married. Standing five feet eleven inches tall, with blonde hair and hazel eyes, he was tellingly portrayed by his friend Gertrude Stein in her *Autobiography of Alice B. Toklas*: in the early days, "holding his head a little on one side and with his tow-colored hair, he looked like a lamb. Sometimes in the latter days as [she] told him the lamb turned into a wolf."

Because Hopwood's talents were given to popular drama as distinct from the literary drama during the period of innovation in the 1920s, his plays and his career have been almost totally eclipsed. Today he is chiefly remembered on the campus of his alma mater as benefactor of the Avery Hopwood and Jule Hopwood Creative Writing Awards—awards that encouraged such writers as Betty Smith, Marge Piercy, John Ciardi, Robert Hayden, and Arthur Miller, to name but a few. Dissatisfied with his own contribution to writing, he wished to encourage in others, in the words of the bequest, "the new, the unusual, and the radical." Hopwood had always wanted to write good fiction, "something," he once told a newspaper reporter, "which an intelligent man can sit down and read and think about." Although Hopwood worked on such a book throughout his career, he only succeeded in completing a rough draft, which disappeared shortly after his death. Rumored to be a "devastating theatre exposé," the work was uncovered in 1982. It is a semiautobiographical novel that sheds significant light upon Hopwood's life, career, and why he wanted to encourage young writers.

• Letters from Hopwood are in the Avery Hopwood Papers in the Department of Rare Books and Special Collections at the University of Michigan; in the Archie Bell folder in the Literature Department of the Cleveland Public Library; in the Mary Roberts Rinehart Collection in the Hillman Library Special Collections at the University of Pittsburgh; and in the Gertrude Stein Collection in the Beinecke Rare Book and Manuscript Library at Yale University. A carbon transcript of his unpublished semiautobiographical novel is in the files of Hollywood Plays, Inc., Glen Rock, N.J. Copies of his unpublished plays are in the Billy Rose Theatre Collection in the New York Public Library at Lincoln Center. Newspaper clippings are in the Robinson Locke Collection in the Billy Rose Theatre Collection at the New York Public Library at Lincoln Center. A collection of dramatic reviews and biographical materials, compiled by Arno L. Bader, is in the Department of Rare Books and Special Collections at the University of Michigan. The standard biography, which includes an extensive bibliography, is Jack F. Sharrar, *Avery Hopwood: His Life and Plays* (1989). See also Gertrude Stein, *The Autobiography of Alice B. Toklas* (1933) and *Everybody's Autobiography* (1937); Alice B. Toklas, *What Is Remembered* (1963); and Mary Roberts Rinehart, *My Story* (1948). Obituaries are in *Variety* and the *New York Times*, 2 July 1928.

JACK F. SHARRAR

HORLICK, William Alexander (23 Feb. 1846–25 Sept. 1936), manufacturer, was born in Ruardean, Gloucestershire, England, the son of James Horlick, a saddler, and Priscilla Griffiths. Educated in local schools and at Candover boarding school, near Winchester, William was apprenticed to a harness maker before opening his own shop. Immigrating to the United States in November 1869, he settled in Racine, Wisconsin, where he worked for James A. Horlick, a relative who had resided there since 1844. The following year William married James's daughter, Arabella Rozelia Horlick, with whom he had four children.

In 1873 Horlick moved to Chicago, where he later was joined by his brother James, a chemist, and began to manufacture food products, beginning with J. and W. Horlick's New Food for Infants, Dyspeptics and Invalids. Produced by macerating wheat flour and malted barley with water, removing the water, and pulverizing the resultant solid matter, thereby converting the starch into maltose and dextrine, Horlick's New Food was endorsed by a group of Chicago physicians as a means of reducing infant mortality because it contained fewer carbohydrates. In 1876 the Horlick brothers relocated their operations to Racine to be closer to needed supplies of milk and grain while they experimented with related processes. The chief result of these investigations was the discovery of "malted milk," a nutritive extract of malted grain combined with cow's milk in powdered form that, flyers claimed, would "keep indefinitely in any climate, agree with the most delicate stomach, and is instantly prepared for use by dissolving in water only."

Within a few years the company began producing malted milk in tablet form and introduced Diastoid, pure extract of malt in the form of powder. The "Malted Milk" trademark, registered in 1887, rapidly became nationally and internationally renowned, becoming a common noun and remaining synonymous with the Horlick family name for over half a century. By the early 1890s, Horlick's Food Company, incorporated in 1883, had established branches in New York City and in England, through which it supplied both European and British Empire markets. Reorganized as Horlick's Malted Milk Company in 1906 (and later, in 1925, as Horlick's Malted Milk Corporation), the new corporation's English-style plant and offices quickly became one of the architectural landmarks of the western Great Lakes region. After serving as treasurer of the company until James's death in 1921, William acceded to the presidency, a post he held until his death fifteen years later. By 1953 the company was known simply as Horlick's Corporation. Purchased by Beecham Group Ltd. in 1961, it ceased U.S. production in 1975.

Over the years, Horlick products gained considerable prestige and publicity from their use by the United States military and by various explorers. First utilized by the Union army during the Civil War, Horlick's malted milk tablets became a dietary staple of the armed forces during the Spanish-American War and both world wars. During the Second World War they became a standard component of the Army's K ration supplies as well as of the survival kits issued to air corps and navy personnel. Readily portable and resistant to spoilage, Horlick's malted milk products accompanied Robert E. Peary's expedition to the North Pole, Raold Amundsen's discovery of the South Pole, and Richard E. Byrd's exploration of both poles. For his support of Amundsen's journey and the scientific investigations of Carl Lumholz, Horlick was knighted as a member of the Royal Norwegian Order of St. Olaf by King Haakon in 1922. He was also the first honorary member of the Order of Sons of St. George and a member of the American Pharmaceutical Association, the Union League Clubs of Chicago and New York, the Explorers Club, the Hamilton Club of Chicago, and the Milwaukee Club.

During his long tenure in Racine, Horlick was a noted contributor to a variety of civic and philanthropic causes. Among his contributions to the city were the 33-acre Horlick Park, the 5-acre Horlick Athletic Field, and the 17-acre site and athletic field of the William A. Horlick High School. He was the leading contributor to and organizer of Memorial Hall, built after the First World War to serve as a meeting place for patriotic societies and to house war records and memorabilia. A generous patron of the American Legion, Young Men's Christian Association, and the Boy Scouts of America, Horlick was especially generous in his gifts to Racine's St. Luke's Hospital, which he also presented with the Alice Horlick Memorial and the Alice Horlick Maternity units in memory of his daughter who had died in childhood. He died at his home in Racine. His funeral was reputed to be the largest in the city's history. In his will Horlick enjoined his beneficiaries to manifest "the same industry, intelligence and frugality that he had."

• The Horlick's Corporation Records (1873–1974) are housed in the Area Research Center of the University of Wisconsin-Parkside. They consist of six boxes and two microfilm reels of testimonial and promotional materials, corporate minutes books, advertisements, scrapbooks, diagrams, and postcards and include historical and biographical information on the Horlick family and business. Brief sketches are in C. W. Butterfield, *History of Racine and Kenosha Counties, Wisconsin* (1879), pp. 590–91; *Biographical Dictionary and Portrait Gallery of Representative Men of Chicago, Wisconsin and the World's Columbian Exposition* (1895), pp. 312–13; E. B. Usher, ed., *Wisconsin: Its Story and Biography, 1848–1913*, vol. 4 (1914), pp. 920–21; State Historical Society of Wisconsin, *Wisconsin Necrology* (1984), vol. 36, p. 169, vol. 37, p. 187, and vol. 42, pp. 223–24; Fanny S. Stone, ed., *Racine: Belle City of the Lakes and Racine County, Wisconsin*, vol. 1 (1916), pp. 249–50; Fred L. Holmes, ed., *Wisconsin: Stability, Progress Beauty*, vol. 3 (1946), pp. 41–43; and U.S. Patent Office, *Official Gazette*, 8 Oct. 1926. Obituaries are in the *Milwaukee Journal*, 25 Sept. 1936, and the *Racine Journal-Times*, 25 Sept. and 8 Oct. 1936.

JOHN D. BUENKER

HORMEL, George Albert (4 Dec. 1860–5 June 1946), businessman, was born in Buffalo, New York, the son of John Godfrey Hormel, a tanner, and Susanna Decker. His parents were German immigrants. The third of twelve children in a family of modest means, Hormel sought work upon completing the sixth grade. He held several menial jobs before he left home at the age of seventeen for Chicago, where he found employment first in his uncle Jacob Decker's meat market

and then at the Philip D. Armour meatpacking house. While at Armour he came into contact with Edward A. Cudahy and Gustavus F. Swift, who, like Hormel, learned the trade from Armour before creating successful meat companies of their own. Following his tenure at Armour, Hormel worked a series of jobs in the meatpacking business and the wool and hides trade. He took a regional post in southern Minnesota that enabled him to develop a network of friends and business relations in the meat industry. In 1887 he became co-owner of the Friedrich and Hormel butcher shop in Austin, Minnesota. By 1891 the partners' diverging interests led to the dissolution of the company into a meat market, operated by Friedrich, and a packinghouse, run by Hormel, that grew into Hormel and Company. The following year Hormel married a local teacher, Lillian Belle Gleason; the couple had one son.

Under Hormel's guidance the company grew steadily, expanding output, product lines, physical plant, and market after the turn of the century. He developed a reputation for demanding high quality and setting goals of perfection for his products. Keenly aware of how the giants in the industry such as Swift and Armour conducted business, Hormel believed that higher quality meats would enable his company to improve its market share in an industry where quality was unreliable at best. Equally uncharacteristic of the meatpacking industry in this era, Hormel placed a high value on sanitary conditions, constantly finding means to improve cleanliness in the plant. The success of the giant Chicago packinghouses, combined with their ruthless business practices, forced most smaller or newer competitors out of business. Hormel succeeded where others failed, in part by giving his employees a stake in the company's prosperity. He offered employees shares of company stock as a means of providing them with an incentive to help make the business thrive.

Hormel flourished by taking advantage of new markets. He recognized and took advantage of the changes wrought by urbanization, the increased importance of railroads, and the new immigrants coming into the country. The markets among immigrants and people new to the cities meant that new products, such as Genoa sausage, would sell well in New York and other places. In addition, people began to purchase according to brand recognition. In response, Hormel launched national advertising efforts. The company made heavy use of railroads and new refrigerated cars to ship their products throughout the nation. Hormel's son, Jay, took the reins of the company in 1927, after his father made him learn the business from the cutting floor up. In the later 1920s Hormel, along with his son, introduced the first canned ham in the country. They quickly followed this with other canned meats and soups. During the Great Depression the company focused on the working-class market and introduced both the Dinty Moore brand of ready-to-eat canned foods and their most famous product, the can of spiced pork shoulder called Spam.

The lowest point for the Hormel company came in 1921 when the company discovered that the assistant comptroller, Cy Thomson, had embezzled more than a million dollars during a ten-year period. This financial debacle came at a bad time for the company. Sales had fallen, and fluctuations in stock prices left the company mired in debt. Hormel authorized the selling of company bonds to release the company from its creditors. The plan worked, and in the final years of Hormel's presidency the business expanded into every corner of the nation and prospered financially.

During the depression of the early 1930s, the company weathered more economic uncertainty. In 1933 workers joined together to form Local P-9, a union affiliated with the Congress of Industrial Organizations. Hormel revealed that, while he did not approve of unions, he and his son would accept one. Workers struck for three days before their wage demands were met. Hormel clearly thought about his employees and working people and expressed his vocal support for unemployment benefits during the time. However, he liked to consider himself a benevolent employer and never wholly approved of union efforts in the company.

Upon retirement, George Hormel and his wife relocated to Bel Air, California, and he remained chief executive officer of the Hormel Company until his death in Bel Air.

• The Hormel Foods Corporation archives contain Hormel's personal papers and his unpublished autobiography, "The Open Road." A company-produced monograph, Doniver A. Lund, *The Hormel Legacy: 100 Years of Quality* (1991), details much of his life and career. See also Richard Dougherty, *In Quest of Quality* (1966), and "The Name Is HOR-mel," *Fortune*, Oct. 1937, pp. 127–32. Obituaries are in the *New York Times*, 6 June 1946, and *Newsweek*, 17 June 1946.

JAMES H. TUTEN

HORMEL, Jay Catherwood (11 Sept. 1892–30 Aug. 1954), meatpacking executive, was born in Austin, Minnesota, the son of George Albert Hormel, the owner of the meat-packing firm Hormel & Co., and Lillian Belle Gleason. He attended Austin public schools and the Shattuck Military School for Boys in Faribault, Minnesota. He first began working at age ten, assisting his uncle Herman Hormel in the Hormel Provision Market. On 29 March 1907 he went to work in the Hormel packing house, learning about by-products in the lard room. When he went to Princeton University in 1911, he opened his own business, a laundry. An indifferent student, he left after three years, in 1914, to work full time at Hormel & Co. He became a director on 17 November 1914 and worked in the plant first as a foreman, then as a superintendent. In 1916 he was appointed a first vice president.

In September 1917 Hormel was drafted and inducted into the army. He went to France as a first lieutenant in the Quartermaster Corps. A skilled manager, he made a valuable contribution to the war effort, developing a plan to bone beef before shipping it from the United States. This saved 40 percent on shipping space, which was critical because German U-boats had diminished Allied shipping capacity. Discharged on 18 December 1918, he returned to Austin and Hormel & Co. In 1922 he traveled to France to marry Germaine Dubois, with whom he had three sons.

Hormel literally saved the company in 1921. On 9 July of that year he stumbled on an odd item in the accounting office. He soon discovered that an old, trusted employee, Cy Thompson, the assistant comptroller, had embezzled from the company more than a million dollars. The loss nearly forced the company into bankruptcy. With his father, Jay Hormel personally confronted a committee of creditors. The Hormels pledged all their personal property to secure loans from Chicago banks, and the creditors imposed a supervisory committee that had oversight authority on the business. As soon as they could, the Hormels floated a $1.5 million bond issue, retired the debt, and freed themselves from the creditor committee supervision. Jay Hormel then redesigned the accounting system so that such diversion of funds could never happen again. In 1923 he was appointed company treasurer.

Hormel was increasingly active in shaping the work of the company. He initiated an executive training program that sought systematically to attract talented people into managerial levels, worked with his father to clarify and simplify lines of managerial authority, and as a member of the executive board pressed successfully for investments in marketing research and product development. He took a direct hand in research and development, initiating an unprecedented $.5 million advertising campaign in 1926 and ordering experiments with canning sauerkraut and frankfurters. When he learned of Paul Jorn's work in Germany on canning hams, Hormel persuaded Jorn to move to Austin. With his aid, the Hormel company soon offered an array of successful canned products, from ham and spiced ham to chicken, under its "Flavor-Sealed" brand. But larger competitors soon moved in on the markets Hormel pioneered, pushing it into a secondary position. Then in 1935 the company perfected a new product that was part pork shoulder, which meant that federal regulations prohibited labeling it "ham." Hormel searched for a new name and came up with "Spam." Released in 1937 with dramatic success, the copyrighted Spam brand name meant no competitor could take this market from Hormel.

On 19 November 1928 George Hormel moved to the position of chair of the board and effectively retired from active management. Jay Hormel became president that year. In 1929 he began an administrative reorganization, creating four divisions. More critically, he initiated a product diversification strategy that led the industry. His most enduring introductions were Dinty Moore Beef Stew in 1935, Hormel Chili in 1936, and Spam luncheon meat in 1937, along with a variety of canned chicken, luncheon loaf, and chili con carne products. Hormel pushed these products with innovative marketing, sponsoring the "George Burns and Gracie Allen" radio show and creating Spammy the pig to advertise Spam. He introduced some of the first singing commercials, using the Hormel Chili

Beaners, a twenty-member troupe of Mexican song-and-dance women, to advertise chili con carne, and he hired an all-male crew to peddle Spamwiches and milk throughout Chicago, even offering "bribes" of a dollar or two to entice customers. Demand for canned products increased dramatically. In 1937 only 18 percent of urban Americans used canned meats; by 1940 70 percent did. Spam was the leading product, outselling competitors 2 to 1. After World War II, during which Spam was widely used, advertising played on Spam's patriotic role by using the American Legion Spam Post No. 750 and "Hormel girls."

Hormel confronted a bitter labor strike in 1933. Recognizing the validity of some of the workers' complaints, he introduced an annual wage plan, profit sharing, merit pay, pensions, and an employment guarantee with a one-year notice for layoffs. In 1938 he extended this approach, creating a joint earnings plan that enabled workers to supplement regular income with employees' stock, which earned dividends the same as common stock. These efforts were notably successful, raising average weekly employee earnings nearly 40 percent between 1929 and 1940. Hormel could make such improvements because the company, bucking economic conditions and building on Jay Hormel's process and product innovations, more than doubled in size in the same period. Nationally, Jay Hormel became a leading proponent of stable employment and reasonable benefits for workers.

In 1946 the company was the largest independent meat processor in the United States. That year George Hormel, still nominally chair of the board, died. Jay Hormel then took over as chair, and H. H. Corey was appointed president. From his new position, Hormel oversaw the company's expansion nationally and a product diversification program, moving into spreads, frozen foods, and the manufacture of by-products. He also gave attention to long-range planning and supported innovative programs to improve agriculture on the state and local levels.

Hormel founded the Hormel Foundation, which funded the Hormel Institute, a center at the University of Minnesota to promote research on foods, especially fats and other lipids. He was also chair of the American Legion Employment Committee (c. 1935–1940). At the time of his death at his home in Austin, his company employed 9,000 workers in three plants and had twenty branches covering the nation. Under his leadership, Hormel & Co. had redefined competition in meat products with its innovative introductions and marketing techniques.

• The Hormel Foods Corp. of Austin, Minn., has a large collection of Hormel family records and business correspondence. See also Fred H. Blum, *Toward a Democratic Work Process: The Hormel-Packing-House Workers' Experiment* (1953); Jack Chernick, *Economic Effects of Steady Employment and Earnings: A Case Study of the Annual Wage System of Geo. A. Hormel & Co.* (1942); Richard Dougherty, *In Quest of Quality: Hormel's First 75 Years* (1966); Doniver Adolph Lund, *The Hormel Legacy: 100 years of Quality* (1991); Frances Levison, "Hormel: The Spam Man," *Life*, 11 Mar. 1946, pp. 63–66; and *Fortune*, Oct. 1937, pp. 127–41. An obituary is in the *New York Times*, 31 Aug. 1954.

FRED CARSTENSEN

HORN, George Henry (7 Apr. 1840–24 Nov. 1897), entomologist and physician, was born in Philadelphia, Pennsylvania, the son of Philip Henry Horn, a pharmacist, and Francis Isabella Brock. Upon completion of his elementary education in Philadelphia in 1853, Horn enrolled in the city's Central High School, from which he received the bachelor of arts degree five years later. Soon thereafter he entered the medical program of the University of Pennsylvania and was awarded the M.D. degree in 1861. During his days as a medical student Horn developed an interest in living and fossil marine invertebrates, and in 1860 he presented a paper before the Academy of Natural Sciences of Philadelphia, in which he described three species of gorgonian corals. Over the next two years he published three papers on recent and fossil scleractinian corals. Meanwhile Horn had joined the Entomological Society of Philadelphia (later the American Entomological Society), before which, in 1860–1861, he presented three papers, the most significant of which was a presentation describing seven new species of Coleoptera, or beetles.

Horn traveled to California in June 1862 and seven months later accepted a commission as assistant surgeon in the California Volunteers. Shortly after the expiration of his commission in December 1864, he reenlisted. By mid-1865 Horn had risen to the rank of major and surgeon, which position he held until the end of his enlistment in April 1866. Essentially unaffected by the events of the American Civil War, Horn used much of his time in the army to collect insect specimens in upper California, Nevada, and Arizona. He returned to Philadelphia in 1866, established a medical practice, and resumed his activity in the Entomological Society.

Dependent upon his medical practice for livelihood, Horn was constantly occupied with his work, especially because he attended a considerable number of obstetric cases. Nevertheless, he devoted the better part of his free hours to entomological inquiries. Indeed, he found little time for cultural or recreational pursuits, except for occasional fishing trips. Never married, the prodigious worker frequently labored until late at night in his cluttered study, examining specimens and writing descriptions of them. Despite his heavy load of patients and his activity in professional organizations, Horn managed to publish an average of nine articles during each year of his productive life. Through the development of a personal and professional relationship with John Lawrence LeConte, the renowned authority on North American beetles, Horn became especially interested in coleopterology. In his initial work in entomology, he essentially served an apprenticeship with LeConte, but he eventually surpassed his mentor in attention to the anatomical details of species and to similarities of characteristics among certain Coleoptera. Horn's concentrated investigations led to revision of several of LeConte's descriptions. In addition to contributing a 100-page section to LeConte's lengthy monograph "The Rhyncophora of America North of Mexico," published in 1876, Horn collaborated with LeConte in classifying the beetles of North America, which, upon its publication in 1883, represented the most thorough taxonomic work in American entomology to that point.

On his own, however, Horn was extraordinarily productive, publishing independently nearly 250 papers in entomology, of which the vast majority dealt with taxa and descriptions of Coleoptera. Of the more than 11,000 species of beetles he described, almost 1,600 were new to science. Horn also established over 150 new genera of Coleoptera. Among his most significant papers were those on the ground beetles (Carabidae) and the carrion beetles (Silphidae), both of which attracted attention in Europe. From the beginning of his study of beetles, Horn manifested a keen interest in their life history. He also demonstrated a desire to study non-American species, and in 1874, 1882, and 1888 he went to Europe to examine collections and to converse with noted entomologists. An honorary member of ten foreign entomological societies, Horn was, until the 1890s, one of only two Americans selected by several of those societies, and he was one of only a dozen honorary members in two of the most prestigious European entomological societies.

A man of warm and genial character, Horn shunned rancorous argument, once saying, "No literary work is more distasteful to me than controversy, especially when there is a personal element." Even when he felt aggrieved over the failure of a noted entomologist to credit him with a certain discovery, Horn tempered his criticism in a professional journal and expressed his indignation in a privately published pamphlet. On the other hand, he readily defended his position in any argument in which he believed that an important principle of scientific inquiry was at stake. In particular, while he followed his associates LeConte and E. D. Cope in accepting the theory of evolution, he depreciated certain generalizations about the inheritance of acquired characteristics because supporting evidence was problematic.

Although reared in the German Reformed church, Horn eschewed any ecclesiastical affiliation during his adult life, but he never expressed any antireligious sentiments. Highly regarded by his Philadelphia peers, he served as president of the American Entomological Society from 1866 to 1868 and from 1883 to 1897 and as vice president of that organization from 1869 to 1883. In addition, he served as vice director of the Entomological Section of the Academy of Natural Sciences of Philadelphia from 1876 to 1883 and as director of that group from 1883 to 1897. During the last two years of his life, however, his poor health greatly curtailed his activity. Soon after he suffered a stroke in 1896, Horn moved to a small resort on the coast of New Jersey, where he died a few months later.

Successor to John Lawrence LeConte as America's leading coleopterist, Horn advanced the field significantly through his meticulous and accurate descriptions of hundreds of beetles, his service to the profession of entomology, and his high standards for taxonomic work.

• Most of Horn's papers, which are not numerous, are located in the archives of the American Philosophical Society and the Academy of Natural Sciences of Philadelphia. The portion contributed by Horn to John Lawrence LeConte's "The Rhyncophora of America North of Mexico" was published in the *Proceedings of the American Philosophical Society* 25 (1876): 13–112; the work he coauthored with LeConte, "Classification of the Coleoptera of North America," originally appeared in the *Smithsonian Miscellaneous Collections* 26 (1883): 1–567. Horn published the largest number of his papers in the *Transactions of the American Entomological Society*. Late in his career he also published several papers in the Brooklyn Entomological Society's *Bulletin* and in its *Entomologica Americana*. Philip P. Calvert, an associate of Horn, who wrote a biographical sketch of him soon after his death, included information that he obtained from some of Horn's closest acquaintances. Calvert's account is in the *Transactions of the American Entomological Society* 25 (1898): appendix, i–xxiv. Accompanying it (pp. xxv–xxxvii) is a list of "The Entomological Writings of George Henry Horn" by Samuel Henshaw. An "Index to the Genera and Species of Coleoptera" described by Horn follows the list (pp. xxxvii–lx). A useful anonymous sketch of Horn is in the *Proceedings of the Academy of Natural Sciences of Philadelphia* (1897), pp. 515–18. An evaluation of Horn's work by a contemporary, the able entomologist C. V. Riley, appears in *Psyche* 8 (1897–1898): 159–60. Arnold Mallis pays tribute to Horn in his *American Entomologists* (1971), pp. 248–52. In his "Systematics Specializes between Fabricus and Darwin, 1800–1859," in *History of Entomology*, ed. Ray F. Smith et al. (1973), pp. 119–54, Carl H. Lindroth mentions Horn only once, but his overview of developments in European entomology helps to set Horn in context.

LESTER D. STEPHENS

HORN, Tom (21 Nov. 1860–20 Nov. 1903), scout, detective, and assassin, was born near Memphis, Scotland County, Missouri. His parents, whose names are no longer known, were farmers. He attended school irregularly during winter months, did hard farm work, enjoyed hunting, and became an excellent marksman. At about age fourteen and after an argument and violent fight with his father, he ran away to Santa Fe and may have worked as a stage driver. While in that region, he learned to speak Spanish. In 1876 or so he went to Prescott, in Arizona Territory, where he met Al Sieber, the famous civilian chief of scouts for various U.S. Army units in the San Carlos area. Little is known of Horn's activities for the next several years. In 1882, according to Sieber, Horn worked as an army packer. He undoubtedly participated in the army pursuit of Apaches fleeing from the San Carlos Reservation. American cavalry units commanded by Tullius Cicero Tupper and William Augustus Rafferty, both captains, followed the Apaches into northwest Chihuahua, Mexico, and engaged them in April 1882 in a standoff at Sierra Enmedio, in Sonora.

In his autobiography, Horn claims that he learned to speak Apache fluently, but this assertion—often recorded as historical fact, like other boasts of his—may be doubted. In any event, he was one of some seventy-six packers with General George Crook during his 1883 expedition into the Sierra Madre mountains of Mexico, resulting in the return of the Apaches to the reservation. Although in his autobiography Horn contends that he played an important combat role under Crook, his name is not mentioned in any official report concerning the expedition. He evidently did, however, continue to work well under Sieber, who occasionally placed him in command of army scouts when he himself was absent. In 1885 Captain Emmet Crawford appointed Horn chief of scouts during the army's pursuit of Geronimo into the Sierra Madres. Mexican irregulars killed Crawford and wounded Horn in January 1886. Geronimo surrendered in September to Lieutenant Charles B. Gatewood, under General Nelson Appleton Miles's command, during which Horn was present. Although Horn later wrote that he was of central importance at the surrender, Gatewood reported that Horn acted only as a Spanish-English interpreter.

Once Geronimo was captured, Horn was no longer needed as a scout or an interpreter and became a prospector for gold in Aravaipa Canyon, Arizona. He says that he played a major role in the bloody Pleasant Valley War of 1886–1892. It involved fights by rival Tèwksbury and Graham family members and their riders over cattle- and sheep-grazing lands in central Arizona. Horn says that he was ordered into the region to mediate the feud by Buckey O'Neill, sheriff of Yavapai County, and also that he was deputized by Commodore Perry Owens and Glenn Reynolds, sheriffs, respectively, of nearby Apache and Gila counties. However, O'Neill was not the Yavapai sheriff then, and there is no record that either Owens or Reynolds ever deputized Horn. In any event, he sided with the Tèwksburys in 1887 and may have been responsible for the murder in July of Mart Blevins, a Graham man. Next, Horn is known to have won steer-roping events at rodeos in 1888 in Globe, Arizona, and in 1890 or so in Phoenix.

From 1890 to 1894 Horn was employed by the Pinkerton Detective Agency in Denver as a loner to track outlaws preying on banks, railroads, and mine payrolls. In 1894 the Swan Land and Cattle Company of Wyoming hired him as a stock detective. By this time, if not a little earlier, he may have become a hired gun. He boasted that in 1895 he killed two small-time ranchers near Laramie, Wyoming, for $600 each. After these jobs, he avoided possible legal consequences by working for a while as a ranch supervisor in Aravaipa. It is known not only that he wrote a letter late in 1896 to a Tucson marshal offering to destroy William Christian's gang of rustlers for pay, but also that William Christian was killed early in 1897 and Robert Christian disappeared permanently later the same year. During the Spanish-American War, Horn was employed as a packer in Tampa, Florida, from April to September 1898. Hired in 1900 as little more than a paid killer (now alias James Hicks), he waged a one-man war on suspected cattle rustlers in Brown's Hole, Colorado, shooting to death Madison M. Rash, a Cold Spring Mountain rancher, in July, and Isom Dart, an African-American rancher at Summit Spring, in October. By these acts he succeeded in scaring other possible rustlers out of the region.

In 1901 Horn resumed his work as a Wyoming stock detective. On 19 July William Nickell, age fourteen, was shot to death from long range in Wyoming's Iron Mountain area, and a few days later his father, Kels P. Nickell, was wounded, also by an unknown assailant. Horn, for some time an employee of John C. Coble of Iron Mountain, was a suspect in both incidents, but there was no proof. In January 1902 U.S. deputy marshal Joe LeFors baited Horn in Cheyenne about a possible job to rid rustlers from an area in Montana and enticed him to boast about his marksmanship. Horn, possibly drunk, hinted that he had killed the Nickell boy from a distance of 300 yards. Charles J. Ohnhaus, a court stenographer, was concealed in the next room and took down the "confession," which was used as evidence in Horn's subsequent trial for murder. Despite substantial defense funds from a never-identified source, Horn was convicted, and the Supreme Court of Wyoming upheld the verdict. In August he escaped, was quickly recaptured, and was executed by hanging. He never implicated his corrupt employers, either during his imprisonment or in the autobiography he wrote while awaiting execution.

Tom Horn has become a legendary figure of the Old West, part courageous hero, part brutal assassin, about whom the truth will never be known. In September 1993 a serious retrial was staged in Cheyenne by collateral descendants of Horn, who never married, and by forensic experts and Amnesty International. After detailed evidence was carefully presented, Horn was declared not guilty of killing the Nickell boy.

• Documents by and relating to Tom Horn are in the First Judicial District of Wyoming, Laramie County Courthouse, Cheyenne; the Archives and Western History Library of the University of Wyoming, Laramie; and the James Covington Hancock Papers and the John Pleasant Gray Papers at the Arizona Pioneers' Historical Society Collections, Tucson. *Life of Tom Horn, Government Scout and Interpreter, Written by Himself Together with His Letters and Statements by His Friends: A Vindication* (1904) is fictitious in many parts. The following works concern Horn centrally or tangentially and often contradict one another: Britton Davis, *The Truth about Geronimo* (1929); Joe LeFors, *Wyoming Peace Officer: The Autobiography of Joe LeFors* (1953); Dean F. Krakel, *The Saga of Tom Horn: The Story of a Cattlemen's War, with Personal Narratives, Newspaper Accounts and Official Documents and Testimonies* (1954), with many photographs; John Rolfe Burroughs, *Where the Old West Stayed Young* (1962); Lauran Paine, *Tom Horn, Man of the West* (1963); Dan L. Thrapp, *Al Sieber: Chief of Scouts* (1964); "'No Cure, No Pay,' a Tom

Horn Letter," ed. Larry D. Ball, *Journal of Arizona History* 8 (1967): 200–202; *Chasing Geronimo: The Journal of Leonard Wood, May–September 1886*, ed. Jack C. Lane (1970); Doyce B. Nunis, Jr., *The Life of Tom Horn Revisited* (1992); "Tom Horn's Second Chance," *Economist*, 25 Sept. 1993, p. 37; Chip Carson, *Joe LeFors: 'I Slickered Tom Horn': The History of the Texas Cowboy Turned Montana-Wyoming Lawman—A Sequel* (1995); and William Hafford, "The Life and Legend of Tom Horn," *Arizona Highways* 72 (May 1996): 18–23. An obituary is in the *New York Times*, 21 Nov. 1903.

ROBERT L. GALE

HORNADAY, William Temple (1 Dec. 1854–6 Mar. 1937), conservationist and naturalist, was born near Plainfield, Indiana, the son of William Hornaday and Martha Varner Miller, farmers. When he was three, his family moved to Knoxville, Iowa. Although lacking a high school education, he enrolled at Oskaloosa College in 1870 for a program of preparatory studies. In the spring of 1872 he became a freshman at Iowa State Agricultural College. After working in the museum at Iowa State, Hornaday became committed to becoming a taxidermist, a program of study that was not offered by this college. In November 1873 he obtained a position at the nation's center for the practice of taxidermy at Henry Augustus Ward's Wards Natural Science Establishment in Rochester, New York.

Ward played a significant role in Hornaday's advancement by allowing him to develop his skills as a taxidermist and by providing support for collecting trips to Florida, Cuba, and the Bahamas in 1874 and for a trip around the world from 1876 to 1879, during which he made extensive collections in India, Ceylon, the Malay Peninsula, and Borneo. Hornaday's experiences on this arduous trip, which he made essentially alone on limited funds, are vividly chronicled in *Two Years in the Jungle: The Experience of a Hunter and Naturalist in India, Ceylon, the Malay Peninsula, and Borneo* (1885), a work that established his reputation as an author of wildlife adventures. Often exhausted and ill from the demands of this journey, he made some of the most extensive collections of elephant, crocodile, orangutan, monkey, and bird skins, skulls, and feathers yet obtained from India and Southeast Asia. While on this trip, he developed his skills as a field naturalist and became convinced of the importance of displaying prepared specimens in their natural habitat. After his return to the United States in 1879, he married Josephine Chamberlain of Battle Creek, Michigan. They had one child.

As Hornaday began to prepare the many specimens he had obtained for mounting, he became even more convinced of the need to improve the standards in taxidermy. In March 1880 he founded the Society of American Taxidermists to improve the practice of taxidermy and to hold competitive exhibitions in this field that would demonstrate the growing refinements in the profession. Although this society existed for only four years, during that period Hornaday served as its secretary from 1880 to 1883 and its president from 1883 to 1884. By 1884 the society had accomplished its goal of establishing higher standards for the display of mounted specimens in museums and subsequently ceased its activities. It contributed substantially to the growing professionalization of museum taxidermy. While a few others had mounted animals in limited, and occasionally theatrical, natural habitats, Hornaday began to present animals not only in appropriate natural habitats but also in family groupings in which males, females, and offspring could be seen. With much public acclaim, two of Hornaday's habitat groups of orangutans were obtained by the American Museum of Natural History and the U.S. National Museum. Within a decade, large family groups in natural habitats became the expected method of presenting mounted animals in natural history museums.

As a result of his growing skills and willingness to experiment with new methods and materials in the preparation of animal specimens, Hornaday became in 1882 the chief taxidermist of the U.S. National Museum, a branch of the Smithsonian Institution. Bringing enthusiasm, knowledge, and a high level of technical skills to this position, he began immediately to remount existing specimens at the museum and to establish new procedures for the practice of taxidermy there so that mounted animals would have a more lifelike appearance.

With the rapid decline of the American bison because of hide hunters in the 1870s and 1880s, concern about this animal's future became pronounced. In 1886 Hornaday led an expedition to Montana to kill and collect specimens for display in the museum. This western expedition led not only to elaborately mounted habitat groups of bison but also to Hornaday's lifelong interest in the American bison and his significant 1887 study of their fate, *The Extermination of the American Bison*. Concerned about both the future of American wildlife and the need to develop methods for more effectively displaying living animals to the general public, Hornaday was the primary force for the development of the National Zoological Park and drafted the plans for its establishment. After being appointed its initial director in 1889, he resigned in frustration in 1890 when the secretary of the Smithsonian dramatically altered his plans. For six years he sold real estate in Buffalo, New York.

Deeply committed to museums, taxidermy, and zoological collecting and to displaying the wealth and variety of the animal world to the American public, Hornaday eagerly accepted in 1896 the position of director of the New York Zoological Park, a post he held for the next three decades. As director he had the opportunity to plan, build, and supervise the development of a zoo where the public could view animals safely maintained in ingeniously created natural environments. Even as his family habitat groups became the standard for museum displays of mounted animals, so the 261 acres of the New York Zoological Society's Bronx Zoo became the world's exemplar for the exhibition of living wildlife. The mission of the zoo also included the preservation and propagation of animal species that were endangered, the publication of information for the general public about wildlife, the development of a research library, and the creation of a gallery and studio for wildlife artists.

Sensitive to the declining numbers of American wildlife in the early decades of the twentieth century, Hornaday became a vigorous and strident advocate for the preservation of the nation's native fauna. In 1913–1914, with $100,000 in support from private contributors, he established the Permanent Wild Life Fund to protect North America's diminishing wildlife. Deeply committed to this goal, Hornaday spoke and wrote forcefully on the topic, maintaining that for

educated, civilized Man to exterminate a valuable wild species of living things is a crime. It is a crime against his own children, and posterity. No man has a right, either moral or legal, to destroy or squander an inheritance of his children that he holds for them in trust. And man, the wasteful and greedy spendthrift that he is, has not created even the humblest species of birds, mammals, and fishes that adorn and enrich this earth. (*Our Vanishing Wild Life* [1913], p. 7)

Hornaday played an active and sustained role in the preservation of Alaska's fur seals, the American bison, and American waterfowl and songbirds and provided frequent warnings of animals that were faced with extinction. His numerous books and articles alerted Americans to the consequences that industrialization and negligent human behavior had on animal populations. He was singularly effective in presenting programs for the preservation of the American bison and in 1905 helped establish the American Bison Society; he served from 1905 to 1907 as its president. Sensitive to the impact of unrestrained market hunting for wild game, he worked diligently to pass the Bayne Law in New York in 1911, which prohibited the sale of game in that state. He also lobbied extensively for the passage of the Migratory Bird Law of 1913, which placed migratory birds under federal supervision. The author of hundreds of articles on wildlife conservation, Hornaday also authored the conservation section in the Boy Scout *Handbook for Boys*. Abstemious in his personal behavior, he authored in 1887 for the Woman's Christian Temperance Union a book against the sale of rum to African natives. He died in Stamford, Connecticut.

In a career of almost six and a half decades, Hornaday made distinctive contributions to the professionalization of museum taxidermy and its procedures, to the organization and display practices of natural history museums, to the development of zoos with ecologically correct habitats, and to the preservation of North American wildlife.

• Substantial collections of Hornaday's correspondence and personal papers are in the William Temple Hornaday Memorial Trust, the William T. Hornaday Papers in the Manuscript Division of the Library of Congress, the Smithsonian Institution Archives, the New York Zoological Society, and in collections in the Rush Rees Library of the University of Rochester, the Conservation Center at the Denver Public Library, Yale University Library, the Huntington Library, and the Theodore Roosevelt Papers in the Library of Congress. Hornaday's most significant publications not mentioned in the text include *Free Rum on the Congo, and What It Is Doing There* (1887), *Taxidermy and Zoological Collecting* (1891), *The American Natural History* (1904), *Campfires in the Canadian Rockies* (1906), *Campfires on Desert and Lava* (1908), *Wild Life Conservation in Theory and Practice* (1914), *Old Fashioned Verses* (1919), *Tales from Nature's Wonderlands* (1924), *A Wild Animal Round-Up* (1925), *Wild Animal Interviews* (1929), *Minds and Manners of Wild Animals* (1930), and *Thirty Years War for Wild Life* (1931). Although focusing primarily on the first forty years of Hornaday's life, James Andrew Dolph, "Bringing Wildlife to Millions: William Temple Hornaday, the Early Years: 1854–1896" (Ph.D. diss., Univ. of Massachusetts, 1975), is the most complete and balanced study of his career and accomplishments. This work may be augmented by John Ripley Forbes, *In the Steps of the Great American Zoologists: William Temple Hornaday* (1966). Additional insight into his career is in Peter Wild, "William T. Hornaday: Warrior for Wildlife," in his *Pioneer Conservationists of Eastern America* (1986). An obituary is in the *New York Times*, 7 Mar. 1937.

PHILLIP DRENNON THOMAS

HORNBECK, Stanley Kuhl (4 May 1883–10 Dec. 1966), State Department official, was born in Franklin, Massachusetts, the son of Marquis D. Hornbeck, a Methodist minister, and Lydia M. Kuhl. He spent much of his adolescence in Colorado. He attended the University of Colorado but after two years transferred to the University of Denver, from which he graduated in 1903 with Phi Beta Kappa honors. After teaching Latin for one year at Golden (Colo.) High School, he became his state's first Rhodes Scholar.

From 1908 to 1909 and again from 1914 to 1917, Hornbeck was a member of the political science department of the University of Wisconsin, reaching the rank of associate professor in 1917. He received his doctorate there in 1909. His published dissertation, titled *The Most-Favored-Nation Clause in Commercial Treaties* (1910), was long the definitive work on the subject. From 1909 to 1913 Hornbeck taught in China, first at Chekiang Provincial College in Hangchow and then at Fengtien Law College in Mukden, experiences that developed in him an interest in the Far East and then an expertise that he never lost. In his book *Contemporary Politics in the Far East* (1916), Hornbeck warned of Japanese expansion. China, he was soon saying, needed American loans and the nationalization of its railroads; spheres of influence should be abolished. To Hornbeck the United States had special moral obligations to that nation, ones that would eventually pay off in a thriving market. Yet unlike many China partisans, he favored retention of American extraterritorial privileges as long as the Chinese could not protect Western rights.

In 1917 Hornbeck joined the newly established federal Tariff Commission but entered the army the following year as a captain in ordnance. Almost immediately he was detailed to President Woodrow Wilson's inquiry on peacemaking, where he supervised research on Far Eastern issues. In 1919 he served as the technical expert on the Far East at the Paris Peace

Conference. In that capacity, he represented the United States on the commission studying the disposition of Tientsin, and he unsuccessfully opposed Japanese retention of the Chinese province of Shantung. In 1920 he was again a special expert with the Tariff Commission. From 1921 to 1924 Hornbeck was a drafting officer in the State Department's Office of Economic Advisers, a post he left to join the Harvard faculty as a lecturer on Far Eastern government and politics. He also participated in the Washington Naval Conference (1921), the Peking Tariff Conference (1925), and the Commission on Extraterritoriality (1926).

From 1928 to 1937 Hornbeck was chief of the State Department's Far Eastern Division, and from 1937 to 1944 he was one of four special advisers on political questions to Secretary of State Cordell Hull. In both offices he became known as the department's leading foe of Japanese expansion. Within months after the Manchurian crisis broke out in September 1931, Hornbeck claimed that Japan could be brought to terms within six months through an economic boycott, even as Japan was taking over Manchuria and establishing the puppet state of Manchukuo. Always denying that moral suasion or world public opinion were effective diplomatic instruments, he opposed the nonrecognition policy of Secretary of State Henry L. Stimson. His own remedies included naval superiority and an embargo on private loans to Japan. When in late January 1932 a Japanese admiral, acting without authorization, occupied Chapei, the Chinese section of Shanghai, Hornbeck offered a host of suggestions, including the establishment of demilitarized zones, League of Nations sanctions, and negotiation by the Shanghai Municipal Council. He also advised invoking the Nine Power Treaty on China (1922), under which the signers—including the United States and Japan—pledged to maintain the open door of commercial equality and territorial and administrative integrity. Until the Truce of Tangku on 31 May 1933, Hornbeck continued with a battery of proposals, including a Western boycott of Japanese goods, a defensive alliance in the Pacific, and keeping the American fleet in the Pacific.

From 1933 to 1938 Hornbeck opposed U.S. intervention in East Asia. During this time he urged an evenhanded policy between China and Japan. In 1933, for example, he told Secretary of State Hull that while Japan was a "war-minded" nation, the United States would never possess vital interests in the Far East and should take no action that would further aggravate relations. Hence, for at least three years he opposed any unilateral financial assistance to the Chinese Nationalist government. In 1934 he opposed the presence of any American military advisers to the Chinese government. In 1936, in continuing to recommend American passivity concerning Japanese encroachments in China, he hoped that in time Japan itself would realize that it lacked the financial resources to underwrite all the economic development needed in China. Hornbeck, however, always sought a navy second to none,

believing that American naval strength in the Pacific was the greatest deterrent to war with Japan.

Once the Japanese attacked Marco Polo Bridge in China in July 1937, Hornbeck claimed that a Sino-Japanese war of attrition might preserve the immediate interest of other powers by allowing both China and Japan to exhaust themselves. Yet by September he wanted pressure on Japan, recommending such policies as sending heavy cruisers to China to protect American interests, constructing three new battleships, and issuing a presidential order banning all American merchant vessels from the China coast. In November 1937 he attended the Nine Power Treaty Conference in Brussels, where he wanted the great powers to guarantee Japan's access to raw materials and markets in return for Japanese agreement to an armistice.

In 1938 Japanese violations of American rights and interests in the Far East, as well as the new order espoused by Japanese premier Konoye Fumimaro, made Hornbeck far more militant; he was soon espousing a vastly increased navy, economic support of Chinese ruler Chiang Kai-shek, and ever-tightening commercial restrictions on Japan. Not desiring war, Hornbeck believed that economic sanctions offered the best way to avoid it. That same year he married Vivienne Barkalow Breckenridge, dean of women at American University; the couple had no children.

In 1941 all Japanese peace proposals underwent Hornbeck's scrutiny, and not surprisingly, he found all wanting. Japan, he believed, should not be allowed even to retain part of Manchuria. In January 1941 he endorsed an oil embargo of Japan, simultaneously becoming the leading proponent for freezing Japanese funds. In August 1941 he opposed a summit meeting between President Franklin D. Roosevelt and Prime Minister Konoye. Hornbeck's only peace proposal, made on 12 November, would have involved a relaxation of the U.S. trade embargo for an end to all Japanese military operations. In late November 1941, knowing that negotiations with the Japanese had reached a standstill, Hornbeck found the odds five-to-one that Japan would not be at war with the United States by 15 December. (He later claimed that he thought the Japanese fleet, which attacked Pearl Harbor on 7 December, was still in home waters.) Always failing to assess realistically the risks of war with Japan, he believed that Japan would never retaliate against American economic pressure. Three days before the Pearl Harbor attack, Hornbeck called for a preventive strike against the Japanese navy.

All during World War II Hornbeck called for unconditional support of the Chiang regime, in the process bristling at Foreign Service officers who recommended aid to the Communist forces. In 1944 he was made director of the new Office of Far Eastern Affairs and then named ambassador to the Netherlands, a post he held for three years. Also in 1944 he was an American delegate to the Dumbarton Oaks Conference. In 1947 Hornbeck retired from the State Department, after which he lacked major influence. Bitterly anti-Communist during the Cold War, he backed American military efforts in Korea and Vietnam. He opposed recognition of Communist China and its admission to the United Nations. In one sense Hornbeck was simply remaining faithful to his lifelong belief in the Open Door. In another sense, he saw Soviet ambitions replacing Japanese ones.

Hornbeck was a lively man of medium build and height, possessing a slight paunch and an acerbic personality. He was a tireless worker whom subordinates found both autocratic and pedantic. Though he was never the determining policymaker in United States–Japanese relations, historians still debate his role. Jonathan G. Utley writes that in 1941 "Hornbeck became vociferous but his recommendations were rarely followed." Conversely Kenneth G. McCarty, Jr., claims that "by 1941 Washington had implemented most of his recommendations." There was no question that his detailed knowledge of Asian history and politics coupled with adept bureaucratic maneuvering forced the State Department always to contend with his views. He died in Washington, D.C.

• The papers of Stanley K. Hornbeck are located in the Hoover Institution of War, Revolution and Peace, Stanford University. See also U.S. State Department, *Papers Relating to the Foreign Relations of the United States*, and Justus D. Doenecke, comp., *The Diplomacy of Frustration: The Manchurian Crisis of 1931–1933 as Revealed in the Papers of Stanley K. Hornbeck* (1981). For more of Hornbeck's views see his *China Today—Political* (1927) and *The United States and the Far East: Certain Fundamentals of Policy* (1942). Major studies of Hornbeck include Kenneth G. McCarty, Jr., "Stanley K. Hornbeck and the Far East, 1931–1941" (Ph.D. diss., Duke Univ., 1970), and K. Marlin Friedrich, "In Search of a Far Eastern Policy: Joseph Grew, Stanley Hornbeck, and American-Japanese Relations 1937–1941" (Ph.D. diss., Washington State Univ., 1974). Important articles include McCarty, "Stanley K. Hornbeck and the Manchurian Crisis," *Southern Quarterly* 10 (1972): 305–24; Thomas M. Leonard, "Stanley K. Hornbeck: Major Deterrent to America-Japanese Summitry, 1941," *Towson State Journal of International Affairs* 8 (1974): 113–21; Richard Dean Burns, "Stanley K. Hornbeck: The Diplomacy of the Open Door," in *Diplomats in Crisis: United States–Chinese–Japanese Relations, 1919–1941*, ed. Burns and Edward M. Bennett (1974); Russell D. Buhite, "The Open Door in Perspective: Stanley K. Hornbeck and American Far Eastern Policy," in *Makers of American Diplomacy: From Benjamin Franklin to Henry Kissinger*, ed. Frank J. Merli and Theodore A. Wilson (1974); and Michael Barnhart, "Hornbeck Was Right: The Realist Approach to American Policy toward Japan," in *Prologue to the Pacific War*, ed. Hilary Conroy and Harry Wray (1990). Jonathan G. Utley, *Going to War with Japan, 1937–1941* (1985), stresses Hornbeck's lack of influence. An obituary is in the *New York Times*, 12 Dec. 1966.

JUSTUS D. DOENECKE

HORNBLOW, Arthur, Sr. (1865–6 May 1942), editor, author, and dramatist, was born in Manchester, England, the son of William Hornblow and Sarah Jane Rodgers. Little is known of Hornblow's childhood; however, he studied literature and painting in Paris

before coming to the United States in 1889. While in Paris, Hornblow acted as a correspondent for both English and American newspapers.

Once in America Hornblow's first job as a journalist was at the *Kansas City Globe*. A year later he joined the staff at the *New York Dramatic Mirror*, where he worked for two years while also becoming an assistant play reader for A. M. Palmer, manager of the Madison Square Theatre in New York. In 1892 Hornblow married Natalie Lambert, and a son, Arthur Hornblow, Jr., was born a year later. (Hornblow, Jr., became a successful motion picture producer in Hollywood.) Looking for a better job to support his family, Hornblow left the *New York Dramatic Mirror* and in 1894 became the assistant foreign editor for the *New York Herald*; within a year he was promoted to editor. He served as a staff member of the Paris edition from 1896 to 1897 and as the assistant cable editor in London from 1897 to 1899. In 1899 he moved from the *New York Herald* to the *New York Times* copy desk.

From 1901 to 1926 Hornblow served as editor and principal critic for *Theatre Magazine*. Founded only a year earlier as a pictorial quarterly under the title *Our Players*, its title was changed to *The Theatre* when Hornblow took over in May. He also began to publish the magazine monthly rather than quarterly. The magazine went through several subtle name changes, becoming known as *Theatre Magazine* and, finally, *Theatre*. Over the next twenty-five years Hornblow made *Theatre Magazine* into the most acclaimed of the monthlies devoted to the popular theater. He separated it from the gossip magazines with his insightful reviews and critical commentary without allowing it to become a journal for intellectuals like its contemporary, *Theatre Arts*. The magazine did not last long after Hornblow's retirement—its final issue was printed April 1931. After leaving the magazine he served as dean of the John Murray Anderson–Robert Milton School of the Theatre and Dance in New York during 1927–1928.

In the 1890s Hornblow began translating and writing with regularity, and it was in this area that he achieved financial success. His translations of Marcel Prévost's *The Demi-Virgins* (1895) and *Letters of Women* (1897) and of Gabriele d'Annunzio's *The Triumph of Death* (1897) and *The Intruder* (1898) brought him widespread popularity. His translation of Georges Dorys's *The Private Life of the Sultan* (1901) appealed to a limited audience. Hornblow's interest in the stage also led him to write a number of plays. He wrote adaptations of Guy de Maupassant's *Musotte* (1894) and *Strolling Players* (1906). He also wrote several original scripts, including *Twilight* (1896) and *The System of Dr. Tarr* (1905).

Hornblow enjoyed the most success from his novelization of popular plays, often in collaboration with the play's author. The first and most popular of these adaptations was *The Lion and the Mouse* (1906), based on Charles Klein's successful play of the same name. According to his obituary in the *New York Times*, Hornblow bought a summer home from the royalties from this novel. Other novelizations include *The End of the Game* (1907), *By Right of Conquest* (1909), and *The Third Degree* (1909). *John Marsh's Millions* (1910), *The Gamblers* (1911), and *The Money Makers* (1914) were all written in collaboration with Klein. *The Easiest Way* (1910) was written with playwright Eugene Walter; *Bought and Paid For* (1912) with playwright George Broadhurst; *The Talker* (1912) with playwright Marion Fairfax; *The Argyle Case* (1913) with playwrights Harriet Ford and Harvey J. O'Higgins in cooperation with William J. Burns; and *The Price* (1914) again with Broadhurst.

In addition to plays and novels, Hornblow published *Training for the Stage* (1916), in which he admonishes actors who come to the stage without proper training. In 1919 he published a two-volume *History of the Theatre in America, from Its Beginning to the Present Time*, one of the first truly scholarly attempts to document America's theatrical history. The next serious studies of the American theater did not appear for another twenty years, making Hornblow's study a standard reference book for theater historians for many years. The *New York Times* review called the book "a stupendous collection of facts and chronologies which affords a panoramic view of our stage" (3 May 1919).

Hornblow's wife died in 1912, and two years later he married Nora Marie Geoghegan. The couple had one son, Herbert, who became a flight lieutenant in the Royal Air Force. In 1929 Hornblow moved to London and lived there until returning to the United States shortly before his death in Asbury Park, New Jersey.

Hornblow's primary contributions to the American theater were his editorship of *Theatre Magazine* and his *History of the Theatre in America*. His magazine brought theater criticism into the lives of the theatergoing public without sacrificing scholarship. He made ideas understandable to the lay reader in the magazine, and its popularity helped to increase the popularity of the theater it reported on and critiqued. In addition, Hornblow was publishing *Theatre Magazine* at a transitional period in American theater: though the Syndicate, a corporation that had had a monopoly on theatrical ventures for decades, still held sway over the touring circuits, David Belasco and others were introducing a new realism to the American stage, and the experimental theater movement had finally reached the United States from Europe resulting in the growth of small theater groups such as the Provincetown Players and the Theatre Guild, which altogether changed the state of American theater. Hornblow watched and reported on these changes in *Theatre Magazine* with the same enthusiasm for innovation as those making the changes. Although supportive, Hornblow was also objective: looking for quality in art in any form it took and not hesitating to criticize when his standard of quality was not met. In addition, through his *History of the Theatre in America*, he told the story of an American stage coming into its own and educated the theater-going public about the changes taking place around it.

• Hornblow is included in the *Oxford Companion to American Theatre* (1984). An obituary appears in the *New York Times*, 7 May 1942.

MELISSA VICKERY-BAREFORD

HORNBLOWER, William Butler (13 May 1851–16 June 1914), lawyer, was born in Paterson, New Jersey, the son of Reverend William Henry Hornblower, a Presbyterian minister, and Matilda Butler. He graduated from Princeton in 1871 and from Columbia Law School in 1875. From then until his death he was an active member of the New York bar. In 1882 he married Susan Sanford of New Haven. They had three children before her death in 1886. Hornblower's second wife was Mrs. Emily Nelson, a widow; they married in 1894.

In 1893 President Grover Cleveland nominated Hornblower to the U.S. Supreme Court. The Senate rejected the appointment because of opposition from New York's senators. Their opposition was both the outcome of political disagreements with Cleveland and a retaliation for Hornblower's efforts in the defeat of a candidate for the New York Court of Appeals.

Hornblower's distinguished career was dominated by corporate practice, including cases in the New York Court of Appeals and the U.S. Supreme Court. Among his clients were the New York Life Insurance Company, a number of railroads, and Joseph Pulitzer. In spite of the nature of his practice, Hornblower believed that the bar had a special role in mediating the conflicts between extreme ideologies such as "imperialism, plutocracy, populism and bossism" (commencement address, Dickinson College School of Law, 7 June 1898) which he saw arising in the late nineteenth century. He accepted some of the changes in the practice of law that had come about in the late nineteenth century, including the greater organization of the profession and the trend away from sole practitioners in favor of firms. He did not, however, go so far as to favor codification, one of the most significant movements for legal reform at the turn of the century. Instead, reflecting his leanings toward corporate and commercial practice, he called for greater certainty in the law. He opposed codification because it created different laws for each state, thereby tending to "denationalize" the law. Even though codes seemed to offer the certainty needed for commercial practice, Hornblower favored the "common sense" of the common law: "Judge-made law, on the whole, tends to conform itself to the principles of common sense, right reason and justice. Statutory law, on the other hand, tends to become technical and arbitrary." In Hornblower's opinion, the common law was preferable to a code drafted by inept legislators and subject to the uncertainties of interpretation.

Hornblower served as president of both the New York State Bar Association (1901–1902) and the Bar Association of the City of New York (1913–1914). Between 1904 and 1909 he served on a committee charged with revising the laws of New York. He was appointed to the New York Court of Appeals, along with Benjamin Cardozo, in February 1914, but he served only a week before illness forced him to retire. He died four months later of myocarditis, at his summer home in Litchfield, Connecticut.

Following in the footsteps of other members of his family, Hornblower's life reflected a patrician dedication to public service. His grandfather had served as chief justice of New Jersey for fourteen years; his uncle was Joseph P. Bradley, justice of the U.S. Supreme Court. His career therefore represents an approach to life that was to decline with the societal changes following World War I.

• The most accessible of Hornblower's speeches are the following: "Appellate Courts," *Columbia Law Times* 5 (1892): 151; "The Supreme Court," *Report of the New York State Bar Association* 26 (1893): 76; "Has the Profession of the Law Been Commercialized?" *The Forum* 18 (1895): 679; "Address at the Opening of the College of Law of Syracuse University," *The Counsellor* 5 (1895): 31. A lengthy account of his life is in Benjamin Cardozo, "Memorial of William B. Hornblower," *The Association of the Bar of New York, Year Book 1915* (1915): 186. Obituaries are in the *New York Times*, 7 June 1914; *Report of the New York State Bar Association* 38 (1915): 831; and *Case and Comment* 21 (1914–1915): 258.

WALTER F. PRATT, JR.

HORNBOSTEL, Henry (15 Aug. 1867–13 Dec. 1961), architect, was born Henry Fred Hornbostel in Brooklyn, New York, the son of Edward Hornbostel, a stock broker, and Johanna Cassebeer. Although Hornbostel's father steered him toward the silk trade, a high school teacher observed his drawing talents and encouraged him to study architecture at Columbia University. He graduated at the head of his class with a bachelor of philosophy in 1891. Hornbostel then went to work for New York architects Wood and Palmer (a firm whose later iterations were Wood, Palmer and Hornbostel; Palmer and Hornbostel; and Palmer, Hornbostel and Jones). Beginning in 1893 he studied architecture for four years at the École des Beaux-Arts in Paris. In addition to his studies, he sought out sculptors and painters, as well as other artisans and workmen, to develop skills that would serve his architectural designs. Hornbostel's colleagues dubbed him "l'homme perspectif" for his dramatic perspective drawings, works that contrasted with the traditional Beaux-Arts plans, sections, and elevations. During this period Hornbostel also began wearing the red silk ties that became his trademark.

Hornbostel returned to New York in 1897 to a variety of architectural activities. As a freelance delineator, he worked for some of the preeminent American firms of the period: McKim Mead & White; Carrère and Hastings; and G.B. Post. He also produced renderings for some architects of the Paris Exposition of 1900. Between 1903 and 1917, working for the Board of Estimate and Apportionment in New York, he designed the Queensborough, Manhattan, Pelham Park, and Hell Gate bridges and earned considerable professional acclaim for his renderings of them. Hornbostel also taught architecture at Columbia, first as an assistant,

then as a lecturer. In 1899 he married Martha Armitage; they had two children.

In a period when design competitions enjoyed widespread popularity among prestigious clients, Hornbostel excelled in them. In temporary association with Howells & Stokes, he designed the well-received second-place entry in the 1899 Phoebe Hearst competition for the buildings of the University of California. More important, as a partner in Palmer and Hornbostel, he won the competition to design a new campus for Pittsburgh's Carnegie Institute of Technology in 1903. Although his scheme was steeped in the Beaux-Arts tradition of Roman, Renaissance, and French architecture, Hornbostel gave it clarity and personality. His plan deftly reconciles a complex program with difficult topography, while his details allude to technology with pragmatism and wit. The Paris-trained Hornbostel even convinced industrialist and patron Andrew Carnegie to include a department of fine arts in the new engineering school. For his efforts, he became the first head of Carnegie Tech's School of Architecture.

Palmer & Hornbostel moved their practice to Pittsburgh, even as the firm maintained its national profile. With Hornbostel as chief designer, the firm produced monumental works in the Beaux-Arts style, including city halls for Oakland, California (1910), Wilmington, Delaware (1910), and Hartford, Connecticut (1911). Hornbostel continued to be a presence on university campuses as well, designing buildings for Emory and Northwestern Universities. Meanwhile, his bridges in New York reached completed construction, culminating with the Hell Gate Bridge of 1917.

At the same time, Hornbostel's buildings made a profound mark on Pittsburgh. In the city's Oakland area alone, he designed the Rodef Shalom synagogue, the Schenley Hotel, the University Club, and the Upper Campus of the University of Pittsburgh. He also won the competition to design the Soldiers and Sailors Memorial (1910). The urbanity of these designs, separately and severally, helped transform a collection of foundling and relocated institutions into the city's center of culture and higher learning. Nationally known as a competition-winning pillar of Beaux-Arts architecture, Hornbostel became a Pittsburgh personality, adding a dash of refined color to the architecture and the social scene of what was then a grim industrial city. He also matched his design output with a visible professional profile. He was active as a member of the American Institute of Architects, the National Sculpture Society, the Architectural League of New York, and the Society of Beaux-Arts Architects, of which he was the president in 1916.

During World War I Hornbostel was commissioned as a major and served as first assistant gas officer in the Twenty-sixth Division of the U.S. Army in France. Although his sophisticated manners and Van Dyke beard clashed with military custom, he discharged his duties successfully and with notorious good humor before his safe return to the United States. With his postwar return to architecture, Hornbostel dissolved his partnership with Palmer and embarked upon increasingly modern designs. His Smithfield Street Congregational Church in Pittsburgh is an early and innovative use of architectural aluminum, while his Grant Building is an Art Deco essay of unapologetic abstraction.

The Great Depression brought Hornbostel personal and professional turmoil. In 1932, his first marriage having ended, he was married to Maybelle Weston. During this period, he saw a drastic reduction in commissions brought about by the economic decline. Hornbostel was, however, able to secure a position as director of Allegheny County Parks beginning in 1935. In 1939 he retired, first to Connecticut, then to Melbourne, Florida, where he lived in a modern house of his own design until his death.

Hornbostel, who was best known for his Beaux-Arts work, had the misfortune to die when the style was at a low point in popularity, eclipsed by Modernism. The professional press, which had once adored him, barely noted his passing. Subsequently, the historical curiosity that accompanied postmodern architecture helped revive Hornbostel in the professional consciousness. Later twentieth-century devotees rediscovered, in addition to the monumentality and historical pedigree that they expected in Beaux-Arts buildings, a technologically and artistically progressive oeuvre with far-reaching affinities.

• Significant repositories of Hornbostel's papers and drawings reside in the Avery Architectural and Fine Arts Library at Columbia University and the Architecture Archives at Carnegie-Mellon University in Pittsburgh. The latter collection also contains a comprehensive collection of articles on Hornbostel's work from the professional press, the forum that has seen the most thorough coverage of his accomplishments. These include Francis S. Swales, "Master Draftsmen XVII—Henry Hornbostel," *Pencil Points*, Feb. 1926, pp. 73–92, a well-illustrated biographical assessment of the architect at mid-late career. James D. Van Trump, *Life and Architecture in Pittsburgh* (1983), contains three articles on Hornbostel's life and work, including a detailed obituary. Clark V. Poling, *Henry Hornbostel, Michael Graves: An Exhibition of Architectural Drawings, Photographs and Models* (1985), uses buildings at Emory University as a lens through which to view the careers of Hornbostel and postmodern architect Michael Graves.

CHARLES ROSENBLUM

HORNER, William Edmonds (3 June 1793–13 Mar. 1853), physician, teacher, and author, was born in Warrenton, Fauquier County, Virginia, the son of William Horner, a merchant, and Mary Edmonds. Slender in build and frail in health as a child, Horner found companionship in books rather than in other children. At the age of twelve Horner was sent to the private academy in Warrenton of the Reverend Charles O'Neill, an Episcopalian clergyman, where he spent four years.

In 1809 Horner was apprenticed to John Spence, a Dumfries, Virginia, physician who had been born in Scotland and educated in Edinburgh. After three years with Spence, Horner traveled to Philadelphia to attend the medical school at the University of Pennsyl-

vania. In July 1813, during his first year of medical studies, Horner applied for and received a commission as a surgeon's mate in the U.S. Army. Attached to the Ninth Military District in the state of New York, he was in charge of a hospital near the Canadian border. A furlough from the army enabled Horner in 1814 to complete his medical school education at the University of Pennsylvania, with a thesis on gunshot wounds. Seeing little chance for advancement in the U.S. Army after the War of 1812 had ended, Horner resigned from the service in 1815. The surgical experience Horner gained in the war, which he described later in the journal article "Surgical Sketches," was an invaluable asset to his fledgling medical career.

After his discharge, Horner returned to Warrenton to practice medicine. He soon realized that the town held few opportunities and wrote that "Virginia is a fine nursery for young men, but a poor theater for the display of their abilities" (Walsh and Goudiss, 1903). Failing to obtain a surgeon's post on a ship bound for India, Horner decided to move to Philadelphia.

With a small legacy from his grandmother, Horner arrived in Philadelphia in December 1815. While attempting to establish a private practice, he attended two sessions of courses at the medical school of the University of Pennsylvania. He was attracted particularly to anatomy, and his enthusiasm for this subject as well as his skill in dissecting came to the attention of professor of anatomy Caspar Wistar, who in March 1816 offered Horner a position as his dissector (at $500 per year). A great friendship developed between the professor and his assistant, and out of loyalty to Wistar, Horner later that year turned down an opportunity to realize a childhood dream of becoming a surgeon on a ship bound for India.

John Syng Dorsey, who succeeded Wistar as professor of anatomy in 1818, immediately appointed Horner as his demonstrator. When Dorsey died suddenly, his uncle Philip Syng Physick took over his course and retained Horner as demonstrator; the latter did much of the teaching. The next year, Physick resigned the professorship of surgery to assume that of anatomy, and Horner was named adjunct professor of anatomy. In 1820 Horner married Elizabeth Welsh, the daughter of John Welsh, a prominent Philadelphia merchant; they had ten children.

In 1822 Horner was appointed dean of the University of Pennsylvania medical faculty, a post that he would hold for the next three decades. During his tenure as dean, Horner raised the educational standards of the institution by requiring a third year of lectures beyond the customary two-year course offered by virtually every medical school at the time. When Physick resigned from the faculty in 1831, Horner was appointed professor of anatomy, a position he held for the next twenty-two years. Though not known as an inspiring lecturer, Horner was a popular teacher. His lectures were conducted entirely by demonstration.

By the 1830s Horner's practice and his personal wealth had expanded considerably. Additional appointments recognized and enhanced his reputation.

From 1832 to 1834 he served on the surgical staff of the Philadelphia Almshouse. He was elected to membership in the Philadelphia Medical Society and the American Philosophical Society. When cholera appeared in Philadelphia in 1832, Horner played a key role in the city's response. He was a member of Philadelphia's sanitary board and was in charge of one of the city's cholera hospitals. Horner's extensive publications won him a reputation as one of America's leading anatomists. In 1823 he edited the third edition of Wistar's *System of Anatomy* (1811–1814), the first American textbook on the subject. Horner's own *Treatise on Special and General Anatomy* (1826) replaced Wistar's as the most popular textbook of anatomy in the United States; it was used in virtually every American medical school. Published in 1843 under the title *Special Anatomy and Histology*, Horner's anatomy textbook went through eight editions. His *Lessons in Practical Anatomy, for the Use of Dissectors* (1823) appeared in five editions.

Horner's *Treatise on Pathological Anatomy* (1829) was the first textbook on pathology published in the United States. Horner had traveled to France eight years earlier and was impressed by the advances made by French physicians in pathology. He returned determined to write a textbook on the subject that would introduce its study into America's medical schools. Horner's pathology text, which went through three editions, was based on the work of leading French physicians such as Xavier Bichat, Pierre Louis, and Gabriel Andral, as well as on his own extensive postmortem experience, which he had gained primarily at the Philadelphia Almshouse. This work became the standard text in its field for at least a decade.

Although outwardly calm and composed, Horner suffered in private for many years from depression and ill-health and once stated that he had been afflicted by a dull headache for most of his adult life. Deeply religious, Horner read the Bible daily. Inspired by the charitable work of the Roman Catholic nuns and priests during the 1832 cholera epidemic, Horner, raised an Episcopalian, converted to Catholicism in 1839. In 1849 Horner was one of the founders of Saint Joseph's Hospital, the first Catholic hospital in Philadelphia, which he served as chief physician, surgeon, and president.

After 1848 Horner suffered constant physical discomfort yet carried out his responsibilities as dean and continued to teach almost to the end, presenting his final lecture in January 1853. He died in Philadelphia.

Horner's contributions to anatomy and pathology have largely been forgotten. Although he was not a brilliant thinker, Horner should be remembered for introducing modern pathology into the curricula of American medical schools. His other contributions to medicine include the first description of the tensor tarsi muscle—also known as Horner's muscle—of the eye, a report of the first successful method for cure of a ruptured Achilles tendon, and the first descriptions of the vocal membrane of the larynx and the cartilages of the bronchi. Horner was also the first to describe the Z-plasty procedure used in plastic surgery. After Wistar's death, Horner supervised and expanded the anatomical museum that Wistar had left to the University of Pennsylvania. By the time of Horner's death, two-thirds of the museum's preparations were from Horner's own collection.

• Horner bequeathed his personal papers and library to Saint Joseph's Hospital, but apparently they have been lost. The Archives and Records Center of the University of Pennsylvania holds material that documents Horner's career with the university's medical school. In addition to those cited in the text, Horner's writings include, in the *Philadelphia Journal of the Medical and Physical Sciences*, "Description of a Small Muscle at the Lateral Commissure of the Eyelids," 8 (1824): 70–80, and "Observations on a Case of Ruptured Tendo-Achilles, and the Method Adopted for Its Cure," 12 (1826): 407–9; and "On the Anatomical Character of Asiatic Cholera with Remarks on the Structure of the Muscle Coat," *American Journal of the Medical Sciences* 16 (1835): 58–81, 277–95. [Cato], "Sketches of Eminent Living Physicians. No. XI. William E. Horner," *Boston Medical and Surgical Journal* 42 (1850): 114–18; Samuel Jackson, "A Discourse Commemorative of the Late William E. Horner, M.D." (1853); and [William Horner (son)], "William E. Horner," in *Lives of Eminent American Physicians and Surgeons of the Nineteenth Century*, ed. Samuel D. Gross (1861), pp. 697–721, are the best contemporary accounts of Horner's life. J. Walsh and C. H. Goudiss, "Notes on the Life of William Edmonds Horner," *Records of the American Catholic Historical Society* (1903): 275–98, 423–37; William Shainline Middleton, "William Edmonds Horner (1793–1853)," *Annals of Medical History* 5 (1923): 33–44; and David Y. Cooper, "William Edmonds Horner (1793–1853), America's First Clinical Investigator," *Transactions & Studies of the College of Physicians of Philadelphia*, ser. 5, 8 (1986): 183–200, are the most useful modern accounts of Horner's life and career. See also Esmond R. Long, "The First Text of Pathology Published in America," *Archives of Pathology* 9 (1930): 898–909; Alfred Rives Shands, Jr., "William Edmonds Horner, 1793–1853," *Transactions & Studies of the College of Physicians of Philadelphia*, ser. 4, 22 (1955): 105–11; and A. F. Borges and T. Gibson, "The Original Z-Plasty," *British Journal of Plastic Surgery* 26 (1973): 237–46.

THOMAS A. HORROCKS

HORNEY, Karen Theodora Clementina Danielsen (15 Sept. 1885–4 Dec. 1952), psychoanalyst, was born near Hamburg, Germany, the daughter of Berndt Wackels Danielsen, a sea captain, and Clothilde Marie van Ronzelen. Among the first to benefit from the gradual opening of German education to women, Karen Danielsen entered a girls' Gymnasium in Hamburg in the first year of its existence and embarked on medical studies at the University of Freiburg just six years after its doors opened to women. In 1909 she married Oskar Horney, a doctoral student she had met in Freiburg who was embarking on a career as an executive in the Stinnes Corporation in Berlin. In Berlin, Horney continued her medical studies in the field of psychiatry and obtained her medical degree in 1915. By that time she had become deeply engrossed in a new and little-known discipline called psychoanalysis, imported to Berlin by Karl Abraham, a follower of Sigmund Freud.

In 1910 Horney's own unhappiness as well as her curiosity led her to undertake personal analysis with Abraham, Freud's only disciple in Berlin at the time. Within two years she had become a participant in Abraham's seminars on psychoanalysis, and within seven years she was lecturing on the techniques used in psychoanalytic treatment. While overseeing the rearing of her three daughters and running a bourgeois household in the Berlin suburbs, Horney developed a psychoanalytic practice of her own and became a prominent member of the growing Berlin Psychoanalytic Institute with particular responsibility for psychoanalytic education. In 1926 her marriage, which was troubled by infidelities on both sides and the collapse of the German economy, ended in separation. Around the same time, Horney began to write and publish a series of papers of enduring significance.

In a 1922 paper, "On the Genesis of the Castration Complex in Women," Horney first took issue with Freud's psychology of women. According to Freud, women are powerfully affected by the early realization that they do not possess a penis. Because the vagina is not seen or known in childhood, the girl concludes that the male organ is the norm, that she once had a penis but lost it through castration. Envy of the male takes hold and is likely to last a lifetime. If a woman bears children, they will be experienced as a compensation for this profound deprivation.

Horney suggested a very different interpretation of male and female experience. In "Genesis" she wrote that "we have assumed as an axiomatic fact that females feel at a disadvantage because of their genital organs. . . . Nevertheless, the conclusion so far drawn from the investigations—amounting as it does to an assertion that one half of the human race is discontented with the sex assigned to it . . . is decidedly unsatisfying, not only to feminine narcissism but also to biological science."

In "The Flight from Womanhood" (1926), Horney suggested that "penis envy" is in fact a male invention, based not on what little girls truly experience, but on what males suppose they must experience. Boys, for instance, are troubled when they discover that girls do not have a penis. Girls, as Freud concluded, must be similarly disconcerted. Horney suggested, however, that the concept of penis envy may be a male construct, a product of "a one-sidedness in our observations, due to their being made from the man's point of view." Horney further asserted that women's bodies bring with them certain advantages, such as the "bliss" of bearing a new life and the "deep pleasurable feeling" of nursing and caring for a new baby, and she suggested that motherhood gives women "a quite indisputable . . . physiological superiority." There is reason, in fact, for men to envy women.

Horney did not coin the phrase "womb envy," but she was the first within psychoanalysis to argue for its existence. She also argued, in this and subsequent essays, that women's feelings of inferiority, which often are real enough, have more to do with society than with inherent, biological constraints. "Our culture," she wrote in "Inhibited Femininity" (1926), "is a male culture, and therefore by and large not favorable to the unfolding of woman and her individuality." The fourteen papers Horney wrote between 1922 and 1935 constitute an impressively full and persuasive challenge to Freud. Although he acknowledged Horney's essays, Freud did not substantially change his own views of what he called the "riddle of femininity." Had she written nothing else these papers would have earned Horney a place of importance in the history of psychoanalysis.

In 1932, lured by the promise of a position at the newly formed Chicago Psychoanalytic Institute and troubled by early signs of fascism in Germany, Horney left Berlin for the United States. She settled with her youngest daughter in Chicago, where she served as second in command to the somewhat younger Franz Alexander, a Hungarian who had trained at the Berlin Psychoanalytic Institute. She stayed at the Chicago Institute for two years, during which time she won the admiration of many students but, for unclear reasons, came into conflict with Alexander.

In 1934 she moved to New York City, where she was to live and practice for the rest of her life. She soon became part of a lively circle of intellectuals, including Paul Tillich and Erich Fromm. Like many of the most brilliant refugees from Hitler's Germany, Horney began lecturing at the New School for Social Research in Greenwich Village. Because of her clarity and dramatic flair, the lectures became enormously popular events, remembered for years afterward by many who attended. She had the ability to make listeners feel she was addressing them personally, and speaking of their own personal problems. That same ability contributed to the popularity of her five books, which were written in English. The first, *The Neurotic Personality of Our Time* (1937), went through thirteen printings in a decade. Paperback editions of her books began appearing in the 1960s and have sold over a million copies.

Horney's books address a constellation of themes now grouped under the rubric "narcissistic." They reflect her own difficulties in the area of self-love and love for others, including her lifelong inability to find a lasting, satisfying love relationship. *The Neurotic Personality* describes a particular kind of neurotic: a person who is guided in most situations by a need for love or, more precisely, a need to *be* loved, "an indiscriminate hunger for appreciation or affection." The need is grounded in a profound insecurity that forces the afflicted person to seek constant reassurance. Underlying this need is a deep feeling of anxiety—what Horney called "basic anxiety"—originating in childhood. As in her earlier essays on female sexuality, Horney emphasized the social factors that contribute to neurosis, and she suggested that such neurotic configurations were especially widespread in twentieth-century America, where competition and cravings for outward success left individuals feeling "emotionally isolated."

Because of her popular appeal, Horney was viewed with suspicion at the hierarchical and exclusive New York Psychoanalytic Institute. When she published a second book, which directly challenged some of Freud's basic ideas, her position at the New York Institute became even more problematic. In *New Ways in Psychoanalysis* (1939), Horney credited Freud with genius and vision but suggested that he placed too much emphasis on the scientific values of the nineteenth century. His biological orientation, she argued, led him to place instinct at the center of his theory and to give very little autonomy to the ego. Although Freud had ascribed a far more complex role to the ego and added the superego as his ideas developed over his lifetime, the grounding of psychoanalysis in instinct theory made the id the source of energy and the ego a borrower of it. "As long as the 'ego' is considered to be by its very nature merely a servant and supervisor of the 'id,' it cannot be itself an object of therapy," Horney wrote. She argued that the "'ego,' in its weakness," should be "regarded as an essential part of the neurosis." The analyst should work toward changing the ego, toward the "ultimate goal of having the patient retrieve . . . his 'spiritual self.'"

Horney's focus on the ego, even before *New Ways*, had made her a pioneer in what is now generally referred to as "ego psychology." But the book was greeted by Horney's psychoanalytic colleagues with nearly unrelieved hostility. She was viewed as an upstart who wanted to do away with the essence of psychoanalysis. And her timing gave the appearance of insensitivity: the same year that *New Ways* appeared, Freud died, painfully and in exile, in England. Meanwhile, a controversy was growing at the New York Psychoanalytic Institute about the increasingly popular teachings of Horney and her followers. In the fall of 1939, Horney's presentation of her ideas to the membership caused an uproar, with indignation on both the traditional and the Horney side. Over the next two years the institute grew increasingly hostile to Horney and to students who were drawn to her and other analysts, such as Clara Thompson and Abram Kardiner, who shared some of her views. Students who were sympathetic to Horney complained that they were being harassed and denied advancement in the institute. The institute leaders insisted that this was untrue. Finally, fearing that Horney's popularity and influence was growing beyond its control, the Education Committee of the New York Psychoanalytic Institute voted in the early spring of 1941 to demote Horney. She walked out of the meeting at which the vote was upheld by the membership, followed by Thompson and three younger analysts, and never returned.

During the last nine years of her life, Horney founded her own institute, which continues today as the Horney Institute in New York City. In 1942 she wrote *Self-Analysis*, in which she dealt at length with unhealthy dependency, or "morbid dependency." Her last two books, *Our Inner Conflicts* (1945) and *Neurosis and Human Growth* (1950), systematize her theory of the way in which individuals deal with conflict and suggest a common neurotic defense she calls the "pride system," which interferes with finding a true self. In her final years, Horney developed an interest in Zen. Shortly before her death she traveled to Zen monasteries in Japan with the Zen master D. T. Suzuki. She died in New York City.

Horney's early writings on female sexuality, which were rediscovered by feminists after they were translated into English and compiled under the title *Feminine Psychology* (1967), were ignored for many years because of her later "heresies" against Freudian orthodoxy. But, as Zenia Odes Fliegel noted in the *Psychoanalytic Quarterly* (42, no. 3 [1973], Horney "originated many ideas and observations which reappear in later writings on the subject." The psychologist Robert Coles called Horney "a prophet" who "dared look with some distance and detachment at her own profession, and . . . anticipated . . . a future historical moment" (in Jean Strouse, ed., *Dialogues on Psychoanalytic Views of Femininity: Women and Analysis* [1974]). In her five books Horney not only touched the lives of many people; she also sounded themes that have since been taken up and orchestrated by the ego psychologists and the self psychologists. Without using the term, Horney focused on "narcissistic personality," and her ideas have been echoed in more recent writings by Christopher Lasch and Heinz Kohut. Many of her criticisms of Freud have come to be widely accepted by a majority in her field.

• Horney's papers have been contributed to the Yale University Library. In addition to the books referred to above, Horney edited a series of essays, *Are You Considering Psychoanalysis?* (1946), which continues to be a worthwhile guide to the possibilities and pitfalls of psychoanalysis. *The Adolescent Diaries of Karen Horney* (1980) are a lively reflection of Horney's girlhood intelligence and vigor. *Final Lectures* (edited by Douglas H. Ingram), a transcription of Horney's last talks, address analytic technique. Marcia Westkott, *The Feminist Legacy of Karen Horney* (1986), places Horney's last work in a feminist framework. Janet Sayers, *Mothers of Psychoanalysis* (1991), examines Horney's contributions along with those of other important women in the field of psychoanalysis. There have been two biographies: Jack L. Rubins, *Karen Horney; Gentle Rebel of Psychoanalysis* (1978), and Susan Quinn, *A Mind of Her Own; The Life of Karen Horney* (1987). An obituary is in the *New York Times*, 5 Dec. 1952.

SUSAN QUINN

HORNSBY, Rogers (27 Apr. 1896–5 Jan. 1963), baseball player, was born in Winters, a farming community in west-central Texas, the son of Edward Hornsby, a cattle rancher and farmer, and Mary Dallas Rogers. Hornsby's aptitude for baseball was evident early. He played for high school and semipro teams, and he turned professional in 1914 with Hugo, Oklahoma. When that club disbanded, he played at Denison, Texas, where he appeared in 113 games at shortstop, fielded brilliantly, but batted only .232. With Denison in 1915 he had 119 hits in as many games to improve to a .277 average. Bob Connery, the perceptive scout of the St. Louis Cardinals, was impressed by the gangling youth's intensity during a spring exhibition against the Cards' B squad and purchased him for $600 for fall delivery. Hornsby appeared in a Cardinals' lineup for the first time on 10 September and played 18 games in all, averaging .246.

Manager Miller Huggins, a former infielder, liked Hornsby's hustle but told him he needed more than 140 pounds on his 5′11″ frame. Hornsby, who never did anything by halves, spent the winter on his uncle's farm bulking up on a diet of steak and milk. He arrived at training camp in 1916 weighing 175 pounds. To take advantage of Hornsby's heft, Huggins urged him to adopt a different batting stance. Holding himself erect instead of crouching, swinging the bat full-length instead of choking it, and standing deep in the batter's box, Hornsby responded with stunning results. From the far back corner of the box, he strode into the pitch with a level swing and newfound power that eventually made him the greatest right-handed hitter in baseball history.

During a 23-year career, "the Rajah," a laudatory nickname suggesting his almost regal eminence, compiled an average of .358, second only to Ty Cobb's .367. He led the National League in hitting seven times, six of those seasons in a row. In 1924 he hit .424, the highest average achieved in the twentieth century. To the Cardinals' dismay, his batting mark did not win him the annual Most Valuable Player award, but he captured the honor in 1925, the second of his two Triple Crown years, when he led the league in hitting, runs batted in, and home runs. He batted better than .400 in two other seasons, and between 1921 and 1925 he averaged an unparalleled .402. He led the league nine times in slugging average and seven times in total bases.

In 1922 Hornsby had perhaps the most dominant single season any batter ever enjoyed, leading the National League in ten hitting categories: batting and slugging averages; hits, extra-base hits, and total bases; doubles; home runs and home-run percentage; runs and runs batted in. His 250 hits and 450 total bases are among the highest seasonal marks ever attained.

Hornsby hit line drives to all fields, ran the bases with style and daring, and recovered quickly from his right-handed swing to make the dash to first. His home-run total of 301 is modest but respectable. He led the National League four years in runs batted in, hits, and doubles, two in triples and homers, three in walks, five in runs. His numbers place him among the top twenty-five players in all of these career statistics, except for runs, homers, and bases on balls. At 2,930 hits, he finished his career 70 hits short of the elite 3,000 level, a mark reached by fewer than twenty players. As a contemporary said, "When Rogers Hornsby picked up a bat he was perfect."

He also was a capable fielder, mostly at second base. His career average of .958 compares poorly with the marks now attained with superior, more capacious gloves, and it also was pulled down by expectably lower averages in the 548 games he played at shortstop and third base. His only weakness was his difficulty with high pop flies. Some said he was unfamiliar with them because he personally hit so few.

As a youngster, he was the standout performer on a mediocre team and popular with St. Louis fans. He had dimples, rosy cheeks, and a ready smile. He was thoroughly professional. Bean balls never disturbed his concentration at bat. Arguments with umpires and expulsions from games were rare. He neither smoked nor drank and even abstained from coffee. He avoided reading and the movies, which he believed would impair his vision. Observers called him an iron-assed lobby sitter, who expounded his views on baseball generally and hitting in particular until bedtime at 10 P.M.

He was admirable, and people wanted to like him, but he held them off with a cold eye and an abrasive manner. He was a loner who refused to have a road roommate and viewed women as an occasional distraction from his disciplined schedule. In dugout or locker room he blistered anyone who did not play to the maximum of his ability, and he spoke the bitter truth as he saw it to sportswriters seeking a quote for publication. He was contemptuous of his managers, and he often clashed with front-office executives and club owners, usually for daring to criticize his players or his managerial maneuvers. Or sometimes for his persistent betting on horse races. Gambling was frowned on by baseball authorities, only recently scorched by the Black Sox scandal, as threatening the game's integrity. But Hornsby was unmoved by threats or pleas from Commissioner Kenesaw Mountain Landis or anyone else. What he did with his own money on his own time, he told them, was his own business. Even so, his superstar quality and the magnetism of that implacable temperament persuaded clubs again and again that he was just what they needed to win a pennant.

Actually, as baseball analyst Bill James has pointed out, Hornsby's heroics did not make him a consistent winner. He succeeded Branch Rickey as manager of the Cardinals in 1925 and lifted the club from last to fourth. In 1926 he led them to the city's first National League pennant while personally having an off year. He was injured in a collision at second base and, although he played 134 games, saw his batting fall off to .317. The Cardinals triumphed over the New York Yankees in a seven-game World Series, aided by the spectacular pitching of Grover Cleveland Alexander.

Hornsby, whose three-year contract at $18,000 had ended, was offered $50,000 for a single year by Sam Breadon, the club's parsimonious owner. Hornsby insisted on a three-year term; Breadon refused; harsh words were spoken, and in December the star of St. Louis was traded to the New York Giants for second-baseman Frankie Frisch and pitcher Jimmy Ring, a better deal for the Cardinals than it first appeared.

During spring training in 1927 a problem arose over Hornsby's ownership of 1,167 shares of stock in the Cardinals. Originally Rickey's, they were transferred by Breadon to Hornsby for $43 a share when he became manager. They represented a one-eighth interest in the club. John A. Heydler, National League president, decreed that Hornsby could not play for the Giants while being financially involved with another team. Breadon offered to buy back the stock for $60 a share. Hornsby demanded $105. The wrangle ultimately involved the whole league and was not settled until three days before the season opened. Hornsby accepted $112,000. Breadon paid $86,000, the seven other National League clubs $2,000 each, and the Giants also picked up $12,000 in legal fees. That winter the league enacted rules to prevent such situations from developing again.

Hornsby had a sterling year with New York, batting .361 and getting along well with imperious John J. McGraw, in whose absence he managed the team to a 22–10 record and a third-place finish. He was sharp with players, however, tongue-lashed a critical team official, and offended owner Charles A. Stoneham. In January 1928, after signing a two-year contract at $40,000, he was traded to the Boston Braves.

At Boston, Hornsby had another banner year, winning his seventh league batting title with a .387 average. Within six weeks, as expected, he also supplanted the Braves' inoffensive manager, Jack Slattery. It made no difference. A chronically weak team, the Braves finished seventh.

The Chicago Cubs, backed by the Wrigley chewing-gum fortune and on the verge of a championship after a dozen aimless years, decided that Hornsby was the one missing piece in a powerful lineup. Boston was happy with Hornsby but needed Chicago's $200,000, plus five mediocrities, more. In 1929 the Cubs did win the pennant, then lost the World Series. Hornsby hit a solid .380 and won his second MVP award, but it was his last great season. In 1930 he appeared in only 42 games after breaking an ankle, and he became manager when Joe McCarthy resigned. As playing manager in 1931, he hit .331 in 100 games, although hampered by a heel spur, and he led the Cubs to a third-place finish. In 1932 he had the team in second place in August when he was fired. Rumors swirled: Hornsby was in conflict with his players, he had borrowed betting money from them, his gambling was getting out of hand.

The real reason was a prolonged battle about pitching strategy with club president William L. Veeck, Sr. Blunt, barbed-wire Hornsby language had ruined another opportunity. Under first-baseman Charlie Grimm the Cubs won another pennant, but the players made clear their feelings toward the deposed Hornsby by pointedly failing to vote him any share of the postseason money.

Rickey took him back with the Cardinals in 1933, and in 46 games fans got a few glimpses of the old Hornsby. Batting .325, he excelled as a pinch hitter—in one stretch going five for five. At midseason he was appointed manager of the St. Louis Browns of the American League, a hopeless team he did nothing to improve. He lasted until 1937, his teams never rising higher than sixth place in the final standings; then he was cast adrift after arguing with owner Donald Barnes.

Thereafter, Hornsby wandered from job to job, always in demand, sometimes a success, yet never a fixture. He was a batting instructor, coach, manager, general manager, scout, and—briefly, given the harshness of his opinions—TV commentator. He toured the minor leagues, often in the familiar Texas-Oklahoma area, but also in Mexico and in Puerto Rico's winter league.

In 1942 he was voted into the Baseball Hall of Fame at Cooperstown, New York. In 1950 and 1951 he won pennants at Beaumont, Texas, and Seattle. Impressed, Bill Veeck, Jr., now owner of the Browns, gave him a three-year managerial contract. Veeck and Hornsby lasted about three months together, until Hornsby's disgust at Veeck's goofy promotional schemes and what he saw as meddling in managing set off another explosion. Parts of two slack years as manager at Cincinnati, a team with glory days long gone and yet to come, was Hornsby's last stint in the major leagues.

Only with young boys eager to learn baseball could this hard and caustic man be patient and pleasant. Between 1945 and 1948, and again between 1954 and 1957, Hornsby was the director of free baseball schools in Chicago. He never found another Hornsby, but he taught thousands of youngsters the art of hitting baseballs, while sharing with them his rigorous vision of the game.

Otherwise, Hornsby went his contentious way to the end, outspokenly bigoted, racist (he had told sportswriter Fred Lieb long ago of his membership in the Ku Klux Klan), and ever scornful of the baseball establishment. He was married three times, to Sarah E. Martin, Jeannette Pennington Hine, and Marjorie Bernice Frederick—and divorced twice. He had two sons, one of whom briefly played minor league baseball. He died in Chicago. At the last, he spurned floral tributes. His stepdaughter explained: "He didn't like flowers."

• The National Baseball Library in Cooperstown, N.Y., has a Hornsby file. The New York Public Library has newspaper holdings that are particularly informative, including the recollections of Red Smith, who wrote for the *St. Louis Star* in 1926 (Hornsby's last year with the Cardinals) and reported on baseball for the *New York Herald Tribune* from 1945 to 1967; see also the library's holdings of other New York papers of the late 1920s and early 1930s—the *Evening World,* the *Times,* and the *Sun.* Bob Broeg has a good account of Hornsby's life and career in the *Sporting News,* 22 Feb. 1969. Charles C. Alexander, *John McGraw* (1989), is authoritative on Hornsby's tumultuous year in New York. Harold Seymour, *Baseball: The Golden Age* (1971), explains the sale of Hornsby's shares in the St. Louis club. Donald Honig, *Baseball America* (1985), provides the best effort to describe him subjectively. Bill Surface, "The Last Days of Rogers Hornsby," *Saturday Evening Post,* 15 June 1963, is a vivid description of his passion for betting and of his long-held negative views. Frederick G. Lieb, *Baseball as I Have Known It* (1977), discusses Hornsby's Klan membership. *The Bill*

James Historical Baseball Abstract (1986) includes an evaluation of Hornsby. His statistics are in *The Baseball Encyclopedia*, 9th ed. (1993); John Thorn and Pete Palmer, eds., *Total Baseball*, 3d ed. (1993); and Richard M. Cohen et al., *The World Series* (1986). Hornsby died during the New York newspaper strike of 1963, but Red Smith's memorial column was published on 7 Jan. in the *International Herald Tribune*; an obituary by F. G. Lieb appears in the *Sporting News*, 19 Jan. 1963.

A. D. SUEHSDORF

HOROWITZ, Vladimir (1 Oct. 1903–5 Nov. 1989), classical pianist, was born in Berdichev, Ukraine, the son of Samuel (or Simeon) Gorovitz (the Russian form of the name), an electrical engineer and businessman, and Sophie Bodick. Horowitz grew up in Kiev. His family was well-to-do, and he and his three siblings were educated by governesses and private tutors. Horowitz began piano lessons with his mother at about five years of age and, though he was not exploited as a child prodigy, made rapid progress. He entered the Kiev Conservatory of Music in 1912. He proved to be a difficult student, much preferring to read through the piano literature and orchestral and operatic scores than to practice the scales and technical exercises that were the normal conservatory fare. Nevertheless, he soon became recognized as the most promising pianist at the conservatory. In 1919 he became a student of the pianist, composer, and conductor Felix Blumenfeld, who was not only his last teacher but the one who most influenced him. Horowitz graduated from the conservatory in 1920.

That same year the Russian Revolution reached Ukraine and Horowitz's formerly prosperous father soon became destitute. The young pianist perforce became the family breadwinner. He gave his first public concert in Kiev on 30 May 1920 and was soon performing all over Ukraine, first under the management of his uncle and later under the auspices of a Soviet concert bureau. In 1921 he and the violinist Nathan Milstein began giving joint recitals in many parts of the Soviet Union. Horowitz made his Moscow orchestral debut in 1923, playing the Rachmaninoff Third Piano Concerto (which was to become one of his signature pieces) with the conductorless Persimfans orchestra. He soon became a musical star, performing all over Russia.

In early 1925 Moscow concert impresario Alexander Merovitch persuaded Horowitz and Milstein to leave Russia and make their careers in the West under his management. Horowitz secured a visa to go to Berlin on the pretext that he wished to complete his studies there. He and Merovitch departed from Leningrad for Germany in September 1925; he was not to return to Russia until more than sixty years later. He made his Berlin debut in a recital on 2 January 1926 and followed it with two more recitals and an orchestral debut during the same month. He then played three concerts in Hamburg, including an appearance as a last minute substitute for a scheduled soloist in the Tchaikovsky First Piano Concerto that was a spectacular triumph.

He moved on to Paris where he made his recital debut on 12 February and played numerous concerts during the remainder of 1926. He became a great favorite with French audiences and made Paris his headquarters for the next few years. In the late 1920s he concertized throughout western Europe.

On 12 January 1928 Horowitz made his debut in the United States in a concert with the New York Philharmonic at Carnegie Hall in which he performed the Tchaikovsky First Piano Concerto. The performance was controversial in a way that was to typify much of Horowitz's long career. He and the conductor, Sir Thomas Beecham, had disagreed over the basic tempos of the work in rehearsal. Though Beecham by tradition and courtesy should have deferred to his soloist in this matter, he proceeded to conduct the concerto at the concert in his preferred slow tempos. Horowitz, frantically eager to make a big impression with the audience and critics, gradually began to speed up the pace and concluded the final movement in a blaze of rapid notes that left conductor and orchestra several bars behind at the end. The audience went wild with enthusiasm, but most of the newspaper critics, while lauding Horowitz's virtuosity, took him to task for his undisciplined race with the conductor. The most telling criticism came from the great composer and pianist, Sergei Rachmaninoff, who declared that Horowitz had "won the octaves race" but that it "was not musical" (Schonberg, p. 109). This did not prevent the two artists from beginning a close friendship that lasted until Rachmaninoff's death in 1943. Horowitz followed his debut with several highly successful solo recitals at Carnegie Hall and with a lengthy and triumphant tour of many major cities of the United States. He toured widely both in Europe and the United States until 1936.

In April 1933 Horowitz began a very important professional relationship when he performed the Beethoven Fifth Piano Concerto with the New York Philharmonic under the baton of Arturo Toscanini, then widely considered to be the greatest of all conductors. The relationship acquired a personal dimension when Horowitz courted and then married Toscanini's daughter Wanda in December of that year. Wanda Toscanini Horowitz had inherited some of her father's notoriously volatile temperament, and the marriage proved to be a tempestuous one, including at least one lengthy separation. The Horowitzes had one child, a daughter born in 1934 who had a very unhappy life and died, a possible suicide, in 1975. Toscanini himself dominated all members of his family and this tended to accentuate the insecurities and neuroses that began to appear in Horowitz soon after his marriage. Horowitz's personal problems were compounded by the fatigue caused by his heavy schedule of concerts in the United States and Europe. Triggered by complications following a probably unnecessary appendectomy in 1936, Horowitz suffered both a physical and mental collapse and ceased performing in public for two years, the first of three lengthy retirements from the concert stage during his life.

Horowitz resumed his concertizing in the autumn of 1938 with a series of performances in Europe that extended into the summer of 1939. The beginning of World War II forced him to return to the United States, and he did not appear in Europe again until 1951. He became a patriotic resident of the United States and played numerous concerts, including several with Toscanini, to sell war bonds and raise money for war-related charitable activities. He applied for American citizenship in 1942 and became a citizen in 1945. In 1945, to celebrate the end of the war, he introduced the latest in a series of virtuoso transcriptions of famous pieces, a spectacularly complex version of John Philip Sousa's march "The Stars and Stripes Forever," which he frequently played to conclude a concert.

Horowitz continued a busy career of performing and recording both in America and Europe until 1953. In that year he once again abandoned the concert stage; this time the hiatus was to last for twelve years. Though never fully explained, the causes of this long silence were clearly very complex, including fatigue and boredom after thirty-three years of performing and touring, ill-health (especially colitis), problems with his marriage, and some devastatingly critical reviews that suggested that he was far more a superhuman virtuoso than a profound musician. He spent much of his time during this period secluded in his New York townhouse. After about two years, he did begin to make new commercial phonograph recordings, insisting that the recording crews come to his home for the purpose. These recordings kept his name before the public, and they revealed new musical depths in his playing. By 1965 he finally felt ready to perform again in public, and on 9 May of that year he played a successful and highly publicized concert at Carnegie Hall. His long absence had made him even more of a legend, and he was to have wildly enthusiastic audiences wherever and whenever he chose to perform for the rest of his life.

Horowitz was highly selective in the number and location of concerts that he gave from 1965 onward. He traveled away from New York only sparingly and with elaborate preparations for his personal comfort. He took another lengthy sabbatical from the concert stage from 1969 to 1974, allegedly triggered by an unfavorable review in Boston. Beyond that, however, he performed fairly regularly in his later years, though he often cancelled concerts at the last moment, as he had done throughout his life. Highlights of this period included a recital for American television in 1968, a concert with Eugene Ormandy and the New York Philharmonic in 1978 to celebrate the fiftieth anniversary of his American debut, a televised appearance at the White House in the same year, a film titled *Vladimir Horowitz: The Last Romantic* in 1985, and, above all, a triumphant return to Russia in April 1986, during which he played concerts in Moscow and Leningrad. His last public concert was in Hamburg, Germany, on 21 June 1987. He continued to make commercial recordings at his home in New York; his final recording

session took place four days before his death. He was buried in the Toscanini family crypt in the Cimitero Monumentale in Milan, Italy.

Horowitz was unquestionably one of the great piano virtuosos of all time, certainly the equal of any twentieth-century pianist and often ranked with legendary nineteenth-century figures such as Franz Liszt and Anton Rubinstein. Yet his repertoire was surprisingly small and selective. He performed perhaps a dozen different piano concertos during his entire career. Actually, he much preferred recitals to concerto performances. However, even in that field, he played relatively few works: seven or eight of the thirty-two Beethoven piano sonatas, for example, and only a handful of the vast number of works composed by Franz Liszt, a composer to whom he was temperamentally well suited. But the great critical controversy over Horowitz centered not on the size of his repertoire but on the question of whether or not his admittedly staggering technical powers at the piano came even close to being equaled by musical insight into the compositions that he chose to perform. "Horowitz," wrote the critic Michael Steinberg, "illustrates that an astounding instrumental gift carries no guarantee about musical understanding." Harold C. Schonberg, the critic and biographer, was much more sympathetic to Horowitz's virtuosity and musicianship, but even he believed that there was always a "chasm between what Horowitz was and what he secretly wanted to be." "Horowitz," he said, "wanted more than anything . . . to be accepted as a great musician rather than a flashy virtuoso" (Schonberg, p. 177). However, the concluding words of Schonberg's biography were positive: "Horowitz remained the archetype of the Romantic pianist. . . . He was unique, the last of his kind; and when he died there was nobody to replace him" (p. 315).

• Horowitz's music library, recordings of many of his concerts, correspondence, newspaper clippings, and other memorabilia are at Yale University, New Haven, Conn. Most of his many commercial recordings continue to be available. Glenn Plaskin, *Horowitz: A Biography of Vladimir Horowitz* (1983), was the first attempt at a full, carefully documented biography, based on printed source material together with many interviews with persons who knew Horowitz. Harold C. Schonberg, *Horowitz: His Life and Music* (1992), covers the artist's entire life and has more depth and perspective than Plaskin's book. David Dubal, *Evenings with Horowitz: A Personal Portrait* (1991), offers transcriptions of notes and tapes of the author's conversations with Horowitz. David Dubal, comp. and ed., *Remembering Horowitz: 125 Pianists Recall a Legend* (1993), consists of brief and, almost without exception, laudatory comments. See also Michael Steinberg's entry on Horowitz in *The New Grove Dictionary of Music and Musicians*, ed. Stanley Sadie, vol. 8 (20 vols., 1980), pp. 722–23. A lengthy obituary is in the *New York Times*, 6 Nov. 1989.

JOHN E. LITTLE

HORROCKS, James (c. 1734–20 Mar. 1772), college president, was born in Wakefield, England, the son of James Horrocks. (His mother's identity is unknown.)

Horrocks matriculated in 1751, at the age of seventeen, as a sizar (on fellowship) at Trinity College, Cambridge. He earned his A.B. degree in 1756 and became a fellow of Trinity that year. Horrocks's tutor at Cambridge was Stephen Whisson, who later became senior bursar and university librarian and thus was a man of some influence. In 1757 Horrocks became an usher (i.e., assistant teacher) in the Wakefield School, where he taught several prominent Virginians, including Robert Beverley, Theodorick Bland, and Richard Henry Lee. Horrocks's M.A. was confirmed in 1758, and three years later he received twenty pounds from the British government for passage to Virginia. He became licensed to preach in Virginia and served Petsworth and Kingston parishes in Gloucester County from 1762 to 1764; a sermon, "Upon the Peace," survives from that period. In it he outlined proper behavior, encouraging dutiful obedience to the laws and to God, condemning the evils of slavery, and recommending a good education. In 1763 he became master of the grammar school connected with the College of William and Mary.

Horrocks was elected as the sixth president of the college in 1764, the beginning of the turbulent period leading up to the outbreak of the American Revolution, and he immediately became involved in various controversies, both political and ecclesiastical. One involved the division of power between the board of visitors and the professors. The Statute of 1763 had granted the visitors authority over the professors, that is, the right to remove, at their pleasure, and to replace, at will, faculty members; the statute also required all professors to reside at the college, and it forbade them to practice any profession outside of it. Upon discovering that only Horrocks was willing to accept these conditions, the visitors quickly elected him president. At his swearing in, Horrocks vowed to adhere to the very rules he had earlier protested. Feeling contrite, Horrocks called the masters together and explained that he had not changed his mind about the statute and that he wished he had obtained the presidency on better terms. As president, however, he remained more loyal to his colleagues than to his employers; reversing his earlier stand, he refused, as had his predecessor, William Yates, to seek English help against the statute. Horrocks later worked to overthrow the visitors.

Another controversy in which he was involved, known as the Parson's Cause, concerned the colonial assembly's attempt to decrease the salary payment of the clergy and all public officials. The legislature, during a time of rising tobacco prices, fixed the rate at which the legally established payments in pounds of tobacco could be commuted to paper money. The ordinarily underpaid ministers were thus deprived of a substantial increase in their payment, and some brought suit against their vestries. John Camm, professor of divinity at the college, whose appeal to England was seen as the test case, went before the king declaring the legislature's suspension of the royal act an "act of treason." After a protracted battle the clergy's cause was lost.

Horrocks was more directly involved in the contentious issue over whether or not to establish an American episcopate, something the majority of the Virginia clergy did not support. As commissary to the Bishop of London for Virginia, a post he had held since 1768, Horrocks called a convention of the clergy, set for 4 June 1771, to consider "the Expediency of an Application to proper authority for an American Episcopate." However, out of almost one hundred clergymen, only twelve appeared to answer his call for convention; eight voted in favor of preparing an address to the king asking him to appoint a bishop for Virginia, whereas four of the attendants, including Rev. Thomas Gwatkins and Rev. Samuel Henley, professors at the college, were opposed. The proposition created a great stir, especially in the newspapers, but in the end, nothing came of the "Virginia schism." In July the House of Burgesses put an end to it—at least publicly—by voting unanimously against the expediency of an American episcopate and by returning their thanks to the four clergymen who had opposed the measure.

A few days after the clergy convention Horrocks left for England, ostensibly because of failing health. He put Camm in charge of the college and of the defense of the proposed episcopate. Richard Bland (who in 1770 had objected to Horrocks's appointment as councilor of state because he was a clergyman) accused Horrocks of opportunism, claiming that his real reason for going to England was to lay the foundation of the established church in America so that he could become the "First Right Reverend Father" of it. Bland also asserted about Horrocks that "neither his address or abilities can possibly recommend him to so high an office." Horrocks set sail for England on the *Savannah la Mar* with his wife, Frances (maiden name unknown). On the way, at Oporto, Portugal, he died (cause unknown). Because he left no will or children, his widow received one half of his personal estate and one third of his slaves for the rest of her life. The remainder of his estate went to his brother, Thomas, who lived in Great Britain. Mrs. Horrocks died the following year, on 26 December 1773, in Virginia at the age of twenty six. In the archives of the College of William and Mary is a scrap of paper that lists a few books from Horrocks's library that were purchased after his death and received on 8 December 1772. The titles attest to Horrocks's regard for mathematics, as does his obituary in the *Virginia Gazette*.

While he was president of the College of William and Mary, Horrocks was elected by the vestry of Bruton Parish Church to the office of rector. He was thus the last of the college's colonial presidents who combined that post with appointment as commissary to the Bishop of London and election as rector of Bruton Parish. His tenure was marked by the turbulent times of the revolutionary period.

• Horrocks's papers are in the William and Mary Manuscript Library, Faculty Alumni File, and in the papers *Relating to the History of the Church in Virginia* and the *Alumni Association Newsletter*, 15 Mar. 1932. The Fulham papers in the Lambeth Palace Library, London, contain letters between Horrocks and the Bishop of London; they are also on microfilm at the Virginia Theological Seminary, the Virginia Colonial Records Project at the Library of Virginia, the University of Virginia Library, and the Colonial Williamsburg Foundation Library. The Virginia Historical Society has his sermon "Upon the Peace," 25 Aug. 1763, as well as the Bland papers. The *William and Mary Quarterly*, ser. 1, vols. 5, 6, 13, 16, 19, and ser. 2, vol. 6, contain detailed minutes of college meetings held by Horrocks. As an alum of Cambridge he is mentioned in J. and J. A. Venn's *Alumni Cantabrigienses* (1922). The episcopacy controversy is discussed in Richard L. Morton, *Colonial Virginia: A History* (1960), chapters 27–30, as well as in Rhys Issac, *The Transformation of Virginia* (1982), pp. 181–89. The struggles between the faculty and visitors within the college is covered by Robert Polk Thomson in "The Reform of the College of William and Mary, 1763–1780," *Proceedings of the American Philosophical Society* 115: 187–213. R. C. Simmons and Peter Thomas, ed., *Proceedings and Debates of the British Parliament Respecting North America 1756–1783*, vol. 3 (1986), p. 179, discusses the payments made to clergy to come to the American colonies. Frances Mason, *John Norton and Sons: Merchants of London and Virginia* (1937), contains personal letters. An obituary is in the *Virginia Gazette*, 23 July 1772.

LINDA KAREN MILLER

HORSFALL, Frank Lappin, Jr. (14 Dec. 1906–19 Feb. 1971), clinician, virologist, and administrator, was born in Seattle, Washington, the son of Frank Horsfall, a physician, and Jessie Laura Ludden. Horsfall first wanted to become an engineer, but by the end of four years of college at the University of Washington, his interests had switched to medicine, and he entered McGill University Medical School in Montreal, Canada, in 1927.

After receiving his medical degree in 1932, Horsfall served a year as a house officer in pathology at the Peter Bent Brigham Hospital in Boston, Massachusetts, where he found out that he was extremely sensitive to formaldehyde. He made an experimental study of formaldehyde hypersensitivity, resulting in two scientific papers. After a year as a resident physician and surgeon in Montreal, he moved in 1934 to the hospital of the Rockefeller Institute for Medical Research in New York City, where he received training in the basic sciences of bacteriology, immunology, and physiology. Thereafter Horsfall always coupled his basic research with clinical activities and, if possible, sought therapeutic applications for the results of his studies.

At the Rockefeller Institute, Horsfall joined the staff of the pneumonia unit, where type I pneumonia was being treated with specific antipneumococcal horse serum. He did experimental studies on the fundamental aspects of the immunological reactions involved and was the driving force behind the switch in 1936–1937 from horse to the more effective rabbit antiserum.

In 1937 Horsfall resigned from the Rockefeller Institute hospital and accepted a staff position with the International Health Division of the Rockefeller Foundation, which was housed at the Rockefeller Institute. In that year he married Norma E. Campagnari; they had three children.

The International Health Division was particularly strong in virus research, being successful in the battle against yellow fever. Horsfall was the successor of Thomas Francis, Jr., who had set up a laboratory for the study of influenza virus. Horsfall now made use of his earlier interest in constructing and engineering, in that he designed several mechanical projects, such as a low-temperature storage cabinet and a complicated ventilation system for housing infected animals in a single room without cross-infection. Horsfall worked on the production of a "complex" vaccine containing both influenza and distemper virus in the belief that the combination might have a synergistic effect. The vaccine was tested under well-controlled circumstances, using large numbers of volunteers and closely monitoring the influenza antibody titers. However, the results regarding the prevention of influenza were disappointing. Ironically, several of his attempts to apply his findings to the cure and prevention of infectious disease were soon overtaken by more successful approaches. After Horsfall had left the pneumonia unit in 1937, the type-specific serotherapy of pneumonia was replaced by chemotherapy (e.g., sulfonamide), and his influenza vaccine studies were overtaken by the use of influenza vaccines based on virus stocks concentrated by the Sharples ultracentrifuge.

In the early 1940s Horsfall returned to the Rockefeller Institute hospital to take over its Department of Virology. There he studied atypical pneumonia (later shown to be caused by a mycoplasm) and pneumonia virus of mice (PVM). The applied nature of Horsfall's research showed itself in his study of the therapeutic activity of certain high-molecular-weight carbohydrates on PVM. He also, with Igor Tamm, initiated various series of chemotherapeutic experiments using the benzimidazoles and their derivatives against influenza virus infection. Furthermore, he studied antigenic strain differences of influenza virus, as well as the general phenomenon of viral interference.

During the 1940s Horsfall's qualities as an administrator came to the fore, eventually resulting in his becoming vice president and physician in chief of the hospital of the Rockefeller Institute. From 1949 to 1953 he was a member of the Board of Scientific Consultants of the Memorial Sloan-Kettering Institute for Cancer Research in New York. In 1959 Horsfall succeeded Cornelius P. Rhoades as director of the Sloan-Kettering Institute, resulting in a notable change in the direction of the research conducted at that institution. While Rhoades had led the research done at the Sloan-Kettering Institute in the direction of fundamental studies of chemical carcinogenesis and chemotherapy, with the arrival of the virus-oriented Horsfall, research began concentrating on the viral etiology of cancer and on molecular biology. The possibility of the involvement of viruses in human cancer found a rationale in the discovery of many cancer viruses in experimental animals. The hypothesis of a viral etiology of human cancer was attractive to Horsfall because it implied strategies for the early diagnosis and the prevention of cancer through appropriate immunization procedures (see, for example, his "Heritance of Acquired Characters: A Unifying Concept Is Developed in Relation to the Genesis of Cancer," *Science* 136 [1962]: 472–76). Together with T. M. Rivers, Horsfall edited the third edition of the standard work *Viral and Rickettsial Infections of Man* (1959) and, together with Tamm, the fourth edition (1965) of the same. He died in New York City.

Although Horsfall's prophesy of the use of viral vaccines against cancer materialized only to a limited extent, his general support of work on tumor viruses stimulated greatly the discovery of the (anti-)oncogenes, which lie at the heart of the process of cancer formation.

• A biography by G. K. Hirst, "Frank Lappin Horsfall, Jr.— December 14, 1906–February 19, 1971," National Academy of Sciences, *Biographical Memoirs* 50 (1979): 233–67, includes a bibliography of Horsfall's publications. Some of the more important include "Formaldehyde Hypersensitiveness: An Experimental Study," *Journal of Immunology* 27 (1934): 569–81; with K. Goodner and R. J. Dubos, "Type Specific Antipneumococcus Rabbit Serum for Therapeutic Purposes," *Journal of Immunology* 33 (1937): 279–95; with E. H. Lennette, "A Complex Vaccine Effective against Different Strains of Influenza Virus," *Science* 91 (1940): 492–94; with J. H. Bauer, "Individual Isolation of Infected Animals in a Single Room," *Journal of Bacteriology* 40 (1940): 569–80; "Chemotherapy in Viral Infections (The Musser Lecture)," *American Journal of Medical Sciences* 220 (1950): 91–102; and with I. Tamm, "Chemotherapy of Viral and Rickettsial Diseases," *Annual Review of Microbiology* 11 (1957): 339–70.

TON VAN HELVOORT

HORSFIELD, Thomas (12 May 1773–24 July 1859), naturalist, was born in Bethlehem, Pennsylvania, the son of Timothy Horsfield, Jr., and Juliana Parsons. His early education was in the Moravian schools at Bethlehem and Nazareth, and he then engaged in studies in pharmacy and botany. He continued his education as a medical student at the University of Pennsylvania and graduated in 1798. As a "medical apprentice" at the Pennsylvania Hospital from 1794 to 1799, he was a student of Dr. Benjamin Smith Barton. Horsfield's graduation thesis on the toxic action of poisonous plants was considered to be a significant contribution in the history of experimental pharmacology because of its accurate clinical descriptions of toxic symptoms and its excellent experimental data.

In late 1799 Horsfield signed on as surgeon on the merchant ship *China*, sailing from Philadelphia and arriving in Java in 1800. The few months that Horsfield spent on the island so impressed him that he resolved to return as an explorer of its natural history. Back in Philadelphia, he assembled a collection of books and instruments and sailed back to the East Indies in 1801. The Dutch colonial authorities gave him permission to remain in Java, and in 1802 he was appointed chief surgeon in the Dutch Colonial Army and was assigned the special task of investigating plants that were known by the native population to be useful in the treatment of diseases. His biographer James B.

McNair wrote, "This was the beginning of eighteen years of study which linked his name inseparably with the natural history and especially the botany of Java" (p. 3).

At first, Horsfield's researches in natural history were made in the vicinity of Batavia, but after 1804 he widened the geographical scope of his activities. He visited all of the regions of Java and also made trips to neighboring islands. His work included botanical collecting, studies in zoology, observations of agriculture and local industries, examination of ancient Javanese monuments, and geological work, such as mapping of volcanic craters. His 1806 report to the scientific society at Batavia was typical of his accounts of his extensive activities that he regularly forwarded to the authorities. In it he described his travels and noted that he had spent part of his time writing about Javanese quadrupeds, birds and insects, mineralogical history, and antiquities. He had also supervised his two Javanese assistants in preparing drawings of more than 200 plants to be sent, along with the dried specimens, to Europe. He had not neglected his earlier assignment, for he wrote of examining medicinal plants used by the indigenous population and of preparing "a fairly large collection of dried plants between paper" (Bastin, p. 23). The colonial government thought highly of his work. Even though he was not a Dutch citizen, he had unlimited freedom of travel, a salary, which by 1808 amounted to 300 silver Rijksdaalders a month, and a spacious house in Surakarta, which became a favorite place of call for European visitors.

The political situation in Java changed in 1811 when the British conquered the island and put it under the administration of the East India Company. The new governor, Sir Thomas Stamford Raffles, was a man of many talents, and he developed a strong interest in Horsfield's work. The two men became close friends, and Raffles later wrote in his *History of Java* that his knowledge of the natural history of Java came entirely from Horsfield, who was able to continue his work on an enlarged scale with a generous salary and a number of assistants. One of the results was that Horsfield began to acquire a reputation in England. As shipments of dried plants, seeds, and other natural history collections such as birds were received in the home country, leading scientists, particularly Sir Joseph Banks, became impressed with Horsfield. Banks began corresponding with Horsfield, who with the continuous encouragement of Raffles, sent increased collections to Banks.

In 1816 Java was returned to Dutch rule; with British administration at an end, Raffles sailed to England. Two years later, he was back in the East as lieutenant governor of West Sumatra, and Horsfield joined him there before sailing to England in 1819. He had letters of introduction (from Raffles) to James Cobb, secretary of the East India Company, Sir Charles Wilkins, head of the library and museum of the Company, and to Joseph Banks. Raffles's letter to Banks cited Horsfield's sixteen years of work in the East Indies and his ability to provide for publication of a catalog of the quadrupeds of Java, outlines of the mineralogy of Java, and a description and geography of the plants of Java, including climatological information, as well as descriptions of travel throughout the islands. As to Horsfield's character, Raffles wrote, "most estimable; he has deservedly acquired the esteem of every one, and is universally respected in this part of the world."

In 1819 Horsfield was appointed curator of the East India Company Museum, and in 1836, superintendent, a post he held until 1858. These years were spent in managing the affairs of the museum and in working on his own collections and publications. The latter included *Zoological Researches in Java, and the Neighbouring Islands* (1821–1824), of which it was said, "The book established Horsfield's scientific reputation" (Bastin, p. 76). Other publications were *A Catalogue of the Mammalia in the Museum of the Hon. East-India Company* (1851); *A Catalogue of the Birds in the Museum of the Hon. East-India Company* (1854, 1858); and *A Catalogue of the Lepidopterous Insects in the Museum of the Hon. East-India Company* (1858–1860), the last two in collaboration with Frederic Moore. A large botanical work, which was undertaken in 1821, was not completed until 1852. *Plantae Javanicae Rariores* was intended to be a comprehensive flora of Indonesian plants, but owing to the procrastination and lack of cooperation of his collaborator, Robert Brown, keeper of Banks's Herbarium and Library, the book, although beautiful, was a scientific disappointment.

Horsfield received many honors in his lifetime. He was one of the few Americans to become a fellow of the Royal Society of London and was a member of the Batavian Society, the Zoological Society of London, the Geological Society of London, and a fellow of the Linnean Society. Three genera of plants have been named Horsfieldia in his honor. He was the first American to study the natural history of Java and Sumatra, and the first naturalist to bring large Indonesian collections to the United Kingdom. He was a longtime resident of London and died there, leaving a wife and his two children.

• The main body of primary materials for Horsfield is in *Manuscripts in European Languages* in the India Office Library and Records, London. Most of his natural history notes, diaries, and papers were destroyed by the executors of his will, but some letters may be found at the Linnean Society in London, the Royal Botanic Gardens, and elsewhere. The "Horsfield Papers on the Flora of Java" are in the Botanical Library of the British Museum (Natural History). John Bastin's biographical memoir in Horsfield's *Zoological Researches in Java, and the Neighbouring Islands* (1824; repr. 1990) is very complete and includes a full bibliography. James B. McNair, "Thomas Horsfield—American Naturalist and Explorer," *Torreya* 42 (1942): 1–9, is a biographical sketch with references and a list of Horsfield's publications. See also Fraus Stafleu, *Taxonomic Literature*, vol. 2 (1979), and Howard A. Kelly and Walter L. Burrage, *American Medical Biographies* (1920).

ROBERT F. ERICKSON

HORSFORD, Eben Norton (27 July 1818–1 Jan. 1893), chemist, was born in Moscow (now Livonia), New York, the son of Jerediah Horsford and Maria Charity Norton, farmers and missionaries. Growing up on the frontier, Horsford witnessed the completion of the Erie Canal in 1825. The canal opened up markets for wheat grown in the Genesee Valley, but by the 1830s progressive farmers such as Horsford's father recognized that intensive agriculture had resulted in "worn-out soil."

Horsford entered the Rensselaer School (now Rensselaer Polytechnic Institute) in 1837 and graduated the following year with a B.S. in civil engineering. Following graduation, he worked for the New York State Geological Survey and from 1838 to 1839 taught a yearly lecture course in chemistry at Newark College in Delaware. While teaching mathematics and natural history at the Albany Female Academy from 1840 to 1844, Horsford fell in love with a student, Mary L'Hommedieu Gardiner. Her father, however, refused to assent to their marriage unless Horsford improved his station.

Probably on the advice of his friend, the Harvard chemist John White Webster, Horsford set a goal of obtaining a teaching position at Harvard University. In order to enhance his education, Horsford set off in 1844 on borrowed money for the nation of Hessen-Darmstadt (now part of Germany) to study agricultural chemistry with Justus Liebig. Liebig had become world famous following the publication of his book, *Organic Chemistry in Its Applications to Agriculture and Physiology* (1840), which was especially popular in the Genesee Valley region, and Horsford's friend Webster had translated the first American edition. Liebig's laboratory at Giessen was, consequently, at its peak, attracting advanced students from all over the world.

Horsford was at the leading edge of a wave of American students who studied with Liebig in the late 1840s. He worked at Giessen from November 1844 to November 1846 and was admitted to Liebig's laboratory for advanced students during the latter part of that period. His advanced research was on the relative protein content, and presumably therefore the nutritive value, of various grains. Though best known for promoting professional chemical education, Liebig was also a zealous advocate of applying chemistry to industrial development; in both respects, his example shaped Horsford's career.

On returning to the United States in early 1847, Horsford received an appointment to the Rumford chair at the newly founded Lawrence Scientific School at Harvard University. In August 1847 he married Mary Gardiner; they had four children. Endowed by Boston industrialist Abbott Lawrence, the new school was part of a general reform movement that was aimed at making American higher education more responsive to the needs of business and industry. At Harvard, Horsford attempted to model chemical instruction on the paradigm of Liebig's laboratory at Giessen, which had assistants to teach introductory courses, perform lecture demonstrations, provide initial laboratory instruction, and oversee the stockroom and monitor inventory. Horsford's new school, however, was underendowed to achieve anything on this scale, and by 1853 Horsford had worked himself ill in the attempt to do everything himself. Low enrollment confounded his efforts to gain better funding.

After 1853 Horsford put less effort into teaching and administration and more into the industrial applications of chemistry. His efforts to develop patentable and marketable chemical commodities paid off, especially with "artificial yeast," a phosphatic baking powder. He resigned from Harvard in 1863 to devote himself full time to the Rumford Chemical Works. Founded in 1856 by Horsford and industrialist George Wilson, the company was a great success, and Horsford made a modest fortune, largely from contracts with the army for baking powder and other commodities during the Civil War. Horsford also improved condensed milk and scientifically proportioned marching rations for the army, and worked on vulcanized rubber and methods to avert the potential contamination of water that flowed through lead distribution pipes.

Late in life, Horsford took up anthropological studies of American Indian languages and of the evidence for pre-Columbian Viking settlements in North America. He was also an active supporter of Wellesley College after it was founded in 1870. Two years after the death of his first wife in 1855, he married her sister, Phoebe Dayton Gardiner, with whom he had one child. He died in Cambridge, Massachusetts.

In many ways, Horsford was a victim of his times. As a hard-working social climber, he made chemistry his ladder, but his career predated the formation of institutional science in America. Emulating the German model, he tried to establish an advanced school of chemistry but did so before there was a market for professional chemists. Although he accomplished little original scientific work, through his position at the Lawrence Scientific School he trained a subsequent generation of American scientists, who were able to establish a firm institutional basis for chemistry in the United States. These students included George Chapman Caldwell and Charles Frederick Chandler, who built significant programs at Cornell University and Columbia University respectively. Horsford was an early member of the American Chemical Society, despite his initial opposition to its formation. Driven to succeed by the expectations of his father-in-law, and perhaps by his own expectations as well, Horsford was fortunate to find that some of his chemical ideas were readily translated into business profits.

• Most of Horsford's papers are in the archives of Rensselaer Polytechnic Institute. Others are in the family home, "Sylvester Manor," at Shelter Island, N.Y., and in *Harvard College Papers*, 2d ser., 13 (1845–1846), Harvard University Archives. Horsford's publications include "Untersuchungen über Glycocoll," *Annalen der Chemie und Pharmazie* 60 (1846); "Value of Different Kinds of Vegetable Food, Based upon Amount of Nitrogen," *Transactions of the Albany Institute* (1846); "On the Relative Resistance Presented by Fluids to Electric Conduction," *American Journal of Science and Arts* 5 (1848); *Problems in Physics* (1860); *The Army Ration* (1864); *The Theory and Art of Bread-Making* (1861); and *A Report on*

Vienna Bread (1875). See also the volume titled "Original Papers" (1851), Rensselaer Archives. Horsford's publications on early Viking settlements in North America, which contain extensive archaeological and historical evidence and detailed maps, include *John Cabot's Landfall in 1497, and the Site of Norumbega* (1886); *Discovery of America by Norsemen* (1888); and *The Discovery of the Ancient City of Norumbega* (1890). Notable secondary works are H. S. van Klooster, "Liebig and His American Pupils," *Journal of Chemical Education* 33 (1956): 493–97; Samuel Rezneck, "Horsford's Marching Rations for the Civil War Army," *Military Affairs* 33 (1969): 249–55; Rezneck, "The European Education of an American Chemist and Its Influence in Nineteenth Century America: Eben Norton Horsford," *Technology and Culture* 11 (1970): 366–88; Margaret W. Rossiter, *The Emergence of Agricultural Science: Justus Liebig and the Americans, 1840–1880* (1975); and Charles E. Rosenberg, *No Other Gods: On Science and American Social Thought* (1976).

PAT MUNDAY

HORSMANDEN, Daniel (4 June 1694–23 Sept. 1778), legislator and New York's last provincial chief justice, was born at Purleigh, in Essex, England, the son of the Reverend Daniel Horsmanden and Susanna Boyer (or Bowyer). Reverend Horsmanden's sister was the mother of William Byrd of Westover. Daniel studied law in London and was admitted to the Middle Temple in 1721 and to the Inner Temple in 1724. He apparently practiced law and unsuccessfully dabbled in stocks before moving to Virginia sometime in 1729. According to the colonial historian William Smith, Jr., Horsmanden "entered into a Partnership with a Chancery Collector and after a short Trial of that Business he fled from his creditors to Virginia" (*Historical Memoirs from 12 July to 25 July 1778*, ed. William Sabine [1958], p. 39). Horsmanden later admitted that "my losses were such in the South Sea Year that I was Oblig'd to leave England."

Through Byrd family connections, Horsmanden was recommended by Micajah Perry, a London merchant, to Thomas Pelham-Holles, duke of Newcastle, and through Newcastle to New York's new governor, William Cosby. Horsmanden was admitted to the New York bar in 1732 and recommended for a seat on the council later that same year. He was characterized at that time as a man "who has no visible estate in this Govern't and [is] in necessitous circumstances." Although he was a Cosby appointee, Horsmanden recognized that a Cosby opposition group was increasing in strength.

A chameleon in his political affiliations, Horsmanden first left and then rejoined the Cosbyites. The governor was engaged in a bitter salary dispute with Rip Van Dam, who had served as an acting lieutenant governor, regarding compensation for the time between Governor John Montgomerie's death in May 1731 and Cosby's arrival at New York in August 1732. Cosby instituted a legal suit against Van Dam to recover £2,000, to which Cosby felt he was entitled. The New York Council granted Cosby's request to create a juryless exchequer jurisdiction in the supreme court to hear his complaint. The three judges could be identified by their factional affiliations. Chief Justice Lewis Morris sided with Van Dam, while the other two, James DeLancey and Frederick Philipse, supported the governor. The case was heard on 9 April 1733. When Morris accepted the argument presented by Van Dam's attorneys, William Smith and James Alexander, that this extraordinary court procedure was predicated on the fact that it was Cosby's creation, Cosby summarily dismissed Morris in August 1733 and appointed DeLancey in his stead.

Morris openly joined the Cosby opposition. A major instrument used to spread the anti-Cosby message was the creation in November 1733 of the *New York Weekly Journal*, edited by John Peter Zenger. To silence this opposition libel charges were brought against Zenger by DeLancey before the New York County grand jury in January and again in October 1734. On 17 November 1734, Zenger was imprisoned on a warrant from the council. Horsmanden was named to a joint assembly-council committee to "point out . . . the particular Seditious paragraphs in Said Journalls." As a Cosby stalwart, Horsmanden was rewarded in 1734 with a license to purchase 6,000 acres on the east side of the Hudson River near Albany.

After Cosby's death in 1736, George Clarke assumed the acting governorship. Clarke elevated Horsmanden to the position of judge in the Vice Admiralty Court of New York, New Jersey, and Connecticut and in 1737 as third judge of the supreme court of judicature.

The event that brought Horsmanden to prominence as an author was the so-called "Negro Plot" of 1741. In his capacity as city recorder, Horsmanden acted as legal counsel for the city government and presided at the meetings of the common council in the absence of the mayor or deputy mayor. Following a robbery in February and a number of fires in the next two winter months, suspicion grew that a major plot had been hatched against the white inhabitants of the city. Appearing before the common council in April 1741, Horsmanden asserted that a plot existed, and he proposed that the council offer a reward for information leading to the instigators.

Horsmanden, as a member of the provincial supreme court, subsequently heard the cases brought before the court and passed sentence on the accused plotters, including an individual supposedly a Catholic priest. There were, however, city residents who doubted the existence of a major conspiracy. In order to quell such doubts, to bolster his earlier claims, and to support his subsequent actions as a justice in sentencing four white persons and seventeen slaves to hanging (and thirteen others to be burned at the stake), Horsmanden published his version of the events under the title *The New-York Conspiracy, or a History of the Negro Plot*. In a letter to Cadwallader Colden, physician, merchant, and council member, Horsmanden summarized the "plot" as a "most horrible and Detestable piece of Villany a Scheme [which] must have been brooded in a conclave of Devils, & hatcht in the Cabinet of Hell."

Horsmanden's career took another turn in 1743 with the appearance of George Clinton as New York's next governor. A bitter rivalry developed between Clinton and James DeLancey. Seeking vengeance on his political rivals in 1747, Clinton ousted Horsmanden from his positions as a justice of the supreme court and as recorder for New York City while suspending him from his seat on the council. Clinton characterized Horsmanden as "the principal Actor in the opposition, and in forming the Faction against all Measures, which I have thought necessary for his Majtys service." Politically in limbo, Horsmanden at age fifty-four found it expedient in 1748 to marry Mary Reade Vesey, widow of the late rector of Trinity Church. They had no children. Always a trimmer, he again ingratiated himself with Clinton so that in 1753 he was restored as third judge of the supreme court "during good behavior." By 1755 Horsmanden again sat on the council under Governor Charles Hardy. In July 1760 he was left a widower.

In March 1763 then-governor Robert Monckton named Horsmanden as chief justice, a position he held until his death. At the age of seventy Horsmanden married Ann Jevon. The New York merchant John Watts would write: "Would you beleive [*sic*] it Daddy Horsmanden has entered the Lists with Miss Jevon . . . & is as Juvinile a Bridegroom as you could desire to see of above three score and ten."

With shifting political tides, Horsmanden by then was a follower of the Livingston faction. Perhaps out of personal and political expediency, Horsmanden did not attempt to reopen the court during the Stamp Act crisis. Horsmanden was called on to play a role in the *Gaspee* affair.

A British revenue schooner, *Gaspee* ran aground while chasing an American vessel on 9 June 1772, just south of Providence, Rhode Island. It was then attacked and sunk by a group of Rhode Islanders. The Crown's response was to offer rewards for information and to send a royal commission, including Horsmanden, to investigate and report their findings. Horsmanden's recommendation was to consolidate Rhode Island and Connecticut under one royal government.

The last term of the supreme court in which Horsmanden sat met in October 1775. In April 1777 his second wife died. Horsmanden died the following year at his country home in Flatbush, Kings County. William Smith noted, "He had taken a ride as well as usual but was struck by a Palsy in the Evening and continued speechless from that Moment." Horsmanden left a farm in Goodhurst, Kent, England, to be sold, and made bequests to Trinity Church, to St. Paul's Chapel, and to King's College. He was buried in Trinity's churchyard. Characterized by the *Royal Gazette* (as cited in McManus, p. 224) as a "gentleman of a most respectable character," he was viewed with suspicion by New York's provincial leaders because of his chameleon-like ability to switch allegiance depending on immediate circumstances and for his self-serving account of the Negro Plot.

• The manuscript collections of the New-York Historical Society are invaluable sources, including the Horsmanden, DeLancey, and Morris papers. The published Cadwallader Colden Papers in *The Collections of the New-York Historical Society* also are rich in material relating to Horsmanden, which may be found in vols. 9, 10, 50–56, and 67–68. For further material on Horsmanden's career, see Sister Mary Paula McManus, "Daniel Horsmanden, Eighteenth Century New Yorker" (Ph.D. diss., Fordham Univ., 1960). Disagreeing with some of her conclusions regarding the Negro Plot is Thomas J. Davis, *A Rumor of Revolt: The "Great Negro Plot" in Colonial New York* (1985). Horsmanden's account was published under several titles. The most complete one was *The New-York Conspiracy, or a History of the Negro Plot, with the Journal of the Proceedings against the Conspirators at New-York in the Years 1741–2* (1744; repr. 1810). Horsmanden's role as jurist is discussed in James Alexander, *A Brief Narrative of the Case and Trial of John Peter Zenger, Printer of the New York Weekly Journal*, ed. Stanley N. Katz (1963), and Katz, *Newcastle's New York: Anglo-American Politics, 1732–1753* (1968). Contemporary material is in William Smith, Jr., *The History of the Province of New-York*, ed. Michael Kammen (2 vols., 1972).

JACOB JUDD

HORST, Louis (12 Jan. 1884–23 Jan. 1964), composer, arranger, dance critic and pedagogue, and publisher, was born in Kansas City, Missouri, the son of German immigrants Conrad Horst, a cornet player, and Corline "Lena" Nickell. Horst's family traveled to San Francisco, California, in 1893, where Louis studied violin and piano. From about 1900 to 1914 he worked as a pianist in pit orchestras and for silent films. While working at a summer resort he met and subsequently married in 1910 eighteen-year-old Bessie (called Betty) Cunningham. They had no children. In 1911 they went to New York City, where he continued to work as a part-time musician and studied composition and piano, but they returned to San Francisco by 1914.

In 1915 Horst was contacted by the visiting Denishawn dance company, which was in need of a pianist for its San Francisco engagement. Horst was hired and stayed on as a rehearsal and tour pianist, remaining with the company for a decade. At the same time, Betty was also engaged as a dancer in the company, but their marriage was already flagging. Horst became a right-hand man to the company's directors, the dancer-choreographers Ruth St. Denis and Ted Shawn, and helped train many of their dancers, including a promising young student of Shawn's named Martha Graham. The school and company had its home base in Hollywood in 1916, although the company continued to tour extensively, including a trip to England in the early 1920s. By 1922 the company had settled in New York City, and many of its younger members began giving recitals on their own, usually calling on Horst to arrange and perform the music. His repute was such that established choreographers, such as Agnes de Mille, Ruth Page, and Helen Tamiris, regularly hired him.

In 1925 both Graham and Horst broke away from Denishawn to establish themselves as independent agents. Horst worked for the Graham company through 1948, although he was most actively involved with her in the mid-1920s through the 1930s. While still married to Betty, whom he never divorced, he became a close confidant—and probably lover—of Graham's and helped her to hone her choreographic technique. He encouraged her to visit the Southwest, sparking an interest in American themes that would become pronounced in her work of the 1930s. In addition to arranging music and introducing Graham to prominent composers whose music she would eventually use, such as Aaron Copland and Wallingford Riegger, Horst composed music for some of Graham's better-known works. His best-known score was written for her *Primitive Mysteries* (1931), which was based on Native American rituals.

As a tireless promoter of Graham and her work, Horst founded in 1934 the journal *Dance Observer* to promote modern dance. That same year, he was hired by the newly formed summer school of dance at Bennington College, where he began teaching his famous choreographic techniques course; he continued to teach at Bennington through 1945, then at Columbia University Teachers College (1938–1941), and finally at the Juilliard School of Music (1958–1963) as well as at the Neighborhood Playhouse and other New York City schools of dance. He was revered for his ability to spot talent in young dancers and develop it.

Horst had difficulty adapting to changes in the dance world and became somewhat of a gadfly and curmudgeon on the scene by the late 1950s. Most infamously, he reviewed a Paul Taylor dance solo, *Private Domain*, in *Dance Observer* with a single, blank page, signed "L.H." The furor this created among the younger dancers was legendary, although it ultimately only enhanced Taylor's popularity and fame.

Horst continued to teach at Juilliard and at other dance schools in New York City until his death there.

• Scrapbooks of articles and clippings are maintained at the New York Public Library for the Performing Arts Dance Collection, Lincoln Center. Horst wrote two books on choreographic theory, *Pre-Classic Dance Forms* (self-published in 1937) and *Modern Dance Forms* (1961), coauthored with Carroll Russell. Both books were meant to offer an alternative to the theoretical basis of ballet and to show that modern dance had its own unique language of movement. The books, with new introductions by Janet M. Soares, were reissued in 1987. Soares has also written a complete biography of Horst, *Louis Horst: Musician in a Dancer's World* (1992).

RICHARD CARLIN

HORTON, Douglas (27 July 1891–21 Aug. 1968), minister and ecumenical leader, was born in Brooklyn, New York, the son of Byron Horton and Elizabeth Swaim Douglas. After graduating from Princeton University in 1912, Horton studied abroad for a year at Edinburgh, Oxford, and Tübingen. He returned to the United States in 1913 and entered Hartford Theological Seminary, from which he received a bachelor's degree in divinity two years later. He was ordained to the Congregational ministry and called as assistant minister of the First Church in Middletown, Connecticut, in 1915. He became the senior minister of the church in 1916 and held that position until 1925. In May 1916 Horton married Carol Scudder Williams, with whom he had four children. During World War I he served briefly as a navy chaplain in 1918 and 1919.

In 1925 Horton accepted the pastorate at the Leyden Congregational Church in Brookline, Massachusetts. Three years later he won widespread attention with the publication of his translation (entitled *The Word of God and the Word of Man*) of Swiss theologian Karl Barth's *Das Wort Gottes und Die Theologie.* Horton was fascinated both by the seriousness with which Barth approached the Bible and by his insistence on the radical "otherness" of God—hallmarks of the neoorthodox theology that Barth and other European thinkers were championing. Since Horton then regarded himself not as a scholar but as a parish minister, he translated Barth's work in order to introduce his theological ideas to a nonacademic English-speaking audience.

In 1931 Horton left Brookline to become pastor of the United Church of Hyde Park in Chicago. In 1933 he also started teaching on a part-time basis at Chicago Theological Seminary. As a lecturer in practical theology at the seminary, he was given the opportunity to combine his knowledge of both the theory and the practice of ministry. During this period he also edited *The Basic Formula for Church Union* (1938), which was published jointly by Chicago Seminary and Seabury-Western Seminary, an Episcopal school in Evanston, Illinois. This document was written by a group of Congregational and Episcopal clergymen in Chicago, and its discussion of the future reunion of Protestant denominations is now regarded as one of the classic texts of the early ecumenical movement.

In 1938 Horton was chosen to become minister and secretary of the General Council (the biennial national assembly) of the Congregational and Christian Churches, a position that enabled him to function as the chief ecclesiastical and executive officer of his denomination. In that year, representatives of the Evangelical and Reformed Church and of Horton's denomination first gathered to consider the merger of their two bodies. Because of his strong interest in ecumenism, Horton soon joined those talks, and he became a leading figure in the effort they promoted. The Evangelical and Reformed Church represented the Reformed (or Calvinist) tradition that had been brought to the United States by immigrants from Germany beginning in the late seventeenth century, while the Congregational and Christian Churches were heirs of the New England Puritan tradition. While significant ethnic and sociological differences initially divided the two denominations, their common Calvinist theological heritage and the advocacy of Horton and others for a merger eventually facilitated their rapprochement in the early 1940s. Although his wife died in 1944, Horton continued to press representatives of the two bodies to move toward union. He married Mildred Helen McAfee, a noted educator, in 1945; they did not have children.

Horton believed in the need for a larger, more coordinated church government than his denomination possessed at that time. The decentralized model of seventeenth-century Congregationalism was no longer adequate, he reasoned, to meet the challenges of the modern age, when bureaucratic efficiency was essential in all organizations. In a series of lectures delivered in England in 1951 and published the next year as *Congregationalism: A Study in Church Polity*, Horton further refined his ideas about church governance and Christian reunion. He argued that Congregationalism was the key to future ecumenical ventures, for it represented Catholicism freed from the authoritarianism too often associated with both Episcopal and Presbyterian church government. At the same time, he emphasized the need for individual congregations to remain in fellowship with one another on the local, national, and international levels. Although Horton left his denominational position to become dean of Harvard Divinity School in 1955, his efforts and ideas proved to be major factors in the creation of the United Church of Christ, the new denomination formed by the merger of the Evangelical and Reformed Church and the Congregational and Christian Churches in June 1957.

Nathan Pusey, the president of Harvard, chose Horton as dean of the divinity school because he believed Horton's broad ecumenical vision and experience would help revive the study of religion in the university. Despite his relatively short service at Harvard, Horton was able to put his beliefs into practice by overseeing the establishment of a professorship in Roman Catholic studies—the first such academic chair endowed at a traditionally Protestant divinity school. After retiring from Harvard in 1959, he remained active in ecumenical affairs throughout the rest of his life. He served as chairman of the Faith and Order Commission (the group designated to discuss theological issues dividing Christians) of the World Council of Churches between 1957 and 1963. Horton represented the International Congregational Council at the Second Vatican Council of the Roman Catholic Church, an experience he described in a four-volume series, *Vatican Diary* (1964–1966). He also produced a study of the denomination that he helped establish, *The United Church of Christ: Its Origins, Organization, and Role in the World Today* (1962). And his final book, *Toward an Undivided Church* (1967), with a foreword by Richard Cushing, the Catholic archbishop of Boston, outlined his hopes for the ultimate reunion of all Christian churches. Horton was a resident of Randolph, New Hampshire, at the time of his death.

One of the leading ecumenical figures of the mid-twentieth century, Horton contributed to American church life as an administrator, theorist, and practical theologian. As an ecumenist, he argued that Christians needed to overcome the ancient racial and national distinctions that separated them and emphasize the common elements that bound them together in faith in God and Jesus Christ. Horton articulated a religious vision that not only contributed to the merger of two important Protestant denominations in the United

States but also spurred the movement for worldwide Christian unity.

• Manuscript papers relating to Horton's work with the Congregational and Christian Churches are available at the Congregational Library in Boston, and papers from his years at Harvard Divinity School are found in the archives of Harvard University. Louis H. Gunnemann, *The Shaping of the United Church of Christ: An Essay in the History of American Christianity* (1977), provides a full description of his efforts in the creation of the United Church of Christ. Useful obituary notices are in the *New York Times*, 23 Aug. 1968, and in the *Harvard Divinity Bulletin* 2, no. 2 (Autumn 1968): 2.

GARDINER H. SHATTUCK, JR.

HORTON, George Moses (1797?–1883?), poet, was born a slave in Northampton County, North Carolina, and grew up on a Chatham County plantation. He composed poems before teaching himself to read and, much later, learning to write. While selling vegetables in nearby Chapel Hill he also sold verses, often dictating to University of North Carolina students love lyrics ordered for girl friends. With fees from such commissions and from domestic work, he paid his second and third owners—son and grandson respectively of his original owner—to permit him to live mostly in Chapel Hill, where he became a legendary figure.

In 1828 two of Horton's antislavery poems appeared in the Massachusetts weekly *Lancaster Gazette* through the encouragement of Caroline Lee Hentz, a professor's wife. The first antislavery works by a slave ever published, they were included in a book of twenty-one poems by Horton, *The Hope of Liberty*, published in Raleigh in 1829. The book was announced for sale to raise money to buy Horton's freedom and passage to Liberia. Sales were few, however, and philanthropic offers to purchase his freedom were rejected, but the book was reprinted as *Poems by a Slave* both in Philadelphia and Boston in 1837, the second time appended to works of Phillis Wheatley. The next collection, containing more than forty pieces, *The Poetical Works of George M. Horton, the Colored Bard of North Carolina* was published in 1845 by subscription. A prefatory autobiography touches on the boyhood rivalry of Horton's one younger brother among ten siblings, his diligent study of gift books of poetry, and a possible drinking problem. Not going beyond 1830, it throws no light on Horton's evidently unhappy marriage to a woman belonging to nearby farmer Franklin Snipes. Of this marriage, there were two children, who, like their mother, bore their master's surname.

A final collection, *Naked Genius* was published in 1865 under the enthusiastic supervision of Will H. S. Banks, a cavalry captain in Sherman's army. Of 133 pieces, ranging in form from ballad stanza to blank verse—treating love, religion, morality, patriotism, slavery, or death—forty-one are reprintings. Overt antislavery poems are few. (However, William Carroll notes the pervading imagery of liberty and flight in many poems, regardless of subject.) Earthy folk humor is evident in some of Horton's verse, as is a shrewd sense of the comic in a poem on a spendthrift

dandy and one on Jefferson Davis. J. Saunders Redding observes they were "not unworthy of an Oliver Wendell Holmes."

After the Civil War Horton went to Philadelphia, perhaps (as always) in search of sponsorship. No longer a local celebrity or an object of humanitarian concern, he faded from view; one report places him as still living there in 1883, but the place and date of his death are unknown.

Biographer Richard Walser's view of Horton as a vain man who curried favor is countered by Merle A. Richmond's emphasis on his strength in persisting in his art without the moral support of a literate black community. Noticed in the past for his antislavery verse, Horton is now seen as a writer of hard-won technical competence and an important early figure in the black tradition, well deserving of inclusion as a good minor poet in the mainstream of American literature.

• Horton's manuscripts, letters, and printed materials are in a collection at the University of North Carolina at Chapel Hill. *The Hope of Liberty* was reprinted in 1973. *Naked Genius* is available in photofacsimile at the Chapel Hill Historical Society. The most comprehensive biography is Richard G. Walser, *The Black Poet: The Story of George Moses Horton* (1966). Good evaluations are William G. Carroll, "George Moses Horton," in *Afro-American Writers before the Harlem Renaissance: Dictionary of Literary Biography* 50 (1986), pp. 190–201; Joan R. Sherman, *Invisible Poets: Afro-Americans of the Nineteenth Century* (1974), pp. 5–19; and James A. Emanuel, "George Moses Horton," *Dictionary of American Negro Biography* (1982), pp. 327–28. Among other important studies are Blyden Jackson and Louis D. Rubin, *Black Poetry in America: Two Historical Studies in Interpretation* (1974); J. Saunders Redding, *To Make a Poet Black* (1939; repr. 1988); and Merle A. Richmond, *Bid the Vassal Soar: Interpretive Essays on the Life and Poetry of Phillis Wheatley and George Moses Horton* (1974). Representative Horton poems are included in college texts such as Arthur P. Davis and J. Saunders Redding, eds., *Cavalcade: Negro American Writing from 1760 to the Present* (1961), and Richard A. Long and Eugenia Collier, eds., *Afro-American Writing: An Anthology of Prose and Poetry* (1972; rev. ed., 1985).

VINCENT FREIMARCK

HORTON, Johnny (30 Apr. 1925–5 Nov. 1960), musician, was born John LaGale Horton in Los Angeles, California, the son of John "Lolly" Horton, Sr., an itinerant worker who flitted between east Texas and southern California, and Ella Claudia Robinson. There was some musicality in the family. Horton's mother taught piano, his father played guitar, and there was a tradition of singing around the house. The family returned to Tyler, Texas, in 1933, subsequently moving to Rusk, thirty-five miles north of Tyler, in 1935, and then to Jacksonville, thirty miles south of Tyler, a few years later. Show posters would later bill Horton as "Tyler's Own," and it was as close as he came to a hometown.

Horton graduated from high school in 1944 and briefly attended Lon Morris Junior College in Jacksonville, Texas, on a basketball scholarship. Lon Morris was a methodist seminary, and Horton probably attended with the intention of becoming a preacher. Later he attended Kilgore College, then Baylor University in Waco, although he was probably at the latter no more than ten days.

Horton went back to California, and by 1947 he was working in the mail room at the Selznick studios. He and his brother Frank decided to enroll at the University of Washington at Seattle for the fall 1948 semester to study geology, but they both dropped out after a few weeks. The brothers headed to Florida and then backtracked to California. After working at a fruit-packing plant, Horton went to Alaska to work on construction sites.

Horton returned to east Texas in 1950 and won a music talent contest at the Reo Palm Isle club in Longview. This success probably gave him the impetus to try a career in music when he headed back to California late in 1950. Music was never an avocation for Horton; it was just something else he tried.

Horton entered talent contests in California and was spotted by country-music promoter Fabor Robison, who became his manager and placed him with the small Cormac record company. Robison also got Horton a regular spot on "Hometown Jamboree" on KXLA-TV, Pasadena, every Saturday night. Later, he got his own show on KXLA-TV, where he appeared as the "Singing Fisherman," and he guested regularly on "Hacienda Party Time" on KLAC-TV in Los Angeles. At the same time, he was a professional fly-tester for a tackle manufacturer and an assembly-line worker for an aircraft manufacturer.

Horton's Cormac record was issued in the summer of 1951, but the label folded later that year, and Robison started Abbott Records with the purpose of recording him. By November 1951 there were already six Horton records available on Abbott, two of them reissued from Cormac. Most of Horton's Abbott recordings were firmly in the western tradition. He had a light, pleasant voice, and most of the songs idealized a mythical West. The little flash of falsetto at the end of a line—a trademark Horton would use until his death—was a feature from the beginning, as was the amiable quality that always characterized his music.

At the end of 1951 Horton married Donna Cook. They decided to move back to east Texas or Shreveport (La.) so that Horton could make regular appearances on the "Louisiana Hayride," which was broadcast over KWKH in Shreveport. In June 1952, at roughly the same time that Robison secured a place for Horton on the "Hayride," he sold Horton's recording contract to Mercury Records.

At Mercury, Horton was produced by Walter "D" Kilpatrick, but these recordings made little impact, and Horton's wife left him in Shreveport. He eked out a living fronting a band called the Roadrunners. On 26 September 1953 Horton married the widow of Hank Williams, Billie Jean Jones. By then, Horton and Robison had parted company, and it is likely that Horton quit the music business altogether for a period in 1954 when his wife was pregnant with their first child.

(Altogether Horton fathered three children.) He continued to record occasionally for Mercury, but his records lacked a commanding artistic vision and veered uneasily between different styles.

Horton had seen Elvis Presley on "Louisiana Hayride," and after his management was taken over by Tillman Franks in early 1955, Horton reoriented himself toward rockabilly music. Franks's first step was to extricate Horton from his Mercury contract. Kilpatrick had an aversion to rock 'n' roll, so Franks arranged for Horton to be signed by Columbia Records in Nashville. At his first Columbia session, on 11 January 1956, Horton recorded "Honky Tonk Man." Presley's bass player Bill Black was used on the session to give the song much of the drive of Presley's recordings.

Franks, on bass, formed a new trio with himself, guitarist Tommy Tomlinson, and Horton. By May 1956 "Honky Tonk Man" was selling briskly in every major country market, and after five years as a professional entertainer, Horton finally broke through.

For a short period, Horton found success with rockabilly music. He recorded "I'm a One Woman Man," "I'm Coming Home," and "Honky Tonk Mind." Then his career went cold again. Before he returned to the charts with saga songs in 1959, he had just one charted hit, "All Grown Up," which peaked at number eight on *Billboard*'s country charts.

Music was only one side of Horton's life. He is remembered as one of the finest freshwater fishermen and outdoorsmen of his day. He only continued to play music because it provided him with a better living than he could have had as a professional sportsman. Those who worked with him maintain that he did not have the deep psychological need for applause that most performers have and that he preferred to stay in Shreveport and fish rather than move to Nashville to grapple with music business politics.

Throughout Horton's last years his fascination with spiritualism grew. He became a devotee of spiritualist Edgar Cayce. After moving to the Shreve Island subdivision of Shreveport, Horton built a meditation shed on the back of his property. Horton's fascination divided those close to him; his wife was dismissive, as was Franks, but it was a passion that several of Horton's friends, especially Johnny Cash, shared.

The spiritual side of Horton was connected to his love of Native-American lore. He frequently played American Indian reservations in New Mexico and was made an honorary chief of some bands. He espoused native rights long before it was fashionable to do so and wrote a chant called "The Vanishing Race" that Johnny Cash later cut on his *Bitter Tears* album. Horton identified with the First Nations' value system, which placed man in a broader context of animal and plant life.

Horton's career was on a downturn by late 1958, but it rebounded with the release of "When It's Springtime in Alaska," a song that fitted the vogue for pseudo–folk music that had been spearheaded by the Kingston Trio. Recorded on 10 November 1958, "When

It's Springtime in Alaska" was released shortly before the end of the year and spent almost half of 1959 among the country music bestsellers. It held the number one position for one week and became Horton's most successful record to that point.

Searching for a followup in the same vein, Horton chose to record "The Battle of New Orleans," a song by country songwriter Jimmie Driftwood that first appeared as a five-minute folk song on Driftwood's *Newly Discovered American Folk Songs* album in 1957. It was set to the fiddle tune "The Eighth of January." On 27 January 1959 Horton recorded a truncated version of "The Battle of New Orleans" in Nashville. Columbia rush-released it in mid-April, and it peaked at number one on the pop and country charts. On 7 June 1959 Horton performed "Battle of New Orleans" on Ed Sullivan's "Talk of the Town."

Horton tried to combine his love of fishing with his recharged career in music by funding the Cane River Bait Company in Natchitoches, Louisiana, but it was an ill-fated enterprise that drained his income. Under pressure from his wife, Horton closed the venture.

"Johnny Reb" did well as a followup to "The Battle of New Orleans," as did "Sink the Bismarck," a song inspired by the movie of the same name. Horton also recorded "Johnny Freedom," a song designed to coincide with the opening of the Freedomland USA Exposition in the Bronx, New York, on 19 June 1960. In conjunction with the exhibition, Columbia Records shipped an album titled *Johnny Horton Makes History* that cemented his reputation for saga songs.

Horton's last hit while he was alive was "North to Alaska," written as the theme song to the John Wayne movie of the same name. Horton had had premonitions that he would die a premature and violent death, and as early as July 1960 he began visiting those close to him to—in effect—say goodbye. Paradoxically, Horton seems to have accepted this fate but also tried to avoid it: he backed out of attending the premiere of *North to Alaska* and even tried to cancel what became his last show, in Austin, Texas, on 4 November 1960.

After the show, Horton drove back toward Shreveport, intending to go duck hunting the next day, but he was killed en route in a head-on collision on a bridge near Milano, Texas. If nothing else, Horton's career is an object lesson in survival in the music industry. He was a pleasant singer with a distinctive voice, but his greatest asset was probably his adaptability and malleability.

• Michael LeVine, *Johnny Horton: Your Singing Fisherman* (1982), is woefully inaccurate. An extended biographical portrait by Colin Escott is in the booklet accompanying *Johnny Horton 1956–1960* (Bear Family Records, BCD 15470; 1990).

COLIN ESCOTT

HORTON, Lester (26 Jan. 1906–2 Nov. 1953), choreographer and teacher, was born in Indianapolis, Indiana, the son of Iredell Horton, a laborer, and Annie Lauders. Horton began a lifelong interest in American In-

dian traditions during elementary school and at eighth grade commencement was honored with a request to read his composition "The Indian in His Native Art." While a high school student in 1922–1923 Horton saw performances of the American dance pioneers Ruth St. Denis and Ted Shawn and their Denishawn company. He was fascinated by the dancers' movements and felt this was a creative medium he wanted to explore. Soon dance and parallel interests in jewelry- and pottery-making, Indian stories, songs, chants, and dances became so consuming that Horton dropped out of high school in his senior year.

Horton began training with Theo Hewes, who had studied ballet with Andreas Pavley and Serge Oukrainsky in Chicago. After one year of study with Hewes, she assigned him teaching duties with the younger children on Saturday mornings. Horton's first professional dance experience occurred in 1925 when a former Denishawn dancer, Forrest Thornburg, chose him for a small touring company. Shortly after, in 1926, he was invited by Clara Nixon Bates (a founder, with her late husband, of the Indianapolis Theatre Guild) to participate in *The Song of Hiawatha*, an outdoor pageant produced in Indianapolis in 1926 and 1927 and on tour throughout Indiana and Ohio in 1927 and 1928. In 1929 Bates accepted an invitation from a friend to bring *Hiawatha* to Los Angeles and the program listed Horton as director, with music by Charles Wakefield Cadman, Homer Grunn, and Sol Cohen. Los Angeles was to become Horton's permanent home. By 1929 he was ready to launch an independent career.

In July and August 1929 Horton studied and performed with the Japanese choreographer and teacher Michio Ito and by 1931 he was beginning to create his own dances and soon was also teaching. Working with a group of students from Glendale High School in 1932 he staged another pageant, *Takwish, the Star Maker*, and presented his first group choreography at a special Olympic Dance Festival held at the Philharmonic Auditorium. The festival's six evenings featured dancing of all kinds—tap, modern, ballet, interpretive ballroom, ethnic, and folk—and provided the young artist with an opportunity to see numerous other choreographers and absorb their ideas. His offering, *Voodoo Ceremonial*, allowed him to explore concepts of theatricality and ritual that were to be important in later work. At the Shrine Auditorium in 1934 announcements noted that "Lester Horton's California Ballets" would present the first evening devoted entirely to his own work and performed by the group he had trained. From 1934 to 1937 Horton and his company gave concerts at the Tuesday Afternoon Club of Glendale, the Philharmonic Auditorium, the Pasadena Playhouse, and the Hollywood Concert Hall.

In summer 1937 Horton was asked to create a ballet for the Hollywood Bowl. Horton presented *Le Sacre du Printemps* set to music by Igor Stravinsky, making him the first American choreographer to use this score for dance. There, on a large stage for an audience of almost 20,000, Horton demonstrated his originality in conceiving and executing dance and theater presentations. The movement was broad and the energy was high. The vocabulary was sensuous, erotic, weighted, and forceful. There was considerable use of upper back, torso, and hips; legs reached high into space or were planted in a wide stance. The original costume designs displayed vibrant earth colors and bare midriffs, which strongly suggested American Indian dress. This milestone in Horton's career significantly marked his recognition as an original creative artist in his adopted city.

During the next decade Horton continued his concert work and teaching in Los Angeles and accepted invitations to do the same in San Francisco. While the early dances drew heavily from his fascination not only with American Indian but also Japanese, Chinese, African, Polynesian, Hebraic, and Mexican cultures, in the mid-1930s Horton began exploring social issues and contemporary concerns in his work. Among these were *Mound Builders* (1935), which a critic noted had "oppressed groups come together . . . and demand the rights of the people"; *Dictator* (1935), an antifascist piece; *The Mine* (1935), inspired by a newspaper article about a mine disaster; *Chronicle* (1937), which, according to the program notes, was "a record of the forces and trends in American society" and ended with a strong indictment of the Ku Klux Klan; *Pasaremos* (1938), inspired by the Spanish Civil War; and *Warsaw Ghetto* (1949), a strong Holocaust commentary.

Although Horton's financial situation was always precarious, World War II's harsh conditions contributed to his accepting invitations to do movie choreography. From 1942 to 1953 he worked on nineteen films, most between 1942 and 1946. Among them were *Moonlight in Havana* (1942), *Rhythm of the Islands* (1943), *Ali Baba and the Forty Thieves* (1944), *Salome, Where She Danced* (1945), and *Tangier* (1946). He also took dancers to New York in 1943 to perform for the opening of the Folies Bergères nightclub, and in 1946 he became involved in a musical, *Shootin' Star*, which unfortunately never made it to Broadway.

After two years of planning, Horton and three associates (William Bowne, Bella Lewitzky, and her husband Newell Reynolds) opened Dance Theater in 1948, a specially designed studio/theater devoted to all aspects of dance: performance, teaching, and production. Although by 1950 Horton's associates had left the venture, Dance Theater became a vital modern dance center in Los Angeles, a place charged with audience and student excitement about dance. Horton renewed himself creatively there through the support of a new partner, the critic Frank Eng, and set about codifying his technique. He produced a wide variety of dances; some were light, funny, sensual, and full of blazing energetic movement; others returned for inspiration to a variety of ethnic sources. He crafted intense theatrical dramas with strong emotional statements and dances that had magnificent commentary about social and contemporary issues. *The Beloved* (1948), one of only two Horton dances performed into

the 1990s, is based on a news story about a woman beaten to death with a Bible by her husband because of suspected infidelity. It is a supreme example of Horton's ability to make powerful commentary and capture emotional essence. *To José Clemente Orozco* (1953), the other Horton work that continues in production, is a poignant duet in which a man and a woman march—advancing and retreating—downtrodden by forces beyond their control as they attempt to maintain their caring and dignity. Horton died of a heart attack at his home in Los Angeles.

Horton was a seminal American artist whose choreography was not widely recognized for many years because it was not seen outside of California until 1953, when the company performed at one of New York's most important dance venues, the Kaufmann Auditorium of the 92nd Street YMHA. Upon seeing the concert the critic Margaret Lloyd wrote, "Out of an embracive cultural background come choreographies of wide spatial values, voluminous spiral turns, horizontal swoopings across the floor, oblique swervings and circlings over an assortment of stage levels. . . . Now the torso leans backward or sideward from the knees at an impossible angle and suddenly goes off in another tangent. The movement is broad and sustained . . . it unfolds with logical unpredictability."

Many who trained and worked with Horton went on to significant careers in dance, including Alvin Ailey, Janet Collins, Carmen de Lavallade, Bella Lewitzky, James Mitchell, Joyce Trisler, and James Truitte. Horton welcomed ideas and people from all cultures and his companies always had individuals of different ethnic origins—Asian, African-American, Jewish, Hispanic. A man of vibrant creative energy Horton's influence permeates contemporary dance internationally through those who have passed on his philosophy and teaching.

• The Dance Collection of the New York Public Library for the Performing Arts at Lincoln Center has files on Horton and he is mentioned in the Joyce Trisler file and in audiotapes with Alvin Ailey. There is one biography of Horton by Larry Warren, *Lester Horton, Modern Dance Pioneer* (1977, repr. 1991). A book and a video on Horton's technique are also available. Marjorie Perces, Ana Marie Forsyth, and Cheryl Bell wrote *The Dance Technique of Lester Horton* (1992), a book on his technique, and Forsyth and Perces also collaborated on a video, *Lester Horton Technique: The Warm Up* (1992). Two books by Naima Prevots contain significant material on Horton, *Dancing in the Sun, Hollywood Choreographers 1915–1937* (1987) and *A Movement for Art and Democracy* (1990). One of Horton's works is treated in depth in Jana Ellen Frances-Fischer, "A Choreographic and Freudian Analysis of *The Beloved* by Lester Horton" (M.F.A. thesis, Univ. of Calif., Irvine, 1987). Also see Richard Bizot, "Lester Horton's *Salome* 1934–1953 and After," *Dance Research Journal* 16 (Spring 1984): 35–40, and Elizabeth Zimmer, "L.A. Dance Celebrated 1986," *Dance Magazine* 60 (Feb. 1986): 5. There are also informal comments on Lester Horton by Bella Lewitzky, "Keynote Address," *Proceedings, Society of Dance History Scholars*, Twelfth Annual Conference, Arizona State Univ., 17–19 Feb. 1989. Obituaries are in the *New York Times*, 3 Nov. 1953, and in *Dance Observer*, *Dance News*, and *Dance Magazine*, all of Dec. 1953.

NAIMA PREVOTS

HORTON, Walter (6 Apr. 1918–8 Dec. 1981), blues harmonica player and vocalist, known variously as "Big Walter," "Shakey," "Mumbles," and "Tangle-eye," was born in Horn Lake, Mississippi, just south of Memphis, Tennessee, the son of Albert Horton, Sr., and Emma McNaire. When he was five his father bought him a harmonica, or mouth harp, and he began teaching himself to play. Guitarist Johnny Shines first encountered Horton around 1930 and recalled that he was a serious musician, constantly working on new techniques, even as a preteen. After Horton's father got a job as a handyman with the city of Memphis, his family moved there, giving Horton ample opportunity to further his musical education.

Various stories, some passed along by Horton himself, have him recording with the Memphis Jug Band as early as 1927 or 1928, but evidence suggests otherwise. It is more likely that he simply played with the group or with various members such as harmonica player Will Shade. After his father's death Horton became active as a Memphis street musician to help support his mother. In his early teens he played with guitarist Floyd Jones, working crowds in Church Park, since renamed in honor of composer W. C. Handy. Through the 1930s Horton also played with guitarists Little Buddy Doyle (with whom he also may have recorded), Homesick James, Big Joe Williams, Johnny Shines, David Honeyboy Edwards, and other blues musicians, sometimes on the road, sometimes in Memphis. Edwards recalled the Memphis street scene in the mid-1930s:

Me and Walter, we used to go down on Front Street. . . . That 's where all the hustling women lived. And we come along playing the blues late at night, you know, hittin' the blues, just me and him. . . . "Come on in here, come on play us some blues. Why, here's a quarter—I'm gonna give him a quarter. You give him a quarter." And we started playing and the women would bring us a big pint of white whiskey. We'd play there and get drunk and go on downtown on Beale Street to one of them cafes, sit in there all night and drink that nickel mug of beer. It was a rough time, but we made it good.

From the mid-1930s through the late 1940s Horton alternated between the life of a traveling musician and various nonmusical jobs—cook, cab driver, ice hauler. Working with Edwards in Jackson, Mississippi, in 1940, Horton supposedly became one of the first musicians to play amplified harmonica. Around 1949 he hooked up with guitarists Eddie Taylor and Floyd Jones for a stint in Chicago.

By 1951, however, Horton was back in Memphis, broadcasting over WDIA radio with pianist Willie Love, guitarist Joe Willie Wilkins, and drummer Willie Nix, catching the attention of Sam Phillips, who had recently opened the Memphis Recording and Sound Service. Phillips, who would later found the Sun label, was then recording southern blues talent for two West Coast labels owned by the Bihari brothers and for the Chicago labels owned by the Chess brothers. Phillips recorded Horton and guitarist-percussionist Joe Hill Louis in January and February 1951. The resulting single, issued on the Bihari-owned Modern label, featured "Little Boy Blue," a reprise of a Robert Junior Lockwood blues, and "Now Tell Me Baby." Inexplicably, Horton was identified only as "Mumbles" on the release.

A June session with a more conventional blues band produced Horton's second record, this one on the R.P.M. label, also owned by the Biharis. Again Horton was identified as "Mumbles." A 1952 record for Phillips, featuring Horton and Jack Kelly, was credited to "Little Walter" and "Jackie Boy." Horton recorded for Sun in 1953, accompanied by guitarist Jimmy DeBerry, a long-time sideman. These sessions produced some fine music—the title "Easy" became a classic, for example—but none of the Sun material was released then.

In 1953 Horton rejoined Eddie Taylor in Chicago. Their musical reunion lasted only a few weeks, though, because when harp player Junior Wells was drafted for military service, Horton was invited to take his place in the Muddy Waters band. Because of health problems, especially the after-effects of pneumonia and alcohol-related disabilities, which would plague him throughout life, and also because he was said to be undependable, Horton did not have a long run with Waters, though he did record with the band in 1953 and 1954.

After backing Johnny Shines at a session for the JOB label, Horton recorded under his own name for Chicago's States label at a 1954 session supervised by bass player, song writer, and arranger Willie Dixon. The session yielded "Hard Hearted Woman," issued in 1955, probably Horton's best-known song. In 1956 he again collaborated with Dixon for the Cobra label, producing "Have a Good Time," featuring Otis Rush on guitar. As with "Hard Hearted Woman," it is now considered a classic recording, but at the time it did little to advance Horton's career. That same year he backed fellow Muddy Waters bandmate Jimmy Rogers on his hit, "Walking by Myself."

Through the 1950s into the 1960s Horton continued club work with artists, including Johnny Shines, Jimmy Rogers, and Johnny Young. In 1964 he recorded an album, *Shakey Horton: The Soul of Blues Harmonica*, for Argo, a Chess subsidiary. The album was co-produced by Dixon and included fine musicians such as guitarist Buddy Guy, but there was little commercial interest in it.

In Chicago, as earlier in Memphis, Horton's innovative techniques exerted a strong influence on other harp players. Horton always bragged that he'd taught every player from Sonny Boy Williamson to Little Walter to Carey Bell. "To me, it sounded like another one of his stories," said Charlie Musselwhite, a harmonica player who often worked with Horton in Chicago, "but as the years went by, I kept hearing it from other people—that it was true. And now . . . I do believe it. He might not have taught them every note they played, but he got them going." Musselwhite, who considered himself one of Horton's students, said Horton was seldom willing to explain particular techniques; he preferred to teach by example:

I remember going over to his house one day, just for a harmonica lesson. We just ended up talking mostly, and drinking, and going around to see old friends and things, and just having little jam sessions here and there—in the alley, in the liquor store, in different people's homes. And that was good enough for me. I learned plenty doing that.

During the mid-1960s Horton became a regular on the blues-revival festival circuit, touring Europe in 1965, 1967, and 1970. He also continued to work the club scene and recorded as a sideman for Vanguard, Testament, and Arhoolie. He toured and recorded with Willie Dixon's Chicago Blues All Stars and in 1972 was featured on an Alligator album, *Big Walter Horton with Carey Bell*. Bell was Horton's protégé. The album also featured Horton's long-time companion, Taylor. Other session work followed in the 1970s, including records with Johnny Winter and Muddy Waters, along with more club and festival dates. But he was showing the effects of his chronic health problems, domestic strife, and heavy drinking. After a return from Europe in 1981 he began drinking and was later found dead in a Chicago neighbor's apartment, the victim of heart failure and acute alcoholism. His wife Anna Mae Horton (they married probably in the early 1960s; her maiden name is unknown) and five children survived him.

Although Horton was not particularly successful as a vocalist or recording artist, his instrumental skills were unsurpassed. He had what fellow musicians called "deep tone" and could play in up to five different "positions," or keys, on a single harmonica. Long-time musical partner Willie Dixon, in his book *I Am the Blues*, wrote, "Little Walter was a very good player, but Big Walter . . . was a helluva harmonica player." Horton's musical career was littered with obstacles: alcoholism, poor health, partial paralysis (the result of several shooting scrapes), and a reputation for being undependable. But when he was on, said Musselwhite, "there'd be no stopping him. There'd be chorus after chorus of just brilliant playing—things you'd never, ever heard before, even from him."

Horton will be remembered in pop culture for a brief appearance in the film *The Blues Brothers*. In his lifetime he was a true "blues brother" to musicians like Eddie Taylor, Floyd Jones, Jimmy Rogers, Johnny Young, and Johnny Shines. From their perspective he was the best of all harmonica players. As Shines put it in Peter Guralnick's *Feel Like Going Home*, "This harmonica blowing is really a mark for Walter—it's not something he picked up, he was born to do it." Along with John Lee Williamson, Aleck Miller, and Little Walter, Horton is now recognized as one of the architects of modern blues harmonica. Horton was inducted into the Memphis-based Blues Foundation Hall of Fame in 1982.

• For more biographical information on Horton, see Sheldon Harris, *Blues Who's Who: A Biographical Dictionary of Blues Singers* (1979; repr. 1989); and Mike Leadbitter, ed., *Nothing but the Blues* (1971). For discographical information, see Leadbitter and Neil Slaven, *Blues Records 1943–1966* (1968), and Paul Oliver, ed., *The Blackwell Guide to Blues Records* (1989). For a sample of his music, try *Walter "Mumbles" Horton: Mouth Harp Maestro* (Flair V2-86297), *Shakey Horton: The Soul of Blues Harmonica* (Argo 4037), and *Big Walter Horton with Carey Bell* (Alligator 4702). An obituary is in *Living Blues* 52 (Spring 1982): 52–53.

BILL McCULLOCH
BARRY LEE PEARSON

HORTON, Walter Marshall (7 Apr. 1895–22 Apr. 1966), theologian, was born in Somerville, Massachusetts, the son of Walter Emery Horton and Clara Powers Marshall. He graduated summa cum laude from Harvard University in 1917 with fields of distinction in classics and philosophy as well as Greek and French literature.

In 1919 Horton married Lidie Loring Chick at his home congregation, the First Baptist Church in Arlington, Massachusetts; the couple had no children. That same year he received ordination at the church. He earned a B.D. (summa cum laude) in 1920 from Union Theological Seminary in New York City. He also received an M.A. from Columbia University in 1920 and an S.T.M. in 1923 from Union Theological Seminary. During the course of his postbaccalaureate education, he also studied at the Universities of Strasbourg and Marburg and at the Sorbonne in Paris. In 1926 Columbia University granted Horton a Ph.D. in philosophy. His doctoral dissertation dealt with the philosophy of the Abbé Bautain. While pursuing advanced degrees, Horton taught at several institutions of higher education, including Union, Columbia, Barnard College, and Hartford Theological Seminary.

In 1925 the Oberlin College Graduate School of Theology appointed Horton to the position of Fairchild Professor of Theology. Horton flourished as a writer and teacher at the Ohio institution. He contributed articles to a wide variety of periodicals, including the *Christian Century*, *Religious Education*, the *Journal of Religion*, and *Theology Today*. He also produced approximately one dozen books, some of which were featured by the Religious-Book-of-the-Month Club. In his publications, Horton displayed a keen ability to interpret theological trends in Continental and English Protestantism, Roman Catholicism, and Orthodoxy for an American audience.

In "Rough Sketch of a Half Formed Mind" (*Contemporary American Theology*, 1932), Horton reviewed his intellectual development. His parents were both Baptists of nondogmatic temperament. As a member of the First Baptist Church of Arlington, he had come under the influence of the pastor, Nathan E. Wood. In his advanced theological and philosophical education, Horton encountered several of the most important intellectuals of the early part of the twentieth century, including A. C. McGiffert and Eugene W. Lyman.

Both events in Europe and new theological emphases flowing primarily from Germany and Switzerland led Horton in the early 1930s toward a theological orientation that he characterized as Realistic Theology or Neo-Liberalism. In his contribution to a symposium titled "How Barth Has Influenced Me" (*Theology Today*, Oct. 1956), he articulated his agreements and differences with the influential Swiss theologian, Karl Barth. Horton acknowledged the importance of Barth's emphasis on divine revelation, judgment, and redemption; he rejected, however, Barth's vigorous polemic against natural theology and natural religion. Horton concluded that the "'neo-liberalism' I now champion differs from the old liberalism I repudiate precisely because it passed through Barth's thunder and lightning."

As a mature theologian, Horton became increasingly involved in and shaped by the ecumenical movement. He participated in ecumenical conferences at Oxford, England (1937); Madras (now Tamil Nadu), India (1938); Amsterdam, the Netherlands (1948); Lund, Sweden (1952); and Evanston, Illinois (1954). Horton's 1955 volume, *Christian Theology: An Ecumenical Approach*, demonstrated his theological catholicity.

Horton's theology and personal life displayed a concern for ethics. As a student at Harvard, he participated in the Cosmopolitan Club, exploring international issues and making friends with persons of differing races and nationalities. During World War I he adopted a pacifist position and declared himself a conscientious objector. During the 1920s and 1930s he supported the movement for world government. Horton advocated the type of pacifism that worked for an improved world order. In the struggle against totalitarianism, he supported the war effort of the United States.

Horton's wife died in September 1961, and in August the following year he married Marie Rankin, an emeritus professor of education at Oberlin College. In 1962 he also retired from Oberlin. Following the termination of his faculty responsibilities, Horton served as a visiting professor at the United Theological College in Bangalore, South India, and at the Chicago Theological Seminary. The prominent theologian died in Oberlin, after thirty-seven years on the faculty and four years of active retirement.

Students and colleagues at Oberlin College remembered Horton as an effective teacher who was personally modest and somewhat shy. He was committed to assisting students to develop their own theological perspectives rather than adopting the viewpoints of their internationally known mentor. Associates praised his intellectual honesty in engaging intellectual changes of the mid-twentieth century. In the classroom, in his many publications, and in his pioneering work in the ecumenical movement, Horton served as an interpreter of theological currents and a mediator of divergent intellectual traditions within the Christian church.

• Horton's papers are in the Oberlin College Archives. Helpful autobiographical snapshots appear in Vergilius Ferm, ed., *Contemporary American Theology: Theological Autobiographies*, vol. 1 (1932); "Between Liberalism and the New Orthodoxy," *Christian Century*, 17 May 1939, pp. 637–40; and "Ten Revolutionary Years," *Christian Century*, 20 Apr. 1949, pp. 490–92. For an interpretation of his theology, see J. William Lee, "Walter Marshall Horton: Theology as Summons to Dialogue," *Religion in Life* 34 (Autumn 1965): 526–33.

CHARLES E. QUIRK

HOSACK, David (31 Aug. 1769–22 Dec. 1835), physician and botanist, was born in New York City, the son of Alexander Hosack, a merchant, and Jane Arden. His early education was at private academies in Newark and Hackensack, New Jersey, and he entered Columbia College in 1786 as a liberal arts student. His principal interest, however, was in medicine, and he began as an apprentice under Richard Bayley and then transferred in 1788 to the College of New Jersey in Princeton, graduating in 1789 with a B.A. Hosack then returned to New York to the private medical school of physician Nicholas Romayne and next enrolled in the Medical School of the University of Pennsylvania, graduating with an M.D. in 1791. That year he married Catherine Warner; they had one child. After a brief stay with his wife and child in Alexandria, Virginia, he sailed to Europe in 1792 with the intention of studying in both Edinburgh and London. His explanation for this move was that Americans at that time made a definite distinction between physicians who had studied abroad and those whose education had been restricted to the United States, and success depended on being one of the former.

Hosack spent two years abroad, attending lectures by noted physicians and doing hospital work in the two cities. During this period he developed his interest in botany, which, he discovered in England and Scotland, was considered to be a necessary part of a gentleman's education. In London, Hosack was fortunate in making the acquaintance of William Curtis, author of *Flora Londinensis*, who had just completed his botanical garden at Brompton and who became his botanical mentor. He was fortunate also in gaining permission to examine the extensive collections of the Linnaean Herbarium and in having the friendship of Sir James Edward Smith, president of the Linnaean Society, and of Sir Joseph Banks, president of the Royal Society. Before Hosack left London in August 1794, he had been elected a fellow of the Linnaean Society. Along with this honor, he returned home with a large number of duplicate Linnaean specimens and an extensive library in natural history.

Settling in New York City, Hosack opened a medical practice in which he would continue for the next forty-one years. In 1795 he was appointed professor of botany and in 1796 professor of materia medica at Columbia College medical school. Following the death of his wife that same year, he married Mary Eddy in

1797; they had seven children. In 1798 he became a partner of Samuel Bard, a famous New York physician and one of the founders of the King's College medical school. One of Hosack's earliest experiences with the problems of disease treatment came during the terrible yellow fever epidemics of 1795–1799. During this disaster, thousands of residents of New York City died. At that time, no physician knew the cause of yellow fever (it was not discovered until the end of the next century), and the medical profession had only a number of conflicting theories to consider. Hosack's view was that the fever was a disease of the tropics—not developed locally—and that it was contagious. In his program of treatment, he avoided the drastic purges and harsh prescriptions of others of the medical profession and emphasized mild baths and good nursing care with plenty of liquids. In 1812 he incorporated his theories of disease into a paper, "Observations on the Laws Governing the Communication of Contagious Diseases," which was read at a meeting of the American Philosophical Society. Hosack believed that diseases differed in their means of transmission and could be classified on that basis. As did many contemporary physicians, he noted that many diseases were associated with filth, impurities in the atmosphere, and unsanitary living conditions. He therefore urged many practical steps for the prevention of epidemics, including domestic cleanliness and ventilation; provision of areas of sunshine and quiet in large cities; removal of noxious materials from streets and buildings; city planning for the elimination of narrow streets and alleys; laws to enforce cleanliness; common sewer systems; and city beautification. All of these suggestions were included in an 1820 address to medical students and members of the New York City Board of Health, which viewed the proposals as far beyond its authority and resources. Hosack's ideas nevertheless constituted "a blueprint for the sanitary development of New York" (Robbins), and many of them were eventually adopted.

As his career continued, Hosack turned more of his attention to the teaching of medicine, from which he gained a sizable income. Some of his students were private pupils, but he also lectured at Columbia's medical school, which was absorbed into the College of Physicians and Surgeons in 1807. At the latter school, by 1817 he "was the most prominent man in the affairs of the College" (J. C. Dalton, *A History of the College of Physicians and Surgeons in the City of New York* [1888], p. 39). However, Hosack resigned from the college in 1826 following a series of protracted internal disputes. His next association was with a new school, Rutgers Medical School in New York City, which opened in 1826, and he became its first president. Here too, however, there was controversy and opposition from the College of Physicians and Surgeons, which feared competition from a new medical school; as a result, Rutgers Medical School closed in 1830. This ended Hosack's teaching career, and he resolved to limit his medical practice to the winter months and to spend his summers practicing agriculture and horticulture at the 700-acre country estate he had purchased in 1828 at Hyde Park on the Hudson.

This decision reflected not only his advanced age but also the strong interest in botany he had developed in his student days at London and Edinburgh. Hosack had subsequently taught botany at Columbia College but had found himself handicapped by the lack of a botanical garden. Using his private funds, in 1801 he bought twenty acres of land and established the Elgin Botanic Garden at the site now occupied by Rockefeller Center in New York. The garden, the first public botanical garden in North America, when completed included a nursery, a forest belt, a greenhouse, and an extensive herbarium. All of this was very costly, and Hosack was forced to ask the New York state legislature for a loan. Though this was not obtained, the state in 1810 agreed to purchase the garden; no funding for maintenance was provided. The result was a rapid deterioration of the garden's assets, including its botanical specimens and its physical structures. The property was given in 1814 to Columbia College and became one of the richest parts of its endowment.

Hosack's position in the intellectual and cultural life of the early republic was extraordinary. He was a friend and acquaintance of individuals such as David Douglas, John Torrey, Gouverneur Morris, Washington Irving, DeWitt Clinton, Thomas Cole, John Trumbull, and Alexis de Tocqueville, who described him as "noted for his mastery of medicine, surgery, botany, philanthropy and society." He was a member of numerous organizations, including the New-York Historical Society, the American Philosophical Society, the New York Horticultural Society, and the American Academy of Arts and Sciences; in 1816 he was elected a fellow of the Royal Society of London. His published works include *A System of Practical Nosology* (1818), *Lectures on the Theory and Practice of Physic* (1838), *Memoir of the Late DeWitt Clinton* (1829), *Essays on Various Subjects of Medical Science* (1824), and *A Catalogue of Plants Contained in the Botanic Garden at Elgin* (1806), and he was cofounder of the *American Medical and Philosophical Register* (1810–1814). After the death of his second wife in 1824, he married a widow, Magdalena Coster, who had seven children from her first marriage. Hosack died in New York City.

• Much of Hosack's correspondence is at Columbia University, the New York Public Library, and the Library Company of Philadelphia. The most important single reference, Christine Chapman Robbins, *David Hosack: Citizen of New York* (1964), contains a bibliography of published and unpublished sources and family portraits. A shorter reference is Howard A. Kelly, *Some American Medical Botanists* (1977). Andrew Denny Rodgers III, *John Torrey: A Story of North American Botany* (1942), contains considerable material on Hosack and the Elgin Botanic Garden. Older works include Samuel D. Gross, *Lives of Eminent American Physicians and Surgeons* (1861), and John Wakefield Francis, *Old New York: Reminiscences of the Past Sixty Years* (1865). Further biographical and bibliographical information is in Frans Stafleu, *Taxonomic Literature* 2 (1976): 337–38.

ROBERT F. ERICKSON

HOSCHNA, Karl L. (16 Aug. 1877–23 Dec. 1911), composer and oboist, was born in Kuschwarda, Bohemia. His parents' names are not known. When he received a scholarship to the Vienna conservatory for his musical education, he was required to select a band instrument to study, and he chose the oboe. He did well enough in his studies to graduate with honors and upon completion of his studies was an oboist in the Austrian Army band for several years.

In 1896 Hoschna immigrated to the United States and for two years played the oboe with one of Victor Herbert's orchestras. Suddenly obsessed with the idea that the vibrations from the oboe's reeds would have lasting effects on his mind, Hoschna wrote the Whitmark company, a music publisher, asking for any job, no matter how menial and what the salary. Whitmark responded to Hoschna's inquiry first by hiring him as a copyist, after which he soon became an arranger and then eventually was asked to be Isidor Whitmark's adviser, even aiding him in deciding which songs should be published. During this period of working for Whitmark, Hoschna began writing and arranging his own songs.

In 1903 Hoschna met Otto Hauerbach (later Harbach), an advertising executive with a desire to write lyrics for the musical theater. The two began a partnership and soon finished *The Daughter of the Desert*, even rewriting it several times when interest was shown in producing it. However, something always blocked the production. Hoschna did finally debut in the musical theater with three operettas written between 1905 and 1908. The first of these, *The Belle of the West*, with lyrics by Harry B. Smith, was produced in 1905. Not only did it fail but its two successors did as well.

In 1908, however, Hoschna began to achieve some critical success. That year Isidor Whitmark told him that he was looking for someone to compose the music for a musical adaptation of the play *Incog*, based on a novel by Charles Dickson. Hoschna not only accepted but convinced Whitmark to hire Hauerbach to write the lyrics. Together, Hoschna and Hauerbach created the musical *The Three Twins*, which made its successful debut on Broadway on 15 June 1908. Two of Hoschna's most successful songs from this operetta were "Yama Yama Man" and "Cuddle Up a Little Closer."

With their first success behind them, Hoschna and Hauerbach collaborated during the next two years to produce three more Broadway successes. The first two, *Bright Eyes* (1909) and *The Girl of My Dreams* (1910), were moderately well received, but it was the 1910 production of *Madame Sherry* that received the most praise. An adaptation of a French vaudeville farce, this musical included several successful songs, including "Every Little Movement" and "The Birth of Passion." These productions were followed by *Wall Street Girl*, which Hoschna wrote with lyricist Hapgood Burt. Premiering in April 1912 and starring Blanche Ring and Will Rogers, *Wall Street Girl* made famous songs such as "I Want a Regular Man" but did not achieve the popularity of the earlier *Madame Sher-*

ry which continued to tour and draw large crowds. Hoschna did not live to see *Wall Street Girl* on the stage, having died suddenly and unexpectedly the previous December at the age of thirty-four.

Hoschna's music and musical arrangements characterized the popular music of his time with their simple harmonies and recurring melodic patterns. His musical style included adaptations of waltz, ragtime, and other dance rhythms in his vocal scores and, in his operettas, Spanish and African-American influences. Though best remembered for his Tin Pan Alley style, he proved he could write in various musical forms appropriate for the Broadway stage. Some of his ballads, dance music, and vaudeville songs, such as "Cuddle Up a Little Closer," are still heard in various forms today.

• For biographical information about Hoschna, see David Ewen, *Complete Book of the American Musical Theater* (1958), and Ewen, comp. and ed., *Popular American Composers from Revolutionary Times to the Present: A Biographical and Critical Guide* (1962, suppl. 1972).

DONNA H. LEHMAN

HOSKINS, Roy Graham (3 July 1880–5 Nov. 1964), biomedical investigator, was born in Nevinville, Iowa, the son of William Henry Hoskins, a tradesman, and Sarah Graham. As a child, Roy moved by covered wagon with his family to Broken Bow, Nebraska, where newly turned sod became the family's shelter and livelihood. Parental teaching, extensive Bible reading, and "The Youth's Companion" were his sole sources of enlightenment. When Roy was seven the Hoskinses moved to Mullen, Nebraska, but failing family fortunes prompted another move to Fairfield, Nebraska—over land that was unsurveyed and populated with grouse, prairie chickens, and pronghorns, much to Roy's fascination. In Mullens, Hoskins was gainfully employed collecting buffalo bones to be used as boneblack in making sugar. In Fairfield his father returned to carpentry and Hoskins got his first experience with formal education. The outcome was a straight-A record throughout five years of high school, which in 1900 enabled him to matriculate at the University of Kansas. There Hoskins had the good fortune to be associated with seven of this country's most prominent naturalists in both the plant and animal sciences. He also took part in a variety of extracurricular activities, winning the pentathlon and singing with many different groups. He graduated Phi Beta Kappa with an A.B. in 1905.

From 1907 to 1910 Hoskins taught high school at Chanute, Kansas, whereupon an anatomist friend, Ida Hyde, persuaded him to accept an Austin Teaching Fellowship for graduate study with the renowned Walter B. Cannon of the Harvard Medical School. Hoskins wrote his doctoral thesis in 1910 on the functional interrelationships between the endocrine glands. Cannon was so intrigued that he largely abandoned his own work on motor function of the gastrointestinal tract and went on to win international acclaim as an endocrinologist.

Backed by documented talent, Hoskins was immediately hoisted to the top of the academic ladder with successive appointments to professor and chairman in physiology at two midwestern universities between 1910 and 1918. Initially at Starling-Ohio Medical School in Columbus, he moved on to Northwestern University Medical School in 1913. During World War I he served in the Sanitary Corps of the U.S. Army, rising from captain to major. In 1920 Hoskins became an associate in physiology with advanced standing (third year class) at the Johns Hopkins Medical School and graduated that same year with his M.D. degree.

Over the next seven years Hoskins built a strong Department of Physiology at Ohio State with his own interests turning to the role of endocrines in mental diseases (especially *dementia praecox*, schizophrenia, and psychosomatic disorders). This pioneering adventure led to his appointment as director of research of the Memorial Foundation for Neuro-Endocrine Research, in affiliation with Cannon's department at Harvard, and close liaison with the Worcester (Mass.) State Hospital from 1927 to 1947. Herewith Hoskins pioneered the development of a new discipline that had an enormous impact on the care and treatment of the mentally ill. A host of research workers came under his guidance during the twenty years that he was director of the foundation.

Very early in his career (1917), Hoskins rallied a small group of colleagues to form a new organization, the Association for the Study of Internal Secretions, and published a new scientific journal, *Journal of Endocrinology*, of which he became the editor in chief. His briefcase was the editorial office for a few years while he struggled mightily to keep the journal afloat for want of suitable copy. The journal survived as a monument to Hoskins's adroit editorial labors over a 25-year period. In 1942 he engineered the creation of the *Journal of Clinical Endocrinology* and served as managing editor for three years.

What brought Hoskins acclaim was his popularization of the study of the glands of internal secretion through his research, writings (he published two books and 150 or more articles in quality journals), and oratory, often laced with wit and humor. He came upon the scene at a time when the study of the glands was at low ebb in terms of respect. Clinicians were, with a few sparkling exceptions, engaged in disreputable practices for monetary gain (note the likes of John R. Brinkley, the goat-gland specialist of the 1920s, with royalty at his doorstep seeking rejuvenation). In the words of Nobel laureate E. A. Doisy, Hoskins's "guidance as Editor and counsel as a scientist have played an important role in establishing endocrinology on its present sound basis." In like vein, the eminent physiologist C. N. H. Long commented, "It took real insight and a certain amount of courage to enter the uncharted and turbulent seas of endocrinology" at the time he commenced his work. His mastery of the entire field of endocrinology was made explicit in his two books: *The Tides of Life: The Endocrine Glands in Bodily Adjustment* (1933) and *Endocrinology, the Glands and Their Functions* (1941), which brought together his own research findings and much of the information then available in the literature.

Following his retirement in 1947, Hoskins served as either consultant, trustee, or lecturer to a variety of institutions and held an appointment as research professor of physiology at Tufts College (later Tufts University) from 1950 to 1963. From 1948 to 1963 he also was a consultant at the Boston, Massachusetts, branch of the Office of Naval Research. In 1963 he received the U.S. Navy's Superior Civilian Service Award (the navy's second-highest civilian honor). Hoskins served as president of the Association for the Study of Internal Secretions (1926), the Society for the Research of Psychosomatic Problems (1945), and the Gerontological Society (1946).

Hoskins died in Santa Barbara, California. He had been married twice: in 1926 to Agnes Seamans, who died the following year; and in about 1928 to Gertrude Austin Pavey. He had a son with his first wife and a stepdaughter by his second marriage. Hoskins was in many ways a man apart. He was uniquely qualified to lead, as he did, a major advance in a field of study that had a significant impact on the entire spectrum of medical research.

• There is no known list of Hoskins's scientific publications. In addition to the books noted in the text, he published in 1946 the *Biology of Schizophrenia*, a condensation of his Salmon Memorial Lectures before the New York Academy of Medicine. He also edited the two-volume *Endocrinology and Metabolism*, with L. F. Barker and H. O. Mosenthal (1922). A posthumous account of his life and work appeared in *Endocrinology* 76 (1965): 1007–11. An obituary is in the *New York Times*, 6 Nov. 1964.

ROY O. GREEP

HOSMER, Harriet Goodhue (9 Oct. 1830–21 Feb. 1908), sculptor, was born in Watertown, Massachusetts, the daughter of Hiram Hosmer, a physician, and Sarah Grant. Sarah Hosmer died when her daughter was four years old. Hiram Hosmer raised Harriet, providing her with physical and intellectual training well beyond the limits imposed on most middle-class girls of the time. Hosmer grew up renowned in her community for fearlessness and unconventional behavior, especially in regard to outdoor sports involving riding and shooting.

Courage in pursuing her goals and disregard for orthodoxy marked her academic life and her artistic career. When as an aspiring artist in 1850 she desired to obtain a knowledge of anatomy, she determinedly went to live with an old schoolmate and studied at Washington University, St. Louis, having been denied entrance to Boston area medical schools. Back in Watertown, she laboriously carved a bust of Hesper (Watertown Free Public Library), and when she went to Rome in 1852 she used it to persuade the British neoclassical sculptor John Gibson to accept her as a student in his studio. She became a well-known sight around the city, for she wore her hair—and sometimes her skirts—short, rode her own horse wherever and whenever she pleased, and frequently carried pistols or a steel-tipped umbrella for protection. A member of the actress Charlotte Cushman's circle of sophisticated professional women, Hosmer lived a strikingly independent existence.

Early scholars of her work tended to minimize the relationship between her mode of life and the subject matter of her strongest work, such as the life-sized figures of the tragic heroines Beatrice Cenci (1853–1855, St. Louis, Mo., Mercantile Library) and Zenobia, Queen of Palmyra (c. 1857, Hartford, Conn., Wadsworth Atheneum). Instead, thanks in part to pages in Nathaniel Hawthorne's *Marble Faun* (1860) and *Passages from the French and Italian Notebooks* (1871), condescending perceptions of Hosmer's spirited personality as "cute" mixed with the era's generally patronizing attitude toward women artists, creating the image of a "tomboy" maker of frivolous or derivative sculpture. Conceits such as the frequently replicated *Puck* (1856, Washington, D.C., National Museum of American Art) and *Will-o'-the-Wisp* (n.d., Piermont, N.Y., private collection), brought Hosmer attention from the highest circles of European society and formed the basis of her income. Small and charming, if arch, *putti*, these conceits must have appeared to be the very embodiment of "women's work" in sculpture. In contrast, the neoclassic *Sleeping Faun* (Boston, Museum of Fine Arts), exhibited in Dublin in 1865 almost as soon as it left the artist's studio, won instant acclaim for the muscular strength and beauty of the sleeping young man/animal.

Hosmer's recognition in the United States never attained the heights of popularity she reached among the international set in Europe. Derided for using male assistants to carve the marble versions of her clay models—in fact a common practice for all nineteenth-century sculptors of marble—Hosmer fought back in "The Process of Sculpture," published in the *Atlantic Monthly* (Dec. 1864), but her reputation was at least temporarily tainted. One of the few American sculptors who actually *could* carve, Hosmer produced a body of work known for its sensitive handling of drapery and anatomy, its clarity of design, and its highly polished yet delicate surfaces. Her moving images of youth are epitomized in her monument to Judith Falconnet in San Andrea delle Fratte, the first commission awarded to an American sculptor in a Roman church. Art historical scholarship on Hosmer during the latter part of the twentieth century has concentrated on iconographic features of her work and on the exemplary aspects of her career in relation to the history of women artists. She is frequently grouped with other American women artists who worked in Italy, such as Louisa Lander, Emma Stebbins, and Edmonia Lewis, but the quality of her work, from an artistic and technical standpoint, places Hosmer on a level of her own. She died in Watertown, Massachusetts.

• Hosmer's correspondence and reminiscences can be found in Cornelia Carr, ed., *Harriet Hosmer: Letters and Memories* (1913). An early biographical essay by Ruth Bradford, "The Life and Works of Harriet Hosmer," *New England Magazine* 77/n.s. 14 (Aug. 1871): 245–46, has been superseded by Dolly Sherwood, *Harriet Hosmer: American Sculptor, 1830–1908* (1991). For Hosmer in context, see also Margaret Thorp, *The Literary Sculptors* (1965), and Joy Kasson, *Marble Queens and Captives* (1990).

BARBARA GROSECLOSE

HOSMER, Hezekiah Lord (10 Dec. 1814–31 Oct. 1893), judge and author, was born in Hudson, New York, the son of Hezekiah Lord Hosmer and Susan Throop. He was educated in Oxford, New York, and in 1830 moved west to Cleveland, Ohio, to reside with his kinsman John W. Allen, under whose tutelage he read law. Hosmer was admitted to the Ohio bar in 1835 and began the practice of law in Willoughby, later moving to Painesville. Following the onrush of settlers to the Maumee Valley of northwestern Ohio, he moved to Maumee City and then to Perrysburg, where as a young lawyer he rode the circuit of seven or eight counties in northwestern Ohio. It was also during this time that Hosmer began to devote a portion of his time to journalistic pursuits.

In 1844 Hosmer moved again, settling in Toledo, where he became editor and part-owner of the *Toledo Blade*, to which he was closely connected until 1855. In that year he once again turned to the practice of law; however, he continued to write, publishing the *Early History of the Maumee Valley* in 1858 and his only novel, *Adela, the Octoroon*, in 1860. This latter work is noteworthy for several reasons, not the least of which is that it is often cited as one of the plot sources for Dion Boucicault's famous play *The Octoroon*. Set on the Mississippi plantation of Adela's father, the novel is very strong propaganda for abolition; it also distinctly advocates Liberian colonization, carefully detailing through involved subplots the tragedies of freed blacks who suffer in the "free states" in contrast to the accounts of other former slaves who almost effortlessly thrive in the relatively new colony of Liberia. Although it is one of a number of "tragic octoroon" stories of the time, it is one of only a small handful of antislavery novels to solve the slavery/race dilemma through amalgamation, when the hero of the novel, a young lawyer named Frank Thornton, marries the mixed-race Adela and moves to California, where it is implied that the couple can live in some sort of racial obscurity.

In spite of his literary interests, Hosmer continued to practice law in Toledo. He also entered the Masons, becoming deputy grand master and grand orator of the state of Ohio and continuing his Masonic pursuits very actively for the rest of his life. A loyal Whig while the party lasted, he aligned himself with the Republican party in 1860, strongly supporting Abraham Lincoln for the presidency and remaining loyal to the Republican party throughout his life. In 1861, after Lincoln entered the White House, Hosmer moved to Washington, with the ambition of being appointed congressional librarian. While he was unsuccessful in this aspiration, he was able, through the efforts of James M. Ashley, a representative from his district in Ohio who chaired the House Committee on Territories, to acquire a position as secretary of that important committee. This post undoubtedly positioned him advantageously, for in 1864 Lincoln appointed him chief justice of the supreme court of the newly formed territory of Montana, which, as secretary of the House committee, Hosmer had helped organize. However, the organic act that formed the new territory of Montana from the eastern area of the Idaho Territory provided no system of jurisprudence for Montana. Further, when Hosmer arrived in Virginia City in October 1864, the territorial legislature had not yet met to pass any system of law. Thus, when Hosmer opened the district court of the First Judicial District of the territory of Montana in the dining hall of the Planters' House in Virginia City on 5 December 1864, there was "no civil or criminal code, nor any practice act or statute that authoritatively applied to the territory" ("Biographical Sketch," p. 291).

Because Montana Territory had been carved out of Idaho, Hosmer decided to use the Idaho statutes as a guide until the Montana legislature could meet to establish statutes for the territory. This worked well until several cases involving mining claims and water rights forced Hosmer, who knew little law concerning mining litigation, to adopt the California rule, which was replete with mining decisions because of a plethora of cases following the Gold Rush. However perplexing the lack of a civil or criminal code must have been for Justice Hosmer, perhaps the most difficult impediment he faced in establishing justice in the territory was the existence of highly organized vigilantes, who, now that law was coming to the territory, "have fulfilled their work," as Hosmer states in his charge to the territory's first grand jury. While in his charge to the grand jury Justice Hosmer gave credit to the vigilantes for restoring at least a semblance of harmony to a society void of law, he soundly denounced them, noting that in a society organized through law "any subversive organizations are criminal in themselves, and should be among the first subjects to arouse the jealousy and stimulate the investigations of a grand jury." In addition to these problems, the staunchly Republican judge faced political opposition from an almost unanimously Democratic territorial legislature, resulting in a legislative resolution requesting that he resign. Hosmer ignored the resolution, finishing out his term as chief justice but not applying for reappointment.

Upon completing his term as chief justice at the end of 1868, Hosmer retired from public life, accepting an appointment as postmaster at Virginia City, a position he held until he left Montana for San Francisco in 1872, residing there until his death. In San Francisco Hosmer at various times held positions in the State Mining Bureau and in the Custom House, never returning to the bench or practicing law after his Montana judgeship. During this period he devoted much of his time to Masonic interests, reaching positions simultaneously as prelate of Golden Gate Commandery at San Francisco and grand prelate of the Grand Commandery of California. During this period Hosmer continued his literary pursuits, in 1887 publishing *Bacon and Shakespeare in the Sonnets*, in which he posits that the sonnets are a cipher poem in which Bacon explains his authorship of Shakespeare's plays.

Hosmer's life and achievements represent several important aspects of nineteenth-century American life and culture, not the least of which is the sheer diversity of his accomplishments. He was a successful attorney and journalist, and he was a very progressive antislavery novelist, particularly in his acceptance of interracial marriage. Further, he was a highly successful chief justice, one who diligently and steadily brought law and order to the literally lawless frontier of the Montana Territory.

• Hosmer's letters and papers are included in two collections, the Hezekiah Lord Hosmer Manuscripts in the Western Americana Collection at Yale University and the Hezekiah Lord Hosmer Letters at the Montana State Historical Society. Hosmer's letters to Wilbur F. Sanders, which are located in the Sanders papers at the Montana State Historical Society, provide important insight into Hosmer's attitude toward Montana jurisprudence. The only Hosmer biography is the brief "Biographical Sketch of Hezekiah L. Hosmer," *Contributions to the Historical Society of Montana* 3 (1900): 288–99. For a brief discussion of the theme of interracial marriage in *Adela*, see James Kinney, *Amalgamation!: Race, Sex, and Rhetoric in the Nineteenth-Century American Novel* (1985). Hosmer's inaugural charge to the grand jury was printed in the 10 Dec. 1864 issue of the *Montana Post* but is more easily accessible in *Contributions to the Historical Society of Montana* 5 (1904): 235–41. On Hosmer's tenure as a Montana chief justice, see also John D. W. Guice, *The Rocky Mountain Bench: The Territorial Supreme Courts of Colorado, Montana, and Wyoming, 1861–1890* (1972), and Clark C. Spence, "The Territorial Bench in Montana: 1864–1889," *Montana: The Magazine of Western History* 13 (Jan. 1965): 25–32, 57–65. An obituary is in the *San Francisco Morning Call*, 1 Nov. 1893.

VERNON G. MILES

HOSMER, William Howe Cuyler (25 May 1814–23 May 1877), poet, was born west of Rochester, New York, in a community called Avon, the son of George Hosmer, a lawyer, and Elizabeth Berry. Hosmer graduated from Geneva College (now Hobart College), in Geneva, New York. He later received honorary M.A. degrees from Hamilton College and the University of Vermont. Shortly after his graduation from Geneva College in 1837, Hosmer married Stella Hinchman Avery of Owego, New York, in October 1838. They had two sons.

Hosmer joined his father's law practice and spent most of his life there. His mother was fascinated by Native American life, an enthusiasm that he came to share, and she taught him several different languages and dialects. It is not surprising then that he studied tribal customs and legends not only in his native New York but also in Wisconsin (1836) and Florida (1838–1839). Much of his poetry, which he began writing when he was a student, contained Indian themes. In 1830 he wrote a play titled *The Fall of Tecumseh* and subsequently numerous other works of verse. *The Themes of Song* was published in 1842, and *The Poetical Works of William H. C. Hosmer* appeared in two volumes in 1854.

Yonnondio; or, Warriors of the Genesee: A Tale of the Seventeenth Century (1844), the longest and best known of Hosmer's works, relates the attempt of the marquis de Nonville to claim the land of the Seneca for King Louis XIV in 1687 in defiance of a treaty between the English and the French that said both countries would be free to trade in the area. Written primarily in octosyllabic couplets, the verse suggests the oral tradition from which it came. Hosmer states in the preface to his *Poetical Works* that the information he imparts comes from authentic sources. He continues by praising the Indians' "marvellous religious ceremonies, the feast, the dance—his sagacity in the chase, and on the war-path—his self-reliance in adversity in extreme peril."

Hosmer put the legends of the Seneca into verse so that the tribe's traditions and lore would not be forgotten. He versified the Seneca myth of the tribe's origin in "Genundewah," written in 1846. The poem tells the story of how a huge snake destroys all but two inhabitants of an ancient fort; the young couple, saved by the Great Spirit, become ancestors of the Seneca.

With *The Months* (1847) and "Bird Notes" (included in *Poetical Works*) Hosmer moved away from his emphasis on Native Americans and concentrated on accurate descriptions of nature. These poems, again mainly written in couplets, are meant to aptly display his love of upstate New York and its wildlife. Hosmer states in the preface of his *Poetical Works* that his purpose in "Bird Notes" was to "outline a few American birds with their classical and legendary associations." Although Griswold thought that Hosmer described the birds as clearly as an Audubon painting, an analysis of the verses reveals that Hosmer captured the spirit of how he felt about the different species rather than a physical description.

Hosmer stopped writing when he began serving as a clerk in the New York Custom House between 1854 and 1858. On 12 November 1862 Hosmer enlisted in the Twenty-sixth Battery of New York Volunteers as a private. He was not deemed physically fit for battle but did accompany the battery to Louisiana. It was during this time that Hosmer's wife and two sons died. One son, William, was drowned, and the other, Charles, was killed at the battle of Chancellorsville in 1863; Hosmer's wife died in 1864. Stricken with dysentery, Hosmer returned to his home in Avon, where he practiced law until his death.

While Hosmer's poetry was unique in its treatment of Native Americans, he was not considered a major poet during his lifetime. The study of Hosmer's work has continued to be generally neglected despite its historical significance.

• Rufus Wilmot Griswold, *The Poets and Poetry of America* (1842), is of dubious value as a starting point for further information on Hosmer. A more reliable overview appears in Stanley Kunitz et al., eds., *American Authors 1600–1900* (1938). A complete bibliography of Hosmer's separate works, along with a list of original reviews, may be found in *Literary Writings in America: A Bibliography*, vol. 4 (1977).

DIANE LOOMS WEBER

HOTELLING, Harold (29 Sept. 1895–26 Dec. 1973), economist and statistician, was born in Fulda, Minnesota, the son of Clair Alberta Hotelling, a hay merchant, and Lucy Amelia Rawson. When Hotelling was about nine years old, the family moved to Seattle, Washington, which offered educational opportunities not available in Fulda. Hotelling attended high school there and then went on to study at the University of Washington, where he majored in journalism. His studies were interrupted by World War I army service, from which he was discharged early in 1919. He completed his degree in that same year. His undergraduate studies had included mathematics, science, and economics as well as journalism. Later, when he was a professor of economics, he was to exaggerate the amount of that subject he had taken (only three courses), probably because he was sensitive about the relatively little formal training he had received in it.

After receiving his B.A. degree, Hotelling joined the staff of a local paper. He decided almost immediately that journalism and he were not well matched (apparently he wrote too slowly), and he returned to the university after only one semester to study graduate-level mathematics. He had been encouraged to do so by Eric Temple Bell, a mathematician of some note then on the University of Washington faculty. In 1920 he married Floy Tracy; they had two children. Upon receiving his M.A. in 1921, Hotelling applied for a graduate fellowship in economics at Columbia University. Ironically, in the light of his later career, he was rejected. He accepted a fellowship in mathematics at Princeton, hoping to develop his understanding of both mathematical economics and statistics while pursuing the studies in pure mathematics that he considered the necessary basis for both of these. He was to write later that he "found no one there who knew anything about either subject," and so he devoted himself to the mathematics alone, in which he obtained his Ph.D. in June 1924.

Hotelling worked from 1924 to 1927 as a research associate in the Food Research Institute at Stanford University and also taught some courses in the mathematics department of the university. In 1927 he joined Stanford's mathematics department as a full-time assistant professor and remained at that post until 1931, when he accepted an offer from Columbia to join its economics department. As part of the offer, he would teach courses in mathematical economics and statistics, the subjects he had hoped to study ten years earlier. Although Hotelling had received no formal training in mathematical statistics, he had studied the work of the Englishman Ronald A. Fisher, one of the giants in statistics, and he had spent a semester's leave in England working with Fisher.

Hotelling moved to Columbia in 1931 and remained there for the next fifteen years, even though the economics department of the time was not very receptive to theory in general and the university was not receptive to his goal of establishing statistics as a separate discipline with its own institute. A considerable part of his failure to establish such an institute was no doubt his lack of skills in academic politics and fundraising. Gertrude Cox at the University of North Carolina did possess these skills and was able to attract Hotelling by offering him the codirectorship of the newly created Statistical Institute.

Hotelling's years at Stanford and Columbia were very productive, and he made major contributions to both economics and statistics. In economics he wrote seminal papers on spatial competition, the economics of exhaustible resources, marginal cost pricing, and the properties of supply and demand functions. Hotelling's rule (that the rate of increase in the unit value of the remaining stock of a depletable resource like oil will equal the rate of interest under competition) and Hotelling's lemma (a mathematical relationship between a firm's profit function, its supply function, and its demand for inputs) became part of the economics literature. In statistics he was a major pioneer in multivariate analysis, with papers on the generalization of the t-distribution (Hotelling's T^2), the estimation of differential equations subject to error, principal components, and canonical correlations. A special feature of Hotelling's work, in addition to its extraordinary high average quality, was its originality and farsightedness. A considerable portion of his ideas (on spatial competition, exhaustible resources, stochastic differential equations, demand function properties, for example) have proved even more fruitful after fifty or sixty years than they seemed when he wrote them. Besides his academic work, Hotelling was a consultant to many government agencies. During World War II, he organized the Statistical Research Group at Columbia, which carried out defense-related research from 1942 to 1945. Floy had died in 1932, and then in 1934 he married Susanna Porter Edmondson. They had six children, one of whom died in childhood. Susanna was a renowned hostess at Columbia, and later at North Carolina, organizing the famous "Hotelling Teas" (intentional pun on the T^2 statistic) for students, colleagues, and friends.

In 1946 Hotelling moved to his new post in Chapel Hill, North Carolina, where he was the key figure in developing the Department of Statistics. He formally retired as professor of mathematical statistics in 1960 but was then appointed Kenan Professor of Economics and continued to teach at North Carolina until 1966. His years at North Carolina were less productive academically than his Stanford or Columbia periods had been, but his influence was great.

Hotelling received recognition as a statistician and mathematical economist reasonably early. He was a founding member of both the Econometric Society and the Institute for Mathematical Statistics, becoming president of the former in 1936 and of the latter in 1941. Recognition by the general economics profession came only in 1965, when the American Economics Association elected him as one of its first two distinguished fellows. It is interesting that the other was Edward Chamberlin of monopolistic competition fame, since the theory of product differentiation has come to be based on the work of both. In his later years he received many honors, including two honorary degrees and election to the National Academy of Sciences in 1970.

In 1965 Hotelling went to Buenos Aires to help develop a statistics program at the Institute of Statistics. He became ill, underwent an unsuccessful operation, and was obliged to return to Chapel Hill before completing his mission. He remained in poor health and, in 1972, suffered a stroke during a family lunch, from which he never recovered. Nursed by his wife for the next nineteen months, he died in Chapel Hill.

• Hotelling's economic papers (but not his statistical ones) have been brought together in *The Collected Economics Articles of Harold Hotelling* (1990). The editor, Adrian Darnell, supplies an introduction with biographical details and a survey of Hotelling's economics contributions. The volume also supplies a list of all Hotelling's writings, in statistics and mathematics as well as economics. The entry for Hotelling in John Eatwell, Murray Milgate, and Peter Newman, eds., *The New Palgrave*, was written by Kenneth J. Arrow, who had been a student of Hotelling at Columbia. Darnell also wrote an obituary article for *Statistical Science* 3 (1982): 57–61. Another obituary article, by Walter L. Smith in *The Annals of Statistics* 6 (1978): 1173–83, places more emphasis on Hotelling the statistician and on his North Carolina years.

KELVIN LANCASTER

HOTZE, Henry (2 Sept. 1833–19 Apr. 1887), Confederate propagandist, was born in Zurich, Switzerland, the son of Rudolph Hotze, a captain in the French Royal Service, and Sophie Esslinger. Educated by the Jesuits, Hotze emigrated as a youth to the United States. In 1855 he became a naturalized citizen in Mobile, Alabama, where his intelligence, manners, and racial views (he translated Joseph Arthur, Comte de Gobineau's *Essai sur l'inégalité des races humaines* [1854–1855] in 1856) won him acceptance within powerful circles. In 1858 he attended the southern commercial convention in Montgomery as a Mobile delegate. He served as secretary to the U.S. legation in Brussels in 1858–1859, then became associate editor of John Forsyth's influential but moderate Mobile *Register*.

On the outbreak of the Civil War, Hotze joined the elite Mobile Cadets. On 30 May 1861 he was made a clerk to the adjutant general and stationed in Richmond. Confederate secretary of war L. P. Walker sent Hotze on a special mission to London to oversee the financing of Confederate agents in Europe and the purchase of munitions. Hotze traveled via the North and Canada, collecting intelligence on the Abraham Lincoln administration's war mobilization. He arrived in London on 5 October and became convinced of the South's urgent need for a full-scale diplomatic and propaganda offensive in Europe. On his return to Richmond he put this case to the southern leadership, and on 14 November he was appointed by Secretary of State R. M. T. Hunter as commercial agent to Britain, arriving in London on 29 January 1862. His real mission was to convince British public opinion that the Confederacy was viable and worthy of recognition by the great powers. For the rest of the war, despite a shortsighted failure by Richmond adequately to finance his activities, Hotze spent prodigious time and energy, almost wrecking his health and eyesight, in a great range of propaganda efforts.

Hotze was always the realist (in contrast to some other Confederate agents abroad). He perceived that Britain, fearing war with the North, was lukewarm about any intervention in the Civil War. He was also aware that stockpiling and price speculation were diluting the impact of the Confederacy's cotton embargo. By withholding cotton from Europe, the South hoped to force the powers to intervene against the North. Hotze planned to counter British caution and antislavery sentiments by an appeal to British self-interest in dividing a rival United States and in preserving British naval and neutral rights. He appealed also to liberal sympathies for the rights of small nationalities to independence. Cultivating opinion makers within "polite society" and the establishment press, he employed English journalists to write for the southern cause in London newspapers, and Hotze himself wrote leaders for the *Morning Post* (mouthpiece of the Liberal prime minister Lord Palmerston), the London *Standard*, the *Herald* (organ of the Conservative opposition leader Lord Derby), and gained entry to the financial weekly *Money and Market Review*.

Hotze's most enduring achievement was to set up in May 1862 a weekly journal, the *Index*, which he maintained as probably the most effective publicity outlet for the Confederacy until August 1865. It was financed on a shoestring, initially by wealthy southerners and Hotze himself then, grudgingly, from President Jefferson Davis's secret service fund. With a circulation of about 2,000, the *Index* was distributed mainly in Britain but also in France, Ireland, and the Union. Confederate secretary of state Judah P. Benjamin praised as "judicious and effective" Hotze's plan of engaging the services of "writers employed in the leading daily papers and thereby securing not only their cooperation but educating them into such knowledge of our affairs as will enable them to counteract effectually the misrepresentation of the Northern agents" (Benjamin to Hotze, 16 Jan. 1863). Hotze deliberately adopted a "tone of studied moderation" in the *Index*, refusing to alienate the Palmerston administration by intemperate criticism of its policy of nonintervention or by injudicious meddling in English party politics. This caution, as he said, "was mistaken by many of our countrymen for lukewarmness, timidity, or lack of spirit" (Hotze to Benjamin, 17 Jan. 1863). For such reasons, and also because of his foreign origins, Hotze's relations deteri-

orated with firebrand rebel agents in Europe, such as Edwin De Leon, John Slidell, and Paul Pecquet du Bellet.

Hotze energetically supported every effort of the "southern lobby" in England to aid the rebel cause. He helped to write Lord Campbell's speech denouncing the blockade in the House of Lords on 10 March 1862. Rebel hopes for recognition by the powers rode high after Confederate military successes in Virginia that summer. With Palmerston and Foreign Minister John Russell warming to the idea of a joint armistice proposal by Britain, France, and Russia, William Gladstone became the cabinet's chief proponent of mediation. Hotze reassured Gladstone, over an intimate dinner on 30 July, that any boundary difficulties between the Union and an independent Confederacy would be negotiable (Gladstone papers, memo 31 July 1862). On 4 August Russell rejected southern demands for recognition, however, and by late October prospects of British intervention had peaked and waned, given cabinet rifts, Tory opposition, Robert E. Lee's setback at the battle of Antietam, and the publication of Lincoln's preliminary Emancipation Proclamation. Hotze faced mounting antislavery demonstrations, while Richmond focused its diplomatic efforts on France. Benjamin increased Hotze's budget in January 1863, but on 23 March Russell rebuffed Campbell's motion for rebel recognition in the House of Lords. Hotze reported home (9 May) that, even though the "masses of intelligence and respectability" wished the South well, "the public mind has settled down into a state of quiescence on American affairs which resembles stagnation." However, Thomas "Stonewall" Jackson's death in May evoked widespread sorrow in England. Hotze helped organize and publicize a series of large prosouthern meetings in late May at Manchester, Sheffield, Preston, and other towns to bolster J. A. Roebuck's House of Commons motion of 30 June for recognition. It was mismanaged and withdrawn on 13 July. Hotze lamented: "Now, all hope of parliamentary action is past. Diplomatic means can now no longer prevail, and everybody looks to Lee to conquer recognition." In July came the crushing news of the decisive Union victories at Vicksburg and Gettysburg. When Richmond withdrew its unofficial envoy to Britain, James M. Mason, Hotze remained as the South's only representative. His main activity now was to exploit Anglo-northern frictions, caused by Confederate efforts to build an ironclad naval force in British shipyards and aggravated by the Union navy's interference with neutral shipping. By September 1864 more than 300,000 signatures were obtained for peace petitions sent from the people of Britain to those of America. Also in 1864 Hotze successfully infiltrated French newspapers, providing them with prosouthern telegraphic news reports via the Havas Agency.

As northern victory seemed to become inevitable, Hotze's task became impossible and his rhetoric less temperate. His deep commitment to slavery inhibited his flexibility and led to some uncharacteristically flawed moves. In January 1864 he was instrumental in having removed from his post as Confederate financial agent one of the South's warmest defenders in Britain, the author James Spence, mainly because Spence was making "unnecessarily large concessions to the anti-slavery prejudice" (Hotze to Benjamin, 21 Nov. 1863). Hotze felt unable to give full allegiance to Richmond's desperate proposal late in 1864 to emancipate its slaves in return for foreign recognition. After the war Hotze refused to accept "the Africanization of the Union" and stayed in Europe. He married Ruby Senac, daughter of a Confederate navy paymaster, in Paris in 1868; they had no children. Few records survive about Hotze's later career as a journalist, mainly stationed in Paris. He died of cancer in Zug, Switzerland.

Hotze is generally held to be one of the Confederacy's best and most intelligent agents abroad. His ultimate failure reflected the oppressive parameters within which southern diplomacy labored. Goals such as recognition or direct intervention by the great powers were achievable only if they suited the vital political interests of those powers and only if the south won decisive field victories. These conditions were never met.

• Hotze's papers, including letterbook and dispatches, and the *Index* are in the Library of Congress. Dispatches to and from Hotze are published in *The Official Records of the Union and Confederate Navies in the War of the Rebellion*, ser. 2, vol. 3 (30 vols., 1894–1922) and in other official publications. For his time in the Mobile Cadets see Hotze, *Three Months in the Confederate Army*, ed. R. B. Harwell (1952). An attack on Hotze by a fellow rebel agent is in Paul Pecquet du Bellet, *The Diplomacy of the Confederate Cabinet of Richmond and Its Agents Abroad: Being Memorandum Notes Taken in Paris during the Rebellion of the Southern States from 1861 to 1865*, ed. with an introduction by William Stanley Hoole (1963). The best modern account of Hotze's work is Charles P. Cullop, *Confederate Propaganda in Europe, 1861–1865* (1969). See also Brian Jenkins, *Britain and the War for the Union*, vol. 2 (1980); J. F. Jameson, "The London Expenditure of the Confederate Secret Service," *American Historical Review* 35 (1930): 811–24; Stephen B. Oates, "Henry Hotze: Confederate Agent Abroad," *Historian* 27 (1965): 131–54; and Robert Trumbull Smith, "The Confederate *Index* and the American Civil War" (M.A. thesis, Univ. of Washington, 1961). For the international context of Hotze's career see D. P. Crook, *Diplomacy during the American Civil War* (1975), and Howard Jones, *Union in Peril: British Intervention in the Civil War* (1992). An obituary is in the *Mobile Daily Register*, 11 May 1887.

D. P. CROOK

HOUDINI, Harry (24 Mar. 1874–31 Oct. 1926), magician and escape artist, was born Ehrich Weiss in Budapest, Hungary, the son of Rabbi Mayer Samuel Weiss and Cecelia Steiner. In 1878 the family immigrated to Appleton, Wisconsin. The town's small Jewish congregation hired Mayer Samuel as its rabbi but released him after four years. He began a hapless twelve-year search for a settled rabbinical post to support his wife and seven children and was reduced to accepting provisions from a relief society and selling part of his scholarly library. Young Ehrich once ran away from home and later recalled the period as "hard and cruel years when I rarely had the bare necessities of life."

About 1890, in New York City, Ehrich and a friend formed a magic act called "The Brothers Houdini." Which partner coined the name is unknown, but it invoked the celebrated French conjurer Jean Eugène Robert-Houdin. Ehrich's nickname, "Erie," meanwhile modulated into Harry. In 1894 he married Wilhelmina Beatrice Rahner, a diminutive German Catholic from Brooklyn. Known as "Bess," she became his partner in an act renamed "The Houdinis." They had no children.

Until the turn of the century the Houdinis scrounged a living from the lowliest venues of show business: dime-museums, medicine shows, small circuses, and burlesque. They featured "Metamorphosis," an illusion in which Houdini, tied in a sack and locked inside a trunk, changed places with Bess, who seconds later was found inside the same locked trunk, inside the same tied bag. Late in 1895 Houdini introduced a sensational publicity stunt. Before opening in some town, he would visit the local newspaper office or police station offering to escape from any number of regulation handcuffs locked on his wrists and arms, which he often did in less than a minute.

Houdini soon made the handcuff escape a part of his act, which became essentially a solo performance. In the spring of 1899 he gained the attention of Martin Beck, a prominent manager who booked him into the leading American vaudeville houses. Within a year Houdini created three more headline-grabbing escapes. In Los Angeles, for the first time he wriggled free of a tightly strapped straitjacket. Some six weeks later he jumped from a bridge, shackled with handcuffs and ankle irons, and surfaced from the water in a few moments with the restraints opened. In April 1900, after being strip-searched for picks and keys, he broke out of a locked jail cell in just three minutes. The new escapes became mainstays of his repertoire.

Houdini spent most of the next four and a half years in Great Britain, Europe, and Russia. Wildly enthusiastic audiences established him as an international star, the "King of Handcuffs." He upheld his title by escaping in Moscow from a steel high-security van used to transport prisoners to Siberia. At the London Hippodrome he submitted himself to a theoretically unpickable pair of handcuffs that reportedly had taken five years to manufacture, secured by complex locks-within-locks-within-locks. He released himself in an hour and ten minutes. His successes brought hordes of imitators. By 1903 he counted in England alone fifty-five "Kings of Handcuffs."

Intent on standing out as unique and determined not to repeat his father's failure, Houdini dealt with the competition by keeping ahead of it. In the decade before the First World War he invented a succession of ever riskier and more dumbfounding escapes. Late in 1907 he introduced an escape in under three minutes from a sealed milk can filled with liquid. In July 1912 he got out of a locked, roped packing case submerged in New York Harbor. In September of the same year he unveiled his Water Torture Cell, a telephone-booth-size aquarium in which he was suspended upside-down by his ankles. In October 1915 he freed himself from a straitjacket while dangling head first from a skyscraper. He repeated these feats often; the straitjacket escape drew outdoor crowds of up to 100,000.

During the same decade Houdini perfected his so-called "challenge" act, daring audiences to confine him in any sort of restriction they could muster. They nailed him face down to a door or put him into, among other things, four vises, the largest and strongest ever built; a freakish sea creature, its sliced-open belly laced with chains; one roped and padlocked box within another roped and padlocked box; a body-encircling web of waxed fishing line, the knots tightened with a marlin spike; a rolltop desk, zinc piano box, Postal Service mailbag, five-by-ten-foot manila envelope, giant football, and an iron steamboiler, riveted shut. Each restraint was found, after his escape, to be intact and still locked or sealed as at first.

Headlining every bill and earning up to $2,500 weekly, Houdini became the subject of innumerable feature stories and interviews. Yet he often thought of quitting show business. The exhausting escapes left his carefully conditioned body bruised and cut and sometimes ruptured or fractured. Moreover, he had many other interests. Poorly educated but the son of a learned rabbi, he aspired to be a writer and scholar. He edited a magic journal, *The Conjurers' Monthly* (1906–1908), turned out dozens of articles and short stories, and published six books, notably *The Unmasking of Robert-Houdin* (1908), an attack on his progenitor's reputation for originality in the form of a history of modern magic. Much that appeared under Houdini's name was thoroughly revised or even ghostwritten by others, although based on his extensive research done mostly in the personal library that overflowed his fourteen-room Harlem brownstone. He amassed a huge collection of rare theater memorabilia and probably the largest library of magic books in the world.

Houdini's fascination with modern technology drew him farther from the stage. He bought a Voisin biplane and on 18 March 1910 made three brief ascents near Melbourne, becoming the first person to fly in Australia. Drawn to motion pictures as well, in 1916 he launched his own film processing company. He spent time before the cameras also, starring in five features or serials beginning with *The Master Mystery* (1918). The movies attained only middling financial and artistic success but brought him before audiences in India, Japan, and South America.

The aftermath of the First World War redirected Houdini's career. The crisis of faith that followed the war's slaughter produced many new adherents to Spiritualism, the belief that the dead can contact the living through the aid of human mediums. Beginning about 1920 Houdini became absorbed in examining table levitations, slate-writing, and similar Spiritualist phenomena. With his unmatched knowledge of conjuring methods, he scorned claims of supernatural influence. But he also retained some hope-against-hope of contacting his beloved mother, whose death in 1913 he continued to mourn.

Houdini attended scores of séances in the United States and England and befriended Sir Arthur Conan Doyle, a leading evangelist for Spiritualism. During a séance in June 1922, Lady Doyle—a medium herself—produced supposed spirit messages from Houdini's deceased mother. Houdini discredited them, however, and quarreled rancorously with Sir Arthur Doyle in the press. From an investigator of Spiritualism, Houdini soon became an all-out crusader against it. Early in 1924 he began lecturing throughout the United States on fraudulent mediums. In city after city he attended séances in disguise, exposing frauds on the spot and sometimes securing their arrest, aided by his personal squad of detectives. The raids brought him huge publicity as well as a million dollars in lawsuits.

Houdini met his wiliest opponent in July 1924 while serving on a committee sponsored by *Scientific American*. The magazine offered a $2,500 prize to any medium who could produce psychic manifestations under test conditions. The chief contender was a well-to-do young Boston medium nicknamed "Margery." From the first, Houdini was convinced he had grasped the subtle methods by which she lifted tables, hurled objects, and rang a bell even while the committee members held her arms and legs. Largely on his insistence, but after bitter and much-publicized wrangling, the committee denied her the prize.

On 5 August 1926 Houdini performed one of his most astonishing feats. In the swimming pool of New York's Hotel Shelton he stayed underwater enclosed in an iron casket for an hour and a half. Meanwhile, although celebrated as an escape artist, he had designed a full-evening show featuring an hour of traditional magic. On tour in Montreal at the start of his 1926–1927 season he entertained some students from McGill University in his dressing room. One punched him several times in the abdomen to try his much-boasted strength. Houdini probably had already been suffering in silence from appendicitis, for the blows ruptured his appendix and produced peritonitis, from which he died at Grace Hospital in Detroit some ten days later, on Halloween. After a thronged, traffic-stopping funeral near Times Square, he was buried in a brass replica of the iron casket, his head pillowed on a bundle of his mother's letters to him.

Nervy, muscular, intelligent, Houdini was a unique figure in the history of entertainment—a consummate magician, showman, and publicist with a comprehensive knowledge of security mechanisms. Concerning how he gained that knowledge he gave many conflicting accounts. Concerning its deepest secrets he said nothing. Some of his methods are known but most remain intriguing mysteries, and speculation about them continues. The tantalizing uncertainty has made Houdini a hero of legend and folklore.

• The main public collections of Houdini's papers and apparatus are at the Library of Congress; the Houdini Historical Center of the Outagamie County Historical Society, Appleton, Wis.; and the Harry Ransom Humanities Research Center, University of Texas, Austin. Much else is privately owned. Notable among Houdini's published works are *Handcuff Secrets* (1909), *Miracle Mongers and Their Methods* (1920), and *A Magician among the Spirits* (1924). His fiction has been gathered in *Houdini's Strange Tales*, ed. Patrick Culliton and T. L. Williams (1992). The most informative biographies, studies, and collections include Bernard M. L. Ernst and Hereward Carrington, eds., *Houdini and Conan Doyle* (1932); Milbourne Christopher, *Houdini: The Untold Story* (1969); Walter B. Gibson, *The Original Houdini Scrapbook* (1976); Bernard C. Meyer, *Houdini: A Mind in Chains* (1976); Doug Henning and Charles Reynolds, *Houdini: His Legend and His Magic* (1977); and Kenneth Silverman, *HOUDINI!!!* (1996). An obituary is in the *New York Times*, 1 Nov. 1926.

KENNETH SILVERMAN

HOUDRY, Eugene Jules (18 Apr. 1892–18 July 1962), chemical engineer, was born in Domont, France, the son of Jules Houdry, a steel-mill owner, and Émilie Thaïs Julie Lemaire. He studied mechanical engineering at the École des Arts et Métiers in Paris and in 1911 received his degree, as well as a gold medal from the French government for graduating first in his class. He then went to work with his father as a junior partner and engineer and developed a keen interest in the fledgling sport of automobile racing. Drafted into the French army at the beginning of World War I and assigned to the tank corps, Houdry rose to the rank of lieutenant; in 1917 he was badly wounded while repairing a damaged tank in the middle of a battle. He received the croix de guerre for bravery under fire and was made a chevalier in the Legion of Honor.

After the war Houdry returned to the steel business and eventually became a director of several companies, including an automobile parts manufacturer. As he involved himself increasingly in the partmaker's affairs, his interest in auto racing grew. He attempted to make race cars run faster by experimenting with methods to improve the quality of gasoline. In 1922 he visited the Ford Motor Company plant in Detroit, Michigan, and attended the Indianapolis 500 auto race. Shortly after his return the same year, he married Geneviève Marie Quilleret, with whom he had two children.

Houdry was invited by the French government to develop a way to synthesize petroleum, which was in short supply in France, from bituminous and lignite coal, which the French possessed in abundance. In 1925 he developed a catalyst capable of chemically changing lignite into low-grade crude oil; however, it cost more to make petroleum in this manner than it did to import oil, so the project was officially abandoned.

At the time gasoline was derived from petroleum via thermal cracking, a process in which crude oil is heated until it breaks down into various heavy and light oils, gasoline being one of the latter, and a variety of hydrocarbon gases. Having cracked lignite catalytically, Houdry believed that catalysis could produce the high-quality gasoline he had been seeking, and he gave up his situation at the steel mill to concentrate on this line of research. His faith was rewarded in 1927 when he discovered that a clayey compound of aluminum oxide and silicon dioxide caused low-grade crude oil to break down more completely than did thermal cracking. One of the light oils produced by catalytic cracking was a gasoline with a considerably higher octane rating (the ratio of isooctane, an ingredient that permits an automobile motor to run smoothly because it inhibits engine knock, to heptane, the ingredient that causes engine knock) than could be obtained by thermal cracking. Low-octane fuel had limited the development of engines with higher compression and more power; generally, the production of higher-octane fuels and more powerful engines went hand-in-hand.

Unable to convince any French petroleum refineries to adopt his catalytic process, in 1930 Houdry moved to the United States at the invitation of the Vacuum Oil Company. In 1931 he became founder, president, and director of research of the Houdry Process Corporation (HPC), which he funded by selling a one-third interest to the Socony-Vacuum Corporation that same year and a one-third interest to the Sun Oil Company in 1934. In 1936 HPC began cracking petroleum catalytically at the Socony-Vacuum refinery in Paulsboro, New Jersey, and by the end of the year the plant was producing 2,000 barrels of high-octane gasoline a day. In 1937 HPC converted the gigantic Sun Oil refinery in Marcus Hook, Pennsylvania, to the catalytic process. By 1940 fourteen refineries in the United States belonging to Socony-Vacuum and Sun Oil were refining petroleum via the Houdry process. Their high-octane aviation fuel was an important resource during World War II.

In 1940 Houdry founded France Forever, an American-based organization to support the Free French in their struggle against Nazi occupation. In 1942 he became an American citizen. That same year he developed a catalytic process to change butane, a hydrocarbon gas produced in great quantities during catalytic cracking, into butadiene, the principal constituent of synthetic rubber.

The next year Houdry devoted some of his company's research capabilities to cancer research and in the process became convinced that hydrocarbon pollutants released into the atmosphere by automobiles and factories were largely responsible for the increase in lung cancer in the twentieth century. In 1948 he resigned as president of HPC to conduct further research into the catalytic purification of automobile exhaust, and in 1949 he founded the Oxy-Catalyst Company to address this problem. His most important invention in this connection was the first catalytic converter for greatly reducing harmful emissions from automobile exhaust.

Houdry received a number of awards for his contributions to the petroleum industry, including the Franklin Institute's Potts Medal in 1948, the Society of the Chemical Industry's Perkin Medal in 1959, and the American Chemical Society's Award in Industrial and Engineering Chemistry in 1962. He also received the John Scott Medal of the Philadelphia Board of City Trust. He died in Upper Darby, Pennsylvania.

Houdry, known in chemical and petroleum circles as "Mr. Catalysis," was awarded patents for more than 100 devices and processes. In addition to providing high-octane gasoline for peacetime pursuits, his catalytic processes made available to the United States and its allies during World War II superior supplies of higher-quality fuel and synthetic rubber. By inventing the catalytic converter, he helped to reduce the damaging effects of air pollution from automobile emissions.

• Houdry's papers are located in the Manuscript Division of the Library of Congress. A good biography is David E. Newton, "Eugene Houdry," in *Notable Twentieth-Century Scientists*, ed. by Emily McMurray (1995), pp. 956–57. Obituaries are in the *New York Times*, 19 July 1962, and *Chemical and Engineering News*, 30 July 1962.

CHARLES W. CAREY, JR.

HOUGH, Emerson (28 Jun. 1857–30 Apr. 1923), novelist, was born in Newton, Iowa, the son of Joseph Bond Hough, a farmer, clerk, surveyor, merchant, and schoolteacher, and Elizabeth Hough. The couple were distantly related through their Quaker forebears. After graduating from Newton High School with three classmates in 1875 and teaching one term in a country school, Hough in 1876 entered the State University of Iowa (now the University of Iowa), where he distinguished himself as a student of literature, edited the college newspaper, and graduated in 1880. When his father suggested that he become a lawyer, he reluctantly studied and was admitted to the bar in 1882. He published an article on outdoor life in *Forest and Stream* (17 Aug. 1882) and yearned for a writing career, so he went to White Oaks, a small mining and cattle community in New Mexico Territory, the following spring, letting *American Field* finance his travel in exchange for his sending back essays on the Southwest. With a friend, he halfheartedly practiced law in White Oaks; he also published several sketches in *American Field* (1883–1884) and wrote for the White Oaks weekly newspaper. In 1884 he returned to the Midwest to become a business manager for the *Des Moines Times* in Iowa and then associate editor of the *Sandusky Register* in Ohio.

The next several years were frantic for Hough. He published more sketches in *American Field*, sent humorous stories to the McClure-Phillips publishing syndicate, wrote articles illustrated by a friend on western county and city histories (sold by subscription), and bought a half-interest in the Wichita newspaper that failed because of a dishonest partner. Beginning in 1889 he was the western editor of *Forest and Stream*. Based in Chicago, he could happily travel for information and fish, boat, and hunt as far west as Wyoming and as far south as Texas; he also freelanced for newspapers and syndicates. His well-publicized 1893 skiing and snowshoe trip through Yellowstone Park helped save the buffalo herd there by inspiring a congressional act in 1894 extending federal protection. Although he published a play about the Spanish conquest of the Aztecs in 1889 and a collection of children's stories in 1895, his literary career effectively began only with *The Story of the Cowboy* in 1897. Unsolicited letters from Theodore Roosevelt and Hamlin Garland praising the book encouraged Hough. He married Charlotte Amelia Cheesebro of Chicago that same year (the couple had no children) and turned to novel writing—at night, while continuing full time at *Forest and Stream*. *The Girl at the Halfway House* (1900) was mediocre, but *The Mississippi Bubble* (1902) became a bestseller and launched Hough as a writer of fiction. Later he lamented that his early years were "all wrong" and that his wife was his personal and professional salvation. Hough quit *Forest and Stream* in 1903, edited for *Field and Stream* until 1905, and then turned exclusively to fiction writing.

From 1903 through 1923 Hough produced one, two, or three books—mostly novels—per year (with the exception of 1920) and, in addition, more than two hundred short stories and articles for popular magazines such as *Century*, *Collier's*, *Cosmopolitan*, *Everybody's*, *Frank Leslie's Popular Monthly*, *Harper's Weekly*, *Outing*, and the *Saturday Evening Post*. Obviously, he wrote too fast and merits criticism in other ways as well. *The Way to the West* (1903), about Daniel Boone, Kit Carson, and Davy Crockett, is sloppy; and *The Law of the Land* (1904) is marred by pronouncements demonstrating an animus against African Americans. His *Heart's Desire* (1905), concerning the lost-Eden theme, lost money, although it is now regarded as his most artistic production. In 1905 Hough became ill with typhoid fever and pneumonia. In 1906 he started "In the Open," a *Post* column later titled "Out of Doors." Of his next books, *The Story of the Outlaw* (1907) and *54-40 or Fight* (1909) are noteworthy. To help prepare the former, Hough hired Pat Garrett, who shot Billy the Kid, as a consultant, but he still lost money on the project. The latter, a bellicose historical romance based on the Oregon boundary dispute of 1846, turned a profit. In 1909 Hough and his wife visited Europe, which he trivialized as "little" compared to the Far West. A naturalistic novel, *John Rawn* (1912), with a contemporary setting and featuring a ruthless antihero, failed critically. That same year Hough campaigned for his friend Theodore Roosevelt, the unsuccessful candidate for president on the Bull Moose ticket. He also went on a trip during which he argued with his fellow outdoors men; he quit at Fort Yukon, short of their goal—the Arctic.

When World War I began, American neutrality irked Hough. He published selections of *Post* columns as *Out of Doors* (1915) and *Let Us Go Afield* (1916). *The Magnificent Adventure* (1916), his historical romance about Lewis and Clark, also proved popular. In 1919 Hough was commissioned in the army reserve. He opposed the political and social excesses of the Roaring Twenties. As he grew more reactionary, he thought more about the Old West and eventually produced the novel by which he is best remembered—*The Covered Wagon*, serialized in the *Post* (1 Apr.–27 May 1922) and then published that year in book form. Hough, severely ill in 1922, dictated part of the novel while hospitalized in Denver. Early in 1923 he attended a benefit screening of the epic, standard-setting motion picture made from *The Covered Wagon*; he died a few months later in Evanston, Illinois. *North of 36*, his popular trail-drive novel—Texas to Abilene—appeared posthumously in 1923.

Sufficiently representative of Hough at his best are two books. *Let Us Go Afield* offers ever timely advice to the young to be participants in rugged activities and not mere spectators and to young and old alike to conserve American resources and never be wasteful. *The Covered Wagon* is a formulaic western, narrating the adventures of a wagon train proceeding from Missouri across the western plains to Oregon in 1848. Hough uses the standard recipe: hardships and arguments, historical figures (Jim Bridger and Kit Carson), rivals (one good, one bad) for the hand of the pretty heroine, fights with Indians, danger from prairie fires and swollen rivers, and an old-timers' *ubi sunt* dirge for "the ol' days." News of the discovery of gold in California divides the wagon train. Hough's descriptions of western scenes are fine, but Anglo-Saxon hardihood is overly lauded. Hough continued the tradition of the formulaic western, produced solid if not outstanding nonwestern fiction as well, and was a tireless spokesman early in the long-overdue conservation movement.

• Most of Hough's papers are in the Iowa State Department of History and Archives, Des Moines, and at the University of Iowa. Some of his other correspondence is at the Newberry Library, Chicago; the Knox College library, Galesburg, Ill.; and the University of Michigan, the University of Oregon, and the University of Virginia. Hough's informative autobiography is *Getting a Wrong Start: A Truthful Autobiography* (1915). Lee Alexander Stone, *Emerson Hough: His Place in American Letters* (1925), is an affectionate tribute by a friend. Edwin W. Gaston, Jr., *The Early Novel of the Southwest* (1961), treats Hough's *Heart's Desire* briefly but well. Dorys Crow Grover, "W. H. D. Koerner and Emerson Hough, a Western Collaboration," *Montana: The Magazine of Western History* 29 (Apr. 1979): 2–15, discusses Hough's work with the famous *Saturday Evening Post* illustrator. Delbert E. Wylder, *Emerson Hough* (1981), is a balanced study of unique value, especially for biographical information and commentary on films made from Hough's works. An obituary is in the *New York Times*, 1 May 1923.

ROBERT L. GALE

HOUGH, Franklin Benjamin (22 July 1822–11 June 1885), forester, was born Benjamin Franklin Hough in Martinsburg, New York, the son of Horatio Gates Hough, a physician, and Martha Pitcher. When he was eight years old he discovered a cousin with the same name and reversed his given names, styling himself Franklin B. Hough. His father died when Hough was eight years old. He entered Lowville Academy in 1836. Early in his career, local residents became aware

of his fascination with rocks and minerals. He continued his education at the Black River Literary and Religious Institute at Watertown, New York, and then in 1840 he entered Union College in Schenectady and graduated three years later.

Hough financed his education at Union College by teaching school in the vicinity. After graduation he continued teaching and helped organize the Society for the Acquisition of Useful Knowledge in April 1843. A lack of interest led to the society's demise in September 1848, but it did give the young teacher an opportunity to provide lectures on his growing interests: mineralogy and botany. He also supplied the local press with a large number of articles on subjects as diverse as "Gold in Lewis County" and "Teachers Calling."

With his graduation, Hough left the area to become the principal of Gustavus Academy in Cleveland, Ohio. There he entered the Cleveland Western Reserve Medical College, where he received his M.D. in 1848. While there, he married Maria Eggleston of Champion, New York, in the summer of 1846. They had one child, a daughter, but because of ill health Hough's wife returned with the child to her parents' home in Champion, where she died in June 1848. The child was raised by her maternal grandparents.

In 1849 Hough married Mariah E. Kilham, a schoolteacher in Turin; she had been his student when he taught there. They had four sons and four daughters.

After his graduation from medical school, Hough sold his mineral collection to the Cleveland Western Reserve Medical College. He purchased a house and a medical practice in Somerville, in upstate New York. His continuing botanical interests were reflected in a pamphlet, *A Catalogue of Indigenous, Naturalized and Filicoid Plants of Lewis County, New York*, published in 1846. In Somerville, Hough's practice flourished. Again he continued his habit of writing for the local press as well as presenting lectures on mineralogy and botany. He received no compensation for these efforts, but he did become reasonably well known in the area. He continued the collection of minerals and rocks and continued his study of the flora and fauna of the upstate area. He began corresponding with a number of leading scientists, including Louis Agassiz, Charles Shepard, and Henry Boche. In 1852 he left his medical practice and went to Albany to carry on historical research.

In Albany Hough completed *A History of St. Lawrence and Franklin Counties, New York* (1853) and the following year *A History of Jefferson County, New York*. At the same time he served as an editor for the publisher Joel Munsell. He then became a full-time assistant to the newly elected secretary of state, Joel Headley. That led to his selection as the superintendent of the New York State Census in 1855. He was the first to include agricultural and industrial records in the state census. His use of statistics followed the pattern set in England by Sir William Wilde in 1851.

In Albany Hough became a busy civil servant; at the request of the state, he was involved in and published a number of studies concerning Indian treaties, treasury records, educational affairs for the Board of Regents, and meteorological records. He also created the first civil list. As usual, he continued his lectures, this time at the Albany Institute. In 1860 he published his *History of Lewis County, New York*.

In 1861, tiring of life in Albany, Hough and his growing family left the city and built a house in Lowville. The outbreak of the American Civil War, however, brought him back first as a sanitary inspector for the privately run U.S. Sanitary Commission, then as a surgeon for the Ninety-seventh New York Regiment. He then was transferred to the Bureau of Military Statistics where he remained for fourteen months. He left the army in 1864 and accepted the superintendency of the New York State Census in 1865. He then became involved in the preparations for the New York State Constitutional Convention of 1867. He became superintendent of the census in Washington, D.C., in 1867 and then sought and was appointed director of the U.S. census in 1870.

Hough's involvement as superintendent of the census of 1870 and his use of statistical data in the census exercises of 1856, 1865, and 1867 prepared him to analyze agricultural data for changes, and he began his role as protector of the forests. He noticed that the national production of lumber was increasing and that the lumber industry was migrating westward. He also found a noticeable decline in the value of lumber cut in New York State from $13 million in 1860 to $9 million in 1870. He realized that what had happened in New York would occur elsewhere. In 1872 he was appointed a member of the committee to establish a state forest park in the Adirondack Mountains.

In 1873 Hough presented a paper at a convention of the American Association for the Advancement of Science in Portland, Maine. In his paper, published as *Duty of Governments in the Preservation of Forests*, he called attention to the deforestation that had occurred in other areas of the world, notably in the Mediterranean and Middle Eastern countries. He called on agricultural societies and horticultural groups to alert landowners and others to the need to preserve forest resources. He embraced the idea of schools of forestry and outlined legislation that could help protect forests. He recommended practices that states could take to encourage better forest use. He urged the association to bring this problem to the attention of state and local governments.

The association then appointed Hough and a Harvard botanist, George B. Emerson, to prepare a petition for Congress on the subject of forest protection, especially in the territories. Both men went to Washington, D.C., in February 1874 to gain support for their plan and petition. They met and spoke with a number of people, including the agriculture commissioner, Frederick Watts, and President Ulysses S. Grant. Grant forwarded their report to Congress on 19 February 1874. But the Grant scandals and the impact of the panic of 1873 did not augur well for their plea. Emerson had to return to Boston, and Hough was left to carry on the campaign.

Hough found a kindred spirit in Representative Mark Hill Dunnell of Minnesota, who had been a teacher and school superintendent in Maine before his move to Minnesota in 1865. Their ages were similar, and Dunnell clearly recognized the validity of Hough's warnings when he learned what had happened in Maine and recognized what was then taking place in Minnesota. With Dunnell's help in the House Public Land Committee, it seemed that effective legislation might be enacted, but the bill died in committee.

Hough was not deterred. He then began a study on how other nations handled deforestation. Encouraged by Professor Emerson, Hough presented a series of lectures on forestry at the Lowell Institute of Boston. Material from the lectures was published in 1875 and stressed the health benefits of forest preservation.

Hough kept in touch with Dunnell, who in 1876 reintroduced the forestry bill. Hough went to Washington to testify for the measure before the Public Lands Committee. The bill again died in committee, but Dunnell was able to add a rider to the Department of Agriculture appropriation bill authorizing $2,000 for a forest study. When this passed, Agriculture had the funds to appoint a forestry agent to handle the forest study, and Hough received the appointment. He had just published a report for the state of New York, *On the Preservation of Forests and the Planting of Timber*. He completed his first report in December 1877.

In 1881 Congress increased his funding, which enabled him to travel to Europe to study the European system of forest preservation. The German system he found especially impressive. Between 1881 and 1883 he completed his second and third forestry reports, which gained him a wide audience among forestry experts in Europe. He was commended for his work by the American Association of the Geographical Congress, which met in Venice. In addition, the Prussian forestry expert Bernhard Fernow enthusiastically endorsed Hough's work.

In 1883 Nathaniel H. Egleston, a Congregational minister from Massachusetts, was appointed chief of the division of forestry. Hough remained as forestry agent. Undaunted, he drafted a fourth federal report and continued to lecture on the importance of forest preservation. In 1884 he helped the state of New York establish a commission to study the need for a forest reserve. He continued his work in Albany but became ill. Though a competent physician, he ignored his own symptoms. A cold led to lung inflammation, then pneumonia, and finally heart complications. He left Albany and returned to Lowville, where he died.

Hough had many accomplishments to his credit, but he was best known as the father of American forestry. He was a practical reformer. He understood the need to educate the public and even the lumber industry itself to the needs of reforestation. Never strident, he was a gentle man and pleasant to be with. He had a questing, questioning mind and boundless energy, coupled with a firm sense of public duty, while always stressing the positive. In his report, completed by Verplanck Colvin for the Commission on State Parks, he emphasized the necessity of returning the watershed forests to conserve the state's water resources.

• Some of Hough's papers are in the Hough Family Collection at the Lewis County Historical Society Museum in Lyons, N.Y. A genealogical history of the family plus some Hough letters are in Hough Family Collection of the Regional History Collection at the Cornell University Library in Ithaca, N.Y. The William Pierrepont White Collection, also in the Regional History Collection at Cornell, contains a number of Hough's letters. The Benjamin Franklin Hough Papers in the Burton Historical Collection at the Detroit Public Library are mainly manuscripts that deal with a proposed study of higher education. A partial list of Hough's written publications are in the *National Union Catalog Pre-1956 Imprints* (1973) at the Library of Congress.

Edna Jacobsen completed only a short piece before her death, "Franklin B. Hough: A Pioneer in Scientific Forestry in America," *New York History* 15 (1934): 311–25. A short biographical study is Edith Pelcher, "Biography of Franklin B. Hough," in *With Hand and Heart: The Courtship Letters of Franklin B. Hough and Mariah Kilham, January through May, 1849,* ed. Vivian G. Smith (1993). Other short studies are Frank J. Harmon, "Remembering Franklin B. Hough," *American Forest* 83 (1977): 34–37, 52–54; C. E. Randall, "Hough, Man of Approved Attainments," *American Forest* 67 (1961): 10–11, 41; and Ralph S. Hosmer, "Franklin B. Hough: Father of American Forestry," *North Country Life* 6 (1952): 16–20. Additional information on Hough is in Bernhard E. Fernow, *A Brief History of Forestry* (1911), and John A. Haddock, *History of Jefferson County, New York from 1793–1894* (1894).

THOMAS J. CURRAN

HOUGH, George Washington (24 Oct. 1836–1 Jan. 1909), astronomer, was born at Tribes Hill, Montgomery County, New York, the son of William Hough and Magdalene Selmser. His father, described as "a man of pronounced mechanical ability," was probably a farmer and implement repairman. George Hough attended school near his home in Waterloc and went on to the Seneca Falls Academy, where he did excellent work in mathematics. He then entered Union College in Albany, New York, where he received an A.M. in 1856. Hough was principal of a public school in Dubuque, Iowa, for two years; he then spent one year as a graduate student in mathematics and science at Harvard. In 1859 he became assistant astronomer at the Cincinnati Observatory under Ormsby M. Mitchel, its director.

A year later Mitchel accepted the directorship of Dudley Observatory in Albany, and Hough went there as his assistant. When the Civil War broke out, Mitchel, a West Point graduate, returned to the colors, leaving Hough in charge of Dudley Observatory. In 1862 Mitchel, a general commanding the Union Army troops campaigning along the South Carolina coast, was stricken with yellow fever and died; Hough remained acting director of the observatory until 1865, when its trustees officially elected him director. From 1862 to 1874 he divided his efforts between astronomical and meteorological research. With the transit circle and eleven-inch telescope of the observatory, neither particularly well-made, Hough measured the positions of stars. He invented and developed various meteorological instruments, including a recording and printing barometer, a "meteorograph" combining a barometer and wet- and dry-bulb thermometers, and an anemometer (for measuring wind direction and speed), all using electrical circuits to collect and record the data automatically at regular intervals. At the solar eclipse of 7 August 1869 he and Lewis Swift confirmed the briefly-appearing phenomenon known as "Baily's beads" and timed its duration accurately with a recording chronograph of Hough's design. Their measurement helped to establish that this phenomenon occurs as the last rays of the sun, reaching the earth between mountains at the edge of the moon's horizon, are cut off at the instant of totality.

In 1870 Hough married Emma C. Shear of Albany; they had two children. In 1873, with the finances of Dudley Observatory at low ebb, its trustees agreed to amalgamate it into Union University and suspended all astronomical research to build up the endowment. Hough thus lost his position in 1874 and had to enter the world of business, probably as an engineer.

Sometime between 1874 and 1878 Hough moved to Chicago; in 1879 he was appointed director of Dearborn Observatory in that city, and professor of astronomy at the old Chicago University, a Baptist institution which had begun operations in 1858. The observatory and the university were in poor financial condition and began paying Hough a salary only in 1881. Dearborn Observatory had been founded under the auspices of the Chicago Astronomical Society, and its telescope, an 18½-inch refractor built by Alvan Clark & Sons, had been the largest in the world when it was mounted in 1866. It was an excellent instrument, and with it Hough observed double stars and began a regular program of visual observations of the planets, concentrating on Jupiter. He invented an observing chair, sliding on inclined ways mounted on a wooden, wheeled structure, and counterbalanced so that the astronomer could easily raise, lower, and move it in the dark to keep himself in a comfortable position at the eyepiece of a long-focus telescope, no matter where it was pointed. It was extremely practical and was soon adopted at observatories everywhere.

Chicago University's land and buildings, including the observatory dome, were heavily mortgaged, and in 1886 it went bankrupt and ceased to exist as an educational institution. However, the telescope and other instruments of Dearborn Observatory were ruled to be the property of the Chicago Astronomical Society, which in 1887 handed them over to Northwestern University. A new Dearborn Observatory, for which Hough designed many features of the dome, was built on the Northwestern campus in Evanston, just north of Chicago. He planned and supervised the move and started observing with the telescope there in 1889. Hough remained observatory director and also became professor of astronomy at Northwestern. There he continued the program of visual observations of the planet Jupiter he had begun in 1879, measuring the positions of the spots, belts, and other visible features on its disk. Within a few years he had seen that, contrary to earlier belief, these are long-lived structures. He mapped the ways in which they formed, developed, and decayed as they were carried around by Jupiter's rapid rotation. Hough interpreted these features as phenomena in the deep atmosphere (which he thought of as semiliquid) of the giant planet, affected by strong winds, rotation, and the general circulation driven by solar heating. He became an acknowledged world expert on Jupiter. The Royal Astronomical Society in London elected him a foreign associate (honorary member) in 1903.

As the leading professional astronomer in the Chicago area, Hough was named president of the World Congress on Astronomy and Astrophysics, one of the hundred world congresses held in connection with the 1893 World Columbian Exposition, more commonly known as the World's Fair. Young George Ellery Hale, later the greatest organizer and fundraiser in American science, was the secretary who tirelessly persuaded leading astronomers and astrophysicists from all over Europe and America to take part in the first world astronomy meeting held in the United States; the dignified, respected, grandfatherly Hough presided over it. He had seen two observatories closed down for financial reasons but had continued his astronomical research and had helped to bring a third one into existence. Hough died in Evanston, active up to the end as director, observer, and professor.

• Of Hough's many publications on his research, the most important are "Jovian Phenomena," *Astrophysical Journal* 6 (1897): 443–6; "Observations of the Planet Jupiter, Made at the Dearborn Observatory," *Monthly Notices of the Royal Astronomical Society* 60 (1900): 546–65; "On the Physical Constitution of the Planet Jupiter," *Popular Astronomy* 11 (1903): 63–74; and "Our Present Knowledge of the Condition of the Surface of Jupiter," *Popular Astronomy* 13 (1905): 19–30. He described the observing chair he invented in "Observing Seat for Equatorial," *Sidereal Messenger* 1 (1883): 23–26. The most accessible published account of his life and career is an adulatory obituary by his son, George J. Hough, "George Washington Hough," *Popular Astronomy* 17 (1909): 197–200, also published in *Science* 29 (1909): 690–93, but some of the dates and statements in it are incorrect. More factual accounts of Hough's work at Dudley and Dearborn observatories, respectively, are in Benjamin Boss, *History of the Dudley Observatory 1852–1956* (1968), and Philip Fox, "General Account of the Dearborn Observatory," *Annals of the Dearborn Observatory* 1 (1915): 1–20. An obituary is in the *New York Times*, 3 Jan. 1909.

DONALD E. OSTERBROCK

HOUGH, Henry Beetle (8 Nov. 1896–6 June 1985), newspaper editor and author, was born in New Bedford, Massachusetts, the son of George Anthony Hough, Sr., a newspaper editor, and Abby Louise Beetle, formerly a nurse. He earned a bachelor of literature degree in 1918 at the Columbia University

School of Journalism, where he was active in liberal causes and, with Minna Lewinson, won a Pulitzer Prize for the best "History of the Services Rendered to the Public by the Press in 1917." He served in the Office of Naval Intelligence in Washington, D.C., and worked briefly in public relations with the Institute of American Meat Packers in Chicago. In 1920 he married Elizabeth Wilson Bowie, whom he had met at Columbia; they had no children. His father, managing editor of the *New Bedford Evening Standard*, gave the couple the *Vineyard Gazette* as a wedding present.

Hough had ancestral roots on Martha's Vineyard, his mother the daughter of a sea captain, his paternal grandfather a doctor in Holmes Hole (Vineyard Haven) before moving to New Bedford. From early childhood Hough had been making trips to his family's North Tisbury home "Fish Hook." Except for a brief detour at Western Electric Company in New York City, he and Betty devoted their lives to the island newspaper. After his wife died in 1965, Henry continued to own and publish the *Gazette* until 1968, when he sold it to James and Sally Reston, though he still served as editor almost until his death. In 1979 he married Edith Sands Graham Blake, a *Gazette* reporter; they had no children. Hough received numerous honorary degrees and awards for excellence in journalism and in conservation.

Hough's first book, *Country Editor* (1940; rev. ed. 1996), quickly became a classic of its genre. The basic theme was that "small things" are "mature, complete specimens" unappreciated in an age of "bigness" (pp. 2–3). Forces of centralization and development, he thought, have overwhelmed the innocence of earlier generations, with big advertising stifling journalistic diversity. A liberal, he favored government help for the oppressed, but he saw greatest hope in "a striving toward greater dignity and integrity for the individual and his spirit" (p. 272). Though he held that the most precious elements of life cannot be captured by journalism, his depiction of work on a human scale, with a sense of community and in tune with the rhythms of nature, seemed the very image of a "country editor." But Hough never sentimentalized such a life. *Country Editor* recounts endless, necessary accommodations with production machinery. And as he wrote in *Once More the Thunderer* (1950), a sequel to *Country Editor*, he and Betty sometimes "hated" the *Gazette* for inflicting "the fatigue, the anxious responsibility . . . and the long hours" (p. 140). A country weekly, Hough explained in his memoir *Mostly on Martha's Vineyard* (1975), was neither a forum to crusade for international issues, nor a sanctuary: "The *Gazette* had Island affairs to look after, but always with a sense of the world outside and what the world was doing" (p. 273). Indeed, Hough commented on social matters from the snobbery of summer residents to anti-Semitism and racism, from phone rates to the threat of McCarthyism.

Hough's writings include short stories and essays in regional and national magazines on topics ranging from history to roses; introductions to books on the

Vineyard, whaling, and cooking; and eight novels with mainly local or regional themes: *That Lofty Sky* (1941), *All Things Are Yours* (1942), *Roosters Crow in Town* (1945), *Long Anchorage* (1947), *The New England Story* (1958), *Lament for a City* (1960), *The Port* (1963), and *The Road* (1970). Active in the Dukes County (now Martha's Vineyard) Historical Society, he wrote *Martha's Vineyard, Summer Resort 1835–1935* (1936, repr. 1966); *Wamsutta of New Bedford, 1846–1946: A Story of New England Enterprise* (1946); *Whaling Wives* (1953), written with Emma Mayhew Whiting; and *Far Out the Coils* (1985), a personal history of Vineyard culture.

His seafaring heritage inspired two books for young readers, *Great Days of Whaling* (1958) and *Melville in the South Pacific* (1960), and his particular admiration for Henry D. Thoreau led to a popular biography, *Thoreau of Walden: The Man and His Eventful Life* (1956). Hough, who in his own works alludes frequently to Thoreau and who served as president of the Thoreau Society (1968–1969), resembles Thoreau in his crisp style, ironic tone, and commitment to the integrity of words, as well as in his love of the seasons and keen observation of nature, particularly his sense that angle of perception makes all the difference. Like Thoreau's, Hough's distaste for travel was balanced by his dedication to walking, usually with one of his beloved collies, and his understanding of life derived from attention to all things local—nature, history, daily events, stories, characters.

Author John Hersey observed in a memorial tribute that Hough's main theme, like Thoreau's, was the "essentially moral choice" of "quality of life" (*Vineyard Gazette*, 7 June 1985). Choosing and defending that quality of life came increasingly to mean preservation and land conservation. In 1959 the Houghs obtained a charter for the Sheriff's Meadow Foundation and presented the foundation with a gift of a pond and land purchased with earnings from his books. Hough's last book, *Far Out the Coils*, deromanticizes whaling (the "unspeakable horror and cruelty of killing whales" [p. 89]) and foresees in the corruption of Waikiki the destiny of the Vineyard. What had always been a stubborn resistance to modern forces of conformity, centralization, and mass communication focused in later years on sometimes bitter battles with rapacious developers. *Soundings at Sea Level* (1980) chronicles struggles to protect fragile wetlands and to keep the McDonald's restaurant franchise off the island. The damages of unchecked growth and pollution combine with a pressing awareness of mortality to lend an elegaic tone to much of Hough's later writing.

Even with this growing sense that a way of life is passing, some of Hough's best writing weaves a sense of personal loss with an unyielding appreciation of the natural forces that had always defined the Vineyard. In *To the Harbor Light* (1976), a meditation on aging as he approached seventy-nine, Hough juxtaposes shrewd insights into the effects of change with wry self-appraisal. In modern development, "coyness and artifice take the place of inner reality," "but I am also

old and cranky. Which is the greater truth makes no difference" (p. 27). He insists on treating language and aging honestly but is still open to surprise—a firefly lighting on his collie is an epiphany of nature's unhurried example—and his rich texture of time and memory evokes haunting intimations of the past in the present. Hough's essays accompanying photographs by Alison Shaw in *Remembrance and Light* (1984) remind us that we are "guests" in nature, our hurry obscuring the eternity in the here and now. Martha's Vineyard here is a "destination" not simply as a summer haven but as a symbol of renewal and self-knowledge to which Hough, as in all his writings, kept returning. After Hough's death in Edgartown, Massachusetts, television news anchor Walter Cronkite called him "the heart and soul of our Island" (*Vineyard Gazette*, 7 June 1985).

• Hough's papers are deposited in the Butler Library archives at Columbia University. Records relating to the *Vineyard Gazette* are in the library at the newspaper office in Edgartown, Mass. The library of the Martha's Vineyard Historical Society has books and articles by Hough as well as an extensive collection of clippings and memorabilia. Other books by Hough include *An Alcoholic to His Sons, as Told to Henry Beetle Hough* (1954) and four collections: *Singing in the Morning and Other Essays about Martha's Vineyard* (1951); *Vineyard Gazette Reader* (1967); *Martha's Vineyard* (1970), with photographs by Alfred Eisenstaedt; and *Tuesday Will Be Different: Letters from Sheriff's Lane* (1971). A profile by Joseph Chase Allen, a *Gazette* staff writer, appears in *Thoreau Society Bulletin*, no. 106 (Winter 1969): 5; Hough's Thoreau Society presidential address, "Thoreau in Today's Sun," is reprinted from the *Concord Journal* in *Thoreau Society Bulletin*, no. 108 (Summer 1969): 2–4. Obituaries are in the *Vineyard Gazette*, 7 June 1985, which also includes many editorial and guest tributes, and the *New York Times*, 7 June 1985.

WESLEY T. MOTT

HOUGH, Walter (23 Apr. 1859–20 Sept. 1935), ethnologist and museologist, was born in Morgantown, West Virginia, the son of Lycurgus S. Hough, an attorney, and Anna Fairchild. He was trained in chemistry and geology at West Virginia University (B.A., 1883; M.A., 1894; and Ph.D., 1894).

Hough taught school at Alton, Illinois, from 1883 to 1885 and then accepted an appointment as copyist in the Division of Ethnology of the Smithsonian Institution U.S. National Museum. In 1887 he became an aid and, in 1894, an assistant curator there. In 1908 he became acting curator of ethnology and acting head curator of the U.S. National Museum's Department of Anthropology. In 1910 he was appointed the museum's curator of ethnology, and in 1923 he became the head curator while retaining the position of curator of ethnology.

Hough's main mentor in anthropology was his predecessor as head curator, Otis T. Mason. In certain respects the two men's careers are similar. Like Mason, Hough followed the evolutionary theory of culture accepted at the Smithsonian but beginning to be questioned by others in ethnology. During his tenure, the comparative exhibits typical of evolutionary museology continued to appear in Smithsonian exhibit halls alongside dioramas and other exhibits that were culture-specific.

Hough spent much of his time directly occupied with cataloging and caring for the ethnological specimens that entered the museum and with preparing exhibits from the collections. Both types of work required knowledge of ethnological literature, correspondence with professional curators and amateurs around the world, and experimentation to find how things were made and how they worked. Out of such activities came many of Hough's publications, generally descriptive articles that sometimes support a belief in the general progressive nature of man's inventiveness; these articles were published by the *American Anthropologist* and by the U.S. National Museum, among other sources.

Hough's tenure coincided with a period during which the Smithsonian enlarged its holdings as a result of acquisitions from several international expositions, American political ventures abroad, and the entrance of American anthropologists into many distant lands abroad. Thus Hough's research and writings concern cultures of such far-flung regions as Asia, Africa, North and South America, and Oceania. The subjects he dealt with were varied and included such matters as the punishment of wrongdoers, swords, armor, balances, blowguns, social organization, dolls, and beverages.

Hough's efforts were not, however, confined to the museum or to his daily labors. He worked on behalf of several international expositions and had an especially important role in the Columbian Historical Exposition in Madrid, Spain, in 1893. There Hough installed the U.S. government exhibit, for which he published a catalog. For his work, the Spanish Queen Regent made him a Knight of the Royal Order of Isabella the Catholic.

Hough also undertook work in the field. In 1896 he joined Jesse Walter Fewkes in the American Southwest. During the following year, he married Jennie Myrtle Zuck, of Holbrook, Arizona; they had three children. In 1899 he joined J. N. Rose on an ethnobotanical expedition to Mexico. Thereafter, his field work was devoted to his own interests in the Southwest. Between 1901 and 1905 he participated in the so-called Gates-Museum expeditions, sponsored by Peter Goddard Gates, of Pasadena, California, and concentrated on ethnology and archeology in New Mexico and Arizona.

Hough developed a special interest in man's use of fire and lighting. For this work he compiled data about artifacts already in the Smithsonian collections and others he had added, analyzed items and uses described in literature, and made discoveries through contacts with other museum curators. The work led to several publications and exhibits in the U.S. National Museum.

Hough was a founding member of the American Anthropological Association and served as its president in 1924. He was also president of the Anthropo-

logical Society of Washington. Hough died in Washington, D.C.

In his own day, Hough was known as an extremely devoted worker and a kind and patient administrator. He also enjoyed a degree of fame, mainly because the position he occupied still carried considerable prestige and because some of his interests caught the public fancy. However, by the time Hough came into his own, the driving forces of ethnology had passed from museums to the universities, and the study of material culture had passed into questioned respectability for the serious ethnologist. Thus, it is not surprising that Hough, a man of modest ability to begin with, has been largely forgotten by anthropologists.

• Hough's research papers are in the Smithsonian Institution National Anthropological Archives. Most of his administrative material is in the Smithsonian Institution Archives. Much of his research and administrative work are described in the *Annual Report of the Smithsonian Institution*. A brief sketch of his life and a bibliography are provided in Neil M. Judd's obituary in the *American Anthropologist* 38 (1936): 471–81.

JAMES R. GLENN

HOUGHTON, Alanson Bigelow (10 Oct. 1863–16 Sept. 1941), congressman, diplomat, and manufacturer, was born in Cambridge, Massachusetts, the son of Amory Houghton, a glass manufacturer, and Ellen Ann Bigelow. After operating a glass factory in Cambridge, Massachusetts, his grandfather, Amory Houghton, Sr., and his father operated the Brooklyn Flint Glass Company in New York (1864–1868). The company's operations were then transferred to Corning, New York, and the company was renamed Corning Flint Glass Company; it was incorporated as the Corning Glass Works in 1875. After early education in Corning and St. Paul's School in Concord, New Hampshire, Alanson Houghton graduated magna cum laude from Harvard College with an A.B. in 1886. He undertook graduate study at the Universities of Göttingen, Berlin, and Paris, with a focus on political economy. Before 1890 he also published articles on Italian finance in the *Quarterly Journal of Economics* (Jan. and Apr. 1889) and did background research for James Bryce, who was completing *The American Commonwealth* (1888). Houghton returned to Corning to learn the family business when his father became ill in 1889. In 1891 he married Adelaide Louise Wellington; they had five children.

Houghton had three careers. At Corning Glass Works, he started as a shipping clerk, became second vice president for sales in 1903, president in 1910, and chairman of the board in 1918. As a result of his leadership and emphasis on research and development, Corning Glass Works became a major industry during World War I and in the 1920s, developing railroad signal glass in one of the nation's first research labs in industry. He became a generous contributor to local education, the Episcopal church, and the Republican party.

Handsome and well respected within his party and other circles, Houghton represented the thirty-seventh District of New York from 1919 to 1922 in the House of Representatives, where he served on the Foreign Affairs and Ways and Means committees. In 1922 President Warren G. Harding appointed him the first postwar U.S. ambassador to Germany, a position that offered new opportunities for influence. In Berlin Houghton revealed pro-German attitudes and interacted often with the German people as they struggled to adapt to peace, democracy, and economic pressures caused by war reparations and inflation. He exhibited a more conciliatory viewpoint on reparations as France struck a hard line. Since he had at first planned on a scholarly career, his European education, fluency in German, and interest in economic problems prepared him for his diplomatic career in Weimar Germany. However, he was disappointed in his failure to prevent the 1923 Ruhr crisis or to secure U.S. and French support for a peace and security plan, offered at his urging by Germany's chancellor Wilhelm Cuno. Houghton advocated that the major nations of Europe should agree on a fifty-year peace pledge involving disarmament and popular referenda on war declarations. He also advocated a war debts–reparations settlement as a first step toward European recovery and hoped the United States would serve as "trustee" in these arrangements. Although such a comprehensive plan met with U.S. disfavor, he did succeed in helping to persuade the Weimar government to accept the more limited Dawes Plan, which provided private bank credits for Germany.

In 1925 President Calvin Coolidge appointed Houghton ambassador to Great Britain, where he fared better. He worked diligently for an understanding with Great Britain and for a broad peace program for Europe. Although Houghton remained an outspoken diplomat, he was far less so than his earlier predecessor, Ambassador George Harvey. Houghton offered background assistance on behalf of the Locarno agreement of 1925 by pressuring both France and Germany into a rapprochement on European security. Nevertheless, he believed this peace pact was incomplete without his peace by referendum plan. Addressing Harvard graduates in 1927 and in Senate campaign speeches into the thirties, he focused national and international attention on the war referendum idea and expressed his continuing hopes for world peace. In 1928 he failed to win election to the U.S. Senate, and he resigned his diplomatic post the next year, returning to his business, scholarly, and religious interests.

Houghton spent the years following his resignation as ambassador at Corning and in trying to improve the Republican party image and prospects in 1931–1932. He was a trustee and treasurer of the Carnegie Endowment for International Peace, a trustee of the Brookings Institution, and, in 1934, chairman of the board of directors of the Princeton University Institute for Advanced Study. He continued to speak for the war referendum idea at several universities, and he became president of the Academy of Political Science. In 1932

he attended a Paris disarmament conference of religious and peace groups prior to the 1932 Geneva Disarmament Conference. Houghton witnessed both the unsuccessful attempt by Representative Louis L. Ludlow (D.-Ind.) to secure the war referendum amendment to the U.S. Constitution (1935–1941) and the outbreak of the European war he had predicted and had tried to prevent. He died at his summer home in South Dartmouth, Massachusetts.

• Houghton's papers remain in the possession of the family in Corning, N.Y. His official diplomatic correspondence and other papers are in the State Department's decimal files in the National Archives and in relevant volumes for the 1920s in the department's *Papers Relating to the Foreign Relations of the United States* series. An early biographical account is in Beckles Willson, *America's Ambassadors to England* (1928). The most thorough and scholarly treatments of Houghton include Kenneth Paul Jones, "Alanson B. Houghton and the Ruhr Crisis: The Diplomacy of Power and Morality," in *U.S. Diplomats in Europe 1919–1941* (1981), and Ernest C. Bolt, Jr., *Ballots before Bullets: The War Referendum Approach to Peace in America, 1914–1941*, chap. 6 (1977). See also Sander A. Diamond, "Ein Amerikaner in Berlin: Aus den Papieren des Botschafters Alanson B. Houghton, 1922–1925," *Vierteljahrshefte für Zeitgeschichte* 27 (July 1979): 431–70; and Hermann J. Rupieper, "Alanson B. Houghton: An American Ambassador in Germany, 1922–1925," *International History Review* 1 (Oct. 1979): 490–508. An obituary is in the *New York Times*, 16 Sept. 1941.

ERNEST C. BOLT, JR.

HOUGHTON, Amory (27 July 1899–21 Feb. 1981), business executive, was born in Corning, New York, the son of Alanson Bigelow Houghton, a glassworks manager, and Adelaide Louise Wellington. After he graduated from Harvard University in 1921, Houghton married Laura DeKay Richardson of Providence, Rhode Island, with whom he had five children. In the year of his marriage, Houghton became a fourth-generation glassmaker, joining the staff of his family's firm, Corning Glass Works.

Houghton inherited a family tradition of glassmaking rooted in flexible production and a loosely defined canon of "science." Houghton's great-grandfather, the first Amory Houghton, founded the glassworking dynasty by operating a series of factories in Somerville, Massachusetts, and Brooklyn, New York, starting in 1851. In 1868 the patriarch and his sons, anxious to free themselves of union labor, moved to Corning in upstate New York, where citizens were seeking industrial development. After a series of failures, Corning Glass Works passed into the hands of Amory Houghton, Jr., and his brother, Charles F. Houghton, who built a portfolio of clients among the nation's railroads and electrical manufacturers. While contemporaries clung to rule-of-thumb methods, the Houghtons experimented with new batch formulas and product designs, consulting with research scientists on a job-by-job basis to establish important university ties. The next generation, Alanson B. and Arthur A. Houghton, continued to pursue a mixed-output product strategy and added professional scientists to their staff, diversifying into consumer, automobile, and laboratory markets after the development of thermally and mechanically stable glasses—including Pyrex-brand glassware—by factory scientists before World War I.

Following family custom, Houghton spent his early career at Corning Glass Works in a series of hands-on jobs in manufacturing and sales before assuming executive positions. Throughout the 1920s, Houghton worked under the company's attorney-turned-president, Alexander D. Falck, a creative manager who pioneered joint ventures, widely licensed the firm's patents, nurtured the invention of continuous-flow glassmaking equipment, and strengthened the company's commitment to science. When elected president in 1930, Houghton assumed leadership of a sound firm that fused batch and quantity production methods to make a spectrum of products for diverse markets, from household to electrical glassware.

Houghton's tenure as president coincided with the Great Depression and the early years of World War II, which constituted an era of expansion and modernization for Corning. The glassworks was the world's largest manufacturer of envelopes and filament tubing for light bulbs, and making huge quantities of products for electrical manufacturers kept the firm in the black during the depression. Depending on this lucrative business for profits, Houghton built on the traditions pioneered by his forebears to make Corning a world leader in glassmaking science while fostering the development of still more automatic manufacturing processes. The firm's research-based accomplishments in high-temperature glasses—borosilicate, aluminosilicate, and silica glasses—convinced Houghton that laboratory work would yield knowledge essential to successful product and process innovation. He called his investment in research "patient money." During the late 1930s he opened a large research and development facility staffed by professional scientists and modeled after laboratories in leading science-based industries. Symbolic of Houghton's commitment to science at large, Corning cast the world's largest telescope mirror from Pyrex-brand glassware—the 200-inch blank for the Mount Palomar telescope—in 1934.

As president, Houghton also broadened Corning's portfolio of equity ventures to increase the firm's share of markets for "high-technology" products. In 1937 Houghton formed the Pittsburgh Corning Corporation with the Pittsburgh Plate Glass Company to make and sell architectural blocks, and in 1938 he created the Owens Corning Fiberglass Corporation with the Owens-Illinois Glass Company for the production and distribution of fiberglass products. In 1943 Corning entered a joint venture with the Dow Chemical Company, the Dow Corning Corporation, to develop silicones created under Houghton's direction in the early 1930s. In these joint ventures Corning provided technical know-how, while partners contributed marketing expertise. These equity ventures were models for similar endeavors developed by subsequent generations of managers at Corning.

During World War II Houghton undertook a series of government appointments, acting as a liaison between American manufacturers and federal agencies. As a "dollar-a-year man," Houghton held executive positions in the Office of Production Management and the War Production Board. Houghton's wartime career was short-lived, for he withdrew from government service in the light of publicity surrounding an antitrust suit against the Hartford-Empire Company, a manufacturer of glassmaking equipment partially owned by his family. From 1943 to 1945 Houghton returned to war work when President Franklin D. Roosevelt appointed him deputy chief of the U.S. Mission for Economic Affairs in London; from this position, Houghton coordinated shipments of American matériel to Great Britain and Allied fronts. Years of executive experience combined with government service groomed Houghton for diplomacy, and he was U.S. ambassador to France from 1957 to 1961.

During Houghton's first fifty years at Corning, the firm witnessed tremendous growth from a two-factory operation with 2,500 employees in 1921 to a seventy-plant operation with more than 25,000 employees throughout the world in 1971. Houghton's executive accomplishments include expansion of Corning's research and development facilities, the founding of important joint ventures, the broadening of overseas interests, and key product innovations, from fiberglass to silicones. Houghton served Corning Glass Works as a director (1928–1941), executive vice president (1928–1930), president (1930–1941), chairman of the board (1941–1961), chairman of the executive committee (1961–1964), honorary chairman (1964–1971), and chairman emeritus (1971–1981). After his retirement as president, he continued to influence decision making at Corning through a forceful personality that shaped the ideas and actions of family members under his tutelage. His accomplishments as chairman included the construction of Corning Glass Center, an educational center devoted to the science and technology of glassmaking, and the founding of the Corning Museum of Glass, an institution dedicated to collecting and preserving historical glass artifacts. His many philanthropic interests included the Boy Scouts of America, while his belief in higher education materialized as gifts to numerous institutions, from Corning Community College to Harvard University. Houghton died in Charleston, South Carolina.

• The main repository for primary sources relating to Houghton is the Department of Archives and Records Management, Corning Incorporated, Corning, N.Y. Corning's extensive holdings include business records and family papers that illuminate the life and work of members of the Houghton family. For the firm's operations from 1868 to 1965 with reference to early research activities and consumer products, see Regina Lee Blaszczyk, "Imagining Consumers: Manufacturers and Markets in Ceramics and Glass, 1865–1965" (Ph.D. diss., Univ. of Delaware, 1995).

REGINA LEE BLASZCZYK

HOUGHTON, Arthur Amory, Jr. (12 Dec. 1906–3 Apr. 1990), glassworks company executive, was born in Corning, New York, the son of Arthur Amory Houghton, a glassworks company executive, and Mabel Hollister. Houghton attended St. Paul's School (1920–1925) and graduated from Harvard University in 1929. He was married four times and had three children. Houghton married his first wife, Jane Olmstead, in 1929. He married Ellen Crenshaw in 1939. His third wife was Elizabeth Douglass McCall, whom he married in 1944. These three marriages ended in divorce. He died in Venice, Florida, survived by Nina Rodale, whom he had married in 1973.

Houghton joined his family's Corning Glass Works firm in 1929. His great-grandfather founded the firm in 1851 and moved its operations from Brooklyn to Corning in 1868. Houghton was in the treasurer's department in 1929–1930, assistant to the president in 1930–1932, vice president in 1935–1942, and a director of the company for more than fifty years until his death. However, he was better known as chief executive of Steuben Glassworks, of which he was president from 1933 to 1972 and chairman from 1972 to 1978.

Frederick Carder founded Steuben Glass in 1903 in Corning; it became a part of Corning Glass Works in 1918. Carder was a talented, self-taught technician, artist, and craftsman. The division's weakness, despite Carder's genius, seems to have been its indefinable style of glassmaking; it produced many different kinds of glass and marketed haphazardly. Corning Glass Works considered liquidating the Steuben Division in 1933 because of poor profits. But Houghton, the youngest member of the board, asked if he might be given control of the division. The board agreed, and Steuben Glass, Inc. (wholly owned by Corning Glass Works) was formed as a new subsidiary.

Several factors were important in Steuben's success. Most important, Houghton wanted to "produce crystal in the highest standards of design, quality and workmanship, glass which would rank in history among man's greatest achievements." He asked John Gates to join him as the design leader, and Gates invited Sidney Waugh, a sculptor, to become the first designer. All three men were in their twenties. Historically, glassmakers had used their own designs, which became more extravagant as they matured. Steuben's use of independent designers thus brought a discipline to glassmaking that had been lacking. To prove that he was serious in his desire to produce quality glass, Houghton, with Gates, smashed every piece of glass (over 20,000 pieces valued at $1 million) in the Steuben warehouse about one month after assuming control. Another factor in Steuben's success was the Corning Glass Works discovery in 1932 of a formula for making a very pure crystal glass, which Steuben began using after Houghton took over. "From ash can to museum in half a generation" became the company's slogan.

Houghton believed that the company's success depended on what he called the "Steuben Trilogy," which he described as "Material, workmanship, and design. If any of these three elements is deficient, perfect glass cannot be achieved." Steuben glass had a high index of refraction compared to conventional glasses. This contributed to its high reflective quality. Transparent crystal replaced the colored glass of the Carder era. Houghton positioned the company for commercial success by opening retail shops on Fifth Avenue in New York City and in Corning, and he established Steuben-controlled shops in a few high-quality stores.

Beginning in the late 1930s several renowned artists were commissioned to make drawings to be engraved on Steuben glass. In a short time Steuben became known as *the* American glass and was compared favorably to the best European glass. By the late 1940s Steuben's outstanding reputation for its glass prompted both Presidents Truman and Eisenhower to present Steuben glass to other heads of state.

Houghton maintained a heavy schedule of cultural activities throughout his life. He belonged to more than 100 organizations devoted to education and the arts. Houghton was the curator of rare books at the Library of Congress from 1940 to 1942. He had accepted this position because he was an avid collector of original manuscripts and letters of writers such as Samuel Pepys, John Keats, Robert Browning, and Elizabeth Barrett Browning. He donated his Keats collection to Harvard University, and he endowed the Houghton Library at Harvard in 1942 as the repository for the university's collection of rare books and manuscripts. Houghton joined the board of the New York Philharmonic Symphony Society in 1952 and served as chairman from 1958 to 1963. During this time the Philharmonic moved its permanent home from Carnegie Hall to the Lincoln Center for the Performing Arts.

He was a board member of the Metropolitan Museum of Art from 1952 to 1974 and its president from 1964 to 1969. When he became president, the *New York Times* reported that he was "one of the most impressive joiners in town. . . . he does not join for sociability, status, or solvency, [but] because he believes things should be done and because he is interested." During his term he helped to modernize the museum's administration and curatorial system. He was especially active in bolstering its primitive-art collection. Houghton was also a vice president of the Pierpont Morgan Library, president of the English-Speaking Union of the United States, chairman of the Parsons School of Design, chairman of the Institute of International Education, and vice chairman of the Fund for the Advancement of Education. Houghton helped to create the Corning Glass Center (with his cousin Amory Houghton), which opened in 1951 and later became the Corning Museum of Glass. He donated his estate on Maryland's eastern shore to the Aspen Institute and transferred its breeding herd to the University of Maryland, and in 1973 he donated the land for Corning Community College.

Arthur A. Houghton, Jr., served both the community through his cultural activities and the family firm through his management of Steuben Glass. It is likely that his fame will rest on the latter activity. James S. Plaut, describing the "special ethos" of the Houghton years at Steuben, said it was based on "first, the vision and courage to start a new enterprise based on personal conviction; second, his insistence upon the use of a gloriously beautiful material and his staunch refusal to permit any deviation from it toward other kinds of glass; third, his fierce ambition to make Steuben *the* American glass, without peer; fourth, his laudable desire to use Steuben as a vehicle for the creative unification of the major artistic resources of his time; fifth, but by no means last, his awareness that any business enterprise must be viable, since consistent financial losses would erode the creative effort and lead ultimately to Steuben's extinction."

• Paul N. Perrot et al., *Steuben: Seventy Years of American Glassmaking* (1974), provides the most complete information on Steuben. Other sources include "The Houghtons of Corning," *Fortune*, July 1945, pp. 129–32 and 253–60, and Robert Ankli, "Corning: Corning Incorporated," in *International Directory of Company Histories* (1991). An obituary is in the *New York Times*, 4 Apr. 1990.

ROBERT E. ANKLI

HOUGHTON, Douglass (21 Sept. 1809–13 Oct. 1845), geologist and physician, was born in Troy, New York, the son of Jacob Houghton, a lawyer and later a county judge, and Mary Lydia Douglass. Raised in a close-knit, cultured home in Fredonia, New York, Douglass was a small person with a nervous, active temperament inclined toward the practical and scientific. He exhibited early his lifelong interest in the natural world, and in spite of a slight speech impediment and facial scarring from a youthful experiment with gunpowder he was at ease with all levels of society.

In 1829 Houghton entered the Rensselaer School at Troy, New York (later Rensselaer Polytechnic Institute), where, under the direction of Amos Eaton, scientific training was emphasized, particularly in geology. That same year he received both the bachelor's degree and a teaching appointment in chemistry and natural history there. He also studied medicine with a doctor friend of his family and was licensed to practice in 1831. His association with the Michigan Territory began the previous year, when the city fathers of Detroit took their search for a public lecturer on science to Eaton, who strongly recommended Houghton. His enthusiastic reception in Detroit was followed by his participation as physician-naturalist on expeditions led by Henry Rowe Schoolcraft through Lake Superior and the upper Mississippi valley in 1831 and 1832. On these Houghton did extensive botanical collecting, investigated the Lake Superior copper deposits, and provided medical services to the Indian tribes he encountered. In 1833 he married his childhood friend Harriet Stevens, with whom he had two daughters. The establishment of a flourishing medical practice in Detroit earned him the affectionate designation, "the little doctor, our Dr. Houghton"; but by 1836 he had largely set aside the medical profession to concentrate on real estate speculation.

His scientific interests remained strong, however, and as Michigan achieved statehood in 1837 he organized the first state geological survey, following a pattern already established in other states. His appointment as state geologist, a role he filled for the remainder of his life, was unanimously hailed. In 1839 he was also named the first professor of geology, mineralogy, and chemistry at the University of Michigan in Ann Arbor, but he continued to reside in Detroit. He and his survey assistants spent many weeks in the field each season, mapping and evaluating Michigan's natural resources, and his personal influence with state legislators kept the project moving in the face of many financial difficulties. His fourth annual report, based on fieldwork done in 1840, appeared in February 1841. It helped trigger the first great mining boom of American history and earned him the title of "father of copper mining in the United States" (Joralemon, p. 50). He was a founding member and treasurer of the Association of American Geologists and Naturalists (the predecessor of the American Association for the Advancement of Science) and served on several of its committees. A lifelong Episcopalian and staunch Democrat, he was elected to a term as mayor of Detroit in 1842, apparently against his wishes, but his competent administration raised the possibility of higher political office. In 1844, with the state survey moribund because of the lack of funds, Houghton organized a combined linear and geological survey of the Lake Superior region that was funded by the federal government. While working on that survey he and two companions were drowned in Lake Superior near Eagle River when their small boat was swamped in a storm. Neither survey was completed.

Following his death, an enduring tradition arose claiming that many of Houghton's geological insights had been notably in advance of those of his contemporaries. Specifically, it has been repeatedly asserted over the years that he was the first geologist to recognize that the unique native copper deposits on Lake Superior could be profitably mined, contrary to what all previous mining experience would have suggested. These claims, however, cannot be supported by the available evidence, which indicates, rather, that his geological conclusions did not differ significantly from those of his professional colleagues.

Houghton's place in history is somewhat problematic. Although he was the state geologist of Michigan for eight years, for reasons not entirely clear he never wrote the long-anticipated final report that had been the goal of the state survey from its inception and that could have established his scientific reputation. His multiple abilities were ideally suited to the needs of the society of his day, but he was not always successful in reconciling the conflicting demands of the various roles he filled. As a scientist his potential seems to have been considerable, but his tragic death prevented that potential from being fully realized.

• Significant Houghton papers are in the Michigan Historical Collections of the University of Michigan in Ann Arbor, and in the Clarke Historical Library of Central Michigan University in Mt. Pleasant. His annual geological reports are compiled in *Geological Reports of Douglass Houghton 1837–1845* ed. George N. Fuller (1928). Laudatory biographies are Alvah Bradish, *Memoir of Douglass Houghton: First State Geologist of Michigan* (1889), and Edsel K. Rintala, *Douglass Houghton: Michigan's Pioneer Geologist* (1954). Ira B. Joralemon, *Copper: The Encompassing Story of Mankind's First Metal* (1973), provides a brief introduction to Houghton and the Lake Superior copper deposits. A revisionary analysis of Houghton's work is found in David J. Krause, "Testing a Tradition: Douglass Houghton and the Native Copper of Lake Superior," *Isis* 80 (1989): 622–39, and, more fully discussed, in Krause, *The Making of a Mining District: Keweenaw Native Copper 1500–1870* (1992).

DAVID J. KRAUSE

HOUGHTON, George Hendric (1 Feb. 1820–17 Nov. 1897), Episcopal priest, founder of the Church of the Transfiguration in New York City, and leader of the Anglican Catholic movement in the Episcopal church in the United States, was born in Deerfield, Massachusetts, the son of Edward Clarke Houghton, a merchant, and Fanny Smith, a schoolteacher. Born into a Congregationalist home, Houghton moved in 1834 to New York City, where he worked fifteen hours a day while also a student to support his widowed mother. He graduated from the University of the City of New York in 1842 and studied theology at the General Theological Seminary in Manhattan. In 1845 he was ordained a deacon in the Episcopal church by Benjamin Onderdonk, bishop of New York. In 1846 he was ordained a priest, after which he served as curate of the Church of the Holy Communion, founded the same year in New York City by William Augustus Muhlenberg, a High Church Episcopal leader and social and liturgical reformer. He married Caroline Graves Anthon.

In 1848 Houghton founded the Church of the Transfiguration in Manhattan as one of the earliest parochial outposts in the New World of the catholic revival in the Anglican communion. This revival began in England and was associated with the Oxford movement, whose teachings first arrived in the United States in about 1839. In response to the Age of Revolution in England, which included the Industrial Revolution, democratic reform, and urbanization, the leaders of the Oxford movement asserted that the churches of the Anglican communion were part of the One, Holy, Catholic, and Apostolic Church of Jesus Christ. In this proclamation they looked backward to the primitive church of the persecuted and oppressed, gathered as a eucharistic community; this primitive model was a model for the modern church. One of the Oxford movement leaders, Edward Pusey, urged in particular that the Anglican Catholic revival should focus on modern cities, such as London and New York, rather than on areas of former population concentration and the picturesque countryside where the comfortable parishes were located.

Houghton concluded, on the basis of his own experience and Pusey's teaching, that for the first time Episcopalians in New York City should build a parish church in which all would be welcomed, to establish a place "where the Church should be free to all, where charitable institutions for the afflicted of all sorts and conditions are made available for all." Houghton set out to do something new in the Episcopal church, create a visible worshiping community in an urban setting that would welcome all classes, all races, and particularly those marginalized by society for whatever reason, including actors and African Americans, who had theretofore been on the fringes of both society and the Episcopal church. He established a number of charitable societies to help carry out his vision. The Oxford movement had restored the centrality of the Sunday celebration of the Holy Eucharist as the regular form of worship for Episcopalians, and from its foundation Transfiguration was one of the first Episcopal churches in the United States to carry out this eucharistic focus. From 1880 onward a regular daily mass was celebrated in the church.

His long interest in the abolition of slavery led Houghton to found the first black Sunday school in New York City and to harbor runaway slaves as part of the Underground Railway. During the draft riots of July 1863, angry mobs trying to get at former slaves who had found sanctuary within the church twice thronged the gates of the churchyard. With resolution and strong words, Houghton staved off the unruly mob with only a processional cross held before him, and the African Americans in the church remained safe for several more days.

Seven years later a single striking event led the Church of the Transfiguration into the secular as well as religious history of the United States as "the Little Church around the Corner." In December 1870 an actor named George Holland died. His friend Joseph Jefferson, the leading comic actor of the day, went to the rector of the Church of the Atonement on Madison Avenue to see about the funeral. On learning that Holland had been an actor, William T. Sabine, the rector of the Church of the Atonement, refused to take the service. Jefferson recorded what followed in these words:

I paused at the door and said, "Well, sir, in this dilemma is there no other church to which you can direct me, from which my friend can be buried?" He replied that "there was a little church around the corner" where I might get it done; to which I answered, "Then God bless 'the little church around the corner,'" and so I left the house.

News stories, editorials, and songs gave emphasis to the incident, and so Transfiguration became a shrine to the acting profession. More then ten thousand couples came to be married at the altars of the church after that event.

This ideal of catholic inclusivity in the Episcopal church, for which the Church of the Transfiguration stood perhaps more than any other in the United

States in the nineteenth century, caused "the Little Church around the Corner" to be immortalized throughout the nation. Houghton entered into the hagiography of the Episcopal church, where he remained after his death in New York City.

• Houghton's papers, including manuscript sermons, are in the library of the General Theological Seminary in New York City. The most recent historical account of Houghton and the parish he founded is in Zulett M. Catir, *A Parish Guide to the Church of the Transfiguration: The Little Church around the Corner* (1996). A short biographical account of Houghton's life is Harry L. Bodley, *The Rev. George Hendrick Houghton* (1898). Three other sources for the life of Houghton are George MacAdam, *The Little Church around the Corner* (1925); J. H. Randolph Ray, *My Little Church around the Corner* (1957); and Ishbel Ross, *Through the Lich-Gate: A Biography of the Little Church around the Corner* (1931). An obituary is in the *New York Times*, 18 Nov. 1897.

R. WILLIAM FRANKLIN

HOUGHTON, Henry Oscar (30 Apr. 1823–25 Aug. 1895), printer and publisher, was born in Suffolk, Vermont, the son of William Houghton, a sometime tanner and farmhand, and Marilla Clay. His early years were spent in the hardscrabble poverty of a large family in the hill country of northern Vermont. His numerous older siblings soon scattered but continued to provide support at critical points in his life. Through his brother Daniel, who was working his way through the University of Vermont at the Burlington *Free Press*, Houghton was apprenticed at age thirteen to the paper's owner in return for room, board, and clothing. Houghton had only three years of formal education before his apprenticeship, but Daniel organized lessons in Greek, Latin, and mathematics for the apprentices and encouraged Henry to follow him to the University of Vermont, which he entered in 1842.

Poorly prepared by sporadic formal education and possessing a lean, Lincoln-like frame and rural Yankee social awkwardness, Houghton was, as a classmate later described him, "an earnest, honest, unsophisticated Yankee boy." But his characteristic self-discipline and self-reliance gained the respect of classmates and professors. Determined to succeed, he graduated third in a class of twenty, despite the need to work long hours at the press to pay his way. Partly to overcome a lack of confidence and fluency in public speaking, he engaged frequently in debates. Houghton began to articulate political and social convictions that were generally Whig conservative. He favored sound currency and the protective tariff but also viewed public education as essential to both economic self-sufficiency and independent citizenship.

Three hundred dollars in debt on graduation, Houghton found work in Boston as a compositor and later as a proofreader in the printing house of Freeman and Bolles. In 1849 Houghton entered his first of many partnerships. With the help of friends and family, he bought half the office from the retiring John Freeman for $3,100 in annual payments of $250. In 1852, again with borrowed capital, he bought out the

remaining partner, Bolles, and founded H. O. Houghton and Company. In the same year he also established the Riverside Press on the banks of the Charles River in Cambridge, Massachusetts. Between 1849 and 1863, despite financial panic and war, the printing company expanded steadily, growing from sixteen to ninety-six employees kept in continuous employment by a regularly renewed contract with the publisher Little, Brown, as well as contracts for printing the *Atlantic Monthly* and Webster's dictionary.

In 1864 the cancellation of his printing contract with Little, Brown led Houghton to believe that over the long run he could keep his employees and presses supplied with constant work only by becoming a publisher as well as a printer. Partnership with Melancthon Hurd brought capital as well as publishing contracts. In 1872 subsequent partnership capital from his brother Albert Houghton allowed him to triple the capacity of the Riverside Press to twenty power presses, with 300 employees. In 1878 a brief, troubled partnership with the publisher James Osgood, from whom Houghton had bought the *Atlantic Monthly* in 1873, allowed the company to acquire copyrights to the works of the major New England authors including Ralph Waldo Emerson, Nathaniel Hawthorne, Oliver Wendell Holmes, Henry Wadsworth Longfellow, James Russell Lowell, Henry David Thoreau, and John Greenleaf Whittier. The partnership also established Houghton as the literary successor to the publishing house of Ticknor and Fields. The dissolution of Houghton, Osgood in 1880 led to the formation of Houghton, Mifflin and Company with George Mifflin, a young Boston blueblood whom Houghton had reluctantly taken into the business in 1868 but who had subsequently proved his merit. At Houghton's death, Mifflin succeeded him as senior partner of the house Houghton had built.

Houghton was fortunate to enter the printing and publishing businesses at a time of rapid expansion due to major increases in literacy rates, public education, transportation, national distribution systems for books, publicity, and technical advances such as electrotyping, the rotary press, and stereotype plates that allowed storage for reuse. But character as well as circumstance enabled him to found a house that lasted while the businesses of others, such as his sometime partner and rival Osgood, failed. A convincing case has been made that his life and character were the model for W. D. Howells's Silas Lapham, and his trajectory from poverty to business success and civic responsibility recalls that of an earlier printer, Benjamin Franklin. Houghton, like Franklin and Lapham, had a Yankee work ethic, self-discipline, attention to detail, pragmatism, shrewdness in judging character, and long-range perspective.

While quite capable of rationalizing self-interest as principle, Houghton's long horizon enabled him frequently to make them serve each other. Genuinely interested in the aesthetics of printing, he preferred clean, simple styles in both typeface and binding over the prevailing Victorian taste for ostentatious decoration and was willing to found his press's reputation on this preference. Because he felt it brought prestige and authors to the house of Houghton, Mifflin, he was willing to sustain the *Atlantic Monthly* through twenty years of dwindling circulation and revenue loss without intervening in its editorial policies. Both before and after Houghton acquired the copyrights and stereotype plates to the works of the major New England authors, he actively advocated a specifically American literature as representative of American values. His personal convictions and his economic interests also made him an important force in winning international copyright for American authors.

Beyond his Yankee business sense, Houghton had a strong attachment to and satisfaction in family. In 1854 he had married Nanna Manning, a schoolteacher, with whom he had four children. A son, a brother, and nephews became partners in the business. He also found satisfaction in a nondogmatic Methodism, serving the church as warden and Sunday school superintendent. He took pleasure in driving spirited horses and in his later years from donating anonymous charitable gifts. His sense of civic responsibility and the confidence of others in his judgment were reflected in his election as councilman, school board member, and mayor of Cambridge, as well as in his participation in founding the Boston Museum of Fine Arts and his service as a trustee of Boston University and various charitable institutions. Houghton died in North Andover, Massachusetts.

• Houghton's papers are among the collection of Houghton Mifflin Papers at the Houghton Library of Harvard University. This unusually large publishing archive includes payroll books, cost books, account books, copyright books, private journals, and letter books of correspondence. Ellen Ballou, *The Building of the House: Houghton Mifflin's Formative Years* (1970), gives a complete account of Houghton's accomplishment. This may be supplemented by several narratives of Houghton Mifflin's history issued by the firm itself (1889, 1899, 1921, 1930). Horace Scudder, *Henry Oscar Houghton: A Biographical Sketch* (1897), is a sympathetic contemporary account by an associate. *Publishers Weekly*, 7 Sept. 1895, pp. 307–9, has an extended obituary.

ELLERY SEDGWICK

HOUGHTON, Henry Spencer (27 Mar. 1880–21 Mar. 1975), medical administrator, was born in Toledo, Ohio, the son of Albert Charles Houghton, a lawyer, and Amy Twitchell. Reared in Ohio and Minnesota, Houghton entered Ohio State University in 1896. With a brief period out for military service at the time of the Spanish-American War, he graduated with a Ph.B. in 1901.

At age twenty-one Houghton moved east to enter the Johns Hopkins Medical School, then still in its infancy. Houghton's mentors included many of the original department heads at Hopkins. More than any other single element in Houghton's formative years, the period in Baltimore at the turn of the century left a lasting stamp on his intellectual and professional outlook. After receiving the M.D. in 1905, he moved to New York City for a postgraduate year as assistant to Simon Flexner, director of the Rockefeller Institute for Medical Research, recently established in 1901 and the first institution in the United States devoted solely to biomedical research. In June 1906 Houghton married Caroline Martha Carmack, a high school classmate. They had four children.

In the autumn of 1906 Houghton, imbued with a spirit of Christian social service, made his first Pacific crossing to China, where he was to spend the bulk of his professional career. In 1889 the Methodist church had opened a small hospital at Wuhu, 250 miles upriver from Shanghai. It was at Wuhu General Hospital that Houghton had his first direct contact with parasitic diseases and where he initiated early scientific studies of schistosomiasis, the chronic blood and organ infection then endemic in the lowlands near the Yangtze and a menace to all rice-producing peasants. Not least important, it was during his tour of duty at Wuhu that he gained a solid knowledge of the modern Chinese language.

At the time of the republican revolt of 1911 in China, Houghton was temporarily in Shanghai. There a chance encounter led to a new appointment. With impetus from Cambridge, plans developed to create a small Harvard Medical School of China, with faculty and students in Shanghai and trustees in Massachusetts. While Houghton lacked Harvard degrees or prior affiliation, his credentials were sufficiently solid to warrant his appointment in 1912 as dean and professor of tropical medicine. The Harvard school in Shanghai lasted only until 1917, but several of its faculty later played important roles in the development and spread of Western medicine in China.

During the years of the First World War, when the Rockefeller Foundation in New York City focused its energies on Western medical education in Asia, Houghton became increasingly involved in that enterprise. In China he worked closely with the new China Medical Board of the Rockefeller Foundation in the planning and construction of the teaching hospital that in September 1921 was formally dedicated as the Peking Union Medical College (PUMC). The PUMC was then the only full-time academic medical college in Asia, handsomely equipped for both clinical service and scientific research. Houghton was named director of the college at Peking during its seminal years from 1921 to 1928.

An unusually talented international faculty recruited from both North America and Western Europe was at PUMC. At the same time Houghton made strong efforts to recruit young Chinese doctors with high-quality Western medical backgrounds, notably J. Heng Liu (Harvard), Wu Hsien (Harvard), and Robert K. S. Lim (Edinburgh), who became the first Chinese professors at PUMC. In addition, the local faculty was enriched by a constant flow of short-term visiting professors on leave from major American medical schools.

After more than twenty years in China, Houghton, with stimulus from the Rockefeller organization, ac-

cepted new responsibilities in the United States. He
left Peking in December 1927 with the immediate task
of guiding the reorganization and rejuvenation of the
college of medicine at the State University of Iowa. He
moved directly from north China to Iowa City to become dean and director of clinical services.

In the depression years of 1931–1932 Houghton was
on leave from university responsibilities as a member
of a select twelve-member commission charged with
conducting a so-called Laymen's Inquiry to review the
work of Protestant Christian missions in Asia after a
century of activity. An unanticipated result of this year
abroad was an invitation to join the faculty of the University of Chicago. Houghton thus spent two years,
1932 to 1934, at Chicago as director of clinical services
and associate dean of biological sciences.

The 1930s brought new and grave problems both
for China and the PUMC. On one hand, Japanese aggression on the mainland, beginning in Manchuria in
1931 and marked by growing pressure on the provinces of north China after 1935, cast ominous shadows
over Western interests. On the other, increasing nationalism in China created suspicion of American philanthropic institutions as tools of imperialism. Late in
1934 John D. Rockefeller, Jr., who had long had a
keen interest in medical education in China as well as
personal knowledge of Houghton's record, invited
him to return to the team and to allot to the Rockefel-
lers the final full decade of his working career. From
mid-1935 Houghton was again in Peking to replace
Roger S. Greene, his friend of many years, as special
representative of the China Medical Board. Problems
of substance, standards, and teaching style demanded
attention. In July 1937, when full-scale war between
China and Japan erupted, Houghton resumed the acting directorship of the PUMC, the post he had previously held in the 1920s. During the ensuing months of
tension and uncertainty, when Peking and north China were under effective Japanese occupation, his good
judgment and coolness under pressure did much to
sustain discipline and spirit in the college.

In the 1920s the discovery in north China of the collection of fossil remains that had come to be labeled
"Peking Man" was indisputably one of the major
events in modern archaeology. With Houghton's initiative, Rockefeller funds were secured for the study of
these hominid remains. Davidson Black, Canadian
anatomist at PUMC and close personal friend of
Houghton, edited a pioneering monograph, *Fossil
Man in China*, published in Peking in 1933. During
the late 1930s leading Chinese scientists, in company
with an international galaxy of Western physical anthropologists, geologists, and paleontologists, continued to make impressive progress in this work. Late in
1941, after consultation with Chinese authorities, a
high-level decision was made to move these unique
fossils to safety outside the war zone in China. Houghton delivered the bones to American military officers
in Peking for safe transport to the United States. In the
confusion of that period, the bones were inexplicably
lost, and the mystery of their fate remains unsolved.

The outbreak of the Pacific war also ended Houghton's professional career. In early December 1941 the
Japanese army detained him as a political prisoner and
hostage, holding him in Peking for almost four years.
No charges were brought, but in retrospect it appears
likely that Tokyo estimated that these American-con-
trolled institutions in China were covers for intelligence and espionage operations. During this long period of isolated confinement, Houghton knew he needed
intellectual and physical exercise, and he thus kept a
detailed log of his confinement.

Released at the end of the war, Houghton left mainland China for the last time in the autumn of 1945, almost forty years after he first arrived at Shanghai.
After reporting to the China Medical Board in New
York, he retired in the spring of 1946. For the next
seventeen years he lived on the West Coast in a house
near Carmel, California. In 1963 Houghton moved to
Nashville, Tennessee, where he resided quietly until
his death there.

Houghton's long identification with the medical education work sponsored by the Rockefeller Foundation is a matter of record. While both the objectives
and the impact of that major philanthropic enterprise
in China remain debatable, several facts deserve attention. During the republican period in China, the role
of PUMC in the spread of modern medical science and
practice, the stimulation of public health work, the
creation of nursing as a respected profession for Chinese women, and the building of the best medical library and clinical records archive in Asia remains an
important segment of the record of American relations
with that proud but disadvantaged country. Of parallel importance was the role of the college, the leading
medical center of East Asia, as training ground for
many people who later became leaders in academic
medicine at institutions in the United States. In 1951
PUMC was taken over by the Chinese authorities of
the People's Republic. In 1962 the distinguished Toronto neurosurgeon Wilder Penfield visited Peking
and recorded his opinion that no Rockefeller project
had done more to promote the "well-being of mankind
throughout the world" than PUMC.

• Houghton's papers, including typescripts of his prison dia-
ries (1942–1945), are in the possession of his daughter, Mary
Houghton Boorman in Nashville, Tenn. For family history,
the principal source is *The Houghton Genealogy* (1912), comp.
John W. Houghton of Wellington, Ohio. To mark the centennial of Methodist medical work in southern Anhwei, Elsie
Hayes Landstrom prepared a useful record, *Wuhu General
Hospital, 1889–1949* (1989). The Harvard Medical School of
China is documented in the *Annual and Hospital Reports*
(1911–1916), collected and bound by its executive committee
(1918). Jean A. Curran gives an informal summary of the
Shanghai years in the *Harvard Medical Alumni Bulletin* (Dec.
1963). The opening of PUMC is handsomely covered in *Addresses and Papers, Dedication Ceremonies and Medical Conference, Peking Union Medical College, September 15–22, 1921*
(1922).
Four books discuss aspects of Houghton's connection with
the college, I. Snapper, *Chinese Lessons to Western Medicine*
(1941), is a detailed professional account; Mary E. Ferguson,

China Medical Board and Peking Union Medical College, 1914–1951 (1970), is a basic history of the administrative relations among the organizations responsible for the operations of the college; John Z. Bowers of the Josiah Macy Foundation discusses personnel and programs fully in *Western Medicine in a Chinese Palace* (1972); and Mary Brown Bullock, *An American Transplant: The Rockefeller Foundation and Peking Union Medical College* (1980), is a solid critical study based on thorough archival research. An obituary is in the *New York Times*, 24 March 1975.

HOWARD LYON BOORMAN

HOURWICH, Isaac Aaronovich (26 Apr. 1860–9 July 1924), author, lawyer, and statistician, was born in Vilna, Russia, the son of Adolph Hourwich and Rebecca Sheveliovich. Although his father's occupation is unknown, it is known that Hourwich was born into a middle-class Jewish family and that his father was a well-educated man.

Hourwich entered the Saint Petersburg Academy of Medicine and Surgery in 1877 but soon gave up his plan of becoming a doctor and enrolled in the University of St. Petersburg to study mathematics. He became interested in politics and joined a revolutionary socialist circle. In 1879 he wrote a pamphlet titled *What Is Constitutionalism?*, which led to his arrest on a charge of treason. After serving a nine-month sentence, he was exiled to Siberia, where he researched and wrote about peasant migration in a study titled *The Peasant Immigration to Siberia* (1888). His imprisonment and exile heightened his beliefs, and after his release he became an active revolutionary leader. He entered the Demidov Juridical Lyceum in Yaroslavl and received his law degree in 1887.

He moved to Minsk, began to practice law, and continued his revolutionary activities. To avoid being arrested again, Hourwich fled to Sweden, and then went to New York City in 1890. Between 1891 and 1893 he edited a Russian language newspaper while earning a Ph.D. in political science at Columbia University. His dissertation, "The Economics of the Russian Village," was published in the United States in 1892. This work explores the differences between individual and collective landholding by the peasants.

Hourwich taught statistics at the University of Chicago for two years but returned to New York City in 1895 after being forced to resign because of his political activities. He was admitted to the bar and practiced law for several years. He left for Washington, D.C., in 1900 and began a career in government service: he worked as a translator for the U.S. Bureau of the Mint and then as a statistician for the Bureau of the Census. During that time, he also taught at George Washington University, wrote articles on economics, and contributed to several Russian and Yiddish newspapers.

After the Russian Czar declared an amnesty for political prisoners in 1905, Hourwich returned to his homeland. He ran as a candidate in elections for the Duma, but this time he was a member of the Democratic People's Party, an affiliation that angered many of his former Socialist colleagues. When his election was annulled and the Duma was dissolved amidst a period of political repression, Hourwich returned to the United States. He was employed with the Public Service Commission in New York from 1908 to 1909, and then he returned to the Bureau of the Census.

In 1912 his most famous work, *Immigration and Labor*, was published. This book, which is an economic analysis of immigration, was written in reaction to the *Reports of the United States Immigration Commission* (1911). The commission argued that restrictions on the immigration of unskilled laborers would slow down industrial expansion, leading to higher wages for native workers. Hourwich disagreed with these conclusions and tried to counter the commission's arguments with his own statistical analysis and economic reasoning. He maintained that the immigration of unskilled laborers was dependent on the availability of jobs, and that it had no negative effect on the wages or employment levels of native workers. *Immigration and Labor* was at the time a very controversial book, and much was written both for and against Hourwich's arguments. A second edition of the book was published in 1921, and it has since become a classic in American economics literature.

In 1912 Hourwich ran for Congress in one of New York's predominantly Jewish districts. He was running under Theodore Roosevelt's Bull Moose party because he believed that in order to get elected and be able to carry out social reform, the Socialists had to form an alliance with the middle class. This alienated many of his Socialist friends and supporters, and he lost the election.

One year later, he left the Bureau of the Census, began working with labor unions, and continued writing in Yiddish. In addition to the many newspaper articles he contributed, Hourwich wrote *Mooted Questions of Socialism* (1917) and translated Karl Marx's *Das Kapital* into Yiddish (1919).

In 1918 Hourwich became the counsel to the Russian Soviet Government Bureau in New York. He supported the recognition of the Soviet Union but did not defend the actions of the Bolsheviks. A trip to the Soviet Union in the early 1920s left him extremely disillusioned, and he began writing articles denouncing the Communist party. In retaliation, a Communist Jewish newspaper published scathing articles about him.

Little has been written about Hourwich's family life, but it is known that he was married twice and had at least two children. His first marriage was to Helen Kushelevsky of Minsk in 1881, and his second was to Louise Joffe of New York in 1893.

Hourwich became quite ill with diabetes. Realizing that his time was short, he further embraced his Jewishness and concentrated on his work with various Jewish organizations. When he died in New York City, he left behind an unfinished autobiography titled *Memoirs of a Heretic*.

Many of Hourwich's contributions were in the form of public service; he spent several years working for the United States government and teaching at universities. He was deeply involved in politics both in the

United States and Russia. But he is most well known for his writing—*Immigration and Labor* was a significant work that brought forth a debate on the economic aspects of immigration. His many articles inspired spirited discourse, both in academia and in Jewish intellectual circles. Hourwich was always a Socialist and an individualist and did not believe in compromise. Robert Karlowich aptly summed up these defining characteristics, "Known as a man of integrity, honesty, intelligence and stubbornness, Isaac Hourwich was an active socialist all his life, but always remained independent of movements and parties. He joined them, but he never felt himself bound by their tenets" (Karlowich, p. 110).

• Hourwich's personal papers are held at the Houghton Library at Harvard University and at the Yivo Institute for Jewish Research. Cornell University's School of Industrial and Labor Relations Library has papers relating to Hourwich's work as an arbitrator for the labor unions. The Schlesinger Library at Radcliffe College owns the letters that Hourwich wrote to Alice Stone Blackwell. Biographical background information and anecdotes can be found in the sections on Hourwich in two of Melech Epstein's works: *Profiles of Eleven* (1965) and *Jewish Labor in USA* (1969). For information on Hourwich's life and publishing activities, see Robert Karlowich's *We Fall and Rise: Russian-Language Newspapers in New York City, 1889–1914* (1991). George Kennan's article on Hourwich in the *Outlook* (26 July 1913) also provides some insight. For a review of *Immigration and Labor*, see R. F. Foerster in the *Quarterly Journal of Economics* 27 (Aug. 1913): 656–71. An obituary is in the *New York Times*, 11 July 1924.

KATHLEEN A. SHANAHAN

HOUSE, Edward Mandell (26 July 1858–28 Mar. 1938), presidential adviser, was born in Houston, Texas, the son of Thomas William House, a wealthy merchant, banker, and landowner, and Mary Elizabeth Shearn. He led a privileged youth, meeting many prominent people, who visited the large family homes in Galveston and Houston, and enjoying the colorful life of his father's sugar plantation. As a boy he rode and hunted, roaming the vast coastal plains near Houston.

In the autumn of 1877 House entered Cornell University, where he remained until the beginning of his third year, when he returned home to look after his ill father. When the great merchant died in January 1880, House decided to stay in Texas and help manage his father's estate, which was to be divided among the five surviving children. In 1881 House married Loulie Hunter; the couple had two children. House supervised the family's extensive landholdings scattered throughout Texas. In the autumn of 1885 he moved to Austin to escape the heat of Houston and to be closer to his cotton plantations. In the late 1880s and early 1890s House pursued a variety of business activities, including farming and land speculation.

House was drawn into state politics through his friendship with Governor James Stephen Hogg, who in 1892 faced a formidable challenge from both conservative Democrats and Populists. House directed Hogg's successful reelection campaign, creating a network of local, influential Democratic leaders, manipulating the electoral machinery, and bargaining for the votes of blacks and Mexican Americans. Hogg rewarded House with the title of colonel.

Concerned more with the process of politics than with the substance, House proceeded to build his own powerful faction—"our crowd," as he called it—in Texas politics. He was an ambitious political operator, working largely behind the scenes, developing ties of loyalty and affection with his close associates, and using patronage to rally party workers behind his candidates. From 1894 to 1906 House's protégés served as governors of Texas.

By the turn of the century House was bored with his role in state politics and was restlessly searching for broader horizons. Seeking further wealth, he attempted to profit from the discovery of oil at Spindletop in 1901 and in 1902, with the backing of eastern financiers, formed the Trinity and Brazos Valley Railway Company. For years he had summered on Boston's North Shore, and gradually he began to winter in New York, severing most of his ties with Texas and only occasionally visiting the state.

House had long yearned for a place on the national political stage. A conservative, sound-money Democrat, he disliked the platform of William Jennings Bryan and in 1904 supported Alton B. Parker for the nomination. Discouraged by the prospects of the Democratic party after Parker's defeat in 1904 and Bryan's in 1908, House found solace in leisurely tours of Europe and in spiritualism. He continued his search for a Democratic presidential candidate amenable to his advice. In November 1911 he met Woodrow Wilson, forming a close friendship. House was on the periphery of Wilson's campaign for the Democratic nomination and the presidency, but after Wilson's election, House played a key role in patronage decisions, eventually placing five friends in the cabinet.

During the winter of 1912–1913 House joined the circle of intimates around the president who were dedicated to advancing his political career and to maintaining his physical health and emotional stability. House was a shrewd and crafty political infighter, one who enjoyed and motivated people. He performed all sorts of political tasks the president found distasteful. House also catered to many of Wilson's personal needs, recognizing his yearning for male companionship and his vulnerability to emotional stress. House's gentle, deferential manner, his lack of an assertive masculinity, and his frequent assurances of affection and support helped to satisfy some of the president's deepest desires. "My dear friend," Wilson soon told House, "we have known one another always."

House developed a deep and genuine admiration for Wilson, both as a person and as a political leader. He believed that inspired leadership could solve the nation's problems and bring its spiritual regeneration, and in Wilson he found a leader who embodied his moral and political values and who could move the American people toward these larger goals. The two men's conversations moved far beyond the realm of politics, as the president confided his dreams, fears, aspirations, and family problems. The president's first wife, Ellen Axson Wilson, had a keen insight into her husband's emotional makeup and a wise tolerance of his political associates. She had welcomed House into her family, seeking his advice on both personal and political matters. Her death in August 1914 left Wilson in a state of despair and caused him to lean even more heavily on House for companionship and emotional support.

Edith Bolling Galt, whom Wilson met in March 1915 and married in December, was a different sort of person. She was lively and attractive but poorly educated and intolerant of some of the president's closest advisers, including House. Wilson imprudently drew her into his work, showing her House's letters and many important state papers and encouraging her to believe that her judgment was as good as that of his experienced advisers. In turn, House resented Wilson's transference of affection to Edith and the extent to which she changed his relationship with the president. After Wilson's marriage, the remarkable intimacy between the two men lessened. They remained dependent on one another, but the extraordinary closeness of these early years gradually faded away.

In 1913 and 1914, as Congress considered Wilson's New Freedom programs, House intervened in Democratic disputes and negotiated compromises to find an acceptable legislative agenda. He collaborated with Wilson in moving the Democratic party away from its traditional advocacy of states' rights and limited government toward an extension of federal authority over the nation. House's visits to the White House excited much speculation, as journalists labeled him a silent man of mystery and exaggerated his political influence over the president.

With the outbreak of World War I House was the first member of the administration to inform himself about the complexities of the struggle and to seriously consider its implications for the United States. As Wilson came to grips with the magnitude of the conflict and the difficulties of America's position, he turned to House for advice and also chose him as his chief emissary to the European capitals. Although firmly pro-Allied, House felt that, to achieve peace, the warring parties had to abandon aims of complete victory. He based American negotiations on prior understandings with the Allies and anticipated moderate Allied success.

Pursuing his own ambitions as well as an end to the war, House was both adept and naive. During his wartime missions to Europe, House sent back vivid, detailed letters, full of valuable information on every phase of the war, but he also exaggerated his role and his influence. While seemingly realistic, he frequently misinterpreted British and French leaders and assumed that reason would prevail over the passions generated by the war.

House made two trips to Europe before the United States entered the war. During the first, from January to June 1915, he realized that the Allies were not prepared to think seriously about ending the conflict and sought to cultivate their goodwill. After the sinking of the *Lusitania* on 7 May, tension intensified between the United States and Germany, and Wilson and House realized the precariousness of American neutrality. House came to view the war as a conflict between democracy and autocracy and was convinced that American involvement was inevitable. While House wanted to secure a limited Allied victory, Wilson still believed that the United States might remain neutral and was not willing to use the American military to guarantee an Allied triumph.

During his second trip, from January to March 1916, House negotiated with British foreign secretary Sir Edward Grey a memorandum, in which the two statesmen agreed that, on a signal from the Allies, Wilson would propose a peace conference to put an end to the war. If Germany refused to attend the conference or, once there, insisted on unreasonable terms, the United States would probably enter the war on the side of the Allies. Since the Allies refused to invoke the House-Grey Memorandum, the scheme embodied in it was never put to the test, and the differences between House and Wilson never rose to the surface. Germany's announcement that all vessels, enemy and neutral, found near British waters would be attacked ended all hopes for peace and virtually assured U.S. entry into the war on 6 April 1917.

After American intervention, House advised Wilson on foreign policy and peace plans and served as a special presidential emissary. In September 1917 Wilson directed House to assemble a group of experts, eventually known as the Inquiry, to study war aims and to plan for peace negotiations. In late October House returned to Europe for inter-Allied military and war aims conferences. In September 1918 Wilson assigned House the responsibility for preparing a constitution for a League of Nations, which they called a covenant, and he and the president exchanged drafts in ensuing months. In October, when Germany petitioned for peace based on the Fourteen Points, Wilson charged House with negotiating an armistice with the Allies. Convinced by these successful efforts, Wilson and House misjudged American influence and remained idealistic about the emergence of a new community of nations.

The Paris Peace Conference revealed the differences between the president and his confidential adviser. As House dominated the discussions, his self-serving ambition became evident to Wilson and to other members of the American Commission to Negotiate Peace. Although House and Wilson collaborated on the initial drafts of the covenant, House lost touch with Wilson's ideas when Wilson returned to the United States in mid-February and House took his place on the Council of Ten. Lacking commitment to the president's convictions, House was more willing to accept British, French, and Italian demands. Contrary to the president's instructions, House accelerated the negotiations, severely weakening Wilson's position. In mid-March, when Wilson returned to Paris and became cognizant of House's conduct, he lost confidence in him. For the remainder of Wilson's presidency, House found himself on the sidelines.

During the 1920s House made frequent trips to Europe and energetically supported U.S. membership in the League of Nations and the World Court. He also sought to mediate the bitter quarrels within the Democratic party and to strengthen the party's organization. In 1932 he supported Franklin D. Roosevelt for the presidential nomination and, with Roosevelt's election, sought to reestablish his role as a presidential confidant. While House influenced some diplomatic appointments, he was excluded from the president's inner circle and became increasingly unsympathetic with the New Deal. He died in New York City.

• House's papers, including his voluminous diary, are in the Yale University Library, but they are weak on his Texas years and should be supplemented with material in the Austin–Travis County Collection of the Austin Public Library. House revealed his own ambitions in his *Philip Dru: Administrator, a Story of Tomorrow, 1920–1935* (1912). Charles Seymour, ed., *The Intimate Papers of Colonel House* (4 vols., 1926–1928), contains long extracts from his letters, diaries, "Memories," and "Reminiscences," as does Arthur S. Link et al., eds., *The Papers of Woodrow Wilson* (69 vols., 1966–1993). Rupert Norval Richardson, *Colonel Edward M. House: The Texas Years, 1858–1912* (1964), is a reliable account of his early life, but Lewis L. Gould, *Progressives and Prohibitionists: Texas Democrats in the Wilson Era* (1973), and Charles E. Neu, "In Search of Colonel Edward M. House: The Texas Years, 1858–1912," *Southwestern Historical Quarterly* 93 (1989): 25–44, offer a different perspective on his career in Texas politics. Alexander L. George and Juliette L. George, *Woodrow Wilson and Colonel House: A Personality Study* (1956), is a controversial analysis of the House-Wilson relationship. For a different view, see Neu, "Woodrow Wilson and Colonel House: The Early Years, 1911–1915," in *The Wilson Era: Essays in Honor of Arthur S. Link*, ed. John Milton Cooper, Jr., and Neu (1991). Three important studies of Wilson offer insights into House and his role as a confidential adviser: Edwin A. Weinstein, *Woodrow Wilson: A Medical and Psychological Biography* (1981); Cooper, *The Warrior and the Priest: Woodrow Wilson and Theodore Roosevelt* (1983); and August Heckscher, *Woodrow Wilson* (1991). House's activities at the Paris Peace Conference can be traced in Inga Floto, *Colonel House in Paris: A Study of American Policy at the Paris Peace Conference 1919* (1980); Arthur Walworth, *Wilson and His Peacemakers: American Diplomacy at the Paris Peace Conference, 1919* (1986); and Thomas J. Knock, *To End All Wars: Woodrow Wilson and the Quest for a New World Order* (1992). An obituary is in the *New York Times*, 29 Mar. 1938.

CHARLES E. NEU

HOUSE, Royal Earl (9 Sept. 1814–25 Feb. 1895), inventor, was born in Rockingham, Vermont, the son of James N. House and Hepsibah Newton. The family moved to Susquehanna, Pennsylvania, soon after he was born. Though little is known of his early life, House apparently had a fondness for mechanisms and an ability for mentally conceiving machinery. He patented his first invention, a machine for sawing barrel staves, in 1839. Also around this time he devised a

waterwheel on the turbine design. His inventions did not lead to financial reward, and he went to Buffalo about 1840 to study law with a relative.

Early in his legal studies, while reading books on natural philosophy, House became interested in the subject of electricity. This led him to the subject of telegraphs, which were then being introduced in Britain by Charles Wheatstone and William Cooke and in the United States by Samuel Morse. In 1844, the same year Morse built his first line between Washington, D.C., and Baltimore, Maryland, House produced his first telegraph instrument. Although he had modest funds, House had parts for his printing telegraph made in New York City machine shops. After assembling the machinery himself, he exhibited it that same year at the American Institute Fair in New York. This successful demonstration enabled House to acquire support that allowed him to continue improving the design. While in New York City in 1846 House married Theresa Thomas of Buffalo; they had one adopted child.

House's printing telegraph differed significantly from Morse's. Unlike the Morse system, which recorded messages in a code that had to be deciphered, House designed his telegraph to print messages in roman letters. His telegraph incorporated a transmitting keyboard, with an individual key for each letter, which sent electrical impulses to a receiving instrument. There the impulses activated a typewheel to print messages on paper strips. Messages transmitted at about fifty words a minute could be delivered immediately to the recipient without further processing.

In 1847 several telegraph entrepreneurs purchased rights to House's telegraph to use in competition with Morse lines. Two years later they put the first House line into service between New York and Philadelphia with House assisting in the construction and the solving of technical problems. He also designed a glass insulator for line wires and the machinery to manufacture it. The group successfully defended the House system against an infringement suit brought by the Morse interests, leaving it as the most important competing system. The House telegraph proved crucial to the growth of the Western Union Telegraph Company, which used it to compete with and acquire Morse lines and patent rights. Western Union began as a House company known as the New York and Mississippi Valley Printing Telegraph Company (incorporated in 1851). In early 1854, after the company's president, Hiram Sibley, and Isaac Butts, a company director, acquired controlling interest in the House patent rights, the company reorganized and embarked on a plan of expansion. The primary vehicle for expansion was a series of favorable contracts that Sibley and general superintendent Anson Stager negotiated with railroad companies, which agreed to construct and equip telegraph lines along their rights-of-way in exchange for free priority use for railroad business. New York and Mississippi Valley's rapid expansion allowed it to compete with and acquire Morse lines, which also provided access to Morse patent rights. These rights proved important to the company, reincorporated in 1856 as Western Union, because the House system had a limited transmission range and was prone to breakdowns because of the mechanical complexity of its instruments as well as poor synchronism between transmitter and receiver. By 1860 these problems led to the virtual abandonment of the House printing telegraph in favor of the simpler Morse instruments, especially after the introduction of sounders on the latter system enabled operators to write out the messages as they were received.

House profited substantially from his invention and moved to Binghamton, New York, where he continued to experiment with electricity. He patented several other telegraph inventions, although none found much commercial use. House moved to Bridgeport, Connecticut, in 1885, where the Postal Telegraph Company was apparently using a version of his 1868 "telephonic" telegraph sounder modified by his nephew Henry A. House, who was superintendent of the company's experimental department. House died in Bridgeport.

• Letters and documents by House are in the Henry O'Reilly Papers, New-York Historical Society Library; and in National Archives Record Group 241, Records of the U.S. Patent Office. Information about House appears in H. C. Hovey, "Royal E. House's Telephone of 1868," *Scientific American* (1886): 303 and "Royal E. House: The Electrician," *Scientific American* (1888): 391; Franklin L. Pope, "Royal E. House and the Early Telegraph," *Electrical Engineer* (1895): 221–22; George B. Prescott, *History, Theory and Practice of the Electric Telegraph* (1860); James D. Reid, *The Telegraph in America* (1879); and Robert L. Thompson, *Wiring a Continent: The History of the Telegraph Industry in the United States, 1832–1866* (1947). An obituary is in the *New York Times*, 27 Feb. 1895.

PAUL B. ISRAEL

HOUSE, Son (21 Mar. 1902?–19 Oct. 1988), blues musician, was born Eddie James House, Jr., in the Mississippi Delta plantation community of Riverton, north of Clarksdale in Coahoma County, Mississippi, the son of Eddie House and Maggie (maiden name unknown). His parents worked as farm laborers in Mississippi and Louisiana. In later interviews, House said his father was also a musician who performed on weekends until he put secular music aside and joined the Baptist church. House, also active in the church, showed little interest in secular music as a youth. He supposedly preached a sermon while still in his midteens and later became a Baptist pastor.

Following his parents' separation and then his mother's death, House turned to a life of rambling. He traveled through Mississippi, Arkansas, and Louisiana, taking seasonal work on farms and cattle ranches, and serving as a pastor in Lyon, Mississippi, near Clarksdale. When he was about eighteen, he married Carrie Martin, a woman fourteen years his senior (assuming he was born in 1902 and not earlier as some researchers suspect). They left Mississippi and moved to northern Louisiana. Although the chronology is uncertain, due to his own varying accounts, House spent some time, perhaps six months, as a steel worker in St. Louis. After returning to Louisiana, probably around 1926, he and his wife separated. House moved back to the Clarksdale area.

By 1927 the church no longer dominated his life, though it would remain a source of inner conflict until his death. Inspired by guitarist Willie Wilson, whom he met in the town of Mattson, below Clarksdale, House decided to take up guitar. Accounts vary as to his musical education. On one occasion, he said he learned from Wilson; on other occasions, he insisted he was self-taught. According to researcher Dick Waterman, House bragged that he bought a guitar on a Wednesday and was playing that weekend. In any case, he was a quick study, picking up repertoire and technique from local musicians, particularly Reuben Lacey, and playing house parties by 1928. At a house party near Lyon that year, he shot and killed a man, supposedly in self-defense, and was incarcerated. After about two years, however, his case was reconsidered, and he was set free on condition that he leave the Clarksdale area.

He then settled in Lula, Mississippi, where he came in contact with Charley Patton, often regarded as the father of Delta blues, and was soon performing with Patton and Patton's partner, Willie Brown. In the spring of 1930 when H. C. Spier, a representative of Wisconsin-based Paramount Records, contacted Patton about a recording session, Patton suggested that the session also include House, Brown, and barrelhouse pianist Louise Johnson (probably Patton's girlfriend at that time). The four blues artists and gospel singer Wheeler Ford drove to Grafton, Wisconsin, for what would be one of the most important sessions in blues history. For House, the 28 May 1930 session was distinguished by three songs, each long enough to take both sides of a 78 rpm record and each considered a classic: "My Black Mama," "Preachin' the Blues," and "Dry Spell Blues." Paramount listed several other sides for House, but only one of them, "Walking Blues," was ever recovered. House claimed he received forty dollars for the session, which he considered reasonable.

Returning to Mississippi, he continued to associate with Patton and Brown. With Patton's death in 1934, House and Brown became a duo. Working out of Robinsonville, Mississippi, they ranged as far as Memphis, encountering and influencing a young Robert Johnson along the way. In 1934 House married Evie (maiden name unknown).

In August 1941 folklorist Alan Lomax recorded House, accompanied by Brown on guitar, Fiddlin' Joe Martin on mandolin and washboard, and Leroy Williams on harmonica, at a country store near Lake Cormorant. Lomax, working on a survey of African-American music for the Library of Congress, returned the following summer for a second solo session with House.

Around 1943 House moved to upstate New York in search of steady work. He eventually settled in Rochester and got a job as a Pullman porter on the Empire State Express, one of the top passenger trains of that era. (House later confided that he lied about his age to get the job, fueling speculation that he was born earlier than his listed birth date.) During this time, he made music when he visited Brown in Mississippi or when Brown came to Rochester, but after Brown's death around 1952 he gave it up.

In 1964 Dick Waterman and two other blues enthusiasts traced House to Rochester and urged him to try for a second musical career. Although his guitar playing was affected by a senile tremor, his voice remained exceptionally strong, and he made his return that year, appearing on the festival circuit and recording for Blue Goose, a Washington, D.C., label. Signing on with Waterman's booking agency, Avalon Productions, he toured with fellow blues rediscoveries "Mississippi" John Hurt and Skip James, appeared at major festivals, including the Newport Folk Festival, the Philadelphia Folk Festival, and the Ann Arbor Blues Festival, and recorded for several labels, most notably Columbia in New York City, where he was produced by John Hammond. He toured Europe several times through 1970 and was the subject of a short film. By 1971, though, his health was failing and he curtailed his appearances. In 1976 he moved to Detroit, where he died twelve years later in Harpers Hospital. He was inducted into the Memphis-based Blues Foundation Hall of Fame in 1980.

With his highly rhythmic, fully supportive slide guitar playing and his impassioned vocal style, House was one of the seminal figures in Mississippi Delta–style blues, ranking with such greats as Patton and Tommy Johnson. Although he never truly reconciled his church background with his music, he merged the traditions of the folk sermon and the blues singer, preaching the blues with great depth of feeling and a riveting on-stage delivery. According to some sources, he actually did preach in country juke joints on occasion as Saturday night became Sunday morning—then would pick up his guitar and return to "jooking."

• For discographical information, see Robert M. W. Dixon and John Godrich, *Blues and Gospel Records: 1902–1943* (1982); Mike Leadbitter and Neil Slaven, *Blues Records 1943–1966* (1968); Paul Oliver, ed., *The Blackwell Guide to Blues Records* (1989); and *Blues Records, 1943 to 1970: A Selective Discography*, vol. 1 (1987). For more biographical details, see Samuel Charters, *The Blues Makers* (1991; a repr. of *The Bluesmen* [1967]).

For interviews, see Son House, "I Can Make My Own Songs," interview with Julius Lester, *Sing Out* 15, no. 3 (July 1965): 38–45; Jeff Titon, "Living Blues Interview: Son House," *Living Blues*, no. 31 (Mar.–Apr. 1977): 14–22. For a description of his encounter with Lomax, see Alan Lomax, *The Land Where the Blues Began* (1993). His early Paramount recordings are on *Masters of the Delta Blues* (Yazoo 2007); for the Lomax recordings, try *Son House: Delta Blues/The Original Library of Congress Sessions from Field Recordings, 1941–1942* (Biograph BCD 118ADD); and for a sample of his revival phase, *Son House: Father of the Delta Blues/The Com-*

plete 1965 Sessions (Roots 'N' Blues, Columbia Legacy, C2K 48867). An obituary is by Dick Waterman in *Living Blues*, no. 84 (Jan.–Feb. 1989): 48–50.

BILL MCCULLOCH
BARRY LEE PEARSON

HOUSEMAN, John (22 Sept. 1902–31 Oct. 1988), producer, director, and actor, was born Jacques Haussmann in Bucharest, Romania, the son of Georges Haussmann, a Jewish-Alsatian grain merchant, and May Davies, a British woman of Welsh and Irish descent. As a small child Houseman spoke English to his mother, French to his father, German to his governess, and Romanian to the household staff. When Houseman was five years old, the grain business run by his father's family went bankrupt, and he moved with his parents to Paris, where his father became a broker in commodities. At age seven Houseman was sent to the Clifton School in Bristol, England. Summer vacations and holidays were spent with his parents in France. His father died in 1917. After completing his studies at Clifton in December 1920, Houseman lived for a year in Argentina, working on a cattle ranch and as a clerk at the Dutch Bank of South America. Returning to England, he turned down a scholarship to Cambridge University in order to help support his mother and became an apprentice at an international grain brokerage in London.

In his spare time Houseman read widely, attended the theater, and wrote a book of short stories. Through friends from his school days, he became acquainted with London's literary society, and some of his stories and reviews were published in the *New Statesman*. These writings, and all of his literary and theatrical activities, were done under the name John Houseman. In the business world he continued as Jacques Haussmann. His name was legally changed to John Houseman in 1943 when he became a naturalized U.S. citizen.

In November 1925 Houseman moved to New York City to work for the North American office of the Continental Grain Corporation. The following spring he became a traveling representative of the company, making rounds through the grain markets in Chicago, Kansas City, Winnipeg, and other cities. In 1928 he joined the newly founded Oceanic Grain Corporation and moved back to New York. Through friends connected with the theater, he met actress Zita Johann, whom he wed in 1929. Houseman had made a small fortune in the grain business, and the couple, who had no children, resided in a luxurious Manhattan penthouse apartment.

The stock market crash in October 1929 ruined Houseman financially. The Oceanic Grain Corporation was dissolved in early 1930, leaving him unemployed and broke. Houseman used his business failure as an opportunity to pursue his interests in writing and the theater. With Johann he wrote the drama *The Lake*, about lonely visitors to a summer resort. The play was produced in the summer of 1930 at the Berkshire Playhouse in Stockbridge, Massachusetts, with Johann in the lead role. Although the play did not draw much attention, Houseman continued writing for the theater. His plays *Three and One* (1933), a translation of a French farce, and *And Be My Love* (1934), coauthored with Lewis Galantiere, had short Broadway runs. Houseman was divorced from Johann in 1932.

Houseman achieved some notoriety in the theater when he directed the original production of the opera *Four Saints in Three Acts*, with music by Virgil Thomson and libretto by Gertrude Stein. Sponsored by a group called the Friends and Enemies of Modern Music, the opera premiered at the Wadsworth Athenaeum in Hartford, Connecticut, in February 1934. Although he had no experience as a director, Houseman was given the job of staging the opera after meeting Thomson at a New York social gathering and agreeing to follow the composer's vision of how the play should be presented. Using an African-American cast, the opera's Hartford performances were well received, and the production was presented in New York later in the year. Houseman's social contacts, his almost indefatigable energy, and his willingness to accommodate the creator's vision earned him the directorial duties on the plays *Valley Forge* (1934), by Maxwell Anderson, and *Panic* (1935), by Archibald MacLeish.

In 1935 Houseman was named comanager, with actress Rose McClendon, of the New York Negro Theatre Unit of the Federal Theatre Project, a government relief program sponsored by the Works Projects Administration (WPA). When McClendon died in early 1936, Houseman became the company's sole manager. During his tenure at the Negro Theatre, which was based at the Lafayette Theatre in Harlem, the company presented Frank Wilson's *Walk Together Chillun!* (1936), Rudolph Fisher's *Conjur Man Dies* (1936), Gus Smith and Peter Morrell's *Turpentine* (1936), and an extremely successful version of Shakespeare's *Macbeth* (1936) set in early nineteenth-century Haiti. Often referred to as *Voodoo Macbeth*, the production starred Jack Carter and Edna Thomas and was directed by Orson Welles, whom Houseman had brought in as a guest member of the company. *Voodoo Macbeth* played to sold-out houses in Harlem for ten weeks before moving to Broadway for a two-month run and then touring in WPA theaters across the nation.

In the autumn of 1936 Houseman left the Negro Theatre to direct Leslie Howard in a Broadway mounting of *Hamlet*. He then joined Welles in organizing a classical theater unit of the Federal Theatre Project. Housed at Maxine Elliott's Theatre in New York, the classical unit, officially known as Project 891, produced *Horse Eats Hat* (1936), an updating of Eugene Labiche's *An Italian Straw Hat*, and Christopher Marlowe's *Doctor Faustus* (1937). Abandoning its commitment to classical theater, Project 891 produced Marc Blitzstein's anticapitalist musical *The Cradle Will Rock* (1937). When the WPA, fearing Communist involvement, asked for a "postponement" of the controversial show, Houseman and Welles refused to comply. On opening night, after WPA officials closed down the government-funded theater, Houseman and Welles transferred the cast and audience to the Venice Theatre, which was rented at the last minute with private funds.

After the dissolution of Project 891 in mid-1937, Houseman and Welles formed the Mercury Theatre, which specialized in classical plays done with an irreverently modern sensibility. Their first production was a highly acclaimed modern-dress version of *Julius Caesar* (1937), directed by Welles, who also played the role of Brutus. The Mercury also had a major success with Thomas Dekker's bawdy Renaissance comedy *The Shoemaker's Holiday* (1938). Its productions of Shaw's *Heartbreak House* (1938) and Georg Buchner's *Danton's Death* (1938) received mixed reactions. The Mercury Theatre continued Project 891's practice of selling tickets well below normal Broadway prices even though it was without the government funding that Project 891 had enjoyed. As a result, the Mercury was continuously in debt despite packed houses. In conjunction with Theatre Guild, the financially strapped Mercury Theatre produced *Five Kings*, an amalgam of several of Shakespeare's history plays directed and devised by Welles. The sprawling production closed before reaching New York in the spring of 1939 and was the final stage venture of the Mercury Theatre. When Welles signed a film contract later in 1939, the company moved its base to Hollywood.

From 1938 to 1940 the Mercury Theatre performed on radio as the "Mercury Theatre of the Air," offering condensed versions of literary classics. Its most notable effort was H. G. Wells's Martian invasion story *The War of the Worlds* presented as a contemporary news report. Houseman was associated with the radio program as writer, editor, and associate producer until December 1939. With the exception of numerous scripts he wrote for the "Mercury Theatre of the Air," Houseman's contribution to his projects with Welles were primarily administrative and advisory. "The best way to work is to influence work," he said. Acting as business manager, he handled finances and other practical matters, while artistic decisions were left to Welles. The outspoken and self-assured Houseman frequently battled with the talented but erratic Welles, and their personal relationship deteriorated. Houseman ended his official connection to the Mercury Theatre in December 1939 after a violent argument with Welles in Chasen's restaurant in Hollywood. Despite this acrimony, a short time later Welles hired Houseman to edit Herman J. Mankiewicz's screenplay to the film *Citizen Kane* (1941). Houseman received no official credit for his work on the legendary film.

After leaving the Mercury Theatre, Houseman returned to New York to direct Phillip Barry's antifascist play *Liberty Jones* (1941). He then reunited with Welles to coproduce a stage version of Richard Wright's novel *Native Son* (1941), starring Canada Lee. Named vice president of David O. Selznick Productions in late 1941, Houseman returned to Hollywood and worked on the screenplays to *Jane Eyre* (1944) and *The Saboteur* (1942). Selznick did not produce either picture but sold the prepared projects, including director and script, to other studios for a high price. Houseman also directed West Coast stage productions featuring Selznick contract performers, most notably Ingrid Bergman in *Anna Christie* in 1941.

In January 1942 Houseman left Selznick to join the Overseas Branch of the U.S. Office of War Information as chief of multilingual radio broadcasts for the Voice of America. The operation was based on Madison Avenue in New York. In July 1943 Houseman resigned from the government post and became a producer for Paramount Pictures in Hollywood. For Paramount he produced *The Unseen* (1945), *Miss Susie Slagle's* (1945), and *The Blue Dahlia* (1946). When his Paramount contract ended in 1946, Houseman returned to New York to direct the musical *Lute Song* (1946), starring Mary Martin and Yul Brynner, and *Beggar's Holiday* (1946), a reworking of *The Beggar's Opera* with music by Duke Ellington (he quit the latter show during out-of-town tryouts).

In 1947 Houseman returned to Hollywood as a producer for Radio-Keith-Orpheum (RKO) Pictures, where he oversaw production on *They Live by Night* (1948), *The Company She Keeps* (1950), and *On Dangerous Ground* (1951). For the independent Rampart Productions he produced *Letter from an Unknown Woman* (1948), directed by Max Ophuls and starring Joan Fontaine. In 1950 Houseman married British-born Joan Courtney, a former fashion model and personal assistant to architect Philip Johnson. They had two children.

Unhappy with the quality of scripts at RKO, Houseman moved to Metro-Goldwyn-Mayer (MGM) Pictures. Before commencing work at MGM in January 1951, he directed a stage production of *King Lear*, starring Louis Calhern, which opened at Broadway's National Theatre in December 1950. Among the films Houseman produced for MGM are *The Bad and the Beautiful* (1952); *Julius Caesar* (1953), with Marlon Brando; *Executive Suite* (1954); and *Lust for Life* (1956), with Kirk Douglas. Despite Houseman's success as a film producer, the theater remained his primary interest. He kept in touch with the stage by directing Robert Ryan as *Coriolanus* at the off-Broadway Phoenix Theatre in early 1954.

Leaving MGM in December 1955, Houseman became artistic director of the American Shakespeare Festival in Stratford, Connecticut. He personally directed festival productions of *King John* (1956), *Measure for Measure* (1956), *Othello* (1957), *Much Ado about Nothing* (1957), *Hamlet* (1958), and *The Winter's Tale* (1958). Differences of opinion with the festival's board of trustees caused Houseman to end his association with the Stratford company in August 1959. Returning to California, he produced the films *All Fall Down* (1962) and *Two Weeks in Another Town* (1962) for MGM and *This Property Is Condemned* (1965) for Seven Arts Productions. He also served as artistic director of the Theatre Group at the University of California at Los Angeles.

In 1965 Houseman was asked to organize a drama division at New York's Juilliard School of Music. The Juilliard drama division opened in September 1968, and Houseman served as its director until 1976. In 1972 he established the Acting Company, a repertory company made up of graduates of the Juilliard program, which toured with productions of classic plays to universities and small theaters across the country. Houseman continued as artistic director for the Acting Company, on either a full- or part-time basis, until 1987. He considered his work at Juilliard and his founding of the Acting Company as the crowning achievements of his career. Houseman returned to Broadway to direct a successful revival of Clifford Odets's *The Country Girl*, with Jason Robards and Maureen Stapleton, in 1971, and David Rintels's *Darrow*, a one-man show starring Henry Fonda as lawyer Clarence Darrow, in 1974.

Houseman's first major acting role was that of tyrannical Professor Kingsfield in *The Paper Chase* (1973), a popular comedy/drama about the pressures of law school. His only previous acting experience was a brief turn as an admiral in the Cold War suspense drama *Seven Days in May* (1964). *The Paper Chase* earned Houseman an Academy Award for best supporting actor. Houseman parlayed his success in the film into a lucrative career as a movie and television performer. His other films include *Rollerball* (1975), *Three Days of the Condor* (1975), and *Ghost Story* (1981). On television he revived his Professor Kingsfield role in the small-screen version of "The Paper Chase" (1978–1979) and played an imperious millionaire grandfather on the situation comedy "Silver Spoons" (1982–1986). He also lent his distinguished, British-public-school-accented voice to numerous television commercials, most notably for the Smith, Barney brokerage firm. Houseman's work in film and television made him instantly recognizable to audiences who were unaware of his long career in the theater and of his work as a film producer. Houseman died at his home in Malibu, California.

• Information on Houseman's involvement with Project 891 can be found in the papers of the Federal Theatre Project, George Mason University, Fairfax, Va. The New York Public Library for the Performing Arts has a clippings file on Houseman. Houseman's memoirs are *Run-Through* (1972), *Front and Center* (1979), and *Final Dress* (1983). His other books are *The American Shakespeare Festival: The Birth of a Theatre* (1959), coauthored by Jack Landau, and *Entertainers and the Entertained* (1986), a collection of essays on theater, film, and television. Articles on Houseman include "The Moonlighter," *Time*, 26 Jan. 1962, p. 80; Mel Gussow, "At 70, Houseman Is Active and Visible," *New York Times*, 14 Mar. 1972; Chris Chase, "Suddenly They're All Sending for Houseman, *New York Times*, 21 Apr. 1974; Brad Darrach, "John Houseman," *People*, 17 Jan. 1983, pp. 57–65; Robert Brustein, "Memoirs of a Moonlighter," *New Republic*, 5 Sept. 1983, pp. 26–28; and James Bridges, "John Houseman: Actor, Producer, Inspiration," *New York Times*, 6 Nov. 1988. An obituary is in the *New York Times*, 1 Nov. 1988.

MARY C. KALFATOVIC

HOUSTON, Charles Hamilton (3 Sept. 1895–22 Apr. 1950), lawyer and professor, was born in the District of Columbia, the son of William LePre Houston, a lawyer, and Mary Ethel Hamilton, a hairdresser and former schoolteacher. Houston graduated Phi Beta Kappa from Amherst College in 1915. After a year of teaching English at Howard University in Washington, D.C., he served during World War I as a second lieutenant in the 351st Field Artillery of the American Expeditionary Forces. Having experienced racial discrimination while serving his country, Houston "made up [his] mind that [he] would never get caught . . . without knowing . . . [his] rights, that [he] would study law and use [his] time fighting for men who could not strike back." He entered Harvard Law School in 1919, where he became the first African American elected as an editor of the *Harvard Law Review,* and in 1922 he earned an LL.B. cum laude. In 1922–1923 he studied for the doctorate in juridical science, becoming the first African American to be awarded the S.J.D. at Harvard. Following an additional year of study with a concentration on civil law at the University of Madrid, Houston passed the bar examination for the District of Columbia in 1924. In that year he married Margaret Gladys Moran. They divorced in 1937, and Houston married Henrietta Williams, with whom he had one child.

Houston practiced law as a partner in the District of Columbia firm of his father (Houston & Houston; later Houston, Houston, Hastie & Waddy) from 1924 to 1950, with occasional leaves of absence. He also taught law and became an academic administrator at Howard University Law School, serving on its faculty from 1924 to 1935. His accomplishments at Howard were remarkable. From 1929 to 1935 he provided leadership during the transformation of the then nonaccredited evening school to a highly respected, full-time, American Bar Association–accredited day law school that enjoyed membership in the Association of American Law Schools. Directing the work of the law school as vice dean and chief administrative officer (1930–1935), Houston inspired the faculty and students with a sense of urgency and a spirit of boldness regarding the duty of African-American lawyers as advocates of racial justice. Houston expounded a philosophy of "social engineering," which was grounded in the beliefs that law could be used effectively to secure fundamental social change in society and that the law was an instrument available to minority groups who were unable to use fully the franchise or direct action to achieve recognition of their rights and equality. Among his students during this period were Oliver Hill, William Bryant, and Thurgood Marshall, each of whom would become distinguished civil rights litigators and the latter two of whom would achieve national renown as federal jurists.

Houston's civil rights advocacy primarily focused on achieving recognition of African Americans' equal rights under law through the elimination of legally enforced racial discrimination. He argued that the status of African Americans as an oppressed minority necessitated the "complete elimination of segregation" through a protracted struggle including a legal campaign supported by a "sustaining mass interest," with "leadership . . . develop[ing] from the aspirations, determinations, sacrifices and needs of the group itself." He served as the first full-time, salaried special counsel of the National Association for the Advancement of Colored People (NAACP) from 1935 to 1940. He proposed in 1934 and thereafter implemented a strategy for overturning the "separate but equal" precedent of *Plessy v. Ferguson* (1896) to the end that racial discrimination and segregation might be declared unconstitutional by the U.S. Supreme Court. In recognition of courts' reliance on *stare decisis* and of widespread racism, Houston developed a long-range strategy of building favorable precedents over time until a direct attack on segregation per se could be made based upon such precedents rather than following one proposed earlier by Nathan Margold to make an immediate attack on segregation. Houston's strategy was implemented by the NAACP and later its Legal Defense and Educational Fund under Thurgood Marshall's direction. While the NAACP and its Legal Defense Fund were concerned about various manifestations of racial discrimination, a special grant from the American Fund for Public Service was primarily devoted to funding cases involving discrimination in education because of its relation to the fundamental problem of white supremacy. According to Houston in 1935, "Apparent senseless discriminations in education against Negroes have a very definite objective on the part of the ruling whites to curb the young and prepare them to accept an inferior position in American life without protest or struggle."

As special counsel and later adviser to Thurgood Marshall, Houston emphasized for the sake of "effectiveness" both the importance of the use of African-American lawyers and the commitment to a program of "intelligent leadership plus intelligent mass action." Houston worked with local African-American attorneys and argued before the U.S. Supreme Court *Missouri ex rel. Gaines v. Canada* in 1938, the first major Supreme Court case in the groundwork laid for *Brown V. Board of Education* (1954), which declared segregation in public schools unconstitutional. He thereafter shaped with Marshall many of the essential legal precedents leading to *Brown,* including *Sipuel v. Oklahoma State Board of Regents* (1948), *McLaurin v. Oklahoma State Regents* (1950), and *Sweatt v. Painter* (1950). For African Americans in the Consolidated Parent Group of the District of Columbia, Houston initiated litigation against inequality in public schools, which under James Nabrit was later transformed and ultimately led to *Bolling v. Sharpe* (1954), the companion case to *Brown* declaring segregation in the District's public schools unconstitutional.

Houston's historical significance is chiefly derived from his role as strategist, legal counsel, and adviser in the struggle against racial discrimination in public education. It is noteworthy, however, that while he was among the first to emphasize the importance of training lawyers to change law and to participate in dissent regarding fundamental policy and practice of the government, he recognized that the judicial process was slow and not designed to change, but rather to uphold the status quo. Because of these "limitations," he cautioned those who would rely on the courts alone and encouraged African Americans to "do [their] own fighting and more of it by extra-legal means," that is, boycotts, demonstrations, and the like.

Houston's contributions to eliminating legal validation of racial discrimination extended into other areas, particularly the struggles for fairness in employment, housing, and the rights of the accused. He served, for a time, on the President's Fair Employment Practices Committee and in 1944 successfully argued before the U.S. Supreme Court in *Steele v. Louisville and Nashville Railroad* as well as *Tunstall v. Brotherhood of Locomotive Firemen and Engineers* the duty of fair representation regardless of race or union affiliation. In regard to housing discrimination, Houston assisted the NAACP in its preparation for *Shelly v. Kraemer* (1948) and was chief counsel before the U.S. Supreme Court in the companion case, *Hurd v. Hodge* (1948), in which the Court barred racially restrictive covenants in the states and the District of Columbia. With respect to the rights of persons accused of crimes, Houston litigated *Hollins v. Oklahoma* (1935) and *Hale v. Kentucky* (1938), in which the U.S. Supreme Court overturned the convictions and death sentences of African-American defendants who had been tried by juries from which African Americans had been excluded on the basis of race.

An active participant in the civil rights struggle of African Americans beyond the courtroom, Houston engaged in a variety of expressions of political activism during his lifetime, including marching during the 1930s for the freedom of the "Scottsboro Boys," writing a regular column of political commentary in the *Afro-American,* and testifying before Congress against lynching and other forms of racial injustice. His analysis and experiences compelled him in 1949 to urge African Americans not simply to be "content . . . with . . . an equal share in the existing system," but to struggle to establish a system that "guarantee[d] justice and freedom for everyone."

Charles Hamilton Houston's grueling pace in the struggle for racial justice eventually resulted in a heart attack from which he died in Washington, D.C. He was buried in Lincoln Memorial Cemetery in Suitland, Maryland.

• Letters and papers of Houston may be found in the records of the NAACP and the William L. Houston Family Papers in the Library of Congress, in the records of the Fair Employment Practices Committee at the National Archives, and in the Charles H. Houston vertical file, the Consolidated Parent Group Records, and the C. H. Houston Collection at the Moorland-Spingarn Research Center, Howard University. Genna Rae McNeil, *Groundwork: Charles Hamilton Houston and the Struggle for Civil Rights* (1983), is a full-length biography, while Geraldine Segal, *In Any Fight Some Fall* (1975), is a shorter study of Houston's life. Recollections of Thurgood

Marshall's relationship with Houston appear in "College Honors Charles Houston '15," *Amherst Magazine,* Spring 1978, and Kenneth Gormley, "The Man Who Won't Retire with Thurgood Marshall," *ABA Journal* 78, no. 6 (1992): 62–66. The recollections of Houston's colleague Spottswood Robinson III and his cousin and former law partner William H. Hastie are published in "No Tea for the Feeble," *Howard Law Journal* 20 (1977): 1–9. Houston may be seen and heard in *The Road to Brown* (1990), an audio-visual production produced by William Elwood and Mykola Kulish. Conrad Harper's particularly useful biographical entry incorporating excellent summaries of Houston's major legal cases appears in the *Dictionary of American Negro Biography* (1982). Compare Richard Kluger, *Simple Justice* (1976), and Mark Tushnet, *The NAACP Legal Strategy against Segregated Education, 1925–1950* (1987), for different interpretations on Houston's role as strategist. See also Clement Vose, *Caucasians Only* (1959), and G. R. McNeil, "'To Meet the Group Needs': The Transformation of Howard University School of Law, 1920–1935," in *New Perspectives on Black Educational History,* ed. V. P. Franklin and James Anderson (1978). Lengthy obituaries are in the *Afro-American,* 29 Apr. 1950, and the *Pittsburgh Courier,* 6 May 1950.

GENNA RAE MCNEIL

HOUSTON, David Franklin (17 Feb. 1866–2 Sept. 1940), cabinet officer and university president, was born in Monroe, North Carolina, the son of William Henry Houston and Cornelia Anne Stevens, farmers. When he was six, his family moved to Darlington, South Carolina, where his father farmed unsuccessfully and later bought and sold horses. David graduated from the College of South Carolina in 1887, pursued graduate work there, and was the superintendent of public schools in Spartanburg, South Carolina, between 1888 and 1891. Houston then attended Harvard where he received an A.M. degree in economics and political science in 1892. He followed politics closely, but no one "commanded my admiration or aroused my enthusiasm" until the emergence of Grover Cleveland as the Democratic presidential candidate in 1884 (*Eight Years,* vol. 1, p. 2). Houston responded to Cleveland's candidacy because the New York Democrat emphasized economy in government and sound money. When Cleveland ran for a second, nonconsecutive term, Houston wrote the section of the Democratic campaign textbook in 1892 that dealt with the currency issue.

In 1894 Houston was appointed to teach political science at the University of Texas in Austin. He married Helen Beall the next year; they had five children. In 1896 he published *A Critical Study of Nullification in South Carolina.* He was named dean of the faculty at the University of Texas in 1899. In 1902 he became the president of Texas Agricultural and Mechanical College. Three years later he returned to the University of Texas as its president, and during his tenure he raised faculty salaries and academic standards. He was appointed the chancellor of Washington University in St. Louis in 1908. By now he was "considered one of the strongest younger University presidents in the country." He carried forward educational reforms in his new position during the four years that followed.

While in Austin, Houston became friendly with Edward M. House, who emerged as an important figure in shaping the cabinet appointments for the administration of President Woodrow Wilson. House introduced Houston to Wilson in 1911 and lobbied strongly for Houston's appointment to the cabinet in 1912. By February 1913 Wilson had decided to name Houston as secretary of agriculture, although the two men did not meet again before the selection was made. Houston recalled that he had been "more or less in touch with the Department of Agriculture for a number of years, and had been dealing with the problems which it had to consider" (*Eight Years*, vol. 1, p. 15). He had been a member of the General Education Board that John D. Rockefeller had used to direct money into the education of rural southerners, and that gave Houston some expertise in farm problems.

Houston brought the perspective of a Cleveland-era Democrat to the Wilson administration, and that conservatism was often reflected in the policy positions of his department. He resisted efforts by farmers to have the federal government extend financial credit to rural areas. He declared against proposals "that would take the money of all the people . . . and lend it to the farmers or any other class at a rate of interest lower than the economic conditions would normally require" (Clements, p. 64). Like President Wilson, however, Houston accepted the system of rural credits that was established in 1916 and made it work successfully.

Houston had greater influence in the enactment of a federal farm demonstration program through the 1914 Smith-Lever Act, which provided for government funding for extension agents and demonstration activities. The secretary also devoted much attention to improved marketing of farm products, encouraging foreign sales of American agricultural products, and he worked for regulations that would allow farmers to get a fair price for their crops, but he consistently opposed price supports. These policies were embodied in such laws as the Cotton Futures Act (1914), the Grain Standards Act (1916), and the United States Warehouse Act (1916). Houston also worked diligently, and with some success, to improve the organizational structure of the Department of Agriculture.

As a member of Wilson's cabinet, Houston confined his work to the duties of his own department. He was a critic of the submarine policy of the German government during World War I and told the president in February 1917, when unrestricted submarine warfare was declared, that "Nothing worse can ever befall us than what Germany proposes, and no greater insult can be offered to any people." (*Eight Years*, vol. 1. p. 230).

During World War I, Houston ran his department effectively but was overshadowed in the popular mind by the work of Herbert Hoover, the food administrator. After the war, an ailing Wilson named Houston as secretary of the treasury in February 1920. In that post and as chairman of the Federal Reserve Board, Houston followed interest rate policies that contributed in part to the precipitous drop in farm prices during the summer of 1920. He served until the end of the Wilson presidency on 4 March 1921.

Houston left public service for the business world and held a number of corporate positions during the remainder of his life. He was president of Bell Telephone Securities Company and later vice president of American Telephone and Telegraph. He served as president of the Mutual Life Insurance Company from 1927 to 1940 and was on the executive boards of Harvard University and Columbia University. He died in New York City.

Houston was normally quiet and reserved. A newspaperman said of him that "before reaching a conclusion he rolls a thought over and over in his mind, much as a cow chews a cud" (Hemphill, p. 905). His discretion and tact appealed to Wilson, who relied on Houston for advice about important issues during the White House years. In 1916 the president said of his cabinet colleague, "His services are of a very unusual quality and there is no one among my advisers whose advice and judgment I more confidently rely upon" (Link, vol. 40, p. 216). Houston provided significant service in the development of the federal government's policies toward agriculture during the early twentieth century and merits greater historical recognition than he has received.

• Houston's personal papers are at Harvard University, and the period of his cabinet service can be followed in the Records of the Office of the Secretary of Agriculture, National Archives. The papers of Edward M. House, Yale University, and Albert S. Burleson, Library of Congress, are also useful for Houston. There is a biographical file about his service at the University of Texas at the Center for American History there. For his tenure in the Wilson administration, Arthur S. Link et al., eds., *The Papers of Woodrow Wilson* (65 vols. 1966–1994), is indispensable. Houston published *Eight Years with Wilson's Cabinet* (2 vols., 1926). For his writings in the cabinet, see "Better Roads Make Better Neighbors," *Independent* 76 (20 Nov. 1913): 337. J. C. Hemphill, "A Great Farmer: David Franklin Houston," *North American Review* 205 (June 1917): 905–14, is a contemporary evaluation. John Weston Payne, "David F. Houston: A Biography" (Ph.D. diss., Univ. of Tex., Austin, 1953), is the only biography. Kendrick A. Clements, *The Presidency of Woodrow Wilson* (1992), has a good chapter on Houston's administration of the Agriculture Department. An obituary is in the *New York Times*, 3 Sept. 1940.

LEWIS L. GOULD

HOUSTON, Edwin James (9 July 1847–1 Mar. 1914), educator and electrical engineer, was born in Alexandria, Virginia, the son of John Mason Houston and Mary Larmour. Houston attended public grammar schools and Philadelphia's Central High School, actually an undergraduate college, from which he graduated in 1864 with a bachelor of arts degree. He taught at Philadelphia's Girard College, where he was prefect in 1865, for a year. He then went to Europe, where he studied at the Universities of Heidelberg and Berlin for the following two years. In 1867 he returned to

Philadelphia to take the chair of the newly organized civil engineering and physical geography department at Central High School.

Known as an earnest and persistent worker, Houston developed the curriculum for his department. In mapping out the coursework, he found the existing natural science textbooks sorely inadequate. He remedied this by writing textbooks for the classes, including *Elements of Physical Geography* (1875), *Elements of Natural Philosophy* (1879), *Elements of Chemistry* (1879), *Primer of Electricity* (1879), and *Outlines of Forestry* (1893). He also saw to it that Central High School became equipped with a laboratory.

At Central High School Houston came to know Elihu Thomson, an outstanding student who was asked to join the faculty as an assistant to a chemistry professor in 1870. Thomson and Houston, both drawn to the science of electricity, soon became associates and friends. Houston suggested that they form a partnership to carry out electrical research; Thomson would perform the experimental work, and Houston would document the experiments and their findings for publication.

In 1877 the Franklin Institute made plans to purchase an arc-light dynamo; Houston and Thomson were assigned to test the three dynamos submitted for purchase and select the one with the best design and construction. The two men gained a comprehensive understanding of the electrical principles involved in the makeup of an effective dynamo and went on to produce an arc-lighting system of their own design. Their system was the first to maintain a constant level of current in the circuit by automatically shifting the brushes of the generator as the load varied. Thomson and Houston demonstrated their arc-light system at the Franklin Institute during the fall and winter of 1878 and 1879 and attracted wide notice. In March 1881 they received a patent for this device; their paper "On the Transmission of Power by Means of Electricity" appeared in the *Journal of the Franklin Institute* in January 1879. In this paper Thomson and Houston argued that the long-distance transmission of power from Niagara Falls was feasible, a claim not entirely substantiated until 1896.

Also in 1879 Thomson and Houston sold their first lighting system to a Philadelphia baker. The success of their arc light led to the establishment in the fall of 1879 of a factory to manufacture arc-lighting dynamos, lights, and other accessories, producing about three dynamos and fifty lamps a week. The following July the American Electric Company was organized with a capital stock of $125,000 to promote and market the Thomson-Houston arc-light system. Thomson left his position at Central High School to work as an electrical engineer for this company, which underwent several reorganizations, becoming the Thomson-Houston Electric Company in 1883 and in 1892 consolidating with the Edison General Electric Company to form the General Electric Company. Unlike Thomson, Houston remained with Central High School and became disassociated from the company after 1882.

In spite of Houston's achievements in the commercial electrical field, he regarded educational and scientific work as his primary calling. In 1884 he served as a member of the U.S. Electrical Commission, which met in Philadelphia, and presented a paper on high-vacuum phenomena in incandescent lamps (the "Edison effect") at the first meeting of the American Institute of Electrical Engineers. That same year Houston served as the chief engineer of the International Electrical Exposition in Philadelphia; in 1893 he was president of the International Electric Congress's Section C in Chicago. He was a charter member of the American Institute of Electrical Engineers, serving as its president in 1893 and 1894, and was also a member of the American Philosophical Society. Houston was elected to life membership in the Franklin Institute in 1868; over his lifetime, he served on many of its committees, including the lecture and meeting committees. He was also the first president of the Franklin Institute's Electrical Section, editor of its journal, and emeritus professor of physics at the institute.

In 1894 Houston resigned from Central High School and established a consulting electrical engineering partnership in association with Arthur Edwin Kennelly. They wrote what were probably the first elementary electrical textbooks. The ten-volume set, the Elementary Electro-Technical Series (1895–1906), covered electric heating, street railways, telegraphy, incandescent lighting, and arc lighting, as well as other fundamental electrical topics. Houston also wrote *Electricity in Electro-Therapeutics* (1896), an exploration of the role of electricity in medicine, and *Franklin as a Man of Science* (1906). In his later years he wrote many adventure books for boys, such as *In Captivity in the Pacific* (1908). Houston, a bachelor, died in Philadelphia.

Houston played an important role in the early years of electrical engineering, not only on a practical level with his pioneering work in arc-lighting systems, but also in his role as an educator. Many future electrical engineers received their guidance from Houston or his textbooks.

• Besides the works mentioned above, Houston's publications include "Notes on Phenomena in Incandescent Lamps," *Transactions of the American Institute of Electrical Engineers* 1 (1884): 1–8. Harold C. Passer, *The Electrical Manufacturers: 1875–1900* (1953), provides an understanding of the context within which Thomson and Houston developed and marketed their arc-lighting system. Detailed obituaries of Houston are in the *Journal of the Franklin Institute* (Apr. 1914); *Electrical World* (N.Y.), 7 Mar. 1914; *Electrical Review* (London), 20 Mar. 1914; and the *New York Times*, 2 Mar. 1914.

DANIEL MARTIN DUMYCH

HOUSTON, George Smith (17 Jan. 1811–31 Dec. 1879), governor of Alabama and U.S. senator, was born in Williamson County, Tennessee, the son of David Houston, a planter, and Hannah Pugh Reagan. Moving with his family to Lauderdale County, Alabama, in 1821, Houston eventually read law in Florence, and completed his studies by attending a law school conducted by U.S. District Judge John Boyle in Harrodsburg, Kentucky. He was admitted to the bar in 1831 and was elected to the state house of representatives in 1832. In the legislature he voted for resolutions condemning South Carolina's attempt to nullify the operations of the federal tariff within that state. In 1833 Governor John Gayle gave Houston a recess appointment as circuit solicitor, and in December Houston unsuccessfully sought election to the office. He moved the following year to Athens, the county seat of Limestone County, where he resided for the rest of his life. In 1835 he married Mary Beatty; they had eight children, four of whom survived to adulthood.

In 1837 the legislature elected Houston circuit solicitor. He served until 1841, when he was elected on the Democratic general ticket to Congress. Except for a period between 1849 and 1850, Houston served in the House for the next twenty years. He was a leading advocate of Democratic proposals to graduate and reduce the price of public lands, and he strongly opposed protective tariffs. He was a close friend and advisor of James K. Polk and also vigorously defended the policies of Franklin Pierce. He supported John Tyler's (1790–1862) efforts to annex Texas and championed the Gadsden Purchase. He served as chairman of the Ways and Means Committee from 1851 to 1855 and as chairman of the Judiciary Committee from 1857 to 1859.

Houston persistently sought to suppress the emerging sectional conflict. His refusal to sign John C. Calhoun's Southern Address calling for bipartisan unity against the Wilmot Proviso was so unpopular in his district that he decided not to seek reelection in 1848, but his constituents' general acceptance of the Compromise of 1850 allowed him to return to the House in that year. He was a leader in the search for a satisfactory resolution of the Kansas question, ultimately supporting the 1858 English Bill for a popular referendum to determine if Kansans would accept a smaller federal land grant in return for statehood under the proslavery Lecompton constitution. He campaigned for Stephen A. Douglas in the presidential election of 1860. In the winter of 1860–1861 he supported the creation of, and represented Alabama on, the committee appointed to draft compromise proposals. But when Alabama adopted a secession ordinance, he joined his colleagues in resigning from Congress. In the summer of 1861 he toured the hill counties of North Alabama to urge loyalty to the Confederacy. Two of his sons served in the Confederate army.

During the Civil War, Houston devoted himself to his law practice. In April 1861, now a widower, he married Ellen Irvine of Florence; they had two daughters. Investing rather extensively in real estate, Houston saw his real property increase in value (to $100,000) between 1860 and 1870. At the same time, emancipation greatly reduced the value of his personal property, and in 1870 his personal property was worth only one-tenth of its 1860 value of $150,000. In No-

vember 1865, the legislature elected Houston to a short term in the U.S. Senate. But a year later, after a heated contest, Houston was defeated for a full term by former governor John A. Winston. Both of these elections proved meaningless, however, as the Congress refused to seat the southern members chosen by the Presidential Reconstruction regimes. For the next eight years Houston maintained a law partnership with Luke Pryor, a wealthy planter and railroad director, and in 1868 Houston himself became a director of the Nashville & Decatur Railroad. In 1874, at a time when the Democrats were seeking a gubernatorial candidate who could unite all white men in the effort to overthrow the state's Republicans, Houston seemed the ideal choice; his Jacksonian background made him popular among North Alabama's small farmers, and his new ties with the railroads made him acceptable to South Alabama's former Whigs. After a bitter election marked by widespread violence, massive fraud, and highly suspect returns, Houston was declared the victor over the Republican incumbent, David P. Lewis.

Houston's governorship was dominated by questions arising from the Reconstruction state debt. Agrarian Democrats wished to see a sharp reduction of property taxes and supported a general repudiation of the debt, while railroads and business interests opposed this course. Struggling to hold together the tenuous Democratic alliance, Houston induced the state's bondholders to swap their bonds for new securities bearing lower interest rates, rather than see them repudiated entirely. He also paid off some of the railroad bonds with public lands and eliminated the state's contingent indebtedness for other railroad bonds by abandoning the state's mortgages on the railroads. Then, by reducing Alabama's support for schools and other state services to genuinely niggardly levels, he managed to lower taxes. Both elements of the Democratic coalition emerged from this process reasonably satisfied with the arrangements. In the meantime, Democrats cooperated smoothly in securing the victory of white supremacy, the one goal upon which they all agreed. The state's new constitution of 1875 raised the racial segregation of public schools to a constitutional requirement. And the elective county governments that remained in Republican hands were abolished in favor of gubernatorially appointed county boards. On Houston's final day as governor in 1878, a grateful legislature elected him to the U.S. Senate. Plunging actively into Senate proceedings in 1879, he endorsed the free coinage of silver on an equality with gold and sought to require partisan balance in federal court jury venires. In the fall, however, Houston's health suddenly failed, and he died in Athens, Alabama.

• Houston's papers, principally from his antebellum congressional career, are held by the Duke University Library, Durham, N.C. His gubernatorial correspondence is at the Alabama Department of Archives and History in Montgomery. Surprisingly little scholarly work has been done on Houston, but see Ralph B. Draughon, Jr., "George Smith Houston and Southern Unity, 1846–1849," *Alabama Review* 19, no. 3 (1966): 186–207; Edward C. Williamson, "The Alabama Election of 1874," *Alabama Review* 17, no. 3 (1964): 210–18; Allen J. Going, *Bourbon Democracy in Alabama, 1874–1890* (1951); and Virgil P. Koart, "The Administrations of George Smith Houston, Governor of Alabama, 1874–1878" (Master's thesis, Auburn Univ., 1963).

J. MILLS THORNTON III

HOUSTON, Henry Howard (3 Oct. 1820–21 June 1895), entrepreneur and early suburban developer, was born in Wrightsville, Pennsylvania, the son of Samuel Nelson Houston, a small landowner and farmer, and Susan Strickler. Houston's father was an inadequate provider and may have suffered from alcoholism. Henry attended public school, discontinuing his formal education at age fourteen in large part because the local system did not continue beyond the eighth grade, and there were insufficient family funds to send him for further education. Houston then worked for several years at a general store in Wrightsville, and in 1840 he became the clerk of the Lucinda iron furnace in Clarion County, Pennsylvania, which was owned by his father's friend (and future president of the United States), James Buchanan. In 1843 Houston joined with a young associate to rebuild and operate the Horse Creek furnace in Venango County, Pennsylvania.

With these early experiences in business, Houston moved to Philadelphia in 1851, where he became a freight agent for David Leech and Company, a leading canal and railroad transportation firm. Houston's success with this establishment brought him to the attention of the recently formed Pennsylvania Railroad, which hired him as its general freight agent in 1851. As such he was in charge of developing and managing all the freight operations of the Pennsylvania, which soon became the most important railroad in the United States. After five years in this position Houston found himself well enough established to marry. In 1856 he wed Sallie Sherrerd Bonnell of Philadelphia; the couple had three children who survived to adulthood.

Houston began to amass large amounts of money during the Civil War, when he and several other men associated with the Pennsylvania Railroad founded the Union Freight Line, a "fast freight" company that used "through bills of lading" (freight loading receipts) to speed shipments along the Pennsylvania and connecting routes, a technique that was then being adopted by competing railroads as an efficiency measure during the Civil War. Houston's income soared from approximately $5,000 per year in 1860 to $114,000 in 1865. Following the war he invested much of this money in a variety of undertakings, including railroads, steel mills, coal mines, oil refining and transporting systems, stockyards, lake freighters, and a transatlantic steamship line. One of these enterprises, the so-called Green Line, pioneered in the development of oil tank cars for hauling petroleum from the Pennsylvania oil fields. The Empire Line, with which he was also associated, was the first such concern to consolidate oil pipelines onto a rational system of transport.

Houston's increasing wealth and absorption in so many business activities led him to retire as the Pennsylvania Railroad's general freight agent in 1867, at a time when he was widely considered to be the leading transportation expert in the United States. In 1881 he was made a director of the Pennsylvania, a position that he held for the rest of his life. At the time of his death he left an estate of just over $14 million.

As early as 1853 Houston began investing in Philadelphia real estate. However, it was his residential development in the Chestnut Hill section of the city, located some ten miles northwest of downtown, that has given him the reputation as one of the earliest and most successful suburban planners in the United States. In executing this project he amassed about 3,000 acres of largely contiguous land, beginning in 1879 and continuing virtually to the time of his death.

Houston named his Chestnut Hill development Wissahickon Heights after the Wissahickon Creek that borders it on the west side. To connect Wissahickon Heights to downtown Philadelphia, Houston used his considerable influence with the Pennsylvania Railroad to have built a commuter line into the west side of Chestnut Hill, an undertaking that was completed in 1884. Clustering near the railroad station were several institutions that became integral parts of the development. These were the Wissahickon Inn, a summer resort hotel built by Houston and opened in 1884; the Philadelphia Cricket Club, erected on land donated by Houston and also completed in 1884; and St. Martin-in-the-Fields Episcopal Church, built and furnished by Houston and inaugurated in 1889. (Several Houston heirs would subsidize private schools in the neighborhood as yet another convenience to residents.)

Meanwhile Houston commissioned about a hundred houses, most of them designed in the Queen Anne style by the architect brothers, George W. Hewitt and William D. Hewitt. Houston rented rather than sold most of these dwellings in order to select the residents of Wissahickon Heights and to maintain control of the properties. He preferred young businessmen and professionals, invariably white, upper-middle-class Protestants, who would settle on the Heights and rear their families there. For his own family he had the Hewitt brothers design a thirty-room castellated mansion, called "Druim Moir" (1886), located on a bluff overlooking the steep and dramatic Wissahickon gorge. During the first four decades of the twentieth century Houston's son-in-law, George Woodward, M.D., would commission about 180 more houses in the area, likewise renting rather than selling the dwellings. However, in 1906 Woodward changed the name of the development from Wissahickon Heights to St. Martin's, in honor of St. Martin's Church.

The Wissahickon Heights/St. Martin's development thus represents one of the country's early planned suburbs. Although Houston was not able to supersede the grid pattern of streets that was mandated by the city of Philadelphia, he did use his influence to rename numbered streets after various Native American tribes, an idea attributed by oral tradition to his daughter, Gertrude Houston Woodward. The development thus combined Houston's passion for order and system (a characteristic that he had exhibited in creating and then presiding over the Pennsylvania Railroad's freight lines and other transportation enterprises) with the antiurban attitudes of many well-to-do Americans like Houston himself, who sought to escape the more unsavory aspects of urban life. His residential enclave in Chestnut Hill also provides a superb example of the late nineteenth- and early twentieth-century railroad suburb. Although earlier assessments of Houston have emphasized his activities as an important player in America's industrial revolution, his role as an early suburban planner may have more lasting significance. This is particularly true in light of the fact that the Pennsylvania Railroad no longer exists as a corporate entity, while the Wissahickon Heights/St. Martin's development continues to flourish as an attractive suburban enclave within the municipal limits of Philadelphia.

Houston was a private and reserved individual, who with a quiet persistence pursued his goals, including a number of charitable interests. Frank J. Firth, one of Houston's younger associates at the Pennsylvania Railroad, wrote in his unpublished diary that Houston "was not an easy man to become intimate with." He was an "able, generous gentleman," the diarist continued, "a patient, even tempered man with an amazing tenacity of purpose." Houston died at his home on Wissahickon Heights in Philadelphia after having returned on the train, as usual, from his office downtown.

• Only a few fragments of Houston's personal papers have survived. These are in the Houston collection at the American Philosophical Society in Philadelphia. The Houston Estate Papers are deposited at the Pennsylvania State Archives in Harrisburg. The board minutes and other records of the Pennsylvania Railroad, which shed light on Houston's work with the railroad as well as on his real estate development in Chestnut Hill, are located at the (Hagley) Elutherian Mills Historical Library near Wilmington, Del. Materials relating to Houston's life and work also are in the Houston Estate File at the Architectural Archives of the University of Pennsylvania and in the Alumni Records collection at the University of Pennsylvania Archives. The most complete biography of Houston appears in David R. Contosta, *A Philadelphia Family: The Houstons and Woodwards of Chestnut Hill* (1988), pp. 3–35. Also helpful in understanding Houston's real estate ventures is Contosta, *Suburb in the City: Chestnut Hill, Philadelphia* (1992), pp. 78–117. Both works by Contosta include photographs of Houston and of the Wissahickon Heights/St. Martin's development, along with a more extensive bibliography concerning Houston's life and works. A substantial obituary is in the *Philadelphia Public Ledger*, 22 June 1895.

DAVID R. CONTOSTA

HOUSTON, Sam (2 Mar. 1793–26 July 1863), president of the Republic of Texas and U.S. senator, was born Samuel Houston in Rockbridge County, Virginia, the son of Samuel Houston and Elizabeth Paxton, well-to-do planters of Scotch-Irish descent. Houston's father died in 1806, and he moved with his mother and eight siblings to Blount County, Tennessee, in 1807.

Sam Houston had little formal education and showed no interest in school or farming. When put to work in 1809 as a store clerk, he responded by leaving home to live most of the next three years with the Cherokees. He translated the name given to him by his adoptive father, Chief Oo-loo-te-ka, as "The Raven."

Houston left the Cherokees in 1812, spent eight months teaching school in Maryville, Tennessee, and on 24 March 1813, enlisted in the army. He fought in Andrew Jackson's campaign against the Creek Indians in Alabama, and at the Battle of Horseshoe Bend on 27 March 1814 was wounded three times. After recovering he remained in the army, receiving a promotion to first lieutenant on 1 May 1817 and an appointment as subagent to the Cherokees on 18 October 1817. However, following a dispute with Secretary of War John C. Calhoun while visiting Washington with a delegation of Cherokees in the spring of 1818, Houston resigned from the army and as Indian subagent.

Houston moved to Nashville in June 1818, read law, and was admitted to the bar. He then opened an office in Lebanon, Tennessee. In October 1819 he was elected attorney general for Davidson County. He resigned that position a year later and in 1821 was elected a major general in the Tennessee Militia. A strong Jacksonian, Houston was elected to the U.S. House of Representatives in 1823; he was reelected in 1825. When his second term ended, he ran successfully for governor of Tennessee and was sworn in on 1 October 1827.

On 22 January 1829 Houston married eighteen-year-old Eliza Allen, daughter of a prominent Gallatin, Tennessee, family. Less than three months later, for reasons that remain unknown, his wife went home to her family. Although his term had been successful to that point, the separation caused a public furor, and Houston resigned the governorship on 16 April 1829.

Houston left Nashville on 23 April 1829 and went into exile with the Cherokees in present-day Oklahoma. On 21 October he became a member of the Cherokee Nation. During the summer of 1830 he married Tiana Rogers Gentry, who was one-quarter Cherokee. Houston had long been a heavy drinker, and in 1830 and 1831 his weakness for alcohol gained the upper hand. Some of the Cherokees called him "Big Drunk." In 1831 he ran for a seat on the national council of the Cherokee Nation and lost.

As early as 1829 rumor had Houston intending to go to Texas and create a revolution there. Such stories made good gossip then, and they have made good reading ever since. However, the truth of these tales is questionable. When Houston first departed for Texas in 1832, his official reason was to seek an arrangement with the Comanches that would facilitate the peaceful settlement of the southeastern tribes in the Indian Territory. Houston also had determined to end his exile with the Cherokees, and the land to the southwest held the promise of financial opportunity and perhaps even a return to public life. He arranged a divorce from Tiana, rode southwestward, and crossed the Red River at Fort Towson on 2 December 1832.

Legal migration by Anglo-Americans into Mexican Texas had begun in 1821 under the terms of a contract granted by Spanish authorities to Moses Austin and confirmed to his son, Stephen F. Austin, and the essential ingredients for revolution were in place well before Houston entered the province. When the central government in Mexico City attempted to levy customs duties in the spring of 1832, settlers in east Texas created violent disturbances and held a convention that adopted resolutions calling for making Texas a separate state in Mexico's federal union. Mexican authorities refused to accept the petition, but the Texans called another convention for April 1833. In the interval Sam Houston arrived in Texas.

Houston met with the Comanches at San Antonio, securing a promise of talks with the United States and the southeastern Indians; visited San Felipe and applied for a land grant in Stephen F. Austin's colony; and went to Nacogdoches where on 1 March 1833 he was elected a delegate to the April convention. At this meeting he supported the call for separate statehood and served on a committee that drafted a constitution for the Mexican state of Texas. Austin was given the task of taking this request to Mexico City, an assignment that would take more than two years. In the meantime, Houston settled in Nacogdoches and practiced law.

Texas remained relatively quiet until the spring of 1835. Then, as the president of Mexico, General Antonio Lopez de Santa Anna undermined the federal constitution of 1824 and moved toward assuming dictatorial powers over the central government in Mexico City, conflict developed over the collection of customs duties and the threatened arrest of outspoken opponents of his regime. Anglo-Texans called for a consultation of representatives of all the province's municipalities to meet in the fall. Houston was elected a delegate from Nacogdoches.

The consultation rejected independence, protested loyalty to Mexico's federal system, and established a provisional government for the Mexican state of Texas. On 12 November 1835 Houston was appointed commander in chief of the Texas army. The Texans took San Antonio in December, but aggressive militarists then ignored Houston's pleas for caution and planned an attack on Matamoros on the Rio Grande. Disgusted, he asked in January 1836 for a furlough until 1 March, when a new convention was scheduled to meet. Houston was elected as a delegate from Refugio, a small Texas settlement he had visited while opposing the Matamoros campaign.

The convention adopted a declaration of independence on 2 March 1836. Two days later Houston was again chosen commander in chief as attention focused on the Alamo in San Antonio where Santa Anna's army besieged a small force of Texans. Houston was at Gonzales, fifty miles east of San Antonio, when he received confirmation on 13 March that the Alamo had fallen. He then began a retreat eastward that lasted for more than a month. It was not a headlong flight but rather a controlled movement away from a numerically superior enemy while building strength and waiting for an opportunity to strike an effective blow. In early April Santa Anna gave Houston that opportunity by stopping immediate pursuit of the Texas army and moving ahead of his main army with a smaller force in an effort to capture Texas's ad interim government. Houston rushed to block Santa Anna before he could cross the San Jacinto River north of Galveston Bay, and on 21 April 1836 the Texas army routed the Mexican force in an eighteen-minute battle that cost the Mexicans 630 lives and 730 prisoners; the Texans suffered only 25 casualties. Houston was one of the wounded: a musket ball shattered the front part of the tibia just above his right ankle.

Two weeks after the battle Houston went to New Orleans to seek medical attention for his wound. He returned to Texas in the summer of 1836 and on 5 September was elected president of the Republic of Texas. He served from 22 October 1836 until 10 December 1838, facing numerous difficulties in establishing his new nation's domestic and foreign policies. His administration gained diplomatic recognition from the United States in March 1837, but efforts toward annexation to the United States failed.

Houston was ineligible for reelection under the Texas Constitution, but in 1839, soon after leaving office, he was elected to represent San Augustine County in the Fourth Texas Congress. In congress Houston distinguished himself by attacking the administration of his successor, Mirabeau B. Lamar, for its aggressive policy toward the Cherokees in East Texas and its large public expenditures.

On 9 May 1840 Houston married twenty-one-year-old Margaret Lea, the daughter of a wealthy Alabama family, whom he had met while on a business trip in 1839. His wife persuaded him to stop drinking and eventually to join the Baptist church. They had eight children, the last born in 1860 when Houston was sixty-seven.

Houston entered the presidential contest in 1841 to win vindication for his opposition to the Lamar administration. His opponent was Vice President David G. Burnet, a bitter enemy who had called Houston a coward for retreating from the Mexicans in 1836. In a campaign marked by extreme personal vituperation, Houston was elected by an overwhelming margin.

Houston's second administration was marked by retrenchment in public finances, treaty negotiations with Texas Indians, and a search for peace with Mexico. These policies were only sensible for a republic with no money and virtually no armed forces, but peace was not popular, especially after Mexico twice invaded Texas in 1842. In 1843 Houston renewed efforts for annexation to the United States. A treaty was signed in April 1844, but it became entangled in sectional politics in the United States and did not win Senate approval. Unable to succeed himself in the

Texas presidency, Houston left office in December 1844. He supported annexation when it came in 1845.

The Texas legislature elected Houston to the U.S. Senate on 21 February 1846. He drew a two-year term upon entering the Senate but was elected to a full term in December 1847. As sectional animosity over slavery increased, Houston took what would become an unalterable stance against extremism and in defense of the Union. Houston's moderate views on slavery supported his determination to preserve the Union. He owned slaves throughout his life and did not see the institution as a compelling moral issue; he defended it as a practical necessity, a way of providing labor and race control, and rejected the more aggressive view associated with John C. Calhoun and other extremists that slavery was a "positive good." Time would deal with the institution, he hoped, if fanatics would leave it alone. He voted in 1848 for organizing the Oregon Territory with a prohibition on slavery, and he refused to sign John C. Calhoun's 1849 "Southern Address," which called for sectional unity in defense of southern rights. He voted for all parts of the Compromise of 1850. Houston was elected to a third term in the Senate in January 1853, but his unionism began to injure his political career seriously in 1854 when he voted against the Kansas-Nebraska Act. Many of his constituents never forgave what they regarded as an antisouthern act. In 1855 the state legislature officially condemned his vote and indicated that he would not be reelected when his term expired in 1859. Houston identified with the Know-Nothing party in 1855–1856 and ran for governor of Texas in 1857. In that contest he suffered the only electoral defeat of his career, losing to Hardin R. Runnels, an ultrasoutherner.

When Houston's Senate term ended in 1859, he again ran for governor of Texas against Runnels. Unionism was the primary issue, and this time Houston won, becoming governor in December 1859. Unionists talked of nominating Houston for president of the United States in 1860, but he never became a major contender for the nomination. When Abraham Lincoln won the election, and leading Texans called an extralegal secession convention to meet in January 1861, Houston sought to head off disunion by calling the state legislature into session. However, the legislature endorsed the convention, which then met and adopted an ordinance of secession. A referendum on 23 February 1861 resulted in overwhelming support for disunion. Houston accepted these actions as the will of the people, but when the secession convention adopted an ordinance uniting Texas with the Confederate States of America, he objected on the grounds that the public had not approved that step. On 16 March 1861 he refused to take an oath of loyalty to the Confederacy and was removed as governor by the convention.

Houston did everything possible to prevent secession and war, but his first loyalty was to Texas—and the South. Houston refused offers of troops from the United States to keep Texas in the Union and announced on 10 May 1861 that he would stand with the

Confederacy in its war effort. He soon retired to Huntsville where he died.

• Major collections of Houston's letters and documents are in the Barker Texas History Center at the University of Texas and in the Library of Congress. Most of his papers are published in Amelia Williams and Eugene C. Barker, eds., *The Writings of Sam Houston, 1813–1863* (8 vols., 1938–1943), although some important letters and documents have been discovered since the appearance of this work. The most readable study of Houston is Marquis James, *The Raven: A Biography of Sam Houston* (1929), which won a Pulitzer Prize. However, James's study is marked by a great emphasis on the colorful and romantic in Houston's life and a seemingly uncritical reliance on the personal recollections of family members. In places, it resembles semi-fictionalized biography more than a scholarly study. M. K. Wisehart, *Sam Houston: American Giant* (1962), is the most detailed and judicious account of Houston's life. Llerena Friend, *Sam Houston: The Great Designer* (1954), is the best political biography. Friend's research is excellent, and her conclusions are balanced and reasonable, except when she tries to force Houston into the mold of her colorful title by interpreting his career as a Unionist during the 1850s as part of a design to win the presidency of the United States.

RANDOLPH B. CAMPBELL

HOUSTON, William Churchill (1746–12 Aug. 1788), public official and New Jersey delegate to the Constitutional Convention, was born in the Sumter district of South Carolina, the son of Archibald Houston and Margaret (maiden name unknown), small planters. In the early 1750s the family moved to Anson County in the North Carolina piedmont. During the mid-eighteenth century a number of Presbyterian ministers, trained at the College of New Jersey (later Princeton), established churches in the Carolina piedmont among the Scotch-Irish settlers and began schools. Houston probably attended one of these schools, most likely Crowfield Academy, and was then sent on to Princeton. He graduated with the class of 1768; while a student, he helped support himself by teaching at the college's grammar school.

After graduation Houston became master of the grammar school, and in 1771 the college's trustees appointed him to the new professorship of mathematics and natural philosophy. During the first years of the revolutionary war, with the college's president John Witherspoon active in the Continental Congress, Houston not only taught at the school but also assumed many of the administrative responsibilities for the institution and despite an active political career remained on the faculty until 1783.

It was probably Houston's connection with Princeton and Witherspoon that drew him into politics as the Revolution approached. John Adams, who met Houston in 1774, applauded him as among the Sons of Liberty, and in the winter of 1775 Houston traveled to Boston, possibly for the Continental Congress. In February 1776 the New Jersey Council of Safety recorded his election as an officer in the Somerset County militia; he resigned that summer to return to the college but apparently took up his commission again in the fall, when British forces moved on Princeton. He may have seen active combat during the winter campaigns in central New Jersey.

Houston's most significant contributions to rebellion came not as a soldier, however, but as a public official in New Jersey and in the revolutionary confederation government. In March 1777 he was elected to the position of deputy secretary of the Continental Congress, serving under Charles Thomson, and continued in the post until September, when Somerset County sent him to the New Jersey General Assembly as one of its three representatives. He remained active in the assembly, gradually gaining greater and greater committee responsibilities, until May 1779, when he and Abraham Clark were elected as New Jersey representatives to the Continental Congress. Houston played a particularly active role in Congress through July 1781, when he became seriously ill, and he then served intermittently through the winter of 1785.

Given Houston's professorship in mathematics and natural philosophy, it is not surprising that his most significant responsibilities were in dealing with the financial problems of the confederation. Lacking the power to tax to raise revenue for the war effort, the Continental Congress printed ever larger quantities of paper money, offered bonds issues, and authorized agents to seize goods and pay in federal certificates. All these issues depreciated rapidly, and by the time Houston arrived at the Continental Congress, the confederation faced a financial crisis as representatives desperately tried to find a way to continue paying for the war. Houston directed his energies to this crisis. He helped draft a report to the Congress in March 1780 on the repayment of loan office certificates and in May of that year brought in a recommendation to allow certificates, issued by agents of the commissary general for the seizure of provisions, to be used to pay taxes.

In September 1781 Congress recognized his contribution by electing him comptroller of the treasury, a position he declined; then in April 1782 Robert Morris, the superintendent of finance, appointed him receiver of Continental taxes in New Jersey. Congress had authorized Morris to appoint state receivers to coordinate the collection of money paid by the states to Congress and in anticipation of authorization that never came, to levy direct taxes. Houston held the position from 1782 to 1785, and, judging from his papers, he devoted a considerable amount of time to his responsibilities.

As the crisis of 1780–1781 subsided and the victory of the revolutionaries seemed more assured, Houston, like many of those who had struggled to maintain the war effort and had become increasingly disillusioned with what they perceived in their fellow citizens as a corrupt pursuit of self-interest, became less active in the Continental Congress. His decision may have been quickened by poor health and by the fact that about this time he married Jane Smith, with whom he had five children. He had also taken up the study of law with Richard Stockton and in 1781 was admitted to the bar and appointed clerk of the New Jersey Supreme Court. The next year he resettled in Trenton, became a leader in the local Presbyterian church, and began to practice law, litigating cases in the Hunterdon, Burlington, and Monmouth county courts.

In 1782 Houston was among the lawyers who supported the East Jersey proprietors in their dispute before the New Jersey Assembly with the West Jersey proprietors over location of the division line between the two sections of the state. Still a member of Congress, but now less active, he was also appointed in 1782 to a commission to resolve the conflicting claims of Connecticut and Pennsylvania to the Wyoming lands (the commission resolved the dispute in favor of Pennsylvania), and in his last term in Congress he took some interest in John Fitch's efforts to promote his plans to build a steamboat.

During the early 1780s Houston wrote a number of brief essays on political and economic topics. Some were probably crafted for law cases; others may have merely been private reflections on matters with which he was dealing in Congress. None were ever published. Among them were "Detached Thoughts on the Subject of Money and Finance" from January 1781 (arguing against paper money and price controls), "Whether It Would Be a Good Policy to Erect Corporations of Any Kind in the State and If So of What Kind?" from January 1782 (arguing against civic corporations), an "Essay on Taxation" from May 1782 (which denounced slavery and proposed greater taxes on luxury goods), and an extended opinion on free speech from March 1784 (that argued that a statement was libelous only if it was intentionally false and clearly malicious).

Houston was among the representatives sent by New Jersey to the Annapolis Convention of 1786 to consider how the states might cooperate in trade policy. From the Annapolis meeting came the call for a new convention to consider amending the Articles of Confederation. Houston was appointed to the New Jersey delegation for the Philadelphia Convention of 1787—but now very ill, he left little mark on the meeting. Shortly thereafter Houston died, probably in Frankford, Pennsylvania, from tuberculosis. His personal estate, land excluded, was inventoried at a modest but comfortable £355; at the time of his death, he owned a substantial law library and a young slave woman.

Houston was a second-rung public leader during an era of extraordinary circumstances. In the revolutionary politics and the state-building activities of that era, his accomplishments were not on the same order as those of New Jersey leaders such as William Paterson, John Witherspoon, or William Livingston, but he played key roles in guiding the College of New Jersey through difficult times and in serving in the Continental Congress. While he left little in the way of a written legacy, Houston shared the sentiments, borne of his wartime experience, of those who worked to create a stronger, more centralized national government.

• The Princeton University Library has the most significant collection of Houston's papers; these deal with his legal practice, his activities as receiver for Continental taxes, and the settlement of his estate. Additional papers are at the New Jersey Historical Society, Trenton; the Historical Society of Pennsylvania, Philadelphia; and the Rutgers University Library, New Brunswick. Thomas Allen Glenn, *William Churchill Houston, 1746–1788* (1903), is an extended biography but should be supplemented by the essay on Houston in James McLachlan, ed., *Princetonians, 1748–1768: A Biographical Dictionary* (1976), pp. 643–47. His schooling is mentioned in William Henry Foote, *Sketches of North Carolina, Historical and Biographical, Illustrative of the Principles of a Portion of Her Early Settlers* (1846). On the question of Houston's service at the Philadelphia Convention, compare Glenn with Richard P. McCormick, *Experiment in Independence: New Jersey in the Critical Period, 1781–1789* (1950), which is also extremely useful for placing Houston's many activities in the context of New Jersey politics. His activities can be traced in several document collections: Edmund Cody Burnett, ed., *Letters of Members of the Continental Congress* (8 vols., 1921–1936); Carl E. Prince et al., eds., *The Papers of William Livingston* (5 vols., 1979–1988); E. James Ferguson et al., eds., *The Papers of Robert Morris, 1781–1784* (6 vols., 1973–1984); the *Journals of the Continental Congress* (34 vols., 1904–1937); and *Votes and Proceedings of the New Jersey General Assembly*.

PAUL G. E. CLEMENS

HOUSTON, William Vermillion (19 Jan. 1900–22 Aug. 1968), physicist and science administrator, was born in Mount Gilead, Ohio, the son of William Houston, a Presbyterian minister, and Lena Vermillion. Houston spent much of his childhood and early years in Columbus, Ohio, where he completed secondary school and in 1920 obtained a B.A. and a B.S. from Ohio State University. After teaching at the University of Dubuque for a short period, Houston undertook graduate studies in physics at the University of Chicago. There he studied under Robert A. Millikan and Albert A. Michelson, two of the most prominent American physicists at the time. Both experimentalists, they exerted a strong influence on Houston's scientific approach and career. Houston received a master's degree in physics at Chicago before returning to Ohio State to complete his doctorate. He received his Ph.D. in physics in 1925 for work conducted under the supervision of A. D. Cole in spectroscopy. In 1924 he married Mildred White; they had one child.

In 1925, with a fellowship from the National Research Council, Houston headed west to the California Institute of Technology, a rising scientific center under the direction of his former teacher Millikan. There Houston continued to work on atomic spectroscopy, conducting experiments and teaching on the topic. In 1927 Houston, now an assistant professor of physics at Caltech, won a Guggenheim Fellowship, which enabled him to study with Arnold Sommerfeld in Munich, Germany. A great authority in the field of atomic spectroscopy, Sommerfeld was a masterful teacher to many of the young stars of the quantum revolution in physics, such as Werner Heisenberg and Wolfgang Pauli.

During his half-year stay at Munich, Houston made his best-known scientific contribution, a quantum mechanical explanation of electrical resistance. Deviating from his original plan to study the theory of the spin of electrons within the atom, Houston, at Sommerfeld's direction, investigated the mean-free path of electrons in metals, which was a crucial indicator of a metal's electrical conductivity. Applying the new wave mechanics, Houston treated the electron as a wave and found not only a way to calculate the mean-free path for electrons in metals but also, more important, a proportional relationship between electrical resistivity and temperature at high temperature. This work, which Sommerfeld called "the first decent treatment of the electrical resistance law," represented a significant step in the application of quantum mechanics to metals and in the rise of solid-state physics. In the spring of 1928 Houston moved to Leipzig to work with Heisenberg. At the latter's suggestion, Houston reverted to his original interest in atomic spectra and examined the interaction between the spin and the orbital motion of electrons in a two-electron atom and the resultant spectra.

Returning to Caltech in 1928, Houston resumed his experimental work on spectroscopy while keeping an active interest in the theoretical front of electrons in atoms and solids. He made more precise measurements on the Zeeman effect (changes in spectra caused by the presence of a magnetic field), which led to a correction of the value of the ratio between the electron's electrical charge and mass. In the field of solid-state theory, Houston continued to work on electrical resistance. In 1929 he showed that quantum statistics, combined with the conservation of energy, gave rise to an electrical resistance proportional to T^5 (T stands for temperature) at low temperature, a result independently derived at by Houston's friend the physicist Felix Bloch. In 1931 Houston became full professor at Caltech. Three years later, he wrote *Principles of Mathematical Physics*, which was based on his popular introductory course on the subject at Caltech and which became a widely used text.

When World War II broke out, Frank B. Jewett, president of Bell Laboratories and the National Academy of Sciences, persuaded Houston to move to the Columbia University Division of War Research to work on antisubmarine warfare. There Houston led a group in developing a homing antisubmarine device. The device proved effective in the battle of the Atlantic and brought Houston a Medal of Merit from the U.S. Navy at the end of the war. The war transformed Houston from a competent and versatile physicist into a skilled science administrator. He was elected to the National Academy of Sciences in 1943 and later served on its council for several years. In 1945 he succeeded Millikan as chairman of Caltech's division of physics, mathematics, and electrical engineering.

Houston's outstanding administrative qualities and scientific stature at Caltech led to his appointment as the second president of Rice University at Houston, Texas, in 1946. For the next fifteen years, Houston oversaw a considerable expansion of the university in both the sciences and the humanities. Among his innovations at Rice was the development of a residential college system modeled after those of Oxford, Cambridge, and Yale Universities. When a serious illness in 1961 forced Houston to retire from the presidency of Rice, he continued as professor of physics there. The next year, he was elected president of the American Physical Society. Before he died in Edinburgh, Scotland, Houston also received numerous honors from a variety of academic and scholarly organizations.

As one of the few American physicists who made significant contributions to the quantum revolution and to the development of solid-state physics, Houston distinguished himself by his competence in both experiment and theory. As both a major scientific organizer during World War II and a successful university president during the postwar period, Houston had a scientific and academic career that reflected the increased interaction between American science and society in the twentieth century.

• Houston's papers, both personal and professional, are deposited in Rice University's Fondren Library. See Harold E. Rorschach, "The Contributions of Felix Bloch and W. V. Houston to the Electron Theory of Metals," *American Journal of Physics* 38 (1970): 897–904, and Lillian Hoddeson et al., eds., *Out of the Crystal Maze: Chapters from the History of Solid-State Physics* (1992), for discussions of Houston's scientific work. The best obituary, by Kenneth S. Pitzer, Houston's successor as president of Rice, and Harold E. Rorschach, Jr., a former physics colleague, is "William Vermillion Houston," National Academy of Sciences, *Biographical Memoirs* 44 (1974): 126–37, which includes a bibliography of Houston's publications.

ZUOYUE WANG

HOUSTOUN, John (1750?–20 July 1796), lawyer, soldier, and politician, was born in St. George's Parish, Georgia, the son of Sir Patrick Houstoun, a baronet, registrar of grants and receiver of quit rents for the colony, and Priscilla Dunbar. He studied law in Charleston and practiced in Savannah, where he early became involved in the protests against Great Britain prior to the Revolution and was probably a member of the Sons of Liberty. In 1775 he married Hannah Bryan, the daughter of Jonathan Bryan, a prominent planter, a former member of the governor's council, and one of the leaders of Georgia's Whig movement; they apparently had no children. In July 1774 he joined Archibald Bulloch, Noble W. Jones, and George Walton in calling for a meeting to discuss the British Intolerable Acts and prepare a response to them. Attending this and subsequent extra-legal meetings, he was appointed to a committee to raise money for the people of Boston when that port was closed by the Intolerable Acts. Georgia's first provincial congress selected him (along with Jones and Bulloch) as representatives to the Continental Congress, but since the Georgia body did not contain representatives from every parish in the prov-

ince they declined to attend. Houstoun, however, stayed active in the liberty movement and in the summer of 1775 helped organize a local council of safety.

The provincial congress met again on 4 July 1775 with all but two parishes represented, and that body elected Houstoun, the Reverend John J. Zubly, and Archibald Bulloch as delegates to the Continental Congress. Houstoun left shortly for Philadelphia and by all accounts would have been there to sign the Declaration of Independence the next year had he not felt the need to come home to work against Zubly, who by now was opposed to separation from Britain. Back in Georgia by January 1776, he served on the council of safety and was part of the effort to arrest Royal Governor James Wright, which resulted in Wright's flight from the province. Though reelected to the Congress, Houstoun decided to remain in Georgia. The next summer he was elected a member of the executive council and on 10 January 1778 he was chosen as governor of the state.

Governor Houstoun led the Georgia militia on an ill-fated expedition against St. Augustine in the summer of 1778. The mission failed because of divided command between state and continental forces, poor coordination, a lack of supplies, and inadequate transportation, all compounded by an outbreak of malaria. That disaster was followed, in the fall, by a successful British attack on Savannah. When the city fell, Houstoun fled to his brother's plantation and then to Augusta, where the state government had been transferred. The enemy followed him upriver and took Augusta, and Houstoun fled again, this time to Purryburg, South Carolina, and then to Charleston. At that point resistance to the British presence in Georgia crumbled and for nearly a year there was not a Whig government to speak of in the province. When the Georgia revolutionary government was finally restored, Houstoun, whose term as governor had expired, was selected once again as a member of the Continental Congress, but in those unsettled times he did not attend. As an indication of his importance, at least in British eyes, his name headed the list of those proscribed by the Disqualifying Act passed by the restored royal assembly. But that notice did not keep him from serving on the staff of General Lachlan McIntosh in Charleston and later being elected to the House of Assembly from Chatham County, a body that initially elected him Speaker.

When the British evacuated Georgia he returned to his plantation "White Bluff" on the Little Ogechee River but later built a home in Savannah. In 1784 Houstoun was once again elected governor. During his term he dealt with land and American-Indian problems and a boundary dispute with South Carolina and was chosen a trustee of the college that would eventually become the University of Georgia. After he left office he served in the state legislature (1785), as commissioner to settle the boundary dispute with South Carolina (1787), and as a justice for Chatham County (1787). He also turned down appointments as chief justice (1786) and as a member of the state constitutional convention (1787). He lost a close election for governor to Edward Telfair (1789) and was disappointed in an attempt to obtain an appointment to the federal bench. Still he remained politically active. In 1790 he became the first mayor of Savannah; the next year he was appointed to the state superior court; in addition he served as Christ Church vestryman and on the board of trustees of Chatham Academy.

Houstoun left the bench in 1793 and spent his remaining years in law practice and tending to family business, which included planting rice and owning slaves. He died of natural causes at his plantation.

• Most of Houstoun's career is covered in Edith D. Johnston, *The Houstouns of Georgia* (1950). For general treatment of the period see Kenneth Coleman, *The American Revolution in Georgia* (1958), Harvey H. Jackson, *Lachlan McIntosh and the Politics of Revolutionary Georgia* (1979), and Allen D. Candler, ed., *The Revolutionary Records of the State of Georgia* (1908).

HARVEY H. JACKSON

HOVE, Elling (25 Mar. 1863–17 Dec. 1927), Lutheran pastor and theologian, was born near Northwood, Iowa, the son of Ole Hove and Kari Olson, farmers. At the age of fifteen, he entered Luther College in Decorah, Iowa, in 1877, graduating with a B.A. in 1884. He then attended Concordia Seminary in St. Louis, Missouri, from which he received his certificate in theology in 1887. Ordained into the Norwegian Synod that same year, he served a congregation in Portland, Oregon, from 1887 to 1889, and then served in Astoria, Oregon, from 1890 to 1891. His next call was to one of the most important congregations in the synod, First Lutheran, in Decorah, Iowa, which he served from 1891 to 1894. During his time in Decorah he also taught courses in religion at Luther College and served as the college pastor. In 1893 Hove married Ottine Didrikke Wulfsberg; they had two sons. In 1894 he accepted a call to a congregation in Mankato, Minnesota, where he served until 1901.

Hove's training and interest lay in the field of systematic theology; he specialized in detailed and painstaking work on fundamental theological doctrines. He was called in 1901 to become professor of theology at Luther Seminary in St. Paul, which was the seminary of the Norwegian Synod. Known for his skills in languages, he read theology in the original languages (German, Latin, and Greek) and lectured at Luther Seminary in both English and Norwegian. He was also a prominent and powerful preacher who spoke in Norwegian churches around the country. Hove served the Norwegian Synod as a member of its board of education from 1908 to 1909 and again from 1912 to 1913. He also served on the synod's important Union Committee from 1905 to 1910, negotiating with other Norwegian-American Lutheran synods for the union of these groups.

In 1912 the Norwegian Synod and the other synods, looking for a way to merge together, reached a theological compromise called the Madison Agreement, or *Opgjør* ("settlement"), which settled certain outstanding theological differences, including the long contention over the doctrine of election. The divisive debate about election within Norwegian-American Lutheranism involved the question of how God predestined or "elected" believers to salvation. The Norwegian Synod (following the Missouri Synod) stressed that God predestined believers to salvation before they were born. Hove, trained at the Missouri Synod seminary, held this view of election. Other Norwegian-American Lutherans, however, suggested that God had foreknowledge of how a person would act, and in this way the believer was reckoned as one of God's elect. The *Opgjør* settled the long debate by suggesting that as long as certain non-Lutheran extremes on both sides were avoided, both formulations were acceptable.

Hove belonged to a vocal minority within the Norwegian Synod opposed to the *Opgjør*. He suggested that the agreement masked the real theological differences between the two positions and insisted that complete doctrinal agreement must be reached before merger could be considered. In 1913 Hove, along with two other Luther Seminary professors, issued an anonymous document known as "The Petition" or "*Bønskrift*," which raised these theological objections to the *Opgjør* settlement. Later that year, in response to criticisms of the anonymity of the document, Hove and the others revealed their authorship. At the Norwegian Synod convention in 1913, Hove signed a minority committee report that again suggested that the *Opgjør* settlement was an unsatisfactory resolution to the election controversy.

Whatever his reservations about the theological bases of the settlement, when the Norwegian Synod united with the other Norwegian-American denominations in 1917 to form the Norwegian Lutheran Church in America (NLCA), Hove remained in the new NLCA and did not join with Norwegian Synod dissenters in forming an independent synod. He was also retained as theological professor when Luther Seminary merged with the seminaries of the other synods in 1917 to form the NLCA's Luther Theological Seminary in St. Paul. He served at this new institution until poor health caused him to retire in 1926. He died in Hudson, Wisconsin.

Hove's theological work led him to produce detailed notes on many theological questions, but his manuscripts remained unpublished at the time of his death, although he had translated them from Norwegian into English. His son, O. Hjalmar Hove, completed his father's manuscript, and in 1930 the 500-page work was published under the title *Christian Doctrine*; it is an important summary of the theological questions within Norwegian-American Lutheranism, which generally summarized and represented the doctrinal positions taken by the Norwegian Synod. In spite of the merger, Hove continued to press the question of election and other disputed issues.

Hove was known among his contemporaries for his single-minded devotion to his theological calling and for his keen intellect. During his long service to the

Norwegian Synod he ably represented its institutions and its theological positions, continuing to press this cause with the new Norwegian Lutheran Church in America after its formation in 1917. He was remembered by his students and contemporaries as a careful and forceful teacher who was dedicated to his students and his work.

• Hove's papers are in the Archives of the Evangelical Lutheran Church in America, Chicago, Ill. Hove is also listed in Rasmus Malmin et al., *Who's Who among Pastors in All the Norwegian Lutheran Synods of America, 1843–1927* (1928). Gerhard L. Belgum, "Elling Hove," *Luther Theological Seminary Review* 9, no. 2 (Nov. 1970), is a personal remembrance. For information on the merger process that led to the formation of the NCLA in 1917 and Hove's role in that process, see E. Clifford Nelson and Eugene Fevold, *The Lutheran Church among the Norwegian-Americans* (2 vols., 1960). An obituary is in the *Lutheran Church Herald*, 10 Jan. 1928.

MARK GRANQUIST

HOVENDEN, Thomas (23 Dec. 1840–14 Aug. 1895), painter, was born in Dunmanway, Cork County, Ireland, the son of Robert Hovenden, a prison warden, and Ellen Bryan. The family lived modestly but comfortably in a rural, one-street farming community until 1846, but during the height of the disastrous potato famine both parents died, and the six-year-old Thomas was placed in an orphanage in the city of Cork. It was there that he first started to draw. At fourteen he began a seven-year apprenticeship to a carver and gilder in Cork, who sent him to the Kensington Department of the Cork School of Design in 1858 to learn the crafts of frame-making and gilding. Although the school trained artisans in the decorative arts, Hovenden nevertheless learned to revere what were then considered to be the "higher" aims and nobler ideals of painting and the use of the heroic figure as a way to portray those ideals. The school had an excellent collection of plaster replicas of Greek and Roman gods and goddesses, which he used as models to refine his figure drawing.

Hovenden completed his apprenticeship in 1863 but faced limited prospects as a frame-maker in Cork County. His older brother was living in New York City, and he decided to join him. He found a cheap apartment in Greenwich Village, worked as a frame-maker and gilder, and attended evening classes at the National Academy of Design in New York. He also found work as a lithographer and illustrator for *Harper's Magazine* and as a colorist of photographs. The combination of his early and sudden orphaning, his training as a frame-maker, his exposure to heroic figures and the noble ideals of painting, and his experience coloring photographs and composing lithographs all served to influence his "romantic realism" as a painter. He became famous for his ornately framed canvases (the frames were often his own) that depicted heroic figures affirming the ideals of family, hearth, and home portrayed in a style that art historian Lee Edwards called "quasi-photographic realism" (p. 5).

During his first few years in New York Hovenden shared a studio with Hugh Bolton Jones, a landscape painter who became a lifelong friend. He exhibited his first painting at the National Academy of Design in 1867 while still earning a living as a frame-maker and part-time illustrator. The exhibition gave him the confidence to make a career of painting, and the following year he moved to Baltimore with Jones and set up a studio in Jones's family home. He continued to exhibit at the National Academy of Design, and in 1872 his work attracted the attention of the Baltimore business partners and art collectors William T. Walters and John McCoy. Their generous patronage and support allowed him to study in France, which was then considered a crucial source of training for an aspiring artist.

Hovenden reached maturity as an artist during the six years he spent in France, from 1874 until 1880. He worked briefly with Jules Breton, whose romantic scenes of French peasant life were then quite popular with American viewers. He then met Alexandre Cabanel, the famous Parisian history painter and portraitist, and was admitted into the prestigious École des Beaux-Arts, where Cabanel taught. It was primarily from Cabanel that Hovenden learned to paint figures with almost photographic precision and to endow his paintings with noble design and historic purpose. In 1875 he joined the art colony in Pont-Aven, Brittany, and became a close friend of Robert Wylie, a well-known American painter and the colony's "guiding spirit." During the five years he lived at the colony he fell in love with Helen Corson, an animal painter and Quaker from Plymouth Meeting, Pennsylvania, who was also studying at Pont-Aven. His paintings from the colony focused primarily on the local peasant life; and two images, *The Vendéan Volunteer* (1878; also titled *Breton Interior*) and *In Hoc Signo Vinces* (1880; In this sign shalt thou conquer), which heroically depict the peasant uprisings of the French Revolution, established his reputation as a figure and history painter of the first order. An American critic, upon seeing *In Hoc Signo Vinces*, boasted of Hovenden as an American "who is really able to walk in the highest walk of art" (Anne Gregory Terhune, "Thomas Hovenden: Images of Heritage and Hope," *Thomas Hovenden [1840–1895]: American Painter of Hearth and Homeland*, p. 24).

After returning to the United States Hovenden spent a little over a year in New York City. He leased a studio and completed *Elaine* (1882), a highly romantic period piece based on a scene from "Lancelot and Elaine" in Alfred Lord Tennyson's *Idylls of the King* (1852). The painting met with enormous critical success and was exhibited at the National Academy in New York in 1882 and then in Philadelphia and Baltimore. The critic for the *Baltimore Sun* called it "the best of any, in composition, grouping and technique, that has yet come from the easel of an American painter" (quoted in Edwards, p. 14). Based primarily on the critical acclaim of *In Hoc Signo Vinces* and *Elaine*, Hovenden was elected a full member of the National

Academy of Design. Despite these successes, however, his patron John McCoy encouraged him to pursue American history themes and genre paintings (scenes of everyday life) to gain broader popular appeal: "Go to work on pictures *that you can get material for & that will sell at proper prices*," McCoy urged (quoted in Terhune, "Thomas Hovenden [1840–1895] and Late-Nineteenth-Century American Genre Painting," p. 25).

Hovenden found it practical to follow McCoy's advice. American history scenes, especially those of the Civil War, were in great demand; and Hovenden's attention to realistic detail facilitated a turn to American subject matter. He was meticulous about choosing models, costumes, and props that fit his subject matter. His friend Thomas Eakins recalled that he "made up his mind so thoroughly and mapped out his work so completely before he began to paint that it came to be simply a matter of so many square feet of execution" (*Philadelphia Express*, 17 Aug. 1895).

Hovenden married Helen Corson in 1881; they had two children and settled on her family's century-old homestead in the quiet Quaker community of Plymouth Meeting, Pennsylvania. He used for his studio an old "antislavery hall" that had been built by his father-in-law, a fervent abolitionist during the Civil War. Hovenden often said he heard "the voices of Lucretia Mott, Fred Douglass, and many other famous people" resonating "within its old walls time and again" (*Philadelphia Times*, 23 Feb. 1891). He soon replaced European scenes of domesticity and heroism with American ones; instead of his earlier motifs of European peasant life and chivalric knights he chose for his subjects American reformers, military heroes, farmers, and African Americans, whom he portrayed with sensitive and empathic dignity.

It was in the old antislavery hall, with the voices of black heroes echoing within its walls, that he painted his most popular and enduring history painting as well as his personal favorite, *The Last Moments of John Brown* (1884). The painting was commissioned in 1882 by Robbins Battell; Hovenden spent two years researching the background of John Brown's infamous 1859 raid on the federal arsenal at Harpers Ferry, Virginia, in an attempt to commence a revolution to end slavery. Brown was executed for treason before his plans could be carried out, but he was hailed as a martyred hero by abolitionists and intellectuals throughout the North. Hovenden researched the design of the militia uniforms, visited the jail where Brown had been held before his execution, and interviewed Brown's jailor. He consulted photographs of Brown to obtain an exact likeness of his subject. Against these details of historical accuracy, however, his painting depicts a fictive scene that stemmed from an 1859 *New York Tribune* story in which John Brown, on his way to the gallows, stooped to kiss a black baby whose slave mother was holding the infant out to him. Hovenden acknowledged that the story might be apocryphal, but he argued that "it is true in spirit if not in fact, and it is consequently a fit subject for treatment in a picture which aims to have a high historical value" (*Evening Telegraph*, 12 Jan. 1884).

By the early 1890s Hovenden's paintings of realistic people acting out grand historic and mythic themes were becoming the most popular of any in the United States. *In the Hands of the Enemy* (1889) portrays a family of honorable Pennsylvania farmers during the battle of Gettysburg caring for a wounded Confederate soldier who had found himself "in the hands of the enemy." The painting was voted the "star picture" of more than 500 entries at the National Academy in 1889, and it sold for a record $5,000. A year later Hovenden completed *Breaking Home Ties*, a sentimental portrayal of a young rural lad respectfully facing his mother with hat in hand, about to venture into the world to seek his place and become a man. *Breaking Home Ties* received enormous critical and popular acclaim; the critic for *Harper's Weekly* called it "one of the best scenes of American life yet painted by anybody." It was exhibited at the 1893 Columbian Exposition in Chicago and was declared the popular favorite of the thousand or so on exhibit.

Hovenden lived out the "noble domesticity" he so often portrayed in his paintings. Despite his growing wealth and fame, he and Helen and their two daughters lived simply, shunned pomp and extravagance, and were active in the local Meeting of the Society of Friends. "Everybody liked Hovenden," Thomas Eakins remembered, "He bore his honors very quietly and his success did not seem to affect him as it does many" (*Philadelphia Express*, 17 Aug. 1895). Hovenden also devoted time to young, aspiring artists; beginning in 1886 he succeeded Eakins as an instructor at the Pennsylvania Academy of the Fine Arts and Robert Henri became his most famous pupil.

Throughout his career Hovenden retained his belief in the romantic notion of art as an ennobling and moral ideal and a benchmark of social virtue. In 1895 he denounced the emergence of impressionism and the modernist aesthetic that embraced "art for art's sake" and dispensed with romantic ideals as anachronistic in a modern world: "The practice of art for art's sake to the exclusion of art's highest mission," he argued, "becomes self-centered and tends towards self-worship" (*Morristown Daily Herald*, 9 Feb. 1895). He died acting out the heroic ideals he affirmed in his art. On 14 August 1895, while waiting to cross a busy railroad crossing near his home, he saw a small girl venture across the tracks as a freight train bore down on her. He dove in front of the speeding locomotive in an effort to save the child, but they were both instantly killed. Over the following weeks and months, newspapers throughout the country hailed him as a martyred hero and one of America's preeminent painters. But within five years, as modernism became the standard-bearer of value in art, his work was largely forgotten. For sixty years beginning in 1900 there were no Hovenden exhibitions; the first retrospective of his work was a centennial exhibition in 1995 at the Woodmere Art Museum in Philadelphia.

• Hovenden's papers are available on microfilm at the Archives of American Art, Smithsonian Institution. The exhibition catalog *Thomas Hovenden (1840–1895): American Painter of Hearth and Homeland* (1995), from the Woodmere Art Museum in Philadelphia, is excellent. Anne Gregory Terhune, "Thomas Hovenden (1840–1895) and Late-Nineteenth-Century American Genre Painting" (Ph.D. diss., City Univ. of New York, 1983), is also helpful. Two excellent essays that address Hovenden's "romantic realism" are Lee M. Edwards, "Noble Domesticity: The Paintings of Thomas Hovenden," *American Art Journal* 19, no. 1 (1987): 5–38; and Sarah Burns, "The Country Boy Goes to the City: Thomas Hovenden's *Breaking Home Ties* in American Popular Culture," *American Art Journal* 20, no. 4 (1988): 59–73; on Hovenden's *The Last Moments of John Brown*, see Natalie Spassky, *American Paintings in the Metropolitan Museum of Art*, vol. 2 (1985).

JOHN STAUFFER

HOVEY, Henrietta (6 Apr. 1849–16 Mar. 1918), Delsartean teacher, was born Henriette Knapp in Cooperstown, New York, the daughter of Edgar Knapp and Catharine Tyler. Hovey's lifelong interest in clothing reform is traced to an early experience when a doctor, to combat her frailty and ill-health, prescribed loose-fitting garb that would allow easy breathing and free motion. By her early twenties, Hovey was designing her own unique uncorseted costumes—subtly colored flowing gowns that became her hallmark—and lecturing on the aesthetic and health aspects of dress. To improve her speech for such presentations, she entered the Boston School of Oratory in the early 1870s where she was introduced to the system of expression developed by François Delsarte (1811–1871), a French theorist and teacher of acting, voice, and aesthetics. Delsarte's theory was an elaborate derivation of his personal interpretation of the Christian Trinity and featured particular attention to the relationship between body, mind, and spirit in the practical work of expression in any of the arts. Hovey's interests expanded to include physical culture and expression, and she traveled to Paris where she met Delsarte's widow and studied with his son Gustave before the latter's death in February 1879. In the late 1860s or 1870s she married Edward B. Crane; their son was born on 21 April, probably in 1878—possibly in 1867.

After Hovey's return to the United States she was recognized as a major Delsartean exponent and taught at various locations in New York and elsewhere. She also began to develop a following among society women who would gather at one another's homes for lessons in aesthetics, expression, and physical culture. Her first marriage over, she became involved in 1884 with Edmund Russell, an artist and poet who had come to her for instruction in the Delsarte "science and philosophy of art." Their son was born in July 1885; they were married probably in late 1885. Russell soon became co-teacher as well as mate, and the couple were characterized as the "high priest and priestess of Delsarte" as they moved gracefully among the wealthy and socially prominent.

In late June 1886 the Russells traveled to London where they offered instruction in their greatly expanded range of Delsartean topics including "art-study and criticism, color and house decoration, dress, grace, gesture and expression in oratory, acting, painting, and sculpture" (*Delsartean Scrap-book*, p. 107). They shared with the English Arts and Crafts movement the mission of infusing all of life with beauty and harmony. Although most of their teaching was at private social and artistic gatherings, they also gave public lecture-demonstrations and appeared in two plays to promote the Delsarte system.

In 1889 the Russells returned separately to the United States. From then through the 1890s Henrietta taught and lectured from the East Coast to as far west as Kansas. Frequent society-page news items attest to her popularity among the fashionable women who provided most of her employment. Of particular note were extensive summer engagements at Newport, Rhode Island (1891), and Bar Harbor, Maine (1892), where the summer residents were enthralled with Henrietta's exotic dress and "Delsartism." For her first appearance at Newport (for which she was paid $100), she lectured on "grace," wearing an "aesthetic gown of yellow and silver, sheeny and soft, clasped with Indian ornaments of dead gold" (*Sunday Advertiser*, 12 July 1891). Other sessions featured Delsartean aesthetics and training in relaxation and graceful ways to sit, stand, walk, bow, and fall down. In 1891 she published *Yawning*, a book lauding the yawn as "nature's gymnastic." This was the first part of a projected multivolume work on the Delsarte system that was never completed. The manuscripts for the unpublished volumes as well as the voluminous notes and letters left by Hovey attest to a level of intellectual depth and rigorousness that contrasts with the impression given by *Yawning* and her many society clippings.

During 1890–1891, Henrietta became increasingly close to the young poet and critic Richard Hovey, who would become her third and last husband. Their son was born on 9 February 1892 in France to avoid scandal; they were married in 1894. In addition to Henrietta's other travels, after their marriage the Hoveys spent extended periods in Nova Scotia, England, and France where she also taught and lectured. Recognized nationally as a leader in clothing reform, she was invited to speak at the Department Congress of the National Council of Women of the United States as part of the World's Congress of Representative Women at the Chicago World's Columbian Exposition in 1893.

After Hovey's death in 1900, Henrietta remained in New York but discontinued her teaching. At first she devoted her time to the editing and publication of Hovey's writings. In 1904 she—along with Edmund Russell—helped found and worked with a socialist-leaning theater group called the Progressive Stage Society. In 1909 she moved to the Los Angeles area, where she resumed her Delsartean work and gained prestige and popularity again among a fashionable elite. In 1915 Hovey met the American dance artist

Ted Shawn, who studied with her himself and engaged her to teach the Delsarte system at the Denishawn School where he and Ruth St. Denis were laying the foundations of a new American concert dance art.

Hovey's teaching and influence took place in both social and professional contexts. Her society teaching generated the most publicity because her pupils were newsworthy and their Delsarte activities somewhat titillating. Under Hovey's tutelage respectable women were paying attention to their bodies, exploring aesthetic expression, and falling down stairs—as an exercise! What was less noticed during her lifetime was her ongoing work with students and professionals in the arts and in oratory and physical expression. Her most significant contribution to the arts came later in life through her work at Denishawn. Hovey was one of the major conduits through which the American adaptations of Delsartean theory and practice influenced what has come to be known as modern dance.

Hovey supported woman suffrage and other causes advocating women's rights. Although she made no statements supporting free love, she practiced it discreetly. Despite her pregnancies before marriage, no hint of scandal touched her name, and the elite society never seemed to know that her social behavior was anything but appropriate.

• Most of Hovey's papers are in the Richard Hovey Collection, Dartmouth College Library. Her unfinished Delsarte manuscript as well as some of Shawn's references to her are in the Ted Shawn Collection, Dance Collection, New York Public Library for the Performing Arts. Frederic Sanburn, comp., *A Delsartean Scrap-book: Health, Personality, Beauty, House Decoration, Dress, Etc.* (1890), is a collection of articles and clippings featuring the Russells and Delsartism in England and the United States. A modern assessment is Richard A. Meckel, "Henrietta Russell: Delsartean Prophet to the Gilded Age," *Journal of American Culture* 12, no. 1 (Spring 1989): 65–78. Additional material is in Allan Houston MacDonald, *Richard Hovey: Man and Craftsman* (1957).

NANCY LEE CHALFA RUYTER

HOVEY, Otis Ellis (9 Apr. 1864–15 Apr. 1941), civil engineer, was born in East Hardwick, Vermont, the son of Jabez Wadsworth Hovey, a teacher and dairy farmer, and Catherine Montgomery. Hovey was first introduced to the field of civil engineering by his father, an amateur surveyor with an avid interest in railroad construction. The economic considerations of raising a family discouraged Hovey's father from changing careers to enter the booming railroad business of the time. He satisfied himself instead by taking his young son out to watch survey crews at work. In his later years, Hovey reminisced that "the mysteries of the shining instruments on top [of the tripods], and the wonderful rod up and down which a beautiful red and white target could be made to slide, bewitched me. Then and there, I knew that I must learn more about them, why they were used and what they accomplished." Pursuing this quest for greater understand-

ing, Hovey enrolled in Dartmouth College's Chandler Scientific Department, receiving a bachelor's degree in 1885.

Before continuing for a postgraduate degree, Hovey took a position as engineer for a thirteen mile-long railroad under construction by the Hoosac Tunnel and Wilmington Railroad from Hoosac Tunnel, Massachusetts, to Readsboro, Vermont. His first practical experience with bridge design came in 1886, when he was faced with the problem of building an eighty-foot-long highway bridge. Although hampered by an inadequate background for the task, Hovey nevertheless produced an effective design for a wooden Towne through lattice truss. Bolstered by his success, and eager to become more skilled at bridge planning, Hovey left the railroad for employment as a draftsman with the Edgemoor Iron Company, a bridge fabrication firm based in Wilmington, Delaware. Less than a year later, in the fall of 1887, he returned to Dartmouth to continue his formal education, entering the Thayer School of Civil Engineering. Always on the lookout for new opportunities, Hovey secured a position during his class break in the summer of 1888 as an assistant engineer on a masonry dam construction project in Chicopee, Massachusetts. In addition to working at the dam site, he was put in charge of improvements at several paper mills in the area. In February 1889 the director at Thayer, Dr. Robert Fletcher, recommended Hovey for a civil engineering instructor's position at Washington University in St. Louis. Impressed with his abilities and experience, Fletcher allowed Hovey to continue his studies by mail until he completed his degree in June 1889.

Hovey stayed at Washington University, teaching and managing the department's testing laboratory among other duties, until April 1890 when he truly embarked upon his professional career of bridge engineering. Hovey had maintained contact with George S. Morison, a well-known bridge engineer, since his days at Edgemoor, and he used this past acquaintance to obtain an engineering position at Morison's company in Chicago. After an initial assignment in Detroit, surveying for a proposed railroad bridge over the Detroit River, he was appointed head of the Chicago office. In 1891 he married Martha Wilson Owen; they had two children. Over the next five years, Hovey worked closely with Morison, designing several bridges and structures. One especially notable project was the Bellefontaine Bridge, completed in 1893. The main structure consisted of four 440-foot steel pin-connected Baltimore through trusses carrying the tracks of the Chicago, Burlington and Quincy Railroad across the Missouri River near Alton, Illinois. Hovey was responsible not only for the design of the bridge's superstructure but also for the planning of a street bridge and two stations near the railroad's yard, about fifteen miles to the south in St. Louis. As his last undertaking for Morison, he designed a four-track bascule (movable) bridge across the Chicago River.

In 1896 Hovey took employment as an engineer for the Union Bridge Company, running its shop facility in Athens, Pennsylvania, until 1900, when the firm joined several others nationwide in forming the American Bridge Company. Hovey stayed with the new organization, first as a design engineer and then as assistant chief engineer, working in its Pencoyd, Pennsylvania, office from 1900 to 1904 and in New York City from 1904 to 1931. In 1931 he started his own consulting firm.

During his time with the American Bridge Company and after, Hovey maintained an active presence within academia, sitting on Thayer's board of overseers from 1916 until his death, receiving an honorary doctorate in engineering from Dartmouth in 1927, and lecturing on bridge design at Yale and Princeton Universities. Within the engineering field at large, he was a member of such groups as the American Society of Civil Engineers, the American Society of Mechanical Engineers, and the American Railway Engineering Association; he served as the director of the Engineering Foundation after 1935.

Hovey's wide experience led him to be regarded as an expert in bridge design. Through his constant design work and the publication of several technical articles, he gained particular recognition as an authority on the subject of movable bridges, a span type that came to mature form in the United States during the period from roughly the 1880s to the 1920s. From his first experience in 1891 designing swing-bridge components, he became interested in the problem of simplifying and standardizing machinery for movable bridges. His best-known work on the subject was the well-received *Movable Bridges*, a two-volume work issued in 1926 and 1927, intended as a "practical treatise" for "practicing engineers and advanced students in engineering schools." He died in New York City.

• Hovey's reminiscences about his professional life are recorded in an autobiographical article, "A Bridge Builder Looks Back," *Civil Engineering* 9 (Aug. 1939): 483–86. Hovey published several articles, particularly during the 1930s, on a wide range of topics concerning bridge and dam construction; these have been indexed and annotated by the *Engineering Index*. An important precursor to his two-volume work on movable bridge forms is "Movable Bridges," *Civil Engineering* 7 (Apr. 1931): 595–600. Hovey's single book on dam construction was *Steel Dams* (1935). An excellent source of information on the Bellefontaine Bridge project is George S. Morison, *The Bellefontaine Bridge* (1894), which includes specifications and plans. An obituary is in the *New York Herald Tribune*, 16 Apr. 1941.

SHAWN P. ROUNDS

HOVEY, Richard (4 May 1864–24 Feb. 1900), poet, was born in Normal, Illinois, the son of General Charles Edward Hovey and Harriette Spofford, educators. General Hovey, a native of Vermont and graduate of Dartmouth, had been a teacher and administrator in Massachusetts schools before migrating to Illinois. In 1857 he was chosen to be president of a new normal college located at Bloomington (today Illinois State University). When the Civil War broke out he recruited a regiment of teachers and students. He was dis-

charged in 1865 as major general, having been wounded several times. He then located in Washington, D.C., where he began a practice in law.

Charles Hovey had met Harriette Spofford at Framingham Academy in Massachusetts, where she taught under his administration. In later years she would serve as French translator for the U.S. Bureau of Education. During the War Mrs. Hovey converted the Hovey home at the new town of Normal into a hospital for the wounded. After the war she took the infant Richard and his older brother to her family home in Massachusetts until the general's law practice was established.

Most of Richard Hovey's early education came from his mother. His only formal schooling was two years of Greek, Latin, and mathematics at prep school. He showed an early interest in writing poetry and printed a chapbook of his poems when he was sixteen. These poems indicate the influence of Lord Byron, John Keats, Algernon Charles Swinburne, Walt Whitman, and Edgar Allan Poe. The strongest influence was the musicality of Sidney Lanier, who was living in nearby Baltimore.

In 1881 Hovey entered Dartmouth, where he imitated the fashions of Oscar Wilde's Aesthetic Movement. But he was not an alienated radical. He wrote essays and poems for the newspaper, edited the yearbook, and pledged Psi Upsilon fraternity. He was the only member of the class of 1885 to graduate cum laude. In later years Hovey wrote several poems praising Dartmouth and fraternity life. The "Hanover Winter Song," for example, set to music by Frederick Field Bullard, celebrates the Winter Carnival.

The years after graduation were restless ones. Hovey repeatedly tried to get a teaching job, but his full beard and outlandish dress alienated superintendents. He worked as an extra in theatrical companies and spent a year in an Episcopal seminary. He accompanied Canadian poet Bliss Carman on walking trips, sometimes paying for bed and board by reciting verses. In 1894 the two poets brought out *Songs from Vagabondia*, which was instantly popular. *More Songs from Vagabondia* appeared in 1896, and *Last Songs from Vagabondia* (1901) was published after Hovey's death.

Hovey experimented considerably with free verse. His lines are often short, with varied and syncopated rhythms. The poems, often employing internal and interlocking rhymes, have a strong lyrical quality. They seem as though the works of Whitman had been revised by Rudyard Kipling. However, Hovey's most famous works—"The Sea Gypsy," "At the Crossroads," "A Stein Song," "Comrades," and "Unmanifest Destiny"—follow a regular metrical pattern. The typical Hovey poem is a protest against safe, middle-class values and a eulogy of the daring and adventurous. His heroes are poets, rebels, even outlaws. Hovey's poems were what the public expected from literary bohemians.

In the winter of 1889–1890 Hovey met Mrs. Henrietta Russell, who was sixteen years years older than he. Mrs. Russell taught classes in Delsartism, a system of elocution involving breath control and body movement. Richard accompanied her to Europe in 1891, and their son was born in France in 1892. The couple was married in 1894 after Mrs. Russell obtained a divorce.

Hovey was one of the first Americans to become aware of the Symbolist poets in France. He wrote essays and gave lectures about the movement and translated poems of Stéphane Mallarmé and Paul Verlaine. He also translated two volumes of the *Plays of Maurice Maeterlinck* (1894 and 1896). He was critical, however, of the pessimism and dissipation of the Symbolists; what attracted him to the movement was their belief in individuality. Although Hovey's own poetry has little in common with Symbolism, he served as a publicist for the movement in America.

Early in his career Hovey conceived a series of masques and blank verse dramas on the Arthurian legends. He completed four works: *The Quest of Merlin: A Prelude* and *The Marriage of Guenevere: A Tragedy* (1891), *The Birth of Galahad* (1898), and *Taliesin: A Masque* (1890). Hovey's intent was to deal with "woman in a new way." His Guenevere was bold and courageous, quite different from Lord Tennyson's. Hovey believed that the modern practice of divorce could solve the eternal triangle, as it had in his own case.

Although Hovey's last years were marred by an oppressive poverty, his spirit, as reflected in *Along the Trail: A Book of Lyrics* (1898), remained strong. This volume is most representative of his work; it contains some juvenilia, the Dartmouth lyrics, and patriotic poems of the Spanish-American War. Hovey did have a temporary teaching job at Barnard College in 1899. He died suddenly during an operation on a testicle. Mrs. Hovey edited unpublished Arthurian material in *The Holy Graal and Other Fragments* (1907), with an introduction by Carman. In 1908 she edited *To the End of the Trail*, which contains early poems, translations, and a modernization of Lord Byron's unfinished epic, *Don Juan*.

• The Dartmouth College Library has an extensive collection of Hovey's works, letters, and memorabilia. Milner Library at Illinois State University has a collection of material about the Hovey family. *Dartmouth Lyrics*, edited by Edwin Osgood Grover, was published in 1924. The standard biography is Allan Macdonald, *Richard Hovey: Man and Craftsman* (1957). Obituaries and reviews of Hovey's career are in the *New York Times*, 25 Feb., 27 Feb., and 3 Mar. 1900.

WILLIAM R. LINNEMAN

HOVING, Walter (2 Dec. 1897–27 Nov. 1989), corporate executive, was born in Stockholm, Sweden, the son of Johannes Hoving, a surgeon, and Helga Adamsen, an opera singer. In 1903 he went with his parents to New York City, where he graduated from DeWitt Clinton High School before earning his Ph.B. from Brown University in 1920. Four years later he found his metier while in a training program for R. H. Macy & Company, where by 1928 he had become a vice president. During this period he refined his artistic tastes by attending Metropolitan Museum classes for four years in areas such as textile design, painting, and antique silver and furniture. In 1924 he married Mary Osgood Field, with whom he had two children, one of whom, Thomas Hoving, became a director of the Metropolitan Museum. In 1937, a year after his first marriage had ended in divorce, Walter Hoving married Pauline Vandervoort Rogers. They had no children.

Hoving was a vice president in charge of sales at Montgomery Ward & Company from 1932 to 1936; one of his first decisions was to redesign its catalog. Next he was president of Lord & Taylor from 1936 to 1946. Enjoying his own meteoric rise, he decided business was "the great adventure of modern life" and in 1940 published *Your Career in Business* to help others give some "intelligent thought" to their future. In this common sense book Hoving stressed the importance of speaking clearly and developing one's imagination, maturity of mind, and sense of humor. He defined personality "as those qualities and skills which enable one person to reach others, plus the courage to do so" (p. 86). He called aggressiveness "an affirmative" trait, "essential for the man who aspires to responsibility" and warned the introvert not to try to do the work of an extrovert, adding encouragingly: "Most of the imaginative, creative work in business is done by the introvert" (pp. 91, 201).

Leaving Lord & Taylor, Hoving founded the Hoving Corporation, which he operated from 1946 to 1960. Hoving Corporation properties beginning in 1950 included the department store Bonwit Teller. In 1955 he purchased control of Tiffany & Company, which was foundering. As the chair of its board, he succeeded in revitalizing the company by advocating aesthetics and good design. He began with a giant sale to rid the store of merchandise that did not meet his standards, including a $29,700 emerald brooch. When he brought in his own merchandise, there were no diamond rings for men, no silver plate, and no plastic; cellophane tape was not allowed on gift packages. "Design what you think is beautiful," he instructed his artists, on the assumption that customers would like what Tiffany liked. They did. During his command of the store, which lasted until 1980, yearly sales rose from $7 million to $100 million. Tiffany salespeople were told to treat everyone—even gawking sightseers—as potential customers, but those who were rude to the salespeople were not allowed charge accounts.

Hoving gave a Tobe lecture at the Harvard Graduate School of Business Administration in 1959. After expanding this talk, he published it as *The Distribution Revolution* (1960). Fearing that mass production without mass distribution would "end up in a mass production jam," he traces in this book, from an economic viewpoint, the intricacies and interrelated factors of distribution.

For Hoving, design was all important. During interviews with job-seekers, he asked them to choose between well designed and badly designed objects. Finding American business bankrupt "in terms of design," he sponsored seven Tiffany-Wharton Lectures on Corporate Design Management at the University of Pennsylvania, which were published in 1975. "Most people walk in ugliness in terms of architecture and merchandise," he complained, while lamenting that the storekeeper's and manufacturer's taste lagged far behind the public's taste. His formula for creating "a high standard of design" was to help future corporate executives "think fundamentally about design" by teaching them "something about aesthetics" as well as marketing, advertising, merchandising, and finance (Schutte, pp. 1, 4).

An Episcopalian who believed that God had guided him during his entire career, Hoving was named Churchman of the Year in 1974 by Religious Heritage America. He received numerous other awards—some of them international—and honorary doctorates. He was active in national and community organizations. Among his many positions, he was the chair of the United Service Organizations (USO) board and of its camp shows from 1941 to 1948, president of the Salvation Army Association of New York from 1939 to 1960, and the national chair of the United Negro College Fund in 1944, the same year that he was the assistant campaign manager of Thomas E. Dewey's presidential campaign. When Hoving died in Newport, Rhode Island, he was survived by his third wife, Jane Pickens Langley, whom he had married in 1977, a year after the death of his second wife.

• Hoving papers are in the Tiffany & Company Archives, New York City. In addition to Hoving's two books listed above, see his "Are We Underdeveloped In Design?" *New York Times Magazine*, 18 Nov. 1962, and his foreword and lecture in *The Uneasy Coalition: Design in Corporate America*, ed. Thomas F. Schutte (1975). An obituary is in the *New York Times*, 28 Nov. 1989.

OLIVE HOOGENBOOM

HOVLAND, Carl Iver (12 June 1912–16 Apr. 1961), psychologist, was born in Chicago, Illinois, the son of Ole C. Hovland, a telephone engineer, and Augusta Anderson. Hovland entered Northwestern University in 1929, receiving a B.A. "with highest distinction" in 1932 and an M.A. in psychology in 1933. The psychophysiological studies carried out during 1932–1933 under the direction of G. L. Freeman (a former student and follower of E. B. Titchener) generated Hovland's first published articles in 1934 and 1935.

In 1933 Hovland entered the graduate program in psychology at Yale University and at the end of his first year accepted a fellowship to continue his doctoral work there. For his dissertation work, Hovland elected to join Clark L. Hull's ambitious and personally directed program of experimentation on the conditioned reflex, research that eventually established Hull as the preeminent learning theorist of the 1940s and early 1950s. This work secured for Hovland a Ph.D. in 1936 and an instructor's post at Yale for 1936–1937. It also resulted in four journal articles on the sensory generalization of conditioned responses in humans that achieved the status of classics, not least because of the use Hull made of them (especially Hovland's "The Generalization of Conditioned Responses: I. The Sensory Generalization of Conditioned Responses with Varying Frequencies of Tone," *Journal of General Psychology* 17 [1937]: 125–48) to support his own theories.

Although tempting offers came from other institutions, Yale retained Hovland's services by promoting him to assistant professor in 1937. Hovland's subsequent progress through the academic ranks was meteoric: he was appointed director of graduate studies in 1941, associate professor in 1942, and professor in 1945. He was awarded a prestigious Sterling Professorship in 1947 (the same year that Hull, almost thirty years his senior, was similarly honored). Hovland married Gertrude Raddatz in 1938; they had two children.

After joining Yale's faculty, Hovland was chiefly associated with the experimental side of Hull's attempts to develop an axiomatic system for human rote learning, publishing several journal articles and contributing in a minor way to the complex and difficult book by Hull and others, *Mathematico-Deductive Theory of Rote Learning* (1940). In 1942, however, Hovland took a leave of absence from Yale when the sociologist Samuel A. Stouffer succeeded in recruiting him to head the newly created Experimental Section of the Research Branch of the War Department's Information and Education Division in Washington, D.C.

In Washington, Hovland's work focused on training, morale, and persuasion; he was to pursue this last theme for the rest of his life. Although they appear to break with his previous research, Hovland's published studies in communication, beginning with those from his War Department days, show a continuing concern with controlled experimentation, the use of quantitative analyses, and a willingness to incorporate many aspects of learning theory and psychophysical measurement into social psychology. Free of the intellectual and personal influence of Hull, Hovland now had a chance to develop a more cooperative and less hierarchically organized research team, and also to break away from a narrowly behaviorist vision of psychology.

On returning to Yale in 1945, Hovland served as chairman of the Psychology Department for the next six years. He also brought together several of his wartime co-workers, as well as numerous research fellows and assistants, into what became the Yale Communication and Attitude Change Program. From 1947, the Yale program, directed by Hovland, was funded mainly by the Rockefeller Foundation's Social Science Program.

The 1940s and 1950s were particularly active times for new empirically oriented thinking about personality, attitude change, and social psychology in general, substantive areas that readily lent themselves to the kind of tightly controlled laboratory research favored by Hovland and his many collaborators. Most clearly articulated in the introductory chapter of *Communication and Persuasion* (1953) by Hovland, Irving L. Janis, and Harold H. Kelley, this new laboratory-based approach generated many articles and the four volumes of *Yale Studies in Attitude and Communication* published under Hovland's general editorship between 1957 and 1961, beginning with the influential *The Order of Presentation in Persuasion* (1957). As well as investigating order effects in presenting persuasive material, these volumes covered experiments on the relationship between personality and persuasibility, the consistency of attitudes, and sophisticated aspects of the scaling of social judgments.

From 1952 onward, with grants from the Ford Foundation and Bell Telephone Laboratories, Hovland also undertook a systematic exploration of human thinking and problem solving, which culminated in a series of articles on the computer simulation of concept formation and reasoning. These included, with Walter Weiss, "Transmission of Information Concerning Concepts through Positive and Negative Instances," *Journal of Experimental Psychology* 45 (1953): 175–82, and Hovland's "Computer Simulation of Thinking," *American Psychologist* 15 (1960): 687–93. The pace of this work had begun to accelerate in the two years before his early death from cancer at the age of forty-eight at Hamden, Connecticut.

During his academic career, Hovland published over seventy articles and chapters, and he was editor or coauthor of seven books. He served as consultant to many research foundations, industrial organizations, and government agencies, and was a member of several distinguished bodies including the American Academy of Arts and Sciences, the American Philosophical Society, and the National Academy of Science. He received a Distinguished Scientific Contribution Award from the American Psychological Association, of which he was a fellow, in 1957, and the Warren Medal of the Society of Experimental Psychologists in 1961.

Hovland's successful transition from hard-nosed learning theorist to laboratory-based social psychologist secured his place among the pioneering investigators of those forms of human communication known as persuasion or rhetoric. His achievements were due in no small part to his skills in creating, sustaining and funding, over some fifteen years, a large-scale research network of the leading young social psychologists of the day. Although, in retrospect, Hovland's research on communication and persuasion should be judged as his chief legacy to psychology, his concept formation work, cut so tragically short, might well have become his third major contribution to twentieth-century psychology.

• The Carl Iver Hovland Papers, which include correspondence, research records, and reports mostly relating to the 1940s onward, are held in Manuscripts and Archives, Yale University Library. Among his works not already mentioned are "Experimental Studies in Rote-learning Theory: V. Comparison of Distribution of Practice in Serial and Paired-associate Learning," *Journal of Experimental Psychology* 25 (1939): 622–33, on learning theory; with Arthur A. Lumsdaine and Fred. D. Sheffield, *Experiments on Mass Communication* (1949), which describes aspects of his wartime research; and, with Muzafer Sherif, *Social Judgment: Assimilation and Contrast Effects in Communication and Attitude Change* (1961), the fourth volume of the *Yale Studies in Attitude and Communication*. Bibliographies of Hovland's publications can be found in "American Psychological Association Distinguished Scientific Contribution Awards 1957," *American Psychologist* 13 (1958): 158–62, and appended to an assessment of Hovland's research by one of his collaborators, Irving L. Janis, in the *International Encyclopedia of the Social Sciences* (1968), pp. 526–31. Obituaries by Robert R. Sears, *American Journal of Psychology* 74 (1961): 637–39, and Walter R. Miles, *American Philosophical Yearbook 1961* (1962): 121–25, provide biographical material as well as more personal impressions and reminiscences about Hovland.

ALEXANDER D. LOVIE
PATRICIA LOVIE

HOWARD, Ada Lydia (19 Dec. 1829–3 Mar. 1907), educator, was born in Temple, New Hampshire, the daughter of William Hawkins Howard, a farmer, and Lydia Adaline Cowden. Her father had scholarly and scientific interests and tutored her at home before she attended nearby New Ipswich Academy and Lowell High School. In 1850 she enrolled at Mount Holyoke Seminary, from which she graduated in 1853. After teaching in Downington, Pennsylvania, and Warren, Massachusetts, she returned to Mount Holyoke, where she served as an instructor from 1858 to 1861. The following year she taught at the Western Female Seminary in Oxford, Ohio, one of Mount Holyoke's "daughter" institutions.

In 1866 Howard became principal of the Female Collegiate Department at Knox College in Galesburg, Illinois. Its eastern-educated president, William S. Curtis, looked unfavorably on the western practice of mixing men and women in the classroom, and sought instead to reorganize women's education to conform with the seminary model of Mount Holyoke, the alma mater of both Howard and his wife. Under his direction, Howard became principal of the newly resegregated female seminary in 1867. Apparently well liked by students and faculty, Howard also served as instructor in moral philosophy, and in historic and literary criticism. In 1868 she came into conflict with Curtis over a variety of matters, which included her heavy administrative load and the pay cuts that he had decreed for female teachers. Difficulties peaked when, in a dispute over catalogue copy for the coming year, Curtis seized Howard by the wrists to secure the disputed proofs, which were destroyed in the tussle. In response, Howard and two other seminary faculty members tendered their resignations. Charging that Curtis had "by his opprobrious conduct insulted our beloved Preceptress and disgraced the entire Institution," seminary students called for him to resign instead. College students supported the women, undertaking a noisy boycott of classes. In the end, Curtis was dismissed from the presidency. Howard left the following year. In 1870 she established her own private school, Ivy Hall, in Bridgeton, New Jersey, where she remained until 1875.

In the spring of 1875, Wellesley College founder Henry Fowle Durant met Howard. Committed to staffing his college for women with women faculty and administrators, and impressed both by Howard's strong Christian faith and her academic experience, Durant proposed her selection as president of the college. "I look upon her as appointed to this work not by the trustees, but by God, for whom the College was built," Durant reported. With the opening of Wellesley in September 1875, Howard officially became the first woman college president and oversaw approximately thirty faculty members and 314 female students, who were mostly enrolled in its preparatory program. Howard shouldered a substantial administrative burden and played a significant role in setting the social and academic tone for the new institution. She presided over the graduation of the first class in 1879 and the closing of the preparatory department in 1881. Ultimately, however, her students recognized that "she was in the difficult position of the nominal captain, who is in fact only a lieutenant." Durant retained primary authority throughout his lifetime and dictated everything, as one student wrote in 1875, "from the amount of Latin we shall read to the kind of meat we shall have for dinner."

Students remembered Howard as the archetypal Victorian gentlewoman, "with her young face, pink cheeks, blue eyes, and puffs of snow-white hair, wearing always a long trailing gown of black silk, cut low at the throat and finished with folds of snowy tulle." Howard regularly addressed students at the required chapel services and spoke on deportment, appropriate costume, and religious issues. Beginning with the hope that she could achieve the restraint of students through deployment of influence rather than regulation of behavior, she nonetheless became associated in the minds of many with seminary rules and restraint rather than collegiate progress. Plagued by illness throughout her term in the college presidency, she retired from her position in 1881, only one month after the death of the founder, and was replaced by dynamic, college-educated Alice Freeman (Alice Freeman Palmer). Howard's lasting influence on Wellesley was, by all accounts, limited, but loyal alumnae did rally to provide the otherwise impecunious president emeritus with an annuity. She visited the campus regularly after her retirement first to nearby Methuen, Massachusetts, and later to Brooklyn, New York. After she died in Brooklyn, funeral services were held in the Wellesley College Chapel, and she was buried on the grounds of the college.

Howard participated in the transition of women's higher education from the seminary model that was pioneered at Mount Holyoke to the emergent collegiate standards represented by Wellesley's growth. Evidently an able administrator, if not a visionary, she contributed to the institutionalization of women's higher education.

• Primary sources on the life of Howard are extremely limited, but the Wellesley College Archives contain some personal letters as well as college records that detail her term as president. Additional published materials on her Wellesley role can be found in Florence Converse, *The Story of Wellesley* (1915); Alice Payne Hackett, *Wellesley: Part of the American Story* (1949), and Jean Glasscock, ed., *Wellesley College, 1875–1975: A Century of Women* (1975). Hermann Muelder, *Missionaries and Muckrakers: The First Hundred Years of Knox College* (1984), describes the Knox contretemps.

CAROL LASSER

HOWARD, Benjamin (1770?–18 Sept. 1814), soldier and territorial governor, was born in Virginia, the son of John Howard, a farmer and land speculator, and Mary Preston. Howard's birth is often dated 1760; however, the fact that he was the fourth child of a 1764 marriage along with his letters from college offer convincing evidence that 1760 is at least a decade too early. Howard's father, by living to be 103 years old, eventually became a celebrated Kentucky figure. His mother belonged to a powerful western Virginia clan. Benjamin Howard had an unsettled and difficult childhood. A disastrous manager and a sometimes violent husband, John Howard in 1779 was judged, in a court controlled by his wife's connections, to have been "for some time past in a State of Insanity." Throughout Benjamin's boyhood and youth, his father spent long periods in Kentucky, where adventure and military bounty lands drew him, while his mother, often calling on her kin for help, struggled in Virginia to fix the family's tangled affairs so that they could migrate to Kentucky. The fact that Benjamin Howard so often found himself under the care and tutelage of his maternal kin was formative.

By 1789 Howard was in Kentucky, where a cousin found him living alone "in his little hut," waiting for his family to join him. They arrived in Fayette County, Kentucky, around 1790 and began to develop a farm called "Howard's Grove." Always an eager student, Howard had hoped as early as 1787 to enter the College of William and Mary, but five years later in Kentucky the family were still scrabbling for funds. During this time, his mother also reported that he spent "almost half his time after the Indians." He joined many militia expeditions and commanded a band of volunteers attached to General Anthony Wayne's forces.

Clerking for a cousin, James Brown, who was secretary of the state, Howard was introduced to Kentucky politics. He was not impressed. During the first session of the state assembly, he complained of the "Set of Novices at the helm that has got entangled in politics and knows not how to extricate itself." For the next few years he clerked in the law office of another cousin, John Breckinridge, conducted land business for his Virginia kin and connections, and took an avid interest in western land speculations. Though Howard still worried that the federal establishment was "improper and ineffectual" to "subdue the Indians," expeditions against them ceased after the 1795 Greenville Treaty.

Suddenly Howard had more leisure to consider his options. At last, he entered the College of William and Mary, studying law and politics with St. George Tucker in 1796–1797 and again in 1798–1799. The intervening year he spent in Botetourt County, reading in a cousin's law library and conducting an illicit affair. Facing down the local scandal, Howard made a point of practicing briefly in Botetourt before returning to Kentucky in 1801. Among friends, at least, Howard saw himself and his new profession with cynical humor, calling himself in 1799 a "right sharp chunk of a Lawyer."

Howard represented Fayette County in the state legislature in 1801 and 1802, but he took a dim view of Kentucky's democratic politics. He complained that "the popular mind" often elected their own, "in preference to rich men," to state office. If Howard was never a rich man himself, he was kin to some of the most prominent men in the state, including his first cousins John Brown and John Breckinridge, who were Kentucky's U.S. senators, and now he was educated to take his place among them. With their firm "republican principles" and their disgust for the broils of state politics, such men naturally gravitated toward national office. By 1803 Howard considered running for Congress. Elected to the Tenth and Eleventh Congresses (1807–1810), he espoused a national outlook that coincided with the needs and interests of the western country, advocating a larger army and more aggressive protection of the frontiers. Though he left Congress too soon properly to be called a "War Hawk," it was his military bent that finally elevated him to high civil and military office.

In 1810, recommended to President James Madison as a man with "a perfect knowledge of Indians," Howard was appointed governor of the District of Louisiana, renamed the Territory of Missouri in 1812. When Howard arrived in Missouri five months later, the territory was anxiously expecting trouble from the Indian tribes of the region. He organized local militia and coordinated his efforts with the governors of the adjacent territories. Like many early territorial governors, he actually spent little time in residence. During an eight months' absence in 1810–1811, he was married in Virginia to Mary Thomson Mason, daughter of Jeffersonian statesman Stevens Thomson Mason. The following summer he was in Missouri to inspect the northern frontier and oversee local defenses before returning to Kentucky, where his parents deeded to him Howard's Grove, their Fayette County property.

The outbreak of war in 1812 found the Missouri Territory still in an anxious and defensive position. Howard continued to organize militia companies, including one known as Howard's Rangers, who patrolled the territory and established forts along the Missouri.

On 12 March 1813 Howard resigned his governorship to accept the office of brigadier general of the army in charge of the Eighth Military District, the forces west of the Mississippi. He saw little action before his death the next year in St. Louis. Howard's young wife had died in 1813, and there were no children. Benjamin Howard's individual talents and even his public achievements are now mostly lost to the his-

torical record. But his achievement, albeit a collective one, stands: he was one of hundreds of men of the postrevolutionary generation whose training and prospects, for better or for worse, exactly fitted them to effect the extraordinary expansion of the Early American Republic.

• Though no single collection of Howard's papers has survived, some of his correspondence and many references to him are scattered through the various archives of the Preston clan of Va. and Ky., notably in the Preston papers of the Lyman C. Draper Collection at the State Historical Society of Wisconsin; the Preston Davie Collection at the Virginia Historical Society; the Preston Family Papers, Joyes Collection, at the Filson Club; and the Campbell-Preston-Floyd Papers and the Breckinridge Family Papers in the Library of Congress. For Howard's college experience, see "Letters from William and Mary, 1795–1799," *Virginia Magazine of History and Biography* 29 (1922): 228–30, 248–49. Official correspondence and many references to his governorship and last military assignment are in Clarence Carter, ed., *Territorial Papers: The Territory of Louisiana-Missouri, 1806–1821* (1949). John Frederick Dorman, *The Prestons of Smithfield and Greenfield in Virginia* (1982), is useful. Howard's brief territorial career is described in William E. Foley, *The Genesis of Missouri: From Wilderness Outpost to Statehood* (1989).

MARION WINSHIP

HOWARD, Benjamin Chew (5 Nov. 1791–6 Mar. 1872), lawyer and legislator, was born at "Belvedere" in Baltimore County, Maryland, the son of John Eager Howard, an officer in the revolutionary war, and Peggy Oswald Chew of Pennsylvania. His maternal grandfather was Benjamin Chew, prerevolutionary president of the Pennsylvania Court of Errors and Appeals. After an elementary education in Baltimore, Howard earned his A.B. in 1809 and A.M. in 1812, both from Princeton (then called the College of New Jersey). His subsequent law studies in a Baltimore office were interrupted by the 1812 war with Britain, during which he organized troops for the defense of Baltimore and commanded the Mechanical Volunteers military unit at the battle of North Point on 12 September 1814. Howard was later commissioned brigadier-general in the Maryland Militia. He married Jane Grant Gilmor in 1818; the number of their children, if any, is unknown.

Admitted to the Maryland bar about 1816, Howard carried on a prosperous law practice while actively participating in politics and public affairs. A Democrat, Howard was elected to the Baltimore City Council in 1820 and to the Maryland House of Delegates in 1824. He was a member of the public committee that formally proposed the construction of a railroad between Baltimore and the Ohio River for the extension of trade to the western territories. Howard was a presidential elector for Maryland in 1828.

Elected from Maryland to four terms in Congress, Howard served in the House of Representatives from 1829 to 1833 in the Twenty-first and Twenty-second Congresses, and from 1835 to 1839 in the Twenty-fourth and Twenty-fifth Congresses, chairing the House Foreign Relations Committee during his second set of terms. As chair of the Foreign Relations Committee, Howard drew up the congressional report on the question of the northeastern boundary between Canada and the New England states. Howard also served at President Andrew Jackson's direction as a "peace commissioner" in the volatile "boundary war" between Michigan and Ohio in 1835. The intervention resulted in a compromise under which Michigan gave up its claims to the city of Toledo in exchange for acquiring what is now the state's upper peninsula. After his congressional service ended Howard returned to the Maryland legislature, representing Baltimore in the Maryland Senate for a term in 1840–1841.

Howard's long association with U.S. Supreme Court Chief Justice Roger Taney, a fellow Maryland lawyer, apparently gained Howard the position of reporter of decisions of the Supreme Court in 1843, although there is no evidence to suggest that he sought the job or intrigued before the summary discharge of his predecessor, Richard Peters. Howard's twenty-four volumes of case reports, officially called "Howard's Reports" (also denominated volumes 42–65 of the United States Reports series), were praised in the legal community as clear, thorough, and well written. In pointing out what was perhaps Howard's only obvious editing mistake in his reports, Justice Peter Daniel did complain on one occasion that his name had been omitted before a dissenting opinion.

After serving as a Unionist Maryland delegate to a peace conference in February 1861, which unsuccessfully attempted to avoid civil war, Howard resigned as reporter of decisions between terms of the Supreme Court in that year to run as Democratic candidate for governor of Maryland. The unconditional Unionist candidate Augustus W. Bradford, however, defeated Howard in the election. Howard died in his native Baltimore after a long illness.

Howard exhibited an almost breathless energy in long and varied service to his home city, state, and country in numerous important public positions. From his youth to nearly the end of his life he capably performed an extraordinary range of duties in response to the needs of his time. His legacy includes the admirably edited volumes of U.S. Supreme Court case reports he compiled and published and the present boundaries of the states of Michigan and Ohio.

• Entries about Howard appear in the *Biographical Directory of the American Congress* (1989); in *Wallace's Reports*, vol. 13, p. vii; and in the *Maryland History Magazine*, Sept. 1914, Mar. 1920, and Sept. 1922. An obituary is in the Baltimore *Sun*, 7 Mar. 1872.

FRANCIS HELMINSKI

HOWARD, Blanche Willis (21 July 1847–7 Oct. 1898), novelist, journalist, and editor, was born in Bangor, Maine, the daughter of Daniel Mosely Howard, an insurance broker, and Eliza Anne Hudson. She graduated from the local high school and later attended a boarding school in New York City. Her first novel *One Summer* was published in 1875. The novel, set in her home state, met with instant success, eventually going through several editions and launching her career as both a novelist and journalist. Later that year, she left for Europe as a travel correspondent for the *Boston Transcript*. Her residence abroad would prove to be permanent.

Howard settled in Stuttgart, Germany, where she established a residence and offered herself as a paid chaperone and guide to American girls studying abroad. This arrangement provided her with the financial resources to continue her writing career while pursuing independent studies in philosophy, science, and music. Beginning in 1878 she also acted as the English language editor for *Hallberger's Illustrated Magazine*, which reprinted excerpts from British and American literature for a German audience.

The years following the publication of *One Summer* were fruitful. Howard's works from the next two decades include: *Aunt Serena* (1881), *Guenn: A Wave on the Breton Coast* (1884), *Aulnay Tower* (1885), *Tony the Maid* (1887), *The Open Door* (1889), *A Battle and a Boy* (1892), *No Heroes* (1893), *Seven on the Highway* (1897), *Dionysius the Weaver's Heart's Dearest* (1899), and *The Garden of Eden* (1900) (the last two were published posthumously). Another novel, *A Fellowe and His Wife* (1892), was an epistolary novel written with William Sharp, with Howard writing the letters from the husband and Sharp writing those from the wife. She wrote one nonfiction book, *One Year Abroad* (1877), which recorded her travels with a group of friends through Germany and Switzerland. She also translated *The Humming Top; Or, Debit and Credit in the Next World* (1890), a Christian children's story by Theobald Gross.

Howard was married to Julius von Teuffel, the personal physician to the King of Wurttemberg, from 1890 to his death in 1896. The marriage was reported by contemporaries to be happy, in spite of its brevity and von Teuffel's rumored insanity. The couple had no children. Because von Teuffel was a member of the German aristocracy, Howard's marriage to him considerably enhanced her social status. She remained in Stuttgart after his death. She died, following an unidentified illness, two years later in Munich.

Howard's conventional romantic plots and romanticized settings were both the secret of her success with her audience and the bane of her critics. In her earlier and weaker novels, in particular, the settings are simply attractive backdrops for the love stories of young, handsome, and charming characters. Her first novel, for example, is a sketch of the romantic foibles of a group of wealthy young people on vacation in Maine. By contrast, for contemporaries such as Harriet Beecher Stowe and Sarah Orne Jewett, the rugged landscape of northern New England served as a reflection of the careworn existences and moral strength of their characters. Howard's transplantation to Europe initially affected her fiction simply by providing her with settings that were new and more exotic to an American audience. Her interest in romances of the well-born persists in later novels such as *Aulnay Tower*, though in that book she exchanged the vacationing Mainers for European aristocrats, and her romantic obstacle is now the Franco-Prussian War, not a case of mistaken identity. Still, it is noteworthy that although most of her heroines are conventionally beautiful and irresistible to men, their opinions often reflect her own progressive views on women's rights and women's abilities.

Yet critics also noted that Howard's later works revealed an increasingly insightful portrayal of human nature, particularly with regard to her lower-class characters. As her early travel writings show, Howard had always been more interested in the people she encountered than in the landscape, and as her writing developed, her characterizations became less condescending and more sympathetic. In *Guenn* and *Dionysius the Weaver's Heart's Dearest*, the works usually cited as her best, Howard treats the European peasantry with tact and understanding. She is reported to have said, speaking of her method of gathering material for her books, "I go about among the German peasants and working people and fisherman on the Baltic, and mountaineers in the Tyrol, but with no ulterior motive, and certainly not with a notebook in my hand" (*New York Times*, 16 July 1898). This statement suggests that she eventually strove to distinguish herself from artists like the egotistical male painter in *Guenn*, who exploits the peasant girl who models for him.

The popularity of her European-based works undoubtedly was fueled by the increasing interest in Europe and European travel among postbellum Americans. By encouraging this interest, it may be said that she broadened the horizons of her audience and may even have helped prepare readers for more artistic treatments of similar subject matter by contemporaries such as Henry James.

• Two letters (dated 20 Apr. 1883 and 21 Feb. 1890) Howard wrote to Edward F. Strickland are in the Schlesinger Library's Strickland Collection, Radcliffe College; another (dated 23 Mar. 1887) she wrote to Ben W. Austin is in the Cairns Collection at the University of Wisconsin at Madison. Howard's obituary in the *New York Times*, 10 Oct. 1898, and the biographical sketch (with picture) in Frances E. Willard and Mary A. Livermore, *A Woman of the Century* (1893), are the best contemporary sources of biographical information. Margaret Hubbard Ayer and Isabella Taves, *The Three Lives of Harriet Hubbard Ayers* (1957), contains an extensive, though apparently biased and possibly inaccurate, account of Howard.

ANNE SHEEHAN

HOWARD, Bronson Crocker (7 Oct. 1842–4 Aug. 1908), playwright, was born in Detroit, Michigan, the son of Charles Howard, a prosperous commission merchant who became mayor of Detroit (1849), and Margaret Vosburgh. Howard attended Detroit public schools until 1858, when he was sent to Russell's Institute in New Haven, Connecticut. In 1861 he enrolled at Yale University, but an eye ailment forced him to withdraw during his freshman year. He returned to Detroit and began work as a drama critic for the *Free Press*. Howard's first play, *Fantine*, based on an episode in Victor Hugo's *Les Misérables*, was produced in Detroit in 1864. The following year he moved to New York City, where he supported himself as a reporter for the *Mail*, the *Tribune*, and the *Evening Post* while devoting his spare time to writing plays. Howard continued to work occasionally as a journalist until 1876, several years after he had established himself as a playwright.

Howard's first New York play, *Saratoga*, a satiric comedy about life in the fashionable resort town, opened at Augustin Daly's Fifth Avenue Theatre on 21 December 1870, with Fanny Davenport and James Lewis in the cast; the play enjoyed a lengthy run. Although similar in construction to other comedies of its time, *Saratoga* showed Howard's aptitude for dialogue and his eye for detail. *Brighton*, a British adaptation of *Saratoga*, was successfully produced in London in 1874. The London production starred Sir Charles Wyndham. Howard married Wyndham's sister Alice in 1880; they had no children.

After three commercial failures—*Diamonds* (1872), *Moorcroft* (1874), and *Hurricanes* (1878)—Howard had another major success with *The Banker's Daughter* (1878). The comedy was a reworking by Howard and A. R. Cazauran (producer A. M. Palmer's "play doctor") of an earlier Howard play, *Lillian's Lost Love*, which had a brief run in Chicago in 1873. A third version of the play, called *The Old Love and the New*, was crafted by Howard and James Albery and produced in London in 1879. Howard recounted the play's metamorphosis and expressed his ideas about dramatic construction in a notable lecture to the Harvard University Shakespeare Club in 1886, which was published as *The Autobiography of a Play* in 1914. Howard based his rules of dramatic technique on audience expectation and reaction. Later critics faulted Howard for assuming that the attitudes of theatergoers of his time represented universal and unchangeable responses. Accordingly, Howard's plays are generally considered to have little enduring dramatic worth, but they are valuable indicators of the concerns and opinions of Gilded Age audiences.

Howard's next important play was *Young Mrs. Winthrop*, a drama about the breakup of a marriage due to a husband's obsession with business and his wife's preoccupation with social life. The play, which opened at the Madison Square Theater in October 1882 with George Clarke and Carrie Turner in the lead roles, signaled a shift by Howard away from farces and toward relatively realistic examinations of contemporary society. A critic in the *New York Times* (10 Oct. 1882) noted, "Mr. Howard's talent and courage are now unmistakable. He has made a play which should be accepted as a model by those young and honestly ambitious dramatists who are willing to put art first and the theatre last." *Young Mrs. Winthrop* was successfully produced, without alteration, in London in November 1882.

Howard was especially interested in examining how the rise of big business and the accumulation of great personal fortunes were affecting the American character. In *One of Our Girls* (1885), the daughter of a newly rich American millionaire visits her upper-class relatives in France—those who had once scorned her mother for marrying a penniless Yankee. The play starred Helen Dauvray and E. H. Sothern and was the biggest nonmusical hit of the season. Even more successful was *The Henrietta* (1887), about a Wall Street financier whose greed and philandering cause his family to suffer. Blending drama and comedy in equal measure, the popular play utilized modern devices such as ticker tape machines and telephones. Comic touches were primarily derived from confusion over the name Henrietta, which referred to a mining company, a racehorse, and an actress of ill repute. A successful updated version, eliminating soliloquies and asides, opened in New York in December 1913 as *The New Henrietta* starring Douglas Fairbanks. The screen version of the updated play was *The Saphead* (1920), starring Buster Keaton and William H. Crane (Crane had appeared in both stage versions).

Howard's most commercially successful play was the Civil War epic *Shenandoah*. The sprawling play was poorly received at its premiere in Boston in 1888, but Charles Frohman, then a young road company advance agent with producing aspirations, saw possibilities in it and obtained financing to mount a slightly rewritten version in New York City. The play opened at the Star Theatre in September 1889 featuring Henry Miller, Wilton Lackaye, Viola Allen, and John E. Kellerd in the central roles and became one of the biggest hits of its time. It established Frohman as an important producer. A grandly theatrical crowd pleaser featuring huge assemblies of troops, rousing bugle calls, and a galloping horse, *Shenandoah* received a mixed reception from critics, many of whom found its plot contrived and confusing. In November 1890 Frohman moved the play to the larger Grand Opera House so that its lavish production values could be better appreciated. Although *Shenandoah* may have been of little dramatic merit, it enhanced Howard's reputation as a playwright who tackled American subjects at a time when the American theater was dominated by British and French imports.

After writing *Shenandoah*, Howard's creative energies appear to have slowed, and only two more new plays of his were produced: *Aristocracy* (1892), a moderately successful comedy about an American family's involvement with titled Europeans that starred Viola Allen, Wilton Lackaye, and William Faversham; and *Peter Stuyvesant* (1899), a lackluster vehicle for William H. Crane, written in collaboration with Brander Matthews. His last play, *Kate*, was published in 1906 but never produced. After the turn of the century, Howard's plays began to seem dated; however, Howard was still held in high esteem by his colleagues, and his major works were regularly performed by regional stock companies until the World War I era.

The dapper, mustachioed Howard, who was not an especially imaginative writer, spent much time on preparatory study in order to obtain ideas for his plays. As he stated in *Theatre Magazine* (Apr. 1906), "a dramatist must completely saturate himself with his subject before he begins to write. In writing a play he must assimilate about fifty times as much knowledge as he can use. It is the only way that what one does use will flow freely and spontaneously." Howard also did a great deal of rewriting, sometimes with a collaborator, and he usually heeded the advice of producers on how to make a play work better on stage. He believed that a play's value was primarily dramatic, not literary.

One of Howard's chief concerns was the development of writing plays as a profession rather than as a sideline of actors, producers, or "men of letters." In 1891 he founded and became the first president of the American Dramatists Club (later the Society of American Dramatists and Composers), which successfully lobbied for reform of copyright laws to put an end to script pirating. The highly respected Howard, who was often called the "Dean of American Playwrights," was long considered to be the first American to make a living exclusively as a playwright, but that distinction can be more correctly accorded to one of a number of more obscure figures from earlier in the nineteenth century. Despite his association with American-themed plays, Howard spent much of his time abroad. He had homes in New York City, California, and London. He died in Avon-by-the-Sea, New Jersey.

• Howard's papers, including correspondence, bibliography, and autobiography, are at the Detroit Public Library. Grace Hortense Tower, "Bronson Howard: Dean of American Dramatists," *Theatre*, Apr. 1906, pp. 99–102, offers an interview with Howard. A bibliography by Barbara C. Gannon is in *American Literary Realism, 1870–1910* (Spring 1982): 111–18. Also see Charles John Boyle, "Bronson Howard and the Popular Temper of the Gilded Age" (Ph.D. diss., Univ. of Wisconsin, 1957), and Lloyd A. Ferrer, "Bronson Howard: Dean of American Dramatists" (Ph.D. diss., Univ. of Iowa, 1971). Additional information is in Montrose J. Moses, *The American Dramatist* (1925), Arthur Hobson Quinn, *A History of the American Drama from the Civil War to the Present Day*, vol. 1 (1927), and Jack A. Vaughn, *Early American Dramatists from the Beginnings to 1900* (1981). An obituary is in the *New York Times*, 5 Aug. 1908.

MARY C. KALFATOVIC

HOWARD, Charles Perry (14 Sept. 1879–21 July 1938), labor leader, was born in Harvel, Illinois, the son of Lewis Pontius Howard, a lawyer, and Mary M. Williamson. After moving to Kansas as a young boy, Howard left school at the age of thirteen. He spent the next fifteen years moving from job to job, laboring as a railroad worker (1897–1899), miner (1900–1903), and finally learning the printing trade in a series of small shops. In 1907 he joined an International Typographical Union (ITU) local in Tacoma, Washington. Shortly thereafter he moved to Portland, Oregon, and joined the Multnomah Typographical Union there.

He became president of the local in 1914 and represented it on Portland's Central Labor Council, which he headed from 1916 to 1918.

Howard's labor activities soon extended beyond Portland. He represented his local at the ITU's national convention in 1916, spent 1918 in Washington, D.C., as commissioner of conciliation at the U.S. Department of Labor, and then worked for three years as editor of the *Railway Maintenance of Way Employees' Journal*. In 1920 he attended his first annual convention of the American Federation of Labor (AFL) as a member of the ITU delegation. Meanwhile he was also rising within the ITU. This union had an unusual two-party system like that of national politics. As a candidate of the more militant Progressive party, Howard was elected vice president in 1922, and when the president died in office a year later, Howard succeeded him. He was defeated for reelection in 1924 but won in 1926 and remained in office for the rest of his life.

During the 1930s Howard became increasingly active in the AFL, serving first as a member and then as secretary of its powerful Resolutions Committee. In this position he was soon drawn into the lacerating debates over whether to experiment with industrial unionism, under which whole industries would be organized as single units. By 1933 Howard had come to agree with the leader of the industrial unionists, John L. Lewis, that the traditional arrangement of having a separate union for each craft was too narrow and fragmented to meet the AFL's most immediate challenge: organizing mass production industries. The AFL leadership strongly preferred craft unions, and a proposal by Howard at the 1933 convention to permit some industrial organizing was defeated. At the 1934 AFL convention he helped negotiate a compromise that permitted a limited number of mass production industries to be organized on "a different basis" by new so-called federal unions structured along industrial lines. The federal unions were weak, but the arrangement seemed like a promising beginning.

When the AFL convened in October 1935, it became clear that the 1934 compromise satisfied neither side. The resolutions committee's majority report defended the limitations on the federal unions' power and implied that perhaps they should be weakened further. The minority report, presented by Howard, maintained that the unions should be strengthened. Pointing out that mass production industries included many workers who could not qualify for membership in any craft union, while other workers' duties qualified them for more than one, inviting jurisdictional disputes, Howard concluded: "industrial organization is the only solution." After hours of bitter debate, the existing system was supported by a majority vote of nearly two to one. At breakfast the next morning Howard, Lewis, and six other industrial unionists agreed that they must pursue the matter on their own. A month later, at a press conference in Washington, D.C., they announced the formation of a new Committee for Industrial Organizations (CIO) to "encourage and promote organization of the workers in the mass production and unorganized industries." Lewis would chair the committee and Howard would be its secretary.

As spokesman for the CIO, Howard denied accusations by the AFL Executive Committee that the new organization represented dual unionism; he insisted that, although self-appointed, it could function harmoniously within the AFL. The executive committee saw matters otherwise, however, and in January 1936, after listening unsympathetically to a final presentation by Howard, they ordered the CIO to dissolve. Lewis immediately began a series of belligerent speeches that widened the breach. Howard regretted Lewis's tone, feeling that it might still be possible to achieve reform from within the AFL, but he joined the rest of the CIO leadership in refusing to disband. In August 1937 the CIO unions were ejected from the AFL. Representatives from both sides, including Howard, met periodically that fall, but the break was final. By the following year Howard was encouraging the CIO to broaden its organizing efforts, even among trades already affiliated with the AFL.

Howard's participation in the CIO was somewhat different from that of his fellow insurgents because his own union had not followed him into the new organization. Nevertheless the ITU reelected him by a large majority in May 1936 and at its convention that fall pledged both moral and financial support to the CIO's organizing drives. Howard faced greater difficulties, however, as he prepared to run again two years later. By then he had been expelled from the 1937 AFL convention, which he attended as an ITU delegate, because of his CIO connections. Even though his union refused to pay a special assessment to fund the AFL's battle against the rebels, Howard's CIO involvement caused him problems with the ITU's more conservative wing, while critics from the left attacked his reluctance to share work with unemployed members. In May 1938 he was decisively defeated. He was completing his final term when he died of a heart attack while attending the board meeting of an ITU retirement home in Colorado Springs, Colorado. He was married to Margaret McPhail; they had no children.

If Howard had died in 1933 he would be remembered as a progressive but unexceptional trade unionist. In the last five years of his life, however, his career was transformed. A man of accommodating style, he would have preferred to keep the CIO inside the AFL, but when that proved impossible he stuck to his faith in industrial unionism, even though it cost him the professional associations of a lifetime and ultimately helped lose him the ITU presidency. His central role in launching the CIO earned him an important place in the labor history of his times.

• The papers of the International Typographical Union are in the Southern Labor Archives at Georgia State University. See Gary Fink, *Labor Unions* (1977); Saul Alinsky, *John L. Lewis: An Unauthorized Biography* (1949); Melvyn Dubofsky and Warren Van Tine, *John L. Lewis: A Biography* (1977); Walter Galenson, *The CIO Challenge to the AFL: A History of the*

American Labor Movement, 1935–1941 (1960); Charles A. Madison, *American Labor Leaders* (1950); Sidney Lens, *The Labor Wars: From the Molly Maguires to the Sitdowns* (1974); and Milton Derber and Edwin Young, eds., *Labor and the New Deal* (1957). An obituary is in the *New York Times*, 22 July 1938.

SANDRA OPDYCKE

HOWARD, Curly. *See* Three Stooges.

HOWARD, Elston Gene (23 Feb. 1929–14 Dec. 1980), baseball player, was born in St. Louis, Missouri, the son of Wayman Hill Howard, a high school principal, and Emmaline Webb, a dietician. A three-sport star in high school, Howard received twenty-five scholarship offers to play intercollegiate football and basketball. Instead, inspired by Jackie Robinson's recent breaking of the color ban in Organized Baseball, Howard signed in 1948 to play with the Kansas City Monarchs of the Negro American League.

While with the Monarchs, a team that eventually graduated far more players to the major leagues than any other Negro League club, he caught the attention of New York Yankees' scouts, and in 1950 he signed a contract to play with Muskegon, Michigan, in the Class A Central League. After an army hitch in 1951–1952, Howard spent 1953 with the Kansas City Blues of the Class AAA American Association. He had a strong season and decided to play winter baseball in Puerto Rico as a prelude to making the Yankee roster. But during spring training the Yankees switched him from the outfield to catcher under the tutelage of Hall of Fame receiver Bill Dickey and then assigned him to Toronto of the Class AAA International League. Howard quickly mastered his new position. Named the league's Most Valuable Player for 1954 after hitting .330 with 22 home runs and 109 runs batted in, he joined the Yankees in 1955, the first black to play for baseball's most storied franchise. To those who charged that his promotion had been delayed because of race, Howard replied only: "I am playing for the greatest baseball team in the history of the game."

Howard's successful pioneering was based on temperament as well as talent. Indeed, it was likely his ingratiating personality and gentleman's demeanor as much as his athletic ability that prompted the Yankees to select him in preference to some more unpredictable player to integrate the club. Still, his early years with the Yankees were trying. While not directed toward him personally, the racist attitudes and epithets of general manager George Weiss and field manager Casey Stengel were hard for the mild-mannered and soft-spoken Howard to endure. He knew that the Yankees had been severely criticized since the early 1950s for fielding lily-white teams and that his presence was especially conspicuous in contrast to the significant number of black players on the crosstown Brooklyn Dodgers and New York Giants. The failure of the Yankees to promote other African Americans did not help matters; six years later, there were only two other blacks, one of them a Panamanian, on the club. More-

over, because Stengel considered him to be the consummate utility player, Howard bounced between three positions during his first five years with the Yankees. While serving as backup to Yogi Berra, the team's fixture at catcher, Howard played mostly in left field and occasionally at first base. Things changed when Ralph Houk, a former catcher, replaced Stengel as manager after the 1960 season.

In 1961, at age thirty-two, rather old for the position, Howard finally became the team's regular catcher. Perhaps not coincidentally, he hit a career-high .348 with 21 home runs and 77 runs batted in. The next year 21 homers and 91 RBIs brought him little national recognition, but in 1963, following injuries to sluggers Mickey Mantle and Roger Maris, Howard assumed leadership of the Yankees. Refusing to allow racist hate mail to mar his performance, he was voted the league's Most Valuable Player after batting .287 with 28 homers and 85 RBIs. After hitting .313 with 84 RBIs in 1964, his batting skills deteriorated badly, and in early August 1967 the Yankees traded him to the Boston Red Sox, then involved in a close pennant race. Although he hit only .147 for the Red Sox (.178 overall), Howard played a major role in the team's league championship by providing leadership and effectively handling the young pitching staff. He also caught six of seven games in Boston's loss to St. Louis in the World Series.

Howard retired as a player after the 1968 season, returning to New York as the first black coach in the American League. He coached first base and worked with catchers, and he was frequently mentioned as a possible manager. He resigned after the 1978 season, perhaps because of resentment at never having the opportunity to manage a major league team. Out of baseball in 1979, he rejoined the Yankees in the following year as an administrative assistant to principal owner George Steinbrenner.

In fourteen seasons, twelve and one-half of them with the Yankees, Howard never led the league in any offensive category and posted solid albeit unspectacular statistics—a lifetime .274 batting average, 167 home runs, 619 runs, 762 RBIs. But the true indicator of his excellence—his ability to play several positions and his defensive prowess as a catcher as well as his knack for handling pitchers—is his being named nine times to the American League All-Star team. He also twice won the Gold Glove for fielding (1963 and 1964). He appeared in ten World Series, nine with New York, earning the Babe Ruth Award as the outstanding player in the 1958 Series after leading the Yankees to a three-game comeback win over the Milwaukee Braves. In 1963 he became the first African American to be named Most Valuable Player in the American League.

Howard married Arlene Henley in 1954; they had three children. When he died unexpectedly in New York from myocardinitis, Yankee executives departed from convention in praising the man more than the player. Executive vice president Cedric Tallis declared that the self-effacing Howard "was one of the most popular Yankees of all time." Owner Steinbrenner said: "If indeed humility is a trademark of many great men, with that as a measure, Ellie was one of the truly great Yankees." In 1984 the Yankees retired Howard's uniform number (32) and placed his name on the center-field honor plaque at Yankee Stadium.

• A clipping file on Howard is in the National Baseball Library, Cooperstown, N.Y. For his playing statistics, see Macmillan's *Baseball Encyclopedia*, 9th ed. (1993), and John Thorn and Pete Palmer, eds., *Total Baseball*, 3rd ed. (1993). Biographical accounts are Maury Allen, "Elston Howard: Portrait of a Key Yankee," *Sport*, May 1965, pp. 24–27; Al Hirshberg, *Baseball's Greatest Catchers* (1966); John L. Pratt, ed., *Baseball's All-Stars* (1967); Jack Zanger, *Great Catchers of the Major Leagues* (1970); Dave Masterson and Timm Boyle, *Baseball's Best: The MVPs* (1985); and Dom Forker, *Sweet Seasons: Recollections of the 1955–64 New York Yankees* (1990). See also Elston Howard, "It's Great to Be a Yankee," *Ebony*, Sept. 1955, pp. 50–54; Barry Stainback, "Have the Yankees Held Back Howard?" *Sport*, Dec. 1961, pp. 46–47ff.; Peter Golenbock, *Dynasty: The New York Yankees, 1949–1964* (1975); and Art Rust, Jr., *"Get That Nigger Off the Field"* (1976). Noteworthy obituaries are in the *New York Times*, 15 Dec. 1980, and the *Sporting News*, 3 Jan. 1981.

LARRY R. GERLACH

HOWARD, Francis (baptized 17 Sept. 1643–30 Mar. 1695), fifth baron Howard of Effingham and Virginia governor, was born in Surrey, England, the son of Sir Charles Howard and Frances Courthope, both members of important gentry families. This particular branch of the Howard family supported the Crown and embraced the Church of England during the English Civil War era. In keeping with his social status, Francis attended Magdalen College, Oxford, for about a year beginning in 1661. When Sir Charles Howard died in 1673, Francis inherited the family estate, enabling him to marry Philadelphia Pelham later that year. They had eight children in ten years, though only three survived childhood. With the help of an extensive family network, Howard became deputy county lieutenant and justice of the peace for Surrey. When his cousin Charles Howard died without an heir in 1681, Francis succeeded to the barony of Effingham. His new title enabled him to meet the most influential government officials, including the Duke of York and King Charles II. When Charles II decided to replace Virginia governor Thomas Culpeper in 1683, he commissioned Howard. Since Howard lacked any real political expertise or service to the Crown, the king probably named him because of his family connections. The Restoration kings—Charles II and his successor James II—maintained a decidedly different vision for the American colonies than their predecessors had held. Instead of the haphazard governance that often verged on colonial autonomy, the Crown sought to pursue an efficient, centrally controlled empire to serve the needs of England.

Howard's loyalty to the Crown's vision of empire and his willingness to accept the modest £2,000 yearly salary made him a good choice for bringing the Virginians under control. He left for the colony in November 1683 with one young daughter and his aunt. Philadelphia and five small children remained in England with Howard's sister, Jane Howard Methwould, and journeyed to Virginia a year later. Howard's letters to Philadelphia during their separation offer a rare glimpse into his personal life and intense love for his wife and children. When he arrived in Virginia on 10 February 1684, he seemed pleased with the social gatherings staged to both welcome and assess him. He suffered throughout his life with chronic kidney stone attacks, but, largely unimpeded by his poor health, he embarked on his royal mission to squelch Virginia's near autonomy.

Howard's efforts to wrestle power away from the elites of the colony began when he established himself as the bestower of offices, allowing him to manipulate local politics and decrease the power of established gentry families. He denied the county magistrates in Virginia their right to appoint sheriffs, a powerful and often lucrative position, and removed Robert Beverley, naming a new House of Burgesses clerk. Howard further rebuked gentry families by dismissing several other distinguished gentlemen from holding any public office. An officeholder who spoke out against the governor found himself stripped of his lucrative government post and personally persecuted.

Howard attempted to control lawmaking in the colony. The new House of Burgesses clerk, Captain Francis Page, served as the governor's envoy. Acting on royal instructions, Howard divested the colonial legislature, the general assembly, of its privilege of accepting appeals from the General Court. Appeals now had to go directly to the king, and the colonial assembly never regained this power. He reduced the assembly's authority further when he vetoed legislation, issued his own proclamations, altered the assembly's control over some revenues, and dissolved the assembly of 1685–1686. While Howard merely reintroduced English custom and the royal prerogative, colonists saw these and many of his other changes, such as imposing new fees and raising old taxes, as a threat to their own power and well-being.

Virginians did not disdain all of Howard's actions. He negotiated an important and effective peace treaty with the Iroquois in Albany, New York, that was ratified in 1685. However, the threat of attacks by Native Americans on the Virginia frontier provided Howard with the justification for reforming the militia. His plans included a standing army, yet another repugnant idea to the colonists. In August 1685 the death of his wife, probably from scurvy as a result of her voyage to Virginia, dampened Howard's enthusiasm for royal reforms. He returned to England in March 1689.

One of the gentlemen Howard had dismissed from office in Virginia, Philip Ludwell, went to England to press charges against the governor. Virginia's representative maintained that the governor had misused his power by reinstating a repealed act of the assembly, imposing unwarranted fees upon the colonists, and appropriating money paid in fines to the county courts for the use of the provincial government. From

May to October 1689 Howard refuted the accusations of mismanagement, arguing that he merely followed the Crown's instructions, to the satisfaction of the Privy Council. The support of the Privy Council and the Crown for Howard's colonial policies sent a clear message to Virginians. In 1690 Howard married Susannah Felton Harbord, and his interest in colonial affairs waned. He never returned to Virginia, though he remained governor and collected a portion of his salary until he resigned in February 1692. Beginning in 1690, Lieutenant Governor Francis Nicholson served the colony in Howard's stead until William and Mary named Sir Edmund Andros the new governor in 1692. Howard died in London.

Before historian Warren Billings began writing about Howard in the 1980s, historians had portrayed him as an unscrupulous, rapacious, and tyrannical Virginia governor in the tradition of his predecessor Culpeper. Billings meticulously collected all the known correspondence of Howard and found a more human and somewhat tragic figure, while also correcting erroneous information about him. Earlier interpretations argued that Howard's governorship contributed to the success of the American Revolution, as it forced colonists to work together in resisting the threat to their political autonomy. While Billings argued that Howard's historical significance principally rests with the transformation of Virginians into a more docile lot under the Crown's control, he qualified this by acknowledging the older interpretation, in which Howard inspired oppositional unity that ultimately proved detrimental to royal authority.

• Warren M. Billings, comp., *The Papers of Francis Howard: Baron Howard of Effingham, 1643–1695* (1989), includes letters and directives concerning the governance of the colony, quarrels with Md., and his ambitious attempt to gain control of Md. and Carolina, in addition to letters to his wife and his last will and testament. Billings wrote a complete biography, *Virginia's Viceroy: Their Majesties' Governor General: Francis Howard, Baron Howard of Effingham* (1991). For earlier biographical interpretations, refer to Philip Bruce, *Institutional History of Virginia in the Seventeenth Century* (1910), and Thomas J. Wertenbaker, *Virginia under the Stuarts, 1607–1688* (1914).

DEBRA A. MEYERS

HOWARD, George Elliott (1 Oct. 1849–9 June 1928), historian and sociologist, was born in Saratoga, New York, the son of Isaac Howard and Margaret Hardin (occupations unknown). In 1868 Howard traveled in a covered wagon to Nebraska, where he graduated from State Normal School at Peru in 1870. After receiving an A.B. from the new University of Nebraska in 1876, he traveled to Munich and Paris to study history and Roman law for two years. He married a classmate, Alice May Frost of Lincoln, Nebraska, in 1880; they were childless.

Howard's interests in history and law led him to accept a position as the first instructor of history at the University of Nebraska in 1879 and to found the Nebraska State Historical Society, for which he served as secretary for several years. Howard believed that the role of the university as an evolving social institution was to assist humanity to transcend their environment through education. In particular, he advocated educational equality for men and women as a step toward the political and economic emancipation of all Americans. Howard first set out his beliefs about modern education in *Evolution of the University: First Annual Address before the Alumni Association of the University of Nebraska, June 11, 1889* (1890). His publications from this time also indicate his interests in legal and social history. *An Introduction to the Local Constitutional History of the United States: Development of the Township, Hundred, and Shire*, one of the Johns Hopkins University Studies in Historical and Political Science, appeared in 1889. His work "On the Development of the King's Peace and the English Local Peace-Magistracy" (*University Studies* 1, no. 3 [1890]: 235–99), proved to be a significant contribution to understanding the social and legal underpinnings for this time period. Howard also advocated the importance of history as a subject in education as illustrated in "The Study of History in Schools" (*Educational Review* [Mar. 1900]: 257–68).

Howard left the University of Nebraska in 1891 when he was chosen to be among the original fifteen professors to organize a department of history at the new Leland Stanford Junior University in Palo Alto, California. There, in addition to demonstrating administrative leadership, Howard was an inspiring lecturer. In 1893 he accepted an invitation to deliver Stanford's second commencement address, which was published that year as *The American University and the American Man: Second Commencement Address, Leland Stanford Junior University, May 31, 1893*.

In this speech, Howard revealed his belief that the new American universities appearing nationwide were products of a nineteenth-century renaissance and argued that these modern institutions had several roles: to support the free differentiation of departments; to include in their curriculum the scientific study of the family, marriage, and divorce; and to work for the betterment of society as a whole. His ideas, while liberal for his time, reflected the social Darwinism of the day and placed modern man and all of his institutions as somehow closer than his ancestors to the ideal form of society. Like other scholars of this time, Howard borrowed from theories of biology to create a model for science and the forces active in basic human processes: "Man beholds himself in the actual process of evolution. His ideas and passions, his virtues and vices, are the product of environment, selection and heredity. He perceives that social institutions are living beings as much as are plants and animals" (p. 10). His ideas for the active and self-reflective role of sociology for the betterment of humanity heralded what was to become the pragmatist and reformist perspective typified in the early years of sociology at the University of Chicago (1890–1920) and formed a solid foundation for Howard's lifelong goals:

society itself is seen to be a vast organization, a complex animal, obeying the same law as do individuals or "self-conscious" cells which compose it. Therefore, since the conditions of social growth and decay may be understood, it is inevitable that sociology should become dynamic. Perceiving that our destiny is pretty largely in our own hands, we are beginning to realize that it is the supreme function of culture to lift humanity upward. At last society has become self-conscious. This is the philosophy of the new utilitarianism; this, the secret of the humanism of the Nineteenth Century Renaissance. (P. 10)

Howard was an eclectic scholar who combined views parallel to those of emergent sociology with a strong belief in the importance of history at a time when other intellectuals were more ahistorically oriented. He received his Ph.D. from the University of Nebraska in 1894 and in 1899 continued his interest in legal social history with the publication of "British Imperialism and the Reform of the Civil Service" (*Political Science Quarterly*, 14, no. 2).

A man of strong convictions, Howard resigned from Stanford in 1901 in protest over the dismissal of Professor Edward A. Ross, a sociologist. Howard perceived that Stanford's dismissal of Ross for his public stand against the use of Chinese labor in railroad construction was a violation of academic freedom. After ending his outstanding teaching career at Stanford, Howard served as a professor of history at Cornell University during the summer of 1902 and accepted a post as professorial lecturer in history at the University of Chicago from 1903 to 1904. His interests in political and social history are reflected in the collections of lectures published from this time.

While at Chicago, Howard published his three-volume work on marriage and divorce, *History of Matrimonial Institutions: Chiefly in England and the United States with an Introductory Analysis of the Literature and the Theories of Primitive Marriage and the Family* (1904). The general focus for this work was a continuation of his argument that the family and its cognate institutions should be part of systematic social training and scientific recognition. In addition, he included a review of the social evolutionary theories of matrimonial institutions and a historical record of legislation on marriage and divorce in England and the United States. Howard predicted that "the family will, indeed, survive; a family of a higher type" would evolve (vol. 3, p. 259). He also countered the popular argument that women's work in the public sphere was a threat to the nation in his statements that women should be economically and socially free. His concern for the equality of women in education is reflected in his later mentoring and support of Hattie Plum Waters at the University of Nebraska.

Several other publications appeared from 1904 to 1907 that complemented Howard's *History of Matrimonial Institutions* and contributed to his reputation as a scholar of social institutions. These include several encyclopedia articles; "The Problem of Uniform Divorce Law in the United States" (*The American Lawyer* 14 [1906]: 15–17); and "Social Control and the Function of the Family" (*Congress of Arts and Science* 7 [1906]: 699–708).

In 1904 Howard followed Ross to the University of Nebraska, where Howard became a professor of institutional history. In 1905 he published *Preliminaries of the American Revolution 1763–1775* (vol. 8 of the collection *The American Nation: A History*, ed. Albert Bushnell Hart), which explored the social, legal, and political underpinnings of the Revolution from both the British and American perspectives. In addition to providing a good overview of historical sources for this significant time period in U.S. history, Howard included a discussion of the influence of the Anglican Episcopate on the Revolution and, reflecting the arguments of the progressive historians of the late 1800s, heralded the first appearance of the western frontier as a distinct factor in American national consciousness.

When Ross moved to the University of Wisconsin in 1906, Howard became head of the newly formed department of political science and sociology at the University of Nebraska, where he again exercised his abilities to organize and influence a community of scholars. Howard credited the focus of his lectures on general sociology at Nebraska to the influence of Ross. His publications of this time continue to reflect his interest in social institutions. In particular, Howard advocated the application of science to the improvement of social life through the use of a "pure and applied" sociology in the treatment of social processes. His "Biographical Preface" in Amos G. Warner's *American Charities* (1908) illustrated Howard's use of sociology to aid man in transcending his environment and his evangelical stance on philanthropy.

Howard was president of the American Sociological Society in 1917. Under the auspices of this society he published two articles that help illustrate the larger dimensions of his social concerns: "The Social Cost of Southern Race Prejudice" (*American Journal of Sociology* 22, no. 5 [Mar. 1917]: 577–93) and "Alcohol and Crime; A Study in Social Causation" (*American Journal of Sociology* 24, no. 1 [July 1918]: 61–80).

Howard's abilities as an advocate of human welfare and the scientization of studies of family and marriage, as a legal social historian, and as a social feminist were recognized and rewarded by an honorary vice presidency of the Institut International de Sociologie. He retired from teaching in 1924 and died in Lincoln, Nebraska.

• With the exception of Floyd Nelson House, *The Development of Sociology* (1936), pp. 247–48, there is little discussion of Howard and his work in the sociological literature until 1988, when a renewed interest in Howard and the University of Nebraska school of sociology appears in a special volume of the *Mid-American Review of Sociology* 13, no. 2.; the scholars who reexamine Howard and sociology at Nebraska place Howard's pragmatic and reformist perspective within an historical context of empirically rigorous sociology. See Michael R. Ball, "George Elliott Howard's Institutional Sociology of Marriage and Divorce," pp. 57–68; Michael R. Hill, "Sociology in the University of Nebraska, 1898–1927," pp. 3–19;

and Hill, "The Intellectual Legacy of Nebraska Sociology: A Bibliographical Chronology of Separately Published Works (1887–1989)," pp. 85–103. In addition, Howard's support for the equality of women in higher education is discussed in Hill, "Research by Bureaucracy: Hattie Plum Williams and the National Commission on Law Observance and Enforcement, 1929–1931," pp. 69–84. Obituaries are in the *American Journal of Sociology*, Jan. 1929; *Sociology and Social Research*, Sept.–Oct., Nov.–Dec. 1928, and Jan.–Feb. 1929; the *Omaha Bee-News*, 10 June 1928; and the *Nebraska State Journal* (Lincoln), 11 June 1928.

PAMELA R. FRESE

HOWARD, Jacob Merritt (10 July 1805–2 Apr. 1871), congressman and senator, was born in Shaftsbury, Vermont, the son of Otis Howard and Polly Millington, farmers. He graduated from Williams College in 1830 and then studied law in Ware, Massachusetts. Two years later he moved to Detroit, Michigan, where he was admitted to the bar in 1833. In 1835 he married Catherine A. Shaw, with whom he had five children.

In 1838 Howard was elected as a Whig to the lower house of the state legislature, where he was active in revising the state's legal code, in investigating Michigan's wildcat banks, and in drafting railroad legislation. In 1841 he was elected to Congress. Throughout his tenure as a congressman, Howard was an outspoken opponent of slavery. After completing his term, he returned to private practice in Michigan. In 1850, when arguing a fugitive slave case before the U.S. circuit court, he publicly denounced the Fugitive Slave Law and predicted that the country would eventually come to armed conflict over the issue of slavery.

In 1854 Howard joined the new Republican party. He was one of the leading members of the Jackson, Michigan, convention held on 6 July that organized the new party. As chair of the Committee on Resolutions, Howard drafted the party platform, which deplored slavery as a social evil and opposed its expansion into the territories. He was reputed to have given the new party its name. The same year he was elected the state attorney general as a Republican. Howard served in this position from 1855 to 1861, when he was elected U.S. senator to replace Kinsley S. Bingham, who had died in office.

Known in Michigan as "Honest Jake," Howard was considered to be one of the "better constitutional lawyers in the [Senate] chamber." In the wartime debates in the Senate, Howard consistently voted for Radical measures, approved President Abraham Lincoln's emergency actions during the secession crisis, and advocated "severe, exemplary, and speedy punishment" of the rebels. He was especially vocal on all matters pertaining to the confiscation of rebel property and the emancipation of slaves. He was also one of the most forceful advocates of the 1863 Conscription Act, and he served on the Committee on Military Affairs. As a member of the Committee on the Judiciary, he drafted a portion of the Thirteenth Amendment. He also made several important speeches in favor of the Civil Rights Act of 1866.

Howard opposed President Lincoln's Reconstruction program to readmit southern states on the "10 percent plan" (1863), which stipulated that 10 percent of the state's population had to take an oath of loyalty to the government to qualify for readmission. Howard contended that the federal government had a right to extend military rule over the defeated southern states and advocated extreme retaliatory measures. He argued forcefully that Congress, and not the president, had the power to judge the proper time and manner of readmitting the seceded states and that Congress also possessed the power to reorganize the states upon readmission.

Howard served on the Joint Committee on Reconstruction and traveled to Virginia, North Carolina, and South Carolina to investigate postwar conditions there. Upon Howard's return to Washington, the committee submitted a proposal to Congress to amend the Constitution. The committee's proposals, actively supported by Howard on the Senate floor, passed both Houses of Congress as the Fourteenth Amendment.

Although Howard had confidence in Andrew Johnson during the first year of Johnson's term, he soon lost faith in the president. When Johnson tried to remove Secretary of War Edwin B. Stanton, Howard reacted with outrage and authored the committee's report censuring the decision. During President Johnson's impeachment trial, Howard voted to convict.

Howard chaired the Committee on the Pacific Railroad from its creation in 1864 until 1871. President Ulysses S. Grant offered him the presidency of the Southern Claims Commission, but he declined the post. At the end of his congressional career in 1871, Howard returned to Detroit, where he died.

In public, Howard's image was grave and somewhat portly; his speaking style, according to his eulogist, Chief Justice John A. Campbell, was eloquent but ponderous. Privately, however, he was a genial, pleasant man with a keen sense of humor. According to George W. Julian, in reminiscences about the Senate during the Civil War, Howard "ranked among the first lawyers and most faithful men in the body, and no man had a clearer grasp of the issues of the war."

• Howard's papers are in the Burton Historical Collection of the Detroit Public Library. He published his translation of the *Historical and Secret Memoirs of the Empress Josephine* (1848). Howard's son, Hamilton Gay Howard, wrote a biography entitled *Civil War Echoes: Character Sketches and State Secrets* (1907). See also Elsa Holderried, "Public Life of Jacob Merritt Howard" (M.A. thesis, Wayne State Univ., 1950). For a discussion of Howard's role in the formation of the Republican party, see William E. Gienapp, *The Origins of the Republican Party, 1852–1856* (1987). Allan G. Bogue, *The Earnest Men: Republicans of the Civil War Senate* (1981), discusses Howard's Senate career during the Civil War. Obituaries are in the *New York Times*, 3 Apr. 1871, and the *Detroit Free Press*, 3 and 5 Apr. 1871.

SILVANA SIDDALI

HOWARD, Joe (12 Feb. 1867–19 May 1961), singer and composer, was born Joseph E. Howard in New York City, the son of a Mulberry Street saloon keeper. His parents' names are unknown. He was orphaned by the age of seven and spent some time in a Roman Catholic orphanage from which he escaped frequently (he later claimed to have spent much of his time singing for pennies on street corners and in saloons). By the time he was eleven, Howard had debuted in vaudeville as a boy soprano. As a teenager, he finally escaped the orphanage for good and hopped a freight train for St. Louis, Missouri, where he sold newspapers before landing a singing job in McNigh, Johnson, and Slavin's Refined Minstrels.

Howard next teamed with a professional wrestler, William Muldoon, on the minstrel circuit. He took up boxing himself and subsequently joined Bob Fitzsimmons, another heavyweight boxer, as a singer in Fitzsimmons's troupe. Howard's first modest successes as an entertainer came with the emerging popularity of ragtime. Performing George Rosey's "Handicap March," Howard amused audiences by playing the roles of fifteen horses, their jockeys, two bookies, and the grandstand crowd. As he gained widespread popularity in the 1890s as both a performer and a songwriter, he billed himself as Joe Howard.

As a songwriter, Howard teamed frequently with Will Hough and is credited with the composition of several of the most popular songs of the Gilded Age, including "Hello, My Baby," "Goodbye, My Lady Love," "I Wonder Who's Kissing Her Now," "A Boy's Best Friend Is His Mother," and "What's the Use of Dreaming." "I Wonder Who's Kissing Her Now" became the most popular of these and is believed to have sold in excess of 3 million copies of sheet music in the first of its releases. The song attained fresh popularity after World War II. Fellow vaudevillian George Jessel produced a highly fictionalized screen version of Howard's life for 20th Century–Fox in 1947 under the title *I Wonder Who's Kissing Her Now*, featuring Mark Stevens as Howard. A lawsuit ensued questioning the true authorship of the title song. The suit suggested that Howard had purchased the tune from another composer, Harold Orlob, giving credence to the appellation "opportunist of song" applied to him by music publisher Edward B. Marks.

Howard's songwriting was so successful that he bought his own theater in Chicago and composed music for several pre–World War I musical comedies, including *His Highness the Bey* (1904); *The Isle of Bong Bong* and *The Umpire* (both 1905); *The District Leader* and *The Girl Question* (both 1906); *The Land of Nod* (1907); and *Honeymoon Trail* and *A Stubborn Cinderella* (both 1908), the latter of which featured John Barrymore. Sentimental, naive, and melodic, these shows perfectly embodied the early twentieth-century audience's tastes, as did *The Flower of the Ranch* (1908); *The Flirting Princess* and *The Prince of Tonight* (both 1909); and *The Goddess of Liberty* and *Miss Nobody from Starland* (both 1910). The most popular of all Howard musicals, *The Time, The Place and the Girl* (1907), set a long-run record for Chicago and was revived successfully in 1942. A few of these Chicago shows were transferred to Broadway, but they met with scant popularity. Howard claimed credit for writing more than 500 songs and twenty-eight musicals. He continued writing songs until close to the end of his life and had one success in the 1940s with "Remember Pearl Harbor."

A seasoned performer by the 1910s, Howard began to wear immaculately tailored evening clothes, which would become his trademark, and he developed a persona as a man about town and lady killer. During this period he frequently worked with women partners, including Ethelyn Clark and Anita Case. By the 1920s, Howard, then teamed with Case, was a staple of the vaudeville circuit. In 1926 *Variety* called them "sure fire in front of any audience."

In 1927 Jerome Kern and Oscar Hammerstein II interpolated Howard's song "Goodbye My Lady Love" into their epic musical *Show Boat* as a perfect evocation of the 1890s popular stage. As time passed, Howard himself became a living link with that era. Although the public's taste for his songwriting style waned in the 1930s, Howard's performing remained popular in cabarets and nightclubs. In 1938 he headlined a highly successful act at Billy Rose's Diamond Horseshoe nightclub. During World War II, when a renewed interest in the nostalgic songs of the past began to surface, Howard capitalized on the interest by hosting his own radio show, "Gay Nineties," billing himself as the "Mayor of the 1890s."

In the 1950s, Howard retired to a home in Fort Lauderdale, Florida. He occasionally returned to the stage, despite his advanced age, for benefits or television appearances. It is believed that he had squandered vast sums of money during his career on various amorous adventures, but the continual income from his early song successes kept him solvent. Howard collapsed and died onstage at Chicago's Civic Opera House following a benefit performance he had just completed at the age of ninety-three. He had been married nine times, and his last wife, Miriam, was in the audience at the time of his death.

• For information on Howard, see Robert Lissauer, *Lissauer's Encyclopedia of Popular Music in America: 1888 to the Present* (1991); Anthony Slide, *The Encyclopedia of Vaudeville* (1994); and *Variety*, 25 Aug. 1926. An obituary is in the *New York Times*, 21 May 1961.

JAMES FISHER

HOWARD, John Eager (4 June 1752–12 Oct. 1827), revolutionary soldier, governor of Maryland, and U.S. senator, was born at "The Forrest," in Baltimore County, Maryland, the son of Cornelius Howard and Ruth Eager. His English ancestor, Joshua Howard, had emigrated to Maryland after serving in the army of James II during Monmouth's Rebellion in 1685 and had received a grant of land in Baltimore County. Because subsequent generations had added to this plantation, Cornelius could provide John with a good education under private tutors. John served in Maryland's militia for the duration of the War of Independence, first as captain in the "Flying Camp" of 1776, as major of the Fourth Regiment from late February 1777 onward, then as lieutenant colonel of the Fifth Regiment after early March 1778, until transfer to the Second Regiment in October 1779. He served in the battles of White Plains, Germantown, and Monmouth in the North and Camden, Guilford Court House, Hobkirk's Hill, Cowpens, and Eutaw Springs in the South, where he was severely wounded on 8 September 1781 and was forced to resign his commission and return home. Singled out for a heroic charge at Cowpens, Congress awarded him a silver medal, which he wears in a portrait by Charles Willson Peale, painted in 1792. In 1787 he married Margaret Oswald Chew, daughter of Benjamin Chew, chief justice of the Pennsylvania Supreme Court. They had eight children.

Following recuperation and the end of the war, Howard served in various local and federal offices: as justice of the Baltimore County Court from 1785 through 1787, as senatorial elector from Baltimore County and justice of the Baltimore County Orphans' Court in 1786, and as one of Maryland's representatives to Congress under the Articles of Confederation during 1787 and 1788. On 21 November 1788 he was elected governor of Maryland, the first to be identified with a political party (the Federalists). During his first year as governor, Maryland granted the ten-mile section of land to become part of the District of Columbia as well as other bounty lands west of Cumberland, Maryland, to Continental army veterans. During his second year the state ratified the Bill of Rights and during his third approved the manner of holding both congressional and presidential elections.

Howard was elected to the state senate in September 1791 and reelected in 1796. In 1792 he served as a presidential elector for the reelection of George Washington and John Adams (1735–1826), and also acted as commissioner of the most rapidly expanding seaport in the United States, Baltimore. Two years later Howard declined President Washington's offer of appointment as secretary of war, but in the following year the Maryland General Assembly elected him to fill the (U.S. Senate) seat Richard Potts had resigned. He was elected to a full term in 1797 and served until 1803. Howard declined President Adams's offer of a brigadier generalship during the "Quasi-War" with France from 1798 to 1800.

In 1803 Howard again returned home to serve in local offices, including commissioner of the state penitentiary, overseeing construction of a new prison. He was nominated three more times for the U.S. Senate, but the state legislature failed to elect him, primarily because after 1801 the Republicans became the majority party. During the War of 1812 he raised a regiment of veterans, but they were not called into service. He also served on Baltimore's Committee of Supply, which raised money and supplies for defense, particularly against the British invasion of September 1814.

Identified with the Federalist party since the late 1780s, Howard was nominated as Rufus King's (1755–1827) vice presidential running mate in 1816.

Following his defeat in this election, Howard retired to his estate, "Belvedere," in Baltimore City, where he spent his remaining years as an elder statesman, philanthropist, and gentleman. He donated many tracts of land to the city for the construction of churches, a cemetery, a market house, and the Washington Monument.

Howard's death at Belvedere coincided with the passing of the Federalist era and the beginnings of the Industrial Revolution. Prominent leaders from President John Quincy Adams down through the ranks of local dignitaries attended his funeral. His plantation lands were divided among his several sons; the most notable were Benjamin Chew Howard, a future Supreme Court reporter, and George Howard, governor of Maryland from 1831 to 1833.

Howard represented that waning class of large-scale landowners in the Upper South who redefined their inherited British traditions during and after the Revolution and who found themselves increasingly out of place in the more democratic, commercial, and specialized world that America became during the 1790s. Bred in the Anglo-American code of the landed gentry, his lingering federalism continued its eighteenth-century characteristics of personal initiative through form and order, of changing custom but preserving tradition, and of faith in man's reason and the rationality of the universe. To this degree the sum of his life added up to more than personal fulfillment; it served as example.

• Howard's papers, including a room by room inventory of Belvedere at the time of his death, are in the Maryland Historical Society. No full-length biography of Howard exists; the closest is Cary Howard, "John Eager Howard, Patriot and Public Servant," *Maryland Historical Magazine* 62 (1967): 300–17. Edward C. Papenfuse et al., eds., *A Biographical Dictionary of the Maryland Legislature, 1635–1789* (2 vols., 1979), contains the most detailed and instantly useful information about Howard, and Frank F. White, Jr., *The Governors of Maryland, 1777–1970* (1970), presents a brief overview of Howard's life. Otherwise, one can piece together information about Howard in Whitman H. Ridgway, *Community Leadership in Maryland, 1790–1840: A Comparative Analysis of Power in Society* (1979); Gary Lawson Browne, *Baltimore in the Nation, 1789–1861* (1980); and Frank A. Cassell, *Merchant Congressman in the Young Republic: Samuel Smith of Maryland, 1752–1839* (1971). *A Memoir of the Late Col. John Eager Howard* appeared in the Baltimore *Gazette*, 15 Oct. 1827.

GARY BROWNE

HOWARD, Leland Ossian (11 June 1857–1 May 1950), entomologist, was born in Rockford, Illinois, the son of Ossian Gregory Howard, a lawyer, and Lucy Dunham Thurber, a music teacher. His parents, both natives of upstate New York, moved from Illinois to Ithaca, New York, when Howard was an infant. On one of the boy's frequent outings collecting insects, he encountered John Henry Comstock, the young entomology professor of nearby Cornell University. Comstock became Howard's mentor. Howard received his B.S. from Cornell in 1877 and prepared to study medicine.

On Comstock's recommendation, however, Howard became assistant to new U.S. Department of Agriculture (USDA) entomologist Charles Valentine Riley in 1878. The temperamental Riley soon resigned and was replaced by Comstock for two years before returning in 1881. Howard remained in the USDA and rose to chief entomologist upon Riley's second resignation in 1894. He married Marie Theodora Clifton in 1886. They had three children.

While in the USDA, Comstock began extensive study of the scale insects. Howard then moved into what would become his specialty, the taxonomy of parasitic wasps, particularly those attacking scale insects. Howard advocated the use of parasitic wasps in the biological control of pests after USDA agents under Riley's direction introduced Australian insects that controlled cottony-cushion scale in California in 1889. Howard inherited Riley's rivalry with California officials over credit for that achievement, which became the textbook case of biological control.

Between 1889 and 1898 four other events occurred that shaped the history of applied entomology (often called "economic entomology") and the course of Howard's career. The gypsy moth, San Jose scale, and boll weevil, all foreign to the United States, became serious pests, and insects were proven for the first time to transmit human disease. Howard established a large entomological presence in the South, although his staff largely failed to persuade farmers to adopt cultural methods against the boll weevil. The San Jose scale spurred other nations to enact quarantine laws against American produce, leading eventually to the first federal plant quarantine legislation in 1912. Howard's grandest project was a long-term concerted effort, beginning in 1905, to control gypsy moths in New England with parasites. Many were introduced from Europe; none controlled the moth. In connection with the gypsy moth work, Howard and William F. Fiske produced one of the earliest articulations of what came to be called density-dependent mortality in populations, a concept ecologists debated hotly in later years. Density-dependent mortality is mortality caused by factors that intensify as the population increases, presumably including predation, parasitism, and competition for food. Since this concept received widespread attention in the 1930s, some ecologists (including advocates of biological control) have claimed that only density-dependent factors can regulate population levels. Others have argued that density-independent factors, particularly climatic elements, are far more important, or that populations are not regulated at all but fluctuate irregularly. Howard never participated in the debate, which erupted after his retirement.

Howard, who had received an M.S. from Cornell in 1883, in part for his abbreviated medical studies, also became a spokesman for medical entomology after insects were found to transmit malaria and other diseases. He wrote books on the dangers of mosquitoes and houseflies and made "Swat the Fly" a nationwide slogan. In addition to his descriptions of 272 new species of parasitic wasps, Howard collaborated in naming 22 species of mosquitoes.

The small office Howard had taken over in 1894 became the Bureau of Entomology in 1904. He organized it into divisions on the basis of crop groups. In his thirty-three years at the helm, the USDA budget for entomology grew a hundredfold, to $3 million annually. Howard became by far the largest employer of entomologists during a period of rapid growth and professionalization of that scientific discipline.

Howard's manner contrasted sharply with that of his predecessor. Harold Compere, an entomologist who knew Howard late in his career, wrote, "Unlike Riley, Howard was a loveable character and a smooth, suave, polished gentleman. Where Riley used a battle axe or bludgeon, Howard used a stiletto if the occasion warranted" (letter to Edward Steinhaus, 11 May 1959; Compere's papers, Univ. of California, Riverside.) Preaching that insects threatened to doom civilization as both agricultural and public-health pests, Howard constantly lobbied politicians and the general public for support of economic entomology.

Considered the international leader in his field during his lifetime, Howard was very much an insider among the Washington, D.C., intelligentsia. He helped found the American Association of Economic Entomologists, over which he presided in 1894, and was an officer of several other scientific organizations. He served as permanent secretary of the American Association for the Advancement of Science for twenty-two years, until that body rewarded him with its presidency in 1920. Six universities, beginning with Georgetown in 1896, awarded him honorary doctorates. In Washington, Howard spent part of nearly every day at the Cosmos Club, where he served as president in 1909.

Howard traveled extensively, regularly touring Bureau of Entomology facilities throughout the country and visiting Europe nearly every year. He used foreign travel in part to set up exchange of beneficial insects for biological control projects. Some thirty national entomological societies made him an honorary member. He presided over the Fourth International Congress of Entomology in his hometown of Ithaca in 1928.

After stepping down as bureau chief in 1927, Howard remained in USDA service another four years as principal entomologist. He wrote on the history of entomology and continued to warn the public against what the title of his 1931 book proclaimed as "the insect menace." He spent his last years as a revered elder statesman of his discipline. He died in Bronxville, New York.

Howard's importance lies primarily in his work as administrator and spokesman for the field of entomology. His taxonomic papers were of the typological, strictly morphological style that went out of fashion during his lifetime, and they are not widely admired. He did little original research in medical entomology but brought great publicity to that field. The biological control projects begun under his administration, including that on the gypsy moth, accomplished little of practical value. His bureau's organizational structure, while highly successful in attracting funds and building a reputation for economic entomology, severely retarded progress in biological control. The few experts in that specialty were scattered among the various crop divisions. Howard meanwhile worked to prevent state organizations from following the lead of California and introducing parasites and predators from abroad themselves. Despite his advocacy of this use of beneficial insects, Howard did more than anyone else to convince the public that insects in general were a menace to be vigorously fought. He thus contributed to the insecticidal orientation of economic entomology, which became controversial after his death because of threats to public health and the environment posed by the use of insecticides.

• Howard's personal papers are scattered under several entries in Record Group 7 (Bureau of Entomology and Plant Quarantine) of the National Archives in Washington, D.C. His major publications include *The Insect Book* (1901); *Mosquitoes* (1901); *The House Fly—Disease Carrier* (1911); "The Importation into the United States of the Parasites of the Gipsy Moth and the Brown-tail Moth," *U.S. Bureau of Entomology Bulletin* 91 (1911), with William F. Fiske; *Mosquitoes of North America* (1912–1917), with Harrison Gray Dyar and Frederick Knab; *A History of Applied Entomology* (1930); and *The Insect Menace* (1931). He published his autobiography, *Fighting the Insects: The Story of an Entomologist*, in 1933. Among other accounts of his life, the most detailed are an unsigned obituary in the *Journal of Economic Entomology* 43 (1950): 958–62 and another by A. B. Gahan et al., *Proceedings of the Entomological Society of Washington* 52 (1950): 224–33 as well as accounts by John E. Graf and Dorothy W. Graf, "Leland Ossian Howard," *Biographical Memoirs, National Academy of Sciences* 33 (1959): 87–124 and Arnold Mallis, *American Entomologists* (1971), pp. 79–86. The article by Graf and Graf lists some 400 of Howard's more than 1,000 publications. On Howard's role in biological control, see Richard C. Sawyer, "Monopolizing the Insect Trade: Biological Control in the USDA, 1888–1951," *Agricultural History* 64, no. 2 (1990): 271–85.

RICHARD C. SAWYER

HOWARD, Leslie (3 Apr. 1893–1 June 1943), stage and screen star, was born Leslie Howard Stainer in London, England, the son of Frank Stainer, an office worker who later became a stockbroker, and Lilian (maiden name unknown). Shortly after his birth, the family moved to Vienna, Austria, for several years. Upon their return to England, they settled in the London suburb of Upper Norwood.

Howard, a shy, extremely nearsighted boy, disliked school but found escape in writing plays, producing a number of musical comedies with two close school friends. His mother, a would-be actress, encouraged his interests by organizing the Upper Norwood Dramatic Club as an outlet for his dramatic products, in some of which she appeared with him.

When Howard reached nineteen, his father decided that his son was not preparing himself adequately to make a living and had him removed from Dulwich College and placed in a bank job. The unpleasant prospect of a lifetime in this type of work was solved by the outbreak of World War I, which provided him, as it did countless other young men caught in unsatisfying situations, the needed escape. Enlisting in the army, he obtained a cavalry assignment despite a limited knowledge of riding. In the training process he acquired a love of horsemanship expressed in his later enthusiasm for polo.

Assigned to a base near Colchester, Howard met a young woman named Ruth Martin. They were married in the spring of 1916 shortly before the departure of his regiment for France.

After a year of combat Howard returned home with a severe case of shell shock. When he recovered, his father wanted him to return to bank work, but his mother prevailed in encouraging him to seek a career in the theater.

Following initial setbacks, Howard found an agent who was impressed by his voice and obtained for him a role in a road company of *Peg o' My Heart* in 1917. A second tour that same year in *Charley's Aunt* determined him to pursue further opportunities in London. He subsequently was hired by actor-manager Matheson Lang as his secretary and later played the juvenile lead on the road in one of Lang's productions. Minor roles in productions under other managements followed, including A. A. Milne's *Mr. Pim Passes By*.

In 1918 Howard organized Minerva Films, Ltd., in partnership with director Adrian Brunel. The company used the writing talent of Milne and the acting of C. Aubrey Smith and Howard, with Howard as managing director, in several short satirical comedies. Although the enterprise failed, it introduced Howard to the fascinations of producing and directing.

In 1920 Howard was given the opportunity by American producer Gilbert Miller to appear on Broadway in A. E. Thomas's *Just Suppose*, a romantic comedy. It was his first experience in a light comedy role.

Parts in other American productions followed. Howard appeared in Tarkington's *The Wren* with Helen Hayes (1921) and played the juvenile lead in Milne's *The Truth about Blayds* (1922). He performed with Margalo Gillmore in Sutton Vane's fantasy drama *Outward Bound* (1924), about a pair of suicidal lovers aboard a mystery ship; the cast also included Alfred Lunt. In 1930 Howard made his American film debut in the screen adaptation of the play.

In September 1924 Howard and Gillmore appeared with Katharine Cornell in *The Green Hat*, Michael Arlen's adaptation of his bestselling novel about a willful young woman who leads an amoral life after being denied the one man she really wants. Howard detested his role as the object of her desire, but his performance won him further adulation from female playgoers.

Howard next appeared in *Her Cardboard Lover*, the adaptation of a French farce, produced in March 1927. Although Laurette Taylor, who played the female lead, and Jeanne Eagels, who succeeded her, were miscast, the play gave Howard an ideal opportunity to exhibit his talent. His triumph in the New York production was followed by an equally successful appearance in the London production the following year, in which his leading lady was Tallulah Bankhead. However, his popularity in the United States had given him a reputation in England as an American actor with an English accent.

In March 1929 he was again onstage in London, this time as coproducer with Gilbert Miller of John Balderston's *Berkeley Square*. In it he played young American Peter Standish, who takes over a family home in London and is transported in spirit to the time in the late eighteenth century when his ancestor of the same name arrived from the former colonies and fell in love with one of his English cousins. The double role proved ideal for Howard, who repeated it on Broadway to great acclaim in November, once more opposite Margalo Gillmore.

The following year Howard began his Hollywood career with the film version of *Outward Bound*. He did not like the film capital and quickly escaped with his family (his son was born in 1918 and his daughter four years later) to England, where they acquired a much-loved home in Surrey, Stowe Maries.

In 1932 he appeared in Philip Barry's *The Animal Kingdom*; he repeated his role in the film version later in the same year with Ann Harding and Myrna Loy. Other film appearances in this period included *Smilin' Through*, with Norma Shearer, and *Secrets*, with Mary Pickford.

His first important screen role came in 1934, when he played opposite Bette Davis in the screen adaptation of Somerset Maugham's *Of Human Bondage*. He scored a similar hit in the English production of *The Scarlet Pimpernel*, which won him the Picture Goer Gold Medal for 1934, his long-sought recognition by the public at home as one of their own.

In 1935 he solidified his position as a versatile Broadway actor with Robert Sherwood's *The Petrified Forest*, in which his performance as the doomed intellectual Alan Squier was matched by Humphrey Bogart's equally memorable portrayal of the hunted gangster Duke Mantee. Both actors reprised their stage roles in the 1936 film adaptation of the play.

Howard played Romeo to Norma Shearer's Juliet in the 1936 MGM version of Shakespeare's immortal romance. He thought he was too old for the role, but the film was well received. Later that year he portrayed Hamlet on Broadway. Despite a handsome production codirected by John Houseman with music by Virgil Thomson and choreography for the players scene by Agnes de Mille, Howard's interpretation of the title role was unfavorably compared with that of John Gielgud in a concurrent production.

Howard returned to the screen in 1938 in the English production of Bernard Shaw's *Pygmalion*, which he codirected with Gabriel Pascal. The first film version of one of Shaw's plays that the author authorized, the production gave new scope to Howard's acting abilities in his performance as Henry Higgins while elevating Wendy Hiller to stardom for her portrayal of Eliza Doolittle.

The film version of Margaret Mitchell's bestselling novel about the Civil War, *Gone with the Wind* (1936), was produced in 1939 and featured an all-star cast headed by English actress Vivien Leigh as Scarlett O'Hara, Clark Gable as Rhett Butler, Olivia de Havilland as Melanie Wilkes, and Howard as her husband Ashley. It became one of the biggest box-office hits of all time, winning nine Academy Awards, including best picture. Although Howard's portrayal of Ashley was one of his most famous roles, despite his personal dislike for it, it was eclipsed in importance by his performances in *Berkeley Square*, *The Scarlet Pimpernel*, *The Petrified Forest*, and *Pygmalion*.

Gone with the Wind was followed by Howard's final American film, the Hollywood version of *Intermezzo* (1939), in which Ingrid Bergman repeated the role of the young pianist that had won her acclaim in the Swedish original. He and his family went home to England at the end of August 1939 expecting to return later to the United States, but the outbreak of World War II canceled these plans.

Howard participated in an ideas committee of the Ministry of Information for fresh propaganda approaches and did a cameo role in the semidocumentary film *Forty-ninth Parallel*. He produced two feature films of his own related to the war effort, *Pimpernel Smith* (1941) and *The First of the Few* (1941), the latter about the designer of the Spitfire fighter plane, which saved England in the battle of Britain. At the height of that crucial struggle he began a weekly series of radio broadcasts to the United States titled *Britain Speaks*, in which he interpreted Britain's heroic fight to his American listeners.

In the spring of 1943 Howard delivered a series of lectures in neutral Spain and Portugal. On the trip back from Lisbon, where he had stayed over for the Portuguese premiere of *The First of the Few*, the commercial airliner on which he was a passenger was attacked over the Bay of Biscay by a squadron of German fighter planes and was shot down. It was suggested later that the Nazis thought Winston Churchill, who was en route home from Algiers, was one of the passengers, but in his memoirs Churchill scoffed at the idea that anyone in authority would believe a person in his position would take an unprotected mode of transportation.

Howard's personal grace and charm lent distinction to a number of well-loved plays and films of the 1920s and 1930s. He considered himself a technical actor, but the force of his personality and intellect made all his performances enjoyable and the main ones truly memorable.

• Leslie Ruth Howard has written charmingly and perceptively about her father's human side, in addition to covering his career in careful, objective detail, in *A Quite Remarkable Father* (1959). A similarly perceptive, sympathetically candid account of Howard's final years was contributed by his actor-writer son Ronald in his memoir *In Search of My Father: A Portrait of Leslie Howard* (1982). Sheridan Morley, *Tales from the Hollywood Raj: The British, the Movies, and Tinseltown* (1983), discusses British actors, including Howard, in Hollywood. *Forty-ninth Parallel* and *Pimpernel Smith* receive detailed treatment in Anthony Aldgate and Jeffrey Richards, *Britain Can Take It: The British Cinema in the Second World War* (1986). On *Gone with the Wind*, see Herb Bridges and Terryl C. Boodman, *"Gone with the Wind": The Definitive Illustrated History of the Book, the Movie, and the Legend* (1989), and Gavin Lambert, *GWTW: The Making of "Gone with the Wind"* (1973). A concise overview of Howard's career, with the basic credits for all his films, is Homer Dickens, "Leslie Howard," *Films in Review*, Apr. 1959, pp. 198–207. An obituary is in the *New York Times*, 3 June 1943; a supplementary article, "A Symbol of England," by C. A. Lejune, appears in the drama pages of the 27 June 1943 issue.

ALBERT O. WEISSBERG

HOWARD, Martin (c. 1725–4 or 24 Nov. 1781), Loyalist and chief justice of North Carolina, was born either in Rhode Island or England. Since his father, Martin Howard, Sr., was admitted as a freeman of Newport, Rhode Island, in 1726, it is probable that Howard was born and grew up there. His mother's name is unknown. At least one biographer said he was educated at an Inn of Court in London, but he is not listed in Jones's *American Members of the Inns of Court*. At any rate, he read law in Newport under James Honyman, Jr., and began the practice of law there. In 1749 he married Ann Brenton Conklin of South Kingstown, Rhode Island. They had three children. Although Howard was reared as an Anabaptist, he regularly attended the Anglican Trinity Church in Newport, but he was not baptized as an Anglican until 1770 in North Carolina. In 1754 the Rhode Island legislature chose him as a delegate to the Albany Congress to negotiate with the Six Nations of the Iroquois Confederacy before the French and Indian War. Howard was elected to the Rhode Island assembly in 1756. He was a member of a committee revising the colony's laws in 1760.

While serving as a member of the Newport Club, Howard and Thomas Moffat engaged in a newspaper campaign supporting a movement to have the colony's charter revoked and replaced by royal government. While thus engaged he began corresponding with Benjamin Franklin, who was seeking the same thing in Pennsylvania. In 1765 Howard wrote a pamphlet titled *A Letter from a Gentleman at Halifax to His Friend in Rhode Island*, in which he asserted that Parliament had the power to tax the colonies.

This pamphlet and Howard's appointment as a stamp tax collector made him a prime target in the Stamp Tax riots a few months later. He awakened on 27 August 1765 to learn that he and two other collectors had been hanged in effigy. While he was walking that evening with John Robinson, a customs officer, Robinson was attacked by a small mob. Howard went to his friend's assistance. The following evening, a mob of disguised men, armed with broad axes, attacked Howard's house. They demolished furniture, smashed doors, floors, and windows, and even cut down the trees in his front yard. Concerned for their own safety, Howard and his family fled to England, arriving in October 1765. A few months later the Crown appointed him chief justice of North Carolina.

When he arrived in January 1767 he found himself in the midst of the Regulator upheaval, in which farmers were protesting what they considered exorbitant court fees. The protest culminated in a pitched battle in which the Regulators were routed. Several of their leaders were arrested, and Howard presided over trials at which twelve were convicted and six were hanged. Howard won a reputation for fairness—even among the Regulators. When the Regulators planned to disrupt court sessions at Salisbury in 1771, they urged their followers not to hector Howard. Meanwhile, following the death of his first wife, Howard had married Abigail Greenleaf, daughter of the sheriff of Suffolk County, Massachusetts. The couple had one child.

Speaking to a grand jury in 1771, Howard roundly criticized slavery. This took courage because many white North Carolinians at that time owned slaves. Howard's diatribe, published by the *Wilmington Cape Fear Mercury* on 12 February 1772 and by the *Newport Mercury* three months later, was prompted by the refusal of the grand jury to indict a white man accused of murdering a black slave. Howard, who owned slaves himself, said that "slavery is not a natural state. The bodies and souls of negroes are of the same quality with ours—they are our own fellow creatures, tho' in humbler circumstances." He added that while slavery was legal in North Carolina, "I am not alone in my opinion, that slavery is not only in itself a great evil, but produces the worst effect upon our manners." Howard could not resist pointing out how inconsistent it was for North Carolinians to take from slaves "every right and privilege of humanity," but when "they imagine their own liberty is in the least invaded, they will gravely, and without blushing, quote every writer upon government and civil society to prove, that all men are by nature equal and by nature free." Howard's powerful indictment probably prompted the North Carolina assembly in 1773 to enact a law providing fines and other punishment for killing slaves.

When the Revolution broke out, Howard was permitted to withdraw to "Richmond," his plantation on the Neuse River near New Bern. When he refused to take a loyalty oath to the state in 1777, he was permitted to move to New York with his family. From there they went to London where he died.

• Documents relating to Howard are in the Loyalist Claims Commission Transcripts, North Carolina Division of Archives and History, Raleigh, and William L. Saunders, ed., *Colonial Records of North Carolina*, vols. 8–10 (1890). Information on Howard's life is in William S. Powell, ed., *Dictionary of North Carolina Biography*, vol. 3 (1988); Samuel A. Ashe, *Biographical History of North Carolina*, vol. 3 (1906); Bernard Bailyn, ed., *Pamphlets of the American Revolution, 1750–1776*, vol. 1 (1965); John R. Bartlett, ed., *Records of the Colony of Rhode Island and Providence Plantations in New England*, vols. 4–6; Henry Herbert Edes, *Martin Howard, Chief-Justice of North Carolina and His Portrait by Copley* (1903); and Don Higginbotham and William S. Price, Jr., eds., "Was It Murder for a White Man to Kill a Slave? Chief Justice Martin Howard Condemns the Peculiar Institution in North Carolina," *William and Mary Quarterly* 36 (Oct. 1979).

Also see G. J. McRee, ed., *Life and Correspondence of James Iredell*, vol. 1 (1857–1858); Edmund S. Morgan and Helen M. Morgan, *The Stamp Act Crisis: Prologue to Revolution* (1995); and Lorenzo Sabine, *Biographical Sketches of Loyalists in the American Revolution* (1864; repr. 1966).

NOEL YANCEY

HOWARD, Moe. *See* Three Stooges.

HOWARD, Oliver Otis (8 Nov. 1830–26 Oct. 1909), soldier, government official, and educator, was born in Leeds, Maine, the son of Rowland Bailey Howard and Eliza Otis, farmers. As a boy Howard worked in the company of a young black farmhand, an experience to which he later attributed his broadmindedness in racial matters. Howard graduated from Bowdoin College in 1850 and entered the U.S. Military Academy. He graduated from West Point in 1854, ranked fourth in his class. In 1855 Howard married Elizabeth Ann Waite; the couple had seven children. He first served at the federal arsenals in New York and Maine and then as an ordnance officer in Florida. In 1857 Howard returned to West Point to teach mathematics. The same year he experienced the religious conversion that would earn him such sobriquets as "the Christian Soldier." His distaste for alcohol and profanity hardly endeared him to many of his fellows. Joseph Hooker, who had other reasons to dislike him, grumbled that if Howard "was not born in petticoats he ought to have been, and ought to wear them" (Carpenter, pp. 24–25).

A first lieutenant when the Civil War erupted in 1861, Howard became colonel of the Third Maine, a volunteer regiment. In command of a brigade at Bull Run (Manassas) in July, he was promoted to brigadier general two months later. The next spring his right arm was badly shot up at Fair Oaks, and most of it had to be amputated. Howard returned to service in August 1862 and commanded troops at Antietam and Fredericksburg. Promoted to major general of volunteers in November 1862, Howard replaced Franz Sigel at the head of the XI Corps the next spring, much to the chagrin of many of its German-American troops. It was Howard's corps that Thomas "Stonewall" Jackson surprised and routed with his flank attack at Chancellorsville on 2 May 1863. Howard later claimed never to have received Union commander Hooker's warning of danger from the west. Whatever the case, both men had misread Robert E. Lee's daring division of his army, and neither adequately prepared the Union forces for an onslaught. Less than two months later Howard's men were again manhandled during the early stages of the battle of Gettysburg. Stampeded by Confederate forces north of town, they fell back to Cemetery Hill, where Howard, for a time the senior officer on the field, had left a unit in reserve and some artillery. The Confederates hesitated before the heights, allowing Winfield Scott Hancock, who took charge from a reluctant Howard, to construct the strong defensive line that sustained Union forces through the next two days.

Transferred west that autumn, Howard and his corps began to refurbish their reputations. Though not in the thick of things, they performed well in the fighting around Chattanooga, Tennessee, and in early 1864 Howard took command of the IV Corps in the Army of the Cumberland. Howard participated in William T. Sherman's advance on Atlanta, his being among the troops ill used in the frontal assault at Kennesaw Mountain. After James McPherson's death at the battle of Atlanta, Sherman selected Howard to head the Army of the Tennessee. His men held off the Confederates at Ezra Church and then played a key role in severing Atlanta's remaining rail connections, forcing the abandonment of the city to Sherman. The Army of the Tennessee formed the right of Sherman's combined force as it made its destructive way to the coast and then north through the Carolinas. In March 1865 Howard was promoted to brigadier general in the regular army.

At the war's end, President Andrew Johnson appointed Howard to a command unlike any previously exercised by an American army officer or civilian—the leadership of the newly chartered Bureau of Refugees, Freedmen, and Abandoned Lands. Better known as the Freedmen's Bureau, this federal agency was given a mandate of unprecedented scope, to manage southern lands abandoned during wartime or confiscated by federal authorities, to arrange for its distribution to emancipated slaves, and to govern "all subjects relating to refugees and freedmen from rebel states." These latter responsibilities came to include the provision of emergency food, shelter, and medical care, the superintendence of the terms by which former slaves labored for former masters, the promotion of education, and the administration of justice where it could not otherwise be obtained for freedpeople. Howard had not earned the appointment by any especially prominent identification with the cause of emancipation, however. Instead, his high rank suited a branch of the War Department that would be staffed largely by army officers, while his conspicuous Christianity appealed to many in the private freedmen's aid societies that would do much of the actual work of relief and education.

Howard immediately grasped the importance of providing former slaves with their own land and drew up orders looking toward the distribution of over 850,000 acres under Bureau control in forty-acre plots. Johnson's liberal pardon policies soon undermined him, though. The president ordered not only much of the Bureau's unallotted holdings restored to their former owners but also land already being cultivated by black families. Howard increasingly touted the virtues of wage labor of the sort that the Bureau was already helping to establish through much of the plantation South. He hoped that by hard work and thriftiness freedpeople might eventually be able to purchase their own plots, but most could earn only meager returns. Some were compelled by necessity or by the Bureau to work for white landlords on the most restrictive terms. Black southerners made plain to him their doubt that true freedom could be achieved in such lopsided arrangements, so Howard continued to urge Congress to make good on the promise of proprietorship, but to little avail. The Bureau's efforts to provide relief, protection, and justice for black people denied them by civil authorities were likewise hampered, and not only by scant funding, rapid turnover in staff, and a decided lack of sympathy for the Bureau's constituency among many military officers. Howard and many of his Republican allies believed that federal aid could be quickly curtailed because reconstructed states' formal recognition of black citizenship would necessarily end discrimination in the provision of services. Indeed, by the end of 1868 Congress had all but closed the Bureau down except for its support for education, which continued into 1870, and for black veterans, which continued to 1872. This educational work surely counts as Howard's least compromised achievement. The Bureau helped maintain thousands of primary schools in the South as well as a smaller number of black colleges and normal schools.

Howard clearly saw his mission to African Americans as extending beyond the statutory confines of freedmen's legislation. At the same time that he headed the Bureau he engaged in private endeavors, ranging from the sale of small plots of land to black Washingtonians to the unseating of his church's pastor, who was believed to be hostile to the congregation's integration. Howard also cofounded Howard University in Washington in 1867 and served as its president from 1869 to 1874. He began the work of building a campus, raised funds, and insisted that the maintenance of high academic standards would demonstrate the capacity of African-American students. Both in these efforts and at the Bureau, Howard's zeal for uplift was not always matched by a strict attention to the letter of the law or the activities of his subordinates. He was not above playing shell games with Bureau money to fund good causes not explicitly provided for by Congress. Only in the case of his interest in a firm that sold construction material to Howard University and, in turn, received Bureau funds, might Howard's propriety be called into question, however. His spending inspired a congressional investigation in 1870, while seeming malfeasance and incompetence in the Bureau's payments to black veterans inspired a military inquiry four years later. Both panels cleared Howard of wrongdoing, but his casual administration had allowed enemies to cloud both the Bureau's reputation and his own.

Historians hostile to Reconstruction often focused on these lapses, charging Howard with being blind to or even a party to what they took to be the Bureau's and Reconstruction's cardinal sins: corruption, governmental incompetence, and the politicization of black southerners. By the 1960s, however, scholars friendlier to freedpeople's aspirations emphasized other failings, chiding Howard for acquiescing to the defeat of land reform, the sacking of the Bureau's most committed officers, and a flaccid paternalism and shortsightedness that failed to lay a groundwork for black self-sufficiency. Certainly Howard was not so extraordinary a man as to be able to defy the explicit wishes of his commander in chief, his era's understanding of the proper role of government and public relief, or his own and many of his white Republican allies' sometimes formalistic notions of freedom. Yet, for a white man of his time, he might be recognized as, in many respects, exceptional. The energy, scope, and persistence of his commitment to African-American welfare and the equanimity with which he greeted the prospect of racial integration were by no means typical, even amongst Radical Republicans. It was, perhaps, these complexities of character that led W. E. B. Du Bois to conclude, "Howard was neither a great administrator nor a great man, but he was a good man" (*Black Reconstruction in America* [1935], p. 223).

This same quality of being atypical but not extraordinary manifested itself in Howard's post-Bureau career in the American West. Though less bloodthirsty and more willing to acknowledge the injustices done Native Americans than many of his white contemporaries, Howard hardly possessed the sort of cultural relativism that might have caused him to question the goals of American Indian subjugation and assimilation, nor would he defy government policy to indulge his humanitarianism. In 1872 he traveled to the Southwest to negotiate an end to Apache raiding. Unaccompanied by troops, he met with the Chiricahua leader Cochise, who agreed to take his people to a reservation to be established in southeastern Arizona. Some criticized Howard for not providing for closer supervision of the Chiricahua. In 1874 Howard was placed in command of the Department of the Columbia, headquartered in Portland and encompassing Oregon, Washington, Alaska, and parts of Idaho. Three years later he led the army's efforts to run down Chief Joseph's band of Nez Percé, who had balked at confinement on a reservation. Howard's sometimes faltering pursuit took his men through Idaho and Montana, over many hundreds of miles of mountains and plains. Other troops actually intercepted the Nez Percé and secured their surrender, but Chief Joseph addressed to Howard his famous declaration, "I will fight no more forever." The following year Howard again directed a pursuit of recalcitrant Indians, in this case Bannocks and Paiutes, across rugged country in the Northwest.

By the 1880s Howard was no longer called upon to fight the battles that shaped the nation's character. After an uneventful tenure in 1881–1882 as superintendent of West Point, he moved to Omaha to head the Department of the Platte. Promoted to major general, Howard in 1886 took command of the Military Division of the Pacific but played little part in the operations against Geronimo. Moving from San Francisco to New York in 1888, Howard headed the Military Division of the Atlantic and, after a reorganization in 1891, the Department of the East. He left the army in 1894 and settled in Burlington, Vermont. He had already begun to publish, and his oeuvre came to include juvenile tales, biographies of Zachary Taylor and Queen Isabella, and several volumes of memoirs.

In retirement he again turned his energies to educating a neglected population, that of southern Appalachia. The funds he raised helped establish Lincoln Memorial University in Harrogate, Tennessee. Howard died in Burlington, Vermont.

• The largest collection of O. O. Howard Papers is at Bowdoin College in Brunswick, Maine. Smaller collections are at Howard University in Washington, D.C.; Lincoln Memorial University in Harrogate, Tenn.; and the University of Vermont in Burlington. Selected wartime correspondence and reports are reprinted in *The War of the Rebellion: A Compilation of the Official Records of the Union and Confederate Armies* (128 vols., 1880–1901). The records of the Bureau of Refugees, Freedmen, and Abandoned Lands are at the National Archives (RG 105). Howard's reports as commissioner of the Freedmen's Bureau between 1865 and 1871 were published as House Executive Doc. in the U.S. serial set (#1255, 1285, 1324, 1367, 1412, 1446, 1503). For Howard's own account of his career, see *Autobiography of Oliver Otis Howard, Major General United States Army* (1907) and *My Life and Experiences among Our Hostile Indians* (1907). John Carpenter, *Sword and Olive Branch: Oliver Otis Howard* (1964), is a sympathetic but scholarly biography. William McFeely's study of Howard's work with the bureau, *Yankee Stepfather: General O. O. Howard and the Freedmen* (1968), is considerably more critical. For a brief but finely balanced treatment of Howard and the Freedmen's Bureau, see Eric Foner, *Reconstruction: America's Unfinished Revolution, 1863–1877* (1988). A prominent frontier historian who offers an overview of Howard's career in the West is Robert Utley, "Oliver Otis Howard," *New Mexico Historical Review* 62 (1987): 55–63. Many studies of the battles of Chancellorsville and Gettysburg, Sherman's campaigns in Ga. and the Carolinas, and the pursuit of the Nez Percé discuss Howard. See Stephen Sears, *Chancellorsville* (1996); Shelby Foote, *Stars in Their Courses: The Gettysburg Campaign, June–July 1863* (1994); Albert Castel, *Decision in the West: The Atlanta Campaign of 1864* (1992); and Alvin Josephy, *The Nez Percé Indians and the Opening of the Northwest* (1965).

PATRICK G. WILLIAMS

HOWARD, Roy Wilson (1 Jan. 1883–20 Nov. 1964), newspaper journalist and executive, was born at Gano, Ohio, sixteen miles from Cincinnati, in a turnpike tollhouse presided over by his grandmother. His father was William A. Howard, a railroad brakeman on the nearby Big Four Railroad, and his mother was Elizabeth Wilson. When Howard was a boy, the family moved to Indianapolis, where he became a carrier for the *Indianapolis Star* and the *Indianapolis News*. He was still a pupil at Manual Training High School when the *News* began paying him for articles. On graduation from Manual in 1902, he was hired as a full-time reporter at $8 a week.

In 1904 Howard went east, where he tried unsuccessfully to get a job at the *New York World*. He returned to the Midwest and worked briefly as sports editor of the *Indianapolis Star* and assistant telegraph editor of the *St. Louis Post-Dispatch*. From there he took a position as an editor of the *Cincinnati Post* in 1905. In 1906, at the age of twenty-three and four years out of high school, he left to become a New York correspondent of the Scripps-McRae newspapers.

In 1907 E. W. Scripps merged several small news agencies to form the United Press, and after interviewing Howard at his ranch, "Miramar," in California in February 1908, Scripps hired him as the first general news manager of the United Press. Scripps described Howard later as "a striking individual, very small of stature, with a large head and speaking countenance, and eyes that appeared to be windows for a rather unusual intellect. His manner was forceful, and the reverse from modest. Gall was written all over his face. . . . There was ambition, self-respect and forcefulness oozing out of every pore of his body. . . . However, so completely and exuberantly frank was he that it was impossible for me to feel any resentment on account of his cheek" (McCabe, p. 219).

In 1909 Howard went to Europe to study and reorganize the continental bureaus, which the United Press had taken over from the Scripps-McRae Publishers Association. In June 1909, Howard married Margaret Rohe, an American from Lawrence, Kansas, in London, where she was writing for *Munsey's* magazine and acting in an American comedy. That same year the Howards returned to live in New York, where their two children were born.

In 1912, at age twenty-nine, Howard became the United Press's first president and general manager in charge of both editorial and business operations. During the winter of 1915–1916 Howard traveled to South America to break the news monopoly in that region held by Havas, the French news agency. He signed up leading newspapers in many of the South American capitals, including *La Prensa* in Buenos Aires, and set off an international news agency war. In 1918 Reuters and Havas cut off the United Press's quota on the British cables from Europe, the only direct telegraphic link between Europe and Latin America. Howard took a ship from Brazil to Britain, presented his case to the British Home Office, and had the United Press quota restored.

Howard also broke the story from France announcing the armistice of World War I in November 1918, even though his dispatch was premature, exactly four days too early. He took this error in stride, remarking, "No real reporter could have or would have done otherwise in the circumstances." Admiral Henry Braid Wilson, commander of American naval forces in France, later confirmed that he thought the armistice had been official and had given permission to Howard to use this news on 7 November 1918.

E. W. Scripps did not hold the miscommunication against Howard, and in 1920 Howard left United Press to become associated with Robert P. Scripps in the management of the Scripps newspapers. In 1922 E. W. Scripps changed the company's name to Scripps-Howard Newspapers, and Howard was named chairman of the board. In 1931 Howard bought the *New York World* and the *Evening World* for $5 million and consolidated them with the *New York Telegram*, which he had acquired in 1927. His *New York World-Telegram* won the Pulitzer Prize for public service in 1933 for four series published in 1932 on irregularities in the handling of real estate bonds, lottery frauds, extravagances in administering veterans' relief, and corruption in the campaign for mayor of New York. Howard not only directed the newspaper's attack on the powerfully entrenched Tammany Hall but also strongly supported Fiorello H. La Guardia, the reform candidate for mayor. In 1937 and 1947 Scripps-Howard Newspapers won two more Pulitzer Prizes.

Throughout his career Howard maintained a keen interest in reporting and obtained exclusive interviews with various world leaders, including Britain's minister for war David Lloyd George, the Japanese emperor Hirohito, and Soviet leader Josef Stalin. Howard traveled to Manchuria in 1933 along the fronts of the Sino-Japanese war, covering it first from the Japanese side and later with the Chinese forces. He obtained an interview with Hirohito, the first ever granted to an American newspaper journalist. After his return to the United States, Howard urged a larger U.S. Navy to defend against the Japanese military.

Howard also obtained an exclusive interview with Stalin in the Kremlin in Moscow in 1936 regarding Soviet foreign policy. The interview lasted more than three hours, and a Russian interpreter decided to "improve" some of Stalin's more forthright statements over Howard's protests. The next day Stalin saw the story draft and ordered all the original language restored, much to Howard's satisfaction. Howard became president of Scripps-Howard Newspapers the same year.

The *New York Times* credited Howard with being a major influence in the election of Franklin D. Roosevelt in 1932. Howard backed Roosevelt's second term after failing to get Newton D. Baker the presidential nomination at the Democratic convention in 1932, but he later withdrew his support during Roosevelt's second term because he disapproved of Roosevelt's plan to increase the number of Supreme Court justices. To Howard, this "court packing" with justices favorable to Roosevelt's New Deal policies meant substituting "government by bureaucracy" for the Scripps concept of government by liberalism.

In 1938 Howard was charged by press critic George Seldes with changing the policies of Scripps-Howard Newspapers "from liberal to phony-liberal and eventually to a more honest anti-liberalism" (p. 322). Howard emphatically denied the charge in a May 1944 issue of *Look* magazine, where he wrote that the Scripps-Howard papers had supported all legislation designed to improve the lot of workers and had fought legislation designed to foster corrupt labor leadership.

Howard retired officially in 1953 but continued to serve as chairman of the executive committee of Scripps-Howard Newspapers until his death of a heart attack in his New York office. Informed of Howard's death at his ranch in Texas, President Lyndon B. Johnson said, "I deeply regret the passing of this outstanding newspaperman, who played such a major role as the leader of one of the world's largest newspaper chains. He was already a legend in his profession and will go down in the history of journalism as one of its commanding figures" (*New York World-Telegram and The Sun*, 21 Nov. 1964, p. 1).

Roy Howard, known for his colorful clothes, including matching shirts and bow ties of various checks and stripes, and a Park Avenue office furnished with oriental antiques, made a strong and lasting impression in several areas of American journalism during the twentieth century, including the reporting of politics and foreign affairs, the building of the United Press wire service, and the management and growth of Scripps-Howard Newspapers.

• Howard's papers have been deposited in the Roy W. Howard Archive at Indiana University's School of Journalism at Bloomington and also in the Library of Congress. His family, longtime secretary Naoma Lowensohn, and the Scripps Howard Foundation have endowed both the archive and the Roy W. Howard Research Chair at the School of Journalism. Other references that provide information on Howard include Charles R. McCabe, ed., *Damned Old Crank: A Self-Portrait of E. W. Scripps Drawn from His Unpublished Writings* (1951), especially chap. 21; Edwin Emery and Michael Emery, *The Press and America* (1978); and Vance H. Trimble, *The Astonishing Mr. Scripps* (1992). Other sources are A. J. Liebling, "Publisher," a four-part series in the *New Yorker*, 2, 9, 16, and 23 Aug. 1941; George Seldes, "Roy Howard and His Papers," *New Republic*, 27 July 1938, pp. 322–25; Seldes, *Lords of the Press* (1938); Robert Bendiner and James Wechsler, "From Scripps to Howard," *The Nation*, 13 and 20 May 1939; Frank Luther Mott, *American Journalism* (1969); Leland Stowe, "Roy Howard: Newspaper Napoleon," *Look*, 30 May 1944; Lee Wood, "The Most Unforgettable Character I've Met," *Reader's Digest*, Nov. 1965, pp. 82–86; and Forrest Davis, "Press Lord," *Saturday Evening Post*, 12 Mar. 1938. Obituaries are in the *New York Times* and the *New York World-Telegram and The Sun*, 21 Nov. 1964, and in *Newsweek*, 30 Nov. 1964, and *Editor & Publisher*, 28 Nov. 1964.

DAVID H. WEAVER

HOWARD, Shemp. *See* Three Stooges.

HOWARD, Sidney Coe (26 June 1891–23 Aug. 1939), playwright and screenwriter, was born in Oakland, California, the son of John Lawrence Howard, a steamship executive, and his second wife, Helen Louise Coe, a professional organist and piano teacher. Howard attended public schools and traveled in the Sierras, British Columbia, Mexico, and Europe. Tuberculosis in his teens sent him to Ojai Valley near Los Angeles and, in 1910, to a sanatorium in Switzerland.

Because his father was ill, Howard enrolled at the nearby University of California at Berkeley, instead of at Harvard. His first pageant play was produced in 1914 by an artist's colony at Carmel. In 1915 he received his B.A. in English and classical literature and began working on a master's degree at Harvard. While earning money writing freelance and syndicate newspaper articles, he was also a drama student in George Pierce Baker's famous 47 Workshop at Harvard. As payment for odd jobs at *The Transcript*, a daily newspaper, Howard received gallery admissions to Boston theaters. In 1916 he was contracted by a Detroit millionaire to write and act in a play performed at his private theater. Howard finished the play, collected $500, but avoided acting by boarding a submarine-dodging liner destined for Europe.

For more than two years Howard was an ambulance driver on the French and Balkan fronts. When the U.S. joined World War I he enlisted as an aviator for French and U.S. forces, eventually becoming a captain. After the war, in January 1919, Howard joined the editorial staff of *Life*, a weekly humor magazine, in New York City, and within three years moved from joke-reader to literary editor. Between 1920 and 1924 he gained a reputation as a radical reporter and feature writer for the *New Republic* and *Hearst's International Magazine*, investigating Communist witch hunts, stock and oil swindles, and labor disputes. Howard's interest in social issues did not stop when he turned full time to fiction and playwriting. Throughout his career he fought censorship, defended minorities, and supported the American Civil Liberties Union. An advocate of Woodrow Wilson, Howard believed in the ideal of America's service to, rather than conquering of, humanity.

Howard's first short story in *Collier's Weekly* in 1920 was followed by "The Homesick Ladies," published in *Scribner's Magazine* and winner of the second prize in the O. Henry short story competition, after Dorothy Parker's "Big Blonde." His translation of D'Annunzio's *Fedra* into a pageant play led to Howard's first New York production, *Swords*, an imaginative poetic drama that opened in September 1921. Though the play failed, Howard's courtship of the leading actress, Clare Jenness Eames, was a success. They married in June 1922 and had one child. After translating Charles Vildrac's *S.S. Tenacity* from the French in 1922, Howard moved toward realism. His most successful play, *They Knew What They Wanted* (1924), was about an Italian-American bootlegger with California vineyards who prospers during Prohibition and desires a mail-order bride. It starred Pauline Lord and Richard Bennett and gained Howard international fame and a Pulitzer Prize in 1925. Producing play after play, Howard established himself as "an institution in the theatre—just like the war tax" (*New York Times*, 5 Dec. 1926), garnering success from such gangster-world plays as *Ned McCobb's Daughter* (1926).

In 1928 Howard and his wife separated. She moved to London, while he and their daughter lived with his sister in Berkeley for two years. Though he openly criticized Hollywood, in 1929 Howard was persuaded by Samuel Goldwyn to write screenplays. As the highest paid screenwriter of his time, with ten of his thirteen screenplays produced, the only drawback for Howard was having periodically to leave the East Coast and his family for his work. Howard's first screenplay, *Bulldog Drummond* (1929), was voted one of the "Ten Best" by the *New York Times*. In 1931 he received an Academy Award for his screen adaption of Sinclair Lewis's *Arrowsmith*. In March 1930 Howard's divorce from Clare was official; later that year she died

in a London nursing home. The next January he married Leopoldine Blaine Damrosch, daughter of conductor Walter Damrosch. They had three children.

In 1934 Howard, long praised for his innovation, his heroic female characters, energetic writing, and portrayals of a modern morality, was deemed by *Time* second only to Eugene O'Neill in U.S. playwriting. He referred to himself in a letter to longtime friend Barrett H. Clark as an "earthbound pragmatic stoic without any aptitude for the empyrean" who believed "whatever a healthy and normal human being feels to be right, is right." Howard teamed up with Sinclair Lewis for a second time and produced his best stage adaptation with *Dodsworth* (1934). His screenplay of *Dodsworth* for the 1936 movie made the *New York Times* "Ten Best" list.

Already a member of the National Institute of Arts and Letters (inducted 1927), in 1935 Howard became a member of the American Academic Arts and Letters and was elected president of the Dramatists Guild of the Author's League of America, serving two years. The same year he bought a 500-acre woodland and dairy farm in Tyringham, Massachusetts, where he went to relax by plowing and gardening. In 1936 independent producer David O. Selznick hired Howard for the daunting task of converting the 1,037-page *Gone with the Wind* into a screenplay. Howard succeeded, and except for some changes made while shooting, Selznick followed Howard's script. The movie premiered in 1939 and won ten Oscars, including one for best screenplay. In 1977 the American Film Institute voted *Gone with the Wind* the greatest film made in the United States. Concerned for young playwrights, in 1938 Howard joined Robert Sherwood and Elmer Rice, among others, to form the Playwrights' Producing Company to challenge commercial theater by producing their own plays. Howard's last play, a female version of Faust titled *Madam, Will You Walk?* was completed in 1939, but was not staged until 1953.

In addition to the publication of several short stories, journalistic pieces, and two pageants, Howard had twenty-seven plays—adaptations, translations, and original scripts—produced in New York City. According to lifelong friend Barrett Clark, who believed Howard's "voice was American," Howard was shy yet arrogant when it came to meeting people, preferring an audience of children to adults. He did not consider himself an intellectual dramatist and was more pleased by a popular play than one hailed by highbrow critics. On 24 August 1939 a *New York Times'* front-page headline notified the nation that "Sidney Howard Killed by Tractor on Estate." A freak accident on the Tyringham farm ended the life of one of the most successful dramatists and the highest-paid film scenarist of the 1920s and 1930s.

• The Sidney Howard Collection is housed at the University of California, Berkeley. His correspondence is in the Princeton University Scribner Archives and in the James Branch Cabell and Walter Prichard Eaton Collections at the University of Virginia Library. Various press books and clipping files are at the Yale University Library and the Billy Rose Theatre Collection of the New York Public Library for the Performing Arts, Lincoln Center. Sidney Howard White, *Sidney Howard* (1977), has a detailed overview of Howard's life and work and lists all his plays and publications. Other biographical pieces include "Both Sides of the Footlights—An American Playwright, the Recurrent Sidney Howard," *New York Times*, 5 Dec. 1926, and Barrett H. Clark, "His Voice Was American," *Theatre Arts*, Apr. 1949, pp. 27–30. Clark also published some of his correspondence from Howard between 1919 to 1939, with biographical notes, in "Letters from Sidney Howard," *Theatre Arts*, Apr. 1941. A discussion of the adaptation to screen of *Gone with the Wind* is in *Cinema: The Novel into Film*, ed. Frank N. Magill (1980). For references to Howard's Hollywood career see Alvin H. Marill, *Samuel Goldwyn Presents* (1976). An obituary is in the *New York Times*, 24 Aug. 1939.

BARBARA L. CICCARELLI

HOWARD, Timothy Edward (27 Jan. 1837–9 July 1916), professor, legislator, and judge, was born in Ann Arbor, Michigan, the son of Martin Howard and Julia Beahan, farmers. Howard enrolled in the University of Michigan after attending "common schools" and a seminary in Ypsilanti but left during his sophomore year because of an illness in his family. He taught in rural Michigan schools for two years before entering Notre Dame in 1859. In February 1862, before he had graduated, he enlisted in the Twelfth Michigan Infantry. His friends would later recall that he had enlisted without telling anyone at Notre Dame. He served only two months before he was seriously wounded in the battle of Shiloh. Although he recovered, the wound was so severe that he was discharged as unfit for further service.

In 1862 Howard returned to Notre Dame, received his degree, and joined the faculty. His first teaching responsibilities tell as much about his eclectic interests as about the nature of the school: appointed as a professor of rhetoric and English literature, he also taught classes in history and astronomy, and at the same time began the study of law. He received an M.A. from Notre Dame in 1864, and a law degree in 1873. In the same year he married Julia A. Redmond; they had ten children. He was a professor at Notre Dame until 1878, and between 1908 and 1916 he taught courses in the law school.

Howard began public service in 1878, when he was elected to the South Bend, Indiana, city council and to the clerkship of the St. Joseph County circuit court. He was the Democratic nominee for both offices. Among his accomplishments was the establishment of the city's first park, which was later named after him. In 1883 he was admitted to the Indiana bar. Three years later he was a successful Democratic candidate for the state senate, where he served until 1893, when he was elected to the state supreme court. His unassuming manner made him a favorite among politicians of all parties. While in the senate he sponsored a number of laws, including the creation of an intermediate state appellate court, the revision of the state's tax law,

and the modification of election laws. After leaving the supreme court in 1899, he practiced law in South Bend and continued to serve the public as president of the Northern Indiana Historical Society, chair of a commission to codify the laws of Indiana, and author of two histories, *The Indiana Supreme Court: With Some Account of the Courts Preceding It* (1900) and *A History of St. Joseph County, Indiana* (1907). He also wrote a volume of poetry, *Musings and Memories* (1905); a collection of essays on proper behavior for young men in boarding schools, *Excelsior; or, Essays on Politeness, Education, and the Means of Attaining Success in Life* (1868); and a book on grammar, *Outlines of Composition* (1871). In 1898 Notre Dame recognized his contributions by awarding him its most prestigious award, the Laetare Medal, for outstanding contributions as a Catholic layman. Notre Dame students showed their continued affection for Howard by dedicating the 1913 yearbook to him.

Howard's judicial opinions are notable for their attention to the pleadings and to the facts. Written as though they were classroom lectures, his opinions began with a recital of the pleadings and frequently quoted them in their entirety. He then recounted the facts, often in far greater detail than was necessary to explain the decision. His prose was sparse; he concentrated on reciting precedent and made only occasional excursions into considerations of policy. When he made such an excursion, it was most likely in an effort to protect children. In *Hardesty v. Hine* (1893), he criticized a bar owner who allowed children near a pool table with the observation that "[f]ew greater crimes against society can be conceived than that of the moral pollution of our youth." In other rare instances, he revealed his approval of development and once wrote that "the great interests of mankind must go on unhampered. Railroads must reach cities; the treasures of the earth must be drawn from the mines; factories and mills must send forth noise, dust, and smoke. Inconveniences resulting from such causes must be endured by individuals for the general good, otherwise we should have to forego a multitude of the blessings of modern civilization" (*Barnard v. Sherley* [1893]). Usually, though, he remained focused on the case before him, as a matter of Indiana law. He wrote equally conscientious opinions no matter whether the issue was a complex matter of pleading, an intricate real estate transaction, or a suit for damages caused by accidental death. Even the most obtuse lawyers could count on a kind word from Howard in most opinions.

Howard died in South Bend, Indiana. His life was a model of dedication to public service at all levels of Indiana government. His unassuming manner made him a favorite of all political parties.

• Howard's opinions are reported in volumes 133–52 of the *Indiana Reports*. An obituary is in the *South Bend Tribune*, 10 July 1916.

WALTER F. PRATT, JR.

HOWARD, Willie (13 Apr. 1886–12 Jan. 1949), theatrical performer, was born William Lefkowitz in Neustadt, Germany, the son of the Reverend Leopold Lefkowitz, a cantor, and Pauline Glass. In 1886 the family emigrated to the United States, settling in Harlem, New York City. Howard was educated in the New York City public schools. Expelled from school in 1897 for telling jokes, he decided to follow in the footsteps of his older brother Eugene and pursue a career on the stage. Owing to his great comic talent, Howard was soon picking up nickels and dimes clowning and singing his way from one end of the city to the other. He obtained his first regular job at the age of fourteen, as a boy soprano for Harry Von Tilzer, a composer of popular songs, at Proctor's 125th Street Theater. In 1901 the publishing firm M. Witmark and Sons hired Howard as a song plugger, singing and promoting their songs, at five dollars a week. Theatrical producer Florenz Ziegfeld heard Howard sing and hired him to perform in *The Little Dutchess* (1901), starring Anna Held. Howard sang in the chorus, which performed a refrain from one of the theater boxes, as was then customary. Unfortunately, Howard's voice was changing, and he developed into a "bullfrog coloratura" almost overnight; he soon found himself among the unemployed. There followed a brief stint as a mimic in Huber's Museum on Fourteenth Street, impersonating David Warfield, Sam Bernard, and other stars of the theater.

In 1903 Willie joined his brother Eugene in vaudeville. Adopting the stage name "Howard," the brothers toured the country for nine years as "Howard and Howard." Willie was the comedian and Eugene the straight man. They soon became one of the most successful comedy teams in vaudeville. Diminutive Willie, with his hooked nose, sallow cheeks, and shock of unruly hair, was the star of the act. Around his physical features, using all sorts of wigs and moustaches, he built a comedy act with universal appeal. Eugene, tall and dapper, made the ideal straight man. By 1906 their act *The Messenger Boy and the Thespian* had become well known on the vaudeville circuit. In one of their famous turns, "French Taught in a Hurry," Willie played a foreign language teacher whose French contained more Yiddish and broken English than it did French. His "Rigoletto" routine, in which he constantly leered at a buxom woman singing an aria, was a favorite among audiences. Willie Howard was a master of dialect comedy; he regularly did skits using Russian, German, French, or Yiddish dialects. This type of act was developed primarily to please the various immigrant groups that were often the bulk of spectators in a vaudeville theater, especially from the 1890s to the 1930s. By 1910 Willie and Eugene had become headliners on the Orpheum Circuit, the major vaudeville circuit between Chicago and the West Coast. In 1912 the Howards left vaudeville for revue and musical comedy. They did not return to vaudeville until 1924, when they played the Palace Theater in New York for $2,500 a week, as opposed to the $450 per week they had received in their vaudeville days.

When in 1912 the Shubert brothers, Lee and Jacob, revived the nineteenth-century revue *The Passing Show*, with the intent of creating competition for Ziegfeld's popular *Follies*, they hired the Howards as their lead comedians. The first *Passing Show* was a great success, and the Howard brothers appeared in six more Shubert revues, all of them at the Winter Garden Theater in New York. In a typical exchange from the first *Passing Show* in 1912, Willie, in dialect, is applying for a job as a singing waiter and Eugene is inquiring about his musical background:

WILLIE: I was the leader of a circus orchestra.
EUGENE: How many pieces were in the orchestra?
WILLIE: Six pieces—fife and drum.

Around 1922 Willie married Emily Miles of Chicago; they had no children. Also in 1922, after the last *Passing Show*, the Howards appeared in a number of successful musical comedies for other producers. Among them was *George White's Scandals of 1931*, in which the brothers displayed some of their best dialect gags. Here Willie appears as a celebrity being interviewed by a newspaper reporter:

WILLIE: I bagged a lion in Africa.
REPORTER: You bagged a lion?
WILLIE: I bagged him and I bagged him but he wouldn't go away.

Throughout the 1930s the Howards' careers flourished in shows such as George Gershwin and Ira Gershwin's *Girl Crazy*, the *Ziegfeld Follies of 1934* with Fanny Brice, and Vincente Minnelli's *The Show Is On*.

In 1940 Eugene Howard decided to retire, and Willie never again enjoyed real success in a Broadway musical comedy or revue, though he continued to perform for several years. He and Eugene appeared together only twice after Eugene's retirement and then only briefly. Howard made his last stage appearance in June 1948 in an unsuccessful revival of the musical *Sally*. He died in New York City.

Howard did little work in radio, and his style of comedy was considered too broad for motion pictures, though he did make a few appearances in films during the 1930s, primarily shorts. He also did some nightclub work in his later years. But it was as a dialect comedian—be it Yiddish, French, or Spanish—that he is best known. His wit and timing were models for other comedians, and his impersonations of great performers such as Eddie Cantor, Al Jolson, and George Jessel became classics.

• The best source of information on Howard is Stanley Green, *The Great Clowns of Broadway* (1984). Also useful are Abel Green and Joe Laurie, Jr., *Show Biz: From Vaude to Video* (1951); Laurie, Jr., *Vaudeville: From the Honky-Tonks to the Palace* (1953); Brooks McNamara, *The Shuberts of Broadway* (1990); Charles Samuels and Louise Samuels, *Once Upon a Stage: The Merry World of Vaudeville* (1974); Anthony Slide, *The Vaudevillians* (1981); Jerry Stagg, *The Brothers Shubert* (1968); and Isidore Witmark and Isaac Goldberg, *From Ragtime to Swingtime* (1939). An informative article is Nat Kahn, "Willie Howard," *Variety*, 19 Jan. 1949, pp. 2–3. See also Murray Schumach, "Willie Howard: The World's His Straight Man," *New York Times Magazine*, 2 May 1948. An obituary is in the *New York Times*, 13 Jan. 1949.

CHARLES W. STEIN

HOWE, Edgar Watson (3 May 1853–3 Oct. 1937), author and journalist, was born in Treaty, Indiana, the son of Henry Howe, at the time a farmer, and Elizabeth Irwin, who was Henry Howe's second wife. The Howe family moved west and settled in Bethany, Missouri. Edgar had only fragmentary schooling and worked as a printer's devil for his father, with whom he went out on "circuit rider" expeditions into northern Missouri and Iowa. Edgar Howe became a tramp printer in the Midwest and the Rocky Mountains, including time on the *Deseret News* in Salt Lake City.

In 1877, with the help of his half brother Jim, Howe picked Atchison, a Kansas town on the Missouri River, as a likely place to succeed with a small daily paper and founded the *Atchison Daily Globe*. He faced formidable competition from such papers as the *Champion* but gradually, through his enterprise, his sharp wit, and his telling observations, made the *Globe* not only the leading paper in Atchison but the best-known small-town paper in the United States. The *Globe*'s circulation was not significant, but the paper gained importance because Howe's frequently bitter "Globe Sights" were picked up and reprinted by papers all across America. He became known for his caustic comments about the frailties of women and about town loafers who could not understand "the blessings of business," and he made observations like these:

There are two ways of raising boys, but judging from the men turned out, both ways are wrong.
No man ever loved a woman he was afraid of.
An Atchison girl has such a good time single, that no one can understand why she intends to get married.
This Freedom you hear so much about; there's mighty little of it in this country: Think it over: how much Freedom have you? Isn't there someone standing over you with a club night and day?

At night, after getting off work at the paper, Howe began to write *The Story of a Country Town*, a novel about a little family, a father who leaves home with "another woman," and a hero and his love for a girl who, unfortunately, has been engaged before, making her quite unacceptable to the boy. The book was published in 1882, came to the attention of William Dean Howells and Mark Twain, received national attention, and over the years attained the standing of an at least minor classic of naturalism. Much of the story was autobiographical, the wayward father being a direct copy of Howe's own father. Though the book became known as an iconoclastic attack on small-town values, Howe was never an enemy of the small town. He was, if anything, a booster, a promoter of Atchison, business enterprise, and his famous Corn Carnival, an annual festival started in the 1890s and imitated in other towns.

Howe followed *The Story of a Country Town* with other novels, but they were unsuccessful. He also wrote for the mass magazines of the time—the *American* and the *Saturday Evening Post*—articles and sketches about success, the frailties of women, and the conservative business leaders of his time. In 1929 he published *Plain People*, a warm and engaging autobiography that reveals little of the bitterness and cynicism attributed to him and that also virtually ignores his own disastrous marriage in 1875 to Clara L. Frank, whom he divorced in 1901. They had three children: Eugene became famous as an Amarillo, Texas, editor; James was a foreign correspondent for the Associated Press; and Mateel wrote light fiction, some of which commented on her father and the family. Howe achieved a national reputation, became a friend of such people as H. L. Mencken and William Allen White, continued his "paragraphing," and retired from the *Globe* in 1911, leaving it in the hands of his son Eugene.

In 1912 Howe launched a little magazine that turned into a four-page newspaper, *E. W. Howe's Monthly*, devoted entirely to his wit, diatribes, and commentaries about human nature, national affairs, and politics, although he always claimed to have no interest in political matters. In 1933 he suddenly gave up the *Monthly* and retired, by then a senior citizen widely respected not only in the hometown he had so often criticized but also throughout Kansas and among American journalists. In his time he was the most important country editor in the United States, but most of his journalism has been forgotten. He is best known for *The Story of a Country Town*, which has gone through many editions.

Howe died on his farm, "Potato Hill," a short distance from Atchison. His *Story of a Country Town* is his one lasting legacy. Still considered a pioneering novel in the naturalistic vein, it can be seen as a forerunner of Edgar Lee Masters's *Spoon River Anthology* (1915) and Sinclair Lewis's *Main Street* (1920).

• Among Howe's other published writings are two volumes on his travels, *Daily Notes of a Trip around the World* (1907) and *The Trip to the West Indies* (1910), plus *Success Easier Than Failure* (1917) and *The Blessings of Business* (1918). For biographical details and insight into his character, see Calder M. Pickett, *Ed Howe: Country Town Philosopher* (1968), and Gene Howe, "My Father Was the Most Wretchedly Unhappy Man I Ever Knew," *Saturday Evening Post*, 28 Oct. 1941.

CALDER PICKETT

HOWE, Elias (9 July 1819–3 Oct. 1867), inventor, was born in Spencer, Massachusetts, the son of Elias Howe and Polly Bemis, farmers. Howe's father also owned a small gristmill and a sawmill, and from an early age young Howe worked at the mills as well as on the family farm. He was able to attend school from time to time each winter, but he was more interested in tinkering with the machinery at the mills. Poverty forced the elder Howe to hire out his son to a neighboring farmer when Elias was twelve years old, but poor health made the boy unsuitable for heavy farm-work. He returned to his family after a year and began working full time in the mills.

At age sixteen Howe became an apprentice in a factory in Lowell, Massachusetts, that manufactured cotton-spinning machinery. When the firm folded two years later, he worked briefly in a Cambridge, Massachusetts, machine shop as an operator of a hemp-carding machine, which had recently been invented; then he became an apprentice to Ari Davis, a Boston watchmaker who also made surveying instruments and scientific equipment for professors at Harvard University.

Under the tutelage of Davis, an ingenious creator and repairer of mechanical devices who was frequently consulted by inventors and businessmen, Howe became a proficient machinist and was hired by Davis at a salary of $9 a week. In 1841 he married Boston resident Elizabeth J. Ames; the couple had three children.

Around the time of Howe's marriage, a chance remark inspired him to begin what would become his life's work. Howe overheard a conversation between Davis and a visitor to his shop, during which one of the men observed that a great fortune awaited whoever could perfect a mechanical sewing device. From that day forward, Howe was determined that he would invent such a machine. Although their existence was not widely known, several versions of sewing machines had already been invented in England and France, beginning in the late eighteenth century, but they were crude devices that had never become popular. In 1834 a New York inventor named Walter Hunt, apparently without knowledge of these English and French inventions, became the first American to build a sewing machine; when the machine failed to arouse interest, Hunt turned his attention to other inventions. When he finally applied for a patent in 1853, his application was denied on the grounds that he had abandoned his invention decades earlier.

Elias Howe was apparently unaware of these earlier inventions when he began his tinkering in the early 1840s. Believing that any sewing machine had to replicate the motions of the human hand, Howe spent many hours observing his wife sewing clothes for their own household as well as hired work she took on to help support their poverty-stricken family.

The first machine Howe constructed had a double-pointed needle with a hole in the middle of the shank, but this proved a failure. Frustrated and often exhausted after twelve-hour workdays in Davis's shop, Howe nevertheless persisted in an effort to perfect his machine. A breakthrough occurred in 1844, when he constructed a model that combined an eye-pointed needle and two threads with a shuttle. Later Howe claimed that a dream had inspired him to invent the special needle: in the dream he was surrounded by African warriors who carried sharp-pointed spears with eye-shaped holes at their tips.

Eager to devote himself full time to his invention, Howe was able to leave his job at Davis's shop late in 1844 when friend and former schoolmate George Fisher, now a prosperous wood and coal merchant, offered him short-term support. In April 1845 Howe was able to sew a seam on his new machine, and three months later he stitched together two men's suits, one for Fisher and one for himself.

To convince the public that his invention had commercial value, Howe took it to the Quincy Hall Clothing Manufacturing Company in Boston, where he demonstrated that it could sew faster and more reliably than the best hand stitchers. Nonetheless that factory and others declined to buy his machine, saying that it would be too expensive to manufacture in quantity and would also create discord by putting hand stitchers out of work.

Still hopeful that his invention would prove successful, Howe was determined to secure a patent, and he constructed a second machine, as required by law, for submission to the U.S. Patent Office; his patent was issued in September 1846. When American manufacturers continued to ignore Howe's invention, Howe's brother Amasa suggested that he try to interest British clothing makers in the machine. Aided by a loan from their father, Amasa sailed to England in steerage, carrying with him a third model built by Elias.

After much searching, Amasa Howe was able to persuade a London corset manufacturer, William Thomas, to buy the machine and the rights to its future manufacture, as well as the right to patent it in England, for a sum of £250. As part of the bargain, Thomas agreed to hire Elias Howe to adapt the machine to the manufacture of corsets at a salary of £3 a week and promised to pay Howe £3 for every machine sold under English patent.

In February 1847, with money advanced him by Thomas, Elias Howe, along with his wife and children, moved to London to begin working for Thomas, taking with him his first machine and his patent papers. Although Howe was able to construct a machine suitable for Thomas's factory, he found working conditions dismal; when he asked for improvement, he was dismissed from Thomas's employ. Thomas never paid Howe royalties on his sewing machine and eventually made an estimated $1 million from Howe's invention.

Out of work and short of funds, Howe sent his ailing wife and children back to his father's house in Massachusetts while he remained in London. He rented a small workroom where he constructed a fourth sewing machine but was able to sell it for only £5. Howe was forced to pawn his first machine and his patent papers to raise enough money to pay his debts and purchase return passage to America. He arrived in New York in April 1849 and found work in local machine shops. Not long after his return, his wife died of tuberculosis. Several years later Howe remarried; his second wife's name and the year of their marriage cannot be ascertained. It is known that the couple lived in New York City and also maintained a residence in Bridgeport, Connecticut, after 1860.

Working in his spare time on the construction of a fifth sewing machine, Howe learned that during his two-year absence from America public interest in a mechanical sewing device had increased. Versions of his invention had been manufactured and exhibited around the country, though he himself had received no credit, and sewing machines using devices covered under his patent were in daily use in several Boston factories. With the help of his father and several friends, Howe began a series of lawsuits for patent infringement, even as other manufacturers continued to create new machines based on Howe's invention. While Howe battled his competitors in the courts, he was also able to compete in the marketplace. He supported himself by manufacturing and selling his machines in New York City.

Howe's primary lawsuit was filed against Boston inventor Isaac M. Singer. In 1850 Singer made substantial improvements in Howe's device and started selling the new machine under his own name. The longest court case in U.S. history up to that time ended in 1854, when an initial settlement forced Singer to pay Howe $15,000 in royalties for machines sold by him up to that time. Additional lawsuits against Singer as well as other infringers of Howe's patent were also decided in favor of Howe, with the result that all American manufacturers of sewing machines were required to pay a royalty of $25 per machine to Howe until 1867, when his patent expired. For nearly thirteen years, Howe's royalties were estimated to average about $4,000 a week.

Although this dramatic improvement in his financial status meant that Howe could retire, he continued to tinker with his invention. During the Civil War, he used his fortune to underwrite the cost of a private regiment that he organized and maintained in Connecticut; he served as an enlistee while paying the cost of the unit's salaries, uniforms, and equipment. In 1863, along with his brother Amasa, he founded the Howe Machine Company in Bridgeport, Connecticut, to manufacture and sell sewing machines, putting himself in direct competition with Singer's company, the industry leader. One model made by Elias Howe at the Bridgeport factory was awarded a gold medal at the Paris Exhibition of 1867. The Howe Machine Company operated successfully for twenty years, until it was destroyed by fire in July 1883.

Howe died in Brooklyn, New York, leaving a legacy in public memory as "the inventor of the sewing machine." More accurately, he should be remembered as the first person to secure a U.S. patent on a sewing machine. The first two machines that he built are at the Smithsonian Institution in Washington, D.C.

• There is no known repository of Howe's papers. Accounts of his life and work are in Charles Greeley Abbot, *Great Inventions*, vol. 12 of the Smithsonian Scientific Series (1932); Waldemar Kaempffert, ed., *A Popular History of American Invention*, vol. 2 (1924); and George Iles, *Leading American Inventors* (1912). An account of Howe's life and work in Connecticut is included in Samuel Orcutt, *The History of the Old Town of Stratford and the City of Bridgeport* (1896). Obituaries are in the *New York Times* and the *New York Tribune*, both 5 Oct. 1867.

ANN T. KEENE

HOWE, Frederic Clemson (21 Nov. 1867–3 Aug. 1940), lawyer and reformer, was born in Meadville, Pennsylvania, the son of Andrew Jackson Howe, a furniture manufacturer, and Jane Clemson. He graduated with an A.B. from hometown Allegheny College in 1889, studied at the University of Halle in Germany, and received his Ph.D. from Johns Hopkins University in 1892 with a dissertation on the "History of the Internal Revenue System." He married Marie H. Jenney, a Unitarian minister, in 1904; they had no children.

Although Howe's ambition from boyhood was journalism, his failure to find a newspaper job after finishing his Ph.D. led him to switch to the law. After a year at New York Law School, he became secretary of the Pennsylvania Tax Commission and passed the bar examination. In 1894 he moved to Cleveland, Ohio, where he became associated with the law firm of Harry Garfield and James R. Garfield, the sons of the former president. A specialist on tax questions, he wrote the comprehensive *Taxation and Taxes in the United States under the Internal Revenue System 1791–1895* (1896).

Impelled by a gospel of service from his Methodist-Quaker family background, Howe was active in social settlement work in Cleveland. He was secretary of the city's good-government organization, the Municipal Association, and was elected in 1901 to a two-year term on the city council. Although elected as a Republican, he became a lieutenant of Democratic mayor Tom L. Johnson. Under Johnson's influence, Howe was converted to Henry George's (1839–1897) single-tax philosophy and championship of municipal ownership of public utilities, such as the streetcar lines. He studied cities in this country and abroad and published a series of books—starting with *The City: The Hope of Democracy* (1905)—setting forth his vision of economic, cultural, and moral improvement through municipal planning and an activist city government.

Howe was a member of the Ohio State Senate (1906–1908) and the Cleveland Board of Tax Assessors (1909–1910). Having become financially independent, Howe retired from his law practice in 1910 and moved to New York City. He was director for three years of the People's Institute, which carried on a program of educational and cultural activities aimed at the city's poor. He was part of the artistic and political ferment centered in Greenwich Village. In 1911 he became secretary of the National Progressive Republican League in support of the presidential bid of Wisconsin senator Robert M. La Follette (1855–1925), and he wrote an admiring account of La Follette's achievements in *Wisconsin, an Experiment in Democracy* (1912). After La Follette failed to win nomination, Howe, admiring neither Progressive Theodore Roosevelt (1858–1919) nor Republican William H. Taft, supported Democrat Woodrow Wilson for president in 1912. In 1914 Wilson appointed him commissioner of immigration for the Port of New York. In that post, he labored to humanize the treatment of immigrants and to protect the newcomers from exploitation.

Howe moved to the left politically during the Wilson years. He blamed World War I on economically motivated and upper-class-driven imperialist rivalries among the European powers. He joined with social philosopher John Dewey and reformer George L. Record in organizing the Association for an Equitable Federal Income Tax to push for higher taxes on the wealthy to pay for military preparedness. He attended the Paris Peace Conference in 1919 as a consultant on the eastern Mediterranean but was so disillusioned with what he thought was Wilson's betrayal of his anti-imperialist ideals that he attacked the League of Nations as "an international sanction to make permanent the conquests of the war."

Howe resigned his immigration commissionership in September 1919 rather than carry out the deportation of alien radicals in the postarmistice "red scare." He became executive director of the Conference on Democratic Railroad Control to promote the railroad brotherhoods' Plumb Plan for government ownership of the railroads. In *Denmark: A Cooperative Commonwealth* (1921), he extolled the Danish network of cooperatives as a democratic alternative to the wage system. In 1922 he was involved in the formation of the Conference for Progressive Political Action to mobilize the labor and farmer vote in that year's congressional elections. When the conference took the lead in launching the Progressive party in 1924, Howe was research assistant for the new party's presidential nominee, La Follette.

Howe published his autobiography, *The Confessions of a Reformer*, in 1925. In it he portrayed the small-town society in which he was reared—"a comfortable little world, Republican in politics, careful in conduct, Methodist in religion"—and his efforts to unlearn its values and prejudices. He was perceptive about the tensions within himself between his conscience and his attraction to the comforts and status that money and professional success offered. Politically he remained under the sway of the "evangelistic psychology" of his youth. He viewed the world in terms of moral absolutes—the people versus the privileged, producers versus nonproducers, good versus evil.

After 1924 Howe spent his winters traveling in Europe and summers running a self-styled "School of Opinion" on Nantucket Island, Massachusetts, at which reform-minded intellectuals and academics gathered for informal discussions. He supported Franklin D. Roosevelt for president in 1932 and was rewarded with appointment as consumer's counsel for the Agricultural Adjustment Administration (AAA). His efforts to organize consumers to resist food profiteers antagonized processors and distributors. In the reshuffle of the AAA in 1935, he was edged out of his post and given the token title of special adviser to the secretary of agriculture. In 1937 he became adviser to the Philippine government on farm tenancy and coop-

eratives. After his return to the United States he served as an expert consultant on agricultural commodities to the Temporary National Economic Committee set up in 1938 at Roosevelt's behest to investigate the problem of monopoly. He was finishing up a study of European banking when he died in Oak Bluffs, Massachusetts.

• Howe left no personal papers. His autobiography is at times vague on details and at other times suffers from lapses of memory. Howe was a prolific writer. In addition to works noted above, his books include: *The Confessions of a Monopolist* (1906), *The British City: The Beginnings of Democracy* (1907), *Privilege and Democracy in America* (1910), *European Cities at Work* (1913), *The Modern City and Its Problems* (1915), *Socialized Germany* (1915), *Why War* (1916), *The Only Possible Peace* (1919), and *Revolution and Democracy* (1921). Howe's life and career are discussed in Robert H. Bremner, "Honest Man's Story: Frederic C. Howe," one of several articles in the series "The Civic Revival in Ohio," *American Journal of Economics and Sociology* 8 (July 1949): 413–22, and John Braeman's "Introduction" to the Quadrangle Books reprint edition of *The Confessions of a Reformer* (1967).

JOHN BRAEMAN

HOWE, George (6 Nov. 1802–14 Apr. 1883), Presbyterian clergyman and professor, was born in Dedham, Massachusetts, the son of William Howe, a tavern owner and later a cotton mill superintendent, and Mary Gould. In 1822 he graduated with first honors from Middlebury College and entered Andover Theological Seminary, an institution established to combat the growing influence of Unitarianism in New England and to advocate a united front by orthodox Calvinists.

On graduating in 1825, Howe was appointed Abbott scholar of Andover, a position that allowed him to continue his theological studies. He was named the Phillips Professor of Sacred Theology at Dartmouth College in 1827. Sickness forced him to seek a warmer climate, and in 1830 he sailed for Charleston, South Carolina. He was invited to become the pastor of the First (Scots) Presbyterian Church in the city, but he accepted a call from the Presbyterian Synod of South Carolina and Georgia to be an instructor of oriental languages and literature at the newly established Presbyterian seminary in Columbia, South Carolina. In 1831 Howe married Mary Bushnell, the daughter of the Reverend Jedediah Bushnell of Cornwall, Vermont. The couple had no children. In 1832 he was inaugurated as professor of biblical literature at the seminary, a position he held until his death.

In 1836, four years after his first wife's death, Howe married the widow Sarah Ann Walthour McConnell of Walthourville, Georgia. They had six children, four of whom lived to maturity. With his wife Sarah, he owned several plantations in Liberty County, Georgia, and through her he was connected to a wide and influential web of southern families. He was, with his wife, a slave owner.

The year of his second marriage, Howe declined a professorship at Union Theological Seminary in New York City, declaring, "It appears still my duty to cast in my lot . . . with the people of the South, among whom I have made my home." He wrote that he had originally accepted the professorship at Columbia "with the hope that I might be the means of building up the wastes, and extending the borders, of our Southern Zion." Howe believed that though Columbia was small, "it is necessary, whatever be the fate of our beloved country, that this seminary should live" (Louis C. LaMotte, *Colored Light: The Story of the Influence of Columbia Theological Seminary, 1828–1936* [1937], all quotes in this paragraph from p. 43). Howe, while not the first professor, was the real founder of Columbia Theological Seminary. Columbia's institutional character followed the example of Andover and Princeton theological seminaries—a graduate professional institution with a full-time faculty, capital funds, a campus, a library, a resident student body, a board of trustees, and a three-year curriculum. The requirement of a bachelor of arts degree for entrance to Columbia was intended to ensure that its students had both the philosophical and linguistic background provided by a collegiate education and the general culture and manners taught in the colleges.

The three-year curriculum Howe introduced at Columbia was organized around three areas—philosophical theology; historical theology, which included biblical studies and church history; and practical theology, which included rhetoric and homiletics. Howe also served as seminary librarian and played a major role in securing the majority of the library of the Reverend Thomas Smyth of Charleston for the seminary. His reputation as a scholar helped to attract numerous theological students from New England and the Northeast to Columbia.

In 1844 Howe published *A Discourse on Theological Education*, in which he emphasized the importance of a critical hermeneutic for theological studies and the need for theological seminaries to nurture in their students a disciplined use of the mind. When he first moved to Columbia, his New England background caused some to wonder if he were influenced by the more liberal New School Presbyterian theology. However, by the time of the Old School–New School split of the Presbyterian church in 1837, he was firmly identified with the Old School position.

Howe was part of a circle of Presbyterian intellectuals in Columbia that included James Henley Thornwell, Benjamin Morgan Palmer, Joseph LeConte, and Louisa Cheves McCord. With Thornwell and Palmer, he established in 1847 the *Southern Presbyterian Review*, perhaps the most influential and certainly the most scholarly religious journal published in the South for the next thirty-eight years. Articles in the review were noted for their support of the religious instruction of slaves, for their advocacy of a moderate "middle way" in regard to politics, and for their opposition to the centralization of Presbyterian polity, especially as encouraged by Charles Hodge and Old School theologians associated with Princeton Theological Seminary.

Howe published sermons, eulogies, and addresses, in addition to numerous articles and reviews in the *Southern Presbyterian Review*. He is best remembered, however, for his two-volume *History of the Presbyterian Church in South Carolina* (1870–1883). The Synod of South Carolina had commissioned him in 1849 to write the history of Presbyterianism in that state, and he completed it in 1883 after extensive travel to archives as distant as Boston. The study, organized largely by decades, lacks grace but is a rich resource for students of South Carolina social and religious history. Of particular importance is his inclusion of early records that are no longer available and his careful recording of oral traditions.

Howe moved in conservative Whig and Unionist circles, although he did not often engage publicly in the political and social issues of his day. He did join those who denounced Louis Agassiz and the southern radicals who claimed a dual origin of the races. Agassiz and his supporters insisted on a dual origin of the races because, they said, the physical differences between the "negro and Caucasian" races were great and because one type always remains the same in nature. Howe supported two Charleston clergymen—Thomas Smyth and John Bachman—who wrote large volumes arguing for the unity of the races. Howe was an advocate for the evangelization of slaves and for reforms within the slave system that were suggested by his friend and sometime colleague Charles Colcock Jones, Sr. With the coming of the Civil War, Howe abandoned his Unionist position and became a strong supporter of the Confederate cause. His sons George and William served in the Confederate army.

Columbia Seminary and the Howe home escaped the fires that swept the city with the arrival of Union troops. Howe reopened the seminary in 1865 with faculty colleagues James Woodrow and John Adger. In that year he was elected moderator of the Southern Presbyterian church, the highest elected office in the denomination. He died in Columbia and was buried in the First Presbyterian Churchyard.

• Numerous letters from Howe are in Robert Manson Myers, ed., *Children of Pride: A True Story of Georgia and the Civil War* (1972). Myers's book also contains biographical sketches of Howe and many of his associates. William Childs Robinson, *Columbia Theological Seminary and the Southern Presbyterian Church, 1831–1931* (1931), provides insights into the character of Howe's leadership at Columbia. The social context for Howe's life and work and the intellectual world of which he was a part are given in Erskine Clarke, *Our Southern Zion: Calvinism in the South Carolina Low Country, 1690–1990* (1996). See also John L. Girardeau, "Eulogy on Professor George Howe," *Memorial Volume of the Semi-Centennial of the Theological Seminary at Columbia, South Carolina* (1884), and Ernest Trice Thompson, *Presbyterians in the South*, vols. 1 and 2 (1973). An obituary is in the (Charleston, S.C.) *News and Courier*, 16 Apr. 1883.

T. ERSKINE CLARKE

HOWE, George (17 June 1886–17 Apr. 1955), architect, was born in Worcester, Massachusetts, the son of James H. Howe, a gentleman from a prestigious and wealthy New England family, and Helen Fisher Bradford of Philadelphia. After James H. Howe's death, Helen Howe took her son to live in France, where he soon became fluent in French, German, and Italian. An encounter with John Stewardson of the venerable Philadelphia firm of Cope & Stewardson confirmed the idea in both mother and son that architecture should be Howe's chosen career path. After a few years in a boarding school in Switzerland, Howe returned with his mother to the United States, where he was soon enrolled in the prestigious Groton School. From Groton Howe went on to Harvard University, receiving his B.A. with an honorable mention in fine arts in 1907 and almost immediately thereafter marrying Marie Jessup Patterson of Philadelphia. (The couple later had two daughters.) Like many young American architectural students, he then journeyed back to Paris, where he entered the École des Beaux-Arts in the atelier of Victor Laloux in 1908.

Graduating in 1912, Howe decided to return to Philadelphia to settle with his mother's family nearby. Almost immediately he entered the office of Furness, Evans & Co., and in 1913 he was offered a partnership in the firm. By 1914 Howe was occupied with the design of his own house, "High Hollow," in Chestnut Hill, Philadelphia. In 1916, however, Howe decided to change firms, transferring his loyalty to Walter Mellor and Arthur I. Meigs and the firm of Mellor & Meigs. These younger men had already achieved a reputation in what was being called the "Pennsylvania School" with their colonial, Cotswold, and Tudor revival residential designs. Just as Howe was ready to join this firm, however, World War I broke out; and he left the United States to serve in the reserve corps of the Pennsylvania Hospital Medical Unit. He did not return until 1919.

The years following Howe's return to Mellor, Meigs & Howe were ones of considerable industry as the firm's national reputation for tasteful residential design increased. During these boom years the firm was awarded gold medals both locally, from the Philadelphia Chapter of the Architectural Institute of America, and in the New York exhibitions of the Architectural League. Their designs for the Robert McCracken House in Germantown, as well as the larger Newbold Estate property in Laverock, Pennsylvania, received considerable attention from local and national architectural presses. By the mid-1920s the firm was also engaged in the design and construction of Goodhart Hall on the Bryn Mawr College campus. Howe, unfortunately, was not comfortable with the kind of design with which the firm was identified, although his own work for the Philadelphia Savings Fund Society branch offices, really the only commercial work that the firm sustained, also demonstrated considerable reliance upon his Beaux-Arts training. In 1928 Howe resigned from the firm, taking the prestigious and lucrative Philadelphia Savings Fund Society account with him.

In the years that followed Howe characterized the work of Mellor, Meigs & Howe and those of their architectural persuasion as "Wall Street Pastorale," a style that was irrelevant to the modern industrial and commercial world. He actively engaged in the argument then current between so-called modernists and traditionalists regarding the proper styles for modern architecture, and he was a catalyst in the acceptance in the United States of the form of modernism known as the International Style. By 1930 Howe and Swiss architect William Lescaze, with whom he had formed a partnership in 1929, were engaged in creating an office tower for the Philadelphia Savings Fund Society, to stand at Twelfth and Market streets in Philadelphia. This building, with its first-floor retail space, second-floor banking offices, and speculative rental tower was at the center of controversy regarding the International Style, a descriptive term coined by Henry-Russell Hitchcock and Philip Johnson in their landmark "Modern Architecture: International Exhibition," held at the Museum of Modern Art in 1932. Lacking the traditional styles associated with bank buildings, the popular art deco and the modern classical designs of such Philadelphia architects as Paul P. Cret and John T. Windrim, the PSFS tower was constructed without visible references to past styles and the usual architectural ornament, prompting critic Douglas Haskell to label it "The Filing-Cabinet Building" in his 1932 article in *Creative Art*. Designs for this building appeared in the T-Square Club's *Journal*, as did an article by Howe titled "A Further Vague Pursuit of Truth in Architecture" (1 [Feb. 1931]: 13), and in 1931 the rendering and model for the PSFS Building were exhibited at the annual show of the Architectural League in New York. But by 1932, the year the building was completed, Howe & Lescaze had their three submissions, "A Skyscraper for New York," the Arthur Peck residence in Philadelphia, and a residence for William Burlee Curry in England, rejected by the Architectural League Exhibition Committee just at the time that their work was featured in Philip Johnson and Henry-Russell Hitchcock's show of modernism at the Museum of Modern Art.

Back in Philadelphia, controversy regarding the PSFS Building did not cease, but Howe continued to prosper. In 1930 he had assumed the role of president of the T-Square Club, and by 1932 he was financially supporting the journal *T-Square*, now independent of the club but still under the editorial leadership of Max Levinson. In April 1932 the name of the journal would change again, becoming *Shelter* and actively pursuing the controversial subject of what should be called "modern" in American architecture. In 1935 Howe and William Lescaze formally dissolved their firm.

By 1940 Howe had become involved with the problems of public housing, associating on the design of housing developments with Louis Kahn and Oscar Stonorov, but in 1942 Howe's career took yet another turn. In February of that year he was appointed supervising architect of the Public Buildings Administration. During his years associated with the federal government he was accorded the honor of being made a fellow of the American Institute of Architects, perhaps the first American modernist to achieve this status. Howe, nonetheless, was unhappy in Washington, D.C., and in 1945 he resigned from his post. In his later years he concentrated on education, serving as resident architect at the American Academy in Rome from 1947 until 1950, the year in which he was appointed chair for the Department of Architecture at Yale University. During his tenure at Yale, Howe was instrumental in bringing the services of Louis Kahn to play in the design of Yale's Art Gallery and in inaugurating *Perspecta: The Yale Architectural Journal*. After his retirement from Yale in 1954 Howe returned to Philadelphia and to his practice with Robert Montgomery Brown, a younger architect with whom he had been associated since 1939. During the 1950s the designs for the WCAU television station on City Line Avenue in Philadelphia (1952) and for the Evening Bulletin Building at Thirtieth and Market streets (1954–1955) were completed. In his final years in Philadelphia Howe was engaged in the controversial battle for the design of Penn Center, the area around Philadelphia City Hall, a battle that he undertook alongside Edmund Bacon, then chair of the Philadelphia Planning Commission. Equally controversial was his involvement with plans for Independence Mall Historical Park. Voicing the unpopular and eventually unsuccessful view that the nineteenth-century buildings adjacent to the Independence Mall should be saved, in 1955 Howe spoke out against the imposition of a Colonial style on surrounding buildings. His voice was unheeded, and such landmarks as Frank Furness's Guarantee Trust and National Bank of the Republic were lost. When he died in Philadelphia, Howe was still involved in architectural education; he was engaged, along with G. Holmes Perkins, to establish an architectural school under the auspices of UNESCO in Turkey.

As a modern architect, architectural educator, and city planner, George Howe occupied a pivotal role in the acceptance of the International Style in the United States. He was a leader in his profession, lecturing and writing about the changing practice of architecture in the early to mid-twentieth century. Furthermore, according to biographer Robert A. M. Stern, he was a member of that important group of architects who have become known as the Philadelphia School, a group beginning with Frank Furness and proceeding to Louis I. Kahn and eventually Robert Venturi.

• Architectural records for Mellor, Meigs & Howe can be found at the Athenaeum of Philadelphia and the University of Pennsylvania Architectural Archives. Other records documenting the work of George Howe are in the Avery Architectural Library, Columbia University, and at Yale University. PSFS archives are now housed at Hagley-Eleutherian Mills. For a complete biographical treatment of Howe as well as a comprehensive approach to bibliography regarding Howe, the buildings that he designed, and the organizations in which he was a member, see Robert A. M. Stern, *George Howe: Toward a Modern American Architecture* (1975). For a more complete list of works to 1930, see S. L. Tatman and Roger W. Moss, *Biographical Dictionary of Philadelphia Architects* (1985).

Sandra Tatman

HOWE, George Augustus (1724–6 July 1758), British general, was born in Langar, Nottingham, England, the son of Emanuel Scrope Howe, second Viscount Howe of the Irish peerage and a royal governor of Barbados, and Maria Sophia Charlotte, daughter of Baron von Kielmansegge. In 1735 he succeeded to the title of third Viscount Howe and twelve years later was elected to his father's seat in Parliament as representative of Nottingham borough. Choosing the army as a career, Howe entered the Grenadier Guards in 1745 as an ensign. He rose rapidly through the ranks because he was supported by patrons but also because he was an unusually able soldier with a particularly appealing personality. In 1746 he was promoted captain, and during the War of the Austrian Succession served for two years as an aide-de-camp to the Duke of Cumberland. He also fought in the battle of Laufeldt. In 1749, a year after the war concluded, he achieved the rank of lieutenant colonel. During his military service on the continent, Howe acquired a reputation as one of the ablest young soldiers in the British army, destined for great things because of his ability and natural charm.

In 1757, during the Seven Years' War, Howe was given command of the 3d Battalion of the 60th Regiment, the Royal Americans, and ordered to America. In July he arrived at Halifax, Nova Scotia, bearing a letter from the duke of Cumberland to John Campbell, earl of Loudoun, commander in chief in America, recommending Howe as "an intelligent, capable & willing officer" who was highly qualified "to command one of the *Batts.* that will be employ'd upon Servies." Loudoun and his second in command, James Abercromby, quickly came to agree with Cumberland's assessment, and both men began to rely upon their subordinate for a wide range of services. Proceeding on to Fort Edward where his troops were located, Howe joined Major General Daniel Webb. Shortly thereafter he was advanced to the permanent rank of colonel and given command of the 55th Regiment. In November he led a detachment to German Flats, where the French were attacking, but arrived too late to render assistance. The following month Loudoun ordered him to conduct winter operations against Forts Crown Point and Ticonderoga, but his inability to secure snowshoes, in addition to other problems and impediments, finally ended that project. Meantime, he immersed himself in a study of the peculiarities of frontier warfare, paying particular attention to the tactical innovations of Robert Rogers, a ranger. He also worked to improve the personal appearance of his soldiers and encouraged his officers to dress and eat in the same style as the privates. Because of these reforms he was idolized by his men.

In March 1758 Howe learned that William Pitt had recalled Loudoun, appointed Abercromby commander in chief, and elevated Howe to second in command with the rank of brigadier general. Pitt ordered Abercromby and Howe to carry out a major expedition against Canada during the summer of 1758, proceeding by way of Lakes George and Champlain and capturing Fort Ticonderoga on the way. By 4 July the army of 16,000 men was organized. On that day it embarked in 900 bateaux, 135 whale boats, and rafts carrying 40 artillery pieces and proceeded down Lake George toward Ticonderoga. On the night of 5–6 July, the army landed on the west side of the lake a few miles from the fort, where to the considerable consternation of the British commanders they learned that the French had constructed formidable defenses across the only approaches to the bastion. These defenses, consisting of strong entrenchments in front of which was an abatis of parallel tree trunks with sharpened branches pointing toward the enemy, were constructed to a depth of one hundred yards. Nevertheless, the French were in a precarious position, for they were outnumbered five to one; also, Abercromby had forty cannons that he might place on lofty Mount Defiance, a hill commanding the fort, and compel their surrender or retreat.

Early on 6 July Howe set out at the head of one column of British troops, while Abercromby commanded another, to approach Fort Ticonderoga. As they marched forward Howe's column suddenly collided with an enemy reconnaissance force, which it soon routed, killing 100 Frenchmen and taking another 150 prisoners. But the British had lost 87 troopers killed and 230 wounded. Among the slain was Lord Howe, "the soul of General Abercromby's army," according to Thomas Mante, a contemporary historian. On 8 July the commander in chief tried a disastrous assault against the French defenses rather than emplacing his cannon upon Mount Defiance and making the fort uninhabitable. After suffering enormous casualties, Abercromby was compelled to withdraw up Lake George, and in 1759 he was replaced by Jeffery Amherst.

As the army retreated, it bore Lord Howe's body back to Albany, where he was interred in St. Peter's Church. But the popular officer was not forgotten by Americans. Four years after his death, he was paid a unique tribute by the general court of Massachusetts, which appropriated £250 for the erection of a monument to his memory in Westminster Abbey. He never married and had no children. His brother, Richard Howe, succeeded him as fourth Viscount Howe and went on to fame as a talented British admiral. Another brother, William Howe, was a somewhat less successful army officer. Ironically, in light of the adulation that colonial Americans showered on the third Viscount Howe, both Richard and William Howe found themselves seventeen years later propelled by the vicissitudes of fate and politics into a fight against Americans during the Revolutionary War.

• References to Howe are found in the Abercromby and Loudoun papers in the Henry E. Huntington Library, San Marino, Calif. Important information on his career is also in Gertrude Selwyn Kimball, ed., *Correspondence of William Pitt When Secretary of State with Colonial Governors and Military and Naval Commissioners in America* (2 vols., 1906); Stanley Pargellis, ed., *Military Affairs in North America, 1748–1765: Selected Documents from the Cumberland Papers in Windsor Castle* (1936); Alfred Proctor James, ed., *Writings of General John Forbes, Relating to His Service in North America* (1938); and E. B. O'Callaghan, ed., *Documents Relative to the Colonial History of the State of New York . . .*, vol. 9 (1858). See also Robert Rogers, *Journals . . .* (1765). Background information on the Howe family is in Ira D. Gruber, *The Howe Brothers and the American Revolution* (1972). Howe's American service is discussed and evaluated in Thomas Mante, *The History of the Late War in North-America . . .* (1772); Lawrence Henry Gipson, *The British Empire before the American Revolution*, vol. 7 (1949); Howard H. Peckham, *The Colonial Wars, 1689–1762* (1964); and Douglas Edward Leach, *Arms for Empire: A Military History of the British Colonies in North America, 1607–1763* (1973).

PAUL DAVID NELSON

HOWE, Helen (11 Jan. 1905–1 Feb. 1975), writer and monologuist, was born in Boston, Massachusetts, the daughter of Mark Antony De Wolfe Howe, a writer, and Fanny Huntington Quincy, also a writer. Though the children did not want to listen, their father tried to read poetry to them on Sunday afternoons. Helen and her brothers preferred the times he sat at the piano to lead them in hymn sings. The family also participated together in tennis, sailing, swimming, and clambakes. Howe was so attached to her parents that, when they sent her to a boarding school only twelve miles away, she became homesick and stayed in bed three days. She graduated from Milton Academy in 1922, after which she attended Radcliffe College for one year only (1923–1924). At Radcliffe, she acted in college plays and decided to work and study toward becoming an actress. Her favorite authors were Jane Austen, Charles Dickens, Henry James, and Marcel Proust.

Howe's desire to act led her to emulate Ruth Draper and Cornelia Otis Skinner, who were pioneer monologuists. Howe made her debut as a monologuist in 1933 after ten years of study, and she wrote all of her own scripts, which were character sketches. She played one-woman shows in forty-five states, in theaters in London and New York, and in supper clubs; a favorite, repeat performance was at the Blue Angel nightclub in New York. She was invited twice to perform at the White House. She enjoyed reading and telling fairy stories to underprivileged children at a recreation center in New York.

When she began writing, Howe said she was the only member of her family not to have published a book. Her father had over forty books to his credit, most of them biographies. Her brother Quincy Howe, a radio commentator, was also a writer, and her other brother Mark DeWolfe Howe, was a professor at Harvard Law School and editor of two books of Holmes letters. Her mother wrote several volumes of literary essays and contributed regularly and anonymously to the *Atlantic Monthly*.

Reviews of Howe's *Whole Heart* (1943), published by Simon and Schuster, included such phrases as "outstanding woman's novel" and "remarkable first novel, funny, shrewd, sinister." Her second book, *We Happy Few* (1946), was about a group of Harvard professors and their families in the 1940s and 1950s. A *New York Times* critic praised it as "satirizing intellect and snobbery, hot-house preciousness, and elaborate personalities," and Bernard DeVoto thought that her skill had increased. *The Circle of the Day* (1950) first appeared in a woman's magazine and was a monthly selection of the Literary Guild. Howe chose to describe a day in the life of a woman on her tenth wedding anniversary. The protagonist had to decide what to do about her unfaithful husband. The *Christian Science Monitor* described her novel as "tight, unified, satisfying." The novel *The Success* was published in 1956. Her last two books, *Fires of Autumn* (1959), a biography, and *The Gentle Americans* (1965), a biography of her father, were published by Harper. In the last book, Howe described old Boston social life and her father's friendships with Alfred North Whitehead, Justice Felix Frankfurter, Robert Frost, Van Wyck Brooks, and John Marquand. The elder Howe had also known William and Henry James, Sara Orne Jewett, and Julia Ward Howe.

A Democrat and an Episcopalian, Helen Howe married Alfred Reginald Allen, then a curator of a library collection, on 31 May 1946. They moved from New York to Hollywood, where Allen was the West Coast representative for the J. Arthur Rank Organization. When they returned to New York, where he was the assistant manager of the Metropolitan Opera Company, they bought a vacation home in Somesville, Maine, on Mount Desert Island. A petite woman, Howe liked to sail, climb, and walk her dogs. After her death she was interred in the Mount Wollaston Cemetery in Quincy, Massachusetts.

Perhaps one reason Howe's books are not read today may lie in a criticism that appeared in the *Atlantic Monthly*: "She doesn't trust herself as a novelist, and she depends on her ability as a monologuist." Another may be that she allowed herself to be called a woman's novelist.

• A source for personal information is Helen Howe's *The Gentle Americans: Biography of a Breed* (1965). See also Durward Howes, ed., *American Women, 1935–1940* (1981). Obituaries are in the *New York Times*, 2 Feb. 1975, and the *Washington Post*, 3 Feb. 1975.

SUE LASLIE KIMBALL

HOWE, Henry Marion (2 Mar. 1848–14 May 1922), metallurgist, was born in Boston, Massachusetts, the son of Samuel Gridley Howe, a physician, historian of the Greek revolution, and founder of the Perkins Institution for the Blind, and Julia Ward, a poet best known for her composition of the lyrics of "The Battle Hymn of the Republic." Like many children of Boston's elite, Howe received a classical education and attended Harvard College, where he took a bachelor's degree in 1869. Less typical was his decision to follow up on these studies by enrolling in a small technological institute that had recently opened in Boston, the Massachusetts Institute of Technology, where he completed a second bachelor's degree, in geology and mining engineering. After graduating in 1871, Howe traveled to Troy, New York, site of one of the first Bessemer steelworks in the United States, apparently to obtain the experience with equipment and workers that no school could offer. Thus initiated, Howe entered a field that was in the midst of an unprecedented boom. Despite his youth and modest experience, he quickly found employment as a plant superintendent, first for the Joliet Iron and Steel Company and then for the Blair Iron & Steel Works of Pittsburgh. Confident that he had found a career, Howe married Fannie Gay of Troy in 1874 and took his bride on an extended European tour. The couple had no children.

Howe was not alone in recognizing opportunity in the iron and steel industry. After returning to the United States early in 1876, he found "the market fearfully overstocked with young metallurgists and chemists." He wrote a friend in California, "Do you know of any chance for a metallurgical chemist to earn his salt in your region whether by teaching chemistry, mathematics, physics, metallurgy, or geology, by analyzing, by assisting a professor or chemist or manager of works, by starting a manufacturing works or by any other means? If you do, I am your man." Eventually, in late 1876 or 1877, he did find work, not in iron and steel, where his experience lay, but in copper. In quick succession, he served as a works engineer in Chile in 1877, designed and built smelting plants in New Jersey and Quebec (1879–1882), and became manager of the Pima Copper Mining & Smelting Company of Arizona (1882).

Howe's *wanderjahren* afforded him a superb training in metallurgy, both ferrous and nonferrous. The hardships of work in remote areas and the day-in, day-out responsibilities of management, however, did not long prove congenial. In 1883 he accepted a lectureship in metallurgy at MIT that offered him opportunities both to write and to develop a consulting practice. Drawing on his extensive experience, he published a monograph, *Copper Smelting* (1885), undertook short-term consulting assignments, and became a partner in the Taylor Iron and Steel Company, a manufacturer of steels for armor-piercing projectiles and other special purposes.

More important, both for Howe's career and his science, he used the freedom afforded by his position to undertake a thorough exploration of new ideas and techniques that were beginning to make their way into metallurgy in the 1880s. Europeans, especially Floris Osmond and William Roberts-Austen, were beginning to make good use of the microscope to study the fine structure of metals. Such examination revealed great complexity and changes in grain shape, size, and distribution as metals underwent mechanical and heat treatment. Others, most notably Henry Le Châtelier, were improving techniques for controlling and measuring high temperatures. With devices such as the thermocouple pyrometer it became possible to detect arrests in the rate at which alloys cooled. These arrests, caused by the liberation of heat, marked changes in phase that often could be associated with changes in microstructure. At the same time physical chemists Jacobus van't Hoff and H. W. B. Roozeboom were developing conceptual tools, especially a theory of solutions and chemical thermodynamics, that would prove useful in analyzing thermal data. These developments, packed tightly into the 1880s, yielded new understanding of traditional craft practices such as annealing and quenching. They also generated intense controversies over the relative importance of microstructure and chemical composition in explaining the physical properties of iron, steel, and other metals.

Although Howe made only modest contributions to the experimental science of this period, he was a masterful expositor and synthesizer. His *Metallurgy of Steel* (1890) was among the first books to integrate the research of the 1880s and relate it to industrial practice. Making abundant use of illustrations and equilibrium diagrams, but little use of mathematics, Howe skillfully led readers by modest steps into the central issues of his subject. Students and practicing metallurgists were delighted by Howe's lucid prose and constant attention to practical problems; researchers in the United States and abroad valued his judicious exploration of the most recent science. The book established Howe as one of the world's leading authorities on iron and steel.

In 1897 Howe became head of the department of metallurgy at the School of Mines of Columbia University, a position in which he remained until 1908, when he withdrew from administrative duties to concentrate on his research and writing. Howe's impact on the School of Mines was considerable. He had a shrewd sense of his subject and a discriminating eye for young talent, and his international reputation gave him the leverage to exercise these skills. He supervised the equipping of new facilities in metallurgy when the School of Mines relocated from Forty-ninth Street to Morningside Heights, expanded the faculty and course offerings of his department, and helped make Columbia a center for metallurgical research with few rivals in the United States. Howe's influence extended beyond his own tenure in the department, most especially through his protégé, William Campbell, an Englishman who attended Columbia to study under Howe and later occupied a chair named in Howe's honor.

As was customary for engineers in academia, Howe maintained an active consulting practice during his years at Columbia. He estimated the value of copper mines for investors, evaluated new technologies for concentrating ores, advised clients on the design of smelters and metal fabrication plants, and identified the causes of mysterious failures in wheels, rails, and other products. His broad experience, clarity of expression, and reputation for probity made him a much sought-after "expert witness" in patent litigation. Howe enrolled students and colleagues in these projects as assistants and associates; in so doing he helped propagate his conviction that an understanding of the fundamental principles of metallurgy would grow best when coupled with practical experience in industrial practice.

Howe retired from teaching and most of his industrial commitments in 1913, although he served in the engineering division of the National Research Council during World War I and, later, as a consulting metallurgist to both the Bureau of Standards and the Bureau of Mines. Working with a paid assistant at "Green Peace," his home in Bedford Hills, New York, Howe continued to pursue his passion for steel, sometimes trading advice for equipment and materials for his personal laboratory. He died in Bedford Hills.

Howe was widely recognized during his lifetime as the dean of American metallurgists. He served as president of the American Institute of Mining Engineers in 1893 and president of the American Society for Testing Materials from 1900 to 1902 and again from 1909 to 1912. Howe received medals from a half-dozen professional organizations at home and abroad, including the Bessemer Medal of the Iron and Steel Institute of Great Britain and the John Fritz Medal of the American Institute of Mining Engineers. Howe commanded wide respect in both industrial and academic circles in Europe, in part through the translations of his books into French and Russian. In recognition of his contributions, he was made a knight of the Order of St. Stanislaus of Russia and a chevalier of the French Legion of Honor.

An influential teacher, accomplished engineer, and gifted writer, Howe's major contribution was as mediator between industrial practice and the emerging science of metals. He showed, by precept and example, how industrial research could sharpen and focus scientific inquiry and how academic research could illuminate traditional methods for producing and working metals.

• The modest collection of Howe's papers in the University Archives of Columbia University contains copies of some of his consulting reports, courtroom testimony, and professional correspondence. Howe described his search for a job in a letter of 6 Sept. 1876 to George Ferdinand Becker, located in Box 15 of the Becker papers at the Library of Congress. Howe's other principal writings include *Iron, Steel, and Other Alloys* (1903) and *The Metallography of Steel and Cast Iron* (1916). A useful biographical sketch of Howe is George K. Burgess, "Henry Marion Howe," in National Academy of Sciences, *Biographical Memoirs* 21 (1926); it includes a partial bibliography of Howe's publications. Of lesser value is Arthur L. Walker, "Henry Marion Howe," *School of Mines Quarterly* 34 (1913): 301–4. Maxwell Gensamer, "Henry Marion Howe's Contributions to Metallurgy," in *The Sorby Centennial Symposium on the History of Metallurgy*, ed. Cyril Stanley Smith (1965), pp. 59–66, offers valuable insights into Howe's research. Also see Smith, *History of Metallography* (1960), and R. F. Mehl, *A Brief History of the Science of Metals* (1948), on the historical context of Howe's work on iron and steel.

JOHN W. SERVOS

HOWE, Irving (11 June 1920–5 May 1993), literary critic and historian, was born in New York City, the son of David Howe and Nettie Goldman, grocery store operators and later garment workers. Irving Howe was married twice, first to Arien Hausknecht, with whom he had two children, and later to Ilana Wiener.

Howe became a socialist at fourteen, joining a faction led by Leon Trotsky. He graduated from City College of New York in 1940, claiming that he spent more time talking to fellow radicals than he spent in class. He completed a year and a half of graduate study at Brooklyn College before being drafted into the army in 1942; he served in Alaska for two or three years. When he returned to New York after the war, he began to publish articles in the *Partisan Review*, *Commentary*, and the *Nation*. In 1953 he founded *Dissent*, a political and literary journal that he edited for many years. In that year he became an associate professor of English at Brandeis University and also was appointed a *Kenyon Review* fellow. Leaving Brandeis in 1961, he spent 1961 to 1963 as a professor of English at Stanford University. From 1963 to 1970 he was professor of English at Hunter College of the City University of New York, where he was named in 1970 Distinguished Professor of English.

Howe wrote or contributed to more than forty books, the most noteworthy of which are works of literary criticism. His first study, *Sherwood Anderson* (1952), was an analysis of Anderson's work and a rebuttal of Lionel Trilling's assault on the realist movement in modern literature. Howe reveals himself as a capable historian in his portrait of Anderson's childhood in Ohio, and he is charitable in dealing with Anderson's indistinctness and sentimentality. Howe's next book, *William Faulkner: A Critical Study* (1952), provides a sensible and balanced preface to Faulkner. Another high point of Howe's literary career is *Thomas Hardy: A Critical Study* (1967), particularly his interpretation of Hardy's *Jude the Obscure*.

Howe's political writing includes a wide variety of subjects: *Politics and the Novel* (1957); *The Critical Point: On Literature and Culture* (1973); *Trotsky* (1978); and *The American Newness: Culture and Politics in the Age of Emerson* (1986). Based on three lectures on Emerson that Howe gave at Harvard University in 1985, *The American Newness* reflects his earlier optimism and pays tribute to some of his heroes such as Marx, Trotsky, and Ben-Gurion. One of Howe's most enduring pieces is an essay published in *Commentary* in 1968, "The New York Intellectuals." It is a history of Howe's circle of associates in which he describes the radical experience, including nontraditional attitudes and Communist sympathies, and the immigrant Jewish experience.

Howe edited, along with Yiddish poet and translator Eliezer Greenberg, several important anthologies of Yiddish writing in English translation, including *A Treasury of Yiddish Poetry* (1969) and *World of Our Fathers: The Journey of the Eastern European Jews to America and the Life They Found and Made* (1976), the latter coauthored with Kenneth Libo. *World of Our Fathers* describes Eastern European Jewish society of the late 1800s and early 1900s in New York City; it realized an unusual popular success, and in 1977 Howe was awarded the National Book Award for it. Howe received the Longview Foundation prize for literary criticism, the Bollingen Award (1959–1960), the National Institute of Arts and Letters Award (1960), Guggenheim fellowships (1964–1965, 1971), the Jewish Heritage Award (1975), and the Brandeis University Creative Arts Award (1975–1976). He died in New York City.

• Howe's interests were varied. He wrote or edited a number of books about politics, including *The American Communist Party: A Critical History, 1919–1957* (1957); *Steady Work: Essays in the Politics of Democratic Radicalism, 1953–1966* (1966); *Essential Works of Socialism* (1970); and *Socialism and America* (1985). Howe, however, is probably better known for his literary criticism. In addition to those works already mentioned, his books include *Modern Literary Criticism: An Anthology* (1958); *Edith Wharton: A Collection of Critical Essays* (1962); "*Nineteen Eighty-four*": *Text Sources, Criticism* (1963); *Saul Bellow's Herzog: Text and Criticism* (1976); and *The Portable Kipling* (1982). Howe's books also cover Yiddish literature, such as *Jewish-American Stories* (1977); *The Best of Sholom Aleichem* (1979); and, with Ilana Wiener, *Short Shorts: An Anthology of the Shortest Stories* (1982). In addition to poetry and short stories, he edited *Voices from the Yiddish: Essays, Memoirs, Diaries* (1972). His obituary is in the *New York Times*, 6 May 1993.

SHIRLEY LAIRD

HOWE, James Lewis (4 Aug. 1859–20 Dec. 1955), chemist and bibliographer of the platinum metals, was born in Newburyport, Massachusetts, the son of Francis Augustine Howe, a physician, and Mary Frances Lewis. The Howe family was noted for its progressive and liberal outlook. Howe originally intended to become a physician like his father, but during high school in Newburyport he became interested in chemistry. He received his B.A. degree in 1880 from Amherst College, his father's alma mater.

As was then customary, Howe went to Germany after graduation to complete his studies. From 1880 to 1882 he studied at the Universität Göttingen under Hans Hübner, J. Post, and the legendary Friedrich Wöhler. In 1882 he was awarded his Ph.D. with the dissertation "On Ethyl Derivatives of Anhydrobenzdiamidobenzene and Its Nitrile" ("Ueber die Aethylderivate des Anhydrobenzdiamidobenzols und über ein Nitril desselben"), carried out under Hübner's direction. Published as two short, separate papers, they constitute both his first publications and his only works in organic chemistry. On his return to the United States, Howe became instructor of science at Brooks Military Academy, Cleveland, Ohio (1882–1883); professor of chemistry (later of physics and geology as well) at Central College, Richmond, Kentucky (1883–1894); and finally in 1894 professor of chemistry and head of the chemistry department at Washington and Lee University, Lexington, Virginia, one of the South's leading liberal arts colleges for men, where he remained for almost half a century. In December 1883, Howe married Henrietta Leavenworth Marvine of Scranton, Pennsylvania. The couple had three children, one of whom, James Lewis, Jr., became a chemist. In 1886 Howe received an honorary M.D. from the Hospital College of Medicine in Louisville, Kentucky, where he was professor of medical chemistry and toxicology.

Nothing in Howe's background indicated that he would go against the mainstream of the time and leave organic chemistry, which was at the zenith of its development while inorganic chemistry languished in the doldrums. Then, at a meeting of the American Association for the Advancement of Science, he happened to mention to Frank Wigglesworth Clarke, the eminent geochemist, that he was looking for a new research topic. Clarke told him that he could not understand why chemists persisted in devoting themselves so exclusively to carbon, an element with so few oxidation states, when so much more real chemistry could be learned from the elements of the platinum group, some of which possess as many as eight different oxidation states. This chance remark made a deep impression on Howe, who began eagerly to read the literature of the platinum metals. Within a remarkably short time, Howe became not only the outstanding American authority on and bibliographer of the platinum metals in general but also the undisputed world authority on the chemistry of ruthenium, one of the least known platinum metals, in particular.

Despite his fundamental research on the chemistry of ruthenium, Howe's *magnum opus* is his *Bibliography of the Metals of the Platinum Group*, which covers the literature from 1748, when platinum was first described, to the end of 1950. This monumental bibliography was cited as the major basis on which he was awarded in 1937 the American Chemical Society, Georgia Section's Charles H. Herty Medal for the advancement of science in the southern states. Professor M. Guy Mellon of Purdue University, long a recognized authority on the literature of chemistry, referred to Howe's work as an ideal bibliography.

Howe completed the first volume of his bibliography (covering 1748–1896) less than three years after publishing his first research paper on ruthenium, a remarkable achievement in view of the painstaking and meticulous care expended in its compilation. It contains 2,438 separate entries by more than 1,300 authors. Many of these entries contain more than one reference citation, some as many as two dozen. Dissertations as well as journal articles are included, and many entries contain citations of reviews and abstracts of articles. Howe's bibliography and his position as the leading American authority on the platinum metals led to his appointment in 1917 as chairman of a special subcommittee on platinum of the National Research Council, and he received three presidential appointments to commissions for assaying the coinage of the United States.

A member of and participant in many professional and honorary organizations, Howe also engaged in numerous civic and fraternal activities. He was active in the Presbyterian church and ranked religion equal to science in his life. Although he retired from teaching in 1938, he continued to work on his bibliography. During World War II he was recalled from retirement to teach chemistry and German. He retired for a second time in 1946. At the time of his death in Lexington, Virginia, Howe was one of the American Chemical Society's oldest members. A transitional figure in chemistry, he was born one year after German chemist Kekule von Stradonitz proposed the self-linking of carbon atoms, yet he lived to witness the hydrogen bomb.

• Howe was the author of two textbooks, *Inorganic Chemistry according to Periodic Law* (1898), with Francis P. Venable, and *Inorganic Chemistry for Schools and Colleges* (1907; 2d ed., 1920). His major work appeared in several parts as *Bibliography of the Metals of the Platinum Group: Platinum, Palladium, Iridium, Rhodium, Osmium, Ruthenium, 1748–1896*, in *Smithsonian Miscellaneous Collections* 38, part 6, no. 1084 (1897); *Bibliography of the Metals of the Platinum Group: Platinum, Palladium, Iridium, Rhodium, Osmium, Ruthenium, 1748–1917*, in *Bulletin of the U.S. Geological Survey*, no. 694 (1919), comp. with H. C. Holtz; *Bibliography of the Platinum Metals 1918–1930* (1947), comp. with the staff of Baker and Co.; *Bibliography of the Platinum Metals 1931–1940* (1949); and *Bibliography of the Platinum Metals 1941–1950* (1956). For discussions of Howe's life and work see George B. Kauffman, "Platinum Metal Pioneer: James Lewis Howe (1859–1955)," *Journal of Chemical Education* 45 (1968): 804–11, and "The Work of James Lewis Howe: Bibliographer of the Platinum Group Metals," *Platinum Metals Review* 16 (1972): 140–44. Obituaries are in the *Lexington* (Va.) *Gazzette*, 21 Dec. 1955; the Washington and Lee University *Alumni Magazine*, Jan. 1956; and *Chemical and Engineering News*, 30 Jan. 1956.

GEORGE B. KAUFFMAN

HOWE, James Wong (28 Aug. 1899–12 July 1976), motion picture cinematographer, was born Wong Tung Jim How in Kwantung (Canton), China, the son of Wong How. His mother's name is unknown. He moved to the United States in 1904 to join his father and his stepmother (who had immigrated months after his birth) and was raised in Pasco, Washington. His name was changed to James Wong Howe on his first day at school. His father died in 1914, and the family general store business failed. Howe left and moved to Ferndale, Oregon, where he attended high school and worked for a friend of his late father's, Smith O'Brian.

Soon thereafter Howe quit school and moved to live with an uncle in Astoria, Oregon. There he became a professional boxer, fighting in clubs in and around Portland, Oregon. Moving once again, this time to San Francisco, he struck out on his own and became a delivery boy for a commercial photographer. He ceased his journeys in either 1916 or 1917, when he moved to the environs of Los Angeles, working as a bellhop at hotels in Pasadena and Beverly Hills.

It was from this southern California base that Howe entered the movie business in 1917. Although few took him seriously, he quickly graduated from editing assistant to assistant cameraman for Cecil B. DeMille. Howe's break came with DeMille's *Male and Female*

(1919), when he was drafted as a camera operator for a scene that required multiple simultaneous shots of the same action.

Known as "James Howe," by 1922 he had moved up the ranks from assistant to principal cinematographer, gaining a reputation as an efficient and meticulous master of lighting. By the mid-1920s, despite some heckling about his five-foot stature, Howe had earned a reputation as an efficient studio worker. His most noted silent film credits include *Peter Pan* (1924), *Mantrap* (1926), and *The Rough Riders* (1927). Despite a number of instances of outright prejudice against him as an Asian American, Howe earned an early degree of fame for his exquisite, careful lighting of the eyes of actresses, in particular Mary Miles Mintner. Later he would photograph and help glamorize such stars as Marlene Dietrich, Myrna Loy, Joan Crawford, and Loretta Young.

In film industry circles during the 1930s Howe was known as "Low-key Howe" for his penchant for cinematography with little light. For *Transatlantic* (1931) Howe utilized wide-angle lenses, deep-focus lighting, and a deep space style, a decade before Orson Welles and Gregg Toland made that look world famous in *Citizen Kane* (1941).

In the 1930s the MGM publicity department "changed" his name to James Wong Howe to connote an image of exoticism. Howe fashioned *The Criminal Code* (1931), *The Power and the Glory* (1933), *The Thin Man* (1934), *Manhattan Melodrama* (1934), *The Prisoner of Zenda* (1937), *The Adventures of Tom Sawyer* (1938; his first film in Technicolor), and *Algiers* (1938), which earned him his first Academy Award nomination.

By the early 1940s Howe was one of the most famous Hollywood cinematographers, commanding a salary of $500,000 per week. Howe's signature style was acknowledged in the twenty-six films he made for Warner Bros. between 1938 through 1947, including *Dr. Ehrlich's Magic Bullet* (1941), *Strawberry Blonde* (1942), *King's Row* (1942), *Yankee Doodle Dandy* (1942), and *Objective Burma!* (1945). Howe experimented with hand-held cameras. For *Body and Soul* (1947), a boxing drama, he got into the ring on roller skates and rolled around as the actors fought. And in *He Ran All the Way* (1951) Howe strapped a camera to himself, jumped in a pool, and captured the drama of a swimming event. In time Howe became known even to general film fans—one of a handful of cinematographers ever actually followed by the moviegoing public.

Racial prejudice always dogged Howe. To escape anti-Japanese prejudice during the Second World War he took to wearing a pin that proclaimed: "I am Chinese." When he married novelist Sanora Babb, a white woman, in 1949, they had to obtain a license outside Los Angeles County, where laws against miscegenation were strictly enforced. The marriage was childless.

In 1948 Howe began work in China on the background for a film to be titled *Rickshaw Boy*, but the project was never completed because of the Red Chinese takeover of mainland China. This work in China caused Howe to be investigated by the House Un-American Activities Committee in the early 1950s, which, coupled with his close association with John Garfield, Robert Rossen, and a number of other Warner Bros. employees, led to Howe having a difficult time finding work in the era of blacklisting in the 1950s.

Howe survived this ordeal, and in the late 1950s and 1960s he reached the height of his cinematic powers. The visual beauty of *The Sweet Smell of Success* (1957), *Bell, Book, and Candle* (1959), and *Seconds* (1966) can only be described as stunning. He also completed a small amount of television work during that same period, including several episodes of "Checkmate," a number of documentaries, and ads for Texaco and Eastern Airlines.

Throughout his life Howe harbored ambitions of being a director, but Hollywood producers were satisfied with his role as ace cinematographer. Howe's lone solo directing credit was for the story of the Harlem Globetrotters basketball team in *Go, Man, Go* (1954); with John Sledge he co-directed *The Invisible Avenger* in 1958. It is reported that he produced, directed, and photographed a Japanese-language film (title unknown) to specialized markets in the United States during the early 1930s. The film was never completed, but the footage was used for Josef von Sternberg's *Shanghai Express* (1932).

In his more than fifty years behind the camera Howe was nominated for sixteen Academy Awards, earning Oscars for *The Rose Tattoo* (1955) and *Hud* (1963). In his day Howe worked with a number of the best filmmakers the cinema offered: Howard Hawks, Victor Sjostrom, Busby Berkeley, William Dieterle, Raoul Walsh, Fritz Lang, and Sam Fuller. He was one of the greatest cinematographers in the history of motion pictures. He died at his home in West Hollywood.

• The major biographical study of Howe is Tedd Rainsberger, *James Wong Howe: Cinematographer* (1981), which offers a complete critical examination. See also the chapter on Howe in Charles Higham, *Hollywood Cameraman* (1970); the entry in *Current Biography* for 1943; Harry Burdick, "James Wong Howe—An Uncommon Artist," *American Cinematographer*, Aug. 1935, pp. 334ff.; and George Blaisdel, "James Wong Howe Wins Honors for His Photography in *Algiers*," *American Cinematographer*, Aug. 1938, pp. 312–15. Obituaries are in the *New York Times*, 16 July 1976, and *Variety*, 21 July 1976.

DOUGLAS GOMERY

HOWE, John Homer (12 Sept. 1822–3 Apr. 1873), jurist and soldier, was born in Riga, New York, the son of Joseph Howe and Eunice Smith, farmers. After working for a time on the Erie Canal, Howe migrated along the lakefront to Kingsville, Ohio, where he completed his legal studies. He was admitted to the Ohio bar and in 1845 married Julia Anna Castle in Ashtabula, Ohio. They had four children.

During his law practice in Ashtabula, Howe became a member of the local Whig party. In search of wider opportunity, he considered moving his family west to Kansas, but the antislavery violence there caused him to change his plans. In 1855 he settled in the newly formed town of Kewanee in western Illinois. There Howe practiced law, edited a local newspaper, and joined the new Republican party, campaigning for John C. Frémont in the 1856 presidential election and for Abraham Lincoln in 1860.

In that year Howe, a stirring public speaker, was elected judge of the Sixth Judicial District of Illinois. In this capacity he acquired a reputation for rendering decisions favoring the expansion of local and transcontinental railroads. In 1862, after the outbreak of the Civil War, the 124th Illinois Volunteers Regiment was formed. Howe was elected lieutenant colonel, second in command.

The 124th Illinois took part in the Union army's western campaigns under Ulysses S. Grant and William T. Sherman, which focused on gaining control of the Mississippi River. By the time Vicksburg, Mississippi, came under Union siege, Howe had assumed command of the regiment. The 124th was responsible for tunneling under the Confederate works near the city's outskirts. Leading a group of volunteer ex-miners from Kewanee nicknamed "the Mad Moles," Howe apparently contracted tuberculosis during the days underground.

After Vicksburg's fall on 4 July 1863, which, coincidental with the triumph at Gettysburg, turned the war in the Union's favor, the regiment generally remained in Vicksburg, where Howe administered the conquered area. He left the army in 1865 as a brevet brigadier general, resuming his judicial duties in Illinois.

After the Republican Grant was elected president in 1868, Howe, supported by the Republican governor of Illinois, successfully applied to Grant and was appointed chief justice of the Wyoming Territory in April 1869. As a Republican, Howe had supported African-American emancipation and suffrage; in Wyoming, however, he was required to deal with a different sort of liberation. Overriding the Republican governor's veto, Wyoming's all-Democratic territorial legislature gave women full rights to vote and hold office. It fell to Howe, who denied any involvement in the woman suffrage movement, to rule on that action's legality as it related to jury duty.

In Laramie in 1870 Howe upheld this aspect of the law. In a murder case he empaneled six women in the first jury in the United States to break the gender barrier. Local newspapers reported that Howe's persuasion overcame the women's initial hesitancy to serve. It was theorized by many that women would avoid imposing harsh punishment; however, while the six women preferred a first- or second-degree conviction, three of the men voted for acquittal. A compromise manslaughter conviction was reached. Howe commended the women: "These women acquitted themselves with such dignity, decorum, propriety of conduct, and intelligence as to win the admiration of every fair minded citizen of Wyoming" (Larson, p. 3).

The trial briefly set a historical legal precedent. The editor of the *Laramie Sentinel* later wrote, "It would be impossible to describe . . . the excitement which this event created, and the fact was telegraphed, not only throughout the country, but over the whole civilized world" (Larson, p. 3). But after Howe left office, the next Wyoming chief justice held that jury service was not a necessary adjunct of suffrage, and no more women served. Wyoming women maintained the right to vote until the territory became a state in 1890.

A sometimes imperious man willing to be unpredictable and controversial, Howe also proved that he was not an unwavering railroad man when he allowed Laramie County to tax the Union Pacific. In an anti–Native American action, Howe traveled to Washington, there successfully arguing that the Big Horn Mining Expedition should be permitted to seek gold on Sioux reservations.

Howe remained chief justice of Wyoming until 1871, when failing health caused his resignation. He returned to Illinois and private practice but sought appointment to warmer climates. In 1873 he became secretary to the U.S.–Mexican Border Commission, charged with permanently setting the border. While traveling the disputed boundary, Howe fell ill of tuberculosis and died in Laredo, Texas.

• Howe's papers are held by family members in Ariz. and Calif., as well as by the Kewanee Historical Society, Kewanee, Ill. Over the years many articles relating to Howe appeared in the *Kewanee Courier-Journal*. His service in the Civil War is documented in R. L. Howard, *The History of the 124th Regiment, Illinois Volunteers, Also Known as the Hundred Two Dozen* (1880). Excellent sources on Wyoming woman suffrage are Sidney Howell Fleming, "Solving the Jigsaw Puzzle," *Annals of Wyoming* 62, no. 1 (Spring 1990): 23–72, and T. A. Larson, "Wyoming's Contribution to Regional and National Women's Rights Movement," *Annals of Wyoming* 52, no. 1 (Spring 1980).

MARK R. WILLIAMS

HOWE, Julia Ward (27 May 1819–17 Oct. 1910), poet, author, and woman suffrage leader, was born in New York City, the daughter of Samuel Ward, Jr., a Wall Street stockbroker, and Julia Rush, a poet. Julia was five when her mother died of tuberculosis. She was educated both by tutors at home and at schools for young ladies until the age of sixteen. Her father died in 1839. Visiting Boston in 1841, she met Dr. Samuel Gridley Howe, head of the Perkins Institute for the Blind; in 1843 they married, despite an eighteen-year age difference. Julia gave birth to the first of six children eleven months later while honeymooning in Europe; she bore her last child in 1859 at the age of forty.

In South Boston Howe cared for her household and children while her husband participated in prison reform, school reform, education for the "feeble-minded," Greek and Armenian foreign relief, and abolitionism. Unhappy in her new surroundings and prohibited by her husband from participating in public reform work, she attended lectures, privately studied foreign languages, religion, and philosophy, and wrote poetry and drama. Her husband's resistance to her growing public life and reputation, and his resentment of her income-generating inheritance, led to difficulties in their marriage. In 1850 she spent a year in Rome with her children while Samuel Howe remained in Boston. In 1854 and again in 1857 she contemplated divorce.

Although she had published essays on Goethe, Schiller, and Lamartine in the *New York Review* and *Theological Review* before her marriage, Julia Ward Howe's literary career began in earnest in Rome. She wrote her first collection of poems, *Passion-Flowers*, in 1850; it was published anonymously four years later. Her second anonymous collection, *Words for the Hour*, appeared in 1857. Both contained allusions to her stultifying marriage, a subject she also wrote about in plays, *Leonora; or, The World's Own* and *Hippolytus*. Although the latter was not published until 1941, the former, a story about a woman whose lover abandons her and prompts her suicide, was performed for one week in 1857 before it succumbed to hostile New York reviews. Among her other literary endeavors were an 1860 book, *A Trip to Cuba*, describing an 1859 vacation, and several letters on Newport high society published in the *New York Tribune* in 1860.

By far Howe's most famous work, the "Battle Hymn of the Republic," was published in the *Atlantic Monthly* in February 1862. She wrote the poem in 1861 while in Washington, D.C., with her husband, who was helping distribute supplies to Massachusetts regiments. Set to the music of "John Brown's Body," her poem became the rallying song for the North during the final year of the Civil War.

The "Battle Hymn" also brought Howe the fame required to more actively pursue a writing career. In 1867 she produced eleven issues of a literary magazine, *Northern Lights*. That same year she wrote about her European travels in *From the Oak to the Olive* (1868). In 1870 she founded the weekly *Woman's Journal*, a successful, widely-read suffragist magazine to which she contributed for twenty years. She edited a defense of coeducation titled *Sex and Education* in 1874 and brought out a collection of her own addresses, *Modern Society*, in 1880. She published a biography of Margaret Fuller in 1883, and another collection of lectures, *Is Polite Society Polite?*, in 1895. Her popular memoirs, *Reminiscences*, appeared in 1899. Indeed, Howe continued to write lectures, poems, and articles until her death.

By 1868, when Howe's husband no longer opposed her involvement in public life, she seized the opportunity to become active in reform after years of relative isolation. That year she helped found the New England Women's Club and the New England Woman Suffrage Association; she served as president of the latter for nine years beginning in 1868. In 1869 she became co-leader (with Lucy Stone) of the American Woman Suffrage Association, one of two national suffrage organizations to appear in the wake of a Civil War–related schism in the women's movement. In 1870 she began a seven-year term as president of the Massachusetts Woman Suffrage Association and almost lifelong service as president of the New England Women's Club. That same year she wrote "Appeal to Womanhood throughout the World," an attempt to rally a women's peace movement in response to the Franco-Prussian War. Two years later she organized a poorly-attended Woman's Peace Congress in London.

In January 1876, when her husband died, Howe's public involvement expanded rapidly. She immediately embarked upon her first speaking tour to advance a national women's club movement; she addressed women's groups throughout the Midwest and helped found clubs such as the Wisconsin Women's Club. She then embarked on a two-year tour of Europe and the Middle East.

The whirlwind continued into the 1880s. In 1881 Howe was elected president of an organization she founded eight years earlier, the Association for the Advancement of Women, a group dedicated to improving educational and professional opportunities for women. She became director of the Woman's Department of the New Orleans Cotton Exposition in 1884. Four years later she embarked on a speaking tour of the Pacific Coast and founded the Century Club of San Francisco. In 1890 she helped found the General Federation of Women's Clubs as a means of reaffirming the Christian values of frugality and moderation. From 1891 to 1893 she again served as president of the Massachusetts Woman Suffrage Association, and from 1893 until her death once more presided over the New England Woman Suffrage Association. From 1893 to 1898 she directed the General Federation of Women's Clubs, and she also headed the Massachusetts Federation of Women's Clubs, founded in 1893.

Although her best-known contribution to American history was providing the lyrics for the "Battle Hymn of the Republic," a song that contended for the national anthem until 1931, Julia Ward Howe's most substantial contribution lay in women's rights. When she died in Oak Glen, Massachusetts, at the age of ninety-one, she was the acting president and guiding light of the New England Woman Suffrage Association. She founded and presided over numerous organizations dedicated to improving opportunities for women in education, politics, and the professions. She single-handedly laid foundations for woman's rights groups while asserting her own right to participate in public life against formidable opposition, both at home and in the broader community.

Howe's written response to Francis Parkman's analysis of "The Woman Question" in 1879 reveals much about her belief in the need for advances in women's rights. Writing that suffrage was the only way women's interests would be represented at the polls, she explained that

sex is certainly an important agent in human affairs, but not the most important. Its influence is easily exaggerated and lost. Men and women may have too much sexuality as well as too little. Society, if impoverished by the insufficiency of this quality, is also degraded by its excess. In men or in women sex is a power only when it is made subservient to reason, when thought and duty common to both sexes are brought forward and dwelt upon, uplifting both alike to self-forgetfulness and self-sacrifice. ("The Other Side of the Woman Question," *North American Review* 272 [Sept. 1987]: 36)

• Howe's memoirs, essays, lectures, and letters can be found in the Julia Ward Howe collections at the Library of Congress and at the Houghton Library of Harvard University. Florence Howe Hall, *Julia Ward Howe and the Woman Suffrage Movement* (1913), contains selections of Howe's speeches and essays. Howe's published works not mentioned above include *At Sunset* (1910), *From Sunset Ridge: Poems Old and New* (1898), and *Later Lyrics* (1866). A book-length biography is Mary H. Grant, *Private Woman, Public Person: An Account of the Life of Julia Ward Howe from 1819 to 1868* (1994). Valuable for its insights into Howe's writing of the "Battle Hymn of the Republic" is a brief article by Debbie Williams Ream, "Mine Eyes Have Seen the Glory," *American History Illustrated* 27 (Jan.–Feb. 1993): 60–64. Other informative works are Deborah Pickman Clifford, *Mine Eyes Have Seen the Glory* (1979); Louise Tharp, *Three Saints and a Sinner* (1956); and Laura E. Richards and Maud Howe Elliott, *Julia Ward Howe, 1819–1910* (2 vols., 1915). An obituary is in the *New York Times*, 18 Oct. 1910.

SANDRA VANBURKLEO
MARY JO MILES

HOWE, Lois Lilley (25 Sept. 1864–13 Sept. 1964), **Eleanor Manning** (27 June 1884–? 1973), and **Mary Almy** (23 July 1883–? 1967), architects, who as Howe, Manning & Almy constituted the only all-female architectural firm in Boston between 1895 and 1937, although Howe had begun her career in 1893. With some notable exceptions, all of the partners focused their professional work on house designs for suburban clients, and nearly 500 projects were executed during the life of the firm, mostly in the wider Boston area.

Lois Lilley Howe was born in Cambridge, Massachusetts, the daughter of Estes Howe, a real estate speculator, and Lois Lilly White. She received an equivalency certificate from Cambridge Public High School and then studied design at the School of the Boston Museum of Fine Arts from 1882 to 1886. On the death of her father in 1887, Howe had the opportunity to witness the construction of a new family home and determined to become an architect. In 1888 she entered the Massachusetts Institute of Technology (MIT), which as a land-grant college was obliged to admit qualified women to all of its courses. Howe, the only woman among sixty-five male classmates, completed the special two-year Partial Architecture course in 1890. This "nuts-and-bolts" program did not result in an MIT degree but concentrated on the rendering and construction of buildings as well as a firm grounding in architectural history.

For two years after graduation, Howe served as a draftsman for Boston architects Allen & Kenway; in 1892 she became nationally recognized by receiving the $500 second prize in the design competition for the Woman's Building to be constructed for the 1893 World's Columbian Exposition in Chicago. The Board of Lady Managers had called for entries by women architects, and the commission was ultimately awarded to Sophia G. Hayden, who had just become the first woman to complete MIT's four-year degree course in architecture. Howe spent her prize money traveling in Europe with her mother and sisters. Back in Boston, Howe designed her first house in 1894, in association with Joseph Prince Loud. By 1895, while working part time as an architecture librarian at MIT, Howe, supported at first by commissions from friends, had opened her own architectural office on Clarendon Street.

In 1900 Howe moved her office to Tremont Street and briefly had two (unidentified) male partners. After they left the firm at the end of the year, leaving Howe "high and dry," she began to specialize in the design and renovation of suburban houses in period styles throughout the Boston area. She became an expert on the colonial domestic architecture of New England by traveling widely in the region and by making measured drawings of interiors and exterior details, which were published, in collaboration with MIT alumna Constance Fuller, as *Details from Old New England Houses* (1913). Howe's own designs were influenced by this study of styles and use of materials, but the houses she designed were never directly copied from historical examples. Her design for the house of Mrs. A. A. Burrage in Brookline, published in 1905 in *American Architect and Building News*, demonstrated Howe's inclination toward designs with "the English suggestion" but with a distinctive simplification of surface and form. Burrage's house was featured in 1907 articles by Frank Chouteau Brown on "Exterior Plaster Construction" and "Boston Suburban Architecture," the latter placing Howe's work in the company of noted regional firms.

During her extraordinarily long career, Howe was active in many professional and artistic organizations: She served on the Council of the Boston Museum School in 1897, presided over the Business Women's Club of Boston during World War I, and was director of the Boston Society of Arts and Crafts from 1916 to 1919. With the support of Boston architect Robert Swain Peabody, Howe was elected to the American Institute of Architects (AIA) in 1901, at a time when women practitioners were generally unwelcome in the institute. (Howe's application apparently succeeded because some AIA members thought the petitioner was male.) She was not admitted to the Boston Chapter of the AIA until 1916. After serving on the Architects' Small House Service Bureau in 1925–1926, Howe was elected an AIA Fellow in 1931; the citation mentioned her "strong personality . . . which has in many ways indicated the capacity of her sex in the profession of architecture." Howe and Louise Bethune would be the only women so honored by the AIA until 1955.

In 1913 Howe established a partnership with Eleanor Manning, who had served as a draftsman in the office for five years. Manning, who was born and raised in nearby Lynn, Massachusetts, the daughter of

James Edward Manning and Delia Josephine Grady, had graduated from MIT with an architecture degree in 1906. After a period of travel, she had joined Howe's office in 1908, bringing to the practice an avid concern for housing at all social levels along with connections to women's reform activities in Boston. Manning served on the Lynn city planning board from 1923 to 1930 and became a noted consultant to state, regional, and federal housing committees. In addition to her architectural practice, she also held a teaching position at Simmons College in Boston.

Between 1913 and 1926 Howe & Manning served the housing needs of suburban clients by creating "comfortable" designs that emphasized the functional spaces and lighting within the house, the relationship of house to site, and the understated use of the period styles favored among their clients. The firm tended to use traditional building materials, such as wood, brick, and stucco, but did experiment with industrial materials and construction techniques. Much of the firm's business consisted of what Manning called "renovising," updating buildings for new or more effective uses. However, during 1918 Howe & Manning designed several structures dedicated to the war effort, including the Army & Navy Canteen for Boston Common and the Lucy Stone Hospital in Dorchester. After the war the firm continued to design structures for cultural and social organizations, including art centers in Concord and Fitchburg, and for women's business and political clubs in Boston.

Prompted by Manning's social consciousness and interest in public housing, the firm sought and won commissions to design two "garden city" residential communities. In 1923 Howe & Manning provided the layout and house designs for Denny Place in Mariemont, Ohio, on the outskirts of Cincinnati. Intended as a planned community for middle-class commuters, eventually to include commercial and institutional buildings, the Mariemont project engaged twenty-six architectural firms. Completed in 1924, Denny Place grouped together seven single-family cottages and two double-houses of differing sizes, all picturesque in character but relatively simple in form and used local limestone for a rustic effect. Drawings and photographs of these houses appeared in *Architecture* in 1926. Because of her reputation in housing matters, Manning was chosen to represent the firm as one of the Seventeen Associated Architects who designed Old Harbor Village (now Mary Ellen McCormack Housing Development) in South Boston. Constructed between 1935 and 1940, Old Harbor Village was the first public housing project built in Boston; part of the larger federal program of mass housing, it was nonetheless distinctive because of its humane site planning and low-scale residences.

As of 1926, the firm included Mary Almy. Born in Beverly, Massachusetts, the daughter of Charles Almy and Helen Jackson Cabot, Almy had graduated from Radcliffe College in 1905, taught at several private schools, and then earned a degree in architecture from MIT in 1920, after designing a family home and recovering from the lingering effects of polio. Almy's strengths lay in the areas of business management and landscape design, though she is also credited with several house designs, including a Cambridge residence for family members Charles and Elizabeth Almy in 1926, the year she was promoted from draftsman to partner.

The depression curtailed most of the firm's business, except for renovation projects and the federally funded Old Harbor Village. Nevertheless, Manning in particular remained prominent during the 1930s, publishing several topical articles, such as "Building for National Welfare" (*National Altrusan*, Mar. 1935, pp. 5–6), which concerned government slum clearance and housing projects, and "Architecture as a Profession for Women" (*Simmons College Review* [Apr. 1934]: 71–75). In the latter essay, Manning observed, "Women find themselves very much at home with every phase of housing for the whole vertical cross section of society . . . work in which they are expected to perform credibly and in which they have often achieved distinction."

When the partnership of Howe, Manning & Almy was dissolved in 1937, Lois Howe was seventy-three years old; she lived virtually to her one hundredth birthday and was an active participant in Cambridge community life until her death there. Mary Almy entered the practice of landscape architect Henrietta Pope. Almy and Howe had never married. Eleanor Manning, who in 1929 had married Johnson O'Connor, founder of the Human Engineering Laboratories, maintained her architectural and teaching activities into the 1960s. The places of death for Manning and Almy are unknown.

• The MIT Archives has papers related to Howe, Manning & Almy; the Daniel H. Burnham Papers at the Art Institute of Chicago has papers related to Howe's design for the World's Columbian Exposition; Schlesinger Library at Radcliffe College has a biographical file on Howe, as does the MIT Museum and Historical Collections. Lois Lilley Howe's other publications are "Serving Pantries in Small Houses," *Architectural Review* 14 (Mar. 1907): 31–33, and *An Architectural Monograph: The Colonel Robert Means House at Amherst, New Hampshire* (1927). Additional sources on Howe, Manning, and Almy are cited in Lamia Doumato, ed., *Architecture and Women: A Bibliography* (1988). The major sources of information on Howe, Manning & Almy are Doris Cole and Karen Cord Taylor, *The Lady Architects: Lois Lilley Howe, Eleanor Manning and Mary Almy, 1893–1937* (1990); Elizabeth W. Reinhardt, "Lois Lilley Howe, FAIA, 1864–1964," *Cambridge Historical Society Publications* 43 (1980): 153–72; and "An Alumna's Architectural Career," *Technology Review* 66 (Dec. 1963): 21, 38. For women in architectural practice see Mathilda McQuaid, "Educating for the Future: A Growing Archive on Women in Architecture," in *Architecture: A Place for Women*, ed. Ellen Perry Berkeley and Mathilda McQuaid (1989), and Susana Torre, ed., *Women in American Architecture: A Historic and Contemporary Perspective* (1977). For the firm's work at Mariemont, Ohio, see Warren W. Parks, *The Mariemont Story* (1967). A short death notice for Howe is in *Progressive Architecture* 45 (Oct. 1964): 118.

LISA B. REITZES

HOWE, Louis McHenry (14 Jan. 1871–18 Apr. 1936), political operative and presidential adviser, was born in Indianapolis, Indiana, the son of Edward Porter Howe, an insurance executive and small-time newspaper publisher, and Eliza Blake Ray. Short and slight, Howe survived a precarious childhood. His father failed financially twice, once in the insurance business in Indiana, and again as owner of the Saratoga (N.Y.) *Sun*, and he himself was plagued by a mysterious amalgam of ailments and accidents that included asthma, a possible heart condition, bronchitis so severe he had to wear a truss all his life to counteract the damage coughing had caused, and a fall from a bicycle that drove gravel and dirt deep into his face, permanently scarring it.

Howe was sent to the Temple Grove Seminary for young women in Saratoga, because his parents feared he was too frail for the rough-and-tumble of ordinary school. He never got to college, working instead at age seventeen as a reporter and salesman for his father's newspaper and print shop and picking up a little extra money gathering society items during the Saratoga racing season as a stringer for the New York *Herald*. "Getting a respectable showing of Society," he remembered, was "like marching 6 supers 'round and 'round the stage to represent an army" (Ward, p. 193). He did score one celebrated beat; he was the first newspaperman to report Theodore Roosevelt's (1858–1919) furious buckboard ride down from Lake of the Clouds, New York, to Buffalo after William McKinley's assassination in 1901. In 1898 he married Grace Hartley; they had two children.

In 1906 Howe began covering the New York state legislature in Albany for the New York *Herald* and quickly won a reputation for political savvy and cynical wit. He was fascinated from the first with the winning and wielding of political power. He was not a prepossessing figure—gruff, diminutive, frequently dusted with cigarette ash, his clothes often unwashed and always unpressed, and so homely that he sometimes answered his telephone, "Medieval Gnome, here" (Ward, p. 229).

His interest gradually shifted from covering politics to politics itself. Howe "had an enormous interest in . . . having power," Eleanor Roosevelt once told an interviewer, "and [since] he could not have it . . . himself, he wanted it through someone he was influencing. I think he loved power" (Ward, p. 230).

Howe first went to work as personal assistant to Mayor Thomas Mott Osborne of Auburn, an anti-Tammany reformer who then seemed destined for great things. Osborne's career foundered in 1910, when he failed to win his party's nomination for governor, and Howe's hopes winked out with his.

Then Franklin Delano Roosevelt arrived to take his seat in the state senate in 1911. Young, handsome, hugely ambitious, and blessed with a famous name, he became a leader of a rebellion against Tammany Hall's nominee for the U.S. Senate. Roosevelt's revolt failed, but Howe was impressed by his magnetism and progressive spirit. In 1912, when Roosevelt fell ill with typhoid in the midst of his reelection campaign and asked Howe, now out of a job, to run his campaign in his enforced absence, the would-be political operative jumped at the chance. Soon Howe was addressing his new employer, only half in jest, as "Beloved and Revered Future President." From then on there would be no line dividing Roosevelt's ambition from Howe's; their political partnership would last until Howe's death.

When Roosevelt went to Washington in 1913 to serve as assistant secretary of the navy, Howe went with him as his chief of staff. He steeped himself in naval matters and kept a sharp eye on how the navy yards were run. He enjoyed the fact that the admirals called him "Roosevelt's gumshoe" (Ward, p. 234), but his primary concern, as always, was the furtherance of Roosevelt's career. He drafted Roosevelt's speeches, saw to the details that bored his restless boss, and served as Roosevelt's link to the Democratic party back in New York State, doling out federal patronage to his allies and denying it to his enemies. Roosevelt's superior at the Navy Department, Josephus Daniels, later recalled that Howe "would have sidetracked both President [Woodow] Wilson and me to get Franklin to the White House" (Ward, p. 229).

In 1920 Howe accompanied Roosevelt on his hectic cross-country campaign for the vice presidency. The Democratic ticket lost, and Howe planned to go into business until Roosevelt would again need his services. Then in 1921 his candidate was felled by infantile paralysis. The conventional wisdom was that Roosevelt was finished in politics, and a less devoted aide might well have abandoned him. Howe remained faithful to his fallen chief, and for the next seven years, as his boss struggled in vain to regain his feet, he did his best to keep Roosevelt's name alive. He orchestrated statements for Roosevelt on public issues, wrote magazine articles for him to sign, encouraged Eleanor Roosevelt to become a public person in her own right, even brokered a peace between Roosevelt and his old nemesis, Tammany, that paved the way for Roosevelt's dramatic appearance on behalf of the presidential candidacy of New York governor Alfred E. Smith at the 1924 Democratic convention.

Smith's urgent, last-minute call for Roosevelt to run for governor of New York in 1928 came as a surprise to Howe and Roosevelt alike. They had not planned to return to active politics for another four years, and at first Howe urged his boss to turn Smith down. However, he quickly rallied and was instrumental in planning the whirlwind three-week campaign that convinced voters Roosevelt's illness should not bar him from public office.

All through Roosevelt's four years in Albany as governor, Howe remained quietly in New York, working to secure for him the Democratic presidential nomination in 1932. He was "indifferent to political ideology," wrote Arthur M. Schlesinger, Jr., in *The Crisis of the Old Order* (1951), "beyond a commitment to the Democratic party and a newspaperman's contempt for stuffed shirts; but he was a master of political technique" (p. 341).

Roosevelt's presidential triumph represented the fulfillment of the dream he and Howe had long shared, but it also became a source of considerable frustration for the little man who had helped make it all possible. He moved into the White House to serve as the president's secretary, still had unrivaled access to Roosevelt, and remained the sole person who could get away with telling him "you're a damned fool . . . a damned, idiotic fool!" (Ward, p. 230) when the two men disagreed. "Howe was the only one who dared to talk to him frankly and fearlessly," Harold Ickes remembered. "He could not only tell him what he believed to be the truth, but he could hang on like a pup to the root until he got results" (Arthur M. Schlesinger, Jr., *The Coming of the New Deal* [1958], p. 515). However, Howe was no longer Roosevelt's sole adviser, his views were far more conservative than those of many of the others who now had the president's ear, and he bitterly resented having to take his turn among other competing counselors with deeper knowledge of the complex challenges Roosevelt now faced. By the time of Howe's death in Washington, D.C., he had largely been supplanted in the president's inner circle by other advisers, but Roosevelt saw to it that he was given a state funeral in the East Room of the White House.

Roosevelt provided Howe with proximity to the political power his own limitations denied him. Howe, in turn, provided Roosevelt with shrewd counsel, absolute loyalty, and a willingness to perform almost any task that would move them closer to the pinnacle of power that was their common goal. Without him, Roosevelt might never have made it to the White House.

• Howe's papers are in the Franklin D. Roosevelt Library at Hyde Park, N.Y. The standard work on Howe and his complicated relationship with his famous patron is Alfred B. Rollins, Jr., *Roosevelt and Howe* (1962). Lela Stiles, *The Man behind Roosevelt: The Story of Louis McHenry Howe* (1954), is an anecdotal account written by his admiring secretary. See also Geoffrey C. Ward, *A First-Class Temperament: The Emergence of FDR* (1989).

GEOFFREY C. WARD

HOWE, Mark Antony DeWolfe (23 Aug. 1864–6 Dec. 1960), author and editor, was born in Bristol, Rhode Island, the son of Mark Antony DeWolfe Howe, rector of an Episcopalian church in Philadelphia, and Eliza Whitney. In 1872 Howe, who was his father's seventeenth of eighteen children by three wives, moved with his big family to Reading, Pennsylvania, where his father had been appointed bishop of central Pennsylvania. There Howe attended Selwyn Hall and in 1882 enrolled at Lehigh University, where his father was president of the board of trustees. Howe would probably have trained for the clergy but for a persistent stammer. His closest friend at Lehigh was Richard Harding Davis, later a war correspondent and novelist. Howe and Davis wrote and did editorial work for the *Lehigh Burr*. After graduating in 1886 with a B.A.,

Howe began graduate work in English literature at Harvard University, where he earned a second B.A. in 1887 and an M.A. in 1888. His most influential professors at Harvard were Francis James Child and Barrett Wendell.

In 1888 Howe applied to Horace Elisha Scudder, editor of the *Atlantic Monthly*, for a job. Lacking an opening, Scudder recommended Howe to the editor of the *Youth's Companion*, for which Howe worked as an associate editor for the next five years. He easily made friends in the Boston area with many persons of note, among them Harvard faculty members George Pierce Baker, Charles Townsend Copeland, Charles Eliot Norton, and George Santayana, musician Francis Boott, playwright Clyde Fitch, and Boston mayor Josiah Quincy. In 1893 Howe privately published *Rari Nantes*, his first book of competent but conventional verse, and declined an offer to work for *Harper's Monthly* in order to became assistant editor of the *Atlantic* under Scudder. Beginning to experience severe eye trouble, Howe traveled to Europe briefly in May 1893 and again in November 1894, the latter time specifically to see the mayor's sister Fanny Huntington Quincy, then in England, whom Howe wished to marry. In 1895 his eyesight grew worse; so he resigned from the *Atlantic* and moved to his parents' home in Bristol to do farm work. In 1897 he published *Shadows*, another book of poetry, and two years later his first biography, that of Phillips Brooks, the gifted, recently deceased Episcopal bishop. Early in 1899 Howe's sight improved when a surgeon removed part of his upper nasal bones. Later that year he and Fanny Quincy were married; the couple had three children.

From 1899 to 1913 Howe helped edit *Youth's Companion*. In his ample spare time, he also edited the Beacon Biographies Series (31 vols., 1899–1910) and wrote the often reprinted 397-page *Boston, the Place and the People* (1903), *Life and Letters of George Bancroft* (2 vols., 1908), and *Harmonies: A Book of Verse* (1909). The Beacon Biographies, slim books of about 120 pages each, began in 1899 with Howe's own *Phillips Brooks* and four other titles. Howe considered Owen Wister's *Ulysses S. Grant* (1900) the best of the series. Preparation was arduous for Howe's biography of Bancroft, which was commissioned and financed by the late historian's family. Howe spent four years reading Bancroft papers deposited in three large trunks. Norton wrote Howe that Bancroft was "happy in having such a biographer" and praised Howe's display of skill, taste, tact, discretion, and judgment in the finished work.

Despite his Rhode Island and Pennsylvania background, Howe quickly became and permanently remained foremost a Bostonian. His 1903 book on Boston was followed by his *Boston Common: Scenes from Four Centuries* (1910), *The Boston Symphony Orchestra* (1914), and *Boston Landmarks* (1946). In addition, he wrote books about the Massachusetts Humane Society (1918), a history of the *Atlantic Monthly* (1919), and what he called a "town biography" of Bristol, Rhode Island (1930).

Howe gained preeminence as a biographer. Even before his early work on Brooks and Bancroft, he wrote, while living at Bristol and having difficulty with his vision, essays for the *Bookman* magazine, which he assembled as *American Bookmen: Sketches, Chiefly Biographical, of Certain Writers of the Nineteenth Century* (1898). Unfortunately, many subjects to whom he devoted his biographical talents were notable in their time but have since become obscure. His *Life and Labors of Bishop [William Hobart] Hare, Apostle to the Sioux* (1911) concerns a missionary to the Sioux Indians in the Dakotas; *George von Lengerke Meyer: His Life and Public Services* (1919), his longest book at 556 pages, chronicles the life of a Bostonian who was an ambassador and a member of the cabinets of presidents Theodore Roosevelt and William Howard Taft; *Portrait of an Independent, Moorfield Storey, 1845–1929* (1932) extols the reformist Boston lawyer; *The Children's Judge, Frederick Pickering Cabot* (1932) details the jurist's attempts to better the lot of juvenile delinquents in Boston; and *John Jay Chapman and His Letters* (1937) concerns an American literary critic versatile in his day but now nearly forgotten. Better remembered are the subjects of Howe's *Memories of a Hostess: A Chronicle of Eminent Friendships Drawn Chiefly from the Diaries of Mrs. James T. Fields* (1922), about Annie Adams Fields, wife and then long-lived widow of the hospitable Boston publisher; *Barrett Wendell and His Letters* (1924), for which Howe won the 1924 Pulitzer Prize for biography; *James Ford Rhodes, American Historian* (1929); and *[Oliver Wendell] Holmes of the Breakfast Table* (1939). Howe, who knew most of his subjects personally, made it a point to let them reveal their own lives, as far as possible, by extensively quoting from their own writings. Thus, for his book about Annie Fields, he combed through the more than fifty small diaries she kept and then presented in five separate chapters her comments on Oliver Wendell Holmes, visitors from Concord and Cambridge (including Ralph Waldo Emerson, Nathaniel Hawthorne, and Henry Wadsworth Longfellow), Charles Dickens, theatrical people (notably Edwin Booth and Charlotte Cushman), and fiction writer Sarah Orne Jewett. Among the books Howe edited are six separate volumes containing the writings of General William Tecumseh Sherman (1909); Charles Eliot Norton (1913); Francis James Child (1920, 1952); Charles William Eliot, president of Harvard (1924); and James Russell Lowell, author and ambassador (1932, 1952).

A gentle, affable person of almost boundless energy, Howe found time for much besides his writing. He was a member of Boston's Trinity Church, a trustee in 1906 of the Boston Athenaeum and later its library director (1933–1937), vice president of the Atlantic Monthly Company (1911–1929), a trustee of the Boston Symphony Orchestra (1918), an "overseer" of Harvard University (1925–1931, 1933–1939 [in 1932 he was at the Henry E. Huntington Library in Calif.]), and a consultant to the Library of Congress on biography (1929–1931). Also a member of several convivial clubs, he came to be known as the "dean of Boston's literary world." Howe continued writing almost to the end of his life and died in Cambridge, Massachusetts.

Howe was a member of and a spokesman for the genteel tradition, particularly the old-fashioned Boston variety, which has since come under attack by revisionist historians and modernist critics. For that reason, his work is regarded as having been sincere and distinguished in its time but as having become passé.

• Most of Howe's voluminous papers are in the Houghton Library, Harvard University. Others are in the Archives and Historical Collections of the Episcopal Church, Austin, Tex. Some others are in libraries at Columbia University, the University of Pennsylvania, and Yale University. Howe's autobiography is *A Venture in Remembrance* (1941); see also his "Nearing Ninety," *Atlantic Monthly*, Dec. 1953, pp. 71–74. The best biography of Howe, by his daughter Helen Huntington Howe, is *The Gentle Americans, 1864–1960: A Biography of a Breed* (1965), which also lists Howe's fifteen books of biography, his twelve historical books, his eight books of poetry, and the thirteen works he edited. Arthur S. Pier, "Mark Antony DeWolfe Howe," *Proceedings of the Massachusetts Historical Society* 72 (Oct. 1957–Dec. 1960): 403–8, is a fine biographical sketch. Ellery Sedgwick, *The "Atlantic Monthly" 1857–1909* (1994), discusses Howe's relationship with Scudder and the *Atlantic*. An obituary is in the *New York Times*, 7 Dec. 1960.

ROBERT L. GALE

HOWE, Mark De Wolfe (22 May 1906–28 Feb. 1967), legal historian and civil rights activist, was born in Boston, Massachusetts, the son of Mark Antony De Wolfe Howe, a noted biographer, and Fanny Huntington Quincy. Howe lived in the Boston-Cambridge area all of his life. He attended prestigious Phillips Andover Academy and received his B.A. from Harvard in 1928, then his LL.B. from Harvard Law School in 1933. In 1935 he married Mary Manning, with whom he had three children.

After Howe graduated from law school, his family connections continued to present opportunities for him, and he served for one year as law clerk for Oliver Wendell Holmes, Jr., who by that time had retired from the U.S. Supreme Court. Following his clerkship with Holmes, Howe joined a Boston law firm but was persuaded by his friends Felix Frankfurter and Louis Brandeis to follow his academic leanings. He joined the University of Buffalo Law School as a professor of law and in 1941 became dean. His scholarly career was interrupted, however, by World War II. He served as an officer in North Africa, Sicily, and southern France and received the Legion of Merit and the Distinguished Service Medal. In 1945 he was discharged with the rank of colonel.

After the war Howe followed in his father's footsteps and joined the faculty of Harvard Law School. He was a popular teacher who, unlike many on the Harvard faculty, was accessible to both undergraduate and graduate students. During his Harvard years he wrote his most significant books. Inspired by his year with the former chief justice, Howe produced a large body of work on Holmes, including *Touched with Fire*

(1946), Holmes's Civil War letters and diary; *The Holmes-Laski Letters* (2 vols., 1953); *The Shaping Years* (1957); *The Proving Years* (1963); and an annotated edition of Holmes's *The Common Law* (1963).

The two-volume biography of Holmes, comprising *The Shaping Years* and *The Proving Years*, has been of most service to historians. The first volume tracks Holmes's intellectual development during his youth and through the trials of the Civil War. Howe provides a solid contribution to the history of ideas as he traces the influence that a variety of thinkers, especially Herbert Spencer and John Stuart Mill, had on the young Holmes and the further maturation of his thinking during the ordeal of war. The second volume departs from the themes of youth and war and concentrates even more squarely on Holmes's development as an architect of legal thought.

In his teaching, Howe sought to develop courses that approached the study of the past to illuminate problems of his time. Without skewing the interpretation of the past to fit a present agenda, he tried to use current problems to frame the questions that he wanted his students to ask of history. The most pressing matter of his time, he believed, was how to bridge the fissure between American ideals and social reality. Racial inequality, he maintained, was the central evil of American society. He argued that the Supreme Court had both a legal and a moral imperative to eradicate structural inequality. Howe wrote:

It is not, I submit, of crucial significance that no evidence tells us conclusively that the draftsmen of the Fourteenth Amendment intended to outlaw separate but equal facilities for Negro citizens. It is enough to know that they meant to prohibit state action which supports a caste system. No honest observer of American life can deny, I think, that when the state puts Negroes in separate railroad cars, in separate slums, in separate schools, in separate jobs, the nation's promise of equality has been violated. (Pollak, p. 1635)

In his classes Howe taught his students how to use the law and legal institutions to challenge state actions that circumvented the Fourteenth Amendment's original intent to create a society based on racial equality. This found expression in 1966, when Harvard law students published the pioneering *Harvard Civil Rights–Civil Liberties Law Review*.

Howe's strong dedication to civil rights led him to become a member of the National Association for the Advancement of Colored People (NAACP) Legal Defense Fund. In this capacity he helped prepare many southern trial lawyers for civil rights litigation. He also went to Mississippi and fought in the courts for the rights of blacks. In 1967, shortly before his death, Howe was appointed chairman of the Massachusetts Attorney General's Committee on Civil Rights and Civil Liberties. He died at his Brattle Street home in Cambridge, Massachusetts.

• Howe's papers are in the Harvard Law School Library. See also Louis Pollak, "Mark De Wolfe Howe and the Fight for Racial Equality," *Harvard Law Review* (June 1967). Obituaries are in the *New York Times*, 1 Mar. 1967, and *Newsweek*, 13 Mar. 1967.

MICHAEL JOHNSON

HOWE, Mary (4 Apr. 1882–14 Sept. 1964), composer, pianist, and music activist, was born Mary Carlisle in Richmond, Virginia, the daughter of Calderon Carlisle, a lawyer, and Kate Thomas. Howe was educated at home by tutors, including a piano teacher, Herminie Seron, who provided her with a thorough grounding in music theory and piano. Howe traveled abroad frequently with her family. During a visit to Europe in 1904 with her mother, she studied piano for a brief and intense period of time with Richard Burmeister in Dresden, Germany. In 1910 she began studying with Ernest Hutcheson and Harold Randolph at the Peabody Conservatory of Music in Baltimore and, at Hutcheson's suggestion, studied composition with Gustav Strube. In 1922 Howe earned a diploma in composition from Peabody, for which she presented a full program of her own works. The concert featured her Sonata for Violin and Piano, several piano solos, choral works, and a group of songs, including "If I Am Slow Forgetting," "Cossack Cradle Song" (later renamed "Berceuse Cossaque"), "There Has Fallen a Splendid Tear," and "O Mistress Mine."

In 1912 Howe married Walter Bruce Howe, a Washington lawyer. They had three children. When interviewed by Grace Perkins Oursler in the April 1955 issue of *Guideposts* magazine, Howe was asked how she managed to write music while carrying the responsibilities of home, children, concert performances, and other community commitments. Howe responded, "I use the chinks of time and fill each day to the brimming. It's the only way I know to be happy." She was vibrant, energetic, and well organized, and with the help of a network of family, friends, and domestic personnel, she successfully juggled several careers.

Although Howe composed throughout her adolescent years and early adulthood, it was not until 1924, after leaving Peabody, that she began to compose in earnest. In her own words, "I can only say it was because gates had been opened and I wanted to go into those fields and pastures and towards those hills and mountains that had always seemed the property of other people . . . I began to compose. I felt I had a *right* to be there doing it, because what I worked on was *myself*" (*Jottings*, pp. 87–88). In 1933 Howe spent a brief but worthwhile period of coaching in Paris with Nadia Boulanger, the renowned teacher of composition. Boulanger examined some of Howe's manuscripts, gave her some suggestions on orchestration, and recommended that Howe develop a more modern métier.

Early in her life, Howe had developed considerable skill as a pianist who played by ear and sight. She was consequently in demand as an accompanist and accompanied singers Myron Whitney and Helen Howison, and violinists Henri Sokolov and Roman Totenberg. She played with the National String Quartet in the chamber music ensemble, performed solo recitals, and gave two piano recitals with her colleague Anne Hull, who in later years became Howe's manager.

At home, Howe entertained her family with an extensive piano repertoire that ranged from Beethoven to ragtime, accompanied a friend in Broadway show tunes, and created musical parodies. Around 1930 Howe and her three grown children formed a vocal group they called the "Four Howes," which presented programs of madrigals and early music for recorder and virginals. Among other activities, the group performed for a brief period to raise money for the MacDowell Colony, a retreat for composers, artists, and writers in Peterboro, New Hampshire. Howe often used the group as a touchstone on which she tested some of her musical ideas, and she collaborated with her children in matters of text selection, recordings, and choreography. As a woman "smitten by music," according to Celius Dougherty, a colleague and mentor, Howe endeavored throughout her lifetime to develop music audiences and to build music institutions.

During the 1920s Howe helped to found the Chamber Music Society of Washington, in collaborations with other dedicated musicians, including Carl Engel, then the chief of the music division in the Library of Congress. In 1928 the membership was opened to a wider public, and the society was reorganized as the Friends of Music in the Library of Congress. At the request of Amy Beach, America's best-known woman composer, Howe joined Beach and other female composers in 1925 to form the Society of American Women Composers. Together they sought to gain greater recognition in the musical community and to have their works performed in public.

From 1931 to 1948 Howe worked as a fundraiser, organizer, and member of the board of directors on behalf of the National Symphony Orchestra, which she helped to found with her husband and prominent figures in Washington, D.C. Not only was she active in the effort to raise funds to finance the orchestra, but she also organized committees to solicit support for the orchestra and its first conductor, Hans Kindler. As national chairman of orchestras in the National Federation of Music Clubs, Howe pursued her lifelong goals of promoting the performance of American music and developing understanding and knowledgeable audiences through performances, lectures, and radio and television programs. Most of her life was spent in Washington, D.C., although she traveled frequently, both throughout the United States and abroad. Howe died at her home in Washington.

Howe produced more than 200 original compositions in many genres, including orchestral works, chamber music, music for solo voice and chorus, ballet music, and pieces for two pianos. Notable works include the orchestral scores *Stars* (1927), *Sand* (1928), and *Rock* (1954); the songs "When I Died in Berner's Street" (1936), "Viennese Waltz" (1938), "Liebeslied" (1931), and "Die Jahre" (1940); *Ballade Fantasque* (1927) for cello and piano; *Interlude between Two Pieces* (1942) for alto recorder and harpsichord;

Castallano (1930) for two pianos and orchestra; and *Sheep May Safely Graze* (1932), a transcription for two pianos of the original by J. S. Bach. Many of Howe's pieces were performed, to great acclaim, throughout her lifetime. Her musical language is essentially tonal, although she developed a style of composition that reached from the past through the contemporary. Her use of dissonance, rhythmic subtlety, and melodic invention, particularly in the setting of texts, produced a thoroughly fascinating oeuvre.

A gap in American music history (the countless number of women composers who have been ignored) is partially filled when we give due recognition to Mary Howe, a musician whose compositions enriched the body of music literature, a pianist who successfully made the transition from amateur to professional status, and a community activist whose energetic and enthusiastic efforts helped to promote and sustain music and the institutions dedicated to it.

• Most of Howe's manuscripts, programs, correspondence, scrapbooks, and newspaper clippings can be found in the New York Public Library for the Performing Arts in Lincoln Center. Her book of memoirs, *Jottings*, was privately published in 1959. A complete, annotated catalog of her works has been compiled by her son Calderon Howe and is in his possession in Newport, R.I. In addition to the entry on Howe in *The New Grove Dictionary of Music and Musicians* (1980), the following represent the most recent surveys of Howe's life and work: Dorothy Indenbaum, "Mary Howe: Composer, Pianist and Music Activist" (Ph.D. diss., New York Univ., 1993); Sandra Clemmons McClain, "The Solo Vocal Repertoire of Mary Carlisle Howe with Stylistic and Interpretive Analyses of Selected Works" (Ph.D. diss., Columbia Univ., 1992); and Denise N. Allen, "The Works of Mary Howe: A Survey of Performance History & Critical Response" (master's thesis, George Washington Univ., 1992). Obituaries are in the *Washington Post* and the Washington, D.C. *Evening Star*, both 18 Sept. 1964.

DOROTHY INDENBAUM

HOWE, Percy Rogers (30 Sept. 1864–28 Feb. 1950), dental educator and scientist, was born in North Providence, Rhode Island, the son of James Albert Howe and Elizabeth Rachel Rogers. His father was a Baptist minister who became dean of the Cobb Divinity School at Bates College in Lewiston, Maine, where Percy spent his childhood and attended the Nichols Latin School and Bates College, from which he graduated with a B.A. in 1887. Not wishing to enter the ministry, he accepted an offer to apprentice with a family dentist; afterward, having decided on a dental career, he entered the Philadelphia Dental College, earning a D.D.S. in 1890. Having established a successful practice in Lewiston, he moved in 1903 to Boston, where once again his practice flourished. He had married Rose Alma Hilton in 1891; they had two sons.

During his initial practice Howe had taught himself the rudiments of basic scientific research, and in 1915 the trustees of the newly opened Forsyth Dental Infirmary for Children in Boston invited him to create a small research facility at Forsyth. Some of his early work at the infirmary disproved British physician William Hunter's focal infection theory, which cited poor oral hygiene as a source of infection throughout the body, a thesis that had resulted in the extraction of too many teeth. Howe also pioneered the use of ammoniated silver nitrate as a caries inhibitor, a method that was adopted nationally and also resulted in the avoidance of many extractions.

Howe and a growing number of dentists both in the United States and abroad recognized the need for additional training in the basic sciences and in research methodology if the dental profession was to be upgraded and achieve its potential. By 1923, Howe had embarked on preliminary studies with the Harvard biochemist Otto Folin, who was known for his microchemical quantitative testing of urine and blood and had become interested in the excreted metabolites of saliva. Folin and Howe speculated that saliva might be the indicator of general body conditions by which the teeth, in turn, might be affected. Howe was searching for an additional etiology of dental caries, which he thought might be caused by an imbalance in general bodily functioning.

When William J. Gies, an early dental biochemist and founder of the International Association of Dental Research, visited Forsyth in 1925, he noted that it was the only dental facility in Boston where endowed dental research was being done. (This contrasted with the Harvard and Tufts dental schools, where research was not endowed and was usually conducted as an avocation by staff members.) In 1925 Howe was named the Thomas Alexander Forsyth Professor of Dental Science at the Harvard Dental School, a post he held until 1940; and in 1928 he was named director of the Forsyth Dental Infirmary. During these years, he forged important research links with S. Burt Wolbach and Otto Bessey at the Harvard Medical School. Wolbach was one of the nation's early workers on vitamin deficiencies, and he and Howe published a series of papers exploring changes in bone, teeth, and soft tissue in animals deprived of adequate amounts of vitamins A and C.

As an educator, Howe advanced the dental profession in three ways. First, he was instrumental in teaching scientific thinking processes to Forsyth's many interns, who in turn carried his message to many parts of the United States as well as to Europe and Asia. Second, he pointed out the opportunities of research to the many luminaries who visited Forsyth from the 1920s on. Finally, he was one of a small group chosen by Harvard president James Conant to create the Harvard School of Dental Medicine, which would replace the original Harvard Dental School. Conant wanted the new Harvard facility to follow the patterns established at Harvard's medical school, with primary focus on basic medical science and research centered on multidisciplinary studies at the graduate level, enabling researchers to discover the cause and mechanisms of dental disease and develop preventive therapy.

Under Howe, Forsyth had become by the largest and best equipped private dental center in the world.

To maintain its research presence, however, Howe realized that the institution would have to become a multidisciplinary research center similar to that which was being attempted at Harvard, which the exigencies of World War II made impossible at the time. In the decade following World War II, Forsyth was no longer the first choice of American dental graduates seeking pediatric training. Other dental schools had introduced pediatric dentistry into their curricula, and Forsyth did not award graduate degrees, which were becoming important to dentists in furthering their careers. Forsyth's research capability and output had fallen behind, and its future was uncertain, when Howe died.

Nonetheless, Howe's foresight would strongly influence later events bringing Forsyth into university education. In 1944 Howe had invited Howard Marjerison, a graduate of Tufts College Dental School and a member of Forsyth's first class of dental interns in 1916, to join the Forsyth faculty as an associate researcher. Succeeding Howe as the facility's director in 1950, Marjerison used his skills as an administrator and parliamentarian to effect an affiliation between Harvard and Forsyth in 1955; and despite the fact that the affiliation's existence was checkered, with disaffiliation occurring in 1967 and reaffiliation in 1993, Forsyth continued as a leading institution in the education of scientific dentistry, training a limited number of national and international postdoctoral students in a variety of research programs, and continuing to be represented by its faculty at scientific meetings worldwide.

Howe's important role in advancing dental education was matched by his lifelong interest in promoting dental research. His work on the chemistry of saliva and its relation to dental disease resulted in Forsyth's researchers becoming leaders in human salivary chemistry, with the mouth being used as a model for systemic research. Saliva later became routinely used to monitor genetic diseases, AIDS metabolism, and a variety of systemic diseases. His research work on diet, nutrition, and vitamins and their relation to preventive dentistry and systemic well-being would be done within the newly created Department of Nutrition, a joint venture of the Harvard schools of Medicine and Public Health, in 1942. Howe published more than 100 scientific papers, a great rarity for a dentist of his day. His wife had died in 1943, and later that year he had married Ruth Loring White, a nutritionist and his longtime assistant at Forsyth. He died in Belmont, Massachusetts.

• Howe's papers, including his letters, are located in the Forsyth Dental Center Archives, Cambridge, Mass. A complete list of his research publications are listed in Rollo Walter Brown, *Dr. Howe and the Forsyth Infirmary* (1952), pp. 169–82. A modern assessment of Howe's place in dental research and at Forsyth is Charles Millstein, "The Forsyth Dental Center: 1914–1991" (1991), an unpublished thesis stored in the Rare Books Room of the Countway Library in Boston. A memorial tribute composed by his Harvard colleagues was recorded in the *Thirty-Fifth Annual Report of the Forsyth Dental Infirmary for Children* in 1950.

CHARLES B. MILLSTEIN

HOWE, Quincy Huntington (17 Aug. 1900–17 Feb. 1977), journalist, was born in Boston, Massachusetts, the son of Mark Antony De Wolfe Howe, an editor and biographer, and Fanny Huntington Quincy. He attended the Country Day School for Boys in Boston and St. George's School in Newport, Rhode Island, and went on to Harvard University, where he received a bachelor's degree magna cum laude in 1921. He studied for a year in England at Christ College, Cambridge University.

On his return, he went to work for the Atlantic Monthly Company in Boston, where his father was a vice president: "I figured the best way to get your first job is to use pull," he later conceded. He was placed with a company subsidiary, the *Living Age*, a magazine of reprints and translations from the foreign press. Initially assigned to the circulation department, he moved to the editorial side as a translator and editor. In 1928 the magazine was sold, and Howe found himself out of work. He moved to New York, propelled by his feeling that he had to "get out from under" his Bostonian upbringing. He worked briefly in advertising but soon returned to the *Living Age*, which had also moved to New York, as editor. In 1932 he married Mary L. Post; they had two children.

As editor of the *Living Age*, Howe made his mark with an exposé of the international arms traffic, one of several that led to a congressional investigation of munitions makers in 1935. In monthly editorial essays Howe began also to stake out an isolationist position, designed to warn the United States against becoming involved in the growing European crisis. In 1935 he was named chief editor by the New York publisher Simon & Schuster. There his work was perceived as anti-British, not only for books he accepted as an editor but, in 1937, for his own *England Expects Every American to Do His Duty*, a tract he subsequently dismissed as a lampoon of American Anglophiles.

But his other writings pursued isolationism more seriously, placing him at odds with the internationalist stance of much of the liberal and moderate press, most notably when he began to contribute to the *North American Review*. In the Spring–Summer 1938 issue he urged that the United States "adopt a strictly isolationist line" in relation to British interests. Curiously, the *North American Review* and the *Living Age* were bought in 1938 by Joseph Hilton Smyth, who was later found guilty of accepting Japanese government subsidies for the publications. There is no indication that Howe knew of this link at the time, but he stopped contributing to *North American Review* after the start of World War II in September 1939. His opinions were little changed, however, as could be seen in his 1940 book, *The News and How to Understand It*, a thinly disguised attack on "Anglophiles" and "warmongers."

The war offered Howe a new medium: radio. The Mutual Broadcasting System hired him as one of its commentators during the Munich crisis of September 1938, and a year later WQXR, the radio station of the *New York Times*, hired him for war analysis. His sharp, direct New England inflections and his pointed opinions were well suited to success in radio commentary, which hinged not only on content but on a distinctive voice. He believed that his experience as a lecturer and his grounding in world affairs while an editor also prepared him for his new role. Although he was still warning against close ties with Britain in mid-1941, he abandoned his isolationism after the United States entered the war late that year and was hired in June 1942 to do commentary for the most important news network, the Columbia Broadcasting System.

His broadcasting career did not run smoothly after the war. In 1947 he was bumped from his broadcast time because a commercial sponsor wanted a different commentator, generating a controversy that was aired in the *New York Times*. But his low-keyed approach made it possible for him to move to television while more bombastic radio commentators fell by the wayside. Even so, he never considered broadcasting a full-time occupation. In 1950 he left New York to teach journalism at the University of Illinois and continued to broadcast comment from the campus. In 1954 he returned to New York and was hired by the American Broadcasting Company, an affiliation he maintained until 1968. As an ABC correspondent, he moderated the last of the John F. Kennedy–Richard M. Nixon presidential debates of 1960 and covered the trial of Adolf Eichmann in Israel in 1961. His part-time broadcast commitments left him time to write for the *Saturday Review of Literature* and to work on his ambitious project, *A World History of Our Times*, the first volume of which appeared in 1949 and the third and last in 1972.

A strong concern for civil liberties and free speech ran through his career. In 1932 he joined the mission of leftists and liberals that went to Kentucky to aid coal miners in Harlan County. He served on the board of the American Civil Liberties Union (1932–1940). Later, as head of the National Council on Freedom from Censorship, he opposed New York City's effort to drive "objectionable" magazines from the newsstands. In the postwar years he criticized government loyalty-security programs and censorship of libraries as well as Soviet repression of writers.

In 1961 he returned to his beginnings when he was hired as editor of *Atlas*, a monthly devoted, like the *Living Age*, to material from the foreign press. He saw *Atlas* through its first four years before yielding to a younger editor. He died in New York City.

Howe, always modest about his own achievements, is remembered primarily as a broadcaster, largely for his commonsensical, dry manner. Although he worked with notable broadcast journalists such as Edward R. Murrow, he was not considered to be in the top echelon, and his influence on politics was in fact probably greatest in the years when, as a book and magazine editor, he argued for isolationism and pacifism.

• Materials relating to Quincy Howe can be found in the M. A. De Wolfe Howe Papers, Houghton Library, Harvard

University, and in the CBS Library and Special Projects Division Records, Broadcast Pioneers Library, Washington, D.C. The Oral History Collection, Columbia University, has a brief memoir (1962). His books include *World Diary: 1929–34* (1934) and *Blood Is Cheaper Than Water* (1939). Information on the magazines he edited can be found in Theodore Peterson, *Magazines in the Twentieth Century* (1964). His career through 1939 is summarized in the *Current Biography* yearbook for 1940. Only scattered references to his work in broadcasting appear in histories or biographies in the field. An obituary is in the *New York Times*, 18 Feb. 1977.

JAMES BOYLAN

HOWE, Samuel Gridley (10 Nov. 1801–9 Jan. 1876), educator of the handicapped and social reformer, was born in Boston, Massachusetts, the son of Joseph Neals Howe, a prosperous maker of ropes and cordage, and Patty Gridley. During the War of 1812, Joseph Howe lost money by selling cordage to the federal government for which he received in payment useless treasury notes, leaving his family in straitened circumstances during Samuel Howe's boyhood.

The family did not have enough money to send three sons to college. To decide which one should go, Joseph Howe had each son open the family Bible and read a chapter. "The one who reads the best," he announced, "shall go to college!" Sam read the best. He entered Brown University in 1817 because Harvard University was strongly Federalist, and Howe's father was an ardent Democrat. He graduated in 1821 and entered the Harvard Medical School. After graduating in 1824, he spent a few months practicing medicine in Boston and then decided to fight in the Greek war of independence, arriving in Greece in January 1825. In later years he said, "I think that I was impelled in . . . going to Greece, rather by thoughtless indifference, perhaps ignorance of what course would have been profitable to me. Lacking prudence and calculation, I followed an adventurous spirit."

Howe returned to Boston in 1831 after serving as a soldier and doctor with the Greeks and sought a new profession. One day shortly after his return, he met an old friend from Brown University, John Dix Fisher. Fisher was the principal founder in 1829 of what at that time was known as the New England Asylum for the Blind (now the Perkins School for the Blind). The school had no students, no buildings, and no director. Fisher offered Howe the directorship, which he accepted.

There being no schools for the blind in either North or South America, Howe was directed by the trustees to visit schools for the blind in Europe to observe their programs and obtain educational aids and appliances. He was also instructed to hire two teachers to assist him. In Europe he visited all the major institutions for the blind and noted that institutions supported by individual and public benevolence tended to be overprotective of their pupils and to treat them as objects of charity. Howe was determined that his school would not make the same mistakes.

Howe returned to Boston in July 1832 with two highly competent blind teachers, Emile Trencheri,

from the school for the blind in Paris, and John Pringle, from the school in Edinburgh. He opened the school in his father's home with two young sisters, Sophia and Abigail Carter from Andover, Massachusetts. Within a month the enrollment had reached six students, ranging in age from six to twenty years. Because Howe needed a larger place, Thomas H. Perkins, a wealthy Bostonian and one of the school's trustees, offered his house. The school moved again in 1839 to the Mount Washington House Hotel in south Boston and changed its name to the Perkins Institution for the Blind.

During those early years, Howe developed his philosophy of education of the blind. He was aided by his friend Horace Mann. "You must not think because you are blind," he advised students, "that you cannot learn as much as other children." Armed with equal education ideals, he believed that the blind should no longer be doomed to inequality, to becoming only "mere objects of pity." During his first years as director, he visited seventeen states, establishing schools in Ohio, Tennessee, Kentucky, and Virginia. He also developed an embossed-letter system for the blind to read, first known as Howe Type, and later as Boston Line Type. It was used at Perkins until Braille came into common usage at the turn of the century.

In 1837 Howe began an experiment in education that would bring him to the attention of the world, that of educating Laura Bridgman, a girl who had become deaf-blind from scarlet fever at the age of two. His success in educating her proved that it was possible to educate a deaf-blind person.

Howe also became involved in the education of the mentally retarded. In 1839 he worked with a "Blind idiot child, unable to walk." In 1848 he started the first public institution in the United States to educate the mentally retarded. He also became involved in deaf education, helping to establish the Clarke Institution for Deaf Mutes (now the Clarke School for the Deaf) in Northampton, Massachusetts, in 1867. He has rightly been called the most significant and foresighted figure in the American history of special education. He also participated in the reform of public school education with Horace Mann, in prison reform, in helping the mentally ill with Dorothea Dix, and in the antislavery movement.

In 1843 Howe married Julia Ward, a young woman from a wealthy New York City banking family. They met while she was visiting Perkins with Henry Wadsworth Longfellow and Charles Sumner. The Howes had six children, but it was not the happiest of marriages. Howe was constantly on the go, often leaving his wife to take care of a household and raise their children. The Howes became editors in 1851 of the *Boston Commonwealth*, an abolitionist paper. They entertained many prominent antislavery figures, including John Brown in 1857, although Howe did not support Brown's efforts to end slavery with arms. During the Civil War, Howe joined the Sanitary Commission on a trip to Washington, D.C., to inspect the sanitary conditions of the Grand Army of the Potomac. While on that trip with him, Julia Ward Howe wrote "The Battle Hymn of the Republic."

After the Civil War, Howe resumed his work at Perkins. He developed the "cottage system," which allowed students to live in family units, but the plan was not fully put into practice until 1912. He again took an active role in the struggle of the Greek people. In 1867 Crete, still under the rule of the Turks, rose in revolt. Howe took supplies of food and clothing to Greece for the Cretan refugees in camps near Athens. In 1868 he brought his young secretary, Michael Anagnostopoulos, to the United States.

In 1871 Howe accepted President Ulysses Grant's request to be on a three-man commission to visit and annex Santo Domingo. Howe loved the country and saw a chance to make money through the Samana Bay Company. Congress did not approve the recommendations for annexation by the commission. Howe not only lost money, but he also lost his crusading spirit. As his health and interest in Perkins declined, Michael Anagnos (as he became known after his marriage to Julia Romana Howe in 1870) took on the responsibilities of running the institution. In a period characterized by resurgent imperialism, when the leading nations of Europe led in the looting of the world's backward areas, Howe had sought to bring enlightenment and the "American Way of Life" (which he thought meant democracy, liberty, and social justice) to an "unprogressive" society. However, as Harold Schwartz writes, "Howe the teacher, Howe the journalist, Howe the abolitionist, and Howe the patriot, in all of these he attained great distinction; but as Howe . . . the adviser of presidents, he was a wretched dupe and miserable failure" (p. 320).

In his seventies Howe still worked on the affairs of Perkins and the Massachusetts School for Idiotic and Feeble-Minded Children, which, founded in 1850, had its genesis in 1848 as an experimental school housed in Perkins. He was also a trustee of the Massachusetts General Hospital and the Insane Asylum at Somerville. He died in Boston.

Howe's friend Ralph Waldo Emerson once said: "Every great institution is the lengthened shadow of a single man." Howe was certainly such a man. His work in the field of special education was outstanding, unequaled by any other. Today he is regarded as one of the first to advocate for inclusion of handicapped children into regular classes.

• The largest collection of Howe's papers are in the Howe papers, Houghton Library, Harvard University. Papers, writings, and reports relating to his directorship of the Perkins School for the Blind are in the archives of the Perkins School for the Blind, Watertown, Mass. Material relating to his work with the mentally retarded is in the Howe Library, Walter E. Fernald School, Waltham, Mass. See also *Letters and Journals of Samuel Gridley Howe: The Greek Revolution*, ed. Laura E. Richards (1906); *Letters and Journals of Samuel Gridley Howe: The Servant of Humanity*, ed. Laura E. Richards (1909); Deborah Pickman Clifford, *Mine Eyes Have Seen the Glory: Julia Ward Howe* (1978); Edward J. Renehan, Jr., *The Secret Six: The True Tale of the Men Who Conspired with John Brown* (1995); F. B. Sanborn, *Dr. S. G. Howe, the Philanthropist* (1981); and Harold Schwartz, *Samuel Gridley Howe, Social Reformer* (1956). Obituaries are in the *Boston Transcript* and *Boston Herald*, 10 Jan. 1876.

KENNETH STUCKEY

HOWE, Timothy Otis (24 Feb. 1816–25 Mar. 1883), senator and postmaster general, was born in Livermore Falls, Androscoggin County, Maine, the son of Timothy Howe, a doctor, and Betsy Howard. He attended local public schools, worked on a farm, and graduated from the Maine Wesleyan Seminary. After studying law, he was admitted to the bar in 1839 and practiced in Readfield, Maine, where for a short time he was postmaster. In 1841 he married Linda Ann Haynes, with whom he raised two children. An ardent Whig, Howe served in the state legislature in 1845. The next year he relocated to Green Bay, Wisconsin, for health reasons. Although he ran unsuccessfully for a seat in the U.S. House of Representatives in 1848, Howe succeeded two years later in winning election as judge of the Fourth Circuit Court, which meant he also sat on the state supreme court and for one year occupied the chief justiceship. While serving as circuit judge, he presided at the locally celebrated murder trial of Ann Wheeler in Kenosha. He held this judicial position until 1855, when he resigned to return to his law practice.

Howe remained a Whig until the partly collapsed after the 1852 elections, but two years later he was drawn to the new Republican party by its antislavery stand and Whiggish economic policy. In 1856 he sought a seat in the U.S. Senate, but he lost the Republican party's senatorial nomination to James R. Doolittle, a Racine lawyer, largely because he opposed abolitionist efforts to nullify the federal Fugitive Slave Act by means of a state sovereignty act. Though unsympathetic to slavery, Howe denounced any action by the Wisconsin courts or legislature to defy federal laws. His disinclination to acquiesce in the extreme views of the abolitionists temporarily postponed his political career. In 1861, however, he was elected to the U.S. Senate, where he served until 1879.

Howe's senatorial career was noteworthy in several respects. An unwavering Union politician during the Civil War, he supported President Abraham Lincoln's endeavors to prosecute the conflict to a successful conclusion. At the same time, he was somewhat in advance of Lincoln on the questions of emancipation and black suffrage. He was an early sponsor of African-American suffrage in the District of Columbia. In a Senate speech on 5 May 1862, the year in which he was a candidate for the Supreme Court appointment that went to David Davis of Illinois, Howe urged the confiscation of rebel property, called for the emancipation of the slaves, and argued the right of the federal government to consign the South to territorial status, giving national authorities extensive authority in conquered areas. After the war, he spoke of the supreme and absolute authority of the nation, insisting upon the subordinate and conditional status of the states. Accordingly, Howe denounced President Andrew Johnson's plan of Reconstruction and supported stronger congressional measures. Drawn into opposition by Johnson's recalcitrance, he voted for the president's conviction and removal in the impeachment trial in 1868.

Howe was an equally active senator with respect to other issues. He introduced bills to establish postal routes, to repeal the law restricting the number of national banks, to incorporate railroads in the territories, to improve the Wisconsin and Fox rivers, and to facilitate telegraphic communication between the United States and foreign countries. These measures demonstrated his interest in economic development and constituent service. Howe was an important member on the Judiciary, Finance, Appropriations, Pensions, Commerce, and Foreign Relations committees. He served as a commissioner for the purchase of the Black Hills territory from Native Americans, and President Ulysses S. Grant selected him as a member of the Board of Visitors to West Point in 1874. Although Grant offered him a position on the U.S. Supreme Court and on another occasion the ambassadorship to Great Britain, Howe declined both offers, knowing that either the Democratic state legislature or the Democratic governor of Wisconsin would fill the vacancy in the Senate with a Democrat. In 1879 Howe was defeated for reelection in a three-way race by Matthew H. Carpenter, a Milwaukee Republican and former U.S. senator.

Howe belonged to the Stalwart faction of the Republican party in the 1870s and early 1880s, cultivating personal and political relations with Senator Roscoe Conkling of New York, a powerful Republican leader. He entertained no commitment to civil service reform, believing essentially in spoils politics. To Howe, senatorial patronage revolved around senators naming the officeholders and officeholders in turn making senators. At the Republican National Convention in Chicago in 1880, Howe joined forces with Conkling in favoring former president Grant, a political ally, for the presidential nomination. That honor went instead to Congressman James A. Garfield of Ohio, who belonged to the Half Breed or anti-Conkling wing of the party. To placate Conkling, President Garfield appointed Howe a delegate to the International Monetary Conference in Paris in 1881. The president also considered Howe for a cabinet portfolio but dropped him when Senator John Sherman of Ohio criticized Howe for an absence of business acumen.

When Postmaster General Thomas L. James resigned his position three months after the death of President Garfield in 1881, President Chester A. Arthur immediately appointed Howe postmaster general. Arthur thereby named a fellow Stalwart to an office prominent in the distribution of patronage plums. Howe had already proved himself to be an Arthur loyalist. He had opposed Arthur's removal as collector of customs for the Port of New York by President Rutherford B. Hayes in 1878, and he had endorsed Arthur as Garfield's vice presidential running mate in 1880.

Although he had long supported Arthur, Howe came to appreciate more fully the president's qualities as a leader while watching him discharge his official duties. Following a dinner with the president in early 1882, Howe wrote to his niece: "General Arthur is a much more accomplished man than I had supposed. He has more tact and more general culture than any man I have seen in the White House."

After his confirmation by the Senate, Howe entered upon his duties as postmaster general on 5 January 1882. During his brief period in office, he demonstrated administrative capabilities. He approved a reduction of postal rates and sought to improve mail facilities across the nation, among other reforms. He died in Kenosha, Wisconsin.

• Howe's papers are in the State Historical Society of Wisconsin at Madison. Some of his letters are in the papers of Abraham Lincoln, Ulysses S. Grant, James A. Garfield, and Chester A. Arthur in the Library of Congress and the papers and diaries of Rutherford B. Hayes at the Hayes Presidential Center in Fremont, Ohio. His speeches are in the *Congressional Globe* and *Congressional Record* from 1861 to 1879. Information relating to Howe is in Thomas C. Reeves, *Gentleman Boss: The Life of Chester Alan Arthur* (1975); George Frederick Howe, *Chester A. Arthur: A Quarter-Century of Machine Politics* (1934); and Dorothy Ganfield Fowler, *The Cabinet Politician: The Postmasters General, 1829–1909* (1943). An obituary is in the *Milwaukee Sentinel*, 26 Mar. 1883.

LEONARD SCHLUP

HOWE, William (10 Aug. 1729–12 July 1814), commander in chief of the British army in the war for American independence from 1775 to 1778, was the son of Emanuel Scrope Howe, second viscount Howe, and Mary Sophia Charlotte Kielmansegge of Langar, Nottinghamshire, England. His place of birth is unknown. Howe's career in the British army began auspiciously. His family used its wealth and connections to see that he had a good basic education (tutors and four years at Eton) and that he entered the army in 1746 in the prestigious Duke of Cumberland's Light Dragoons. During the next ten years, Howe established himself as a brave, knowledgeable officer who trained and led his men with unusual care. Early in the Seven Years' War (1756–1763), he became lieutenant colonel commanding the Fifty-eighth Regiment of Foot in the conquest of Canada. He distinguished himself in the successful siege of Louisbourg (1758), the capture of Quebec (1759), and the advance on Montreal (summer of 1760). He subsequently won praise as a brigade commander at the siege of Belle Isle on the coast of France in the spring of 1761 and as adjutant general of the British army that captured Havana in 1762. By the end of the war, Howe was considered one of the best young officers in the British army.

During the ensuing years of peace—the dozen years between the Seven Years' War and the American War of Independence—Howe's career continued to flourish. He received steady promotions and military favors, becoming colonel of the Forty-sixth Regiment of

Foot in 1764, lieutenant governor of the Isle of Wight in 1768, and major general in 1772. He also took a leading part in the army's summer maneuvers; at Salisbury in 1774 he taught light infantry tactics. By the winter of 1774–1775, Howe was among the few general officers being considered for service against the rebellious colonists in North America. He did not welcome the prospect of leading troops against his former comrades in arms, but he hoped that he might succeed to the command in North America and have an opportunity to promote a negotiated settlement.

Howe went to Boston as second in command in the spring of 1775, led the costly assault on Bunker Hill (17 June), and succeeded Thomas Gage (1721–1787) as commander in chief in October. Although Howe had gained the command he sought, he never received authority enough to negotiate a settlement. In the spring of 1776, he took his army from Boston to New York, expecting that he would have to destroy the Continental army to end the rebellion. But his brother, Admiral Richard Lord Howe, who arrived in July to take command of the North American squadron, persuaded him to put conciliation before coercion. Howe devoted the remainder of the campaign to a series of flanking maneuvers that were designed to turn the Americans out of their positions in New York, create the impression of British invincibility, and complement peace overtures. These cautious maneuvers brought partial victories at Long Island (27 Aug.), Kip's Bay (15 Sept.), White Plains (28–29 Oct.), and Fort Washington (15 Nov.); they also drove the rebels progressively from Long Island, Manhattan, New Jersey, and Rhode Island. But when George Washington managed to surprise Howe's detachments at Trenton (26 Dec.) and Princeton (2–3 Jan.)—winning victories that restored American morale—Howe's conciliatory strategy collapsed.

That collapse blighted the remainder of his command in America. No longer confident that steady advances and conciliatory gestures would bring success, Howe seemed unable to pursue any strategy consistently. He spent the winter and spring of 1777 in New York planning to recover territory piecemeal. He would go to Pennsylvania by sea, evict rebel forces, and rely on Loyalists to help restore royal government. (He would not provide significant support for another British army that was to advance from Canada to operate on the upper Hudson River because he was unwilling to jeopardize his own efforts in Pennsylvania.) Yet before Howe sailed from New York, he spent much of June trying to lure the Continental army into a decisive battle in New Jersey; and he did not reach Pennsylvania by way of the Chesapeake Bay until early September. Then, finding that the people were not as loyal as he had hoped, he sought once again to end the war with a climactic battle. He defeated the Continental army at Brandywine Creek on 11 September, but the battle was not decisive, and he returned once more to a strategy of securing territory. In the next two months he parried an American attack at Germantown (4 Oct.), opened the Delaware River to British ship-ping, and fortified Philadelphia. During that time he also came under increasing criticism from the ministry for his conciliatory efforts as well as his failure to crush the rebels; he also knew that he would be made partially responsible for the loss of the Canadian army at Saratoga on 17 October. He decided, therefore, to resign his command and confront his critics. He made one further effort to engage the Continental army—at Whitemarsh in early December—but did little else before giving up his command to Sir Henry Clinton in May 1778.

Howe was not honored for his service in the American Revolution, and he did not again command against an enemy. But after returning from America he gradually regained some of his standing in the British army. His efforts to answer his critics and to blame the ministry for his failure to end the rebellion resulted in an inconclusive parliamentary hearing from April to June 1779 and an extended exchange of charges in newspapers and pamphlets. Howe defended himself by saying that campaigning in America had been unusually difficult, that he had never allowed his hopes for peace to interfere with his conduct of the war, and that he had made every reasonable effort to destroy the Continental army and end the rebellion. Once his enemies left the ministry, he again received promotions and military honors: the lieutenant generalcy of Ordnance (1782–1804), the colonelcy of the Nineteenth Light Dragoons (1786–1814), a generalcy in the army (1793), and the governorships of Berwick (1795–1808) and Plymouth (1808–1814). He was also given command of an expeditionary force raised during the Nootka Sound Controversy in 1790 and of several other defense forces during the French Revolution. He died at Plymouth, survived by his wife of forty-nine years, Frances Conolly (c. 1742–1817). They had no children.

• There is no known collection of Howe's private correspondence. There are a few of his letters among the Clinton, Germain, and Howe papers at the William L. Clements Library in Ann Arbor, Michigan; the Dartmouth papers in the William Salt Library in Stafford; and the Percy papers at Alnwick Castle, Alnwick, Northumberland. His official correspondence with the American secretary is in the Colonial Office Papers, the Public Record Office, Kew, England. For information on his parliamentary hearing, see *The Narrative of Lieut. Gen. Sir William Howe in a Committee of the House of Commons . . .* (1780). For accounts of his activities during the Revolution, see Ira D. Gruber, *The Howe Brothers and the American Revolution* (1972), and Troyer S. Anderson, *The Command of the Howe Brothers during the American Revolution* (1936).

IRA D. GRUBER

HOWE, William Wirt (24 Nov. 1833–17 Mar. 1909), jurist, was born in Canandaigua, New York, the son of Henry H. Howe, an educator, and Laura Merrill. Born in the year after the presidential election of 1832, Howe was named after William Wirt, candidate of the Anti-Masonic party, the first presidential candidate to be nominated by convention. After graduating in 1853 from Hamilton College, where he was valedictorian and elected to Phi Beta Kappa, Howe read law in St. Louis. He then settled in New York City, where he became a member of the bar. Howe was married to Frances A. Gridley; they had three children.

During the Civil War, Howe served as a lieutenant in the Seventh Kansas Cavalry and eventually became adjutant-general on the staff of General A. L. Lee. In 1865 Howe moved to New Orleans. During Reconstruction he served in several judicial posts, first as judge of the chief criminal court and then as an associate justice of the Louisiana Supreme Court. In 1872 Howe returned to private practice and became legal counsel to the Texas and Pacific Railway Company, the New Orleans Board of Trade, and the Louisiana Sugar Refining Company. He was a senior partner in the New Orleans law firm of Howe, Fenner, Spencer and Cocke. In 1900 President William McKinley appointed Howe as the U.S. attorney for the eastern district of Louisiana, a position he held until 1907.

A prominent citizen of New Orleans, Howe was president of the Louisiana Historical Society from 1888 until 1894, succeeding Charles E. A. Gayarée, the distinguished Louisiana historian. He was also treasurer of the University of Louisiana, an incorporator of the New Orleans Art Association, and a member of the New Orleans Chamber of Commerce and the New Orleans Board of Trade. He served as president of the New Orleans Board of Civil Service Commissioners, administrator of the New Orleans Charity Hospital, incorporator and trustee of the Eye, Ear, Nose and Throat Hospital, and founding member of the Society for the Prevention of Cruelty to Animals. He was also a vestryman of Christ Church Cathedral. Howe achieved national prominence when he became president of the American Bar Association in 1898. As a leader of the nation's organized bar, Howe lectured before numerous law schools and state and local bar associations.

He was also a productive author. His first book, *the Pasha Papers* (1859), was a satire on American society, culture, law, politics, the press, religion, and government. Howe's later published works were more erudite and serious. He wrote chiefly on legal subjects and history. He was one of a distinguished line of American lawyers (which included Edward Livingston, George Mathews, and Alexander Porter) who, after settling in Louisiana, became recognized authorities on civil law. The dominant legal system of continental Europe, civil law is based on Roman law and is to be contrasted with the common law system, which is derived from the English legal tradition. Howe's major contributions in this field, *Studies in the Civil Law* (1896), was prepared for the Storrs Lectures at Yale University. In numerous articles, Howe wrote of the importance of civil law in American legal culture. With the acquisition of important Spanish-speaking possessions (Puerto Rico and the Philippines) after the Spanish American War, he advocated greater education of the American bar in the civil law tradition. Howe had particular admiration for the Spanish legal system even though he criticized the manner of its administration in Spain's American colonies. A legal system, he said, must be administered "with fidelity and honor, without which the best legal system is a mockery." Howe hoped that "no effort will be made to disturb the general system of law in our new possessions so far as it concerns civil matters." He argued that the differences between English common law and Roman civil law were superficial and that "in those elementary principles which are essential to the administration of justice between man and man" they were the same. Drawing upon his deep knowledge of Louisiana's "Franco-Spanish" legal tradition, Howe recommended the study of civil law to the American common lawyer. He also stressed the importance of historical studies in legal education because "law is a vital growth; the roots of its present lie deep in the past."

As ABA president, Howe focused on the professional ethics of lawyers. He likened the practice of law not to science, but to "artistic expression," which he defined as "a capacity for taking infinite pains." He called this "intellectual conscience." Howe held a broad vision of professional ethics. He summarized the qualities of the great advocate as "fidelity, eloquence and courage." He defended corporate law practice and shared the prejudices of the bar's elite toward what he called "little shysters and calaboose lawyers . . . on the edge of the profession." Howe was critical of much judicial writing. He questioned the utility of the West Publishing Company's voluminous production of judicial opinions "in which two grains of judicial wheat must be sought for in two bushels of chaff."

Howe wrote scholarly articles on Roman law, Spanish law, and law in the Louisiana Purchase as well as historical pieces on ancient and medieval law schools and the history of New Orleans. His printed works appeared in early editions of the nation's leading law journals. He died in New Orleans but was buried in Canandaigua.

• A list of Howe's major articles can be found in vol. 2 (1887–1899) and vol. 3 (1898–1907) of the *Index of Legal Periodicals*. His "Municipal History of New Orleans" was published in the *Johns Hopkins University Studies in History and Political Science*, 7th ser., 4 (1889): 5–33. A brief sketch with a portrait of Howe appears in the *American Law Review* 43 (1909): 116. Obituaries are in the New Orleans *Times-Democrat* and the New Orleans *Daily Picayune*, 18 Mar. 1909.

GEORGE DARGO

HOWELL, Clark (21 Sept. 1863–14 Nov. 1936), newspaper editor and politician, was born on a plantation in Erwinton, Barnwell County, South Carolina, the son of Evan Park Howell, a lawyer and Confederate army officer, and Julia A. Erwin. When Union troops first threatened Georgia, Julia Howell fled to her South Carolina home and gave birth to her son there. When the war ended, Evan Howell moved his family to Atlanta, Georgia, which was his home. He cut and sold timber, was a reporter and an editor, practiced law, and was elected a state solicitor and senator. In 1876 he bought a half-interest in the *Atlanta Constitution* and engaged Henry Woodfin Grady and Joel Chandler Harris as editors. Grady, a brilliant newspaperman, soon made the *Constitution* a major Democratic party voice. Grady called for the "New South" to rebuild, advocating advantageous protective tariffs and laws to promote railroad development. He also hoped rationally to resolve problems attendant on the enfranchisement of African Americans.

Clark Howell attended the University of Georgia, graduating in 1883, and served a one-year apprenticeship as a reporter for the *New York Times* and then the *Philadelphia Press*. Returning to Atlanta, he became night editor of the *Constitution*, overseeing production, editing, and makeup. He admired Grady enormously, adopted most of his ideas, and welcomed his professional and personal advice, as well as that of his father.

In 1884 Howell started to combine a political career with his journalistic one. He was elected to membership in the Georgia House of Representatives and served from 1886 to 1891. In 1887 he married Harriet Glascock Barrett of Augusta, Georgia; they had one child. In 1888 he became assistant managing editor of the *Constitution*. Grady died in 1889, and Howell became the editor. He served as Speaker of the Georgia house (1890–1891), and in 1892 he began thirty-two years as a Democratic national committeeman, representing Georgia.

By 1895 Howell, who always worked congenially with his father, was in charge of setting editorial policy for his newspaper. He editorialized in favor of regularizing and limiting the use of convict labor by private businessmen. He opposed Prohibition and the Ku Klux Klan. In 1896 he was named a trustee of the University of Georgia, a position he held until 1927. Howell's father retired from work on the *Constitution* in 1897 and sold his interest in it, partly to Howell. By 1901 Howell exercised complete financial and editorial control. In 1900 Howell became a member and president of the Georgia Senate, serving six years. He also became a director of the Associated Press, established that year; he held that position until his death. His wife having died in 1898, in 1901 Howell married Annie Comer, the daughter of a railroad president in Savannah; they had three children.

Howell was much in demand as a public speaker even outside the South. In 1906 he ran for governor of Georgia. The main issue was a state constitutional amendment sponsored by Hoke Smith, his opponent, to ban most African Americans from voting by instituting property and literacy requirements. Howell thought that the amendment would also disfranchise poor whites and would soon be struck down as unconstitutional. Smith, with the backing of the rebellious agrarian populist Thomas Edward Watson, attacked Howell's position on the amendment, criticized his favoring corporations and railroads, and coasted to an easy victory.

Although Howell never sought another elective office, he remained a significant force in state and national politics. He wrote *Eloquent Sons of the South: A Handbook of Southern Oratory* (1909) and "Aftermath of Reconstruction" (*Century*, Apr. 1913). His opinions were sought and valued by presidents; Warren Harding, though a Republican, appointed Howell to the National Coal Commission in 1921. Annie Howell died in 1922, and in 1924 Howell married Margaret Cannon Carr of Durham, North Carolina; they had no children. That same year he was defeated as a Democratic national committeeman because he eloquently supported Alfred E. Smith's candidacy for president and opposed the Ku Klux Klan. He wrote a four-volume *History of Georgia* (1926). In 1931 the *Constitution* was awarded a Pulitzer Prize for exposing a graft ring of Atlanta City Hall officials.

Over the years, Howell's closest presidential friend was Franklin D. Roosevelt. In 1930 Howell established one of the first "Franklin Delano Roosevelt for President" clubs in the United States. When in the winter of 1931–1932 Roosevelt and Smith were vying for the Democratic nomination for president, Howell privately conferred with Smith and reported the results to Roosevelt. Once elected, Roosevelt offered to make Howell ambassador to Brazil or Argentina, then to Turkey or Poland, but Howell wanted a more significant post and declined. In 1934 Roosevelt named him chair of the newly formed Federal Aviation Commission. Howell conducted hearings and visited airfields before making recommendations on aviation policy.

Howell was an honorable journalist, an able politician, and a skillful orator. His position was that of a moderate Democrat in the turbulent years of the post-Reconstruction South. Later times, however, censured his steady espousal—perhaps understandable, given his background and the times—of "separate but equal" racial policies. He died in Atlanta.

• Howell's papers are in the Atlanta Historical Society and in the libraries of Emory University and the University of Georgia. Albert Berry Saye, *A Constitutional History of Georgia, 1732–1945* (1948), places Howell in the context of state politics. Joel Chandler Harris, "The New Editor-in-Chief of the *Constitution*," *Review of Reviews* 15 (May 1897): 558–60, genially sketches Clark Howell, Evan Park Howell, and Henry Woodfin Grady. Wallace B. Eberhard, "Clark Howell and the *Atlanta Constitution*," *Journalism Quarterly* 60 (Spring 1983): 118–22, sketches his careers as journalist and politician. Incidental information on Howell is in C. Vann Woodward, *Tom Watson: Agrarian Rebel* (1938; 2d ed., 1973); Raymond B. Nixon, *Henry W. Grady: Spokesman of the New South* (1943); Paul M. Cousins, *Joel Chandler Harris: A Biography* (1968); and Harold E. Davis, *Henry Grady's New South: Atlanta, a Brave and Beautiful City* (1990). Howell's friendship with Roosevelt is touched on in Frank Freidel, *Franklin D. Roosevelt: The Triumph* (1956), and Freidel, *Franklin D. Roosevelt: Launching the New Deal* (1973). An obituary is in the *New York Times*, 15 Nov. 1936.

ROBERT L. GALE

HOWELL, Evan Park (10 Dec. 1839–6 Aug. 1905), newspaper editor, soldier, and public official, was born in Warsaw, Georgia, the son of Clark Howell, a farmer, and Effiah Jane Park. The family moved to Marthasville—which soon was renamed Atlanta—where Howell grew up. He learned telegraphy, completed a two-year course at Georgia Military Institute in Marietta, studied law in Sandersville, Georgia, and enrolled in Lumpkin Law School (which later became the law department of the University of Georgia) in Athens. He was admitted to the bar in 1859 and returned to Sandersville to practice. Howell married Julia A. Erwin in 1861; they had seven children.

Howell enlisted in the Confederate army as an orderly sergeant in the First Regiment, Georgia volunteers. He soon was promoted to lieutenant and then to first lieutenant. When the regiment was discharged at the expiration of its enlistment in May 1862, Howell helped reorganize the unit as an artillery company. He eventually rose to the rank of captain of what became known as "Howell's Battery." The unit played a prominent role in the battle of Chickamauga and in the engagements in and around Atlanta when General William T. Sherman overwhelmed Confederate forces in his "March to the Sea." During the battle of Atlanta, Captain Howell's horse was shot from under him and he lost almost half of his men, but his soldiers nevertheless captured a Union battery that was pounding Confederate forces.

After the war Howell returned to his father's land and spent the next two years cutting and selling timber for the rebuilding of Atlanta. He viewed reconciliation between North and South as essential for the economic revitalization of the former Confederate states. In 1867 he took a job as a reporter and then as city editor for the *Atlanta Intelligencer*. After a year with the newspaper he resumed his law career. He also served on the Atlanta City Council and was elected solicitor general of the Atlanta judicial circuit, developing a reputation as a tough prosecutor. He served three terms as a state senator and was a delegate to four Democratic National Conventions.

While in the private practice of law, Howell was retained by the *Atlanta Constitution*, which was having financial difficulties despite its growth in reputation and circulation. When he was asked to examine the newspaper's books and make recommendations, Howell recognized the property as a valuable one and purchased a one-half interest in October 1876. He immediately became editor in chief. The next day he hired reporter Henry W. Grady, who would become Howell's partner in journalism as the *Constitution* developed a national reputation, built in part on their efforts to bring North and South together. Grady eventually became managing editor and bought a one-quarter interest in the paper. On Grady's recommendation, Howell next hired Joel Chandler Harris away from the *Savannah Morning News*. Harris, best known for his "Uncle Remus" stories, became the *Constitution*'s editorial writer.

"With Howell and Grady on the 'inside' of virtually everything of significance going on in Georgia, it was seldom that the paper was 'beat' on an important story," wrote Raymond B. Nixon in his biography *Henry W. Grady: Spokesman of the New South* (1943). Although Grady was the better-known journalist, Howell played a prominent role as a civic leader and shares credit for establishing the *Constitution* as perhaps the most influential voice of the South. "He made the *Constitution* the mouthpiece of the common people and he had a voice for or against every public measure that was passed or proposed," Harris said. "He made the newspaper very successful, for when he gained control, it was a sorry affair, even as newspapers went in that day" (*Constitution*, 7 Aug. 1905).

Howell and the *Constitution* led the effort to write a new state constitution in 1877 and to establish a railroad commission. Howell was a strong and successful advocate for locating the state capital in Atlanta and served on the commission that built the Capitol building for less than the legislative appropriation. He helped bring an international cotton exposition to Atlanta in 1881 and in so doing proclaimed to the nation the South's industrial growth. Howell and Grady seldom disagreed, the one noteworthy exception being an 1887 vote to prohibit liquor in Atlanta. Howell supported the "wets" and Grady the "drys." The newspaper did not take an editorial position, but it covered the issue thoroughly.

When Grady died in 1889, Howell promoted his own son Clark to managing editor, and the father-son team continued the *Constitution*'s progressive editorial policies. They supported public education and opposed exorbitant railroad rates (although Howell was a promoter of rail lines and served as director of several). They also supported antilynching legislation and reconciliation of the races, but nevertheless endorsed Jim Crow laws.

Howell retired as editor of the *Constitution* in 1897, and his son replaced him as editor in chief. Howell did not, however, retire from public life. President William McKinley appointed him to a special commission to investigate the conduct of the Spanish-American War; he served a term in the Georgia House of Representatives; and he was the mayor of Atlanta in 1903–1904. In a 1917 article, the *Georgia Historical Quarterly* called Howell "a political 'Warwick' whose force in the shaping of any public question perhaps exceeded that of any other individual in the state." He died in Atlanta.

• Transcripts of Howell's Civil War letters, as well as a scrapbook with his obituary, are in the Clark Howell Papers, Woodruff Library, Emory University, Atlanta. Other material relating to Howell is in the Clark Howell Papers, Hargett Rare Book and Manuscript Library, University of Georgia Libraries, Athens, Ga., and in the Howell-Foreman Families Papers, Atlanta Historical Society. Two of the better accounts of Howell's life are in Wallace B. Eberhard, *American Newspaper Journalists, 1873–1900* (1983), and the *Georgia Historical Quarterly* 1, no. 1 (Mar. 1917): 52–57. A lengthy obituary is in the *Atlanta Constitution*, 7 Aug. 1905, as is a story on his military, civic, and public career and a commentary by Joel Chandler Harris.

DANIEL J. FOLEY

HOWELL, John Adams (16 Mar. 1840–10 Jan. 1918), naval officer and innovator of ordnance weapons systems, was born in Bath, New York, the son of William Howell and Frances Adelphia Adams. His parents' occupations are unknown. He was appointed to the U.S. Naval Academy from the Twenty-eighth New York Congressional District in 1854 and graduated second in his class as a midshipman in 1858.

Howell was assigned to the sloop *Macedonian* of the Mediterranean Squadron (1858–1859) and then to the *Pocahontas* and the *Pawnee* (1860). He was promoted on 19 January 1861 to passed midshipman and to lieutenant on 18 April 1861, less than one week after the shots at Fort Sumter that opened the Civil War. During that war he served as a lieutenant aboard the steam sloop *Ossipee* with the blockade of the western Gulf of Mexico (1863–1865). He participated in the battle of Mobile Bay on 5 August 1864 as executive officer of the *Ossipee*. After the war, he had sea duty aboard the *De Soto* as lieutenant commander. In 1867 he married Arabella E. Krausé; they had three children.

Howell's postwar alternation between sea and shore duty reflected his growing technical and scientific interests. He served at the Naval Academy from 1867 to 1871 and again from 1874 to 1878, in both terms heading the Department of Astronomy and Navigation. His blue-water assignments took him aboard several exploration vessels working with the Coast and Geodetic Survey, including service with the *Bache* and the *Blake* (1871–1874). In 1881 he was an assistant at the Bureau of Ordnance, and he served from 1881 to 1884 as inspector of ordnance at the Washington Navy Yard. Promoted to captain in 1884, he commanded the first of the new navy steel ships, the *Atlanta*, from 1888 to 1890.

As a specialist in ordnance, Howell's most important innovation was the invention of the self-steering torpedo, patented about 1885. Between 1885 and 1892 he also patented gyroscopes for the guidance of torpedoes, torpedo launchers, explosive shells, a disappearing gun carriage for shore defense emplacement, and an amphibious lifeboat. The Howell self-propelled or "automobile" torpedo, the first with gyroscopic guidance, became the basis for later advances in American torpedo design.

Howell next served as inspector of steel and from 1893 to 1896 as commandant of the Washington Navy Yard. He then became commandant of League Island, Philadelphia, from 1895 to 1898. At the same time he served on the Steel Board, which was in charge of the purchase of armor plate for the navy, and was president of the board from 1891 through 1894.

During the war with Spain in 1898 Howell commanded the North Patrol Fleet headquartered at Provincetown, Massachusetts, and the First Squadron, North Atlantic Fleet, blockading the north coast of Cuba. He served as commander in chief of the North Atlantic Fleet in the absence of Admiral William T. Sampson. After the Spanish-American War, he presided over the Naval Examining Board until 1900 and over the Retiring Board until his own retirement,

overseeing officer promotion decisions. Howell retired on 16 March 1902 with the rank of rear admiral after more than forty-five years of varied active duty. Following his retirement, he lived at the home of one of his children in Warrenton, Virginia, where he died.

During both his sea and shore appointments, Howell reflected the qualities of the professional officer class of the new navy, bringing scholarship and an inquiring, innovative, and scientific approach to his work. While teaching at the Naval Academy, he prepared several textbooks, and during his exploratory voyages he conducted astronomical observations and prepared documented accounts of his findings.

Howell's post–Civil War career followed a path similar to that of many other U.S. Navy officers who had served in the war. He earned a reputation for competent leadership under fire and steady promotion. At first, the peacetime navy concentrated on hydrographic, arctic, and coastal exploration and then, with encouragement and funding from Congress in the 1880s, on expanding the navy's technical capabilities with new steel ship construction, innovation of new weapons and auxiliary systems, and improvements in the technical training of future officers. Howell, by temperament, background, and inclination, was well suited to these opportunities.

• Howell's publications include *A Textbook on Surveying, Projection and Portable Instruments for Use at the Naval Academy* (1876); *The Mathematical Theory for the Deviations of the Compass Arranged for the Use of the Cadets at the U.S. Naval Academy* (1879); *Report of the Armor Factory Board* (1897); and a five-page scientific paper, *Observations for Dip Taken on the U.S. Steamer "Adams"* (1882), prepared off the coasts of California, Mexico, and Peru. Information on Howell is in William Cogar, *Dictionary of Admirals of the U.S. Navy* (1989). An obituary is in the *New York Times*, 12 Jan. 1918.

RODNEY P. CARLISLE

HOWELL, Richard (25 Oct. 1754–28 Apr. 1802), revolutionary war officer and governor of New Jersey, was born in Newark, Delaware, the son of Ebenezer Howell and Sarah Bond, farmers. The parents emigrated from Wales. Richard Howell was one of eleven children; his twin brother, Lewis, was an army regimental surgeon. Richard attended school in Newark until a short time after his family moved to a farm near Bridgeton, New Jersey, in 1774. Howell excelled in sports as a youth, particularly boxing and leaping. He did not attend college. Before the war, however, he began the study of law. Originally a Quaker, Howell became an Episcopalian.

Howell participated in the Greenwich, New Jersey, "Tea Party" in November 1774. He and about forty others, disguised as Indians, seized tea from the ship *Greyhound*, took the cargo to a cellar, and burned it in a field the next day. Howell joined a militia company recruited from Salem and Cumberland counties as a subaltern officer. When the group became the Second New Jersey Regiment in the Continental army, Howell, on 29 November 1775, was commissioned a captain; he was promoted to major on 28 November 1776.

As part of Colonel William Maxwell's Second New Jersey Regiment, Howell and his company linked up with the remnant northern army that was still hovering about Quebec after its disastrous assault on that city, 31 December 1775–1 January 1776. The New Jersey and other American troops made a fainthearted attempt to attack Quebec from the Plains of Abraham on 3 May 1776. The British general, Guy Carleton, ordered a sortie against the American lines, which broke and fled. The American general, John Thomas, had his troops retreat. Howell wrote his brother Lewis afterward that "I had the honor to fire the first gun on the plains of Abram, before the retreat." The arrival of large British reinforcements forced the American army up the St. Lawrence and across to its south bank, up the Richelieu River, and then along the shores of Lake Champlain. Being sick, Howell did not join his New Jersey comrades in the ill-fated attack (8 June 1776) on the British encampment at Three Rivers, on the north bank of the St. Lawrence.

Howell subsequently served at Crown Point, Ticonderoga, and Mount Independence on Lake Champlain. By late fall 1776 the British halted their invasions, and Howell and the New Jersey troops returned to their state in early December 1776. Posted briefly at Morristown, the New Jersey Brigade did not see action at Trenton. During winter and spring 1777 the New Jersey Continentals harassed British troops, particularly in their foraging expeditions out of their posts at New Brunswick and Amboy.

At the battle of Brandywine, Howell saw action during the initial phase, contesting the British advance to Chad's Ford, and afterward, covering the American retreat. At Germantown, he and the New Jersey troops fought to dislodge a British regiment from the thick-walled Chew House. Howell spent the winter and spring of 1778 at Valley Forge. Just before the battle of Monmouth (28 June 1778), being informed that he could attend to his dying brother Lewis at the Blackhorse Tavern near Trenton, he elected to stay and fight.

Howell resigned from the army on 7 April 1779, owing primarily to two considerations. He was licensed as an attorney by the New Jersey Supreme Court during its April 1779 term, and George Washington requested that he go behind enemy lines in New York City as a civilian to gain intelligence. On his return to New Jersey, Howell was arrested on the charge of treason. At his arraignment before Chief Justice David Brearly in the state supreme court, Howell pulled from his pocket Washington's orders for the spy mission; he was immediately discharged, and the case was expunged from the court's minutes.

In November 1779 Howell married Keziah Burr, of Burlington County, New Jersey. They had nine children; a son later moved to Mississippi and was the father of Varina Howell, who married Jefferson Davis. After his army service Howell practiced law. On 18 September 1782 Congress elected him judge advocate for the army, an appointment Howell declined. The Howells made their residence in Trenton. On 21 April 1789 Howell had the chief responsibility for the festivities in Trenton welcoming Washington as he made his way to New York City for his inauguration as president; Howell composed an ode for the occasion. By legislative appointment, Howell served as clerk of the New Jersey Supreme Court, 1778–1793. He was a member of the Society of the Cincinnati and was a vestryman for St. Michael's Church in Trenton, 1790–1793.

On 3 June 1793 the New Jersey legislature elected Howell governor, replacing William Paterson who was named to the U.S. Supreme Court. Howell was reelected eight times, serving as governor until 1801. A Federalist, he faced opposition only in the 1798 and 1799 elections. With the Democratic-Republican sweep at the polls in 1800, Howell relinquished his office to a friend, Joseph Bloomfield, who had left the Federalist fold for the Democratic-Republican party.

Lacking a veto power and without patronage for his independent distribution, Howell's authority as governor was limited primarily to the areas of the judiciary, such as pardons, and the military. Howell thought of himself more as a soldier than as a politician. He helped raise four companies of infantry, "the New Jersey Battalion," to serve for six months in the western Indian campaign of Major General Arthur St. Clair in 1791. As "captain-general and commander in chief " of the New Jersey militia, Howell personally led 1,500 New Jersey troops into western Pennsylvania during the Whiskey Rebellion of 1794. Washington gave him command of the right wing of the army (N.J. and Pa. militia), which traveled by way of the Forbes Road; the left wing marched along Braddock's Road. When Washington came to Carlisle to review the troops, Howell hosted a dinner for the president. The New Jersey troops were on the verge of mutiny, having second thoughts about making war on their countrymen. But any major mishap was prevented. To shore up morale, Howell wrote a marching song, which was to become very popular among the public and students at the College of New Jersey (now Princeton). The first of the song's many stanzas is:

> To arms, once more our hero cries,
> Sedition lives and order dies.
> To peace and ease then bid adieu,
> And dash to the mountains, Jersey Blue.

The Whiskey insurgents submitted to federal commissioners on 24 October 1794, and Howell and the militia army had no one to fight. As soon as they arrived at Pittsburgh, on 17 November 1794, they headed for home.

Howell fully supported the Alien-Sedition measures passed by Congress in 1798 to quash dissent during the Quasi-War with France. Two editors of the *Newark Centinel of Freedom*, a weekly newspaper, were arrested for refusing to reveal their sources for an article attacking Howell. Although Howell did not personally take action against New Jersey's "French Tories" (Republicans), he obtained from Governor Thomas Mifflin of Pennsylvania a commitment to examine and detain "suspected strangers" before they crossed into New Jersey. Howell's declining health was a factor in his decision to leave the government arena. He died in Trenton.

Howell was well liked and very popular during his career, despite an aristocratic bearing. Fond of good horses and athletics and of military disposition, he may be compared to an English cavalier of the seventeenth century. He always sat upright in a chair, never crossing his legs. Although a staunch Federalist, Howell had a personal appeal that bridged party lines.

• Howell papers are in several collections at the New Jersey Historical Society, Newark; for military correspondence see the Papers of George Washington, Library of Congress, and the Dreer collection, at the Historical Society of Pennsylvania. Biographical notices are found in Lucius Q. Elmer, *The Constitution and Government of the Province and State of New Jersey* (1872), pp. 102–13; Daniel Agnew, "A Biographical Sketch of Governor Richard Howell, of New Jersey," *Pennsylvania Magazine of History and Biography* 22 (1898): 221–30; and Hamilton Schuyler, *A History of St. Michael's Church, Trenton* (1926), pp. 101–2. For Howell's role in the Whiskey Rebellion, see Leland D. Baldwin, *Whiskey Rebels: The Story of a Frontier Uprising* (1976 ed.), and "Journal of Capt. David Ford, during the Expedition into Pennsylvania in 1794," New Jersey Historical Society, *Proceedings* 8 (1856–1859): 75–88. Howell as governor is discussed in Rudolph J. Pasler and Margaret C. Pasler, *The New Jersey Federalists* (1975), and Carl E. Prince, *New Jersey's Jeffersonian Republicans: The Genesis of an Early Party Machine, 1789–1817* (1964). An obituary is in the *Philadelphia Gazette & Daily Advertiser*, 5 May 1802.

HARRY M. WARD

HOWELL, Robert Boyte Crawford (10 Mar. 1801–5 Apr. 1868), Baptist minister, was born in Wayne County, North Carolina, the son of Ralph Howell and Jane Crawford, farmers. Reared in the Episcopal church, he became a Baptist in 1821. He briefly attended Columbian College, a Baptist school in Washington, D.C., but left after the 1825–1826 school year to become a lawyer in his native North Carolina. A religious experience in Portsmouth, Virginia, influenced his decision to become a missionary. He was ordained to the Baptist ministry in January 1827 and became pastor of Cumberland Street Baptist Church, Norfolk, Virginia. He married Mary Ann Morton Toy in 1829. They had ten children, two of whom died in infancy.

In 1834 Howell accepted appointment as a home missionary to Nashville, Tennessee, as a representative of the American Baptist Home Mission Society. He also became pastor of the First Baptist Church, a congregation torn by schism over the restorationist teaching of Alexander Campbell. Campbell's belief that he and his followers had restored the true church of Christ in its New Testament form led many to desert the Baptists for the Restorationist movement. The so-called Campbellite schism in the First Baptist Church led to the loss of the pastor, a majority of the members, and the church's property to the Campbellite or Christian movement.

In an effort to reclaim Baptist influence in Tennessee, Howell led in rebuilding First Baptist Church, dedicating a new facility for the congregation during the years 1837–1838. He reorganized a Sunday school in the First Baptist Church in 1835 (earlier efforts had not been successful), at that time the only Sunday school in the Tennessee region. Also in 1835 he founded *The Baptist*, a Tennessee periodical that continues today as the *Baptist and Reflector*, the official state paper of Tennessee Baptists. The paper helped to unite Baptists in the region, publishing news from the churches, sermons, and Bible study materials. Editorials addressed concerns and controversies in the church and the society.

From 1836 to 1841 Howell helped to establish numerous Baptist societies for mission work, ministerial education, colportage (providing missionaries on trains), publication, and Bible distribution. He participated in the founding of the Southern Baptist Convention (SBC) in 1845, serving as president of the denomination from 1851 to 1859. During his ministry he also served as president of the Southern Baptist Foreign Mission Board, the Bible Board, and the Sunday School Board. Howell was instrumental in the establishment of Union University, an early Tennessee Baptist school located in Jackson. His concern for the development of theological education for Baptist ministers influenced the founding of the Southern Baptist Theological Seminary in Greenville, South Carolina, in 1859.

As a leader of the nineteenth-century Southern Baptists, Howell confronted numerous denominational controversies. He opposed Campbellite Restorationism and frequently debated Christian preachers in the pulpit and the press. An advocate of missionary endeavors and the use of mission boards, he opposed the antimission forces inside and outside the Baptist fold. Perhaps his most intense altercation was his dispute with J. R. Graves and the forces of Old Landmarkism, an effort to trace Baptist origins all the way back to Jesus' baptism by John the Baptist in the Jordan River.

In 1850 Howell accepted the pastorate of the Second Baptist Church, Richmond, Virginia, and remained there until 1857, when he returned to the First Baptist Church, Nashville. During his absence, Graves became editor of *The Baptist*, promoting Landmark views in the Nashville region, even among the membership of the First Baptist Church. In response to Campbell's claim to have restored the true New Testament church, Landmarkists insisted that they could trace a succession of true Baptist churches across church history to the first-century Christian community; thus there was nothing to restore since Baptists had retained the "landmarks" of the true church from the beginning of Christianity. These marks included immersion baptism of believers, congregational autonomy, the Lord's Supper for church members only (closed communion), and the proper ministerial authority. Landmark supporters demanded that Southern Baptist churches conform to Landmark doctrines as the only valid Baptist theology.

Howell returned to the Nashville church, resisting Graves and the Landmarkers at every turn. He opposed Graves's efforts to establish the Southern Baptist Sunday School Union as a competing agency with the denomination's Publication Society. Graves attacked Howell and challenged him for the leadership of the First Baptist Church. Howell's supporters brought disciplinary charges against Graves, charging him with "sundry foul and atrocious libels" against the pastor. Subsequent trials led to Graves's dismissal from the congregation. The controversy raged throughout the Baptist system as Graves and his followers claimed to be the "true and orderly First Baptist Church" (McBeth, p. 456) and sought recognition as such by the Southern Baptist Convention in 1859. The convention rejected their claims and reelected Howell convention president on the first ballot. Howell promptly accepted then resigned the office in the interest of denominational harmony. While that action prevented a schism in the fledgling denomination, his election kept Landmarkism from dominating the theology and polity of the SBC.

When the Civil War led to Union occupation of Nashville in 1862, Howell and a group of other ministers were imprisoned for two months by Andrew Johnson, the military governor, because of their failure to take an oath of allegiance to the U.S. government. Howell remained pastor of First Baptist Church until 1867, resigning because of declining health. He died a year later in Nashville.

Howell published several books on Baptist doctrine and practice, including *Terms of Sacramental Communion* (1841), a study of the doctrine of the Lord's Supper; *The Deaconship* (1846), a discussion of the office of deacon in Baptist churches; and *The Way of Salvation* (1849), a description of the Baptist idea of conversion. He also wrote polemical works, including *The Evils of Infant Baptism* (1851), a response to what Baptists then called "pedo-baptist" churches. These books set forth a Baptist response to significant theological issues, articulating a denominational identity for churches and individuals in the Southern Baptist Convention. Howell also produced a two-volume unpublished manuscript, "A Memorial of the First Baptist Church, Nashville, Tennessee, from 1820 to 1863," a history of the church during his lifetime.

Howell's theology reflected a modified or evangelical Calvinism, which encouraged missionary activity and preaching as a means of awakening the elect and bringing them to conversion. He preached as if all could be saved, believing that preaching would awaken the hearts of the elect. His work as pastor and denominationalist shaped the Southern Baptist Convention in the last half of the nineteenth century by helping to form the more connectional convention organization and by helping to keep Landmarkism from dominating convention theology and polity.

• A recent biography of Howell is Joe W. Burton, *Road to Augusta: R. B. C. Howell and Formation of the Southern Baptist Convention* (1976). A discussion of his conflict with J. R.

Graves is found in Leon McBeth, *The Baptist Heritage* (1987), pp. 455–57. Lynn May, *A History of First Baptist Church, Nashville* (1970), also has substantial information about Howell's years as pastor. An obituary is in the *Nashville Republican Banner*, 7–8 Apr. 1868.

BILL J. LEONARD

HOWELL, William Henry (20 Feb. 1860–6 Feb. 1945), physiologist, was born in Baltimore, Maryland, the son of George Henry Howell, a businessman, and Virginia Teresa Magruder. Both the Howell and Magruder families had lived in the southern Maryland counties of Charles and Prince Georges since 1651, and, as children, Howell and his four siblings spent much time on the family's considerable land holdings in Prince Georges County. After attending City College, a Baltimore public high school, Howell entered the Johns Hopkins University in 1878, earning in 1881 an A.B. for completing the chemical-biological course intended to prepare students for medical school.

Although Howell did go on to take some medical courses at the University of Maryland, he never attended medical school, choosing instead to pursue graduate study in physiology at Johns Hopkins. For his dissertation, "The Origin of the Fibrin Formed in the Coagulation of Blood," completed under H. Newell Martin, Howell was awarded a Ph.D. in 1884. Howell's dissertation research conclusively demonstrated that only the chemical factors fibrinogen and thrombin—not fibrinogen and protein globulin as previously thought—were needed to mediate blood coagulation. The chemical and physiological mechanisms underlying the phenomenon of blood clotting remained for Howell the central research problem of his lengthy professional career of nearly sixty years.

Upon graduation in 1884, Howell was appointed assistant professor of biology at Johns Hopkins, where he continued to work in the physiology department as Martin's chief assistant and as head of the physiology laboratory course. A year after his marriage in 1887 to Anne Janet Tucker of Baltimore (with whom he had three children), Howell was promoted to associate professor of physiology. Howell's teaching responsibilities, after his promotion, expanded to include animal morphology, vertebrate histology, mammalian anatomy, and animal physiology. Although it provided him with valuable experience for his later career, the burdens of administration and teaching left Howell with little time to perform original research, resulting in his publishing only three brief papers from 1885 to 1889 on the blood's properties.

Howell left Johns Hopkins in 1889 to succeed Henry Sewall as lecturer (and later professor) of physiology and histology at the University of Michigan, Ann Arbor, where in 1891 he instituted the first required physiology laboratory course in an American medical school. Leaving the Michigan professorship in 1892, Howell joined the physiology department at Harvard Medical School, which was then under the direction of Henry Pickering Bowditch. Howell's research matured while at Michigan and at Harvard, leading to seminal work on the processes of nerve degeneration and regeneration and demonstrations that inorganic salts (rather than albumin/protein serum) were needed to sustain the heartbeat. In 1893 he returned to Johns Hopkins to become the first professor of physiology at the university's new medical school and to succeed his mentor Martin as chairman of the physiology department. Notably, Howell was the only one of the four preclinical department heads not to have research experience in a European laboratory. Unlike nearly all American physiologists of the late nineteenth century, Howell did not travel to study in European laboratories of physiology. He did briefly visit Carl Voit's laboratory in Munich and Wilhelm Kühne's laboratory in Heidelberg but did not undertake any research at either site. Howell remained until his death at Johns Hopkins, where from 1899 to 1911 he served as dean of the medical faculty and from 1926 to 1931 as director of the School of Hygiene and Public Health, which he had cofounded in 1916 with William Henry Welch.

Howell's research after his return to Johns Hopkins can be divided into two phases. In the first phase, extending to 1909, Howell pursued a variety of research interests, including neurophysiology and the physiology of sleep. In addition to demonstrating that the nerve impulse could be artificially obstructed with chemical inhibitors, Howell also made important observations on the responses of intracranial vasomotor nerves to chemical and electrical stimuli, showing the mechanical sensitivity of the brain's dura. While studying the physiological mechanics of sleep, Howell established the linear relationship between arterial pressure and blood flow in the brain. Another of Howell's research projects demonstrated that potassium was a chemical mediator of the vagus nerve's actions on the heart, as stimulation of the vagus released potassium at levels capable of stopping the beating heart. A final contribution from Howell during this period determined that the two lobes of the pituitary gland were functionally different.

After 1909 Howell investigated almost exclusively the physiology and the pathophysiology of blood. All but four of his thirty-eight research papers published after 1909 were about the physiology of blood. Recognizing that the mechanism of blood coagulation involved poorly known physicochemical reactions and substances, Howell devoted considerable time and energy to isolating and purifying the substances. In 1912 Howell showed that, unlike that of other vertebrates, mammalian plasma contained an inherent source of thromboplastin, a chemical factor necessary for clotting, and that the presence of another factor, antithrombin, prevented the clotting of intravascular blood. Intending to find a factor that could induce clotting, Howell's later research instead isolated, in 1918, an anticoagulant produced by the liver, which he named heparin. Heparin became an important clinical treatment in illnesses that threatened to spawn life-threatening blood clots. The pathophysiology of hemophilia was another of Howell's clinical interests, and in 1926, aided in his laboratory by three hemo-

philiac brothers, he suggested that the slow release of thromboplastin was responsible for the hemophiliac condition.

An impressive career as an administrator, teacher, and statesman of science complemented Howell's research accomplishments. While serving as dean of the medical faculty, Johns Hopkins considerably expanded its facilities and staff for teaching and research and began discussing the creation of a full-time plan of teaching and research appointments. Although he did no research in the field of hygiene and public health, Howell's skills in planning and organization were critical to the founding of the School of Hygiene and Public Health in 1916. As a teacher, Howell served as general editor of the collaborative effort of American physiologists to produce *An American Textbook of Physiology* (1896), which appeared in an even larger second edition in 1900. Howell completed his highly influential and popular *Textbook of Physiology for Medical Students and Physicians* in 1905. Howell's textbook went through fourteen editions by 1945 and was used by two generations of American medical students.

Soft-spoken, unassuming, and thoughtful, Howell was widely admired by his colleagues and his students. Three of his students—Joseph Erlanger, Herbert S. Gasser, and George H. Whipple—later received Nobel Prizes in physiology or medicine. His peers recognized his many accomplishments by electing Howell to the American Philosophical Society (1903) and the National Academy of Sciences (1905). Howell's experienced and sagacious leadership was called upon to guide the American Physiological Society (1905–1910), the National Research Council (1932–1933), and the International Physiological Congress (1929). By his achievements as an administrator, educator, and scholar, he played a profound role in shaping twentieth-century American physiology and medical education during a period of intense reform. Howell died in Baltimore.

• Howell's papers, consisting principally of drafts of articles and speeches, are in the Alan Mason Chesney Medical Archives at The Johns Hopkins University School of Medicine. Among his most important publications are, with G. Carl Huber, "A Physiological, Histological, and Clinical Study of the Degeneration and Regeneration in Peripheral Nerve Fibres after Severance of Their Connection with the Nerve Centers," *Journal of Physiology* 13 (1892): 335–406; "An Analysis of the Influence of the Sodium, Potassium, and Calcium Salts of the Blood on the Automatic Contraction of the Heart Muscle," *American Journal of Physiology* 6 (1901): 181–206; "The Preparation and Properties of Thrombin Together with Observations on Antithrombin and Prothrombin," *American Journal of Physiology* 26 (1910): 453–73; "The Condition of the Blood in Hemophilia, Thrombosis, and Purpura," *Archives of Internal Medicine* 13 (1914): 76–95; "Prothrombin," *American Journal of Physiology* 35 (1914): 474–82; "The Coagulation of Blood," *The Harvey Lectures*, ser. 12 (1916–1917): 273–324; with L. Emmett Holt, Jr., "Two New Factors in Blood Coagulation, Heparin and Proantithrombin," *American Journal of Physiology* 47 (1918): 328–41; "The Purification of Heparin and Its Presence in Blood," *American Journal of Physiology* 71 (1926): 553–62. The best available biographical study, by his student and Nobel laureate Joseph Erlanger, in National Academy of Sciences, *Biographical Memoirs* 26 (1951): 153–80, includes a complete list of Howell's extensive publications. A. McGehee Harvey details Howell's physiology career at Johns Hopkins in *Adventures in Medical Research: A Century of Discovery at Johns Hopkins* (1976). Howell's involvement with the School of Hygiene and Public Health is discussed by Elizabeth Fee in *Disease and Discovery: A History of the Johns Hopkins School of Hygiene and Public Health, 1916–1939* (1987) and "William Henry Howell: Physiologist and Philosopher of Life," *American Journal of Epidemiology* 119 (1984): 293–300.

D. GEORGE JOSEPH

HOWELLS, Elinor Mead (1 May 1837–7 May 1910), artist, was born in Chesterfield, New Hampshire, the daughter of Larkin Goldsmith Mead, a lawyer, and Mary Jane Noyes. Her parents settled the family in Brattleboro, Vermont, when Elinor was two years old, where they were highly respected for their community service and considered part of the "'intellectual aristocracy' of New England" (Cady, *Road*, p. 75). Elinor's father, called "Squire" Mead in admiration of his public works, founded Vermont's first savings bank and helped to create the town library and high school. Along with most of her eight siblings, Howells was educated at the Brattleboro High School, where she was a superior student. She grew up in a home where the sitting room table was always equipped with brightly colored paints, ready for any member of the family to use—and she was one of many Mead children who followed artistic callings in their adult lives. From March through June of 1862, on the invitation of her former teacher Clara E. Nourse, Howells taught at Nourse's English and French Family and Day School for girls in Cincinnati.

Elinor pursued painting in earnest after graduating from high school. Her brother, renowned sculptor Larkin Mead, quoted the well-known artist George Fuller as saying that Elinor "will, if she chooses, make a great painter" (Merrill and Arms, p. 3). Howells's artistic nature, as well as her characteristic wit, were evident in her first meeting with her future husband at a dance in Columbus, where she drew a caricature of sculptor J. Q. A. Ward on her fan, "convulsing" fellow revelers "by flashing and then concealing it in the folds of her fan" (Cady, *Road*, p. 75). She married aspiring writer William Dean Howells in 1862 and had three children. From the time of their marriage until July of 1865, the couple lived in Venice, Italy, where Howells's interest in art blossomed. She studied and copied several Venetian paintings, and she painted and sketched at Venetian street corners, buildings, and palaces. Some of her works were published as illustrations for her husband's writing, including his poem "Saint Christopher," published in *Harper's Monthly* in December 1863, as well as his Venetian poem *No Love Lost* (1869). Upon their return to the United States, the Howellses settled eventually in Cambridge, Massachusetts, where they lived from 1866 to 1878. Howells continued her artistic pursuits, receiving instruction in Boston in 1869; painting a portrait of her

mother-in-law, Mary Dean Howells, some time before June of 1871 as well as a watercolor of her children in 1874; and often incorporating numerous sketches into her letters. Howells was also the architect and interior designer for the Howellses' house on 37 Concord Avenue in Cambridge in 1872–1873 and was thoroughly involved in the building of their home in Belmont, Massachusetts, where they lived from 1878 to 1882. After a trip to Europe in 1882, the Howellses undertook an increasingly nomadic existence, moving among various cities in Massachusetts and New York. Though Howells painted less frequently in these later years than she had before, her interest in art endured throughout her life.

The strength of Howells's personality and intellect was noted by many who knew her, and made her a formidable critic of her husband's literary works. Her cousin Rutherford B. Hayes, the nineteenth president of the United States, said of Howells in 1858 that some thought her "'sarcastic,' but as she is not ill-natured in her satire, I like it" (Merrill, p. 24). Though she appeared to some in Columbus as "hyperintellectual and thus raised the Victorian specter of the 'advanced' woman in their minds" (Cady, *Road*, p. 76), William Dean Howells defended her to his family, saying in 1862 that "she has artistic genius, and a great deal of taste" (*Selected Letters*, vol. 1, p. 120). Calling Howells his "terriblest critic," her husband admitted that "there was never such insight as hers for truth of character, and fidelity to nature, and she held me to both unsparingly" (*SL*, vol. 2, p. 18; vol. 5, pp. 113–14). Not only did he discuss all of his most important literary ideas with Howells but she also read (or had read aloud to her) all of her husband's work before it was sent to the printer, perusing the proofs as well. This collaboration is quite significant given her husband's renown as a writer, editor, and shaper of American literary realism—indeed, his status as "dean of American letters" owes a great deal to the intellect and insights of his wife. Her husband described this "literary partnership, probably unique in the period" (Merrill and Arms, p. xxx), in *My Mark Twain* (1910) and *Years of My Youth* (1916). In addition to its expression in her husband's works, Howells's voice can be heard in her many extant letters, her unpublished *Venetian Diary* (1863–1869), and her pocket diary (1862–1866). Though she clearly enjoyed her involvement in her husband's literary career, and though her husband supported her artistic pursuits, Howells seemed to be aware of the fact that she was expected to put his work ahead of her own. In a letter to her father-in-law, William Cooper Howells, in 1863, she confesses that her husband "keeps me writing from morning till night you see. . . . I begin to think I'm rather more his *secretary* than his wife" (Merrill and Arms, p. 18).

In keeping with the expectations of nineteenth-century middle-class New England, Howells devoted much of her life to her husband and children. Yet throughout her life, she worked as a painter and sketch-artist and also served as an indispensable editor and critic of her husband's writing. In contributing to

William Dean Howells's illustrious career, she had a significant influence on American literary history; and in pursuing her talents as an artist, she was able to express more explicitly her own sensibilities. After suffering on and off from various ailments later in her life, she died in New York City.

• Many of Howells's papers are collected at the Houghton Library, Harvard University, as well as at the Massachusetts Historical Society and the Herrick Memorial Library, Alfred University. Some of her sketches, correspondence, photographs, artwork, and other miscellany can also be found at numerous other locations detailed meticulously in Ginette de B. Merrill and George Arms, eds., *If Not Literature: Letters of Elinor Mead Howells* (1988), which offers a detailed consideration of the subject's life and includes both a biographical introduction and a number of previously unpublished materials. See also Merrill's "The Meeting of Elinor Gertrude Mead and Will Howells and Their Courtship," *Old Northwest* 8, no. 1 (1982): 23–47. John W. Crowley explores the important topic of the Howells family dynamic of illness in "Winifred Howells and the Economy of Pain," *Old Northwest* 10, no. 1 (1984): 41–75. Both of these articles contain detailed footnotes that point the reader to many other sources on Howells.

A number of sources primarily designed as studies of the life and work of her husband also offer useful insights into Elinor Howells's life. See *Life in Letters of William Dean Howells*, ed. Mildred Howells (2 vols., 1928), and *Selected Letters of W. D. Howells*, ed. George Arms et al. (6 vols., 1979–1983). Two biographies written by Edwin H. Cady are also extremely useful: *The Road to Realism: The Early Years, 1837–1885* (1956), and *The Realist at War: The Mature Years, 1885–1920* (1958). Also useful is Kenneth S. Lynn, *William Dean Howells: An American Life* (1971).

JENNIFER S. TUTTLE

HOWELLS, William Dean (1 Mar. 1837–11 May 1920), author, was born in Martin's Ferry, Ohio, the son of William Cooper Howells, a "country printer," and Mary Dean. He was named for his uncle William Dean, a noted Ohio River steamboat pilot. All his life he felt ethnically different: "American," not "Anglo-Saxon." The Howellses were Welsh immigrants with Quakerish and radical leanings. In proslavery southern Ohio the father's radical notions (Swedenborgian, utopian, egalitarian, antislavery) cost him his newspaper in Hamilton, scene of *A Boy's Town* (1890), and in 1848 plunged the family into painful poverty and a struggle to recover that did not entirely succeed before the Civil War.

They were rescued in 1852 by radical allies from Ashtabula County, Ohio, which sent an antislavery congressman, Joshua Giddings, to Washington. The family printed the *Ashtabula Sentinel*, "the voice of Giddings," in Jefferson, Ohio, and slowly paid for their property.

Howells learned sympathy for liberty and social justice at home. Beginning to set type in childhood he acquired habits of hard work that remained to his deathbed. *My Literary Passions* (1895) and *Years of My Youth* (1916) tell how the autodidact, schooled largely in the printshop, mastered languages and literatures. Toiling furiously during the hours after he had set a

man's daily stint of type, he read English literature and got a literary use of Spanish, Latin, French, and German. Bewitched by the ironies of Heinrich Heine, he distanced himself from earlier passions for Alfred Lord Tennyson and Henry Wadsworth Longfellow. He would always feel ambivalent toward romantic and antiromantic sensibilities, though to think and write according to his antiromantic vision made him distinctively Howells.

In all, Howells wrote "about 200 books wholly or in part," say Gibson and Arms. His first publication, a poem, came in 1852. Between 1860 and 1921 appeared thirty-six novels, twelve books of travel, ten volumes of short stories and sketches, seven of literary criticism, five of autobiography, four of poetry, three of collected drama, and two presidential campaign biographies. There were many hundreds of essays, reviews, editorials, speeches, poems, farces, and miscellanea—some of them collected. He published in sixty-four magazines and nineteen newspapers and conducted eight different serial columns. At a time when the media were predominantly literate, Howells was the major presence. This was especially true during the 1890s.

Country newspapers before the Civil War served political interests. In the family shop Howells breathed politics, and he succeeded as a legislative reporter to a Cincinnati newspaper before he was twenty. In 1858 he jumped to an editorial post on the Republican *Ohio State Journal* in Columbus and became a poet and critic and man-about-town in the city. By 1861 he had placed poetry, fiction, and criticism in nationally conspicuous magazines (*Knickerbocker, Saturday Press, Atlantic Monthly*) and had published a collection of verse (*Poems of Two Friends*, 1860) and a campaign biography of Abraham Lincoln. In 1861 Lincoln's secretaries John George Nicolay and John Milton Hay helped this deserving Republican win appointment as the U.S. consul in Venice.

On 24 December 1862 Howells married Elinor Mead, a painter and illustrator, at the American embassy in Paris. As Merrill and Arms say, "Their marriage was fulfilling and their life together brimming with fun." She sprang from an extraordinary tribe: John Humphrey Noyes was an uncle and Rutherford B. Hayes a cousin; among her brothers were Larkin Mead the sculptor and William Mead the architect. The Howells had three children, and all were artistically gifted. John Mead Howells became a leading architect.

Elinor Mead Howells seemed to her husband to possess as a critic something akin to absolute pitch. In the retrospect of *Years of My Youth* he said that "she became with her unerring artistic taste and conscience my constant impulse toward reality in my work." Through the insights of Ginette de B. Merrill it is clear that Elinor Mead was one of the significant women of her era.

It is not true, though H. L. Mencken casually said it was, that Howells's books had "no . . . ideas in them." Perhaps Howells was too sensitive for Mencken. "Mr. Howells," wrote Hamlin Garland in 1892, "has come to stand for the most vital and progressive principle in American literature" and speaks to "the more radical wing of our literary public." Garland's Howells had begun to emerge with *Venetian Life* (1866). In Venice the Western radical and Heinesque ironist recognized that the contemporary common life of the people in a ruined and antiromantic city groaning under Hapsburg tyranny interested him, not the dreams of Lord Byron, James Fenimore Cooper, or John Ruskin. The charm of his book has kept it alive to this day. By the time Mark Twain published *The Innocents Abroad* (1869) he would find Howells, already master of much the same reductive vision, waiting to review the book and applaud him. It began a friendship good for life.

Home from Italy, Howells discovered that the same vision succeeded when he applied it to American realities (*Suburban Sketches*, 1871; *Their Wedding Journey*, 1872). Success led him to thoroughly fictional narrative in *A Chance Acquaintance* (1873) and to paired discoveries. He wished, as he told his friend Henry James (1843–1916), to confront one American sort, the "unconventional"—the native, common, democratic—with the "conventional"—the Europeanized, urban, aristocratic—American type. And, as he wrote his father, his preference for the "unconventional" American elated him: it proved that he felt "the true spirit of Democracy."

Howells experienced that elation, that adventure in ideas, at a time when some critics have believed that he was smothered under the conventionalities of Boston and Cambridge. In fact he had launched what Annie R. M. Logan called in 1890 "A series appropriately entitled 'Boston Under the Scalpel' or 'Boston Torn to Tatters.'" When he came home after the Civil War, Howells went to New York to establish a literary career. He was scarcely settled into a job on E. L. Godkin's *Nation* when James T. Fields came to recruit him as assistant editor of the *Atlantic Monthly*.

That was the best job in the world for Howells. He began work on 1 March 1866, his twenty-ninth birthday. The literary nation took note. A western phenomenon, poet, critic, and authority on contemporary Italian literature was now second in command of the flagship American magazine. He lived in Cambridge, close to the press to which proof corrections took him. In truth, Howells hardly ever lived in Boston: only a relatively few months in 1883–1884 and again in 1890–1891 before he moved to New York on 8 November 1891.

For about a dozen years, from 1866 to 1878, Cambridge seemed "the perfect home." The Howells family moved around in it so regularly that they appeared nomadic. The Fireside Poets Oliver Wendell Holmes (1809–1894), Henry Wadsworth Longfellow, and James Russell Lowell were Harvard professors with national reputations. Howells, with his gift for friendship, won theirs and would focus *Literary Friends and Acquaintance* (1900) on them because by that time they and Old Cambridge were dead, and decorum allowed

him to stand as a privileged witness. Longfellow admitted Howells to the weekly sessions of the Dante Club. Holmes gave him spiritual counsel. Lowell took him on long walks and talked for hours on end about literature and how to build a career. Only hints, however, of other, more important associations in Cambridge appear in *Literary Friends*. At that moment the town sparkled as one of the most exciting intellectual centers in the United States.

Fields assigned Howells to recruit new writers for the *Atlantic*; Howells obliged, and his coevals felt gratified. Business aside, he formed friendships with three older men: Henry James, Sr. (1811–1882), Charles Eliot Norton, and Francis Child. But the true galaxy consisted of people about his own age: William James, Henry James (1843–1916), and Alice James; Henry Adams (1838–1918) and Brooks Adams; John Fiske (1842–1901); and the younger Oliver Wendell Holmes (1841–1935).

In Cambridge, Howells learned to deal with the chief ideas of his day. The intellectual atmosphere was intense, stimulating, international: philosophic and scientific as well as aesthetic. New thought, especially Darwinism in its permutations, agitated the town and forced its way into the book reviews in the *Atlantic*—of which Howells had charge and wrote many. His fiction became increasingly sophisticated in fine novels like *A Foregone Conclusion* (1875) and *The Undiscovered Country* (1880), as he learned techniques and stances from new literary passions like Turgenev. He began to write a novel a year.

In 1881 Howells resigned his editorship to devote himself to fiction. His vision deepened and darkened in works like *A Modern Instance* (1882), *The Rise of Silas Lapham* (1885), and *Indian Summer* (1886). Losing the moral euphoria of the postwar years and uneasy about industrializing, urbanizing America, Howells and his generation felt qualms about romantic, democratic American life. His work began to look to humane values: the ethics of "the economy of pain" *(Lapham)* and "complicity" (*The Minister's Charge*, 1887) and "solidarity" (*Annie Kilburn*, 1889). Tolstoy hit him with a force almost equal to religious conversion. In *A Hazard of New Fortunes* (1890), he discovered another basis for his concern with ethical principles. It may be that the sins of evil persons find vicarious atonement in the suffering of the good.

The years 1886 to 1891 were a time of "black care" for Howells despite the fact that the period began with a stroke of wonderful professional luck. The good luck came in the contract he signed with Harper & Brothers in 1885. For an annual salary of $10,000 he was to write a novel a year to be serialized in *Harper's Monthly*, plus a monthly column on subjects of his choosing. The money and security were, he said, "incredibly advantageous." "The Editor's Study" began in January 1886 with a bang. Soon Howells became a fighting critic who espoused the modern, the democratic and common, even contending for "the superiority of the vulgar" over Matthew Arnold and against British resistance to international literary realism. He argued for sociopolitical compassion and reform even to the point of socialism. The wide public for *Harper's Monthly* discovered in the "Study" Edward Harrigan and James A. Herne, Dostoyevsky, Emily Dickinson, Hamlin Garland, William James, Harold Frederic, and the contemporary Spanish realists. Howells praised American women local colorists and George Washington Cable, Henry James, Emile Zola, Mark Twain, John William De Forest, and, of course, Tolstoy. The "Study" employed terms like "neo-romantic" and "effectism." Opponents both native and transatlantic fired back a barrage of often slanderous retort.

The last "Study" appeared in March 1892, but during its course Howells passed through events so momentous they made the troubles of his critical controversies trivial by comparison. His daughter Winifred was stricken with a mysterious illness and died in 1889. Her health had been blighted for nine years, and she spent most of the years after 1886 in sanatoriums.

Simultaneously, Howells faced the most menacing crisis of conscience in his life. On May Day 1886 American labor unions went on strike for an eight-hour workday. In Chicago the police were murderously violent in putting down the strike. On 4 May police tried to break up a mass protest in the Haymarket Square. Someone threw a bomb, and several policemen were killed. With no actual suspects available, authorities rounded up eight Anarchists, tried them for murder on charges of advocating and inciting to violence, found them guilty, and sentenced seven of them to be hanged. Howells felt morally outraged: they were to be hanged for expressions of opinion. He thought their opinions "frantic" but considered the miscarriage of justice intolerable. He published letters in the *New York Tribune* and the *Chicago Tribune* in which he argued for gubernatorial clemency to commute the death sentences.

Howells stood alone among American celebrities in this act of conscience and common sense. The press ridiculed and damned Howells and rejoiced when four Anarchists were hanged on 11 November, a fifth having committed suicide. Howells risked his professional reputation for a moral principle. Luckily he lost only his fight for liberty of speech and conscience, not his livelihood. The popular success of *A Hazard of New Fortunes*, which dealt with issues of wealth and poverty, capital, labor, socialism, urban crisis, and violence, vindicated him.

Many students of Howells have ignored all or most of his last thirty years. Yet much of his best work, including a number of developments and departures, took place during these years. Howells stepped forward into the nascent modernist movement. Between 1890 and 1900 he published thirteen novels, four memoirs, and a book each of poetry, criticism, and collected essays. He ran three series of columns. He championed Charlotte Perkins Gilman, Stephen Crane, Frank Norris, Paul Laurence Dunbar, Charles Chesnutt, Abraham Cahan, Thorstein Veblen, Henrik Ibsen, and George Bernard Shaw, demolished Max Nordau, and defended *Anna Karenina* and *The Kreutzer Sonata*. He developed as a feminist, an anti-imperialist, an egalitarian, and a socialist. He moved toward psychological realism and produced utopian romances.

Other important books from the 1890s are: *The Shadow of a Dream* (1890), a pre-Freudian study of a complex sexual triangle; *A Boy's Town* (1890), which fascinated Dr. S. Weir Mitchell for its insights into childhood terror; *An Imperative Duty* (1893), a miscegenation novel praised by W. E. B. Du Bois; *The Quality of Mercy* (1892), the study of a business man turned fugitive embezzler; *A Traveller from Altruria* (1894), a utopian romance; *Stops of Various Quills* (1895), a collection of dark, modernist poetry; and *The Landlord at Lion's Head* (1897). During the 1890s Howells was virtually a literature in himself.

Psychic motives partly spurred Howells's prodigious output. Against the Haymarket crisis and the "Study" fight he reacted with creative indignation. His daughter's illness and death almost silenced him, but he rebounded because work was his solace and refuge. He carried a message to the disintegrating world: *The World of Chance* he called it in an interesting novel of 1893. New personal economic realities also motivated him. With other publishers wooing him, Howells and the Harpers agreed to disagree before his contract expired. On 1 January 1891 he became a freelancer. At the end of the year he moved to New York to edit *Cosmopolitan* magazine, owned by a reform-minded millionaire. Howells hoped, as he said, "to do something for humanity as well as the humanities." But he and the millionaire had misunderstood each other, and Howells was free again by June.

Howells's work was serialized in various periodicals, but Harper & Brothers published his books. Howells was shocked, then, when Harper & Brothers failed in November 1899. As soon as he could, however, George Harvey, the new head of the firm, struck a bargain with Howells. This new contract was much like the original: he was to produce a book a year and conduct the famous "Editor's Easy Chair" column monthly. The Harpers were to have first refusal of everything he wrote, but he could publish for extra pay in their *Weekly* or *Bazar* or in the ancient *North American Review*, which Harvey owned personally. Howells did place editorials in the *Weekly*, major criticism in the *North American*, and material especially for women in *Bazar*. He also recruited novelists, among them Edith Wharton, Robert Herrick, Henry B. Fuller, George Ade, and of course Henry James, for a new Harper stable.

Though the fighting realist, social critic, and anti-imperialist tended to appear in the *North American* and the *Weekly*, it is not true that pungency deserted "The Editor's Easy Chair" under Howells. The best of his literary criticism and his best poetry appeared in the period 1900–1916. Among the novels of the last decades, *The Kentons* (1902); *The Son of Royal Langbrith* (1904); *Through the Eye of the Needle* (1907), the sequel to his utopian romance; *The Leatherwood God* (1916); and *The Vacation of the Kelwyns* (1920) have notably caught the attention of critics in later generations. *Questionable Shapes* (1903) and *Between the Dark and the Daylight* (1907) gathered excellent short stories, mainly supernatural, but including "Editha," a favorite choice of classroom anthologies. The travel books of the period, especially *London Films* (1905), *Certain Delightful English Towns* (1906), and *Seven English Cities* (1909), draw present-day interest. *My Mark Twain* (1910) is a unique literary memoir. *The Mother and the Father* (1909), with its sinewy blank verse, seems always about to be rediscovered.

With the younger generation he tried to lead into a new realism Howells had bad luck. The best died tragically young, a "generation lost": Frederic in 1898, Crane in 1900, Norris in 1902. He never hit it off with Theodore Dreiser, though Howells put "The Lost Phoebe" into his *Great Modern American Stories* (1920). A third of the pieces anthologized in that volume were written by women, including some by older friends like Sarah Orne Jewett, Mary Wilkins Freeman, and Alice Brown, and others by newer friends like Edith Wharton, Edith Wyatt, and Charlotte Perkins Gilman. Gilman's "The Yellow Wall Paper" was a special case: Howells had secured its first publication in 1892 and was first to reprint it.

Honors were heaped on Howells as he aged. An evanescent town and a five-cent cigar took his name. He presided over the first meeting of the National Institute of Arts and Letters in 1900 and served as its president until 1904. He then became a charter member of the American Academy of Arts and Letters and its president for life. He played a leading role in founding the National Association for the Advancement of Colored People. The celebration of his seventy-fifth birthday was a national event; President William H. Taft attended. Howells died in New York City. To mainstream America, so far as it cared, he became an icon—required reading in many high schools. And a new professional generation took him as a target for iconoclasm.

In his time Howells was famous for the personality that still shines through his letters and his art. Who else could have been the intimate friend of both Henry James and Mark Twain? Howells charmed women and men with wit, extraordinary verbal facility, kindness, and gentleness. Yet to overlook his mastery of every mode of irony is to overlook Howells. Irony requires plural habits of thought and complex vision. With a deep capacity to suffer, he forged his personality in the fires of inner conflict. His ironies could be delightfully funny; "droll" was a word he loved so well that he used it as a verb. He consciously released aggressions and resentments into critical irony. His dark ironies were deadly, and he knew the power of tragic irony. Nevertheless, to fail to grasp the implications of his self-irony, his self-deprecation, is to lose Howells altogether.

He realized that he might have been a greater artist had he written less. But he could hardly have helped being Howells as he was. The great reputation that declined disastrously during the last decade of his life began to revive at the centennial of his birth in 1937. His name has risen slowly but steadily since. His place in literary and cultural history is established. Editing of his work and his correspondence has become a minor industry.

At the low point of Howells's reputation modernist critics condemned him as "feminine" and "shallow" and "smiling" and "squeamish" to the point of ignoring sexuality. During the second half of the twentieth century, however, revisionist studies challenged such notions, and taste changed over time. The "feminine" came to be seen as a good in itself. "Shallow" Howells disappeared before perception of the serious social and moral critic, a prescient and complex ironist. "Smiling" Howells was set beside a man often conflicted and anguished, with his own sort of tragic vision. In place of the "squeamish" Howells, readers recognized an artist in whose work sexuality, carefully coded, is richly present.

The late twentieth-century essays on Howells by Gore Vidal and John Updike are a milepost. In "'The Peculiar American Stamp'" (*New York Review of Books*, 27 Oct. 1983), Vidal characterizes him as "a master of irony" who "wrote a half-dozen of the Republic's best novels" with an "avant-garde realism" in which may be found "a darkness sufficiently sable for even the most lost-and-found of literary generations." In "A Critic at Large: Howells as Anti-Novelist" (*New Yorker*, 13 July 1987) and "Rereading *Indian Summer*" (*New York Review of Books*, 1 Feb. 1990) Updike sees an artist who is not only postmodern, but avant-garde: a natural antinovelist. Where Vidal is struck by Howells's "lapidary" sentences, Updike responds to the "felicity" of the style—as Twain and James did a hundred years before. Updike finds Howells "fascinated and truthful" about sex. Sex in Howells's novels, says Updike, "surfaces in sudden small gestures or objects of fetishistic intensity." Most of all, "today's fiction . . . has turned, with an informal—a minimalist—bluntness, to the areas of domestic morality and sexual politics which interested Howells. . . . Howells' agenda remains our agenda."

• The central collection of Howells's papers is held by the Houghton Library, Harvard, though important collections exist in many places. *A Bibliography of William Dean Howells*, ed. William M. Gibson and George Arms (1948), marks the beginning of serious Howells studies, and it remains the standard. Also indispensable are the major collections of published letters: *Life in Letters of William Dean Howells*, ed. Mildred Howells (1928); *Mark Twain-Howells Letters*, ed. H. N. Smith and Gibson (1960); *W. D. Howells: Selected Letters*, ed. C. Lohmann et al. (6 vols., 1978–1983); and *If Not Literature: Letters of Elinor Mead Howells*, ed. Ginette de B. Merrill and Arms (1988). The nineteen volumes thus far published of *A Selected Edition of W. D. Howells* are important for their editorial materials as well as the texts. Significant other collections of Howells's writings are *The Complete Plays of W. D. Howells*, ed. Walter J. Meserve (1960); *W. D. Howells as Critic*, ed. Edwin H. Cady (1973); and *The Early Prose Writings of William Dean Howells (1853–1861)*, ed. Thomas Wortham (1990). Also see *Critical Essays on W. D. Howells, 1866–1920*, ed. E. H. Cady and Norma W. Cady (1983).

The main biographies are Edwin H. Cady, *William Dean Howells: Dean of American Letters* (1958); Van Wyck Brooks, *Howells: His Life and World* (1959); and Kenneth S. Lynn, *William Dean Howells: An American Life* (1971). Studies mainly focused on the early life include James Woodress, *Howells and Italy* (1952); Olov Fryckstedt, *In Quest of America: A Study of William Dean Howells' Early Development* (1958); John W. Crowley, *The Black Heart's Truth: The Early Career of W. D. Howells* (1985); Cady, *Young Howells & John Brown: Episodes in a Radical Education* (1985); and Rodney D. Olsen, *Dancing in Chains: The Youth of William Dean Howells* (1991).

Among the major critical volumes are O. W. Firkins, *William Dean Howells: A Study* (1924); Everett Carter, *Howells and the Age of Realism* (1954); George N. Bennett, *William Dean Howells: The Development of a Novelist* (1959); George C. Carrington, *The Immense Complex Drama: The World and Art of the Howells Novel* (1966); Kermit Vanderbilt, *The Achievement of William Dean Howells* (1968); George N. Bennett, *The Realism of William Dean Howells, 1889–1920* (1973); and Elizabeth S. Prioleau, *The Circle of Eros: Sexuality in the Work of William Dean Howells* (1983). The best obituary is by Booth Tarkington, "Mr. Howells," *Harper's Monthly*, Aug. 1920.

EDWIN H. CADY

HOWETSON, James (?–4 July 1777), was a New York Loyalist and commander of the Loyal Volunteers. There are many variant spellings of Howetson's name. One of many versions is his wife's, who spelled it Hewetson (which is probably how it was pronounced). Little is known about Howetson's background, save that he was a retired lieutenant of the British army on half pay. Before 1776 he settled in Lunenburgh, located in the Coxsackie district of Albany County, New York.

As early as January 1776, the patriot committee of Coxsackie was watching him closely. On 30 April 1776 the Albany committee forced him to sign a parole, which was meant to restrict his activities. He agreed to stay in Coxsackie and not communicate in any way with Loyalists to oppose the Revolution.

Clearly, however, Howetson had no intention of honoring his parole. During August 1776 he had violated his agreement in some fashion. The patriots, rather mildly, advised him to behave himself. Nonetheless, he was probably involved in the Tory activities of October 1776 that occurred in Coxsackie.

The capture of New York City by the British (Sept. 1776) had to have emboldened him. If what New England minister Ezra Stiles stated in his *Literary Diary* (vol. 2 [1901], p. 160) is correct, Howetson was communicating with the British by a roundabout Tory network. Loyalists of western Massachusetts brought him a commission as the colonel of the "Loyal Volunteers," who were supposed to be raised from Tories of Albany County.

This Loyalist battalion had the blessing of the British high command, New York's royal governor, William Tryon, and Sir John Johnson, who was already trying to raise a Tory regiment. Unlike other Loyalist military units, which were created in British-controlled areas, the Loyal Volunteers had to be formed secretly, as it was operating deep within rebel territory. Before any potential recruit would be told about the Loyal Volunteers, he had to swear to complete secrecy. Recruits were offered terms akin to what other Tory soldiers obtained, including bounty land. To protect Howetson, documents stated that he was the commander, but they only gave his initials.

Exactly what Howetson and his soldiers were supposed to do, aside from eventually joining the British and overcoming the patriots, is unclear. There was talk among themselves of an attack to free confined Tories. More grandiose ideas included capturing the Albany jail, the patriot supply of gunpowder in Albany, and even the city itself. But, apparently, the only thing Howetson's men ever succeeded in doing was disarming some patriot militia.

Howetson and his hopeful officers scoured the countryside looking for men willing to join them. One of their richest recruiting grounds was the King's District section of New York, which was populated by New Englanders, some of whom were Anglicans. Howetson then moved into Livingston Manor, where some of the tenants enlisted. One of them, Aernout Viele, allegedly became an industrious recruiter. A number of these tenants seem to have joined Howetson's force because they had been told that some of the aristocratic Livingston family, who owned Livingston Manor, were involved with it.

On 2 May 1777 Howetson and his Loyal Volunteers were attacked near Livingston Manor's border with Massachusetts by patriot militiamen from both New York and New England. Small-scale fighting also occurred during 3 May, but the Loyalists were easily defeated. Howetson, Viele, and others were captured. A number of his recruits managed to evade their pursuers and remained in the area, committing robberies, for some time. Finally driven away, these survivors, led by Thomas Garnett, linked up with Johnson's troops in September 1778.

Howetson had already met his fate by that time. The Loyalists were tried by court-martial for "traitorously" recruiting for the British while subject to New York State. Howetson's trial, which took place on 14 June 1777, was quick, despite his claim of innocence. The prosecution produced witnesses who detailed the various steps taken by the Loyalists to enlist men. One witness stated that Howetson had declared that the initials J. H., which indicated the commander in the documents, stood for himself. The Tory's defense was a feeble one. He was found guilty and was condemned to death. Howetson remained unrepentant. His coffin had on it a crown, the king's initials, and, to symbolize the Loyalist's love for the monarch, a heart. Viele would also suffer the death penalty.

After the hanging of Howetson in Albany, his wife, Catherine—who had tried, unsuccessfully, to save his life—took her children to New York City. When General Guy Carleton was in command, he showed her much kindness. In 1783 after she petitioned him, Carleton awarded her twelve-year-old son an ensign's commission, which, even on half pay, provided for his schooling.

• There are no James Howetson letters. His wife's letter of 2 Oct. 1783 to Carleton is in the British Headquarters Papers, no. 9772, New York Public Library. The Haldimand papers, British Museum Additional Manuscript 21818, has two lists of his men; the Library of Congress has transcripts. The record of his trial is in *Calendar of Historical Manuscripts Relating to the War of the Revolution in the Office of the Secretary of State*, vol. 2 (1868), pp. 225–29. Other information is in *Minutes of the Albany Committee of Correspondence* (2 vols., 1923–1925), and William H. W. Sabine, ed., *Historical Memoirs from 12 July 1776 to 25 July 1778 of William Smith* (1958). There is no biography. The only account of Howetson is in Philip Ranlet, *The New York Loyalists* (1986).

PHILIP RANLET

HOWEY, Walter Crawford (16 Jan. 1882–21 Mar. 1954), journalist and inventor, was born in Fort Dodge, Iowa, the son of Frank Harris Howey, a helper in a drug, paint, and wallpaper store and later a businessman, and Rosa Crawford. He attended public schools and, ambitious to become an artist, took classes at the Chicago Art Institute in 1899 and 1900. Returning to Fort Dodge, he was hired as editor of the *Fort Dodge Chronicle* in 1900. He scooped the nation in 1901 by writing up the death of President William McKinley before it had quite occurred. He had the report set in type, bribed by telephone a servant near the wounded president to notify him the instant McKinley died, and rushed the report onto the streets. In 1902 and 1903 he worked for the rival *Fort Dodge Messenger*. In 1903 he moved to Des Moines, Iowa, and briefly reported for the *Des Moines Daily Capital*. Ambitious to be a big-city reporter, he went to Chicago, fibbed about his experience and knowledge of Chicago, and got a job with the *Daily News*. On 30 December 1903 he chanced to see an event that made Chicago newspaper history. He observed a knight in armor and three elves with wings emerge from a manhole. They were part of a group of actors, followed by other people, escaping the horrible Iroquois Theater fire by an underground passage. But 602 people were burned or trampled to death. Howey telephoned the story in from a nearby store. He was hired by the *Chicago American* in October 1904 and within two weeks was promoted to assistant city editor.

Howey stayed with the *Chicago American* until 1906. He was city editor of the *Inter-Ocean* (1906–1907), the youngest in such a position in the United States at that time. He moved to become city editor of the morning *Chicago Tribune* in 1907 and remained there a decade. In 1917 he argued with Joseph Medill Patterson, the *Tribune* copublisher, and quit his position, which paid $8,000 annually. According to legend, he walked straight over to the rival morning paper, the *Herald-Examiner*. William Randolph Hearst, the owner and an admirer of Howey, offered him $35,000 on the spot to be his managing editor. Howey worked for the next five years in Chicago for Hearst, whom he always esteemed. He scooped rival papers both by ability and

by trickery. He ordered his reporters to find news, introduce their stories dramatically, write well, and vary their styles. He often condensed the results himself to bare-bones excitement. In 1919 the *Herald-Examiner* was the only newspaper to endorse William Hale Thompson, who successfully ran for mayor of Chicago. In gratitude for the support, Thompson posted city policemen in Howey's office with orders to escort his reporters to crime scenes, keep rival photographers away, and let only Howey's men into private interrogation rooms. The *Herald-Examiner* naturally obtained many exclusives. Howey's envious competitors often complained to city officials—but always in vain, because they were aware that Howey knew about the criminal conduct of many of them and would expose them if need be.

In 1922 Howey went to Boston as managing editor of Hearst's faltering *American* and immediately improved its circulation, often by sensationalizing the news. Two years later he left Boston, studied journalistic techniques in England for a few weeks, and then, on short notice, founded Hearst's notorious tabloid the *New York Mirror*. Howey was attuned to tabloids since his style always was to present sensational news to the eager public in crisp form, complete with garish pictures.

In 1928 Charles MacArthur, one of Howey's former general assignment reporters and a budding playwright, teamed up with Ben Hecht, the prolific Chicago reporter and author, to write *The Front Page*. Opening in New York City, it was the first realistic American newspaper drama and enjoyed a rollicking nine-month run. Walter Burns, the hard-driving, shrewd, cynical editor, was closely based on Walter Howey, whom both MacArthur and Hecht knew well. Some reviewers regarded the play as too sensational to be credible, but the playwrights insisted that they restrained themselves. In *Charlie*, his biography of MacArthur, Hecht says that "the Howey and MacArthur of the *Examiner* office in 1919 would have made too eerie a tale for any theatre." MacArthur affectionately called Howey "Mister Front Page."

In 1931 Howey invented and patented an automatic photoelectric engraving machine. Four years later he developed the so-called soundphoto method of transmitting half-tone pictures over telephone lines. The device used a photoelectric cell to transform light-volume variations into sound-volume variations and could send an $8'' \times 10''$ picture in fourteen minutes. A device at the receiving end reversed the procedure by use of a synchronized tuning fork. Howey hastened the use of wirephotos throughout the newspaper industry. He ultimately owned seventeen patents.

Howey returned to Boston in 1939 and became the editor of the *Boston Record-American* there. Ever restless, he went to Chicago and edited the *Herald-American* (1942–1944) and also became Hearst's special editorial assistant (1944–1951). When Hearst died in 1951, Howey became the executive editor of three Boston newspapers—the *Boston Evening American*, the *Boston Daily Record*, and the *Boston Sunday Advertiser*.

During his last years, he mellowed somewhat and displayed less bravado.

Little is known about the personal life of Walter Howey, this old-style, expert newsman who was so brash and noisy in public. He was twice wed. In 1900 he married Elizabeth Board. They had no children, and she died in 1935. A year later he married Gloria Ritz. They had one child, whom they named William Randolph, after William Randolph Hearst. In January 1954 Howey was badly injured when a taxi skidded and plowed a mailbox on top of him. Ten days later, while he was still in the hospital for treatment, his wife died of pneumonia. He was apparently on the road to recovery when, continuing to manage his professional duties, he suddenly died at his home in Boston. Howey epitomizes many a hard-driving, zany, ruthless big-city editor of the frenzied decades between World War I and World War II, when to gain a scoop it was considered legitimate to steal and publish evidence, plant or even print false stories to discomfit rival reporters, bribe the police, and blackmail political officials.

• Paul H. Stevens, "Walter Crawford Howey: Fort Dodge's Most Famous Journalist," *Palimpsest* 56 (Jan.–Feb. 1975): 22–31, is a short, detailed biography and mentions several hoaxes Howey staged. Alfred McClung Lee, *The Daily Newspaper in America: The Evolution of a Social Instrument* (1937), and Frank Luther Mott, *American Journalism, a History 1690–1960*, 3d ed. (1962), provide details of Howey's two main inventions. Stephen Bates, *If No News, Send Rumors: Anecdotes of American Journalism* (1989), discusses Howey, his trickery, and the character based on him in *The Front Page* by Charles MacArthur and Ben Hecht. Hecht, *Charlie: The Improbable Life and Times of Charles MacArthur* (1957), and John L. McPhaul, *Deadlines & Monkeyshines: The Fabled World of Chicago Journalism* (1962), provide details of Howey's journalistic work in Chicago. W. A. Swanberg, *Citizen Hearst: A Biography of William Randolph Hearst* (1961), touches on Howey's association with Hearst. Obituaries are in the *Boston Record-American* and the *New York Times*, both 22 Mar. 1954.

ROBERT L. GALE

HOWISON, George Holmes (29 Nov. 1834–31 Dec. 1916), philosopher and teacher, was born in Montgomery County, Maryland, the son of Robert Howison, a landholder and farmer, and Eliza Holmes. At age four Howison moved with his family to Marietta, Ohio, where he spent the remainder of his youth. In 1849 Howison entered Marietta College after studying the first half year of his freshman course under his secondary school teacher. Graduating from Marietta in 1852, he enrolled in Lane Theological Seminary in Cincinnati. Although he finished the program, Howison decided against taking a pastorate and embarked instead on a teaching career. He at first served as an itinerant high school teacher, working in four different towns in Ohio before moving to Salem, Massachusetts, in 1854.

While at Salem, Howison married in 1863 another schoolteacher, Lois Thompson Caswell, niece of the president of Brown University. The couple did not have children. In 1864 the two moved to St. Louis.

There Howison became professor of mathematics at Washington University. Later, he also taught both political economy and Latin. While in St. Louis, Howison's interest in philosophy, which had begun to develop in Salem, received further impetus from his association with the St. Louis Philosophical Society. The leaders of the society, William Torrey Harris and Henry Brokmeyer, interested Howison in German idealism and in particular the writings of Immanuel Kant and G. W. F. Hegel. These philosophers established the groundwork from which Howison's own personalistic idealism later emerged. Howison also came under the sway of Ralph Waldo Emerson and Bronson Alcott when they came west to lecture to the philosophical society.

In 1869 Howison published his first book, *A Treatise on Analytic Geometry*. His teaching at Washington University was very successful, but he was interested in moving to the East to be closer to the center of intellectual activity. In 1871, therefore, the Howisons moved to Boston; later in that year the Massachusetts Institute of Technology offered him a professorship in logic and the philosophy of science. Initially things went well: Howison continued to publish and lecture in philosophy, and he enjoyed participating both in the Harvard Philosophical Club and in Cambridge's informal Metaphysical Club with the likes of Thomas Davidson, Charles Peirce, William James, and John Fiske. In 1878, however, MIT suffered financial difficulties and was forced to eliminate Howison's position. From 1879 to 1884 Howison worked in a variety of capacities. He received a one-year appointment at Harvard Divinity School, studied in Europe, lectured several times at the Concord School of Philosophy, and spent a year in private tutoring in Boston. When it appeared that Howison's options were beginning to run out, he was offered a professorship at the University of California. Although he was at first uncertain about moving to the West Coast, Howison accepted the Mills Chair of Mental and Moral Philosophy and Civil Polity, a position he held until 1909. It was in this last stage of his career that he had his greatest successes as a teacher and philosopher.

Howison had already achieved international recognition for his philosophical ability, and while at California he came to serve on the editorial boards of *Psychological Review*, *Kantstudien*, and the *Hibbert Journal*. He continued to publish essays and reviews. Moreover, for years he worked on the papers that were to constitute his single important philosophical book, *The Limits of Evolution and Other Essays*, which appeared in 1901. Howison challenged absolute idealism because it negated human freedom and agency; in its place he offered a personal idealism in which what is real is dependent on the community of minds in the universe. Howison also brought attention to himself and the University of California through the Philosophical Union that he established. The union held yearly conferences with major philosophers; two such conferences were of special importance. In 1897 Howison arranged for Josiah Royce to lecture on "The

Conception of God," with commentary offered by Howison, Sidney Edward Mezes, and Joseph LeConte. The debate was published and helped mark the transition from absolute to finite idealism within the American tradition of philosophy of religion. In 1898 William James first identified "pragmatism" in his lecture for the union titled "Philosophical Conceptions and Practical Results."

Despite his success as a philosopher, Howison was better known for his teaching. "His chief influence, for all the value of his publications, was upon those whom he taught in person, visibly and by living voice" (Buckham and Stratton, p. 3). By all accounts he was a dynamic lecturer and an inspiration to students over the course of their college years. He sent a number of students on to teach philosophy in the United States, including A. O. Lovejoy. Thus, Howison's legacy is twofold, embracing both the work he published and the philosophers he educated. He died in Berkeley.

• Howison's papers are at the University of California, Berkeley. The best biography available is John Buckham and George Stratton, *George Holmes Howison, Philosopher and Teacher: A Selection from His Writings with a Biographical Sketch* (1934). Further information can be found in G. Watts Cunningham, *The Idealistic Argument in Recent British and American Philosophy* (1933); William Goetzmann, *The American Hegelians* (1973); and Henry A. Pochmann, *New England Transcendentalism and St. Louis Hegelianism* (1948). An obituary is in the *San Francisco Chronicle*, 1 Jan. 1917.

DOUGLAS R. ANDERSON

HOWKINS, Elizabeth Penrose (1 Apr. 1900–10 Jan. 1972), journalist, was born Elizabeth Webb Penrose in Johnson County, Wyoming, the daughter of James Norman Penrose and Julia Corcoran. Although her family lived in Philadelphia, Wyoming was their summer home. She was educated at Mount St. Joseph and Chestnut Hill College in Philadelphia and arrived in New York in 1924, seeking work in publishing. She was hired by the publishing firm of E. P. Dutton & Co., where she worked in the publicity department, and then she moved to James McCreery & Co., where she worked until 1931.

Her first journalistic job was as merchandise editor of American *Vogue* magazine, where she worked from 1931 to 1933. She joined the staff of British *Vogue* in London in 1933 and served as editor from 1935 until 1941. In eulogizing her, Alexander Liberman, editorial director of *Vogue*, assessed Howkins's contribution to the magazines: "She did an outstanding job. She was always immensely sensitive to the creative effort, extraordinarily generous toward talent and other people's creativity" (*New York Times*, 12 Jan. 1972).

Penrose found herself stranded in New York in the summer of 1940, unable to return to England because of the war. She was named associate managing editor of *Vogue*, but the following March she was appointed managing editor of the fledgling *Glamour* magazine, created by the fashion and society publisher Condé Nast. *Glamour of Hollywood*, as the magazine was called when it was first introduced in 1939, usually numbered about 100 to 150 pages and was Nast's attempt to appeal to the woman interested in fashion but not in the haute couture of *Vogue*. The magazine was aimed at the working woman who was interested in movie stars and their fashions. Penrose's name first appeared in the editorial box in May 1941, and that same month the magazine dropped the "Hollywood" from its title. The new subtitle was "For Young Women—The Way to Fashion, Beauty and Charm." In August 1943 the subtitle again changed, this time to "For the Girl with a Job," an emphasis that Penrose maintained throughout her tenure there. Penrose told readers in February 1942 that she thought it necessary to "adjust the editorial formula of a feminine magazine from a peace-time to a war-time tempo." She had made a similar adjustment in British *Vogue* when England declared war on Germany in 1939. Then, at *Glamour*, Penrose reminded each reader of her duty to "flaunt your lipstick bravely" to maintain morale. "It is up to people like you—the career girls of the United States—and to people like us, the women journalists of the country—to keep the fighting spirit of America high and healthy." Throughout the war the magazine featured patriotic stories and articles for women who were working to help the war effort.

In 1947, when the magazine had about three million readers, Penrose instituted a monthly feature, "Dear Reader," in which she highlighted the month's articles and chatted with readers about her own concerns. After her death Liberman noted, "She gave *Glamour* a mass concept of quality."

Penrose was appointed to the New York Woman's Council in 1945 and then was elected to the board of Condé Nast Publications in 1947. Her first marriage, in 1928 to Lloyd B. Averill, had ended in divorce. In 1952 she married Colonel Walter Ashby Howkins, a retired British army officer turned financial consultant.

Howkins remained at the helm of *Glamour* until 1954, when ill health forced her into semiretirement. Then, restored to health, she joined the staff of the *New York Times* in 1955 as the women's news editor. She expanded the *Times*'s coverage of fashion, food, home decor, and other areas of traditional women's news and also increased the number of photographs and art work that appeared on her pages. When she came to the *Times*, she had little knowledge of how newspapers worked, but she distinguished herself as an editor who could spot talent. One former staffer from *Glamour* said in Howkins's obituary in the *Times* that Howkins had hired her with no experience because it was clear that she had "style, and that's the only thing we can't teach you."

At the *Times* Howkins surrounded herself with young reporters who ultimately distinguished themselves in careers at the newspaper, including Pulitzer Prize–winner Nan Robertson, editor Charlotte Curtis, and food writer Craig Claiborne. Howkins staunchly defended her decision to hire Claiborne for a job that was traditionally held by women because, she said, the best chefs had always been men. Claiborne went on to become one of the best-known food writers in the country.

Howkins retired because of ill health in 1965. She died in New York City.

Howkins firmly established *Glamour* as an important and popular magazine for young working women and later, at the *Times*, exhibited an uncanny ability to spot writing talent. During her tenure the women's section of the newspaper flourished, and she retired before the second wave of the women's rights movement forced newspapers to eliminate the women's section and change the focus of coverage aimed at women.

• Howkins is mentioned in Nan Robertson, *The Girls in the Balcony: Women, Men and the New York Times* (1992). An obituary is in the *New York Times*, 12 Jan. 1972.

AGNES HOOPER GOTTLIEB

HOWLAND, Emily (20 Nov. 1827–29 June 1929), educator, suffragist, and philanthropist, was born in Sherwood, New York, the daughter of Slocum Howland, a wealthy merchant and landowner, and Hannah Tallcot. Her ancestors were members of the Society of Friends (Quakers), and it was in that strict tradition of speech, dress, and conduct that Emily was raised.

Howland attended school until she was sixteen. Because of her mother's poor health and because she was a girl, she left school to take on household responsibilities full time, a life she found boring and uneventful. During this time she began to rebel and became impatient with the strictness of Quaker life, although she remained in the faith and reconciled with it later in her life.

Howland's enthusiasms were kindled by the antislavery movement. Her father was a Garrisonian abolitionist and William Lloyd Garrison was a frequent visitor to the Howland home, which became a station on the underground railroad. Howland frequently attended antislavery conventions with her father. In addition to abolitionism, she also took up the causes of education, woman suffrage, and the promotion of peace.

In 1857 Howland convinced her parents to allow her to go to Washington, D.C., where she taught in the Miner School for Colored Girls opened in 1851 by Myrtilla Miner. Howland assumed the role of director and teacher after Miner became ill. Howland believed in the equality of all persons and did not appear to share the paternalism and racism that Miner demonstrated toward the girls. She befriended many of the girls, corresponding with them for decades. While working at the Miner School, Howland was more fully exposed to issues of social reform, including women's rights and abolition.

Howland went back to Sherwood in 1859, but she returned to Washington four years later. She worked in the refugee camps that housed more than one thousand newly freed blacks. She served as both a teacher and a nurse. She initially worked in the Washington Contraband Camp (Camp Barker), where she organized efforts to secure clothing, food, bandages, bedding, and other needed supplies. Howland helped to devise a method for distribution of the supplies, but it was during this stage that Howland's paternalism and prejudices toward blacks surfaced. She often referred to the refugees as "her people," and she expressed disdain for Africanisms. After Camp Barker closed, she moved on to work at Camp Todd in Arlington for a short period of time.

At the end of the Civil War, Howland convinced her father to buy four hundred acres of land in Northumberland County, Virginia. In 1866 she opened a school in Heathsville and began to settle former slave families on the land. In doing so, she became part of a broader movement to educate the freed people. Howland called the project Arcadia, envisioning the area as a promised land for those who followed her. She left shortly after the opening of the school to return to New York to nurse her mother but she returned to Arcadia in 1867 to fully develop the project. The Howland School became one of the first to educate poor white children and black children together. The school remained free of sectarian, military, and political control because Howland's father financed the project. When Howland had to leave once again because of her mother's illness, she put her good friend Sarah Goodyear in charge of the school.

Howland became responsible for managing the family home in Sherwood after her mother died in September 1867. She traveled back and forth between Virginia and Sherwood, eventually opening another school in Westmoreland County, Virginia, in 1869. She returned to New York in February 1870 because of her father's health and ultimately had to make a choice between her father and her Virginia projects. She chose to remain in New York, effectively ending her physical involvement in Virginia. She supported the Howland School financially until it was incorporated into the Virginia public school system in 1921.

Howland nursed and cared for her father until his death in 1881. She managed the family estate, which included two local farms, the Virginia property, and the Sherwood homestead. In 1882 she financed the enlargement of the Sherwood Select School, founded by Quakers in 1871, serving as its patron until it was taken over by the state of New York in 1927. The school was then renamed the Emily Howland School.

Howland supported women's rights and the temperance movement. She was a personal friend of Susan B. Anthony and Elizabeth Cady Stanton and was a regular delegate and occasional speaker at the National Woman Suffrage Association conventions during the 1880s and 1890s. She served as president of the Cayuga County Suffrage Society and was also a member of the Woman's Christian Temperance Union. In 1890 Howland was appointed a director of the Aurora National Bank, a position she held for thirty-one years. She was the first woman bank director in the state of New York. In 1903 she attended the International Women's Rights Convention in London.

Interviewed in 1927 on the occasion of her 100th birthday, Howland noted that she had lived to see many changes in her lifetime. She pointed out specifically that women in her day were supposed to be seen and not heard but that in contemporary times women were taking their places in the world and were much better for it. She said that she hoped to see "the dawn of uninterrupted international peace." Howland died at her home in Sherwood. She left an estate valued at $239,300, much of which was left to charitable and educational institutions.

Although Howland promoted women's education, often providing interest-free college loans for women to attend Cornell University, her primary interest was in black education. She was the major supporter of the Howland School in Virginia. She financed the education of many black girls to attend Oberlin College or Howard University and made regular contributions to more than thirty schools, including Booker T. Washington's Tuskegee Institute and Laurence Jones's Piney Woods.

• Manuscript collections include the Emily Howland Papers, Manuscript Division, John Olin Library, Cornell University, and the Howland Family Papers, including the Phebe King Collection, Friends Historical Library, Swarthmore, Pa. Scattered references to Howland and the Howland family also appear in histories of Cayuga County, N.Y. A definitive work on Emily Howland is Judith Colucci Breault, *The World of Emily Howland: Odyssey of a Humanitarian* (1976). A biographical sketch and photograph are in Frances Willard and Mary Livermore, *American Women*, vol. 1 (1897; repr. 1973). Dorothy Sterling, *We Are Your Sisters: Black Women in the Nineteenth Century* (1984), contains a number of letters to Howland from former students and fellow teachers. See also an interview with Howland in the *New York Times*, 20 Nov. 1927. An obituary is in the *New York Times*, 30 June 1929, as is a notice of the probate of her will, 21 July 1929.

MAMIE E. LOCKE

HOWLAND, John (3 Feb. 1873–20 June 1926), pediatrician and medical educator, was born in New York City, the son of Henry E. Howland, a judge, and Sarah Louise Miller. He was a direct descendant of John Howland of the Mayflower Company. Howland attended some of the finest private schools in the United States, including the Cutler School, the King's School of Stamford, Connecticut, and the Philips Exeter Academy, where he graduated in 1890. From Exeter, Howland went on to Yale University, where he was best known for his athletic prowess. At Yale he became the intercollegiate champion in tennis. He was also a member of the Yale crew team, editor of the *Yale Daily News*, and a member of the secret society Skull and Bones. He graduated from Yale in 1894 and went on to the New York University Medical School, where he received his medical degree in 1897. Howland served an internship from 1897 to 1899 at the Presbyterian Hospital, followed by another year of postgraduate training at the New York City Foundling Hospital. During this same period Howland entered the Cornell Medical School, where he received a second

M.D. in 1899. During the Spanish-American War, Howland was an Army surgeon on hospital ships that transported soldiers from Cuba who had been stricken with typhoid fever.

It was at the New York Foundling Hospital that Howland came under the influence and mentorship of Luther Emmett Holt, one of the country's most prominent pediatricians. After his sojourn at the Foundling Hospital, Howland traveled to Berlin and Vienna, where he studied pathology and clinical pediatrics. He returned to New York City in 1901 and began a professional association with Dr. Holt that would continue throughout his career. In New York City, Howland acted as an attending pediatrician at the Babies Hospital (which was directed by Holt), the Willard Parker Contagious Disease Hospital, St. Vincent's Hospital, and the New York Foundling Hospital. He was also an instructor in pediatrics at the College of Physicians and Surgeons. In 1903 Howland married Susan Morris Sanford of New Haven, Connecticut. They had four children.

In 1908 Howland was appointed director of the children's clinic at Bellevue Hospital. He soon grew weary of this post and the strains of a burgeoning private practice and in 1910 accepted the professorship of pediatrics at Washington University in St. Louis. Before moving to St. Louis, however, Howland insisted on taking an additional year of study under Adalbert Czerny, one of the world's leading pediatricians and an expert on infant nutrition and gastrointestinal disorders. During this period Howland began to focus his own research on the nutritional disorders of infancy and the administration of a university-based pediatrics clinic. He arrived in St. Louis in 1911 but only remained there one year. In 1912 he was called to the professorship of pediatrics at the Johns Hopkins Hospital and Medical School, where he succeeded Clemens von Pirquet.

Howland is largely credited with creating at Johns Hopkins the first full-time, academic, university-based pediatrics department in the United States. At the time of Howland's arrival in Baltimore, Johns Hopkins had just opened its children's hospital, the Harriet Lane Home. Howland's brilliance as a clinician, teacher, and investigator soon attracted some of the finest medical graduates in the country, and the pediatrics staff under Howland included such medical luminaries as Kenneth Blackfan, Edwards A. Park, James Gamble, W. McKim Marriot, Benjamin Kramer, Thomas Rivers, and Wilburt Davison. Howland was widely respected by his medical students as the best teacher at Johns Hopkins. Nationally he was widely regarded as a teacher of pediatrics when he collaborated with his former mentor, L. Emmett Holt, on the seventh and eighth editions of the well-known textbook *Diseases of Childhood and Infancy*. He died before completing the revision of what would have been the ninth edition.

In order to create more clinician-investigator-teachers, Howland insisted that his associates spend at least half their time in the clinics or wards and the other half in the laboratory. Like Howland, many of the young investigators at the Harriet Lane Home explored the importance of chemistry in the investigation of the diseases of childhood. Among some of Howland's greatest contributions to the study of the diseases of infancy and childhood were the effects of chloroform poisoning on the liver, chemical aspects of childhood rickets and infantile tetany, the metabolic derangements incurred by infantile diarrhea, and the energy metabolism of sleeping infants.

Howland's work on rickets brought him his greatest scientific fame. Rickets is a defect in the mineralization of growing bones and cartilage that can lead to soft bones and a "bowing out" of the long bones that bear weight, such as the bones of the leg. Howland, along with E. V. McCollum and Edwards A. Park, demonstrated the derangement of blood levels of calcium and phosphorus in children with rickets; they were also able to ameliorate this condition with the use of ultraviolet light and doses of cod liver oil. Subsequent work by Howland, McCollum, and Park led to the discovery that a dietary deficiency of vitamin D was the cause of rickets. They concluded that cod liver oil, which is rich in vitamin D, and ultraviolet light, which breaks down inactive forms of vitamin D into an active form that can be used by the body, work together to balance calcium and phosphorus levels in the blood and thus aid in the development of a healthy skeletal system.

As an administrator, Howland was known as a highly controlling and heavily involved chief. He was also well known for his ability to stretch a dollar—not an insignificant quality for a chief of a university children's hospital. The medical staff's salaries at the Harriet Lane Home were described by many of its recipients as "skimpy," yet each year during Howland's tenure as chief of pediatrics at Johns Hopkins, he turned back a large amount of unexpended monies to the medical school. In an article penned for the book *Pediatric Profiles*, Howland's former resident, colleague, and friend Wilburt Davison (who later became founding dean of the Duke University Medical School) illustrates Howland's well-developed sense of thrift: "[Howland] hated to waste money. A good example was his invariable custom at lunch in Child's restaurant at Atlantic City. The menus in those days had the prices and calories in parallel columns; Howland would study the two sets of figures until he could find the article which gave the most calories for the least money. The result was always hot cakes, syrup, and sausage."

Six months before his untimely death at the age of fifty-three, Howland developed a painful and protracted episode of hiccoughs and stomach pain. It turned out that he was suffering from cirrhosis of the liver and the resultant pressure on his phrenic nerve. Although Howland was a lifelong teetotaler and was in otherwise good health, he did suffer an episode of typhoid fever and jaundice as a college student at Yale. In retrospect, it seems likely that Howland suffered from chronic active hepatitis. He died of the complications of this condition in London, England.

John Howland remains a prominent figure in American pediatrics, and his life and career are commemorated annually by the presentation of the John Howland Award of the American Pediatrics Society, the highest honor bestowed on an American pediatrician. Indeed, the list of Howland awardees since its creation in 1951 represents a pantheon of American pediatrics.

• Papers pertaining to Howland's tenure as chair of pediatrics at Johns Hopkins are in the Alan Mason Chesney Archives of the Johns Hopkins Medical Institutions in Baltimore, Md. For additional information see Wilburt C. Davidson, "John Howland, 1873–1926," in *Pediatrics Profiles*, ed. Bordon Veeder (1957); Harold K. Faber and Rustin McIntosh, *History of the American Pediatric Society* (1966); Edwards A. Park, "The History of the Harriet Lane Home," in *A Symposium on the Child*, ed. J. A. Askin et al. (1967); and Alan Mason Chesney, *The Johns Hopkins Hospital and the Johns Hopkins University School of Medicine* (3 vols., 1948–1963). An obituary is in the *New York Times*, 21 June 1926.

HOWARD MARKEL

HOWLAND, Marie (23 Jan. 1836–18 Sept. 1921), women's rights advocate, utopian socialist, and writer, was born Hannah Marie Stevens in Lebanon, New Hampshire, the eldest daughter of poor farmers whose names are unknown. As a young girl, Howland insisted that her parents allow her to attend school, just like her brother, and she excelled at her studies. When she was twelve, however, her formal education came to an abrupt end with the death of her father. Left destitute, the family had to separate in order to survive. Her mother had always worked hard on the farm but without wages. Howland learned, at an early age, what economic dependence meant for women.

Howland's first wage-earning job was in the textile mills of Manchester, New Hampshire. She moved to Lowell, Massachusetts, in about 1850 and obtained work as a weaver. The "golden age" of the Lowell textile mills was long over and, along with many other immigrant and native-born workers, she endured low wages and long hours. Shop-floor organizing was at an all-time low after the defeat of the ten-hour movement. Howland did witness, however, the establishment of cooperative stores that were loosely based on the utopian socialist philosophy of Charles Fourier.

Although proud of her work as a weaver, Howland did not want to be a factory worker all her life. After some years at Lowell, she moved to Boston, where she learned phonography, a type of shorthand hailed by reformers as a shortcut to literacy. She used her new skill while working for the famous phrenologists Lorenzo N. Fowler, Orson S. Fowler, and Samuel R. Wells, who studied head shapes in order to determine and reform personality traits.

At the age of nineteen Howland left Boston for New York City, where she obtained a teaching job in the poverty-stricken Five Points district in lower Manhattan. No stranger to poverty herself, Howland was nonetheless appalled by the vast disparities in living standards that she encountered within a few city blocks. She started to examine the social and economic structures of the emerging capitalist order, seeking a deeper understanding of what Henry George would later identify as the central problem and paradox of the nineteenth century: progress and poverty. In 1859, as Howland continued to teach in Five Points, she earned her normal school diploma. Proud of her achievement because she placed a high value on education and because it gave her the means to be economically independent, she treasured her diploma and what it signified for the rest of her life. Shortly after receiving her degree she became the principal of a public school.

During this time Howland began to socialize in freethinking circles. Her friends and acquaintances Albert Brisbane, Stephen Pearl Andrews, and Ada Clare McElhenney were avid followers of Fourier and/or advocates of free love. In this group Howland met her first husband, Lyman Case, a radical lawyer. Shortly after their marriage in 1857, they moved into the Unitary Household, an experimental urban community that attempted to apply the Fourierist principles of equitable class relations and cooperative domestic arrangements. Here she met her soul mate, Edward Howland, whom she eventually married in 1865 after obtaining an amicable divorce from Case. Edward Howland, a friend and Harvard classmate of Case's, adhered to the dictum "Once a Fourierist always a Fourierist." Edward and Marie remained a devoted couple until his death in 1890. As a free-love advocate, Case supported their union and remained a lifelong friend. Howland had no children from either marriage. On the eve of the Civil War Howland and her husband left for Guise, France, to visit the Familistère, a famous and successful Fourierist community founded by Jean-Baptiste André Godin.

After returning to the United States, shortly after the Civil War, Howland and her husband lived more or less self-sufficiently on a New Jersey farm for twenty years. There she translated Godin's book *Social Solutions* (1871), which laid out the theory and practice behind the Familistère; her translation was published in 1886. Howland connected her own life experiences with the theories of Fourier and free love in her novel, *Papa's Own Girl* (1874), which offered a searing critique of nineteenth-century gender and class relations, arguing for women's liberation through economic independence and the reform of domestic life. Reprinted three times during Howland's life, it was an immensely popular novel appealing to a diverse reading public hungry for alternatives to the emerging industrial order. Howland advocated communitarianism as an alternative to unhappy marriages, economic dependency, and the isolation that most women faced in nuclear families; she argued for a society in which women would have control over their lives and livelihoods. The book received enthusiastic appreciation from women's rights activist Elizabeth Cady Stanton who stated that she "would rather be the author of *Papa's Own Girl* than the mother of half the children of America" (*Woman's Tribune*, May 1892). *Harper's Monthly* also hailed Howland's novel for "bearing upon the great social questions of the day—the posi-

tion of women and the conditions of labor" (Aug. 1874), but the Boston Public Library banned her book from its shelves. Although undoubtedly a popular novel, Howland's ideas were not universally acclaimed.

Throughout her life Howland critiqued conventional domestic arrangements, questioning the separation of private and public spheres. As she wrote in *Papa's Own Girl*, "No woman knows her strength until she has had to battle with the cry of 'strong-minded,' 'out of her sphere,' 'unfeminine,' and all other weapons of the weak." Although Howland respected the ideal of the family, she attacked its conventional structure, which kept women separated from one another, economically dependent on men, and burdened with unpaid and undervalued domestic work. Her alternative vision sought to remove "women's work" from the isolated household and pay it a wage. By socializing domestic work, including cooking, laundry, and child care, Howland aimed to remove the barriers to women's economic independence. Indeed, her architectural plans for cooperative kitchens and kitchenless homes preceded those of Charlotte Perkins Gilman. She also recognized that economic independence was fundamental to egalitarian relations between the sexes. With financial means, women could remain single, choose to marry for love rather than economic necessity, and leave a bad marriage without the threat of destitution.

Howland's radical challenge to nineteenth-century domestic and economic relations was limited by her failure to see race as an equally important social marker, a failing she shared with most of her white contemporaries. To a great extent she embraced popular misunderstandings of Charles Darwin's theories. Although she believed that environmental influences shaped human character, she also believed that racial differences predestined individuals to higher or lower socioeconomic roles. She challenged the poor treatment of African Americans on humanitarian grounds but failed to question the racism that limited their opportunities.

In the late 1880s Howland and her husband attempted to put their beliefs into practice by organizing and participating in a utopian socialist community in Topolobampo, Mexico. In 1893, three years after her husband's death there, Howland moved to Fairhope, Alabama, a single-tax community, where she lived until her death. As a friend observed at her funeral, "She was a noble unselfish soul ready to spend and be spent for any high cause which enlisted her sympathy and support . . . devoting a long and active life to the welfare of her fellows" (*Fairhope Courier*, 23 Sept. 1921). Relentless in her challenge of household and economic structures that kept women dependent on men, Howland represents an important, yet often ignored, radical tradition in the United States.

• Primary sources for Howland include the Edmund Clarence Stedman Papers at Columbia University, the Marie Howland Collection at the Library of Congress, the Marie

Howland Correspondence regarding Topolobampo at California State University in Fresno, and holdings in the Fairhope, Ala., public library and single-tax archives. Howland wrote for and edited the *Credit Foncier*, the organ of the Topolobampo community; she also edited and wrote a regular column in the *Fairhope Courier*, the newspaper of the single-tax community. Throughout her life, she published many articles and short stories in *Harper's New Monthly Magazine* and *Lippincott's Magazine of Popular Literature and Science*. She significantly influenced the writing of *Integral Cooperation: Its Practical Application* (1885), by Albert Kimsey Owen, the cofounder of the Topolobampo, Mexico, community. Secondary sources include chapters on Howland in Paul M. Gaston, *Women of Fairhope* (1984); Dolores Hayden, *The Grand Domestic Revolution* (1985); Ray Reynolds, *Cat's Paw Utopia* (1972); Carol Farley Kessler, ed., *Daring to Dream: Utopian Fiction by United States Women before 1850* (1995); and Vicki Lynn Hill, "Strategy and Breadth: The Socialist-Feminist in American Fiction" (Ph.D. diss., State Univ. of New York, Buffalo, 1979). See also Susan Lynch Foster, "Romancing the Cause: Fourierism, Feminism, and Free Love in *Papa's Own Girl*," *Utopian Studies* (Winter 1997). For briefer references see Carl Guarneri, *The Utopian Alternative: Fourierism in Nineteenth-century America* (1991); Robert S. Fogarty, *All Things New: American Communes and Utopian Movements, 1860–1914* (1990); and Edward K. Spann, *Brotherly Tomorrows: Movements for a Cooperative Society in America 1820–1920* (1989). An obituary is in the *Fairhope Courier*, 23 Sept. 1921.

HOLLY BLAKE

HOWLAND, William Dillwyn (27 Mar. 1853–23 Apr. 1897), textile manufacturer, was born in New Bedford, Massachusetts, the son of Matthew Howland, a whaling merchant, and Rachel Collins Smith. Howland was raised in one of New Bedford's wealthiest and most prominent families. He graduated from Brown University with a bachelor of philosophy degree in 1874. After college Howland worked in his father's whaling firm. In 1875 he married Caroline Thomas Child, with whom he had two children. Howland was hired in 1877 to work in the office at the Wamsutta Mills, the largest of a number of textile mills that transformed New Bedford in the late nineteenth century from a whaling port into one of the major cotton textile manufacturing centers of America.

In 1881 Howland moved to another local textile corporation, the Potomska, where he helped draw plans for a new mill. Howland now had experience in the textile business and access to the vast pool of capital that his family and other New Bedford whaling merchants hoped to transfer to manufacturing. Accordingly, in 1882 he organized his own yarn mill, the New Bedford Manufacturing Company. Six years later he opened the Howland Mills Corporation, also a yarn mill, and in 1892 he established the Rotch Spinning Company.

The first indication that Howland would follow a path in labor relations different from his manufacturing colleagues came with the construction of housing for workers at the Howland Mills in 1889. Vastly different from housing usually found in mill villages, it was designed by prominent Boston architects. It consisted of large, single-family houses of varied architectural styles, with indoor plumbing and bathtubs. The village was laid out with winding roads and houses irregularly placed to provide diversity. Management kept rents low enough so workers at all levels in the mills could afford the houses.

In the early 1890s Howland took other actions that enhanced his reputation as New Bedford's model employer. In 1892, when the state passed a law reducing the number of hours that women and children could work, the other New Bedford manufacturers lowered wages, but Howland did not.

During the depression of 1893–1894, the city's textile industrialists levied two pay cuts that amounted to 20 percent to 28 percent of wages. After the second cut, on 20 August 1894 New Bedford's textile workers went out on strike, except for those in the Howland mills. The next day Howland confirmed the expectations of his workers and announced he would not go along with the cuts. The secretary of the spinners' union stated that Howland was "almost worshipped by the operatives" for his stand. Even after a state arbitration board worked out a compromise 5 percent cutdown, Howland continued at the old rates. In succeeding years Howland would continue to pay his workers higher wages than his fellow local mill owners. In 1895 labor union leaders initiated a plan for meeting with local textile manufacturers; the first and probably the only one to meet with the workers' representatives was Howland.

Observers outside of New Bedford praised Howland's experiment. The *Cleveland Plain Dealer* in 1891 published an enthusiastic article on the housing, wages, and other benefits of Howland's workplace, such as the annual excursion to Martha's Vineyard. The newspaper spoke of the manufacturer's plans to develop for his workers a cooperative insurance company, gymnasium, library, and evening school. The trade paper, the *Wool and Cotton Reporter and Financial Gazette*, noted in 1894 that the Howland mills along with two other American mill complexes were places where "a strike is as much an unknown incident in their whole career as an impairment of their credit."

Howland denied philanthropic reasons for his programs, citing practical business considerations. The industrialist's mills were originally located in an undeveloped part of the city, suggesting the need for company housing. And Howland's mills produced fine yarn goods that required a more skilled and difficult-to-find work force than was needed in most textile mills.

Yet other factors are required to explain Howland's approach to labor relations. Like much of New Bedford's elite, Howland came from a Quaker background, and his family was exceptionally imbued with the social ethos of that religion. His grandmother had been active before the Civil War in movements for abolition, prison reform, aid to Native Americans, and education. His father had a reputation for treating the seamen on his whaling ships better than many of his competitors. And his mother, widely known for her leadership of charitable organizations, had personally mediated and arranged a settlement that helped end a major strike at the Wamsutta Mills in 1867.

The importance of this background of social activism as opposed to business concerns in motivating William Howland became evident in 1897. On 15 April New Bedfordites learned of financial irregularities, including embezzlement, in the operations of two New Bedford yarn mills not owned by Howland. Eight days later Howland went to a local bank to request a loan of $200,000. In light of the other mills' problems and rumors about the financial well-being of the Howland mills, the bank refused to make the loan until it could examine the Howland financial records.

The manufacturer returned to his office and expressed his desperation to his bookkeeper. He then walked down to the New Bedford piers where his family's whaling fortune was made; on 6 May his body was found under one of the docks.

Soon after Howland's suicide, outside auditors found that he had hidden the seriousness of the three mill corporations' indebtedness. He had done this not for personal profit but to preserve his reputation for financial acumen and, more important, his extraordinary relationship with his workers. The disaster brought on the financial collapse of the Howland corporations as well as other financially interconnected New Bedford businesses.

Howland was one of a few late-nineteenth-century manufacturers who tried to provide a marked alternative to the usual alienation of workers and industrialists. His efforts were early examples of what would be called welfare work in industry at the turn of century. Welfare work consisted of various programs that provided amenities such as housing, recreation, education, and profit-sharing for workers.

Many proponents of this concept, such as George Pullman in Illinois, sought to use these programs to control their workers and to impart to them values such as hard work, sobriety, employer loyalty, and aversion to unions. While Howland had practical business considerations, he also possessed a genuine humanitarian concern for his workers. Idealistic examples of welfare work, like Howland's, were rare. The more common self-serving manifestations of the concept were joined at the time of World War I with the Taylor scientific management movement to form the new field of personnel management.

William D. Howland's career, with its tragic end, evinced the enormous difficulty in combining social and humanitarian concerns with the harsh realities of industrial capitalism.

• Some correspondence of William Howland from 1878 to 1884 is in the possession of Llewellyn Howland, Jamaica Plain, Mass. The only modern assessment is Thomas A. McMullin, "Lost Alternative: The Urban Industrial Utopia of William D. Howland," *New England Quarterly* 55 (1982): 25–38. For discussion of Howland's parents and the milieu in which he was raised, see Everett S. Allen, *Children of the Light: The Rise and Fall of New Bedford Whaling and the Death of the Arctic Fleet* (1973). The files of the *New Bedford*

Evening Standard are the best source of information on Howland's career; see particularly his obituary and related stories, 6 May 1897. For the general context of labor-management relations in New Bedford in the late nineteenth century, see McMullin, "The Immigrant Response to Industrialism in New Bedford, 1865–1900," in *Massachusetts in the Gilded Age: Selected Essays*, ed. Jack Tager and John W. Ifkovic (1985).

THOMAS A. McMULLIN

HOWLEY, Richard (1740–30 Dec. 1784), lawyer and governor, was born near Savannah, Georgia; his parents are unknown. Few records of his early life survive, but he apparently studied law and moved to Sunbury, St. John's Parish, as a young man. In 1775 he married Sarah Fuller of Charleston, South Carolina, the widow of William Fuller and mother of two daughters. Subsequently, the couple had two daughters of their own, one of whom reached adulthood. When the Revolution began, Howley was practicing law at Sunbury, where he also owned a small plantation and a few slaves. He was not prominent in the early stages of the Revolution in Georgia. Apparently, he did not attend early Whig meetings in Savannah during 1774–1775, nor was he a member of the provincial congress. Savannah fell to the British on 29 December 1778, and Colonel Augustine Prevost began a siege of Sunbury. When Fort Morris surrendered in January 1779, Howley fled to Augusta.

The British occupied eastern Georgia again, and fighting moved into the backcountry. Georgia Whigs—openly divided into radical and conservative factions since the infamous duel in May 1777 between patriot leader Button Gwinnett and Lachlan McIntosh, a general in the Continental army—vied for political leadership as they tried to convene a new assembly in Augusta. After selecting a supreme executive council to govern the sections of the state still under Whig control, this council, dominated by conservative Whigs, elected John Wereat president on 6 August 1779. Howley, long associated with the radical Whig faction, was a close ally of George Walton who, after the joint American and French siege of Savannah failed in October 1779, was sent to Augusta to hold new elections. Backed by Howley, George Wells, and their backcountry supporters, Walton organized a rival assembly in November 1779. This body elected Walton governor and Walton, Howley, and three others delegates to the Continental Congress, in effect ousting Wereat from power. Within two months, Walton departed for Philadelphia. The assembly elected Howley governor on 4 January 1780 and empowered him to act on behalf of the government even if forced into exile. During these uncertain times he called on Georgians to be steadfast in their support of independence. As British raids increased, the council directed Howley to flee to the Carolinas. Howley and several council members transported the state archives and some paper money to New Bern, North Carolina. On 1 July 1780 he was among those listed under the British Disqualifying Act.

Howley took his seat in Congress in July 1780. He assisted in obtaining a new loan from France. His primary interest, however, was to guard against peace proposals that would allow Britain to retain control of Georgia. With Walton and William Few, he published *Observations upon the Effects of Certain Late Political Suggestions by the Delegates of Georgia.*

Controversy surrounding the return of a command to General McIntosh continued while Howley was in Congress. Howley's experience in the Georgia assembly, where he had believed McIntosh to be a cause of conflict, led him to testify before a congressional committee that a letter calling for McIntosh's removal written by William Glascock, Speaker of the assembly, was not a forgery as the author insisted. Instead, it was authentic and accurately reflected the sense of the Georgia assembly. Congress stripped McIntosh of the southern command in response to the recommendations of Howley and Walton. After the conservative Whigs regained political power in 1781, however, Howley and Walton lost their seats in Congress.

Howley returned to Georgia and was elected to the assembly in 1782. He was able to acquire confiscated Tory property being sold in Chatham and Liberty counties. Aedanus Burke of South Carolina turned down an offer to become chief justice of Georgia, and in October 1782 Howley was appointed pro tempore chief justice. He represented Liberty County in the assembly during 1783 and 1784, after which he moved his residence to Savannah.

A devout Catholic, Howley journeyed to St. Augustine in December 1784 to receive sacraments of penance and holy communion that were not available in Georgia. While there, he wrote to Bishop Echevarrio of Cuba requesting that priests from Florida be sent to administer sacraments to his co-religionists in Georgia. Apparently ill when he returned from Florida, Howley died at his residence in Savannah.

Thomas Rodney of Delaware, a contemporary delegate to the Continental Congress, recorded in his diary that Richard Howley was among the sixteen most noteworthy delegates at the Congress in 1781. "The rest of the House," Rodney observed, "may be thrown into one group of inferior talents" (*Letters of Members of the Continental Congress*, vol. 6, pp. 19–21). He described Howley as a man of great reading and knowledge, which he generally displayed without system or design; consequently, his listeners were often confused as to what side of the question he really supported. According to Rodney, the Georgian was loud but not very eloquent; he excelled in declamation rather than argument and was not closely followed except when he entertained the Congress with his wit and knowledge. Rodney concluded that Howley would have shone more in a democratic assembly.

• The most useful collection of documents is Allen D. Candler, comp., *The Revolutionary Records of the State of Georgia* (1908). For discussion of Howley and the political developments in which he was involved, see Edward J. Cashin, Jr., "'The Famous Colonel Wells': Factionalism in Revolutionary Georgia," *Georgia Historical Quarterly* 58 (1974): 137–56; Cashin, "George Walton and the Forged Letter," *Georgia Historical Quarterly* 62 (1978): 133–45; Cashin and Heard Robertson, *Augusta and the American Revolution: Events in the Georgia Back Country, 1773–1783* (1975); and Kenneth Coleman, *The American Revolution in Georgia, 1763–1789* (1958). Also see Dolores B. Floyd, "Georgia's Catholic Delegate to the Continental Congress," unpublished paper in the D. B. Floyd Papers, Georgia Historical Society, Savannah; Harvey H. Jackson, *Lachlan McIntosh and the Politics of Revolutionary Georgia* (1979); Charles C. Jones, Jr., *Biographical Sketches of the Delegates from Georgia to the Continental Congress* (1891); and Alexander A. Lawrence, "General Lachlan McIntosh and His Suspension from Continental Command during the Revolution," *Georgia Historical Quarterly* 38 (1954): 101–41.

R. F. SAUNDERS, JR.

HOWLIN' WOLF (10 June 1910–10 Jan. 1976), musician, was born Chester Arthur Burnett on a plantation around West Point, Mississippi, the son of Dock Burnett and Gertrude (maiden name unknown), farmers. In 1923 the family moved to Young and Morrow's plantation near Ruleville. There Burnett farmed, sang in the Life Board Baptist Church choir, and encountered the music of legendary bluesman Charlie Patton, who lived on the neighboring Dockery's plantation. Inspired by Patton's rough-hewn voice, percussive guitar style, and showmanship, Burnett began playing on 15 January 1928 with a guitar and harmonica his father bought him. Soon Burnett began to play with local musicians Dick Banks and Jim Holloway, already billing himself as Howlin' Wolf (though he was also called "Bull Cow" and "Big Foot"), a nickname he seems to have acquired either because of childhood prankishness, his fearsome size and feral demeanor, or his familiarity with the work of J. T. Smith, a blues singer who also used that nickname and wrote a song with that title.

Working as a farmer in Mississippi and Arkansas during the depression, Wolf was also influenced by the records of the Mississippi Sheiks and Tommy Johnson. He recorded songs from both repertoires and adapted the falsetto leap heard in Johnson's work and the blue yodel of country singer Jimmy Rodgers into his own traditional howl. In 1933, when Wolf was on Nat Phillips's plantation in Twist, Arkansas, farming with his father, Rice Miller (Sonny Boy Williamson No. 2) gave him some harmonica lessons while Miller was courting Wolf's stepsister Mary, and Wolf formed a trio with Sonny Boy and guitarist Robert Johnson that played together for a couple of years. Also during the 1930s, Wolf married a sister of bluesman Willie Brown, but she died soon thereafter. In 1938 he moved to Doddsville, Mississippi, farming and playing until he was drafted into the army on 8 April 1941. After serving most of his four years in the army signal corps in the Pacific Northwest, primarily Seattle, Washington, he returned to the Phillips plantation but left in 1946 to farm on his own in Penton, Mississippi.

By 1948 the musically confident Wolf had moved to West Memphis, Arkansas, with his second wife, Lillie

Handley; the couple had four children. He began broadcasting daily on and selling ads for radio station KWEM. Wolf formed a band that included, at various times, guitarists Willie Johnson, Pat Hare, or M. T. Murphy, harpists Junior Parker or James Cotton, drummer Willie Steele, and pianists Bill Johnson or Albert Williams. Their mixture of traditional Delta blues and explosive electrified sound, combined with Wolf's connections at KWEM, helped land Wolf a recording contract. Although Wolf and record company owner Leonard Chess both claimed that Wolf made some audition tapes for Chess in 1948, Wolf's first traceable recordings were made around either May 14 or July in 1951 at Sam Phillips's Memphis Recording Service. Phillips seemed to have an arrangement with the Bihari Brothers of Modern Records to send them promising audition dubs, but in August 1951 Chess Records released Wolf's "How Many More Years." Modern responded by sending talent scout/musician Ike Turner to record Wolf at KWEM in West Memphis, releasing "Riding in the Moonlight" and "Moaning at Midnight" also in 1951 and cutting more sessions with Wolf in Memphis before the year was out. Following contractual disputes involving Wolf and Roscoe Gordon, both of whom had recordings issued for Chess and Modern, the Chess Brothers and the Biharis settled on Wolf going to Chess and Gordon to Modern. Wolf remained with the Chess Label for the rest of his life, recording more than 100 sides at more than twenty-five sessions through 1973.

In 1952, after a six-month show on KXJK in Forrest City, Arkansas, Wolf left the South to live in Chicago. He recorded frequently for Chess Records there, becoming a dominant performer and major attraction rivaling ruling Chicago blues kingpin Muddy Waters and playing clubs like the 708 Club, the Club Zanzibar, and Sylvio's. By 1957 Hubert Sumlin, who Wolf had unofficially "adopted" in West Memphis before coming to Chicago, was a major part of Wolf's sound, providing a fleet-fingered guitar sound with a wide vibrato and helping to provide Wolf's traditional sound with a contemporary edge. By 1961 Wolf added the international festival circuit to his itinerary, playing jazz, folk, and blues festivals in England, Germany, Poland, and Canada, as well as in the United States as the white market became more appreciative of his sound. He always returned, though, to Chess Records and to Chicago, where he appeared on the "Big Bill Hill Show" on WOPA radio in the 1960s, on "For Blacks Only" on Chicago TV around 1968, and in a short film called *Wolf* (1971). He recorded at the 1972 Ann Arbor Jazz and Blues Festival for Atlantic and in England in 1974 with a number of his British blues "disciples."

By this time Wolf was into litigation with Arc Music, the music publishing wing of Chess, regarding royalties he alleged they owed him, and he experienced a series of heart attacks in the early 1970s that slowed but did not stop his performing. A 1973 car accident in which he was pitched through the windshield precipitated kidney problems that plagued him the

rest of his life. He recorded his last album, *The Back Door Wolf*, in 1973 but continued to perform through 1975. He died during surgery for an aneurysm at Chicago's Veteran's Administration Hospital.

Howlin' Wolf is one of the true giants in the history of the blues. Like others of his time and place, he was rooted in the traditional Delta blues of artists like Charlie Patton and Tommy Johnson, but Wolf was able to fashion a persona so perfectly matched to his awesomely fierce voice, and to find accompanists who could provide a driving, slashing accompaniment, that he attained legendary status. He not only gave birth to Chicago blues of the 1950s and rock music of the 1960s but in some ways helped anticipate the piledriving style of heavy metal. In the 1930s blues artists such as Johnny Shines were already held spellbound by his brooding Delta drones and deep blues feeling. Sam Phillips of Sun Records felt Wolf was his greatest discovery (rather than Elvis Presley or Jerry Lee Lewis), commenting, "When I heard him, I said 'This is for me. This is where the soul of man never dies'" (Palmer, p. 233). The list of songs he recorded, often either traditional or written by himself or Willie Dixon, reads like a countdown of the blues's greatest hits. "I Ain't Superstitious," "Spoonful," "Back Door Man," "Forty-Four," "Killing Floor," "Smokestack Lightning," and many others, all done distinctively and definitively by Wolf, influenced other blues singers such as Floyd Jones, Junior Wells, John Littlejohn, and imitators like Tail Dragger and Little Wolf, as well as rock musicians such as Paul Butterfield, John Fogerty, the Yardbirds, the Rolling Stones, Captain Beefheart, and Cream. The Stones even arranged for an appearance by Wolf on the rock TV show "Shindig" in 1965, introducing an unsuspecting generation of teen rockers to the unadulterated real thing. He was awarded an honorary doctor of arts degree from Columbia College in Chicago in 1972, won the 1975 Montreux Festival Award for his album *The Back Door Wolf*, is included in the W. C. Handy Awards Blues Hall of Fame, and appears on a stamp issued by the U.S. Postal Service in 1994. "The only artist to share the surreal darkness of Robert Johnson," wrote fellow Memphis musician Jim Dickinson. "His singing is so powerful that between the vocal lines the compressor-limiter through which the mono recordings were made sucks the sound of the drum and the French harp up into the hole of the audio mix. . . . He is a Primitive-Modernist, using chants and modal harmonies of the dark ritualist past brought up from mother Africa and slavery through electric amplifiers." His recordings are a monument to the soul, will, and imagination of Chester Burnett.

• Nearly all of Howlin' Wolf's recordings from 1951 to 1969 were released on *Howlin' Wolf: The Complete Recordings 1951–1969* (Charly CD Red Box 7), which features extensive booklet notes and a discography by Les Fancourt. Wolf's Memphis recordings, included on the Charly set, are also available on Bear Family 15460 (with strong booklet notes by Sun expert Colin Escott) and 15500 (with evocative notes by Jim Dickinson). Wolf's Modern sides from 1951 to 1952, not on the Charly set, were rereleased on *Howling Wolf Rides Again* (Flair/Virgin CD V2-86295). A number of sides recorded from 1964 on were released on Chess and other labels. Pete Welding's interview, "I Sing for the People," *Down Beat*, 14 Dec. 1967, is a valuable early resource, as are Mike Leadbitter, "Still Worried All the Time," *Blues Unlimited* 90 (April 1972): 12–14; Peter Guralnick, *Feel Like Going Home* (1971) and *Lost Highway* (1979); Sheldon Harris, *Blues Who's Who* (1979); Robert Palmer, *Deep Blues* (1981); and Ed Ward's chapter on Wolf in *Bluesland*, ed. Pete Welding and Toby Byron (1991). An obituary is in the *New York Times*, 12 Jan. 1976.

STEVEN TRACY

HOXIE, Vinnie Ream (25 Sept. 1847?–20 Nov. 1914), sculptor, was born in Madison, Wisconsin, the daughter of Robert Lee Ream, a surveyor, and Lavinia McDonald. Most sources give 1847 as the year of Vinnie Ream Hoxie's birth. However, the 1850 census for Dane County, Wisconsin, lists an L. E. Ream as the nine-year-old daughter of R. L. Ream, and in 1857 L. E. Ream was listed as an undergraduate at Christian College in Columbia, Missouri. Vinnie Ream did attend Christian College, although most sources contend that she was only ten years old in 1857. If true, she would have been enrolled in Christian College's academy and would not have been an undergraduate (Hale, p. 57). At Christian College the gifted young woman wrote sophisticated poems and painted a portrait of Martha Washington, which has been preserved at the college, now called Columbia College. While at Columbia, she became a favorite of James Sidney Rollins, a prominent Missouri political figure and one of the founders of the University of Missouri.

Ream's career began in Washington, D.C., during the Civil War. Robert Lee Ream moved his family to the nation's capital in 1861, hoping to earn a living as a map maker. Senator Edmund G. Ross of Kansas, an old acquaintance, boarded in the Ream household, helping the family financially. Vinnie Ream obtained a clerical job at the U.S. Post Office in order to support herself. At this time Rollins introduced her to the sculptor Clark Mills, who accepted her as an apprentice. In December 1864 Ream made several sketches and probably a bust of President Abraham Lincoln.

In 1866 Ream entered a competition and won the coveted $10,000 commission from Congress to create a life-sized marble statue of Lincoln for the rotunda of the U.S. Capitol. Her competitors in the bitter fight for the commission included her teacher Clark Mills and another female sculptor, Harriet Hosmer. Jane Grey Swisshelm, a supporter of women's rights, championed Hosmer and commented acidly on Ream's alleged use of beauty and feminine charm to win the job. On July 27 Senator Charles Sumner vehemently opposed awarding the contract to such a young woman in these words: "You might as well place her on the staff of General Grant, or put General Grant aside and place her on horseback in his stead. She cannot do it" (*Congressional Globe*, 27 July 1866). Nevertheless, the Senate voted twenty-three to nine to give her the commission, even though she had never completed a statue before.

Ream sculpted her full-length model of Lincoln in a workshop in the Capitol basement. In 1868, amid the nasty political battles surrounding Andrew Johnson's impeachment crisis, Ream finished her work and packed it off to Rome to be carved in marble. She followed the statue to Europe, selecting the marble slab herself. While in Italy in 1870, she sat for a portrait by G. P. A. Healy. That portrait is now housed in the National Museum of American Art, Washington, D.C. On 25 January 1871 Congress unveiled the first commissioned statue of Lincoln to generally favorable reviews, and General William Tecumseh Sherman introduced the sculptor to a cheering crowd.

The *Washington Evening Star* (7 Jan. 1871) reported that officials who previewed the statue appreciated the realistic and unpretentious qualities of the work of the "little sculptor-girl." After the unveiling Senator Matthew Carpenter of Wisconsin praised his fellow Wisconsonian for her achievement. He said her sculpture was a remarkable likeness of Lincoln "as he appeared in the White House" (Hall, p. 99).

Admirers sent poems, tributes, love letters, and new commissions to Ream. Her most notable works included statues of Thaddeus Stevens and Gustave Dore and portrait busts and medallions of General Ulysses S. Grant, General John C. Frémont, Horace Greeley, and others. She created romantic figures of *The Spirit of the West* (Wisconsin State Capitol), and *Sappho* (Smithsonian). General Albert Pike, lawyer and poet, posed for her in her Washington studio. During their long friendship, Pike produced five manuscript volumes of "Essays to Vinnie." General Sherman sat on a committee that awarded her the commission to create a statue of Admiral David Glasgow Farragut to be erected in Washington, D.C.

In 1876 Ream met the artist George Caleb Bingham, then serving as Missouri's adjutant general. Bingham was in Washington settling some of the state's war claims, and his close friend Rollins introduced him to Ream. Bingham painted a magnificent portrait of her, which is now in the collection of the State Historical Society of Missouri in Columbia. Although she was probably thirty-five years old at the time, he painted her as a young girl with long, flowing curls.

While executing the Farragut commission, Ream met Lieutenant Richard Leveridge Hoxie of the U.S. Army Corps of Engineers, a friend of the Farragut family. Ream and Hoxie were married in 1878. In 1880 she delivered the Farragut model to the Navy Yard in Washington to be cast in bronze and with great fanfare, the bronze statue was unveiled in Farragut Square on 25 April 1881. The wealthy Hoxie discouraged his wife from continuing her career, and she believed the Farragut statue would be her final work.

Vinnie Ream Hoxie worked very little after her marriage, and she suffered chronic poor health after her son, Richard Ream Hoxie, was born in 1883. However, in 1906 a friend persuaded her to create a statue of Iowa's Civil War governor, Samuel Jordan Kirkwood, which was finally unveiled in 1927. Her statue of the Cherokee leader Sequoyah was completed by George Julian Zolnay and unveiled in the National Statuary Hall in the U.S. Capitol in 1917, three years after her death in Washington, D.C. Her husband placed a bronze copy of her statue of Sappho over her grave in Arlington National Cemetery. On her gravestone is a Zolnay medallion depicting her as the young girl who sculpted Abraham Lincoln.

• The Hoxie Family Papers are in the Library of Congress. The Letters of George Caleb Bingham to James S. Rollins, containing references to Vinnie Ream Hoxie, are housed at the Joint Collection of Western Historical Manuscripts and the State Historical Society of Missouri Manuscripts in Columbia, Mo. The State Historical Society of Wisconsin has a collection of pertinent items, and Albert Pike's "Essays to Vinnie" are housed in the University of Texas Library, Austin. The Christian College Historical Collection at Columbia College, Columbia, Mo., has material relating to her education. Allean Lemmon Hale, *Petticoat Pioneer: The Story of Christian College* (1956), is another useful source. Georg Brandes, *Reminiscences of My Childhood and Youth* (1906), contains a personal recollection of young Vinnie Ream. Gordon Langley Hall, *Vinnie Ream: The Story of the Girl Who Sculptured Lincoln* (1963), is a full-length biography. Also see Mary Ellen Kulkin, *Her Way: A Guide to Biographies of Women for Young People* (1976). An obituary is in the *Washington Post*, 21 Nov. 1914.

BONNIE STEPENOFF

HOYER, Linda Grace (20 June 1904–11 Oct. 1989), fiction writer, was born in Plowville, Pennsylvania, the daughter of minister John Franklin Hoyer and Katherine Ziemer Kramer, farm owners. When lightning killed two men at the Plowville Tavern on 2 June 1895, her father survived; Linda Hoyer called this a miracle, for it enabled her to be born nine years later. In 1916 she went to Keystone Normal School (later Kutztown University) in Kutztown, Pennsylvania, graduated in 1918, and attended Ursinus College in Collegeville, Pennsylvania, in 1919. She played and managed hockey, was class secretary, and majored in English and history, earning a B.A. in 1923. Her only child, John Hoyer Updike, noted that "she found her intellectual focusing there, as well as her husband," since on her first day there she met Wesley Russell Updike. They married in 1925, after she earned an M.A. from Cornell the same year. While the Updike family lived in Shillington, Pennsylvania, with Hoyer's parents, Updike quit his job as a telephone line tester and began teaching high school science in 1934. Hoyer worked as a saleswoman at Pomeroy's Inc., but when John returned one day from school beaten, she decided, "I'm going to stay home and become a writer." In 1945 she purchased her parents' Plowville farm and eighty-three acres, and the extended family moved there. After her parents died in this house in the mid-1950s she felt freer to pursue a writing career.

Encouraged by Cornell professor Lane Cooper, Linda Hoyer began to write seriously. In the 1940s she took a correspondence course from Thomas H. Uzzell, and though *Scribner's*, *Collier's*, and *Story* rejected her work, their encouragement prompted her to begin one novel about twelve critical days in a woman's life and another about Ponce de Leon; though she researched the book on three trips to Spain, the work went unpublished. The *New Yorker* published "Translation" (13 Mar. 1965), the first of many stories—collected in *Enchantment* (1971)—to center on her alter ego Belle Minuit. Stories like "The Mantle and Other Blessed Goods" show, as she said, the terror and astonishment any autobiographical writer feels. Anxious that her son pursue the arts, she arranged drawing lessons and encouraged his high school fiction, poetry, and film reviews. Since she feared he would be trapped in despised Shillington, she followed a lead from a fiction anthology that suggested to her that Harvard University spawns great writers. So John enrolled in Harvard in 1950.

Enchantment and, later, *The Predator* (1990) use a pattern in which reflection on some present action encloses memories of childhood, parents, husband, and her son. As the heroine moves forward in *Enchantment*, reclaiming the family farm, protecting her husband from ridicule, and enabling her son to become the artist she longed to be, she carries with her formative parental images composed of her father's proverbs, her mother's thoughtlessness, and her aunt's conviction that she would create trouble. The pattern produces uncommon power for subjects that treat the death of her parents, her education and marriage, and the birth and development of her son—Eric Minuit in *Enchantment* and Christopher Gibson in *The Predator*. His birth is her destiny; his success validates it.

The stories form a connected cycle in the manner of Sherwood Anderson's *Winesburg, Ohio*, and they are linked together by the thematic image or motif that titles the collection, enchantment. In the first story Belle Minuit announces that she plans to tell her story from the viewpoint of Halloween, since her mother thought her a "witch" because she weighed fourteen pounds at birth ("A Halloween Story"). The theme is continued through the eerie arrival of Halley's comet when she was six, more frightening than the Christmas elf, the Belsnickle. Of more lasting "enchantment" is her parents' "hex" from their fear she will always be ugly, her Aunt Hester's pronouncement that "she'll never be right," and a teacher's stamping her foot, which casts a spell over Belle ("A Halloween Story," "A Time of Tribulation," and "A Predisposition to Enchantment"). The motif is dramatized by her father's miraculous escape from a lightning bolt that killed two other men, which she calls "perhaps the only magic I have ever known" ("A Time of Tribulation" and "A Predisposition to Enchantment"). In "Hindsight and Foresight" she casts her meeting with her future husband as resembling "Beauty and the Beast," and in this story she sees her life mystically justified by Eric's birth.

As Belle "quite unconsciously" draws her ideal homestead, her parents' house, surrendered during the depression, comes on the market in 1946 as if by supernatural action, and she buys it ("Locked into a Star"). When Belle's father dies, Eric seems to have known telepathically ("A Woman's House"). She is certain Eric will be famous ("An Arabian Beauty"), that his very name is magic ("A Job's Daughter" and "A Predisposition to Enchantment"). Yet grandmotherhood may make her a witch ("A Predisposition to Enchantment"). A specific use of "contradictory magic for its undoing" is dramatized when, after her father's "burning bush" is destroyed, Belle plants another for her grandchildren, passing along "the child she used to be" ("The Burning Bush"). Similarly, when she queries her son about his divorce he replies with his form of "contradictory magic": "I'm not running *away*. I'm running to something" ("Dropouts in September"). Reviewers unkindly suggested that *Enchantment* was published only because John Updike was her son, but the pleasure of the anecdotal stories, the variety of concrete portraits, and the richness of Belle Minuit enable these stories to stand as successes. No doubt she felt some jealousy toward her son's fame, for when asked if she was happy for his international renown, she said, "I'd rather it had been me."

Six more of Hoyer's stories for the *New Yorker* were collected in a story cycle—which she called a novel— *The Predator*. The sustaining power of love through the trials of old age (which she personifies as "predators") is the main theme of this work. Hoyer's alter ego Ada Gibson announces the apparent motto of the book in the title story, "for each of us there is a predator and the game of life is nothing more than an attempt to postpone the day when predator and prey meet." One such predator is loneliness, but when death captures her husband, his memory keeps her warm ("Primal Therapy"). Another predator, time, is constantly present in the turning seasons, but in "The Papier-Mâché Santa Claus" Ada's son Christopher deflects time's ravages when he returns to her the fantasy her father had deprived her of when he unmasked Santa Claus. Though she is tough enough to adopt her father's slogan "we must carry our own hides to market" ("A Week of Prayer"), she also knows that symbolic gifts can forestall the predator Death, as when she and Christopher exchange presents of graphic arts, emblematic of their symbiotic lives as artists ("Gift of Time"). Even minor hurts can be tended by the dead, as when, in "Solace," directions left by her dead husband help her treat burns from her careless igniting of Christmas wrappings. Such simple, realistic accounts, told with what a critic called "deadpan wit," depict the reliance with which a feisty, loving woman can face the predator, the trials of decline.

On 16 March 1985 Linda Hoyer received the Distinguished Alumni Service Plaque from Kutztown University. When John Updike deposited more than 600 letters, nearly 200 of her short story manuscripts, and six novels at Ursinus College in 1989, he knew she would have been "amazed, amused and pleased." She died in Plowville.

• Hoyer's papers are at Myrin Library, Ursinus College, Collegeville, Pa. Biographical treatments include Burt N. Corbett, "Lightning Bolt Led to Author Updike," *Reading Tri-County Shoppers News*, 3 Feb. 1987; "Kutztown University to Honor John Updike and Mother," *Allentown Morning Call*, 16 Mar. 1985; John Updike, "Safe in the Bosom of Ursinus," *Ursinus Bulletin* 84 (Spring 1991): 10; and Jon Volkmer, "A Morning with Linda Grace Hoyer," *Ursinus Bulletin* 84 (Spring 1991): 11–13. An obituary is in the *Reading (Pa.) Eagle*, 12 Oct. 1989.

JACK A. DE BELLIS

HOYT, Beatrix (1880–14 Aug. 1963), early golfer, was born in Westchester County, New York, the daughter of William Sprague Hoyt and Janet Ralston. She was the granddaughter of Salmon P. Chase, secretary of treasury in the Lincoln administration and later chief justice of the U.S. Supreme Court. Virtually no biographical information on Hoyt's family or her childhood is available. Hoyt made her mark as the first prominent woman golfer in the United States when golf, in its infancy in the 1890s, was essentially a man's game. She took her first lessons early in the 1890s at the Shinnecock Hills Club on Long Island from Willie Dunn, the Scottish architect and professional golfer who had laid out the twelve-hole course in 1889. Shinnecock was the first incorporated golf club in the nation, and with its opulent clubhouse as a hallmark it became a model for clubs springing up at Newport, Philadelphia, and elsewhere in the East.

Women played at these clubs largely at the sufferance of men, who permitted them to play only on certain afternoons. Men argued that the game developed "unbecoming muscles" in women and alluded to dangers awaiting women on holes remote from clubhouses. Women played golf in a social milieu in which they were effectively hostages to the demands of femininity and the environment of the plush clubhouse. F. Johnston Roberts, writing for the Illustrated Weekly Magazine of the *New York Times* in 1897, a year when Hoyt won a national title, portrayed women at the clubs near New York City as social creatures. Women were playing, he noted, "matches galore" in "golf gowns designed to best set off women's charms." Roberts spoke of women at golf lunches and afternoon teas. He saw at Shinnecock a "mighty spinning of wheels, a great glitter of harness, and a blaze of gay costumes along the white road leading to the clubhouse."

Nonetheless, he detected a new outlook animating the clubhouse, saying that "society folk have determined to develop the game more than ever." Indeed, two years earlier, thirteen "enterprising" women had gathered at the Meadow Brook Club on Long Island to compete for the first U.S. Golf Association Women's Amateur championship. Constricted by the clothing of the day—heavy shoes, skirts reaching the ankles, multiple petticoats, long-sleeved blouses—they hit away at golf balls made of gutta-percha, the winner in medal play posting a score of 132. The next year twenty-nine women entered the tournament, now a match-play event, at the Morris County Golf Club in New Jersey. Her pigtails emblematic of her youth, the sixteen-year-old Hoyt took the qualifying medal with a round of 95 and then won the championship, the youngest winner in its history. She claimed the title again in 1897 and 1898, as well as the qualifying medals.

According to John Allen Krout, a sports historian writing in the 1920s, Hoyt had an innate and acquired capacity for golf as well as a natural aptitude for competition. Using a brassie from the tee, she hit long, accurate drives. Her swing moved in a low, round arc and concluded with a "beautiful follow-through." For all her ability, she enjoyed only a brief dominion in women's golf. At the Philadelphia Country Club in 1899, as the *New York Times* reported, "The colors of Miss Hoyt were lowered" when she lost an early match. Her play on the greens was "somewhat indifferent." After 1900, when she failed for a second time to win her fourth national championship, she played in no more tournaments.

Hoyt left no lasting impress on women's golf. She received little publicity for success beyond the East Coast; she did not inspire large numbers of women to take up competitive play; and her swing, although excellent, set no new standard for women to emulate. The leading women golfers following her before World War I—Margaret Curtis and Harriot Curtis, for example—owed her no debt.

Apparently within a few years after giving up competitive play, Hoyt went to France to study painting. Never married, she became a landscape painter and sculptor of animals, finding occasional buyers for her work. Sometime in the 1920s she moved to Thomasville, Georgia, living there with her sister Placidia White, the wife of an Episcopalian minister. For many years Hoyt operated an antique shop in the community. She played golf occasionally, but more often she rode horseback for recreation. She and her sister earned some notoriety as the only women in Thomasville who wore pants in public. In 1950, in recognition of her achievement in winning three consecutive national amateur championships, the Ladies' Professional Golf Association selected Hoyt as one of the seven charter members of the Ladies' Golf Hall of Fame. She died in Thomasville.

• Limited information on Hoyt and women's golf in the 1890s can be found in several secondary sources: David L. Porter, ed., *Biographical Dictionary of American Sports: Outdoor Sports* (1988); Will Grimsley, *Golf: Its History, People and Events* (1966); John Allen Krout, *Annals of American Sport* (1929); Benjamin G. Rader, *American Sports: From the Age of Folk Games to the Age of Spectators* (1983); John M. Ross, ed., *Golf Magazine's Encyclopedia of Golf* (1979); Herbert Warren Wind, *The Story of American Golf: Its Champions and Its Championships*. For two contemporary accounts of Hoyt, one portraying her at Shinnecock and the other describing her defeat at Philadelphia in 1899, see F. Johnston Roberts, "Woman's Prowess on Golf Links," *New York Times*, 3 Oct. 1897, and "Golf Queen Dethroned," *New York Times*, 12 Oct. 1899. For comments on her life in Thomasville, this essay depends, in part, on the author's interview on 11 Sept. and 15 Sept. 1992 with Hoyt's acquaintance Mary Upchurch. An obituary is in the *New York Times*, 15 Aug. 1963.

CARL M. BECKER

HOYT, Charles Hale (26 July 1859–20 Nov. 1900), playwright, journalist, and theater director, was born in Concord, New Hampshire, the son of George W. Hoyt, a hotel manager and mail clerk, and Mary Ann Hale. He attended private school and the Boston Latin School before becoming a law student in Boston. Hoyt had a successful career writing "All Sorts," a local-color column for the *Boston Post*, in which he depicted genial American portraits that later became prototypes for roles in his plays.

Between 1883 and 1899 he wrote twenty comedies and one comic opera, satirically deriding daily life in various parts of the United States. His sharp observations covered contemporary topics such as hotel management (*A Bunch of Keys* [1883]), sporting crazes (*A Rag Baby* [1884]), urban life (*A Tin Soldier* [1885]), railroads (*A Hole in the Ground* [1887]), superstition (*A Brass Monkey* [1888]), rural life (*A Midnight Bell* [1889]), national politics (*A Texas Steer* [1890]), temperance (*A Temperance Town* [1895]), small-town militia (*A Milk White Flag* [1894]), and baseball (*A Runaway Colt* [1895]). His last series of plays scrutinized social considerations more than it satirized city and rural character types. American manners are the subject of *A Black Sheep* (1896); women's suffrage, *A Contented Woman* (1897); café society, *A Stranger in New York* (1898); and big business, *A Dog in the Manger* (1899).

A Trip to Chinatown (1891), his best-known work, opened at Hoyt's own Madison Square Theater to play 657 performances and subsequently to tour for more than two decades. This "laughing farce," as Hoyt called it, utilizes a plot similar to that of *The Matchmaker* (1955) by Thornton Wilder, both men having borrowed from the same sources: Johann Nestroy and John Oxenford. This early musical contains three songs of lasting popularity: "The Bowery," "After the Ball," and "Reuben, Reuben, I've Been Thinking." *A Trip to Chinatown* was revived at Rutgers University in 1962 in an adaptation by Lowell Swortzell in which Hoyt himself became a character in a framework showing how the play evolved on its long road to New York.

Realizing that his business talents were mediocre, Hoyt formed a partnership with Charles W. Thomas that lasted from 1883 until Thomas's death in 1893. His second business manager, Frank McKee, survived Hoyt and administered his estate. Having written and directed a new play each season for twenty years, Hoyt died a rich man. His practice of keeping a production on tour for as long as a year while he monitored audience reactions, rewrote, and recast until he had polished the comic business to his satisfaction accounted for much of his success as a producer.

Hoyt married twice. Both of his wives were actresses noted for their beauty. He married Flora Walsh in 1887. After her death in 1893, he married Caroline Miskel (1894), who died four years later in childbirth. Soon thereafter, both physically frail and emotionally despondent, he was committed to an insane asylum in Hartford, Connecticut. Later released, he died at home in Charleston, New Hampshire, where he is buried next to both wives.

Hoyt was one of the most popular nineteenth-century playwrights and producers. In addition to being a noteworthy social critic, he was a favorite humorist. Unlike his predecessors in farcical satire, Edward Harrigan and Tony Hart, who wrote sketches involving blacks and certain New York immigrant types, Hoyt created a complete cross section of American portraits. Not only did he portray city and country types drawn from all walks and ages of life; he also went beyond farce to give sympathetic insight into small-town New England values in *A Midnight Bell* and into the political emergence of women in *A Contented Woman*. His purpose was to have both the exploiters and the exploited recognize each other in his plays so that his audiences thereby could better meet the challenges of a changing age. "A harmless sort of satire that pokes fun" is as close as he came to defining his work, but his enormous success paved the way for the exploration of American life in much the same way by George M. Cohan, George Ade, and the team of George S. Kaufman and Moss Hart.

• "The Dramatic Works of Charles H. Hoyt, Printed in Conformity with the Provisions of His Last Will and Testament under the Directions of Its Executors," 3 vols., n.d., exists as follows: one set in the Lambs Club Library, New York City; one set in the Rare Book Collection of the New York Public Library; one at the Actor's Club of America; and one at the Charlestown, N.H., public library. Vol. 9 of *America's Lost Plays*, ed. Douglas L. Hunt (reissued 1964), contains *A Bunch of Keys*, *A Midnight Bell*, *A Trip to Chinatown*, *A Temperance Town*, and *A Milk White Flag*. Arthur H. Quinn cites Hoyt's importance in *A History of the American Drama: From the Civil War to the Present Day* (1937), as does T. Allston Brown in *A History of the New York Stage from the First Performance in 1732 to 1901* (1903). Nancy Foell Swortzell, "The Satire of Charles Hoyt" (Ph.D. diss., Yale Univ., 1964), discusses the unique qualities of his comedies in the development of satire in American drama.

NANCY FOELL SWORTZELL

HOYT, Henry E. (?1834–30 Dec. 1906), theatrical scene painter and designer, was born in New Hampshire; other details of his early years and personal life outside his theatrical career are not documented. Hoyt's career spanned a period of drastic change in the business arrangements of New York's commercial theater. Theater managers abandoned the "stock company" approach of hiring a company of actors and a design staff to produce an entire season of plays, opting instead for "combination" production, that is, hiring actors for the run of a single play and contracting out sets and costumes to the lowest bidder among designers working for competing commercial studios. Judging from his major credits, Henry Hoyt seems to have

preferred to continue working as a freelancer and was fortunate in having developed relationships with managements that continued to use the old production system.

Hoyt's work appeared regularly on the stage of the Casino Theatre, the first New York theater specifically built for the production of popular musicals. Its opening in October 1882 coincided with the beginning of Hoyt's most productive period. But Hoyt's name was most frequently associated with the newly formed Metropolitan Opera Company, established in 1883 right across the street from the Casino Theatre at Broadway and Thirty-ninth Street. The Metropolitan Opera's *Annals* credit Hoyt as the designer of eight of the company's earliest productions, all U.S. premieres or first productions by the Metropolitan. Hoyt designed Goldmark's *Die Königen von Saba* (opened 2 Dec. 1885), Wagner's *Die Meistersinger* (4 Jan. 1886), Verdi's *Aida* (12 Nov. 1886), Goldmark's *Merlin* (3 Jan. 1887), Spontini's *Fernand Cortez* (6 Jan. 1888), Meyerbeer's *L'Africaine* (7 Dec. 1888), Franchetti's *Asreal* (26 Nov. 1890), and Smareglia's *Il Vassalo di Szigeth* (12 Dec. 1890).

As chief scenic artist for the company, Hoyt probably also designed and painted parts of other productions, since the typical practice of the period was to employ several painter/designers on a many-scened production, one for each scene. The recognition of Hoyt as the sole designer of so many major productions was unusual, and newspaper reviews of work he did for other managements soon referred to him as "Hoyt of the Metropolitan Opera."

All Hoyt's Metropolitan Opera sets were destroyed in a fire that gutted the stage and auditorium on 27 August 1892. After some reports blamed the fire on "highly combustible paints used by scenic artists," Hoyt refuted them in a long interview published in *The World* on 11 September, pointing out that scene painters used only water-based "distemper" paints. This unique moment of public interest allowed Hoyt to expound on his profession. Although rambling and poorly written, this report is the only record we have of the 58-year-old designer's views. "Scene painting may almost be termed a combination of all the arts," he asserted, describing the designer's need to observe, study, and sketch every potential scenic element from "a heap of stones . . . to the mechanism of a locomotive," all in advance of any particular assignment, for the actual design and execution of sets was done very quickly to meet tight production schedules. These were the views of a practical professional informing the public about what went into their entertainments; he did not enunciate any aesthetic theory, such as those of Adolphe Appia and Gordon Craig, which began to revolutionize theatrical production a decade after this interview. But Hoyt clearly was proud to be one of only 150 accomplished scenic artists he estimated were working in the United States in 1892.

Some of Hoyt's most highly praised work was done for Augustin Daly. A critic and playwright, Daly founded, managed, and directed his own theater for a number of years. His theater was famed for ensemble acting (unusual at that time) and for the excellence and beauty of Daly's classical revivals. Hoyt was assisting Daly's chief designer James Roberts at least as early as January 1886, when he was credited as co-designer of Daly's revival of *The Merry Wives of Windsor.*

Daly's spectacular revival of *A Midsummer Night's Dream* in 1888, with scenery designed by Hoyt, "surpassed Daly's own previous achievements as well as those of other managers" and presented "the most beautiful setting of Shakespeare ever seen on the New York stage" (undated clippings in Daly scrapbook). Twice during the performance the first-night audience (31 Jan.) called Daly and Hoyt before the curtain to acknowledge the enthusiastic applause. Newspapers devoted long descriptive articles to the spectacle, especially lauding the elaborate scenic sequence Daly had added to the end of Shakespeare's fourth act: a barge trip in which Theseus brought the lovers out of the forest and back to his palace. For this effect, Hoyt had painted a moving panorama backdrop and moving set pieces in several planes around the royal barge, creating a three-dimensional effect that one reviewer called "the most luxurious and beautiful work of this kind that has been shown upon our stage."

Hoyt was famous for moody forest effects, which made him the ideal designer for Daly's *Dream* and probably explains his contribution, as one of five designers, to Daly's *As You Like It* (1889). Shortly after James Roberts's death in 1891, Hoyt's specialty was used again when he and three others created the sets for Daly's production of *The Foresters,* Tennyson's new play about Robin Hood. In 1893 Hoyt designed all the scenes for Daly's *Twelfth Night,* and he seems to have been Daly's chief designer for the entire 1896–1897 season, creating a brand new set of scenes for *The Tempest* (6 Apr. 1897).

Hoyt designed single productions for other managements. In 1890 Fanny Davenport, a popular star who had been part of Daly's first ensemble, commissioned him to design her production of Sardou's *Cleopatra;* in 1891 he designed *Apollo* for musical stage prima donna Lillian Russell. He also designed the 1891 U.S. premiere of *Cavalleria Rusticana,* produced as a Broadway theater attraction rather than in an opera house.

Among Hoyt's other admired works in the 1890s were a front curtain for the New Park Theatre in Brooklyn and the curtain for the refurbished Metropolitan Opera House, the only work mentioned in his three-line obituary notice in *American Art Annual* (vol. 6, p. 110). Hoyt retired to Germantown, Pennsylvania, where he died.

Newspaper reports and theater program credits place Hoyt in the highest ranks of his profession from about 1880 until his retirement around the turn of the century. But unlike some designers, Hoyt left no memoirs or collections of drawings to attract theater scholars, so the career of this hard-working and much-admired theatrical artist has not received the attention it deserves.

• Most of the information on Hoyt comes from the clippings files of the Billy Rose Theatre Collection of the New York Public Library for the Performing Arts at Lincoln Center and from scrapbooks of Augustin Daly's theater in that collection. Orville Larson's *Scene Design in the American Theatre, 1915–1960* (1989) briefly describes and reproduces in its introductory chapter two photographs of the barge sequence from Daly's *Midsummer Night's Dream* production, but the designer is not identified.

DANIEL S. KREMPEL

HRDLIČKA, Aleš (30 Mar. 1869–5 Sept. 1943), physical anthropologist, was born in Humpolec, Bohemia (now the Czech Republic), the son of Maximilian Hrdlička, a master joiner, and Karolina Wagner. Hrdlička spent the first twelve years of his life in Humpolec. In 1881 his family moved to the United States. They settled in New York City, where he completed his secondary education and in 1889 began his medical studies at the New York Eclectic Medical College. He graduated with honors and in 1892 entered general practice on the Lower East Side, while continuing his medical education at the New York Homeopathic College (1892–1894).

On completion of his studies at the Homeopathic College, Hrdlička quit private practice to take a position as a junior physician at the Middletown (N.Y.) State Homeopathic Hospital for the Insane. During this time he became interested in the application of anthropometry to medicine, and as a direct result of the research conducted at Middletown he was invited two years later to join a multidisciplinary research team of scientists being assembled by the histologist Ira Van Gieson to staff the newly created Pathological Institute in New York City. To prepare for this new post, Hrdlička spent the winter of 1896 studying anthropology, and in particular anthropometric techniques, at the École d'Anthropologie and the Laboratoire d'Anthropologie de l'École pratique des Hautes Études in Paris.

In the winter of 1898, while still attached to the Pathological Institute, Hrdlička accompanied the Norwegian ethnologist Carl Lumholtz on an expedition to northern Mexico for the American Museum of Natural History. As he later wrote in his unpublished memoir "My Journeys," this field trip "seemed more like a rich rare dream than reality." Following this seminal experience, his career moved progressively toward a total immersion in anthropology. In 1899 he resigned his position at the institute and signed on as an unsalaried field anthropologist attached to the American Museum of Natural History, where he worked under the direction of the Harvard anthropologist Frederic Ward Putnam. Between 1899 and 1902 he conducted four intensive anthropometric surveys among the Indians of the American Southwest and northern Mexico. Based largely on his field experience and expanding publication list, he successfully competed against two other candidates, namely George Grant MacCurdy from Yale and William Curtis Farabee from Harvard, to head the newly created Division of Physical Anthropology (DPA) at the National Museum of Natural History (Smithsonian Institution) in Washington, D.C.—a position he held for the next forty years.

During his tenure at the National Museum, Hrdlička built the DPA into a major research center housing one of the finest human osteological collections in the world. He also did much to promote physical anthropology as an independent discipline. Although his dream of transforming the DPA into an American Institute of Physical Anthropology and to organize the discipline along the lines Paul Broca had taken with French anthropology were never realized, he nevertheless did succeed in founding the *American Journal of Physical Anthropology* in 1918 and the American Association of Physical Anthropologists, which held its inaugural meeting in Charlottesville, Virginia, in April 1930. He also did much to assist the development of the discipline in his native land. In particular, an endowment he established at Charles University in Prague provided not only valuable financial support for Jindřich Matiegka's fledgling journal, *Anthropologie*, but also the establishment of the Museum of Man at Charles University.

Although Hrdlička's interests spread over the entire spectrum of the discipline, the primary focus of his scientific endeavors was the origin and antiquity of the aboriginal population of the Americas. Then, as now, the question of when the first humans entered the New World was controversial. Hrdlička's investigations during the early 1900s (and subsequently) of the skeletal evidence from North and South America that had been used to support the case for the early arrival (i.e., either before or during the Glacial Epoch [Pleistocene]) of human beings in the New World did not stand up to rigorous scientific scrutiny. His initial studies, summarized in two monographs published in 1907 and 1912, served to bolster his view that the continent had been peopled sometime during the terminal stages of the Pleistocene and the commencement of the Holocene (Recent) epochs.

At this juncture Hrdlička turned his attention to the problem of the origin of *Homo sapiens* in the Old World. Specifically, it was his growing conviction that anatomically modern (a.m.) *Homo sapiens* had evolved from an essentially Neandertaloid population that had initially been restricted to Africa and Europe. He contended that as these hominids slowly spread eastward into Asia, they (like their counterparts in Africa and Europe) underwent progressive transformation to a.m. *Homo sapiens*. He envisioned that by the close of the last glaciation these early modern humans had reached northeast Asia from where they ultimately entered the New World via a land bridge that was thought to have existed at that time linking the North American continent with Asia. Following in the wake of the retreating glaciers in the northern hemisphere this land bridge became submerged—thereby sealing these itinerant Asian hominids in the New World. The following ten thousand or more years that constitute the Holocene Epoch, Hrdlička believed, was more

than enough time to account for the evolution of the biological and cultural diversity encountered in the Americas. His subsequent study of the shovel-shaped incisor trait, which in part was based on work conducted in Japan and China in 1920, served to reinforce his conviction that the Neandertals of the Upper Pleistocene had been the direct ancestors of modern humans. It was in this context that Hrdlička became a vocal critic of the now infamous Piltdown remains, which at the time had been used to support a completely different evolutionary scenario. The direct-ancestry idea was developed in a series of papers published during the early 1920s and culminated with his case for "The Neanderthal Phase of Man," which was presented in his Huxley Memorial Lecture to the Royal Anthropological Institute in London in 1927.

The remaining years of Hrdlička's life were spent pursuing documentary evidence to support the thesis of an Asiatic origin of the American Indians. This work took him initially to the Yukon and Alaska (1926–1930) and then to Kodiak Island (1931–1935) and the Aleutian and Commander islands (1936–1938). The primary objective of his work in the Commander and Aleutian islands was to test the hypothesis that they had served as kind of stepping stones from Kamchatka to the North American mainland. Unable to substantiate this idea, he concluded that the early inhabitants must have entered this chain of islands from the direction of Alaska rather than the Asian mainland. At this juncture he began formulating plans for a program of research on the Siberian mainland, but with the outbreak of World War II these plans were never realized. Hrdlička died at his home in Washington, D.C.

Hrdlička was married twice but had no children. His first marriage, in 1896, was to Marie Strickler (originally from Alsace-Lorraine), who had inherited a small estate from her mother and before her marriage had been a live-in companion to a Madame M. Fogarty who was a New York haute couturiere. From their surviving correspondence, it is clear that Hrdlička was devoted to Strickler and that throughout their marriage she had exerted an important influence on him. Indeed it was largely her financial independence that provided him with the means to take the unsalaried position at the American Museum and undertake many other subsequent ventures. His relationship with Strickler is important for other reasons. In particular, the picture that emerges from their correspondence contradicts the reports that appeared after his death in which he is portrayed as an unyielding autocrat who regarded women as inferior beings. From all accounts Strickler's health had been a source of continual anxiety for Hrdlička, and when she died of diabetes in 1918 he continued, long after his marriage to Vilemína "Mina" Mansfeld in 1920, to frequent spiritualist meetings in an effort to contact his deceased wife. His second marriage seems to have been more a contract of convenience than "an affair of the heart." In fact it has been conjectured that this relationship gave birth to the posthumous anecdotes regarding his attitude toward women. From the financial foundations supplied by Strickler and through careful investment in property and bonds, Hrdlička accrued a sizable estate that provided the basis of the Aleš and Marie Hrdlička Fund he established at the Smithsonian Institution to promote research and publication in physical anthropology.

Although Hrdlička's ideas, particularly with regard to his views on the evolutionary significance of the Neandertals, are currently under siege, it is still impossible on the basis of current evidence to predict what the final outcome of this controversy will be. But whatever the ultimate fate of this and other details of his grand synthesis, there is little question that a century from now he will still be seen as an influential figure who did much to shape the institutional and intellectual contours of American physical anthropology during the twentieth century.

• Hrdlička's private and professional papers are preserved in the National Anthropological Archives, National Museum of Natural History, Smithsonian Institution. During his career he published several hundred articles and books. Much of the work he conducted during the Middletown and Pathological Institute periods can be found in the *Annual Report of the Middletown State Homeopathic Hospital* (1895, 1896), and the *New York State Hospital Bulletin* (1896, 1897). A summary of his fieldwork between 1899 and 1906 is summarized in *Physiological and Medical Observations among the Indians of Southwestern United States and Northern Mexico* (1908). In addition to *The Skeletal Remains Suggesting or Attributed to Early Man in North America* (1907) and *Early Man in South America* (1912), his report, "The Most Ancient Skeletal Remains of Man," in the *Annual Report of the Smithsonian Institution* (1914), provides further information on his field activities and developing views on human antiquity in the New World. His article "Shovel-shaped Teeth," *American Journal of Physical Anthropology* 3 (1920): 429–65, along with a series of articles published in the same journal in 1922, 1923, and 1924, document his opposition to the monistic interpretation of the Piltdown remains and his developing views on human evolution that culminated with the publication of "The Neanderthal Phase of Man," *Journal of the Royal Anthropological Institute of Great Britain* 57 (1927): 249–74. For further insights into his views on human paleontology, see *The Skeletal Remains of Early Man* (1930). His fieldwork after 1926 is summarized in two posthumously published volumes: *The Anthropology of Kodiak Island* (1944) and *The Aleutian and Commander Islands and Their Inhabitants* (1945). For a more detailed exposition and complete bibliography of Hrdlička's work, see Frank Spencer, "Aleš Hrdlička M.D., 1869–1943: A Chronicle of the Life and Work of an American Physical Anthropologist" (Ph.D. diss., Univ. of Michigan, 1979).

FRANK SPENCER

HUBBARD, Cal (31 Oct. 1900–17 Oct. 1977), football player and baseball umpire, was born Robert Cal Hubbard near Keytesville, Missouri, the son of Robert Porter Hubbard and Sarah Elizabeth "Sallie" Ford, farmers. After graduating from Keytesville High School in 1919, Hubbard, a four-sport letterman, played football for a year at Chillicothe (Mo.) Business College and then worked on the family's three farms and at odd jobs until he was enticed in 1922 to Shreve-port, Louisiana, by coach Bo McMillin to play football at Centenary College. When McMillin moved to Geneva College after three years, Hubbard sat out a year and then transferred to the Beaver Falls, Pennsylvania, school where he earned All-America honors in 1926 as a lineman. At 6'3" and 250 pounds, Hubbard had the strength, speed, and agility that allowed him to play both tackle and end in college and professional ball.

After receiving a bachelor's degree in 1927, he signed to play with the New York Giants of the National Football League. Hubbard was an immediate sensation among the pros, teaming with tackle Steve Owen to help carry the Giants to a 11–1–1 record and the NFL championship that year. Relatively old for a rookie at twenty-seven, he used quickness to revolutionize defensive tactics by playing behind the line of scrimmage, thereby becoming the first linebacker. After the 1928 season Hubbard, always a country boy at heart, demanded to be traded to the Green Bay Packers. His acquisition proved critical, as the Packers went 12–0–1 and won the first of three consecutive NFL titles (1929–1931). The six-time All-Pro (1928–1933) was line coach at Texas A&M in 1934, but he returned to Green Bay in 1935 and finished his football career splitting the 1936 season with the New York Giants and the Pittsburgh Pirates. Green Bay coach Curly Lambeau proclaimed Hubbard, who served as head football coach at Geneva College in 1941–1942, "the best lineman I ever saw on both offense and defense"—a sentiment echoed by George Halas of the Chicago Bears. In 1969 the board of selectors of the Pro Football Hall of Fame named Hubbard the NFL's "greatest tackle" during its first fifty years.

Hubbard's retirement from professional football coincided with the beginning of his career as a major league baseball umpire. He had begun umpiring local games after graduating from high school and entered the professional ranks in 1928 to supplement his football income. He advanced rapidly through the minor leagues, reaching the International League in 1931. Promoted to the American League in 1936, Hubbard was acclaimed by veteran umpires as the finest newcomer in memory. The "gentle giant," as Hubbard was known, combined an imposing physical presence with an encyclopedic knowledge of the rules to become one of the most respected and authoritative umpires in baseball history. To Hubbard, who rarely was argumentative or aggressive, the two keys to umpiring were simply "maintaining discipline and knowing the rule book." Always a strict enforcer of the rules, he became the first umpire to eject a pitcher for throwing a spitball when he tossed Nelson Potter of the St. Louis Browns in 1944. He was named to work the 1938 World Series after only three years in the league, and he went on to umpire the 1942, 1946, and 1949 postseason classics. Hubbard also umpired three All-Star games—1939, 1944, and 1949.

His umpiring career ended prematurely after the 1951 season when a hunting accident impaired the vision in his left eye. League president Will Harridge then appointed him as an assistant to supervisor of umpires Tommy Connolly; when Connolly retired in 1954, Hubbard, well known for his cooperation with his superiors, replaced him and served as the league's umpire supervisor until 1969. During his fifteen-year tenure, Hubbard transformed the nature of American League umpires by imposing his personal preferences. Partial to "strong, silent types," he hired men with "size" and insisted that they adopt a low-key demeanor and make calls with understated gestures. From 1959 through 1969 he was a member of the Official Playing Rules Committee, and during the late 1960s he wrote a nationally syndicated feature, "Cal's Column," on rules interpretations.

Hubbard, who insisted that his middle name was "Cal" despite it being written as "Calvin" in the family Bible, married Ruth Frishkorn in 1927 and had two children. She died in 1964, and in 1966 Hubbard married Mildred Freeman. Elected in 1962 to the College Football Hall of Fame, his subsequent enshrinement as a charter member of the Pro Football Hall of Fame (1963) and the Baseball Hall of Fame (1976) earned him the distinction of being the only person named to three national sports shrines.

• Noteworthy are the Hubbard files in the National Baseball Library, Cooperstown, N.Y., and the Pro Football Hall of Fame, Canton, Ohio. Mary Bell Hubbard's hagiographic *Strike 3! and You're Out!! or the Cal Hubbard Story* (1976) is the only full-scale biography. For Hubbard's football career, see Chuck Johnson, *The Greatest Packers of Them All* (1968); George Sullivan, *Pro Football's All-Time Greats: The Immortals in Pro Football's Hall of Fame* (1968); and Alexander M. Weyand, *Football Immortals* (1962). For his baseball career, see Martin Appel and Burt Goldblatt, *Baseball's Best: The Hall of Fame Gallery* (1977); James M. Kahn, *The Umpire Story* (1953); Daniel M. Daniel, "An Umpire Is Born!" *Baseball Magazine*, May 1938, pp. 535–36; and Stanley Frank, "Strong Silent Man," *Colliers*, Apr. 1939, pp. 55–57. Important obituaries are in the *New York Times* 18 Oct. 1977, and the *Sporting News*, 5 Nov. 1977.

LARRY R. GERLACH

HUBBARD, Elbert Green (19 June 1856–7 May 1915), author and publisher, was born in Bloomington, Illinois, the son of Dr. Silas Hubbard, a physician, and Juliana Frances Read. After Elbert's birth, the family moved to rural Hudson, Illinois. Elbert's childhood was ordinary enough. He paid as little attention to school as possible, but he couldn't avoid religion, which he got in triple doses from his father's family prayers, the nearby Baptist church, and from the Bible readings that formed a part of the school curriculum of the day. He never submitted to baptism and in his later writings took the position that religion was a crutch that lessened a man's self-reliance. Although he tried to avoid as much religion and school as possible, Hubbard could not stay away from horses. The first twelve dollars he saved from his chores went to purchase a horse, and in his later writings he often said that he preferred the company of a good horse to that of many a man he had met.

Hubbard left school in his sixteenth year and became a door-to-door salesman for his cousin, Justus Weller, a nephew of Dr. Silas, and operator of a soap business with partner John Larkin. Within three years Hubbard was so successful a salesman that he had hired sales teams of his own to canvass the local farms while he concentrated on the shopkeepers of his territory. He was personable, good looking, and a good storyteller. He personified the commercial traveler in his dress, but, unlike his fellow drummers who sat around hotel lobbies and saloons, Hubbard sought out the local lecture halls and book stores and began to absorb the Midwest populist philosophy. In 1875 the Weller-Larkin partnership broke up, and Hubbard chose to work at the reorganized Larkin Company in Buffalo, New York. In 1881 he married Bertha C. Crawford, who soon gave birth to their first child. In 1884 the family moved from Buffalo to the rural, horse-raising suburb of East Aurora, where Hubbard could indulge his love for horses. He also began to be involved in the local book circles that came out of the Chautauqua movement in western New York and started to submit short pieces to the weekly newspaper.

In 1890 Hubbard started writing seriously. His first book, *The Man: A Story of Today* (1891), was written under the name Aspasia Hobbs and was published by J. S. Ogilvie as part of their Sunnydale Series. It was awful, though it contained hints of the changes in Hubbard. The author(ess) expounds on many topics, including the basic goodness of women, but not wives. This woman/wife dichotomy signals the partition in Hubbard's mind between his wife Bertha and Alice Moore, one of his literary circle acquaintances. In 1892 Hubbard sold his share of and resigned from the Larkin Company and enrolled in Harvard University as a special student. He failed as a student, but while in the Boston area he established a relationship with the Arena publishing house, which published his second book, *One Day: A Tale of the Prairies* (1893), and was exposed to the new small publishing movement and the new, small monthly magazines.

Hubbard was still living in Boston when a situation that had started in East Aurora came to a head. Alice Moore moved to Boston and soon was carrying Hubbard's child. To gain time before facing the consequences of this liaison, Hubbard journeyed to England. Here one of the self-generated Hubbard myths has its foundation. Hubbard always claimed that he visited with William Morris and that Morris explained the operation of the Kelmscott Press, encouraging him to return and start the American Kelmscott with Hubbard as the American William Morris. In fact, when Hubbard visited Kelmscott, Morris was gravely ill, and Hubbard got the standard tour. He never met Morris, and what he really took from Kelmscott was the sense of Morris's great stature and the realization that there was money in producing fine books.

The year 1894 was the turning point in Hubbard's life. In that year he fathered two daughters: Katherine, by his wife Bertha; and Miriam, by Alice Moore. Child support payments were arranged, and Miriam was sent to Alice's relatives in Buffalo while she left for Denver, Colorado. With this sticky situation temporarily resolved, Hubbard used the journal of his English trip to write the first *Little Journey* biographical booklet and made the rounds of publishers without success. A local acquaintance from his advertising days, Harry P. Taber, suggested that Hubbard have the piece printed in a way that would show it in a finished, printed form. Hubbard made the rounds again with the printed samples, and this time Putnam and Sons accepted the series and contracted for one *Little Journey* booklet a month. Hubbard had also started writing essays for Taber's *The Philistine* magazine, and when Taber decided to produce a book through his Roycroft Printing Shop, he invited Hubbard to participate. The first book, *The Song of Songs*, with an introductory essay by Hubbard, was published, and a second title, *The Journal of Koheleth*, again with an introductory essay by Hubbard, followed. Neither book had much literary or aesthetic merit, but Hubbard had found a new role as a writer and as a publisher. Producing a few issues of *The Philistine* and Hubbard's two books had exhausted Taber's financial resources, and in 1895 he sold the rights to the Roycroft Printing Shop, *The Philistine*, and his interest in White and Waggoner's printing shop to Hubbard for one thousand dollars. The first two titles and most of the early numbers of *The Philistine* came along as unsold stock. The books were crudely done, but *The Philistine* had attracted some good material from contemporary writers.

Hubbard quickly turned the little literary magazine into his own platform and brought well-trained craftsmen into the Roycroft Printing Shop. Hubbard was not a creative writer in the literary sense, but he was an advertising genius and used his copywriting and promotion skills to turn the early, unsalable *The Philistine* press run of 2,000 in 1895 into a press run of 110,000 at its peak in 1902. The rapid early increase in circulation was mostly the result of an untitled essay Hubbard included in the March 1899 *Philistine*. It spoke of doing your job without question and about loyalty and the rewards of work well done. It was about the message to Garcia carried by Lt. Rowan during the Spanish-American War. Orders for this issue of *The Philistine* poured in and Hubbard gave permission to George H. Daniels of the New York Central Railroad to republish the essay as one of the railroad's promotional pieces. This little essay, titled *A Message to Garcia*, brought Hubbard his audience of independent farmers, small businessmen, and company executives, and it is probably the only work written by Hubbard that has remained in print. When Hubbard had new presses ready he took over the printing of the essay as a booklet, and it gave him the financial as well as the ideological base for expansion.

Within five years the little printing shop grew into the multibuilding Roycroft campus, and the Roycroft enterprise became the largest and most complex exponent of the American arts and crafts movement. It had shops for printing and binding and for furniture, metal, and leather work; it also established training schools for the local youth in drawing, watercolor, and bookbinding. Hubbard did not follow the philosophy of the arts and crafts movement that the "heart" (the humanistic spirit) and hand of the craftsman had to be the tools of creation and not subservient to the machine and mass production. Indeed, he mechanized as much of the entire Roycroft enterprise as was possible. Although he constantly proclaimed the arts and crafts philosophy of hand crafting in his promotional advertising for the books produced, the printing shop was among the largest and most mechanized on the East Coast.

Despite or perhaps because of the fact it was mechanized, the printing shop attracted some of the best creative and craft talent. Hubbard allowed free experimentation and never questioned the cost throughout the shops. Designers and craftsmen could work out ideas and, if unsuccessful, just start over. There were never deadlines for the books or prohibitions on design motifs. Hubbard's only prohibition was idleness, and his only requirement for employment was acceptance of Elbert Hubbard as the guiding patron, "the Fra." The material produced by the print shop and bindery from 1896 to 1912 was always of high quality. By 1912 most of the best designers, such as Dard Hunter and the binder Louis Kinder, had left to establish their own enterprises.

On the literary side, a young writer like Stephen Crane gladly sent material to his friend Hubbard, and established authors such as George Bernard Shaw gave permission to reprint pieces. Crane had offered Hubbard *The Black Riders* (1895), which Hubbard rejected as poor work. Hubbard ridiculed Crane's work in *The Philistine* and edited Shaw's *On Going to Church*, for which Shaw became Hubbard's lifelong enemy and critic. Hubbard explained to his readers that he had really improved these pieces, but soon no serious author would work with or for him. Although Hubbard later stated in *The Philistine* that Crane's *The Red Badge of Courage* would put the young author among the best writers of the age, Hubbard's treatment of true talent destroyed the chance of the Roycroft shop to be a literary fountainhead of the early twentieth century. By 1903 the output of the Roycroft shop became either Hubbard's own titles (more than thirty books by 1915) or the works of those few authors whose outlook he shared. The other names in the annual catalogs of titles continued to be those who would pay for their exposure in print.

As the shops increased in size and operating expenses soared, Hubbard began to accept commercial writing assignments. He would write an essay for any client and print it as a *Little Journey*. Soon, these exploitive pieces along with his lecturing took all of his time. The time he had regained in the public conscience with *A Message to Garcia* was running out. He had survived the exposure of his love child in 1901, his divorce from Bertha in 1903, and his marriage to Alice the following year. The essay had spoken of loyalty and getting the job done, not asking why it had to be done or why someone else shouldn't do it. Hubbard's audience of small businessmen and farmers understood that statement of self-reliance. Even though Hubbard had changed from a high-collared business executive with slicked down hair to an aesthete who wore a leather thong to keep long hair in place and who favored an artist's flowing bow tie, he still spoke their language. They were ready to forgive him as an eccentric who shared their roots. But Hubbard had saturated that audience with the same message over the years, and he could not gain new audiences. He spoke for big business when big business was becoming suspect in the public's mind. He defended Standard Oil from Ida Tarbell's attack because John D. Rockefeller was a friend who had a right to conduct his business in his own way. But his old audience did not consider Standard Oil to be a friend. In 1915 the Roycroft enterprise was floundering. The print shop had become just a large commercial printer, and all of the other shops that had produced the craft items were long shut down. The Hubbards announced that they were going to Europe, and Hubbard's last note to his employees said that they "would be gone two months or longer." Elbert and Alice Moore Hubbard died together on the *Lusitania*, which was sunk by a German submarine off the coast of Ireland.

Hubbard was a paradox. He insisted on being recognized as the guiding genius of Roycroft, but he never interfered in a creative experiment or overruled an employee's decision. He established one of the most pleasant working environments of the time. He paid competitive salaries, instituted morning and afternoon work breaks, and led the workers in physical exercise. He formed and financed a band, a baseball team, and a bank for his employees. He never fired people he deemed unsuitable for his purposes but would give them their pay and a railroad ticket with the suggestion that their career rewards were elsewhere.

The best analysis of Hubbard's influence on his time was made by his friend William Marion Reedy: "It has been said, by myself and others, that Hubbard's appeal is to the half-baked. Culture is relative. People who follow Hubbard do not stay half-baked. They come out of it: he makes lovers of books out of people who never knew books before."

• Elbert Hubbard's papers are held by the Elbert Hubbard Museum, East Aurora, N.Y. Material related to Elbert Hubbard and the Roycroft shops is in the Rare Book Room, Buffalo and Erie County Public Library, Buffalo, N.Y. Hubbard authored or coauthored more than thirty books plus the monthly *Philistine*, *Fra*, and *Little Journey* magazines. Some additional works by Hubbard include *As It Seems to Me* (1898); *Little Journeys to the Homes of Famous Women* (1898); *The City of Tagaste* (1900); *Contemplations* (1902); *The Man of Sorrows* (1904); *Respectability: Its Rise and Remedy* (1905); *White Hyacinths* (1907); *William Morris Book* (1907).

The best biographies of Elbert Hubbard are Charles Hamilton, *As Bees in Honey Drown* (1973), and F. Champney, *Art And Glory* (1968). There is also interesting information in Mary Hubbard Heath, *The Elbert Hubbard I Knew* (1929), and H. K. Dirlam and E. Simmons, *Sinners, This Is East Aurora* (1964). The best history of Elbert Hubbard and the Roycroft Printing Shop is Paul McKenna, *A History and Bibliography of the Roycroft Printing Shop* (1986).

PAUL McKENNA

HUBBARD, Gardiner Greene (25 Aug. 1822–11 Dec. 1897), businessman and civic leader, was born in Boston, Massachusetts, the son of Samuel Hubbard, a justice of the Massachusetts Supreme Court, and Mary Anne Greene. Hubbard was named for his mother's father, who had come, modestly wealthy, from Ireland and had become one of the richest men in Boston. After Hubbard's graduation from Dartmouth in 1841, he studied law for a year at Harvard before entering a prominent Boston firm. He married Gertrude McCurdy in 1846 and moved with her to Cambridge. Of their six children, two died in infancy.

Hubbard was energetic in his devotion to public service. In order to promote quicker transit between Cambridge and Boston, a cause also of personal significance to himself as a commuter, he founded the Cambridge Horse Railroad Company, then the only street railway system outside New York. Another Boston entrepreneur planned to start a commuter rail at the same time, but Hubbard rushed to open his first. His train's cars bore witness to his haste: bought used from Brooklyn, they still had the destination "Greenwood Cemetery" painted on their sides. Hubbard's civic projects also included a water system for Cambridge and the creation of the Cambridge Gas Light Company.

Working on patent cases in his law office, Hubbard became interested in mechanical and electrical inventions, particularly telegraphy. In 1850 he considered investing in a telegraphic device proposed by a Boston man but decided against it. Still, he recognized the vital role of rapid communication in a quickly expanding industrial society, and he maintained his active interest in that area.

Closer to home, Hubbard faced a different problem of communication when scarlet fever left his five-year-old daughter Mabel totally and permanently deaf in 1862. Determined that the bright little girl not be limited to sign language in her dealings with others, he investigated European successes in teaching speech and lipreading to the deaf, and he engaged a teacher who made impressive progress in repeating them with Mabel. In 1867, using Mabel's achievements as a model, Hubbard organized and became first president of the Clarke Institution for Deaf Mutes, a Massachusetts school using the oral method exclusively. It was there in 1872 that he first met a young visiting teacher of the deaf, Alexander Graham Bell, a recent immigrant from Scotland. Bell shared Hubbard's faith in the feasibility of teaching speech and lipreading to the deaf. He demonstrated that feasibility during his brief visit to the school. Later that year Bell began taking private pupils in Boston, and in the fall of 1873 Mabel Hubbard, having returned from European study, became one of them.

By the fall of 1874 a close personal friendship had developed between teacher and pupil. Bell paid a social call on the Hubbards one day and after tea consented to play the piano, at which he was accomplished. When he demonstrated the trick of sounding a piano string by singing its pitch, Hubbard asked what value was in that, to which Bell replied that a tuned string or metal reed could be sounded by exciting an electromagnet with an intermittent electric current of the tuned frequency. By superimposing several frequencies over a single wire, as many tuned reeds could be selectively sounded. Thus several telegraphic messages could be sent simultaneously over a single wire. Bell remarked that he was well along in perfecting such a multiple or harmonic telegraph.

To Bell's surprise, this revelation galvanized Hubbard. Several years previously Hubbard had campaigned for a federally chartered telegraph company in conjunction with the post office department to challenge Western Union and cut rates in half. But President William Orton of Western Union countered by acquiring rights to Thomas Edison's quadruplex telegraph, which sent two telegrams each way simultaneously. Bell's plan envisioned outdoing Edison five or six times over.

After checking with the Patent Office to confirm the novelty of Bell's idea, Hubbard agreed to join with a Salem businessman, Thomas Sanders, to finance Bell's research and development in return for a share in patent rights. On 27 February 1875 Bell, Sanders, and Hubbard put their oral agreement in writing, providing that, if a corporation were organized, each of the three would get a third of the stock. Thus began what would one day become the largest single business enterprise in history to that point. Bell and Hubbard treated Orton to a successful demonstration of the perfected system, but Orton, having the rival inventor Elisha Gray in reserve as well as the legal resources of a great corporation, declined to deal with any scheme that would benefit his longtime adversary Hubbard.

Among the ideas covered by the agreement was one that Bell had conceived the preceding summer, a system for transmitting vocal and other sounds over an electrical circuit. Bell himself had not yet tested his theory, and Hubbard brushed it aside in favor of pushing on with the multiple telegraph and an adaptation of that instrument for sending facsimiles of written messages, an "autograph telegraph." These, he felt, had been secured with patents and promised quicker, surer, and larger profits than did the "telephone," as Bell was calling his new idea. Nevertheless, as problems cropped up in perfecting the autograph telegraph, Bell's enthusiasm focused more and more on the telephone concept. Hubbard insisted on priority for the autograph telegraph, even after Bell triumphantly tested the telephone principle on 2 June 1875. That summer Bell avowed his love for Mabel, despite her parents' opposition on the grounds that Mabel was only seventeen, almost eleven years younger than Bell. In August Bell at last won the Hubbards' consent to court their daughter, whom he eventually married. This and other distractions kept Bell from preparing an application for a patent on the telephone until January 1876. Even then he held back from filing it so as not to interfere with filing one in England.

Though Hubbard still put the autograph telegraph first, he had now begun to see possibilities in the telephone. Impatient with Bell's delay, Hubbard took it upon himself to file the telephone patent application on 14 February 1876, just in time to forestall an interference with a caveat entered by Gray that same day. Priority in the concept was not at stake. Bell's priority was unquestionable. However, any delay in the issuance of Bell's patent would have greatly increased the risk that Western Union's stable of lawyers would litigate Bell's infant enterprise into selling out cheaply. Hubbard's decisive step was his first great contribution to the growth of what would become the mighty Bell telephone system.

Others soon followed. Bell's transmission of the first intelligible speech by telephone on 10 March 1876 so impressed Hubbard that he pressured Bell into demonstrating it at the Philadelphia Centennial Exhibition in June. This helped bring the telephone to the world's attention. By year's end the telephone had displaced the autograph telegraph in Hubbard's mind, and he began shaping the nascent industry. Having been an attorney for a shoe machinery company that profited hugely from leasing rather than selling its product, Hubbard applied that policy to telephones, thereby laying the foundation for standardized equipment, authorized repair, wide-ranging interconnection, and eventually a single dominant corporation.

In the fall or winter of 1876–1877 Hubbard had offered to sell Western Union the rights to the telephone for a mere $100,000. Orton refused, since Edison was confident of inventing around the Bell patent. By then Hubbard had no regrets, though capital and cash flow problems grew increasingly critical. When a six-month safari in pursuit of investors fell short, Hubbard in June 1877 began franchising local agents, who leased telephones to subscribers for a commission and paid for plant, operations, and marketing. In the spring of 1878 he persuaded Theodore N. Vail, the young superintendent of the Railway Mail Service, to become general manager of the telephone company. Some have seen this coup as Hubbard's greatest service to the enterprise, since Vail's brilliant policies and management proved to be a major factor in its success.

Hubbard's faith that what was theoretically attainable in a distant future might be considered as money in the pocket today and spent forthwith, brought him into conflict with Sanders, the company's treasurer, who propped up the cash-starved business by exhausting his own fortune and credit. Hubbard doggedly resisted surrendering his control even to save the company. At last Bell, his son-in-law, negotiated a compromise whereby the company was reorganized in

1878 as a new corporation in which Hubbard was given a place on the board, and enough stock was sold to put the new corporation on a sound footing. Though for some years Hubbard occasionally gave the new company astute advice (not always heeded), in 1879 he moved to Washington, D.C., and gave play to his promotional zeal in civic ventures, supported by the substantial fortune that his telephone interests yielded him under the brilliantly successful regime of Vail.

To the day of his death Hubbard served on the board of the Clarke School and, beginning in 1890, as vice president of the American Association to Promote the Teaching of Speech to the Deaf, founded by Bell that year. For twelve years he was a trustee of the Columbian (now George Washington) University. He also was active in the cause of science. In 1882 he joined with Bell in rescuing the foundering journal *Science*, incorporating it and helping Bell to support it financially until the American Association for the Advancement of Science adopted it as its official journal in 1900. In 1888 Hubbard led in founding the National Geographic Society and became its first president, 1888–1897. He died at "Twin Oaks," his Washington home.

• The papers of Hubbard and his family are included in the Alexander Graham Bell Papers at the Library of Congress. The fullest modern overview of Hubbard's life is given in Robert V. Bruce, *Bell: Alexander Graham Bell and the Conquest of Solitude* (1973; 2d ed., 1990). Further details of his activities in the telephone industry are in Rosario J. Tosiello, "The Birth and Early Years of the Bell Telephone System, 1876–1880" (Ph.D. diss., Boston Univ., 1971), and Robert W. Garnet, *The Telephone Enterprise: The Evolution of the Bell System's Horizontal Structure, 1876–1909* (1985). An obituary is in the *Washington* (D.C.) *Evening Star*, 11 Dec. 1897.

ROBERT V. BRUCE

HUBBARD, George Whipple (11 Aug. 1841–22 Aug. 1924), medical educator and physician, was born in Charlestown, New Hampshire, the son of Jonathan B. Hubbard, a minister, and Annie Whipple. Hubbard was educated at the Pomfret (Vt.) Academy, New Hampshire Methodist Conference Seminary, and the New London Literary and Scientific Institution. He graduated from the medical department of the University of Tennessee in 1876 and the medical department of Vanderbilt University in 1879.

Hubbard moved south, to Nashville, Tennessee, while a delegate of the Christian Commission, having served with the Army of the Potomac before taking up the same work with the Army of the Cumberland. Having taught in a missionary school in 1864–1865, Hubbard, who was white, was employed as an instructor by the 110th U.S. Colored Infantry in 1865–1866. During his service as principal of the Belle View Public School for black pupils from 1867 to 1874, Hubbard published comparative studies of the intellectual abilities of white and black pupils. He married Sarah A. Lyon, of Allegheny City, Pennsylvania, in 1869.

In 1876 Hubbard was appointed by the Freedmen's Aid Society of the Methodist Episcopal Church to organize a medical department at Central Tennessee College, which the church had founded in 1866 as a missionary school for freed people. He was appointed dean, professor of chemistry, materia medica, and therapeutics in the new department, named Meharry for its chief benefactors. From that position he called for public health improvements in disease-ridden Nashville.

In an 1878 address, "Practical Hygiene," Hubbard expressed his goal for Meharry and its commitment to Christian service.

Well educated colored physicians are needed throughout the South, and a most promising field of usefulness is open before them. They know the habits, peculiarities and superstitions of their own people, and their warnings and admonition will be listened to and treated with respect. . . . We hope in years to come to send out from this institution a constantly increasing number of carefully trained and well prepared young men, who will not only be animated with a desire to succeed in their profession, but will also be inspired with the purpose of being useful to their own race, and, like our common Master, spend their lives going about doing good.

Hubbard oversaw the creation of departments of dentistry (1886), pharmacy (1889), and nursing (1910) at Meharry, all under his administration. These programs afforded opportunities for black students, ordinarily denied admission to white institutions, to obtain sound training and professional credentials in the health sciences. Hubbard also served as acting president of Walden University, the successor institution to Central Tennessee College, in 1900–1901.

Hubbard's diligent fundraising and scrupulous management of the departments' resources bought new facilities and equipment and paid an able faculty, many of whom were alumni. Meharry treasurer George W. Claridge noted that Hubbard "had but a small amount of money at his command but with it he did a great amount of good. He established a coveted credit for Meharry. . . . He directed its bills to be paid with unfailing regularity. He never closed a year with a deficit."

Dr. Charles V. Roman (Meharry, 1890) called Hubbard "a natural born leader of men, a gifted teacher and a cautious and tactful administrator. Large of body, slow of speech, with a furtive though penetrating look . . . he was canny but kind; non-combative but persistent; always yielding but continually advancing." However, he was little inclined to share authority. "From the first lesson in 1876 until his last order . . . Dr. Hubbard was an absolutist," Roman recalled. Hubbard arrived at his conclusions and then issued them as edicts. He convened the faculty only to announce, never to discuss or debate. No faculty member held an administrative title.

Hubbard guided Meharry through a period when national standards were evolving for education in the health professions, standards he oversaw at Meharry. These included more stringent admissions requirements, lengthened time of study, and, especially, clinical training. Meharry's first teaching hospital, named the George W. Hubbard Hospital, opened in 1912 with money raised from alumni and friends.

Hubbard had also won support from the Carnegie and Rosenwald funds to help build the hospital. They and other private foundations endorsed the recommendation in the Flexner Report (issued in 1910) that organized philanthropy contribute to Meharry and Howard, while allowing the nation's five other black medical schools to close because of alleged poor quality. Carnegie and the General Education Board offered to assist in creating an endowment, provided that the institution be reorganized in keeping with standards advocated by Flexner and the American Medical Association's Council on Medical Education. The Methodist church, seeing that it could not financially carry a modern medical school, allowed the institution to separate itself from the failing Walden University in October 1915.

At age seventy-five, Hubbard became president of the newly independent Meharry Medical College, which had graduated 2,000 students since its founding. According to contemporaries, however, he was beset with mental and physical infirmities that led to serious problems of administrative inefficiency and low morale at the institution. The trustees accepted his resignation in the winter of 1920, awarded him the title president emeritus, and built a residence for him on the campus, where he lived out the remainder of his life.

As one of the pioneers and the first leader of Meharry Medical College, Hubbard deserves a foremost place of honor in its history. Approximately half of the nation's black physicians who practiced during his lifetime were trained at Meharry during Hubbard's years at its helm. The faculty of black physicians, dentists, pharmacists, and nurses whom Hubbard trained and then associated with himself, won the respect of their students and of college benefactors. Hubbard's life's work ostracized him from many whites. Yet others, such as AMA president John A. Witherspoon, praised Hubbard for Meharry's adherence to high standards and the idealism he instilled in its graduates.

• Hubbard's few surviving papers are in the archives at the Meharry Medical College Library. His published works include "The Education of Colored Physicians, Dentists, and Pharmacists," *Christian Century* 2 (1891): 155–62, and "Historical Sketch of Meharry Medical College," *Meharry Annual and Military Review* (1919): 12–16. The main facts of Hubbard's life are detailed in "Dr. George W. Hubbard Retires," *Journal of the National Medical Association* 13 (1921): 30–31. See also T. Manuel Smith, "The Pioneering Influence of Dr. George W. Hubbard on Medical Education," *Journal of the National Medical Association* 45 (1953): 427–29. Charles Victor Roman, *Meharry Medical College: A History* (1934), provides valuable insights about Hubbard from one who was his protégé and confidant. Hubbard's career receives a modern assessment in James Summerville, *Educating Black Doctors: A History of Meharry Medical College* (1983).

JAMES SUMMERVILLE

HUBBARD, Gurdon Saltonstall (22 Aug. 1802–14 Sept. 1886), fur trader and pioneer Chicago businessman, was born in Windsor, Vermont, the son of Elizur Hubbard, a lawyer and businessman, and Abigail Sage. Young Hubbard attended the local common school. In 1816 his father moved the family to Montreal, Quebec. Both father and son eventually went to work for the American Fur Company (AFC), the father drawing up contracts for John Jacob Astor and the son signing, in 1818, a five-year contract as a clerk for the company. After working for several months in a company warehouse on Mackinaw Island in Lake Michigan, Gurdon Hubbard was reassigned to the Illinois Brigade of the AFC and saw Fort Dearborn (now Chicago) for the first time in November 1818. His early relations with the Native American population were close, and he came to be known as "Papamatabe" or "Swift Walker." Various accounts claim an early, secret marriage to Watseka, niece of the Kankakee chief, Tamin, in the winter of 1821–1822 that dissolved after the death of their only child.

During the next sixteen years Hubbard prospered with the fur trade and the white settlement in Illinois and eastern Indiana. Although his operations were based primarily in the Iroquois River area, he was a regular and well-known visitor to Chicago in the years after 1822. In 1823 he was appointed superintendent of all the AFC posts in Illinois and in 1826 was made a partner in the company. In 1827 Hubbard purchased the company's interests in Illinois and operated trading posts from Fort Dearborn through his headquarters in Danville, Illinois, to Fort Vincennes, Indiana, along what came to be known as Hubbard's Trail. He participated in the various Indian wars, securing help for settlers in the Winnebago War of 1827 after a dramatic all-night ride and serving as a scout in the Blackhawk War of 1832. He served in the Illinois state legislature as a representative from Vermillion County. He introduced the first unsuccessful bill to build a canal linking Lake Michigan and the Mississippi River and, when that failed, introduced a bill to build a railroad. Eventually, when the Illinois and Michigan Canal was approved in 1836, he served on its initial board of trustees and dug the first spadeful of dirt in its construction.

In 1831 Hubbard married Elenora Berry, with whom he had one child who lived to adulthood. In January 1834 he and his wife moved permanently to Chicago, where he quickly became one of the village's most prominent citizens, a position reflected in his election as a village trustee that year. Their home served as an early center of Chicago society. His biggest contribution to Chicago, however, was in his various trading and business activities, which led city historian A. T. Andreas to label him the single man most identified with the modern trade and commerce of the city.

Hubbard recognized Chicago's potential as a meat-packing center. On his arrival he opened one of the city's first pork- and beef-packing houses, which grew to be one of the largest in the West. The building he built for its operations temporarily housed Chicago's first bank, of which he was director. In 1836 he built a larger warehouse for what had become Hubbard and Company on the Chicago River in his new addition to the city. There, in partnership with Pratt, Taylor and Company of Buffalo, New York, he established the Eagle Line of vessels and steamers, the first systematic shipping service between Chicago and Buffalo and between Chicago and Lake Superior. Elenora Hubbard and their infant son died in 1838. In 1843 Hubbard married his cousin Mary Ann Hubbard.

Hubbard's other activities serve as a virtual list of Chicago firsts. He ordered Chicago's first fire engine in 1835 and served with its volunteer fire department. He helped raise money to build St. James Episcopal Church. In 1836 he was one of the original incorporators of the Chicago Hydrolic Company, founded to construct the city's first water works, which was subsequently bought by the city. He reportedly wrote the first insurance policy in the city and served as the first president of the Chicago Board of Underwriters. Perhaps more important, he was an organizer and original director of the Chicago Board of Trade. A Whig and then a Republican and a friend of Abraham Lincoln, Hubbard was also instrumental in 1860 in attracting the Republican party to Chicago, where it nominated Lincoln as its candidate for the presidency of the United States in the famous Wigwam, a structure Hubbard helped to build. During the Civil War he served as a captain in the Second Board of Trade Regulars (the Eighty-eighth Illinois Volunteers).

A series of setbacks affected Hubbard's businesses in his later years. One of his ships, the *Lady Elgin*, was rammed by a lumber vessel in 1860, and more than 290 lives were lost when it sank. In 1868 a fire destroyed the Hubbard Packing Company. The final collapse of his fortune came with the fire that devastated much of Chicago in 1871. The fire destroyed his business and more than 200 buildings that he owned. It also generated massive claims on the insurance policies he had written, claims that he felt he needed to repay. He never actively reentered business thereafter, as the city's social and economic leadership passed to a new generation of Chicagoans. Hubbard died in Chicago.

• The *Autobiography of Gurdon Saltonstall Hubbard* (1911) presents his version of his life story. Hubbard's *Incidents and Events in the Life of Gurdon Saltonstall Hubbard*, arr. Henry E. Hamilton (1888) and Hamilton, "Biographical Sketch of Gurdon Saltonstall Hubbard," Chicago Historical Society, *Proceedings* (1908), offer near-contemporary histories. Lloyd Wendt, *Swift Walker* (1986), is the most comprehensive study of Hubbard's life. Hubbard's life is well documented in most histories of Chicago and in biographical sketches of its most prominent people.

JANICE L. REIFF

HUBBARD, Henry Vincent (22 Aug. 1875–6 Oct. 1947), pioneering landscape architect and planner, was born in Taunton, Massachusetts, the son of Charles Thacher Hubbard, a physician, and Clara Isabel Reed. Hubbard attended Harvard College, as had five generations of Hubbards before him, and graduated in 1897. Hubbard studied at MIT in 1897–1898, completing in one year the first two years of the course in architecture and hoping to continue study in landscape architecture. Since instruction in this subject was not available in any school in the United States at that time, he enrolled at the Harvard Graduate School, where he studied under the direction of Frederick Law Olmsted, Jr., the son of the founder of the profession. He received an A.M. in 1900 and an S.B. in 1901, both in landscape architecture, from the newly established Lawrence Scientific School of Harvard; the degree was the first in the United States to be conferred in landscape architecture as an independent professional study.

In 1901 Hubbard entered the office of Olmsted Brothers, Landscape Architects and Site Planners in Brookline, Massachusetts, and in 1902 he traveled in France and Germany for professional study with Olmsted, Jr. Travel abroad has long formed part of the American landscape architect's education, and Hubbard had already traveled in England and on the continent in 1899. Again in 1913 he traveled to Europe, this time to study in Italy.

In 1906 Hubbard set up an independent practice in Boston with H. P. White and J. S. Pray, known as Pray, Hubbard and White. He was called to Washington, D.C., in 1917 to serve as a designer in what became the Cantonment Branch of the Construction Division of the U.S. Army. He served successively as "expert" with the Housing Commission of the Council of National Defense, as designer for the U.S. Shipping Board, as assistant manager and for a time acting manager of the Town Planning Division of the U.S. Housing Corporation, and finally as editor of a volume on technical design for the report of the Housing Corporation after the World War I armistice.

In 1918 the firm of Pray, Hubbard and White was dissolved, its "good and interesting" practice "squelched," as Hubbard put it, by World War I. He returned to the office of Olmsted Brothers and in 1920 was made a partner, which he remained until his death. He served as a planning consultant to the cities of Boston, Baltimore, and Providence, as well as to the Federal Housing Authority, the Tennessee Valley Authority, and the National Park Service. He was president of the American Society of Landscape Architects from 1931 to 1934 and was a member of the National Capital Park and Planning Commission from 1932 to 1947.

Hubbard began teaching landscape architecture at Harvard in 1906, as an instructor in what was then called the Graduate School of Applied Science. He was appointed assistant professor in the Harvard School of Landscape Architecture in 1911 and was appointed professor in 1921. Subsequent to a conference at Columbia University in 1929 on whether city planning should be taught in the United States, Harvard established a program of instruction and research in planning, with funding from the Rockefeller Foundation. Almost simultaneously, the Charles Dyer Norton Professorship in Regional Planning was established at Harvard and was awarded to Hubbard. The Rockefeller Foundation funding ended after seven years, and to Hubbard's disappointment the university did not continue instruction in the subject during his tenure there. Hubbard retired from teaching in 1941.

In 1910, with Charles Downing Lay and Robert Wheelwright, Hubbard founded *Landscape Architecture*, the (then quarterly) magazine of the American Society of Landscape Architects. In the face of financial difficulties brought about by the war years of 1917–1918, Wheelwright and Lay resigned, and Hubbard remained sole editor of the publication until his death. In volume 1, number 1, published in October 1910, Hubbard wrote that "only within the last two decades has there been any widespread general realization of our need for beauty in land adapted to our use—beauty, not merely as a luxury, but as a practical necessity and as a matter of course."

In 1917 Hubbard and Theodora Kimball, the librarian of the Harvard School of Design, published *An Introduction to the Study of Landscape Design*, the first and for a long time the standard text in landscape architecture. The work was revised in 1929 and was reprinted many times, most recently in 1959. In 1929 the authors wrote, "We take an esthetic theory which seems—to us at least—consistent and capable of general application, and use it as the basis of an organization of the subject matter of the field of landscape design." Hubbard and Kimball married in 1924; they had no children.

Kimball and Hubbard also founded and edited the journal *City Planning* (beginning 1925) and collaborated on *Our Cities To-day and To-morrow: A Survey of Planning and Zoning Progress in the United States* (1929). Hubbard collaborated with John Nolen on two important planning studies, *Airports* (1930) and *Parkways and Land Values* (1937). Hubbard wrote, "Regional planning is based first on a recognition of the topography, the economics, the law, the political machinery, the predispositions and backgrounds of the people who are to be served, or, more properly, who are to be enabled to serve themselves" ("Official Minute," Jan. 1948). His first wife having died in 1935, Hubbard married Isabel F. Gerrish in 1937; they had no children. Hubbard made his contributions to the field of planning at a time when its significance was not widely recognized, and with a few other pioneers he prepared the way for its acceptance as an essential function of government. He is remembered chiefly for his teaching, his many writings, and his editing of city planning studies and professional journals. Hubbard died in Milton, Massachusetts. In 1953 the Hubbard Educational Trust was founded in his memory with the purpose of furthering the understanding and appreciation of landscape architecture with support for its education and history.

• Hubbard's personal papers have not been located. Autobiographical material can be found in the Harvard Class of 1897 Notes. Miscellaneous correspondence and reports pertaining to Hubbard's role as partner in Olmsted Brothers are held at the Frederick Law Olmsted National Historic Site of the National Park Service, Brookline, Mass. Biographical notes, many from Hubbard's own writings, are joined with tributes to his achievements in "Henry Vincent Hubbard: An Official Minute on His Professional Life and Work," *Landscape Architecture* 38 (Jan. 1948): 47–57, which was authored by twelve people.

KAREN MADSEN

HUBBARD, L. Ron (13 Mar. 1911–24 Jan. 1986), writer and founder of Dianetics and Scientology, was born Lafayette Ronald Hubbard in Tilden, Nebraska, the son of Harry Ross Hubbard, an officer in the U.S. Navy, and Ledora May Waterbury de Wolfe. Hubbard spent much of his youth with his maternal grandfather in Montana due to his father's service in the navy. In 1923–1924 and again after 1929 Hubbard lived in Washington, D.C., graduating from high school there in 1930. Between 1927 and 1928 Hubbard traveled throughout the Far East. In 1930 he entered George Washington University but left before graduating, leading two expeditions to Central America (1932–1933) and a later one to Alaska (1940). While at the university, he conducted independent experiments on small energies (atomic and molecular physics). These experiments led directly to his research into the workings of the human mind.

Hubbard spent some of the early 1930s as an aviator and aviation correspondent. His major vocation by 1934, however, was as a prolific and increasingly successful fiction writer. His stories of the 1930s and 1940s were predominently action and adventure and included westerns and science fiction.

Hubbard married Margaret Louise Grubb in 1933 but divorced shortly after the war. In 1952 Hubbard married Mary Sue Whipp. He had a total of six children.

During World War II he was a navy lieutenant, serving in both the Pacific and Atlantic, and he spent time in 1943 and 1945 as a patient in a naval hospital for ulcers and injuries to eyes and hip. In 1945 he conducted independent studies in endocrinology, concluding that the mind could influence the functions of the body. In 1950 he published his most famous book, *Dianetics: The Modern Science of Mental Health*. This work became an instant bestseller, generating numerous articles, discussion groups, and conversations.

The basic concept in *Dianetics* is that the mind has two very distinct parts. Hubbard called the conscious part the analytical mind. The second, termed the reactive mind, comes into play when the individual is "unconscious"—in full or in part. Unconsciousness could be caused by the shock of an accident, the anesthetic used for an operation, the pain of an injury, or the deliriums of illness. According to Hubbard, the reactive mind stores particular types of mental images he called engrams. Engrams are a complete recording of every perception present in a moment of partial or full unconsciousness. This part of the mind can cause unevaluated, unknowing, and unwanted fears, emotions, pains, and psychosomatic illnesses. Through "auditing"—the application of Dianetics and Scientology processes and procedures—one can rid oneself of the reactive mind.

As a result of the popularity of *Dianetics*, the Hubbard Dianetics Research Foundation was established in May 1950 in Elizabeth, New Jersey, with offices in Los Angeles, Chicago, Honolulu, and Washington, D.C. *Dianetics* was opposed by the medical, psychological, and psychiatric professions, which all published articles discouraging its use. Despite these attempts, by late September 1950 over 750 Dianetics groups were established with over 250,000 individuals applying the techniques described in *Dianetics*.

In the fall of 1951 Hubbard felt he had isolated "life energy" or "life source"—the individual himself, which he termed the thetan (the human soul). From his research Hubbard concluded that the thetan was able to leave the body and exist independently of the flesh. In March 1952 he moved to Phoenix, Arizona, where he publicly announced this discovery. At that time he also announced the establishment of the Hubbard Association of Scientologists International. In 1954 Scientologists and Dianetics practitioners in Los Angeles formed the Church of Scientology. Scientology expanded rapidly in the United States and abroad, with hundreds of churches and centers appearing after 1954 and with millions of persons having passed through Scientology classes and counseling. Between 1951 and 1954 Hubbard wrote some twenty Scientology books and gave more than 1,100 lectures.

In 1959 Hubbard moved to England, where he started the Hubbard College of Saint Hill, in Sussex. At the college, he lectured and supervised the education of "auditors"—persons trained to deliver and apply Dianetics and Scientology processes and procedures. He also developed his ideas on the "operating thetan (OT)," Hubbard's concept of the state of spiritual freedom (and the ultimate goal of Scientology processing).

In 1966 Hubbard resigned all administrative positions in the church. In 1967 he set to sea with a handful of veteran Scientologists, called the Sea Organization, with the goal of researching and developing procedures for achieving the state of OT. In 1975 he settled in Dunedin, Florida, and a year later moved to a southern California desert ranch in La Quinta. In 1982 Hubbard retired to a private life in San Luis Obispo County, California, devoting the majority of his time to writing and completing research on the state of OT. He died in Creston, California.

L. Ron Hubbard and the Church of Scientology have generated considerable controversy. The United States and several other governments have taken legal action against Scientology, largely based on claims made by critics of excessive fees, intimidation and harassment of critics, and deceptive marketing practices. The church in turn has claimed government vendettas against its religious freedom and has in the end won most of its legal battles. On 1 October 1993 the IRS granted the Church of Scientology and more than 150 of its corporate entities tax-exempt status, ruling that they are charitable religious organizations. Critics have alleged that official biographies of Hubbard published by the church contain false claims, but supporters counter that the very success of Hubbard and Scientology has engendered the criticism. In any case, L. Ron Hubbard, a man of rich creativity, started one of the most successful and widely publicized new religious movements of the twentieth century.

• The Church of Scientology maintains a major archive on the life and teachings of Hubbard. The church has also published such booklets as *L. Ron Hubbard: A Profile* and a series of publications describing Hubbard's early travels, his research into the mind, and his achievements in education, drug rehabilitation, and social reform. The existing book-length biographies authored by non-Scientologists—Bent Corydon and L. Ron Hubbard, Jr., *L. Ron Hubbard: Messiah or Madman* (1987), and Russell Miller, *The Bare-Faced Messiah* (1987)—are polemical works. Both were later shown to contain inaccurate and incomplete information, with L. Ron Hubbard, Jr., retracting all his statements and demanding that his name be removed as author. A short introduction to Hubbard can be found in *Contemporary Authors*, New Revision Series, vol. 22, which lists all of Hubbard's works as well as a selection of secondary sources. Also refer to the Hubbard entry in J. Gordon Melton, *Religious Leaders of America* (1991), and to his obituary in the *New York Times*, 29 Jan. 1986.

JAMES R. LEWIS

HUBBARD, William (1621–14 Sept. 1704), Puritan minister, was born in Ipswich, Suffolk, England, the son of William Hubbard, a husbandman, and Judith Knapp. Hubbard came to New England with his family in 1635 and settled the same year in Ipswich, Massachusetts. He attended Harvard, studied medicine in addition to the standard curriculum, and graduated in 1642 with the first graduating class. He married Margaret Rogers in 1646; they had three children. Hubbard became a full church member and freeman in 1653. In 1656 he joined Rev. Thomas Cobbett as a ministerial colleague in the Ipswich church and was ordained in 1658.

Hubbard was a leading political and religious moderate in late seventeenth-century Massachusetts. In 1671 he and several other ministers defended Boston's Third Church against a General Court censure. The Third Church was composed of a group of disgruntled First Church members who had supported adoption of the Half-Way Covenant as a means of expanding church membership. The covenant allowed the children of any baptized person, even those who had not been admitted to full communion in the church, to be baptized. The dissidents broke off to form their own congregation when the majority of First Church members voted to hire John Davenport, a vehement opponent of the covenant, as minister. Hubbard also urged the colony to adopt a more accommodating policy toward religious dissenters, arguing they should be tolerated as long as they did not disturb the public peace.

Hubbard rejected the view promulgated by Increase Mather and other ministers in the jeremiads that New England had lost sight of its original purpose and had become corrupt and worldly, caught in a downward spiral of declension. In his 1676 election sermon, "The Happiness of a People in the Wisdom of Their Rulers," he contended that the religious and social changes besetting New England, while disturbing, were not unique omens of impending doom. Rather, they were just the latest expressions of the adversity Christians always had to counter when facing the temptations of prosperity. Similarly, he rejected Mather's portrait of the colony's youth, the "rising generation," as morally degenerate. He argued that there were abundant signs of moral regeneration among Puritan youth that offered true hope for the future. Hubbard's was a more rational, tolerant view of human nature and social change. While Hubbard agreed that King Philip's War did indeed have some spiritual significance as a judgment from God, for instance, he also contended that the colonists defeated Philip because of the superior strength of their mind and will—and that their defeats along the way were due entirely to secular weaknesses (*Narrative of the Troubles with the Indians in New-England* [1677]).

During the 1670s and 1680s Hubbard was closely identified with the moderate wing of Massachusetts politics—those individuals who supported some accommodation to England's demands that Massachusetts allow freedom of religion and obey the Navigation Acts. In 1685 he counseled the General Court to proceed cautiously if the colony's charter were repealed. Yet here as elsewhere Hubbard's tolerance would only go so far. In 1687 he helped lead the Ipswich resistance to the burdensome taxes imposed by Sir Edmund Andros, governor of the Dominion of New England.

Hubbard continued to espouse moderation in his religious views as well, as evidenced by his 1684 sermon, "The Benefit of a Well-Ordered Conversation," a funeral oration delivered upon the death of his close friend and political moderate, Daniel Denison. Here he expressed greater faith in the abilities of human reason than did more traditional Puritan ministers; indeed, he seemed to come perilously close to Arminian views in arguing that God would grant salvation to those who led righteous lives. Men caused their own problems, Hubbard felt, by failing to employ their God-given reason, and they could thus effect their own solutions. There were limits, though, to Hubbard's accommodationist view in religion as well as in politics. Later in the century he joined Increase and Cotton Mather in opposing Benjamin Colman's Brattle Street Church, a congregation that abandoned the church covenant and conversion narrative and allowed all who were baptized to become full church members.

Hubbard received official recognition of his talents several times. In 1682 the General Court commissioned him to write a history of the colony. The result, *A General History of New England from the Discovery to MDCLXXX* (pub. in 1815), was not very original; Hubbard relied heavily on William Bradford's (1590–1657) *Of Plymouth Plantation* and John Winthrop's (1588–1649) *Journal*. The General Court also twice appointed him temporary president of Harvard—in 1684, when President John Rogers (1648–1721) (his wife's grandfather) was ill, and again in 1688 while Increase Mather was in England seeking the return of the colony's charter.

During the last decades of his life Hubbard continued to pursue truth in a quiet, moderate fashion. He resisted the Salem witchcraft hysteria in 1692, testifying to the good character of one of the accused, and in 1703 he joined several others in petitioning the General Court on behalf of survivors of the trials who were still under legal restrictions. He seems to have made the greatest stir in his old age, though, when in 1694 he married his housekeeper Mary Pearce after his wife had died. His action shocked his parishioners, but it is further evidence of his unpretentious, sober character. Hubbard died in Ipswich.

• There is no book-length study of Hubbard's life. In addition to his own writings, see the following works for biographical information and analyses of his religious and social thought: J. L. Sibley, *Biographical Sketches of Graduates of Harvard University,* vol. 1 (1873); T. H. Breen, *The Character of the Good Ruler: A Study of Puritan Political Ideas in New England, 1630–1730* (1970); Emory Elliott, *Power and the Pulpit in Puritan New England* (1975); Perry Miller, *The New England Mind: From Colony to Province* (1953); Richard Slotkin, *Regeneration through Violence: The Mythology of the American Frontier, 1600–1860* (1973); and Stephen Foster, *The Long Argument: English Puritanism and the Shaping of New England Culture, 1570–1700* (1991).

RONALD P. DUFOUR

HUBBARD, William DeHart (25 Nov. 1903–23 June 1976), first African American to win an individual Olympic Games gold medal, was born in Cincinnati, Ohio, the son of William A. Hubbard. Olympic historians know nothing of his father's occupation nor his mother's full name at the time of her marriage. After excelling in both academics and athletics at Walnut Hills High Schools between 1918 and 1921, Hubbard entered the University of Michigan. As a freshman he tied the school record in the 50-yard dash, set a school record of 24'6¾" in the long jump, and won two U.S. National Amateur Athletic Union (AAU) Championships in the long jump (24'5½") and triple jump (48'1½"). He won All-American honors in 1922, and until his graduation in 1925, his exploits reserved for him recognition as the greatest combination sprinter-jumper of the 1920s.

Hubbard was a compact, 150-pound world-class sprinter, and no one before his time nor during his career was able to "run off" the wooden toeboard with the same speed as "King Hubbard." His speed and technique not only won him American, world, and Olympic honors, but he was the precursor of the even greater sprinter-jumpers of the next generation. The British expert, Colonel F. A. M. Webster, watched

Hubbard, his speed, and jumping prowess and called Hubbard "a regular pinch of dynamite." Hubbard won AAU long jump titles six times, 1922–1927, "an astonishing achievement," wrote historian Roberto L. Quercetani. "His style included a run of less than 30 meters, a remarkable acceleration and a single, fast kick of the lead leg."

Hubbard qualified as an American Olympic team member for the 1924 Games in Paris; despite an injured leg, he won the gold medal with a 24′5⅛″ leap. Returning home to his studies and his athletics, Hubbard dominated the jumps and sprints at the prestigious National Collegiate Athletic Association (NCAA) Championships. He had won the 1923 NCAA jump title, and at the 1925 competition he literally hurled himself out of the sand pit with a world record leap of 25′10⅞″, having already won the 100-yard dash. The Associated Press release on 13 June 1925 shouted, "Hubbard approaches 26 feet, a long jump record that may stand for all time."

In 1926 Hubbard ran 100 yards in 9.6 seconds, tying the world record. He had recently graduated from Michigan, "one of only eight blacks in a class of 1,456" (Ashe, p. 79). Injuries plagued Hubbard, slowing him down so much that at the 1928 Olympic Games in Amsterdam he finished in eleventh place. His athletic career was finished, and with a degree in physical education, Hubbard accepted a position with the Cincinnati Recreation Department. For fifteen years he supervised Negro athletic leagues in that city and persisted in efforts to improve housing for blacks. In 1943 Hubbard moved to Cleveland and served as race relations adviser to the Federal Housing Authority, remaining in that position for many years. Hubbard died in Cleveland. His wife, Audrey, and three children survived.

• For additional information on Hubbard, see Arthur R. Ashe, Jr., *A Hard Road to Glory: A History of the African-American Athlete*, vol. 2 (1988), pp. 78–79; and Roberto L. Quercetani, *A History of Modern Track and Field* (1990), p. 73. See also Bill Mallon et al., *Quest for Gold* (1984), pp. 309–10. For a vivid account, see F. A. M. Webster, *Athletics of To-Day* (1929), pp. 206–7. American newspapers covered every aspect of Hubbard's athletic career; for example, see the *New York Times*, 14 June 1925 and 6 July 1926; the *Chicago Sunday Tribune*, 14 June 1925; and the *New York Herald Tribune*, 9 July 1924 and 6 July 1926. Obituaries are in the *New York Times*, 25 June 1976, and *The Times* (London), 26 June 1976.

JOHN A. LUCAS

HUBBELL, Carl (22 June 1903–21 Nov. 1988), baseball player, was born Carl Owen Hubbell in Carthage, Missouri; the names of his parents cannot be ascertained. Hubbell grew up in Meeker, Oklahoma, where he picked pecans and cotton as a child. He began pitching in Meeker High School and then worked in the Oklahoma oil fields. He played for local teams before signing in 1923 with Cushing in the Oklahoma State League. In 1925 he was promoted to Oklahoma City of the Western League.

The left-hander augmented an adequate fastball and curveball and good control with a reverse curveball, a pitch that broke away from right-handed hitters and broke in on left-handed hitters. The unorthodox, hard-to-control delivery was labeled a "screwball" by a veteran minor league catcher, who called it the "screwiest damn pitch I ever saw." Christy Mathewson also threw a reverse curve, which was called a "fadeaway."

The Detroit Tigers purchased Hubbell in 1925 but discouraged him from using the potentially arm-damaging screwball. The arm and wrist motion involved in the screwball runs contrary to the normal across-the-body twist involved in throwing an orthodox curveball. Hubbell's pitching performance declined, causing the Tigers to option him early in the season to Toronto of the International League. He did not pitch for the Tigers during three years with their organization and played for Beaumont of the Texas League for part of 1928.

Dick Kinsella, a friend of New York Giants' manager John McGraw, saw Hubbell pitch in June 1928 and persuaded the Giants to purchase him. Hubbell compiled a 10–6 won-lost record in the final half of that season for New York, baffling hitters with his screwball and impressing the baseball establishment with his coolness and all-around pitching mastery. He led McGraw's pitching staff from 1929 until 1932.

Hubbell attained superstar status in 1933 as new Giants' manager Bill Terry's club surprised the baseball world by winning the National League pennant and defeating the Washington Senators in the World Series. Hubbell's splendid 1933 season included a 23–12 won-lost record, a remarkable 1.66 earned-run-average, and the National League Most Valuable Player award. The Giants' "Meal Ticket," as the writers nicknamed him, won 21 or more games in each of the next four seasons, helping the Giants win pennants in 1936 and 1937.

Beset by painful arm injuries, attributable largely to the punishing screwball, Hubbell struggled to a 13–10 record in 1938 before undergoing elbow surgery. He won a relatively modest 11 games in each of the next four seasons and then retired after the 1943 season. Well fixed financially through oil investments, he took over as the Giants' farm system director in 1944, a position he held for thirty-five years.

Through his playing career, "King Carl" was responsible for some striking pitching feats, beginning with a no-hit, no-run victory over the Pittsburgh Pirates on 8 May 1929. On 2 July 1933 he shut out the St. Louis Cardinals' "Gas House Gang" 1–0 in eighteen innings, striking out 12 hitters and walking none. He held opponents scoreless over 46⅓ innings in one stretch during the same year. Hubbell's incredible control was best exemplified in a 2–0 shutout win in 1933. In that game he did not walk a hitter or even reach a three-ball count against any batter. He won his last 16 decisions in 1936 and his first eight decisions in 1937 (although he lost a 1936 World Series game to the New York Yankees), setting a long-standing record of 24 consecutive regular season wins. His most celebrated accomplishment came during the 1934 All-Star game, when he struck out consecutively five future Hall of Famers (Babe Ruth, Lou Gehrig, Jimmie Foxx, Al Simmons, and Joe Cronin). Hubbell appeared in three other All-Star games—1936, 1937, and 1940. From 1933 through 1937 he compiled a 115–50 record, saved 20 games in relief of other pitchers, and averaged almost 300 innings pitched per season. Hubbell's imposing career totals include a 253–154 won-lost record, a 2.98 ERA, 36 shutouts, a 4–2 mark with a 1.79 ERA in three World Series, and Most Valuable Player awards in 1933 and 1936. In 1947 he was elected to the National Baseball Hall of Fame.

Hubbell, colorless except for the curiosity of his misshapen left arm (hopelessly twisted inward by years of throwing the screwball) and his custom of wearing his uniform knickers long (claiming that he had no backside to hold them higher), remained a quiet, modest, unfailingly composed man. He was rivaled only by Lefty Grove as the most respected pitcher of his era.

National Baseball Hall of Famer pitcher Waite Hoyt, a perceptive observer of the era, commented: "Hubbell is one of the great pitchers, yet he presents no mystery to the onlooker. The source of his skill is his matchless control in using his curveball to set up his screwball. Emotions, if he has any, never affect him. His timing, his conservation of energy, and influence on the ballclub are other factors in rating him among the great pitchers of all time."

Hubbell married his high school sweetheart, Lucille Herrington, in 1930 and had two children. Widowed in 1964, he married Julia Stanfield in 1970 and resided in Mesa, Arizona, until his death following an automobile accident.

• See the Carl Hubbell file, National Baseball Hall of Fame Library, Cooperstown, N.Y. Authoritative biographical material can be found in Bob Broeg, *Super Stars of Baseball* (1971); Gene Karst and Martin J. Jones, Jr., *Who's Who in Professional Baseball* (1971); David L. Porter, ed., *Biographical Dictionary of American Sports: Baseball* (1987); and Walter M. Langford, *Legends of Baseball—An Oral History of the Game's Golden Age* (1987). Hubbell's career is detailed in Fred Stein, *Under Coogan's Bluff* (1979), and in Fred Stein and Nick Peters, *Giants Diary—A Century of Giants Baseball in New York and San Francisco* (1987). The most up-to-date compilation of his playing records appears in John Thorn and Pete Palmer, eds., *Total Baseball*, 3d ed. (1993). Obituaries are in the *New York Times*, 22 Nov. 1988, and the *Sporting News*, 5 Dec. 1988.

FRED STEIN

HUBBELL, Jay Broadus (8 May 1885–13 Feb. 1979), university teacher and literary historian, was born in Smyth County, Virginia, the son of David Shelton Hubbell, a Baptist minister, and Ruth Eller. He was educated at Richmond College (B.A., 1905), Harvard University (M.A., 1908), and Columbia University (Ph.D., 1922), teaching in the meantime at the University of North Carolina (1908–1909), Wake Forest College (1911–1914), and Southern Methodist University (1915–1927), with time out for service in World War I as a first lieutenant in the field artillery (1918–1919). In 1918 he married Lucinda Smith of Dallas, Texas, one of his students at Southern Methodist University (SMU) and the daughter of a well-known attorney. The couple had two sons, Jay Broadus Hubbell, Jr., who frequently served as his father's research assistant, and David Smith Hubbell, a physician. After his return from the war, Hubbell became chair of the Department of English and E. A. Lilly Professor of English at SMU and edited the *Southwest Review* from 1924 to 1927. In the latter year he went to Duke University as professor of English (eventually as professor of American literature) and remained—except for infrequent stints teaching summer sessions at the University of Colorado, the University of Texas, Columbia University, and the University of California at Los Angeles and for visiting professorships at the University of Vienna (1949, 1950) and the University of Athens (1953)—until he retired in 1954. Subsequently, he taught at the University of Virginia (1954–1955), Clemson University (1956), Columbia University (1957–1958), Texas Technological University (1960), and the University of Kentucky (1961). He was also Smith-Mundt Professor of American Literature at Hebrew University, Jerusalem (1956), but his tenure was interrupted by the Suez War, and he was ordered home by the U.S. State Department in October 1956.

Hubbell pioneered the scholarly study of and the direction of graduate work in American literature during his tenure at Duke. An early member and chair (1924–1927) of the American Literature Group (later the American Literature Section) of the Modern Language Association (MLA), he became founding editor of the group's semiofficial organ *American Literature*, the first scholarly journal and still a vital factor in the field, and served as chair of the board of editors until his retirement in 1954. Use of his *American Life in Literature* (2 vols., 1936) was widespread, and the anthology was reprinted on three occasions for the U.S. Armed Forces Institute (1944, 1945, 1947) and twice after the war for college audiences (1949, 1951). Hubbell's position in the profession at large was recognized by his election to the executive council of MLA (1946–1949) and as vice president in 1951. His articles and reviews, his direction of graduate work (especially dissertations), and his full-scale study of southern literature to the twentieth century, *The South in American Literature* (1954), still indispensable to a serious consideration of the field, all contributed to his reputation as a leading authority on southern and American writing. Two books published in his later years, *South and Southwest* (1965), a collection of new essays and a number of revised and reprinted articles and reminiscences, and *Who Are the Major American Writers?* (1972), a topic he first examined in 1955 and by the 1990s a focus of much controversy, testified anew to his stature in each area. His professional position was recognized by the institution in 1964 of the Jay B. Hubbell Medallion, awarded by the American Literature Section of the MLA to honor significant lifetime contributions to

American literary scholarship (Hubbell was the initial recipient); by *Essays on American Literature in Honor of Jay B. Hubbell* (1967), a Festschrift containing twenty-three essays; and subsequently by the establishment in 1976 of the Jay B. Hubbell Center for American Literary Historiography, Duke University, to house the professional papers of eminent scholars who sought "to promote studies in the history of American thought" through an examination of American literary history, criticism, and bibliography. In addition to these honors, Hubbell was a member of Phi Beta Kappa.

No consideration of Hubbell's contribution to the profession should fail to include his pioneering efforts to promote the teaching of literature to undergraduates. In addition to his *American Life in Literature*, he edited widely adopted anthologies in collaboration with John O. Beaty titled *An Introduction to Poetry* (1922) and *An Introduction to Drama* (1927), compilations that sought to present to college readers the work of new poets and playwrights as well as that of established writers, an interest that resulted in friendships and correspondence with diverse artists such as Robert Frost, Carl Sandburg, and John Hall Wheelock, among others.

Hubbell, indeed, was a pioneer in the study of many branches of literature. It would be difficult to overestimate his importance to the serious consideration of American and southern literature on the university level. As a teacher and distinguished authority in these areas for many years, he set an example in and out of the classroom and in his scholarship that is still being followed and passed on by generations of his students and their successors. His critical judgments generally reflect a literary historian's full knowledge of a writer's output, from individual work to entire corpus, within the context of the period involved and of the writing of the past. Yet his approach is also open to the insights of critical and psychological analysis, among other avenues, without being captive to them or becoming eclectic in standards. He sought to open the study of literature to all, to make it accessible and understandable to those who were willing to examine it, and, accordingly, he eschewed the use of arcane language and restricted point of view. His angle of vision, after all, was to see literature (and American and southern writing in particular) as a vital and significant aspect of the cultural life of a people, as an essential part of their heritage and future, as an "expression of American thought and as a record of American life" (*American Life in Literature*, vol. 1, rev. ed. [1949], p. xv). These principles are admirably embodied in his most important book, *The South in American Literature*, which, despite some recent additions and modifications offered in works such as *The History of Southern Literature*, edited by Louis D. Rubin and others (1985), seems destined to last as a monument to thorough research and mature scholarship. Hubbell died in Durham, North Carolina.

• The major collection of Hubbell's papers is in the Hubbell Center, Perkins Library, Duke University. Books and parts of books not mentioned in the text include *Virginia Life in Fiction* (1922); *The Enjoyment of Literature* (1929); *The Last Years of Henry Timrod, 1864–1867* (1941); *Southern Life in Fiction* (1960), the Lamar Memorial Lectures delivered at Mercer University in 1959; and the bibliographical essay on Edgar Allan Poe in *Eight American Authors: A Review of Research and Criticism*, ed. James Woodress (1956; rev. ed., 1971). For Hubbell's own listing of his publications (excluding numerous book reviews in scholarly journals, magazines, and newspapers), see *South and Southwest* (1965), pp. 365–69, and for a resume in outline form, see Ray M. Atchison in *Essays on American Literature in Honor of Jay B. Hubbell*, ed. Clarence Gohdes (1967). A brief appraisal of Hubbell as teacher and man appears in Rayburn S. Moore, "Jay B. Hubbell: A Memorial Tribute," *Southern Literary Journal* 12 (1979): 92–95.

RAYBURN S. MOORE

HUBBELL, John Lorenzo (27 Nov. 1853–12 Nov. 1930), trader to the Navajos, was born in Pajarito, New Mexico Territory, the son of James (Santiago) Lawrence Hubbell and Julianita Gutierrez. His father, from Salisbury, Connecticut, settled in New Mexico in 1848 following the Mexican War and became a government contractor, buying and selling cattle, and a freighter. His mother's antecedents were Spanish pioneers in New Mexico and had held papers to the Pajarito Land Grant since 1739. Lorenzo, as he was called, was raised a Catholic and was first taught, in Spanish, by a tutor. At twelve, he was sent to Farley's Presbyterian School in Santa Fe, where he learned English. After completion of his education, Hubbell became a clerk in an Albuquerque post office. However, "craving romance and adventure," he set out for Utah Territory, arriving in Kanab in 1872, where he served as a clerk in a Mormon trading post. Following what Hubbell later called "difficulties" in Panguitch, Utah, in which he was seriously wounded, he fled south, where he was cared for by Paiutes. He then swam across the Colorado River at the bottom of the Grand Canyon on his way to the Hopi villages in northeastern Arizona. While there in the summer of 1873 he was, perhaps, the first white man to observe the Snake-Antelope Ceremony.

During the next several years Hubbell was employed at a trading post near Fort Wingate, New Mexico, and at the Navajo Agency at Fort Defiance, Arizona. Because of his skills with the Navajos, he served as Spanish interpreter in negotiations between Navajo leaders and agent W. F. M. Arny in 1874. By 1876 he moved to the Hispanic settlement of St. Johns, Arizona, and established a trading post about 100 miles north at Pueblo Colorado Wash. In 1878 he purchased William Leonard's nearby trading post. Because of the confusion with Pueblo, Colorado, Hubbell had the name changed to Ganado in honor of his friend, the Navajo headman Ganado Mucho. In 1880 the Pueblo, Colorado, area was added to the Navajo reservation, but it was not until 1908 that Hubbell's prior homestead rights were acknowledged by patent. For the next fifty years, Hubbell was associated with the trading post at Ganado, since 1967 preserved as Hubbell Trading Post National Historic Site.

In 1879 Hubbell married Lina Rubi, daughter of Cruz and Tàfoya Reyes Rubi of Cebolleta, New Mexico; four children were born to them. While St. Johns served as the family home, Hubbell expanded his trading operations by establishing posts at Chinle, Black Mountain, Cornfields, Nazlini, Keams Canyon, Oraibi, and Cedar Springs—all in Arizona—and purchased a large warehouse in Winslow. In 1882 he was elected to the first of two terms as sheriff of Apache County. During this time, the grazing lands in the St. Johns area were the subject of a bloody conflict between Hispanic sheepherders and Texas cattlemen, with Hubbell siding with the sheepmen because, he said, "the country was better suited to sheep." Hubbell served two terms in the territorial legislature. In "Fifty Years an Indian Trader," Hubbell reflected on his political career: "I went into politics in this Territory as one of the first and few men who had the courage to tell certain politicians that they were a lot of damned rascals." Hubbell also served the Republican State Central Committee as chair for four years and was a member of the first state legislature, but he failed in a bid to become a U.S. senator in 1914.

Toward the end of his first term as sheriff (1885), Hubbell went into partnership with Clinton N. Cotton, who operated his trading post at Ganado for the next ten years. While early trade was based on wool and hides, Cotton saw commercial possibilities in Navajo silverwork and, with Hubbell's approval, brought Mexican silversmiths to Ganado. By the time of Hubbell's first mail order catalog in 1902, Navajo concho belts and turquoise bracelets had become significant craft items. Cotton, too, saw an economic potential in Navajo weaving, but it was Hubbell who made a lasting imprint on the "Ganado blanket." As early as 1886–1887 Hubbell rejected—except for red—the bright aniline dyes that were being introduced at other trading posts in favor of colors and designs that he felt had more market potential, and he discouraged the use of cotton warp because it was subject to shrinkage. In the early 1900s he had E. A. Burbank, an artist and frequent visitor to Ganado, make small-scale paintings of fifty or sixty of the best blankets brought to the trading post, to which Hubbell referred both less talented weavers and customers seeking a traditional Ganado-style blanket. At about this time, the Fred Harvey Company made an agreement to buy all of the better quality blankets, most of these going to the Harvey Indian Room in Albuquerque's new Alvarado Hotel. Frank McNitt (p. 209, n. 17) summarized, "All authorities agree that Hubbell did as much as any trader, and more than most, to improve the quality of Navaho weaving."

Hubbell's success as a trader was due to his knowledge of Navajo language and culture; his fairness and honesty in his business dealings; his friendships with various local Navajo headmen, notably Ganado Mucho, Manuelito, Many Horses, and Henry Chee

Dodge; and his sense of responsibility to the community of which he was a part. Hubbell reviewed his philosophy in "Fifty Years an Indian Trader": "The first duty of an Indian trader, in my belief, is to look after the material welfare of his neighbors; to advise them to produce that which their natural inclinations and talent best adapts them; to treat them honestly and insist upon getting the same treatment from them . . . to find a market for their production of same, and advise them which commands the best price. This does not mean that the trader should forget that he is to see that he makes a fair profit for himself, for whatever would injure him would naturally injure those with whom he comes in contact." When political activists of the 1960s protested the abuses of many modern traders, John Lorenzo Hubbell was cited as an example of a good trader worthy of emulation.

Known to Navajos as Nak'eznilih, Double Glasses, because of his appearance, and later in life as Naakaii Saani, Old Mexican, out of respect, Hubbell was known to visiting travelers, scientists, artists, writers, missionaries, politicians, and others as Don Lorenzo or, in Hamlin Garland's phrase, "Don Lorenzo the Magnificent," for his hospitality and generosity. In 1900 the Presbyterian church sent Charles Bierkhemper and his wife to serve as missionaries to the Navajos. Hubbell provided living quarters for them for two years while the first mission buildings were constructed nearby. Generals Lew Wallace, Hugh Scott, and Nelson A. Miles visited the Hubbells, as did anthropologists Adolph Bandelier, J. Walter Fewkes, Steward Culin, and Sylvanus G. Morley. Hubbell met every president from Grover Cleveland to Warren G. Harding, and Theodore Roosevelt (1858–1919) stayed with him for a week in 1912 en route to see a Hopi "Snake Dance." Hubbell died at his Ganado trading post. He was succeeded in business by his sons Lorenzo, Jr., and Roman.

In its distinctive designs and colors, the Ganado blanket (now a rug or wall tapestry) reflects something of the lasting contribution John Lorenzo Hubbell made to the social and economic development of northern Arizona.

• Hubbell's personal and business papers are in the University of Arizona Library, Tucson. His "Fifty Years an Indian Trader" (as told to John Edwin Hogg), *Touring Topics* 22 (Dec. 1930): 24–51, has long served as the basic source of biographical information. Assessment of his importance as a trader to the Navajos is in Frank McNitt, *The Indian Traders* (1962). More recent scholarship has benefited from the availability of the Hubbell papers. For Hubbell's Hispanic heritage, see Charles S. Peterson, "Big House at Ganado: New Mexican Influence in Northern Arizona," *Journal of Arizona History* 30 (1989): 51–72. See David M. Brugge, *Hubbell Trading Post National Historic Site* (1993), for a history of the trading post. Several scholars have studied Hubbell's influence on Navajo silverwork and textile arts. See Joann F. Boles, "The Navaho Rug at the Hubbell Trading Post, 1880–1920," *American Indian Culture and Research Journal* 5 (1981): 47–63, and Nancy J. Blomberg, *Navajo Textiles: The*

William Randolph Hearst Collection (1988). An obituary by Joseph Emerson Smith is in the *Denver Post*, 23 Nov. 1930, and is reprinted in *El Palacio* 29 (1930): 371–77.

LOUIS A. HIEB

HUBBERT, M. King (5 Oct. 1903–11 Oct. 1989), geophysicist, was born Marion King Hubbert in San Saba, Texas, the son of William Bee Hubbert, a farmer and mechanic, and Cora Virginia Lee, a teacher. Hubbert's mother imparted to him a strong devotion to learning and a great deal of self-confidence, and when Hubbert was four she organized a school for neighborhood children. In 1908 his family moved to the Fort Stockton area, where his father temporarily found work as a ranch foreman and farmer; subsequently the family returned to San Saba. Hubbert attended county schools in Fort Stockton and San Saba before enrolling in a private high school. Inquisitive and gifted, Hubbert read popular science magazines and became deeply interested in steam engines and telephones, still a novelty in rural Texas.

Hubbert attended Weatherford Junior College between 1921 and 1923. Desiring greater intellectual challenges, Hubbert set out unannounced for the University of Chicago on the recommendation of a Weatherford instructor. Gaining probationary admission, Hubbert excelled at Chicago, earning a B.A. in 1926 and an M.S. in 1928, both in geology and physics. Broadly interested in the physical sciences, Hubbert then undertook comprehensive graduate studies in classical physics and sought to integrate physical concepts into structural geology, then a particular strength of Chicago geologists.

While preparing his dissertation, Hubbert was hired to teach structural geology and geophysics at Columbia University, a respected center for traditional field geology. He remained at Columbia from 1930 to 1940, formally receiving his Ph.D. from Chicago in 1937. During summer months, Hubbert took on assignments at the Amerada Petroleum Corporation in Oklahoma, the Illinois State Geological Survey, and the U.S. Geological Survey, addressing a variety of geophysical problems. In 1938 he married Miriam Graddy Berry; they had no children.

Most of Hubbert's professional career was spent not in higher education, but in industrial and government service. After leaving Columbia, where his research in geophysics was not well appreciated by traditionally trained geologists within his department, Hubbert served briefly as a senior analyst at the Board of Economic Warfare in Washington, D.C. Leaving that post in 1943 to join the Shell Oil Company, Hubbert soon took direction of its company-wide research laboratory in Houston, Texas, making it a center for fundamental geophysical studies. He studied many fields of solid-earth geophysics and fluid dynamics and imposed high academic standards on the lab. It became a significant research center and not simply a place where limited, strictly "applied" studies were carried out. In 1964, reaching Shell's mandatory retirement age, Hubbert joined the U.S. Geological Survey as a senior research geophysicist, a position he retained until 1976.

Hubbert made numerous important contributions to geophysics, ranging from fundamental scientific investigations to extensive evaluations of petroleum and natural gas reserves, developments of immense practical significance. In 1937 Hubbert resolved a puzzling, long-standing paradox involving the apparent strength of materials forming the crust of the earth, since such rocks—despite their evident strength—often show signs of plastic flow (the ability of a solid under great pressure to deform). Hubbert's mathematical analysis showed that even the hardest of rocks, subjected to the immense pressures that exist across large areas, render, as if they were soft muds or clays. By the early 1950s Hubbert introduced far-reaching revisions to theories regarding the flow of underground fluids; his work, which showed that fluids can become entrapped under circumstances previously thought impossible, led petroleum corporations to fundamentally reassess their techniques to locate oil and natural gas deposits. In addition, working with William W. Rubey, a highly respected geologist at the U.S. Geological Survey, Hubbert interpreted the origin of overthrust faults, created by the displacement of enormous blocks of materials, as a consequence of fluid pressures. How these blocks had shifted was a major challenge of geology, one that had puzzled American and European researchers alike.

Hubbert is perhaps best known for his investigations of world reserves of oil and natural gas, a subject that first intrigued him while a student in Chicago in the 1920s. In 1949 Hubbert used physical and statistical methods to calculate the total worldwide volume of oil and natural gas, then documented accelerating consumption of these resources. By the mid-1950s he predicted that the peak of crude oil production in the United States would occur between 1966 and 1971. Although Hubbert's figures were later judged as essentially correct but somewhat low, his estimates of future reserves were far below those then endorsed by leaders of several major petroleum corporations and the U.S. Geological Survey, and became a matter of intense controversy. Increasingly consulted on natural resource issues, Hubbert accepted membership in various government panels, including several that addressed the disposal of nuclear wastes, and a National Academy of Sciences–led study of the natural resources of the United States, requested by President John F. Kennedy. In evaluating nuclear waste policy Hubbert came into conflict with advocates of peaceful applications of nuclear explosions, leading to public criticisms of the noted physicist Edward Teller.

Hubbert also influenced university programs in the earth and environmental sciences. Dissatisfied with conventional geology departments, which placed limited emphasis on physics and mathematics, Hubbert actively participated in committees on geophysical education sponsored by the American Institute of Mining, Metallurgical, and Petroleum Engineers, the National Research Council, and the Geological Society of

America. He also served on numerous national committees and toured as the Distinguished Lecturer of the American Association of Petroleum Geologists. At Stanford University, where he served as visiting professor from 1962 to 1968, Hubbert helped create its new earth sciences program, arguing that "integration of the traditional and areal aspects of the solid earth and its biological inhabitants" with the earth's physical and chemical aspects was a positive, progressive development (letter to members of the Department of Geology, Stanford Univ., 20 Mar. 1967, C. Hulett Dix Papers, California Institute of Technology archives). By the late 1970s environmental science curricula of this kind had been replicated at other American universities.

Hubbert was also active in social causes. In the 1930s he became involved in the Technocracy movement, a group dedicated to applying scientific principles to economic and social phenomena, which, in addition to its founder, engineer Howard Scott, had attracted economist Thorsten Veblen and physicist Richard Tolman. Hubbert became director of Technocracy's Division of Education and wrote a short work, *Manpower and Distribution* (1940), to explain Technocracy's concern with industrial policy; his later concern for the economics of natural resources took early form in this work. He became a strong advocate of civil rights during his residence in Houston.

Hubbert received numerous medals and honorary awards for his geophysical research and studies of natural resources. In addition to the 1954 Arthur L. Day Medal of the Geological Society of America, Hubbert received the prestigious Penrose Medal of the GSA in 1973, the William Smith Medal of the Geological Society of London in 1978, and a $10,000 Rockefeller Public Service Award for his contributions to U.S. petroleum estimates. In 1981 Hubbert was given the $50,000 Vetlesen Prize of Columbia University in recognition of his achievements in the earth sciences.

After his formal retirement from research and teaching, Hubbert continued to consult and write from his home in Bethesda, Maryland, where he died.

Hubbert exercized considerable influence over the intellectual and professional development of geophysics in mid-twentieth century America. His contributions to conservation and environmental science, though recognized during his lifetime, have been increasingly appreciated after his death.

• Hubbert's papers are at the Western Heritage Center, University of Wyoming; a transcribed, edited oral history interview, more than thirty hours in length, is at the Niels Bohr Library, American Institute of Physics, College Park, Md. No comprehensive assessment of Hubbert's career yet exists; brief reviews appear in citations and responses when Hubbert received the Penrose Medal (*Geological Society of America Bulletin* 85 [1974]: 1341) and the Vetlesen Prize (*Journal of Geological Education* 31 [1983]: 42–44). An obituary is in the *Washington Post*, 14 Oct. 1989.

RONALD E. DOEL

HUBBLE, Edwin Powell (20 Nov. 1889–28 Sept. 1953), astronomer, was born in Marshfield, Missouri, the son of John Powell Hubble, an insurance agent, and Virginia Lee James. In 1898 John Hubble transferred to the Chicago agency of his company, and the family moved to Evanston, and then to Wheaton, Illinois. The young Hubble went to the University of Chicago on an academic scholarship in 1906. There he took courses in physics, chemistry, mathematics, astronomy, French, Greek, and Latin. He was a star athlete, winning letters in track and basketball. He was also vice president of his senior class.

Hubble graduated in 1910 and went on to Queens College, Oxford, as a Rhodes scholar. Since both his father and grandfather wanted him to become a lawyer, he studied jurisprudence. He participated vigorously in sports and traveled widely on the continent during vacations. He also adopted the language and manners of the English upper class, traits that later annoyed colleagues.

After returning from Oxford in 1913, Hubble passed the Kentucky bar examination (his family had moved to Louisville). But he seems never to have practiced law. Instead, he taught Spanish and physics at the New Albany, Indiana, high school, across the Ohio River from Louisville, where he also coached the basketball team.

Not satisfied with high school teaching, Hubble decided to go back to school. His astronomy professor at Chicago recommended him for a scholarship at the university's Yerkes Observatory.

When the United States declared war on Germany in 1917, Hubble hurriedly patched together a dissertation, passed his final examination, and reported for officers' training camp. Commissioned a captain in the infantry, he served as commanding officer of a battalion in a training division. He was promoted to major in 1918 and later that year attended an advanced combat training school in France, but the war ended before his division entered into combat.

Discharged in 1919, Hubble immediately took up a prewar offer of a position at the Mount Wilson Observatory. He worked there for the rest of his life, except for service from 1942 to 1946 at the U.S. Army's Aberdeen Proving Ground in Maryland as chief of ballistics and director of the Supersonic Wind Tunnels Laboratory. He was awarded the Medal for Merit for this work.

On 26 February 1924 Hubble married Grace Burke Leib, the widow of Earl Leib, a geologist, who had died of asphyxiation in a coal mine in 1921. The Hubbles had no children.

Hubble's scientific achievements made him the foremost observational astronomer of the twentieth century and one of the most influential scientists of all time in changing our understanding of the universe. First, he showed that certain types of "nebulae" long suspected of being galaxies beyond the boundary of our own galaxy are indeed independent "island universes." He also developed the basic classification scheme for galaxies. Next, he shattered the long-held assumption that the universe was static, with evidence that the more distant a galaxy is, the greater the speed with which it is receding from us (the velocity-distance relation, now also known as the Hubble law).

With the velocity-distance relation firmly established, Hubble turned to a theoretical interpretation of the empirical relationship, bringing together observers and theorists and thus making cosmology—for centuries consisting of speculation based on a minimum of observational evidence and a maximum of philosophical predilection—an observational science. Despite contradictory observations, he championed the relativistic, expanding model of the universe.

Hubble's research interests were evident, in embryonic form, in his doctoral dissertation completed at Chicago. As he noted in his photographic investigation of nebulae, "extremely little is known of the nature of nebulae . . . " To the 76 known "nebulae" in clusters, Hubble industriously added 512 more. The rapidly increasing number of "nebulae" observed and the estimated 150,000 within reach of existing instruments emphasized the need for a classification scheme, especially since "no significant classification has yet been suggested; not even a precise definition has been formulated." Hubble's classification scheme was announced in the 1920s, contemporaneously with his demonstration that the "nebulae" are galaxies, and his diagram of the sequence of nebular types became famous in the 1930s.

Centuries of speculation over the possible existence of island universes similar to our galaxy was finally resolved by Hubble. Using the new 100-inch telescope at Mount Wilson, he found Cepheid variable stars in spiral nebulae. Next, he used the period-luminosity relation for Cepheids to calculate the luminosities of such stars from their observed periods (the length of time for such a star to go from maximum luminosity to minimum and back to maximum). Then Hubble compared these estimated intrinsic luminosities to the observed luminosities (diminished owing to the distances of the nebulae in which the Cepheid stars were embedded) and derived distances that placed the spiral nebulae far beyond the boundary of our galaxy.

With the benefit of hindsight, Hubble's work seems inevitable. But no contemporary scientist showed such vision. Considerable courage—even lack of normal scientific prudence—was required. Some of his working assumptions were wrong. For example, the Cepheids he studied in spiral nebulae are not the same as Cepheids found in our galaxy, and Hubble's distance estimates had to be doubled when this fact eventually was recognized, in 1952. Yet the assumption was necessary if his plan of scientific investigation was to proceed by extrapolating from the known to the possibly knowable.

Hubble further strengthened his case for the existence of island universes with evidence from novae, from the observed colors of the brightest stars, and from star counts. A good part of Hubble's genius and the extent to which his revolutionary conclusions commanded acceptance are to be attributed to voluminous and thorough studies carried out in meticulous detail over many years.

Establishing that spiral nebulae are island universes was but a starting point for Hubble. He seized upon distances to a few nebulae to open a new phase of astronomical investigation that culminated in the notion of an expanding universe. Early in the twentieth century the universe was generally believed to be static, and with the rise of relativity theory astronomers initially sought only static solutions to Albert Einstein's field equations. The Dutch astronomer Willem de Sitter described a static model with an apparent—but not real—velocity of recession greater for objects at greater distances. Velocities for some spiral nebulae were known, but distances were yet to be determined. Both velocities and distances were known for globular clusters, on which an ill-judged attempt was made to demonstrate a velocity-distance relation. Although critics were careful to distinguish between the soon-discredited work and the general hypothesis of a velocity-distance relation, theoretical preconceptions of a velocity-distance relation nonetheless had become suspect.

Although Hubble was aware of de Sitter's cosmological model and its predicted velocity-distance relation, he did not, at first, grasp its relevance. After discussions at the 1928 International Astronomical Union Meeting in Holland, however, Hubble returned to Mount Wilson determined to test de Sitter's model. He directed Milton Humason, a careful, skilled, and gifted observer, to systematically observe faint and more distant galaxies to determine if their velocities were greater than those of closer galaxies.

Step by systematic step, Hubble estimated distances to increasingly more distant galaxies and established an empirical velocity-distance relationship. From the period-luminosity relation for Cepheids, he first determined distances directly to five galaxies and indirectly to a sixth, a physical companion of one of the five. Then he calibrated the intrinsic luminosity of the brightest stars in the six galaxies and, from observations of the observed luminosities of the brightest stars in fourteen more galaxies, estimated their distances. Next Hubble found an average intrinsic luminosity for all twenty galaxies and compared that value to the observed luminosities of four galaxies in the Virgo Cluster of galaxies, thus obtaining distances to them. The distances combined with velocities showed that the velocity-distance relation was linear. For the remaining twenty-two galaxies with known radial velocities but unknown distances, but which were too distant to allow observations of Cepheids or bright stars, Hubble measured the observed luminosity of each, calculated a mean observed luminosity for all twenty-two galaxies, and compared that value to the mean intrinsic luminosity for galaxies whose distances were known, thus obtaining a mean distance for the twenty-two galaxies. He was then able to show that the mean distance and the mean velocity of the twenty-two galaxies agreed well with the velocity-distance relation he had calculated from the first twenty-four galaxies. Though he had obtained a relatively small amount of data, and the details of his interpretation were a bit vague, it was a brilliant and bold extrapolation.

Not until the final paragraph of his 1929 paper reporting these results did Hubble mention de Sitter or theory, and then he simply noted that the velocity-distance relation might represent the de Sitter effect and might be useful in cosmological discussion. In this understated manner, Hubble revealed the key to the scientific exploration of the universe.

Though begun in a climate of skepticism and suspicion, Hubble's effort to establish a velocity-distance relation proceeded smoothly and quickly. By 1935 he and Humason had calculated velocities for 100 additional galaxies at distances as much as thirty to forty times farther than the Virgo Cluster. A solid scientific case was now in hand.

With the velocity-distance relation firmly established, Hubble turned to a theoretical interpretation of the empirical relationship. It would be a joint scientific effort. Cooperation was a distinctive feature of nebular research at Mount Wilson. Working with colleagues at the California Institute of Technology, the scientists combined resources for some investigations and interpreted their results in the light of constructive criticism from the whole group. Mrs. Hubble later recounted how scientists came to her house in the evening. "They brought a blackboard from Cal Tech and put it up on the living-room wall. In the dining-room were sandwiches, beer, whiskey and sodawater; they strolled in and helped themselves. Sitting around the fire, smoking pipes, they talked over various approaches to problems, questioned, compared and contrasted their points of view—someone would write equations on the blackboard and talk for a bit, and a discussion would follow."

Discussions, at Hubble's home or elsewhere, no doubt were enlivened by the emergence of new cosmological models elicited in the early 1930s by a crisis in astronomy. Hubble's velocity-distance relation ruled out Einstein's static model, while de Sitter's alternative model was excluded by new estimates of the density of the universe. The Belgian astronomer Georges Lemaître proposed to account for the observed velocity-distance relation with a relativistic, expanding space carrying along the galaxies. An alternative was the English astronomer E. A. Milne's proposal of an initial group of galaxies moving in Euclidean space in random directions with different velocities, the galaxies of highest velocity naturally receding farthest from the starting point. And Fritz Zwicky, a physicist at the California Institute of Technology, suggested that the universe might not be expanding, nor the galaxies moving, but that the observed redshifts could be the result not of real motions, but of interactions between light quanta and matter in space increasingly affecting the light from increasingly distant galaxies.

Hubble ostensibly took up the problem of discriminating, on the basis of observations, among Lemaître's, Milne's, and Zwicky's possible models of the universe. He was joined by Richard Tolman, a theoretical physicist at the California Institute of Technolo-

gy, who had developed the mathematical foundations of relativistic cosmology. Hubble and Tolman formulated methods for interpreting their evidence, but, given the many observational problems, any conclusion could only be tentative. Also, there were philosophical issues to consider.

Writing on the philosophy of science, Hubble stated that a scientist "naturally and inevitably . . . mulls over the data and guesses at a solution." The scientist then proceeds to "testing of the guess by new data—predicting the consequences of the guess and then dispassionately inquiring whether or not the predictions are verified." Science dealt with facts and events on which it was possible to obtain universal agreement, and the necessity for such agreement completely barred science from the great world of values.

In practice, however, notwithstanding Hubble's expressed allegiance to observations, theory had an independent authority, and human values were not entirely excluded. The number of logically consistent systems to be compared against observations could be reduced by the application of fundamental principles: the general theory of relativity and the cosmological principle. The former posited both an unstable universe, either expanding or contracting, and a universe whose space was curved in the vicinity of matter. The latter, acknowledged by Hubble to be "pure assumption," stated that, on a grand scale, the universe will appear the same from any position, homogeneous and isotropic, with neither center nor boundaries.

Milne's and Zwicky's models were logically consistent systems, but each contradicted beliefs held by Hubble to be fundamental. As for Lemaître's model, favored by Hubble, initially it was contradicted by observations. Hubble found that the age of the universe calculated from the rate of expansion was less than the age of the earth. Either the data were unreliable or the redshifts were not the result of velocities of recession in an expanding universe, Hubble conceded.

It is possible to distinguish science from pseudoscience by the former's ability to test a theory against physical evidence. The criterion of falsifiability is often taken to be a necessary and sufficient condition for being scientific. Yet there is also a long tradition of some scientists refusing to accept falsification of their theories by contrary evidence. Einstein wrote: "I do not by any means find the chief significance of the general theory of relativity in the fact that it has predicted a few minute observable facts, but rather in the simplicity of its foundation and in its logical consistency." In this spirit Hubble refused to accept the falsification by observations of the relativistic, expanding, homogeneous model of the universe. Instead, he pursued unrelentingly his scientific vision.

World War II interrupted Hubble's work on cosmology, and his life ended in 1953, soon after the 200-inch telescope was completed on Palomar Mountain and too soon for conclusive answers from the research program planned by Hubble. Subsequent results have removed much of the doubt surrounding his choice of a relativistic, homogeneous, expanding model of the universe. His work, though, is not to be judged primarily on the basis of some number of answers currently believed to be correct. Hubble's cosmology should be appreciated more for the assumptions it overthrew, for the vistas it opened, and as one of the great accomplishments of the human intellect.

Recognition of Hubble's achievements and stature included invitations to present prestigious lectures: the Halley Lecture of the Royal Astronomical Society in London in 1934, published as *Red-Shifts in the Spectra of Nebulae* (1934); the Silliman Lectures at Yale University in 1935, published as *The Realm of the Nebulae* (1936); and the Rhodes Memorial Lectures at Oxford in 1936, published as *The Observational Approach to Cosmology* (1937). He was a member of the National Academy of Sciences, received the Gold Medal of the Royal Astronomical Society and the Bruce Gold Medal of the Astronomical Society of the Pacific. More popular indices of Hubble's fame are the appearance of his face on the cover of *Time* magazine in 1948 and the attachment of his name to the space telescope in 1990.

• Hubble's personal and scientific papers are at the Henry E. Huntington Library, San Marino, Calif. See R. S. Brashear, "History of Modern Astronomy Sources at the Henry E. Huntington Library," *American Institute of Physics History Newsletter* 23, no. 2 (1991): 3–5. Hubble summed up much of his work in *The Realm of the Nebulae* (1936). For an overview see also N. Hetherington, "Edwin Hubble's Cosmology," *American Scientist* 78 (1990): 142–51, and *The Edwin Hubble Papers: Previously Unpublished Manuscripts on the Extragalactic Nature of Spiral Nebulae, Edited, Annotated, and with an Historical Introduction by Norriss S. Hetherington* (1990). Major biographical sketches are N. U. Mayall, "Edwin Powell Hubble," *Biographical Memoirs, National Academy of Sciences* 41 (1970): 175–214, and H. P. Robertson, "Edwin Powell Hubble, 1889–1953," *Publications of the Astronomical Society of the Pacific* 66 (1954): 120–25. Colleagues and friends of Hubble, Mayall and Robertson accepted uncritically stories he told about his early years and embellishments added by his widow, Grace B. Hubble. Her unpublished manuscript, "Edwin Powell Hubble, a Biographical Memoir," is at the Huntington Library, along with her "diaries" (perhaps more accurately characterized as memories). For a reliable account of Hubble's early years, see D. E. Osterbrock, R. S. Brashear, and J. A. Gwinn, "Self-Made Cosmologist: the Education of Edwin Hubble," in *Evolution of the Universe of Galaxies: Edwin Hubble Centennial Symposium*, ed. R. G. Kron (1991).

NORRISS S. HETHERINGTON

HUBBS, Carl Leavitt (18 Oct. 1894–30 June 1979), ichthyologist and naturalist, was born in Williams, Arizona. His father, Charles Leavitt Hubbs, who worked as a farmer, a merchant, and a newspaper editor in various western states, was doing placer mining at the time of Hubbs's birth. Carl's mother, Elizabeth Goss (Johnson, by way of a brief marriage), was at times a teacher of art. The family settled in San Diego, California, in 1896 until the parents divorced in 1907. Carl then lived with his mother and later also with his stepfather, Frank Newton, in various places in California,

graduating from high school in Los Angeles. Carl developed an early interest in natural history, collecting seashells and identifying birds. He later recalled that in high school he had "plunged into nature study with a vengeance." A teacher in Los Angeles introduced him to the fishes of nearby streams and urged him to attend Stanford University, then the nation's center of ichthyology. His primary mentor there was Charles Henry Gilbert, who assigned the young man as curator of the university's large collection of preserved fishes. Also while a student, Hubbs accompanied Stanford zoology professor John Otterbein Snyder on a summer trip in 1915 to the Bonneville Basin in Utah, which led to a lifelong interest in the isolated fishes of the Great Basin. Hubbs had a great admiration for David Starr Jordan, ichthyologist and president of Stanford, and he was always gratified to have coauthored papers with him.

After graduation from Stanford (A.B., 1916) and a semester of graduate work there (M.A., 1917), Hubbs became assistant curator in charge of fishes, amphibians, and reptiles at the Field Museum of Natural History in Chicago. He married Stanford classmate Laura Clark in 1918; they had three children. In 1920 Hubbs accepted a position at the University of Michigan, as assistant professor and curator of fishes in the Museum of Zoology. There in 1927 he was awarded a Ph.D. on the basis of his many published papers, one of which was selected as his thesis. At that university, he advanced to associate and full professor (1940), and he increased enormously the museum's collection of fishes.

His means of adding to the museum's holdings included field trips with his students and family and receiving duplicate specimens from others when he made the identifications for them. The emphasis in the collection was on freshwater fishes, but it also included marine ones. The classification of fishes was Hubbs's primary interest, but, scorning those who defined new species from one or two specimens, he felt obliged to collect large series of specimens for detailed analysis.

During eight summers from 1922 to 1943, Hubbs concentrated on the Great Basin, especially Nevada, where the fishes were relics from a time of greater precipitation and extensive lakes. During a visit to Japan in 1929, after the Fourth Pacific Science Congress in Java, he visited various museums and acquired five tons of specimens for the museum at Michigan. In 1935 he collected freshwater fishes in remote areas of Guatemala. On all trips he collected many creatures other than fishes and gave them to appropriate museums. In his field notes he included many observations on the habitats of the fishes and other animals.

When the University of Michigan and the Michigan Department of Conservation jointly established the Institute for Fisheries Research in 1930, Hubbs became its first director for five years. This group inventoried the life of many of the state's lakes and streams, investigated fish mortalities and pollution, and developed ways to improve lake and stream habitats. With Karl

F. Lagler, Hubbs wrote *Guide to the Fishes of the Great Lakes and Tributary Waters* (1941), which has been reprinted and expanded several times.

Hubbs's recognition of what appeared to be hybrid fishes in nature led to an extensive program of hybridization of living fishes in the laboratory, assisted by his wife Laura. This study clarified the taxonomy of various fishes.

In 1944 Hubbs became professor of zoology at Scripps Institution of Oceanography, a unit of the University of California in La Jolla, California. There he promptly expanded his researches in marine fishes, off California and Baja California, Mexico. He also began enlarging the collection of preserved fishes at Scripps. In 1947 a major fisheries program began in California to determine the reasons for the decline in the catch of sardines. Hubbs was among the scientists at Scripps Institution who were involved in the program, which led to the development of new collecting gear—and so, many more specimens of fishes and invertebrates. The study established the definition of many problems in fishery resource management.

His interest in Baja California led to three major contributions: a fourteen-year record of the ocean temperatures along its remote west coast for 225 miles; the collection and analysis of the shell refuse of prehistoric human populations, dated by radiocarbon from recent times as far back as 7,000 years before the present; and studies of the marine mammal populations off the coast. Through his acquaintance with Mexican scientists and officials, he persuaded that nation to protect the gray whale, the Guadalupe fur seal, and the elephant seal in Baja California.

Recognized as a powerful force in many conservation groups, he convinced the National Park Service to establish a refuge for the Devil's Hole pupfish as an adjunct of Death Valley National Monument (1952), and he found locations on protected land to save other endangered fishes of the Great Basin, working through the American Society of Ichthyologists and Herpetologists.

Hubbs published about 700 scientific papers, half of them on fishes and the remainder on his other interests: marine mammals, prehistoric peoples and ancient climates, and the history of science—the last in the form of memorials and summaries. His most intense concentration was on cyprinodont fishes, on whose taxonomy, distribution, and habits he wrote a series of papers from 1924 to 1978, many in collaboration with his son-in-law Robert Rush Miller. His longest work summarized the Great Basin studies: *Hydrographic History and Relict Fishes of the North-central Great Basin* (1974), coauthored with his wife and with Miller.

Hubbs was elected to the National Academy of Sciences in 1952 and received a number of other awards. He was a self-confident, forthright person, much interested in people. Highly admired by his students, he was also considered by them and his colleagues as remarkably energetic, practically indefatigable, in the field and in the office. Still active in researches until the end, he died in La Jolla, California.

• Hubbs's papers, including considerable biographical material, are in the Archives of Scripps Institution of Oceanography in La Jolla, Calif. Frances Hubbs Miller compiled a complete bibliography of her father, *The Scientific Publications of Carl Leavitt Hubbs: Bibliography and Index* (1981). Kenneth S. Norris summarized Hubbs's life and personality in "To Carl Leavitt Hubbs, a Modern Pioneer Naturalist on the Occasion of His Eightieth Year," *Copeia* (1974): 581–94. A final biography is by Elizabeth N. Shor et al., *Biographical Memoirs of National Academy of Sciences* 56 (1987): 215–49.

ELIZABETH NOBLE SHOR

HUBERMAN, Leo (17 Oct. 1903–9 Nov. 1968), teacher, writer, and publisher, was born in Newark, New Jersey, the son of Joseph Huberman, a painter and decorator, and Fannie Kramerman. After graduating in 1922 from Newark State Normal School he taught in the Newark public schools (1922–1926). Huberman received a B.S. in education in 1926 and later an M.S. in 1937 from New York University. During summer vacations he gained valuable industrial experience (beginning at age eleven) by working in a celluloid factory, a glass factory, as a post office clerk, and as a runner on Wall Street.

Huberman married Gertrude Heller, a teacher, in 1925; they had no children. On their honeymoon that summer they hitchhiked back and forth across the continent, traveling 8,350 miles for $500, visiting stockyards, mines, and farms, as well as the usual scenic spots, and talking with a vast assortment of fellow Americans. His early jobs and the trip—a pioneering venture when there were so few automobiles and when women's lives were much more restricted—helped to determine the elements that came to define Huberman's career: his interest in the workings of economics and history from the bottom up; his concern for the common people; his talent for relating to people of every social level; and his willingness to accept risks. His gifts for relating to people were already evident in his work as a teacher, and in 1926 he was invited to teach at City and Country, a private experimental school in New York City.

Huberman's history classes at City and Country became famous and led to Harper and Brothers asking him to write a children's history of the United States. The result, *We, the People* (1932), is a text for young people that puts the emphasis, in Huberman's words, "on the workers, not the wars; on the common man, not the 'leaders.'" The work was greeted with immediate acclaim: in his "Conning Tower" column, F. P. Adams wrote: "Ring bells from this here Conning Steeple / For Leo Huberman's *We, the People*," and the *New York Times* called it "stirring and thrilling." The book was later revised for adults and in 1947 was named a Book Find Club selection. Translated into many languages, including Japanese, Huberman's text became one of Japan's bestsellers.

Huberman left City and Country in 1932 to do graduate work for a year at the London School of Economics. When he returned to the United States the country was undergoing enormous social and economic changes caused by the depression, and Huberman saw a need to reach beyond the ordinary classroom to facilitate public understanding of the historic moment. In response, he wrote *Man's Worldly Goods* (1936), a work that sold widely and won high praise for rendering economic theory intelligible to the layperson by linking it with lively human history. Huberman served for 1938–1939 as chair of the Department of Social Sciences at New College, Columbia University. The American labor movement was reactivated by the economic crisis and by supportive New Deal labor laws, and Huberman became involved in workers' education and began, as a journalist, reporting to the public on labor issues.

In 1940 Huberman served as labor editor for the New York newspaper *PM*, and the next year he worked as a columnist for the magazine *U.S. Week*. He taught at the Bryn Mawr Summer School for Women Workers in Industry and at the Southern Summer School for Workers. From 1942 to 1945 Huberman directed a leadership training program at the National Maritime Union, of which *Time* magazine took note, reporting that the union pamphlets produced there were "some of the slickest trade union literature in the world, most of it the work of Leo Huberman." Union members in the program, the report continued, were "laboriously trained in procedures. Skippers have learned to respect and fear the shipboard committees who handle seamen's beefs." Between seamen and teacher there developed mutual respect and admiration.

By 1949, however, labor and the left in general were in decline; the Cold War had begun. "For the great majority of Americans," Huberman wrote in that year, "socialism is little more than a dirty word." He and a few other veterans of the left sought to provide a vehicle for intelligent discussion of the subject. With Huberman and economist Paul Sweezy as editors, *Monthly Review* was founded that year as "an independent magazine devoted to analyzing, from a socialist point of view, the most significant trends in domestic and foreign affairs." Beginning with only a small list of subscribers, the magazine became increasingly influential as one of the world's leading Marxist journals, appearing also in Spanish and Italian translations. In 1966 Huberman and Sweezy went to Italy to receive the Omegna Award, a literary prize given by a committee of former Italian resistance fighters. The award citation stated, "The fundamental genius of these two writers lies in a Marxist humanism."

In 1953, however, Marxist humanism was not highly regarded in Washington, D.C. That summer Huberman was summoned to appear before the McCarthy committee on the pretext that several of his works had been found in State Department libraries abroad. He believed that the hearings represented an attempt to silence dissent and to deny an author the right to pursue his trade without interference. Huberman freely stated he had never been a communist. As for his socialist and Marxist principles, he had never made a secret of them. But to any further queries concerning what he thought or believed or with whom he associated, he would not answer, citing the First Amendment. Those questions, he stated at the hearing, are "my own business—to be discussed only with whom I choose. I do not choose to discuss it with the McCarthy committee."

In 1952 the influence of *Monthly Review* had been greatly extended when the editors founded Monthly Review Press to print texts that more conventional publishers avoided. Their first book published was I. F. Stone's *Hidden History of the Korean War*. Huberman directed the press through the next fifteen years, while the annual list grew from a few titles to twenty-five a year in 1968. He continued to coedit the magazine, write prolifically himself, and fill many speaking engagements both at home and abroad. Huberman and Sweezy traveled widely in Europe, India, Japan, and China. As *Monthly Review* began to examine incipient guerrilla struggles in Latin America, both editors turned their attention in that direction. No sooner had Fidel Castro triumphed in Cuba in 1959 than Huberman and Sweezy flew there. Their *Cuba: Anatomy of a Revolution* (1961) introduced the Cuban revolution to the American public, and their subsequent *Socialism in Cuba* (1969) assessed its successes and failures.

When Huberman died suddenly in Paris, he was in full harness, as he had always been. He and Sweezy were there to arrange for French and German editions of *Monthly Review*, and Huberman had just come from Oxford, England, where he talked with a group of Oxford students.

A 1963 *Business Week* interview with Huberman noted his skill "as a writer and popularizer." Huberman's abilities were critical for an informed public. He was perhaps the best synthesizer and communicator in the United States of essential facts regarding history and economics.

• Huberman's papers, including manuscripts of books, pamphlets, and speeches, as well as books from his library, are collected in the University of Oregon library. His major publications, in addition to those mentioned in the text, include *The Labor Spy Racket* (1937); *America Incorporated* (1940); *The Great Bus Strike* (1941); *The Truth about Unions* (1946); *The Truth about Socialism* (1950); *The ABC of Socialism*, with Sybil H. May (1953); and *Introduction to Socialism*, with Sweezy (1968). Books coedited with Sweezy include *F. O. Matthiessen (1902–1950): A Collective Portrait* (1950); *Whither Latin America?* (1963); *The Communist Manifesto*, including Engels's "Principles of Communism" and an essay by the editors, "The Communist Manifesto after 100 Years" (1964); *Paul A. Baran (1910–1964): A Collective Portrait* (1965); *Fifty Years of Soviet Power* (1968); and *Regis Debray and the Latin American Revolution* (1968). Huberman also wrote hundreds of magazine articles and pamphlets. Obituaries are in the *New York Times*, 10 Nov. 1968, and in the *Guardian*, Dec. 1968.

ELIZABETH HUBERMAN

HUBLEY, John (21 May 1914–21 Feb. 1977), animated filmmaker and producer, was born in Marinette, Wisconsin, the son of John Raymond Hubley, a businessman, and Verena Kirkham, an amateur painter. After studying art at the Los Angeles Art Center School, Hubley began to train in animation at the Disney studio in 1935. He painted backgrounds for *Snow White and the Seven Dwarfs* (1937) and did layout on *Pinocchio* (1940), *Fantasia* (1940), *Dumbo* (1941), and *Bambi* (1942). Active in the 1941 strike at the studio, he left Disney's employ after it ended.

Like many Disney strikers, Hubley was hired by Columbia's Screen Gems Studio, newly reorganized under ex–Warner Bros. animator Frank Tashlin, who initiated a short-lived innovative period there. Hubley codirected *The Dumb Conscious Mind* (1942), *The Vitamin G-Man* (1943), and *Professor Small and Mr. Tall* (1943) for Columbia's "Color Rhapsody" series, moving from the mimetic Disney style to one utilizing illogical narratives, flattened perspective, and brighter colors.

Hubley became politically active because of his strike experiences and joined a communist discussion group that included animation artists Phil Eastman, Zachary Schwartz, Eugene and Bernyce Polifka Fleury, and Bill and Edwina Pomerance. In 1942, with Eastman and Eugene Fleury, Hubley founded *The Animator*, a magazine devoted to promoting animation both as a social medium and as a form for artistic experimentation. At the 1943 University of California at Los Angeles (UCLA) Writers' Congress, Hubley outlined his thoughts on animation, maintaining that the relationship between storytelling and graphics formed the key artistic challenge to animators. Cartoons had "drifted away from the cartoon's original role as a commentary on the contemporary scene." He argued that the Disney studio had abandoned social concerns and called for animated films to marry abstract visual symbolism with "stories . . . written in terms of human behavior and broad social caricature" ("The Writer and the Cartoon," pp. 105–6). During this period, Hubley also worked outside animation, most notably as director Joseph Losey's production designer for the 1947 staging of Brecht's *Galileo*.

In 1943 Hubley joined the Air Force First Motion Picture Unit in Culver City, California, spending the remainder of the war producing training films and the "Trigger Joe" series in which he experimented with the use of photo collage and flat painting. Moonlighting with Eastman and Bill Hurtz, Hubley prepared the storyboard for an animated film short used in Franklin D. Roosevelt's election campaign commissioned for the August 1944 Democratic convention by the United Auto Workers. The film, *Hell Bent for Election* (1944), eventually was produced by a company formed by David Hilberman and Zachary Schwartz called Industrial Films and Poster Service, later reorganized into United Productions of America (UPA), with Hubley as vice president and supervising director. Hubley was considered a prime contributor to the UPA style, which incorporated modernist graphics, flattened perspective, and greater attention to color design, with narratives that were either impressionistic or based on literary properties. Hubley worked on such films as *Flat Hatting* (1945), *Robin Hoodlum* (1948), *The Magic Fluke* (1949), and *Rooty Toot Toot* (1952). He also created the animated sequences of the feature film *The Fourposter* (1952). In 1949, with writer Millard Kaufman, Hubley devised UPA's most successful series character—the nearsighted Mr. Magoo. As coworker Bill Melendez recalled,

Hub could draw like nobody else—very expressive drawings that would capture the essence of almost anything, in a style that was completely opposite of what was at Disney and the rest of the industry. I always felt that it was Hub that started us in the direction of caricaturing humans, rather than animals. (Solomon, pp. 215–16)

The dramatic change in the political climate after 1945 affected the careers of many leftists in the film industry. Congress investigated a number of Hubley's colleagues, some of whom became government informants. Hubley, called before the House Un-American Activities Committee on 5 July 1956, refused to name names and subsequently resigned from UPA.

Having created television commercials at UPA since 1948, Hubley formed Storyboard Productions to animate commercials in Los Angeles in 1955 (dissolved and reformed in New York City in 1956). Yip Harburg, producer of *Hell Bent for Election*, hired Hubley as animation director of the feature film *Finian's Rainbow* and hired Faith Elliott (a script supervisor and film and music editor) as Hubley's assistant. After a year, the project was abandoned when the backers ran out of money.

In 1941 Hubley married Claudia Ross Sewell. This marriage produced three children and ended in divorce in 1955. That same year Hubley married Faith Elliott; they had four children. John and Faith Hubley relocated Storyboard Productions to New York, where they produced animated commercials, the most successful being the "Marky Maypo" cereal commercials (1956–1957).

The Hubleys resolved to make at least one noncommercial animated film annually. Their first, *The Adventures of an* (1956), sponsored by the Guggenheim Foundation, presented the asterisk's adventures as a symbolic journey through a human's life. This concern for the stages of life, as well as the Hubley tendency to personalize their films, led to a series of shorts based on the fantasies of children, such as the Academy Award–winning *Moonbird* (1959), as well as *Windy Day* (1967) and *Cockaboody* (1973). The Hubleys' political preoccupations were apparent in films displaying concerns about war (*The Hat*, 1964), nuclear holocaust (*The Hole*, 1963, winning them a second Academy Award), women's rights (*Windy Day*, which won an Academy Award in 1968), and overpopulation (*Eggs*, 1971). These films often were based on soundtracks improvised by Hubley family members or friends. The Hubleys drew upon the talents of many important figures in animation, such as Art Babbitt, Bill Littlejohn, and Shamus Culhane.

The Hubleys' films tended to eschew the use of outlined figures, favoring multilayered images produced by multiple exposures. Backgrounds often were visible through the characters. The Hubleys also experimented in the use of watercolors and pastels, rather than the conventional cel paints used in most animation studios. Some of the Hubley noncommercial work was done on commissions from foundations; some of it they funded with earnings from television commercials and their work as animators for *Sesame Street* and *Electric Company*. Through self-sponsorship, the Hubleys completed their first feature film, *Of Stars and Men* (1962).

In 1966 John Hubley became president of ASIFA, the International Association of Animated Film Makers, and became a visual consultant to the educational television station WNET in New York. The Hubleys abandoned animating television commercials in favor of television commissions that provided sponsorship for their projects. For example, Storyboard Productions adapted psychoanalyst Erik H. Erikson's work on the psychological crises associated with stages of life into the feature *Everybody Rides the Carousel* (1976) for CBS. In 1976 the Hubleys began teaching a course at Yale called "The Visualization of Abstract Themes" and began production of *A Doonesbury Special* for NBC. In 1977, in the midst of both projects, John Hubley was hospitalized with a heart ailment and died during heart surgery in New Haven, Connecticut.

Hubley will be remembered as a key figure in the postwar reconfiguration of American animation as a medium for personal artistic expression and the transmission of intellectual thought. His career left marks in studio animation, independent animation, commercials, educational television, and children's broadcasting.

• Considerations of John Hubley's career can be found in Holly Allen and Michael Denning, "The Cartoonists' Front," *South Atlantic Quarterly* 92, no. 1 (Winter 1993): 89–117; John Canemaker, "The Happy Accidents of the Hubleys," *Print*, Sept.–Oct. 1981, pp. 55, 58–59, 62, 96; and Leonard Maltin, *Of Mice and Magic: A History of American Animated Cartoons* (1980). See also Charles Solomon, *Enchanted Drawings: The History of Animation* (1989). An obituary is in the *New York Times*, 23 Feb. 1977.

MARK LANGER

HUBNER, Charles William (16 Jan. 1835–3 Jan. 1929), poet, was born in Baltimore, Maryland, the son of Johh Adam Hubner and Margaret Semmilroch, who were both from Bavaria. John prospered in real estate, and when Charles was eighteen, he accompanied his mother to Germany, where he remained for six years studying art, music, and poetry (poetry had been his earliest love). He returned to the United States in 1858 and took a position as a music teacher at the Tennessee Female Academy in Fayetteville. With the onset of the Civil War, Hubner's mother returned to Bavaria, where she remained after her husband died at the bat-

tle of Shiloh, fighting for the Union army. Charles adopted the cause of his Tennessee neighbors and joined the Confederate army, where he rose to the rank of major and was in charge of the telegraph corps at the battle of Atlanta. After the war he worked as a freelance journalist for Atlanta newspapers and for the *Christian Index*, was employed as associate librarian for the Young Men's Library Association, and, beginning in 1873, wrote several books. About 1865 he married Ida Ann Southworth of Memphis. She died about 1877, and shortly thereafter he married Mary Frances Whitney of Atlanta, Georgia; she was the mother of their two children and the stepmother of his three children with his first wife. In 1895 he became assistant librarian at the Carnegie Public Library of Atlanta, where he remained for twenty years.

Hubner had begun writing at the age of ten and published a poem, "A Threnody on the Death of Thomas Moore," in a Boston periodical when he was thirteen (1848). His first book, a biography, was *Historical Souvenirs of Martin Luther* (1873). In 1880 he published an essay on Marxist theory, *Modern Communism*, and in 1896 he edited an anthology, *War Poets of the South*, followed in 1906 by his still useful *Representative Poets of the South*. Hubner's earliest book of poetry, *Wild Flowers* (1877), also included a play in blank verse, *The Maid of San Domingo*. These poems, like his others, are light, conventional magazine verse on traditional, romantic subjects: "sunset roses, supernal splendor, music tender, beauty and Duty"; more interesting are his lyrics in praise of fellow poets, including Sidney Lanier and Walt Whitman. More philosophical, but quotidian, is his last collection, *Poems of Faith and Consolation* (1927). John Greenleaf Whittier and Henry Wadsworth Longfellow are listed among Hubner's admirers. As a critic he was discriminating and kind. He is also the author of the brief biography of Frank L. Stanton for *The Library of Southern Literature*. His style in poetry and prose is simple, strong, and traditional; his subjects are many and varied but mostly involve art, beauty, and the ideal. While he had some international reputation, he is best remembered as a southern writer. In the last year of his life, he was given the honorary title of poet laureate of the South by the regional poetry society. Hubner died in Atlanta.

• Hubner's letters and papers are collected in the Hubner-Whitney papers of the Atlanta Historical Society. Other significant titles include *Cinderella: or, The Silver Slipper*, a drama (1979); *Poems and Essays* (1881); *Prince and Fairy; or, Magic Wonder Stone* (1883); *Poems* (1906); and *For Love of Burns: Poems* (1910). Mary Hubner Walker has written *Poet Laureate of the South* (1976). Articles and commentaries are in A. D. Chandler and C. A. Evans, *Georgia* (1906), and M. L. Rutherford, *The South in History and Literature* (1907). Obituaries appear in the *Atlanta Journal*, 3 Jan. 1929, and the *Atlanta Constitution*, 4 Jan. 1929.

GERALD M. GARMON

HUCK, Winnifred Sprague Mason (14 Sept. 1882–24 Aug. 1936), congresswoman and journalist, was born in Chicago, Illinois, the daughter of William Ernest Mason, an attorney, state legislator, and, later, congressman and U.S. senator, and Edith Julia White. After attending public schools in Chicago and Washington, D.C., she graduated from Central High School in the nation's capital. In 1904 she married Robert Wardlow Huck, a steel company executive. The mother of four children, Winnifred Huck played an active role in Chicago's social community.

Huck's interest in politics developed at an early age. As the daughter of a public figure, she was familiar with the Capitol and with the life of a politician. Upon her father's death in 1921 during the first session of the Sixty-seventh Congress, Huck publicly announced her intention to succeed him in office. She felt it was her duty to assume this position.

Illinois state officials procrastinated in filling Mason's seat. Not until shortly before the general election in 1922 was Huck named as the Republican party's candidate for her father's representative-at-large seat. Conducting an energetic campaign, she easily defeated Allen D. Albert, the Democratic opponent, on 7 November, for the remainder of the unexpired term. This victory earned Huck the distinction of being the third woman elected to Congress (following Jeannette Rankin of Montana and Alice Mary Robertson of Oklahoma) and the first woman to represent Illinois in the national legislature. She was also among the first of several dozen women who, in the following decades, first reached Congress as successors to male relatives (more typically these were widows). In addition, Huck was the only successful female congressional candidate in the second election after the adoption of the Nineteenth Amendment to the Constitution. Elected to complete the short time left in Mason's term in the Sixty-seventh Congress, Huck failed to secure the party's regular nomination that year to retain the seat in the Sixty-eighth Congress, losing to Henry R. Rathbone, a Chicago lawyer.

Huck served in the U.S. House of Representatives from 20 November 1922 to 3 March 1923. Because state officials in Springfield had not yet processed her formal certificate of election, Huck arrived in Washington without her credentials. Republican congressman James R. Mann of Illinois explained the situation to members of the House, who unanimously consented to allow her to take the oath of office with the other congressmen-elect.

During her fourteen weeks in the House of Representatives, Huck was guided by her father's legislative agenda. These included the finalizing of a peace treaty between the United States and Germany and Austria (its World War I antagonists), the adoption of a constitutional amendment restricting child labor, and independence for the Philippine Islands and for Cuba. An advocate of women's rights, Huck also wanted to see an end to legal discrimination against women. She served on the committees dealing with civil service reform, woman suffrage, and expenditures in the Department of Commerce.

On 16 January 1923 Huck delivered her most significant speech as a member of the House. Like her father, she advocated a constitutional amendment to provide for a national referendum on any declaration of war. Her goal was to make war impossible except by a direct affirmative vote of the American people. This issue concerned Huck, for her father had been accused of treasonous tendencies for his arguments in opposition in 1917 to U.S. involvement in World War I. Huck's plebiscite resolution for world peace was presented and soon forgotten, but she subsequently supported the movement for the outlawry of war, culminating later that decade in the Kellogg-Briand Peace Treaty.

Despite her avowed opposition to war, Huck voted for the Ship Subsidy Bill. She also appointed her son, Wallace, to the U.S Naval Academy in Annapolis, Maryland. She defended her action by pointing out that until her war referendum resolution was achieved, the nation would need "a splendid army and an efficiency navy." In 1923 she wondered if "this rumbling of war along the Ruhr is only a passing storm that will soon blow over. Or does it portend another outburst of hatred of such force and magnitude that the killing of human beings will be, as it was in the last war, but a small incident in its path of destruction?" Huck hoped that America was inoculated against the war fever.

Huck enjoyed her brief tenure in Congress. She especially liked associating with people from different regions of the country who held a variety of views but labored for the common interests of the nation. Although noting that the Senate was more quiet and dignified than the noisy House, Huck referred to her colleagues as tireless workers. "To me these men are truly great, for with all the different opinions backed by strong wills that are brought here to the House of Representatives, there is, I believe, no personal bitterness, and to work among such people makes work a joy."

In February 1923 Huck was defeated in another Republican primary, this one to fill the vacancy caused by the death of Representative James R. Mann, a Chicago Republican and former minority floor leader. Huck charged that her successful Republican opponent, Morton D. Hull, a Chicago lawyer and manufacturer, had spent $100,000 to win the nomination. Although she requested a congressional investigation, Hull was seated without incident.

In her postcongressional career, Huck engaged in numerous activities. She joined the National Woman's Party's political council in an endeavor to advance its goal of electing women to office at all levels of government. She also lectured and wrote syndicated articles for the Newspaper Enterprise Association. Pursuing an interest in penology, Huck in 1925 persuaded Governor Vic Donahey of Ohio to permit her to investigate the treatment of women in prison. To pursue this assignment, she assumed the name of Elizabeth Sprague and committed a petty theft for which she was tried and sentenced to Marysville Prison, a penal institution for women, for six months. After serving one month, the time needed to complete her study of prison and incarceration, Huck was pardoned by the governor as part of their prearranged agreement. Following her release, she explored employment opportunities for former convicts. She secured work as a housemaid, a hotel chambermaid, and a factory employee, living on the wages she earned in each position. Later, in 1928 and 1929, Huck worked as a staff writer for the *Chicago Evening Post*.

Huck died in Chicago after surgery for ulcerative colitis. The first mother to sit in Congress, she was a woman of compassion who met high standards for herself. Fiercely militant in her opposition to war and unwaveringly loyal to her father's traditions, Huck never hesitated to express her opinions or journey into arenas once reserved for men. She epitomized the new woman of the 1920s.

• Neither Huck nor her father left any personal papers. Huck recorded her congressional experience in Winnifred Mason Huck, "What Happened to Me in Congress," *Woman's Home Companion*, July 1923, pp. 4, 100. See also the *Congressional Record* for the Sixty-seventh Congress. Additional information is in Anna Steese Richardson, "What About the Ladies?" *Collier's*, 27 Sept. 1924, pp. 18–19, 39; *Literary Digest*, 25 Nov. 1922, p. 11; the *Chicago Tribune*, 8 Nov. 1922; and *Time*, 13 July 1925, p. 4. Obituaries are in the *Chicago Tribune*, 25 Aug. 1936, and the *New York Times*, 26 Aug. 1936.
LEONARD SCHLUP

HUDDE, Andries (1608–4 Nov. 1663), New Netherland commissary and public official, was born in Kampen, the Netherlands, the son of Hendrick Hudde and Aeltje Schinckels. Nothing is known of his early life. In 1629 he moved to New Netherland, and in 1632 he was appointed commissary of stores. Hudde also served in the council of the Dutch colony and as provincial secretary. In 1636 Hudde, in partnership with others, purchased 3,600 acres on Long Island (Coney Island area) and two years later acquired land in Manhattan. He also bought a farm in Harlem, where, hiring laborers, he attempted to establish a tobacco plantation. Visiting Amsterdam, the Netherlands, in January 1639 Hudde married Geertruyt Bornstra, the widow of Hendrick de Forest. The number of their children, if any, is unknown.

After returning to New Netherland in 1639, Hudde discovered that his Harlem farm had been foreclosed and sold. Hudde resumed government service as surveyor of Manhattan. He and his wife resided in New Amsterdam. In 1644 Hudde was appointed commissary for the South (Delaware) River and was stationed at Fort Nassau, on the east side of the river, opposite from present-day Philadelphia. Hudde had to contend with efforts by the governor of New Sweden, Johan Printz, to cut off the Dutch from trade along the Delaware. But the Dutch persisted in their rivalry with the Swedes. On behalf of the New Netherland government, Hudde purchased land from the Indians on the present site of Philadelphia and then presided over the building of Fort Beversreede at the mouth of the Schuylkill River. He established friendly relations with the Minqua Indians on the west side of the Delaware but was turned away by Indians on the east side

of the river because the Swedes had spread rumors among them that the Dutch intended to murder all Indians.

Hudde was frustrated in trying to develop Dutch-Indian trade along the Delaware because of a lack of support from the authorities in New Amsterdam. The Swedes effectively controlled the river. Besides Fort Christina (Wilmington), the Swedes built Fort Elfsborg at the mouth of Varkens Kill (Salem Creek), which obstructed the Dutch at Fort Nassau from access to the sea.

In 1644 Hudde had sent a petition to the West India Company in the Netherlands to ask for the recall of Wilhelm Kieft, the director general in New Netherland, because of Kieft's alienation of the Indians. Hudde, however, formed a better relationship with Kieft's successor, the feisty and aggressive Peter Stuyvesant. In November 1648 Hudde sent Stuyvesant a long appraisal of the Swedish interference along the Delaware, "A Brief, but True Report of the Proceedings of Johan Printz, Governor of the Swedish forces at the South River of New Netherland."

In 1651 the Dutch erected Fort Casimir (Newcastle, Del.) several miles below the Swedish post, Fort Christina, and abandoned Fort Nassau and Fort Beversreede. Hudde served as commissary at Fort Casimir, with authority to detain any passing ships. Hudde, however, became very friendly with the new Swedish governor, Johan Rising, even making maps for him. Brought to New Amsterdam to answer the serious charge of deserting from Dutch rule, Hudde was found guilty but was cleared of charges and released as a result of the intervention of friends. From 1652 to 1654 Hudde lived in New Amsterdam. He received a license to conduct a school but appears not to have pursued this career. His first wife having died, about 1655 Hudde remarried (the name of his second wife is unknown); they had at least one child.

Hudde continued to experience financial difficulties and in 1655 mortgaged his land on Long Island and his house on the South River to secure his debts. Fortunately, in that year, with the capitulation of the Swedes on the Delaware, Hudde was appointed secretary and schout-fiscal (equivalent to a sheriff or attorney general) to the new vice director of the Dutch colony along the Delaware. When the city of Amsterdam bought out the West India Company's claim to the Delaware it created a new colony called New Amstel. In addition to being commissary, Hudde served the new government as clerk, sheriff, surveyor, and as a member of the local court for the trying of civil and criminal cases. He resided at Altena (formerly Fort Christina). In 1657 Hudde briefly served as director for the colony after the dismissal of Jean Paul Jacquet from that post. The new director, Willem Beeckman, made Hudde his secretary and also sexton of the church at Altena, positions Hudde held until 1663.

Hudde made little income from these offices and lived on the edge of poverty. Indians robbed him of trading goods. To better seek a fortune Hudde decided to establish a brewery in Maryland. Resigning his posts at Altena, Hudde, with his family, headed for their new home. Before reaching it, however, he died from "an ardent fever" at Apoquinamingh (Del.). Hudde was a capable and energetic servant for the West India Company and New Netherland.

• Hudde's life in America can be gleaned from the published records relating to New Netherland. See particularly *Documents Relative to the Colonial History of New York*, vol. 1, *Holland Documents, 1603–1656*, ed. E. B. O'Callaghan (1856), and vol. 12, *Documents Relating to the History of the Dutch and Swedish Settlement on the Delaware River*, comp. Berthold Fernow (1877). Charles T. Gehring, trans. and ed., *New York Historical Manuscripts*, vols. 18–19 (1981), contains "Delaware Papers (Dutch Period, 1648–1664)." Some biographical information is found in Emily J. de Forest, *A Walloon Family in America: Lockwood de Forest and his Forbears [sic], 1500–1848* (2 vols., 1914), and I. N. Phelps Stokes, *The Iconography of Manhattan Island*, vol. 2 (1916). Hudde's career on the Delaware is covered in Samuel Hazard, *Annals of Pennsylvania from the Discovery of the Delaware, 1609–1682* (1850), Israel Acrelius, *A History of New Sweden, or the Settlements on the River Delaware* (1874); O'Callaghan, *History of New Netherland* (2 vols., 1848); Amandus Johnson, *The Swedish Settlements on the Delaware: Their History and Relation to the Indians, Dutch and English* (2 vols., 1911); and C. A. Weslager, *Dutch Explorers, Traders and Settlers in the Delaware Valley, 1609–1664* (1961).

HARRY M. WARD

HUDSON, Claude Silbert (26 Jan. 1881–27 Dec. 1952), chemist, was born in Atlanta, Georgia, the son of William James Hudson, a business man, and Maude Celestia Wilson. His years before college were spent in Mobile, Alabama, where his father was in the phosphate mining business. In 1901 he earned a bachelor's degree at Princeton, where his lifelong fascination with science began, sparked by the chemistry lectures of L. W. McKay. He abandoned his original plan to enter the ministry and pursued graduate work in physics at Princeton, making a physicochemical study of the forms of lactose (milk sugar), suggested by a chance observation of his. He earned an M.S. in 1902 and then spent the next year in Göttingen working with Walther Nernst on the change of rotation (mutarotation) of lactose. During the summer of 1903, he worked in Jacobus H. van't Hoff's laboratory in Berlin on physical measurements on sugar solutions.

His father's business reverses prevented Hudson from studying in Europe for three years, as originally planned, so he returned to a research assistantship in Arthur A. Noyes's laboratory at the Massachusetts Institute of Technology (1903–1904). Thereafter he was physics instructor at Princeton (1904–1905) and at the University of Illinois (1905–1907). He married Alice Abbott, the first of his four wives, in Urbana in 1906, and they had a son and two daughters. His second wife was Olive Gale; his third was Mavel Felix Hazard. Hudson was personally convivial, sometimes to excess. Of his four marriages, he once said, "I must regretfully record that the first three . . . ended in divorce." In 1942 he married his fourth wife, Erin Gilmer Jones, a widow and childhood sweetheart.

He received the Ph.D. magna cum laude from Princeton in 1907. After a few months as assistant physicist at the U.S. Geological Survey, and five months analyzing asphalt at a plant near Perth Amboy, New Jersey, he became a chemist aid in the Bureau of Chemistry in Washington, D.C. (1908). Here he did analyses for Harvey W. Wiley, the crusader for pure food. In his spare time he read carbohydrate chemistry, and later, after Wiley's departure, started full-time research on the hydrolysis of common sugar (sucrose) by the enzyme invertase.

Beginning in 1912, Hudson headed a carbohydrate laboratory in the Bureau of Chemistry, where he pushed fundamental studies of sugars. During World War I, he developed syntheses of rare sugars, such as xylose, arabinose, and raffinose, which were no longer available from Germany. He contributed his knowledge of adsorbent charcoal to the development of gas masks and became an independent consultant in this field from 1918 to 1923. He joined the Bureau of Standards in 1923, then transferred in 1929 to the Hygienic Laboratory of the U.S. Public Health Service (later part of the National Institutes of Health), where he remained until his retirement in 1951.

Hudson's life work was the study of the chemical and physical properties of the simple sugars. Sugars are compounds of fundamental importance in the processes of living systems. They are the unit structures of polysaccharides, such as starch and cellulose, and are present in the nucleic acids (DNA and RNA) as well as in many antibiotics. Hudson's efforts to elucidate the rules of optical rotation—the shift in plane of polarization experienced by plane-polarized light as it passes through a solution of sugar (or other optically active compound)—were to become a major contribution to carbohydrate chemistry and a continuing theme of his research.

As early as 1909, he empirically noted regularities in the optical rotation of closely related sugars, which allowed him to assign configurations—that is, the three-dimensional arrangements of constituent atoms—to many sugar derivatives. His background in physical chemistry was invaluable to this work, especially in dealing with mutarotation and enzymatic hydrolysis. He and his collaborators developed great skill in the often difficult and frustrating task of obtaining crystalline samples. In one case where his "isorotation rules" led to an incorrect answer, Hudson developed the Malaprade reaction—whereby periodate accomplishes oxidation—into a valuable tool of sugar chemistry. Periodate was a frequently used reagent in his laboratory from 1937 on, and it represented a great advance over existing methods.

Hudson's work was invaluable in providing knowledge of the simple sugars and working out methods for discovering structures of sugar components of nucleic acids. He was the first to isolate the seven-carbon sugar sedoheptulose and study its reactions. This sugar was later (1952) found by Melvin Calvin to be a key intermediate in photosynthesis.

Hudson's laboratory became a world center for carbohydrate research, and his nearly 275 papers show very careful and laborious work. His insistence on a high standard of performance gave his collaborators excellent training. His eminence helped establish the Public Health Service as an outstanding research center. He was honored by election to the National Academy of Sciences in 1927, and was awarded the Nichols, Gibbs, Richards, and Borden medals, among others. He died in Washington, D.C.

• Hudson's personal papers were destroyed after his death. His published papers through 1945 are collected in R. M. Hann and N. K. Richtmyer, *The Collected Papers of C. S. Hudson* (2 vols., 1946); volume 1 contains an autobiographical account. He published over sixty research papers after 1945. A complete bibliography and account of his career is given by L. F. Small and M. L. Wolfrom in *National Academy of Sciences, Biographical Memoirs* 32 (1958). Other accounts include those by M. L. Wolfrom in *Advances in Carbohydrate Chemistry* (1954), an annual volume of reviews.

D. STANLEY TARBELL

HUDSON, Daniel Eldred (18 Dec. 1849–12 Jan. 1934), Roman Catholic priest and magazine editor, was born at Nahant, Massachusetts, the son of Samuel Henry Hudson, a fisherman, and Mary Hawkes, a domestic servant. The third of ten children, Hudson received his early education in public school. At fourteen he went to work at the Burnham Antique Boke Shop in Boston, a bookstore that stocked more than 500,000 books and pamphlets. The following year he found employment at the Boston publishing house of Lee and Shepherd, where he came into contact with several leading New England literary figures; Henry Wadsworth Longfellow, in particular, was on cordial terms with him.

In 1868 Hudson left Boston to enroll in the College of the Holy Cross, a Jesuit school in Worcester, Massachusetts. In 1870 he decided to become a monk and set out for the Trappist monastery in New Melleray, Iowa. On the train west he met Paul Gillen, a priest of the Congregation of Holy Cross, who persuaded him to stop at South Bend, Indiana, and visit the University of Notre Dame. He stayed there for the rest of his life.

Hudson joined the Congregation of Holy Cross at Notre Dame as a novice in 1871, professed vows the following year, and was ordained a priest in 1875. His first—and only—assignment after ordination was as editor of *Ave Maria* magazine, a Catholic weekly founded by Edward Sorin in 1865 and published by the Holy Cross community at Notre Dame. When Hudson took over as editor the magazine had a circulation of 8,000. At the end of his tenure, fifty-four years later, it had a reported circulation of 36,000 and had become the most widely circulated Catholic magazine in the English language. Under Hudson, the *Ave Maria* was noted for its excellent English and for the breadth of its articles on Catholic culture and piety. By 1890, when the magazine celebrated its silver jubilee, almost every important Catholic writer had contributed to its pages.

As editor, Hudson ended the practice of reprinting pieces from European publications and worked to develop American writers of quality. He was a vigorous supporter of Catholic schools and encouraged the publication of useful Catholic books. One of the first to draw attention to the missionary priest Father Damien De Veuster's work among the lepers on Molokai, he directed a retreat in 1886 for Ira Barnes Dutton (1843–1931), who determined to join De Veuster. When De Veuster died in 1888, Dutton, then known as Brother Joseph, carried on his work with the lepers. Hudson promoted Marian devotions, the shrine at Lourdes in particular, and championed the canonization of John Vianney, the curé of Ars.

From the time he came to Notre Dame, Hudson seldom spent a night elsewhere. So total was his concentration on his work that he never attended conventions, made speeches, or took vacations. His asceticisms included the use of none but straight-backed chairs and no food or drink between meals. When illness forced his retirement as editor in 1929, he never again read *Ave Maria*, lest it seem that he was judging the work of his successor.

Despite his reclusive habits, Hudson was widely consulted by members of the Catholic hierarchy and was credited by Pope Pius XI with explaining and defending Catholic teaching and Catholic life "with choice literary grace and penetrating grasp of present conditions." He died at Notre Dame.

• Hudson's papers, consisting of more than 7,500 items, fill 8.5 linear feet in the University of Notre Dame Archives. While he has yet to find a biographer, Hudson's life and work have been sketched by John W. Cavanaugh in *Ave Maria*, 27 Jan. and 3, 10, and 17 Feb. 1934. Thomas T. McAvoy described Hudson's place in the history of the magazine he edited in "The *Ave Maria* after 100 Years," *Ave Maria*, 1 May 1965.

JAMES T. CONNELLY

HUDSON, Frederic (25 Apr. 1819–21 Oct. 1875), journalist, was born in Quincy, Massachusetts, the son of Barzillai Hudson, a sea captain and businessman, and Rebecca Eaton. Hudson was educated in the public schools of Concord, Massachusetts. He left home in 1836 following the death of his mother and accepted a position in New York City with Hudson's News Rooms, a news-gathering agency run by his older brother Edward.

The young man worked the docks, gathering information from incoming ships and earning a reputation for speed and accuracy as a reporter. As Hudson made his rounds, he met James Gordon Bennett, who offered Hudson a position on his newspaper, the *New York Herald*. At eighteen Hudson became the third staff member for the newspaper.

Hudson, hired solely as a reporter, spurred Bennett to make innovative use of technology in collecting information. These innovations reflected Hudson's previous work with his brother's News Rooms, and each involved greater speed and accuracy in gathering and printing news. The *Herald* ran news boats out to meet ships approaching the harbor. Hudson used horse expresses, trains, and the telegraph to move information from its source to the *Herald*. During the Mexican War he used all three to establish communication lines with New Orleans, which meant that northern readers could receive news of the war in as little as two weeks. The *Herald* also sent engravers to war sites to prepare maps for use with stories. Other newspapers in New York, Boston, and Philadelphia quickly followed the *Herald*'s methods of covering the war.

As the *Herald* grew, Bennett increasingly left New York on business trips, and Hudson's role with the newspaper expanded. At first Bennett unofficially placed Hudson in charge of the *Herald*'s operation, but in 1840 Bennett named Hudson the newspaper's managing editor, a new concept in newspaper organization. Most newspaper printers at the beginning of the nineteenth century still served as editors, reporters, typesetters, and press operators. They also sold advertisements and were responsible for circulation. In the 1820s and 1830s printers began to add reporters and created staffs to handle newspaper operations, but there was no coordination of their activities. As managing editor, Hudson took the concept of editor and expanded it into one that directed the activities of reporters, managed and edited copy, and oversaw the daily operations of the newspaper. Hudson held this position until his retirement.

In 1848 Hudson became the *Herald*'s representative to the newly formed New York Associated Press, the predecessor to the Associated Press. Hudson served on the NYAP's first executive committee. He helped manage the organization for fifteen years, developing its news collection capabilities and gaining special use rates and privileges from the Western Union Telegraph Company in 1855. By the outbreak of the Civil War, Hudson's knack for news gathering had made the *Herald* the most widely read newspaper in the United States, claiming 77,000 subscribers. Hudson's news collection concepts culminated in the *Herald*'s coverage of the dissolution of the Union. The *Herald*, Hudson boasted, anticipated the trouble in the South and "dispatched half a dozen correspondents to the infected districts." By 1865 the *Herald* had approximately forty reporters sending news of the war back to New York, and the newspaper spent nearly one-half million dollars to provide that coverage. In his history Hudson recalled that "with the organization of the first army, the *Herald* corps of army and navy correspondents were organized. With every division marched a young representative of that establishment. At every fight one of its correspondents was an eye-witness. There was a *Herald* tent and a *Herald* wagon with army corps."

Following the Civil War, James Gordon Bennett, Jr., assumed ownership of the *Herald*. In 1866 Hudson resigned and took his ailing wife, Eliza Woodward, whom he had married in 1844, and their son to Concord, Massachusetts, where Eliza had been a schoolteacher before the couple's marriage. While caring for his invalid wife, Hudson wrote his history of American journalism, the first to approach journalism as a news-gathering institution and the first major work on the press in America since Isaiah Thomas's *History of Printing* in 1812. Hudson's *Journalism in the United States, from 1690–1872* was published in 1873. He planned to produce a second and third edition of the work, but he died in a train accident in Concord two years after the text's release.

Hudson's history received mixed reactions in American newspapers. Most reviewers acknowledged the importance of Hudson's work in gathering information about the development of American journalism, a topic neglected by historians. But reviewers also condemned the text for inaccuracies and its thesis that the *New York Herald* was the model for newspapers and information gathering of the 1800s. The *New York World* caustically referred to the book as "a rag bag of shreds and patches" following Hudson's death. Despite contemporary reaction, Hudson's text was cited as authoritative by media historians for the next fifty years.

Hudson believed that newspapers needed to remain objective and nonpolitical in order to gather and disseminate information as quickly as possible. Despite his beliefs, Hudson could not completely steer the *Herald*—and its fiery publisher Bennett—away from turmoil and partisanship. The paper became a Democratic party organ in the 1850s, sympathizing with the southern cause and opposing the election of Abraham Lincoln. Once war began, however, the *Herald* adopted a stance of support for the Union and endorsed Lincoln's 1864 reelection campaign.

In an 1875 interview published in the *Herald*, Hudson speculated that electricity would in the future do all of the work of news gathering; no doubt he envisioned an expansion of technology and its use by newspapers to collect and disseminate information. Following his death, the *Springfield* (Mass.) *Republican* credited Hudson with having more to do with the organization and collection of news than any other individual of the period, and the *Herald* credited him as being "the father of American journalism" in relation to news-gathering practices.

• Information about Hudson's life and news practices is in Louis M. Starr, *Bohemian Brigade: Civil War Newsmen in Action* (1954). The changes Hudson brought to journalistic practices in the nineteenth century are in Frank Luther Mott, *American Journalism: A History, 1690–1960* (1962). References to Hudson are in Isaac C. Pray, ed., *Memoirs of James Gordon Bennett and His Times* (1855), and Don C. Seitz, *The James Gordon Bennetts* (1928). The reaction to Hudson's journalism history is discussed in William J. Thorn, "Hudson's History of Journalism Criticized by His Contemporaries," *Journalism Quarterly* 57 (1980): 99–106. Obituaries are in the *New York Herald* and the *Springfield* (Mass.) *Republican*, both 22 Oct. 1875.

DAVID A. COPELAND

HUDSON, Henry (?–c.23 June 1611), English navigator and explorer, was evidently a Londoner by birth and was probably trained in the service of the Muscovy Company, but his early life has not been documented. He is known to have married Katherine (maiden name unknown) and to have had three sons: Oliver, who was of marriageable age by 1608, Richard, and John. His career can be followed only from 19 April 1607 to 23 June 1611, shortly after which he died at sea in Hudson Bay. The Muscovy Company, seeking a route to Asia, sent him on the earliest known polar expedition to investigate the possibility of open water between Spitzbergen (Svalbard), recently explored by the Dutch, and the northern shore of Greenland. Leaving the Thames on 1 May 1607, he sailed successfully north until he reached his remarkable estimated latitude of 81°23′ (actual 80°23′) by 15 August before being turned back by ice. He investigated the western shores of Spitzbergen and Bear Island and on the return was the first Englishman to discover what was to be Jan Mayen Island. He reached the Thames on 15 September after a successful pioneer exploration of these northern waters.

On his second expedition for the same sponsors Hudson searched the northeast for a possible channel between Spitzbergen and Novaya Zemlya that would open into a Northeast Passage to China. The *Hopewell* cleared the Thames on 22 April 1608. With Robert Juet serving as master's mate, the crew sighted North Cape on 3 June and sailed northeastward to an estimated latitude of 75°29′ before being blocked by ice. There was clearly no passage this way. Hudson explored the western shore of Novaya Zemlya southward but was not equipped to attempt the hoped-for voyage to China by the Strait of Viagach. He returned safely to the Thames on 20 August.

Having served the immediate objectives of the Muscovy Company and gained an outstanding reputation for his skill in navigating arctic waters, Hudson was approached by the Amsterdam Chamber of the Dutch East India Company to make a Northeast Passage voyage by the Strait of Viagach. He left Amsterdam with a crew of experienced and inexperienced men, though with Juet as mate, on 25 March 1609 (NS), passing North Cape on 5 May (NS). He soon found that the ice had not cleared, so he determined to show his independence by sailing westward, skirting the Faröes and landing briefly in western Iceland but making no attempt on the Northwest Passage. Instead he turned south, having seen in London a first draft of the map of Virginia prepared by John Smith (1580–1631) and being curious to know what lay between Labrador and Virginia, in particular whether there was a passage through the mainland.

He made his landfall at about 50° N on Labrador, worked down past Newfoundland, and coasted New England, turning southwest to reach Virginia. He overshot the Chesapeake but worked his way up to the entry to Chesapeake Bay, entering it to make sure that this was where the English colony had been founded. He then coasted the Eastern Shore and located the mouth of a major river (the Delaware) but could not enter on account of shoals. Farther north, Hudson encountered a complex of islands through which he worked his way into lower New York Bay. From there he probed inland and found the wide river to which his name was to be given. This might be, he thought, the passage through the continent. Sailing upstream, he was attacked by arrows from a canoe belonging to a Delaware band and replied with gunfire. His further progress to a site below present-day Albany was without incident, but a boat reconnaissance farther upstream revealed shoaling and therefore no passage, so he decided to return, but not before making friendly trading contacts with a Mahican group. Downstream, he was again attacked from canoes and replied with handgun and cannon to deadly effect. However, on the left bank, at the island of Mannahata, he had a friendly reception from the Delaware band living there.

Hudson had an uneventful return voyage to Dartmouth, which he reached on 2 November 1609 (OS). The mayor wrote at once of his arrival to Lord Salisbury (Robert Cecil) telling him what he had discovered. Salisbury immediately put the official machine in motion to prevent Hudson's leaving the country, with the result that Hudson's charts and Juet's journal fell into English hands even though it was the Dutch who were to exploit the Hudson River.

Hudson's next and final journey—an attempt at a Northwest Passage—was undertaken at the request of a group of London merchants and headed by Sir Thomas Smith (of Virginia and East India Company fame). The bark *Discoverie* left the Thames on 22 April 1610 (OS), sighting Greenland at the beginning of June. By 15 June, Hudson was within sight of Cape Chidley. He entered Hudson Strait in the days following, plying westward against the outflowing current and making slow progress through fog and drifting ice. He reconnoitered Ungava Bay and the north shore of Ungava Peninsula, clearing the strait by 3 August. He named the southern cape at the exit Cape Wolstenholme and the southern Cape Digges (actually the tip of Digges Island).

Then began what the narrator of the voyage, Abacuc Prickett, called "three months in a labyrinth without end" in the body of water that was to be named Hudson Bay. Hudson worked first westward and then northward without finding land or a further channel and finally turned south along the eastern shore of Hudson Bay until he reached the end of James Bay at the mouth of the Grand River. Attempting to turn back, he was checked by ice on 10 November and forced to lay up for the winter. The men built a house on shore and survived on limited rations, supplemented for a time by ptarmigan and, much later, by fish. A solitary Cree Indian promised to return but did not. There had been discontent aimed at Hudson since August 1610, and this now broke out in recriminations about the hoarding of food and other complaints. Juet may have planned a mutiny, but it was led by crew members Greene and Morgan. They decided to rid themselves of Hudson, his son John, several sick men, and one volunteer—nine in all—in the hope of survival for the rest. The nine were forcibly placed in the shallop without warm clothing and with only some biscuits and an axe as nominal supports. In effect, they were left to die. The remainder of the company claimed that this happened so quickly that they knew nothing until the shallop had been cast off on 23 June. With few resources, but under capable leadership from Juet, the crew reached Digges Island. Going ashore to take birds, they encountered a large concentration of Inuit, who attacked their boat, killing two and mortally wounding two others. The boat, however, did succeed in returning to the *Discoverie*. They continued on starvation rations, Juet dying and being replaced by Bylot, who somehow got the ship to Berehaven, Ireland. There they managed to buy food and hire a few men so that they reached Dartmouth and ultimately, early in October 1611, the Thames.

The nine survivors were interrogated by the masters of Trinity House on 24 October. They all pleaded dire necessity for their actions (and ignorance of the preliminaries of the 23 June action): also they could show Hudson's charts of his great discovery and Prickett's narrative. Suspected of mutiny by the High Court of Admiralty and imprisoned for a time, they were released (and Bylot at least was employed on further Hudson Bay voyages), but suspicion lingered. Samuel Purchas, in his *Purchas His Pilgrimage* (2d ed., 1614), produced evidence against them, as apparently did others. Eventually, Prickett, Bylot, and two others were charged with murder before the criminal branch of the Admiralty Court in 1618 but were acquitted. An expedition in 1612 found no trace of Hudson.

Hudson's contributions to discovery were outstanding. He pioneered the exploration of polar waters, discovered and gave his name to the Hudson River, a vital element in the exploration of eastern North America, and was the first European to land on the island that was to become first New Amsterdam and then New York. He passed the Hudson Strait, to which he gave his name, and perhaps most important entered Hudson Bay, although he did not explore it to its western limits. The bay became a highway for commerce and the crucial opening for the long and often painful search for the Northwest Passage for some three centuries. Hudson's dramatic and tragic end has fascinated and appalled subsequent generations.

• Among the sources to consult are Samuel Purchas, *Hakluytus Posthumous* (the final revision of *Purchas His Pilgrimage*), vol. 3 (1625), pp. 531–611, which prints Prickett's narrative; G. M. Asher, ed., *Henry Hudson the Navigator* (1860), which reproduces the basic documents; Henry C. Murphy, *Henry Hudson in Holland* (1909), which has something from Dutch sources; L. P. Kirwan, *A History of Polar Exploration* (1959); Llewelyn Powys, *Henry Hudson* (1928); *Juet's Journal*, ed. Robert M. Lunny (1959), which contains an edited version of the 1608–1609 document; Historical Manuscripts Commission, *Salisbury Papers*, vol. 21 (1970), p. 152, which mentions the return of survivors from the 1610–1611 expedition; and David B. Quinn et al., eds., *New American World*, vol. 4 (1979), pp. 278–97, which prints a selection of the sources.

DAVID B. QUINN

HUDSON, Manley Ottmer (19 May 1886–13 Apr. 1960), legal educator and judge, was born in St. Peters, Missouri, the son of David Ottmer Hudson, a physician, and Emma Bibb. After graduating from William Jewell College in Liberty, Missouri (B.A., 1906; M.A., 1907), he entered Harvard Law School, where he obtained an LL.B. degree in 1910. From 1910 to 1918 he taught on the faculty of the University of Missouri Law School, published several essays on real property law and conveyancing, and edited the *Missouri Law Bulletin* (1914–1917). When World War I broke out, he joined the local antiwar movement and served as secretary of the Missouri Peace Society. He also completed research for an S.J.D. degree, which he received from Harvard in 1917.

Hudson traveled to Paris with the international law division of the American Commission to Negotiate Peace in November 1918 and became an enthusiastic supporter of the new peace-keeping machinery established by the Treaty of Versailles. He worked from 1919 to 1921 in the legal section of the League of Nations Secretariat and accepted a teaching position at Harvard Law School in 1919. In 1923 he became Bemis Professor of International Law at Harvard and thereafter divided his time between classroom instruction and practical assistance to international organizations. The donor of his endowed chair, George Bemis, had prescribed just such a dual role, noting in his bequest that he preferred "not merely a professor of the science, but a practical co-operator in the work of advancing knowledge and good-will among nations and governments." In 1930 Hudson married Janet Norton Aldrich; they had two sons.

From the beginning of his postwar academic career, Hudson took a special interest in the work of the Permanent Court of International Justice, the judicial arm of the League of Nations. He published an authoritative review of the court's activities each year in the *American Journal of International Law* from 1923 to 1940 and campaigned vigorously, but unsuccessfully, for American acceptance of the court's jurisdiction in the 1920s and 1930s. His book, *The Permanent Court of International Justice* (1934; rev. ed., 1943), quickly became the standard work on the subject, noted for its clarity and meticulous documentation. Hudson also edited four volumes of *World Court Reports* from 1934 to 1943, covering all decisions that were handed down by the tribunal before 1940, when the onset of World War II caused it to suspend operations. Elected to the court in October 1936 to succeed Judge Frank B. Kellogg, he wrote separate opinions in six of the ten cases that reached the bench in the late 1930s. Particularly notable was his concurring opinion in a 1937 dispute between Belgium and the Netherlands over the diversion of water from the river Meuse, in which he offered an enlightening exposition of the role of equity in international law.

His pragmatic and fact-based approach to adjudication owed much to the positivist temper of the social sciences in the 1920s. Convinced of the need for accessible official texts to guide students and practitioners of international law, he compiled nine volumes of *International Legislation* (1931–1950). The series provided in a convenient format authenticated texts of 670 important treaties signed between 1919 and 1945. Careful analysis of such documents, along with the *World Court Reports*, would, Hudson believed, acquaint students with the methods of contemporary dispute resolution and thus establish an essential foundation for the further development of international law. An emphasis upon documentary precision would also enhance the status of law teachers, who could now claim that their international law courses were as "scientific" and "tough-minded" as any other course offerings.

Hudson's insistence upon technical proficiency culminated in the work of the Harvard Research in International Law project, which he organized and directed from 1927 to 1939. Funded by the Carnegie Endowment for International Peace, this project brought together about fifty leading American experts in international law each year to assist the codification efforts of the League of Nations. Within a decade the group published thirteen draft conventions, with documentation and commentary, on such subjects as nationality, extradition, and diplomatic privileges and immunities. The impressive learning and painstaking draftsmanship that characterized these texts made them valuable models for later codifiers.

During World War II Hudson continued to urge the need for stronger international organizations to maintain world peace in the future. He formulated proposals to revise and improve the workings of the old court, especially by expanding its jurisdiction over international disputes, and at the 1945 United Nations conference in San Francisco he helped draft the statute of a new judicial body, the International Court of Justice. Once the statute had been approved, he and the other judges of the old court collectively resigned in January 1946. Thereafter he resumed his annual review of the court's activities in the *American Journal of International Law*, continuing the role of chronicler he had undertaken for its predecessor in the 1920s and 1930s. He also served on the United Nations International Law Commission from 1948 to 1953. As the first chairman of this group, he did much to establish its agenda, particularly with reference to further codification efforts.

Although failing health forced Hudson to resign his Harvard professorship in 1954, he continued his writing and consulting work at his home almost until his death. In 1956 he became the first recipient of the Manley O. Hudson Gold Medal, the highest award of the American Society of International Law, which had been created to honor his achievements as teacher, scholar, and judge. A demanding, and sometimes abrasive, individual, Hudson nevertheless impressed his contemporaries as a generous idealist who labored tirelessly to improve the institutions of international law. While he displayed little interest in philosophical issues and never wrote a comprehensive treatise on international law, his voluminous publications explored a broad range of subjects and helped to establish the institutional foundations on which later generations have built. As the distinguished international legal scholar Quincy Wright observed at the award ceremony in 1956, "Those of us who have been associated with him recognize that without his energy, ability and devotion, International Law and the institutions which have been established since the first World War to develop, maintain and apply it, would have been less effective." Hudson died in Cambridge, Massachusetts.

Of all Hudson's achievements, his pioneering work as a reporter of the decisions handed down by the Permanent Court of International Justice constitutes his most enduring legacy to later generations of legal scholars and advocates of a peaceful world order. Like the early decisions of the United States Supreme Court, his *World Court Reports* provide a permanently valuable record of a major judicial institution during its formative years.

• Letters from Hudson are in the Manley O. Hudson Papers, the Louis D. Brandeis Papers, and the Louis B. Sohn Papers, all in the Harvard Law School Library; and in the Elihu Root Papers and the Philip C. Jessup Papers in the Library of Congress. Julius Stone, a former student and colleague, provides an appraisal of Hudson's career in "Manley Hudson: Campaigner and Teacher of International Law," *Harvard Law Review* 74 (1960): 215–25. The only full-length study is J. T. Kenny, "The Contributions of Manley O. Hudson to Modern International Law and Organization" (Ph.D. diss., Univ. of Denver, 1976), which contains a comprehensive bibliography of Hudson's writings. Valuable obituaries appear in *American Journal of International Law* 54 (July 1960): 603–4, and *Proceedings of the American Society of International Law* (1960): 223.

MAXWELL BLOOMFIELD

HUDSON, Rock (17 Nov. 1925–2 Oct. 1985), film and television actor, was born Roy Scherer, Jr., in Winnetka, Illinois, the son of Roy Scherer, an automobile mechanic who abandoned his family, and Kay Wood, a telephone operator. During the depression the family experienced financial hardships. His mother married Wallace Fitzgerald when Hudson was eight. Reportedly, the boy's memories of his stepfather, whose surname he took, were less than favorable. The marriage lasted nine years. Starting at age ten, the shy, reclusive Hudson took odd jobs to help support the financially strapped family. He sang in school glee clubs and in church choirs and harbored a strong desire to act; however, in trying out for school plays at New Tier High School, he invariably failed to get parts because of his inability to remember lines. According to one report, the closest he came to his goal at this time was "playing the part of one of the Three Wise Men in the annual Christmas pageants" (*Current Biography*,

Oct. 1961). His childhood was reportedly so normal and wholesome that one of his high school friends recalled that "it looked like apple pie and ice cream to me" (*Time*, 14 Oct. 1985).

Upon graduating from high school in 1944, Hudson joined the navy and served as an airplane mechanic in the Philippines. He was discharged in 1946 and returned to Winnetka, where he worked as a piano mover and mail carrier. Still determined to act, he moved to Los Angeles, where he lived with his remarried biological father (now the owner of an electrical appliance store). His application for admission to the University of Southern California to study drama was rejected because of his low grades. He later took a truck-driving job for a food company, between deliveries spending most of his time standing in front of various studio gates waiting to be discovered. For several months no one noticed him; then, upon the advice of friends, he bought the first complete suit he had ever owned and invested $25 in photographs of himself. He sent these photos to various producers along with personal information.

Hudson's first big break came in September 1947, when Henry Willson, a talent agent for the Selznick Studio, was favorably impressed by Hudson's photographs and asked him in for an interview. Reportedly Willson began, "You're not bad looking. Can you act?" Hudson replied, "No . . . I can't act." To which Willson replied, "Good. I think I can do something for you" (*Time*, 14 Oct. 1985). Agreeing to place himself professionally in Willson's hands, he changed his name to Rock Hudson ("Rock" for the Rock of Gibraltar and "Hudson" for the Hudson River) and went to various studios. Years later the actor confided to an interviewer that he hated the name. Initially, Hudson failed to make much of an impression, owing to his inordinate shyness. In fact, his 20th Century–Fox screen test was so poor that it was later used in acting classes as a classic example of bad acting. However, through Willson, Hudson met director Raoul Walsh, who invested some $9,000 for living expenses and acting lessons in the introverted actor. Walsh also cast Hudson in his first film role, a small part in *Fighter Squadron* (1948). In 1949 Universal–International Pictures bought Hudson's contract from Walsh and paid the struggling actor $125 a week. During the next six years, twenty-five films followed. Hudson typically portrayed uncomplicated, easy going characters. When his first big role came along in 1954—the wealthy playboy-turned-surgeon Bob Merrick in *The Magnificent Obsession*, opposite Jane Wyman—Hudson found his film personality: steady, likable, a man among men. The film earned the studio $5 million and made Hudson Universal's top star.

Universal secured Hudson's star potential by again pairing him with Wyman in *All That Heaven Allows* (1955) and casting him as Colonel Dean Hess in *Battle Hymn* (1956). However, the film that firmly established him among Hollywood's top male stars was the 1956 adaptation of Edna Ferber's *Giant*, which paired him with Elizabeth Taylor and James Dean. His performance in *Giant* was the high point of Hudson's career. Under George Stevens's direction, Hudson provided emotional depth to his portrayal of Texas rancher Bick Benedict. He was nominated for an Academy Award for best actor in 1956.

After his success in *Giant*, Hudson displayed a talent for light romantic comedy, particularly in his films with Doris Day—beginning with *Pillow Talk* in 1959 and followed by *Lover Come Back* in 1962 and *Send Me No Flowers* in 1964. It was also evident in his successful 1970s NBC television series, "McMillan and Wife." Hudson not only had a sure sense of timing but conveyed a natural, self-deprecating attitude that allowed him "to have fun with sex without putting audiences off by actually having fun with sex" (*Time*, 14 Oct. 1985).

Hudson starred in sixty-five films, including *A Farewell to Arms* (1958), *Twilight for the Gods* (1959), *Come September* (1961), *The Spiral Road* (1962), *Ice Station Zebra* (1968), and *Darlin' Lili* (1969). In 1981 he starred in his last TV series, "The Devlin Connection" (which was interrupted by Hudson's heart surgery and five heart bypasses). He had a recurring role on ABC's "Dynasty" in 1984.

The public Rock Hudson was a romantic star adored by millions of women; however, the private Rock Hudson was a homosexual who had to live by a double standard that made him both cynical and resentful. His 1955 marriage to Willson's secretary Phyllis Gates was hastily arranged by Universal Studios to counter rumors that the actor was homosexual. The marriage ended in divorce in 1958. Hudson's secret became public in July 1985, when he flew to Paris for treatment with an experimental drug for AIDS. When he returned to Los Angeles in September, his illness had progressed to the point that Hudson openly acknowledged his condition as well as his homosexuality. His forthrightness and dignity in the face of physical deterioration and impending death aroused widespread sympathy and admiration. Hudson attempted to channel this good will into a campaign to find a cure for AIDS. Too ill to appear at a Hollywood AIDs benefit on 19 September 1985, Hudson released a statement: "I am not happy that I am sick. I am not happy that I have AIDS. But if that is helping others, I can at least know that my own misfortune has had some positive worth."

Hudson died in Los Angeles. Marc Christian, his lover and companion, successfully sued the Hudson estate, claiming that the actor had exposed him to AIDS by not revealing his condition to him.

• Significant information is in Hudson's autobiography, written with Sara Davidson, *Rock Hudson: His Story* (1987). Other helpful sources include Phyllis Gates, with Bob Thomas, *My Husband, Rock Hudson* (1987); John Parker, *Five for Hollywood: Their Friendship, Their Fame, and Their Tragedies* (1991); and Jack Vitek and Jerry Oppenheimer, *Idol: Rock Hudson* (1987). Obituaries are in the *New York Times*, 3 Oct. 1985, and *Time*, 14 Oct. 1985.

JAMES YATES

HUEBNER, Solomon Stephen (6 Mar. 1882–17 July 1964), professor of insurance, was born in Manitowoc, Wisconsin, the son of Frederick August Huebner and Wilhelmina Dicke, wealthy farmers. Huebner's character was first shaped by the values incorporated in his family's religious evangelicalism and political progressivism. After graduating as valedictorian of his high school class in 1898, Huebner enrolled at the University of Wisconsin, where he studied social sciences under the tutelage of such eminent scholars as economist Richard T. Ely and historian Frederick Jackson Turner. He satisfied the requirements for a bachelor of letters degree in 1902. The following year he continued at Wisconsin, completing a master's thesis on stockholding in American railroads under the direction of economist Balthesar Meyer. Although he had intended to enroll at the University of Berlin that same year, he abandoned this plan on learning of his selection as a Harrison fellow at the Wharton School of the University of Pennsylvania. There he completed, in 1904, the requirements for a doctorate in economics, writing a dissertation on marine insurance under the direction of Emory R. Johnson. That same year he began a lifelong career at Wharton. In 1908 the young scholar married Ethel Elizabeth Mudie; the couple had four children.

Huebner's academic interests were highly concentric with the broad goals of promoting pragmatic, professional education in business that had been envisioned by the school's founder and chief benefactor, Joseph Wharton. The Wharton School's program had been influenced by the example of the University of Halle, where many of its first generation of scholars had received their training. As at the German institution, which had emerged as a leading center of applied economics, the objective at Wharton was to establish a practical course of studies that would provide a better grounding in the knowledge necessary for careers in specialized business functions than was possible to attain through traditional apprenticeships. Thus, the Wharton School had developed capacities by 1900 for the training of specialists in such fields as accounting, finance, and transportation—capacities that Huebner later extended to additional fields of learning. This approach differed markedly from the case study system begun at Harvard University in 1908 that sought to train generalists who were capable of evaluating all business problems. It also differed from the patterns followed by contemporary liberal arts colleges, which generally sought to impart an understanding of theoretical rather than pragmatic issues in their economic pedagogy. The Wharton model soon became the standard most widely imitated by other American universities establishing business curriculums in the early decades of the twentieth century. This result came about partly from the recruitment of key Wharton leaders such as Dean Edmund J. James as president of the University of Illinois and Professor Joseph French Johnson as dean of the School of Commerce at New York University. It was also a consequence of Wharton's early commitment to doctoral studies in business

and the influence of its alumni in the growing ranks of the business professoriate.

Huebner's success at Wharton derived in large part from his achievements in extending the school's teaching capabilities in yet another business specialization—insurance. Although this topic had been included in the curriculum in 1896, it was not regularly offered until Huebner began teaching in 1904. His choice of specialization was propitious for several reasons. The insurance industry ranked among the nation's largest financial intermediaries, and some of its leading concerns were based in Philadelphia. Moreover, the public image of the industry was in need of restoration because of the negative findings of critical public inquiries. In 1905 shortcomings in the practices of some of the largest life insurance companies were revealed in the investigation undertaken by the New York State legislature's Armstrong committee, led by its reformist chief counsel, Charles Evans Hughes. Huebner's developing program was helpful in bolstering public confidence. His training programs, for example, made credible insurance's claim to be a learned calling requiring the mastery of special knowledge for competent performance. In addition, his teaching had a strongly positive bias emphasizing the constructive ways that insurance underwriting could protect business and the public from losses due to unexpected adversities. This activism helped Huebner advance to the rank of professor by 1908. Five years later he became the first chair of the newly organized insurance department. The reputation of the Wharton School as a center for insurance education was further extended by Huebner's subsequent publication of several seminal textbooks in this field, including *Property Insurance* (1911), *Life Insurance* (1915), *Marine Insurance* (1920), and *The Economics of Life Insurance* (1927).

Huebner also contributed to Wharton's growing reputation as a center for scholarship in finance. In 1904 he had begun to teach a course on financial and commodity markets. Investment banking had become well established on the American financial scene during the nineteenth century primarily because of the enormous capital requirements of the expanding railroads. However, the public image of this industry, like that of insurance, had been tarnished by the depressing revelations of unethical practices in the aforementioned Armstrong committee hearings as well as the 1911 money trust investigation conducted by the Banking Committee of the House of Representatives. In 1918 the Investment Bankers Association engaged Huebner to develop a curriculum to prepare candidates for careers in their field. This eventually led to the publication by Huebner of another important textbook, *The Stock Market*, in 1920.

Like many contemporary scholars in new fields of expertise, Huebner sought to publicize the benefits of his specialized knowledge by serving as an adviser to government on difficult public policy issues. In two early instances of such advocacy, Huebner revealed a strong preference for administrative rather than judicial solutions for economic problems, particularly those involving issues of industrial concentration. This was evident in his recommendations to the House Merchant Marine and Fisheries Committee about how the federal government should address agreements formed between domestic railroads and international shipping companies. Although some of these treaties seemed monopolistic, Huebner believed that they should be regulated in the public interest, the general practice followed in controlling natural monopolies, rather than challenging them in the courts as probable violations of antitrust laws. This perspective proved influential in the drafting of the U.S. Shipping Act of 1916. Later, after the 1918 armistice, the same congressional committee engaged the Wharton professor to formulate a plan for reestablishing American firms in the maritime insurance business after the devastating losses they had experienced in the war. After five years of study Huebner drafted a model marine insurance law and a plan that won congressional approval that allowed the formation of insurance syndicates exempt from the strictures of the antitrust laws. In addition to these assignments, Huebner served as an adviser to the Civil Aeronautics Board, the Department of Commerce, and the War Department.

In the 1920s Huebner began to devote much of his attention to the professionalization of insurance underwriting. He played a leading role in forming qualifying associations for those who aspired to pursue careers in specialized aspects of insurance. In 1927 he helped organize the American College of Life Underwriters and establish the Chartered Life Underwriters (CLU) certification as well as the master of science in financial services. In 1932 he helped organize the American Association of University Teachers of Insurance (later the American Risk and Insurance Association) and, in 1942, the American Institute for Property and Liability Underwriters.

Beginning in the 1920s Huebner also began to promote the "human life value concept" to provide a basis for analyzing the insurable value of an individual life. Embedded in this notion was the recognition that human capital was an important factor in creating economic value in a complex urban-industrial society. Thus, a key to life underwriting was the assessment of the economic worth of the insured's knowledge, skills, and other capabilities that could contribute to his or her lifetime earnings power. The complexities of making this determination from the perspectives of surviving family, employers, business partners, and other insurable interests were distinguishing features of the later editions of Huebner's life insurance textbooks. He died at Merion Station, Pennsylvania.

Huebner's primary contribution involved the successful integration of insurance as a fundamental subject in collegiate business curriculums and the establishment of associations and qualifying standards that helped to professionalize insurance underwriting in the United States.

• The two most comprehensive works about Huebner and his achievements are by Mildred F. Stone, *The Teacher Who*

Changed an Industry: A Biography of Dr. Solomon S. Huebner (1960) and *A Calling and Its College: A History of the American College of Life Underwriters* (1963). Two briefer pieces by close associates include David McCahan, "Solomon Stephen Huebner—World's Foremost Insurance Educator," *Life Association News*, July 1940, and McCahan and D. W. Gregg, "A Collection of Huebnerian Philosophy," *Journal of the American Society of Chartered Life Underwriters* (June 1952). Huebner's contributions to the Wharton School are documented by Steven A. Sass in *The Pragmatic Imagination: A History of the Wharton School, 1881–1981* (1982). An obituary is in the *New York Times*, 18 July 1964.

PAUL J. MIRANTI, JR.

HUEBSCH, B. W. (21 Mar. 1876–7 Aug. 1964), publisher, was born Benjamin W. Huebsch in New York City, the son of Adolph Huebsch, a rabbi, and Julia Links. His father, who had immigrated to the United States from Germany, died when Benjamin was eight years old. Much of Huebsch's early education was received at home through tutoring by his uncle Samuel Huebsch, who lived with the family.

When Huebsch was thirteen, he studied for several months at a business school and then became an assistant at the New York Engraving and Printing Company. Less than a year later, in June 1890, he was hired as an apprentice lithographer with another printing firm, Joseph Frank and Sons, and remained there for nearly four years. During this time he developed an interest in classical music and studied the violin privately with Sam Franko, a well-known conductor and teacher. He also attended night classes in art at Cooper Union. In his late teens Huebsch stopped using his given first name and became known as "B. W."

In 1894 Huebsch joined D. A. Huebsch and Company, a printing firm founded several years earlier in New York City by his older brother Daniel and their uncle Samuel. The firm printed appointment books and diaries, which it advertised and distributed nationally, and B. W. Huebsch took over the promotional side of the business while continuing to pursue his interest in classical music. In the late 1890s he served as music critic of the *New York Sun*.

In 1900, through B. W. Huebsch's efforts, D. A. Huebsch and Company printed and distributed its first trade book, *The New Humanism*, by E. H. Griggs. About this time both Samuel and Daniel Huebsch left the firm, and B. W. Huebsch decided to get out of the printing business and become a book publisher. In April 1901 he announced that the firm would henceforth be known as B. W. Huebsch and Company. During a four-year transition period Huebsch published several other works by Griggs while continuing to distribute the appointment books; he augmented his income by acting as a part-time printing contractor.

By 1906 Huebsch had begun publishing books by other authors, including humorist Gelett Burgess. In less than a decade he became established as a major publisher of fiction and nonfiction by important writers of the period, including works by H. G. Wells and William Ellery Leonard, and translations of Maxim

Gorky, Gerhart Hauptmann, and August Strindberg. Huebsch's list of authors and their subjects reflected his own interests in socialism, radical political theory, and the new science of psychoanalysis. He was personally involved in every aspect of publication, including design, and created the company's well-known logo, a seven-branched candelabrum combined with the initials B. W. H.

In the second and final decade of the company's existence, from 1915 to 1925, Huebsch added other distinguished authors to his roster, publishing works by Van Wyck Brooks, George Jean Nathan, James Joyce, D. H. Lawrence, Thorstein Veblen, Sherwood Anderson, and Randolph Bourne. From 1920 to 1924 Huebsch also published a widely read radical weekly called *The Freeman*. In 1920 Huebsch married Alfhild Lamm; the couple had two children.

B. W. Huebsch and Company had published more than 400 different titles by August 1925, when it was bought by publishers Harold K. Guinzburg and George S. Oppenheimer, who had recently founded the Viking Press. Under the acquisition agreement, Viking, which had not yet published a book, thereby inherited the Huebsch backlist, and Huebsch himself became Viking's vice president and editorial director. In addition to retaining most of the authors he had published earlier, he attracted other distinguished writers to Viking, including Sylvia Townsend Warner, Harold Laski, Franz Werfel, Stefan Zweig, and Upton Sinclair. Huebsch's virtually unique mastery of all aspects of book publishing—editing, printing, production, and promotion—earned him a reputation as a giant in the field during his four-decade association with Viking, and from the 1940s onward he was regarded as an elder statesman in the industry.

Huebsch was well known not only for his accomplishments at B. W. Huebsch and Viking but also for his strong support of book publishing generally. He encouraged efforts to improve the retail distribution of books nationwide, advocated educational programs for booksellers, and worked for the creation of a national book center. Huebsch also proposed and helped found the National Association of Book Publishers. He was a member of the executive committee of P.E.N., the international association of writers, editors, and publishers, and served as the delegate of the U.S. book industry to UNESCO (United Nations Educational, Scientific, and Cultural Organization) in 1949–1950. Huebsch contributed numerous articles to professional journals and translated a Stefan Zweig novel with the English title *The Royal Game* (1944). A memoir, *Busman's Holiday*, was published in 1959.

As an outspoken supporter of freedom of expression, Huebsch was active in liberal political causes throughout his adult life. An opponent of militarism, he traveled to Europe with Henry Ford's Peace Expedition in 1915–1916 and edited a daily newspaper aboard ship. During World War I he was also a leader of the American Neutral Conference, which sought an end to the fighting. He helped found the American

Civil Liberties Union in 1920 and served for more than thirty years as its treasurer.

Although Huebsch retired as editorial director at Viking in the late 1950s, he continued to be active as a consulting editor at the firm. In June 1964 the *New York Herald Tribune* awarded him its first Irita Van Doren Literary Award, citing him for "exemplifying in the highest degree the best qualities of responsible editing and publishing." Huebsch died suddenly while on a business trip to London.

• Most of Huebsch's papers are housed in the Manuscript Division of the Library of Congress; for a description, see the library's *Information Bulletin*, 31 Aug. 1964. Some of his letters as well as several hundred books owned by Huebsch are deposited at the Columbia University library. Articles by Huebsch include "Reflections on Publishing," *Publishers Weekly*, 25 Apr. 1936, pp. 1677–81, and "Footnotes to a Publisher's Life," *Colophon*, ns., 2, no. 3 (1936–1937): 406–26. Biographical information on Huebsch can be found in Charles A. Madison, *Book Publishing in America* (1966); John Tebbel, *A History of Book Publishing in the United States*, vol. 3 (1978); and Ann McCullough, "A History of B. W. Huebsch, Publisher" (Ph.D. diss., Univ. of Wisconsin, 1979). Biographical material is also contained in a series of interviews with Huebsch conducted by Louis Starr in 1954 and 1955 and interviews with Marshall Best, Huebsch's protégé at Viking; this material is in the Oral History Collection at Columbia University. An obituary is in the *New York Times*, 8 Aug. 1964.

ANN T. KEENE

HUFFMAN, J. C. (1869?–22 June 1935), theatrical director, was born Jesse C. Huffman in Bowling Green, Ohio, the son of a Civil War general. His parents' names are unknown. He found his way into the theater at the age of twelve as an actor. When he reached adulthood, Huffman became more interested in stage direction when he assumed a directorship of the Harry Davis Stock Company in Pittsburgh, Pennsylvania. The celebrated actor Richard Mansfield brought Huffman to the attention of the New York theater, and as a result, Huffman subsequently worked with American stage luminaries such as Julia Marlowe, E. H. Sothern, and Mrs. Leslie Carter.

In 1911 Huffman became a director with the Shubert Bros. producing organization in New York City. Although he had many successes with straight dramas, including *Whispering Wives* (1922), Huffman became best known for directing many of the popular musicals and operettas of the first twenty-five years of the century.

For the Shuberts, Huffman directed several editions of their annual *Passing Show* revue, a vulgarized imitation of the more prestigious *Follies* produced annually by Florenz Ziegfeld. Huffman also directed many of the numerous interchangeable musical comedies starring the Shubert's most popular star, Al Jolson. These included *La Belle Paree* (1911), Jolson's first Shubert show, in which he was overlooked on opening night because his appearance was scheduled late in the performance, and most of the critics had already departed. The Shuberts and Huffman reorganized the show, and Jolson, appearing earlier in the evening, scored a personal triumph. Huffman also directed Jolson in *Dancing Around* (1914), *Robinson Crusoe, Jr.* (1916), *Sinbad* (1918), *Bombo* (1921), and *Big Boy* (1925). These shows were all typical musical comedies of the first decades of the twentieth century: the librettos were merely elaborated, loosely constructed sketches designed to permit ample opportunities for star turns, decorative chorus numbers, and broad comic interludes. Reviewing *Sinbad*, the quintessential Jolson show, a critic for the *New York Dramatic Mirror* ably described the task Huffman typically had in creating a production to surround his egocentric star: "A wealth of scenic detail has been prepared for this newest Winter Garden spectacle, affording opportunities to the principals to wend their way to the Baghdad of the 'Arabian Nights,' to mythical islands on storm-swept seas and to Long Island golfing grounds. . . . an attractive entertainment." Jolson played Inbad, a servant (in minstrel-style blackface) to Sinbad; Inbad was simply a variation on Gus, the blackfaced servant Jolson portrayed in most of his stage musicals. Despite this broad characterization, Jolson tended to view his vehicles as mere excuses for his presence on stage. When the mood struck him, he abandoned the show in mid-performance and turned the evening into a Jolson concert, leaving his fellow actors and the chorus on the sidelines. Songs from the show's score were frequently eliminated, and Jolson interpolated at will other popular songs, many of which became standards despite the fact that (or perhaps because) they had no connection with the plot of the show. What Huffman thought of all this is unrecorded, but he undoubtedly accepted it since it was the standard practice of the time. Audiences preferred Jolson to the shows themselves, and the success of the Jolson shows ensured Huffman's position with the Shuberts.

Huffman made a more personal mark staging a series of popular operettas for the Shuberts. Heavy on romance, pseudoserious music, and exotic foreign settings featuring European nobility, these fanciful musical entertainments had quite a vogue in the 1920s. A departure from the more vulgar entertainments of which the Jolson shows were the superior examples, these operettas were both a step forward in the evolution of the musical stage and a throwback to the operettas of the nineteenth century. Huffman was widely considered one of the finest directors of Broadway operettas and was much sought after to stage them. Those he directed for the Shuberts included classics of the genre such as *Blossom Time* (1921), *Countess Maritza* (1926), and *My Maryland* (1927). The best, and most lastingly popular, was *The Student Prince* (1924), a significant triumph for Huffman. Critic Arthur Hornblow declared it was "of transcendent worth, beautifully sung, acted, staged and costumed." It is frequently revived and generally regarded as the prototype of the Broadway operetta.

Huffman's career was not without its difficulties. It was not always pleasant to work with the demanding and eccentric Shubert brothers. They fought with each other, often catching their employees in the cross fire, and attempted to intimidate their performers and production personnel. J. J. Shubert, who fancied himself a director, often "personally supervised" the productions that Huffman actually directed. Always with an eye on boosting box office, Shubert demanded scanty costumes (even frequent nudity) for chorus girls, and he tended to scrimp on production values. Despite this, Huffman worked for the Shubert organization for most of his career, which was slowed in the mid-1920s by bouts with heart disease resulting, at least in part, from many years of stressful work. Huffman retired, but he was lured back to the stage one last time to direct *Nina Rossa* in 1929. The strain of it, coupled with the production's tepid critical response, brought an end to Huffman's directing work. In all, Huffman is credited with directing more than 200 Broadway shows.

Huffman was adept at stage lighting and wrote several monographs on theatrical practices that were frequently used in the 1920s and 1930s as texts in stagecraft classes at academic institutions such as Columbia University and Harvard University. Huffman was clearly a key player in the Broadway stage of the first third of the twentieth century and in the making of the legendary Shubert organization. A lifelong bachelor, Huffman died in New York's St. Luke's Hospital.

• For information on Huffman, see Gerald Bordman, *American Musical Theatre: A Chronicle* (1992) and *The Oxford Companion to the American Theatre* (1984); James Fisher, *Al Jolson: A Bio-Bibliography* (1994); Herbert G. Goldman, *Jolson: The Legend Comes to Life* (1988); Brooks McNamara, *The Shuberts of Broadway: A History Drawn from the Collections of the Shubert Archive* (1990); *New York Times*, 9 July 1935; and Jerry Stagg, *A Half-century of Show Business and the Fabulous Empire of the Brothers Shubert* (1968). An obituary is in the *New York Times*, 23 June 1935.

JAMES FISHER

HUGGINS, Miller James (27 Mar. 1879?–25 Sept. 1929), baseball player and manager, was born in Cincinnati, Ohio, the son of English immigrants James Thomas Huggins, a grocer, and Sarah Reid. Huggins was an excellent student who received a law (and probably a bachelor) degree from the University of Cincinnati, and he passed the Ohio bar examination in 1902, although he never pursued a law career.

In the 1890s Huggins played semiprofessional and college baseball in Cincinnati as well as for the Mountain Tourists in Fleishmanns, New York, a team organized by Julius Fleishmann, the gin and yeast magnate and part-owner of the Cincinnati Reds. Huggins played under the name of Procter to protect his amateur eligibility and possibly because his father disapproved of Sunday baseball. He altered the spelling to Proctor in his first professional season at Mansfield, Ohio, in the Inter-State League in 1899.

Known as the Mighty Mite because he was 5'6" and 140 pounds, Huggins was quickly recognized as a talented second baseman, base stealer, and leadoff man. From 1901 through 1903 he played for St. Paul in the

American Association, and he hit above .300 each of the three seasons. He joined Cincinnati of the National League in 1904, after the Reds purchased his contract from St. Paul. In six seasons with Cincinnati he established himself as an excellent defensive second baseman; he was a major league leader in walks and stolen bases, which made him a good leadoff man. His highest batting average with the Reds was .292 in 1905.

In February 1910 Huggins was traded to the St. Louis Cardinals as part of a five-player deal. There his hitting slightly improved (.304 in 1912), and he continued to upgrade his ability to get on base, becoming an excellent leadoff batter and outstanding defensive player. Many baseball historians and writers consider him to be one of the top second basemen of his day.

Huggins was made player-manager of the Cardinals in 1913, retiring as a player after the 1916 season. Taking over a last-place team, he led the Redbirds to third-place finishes in 1914 and 1917, the highest the Cardinals had finished since 1876. Huggins replaced himself at second base with future Hall of Famer Rogers Hornsby.

A change in the Cardinals' ownership led to the appointment of Branch Rickey as manager in 1918, as he moved across town from the Browns of the American League. In retaliation American League President Ban Johnson encouraged Yankee owner Jacob Ruppert to hire Huggins as the Yankees' manager. With Ruppert's co-owner Tillinghast Huston in France, Ruppert was able to appoint Huggins as manager despite Huston's preference for Wilbert Robinson of Brooklyn.

After finishing fourth and third in 1918 and 1919, Huggins and Yankees general manager Ed Barrow began to reconstruct the team. The first move, encouraged by both men, was the acquisition of Boston Red Sox pitcher-outfielder Babe Ruth. The Yankees won consecutive American League pennants from 1921 through 1923 and the World Series in 1923. This early success was usually attributed to the willingness of Yankee management to spend their money for players, rather than to the skills of Huggins as manager.

Following a second-place finish in 1924, the team fell apart in 1925, finishing seventh. It was also in 1925 that Huggins fined Ruth $5,000 and suspended him, thus firmly establishing his authority. Huggins and Barrow built up the team again, winning the pennant in 1926 with six of eight starters who had no previous major league experience. This achievement finally led people to give Huggins full credit as manager.

In 1927 and 1928 the Yankees repeated as pennant winners and swept the World Series both seasons, the first time that had been done. Many rate the 1927 Yankees, put together and led by Huggins, the greatest team in baseball history. During his twelve seasons as manager Huggins led the Yankees to six American League pennants and three World Championships, and his teams only twice finished lower than third place.

Late in the 1929 season Huggins developed an infection under his eye, which led to complications. Feeling weak and tired, with eleven games remaining in the season, he checked into a New York hospital. Blood poisoning was diagnosed, and despite transfusions Huggins slipped into a coma and five days later died there of erysipelas.

Outside baseball, Huggins led a quiet life of fishing, golf, and reading. He liked books and good conversation. He lived much of the off-season in St. Petersburg, Florida, where he successfully invested in real estate. He did not marry.

The first monument in center field at Yankee Stadium was dedicated to Huggins in 1932, and in 1964 he was elected to the National Baseball Hall of Fame by the Veterans' Committee. As a manager, he was considered a master psychologist, architect of the first great Yankee dynasty, creator of the new style of power baseball during the 1920s, and one of baseball's greatest managers.

• Both the *Sporting News* and the National Baseball Hall of Fame Library at Cooperstown, N.Y., have files on Huggins. There is no standard biography of Huggins, but several good secondary works include material on him, including Frank Graham, *New York Yankees, an Informal History* (1948); Edwin Pope, *Baseball's Greatest Managers* (1960); Bob Broeg, *Redbirds: A Century of Cardinal's Baseball* (1981); Mark Gallagher, *The Yankee Encyclopedia* (1982); Lowell Reidenbaugh, *Cooperstown: Where Baseball's Legends Live Forever* (1983); and Leonard Koppett, *The Man in the Dugout* (1993). In addition, Leo Durocher's autobiographical *Nice Guys Finish Last* (1975), and Gerald Eskenazi's biography of Durocher, *The Lip* (1993), contain extensive comments on Huggins and his influence on Durocher. Fred Lieb, *Baseball As I Have Known It* (1977), also offers evaluative material on Huggins. An obituary is in the *New York Times*, 26 Sept. 1929, along with a column by John Kieran.

RICHARD C. CREPEAU

HUGHAN, Jessie Wallace (25 Dec. 1875–10 Apr. 1955), pacifist, socialist, and teacher, was born in Brooklyn, New York, the daughter of Samuel Hughan, an accountant and librarian, and Margaret West. Both parents were religious seekers and followers of Henry George's Single Tax theory. Hughan attended Barnard College, graduating in 1898 with an A.B. in economics. A year later she received an A.M. from Columbia University with a thesis on Henry George's economic theories. In 1910 she was awarded a Ph.D. from Columbia; the title of her dissertation was "The Present Status of Socialism in America." Having become acquainted with Socialist party members through her research, she herself became a socialist in 1907. The Socialist party recognized her leadership potential and appointed her to its executive committee and that of the Inter-Collegiate Socialist Society, later the League for Industrial Democracy. She also ran as a socialist candidate for a number of offices, including the U.S. Senate in 1924.

By the time of World War I, Hughan had added pacifism to her faith in a socialist future. It was then that she began her lifelong crusade to end war. In 1915 she took the lead, along with Francis Witherspoon,

Tracy Mygatt, and John Haynes Holmes, in organizing the Anti-Enlistment League. The league pledged its members not to enlist for any military service. Operating from Hughan's home, the league enrolled 3,500 men and women before disbanding because of dissension among members and government harassment.

Hughan continued her work as a militant pacifist, joining the religiously oriented Fellowship of Reconciliation (FOR) as a charter member in 1915. A lifelong Unitarian, she believed that spreading the message of nonviolence was part of her religious responsibility. Pacifism, she believed, was not only for Christians, and she worked diligently to persuade the FOR to set up a separate pacifist recruitment committee. In 1923 her dream became reality with organization of the War Resisters League (WRL), which enrolled members willing to sign its declaration: "War is a crime against humanity. I therefore am determined not to support any kind of war, international or civil, and to strive for the removal of all causes of war." Hughan's determination to provide a home for the non-Christian and nonreligious pacifists had borne fruit.

For all practical purposes, in the early years Hughan *was* the WRL, with headquarters in her apartment. She was recording secretary until 1928, when she and her sister hired and personally paid a half-time staffperson. Her work for WRL included signing up war resisters, public speaking, and writing tracts explaining the potential of individual war resistance for eliminating war. Hughan also organized and participated in many protest actions, including a number of "No More War" parades.

Hughan joined other antiwar leaders in attempting to defeat the 1940 conscription bill. After its passage she protested the law's provisions, which denied legal recognition of absolutists who refused to register, defined narrowly the classification of conscientious objectors, and established camps in which they must work without pay. Under her leadership, WRL supported all objectors, whatever position they took on the draft. In 1945 she stepped down as secretary and became honorary secretary.

Hughan paid a price for her strong personal stand against war. As a public school teacher of English, she barely managed to hold on to her teaching position during World War I, when she received warnings that her pacifism might cause her dismissal. She refused to back down when called before the New York legislature's Lusk Committee for adding to the teacher's loyalty oath the words "This obedience being qualified always by dictates of conscience." The committee denied her its certificate of character and loyalty. During World War II she helped organize the Pacifist Teachers League, whose members refused to register young men for selective service.

The American war resistance movement owes much to the life and work of Jessie Wallace Hughan. The WRL and many post–World War I peace actions grew out of her persistent efforts. Her writings made substantial contributions to the literature of nonviolent action and democratic socialism. Her life, combining professional teaching and social activism, provided a model and inspiration for many World War II resisters. Hughan never married. She died in her Manhattan home.

• Jessie Wallace Hughan's papers are in the possession of her family. Her publications include her doctoral dissertation published under the title *American Socialism of the Present Day* (1911); *The Facts of Socialism* (1913); *A Study of International Government* (1923); and *What Is Socialism?* (1928). *The Challenge of Mars and Other Verses* (1932) contains some of her poetry. WRL pamphlets include *If We Should Be Invaded: Facing a Fantastic Hypothesis* (1940); *Three Decades of War Resistance* (1942); and *New Leagues for Old: Blueprints or Foundations?* (1947). See also Michael David Young, "Wars Will Cease When Men Refuse to Fight: The War Resisters League, 1925–1950" (M.A. thesis, Brown Univ., 1975), and Frances E. Early, "Revolutionary Pacifism and War Resistance: Jessie Wallace Hughan's 'War against War'" *Peace and Change* 20 (1979): 307–28. Her obituary in the *New York Times*, 11 Apr. 1955, emphasizes her work with the Socialist party.

LARRY GARA

HUGHES, Charles Evans (11 Apr. 1862–27 Aug. 1948), governor of New York, secretary of state, and chief justice of the U.S. Supreme Court, was born in Glens Falls, New York, the only son of Mary Catherine Connelly and David Charles Hughes, a Baptist (formerly Methodist) preacher who had immigrated to the United States from England in 1855. Tutored primarily at home until the age of fourteen, Charles Evans Hughes attended Madison University, later renamed Colgate (1876–1878), and received a B.A. from Brown University, which he attended from 1878 to 1881. In 1884 he received an LL.B. with honors from Columbia University Law School, passed the New York County bar exam, and joined the prestigious law firm of Chamberlain, Carter & Hornblower in New York City. He taught law on a visiting basis at Cornell University Law School (1891–1893) and remained in private practice until 1905. He married Antoinette Carter in 1888; they had one son and three daughters.

Hughes first won public recognition as special counsel for committees of the New York State legislature that were investigating irregularities in the gas, electric, and life insurance industries of New York (1905–1906). As the Republican candidate for governor of New York in 1906, he narrowly beat the Democratic candidate, William Randolph Hearst. During his two terms as governor (1907–1908, 1909–1910), Hughes embraced reform measures, including a bill providing for worker safety and another outlawing racetrack gambling. He vetoed a law giving women equal pay in New York City, however, on the grounds that the matter should be handled locally.

An unconventional politician, Hughes never actively sought office for himself. His nominations for governor of New York in both 1906 and 1908 were pushed upon reluctant Republican conventions by President

Theodore Roosevelt. As governor, Hughes refused to advise party leaders of the New York State legislature on the selection of committee chairs, and he ignored the recommendations of Republican party organizations on appointments. When the Brotherhood of Locomotive Firemen and Engineers asked him to appoint a labor representative to one of the public service commissions, he rejected their suggestion on the grounds that appointments should be made on the basis of merit. He vetoed a bill, backed by Italian Americans in New York, making Columbus Day a legal holiday because he considered it poorly drafted. He believed political decisions should be based on reason, not extraneous considerations such as group pride or political rewards and punishments. His preferred political technique was to build popular pressures for the measures he backed.

Hughes's distrust of the politician's craft sometimes hurt him. In his 1908 reelection campaign he carried the state by only 69,462 votes as contrasted to the presidential vote in the state for William Howard Taft of 201,855. In 1910 he was saved from the probable defeat of his direct primary bill in the New York State legislature by his appointment as associate justice to the U.S. Supreme Court. In the next six years he distinguished himself as a moderate jurist—arguing for the expansion of national and state power to regulate commerce and relatively broad interpretations of First Amendment and equal protection clauses of the Constitution. In the *Minnesota Rate Cases* (1913), for example, he argued that states could regulate intrastate commerce in instances where it did not conflict with the federal authority; in the *Shreveport Rate Case* (1914) he argued that the nation could regulate intrastate commerce whenever that commerce was in fact commingled with interstate commerce.

In 1916 Hughes was an obvious choice for the Republican presidential nomination. As a member of the U.S. Supreme Court, Hughes had not had to take a stand in 1912 at the time of the Bull Moose Revolt from the Republican Convention. This, plus his moderately progressive record as governor of New York, led former president Taft and Republican National Committee chairman Frank Hitchcock to back him as the obvious candidate to heal the rift in the party. Nominated once again without any effort on his part, Hughes resigned from the Supreme Court only after the nomination had been secured. After Theodore Roosevelt turned down a nomination from the Progressive party, its executive committee endorsed Hughes.

Hughes's campaign was designed to keep both progressive and conservative Republicans in his camp. At first he emphasized his support for rural credits, efficient administration of government, the merit system in the civil service, and the protection of the just interests of labor. Later he backed a national suffrage amendment to give women the right to vote, and he hammered away at Woodrow Wilson's support for the Adamson Act, which had established an eight-hour day for railroad workers. His appeal to "Americanism"

and an emphasis on American neutral rights was an attempt to keep both Republican nationalists (led by Theodore Roosevelt) and Americans of German and Irish extraction in his camp.

Hughes lost the election by 254 electoral votes to Woodrow Wilson's 277—a thirteen-vote margin. The final popular tally showed Hughes with 8,538,221 votes to Wilson's 9,129,606. This outcome was, in part, the result of Wilson's peace campaign and the president's ability to secure the passage, in the summer of 1916, of several progressive measures that had been in the Republican and Progressive party platforms. Hughes's inability to find a stirring campaign theme and his distrust of organizational politics also contributed to his defeat. Bypassing political professionals, he appointed an old Union League Club friend as campaign chair. Mistakes included Hughes's trips into Ohio and California during bitter factional fights. The latter trip was managed by Republican regulars, and plans to meet the Progressive governor and candidate for the U.S. Senate, Hiram Johnson, were never worked out. Hughes decided to address a luncheon at the Commercial Club in San Francisco, despite a waiters' strike in the area. He was served his food by strike breakers in a room displaying anti-union signs.

If Hughes had won either Ohio or California, he would have been president. California was a particularly close race: Hughes lost by 3,775 votes. It cost him 13 electoral votes, the margin of his electoral college defeat. Hiram Johnson, running for the Senate on the same ticket as Hughes, won by 300,000 votes. The Progressive Republicans had won the Senate nomination and control of the party in the state, and Hughes paid the price for his apparent neglect of them. Hiram Johnson formally endorsed Hughes, but he Progressives as a whole did not engage in a major effort to get out the vote for Hughes.

Returning to the private practice of law in New York, Hughes's major political activities from 1917 to 1920 were confined to his support for U.S. adherence to a modified League of Nations and a protest of the expulsion of five Socialists from the New York State legislature. As secretary of state under Warren Harding and Calvin Coolidge from 1921 to 1925, Hughes took the initiative in adapting American policies to the postwar world. Usually he formulated his policy choices and then presented them to the president for approval. Philosophically he was guided by a view of the world that suggested reason governs human affairs and is progressively embodied in customs and laws. Traditional notions of American national interest—isolationism, the Monroe Doctrine, the Open Door, and the territorial integrity of China—provided guidance for his policies toward various regions of the world. But where there were no clear precedents, he could strike out on his own. Tactically, he showed considerable finesse in his dealings with a Senate suspicious of the new League of Nations and hesitant to embrace even diplomatic negotiations with former allies. Avoiding some of the mistakes he had made as governor, Hughes wooed senators who might come over to his side. Sometimes he cut around the Congress, and on rare occasions, when he had public opinion strongly behind him, he would confront that body.

In his policies toward Europe, Hughes followed an approach of enlightened isolationism. Rejecting any permanent alliances with European powers, he nevertheless used diplomatic means to resolve problems resulting from World War I. The Treaty of Berlin (1921) was negotiated to bring a formal end to the war between the United States and Germany. A German-American Claims Commission was established to settle American claims against Germany arising out of the war. The Dawes Plan, which Hughes played a central role in bringing to fruition, provided a means for the Allies to repay their war debts. Germany was given a large private loan, the Reichsbank was organized under Allied supervision, and a schedule for German reparations payments was drawn up.

Hughes had greater difficulty in coming to terms with the existence of the Soviet Union. Insisting that the United States would not recognize the Soviet government until such time as it unambiguously recognized the rights of private property, free labor, and the sanctity of contract, his policies set an unfortunate precedent. In extending nonrecognition policies to a major power it found noxious, the United States impeded its abilities to deal directly with influential actors on the world scene.

Hughes's major accomplishments were in the field of arms control and Far Eastern policies. His dramatic speech at the opening session of the Washington Conference on the Limitation of Arms signaled U.S. commitment to bringing about an end to the world naval race then under way. As chief negotiator for the United States, he brought to fruition the Five-Power Naval Treaty (United States, Great Britain, Japan, France, Italy), which provided for the limitation of capital ship strength of the major naval powers at a ratio freezing the status quo. In Article Nineteen of that treaty, the powers also agreed that they would not fortify any of their possessions in the Pacific. In the Four-Power Treaty, the United States, Great Britain, Japan, and France recognized one another's rights to their insular possessions and dominions in the Pacific and agreed to consult should any threat to that status quo arise. In the Nine-Power Treaty, Hughes also obtained, for the first time in treaty form, an international commitment to traditional American policies for the Far East. In their relations with China, the signatories agreed to respect the principles of the Open Door and territorial integrity of China.

Critics have noted that the Washington Conference treaties did not suffice to contain Japanese imperialist expansionism in the 1930s. Yet it can be argued that Hughes accomplished as much as was possible, given the political circumstances in which he was operating. Japan legally could build its auxiliary craft because there had been no agreement to limit such arms. But Hughes's attempts to limit such craft at the Washington Conference had foundered on France's insistence on a submarine capability that the other nations would

not accept. Article Nineteen of the Naval Agreement set a legal framework in which Japan could assert its naval superiority in the Pacific West of Hawaii, but Congress in the 1920s was not willing to increase U.S. fortification of Guam and the Philippines. Contrary to Hughes's advice, the United States did not even maintain its naval strength at the level permitted by the Washington treaty. The Four-Power Treaty was merely an agreement to consult, not a guarantee of the status quo in the Pacific. But it did enable Great Britain to back out of its alliance with Japan gracefully. Moreover, given the attitudes of the U.S. Senate and the prevailing political climate in the country, no stronger guarantee could have been given. As it was, various senators raised objections to the Four-Power Treaty as a form of alliance, and it passed the Senate only after a specific reservation had been inserted that the treaty involved "no commitment to armed force . . . no obligation to join in any defense."

In his dealings with Latin America, Hughes resisted any attempts to multilateralize interpretations of the Monroe Doctrine. The doctrine of the two spheres, moreover, was evident in his earlier insistence on a special reservation protecting the American system from peaceful settlement efforts in the League of Nations. Although U.S. interventions in the Caribbean were justified on the grounds of national security and a broader moral responsibility, and U.S. troops remained in Haiti, withdrawals from Nicaragua and Santo Domingo were negotiated during Hughes's terms of office; and though Hughes insisted on the protection of American property rights as a condition for any U.S. recognition of the Obregón government in Mexico, he never considered any form of military involvement in that country.

For Hughes, American leadership in the Western Hemisphere brought responsibilities as well as rights. As an alternative to League of Nations action, he offered the services of the United States as a peacemaker. Hughes helped settle disputes between Panama and Costa Rica (1921); Honduras, Nicaragua, and El Salvador (1922); Brazil, Colombia, and Peru (1925); and Peru and Chile (1922–1925). He also sought to breathe life into the principle of hemispheric unity associated with Pan-Americanism. His efforts contributed to the passage in 1921 of the treaty negotiated by Wilson to pay Colombia $25 million for the Panama Canal Zone. In a treaty with Cuba (1924), all U.S. claims to the Isle of Pines were renounced.

Hughes's orientation toward the new world order was a reflection of his views about the nature of the historical process and the political climate in which he operated. His failure to seek U.S. entry into the League of Nations was the result of the domestic political climate of the time and his own intellectual reservations about Article 10 of the League of Nations Covenant. He saw the guarantee to the territorial status quo in that article as creating a legal commitment that was too far removed from the actual practice of states. Gradually, Hughes and the State Department finally came to recognize the League as a corporate entity, and unofficial observers were sent to League meetings in which the United States had an interest.

Hughes's support for U.S. adherence to the World Court Protocol was based on his assumption that the Court, unlike the League, would not require radical changes in national behavior. William E. Borah and several other senators, however, attached a reservation to the document that would have given the United States a veto over Court advisory opinions. The condition killed the project. When President Coolidge made an absolute commitment to that condition, it ended all possibility of U.S. adherence to the World Court.

After his return to private life in 1925, Hughes continued to promote what he called the "institutions of peace." He headed the U.S. delegation to the Sixth Pan-American Conference at Havana in 1928 and in a follow-up conference at Washington negotiated a treaty in which several Latin American nations agreed to compulsory arbitration of all differences that were not resolved by diplomacy and were judicial in their nature. For political questions, another treaty provided for conciliation arrangements.

In 1930 President Herbert Hoover nominated Hughes to serve as chief justice of the U.S. Supreme Court. Several Progressives opposed his nomination on the grounds that his legal representation of corporate interests ill suited him to the times. His appointment was approved by a Senate vote of 52 to 26.

For the next ten years Hughes led the Court into an increasingly active use of the Bill of Rights to protect personal liberties. Earlier, as an associate justice of the Supreme Court, he had joined Oliver Wendell Holmes (1841–1935) in dissents in several civil liberties cases. In the 1930s the Court adopted the "selective incorporation" theory in which the states, under the due process clause of the Fourteenth Amendment, were bound to recognize certain basic rights guaranteed in the Bill of Rights. These included freedom of press (*Near v. Minnesota ex rel. Olsen*, 1931), religion (*Hamilton v. Regents of University of California*, 1934), and assembly (*De Jonge v. Oregon*, 1936). In the Scottsboro cases, Hughes argued that defendants in capital cases have the right to counsel (*Powell v. Alabama*, 1932) and the right to a trial from which black people have not been systematically excluded (*Norris v. Alabama*, 1935).

As chief justice, Hughes also played a key role, albeit after some hesitation, in adapting constitutional doctrine to political demands for greater governmental intervention in the economy. At first the Court invalidated several of the more hastily drawn New Deal measures. A section of the National Industrial Recovery Act was knocked down by an 8 to 1 vote on the grounds that it constituted an unconstitutional delegation of power to the president (*Panama Refining Co. v. Ryan*, 1935). In May 1935 Hughes led a unanimous court in striking down three New Deal measures: the National Industrial Recovery Act (*Schechter Poultry Corp. v. United States*), the Frazier-Lemke Act providing for relief of farm debtors (*Louisville Joint Stock Land Bank v. Radford*), and the Federal Home Owner's Loan Act of 1933 (*Hopkins Federal Savings &*

Loan Assn. v. Cleary). In his opinion in the *Schechter Poultry* case, Hughes argued that the NIRA was based on an unconstitutional delegation of power to the chief executive. The federal government, moreover, could not regulate local transactions, except insofar as those activities had a direct (as contrasted to an indirect) effect on interstate commerce. In another case, *Humphrey's Executor v. the United States* (1935), the Court ruled that the president could not remove a member of a regulatory commission unless Congress gave him authority to do so.

These decisions were followed by several more controversial opinions and split votes. Hughes and Owen J. Roberts, at the center of the Court, were able to assemble majorities by shifting either to join four members on the right (Willis Van Devanter, James C. McReynolds, George Gutherland, Pierce Butler) or the three on the Left (Benjamin Cardozo, Harlan Stone, and Louis Brandeis). In 1936 Hughes and Roberts joined the conservatives in declaring the Agricultural Adjustment Act (1933) unconstitutional (*United States v. Butler*) on the grounds that the provision for governmental control of acreage was an improper extension of governmental power under the general welfare clause of the Constitution. This same coalition rejected the Guffey Bituminous Coal Conservation Act of 1935 on constitutional grounds (*Carter v. Carter Coal Co.*, 1936). In a separate opinion, Hughes noted that the provisions regarding labor were invalid because of the broad delegation of legislative power, though he differed with others in finding the price-fixing section of the act inoffensive.

Hughes also played a role in the defeat of Franklin Roosevelt's Court Reorganization Plan of 1937. The president's proposal would have permitted the appointment of a possible six new justices (for every one over seventy who refused to retire). Though the effort was clearly a measure to save the New Deal by changing the makeup of the Court, the president's public rationale was that the change was needed to help the Court meet its workload. In a letter to the Senate Judiciary Committee, Hughes countered that rationale, indicating that the Court was not behind in its work. It was a devastating blow to the Roosevelt proposal. Robert H. Jackson, one of the president's aides in the Court fight, later noted that Hughes's letter "did more than any one thing to turn the tide in the Court struggle."

Earlier, Hughes had warned in his writings that a Court out of tune with broad trends in public opinion could inflict injuries on itself. Certainly, the Court's tendency to set up an arena in which neither the national government nor the states could act was of concern to him. As an associate justice he had supported an Oregon minimum wage law. As chief justice he dissented when the Court struck down New York's minimum wage law for women. Freedom of contract, he argued, could not override all attempts at state regulation, especially when one side had no real bargaining power (*Morehead v. New York ex rel. Tipaldo*, 1936). Moreover, he understood that even national authority must evolve in response to deeper changes in public opinion. In 1935 he upheld the government's right to forbid payment of public and private debts in gold (*Norman v. Baltimore & Ohio Railroad Co.*; *Nortz v. United States*). He also wrote a strong dissent to the Court's opinion striking down the Railroad Retirement Act that had provided for a compulsory retirement and pension system for railway employees. (*R.R. Retirement Board v. Alton R.R. Co.*, 1935). The power of the U.S. Congress to regulate interstate commerce, he wrote, "implies a broad discretion."

In the spring of 1937 Hughes led the Court into the switch that would avoid a constitutional crisis. One week after his letter to the Judiciary Committee was made public, Hughes presided over the Court when it sustained a Washington State minimum wage law (*West Coast Hotel Co. v. Parrish*). In this case, Roberts made the shift, though Hughes's arguments in the Tipaldo case may have convinced him to do so. The next week the Court, in a 5 to 4 decision, upheld the establishment of the National Labor Relations Board (*NLRB v. Jones and Laughlin Steel Corp*). In the next three years Hughes voted with the majority to uphold the constitutionality of other New Deal measures such as the Social Security Act of 1935, the Public Utilities Act of 1935, the Bituminous Coal Act of 1937, the revised Agricultural Adjustment Act, and the Fair Labor Standards Act of 1938.

Scholars have differed as to whether or not Hughes had actually shifted his legal doctrine at this time. Merlo J. Pusey contends that the difference in Hughes's opinions was a result of the fact that the Court was dealing with different laws. Most had been written so as to avoid some of the constitutional issues apparent in the earliest cases. Alpheus Mason, however, argues that in *NLRB v. Jones and Laughlin Steel Corp.* Hughes did change the interpretation of the interstate commerce clause he had offered in the *Schechter Poultry* and *Guffey Coal Act* cases. From a nearly absolute distinction between direct and indirect effects on interstate commerce, he came to the view that the distinction was a matter of degree. In the *Guffey Coal Act* case, for example, Hughes had argued that only commerce directly related to interstate commerce could be regulated, and he declared that the Tenth Amendment was a barrier to the exercise of national power. In upholding the establishment of the NLRB, however, he argued that the power of Congress to regulate interstate commerce is not limited to those transactions that can be deemed essential to the flow of interstate or foreign commerce. National corporations organized on a national scale cannot turn their labor relations into a forbidden area in which Congress may not enter.

Hughes's shift can best be understood in terms of his broader philosophic orientation. Law, as he saw it, must evolve if it is to meet changing conditions in society. If the Court sets itself up as a barrier to broad and deep trends in public opinion, it undermines its credibility as an institution of government. Yet changes in Court doctrine should occur through the reinterpreta-tion of precedents rather than by overruling them. Otherwise, the Court's opinions would lack legitimacy. His opinion in the *Jones and Laughlin Steel* case can best be seen as a reinterpretation of the law along these lines.

Whether adapting to new conditions or preserving its integrity against radical change, Hughes was concerned that the Court act in ways so that it appeared to be above ordinary political passions. As chief justice he tried to secure strong majorities for controversial decisions. The early decision overthrowing such New Deal measures as the National Recovery Act and the first Agricultural Adjustment Act were unanimous or near-unanimous decisions. To increase the credibility of the Court's decisions, he also assigned opinions to members of the Court who might at first glance seem to be philosophically opposed to the decision at hand. He assigned the opinions in at least three cases striking down New Deal measures to liberal members of the Court.

Hughes resigned from the Supreme Court in July 1941. He died in Cape Cod, Massachusetts.

In some respects Hughes was a puzzling individual. His personality and world view created problems for him as a politician. Extraordinarily disciplined and suspicious of strong emotions, he was inclined to ignore the role of passion and pride in politics. His view that reason had been incorporated in American political institutions made it difficult for him to understand political groups that felt the rules did not really reflect their concerns. Yet his personal qualities contributed to his success as a member of the Supreme Court. His idea that institutions do evolve in accord with rational principles provided an ideal framework for interpreting the law. His intellectual brilliance made his arguments persuasive. His personal integrity contributed to his credibility as a neutral participant in the legal process. Perhaps the lasting testament to his career came from Judge Learned Hand at the time of Hughes's retirement: "The Court will look back to him as one of its greatest figures."

• Hughes's papers are at the Library of Congress in Washington, D.C. In 1933–1934 William C. Beerits, under Hughes's direction, provided a guide to the collection as well as a brief overview of his career. The Oral History Collection at Columbia University includes interviews with individuals affiliated with Hughes in New York politics and the Department of State. For collections of Hughes's speeches and works by him see *Public Papers of Charles E. Hughes, Governor* (4 vols., 1908–1910); *Addresses and Papers of Charles Evans Hughes, 1906–16*, with an introduction by Jacob Gould Schurman (1916); *Condition of Progress in Democratic Government* (1910); *Our Relations to the Nations of the Western Hemisphere* (1928); *The Permanent Court of International Justice* (1930); *The Pathway of Peace: Representative Addresses Delivered during His Term as Secretary of State, 1921–25* (1925); *Pan American Peace Plans* (1929); and *The Supreme Court of the United States: Its Foundation, Methods and Achievements; an Interpretation* (1928).

A major biography is Merlo J. Pusey, *Charles Evans Hughes* (1951). Betty Glad, *Charles Evans Hughes and the Illusions of Innocence* (1966), focuses more on the shaping of

Hughes's character and world view and the impact of these factors on his early political career and his conduct of foreign policy. For specialized works on various phases of his career see Robert F. Wesser, *Charles Evans Hughes: Politics and Reform in New York, 1905–06* (1967); William L. Ransom, *Charles E. Hughes, The Statesman, as Shown in the Opinions of the Jurist* (1916); S. D. Lovell, *The Presidential Election of 1916* (1980); Alpheus Thomas Mason, *The Supreme Court: From Taft to Burger*, 3d ed. (1979); and Samuel Hendel, *Charles Evans Hughes and the Supreme Court* (1951). An obituary is in the *New York Times*, 28 Aug. 1948.

BETTY GLAD

HUGHES, Christopher, Jr. (11 Feb. 1786–18 Sept. 1849), diplomat, was born in Baltimore, Maryland, the son of Christopher Hughes, Sr., a merchant, and Margaret Saunderson. Having attended preparatory schools in Annapolis, he entered the College of New Jersey (now Princeton University) in January 1803 and received legal degrees there in 1805 and 1809. However, Hughes displayed little interest in pursuing law and instead entered politics. He joined the political circle of Baltimore's influential Republican senator, Samuel Smith, and, despite his reputation as a dilettante, he became a trusted aide. It was in this capacity that Hughes met and fell in love with Laura Sophia Smith, the senator's daughter. Despite their affiliation, Smith regarded his prospective son-in-law as a ne'er-do-well who was unfit to join the family. The two married over family objections. They had three children. Hughes then endured a period of political ostracism, broken only by the onset of war with England in June 1812.

For several months Hughes found employment as a captain of militia artillery at Fort McHenry. He also applied to the Madison administration for an appointment to the federal government. President James Madison, who was acquainted with Hughes and favorably impressed, proffered the post of secretary of the forthcoming mission to negotiate peace with England on 2 February 1814. Congress quickly assented, and, accompanied by Henry Clay and Jonathan Russell, Hughes departed New York aboard the USS *John Adams* for Europe.

Hughes tarried several weeks in London and Göteborg, Sweden, before joining John Quincy Adams and Albert Gallatin in Ghent, Belgium. Throughout arduous negotiations with British ministers, he deciphered State Department communiqués, made fair copies of diplomatic documents, and attended to related administrative matters. Hughes acquitted himself well in these duties and enjoyed his exposure to the rigors and nuances of international diplomacy. Both Clay and Adams made particularly strong impressions on him; they became lifelong friends and political allies. Peace was successfully concluded on 24 December 1814, and Hughes was entrusted to take a copy of the treaty to Washington for ratification. Poor weather detained him until after the arrival of Henry Carroll with a duplicate copy, but Clay and Adams relayed their approval of Hughes's performance to Secretary of State

James Monroe. Hughes returned to Baltimore in the spring of 1814 with a measure of public celebrity.

Hughes's newfound reputation led to partial reconciliation with his father-in-law, who encouraged him to enter politics. In July 1815 he gained election to the Maryland General Assembly, representing Baltimore. He served only one term, however, before Monroe appointed him as special agent to resolve an incident in Cartagena, New Granada (Colombia). Spanish authorities there had seized several vessels and crews from Baltimore for technical violations of a paper blockade. On 6 June 1816 Hughes conferred with the governor-general and arranged for the release of fifteen captives. Consequently, Monroe rewarded Hughes with appointment as the secretary to the American legation in Stockholm, Sweden. He reported for duty in April 1817 and for two years fulfilled the mundane but essential duties of his post. Hughes then succeeded Jonathan Russell there as chargé d'affaires in June 1819 and spent several years facilitating settlement of American claims against the Swedish government. He was also diligent in befriending foreign dignitaries and passing along political information to superiors in Washington.

In 1825 Hughes requested transfer to a warmer climate to preserve his wife's health, and Adams, now president, arranged for his appointment as a chargé to the court of the Netherlands. Concurrently he was dispatched as a special agent to Denmark to settle claims of American merchants against that government and to request appointment of a U.S. consul on the island of St. Thomas. Hughes succeeded on both counts, and in 1828 Adams nominated him for promotion to full minister. However, Congress was then engaged in cost-cutting measures and refused to elevate the level of representation at The Hague. Hughes resumed his activities as chargé in competent, if undramatic, fashion and concluded the assignment in 1828.

In 1829 a new president, Andrew Jackson, reassigned Hughes to his old position in Stockholm. For the next twelve years he successfully addressed a number of trade and commerce issues between the two nations. In 1832 his wife died, but Hughes continued conducting himself with his usual good humor and dignity. In 1842 the State Department shifted him back to the Netherlands, where he remained for three years. In 1845 President James K. Polk effectively ended Hughes's diplomatic career by recalling him in favor of a political supporter, Auguste Davezac. Hughes then lived in retirement in Baltimore, where he died.

Hughes was an effective diplomat who labored more than three decades promoting and safeguarding U.S. interests in northern Europe. Although he never attained the coveted rank of full minister and never negotiated a treaty, his competent handling of claims and trade disputes did much to promote goodwill and harmonious relationships.

• Hughes's official correspondence is in the National Archives, Records of the Department of State, Foreign Service

Posts, RG 84. Collections of his personal letters are in the Clements Library at the University of Michigan; the Henry Clay Papers at the Library of Congress, Manuscript Division; the William H. Smith Papers at the Ohio Historical Society; the Adams Family Papers at the Massachusetts Historical Society; and the William H. Crawford Papers in the Perkins Library at Duke University. For materials located abroad consult John W. Raimo, *A Guide to Manuscripts Relating to America in Great Britain and Ireland* (1979). See also Chester G. Dunham, "Christopher Hughes, Jr., at Ghent," *Maryland Historical Magazine* 66 (Fall 1971): 288–99; Jesse S. Reeves, "A Diplomat Glimpses Parnassus: Excerpts from the Correspondence of Christopher Hughes," *Michigan Alumnus* 41, no. 1 (1934): 189–201; and Emily Stone Whiteley, "Between the Acts at Ghent," *Virginia Quarterly Review* 5 (Jan. 1929): 18–30. A biographical treatment is Dunham, "The Diplomatic Career of Christopher Hughes" (Ph.D. diss., Ohio State Univ., 1968), and additional information is in Brynjolf J. Houde, *Diplomatic Relations between the United States and Sweden* (1921). A detailed obituary is in the *Baltimore Patriot and Commercial Gazette*, 18 Sept. 1849.

JOHN C. FREDRIKSEN

HUGHES, Emmet John (26 Dec. 1920–19 Sept. 1982), journalist, author, and government official, was born in Newark, New Jersey, the son of John L. Hughes, a Union County (N.J.) judge, and Grace Freeman. Reared in Summit, New Jersey, he attended Princeton University, where he was a member of Phi Beta Kappa and was graduated *summa cum laude* in 1941. His senior honors thesis was expanded into a book and published as *The Church and the Liberal Society* in 1944.

After graduation from Princeton, Hughes received a fellowship from Columbia University, where he studied under Professor Carlton J. H. Hayes in the history department. Hughes's graduate career was interrupted in 1942 when Hayes was appointed ambassador to Spain and invited Hughes to be his press attaché. While serving at the American embassy in Madrid, Hughes enlisted in the U.S. Army as a private in the Office of Strategic Services and was appointed to the Office of War Information. After the war he remained in Spain until 1946. His second book, *Report from Spain*, a study of Spanish life under the dictatorship of Francisco Franco, was published the following year.

While in Spain, Hughes came to the attention of Time-Life, Inc., and soon joined the Henry Luce publishing concern. From 1947 to 1948 he was Time-Life bureau chief in Rome. He then moved to Berlin, where he served as bureau chief from 1948 to 1949. That same year he was appointed articles editor for *Life* magazine in New York City.

In 1952 Hughes took a leave of absence from *Life* and joined the Republican presidential campaign of Dwight D. Eisenhower as a speech writer. Hughes's speeches, which William Bragg Ewald claimed turned Eisenhower's thoughts and ideas into "fused vibrant rhetoric," were some of the most noteworthy of the campaign. They included the famous speech in which Eisenhower was to denounce Senator Joseph McCarthy's red-baiting tactics as well as defend General George C. Marshall from charges that he was a Communist. At the behest of Wisconsin politicians, however, Hughes's text defending Marshall was deleted before Eisenhower gave the speech, and the cut resulted in controversy. The criticisms of McCarthy were also cut, but the press was given copies of the speech containing the critical passages. Near the end of the campaign, Hughes wrote the speech in which Eisenhower declared, "I shall go to Korea." Given in the midst of negotiations over the Korean war stalemate, the speech was a huge success. Coming just days before election day, it helped propel Eisenhower to victory.

After Eisenhower became president, Hughes began working in the new administration as an assistant to the president with primary responsibilities as a speech writer. He helped draft Eisenhower's first inaugural address as well as "The Chance for Peace" speech delivered in 1953 at the American Society of Newspaper Editors meeting in Washington. Scholars have since given high marks to the speech for its foresight and its attempt to forestall the nuclear arms buildup. By September 1953, Hughes, who claimed that he had never intended to stay on past the election, had returned to Time-Life as special European correspondent.

In 1956 Hughes returned briefly to aid in Eisenhower's reelection campaign, once again as a speech writer. After Eisenhower won the election, Hughes considered remaining with the administration. He hoped to play an operational role in foreign affairs as a policy adviser, but Secretary of State John Foster Dulles would not permit him to take a major position in the State Department. As a result, in 1957 Hughes left the administration and returned to its service only occasionally to spruce up a speech.

Hughes's desire for a State Department position and Dulles's blockage of his aims evolved into two books critical of Dulles and Eisenhower. The first, *America the Vincible* (1959), criticized the direction of American foreign policy during Eisenhower's second term and was particularly critical of the role played by Dulles. The second and more widely read book was *The Ordeal of Power: A Political Memoir of the Eisenhower Years* (1963), an account of the internal workings of the Eisenhower administration published two years after the president left office. Based on Hughes's diary entries while working for the administration, the book describes his frustrations with the president and others in the administration and sums up its success as "so modest an achievement in so crucial a cause" (p. 142). The now-common practice of presidential aides publishing inside descriptions of an administration was unheard of in 1963. *The Ordeal of Power* thus gained notoriety because it was the first political memoir to describe in a critical fashion the inner workings of a presidential administration. Not surprisingly, Hughes became persona non grata with Eisenhower and other administration officials. Otherwise, the critical response to the book was good, and it enhanced Hughes's reputation, although historians now see it as flawed.

After leaving the White House, Hughes returned to Time-Life and remained with the company until 1960. He then joined the Rockefeller family as a policy adviser, a position he held until 1963, and simultaneously served as a special assistant to New York governor Nelson Rockefeller. From 1963 to 1970 Hughes was a columnist and editorial consultant for *Newsweek*.

In 1968 Hughes joined Rockefeller's unsuccessful presidential campaign and remained as an aide to the governor until 1970. He then joined the Eagleton Institute at Rutgers University, where he continued to write and taught classes. Hughes's final book, *The Living Presidency: Resources and Dilemmas of the American Presidential Office*, was published in 1973. A study of how character and public perception shape American leaders, the book appeared just as the nation was entering the throes of the Watergate scandal.

Hughes was married three times, first to Marifrances Hughes, with whom he had one child, then to Eileen Lanouette, with whom he had two children, and then to Katherine Nouri, with whom he also had two children. The first two marriages ended in divorce. He died in Princeton, New Jersey.

• The papers of Emmet John Hughes are in the Seely G. Mudd Library at Princeton University. Most information on Hughes is associated with the presidential administration of Dwight Eisenhower. Among the useful secondary sources are Stephen E. Ambrose's two-volume biography, *Eisenhower: Soldier, General of the Army, President-Elect, 1890–1952* (1983) and *Eisenhower: The President* (1984); William Bragg Ewald, Jr., *Eisenhower the President, Crucial Days: 1951–1960* (1981); and Townsend Hoopes, *The Devil and John Foster Dulles* (1973). Reaction to *The Ordeal of Power* can be found in Henry Brandon, "Witness in the White House," *Saturday Review*, 16 Mar. 1963, pp. 85–86, and Richard Rovere, "Tales Out of School," *New Yorker*, 16 Mar. 1963, pp. 195–204. Obituaries are in the *New York Times* and the *Washington Post*, both 21 Sept. 1982.

MARK E. YOUNG

HUGHES, Hatcher (12 Feb. 1881–17 Oct. 1945), dramatist, was born Harvey Hatcher Hughes in Polkville, Cleveland County, North Carolina, the son of Andrew Jackson Hughes and Martha Gold, farmers. He was educated in a typical rural mountain schoolhouse, and while visiting his relatives during vacations he learned the dialects that undoubtedly influenced the language of some of his later dramas. After graduating from high school in Grover, North Carolina, Hughes worked at several jobs (including writing for newspapers) to earn money for college. In 1901 he entered the University of North Carolina, earning his A.B. in 1907. During his college years Hughes belonged to literary clubs, wrote for campus publications, served as editor of the yearbook, and became an instructor of English in his senior year. He continued his studies at North Carolina, receiving his M.A. in 1909. He then left for Columbia University with the intention of earning a doctorate, but he abandoned this plan when he was appointed as a lecturer there in 1910. At Columbia Hughes instituted a course in practical playwriting and organized the Morningside Players, directing many of their productions.

During World War I, Hughes served as a captain in the army and saw action as a member of the American Expeditionary Force in France. Upon his return to Columbia, he continued to teach classes that were well received. Hughes was also active in theater affairs, serving at one time as chairman of the National Council on Freedom from Censorship. In 1928 he was made an assistant professor and served in that capacity until his death.

Hughes wrote his first play, *A Marriage Made in Heaven*, in 1918; it was produced in 1927 with the title *Honeymooning*. His first produced play, *Wake Up, Jonathan* (1921), written in collaboration with Elmer Rice, told of strategems employed by a clever wife to bring about a reconciliation with her husband. It had originally been written as a vehicle for actor David Warfield, but it was later revised for the well-known actress Minnie Maddern Fiske. The play was characterized in the *New York Times* as a "fair-to-middling whimsey" but it enjoyed two successful seasons with Fiske in the starring role.

Hughes's *Hell-Bent fer Heaven* (1924) was much more enthusiastically received. This play was based on impressions from Hughes's youth and on fresh observations made from vacations in the early 1920s, during which Hughes hiked through the North Carolina mountains and mingled with the local people. It dealt with religious fanaticism among the southern Appalachian people, and it corresponded well with the strong interests in folk drama that existed during the 1920s. Alexander Woolcott in the *Sun* described it as a "capitally acted and intensely interesting comedy of the Blue Ridge mountains," and John Corbin in the *New York Times* praised it as "one of the most original and vividly colored pieces in the contemporary drama." Other critics commented that the play's structure was faulty and that it was at times overlong, but on the whole the reviews were good to excellent. The play ran for 122 performances on Broadway, and it was awarded the Pulitzer Prize on 11 May 1924, the day after it closed. The circumstances surrounding the prize were somewhat controversial; the Pulitzer Drama Jury had selected George Kelly's comedy, *The Show-Off*, but Professor Brander Matthews of Columbia wrote to the president of the Pulitzer Advisory Board to protest this decision and recommend *Hell-Bent fer Heaven*. The jury's decision was reversed by the board amid accusations of undue influence by the Columbia University faculty favoring one of its own.

Hughes's next drama was *Ruint* (1925), a comedy in which the mountain people take revenge on a northern visitor believed to have "ruint" a local girl, when in fact he had only kissed her. It was reviewed in the *New York Times* as "less of an achievement dramatically than *Hell-Bent fer Heaven* . . . but its material is alive and promising." Less successful were the three farcical comedies that followed: *Honeymooning* (1927), which the author referred to as "a silly play for serious people" that portrays newlyweds who learn that their marriage is not legal; *It's a Grand Life* (1930), a study of a self-satisfied woman who ignores problems around her, written in collaboration with Alan Williams and again starring Fiske; and *The Lord Blesses the Bishop* (1934), a farce about paternity out of wedlock, which the *New York Times* described as "not up to the author's best." Hughes married Janet Ranney Cool in 1930; they had one child. Shortly before his death, he completed an unnamed comedy about contemporary life.

Hughes is best remembered as a professor of drama and for his folk plays *Ruint* and, particularly, *Hell-Bent fer Heaven*. These two plays overshadow the lighter farcical comedies, which are described as unsuccessful by most reviewers and biographers. Hughes died at his home in New York City.

• Hughes's papers, which include letters to his mother (1917–1924) and a brief biographical sketch, are in the Southern Historical Collection at the University of North Carolina, Chapel Hill. *A History of the Pulitzer Prize Plays* (1967) contains information about the controversy surrounding his award. An obituary is in the *New York Times*, 20 Oct. 1945.

ANN S. PERKINS

HUGHES, Howard (24 Dec. 1905–5 Apr. 1976), aviator, manufacturer, and film producer, was born Howard Robard Hughes, Jr., in Houston, Texas, the son of Howard Robard Hughes, a mining engineer, and Allene Gano. Hughes was three years old when his father devised a drilling bit that revolutionized oil drilling, resulting in a great profit for his tool company. While his parents were gregarious socialites, Hughes as a boy was quiet and introspective, showing little interest in school other than a leaning toward mathematics and an ability to build things with wires and scraps of metal. Greatly attached to his devoted mother, he stood in awe of his personable father. Those who came to know him years later claim that Hughes never considered himself his equal. At the age of fourteen, Hughes was enrolled in the Fessenden School in West Newton, Massachusetts. During a vacation at home his mother denied him a motorcycle, believing it to be unsafe. He then turned his bicycle into a motorized vehicle by using parts from a car starter and batteries. On another occasion, when his father promised him he could have his choice of present, Hughes chose a ride in a flying boat. With that he discovered the joy of aviation, a joy that soon became obsessive.

The Hughes drilling bit had a profound effect on the American oil industry. Spending more and more of their time in California, Hughes's parents sent him to the Thacher School in Ojai, some seventy miles northwest of Los Angeles, in September 1921. Hughes's uncle Rupert Hughes was a leading scenarist in Hollywood, and through him the family became acquainted with the upper strata of Hollywood society. Tragedy struck in the spring of 1922 when his mother died after surgery. Father and son returned to Houston, where Hughes, Sr., was stricken with a fatal heart attack while conducting a sales meeting in 1924. The loss of his parents in the prime of their lives had a profound

effect on the lonely, withdrawn Hughes. At the age of eighteen Hughes began to be a hypochondriac, fearful of death and panicky about germs. A student at the Rice Institute in Houston at the time, he decided to end his education and enter the world of business. Not content with inheriting 75 percent of his father's business assets, he bought out the other 25 percent dispersed among relatives. The agreements with his relatives were bitterly arrived at and caused a permanent rift, one that seemed to bother Hughes very little. He declared that in order to take command it was necessary to be tough with people, and it was an attitude from which he never wavered.

With no liking for the administrative side of business, Hughes hired men who knew how to operate with little direction from him. His judgment was sound and the company prospered, leaving him to indulge his fascination with a Houston socialite, Ella Rice, whom he married in 1925. They settled in Los Angeles, where Hughes set about becoming a film producer.

Hughes was a man impossible to advise. He did whatever he wanted. His first film, *Swell Hogan*, was so bad that it was never released, but he did better with his next, *Everybody's Acting* (1926), and with *Two Arabian Knights* (1927), directed by Lewis Milestone and starring William Boyd. It brought Milestone an Academy Award for best comedy director. Hughes's next films, *The Mating Call* and *The Racket* (both 1928), did well enough to inspire him to undertake an epic about aviation in World War I—*Hell's Angels*, which was two and a half years in production. Hughes spent lavishly buying airplanes and hiring pilots, virtually operating his own little air force in the San Fernando Valley. The cost ran to $4 million, an astonishing sum for its time, and Hughes ended up with 300 times as much footage as the film needed. Released in the summer of 1930, during a time of national depression, the film was well received but took a long time to recover its costs.

Among the costs was Hughes's marriage. Ella Rice Hughes returned to Houston, claiming it was impossible to be married to a man who was obsessed with his work and seldom home. Hughes then fell in love with actress Billie Dove and starred her in his next two films, *The Age for Love* and *Cock of the Air*, both made in 1931. Neither was successful, nor was the romance with Dove, which proved to be the first in a long line of affairs with actresses. Hughes returned to World War I aviation with *Sky Devils* (1931), starring Spencer Tracy, but it failed to come close to the merits of *Hell's Angels*. He did far better with *The Front Page* (1931) and *Scarface* (1932), both considered minor classics.

Hughes announced that his next film would be about zeppelins, but those who ran the Hughes Tool Company bore down on him to avoid sinking money in another film epic. He took their advice even more than they expected and turned his back on the picture business. In 1933 he founded the Hughes Aircraft Company in Glendale, California. Nine years later he relocated it to Culver City, where it grew into one of the most profitable aircraft production companies in the world.

Hughes's personal triumph as an aviator began early in 1934 when he received a trophy at the All-American Air Meet in Miami, flying a Boeing pursuit plane he had bought from the U.S. Army and turned into a racer. In September 1935 he set a new land speed record in a car he had designed, and the following January he set a new transcontinental speed record, flying from Los Angeles to Newark, New Jersey, in nine hours and twenty-seven minutes. His aerial adventures made him a popular figure in the press and on the airways, especially in 1938 when, with a remodeled twin-engine Lockheed 14 and a crew of four he flew around the world in three days, nineteen hours, and twenty-eight minutes. In May 1939 Hughes acquired stock in what later became Trans World Airlines, placing him in commercial aviation, and in the fall of that year his company began designs for new kinds of military aircraft in the event of America's possible involvement in war.

In the 1940s Hughes set up another film production company. He announced he would make a film about Billy the Kid, using unknown actors for the parts of Billy and his girlfriend. For the latter he chose nineteen-year-old Jane Russell, clearly because of her well-developed bust, a factor that caused the picture, *The Outlaw* (1943), to become a cause célèbre in film censorship. Hughes himself directed the film. After first being banned by the censors, Hughes finally received approval to show it, but he shrewdly allowed two years to go by, allowing public curiosity to build. Rightly condemned as a ludicrously bad film, *The Outlaw* nevertheless made millions for Hughes.

Much else happened during the years *The Outlaw* was in production. In 1943 he joined forces with shipbuilder Henry J. Kaiser and won a government contract to build three huge flying boats. Only one was completed, the famous Spruce Goose. The government contract for the flying boats was canceled when it became obvious they could not be completed in time for use in the war. Other contracts for planes were also canceled.

Always unusual in his habits and behavior, Hughes became ever more eccentric. He nonetheless possessed amazing luck in surviving accidents. On 7 July 1946, while on a test flight of his XF-11, the engines malfunctioned. He crashed in Beverly Hills, and the plane exploded and burned. Hughes was dragged from the wreckage with a crushed chest, collapsed lung, and broken ribs. It was doubted he would live. However, he recovered in a month and was soon flying again. Few knew that in order to tolerate his pain he had become addicted to codeine.

Despite his pain and the problems in running an aircraft corporation, Hughes again turned to the movie business, possibly because of the profits and the publicity stirred up by *The Outlaw*. He signed contracts with two famous Hollywood figures, Harold Lloyd and Preston Sturges, to produce the comedy *Mad Wednesday* (1947), but it was a flop. Then, being in love with 22-year-old Faith Domergue, he starred her in the costumed drama *Vendetta* (1948). Even Hughes realized it was bad and shelved it for two years.

Concurrent with these films Hughes had other problems, one being his compulsion to rebuild the XF-11 and prove it airworthy, which he did on a flight on 5 April 1947. Four months later he testified before the Senate War Investigating Committee, which had probed into his work as a defense contractor. Hughes had made enemies in the fiercely competitive war years, and he had not been as successful as he had hoped. Hughes Aircraft had not become the giant he had planned—that would come later, in the Space Age. Building the massive Spruce Goose brought charges it was not airworthy, which he then disproved by flying it for a few minutes above the waters of Long Beach Harbor on 2 November 1947.

Obsessive-compulsive by nature, Hughes was not a man who could accept defeat. In 1948 he bought the RKO Studios in Hollywood. He owned and managed it for five years, while maintaining his office at the Goldwyn Studios and only once setting foot on RKO property. Few of the films made during these years were financial winners, and every producer, director, and writer for RKO complained about never getting to see Hughes to discuss their problems. Eventually he said, "I need RKO like I need the plague," and he sold the studio for $25 million, $6 million of which were his after the stockholders and lawyers had been paid off.

Hughes's interests in other enterprises, especially aviation, grew during the RKO years, and his wealth amassed by the millions. It was at this time that he founded the Howard Hughes Medical Institute in Florida, stating his concern about germs and disease. He said he wanted the institute to inherit most of his wealth and accomplish something good in his name. Always a loner, he became ever more reclusive, eventually seeing almost no one other than his closest business executives. In 1957 he married actress Jean Peters, but the marriage was unconventional, with its partners seldom living together. They divorced in 1971.

Whatever his failures in marriage or in making films, Hughes's success in building jetliners and military aircraft burgeoned. However, the strain of all these endeavors caught up with him in 1958, and he suffered a nervous breakdown. He was constantly at odds with the government over his taxes, eventually leaving California and settling in Nevada. In 1967 he bought the Desert Inn in Las Vegas, to make it his home and the headquarters of his Nevada enterprises. He sold TWA in 1966 for $566 million. Four years later he bought Air West.

In November 1970 Hughes moved to the Britannia Beach Hotel on Paradise Island in the Bahamas, again to avoid taxes. He never returned to the United States; the last six years of his life were those of an itinerant exile, moving from one luxurious hotel to another. He became a total recluse, living behind closed curtains. He moved to Manangua, Nicaragua; from there on to

Vancouver; London; Freeport in the Bahamas; and finally Acapulco, Mexico. In 1972 he sold Hughes Tool Company for $150 million. The assets of his Summa Corporation, under which all of his businesses were governed, were valued at $2 billion. Despite his wealth, Hughes gave the appearance of a man living in abject poverty. In his last years he refused medical treatment and did not eat properly. He became an emaciated wreck, weighing only ninety-four pounds at the time of his death. He denied his aides the right to tend him, until he finally lapsed into unconsciousness. They then flew him to Houston, but he was dead by the time the plane landed. Howard Hughes had died in an airplane in flight, and it was in the air, and only in the air, that he felt at home. Childless, Hughes left to the world his properties and a name that has become ever more of a legend.

• Several biographies of Hughes were written during his lifetime: John Keats, *Howard Hughes* (1966); Albert B. Gerber, *Bashful Billionaire* (1967); Noah Dietrich and Bob Thomas, *Howard: The Amazing Mr. Hughes* (1972); and Joe Davenport and Todd S. J. Lawson, *The Empire of Howard Hughes* (1975). Many biographies explore Hughes's reclusiveness: Jerry Bell, *Howard Hughes: His Silence, Secrets and Success* (1976); James Phelan, *Howard Hughes, the Hidden Years* (1976); and Charles Higham, *Howard Hughes: The Secret Life* (1993). Some of the more reliable biographies written after his death are Donald L. Barlett and James B. Steele, *Empire: The Life, Legend and Madness of Howard Hughes* (1979); Michael Drosnin, *Citizen Hughes* (1985); Robert Maheu with Richard Hack, *Next to Hughes: Behind the Power and Tragic Downfall of Howard Hughes* (1992); and Mark Hurwitz, *Howard Hughes' Final Years* (1977). Many book-length treatments focus on one or another of the complex events and rumors surrounding Hughes's character, life, and death: Omar V. Garrison, *Howard Hughes in Las Vegas* (1970); Stephen Fay et al., *Hoax: The Inside Story of the Howard Hughes–Clifford Irving Affair* (1972); David B. Tinnin, *Just about Everybody vs. Howard Hughes: The Inside Story of the Hughes–TWA Trial* (1973); Stuart M. Kaminsky, *The Howard Hughes Affair* (1979); Harold Rhoden, *High Stakes: The Gamble for the Howard Hughes Will* (1980); Terry Moore, *The Beauty and the Billionaire* (1984); and Tony Thomas, *Howard Hughes in Hollywood* (1985).

TONY THOMAS

HUGHES, Howard Robard, Sr. (9 Sept. 1869–14 Jan. 1924), inventor and manufacturer, was born in Lancaster, Missouri, the son of Jean Amelia Summerlin and Felix Turner Hughes, a lawyer. The family moved to Keokuk, Iowa, about 1880, and according to his brother Rupert Hughes Howard showed a "marked genius" at an early age for taking apart clocks and small engines "to see what made them go" (Bartlett and Steele, p. 27). He was also prone to mischief and was sent to military academies in Morgan Park, Illinois, and St. Charles, Missouri. Accepted to Harvard in 1893, he dropped out in less than two years, moved home, and began studying law at the University of Iowa. Too impatient to finish the program, he took the state bar examination, passed it, and joined his father's practice. He soon found the law "too-exacting a mis-

tress" (Harvard College Class of 1897, Fourth Report, p. 218), however, and briefly was a telegraph operator before leaving Keokuk to pursue an interest in mining.

Hughes hunted for low-grade silver in the Colorado Rockies and apparently also did a little newspaper reporting while in the area. He next tried zinc mining in the Indian Territory (now Okla.), then lead mining in southwestern Missouri. "If I accomplished nothing more," Hughes recalled, "I, at least, learned something of the art of drilling wells with cable tools." He kept hoping to find a fortune "under the surface of the earth," and when news of the legendary January 1901 Spindletop oil strike in eastern Texas began to circulate, he "heard the roar in Joplin and made for the seat of disturbance." That was Beaumont, Texas, where he "turned greaser and sank into the thick of it" (*Harvard College Class of 1897, Fourth Report*, p. 219).

Like most oil speculators of the period, Hughes's luck ran both good and bad, but he loved the excitement of it all. When he ran out of supplies while drilling one of his first wells, future partner Walter Sharp loaned him what he needed, for which Hughes put up a diamond stud as collateral. Whatever money he made on successful wells in the Spindletop and Sour Lake fields was invested in leases on other plots. He lost a considerable amount when salt water ruined his wells in the Batson field and often had to turn to his father for loans to finance further exploration. During this time he also formed a partnership, dubbed the Moonshine Company, with Dallas oilmen Ed Prather and the brothers Walter Sharp and James R. Sharp. A driller recalled, "Mr. Hughes was quite a character. . . . He was energetic and full of theories and ideas" (Boatright and Owens, p. 126).

Although Hughes enjoyed the boisterous activity associated with the oil chase, he retained the polish from an upper-class background that allowed him to catch the attention of Allene Stone Gano, whose father was a prominent judge in Dallas. They married in 1904, and their $50,000 European honeymoon took all of the money Hughes had. They settled in Houston and had one son, Howard R. Hughes, Jr.

The Hugheses moved to Oil City, Louisiana, and then twenty-five miles south to Shreveport, where Hughes supported his household by working as a postmaster and deputy sheriff while he continued to search for oil. In 1907 he acquired leases in the promising Texas fields of Pierce Junction and Goose Creek, but a granite shelf that no drill bit could penetrate lay between his rigs and the potential strike.

A number of stories exist concerning the origins of the rock drill bit with which Hughes made his fortune. He and Walter Sharp were not the only ones who realized what such an invention could do for the oil industry, and several people in the Texas-Louisiana area had conceived of crude designs. Hughes and Sharp bought the rights to at least a couple of these, and Sharp gave Hughes, described by a colleague as "an excellent engineer," a reported $1,500 to come up with a workable device. Hughes left a third of the money with his wife and boarded a train for Keokuk, where he planned to work on the model while seeking patent advice from his father. Ever the tinkerer, he sat at the same kitchen table where he had once dismantled clocks and designed a bit with 166 rolling, cutting edges. His father put him in touch with Paul Bakewell, a top St. Louis patent lawyer, and on 20 November 1908 Bakewell filed the application for two patents, listing Hughes as the sole inventor.

While awaiting approval of the patents, which came on 10 August 1909, Hughes and Sharp built a prototype and tested it in a Houston warehouse. The bit cut through a ten-inch granite slab and kept going, tearing holes in the table and the concrete floor. In June they took the multiedged bit in a locked wooden box to the Goose Creek field outside of the city and sent the crew away while they put the secret device on the pipe and lowered it into the hole. Word soon circulated that the Hughes bit had penetrated fourteen feet of granite in eleven hours. Rather than just scraping the rock, the new bit ground and pulverized it with multiple turning heads. The design would revolutionize the industry.

Sharp-Hughes Tool Company opened in Houston in 1909 in a shop only twenty feet by forty feet. Within ten years their bits were drilling 75 percent of the world's oil wells. Sharp oversaw their continuing efforts at exploration, while Hughes became the primary salesman for the company's main product, on the road for a majority of the time. Interest in the device grew slowly until Hughes gained the attention of Standard Oil, which eventually had 1,500 of the rollerbits in use. Hughes and Sharp decided not to sell the bits but to lease them for $30,000 per well. In 1910 the company turned a $500,000 profit, and Hughes undertook an extensive international advertising campaign. According to his partner's son, however, Hughes "was spending money faster than the tool company could make it" (Bartlett and Steele, p. 36), living and traveling in high style. Sharp died in 1912, and three years later the business became Hughes Tool Company. Sharp's wife sold her interest in the firm to Ed Prather, whom Hughes bought out in 1918, giving him full control of the corporation.

During World War I Hughes developed a horizontal drilling machine that could be used to plant bombs under enemy trenches, but the conflict ended before production was approved. His company did, however, receive government contracts to make Stokes mortars, molds for dummy bombs, and a training device for airplane gunners.

Hughes continued to refine the rollerbit, patenting twenty-five improvements on it, and also kept experimenting with other implements for oil exploration, gaining a total of seventy-three patents during his lifetime. The advancement of the company often came at the expense of his family, though, as Hughes was rarely at home or in Houston. After his wife's death in 1922, he spent most of his time in Los Angeles, leaving his son in the care of relatives. While visiting Houston in January 1924 to check on the company, he suffered a fatal heart attack during a business meeting. Howard Hughes, Jr., inherited three-fourths of his father's estate, which, because of his father's free-spending ways, was almost entirely in stock. He bought out his uncle and grandparents four months later, giving him full control of Hughes Tool at age eighteen. He parlayed this stake into one of the world's great fortunes.

The company stayed in family hands until going public in 1972. Although it diversified and expanded, its signature product remained the drilling rollerbit in designs still operating on the same principles that Hughes had sketched out in 1908.

• An interview with Granville A. Humason, 7 July 1953, concerning the origins of the rollerbit is in the Oral History of the Texas Oil Industry Collection, tape 102, Barker Texas History Center, University of Texas, Austin. Other interviews from the same collection are published in Mody C. Boatright and William A. Owens, *Tales from the Derrick Floor: A People's History of the Oil Industry* (1970). Hughes outlined the early part of his career in *Harvard College Class of 1897, Fourth Report* (1912) and also contributed to *Harvard College Class of 1897, Twenty-fifth Anniversary Report 1897–1922* (1922). The most thorough research into his life is in biographies of his son, including Donald L. Bartlett and James B. Steele, *Empire: The Life, Legend, and Madness of Howard Hughes* (1979), and Peter Harry Brown and Pat H. Broeske, *Howard Hughes: The Untold Story* (1996). Hughes's brother Rupert Hughes discussed their early life in "My Mother," *American* (Sept. 1924), and "Howard Hughes—Record Breaker," *Liberty* 32 (6 Feb. 1937). Charles Albert Warner, *Texas Oil and Gas since 1543* (1939), has information on Hughes's role in the oil industry. Marguerite Johnston, *Houston: The Unknown City, 1836–1946* (1991), and David G. McComb, *Houston: The Bayou City* (1969), provide details on Hughes's life and operations in that city. Obituaries of Hughes are in the Houston *Chronicle* and the Houston *Post*, both 15 Jan. 1924, and *Mining and Oil Bulletin, Oil Trade Journal, Petroleum World,* and *Oil Age,* all Feb. 1924.

KENNETH H. WILLIAMS

HUGHES, John Joseph (24 Apr. 1797–3 Jan. 1864), Roman Catholic bishop, was born in County Tyrone, Ireland, the son of Patrick Hughes, a small farmer, and Margaret McKenna. In 1817 he joined his father and older brother who had immigrated to America three years earlier, settling in Chambersburg, Pennsylvania. After working several years as a day laborer, he entered Mount St. Mary's Seminary in 1820 and was ordained a priest of the Diocese of Philadelphia on 15 October 1826. He held several pastorates in the diocese and dealt firmly with lay trustees who sought a voice in the administration of the parishes. Hughes quickly became known as a preacher and a major spokesman for the Catholic church on various issues. At a time when there was a great deal of distrust of Catholics among American Protestants, Hughes endorsed Catholic emancipation in Ireland as well as Irish immigration and entered into polemics with various anti-Catholic leaders. He also founded in 1833 the *Catholic Herald* newspaper, which he later turned over to the diocese. His actions drew attention, and he was nominated for the episcopate in 1829, 1833 and 1836. In 1837 he was named coadjutor bishop of New York with the right of succession and was consecrated at old St. Patrick's Cathedral in New York City on 7 January 1838. Hughes became apostolic administrator of the see in 1839 and succeeded to the see on 20 December 1842, on the death of Bishop John Dubois. He became archbishop of New York on 19 July 1850, when it was made an archdiocese.

In the New York diocese Hughes became known for his suppression of the power of lay trustees, very much as he had done as a priest in Philadelphia. A number of Catholic parishes had adopted a corporate structure similar to that of Protestant churches, which vested ownership and control of church property in the hands of lay trustees. Policy differences between trustees and bishop often led to public clashes and litigation in civil courts. For Hughes, American democratic principles, while good for the nation, could not be applied to the internal governance of the church. Disputes over this issue lasted for the greater part of his tenure as bishop.

Hughes also engaged in often bitter polemics with prominent Protestant leaders. No matter how highly placed the figure, Hughes did not hesitate to respond to what he perceived as attacks on the church, for example, in 1843 responding to John Quincy Adams (1767–1848), who, citing the Galileo case, had attacked the Catholic church and the Jesuits as despotic. In 1844, when nativist violence threatened to spread from Philadelphia to New York, he warned municipal authorities that "If a single Catholic Church is burned in New York, the city will become a second Moscow," a not too subtle allusion to the burning of Moscow in 1812. To the mayor's concern that some Catholic churches might be burned, Hughes replied, "I am concerned that some of yours will be burned. We can protect our own." Hughes has been criticized for the level and tone of his rhetoric, but the threatened riots did not take place, and his uncompromising attitude was no doubt instrumental in avoiding the anti-Catholic violence that was prevalent in other major cities at the time.

His struggle in the 1840s with the Public School Society over the issue of teaching the Protestant faith and using the King James Version of the Bible exclusively in the public schools sped the secularization of the public schools and the movement toward the establishment of the parochial school system in the United States. After attempts at compromise initiated by his predecessor had failed, Hughes took the offensive in a series of debates, sermons, and addresses. The Public School Society promised to remove anti-Catholic slurs from textbooks, but this was not enough for Hughes. His opposition quickly denounced the Catholic church as the "enemy of Liberty." Hughes answered the attacks of Protestant ministers and prominent citizens such as Samuel F. B. Morse in kind, on one occasion at an open debate, forcing his critics to listen to a three-and-one-half-hour speech. Hughes then became involved in complicated political maneuvering that led in 1842 to the passage of legislation by the state mandating the creation of an elected board of education in New York City. In the midst of these activities, Hughes developed an acquaintance with New York Governor William H. Seward that would develop into a close friendship and provide Hughes with an entry into higher political circles. His strong stand on the school issue and his uncompromising resistance to anti-Catholic movements made him a recognized and a very controversial figure throughout the nation.

During the Mexican War (1846–1848), at the request of Secretary of State James Buchanan, Hughes assisted the federal government in providing unofficial Catholic chaplains to the U.S. forces. Due to nativist pressure, it was impossible for these chaplains to have official status. Hughes had objected to Catholic soldiers being ordered to attend Protestant services, and he was willing to accept this compromise. His help led President James K. Polk to ask him to undertake a mission to Mexico in 1846 to assure Mexican Catholics that the U.S. government was not hostile to their religion. Hughes initially accepted but then declined when he realized that Polk would not give the mission official status, without which he saw the mission as useless.

At President Abraham Lincoln's request, Hughes visited Europe in 1861–1862 in support of the Union cause. His episcopal status gave him entry into circles that were closed to the American ambassador and while in Paris he was able to plead the Union's case to a skeptical Emperor Napoleon III and Empress Eugenie. Hughes's association of abolition with Protestant divines who also attacked the Catholic church had made him lukewarm to the antislavery movement, however, and for this he was roundly criticized, especially during the Civil War. His last public appearance was a speech delivered from the balcony of his New York residence in which he urged obedience to the conscription acts and an end to the antidraft riots. He died in New York City.

During his tenure as archbishop, in 1858, Hughes began the new St. Patrick's Cathedral at Fifth Avenue and Fiftieth Street, a site then believed to be far out in the country. He introduced many religious communities into his diocese and in 1846 founded the independent New York branch of the Sisters of Charity. In 1840 he founded St. Joseph's Seminary at "Rose Hill" in the Bronx and in 1841, in the same place, established St. John's College, which later became Fordham University under Jesuit auspices. A supporter of the temporal power of the pope in the midst of the Italian Risorgimento, he also was instrumental in the founding of the Pontifical North American College at Rome, a school for American seminarians, in 1859. Although his health was never robust, Hughes made pastoral visits throughout his diocese, often on journeys that took him away from New York City for several months. Citing poor health, he asked Rome on several occasions for permission to resign, but his request was never granted.

Throughout his episcopate in New York, Hughes engaged in lengthy battles with Horace Greeley's *Tribune* and James Gordon Bennett's (1795–1872) *Herald*, both of which indulged in severe criticism of

Hughes and the church. These disputes often took on a very personal tone, from which none of the protagonists shrank. Never far from controversy, Hughes appeared to relish and thrive on it. His opponents called him "Dagger John," a sobriquet derived from the pastoral letters and other documents on which his name was appended as "+John, Bishop of New York," the cross appearing as a dagger when typeset. Autocratic but fiercely devoted to the cause of Catholics and immigrants, Hughes set the style for what Americans would expect in a bishop for almost a century after his death.

• Most of Hughes's papers are in the Archives of the Archdiocese of New York. The collection of his sermons and articles can be found in Lawrence Kehoe, ed., *Complete Works of the Most Rev. John Hughes, D.D.* (2 vols., 1865). The major biographies are J. R. Hassard, *Life of the Most Rev. John Hughes, D.D., First Archbishop of New York* (1866); H. A. Brann, *Most Rev. John J. Hughes: First Archbishop of New York*, 2d ed. (1912); and Richard Shaw, *Dagger John: The Unquiet Life and Times of Archbishop John Hughes of New York* (1977).

ROBERT J. WISTER

HUGHES, Langston (1 Feb. 1902?–22 May 1967), writer, was born James Langston Hughes in Joplin, Missouri, the son of James Nathaniel Hughes, a stenographer/bookkeeper, and Carrie Mercer Langston, a stenographer. Left behind by a frustrated father who, angered by racism, sought jobs in Cuba and Mexico, and also left often by a mother searching for employment, Hughes was raised primarily in Lawrence, Kansas, by his maternal grandmother, Mary Sampson Patterson Leary Langston. In 1915 he went to reside with his mother and stepfather, Homer Clark, in Lincoln, Illinois, later moving with them to Cleveland, Ohio.

Hughes spent the summers of 1919 and 1920 with his father in Mexico, writing his first great poem, "The Negro Speaks of Rivers," aboard a train on his second trip. By the time he entered Columbia University in September 1921, Hughes already had poems published in *Brownies' Book* and the *Crisis*. He left Columbia after one year, traveled as a dishwasher and cook's assistant on freighters to Africa and Holland and at Le Grand Duc in Paris, and later worked as a busboy in Washington, D.C. With financial help from the philanthropist Amy Spingarn, he entered Lincoln University in 1926 as an award-winning poet who had taken first place in an *Opportunity* contest and second and third places in a contest in the *Crisis* the year before. By the time he graduated in 1929, he had published two volumes of poetry, *The Weary Blues and Other Poems* (1926) and *Fine Clothes to the Jew* (1927), and had helped to launch the daring African-American literary journal *Fire!!* He had also completed a reading tour in the South with the writer and anthropologist Zora Neale Hurston, had become friends with other leading lights of the Harlem Renaissance, and had interested white socialites, artists, and patrons in his work.

For developing his artistic and aesthetic sensibilities, however, Hughes credited those people he dubbed admiringly as the "low-down folks." He praised the lower classes for their pride and individuality, that "they accept what beauty is their own without question." Part of the beauty that attracted him most was their music, especially the blues, which Hughes had heard as a child in Kansas City, as a teen in nightclubs in Chicago, Harlem, and Washington, D.C., on his trips through the South, and even as a young man in Europe. To Hughes, the blues were, as he wrote in "Songs Called the Blues" (1941), songs that came out of "black, beaten, but unbeatable throats." They were the sad songs of proud and wise people who, through the mixture of tears and laughter (often their response on hearing the lyrics) demonstrated a vivacity, wisdom, and determination. This inspired Hughes to attempt to capture the pulse and spirit of the blues tradition as a way of interpreting his people both to the rest of the world and to themselves. Hughes was galvanized by the music of his people, whether blues, jazz, or religious. The music provided him with themes, motifs, images, symbols, languages, rhythms, and stanza forms he would use in his writing throughout his career. As early as 1926, he was trying to schedule blues music as part of his poetry readings; in 1958 he recorded his poetry to the accompaniment of jazz groups led by Henry "Red" Allen and Charles Mingus. At Hughes's funeral, a program of blues was performed.

At the beginning of his writing career, Hughes was encouraged by the writer and editor Jessie Fauset; W. E. B. Du Bois; James Weldon Johnson, one of the judges who awarded Hughes his first poetry prizes and later anthologized some of Hughes's work; and Alain Locke, whose 1925 issue of the *Survey Graphic*, later revised into the groundbreaking volume *The New Negro* (1925), included some of Hughes's work. Through both the intellectual leadership of the highbrows and the invigorating atmosphere provided by the low-down folks in Harlem, Hughes found himself encouraged and gaining in fame. Vachel Lindsay's praise in 1925 of poems left by his plate in the Wardman Park Hotel in Washington by a "busboy poet" precipitated a flurry of interest and brought Hughes a wider audience for his poetry. But it was arts patron Carl Van Vechten who gave Hughes's career its biggest boost in the white world by taking Hughes's first book to Knopf and establishing contacts for Hughes that would serve him personally and professionally. Hughes repaid Van Vechten's assistance most directly with his support of and contributions to Van Vechten's novel *Nigger Heaven*; the two remained friends until Van Vechten's death in 1964.

At the end of her review of *The Weary Blues* in the *Crisis* in 1926, Fauset said of Hughes that "all life is his love and his work a brilliant, sensitive interpretation of its numerous facets." Not all reviews of Hughes's first book were so laudatory. Although the white press largely responded positively to Hughes's poetry, some black reviewers, seeking middle-class respectability from their "Talented Tenth" writers rather than Hughes's more realistic portrayal of the range of African-American life, reacted negatively. They particularly opposed the blues and jazz poems of the opening section of the book. In his review in *Opportunity* in February 1926, the poet Countee Cullen characterized the book as "scornful in subject matter" with "too much emphasis here on strictly Negro themes." Hughes naturally identified with the black masses, but at the same time he aligned himself with the modernist predilection for experimentation and frank treatment of themes previously banished from polite literature. Thus Hughes is both avant-gardist and traditionalist in his approach to his art. Surely he must have appreciated Locke's review in *Palms* in 1926, which stated that some of the lyrics "are such contributions to pure poetry that it makes little difference what substance of life and experience they are made of." Clearly, however, the substance of life and experience of which they were made also was paramount to Hughes. The lives and dreams of African Americans found intimate expression in Hughes's poems such as the heritage-laden "The Negro Speaks of Rivers," "Mother to Son," with its doggedly determined narrator, "To Midnight Nan at Leroy's," with its evocation of Harlem nightclub life, and the longingly hopeful "Dream Variation." The volume was an auspicious beginning that established Hughes's ideological and artistic leanings and conflicts that recurred amplified in his later work.

The responses to *Fine Clothes to the Jew* were even more extreme. Hughes realized that the book was, as he told the *Chicago Defender*, "harder and more cynical." He braced himself nervously for the reviews, encouraged by positive responses from Amy and Arthur Spingarn and George Schuyler. Again many black critics believed that Hughes had presented a cheap, tawdry portrait, far from the respectable Negro they longed to see in their literature. The "poet 'low-rate' of Harlem" the reviewer for the *Chicago Whip* dubbed him; "Sewer Dweller" sneered the headline of the New York *Amsterdam News* review; "piffling trash" pronounced the historian J. A. Rogers in the *Pittsburgh Courier*. Attacks on the short-lived *Fire!!* and Van Vechten's *Nigger Heaven*, which Hughes supported and for which he wrote blues lyrics following a lawsuit against Van Vechten for copyright infringement, compounded Hughes's embattled aesthetic consciousness at this time. However, Hughes continued undeterred, in spite of the volume's failure to sell well. In winter 1927, Alain Locke introduced Hughes to "Godmother" Charlotte Mason, an elderly, wealthy widow with a newfound interest in African-American authors, who became his benefactress, offering both financial support and opinions about his work. After reading and lecturing in the South in summer 1927, during which he met up with Hurston in Biloxi, Mississippi, Fauset in Tuskegee, Alabama, and Bessie Smith in Macon, Georgia, Hughes returned to Harlem and the directive of Mason to write a novel, *Not without Laughter* (1930).

Initially Hughes and Mason got along well, but the artistic and social demands she made on him were at times stultifying, and even the stipend she provided placed him in uncomfortable surroundings that impeded his artistic progress. The social "upward mobility," the economic support for his mother and half brother Gwyn Clark, the free apartment, the patron-funded trip to Cuba—all were mixed blessings. After their relationship was ruptured in 1930, Hughes, hurt and angry, wrote about the situation in the poem "The Blues I'm Playing" (1934) and in the first volume of his autobiography, *The Big Sea* (1940). Winning the Harmon Foundation Prize in 1930 brought him welcome cash, and he occupied some of his time by collaborating with Hurston on the play *Mule Bone* and traveling to Haiti, but the break with Mason was both psychologically and physically trying for Hughes.

Hughes dedicated *Not without Laughter* to his friends and early patrons, the Spingarns; his *Dear Lovely Death* was privately printed by Amy Spingarn in 1931. At the same time he was losing Godmother, difficulties with Hurston concerning *Mule Bone* put a chasm between them and a distrust of Locke, who was vying for Godmother's favor, separated Hughes from him as well. Hughes avoided dealing with these personal difficulties by going first to Florida, then Cuba, and on to Haiti, where he met with Haitian poet Jacques Roumain, who, inspired by Hughes, later wrote a poem titled "Langston Hughes" and received a letter of support from Hughes when he was sentenced to prison for alleged procommunist activity. Hughes, of course, had always identified with the masses, and he had a distinct influence on writers like Roumain and Nicolás Guillén, whom Hughes had inspired in 1929 to employ the rhythms of native Cuban music in his poetry. A 1931 reading tour partially sponsored by the Rosenwald Fund reintroduced Hughes to the rigid segregation and racism of the South, as did the much-publicized trial of the Scottsboro Boys. Hughes, the poet who initially had not been radical enough for the Marxist *New Masses* but who later published poems in that journal while at Lincoln, now began writing more controversial and directly political poems, such as "Christ in Alabama," which caused a furor that swelled his audience and increased sales of all his work.

In June 1932 he left for the Soviet Union with a group interested in making a film about race relations in America. Although the film, proposed by Soviet authorities and backed by the black communist James W. Ford, was never made, Hughes's travels in the Soviet Union showed him the lack of racial prejudice he longed for and a peasant class that he sought out and admired. Both *The Dream Keeper* and *Popo and Fifina*, children's books, were released to acclaim while he was in Russia. After visits to Japan, where Hughes was both questioned and put under surveillance because he was a "revolutionary" just come from Moscow, and Hawaii, Hughes returned to wealthy arts patron Noel Sullivan's home in Carmel, where he worked on the short-story collection *The Ways of White Folks* (1934), which was published shortly before his father died in Mexico.

Hughes's interest in drama, as shown by his collaboration on *Mule Bone*, finally bore fruit with the 1935 production of his play *Mulatto* at the Vanderbilt theater on Broadway and the Gilpin Players' 1936 production of *Troubled Island*. He received financial support from a Guggenheim Fellowship in 1935 and worked in Spain as a correspondent for the *Baltimore Afro-American* in 1937. Following the death of his mother in 1938, Hughes founded the Harlem Suitcase Theatre that same year, the New Negro Theatre in Los Angeles in 1939, and the Skyloft Players in Harlem in 1942. During this period he had plays produced in Cleveland, New York, and Chicago, among them *Little Ham* (1936), *Soul Gone Home* (1937), *Don't You Want to Be Free?* (1938), *The Organizer* (with music by James P. Johnson, 1939), and *The Sun Do Move* (1942), and he collaborated on a play with Arna Bontemps, *When the Jack Hollers* (1936). His experience with Hollywood, writing the script for *Way Down South* (1939), was a bitter disappointment. Still, Hughes managed to establish his importance as an African-American dramatist and continued to write plays and libretti for the rest of his career.

The year 1939 found Hughes back in Carmel working on his autobiography, *The Big Sea*, which dealt with his life up to 1931. Positive response to the work was overshadowed by fevered excitement over Richard Wright's *Native Son*, but Hughes did receive a Rosenwald Fund Fellowship at a point when his repudiation of his poem "Goodbye Christ" had turned some of his leftist friends against him. The Rosenwald money allowed Hughes to focus on writing rather than on financial matters. His blues-inflected *Shakespeare in Harlem* (1942) picked up where he had left off with *Fine Clothes to the Jew* in 1927 and provoked the same divided response as the earlier volume. Following an invitation to the writers' colony Yaddo, where he met Carson McCullers, Katherine Anne Porter, and Malcolm Cowley, he contacted the *Chicago Defender* about being a columnist and was hired. In 1943 Hughes created the beloved comic character Jesse B. Semple ("Simple"), the assertive and lively "lowdown" hero who appeared in many of his *Defender* columns over the next twenty years. Also in 1943 he published the prose poem *Freedom's Plow* (introduced with a reading by Paul Muni, with musical accompaniment by the Golden Gate Quartet and later performed publicly by Frederic March) and *Jim Crow's Last Stand*, a leftist, patchwork book of poetry.

In 1945 Hughes began to work on lyrics for Elmer Rice's *Street Scene*, with music by Kurt Weill, which opened to strong reviews in 1947. Hughes, however, opted to work as a visiting writer in residence at Atlanta University that year, seeing his book of lyric poems *Fields of Wonder* released to mixed reviews and the publication of his translation, with Mercer Cook, of Roumain's *Masters of the Dew*. Receiving a regular salary from Atlanta and $1,000 from a National Institute and American Academy of Arts and Letters Award in 1946, plus royalties from *Street Scene*, provided him more financial stability, thus

leaving time for him to edit with Bontemps a reissue of James Weldon Johnson's *Book of American Negro Poetry*. He was also able to publish a translation (with Ben Frederic Carruthers) of Nicolás Guillén's *Cuba Libre* and prepare another collection of poetry, *One-Way Ticket* (1949). A return to jazz- and blues-saturated poetry, this volume contains Hughes's celebrated "Madam" poems and the song "Life Is Fine," trumpeting perseverance and optimism. When the opera *Troubled Island* opened in 1949, Hughes was busy trying to find a publisher for the second volume of his autobiography and a new volume of poems. The production of *The Barrier* (1950), an opera based on the play *Mulatto*, yielded little money, though the collection of Simple stories *Simple Speaks His Mind* (1950) sold 30,000 copies and received general critical acclaim. Hughes was becoming better known, and translations of his work and critical essays were becoming extant.

Yet as success loomed, Hughes's masterful jazz-imbued *Montage of a Dream Deferred* (1951), a book-length poem in five sections depicting the rhythms of bop, boogie, and blues of the urban African-American experience in the context of continued deferment of the promises of American democracy, was critically panned. However, his short-story collection *Laughing to Keep from Crying* (1952) fared better with critics. Prolific throughout his career in multiple genres, Hughes began work on a series of children's books for Franklin Watts, which released *The First Book of Negroes* (1952), *The First Book of Rhythms* (1954), *The First Book of Jazz* (1955), *The First Book of the West Indies* (1956), and *The First Book of Africa* (1960). He also published other historical nonfiction works, *Famous American Negroes* (1954), *Famous Negro Music Makers* (1955), *A Pictorial History of the Negro in America* (with Milton Meltzer, 1956), *Famous Negro Heroes of America* (1958), *Fight for Freedom: The Story of the NAACP* (1962), and *Black Magic: A Pictorial History of the Negro in American Entertainment* (with Meltzer, 1967). The quality and success of these books established Hughes's importance as a popular historian of African-American life. The second volume of his autobiography, *I Wonder as I Wander* (1956), emphasized Hughes's determination to survive and prosper undaunted by the adversity and suffering he had faced in his travels in this country and around the world.

Nevertheless, Hughes found himself increasingly under the siege of McCarthyism and was forced to appear in March 1953 before Joseph R. McCarthy's Senate subcommittee not to defend his poetry but to repudiate some of his zealous leftist activities and work. Hughes's Simple stories continued to draw positive critical response and pleased his readers, although the Simple collections, *Simple Takes a Wife* (1953), *Simple Stakes a Claim* (1957), *The Best of Simple* (1961), and *Simple's Uncle Sam* (1965) did not sell well. The play *Simply Heavenly* began a reasonably successful run in 1957, landing on Broadway and on the London stage. That same year his translation of *Selected Poems of Gabriela Mistral* appeared, followed in

1958 by his selection and revision of his writings, *The Langston Hughes Reader*, and in 1959 by *Selected Poems of Langston Hughes* and his rousing play *Tambourines to Glory*, which he had converted into a novel of the same title in 1958.

Certainly by the sixties Hughes was an elder statesman of his people and a literary celebrity, adding to his publications stagings of his dramas, recordings, television and radio shows, appearances at conferences (in Uganda and Nigeria and at the National Poetry Festival in Washington, D.C., in 1962), jazz clubs, and festivals. He received honorary doctorates from Howard University in 1963 and Western Reserve University in 1964. The poetry was still flowing, with *Ask Your Mama* (1961) and *The Panther and the Lash* (1967) demonstrating that Hughes's satiric and humanitarian impulses were undiminished, as were his dramatic juices, evidenced by the critical success of the gospel play *Black Nativity* (1961). Always eager to help younger writers, he edited *New Negro Poets: USA* (1964).

Indeed, the final years of his life were filled with activity: the production of his play *The Prodigal Son* (1965), a two-month State Department tour of Europe lecturing on African-American writers, work on *The Best Short Stories by Negro Writers* (1967), and trips to Paris (with the production of *Prodigal Son*) and to Africa (as a presidential appointee to the First World Festival of Negro Arts), along with readings and lectures, filled his days. In the midst of this frenetic life, Hughes was admitted to the hospital with abdominal pains, later found to be caused by a blocked bladder and an enlarged prostate. Despite a successful operation, his heart and kidneys began to fail, and Hughes died in New York City.

Langston Hughes praised the "low-down folks" in the essay "The Negro Artist and the Racial Mountain" (*Nation*, 23 June 1926) for furnishing "a wealth of colorful, distinctive material" and for maintaining "their individuality in the face of American standardizations." Hughes's own life and career might be viewed in the same light. The variety and quality of his achievements in various genres, always in the service of greater understanding and humanity, and his specific commitment to depicting and strengthening the African-American heartbeat in America—and to helping others depict it as well—gave him a place of central importance in twentieth-century African-American literature and American literature generally. Hughes sought to change the way people looked not only at African Americans and art but at the world, and his modernistic vision was both experimental and traditional, cacophonous and mellifluous, rejecting of artificial middle-class values, and promoting emotional and intellectual freedom. He demonstrated that African Americans could support themselves with their art both monetarily and spiritually. Hughes published over forty books in a career that never lost touch with the concerns of sharecroppers and tenement dwellers as it provided inspiration for not only African-American writers but for all working people.

• Hughes's papers are in the James Weldon Johnson Memorial Collection, Beinecke Rare Book and Manuscript Library, Yale University. Arnold Rampersad, *The Life of Langston Hughes*, vol. 1 (1986) and vol. 2 (1988), and Faith Berry, *Langston Hughes: Before and Beyond Harlem* (1983), are the standard biographical treatments, to be supplemented by interesting glimpses in the correspondence included in Charles Nichols, ed., *Arna Bontemps—Langston Hughes Letters, 1925–1967* (1980). Thomas A. Mikolyzk, comp., *Langston Hughes: A Bio-Bibliography* (1990), presents annotated references, and *The Langston Hughes Review*, which first appeared in 1982, continues to publish and document important work on Hughes. Important contemporary critical assessments include Onwuchekwa Jamie, *Langston Hughes: An Introduction to the Poetry* (1976); Richard K. Barksdale, *Langston Hughes: The Poet and His Critics* (1977); Therman B. O'Daniel, ed., *Langston Hughes: Black Genius* (1971); R. Baxter Miller, *The Art and Imagination of Langston Hughes* (1989); Edward J. Mullen, ed., *Critical Essays on Langston Hughes* (1986) and *Langston Hughes in the Hispanic World and Haiti* (1977); Steven C. Tracy, *Langston Hughes and the Blues* (1988); and Harold Bloom, *Langston Hughes: Modern Critical Views* (1989). Berry also edited a valuable and fascinating collection, *Good Morning Revolution: Uncollected Writings of Social Protest by Langston Hughes* (1973, repr. 1992). An obituary is in the *New York Times*, 24 May 1967.

STEVEN C. TRACY

HUGHES, Pryce (1686?–?Apr. 1715), promoter of British settlement in the lower Mississippi Valley, was born in Llanllugan, Wales, the son of Richard Hughes, the county clerk of Montgomeryshire and chief steward to the Herbert family of Powis Castle, and Maria Pryce. Hughes had succeeded his father as chief steward to Lord Powis by 1708. Apparently inspired to emigrate by conversations with Thomas Nairne, first colonial Indian agent for South Carolina, Hughes and his brother Richard developed plans for a Welsh settlement near Port Royal. Richard arrived first in the colony, along with several indentured servants, and bought 5,000 acres of land in February 1711. Richard's death from illness at Charles Town by October of that year led Pryce Hughes to settle his affairs in Wales and follow his brother to South Carolina, where he intended to direct the Welsh colonization scheme personally.

By the spring of 1713 Hughes had arrived in Charles Town, where he began a frenetic two years of travels throughout the Southeast, evidently acting as an unofficial agent of Nairne. He first visited the Cherokees, with whom he negotiated the release of two captive French *coureurs de bois*. Hughes then provisioned the Frenchmen and dispatched them to the distant Missouri River tribes, which they were to bring into the British trading sphere. At about this same time, Hughes drafted several letters proposing "a Welsh colony in America," to be located west of the Appalachians, apparently in the area of the Natchez or Yazoo. In order to implement this bold proposal Hughes sought royal support, especially funds, to transport and settle thousands of destitute Welshmen among the French-allied Indians of the lower Mississippi Valley. His letters to the duchesses of Powis and Ormonde asked them to appeal to Queen Anne for the establishment of a new royal colony, to be called "Annarea" in her honor.

Although Hughes never received royal patronage, he continued to pursue vigorously his goal of British colonial expansion through diplomacy and trade with the Native American tribes of the Mississippi Valley. Within a year of his arrival in South Carolina, he was widely acknowledged as an expert on Indian affairs. Hughes almost immediately recognized how traders' abuses undermined Indian relations, and he sought to end the divisive Indian slave trade. His efforts to turn the southeastern tribes from trade with the French earned him command of a force of 2,000 Tallapoosa, Alabama, and Chickasaw warriors and twelve British colonials that marched on the Choctaw homeland in April 1714. Without a battle, the Choctaws agreed to permit British traders in their villages, a decision that temporarily undermined French influence with their most important native allies.

Hughes drafted a map of the Southeast during the summer of 1714; unfortunately it survives only as a crude copy made by Governor Alexander Spotswood in 1720. But that copy suggests that Hughes was acquiring considerable geographical information from his journeys in the region, particularly about areas for potential colonization. His vision of Welsh settlement on the banks of the Mississippi remained foremost in his mind as he set out on his final journey westward from Charles Town late in 1714. Throughout the fall and winter, Hughes traveled methodically from one village to another, visiting with the Alabamas, Chickasaws, and Natchez and engaging in trade from a warehouse in the Choctaw country. By the spring of 1715 he had made his way to the Tensaw village near Manchac and intended to continue to the mouth of the Mississippi River, when he and his English interpreter were arrested on orders of Louisiana governor La Mothe Cadillac.

Hughes was taken to Mobile and interrogated by Commandant Jean-Baptiste Le Moyne de Bienville. For three days Bienville cross-examined "Mr. ÿous," who produced a commission from Governor Charles Craven of South Carolina and, according to Bienville, boasted that "the Queen of England was going to send him five hundred families this autumn to settle on the St. Louis [Mississippi] River." After having watched his own influence with the southern tribes erode steadily over the last two years, largely as a result of Hughes's efforts, Bienville concluded from his interrogation that this man threatened French political and economic interests. Retaining Hughes's commission as evidence of British intentions to seize Louisiana, Bienville released his prisoners. Hughes and his interpreter made their way to Spanish Pensacola, where he remained for another three days before departing alone. On the trail to the Tallapoosas, just north of the forks of the Mobile and Tensaw rivers, the never-married Hughes was captured by a hunting party of Tomeh Indians who "broke his head." According to a legend found on the 1721 Barnwell map, "hereabouts

Esqr. Hughes was murthered by the Indians by Order of the French." The Tomehs' motives remain unknown although, as close allies of the French, they had suffered through years of English-inspired slave raiding. Hughes's death was among the first blows struck in the Yamasee War, which expelled British traders from the interior Southeast and set back British colonization plans for that region for many decades. From the French viewpoint, as expressed by François Le Maire in 1717, "Dieu rompit ce coup, et par la mort du ministre Yousse, le chef de leur ambassade aux Indiens du Mississippi et par le révolte des sauvages des environs de la Caroline" (God struck this blow by the death of the minister Hughes, the leader of their embassy to the Indians of the Mississippi, and by the revolt of the Indians in the vicinity of Carolina). Although the outbreak of the Yamasee War reflects the failure of Hughes's trade reform efforts and a widespread Native American rejection of British Indian policy in the Southeast, historian Verner Crane aptly characterized Hughes as "an authentic prophet of Anglo-American westward expansion."

• Autograph drafts of letters by Hughes are in the Caroliniana Library, University of South Carolina, Columbia. A sketch by Governor Alexander Spotswood drawn in about 1720 of Hughes's map of the Southeast is found in W. P. Cumming et al., *The Exploration of North America, 1630–1776* (1974). Eirlys M. Barker, "Pryce Hughes, Colony Planner, of Charles Town and Wales," *South Carolina Historical Magazine* 95 (Oct. 1994): 302–13, details his Welsh origins and British political connections. W. L. McDowell, ed., *Journals of the Commissioners of the Indian Trade, September 20, 1710–August 29, 1718* (1955), provides a context for the origins of the Yamasee War. Still valid in its political assessment of Hughes's brief career is Verner W. Crane, *The Southern Frontier: 1670–1732* (1929).

GREGORY A. WASELKOV

HUGHES, Revella Eudosia (2 July 1895–24 Oct. 1987), musician, singer, and educator, was born in Huntington, West Virginia, the daughter of George W. Hughes, a postman, and Annie B. (maiden name unknown), a piano teacher and seamstress. At age five Hughes began studying piano with her mother and, at eight or nine, violin with a musician friend of her father's. She attended Huntington's segregated public schools. Disturbed when Hughes was racially harassed, her parents sent her to Hartshorn Memorial College (later part of Virginia Union University) in Richmond, which she attended from 1909 to 1911, graduating with a degree in music and elementary studies. She attended Oberlin High and Conservatory, graduating in 1915. In 1917 she earned a bachelor of music in piano from Howard's Conservatory of Music, where she studied piano with LeRoy Tibbs and voice with conservatory director Lulu Childers. Hughes then taught violin and piano at the Washington Conservatory of Music (1917–1918) and voice, piano, and violin at North Carolina State College. In 1919 she became director of music at A & M College in Orangeburg, South Carolina.

During the early 1920s Hughes pursued a career as a lyric soprano, performing classical art songs, arias, art songs by black composers, and spirituals in New York, New Jersey, and New England. Her vocal gift was recognized by Roland Hayes, who arranged for her to study voice with George Bagby. She lived in New York with family friends, the Adam Clayton Powell, Sr., family. Hughes was featured in Bagby's Sunday morning Memorial Concerts at the Waldorf-Astoria. She also studied with Walter Kiesewetter. She appeared with Harry T. Burleigh, Paul Robeson, and Marian Anderson in separate concerts in 1920. Hailed as a fine lyric soprano, she was dubbed the "Sepia Lily Pons" and the "Colored Nightingale" by the African-American press.

Her concert career short-lived, Hughes turned to musical theater, appearing in *Dumb Luck* (1922) and joining *Shuffle Along* (1921) in 1922, singing "I'm Just Wild about Harry" and "Gypsy Blues." Hughes became the first female Broadway choral director when Noble Sissle and Eubie Blake asked her to direct the chorus of the show's Chicago road company. In 1923 Hughes played in Fess Williams's *And the Band in Padlox* at Chicago's Regal Theatre. She later played the lead in James P. Johnson's *Runnin' Wild*, the show that introduced the Charleston, and in Will Vodery's *Swing Along*. She was one of the Four Bon Bons, a quartet including Georgette Harvey, Musa Williams, and Lois Sparker that first appeared in *Runnin' Wild*. The group disbanded after two years when Hughes became ill and needed surgery. After recovering, Hughes performed as a solo entertainer in black theaters such as the Lafayette and the Alhambra in New York, the Regal and the Metropolitan in Chicago, and the Howard in Washington and on the B. F. Keith vaudeville circuit. She appeared with Duke Ellington, Cab Calloway, Claude Hopkins, Fats Waller, and Eubie Blake. She also recorded for Black Swan and appeared briefly on radio over WHN.

When her mother became ill in 1932, Hughes returned to Huntington to care for her. She worked as supervisor of music of Negro schools and taught elementary school music at Douglass High School for eleven years. While at Douglass, she organized a 128-piece band in 1938–1939 and directed the orchestra and an award-winning fifty-voice choir. Praised for her outstanding work, Hughes received a citation from the Cabell County Board of Education. She was also briefly the director of the piano and violin departments at West Virginia State College. Hughes remained active in Huntington, leading her Society Syncopators, which played dances and society functions throughout West Virginia. During school summer vacations, she attended Northwestern University's Graduate School of Music Education, earning her M. Mus. Ed. from Northwestern University in 1942, the year her mother died. She briefly pursued doctoral studies at Columbia University, though she never finished the degree.

After her mother's death, Hughes returned to New York and show business. In 1949 she adopted the name "Camella Dasche" and performed on the Hammond organ in nightclubs and lounges in the eastern cities of Baltimore, Philadelphia, Albany, Troy, Monticello, and New York's Harlem. She was known for "swinging the classics," a blend of the classical piano and jazz she called "informal music" because, as a classically trained pianist, she did not improvise but performed from written arrangements that she memorized. She rearranged classical, jazz, and Latin American pieces and spirituals, exaggerated the rhythm, and enhanced the harmony. Hughes entertained the U.S. Armed Forces during the 1950s, performing at the Salvation Army Servicemen's Center. In 1953 she toured Europe and the Middle East for fourteen weeks with the Wandering Gypsies in the Gypsy Markoff Celebrity Show, a USO show sponsored by the Entertainment Department of the U.S. Air Force. She played the Hammond organ and piano and was musical director. In 1957 she made a second tour of Europe. After returning to the United States, she resumed playing in clubs. In February 1956, while appearing with Markoff's All Girl Revue in the Beverly Hotel Supper Club Room in New York, Hughes met heiress Evelyn V. "Sally" Adams, the granddaughter of the Adams chewing gum company founder. In July Adams invited Hughes to Europe. The two became lifelong friends, sharing Adams's residence. Hughes retired in the late 1950s but continued performing, playing organ for services at Norman Vincent Peale's Marble Collegiate Church. In 1961 Hughes inherited Adams's $1 million estate.

Honored at age eighty-five by Sarah McLawler's third Women's Jazz Festival, "Salute to Women in Jazz" (1–8 June 1980), Hughes performed on Saturday, 7 June 1980. She appeared at the jazz festival the following year. She was also honored by the Bramwell Mapp Scholarship Fund at the Waldorf-Astoria in 1982 and received Howard's Alumni Achievement Award in 1987. She died in Manhattan, New York.

Though largely forgotten in the last thirty years of her life, Hughes was an important figure in art music, musical theater, and jazz. During the late teens and early 1920s, she was among the ranks of a generation of pioneering African-American concert singers. As a musical theater actress, she appeared in several important trend-setting African-American musicals. Although she did not improvise in the strict sense, she was one of few women who pursued and sustained a career as a jazz and nightclub instrumentalist.

• Hughes's papers are archived at the Moorland-Spingarn Research Center at Howard University, Washington, D.C., and at Marshall University in Huntington, W.Va. The most accurate and extensive biographical article is Doris Evans McGinty, "Conversation with Revella Hughes: From the Classics to Broadway to Swing," *Black Perspective in Music* 16 (1988): 81–104. A discography can be found in Patricia Turner, *Dictionary of Afro-American Performers: 78 RPM and Cylinder Recordings of Opera, Choral Music, and Song, 1900–1949* (1990), pp. 212–14. She was the subject of a documentary produced by New York's Channel 13. An obituary is in the *New York Times*, 27 Oct. 1987.

GAYLE MURCHISON

HUGHES, Robert Ball (19 Jan. 1806–5 Mar. 1868), sculptor, was born in London, England. His parents' names are unknown. At an early age he made small figures and reliefs from candle wax, reportedly undertaking a complex composition copied from a picture of the judgment of Solomon. In 1818 he entered the school of the Royal Academy, following the prescribed study of ancient statues; his copy of the *Barbarini Faun* (1820) received high praise. That same year he modeled one of his earliest surviving pieces, a bust of his father, which is at the Boston Athenaeum. The next year he was apprenticed to a well-known English sculptor, Edward Hodges Baily, a member of the Royal Academy, and he studied the monuments of the celebrated neoclassical sculptor John Flaxman. The titles of the works Hughes exhibited at the academy's annual shows in the 1820s—*Pandora Brought by Mercury to Epimetheus*, a relief awarded a gold medal in 1823, and *Achilles*, inspired by his reading of the *Iliad*, shown in 1825—further reveal the neoclassical bent of his early career.

Hughes and his wife left England and arrived in New York in 1829; the reasons for their emigration are not known. Sculpture was then in its infancy in America, confined mainly to ships' figureheads and wooden shop signs. Although a few Italian sculptors had immigrated earlier, mainly to work at the new U.S. Capitol in Washington, Hughes played an important role in introducing sculpture to Americans. His work helped establish a high standard for the new art form, as seen in his portrait of the Boston merchant and philanthropist Thomas Handasyd Perkins (c. 1832, Perkins School for the Blind, Watertown, Mass.) and the dramatic marble image of the aged painter John Trumbull (1834, Yale University Art Gallery). Naturalism rather than idealizing neoclassicism was the foundation of these works, and in this the sculptor correctly judged the artistic preferences of his American patrons.

Soon after Hughes arrived in America, he modeled a heroic statue of Governor DeWitt Clinton, about which the *New York Mirror* reported on 13 February 1830, " . . . the exquisite accuracy of its execution has so fully satisfied the directors that they have ordered one of marble, larger than life" for Clinton Hall. While it is not known if the second statue of Clinton was ever executed, one representing Alexander Hamilton was completed in 1835; it was one of the first life-size marble statues to be carved in the United States. Unfortunately, only a few months after it was erected in the New York Merchants' Exchange, it was destroyed when fire consumed that building on the evening of 17 December 1835; its appearance is known from a small plaster model that survives in the Detroit Institute of Arts. In the early 1830s Hughes also created a monument to Bishop John H. Hobart, showing the subject in a profile relief portrait, which was erected in New York's Trinity Church.

In 1836 Hughes modeled a portrait bust of Washington Irving, versions of which are at the Pennsylvania Academy of the Fine Arts and at Irving's home in Tarrytown, New York. Hughes moved to Philadelphia in 1838, probably in response to word that the Society of the Cincinnati of that city intended to commission an equestrian statue of George Washington. Hughes's model for that statue, which won the competition but was not executed because of the failure of the U.S. Bank, is housed in the Society for the Preservation of New England Antiquities, Boston. By 1840 Hughes and his wife had settled in Boston. There, his major effort was a bronze life-size seated figure of Nathaniel Bowditch, marking the grave of the famous mathematician and astronomer in Mount Auburn Cemetery, Cambridge, Massachusetts. Hughes had to build his own foundry, there then being no facility existing in the United States that could produce a cast-bronze figure. In 1847 he became the first in the country to cast a sculpture in bronze. Regrettably, his technique was faulty, and by the 1880s it had deteriorated so badly that it had to be replaced by a replica cast in Paris. A plaster version of the *Bowditch* is in the Boston Athenaeum, as is Hughes's life-size plaster group, *Little Nell*, a subject taken from Charles Dickens's popular tale, *The Old Curiosity Shop*.

In spite of the importance of Hughes's role in introducing the art of sculpture to America in the 1830s and the high quality of his work, his life was not happy. Occasionally lecturing on art topics, he spent much of his later life making miniature wax portraits or burning images on wood panels. Often destitute, he frequently wrote to friends or patrons to plead for small amounts of money. He died at his home in Dorchester, where he had lived since about 1842. Hughes's work is not currently well known, largely because so few of his major pieces have survived. Those that do exist, however, reveal the hand of an exceptionally gifted artist.

• For an analysis of Hughes's work, see Georgia Chamberlain, "Portrait Busts of Robert Ball Hughes," *Art Quarterly* 20 (1957): 383–86, and Chamberlain, *Studies on American Painters and Sculptors of the Nineteenth Century* (1965). For Hughes's place relative to the early history of sculpture in the United States see Wayne Craven, *Sculpture in America* (1984), and Lorado Taft, *History of American Sculpture* (1930). Ethel S. Bolton discusses his little wax portraits in *American Wax Portraits* (1929). Hughes's obituary is in the New York *Sun*, 7 Mar. 1868, and in the London *Art Journal*, 1 July 1868.

WAYNE CRAVEN

HUGHES, Robert William (6 or 16 June 1821–10 Dec. 1901), writer and judge, was born in Powhatan County, Virginia, the son of Jesse Hughes, a farmer, and Elizabeth Woodson Morton. In 1822 Hughes's parents died and the infant was taken in and reared by General Edward C. Carrington and his wife. At the age of twelve Hughes was apprenticed to a carpenter in New Jersey but later attended the Caldwell Institute in Greensboro, North Carolina, and in the early 1840s taught school in Hillsboro (now Hillsborough), North Carolina. In the mid-1840s he read law in Fincastle, Virginia, and began his law practice in Richmond in

1846. In 1850 he married Eliza M. Johnston, daughter of Charles C. Johnston, a U.S. congressman; the couple had two children.

By the 1850s Hughes's interest had shifted to writing occasional editorials for the Richmond *Examiner*. When the *Examiner*'s editor, John M. Daniel, moved to Europe in 1853, Hughes became editor until Daniel's return in 1857. By 1855 he had ceased to practice law. In 1857 he moved to Washington, D.C., where he edited the *Washington Union* (from 1859 the *States and Union*) until February 1861. A chronic illness forced Hughes into semiretirement later that year, but he continued throughout the Civil War to write editorials for the Richmond *Examiner* from his home near Abingdon, Virginia. Beginning in 1865 he edited the Richmond *Republic*, the first Republican paper printed in Richmond after the war. In 1869–1870 he founded and edited the Richmond *State Journal*.

Hughes began his editorial career as a staunch advocate of state's rights and secession. Toward the end of the Civil War his hostility to the Jefferson Davis administration and the severe losses suffered by the Confederacy prompted him to write guarded suggestions of peace. At the end of the war he had aligned himself with the Republican party on the grounds that it was best for the South to resume friendly relations with its recent enemies. During Reconstruction his editorials accused prominent whites of inciting the murder of blacks. These charges culminated in his June 1869 duel with William E. Cameron, editor of the Petersburg *Index* and later governor of Virginia. Cameron was wounded but survived.

Hughes's support of the Republican party led to his appointment (by President Ulysses S. Grant) as federal district attorney for the Western District of Virginia (1872) and his nomination for U.S. congress (1872) and for governor (1873). In 1874 Hughes was nominated and confirmed as federal judge for the Eastern District of Virginia. He retired in 1898.

While on the bench Hughes continued writing political pamphlets and biographies in his spare time and also edited ten volumes of court reports (*Reports of Cases Decided in the Circuit Courts of the United States for the Fourth Circuit*, vols. 1–5; and *Transcripts of Decisions [Morrison's] of the United States Supreme Court*, vols. 1–5). His political pamphlets included *A Popular Treatise on the Currency Question Written from a Southern Point of View* (1879) and *The American Dollar* (1885). He also contributed biographies of Generals John B. Floyd and Joseph E. Johnston to Edward A. Pollard's *Lee and His Lieutenants* (1867) and published an autobiography, *A Chapter of Personal and Political History* (1881). Hughes died at his home near Abingdon, Virginia.

In his own time Hughes was probably best known as a newspaper editor who successfully shifted from Democrat to Republican in the waning days of the Civil War. Although he served on the federal bench for twenty-five years and was noted for his leniency toward offenders, he was not known for his judicial craftsmanship. His reports of cases were workman-like, but neither they nor his editorial articles and pamphlets are recognized as critical statements on law or politics.

• Besides the brief entries in major biographical directories, very little has been written on Hughes. A more extended treatment is provided by Lyon Gardiner Tyler in *Encyclopedia of Virginia Biography* (1915). Hughes's obituary in the Richmond *Times*, 11 Dec. 1901, is largely genealogical but does point out that he was a well-respected judge in his later years. Most of his own works are either reports of court cases or polemical articles and pamphlets.

ELIZABETH BRAND MONROE

HUGHES, Rupert (31 Jan. 1872–9 Sept. 1956), author, was born in Lancaster, Missouri, the son of Felix Turner Hughes, an attorney and railroad president, and Jean Amelia Summerlin. He was the third of five children; his brother, Howard Robard Hughes, invented the conical drilling bit, founded the Hughes Tool Company, and sired the eccentric billionaire Howard Hughes. Rupert was a studious boy at a Missouri military boarding school (his nickname was "History"), and he went on to graduate Phi Beta Kappa from Adelbert College (now Western Reserve University) in Cleveland in 1892, where he also got an M.A. in 1894. His early career was somewhat indefinite: he studied music and literature at Yale (M.A., 1899), worked as a reporter for New York newspapers, and—with his father's backing—wrote and produced a musical comedy (*The Bathing Girl*) that opened and closed in one night. In 1895 Hughes married Agnes Hedge; they had one child.

Hughes began to sell his fiction to *St. Nicholas* magazine, principally stories for boys, in 1897; these were collected as his first book, *The Lakerim Athletic Club*, in 1898, inaugurating his long career as an enormously popular writer of commercial fiction. He was to publish his last novel for juveniles, *The War of the Mayan King*, in 1952 when he was eighty. Hughes's Iowa boyhood was romanticized repeatedly in his fiction, and his treatment of small-town life (as in *The Old Nest* [1912]) and forgotten parents induced legions of young Americans to come back to their roots. But he also wrote city stories in the O. Henry tradition, as well as detective fiction, stories about the theater, war stories, historical novels, and dozens of contemporary romantic intrigues. Ephemeral as this material proved to be, it can be read with relish by cultural historians for its depiction of the era's popular values. At his peak—from the early 1900s through the 1920s—Hughes produced fiction almost faster than his publishers could bring it out—some thirty novels and short story collections by 1930. Critics dismissed this productiveness as superficiality, but few literate Americans in the first three decades of the twentieth century had not read some of Hughes's fiction. His work appeared in almost every popular magazine; ninety-six short stories were indexed by 1929. Hughes claimed that he had signed "the highest priced contract given to a short story writer" (Kemm, p. 15) with *Hearst's Magazine* in 1917.

As important as Hughes's commitment to fiction was his concurrent devotion to writing for the American stage. Undaunted by his first theatrical flop, he kept plugging away at playwriting. From 1902 to 1908 Hughes saw eight of his dramas produced in New York, London, and elsewhere. His *Alexander the Great* toured the United States for a year but never succeeded on Broadway. *The Bridge* (1909) was Hughes's first real hit in New York, subsequently touring for three years. *Excuse Me*, a "Pullman car farce," made the Hughes name popular with its long run on Broadway in 1911. This comedy spawned a book version, several touring companies in the United States and abroad, two movie versions, and a 1918 musical comedy adaptation, *Toot-Toot!*, with music by Jerome Kern. Hughes became a fashionable theatrical producer, with a play every other year on Broadway, featuring actors like Douglas Fairbanks and John Drew (1853–1927).

Divorced in 1904, Hughes in 1908 married the star of one of his plays, Adelaide Mould Bissell, a divorcée with two children. By this time, his celebrity was considerable—no more the Grub Street editor who labored for five years on *The Historian's History of the World* in twenty-five volumes for the *Encyclopaedia Britannica*. Hughes turned his interest in music into several successful books on American musical history, including *American Composers* (1900), *The Love Affairs of Great Musicians* (1903), *Songs by 30 Americans* (1904), and *Music Lovers' Encyclopedia* (1913). He composed songs as well. The poetry he wrote at this time appeared as *Gyges' Ring* (1901; reissued in 1949 as *Gyges' Ring and Other Verse*). Concomitantly, he carried on with his military school training by serving with the New York National Guard, where he rose from private to captain, and was among the U.S. troops on the Mexican border in 1916. A slight deafness kept him from service in France during World War I, but he saw duty as a military intelligence officer in Washington, D.C., in 1918. He remained an indefatigable militiaman, retiring as a colonel and regimental commander in the California State Guard at the age of seventy-one.

Service in California was inevitable, for by the 1920s Hughes had become one of Hollywood's most sought-after screenwriters. He had sold his first story to the movies in 1907 (Thomas Edison had planned to use a Hughes play for his first sound film), and by the 1920s he and his second wife were Hollywood luminaries in their own right. After his wife's suicide in 1923, Hughes married Elizabeth Patterson "Pat" Dial, an actress in his 1924 film *Reno*. Pat continued to appear in films, and her husband wrote and directed dozens of movies for Samuel Goldwyn and others. Nearly fifty motion pictures were made from Hughes's work starring such notables as Mary Pickford, Norma Shearer, and Richard Barthelmess. In 1927–1928 Hughes was nominated for an Academy Award for best original story for the film *The Patent Leather Kid* (1927).

As he solidified his position in the film industry and in the military establishment, Hughes became increasingly more active in conservative political causes. Once thought of as somewhat radical for debunking such myths as the fallen cherry tree in his well-researched biography of George Washington (3 vols., 1926, 1927, 1930), Hughes now produced a laudatory biography of Republican politician Thomas Dewey (*Attorney for the People* [1940]), and he anathematized Communists in the film industry as a radio commentator in the 1940s. In his fairy tale castle of a house in Los Angeles, Hughes mourned the death of his third wife from an accidental drug overdose in 1945, but he continued to write for hours each day at one of the five desks in his study.

By 1950 Hughes was being lauded at testimonial dinners sponsored by the Authors, the Lambs, and the Masquers (Hollywood's social clubs for film industry professionals) and attended by politicians and movie stars. The midwestern boy reared in Keokuk, Iowa, had come far. He no longer wrote poetry, and his current fiction was thought most appropriate for junior high school students. But Hughes was a consummate writer: he died at his Hollywood desk at work on yet another novel. He may not be remembered as he was eulogized in the *Los Angeles Examiner*—"a towering figure in the literary life of the nation" (10 Sept. 1956)—but he produced a considerable and honest body of popular entertainment for an American public who kept coming back for more. Hughes was a professional whose myriad of stories, novels, plays, poems, scenarios, and biographies are his monument.

• The best collection of Hughes's papers is at the University of Iowa. A judicious modern assessment is James O. Kemm, "The Literary Legacy of Rupert Hughes," in *Books at Iowa*, Apr. 1985, pp. 10–25. Family recollections include Ruby H. Hughes, with Patrick Mahoney, "Rupert Hughes (1872–1956): Reflections on His Centennial," *Coranto* 8, no. 2 (1973): 25–33.

CHARLES BASSETT

HUGO, E. Harold (8 Aug. 1910–9 Sept. 1985), printer, was born Everett Harold Hugo in Stamford, Connecticut, the son of Otto Hugo, an upholsterer, and Esther Lundstrom, both of whom had recently arrived from Sweden. In 1918 the Hugo family moved to Meriden, Connecticut, to a house not far from the Meriden Gravure Company, where Harold began working at whatever odd jobs were given him after school and on Saturdays. As the years went by his ability to make himself increasingly useful prompted Parker Allen, president of the Meriden Gravure Company, to induce Hugo to return to the company as his fulltime assistant following his freshman year at Northeastern University.

Founded in 1888, the Meriden Gravure Company's principal business was printing catalogs for the numerous silver manufacturers in that city. As the depression set in and business declined, Hugo sought new customers among museums and scholarly publishers. The exceptionally high quality of the collotype process used by Meriden Gravure was admirably suited for illustrations. In 1935 he married Marjorie Ek-berg; they had two children.

In 1942 Allen left to accept a commission in the army, appointing Hugo as general manager of the company. At the same time Meriden Gravure began working for the army's map service, which required printing in the finest possible detail. With this opportunity for technical development under Hugo's persistent leadership, the craftsmen at Meriden constantly improved the quality and efficiency of their printing.

Hugo's capable wartime management of the company earned him the permanent position of manager, from which he eventually rose to become president and, following the merger with the Stinehour Press in 1977, chairman. For the rest of his active career Hugo continued to push the firm toward new levels of excellence. He pioneered the conversion to photo-offset lithography and the development of fine-screen, 300-line halftones, which produced images of exceptionally fine quality at a fraction of the cost of the difficult and relatively slow collotype. He insisted that images be faithful to the originals, that the paper upon which they were printed be of archival quality and appropriate for the job, and that the other elements of the books they produced be of consistent quality. In these ways, Hugo raised the standards of bibliogony in the United States. Indeed, his reputation became international. As Ruari McLean wrote in his London *Times* obituary, the work of the Meriden Gravure Company was "without peer anywhere in the world." That the customers fully recognized the importance of Hugo's ability, imagination, and resourcefulness in attaining such levels of excellence is revealed in the acknowledgments of countless fine volumes, which include appreciative statements about Hugo's work.

Immersed as he was in a world of learned societies, museums, scholars, curators, and collectors, it is not surprising that Hugo became a collector of books and prints. When the Meriden Gravure Company printed an art catalog, Hugo often acquired some of the artist's work. In addition, as one devoted to excellence in typographic design and printing, he collected many examples of fine printing, both historical and contemporary. As much pleasure as he had in these acquisitions, he derived equal satisfaction in giving them to appropriate museums and libraries, always seeking to enhance collections and avoid duplication. The Arts of the Book Collection in the Stirling Library at Yale was a principal beneficiary.

To be a customer of the Meriden Gravure Company was to be a friend of Hugo's. Customers were encouraged to conduct their business before or after the noon hour so they could be taken to the Home Club for a good lunch and conversation. In May, if Hugo knew a visitor was fond of shad roe, he called ahead to make sure it would be available. Upon their return to the company, customers received handsome gifts of the latest products. Even in retirement, Hugo wanted to be informed whenever any of his old friends were expected at the company so he could join them. He was a member of such societies as the American Academy of Arts and Sciences, the American Antiquarian Society, the Massachusetts Historical Society, and the Society of Printers. He also belonged to a number of book clubs including the Columbiad (of which he was the founder), the Club of Odd Volumes, the Grolier Club, and the Double Crown Club of London. Although Hugo's life was filled with work, books, and friends, he was, nevertheless, a good family man. He died in Meriden.

If Hugo did not earn degrees within the walls of universities, he earned them in his printing shop, as Yale acknowledged with an honorary master of arts degree in 1963, and Wesleyan with a doctor of humanities in 1970. The Bookbuilders of Boston conferred the W. A. Dwiggins Award on Hugo in 1984. Twice Hugo was celebrated by publications in his honor. The first was *Thomas Jefferson among the Antiquities of Southern France in 1787—A Tribute to E. Harold Hugo* (1954), the significance of which is explained in the introduction celebrating Hugo's contributions to the lives of others. The second, *A Portfolio Honoring Harold Hugo for his Contribution to Scholarly Printing* (1978), contains thirty-six images and essays by scholars representing organizations with which Hugo was involved. Both of these tributes were, in the words of historian Julian Boyd, "inspired by a sense of gratitude for all that he had done for us and for others." Professor Alvin Eisenman of Yale accurately assessed Hugo's career with the statement, "There has never been anyone who has held the position that Harold does in American scholarly printing."

• The most complete account of Hugo's career is in Walter Muir Whitehill's foreword to *A Portfolio Honoring Harold Hugo*. Memoirs may be found in the proceedings of many of the organizations with which Hugo was affiliated including the *Proceedings of the Massachusetts Historical Society* 92 (1985), and the *Proceedings of the American Antiquarian Society* 96, pt. 1 (1986). Much of the information provided above was acquired in conversation with Harold Hugo.

ELTON W. HALL

HUGO, Richard (21 Dec. 1923–22 Oct. 1982), poet, was born Richard Franklin Hogan in Seattle, Washington, the son of Richard Hogan and Esther Clara Monk. His father abandoned the family when Hugo was only twenty months old, and, lacking any means to support her son, Hugo's teenage mother left him in the care of her parents, who lived in White Center, then a depressed, semirural suburb of Seattle. In 1927 Hugo's mother married Herbert Franklin James Hugo, a naval officer. Although his mother was unable to regain custody of her son, Hugo began to use her husband's name when he was in eighth grade.

Like many of his generation, Hugo was called to military duty in World War II, serving in the army air corps in Italy from 1943 to 1945 as a first lieutenant and bombardier, an experience he would remember later in *Good Luck in Cracked Italian* (1969) and *The Triggering Town* (1979). After receiving the Distinguished Flying Cross, he returned to Seattle to study under the G.I. Bill. He earned both his B.A. (1948) and M.A. (1952) at the University of Washington, where he studied creative writing with Theodore Roethke, whose influence is evident in much of his poetry. In 1951, while in graduate school, Hugo married Barbara Williams; the marriage was childless.

After receiving his M.A., Hugo worked for Boeing Aircraft in Seattle for thirteen years as a document supervisor and industrial writer. His first volume of poetry, *A Run of Jacks* (1961), composed of poems written in the 1940s and 1950s but published while he was at Boeing, helped him secure a position at the University of Montana at Missoula. He remained at Missoula for most of his writing career; he began as a lecturer in 1964 and, by 1971, had been appointed director of the creative writing program. He was visiting poet at several universities, including the University of Iowa (1970–1971), University of Washington (Roethke Chair, 1971), University of Colorado (1974–1975), and University of Arkansas, Little Rock (1980).

A Run of Jacks establishes the subjects and themes that run through Hugo's subsequent volumes. In some regards a populist poet of the Walt Whitman–William Carlos Williams–Carl Sandburg line, Hugo looked to the landscapes, the towns, and the working people of the Pacific Northwest for his subjects. The emphasis on place and on the need of the individual to overcome loneliness and to establish community pervades all of his poetry.

Hugo's treatment of western scenes is not, however, that of a realist. Having cultivated, under Roethke's tutelage, a fine sense of meter and a subtle musical ear, Hugo transformed and defamiliarized his raw material of tugs, waterfowl, damp roofs, and working men. In the later volume *Death of the Kapowsin Tavern* (1965), one continues to hear the influence of Roethke, as much in the moist landscapes peopled with gulls, ferns, and grebes as in the musical iambic lines, often endstopped and distinct as if each declared its separate law. What makes the poem "Port Townsend" peculiarly Hugo's, however, is the subject of the northwest peninsular town itself, decaying, unrecoverable.

Hugo left the Northwest for Italy, once in 1963 with his wife Barbara and again in 1969, three years after their divorce. These visits inspired his third book, *Good Luck in Cracked Italian* (1969). His first effort to set his poems outside the American Northwest, *Good Luck* concentrates on the Italian locales he had known as a soldier. It was followed by *The Lady in Kicking Horse Reservoir* (1973), which was nominated for a National Book Award. The poems in this volume are set in England, Scotland, Spain, and, principally, Montana.

In 1974 Hugo married poet Ripley Schemm and became father to her two children from a previous marriage. Now a family man, he returned to the ghosts of his own childhood in *What Thou Lovest Well, Remains American* (1975), which brought him his second National Book Award nomination, and *31 Letters and 13 Dreams* (1977), which was based on a near breakdown Hugo experienced while in Iowa. In these letter-poems, addressed to contemporary poet-friends, Hugo developed a loose fourteen-syllable line that allowed him to explore a more confessional and often more humorous style than he had hitherto used. Although Hugo claimed that he "didn't much care for" this experiment, these new poems revived his reputation and expanded his audience.

Hugo's standing as a significant American poet was confirmed with the publication of his *Selected Poems* (1979) and *The Triggering Town* (1979), a compilation of essays on the teaching of poetry together with a memoir of his war years in Italy. A year later came *White Center* (1980), invoking his childhood locale. The final volume of poems he published, written on a Guggenheim Fellowship, was *The Right Madness on Skye* (1980), which celebrates the Isle of Skye in Scotland.

The last of Hugo's writings published during his lifetime was a detective novel, *Death and the Good Life* (1981), a re-visioning of the landscapes and characters of Hugo's West in the tradition of Raymond Chandler and Dashiell Hammett. One year after Hugo's death in Seattle, from complications caused by leukemia, another novel, *The Hitler Diaries* (1983), and his last book of poems, *Sea Lanes Out* (1983), were published.

Hugo's other works include *The Real West Marginal Way* (1983), a collection of autobiographical essays edited by his second wife and others; a film, *Kicking the Loose Gravel Home* (1976–1977), made with Anna Smith; *Making Certain It Goes On* (1983), a posthumous collection of his poetry; and numerous sound recordings. Hugo also helped found *Poetry Northwest*, the distinguished University of Washington literary journal. In 1977 he succeeded Stanley Kunitz as judge of the Yale Younger Poets Series.

Although it was often predicted that Hugo would be a major figure in American literature, his poems are infrequently anthologized or taught in modern American literature classes. He has assumed instead the status of an important regional poet.

• Hugo's papers are collected at the University of Washington and the University of Montana. A book-length study is Michael S. Allen, *We Are Called Human: The Poetry of Richard Hugo* (1982). Jack Meyers, ed., *Trout in the Milk: A Composite Picture of Richard Hugo* (1982), is a collection of criticism and tributes by various poets and friends. Donna Gerstenberger's chapbook *Richard Hugo* (1983) examines Hugo's work and includes a helpful selected bibliography. Sanford Pinsker, *Three Pacific Northwest Poets: William Stafford, Richard Hugo, and David Waggoner* (1987), provides a biography and a study of Hugo's themes and techniques. Among the numerous articles on Hugo are Richard Howard's essay "Richard Hugo: Why Track Down Unity When the Diffuse Is So Exacting?" in Howard's *Alone with America: Essays on the Art of Poetry in the United States since 1950* (1969) and Vernon Young's "Two Hedgehogs and a Fox," *Parnassus* 8, no. 1 (Fall/Winter 1979): 227–37. An obituary is in the *New York Times*, 26 Oct. 1982.

JEFFREY GRAY

HUIE, William Bradford (13 Nov. 1910–22 Nov. 1986), journalist and novelist, was born in Hartselle, Alabama, the son of John Bradford and Margaret Lois

Brindley. An eighth-generation heir to the white agrarian culture of the Tennessee Valley in North Alabama, he was educated at the University of Alabama, graduating with an A.B. in 1930.

He subsequently worked as a reporter for the *Birmingham Post* (1932–1936) and associate editor of the *American Mercury* in New York (1941–1943). Serving as a lieutenant in the U.S. Navy (1943–1945), he returned to the *American Mercury* as its editor in 1945. In 1950 he bought the magazine and became both editor and publisher. Still famous for the reputation H. L. Mencken had created for it in the 1930s, the magazine was losing money. In his effort to maintain its solvency, Huie gradually relinquished editorial control, was bought out, and in 1952 was fired. Thereafter, the *American Mercury* suffered a rapid decline, but Huie, who by then had published at least seven books, was largely able to make his living as a freelance writer and novelist, which he did, traveling from his home base in Hartselle. In the 1950s he also worked for the CBS news series *Chronoscope*, interviewing, among others, John F. Kennedy, Senator Estes Kefauver, and Chief Justice Earl Warren. He was married to Ruth Puckett in 1934. His first wife died in October 1973, and he married Martha Hunt Robertson in 1977.

The concerns apparent in the chronology of his published works reflect Huie's experiences as a reporter, as a World War II veteran, and as, in his introduction to *Three Lives for Mississippi* (1964), "an agrarian who may reside temporarily in New York, Washington, Los Angeles, London, or Zürich but who still feels 'at home' only near the ancient churchyards where the generations are sleeping." He was markedly interested in the uneasy and sometimes violent transformation of the South from New Deal–era politics through the Civil Rights movement, as well as in the parallel evolution of national and foreign policy before and during the Cold War. He broached these subjects through both nonfiction and fiction, sometimes inserting the results of his investigative reporting within the parameters of fiction, as he did in his first novel, *Mud on the Stars* (1942), which contains an account of the wrongful execution of Roosevelt Wilson, a black man, for the crime of raping a white woman in Alabama. In its examination of racism in the rural South and the effects of modernization brought on by the creation of the Tennessee Valley Authority and other Roosevelt-era federal projects, *Mud on the Stars* initiates Huie's career-long engagement with the dissonance wrought on individual lives between tradition-bound regionalism and great national transformations.

During the 1940s he wrote in support of the American war effort, celebrating the work of the Seabees in three different documentary books while challenging, in *The Fight for Air Power* (1942) and *The Case Against the Admirals: Why We Must Have a Unified Command* (1946), what he considered to be the antiquated strategic thinking of the military establishment. In the 1950s he began writing about the war in fictional terms, ultimately producing a trilogy of popular novels that were at the time considered risqué—*The Revolt of Mamie Stover* (1951), *The Americanization of Emily* (1959), and *Hotel Mamie Stover* (1962). These novels probed the public relations machinery of the American military while frankly interpreting the evolution of heterosexual relations in a culture marked by heightened postwar mobility and controversy surrounding Alfred Charles Kinsey's studies of human sexual behavior.

Huie was, however, primarily an investigative journalist and pursued his discipline with an eye toward the discrepancies created between public perception of historical events and the individual lives affected by those events. Three war-related works, *The Execution of Private Slovik* (1954), *The Hero of Iwo Jima and Other Stories* (1962), and *The Hiroshima Pilot* (1964), used extensive biographical research to analyze and discredit American jingoism in favor of informed assessments of the transformations occurring in American culture. In *Hero*, for example, he reported the staging of the famous flag-raising photograph at Iwo Jima through the story of Ira Hayes, a Pima Indian who participated in the staging, and whose undistinguished war record was suppressed in favor of a public relations effort to make him a hero. Huie's juxtaposition of the impoverishment by Anglos of Native-American communities against the public celebration and tragic, private demise of Ira Hayes exemplified the writer's attention to the domestic effects of national military policy and, increasingly, racism.

From the mid-1950s throughout the 1960s Huie produced a number of nonfiction books and one novel about race relations in the South. Through contact with Zora Neale Hurston, he began investigating the conviction in Florida of a black woman accused of murdering a white doctor. *The Crime of Ruby McCollum* (1957) is an account of judicial efforts to suppress testimony revelatory of white corruption and coercive race relations existent both within the case and in the community at large. The text also contains Hurston's own brief report on the trial. During the course of his reporting, Huie was jailed in contempt of court for allegedly attempting to influence a psychiatrist who was a witness in the case. His notoriety among southern segregationists increased with his continuing investigations, among them the 1955 lynching of Emmett Till, the 1964 murder of three civil rights workers in Mississippi, and the story of James Earl Ray's 1968 assassination of Martin Luther King. In his novel *The Klansman* (1967) he attempted to account for, as well as castigate, the re-emergence of the Ku Klux Klan among his fellow Alabamians. The publication of this book earned him the enmity of Governor George Wallace and made him the target of harassment and cross-burnings. Yet he remained in the South. In *The Crime of Ruby McCollum* he wrote, "These men are my folks—the snuff-dipping, weak-livered, red-necked, half-witted Anglo-Saxon bastards whom I alternately love and fear." He died at his office in Guntersville, Alabama.

• Huie's papers are in Special Collections at Ohio State University. His other works include *Seabee Roads to Victory*

(1944), *Can Do! The Story of the Seabees* (1944), *From Omaha to Okinawa: The Story of the Seabees* (1946), *Untold Facts in the Forrestal Case* (1950), *Wolf Whistle and Other Stories* (1959), *He Slew the Dreamer: My Search with James Earl Ray for the Truth about the Murder of Martin Luther King* (1977), *In the Hours of the Night* (1975), *A New Life to Live: Jimmy Putnam's Story* (1977), and *It's Me, O Lord!* (1979). Obituaries are in the *Los Angeles Times*, 23 Nov. 1986, and the *New York Times* and *Washington Post*, both 24 Nov. 1986.

JANE CREIGHTON

HULBERT, William Ambrose (23 Oct. 1832–10 Apr. 1882), baseball executive, was born in Burlington Flats, New York, where his parents (names unknown) were wholesale grocers. His family moved to Chicago when he was two. He attended Chicago public schools and in 1851 entered Beloit Academy in Beloit, Wisconsin. Beloit College had just opened its doors in 1846, and Hulbert expected to matriculate at the new college after completing his preparatory work at the academy, but the family business did not do well enough to keep him there, and he was forced to drop out after only two semesters. His formal education ended at that point. He returned to Chicago to help in his father's wholesale coal and grocery business. About this same time he met and married Jennie Murray. He rapidly made a place for himself in the Chicago business community as a highly regarded member of the Board of Trade. He was honest and energetic and was often quoted by his friends as saying that he would rather be a lamppost in Chicago than a millionaire in any other city.

The growing popularity of baseball added a new dimension to Hulbert's life. By the 1860s players had organized themselves enough to establish some national standards of play and guidelines for structuring a team. The Civil War reinforced this interest, and the game spread widely with the end of hostilities. In 1871 the teams made up of paid players created the National Association of Professional Baseball Players, the game's first professional league.

Civic pride pushed Hulbert into helping his home team, the Chicago White Stockings. The Great Fire of October 1871 burned their stadium and shut the team down until 1874. In that year the team was reorganized and built a new stadium at State and 23d streets. Hulbert, apparently not an athlete despite his six-foot, 215-pound bulk, nevertheless wanted to save the team. He helped in the 1874 rebuilding, became a stockholder, then director, and, in 1875, president.

The new NAPBBP experienced many problems that threatened to destroy the league. It had no centralized control; players jumped from one team to another, even in mid-season. The games were accompanied by much gambling, drunkenness, and rowdyism; game-throwing was often suspected, and losing teams frequently did not bother to finish the season. The owners were particularly unhappy with the power exerted by the players. Hulbert determined to effect a change.

At the end of the 1875 season he secretly negotiated contracts with a handful of the game's stars who belonged to other teams—among them Adrian "Pop" Anson, one of the greatest hitters of all time; Roscoe Barnes, league batting champion in 1875; and Albert G. Spalding, the league's best pitcher. With a strong, stable White Stockings team in hand and facing possible censure from the other presidents for stealing players, Hulbert concluded that the future lay in a league of similar teams outside the control of the players. On his own initiative, but with advice from Spalding, he held a secret meeting in Louisville to get the support of the Louisville, Cincinnati, and St. Louis management; he then called a meeting for February 1876 in New York. He invited only the owners of the New York, Boston, Hartford, and Philadelphia teams. Before the others could condemn him, Hulbert pulled a constitution out of his pocket and presented the owners with a plan for a new eight-team league—to be run by the owners. They liked what they saw, abandoned the censure, and created the National League of Professional Baseball Clubs. The players were caught by surprise but were not totally happy with present conditions, and the NAPBBP quickly folded.

Hulbert established a league office with a board and officers. These officials paid the umpires, set regular game schedules, and supervised the signing of tighter player contracts. For the next century the players were employees who had few rights. Hulbert and Spalding selected Morgan G. Bulkely—a banker, future president of the Aetna Life Insurance Company, and president of the Hartford team—to be the first president of the league. Bulkely held the job for one year, and then, apparently by prearrangement, resigned in favor of Hulbert.

Not all went well with the league in the beginning. The White Stockings were too powerful—Spalding won three-fourths of his games. Two teams did not finish the 1876 season and were expelled by Hulbert. His refusal to permit Sunday games cut into profits. Some teams were not well run. A few Louisville players threw some games; the nation's poor economy played its part. Franchise shifting was common, upsetting the very stability that Hulbert had hoped to bring to the sport. But Hulbert's White Stockings, who eventually became the Chicago Cubs, continued to do well. Anson served as field manager, and Spalding, who soon quit pitching to spend more time with his highly successful sporting equipment business, moved up to general manager. Home attendance averaged about 2,500. The National League, as it came to be called, faced strong competition from many other leagues, but Hulbert's work outlasted all except the new American League, founded in 1901, which finally achieved equality with the first World Series in 1903. The National League stabilized at eight teams from 1899 until 1962.

No baseball executive ever again exerted as much authority as Hulbert did. Perhaps his most important contribution was including the infamous reserve clause into players' contracts, virtually tying a player to one team for the length of his career, a policy that survived until the 1970s. He singlehandedly banished teams for violating agreements and permanently outlawed players for gambling or even drunkenness. Hulbert continued as president of both the Chicago team and the National League until he died in Chicago of lingering heart problems. On his death, the league owners resolved "that to him alone is due credit for having founded the National League." Although most of the early baseball administrators were voted into the Baseball Hall of Fame, Hulbert, often called "the savior of baseball," still remained unrecognized by the Hall as of the early 1990s.

• No full biography of Hulbert exists. The best short sketch is by William E. Akin in *Biographical Dictionary of American Sports: Baseball*, ed. David L. Porter (1987). Brief items are to be found in Donald Honig, *The National League* (1983); Joe Reichler, *Ronald Encyclopedia of Baseball* (1962); Jack Selzer, *Baseball in the Nineteenth Century* (1986); Eddie Gold, "Hall Would Be Home for Hulbert," *Baseball Historical Review* (June 1981): 89–91; Peter Levine, *A. G. Spalding and the Rise of Baseball* (1985); Robert L. Tiemann and Mark Rucker, eds., *Nineteenth Century Stars* (1989); *Sport Magazine*, July 1990, p. 56; David Q. Voigt, *Baseball, an Illustrated History* (1987); and a clipping and a letter from the Beloit College office of alumni affairs. For background, see Jay Robert Nash, *Makers and Breakers of Chicago* (1985), and Bessie Louise Pierce, *A History of Chicago* (1937; repr. 1957, 1975).

THOMAS L. KARNES

HULL, Agrippa (1759–1848), revolutionary war soldier, was born a free African American in Northampton, Massachusetts, of unknown parentage. He was taken to Stockbridge, Massachusetts, at the age of six by Joab, an African-American former servant to Jonathan Edwards. When Hull was eighteen years old, in May 1777, he enlisted to fight in the revolutionary war as a private in General John Paterson's brigade of the First Massachusetts Regiment of the Continental army. Free blacks had been allowed by the Continental Congress to enlist in the army since January 1776, but each unit commander determined whether or not he would accept African-American recruits.

Hull served as General Paterson's personal orderly for two years. He then attended General Tadeusz Kosciuszko, the Polish volunteer in the American cause, as an orderly for four years and two months. As an orderly, Hull performed a variety of personal and military duties for the generals, including serving as a surgeon's assistant in South Carolina in 1781. Hull was with Kosciuszko during battles from Saratoga, New York, through the campaign in the South and served with the general until the end of the war. When the Continental army was disbanded at West Point in the summer of 1783, Hull received a discharge signed personally by George Washington, the commander in chief, a document he prized for the rest of his life.

After the war, Hull returned to Stockbridge, Massachusetts, where he eventually owned a small plot of land. As was the case for many free African Americans in New England after the Revolution, Hull was on the economic margins of society, and he eked out a living from a variety of sources. He farmed his land, performed odd jobs around Stockbridge, and occasionally served as a butler and a major-domo to the local gentry.

However marginal his economic position, Hull was very much a part of town life in Stockbridge. The prominent Stockbridge resident and novelist Catherine Maria Sedgwick, whose family was friendly to Hull, called him "a sort of Sancho Panza in the village." He acquired a reputation for understanding the supernatural and was considered something of the town "seer."

Hull married twice and adopted at least one child. His first wife (whom he married sometime before 1790) was Jane Darby, a fugitive slave from Lenox, Massachusetts, whose master, Mr. Ingersoll, tried to seize her after she had married Hull. After Jane Darby died, Hull married Margaret Timbroke. Sometime after the revolutionary war, Hull adopted the daughter of Mary Gunn, a runaway slave from New York.

Like most revolutionary war veterans, Hull was proud of his military service. When General Kosciuszko returned to the United States in 1797 after fighting for Polish independence, Hull traveled to New York to meet with him, and during this trip Kosciuszko directed the Ohio land granted to him by Congress to be sold to pay for a school for African Americans.

One of only several dozen African Americans who applied for revolutionary war pensions, Hull received a veteran's pension from Congress, which he sought to have mailed to his home in 1828. Hull enlisted the help of Charles Sedgwick, who wrote to Acting Secretary of State Richard Rush for assistance with Hull's claim. Hull enclosed his discharge paper as proof of his service but worried that it might not be returned.

Slavery was outlawed by 1790 under the Massachusetts state constitution, but racial divisions in society persisted. Within a restrictive system of racial hierarchy, Hull used his good standing in the community of Stockbridge and his good humor to question the limitations of race. The town historian, Electa F. Jones, who knew Hull, recorded several anecdotes that reveal Hull's racial attitudes. For example, on one occasion he proclaimed: "It is not the *cover* of the book, but what the book *contains*. . . . Many a good book has dark covers."

That Hull was a respected member of Stockbridge society by the end of his life in the 1840s is evidenced by two main facts. The historian Francis Parkman recorded his impressions of Hull after a visit to Stockbridge in 1844, declaring that Hull "looked on himself as father to all Stockbridge." Hull's respectability was also portrayed visually in 1844 in a daguerreotype photograph by Anson Clark, which was copied as an oil painting in 1848. The photograph and painting present an image of Hull as a distinguished, formally dressed old man staring out resolutely and grasping a cane firmly in his left hand. The oil painting of Hull, one of the few formal portraits of an African-American revolutionary war veteran, hangs in the Stockbridge Public Library.

Hull died in Stockbridge. His position in the Continental army was more distinguished than that of most African Americans who were allowed to serve, and as the orderly to generals, he witnessed some of the most important fighting of the war. Hull carried with him for the rest of his life the legacy of his important service to the revolutionary cause, which enhanced his pride as a free African-American man. He stands as an extraordinary example of early African-American military service and as a typical example of the free African Americans who carved a place for themselves in New England society between the revolutionary war and the Civil War.

• Hull's pension application is in the National Archives, Service and Pension Records. Additional information is in the Agrippa Hull Collection in the Stockbridge, Mass., Public Library and in Electa F. Jones, *Stockbridge, Past and Present* (1854; repr. 1994). The best biographical treatment of Hull is in Sidney Kaplan and Emma Nogrady Kaplan, *The Black Presence in the Era of the American Revolution* (1989).

SARAH J. PURCELL

HULL, Albert Wallace (19 Apr. 1880–22 Jan. 1966), physicist, was born in Southington, Connecticut, the son of Lewis Caleb Hull, a dairy farmer and justice of the peace, and Frances Hinman. Hull attended school in Torrington, Connecticut, then returned to the farm for four years before entering Yale College in 1901. He majored in Greek but also excelled in mathematics, and worked at carpentry during vacations. After earning a B.A. in 1905, he spent the summer in Germany, and then took a job teaching French and German at the Albany Academy, a private high school in Albany, New York.

In 1906 he returned to Yale to do graduate work in physics, in which he received a Ph.D. in 1909. He then became an instructor of physics at Worcester Polytechnic Institute, where he rose in 1909 to assistant professor. He carried out research on the photoelectric effect and in 1913 presented a paper on that subject at a meeting of the American Physical Society in New Haven. There he met two researchers from the General Electric Research Laboratory in Schenectady, New York, William D. Coolidge, a physicist who had recently invented the modern form of X-ray tube, and Irving Langmuir, a chemist who was then beginning the research in surface chemistry that would win him the Nobel Prize in 1932.

As a result of this meeting, Hull received an invitation to work at the GE lab for the summer of 1913. In 1914 Hull joined the GE Research Laboratory full time as a research physicist. At the time of his arrival, GE researchers were extending their established knowledge of phenomena inside light bulbs to the new field of vacuum-tube electronics, the basic technology for making devices to control and amplify the flow of electricity in electronic devices such as radios. The re-

searchers were challenged to develop technology not already covered by rival electronic patents, such as the one received by independent inventor Lee De Forest on the three-element vacuum tube. In his first year at GE, Hull invented a vacuum tube based on a new method of control, the dynatron, which used a special spacing of electrodes to cause the current of the tube to decrease with increasing voltage. Though an intriguing idea, it never found practical use. He would go on to obtain ninety-four U.S. patents, mainly in the field of vacuum-tube electronics, and to publish seventy-two papers.

A second new idea emerging in physics in 1914, the scattering of electron beams by crystals, led Hull in another pioneering direction. The original electron scattering concept was applicable only to relatively large single crystals. Hull recognized that the method could, with the proper mathematical treatment, also be applied to powders to determine the structure of the smaller crystals that made up the powder grains. A calculation error by an assistant set back completion of the research slightly, but Hull published the new method in a 1917 paper in the *Physical Review*. By then it had already been independently discovered by two other physicists, Peter Debye and Paul Hermann Scherrer, and today all three are credited for the development of the method, which is now a standard technique for determining the structure of powdered materials.

During World War I, Hull worked on methods for the detection of submarines. After the war, he returned to the problem of helping establish for GE a strong position in vacuum-tube electronics, which was now seen as a key to the emerging business of radio. Resuming the search for an alternative to the control of electron tubes by the electrostatic means covered by the De Forest patent, he explored the control of vacuum tubes by magnetism.

The result was Hull's invention in 1920 of a new type of magnetically controlled vacuum tube, the magnetron. It drew intense but temporary interest for its initial applications to radio and power. Though no immediate practical uses emerged, the magnetron remained a topic of engineering research at many laboratories through the 1920s and 1930s. In the 1940s it found its first major use, when Henry A. H. Boot and John T. Randall of the University of Birmingham, England, developed the cavity magnetron, which became the basis of airborne radar systems. After the war, several investigators, such as Percy Spencer of the Raytheon Corporation, recognized that the cavity magnetron could serve as a means of heating many nonmetallic objects from the inside out. As a result, Hull can lay claim to being a grandfather of the microwave oven.

Hull continued to be a prolific inventor of electron tubes. One of his most valuable patents was of the screen-grid tube, a key component in early commercial radios, in 1921. In the mid-1920s, his attention shifted to the use of vacuum tubes to control sizable amounts of power. He led in the improvement of the thyratron, a pioneering device used to control power in such applications as theater lighting. He made major improvements to glass-to-metal seals. One of his inventions became crucial to the development of the modern fluorescent lamp. During World War II, he invented a way to demagnetize ships so they would not set off magnetic mines, and contributed to uses of the magnetron to jam enemy radar. After the war, with colleague Emmet Burger, he made improvements in glass-to-metal seals and tube design that made possible the use of gaseous cesium as an electricity carrier in a tube for converting alternating to direct current.

Hull became a leader in the physics profession, earning a membership in the National Academy of Sciences in 1929 and serving as president of the American Physical Society in 1942. His major awards included the Potts Medal of the Franklin Institute, and the Liebmann Prize of the Institute of Electrical and Electronic Engineers. His style as scientist and inventor emphasized both optimism and daring. In a 1961 autobiographical sketch he declared that "mistakes are unimportant. There is usually something about the result that leads one to suspect and correct the mistake. The main thing is to make progress and not worry about mistakes."

Hull remained at the GE Research Laboratory for his entire career and served as its assistant director from 1928 until 1950. This position was not managerial; instead, it provided him with an office in which he could sketch out a stream of new ideas for vacuum-tube designs to be built and tried out by assistants and technicians. His optimism and encouragement energized a generation of GE researchers, including the laboratory's post–World War II director, C. Guy Suits.

In 1911 Hull had married Mary Walker, with whom he had two children. His hobbies included golf and serving as president of the Schenectady Museum. He retired from GE in 1950 but continued to serve the GE laboratory as a consultant until his death in Schenectady.

• A good extended account of Hull's career is his 1961 autobiographical sketch, on file at both the GE R&D Center, Schenectady, N.Y., and the American Institute of Physics Niels Bohr Library, College Park, Md. Hull's key papers include "A New Method of X-Ray Crystal Analysis," *Physical Review* 10 (1917): 661–96; "The Magnetron," *Journal of the American Institute of Electrical Engineers* 42 (1923): 715–73; and "Qualifications of a Research Physicist," *Science* 73 (1932): 623–27. The fullest biographical sketch is by C. Guy Suits and James Lafferty, "Albert W. Hull," National Academy of Sciences, *Biographical Memoirs* 45 (1968): 53.

GEORGE WISE

HULL, Clark Leonard (24 May 1884–10 May 1952), psychologist, was born near Akron, New York, the son of Leander G. Hull and Florence L. Trask, farmers. Despite growing up under harsh conditions on the Michigan farm to which the family moved in 1887 and only attending school when he could be spared from farmwork, Hull passed a teacher's examination at the age of seventeen. He taught for a year at a local school before returning to high school and subsequently to the academy of Alma College, Michigan, to prepare for college entrance. Hull graduated from the academy in 1905 but immediately fell victim to typhoid fever in an outbreak traced back to the graduation dinner. A year later, after several months of recovering from his illness and a further spell of school teaching, he enrolled at Alma College for a special two-year physical sciences course that prepared future mining engineers for study at other institutions.

Two months after completing this preliminary training and while working as an apprentice engineer, Hull contracted poliomyelitis that left him, at age twenty-four, with a paralyzed leg and in poor general health. These two serious illnesses had profound and lifelong effects on Hull; a career as a mining engineer was now out of the question, and as can be discerned from the notebooks that he kept meticulously for most of his life, an enduring anxiety about his health brought with it an acute sense that he might not be granted enough time to achieve his goals.

During a year of convalescence and a further two years as a schoolteacher, Hull settled on the idea of a career in psychology. In 1911 he married Bertha Iutzi; they had two children. That same year he entered the University of Michigan, graduating with an A.B. and teacher's diploma in 1913. After a year spent teaching at a normal school in Kentucky and unsuccessful attempts to secure fellowships for graduate work at Yale and Cornell Universities, Hull accepted a part-time post as teaching assistant to Joseph Jastrow at the University of Wisconsin, where he earned an M.A. in 1915 and a Ph.D. in 1918. Remaining at Wisconsin, he rose from instructor in psychology in 1916, to assistant professor in 1920, associate professor two years later, and full professor in 1925.

Hull's dissertation had been a laboratory-based demonstration that concept formation, that is, how appropriate rules for categorizing objects or events develop, could be considered a form of learning; this novel and highly influential research was published as *Quantitative Aspects of the Evolution of Concepts: An Experimental Study* (1920). In the early 1920s Hull's attention turned toward two new areas, psychometrics, that is, the measurement of intelligence and ability, and the experimental study of hypnosis and suggestibility. The former led to *Aptitude Testing* (1928), after which he essentially lost interest in the topic. On the other hand, his work on hypnosis, which eventually led him to conclude that the phenomenon was no more than a form of "hypersuggestibility," expanded into an ambitious ten-year program that not only generated many publications, culminating in *Hypnosis and Suggestibility: An Experimental Approach* (1933), but also demonstrated Hull's ability to organize large-scale research projects. By the latter part of the 1920s, however, several events, some quite unconnected, were instrumental in moving Hull's research in a new direction.

Although familiar with J. B. Watson's variety of behaviorism and his claim that the Pavlovian conditioned reflex would provide the scientific basis for a theory of learning, Hull had never been convinced by Watson's system nor by the counter view put forward by supporters of the Gestalt movement, notably German psychologist Kurt Koffka, a recent visitor at Wisconsin. But on reading Gleb Vasilevich Anrep's 1927 translation of Ivan Petrovich Pavlov's *Conditioned Reflexes*, Hull concluded that Pavlovian thinking, especially through the notions of stimulus irradiation and generalization, could actually advance behaviorism well beyond the state in which Watson had left it.

Another crucial event was Hull's decision in 1929 to accept a post as research professor at Yale University's Institute of Psychology, which soon thereafter became part of the Institute of Human Relations, an interdisciplinary research establishment with generous funding from the Rockefeller Foundation. Because Yale had recruited him as a psychometrician, Hull's insistence on continuing his long-term program on hypnosis and his growing interest in learning and behavior (in particular, the conditioned reflex) inevitably brought him into early conflict with some members of the institute; particularly the chair of the psychology department, Roswell P. Angier. While he reluctantly abandoned the hypnosis studies, Hull managed to continue his work on behavior with the help of an increasing number of research assistants and graduate students. In the mid-1930s, however, discontentment about the lack of cooperative research programs expressed by some members of the institute, and also by the Rockefeller Foundation, led to a "revolution" at the institute that put in place the former executive secretary, Mark A. May, as its full-time director and established Hull as its de facto intellectual leader.

Hull's goal now was to develop an empirically grounded system of fundamental laws of behavior of a Newtonian kind. To achieve this, Hull once again exercised his considerable skills to organize and inspire several generations of research assistants and graduate students, at Yale and elsewhere, to carry out closely supervised experimental work, thus freeing him to concentrate on theory. The first mature expression of Hull's system emerged in 1943 in what he termed his "magnum opus," *Principles of Behavior*. Here, he presented an axiomatic and quantitative account of the elementary mechanisms, such as drive, reinforcement, and generalization of stimuli and responses, through which organisms learn to adapt to their environment; a refined and extended version appeared in *A Behavior System*, published posthumously in 1952. Hull, who had suffered from a serious heart condition for a number of years, died in New Haven, Connecticut, two weeks before his sixty-eighth birthday and intended retirement from Yale.

During his academic career, Hull published more than seventy articles, chapters, and monographs, and was author or coauthor of six books. He served as president of the American Psychological Association in 1935–1936 and was a member of the American Academy of Arts and Sciences and the National Academy of Sciences. He received the Warren Medal of the Society of Experimental Psychologists in 1945. In 1947 he was honored by Yale with the award of a prestigious Sterling Professorship.

Although Hull undoubtedly viewed his behavior system as the crowning achievement of his career and, indeed, his was the dominant voice in the published literature on learning through the 1940s, its rapid eclipse after his death has tended to raise the profile of his pioneering work on concept formation and hypnosis.

• The Clark Leonard Hull Papers, in Manuscripts and Archives, Yale University Library, include research and laboratory notes, class outlines, seminar notes, and a series of twenty-eight notebooks, Hull's "idea books" (1915–1952), in which he recorded research plans, reactions to events and people, and also some personal thoughts. Extracts mainly from the latter, together with a commentary, are given by R. B. Ammons and R. Hays in "Psychology of the Scientist II–IV," *Perceptual and Motor Skills* 15 (1962): 800–882. Among Hull's works not already mentioned are, with C. E. Limp, "The Differentiation of the Aptitudes of an Individual by Means of Test Batteries," *Journal of Educational Psychology* 16 (1925): 73–88, and "Quantitative Methods of Investigating Hypnotic Suggestion. Part I," *Journal of Abnormal and Social Psychology* 25 (1930): 200–23, exemplifying his work on psychometrics and on hypnosis and suggestibility; "Learning: II. The Factor of the Conditioned Reflex," in *A Handbook of General Experimental Psychology*, ed. C. Murchison (1934), pp. 382–455; "Mind, Mechanism, and Adaptive Behavior," *Psychological Review* 44 (1937): 1–32; "The Problem of Stimulus Equivalence in Behavior Theory," *Psychological Review* 46 (1939): 9–30; and, with C. I. Hovland et al., *Mathematico-Deductive Theory of Rote Learning* (1940), which describes aspects of his work on behavior and learning theory. An autobiographical sketch appears in E. G. Boring et al., eds., *A History of Psychology in Autobiography*, vol. 4 (1952), pp. 143–62. A bibliography of Hull's publications is appended to an obituary by F. A. Beach, National Academy of Sciences, *Biographical Memoirs* 33 (1959): 124–41. Other obituaries include those by K. W. Spence in *American Journal of Psychology* 65 (1952): 639–46, and C. I. Hovland in *Psychological Review* 59 (1952): 346–50.

ALEXANDER D. LOVIE
PATRICIA LOVIE

HULL, Cordell (2 Oct. 1871–23 July 1955), secretary of state, congressman, and lawyer, was born near Byrdstown, Tennessee, the son of William Hull, a businessman, and Elizabeth Riley. Hull was raised in middle Tennessee near the foothills of the Cumberland Mountains, along with four other brothers. His mother taught him to read and write so that he could understand the Bible while attending Baptist church services, and he furthered his education by going to local schools. In 1891 he entered Cumberland Law School; after being admitted to the state bar the next year, he practiced law until 1903, when he was appointed circuit judge. From that time on, he was nicknamed "judge," and while that was his profession, his avocation was Democratic politics. He gave his first partisan speech at seventeen, served as chairman of the Democratic county executive committee two years later, and went to the state legislature at twenty-two. Only a captaincy in the Spanish-American War interrupted his rising political star.

Hull won a seat in the U.S. House of Representatives in the 1906 election on a platform of championing the rights of farmers from his district. He passionately preached for the rest of his life that the high protective tariff damaged his constituents, and he therefore sought to lower trade barriers. In pursuit of that objective, he promoted an income tax as a more equitable method to raise revenue for the federal government's operations. Never a charismatic speaker and mindful that House Democrats occupied a minority position for most of his congressional tenure, he depended on his skills as a compromiser to reach political consensus. He won plaudits for his abilities to persuade foes and seemed consumed with his political lifestyle. Despite this intensity, he still found time to court Rosetta "Rose" Frances Witz Whitney, and they were married in November 1917. They were not to have children.

Hull generally supported the policies of President Woodrow Wilson and paid dearly for that loyalty when he and large numbers of Democrats lost in the Republican landslide of 1920. For the next two years, Hull served as chairman of the Democratic National Committee, but during his chairmanship he planned to run again in his congressional district and in fact returned to Congress in 1922, resuming his career as a powerful party member with national exposure. During the 1920s he helped shape the Democratic national agenda and met many influential leaders, including Franklin Roosevelt, who advanced Hull's vice presidential bid in 1928. Four years later, the congressman remembered this advocacy by announcing early his support for Roosevelt's presidential bid.

To pay off a political debt and to reward the South for its role in the 1932 Democratic triumph, Roosevelt offered the post of secretary of state to Hull early in January 1933. Although he lacked any significant skills in foreign affairs, that was immaterial, for Roosevelt expected to play a dominant diplomatic role. Hull mirrored the image of how a secretary of state should look: about six feet tall, lean, with white hair and dark piercing eyes. His attractive appearance and three-piece suits in many ways masked deficiencies. He had virtually no management experience, was unduly sensitive to press criticism, acted indecisively, and had tuberculosis, then menacingly labeled the "White Plague." In addition, his wife—though raised an Episcopalian—had a Jewish father; and to forestall the potentially harmful effects of her background on his career, he refused to address Jewish issues.

Hull managed to stay away from unpopular immigration matters during his first year in office because he spent much of his time abroad. His first foreign assignment was attendance at the London Economic Conference during the summer to try to answer questions on how to solve the worldwide economic depression. He initially hoped to present a resolution to lower trade barriers, but the president squelched that idea. When the secretary arrived in England, each nation offered its own solution to solve the economic chaos, but the conferees, as a whole, could not agree. In the midst of this uncertainty, Roosevelt dispatched Raymond Moley, a member of his "Brain Trust," to present his recommendations, but he arrived without any concrete proposals. As a result, the European delegates turned against the United States and were prepared to blame it for the conference's failure to act. At that critical juncture, Hull asserted his authority, sent Moley home, and deflected antagonism from the Americans. Roosevelt recognized that the secretary had saved him from severe criticism and praised Hull on his return. The secretary vaguely realized that the conference had only the remotest chance of success; instead, he focused his frustration on Moley, who allegedly spied on him at the gathering and so proved his disloyalty.

Hull grossly exaggerated Moley's insubordination and, for the first time in his tenure, demonstrated that he placed personalities above issues. The U.S. failure at the London conference was, according to Hull, principally due to Moley's interference, not to worldwide economic chaos. Shortly after the London meeting, recognizing the secretary's chagrin, Moley submitted his resignation as assistant secretary of state. Hull was elated that he not only could rid his department of an enemy but could also take the occasion to replace him with an old congressional ally, R. Walton Moore.

Hull's second mission that year came in the winter when he traveled to Montevideo, Uruguay, for the Seventh International Conference of American States. The president had persuaded him to become the first secretary of state to attend a pan-American gathering while in office. Initially, the secretary predicted failure because of the anarchical conditions in Cuba. Gerardo Machado, the island's dictator, removed him from power by revolt, but his successor, Carlos Manuel de Céspedes, was soon overthrown. The president and Hull adamantly opposed U.S. intervention, but they agreed to Ambassador Sumner Welles's request not to recognize the provisional government. As Hull later learned, nonrecognition guaranteed Cuban instability and criticism of U.S. interference in the island's domestic affairs. Throughout the fall, the secretary urged Welles to resolve the nonrecognition impasse, but no one found any resolution by the time Hull left for South America. Hull knew that any lasting accomplishments at the Montevideo conference depended on the whim of Carlos Saavedra Lamas, Argentina's volatile foreign minister. Once they agreed to act in concert by backing each other's chief proposal, success was assured: Hull pressed for lower trade barriers, while Saavedra Lamas pushed for a peace resolution. The gathering, however, was best remembered for its nonintervention declaration, in which the United States promised not to intervene in Latin American affairs, thus establishing the so-called good neighbor policy of the Roosevelt administration. The secretary, having scored a badly needed triumph, resumed his lobbying efforts to reduce tariffs after returning to Washington. He saw the trip to South America as the foundation for future bargaining, never understanding that this was a unique situation. The fortuitous convergence of interests resulted in a productive meeting where all sides benefited; such congeniality would not be repeated.

This miscalculation did not dampen Hull's continued push for freer trade, and by the summer of 1934 his dogged perseverance forced the passage of the Reciprocal Trade Agreements Act. The act put into effect the "most-favored nation" policy with trading partners and enabled the president to negotiate tariff agreements without necessarily having to obtain congressional approval. But even after Roosevelt signed it, he did not give the legislation his unequivocal support. Instead, the president had his foreign trade adviser, George Peek, unsuccessfully promote barter agreements; Hull vehemently resented Peek's intrusion into trade policy and painted him as an enemy, similar to Moley, who was trying to derail Hull's economic philosophy for American prosperity. The secretary of state prevailed, forcing Peek to resign in frustration, and eventually won presidential backing. While many opposed the assumptions on which the Reciprocal Trade Agreements Act rested, it remains the foundation for modern American foreign trade policy.

Hull also assumed the duties of shaping East Asian policy. Relying on guidance from the chief of the Division of Far Eastern Affairs, Stanley Horneck, he opposed Japanese interference in Chinese affairs and demanded U.S. access to China's economic markets, where the Roosevelt administration would not accept Japanese domination. Throughout the remainder of the president's first term the secretary worked to decrease the chances of war in East Asia; he tried to build on the good neighbor concept and preached reciprocity. He avoided the divisive issue of the growing number of German Jews who clamored for American visas to escape Nazi persecution.

Much to Hull's chagrin, Roosevelt directed many of the administration's European initiatives, but Hull tolerated White House meddling. The real or imagined interloping of presidential appointees like Moley and Peek was demeaning enough that toward the end of 1935 Hull momentarily considered running for election to the Senate, but eventually he decided to remain in the cabinet.

At the end of Roosevelt's first term, Hull traveled to the Inter-American Conference for the Maintenance of Peace that convened in December at Buenos Aires, Argentina. Roosevelt had initiated the idea of the hemispheric peace gathering, and his secretary of state also anticipated success based on the past cooperation of Saavedra Lamas at Montevideo. Hull did not understand that the Argentine foreign minister had his own imperatives that clashed with the secretary's plans, and by the end of the meeting Hull was so angry that he considered demanding that Argentine president Augustín Justo compel Saavedra Lamas's resignation. Although he did not make the demand, Hull, for the rest of his tenure, staunchly maintained that the Argentine foreign ministry was a personal enemy.

What Hull perceived as a diplomatic affront deeply affected him, but he refused to deal with a bureaucratic battle within his department that had scarring repercussions. When the job of undersecretary of state opened in 1936, both Welles and Moore vied for the post. The former was allegedly the president's choice; the latter was the secretary's. Hull, however, refused to select Moore, and in the spring of 1937, after much intrigue, Welles became undersecretary while Moore became counselor to the secretary. Welles assumed the post with gusto and gradually drew closer to the president; vanquished, Moore turned into a constant critic of both Welles and Hull for the balance of his term.

With Welles actively in charge of managing the departmental bureaucracy, Hull concentrated on the direction of East Asian policy, continually calling for restraint even when Japanese military aircraft flying in China attacked the USS *Panay*, causing two deaths and injuring fifty. When the president, with Welles's encouragement, wanted to hold a disarmament conference in early 1938, the secretary correctly dampened their enthusiasm by pointing out the futility of the project. Hull did welcome another inter-American gathering, held in Peru at the end of the year, as an opportunity to advance the good neighbor policy, and the Declaration of Lima moved the cause of hemispheric solidarity forward by doing just enough to demonstrate unity and condemn foreign aggression.

By the time World War II erupted in September 1939, Hull's personal health was worsening, as was his suspicion concerning Welles's friendship and increasing access to Roosevelt. Shortly after the fighting commenced, the undersecretary advocated enforcing a neutrality zone around the Western hemisphere to prevent the warring parties from deploying their warships in American waters. While Hull seriously doubted the legality of such a policy, he grudgingly accepted it. But when Roosevelt sent Welles on a European mission at the start of 1940, the secretary believed that his subordinate was using the trip to gain exposure for himself at the expense of caution. Welles's journey ended futilely, yet Hull viewed it as concrete evidence that his undersecretary had bypassed him and gone directly to the White House.

Hull endured these slights because he wanted to run for the presidency in 1940. The president, before he broke the two-term tradition, had even encouraged his secretary of state and others to consider the possibility. Hull knew his major liabilities: his wife's Jewish ancestry, his southern background, his age, and his deteriorating health. Despite these drawbacks, he wanted to try, and a successful candidacy depended heavily on Roosevelt's blessing. Once the president announced his intention to run for a third term, Hull fumed but remained silent. He preferred Roosevelt to any Republican.

Hull, who seldom moved boldly, was always consistent. Above all else, he wanted to save the United States from being drawn into another world war. In that effort, he fought energetically for his reciprocity program on the grounds that economic intercourse fostered peaceful relations. He negotiated with the Japanese to halt their expansionist dreams, while he simultaneously tried to bolster the Chinese government. And he acted as the principal spokesman for the good neighbor policy, thereby promoting the cause of inter-American cooperation.

Hull resented White House direction of Anglo-American negotiations and was deeply wounded when Roosevelt, without consulting him, chose Welles to attend the Argentia conference with Winston Churchill in the summer of 1941 off the Newfoundland coast. Once the Atlantic Charter was announced, Hull feigned knowledge, but he played no part in this declaration that called for the collapse of the Nazi regime, a new world organization, freer international trade, and self-determination for all peoples.

Throughout that year Hull worked tirelessly to preserve peace in East Asia by lobbying for solutions to the problems of Sino-Japanese relations under the rule of international law. He tried to minimize friction by refraining from labeling the Japanese as aggressors; at the same time he insisted on recognizing Chinese sovereignty through the recognition of the Chungking government of Chiang Kai-shek and providing it with economic assistance. Hull also fought against the establishment of Japan's East Asia Co-Prosperity Sphere, which made Tokyo the center of the region's trade, thus restricting U.S. commercial opportunities. He even threatened economic sanctions, but this proved ineffectual. Somehow he felt that his initiatives ranging from military threats to economic cooperation would prevent bloodshed. Even after Germany, Italy, and Japan formed the Axis, he hoped to split that alliance by encouraging Japanese moderates to block their militarists. The United States froze Japanese assets during the summer of 1941 to keep a shaky Pacific peace. Throughout the fall Hull tried to resolve irreconcilable differences. In November and early December, he held many secret meetings with Japanese envoys, but the Japanese attack on Pearl Harbor crushed his dream of peace.

Distraught over his failure to prevent war and physically exhausted from his hectic schedule and health complications, the secretary suffered further from unfounded rumors that he somehow had led a conspiracy to withhold essential documents that would have prevented the surprise attack. The overwhelming majority dismissed these rumors, and Hull's popularity soared, for he was to many a symbol of America's stoic wartime strength. But he sometimes made critical blunders, as in the case of the St. Pierre–Miquelon dispute when Charles de Gaulle's Free French forces took three tiny islands from the Vichy government on Christmas Day. Hull demanded that the "so-called Free French" return these islands to Vichy, and the press viciously disapproved, labeling him the "so-called secretary of state." Neither Churchill nor Roosevelt rallied to his side, adding to Hull's humiliation.

Worn out, Hull penciled out his resignation in January 1942 but never sent it to the White House. The United States was at war, and his patriotic duty was to remain at his desk. While Hull tried to cope with wartime diplomacy at the beginning of 1942, Undersecretary Welles journeyed to Rio de Janeiro for an emergency inter-American conference to have Latin America sever its relations with the Axis. Listening to a radio commentator on 23 January, Hull heard that Argentina had refused to break relations and that to win unanimous approval the United States had agreed to a compromise resolution. He exploded. Welles now was guilty of betrayal, and Hull phoned him in Brazil to demand a reversal of policy. When the undersecretary refused, Hull had Roosevelt join in the discussion; but the president sided with Welles. Nevertheless, the secretary decided to remove his subordinate for his disloyalty. The Hull-Welles relationship had moved from cooperation to halting acceptance, resentment, distrust, and finally hatred. Almost immediately after Welles returned to the capital, Hull left Washington for Florida without even exchanging a word with him.

The secretary stayed away from the capital until the end of April and came back well rested, with a promise to his doctor to reduce his workload. Hull resumed control of his department by preventing Vice President Henry Wallace from encroaching on foreign economic policy and stopping Secretary of the Treasury Henry Morgenthau from interfering in diplomatic affairs, especially the controversial issue of Nazi subversion in Argentina. Hull even joined in the debate over a postwar world association by delivering a carefully worded statement on nationwide radio. Although somewhat pessimistic, he advocated a modest beginning rather than unmanageable grandiose plans for an international police force. Hull also began to plot Welles's ouster. The secretary met with his subordinate toward the end of June and ordered him to stop speaking out on postwar planning, especially with regard to the notion that the United States would help police the world. In addition, gossip had reached Hull that Welles had made homosexual advances to porters on a train ride, and the secretary agonized that such stories would become public and create an embarrassing scandal. To confirm the veracity of the rumors, Hull met privately with the director of the Federal Bureau of Investigation, J. Edgar Hoover, at the end of October. He deduced that Hoover had confirmed the rumors.

At the start of 1943, Hull felt that Roosevelt was ignoring his counsel while heavily depending on Welles. Assistant Secretary of State Adolph Berle lamented in his diary that the "antagonism between Secretary Hull and Mr. Welles makes a good deal of difficulty; the Secretary resents Sumner's going to the White House too much but as he does not go very much himself, this leaves the President at the mercy of unskilled advisers" (Beatrice Bearle and Travis Jacobs, eds., *Navigating the Rapids, 1918–1971*, p. 431). As this irritation festered into a serious sore, the secretary called on former ambassador to France William Bullitt and others to demand Welles's removal. By the middle of August, the president decided that Welles had to leave office, and the White House sadly announced his resignation at the end of September.

Hull, free of Welles, initially rejoiced, but his elation quickly faded as he found himself attacked for his part in the removal of his most experienced and capable assistant. Hull had never been engaged in managing his department's bureaucracy and tended to address only those issues of passionate meaning to him. When Edward Stettinius, Jr., replaced Welles, Hull not only did not indoctrinate the new appointee; he left for a vacation. By the time Hull returned, he had decided to head an American delegation to Moscow in mid-October, even though he was coughing a good deal of blood. Arriving in the Russian capital on the eighteenth, he faced severe winter weather, fatigue, and a frantic schedule. Even so, he argued for and won four-power agreement for a postwar international organization.

Hull landed in Washington to a hero's welcome and became the first secretary of state to speak before a joint session of Congress, where he naively predicted that "there will no longer be need for sphere of influence, for alliances, for balance of power, or any other of the special arrangements through which, in the unhappy past, the nations strove to safeguard their security and promote their interests" (*The Memoirs of Cordell Hull*, vol. 2 (1948), p. 1314–15). What he did not tell his audience was that Welles had scripted the U.S. agenda for the Moscow gathering, and Hull had presented the documents prepared by his adversary to accomplish the American objectives.

Hull celebrated his victory through Christmas, but at the start of the new year he was unable to face new challenges because of ever-worsening health problems and the lack of firm direction of his department. The secretary mishandled the response to a Bolivian coup d'état, and his answer to a military revolt in Argentina was clouded by his antipathy toward Argentina leaders, resulting in a unilateral response of nonrecognition rather than a call for hemispheric consultation.

While inter-American relations suffered, Hull worked to make a global peace organization a success. Using the bargaining skills that he developed in Congress, he consulted with powerful legislators to win their cooperation. Hull forged an agreement whereby both presidential contenders consented not to make this foreign-policy question a contentious issue in the electoral campaign. And he lent his personal prestige to his opening address at the Dumbarton Oaks conference on 21 August 1944 to demonstrate the significance he assigned to the formative gathering of the United Nations.

Despite this activity, Hull realized that his tuberculosis and other medical complications were accelerating his need to retire. Throughout the year, he faced a steady decline, and by the spring he offered his resignation. Roosevelt not only refused this request but also asked the secretary to be his vice presidential running mate. Hull declined the offer, agreeing, however, to remain in office until after the election. While he officially stayed at his post until 27 November, Hull went to the White House for the last time on 1 October to repudiate Morgenthau's plan to dismember Germany. On the very next day, his seventy-third birthday, the secretary was confined to bed and became a semipermanent resident of the Bethesda Naval Hospital. Roosevelt personally expressed his deep regrets about Hull's departure, and others, including Saavedra Lamas, voiced their admiration. Hull spent much of his remaining years hospitalized. He took the honorary title of senior delegate to the United Nations conference in San Francisco, but he had virtually no influence in those epic deliberations in the spring and summer of 1945. Later that year, among other accolades, he won the Nobel Peace Prize, but he was too ill to travel abroad and personally receive the award.

Hull devoted most of his time to completing his memoirs. Although Andrew Berding, his ghostwriter, drafted the majority of the text, Hull spent one hour a day, three days a week, reviewing material and presenting his recollections of the events. He avoided his wife's Jewish ancestry and even applauded his department's controversial role in the Holocaust. He distorted his relationships with Welles, Moore, Bullitt, and others to reflect his perspective. He took credit for the accomplishments at the Montevideo conference and the Moscow mission and undeservedly assumed the mantle of father of the United Nations. These memoirs remain the ultimate defense of Hull's diplomatic tenure; and while there are obvious flaws in them, his reminiscences have become, in far too many instances, indisputable fact.

Although rushed to the hospital in late 1944 and placed on the critical list several times, Hull recovered and remained alert until his wife died in 1954. After her passing, he became a semi-invalid. In the summer of 1955, he suffered a major stroke, lapsed into a coma, and died. With 2,000 mourners in attendance at the National Cathedral in Washington, Hull was laid to rest in a crypt beneath the church next to his wife.

Many have minimized Hull's importance for a variety of reasons, largely because of Roosevelt's titanic presence. Hull simply did not rise to the presidential legend. This, however, begs a serious evaluation of his place in history. In many ways, he was petty, particularly in the treatment of Moley and Peek. His fixation on personal insubordination reached its climax with the firing of Welles, which created a void that the secretary could not fill. Hull made substantial mistakes, as in the case of the St. Pierre–Miquelon fiasco and the argument over the Rio declaration. In spite of his errors in judgment, Hull won an enormous following and used his popularity to shape public opinion. He helped to forge support for good neighbor diplomacy and the United Nations. While he worked tirelessly to find a peaceful solution to U.S.-Japanese relations, he could not deflect the assault on Pearl Harbor. His labors to reduce tariff rates still reverberate; more than anyone else, Hull sought to lower trade barriers when this idea was greeted with skepticism. He never relinquished his crusade that increased international commercial intercourse assisted in greater prosperity and therefore created a more peaceful world. His legacy persists.

• The Cordell Hull Papers located at the Manuscript Division of the Library of Congress in Washington, D.C., are incomplete, although they contain a great deal of useful information. The George F. Milton Papers, the only collection that contains significant correspondence from Frances Hull, are in the same repository. For Cordell Hull's medical records, see the Barbara Gellman Papers at the Franklin D. Roosevelt Library, Hyde Park, N.Y. Harold Hinton, *Cordell Hull: A Biography* (1942), published at the beginning of World War II, is laudatory, while Julius Pratt, *Cordell Hull, 1933–44*, vols. 12 and 13 in *The American Secretaries of State and Their Diplomacy*, ed. Robert Ferrell (1964), rearranges Hull's memoirs and adds few insights. Irwin Gellman examines his career in *Secret Affairs: Franklin Roosevelt, Cordell Hull, and Sumner Welles* (1995). Two Ph.D. dissertations focus on Hull's early life: Catherine Grollman, "Cordell Hull and His Concept of a World Organization" (Univ. of North Carolina, 1965), and Cooper Milner, "The Public Life of Cordell Hull: 1907–1924" (Vanderbilt Univ., 1960). His role as secretary of state in East Asia up to the Second World War is definitively explored in Jonathan Utley, *Going to War with Japan, 1937–1941* (1985). Gellman, *Roosevelt and Batista: Good Neighbor Diplomacy in Cuba, 1933–1945* (1973), discusses Hull's conduct during and after the Cuban revolution of 1933. The same author's *Good Neighbor Diplomacy: United States Policies in Latin America, 1933–1945* (1979) surveys Hull's general and specific hemispheric actions. Concerning the bitter and complicated Hull-Welles conflict, Benjamin Welles, *Sumner Welles: FDR's Global Strategist: A Biography* (1997), offers a slanted, sympathetic rationale for his father's actions that should be tempered with Gellman, *Secret Affairs*.

IRWIN GELLMAN

HULL, Hannah Hallowell Clothier (21 July 1872–4 July 1958), peace activist and suffragist, was born in Sharon Hill, Pennsylvania, the daughter of Isaac Hallowell Clothier and Mary Clapp Jackson. The fourth of nine children, Hannah Clothier grew up within the sheltered confines of wealthy Philadelphia society. Her father was a founding partner in the largest dry goods store in the United States, Strawbridge & Clothier, and the family devoted its considerable fortune to Quaker philanthropies, especially Swarthmore College. After attending the Friends' Central School in Philadelphia, seventeen-year-old Hannah attended Swarthmore College for two years, leaving with a B.L. degree in 1891. The family forbade her from seeking paid employment, but she was able to spend five years engaged in volunteer settlement work in Philadelphia. In 1896 and 1897 Hannah resumed her studies in history and biblical literature at Bryn Mawr, and in 1898, at the age of twenty-six, she married William Isaac Hull, an associate professor of history and political science at Swarthmore College.

The Hulls' courtship had coincided with the Spanish-American War, and their shared distrust of that military venture served as the starting point for a forty-year partnership devoted to activist pacifism. In addi-

tion to raising two children, Hannah and William Hull engaged in reform efforts, within and outside the Quaker community, which aimed at creating a peaceful and humane world.

The Hull family was on sabbatical, living at The Hague, at the time of the Second International Peace Conference in 1907. This was a useful introduction to the worldwide peace movement for Hannah Hull, but upon her return to the United States, where she was a faculty wife and the mother of two school-age children, she initially devoted her civic energies to local concerns. Hull served as president of the Swarthmore Woman's Club from 1909 to 1913, vice president of the Pennsylvania Woman Suffrage Association in 1913 and 1914, and chair of the Philadelphia branch of the Association of Collegiate Alumnae between 1916 and 1920. Her ties to both Quaker pacifism and to the woman suffrage movement served to draw her into international peace efforts during World War I, however. Under the leadership of Chicago's premier social reformer, Jane Addams, thousands of suffragist women in 1915 had formed the Woman's Peace party. Hull became president of the Pennsylvania chapter of the Woman's Peace party in 1917, just at the time that the United States was entering the war and many Americans were withdrawing from pro-peace activities.

Taking on this position at the age of forty-five, when the average age of Woman's Peace party members was fifty-nine, Hull represented a new generation of female peace activists. While sympathetic to the nineteenth-century view that maternal nature was inherently pacifist, Hull's own religious and marital experience led her to emphasize sexual equality and to insist that women be allowed to be "complete citizens" so that they could prevent war from diverting money and energy away from social welfare. Her moderate political orientation and self-effacing personal style made her an ideal leader for the women's peace movement during the troubled 1920s.

After World War I, the Woman's Peace party became the Women's International League for Peace and Freedom (WILPF), and Hull continued to serve as president of the league's Pennsylvania chapter, in addition to working with the American Friends' Service Committee on relief to European civilians. In 1924 Hull was recruited to serve as WILPF's national chair. The organization had been in disarray since 1919 when Jane Addams had shifted her attention to the league's international affairs. During these difficult years, conservatives on the outside had been attacking WILPF for being too radical, while radicals on the inside had been rebelling against the organization's perceived conservatism.

Hull stepped into this situation as one member of a triumvirate that stabilized WILPF in the mid-1920s. Along with Dorothy Detzer and Mildred Scott Olmstead, Hull focused WILPF's program and broadened its membership. During these same years, she continued to be active in Philadelphia in the American Friends' Service Committee, the American Association of University Women, the Armstrong Association for Social and Educational Work with Negroes, and the Quaker Meeting.

Hull served as chair of the national unit of WILPF from 1924 to 1928. Following a year of international travel with her husband in 1928 and 1929, Hull returned to WILPF to serve as chair of the national board from 1929 to 1933 and then as president of the U.S. section of the organization from 1933 to 1939. Under Hull's leadership, WILPF called for an end to immigration quotas, repeal of the Platt Amendment, reduction of tariffs, antilynching legislation, an end to military training in the schools, and, above all, an end to government support of the munitions industry. WILPF lobbied heartily for the Kellogg-Briand Pact (1928) outlawing all offensive military actions but chose to focus its political energy on disarmament efforts rather than on efforts to unconditionally outlaw war. As a suffrage leader, Hull had publicized the liquor industry's investment in the antisuffrage movement. As a peace leader, Hull concentrated on the munitions industry's investment in war. In 1934, Hull, Olmstead, and Detzer were instrumental in passage of the bill that funded the Nye Committee's investigations into the relationship between the arms traffic and World War I.

Hull worked with Mabel Vernon in 1932 on WILPF's aggressive drive collecting 500,000 signatures on a petition calling for "total and universal disarmament," which was presented to the League of Nations Conference on Reduction and Limitation of Arms in Geneva. Three years later, she served as chair of the executive committee of the People's Mandate committee, which collected eight million signatures on an international petition calling on governments to end war.

During the tortured debate in WILPF over neutrality in the mid-1930s, Hull sided with those who favored strict and absolute neutrality, but she spoke openly of the debate as a "wholesome sign." She spoke with equal candor of her view that the Munich agreement merely afforded time for allies to arm themselves and noted in a speech in 1936 that "our own country is . . . the chief offender in the illusion that armaments are a means of maintaining peace."

Hull retired from the presidency of the U.S. section of WILPF after her husband died in 1939 but held a post as honorary national president until her death. According to one biographer, she continued to attend Swarthmore football games until the age of eighty-five. She died at her home in Swarthmore.

• Swarthmore College Peace Collection contains some of Hull's writings, speeches, and correspondence related to her work with WILPF. The Peace Collection holdings on Jane Addams and Lucia Ames Mead, as well as on the Woman's Peace party and WILPF, also contain information on Hull. The Swarthmore College Alumni Office has some clippings on Hull. For information on Hull's Quaker background, see Howard Brinton, ed., *Byways of Quaker History* (1944), chap. 1. See Harriet Hyman Alonso, *Peace as a Women's Issue: A History of the U.S. Movement for World Peace and*

Women's Rights (1993); Gertrude Bussey and Margaret Tims, *Women's International League for Peace and Freedom, 1915–1965* (1965); and Charles Chatfield, *For Peace and Justice: Pacifism in America, 1914–1941* (1971), regarding Hull's work in the peace movement. Elizabeth Dilling, *The Red Network* (1934), contains entries on both Hanna and William Hull among its list of subversives.

VICTORIA BROWN

HULL, Henry (3 Oct. 1890–8 Mar. 1977), actor and playwright, was born in Louisville, Kentucky, the son of William M. Hull, a drama critic for the *Louisville Courier-Journal*, and Elinor Bond Vaughn. Hull attended Louisville public schools as a young boy, and in 1904 he enrolled in the College of the City of New York. After two years Hull transferred to the Cooper Union Institute in New York City, remaining there two years before completing his engineering education at Columbia University in 1909. Hull had been working as a mining engineer when his brother Shelley, an actor, secured a small part for him with Guy Bates Post's company; Hull made his stage debut in 1909 in *The Nigger*, under the direction of David Belasco at the Alvin Theatre in Pittsburgh. Hull returned to engineering briefly, and in 1910–1911 he worked as a prospector in Quebec, Canada; however, he had become enchanted with acting and returned to the stage.

Hull made his New York City debut at the Thirty-Ninth Street Theatre on 2 October 1911 as Henry Steele in *Green Stockings*, which starred his sister-in-law Margaret Anglin. He joined Anglin's Greek Repertory Company the following year and toured with them for three years. In 1913 he married Juliet Van Wyck Fremont; they had two children. Hull's first big success came in 1916 when he starred as Henry Potter in *The Man Who Came Back*, which opened at the Playhouse in New York City on 2 September 1916. That same year Hull made his film debut in *The Little Rebel*, and from that time on he alternated between stage and screen.

On the stage he continued his success in *39 East*, playing Napoleon Gibbs (Broadhurst Theatre, 31 Mar. 1919). He then played Carey Harper in *When We Were Young* (Broadhurst Theatre, 22 Nov. 1920). Alexander Wollcott, theater critic for the *New York Times*, said the play "rests heavily upon the likable and engaging qualities of young Henry Hull as a player and a person and it exhibits him agreeably" (23 Nov. 1920). For the next fourteen years Hull played over twenty roles on Broadway, notably Morgan Wallace in *Congratulations* (National Theatre, 7 Feb. 1920), a play that Hull also wrote, and Baron Von Gaigern in *Grand Hotel* (National Theatre, 13 Nov. 1930). As Vincent Armstrong in *The Naked Man* (Broadhurst Theatre, 7 Nov. 1925), Hull's performance, according to the *New York Times*, was "possessed of the forceful repose and naturalness that are characteristic of his work" (8 Nov. 1925). In 1934 Hull played the greatest role of his career, Jeeter Lester in Erskine Caldwell's *Tobacco Road*. The play opened at the Masque Theatre on 4 December and ran for over 3,182 performances—one of the longest runs on Broadway up to that time. His portrayal of the tobacco-chewing farmer won him rave reviews. Brooks Atkinson, theater critic for the *New York Times*, wrote, "As Jeeter Lester, Henry Hull gives the performance of his life. . . . Here is a character portrait as mordant and brilliant as you can imagine" (5 Dec. 1934). Hull continued to act on Broadway in many successful plays until 1959. He also acted at the Shakespeare Festival in Idyllwild, California, in 1954, playing Shylock in *The Merchant of Venice* and Malvolio in *Twelfth Night*.

Although Hull began in silent films, his stage experience allowed him to make the transition to talking films easily. He made forty-six films, including *Little Women* (1919), *Boys Town* (1938), and *The Great Gatsby* (1949). Of his portrayal of Magwitch in *Great Expectations* (1935), *Variety* said, "Henry Hull is by far the stand out performance. Hull has woven a keen understanding of the author's caricature" (29 Feb. 1935). Later in 1935 Hull played his most well known film role: the title role in *The Werewolf in London*. The movie garnered no critical acclaim, but Hull's performance brought him recognition. *Variety* commented that "Hull surmounts most of the hardships with a sterling performance" (15 May 1935). The reviewer compared him to actor Lon Chaney, known for his spectacular makeup and horror caricatures. Hull was also a standout in Alfred Hitchcock's *Lifeboat* (1944), which also starred Tallulah Bankhead, Hume Cronyn, and Canada Lee. He made his last film, *The Chase*, starring Marlon Brando, in 1966. He died in Cornwall, England.

Hull was described in his obituary: "thin and gaunt in stature, he gave the appearance of being a large man and his resonant bass voice embellished that image." In *Great Stars of the American Stage: A Pictorial Record*, the editor commented that Hull had "humor, intelligence, grace, and a modulative voice." Because of his energetic style and genuine love for acting, he appealed both to audiences and to his fellow actors. Hull's versatility and success were due to his natural ability and hard work rather than his training. Likewise, his naturalness and ease of style were the result of his being a feeling rather than a thinking actor.

• An article written by Hull, "Silence Is the Most Effective Censorship," *Theatre* 49 (Feb. 1929): 35, 74, suggests audiences take responsibility for what they patronize. Hull is discussed in *Who Was Who in the Theatre* (1979) and Ephraim Katz, *Film Encyclopedia* (1994). An obituary is in the *New York Times*, 9 Mar. 1977.

MELISSA VICKERY-BAREFORD

HULL, Isaac (9 Mar. 1773–13 Feb. 1843), naval officer, was born at Derby, Connecticut, the son of Joseph Hull, a mariner and farmer, and Sarah Bennett, a farmer. Hull had little formal education, preferring to join his father in sailing ventures on Long Island Sound and in the West Indies. By 1790 he had begun sailing to Europe, and in 1794 he obtained his first command. In 1795 he returned to the West Indies

trade, where he lost several vessels either to French privateers or financial disaster before being appointed, through the influence of his uncle William Hull, a lieutenant in the U.S. Navy, 9 March 1798.

William Hull was a Republican, and so was the captain of the frigate *Constitution*, one of the first ships of the new navy. Isaac Hull's first assignment was as fourth lieutenant of the *Constitution*, serving on it until 1801 and rising to first lieutenant in 1799 under Captain Silas Talbot. *Constitution* made a series of cruises to the coast of Santo Domingo (now Dominican Republic), where in May 1800 Hull led a cutting-out expedition into Puerto Plata, to capture a French privateer schooner, the *Sandwich*, an exploit in which he took great pride.

With a Republican administration in power, Hull survived the Peace Establishment of 1801. There was trouble in the Mediterranean sufficient to keep the navy active and soon expanding again. Hull went there in the summer of 1802 as first lieutenant of the frigate *Adams*. He was too senior for that post and was soon given command of the schooner *Enterprize*, the navy's only surviving small vessel. In 1803 he was promoted, under Commodore Edward Preble, to command of the new brig *Argus*, continuing in that position until his return to the United States in 1806. He participated in Preble's attacks on Tripoli and commanded the naval support for William Eaton's expedition to Derna.

Hull was promoted to master commandant in 1804 and was advanced to captain in 1806, then the highest commissioned rank in the U.S. Navy. The courtesy title of "commodore" was accorded officers who commanded squadrons of vessels on separate service, and quarrels over the title shadowed many professional careers, including Hull's.

By 1806 the Jefferson administration had decided to bolster national defense by building gunboats to protect the coastline. Hull supervised gunboat building from 1806 to 1809 on Long Island Sound and in the Chesapeake. In 1809 he commanded the frigate *Chesapeake* and in 1810 moved to the frigate *President*, where he remained only for a few weeks, because his senior, John Rodgers (1773–1838), who had been assigned to the *Constitution*, found his own command in bad order and requested an exchange. On 17 June 1810, twelve years from the day he had first joined it as fourth lieutenant, Hull took command of, in his words, "that favorite frigate," the *Constitution*.

Hull's fame rests on his years with the *Constitution*, 1810–1812. After a cruise to Europe in 1811–1812, he refitted and recoppered the ship at the Washington Navy Yard, sailing just after the declaration of war to join Commodore Rodgers at New York. He was chased off the port by a British squadron in a long and breathtaking escape and made Boston, where he restored his lost supplies then sailed alone and without orders in pursuit of British shipping. On 19 August 1812, off the Grand Banks, he met the British frigate *Guerriere*, also cruising alone. *Guerriere*, though eager for battle, was destroyed in half an hour. Hull returned with *Constitution* to Boston to find that his was the first capture of a British frigate and the first good news the country had had since war began. It coincided with very bad news from Detroit, which had just been surrendered by Hull's own uncle William Hull.

Feted throughout the country, Hull next assumed command of the Portsmouth (N.H.) Navy Yard to defend the eastern coast and build a line of battleships there. Before traveling to Portsmouth, he married Ann McCurdy Hart in 1813. Though she was a great beauty and he was short and round, the two were devoted spouses for thirty years. They had no children. An acquaintance described Isaac Hull in his maturity: "Hull is as fat and good-natured as ever."

At war's end Hull went briefly to Washington, D.C., as a member of the first Board of Navy Commissioners, but he detested the capital city and naval politics and transferred to the command of the Boston Navy Yard. His years there were marked by quarrels with Captain William Bainbridge (who thought Hull had cheated him of the command) and with other officers over the disputed title of "commodore," to which Hull was technically not entitled while others junior to him in rank were. In 1823 he left the navy yard to take command of the squadron on the Pacific coast of South America, where he served until 1827. In 1829 he became commandant of the Washington Navy Yard, remaining there until 1835. He then spent two years in Europe with his family, but his financial needs forced him to seek a new command in spite of his age and poor health. He commanded the Mediterranean squadron in the new ship *Ohio* from 1839 to 1841. It was a very unhappy period. Hull was isolated from his junior officers by his deafness (nearly total by this time) and by the protective care of his wife, who, with her sister, accompanied him on the cruise. (This was not unusual, but it often created frictions.) Lieutenants, some of them already twenty years older than Hull had been when he became a captain, hoped only to see the old war heroes retire. The attitude of Hull's officers in the *Ohio* can be summarized in this observation from one of them: "Poor old creature! I believe he is more to be pitied than despised."

Hull spent the last year and a half of his life on leave, finally settling in Philadelphia, where he died. He is most clearly remembered for his War of 1812 service in the *Constitution* and for having won the first victory in that war, but perhaps of still greater value was his long career as a founder and builder of tradition in a navy dedicated to the protection of a democratic nation.

• Hull's papers are widely scattered. The largest groups are the family papers, now housed at the USS *Constitution* museum (Boston, Mass.), and collections at the New-York Historical Society and the Boston Athenaeum. The letters quoted in the text are respectively from the Rodgers Family Papers, Library of Congress, and in the private collection of Admiral George W. Emery, USN. The most recent biography is by Linda M. Maloney, *The Captain from Connecticut: The Life and Naval Times of Isaac Hull* (1986).

LINDA M. MALONEY

HULL, John (c. 18 Dec. 1624–30 Sept. 1683), goldsmith, mintmaster, and merchant, was born in Market Hareborough, Leicestershire, England, the son of Robert Hull, a blacksmith, and Elizabeth Storer. He came to Boston with his family in 1635 and was trained as a goldsmith (synonymous with silversmith) by Richard Storer, his half-brother, between about 1639 and 1646.

During his life in Boston, Hull pursued a multifaceted career. One key to his success in Boston was his marriage in 1647 to the well-connected Judith Quincy The couple had five children, but only Hannah, later married to the famous diarist Samuel Sewall, survived infancy. Another important element was his acceptance into membership in the Reverend John Cotton's First Church in 1648. Hull remained a devoutly orthodox Puritan until his death, as revealed by much of his diary and correspondence.

Hull's work as silversmith and mintmaster were intimately connected. The General Court of Massachusetts Bay Colony established the mint in May 1652, placing Hull in charge and allowing him to select Robert Sanderson as his partner in June. The two men operated the mint together for the next thirty years, producing silver coins of various denominations, generally known today as New England, pine-, oak-, and willow-tree shillings, that helped give Massachusetts a stable means of exchange. Hull and Sanderson received one shilling and sevenpence for every twenty shillings coined, a substantial source of income that fueled Hull's other commercial activities.

As silversmiths, Hull and Sanderson produced silver objects largely in a mannerist style derived from contemporary English work, decorated with flat-chasing, engraving, punchwork, matted grounds, and pricked ornaments, and featuring such design elements as twisted-wire and cast-caryatid handles and baluster stems. Surviving objects bearing their marks include beakers, caudle cups, wine cups, dram cups, porringers, a tankard, and tablespoons; documents indicate that they also made gold rings, whistles, and other small wares. Only one piece has survived bearing Hull's mark alone, a small beaker made c. 1650 for the Boston Church. Several apprentices were trained in their shop: including Sanderson's sons, John, Joseph, Benjamin, and Robert, Jr.; Jeremiah Dummer; Samuel Paddy; Daniel Quincy; Timothy Dwight; Samuel Clarke; and probably others. Due to the increasing pressure of his political and commercial activities, Hull probably played a secondary role in the actual fabrication of silver as time passed, leaving much of the day-to-day activity in Sanderson's hands, but he remains significant as a founder of the silversmithing tradition in Massachusetts.

Hull was active in the import-export trade as early as 1650. He was soon sending yearly shipments of furs, timber, salt fish, and other colonial goods to the West Indies, London, and elsewhere and importing textiles, ironware, sugar, cocoa, tobacco, and even goldsmiths' tools. Hull also invested heavily in real estate in Massachusetts and Rhode Island and acquired a share in the Pettiquamscut Purchase in 1657.

Hull served in many town offices, acting as treasurer to the town and colony. In 1648 he was a corporal in the military company of Major Edward Gibbons. Hull was first elected as a Boston selectman in March 1657 and as town treasurer in 1658; he served almost without interruption for the next decade. In 1660 he joined the Ancient and Honorable Artillery Company. In 1662 he traveled to England as part of the team sent to renegotiate the Massachusetts Bay charter in the court of Charles II. In 1669 he again went to England, this time to help select a minister for the Third Church, which had just split off from the First Church. In 1671 Hull moved on from Boston town government to colony positions, becoming a member of the General Court, serving as treasurer on the committee that managed King Philip's War, becoming treasurer of the colony in 1676, and becoming an assistant of the General Court in 1680. As treasurer, many times Hull used his own resources and contacts for the benefit of Massachusetts Bay, often suffering personal financial losses as a result. Hull died in Boston.

In his funeral sermon delivered at Hull's death, the Reverend Samuel Willard of the Old South Church observed: "This Government hath lost a Magistrate; this Town hath lost a good Benefactor; this Church hath lost an honourable Member; his Company hath lost a worthy Captain; his Family hath lost a loving and kind Husband, Father, Master; the Poor hath lost a Liberal and Merciful Friend." Willard noted that "nature hath furnished [Hull] with a sweet and affable Disposition, and even temper; that Providence had given him a prosperous and Flourishing Portion of this Worlds Goods; that the love and respect of the People had lifted him up to places of honour and preferment; this, this outshines them all; that he was a Saint upon Earth." Hull was buried in the Granary Burying Ground in Boston.

• Hull's public and private diaries and a letter-book from 1671–1683 are at the American Antiquarian Society, Worcester, Mass. The diaries are published along with a memoir and other documents as, "The Diaries of John Hull, Mint-Master and Treasurer of the Colony of Massachusetts Bay," in *Archaeologia Americana: Transactions and Collections of the American Antiquarian Society* 3 (1857): 109–316. Five of Hull's account books are at the New England Historic Genealogical Society, Boston, which contains other significant Hull material, as does the Massachusetts Historical Society. The papers of Hull's son-in-law Samuel Sewall in these same repositories contain valuable information concerning Hull's mercantile career. The principal repository of Hull's silver is the Museum of Fine Arts, Boston. Other important examples are in the Yale University Art Gallery, and Winterthur Museum, Winterthur, Del.

The best biographical works on Hull are in Samuel Eliot Morison, *Builders of the Bay Colony* (1930), and Hermann Frederick Clarke, *John Hull: A Builder of the Bay Colony* (1940). Hull's silversmithing career is in Patricia E. Kane, "John Hull and Robert Sanderson: First Masters of New England Silver" (Ph.D. diss., Yale Univ., 1987), and her biographical sketch in *Colonial Massachusetts Silversmiths and*

Jewelers: A Biographical Dictionary Based on the Notes of Francis Hill Bigelow and John Marshall Phillips (1998), which contains a checklist of Hull and Sanderson's work. See also Albert S. Roe and Robert F. Trent, "Robert Sanderson and the Founding of the American Silversmith's Trade," in Jonathan L. Fairbanks and Robert F. Trent, *New England Begins: The Seventeenth Century*, vol. 3 (1982) pp. 480–89. Hull's coinage is discussed in Sylvester S. Crosby, *Early Coins of America* (1875), and in Sydney P. Noe, *The Silver Coinage of Massachusetts* (1973).

GERALD W. R. WARD

HULL, Josephine (3 Jan. 1877?–12 Mar. 1957), actor and director, was born Mary Josephine Sherwood in Newtonville, Massachusetts, the only child of William H. Sherwood, a perfume importer, and Mary Elizabeth Tewksbury. When her husband died in 1886, Mary Sherwood returned to her parents' home in Newtonville, taking up residence with her four unmarried sisters. Although these conservative aunts were distressed by Josephine's choice of an acting career, they were unfailing in their financial and emotional support, and she remained a devoted niece throughout her life.

In 1895 Josephine Sherwood was admitted to Radcliffe College, where she studied with George Pierce Baker, a seminal force in establishing theater as an academic discipline; George Lyman Kittredge, a Shakespearean scholar respected by both theater practitioners and colleagues; and Charles Townsend Copeland, whose classes inspired generations of influential thinkers. Sherwood's energy was prodigious. She acted in college productions, led the glee club, attended professional theater regularly, and wrote and directed two operettas, which earned royalties for years. After graduating magna cum laude in 1899, she enrolled in the New England Conservatory of Music in Boston and studied privately with Kate Reignolds, a noted nineteenth-century actor who became her mentor.

In 1902 Sherwood joined the Castle Square Theater Dramatic Company, a stock troupe in Boston, as an extra. Admiring her dancing, George Ober invited her to tour with his company. Short engagements and some critical acclaim followed. In 1906 she was hired by William Lackaye's company and played Fantine and Cosette in *The Law and the Man*. Three years later, Harrison Grey Fiske signed her on as the ingenue in *The Bridge*, which opened in New York at the Majestic Theatre, opposite Shelley Hull, a gifted leading man. Hull's whole family was stagestruck. His father had been a drama critic, his brothers, Howard and Henry, were performers, and Howard's wife, Margaret Anglin, starred in classical dramas.

Sherwood married Hull in 1910 and retired from the stage. She remained behind the scenes for almost a decade while her husband's career flourished with war melodramas like *Under Orders* (1918), in which he played both the British hero and the German villain, and popular comedies like *The Cinderella Man* (1916) and Jesse Lynch Williams's *Why Marry?* (1917), the first play to be awarded the Pulitzer Prize in drama.

In January 1919 Josephine Hull's life changed drastically; her husband died during the great influenza epidemic. Hull, who was childless, never fully recovered from this loss. She welcomed the invitation in 1921 from Jessie Bonstelle, a gifted theater manager, to direct at the Garrick Theatre in Detroit. A former actor, Bonstelle had become so successful at spotting talent that she was dubbed the "maker of stars." She assigned Jo Mielziner, an art student who would become one of the modern theater's great set designers, to be Hull's assistant and advised the widow, who sorely missed the footlights, to become a character actor.

In 1923 Hull relocated to New York to direct the Equity Players in John Howard Lawson's *Roger Bloomer*. After an absence of thirteen years, she returned to the Broadway stage as Mrs. Hicks in *Neighbors* (1923) and as George's mother in the comedy *Fata Morgana* (1924) for the Theatre Guild. She became a hit as Mrs. Frazier, the comical busybody neighbor, in *Craig's Wife* (1925), George Kelly's Pulitzer Prize–winning drama about a despotic woman.

Despite favorable reviews, Hull experienced a streak of short runs that continued for ten years. Among the plays were *Daisy Mayme* (1926), *The Wild Man of Borneo* (1927), *March Hares* (1928), *Before You're Twenty-five* (1929), *Those We Love* (1930), *After Tomorrow* (1931), *A Thousand Summers* (1932), *An American Dream* (1933), *By Your Leave* (1934), and *Seven Keys to Baldpate* (1935). She did Radio Guild broadcasts, mostly adaptations of classic plays, to keep her budget in the black and was considering a career change when Moss Hart and George S. Kaufman cast her as Penelope Vanderhof Sycamore, the cheerfully eccentric author-sculptor in *You Can't Take It with You*, which opened at the Booth Theatre in December 1936. It ran for two years and won the 1937 Pulitzer Prize. More recognition was to come.

After the short-lived *An International Incident* in 1940, Hull was cast as Abby Brewster, opposite Jean Adair and Boris Karloff, in *Arsenic and Old Lace*. The play opened on 11 January 1941 and ran for 1,444 performances. She re-created the role of the genial geriatric who poisons the elderberry wine of thirteen elderly male boarders and buries them in the cellar in Frank Capra's film version of the play (1941, released 1944) opposite Cary Grant.

Back on Broadway in *Harvey* (1944), Hull was an instant hit as Veta Louise Simmons, the bewildered sister of an alcoholic (Frank Fay, later replaced by James Stewart) who is befriended by a six-foot white rabbit. The Pulitzer Prize comedy by Mary Chase, directed by Antoinette Perry, began its four-year run at the Forty-eighth Street Theatre on 1 November 1944. Playing opposite Stewart in the Universal-International film version, Hull won an Academy Award as Best Supporting Actress in 1951. A short-lived stage production, *The Golden State* (1950), and a movie, *The Lady from Texas* (1951), followed. Critics raved about her performance in *Mistress Leggins* (1951), a stage comedy about an aging couple, never properly married, who liberate the inmates of a home for the aged. Appearances in television dramas became more frequent.

As Mrs. Laura Partridge in *The Solid Gold Cadillac* (1953), Hull received star billing and won a Drama League award. She withdrew from the play after a series of strokes, returned for three weeks, until 24 August 1954, but was forced to retire. She died in St. Barnabas Hospital in New York City. Her exact age is unknown. The actor adopted 1886 as her "public" birth date, and even scholarly records still list that year. Since no birth records exist, Radcliffe College calculated her birth year to be 1877 based on her school attendance.

The "small, roly-poly comedienne [with the] expressively arching eyebrows and a stage manner of matronly determination" (*Boston Herald*, 13 Mar. 1957) invested over thirty years in the theater before she became a star. Critics agreed that never had addlepated women, her specialty, seemed so clever. In 1947 Radcliffe awarded her a Phi Beta Kappa key for "bringing laughter and joy to people." Reviewers adored her even in panned plays. Brooks Atkinson wrote, "Everyone should live in a home presided over by Mrs. Hull. It would wipe out crime, increase industry, sweeten society, and fill the churches on Sunday" (*New York Times*, 12 Dec. 1952). On the set, the classically trained performer was known for her hard work, unflagging courtesy, and genuine human sympathy. "Comedy," Hull observed, "has to have an underlying structure of drama. . . . True comedy needs pathos to shadow it and bring out the highlights."

• Hull's papers—eight file boxes and several folio folders containing letters, diaries, photographs, scripts, scores, scrapbooks, and contracts—are housed in the Arthur and Elizabeth Schlesinger Library at Radcliffe College. Play and movie reviews, articles, photographs, and programs can be found in the Billy Rose Theatre Collection of the New York Public Library, Performing Arts Research Center, Lincoln Center. William G. B. Carson has written a full-length biography, *Dear Josephine* (1963). Also useful is Daniel Blum, *Great Stars of the American Stage* (1952). Obituaries are in the *New York Times*, *New York Herald Tribune*, and *Boston Herald*, all 13 Mar. 1957.

GLENDA FRANK

HULL, William (24 June 1753–29 Nov. 1825), army officer and territorial governor, was born in Derby, Connecticut, the son of Joseph Hull and Eliza Clark, farmers. Hull graduated from Yale College in 1772, studied law, and was admitted to the bar in 1775. At the outbreak of the Revolution, he joined the first company raised in Derby, and he served through the entire war, rising in 1779 to lieutenant colonel in the Massachusetts line of the Continental army. Hull fought in most of the important battles of the northern theater—New York, White Plains, Trenton, Saratoga, Monmouth, Stony Point—and he frequently exercised independent command. Late in the war he commanded the army's advance position in the lines outside New York City, and he won recognition for a daring raid on the British outpost at Morrissania in January 1781. While on leave in 1781, Hull married Sarah Fuller, with whom he had eight children.

Hull left the service in June 1784, on the disbandment of the last units of the Continental army. He took up the practice of law in Newton, Massachusetts, the home of his wife's family. During the winter of 1786–1787, he briefly returned to military service as a major in a Massachusetts regiment added to the Confederation's small peacetime army for the suppression of Shays's Rebellion. In 1793 he undertook a diplomatic mission to Canada in an unsuccessful effort to procure British cooperation in negotiating a treaty with the Indian tribes that were resisting federal occupation of the Northwest. Hull also held a number of state and local offices during the late 1790s and early 1800s: judge of the county court of common pleas, state representative and senator, member of the council, and major general of militia.

Although not an ardent partisan, Hull was a Democratic Republican, and in 1805 Thomas Jefferson appointed him to be governor of the newly formed Michigan Territory. He arrived in the remote and thinly populated region in July 1805, soon after a fire had destroyed most of the tiny territorial capital of Detroit. Much of his early administration was devoted to easing the burdens of the homeless inhabitants, sorting out land titles, and rebuilding the town. With the territorial judges, he organized judicial districts and gradually developed a code of law. As was true of all territorial governors, Hull was superintendent of Indian affairs within his jurisdiction, and he worked to implement the combination of paternalism and expropriation that characterized the administration's Indian policy. In 1807 he negotiated a treaty with the Wyandot, Ottawa, Chippewa, and Potawatomi tribes that ceded a large portion of southeastern Michigan to the federal government. During the war scare with Great Britain that followed the *Chesapeake-Leopard* incident of 1807, Hull labored to strengthen the territory's defenses and place its militia on a firmer footing, a task made difficult by the diffuse and heterogeneous character of the population. Beginning in 1806 Hull's administration was plagued by bitter quarrels involving the leading territorial officials—the governor himself engaged in a feud with Judge Augustus B. Woodward—and Hull's efforts to establish a territorial bank and thus attract eastern capital ended in failure. Hull appears to have been a conscientious and honest administrator, but a man whose eastern background was not entirely suited for governing an ethnically diverse frontier society.

Early in 1812, as war with Great Britain again threatened, Hull journeyed to Washington, D.C., to consult with the Madison administration on defense measures. In April the president appointed him brigadier general in the U.S. Army, a position he was to hold simultaneously with his governorship, and ordered him to take command of a force of 1,200 Ohio volunteer militia and some regulars gathering in western Ohio for the reinforcement of the Northwest. From the start Hull's command was plagued with difficulties. The citizen soldiers lacked training and discipline, and the volunteer colonels clashed with the commander of the regular contingent over precedence. The administration's failure to plan for war, especially its neglect of naval strength on the Great Lakes, left Hull's logistical lifeline vulnerable to British and Indian attack.

Hull's army completed the arduous march to Detroit in early July, soon after news had arrived of the declaration of war. Acting on administration orders, Hull crossed the Detroit River into Upper Canada, issuing a proclamation that promised the inhabitants security if they supported the American cause. However, the British and their Indian allies soon cut his tenuous supply link to the south. Because of Hull's concerns about the unreliability of the volunteers and rumors of approaching British and Indian reinforcements, the general abandoned his plan to attack the vulnerable British bastion of Fort Malden, at Amherstburg. Moreover, other American offensives planned against the Niagara peninsula and Montreal, which might have distracted the British and relieved the pressure on the Northwest, were slow to get under way. Early in August Hull withdrew his army into Detroit; the British, now led by an able and aggressive commander, Major General Sir Isaac Brock, followed and began to bombard the town from batteries on the Canadian shore. In a final attempt to break the tightening noose, Hull divided his command, dispatching 400 volunteers to establish contact with the American supply depot on the River Raisin. Brock was aware of Hull's predicament because of captured mail, and on 16 August he ordered his forces across the river. Locally outnumbered, short on supplies, unsure of his ability to defend the town against an assault backed by artillery, and fearful of a massacre of noncombatants by Brock's Indian allies, Hull surrendered his entire command on the same day.

The surrender of Detroit shocked the American public and cast Hull into disgrace. Paroled in October, the unfortunate general requested an investigation of his performance. A court-martial ordered for early 1813 was cancelled by President James Madison, but a second tribunal convened in January 1814 and, acting mainly on the testimony of the Ohio volunteer officers, convicted Hull of cowardice and neglect of duty. He was sentenced to be shot, but the president commuted the sentence on the basis of his revolutionary services. In fact, the loss of Detroit was far more the product of general problems plaguing the early stages of the American war effort—the lack of planning and coordination by the administration, the indiscipline of the militia and volunteers, the inexperience and bickering within the military command structure—than it was the result of Hull's personal shortcomings. Dismissed from the army and financially strapped, the former general spent his later years cultivating a farm in Newton and attempting to redeem his name—a task at least partially accomplished by his publication in 1824 of a defense of his leadership. He died in Newton.

• Collections of Hull's papers are preserved in the Burton Historical Collection at the Detroit Public Library, at the Georgia Historical Society, and at Houghton Library, Harvard University. A modern full-length biography of Hull has yet to be published, but see Samuel C. Clarke, "William Hull," *New-England Historical and Genealogical Register* 47 (1893): 142–53, 305–14, and Maria Campbell and James F. Clarke, *Revolutionary Services and Civil Life of General William Hull; . . . Together with the History of the Campaign of 1812 and Surrender of the Post of Detroit* (1847). The latter is a defense of Hull by his daughter and grandson, but it is based on his personal papers. On Hull's career as territorial governor, see Alec R. Gilpin, *The Territory of Michigan (1805–1837)* (1970), and Clarence E. Carter and John P. Bloom, eds., *The Territorial Papers of the United States*, vol. 10 (1942). The most complete and balanced account of the Detroit campaign is Gilpin, *The War of 1812 in the Old Northwest* (1958), but see also John K. Mahon, *The War of 1812* (1972); George F. G. Stanley, *The War of 1812: Land Operations* (1983); and other military histories of the War of 1812. For the transcript of Hull's court-martial, see James G. Forbes, *Report of the Trial of Brig. General William Hull: Commanding the North-Western Army of the United States* (1814). Hull defended his leadership in *Memoirs of the Campaign of the North Western Army of the United States* (1824).

WILLIAM B. SKELTON

HULLIHEN, Simon P. (10 Dec. 1810–27 Mar. 1857), oral and plastic surgeon, was born in Point Township, Northumberland County, Pennsylvania, the son of Thomas Hullihen, a farmer, and Rebecca Freeze. At the age of nine he suffered severe burns on his feet as a result of an accident. This incapacitated him for two years, and after recovery he suffered permanent lameness throughout life. He attended his local public school and then matriculated in the medical department of Washington College at Baltimore, Maryland, from which he received an M.D. in 1832. While a student there he gained experience in extracting teeth and in the art of mechanical dentistry. This led to his entry into dentistry and oral surgery in Canton, Ohio. Two years later he married Elizabeth Fundenberg at Pittsburgh, Pennsylvania, and moved to Wheeling, Virginia (now West Virginia). He and his wife had five children.

In Wheeling, Hullihen gained an enviable reputation as an oral surgeon. His manual dexterity, anatomical knowledge, and expertise in operative technique earned him recognition as an authority in the field. His operations for cleft lip, cleft palate, and maxillary antrum and his reconstructive surgery of the eyes, nose, and lips numbered in the hundreds and put him in the foreground of dento-facial surgery. These procedures were considered by his contemporaries at home and abroad as unprecedented and extraordinary.

As Hullihen's reputation grew, patients traveled long distances to be treated. In order to meet the exigencies of his practice he established a private infirmary at East Wheeling in 1850. Finding this inadequate, he sought and received the aid of the diocese of the Catholic church in establishing the Wheeling Hospital, chartered on 12 March 1850.

Hullihen also found time for active participation in civic and professional societies. He was a member of the American Society of Dental Surgeons, the Ohio County Medical Society, and the Mississippi Valley Association of Dental Surgeons. He presented important lectures before dental societies and published the results of his experiences in professional journals such as the *Dental Register of the West*, of which he was a founding member. Committed to raising the standards of his profession, Hullihen believed that dentistry should be an integral part of medical science. He died in Wheeling of typhoid pneumonia.

• Among Hullihen's more important articles are "Observations on Abscess of the Antrum Maxillary," *American Journal of Dental Science* 2 (1842): 179; "Harelip and Its Treatment," *American Journal of Dental Science* 5 (1845): 166; and "Observations of Such Diseases of the Teeth as Induce Facial Neuralgia or Tic Douloureux," *Dental Register* 3 (1850): 64. Sources for general biography include William A. Bruce, *A Biography of Simon P. Hullihen* (1942), available at the archives of the University of Maryland Dental School; "Simon P. Hullihen, M.D., D.D.S.," *Dental Radiography and Photography* 22 (1949): 79–80; and Charles R. E. Koch, ed., *History of Dental Surgery*, vol. 3 (1909). For his contributions to dentistry and oral surgery, see Milton B. Asbell, *Dentistry— A Historical Perspective* (1987); Asbell, "Hospital Dental Service in the United States—A Historical Review," *Journal of Hospital Dental Practice* 3 (1969): 34–36; Edward C. Armbrecht, "Hullihen, The Oral Surgeon," *International Journal of Orthodontia and Oral Surgery* 23 (1937): 377–86; and James R. Hayward, "The Legacy of Simon P. Hullihen," *Journal of Hospital Dental Practice* 10 (1976): 73–74.

MILTON B. ASBELL

HULMAN, Tony (11 Feb. 1901–27 Oct. 1977), businessman and owner of the Indianapolis Motor Speedway, was born Anton Hulman, Jr., in Terre Haute, Indiana, the son of Anton Hulman, a local wholesaler, and Grace Smith. By the time of his birth, his father had built Hulman & Company an enterprise started by Hulman's German immigrant paternal grandfather in 1849, into a thriving wholesaling firm. His family's prosperity enabled Hulman to attend prestigious educational institutions throughout his youth. He attended the Lawrenceville Academy in New Jersey and Worcester Academy in Massachusetts in preparation for taking an engineering degree at Yale University in 1924. During his school years Hulman was an outstanding athlete. He was named to the All-American Scholastic Team in 1919 and 1920 for track and field and played on the undefeated 1923 Yale football team. Before attending Yale, Hulman served in the American Red Cross Ambulance Corps during World War I.

Upon his graduation from Yale, Hulman joined the family business as vice president in charge of the Clabber Girl Baking Powder Division, the firm's most successful product. In 1926 he married Mary Fendrich, the daughter of a wealthy cigar manufacturer from Evansville, Indiana; the couple had one daughter. After the death of his father in 1942, Hulman assumed the presidency of Hulman & Company and continued the process of product diversification he began earlier as vice president. By the 1950s Hulman & Company was wholesaling a wide variety of grocery items, hardware, and notions.

Hulman's success with his family's business attracted other Indiana and midwestern firms in search of executive board members. During his long business career he served in executive positions, from board member to president, for a wide variety of companies, including the Richmond (Ind.) Gas Corporation; WTHI, a Terre Haute radio and television station; Princeton Mining Corporation; Indiana Gas and Chemical Corporation; Terre Haute Gas Corporation; F. W. Cook Brewing Company; Southern Indiana Gas and Electrical Corporation; Public Service Company of Indiana; Chicago and Eastern Illinois Railroad; Citizens Independent Telephone Company; Terre Haute First National Bank; and Terre Haute Realty Company. Hulman also devoted much time, energy, and money to charitable and educational institutions. He served as a trustee to the Indiana State University Foundation. Rose Polytechnical Institute in Terre Haute was renamed Rose-Hulman Institute of Technology after Hulman gave the engineering school a gift of $14 million.

Throughout his career Hulman remained an avid sportsman. His love of sports and business acumen converged in 1945 when, on the suggestion of former race car driver Wilbur Shaw and Indianapolis businessman Homer Cochrane, Hulman purchased the Indianapolis Motor Speedway from Colonel Eddie Rickenbacker. The speedway had hosted the Indianapolis 500 since 1911, and, except during World War I when racing was suspended, had quickly become recognized as the location of the premier automobile race in the United States. During World War II the 500-mile race was suspended once again, and the track fell into disrepair. Weeds grew on the track itself and the grandstands were in danger of collapsing. Believing that the Indianapolis 500 was both a tradition worth saving and a sound business investment, Hulman, Shaw, and Cochrane purchased the dilapidated track for $700,000 and began to resurrect the race to its former glory.

One of Hulman's first accomplishments as the speedway's owner was to increase the prize money for the race to attract top race drivers and teams. Although warned by Rickenbacker not to let the prize money exceed $75,000 unless he wanted to risk financial ruin, Hulman increased the stakes to $116,000 in 1946, setting the precedent for consecutively more lucrative prizes in the following years. Physical improvements to the massive facility on the west side of Indianapolis came next. Beginning in 1947 Hulman replaced the fire-prone wooden grandstands with concrete and steel structures. A new and safer pit area, an updated and technologically advanced control tower, new entrances to the speedway, and improved parking facilities all were completed under Hulman. Except for a narrow strip at the starting line, the fabled brick track was paved, increasing the speed of the cars. The

Indianapolis 500, under Hulman's shrewd business sense, soon returned to its place as the premier American automobile race, earning the nickname "the greatest spectacle in racing." Attendance at the race grew from 175,000 in 1946 to approximately 500,000 at the time of Hulman's death in Indianapolis.

Hulman's love of automobile racing, particularly the tradition surrounding the Indianapolis 500, combined with his business and promotional skills to save one of the most well-known sporting events in the United States. The condition of the speedway in 1945 had made it a prime candidate for razing to make room for the postwar suburban housing boom taking place in Indianapolis. Under Hulman's direction the Indianapolis Motor Speedway was preserved, and the Indianapolis 500 became one of the truly unique American sporting events of the twentieth century.

• There are no known manuscript collections. Hulman was a favorite subject for the Indianapolis newspapers, especially when the Indianapolis 500 took place each May. The best feature articles about Hulman are Nancy L. Comiskey, "The Hulman Legacy," *Indianapolis Monthly*, May 1982, pp. 60–64; and Fred D. Cavinder, "Tony Hulman: Hoosier in Profile," *Indianapolis Star Magazine*, 28 May 1972, pp. 6–13. Also useful but less detailed is an entry on Hulman in John D. Barnhart and Donald F. Carmony, *Indiana: From Frontier to Industrial Commonwealth*, vol. 4: *Family and Personal History* (1954), pp. 353–54. An obituary is in the *New York Times*, 29 Oct. 1977.

ALEXANDER URBIEL

HUMBERT, Jean Joseph Amable (22 Aug. 1767–2 Jan. 1823), French general and military adventurer, was born in Saint-Nabord, Vosges, France, the son of Jean Joseph Humbert and Catherine Rivat, occupations unknown. Older sources list his birthdate as 22 November 1755. Orphaned at an early age, Humbert enlisted as a sergeant in the National Guards when the French Revolution erupted in 1789. Three years later he had risen to lieutenant colonel, Thirteenth Battalion, Vosages Volunteers, and distinguished himself in suppressing peasant rebellions in the Vendée region of western France. A man of indefatigable action, Humbert also campaigned on the Rhine under Jean Charles Pichegru, Jean Victor Moreau, and Charles Dumouriez, and he became brigadier general on 9 April 1794 at the age of twenty-seven. In 1795 he accompanied the famous general Louis Lazare Hoche on a campaign against Royalists on the Quiberon peninsula, Brittany. A British-backed beachhead was crushed on 16 July, and Hoche thereafter accepted Humbert as a personal confidant. Hoche died in 1797, but he was undoubtedly instrumental in having his aide promoted to lieutenant general and entrusted to command an expeditionary force sent to support an Irish insurrection.

Humbert sailed from Brest with four ships, 1,000 men, and three cannons on 6 August 1798. Unfavorable winds forced him to land at Killala Bay, County Mayo, on 22 August, but local inhabitants flocked to his standards. Humbert immediately pushed inland and on 27 August encountered a larger Anglo-Irish force under General Gerard Lake at Castlebar and routed it. Consequently, Charles, Lord Cornwallis advanced on the invaders with 13,000 men, forcing Humbert to withdraw northward toward Collooney. There Humbert defeated another British force on 5 September but was overpowered at Ballinamuck three days later. Humbert and his officers were taken to Dublin and well treated, although the British exacted fierce reprisals against his Irish supporters.

Following his exchange, Humbert joined the army of Masséna in Switzerland and fought at the battle of Zurich on 4 June 1799. The Austrians under Prince Charles were defeated, but Humbert sustained serious injuries and recuperated for several months. In 1801 he accompanied General Charles Victor Emmanuel LeClerc, Napoleon's brother-in-law, on an expedition against Santo Domingo. He served as governor general of Port-au-Prince and, after savage fighting, assisted in the capture of Haitian patriot Toussaint L'Ouverture. When General LeClerc and thousands of his soldiers died of yellow fever in 1802, Napoleon canceled the operation, and Humbert returned to France.

Humbert was coldly received by Napoleon, seemingly over his tryst with LeClerc's widow, Caroline Bonaparte. More likely, Humbert's staunch republican sympathies clashed with the first consul's ambitions. Accordingly, Humbert was stripped of his rank on 13 January 1803 and exiled. The former general retired to his castle at Crevey, Brittany, which he had acquired in 1796. Beset by financial hardships, Humbert besieged the war ministry for a military assignment, and in 1809 he served briefly with General Henri Clarke in Holland. Nonetheless, Humbert grew weary of seclusion and in 1812 received Napoleon's permission to emigrate to the United States.

The exact date of Humbert's arrival in the United States is unknown, but in 1813 he spent several weeks in Washington, D.C., seeking a military commission and offering to establish a military college. Thwarted, he left Philadelphia on 12 August 1813, headed to the former French colony at New Orleans, and embroiled himself in filibustering schemes with Mexican revolutionaries. Humbert also became a regular consort of the notorious Lafitte brothers. He tendered his service to the United States during the British invasion of Louisiana in December 1814 and was assigned to General Andrew Jackson's staff. Humbert became celebrated for his daily reconnaissance of British lines, and during the battle of New Orleans on 8 January 1815 Jackson sent him to reinforce the endangered right flank. He crossed the Mississippi River as ordered but when the commanding general, David B. Morgan, refused to follow the orders of a foreigner, Humbert withdrew. He spent several weeks after the battle trying to organize a battalion of British deserters. Despite these minor roles, Jackson was pleased with the old soldier and publicly commended him in his general orders of 21 January 1815.

Back in New Orleans, Humbert resumed his filibustering activities and raised an army of 1,000 volunteers for revolutionary José Alvarez de Toledo. In 1816 he led de Toledo's force as far south as El Puente, between Puente del Rey and Veracruz, before the rebellion collapsed. Humbert disbanded his army in 1817 and retired in obscurity at New Orleans. He found employment teaching at a French college there while concurrently receiving a small stipend from the French government. Humbert died at New Orleans of dysentery and dissipation. It is not known if he ever married or had children.

In an age of heroes, Jean Humbert enjoyed one of the most meteoric careers in French military history. Reckless and impetuous, he fought with distinction on battlefields across Europe, Haiti, and Louisiana. He nonetheless sacrificed military glory and possibly a marshal's baton under Napoleon to remain true to his republican precepts. His reputation as a quixotic adventurer notwithstanding, one stern judge of soldiers, Andrew Jackson, pronounced him "a man in whose bravery I have unbounded confidence" (*Jackson Papers*, vol. 3, p. 238).

• Humbert's official correspondence is at the Archives Nationales, Paris. A large cache also exists in the Andrew Jackson Papers, Manuscript Division, Library of Congress. See also Harold D. Mosher, ed., *The Papers of Andrew Jackson*, vol. 3 (1980). Modern biographies are Jacques Baeyens, *Sabre au Clair* (1981), and Marie-Louise Jacotey, *Un volontaire de 1792* (1980). Details on his military operations can be gleaned from Michael C. Ross, *Banners of the King* (1975); Thomas O. Ott, *The Haitian Revolution, 1789–1803* (1973); Thomas Pakenham, *The Year of Liberty* (1972); and Hough Gough and David Dickson, eds., *Ireland in the French Revolution* (1990). Humbert's American affairs are amply treated in Alexander Walker, *Jackson and New Orleans* (1856), and Harris G. Warren, *The Sword Was Their Passport* (1943).

JOHN C. FREDRIKSEN

HUME, David Milford (21 Oct. 1917–19 May 1973), surgeon, was born in Muskegon, Michigan, the son of Wallace Colton Hume, a wholesale grocer, and Fay Hill. He received his B.S. from Harvard University in 1940 and his M.D. from the University of Chicago in 1943. That same year he married Martha Emily Egloff, with whom he had four children. After spending the next two years as an intern and assistant resident in surgery at Peter Bent Brigham Hospital in Boston, Massachusetts, he served for a year as a lieutenant in the U.S. Navy Reserve Medical Corps, then returned to Brigham as assistant resident. He was promoted to chief resident in 1950, junior associate surgeon in 1951, and associate surgeon in 1955. During this period he was also affiliated with Harvard Medical School as an assistant in surgery from 1944 to 1948 and as Harvey Cushing Fellow from 1948 to 1950; he became an instructor in surgery in 1950 and was promoted to assistant professor in 1955. From 1952 to 1956 he also conducted research as an American Cancer Society scholar.

Hume specialized in surgical procedures involving the kidney, and in 1947 he and his colleagues at Brigham performed one of the first kidney transplants. He became interested in the possibility of transplanting healthy kidneys from cadavers into patients dying from kidney failure, and in 1950 he succeeded in performing this procedure. In 1952, the year after he was appointed director of Harvard's laboratory of surgical research, he performed the first kidney transplant ever undertaken at Harvard. In 1956 Hume resigned from Brigham and Harvard to become Stuart McGuire Professor of Surgery and chairman of the surgery department of the Medical College of Virginia (MCV; later part of Virginia Commonwealth University [VCU]), positions he held until his death. The next year he performed the first successful kidney transplantation involving twins. Under his leadership MCV/VCU developed a surgical research laboratory that became one of the world's foremost research centers for kidney transplants.

The earliest kidney transplants involved removing the recipient's failed kidney to make room for the donor kidney. Hume developed a simpler technique that involved leaving the failed kidney in place and implanting the donor kidney in the iliac fossa, a cavity in the small of the back. He then connected the donor kidney's artery and vein to the iliac's artery and vein and attached the ureter from the donor kidney directly to the bladder. Although this procedure is a relatively uncomplicated one (the kidney was the first organ to be transplanted successfully), early transplants were often unsuccessful because the recipient's immune system rejected the donor kidney. Hume set out to investigate the physiological mechanism that causes organ rejection and in the process performed much useful work concerning the role played by the brain and the endocrine system in response to bodily injury. His investigations concerning the way in which the pituitary gland controls the secretion of adrenocorticotropic hormone, the substance that regulates the secretion of anti-inflammatory hormones by the adrenal cortex, led indirectly to the development in 1963 of azathioprine, an immunosuppressive drug that increased significantly the success ratio of organ transplants.

Hume also investigated the transplantation of other vital organs, and in 1968 he and a VCU colleague performed the world's sixteenth heart transplant. He also developed a portable device that could sustain the life of a patient who had lost most of his intestines, devised a method to treat severe cases of obesity surgically, and developed a procedure whereby a human patient could be hooked up to a baboon in such a way that the baboon's liver filtered the human's blood without the liver having to be removed from the baboon.

Hume published more than 100 scientific papers, most of them related to kidney transplants or the body's defense system, and coauthored *Principles of Surgery* (1969). He served as a member of the National Heart Institute's project committee, the National Institutes of Health's nephrology planning committee and surgery study section, the Atomic Energy Commission's advisory board, the National Kidney Foundation's task force committee, and the Veterans Administration's advisory group on renal transplants. He

was awarded the American Academy of Arts and Sciences' Francis Amory Prize in 1962, the New York Academy of Medicine's Valentine Award in 1970, the University of Chicago's Distinguished Service Medal in 1971, and *Modern Medicine*'s Distinguished Achievement Award in 1972. He died while vacationing in Chatsworth, California.

Hume was a pioneer in the field of organ transplants and the study of the neuro-endocrine system. His method for transplanting kidneys served as the standard procedure for a number of years.

• Hume's papers have not been located. The significance of his work is discussed in Mark M. Ravitch, *A Century of Surgery* (2 vols., 1981). Obituaries are in the *New York Times*, 21 May 1973, and the *Transactions of the American Surgical Association* 92 (1974): 41–43.

CHARLES W. CAREY, JR.

HUME, James B. (23 Jan. 1827–18 May 1904), peace officer and detective, was born near South Kortwright, New York, the son of Robert Hume, Jr., and Catherine Rose, farmers. Hume was a typical farm lad in the Catskills and in Lagrange County, Indiana, where his father migrated with his family when Hume was almost ten years old. The boy seemed destined to follow the plow for the rest of his life, although he rebelled against his dour puritanical parent and threatened to leave home. His father relented and began to treat him as an adult. Hume's only education was that of winters in a one-room rural grammar school, plus only two twelve-week winter quarters sometime between 1841 and 1849 at Lagrange Collegiate Institute, but he continued his learning by zealous reading.

Hume caught the prevailing California gold fever and headed over the plains via the California-Oregon Trail in 1850. For ten years after his arrival in the Sierra Nevada foothills, Hume prospected and mined for gold in the rugged canyons of the mother lode. Although he did only well enough to keep himself in beans and bacon, he stubbornly refused to give up looking for a big bonanza. But, finally, in 1860 he abandoned the miner's life and began a career in public service.

Starting that year as deputy tax collector for El Dorado County, California, Hume became city marshal and chief of police of Placerville (formerly Hangtown), California, in 1862. He finally found his proper niche in life as a lawman. Hume cleaned up the county seat so effectively that the county sheriff appointed him undersheriff, chief assistant. Hume's first major criminal case was the bizarre holdup of two stagecoaches at once, at Bullion Bend in the Sierra east of Placerville in the middle of the Civil War, 30 June 1864. A dual stage holdup was rare enough, but Hume found that the strongboxes had been looted by Copperheads—Confederate sympathizers—raising money for the southern cause in this unusual fashion. The leader of the highwaymen, Ralph Henry, used the alias of Captain R. Henry Ingrim. He identified himself and his gang as a company of Confederate guerrillas. Along with other peace officers, Hume trailed the bandits all over California before running them down in San Jose in 1864.

Because Hume was a (Union) Democrat in a patriotically Republican county, he lost the election when he ran for sheriff in 1865. However, he was reappointed undersheriff and won considerable local renown by putting out of action the Hugh DeTell gang, but not before he was wounded in a gunfight with the bandits near Lake Tahoe in 1867. Such a shootout was not Hume's forte. He preferred to use his brain rather than his revolver. An excellent tracker, he studied the modus operandi of individual criminals at a time and place where fingerprinting and photographing of felons were still unknown procedures. Even the systematic collection of clues was in its infancy. In 1869 he was able to break up the S. D. Emmons (alias Vern Emmons) gang, which had preyed with impunity on Chinese settlers because their testimony was inadmissible in California courts. His expedient was simplicity itself but had not been tried, probably because most lawmen treated the Chinese with—at best—benign neglect. He arrested the weakest member of the gang and pressured him, in isolation, to implicate his partners in crime.

Because of his excellent record, Hume was elected sheriff of El Dorado County in 1868, but, being no politician, he lost in the next election. The *Mountain Democrat* lamented, "Personal spite and sore disaffection in our own ranks have defeated one of the best and most deserving officers this, or any other, county has ever had in its service." The election defeat only propelled Hume to more challenging tasks. First, he was appointed deputy warden to clean up the mess at the Nevada State Penitentiary after twenty-nine convicts escaped in the bloody Big Break of September 1871. After restoring order, morale, and discipline in the prison, he began his career as the first chief of detectives for Wells, Fargo and Company, the leading express and banking firm in the West.

Hume rarely "rode shotgun" as a guard on express stages, but he was often in the field, on the trail of bandits. He established excellent contacts with local peace officers in California and adjoining states, and especially the lawless Arizona Territory, and cooperated in making arrests. Hume compiled a morgue of scrapbooks of newspaper clippings on cases and trials of known criminals; assembled albums of mug-shot photographs of convicted felons; and worked up a statistical *Robbers' Report* (1884) demonstrating the effects of fourteen years of his anticriminal activities in behalf of Wells, Fargo. Also in 1884 he married Lida Munson, with whom he had one child.

The Wells, Fargo detective won his greatest fame for his role in sending the legendary road agent Black Bart to prison by tracing a handkerchief, dropped at the scene of a robbery, to Charles E. Bolton (alias Boles), the "Po-8" who liked to taunt Hume and local law officers by leaving derogatory doggerel at the scenes of his crimes. Hume did not personally snap the handcuffs on Bart, but the arrest was made under his supervision. So ended the career of the road agent who had pulled some twenty-nine stagecoach holdups, most of them successful and lucrative, between 1875 and 1883.

Hume was liked and respected—even by criminals—but he was so honest and so courageous in his convictions, as well as in the physical sense, that he sometimes forfeited public appreciation and support. On several occasions he took the side of felons against decent people whose simplistic idea of justice was a blanket "Good riddance!" Thus, he was vilified by some as a traitor when he tried to appear in court in behalf of William Evans, accused of murdering Hume's friend Mike Tovey, a Wells, Fargo guard, in 1893. From a study of the evidence, the detective was sure that the outlaw was innocent of the crime of which he was charged. Hume lost his fight, however, and Evans was railroaded into prison. Not until 1907 was Hume vindicated when the San Francisco *Call* carried a banner headline, "Innocent Man Will Go Free after 13 Years." But it was much too late for Hume to celebrate. He had died, still in harness, in Berkeley three years before.

• An archive of James B. Hume's detective papers—letters, clippings, telegrams, etc.—is preserved in the history department of Wells, Fargo Bank, in its San Francisco headquarters. The only biography of Hume is Richard H. Dillon, *Wells, Fargo Detective* (1969; repr. 1986). There are many histories of the express and banking concern, notably Lucius Beebe and Charles Clegg, *U.S. West* (1949), and Edward Hungerford, *Wells, Fargo* (1949).

RICHARD H. DILLON

HUME, Robert Allen (18 Mar. 1847–24 June 1929), Congregational minister and missionary, was born in Bombay, India, the son of the Reverend Robert Wilson Hume and Hannah Derby Sackett, missionaries of the American Board of Commissioners for Foreign Missions since 1839. He was the fourth of six children. After his father's death in 1854, his mother returned to the United States with the children to reside first in Springfield, Massachusetts, and later in New Haven, Connecticut. He graduated from Yale in 1868 (B.A.), then taught in General Russell's Collegiate and Commercial Institute, New Haven, in 1868–1869. He studied at Yale Divinity School the next two years and received an M.A. from Yale College in 1871. The following year he taught in the Edwards School in Stockbridge, Massachusetts, and in 1873 he received the B.D. degree from Andover Theological Seminary. He taught again in New Haven during 1873 and 1874. In 1874 he was ordained to the Congregational ministry on 10 May in New Haven and on 7 July was married to Abbie Lyon Burgess, who was also born in India of former missionaries. They had four children.

Hume and his wife were appointed missionaries to India by the American Board and sailed in August 1874 from New York for Bombay, via Glasgow. He was assigned to the Marathi Mission, western India, based in the city of Ahmednagar, during his entire missionary career (1874–1926). In 1878 he founded and headed the Ahmednagar Divinity College (later named Union Theological College), his main responsibility for forty-three years. One of his most notable students at the seminary was the famous Marathi Christian poet Narayan Vaman Tilak. In addition, for forty-three years Hume was superintendent of the Parner mission district near Ahmednagar, an area containing some seventy-five villages. Over thirty buildings—churches, schoolhouses, dormitories, and residences—were built under his administration. He was English editor of *Dnyanodaya*, the mission's Anglo-Marathi newspaper, a position his father held from 1844 to 1854. At various times he served also as principal of the Ahmednagar High School and the Ahmednagar Girls' School; president of the Bombay Christian Council; president of the All-India Christian Endeavor Union for the year 1902 to 1903; delegate to the nonofficial Indian National Congress in 1907; and member of the Municipal Committee of Ahmednagar. He was the first moderator of the United Church of North India when it was formed in 1925, and after his retirement he was a representative of that church to the World Conference on Faith and Order in 1927 at Lausanne, Switzerland. He was appointed by the governor of Bombay as a member of the presidency's committee on problems of religious mendicancy, and he was the only American summoned to testify by the Montagu-Chelmsford Royal Commission concerning problems of political reform in India. For his work during the famine of 1899 through 1901 as administrator of famine relief funds sent from the United States and for care of orphans, Queen Victoria conferred upon Hume in 1901 the Kaiser-i-Hind gold medal for public service in India.

Hume's first wife died at Panchgani, India, in 1881. Hume was married a second time in 1887 to Katie Fairbank, who was born in Ahmednagar and had been a missionary there since 1882. They had four children.

During his first furlough in the United States, in 1885 through 1887, Hume became a central figure in the Andover Controversy, which was centered on the view that a person who had died without knowledge of Christ might have an opportunity in the afterlife for repentance and salvation before facing final judgment. His sympathies lay with the liberal theological views of Andover Theological Seminary professors. He received a D.D. from Yale (in absentia) in 1895. In 1904 and 1905 he was Hyde Lecturer at Andover; in 1910 and 1911 he lectured at the University of Chicago, Oberlin College, Beloit College, and the International College in Springfield, Massachusetts. From 1919 to 1920 he lectured at Union Theological Seminary, New York, and at the Kennedy School of Missions of Hartford Theological Seminary, and he was vice moderator of the National Council of Congregational Churches in the United States of America. He was the author of *Missions from the Modern View* (1905), *An Interpretation of India's Religious History* (1911), and nearly 200 pamphlets in English and Marathi. Five of his children were missionaries to India.

Hume returned to the United States in 1926 and retired in 1927. He died in Brookline, Massachusetts. At his request, his body was cremated, and the ashes were taken for burial in Ahmednagar where a large church seating 1,300 people that was built under his leadership was named after his death the Robert A. Hume Memorial Church.

As he stated in *An Interpretation of India's Religious History* (pp. 174–210), Hume believed that God had always been at work in India; that Hindus had earnestly been seeking after God, without success; that Hinduism was breaking down; and that, through all this, God was preparing India for Christ, who would fulfill the best elements of Hinduism. He predicted that the Hindu doctrine of Karma, and the caste system, would "eventually be discarded entirely." Hume did not suggest that India would accept Christianity as a religion, but that Christ would enter into the life and thought of India; thus India would become Christianized, and through it God would enrich the world. Missionaries were ambassadors of Christ in this plan.

• A series of autobiographical articles, "Hume of Ahmednagar," was published in the *Congregationalist*, vol. 106 (1921). Additional material on Hume may be found in issues of the *Missionary Herald*, 1874–1929, especially Feb. 1925 and Sept. 1929. See also Alden H. Clark, "Hume of Ahmednagar," *Missionary Review of the World* 52 (Nov. 1929), and Fred Field Goodsell, *They Lived Their Faith* (1961). Obituaries are in the *Boston Transcript*, 29 June 1929, and *Yale Obituary Record* (1929).

GERALD H. ANDERSON

HUME, Samuel James (14 June 1885–1 Sept. 1962), scene designer, director, and educator, was born in Berkeley, California, the son of James Bunyan Hume, a law enforcement officer, and Linda Murison. He attended the University of California at Berkeley and became interested in theater. Before completing his degree, Hume went to Europe to study scene design under one of the most outspoken visionaries of the early twentieth century stage, Edward Gordon Craig. Craig insisted that the modern theater had become mired in what he called "photographic realism." He proposed a visual theater that merged action, scene, and voice with scenic pictures that heightened the emotional aspects of the play. Hume studied for nearly a year at Craig's Arena Goldoni School in Florence, Italy, before the outbreak of World War I forced the closing of the school. However, the influence of Craig on Hume was significant enough for him to return to the United States a confirmed devotee of Craig's theories. It became Hume's goal to bring the "New Stagecraft," which was becoming predominant in Europe, to his homeland.

Hume received his undergraduate degree from California in 1913 and his master's degree in 1914 from Harvard University, where he studied under the legendary drama teacher George Pierce Baker. He had married Maude Crawford Izett Dick in 1912; they had no children and were divorced in 1927. That year he married Maurine Theodora Portia; they had no children. In 1914 Hume organized The New Stagecraft Exhibition, an ambitious exhibition that featured his designs and those of others. Most particularly among these was Robert Edmond Jones, who would emerge by the 1920s as America's outstanding innovator in the art of scene design. Hume's exhibition was displayed at Harvard before moving on to New York City, Chicago, and Detroit. The last stop led to Hume's employment as artistic director of the Detroit Arts and Crafts Theatre, which permitted him an opportunity to put his Craig-inspired theories into practice. In particular, Hume popularized Craig's notion of a permanent setting of levels, pylons, walls, fences, and platforms, all of which could be adapted to virtually any play. Through the addition of a few selected properties and evocative lighting, a unique environment could be created with economy and comparative ease. More importantly, this move toward great simplicity and the power of suggestion would have profound influence during the early and middle twentieth century.

Inspired by Craig's controversial concept of the single unifying artist of the theater—that one "master artist" would guide all aspects of a theater production—Hume directed and designed an array of new plays, including *The Tents of the Arabs* (1916), *The Chinese Lantern* (1917), and *Helena's Husband* (1917). As a result, his theater became one of the most interesting of the "little theaters" that were inspired by European developments in stagecraft—such as those by Craig, Adolphe Appia, and others who led the movement away from naturalistic staging practices. One of his productions was *The Wonder Hat* (1916) by Kenneth Sawyer Goodman and Ben Hecht. One of Chicago's little theaters was named for Goodman, who died shortly after the production. The theater, situated at the back of Chicago's famed Art Institute, remains in operation today as a symbol of the little theater movement of which Goodman and Hume were both exemplars. Other important Hume productions included *The Doctor in Spite of Himself*, *The Tragical History of Doctor Faustus*, and *Riders to the Sea*, all in 1918.

Again following Craig's lead, Hume extended his influence on scene design practices through publications. He found financial backing for Sheldon Cheney to open an office at the Detroit Arts and Crafts Theatre where Cheney founded *Theatre Arts Magazine*. Until the early 1960s it remained one of the outstanding theatrical periodicals in the United States. In 1928 Hume also coauthored (with Walter Réne Fuerst) a two-volume study of world scene design (heavily illustrated) titled *Twentieth-Century Stage Decoration*. It focused on the new theories of stagecraft and featured an introduction by Adolphe Appia, who along with Craig was considered the guiding light of the new antinaturalistic theories of scenic practice. (Craig refused to contribute to Hume's book and would not even allow his designs to be reproduced, partly because of his annoyance that his "pupil" was making a livelihood from the theories he had pioneered.)

In the early 1920s Hume returned to the University of California, where he became a professor, taking charge of a Greek theater project (the staging of classic plays in the ancient manner) and founding the dramatic arts department. At the university Hume staged productions of both parts of *Henry IV* (1920), *The Pillars of Society* (1921), *Arms and the Man* (1922), *If* (1923), and *Major Barbara* (1924)—all featuring Hume's neo-Craigian concepts. Another book by Hume, *Theatre and School* (with Lewis M. Foster, 1923) examined the importance of educational theater and developed techniques and theories that would inspire future artists. Following his retirement from the university, Hume died in Berkeley, California.

• Some of Hume's papers are held by the University of California at Berkeley. For further information on Hume see John Seelye Bolin, "Samuel Hume: Artist and Exponent of American Art Theatre" (Ph.D. diss., Univ. of Michigan, 1970); Sheldon Cheney, "Sam Hume's Adaptable Settings," *Theatre Arts Magazine*, Aug. 1917, p. 149; Edward A. Carrick, *Gordon Craig: The Story of His Life* (1968); and Arthur Feinsod, *The Simple Stage: Its Origins in the Modern American Theatre* (1992).

JAMES FISHER

HUME, Sophia Wigington (1702–26 Jan. 1774), religious writer and Quaker minister, was born in Charleston, South Carolina, the daughter of Henry Wigington, a colonial official, and Susanna Bayley. The family was wealthy, and Hume received a genteel education. Though her maternal grandmother was the Quaker minister Mary Fisher and her mother followed the Quaker faith, Hume was raised in the Anglican tradition of her father. She embraced the luxuries of Charleston society, taking delight in clothes, jewelry, and "attendance on balls, assemblies, masquerades, operas, musick-gardens, and vain recreations of all kinds." In 1721 she married the prominent Charleston lawyer Robert Hume, with whom she had two children.

Sophia Hume's life changed radically around 1740. Her husband had died a few years earlier, and Hume suffered two serious illnesses. Faced with these crises, she experienced a profound religious conversion. She began to examine critically Anglican teachings and to contemplate her hopes for salvation. Convinced that her vanity and worldliness were keeping her from grace, she disposed of her finer possessions and committed herself to a life of simplicity. In 1741 she moved to London and joined the Society of Friends.

Near the end of 1747 Hume returned to Charleston. She felt a divine call to warn her former neighbors of the dangers of luxury and vanity. Her message of repentance was not welcomed by most. She found herself "despised by my Acquaintances, Friends and Children" and wrote that "the Novelty of my religious Sentiments, and Meanness of my Appearance, has, I find, render'd me despicable in your Eyes" (*Exhortation*). Nonetheless, Hume began speaking at public meetings and renewed the efforts of the small group of Charleston Quakers. She articulated and defended her views in *An Exhortation to the Inhabitants of the Province of South-Carolina* (1748). To get the treatise printed, she traveled to Philadelphia, where for several months she worshiped with the Quaker community and enjoyed the company of leading Friends. The first of five editions of the book was published in 1748, and Hume sailed back to London.

In the *Exhortation*, Hume displayed the theological views and stylistic techniques that would characterize the rest of her writing career. She emphasized the sinfulness of pride and luxury and urged her readers to discover the finer rewards of faith and simplicity. She grounded her theology in basic Quaker tenets, particularly in the belief that all people possessed inner grace. Yet Hume was careful to address all Christians; she broadened her appeal by quoting extensively from the Bible and from non-Quaker as well as Quaker scholars. While the essay suffered from a lack of clear organization, it gained force from Hume's broad background knowledge and impassioned writing style. She repeatedly used her own conversion experience to demonstrate her arguments, as when she explained, "Having seen and lamented the divers and hurtful Lusts I was obnoxious to, when I was in Possession of a plentiful Estate . . . my Business is to warn and caution you that are rich."

For the next two decades Hume remained in England, where her writing career flourished along with her status in the English Quaker community. She authored several more religious treatises, including *A Caution to Such as Observe Days and Times* (c. 1763) and *Extracts from Divers Antient Testimonies* (1766). The *Caution*, which went through at least five printings, warned of the dangers of formal religious festivals in the same way that the *Exhortation* had condemned finery and frivolity. She appended to this essay a special plea for social and spiritual responsibility, directed to "Magistrates, Parents, Masters of Families, &c." Hume gained the respect of London Friends and was formally recognized as a minister. She continually urged fellow Friends to reform and to resist worldliness, issues that increasingly concerned the Quaker community in the 1760s. *Extracts* was in part a response to this goal; Hume presented the writings of early Quakers such as William Penn and George Fox to inspire and reinvigorate believers.

In 1767 Hume felt another divine call to foster Quakerism in Charleston. She returned to the city to find the old meetinghouse in ruins, frequented by just one remaining Friend. Hume preached her message of repentance at public meetings and sparked some new interest in the Quaker community. She also tried to raise funds for a new Charleston meetinghouse but had no success. Growing increasingly weak and ill, she returned to London in 1768. She apparently maintained a prominent position in the English Quaker community, as the religious leader and abolitionist John Woolman chose her to safeguard his journal in 1772. Hume died presumably in London and was buried in Friends' Burial Ground near Bunhill Fields.

Hume's unwavering dedication to the Quaker faith guided her entire life after her conversion. Her early taste for luxury and her uncommon, far-reaching

knowledge lent a unique perspective to her writing and preaching. She faced additional challenges as a woman and had difficulty reconciling her traditional views of female roles with her own career and public life. She used her higher purpose to justify her actions, and in the same way she persuaded readers not to discount her arguments on the basis of her sex. She wrote, "Neither will the unprejudiced reject christian advice, though it drop from a female pen" (*Caution*). Ultimately, what distinguished Hume was her commitment to the Quaker life and her tenacity in calling others to repentance. She influenced Quaker communities in Charleston, Philadelphia, and London and was remembered as "a ministering Friend of extraordinary character" (Bowden, p. 40).

• Most of Hume's papers are at the Department of Records, Philadelphia Yearly Meeting. Additional correspondence can be found at the Historical Society of Pennsylvania, Philadelphia, and at the Friends House in London. Along with the publications mentioned above, see her *An Epistle to the Inhabitants of South-Carolina* (1754), *A Short Appeal to Men and Women of Reason* (1765), and *The Justly Celebrated Mrs. Sophia Hume's Advice and Warning to Labourers* (1769) for autobiographical information and theological views. Brief sketches of her career and life are in James Bowden, *The History of the Society of Friends in America* (1850), and *The Journal and Essays of John Woolman*, ed. Amelia Mott Gummere (1922).

NANCY NEIMS PARKS

HUMES, Helen (23 June 1909–13 Sept. 1981), jazz, blues, and rhythm-and-blues singer, was born in Louisville, Kentucky, the daughter of John Henry Humes, a railroad worker who became one of the first African-American attorneys in Louisville and then worked in real estate, and Emma Johnson, a schoolteacher. "Well, I was born June 23, 1909, but I put it June 23, 1913. And everybody that's been writing books and things, they got 1913," Humes explained to Helen Oakley Dance. Her mother sang in a Baptist church choir and played piano at home. Humes sang with her mother and then took piano lessons as well. At Central High School her classmates included jazz trombonist Dicky Wells, drummer Bill Beason, and trumpeter Jonah Jones. At age seventeen, before finishing her schooling, Humes traveled to St. Louis to make her first blues records for the OKeh label, pairing "Black Cat Blues" and "A Worried Woman's Blues" in April 1927. Further sessions in New York in November produced "If Papa Has Outside Lovin'," "Do What You Did Last Night," "Everybody Does It Now," and other titles.

Like many famous individuals who are interviewed regularly, Humes developed a story of her life from which the same anecdotes were repeatedly published, including the false account of a fourteen-year-old blues singer. When retelling these anecdotes, Humes routinely contradicted herself; consequently the details of affiliation, location, and chronology are difficult to determine, but there seems to be no confusion over the essential outline of her story.

After graduation from Central High School, Humes worked for her father and took a two-year business course that led to a position as a secretary in a bank, but she quit to work as a waitress. She went to Buffalo on vacation and stayed for two years, singing at the Spider Web club with saxophonist Al Sears's band and at the Vendome Hotel in a band that included violinist Stuff Smith (probably in 1935). After working as a cook in a restaurant in Albany, probably in 1936, she returned home for a few months. She rejoined Sears in 1937 at the Cotton Club in Cincinnati, where Count Basie heard her sing and asked her to join his band. The pay was low and she did not want to travel, so she decided to stay with Sears. Later that same year, Sears himself decided to travel, and Humes went with him to New York City, where jazz promoter John Hammond heard her singing at Vernon Andrade's Renaissance Ballroom. Hammond soon organized trumpeter Harry James's first sessions, using sidemen from the Basie and Benny Goodman bands, and Humes sang on several tracks, including "(I Can Dream) Can't I?" (Dec. 1937), "Song of the Wanderer" (Jan. 1938), and "It's the Dreamer in Me" (Jan. 1938).

On 3 March 1938 Billie Holiday left Basie, and Hammond contrived to have Humes compete in the Apollo Theatre's renowned amateur contest as a means of getting her into Basie's band. Humes finished second to an Ella Fitzgerald imitator, but when that unidentified woman proved unsuitable at an audition, Basie hired Humes. For three years their careers ran together. Humes participated in Basie's rise to fame during a stand at the Famous Door on Fifty-second Street and in his subsequent extensive touring. She joyfully recalled doubling as the band's cook during tours of the South, where the difficulty in finding restaurants that would serve African Americans made her culinary talent especially useful and appreciated.

Although membership in Basie's greatest band was the most significant affiliation of Humes's career, her best recordings were made elsewhere. It was impossible for Basie to assign blues songs to her when he had the magnificent blues singer Jimmy Rushing in the band. The significant exception is "Blues for Helen," recorded on 3 June 1938 with Basie's sextet, including trumpeter Buck Clayton and clarinetist Lester Young. It was not issued until two decades later, when Hammond put the performance into the 1960 *Spirituals to Swing* album, splicing in a fake spoken introduction and applause at the end to make it appear as if it were part of his famous From Spirituals to Swing concert of 23 December 1938. In her work with Basie, Humes sang ballads and pop songs in arrangements that were unfortunately lugubrious, saccharine, or childish. For superior examples of her ballad and swing style from this period, seek out amateur low-fidelity recordings of "Stardust" and "Exactly Like You" made while she sang with Don Byas at Minton's Playhouse in Harlem in May 1941, one month after she tired of touring and left Basie. "Stardust," Eric Townley claimed, is "the greatest vocal version of Carmichael's song" (*Jazz Journal International*, Nov. 1981).

After she left Basie, Hammond secured a job for Humes at Café Society, where from 1941 to 1943 she sang to the accompaniment of the boogie-woogie piano trio of Albert Ammons, Meade Lux Lewis, and Pete Johnson; pianist Art Tatum (who, Humes reported, characteristically played too many notes); pianist Teddy Wilson's band; and clarinetist Edmond Hall's group. In 1942 she also sang at the Three Deuces, at the Village Vanguard with pianist Eddie Heywood, and on a Midwestern tour with trombonist Ernie Fields's band.

In 1944 Humes moved to California, where initially pianist Connie Berry accompanied her at the Streets of Paris in Hollywood. After working in another all-woman group, she sang with the all-star swing and bop conglomerate, Jazz at the Philharmonic. In 1945 Humes recorded "Be-baba-leba," which became a hit in the emerging rhythm-and-blues field. Accompanied by Dizzy Gillespie's big band, she sang in the movie *Jivin' in Bebop* (1947). In August 1950 a live recording of a performance in Los Angeles with Roy Milton's band yielded another rhythm-and-blues hit, "Million Dollar Secret." In October she was reunited with Basie, now leading a small group, for the film shorts *(If I Could Be with You) One Hour* and *I Cried for You*; these performances were used in mid-1950s compilation films, including *Harlem Jazz Festival* and *Stars over Harlem* (both 1955). Accompanied by Dexter Gordon's band in November 1950, she made further rhythm-and-blues recordings, including "Helen's Advice" and "Airplane Blues." Humes's voice was also featured in three movie soundtracks: *Panic in the Streets*, *My Blue Heaven* (both 1950), and *The Steel Trap* (1952). During these years Humes rejoined Jazz at the Philharmonic several times, including concerts in the Northeast in 1946 and a Hawaiian tour in 1951. She married Harlan O. Smith, a navy man, in 1952; they separated permanently in 1960.

In 1956 Humes toured Australia with vibraphonist Red Norvo, and she recorded with his group in March 1958. She then recorded her first albums under her own name, which became classics: *Helen Humes: 'Tain't Nobody's Biz-ness If I Do* (1959), *Songs I Like to Sing* (1960), and *Swingin' with Humes* (1961), and she performed at the Newport (1959) and Monterey (1960, 1962) jazz festivals. She toured Australia again in 1962 and Europe with the American Folk Blues Festival and Rhythm & Blues USA (1962–1963). In 1964 she worked in Australia for ten months. She resumed working in the United States, mainly in Los Angeles, until 1967, when her mother became terminally ill. Humes returned home to Louisville and quit singing to stay with her father and work in a munitions factory. Jazz writer Stanley Dance persuaded Humes to sing with Basie's reunion band at the Newport festival on 3 July 1973. Five days later she began a European tour, during which she recorded the album *Helen Comes Back* in France. The year 1974 witnessed her return to Newport, another European tour, another French album, *Sneaking Around*, and a brief stand at the Half Note in New York. After her father's death, she began an engagement at the Cookery in New York on 31 December 1974. Receiving rave reviews, Humes returned to the Cookery regularly through the late 1970s. In 1975 she recorded yet another fine album, *The Talk of the Town*, featuring tenor saxophonist and clarinetist Buddy Tate, pianist Ellis Larkins, and electric guitarist George Benson. That same year Humes sang in "The World of John Hammond" on the PBS television series *Soundstage*, and she performed at the Nice Jazz Festival in France. In 1976 she sang in a tribute to Louis Armstrong in Rotterdam. She was a guest with Basie's big band on a National Education Television show filmed in San Francisco in 1978, and she returned to the festival in Nice that year. She recorded the album *Helen Humes and the Muse All Stars* in 1979. In 1980 she performed in Japan, in New York, and at Ronnie Scott's club in London. She died in Santa Monica, California.

Humes's voice was centered on a trebly, sweet sound, but it also conveyed gutsiness and had a raspy edge that separated her approach from that of mainstream popular singers and made her suitable for and convincing in the musical context of African-American jazz and rhythm-and-blues bands. Humes repeatedly professed a preference for pop songs, but her finest work is founded on her sparky, clearly enunciated, joyful approach to blues singing, of which a definitive example is "I Don't Know His Name" on *The Talk of the Town*.

• A tape and transcript of Helen Oakley Dance's interview with Humes on 12 May 1981 are in the oral history collection at the Institute of Jazz Studies, Newark, N.J. Published surveys and interviews are by Whitney Balliett, *American Singers* (1979), repr. in *American Singers: Twenty-Seven Portraits in Song* (1988); Stanley Dance, *The World of Count Basie* (1980); John McDonough, "Helen Humes: Still the Talk of the Town," *Down Beat* 43 (20 May 1976): 17–18, 41; Eric Townley, "Million Dollar Singer," *Storyville* no. 64 (Apr.–May 1976): 126–30; Joe H. Klee, "Helen Humes' Home Cookin'," *Mississippi Rag* 6 (May 1979): 1–2; Mike Pinfold, "Beyond the Blues," *Jazz Journal International* 34 (Feb. 1981): 16–17; and Jean Buzelin, "Helen Humes," *Soul Bag* no. 86 (Dec. 1981–Jan. 1982): 4. The fullest chronology of her activities is by Sheldon Harris, *Blues Who's Who: A Biographical Dictionary of Blues Singers* (1979). Further details of her years with Basie are in Chris Sheridan, *Count Basie: A Bio-discography* (1986). See also Gunther Schuller, *The Swing Era: The Development of Jazz, 1930–1945* (1989), and Linda Dahl, *Stormy Weather* (1984). Obituaries are in the *New York Times*, 14 Sept. 1981, and *Jazz Journal International* 34 (Nov. 1981): 22–23.

BARRY KERNFELD

HUMISTON, William Henry (27 Apr. 1869–5 Dec. 1923), organist, conductor, and composer, was born in Marietta, Ohio, the son of Henry Humiston and Margaret Voris. As a child, Humiston moved to Chicago with his family, where he completed high school in 1886. He continued his education at Lake Forest College, graduating in 1891 with a B.A. During these years and even later, he studied piano and harmony with W. S. B. Mathews, and he concurrently studied

organ with Clarence Eddy and R. H. Woodman from 1885 to 1894. Humiston played the organ in a few Chicago churches, including the Lake Forest Presbyterian Church (1889–1891 and 1893–1894) and the First Congregational Church (1891–1893). He then moved to New York City.

From 1896 to 1899 Humiston studied composition at Columbia University with the American composer and pianist Edward MacDowell. Columbia's School of Music had just been created, and MacDowell was the first head of the department. While Humiston pursued his studies at the university, he resumed his career as an organist, initially for the Trinity Congregational Church in East Orange, New Jersey (1896–1906), and then for the Presbyterian Church in Rye, New York (1906–1909). He was also a member of the American Guild of Organists.

In 1909 Humiston expanded his musical activities to include conducting, and for the next couple of years he led several traveling opera companies. In 1912 he was appointed as the editor of the program book of the Philharmonic Society of New York, succeeding Henry Edward Krehbiel. He remained in that position until the Philharmonic merged with the National Symphony Orchestra in 1921. From 1916 until 1921 he also served as the Philharmonic's assistant conductor, and he led the orchestra on several occasions.

Humiston was one of the first members of the Edward MacDowell Colony in Peterboro, New Hampshire, a resort that was established by MacDowell's widow shortly after his death to provide an amenable workplace for composers and other artists. In 1914 Humiston conducted for the MacDowell Club of New York what was in all likelihood the first American performance of Mozart's early one-act singspiel, *Bastien und Bastienne*.

In 1916 Humiston conducted a program called "The Lighter Side of J. S. Bach," which featured the secular *Peasant Cantata*, complete with scenery and costume. In 1918 he led another Bach program, which presented the Triple Concerto in D Minor, as well as numerous solo selections from his cantatas.

In 1921 Humiston became the music critic of the *Brooklyn Daily Eagle*. The following year, he received his M.A. from Lake Forest University in Illinois, and that summer he set sail for Europe to report on the state of music there following World War I. Humiston worked for the *Brooklyn Daily Eagle* until his death in New York City following an exploratory operation that revealed a malignancy.

Although the majority of his career was devoted to performance, music history, and criticism, Humiston was not without his own musical inspirations. His original compositions include the Suite in F-sharp Minor (1911), which was revised in 1915; an overture titled *Twelfth Night* (1916); *Iphigenia*, a dramatic scene for soprano, chorus, and orchestra (1913); and numerous songs.

Humiston received perhaps the most recognition for his work *Southern Fantasy*, which was first performed at a private concert of the Orange Mendelssohn Union in Orange, New Jersey, on 3 May 1906. The New York Philharmonic gave its first performance of the piece on 7 December 1913, during Humiston's tenure as the orchestra's program annotator. The piece was based on two motives: one, a five-note figure of African-American origin, and the other, a fragment borrowed from the introduction to Stephen Foster's *Angelina Baker*. The Philharmonic performance of *Southern Fantasy* was presented under the direction of Josef Stransky, who succeeded Gustav Mahler as the orchestra's music director in 1911.

As a historian, Humiston made exhaustive studies of the music of Bach, Wagner, and MacDowell, and he was regarded as one of the country's leading authorities on each of these composers. Over the years, he accumulated an extensive musical library, which he willed to the MacDowell Colony in Peterboro, New Hampshire.

• Information on Humiston's life and career may be found in *Baker's Biographical Dictionary of Musicians*, 6th ed. (1978); *Grove's Dictionary of Music and Musicians* (1920); and Lawrence Gilman's notes in the New York Philharmonic concert program book, 31 Dec. 1924. Obituaries are in *Musical America*, 15 Dec. 1923, and the *New York Times* and *Brooklyn Daily Eagle*, both 6 Dec. 1923.

CORY SINCLAIR

HUMPHREY, Doris (17 Oct. 1895–29 Dec. 1958), dancer and choreographer, was born in Oak Park, Illinois, the daughter of Julia Ellen Wells, a musician, and Horace Buckingham Humphrey, a composer and hotel manager who was also an amateur photographer. Humphrey began dancing lessons as a young child and was encouraged by her teacher, Mary Wood Hinman. To earn much-needed money for the family, she began teaching social dance in 1913. That year she also performed with a small group that toured to various stations of the Santa Fe Railroad to entertain employees. Four years later she had earned enough money to travel to Los Angeles, where she entered the Denishawn School and soon became a member of the dance company of Ruth St. Denis and Ted Shawn. Her seven years dancing with that company were spent in cross-country tours that climaxed in 1925 with performances in the Orient. Much of the Denishawn repertory was loosely based on exotic models drawn from ancient eras or from foreign countries. In time Humphrey began to feel that dance should deal with the meaning of one's personal experience. She began to choreograph, but the leaders of the company did not approve of her serious, experimental approach. In 1928 Shawn's unsuccessful plea that she join a production of the Ziegfeld Follies led to her resignation from Denishawn.

Joined by former company members Pauline Lawrence and Charles Weidman, Humphrey opened a studio in New York City, where teaching earned funds to produce concerts of new works. The Federal Theatre Project of the Works Progress Administration offered further opportunities for choreographing. With Law-

rence as manager, the Humphrey-Weidman company performed in New York and at colleges throughout the country until 1940, developing audiences for the new art of "modern" dance. Humphrey's summers were spent teaching and choreographing, first at Bennington College and later at Connecticut College. She also taught in New York at the Ninety-second Street Young Men's–Young Women's Hebrew Association Dance Center, eventually becoming its director. In 1945 she retired as a dancer because of arthritis of the hip. She then became artistic director of the company of her former student, José Limón, who under her guidance became an important choreographer. Until her death in New York City, Humphrey continued to create dances for his group as well as for the Juilliard Dance Theatre, which she founded for her students at the Juilliard School of Music in 1955.

Discarding not only the glamorous images of Denishawn but also the traditional vocabulary of classical ballet, with its reliance on narrative structure and virtuoso technique, Humphrey set out to create dances for her own time and her own country. She believed in "moving from the inside out." This meant starting not with fixed positions and steps but with a feeling to be expressed. Then one had to find the movement that would best express that feeling. Complete mastery developed with time, but even the early works revealed her dedication to this principle and her skill in using it. Individual movements and group patterns reflected the emotions she wanted to portray; the tense leaps and percussive thrusts of anxiety and anger were contrasted with flowing sweeps of bodies moving in blithe accord with one another.

While she did not develop a complete system of dance technique, as did her contemporary Martha Graham, Humphrey did establish an important basis for such a development. For her, dance existed in an "arc between two deaths." In one, the body lies prone; in the other, it stands at ease. Both positions are secure; both lack theatrical excitement. Interest is stirred when the body dares to venture into space, defies gravity, and triumphs over it. The theory, which became known as "fall and recovery," was both a pure movement concept and a dramatic idea, a symbol of the eternal human conflict between the longing for security and the lure of adventure.

Though concerned with technique, Humphrey was more interested in teaching approaches to choreography, beautifully described in her book *The Art of Making Dances* (1959). In many years of teaching, particularly in summers at the Connecticut College School of Dance beginning in 1948 and at the Juilliard School of Music from 1951 onward, she developed methods of teaching choreography. Inspired by her, many young people went on to creative careers of their own. She described the ideal choreographer to a 1956 class at Juilliard as one who "never ceases to be curious about the meaning of movement and never stops wondering at the infinite possibilities and gradations of movement." Further, "the choreographer had better have something to say." There did not have to be a "message." A touching emotion about a piece of music or a poem or a simple experience could be expressed, but there had to be excitement about the subject and about the need to communicate the feeling about it. Humphrey never lost sight of the need for "moving from the inside out."

She began her classes with exercises to develop skills in the formal tools: design, dynamics, rhythm, motivation, and gesture. The last involved recognition of the natural movement, which might be social, functional, or emotional but also required techniques of stylization. The handshake, for example, could appear in many guises, depending on the position of the bodies in relation to each other in space; on the rhythm, the tempo, the phrasing, the placement of emphasis, and numerous other formal factors. Any change in such elements would alter the significance of the movement, which could appear sincerely friendly, formally cordial, or downright hostile.

In the end she provided the student with a checklist, which began as follows:

Symmetry is lifeless
Two-dimensional design is lifeless
The eye is faster than the ear
Movement looks slower and weaker on the stage
All dances are too long

The development of approaches to the making of dances constituted one of Humphrey's most important contributions to the art.

The works she choreographed remain significant both for their movement qualities and for the dramatic ideas they express. There were dances based on her fascination with movements in nature, such as *Water Study* (1928) and *Life of the Bee* (1929). She delved into the historical roots of America with *The Shakers* (1931). Her idea of a harmonious society and of the passions that can disrupt it appeared in *With My Red Fires* and *New Dance* (1935–1936). Even a work so apparently abstract as *Passacaglia* (1938), inspired by the music of Bach, meant more than the beauty of its majestic visual patterns. In this time of war, she wrote, she made a dance inspired by "the need for love, tolerance and nobility in a world given more and more to the denial of these things" (*New York Times*, 14 Feb. 1943).

Then there was the poignant *Day on Earth* (1947), which she called "a naive piece of sentiment and simple people." There were just four dancers: a man, his first love, his wife, and their daughter. As each of them leaves him, he finds solace in his work until death unites them all. In the *New York Times* (4 Jan. 1948) John Martin wrote, "It is almost as if she had looked from some other planet and seen things telescoped into a simple arduous pattern of dignity and beauty." Humphrey, he declared, was "a mature artist and a profound one."

Some of the dances she made for Limón were linked to his Spanish heritage. *Lament for Ignacio Sánchez Mejías* (1946) was based on a poem by Federico García Lorca; *Ritmo Jondo* (1953) was set to a scintillating score by Carlos Surinach. But universal themes always returned, as in *Ruins and Visions* (1953), where a mother learns the cost of having isolated her son from the realities of the world around him.

The many facets of her career left Humphrey little time for a personal life. She was married in 1932 to Charles Francis Woodford, a merchant seaman who spent much of his time at sea. Her husband later recalled her saying that she was an artist first and afterward a woman. The couple had one child.

In 1949 Humphrey received a Guggenheim Fellowship to write a book on choreography; in 1954 she received the Capezio Award and in 1958, the Dance Magazine Award. But her life was never easy. Her small company might have made more money had she been willing to compromise her values, which, of course, she would never consent to do. By the 1950s the direction of modern dance was changing as the world around it changed. While Humphrey's arc between two deaths was inherently dramatic, the new trend was toward abstraction. She continued to believe that American dance should comment on contemporary life and that it should affirm the potentially harmonious relationship of people on this earth. She never deviated from her faith in the power of her art.

Humphrey's works are still performed by the Limón company and other, selected groups. In 1995 centennial performances, exhibits, and workshops were held in her honor throughout the United States.

• All of Humphrey's papers, including her personal letters as well as her professional writings and correspondence, are in the Dance Collection of the New York Public Library for the Performing Arts at Lincoln Center. *Doris Humphrey: An Artist First* (1972) contains her unfinished autobiography, edited and completed by Selma Jeanne Cohen. It also includes a number of her own articles and scenarios. A second biography is Marcia B. Siegel, *Days on Earth* (1987). Humphrey's movement theory is discussed by an early member of her company in Ernestine Stodelle, *The Dance Technique of Doris Humphrey and Its Creative Potential* (1978). The Dance Notation Bureau is making available Labanotation scores of Humphrey dances, with notes on their history and style. As of 1992 two volumes, with six scores each, had been published. An obituary is in the *New York Times*, 30 Dec. 1958.

SELMA JEANNE COHEN

HUMPHREY, George Magoffin (8 Mar. 1890–20 Jan. 1970), secretary of the U.S. Treasury, was born in Cheboygan, Michigan, the son of Watts Sherman Humphrey, a lawyer, and Caroline Magoffin. The family moved to Saginaw, Michigan, where Humphrey attended public schools. In 1908 Humphrey entered the University of Michigan, from which he received an LL.B. in 1912.

After receiving his law degree Humphrey joined his father's law firm in Saginaw. In 1913 he married his high school sweetheart, Pamela Stark; they had three children. Humphrey left his father's law firm in 1918 and a year later became general counsel of the M. A. Hanna Company of Cleveland, Ohio. Until 1904 the

Hanna Company had been owned and run by Ohio Republican senator Mark Alonzo Hanna, and at the time Humphrey joined the company its primary interest was the shipping of coal and iron on the Great Lakes. By 1920 Humphrey had become a partner in the company; in 1922 he was promoted to vice president; he served as executive vice president from 1925; and in 1929 he became president.

Humphrey was considered a brilliant businessman, representative of a second generation of financial executives who had inherited capitalist enterprises from their entrepreneurial forerunners. He merged small companies into big ones within the larger Hanna holding company. Among the companies thus formed were the National Steel Company and the Pittsburgh Consolidation Coal Company. Humphrey was given credit for masterminding the vast and profitable expansion of the Hanna Company and was named its chairman of the board in 1952. *Time* quoted one of Humphrey's associates as saying, "If you dropped Humphrey in the middle of the Sahara, he'd come out with a newly organized corporation—on a dividend-paying basis" (1 Dec. 1952).

After World War II Humphrey became involved in public affairs. He was named chair of the Business Advisory Council in 1946 by the Department of Commerce. In 1947 Humphrey played a major role, along with U.S. Steel's Benjamin Fairless, in negotiating the coal industry's 1947 union contract with United Mine Workers president John L. Lewis. In December 1947 President Harry S. Truman appointed Humphrey to represent industry on a twelve-member advisory panel established under the Taft-Hartley labor law. In 1948 the Republican-controlled Eightieth Congress directed the Economic Cooperation Administration (headed by Paul Hoffman) to halt the dismantling of German plants, and Hoffman persuaded Humphrey to chair the five-member Reparations Survey Committee to investigate and report on the situation in West Germany.

In 1948 Humphrey strongly supported Senator Robert Taft's unsuccessful attempt to gain the Republican nomination for president. A traditional conservative, Humphrey also supported Taft's efforts in 1952 to become the Republican nominee; however, the more moderate General Dwight Eisenhower won the nomination. Humphrey was subsequently named chair of the Republican finance committee. When Eisenhower was elected, the new president nominated Humphrey, a man he hardly knew, as his secretary of the treasury. He did so based on the recommendations of General Lucius Clay, the former military governor of West Germany, and Paul Hoffman. Following Senate confirmation, Humphrey took the oath of office on 21 January 1953.

As Eisenhower's chief economic spokesperson, Humphrey was confronted with a number of challenges, one of which was dealing with the national debt, which had risen to $266 billion in 1953. He had only modest success in shifting the federal government's short-term obligations into a system of long-term financing. More successful was the reduction of the deficit of Truman's last budget for fiscal year 1954 (introduced in Jan. 1953) by more than $4 billion. Humphrey's efforts helped to produce small budget surpluses of about $1.6 billion in fiscal years 1956 and 1957. However, he was not able to achieve Eisenhower's campaign goal of reducing federal expenditures from more than $80 billion in fiscal year 1953 to $60 billion by the end of the president's first term. Actual expenditures did reach a low of $64.4 billion in fiscal year 1955, but they then began to increase incrementally and were again more than $80 billion in fiscal year 1959. With the end of the Korean War in July 1953, Humphrey contributed to the lowering of taxes and the codification of tax laws in the Tax Revision Act of 1954. But he was bitterly disappointed that taxes could not be reduced further.

Despite not knowing each other well before 1952, Eisenhower and Humphrey became close friends. They were the same age and shared interests in golf, hunting, and fishing. Both men were committed to balancing the budget, because they feared that an unbalanced budget would lead to inflation. Humphrey became as important an adviser to the president in economic policy as Secretary of State John Foster Dulles was in foreign policy. To better enable Humphrey to reduce defense expenditures, which constituted almost 70 percent of the federal budget in 1953, Eisenhower placed Humphrey on the National Security Council.

As an adviser and executive, Humphrey proved a successful and practical businessman who exuded an air of confidence and decisiveness. This attitude caused Humphrey to have occasional conflicts with other members of the administration, including Arthur Burns, the chair of the Council of Economic Advisers. In response to the 1953–1954 recession, Burns advocated the Keynesian strategy of budget increases and tax decreases to stimulate aggregate demand, while Humphrey urged reliance on markets to ride out the recession. Eisenhower, mindful of President Herbert Hoover's electoral defeat in 1932, sided with Burns.

Humphrey played a role in two of the major budgetary squabbles of the 1950s. At the legislative leaders' meeting on 30 April 1953 Eisenhower outlined his budget for the coming fiscal years to the Republican congressional officials. When Taft, the Republican majority leader, learned that Eisenhower would not be able to balance the budget as soon as expected, he exploded with an emotional outburst against the president. At this critical moment, Humphrey ventured into the debate in support of Eisenhower. His timely intervention successfully prevented a rift between the president and Taft.

The second budget conflict in which Humphrey was involved occurred on 15 January 1957, when Humphrey introduced Eisenhower's fiscal year 1958 budget before a press conference. Reporters were flabbergasted when Humphrey predicted that the nation would suffer a depression that would "curl your hair" if the government continued to tax and spend at its current rate. Humphrey's statement, critical of Eisenhower's budget, dominated the headlines the next day and eroded the bargaining advantages Eisenhower had earned by defeating Adlai Stevenson in 1956. The Humphrey incident made Eisenhower look weak—a president who could not mobilize his own cabinet secretary to support his budget.

On 28 May 1957 Humphrey submitted his letter of resignation as treasury secretary and returned to the business world as chairman of the board of National Steel and honorary chairman of M. A. Hanna, the latter of which was liquidated in 1965. Humphrey died in Cleveland, Ohio.

• The Humphrey papers are in the Western Reserve Historical Society offices in Cleveland, Ohio. See Nathaniel R. Howard, ed., *The Basic Papers of George M. Humphrey As Secretary of the Treasury, 1953–1957* (1965). For summaries of his business career, see [anon.], "Eisenhower's Cabinet: A Gamble about Humphrey," *Business Week*, 29 Nov. 1952, pp. 27–31; James Reston, "G. M. Humphrey to Get Treasury Post," *New York Times*, 22 Nov. 1952, pp. 1, 9; and [anon.], "The New Administration," *Time*, 1 Dec. 1952, pp. 14–15. Three major studies of the Eisenhower presidency that include information about Humphrey's role as treasury secretary are Stephen Ambrose, *Eisenhower: The President*, vol. 2 (1984); Fred I. Greenstein, *The Hidden Hand Presidency: Eisenhower As Leader* (1982); and Elmo Richardson, *The Presidency of Dwight D. Eisenhower* (1979). Three memoirs by members of the Eisenhower administration paint vivid portraits of Humphrey: Sherman Adams, *Firsthand Report: The Story of the Eisenhower Administration* (1961); Emmet John Hughes, *The Ordeal of Power* (1963); and Arthur Larson, *Eisenhower: The President Nobody Knew* (1968). Richard Neustadt's classic study of the modern presidency, *Presidential Power: The Politics of Leadership* (1960), includes a case study of the negative consequences of Humphrey's criticism of the 1958 budget on Eisenhower's power. John W. Sloan analyzes Humphrey's role as an economic adviser in *Eisenhower and the Management of Prosperity* (1991). An obituary is in the *New York Times*, 21 Jan. 1970.

JOHN W. SLOAN

HUMPHREY, Heman (26 Mar. 1779–3 Apr. 1861), educator and Congregationalist clergyman, was born in West Simsbury (now Canton), Hartford County, Connecticut, the son of Solomon Humphrey and Hannah Brown, farmers. As a child he attended district schools and was also privately tutored. At age seventeen he began teaching at local schools in the wintertime, while his summers were filled with farmwork. Desiring further education, Humphrey began an intense period of self-education that, in combination with his teaching duties, prepared him for entrance into the junior class at Yale in his twenty-fifth year. At Yale he was a classmate of Thomas Hopkins Gallaudet, who later led advancements in educational opportunities for the deaf. Humphrey graduated with an A.M. in 1805. He then joined a theological class under the direction of the Reverend Asahel Hooker in Goshen, Connecticut, receiving his license to preach from the Litchfield North Association in 1806.

Ordained at Fairfield, Connecticut, in March 1807, Humphrey ministered to that community for ten years. In 1808 he married Sophia Porter, the daughter of Deacon Noah Porter of Farmington, Connecticut. They had ten children. While still a candidate for the Fairfield post, he became involved in the controversy surrounding the Half-Way Covenant, which allowed church membership to those who had been baptized even though they had not experienced an emotional sense of salvation but withheld from them the privilege of communion and the possibility of holding leadership positions within the church. The Fairfield church supported the tenets of the Half-Way Covenant, but it was regarded by orthodox Congregationalists as heresy. Humphrey refused to sanction the existing beliefs at Fairfield, thereby demonstrating his own orthodoxy. In the third year of his pastorate (1810), he began active proselytizing on behalf of the temperance movement, preaching and writing two books: *Intemperance: An Address to the Churches and Congregations of the Western District of Fairfield* (with Revs. R. R. Swan and W. Bonney; 1813) and *Parallel between Intemperance and the Slave Trade* (1828). In 1817 Humphrey assumed the pastorate at Pittsfield, Massachusetts, where he served as minister of the Congregational church and conducted numerous revivals.

On the basis of his pastoral and temperance work, Humphrey had become well known to the trustees of Amherst Academy (later Amherst College). After the sudden death of the first president of Amherst, Zephania Moore, on 29 June 1823, Humphrey was called to the presidency as his replacement, being formally inaugurated on 15 October 1823. Humphrey's first and most lasting contribution as president of Amherst was the procurement of a charter for the college from the Commonwealth of Massachusetts. The charter (obtained in 1825) gave the college badly needed recognition and was secured despite opposition from Williams College and Harvard, both of which feared the loss of students and revenue to the upstart institution.

The Humphrey administration began with great enthusiasm. Preferring that his students worship as a group, Humphrey started the Church of Amherst College, leading the Congregational services himself. Great emphasis was placed on the spiritual development of the students, with six revivals taking place during the administration. By 1830 he had founded the Antivenenean Society, whose members were required to abstain from alcohol, tobacco, and narcotics.

During the early years of his administration, Humphrey presided over a rapidly growing student body, until the college was second only to Yale in size among New England colleges. The physical plant also was expanded, with the acquisition of new buildings and land. An innovative "parallel course" begun in the fall of 1827 enabled students to study modern languages, English literature, and physical sciences in lieu of more traditional subjects. Although the program was discontinued in the summer of 1829 due to faculty indifference and lack of resources, the experiment foreshadowed later curricular developments in American higher education.

Unfortunately, problems began to arise at the college. Founded with the goal of enabling students of modest means to enter the ministry, the college was successful (over half of the first 765 graduates entered the ministry); however, the percentage of students entering the clerical ranks declined with each graduating class. More wealthy (and worldly) students began entering the freshman classes, and the college's heavy emphasis on personal piety attracted fewer students overall. The debt load from the rapid expansion of the facilities grew burdensome, and potential contributors grew weary of incessant appeals for money. Attempts to obtain financial assistance from the commonwealth repeatedly failed. With the onset of the panic of 1837, enrollments, which were already in decline, dropped precipitously. Tired and discouraged, and sensing a need for a change, President Humphrey resigned his post on 19 January 1844 at a special meeting of the trustees in Worcester, Massachusetts. He retired to Pittsfield, dying there after several active years filled with writing, lecturing, and substitute preaching.

The career of Heman Humphrey in many ways typified the experience of many antebellum college presidents. Chosen more for their piety than for their administrative skills, they were often more successful in founding institutions than in running them. While his resignation from the college was under difficult circumstances, the college soon returned to prosperity, indicating the solid foundation that had been laid by Humphrey—which included the critical granting of the Amherst College charter.

• A limited amount of Humphrey material is held at the Amherst College Archives. The best source of information on the life and career of Humphrey is Claude M. Fuess, *Amherst: The Story of a New England College* (1935). His obituary is in the *Boston Transcript*, 5 Apr. 1861, and the *Springfield Republican*, 6 Apr. 1861.

EDWARD L. LACH, JR.

HUMPHREY, Hubert Horatio (27 May 1911–13 Jan. 1978), thirty-eighth vice president of the United States and U.S. senator from Minnesota, was born in Wallace, South Dakota, the son of Hubert H. Humphrey, Sr., a druggist, and Christine Sannes. He left college in 1931 to help in his father's store in Huron, South Dakota, where he became a registered pharmacist in 1933 and later met and married Muriel Buck in 1936; they had four children. He graduated from the University of Minnesota in June 1939 and earned a master's degree from Louisiana State University in 1940. He returned to Minnesota for a doctoral program but soon left to work in a federal workers' education program.

Minneapolis labor leaders whom he met on the job convinced Humphrey to run for mayor in 1943. His oratory and prolabor stance won him a surprising second place. His political appetite whetted, he played a key role in the 1944 merger of Minnesota's Farmer-Labor and Democratic parties into the Democratic-Farmer-Labor party (DFL) by convincing the recalcitrant on both sides to accept the inevitable. With labor support, and promises of reform and new leadership, Humphrey was elected mayor of Minneapolis in June 1945. He had little real power but used his popularity and the force of his personality to resolve labor disputes, to form citizens groups to combat racism and anti-Semitism, and to create a fair employment practices process.

After his easy reelection in June 1947, Humphrey turned his attention to wresting control of the DFL from its left-wing leaders. In a battle mirroring the split between progressives and anti-Communist liberals nationwide, Humphrey and his allies took control of the DFL in June 1948, and Humphrey won the party's senatorial nomination. He shot to national attention in July with his call for the party to "get out of the shadow of states' rights," rallying delegates at the Democratic National Convention to buck party leaders and pass a strong civil rights plank. In the November elections, Humphrey easily unseated Republican senator Joseph Ball, a cosponsor of the restrictive Taft-Hartley Labor Act.

Humphrey interpreted his own and President Harry S. Truman's electoral victories as a mandate for liberal change and was shocked to discover the hold that southerners and conservative Republicans had on Congress. In 1949 he joined futile attempts to change Senate filibuster rules and push civil rights legislation. His unskillful efforts to repeal the Taft-Hartley Act left it unchanged. Humphrey was at first ostracized by southerners for his civil rights stance and ignorance of Senate rules. An irrepressible speaker, throughout the 1950s he denounced Republican red-baiters, including, at first, Joseph R. McCarthy, in heated arguments. On the defensive, he and other liberals sponsored in 1950 an amendment to an omnibus internal security bill to give the president authority to detain subversives in time of national emergency, a vote Humphrey immediately regretted. Nonetheless, in 1954 he lobbied for passage of an even more stringent measure, the Communist Control Act.

Stung by his early defeats, Humphrey made a determined effort to get to know the Senate leaders and in time dropped his all-or-nothing approach. "I'm not looking for miracles," he told a journalist, but rather "at least inch by inch progress every month" (W. McNeil Lowry, "The Education of a Senator," *The Progressive*, May 1951, pp. 21–23). In search of this progress he took an interest in almost every issue on the liberal agenda. He sponsored or cosponsored dozens of bills every session on civil rights, labor, immigration, health care, education, housing, social security, and tax reform, and he talked them up to whomever would listen. When some progress in any field seemed possible, he accepted compromise, as when he opposed an antidiscrimination amendment to the 1954 Housing Act that would have lost southern supporters and killed the whole program. He pressed

Dwight D. Eisenhower constantly for executive action on ending segregation.

Humphrey focused increasingly on the issue of primary concern to his largely rural constituency—Eisenhower's reduction of farm price support payments. He tried incessantly to restore high price supports and proposed reducing surpluses through a domestic food stamp system and foreign emergency food aid program. His proposal for the purchase of surplus grain for foreign food aid, which became known as P.L. 480 and later Food for Peace, became law in 1954.

Humphrey supported much of Eisenhower's foreign policy, especially growing involvement in the North Atlantic Treaty Organization, but he criticized reductions in troop strength and growing reliance on nuclear weapons. He also was dismayed at Eisenhower's failure to criticize Joseph McCarthy. In August 1954, however, with his own reelection campaign approaching, Humphrey tried to preempt Republican red-baiting with a proposal to outlaw the Communist party, which passed easily. This enraged many liberals but had little effect on his bid for reelection; he won easily.

By this time Humphrey was accepted by the Democratic southern leadership, with whom he allied on agriculture bills, and had become majority leader Lyndon B. Johnson's bridge to the Senate liberals but still kept up pressure for liberal legislation. He made a critical contribution to the passage of the 1957 Civil Rights Act, which created the Civil Rights Commission, with his compromise proposal to make it a civil (rather than criminal) offense to violate federal court orders enforcing voting rights.

He also broadened his foreign policy interests and stepped up pressure for more emphasis on economic assistance in foreign aid. In 1955 he was named chairman of the Senate Subcommittee on Disarmament, whose creation he had urged, and in 1956 and 1958 held hearings that engendered support for an atmospheric nuclear test ban. He represented the U.S. delegation to the U.N. General Assembly in 1956 and to UNESCO in 1958. In this capacity he visited the Soviet Union in December 1958 and there spent eight hours in a private meeting with Nikita Khrushchev, earning a splash of media coverage.

This kind of attention encouraged Humphrey to make a run for president in 1960. He had long harbored ambitions for higher office, mounting a favorite son candidacy for president in 1952 and a more serious bid for the vice presidency in 1956. He was encouraged by labor and liberal colleagues, but his campaign was poorly organized, and he could not overcome the well-financed Massachusetts senator John F. Kennedy. Humphrey pulled out of the race after losing to Kennedy in the Wisconsin and West Virginia primaries. After the convention he threw his efforts into his own Senate reelection campaign and into ensuring Kennedy's success in the November elections.

Humphrey was elected Senate Majority Whip in January 1961, a position that gave him the opportunity to steer through the Senate a variety of administration bills for programs he had been advocating for years, including the Job Corps and the Occupational Health and Safety Administration. His idea of creating a volunteer peace corps to foster international understanding became law in June 1961. Humphrey's advocacy also led to the creation of the Arms Control and Disarmament Agency in the fall of 1961 and advanced the signing and ratification of the Nuclear Test Ban Treaty in 1963.

After Kennedy was assassinated, Humphrey convinced President Johnson to push ahead with passage of the Civil Rights Act of 1964, which outlawed discrimination in schools and public accommodations. As floor leader, and working closely with the president, Humphrey organized the defeat of the southerners' three-month filibuster and convinced Republican leaders to support the bill. Through good organization, constant pressure, and his powers of persuasion, Humphrey managed to see the bill passed with little substantive change. It was his most significant legislative achievement.

This success and his good relationship with Johnson rekindled Humphrey's hopes for higher office. With the vice presidency vacant, Johnson kept Humphrey dangling until the last minute. When Johnson finally asked him to be his running mate in 1964, Humphrey eagerly accepted. He and Johnson swept to victory in November.

Humphrey understood that Johnson wanted loyalty from his vice president, but he was not prepared for the complete subservience Johnson demanded. Humphrey had a busy schedule but no freedom to advance his own programs. A loyal vice president, he was nonetheless often berated for talking about administration bills before Johnson had announced them. He worked with the congressional leadership to ensure passage of the 1965 Voting Rights Act and the Medicare law but played nowhere near as prominent a role as when he was a liberal Senate advocate.

In early 1965, after Humphrey had disagreed with Johnson in a National Security Council meeting over the proposed bombing of North Vietnam, an enraged Johnson excluded him from all discussions of the issue. Humphrey publicly defended Johnson's decision to bomb, which returned him to Johnson's good graces and earned him a trip to the Philippines in December 1965 and then to South Vietnam in February 1966. What Humphrey saw and heard there convinced him that the president's policy was correct. Once converted he became one of the most enthusiastic supporters of the war, shocking his increasingly antiwar liberal friends. They believed that Humphrey was voicing his support only out of loyalty and tried to convince him to break with the president, but Humphrey insisted that he genuinely supported the war. Indeed, Humphrey's support for the war and loyalty to Johnson overwhelmed all else. He was shouted down by increasingly militant antiwar students during college campus appearances to promote Johnson's domestic programs. He was also criticized by conservatives for remarking that if he lived as did slum dwellers he might have "enough spark left in me to lead a mighty good revolt . . . " (*Minneapolis Tribune*, 21 July 1966). Later, however, he was rebuked by Johnson when he called for a "Marshall Plan" for American cities in the wake of widespread rioting in 1967.

The growing antiwar sentiment opened for Humphrey another chance at the presidency when Johnson announced in March 1968 that he would not seek reelection. Humphrey announced his candidacy in April. He avoided the remaining primaries and focused on states where delegates were picked at caucuses and party conventions, while antiwar candidates Eugene McCarthy and Robert F. Kennedy exploited popular opposition to the Vietnam War and President Johnson's leadership style by focusing on states with primaries. By this time Humphrey too questioned the bombing of North Vietnam, but his loyalty to Johnson prevented him from publicly disagreeing. Humphrey's caution angered antiwar Democrats, but his standing with party regulars eventually earned him the nomination. His victory at the August Democratic National Convention in Chicago was marred by charges that he had won through undemocratic methods and by a party deeply divided by the acrimonious debate over the war. As he celebrated his nomination, antiwar demonstrators were being tear-gassed and clubbed by police on the streets below.

Humphrey emerged from the convention far behind Richard Nixon and losing blue collar support to third-party candidate Alabama governor George Wallace. His campaign foundered until 30 September, when Humphrey said that if elected he would halt the bombing of North Vietnam, and his labor union allies won back blue collar support from Wallace. The Democratic campaign strategy of exploiting questions about the competence of Nixon's running mate, combined with President Johnson's bombing halt announcement in October, transformed Humphrey's sagging campaign. He seemed to come alive, campaigning with the exuberance that had been his trademark. He gained steadily in opinion polls throughout October, but the surge came too late. Humphrey lost narrowly, defeated by a growing conservative tide in reaction to urban race riots and violent student-led antiwar demonstrations but also by his own ambivalence over the war and reluctance to break openly with Johnson.

Humphrey's return to Minnesota to teach at Macalester College and the University of Minnesota lasted only until 1970, when fellow Minnesota senator Eugene McCarthy decided not to seek reelection. Humphrey ran for the seat and easily defeated Nixon ally Clark MacGregor. As before in the Senate, his incredible energy encompassed a broad range of issues: he led the fight to limit development of the Anti-Ballistic Missile (ABM) system and to counter President Nixon's refusal to spend appropriated funds on social programs.

Humphrey still had the presidential bug and in January 1972 announced his candidacy, but once again his campaign lacked the organization and financing of his rivals. In the primaries Humphrey lost to George Wallace in Florida and to South Dakota senator George McGovern in Wisconsin and California. In a desperate bid, he challenged California's winner-take-all rules in a damaging credentials fight at the Democratic National Convention. Nonetheless he rallied to McGovern's campaign, but Nixon won reelection in a massive landslide.

Despite these disappointments, Humphrey remained a leading national spokesman for the liberal program. He became chairman of the Joint Economic Committee. In 1975 he introduced the Humphrey-Hawkins Act, which required the government to take action to bring about full employment. Although praised by unions and traditional liberals, the idea was the type of liberal spending program that was coming under increasing attack even from within the Democratic party. Humphrey only flirted with the idea of a presidential bid in 1976 and instead won an easy reelection to the Senate. He was given the post of deputy president pro tempore, created to make him part of the official Democratic leadership.

By the time of his very public death at his home in Waverly, Minnesota, from cancer, Humphrey was seen by critics and admirers alike as the personification of postwar liberalism. In the twenty-six years since he had first come to the Senate, Humphrey had, by his persistence, incredible energy, and legislative skill, contributed significantly to the often incremental but sometimes dramatic expansion of civil rights, social welfare, and foreign aid legislation. He brought to his work an exuberance that was the source of his success, but also of his greatest political problems. He left his stamp on an institution and an era with a body of ideas and laws that affected the lives of millions of Americans.

• Humphrey's papers are at the Minnesota Historical Society. Hubert H. Humphrey, *The Education of a Public Man: My Life and Politics* (1976), are his memoirs. The most complete biography is Carl Solberg, *Hubert Humphrey: A Biography* (1984). Dan Cohen, *Undefeated: The Life of Hubert H. Humphrey* (1978), is also useful. Campaign biographies such as Michael Amrine, *This Is Humphrey: The Story of the Senator* (1960), and Winthrop Griffith, *Humphrey: A Candid Biography* (1965), give favorable assessments, while Robert Sherrill and Harry W. Ernst, *The Drugstore Liberal* (1968), and Allan Ryskind, *Hubert: An Unauthorized Biography of the Vice President* (1968), provide strong criticisms from the left and right. An obituary is in the *New York Times*, 14 Jan. 1978.

MARY T. CURTIN

HUMPHREYS, Andrew Atkinson (2 Nov. 1810–27 Dec. 1883), Union soldier and engineer, was born in Philadelphia, Pennsylvania, the son of Samuel Humphreys and Letitia Atkinson. Humphreys's grandfather, Joshua Humphreys, designed the first warships for the U.S. Navy during the administration of George Washington, and his father served as chief constructor for the navy from 1826 to 1846. Humphreys entered the U.S. Military Academy at West Point at the age of sixteen in 1827 and graduated four years later.

He was commissioned a second lieutenant in the artillery and served with the Second Artillery in Florida, South Carolina, and Georgia. While serving in Florida in the Seminole War, soon after attaining promotion as a first lieutenant, Humphreys became seriously ill from exposure and fatigue. His poor health and the offer of an attractive civilian position induced him to quit the military at the end of September 1836 and to work as a civilian engineer under Major Hartman Bache, a topographical engineer officer. In that position, Humphreys helped prepare plans for the Brandywine Shoal Lighthouse and Crow Shoal Breakwater in the Delaware Bay.

On 7 July 1838 Humphreys received an appointment in the newly established Corps of Topographical Engineers. Subsequently, he superintended improvements of Chicago harbor, surveyed Oswego and Whitehall harbors in New York State, and worked in the Topographical Bureau in Washington, D.C. In 1843 he designed and planned the first expansion of the capitol building. In 1844 Humphreys was detailed to the U.S. Coast Survey Office, where he assisted Alexander Dallas Bache, the superintendent. He remained in that post for six years and was promoted to captain in 1848.

In 1850 Humphreys received an assignment that, over a decade later, resulted in a major contribution to hydraulic engineering. That year Congress appropriated $50,000 to survey the delta of the Mississippi and to recommend a method both to protect the delta from destructive floods and to secure a reliable navigation passage through the mouth of the Mississippi for ships of twenty-foot draft or less. Humphreys attacked the problem with his usual high energy, employing teams composed of both civilian and army engineers. However, in the summer of 1851 he became ill—a combination of sunstroke and mental fatigue—and returned home to Philadelphia. His recuperation was lengthy; by early 1853 he was ready to travel and went to Europe. The excursion afforded Humphreys the opportunity to take notes on river and harbor improvements in several European countries. Upon Humphreys's return to the United States, Secretary of War Jefferson Davis assigned him to supervise the Pacific railroad surveys. Depending on data sent to him from various Corps of Topographical Engineer expeditions in the West, Humphreys's final report described the major railroad routes that eventually would be used to cross the Trans-Mississippi frontier.

In 1857 Humphreys returned to the Mississippi delta project, this time with the help of Lieutenant Henry L. Abbot. Abbot's field work was vital to the report, and in appreciation Humphreys made the young officer his coauthor. In 1861, a few months after the firing on Fort Sumter, Humphreys finally submitted the massive *Report upon the Physics and Hydraulics of the Mississippi River*. It became the most significant contribution made by U.S. Army engineers to hydraulic engineering in the nineteenth century.

Humphreys and Abbot had examined early formulae describing stream flow and found all of them lacking, based on their own research on the lower Mississippi. They devised their own formula for determining discharge in water courses. Based on data from very small channels as well as from the Mississippi, the formula was far more thorough and accurate than earlier ones had been. However, its failure to include a roughness term prevented it from being widely accepted. Still, the report itself was so full of new data that it enormously influenced the development along the Mississippi and other alluvial rivers around the country. Humphreys received academic honors and international recognition for his work. He and Abbot argued that neither cut-offs nor reservoirs were necessary to control flooding on the lower Mississippi, but that levees alone were sufficient. The Corps of Engineers clung to this approach until 1927, when a destructive flood discredited it and led to additional means of controlling floods in the Mississippi delta.

During the Civil War, Humphreys served with distinction. He was promoted to major in August 1861 and assigned to the staff of Major General George B. McClellan (1826–1885). By April 1862 he had advanced to the rank of brigadier general, U.S. Volunteers. He served both as the chief topographical engineer for the Army of the Potomac and as General McClellan's aide-de-camp. In the former capacity he supervised all map-making for the Army of the Potomac during the Peninsula Campaign. Although he impressively discharged his responsibility, he was dissatisfied, wishing for a combat assignment. His desire was realized when, on 30 August 1862, he received the command of the Third Division of Brigadier General Fitz-John Porter's V Corps. Humphreys showed his leadership abilities at Fredericksburg and Gettysburg, although his division's gallant charge at Marye's Heights in Fredericksburg proved enormously costly in dead and wounded. When, shortly after the battle of Gettysburg, Major General George G. Meade renewed an earlier request that Humphreys serve as his chief of staff, Humphreys reluctantly agreed, depressed over his loss of a division command but attracted by the promotion to major general, U.S. Volunteers, which went along with the new position. In the end, the two men worked well together. Humphreys saw action at the Battle of the Wilderness, Spotsylvania Court House, Cold Harbor, and Petersburg. On 25 November 1864 he received command of the II Corps. He led the corps through to the final Confederate surrender at Appomattox, advancing to the rank of brevet major general, U.S. Army, in April 1865, in recognition of his service at the battle of Sayler's Creek.

On 8 August 1866 Humphreys was appointed chief of the U.S. Army Corps of Engineers and brigadier general in the regular army; he served in that position until his retirement on 30 June 1879. He oversaw a corps whose personnel—consisting of only about 100 officers and an equal number of civilian assistants—were greatly taxed by the numerous responsibilities heaped upon them. River and harbor work increased from 49 projects and 26 surveys in 1866 to 371 projects and 135 surveys in 1882. Corps expeditions also surveyed and explored the American West until 1879, when Congress established the U.S. Geological Survey. Humphreys also faced professional challenges from the growing ranks of civilian engineers. In particular, he uncompromisingly defended the conclusions of his Mississippi delta survey. His—and the corps's—credibility suffered when the renowned engineer James B. Eads showed that jetties could provide a reliable navigation passage through the mouth of the Mississippi despite Humphreys's dogmatic assertions to the contrary.

Upon retirement Humphreys devoted his time to writing about the Civil War. He produced two accurate but boring monographs, *From Gettysburg to the Rapidan* and *The Virginia Campaign of '64 and '65*. He died in Washington, D.C.

Humphreys had married his cousin, Rebecca Humphreys Hollingsworth, in 1839. They had two daughters and two sons.

Abbot described Humphreys as "dignified, self-possessed, and courteous" with "a profound contempt for everything which resembled double-dealing or cowardice." However, Humphreys could also be playful, which might account for the demerits that resulted in an unremarkable West Point record. Charles A. Dana thought Humphreys was very pleasant to deal with except when you were against him and added, "He was one of the loudest swearers I ever knew." Clearly, Humphreys drove himself hard and expected no less of others. A man of courage, conviction, and intelligence, with an ego largely untouched by failure, he could be kind and generous to his associates but inflexible and unyielding to all those who challenged him and the Corps of Engineers.

• Humphreys's personal papers (and some official correspondence) are in the Historical Society of Pennsylvania, Philadelphia. The collection contains approximately 16,000 items. Most of Humphreys's official correspondence is in record group 77, U.S. Army Corps of Engineers, in the National Archives and Records Administration. The Office of History, Headquarters of the U.S. Army Corps of Engineers, has a biographical file on Humphreys containing copies of official and unofficial biographies. See also Henry H. Humphreys, *Andrew Atkinson Humphreys* (1924); Martin Reuss, "Andrew A. Humphreys and the Development of Hydraulic Engineering: Politics and Technology in the Army Corps of Engineers," *Technology and Culture* 26, no. 1 (Jan. 1985): 1–33; Henry L. Abbot, "Memoir of Andrew Atkinson Humphreys, 1810–1883," *National Academy of Sciences, Biographical Memoirs* 2 (1886); Todd A. Shallat, "Andrew Atkinson Humphreys," *APWA Reporter* 49, no. 1 (Jan. 1982): 8–9; Harold F. Round, "A. A. Humphreys," *Civil War Times Illustrated* 4 (Feb. 1966): 22–25. The following two items focus on Humphreys's Civil War career: James H. Wilson, "Major-General Andrew Atkinson Humphreys," in *Critical Sketches of Some of the Federal and Confederate Commanders*, ed. Theodore F. Dwight (1895), pp. 71–96; and John Watts De Peyster, "Andrew Atkinson Humphreys," *Magazine of American History* 16 (Oct. 1886): 347–69.

MARTIN REUSS

HUMPHREYS, Benjamin Grubb (26 Aug. 1808–20 Dec. 1882), Confederate general and Mississippi governor, was born in Claiborne County, Mississippi Territory, the son of a planter, George Wilson Humphreys, and Sarah Smith. He entered West Point in 1825 in the same class with Robert E. Lee, but was dismissed following a student riot on Christmas Eve 1826. He returned to Mississippi, became a planter, and studied law. In 1832 he married Mary McLaughlin. The couple had two children, but she died in 1835. In 1839 Humphreys married Mildred Hickman Maury, with whom he had fourteen more children.

In 1838 he entered politics with his election to the lower house of the state legislature; in 1840, as a Whig, he was elected to the state senate and served until 1844. Moving to Sunflower County in the developing Mississippi Delta in 1846, Humphreys, a slaveholder, devoted most of his energies until the Civil War to the management of his plantations.

He vehemently opposed secession and expressed the view that, if they left the Union, the southern states could not sustain their independence. But when Mississippi seceded, he believed that he must offer his services to its defense. In May 1861 he was elected captain of a company of volunteers and was assigned to the Virginia front. Before the end of the year, he had been appointed colonel of a Mississippi regiment. With Lee's army, Humphreys participated in most of the major battles in the eastern theater. He won distinction at the battle of Fredericksburg when his regiment repulsed a Federal charge. At Gettysburg he assumed command of the famous Barksdale Brigade after its commander was killed. He was promoted to brigadier general in August 1863, and his brigade fought with James Longstreet in Georgia and Tennessee, and in the Shenandoah Valley. Humphreys was wounded at Berryville, Virginia, in September 1864.

Humphreys's military popularity and his background as a Union Whig resulted in his election as governor of Mississippi in October 1865. To allow him to serve, President Andrew Johnson, whose conservative Reconstruction policies Humphreys supported, immediately granted him a special pardon. Years later, however, Humphreys expressed regret that the Confederacy had failed. As governor in 1865, he approved the discriminatory "Black Code" designed to maintain a subtle form of slavery, but when a storm of protest erupted in the North against it, he appealed to the legislature to "relax the rigidity" of these laws. At the same time, he opposed ratification of the Fourteenth Amendment. He also promoted policies designed to restore the credit standing of the state and to encourage the extension of northern capital to business and planting enterprises.

When the Republican Congress gained control of Reconstruction in March 1867, Humphreys's authority was severely restricted by a military commander, but he was permitted to continue as governor. Although he disapproved of the congressional Reconstruction program, which included black political rights, Humphreys at first cooperated with the military authorities. However, after he was nominated by the Democrats for governor on a platform denouncing the new political order in the South, General Irvin McDowell forcibly removed him from office on 15 June 1868. He won the election but did not serve because the new state constitution, which was voted on in the same election, was not ratified.

Although he maintained an interest in Reconstruction affairs, Humphreys retired from politics when the Republicans came to power in 1870. In addition to managing his plantations, he served for a time as an insurance agent in Mississippi. He died on his plantation "Itta Bena" in the Mississippi Delta.

• Humphreys's correspondence as governor can be found in the Mississippi State Department of Archives and History, Jackson. A brief autobiography of Humphreys was edited by Percy L. Rainwater and is printed in the *Mississippi Valley Historical Review* 21 (Sept. 1934): 231–55. For Humphreys's role in Reconstruction, see William C. Harris, *Presidential Reconstruction in Mississippi* (1967), and also William C. Harris, *The Day of the Carpetbagger: Republican Reconstruction in Mississippi* (1979).

WILLIAM C. HARRIS

HUMPHREYS, David (10 July 1752–21 Feb. 1818), poet and diplomat, was born in Derby, Connecticut, the son of the Reverend Daniel Humphrey(s), pastor of the Congregational Church in Derby, and Sarah Bowers. With his father instructing him at home in Latin and English grammar as well as in rhetoric, the poet entered Yale College at age fifteen. There he founded a literary society, known as the Brothers in Unity, and met the other writers who would later be known with him as the Connecticut Wits: Timothy Dwight, John Trumbull, and Joel Barlow. After his graduation in 1771, Humphreys became master of a school in Wethersfield, Connecticut, where he remained for two years, simultaneously doing independent study, which earned him a Master of Arts degree from Yale in 1774. He then spent three years as tutor at Philipse Manor in New York, which put him in touch with the polished manners and aristocratic bearing that he would assume for himself throughout his several public careers.

Humphreys's first career was as an officer in the Continental army, which he joined in August 1776 as a captain of the Second Connecticut Regiment. He also served under Generals Israel Putnam and Nathaniel Greene before joining George Washington as aide-de-camp on 23 June 1780. When the siege of Yorktown ended on 19 October 1781, Humphreys carried Washington's official account of the victory as well as the surrendered British standards to Congress in Philadelphia. Between 1781 and 1783 Humphreys remained Washington's trusted aide, accompanying him on travels to Philadelphia; Newburgh, New York; Princeton, New Jersey; New York City; and Annapolis, Maryland, before returning to Mount Vernon in time for Christmas in 1783.

In the summer of 1785 Humphreys became secretary to a European commerce commission, working under Thomas Jefferson, John Adams, and Benjamin Franklin. When he returned home in 1786, Humphreys visited Washington at Mount Vernon for five weeks and then moved in permanently in the fall of 1787. Humphreys accompanied Washington to New York for the first inauguration in April 1789, and he stayed on as Washington's personal secretary until 1790, when Washington sent him on a diplomatic mission to Portugal and Spain. He was named minister resident to the court at Lisbon in 1791, and two years later he became responsible for negotiations with the dey of Algiers for the release of American hostages being held by the Barbary pirates. Despite some complications and frustrations, by early 1796 a treaty was signed under Humphreys's authority, and Washington rewarded Humphreys by naming him America's first minister plenipotentiary to the Spanish court in Madrid. When Jefferson became president in March 1800, he recalled Humphreys for political reasons; Humphreys had long been associated with the Federalist party of Washington, Alexander Hamilton, and John Adams, while Jefferson himself had led the opposition.

Humphreys's last career was as a gentleman industrialist back in Connecticut. He returned from Madrid with a wife, Ann Frances Bulkeley, whom he had married on 8 May 1797; they would have no children. He also brought one hundred merino sheep, a gift from the Spanish court, to begin a woolen manufacturing business in 1802. He managed this business with great success in Rimmon Falls, Connecticut (renamed Humphreysville in 1808), until his sudden death there.

Considering Humphreys's unusually active and accomplished public life and his successful private enterprise, it is all the more remarkable that he was also a prolific and able literary figure—a poet, biographer, and playwright. Among his more important longer works are "Elegy on the Burning of Fairfield" (1780); "Address to the Armies of the United States of America" (1779–1780; revised 1782); "The Glory of America" (1782); "A Poem on the Happiness of America" (1785); a sizable portion of *The Anarchiad* (1786–1787); *An Essay on the Life of the Honourable Major-General Israel Putnam* (1788); *Miscellaneous Works* (1790); "A Poem on Industry" (1792); *Miscellaneous Works* (1804); and *The Yankey in England* (1815).

Each of these works has made its own literary and moral claim to attention. However, only one has continued to interest readers: *The Anarchiad*, which was subtitled *A Poem on the Restoration of Chaos and Substantial Night*. Originally published between 26 October 1786 and 13 September 1787 in the *New-Haven Gazette and Connecticut Magazine*, the poems addressed what Humphreys and Washington in letters agreed was a "levelling principle" that proceeded from the "licentiousness" that characterized the September uprisings in western Massachusetts that came to be known as Shays's Rebellion. The work was a collaboration of Humphreys, Barlow, Trumbull, and Lemuel Hopkins, but only number five—"The Genius of

America," written by Humphreys—was directly traceable to one of the writers. The authorship of the remaining numbers has fostered a low-grade scholarly controversy that persisted in the late twentieth century. (See, for example, J. K. Van Dover, "The Design of Anarchy" [1989], and William C. Dowling, "Joel Barlow and *The Anarchiad*" [1990], both in *Early American Literature*.) Individual authorship aside, however, Humphreys claimed in a November 1786 letter to Washington that the poems met with approval from readers: "In some instances the force of ridicule has been found of more efficacy than the force of argument, against Anti-federalists & Advocates for Mobs" (quoted in Cifelli, *David Humphreys*).

Humphreys's other poems are largely forgotten, probably, because he wrote in an elocutionary and rhetorical style built on epideictic oratory, thus producing very ornamental, laudatory, and patriotic poems. His poems invariably break down, like an epideictic speech, into an exordium, an extended narration, and a peroration. Moreover, Humphreys tried to match his important subjects with an appropriately sublime style that depended on the formulaic use of such things as earthquakes, storms, and cannon volleys, plus the heightened effects made possible by circumlocution, inversion, exclamation, and interrogation. This classical, very formalized poetry suited the intellectual climate of eighteenth-century America because it tied the turmoil of revolution to the stability of classicism. However, neither the epideictic method nor Humphreys's poems long outlived his own era.

Formal and dignified in personal matters, neoclassical in style, and Federalist in politics, Humphreys made several contributions to the literature of the late eighteenth century, to diplomacy during the age of the Barbary pirates, and to the development of a domestic woolen industry. His position, though minor, is secure in American literary history, for Humphreys was one of the figures who tried to establish an American cultural identity during the years of the Revolution and the early national period. Although his poems have not survived in the national memory (except for antiquarian reasons), his openly patriotic verse achieved great popularity in his own time and earned him a contemporary reputation equal to that of Trumbull, Dwight, Barlow, or Philip Freneau. Moreover, as both the originator of *The Anarchiad* and a major contributor to it, Humphreys is rightly remembered as one of the "wicked" Connecticut Wits.

• The largest repository of Humphreys papers is at the Connecticut Historical Society Library; two smaller but sizable collections are at the Massachusetts Historical Society Library and the Beinecke Rare Book and Manuscript Library at Yale University. For a comprehensive list of Humphreys papers in thirty-three repositories plus a complete listing of Humphreys's publications, see Edward M. Cifelli, *David Humphreys* (1982). An honorific, two-volume biography was published by Frank Landon Humphreys in 1917, *The Life and Times of David Humphreys: Soldier-Statesman-Poet, "Belov'd of Washington"* (repr. 1971). For previously unpublished or uncollected Humphreys poems, plus an extensive bibliography of secondary sources, see Cifelli, "David Humphreys: The Life and Literary Career of an American Patriot" (Ph.D. diss., New York Univ., 1977). John Fellows, *The Veil Removed* (1843), shows that David Humphreys was a romantic mythmaker, rather than a historian, in his biography of Putnam. Leon Howard wrote two unsympathetic chapters on Humphreys in *The Connecticut Wits* (1943). For background information on the relationship between epideictic oratory and late eighteenth-century poetry, see Gordon E. Bigelow, *Rhetoric and American Poetry of the Early National Period* (1960), and Theodore Chalon Burgess, "Epideictic Literature," *Studies in Classical Philology* 3 (1902). Providing access to early texts is William K. Bottorff, who was responsible for facsimile editions of *The Anarchiad* (1967) and the 1804 *Miscellaneous Works* (1968). Rosemarie Zagarri, in *David Humphreys' "Life of Washington"* (1991), salvaged what was previously thought to be an interesting but minor fragment that Humphreys left of a biography of George Washington.

EDWARD M. CIFELLI

HUMPHREYS, James (15 Jan. 1748–2 Feb. 1810), printer, was born in Philadelphia, Pennsylvania, the son of James Humphreys, a conveyancer, and Susanna Assheton. In 1763 he entered the College of Philadelphia but left without graduating. He next studied medicine; when this proved unsuccessful he became an apprentice to printer William Bradford. On completion of his apprenticeship, Humphreys set up his own printing business in Philadelphia. The early products of his press reveal his personality and his ambivalent political stance. Humphreys was an ambitious printer. One of his earliest publications was Edward Wetenhall's *Short Introduction to Grammar* (1773), a Greek textbook for students at the College of Philadelphia. Humphreys's interest in learning extended to the sciences, as was partially evidenced by his friendship with Philadelphia scientist David Rittenhouse, whose *Universal Almanacks* he published. Humphreys also printed Benjamin Rush's *Experiments and Observations on the Mineral Waters of Philadelphia* (1773). He capitalized on the popular taste for English belletristic works by printing Oliver Goldsmith's *Vicar of Wakefield* (1773); Laurence Sterne's six-volume *Works* (1774); and Sterne's two-volume *Sermons of Mr. Yorick* (1774), a separate issue of volumes three and four of *Works*. Other items that Humphreys printed suggest that he sympathized with the revolutionary cause: Mercy Otis Warren's *The Group* (1775); Jacob Duché's impassioned sermon before the Continental Congress, *The American Vine* (1775); and Duché's *Duty of Standing Fast* (1775). Based on the large number of his pamphlets that were reprinted throughout the colonies, Humphreys ranked among the most important colonial American printers before the revolutionary war. For example, Humphreys was the original printer for William Smith's *Sermon on the Present Situation of American Affairs* (1775), which was reprinted fourteen times.

While Humphreys's early publications suggest that he supported the revolutionary cause, he was unwilling to commit himself to it and preferred to remain neutral. When he established a weekly paper on 28

January 1775 with the ambitious title *Pennsylvania Ledger; or, The Virginia, Maryland, Pennsylvania, & New-Jersey Weekly Advertiser*, he announced his intentions to conduct the paper "with political impartiality." As the printer Isaiah Thomas noted, "perhaps, in times more tranquil than those in which it appeared, he might have succeeded in his plan," but the *Pennsylvania Ledger*'s impartiality "did not comport with the temper of the times." Shortly after Humphreys proposed his paper, Philadelphia printer Benjamin Towne announced his plans for a rival paper that supported the revolutionary cause. In his *Evening Post*, also first published in January 1775, Towne frequently denounced Humphreys as a Tory. From his nineteenth-century vantage point, Thomas recognized that Humphreys "possessed a candid mind, and was apparently guided by moral principle," while "Towne appeared to be artful, and governed by self interest," but contemporary observers sided with Towne. Humphreys was branded a Loyalist, a label that stuck following his printing of two editions of Charles Inglis's reply to Thomas Paine, *True Interest of America Impartially Stated, in Certain Strictures on . . . Common Sense* (1776). Each edition consisted of several thousand copies that were sold in just a few months.

After the 30 November 1776 issue, Humphreys suspended his paper and left Philadelphia. Once British troops took the city, Humphreys returned there and resumed his business. Besides printing numerous broadsides for the British, Humphreys revived his newspaper as *The Pennsylvania Ledger; or, The Weekly Advertiser*, starting on 10 October 1777. On 3 December 1777 the paper became a semiweekly, published on Wednesday and Saturdays (Philadelphia's market days), and Humphreys changed the title to *The Pennsylvania Ledger; or, The Philadelphia Market-Day Advertiser*. With the revolutionary forces poised to retake the city, Humphreys suspended the *Ledger* on 23 May 1778. He accompanied British forces to New York, where he worked as a merchant until the end of the war. He then went to England, procured a good supply of printing materials, and moved to Shelburne, Nova Scotia. There he established the *Nova Scotia Packet*, which was issued once a week in both folio and quarto formats. His Nova Scotia printing business proved largely unsuccessful, and Humphreys resorted to the merchant trade for the next several years.

Humphreys returned to Philadelphia in April 1797. The following year he published a new paper for approximately six months, the *Philadelphia Weekly Price Current*; apparently no copies survive. His main business was that of printing books, and he undertook many ambitious projects that reveal a cosmopolitan outlook and a wide variety of interests. Besides history, travel, and belletristic works, he printed medical treatises, scientific essays, books on husbandry and gardening, library catalog, and works concerning mercantilism and commerce. The most notable imprints of his later period include the ninth and tenth books of William Robertson's *History of America* (1799), Mungo Park's *Travels in the Interior Districts of Africa*

(1800), Christopher Robinson's five-volume *Reports of Cases* (1800–1807), the first American edition of William Wordsworth's *Lyrical Ballads* (1802), William Wittman's *Travels in Turkey* (1804), Bryan Edwards's four-volume *History . . . of the British Colonies in the West Indies* (1805), Archibald Duncan's *Mariner's Chronicle* (1806), and John Carr's *Caledonian Sketches; or, A Tour through Scotland* (1809). Humphreys remained active until his death in Philadelphia.

Humphreys's career illustrates the difficulties facing printers during the revolutionary period. As Stephen Botein has noticed, Humphreys's intention to keep the *Pennsylvania Ledger* open to both sides of the conflict was naive, and once it proved futile "he became known by default as a Tory." After siding with the British, it was impossible for him to revert to the colonial cause. Humphreys had the ambition and talent to be one of the best American printers during the last third of the eighteenth century, but the political climate effectively subtracted nearly twenty years from his otherwise productive career.

• For Humphreys's eighteenth-century imprints, see Charles Evans, *American Bibliography* (1903–1934). A source locating information concerning Humphreys within Evans's work is Roger Pattrell Bristol, *Index of Printers, Publishers, and Booksellers Indicated by Charles Evans in His American Bibliography* (1961). For additional Humphreys imprints see Bristol, *Supplement to Charles Evans' American Bibliography* (1970), and Ralph R. Shaw and Richard H. Shoemaker, *American Bibliography: A Preliminary Checklist for 1801 [–1819]* (1964–1971). Other sources include Isaiah Thomas, *The History of Printing in America*, ed. Marcus A. McCorison (1970); William McCulloch, "Additions to Thomas's History of Printing," in *Proceedings of the American Antiquarian Society* 31 (1921); and G. Thomas Tanselle, "Some Statistics on American Printing, 1764–1783," in *The Press and the American Revolution*, ed. Bernard Bailyn and John B. Hench (1980). Humphreys's newspapers are discussed in Clarence S. Brigham, *History and Bibliography of American Newspapers 1690–1820* (1947).

KEVIN J. HAYES

HUMPHRIES, Rolfe (20 Nov. 1894–22 Apr. 1969), poet and translator, was born George Rolfe Humphries in Philadelphia, Pennsylvania, the son of John Henry Humphries, a professional baseball player turned high school principal, and Florence Yost, an English teacher. Humphries was educated at home and in the public schools of Towanda, Pennsylvania. By the time he entered Amherst College in 1911, he knew Latin, Greek, German, and French and had read widely in English literature. He graduated a year early from Amherst, in 1914 (retaining his class of 1915 identity) and took a position teaching Latin and coaching football and baseball at the Potter School in San Francisco. Soon he purchased land on Lake Tahoe and opened a summer camp, which he ran until the depression. Humphries was drafted into the army in September 1917 but did not see service overseas. Discharged with the rank of first lieutenant in December 1918, he returned to the Potter School, joined a poetry workshop taught by Genevieve Taggard, and began to publish his poems in little magazines and literary journals.

In 1923 Humphries followed Taggard to New York, where he taught Latin for one year at the Browning School and for the next thirty-two years at Woodmere Academy on Long Island. From late 1923 until 1926 he served on the editorial board of the *Measure*, a magazine founded by Taggard to publish the formally polished, emotionally controlled poetry that she and Humphries favored. Within a year of his arrival, Humphries met poet Louise Bogan, who became a lifelong friend. Bogan later remembered the young Humphries as "belying what was patently a gentle and cultivated nature by flights of rather tough and fanciful humor" (*Letters*, p. 14). In 1925 he married Helen Ward Spencer, a practicing obstetrician and gynecologist; they had one son. Humphries's first book of poems, *Europa and Other Poems and Sonnets*, appeared in 1928 but received little critical notice. By the end of the decade Humphries was publishing poetry and reviews in the *New Republic* and the *Nation*.

In 1934 Humphries met Theodore Roethke. Humphries recognized the younger poet's talent from the outset and, as he had with Bogan, wrote Roethke letters filled with suggestions for revision. By 1935 the progress of fascism in Europe had caused Humphries to experience what Bogan described as "a violent Marxist conversion." He joined the League of American Writers and began to publish in its journal, *New Masses*. As part of his revolutionary duty, Humphries coedited and contributed to . . . *And Spain Sings* (1937), an anthology of poems by Spanish loyalists in English translation. He went on to translate Garcia Lorca's *Poet in New York* (1940) and *Gypsy Ballads* (1953). Humphries, who admitted to translating from Spanish by "looking up every word in the dictionary and calling on a lot of friends" (*Letters*, p. 157), prepared for the Lorca translations by going to Mexico in 1938–1939 on a Guggenheim fellowship, then on to England, France, and Greece on the brink of World War II.

By 1940 Humphries had grown disillusioned with the Communist party, an outcome acknowledged in his poem "With a Resignation, Untendered," and he turned his considerable energy back to poetry. The result was four books in quick succession: *Out of the Jewel* (1942); *The Summer Landscape* (1944); *Forbid Thy Ravens* (1947), awarded the Shelley Memorial Award by the Poetry Society of America; and *The Wind of Time* (1949). Critics such as Randall Jarrell, writing in the *Nation* of 27 March 1948, objected to Humphries's poetry as academic, but at its best it lived up to Bogan's notion, quoted as an epigraph to *Out of the Jewel*, that "minor art needs to be hard, condensed, and durable."

Humphries continued to write poetry in the 1950s. *Poems, Collected and New* appeared in 1954, and *Green Armor on Green Ground*, containing poems in the twenty-four official Welsh meters, was published in 1956. He was elected to the National Institute of Arts and Letters in 1953 and received a fellowship from the Academy of American Poets in 1955. But the decade is more remarkable for Humphries's metamorphosis from a minor poet into a major translator.

Humphries called his translation of Virgil's *Aeneid* (1951) "a quick and unscrupulous job," but it won the praise of reviewers and sold more than 250,000 copies. It was followed by Ovid's *Metamorphoses* (1955) and *Art of Love* (1957), Juvenal's *Satires* (1958), a selection of Martial's *Epigrams* (1963), and Lucretius's *The Way Things Are* (1968). Bogan remembered that the young Humphries "could speak the American vernacular with skill, in a period when American poets were not giving 'slang' much attention" (*Letters*, p. 14). The mature Humphries taught the Latin classics to speak a witty and lucid American vernacular shaped into loose iambic pentameter. Presenting himself to readers as a poet rather than a scholar, Humphries delighted in "perverse and deliberate anachronisms," such as horse races for chariot races in Ovid and haggis for Lucanian sausage in Martial.

Humphries left Woodmere Academy in 1956. After a year at Hunter College, he taught writing and Latin at Amherst from 1957 to 1965. His *Collected Poems* appeared in 1965, the year he retired—a joy tempered by the death of his son in an auto accident. In 1967 Humphries and his wife moved to Woodside, California. He died two years later in nearby Redwood City, California, before the appearance of *Nine Thorny Thickets: Selected Poems by Dafydd ap Gwilym in New Arrangements* and *Coat on a Stick: Late Poems*, both in 1969.

Humphries's poems combine linguistic vigor and intellectual clarity. His reviews and letters, especially those to Bogan and Roethke, form an interesting chapter in the history of twentieth-century American poetry. But it is for his translations of the Latin classics that Humphries will be remembered. There he found the great subject that he never attempted in his own poetry; there the poet and the Latin teacher were one. The result is some of the best poetic translations ever written by an American.

• Humphries's papers are collected at Amherst College Library, as are Bogan's. In addition to the works mentioned above, Humphries coedited and translated many of the poems in *Aragon: Poet of the French Resistance* (1945); he also edited or coedited a number of poetic anthologies: *A Little Anthology of Very Short Poems from the Magazines of 1921* (1921); with Marjorie Fischer, *Pause to Wonder* (1944); with Fischer, *Strange to Tell* (1946); two volumes of *New Poems by American Poets* (1953 and 1957); and *Wolfville Yarns of Alfred Henry Lewis* (1968). Selected letters are collected by Richard Gillman and Michael Paul Novak, eds., *Poets, Poetics, and Politics: America's Literary Community Viewed from the Letters of Rolfe Humphries, 1910–1969* (1992), which also contains a biographical essay by Ruth Limmer. Particularly interesting letters concern Humphries's childhood reading (pp. 278–80) and method of teaching Latin (pp. 237–40). Limmer publishes many letters to Humphries in *What the Woman Lived: Selected Letters of Louise Bogan, 1920–1970* (1973). Specific events in Humphries's career are illuminated by Novak, "Love and Influence: Louise Bogan, Rolfe Humphries, and

Theodore Roethke," *Kenyon Review*, n.s., 7 (1985): 9–20, and Hugh Witemeyer, "The Making of Pound's *Selected Poems* (1949) and Rolfe Humphries' Unpublished Introduction," *Journal of Modern Literature* 15 (1988): 73–91. An obituary appears in the *New York Times*, 24 Apr. 1969, and a brief memorial notice in *Time*, 2 May 1969.

ROGER HILLAS

HUNDLEY, Mary Gibson Brewer (18 Oct. 1897–1 Jan. 1986), educator and civil rights activist, was born in Baltimore, Maryland, the daughter of Malachi Gibson, a lawyer and graduate of Howard University, and Mary Matilda Syphax, a teacher. Hundley was the granddaughter of William Syphax, first superintendent of Colored Public Schools in Washington and Georgetown after the Civil War, and, according to family tradition, a descendant of George Washington Parke Custis, grandson of Martha Custis Washington. She attended the Dunbar High School (then known as the M Street School) in Washington, D.C., and went on to Radcliffe College, where she was the first black student to come from a southern segregated public school. At Radcliffe she was one of a handful of black students, all of whom lived off campus. She enjoyed easy relations with her classmates (writing songs for her class and serving as an accompanist for college musical productions) and relished the opportunity to concentrate in English and study with leading professors in the field. But her college experience was clouded by financial difficulties and by what she later called "the persecution" of Dean Bertha Boody, who insisted that she work her way through college as a maid. Hundley's refusal to do this would have led to her withdrawal from college but for the intervention of President LeBaron Russell Briggs, who arranged a loan for her. Hundley was graduated cum laude in 1918. She later pursued graduate study in French at Middlebury College (A.M., 1929) and the Sorbonne (1928).

Hundley married William Miles Brewer, a Harvard graduate, in 1924 and divorced him in 1935; three years later she married Frederick F. Hundley, a public school art teacher who died in 1955. Neither marriage produced children. She began her teaching career in Baltimore and then moved back to her alma mater, Dunbar High School, where she taught French, English, and Latin (1920–1955). Her pupils remembered her as a demanding but fair teacher whose high standards brought out the best in generations of students. She believed that teaching was a "noble profession," developing "ideals of freedom, tolerance, opportunity, democracy, and citizenship" in future citizens. But a good teacher, she wrote, "must do other things as well." These "other things" for Hundley included organizing after-school enrichment programs, the Coleman and Margaret Jennings Clubs (social service clubs), Le Cercle Français, and the Junior Auxiliary of the Freedmen's Hospital, which provided voluntary nursing aides. As a member of the Guidance Committee and chair of the College Bureau (1943–1949) she was credited with inspiring many students to enroll in Ivy League and other colleges. In

1955 she transferred to Eastern High, an integrated school, where she taught English and Latin, and from 1959 to 1964 she tutored French at Howard University, joining twenty-five of her former pupils on the faculty.

Her pride in Dunbar school and the achievements of its alumni prompted her to write *The Dunbar Story, 1870–1955* (1965), a chronicle of the school, its faculty, and its alumni. Dunbar was the first college preparatory school for African Americans in the nation, and its roster of notable alumni included civil rights lawyer Charles Houston, judge and Harvard law professor William H. Hastie, U.S. senator Edward Brooke, scientist Charles Drew, university professor Eva Dykes, gynecologist Lena Edwards, Secretary of Health Education and Welfare Robert Weaver, and other leading clergy, teachers, administrators, and doctors. In its heyday, 80 percent of students went on to college. Ironically, its success was dependent on a racially segregated education system, and when, after integration in 1955, it became a high school in a deprived neighborhood, the proportion of students attending college dropped to 23 percent. From 1973 to 1977 Hundley led the Dunbar Alumni Association in an unsuccessful campaign to prevent the demolition of the original school building.

In 1941 the Hundleys purchased and moved into a house in Washington with a restrictive racial covenant. Their white neighbors brought suit against them and won the case in December 1941. The Hundleys were enjoined from occupying their house and were evicted in July 1942. The judgment was reversed on appeal in December 1942. The landmark case of *Hundley v. Gorewitz* was one of those cited in *Shelley v. Kraemer* (1947), a U.S. Supreme Court case that established that covenants restricting use and ownership of property to whites violated the equal protection clause of the Fourteenth Amendment and affirmed the right of minorities to live in neighborhoods without regard to race.

Hundley was active in many African-American organizations, including the Links, the Women's Auxiliary of the Freedmen's Hospital, the National Association for the Advancement of Colored People, and the Phillis Wheatley branch of the Washington Young Women's Christian Association. She was a member of the American Association of University Women, the International Federation of University Women, and the Radcliffe Club of Washington D.C. She also was active in St. Luke's Episcopal Church and in Washington organizations that provided guides and interpreters for foreign visitors. From 1974 to 1979 she was a docent at the Renwick Gallery of the Smithsonian.

Although in 1946 she wrote frankly to Dean Mildred Sherman about the prejudice that she had encountered in the Radcliffe Club of Washington D.C., and was critical of the then "unfavorable local conditions" for black students at Radcliffe, she always remained fiercely loyal to her college. In 1979 she received the Radcliffe Alumnae Recognition Award, which honored her dedicated service as an educator and courageous citizen. She died in Washington, D.C.

• An extensive collection of Hundley's papers in the Schlesinger Library consists of family genealogies, records of her teaching career, the *Hundley v. Gorewitz* lawsuit, drafts of *The Dunbar Story*, and biographical data on Dunbar alumni. Her musical compositions, talks, articles, correspondence with former students, and the records of her volunteer activities also are included. The papers of President LeBaron Russell Briggs in the Radcliffe College Archives contain significant correspondence about Hundley's financial situation while at Radcliffe, her loan repayments, and her subsequent teaching career; the archives has a useful biographical file as well. Hundley's other writings include "The Unknown French," *Radcliffe Quarterly* 47 (Nov. 1963): 28–29; "A Case for Color Blindness," *Radcliffe Quarterly* 52 (Aug. 1968): 17–18; two Radcliffe songs in *Radcliffe College Songs* (1923); and the music for a reunion song, "There's a Rainbow over Radcliffe" (1938). Obituaries are in the *Washington Post*, 3 Jan. 1986, and the Washington, D.C., *Afro-American*, 11 Jan. 1986.

JANE KNOWLES

HUNEKER, James Gibbons (31 Jan. 1857–9 Feb. 1921), critic, essayist, and musician, was born in Philadelphia, Pennsylvania, the son of John Joseph Huneker, a prosperous housepainter and decorator, and Mary Gibbons, a schoolteacher. Huneker was introduced to the world of music, drama, and art by his father, who owned one of the largest private collections of prints in the United States; his interest in literature was fostered by his mother, the daughter of the Irish printer and poet James Gibbons. After attending Philadelphia's Broad Street Academy (1865–1872), Huneker began a five-year apprenticeship in law before discovering his chief interest, music. In 1875 he started piano lessons with one of Philadelphia's outstanding teachers, Michael Cross, and began writing music critiques and articles for the *Evening Bulletin*, Philadelphia's leading newspaper.

In the fall of 1878 Huneker sailed to France with the intention of studying music at the Paris Conservatoire. Although his audition was unsuccessful, he was permitted to audit the piano classes of Georges Mathias, Chopin's protégé, at the conservatoire, while absorbing French culture and gathering information for articles for the *Bulletin*. He also studied philosophy for a brief time at the Sorbonne. In July 1879 he returned to Philadelphia, where he studied and taught piano. Beginning in 1885, Huneker wrote articles for *Etude* magazine, an activity he continued for some thirty years.

After moving to New York in 1886, Huneker continued his studies in piano with Edmund Neupert and Rafael Joseffy. In 1888, owing to his vast knowledge of piano literature and considerable pianistic skills, Huneker became Joseffy's assistant and a member of the piano faculty of the prestigious National Conservatory of Music in New York. For the next ten years he taught piano there while simultaneously pursuing his career as a critic and essayist.

In 1887 Huneker began a fifteen-year association with the New York *Musical Courier*, where, primarily as a columnist ("The Raconteur"), he made his reputation as a witty, clever writer of unusual insight, ardent admiration, and frequently passionate expressions. For example, he encapsulated his negative reaction to Richard Wagner's operas by dubbing the composer "Richard of the Footlights" (*Mezzotints*, p. 9). During this period Huneker also worked as a music and drama critic for the New York *Recorder* (1891–1895) and the *Morning Advertiser* (1895–1897), and as a music critic for the weekly magazine *Town Topics* (1897–1902). In 1900 he joined the New York *Sun*, becoming in rapid succession its critic for music (1900–1902), drama (1902–1904), and art and literature (1906–1912), a feat of versatility only paralleled by England's George Bernard Shaw. From 1912 to 1914 Huneker served as a foreign correspondent for the *New York Times*. He then began writing "The Seven Arts," a potpourri column in *Puck* magazine, the oldest humorous weekly in the United States. The column was filled with short stories, humorous sketches, and critiques of literature, art, music, drama, and motion pictures. In 1916 he stopped writing for *Puck* and for a short time rejoined the editorial staff of the *Sun*, primarily as a book reviewer, before becoming a music critic for the *Philadelphia Press* (1917–1918), the *New York Times* (1918–1919), and the *New York World* (1919–1921).

Most of Huneker's twenty-two books consist of reprints of criticisms, essays, and short stories previously published in newspapers and magazines. Hailed by music critic Henry T. Finck as "one of the most readable and at the same time useful books on music ever issued in this country" (*Nation*, 4 May 1899, p. 338), Huneker's first book, *Mezzotints in Modern Music* (1899), successfully established Huneker's writing career in the United States and Europe. In 1900 he published what he called his "magnum opus," *Chopin: The Man and His Music*, a critically acclaimed biography and scholarly analysis of the composer's works. A less successful biography of Franz Liszt followed in 1911.

Other significant books by Huneker that deal with music and musicians include *Melomaniacs* (1902), *Visionaries* (1905), and *Bedouins* (1920). He also authored two autobiographies, *Old Fogy* (1913) and *Steeplejack* (1920); many letters, which his wife Josephine compiled in two collections, *Letters of James Gibbons Huneker* (1922) and *Intimate Letters of James Gibbons Huneker* (1924); and a novel, *Painted Veils* (1920). His *Iconoclasts: A Book of Dramatists* (1905) deals with drama criticism; *Egoists* (1910), with literary criticism; and *Promenades of an Impressionist* (1910), with art criticism. Huneker also edited and published collections of the songs of Brahms, Tchaikovsky, and Richard Strauss, and of the piano music of Chopin.

Because of his ingratiating manner, Huneker, who according to literary critic Alfred Kazin "almost singlehandedly brought the new currents of European art and thought to America and made them fashionable" (*Saturday Review of Literature*, 3 Feb. 1940, p. 11), was able to acquaint more Americans with European composers, artists, and writers than any other critic of his time. He became a crusader for new and neglected artists: in 1899 he touted Brahms as the "last of the immortals" and "our most modern music maker" (*Mezzotints*, pp. 1, 16); he vehemently supported Richard Strauss, naming him "the greatest living musician and the greatest master of orchestration in the history of music" (*Musical Courier*, 25 Dec. 1901, 23–24), and described Strauss's *Also Sprach Zarathustra* (1896) as "a cathedral . . . dangerously sublime . . . with grotesque gargoyles, hideous flying abutments, exquisite traceries, fantastic arches half gothic, half infernal . . . a mighty structure" (*Mezzotints*, p. 153). After hearing one of the first performances of Arnold Schoenberg's *Pierrot Lunaire* (1912) in Berlin, Huneker concluded that "a man who could portray in tone sheer ugliness with such crystal clearness is to be reckoned with in these topsyturvy times. . . . Perhaps he is a superman and the world doesn't know it" (*Ivory, Apes, and Peacocks* [1957], p. 97).

Huneker similarly championed controversial writers and artists: a proponent of Nietzsche, he maintained that the philosopher preached "egoism, individualism, personal freedom, and selfhood" (*Musical Courier*, 6 May 1896, p. 20); Huneker was the first American to write a detailed criticism of the work of Henrik Ibsen and to publish an interview with Joseph Conrad; and, after designating the Salle Cézanne in Paris as "the very hub of the Independents' universe," Huneker wrote in 1906 the first study of Paul Cézanne to be printed in an American newspaper.

Huneker also vigorously applauded American artists of all types. They included the performer Mary Garden; writers Walt Whitman, Edgar Allan Poe, and Henry James; composers Edward MacDowell and Victor Herbert; and a group of painters known as "The Eight": Robert Henri, George Luks, John Sloan, Ernest Lawson, Arthur Davies, Maurice Prendergast, William Glackens, and Everett Shinn. Moreover, Huneker's position as a progressive, crusading critic established a new school of American criticism, whose members included H. L. Mencken, George Jean Nathan, and Benjamin De Casseres.

The French government made Huneker an officer of the Legion of Honor in 1910 in recognition of his service to French literature and art. In addition, he was elected to membership in the Authors' Club of London, the Academy of Natural Sciences of Philadelphia, and the National Institute of Arts and Letters (1918).

Huneker married Elizabeth Holmes in 1878; they divorced in 1891. The couple had two children, both of whom died in infancy. In 1892 he married the sculptor Clio Hinton; they had one child. This marriage ended in divorce in 1899. In 1899 he married Josephine Ahrensdorf Laski, a young widow, and remained with her for the last twenty-two years of his life.

Huneker died at his home in Brooklyn, New York. Four days later, on 13 February 1921, more than 1,200 people representative of the musical and artistic life of New York filled the auditorium of the new Town Hall, while hundreds more stood outside, for Huneker's funeral service, where he was eulogized for his credo of criticism. Believing that criticism was "the adventures of the soul among masterpieces" (*Times*, 10 Feb. 1921), Huneker "never preached aught but the beauty of art; I didn't even spell beauty with a big B. Not that I don't love art, but because I love life the more" (*World*, 10 Oct. 1920).

Even though Huneker's highly impressionistic literary style did not remain in favor and most of his books went out of print, his writings remain among the most significant sources for information about the cultural life of the United States and Europe from the 1880s to the 1920s, and his influence on that cultural life is inestimable. According to journalist and poet De Casseres, "He is the greatest of patriots who raises the intellectual levels of his country; and James Huneker is therefore, to me, the greatest of twentieth century Americans. James Huneker was the end of the nineteenth century and the beginning of the twentieth in America" (pp. 17, 20).

• Huneker's personal papers, including literary manuscripts, notebooks, photographs, correspondence, press clippings, and 175 volumes from his library are in the Huneker collection, Baker Memorial Library, Dartmouth College; 800 books from his library, pamphlets on music and literature, and his scrapbooks are at the New York Public Library at Lincoln Center. A recent publication of selected critiques by Huneker is Arnold T. Schwab, ed., *Americans in the Arts, 1890–1920: Critiques by James Gibbons Huneker* (1985). The most complete modern assessment is Schwab, *James Gibbons Huneker: Critic of the Seven Arts* (1963), which includes a complete list of Huneker's books, an extensive bibliography, and a note on sources. See also Benjamin De Casseres, *James Gibbons Huneker* (1925; repr. 1980), and the obituary in the *New York Times*, 10 Feb. 1921.

SHERRILL V. MARTIN

HUNG, William (27 Oct. 1893–22 Dec. 1980), historian and educator, was born Hung Ngiek in Foochow, Fukien, China, the son of Hung Hsi, a minor official of the Ching Empire, and Lin Fei, daughter of a wealthy tea merchant. Hung was also known as Hung Yeh, Hung Wei-lien, and Hung Cheng-chi. He received a traditional Confucian education before enrolling at a modern school at the age of thirteen in Shantung province. From 1910 to 1915, he attended the Foochow Anglo-Chinese College, which was run by the Board of Foreign Missions of the Methodist Church, where he was converted to Christianity. Impressed by Hung's intelligence, one of the school's American benefactors, Hanford Crawford, offered to pay for Hung's schooling in the United States. Hung graduated magna cum laude and Phi Beta Kappa from Ohio Wesleyan in 1917. He received a master's degree in history from Columbia University in 1919, and an S.T.B. from Union Theological Seminary in 1920. In 1919 he married Rhoda Kong (though the marriage was not announced until 1921). They had three children.

Hung's patriotism was aroused by the Paris Peace Conference of 1919, in which the world powers supported Japan's claims to Chinese territories, and in 1920 he embarked on a lecture tour of the United States to explain his country to Americans. His ability to inform and entertain from the podium led to engagements with the Lyceum and the Community Chautaqua. In 1922 he was recruited by John Leighton Stuart, later the U.S. ambassador to China, to raise money for the newly founded, theologically liberal, Christian Yenching University in Peking. Hung was associated until 1947 with Yenching University, where he served variously as dean of the College of Arts and Sciences (1924–1927), professor of history, chairman of the history department, chairman of the university library, and director of the Graduate Institute of Letters. He played a crucial role in developing Yenching University into one of the leading institutions of higher learning in China. He also helped found the Harvard-Yenching Institute, a nonprofit organization that promotes research, instruction, and publications in Chinese, Japanese, and other Asian cultures. He conceived, developed, and supervised the publication of the Harvard-Yenching Institute Sinological Index Series, which proposed to systematically evaluate the most important books ever written in China and provide them with indices or concordances. This series is viewed by many scholars as the single most important set of research tools to be produced in the first half of the twentieth century for the study of traditional Chinese civilization. Scholars in China and abroad rely on it heavily to this day.

Hung was a member of that small but influential group of Chinese intellectuals who were well grounded in the Chinese classics before they received a Western education in the United States or Europe in the 1910s and were convinced that it was their destiny to lead China into becoming a modern, democratic nation. Those who came after them were inclined to be less confident and more cynical. Although Hung held himself above the fray of politics, many of his close friends, including Hu Shih and Timothy Ting-fang Liu as well as his brother David (Hung Shen), served under the Nationalist government. Hung was incarcerated by the Japanese military on suspicion of anti-Japanese activities for approximately six months between 1941 and 1942. After Japan surrendered, Hung watched with dismay the deterioration of the Nationalist government and the rapid inroads made by the Communists. Although he found the goals of communism appealing, he realized early on that Chinese Communists were highly intolerant of any view of the world other than their own. He felt that under a communist regime, there would be no place for someone like himself, who believed in a spiritual dimension of man that was inexplicable by the terms of science, and who believed that many traditional Confucian values and codes of conduct were applicable to twentieth-century China. In addition, Hung also considered himself a Christian until the end of his life. He felt that his Confucian values were totally compatible with his

Christian faith but was concerned that communism would tolerate neither belief. On this and other matters, Hung was proven prescient; his colleagues were humiliated, tortured, hounded, and some were killed during the various political campaigns that ensued.

Hung was lecturing in the United States when it became clear that communism would prevail in China, and he settled in 1947 in Cambridge, Massachusetts, where he carried on his scholarly work. Notable among his publications after he left China was *Tu Fu: China's Greatest Poet* (1952). Hung lived, however, to see moderation come back into favor in China, his publications reprinted, and many of his students and colleagues restored to positions of power and prestige. He died in Cambridge.

Hung was known not only for his formidable scholarship and the large number of historians that he trained, but also for his great warmth and quick wit. The *Harvard Journal of Asiatic Studies* dedicated its 1963 issue to him on his seventieth birthday, citing his "contribution to the study of Chinese history and letters, and the encouragement and guidance—characterized by both solicitude and the most exacting severity—which he has offered to the generations of scholars and students."

• A partial list of Hung's publications is found in the 1963 issue of the *Harvard Journal of Asiatic Studies*. A collection of Hung's Chinese essays, *Hung Yeh lun-hsueh chi*, appeared in Beijing in 1981. During the last three years of his life, Susan Chan Egan taped his memoirs, which were published as *A Latterday Confucian: Reminiscences of William Hung (1893–1980)* (1987). For other assessments of his life, see Yu Ying-shih, "Ku Chieh-kang, Hung Yeh and Chinese Modern Historiography" (in Chinese), *Ming Pao Monthly*, May 1981, pp. 57–61; a biographical sketch (in Chinese) by Wen Tu-chien et al. in *Chung-kuo shih-hsueh-chia p'ing chuan*, vol. 3 (1985), pp. 1464–72; Wang Yi-tung, "A Short Introduction to a Contemporary Historian, Mr. Hung Yeh" (in Chinese), *Chung-kuo li-shih hsueh-hui hui-hsin*, 22 Sept. 1986, pp. 3–5; Joseph Lau, "Yenching, Harvard, Hung Yeh" (in Chinese), *Chuan-chi wen hsueh* 52.5 (1988), pp. 49–51, and his articles on Hung in the *Lien-he pao*, 1 and 2 Sept. 1988; and Hou Jen-chih, "Four Remembrances of My Mentor, Professor Hung Yeh" (in Chinese), *Hou Jen-chih Yen-yuan wen-hsueh chi*, 1991, pp. 7–30. See also Wang Chung-han, "Mr. William Hung and the Harvard-Yenching Sinological Index Series" (in Chinese), *Hsueh-lin man-lu* 8 (1983): 52–68, and Wang Yi-tung, "Harvard Sinologist Nurtured Asian Studies at Pitt," *Pitt*, Nov. 1981, p. 21. For a history of Yenching University and Hung's role in it, see Philip West, *Yenching University and Sino-Western Relations, 1916–1952* (1976). An obituary is in the *Boston Globe*, 1 Jan. 1981.

SUSAN CHAN EGAN

HUNSAKER, Jerome Clarke (26 Aug. 1886–10 Sept. 1984), aeronautical engineer and aviation pioneer, was born in Creston, Iowa, the son of Walter J. Hunsaker, a newspaper publisher, and Alma Clarke. Hunsaker was raised in Detroit and Saginaw, Michigan. He enrolled in the U.S. Naval Academy and graduated first in his class in 1908. He was then assigned to the naval construction corps, and shortly afterward he was sent by the navy to begin graduate studies at the Massachusetts Institute of Technology (MIT), where he intended to study ship construction. Hunsaker, however, soon became fascinated by the phenomenon of flight and the study of aeronautical engineering. In 1911 he married Alice Porter Avery, with whom he had four children.

For his master's thesis, Hunsaker undertook the task of translating Alexandre-Gustave Eiffel's treatise on wind tunnels. Because of this work, Hunsaker received his master of science degree in 1912. He then left on a two-year tour of Europe to assess the development of aeronautics on the Continent and in Britain. While in Europe, he was given a tour of Eiffel's tower by the designer himself, and he also visited laboratories and wind tunnel facilities in England and Germany. He also hoped to examine the German zeppelin airships, but military restrictions prevented him from an official study. Hunsaker instead booked an excursion on one of the dirigibles and learned as much as he could as a passenger.

Upon his return to the United States in 1914, Hunsaker resumed his studies at MIT. Using a plan that he developed as an improvement on an English wind tunnel, Hunsaker constructed the first wind tunnel with a modern design built on U.S. soil. In this work he collaborated with Donald W. Douglas, who later founded the Douglas Aircraft Company. Hunsaker also convinced MIT to begin a graduate course in aeronautics, which he was allowed to teach. In 1916 Hunsaker was granted his Ph.D. for work on the dynamic stability of flying craft, the first bestowed by MIT in the field of aeronautical engineering.

When Hunsaker completed his academic studies, the navy assigned him to duty as the head of its Bureau of Construction and Repair's aircraft division. With the war in Europe raging, the navy was concerned that the United States be prepared for the possibility of taking an active role in the fighting. In 1915 President Woodrow Wilson had set up a National Advisory Committee on Aeronautics (NACA) to coordinate U.S. efforts in the newly emerging field. Together with his colleague Edwin Bidwell Wilson of MIT, Hunsaker published the first NACA report, "The Behavior of Aeroplanes in Gusts," later that year. When the United States did enter the war in 1917, Hunsaker's position placed him in charge of the design, procurement, and production of all navy aircraft. By the end of 1917 the navy had produced 1,000 flying boats and a new, nonrigid dirigible for antisubmarine missions, some of which went from design to full-scale production in less than one year under Hunsaker's supervision.

The navy also asked Hunsaker to head two specialized projects: the creation of a long-range aircraft capable of crossing the Atlantic, and the design and construction of a large, zeppelin-style airship. After the war, he continued these projects. In 1919 the NC-4 flying boat that Hunsaker had designed made the first successful transatlantic flight from Newfoundland to Portugal. To complete the latter project, Hunsaker once again visited Germany in order to view German zeppelins. After this visit, Hunsaker designed the first large, rigid dirigible built in America, an airship that would be known as the *Shenandoah*. Built from "duralumin," a lightweight alloy, and filled with helium rather than highly flammable hydrogen, this craft made its first flight in 1923.

Hunsaker continued his service with the navy until 1926 in several high-level design and engineering posts. In his role as the head of the Naval Bureau of Aeronautics' material division from 1921 to 1923, Hunsaker developed methods of launching and landing aircraft on the decks of ships. In collaboration with his friend and former MIT assistant Donald Douglas, Hunsaker also aided in the design of one of the first torpedo planes designed to carry out attacks on surface vessels. During this period Hunsaker also was assigned to positions as the assistant naval attaché in London, Paris, Berlin, Rome, and The Hague.

In 1926 Hunsaker resigned from the navy to take a position with Bell Telephone Laboratories to work on aircraft communication systems. His stint with Bell Labs was relatively short, however, because in 1928 he was offered a position as a vice president in the newly created Goodyear-Zeppelin Corporation to supervise the development of a gas-proof fabric for use as a dirigible skin. Hunsaker was eager to take on this assignment because he had high hopes for the potential of commercial applications for large lighter-than-air craft. Goodyear-Zeppelin built two large airships under Hunsaker's leadership, the *Akron* and the *Macon*. The company hoped to begin a transatlantic passenger service modeled on the success of the German *Graf Zeppelin*, which flew more than a million miles in commercial service during the late 1920s and early 1930s. Both Goodyear-Zeppelin ships, however, were lost in storms over the next few years. A series of other disasters that took a number of lives, including the explosion of the R-101 in Beauvais, France, in 1930 and the crash of the Hindenburg in Lakehurst, New Jersey, in 1937, helped put an end to commercial dirigible service. By then, Congress had also refused a proposal to fund a federally subsidized civil airship program, effectively dooming the Goodyear-Zeppelin project.

Due in part to this demise in the commercial potential for lighter-than-air craft, in 1933 Hunsaker returned to MIT as the head of the mechanical engineering department. There, he began teaching the course in aeronautical engineering he had founded nearly two decades earlier. In 1939 MIT created the Department of Aeronautical Engineering, headed by Hunsaker. As the head of this department, Hunsaker presided over the expansion of MIT research into the rapidly evolving field of aeronautics, including the development of supersonic aerodynamics and of jet propulsion.

When World War II broke out, Hunsaker was called back into public service. He was appointed to chair the National Advisory Committee on Aeronautics and coordinated the navy's research and development wing. He worked mostly as an administrator and as an expert counselor to several government agencies.

Although he was not directly involved with the Manhattan Project, Hunsaker firmly opposed the dropping of the A-bomb, contending that the military had little or no appreciation of its destructive power.

Hunsaker continued to chair the NACA until 1956, although he retired from teaching at MIT four years earlier. During the course of his career he garnered numerous awards. For his military service during World War I he was awarded the Navy Cross, and after World War II he received the Presidential Medal for Merit. For his innovations in aeronautics, Hunsaker was awarded the Daniel Guggenheim Medal in 1933, the Wright Brothers Memorial Trophy in 1951, the Gold Medal of the Royal Aeronautical Society, the Godfrey L. Cabot and Langely medals, and the NACA's Distinguished Service Medal. He also served as the first president of the Institute of Aeronautical Sciences and was a fellow of the American Academy of Arts and Sciences and of the American Physical Society.

By the time of his death in Boston, Massachusetts, Hunsaker had lived through and participated in one of the most extraordinary centuries of scientific and technological advances that humanity has ever known. During his long and distinguished career, Hunsaker was a leader in the development of both the theoretical and the practical aspects of aircraft design and manufacture. His career spanned nearly the entire history of aviation, from the early years of flight to the launching of the space shuttle. His contributions to aeronautical engineering and aircraft design and production make him one of the most influential figures in the history of flight.

• A small collection of Hunsaker's papers are held at the Institute Archives and Special Collections of MIT. They include biographical information, a small amount of Hunsaker's correspondence, course notes, articles, speeches, information on the National Advisory Committee on Aeronautics, and photographs. Information on Hunsaker's work is also in the records of the NACA, although these sources are scattered throughout the collection. In addition, the NASA history office maintains a historical file on Hunsaker in Washington, D.C.

Several histories of the early days of aviation and the development of aeronautics in the United States have been published, but they largely focus on the careers of a few individuals. Hunsaker, as a result, does not always receive extensive treatment despite his importance. Two such works are Richard P. Hallion, *Legacy of Flight: The Guggenheim Contribution to American Aviation* (1977), and Theodore von Kármán with Lee Edson, *The Wind and Beyond: Theodore von Kármán, Pioneer in Aviation and Pathfinder in Space* (1967). A useful source of important events in the history of aviation in general is Eugene M. Emme, *Aeronautics and Astronautics: An American Chronology of Science and Technology in the Exploration of Space, 1915–1960* (1961). On the history of the NACA, see Alex Roland, *Model Research: The National Advisory Committee on Aeronautics, 1915–1958* (1985).

Biographical information on Hunsaker is contained in *The Guggenheim Medalists* (1964). There are obituaries of Hunsaker in the *New York Times*, 12 Sept. 1984, and in Margot Levy, ed., *The Annual Obituary 1984* (1985), pp. 482–84.

DAVID A. VALONE

HUNT, Alfred Ephraim (31 Mar. 1855–26 Apr. 1899), metallurgist, inventor, and businessman, was born in East Douglass, Massachusetts, the son of Leander Batchelor Hunt, an iron manufacturer and inventor, and Mary Hannah Hanchett, a leader in the temperance movement. Hunt's family moved to the Boston suburb of Hyde Park by his twelfth birthday. He filled his free moments accumulating and classifying a collection of butterflies, birds' eggs, and postage stamps.

Hunt attended Roxbury High School and went on to attend the Massachusetts Institute of Technology in 1872, where he studied mining engineering with an emphasis on chemistry, metallurgy, and basic engineering. During his senior year Hunt spent afternoons at the Bay State Steel Company in South Boston, where he acquired practical experience by doing chemical analyses and metallurgical work. After graduating in 1876 he stayed on at the company and assisted in the construction of the second open-hearth steel plant built in the United States. During this time he was also sent to the upper peninsula of Michigan and northern Wisconsin on behalf of the U.S. Geological Survey to investigate the newly discovered Michigamme iron ore deposits. His reports played a key role in opening up the Lake Superior iron region to mining.

An attractive offer lured Hunt to Nashua, New Hampshire, in 1877, where he took charge of the chemical and metallurgical work in the Nashua Iron and Steel Company's open-hearth steel department. There his knowledge of steel making grew. There, too, Hunt met Maria Tyler McQuesten, whom he married in October 1878; they had one son.

Hunt received his first patent in June 1880 for a new refractory fire brick for use in open hearth and reverberatory furnaces. Sensing that greater opportunities lay elsewhere, Hunt moved to Pittsburgh in June 1881, where he became a metallurgical chemist and superintendent of the heavy-hammer department for the Park, Brother & Company Black Diamond Crucible Steel Works. These works made both crucible and special purpose open-hearth steels. By that October Hunt, already a member of the Engineers' Society of Western Pennsylvania, was quickly establishing a reputation as an authority in the field of metallurgy.

In 1883 Hunt and chemist George Hubbard Clapp, Hunt's assistant at the steel works, resigned their positions and accepted an offer to operate the chemical department of the recently formed Pittsburgh Testing Laboratory. Hunt proved himself to be not only an excellent metallurgist but also a very good business promoter. In 1887 Hunt and Clapp acquired full control of the laboratory and broadened its scope, renaming it the Hunt and Clapp-Pittsburgh Testing Laboratory. This independent research laboratory was one of the first American firms founded to provide expertise and perform research "for hire," and it played a major role in making Pittsburgh an important and innovative industrial center in the late 1800s. Its staff of consulting engineers, chemists, and metallurgists advised manufacturers, inspected construction and manufacturing works, and served as expert witnesses in lawsuits.

In July 1888 Charles Martin Hall's process for the electrolytic reduction of aluminum ore came to Hunt's attention. Hall had previously attempted to interest the Cowles Electric Smelting & Aluminum Company of Lockport, New York, as well as other investors, in his process, but none foresaw its tremendous potential. Hunt, however, after consulting with friends and close business associates, formed the Pittsburgh Reduction Company with himself as president and George Clapp as treasurer. A plant building was swiftly erected during the latter part of summer and early autumn, and on Thanksgiving Day Hall and new employee Arthur Vining Davis ladled out the company's first aluminum and cast it into small ingots. By November 1889 production of aluminum had reached fifty pounds a day, and by March 1891 five tons were being manufactured each month.

In 1893 Hunt assembled plans for the expansion of the Pittsburgh Reduction Company. He was convinced that increased sales of aluminum could only be achieved by lowering its market price. This led Hunt to establish a new plant at Niagara Falls, where newly available cheap hydroelectric power would significantly reduce his production costs and make cheaper aluminum feasible. The Pittsburgh Reduction Company signed its contract with the Niagara Falls Power Company for 6,500 electric horsepower in June 1893.

The World's Columbian Exposition, held that year in Chicago, was a celebration of American industry and growth. Many companies, among them the Pittsburgh Reduction Company, took advantage of the fair to make potential investors and the public aware of their products. Pittsburgh Reduction's display was impressive enough to be given an award; it included some of the original aluminum pellets created by Hall in his family's woodshed, models of the Hall electrolytic reduction pot, and samples of aluminum products such as bicycle frames, pots, pans, and kettles. Hunt also received an award for the best paper presented before the International Engineering Congress, which was held in connection with the exposition. Hunt's paper, "A Proposed Method of Testing Structural Steel," earned the American Society of Civil Engineers' Norman Gold Medal.

Pittsburgh Reduction's new works at Niagara Falls, which were for a time the largest aluminum works in the world, went into operation in August 1895. The building was 200 feet long and 85 feet wide and contained eighty reduction pots. The results achieved with this plant were so favorable that a second plant was erected and began producing aluminum in November 1896. By 1914 the Niagara Falls plant of the Aluminum Company of America—or Alcoa, as Pittsburgh Reduction would be known after a 1907 reorganization—was the world's largest user of hydroelectric power.

During the Spanish-American War (1898) Hunt served as captain of a National Guard unit. His unit was one of the first to volunteer, and Hunt patriotically set aside his business interests to command the unit. During the war Hunt contracted malaria; this weakened his heart and brought on his unexpected death in Philadelphia, where he was on leave because of his poor health.

Through Hunt's efforts, aluminum, which was at one time a very rare metal, became easily available. Although Hall was the inventor and perfecter of the aluminum-creating process, it was Hunt's enthusiasm, business acumen, and scientific knowledge that made this venture a commercial success and brought about the wide use of this metal.

• Junius Edwards, *A Captain in Industry* (1957), was written using Hunt family records, letters, and scrapbooks as reference materials. Hunt's son Roy also contributed personal recollections, making this an ideal source of information. Charles C. Carr, *Alcoa: An American Enterprise* (1952), recounts the formation of the Pittsburgh Reduction Company and its evolution into Alcoa, as does George D. Smith, *From Monopoly to Competition: The Transformation of Alcoa* (1988), and Margaret Graham, *R & D for Industry: A Century of Technical Innovation at Alcoa* (1990). Hamilton B. Mizer, *Niagara Falls: A Topical History, 1892–1932* (1981), details Pittsburgh Reduction's presence in Niagara Falls. Detailed obituaries are in the *Pittsburgh Dispatch*, 27 Apr. 1899, and the *Niagara Falls Gazette*, 27 Apr. 1899. *Technology Review* (July 1899), also contains an obituary and a lengthy overview of Hunt's life.

DANIEL MARTIN DUMYCH

HUNT, Carleton (1 Jan. 1836–14 Aug. 1921), lawyer, educator, and congressman, was born in New Orleans, Louisiana, the son of Thomas Hunt, a physician, and Aglae Carleton, the daughter of an associate justice of the Supreme Court of Louisiana. Hunt spent his early life in the stimulating surroundings of an upper-class family of professionals and academicians. He took his A.B. degree from Harvard in 1856 and then read law in the office of William Henry Hunt (1823–1884), his uncle, and W. O. Denegre. He received his LL.B. from the University of Louisiana (now Tulane University) in 1858. On 24 December 1860 he married Louise Georgine Cammack, daughter of a commission merchant who dealt in cotton and sugar. They had six children.

The Hunts began their marriage amid the turmoil of the secession crisis that gripped the South in the wake of Lincoln's election. Hunt served as a delegate at the 1860 Constitutional Union Party Convention in Baton Rouge; he actively campaigned for the Bell-Everett ticket and supported the cooperationists in the secession election of 1861. However, when the war began he joined the Louisiana Heavy Artillery as a first lieutenant. "Not to volunteer in the popular cause," he explained to his former Harvard classmates, "was to incur reproach, and to be pointed at by the slow, unmoving finger of scorn." Hunt fought in defense of New Orleans and was taken prisoner at Fort St. Philip in April 1862. After being exchanged, he resigned his commission and spent the remaining years of the war in New York, Philadelphia, and Baltimore. While living in New York, he told his former collegiate companions that his loyalty had always been to the Union and that he "found in reflection, and in the pursuit of congenial studies, an amount of happiness never afforded me by military life."

After the war, Hunt returned to New Orleans, resumed his practice, and in 1866 he began teaching at the University of Louisiana, serving as professor of admiralty and international law (1869–1879), professor of civil law (1879–1883), and dean of the law school (1872–1883). In 1883 he took his seat as a Democrat in the 48th Congress where he served on the Committee of American Shipping and on the Committee on Banking and Currency. Although Hunt's speeches reflected his professional expertise in admiralty, international, and banking law, they tended to be too professorial to gain more than respect from his peers. However, he capably espoused measures that promoted New Orleans as a major national and international port, and he persuasively advocated federal subsidies for Mississippi River improvements, steamships, and the World's Industrial and Cotton Centennial Exposition.

After leaving the House, he returned to the practice of law. Encouraged by promises of municipal reform, Hunt accepted the city council's unanimous vote to the post of city attorney during the administration of Mayor Joseph Shakespeare (1888–1892). In that capacity he gave valuable service to both the state and the city. In the case of *Hope & Company v. Board of Liquidation of State Debt* his arguments saved Louisiana great financial embarrassment at a time when the state's coffers had not recovered from the looting of former treasurer E. A. Burke. His success in the case of *Peake v. New Orleans* absolved the city of liability for a large outlay of funds for the redemption of drainage warrants and faciliated the debt settlement plan of the Shakespeare administration that restored city credit. These triumphs assuaged his disappointment with the reform record of the municipal government. Lawlessness became legend in the city while reform measures fell victim to the ambitions of politicians.

Hunt proved neither politician nor placeman. He refused office as associate justice of the Supreme Court of Louisiana during the notoriously corrupt administration of Governor Louis Wiltz. Researching and arguing cases and serving as mentor to students and aspiring attorneys were tasks that captivated his interest. He participated in most of the important litigation brought before the Louisiana courts over a span of fifty-six years. His public addresses reveal a man secure in the esteem of his fellows, confident of his place in society, and proud of his family's contributions to that society. He died suddenly at his home in New Orleans.

• The printed public addresses of Carleton Hunt, *Fifty Years Experience in Practice at the Bar . . .* (1908) and *Life and Services of Edward Livingston . . .* (1903), are housed in the Special Collections at Louisiana State University Library in Baton Rouge; they contain a delightful blend of wit and scholarship, give insight into Hunt's personality, and provide salient comment on the major figures at the Louisiana bar spanning more than half a century. In the *Report of the Secretary of 1865, Harvard* (1865), Hunt provided a candid view of

a Unionist left without option in the secession crisis of 1860–1861. In the *Memorial of the Harvard College Class of 1856 . . .* (1906), Hunt's devotion to the law and his pride in his legal career are apparent. For biographical sketches see James A. Renshaw, "The Hunt Family: A Sketch of Men of Great Attainment," *Louisiana Historical Quarterly* 5 (1922): and Alcee Fortier, *Louisiana Comprising Sketches of Parishes, Towns, Events, Institutions and Persons, Arranged in Cyclopedia Form* (1914). A record of his Civil War service is found in *Records of Louisiana Confederate Soldiers and Louisiana Confederate Commands* vol. 3, book 1 (1984). An obituary is in the New Orleans *Times Picayune*, 15 Aug. 1921.

CAROLYN E. DE LATTE

HUNT, Ezra Mundy (4 Jan. 1830–1 July 1894), physician, sanitarian, and public health official, was born in Metuchen, New Jersey, the son of Holloway Whitfield Hunt, a Presbyterian minister, and Henrietta Mundy. He graduated from Princeton University in 1849 and enrolled in New York's College of Physicians and Surgeons (Columbia University). While in medical school he was apprenticed to Abraham Coles of Newark, New Jersey, to gain practical experience. Hunt graduated from medical school with an M.D. in 1852. In 1853 he married Emma Louisa Ayres of Rahway, New Jersey; they had five children, two of whom died at an early age. Three years after his wife's death in 1867 he married Emma Reeves of Alloway, New Jersey; the couple had one child.

In 1853 he began his practice of medicine in Metuchen but later that year accepted an appointment as lecturer of materia medica and therapeutics at Vermont Medical College in Woodstock. A year later Hunt declined the position of professor of chemistry, and at the beginning of 1855 he returned to Metuchen to resume his medical practice. During the next few years he became painfully aware of the life-threatening sanitary and environmental conditions under which New Jersey residents lived. The obvious need for public health reform prompted Hunt to become active in the Middlesex County Medical Society and the Medical Society of New Jersey, the only organizations then available through which health reforms might be initiated.

On 9 October 1862, moved by patriotism and humanitarianism, Hunt enlisted as a surgeon in the Twenty-ninth New Jersey Infantry; however, he was forced to resign on 7 January 1863 due to illness. When Hunt returned to civilian life, he resumed the leadership of the campaign for sanitary and health reforms in the interest of preventive medicine. Hunt never tired of reminding physicians that "it is grander to remedy morbid causes instead of morbid effects"— that preventive medicine had a far greater value than therapeutic medicine. While many physicians looked on preventive medicine as a restriction on their earnings, they nonetheless recognized Hunt's contributions to sanitary and public health reforms and elected him to positions of leadership in the field. In his farewell address as president of the Medical Society of New Jersey in 1864, Hunt challenged the social Darwinists when he asserted that old age depended more on socioeconomic conditions than on inherited characteristics and that social trauma caused by unsanitary living and dangerous working conditions affected the life expectancy of people adversely. These were positions from which he never wavered.

In 1866 and again in 1874 cholera epidemics struck New Jersey. Hunt mobilized the medical profession in preparation for the expected onslaught from the dreaded disease. As a result of Hunt's agitation a state sanitary commission was formed in 1866 and a health commission in 1874 to cope with the myriad problems created by the epidemics. Aware that temporary measures were often too little and too late, Hunt and the commission members looked on temporary measures as an expediency and requested that the state legislature establish a permanent state board of health. The commissions' recommendations were ignored; however, Hunt used the findings of both commissions as an agenda to promote sanitary progress.

Disappointed but not discouraged, Hunt rallied the proponents of reforms and established the New Jersey Sanitary Association in 1875 to educate and lobby for reforms. The membership consisted of middle-class and upper-class professionals, educators, engineers, ministers, physicians, lawyers, businessmen, and others who, in the process of removing many of the hygienic deficiencies, overcame many of their class antagonisms. The association was dedicated to the "improvement of the sanitary condition of the people" and "the advancement of their economic and moral interests." For eighty-four years the organization served to educate, disseminate public health information, propose health programs, and lobby for the passage of public-health laws. In 1959 it became the New Jersey section of the American Public Health Association, which Hunt had helped to found in 1872; he also served as the association's tenth president in 1882.

While Hunt welcomed voluntary efforts to bring about improvements, he reminded the humanitarians that their efforts had not been enough to alleviate the misery, degradation, and human sorrow that resulted from unsanitary conditions. He asserted that education and moral persuasion did not negate the need for laws, that it was not reasonable "to expect that good advice will cleanse the loaded air, the reeking gutters, or other sources of disease."

In 1877, after years of diligent effort by Hunt and a handful of other dedicated sanitary reformers and mounting pressure from the state's residents, the state legislature established the New Jersey State Board of Health, with Hunt as the secretary of the board. He was determined that the mission of the board include all aspects of public health that were deemed important for the welfare of the people.

Hunt had the foresight to understand and appreciate the health problems that population growth in New Jersey would engender. He visualized the state as a corridor between two large cities (New York and Philadelphia), eventually becoming a megalopolis where large cities, towns, and villages became inseparable. To minimize the potential rapid spread of epidemic or endemic diseases throughout the state, on the advice of Hunt the legislature enacted a law in 1880 that made it mandatory to establish boards of health in rural areas. Hunt also stressed the need to sanitize farms and to pay closer attention to the risks of transmitting diseases through the sale of tainted farm products. In 1953 the American Public Health Association conducted a national poll of leading public health professionals, and Hunt was chosen as the outstanding pioneer in the modern concepts of rural health services.

Throughout his years as secretary of the board of health, Hunt was editor of the *Annual Report of the New Jersey State Board of Health*. The report served as a forum for the sanitary sciences and was eventually distributed to physicians, sanitary inspectors, social workers, educators, politicians, and public health professionals in more than four hundred New Jersey municipalities. Hunt wrote articles for the report that ranged in subject from adulterated foods to zymotic diseases.

When the germ theory of disease began to gain acceptance within the medical profession during the 1880s and to be glamorized by the commercial press, Hunt warned his colleagues to be careful of accepting theories without adequate proof. He claimed that much that was reported was like "sewage contamination defiling the pure stream of science." Hunt cautioned that in their search for germs, sanitarians should not be diverted from removing the sources, the filth, in which diseases flourished. Hunt's worst fears came to fruition in 1903, only a few years after his death, when the president of the New Jersey Sanitary Association announced that it was no longer necessary to stress the great "bugbears" of sanitary science: filth, filthy water, and filthy air.

During his seventeen-year tenure as the secretary of the New Jersey State Board of Health, Hunt was instrumental in establishing public health institutions, getting laws passed, training health personnel, helping to build a sanitation infrastructure, and creating a program of health education in the state's public school systems. With his death in Metuchen, the nineteenth century's jeremiad against unsanitary conditions in New Jersey lost much of its intensity.

• The written minutes, records, and correspondence of Ezra Mundy Hunt during his tenure as secretary of the New Jersey State Board of Health (aside from a single minute book) and his long association with the New Jersey Sanitary Association are no longer available. The schools from which he graduated, received honorary degrees, or served as a teacher— Princeton University, Lafayette College, College of Physicians and Surgeons, and Trenton Normal College—have only a paucity of information. Hunt wrote three treatises on the Civil War, several religious books, histories of Metuchen, and a text on hygiene for home and school. Some of Hunt's correspondence has been found in the Stephen Wickes, M.D., File at the New Jersey Historical Society. A wide range of articles written by Hunt can be found in the *Journal of the American Medical Association, Public Health Papers and Reports of the American Public Health Association, Annual Report of the Board of Health of the State of New Jersey, Transactions of the Medical Society of New Jersey, Abstracts from Ad-*

dresses and Papers before the New Jersey Sanitary Association (see the annual report of the Board of Health of New Jersey), and other publications here and abroad. Sam Alewitz, *Ezra Mundy Hunt: A Life in Public Health* (1986), is a biography of Hunt. There are several published articles: Alewitz, "Ezra Mundy Hunt, Physician, Writer, Humanitarian," *Journal of the Medical Society of New Jersey* 78 (May 1981): 381–85; Fred B. Rogers, "Ezra Mundy Hunt, 1830–1894: Pioneer in Public Health," *Journal of the Medical Society of New Jersey* 53 (Nov. 1953): 554–58; and Rogers, *Help-Bringers: Versatile Physicians of New Jersey* (1960).

SAM ALEWITZ

HUNT, George Wylie Paul (1 Nov. 1859–24 Dec. 1934), governor of Arizona, was born in Huntsville, Missouri, the son of George Washington Hunt, a livery stable owner and wealthy landowner, and Sarah Elizabeth Yates. Descended of pioneer stock, the family had been wealthy Missouri landowners until forced to flee during the Civil War, losing their property and cattle. Hunt received an ordinary education and at age eighteen ran away from home to pursue his fortune in the West. He worked at a variety of odd jobs in Kansas, Colorado, Texas, and New Mexico, arriving in Globe, Arizona, in July 1881. Globe would be his home for the next thirty years.

Hired as a waiter in Pascoe's restaurant, Hunt worked there until 1884, when he left for a job as a "mucker" shoveling ore in the Old Dominion copper mine. In 1885 he formed a ranching partnership with W. A. Fisher that lasted until 1890. Apparently uninterested in ranching, Hunt spent much of the last years of the partnership working at odd jobs in California. In 1890, back in Globe, he began working for A. Bailey & Company, a general mercantile store, as a deliveryman but was soon promoted to clerk. He quickly demonstrated skill in that position and worked his way up to manager. When A. Bailey merged with the Old Dominion Commercial Company, a larger multifaceted mercantile company with assets over $100,000 and eventually its own bank, Hunt continued his upward progress, becoming secretary in 1896 and president in 1900.

In 1890 Hunt also began his political career, running unsuccessfully for county recorder for Gila County. Two years later he was elected to the house of representatives of the territorial legislature. Hunt served two terms in the house and in 1896 was elected to the upper chamber, or council, where he served during the sessions of 1897, 1899, 1905, 1907, and 1909. During the 1905 and 1909 sessions Hunt was president of the council. With his support for a bill requiring that wages be paid in cash instead of "boletas," company script used in lieu of legal currency, for compulsory education, and for an antigambling law, Hunt soon established a reputation as a liberal, prolabor politician interested in improving conditions for workers. Hunt's identification with labor remained steadfast throughout his political career; at times—such as when he allowed himself to be photographed with a member of the Industrial Workers of the World—he was attacked as a radical.

After a lengthy courtship of fourteen years, in 1904 he married Helen Duett Ellison, daughter of a rancher in the Pleasant Valley region north of Globe. One daughter was born of this union.

In 1910 Arizona's long struggle to gain statehood achieved success with passage of the Enabling Act, which permitted the citizens to elect delegates to write a state constitution. Organized labor saw this as an opportunity to get a progressive, prolabor document and quickly formed a Labor party. Hunt recognized the danger to Democrats in this move. He persuaded labor leaders to dissolve the new party and to support the Democrats, who he promised would control the convention and would create the type of constitution labor wanted. Voters elected Democrats to forty-two of the fifty-two seats available and chose Hunt as president of the convention. He placed Democrats at the head of all committees. Although labor did not get all it desired, Hunt's leadership did provide for a direct primary, the direct election of senators, recall of all officials (including judges), as well as initiative and referendum measures—definitely a progressive constitution.

When Arizona became a state on 14 February 1912, Arizonans elected Hunt governor and reelected him six times between 1912 and 1930. Arizona's constitution established two-year terms for the governor, and Hunt was elected in 1912, 1914, 1916 (he apparently lost this election to Thomas E. Campbell, contested it, and was given the office by court decision in December 1917), 1922, 1924, 1926, and 1930. As governor Hunt established a name for himself as an aggressive supporter of labor and prison reform. Included in the seventeen measures he called for dealing with labor were proposals for an antichild labor law and a workmen's compensation bill. His prison reform measures included bills to establish an "honor system" at the state prison and the use of convicts on public works projects. Believing that "criminals are the product . . . of environment," he made a point of visiting the prison to see how the inmates, "his boys," were being treated. He opposed capital punishment and in 1916 secured repeal of the death penalty in Arizona. In 1917, while contesting Campbell's apparent victory, Hunt was appointed U.S. commissioner of conciliation to mediate the labor strife occurring in Arizona's copper mines in Globe.

In 1918 he did not seek reelection but remained an active observer of Arizona's political scene. In May 1920 President Woodrow Wilson appointed Hunt the U.S. minister to Siam, a position he occupied until his resignation on 1 October 1921. Returning to Arizona he immediately reentered politics and won the governorship from Campbell in November 1922; he was reelected in 1924 and 1926. While continuing his prolabor and prison reform activities—advocating a minimum wage for women and establishing an industrial commission for labor and better facilities and education for those interned at the state school for boys— Hunt's major effort during the 1920s was to oppose the Santa Fe Compact. Drawn up by a seven-state meeting in 1921, the Santa Fe Compact divided the water of the Colorado River between the states west of the mountains and California. Hunt objected to California's claim to the largest share of the lower Colorado River. Although he said he was fighting for Arizona's future, opponents charged him with using the water issue solely to win reelection.

Defeated in 1928 by Republican John C. Phillips, Hunt returned to the governorship in 1930 for his seventh and last term. His administration battled constantly with an increasingly stronger opposition and hostile local newspapers. The sudden death of his wife in 1931 also affected him deeply. Although he ran for reelection in 1932, he lost in the primary for the first time in his political career. In 1932 "The Old Roman," as he liked to be called, retired from politics. Thereafter he lived quietly at his home in Phoenix, corresponding with political friends and family. He died in Phoenix while preparing for Christmas dinner with his daughter.

Though there is general agreement among Arizonans and most scholars that his positions on labor, prison reform, and capital punishment were sincere, Hunt's opposition to the Santa Fe Compact and the division of Colorado River water was perhaps less so. Regardless of his sincerity on that issue, it may be his most important contribution to the development of Arizona. That long battle with California eventually resulted in Arizona's gaining the Central Arizona Project, which now supplies water from the Colorado River to the farmers of central Arizona and the growing populations of Phoenix and Tucson.

• The Hunt manuscript collection is in the Arizona Department of Library, Archives and Public Records, Phoenix, and the Hayden Library, Arizona State University, Tempe. Also available are the Hunt collection, at the Arizona Historical Society in Tucson, and the Hunt scrapbooks, located in Special Collections, University of Arizona, Tucson. The only published biography of Hunt to date is John S. Goff, *George W. P. Hunt and His Arizona* (1973). Additional sources are Sidney Kartus, *The Autobiography of George Wylie Paul Hunt* (1933), transcript and microform in Arizona Department of Library, Archives and Public Records, Phoenix; and Marjorie Haines Wilson, "Governor Hunt, the 'Beast,' and the Miners," *Journal of Arizona History* 15 (Summer 1974): 119–38. A report of Hunt's death, with a detailed account of his life and political activities, is in the *Arizona Republic*, 25 Dec. 1934, pp. 1, 3.

JAMES D. McBRIDE

HUNT, Harriot Kezia (9 Nov. 1805–2 Jan. 1875), physician, humanist, and feminist reformer, was born in Boston, Massachusetts, the daughter of Jaab Hunt, a ship joiner and shipping industry investor, and Kezia Wentworth. Hunt attributed her "happy-cheerful-joyous" childhood home to the fact that her parents had had fourteen years together without children before her birth. The influence of her parents' "enlivened intelligence" caused her to articulate marital ideals for women that she never chose to live herself. Both parents became Universalists and raised their children in this tradition.

Taught first at home and then at private schools, Hunt developed a devotion to learning and later confessed in her autobiography that "I was not a useful child in many of those domestic arts which tend to make others happy" (p. 14). With the blessing of both parents, she began, at age twenty-two, a school upstairs in the family home.

Hunt's life was profoundly affected by the prolonged illness of her sister Sarah. After enduring a year's painful and ineffective treatment for a "women's illness" from a local physician the sisters turned to an English couple new to Boston, the Motts, who diagnosed Sarah with consumption and treated her successfully. Enthused by Sarah's recovery, Harriot relinquished her school in 1833 and moved her family into the Motts' household, where the sisters studied medicine for two years and then began their own practice.

Disillusioned with the harsh allopathic treatments of mainstream medicine, the Hunt sisters concentrated on a more wholistic approach that emphasized physiological living and disease etiology rather than just treatment of symptoms. They stressed diet, bathing, exercise, rest, and sanitation. Harriot told her patients, who were mostly women and children, to throw away their medicines, start a journal, and use their mothers' lives as inspiration. Although barred from hospital practice, the Hunts attracted patients from the "highly cultivated, the delicate, and the sensible." They believed that many of the illnesses of women resulted from their unhappy lives; Harriot was increasingly interested in women's lack of self-nourishment ("internal life") and its connections to mental illness.

In 1840 Sarah married and gave up medical work, but Harriot continued to build up the practice. At this point Harriot also took a more public role, as an advocate of health education, women's financial independence, and social reform. In the belief that ignorance of physical laws caused disease, she organized in 1843 the Ladies Physiological Society in Charlestown, Massachusetts. Children's cases took on new importance to her when Sarah gave birth three years later to Harriot Augusta, Harriot's namesake.

The deaths of her beloved niece (1845) and mother (1847) forced Hunt to reassess her priorities and commitments. She turned in 1845 to Swedenborgian religion, which emphasized the equality of men and women, and soon thereafter reflected that "my patients were my family; and a new purpose to labor more effectively for women, seized my soul . . . I must be wedded to Humanity." This union was publicly and privately sanctified. As one physician recalled on Hunt's sixty-sixth birthday, "Not long since Dr. Hunt celebrated her silver wedding—twenty-five years of wedded devotion to her profession. A ring was placed upon her finger, one thousand five hundred friends offered congratulations; among her patients three generations were represented."

Dr. Hunt's autobiography, *Glances And Glimpses* (1856), records her devotion to humanity but is underscored by intense loneliness. Romance in her life was with "many love attachments with the school girls." The "strong spice of romance in her nature" was never expressed towards the male sex; instead she expressed frustration with men in politics, medicine, and law and criticized fathers and husbands for keeping women ignorant, frivolous, and helpless. Hunt was unable to reconcile the chasm between the marital union she idealized and the "monotonous half-life" of the women she observed daily. She agonized over the sentimentalized view of women's sphere as being the home, when the poverty of so many of her patients denied them even minimal shelter.

Pressing women's right to enter male institutions, she applied to Harvard Medical School in 1847, but her entry was denied as "inexpedient." The following year she made her first of many visits to the Shaker community at Shirley, Massachusetts. These trips solidified her conviction that social reform promised women transcendence of their inferior status. To this end Hunt began in 1849 free lectures in physiology and hygiene and attended in 1850 the first National Women's Rights conference, where she met likeminded women, including Lucretia Mott, Paulina Wright Davis, Lucy Stone, and Antoinette Brown (Blackwell).

In December 1850 Hunt was finally admitted to Harvard by the dean of the medical faculty, Oliver Wendell Holmes. This action infuriated the senior class, which was already outraged because African Americans had been admitted. Most accounts interpret Hunt's decision not to attend as acquiescence to public pressure, but, according to her autobiography, illness kept her from entering the class of 1851. Much publicity followed her acceptance and contributed to her receiving the honorary degree of doctor of medicine from the Female Medical College of Philadelphia in 1853.

Continuing her feminist advocacy, Hunt encouraged women to enter the professions of law, medicine, the clergy, and police work. In 1852 she was the first Massachusetts woman to publicly protest "taxation without representation," on the grounds that women were still denied the vote. The following year she began arguing for women's higher education. In 1868 Hunt hosted the founding meeting of the New England Women's Club. Throughout this period she maintained an active medical practice. At her sixtysixth birthday celebration, Hunt told a young physician, "I have been so happy in my work." She died in Boston.

Sometimes called the first woman to practice medicine in the United States, Hunt prepared the way for women to enter the medical profession. Equally important was her work for women's medical self-knowledge. Through her life and work, she both embodied and inspired women's self-determination in their physical and mental lives.

• The source for biographical information detailing Hunt's childhood development, maturity, and life insights is her autobiography *Glances and Glimpses* (1856). For a contemporary interpretive review and legacy see, Carole Levin, "Harriot Hunt: An Affirmative, Healing Woman," *Women: A Journal of Liberation* 7, no. 3 (1981): 40–41. See also Mary Stafford Blake, *Woman's Journal* 3, no. 47 (1872); Fredrika Bremer, *Homes of the New World* (1853); Emily Faithful, *Three Visits to America* (1884); Bessie Rayner Parkes, *Vignettes* (1866); James Parton et al., *Eminent Women of the Age* (1869); Harriot H. Robinson, *Massachusetts in the Woman Suffrage Movement* (1881); Julia A. Sprague, *History of the New England Women's Club from 1868 to 1893* (1894); and Elizabeth C. Stanton et al., eds., *History of Woman Suffrage* (1881). An obituary is in the *Boston Morning Journal*, 5 Jan. 1875.

ROBERTA HOBSON
SUSAN E. CAYLEFF

HUNT, Helen. *See* Jackson, Helen Hunt.

HUNT, Henry Alexander, Jr. (10 Oct. 1866–1 Oct. 1938), educator and government official, was born in Sparta, Hancock County, Georgia, the son of Mariah and Henry Alexander Hunt, Sr., a tanner and farmer. Mariah, who exhibited some of the fundamentals of an education and had studied music, was a free woman of color; Henry Alexander was white. Available evidence suggests that the couple lived together before the Civil War but maintained separate households afterward. Henry was the fifth of eight racially mixed children. At age sixteen, having completed the formal education available to him in Hancock County, he followed his older sister and enrolled at Atlanta University. A popular campus leader, Hunt was captain of the baseball team, moot court judge, and president of the Phi Kappa Society. In addition to his college course, Hunt learned the builder's trade and, during vacations, worked as a journeyman carpenter to earn money for his education. He graduated with a B.A. in 1890.

Hunt's first job after college was as a teacher in Jackson, Georgia; before completing the term there, he moved to Charlotte, North Carolina, where he became principal of a grammar school. In November 1891 Hunt joined the faculty of Biddle (later Johnson C. Smith) University, where for more than thirteen years he served as superintendent of the industrial department and proctor over the boys, who reportedly idolized him. In 1893, while in North Carolina, Hunt married Florence S. Johnson, his college sweetheart and sister of Edward A. Johnson, the first black assemblyman of New York. The like-minded, devoted couple would have three children.

In February 1904 Hunt became the second person to serve as principal of the Fort Valley High and Industrial School (FVHI). At the time, many of FVHI's administrators, teachers, and students as well as black trustees favored the school's developing liberal arts curriculum, but Hunt—and the white philanthropists who helped fund the school—favored simple agricultural and manual training, the approach taken at both the Hampton Institute in Virginia and Tuskegee Institute in Alabama. In 1906 William Taylor Burwell Williams, a black school inspector for the General Education Board (GEB), reported that there was some "very positive opposition to Mr. Hunt" among "the colored trustees and a set of the young men teachers of the school." In June of that year, believing that such resistance threatened the effective and rapid development of industrial education, the white philanthropists, using their power as a majority of the board of trustees, removed virtually all black trustees who opposed Hunt's educational blueprint. The board named new trustees who held to Booker T. Washington's model of industrial education, among them, William H. Spencer, a leading black educator in Columbus, Georgia, and Edward R. Carter, pastor of the Atlanta Friendship Baptist Church and one of the most-influential black ministers in Georgia. Hunt's brother-in-law, Warren Logan of Tuskegee, also was named to the board. In addition, black board president Lee O'Neal, pastor of Usher's Temple Colored Methodist Episcopal Church, was demoted to vice president and replaced by Theodore J. Lewis, a white Philadelphia man.

At the same time, the FVHI faculty was undergoing its own purge. As historian James D. Anderson later observed, Hunt succeeded in weeding out black teachers who opposed his educational plan. In his 30 June 1908 report to the trustees, Hunt recommended a decrease of "our teaching force for the coming year," noting that "decreased contributions" made the recommendation "not only wise but imperative." In his fifth annual report to the board in 1909, Hunt announced that "our classes are now more closely graded and more attention has been given to the work of accurate records of the student's standing with the result that they are applying themselves more assiduously to their studies than in other years." By 1913 the FVHI program comprised a grammar school and a high school as well as industrial training classes for men—agriculture, carpentry, bricklaying, and so on—for women—cooking, laundering, sewing, dressmaking—and for both—basketry and chair caning. In 1914 a black GEB inspector described FVHI as "the most thorough-going industrial school in Georgia." Between 1904 and 1938 FVHI changed from being an ungraded school to a graded grammar school, high school and junior college. Also under Hunt's leadership the school undertook a major construction program and increased its enrollment from about 145 students in 1904 to about 1,000 in 1938, including 103 junior college students as a result of the institution gaining junior college status by 1928. In 1932 the name was changed to the Fort Valley Normal and Industrial School (FVNI). Hunt's official title, however, remained the same.

The school's first sustained financial support, other than that from local sources, came from the American Church Institute for Negroes of the Protestant Episcopal Church. Support from the American Church Institute began as early as 1913, but FVHI did not officially come under the institute's auspices until 1918. Even then, the Fort Valley school could not be described as a sectarian institution. From 1918 to 1938, the school imposed no religious requirements.

Hunt and his teachers brought scientific farming methods to many farmers in the so-called Black Belt of Georgia. The agricultural instruction and demonstrations at the school and community outreach programs were, in general, deeply constructive forces. Because of this work Hunt gained state and national prominence, and in August 1918 Georgia governor Hugh M. Dorsey appointed him supervisor of Negro economics. Through this position he oversaw state efforts to deal with problems relating largely to agricultural labor. Hunt believed in frankness. Speaking on the subject of the "rural conditions of labor" at the Tenth Anniversary Conference of the National Association for the Advancement of Colored People (NAACP) held in June 1919, he explained that blacks had trouble finding jobs away from southern farms because of bias against them. "In going over this country," he said, "I have yet to find a place where there is not prejudice against the Negro." Hunt also argued, however, that black leaders also should bear some of the blame: "I believe that when our ministers and leaders in our lodges give a little less attention to exploiting the people, taking care of the sick and burying the dead, when they give more attention to the development of the living, helping those who are living to see and understand and to know their rights and privileges, I believe we shall make progress by leaps and bounds."

However overly optimistic Hunt was in assessing the situation of rural black southerners, his naiveté was not born from an ignorance of causes, and he never ceased to search for solutions. In November 1933, at the recommendation of Henry Morgenthau, Jr., governor of the newly activated Farm Credit Administration (FCA), President Franklin D. Roosevelt appointed Hunt as Morgenthau's assistant, thus becoming the FCA's "Negro adviser" in its attempts to address the economic problems faced by black farmers. Hunt's primary function was to keep black farmers informed about credit opportunities available through the federal government. Although he was headquartered in Washington, D.C., most of his time was spent on the road, traveling from state to state advising black farmers about FCA services and helping them form credit unions.

Hunt learned early on that the problems caused by a lack of information were greatly exacerbated by artificial barriers placed by race. Black farmers, for example, could not join the white loan associations that extended credit under the New Deal's decentralized program. Moreover, black farm owners, just as other black farm operators, were at a disadvantage because local appraisers often discriminated against them when setting a value on property to be used as collateral. Nonetheless, Hunt's educational campaigns—he used various methods, including the mass media and public forums—brought about a widespread awareness of the national program. In addition, as a result of their participation in Hunt's educational campaigns, black agricultural agents and vocational agricultural teachers became better-informed public servants of black farmers. The outcome was largely positive. As Hunt's secretary, Martha B. Goldman, informed Lawrence A. Oxley, chief of the Division of Negro Labor in the Department of Labor, in 1936: "Thousands of colored applicants are receiving Farm Credit Administration loans freely from the Federal land banks, the production credit associations, and the emergency crop loan office committees, and these loans are being repaid by the colored farmers without trouble and without delay."

Hunt was also primarily responsible for the establishment of the Flint River Farms, a farm cooperative community located near the town of Montezuma in Macon County, Georgia. The community, made up of 146 units and a similar number of families, was one of thirteen such cooperatives established exclusively for black farmers during the New Deal. In addition, Hunt had a great deal of success getting black workers in various fields and groups of blacks who had "a common bond of occupation" to form credit unions.

During his five-year tenure at the FCA, Hunt had to contend with some serious problems as principal of FVNI. The institution suffered a budget deficit after employing twenty-five new teachers in 1937. Albert J. Evans, a local merchant and chairman of the finance committee, threatened to resign from the board of trustees if the deficit continued. Hunt was being pressured as well by Bishop Robert W. Patton, director of the American Church Institute for Negroes, who objected to Hunt's "absentee management" while away in Washington. In August 1938 Patton wrote to Bishop Henry T. Mikell of the Atlanta diocese and chairman of the board of trustees, saying he believed the institute needed new leadership. "Mrs. Hunt is the real Principal of that school," Patton alleged, "and she acts under general instructions from Hunt. Neither of them is what they used to be. The school is being run by the Hunt oligarchy, and that means tyrannous, like other Negro schools, not of the Institute type." Before any action could be taken, however, Hunt died in Washington, D.C. His death marked the passing of a powerful influence in the black education movement in North Carolina and Georgia during the late nineteenth and early twentieth centuries.

• Letters from Hunt are in various collections, among them: the George Foster Peabody Papers, the Booker T. Washington Papers, and the NAACP Papers, all in the Library of Congress; the Governor of Georgia Letter File II in the Georgia Department of Archives and History; Record Group 16 in the National Archives; the Julius Rosenwald Papers in the University of Chicago Library; the Julius Rosenwald Archive at Fisk University; the Frank S. Horne Papers in the Amistad Research Center; the James Weldon Johnson Papers in Yale University Library; the American Church Institute for Negroes Papers in the Archives of the Episcopal church, Austin, Tex.; the General Education Board Papers in the Rockefeller Archive Center, Tarrytown, N.Y.; and the FVSC Administration Collection in the Henry Alexander Hunt Memorial Learning Resources Center, Fort Valley State College. See also Adele Logan Alexander, *Ambiguous Lives: Free Women of*

Color in Rural Georgia, 1789–1879 (1991); Carolina Bond Day, *A Study of Some Negro-White Families in the United States* (1932); Donnie D. Bellamy, *Light in the Valley: A Pictorial History of Fort Valley State College since 1895* (1996); "Henry A. Hunt and Black Agricultural Leadership in the New South," *Journal of Negro History* 60 (Oct. 1975): 464–79, and "Henry Alexander Hunt's Crusade for Quality Public Education of Black Georgians," *Negro Educational Review* 28 (Apr. 1977): 85–94; W. E. B. Du Bois, "The Significance of Henry Hunt," *Fort Valley State College Bulletin: Founder's and Annual Report I*, Oct. 1940, pp. 5–16; and James D. Anderson, "Philanthropy in the Shaping of Black Industrial Education Schools: The Fort Valley Case, 1902–1938," *Review Journal of Philosophy and Social Science* 3 (Winter 1978): 184–209, and *The Education of Blacks in the South, 1860–1935* (1988). Obituaries include G. A. Kuyper, "Henry A. Hunt: Good Shepherd," *Southern Workman* 67 (Dec. 1938): 375, and Carter G. Woodson, "Henry Alexander Hunt," *Journal of Negro History* 24 (Jan. 1939): 135–36.

DONNIE D. BELLAMY

HUNT, Henry Jackson (14 Sept. 1819–11 Feb. 1889), soldier, was born in Detroit, Michigan Territory, the son of Samuel Wellington Hunt, an army officer, and Julia Herrick. After a youth spent at military posts in the Old Northwest, he was graduated from the U.S. Military Academy at West Point in 1839, ranking nineteenth in a class of thirty-one. His initial active-duty service was along the Canadian border and in seacoast fortifications in Rhode Island and New York as a subaltern in the Second U.S. Artillery. During the war with Mexico, he served in Captain James Duncan's (1811–1849) celebrated battery of light artillery, winning the brevets of captain and major and receiving two wounds.

At the war's end, Hunt returned to garrison service. In 1851, while stationed at Fort Monroe, Virginia, he married Emily De Russy, the daughter of a fellow officer; the couple had two children. Three years after Emily's death in 1857, Hunt wed Mary Bethune Craig, and they had six more children. When not engaged in his regular duties, Hunt sat on boards and commissions to revise artillery tactics. His 1856–1860 collaboration with William F. Barry and William H. French produced a manual, adopted by the War Department, to govern the system of instruction for light artillery. This work and other influential writings on artillery administration and tactics made Hunt a nationally recognized authority on his arm of the service.

In January 1861, as the Civil War approached, Captain Hunt was sent to Harpers Ferry, Virginia, to prevent secessionists from infiltrating the U.S. armory and arsenal. Shortly after his transfer to Washington in April, he took command of a regular battery that accompanied Brigadier General Irvin McDowell's army on its march toward Richmond, via Manassas Junction, Virginia. During the 21 July fight near Manassas, Hunt shored up the Union left, foiling Confederate attempts to gain McDowell's rear. His unit subsequently blocked a Confederate pursuit of retreating Union troops. Hunt helped McDowell's successor, Major General George B. McClellan (1821–1885), organize the Army of the Potomac. Hunt became an early and enthusiastic supporter of "Little Mac," despite the latter's often stormy relations with the administration of Abraham Lincoln. Their friendship may have cost Hunt the rank and authority for which his expertise in artillery command recommended him.

McClellan's high regard for Hunt's abilities resulted in the latter's promotion to colonel of volunteers and his assignment to command the army's Artillery Reserve, consisting of eighteen regular and volunteer batteries. When he took the field during McClellan's Peninsular campaign of spring-summer 1862, Hunt served with great distinction. He won special notice atop Malvern Hill, where the Artillery Reserve covered the retreat of the army as it reeled from blows delivered by General Robert E. Lee's Army of Northern Virginia. On 1 July Hunt's 100 cannon, placed hub-to-hub along the summit, destroyed a series of ill-advised infantry attacks. At day's end 5,000 Confederates lay dead or wounded at the base of the hill, "covering the ground," as one Union officer wrote, "like a ragged gray carpet that lived and made incoherent sounds, and, here and there, moved dreadfully."

On 5 September General McClellan named Hunt to replace Barry as his chief of artillery, with the rank of brigadier general of volunteers. By this point the lanky, grizzled veteran had become the army's leading source of information on artillery's care and handling; hence, his elevation was both logical and popular. The promotion, however, conferred more honor than authority. Though Hunt commanded more than 50 batteries, 320 cannon, and 5,000 officers and men, the majority of the guns in a mid-nineteenth-century American army were attached to infantry brigades or divisions, whose commanders enjoyed effective control of them. Field officers of artillery exercised only a loose authority over their batteries, and general officers such as Hunt were treated as administrators or as technical advisers rather than as field commanders.

At the battle of Antietam, fought twelve days after he became artillery chief, Hunt rose sufficiently above these limitations to direct a devastating fire against many parts of the Confederate line. Three months later, at Fredericksburg, he helped McClellan's successor, Major General Ambrose E. Burnside, remove opposition to the army's crossing of the Rappahannock River. On 13 December his guns made a valiant but futile attempt to support the series of suicidal assaults Burnside directed against Marye's Heights.

After the debacle at Fredericksburg, Burnside's replacement, Major General Joseph Hooker, determined to rejuvenate the Army of the Potomac. However, while "Fighting Joe" streamlined infantry and cavalry administration, he betrayed an ignorance of the problems of artillery command. One of his less-inspired moves was to remand Hunt to staff duty at army headquarters, denying him contact with the batteries and brigades he commanded. Artillery's performance suffered as a result, and Hunt's absence from the field at Chancellorsville (1–4 May 1863) helped ensure Hooker's defeat and subsequent relief.

The new army leader, Major General George Gordon Meade, restored Hunt's authority as artillery commander, providing him with his finest hours as a soldier. At Gettysburg, 2 July, Hunt's inspired shifting of batteries to strengthen vulnerable points along Meade's line on Cemetery Ridge helped stave off Confederate victory. The next day his guns shattered an attempt by 12,500 infantry under Major General George E. Pickett to break the Federal center. The artillery's decisive performance was threatened by infantry commanders who attempted to countermand Hunt's order that his batteries conserve ammunition. Had Hunt's authority not prevailed, the guns on Cemetery Ridge might have fallen silent before the outcome of Pickett's charge was decided.

Throughout the balance of the war, Hunt's fortunes, and those of his army, experienced a decline. At the outset of General in Chief Ulysses S. Grant's Overland campaign, May 1864, impossible terrain prevented the artillery from making a major contribution in battle. By mid-June, when Grant lay siege to Petersburg, heavy, fixed artillery eclipsed Hunt's field batteries. At Petersburg Hunt feuded continually with General Meade over the proper rank and authority of artillery subordinates as well as over the extent of the logistical support to which their units were entitled. Several times Hunt tried to resign his commission, but Grant persuaded him to stay on and placed him in charge of siege operations. Hunt's duties in this capacity were many and burdensome, but he served in a manner that won Grant's approval and respect. By the war's end Hunt had won four brevets for gallantry, including those of major general in both the regular and volunteer service. Later that year, however, he reverted to lieutenant colonel in the Third U.S. Artillery.

Hunt's conservative political orientation harmed his postwar career. Appointed to a series of Reconstruction commands in the occupied South, he was continually criticized by Radical Republicans who considered him too lenient toward ex-Confederates and not sufficiently protective of former slaves under his jurisdiction. Possibly as a result, he rose no higher than colonel.

In retirement, Hunt served from 1885 until his death as governor of the Soldiers' Home in Washington, D.C. He also wrote papers and articles on military history and artillery administration, most prominently a three-article series on the battle of Gettysburg for *Century* magazine, reprinted as the centerpiece of *Battles and Leaders of the Civil War* (ed. Robert Underwood Johnson and Clarence Clough Buel, 4 vols., 1887–1888). In the same work, former Confederate general Daniel Harvey Hill paid Hunt an indirect tribute by arguing that any army composed of Confederate infantry and Union artillery could have defeated the most powerful fighting force on the earth. He died in Washington, D.C. Hunt has retained a legitimate claim to the title of America's greatest artilleryman.

• The largest body of Hunt papers is in the Library of Congress; other diaries, journals, and letters are in the possession of his descendants. The only full-length biography is Edward

G. Longacre, *The Man behind the Guns: A Biography of General Henry Jackson Hunt, Chief of Artillery, Army of the Potomac* (1977). With the exception of his *Battles and Leaders* trilogy, Hunt's best-known literary effort is his treatise on "Artillery," *Papers of the Military Historical Society of Massachusetts* 13 (1888): 89–125. His wartime service is highlighted in several books about Civil War artillery, including L. Van Loan Naisawald, *Grape and Canister: The Story of the Field Artillery of the Army of the Potomac, 1861–1865* (1960), and Fairfax Downey, *The Guns at Gettysburg* (1958). Hunt's pre–Civil War career as well as his service from 1861 to 1865 receive attention in William E. Birkhimer, *Historical Sketch of Artillery* (1884). Obituaries include David Fitzgerald, *In Memoriam: Gen. Henry J. Hunt, 1819–1889* (1889); *Washington Post*, 12 Feb. 1889; and *Army and Navy Journal*, 16 Feb. 1889.

EDWARD G. LONGACRE

HUNT, H. L. (17 Feb. 1889–29 Nov. 1974), Texas oilman and supporter of archconservative political causes, was born Haroldson Lafayette Hunt in Ramsey, Illinois, the son of H. L. Hunt, Sr., and Ella Rose Myers, farmers. Hunt left home at sixteen, working as a laborer in the West. For a short time he attended Valparaiso University in Indiana but went into cotton farming in Arkansas about 1911. He later speculated in land, but the post–World War I recession wiped him out. In 1921 he decided to try the oil business in Arkansas, buying and selling leases but not yet becoming rich. In 1930 he learned that Columbus "Dad" Joiner was wildcatting in East Texas, activity that the experts said would surely fail. It did not. The result was one of the greatest oil strikes in history—the East Texas field. Hunt investigated, decided to buy Joiner out for $95,000, and soon became the largest independent operator in East Texas. He was on the way to accumulating a fortune.

In 1914 Hunt had married Lyda Bunker, his first wife, who bore him seven children, including Nelson Bunker, William, and Lamar. In the 1920s and 1930s he had a long-term, reputedly bigamous relationship with Frania Tye, who bore him four children. Hunt believed the rules (and laws) of normal people did not apply to him.

During the early depression years, like many oilmen, Hunt continually tried to get the state to impose limitations on the frantic drilling practiced in East Texas, a concept called proration whose purpose was to increase the price of oil. It was a difficult fight. Finally, to Hunt's horror, in 1935 the federal government intervened and imposed the limits. Hunt began to diversify in the late 1930s, buying large tracts of farm and ranch land. He eventually owned one million acres. He also became involved in the international oil trade. He moved to Dallas in 1938, buying a replica (only larger) of Mount Vernon.

After World War II Hunt invested in overseas oil exploration and became even richer. In 1948, *Life* and *Fortune* published stories calling him America's richest man. Indeed, he was worth more than $600 million. He became a celebrity who enjoyed his fame and soon sought more. He also used his wealth to advance conservative causes (principally to defeat the Democratic politicians he thought were unduly taxing the oil industry). Wanting to limit all government regulation, he wrote works that advocated his conservative ideas.

In 1951 Hunt created Facts Forum to broadcast his conservative political program over radio and television and to circulate a newsletter. Although Hunt was the main source of its funding, Facts Forum also received private and corporate contributions. Hunt and Facts Forum were strong supporters of Senator Joseph McCarthy. Among his other conservative friends was Douglas MacArthur, whom Hunt hoped to help elect president. Hunt also approved of the John Birch Society, although he never joined it. In the 1960s and early 1970s he regularly wrote letters to the editor and produced a newspaper column "Hunt for Truth." Some of his columns appeared in *Weekly Strength*, a publication of HLH Products Co., a subsidiary of Hunt Oil; others were published in newspapers—thirty-six dailies and twenty-two weeklies at the height of their popularity.

In the 1950s and 1960s Hunt and his sons expanded their businesses overseas with considerable success. Hunt tried but failed to secure an oil concession in Kuwait in 1957. Although his son Bunker's drilling in Pakistan proved a failure, Bunker and his partner, British Petroleum, made a fortune in Libya.

Two years after his first wife's death in 1955, Hunt married Ruth Ray, who already had borne him four children. He gave up gambling (he was rumored to have bet as much as $100,000 on a horse race) and became a fervid fundamentalist Baptist. In 1958 he established Life Line Foundation, which replaced Facts Forum and combined religious fundamentalism and political conservatism. In the early 1960s Life Line claimed to reach five- or six-million listeners on 354 stations. The broadcasts were sponsored principally by HLH Products. Hunt used HLH to market the food products of his vast farmholdings. The company, however, was a constant money loser.

In 1960 Hunt published a novel, *Alpaca*, the story of a conservative's utopia where men of wealth could cast multiple votes and run the government in an altruistic way. *Alpaca Revisited* appeared in 1967. He published seven other books of autobiography and collected writings.

Some of Hunt's money went to publish the hostile "Welcome Mr. Kennedy" advertisement in the Dallas *Morning News* on 22 November 1963. Many Americans blamed Hunt for President John F. Kennedy's death because he and Life Line had allegedly created a climate of hate in the United States. Several theories circulated about Hunt's possible involvement, but none was ever proved.

During his later years Hunt remained active in business, especially in seeking offshore oil leases and in food packing, but he spent most of his time devising ways of attacking liberals such as Congressman Wright Patman and Senator J. William Fulbright. He also created Youth Freedom Speakers to propagandize the young. YFS had small success in that era of student and anti-Vietnam war protests.

In 1971 Hunt liquidated HLH Products, which had lost more than $70 million. Without the company's sponsorship, Life Line had to cut back its airtime. Hunt continued to write his newspaper column, and he produced two volumes of autobiography—*Hunt Heritage* and *H. L. Hunt Early Days*, both published in 1973. He died in Dallas.

• There are no scholarly biographies of H. L. Hunt, but one can consult Stanley H. Brown, *H. L. Hunt* (1976); Harry Hurt III, *Texas Rich: The Hunt Dynasty from the Early Oil Days through the Silver Crash* (1981); and Ardis Burst, *The Three Families of H. L. Hunt* (1988). An obituary is in the *New York Times*, 30 Nov. 1974.

WALTER A. SUTTON

HUNT, John Wesley (Aug. 1773–21 Aug. 1849), pioneer merchant, manufacturer, and financier, was born in Trenton, New Jersey, the son of Abraham Hunt, a merchant, and Theodosia Pearson. Growing up with seven siblings, John probably attended a private school. At a young age he began training in business in his father's general store in the same two-story building as their home in Trenton. His father also taught him about breeding racehorses and about flour milling.

In 1792 Hunt entered business with a partner by opening a store in Richmond, Virginia. He moved to Norfolk, Virginia, in 1794 and took advantage of the expanding shipping trade during the war that began in 1793 between France and England. He invested in a merchant ship that on its first voyage was seized and condemned by the British navy for trading in a French port in the West Indies. Hunt invested his remaining capital in the *Vanstable*, a French privateer that was outfitting in Norfolk when it was seized by the U.S. government on 14 June 1794 for violating American neutrality.

Beginning then and for the rest of his life Hunt demonstrated an uncanny ability to get into and out of business ventures at the right moment; his friends said that everything he touched turned to gold. On 25 July 1795 he opened a store in Lexington, Kentucky, a frontier town on the verge of becoming the economic and cultural center of the area west of the Allegheny Mountains. In partnership with his cousin Abijah Hunt, he traded Philadelphia goods for tobacco, whiskey, and other farm products that he marketed with the army and in New Orleans. In 1797 he married Catherine Grosh; they had twelve children.

In 1801 Hunt sold out and invested in the breeding of racehorses, an industry that was beginning to expand in the Bluegrass region. He purchased English thoroughbreds in New York, brought them to Kentucky, and after a few seasons of breeding usually sold them in Nashville, Tennessee. Horses such as Royalist, bred in England by the prince of Wales (later King George IV), improved the thoroughbred bloodlines and established the area at the top in horse breeding.

Like other rising businessmen, in 1803 Hunt entered manufacturing. Imported hemp netting and rope were used to hold cotton bales together for shipment, and the cotton market was booming. Hemp grew well in Kentucky, and Hunt opened one of the first hemp factories in Lexington, which soon became a hemp manufacturing center. In 1810 he was one of the first to ship hemp and yarn up the Ohio River. In 1813 he sold his factory while there was still a buyer; when peace came after the War of 1812, imports resumed and the business slumped. Meanwhile, in 1810 he had begun a commission business. For a 5 percent commission he marketed other people's hemp and other products, and with his contacts in Philadelphia he made eastern credit available to western merchants.

In 1816, with the stability created by the Second Bank of the United States (BUS), Hunt began investing in banking and finance. That year President James Madison appointed him a commissioner to superintend subscriptions to the bank in Lexington. He served as a director of the Lexington branch and made one of the largest individual investments in the July 1817 subscription of BUS stock. He became a director of the Kentucky Insurance Company, a director of the Bank of Kentucky, and president of the Lexington Fire, Life and Marine Insurance Company. He served as president of the Farmers and Mechanics Bank of Lexington, chartered by the state in 1818. Stressing sound banking and giving attention to details, he made his bank one of the most solid in the country. One of his friends told him: "You are not only an attentive; but a particular man in the execution of business" (quoted in Ramage, *John Wesley Hunt*, p. 99). On 1 January 1819 he reported that the amount of specie (gold and silver) in the vaults was more than double the value of the notes in circulation. "The public are thus assured, that this is literally a *specie* bank, possessing the means and ability of continuing the payment of specie," he declared (quoted in Ramage, *John Wesley Hunt*, p. 84). Within months, when the panic of 1819 forced most such independent banks to suspend specie payment, Hunt continued in operation as usual and paid dividends to stockholders.

Active in community life, Hunt served as Lexington postmaster (1798–1802), as a member of the board of trustees of Transylvania University (1819–1835), and as founder and first chairman of the board of commissioners of Eastern State Hospital for Mental Illness (1824–1844). He died in Lexington.

Hunt was a prototype of the nineteenth-century American entrepreneur. His innovative business career stimulated the growth of the market economy on a sound basis, which tended to lessen the impact of downturns in the business cycle. He contributed to industrial production and economic growth and became known as the first millionaire west of the Allegheny Mountains.

• The largest collection of Hunt's papers, the Hunt-Morgan Papers, held in the Margaret I. King Library, University of Kentucky, contains valuable information on almost every aspect of his life and career. The John W. Hunt Papers at the Filson Club in Louisville, Ky., and the John W. Hunt Papers at Transylvania University provide useful perspective on his business activities. James A. Ramage, *John Wesley Hunt: Pioneer Merchant, Manufacturer and Financier* (1974), is a full biography, and Ramage's "The Hunts and Morgans: A Study of a Prominent Kentucky Family" (Ph.D. diss., Univ. Kentucky, 1972) provides information on Hunt's career and family life.

JAMES A. RAMAGE

HUNT, Lester Callaway (8 July 1892–19 June 1954), governor of Wyoming and U.S. senator, was born in Isabel, Edgar County, Illinois, the son of William Hunt, a railroad station agent, and Viola Callaway. The family moved to Atlanta, Illinois, in 1902, where Lester completed his public school education. He enrolled at Illinois Wesleyan University in 1912 but left after one year. In 1914 he enrolled at St. Louis University and graduated from its College of Dentistry in 1917. While in dental school, Hunt supported himself by working for the Pennsylvania Railroad.

Hunt first practiced dentistry in Lander, Wyoming, and in September 1917 he joined the army's Dental Corps, serving until May 1919. In 1918 he married Emily Nathelle Higby, whom he had met in Lander shortly after completion of high school while pitching for the local baseball team. They had two children. Following military service, he did postgraduate work at Northwestern University in 1919–1920, after which he returned to his practice in Lander. He served as president of the Wyoming Board of Dental Examiners from 1924 to 1928 and was a member of several dental and honor societies.

A Democrat active in local politics in Lander, Hunt was elected to the Wyoming state legislature in 1932 in the Democratic sweep that resulted in response to the Great Depression. In 1934 he was elected secretary of state for Wyoming and was reelected in 1938. His main claim to fame while serving in that position was his selection of the "bucking horse" figure for the state's auto license plates. Hunt successfully challenged incumbent Republican governor Nels H. Smith in 1942, winning by a mere 2,000 votes. A liberal Democrat in a conservative state, Hunt nonetheless stressed issues that appealed to the state's electorate, extolling states' rights over federal controls and warning of the dangers of federal bureaucracy, particularly in voicing his opposition to the creation of a national monument in Jackson Hole. In addition to adopting a states' rights posture, Hunt strongly supported education, state building programs, and a balanced state budget. Reelected over Earl Wright in 1946, he chaired the National Governors' Conference in 1948. Despite his own political successes, Hunt faced an overwhelmingly Republican legislature throughout his tenure, and the strength of that opposition led to the defeat of nearly everything he proposed as governor.

In 1948 Hunt challenged and defeated incumbent Republican senator Edward V. Robertson. In the Senate he served on the Armed Forces Committee and the Kefauver Committee investigating organized crime. A general supporter of President Harry Truman's Fair Deal programs, Hunt considered himself "a liberal and a progressive but not a radical." He supported public housing, federal aid to education, health programs, and most of the Truman administration's foreign policy and aid programs, most notably the North Atlantic Treaty Organization (NATO) and Point Four. He consistently worked with the bipartisan foreign policy bloc in the Senate but refused nomination to the Democratic Senate Steering Committee, arguing that it would limit his ability to vote his conscience. Following the election of Republican presidential candidate Dwight D. Eisenhower in 1952, he consistently supported the president's foreign policy.

During his tenure in the Senate Hunt shared Senator Joseph McCarthy's abhorrence of communism, but he openly criticized the Republican senator's methods and, in the words of his son, developed "a strong distaste for him personally." Hunt's civil liberties concerns led him to endorse legislation to protect the innocent from scurrilous and unfounded allegations made by members of Congress who were immune from prosecution. He was unable to obtain the necessary votes to enact such legislation. Hunt feared that the Communist issue would be raised against him in 1954, as it had been against other liberal Democrats in several other Senate races in 1950 and 1952. That concern plus other factors weighed heavily on him as he faced the prospect of reelection. His brother had committed suicide in 1952, and in June 1953 his son was arrested on a morals charge. Although the evidence is not complete, Hunt claimed to have received an offer stating that his son would not be prosecuted if he did not seek reelection. Angry that such an idea would even be suggested, in April 1954 he declared his intention to seek reelection. Shortly thereafter his son was tried and convicted. Physically and emotionally tired, Hunt reversed his decision in June and withdrew from the race.

After rejecting a Republican offer to take a position with the Federal Trade Commission and steadfastly refusing the pleas of his political friends to reenter the senatorial race, Hunt shot himself with a .22 caliber rifle in his Capitol office. Four letters that he had left on his desk do not adequately explain the reason for his action, although the one addressed to his son assured him that his recent conviction was not the reason. Much speculation followed Hunt's death, which occurred a few hours later, including suggestions that he was seriously, perhaps terminally, ill. Some commentators speculated that Hunt might have been the Democratic senator that Senator McCarthy had claimed was under investigation by the Senate's Permanent Subcommittee on Investigations, a suggestion later denied by Republican senator Karl E. Mundt. Most accounts of Hunt's death attribute his suicide to a combination of factors: the pressures of politics, personal dismay over his son's situation, and his own physical and emotional exhaustion.

• Hunt's personal papers are housed in the Division of Special Collections at the William Robertson Coe Library at the University of Wyoming. Ralph Jerome Woody, "The United States Senate Career of Lester C. Hunt" (M.A. thesis, Univ. of Wyoming, 1964), covers Hunt's Senate years. Two articles in the *Annals of Wyoming* that contain helpful information are Rich Ewig, "The Ordeal of Senator Lester Hunt" 55, no. 1 (Spring 1983): 9–21; and Viola A. McNealey, comp., "Governors of the State of Wyoming, 1943–1965" 37, no. 2 (Oct. 1965): 2234–43. Mabel E. Brown, ed., *First Ladies of Wyoming, 1869–1990* (1990), published by the Wyoming Commission for Women, provides biographical information on Hunt's wife. Hunt's brief career as a baseball player is addressed in Lewis Nordyke, "Pitcher from Peoria," *Rocky Mountain Empire Magazine*, 19 Sept. 1948, pp. 4–5. Obituaries are in the *New York Times*, 20 June 1954, and the *Wyoming State Tribune*, 21 June 1954.

JUSTUS F. PAUL

HUNT, Mary Hannah Hanchett (4 June 1830–24 Apr. 1906), temperance educator, was born in South Canaan, Connecticut, the daughter of Ephraim Hanchett, an ironworker, and Nancy Swift. She attended area schools before enrolling in Patapsco Female Institute in Ellicott City, Maryland, in 1848. After her graduation in 1851, she taught natural sciences at the school alongside its principal, Almira Hart Lincoln Phelps. She married axe manufacturer Leander B. Hunt the following year and eventually settled in Hyde Park, a Boston suburb. They had one child.

Following her marriage, Hunt taught Sunday school and oversaw Hyde Park's Ladies Sewing Society. She subsequently joined the Woman's Christian Temperance Union, rising to vice president of the state WCTU in 1878. That year she prevailed upon her local school board to require instruction in the physiological effects of alcohol. At the invitation of Frances E. Willard, she also addressed the WCTU's 1879 national convention to promote a similar curriculum nationwide. For almost a century American temperance reformers had warned of the dangers of alcohol to the liver, stomach, and nervous system. Hunt proposed to systematize this effort within the public schools, calling on every local WCTU to select "two or more persons" to visit their own school boards and demand "thorough text-book study" in the subject. By 1880, Hunt boasted, boards across America were "in a state of siege at the hands of the mothers." Later that year the WCTU named her national director of its new Department of Scientific Temperance Instruction (STI).

Only a few more districts adopted STI during the next school term. In 1881 the WCTU resolved to seek compulsory state temperance education laws. Commanding a vast army of local WCTU "superintendents," Hunt organized sophisticated petition and letter drives to pressure legislators. She also delivered hundreds of addresses across the country, earning the nickname "Queen of the Lobby." During New York's 1883–1884 STI campaign, for example, Hunt took up residence in the state and made fifty-seven speeches. She spent much of 1886 in Washington, D.C., winning a congressional measure that required STI in federal territories. Progress was somewhat slower in the South, where WCTU membership lagged. But by 1901 every state mandated some form of the temperance instruction advocated by the WCTU.

Still, school districts continued to ignore it. Invoking a strong tradition of local control in American education, they argued that community values—not state officials—should determine curriculum. Resistance was especially strong among immigrants, who comprised growing fractions of school boards and teaching forces. Across the country, then, Hunt sent her lieutenants back into schools to enforce STI. "It is our duty not to take the word of some school official," Hunt wrote, "but to visit the school and carefully and wisely ascertain for ourselves if the study is faithfully pursued." To prepare WCTU women for these encounters, Hunt distributed reams of literature—including a monthly periodical, the *School Physiology Journal*—from her Hyde Park headquarters. She also answered thousands of personal letters, eventually employing five secretaries to assist her. Most of this correspondence focused on textbooks. Insisting that alcohol was a "poison," harmful even in tiny amounts, Hunt recommended only those texts that contained this claim. In response, dozens of publishers produced new "teetotal" books; a few even engaged Hunt as an editor, to ensure that their texts met her specifications.

In the 1890s STI came under fire from a new generation of physiologists, educational administrators, and teachers. Trained in the laboratory, physiologists claimed that Hunt and her "endorsed" textbooks exaggerated the perils of drink. They galvanized around Wesleyan University chemist Wilbur O. Atwater, whose elaborate experiments seemed to show that alcohol was oxidized like other foods. Citing their own advanced degrees in psychology and pedagogy, school administrators charged that STI's scare tactics violated the latest principles of educational practice. Finally, teachers complained that the subject overloaded their schedules and bored their students. In response, Hunt fluctuated between expert and majoritarian appeals. To rebuff Atwater, she enlisted several prominent physiologists who vouched for STI's validity; to train "professional temperance teachers," meanwhile, she sought to establish a graduate "college" in the subject. At the same time, she insisted that laypeople should govern its diffusion. Educators "seem to think they own the schools, that the people, the parents have no right or voice in what should be taught their children," Hunt wrote. Yet in a democracy, she declared, taxpaying citizens remained "the final tribunal" for all such questions.

A proud and determined woman, Hunt also earned numerous enemies within the WCTU's national leadership. In 1884 she broke with Willard over the latter's endorsement of the Prohibition party. Hunt feared that this endorsement would harm her cause among antiprohibitionist Democrats, who frequently supported STI as a "compromise" measure. After 1899 several top officials—including Willard's successor,

Lillian M. Stevens—supported experts' attempts to scale back Scientific Temperance. Between 1900 and 1906 at least a dozen states considered measures that would have diluted their STI laws. Rallying her local lieutenants once more, Hunt repulsed all but one of these challenges. After her death in Dorchester, Massachusetts, however, Scientific Temperance began a rapid decline. Some alcohol instruction continued, but it emphasized the "social" rather than physiological consequences of drink. A decade later the WCTU would rehabilitate Mary Hunt and attribute national Prohibition to her pioneering efforts. Yet the widespread violation and subsequent repeal of Prohibition suggest that Hunt had a negligible impact on American attitudes toward alcohol. Instead, her colorful career highlights the promise and the pitfalls of popular educational movements in an age of expertise.

• Most of Hunt's papers are in the Scientific Temperance Federation Series of the Temperance and Prohibition Papers, Ohio Historical Society. For a description, see Randall C. Jimerson et. al., *Guide to the Microfilm Edition of Temperance and Prohibition Papers* (1977). Other important correspondence is in the Scientific Temperance Federation Papers, New York Public Library, and in the Wilbur O. Atwater Papers, Wesleyan University. Hunt wrote two useful histories of her activities, *A History of the First Decade of the Department of Scientific Temperance Instruction in Schools and Colleges* (1891) and *An Epoch of the Nineteenth Century* (1897). For contemporary attacks on STI, see John S. Billings, ed., *Physiological Aspects of the Liquor Problem* (2 vols., 1903). Contrasting modern assessments of the movement may be found in David Tyack et. al., *Law and the Shaping of Public Education, 1785–1954* (1987), chap. 6; Philip J. Pauly, "The Struggle for Ignorance about Alcohol: American Physiologists, Wilbur Olin Atwater, and the Woman's Christian Temperance Union," *Bulletin of the History of Medicine* 64 (1990): 366–92; and Jonathan Zimmerman, "'The Queen of the Lobby': Mary Hunt, Scientific Temperance, and the Dilemma of Democratic Education in America, 1879–1906," *History of Education Quarterly* 32 (1992): 1–30.

JONATHAN ZIMMERMAN

HUNT, Reid (20 Apr. 1870–10 Mar. 1948), pharmacologist, was born in Martinsville, Ohio, the son of Milton L. Hunt, a banker, and Sarah E. Wright, a schoolteacher. His parents were Quakers who valued education and literature. Hunt's interests focused early on science as he studied chemistry with the town pharmacist. After graduating from high school at age sixteen, he spent one year at Wilmington College and one at the University of Ohio at Athens. He completed his undergraduate studies at Johns Hopkins University in 1891.

Hunt then began graduate studies at Johns Hopkins, first in pathology and then in physiology. In 1892 he traveled to Germany and studied medicine at the University of Bonn. There he developed an interest in pharmacology, but without finishing his medical studies, he returned to Hopkins and continued his work in physiology. Appointed assistant in histology and physiology, he studied the effects of simultaneous stimulation of the vagus nerve (which slows the heart-beat) and the heart accelerator nerve, showing that the relative strength of the two impulses accounted for the net effect on the heartbeat. This work sparked his life-long interest in the physiology of the autonomic nervous system. Hunt was awarded the Ph.D. in physiology in 1896. He had also been attending classes at the Baltimore College of Physicians and Surgeons and received his M.D. that same year.

After a year as tutor in physiology at Columbia University's College of Physicians and Surgeons, Hunt returned to Hopkins in 1898 as an associate in pharmacology in the laboratory of John J. Abel. He began investigating the effects on blood pressure of extract from the suprarenal glands when epinephrine was removed. He noted that one constituent of this extract had a powerful effect in lowering blood pressure, and that it must be closely related in chemical structure to choline. These observations heightened his interest in the relationship between the chemical structure of a compound and its physiological activity. He also discovered the toxic effects of methyl alcohol. In 1901 he was named associate professor of pharmacology.

In the summers of 1902 and 1903 Hunt worked at Paul Ehrlich's Institute for Experimental Therapy in Frankfurt, Germany. This experience was the most important influence on his career. Working from the assumption that a molecule's physiological effect depended on its structure, scientists at the institute modified the molecular structures of compounds and then observed the effects of these new compounds in animals as they searched for effective new medicines. Hunt became excited by this collaborative research model and would later devote much energy to encouraging this type of research in the United States. His work at Ehrlich's institute included the discovery that mice given thyroid extract could tolerate otherwise toxic doses of acetonitrile; this finding formed the basis of the "Reid Hunt reaction," a widely used test for thyroid activity.

In 1904 Hunt was named the first chief of the Division of Pharmacology in the Hygienic Laboratory of the U.S. Public Health and Marine Hospital Service. His responsibilities included establishing the division's capacity to carry out the regulatory functions assigned to the federal government by the 1906 Pure Food and Drugs Act. The division, working closely with the U.S. Pharmacopoeial Convention and the American Medical Association's (AMA) Committee on the Pharmacopoeia, established standards of purity and dosage and tested hundreds of medications for conformity to these standards. Hunt remained involved in these activities throughout his career through appointments to the AMA's Council on Pharmacy and Chemistry (1906–1936) and to the Revision Committee of the Pharmacopoeial Convention in 1910, and as president of the U.S. Pharmacopoeial Convention from 1920 to 1930. He expanded the division's work to include basic research. Collaborating with R. de M. Taveau, he discovered that when an acetyl group was added to the choline molecule, the resulting compound lowered blood pressure significantly.

Hunt helped Abel in founding the American Society for Pharmacology and Experimental Therapeutics and in launching the *Journal of Pharmacology and Experimental Therapeutics*, both in 1908. That year, he married Mary Lillie Taylor of Washington, D.C. The couple had no children.

Hunt's reputation as a research pharmacologist brought him to the attention of officials at Harvard Medical School when they sought to transform its traditional department of materia medica and therapeutics into a research department of pharmacology. Hunt was named first chairman of the newly formed department of pharmacology in 1913. He continued his research on choline derivatives, now collaborating with the chemist R. R. Renshaw. His discovery that acetylcholine's power to reduce blood pressure was 100,000 that of choline foreshadowed later work on the importance of acetylcholine as a neurotransmitter.

Hunt's importance as a promoter of pharmacology in the United States is reflected in his many efforts to promote the model of collaborative research he had observed at Ehrlich's laboratory. During World War I he was one of hundreds of scientists brought into U.S. Army Chemical Warfare Service. After the war he worked with Charles Holmes Herty, editor of the *Journal of Industrial and Engineering Chemistry*, to try to establish an institute for chemical research on new medications (an effort which failed). In 1922 Hunt wrote to the National Research Council to urge that it help build an academic infrastructure for research to develop effective new medications. Progress in this effort was slow, in part because Hunt left the country in 1923 to spend a year as visiting professor at the Peking Medical College in China; but in 1928, when the NRC was offered a substantial grant to investigate opiate addiction, Hunt took the lead in applying these funds to research on identifying a nonaddicting medication that might replace morphine in the treatment of pain. That same year he testified before Congress in support of the Ransdell bill, which, when passed, authorized creation of the National Institute of Health.

Hunt retired in 1936. His career had been notable chiefly for his leadership in building the fledgling discipline of research pharmacology in the United States. Although his shy demeanor kept him from being a charismatic teacher, his encyclopedic knowledge of pharmacology and his skill as a researcher were widely recognized. He died in Belmont, Massachusetts.

• The archives of the Countway Library of Harvard University contain several items pertaining to Hunt, including Hans Zinsser, "Reid Hunt," *Aesculapiad*, Class of 1937, Harvard Medical School; and Otto Krayer, "Letters on Hunt." Hunt's first publication, based on his dissertation research, was "The Fall of Blood Pressure Resulting from Stimulation of Afferent Nerves," *Journal of Physiology* 18 (1895): 381–410. His contributions to the understanding of choline and acetylcholine in relation to blood pressure include two articles with R. de M. Taveau: "On the Physiological Action of Certain Cholin Derivatives and New Methods for Detecting Cholin,"

British Medical Journal 2 (1906): 1788–91; and "The Effects of a Number of Derivatives of Choline and Analogous Compounds on the Blood-Pressure," *U.S. Hygienic Laboratory*, Bulletin 73, 1911. He also wrote "Vasodilator Reactions," a two-part article in *American Journal of Physiology* 45 (1918): 197–230 and 231–67. His collaborations with R. R. Renshaw include "Some Effects of Betaine Esters and Analogous Compounds on the Autonomic Nervous System," *Journal of Pharmacology and Experimental Therapeutics* 29 (1926): 17–34. His experiments in thyroid function were reported in numerous publications, including two with A. Seidell: "Studies on Thyroid. I. The Relation of Iodine to the Physiological Activity of Thyroid Preparations," *U.S. Hygienic Laboratory*, Bulletin 47, 1909; and "Thyreotropic Iodine Compounds," *Journal of Pharmacology and Experimental Therapeutics* 2 (1910): 15–47.

Hunt published many articles on pharmacopeial standards and other aspects of drug regulation. These include "Commercial Thyroid Preparations and Suggestions as to the Standardization of Thyroid," with Seidell, *Journal of the American Medical Association* 51 (1908): 1385–88; and "Some Problems of Pharmacopoeial Revision," *Journal of the American Medical Association* 54 (1910): 173–75. His studies of alcohol toxicity include "The Toxicity of Methyl Alcohol," *Johns Hopkins Hospital Bulletin* 13 (1902): 213–25; and "Studies in Experimental Alcoholism," *U.S. Hygienic Laboratory* Bulletin 33, 1907.

Hunt's life and research career are recounted in E. K. Marshall, Jr., "Reid Hunt, 1870–1948," National Academy of Sciences, *Biographical Memoirs* 26 (1951): 25–44, which includes a complete bibliography. An obituary is in the *New York Herald Tribune*, 10 Mar. 1948.

CAROLINE JEAN ACKER

HUNT, Richard Morris (31 Oct. 1827–31 July 1895), architect, was born in Brattleboro, Vermont, the son of Jonathan Hunt, U.S. congressman, and Jane Maria Leavitt. Following Jonathan Hunt's sudden death from cholera, in Washington, D.C., in 1832, his widow brought her five children back to New England. She eventually settled in Boston so that her eldest son, William Morris Hunt, who later became a noted painter, could prepare for Harvard College.

In 1843, while William was attending Harvard, Jane Hunt decided to take her family to Europe. They first visited Paris and then moved on to Rome, but Richard was soon enrolled in Alphonse Briquet's school in Geneva. Fascinated by building design, he decided on an architectural career, and in 1846 he gained admission to the École des Beaux-Arts in Paris, the first American to be trained there. He was also accepted into the atelier of Hector Martin Lefuel, whom Hunt later assisted in work on the new Louvre. In 1855, by then the best-trained American architect, he returned to the United States to set up an office in New York City. When his first commission for a private house led to a dispute regarding his fee, he went to court and the resultant decision helped establish professional rights for architects.

Hunt's most important early commission was for New York's Tenth Street Studio Building, a structure designed for artists, which on completion in 1858 became the center of artistic life in the city. For a few years Hunt conducted an architectural atelier in the Studio Building, and through his instruction he had a formative impact on subsequent architectural education in the United States. He was also a founding member in 1857 of the American Institute of Architects; as the first secretary (1857–1860), as a New York chapter officer, and as the third national president (1888–1891), Hunt played a prominent role in organizing and establishing standards for his profession.

In 1861 Hunt was married to Catharine Clinton Howland, who came from a wealthy shipping family. Soon after their wedding, the couple sailed to France, where their first child was born. (They had five children in all.) Back in New York, Hunt worked on gates for the southern entrances to Central Park, but the elaborate "French" designs of the gateways were out of keeping with the proposed rustic character of the park, and they were not erected. Named a judge for the fine arts section of the Paris Exposition of 1867, Hunt visited Europe briefly that year. Soon after his return, at the age of forty, he was awarded many commissions, and his reputation soared.

Most of Hunt's new projects were located in New York City. Highly significant were the first true American apartment houses, the Stuyvesant Apartments (1869–1870), modeled on Parisian multifamily dwellings, and Stevens House (1870–1872), originally an apartment house but subsequently converted into the Victoria Hotel. Two commercial stores on Broadway, the Van Rensselaer Building (1871–1872) and the Roosevelt Building (1873–1874), utilized new cast-iron technology on their fronts. The Delaware and Hudson Canal Company Building (1873–1876) and the Guernsey Building (1881–1882) provided offices for commercial tenants. The sizable Presbyterian Hospital (1868–1872), embodying new concepts of hospital design, and the elegant Lenox Library (1870–1877), a large private library, were both commissioned by James Lenox, a wealthy merchant and art collector. The most significant of Hunt's commercial designs was for the towering 260-foot Tribune Building (1873–1876), for a time the tallest building in the city, providing a striking headquarters for a leading New York newspaper. Outside New York, Hunt created in New Haven, Connecticut, East Divinity Hall (1869–1870) for the Yale Divinity School, along with the adjoining jewel-like Marquand Chapel (1870–1871) and, nearby, the Moorish-style Scroll and Key Society Clubhouse (1867–1869). In Matteawan (now part of Beacon), New York, his Howland Circulating Library (1871–1872) was designed in a striking Scandinavian polychrome style.

Important domestic projects also engaged the architect in these years. In Newport, Rhode Island, the Griswold house (1861–1863), an elaborately textured, picturesque residence, was influential in the development of the American "stick style." Hunt also remodeled the then-largest house in Newport, Château-sur-Mer (1869–1879). Elsewhere he designed spacious houses for the philanthropist Martin L. Brimmer in Boston (1869–1870) and for the merchant Marshall Field in Chicago (1871–1873). The press of work took a toll, however, and to recuperate from illness, Hunt went to Europe with his family in 1874–1875, returning for extended visits in 1885–1886, 1889, and 1893.

In the mid-1870s, Hunt was commissioned by James Lenox to design a library (1876–1879) for the Princeton Theological Seminary. At Princeton College he also created the massive, rugged Marquand Chapel (1880–1882) and the austere Chemical Laboratory (1885–1891). About the same time, he commenced his first projects for the wealthy Vanderbilt family: a large country house (1878–1880) at Oakdale, Long Island, for William K. Vanderbilt and the Scandinavian stave-style St. Mark's Church and rectory (1879–1880) at Islip, Long Island. His Fifth Avenue mansion for William K. Vanderbilt (1878–1882), modeled on late-Gothic and early-Renaissance French châteaux, became one of his most widely admired and copied projects. A slightly smaller version was the William Borden mansion in Chicago (1884–1889). A huge mausoleum on Staten Island (1884–1889) and a branch of the New York Free Circulating Library (1887–1888) were other early Vanderbilt commissions.

Hunt worked in a variety of forms and styles, but he especially enjoyed designing large houses, many of them in an early–French Renaissance mode. He came to be recognized as the most fashionable architect of the Gilded Age. Hunt is best known now for his spacious Newport "cottages"—Ochre Court (1888–1892), Marble House (1888–1892), Belcourt Castle (1891–1894), and The Breakers (1892–1895)—and for Biltmore House (1888–1895), the George Vanderbilt mansion in Asheville, North Carolina, the largest private house in the United States. His academic commissions included buildings at Case Western Reserve University (then known as Adelbert College), Harvard University, and the U.S. Military Academy at West Point. He also designed several structures for the U.S. Naval Observatory in Washington, D.C. (1887–1893). At the 1893 Chicago World's Columbian Exposition, for which he served as chairman of the Board of Architects, he was responsible for the monumental, high-domed Administration Building (1891–1893), the centerpiece of the fair and his best-known building to contemporaries. Hunt's final major commission was the Fifth Avenue entrance wing for New York's Metropolitan Museum of Art (1894–1895), completed after his death by his eldest son, Richard Howland Hunt.

Throughout his career, Hunt worked on several important statuary and monument projects, including the Yorktown Monument in Virginia (1880–1884); the Washington (1883), the Pilgrim (1884–1885), and the Greeley statue pedestals in New York City (1881–1890); the Beecher Statue in Brooklyn (1888–1891); and the Garfield Monument pedestals in Washington, D.C. (1884–1887). For Trinity Church in New York, he designed elaborate monumental doors (1890–1894). His most significant sculptural collaboration, however, was on the Statue of Liberty, for which he designed the pedestal base (1881–1886).

For his extensive, important work, Hunt became known to his contemporaries as "the dean of American architecture." Acclaimed nationally and internationally, he was one of the most widely honored of all nineteenth-century Americans. In 1898 a civic monument commemorating Hunt was erected on New York's Fifth Avenue. Strongly committed for inspiration to the European past, he adapted ideas from the past for contemporary uses with discriminating taste. He worked tirelessly to elevate the standards of his profession and for many years was its leading spokesman. Highly skilled, hardworking, well respected, he advanced the maturing of the architectural profession in the United States. Hunt died at his summer home in Newport, Rhode Island.

• Rich accumulations of manuscript materials are included in the Hunt Collection of the American Institute of Architects Foundation in Washington, D.C., and in the Hunt papers privately held by members of the family. The fullest study is Paul R. Baker, *Richard Morris Hunt* (1980), which includes a full listing of manuscript sources. See also Susan R. Stein, ed., *The Architecture of Richard Morris Hunt* (1986), and the important early article by Montgomery Schuyler, "The Works of the Late Richard M. Hunt," *Architectural Record* 5 (Oct.–Dec. 1895): 97–180.

PAUL R. BAKER

HUNT, Robert Woolston (9 Dec. 1838–11 July 1923), metallurgist and consulting engineer, was born in Fallsington, Pennsylvania, the son of Robert A. Hunt and Martha Lancaster. Hunt's father, a retired doctor, had opened a drugstore in Covington, Kentucky, but he died when Hunt was seventeen, leaving the boy unable to afford further formal education. Robert ran his father's business for two years but in 1857 moved to Pottsville, Pennsylvania, where he began working at John Burnish & Company, an iron rolling mill in which his cousin was a partner. Here Hunt was exposed to the practicalities of the iron industry as a puddler and roller. Following a course in analytical chemistry at the laboratory of Booth, Garrett & Reese in Philadelphia, Hunt found employment as a chemist in 1860 with the Cambria Iron Company in Johnstown, Pennsylvania, where he established the first analytical chemical laboratory as an integral component of an American ironworks.

Hunt's career at Cambria was interrupted by the Civil War, during which he served as a captain in the Union army. Upon Hunt's return to Cambria in 1865, the company management sent him to observe the experimental Bessemer steel works in Wyandotte, Michigan, established by a group headed by Eber Ward, a midwestern shipbuilder, industrialist, and iron maker. Daniel Morrell, Cambria's general manager, had a financial interest in the Wyandotte experiment, and a technical interest in anticipating that Cambria would also enter into steel production. Following the departure of several key individuals, Hunt suddenly found himself in charge of steel making at the Michigan works. Hunt, lucky by his own account, was successful with his first "blow" and continued on at Wyan-

dotte for a year, familiarizing himself further with the new process.

In the spring of 1866 Hunt once more returned to Cambria's Johnstown plant. Although the Cambria Company had not yet built its own Bessemer converter, it received steel ingots from the Pennsylvania Steel Company, which at that time had no rolling mill of its own. Hunt was placed in charge of rolling the first commercial batch of steel rails to be produced in America for the Pennsylvania Railroad (1867). In December 1866 he married Eleanor Clark; the couple had no children. In 1870 the Cambria management elected to build its own converter, the sixth in the country. When it was completed the following year, Hunt, who had worked closely with George Fritz, Cambria's chief engineer, and Alexander Holley, the outside consultant and designer of the plant, was placed in charge.

In September 1873 Hunt left Johnstown for Troy, New York, where he took on the superintendency of the Bessemer works of John A. Griswold & Co., later regrouped to become part of the Troy Iron & Steel Co. During his fourteen years there, he made many contributions to the company as well as to the iron and steel industry as a whole. He was responsible for a large-scale reworking of the plant that increased output and made possible new products, including new grades of soft Bessemer steel suitable for drop forging and specialty steels for gun barrels, drills, springs, and carriage axles. In 1884, in cooperation with August Wendel and Max Suppes, Hunt developed and patented a feed table for automatically advancing rail stock in the Troy mill, a design that was subsequently adopted by a majority of American rail mills. He also patented a process for handling and rolling wire rod from iron bar stock.

In 1888, at the age of fifty, Hunt resigned from Troy to establish his own engineering consulting firm in Chicago. Robert W. Hunt & Co. attained a worldwide reputation, especially in the areas of testing and inspection, and established offices in major cities throughout the United States as well as in England, Mexico, and Canada. Hunt proposed the "Special Inspection" involving the close supervision of both steel manufacture and the rolling of rails. He also proposed several new rail designs.

Hunt's long and notable career earned him election as a member of almost every American engineering and technical society. He held memberships in the American Institute of Mining Engineers (president, 1883, 1906), the American Society of Mechanical Engineers (president, 1891), the Western Society of Engineers (president, 1893), the American Society for Testing and Materials (president, 1912), the American Society of Civil Engineers, the United States Iron and Steel Institute, the Canadian Society of Civil Engineers, the Institution of Civil Engineers, the Institution of Mechanical Engineers, and the Iron and Steel Institute of England. In 1912 the major national engineering societies jointly awarded Hunt the John Fritz medal in recognition of his contributions to the early development of the Bessemer process. Hunt also served as a trustee of Rensselaer Polytechnic Institute. After his death in Chicago, the American Institute of Mining and Metallurgical Engineers established the Robert W. Hunt Award, further signifying the importance of his career to the development of the iron and steel industry.

• Hunt was a frequent contributor to the technical journals of his day, but his two most important and well-known papers are "History of the Bessemer Manufacture in America," *Transactions of the American Institute of Mining Engineers* 5 (1877): 201–15 and his ASME presidential address, "Evolution of the American Rolling Mill," *Transactions of the American Society of Mechanical Engineers* 13 (1892): 45–69. No known collection of Hunt's papers exists, and there is no full-scale biography; however, his career can be pieced together by reading William Hogan, *Economic History of the Iron and Steel Industry in the United States* (1971); Jeanne McHugh, *Alexander Holley and the Makers of Steel* (1980); Elting Morison, *Men, Machines, and Modern Times* (1966); and Peter Temin, *Iron and Steel in Nineteenth-Century America: An Economic Inquiry* (1964). See also Paul F. Paskoff, ed., *Iron and Steel in the Nineteenth Century* (1989), which contains biographical sketches of Hunt and related individuals and companies.

STEPHEN H. CUTCLIFFE

HUNT, Thomas Sterry (5 Sept. 1826–12 Feb. 1892), chemist and geologist, was born in Norwich, Connecticut, the son of Peleg Hunt and Jane Elizabeth Sterry, farmers. His early childhood was spent at Poughkeepsie, New York, but on Peleg's death in 1838, Jane and her six children returned to Norwich, where Sterry Hunt (as he preferred to be known) received his only formal schooling. Obliged to work from the age of thirteen, Hunt had a succession of jobs in a printing works, an apothecary's shop, and a bookstore, all the while improving himself by reading and attending popular lectures. He was largely self-taught in science. When the Association of American Naturalists and Geologists held its annual meeting at New Haven in 1845, Hunt reported the event for a New York newspaper, including an interview with the chemist Benjamin Silliman (1779–1864), who was so impressed by Hunt's scientific enthusiasm and knowledge that he arranged for his son, Benjamin Silliman, Jr., a professor of chemistry at Yale, to make Hunt his research assistant. In the eighteen months Hunt spent at Yale he was asked to write the organic chemistry section of the younger Silliman's *First Principles of Chemistry* (1847), basing it largely on the French edition of J. Liebig's *Organic Chemistry*; he was also made to analyze the rocks and minerals that Charles Baker Adams sent to Yale during the Geological Survey of Vermont.

From February 1847 until 1872 Hunt was mineralogist and chemist to the Geological Survey of Canada, which, until 1869, was under the leadership of Sir William Logan. The position, which often involved strenuous fieldwork, also allowed Hunt time to serve as professor of chemistry at the French-language University of Laval, Quebec, during the winter semesters of 1856–1862, and from 1862 to 1868 at McGill University, Montreal. Hunt did not succeed Logan, probably because of his irascibility, egotism, and poor opinion of the politicians upon whom the Geological Survey's fortunes depended.

Hunt resigned from the Canadian Geological Survey in 1872 on becoming professor of geology at the Massachusetts Institute of Technology. At the same time, he became chemist to the Geological Survey of Pennsylvania under J. Peter Lesley. His marriage to a Canadian, Anna Rebecca Gale, in 1878 prompted him to resign from both positions that same year in order to pursue geological consultancy and a literary career. The childless marriage ended in separation within a few years.

Hunt spent the remaining years of his life increasingly isolated from the scientific community, continually rehashing his earlier writings and old controversies in such books as *Mineral Physiology and Physiography* (1886); *A New Basis for Chemistry: A Chemical Philosophy* (1887), which was dedicated to the German-American philosopher Johann B. Stallo; and *Systematic Mineralogy* (1891). At his death, from a heart attack suffered in a New York hotel, he was an embittered and largely forgotten figure. He left his mineral collection to Laval University as well as $10,000 for the advancement of chemistry at the university.

Like many autodidacts, Hunt was prone to take up heterodox positions. Reared as a Congregationalist, he was converted to Roman Catholicism in Canada, only to abandon it for a simple deism. As a young man he was greatly influenced by Stallo, who encouraged him to study Kant, Hegel, and the *Naturphilosophen*. In the same spirit, Hunt was attracted to the writings of the American Transcendentalists, and he introduced Richard Maurice Bucke, Walt Whitman's first biographer, to the poet's writings.

Hunt tended to look for the unity of nature. Inspired by Stallo to reject physical atomism and by Kant to explain chemical change as the interpenetration of species, like the mixing of solutions, Hunt viewed interaction as the key to understanding minerals and their variable and complex compositions. Hunt conceived of silicon as the "carbon" of mineralology and minerals as derivatives of polyacids. Using isomorphism and densities to calculate the equivalent weights of minerals, Hunt exploited Charles-Frédéric Gerhardt's classification of organic compounds into homologous series to deduce composition and to arrange minerals into natural families. Such methods seemed dubious to contemporaries and were doomed to be swept aside in the twentieth century by the advent of x-ray crystallography.

Hunt was more successful as a practical geologist, and he played a significant role in Logan's elucidation of the Laurentian and Huronian systems of Canada. He served as coauthor with Logan on the *Esquisse géologique du Canada* (1855) and *Geology of Canada* (1863). His deep interest in Paleozoic rocks led him to speculate in 1867 about the chemical conditions of the primeval earth. As the earth had cooled, he supposed, today's familiar elements and compounds had condensed from more fundamental entities. The various mineral solutions that permeated surface rocks were then metamorphosed under the still violently hot conditions of the earth's interior, to return, like springs, to the earth's surface for weathering. By this amalgamation of Neptunism and Vulcanism (geological changes induced by water and heat, respectively), Hunt explained the origins of granite, gneiss, and serpentine. Although such an "evolutionary," developmental account of the earth's history was in tune with the spectroscopic speculations of chemists, geologists found Hunt's mechanisms implausible. The details led to protracted and heated controversies with J. Dwight Dana, Logan, and David Forbes. The debate with Forbes in the 1860s, over whether it was more important to be a geological chemist or a chemical geologist, can be seen as laying the methodological foundations of geochemistry as a discipline.

On a more practical level, Hunt was responsible in 1857 for advising the City Bank of Montreal to use an unfadeable green chromium sesquioxide [Cr(III) oxide] ink to make counterfeiting of banknotes by photography difficult. The patent, owned by a Montreal engraver, from which Hunt made little money, was sold to the United States and became the basis of the U.S. "greenback" dollar bill.

Hunt was awarded the Légion d'Honneur after serving as a Canadian juror at the International Exposition in Paris in 1855. He was made a Fellow of the Royal Society of London in 1859 and of the National Academy of Sciences in 1873. He was a founding member of the Royal Society of Canada in 1882. He was also largely responsible for the establishment of international congresses of geologists, beginning with one in Paris in 1878.

• Collections of Hunt's letters are at Columbia University, the Smithsonian Institution, and the Royal Society of London, and letters of his are among the Lyell papers at Edinburgh University, Scotland. Hunt published some 350 scientific papers and a dozen reports and books, many of which are aggressively annotated reprints of his papers. These are listed in the long obituaries by James Douglas, *Proceedings of the American Philosophical Society: Memorial Volume* 1 (1900): 63–121; and F. D. Adams, *Biographical Memoirs of the National Academy of Sciences* 15 (1934): 207–38. The background to Hunt's career is supplied by Morris Zaslow, *Reading the Rocks: The Story of the Geological Survey of Canada 1842–1972* (1975), and G. P. Merrill, *The First One Hundred Years of American Geology* (1924; repr. 1964). William H. Brock, "Chemical Geology or Geological Chemistry," in *Images of the Earth: Essays in the History of the Environmental Sciences*, ed. Ludmilla Jordanova and Roy S. Porter (1979; repr. 1981), pp. 147–70, deals with the Hunt-Forbes debate. Also useful are E. R. Atkinson, "The Chemical Philosophy of T. S. Hunt," *Journal of Chemical Education* 20 (1943): 244–45, and Bahngrell W. Brown, "T. Sterry Hunt, the Man Who Brought Walt Whitman to Canada," *The Southern Quarterly* 10 (1971): 43–48.

WILLIAM H. BROCK

HUNT, Ward (14 June 1810–24 Mar. 1886), associate justice of the U.S. Supreme Court, was born in Utica, New York, the son of Montgomery Hunt, cashier of the Bank of Utica, and Elizabeth Stringham. Hunt graduated from Union College in 1828 and attended James Gould's law lectures at Litchfield, Connecticut, before returning to Utica and completing his preparation for the bar in the office of Hiram Denio. He was admitted to the bar in 1831 and, largely through his father's connections, soon established a flourishing commercial practice. Hunt joined Denio as junior partner in 1836; their association lasted until Denio's election to the New York Court of Appeals, the state's highest court, in 1853. Hunt married Mary Ann Savage in 1837; they had two children before her death in 1845. Eight years later he married Maria Taylor.

Law practice and political activism went together in antebellum New York, and Hunt got an early start. He was elected to the New York legislature on the Democratic ticket in 1838, serving a single term without distinction. He got a great deal more attention in 1844 when, as the newly elected mayor of Utica, he endorsed the "Secret Circular" in which antislavery Democrats pledged to vote for James K. Polk but urged the defeat of congressmen who supported the annexation of Texas. Four years later Hunt took a leading part in the formation of the Free-Soil party; in 1855 he joined the Republicans. Hunt was elected by a large majority to the court of appeals in 1865, replacing Judge Denio who had suffered a stroke. He became chief justice three years later, and President Ulysses S. Grant appointed him to the U.S. Supreme Court in 1872 at the urging of Senator Roscoe Conkling of New York.

Justice Hunt's most important contributions to American constitutional development came in voting rights cases. On circuit in June 1873 Hunt presided at the trial of Susan B. Anthony, who had been charged with illegal participation in a national election by casting a ballot in 1872. Counsel for Anthony, relying on the argument formulated by the National Woman Suffrage Association in 1870, claimed that women had been enfranchised by the Fourteenth Amendment (1868), which not only proclaims that "All persons born or naturalized in the United States . . . are citizens of the United States and of the State wherein they reside," but also bars state governments from "abridg[ing] the privileges and immunities of citizens of United States." Hunt flatly rejected the suffragists' theory of the Fourteenth Amendment. "The right of voting, or the privilege of voting, is a right or privilege arising under the constitution of the state, and not under the Constitution of the United States," Hunt explained. "The qualifications are different in the different states. Citizenship, age, sex, residence, are variously required in the different states, or may be so. If the right belongs to any particular person, it is because such person is entitled to it by the laws of the state where he offers to exercise it, and not because of citizenship of the United States." Hunt directed the jury to find Anthony guilty of the crime and fined her $100.

Hunt's colleagues on the Supreme Court unanimously confirmed his rejection of the citizenship-means-suffrage argument in *Minor v. Happersett* (1875). "[T]he Constitution does not confer the right to vote on anyone," declared Chief Justice Morrison R. Waite for a unanimous bench. According to the opinion, even the newly adopted Fifteenth Amendment (1870) merely prohibited the states from denying voting rights "on account of race, color, or previous condition of servitude." In the landmark case of *Reese v. United States* (1876), however, Hunt dissented when the Court cut the heart out of Congress's first attempt to protect voting rights under the Fifteenth Amendment. Chief Justice Waite, speaking for a majority of the justices, struck down the Enforcement Act (1870) because two key provisions did not "confine their operation to unlawful discrimination on account of race, etc." Hunt complained that Waite's majority opinion brought "to an impotent conclusion the vigorous amendments on the subject of slavery."

Hunt's health began to fail in 1877, and he missed a great many court sessions because of gout. Early in January 1879 he suffered a stroke and never returned to the bench, yet refused to resign. He had served fewer than ten years and was ineligible for a pension under existing law. In January 1882 Congress enacted a special retirement bill for him, and Hunt resigned on the day the bill became law. He died in Washington.

• An excellent brief biography is Stanley I. Kutler, "Ward Hunt," in *The Justices of the United States Supreme Court, 1789–1969: Their Lives and Major Opinions*, ed. Leon Friedman and Fred L. Israel (1969). Obituaries appear in the New York Times and the New York Tribune, 25 Mar. 1886.

CHARLES W. MCCURDY

HUNT, Washington (5 Aug. 1811–2 Feb. 1867), congressman and governor of New York, was born in Windham, New York, the son of Sanford Hunt and Fanny Rose. He attended the common schools in Portage, New York, where his family had moved, and studied law with Lot Clark in Lockport, his final home. He was admitted to the bar in 1834 and married Mary Hosmer Walbridge the same year. They had one child.

Hunt's rise was marked by political involvement and shrewd investments, beginning in real estate but eventually expanding to virtually every type of economic enterprise in western New York. In 1835 Democratic governor William Marcy appointed him a first judge in the Court of Common Pleas in Niagara County, a post he held for five years, and in 1836 he was defeated for Congress as a Democrat. By 1840 he had become disgusted with Democratic policies, which seemed increasingly hostile to the banks and credit he believed necessary for growth, and he abandoned the Jacksonians for the Whig party. In 1842 he was elected to Congress, serving three consecutive terms. In this era the typical congressman served only one term;

Hunt's longevity brought him the chairmanship of the commerce committee by his third term and important political recognition as a loyal and energetic party supporter although not a policy innovator.

Territorial expansion and slavery extension were important issues during Hunt's terms in Congress. Hunt disliked slavery and did not wish it to expand; he was allied with the William H. Seward–Thurlow Weed wing of the state party that was adamant on this point. Yet Hunt feared sectionalism and believed that intersectional political parties like the Whig party were necessary to preserve the Union. These beliefs made him appear more moderate than most Sewardites and a valuable "compromise" candidate. In 1848 party boss Thurlow Weed, with whom he had close ties, secured his nomination for state comptroller, and the legislative selected him for the post the following year. Successful in this post, he ran for governor in 1850. President Millard Fillmore wished Whig state conventions to endorse the recently passed Compromise of 1850; the convention that nominated Hunt endorsed the more antislavery stance favored by Seward, precipitating a walkout by conservatives (the "Silver Grays"). The ensuing election was exceedingly close, Hunt defeating Democrat Horatio Seymour by fewer than three hundred votes. Seymour attributed his defeat, however, to Hunt's endorsement by dissident Anti-Renters. As governor, Hunt called for a costly expansion of the state canal system and took a seemingly nativist stand when he pointed to immigration as a growing problem in New York City. Although his canal bill, which passed but was later declared unconstitutional, divided the Democrats, Hunt faced reelection in a presidential election year teamed with the unpopular Winfield Scott. He lost to Seymour by over twenty thousand votes.

Hunt had hoped to succeed Seward in the Senate, but the continued agitation of the slavery issue made Seward more attractive to most Whigs. Hunt was devastated by the collapse of the Whig party in the 1850s. He steadfastly refused to join the sectional Republican party and became estranged from Seward and Weed, whom he blamed for the Whig party's dissolution. After chairing the Whig party's abortive final assembly in 1856, he drifted into the nativist American party, approving its nationalism as much as its antiforeignism, but was soundly defeated as its candidate for Congress that year. In 1860 he presided over a convention of ex-Whigs that nominated John Bell for president as a Constitutional Unionist. In public and private letters to political leaders, he continually decried sectionalism. Believing only moderation and adherence to the Constitution could reunite the nation, he moved increasingly toward his old foes, the Democrats. In 1862 he supported Seymour, the man he had twice challenged for the governorship, for governor and wrote pamphlets attacking the Republicans for destroying the constitutional principles on which the nation was based. He was a delegate to the Democratic National Convention in 1864 and in 1866 to the National Union convention, an attempt to fuse Democrats and conservative Republicans in support of Andrew Johnson. He was also a lay delegate to many conventions of the Episcopal church. He died in New York City following a long bout with cancer.

• There is a small Hunt collection at the New York State Library (Albany). Letters from Hunt appear in the papers of numerous politicians, including Hamilton Fish (Library of Congress), Thurlow Weed (University of Rochester), John Bell (Library of Congress), and the Burrows family (University of Michigan, Bentley Historical Library). The *New York Times*, 3 Feb. 1867, carried an obituary. See also William R. Cutter, *Genealogical and Family History of Western New York* (1912); vols. 2 and 3 of DeAlva Stanwood Alexander, *A Political History of the State of New York* (1906, 1909); and Mark L. Berger, *The Revolution in the New York Party Systems, 1840–1860* (1973). Biographical sketches appear in *The Biographical Directory of the American Congress* (1928) and Charles E. Fitch, *Encyclopedia of Biography of New York* (1916).

PHYLLIS F. FIELD

HUNT, William Henry (12 June 1823–27 Feb. 1884), U.S. secretary of the navy, jurist, and diplomat, was born in Charleston, South Carolina, the son of Thomas Hunt, a planter, lawyer, and state legislator, and Louisa Gaillard, the sister of U.S. senator John Gaillard. After Hunt's father's death in 1830, his family moved to New Haven, Connecticut. Hunt matriculated at Yale, briefly studying law, but he could not afford to complete his education and did not earn a degree. He moved to New Orleans, where his family had settled, and read law in the offices of his elder brothers. Admitted to the Louisiana bar in 1844, Hunt prospered in his practice. The 1860 census reported that he held $34,000 in property, including one slave.

In 1848 Hunt married Frances Ann Andrews, who succumbed to tuberculosis the following year. In 1852 he wed Elizabeth Augusta Ridgely; the couple had seven children. Elizabeth Hunt was a Yankee, and this, together with Hunt's Connecticut upbringing, his elder brothers' opposition to nullification when they had lived in South Carolina, and the fact that his slave ownership was limited to one or two house servants, may help explain Hunt's decided coolness toward states' rights militancy. As the Whigs foundered in the 1850s, Hunt opted for the more nationalistic of the political alternatives available to white southerners, affiliating first with the Know Nothings and in 1860 with the Constitutional Union party. Though opposed to secession, Hunt reluctantly accepted a commission as lieutenant colonel in the Confederate army. However, his service did not extend much beyond drilling a makeshift soldiery on Basin Street, and he apparently welcomed the fall of New Orleans to Union forces in 1862. At any rate, he received the Union naval commander David G. Farragut, who captured the city, in his home. In the war's aftermath, Hunt continued to practice law in New Orleans and lectured briefly in the law school at the University of Louisiana. His second wife died in 1864, and in 1866 he married Sarah Barker Harrison. This unhappy union ended in divorce in 1870. The following year Hunt married Louise F. Hopkins. Hunt's third and fourth marriages, like his first, were childless.

Hunt embraced the new order ushered in by the Thirteenth, Fourteenth, and Fifteenth Amendments and the Reconstruction Acts of 1867. As an attorney he was, in fact, involved in the early stages of the *Slaughterhouse Cases*, which did so much to shape courts' understanding of the Fourteenth Amendment. The 1873 majority opinion of the U.S. Supreme Court embraced the position that Hunt and his brother Randell Hunt had argued in the Louisiana courts, that the amendment had been passed specifically to protect the rights of freedpeople and not also, in this case, white butchers. Ironically, though, the Court narrowly defined the protected rights and thus undermined federal powers to protect black civil rights.

Hunt did not immediately become active as a Republican in partisan politics, but in 1873 he served as counsel to carpetbag governor William P. Kellogg in an electoral dispute. In 1876 Louisiana Republicans made Hunt their candidate for state attorney general, a post to which he was temporarily appointed the same year to fill a vacancy. He canvassed the state throughout a tumultuous campaign. In the end both parties claimed victory and swore in their putative officers-elect, but in the interests of furthering the Compromise of 1877, Republicans in Washington, D.C., refused to support Hunt and his fellow claimants. Eager in the wake of the disputed election to quit Louisiana, Hunt thereupon solicited a federal appointment. In 1877 he was considered for a place on the U.S. Supreme Court, many feeling that the seat then vacant should be filled by a southerner. Hunt, however, was rated by Associate Justice Samuel Miller "a fierce partizan in politics" and by Chief Justice Morrison Waite as not up to the job, and the seat went instead to John Harlan of Kentucky. Hunt had to content himself with an appointment the following year to the U.S. Court of Claims in Washington.

As a distinguished but "loyal" white southerner, Hunt again became a candidate for federal preferment following the Republican victory in the election of 1880. He was initially considered for postmaster general or secretary of the interior, but the process of placing a southerner in James Garfield's cabinet was greatly complicated by the competition of the "Stalwart" and "Half-Breed" factions for supremacy in the party. When the smoke finally cleared, Hunt had been appointed secretary of the navy. By no means the most obvious choice for the post, Hunt nevertheless proved a dedicated and skilled secretary. Ill funded and poorly administered, the navy had been allowed to deteriorate and grow obsolescent in the decade and a half since the Civil War. At the prompting of Admiral David D. Porter, Hunt appointed an advisory board of officers charged with determining what the navy required to rebuild, specifically the number and sorts of vessels and their probable cost. Hunt took to Congress the board's recommendation of a $30 million program, the core of which would involve the construction of thirty-eight cruisers, eighteen of them steel-hulled. Despite Hunt's earnest lobbying, Congress steadily whittled down the program until it merely authorized construction of a few ships. Nevertheless Hunt's thirteen-month tenure as secretary has been taken to be the seedtime of a new navy. His development of the advisory board and of better working relations with Congress ultimately aided the navy in making its case for the enlargement and modernization of the fleet, and Hunt's successors finally won construction of steel cruisers. The Office of Naval Intelligence was also founded during Hunt's term.

If Hunt had been appointed secretary of the navy for purely political reasons, his stepping down from the post can be similarly explained. Anxious to please James G. Blaine, President Chester A. Arthur named Hunt minister to Russia in 1882 in order to ease a Blaine ally, William E. Chandler, into the navy post. Decidedly miffed, Hunt nevertheless accepted the appointment and journeyed to Russia. Though hobbled by liver disease, he concerned himself with Russian anti-Semitism and, to little avail, protested official persecution of Jews. He died in St. Petersburg.

• A microfilm collection of William Henry Hunt papers is at the Library of Congress, Manuscripts Division, Washington, D.C. The National Archives holds the Records of the Office of the Secretary of the Navy (RG 45 and 80). Hunt's son wrote a biography, Thomas Hunt, *The Life of William H. Hunt* (1922). Additional personal information is in Ted Tunnell, *Crucible of Reconstruction: War, Radicalism, and Race in Louisiana 1862–1877* (1984). For his service as secretary of the navy, see the article on Hunt by Walter Herrick in *American Secretaries of the Navy*, vol. 1: *1775–1913*, ed. Paolo Coletta (1980), and Justus Doenecke, *The Presidencies of James A. Garfield and Chester A. Arthur* (1981). His prospective appointment to the Supreme Court is discussed in Charles Fairman, *Mr. Justice Miller and the Supreme Court 1862–1890* (1939).

PATRICK G. WILLIAMS

HUNT, William Henry (29 June 1869–19 Dec. 1951), foreign service officer, was born near McMinnville, Tennessee. His mother was illiterate and poor. His father was a white southerner who gave the family only his name. Hunt's mother died when he was twenty-one. They were so poor that Hunt did not wear shoes for the first several years of his life, and he never saw his father. Later in his life Hunt observed that he had begun with a "three and two count" against him from the umpire of fate. Poverty forced Hunt to drop out of elementary school in Nashville just months after starting. He worked as a janitor, bellhop, and Pullman porter and developed an interest in the wider world.

Contacts Hunt made through work helped him acquire formal education. Employment as a traveling companion for a wealthy invalid at the end of the 1880s carried him through many countries of East Asia, the Middle East, and Europe. While working as a Pullman porter on the Canadian Pacific Railroad a few years later, he became acquainted with Alfred Oren Jower, the headmaster of the Lawrence Academy, a prep school in Groton, Massachusetts. Jower helped him gain admission at Lawrence in the fall of 1890. Hunt graduated in 1894 and entered Williams College the same year with a scholarship. However, he left after only one year because of what he viewed as racism there. He moved to New York where he worked first as an assistant in a chemical laboratory and later as a messenger for a Wall Street brokerage firm. At the same time he took an active interest in Congregational church social concerns. Among the notable figures he met in the course of these activities were the conservationist Gifford Pinchot and Seth Low, the president of Columbia University.

The path to Hunt's Foreign Service career opened suddenly as a result of the appointment of Mifflin W. Gibbs as U.S. consul at Tamatave, Madagascar, in 1897. Hunt was introduced to Gibbs by his daughter Ida, whom Hunt had met some years earlier, and she persuaded her father to accept Hunt's request to accompany him on his mission. In Madagascar Hunt first worked as a consular clerk. He was appointed vice consul in 1899 and consul in 1901 when Gibbs resigned because of illness.

During a leave of absence to the United States in 1904, Hunt married Ida Gibbs. She subsequently accompanied him to all of his posts during his long career as a U.S. consul. After serving at Tamatave until 1906, he was appointed consul at St. Etienne, France, a rare assignment since black officers were assigned almost exclusively to African or Caribbean posts. Hunt's good relations with the French in their protectorate of Madagascar may partially explain this good fortune. He served at St. Etienne until 1926, when that post was closed. While there he became well known and liked in local society. He became fluent in French, was elected honorary head of several social and cultural organizations, and was prominent in relief efforts during World War I. From France, in the period before the war, he visited North Africa, where he later recalled taking his first airplane flight. This probably placed him among the first of his race to experience this new technology. After his long service in France he was assigned to Guadeloupe in the West Indies then in 1929 to St. Michaels, the Azores. In December 1930 he was appointed secretary in the Diplomatic Service. His final appointment was as consul at Monrovia, Liberia, in January 1931. In August 1932 he was assigned temporarily to the State Department, from which he retired in December of the same year.

Hunt's career literally held him apart from the growing civil rights struggle in which so many of the notable black leaders he knew were engaged. In addition to the geographical separation, his official status carried the restrictions placed on all Foreign Service officers. Some of his letters and reports suggest that he accepted the common European assumptions about the backwardness of the colonized peoples. However, since the students he had met during his prep school summers in Boston included such future civil rights leaders as W. E. B. Du Bois, John Hope, and Clement G. Morgan, there can be no doubt that he was conscious of the critical thinking on national liberation and racial equality. Moreover, his collected papers include materials concerning the Niagara movement, the NAACP, the Association for the Study of Negro Life and History, and Pan-African activities. Ida Hunt, working with Du Bois, led the planning for the Third Pan-African Congress, which met in London in 1923. After retirement Hunt resided in Washington, D.C., continuing the public silence to which he had become conditioned by three decades of government service. He died in Washington.

• The W. H. Hunt Papers are in the Moorland-Spingarn Research Center at Howard University. Other vital materials on his career are in the records of the Department of State. Some of Hunt's extensive official reports attracted the attention of the American press; for example, the *Philadelphia Evening Item*, 31 Mar. 1919, which reviewed his report on Roquefort cheese.

ALLISON BLAKELY

HUNT, William Morris (31 Mar. 1824–8 Sept. 1879), painter, was born in Brattleboro, Vermont, the son of Jonathan Hunt, a landowner and politician, and Jane Maria Leavitt. His father served in the U.S. House of Representatives from 1827 until his death in 1832. Following the settlement of the estate, the family settled first in New Haven, Connecticut, and later in Cambridge, Massachusetts, where Hunt entered Harvard College in 1840. He developed consumption, a condition that plagued him the rest of his life, and left before his senior year. His doctor prescribed a trip to a milder climate, so the Hunt family embarked on a grand tour of Europe that lasted twelve years. It was in Europe that Hunt and his brother Richard, who later became an architect, received their professional training and launched their careers.

As a teenager, Hunt had been taught by the Italian-born painter Spiridione Gambardella, who lived briefly with the family in New Haven. Later he received lessons in carving from the sculptor John Crookshanks King in Boston. Hunt also received instruction from the sculptor Henry Kirke Brown, whom he met in Rome after his family moved there in 1844. It was also in Italy that Hunt met the painter Emanuel Leutze, who urged him to attend the highly regarded Düsseldorf art academy. Hunt spent a year (1845–1846) studying there, noting later that the instruction was the same for the art student as for the student of science— "a grinding, methodical process for the accumulation of a required skill" (quoted in Knowlton, p. 6). In 1846 he left Düsseldorf to rejoin his family, now residing in Paris. Hunt flirted with attending the sculpture program at the École des Beaux-Arts and had made plans to study with James Pradier, then the favorite of King Louis-Philippe.

Hunt experienced an epiphany when he discovered a painting, *The Falconer* by Thomas Couture, in a window of Deforge's art supply store. In a legendary but perhaps apocryphal statement, Hunt declared: "If that is painting, I am a painter!" (Knowlton, p. 7). Al-

though he would do a few more sculptural pieces, including a relief of Couture, he devoted the rest of his life to painting. Couture's technique and method of instruction were based on a synthesis of classical academic training and a newer, more expressive, painterly tradition of the romantics. Later Hunt introduced Couture's method to his Boston students and encouraged them to travel to France to study with the master directly. Couture's influence can be seen in a number of genre paintings Hunt did while still in Paris, several of which, *La Marguerite I* (1851, Louvre, Paris), *The Fortune Teller* (1852, Museum of Fine Arts, Boston), and *The Violet Girl* (1856, Museum of Art, Rhode Island School of Design, Providence), he exhibited at the Paris Salon.

Historically, however, Hunt is more often associated with the Barbizon painter Jean-François Millet, whose work he first saw at the 1850 Salon, where Millet exhibited his most famous work, *The Sower*. Two years later Hunt visited Millet in Barbizon, where he purchased this work. It became the first of a number of paintings by Millet and other Barbizon artists acquired by Hunt; he encouraged Boston friends and collectors to buy such works as well. Hunt remained in Barbizon for two years working alongside Millet, whom he always regarded as the "greatest man in Europe." Commenting in his lectures, reprinted as *Talks on Art* (1875), Hunt described the effect Millet had on him: "I took broader views of humanity, of the world, of life, when I came to know Millet and his work. His subjects were real people, who had work to do. If he painted a hay-stack it suggested life, animal as well as vegetable, and the life of man" (repr. as *On Painting and Drawing* [1976], p. 167). In contrast to the urban genre paintings done in Couture's atelier, Hunt adopted Millet's interest in peasant themes. Among the most notable are *La Marguerite II* (1853, Museum of Fine Arts, Boston) and *The Little Gleaner* (1854, Toledo Museum of Art), both single images of young peasant women rendered in outdoor settings.

In 1855 many of the Hunt family members returned to the United States. Richard Hunt settled in New York and became one of the most influential architects of the late nineteenth century. William Hunt went to Boston, where he married the socially prominent Louisa Dumaresq Perkins in the fall of 1855. He and Louisa settled first in Brattleboro, Vermont, then moved to Newport, Rhode Island, where he created an "American Barbizon." Following the death of their first child, Morris, the Hunts spent the winter of 1857–1858 in Fayal and the Azores, then returned to Newport, where they lived until 1862. They would have five more children.

The late 1850s were productive years for Hunt as he successfully established himself as an important and influential painter. He exhibited regularly at the Boston Athenaeum and at the National Academy of Design in New York. In spite of occasional criticism from the press, in 1859 Hunt received a prestigious commission from the Essex County Bar Association of Salem, Massachusetts, to paint a portrait of Lemuel

Shaw (Peabody-Essex Museum, Salem, Mass.) This handsome canvas, in which the judge is strongly profiled against a light cream background, introduced the new French naturalist style of portraiture into the United States. At the time it won for Hunt "an entering wedge" into the profession. Over the next few years he was invited to paint several portraits of Boston women that remain among his most admired works.

In 1859 Hunt established a summer art school in Newport, where John La Farge and William James and Henry James studied for a short time. This idyll, however, was interrupted by the Civil War. Hunt and his family moved to Milton, a suburb of Boston, where, with the exception of two years in Europe, he lived for the rest of his life. During the Civil War, Hunt created several patriotic lithographic images including *The Drummer Boy* (1862, Museum of Fine Arts, Boston) and *The Bugle Call* or *Bugler* (1863, Boston Athenaeum). He was also commissioned to paint several posthumous portraits of men killed in the war and a standing portrait of Lincoln following his assassination in 1865. However, the painting was destroyed, along with a number of other works by Hunt, in the Boston Fire of 1872.

Throughout his life, Hunt was known as a supportive colleague. In the 1860s he befriended Elihu Vedder, whom he invited to spend a year in Boston. Hunt joined with others in the creation of the Allston Club, an organization devoted to the exhibition of contemporary European and American painting, and he became its first president in 1866. In 1867 Hunt and his wife traveled to Europe with four of their children to attend the Paris Universal Exposition. Hunt was one of twelve American artists invited to exhibit paintings at the world's fair. However, these were not happy years for Hunt. After a year and a half he abruptly left his family in Italy and returned to the United States. Although their fifth child was born shortly after the family's return from Europe, Hunt and his wife were never reconciled. A fellow Boston artist, the sculptor Thomas Ball, was on the same boat from Europe but noted only Hunt's enthusiastic plans to start another art school, which was to be in Boston and open to women. Hunt advertised the commencement of classes in 1868, and during the seven years the school was open, more than fifty women studied with him, including Helen Knowlton, who recorded his lectures, later published as *Talks on Art* (first series, 1875; second series, 1883), and later wrote his biography. *Talks on Art*, a compilation of his lectures to women students on the techniques of drawing and painting was based, to some degree, on the instruction he received from Couture.

Throughout the 1860s and 1870s Hunt continued to paint portraits, but after the Boston Fire in 1872, which destroyed his studio and devastated him psychologically, he traveled a great deal and began to paint landscapes. In Florida, at the winter home of his friend John Murray Forbes, Hunt concentrated on landscapes, translating the fleeting effects of nature first into charcoal and then into oils in such works as *Rainbow Creek* (1873, Museum of Fine Arts, Boston) and *View of St. John's River (Florida Sunset)* (1874, private collection). The architect Leopold Eidlitz invited him to submit ideas for two murals for the Assembly Chamber of the New York State Capitol then under construction.

This was one of the most important building projects of the decade; the renowned architect H. H. Richardson and landscape architect Frederick Law Olmsted collaborated with Eidlitz on the building's final design. With its richly carved and painted interior and Hunt's two murals, the New York State Capitol ushered in a new era for civic architecture in America. However, Hunt had never painted a mural and the only other existing murals by American artists were Emanuel Leutze's *Westward the Course of Empire Takes Its Way* (1862) for the U.S. Capitol and La Farge's contemporary painted decorations for Trinity Church Boston. He had originally proposed two views of Niagara Falls, which he thought an appropriate subject for the state house. The sponsors, however, wanted narrative paintings, and Hunt proposed two themes, one of which he had begun in Europe in the late 1840s. He had worked on *The Flight of Night* for a number of years hoping to create a large-scale allegorical painting that in his brother Leavitt's words would "serve as a pendant to Guido Reni's *Aurora*." This was certainly a project appropriate for mural painting, and although a great deal of the early work and sketches had been lost in the 1872 fire, Hunt was able to resurrect enough of his early ideas to present the commissioners with two versions of *The Flight of Night* (one is at the Pennsylvania Academy of Fine Arts, Philadelphia, and the other at the Museum of Fine Arts, Boston). As a pendant to this baroque-inspired allegory of Night in her chariot speeding across a cloud-filled sky, Hunt offered a same-sized version of *The Discoverer* (now destroyed), an allegorical representation of Columbus's discovery of America. In contrast to the aerial world of *The Flight of Night*, the Discoverer is pictured on a small boat in the middle of the ocean surrounded by the allegorical figures of hope, faith, science, and fortune.

Full of enthusiasm, Hunt went to work and in a matter of months had completed two 18-by-96-foot murals on facing tympanum of the Assembly in time for its opening on 1 January 1879. There was enormously favorable critical reception of Hunt's murals. The murals were also the subject, along with La Farge's paintings for Trinity Church, of an article by architect and writer Henry Van Brunt. In an article titled "The New Dispensation of Monumental Art" in the *Atlantic Monthly*, Van Brunt discussed the importance of each man's work, not only in terms of its meaning but of the murals' relationship to their architectural setting. Reproductions of Hunt's murals were widely circulated, and his seminal contribution to the history of American mural painting has always been acknowledged.

The murals' favorable critical acceptance prompted friends to seek additional work for Hunt in the State

Capitol. However, Governor Lucius Robinson hated the building and refused to hire Hunt for any further work. Disappointed, Hunt returned to Boston, but his depression did not lift. Friends and relatives were concerned for his health and accompanied him on travels to New Hampshire. While visiting the poet Celia Thaxter on her island home on Appledore, Isles of Shoals, off the coast of Portsmouth, New Hampshire, Hunt, either by accident or intent, fell into a nearby pond and drowned.

Most writers concede that Hunt never achieved first rank as a painter and is better known today for advancing the new painterly style of Couture and introducing the work of Millet and the Barbizon school to America. Nevertheless, it can be fairly said that he devoted his life to the pursuit of that elusive moment when paint and canvas, charcoal and paper, were transformed into art.

• Aside from museum records, principally at the Museum of Fine Arts, Boston (which also has the largest collection of his work), and the Richard Morris Hunt archives at the Octagon Museum, Washington, D.C., there is little archival information available on William Morris Hunt. The most comprehensive modern biography is Sally Webster, *William Morris Hunt* (1991). Also of note are two museum catalogs: Museum of Fine Arts, Boston, *William Morris Hunt, A Memorial Exhibition* (1979), and University of Maryland Art Gallery, *The Late Landscapes of William Morris Hunt* (1976). Useful for information on the Hunt family is Paul R. Baker, *Richard Morris Hunt* (1980). On Couture's American pupils see Marchal Landgren, *American Pupils of Thomas Couture* (1970). On the Barbizon school in America see Peter Bermingham, *American Art in the Barbizon Mood* (1975). Indispensable for any study is Helen M. Knowlton, *The Art-Life of William Morris Hunt* (1899).

SALLY WEBSTER

HUNT, Wilson Price (1782?–Apr. 1842), explorer and merchant, was born in Hopewell, New Jersey, the son of John P. Hunt and Margaret Guild, occupations unknown. Little is known of his early life. In 1804 he moved to St. Louis, on the edge of the frontier about to be opened by the Lewis and Clark expedition. Hunt ran a general store in St. Louis until 1809; he became an associate of John Jacob Astor in the new Pacific Fur Company in 1810. Astor named Hunt—one of the few Americans among a number of Canadian associates— to lead an overland expedition to the mouth of the Columbia River, where Astor wanted to establish a fur-trading colony. The ship *Tonquin* carried other members of the expedition by sea.

Hunt went to Montreal in June 1810 and recruited Canadian voyageurs for his party. He proceeded to Fort Mackinac (in present-day Michigan) and then to St. Louis, where he arrived on 3 September. In St. Louis Hunt became embroiled in disputes with the Spanish-American fur trader Manuel Lisa, head of the Missouri Fur Company. Hunt departed from St. Louis on 12 March 1811, and on 21 April he and his party left their winter camp near present-day St. Joseph and headed north on the Missouri River. A memorable

keelboat race ensued when Lisa, 240 miles behind Hunt, made all speed to catch up with the latter so that their two parties could enter the land of the Sioux together. Lisa's heroic energies prevailed, and he caught up with Hunt on 2 June, after a race that has been one of the most celebrated in the history of the West. After a short time with Lisa's group, Hunt and his men left their boats and departed on horseback across the plains toward the Rocky Mountains. They were the first large group of white explorers to take this route. The party encountered some difficulties but made steady progress through the unfamiliar terrain. When they reached the Snake River, Hunt's men built canoes and trusted to the waterway. They canoed straight into disastrous waterfalls and whirlpools at "Caldron Linn" (near present-day Milner Dam, Idaho) and then marched on into almost worse conditions in what has become known as Hell's Canyon, one of the most inaccessible parts of North America. After suffering from intense cold, hunger, and despair, members of the expedition straggled into Astoria in early 1812 (Hunt himself arrived on 15 Feb. 1812). It had been a long and costly journey.

After his arrival at Astoria (in present-day Oregon), which had been built by the members of the seaborne expedition, Hunt became the senior associate in charge of the now-united expedition. Unfortunately, Hunt allowed himself to be diverted from this, his primary task. He sailed on the supply ship *Beaver* on 1 August 1812 for Russian Alaska, where he was subsequently entertained and delayed by Governor Alexander Baranoff. To further complicate the situation, the captain of the *Beaver* refused to return to Astoria in the winter months; the best that Hunt could manage was to be left on the Sandwich Islands (present-day Hawaii) on 1 January 1813. Marooned there while important events took place at Astoria, Hunt chartered the *Albatross* and eventually reached Astoria on 20 August 1813 after a year of "seafaring that might have furnished a chapter in the wanderings of Sinbad" (Irving, p. 473).

Hunt and the Astorians had both learned that war had been declared between the United States and Great Britain. To his surprise and chagrin, Hunt found that his associates at Astoria had decided to sell the post to the British North West Company. Hunt was incensed at first, but then he decided to salvage what he could of Astor's trading goods. Hunt left Astoria aboard the *Albatross* on 26 August 1813 in order to find and charter another ship to carry away the valuable goods. Hunt was taken first to the Marquesas and then to the Sandwich Islands. After a long period of forced waiting, Hunt managed to purchase the brig *Pedlar*, in which he returned to Astoria on 28 February 1814.

Hunt had arrived too late to stave off the sale of Astoria (16 Oct. 1813) and its takeover by a British man-of-war, the *Racoon* (13 Dec. 1813). Powerless to change these events, Hunt and several clerks of the expedition sailed away in the *Pedlar*, determined to make some profit for Astor. In the next two years, they sailed to Alaska twice, California once, the Sandwich Islands twice, and China once. When the *Pedlar* entered New York harbor on 17 October 1816, it carried Chinese teas and silks. Hunt had proved himself to be better as a merchant than as an explorer. Hunt returned to St. Louis, where he again ran a general store (1817–1819) and where he built a gristmill. He served as the postmaster of St. Louis from 1822 to 1840. In 1836 he married Anne Lucas Hunt, his cousin's widow; they had no children. He died in St. Louis.

Hunt's journeys to Astoria and around the Pacific Ocean between 1812 and 1814 on behalf of Astor had been fraught with ill fortune. He had had the bad luck to command a party composed heavily of Canadians, who owed no strong loyalty to the United States. In taking the overland route to and through the Rocky Mountains, Hunt had made errors that are understandable but that fare poorly when compared to the earlier expedition of Lewis and Clark (1804–1806). Nevertheless, the Astorian settlement had good prospects of success until the outbreak of the War of 1812. In the war, Astoria was at risk because of its exposed location, the power of the British navy, and the presence of the North West Company. It was surely a handicap to the Americans at Astoria that Hunt was detained at sea and in Hawaii by unfavorable circumstances and not present during 1813. Although the expedition was a large loss for the Pacific Fur Company, the United States regained control of the mouth of the Columbia River, pursuant to the Treaty of Ghent. Furthermore, large sections of Hunt's route to and across the mountains later became parts of the Oregon Trail.

• There appears to be no comprehensive biography of Hunt. Our knowledge of him comes almost exclusively from sources relating to John Jacob Astor, the Pacific Fur Company, and the Astorian expedition. Washington Irving's classic *Astoria* (1836) is still useful. Important primary sources are in R. G. Thwaites, ed., *Early Western Travels 1748–1846*, vols. 6 and 7 (1904). Hunt's diary of the overland expedition is in Philip Ashton Rollins, ed., *The Discovery of the Oregon Trail* (1935), pp. 281–308. Other useful studies include Kenneth Wiggins Porter, *John Jacob Astor, Business Man* (1931); Hiram Martin Chittenden, *The American Fur Trade of the Far West* (1902); and Dale Van Every, *The Final Challenge* (1964). There are also articles in the *Oregon Historical Quarterly*, notably Porter, "Cruise of Astor's Brig *Pedler*," vol. 31, no. 3: 224–30. For an appraisal of the hazards in the Rocky Mountains, see Alvin M. Josephy, Jr., "Ordeal in Hell's Canyon," *American Heritage* 18 (Dec. 1966): 72–79, 91–95.

SAMUEL WILLARD CROMPTON

HUNTER, Alberta (1 Apr. 1895–17 Oct. 1984), singer, was born in Memphis, Tennessee, the daughter of Charles Hunter, a sleeping car porter, and Laura Peterson, a maid. Hunter attended public school until around age fifteen. Her singing career began after she went to Chicago with one of her teachers. Hunter stated at times that she was eleven or twelve years old when she tricked the teacher into allowing her to ride with her by train on a child's pass. However, other accounts suggest that she may have been in her mid-teens. Until she was able to support herself as a performer in Chicago's South Side clubs, she lived with a friend of her mother's.

Hunter worked hard to keep her personal relationships out of the limelight. Her sudden marriage in 1919 to a Willard Saxbe Townsend was most likely a cover for her lesbianism, although she claimed to love him. The marriage was never consummated, but Townsend did not apply for a divorce until 1923. Hunter's biographer, Frank Taylor, states that sexual abuse in her childhood may account for her abhorrence of any man who attempted to become intimate. Her very close relationship with her mother probably was her most enduring alliance. She is known to have had female traveling companions during her sojourns abroad, but there is scant written evidence of her openly acknowledging her homosexuality in the press, though language in her autobiography implicitly supports her preference for women.

Hunter's first singing job was in a bordello. From there she moved to the small clubs that catered mainly to sporting men—black and white. In 1914 she was tutored by Tony Jackson, a prominent jazz pianist, who helped her to expand her repertoire and to compose her own songs.

The next move put her in the company of and competition with other aspiring young women such as Mattie Hite, Cora Green, Florence Mills, and Ada "Bricktop" Smith. The Panama Club, owned by Isadore Levine and I. Shorr, was one of a number of white-owned clubs with white-only clientele that were gaining popularity in Chicago, New York, and a few other cities. Hunter claimed that her act was in the upstairs room where the music and the action was "kind of rough and ready." The barrelhouse upstairs contrasted with the ballads and fox-trot songs that Mills and others performed downstairs. In this setting Hunter developed as a blues singer for a cabaret crowd that was dramatically different from the audiences in black theaters and clubs. During the second decade of the twentieth century, she and the other women who performed in these surroundings shaped the blues into an insurgent song form that attracted an increasing number of white patrons. "The customers wouldn't stay downstairs. They'd go upstairs to hear us sing the blues. That's where I would stand and make up verses and sing as I go along." Hunter's appeal was based on her extraordinary gift for improvising lyrics to titillate and satisfy the white audience's appetite for ribald or humorous material. Other songwriters, recognizing her ability to promote a song by adding her unique melodic and textual twists, brought their new songs to her. This source of income added to her security as a performer and allowed her to support her mother, who had moved to Chicago.

Hunter moved from one small club to another from 1916 until 1920. She considered herself as having arrived when she got a contract at the Dreamland Café where the fabulous King Oliver band, with the young Louis Armstrong, was playing. Her performances at the Dreamland garnered praise from the local black press, and by 1921 she was recording for the Black Swan label. Her first release—"How Long, Sweet Daddy, How Long?"—established her as a blues singer of substantial quality. By the end of 1922 Hunter already had recorded fourteen blues and torch songs. The Black Swan numbers were recorded with the Dreamland orchestra or the Fletcher Henderson orchestra. The material was rather trite and reflected the label's hesitancy to record what they considered to be raw blues.

She switched to the Paramount label in mid-1922 where she recorded her own creation, "Down-Hearted Blues," which was to become famous when Bessie Smith recorded it a year later for Columbia Records. She was called "The Idol of Dreamland" by Paramount Records when they advertised her releases in the *Chicago Defender*. She cut two sides with Eubie Blake on piano around the same time, including "Jazzin' Baby Blues," a light fox-trot rather than a blues. In 1923, while still working for Paramount, Hunter also recorded for Harmograph Records under the pseudonym May Alix. Hunter is heard as Alberta Prime accompanied by Duke Ellington and Sonny Greer on the Biltmore label by the end of 1924. On Gennett she assumed her sister's name, Josephine Beatty, accompanied by Louis Armstrong and the Red Onion Jazz Babies. There is no question that Hunter is the artist on these numbers because her phrasing and expressiveness are evident. From 1921 until 1929 Hunter recorded at least fifty-two songs under her name and various pseudonyms. Her accompanists included some of the finest jazz artists of that era—Armstrong, Henderson, Blake, Ellington, Fats Waller, and Buster Bailey.

Hunter's career received a decided boost from the record advertisements that appeared in the black press. Unlike most of her blues singing peers, she seldom appeared in vaudeville. She was the darling of the cabaret set who enjoyed their blues in intimate club settings undisturbed by the lively crowds on the Theater Owner's Booking Association circuit. In 1923 she was the star of a touring musical revue, *How Come*, but she quit the company to return to New York after five months. Other shows in which she was featured were *Runnin' Wild* and *Struttin' Time*. In late 1924 she performed along with black artists such as Noble Sissle, Blake, and Fletcher Henderson for a benefit sponsored by the NAACP in New York.

Hunter, augmented by two male dancers and a pianist, presented her new act, Syncopation DeLuxe, in February 1925. It opened at New York's Loewe's Theatre and moved to the Waldorf Astoria in April. She had the only black act on the eighteen-act bill, according to the *Chicago Defender*. She toured the Orpheum circuit in the West and the Keith circuit in the East during that year and went back to New York in January 1926 to record her first release on the Okeh label. In June she and Samuel Bailey formed a duo, which toured on the Keith circuit.

Hunter's first European tour came at the end of 1927 and proved an overwhelming success with appearances at London's Hippodrome, Monte Carlo, and the Casino de Paris. She signed with the London cast in mid-1928 for Jerome Kern's *Showboat*, in which she created the role of Queenie opposite Paul Robeson's Joe. The show remained in London at Drury Lane for nearly ten months, earning accolades for the two actor-singers. When *Showboat* closed, Hunter toured the nightclub circuit in France, Denmark, and Germany. Her petite, shapely good looks were enhanced by fashionable clothes, and her ability to learn languages endeared her to French audiences.

On her return to New York in 1929, Hunter recorded on the Columbia label and formed another song-and-dance act with two young male dancers. Chicago continued to have its pull because of her early successes and her mother's presence, so she often moved between the two cities. New York, however, was where she recorded and performed regularly in clubs in and around the city. She left again for Europe in 1933. That tour included Holland and a stint as a replacement for Josephine Baker at the Casino de Paris. Londoners were particularly fond of Hunter's interpretation of ballads, and she did nightly broadcasts while there. Her first European film, *Radio Parade of 1935*, was produced in England. She was cast as a singing star in an episode depicting African dancers and drummers, but she had no speaking part.

Hunter frequently worked abroad during the 1930s. Her itinerary expanded to include the Middle East, Egypt, and Russia by the mid-thirties. Toward the end of the decade, however, the effects of fascism made Europe less receptive to black performers. She returned to Chicago in 1938, where she broadened her radio audience. She also tried serious drama with a role in *Mamba's Daughters*. From that point she performed mainly in small clubs in Chicago, Detroit, and the Great Lakes region. She made few recordings, and by the end of 1940 she was not to be recorded again on an American label for another forty years. By this time the music scene was dominated by the big swing bands, and opportunities were few for African-American women to record with the major white bands that garnered most of the recording contracts.

Ironically, World War II gave her another performing opportunity when she was attached to a USO unit. Her participation in efforts to entertain the troops ended with a command performance for General Dwight D. Eisenhower in June 1945. After the war Hunter officially retired from the stage and stayed home to care for her ailing mother. She earned a nursing certificate at an age when most women were retiring from the profession. Her habitual lying about her age and her youthful appearance fooled the authorities and enabled her to serve in that capacity until she was eighty-two.

Although she had declared that she would not return to the stage, Hunter was enticed to try the cabaret scene again in the fall of 1977 by Greenwich Village club owner Barney Josephson. This appearance revived her singing career, but this time she concentrated on singing the blues for young patrons who were delighted by the octogenarian's naughty ad-libs. Energetic and bubbly with a wry sense of humor, Hunter embarked again on songwriting and recording with the assistance of Columbia Records producer John Hammond (1910–1987). Together, they produced her album *Amtrak Blues*, which included her compositions—the title song and revivals of the 1920s' "I Got a Mind to Ramble" and "I'm Having a Good Time." She also recorded her songs for the soundtrack of *Remember My Name* (1977) and an album of new and old blues, *The Glory of Alberta Hunter* (1981). Hunter appeared in clubs, on television talk shows and documentaries, in commercials, and at jazz festivals and concerts until her death in New York.

• The author's interview with Sammy Price confirmed the point made above concerning Hunter's implicit acknowledgment of her homosexuality in her autobiography. Sources of extensive information on Hunter are the biography by Frank Taylor, assisted by Gerald Cook, *Alberta Hunter: A Celebration in Blues* (1987); Daphne Duval Harrison, *Black Pearls: Blues Queens of the 1920s* (1988); and taped interviews in the Smithsonian Institution's Performing Arts Collection. Also see Whitney Balliett's profile in *American Singers: 27 Portraits in Song* (1988). An obituary is in the *New York Times*, 19 Oct. 1984.

DAPHNE DUVAL HARRISON

HUNTER, Clementine (Dec. 1886?–1 Jan. 1988), folk artist, was born Clemence Reuben at Hidden Hill Plantation near Cloutierville, Louisiana, the daughter of John Reuben and Antoinette Adams, plantation workers. Her exact birth date is unknown. Most sources agree that she was born either in late December 1886 or early January 1887.

Leaving Catholic school in Cloutierville at a young age because she disliked the discipline of the nuns, Clementine became a cotton picker and field hand at several plantations in the Cloutierville area. In her adolescence her father moved the family to "Melrose Plantation," about fifteen miles south of Natchitoches, Louisiana, in the central part of the state.

Melrose Plantation had a rich history since it had been established in 1796 by a freed female slave, Marie-Therese Coin-Coin, and became one of the most successful African-American–owned plantations in the United States. After the Civil War, ownership transferred to white families, and it became a successful cotton and pecan plantation. Cammie Garrett Henry, the owner from the 1920s until her death in 1948, took over management of the plantation after the death of her husband and encouraged the development of the arts within the community. Clementine was one of the many African-American employees working on the plantation. In the late 1920s she became a servant in the Big House, which had been built by the descendants of the original black owner.

Hunter's first two children were birthed in a common-law relationship with Charlie Dupree from about 1906 until his death in 1914. Her only marriage, to Emanuel Hunter in 1924, produced five children, two of whom died at birth. Emanuel Hunter died in 1944 at Melrose Plantation.

During her employ in the house, Hunter met many painters and writers who were guests of Cammie Henry. Using discarded paints left by one of the artists, Hunter created her first works in the early 1940s on window shades, cardboard, and shoe-box tops. François Mignon, a writer and librarian living on the plantation, recognized her talents in capturing scenes of plantation life and encouraged her experimentation with paints.

With encouragement and supplies from Mignon and his friends, Hunter, over age fifty, began a career that would span almost the next half century. Her paintings captured scenes of everyday plantation life as seen through the perspective of an insider. She documented the routines of life on a large southern plantation as few others were able to accomplish as there was little access to education or the arts by these African Americans.

The subjects of her titled paintings are classifiable into four categories—plantation work, such as *Picking Cotton*, *Wash Day*, and *Gathering Pecans*; recreation, such as *Fishing*, *Saturday Night at the Honky Tonk*, and *Playing Cards*; religion, such as *Black Jesus*, *The Nativity*, and *Baptizings*; and still lifes and special themes, such as *Zinnias*, *The Masks*, and *Uncle Tom in the Garden*.

Hunter's works were repetitious in theme, but no two paintings were ever exactly alike. Many of the plantation jobs depicted in her works, such as manual cotton and pecan harvesting, disappeared after World War II, when mechanization of agriculture developed and blacks migrated from the South to the North to seek better-paying jobs in industry. Hunter claimed she was unable to paint a subject simply by looking at it; instead "it had to come to her head" before she was able to put it in a picture.

The style of Hunter's paintings was almost childlike. Having no formal art instruction, she was self-taught and painted in two dimensions without the perspective of depth. Frequently she would paint an object smaller and place it in the sky in order to show its background position. Her colors were intense and often directly out of the oil paint tubes; any mixing was done on a homemade plywood palette and stirred with her brushes.

In addition to her paintings, Hunter also produced quilts with illustrations sewn onto the fabric. She would cut pieces of fabric into designs and sew them together to produce a picture, similar in style to her paintings of plantation life. Her technique of layering the pieces, taught by her mother, has been cited as a unique example of quilting unlike the traditional method of cutting and sewing a pattern.

A significant aspect of Hunter's painting style was the evolution of her signature. Her earliest works were unsigned. From the late 1940s until the mid-1950s, a reversed *C* became the identifying mark of her work. Hunter said that the reason for using the mark was that the plantation owner, Cammie Henry, also had the initials *C. H.*, and she wanted to make sure people did not confuse her works with Miss Cammie's. Once the *C* was reversed, over the years it then moved over to touch the *H*. At the end of her career the *H* was completely inside the reversed *C*. A person knowledgeable about Hunter's painting periods can approximately date her works by the nature of the signature.

Hunter's largest and most encompassing work was a mural of plantation life completed in 1955 around the walls of the second floor of the African House, one of the original structures built by the family of Marie-Therese Coin-Coin. It depicts many of the activities of Melrose, including church scenes, cotton-picking and ginning, a wedding, a funeral, baptizing, and cooking, as well as the major structures on the plantation.

In 1955 the Delgado Museum (now the New Orleans Museum of Art) featured Hunter in its first one-person show by a black artist. This show and publicity in publications such as *Look* and *Ebony* magazines brought her national recognition. Robert Bishop, director of the Museum of American Folk Art in New York City, called Hunter "perhaps the most celebrated of all southern contemporary painters . . . [who] knows well the black life she so touchingly portrays" (Bishop, p. 171). Clementine Hunter's paintings not only artistically captured scenes of rural plantation life but also documented as cultural history a part of American life that disappeared in the mid-twentieth century. She died in Natchitoches, Louisiana.

• The most complete review of Clementine Hunter's career and paintings is James L. Wilson, *Clementine Hunter, American Folk Artist* (1988). The Louisiana Room of the Watson Library at Northwestern State University in Natchitoches has a collection of papers and letters relating to Hunter's career, including the Mildred Hart Bailey archive, which includes extensive research materials and photographic documentation. Collections of Hunter paintings are at the Riverside Museum (Baton Rouge, La.), the Museum of African-American Life and Culture (Dallas, Tex.) the New Orleans Museum of Art, and the Louisiana State Library and Museum. Citations and reviews related to the artist's career can be found in Robert Bishop, *Folk Painters of America* (1979); Jay Johnson, *American Folk Art of the Twentieth Century* (1983); Alice Rae Yelen, *Passionate Visions of the American South: Self-Taught Artists from 1940 to the Present* (1993); and Frank Maresce and Roger Ricco, *American Self-Taught, Paintings and Drawings by Outsider Artists* (1993). Hunter's quilting is discussed in John Vlach, *The Afro-American Tradition in Decorative Arts* (1978). A catalog published by the Museum of African-American Life and Culture, in conjunction with its 1994 exhibition "Clementine Hunter: American Folk Artist," features both academic essays on her works and biographical information. An obituary is in the Baton Rouge *Morning Advocate*, 2 Jan. 1988.

THOMAS N. WHITEHEAD

HUNTER, Croil (18 Feb. 1893–21 July 1970), airline executive, was born in Casselton, North Dakota, the son of John Croil Hunter and Emma Schulze. Hunter's father, of Scottish-Canadian origin, operated the Fargo Mercantile Company, a wholesale grocery firm, in Fargo, North Dakota. Hunter enrolled at Yale in 1912 but withdrew in 1914, after his father's death, to help carry on the family business. He enlisted in the army in 1917 and served as an artillery captain on the Western Front. In 1919 he returned home and served for nine years as treasurer of the enterprise his father had built. In 1923 he married Helen Floan of St. Paul, Minnesota. They had two children.

Hunter was too able and ambitious to remain permanently in Fargo. In 1928, after attracting the attention of Richard C. Lilly, a prominent St. Paul banker, Hunter was selected by Lilly to manage an installment loan subsidiary that the First Bank Stock Corporation of Minneapolis had established in New York City. Lilly headed a group of Minnesota businessmen who in 1929 had taken control of Northwest Airways, Inc., an airmail and passenger carrier that operated a route system connecting the Twin Cities with places such as Chicago, Milwaukee, Omaha, and Winnipeg. Hunter's performance in New York led Lilly to appoint him traffic manager of Northwest in 1932. Moving to Minnesota, Hunter was promoted to general manager of the line in 1933 after the U.S. Post Office Department awarded it an airmail route to Billings, Montana. Together with Northwest's chief executive officer and chief Washington lobbyist, Lewis H. Brittin, Hunter conducted an aggressive campaign of aerial surveys, airport development, and negotiations with postal officials that resulted in expansion of the company's route system to Spokane in October 1933. Soon thereafter, having won a struggle for operating rights from federal authorities in a bitter contest with United Air Lines, Northwest gained access to Seattle and Tacoma. In the process, Hunter was elevated to vice president for operations.

In 1934 Northwest entered a tumultuous period when, amid a scandal over the way in which the Hoover administration had awarded airmail contracts, commercial airlines temporarily lost the airmail routes that were their chief source of revenue. In addition, Brittin had to resign the presidency of Northwest in February 1934 because he had tried to destroy records subpoenaed by congressional investigators, an act for which he was sentenced to ten days in jail. Under a new chief executive, Minneapolis investor Shreve M. Archer, Hunter administered a shrunken system after the firm regained some of its former routes and reorganized itself in April 1934 as Northwest Airlines, Inc. Later that year the company reacquired the remainder of its previous routes from Hanford Air Lines and began a successful comeback in which Hunter gradually rebuilt its airmail and passenger service. Part of his strategy for increasing revenue involved acquiring new and better planes, including the Lockheed 10-A Electra, a swift ten-passenger ship that was designed with the help of Northwest's engineering staff, and the larger and even faster Lockheed 14-H Sky Zephyr, which seated fourteen passengers and set new speed records between the Twin Cities, Chicago, and Seattle.

Hunter became president of Northwest in 1937, marking the first time that the directors had chosen an operating official instead of an investor to head the line. In 1938 the company completed its prewar route system by winning access to Portland, Oregon. Late that year Hunter took a bold step by deciding to replace the Sky Zephyrs, which had proved accident-prone, with much larger Douglas DC-3s, which seated twenty-one passengers and promised lower unit operational costs. Despite skepticism that the firm could attract enough traffic to justify using DC-3s, Northwest enplaned 136,797 travelers in 1940, marking an elevenfold increase since 1934. In 1941 passenger revenue outstripped airmail receipts for the first time in the company's history.

Meanwhile, Hunter began the work for which he became best known: developing a "Great Circle Route" to the Far East via Alaska. Such an airway would not only be much shorter than the transpacific route pioneered by Pan American in the 1930s, but also safer because it would stay close to islands and land masses where refueling and emergency landing facilities could be maintained. However, survey flights and other preparations for prospective services from New York, Chicago, and Seattle to places such as Tokyo and Calcutta were interrupted by World War II.

Northwest's hopes of winning postwar governmental support for its Great Circle plans were strengthened by its wartime record in operating key military supply routes from the Twin Cities to Anchorage, Fairbanks, and Nome. The airline's role in ferrying warplanes and providing logistical support in flights aggregating 21 million miles made an important contribution to driving the Japanese out of the Aleutian Islands. In 1944 Hunter reached a long-standing goal when the Civil Aeronautics Board (CAB) granted Northwest a route to New York City. After the war, over strong opposition from Pan American's chief executive, Juan Trippe, Hunter won authorization to establish Great Circle routes to Tokyo, Seoul, Taipei, and Manila via Alaska. Service to most of these destinations began in July 1947.

Continuing his commitment to technological progress, Hunter enlarged and modernized Northwest's fleet. In 1949 he began to replace unpressurized Douglas DC-4s, which he had acquired four years earlier, with faster and more comfortable long-range Boeing 377 Stratocruisers. Northwest's experience in operating Great Circle routes proved valuable to the United States in the Korean conflict, during which the company's remaining DC-4s flew approximately 13 million miles for the Military Air Transport Command (MATS), carrying 40,000 fighting men and 12 million pounds of cargo. But the firm incurred financial losses in commercial international service because the Stratocruisers used too much fuel. Meanwhile, on domestic routes, Hunter erred by adopting a new twin-engine plane, the Martin 2-0-2, which proved accident-prone and had to be withdrawn from service.

Seeking a way out of these setbacks, Hunter arranged a merger with Capital Airlines in 1951, but this move collapsed when Northwest's stockholders failed to ratify the deal by the required two-thirds margin. Turning over the reins to a new chief executive officer, Harold V. Harris, Hunter became chairman of the board in January 1953. After a brief, unsuccessful stint as president, Harris resigned in 1954 and was replaced by CAB administrator Donald R. Nyrop, whom Hunter had favored all along. Under Nyrop's tight-fisted leadership, Northwest became highly profitable, and Hunter's judgment was vindicated. Using Boeing 707 and Douglas DC-8 jets, Northwest successfully operated a growing web of Great Circle routes stretching all the way from New York City to faraway places such as Tokyo and Hong Kong. In addition, it won lucrative domestic rights that Hunter had long coveted, including routes to Florida and Hawaii.

After retiring in 1965, Hunter found increased time for varied interests including duck hunting, fishing, playing bridge, and studying history, but he continued to advise Nyrop as chairman of the board emeritus. By the time Hunter died at St. Paul, his visions of a shorter and safer way to fly to the Orient had been amply fulfilled. This achievement remains his chief legacy to the American airline industry.

• For an extended history of Northwest Airlines, containing much material about Hunter, see Kenneth D. Ruble, *Flight to the Top* (1986). Also valuable for illustrative materials are Stephen E. Mills, *More than Meets the Sky* (1972), and Bill Yenne, *Northwest Orient* (1986). Obituaries are in the *St. Paul Dispatch*, 22 July 1970, and the *Minneapolis Tribune* and the *New York Times*, both 23 July 1970.

W. DAVID LEWIS

HUNTER, Dard (29 Jan. 1883–20 Feb. 1966), designer and papermaker, was born William Joseph Hunter in Steubenville, Ohio, the son of William Henry Hunter, a newspaperman and editor, and Harriet Rosemond. The family moved to Chillicothe, Ohio, when Hunter was seventeen. There his father was the editor of the *Chillicothe News-Advertiser*, of which he was also a part owner. Hunter became a staff artist, often signing his work "W. J. Hunter" but occasionally signing as "Dard"—a name of unknown origin that he soon adopted. In 1903 he went on the lecture circuit as a "chalk-artist" with the Phil Hunter Company, a magician's group headed by his brother.

At the New Glenwood Hotel in Riverside, California, Hunter became fascinated with mission architecture and furniture; in July 1904, after correspondence with Elbert Hubbard, he enrolled in the Roycroft School in East Aurora, New York. At least one of his early ceramic productions at Roycroft bears the initials "DH." After only two months Hunter was sent to New York City to study stained-glass window design; he returned to design the windows that continue to grace the Roycroft Inn. He remained at Roycroft until 1908, designing title pages, initials, and tailpieces.

In 1908 Hunter married Edith Cornell, a pianist who was also a Roycroft student; they had two children. Strongly attracted to German design, Hunter and his wife left for Vienna in March 1908. There he admired particularly the Steinhof Church of St. Leopold, designed by Otto Wagner with windows by Koloman Moser. He sought out Moser and through him established an association with the Wiener Werkstatte, run by Moser and Josef Hoffmann. Hunter designed a number of books as well as stained-glass and mosaic products, returning to Roycroft in October 1908. There he soon advanced to the post of art director.

In 1909 Hunter founded the Dard Hunter School of Handicraft, a correspondence school that he operated with the assistance of Roycroft coppersmith Karl Kipp. In 1910, however, Hunter parted company with Roycroft. While he was there he had designed over 200 books.

By September 1910 Hunter was back in Vienna, where he earned a diploma from the Viennese Royal-Imperial Graphic and Experimental Institute in February 1911. He immediately departed for London and found employment as a designer with the Norfolk Studio. However, before long he became so involved in book collecting, printing, and papermaking that he abandoned his designing career to begin a career in papermaking and the printing of fine books. In 1911 he purchased an orchard in Marlborough-on-Hudson, New York, and, between farm chores, set up his own printing establishment—complete with a papermaking mill and a type foundry. One of his neighbors was the type designer Frederick Goudy.

In 1915 Hunter printed his first book, *The Etching of Figures* by W. A. Bradley, using his own typeface and handmade paper. The book was published under the auspices of the Chicago Society of Etchers; in 1916 he published a second book for the same group. In 1919, however, he sold the Marlborough mill and returned to Chillicothe. He used the experience gained at Marlborough to enter another venture in 1928 in commercial papermaking and associated publishing concerns in Lime Rock, Connecticut. That business went into receivership in 1931, and the assets were sold at auction in 1933.

His freedom from the cares of entrepreneurship left Hunter free to travel and to study the art of papermaking as it is practiced all over the world. He published his findings in magnificent volumes, using exotic papers, at intervals of every year or two for the rest of his long life. In 1938, after much consideration, he established the Dard Hunter Paper Museum at the Massachusetts Institute of Technology. The museum was moved in 1954 to Appleton, Wisconsin, and again, in 1990—long after his death—to the Georgia Institute of Technology in Atlanta, where it exists today as the American Museum of Papermaking. Hunter died in Chillicothe.

• Hunter's *My Life with Paper: An Autobiography* (1958) provides details of his life and work. He published prolifically, sharing his insights on the history of papermaking in works including *Hand Made Paper and Its Water Marks* (1916); *Old Papermaking* (1923); *Primitive Papermaking: An Account of a Mexican Sojourn and a Voyage to the Pacific Islands . . .* (1927); *Papermaking through Eighteen Centuries* (1930); *Old Papermaking in China and Japan* (1932); and *The Story of Early Printing* (1941). Other Hunter titles include *A Papermaking Pilgrimage to Japan, Korea and China* (1936), *Chinese Ceremonial Paper: A Monograph* (1937); *Papermaking by Hand in India* (1939); *Romance of Watermarks* (1939); and *Papermaking: The History and Technique* (1943). His later works include *Papermaking by Hand in America* (1950) and *Papermaking in Pioneer America* (1952). Information about Hunter's contributions can be found in Dard Hunter II, *The Life Work of Dard Hunter* (2 vols., 1981–1983), and in Douglas B. Stone and Hardev S. Dugal, *The Dard Hunter Collection at the Institute of Paper Chemistry* (1984). Cathleen Baker, "Dard Hunter—Roycroft Artist," *Arts and Crafts Quarterly* 6, no. 1 (1993): 6–11, is a good article on his work. Obituaries are in the *New York Times*, 22 Feb. 1966, the *New York Herald Tribune*, 22 Feb. 1966, and the *Antiquarian Bookman*, 7 Mar. 1966.

ALFRED H. MARKS

HUNTER, David (21 July 1802–2 Feb. 1886), soldier and businessman, was born in Washington, D.C., the son of Andrew Hunter, a minister, and Mary Stockton. His maternal grandfather was Richard Stockton, a signer of the Declaration of Independence. David entered the U.S. Military Academy at West Point in 1818 and graduated with the class of 1822. He served on the American frontier and was stationed at Fort Dearborn, now the city of Chicago, from 1828 until 1831. He married Maria Indiana Kinzie, the daughter of Chicago's first permanent white resident, John Kinzie. Hunter resigned his army commission in 1836 and pursued business interests, engaging in land speculation in and around Chicago. His efforts in civilian life were not sufficiently rewarding, so he applied for a restoration of his army commission. His application was accepted, and in 1842 he was made a paymaster with the rank of major. For the next eighteen years he served at various frontier posts.

In 1860 Hunter furthered his career through deft manipulation of the newly elected president Abraham Lincoln. From Fort Leavenworth, Kansas, Hunter began a correspondence with Lincoln. His ploy resulted in an invitation from the president to travel aboard the inaugural train from Illinois to the nation's capital. Soon after the Civil War began, Hunter wrangled command of a division even though he was only a colonel in the regular army, having been promoted in May 1861. He participated in the 1861 First Bull Run (First Manassas) campaign, but he was wounded early in the battle and was unable to provide the leadership required to properly orient his forces and press the attack. Nonetheless, Lincoln elevated Hunter to major general of volunteers. Later that year Lincoln persuaded him to serve under General John C. Frémont in a perilous situation in the Mississippi River basin, despite the fact that Hunter outranked the famous explorer.

Hunter's abilities as a general did not improve, nor did he learn from the experience of others. Lincoln relieved Frémont of command in part because of Frémont's attempt to liberate the slaves within his command's span of control. When Hunter was dispatched in March 1862 to the Department of the South, a position of relative obscurity on Union-held islands along the South Carolina coast, he repeated Frémont's political gaffe. On 9 May 1862 he decreed that all slaves inside his lines were "free for ever." Lincoln and Secretary of War Edwin Stanton reacted immediately, revoking Hunter's order. Forced to make his policy absolutely clear, Lincoln stated, "No commanding general shall do such a thing, upon my responsibility, without consulting me." Despite Hunter's faulty assumption of authority, Lincoln still regarded the general as a friend.

Hunter's exploits included some controversial burnings and acts of pillage, which provoked retribution. Commanding forces in the Shenandoah Valley in the spring and summer of 1864, he made a foray into territory within Virginia that had been previously dominated by Confederate defenders. Reaching Lexington, he torched the buildings at the Virginia Military Institute and turned his soldiers loose in the town, where they looted private homes and the library at Washington College. Next, he ordered the burning of the residence of John Letcher, a former Virginia governor. On hearing of this outrage, Confederate general Robert E. Lee summoned one of his subordinates, General Jubal Early, for a conference that resulted in the latter's famous raid deep into Union-held territory in June 1864.

When Early began his attack, Hunter and his forces were low on ammunition, and Hunter chose to retreat in order to avoid being swept away by the Confederates. As a result, Hunter was berated by officials in Washington, who pointed to his superior numbers and demanded a better performance in stopping the southerners. General Ulysses S. Grant, concerned that Hunter's mediocre leadership would result in a Federal withdrawal under the steady battering of Lee's forces before Richmond was captured, quickly proceeded to Hunter's headquarters and asked him to step aside in favor of a junior officer. Hunter, who evidently welcomed a chance to turn over a tough combat situation to someone else, agreed. General Philip Sheridan took command of the Union forces in the Shenandoah Valley, and Federal fortunes took a turn for the better.

Following the assassination of President Lincoln in 1865, Hunter accompanied Lincoln's body to Illinois. Hunter was then selected as the head of the military court that tried those arrested in connection with the assassination. He was likely chosen because of his previous service as presiding officer on a court-martial that convicted a fellow officer, a performance that had not escaped the attention of Judge Advocate General Joseph Holt. Even for a military court of the mid-nineteenth century, the trial of the "conspirators" in May and June 1865 was noted for its lack of attention to any of the defendants' rights. All were convicted, and half were hanged. Hunter retired as a colonel of cavalry in 1866. He died in Washington, D.C.

Hunter was one of a handful of ineffective Union commanders who were professionally trained but owed their high ranks to political, not military, connections. His appointments were owed merely to his self-promotion with a newly elected president and point to a conclusion that Lincoln's many problems with Federal officers in the eastern theater were, on occasion, a result of unwise appointments.

• Hunter's battle record is detailed in *The War of the Rebellion: A Compilation of the Official Records of the Union and Confederate Armies* (128 vols., 1880–1901) and in U.S. Congress, *Report of the Joint Committee on the Conduct of the War*, 3 vols., 38th Cong., 2d sess., 1863. The highlights of Hunter's entire military career are in George W. Cullum, *Biographical Register of the Officers and Graduates of the U.S. Military Academy*, 3d ed., vol. 1 (1891). Hunter's judgeship has interested many Lincoln assassination conspiracy theorists, especially Vaughan Shelton, *Mask for Treason: The Lincoln Murder Trial* (1965).

ROD PASCHALL

HUNTER, Frank O'Driscoll (8 Dec. 1894–25 June 1982), U.S. Army officer, was born in Savannah, Georgia, the son of John Heard Hunter (occupation unknown) and Fanny O'Driscoll. Hunter was given the nickname "Monk" as an infant and kept the moniker because of his mischievous boyhood behavior. He was educated at the Hotchkiss School, Lakeville, Connecticut (1909–1913), and at Lausanne, Switzerland. He then became a broker on Wall Street, a job that reportedly gave him little satisfaction. In May 1917, shortly after the United States entered World War I, Hunter enlisted in the Signal Corps, Aviation Section.

Hunter received his primary flight instruction at Chanute Field, Rantoul, Illinois. The training he received was basic indeed: if the trainee pilot could take off and clear the fence six times running, he qualified; if not, Hunter observed, "They picked up the pieces." He received his commission as first lieutenant on 22 September 1917 and was ordered to France for duty. His first assignment was to the Third Aviation Instruction Center, where he received a course in advanced flight training. Hunter was then assigned to the 103d Pursuit Squadron of the American Expeditionary Forces (AEF), where he was shortly designated deputy flight commander. He served seven months at the front as a pursuit pilot.

Hunter distinguished himself as an ace during the war, being officially credited with the destruction of eight enemy aircraft. He was wounded only once and then managed to return his airplane safely to his home field. In recognition of his "extraordinary heroism in action" over the front, Hunter was awarded the Distinguished Service Cross with four Oak Leaves and the French croix de guerre with palms (1918).

Shortly after his return to the United States, Hunter was honorably discharged from the service as first lieutenant, Aviation Section, Officers' Reserve Corps. The excitement of an aviator's life proved irresistible, however, and in November 1920 he accepted a commission as first lieutenant in the Air Corps, regular army.

Hunter's first assignment as a permanent commissioned officer was to the Observation School at Post Field, Fort Sill, Oklahoma. Upon his graduation on 15 September 1921, he was transferred to the First Pursuit Group, Ellington Field, Texas. Shortly thereafter, he was sent to undertake the one-year course at the Air Corps Tactical School, Langley Field, Virginia, from which he received his graduation certificate on 15 June 1923. He was then posted to duty at Selfridge Field, Mount Clemens, Michigan.

During the latter part of 1923, Hunter was involved in the first of a number of rather serious flying accidents. While returning to Selfridge Field from Mitchell Field, New York, he encountered bad weather, dense fog, and finally engine failure. During a forced landing, the plane entered a spin and crashed. Hunter was hospitalized for a number of months with severe back injuries. Undeterred, he returned to active flight duty at Selfridge Field.

From 1926 to 1930 Hunter served in the Training and Operations Division, Office of the Chief of the Air Corps, Washington, D.C. In December 1930 he was transferred to Rockwell Field, Coronado, California, where he assumed command of the Ninety-fifth Pursuit Squadron. On 29 October 1931 he assumed command of the Seventeenth Pursuit Group at March Field, Riverside, California.

Hunter also held a "third degree" membership in the mythical organization referred to as the Caterpillar Club—that group of flyers who were forced to parachute out of their aircraft ("hit the silk") to save their lives. Though he managed to escape with little more than a singed mustache in his first two jumps, Hunter suffered severe injury when forced to bail out a third time at an altitude of only 150 feet. Striking the ground before the parachute could fully deploy, he sustained injuries so severe that he remained in the hospital for more than nine months. He returned to active duty on 23 September 1933.

Between May and October 1940 Hunter was posted as military observer and assistant air attaché to the American Embassy, Paris, and the American Embassy, London. He arrived in London in time for the Blitz, which he claimed gave him the opportunity to learn from the Luftwaffe's mistakes.

From May 1942 to August 1943 Hunter served as commanding general of the fighter wing of the Eighth U.S. Army Air Force, European theater of operations. During this period he gained recognition for planning and executing the movement of aircraft to Africa, for which he was awarded the Legion of Merit. He went on to direct the deployment of the famous P-47 Thunderbolt, the fighter that primarily served as escorts for the Fortresses and Liberators on their bombing missions from England. Hunter made a name for himself by utilizing the Eighth Air Force Fighter Command as an offensive weapon against Adolf Hitler's forces in northern France. His success did much to expand the role of fighter aircraft beyond that of an escort.

Hunter took over as commanding general of the First Air Force in September 1943 and was promoted to the rank of major general in November 1943. He remained in command of the First Air Force until November 1945 and retired as a major general in March 1946.

Hunter's striking appearance and predilection for sharp clothes and cars added to his dashing reputation. By his own admission, he enjoyed food, wine, and women. He never married. Hunter Airfield in Savannah, Georgia, was named after him and bears the distinction of being the only base to be named after someone still living. He died in his hometown of Savannah, Georgia. Hunter was also decorated with the Distinguished Service Medal, Silver Star, Distinguished Flying Cross, Purple Heart, and Commander of the British Empire.

• The best source of information on Hunter is his service record, now with the Air Force, which can be accessed through the National Personnel Records Center, St. Louis, Mo. A contemporary account of Hunter's role as the commanding general of the Eighth U.S. Army Air Force in Great Britain during the Second World War is given by Porter T. Wood, "Boss of the Big Umbrella," *This Week*, 15 Aug. 1943, pp. 6–7. Hunter is also mentioned in DeWitt S. Copp, *A Few Great Captains* (1980) and *Forged in Fire: Strategy and Decisions in the Air War over Europe, 1940–1945* (1982). An obituary is in the *New York Times*, 27 June 1982.

CHRISTINE A. WHITE

HUNTER, Glenn (26 Sept. 189?–30 Dec. 1945), actor, was born in Highland Mills, New York, the son of Isaiah Hunter, an accountant, and Sarah Glenn. Hunter was secretive about the exact year of his birth, and biographical sources give various dates ranging from 1893 to 1897. He wanted to be an actor from childhood. After finishing his education at the Mount Hermon School for Boys in Massachusetts and briefly taking business courses, he came to New York in 1913, seeking stage work. Soon penniless, Hunter often slept in parks and railroad stations while fruitlessly visiting theatrical offices.

Hunter's breakthrough came when a reporter published a story about his struggle. He was consequently hired by the director of the Washington Square Players. Beginning in 1915 he acted in a series of one-act plays there. He next appeared in small juvenile roles on Broadway and on the road, capitalizing on his boyish appearance. In 1918 he volunteered for war service as an ambulance driver but fell ill with influenza while still in camp and was discharged.

Hunter's first major role was that of the teenage Bobby Wheeler in the long-running *Clarence* (1919). In 1921 he appeared in *The Intimate Strangers*. That same year he also began acting in movies, usually playing a youthfully unsophisticated country boy. Hunter knew that the role of a young, movie-mad store clerk, Merton Gill, in a dramatization of the popular novel *Merton of the Movies* (1922) was one he could play perfectly. The character's earnest, naive nature and early struggles closely paralleled Hunter's own. He approached producer George Tyler, who had bought the dramatic rights, and was cast in the role. Critics and public alike praised his portrayal. A *New York World* review (14 Nov. 1922) said Hunter gave "what seems to us a practically perfect performance." The play ran three years in New York and on tour, and Hunter found himself a major star. In 1924 he played the role in the film version with equal success.

All through the play's run, Hunter continued making movies by day, taking the stage at night. He also spent money as fast as he earned it. An interviewer wrote an article describing the atmosphere in Hunter's backstage dressing room. Although Hunter had the entourage of a star, the writer noted, of the dozen people who came to speak with him at least three were there to collect on bills. In 1924 he ultimately had to declare bankruptcy.

After *Merton* closed, Hunter was offered another starring role that was ideal for his adolescent stage image: a schoolboy in love with his housemaster's wife. The play, *Young Woodley*, proved to be the pinnacle of his career. His performance was called one of "matchless and quiet beauty" (*New York World*, 3 Nov. 1925) and "a splendid portrait of a boy overwhelmed with the complexities of ordinary living" (*New York Times*, 3 Nov. 1925). According to one account, "At the end of the play, the audience . . . threatened to carry him from the theatre on their shoulders" (*New York Herald Tribune*, 3 Nov. 1925). In 1926 Hunter ended his movie career. Depending on his various birth dates, he was only in his late twenties or early thirties. He had appeared in eighteen silent films in six years, while simultaneously starring in two demanding stage plays.

Hunter's next play, *Behold This Dreamer* (1927), was unsuccessful. He began to scramble for parts, appearing as Tony Lumpkin in a revival of *She Stoops to Conquer* (1928) and attempting a role in a musical, *Spring Is Here* (1929). Only with *Waterloo Bridge* (1930), in which he played a naive young American soldier in love with a London prostitute, did he return to critical favor. The *New York Telegraph*'s reviewer wrote, "Mr. Hunter has been a problem for two seasons now, or is it three. . . . [but here gives] a flawless, magnificently paced and affecting portrait, totally at variance with the capers he has been cutting and calling acting for some months" (8 Jan. 1930). Other critics faulted his portrayal of the soldier's mature side; the *New York Herald Tribune* reviewer said "in the boyish bits, he was sometimes very good. . . . [but] less successful in the more grown up moments. . . . [although] he worked hard and the whole performance was a gallant attempt to climb out of his familiar and likable mannerisms [to] show that he could do something more" (7 Jan. 1930).

Waterloo Bridge was Hunter's last success of any kind. Personal difficulties, as newspaper reports indicate, compounded the decline of his career. In 1929 he was in trouble for signing contracts with two different producers at once, and in 1933 he was sued by a jeweler for return of a platinum and diamond cigarette case. After broken engagements to various actresses during

the 1920s, he allegedly became engaged to Mae "Babe" Eagan, a film studio musician he had met on the set of *Merton of the Movies*. Immediately after the engagement was announced, his fiancée, the leader of the Hollywood Redheads, an all-girl orchestra, sailed to Europe for an eight-week cabaret tour. Biographical sources differ on whether any marriage ever took place. As an interviewer noted in *American Magazine*, Hunter's true devotion was to his mother, on whom he lavished gifts.

In the 1930s Hunter appeared in road companies, notably with *The Petrified Forest* (1935) and in stock company productions. His last two Broadway appearances were in *Empress of Destiny* (1938) and a revival of *Journey's End* (1939), both failures. An obituary in the *New York Herald Tribune* (31 Dec. 1945) stated that during the 1930s "he went to Hollywood, where he interested himself in the Jewel Box, a small experimental theatre," but returned to New York City in 1945 to seek radio work. Hunter died there of cancer.

Hunter was slender with blue eyes and light brown hair. His husky voice had "a rather explosive manner of speech [suggesting] the boyishness of youth" (*New York Evening World*, 7 Jan. 1930). Offstage, he was reported to be shy, modest, earnest, and hardworking. His significance in theatrical history is his achievement of stardom in adolescent roles when already in his twenties. Such a paradoxical popularity is unmatched except by Mary Pickford, who went on playing spunky "little Mary" in films for years after she was a married woman. In effect, Hunter was a child star discarded by the public as he matured in appearance but failed to create an adult stage image. The irony of his artistry in youthful roles even as he aged is implied in a review of a 1932 touring revival of *Young Woodley*. The *Boston Transcript* reviewer claimed that Hunter, who was by then approaching forty, nevertheless succeeded in portraying a school youth: "Depending on inflections of his voice and awkward gestures of his limbs rather than general appearance he still contrives illusion . . . [and is] sincere and dramatically effective beyond doubt" (9 Feb. 1932).

• Materials on the life and career of Glenn Hunter are in the Billy Rose Theatre Collection at the New York Public Library for the Performing Arts, Lincoln Center. A list of his stage performances is in *Who Was Who in the Theatre, 1912–1976* (1978). For a list of his films, consult Kenneth W. Munden, ed., *American Film Institute Catalog, 1921–1930* (1971), and John Stewart, *Filmarama*, vol. 2 (1977). Three substantial interviews are Zoe Beckley, "From Park Bench to Stardom," *Theatre Magazine*, July 1926; Homer Croy, "Glenn Hunter—On and Off," *Classic*, Dec. 1923; and Mary B. Mullett, "Glenn Hunter Made His Debut in an Apple Orchard," *American Magazine*, May 1926. Portraits of Hunter in various roles are in Daniel C. Blum, *Great Stars of the American Stage* (1952). Obituaries are in the *New York Times* and *New York Herald Tribune*, both 31 Dec. 1945.

WILLIAM STEPHENSON

HUNTER, Jane Edna Harris (13 Dec. 1882–19 Jan. 1971), autobiographer and black women's rights activist, was born in Pendleton, South Carolina, the daughter of Edward Harris and Harriet Millner, sharecroppers. Following her father's death due to jaundice when she was ten years old, Jane and her three siblings were distributed briefly among the homes of various relatives. His death and the ensuing dispersal of her nuclear family were especially difficult for Jane, in part because she had customarily been "father's ally in his differences with mother" (*A Nickel*, p. 12), but also because she now had to forego formal schooling to earn her keep in Anderson, South Carolina, as a live-in nursemaid and cook. Although treated so poorly by her mistress that white and black neighbors alike protested (*A Nickel*, p. 29), she was taught to read and write by the eldest daughter.

Hunter entered Ferguson-Williams College (then Ferguson Academy) in 1896, graduating four years later. Sometime later that year or early the following spring, yielding to her mother's exhortations, Jane entered into a loveless marriage with Edward Hunter, forty years her senior. Soon after the wedding and with her husband's blessing, she moved to Charleston, South Carolina, where she received formal training in nursing from the Cannon Street Hospital and Training School for Nurses. She also took a year of advanced training in the Dixie Hospital and Training School for Nurses at Hampton Institute in Hampton, Virginia, in 1904. These years of schooling helped Hunter recognize the employment difficulties facing even highly trained young African-American women.

Upon her arrival in Cleveland, Ohio, on 10 May 1905, Hunter faced a dilemma that redirected her life. Her autobiographical account covers those first hours in the city searching for living quarters and stresses "the conditions which confront the Negro girl who, friendless and alone, looks for a decent place to live in Cleveland" (*A Nickel*, p. 67). Although Hunter had moved continually throughout the South, she had never arrived in a new location without an extended family member or a new employer to greet her. During this turbulent period, Hunter was forced to resort to menial cleaning positions while continually attempting to secure employment as a nurse. As Adrienne Lash Jones pointed out, Hunter was faced not only with the initial racial barriers aimed at black nurses by a white medical community but also by the very social structure of a city in which "[t]he YWCA residence was not open to black women" (Jones, p. 40). Despite eventually developing a clientele of wealthy white patients for whom she served as massage therapist or private duty nurse, during periods of temporary unemployment she would invariably have to seek out cleaning or laundry jobs.

Constantly aware that "[a] girl alone in a large city must needs know the dangers and pitfalls awaiting her" (*A Nickel*, p. 77), in September 1911 Hunter brought together seven of her closest friends to discuss some means to alleviate the living conditions facing single black women. Agreeing to pay a nickel each as weekly dues and electing Hunter as president, these eight women founded The Working Girls' Home Association. Despite opposition, largely from other African Americans who believed that this self-segregating organization would further hinder efforts to bring about complete racial integration in such institutions as the YWCA, Hunter's group flourished. In 1912 it changed its name to The Phillis Wheatley Association to commemorate the first known African-American poet.

The following year, after electing an interracial board of trustees, the Association leased a 23-room house. Although many detractors argued that there would be little demand for the Phillis Wheatley Home, "weeks before the formal opening, fifteen young women had already taken up residence" (*A Nickel*, p. 106). Hunter's vision for the Wheatley Home had been that it would become not merely a boarding house but an establishment dedicated to training black women in various professions; her dream had reached fruition. Hunter remained the driving force behind the Phillis Wheatley Association, first arguing against a merger with the YWCA in 1916 and then securing donations to purchase both a new 72-room Phillis Wheatley Home in 1917 and an adjacent two-story building in 1919. In 1925 Hunter passed the Ohio bar, having completed her studies at the Cleveland Law School, and promptly began soliciting funds for an even larger home, a plan she accomplished two years later with the erection of an eleven-story building.

For more than thirty years Hunter helped oversee The Phillis Wheatley Association while dedicating herself and her ability as a superb fund raiser to various peripheral black women's enterprises. Although she officially retired in 1947, she found severing her bonds from her life's work extremely difficult. In 1960 she was found mentally incompetent and was placed in a rest home in Cleveland where she remained until her death.

Her autobiography, *A Nickel and a Prayer* (1940), carefully chronicles the laborious stages leading to the creation of the Association. Although the publication received little attention, the few reviews it did garner were glowing. In her lifetime she received recognition for her efforts from various sources, but "[p]erhaps her most meaningful honor was from Tuskegee Institute, which conferred a Master of Science degree, in recognition of her achievements in the development of the social and vocational program conducted at the Phillis Wheatley Association" (Jones, p. 124).

Hunter devoted herself to the welfare of others and particularly to the assistance of single black women, first in her early pursuit of a nursing profession and then in her role in the foundation and enlargement of the Phillis Wheatley Association in Cleveland, Ohio. This organization fulfilled her dream of providing housing for single black working women and also helping them develop their autonomy by training them in various professions.

• Hunter's collected papers and those of the Phillis Wheatley Association are housed at the Western Reserve Historical Society in Cleveland, Ohio. By far the most comprehensive biography of Hunter is Adrienne Lash Jones, *Jane Edna Hun-*

ter: *A Case Study of Black Leadership, 1910–1950*, vol. 12 of *Black Women in United States History* (1990). Other sources which touch upon her life include Sylvia G. Dannett, *Profiles of Negro Womanhood* (1964); Rebecca C. Barton, *Witnesses for Freedom* (1948); and Gerda Lerner, *The Majority Finds Its Past* (1979). For two brief yet glowing reviews of *A Nickel and a Prayer*, see C. G. Woodson's article in *Journal of Negro History* 26 (Jan. 1941): 118–20; and Everett C. Hughes's review in *American Journal of Sociology* 48 (July 1942): 156.

CHRISTOPHER J. NEUMANN

HUNTER, Robert (Oct.? 1666–31 Mar. 1734), British army officer and royal governor of Virginia, New York and New Jersey, and Jamaica, was born in Edinburgh, Scotland, the son of James Hunter, an attorney, and Margaret Spalding. Lacking land or inherited wealth, Robert Hunter chose a military career. In the November 1688 Glorious Revolution, Hunter formed part of the dragoon bodyguard that escorted Princess Anne from London as she fled her father, James II. An ardent Whig, Hunter continued to serve William III in Cardross's Dragoon Regiment, Colonel John Hill's Regiment, the Royal Scots Dragoons, and Colonel Charles Ross's Irish Dragoons. In the War of the Spanish Succession (1702–1713) Hunter was aide-de-camp to commander in chief John Churchill, duke of Marlborough, a close relationship that brought Hunter into contact with the most influential men in Great Britain. Under Marlborough, Hunter rose to the rank of lieutenant colonel, saw active duty at the battles of Blenheim and Ramillies in 1704 and 1706, and was instrumental in securing the 1706 surrender of the city of Antwerp.

Hunter retired from active duty during 1706 to return to London. A close friend, George Hamilton, earl of Orkney, was awarded the governorship of Virginia. In need of a lieutenant governor, Orkney offered the post to Hunter, who accepted. Although raised as a Presbyterian, Hunter joined the Church of England sometime prior to 1707 to be eligible for the government post. While in London, Hunter married Elizabeth Orby, Lady Hay, the widow of another close friend, John Lord Hay. Lady Hay was the sole heir of her father, Thomas Orby, who had extensive landholdings in England and Jamaica. The couple had five children. Lady Hay died in 1716 in Perth Amboy, New Jersey. Hunter also furthered his friendships with such literary figures as Jonathan Swift, Richard Steele, and Joseph Addison. A talented poet and playwright, Hunter published several pieces in the *Tatler*.

In 1707 Hunter sailed for Virginia but was captured en route by French privateers. Taken to Paris, he was exchanged in 1709 for a French prisoner of equal rank. After his release Hunter applied for the vacant Jamaica governorship so he could oversee the Orby property in Jamaica. The duke of Marlborough and treasurer Sidney Godolphin, who between them controlled colonial patronage, gave the Jamaica governorship to another person. Hunter, with the duke of Marlborough's approval, received the highly profitable joint governorship of New York and New Jersey. Prior to sailing,

Hunter developed a plan to employ some of the thousands of displaced Palatine refugees who found their way to England after being forced out of their homeland by the French army. His suggestion, eagerly accepted by the Whig ministry, was to transport some three thousand Palatines to New York to establish a naval stores project there. The Whig ministry promised financial support.

Hunter sailed for New York in the spring of 1710 with 2,814 refugees. He arrived at his new post on 13 June 1710. In England the next day, the Whig ministry fell and the Tories came to power. The Tory dominance left Hunter without financial support for the Palatine project. Before deciding to end the project in 1712, Hunter, who used his own credit to purchase land, supplies, and food, incurred a personal debt on the Crown's behalf of £21,000. Despite Hunter's continual pleas to the Tory ministry, the money was never repaid.

The Tory ministry was also indifferent to Hunter's problems with provincial politicians. In New York, Hunter's opposition was centered in the assembly, which was intent on increasing its power over money, the province's London agent, and the courts at the expense of the royal prerogative that Hunter represented. Hunter, a committed Whig in England, believed in a limited monarchy and favored the rise of parliamentary authority. Like most royal officials, Hunter abandoned his Whig principles in the colonies, where he represented the royal prerogative. When he refused to concede the assembly's demands, the assembly retaliated by not voting him a salary or raising money for government expenses. To contain the assembly's power, Hunter suggested to the ministry that the British Parliament take direct control of the colonies. His suggestion, one that would be implemented after 1763, was ignored.

Hunter, without backing from the Tory government, worked out his own local solution for his problems with the assembly in 1715. The assembly gave Hunter long-term support for government but in return, Hunter conceded the assembly's demand to retain control of the disbursement of funds. To ensure that the assembly continued to do his bidding, Hunter needed to acquire voter support to place his candidates in that body. He did so through his competence, forcefulness, and a winning personality. He was further assisted in his quest for voter support by writing a satirical play, *Androboros* (1715?), the first play printed in America. In the play Hunter made laughing stocks of his Tory enemies. An amused public read the play and voted for Hunter's assembly candidates in the 1716 election. Hunter achieved a strong proadministration majority in the assembly. From 1716 to the time he left the colony, the assembly was an obedient tool in Hunter's hands. Hunter was also helped by the 1714 accession to the throne of George I and the reestablishment of a Whig ministry in England.

In New Jersey, unlike New York, Hunter met opposition from the council. His solution was to discharge troublesome councilors and appoint new men who were loyal to him. The displaced councilors immediately ran for and achieved seats in the assembly and then tried to halt legislative proceedings by not attending sessions. Hunter solved that problem by hounding dissident leaders out of the province. He then called new assembly elections to achieve a proadministration majority in that body as he had in New York.

Hunter, probably the most effective royal governor to serve in New York and New Jersey, returned to England in 1719 for reasons of health and to look after his deceased wife's estate. In 1720 he exchanged posts with William Burnet (1688–1729), comptroller of customs. In his new post Hunter worked closely with the Whig Robert Walpole, first lord of the treasury from 1722 to 1742. In 1727 Hunter's connections with Walpole, who now controlled patronage, brought him the long-desired post of governor of Jamaica.

Hunter experienced difficulty in governing Jamaica both because of his own advanced age and because Jamaica's absentee landowners gave Hunter a small pool from which to draw allies. Hunter was also hampered because the nature of colonial administration had changed in the seven years since he left his New York–New Jersey post. There was little interference from the home government in colonial affairs as long as trade continued to prosper and there were no overt problems. Hence Hunter had inadequate support from the Walpole ministry.

As in New York, Hunter faced defiance from the politically sophisticated Jamaica assembly, which tried to gain control of the militia and the sole right to frame money bills. Despite this opposition, Hunter was able in 1728 to wrest from the assembly a permanent revenue bill, making him the only eighteenth-century British royal governor to achieve such a victory. Still active in both military and civil affairs, the governor died in St. Iago de la Vega and was buried there.

Robert Hunter, a man of many talents, started life with little wealth. He parlayed his innate ability and his personal connections into successful and prosperous careers as soldier and statesman. Few royal governors were as respected or highly regarded as was Robert Hunter. As a colonial administrator, he realized that much of the opposition he faced was directed not so much at him as at the imperial government he represented. He achieved successful governorships by a judicious blend of conciliation, intimidation, and compromise. Hunter warned the ministry of the possible dire consequences of Britain's immature and inadequate colonial policy. He predicted that if administrative changes were not made in good time the provinces, when mature, would reject British rule. It was during Hunter's New World administrations that the forces that would effect the break between Great Britain and its colonies were put into motion.

• Personal and official correspondence and addresses to and from Robert Hunter are in London's British Library in the Blenheim Papers and Additional MSS; Privy Council Register, Admiralty Papers, Colonial Office, and Probate Office papers in the Public Record Office, London; Stair Muniments, Public Record Office, Edinburgh; United States Letters, Rutgers University Library, New Brunswick; Colonial Documents, New York State Library, Albany; John Jay Papers, Rutherfurd Collection, Hunter Miscellaneous MSS, New-York Historical Society, New York City; Logan Letterbook, Parchment Logan Letterbook, and Simon Gratz Autograph Collection, Historical Society of Pennsylvania, Philadelphia; and Livingston Family Papers, 1664–1780, Franklin Delano Roosevelt Library, Hyde Park, N.Y.

Published correspondence is in E. B. O'Callaghan, ed., *Documents Relative to the Colonial History of New York* (15 vols., 1856–1887); O'Callaghan, ed., *Documentary History of the State of New York* (4 vols., 1849–1851); Charles Z. Lincoln, ed., *Messages from the Governors, 1683–1776* (1909); *Calendar of State Papers Colonial Series, America and West Indies* (1916); Harold Williams, ed., *Correspondence of Jonathan Swift* (5 vols., 1963); William Adee Whitehead, ed., *Documents Relating to the Colonial History of the State of New Jersey* (10 vols., 1880); and *Journal of the Assembly of Jamaica* (1745). For correspondence concerning Hunter see *The Letters and Despatches of John Churchill, First Duke of Marlborough, 1702–1712* (6 vols., 1945); *The Letters of Joseph Addison*, ed. Walter Graham (1941).

For an eighteenth-century account of Robert Hunter's New York administration see William Smith, Jr., *The History of the Province of New York*, ed. Michael Kammen (2 vols., 1972). For a modern biography see Mary Lou Lustig, *Robert Hunter (1666–1734), New York's Augustan Statesman* (1983). On Hunter's struggles with the New York Anglican church see Alison Gilbert Olson, "Governor Robert Hunter and the Anglican Church in New York," in *Statesmen, Scholars and Merchants*, ed. Anne Whiteman et al. (1973). For Hunter's satirical view of his Tory enemies see his *Androboros, A Biographical Farce in Three Acts*, ed. Lawrence H. Leder, *Bulletin of the New York Public Library* 68 (1964): 153–90.

MARY LOU LUSTIG

HUNTER, Robert (10 Apr. 1874–15 May 1942), social worker and reformer, was born Wiles Robert Hunter in Terre Haute, Indiana, the son of William Robert Hunter, a carriage manufacturer, and Caroline Fouts. He graduated from Indiana University with a bachelor of arts degree in 1896.

Motivated by religious convictions about the responsibility of the well-to-do to help the poor, and having witnessed the sufferings of the unemployed and their families in the industrial cities of the Midwest during his adolescence, Hunter took up social work as a profession. His first position was as organizing secretary of the Chicago Board of Charities, a post he held from 1896 until 1902. His social conscience was strengthened during this period by his exposure to the conditions under which the city's needy residents lived and worked. His work brought him in contact with many kindred spirits, particularly from 1899 to 1902 when he lived in America's original settlement house, Hull-House. His thinking and subsequent career also were influenced by his 1899 visit to England's Toynbee Hall (which had inspired the development of similar urban settlement houses in the United States). There British social workers and reformers stimulated his interest in European socialist thought.

In 1902 Hunter moved to New York City to assume a leadership position at University Settlement House. This move introduced him to the philanthropic and social-reform elite of the city. In 1903 he married Caroline Margaretha Phelps Stokes, a member of a family of wealthy reform-minded civic leaders. They had four children. After his marriage Hunter gave up his formal employment and devoted himself to social reform. During 1902–1903 he had served as chairman of the Child Labor Committee that was instrumental in bringing about the passage of progressive child-labor legislation in New York state.

Toward the end of his stay in Chicago, Hunter had directed a study of slum housing that led to his first significant publication, *Tenement Conditions in Chicago* (1901). The attention generated by this work encouraged him to undertake the more comprehensive study that resulted in his most important book, *Poverty*, published in 1904. This ground-breaking work made Hunter well known and highly respected in social-reform circles.

Hunter used census data and other empirical studies to provide estimates of poverty and its correlates across the nation. His methods were rigorous by the standards of the day and, in many ways, foreshadowed later approaches to the study of poverty. He demonstrated that poverty was often a consequence of societal factors rather than personal inadequacy. While acknowledging that some people's poverty was their own doing, Hunter concluded that "the mass of the poor . . . are bred of miserable and unjust social conditions, which punish the good and the pure, the faithful and industrious, the slothful and vicious, all alike" (*Poverty*, p. 63). It was clear to him that the majority of the poor are "brought into misery by the action of social and economic forces . . . [which] is a preventable thing" (*Poverty*, pp. 63–64). This represented a radical departure from prevailing attitudes. Hunter not only compiled and reported hard data on unemployment, low wages, unsafe factories, industrial injuries, and squalid housing but, as a result of his experience in the Charity Organization and Settlement House movements in Chicago and New York, he was able to humanize the cold statistics. Reflecting his increasing attraction to socialism, Hunter decried the way wealth was distributed in the United States, pointing out that the data "indicate an inequality of wealth distribution which should have before now received exhaustive investigation by our official statisticians" (*Poverty*, p. 46).

After embracing socialism in 1905, Hunter rapidly assumed leadership in important socialist organizations, including the executive board of the Intercollegiate Socialist Society (1905) and the National Executive Committee of the Socialist Party (1909–1912). He was a delegate to the socialist international conventions held in Stuttgart, Germany, in 1907 and in Copenhagen, Denmark, in 1910. He ran unsuccessfully for the New York State Assembly (1908) and for governor of Connecticut (1910) as a Socialist. His contacts with leading European socialists led him to write *Socialists at Work* (1908), which enthusiastically described the development worldwide of the socialist movement. Wealthy socialists such as Hunter and his "millionaire socialist" brother-in-law, J. G. Phelps Stokes, believed that concentration of America's wealth and power in the hands of about one hundred persons placed everyone else, themselves included, among the working class. This, they believed, justified their membership in and leadership of the Socialist party.

The center/right wing of the Socialist party to which Hunter belonged was primarily intent on out-reforming the liberal wing of the Democratic party. In *Socialists at Work* he complained that planks of the Socialist platform were constantly being taken up by the progressive wings of the Democratic and Republican parties. In the presidential campaign of 1912 he accused Theodore Roosevelt and the Progressive party of stealing most of the Socialists' program.

Hunter became embroiled in the struggle between the left (or Radical) and centrist/right (or Constructive) wings of the Socialist party during 1909–1912 and subsequently became increasingly exhausted and disenchanted by these struggles. A strong believer in political action to achieve social and economic reform but a strenuous opponent of direct action such as general strikes, violent confrontations, and terrorism, he gave up his membership in the Socialist party in 1914, partly because of his disappointment that European socialists had not more vigorously resisted the start of World War I. He dedicated *Violence and the Labor Movement* (1914) to Eugene Debs. The book argued that the adoption of violence by organizations of workers was usually misguided and counterproductive. In *Labor in Politics* (1915), he described what he thought could be accomplished by organized labor working through the political process in democratic societies.

Exhaustion and failing health prompted Hunter's move to California in 1917. He lectured in English and economics at the University of California at Berkeley from 1918 to 1922. Although now less active in organized social reform efforts, he continued to fret about social, economic, and political injustices and, based on his lifelong religious beliefs, wrote *Why We Fail as Christians* (1919). "How can Christians," he asked, "in a society of their own making, observe without pain and protest, poverty, slums, child labor, low wages, long hours and all the other known evils of our industrial life?" (p. 149).

Toward the end of his life Hunter developed the theory that revolution is not a consequence of economic and political oppression but rather is a result of a combination of factors, the most important of which is the instability that usually follows wars. This theory was expounded in *Revolution: Why, How, and When?* (1940) in which Hunter rejected Marxism and argued, despite the Great Depression, that social justice and harmony are achievable in a democratic free-enterprise system. He died in Montecito, near Santa Barbara, California.

Hunter's opposition to the more radical elements of the labor movement, his withdrawal from social and political activism, and the relative conservatism of his later writings (he was a severe critic of Franklin Roosevelt and several New Deal programs) have all contributed to his diminished reputation as a social thinker and reformer. However, he was an important actor in and a substantial contributor to the social-reform movement of the Progressive Era. He was the friend and ally of key figures of that period (Jane Addams, Florence Kelley, Lillian Wald, Edward Devine, Eugene Debs, Norman Thomas) and many of the reforms (child-labor laws, minimum wages, occupational health and safety, sanitary housing, workers' compensation, widows' pensions, unemployment insurance) that he advocated later became the law of the land. He was a competent scholar and a gifted writer. *Poverty* made a substantial impact in its day and represents an important historical landmark in studies of the nature, causes, and cures of poverty.

• Because no known collection of Hunter's papers exists, one must rely almost entirely on his books to assess the development of his thought over a forty-year period. The absence of a published major biographical work also limits the number of details available on Hunter's career and personal life. His role in the campaign for child-labor legislation is documented in Jeremy Felt, *Hostages of Fortune: Child Labor Reform in New York State* (1965); some of his early activities in the socialist movement are included in Ira Kipnis, *The American Socialist Movement, 1897–1912* (1952), and David A. Shannon, *The Socialist Party of America: A History* (1955). *Poverty*, with the subtitle *Social Conscience in the Progressive Era*, was reissued in 1965 in a paperback series on American history and thought. In his introduction to that edition, the editor, Peter d'A. Jones, summarizes the important milestones in Hunter's life and assesses the significance of *Poverty* and other of his writings. The *New York Times* has an obituary, 17 May 1942, and an editorial, 19 May 1942.

EDWARD ALLAN BRAWLEY

HUNTER, Thomas (19 Oct. 1831–14 Oct. 1915), educator, was born in Ardglass, Ireland, the son of John Hunter and Mary Ewart Norris. After an early education in village schools, he attended the Dundalk Institute and the Santry Science School. These institutions, both Anglican boarding schools, had a profound impact on Hunter and his later views. He considered life at the Dundalk school cruel, even in a day and time when corporal punishment was an unchallenged fact of life in secondary schools. The Santry School, which disallowed excessive use of physical punishment, proved more amenable to Hunter. In May 1849 he left school and assumed the duties of parish clerk and teacher at the Callan School. While at Callan he published political writings, advocating Irish independence from Great Britain and criticizing the Anglican church. Hunter inflamed local government officials, and he left Callan in December 1849.

Hunter sailed for New York on 3 February 1850 and arrived in mid-March at Castle Garden in Manhattan, utterly alone and possessing few physical resources. Several days later he met, by chance, attorney Mortimer De Mott, who introduced Hunter to Dr. Edward L. Beadle, a school trustee of the Fifteenth Ward of New York City. Beadle offered a three-month trial as a drawing instructor at the Thirteenth Street School (now Public School Number 35).

Hunter made good use of his opportunity. A solid classroom instructor, he obtained his teacher's license during the trial period and was appointed the following winter as a regular teacher. He spent the next four years teaching regular classes, all the while continuing his drawing instruction at no charge. When Washington Smith assumed the duties of school principal, he made Hunter his assistant. In 1854 Hunter married Annie McBride, with whom he had four children. Upon Smith's death three years later, Hunter became principal (1857). Under Hunter's leadership the school gained a reputation for solid scholarship and effective discipline.

Hunter gave careful study to the entire school system of New York City as it then existed and soon conceived of an evening high school, which would allow students with full-time day jobs to further their education. He began offering special classes, and in 1866 he founded the first night school in the city. The school opened its doors in 1868 and was so successful that within two weeks of its opening the board of education doubled the staff of assistant teachers. While still principal of the Thirteenth Street School, Hunter became a tireless advocate of the educational reforms that were sweeping the post–Civil War United States, including improved teacher education, greater opportunities for working men to obtain an education, and, most significantly, educational opportunities for women.

Hunter worked closely with other progressive-minded educational leaders, such as Richard Ludlow Larremore, president of the New York Department of Public Instruction (DPI), and board members Isaac Bell and William Wood, and the DPI to found the Female Normal and High School on 17 November 1869. Named as the school's first president, Hunter undertook a fact-finding inspection trip of normal schools in the New England and Mid-Atlantic regions.

The Female Normal school opened its doors on 14 February 1870 in a rented portion of a business establishment at Fourth Street and Broadway. Beginning with four instructors and an enrollment of 1,000, the school, renamed the Normal College of the City of New York on 26 April 1870, grew rapidly and in 1872 moved to a permanent location at Sixty-eighth Street and Park Avenue. The new site included a building designed by Hunter. The college operated a model primary school and in 1871 added the first free kindergarten in the United States. The term of instruction gradually grew to four years, and eventually the curriculum was divided, with some students electing teacher training programs and others a standard academic program. The Normal College was granted full collegiate status in 1902.

Hunter, in addition to serving as president, was also professor of intellectual philosophy and professor of the theory and practice of teaching. He edited (with others) *Home Culture, A Self-Instruction and Aid to Social Hours at Home* (1884), and he wrote *A Narrative History of the United States for the Use of Schools* (1896). His administration witnessed the beginning of such outside student activities as literary societies, a student newspaper (*Echo*), and athletic teams, including basketball, bowling, and tennis.

Hunter resigned as president of the college effective 1 September 1906 and received various honors for his efforts. In 1897 the graduates of Thirteenth Street School had founded the Thomas Hunter Association, which held an annual banquet in recognition of his untiring efforts. Perhaps the greatest honor was conferred on 4 April 1914, when the New York City Board of Education changed the name of Normal College to Hunter College of the City of New York. Hunter lived a quiet life as president emeritus until his death at his home in New York City just five days before his eighty-fourth birthday.

Hunter arrived in the United States as a nearly penniless young man and, in a lifetime of service to his adopted city, grew rich in his personal if not financial rewards. Hunter College, as part of the City University of New York system, stands as his greatest legacy.

• Hunter's papers are at the Hunter College Archives, New York, N.Y. His autobiography, edited by his daughters Anna M. Hunter and Jenny Hunter, was published posthumously in 1931. The best source for information on his life and career is Samuel White Patterson, *Hunter College: Eighty-five Years of Service* (1955). A contemporary article on the "New York Normal College" is in *Harper's Weekly*, 25 July 1874, pp. 617–18. His obituary is in the *New York Times*, 15 Oct. 1915.

EDWARD L. LACH, JR.

HUNTER, Walter Samuel (22 Mar. 1889–3 Aug. 1954), psychologist, was born in Decatur, Illinois, the second son of George Hunter, a real estate salesman, and Ida Weakley. In 1901, following his wife's death, George Hunter became a farmer near Forth Worth, Texas, where Walter Hunter continued his schooling and worked on the farm.

Hunter decided to be a psychologist when he was only seventeen as a consequence of his interest in evolutionary theory and of reading William James's *Psychology, Briefer Course* and one of Noah Knowles Davis's psychological texts. He enrolled as an undergraduate at the University of Texas in 1909, graduating with an A.B. in 1910. His focus on comparative psychology via Margaret Floy Washburn's *The Animal Mind* resulted in his first publication, "Some Labyrinth Habits of the Domestic Pigeon" (*Journal of Animal Behavior* 1 [1911]: 278–304). His graduate research at the University of Chicago (1910–1912), under the supervision of the functionalist Harvey A. Carr) was on the delayed reaction, making him the first experimenter to collect objective data about mental events. Hunter came to the conclusion that raccoons, monkeys, and children could all respond adequately to what were apparently mental representations. He inferred that all the species that he had studied shared the same type of intellectual capacity (all could form symbolic representations of the world).

Immediately following the awarding of his doctorate in 1912, Hunter became an instructor at the University of Texas, starting an active research program the following year. Using rats, he worked on the relationships between visual movement and the aftereffects of retinal streaming; he also worked on audition and continued his work on the delayed reaction. He joined the editorial board of the *Journal of Animal Behavior* in 1914 and had editorial responsibilities at the *Psychological Bulletin* from 1916 onward. In 1916 he accepted a post as a full professor at the University of Kansas. He married Katherine Pratt in 1913. They had one child before Katherine died in 1915. In 1917 he married Alda Grace Barber; they also had one child. Hunter was a member of the U.S. Army mental testing program for sixteen months during 1917 and 1918.

At Kansas, Hunter concentrated on studying habit formation in rats. From his work on the temporal maze (which he invented) and on double alternation problems, he concluded that rats could not retain complex temporal sequences, so that one had to assume that their behavior was guided almost exclusively by external cues. Those findings led him to reinterpret his own conclusions about the delayed reaction and to espouse behaviorism. He claimed that internal representations were always representations of some specific stimulus event and that they had a close functional relationship to the situation in which the stimulus occurred. He treated symbols (words were the most important examples) as derivatives of or preparations for overt actions. Consciousness, including the human capacity to describe its contents, thereby became a set of dispositions controlling behavior.

In 1925 Hunter was appointed as the first G. Stanley Hall Professor of Genetic Psychology at Clark University. He also edited the *Psychological Index* from 1925 until it stopped publishing in 1935 and played a crucial role in creating *Psychological Abstracts*, which he edited from 1926 to 1946.

During his years at Clark, Hunter's most significant contributions to psychology were his editorial work and his amplification of a course in learning he had started at Kansas in 1918. He had created the psychological subject of learning, initially using the educational psychologist Edward Lee Thorndike's *Educational Psychology* and the German associationist psychologist E. Meumann's *The Psychology of Learning* as texts. Like Meumann and Thorndike, he treated learning as performance or work. The study of learning thus became the discovery of those factors that influenced performance and, above all, the development of techniques whereby one could study the precise quantitative effects of those factors. Although Hunter included animal studies in the course, he did not, it would seem, include studies of conditioning (even though he believed that all learning was, ultimately, conditioning).

In his psychology as a whole, Hunter obeyed the behaviorist imperatives: to be objective, to deal only with that which can be measured or counted, and to avoid all mentalist or spiritual language. He coined the term "anthroponomy" (from *anthropos* [man] and *nomus* [law]) to signify that behaviorists intended to treat the human condition comprehensively. In his textbook, *Human Behavior* (1928), Hunter treated society as a collection of individuals whose role was to adapt to the situations in which they found themselves. Hunter divided anthroponomy's subject matter into four areas—comparative psychology, the application of psychological tests, abnormal psychology, and social psychology. Hunter was opposed to behaviorist John B. Watson in his most distinctive research. He was moderate in his claims; for example, he denied that all development was due to learning and did not renounce the concept of instinct. Nevertheless, he molded his psychology into a Watsonian form. The discipline was derived from and based its scientific respectability on biology and the physical sciences in general. Its then-current justification lay in the applied area. Its future lay with proposals to cure society's ills; crucially, those ills resided in failures of individual adjustment. By using ontogenetic techniques derived from comparative psychology and modes of assessment developed by mental testers, psychologists were to act as social technocrats.

In 1936 he accepted an appointment as faculty member and head of the psychology department at Brown University. He resigned the headship in March 1954 but continued as a faculty member until his death. At Brown, Hunter became increasingly involved in administrative responsibilities within the profession and spent less time in the lab. In 1936 he also became chair of the Division of Anthropology and Psychology of the National Research Council, where he concentrated on supporting research in abnormal psychology through the work of the Committee on Problems of Neurotic Behavior (1936–1944); one of the committee's tasks was to establish improved working relationships between psychologists and psychiatrists so that together they could serve the needs of the armed forces. From 1939 onward, Hunter became involved in the preparations for World War II, joining the Emergency Committee on Psychology in 1940 and participating in the introduction of the Army Specialized Training Program. In 1943 he became chair of the Applied Psychology Panel of the National Defense Research Committee; he continued to serve on similar committees until his death. In the civilian sphere, he played a large role in establishing the Educational Testing Service as an adviser to the Committee on Testing of the Carnegie Corporation and the Carnegie Foundation. (He recommended merging existing testing agencies into a single entity.) In 1948 Hunter was awarded the President's Medal for Merit in recognition of his services. He died in Providence, Rhode Island.

As a theoretician, Hunter enunciated the behaviorist creed but did not formulate a distinctive version of it. The one concept that was uniquely his, anthroponomy, did no more than affirm his mistrust for the mind and all allied concepts. By the same token, his major innovation was programmatic rather than substantive. In designing the very first course in learning ever to be given in psychology, he initiated the central role that this topic was to play in the thought and research of such behaviorists as Edward C. Tolman, Clark L. Hull, and B. F. Skinner.

• Hunter's autobiography is in E. G. Boring et al., eds., *A History of Psychology in Autobiography*, vol. 4 (1952). His Ph.D. thesis was published as "The Delayed Reaction in Animals and Children," *Behavior Monographs* 2, no. 1 (1913). The best statements of his behaviorist position are in his "The Problem of Consciousness," *Psychological Review* 31 (1924): 1–31, and his "General Anthroponomy and Its Systematic Problems," *American Journal of Psychology* 36 (1925): 286–302. The content of his course on learning is summarized in his article in Carl Murchison, ed., *The Foundations of Experimental Psychology* (1929). His textbook is *Human Behavior* (1928; first published in 1910 as *General Psychology*). There are two obituaries of Hunter, Leonard Carmichael, "Walter Samuel Hunter: 1889–1954," *American Journal of Psychology* 67 (1954): 732–34, and Harold Schlosberg, "Walter S. Hunter: Pioneer Objectivist in Psychology," *Science* 120 (1954): 441–42.

JOHN A. MILLS

HUNTER, William (1729?–30 Jan. 1777), physician and surgeon, was born in Edinburgh, Scotland. Little is known about Hunter's parents or early life. He claimed to be related to the famous Scottish surgeons William and John Hunter, but this claim cannot be confirmed. In 1745, at the age of sixteen, Hunter served as a surgeon's mate at the battle of Culloden, the last gasp of the Jacobite factions determined to put Charles Stuart on the throne of England and Scotland. His participation on the losing side of this battle did not impede Hunter's future career. Shortly after the battle, he enrolled in a course of medical studies at Edinburgh under the tutelage of the well-known anatomist Alexander Monro the elder. He also pursued studies as a nonmatriculated student at the University of Leyden.

In 1752 Hunter set sail for the New World. He arrived in Newport, Rhode Island, bringing with him an extensive medical library—so extensive, in fact, that it was rumored to be the largest such collection in New England at the time. Titles ranged from seventeenth-century editions of classical texts to the latest medical writings from England and Scotland. As one of the few graduates of a European medical school in the American colonies, Hunter soon found himself with a thriving practice. In addition to his other duties he was the first male practitioner in Rhode Island to attend women in childbirth.

Three years after his arrival in America, Hunter embarked on the project for which he is best known, the first public lectures on anatomy and surgery to be delivered in North America. He placed an advertisement in the *Boston Evening Post* of 20 and 27 January and 3 February 1755 announcing his intention to give a series of lectures on "the structure of the human Body" and concluding with "a Course of Chirurgical Operations." He delivered the lectures at the Newport courthouse to what were apparently large crowds. Those attending included not just the medical community but also members of Newport's elite desirous of extending their knowledge of natural history and philosophy. Hunter enlivened his lectures with a display of his extensive and sophisticated collection of surgical tools. The lectures were such a success that Hunter repeated them in 1756.

In 1755 Hunter was appointed surgeon to the British troops engaged on the North American front in the French and Indian War. He served in the Crown Point expedition, where he cared for the captured French commander Baron Deiskau. He also participated in the campaigns of 1756 and 1757. The general assembly of Rhode Island recognized his service in 1758 and appointed him surgeon general to all Rhode Island troops. Thereafter, he served in the successful Canadian campaign. When he returned triumphant from Quebec in 1760, his practice, already successful, boomed.

Hunter added to his growing prosperity by making an advantageous marriage. In 1761 he married Deborah Malbone, the youngest daughter of the wealthy merchant and landowner Godfrey Malbone. The Hunters had seven children, of whom four survived to adulthood.

The revolutionary war was a turning point in Hunter's life. He remained a staunch Loyalist. The Rhode Island revolutionary Ezra Stiles considered him to be one of the most extreme Tories in all of Newport. When he refused to swear loyalty to the cause of independence in July 1776, Hunter was arrested and detained in Smithfield, Rhode Island, far from his family. His captors allowed him compassionate leave to visit his ailing children in Newport later that year, however. When the British captured Newport in December, Hunter became physician to the British troops. It was this posting that led to his death. While tending soldiers and prisoners of war in Newport, Hunter contracted a "putrid fever." He died in Newport. His wife and daughters subsequently returned to Europe, but his youngest son, who did not share his father's Loyalist leanings, stayed in Rhode Island and later became a U.S. senator from that state.

Hunter was, by all accounts, an urbane, amiable man who was widely liked and respected even by those who despised his Tory politics. He played a major role in establishing elite medical practice in America. His public lectures, extensive practice, and personal library all contributed greatly to the dissemination of European medical knowledge and techniques in the American colonies.

• James Thatcher, in his *American Medical Biography* (1828), includes an entry on Hunter. The most extensive discussion of Hunter's life is E. B. Krumbhaar, "Doctor William Hunter of Newport," which appeared in the January 1935 issue of *Annals of Surgery*, pp. 506–28. Krumbhaar's article also includes a reproduction of a portrait of Hunter and his wife and photographs of the original announcements of Hunter's anatomy lectures. Another article on Hunter is Roland Hammond, "Doctor William Hunter," *Rhode Island Medical Journal* 24 (Nov. 1941): 199–201.

REBECCA TANNENBAUM

HUNTINGTON, Anna Vaughn Hyatt (10 Mar. 1876–4 Oct. 1973), sculptor and philanthropist, was born in Cambridge, Massachusetts, the daughter of Alpheus Hyatt II, a professor of zoology and paleontology at the Massachusetts Institute of Technology and at Boston University, and Audella Beebe, an amateur landscape painter. She attended private schools in Cambridge, but at about age seventeen, she began to show an interest in sculpture. This was encouraged by her family, especially by her older sister, Harriet R. Hyatt, who began sculpting in the 1880s. Anna may have accompanied her sister to the Cowles School in Boston to study drawing with Dennis Miller Bunker and Ernest L. Major. She refuted the often-repeated statement that her earliest formal study of sculptural technique was with Henry Hudson Kitson; she gave full credit for her training to her sister, who had studied with Kitson.

Anna's first serious work, a relief sculpture of a nude youth with his dog, called *The Pride of Our Great Dane* (1895, unlocated), was created in collaboration with her sister. This collaboration continued until 1900 when Harriet married and moved to New York. In the relief Anna modeled the dog, an early demonstration of her love for animals. Dogs and horses were of special interest to her, and almost all of her early works dealt with those animals. (Her family owned dogs, and she became an expert equestrian while visiting "Porto Bello," the Maryland farm of her brother Alpheus Hyatt, Jr.) But she soon began to model wild animals at Bostock's Live Animal Show in Boston and in zoos in that city and, later, in New York. At the zoos, she carefully observed the animals and modeled them on the spot. Later, she recalled that these experiences were "some of my happiest" (quoted in Proske, p. 30).

Around 1900, examples of Hyatt's work began to appear in the windows of the jewelry company of Shreve, Crump and Low in Boston, and in 1902 she had her first one-artist show at the Boston Art Club. Her sculptures attracted the attention of her earliest patron, Boston businessman Thomas W. Lawson, who eventually owned about fifty of her animal pieces. In 1902 she moved to New York, where she registered for classes at the Art Students' League (1902–1904). There, she studied with George Grey Barnard and Hermon Atkins MacNeil, while also benefiting from criticism offered by Gutzon Borglum, whose advice on the modeling of horses was especially useful to Hyatt. She collaborated on several sculptures with Abastenia St. Leger Eberle, with whom she shared an apartment and studio beginning in 1903. In 1904 one of their mutual efforts, *Men and Bull* (destroyed), was shown at the Society of American Artists in New York, and it won a bronze medal at the Louisiana Purchase Exposition in St. Louis. Meanwhile, Gorham Company Founders of Providence, Rhode Island, began casting some of Hyatt's animal sculptures for sale.

In 1907 Hyatt and her sister Harriet went to Auvers-sur-Oise, France, where Anna enlarged several of her animal studies, including *Reaching Jaguar* (Metropolitan Museum of Art and the Bronx Zoo, New York), which she showed at the 1908 Paris Salon. That same year, in Italy, she completed a large sculpture of a lion for one of her earliest public commissions, given by the Decorative Art Association of Steele High School in Dayton, Ohio. She settled in Paris, where she became fascinated with the life of Joan of Arc and, after studying many images of the saint, produced her first major figural work, an equestrian statue of Joan that received an honorable mention at the Paris Salon of 1910.

Hyatt's model of *Joan of Arc* was seen and admired by J. Sanford Saltus, an executive of Tiffany and Company and the chairperson of a committee to erect a monument in New York to mark the 500th anniversary of Joan of Arc's birth. Hyatt returned to New York in 1910 to enter the competition, which she won in 1914. She reworked her earlier conception in her studio at her family's summer home, "Seven Acres," in Annisquam, Massachusetts, where she spent most of her time between 1914 and 1920. The finished bronze was unveiled on Riverside Drive in New York in December 1915 and received universal critical acclaim. Replicas were ordered for Blois, France, and Gloucester, Massachusetts, in 1921. The following year, another image of the Maid of Orleans by Hyatt, this one in stone, was installed in the Chapel of Saint Martin of Tours in the Cathedral of Saint John the Divine, New York, a gift of J. Sanford Saltus. In 1922 Hyatt was made a chevalier of the French Legion of Honor.

Meanwhile, in 1908 she began participating in the annual exhibitions of the National Academy of Design. The Gorham Company was also showing her sculptures in their Fifth Avenue gallery and sponsored a comprehensive display of forty-three of them in 1914. That year, one critic called Hyatt "the greatest woman exponent of animal life in this country" (Elizabeth Lounsbery, "Lares and Penates, Recent Small Bronzes by American Sculptors and Their Intimate Use," *Arts and Decoration* 4 [Apr. 1914]: 229). In 1920 the model for her *Joan of Arc* won the Saltus Gold Medal at the National Academy; in 1922 her *Diana of the Hunt* earned another Saltus Gold Medal; in 1928 *Fighting Bull* was awarded the Julia A. Shaw Memorial Prize; and in 1958 *Fillies Playing* won the academy's Watrous Medal. Hyatt was elected an associate member of the academy in 1916 and a full academician in 1922.

In 1920 Hyatt moved back to New York, where she rented a studio in Greenwich Village with sculptor Brenda Putnam. About the same time, she met scholar, museum founder, and philanthropist Archer Milton Huntington. Having seen and admired her *Joan of Arc*, Huntington asked Hyatt, in 1921, to design the

Mitre Medal, an award for distinction in arts and letters to be given by the Hispanic Society of America that Huntington had established in 1904. Their relationship continued to develop during the early 1920s when they worked together on a large, retrospective exhibition of American sculpture that the National Sculpture Society held at the Hispanic Society in 1923. On 10 March of that year Huntington and Hyatt were married in the sculptor's studio. During the first several decades of their marriage, they lived in Huntington's mansion at 1083 Fifth Avenue and at their camp, "Arbutus," in the Adirondacks. They had no children.

In 1923 Anna Huntington began her second major equestrian sculpture, a monument to El Cid. In 1903 Archer Huntington had produced his major literary work, a translation of the Spanish classic *Poema del Cid*, and he asked Anna to model an over-life-size figure of the epic's hero. The result was *El Cid Campeador*, a cast of which Archer Huntington gave to the city of Seville, Spain, where it was placed in the Glorieta de San Diego in 1927. Two years later, another cast was unveiled in the plaza of Audubon Terrace outside the headquarters of the Hispanic Society in New York. In 1929 the king of Spain awarded Anna Huntington the Grand Cross of Alfonzo XII. Two years later, she was elected to membership in the Academia de Bellas Artes de San Fernando of Madrid.

Anna Huntington was diagnosed with tuberculosis in 1927. Over the next seven years, she and her husband, in hopes of affecting a cure, traveled to North Carolina, Switzerland, Arizona, and elsewhere. Anna continued to work as best she could; in fact, she later attributed her eventual recovery to the fact that she never stopped working. Archer funded another huge sculpture exhibition, again organized by the National Sculpture Society and held in San Francisco at the California Palace of the Legion of Honor in 1929. In 1932 they moved to a new estate, "Rocas," in Haverstraw, New York, where Anna kept a private zoo whose inhabitants she used as models.

By that time, the Huntingtons had begun spending their winters in South Carolina, where in 1930 they purchased several seaside plantations near Murrells Inlet. On one of these they built their winter home, the Moorish-inspired "Atalaya." Nearby, on four former plantations, including the old Alston estate of "Brookgreen," they established America's largest outdoor sculpture garden. They collaborated on the design of the garden, creating paths, fountains, and pools, and began purchasing sculptures by nineteenth- and twentieth-century American sculptors to adorn the area. In 1931 Brookgreen Gardens was opened to the public, and in 1935 the Huntingtons gave it to the state of South Carolina.

By 1936 Anna Huntington was well on the way to recovery from her tuberculosis. That year the American Academy of Arts and Letters, which had already elected her as its first woman member in 1932, held a retrospective exhibition of 170 of her sculptures. Between 1937 and 1939 a large show of her works traveled to twenty-five American cities. A number of the works in both of these exhibitions were cast in aluminum, a nontraditional material for sculpture but one that attracted Huntington due to its light weight and durability.

In 1939 the Huntingtons purchased and moved to a 900-acre estate, "Stanerigg," in Redding, Connecticut, and the following year they donated their house at 1083 Fifth Avenue and adjacent properties to the National Academy of Design, which made the mansion its headquarters. Anna Huntington executed two final, major works for the Hispanic Society: large reliefs of the literary hero Don Quixote (1942) and of Boabdil, the last Moorish king of Granada (1943). She completed two large groups for Brookgreen Gardens, *Don Quixote* (1947) and *Fighting Stallions* (1950). During the early 1950s, Archer Huntington's health began to deteriorate, and after a period of invalidism, he died at Stanerigg in December 1955.

Anna continued to live and work at the Connecticut estate. One of her last monumental works is *The Torch Bearers*, executed for the city of Madrid, with replicas for Havana, Cuba, and Norfolk, Virginia. A bronze cast of her heroic equestrian statue of Cuban patriot José Martí, executed in 1958, was erected at one of the southern entrances to Central Park in New York in 1965, and a portrait statue of General Israel Putnam, a hero of the American Revolution, was unveiled at Putnam Memorial State Park near Redding, Connecticut, in 1969. Anna Huntington died at Stanerigg. The following year, a memorial exhibition of over fifty of her small bronzes was held at the Hispanic Society.

Anna Hyatt Huntington was perhaps the best woman animalier of her day; yet she also created a number of impressive monumental sculptures at a time when women artists were still struggling to overcome professional limitations imposed on their gender by society. Her early success and her lifelong energy and perseverance undoubtedly inspired younger artists, female and male. The idea of creating Brookgreen Gardens stemmed from her desire to promote American sculptors and their work. The gardens became an excuse, in a sense, for commissioning and purchasing the works of American artists, thereby affording the public a place to learn about sculpture while giving financial and moral support to the artists who made it.

• Anna Hyatt Huntington's papers, including letters and diaries, are in the George Arents Research Library for Special Collections, Syracuse University; another important collection of correspondence and photographs is at the Hispanic Society of America, New York; and a smaller group of papers, mostly invoices and receipts for her work, is at the Archives of American Art, Smithsonian Institution, Washington, D.C. The Smithsonian also has a taped and transcribed interview with the artist, conducted by Dorothy Seckler, which is undated but obviously made late in Huntington's life. Letters from both Anna and Archer Huntington to art critic and historian Leila Mechlin are at the Philadelphia Museum of Art and are on microfilm at the Archives of American Art as well. Monographic studies of Anna Hyatt Huntington include Doris E. Cook, *Woman Sculptor: Anna Hyatt Huntington (1876–1973)* (1976), and Susan Harris Edwards,

"Anna Hyatt Huntington: Sculptor and Patron of American Idealism" (M.A. thesis, Univ. of South Carolina, 1979), both of which include useful bibliographies and checklists of Huntington's works. Edwards also includes a history of Brookgreen Gardens. For brief but insightful and accurate summaries of Huntington's life, see Beatrice Proske, "A Sculptor in New York," *SITES: A Literary/Architectural Magazine* 16–17 (1986): 30–36, and Janis Conner and Joel Rosencranz, *Rediscoveries in American Sculpture: Studio Works, 1893–1939* (1989), pp. 71–78. An obituary is in the *New York Times*, 5 Oct. 1973.

DAVID B. DEARINGER

HUNTINGTON, Catharine Sargent (29 Dec. 1887–3 Mar. 1987), actress and director, was born in Ashfield, Massachusetts, the daughter of George Putnam Huntington, a clergyman, and Lilly St. Agnan Barrett. Huntington graduated from Miss Haskell's School in Boston, Massachusetts, in 1906 and then attended Radcliffe College, where she graduated cum laude with her A.B. in 1911. After graduation Huntington began teaching at the Westover School in Middlebury, Connecticut, and remained there until 1917. Huntington's parents instilled in her a strong sense of civic responsibility, which influenced her entire life. When World War I broke out, Huntington left her teaching job to entertain the troops in France, serving as the Radcliffe representative with the Wellesley unit of the Young Men's Christian Association, and in 1919 she served as an aide for Réconstruction Aisne Devastée and the Union des Femmes de France. She returned to the United States in 1920 but continued in the local war recovery efforts.

Huntington's interest in the professional theater became apparent in 1923 when she apprenticed at the Orleans Summer Theatre in Cape Cod, Massachusetts. That fall she was named a member of the board of directors of the Boston Stage Society and became involved at The Barn in Boston, playing Mrs. Popov in *The Boor*, which opened 19 November 1923. Huntington spent the next five years working at The Barn and learning her craft. She made her directoral debut in January 1924 with Anton Chekhov's *The Seagull*, a production in which she also played Masha. She next portrayed Marie Duplessis in *Debureau*, opening 24 March 1924, and Dona Sirena in *Invisible Threads*, opening 21 May 1924. That summer when Huntington decided she needed more training, she attended the summer workshops at the Laboratory Theatre in New York City. She returned to Boston to direct *The Last Night of Don Juan* (15 Dec. 1924), *The Unknown Woman* (9 Feb. 1925), *Wedding Breakfast on the Eiffel Tower* (13 Apr. 1925), *Uncle Vanya* (13 Dec. 1926), and *Buddha's Gardens* (18 Mar. 1927). In addition to directing, Huntington continued acting at The Barn, appearing as Sarah Jennings and the Duchess of Devonshire in *Marlborough Rides Away to the Wars* (26 Feb. 1925) and as Madame des Aubels in *The Revolt of the Angels* (4 Dec. 1925). She held minor roles in *The Unknown Woman* and *Wedding Breakfast on the Eiffel Tower*.

After leaving The Barn, Huntington directed *The Lost Disciple* for the Allied Arts Center in Boston (11 Dec. 1930) and then spent the next five years as a member of Mr. Punch's Workshop, a professional puppeteer company. Beginning in 1938 Huntington associated with a number of professional New England theaters that would define her career: primarily the New England Repertory Company, The Artists Theater, The Poets' Theater, and the Provincetown Playhouse in Provincetown, Massachusetts. In 1938 Huntington helped found the New England Repertory Theatre and served as producer and director of marketing. In addition she portrayed Frau Alden and Mlle. Alaret in *Maedchen in Uniform*, which opened at Huntington Chambers in Boston on 19 November 1938. She played Martine in *The Physician in Spite of Himself*, which opened 7 February 1939 and reprised the role when the company took the play to the Samoset Playhouse in Nantucket, Massachusetts, in July of that same year. She performed Madame Muskat in *Liliom*, which opened back at the Huntington Chambers on 16 May 1939 and Aunt Isabel in *The Inheritors*, which opened at the Peabody Playhouse in Boston on 29 March 1939.

In 1940 the New England Repertory Theatre took over the Provincetown Playhouse on the Wharf and operated there until 1972. Among the standard repertory were the plays of Eugene O'Neill, who had been discovered by the original Provincetown Players on 1916. Beginning in 1940 and for the next three decades, Huntington opened every playhouse season with a play by O'Neill. In 1940 Huntington acted with the Artists Theatre, playing the Lion in *Androcles and the Lion*, Wilson in *Easte Lynne*, Claire Hibbert in *The Vortex*, and Mrs. Chamberlain in *Me and Harry*. From November 1941 to May 1942 she repeated several of her earlier roles at the Joy Street Playhouse, including Mrs. Webb in *Our Town*.

Huntington's strong sense of civic duty came to light again in 1943 when World War II intensified. From 1943 to 1944 she worked in a factory that manufactured Red Cross supplies, and from 1944 to 1946 she became a woodworker's assistant in a South Boston Naval Yard. After she completed her work toward the war effort, she returned to the New England Repertory Theatre. For the next twenty years Huntington acted, directed, and produced plays for the company at Provincetown. Her most notable roles include Amanda in *The Glass Menagerie* (11 Aug. 1947); Mrs. Stockman in *An Enemy of the People* (9 July 1951); Sarah Atkins in *Beyond the Horizon* (1 July 1954); Mrs. Crosby in *Diff'rent* (2 July 1955); Essie Miller in *Ah, Wilderness* (27 Aug. 1956); and Grandma in *The American Dream* (13 Aug. 1962). In 1960 Huntington became president and member of the board of directors for the Provincetown Playhouse on the Wharf, and in 1966 she received the Rodgers and Hammerstein Award, given to "the person who has done the most for the American Theater in the Boston Area" (*Boston Globe*, 9 May 1966). *Boston Globe* columnist Elliot Norton wrote that Huntington had "done much for the

theater in Boston and beyond. . . . Nobody in this part of the country has done more for Eugene O'Neill than Miss Huntington" (11 May 1966). Huntington stayed with the New England Repertory Theatre and the Provincetown Playhouse until her retirement in 1972. She died in Roxbury, Connecticut.

The Rodgers and Hammerstein Award acknowledges Huntington's contribution to the American theater. She helped to build theater in New England at a crucial time in American theater history, when the center of professional theater began to move out of New York City. Her commitment to O'Neill helped to establish him as one of American's foremost playwrights. Her dedication to high quality theater, both as an actress and a producer, have made her an important figure in the American theater, particularly on the East Coast.

• Huntington is discussed in *Biographical Encyclopedia and Who's Who in the American Theatre* (1981) and the *Boston Globe*, 9 and 11 May 1966 and 21 Aug. 1966. Her obituary is in the *Boston Globe*, 3 Mar. 1987.

MELISSA VICKERY-BAREFORD

HUNTINGTON, Collis Potter (22 Oct. 1821–13 Aug. 1900), railroad builder and financier, was born at Harwinton, Connecticut, the son of William Huntington, a farmer and small manufacturer, and Elizabeth Vincent. Huntington's schooling, limited to four months a year, ended when he was thirteen. His marriage in 1844 to Elizabeth T. Stoddard lasted until her death in 1883. Childless, the couple in 1862 adopted the daughter of Elizabeth's deceased sister. In 1884 Huntington married a widow, Arabella Duval Yarrington Worsham, and adopted her only son. Huntington died at Pine Knot Lodge, near (or on) Lake Raquette, New York.

Huntington's early experiences image stereotypes of the nineteenth-century formula for success as well as nineteenth-century genre painting. At fourteen Huntington was apprenticed to a neighboring farmer. Saving all he made his first year, he later claimed, "At the end of that year I was as much a capitalist as I have ever been since." At sixteen, by acquiring a stock of clocks and other easily transportable items, he became the far-ranging Yankee Peddler of Asher Brown Durand's painting "The Peddler Displaying His Wares" (1836). After seven years as partner in his brother's hardware store in Oneonta, New York, he became one of the original Gold Rush "49ers" and sailed for San Francisco by way of Panama. En route, while detained on the isthmus for three months, he turned adversity into income by buying and selling merchandise and in the process walking across the isthmus twenty-four times.

On his arrival in California Huntington faced difficulties. The trading posts he set up east of Sacramento proved unmanageable, and illness for the first time sapped his energy. By 1851 Huntington had brought his wife west and had settled in Sacramento as a hardware merchant. Rebuilding after a fire destroyed his new brick store, he became partner with another burned-out merchant, Mark Hopkins.

The partnership flourishing, the second floor of the Huntington and Hopkins Hardware became the center for meetings of disaffected Whigs and "Know Nothings" like Hopkins and fellow merchant Charles Crocker. From a meeting held at the store in 1856, the Republican party in California was launched. As titular head of the new party, Leland Stanford, also of Sacramento, met frequently with the group. Thus the association of the "Big Four" to build the first transcontinental railroad arose primarily from political, not business, alliances.

Building a railroad over the Sierra Nevada range in eastern California required men to venture their capital on an enterprise with high risks. A brilliant engineer, Theodore Judah, wholly conversant with the new technology and unable to find backing in San Francisco, looked to Sacramento for funds to survey a route over the mountains. Huntington, the first to listen seriously to Judah, soon was able, through his political associates, to raise the money. In 1861, then, the "Big Four" incorporated the Central Pacific not only because the survey had found a route through the mountains on a gradient of not more than 105 feet to the mile but also because at the Comstock Lode in Nevada a mining boom was in progress. In addition, the possibility of government subsidies was strong because President Abraham Lincoln knew California's ties to the North needed strengthening.

After efforts in Washington by Judah, Huntington, and Stanford (elected governor of California in 1861), President Lincoln signed the Pacific Railway Act of 1862, which empowered the Central Pacific to build eastward from the Pacific coast and the Union Pacific westward from midcontinent. Both roads would receive land grants and loans for construction in the form of government bonds. In 1864 another federal act doubled the land grants and improved the loan provisions, and in 1866 Huntington achieved his long-sought goal—permission to build eastward until the Central Pacific met the Union Pacific, regardless of mileage.

In the management of the Central Pacific each of the Big Four contributed "teamwork" (Huntington's term) that made the enterprise successful. Huntington, as financier, planner, and policymaker, moved his office to New York, where he could raise capital and purchase equipment. From there he kept in close touch with Crocker, in charge of construction. Hopkins mastered the necessary corporate accounting details, and smooth-talking Stanford could make the right political connections. These "associates" stayed united until their deaths, despite Stanford's gradual loss of interest in railroad affairs, a development irksome to Huntington. Theodore Judah did not become an associate, for Huntington detested Judah, despite Judah's having initiated the project and having provided the know-how for writing the enabling legislation.

Because earth-moving techniques were still mostly in the "pick and shovel" stage, completing the line over the granite-spined Sierra Nevada required over 2,000 Chinese to dig the tunnels and "cuts" and raise the "fills." Unforeseen expenses were the miles of permanent snowsheds necessary to keep the line open in the winter. Huntington's role in the construction race was indispensable. Because of the difficulty of selling stock in this risky enterprise, Huntington often had to raise money by borrowing on his personal credit. And he had to sell the bonds (which were in little demand), buy the material (subject to wartime inflation and government rationing), and find the ships to haul the freight around the Horn. Typical of Huntington's logistical achievements was his bargaining (at a profit of $450,000) for twenty-three ships to haul most of the consignment of 66,000 tons of scarce American rail that he had just purchased.

The energy that Huntington devoted to financing and to purchasing supplies was matched by his schemes to extend the Central Pacific as far east as possible in its race with the Union Pacific. His unrealistic goal was the Weber Canyon east of Ogden. That the Central Pacific finally managed Ogden itself was due to Huntington's intricate dealings in Washington with government officials and to entreaties to Crocker such as to lay rail "as though . . . Hell was behind you." Although Huntington took no part in the ceremony marking completion of the first transcontinental railroad west of Ogden in May 1869, he did acknowledge the significance of the feat by traveling to the summit of the Sierra Nevada with painter Albert Bierstadt and commissioning his *Donner Lake from the Summit* (1873, New-York Historical Society).

The mercenary aspect of the achievement almost overwhelmed the heroic. In 1867 the Big Four had arranged with the Contract and Finance Company, which the Big Four established and which they owned, to complete construction of the Central Pacific, including its track, depots, roundhouses, and rolling stock. Government investigators (the Wilson Commission) discovered that for the 552 miles constructed, Construction and Finance received something in the region of twice what construction should have cost. No accurate statement of the real cost could be made, however, for the journals and ledgers containing actual cost data had been destroyed. Furthermore, two members of the commission accused Huntington, testifying under oath in 1873, of managing "to halt just short of actual perjury, relying . . . upon a poor memory . . . obfuscate the issue."

Meanwhile, without Huntington actively seeking it, an opportunity arose to expand his rail construction ambitions to east of the Mississippi. In attempting to raise capital to complete the Chesapeake and Ohio as a trunk line between Chesapeake Bay and the Ohio River, its promoters looked to Fisk and Hatch, New York investment bankers, who recommended Huntington. After "roughing it" while inspecting firsthand the proposed mountainous route, Huntington was able to raise most of the capital the promoters had stipulated, and he became president of the railroad in 1869. From his New York office Huntington kept close tabs on construction, which, though more expensive than anticipated, was completed in 1873. Hiring a city planner, Huntington himself selected a site on the banks of the Ohio and established the trunk line's main locomotive shops in this new terminus, which he named Huntington, West Virginia.

Financial panics in 1873 and 1884 played havoc with paying off the debts acquired in building the road. Huntington, however, foresightedly extended his trunk line westward to Cincinnati (1886–1889), where he built a strategic bridge over the Ohio River; in 1882 he had extended it eastward from Richmond to Tidewater on Chesapeake Bay, thereby creating his second new city—Newport News, Virginia. Huntington did not stop with these extensions, however, for he was determined to achieve what no other railroad builder had achieved—a coast-to-coast transcontinental. Building or acquiring the necessary connections from the Southern Pacific at New Orleans through Memphis and Louisville to a connection with the Chesapeake and Ohio proved to be Huntington's undoing, for the holding company (established 1884), which united these connecting lines, went into receivership in 1888. But by a plan of reorganization Huntington's company escaped a foreclosure sale. For a time Huntington had been president of a true transcontinental; however, in the reorganization, even though the C&O itself emerged unscathed, the smaller connecting lines were sold to existing roads that could profitably assimilate them. Thus, by 1888 Huntington had sold out his interests in C&O, retaining only the productive Newport News Shipbuilding and Drydock Company, which he established at the same time he had founded Newport News.

Even before completing the Central Pacific and acquiring the Chesapeake and Ohio, Huntington had begun purchasing twenty-three separate railroads in California. The first step in consolidating these acquisitions was linking the short lines around San Francisco in order to have access to the city. The second was to extend one of the acquired lines, the Southern Pacific, to Los Angeles. Simply achieving a railroad monopoly in California would not suffice, however. For Thomas A. Scott, backed with land grants, was building from Texas to San Diego a southern transcontinental that would destroy the monopoly of the Central Pacific in California. This road, the Texas and Pacific, would cross the Colorado River at Yuma, Arizona. Huntington, at work in Washington, successfully lobbied to get a charter to build the Southern Pacific to Yuma to join the T&P. Then, through complex business and political stratagems, Huntington got the best of Scott, and the Texas and Pacific never extended beyond El Paso, Texas. But Huntington was able to extend the Southern Pacific beyond Yuma by obtaining state franchises so that construction could proceed without federal approval.

The completion of Southern Pacific's Sunset Route to New Orleans reveals better than any other of Huntington's initiatives his boldness. For besides the experienced Scott, Huntington had to fight Congress and his own associates to proceed. His boldest stratagem, in overcoming barriers to progress eastward, was presenting the federal government with a fait accompli: bridging the Colorado River at Yuma. While the secretary of war hesitated over giving either the Southern Pacific or the Texas and Pacific rights to cross the Colorado at Yuma, Huntington, taking the law into his own hands, seized the necessary right-of-way across Fort Yuma and completed the bridge.

After completing the Sunset Route to New Orleans and the Shasta Route to Oregon (1887) and absorbing the Central Pacific in 1885, the Southern Pacific became a strangling "octopus" to its critics. Three developments of the 1880s especially tarnished Huntington's reputation: publication of the Colton letters, the protracted refunding controversy, and hearings of the U.S. Pacific Railway Commission. The Colton letters, published in 1883, covered Huntington's legislative activities in Washington from 1874 to 1878—activities aimed at thwarting the advance of the Texas and Pacific and in gaining concessions for his own Southern Pacific. Over this period Huntington closely corresponded with David P. Colton, whom the associates had hired as California-based "financial director." After learning, at Colton's death in 1878, that he had defrauded them, associates compelled Mrs. Colton to liquidate her husband's interests on terms that she considered unjust. In the litigation that followed, letters read into the record reveal Huntington lobbying so doggedly for his companies' benefit that he paid off newspapers, countenanced bribing congressmen, and otherwise, as the *San Francisco Chronicle* editorialized (23 Dec. 1883), exhibited "arrogance, corruption, and duplicity."

In 1887 President Grover Cleveland empowered the U.S. Pacific Railroad Commission to investigate every aspect of the Central Pacific's and Union Pacific's founding and organization. Huntington, whose testimony filled many pages, evaded direct responses by rambling on and by sarcasm, evasion, and forgetfulness, being almost guilty of perjury in his "almost-denials." The commission concluded that the Big Four had reaped enormous profits at the expense of the government and of minority stockholders (by withholding dividends).

Huntington was such an adroit lobbyist that he could hold up legislation unfavorable to him even while Congress was investigating him. For nearly a decade Huntington kept at bay refunding bills introduced in Congress to require repayment of the immense loans made to the Central Pacific in the form of government subsidy bonds. By the mid-1890s it became clear that Huntington could no longer hold back legislation to force repayment. Testifying evasively once again in Washington in 1896, Huntington saw his own refunding bill defeated and in 1899 a settlement forced on him.

Journalists such as Ambrose Bierce and novelist Frank Norris were ensuring that Huntington, in his old age, would be remembered not as a western pioneer but as a robber baron. Although Norris's *The Octopus* was published a year after Huntington's death, the author created the character Shelgrim to represent Huntington in his fictional indictment of the greed and destructiveness of the Southern Pacific: "No one individual . . . was more hated, more dreaded, no one more compelling of unwilling tribute to his commanding genius . . . than the President and owner of the Pacific and Southwestern."

For Norris, Huntington symbolized "ungovernable forces" in the universe. Less mystically, one can understand Huntington through his combativeness. Muckraker Charles E. Russell wrote, "He was always on the scent, incapable of fatigue, delighting in his strength . . . and full of the love of combat." Metaphors throughout his correspondence substantiate his combativeness: To Crocker, on the race with the Union Pacific—"Buckle on your armor for the fight, for the ground once lost is lost forever." To Hopkins, paraphrasing Shakespeare—"Let the fight go on and damn the man who first cries 'Enough'!" Boasting about his boyhood—"No boy in school ever licked me, or ever could! I could wipe up the floor with half the boys in school all together."

In a milieu characterized by laissez-faire capitalism and Social Darwinism, Huntington's view of life as a battleground encouraged his full self-development. At his death he left a transportation system that unified West with East by shrinking the vast distances of the American continent, and he was instrumental in transforming the vision of the West from Great American Desert to the Golden West.

• Indispensable for research into Huntington's highly involved management of his business affairs are 115 rolls of microfilm titled *The Collis P. Huntington Papers, 1856–1901* (1979). This imposing collection includes all the correspondence, files, and records retained in Huntington's New York office. It is the best single source for Huntington's correspondence, which otherwise resides in collections as scattered as those in the Mariners' Museum, Newport News, Va., the Stanford University Libraries, Stanford, Calif., the Henry E. Huntington Library, San Marino, Calif., and elsewhere. Hubert Howe Bancroft, *Chronicles of the Builders of the Commonwealth*, vols. 5 and 6 (1891), has personal data based on interviews with Huntington. Essential biographies are Cerinda W. Evans, *Collis Potter Huntington* (2 vols., 1954), and David Lavender, *The Great Persuader* (1970). Evans's life, which puts a favorable light on Huntington's business ethics, has the best bibliography extant, both of primary and secondary sources. Lavender, more critical, restricts his sources (needed to update Evans) mostly to chapter endnotes. Essential for mastering Huntington's complex business dealings are Stuart Daggett, *Chapters on the History of the Southern Pacific* (1922; repr. 1966), and Julius Grodinsky, *Transcontinental Railway Strategy, 1869–1893* (1962). Detailing Huntington's role in building the first transcontinental railroad are James McCague, *Moguls and Iron Men: The Story of the First Transcontinental Railroad* (1964); John Hoyt Williams, *A Great and Shining Road* (1988); and George Kraus, *High Road to Promontory: Building the Central Pacific across the High Sierra* (1969). For Huntington's relationship with his associates, see Oscar Lewis, *The Big Four* (1938). C. Vann Woodward, *Reunion and Reaction: The Compromise of 1877 and the End of Reconstruction*, rev. ed. (1956), clarifies Huntington's strategy in defeating Thomas A. Scott and the Texas and Pacific. A three-part obituary is in the *New York Times*, 15, 17, and 18 Aug. 1900.

EUGENE L. HUDDLESTON

HUNTINGTON, Daniel (14 Oct. 1816–18 Apr. 1906), painter, was born in New York City, the son of Benjamin Huntington, a stockbroker, and Faith Trumbull Huntington (his distant cousin). Huntington studied with Horace Bushnell before attending Yale College for a brief period in 1832 and then studied at (but did not graduate from) Hamilton College in Clinton, New York, where a chance meeting with Charles Loring Elliott, then an itinerant portrait painter, fired him with the idea of becoming an artist.

By 1835 Huntington had returned to New York City to study with Samuel F. B. Morse, professor of the literature of art at New York University and president of the National Academy of Design. Huntington worked briefly as an assistant to portraitist Frederick R. Spencer, painting draperies and backgrounds. By 1838 Huntington was exhibiting portraits, landscapes, and humorous genre scenes at the National Academy and was teaching his first pupil, Henry Peters Gray. The following year he traveled to Europe, where he turned his attention to religious subjects, which inspired the most ambitious efforts of his long career. *A Sibyl* (1839), produced during this period, was purchased by the American Art-Union and later engraved for distribution to its membership. Huntington was elected an associate of the National Academy in 1839 and was made a full academician the following year.

Following his return to New York in 1840, Huntington painted the most successful work of his career, *Mercy's Dream* (1841), based on John Bunyan's *Pilgrim's Progress*. In this work and its companion, *Christiana and Her Children in the Valley of the Shadow of Death* (1842–1844), Huntington infused idealized female beauty with Christian sentiment in a formula that appealed strongly to contemporary notions of women as pure repositories of religious faith. Such works established Huntington as one of America's most important young history painters. Both paintings were widely copied and engraved and were acquired by prominent collector Henry Carey of Philadelphia.

In 1842 eye problems forced Huntington to give up painting temporarily. In that year he married Harriet Sophia Richards; they had one child. In 1843 they left for a two-year stay in Europe. There he painted landscapes and history paintings, which he sent home for exhibition and sale to a receptive public. In addition, he created designs for an edition of Henry Wadsworth Longfellow's poems for Philadelphia publisher Edward Carey. Huntington made later visits to England and the Continent in 1851, 1852–1853, and 1857–1858. In 1882–1883 he toured Italy, Spain, and Morocco. These experiences reinforced his early admiration for European precedent and tradition.

On his return to New York in 1845, Huntington established himself as a fixture of the New York art scene. In addition to participating regularly in the National Academy's annual exhibitions, he forged a profitable relationship with the American Art-Union and sent pictures to the annual exhibitions at the Pennsylvania Academy of the Fine Arts and other institutions. During the late 1840s Huntington's personal concern over the crisis in contemporary Protestantism, during a period of shifting denominational identity and the rising influence of Roman Catholicism, found expression in somewhat sensational images of the English Reformation, such as *Queen Mary Signing the Death Warrant of Lady Jane Grey* which was distributed as an engraving by the American Art-Union for its membership premium for 1848.

Throughout his career Huntington pursued subjects that expressed both his deep religious conviction and his belief in the academic ideal of moral didacticism. His numerous religious pictures include conventional treatments of sanctioned biblical subjects, such as *The Tribute Money* (1852) and *The Good Samaritan* (1853), as well as what he called "Christian allegories" of his own invention. Typical of these are *Sowing the Word* (1868) and *Philosophy and Christian Art* (1868), pictorial sermons on lofty themes that juxtapose bearded sages with idealized young women. Huntington also painted sentimental genre paintings, sometimes with a historical gloss, and paintings of literary subjects. He executed only one major work loosely based on American history, *Mrs. Washington's Reception* (1862), which became well known to a wide public through an engraving by Alexander Ritchie.

Despite his success in history painting and his growing reputation for landscape, by mid-century Huntington had established portraiture as the staple of his practice. Huntington's sitters—politicians and professionals, churchmen and businessmen, society matrons and presidents—often belonged to his network of club, church, collegiate, and familial ties, and he associated with them as a social equal. His flattering, conventional likenesses evolved from the smooth handling and delicate color inspired by his early mentors, Elliott and Henry Inman, to looser brushwork and a greater sense of atmosphere that reflected his admiration for Sir Joshua Reynolds and Titian. Like his history paintings, Huntington's portraits sometimes betray his limited training in their awkward drawing, but he never lacked sitters. He is said to have painted over 1,000 portraits during a career that spanned more than sixty years.

Huntington was equally successful as a landscapist, though he tended to depreciate his efforts in comparison to other Hudson River School landscapists, notably his friends Asher Durand and John Frederick Kensett. Huntington spent his summers in such popular locales as Newport, Rhode Island; Lake George, New York; New Hampshire's White Mountains; and the Shawangunk Mountains of lower New York State, where he drew from nature. His fine landscape drawings and nature studies reveal a spontaneity and a fresh and passionate vision that did not often translate into his studio production.

Huntington's involvement with the institutional art world of his day was at least as important and influential as his painting. He served as president of the National Academy from 1862 to 1869 and again from 1877 to 1891; his combined tenure is the longest in that institution's history. He also taught in the academy's schools, served on numerous committees, and was a leading force behind the erection of the organization's new building at Fourth Avenue and Twenty-third Street, completed in 1865. Under his leadership the academy saw considerable growth and faced challenges from newer, rival organizations. Despite his administrative abilities and his devotion to the academy, however, Huntington was not always allied with the forces of progress. A thorough conservative both personally and artistically, he responded to the artistic and institutional changes of the post–Civil War era with pleas on behalf of tradition and in his own work remained loyal to traditional academic ideals. Huntington was also active as a founding member and president (1879–1895) of the Century Association, as a trustee and vice president of the Metropolitan Museum of Art (1871–1903), and as a board member of other institutions. He died in New York City.

Huntington was one of the most successful, versatile, and well-documented of nineteenth-century American painters. His paintings, characterized by an earnest religiosity and informed by a literary turn of mind, are often undermined by his consciously derivative approach, didactic purpose, and indifferent technical grounding. While his works have faded into virtual oblivion, Huntington's career stands as an important representative of the vital persistence of European tradition in American art.

• Huntington's own annotated list of his works is preserved at the National Academy of Design, which also has a collection of eighty sketchbooks by him and other materials. *Catalogue of Paintings, by Daniel Huntington, N. A., Exhibiting at the Art Union Buildings, 497 Broadway* (1850), with an introductory text and notes by Huntington, remains a useful guide to his early work. For a summary biography and bibliography see Natalie Spassky et al., *American Painting in the Metropolitan Museum of Art*, vol. 2 (1980–1986), pp. 56–73. William H. Gerdts, "Daniel Huntington's *Mercy's Dream*: A Pilgrimage through Bunyanesque Imagery," *Winterthur Portfolio* 14 (1979): 171–94, offers a detailed analysis of the cultural and artistic context of Huntington's treatments of themes from Bunyan. For a discussion of Huntington's history painting in general, with particular attention to its biographical and religious setting, see Wendy Greenhouse, "Daniel Huntington and the Ideal of Christian Art," *Winterthur Portfolio* 31 (1996): 103–40. An obituary is in the *New-York Daily Tribune*, 20 Apr. 1906.

WENDY GREENHOUSE

HUNTINGTON, Edward Vermilye (26 Apr. 1874–25 Nov. 1952), mathematician, was born in Clinton, New York, the son of Chester Huntington and Katharine Hazard Smith. He received an A.B. from Harvard College in 1895 and an A.M. from Harvard in 1897.

He was a mathematics instructor at Harvard while working for his A.M. and at Williams College from 1897 until 1899. He then traveled to Europe to study. In 1901 he received a Ph.D. from the University of Strasbourg, then in Germany, with a dissertation on algebra. He returned to Harvard as instructor of mathematics in 1901. He became assistant professor in 1905 and associate professor in 1915. He married Susie Edwards Van Volkenburgh in 1909; they had no children. In 1913 he was elected to the American Academy of Arts and Sciences.

Huntington's earliest postulate theory studies were focused on what would today be called algebraic systems. A much-cited example for boolean algebras is "Sets of Independent Postulates for the Algebra of Logic" (*Transactions of the American Mathematical Society* 5 [1904]: 288–309). In this same vein, but presented more didactically, is "The Fundamental Propositions of Algebra" (in *Monographs on Topics of Modern Mathematics*, ed. J. W. A. Young [1911]). One of Huntington's more interesting postulate sets is in "A Set of Postulates for Abstract Geometry, Expressed in Terms of the Simple Relation of Inclusion" (*Mathematische Annalen* 73 [1913]: 522–59). In this paper he develops geometry using only the two undefined concepts of sphere and inclusion of one sphere within another.

Huntington was named professor of mechanics at Harvard in 1919. The latter title reflected the extensive effort he devoted to mathematics teaching for engineering students. His proposal in "The Logical Skeleton of Elementary Dynamics" (*American Mathematical Monthly* 24 [1917]: 1–16) to treat force as a more fundamental concept than mass in the teaching of dynamics is an example of his characteristic focus on clarifying basic concepts.

He developed a four-place table of logarithms that was crafted for ease of use (published in 1907). This was at a time when such tables were essential for practical calculation. He was the only member of the Harvard Mathematics Department of his day to have a (mechanical) desktop calculator. He was also interested in the mathematical analysis of statistics, which was then unusual for a professor of mathematics. During World War I he served in Washington as a major on the general staff, dealing with statistical problems. He participated in the founding of the Mathematical Association of America, which was intended to complement the more research-oriented American Mathematical Society (he was vice president of the latter in 1924). His presidential address to the Mathematical Association of America called attention to some of the mathematical issues involved in statistics (*American Mathematical Monthly* 26 [1919]: 421–35).

Another noteworthy example of Huntington's "applied" interests is his analysis of the method by which congressional seats are apportioned among the states after a census. The Fourteenth Amendment of the U.S. Constitution requires that "Representatives shall be apportioned among the several States according to their respective numbers." Perfect proportionality, however, is impossible without fractional representatives. Huntington showed in studies in the 1920s that the methods of approximation that had been used, such as simple rounding up or down of the fractional allotments, could lead to undesirable results. For more than twenty years he advocated a method called "equal proportions" until the controversial method of apportionment was finally passed into law in 1941. His method was still used at the end of the century.

In his postulational writings of the 1930s, Huntington focused on analyzing systems of formal logic. Typical of this period is "Independent Postulates for the 'Informal' Part of Principia Mathematica" (*Bulletin of the American Mathematical Society* 40 [1934]: 127–36). A general account of his postulate studies is given in "The Method of Postulates" (*Philosophy of Science* 4 [1937]: 482–95).

Huntington was vice president and chairman of the mathematics section of the American Association for the Advancement of Science in 1926 and was elected to the American Philosophical Society in 1933. After retiring from Harvard in 1941, he continued to live in Cambridge until his death there.

Huntington is most noted for his research into "postulate systems," careful formulations of what would later be called "axiom sets" for mathematical areas such as boolean algebras or the fields of real or complex numbers. Huntington's papers were exemplary in their logical precision; he was careful to list the limited set of undefined terms used in the theory and to introduce all other terms by explicit definition. This made it possible for him to clearly present alternative interpretations of his postulate sets. He proved the logical independence of each of the postulates from the remainder in a given set by exhibiting an interpretation in which that postulate is false while the others are true. His careful distinction between the postulates considered as strings of symbols and the diverse interpretations that could be applied to the symbols served to clarify this central concept of modern logical theory. In *Monographs on Topics of Modern Mathematics* (pp. 171–72), Huntington contrasted his own terminology of *postulates* with the traditional terminology of *axioms* in order to mark two different approaches to mathematical theories. For Huntington, "the term axiom should be applied only to statements of *fact*." Axioms can include "obviously true statements about certain definite operations on angles or distances." Huntington's own postulate sets, however, are not taken to be statements, since they are uninterpreted and apply or do not apply to various "systems" of objects and relations. Huntington wrote that his postulates are "conditions which a given system may or may not happen to satisfy" and not statements that are true or false. This is in close agreement with the present-day approach to formal axiomatic theories.

In conjunction with work by Princeton mathematician Oswald Veblen, Huntington clarified the concept of the "categoricity" of axiom sets. All interpretations satisfying a categorical axiom set are isomorphic. As a result, every possible sentence in the language of the theory is either true in every interpretation satisfying the axiom set or false in every such interpretation. A categorical axiom set can be said to completely describe its subject matter since for each sentence of the language it or its negation is implied by the axiom set. These desirable properties of categoricity and completeness have been extensively studied in the logical subfield of model theory.

Huntington's writings are jewels of clear mathematical exposition that focus on central concepts of the subject. Many of them are well worth reading today. In particular, his book *The Continuum and Other Types of Serial Order* (1917) was a widely read introduction to Cantorian set theory and, although now outdated in method, is still a masterful presentation of the mathematical facts.

• Huntington's "method of equal proportions" is presented in "The Apportionment of Representatives in Congress," *Transactions of the American Mathematical Society* 30 (1928): 85–110. A history of debates on apportionment along with criticism of Huntington's method is in M. L. Balinski and H. P. Young, "The Quota Method of Apportionment," *American Mathematical Monthly* 82 (1975): 701–30. Huntington is defended by G. Birkhoff, "House Monotone Apportionment Schemes," *Proceedings of the National Academy of Sciences* 73 (1976): 684–86. References for Huntington's writings on apportionment can be found in Leroy C. Hardy, comp., *Bibliography of Representation and Redistricting* (1992). There is no comprehensive bibliography of Huntington's writings. More on his investigation of postulate systems is in M. Scanlan, "Who Were the American Postulate Theorists?" *Journal of Symbolic Logic* 56 (1991): 981–1002. An account of Huntington's role in the clarification of the logical notions of categoricity and completeness is in J. Corcoran, "From Categoricity to Completeness," *History and Philosophy of Logic* 2 (1981): 113–19. A good obituary of Huntington by J. H. Van Vleck is in the 1952 *Year Book* of the American Philosophical Society.

MICHAEL SCANLAN

HUNTINGTON, Ellsworth (16 Sept. 1876–17 Oct. 1947), explorer and geographer, was born in Galesburg, Illinois, the son of Henry Strong Huntington, a minister, and Mary Lawrence Herbert. The family moved to Gorham, Maine, after his birth. Huntington was close to his mother, "to whom I owe most," as he later wrote in dedicating a book to her. When he was twelve years old the family moved to Milton, Massachusetts. He graduated near the top of his class at Milton High School and passed his Harvard entrance examinations, but family financial pressures forced him initially to attend the less expensive Beloit College, where he wrote for the college newspaper and yearbook.

In 1897 Huntington graduated from Beloit and was appointed assistant to the president of a missionary school, Euphrates College, in Harput in present-day Turkey. He taught English and Christianity. He studied local geology, ran a weather station at the college, and encouraged others to collect meteorological data in eastern Anatolia. His first articles on meteorology appeared in the *Monthly Weather Review* in 1900–1901.

In April 1901, eager to map the Euphrates River, Huntington journeyed 190 miles down it on a raft of trees. For this feat he received the Royal Geographical Society's Gill Memorial. Shortly afterward, he received a scholarship for graduate studies at Harvard. On the voyage home, he read a book that introduced him to the subject of climate change—James Geikie's *The Great Ice Age and Its Relation to the Antiquity of Man*. Thus began Huntington's lifelong effort to link climate changes to variations in human societies.

At Harvard, Huntington was further inspired by Professor William Morris Davis, a leading geomorphologist, and joined Davis on a field trip to the American West. Later, on an expedition sponsored by the Carnegie Institution, Davis and Huntington explored parts of central Asia. Huntington was struck by the dryness of certain regions. This "dessication," he concluded, had affected the historical evolution of regional civilizations. Over the coming decades he developed a grander global theory that tied societal change to climate change and claimed that climate fluctuations or "pulsations" were caused by variations in the intensity of the sun. He decided to write a book "that shall show the true relation between history and geography as exemplified in Asia [so that] every future historian shall have to take into account the ideas there laid down. That is the sum of my scientific ambition."

On a rigorous fourteen-month trip across the Himalayas and other parts of Asia, Huntington traveled by camel through freezing mountainous terrain. Returning to Harvard, he made the trip and his climate theory the subject of his 25,000-word doctoral thesis. The Harvard Travellers Club gave him its gold medal. In 1907 he failed his final examination for the doctoral degree; one examiner complained that Huntington lacked knowledge of climatology. Late that year his book *The Pulse of Asia* was published. The book was widely praised by reviewers, and the Geographical Society of Paris honored him with a medal.

Huntington accepted a faculty position at Yale, where he lectured and received his Ph.D. in geology in 1909. He grew reclusive and developed a reputation among some students as an uninspiring teacher, although others found him intriguing. He speculated years later, "If I had devoted more time to companionship, I am not sure whether I would have done as much as I have in research" (Martin, p. 73). In 1912 he sought a Yale professorship. The school asked outside scholars to comment on his work, which drew mixed reviews—for example, that he was admirably energetic and imaginative but that "sometimes his thoughts run ahead of the facts" (Martin, p. 86). The school extended his teaching contract but declined to offer a professorship. Apparently unhappy, Huntington temporarily left Yale in 1915 and moved back to his parents' home in Milton. During this and other financially tight periods of his career, he supported himself with abundant, sometimes hasty freelance writing. During his career, he wrote twenty-eight books and hundreds of articles.

Huntington developed his theory of climatic impact on social change partly by studying tree rings for clues to ancient climates of the western United States. He lay atop the enormous stumps of Sequoia trees and measured the rings with a ruler and hand lens. His sweeping conclusions about climatic fluctuations and societal evolution reflected an enthusiasm for metahistorical theorizing typical of the day. In that regard, he admired the doyens of grand historical theory Oswald Spengler and Arnold J. Toynbee. Toynbee repaid Huntington's adulation, writing to him that he was "very deeply indebted to [him]": "I have studied your work for years and it has worked its way right into my own thought" (Martin, p. 216).

Huntington also offered physiological explanations for his proposed correlations between climatic and societal change. He believed in an ideal climate for the human body: 38 degrees Fahrenheit was the ideal temperature for mental activity and 64 degrees Fahrenheit for physical exertion. Because climate varies around Earth, this theory obviously implied that certain regions were more hospitable to mental activity and, hence, to culture and civilization. In "The Handicap of the Tropics" he argued that hot, unchanging climates sapped the desire to work and weakened the prospects for advanced civilizations. Reflecting contemporary stereotypes, he said that the inhabitants of the Yucatan Peninsula in Mexico "are a slow, amiable, lazy lot."

His textbook *Principles of Human Geography* (1920, written with Sumner W. Cushing) was widely printed in several languages. Critics were already complaining, however, that Huntington tended to erect grand hypotheses upon inadequate or questionable evidence. In the journal *Nature*, an otherwise positive review of *Principles* said that his "tendency to lack of due care in generalizing cannot be denied, and there are . . . too many evil consequences thereof" (Martin, p. 133).

In 1917 Huntington married Rachel Slocum Brewer. They had three children. During World War I he served as a captain in the Military Intelligence Division of the General Staff. In that post he interviewed travelers from revolutionary Russia, theorized that German militarism stemmed from cultural energy linked to inconstant climate, and wrote monographs—e.g., "A Plan for Detaching Turkey and Bulgaria from Their German Alliance" (Martin, p. 151). In 1919 he returned to Yale. He spent the rest of his life there as a research associate and occasional lecturer.

Huntington became a leading figure in the "eugenics" movement of the early twentieth century. Broadly defined, the movement hoped to "improve" human beings biologically and psychologically by restricting immigration, discouraging certain social groups from reproducing, and encouraging others to have children. "The whole lesson of biology is that America is seriously endangering her future by making fetishes of equality, democracy, and universal education. They are of great vaue, but only when they have good hered-

itary material upon which to work," Huntington said (Martin, p. 177). He complained of humanity: "He preserves the sick and weakly instead of letting them die; he permits an economic and social system which causes the people with greatest mental power to have the fewest children, while the stupid breed like rabbits" (Martin, p. 236). However, he was not a simple reactionary. During the 1940s he helped sponsor the National Committee to Combat Anti-Semitism and a "citizen's committee" for Harry Bridges, the radical labor unionist. Politically, Huntington was a Republican. His views on eugenics, like the eugenics movement itself, quickly fell out of favor after World War II.

Huntington was a founding member of the Ecological Society of America at Columbia University in 1916. He served as president in its second year. In 1923 he was president of the Association of American Geographers; and from 1934 to 1938, president of the American Eugenics Society. In 1942 the National Council of Geography Teachers gave him its Distinguished Service to Geography Award. His career climaxed in 1945 with the widely read *Mainsprings of Civilization*, a summary of and expansion upon his life's work.

Huntington was a leading popularizer of the science of geography and a prominent early researcher on climate change and its societal impact. His prolific research on and sometimes careless generalizations about climate change and humanity reflected the popularity of grand historical and anthropological theories in the nineteenth and early twentieth centuries. Although a daring explorer and imaginative writer, Huntington's views of foreign cultures often mirrored the national, racial, and ethnic stereotypes of the day; these reemerged later in his writings on eugenics. He stirred interest in the potential societal effects of inconstancies in the planetary ecosystem many decades before debates over "global warming." He died in New Haven, Connecticut.

• A large collection of Huntington's papers is at Yale University Library; it includes correspondence with notables such as Toynbee, Henry Adams, Margaret Sanger, and Frederick Jackson Turner. Huntington was a prolific author of books, scholarly monographs, and popular magazine articles. A bibliography of his writings appears in Geoffrey J. Martin, *Ellsworth Huntington—His Life and Thought* (1973). Huntington's first published article was "Experiments with Available Road-making Materials of Southern Wisconsin," *Transactions of the Wisconsin Academy of Sciences, Arts and Letters* (Sept. 1897). During Huntington's lifetime, some of his most acclaimed books were *Climatic Changes* (1922, with Stephen S. Visher) and *Earth and Sun* (1923). Other works of interest are *The Pulse of Asia* (1907), *Palestine and Its Transformation* (1911), *Civilization and Climate* (1915; rev. ed., 1924), and *The Human Habitat* (1927). His views on race and eugenics are in *The Character of Races* (1925) and *Tomorrow's Children—The Goal of Eugenics* (1935). He studied human ability and birth season in *Season of Birth: Its Relation to Human Abilities* (1938). Critical assessments of Huntington are Stephen S. Visher, "Memoir to Ellsworth Huntington, 1876–1947," *Annals of the Association of American Geographers*,

Mar. 1948; and Robert E. Dickinson, *Regional Concept: The Anglo-American Leaders* (1976). A Soviet Marxist attack on Huntington is B. P. Alisow et al., *Kurs Klimatologii* (in Russian, 1952), which has been translated into German and reprinted in *Lehrbuch der Klimatologie* (1956). See also John E. Chappell, Jr., "Huntington and His Critics: The Influence of Climate on Civilization" (Ph.D. diss., Univ. of Kansas, 1968). David N. Livingstone, *The Geographical Tradition* (1992), criticizes Huntington's "pernicious" use of maps to support ethnocentric ideas. An obituary is in the *New York Times*, 18 Oct. 1947.

KEAY DAVIDSON

HUNTINGTON, Emily (3 Jan. 1841–5 Dec. 1909), educational innovator, was born in Lebanon, Connecticut, the daughter of Dan Huntington, a dry-goods merchant, and Emily Wilson. In 1842 her family moved to Norwich, Connecticut, where she lived until 1872 except for 1856–1858, when she attended Wheaton Seminary in Norton, Massachusetts. Starting in 1859 she took an active part in the mission established by the Second Congregational Church to help the poor in Norwich.

For an increasing number of those in Huntington's generation the most serious challenge to Christian civilization was posed by the great cities, where masses of immigrants seemed unable to sustain either family or community life. In 1872 Huntington moved to New York City and became matron of the Wilson Industrial School for Girls, established twenty years earlier on the Lower East Side. Providing some training in sewing and in general housework, the school enjoyed what the *New York Times* described as "both the confidence and the support of many of the wealthiest and most prominent ladies" (22 Apr. 1876). It was managed by middle-class reformers like Emily Huntington, whom the *Times* described as "a New England woman who has had a large experience in practical work" (25 Nov. 1880). Its clients were girls from poverty-stricken families.

The school had been founded to "repress pauperism" by teaching the girls housekeeping skills that would bring them wages should they go into "service." Huntington, convinced that the failure to love work was "the root of all the misery of the poor," sought to instill in her girls the cheerfulness and efficiency she associated with her New England upbringing. But she was saddened by the "little kitchen girls, with sober, uninterested faces, taking their turn at work that they considered humiliating and tiresome" (*How to Teach Kitchen Garden*, p. 9). When, by chance, she visited a well-run kindergarten, the "mystery" of what to do (she would recall years later) was "all solved." Instead of imposing duties and responsibilities on children, she sought to develop their innate abilities through organized activities that the children would regard as play. She developed teachers' manuals, with carefully graded lesson plans that included songs, marches, and dances as well as drills. The keynotes of her system were discipline and order. Smiles would appear on the children's faces when they sang, "We learned exactly right, for we were taught by rule," or when they mem-

orized the right answer to the question "What is the first thing to do about washing?" (*How to Teach Kitchen Garden*, pp. 49, 90). In these years somewhat similar systems were being experimented with in other American cities, but Huntington's publications established her as the leader of the movement. She coined the curious term "kitchen garden" to reflect the movement's debt to the kindergarten. Huntington soon became convinced that the kitchen-garden system provided the "alphabet" necessary for training older girls in cooking.

Some upper-class women managed to secure kitchen-garden classes for their children, ostensibly so that they would later know what to demand from the cooks and maids they employed. But most classes were intended for the children of the poor, and the program's advocates went to considerable lengths to recruit suitable clients. They regularly proclaimed that domestic service was safer, physically and morally, than a career as a "shop-girl." Disappointed that African-American girls in the North were not entering the program, Huntington for several years trained teachers at the Butler's School of Hampton Institute in the hope of recruiting African Americans throughout the South.

Having never married, Huntington continued to live and work at the Wilson school. The rapid spread of the kitchen-garden movement convinced its upper-class admirers of the need for stronger, more coherent management than Huntington seemed able to provide. In 1879 the Kitchen Garden Association was organized under the leadership of Grace Hoadley Dodge, whom Huntington had introduced to kitchen-garden work. As founder of the association Huntington continued to be regarded as "chief among the members," but its 1881 annual report asserted that "Miss Huntington now does little more than interest herself as one of the volunteer managers who share with her the credit and the responsibility of the work" (quotes from the *New York Times*, 4 May 1881). She was preoccupied with the training of teachers and with writing her manuals, which gave her the pleasant sense, she once wrote, of being "able to teach many pupils, even at a distance" (*Cooking Garden*, p. 11).

Huntington seems to have supported Dodge in the several steps by which, beginning in 1884, the Kitchen Garden Association evolved into the Industrial Education Association, and, five years later, into the New York College for the Training of Teachers, which became Teachers College, Columbia University, in 1892. But there is no evidence that she shared Dodge's desire to move beyond kitchen-garden work into industrial education generally.

In 1892 Huntington resigned from the Wilson school. She became superintendent in 1893 of the New York Cooking School, which had endorsed kitchen-garden methods. Beginning in the summer of 1899 she was one of a small group of women invited to attend annual conferences at Lake Placid, New York. Most of the group shared the desire of Ellen H. Richards, professor of chemistry at the Massachusetts Institute of Technology, to transcend the old idea of "domestic science"—scornfully dismissed as "lessons in cooking and sewing given to classes of the poorer children" (Hunt, p. 267)—in favor of a discipline based on research in nutrition, economics, and sociology. Not surprisingly, Huntington played no part when the Lake Placid group took the lead in the creation of the American Home Economics Association in 1908. She died in Windham, Connecticut.

Huntington adapted kindergarten methods to train the daughters of the urban poor. She did not question—indeed, she gloried in—the cult of domesticity. As Catharine Beecher two generations earlier had tried to help middle-class women fulfill their domestic obligations, so Emily Huntington sought to prepare the children of the poor to be housekeepers, valued for their efficiency by parents and employers alike.

• Huntington's papers have not been collected, but see the Kitchen Garden Association Papers at Teachers College, Columbia University. Among her writings (several of them republished under slightly different titles) were *Little Lessons for Little Housekeepers* (1875), *Kitchen Garden* (1878), *Children's Kitchen Garden* (1881), *Cooking Garden* (1885), *How to Teach Kitchen Garden* (1901), and *Introductory Cooking Lessons* (1901). See also Grace H. Dodge, *A Brief Sketch of the Early History of Teachers College* (1899), three articles by Harriet M. Miller (pseudonym of Olive Thorne) in *St. Nicholas for Boys and Girls*, Apr. 1879 and Sept. 1884, and Caroline L. Hunt, *The Life of Ellen H. Richards* (1912). An obituary is in the *New York Times*, 7 Dec. 1909.

ROBERT D. CROSS

HUNTINGTON, Frederic Dan (28 May 1819–11 July 1904), Episcopal bishop, was born in Hadley, Massachusetts, the son of Dan Huntington, a Congregational minister, and Elizabeth Porter Phelps. He attended Hopkins Academy and then Amherst College from which he graduated in 1839. Huntington went on to Harvard Divinity School, graduating with his B.D. in 1842. In the same year, he was ordained pastor of the Unitarian South Congregational Church in Boston and married Hannah Dane Sargent in 1843.

As a seminarian at Harvard, Huntington assisted at King's Chapel in Boston, where he was attracted to the liturgical worship of that congregation's Unitarian revision of the Book of Common Prayer. At the same time, his training in urban and prison ministry at Harvard appears to have given him a heightened social conscience, which he exhibited in his subsequent career. Between 1845 to 1858 he served as editor of the *Monthly Religious Magazine*. From this influential position and from the pulpit of South Congregational Church, he began to preach a new message that some styled "evangelical Unitarianism."

Huntington's sphere of influence widened further when in 1855 he accepted appointment as the Plummer Professor of Christian Morals and Preacher to Harvard University. Huntington, however, did not satisfy either orthodox Christians or Unitarians. Yet he drew his fiercest criticism from traditional Unitarians who objected to his evangelical message and method. He led meetings at the University Music Hall in 1858 that were considered controversial because they featured revivalistic worship and invitatory preaching. He found little tolerance for these explorations in the direction of Trinitarian orthodoxy. As he put it in a letter in 1857, he found Unitarianism "in peril of being liberal only in its own direction."

Few were surprised when, in 1859, Huntington publicly affirmed an orthodox understanding of the Trinity and the Atonement. The following year he resigned his position at Harvard and began preparing for ordination in the Protestant Episcopal church. Though Manton Eastburn, the Episcopal bishop, did not encourage Huntington's decision to enter the priesthood, he did ordain him in 1861. Huntington helped establish a new mission parish, Emmanuel Church, in the diocese, which he served as rector for eight years. Emmanuel was in a hitherto neglected part of Boston, the Back Bay, and Huntington ministered to both the poor there and to the more affluent parishioners of Unitarian background.

In 1868 Huntington was elected bishop of Maine but declined. In 1869, however, he accepted election as bishop of central New York. The diocese was still in an undeveloped state when its new bishop assumed office and Huntington threw himself into the task with characteristic zeal. As bishop, he was instrumental in founding a seminary, several schools, and scores of new parishes in the diocese. Moreover, he demonstrated a special concern for Native Americans, working among the Onondagas and supporting a mission in their midst. Theologically, Huntington was moderately conservative. His own churchmanship was decidedly "Low," disliking ritualism; as bishop, however, he was rarely confrontational. His concern for the unity of the church made him avoid party polemics. He was convinced that simple apostolic teaching, preserved through an episcopal polity, was the best way to further Christian unity. He died in Hadley, Massachusetts.

Huntington's significance arises from his indefatigable efforts as a missionary bishop within the Episcopal church and his social concerns. Both in Boston and in New York, Huntington took pains to address the needs of the less fortunate. He was committed to the church playing a mediating role in labor disputes, was attracted to Henry George's single-tax movement, and supported woman suffrage. By his efforts, he anticipated the social gospel movement.

• Huntington's letters and related papers are in the Harvard University Archives (under "Harvard University Faculty and Other Officers Deceased before 1940") and in the Robbins collection of Bishops' Papers, 1785–1943, in General Theological Seminary Library, N.Y. Huntington's more notable published works include: *Sermons for the People* (1856), *Divine Aspects of Human Society* (1858), *Human Society: Its Providential Structure, Relations, and Offices* (1859), *Christian Believing and Living: Sermons by F. D. Huntington* (1860), *Helps to a Holy Lent* (1872), *Christ and the World* (1874), *The Fitness of Christianity to Men* (1878), *Christ in the Christian Year and in the Life of Man* (2 vols., 1878–1881), and *Forty Days With the Master* (1891). The standard biographical studies are Arria S. Huntington, *Memoir and Letters of Frederic Dan Huntington* (1906); George C. Richmond, *Frederic Dan Huntington* (1908); and A. L. Bryon-Curtiss, "Bishop Frederic Dan Huntington As I Knew Him," *Historical Magazine of the Protestant Episcopal Church* 25 (1956): 378–90. Also helpful, and mildly critical, is Frederick S. Arnold, *Soldier and Servant: Frederic Dan Huntington, First Bishop of Central New York* (1941). See also Douglas C. Strange, "The Conversion of Frederic Dan Huntington (1859): A Failure of Liberalism," *Historical Magazine of the Protestant Episcopal Church* 37 (1968): 287–98.

GILLIS J. HARP

HUNTINGTON, George (9 Apr. 1850–3 Mar. 1916), physician and discoverer of Huntington's chorea, was born in East Hampton, New York, the son of George Lee Huntington, a physician, and Mary Hoogland. Huntington grew up in a quiet, secluded village on Long Island, New York, and as a child developed a love of music, sketching, nature, and the ocean. He attended the Clinton Academy and at the age of eighteen began an apprenticeship in medicine with his father, followed by study at the College of Physicians and Surgeons of Columbia University in New York. After graduating in 1871, he returned briefly to East Hampton to assist in his father's practice. It was during the summer and fall of 1871, at the age of twenty-one, that he began drafting the paper that later would assure him a place in medical history. In 1874 he married Mary Elizabeth Hackard of Pomeroy, Ohio. They had five children; both of their sons followed Huntington into medicine.

Later in life Huntington recounted how at the age of eight, while riding with his father on his professional rounds, he had encountered a striking medical phenomenon. He and his father saw two women, a mother and daughter, who displayed the graphic symptoms of what clinicians today call chronic degenerative chorea. Witnessing their involuntary bowing, twitching, and grimacing left a strong impression on the young Huntington, one that was recalled when he went to practice medicine with his father in 1871. Drawing on observations compiled by both his father and grandfather, Huntington wrote a paper on chorea and on 15 February 1872 read it to the Meigs and Mason Academy of Medicine at Middleport, Ohio, where he had moved to set up his own private practice. The paper was well received and was sent to the *Medical and Surgical Reporter of Philadelphia*, where it was published on 13 April 1872.

Most of Huntington's article on chorea was taken up discussing the onset, symptoms, and treatment of childhood chorea, or chorea minor. However, at the end of the paper he described a rarer form of chorea, which he called hereditary chorea, and it was this part of his paper that gained the most attention. Huntington argued that there were three important "peculiarities" of this particular form of chorea: its hereditary nature, the tendency to insanity and suicide, and its onset in adult life. Once the symptoms have appeared, he insisted, recovery is out of the question and treatment ineffective.

The hereditary nature of the disease, Huntington contended, derived from a small number of inbred families from the east end of Long Island, where the ordinary form of chorea was unknown. If either or both of the parents exhibit the disease, he continued, one or more of their offspring "almost invariably" will suffer from it. However, if the children go through life without the disease, future generations will be free from it.

This was a noteworthy observation, as Huntington himself pointed out, given commonly held views regarding the inheritance of illness. Beginning in the 1840s Americans increasingly offered hereditarian explanations for antisocial behavior as well as clinical disease. One of the favorite theories of heredity was degeneration, which held that certain families were stigmatized by a flawed nervous system that could manifest itself in a wide range of physical and emotional diseases, including cancer and tuberculosis. The hereditary nature of Huntington's chorea differed from the presumed law of these so-called hereditary diseases in that, as Huntington explained, "one generation may enjoy entire immunity from their dread ravages, and yet in another you find them cropping out in all their hideousness." That the hereditary pattern Huntington saw in chorea was different from this pattern illustrates his refusal to bend his clinical description to fit prevailing views. This is doubly significant given the close clinical ties between insanity and Huntington's chorea as well as the popularity of hereditary theories of mental disease. Because sufferers from Huntington's chorea are sometimes found in institutions, lumped in with patients suffering from a wide range of mental disorders, there were further obstacles to differential diagnosis. On the other hand, because of the growing interest in pathological heredity in Huntington's day, once his paper was published his fame was almost assured.

Although Huntington became well known after 1872, the rest of his life and career was comparatively uneventful. After trying private practice in Ohio, he and his wife moved in 1874 to La Grangeville in the Catskill Mountains of New York, where he settled into the routine of a country practitioner. Huntington preferred this type of medical practice to an urban practice because of his love of the outdoors and his increasingly poor health due to asthma, which often kept him in bed for days at a time. Finally in 1901 his health forced him to move to North Carolina, where after two years he improved. He then returned to the Catskills and became health officer of East Fishkill Township and later visiting physician to the Matteawan General Hospital. In 1915 he gave up his medical practice and went to live with his son Edwin in Cairo, New York. He died there the next year of bronchopneumonia.

The lasting value of Huntington's contribution to clinical medicine was well summed up by Sir William Osler in 1908. "In the history of medicine," Osler wrote, "there are few instances in which a disease has been more accurately, more graphically, or more briefly described." If his place in medicine's past seems less glorious than that of more famous clinical luminaries—such as his French contemporary in neurology, Jean Martin Charcot—it is well to remember that the notoriety of the latter often rests less on solid additions to medical knowledge than on the fleeting influence that their highly publicized but now outdated theories enjoyed in their own day.

• Huntington's paper on chorea is "On Chorea," *Medical and Surgical Reporter of Philadelphia* 26 (13 Apr. 1872): 317–21. The most recent biographical treatment of Huntington is Charles S. Stevenson, "A Biography of George Huntington, M.D.," *Bulletin of the Institute of the History of Medicine* 2 (1934): 53–76.

IAN DOWBIGGIN

HUNTINGTON, Henry Edwards (27 Feb. 1850–23 May 1927), urban developer, railroad executive, and book and art collector, was born in Oneonta, New York, the son of Solon Huntington, a merchant, land speculator, and farmer, and Harriet Saunders. His father was conservative by nature, and it was his uncle, railway magnate Collis Huntington, who became the most influential person in Henry Huntington's life. Huntington was educated at public and private schools in Oneonta. His first business experience was a part-time job in an Oneonta hardware store, and at seventeen he started working there full time. He left the firm in 1869, and after several months at his brother-in-law's hardware store Huntington went to New York City, where he took a job as a porter at Sargent & Co., a hardware manufacturer.

Much of Huntington's free time in New York was spent with his uncle Collis, and a special friendship developed between them. In 1871 Collis Huntington acquired a sawmill in St. Albans, West Virginia, to supply railroad ties for his expanding rail network, and he hired Henry as its manager. Thus, at twenty-one, Huntington began an almost continuous thirty-year relationship with his uncle's enterprises.

Huntington continued as manager and then part-owner of the mill until 1876. After a brief hiatus, he returned to Collis's companies in 1881 as construction superintendent for the Chesapeake, Ohio and Southwestern Railroad. In 1884 Collis transferred him to the Kentucky Central Railroad. First employed as construction engineer, Huntington became the railroad's superintendent in 1885, receiver in 1886, and was the vice president and general manager from 1887 to 1890. After turning the financially troubled company around, Huntington worked for several of Collis's other eastern railroads.

In 1892 Collis, as president of the Southern Pacific Railroad (SP), asked Huntington to act as his assistant at the corporate headquarters in San Francisco. For the next eight years, Huntington held various positions at the railroad. By 1900 he was the firm's first vice president, president of its trolley company, the Market Street Railway, and appeared to be heir apparent to the SP presidency. However, when Collis died in August of that year, Huntington's desire to head the SP was blocked by majority stockholders. Unable to follow in his uncle's footsteps, the fifty-year-old nephew could have retired on his inheritance from Collis's estate, estimated at $15 million. But Huntington was a builder by nature, and he decided to establish his own business empire in southern California.

Originally investing in the region in 1898, when he and a syndicate purchased the Los Angeles Railway, Huntington increased his investments in the Los Angeles basin in 1901 after he sold his San Francisco interests. Huntington understood that real estate served by rail transportation was much more valuable than inaccessible land. Hence his Los Angeles business strategy was to pour vast amounts of his personal fortune into three related businesses important for urban growth: street railways, real estate development, and electric power generation and distribution.

Already controlling the profitable Los Angeles Railway in the heart of the city's business and residential district, Huntington and several investors incorporated the interurban Pacific Electric Railway in 1901. This system was designed to connect many of the basin's small communities, located from ten to ninety miles away, to downtown Los Angeles. Although not a profitable transit system, it served Huntington's larger purpose of promoting the sale of real estate.

Huntington incorporated two other companies to interface with Pacific Electric. He established several land firms to purchase, subdivide, and sell real estate, of which the Huntington Land and Improvement Company, created in 1902, was the most important. In that same year Huntington and investors incorporated the Pacific Light and Power Company, designed to generate and supply electricity for the expanding trolley system as well as distribute excess power to parts of Los Angeles County.

With this triad of companies, Huntington dominated the key sectors of regional development. His street railways held a near monopoly over the basin's public transportation—by 1910 Huntington trolley systems stretched over nearly 1,300 miles of southern California. Huntington's real estate holdings, largely concentrated in the northeastern portion of Los Angeles County, made him one of the area's largest landowners. And by 1913 his power company, besides providing electricity to his streetcars, was supplying 20 percent of the power needs in the city of Los Angeles.

Since local planning commissions had little regulatory power at the time, Huntington became the region's de facto metropolitan planner. By building trolley lines where and when he wanted, Huntington decided the spatial layout of the area. Then, as a large-scale subdivider, he dictated the socioeconomic mix of many suburbs.

Huntington worked in other ways to encourage development in southern California. He was involved in local agriculture, industry, the hotel business, and many leading social and civic organizations. Although always interested in book collecting, Huntington took the hobby more seriously after 1900. Ten years later, he began to disengage himself from his many business concerns and became a serious collector of rare books and paintings. In 1911 he purchased the E. Dwight Church and the Robert Hoe libraries. From 1914 to 1917 he acquired the Kemble-Devonshire collection of English plays, the Frederick Halsey library, part of the Pembroke library, and the Bridgewater library. He eventually held one of the largest collections of English literature in the world. Huntington also assembled a valuable art collection dominated by eighteenth-century paintings by Gainsborough, Reynolds, and Romney. In addition to collecting rare books and art, Huntington built beautiful gardens at the estate he purchased in 1903 in San Marino, a wealthy residential community east of Los Angeles and southeast of Pasadena. Planted with many rare specimens, the grounds included lily ponds, a cactus garden, a palm garden, and a Japanese garden. To preserve his collections and gardens, in 1919 Huntington endowed a trust that established the Huntington Library, Art Collections, and Botanical Gardens at his estate. His mansion housed the art collection, and construction of the library building was completed in 1923. The board of trustees set up a permanent endowment, to which Huntington contributed various securities with a market value of between $9 and $10 million.

Undoubtedly, Henry Huntington's close ties to Collis Huntington were instrumental in his business career, but they were also important in shaping his personal life. Huntington was first married in 1873 to Mary Alice Prentice, the sister of Collis's adopted daughter, and the couple had four children. Divorced in 1906, he married Collis's widow, Arabella Duval Huntington, in 1913. Huntington died in Philadelphia.

Even without the assistance of his uncle, Huntington's determination, drive, and keen sense of timing would likely have made him a successful businessman. Rarely making a poor business decision, Huntington was able to quintuple the market value of the fortune he had received from his uncle's will. In 1928 his estate was appraised at $43 million, a figure that does not include the Huntington Library, Art Collections, and Botanical Gardens (worth about $30 million in 1927) or his boyhood home in Oneonta, New York, which he converted to a library and public park.

Henry Huntington's name remains prominent throughout southern California, as evidenced by Huntington Beach, Huntington Park, Huntington Drive, the Huntington Hospital, and the Huntington Hotel. One of the leading urban developers of the region, Huntington used his wealth and managerial ability to shape the modern contours of greater Los Angeles.

• Family and business correspondence as well as business records are in the Henry E. Huntington Papers, Huntington Library, San Marino, Calif. The Collis P. Huntington Papers, Syracuse University (and on microfilm, Huntington Library), contain letters between Collis and Henry. For information on Huntington the businessman and his impact on southern California, see William B. Friedricks, *Henry E. Huntington and the Creation of Southern California* (1992). Also helpful are Spencer Crump, *Ride the Big Red Cars: How Trolleys Helped Build Southern California* (1962), and Robert M. Fogelson, *The Fragmented Metropolis: Los Angeles, 1850–1930* (1967). For intimate details of Huntington's personal life, see James Thorpe, *Henry Edwards Huntington: A Biography* (1994). Information on Huntington and the library can be found in Ray A. Billington, "The Genesis of the Research Institution," *Huntington Library Quarterly* 32 (Aug. 1969): 351–72; Donald C. Dickinson, *Henry E. Huntington's Library of Libraries* (1995); and John E. Pomfret, *The Henry E. Huntington Library and Art Gallery from Its Beginnings to 1969* (1969).

WILLIAM B. FRIEDRICKS

HUNTINGTON, Jabez (7 Aug. 1719–5 Oct. 1786), politician and general, was born in Norwich, Connecticut, the son of Joshua Huntington, a merchant, and Hannah Perkins. The Huntingtons were one of eastern Connecticut's most prominent families. Jabez's grandfather and great-uncle, Christopher and Simon Huntington, had been among the wealthiest of Norwich's original settlers; his father, Joshua, took advantage of Norwich's strategic location at the uppermost navigable point on the Thames River to become the region's leading merchant. For most of the eighteenth century, Norwich was the second most populous town in the colony, lagging only slightly behind New Haven and standing ahead of urban centers that were to become better known, such as Hartford and New London. Growing up a Huntington in this thriving river port afforded Jabez great opportunities to excel in both politics and business.

As did many young men in his family, Huntington attended Yale College. After graduating in 1741, he returned to Norwich to join his father in trade. He married Elizabeth Backus the following year; they had one son. In 1745 Elizabeth died. In 1746 Huntington married Hannah Williams. They had four sons and two daughters. Four of Huntington's sons played important roles in the Revolution: Jedediah Huntington, the eldest, had a brilliant military career as a major general on Washington's staff, and he was later a delegate to the Constitutional Convention in 1787; Andrew and Ebenezer formed a business firm that financed privateers and acted as a commissary for military supplies; Ebenezer also served in the Continental army, rising to the rank of brigadier general; and Joshua supervised the construction of the thirty-six-gun frigate, the *Confederacy*, the largest naval ship commissioned by the Continental Congress and, because of its size and fire power, one of the technological wonders of the war.

Jabez Huntington's career benefited as much from his energy, ambition, and talent as from his family name. He was elected to the Connecticut General Assembly in 1750 and continued to represent Norwich until 1764, serving as clerk from 1757 to 1760 and as speaker from 1760 to 1764. The freemen elected him in 1764 to the twelve-member Governor's Council. At the same time as he pursued his political career, Huntington achieved parallel success as a merchant and military officer. He expanded the West Indian trading business he had inherited from his father and moved steadily up the ranks of the militia. In 1776, he and David Wooster of New Haven were appointed major generals and commanders of the state militia in the eastern and western regions respectively. When Wooster died the following year of wounds suffered in combat, Huntington became commander for the entire state.

It was during the Revolution, however, as a member of Connecticut's Council of Safety, that Huntington made his greatest contribution. Norwich lay at the heart of Connecticut's eastern region, which was regarded as the most politically radical area of the colony, and Huntington early signaled his Whig sensibilities when he joined six other governor's councilors who walked out of a meeting in 1765 rather than take an oath to enforce the Stamp Act. From this point onward, he was at the forefront of the patriotic cause. In 1769, the elevation to the governorship of his close friend Jonathan Trumbull (1710–1785) further enhanced Huntington's already substantial influence. Trumbull lived in Lebanon, a country town near Norwich and, as did Huntington, made his living in the West Indian provisions trade. Moreover, Trumbull's daughter, Faith, married Huntington's son, Jedediah.

Created by the General Assembly to deal with emergent military matters, the Council of Safety, in consultation with Governor Trumbull, provided the executive leadership for revolutionary Connecticut. Its ten members included three Huntingtons, Jabez and his cousins Samuel and Benjamin, Governor Trumbull, Deputy Governor Matthew Griswold, and five others. The council held over 1,200 meetings in the "war office"—formerly Trumbull's retail store in Lebanon—and from 1776 to 1779, Jabez Huntington exercised a profound influence on it. He combined an unrivaled knowledge of finance, politics, personnel, and the military. As major general of the militia, Huntington did not take the field himself but coordinated military plans and political decisions. The strain of this responsibility coupled with his workload proved too much, and in late 1779 he suffered a physical and mental collapse. Huntington subsequently retired, and he lived the remaining seven years of his life in poor health and spirits as a virtual recluse in Norwich, where he died.

Jabez Huntington was never adequately reimbursed for many of the provisions he procured with his own credit for the troops; it was widely agreed that he sacrificed both health and fortune to the revolutionary cause. He was a devout Congregationalist who was known for his amiability, graciousness, and urbanity. A portrait of Huntington, painted by John Trumbull (1756–1843), is presently hung in the Connecticut State Library.

• No primary collection of Huntington's papers exists. A few personal letters have survived and, along with some official correspondence, are in the Connecticut Historical Society and Connecticut State Library in Hartford, the Sterling Memorial Library at Yale University, and in several other collections, such as the papers of Jonathan Trumbull, General Nathaniel Greene, and William Samuel Johnson. The largest number of letters to, from, and about Jabez are found in the published letters of two of his sons: *Correspondence of the Brothers Joshua and Jedediah Huntington during the Period of the American Revolution*, ed. Albert Bates (1923). No biography exists, but sketches of Huntington appear in several places; among them, E. B. Huntington, *Huntington Memorial* (1863), a genealogy of the family; Francis Caulkins, *History of Norwich, Connecticut* (1873); and Franklin Bowditch Dexter, *Biographical Sketches of the Graduates of Yale College* (1885). For specific discussions of Huntington's role in the Revolution, see Joan Nafie, *To the Beat of a Drum: A History of Norwich, Connecticut during the American Revolution* (1975).

BRUCE C. DANIELS

HUNTINGTON, James Otis Sargent (23 July 1854–10 July 1935), founder of the monastic Order of the Holy Cross of the Episcopal church, was born in Roxbury, Massachusetts, the son of Frederic Dan Huntington and Hannah Dane Sargent. His parents, both of Puritan stock, imbued their children with a strong sense of civic responsibility and particularly with passionate concern for the needy. Huntington was profoundly influenced by his father, who had been a Unitarian minister and professor of moral ethics at Harvard University before joining the Episcopal church. Huntington emulated his father's passionate commitment to trinitarian theology and social justice, although he departed from his father's views in adopting the Catholic tradition of Anglicanism.

Huntington spent his childhood and early adolescence in Massachusetts. After completing his secondary education in Manlius, New York, near Syracuse, where the family moved when his father was elected bishop of Central New York in 1869, he studied at Harvard College, receiving his B.A. in 1875. He studied for the ministry in the Central New York diocesan seminary, St. Andrew's, in Syracuse, and after ordination in 1880 he assumed charge of a small mission, Calvary Church, in Syracuse. In 1881 he moved to New York City to form with two other priests the Order of the Holy Cross. They intended to use the order as a vehicle for evangelism and saw it as an American counterpart to the Society of St. John the Evangelist, an Anglican order founded in England in 1866. The creation of the Order of the Holy Cross also indicated Huntington's dedication to the "High Church" movement, which sought to revive Catholic ideals and practices (such as monasticism) within the Episcopal church. The other founders left the order after a short period. Huntington was the only member for a number of years, and he became its principal molder when it began to grow.

At the same time that he was organizing the monastic order, Huntington served as priest at the Mission of the Holy Cross, conducted by the sisters of St. John the Evangelist in the Lower East Side of Manhattan Island. He quickly gained a reputation as a social crusader, allying himself with Henry George and the single tax program, a proposed means of fighting the inflation of real estate values that victimized the urban poor. Huntington also allied himself with Father Edward McGlynn, a priest of the Roman Catholic church and founder of the Anti-Poverty Society. Huntington, claiming that the "Church is the great Anti-Poverty Society," argued for church involvement in social justice activities. Huntington's theological argument for Christian social action antedated the celebrated social gospel theology of Walter Rauschenbusch by many years.

Huntington promoted his social crusade within the Episcopal church by organizing the Church Association for the Advancement of the Interests of Labor (CAIL), which enlisted many of the influential members of the church, including the majority of the church's bishops. Through CAIL Huntington won church support for the labor movement at a time when many saw labor organizations as contrary to the doctrine of free enterprise. He served as an arbitrator in labor disputes and on one occasion was spectacularly successful in mediating between labor and management in a bitter labor dispute in the mine fields of Illinois in 1889–1890. Along with efforts to organize support for laborers, Huntington sought to identify with the poor and powerless. Garbed as a monk, Huntington addressed rallies in support of the single tax program and preached on behalf of the poor in a church identified with the privileged employers.

In 1892 the order moved to Westminster, Maryland, far removed from the urban scene where Huntington had established his reputation. Following the move, he disengaged himself suddenly and almost totally from the social crusade that had occupied so much of his energy for a decade. In the new setting Huntington redirected his attention to building up the Order of the Holy Cross. He had concluded that the religious formation of the members of the order took precedence over social reconstruction or social welfare activities. This conclusion was no doubt a result of the disappointment he experienced as a social crusader. Most of his supporters, including members of his own order, did not understand, in his judgment, the spiritual principles on which his social concerns were based. To the distress of his former supporters, he concluded that the prevailing spiritual nurturing was inadequate for the task at hand, and inspirational activities displaced social reconstruction as the focus of his ministry, His work within his religious order, his conducting of religious retreats, his establishment of church schools (Kent School, Conn., in 1906 and St. Andrew's School, Tenn., in 1905) reflected this new focus. He did not altogether abandon social reform efforts during these years. For example, he was instrumental in the formation of the Church Mission of Help, an organization designed to assist young people in resolving their own problems rather than having them be dependent on intervention. However, he did not again enter the public fray on behalf of the needy or the labor movement.

The order moved to West Park, New York, in 1904, where Huntington closed his career. He died in New York City.

• The Huntington papers are stored in the Episcopal Church Archives in Austin, Tex. Researchers must obtain permission from the Order of the Holy Cross to gain access to the papers. Among Huntington's publications are *The Work of Prayer* (1921), *How to Preach a Mission: Practical Directions for Mission Services* (1916), and *Philanthropy and Social Progress: Seven Essays* (1893). The major biography is Vida Scudder, *Father Huntington, Christian Social Pioneer* (1940). See also John Fletcher, "Father Huntington, Christian Social Pioneer," in *Pioneer Builders for Christ*, vol. 2, ed. P. M. Dawley (n.d.); J. A. Muller, "Father Huntington and the Beginnings of Religious Orders for Men in the Episcopal Church," *Historical Magazine of the Protestant Episcopal Church* (1941); and Adam McCoy, *Holy Cross: The Order of Anglican Monasticism* (1987).

FRANK SUGENO

HUNTINGTON, Jedediah (4 Aug. 1743–25 Sept. 1818), revolutionary war soldier, was born in Norwich, Connecticut, the son of Jabez Huntington, a merchant, and Elizabeth Backus. His father, who had become prosperous by trading with the West Indies, was well known socially and politically throughout the colony. Hence, when he enrolled in Harvard College, young Huntington was ranked second in his class in terms of status. In 1763 he graduated from Harvard, delivering an oration during the commencement services, and returned home to join his father's business. Firmly establishing himself in the community, he enhanced his position by marrying Faith Trumbull, daughter of Governor Jonathan Trumbull (1710–1785). The date of their marriage and the number of their children, if any, are unknown. As tensions arose over the next few years between Britain and the American colonies, Huntington became an ardent proponent of colonial liberties and began educating himself in military matters. In 1769 he was appointed ensign in a local infantry company raised at the behest of the Connecticut Assembly. Two years later he was promoted to company lieutenant and in 1774 was raised to the rank of captain. Before the year was out, he was chosen by the assembly as colonel of the Twentieth Regiment of the Connecticut militia. On 26 April 1775 he marched with his regiment to Roxbury, there joining the rebel army besieging British troops in Boston. In July he assumed command of the Eighth Connecticut Regiment. On 24 November 1775 his wife, who had become mentally unhinged because of the war, died suddenly. After her funeral, Huntington served at Roxbury until the British evacuated Boston in March 1776, then in April he accompanied General George Washington to New York. En route Huntington entertained Washington and his father-in-law, Governor Trumbull, at his home in Norwich.

At New York Huntington was commissioned a colonel in the Continental army and was given command of the Seventeenth Regiment. On 27 August 1776 he and his regiment fought gallantly and "suffered greatly," according to Washington, in the battle of Long Island. They also were engaged in numerous skirmishes as the American army subsequently was driven from Manhattan. He was ordered to Peekskill, New York, on 3 April 1777 and later in the month was detached to Danbury with fifty men to guard military stores there. On 26 April he retreated when British general William Tryon attacked the town, but the following day he joined Generals Benedict Arnold and David Wooster in harassing Tryon's troops as the British withdrew toward the sea. Impressed by Wooster's fighting spirit, Huntington wrote Washington on 28 April that Wooster had shown "great Spirit, Skill, and Bravery" against Tryon. On 12 May 1777 Huntington was promoted to brigadier general by Congress and that summer served under General Israel Putnam at Peekskill. Although the fighting came near him in October when Sir Henry Clinton seized Forts Montgomery and Independence on the Hudson River, he saw no action. He rejoined General Washington's army near Philadelphia on 11 October. On the 24th he served on the court-martial of General Anthony Wayne, who was charged with dereliction of duty at Paoli, and voted with the majority to acquit him. Huntington remained with Washington the following winter at Valley Forge, suffering with his colleagues the dearth of provisions. He growled to Timothy Pickering on 22 December 1777 that even combat was "preferable to starving."

On 30 May 1778 Huntington's regiment was attached to General Charles Lee's (1731–1782) division, and Huntington was with Lee in the battle of Monmouth, 28 June 1778. A month later Huntington was appointed to a court-martial ordered by Washington to try Lee for refusing to obey orders at Monmouth, for conducting "an unnecessary, disorderly and shameful retreat," and for showing "disrespect to the Commander in Chief." On 12 August Huntington voted with the majority in finding Lee guilty on all counts and suspending him from command for a year. In late 1778 Huntington marched his regiment into winter quarters at Danbury, Connecticut, then went home for an extended visit. In the summer of 1779 he served under General William Heath in the Highlands, and in the following year he was posted at Springfield, New Jersey. On 29 September 1780 he served on a board of general officers that tried Major John André for spying. He and his colleagues, agreeing that André was guilty, declared that the young man "ought to suffer death." Washington approved the sentence, and André was hanged at noon on 2 October. In 1781 Huntington remained on duty in New York while Washington administered the coup de grâce to Charles, Lord Cornwallis at Yorktown, Virginia. The following year he spent most of his time in Connecticut, attempting to recruit his regiment to strength. At the army's last cantonment at Newburgh, New York, in 1783, he helped found the Society of the Cincinnati. Just before his retirement from the army on 3 October, he was promoted to brevet major general by Washington, who expressed "esteem and affection" for his comrade in arms.

Resuming his business career in Norwich, Huntington prospered financially and socially. He was married a second time, to Ann Moore, and entertained many distinguished visitors at his home. The number of their children, if any, is unknown. For a time he was sheriff of New London County, then he was appointed state treasurer. He served as a delegate to a state constitutional convention, was on a board of foreign missions, and zealously supported various charitable institutions. In 1789 he was appointed by President Washington as collector of customs at New London, to which place he and his wife moved. Huntington held the office for twenty-six years and died in New London. Washington considered him to command the Legion army in 1792, praising him as being "sober, sensible and very discreet," but finally chose Wayne. Never a dashing or glamorous man, Huntington was a steady, dependable individual whose basic decency was appreciated and utilized by his fellow citizens.

• Huntington's extensive correspondence with Washington is in the George Washington Papers, Library of Congress. Some of it is printed in John C. Fitzpatrick, ed., *The Writings of George Washington from the Original Manuscript Sources*, vols. 3–31 (1931–1939). His published correspondence is "Letters of Lieut. Jedediah Huntington (1775–1776)," Massachusetts Historical Society, *Collections*, 5th ser., vol. 9 (1885); and "Correspondence of the Brothers Joshua and Jedediah Huntington, during the Period of the American Revolution," Connecticut Historical Society, *Collections* 20 (1923). Sketches of his life are Abel McEwen, *A Sermon Preached at the Funeral of Gen. Jedediah Huntington, of New London . . .* (1818); and Charles W. Heathcote, "General Jedediah Huntington Rendered Patriotic Service for His Country," *Picket Post* 52 (1956): 12–18. Other information is in Elijah Baldwin Huntington, *A Genealogical Memoir of the Huntington Family . . .* (1863); and Huntington Family Association, *The Huntington Family in America . . .* (1915). For his role at Danbury, see James R. Case, *An Account of Tryon's Raid on Danbury in April, 1777, Also the Battle of Ridgefield . . .* (1927). Background information on his life is in G. H. Hollister, *The History of Connecticut . . .*, vol. 2 (1855); and Francis Manwaring Caulkins, *History of Norwich, Connecticut . . .* (1845).

PAUL DAVID NELSON

HUNTINGTON, Samuel (3 July 1731–5 Jan. 1796), signer of the Declaration of Independence, president of the Continental Congress, and governor of Connecticut, was born in Scotland Society, Windham Township, Connecticut, the son of Nathaniel Huntington, a farmer and clothier, and Mehetable (sometimes seen as Mehitabel) Thurston. He was descended from Simon Huntington, who died in passage to America in 1633.

Although he was later to receive honorary degrees from Yale and Dartmouth, Huntington was a cooper's apprentice and was self-taught. He read law with Colonel Jedidiah Elderkin and was admitted to the bar in 1758. Moving to Norwich in 1760, he married Martha Lathrop Devotion, the daughter of a Congregational minister, the Reverend Ebenezer Devotion of Windham, the following year. Although there were no children from this union, the couple raised a nephew and niece.

From this point his career followed a familiar path for New England statesmen. His public service began with his election in 1764 as a representative to the lower house of the general assembly. In 1775 he was elected assistant, one of the twelve members of the governor's council, the upper house. He was reelected to this position until 1784. Simultaneously with his legislative career he served in the judiciary. He was appointed king's attorney for Connecticut in 1768. Opposing the British on the Stamp Act and the Intolerable Acts, Huntington resigned his royal appointment. He was considered a moderate Whig and spoke later of "just rights on the Defensive." He was appointed to the superior court of Connecticut in 1773 and became chief justice in 1784.

Increasingly active in national affairs, Huntington was elected to represent Connecticut in the Continental Congress from 1775 to 1784. During this period he was weakened by an attack of smallpox. One of Connecticut's three signers of the Declaration of Independence, Huntington was elected in 1779 to succeed John Jay as president of the Continental Congress. During the Revolution he was tarred, just as was George Washington, for becoming wealthy by "fleecing his deluded constituents." As president of the Continental Congress he faced difficulties in requisitioning troops and supplies from the states and in raising funds to support the Confederation. He received minor criticism for taking holy water at the de Miralles funeral in 1780, an episode propagandized by Benedict Arnold to encourage anti-Catholic desertions among the Continental troops. In general he was well supported by public opinion.

While not at the national capital, Huntington served on Connecticut's council of public safety and remained active in planning the state's defense. Reflecting Connecticut's interests on the national level, he was primarily concerned with shipping, currency, militia, and territorial questions. Among the controversial issues he faced were the separation of Vermont, which he opposed; the mutiny on the Connecticut ship *Minerva*; Virginia's land claims, which were similar to those of Connecticut; and the problem of recognizing Spain's claims in Florida and thus obtaining free navigation of the Mississippi River in exchange for support for fishing rights in the Grand Banks. He attended the intercolonial meeting at Springfield in 1777 that dealt with price regulation, which he opposed, currency, embargoes, and hoarding. He also took an interest in coastal and admiralty matters.

After his return from Philadelphia, he reentered Connecticut politics in the legislative assembly. In 1783 he drafted the first American copyright law. He was elected lieutenant governor in 1785 and served as governor from 1786 until his death. Selected by the assembly in an election in which no candidate had received a majority, he replaced the incumbent Matthew Griswold in whose political shadow he often had stood. Both contenders were Federalists, but Griswold favored somewhat stronger authority under the Articles of the Confederation. Always popular with his constituents, at one election Huntington received a unanimous vote from his Norwich neighbors. He gar-

nered two "favorite son" electoral votes in the first presidential election.

During his gubernatorial period the principal issues in which Huntington was involved included the Connecticut (large state–small state) Compromise, balancing the powers of the small states in the national Congress; the settlement of Shays's Rebellion in western Massachusetts, in which he assured Governor James Bowdoin of assistance in extraditing insurgents across the still-contested boundary; the Yankee-Pennamite War over settlements by Connecticut's Susquehanna Company in the Wyoming Valley of Pennsylvania, which was resolved by an "act of God" in the form of a flood, according to Pennsylvania; and the development of the western lands, known as the Western Reserve, which Connecticut had retained in Ohio under the Articles for "educational purposes." Samuel Huntington (1765–1817), Huntington's nephew, was to become governor of Ohio, and the Connecticut governor was certainly interested in his state's stake in the western territories as well as in furthering public education. All of these affairs involved the need to resolve disputes among the states and helped prompt Huntington's support for the Constitution. During the later period of his governorship the Connecticut legislature passed a probate act that led to the Supreme Court's decision in *Calder v. Bull* in 1798. The suit established an important precedent regarding ex post facto laws, which allowed the Federalist party to secure the release from prison of some of its leaders by declarations of bankruptcy as of 1783.

Huntington died in Norwich. He was eulogized by his contemporaries, including the marquis de Chastellux, who found the simple modesty of Huntington's life comparable with those of Fabricius and the Philopoemens. Huntington combined traits of both the Puritan and the Yankee. His contributions to the development of American politics during the "critical period" have been underappreciated. He ranks among the founding fathers in a tier just below John Jay and Roger Sherman.

• Relatively few of Huntington's nonofficial papers and letters have survived. The Samuel Huntington Papers are held by the Connecticut Historical Society. Connecticut's American Revolution Bicentennial Commission published Larry R. Gerlach, *Connecticut Congressman: Samuel Huntington, 1731–1796* (1976). Gerlach's book provides the first detailed biography of Huntington. Albert E. VanDusen covers Huntington's career through 1783 in "Samuel Huntington: A Leader of Revolutionary Connecticut," *Bulletin of the Connecticut Historical Society* 19, no. 2 (1954): 38–62. Susan D. Huntington, "Samuel Huntington," *Connecticut Magazine* 6 (May–June 1900): 247–53, provides additional information. There is also a study by Henry Strong Huntington, "The Life of Samuel Huntington," in unpublished form in the Connecticut State Library. Mary E. Perkins, *Old Houses of the Antient* [sic] *Town of Norwich 1660–1800* (1895), along with other local histories provides useful historical and genealogical material. Governor Huntington's proclamations and some transactions are available in Connecticut's public records series.

GILBERT M. CUTHBERTSON

HUNTINGTON, William Reed (20 Sept. 1838–26 July 1909), Episcopal clergyman and advocate of church unity, was born in Lowell, Massachusetts, the son of Elisha Huntington, a physician and politician, and Hannah Hinckley. Both parents were upper-class New Englanders who turned from Congregationalism and became high church Episcopalians. William, their youngest child, was drawn to medicine and in 1853 attended Norwich University, a military preparatory school in Vermont that had a strong scientific department. In 1855 he entered Harvard and became a protégé of Josiah Parsons Cooke, professor of chemistry and mineralogy and a convinced Unitarian. In the circle around Cooke (who was to become Huntington's brother-in-law) were Frederic Dan Huntington, a distant cousin and Unitarian preacher to the college, Charles W. Eliot, who became president of Harvard in 1869, and Francis Ellingwood Abbot, future philosopher and founder of the Free Religious Association. Religion as well as science was a topic of lively conversation in the Cooke circle. Under the influence of F. D. Huntington, William, to the dismay of his family, joined the college's Unitarian chapel. Graduating in 1859, he spent another year at Harvard as a chemistry instructor but in 1860 began studies for the Episcopal ministry, again under F. D. Huntington, who had left Unitarianism and become rector of Emmanuel Church, Boston.

Huntington was exposed to yet another religious viewpoint when in early 1861 he presented himself to the evangelical bishop of Massachusetts, Manton Eastburn, for the preordination examination. Eastburn refused to pass Huntington because he would not subscribe fully to the Thirty-nine Articles of Religion, the central tenets of the Episcopal church. Angered and confused, Huntington traveled to England to talk with John Keble, venerable leader of the Oxford Movement, which rejected the church's traditional, sixteenth-century definition of orthodoxy. Keble confirmed him in his belief that defining *catholicity* was one of the pressing problems of the time. Always an independent thinker, Huntington rejected what for him were Keble's and John Henry Cardinal Newman's too-narrow definitions of catholicity. When he returned to the United States in September 1861, Eastburn relented. Huntington passed a reexamination and on 1 October was ordained deacon. On 3 December 1862 he was ordained a presbyter and became rector of All Saints Church, Worcester, where he remained for the next twenty-one years. In 1863 he married Theresa Reynolds, daughter of a prominent Boston physician. The couple had four children. She died in childbirth in 1872, and he never remarried.

In 1870 Huntington's first book, *The Church-Idea: An Essay towards Unity*, was published. In it Huntington asserted that Christians were not simply private believers, but citizens of both church and state, and of the two, the nation was the crucial, collective historical agent. The national disunity resulting from the Civil War engaged Huntington as much and perhaps more than his experience of religious conflict. In the sermon "American Catholicity," preached at Trinity Church, Boston, in May 1865, Huntington suggested that church unity must follow the restoration of national unity. The question was, who spoke for Christians in the United States? Vatican Council I, with its definition of papal infallibility, declared that the pope did. Not surprisingly Huntington refused that road to unity, but he also questioned the Church of England's claim to catholicity because it had failed to become the spiritual home for the majority of Britons. Neither, in his view, was the present system of the Episcopal church likely to provide such a religious home for Americans. Nevertheless Huntington suggested that there were basic principles in Anglicanism that fitted it to become "America's best hope." These principles were: "1st. The Holy Scriptures as the Word of God, 2d. The Primitive Creeds as the Rule of Faith, 3d. The Two Sacraments ordained by Christ himself, 4th. The Episcopate as the key-stone of Governmental Unity." Huntington substituted this four-sided proposal, or "Quadrilateral," in place of the Thirty-nine Articles. A greatly reduced definition of Anglicanism, the Quadrilateral was accepted by the General Convention meeting in Chicago in 1886 and by the Lambeth Conference of Anglican bishops in 1888. The Chicago-Lambeth Quadrilateral became—and has remained—the official statement of Anglicanism's basic principles.

In the 1870s and 1880s Huntington also sought to reform his church's liturgy, to make it more acceptable to contemporary Americans. (Among other reforms, he wanted to use ordinary English in services, to institute short weekday services for people who worked daily in factories, and to revise the Book of Common Prayer to reflect Americans' needs.) In this regard he was less successful, for his church had been racked for decades by bitter debate and eventual schism (1873) over matters of "churchmanship," that is, its identity as Protestant or Catholic, and these disagreements had come down to issues involving liturgical ritual and ceremonial acts. After Huntington and his friends' reformed Book of Common Prayer of 1886 was rejected, he gave only modest assistance in the preparation of the prayer book of 1892. Not until the prayer book of 1928 were most of his liturgical reforms accepted. During this period, however, his skill in debating made Huntington the acknowledged leader of the House of Deputies of the church's General Convention and eventually led to his being styled "first presbyter" of his generation. In 1883 Huntington was called to one of the leading Episcopal parishes in the nation, Grace Church in New York City, where he remained until his death.

In 1891 Huntington published *The Peace of the Church*, in which he argued that unity could be achieved through the adoption of a "single system" that closely resembled his Quadrilateral. His thinking, however, had taken on a more ecumenical spirit: truth existed in many denominations; his church's mission was to reconcile Christians. The unified church he envisioned would permit a diversity of worship but would insist on an orderly transmission of oversight by bishops. In 1898 *A National Church*, Huntington's blueprint for American Protestant church union, was published. In it, he called on the church to overcome barriers of race, class, and language, but he continued to dignify his own denomination as the agent of reconciliation. In *The Four Theories of Visible Church Unity* (1909), his final address, delivered two months before his death, Huntington declared that unity could be achieved only if the rights of every church were respected.

Huntington was a Christo-centric liberal theologian who, in the heyday of American Protestantism, wanted a nonestablished national church and did not believe that effectual ordination depended on lineal descent from the Apostles. He was also an anti-imperialist who believed that Americans should stay at home and achieve racial and national integration. In the words of Massachusetts Episcopal bishop William Lawrence, Huntington had a "firmness of character exceeded by no Puritan of an earlier day." He was reserved and melancholy, and themes of darkness and the unknown recur in his writings. His abiding interest in religious architecture is demonstrated by All Saints Church, Worcester, and the Cathedral of St. John the Divine in New York City, which he helped erect. He wanted women to have a larger share in the church's ministry and encouraged the revival in the Episcopal church of the order of deaconesses begun in Germany in 1833 by Lutheran pastor Theodore Fliedner. Huntington emphasized service for deaconesses, not celibacy. He was offered college presidencies by Hobart (1871), Kenyon (1874), and Trinity (1883). He was elected bishop of Iowa (1874) and Southern Ohio (1886) and was approached by five other dioceses. He turned them all down. He died in Nahant, Massachusetts.

• Huntington's papers are in the Archives of the Episcopal Church in Austin, Texas; the library of the Episcopal Divinity School, Cambridge, Mass.; and the Archive of Grace Church, New York City; the manuscript of his 1865 sermon "American Catholicity" is in the Morgan Library in New York City. Huntington's other major published works are *Materia Ritualis* (1882), *The Book Annexed: Its Critics and Its Prospects* (1886), *The Spiritual House* (1895), *Psyche: A Study of the Soul* (1899), and *Theology's Eminent Domain, and Other Papers* (1902). Secondary sources include John W. Suter, *Life and Letters of William Reed Huntington* (1925); John F. Woolverton, "William Reed Huntington and Church Unity: The Historical and Theological Background of the Chicago-Lambeth Quadrilateral" (Ph.D. diss., Columbia Univ., 1963); Lesley A. Northup, "The 1892 Book of Common Prayer" (Ph.D. diss., Catholic Univ. of America, 1991); and three articles by Woolverton: "W. R. Huntington: Liturgical Renewal and Church Unity in the 1880s," *Anglican Theological Review*, Apr. 1966, pp. 175–99; "Huntington's Quadrilateral: A Critical Study," *Church History*, June 1970, pp. 198–211; and "Stirring the Religious Pot at Harvard on the Eve of the Civil War: Two Huntingtons and a Cooke," *Anglican and Episcopal History*, Mar. 1989, pp. 37–49. An obituary is in the *New York Times*, 27 July 1909.

JOHN F. WOOLVERTON

HUNTLEY, Chet (10 Dec. 1911–20 Mar. 1974), broadcast journalist, was born Chester Robert Huntley in Cardwell, Montana, the son of Percy Adams "Pat" Huntley, a railroad telegrapher, and Blanche Wadine Tatham, a former schoolteacher. In 1913 his parents claimed a homestead on 960 acres of land near Saco in northern Montana. Chet's earliest memories were of farm chores, and his early schooling was in a one-room schoolhouse built on a corner of his parents' land, where he was taught to read by phonics (sounding out letters), a system he later advocated.

Huntley's maternal grandfather, Bob Tatham, was his hero and source of practical advice. He taught his grandson not to dwell on adversity, and there was plenty of adversity on the ranch as hail, locusts, and wheat rust took their toll on harvests. Huntley learned that farming was risky, yet this did not stop him from later involvement in it.

Huntley's father returned to telegraphy by moving into Saco and taking replacement assignments along the Great Northern Railroad to supplement his income until the farm was sold in 1924 and he returned to work full time with the Northern Pacific Railroad. Thereafter Huntley lived in a succession of railroad towns in southern Montana. His father's telegraphy career in a sense started him in broadcasting: during the World Series, Pat Huntley would write down play-by-play reports as they came over the wire, and Chet would announce the action out the depot window to assembled fans. He announced the Dempsey-Firpo fight in a similar manner.

In 1926 the family moved to Whitehall, Montana, forty miles east of Butte. Chet attended Whitehall High School and graduated in 1929. In high school he had become interested in debate and oratory. He earned a scholarship to Montana State College at Bozeman, where he pursued premedical studies for three years. He then won a scholarship through a national oratory contest to the Cornish School of Arts in Seattle, Washington, where he studied speech and became interested in drama. He transferred to the University of Washington in Seattle, receiving his B.A. in 1934. There he met his first wife, Ingrid Eleanor Rolin; they were married in 1936, had two daughters, and divorced in 1959. While a student Huntley began work at a Seattle radio station, KPCB, and after graduation was hired as program director. He soon moved on to KHQ in Spokane, Washington, as announcer and newscaster, and to KGW in Portland, Oregon, in 1937. He then moved to Los Angeles, California, where he worked for NBC (1937–1939), CBS (1939–1951), and ABC (1951–1955). He acquired a reputation as a conscientious announcer who researched his stories, and developed into a commentator as well as an announcer. His orientation was liberal: he won a George Foster Peabody award in 1942 for writing and producing the series "These Are Americans," which responded to discrimination against Mexican Americans; he also spoke out against the internment of Japanese Americans. In a series of half-hour programs he explored narcotic addiction in Los Angeles and nationwide. He also began to speak out against anti-Communist excesses.

In 1954, when Huntley won his second Peabody award for skill in analyzing the news and talent for mature commentary, he said that his job since World War II had been "trying to stay on the air despite objections of small but powerful vocal pressure groups." Only the week before the 1954 award, a sponsor had dropped him: in 1951 he had left CBS after twelve years because his bosses were unhappy with his liberal commentary, and because he refused to sign a loyalty oath. His battles during the McCarthy era included winning a slander suit against a woman who had called him a Communist. She was forced to write a public retraction and to pay a $10,000 settlement, which Huntley never collected.

Huntley's commentary and awards, coupled with the fact that his show had the highest daytime rating of any ABC news show, caught the attention of NBC scouts in 1954. They were seeking talent to compete with Edward R. Murrow of CBS. Huntley had the requisite serious demeanor, resonant baritone voice, and reputation for courageous commentary. He was hired by NBC in Los Angeles in 1955 and moved to New York a year later, where he did a ten-minute radio commentary, a Sunday afternoon television program called *Outlook*, and a Saturday evening news program. He was teamed with David Brinkley, NBC's Washington correspondent, to broadcast the 1956 national conventions. They worked together so well that NBC teamed them on the fifteen-minute evening news, with Huntley in New York and Brinkley in Washington.

The *Huntley-Brinkley Report* was not an instant success. Of its debut, executive producer Reuven Frank recalled, "It may have been one of the worst news shows in history. We went on with no dry run at all." Frank was responsible for the sign-off, "Good night, Chet. Good night, David," which neither newscaster liked at first: however, it became the show's signature. The program rose in the ratings and a survey found that Huntley and Brinkley were recognized by more adult Americans than the Beatles or John Wayne. The *Huntley-Brinkley Report* won every major news award, including seven Emmy and two Peabody awards. The team's success was due in part to the contrast between the serious demeanor of Huntley and the wit of Brinkley. That contrast was caught by Frank Sinatra and Milton Berle, who, at the presidential inauguration of John F. Kennedy, sang "Huntley, Brinkley/Huntley, Brinkley/One is glum/ The other is quite twinkley ..." to the tune of "Love and Marriage." Huntley wrote a portion of his own script and Brinkley all of his, unlike most newscasters, who mostly read scripts written by others. Huntley had the additional talent of being able to read flawlessly a script he had not seen before, and he carried the bulk of the announcing.

Huntley left the show in 1970 to return to Montana and develop the Big Sky resort. He had presided over an era of technical advances in television, with more remote reporting, and television had surpassed newspapers as a source of news more Americans trusted. Although the *Huntley-Brinkley Report* was surpassed in the ratings by Walter Cronkite in 1967 (perhaps hurt by the AFTRA strike earlier that year, when Brinkley did not cross the picket line and Huntley did), its ratings remained high up to Huntley's departure. The two-person news team was never quite as successful on the national news afterwards. Huntley met his second wife, Lewis Tipton "Tippy" Stringer, in 1959 through the program when he saw her on the monitor in Washington, where she was a weather announcer. Huntley asked if she was married, Brinkley said no, and the two were married about a month later. They had no children.

Huntley stayed active in retirement, broadcasting commentaries, advertising for American Airlines, and contracting with them as sponsor to broadcast a television series, *The American Experience*. He also joined an advertising firm, Levine, Huntley, Schmidt, Inc. He died in Bozeman of cancer, three days before the opening ceremonies for his resort.

• A collection of Huntley's papers (1911–1974) is in the Montana State University Library, Bozeman, and another collection (1957–1974) is at the State Historical Society of Wisconsin. His memoir of his youth is *The Generous Years* (1968). See also David Brinkley, *David Brinkley: A Memoir* (1995); Michael P. Beaubien, ed., *Views on the News* (1994); Barbara Matusow, *The Evening Stars* (1983); and Thomas Fensch, ed., *Television News Anchors* (1993). There are many newspaper and magazine articles on Huntley and the *Huntley-Brinkley Report*; one of the best is in *Newsweek*, 13 Mar. 1961. An in-depth report by William Whitworth is in the "Profiles" section of the *New Yorker*, 3 Aug. 1968. For Huntley's later life, see Robert T. Smith, "The Big Sky Development: A Lesson for the Future," *American West*, Sept. 1975; Don Schanche, "Good Night NBC . . . Hello Montana," *Today's Health*, May 1972; and Thomas Thompson, "Chet Heads for the Hills," *Life*, 17 July 1970. Huntley appeared on the White House "enemies" list for his comment on President Richard M. Nixon in the article by Thompson. Obituaries are in the *New York Times* and the *Washington Post*, both 21 Mar. 1974.

ROBERT T. BRUNS

HUNTON, Addie D. Waites (11 June 1875–21 June 1943), activist, teacher, and author, was born in Norfolk, Virginia, the daughter of Jesse Waites, an oyster and shipping business owner, and Adelina Lawton. Addie attended public school and belonged to the African Methodist Episcopal (AME) church. Her mother died when she was a young child, and she was sent to live with an aunt in Boston. She attended Boston Girls' Latin (High) School and, in 1889, became the first African-American woman to graduate from the Spencerian College of Commerce in Philadelphia, Pennsylvania. She taught for a year in Portsmouth, Virginia, before moving to Normal, Alabama, to teach and later become principal of the State Normal and Agricultural College.

In 1893 Addie Waites returned to Norfolk, where on 19 July she married William Alphaeus Hunton of Chatham, Ontario. He had moved to Norfolk in 1888 to become the first African-American professional youth secretary in the international Young Men's Christian Association (YMCA), and in 1891 he had been appointed administrative secretary of the Colored Men's Department of the International Committee. The Huntons left Norfolk for Richmond, Virginia, then moved to Atlanta in 1899 and had two children.

Hunton worked as a secretary and bursar at Clark University in Atlanta during 1905–1906. When racial riots erupted in Atlanta in 1906 the Huntons moved to Brooklyn, New York. Her husband's career as a YMCA official inspired Hunton to travel with him as his secretary when he attended YMCA conferences. Gradually she became as well known in YMCA circles as her husband was. While in Atlanta, she began to speak publicly against segregation and, beginning in 1904, penned numerous articles on issues relevant to women and, specifically, the African-American woman. In 1907 the National Board of the Young Women's Christian Association (YMCA) appointed her secretary of the South and Middle West regions, which she toured through 1908. In 1909 Addie left for Europe with her children to continue her education. She traveled first to Switzerland, then to Germany, where she studied at the Kaiser Wilhelm University in Strasbourg. When Hunton returned to the United States in 1910, she resumed her work with the YWCA, studied at the College of the City of New York, and cared for her husband, who was suffering with tuberculosis.

After Hunton's husband died in 1916, she volunteered for World War I service by working in Brooklyn canteens designated for "Negro" soldiers. In June 1918 she became one of three African-American women invited to France as YWCA welfare workers. For the next fifteen months she worked with 200,000 racially segregated African-American troops. Her first assignment was near the Loire River at St. Nazaire, a supply and transport center. Desiring to improve on the standard canteen and movies offered at YMCA huts, Hunton introduced a literacy course and a Sunday evening discussion program, each of which gained popularity with African-American servicemen, many of whom felt lonely and demoralized by segregationist practices.

Hunton's second assignment, in January 1919, took her to Aix-les-Bains in southern France, where she helped establish a wide range of activities including religious, educational, athletic, and cultural events for African-American troops. Her final assignment was Camp Pontanezen in Brest, the last YMCA hut for African Americans in France, which was closed by Hunton on 3 August 1919.

When she returned to the United States, Hunton coauthored *Two Colored Women with the American Expeditionary Forces* (1920) with another YMCA volunteer, Kathryn M. Johnson, who, like Hunton, served overseas longer than any other African-American woman. Their book exposed not only the racial discrimination endured by black troops during World War I but also the discrimination perpetrated by white YMCA workers against Hunton and Johnson.

Hunton concentrated her postwar career activities on fighting racism and improving the lives of African Americans and women. She served in numerous leadership positions, on national boards, councils, and organizations including the Council on Colored Work of the YWCA National Board, the International Council of the Women of Darker Races (as president), and the Empire State Federation of Women's Clubs (as president). In 1895 Hunton was a founder and organizer of the National Association of Colored Women, and she was the state organizer for the Georgia Federation of Colored Women's Clubs.

Hunton had been active in the National Association for the Advancement of Colored People (NAACP) almost from its beginning, working as a chapter organizer, lecturer, field worker, field secretary, and vice president. In 1919, working through the NAACP, she addressed the first meeting of the Pan-African Congress in Paris, where she stressed the importance of women in world affairs. She also served as an organizer for the Fourth Pan-African Congress held in New York in 1927. Her interest in peace efforts led to her becoming president of the Circle for Peace and Foreign Relations. In 1926 she traveled to Haiti to observe American occupation of this country, doing so as a member of a six-woman committee for the Women's International League for Peace and Freedom of which she was an executive board member. The committee's observations and findings were published in the book *Occupied Haiti* (1927), in which Hunton coauthored a chapter with the book's editor, Emily Greene Balch. The book condemned American occupation and called for an independent Haiti, although Hunton's chapter was specifically on race relations. Her last public appearance occurred at the 1939 New York World's Fair, where she presided over a ceremony honoring outstanding African-American women. She died of complications resulting from diabetes in Brooklyn, New York.

Addie Hunton dedicated her life to those causes she believed would promote a better life for women and African Americans. She advanced the cause of women's rights as an ardent suffragist, author, and teacher. She wrote and lectured on the need for day-care facilities for working mothers and shelters for homeless children. She worked tirelessly with discriminated soldiers overseas and continued working to raise America's racial consciousness and for the cause of peace well after World War I had ended.

• In addition to her works mentioned above, see her tribute to her husband's life and career, *William Alphaeus Hunton: A Pioneer Prophet of Young Men* (1938). See also Anna V. Rice, *A History of the World's Young Women's Christian Association* (1947).

THEA GALLO BECKER

HUNTON, Eppa (22 Sept. 1822–11 Oct. 1908), soldier and U.S. congressman and senator, was born in Fauquier County, Virginia, the son of Eppa Hunton, brigade inspector of the Virginia militia, and Elizabeth Marye Brent. Educated at a private academy, he taught school, read law, and was admitted to the Virginia bar in 1843. Moving to Brentsville in Prince William County, he pursued his profession and joined the militia. By 1847 he was a general officer of state troops. The following year he married Lucy Carolina Weir; they had one son.

From 1849 to 1861 Hunton served as commonwealth attorney of Prince William County. An avid disunionist, he was a John C. Breckinridge elector in 1860 and the following year was a delegate to the Virginia secession convention. Apparently Hunton believed that Virginia's secession would result in a bloodless restoration of the Union on terms favorable to the South. When he saw that war could not be avoided, he offered his services to Governor John Letcher and in mid-1861 became colonel of the Eighth Virginia Infantry. He commanded the regiment on outpost duty at Leesburg, Virginia, until 18 July, when he led it to Manassas Junction, where troops under Brigadier General P. G. T. Beauregard had gathered to halt a Union advance on Richmond. On the twenty-first Hunton's regiment was held in reserve before moving up to reinforce the Confederate right flank along Bull Run. The timely movement helped thwart an enemy penetration. For his heroics Hunton received the praise of Beauregard and several other superiors.

Despite chronic health problems, including a painful fistula, Hunton distinguished himself at Ball's Bluff, 21 October, where his 400-man regiment chased more numerous Federals into retreat. He ably exercised brigade command at Gaines' Mill, 27 June, after the wounding of Brigadier General George E. Pickett. Hunton led Pickett's brigade during the balance of the Peninsula Campaign and again at Second Manassas, 29–30 August. Returning to regimental command, he served with distinction in the September battles of South Mountain and Sharpsburg. Arduous service on these fields reduced the Eighth Virginia to eleven able-bodied soldiers.

While it recruited its strength, Hunton's outfit was held out of action at Fredericksburg, 13 December, and was lightly engaged during Lieutenant General James Longstreet's Suffolk expedition of April–May 1863. During Pickett's charge at Gettysburg, 3 July, the regiment was again decimated and its commander wounded in the right leg. His long recuperation delayed until 9 August a well-deserved promotion to brigadier general in command of Pickett's old brigade. Transferred to Chaffin's Farm on the James River, the command built defenses and helped foil several raids on the Confederate capital.

Hunton's brigade rejoined the Army of Virginia for the North Anna Campaign of late May 1864. The following month it repulsed several attacks at Cold Harbor, then manned the works between Richmond and Petersburg. There Hunton shared in the hardships of trench warfare. In September the inspector general of Lee's army reported that the brigadier "bivouacs in the trenches with his men, and is active and vigilant in all that is promotive of the comfort and efficiency of his command."

Although incapacitated several times early in 1865, toward the close of March Hunton joined General Pickett on the march to Five Forks, a strategic crossroads southwest of Petersburg. On 1 April his brigade defended Pickett's left flank against irresistible assaults by infantry and cavalry under Major General Philip H. Sheridan. When the untenable position collapsed, Hunton joined thousands of survivors on the road to Appomattox Court House. Although determined to fight to the last, he was captured when the remnant of his brigade was overwhelmed at Sayler's Creek, 6 August. Following Lee's surrender, Hunton was sent to Fort Warren in Boston Harbor, where he was imprisoned for three months. Given his poor health, Hunton feared incarceration would prove fatal. He survived the ordeal thanks partly to comforts provided by Major General George Armstrong Custer, whose troopers had captured Hunton.

Returning to Virginia, Hunton found his Brentsville home in ashes. He promptly relocated to Warrenton, where he resumed his law practice. The old-line Democrat endured the early stages of Reconstruction, rejoicing when his party regained control of state politics in the 1870s. Afterward he was three times elected to the U.S. House of Representatives. Refusing a fourth term, he remained in Washington practicing law. In 1892 he was appointed to fill a vacancy in the Senate. In both houses of Congress Hunton proved himself a vigorous, fair-minded, and forward-looking member of his party. Among other interests, he promoted a reform government for the District of Columbia, a national university, streamlined postal regulations, and improved relations with Canada. In 1877 he was the only southern member of an electoral commission that investigated charges of corruption in the election of President Rutherford B. Hayes. The inquiry helped fashion a political compromise that resulted in the withdrawal of occupation forces from the South. Upon his death at the home of his son in Richmond, Hunton was eulogized as "a gentleman upon whose integrity and moral character no scrutiny can develop the vestige of a stain."

Despite his health problems, his belated appointment to command, and his inability to rise above the brigade level except briefly, Hunton was a highly competent soldier who contributed materially to several Confederate victories. Throughout the war he maintained the respect and confidence of numerous superiors, including the always-discerning Lee. A man of polish, charm, and humor (on occasion he coaxed a chuckle even from the stoical Lee), he could inspire his often-understrength command to stellar performances. Even in demoralizing circumstances, he served to the fullest extent of his physical strength. On the retreat to Sayler's Creek, one of his superiors noted that "the disheartening surrounding influences had no effect" upon Hunton, who kept his "duty plainly in view, and . . . fully performed it."

• Some of Hunton's wartime and much of his postwar correspondence is in several collections in the Virginia Historical Society, including the Robert E. Lee, Elizabeth Byrd Nicholas, and Patton and Pegram Family papers, and in the library of the University of Virginia, including the papers of James Barbour, William E. Bibb, and Joseph J. Halsey. The most illuminating source on Hunton's military and civil careers is his *Autobiography of Eppa Hunton*, ed. his son, Eppa Hunton, Jr. (1933), which provides his unvarnished assessments of a few Confederate leaders. Biographical information is in Clement A. Evans, ed., *Confederate Military History*, vol. 3 (11 vols., 1899); Douglas Southall Freeman, *Lee's Lieutenants* (3 vols., 1942–1944); and Edward G. Longacre, *Pickett, Leader of the Charge* (1995). Hunton is well represented in *The War of the Rebellion: A Compilation of the Official Records of the Union and Confederate Armies* (128 vols., 1880–1901). Obituaries are in the *New York Times* and the *Richmond Times-Dispatch*, 12 Oct. 1908.

EDWARD G. LONGACRE

HUNTON, George Kenneth (24 Mar. 1888–11 Nov. 1967), lawyer and activist, was born in Claremont, New Hampshire, the son of George P. Hunton and Elizabeth Dugan. In 1904 George moved with his family to New York. An Irish Catholic, he finished high school at Holy Cross Prep in 1906 and then entered Holy Cross College. After a year at Holy Cross, he enrolled in Fordham Law School. Hunton graduated from Fordham in 1910 and was subsequently admitted to the New York bar.

Hunton's first job was with the Legal Aid Society in Harlem, where he learned about the life of blacks in the United States. He had been taught early by his parents to be tolerant and respectful of all people, regardless of color. It was his work with the Legal Aid Society that earned him the title "supporter of unpopular causes." He continued to work with the Legal Aid Society until he determined that there was not much of a professional future there. He went briefly into private practice and then entered the military during the First World War, obtaining the rank of sergeant in charge of the Flight Record Office at Scott Field in Illinois. He was discharged in January 1919.

After the war he returned to private practice in Brooklyn and taught moot court at Fordham Law School. Hunton flirted with politics briefly when, in an effort to thwart the political machine in New York, he ran for county judge. He joined forces with the Brooklyn Independent Democratic Committee but lost the election.

The event that dramatically changed Hunton's life was his meeting with the Jesuit priest John LaFarge in 1931, a personal association that lasted more than thirty years. Hunton became involved full time in the Catholic church's interracial movement, working with Father LaFarge in the Clergy Conference on Negro Welfare. This work took him from parish to parish, often confronting unfriendly audiences. He became wholly committed to interracial work, determined to create among Catholics a general climate of interest in the plight of blacks. He also worked with the Layman's Union, a black Catholic laymen's organization.

Hunton assisted Father LaFarge in establishing the Cardinal Gibbons Institute, an industrial school for blacks near Ridge, Maryland. The Institute ultimately failed, and the property was turned over to Archbishop Curley of Baltimore in 1933. It was maintained as a center for various activities of the black community and reopened as a day high school in 1936.

In May 1934 Hunton was among a group of distinguished black and white Catholic laymen who met to consolidate various movements and projects into a specific program for interracial justice. Out of the organizational meeting the Catholic Interracial Council (CIC) was born. Membership in the organization was limited to Catholics, and its purpose was to persuade American Catholics that they were failing to live up to their own principles because of the way they treated blacks. The movement was specifically aimed at removing the barrier of race prejudice and establishing social justice. Hunton saw this effort as a service to the nation, but some blacks in the Federation of Colored Catholics saw it as co-opting and domesticating their more radical critique of racism in the Catholic church and in the country as a whole.

Hunton was elected executive secretary of the CIC and worked with the *Interracial Review* (formerly the *Chronicle* of the Federation of Colored Catholics), St. Louis, Missouri. He was appointed managing editor in 1934, a position he held until 1962. The CIC assumed responsibility for publishing the *Review* after Hunton assumed leadership of the organization. The *Interracial Review* became one of the major sources of news about blacks in the United States, especially in the area of religion and human rights. The CIC was also responsible for hosting the annual Catholic interracial conference.

Hunton saw his task as promoting integration and interracial cooperation among Catholic institutions, including fraternal organizations (for example, the Knights of Columbus), hospitals, nursing schools, and colleges and universities. Much to his delight, Catholic University broke its all-white policy with the admission of black women to the nursing program in 1937.

Hunton also worked to have blacks accepted into seminaries and religious orders and to have black priests accepted into churches. Hunton worked closely with black organizations as well. He was a director with the National Association for the Advancement of Colored People (NAACP) and in 1934 was involved in the Scottsboro Trial through the American Scottsboro Committee, formed to investigate the allegation that nine black boys had raped two girls on a freight train. Several trials resulted in the conviction of the boys, who were given death sentences. The committee conducted a fact-finding mission through the South that led Hunton to the conclusion that the boys were innocent of all charges. Hunton is also credited with soliciting life memberships in the NAACP from two prominent Catholic clergy—Francis Cardinal Spellman of New York and Richard Cardinal Cushing of Boston.

Hunton's work took him throughout the United States and parts of Canada, establishing chapters of the CIC. His work also brought him into contact with many prominent black leaders, including William Du-Bois, A. Philip Randolph, Thurgood Marshall, and Roy Wilkins. Through him, the CIC supported the NAACP's efforts toward school integration in 1954.

Hunton was among a group, led by A. Philip Randolph, selected to meet with President John Kennedy in June 1963 to discuss race matters in the United States. At this meeting plans for a mass demonstration in Washington (the March on Washington in August of that year) were revealed to the president. The CIC of New York, Hunton's branch, chartered and filled five buses that were sent to participate in the march.

Hunton is credited with moving the CIC toward more radical positions on antilynching legislation and other issues relating to social justice. For his work toward interracial cooperation, Hunton received the St. Francis Peace medal in 1961. He never married. At age 78 he was pronounced totally blind. He died two years later.

• There is scant information available on Hunton. The definitive source is his autobiography, *All of Which I Saw, Part of Which I Was* (1967), as told to Gary MacEoin. His booklet *Sermons on Interracial Justice* (1958) was distributed to dioceses throughout the country. His other written work is in the *Interracial Review*; a photograph of him appears in the March 1962 issue.

MAMIE E. LOCKE

HUNZINGER, George Jakob (12 Sept. 1835–1898), furniture designer and manufacturer, was born in Tuttlingen, Germany. The names of his parents, who eventually divorced, are not known. Little is known of his early years in Germany. His family is alleged to have descended from a long line of cabinetmakers who worked near the German-Swiss border. Immigrating to America in 1859 after his father's remarriage, Hunzinger was part of a large mid-nineteenth-century movement of German cabinetmakers who came to Brooklyn and New York City. He married Marie Susanne Grieb, also an immigrant from Tuttlingen, on Christmas Day 1859. They eventually had eight children. Their two sons both followed their father as furniture makers and designers.

In 1866 Hunzinger opened his first cabinet shop at 192 Laurens Street in New York City. To do so, he used money obtained from the successful marketing of three of his patents, which were for designs relating to a folding chair and table combination that he had created. Furniture that could serve multiple purposes was the rage of post–Civil War America, and Hunzinger's designs found a ready market. Just after opening his shop Hunzinger applied for additional patents to protect other design elements on the folding chair/table that he had neglected to cover with his earlier applications.

A disastrous fire on 17 October 1877 destroyed not only his factory but also those of two other prominent New York cabinetmakers, Pierre Hardy and Alexander Roux. The fire was thought to have been caused by a steam engine that all three firms shared. Because he was underinsured, Hunzinger took a year to return to the production of furniture. By July 1878 he was back in business at a temporary headquarters, and his final factory, located at 323–327 West Sixteenth Street in New York, was completed in 1880.

By 1889 Hunzinger's business was so well-established that he turned much of its control over to his sons. Over the next several years he traveled among Paris, London, and New York, trying to expand his furniture markets to Europe. These efforts met with some success, although Hunzinger spent considerable time protecting his patents from illegal use. Following his death in New York City, his family continued in the furniture business until the 1920s. Employee threats of unionization coupled with the effects of the Great Depression eventually led to the closing of the firm.

Hunzinger's greatest contributions to the history of furniture production were in the areas of design and invention. He was awarded nineteen patents during his lifetime and was the unofficial leader of a small group of late nineteenth-century cabinetmakers who set out to revolutionize the design and construction of furniture. These cabinetmakers celebrated technology in their furniture by incorporating innovative industrial components into the designs; in recent years they have been termed "patent" furniture makers because of the large numbers of patents they filed.

Hunzinger devoted much of his energy toward combining the furniture forms of chairs and tables in new and innovative ways. His first and last patents were for improvements on his basic idea of creating a chair that had a built-in writing board. Such forms, although produced by Hunzinger and others during the late nineteenth century, saw their popularity rise with the advent of the Morris chair after the turn of the century. Other patents by Hunzinger included a metal tubing framework used to strengthen seat frames and a wardrobe that could be transformed into a bedstead.

Hunzinger's most famous and commercially successful designs were for platform rockers and fancy folding chairs. The rocking chairs had tremendous appeal for Victorian America's growing middle class. Scholars have argued that the rocker, in many ways, came to symbolize middle-class gentility during this period. The platform rocker that Hunzinger produced was especially popular, because by using springs and hinges there were no sharp runners that could mangle parlor carpets. Similarly, the folding chair appealed to very specific segments of the population. Used at camp meetings and Chautauquas and by military officers, production records show it to have been a mainstay of Hunzinger's production.

Hunzinger's furniture also celebrated the modern world by incorporating spokes, cogs, and fittings into the designs. This inclusion of industrial elements in design was in stark contrast to the various "anti-modern" movements of the late nineteenth century such as the Eastlake, arts and crafts, mission, and art nouveau styles. These movements sought to celebrate nature or historical revivals as a way of distancing the decorative arts from the modern industrial world in which they were produced.

Borrowing elements from the American Renaissance revival style (popular around the time of the 1876 centennial), Hunzinger's industrial-influenced furniture was a unique interpretation of nineteenth-century design. Interestingly, one well-documented parlor set, now at the Strong Museum in Rochester, New York, and patented by Hunzinger in 1869 incorporates animal hooves into the design of the legs. This use of a natural motif is much different from his normal designs and may have been a concession to consumer desires.

Until recently Hunzinger's work has been regarded as an anomaly. Seen in comparison to the mainstream production of his era, his industrial-inspired furniture appears to be only a slight eddy in the overall current of nineteenth-century design. Recent reinterpretations have placed Hunzinger within a larger international body of artisans who anticipated the modern designs of the twentieth century. It is perhaps within that context that the innovations of Hunzinger can best be understood; he was an artisan responding to and celebrating technology.

• Primary sources on Hunzinger are limited to patent records held by the Bureau of Patents (1861–1915) and trade/advertising materials held by the Winterthur Museum and Library. The first specific discussion of Hunzinger's work appears in the landmark catalog *Nineteenth-century America*, published in conjunction with the exhibition of the same name by the Metropolitan Museum of Art in 1970. Richard W. Flint has published most extensively on Hunzinger, including "Prosperity through Patents: The Furniture of George Hunzinger and Sons," *Victorian Furniture*, ed. Kenneth Ames (1983); also see Mary Jean Madigan, "George Hunzinger," in her *Nineteenth-century Furniture: Innovation, Revival and Reform* (1982). For a general discussion of patent furniture designers, see Katherine Grier, *Culture and Comfort: People, Parlors and Upholstery, 1850–1930* (1988), and Robert Bishop, *The American Chair: Three Centuries of Style* (1972; repr. 1983).

PETER SWIFT SEIBERT

HUPFELD, Charles Frederick (c. 1788–15 July 1864), violinist, conductor, and composer, was born in Germany. The identities of his parents are not known. He was probably related to Bernhard Hupfeld, a composer and violinist trained in Italy, who served as director of music at the University of Marburg. Charles Hupfeld was closely associated with Henry Hupfeld, Bernhard's eldest son, who was also a violinist. Charles Hupfeld arrived in Philadelphia as an excellent violinist and probably studied the violin in Germany, but no details of his life there are known.

Many European musicians immigrated to the United States after the colonies became an independent country. Some settled in Philadelphia and taught music and performed in concerts. Hupfeld is frequently named as a violinist in Philadelphia newspapers. He is listed among the principal violins in an announcement in the Philadelphia *Aurora* on 4 June 1810 for "A Grand Selection of Sacred Music from the Oratorios of Handel, Hasse, and Haydn." Besides Charles, another Hupfeld, probably Henry, was named as a principal violinist. Beginning in 1814 Charles Hupfeld is listed in the city directory as a "professor of music," implying that he was a music teacher as well as a concert violinist. He was always associated in advertised programs with the best musicians of the city.

In 1815 Hupfeld married Constantia Hommann, the daughter of violinist John C. Hommann and the sister of violinist and composer Charles Hommann and cellist John C. Hommann, Jr. The couple had at least one child. The families of Hupfeld and Hommann were closely united by marriage and musical performances. At a public performance of a Boccherini quintet in 1826, Hupfeld and Charles Hommann played violin, and one of the cellists was probably John C. Hommann, Jr.

Hupfeld's younger brother John also played the violin and was probably taught by Charles. They played string quartets at popular weekly gatherings during the winter months from 1816 until 1820. The programs included music of Beethoven and Boccherini. Charles Hupfeld was the leader and first violinist; John played second violin and sometimes viola. Occasionally Hommann and his two sons joined the group.

The association of these and other Philadelphia musicians led to the formation of the Musical Fund Society of Philadelphia in 1820. Inspired by the London Musical Fund Society, the organization was established "to present to the public the finest compositions, both sacred and secular" and provide a fund for the relief of "decayed musicians" and their families (Madeira, pp. 61–62). The society brought together the musicians of Philadelphia, both English and German, and promoted quality concerts. Hupfeld served on the committee to draft the organization's constitution, and he was one of twelve directors and eighty-five members who took an active interest in its work. Many distinguished Philadelphia citizens, including lawyer Francis Hopkinson and painter Thomas Sully, became members. The first public concert of the society was given on 24 April 1821 and was repeated on 8 May 1821. The program lists Hupfeld as one of six conductors; he also performed a violin concerto by Pierre Rode.

Hupfeld wrote and published piano compositions that were sold in Philadelphia, Baltimore, New York, and Boston. He published music with his son, and about 1843 they opened a music store. Hupfeld died in Philadelphia. Hupfeld's compositions are stylistically similar to the music of European composers of the time. He is remembered as one of the best American musicians of the first half of the nineteenth century.

• Some of Hupfeld's compositions are located in the Free Library of Philadelphia, including *A Favorite Waltz with Variations for the Piano Forte, Composed and Dedicated to Miss Mary*

Livingston Greenleaf (c. 1820), and *Leaf of an Album in the Form of a Waltz, Composed for the Piano Forte and Dedicated to Miss M. L. Adams.* Also at the library is *Hupfeld's Collection of Easy Duetts for Two Performers on the Piano Forte, Selected from the Works of the Best Composers.* The collection contains seven selections, including a march, a galop, and three polkas. No composers are named. *Hupfeld's Cadwalader's Quick Step Composed for the Piano Forte and Respectfully Dedicated to General George Cadwalader* (1846) is located at the Library Company in Philadelphia. The best secondary source is Louis C. Madeira, *Annals of Music in Philadelphia and History of the Musical Fund Society from Its Organization in 1820 to 1858* (1896).

MYRL DUNCAN HERMANN

HURD, Henry Mills (3 May 1843–19 July 1927), psychiatrist and hospital administrator, was born in Union City, Michigan, the son of Theodore C. Hurd, a physician, and Ellen Hammond. Hurd's father died at age thirty-nine, leaving three small sons. His mother married his father's younger brother, also a physician, who moved the family to Galesburg, Illinois. There Hurd attended school and, at the age of fourteen, entered Knox College, a small liberal arts college known for its antislavery sentiments. Wanting to experience a larger school, Hurd spent the next two years at the University of Michigan, where he was taught philosophy by President Henry P. Tappan and history by Andrew Dickson White, later the founding president of Cornell University. Hurd received an A.B. in 1863 and began to study medicine in the office of his stepfather. He attended medical lectures for a year at the Rush Medical College in Chicago and then returned to Ann Arbor to the University of Michigan's College of Medicine, where he received an M.D. in 1866.

Hurd began his medical career as a dispensary physician in Chicago. In 1870 he became an assistant physician at the Michigan Asylum for the Insane in Kalamazoo, embarking on the work for which he would become best known. A few months after becoming the assistant superintendent in Kalamazoo in 1878, he accepted an offer to become the first superintendent of the newly opened Eastern Michigan Asylum in Pontiac, where for the next eleven years he helped to usher in a new era in the care of the mentally ill. While Hurd was not alone in carrying out such reforms as the abolition of restraints of patients, providing for their employment while hospitalized, improving the nursing services, and generally providing greater comforts for the patients of state hospitals, his work in Pontiac and his publications in the *American Journal of Insanity* established him as a leader in the field that at the time was emerging from the custodial care of the insane to their psychiatric treatment.

When the Johns Hopkins Hospital opened in 1889, its trustees chose Hurd to be the first superintendent and professor of psychiatry for the medical school that was being planned and would open in 1893. Hurd held the hospital position for twenty-two years and was the director of the Department of Psychiatry until 1906. After retiring from the hospital directorship in

1911, he continued in his capacity as secretary to the hospital's board of trustees until the end of his life.

During his years in Baltimore, Hurd's administrative and editorial skills came to the fore. An accomplished writer, he was also an important behind-the-scenes editorial force between 1890 and 1920, serving as the editor of the *Bulletin of the Johns Hopkins Hospital*, beginning with its inaugural number in December 1889. From 1891 he also edited the voluminous *Johns Hopkins Hospital Reports.* His annual reports to the trustees of the hospital were also models of concisely phrased discussions of hospital activities and important administrative, educational, or research issues.

As editor of the *Bulletin*, Hurd not only assured its success, but there is ample evidence that he provided persistent, but gentle, pressure that helped his faculty colleagues, such as William Welch and William Osler, finish their manuscripts so that he could publish them. Hurd's administrative and editorial skills earned these early Hopkins medical publications a wider readership and thus helped immeasurably to build the reputation of the hospital and the medical school. Similarly, his administrative skills helped to facilitate the development of the residency programs in the clinical departments, which would come to be models of their kind.

Hurd's best-known literary effort was the massive, four-volume *Institutional Care of the Insane in the United States and Canada* (1916–1917). He wrote the first volume, which described the history of the Association of the Medical Superintendents of American Institutions for the Insane, later to become the American Psychiatric Association. Hurd served the association as secretary from 1892 to 1897 and as president in 1898–1899. In this first volume he also detailed the history of the *American Journal of Insanity* and described the systems of state and county care in the various regions of the two countries. He edited the other three volumes, which are detailed descriptions of institutions for the care of the insane in North America, Hawaii, and the Philippines.

Hurd married Mary Doolittle in 1874; they had two daughters. He was genuinely liked and admired by his colleagues, a fact that doubtless goes far to explain his great administrative successes. He died in Atlantic City, New Jersey. •

• There are some Hurd Papers in the Alan Mason Chesney Medical Archives of the Johns Hopkins University. Because Hurd played a key role in the first two and a half decades of the Johns Hopkins Hospital, these letters, memos, and reports may be found in several of the Chesney Archives' collections. Long printed extracts of his annual *Reports to the Trustees* have been included in the only biographical attempt to delineate Hurd's career: Thomas S. Cullen, *Henry Mills Hurd* (1920), which contains some of Hurd's own reminiscences. No full biography exists. See also the standard histories of Johns Hopkins Medicine: Alan M. Chesney, *The Johns Hopkins Hospital and The Johns Hopkins University School of Medicine* (3 vols., 1943–1963); Thomas B. Turner, *Heritage of Excellence, The Johns Hopkins Medical Institutions, 1914–1947* (1974); and A. McGehee Harvey et al., *A Model of*

Its Kind: A Centennial History of Medicine at Johns Hopkins, (2 vols., 1989). An obituary is in the *New York Times*, 20 July 1927.

GERT H. BRIEGER

HURD, Jacob (12 Feb. 1703–17 Feb. 1758), silversmith, was born in Charlestown, Massachusetts, the son of Jacob Hurd, a joiner, and Elizabeth Tufts. He served a seven-year apprenticeship, probably with one of the Edwards family of Boston, prior to establishing a shop of his own about 1724. In May 1725 he was married to Elizabeth Mason. They had fourteen children, including Nathaniel and Benjamin, who were trained in his shop, and Elizabeth, who married Daniel Henchman, also an apprentice of Hurd's. Hurd led an exemplary life, serving his community as tithing man (1727), constable (1731), a member of the Ancient and Honorable Artillery Company (1743), and as first sergeant (1745) and later captain in the Boston Regiment until his death in Boston from what the *Boston News-Letter* termed "an Apoplexy."

Hurd's distinguished career as a silversmith was characterized by the quality of his workmanship and design and by his versatility. More than fifty pieces of church silver were made by him and given to Protestant churches by prominent members of towns throughout Massachusetts and occasionally in New Hampshire and Connecticut. Beakers, cups, mugs, and tankards were the most frequent donations, but baptismal basins and alms dishes were also among the church silver he made that was recorded by E. Alfred Jones in *The Old Silver of American Churches* (1913). Hurd's church silver differed little from his domestic work, the two being interchangeable in reformed meetinghouses. Both relied on plain, smooth surfaces, shapely forms, and delicate detailed engraving. Frequently the church silver was engraved with the names of the donors and dates of their presentation. It is likely that this body of church silver helped to establish Hurd's reputation as Boston's leading goldsmith in the second quarter of the eighteenth century, making him the artisan of choice when presentation silver was required.

Four large silver cups with covers (often referred to as loving cups) are known to have been made by Hurd, the most imposing being the cup presented to Edward Tyng, commander of the *Prince of Orange*, by a group of Boston merchants who were grateful to him for his capture of the first French privateer off the coast of Massachusetts on 24 June 1744. Weighing almost 100 ounces, the cup is in the Garvan Collection, Yale University Art Gallery. Its smooth surfaces, pleasing proportions, and elaborately engraved cartouche are characteristic of the finest silver of the period. The presentation inscription is surrounded by a subtly scrolled frame embellished with elaborate vignettes of weapons and British flags. A gleeful mask caps the top of the cartouche. Students at Harvard University turned to Hurd for silver to be presented to their favorite tutors. The globular silver teapot presented *ex dono pupillorum* in 1738 to Henry Flynt, now

at the Museum of Fine Arts, Boston, was inherited by Oliver Wendell Holmes, who used a drawing of the teapot to embellish the pages of his book *Over the Teacups* (1891). Hurd was also chosen by the Massachusetts Admiralty Court to make its ceremonial mace (c. 1740) in the shape of an oar, almost two feet long and engraved with the British Royal Arms.

Among the domestic wares produced by Hurd, the most outstanding is a rare teakettle-on-stand (c. 1735) that is more than fourteen inches high, with a spirit lamp beneath the supporting frame and engraved with the Lowell and Leversedge arms, now at the Boston Museum. The robust round shape of the body of the teakettle and the bird's head spout contrast with a sinuous bail and leafy scrolled legs. A great variety of forms emanated from his shop, from gold rings set with stones, thimbles, snuff boxes, and sword hilts to casters, porringers, spoons, salt dishes, octagonal trays with engraved inner borders, services for tea, coffee, and chocolate, pairs of chafing dishes, and candlesticks. He was without peer among American silversmiths of his generation. Through his sons, his son-in-law, and other apprentices trained by him, Hurd passed on the skills and high standards he set for himself.

• A biography of Jacob Hurd is Hollis French, *Jacob Hurd and His Sons Nathaniel and Benjamin, Silversmiths, 1702–1781* (1939). Examples of his work can be seen in the collections and catalogs of Kathryn C. Buhler, *American Silver 1655–1825 in the Museum of Fine Arts, Boston*, vol. 1 (1975), pp. 201–34; Buhler and Graham Hood, *American Silver, Garvan, and Other Collections in the Yale University Art Gallery*, vol. 1 (1970), pp. 120–37; and Henry N. Flynt and Martha Gandy Fales, *The Heritage Foundation Collection of Silver, with Biographical Sketches of New England Silversmiths, 1625–1825* (1968).

MARTHA G. FALES

HURD, Nathaniel (13 Feb. 1730–17 Dec. 1777), noted silversmith and engraver, was born in Boston, the son of Jacob Hurd, the leading Boston silversmith of his era, and Elizabeth Mason. He was enrolled at the Boston Latin School in 1738 and was probably also apprenticed to his father. Hurd seems to have begun his career in his father's shop in the late 1740s. By 1760 he was working independently at his own shop on the Exchange in Boston, where "he continues to do all sorts of Goldsmith's Work" and "Likewise engraves in Gold, Silver, Copper, Brass, and Steel, in the neatest manner, and at reasonable Rates" (*Boston Gazette*, 28 Apr. 1760). In his brief career, Hurd produced a significant body of silver objects, including hollowware and flatware, of which more than two dozen examples survive. Many are embellished with fine coats of arms and other heraldic devices, testimony to his skill as an engraver.

Hurd is most noted for his substantial body of engraved work, including bookplates (depicting more than fifty-five coats of arms and known in more than 110 varieties and states), seals and dies, trade cards, bills, portraits, provincial currency, and a view of the

Boston courthouse. His activity earned him a position as one of the most important printmakers and print-sellers in prerevolutionary Boston. He cut seals for the Boston Marine Society (1754), Brown University (1765), and Dartmouth College (1773), and he en-graved bookplates and other items for Harvard College. His bookplates, made for prominent families in Boston, New Hampshire, and elsewhere in New England, are generally considered to be his best work and constituted a significant share of his business. Although some examples are in earlier styles, most of his bookplates are in a baroque rococo mode featuring an asymmetrical cartouche surrounded by foliate decoration, C-shaped scrolls, flowing banners, and other exuberant decoration. Hurd was also employed as a specialist to engrave silver objects produced by other makers, including Benjamin Burt.

A portrait of Hurd by John Singleton Copley (c. 1765), the preeminent portrait painter in colonial America, is in the Cleveland Museum of Art. Copley depicted Hurd with two books at his side: John Guillim's *Display of Heraldry* (6th ed., 1724) and a smaller volume that silver scholar Kathryn C. Buhler suggests is Sympson's *A New Book of Cyphers . . .* (1726). These English works were used by American silver-smiths and engravers as inspiration for the heraldic devices they engraved. The Cleveland Museum owns, for example, a teapot, engraved by Hurd for the Gibbs family, with arms derived directly from Guillim.

Hurd never married. He served in several minor town offices in Boston and was a member of the jury at the inquest concerning the murder of Crispus Attucks that occurred during the Boston Massacre in 1770, which found that Attucks was murdered by English soldiers commanded by Captain Thomas Preston.

In his will, Hurd styled himself "Goldsmith & Engraver" and left several bequests to family members. He left his "large Printing Press and some Tools" to his nephew John Mason Furnass because of, as Hurd put it, "the Genius he discovers for the same Business which I have followed & to which I intended to have brought him up to." Hurd died in Boston.

• Examples of Hurd's silver are in the Museum of Fine Arts, Boston; Yale University Art Gallery; Historic Deerfield, Deerfield, Mass.; and Winterthur Museum, Winterthur, Del. The best biography of Hurd is Hollis French, *Jacob Hurd and His Sons, Nathaniel and Benjamin, Silversmiths, 1702–1781* (1939; repr. 1972). For treatment of his engraved work, see Martha Gandy Fales, "Heraldic and Emblematic Engravers of Colonial Boston," in the Colonial Society of Massachusetts' *Boston Prints and Printmakers* (1973), pp. 185–220. Shorter biographical accounts are included in Kathryn C. Buhler, *American Silver, 1655–1825, in the Museum of Fine Arts, Boston* vol. 1 (1972), p. 354; Fales and Henry N. Flynt, *The Heritage Foundation Collection of Silver* (1968), p. 255; and the entry by Fales in the *Brittanica Encyclopedia of American Art* (1973). Hurd's engraved work for other silversmiths is treated in David B. Warren, Katherine S. Howe, and Michael K. Brown, *Marks of Achievement: Four Centuries of American Presentation Silver* (1987), pp. 69–71.

GERALD W. R. WARD

HURD-MEAD, Kate Campbell (6 Apr. 1867–1 Jan. 1941), gynecologist and women's historian, was born Kate Campbell Hurd in Danville, Quebec, Canada, the daughter of Edward Payson Hurd, a physician, and Sara Elizabeth Campbell. Hurd's family moved to Newburyport, Massachusetts, in 1870; there her father, who served as an inspiration to her own medical career, established a medical practice, held a professorship in a Boston medical school, and served on the editorial board of two leading medical magazines. Hurd pursued two years of private tutorials after her 1883 high school graduation in Newburyport before enrolling in the Woman's Medical College of Pennsylvania in Philadelphia. She received an M.D. in 1888, some thirty-seven years after the college awarded its first medical degree to a woman. She interned the following year at the New England Hospital for Women and Children in Boston. This hospital, founded in 1862, had, by Hurd's time, gained a national reputation for being what medical historian Regina Markell Morantz-Sanchez has dubbed the "showplace for quality medical care" administered by women. Under the leadership of Marie Zakrzewska, Hurd worked in an environment designed to offer female interns the opportunity to see women physicians and surgeons in action so "that thereby they may acquire courage and self-reliance, which can never be so completely gained by seeing men acting as physicians and surgeons." She claimed that throughout her internship she was well aware that women physicians "must excel in whatever they do." If, during an "unguarded moment," the female intern was heard "humming a little air or whistling softly at work, or even if her shoe squeaked a trifle, she was taken to task" by some "dignified censor" and "questioned as to her reasons for studying medicine and for her unseemly deportment."

Adept in twelve languages, Hurd pursued postgraduate work in 1889–1890 in Paris, Stockholm, Berlin, and London. In 1890 she accepted an appointment as medical director of the newly founded Bryn Mawr School for Girls in Baltimore and undertook studies at the Johns Hopkins University Medical School. Together with Alice Chapman-Hall, Hurd founded the Evening Dispensary for Women and Girls in Baltimore City, a private institution pioneering in maternal hygiene and infant welfare while concurrently offering supervised postgraduate education for female physicians. Like many female physicians, Hurd restricted her practice to "feminine specialties," which in the view of Morantz-Sanchez, represented a collective hope to "raise the moral tone of society through the improvement of family life."

Confining her practice to women and children did not, however, curtail the realm of Hurd's influence within the medical community. While in Baltimore she attended meetings of the Johns Hopkins Hospital Historical Club, where, according to her own account, physicians William Osler, William Welch, and Howard Kelly, "enthusiastic as they were over the cultural value of the study of medical history," inspired her to "search among the old archives for the story of women's place in the development of medicine." Such a study, she claimed, had "never before been seriously undertaken, and such bits of information on the subject as had appeared in medical histories written by men were meager indeed." Her pioneering determination to resurrect and chronicle hundreds of women's contributions to medicine over the centuries echoed attempts by contemporary social feminists to rescue other hitherto unknown women's achievements from the male-dominated historical record. Hurd's drive to resurrect these historical figures from obscurity coincided with her woman suffrage efforts to provide new liberties for twentieth-century women.

Following her marriage to William Edward Mead, a professor of Early English at Wesleyan University in Middletown, Connecticut, in 1893, Hurd-Mead established a medical practice in Middletown, where, in 1895, she helped incorporate and later served as secretary to the Middlesex County Hospital. In 1904 she traveled to Vienna to pursue additional study of the diseases of women and children. She returned to Connecticut in 1907 as a specialist of women and children's diseases and became consulting gynecologist at the Middlesex County Hospital, a position she held until her retirement.

Gynecology, for Hurd-Mead, was much more than the specialty of treating diseases peculiar to women. As medical historian Rosemary Stevens has noted, Hurd-Mead practiced with the intent of championing women. Beyond concerning herself with women as patients, she furthered her specialist concerns by promoting women physicians as the "natural leaders" in addressing all aspects of maternal and child health care. Like many feminist physicians of her day, Hurd believed that women physicians—because of their innate sensitivity toward womanhood—were ideally suited to understand, nurture, and care for the physical, mental, and social concerns of femaleness. With this idea in mind, she established milk stations for infants and promoted the founding of the Middlesex Hospital Training School for Nurses in 1909, the Middletown District Nurses Association in 1910, and the Hospital Aid Society. Notably, it was her interest in human welfare that led Hurd-Mead to support the eugenic reform movement. As part of the Progressive Era campaigns to curb the onslaught of "unfit" immigrants onto American soil, Hurd wrote the article "Medical Inspection of Schools from the Standpoint of the Physician" (*Woman's Medical Journal* 22 (1912): 281–86), in which she warned:

We are confronted today by problems in a measure unknown a generation ago. Instead of the sturdy Irish and Swedish immigrants of the [18]70's, we have the underfed, undereducated and nervously irritable Italians, narrow chested neurotic Jews, and the half-famished Russians whose suppressed energy may rise in anarchy as soon as it feels the unrestrained freedom of our country. From the children of such parents we must raise a nation strong in mind and body.

Hurd-Mead served as vice president of the State Medical Society of Connecticut in 1913–1914 and later helped coordinate public health and preventive medicine efforts in the state through the Haddam Public Health Association, for which she served as president from 1931 to 1936. During World War I she served in the Volunteer Medical Service Corps, wrote many articles on hygiene and public health for the Council of National Defense, lectured for the Speakers' Bureau, and taught classes for the American Red Cross.

Hurd-Mead also gained nationwide recognition for her medico-social activities. Already a member of the American Medical Association, she became an active and respected member of the Medical Women's National Association, later renamed the American Medical Women's Association, which she served as regional director for New England in 1931, as president in 1923–1924, and for many years as chairman of its committee on history. As an activist in this organization founded in 1915 by feminist physicians who resented their marginality within the medical profession, she helped to organize the Medical Women's International Association in 1919 and served on this group's council in 1924–1925 and as corresponding secretary from the United States in 1929. She tried to alert fellow professionals about the inadequacy of U.S. efforts on behalf of maternal and child welfare in such writings as "Is Infant Mortality an Index to Social Welfare? Scandinavia's Reply" (*Woman's Medical Journal* 27 [1917]: 10–15) and by lobbying for passage of the Sheppard-Towner Act in 1921. This act, one of the first to recognize the importance of preventive medicine, provided states with matching funds to establish prenatal and child-health centers. Hurd-Mead's persistent steps to bolster "alliances with Medical Women all over the world" formed the basis of "Amalgamation, Not Segregation," her Medical Women's National Association presidential inaugural address published in the *Bulletin of the Medical Women's National Association* (4 [1923]: 42–44). Abraham Jacobi, a pioneer in American pediatrics, regarded Hurd-Mead not only as an outstanding medical colleague but also as an exemplary "sanitarian in the councils of the nation" for her efforts through such groups as the Child Welfare Association and the League of Women Voters to support the welfare concerns of all.

In 1925, the year Hurd-Mead retired from active medical practice, she journeyed to London, where she spent two years of research at the Library of the British Museum "seeking authentic information in original documents in Greek, Latin and other languages, and in books now out of print, from which might be compiled as true and as complete a story as possible of the work of women in medicine." With similar intentions, she traveled throughout much of Europe, Asia, and Africa, unearthing manuscript materials and studying pictorial and sculptural representations of women and medicine. After returning to Connecticut in 1929, she and her husband settled at "Sunnymeade," their estate overlooking the Connecticut River in Haddam.

In this setting, Hurd-Mead devoted most of her time to writing. Her "Short History of the Pioneer Medical Women of America and a Few of Their Colleagues in England" was serialized in *Medical Review of Reviews* and appeared in book form as *Medical Women of America* in 1933. She was an active member of the American Association for the History of Medicine and published several shorter medical histories, including *Isis* (1930), which provided valuable insights into Trotula, the eleventh-century woman medical practitioner from Salerno. The first of what was intended to be a multivolume work, *A History of Women in Medicine* (volume one was subtitled *From the Earliest of Times to the Beginning of the Nineteenth Century*) was published in 1938. Hurd-Mead completed the manuscript of the second volume, covering the history of women and medicine in the Eastern Hemisphere (never published), and was in the process of compiling a third volume, to be devoted to women in the Western Hemisphere since the early nineteenth century, when she died at her home in Haddam. Hurd-Mead's endowment to the Woman's Medical College of Pennsylvania, now the Medical College of Pennsylvania, is used to sponsor an annual lectureship in the history of medicine. In addition to her professional activities, Hurd-Mead was an avid gardener and a member of the Garden Club of America as well as the American Association of University Women.

• Hurd-Mead's correspondence and materials collected for a history of British women physicians as well as some gardening and horticultural manuscript materials are in the Archives and Special Collections of the Medical College of Pennsylvania. Her unpublished manuscripts on *A History of Women in Medicine* are preserved in the Schlesinger Library at Radcliffe College in Cambridge, Mass. Hurd-Mead also wrote "Reminiscences of Medical Study in Europe," published in the Woman's Medical College collection *Daughters of Aesculapius* (1897), and an entry on her father's life and career for *American Medical Biographies*, ed. Howard A. Kelly and Walter L. Burrage (1920). Hurd-Mead's sister, Mabeth Hurd Paige, published general family information in her *Lady in Law* (1950). A useful biographical account is Esther P. Lovejoy, "Kate Campbell Hurd-Mead (1867–1941)," *Bulletin of the History of Medicine* 10 (1941): 314–17. Dorothy I. Lansing explored Hurd-Mead's medical histories and the legacy of her medical history lectureship in "Kate Hurd Mead, M.D. (1888) and Her Prestigious Lectures in the History of Medicine," *Journal of the American Medical Women's Association* 33 (1978): 116–23, whereas Rosemary Stevens addressed Hurd-Mead's specialty of gynecology in the 1980 Kate Hurd-Mead Lecture, published as "The Changing Idea of a Medical Specialty," *Transactions and Studies of the College of Physicians of Philadelphia* 2 (1980): 159–77. For a more complete view of Hurd-Mead within the context of feminist activism and female physicians in early twentieth-century America, see Regina Markell Morantz-Sanchez, *Sympathy and Science: Women Physician in American Medicine* (1985).

PHILIP K. WILSON

HURDON, Elizabeth (28 Jan. 1868–29 Jan. 1941), gynecologist and pathologist, was born in Bodmin, England, the daughter of John Hurdon, a linen and woolen draper, and Ann Coom. Soon after her birth, the Hurdons and their two daughters moved to Canada. Not much is known about Elizabeth's early years, but by age thirteen she was attending the Wesleyan Ladies College in Hamilton, Ontario, where in 1886 she received a degree in literature. In 1895 she received a medical degree from the Trinity College of the University of Toronto.

After earning her degree, Hurdon went to the United States to study with Howard A. Kelly, a renowned professor of gynecology at Johns Hopkins University in Baltimore. There Hurdon also received training from William Osler and William H. Welch, two of the leading physicians of the time. From her first days at Johns Hopkins, Hurdon specialized in gynecological pathology. She worked in a laboratory under Kelly's assistant Thomas A. Cullen, who like herself was a graduate of the University of Toronto. In addition, Hurdon, whose friends called her "Lizzie," served as the resident gynecologist in Baltimore's Evening Dispensary for Women and Girls. Not only did she support herself on the salary of that position, she also gained valuable experience on surgical cases, since a local hospital gave the dispensary a bed to use for their patients who needed more care than the dispensary could give.

Despite the fact that Hurdon was a woman and a foreigner, she rose quickly through the medical hierarchy on the coattails of Kelly, whom she had impressed. In 1897 she was appointed assistant gynecologist in Johns Hopkins Hospital's dispensary, and the following year the school named her an assistant professor of gynecology and entrusted their gynecological pathology course to her. With this appointment she achieved the distinction of being the first woman to serve on the staff of the hospital and the first woman faculty member at Johns Hopkins. Like many of her male counterparts, Hurdon also opened a private practice in Baltimore to help support herself.

Hurdon's career continued to flourish. In 1907 she was promoted to instructor in gynecology and the following year became an associate in gynecology. During this period she published a number of articles, which secured her reputation in the medical community outside of Baltimore. Among the several that she coauthored with her mentor Kelly was *The Vermiform Appendix and Its Diseases* (1905). Three years later she contributed a chapter on gynecological pathology to a two-volume set on surgery and gynecology, edited by Kelly and Charles P. Noble. When the American College of Surgeons was founded in 1913, Hurdon was one of only a handful of women elected to the august body.

World War I disrupted Hurdon's work in Baltimore. One year into the war, she requested a leave from Johns Hopkins to join the Royal Army Medical Corps and contribute to her native country's efforts. Named to the rank of captain, she was placed in charge of a dysentery camp in Salonika. She also served in Malta. Accounts of her life disagree about what she did immediately after the war. Some say that after being demobilized in 1919 she returned to Johns Hopkins, while others say she remained with the military corps in 1921, serving at the Royal Herbert Hospital in Woolwich and the Guilford Military Hospital.

On this accounts do agree: in 1921 Hurdon decided to return to Britain, where her family now lived. For five years she was unable to secure a satisfactory hospital appointment, aside for a brief stint as a temporary lecturer in pathology at the University of Liverpool. Later, she would describe her role in that period rather unhappily as a lady of leisure. Her quiet days ended when she heard of the London Association of the Medical Women's Federation's plans to open a hospital specializing in women's cancer and clinical research, to which the Medical Research Council had donated a loan of radium and money for a director's salary.

Hurdon seemed a natural choice. Her years in gynecology had given her the necessary expertise to study cervical cancer, and her years with Kelly, who had been one of the first physicians to employ radium to treat therapeutic diseases, complemented that. In addition, Hurdon's personality turned out to be uniquely suited for the post. A good teacher, Hurdon inspired respect in both her students and subordinates. Friends described her as a fine conversationalist with a sweet manner. She was also a workaholic, with few hobbies other than her family, travel, and her gardening to distract her.

To keep abreast of what others in radiology had done, Hurdon visited almost all of the American and European clinics that were testing the use of radium and X-ray therapy to treat cancer. At home, Hurdon and her colleagues started testing their own theories on patients at the four London's women's hospitals. She and her colleagues started giving these women uniform dosages to abate their cancer but soon realized that every case had to be individualized. With limited radium available—each hospital received one case for one day a week—Hurdon and the committee realized it would be necessary to centralize their efforts. Centralizing the study would not only increase the amount of radium they could use, but would also improve the researchers' ability to consolidate the results from the many cases they saw.

In 1929 the committee opened the Marie Curie Hospital, which would eventually grow to thirty-nine beds, along with therapy rooms, laboratories, and a staff of sixteen women surgeons. Hurdon remained director of the venture, continuing her investigations into radiation and oncological diseases of women. By the mid-1930s doctors at the hospital were treating cancer of the uterus, vagina, vulva, breast, and rectum in women. There was some talk about extending the scope of the hospital to include other maladies, but the staff decided to continue as a research hospital and contain their focus. By 1936 the center had treated more than 500 cases, of which 36.7 percent had survived for five years, according to Hurdon's accounting in a speech before the Medical Women's Society of New York.

At the age of seventy, Hurdon decided to retire. That same year, 1938, King George VI bestowed on her the coveted distinction of the Commander of the British Empire award. Hurdon, who never married, spent the final three years of her life in her home in Exeter, England, working on a book on uterine cancer. She did not live to see its publication in 1942, but died the previous year of cancer of the liver.

• Hurdon wrote a lecture on the founding of the Marie Curie Hospital, reprinted in the *Medical Woman's Journal* (Sept. 1936). For an account of her days at Johns Hopkins, see Alan Chesney, *The Johns Hopkins Hospital and the Johns Hopkins University School of Medicine* (1958). Obituaries are in the *British Medical Journal* (22 Feb. 1941), *The Lancet* (8 Feb. 1941), and *Medical Women's Journal* (Mar. 1941).

SHARI RUDAVSKY

HURLBUT, Stephen Augustus (29 Nov. 1815–27 Mar. 1882), army officer and politician, was born in Charleston, South Carolina, the son of Martin Luther Hurlbut, a Unitarian minister and teacher, and Lydia Bunce. He studied law with prominent Charleston Unionist lawyer James L. Petigru and was admitted to the bar in 1837. During the Seminole wars he served as an adjutant in a South Carolina regiment.

In 1845 trouble seems to have entered the relationship between Hurlbut and his powerful mentor Petigru, possibly as a result of wrongdoing on the part of Hurlbut. Whatever the incident, Hurlbut left Charleston and moved to Belvidere, Illinois, a small settlement on the northern Illinois prairies only a decade or two removed from frontier status. Taking up the practice of law once more, he did well in the new town. In 1847 he married Sophronia R. Stevens; they had two children. Later that same year he was elected a delegate to the Illinois constitutional convention, representing his own Boone County as well as neighboring McHenry County. A staunch Whig, he was a presidential elector for that party in the successful campaign of 1848. In his practice of law in Illinois, he made the acquaintance of fellow Illinois lawyer Abraham Lincoln. In 1858 he was elected to the Illinois legislature as a member of the four-year-old Republican party, and he was halfway through his second term in this office when the Civil War broke out.

During the secession crisis, Hurlbut traveled quietly to South Carolina on behalf of Lincoln to sound the depths of Unionist feeling there. The answer he brought back, of course, was that there was none. Back in Boone County, Hurlbut helped raise a regiment of troops. Partially in reward for his dangerous service in South Carolina and partially because of his political prominence, Hurlbut was appointed brigadier general of volunteers on 14 June 1861, to rank from 17 May. During the rest of that year he served in northern Missouri.

In February 1862 Hurlbut took command of a division in General Ulysses S. Grant's Army of the Tennessee. At the battle of Shiloh, 6–7 April 1862, Hurlbut showed conspicuous courage at the head of his division. He continued to lead his division during the ensuing Corinth campaign. Thereafter he was assigned to the command of widely dispersed occupation troops in West Tennessee. In September 1862 he was promoted to major general, and in December his command was designated the XVI Corps. During the Vicksburg campaign that winter and the following spring and summer, Hurlbut's unglamorous task was managing and protecting Memphis and the surrounding area as the base for Grant's field army.

In February 1864 Hurlbut participated in General William T. Sherman's large raid on Meridian, Mississippi, but in April of that year Sherman, now commanding all Federal forces west of the Appalachians, became dissatisfied with Hurlbut's failure to deal with Confederate cavalry raider Nathan Bedford Forrest. Sherman removed Hurlbut from the sensitive West Tennessee command. Hurlbut waited all summer long for orders and in September 1864 was assigned to the Department of the Gulf.

There things went from bad to worse for Hurlbut. He did not get along with the Reconstruction government in occupied Louisiana, and he was accused of engaging in various corrupt practices, using his official power to make money dishonestly. The same accusation had been made against him in Memphis. Also, Hurlbut was a habitual drunkard and was often scandalously inebriated in public. A special military commission was appointed to investigate the charges, and it recommended Hurlbut's court-martial. His department commander, General Edward R. S. Canby, gave the order for such a proceeding but in so doing reckoned without Hurlbut's political influence. Somehow the whole thing was swept under the rug, and Hurlbut was allowed to resign with such honor as he had left on 20 June 1865.

Charges of drunkenness and corruption continued to crop up throughout Hurlbut's postwar life but did not destroy his political career. He was the first commander in chief of the Grand Army of the Republic (Union veterans organization), holding the position from 1866 to 1868. In 1867 he was elected to the Illinois legislature, and the following year he was a presidential elector. President Grant, his former commanding officer, appointed him U.S. minister to Colombia in 1869, and Hurlbut continued in that post until he was elected to Congress in 1872. (He had run unsuccessfully for Congress in 1870, still retaining his diplomatic position.) He served two terms before being defeated in a bid for reelection. In 1881 President James A. Garfield appointed him U.S. minister to Peru. This proved to be an unfortunate choice, as Peru was then engaged in war with Chile (the War of the Pacific), relations were sensitive, and Hurlbut mishandled the situation rather badly. He was personally favorable to Peru and created the impression that the United States officially favored that country. His performance was the cause of considerable embarrassment and some resentment by Chile.

In Peru Hurlbut was again accused of illegitimate financial dealings, specifically of receiving illicit payments for using his official power improperly to benefit a Peruvian company exporting bat guano (then used to make gunpowder). A congressional committee later cleared him (posthumously) of these charges. He died in Lima, Peru.

Hurlbut remains difficult to assess. Many Civil War and Reconstruction Era politicians gave every indication of being unprincipled opportunists, ready to use politics for personal gain. In some ways Hurlbut fits that mold. Yet he had been, at least at one time, a follower of South Carolina Unionist Petigru, a position that spoke more of principle than of profit. Hurlbut's drunkenness and corruption are still disputed, though the weight of evidence is against him. He was apparently a man of some moral aspirations who was nevertheless plagued by great moral weakness.

• Hurlbut's papers are in the Boone County Historical Society, Belvidere, Ill. Naturally, original source material from his Civil War years can be found scattered throughout U.S. War Department, *The War of the Rebellion: A Compilation of the Official Records of the Union and Confederate Armies* (128 vols., 1880–1901). He has attracted little scholarly attention. Information about him can be gleamed from such general works as Shelby Foote, *The Civil War: A Narrative* (1958–1974), and E. B. Long and Barbara Long, *The Civil War Day by Day: An Almanac, 1861–1865* (1971). He also receives brief mention in Ezra J. Warner, *Generals in Blue: The Lives of the Union Commanders* (1964).

STEVEN E. WOODWORTH

HURLEY, Edward Nash (31 July 1864–14 Nov. 1933), manufacturer, was born in Galesburg, Illinois, the son of Jeremiah Hurley, a railroad mechanic, and Ellen Nash. Both parents were Irish Catholic immigrants. Hurley had little formal education. He quit high school at age fifteen and joined his father and older brothers in the Galesburg machine shops of the Chicago, Burlington and Quincy Railroad. Two years later, in Chicago, he became fireman on a switching engine.

Hurley flirted briefly with labor politics. Promoted to passenger train engineer at age nineteen, he joined the Brotherhood of Locomotive Engineers, lobbied for labor legislation, campaigned for the Democratic candidate for governor of Illinois, and accepted patronage posts in the Cook County Democratic machine. But business, not labor, claimed Hurley's ultimate interest. In 1888 he took a job as traveling salesman for a Philadelphia manufacturer of packing material. Three years later he married Julia Keeley, with whom he had two children.

Eager to strike out on his own, Hurley in 1896 bought the manufacturing and selling rights to a piston air drill invented by a friend from his railroad days. Hurley capitalized on his flair for promotion. He became founding president and treasurer of the Standard Pneumatic Tool Company of Chicago, and by 1899 he was marketing "Little Giant" pneumatic tools, his personal advertising slogan, in both the United States and Europe. Steel shipbuilders, stimulated by the arms race between the British and German navies, clamored for Hurley's pneumatic riveting hammers. By 1902, when he sold his business, Hurley was a millionaire.

Hurley tried early retirement. He purchased a farm in Wheaton, Illinois, a community of wealthy Chicagoans, and joined an elite social circle. His wife Julia, a source of great strength to him in the early, uncertain days of his pneumatic drill business, had died in 1900. On an excursion to Berlin he met his second wife, Florence Agnes Amberg, a music student from Chicago. They married in 1905 and had two children.

But retirement palled, and in 1908 Hurley and his brother organized the Hurley Machine Company to manufacture floor scrapers and other labor-saving devices. The company also experimented with electric washing machines, a product line they expanded after World War I. Hurley also followed national and international economic issues. He joined the Illinois Manufacturers Association and helped found the National Foreign Trade Council in 1914. How to expand America's export markets became a central theme of his public career.

Hurley's connection to Woodrow Wilson benefited that career enormously. In 1910 he worked informally with Princeton University alumni in Chicago to get Wilson elected governor of New Jersey. His support for Wilson in the presidential elections of 1912 and 1916 solidified the tie. In 1914 the administration dispatched Hurley to Latin America to investigate the availability of banking and credit facilities for U.S. exporters. In 1915 the president appointed him to the Federal Trade Commission. Hurley subsequently became its vice chairman and chairman. In 1917 he joined the Red Cross War Council, after resigning from the FTC.

A cooperative vision guided Hurley throughout his Washington service. "Cooperation is the watchword of our day," he wrote in *Awakening of Business*, published in 1917, "cooperation among business men, cooperation between employer and employee, cooperation between business and government" (p. 43). Central principles of Hurley's creed were to relax antitrust enforcement, promote trade associations, and take a strategic approach to international trade. He also championed more sophisticated cost accounting techniques. Their adoption would enhance manufacturing efficiency. The United States should prepare for the trade battles that he and many other business executives anticipated at the end of the European war.

Hurley pressed his views on Wilson and other officials from his post as chairman of the United States Shipping Board, which he held from July 1917 to July 1919. Created by the Shipping Act of 7 September 1916, the board was empowered to regulate waterborne commerce, and, more important, to create a public corporation to purchase, construct, equip, and maintain merchant vessels. The board established an Emergency Fleet Corporation for these purposes on 16 April 1917.

In subsequent months, personality clashes, administrative confusion, and policy differences hobbled the shipbuilding program, and in July 1917 Wilson turned to Hurley for solutions. To facilitate his task, Hurley clarified lines of authority between his office as shipping board chairman and the Fleet Corporation's general manager; he recruited leading business executives for key posts, including Charles Schwab, president of the Bethlehem Steel Corporation; and he decentralized Fleet Corporation offices to get closer to key shipyards.

Congress ultimately appropriated more than $3.5 billion for ship construction, more than twice the value of the world's total commercial fleet before the war, and the Fleet Corporation proceeded to expand U.S. shipbuilding capacity—by direct investment in three huge new shipyards, by liberal distribution of contracts to private owners, and by commandeering all ship construction in the United States under contract to foreign buyers. During the fiscal year ending 30 June 1917, before the program began, American yards produced 664,000 gross tons of merchant ships; during the next year, output rose to 1.3 million tons; and during the second year, ending 30 June 1919, American output reached 3.3 million tons. The merchant marine under American registry jumped from 5,381,147 gross tons in 1913 to 15,997,303 gross tons in 1920.

As board chairman, Hurley left the details of contract negotiations and production operations to others. He focused on policy questions and public relations. The building program raised difficult issues. Who should bear the financial risks of expansion? Who should pay for rising labor costs, for workers' housing? Who should arbitrate labor-management differences? Who should allocate tonnage among civilian and military, American and Allied needs? And what should happen with government-sponsored ships at the end of the war? In grappling with domestic issues, Hurley followed his cooperative principles. He searched for grounds of agreement between labor and management, and between business and government. As a continuing member of the Brotherhood of Locomotive Engineers, Hurley sympathized with Samuel Gompers, head of the American Federation of Labor. He worried about radical challenges to Gomper's leadership. He resisted public pressure for labor conscription. The opportunism of shipyard owners on labor and financial matters appalled him. On the other hand, as a believer in entrepreneurial capitalism and as head of an experiment in mixed enterprise, he also needed management cooperation for expanded production.

Hurley's cooperative approach to domestic policies supported a mercantilist impulse in international affairs. Determined to use the crisis to make the United States "the Mecca of the shipbuilding trade of the world," Hurley regarded the nation's newfound productive capacity as a weapon in wartime diplomacy and as a means to win markets for postwar American exports. On occasion, Hurley's expansive views ran ahead of official policy. In response to British sensitivities and State Department pressure, President Wilson more than once felt compelled to issue a caution.

But Hurley retained Wilson's respect. In March 1918 he joined the president's War Council, composed of key war administrators. And after the Armistice he went to Europe as shipping adviser to the American Peace Commission. He became president of the shipping section of the Supreme Economic Council, and he chaired the Allied delegation that arranged the surrender of the German merchant marine. He also had a place on the Commission for International Labor Legislation. Throughout these activities, Hurley jealously guarded U.S. autonomy in shipping matters and counseled the president against returning requisitioned ships to the British and French until they signed the peace treaty. In February 1919 Hurley returned to Washington and campaigned for a permanent public policy to protect the American shipbuilding industry from postwar decline. He resigned from the Shipping Board in July 1919 but continued to make his case in the popular press and in a book, *The New Merchant Marine*, published in 1920.

After the war, Hurley combined a continuing interest in U.S. trade policy with private business activities. In 1924 president Calvin Coolidge appointed him Democratic member of the World War Foreign Debt Commission. In 1927 he published a ghosted memoir of the war years, *The Bridge to France*, a tribute to colleagues in the shipping program and to Woodrow Wilson above all. In 1930 Herbert Hoover put him on an Advisory Commission on Shipping. Hurley died in Chicago.

Hurley made his major contribution to American public life during the war years. He exemplifies the important policy-making role of business executives during that crisis. He also illustrates the significance of commercial expansion as a critical element of Wilsonian foreign policy.

• Hurley's papers, including fragments of a memoir, are in the University of Notre Dame Archives. Jeffrey J. Safford, *Wilsonian Maritime Diplomacy 1913–1921* (1978), contains important material on Hurley's views of trade policy. For an informative essay on Emergency Fleet Corporation labor policies, see Bernard Mergen, "The Government as Manager: Emergency Fleet Building, 1917–1919," in *Business and Its Environment, Essays for Thomas C. Cochran*, ed. Harold Issadore Sharlan (1987). Useful guides to the U.S. Shipping Board and U.S. shipbuilding program include Jesse E. Saugstad, *Shipping and Shipbuilding Subsidies* (1932); Darrell H. Smith and Paul V. Betters, *The United States Shipping Board* (1931); and Paul M. Zeis, *American Shipping Policy* (1938). Obituaries are in the *Chicago Herald*, 15 Nov. 1933, and the *New York Times*, 15, 16, and 18 Nov. 1933.

ROBERT D. CUFF

HURLEY, Joseph Patrick (21 Jan. 1894–30 Oct. 1967), sixth Roman Catholic bishop of St. Augustine, Florida, was born in Cleveland, Ohio, the son of Irish immigrants Michael Hurley, a steelworker, and Anna Durkin. In 1911 Hurley entered St. Ignatius High School/College in Cleveland, where he received his B.A. in philosophy in 1915. In pursuit of the priesthood, he attended St. Bernard Seminary in Rochester, New York (1915–1916), and then St. Mary's Seminary in Cleveland (1916–1919). At St. Mary's Hurley was

influenced by his mentor, theology professor Edward A. Mooney (later cardinal-archbishop of Detroit), who was impressed by his abilities.

Ordained a priest on 29 May 1919, Hurley was assigned as assistant pastor to St. Columba Parish (Youngstown, Ohio), where he served from 1919 to 1923; to St. Philomena (East Cleveland), from 1923 to 1925; and to Immaculate Conception (Cleveland), from 1925 to 1927. While he was at Immaculate Conception, his former seminary professor, Mooney, was appointed apostolic delegate to India, and in 1927 he called on Hurley to act as his secretary. Hurley took diplomatic and linguistic courses at the University of Toulouse, France, before joining Mooney in India in 1928. In 1931 he left India for Japan, where Mooney had been named apostolic delegate. After Mooney was reassigned in 1933, Hurley remained in Japan for another year as chargé d'affaires of the Vatican delegation. He then was transferred to Vatican City where, from 1934 to 1940, he advised on American matters as attaché to the papal secretariat of state. His international and papal diplomatic experience gave Hurley a sense of self-confidence that remained with him for the rest of his life.

Hurley's career changed direction upon his appointment, on 19 August 1940, as bishop of the Diocese of St. Augustine, which comprised all territory in Florida east of the Apalachicola River. Ordained a bishop in Rome on 6 October, he was installed at St. Augustine's Cathedral on 26 November 1940. For the first five years of his episcopacy, Hurley faced numerous challenges, financial as well as administrative. His predecessor, Patrick Barry, had steered the diocese through the Great Depression but in the process had so mixed his personal finances with those of the diocese that it took half a decade of legal wrangling to disentangle the financial Gordian knot. In addition, nearly twenty years of marriage dispensation forms and other records had been stacked haphazardly in a chancery closet, and it took two years of laborious work for Hurley to put these official documents in order. Responding to the waves of military personnel flowing in and out of Florida during World War II, Hurley, already handicapped by a lack of personnel, temporarily recruited priests from around the country. In a farsighted attempt to ensure the growth of Catholic institutions in the state, Hurley instituted the annual diocesan Catholic Charities Drive in 1944.

Following the end of the war, on 22 October 1945, Hurley was recalled to Vatican diplomatic service, this time as regent of the apostolic nunciature in Yugoslavia, where he worked to protect the interests of Roman Catholicism in the now communist country. While he was there, Hurley became vehemently opposed to communism and extremely distrustful of "religious" priests (priests in religious orders), especially as a result of the 1946 trial of Archbishop (later Cardinal) Aloysius Stepinac on charges of having collaborated with the Nazis, during which Franciscans testified against Stepinac. Afterward, despite his virtually constant need for priests, the bishop allowed few religious priests into his diocese. Hurley was a commanding leader. Even while he was thousands of miles away, he was able to govern his Florida diocese, overseeing even minute matters through intermediaries. From 1945 to 1950 thirteen new churches and twelve new parish schools were constructed. Meanwhile his diplomatic efforts were rewarded in 1949, when Pope Pius XII named Hurley a titular archbishop (a title of honor not jurisdiction).

Returning to Florida in 1950, Hurley took immediate steps to deal with the postwar population boom. He set up the Diocesan Development Fund in 1950 for the support and maintenance of institutional infrastructure. He centralized Catholic high schools in 1952 and promoted parochial schools. He actively recruited Floridians as candidates for the priesthood and enlisted seminarians from Ireland. He also erected twenty-five churches and thirty-nine parochial schools. In response to the increase in the Hispanic migrant population, Hurley encouraged his priests to learn Spanish, recruited diocesan missionaries from Spain, and established, in 1954, three mobile units composed of a total of six Spanish priests and nine Sisters of St. Joseph to serve parishes in South Florida. Hurley's most enduring and prescient action was the establishment, in 1953, of the Missionary Burse Fund, a form of parochial taxation through which Hurley secured Florida real estate for parochial and institutional development.

When the Diocese of Miami was created in 1958, more than one third of Hurley's diocese was subsumed by the new diocese, resulting in a significant loss of diocesan assets and personnel. Hurley battled the new diocese over what he considered to be the fair disposition of property, financial assets, and personnel until 1965, when the matter was finally resolved by a papal commission—in favor of the Miami diocese. In the final years of his episcopacy, Hurley focused on exalting his diocese's rich historical tradition. In celebration of the four hundredth anniversary of the founding of St. Augustine in 1965, the cathedral was refurbished, a new cathedral rectory was built, a large memorial cross was planted on the site of the Spanish landfall in 1565, and the diocese sponsored an academic symposium and commissioned a book on Florida's Catholic history (which was finally realized as Michael V. Gannon's *Cross in the Sand; the Early Catholic Church in Florida, 1513–1870* [1965]).

One of the least known, yet most consistent, aspects of Hurley's episcopacy was his support for Florida's African Americans. In 1941 and 1942 he organized the Convention of Florida Black Catholics, held first in St. Augustine, then in Tampa. He purchased properties in black communities throughout Florida as sites for black Catholic schools and churches. He encouraged religious women and priests to minister to African Americans, and he assigned diocesan priests to pastor black communities in Miami, Fort Pierce, and St. Petersburg. In 1956 the diocese opened two outpatient clinics for African Americans in Miami. And, through Hurley's instigation, blacks were quietly integrated into diocesan high schools and hospitals, in most cases before public institutions were legally desegregated. Over the course of his episcopacy, Hurley established forty-nine parishes, seventy-three Catholic schools, two Catholic hospitals, and several homes for the aged and for disabled children.

Hurley's episcopal motto, *Virtus in arduis* ("virtue in the midst of difficulties"), aptly characterizes his energetic 27-year episcopacy, which had a hugely beneficial impact on the status of Catholicism in Florida. Protective of his authority, Hurley was ill at ease around the laity and was sometimes hard on his priests, but he was respected and admired by both. He died in Orlando, Florida.

• Hurley's official correspondence is in the Archives of the Diocese of St. Augustine. Incidental correspondence can be found in the Archives of the Archdiocese of Baltimore, the Archivio Segreto Vaticano–Secreteria di Stato, the Archives of the Diocese of Detroit, and the Archives of the Diocese of Cleveland. Material on Hurley can be found in Michael J. Hynes, *History of the Diocese of Cleveland* (1953); Richard Pattee, *The Case of Cardinal Aloysius Stepinac* (1953); and in two books by Michael J. McNally, *Catholicism in South Florida, 1868–1968* (1984) and *Catholic Parish Life on Florida's West Coast, 1860–1968* (1996). Hurley's views on World War II are discussed in Gerald P. Fogarty, *The Vatican and the American Hierarchy from 1870 to 1965* (1982); "Catholic Isolationists," *Tablet*, 21 June 1941, p. 484; Michael Williams, "Views and Reviews: Notable Radio Address, July 6, 1941," *Commonweal*, 18 July 1941, p. 303; and "Bishop Hurley's Broadcaste, July 6, 1941," *Tablet*, 16 Aug. 1941, pp. 104–5.

MICHAEL J. McNALLY

HURLEY, Patrick Jay (8 Jan. 1883–30 July 1963), lawyer, diplomat, and secretary of war, was born in the Choctaw nation, Indian Territory, in present-day east-central Oklahoma, the son of Pierce O'Neil Hurley, a coal miner and sharecropper, and Mary Kelly. Hurley was virtually on his own after age eleven. His formal education included classes at a local night school in which he enrolled in 1897. After 1900, though not himself a Native American, Hurley studied at Indian University, a Baptist school for Indians located at Muskogee, where he completed his elementary, secondary, and college work, earning a B.A. in 1905. After serving for two years as a clerk in a law office in Muskogee, Hurley moved to Washington, D.C., and enrolled in National University law school—the only institution in that city that would accept the poorly prepared Oklahoman. He received his LL.B. in 1908.

Hurley then settled in Tulsa, Oklahoma, and began his rise to prominence. A successful law practice, involvement in Oklahoma politics, and service as national attorney for the Choctaws brought him in contact with a number of prominent people both within his home state and in Washington. Service in the Oklahoma National Guard led to an army commission during World War I and indirectly to his meeting Ruth Wilson, daughter of Admiral Henry Wilson. They were married in 1919 and had four children.

During the 1920s Hurley focused on business, law, and politics and became a power in the Republican party both locally and nationally. He had become a Republican largely because of his admiration for Theodore Roosevelt. His party affiliation, though of slight advantage in Oklahoma where Republicans were in the minority, helped him gain national attention. An early backer of Herbert Hoover, he received as his political reward appointment as assistant secretary of war in the Hoover administration. As a member of the subcabinet, he made himself highly visible in Washington—to the point that when Secretary of War James Good died in November 1929, Hurley became the logical successor. From November 1929 until the end of the Hoover administration, Hurley served as secretary of war, gaining national attention primarily for issuing the orders for the expulsion of the Bonus Expeditionary Force and for his unavailing opposition to Philippine independence.

During the 1930s, as he sought to recover a portion of the wealth he had lost in the collapse of the real estate market, Hurley accepted a retainer from the Sinclair Oil Company to negotiate a settlement of Sinclair's claims against the Mexican government after the Mexican expropriation of American oil company properties. The resulting agreement became the model for the settlement of all of the other companies' claims and brought Hurley into closer contact with the Roosevelt administration.

Hurley's association with President Franklin D. Roosevelt, based on Hurley's support of many early New Deal programs, led to a number of diplomatic appointments of major significance during World War II. Roosevelt promoted him to brigadier general (he had been a colonel in the reserves since 1919) and in January 1942 sent him on a mission to arrange the transportation of supplies to General Douglas MacArthur at Bataan. After the impenetrable Japanese military control of the Philippines made this effort impossible to complete, the president appointed Hurley minister to New Zealand, a position he held from April through August 1942. In November and December of that year Hurley completed a goodwill visit of little substance to Josef Stalin, and in 1943 he attended the Teheran Conference, where he wrote the Declaration on Iran, calling for American, British, and Soviet guarantees of Iranian sovereignty and independence.

Nothing Hurley attempted before or after compared in importance to the next assignment he undertook. In September 1944 Roosevelt sent him to China to serve in a liaison capacity between General Joseph Stilwell and Chiang Kai-shek, who were locked in a bitter quarrel over Stilwell's insistence on the improvement of Chinese armies, and to arrange a compromise between Chiang's government and its bitter rivals, the Chinese Communists. The compromise was necessary, Roosevelt believed, not only to bring about a more effective prosecution of the war against Japan but to ensure a strong, stable (and noncommunist) postwar China. After his failure to complete successfully the first of his tasks, Hurley was appointed ambassador to China in November 1944 and worked until his departure to promote a coalition government in which the Communists would play a role—an impossible mission because no outsider was capable of mediating China's internal dispute. He resigned in November 1945, angry and disgusted, blaming his failure not on circumstance but on the disloyalty of some of his subordinates in China and State Department officials in Washington.

Seeking a forum for his anticommunist views as well as a way to feed his oversized ego, Hurley ran for the U.S. Senate from New Mexico, his adopted state, in 1946, 1948, and 1952. He lost each of these contests, two of them (1946 and 1952) by very narrow margins, in part because many voters did not respond to the international issues that he chose to emphasize. His foray into politics showcased his least attractive traits—his short temper, sensitivity to criticism, penchant for self promotion—at the expense of his better ones. Thus he tends to be remembered not as the friendly, gregarious, intelligent lawyer and businessman that he was, but as a failed diplomat and politician who became a common scold. He died in Santa Fe, New Mexico.

• The Patrick J. Hurley Papers are located in the Western History Collection, University of Oklahoma Library. A scholarly biography is Russell D. Buhite, *Patrick J. Hurley and American Foreign Policy* (1973). Other biographical works are Don Lohbeck, *Patrick J. Hurley* (1956), and Parker La Moore, *"Pat" Hurley: The Story of an American* (1932). An obituary is in the *New York Times*, 31 July 1963.

RUSSELL D. BUHITE

HURLEY, Roy T. (3 June 1896–31 Oct. 1971), aviation industry executive, was born in New York City, the son of Edward Hurley and Phoebe King. The product of New York grammar schools, Hurley left school to become an airplane mechanic at the B. F. Sturtevant Company in Hyde Park, Massachusetts, before World War I. Later, when asked how he became an engineer, he answered with typical bluntness: "I took all the correspondence courses and read all the textbooks." Hurley was pleased when the press described him as a "jack knife engineer."

When the United States entered World War I, Hurley became an aircraft inspector for the army air corps. After the war he was hired as chief engineer of the B. G. Aircraft Spark Plug company, where he stayed until 1927. That year he joined the Moto-Meter Company on Long Island as vice president and general manager. In the midst of the depression in 1931, he left to start his own company in New York City, Hurley-Townsend, which he sold to Bendix in 1935.

Hurley went to work for Bendix. Ernest Breech, on becoming the company's president in 1942, took an instant liking to the gruff, self-taught engineer and promoted him to vice president for manufacturing. During World War II Hurley learned his way around defense procurement when he served as deputy chief of ordnance for the army. In 1946 Breech left Bendix to become vice president of Ford, where he helped Henry Ford II rebuild his father's motor vehicle empire. Two years later Breech brought Hurley to Detroit as Ford's vice president of manufacturing. By then Hurley had gained a reputation as a stickler for details and cost-cutting.

In 1949 Hurley became president of Curtiss-Wright, an old-line aircraft manufacturer that had fallen on hard times. When Hurley took over, the company manufactured piston aircraft engines and propellers and was not earning enough profits to pay dividends. Hurley lobbied in Washington, D.C., for more defense contracts, began designing jet engines, electronic devices, and missiles, and by 1953, with the help of Korean war contracts, he had increased sales more than fivefold. Curtiss-Wright started paying dividends out of earnings instead of reserves, and by 1955 the company was paying more than $13 million a year to its stockholders. Hurley also gained a national reputation at Curtiss-Wright for cutting costs, even keeping detailed records on his managers' time away from their desks. When his engineers drew up plans for a circular test facility, Hurley ordered its shape changed because it was cheaper to survey a sixteen-sided figure.

By 1956 Curtiss-Wright was among the hundred largest U.S. corporations with annual net assets of more than $250 million. That year Hurley saw a chance to vastly enlarge his defense contracts by taking over the ailing Studebaker-Packard Corporation. The automaker had idle plant capacity that Curtiss-Wright could use, a huge tax carryback because of its losses, a valuable California missile subsidiary, and a few Pentagon jet and truck contracts. It was a national election year, and the possible loss of 20,000 auto jobs in Studebaker-Packard plants in Indiana and Michigan made Republican political strategists nervous. Hurley offered to take over the carmaker for $1.3 billion in new defense contracts. He had overreached, however, and after six months' negotiations in 1956 he settled for about one-quarter of his demands and signed a management contract with Studebaker-Packard. He was unable to turn the auto company's fortunes around, but over the next two years he signed an agreement with Daimler-Benz that enabled Studebaker-Packard to distribute Mercedes in the United States, and he cut enough costs at South Bend to allow Studebaker to tool its Lark, a subcompact car that kept the company in business for eight more years.

Hurley divorced his first wife Ruth Appleby, whom he had married in 1917 and with whom he had two daughters, and in 1953 he married his executive assistant, Esther Sarchian, with whom he was to have two more children. Professionally active outside his companies, he sat on the boards of General Cable, Manufacturer's Trust, and New York University. He received numerous awards, including the French Legion of Honor in 1957 and the Horatio Alger award in 1956. He retired from Curtiss-Wright in 1961 and moved to Santa Barbara, California, his residence at his death.

An outspoken man, Hurley was one of the dwindling band of American entrepreneurs who rose to the top of the corporate world without benefit of a high school diploma. Physically imposing, he combined his natural mechanical bent with an ability to get along with people, especially those who were in a position to help him. During World War II he learned the niceties of political lobbying and rebuilt Curtiss-Wright through adroit solicitation of Defense Department contracts. Within the company, his rule was unchallenged; he was not a man who liked to delegate responsibility, and he could be ruthless in cutting costs to enhance profits. Paradoxically, this most public of men guarded his privacy. He distrusted newspaper reporters, and he even resented his few lines in *Who's Who in America*. Like many men who rose from humble beginnings, he was reticent to discuss his childhood years.

• There are no Hurley papers, and there is no biography. Information outlining his career may be found in the *New York Times*, 5 Aug. 1956, and in his obituary in the *New York Times*, 6 Nov. 1971. *Automotive News*, 13 Aug. 1956, also ran an article on him, and *Who Was Who* has a synopsis of his life.

JAMES A. WARD

HUROK, Sol (9 Apr. 1888–5 Mar. 1974), impresario and theatrical manager, was born Solomon Isaievitch Hurok in Pogar, Russia, the son of Israel Hurok, a hardware dealer, and Naomi Schream. (According to modern conventions of transliteration from the Cyrillic, the surname would appear as Iurok.) At age sixteen Israel Hurok sent his son to the city of Kharkov with 1,000 rubles to learn the hardware trade and make his fortune. Instead of establishing himself in Kharkov, Solomon used the money to buy a berth on a ship sailing to New York. On his arrival at Ellis Island in May 1906, Hurok had only three rubles to his name. He settled at first in Philadelphia, working as a bottle washer, a streetcar conductor, and a sorter of newspapers for the midnight editions. He soon returned to New York, where he earned his living selling hardware and spent his free time studying English at the Educational Alliance on Manhattan's Lower East Side. He became a naturalized citizen in 1914.

Hurok began his career as an impresario in 1911, when he organized a concert featuring violinist Efrem Zimbalist at the Brownsville Labor Lyceum in Brooklyn. The concert's success encouraged Hurok to organize the Van Hugo Musical Society and to sponsor a series of cheaply priced Sunday night concerts at the Brooklyn Academy of Music. These concerts became enormously popular, and in 1915 Hurok began presenting "Music for the Masses," inexpensive Sunday afternoon concerts featuring well-known performers at the New York Hippodrome. His stars included Mischa Elman, Tito Ruffa, and Alma Gluck. He drew large audiences by advertising in foreign language newspapers.

From these modest beginnings, Hurok went on to manage and promote a wide range of world-famous performing artists. At the Hippodrome he met ballerina Anna Pavlova; he became her manager in 1920. Their collaboration proved hugely successful for both; within four years they shared profits of $500,000. Not all of his productions, however, were popular or financial successes. For the collaborations between Feodor Chaliapin and the Russian Grand Opera, beginning in 1922, Hurok spent $150,000 on lavish productions but suffered a notable flop.

Hurok, nicknamed the "King of Ballet," was one of the leading dance promoters in the United States and is considered instrumental in popularizing dance as an art form in this country. He promoted the American stars Martha Graham, Isadora Duncan, and Katherine Dunham, as well as the Agnes de Mille troupe. He managed the enormously popular British Sadler's Wells Ballet (later the Royal Ballet), which toured the United States with huge success in the 1950s. When the National Broadcast Company (NBC) aired the Sadler's Wells performance of *The Sleeping Beauty* on national television in December 1955, an estimated 37,000,000 people watched. Hurok considered television an exciting and important tool for the popularization of music, calling it the "greatest instrument that has ever been available to bring good music to the country." His other foreign clients included the Ballet Russe de Monte Carlo, London's Festival Ballet, the Royal Danish Ballet, the Paris Opera Ballet, the Bolshoi Ballet, starring Galina Ulanova, the Kirov Ballet, and the Stuttgart Ballet. In addition to ballet Hurok promoted folk and ethnic dance with such companies as the Azuma Kabuki Dancers from Japan, Antonio's Ballets de Madrid, the Festival Polynesia, and the Ballet Folklorico de Mexico.

Hurok's other nickname, the "Mahatma of Music," indicates his deep involvement in the classical music world. In 1933 he discovered the African-American contralto Marian Anderson performing in Paris and brought her to the attention of the American public. Great controversy erupted during an American tour when the Daughters of the American Revolution (DAR) refused to allow Anderson to perform in the DAR-owned Constitution Hall because she was an African American. Hurok secured an alternative venue by persuading the Department of the Interior to allow the singer to perform at Lincoln Memorial, and the concert took place on Easter Sunday, 9 April 1939 (Hurok's birthday), before an audience of over 75,000 people. Hurok's other notable clients included pianists Rudolf Serkin, Arthur Rubinstein, Emil Gilels, and Sviatoslav Richter; guitarist Andrés Segovia; violinists Isaac Stern, Mischa Elman, and David Oistrakh; singers Jan Peerce, Luisa Tettrazini, Patrice Munsel, and Roberta Peters; conductor Pierre Boulez; and the Kolisch String Quartet, the Moscow Cathedral Choir, the German Grand Opera Company, and the Vienna Choir Boys. These were all artists of the first rank, whom any impresario would have wanted to represent.

Hurok was also involved, although to a lesser extent than in dance and music, with dramatic productions, especially with the U.S. tours of foreign theatrical troupes. "S. Hurok Presents" managed such companies as the London and Bristol Old Vic companies, the Théâtre de France, the Théâtre National Populaire, the Compagnie Marie Bell, the D'Oyly Carte Opera Company, the Moscow Art Theater, the Comédie Française, and the company Madeleine Renaud–Jean-Louis Barrault. The Habima Players, whose Broadway debut was entirely in Hebrew, is one example among many of companies that performed entirely in a foreign language.

Hurok was awarded the Légion d'Honneur in 1953 by the French government for his promotion of French culture and was named a commander of the British Empire. He was married twice. He had one child with his first wife (name unknown) and then in 1933 married Emma Runitch, with whom he later separated. He died in New York City.

Sol Hurok is remembered as an effective promoter of the arts who discovered and managed major talents over an impressive number of years. He played a major role in the introduction of Russian and European performing artists, especially ballet dancers, to the American public. Because of his international reputation and impressive client list, he could insist that every venue with which he dealt had to accept all his bookings for any one season. Thus, he helped launch the careers of artists whose chances of receiving notice would otherwise have been slim. While acknowledging Hurok's significant role in bringing about the popularity and visibility of the performing arts in the United States, some have criticized him for his concentration on foreign artists, especially ones from the Soviet Union and Great Britain. As a result of this focus, he may well have contributed to the American tendency during much of the twentieth century of regarding performers from abroad as superior to their counterparts in America.

• Sol Hurok's two autobiographies, *Impresario* (1953) and *S. Hurok Presents: A Memoir of the Dance World* (1953), both ghostwritten, are interesting and informative. Articles on the promoter include John Bainbridge, "S. Hurok," *Life*, 28 Aug. 1944; Ward Morehouse, "S. Hurok," *Theatre Arts*, Feb. 1957; Gerald Goode, "S. Hurok Presents," *Reader's Digest*, Apr. 1958; and Harold C. Schonberg, "Presenting S. Hurok," *New York Times Magazine*, 26 Apr. 1959. Obituaries are in the *New York Times*, 6 Mar. 1974, and *Time*, 18 Mar. 1974.

ELIZABETH ZOE VICARY

HURST, Fannie (19 Oct. 1885–23 Feb. 1968), writer, was born in Hamilton, Ohio, the daughter of first-generation German Jewish Americans Rose Koppel and Samuel Hurst, a businessman. Despite the wide circulation of 19 October 1889 as her birth date, evidence from the census of 1890, her 1905 Washington University matriculation records, and the 1906 St. Louis City Directory indicate that her actual birth date was 19 October 1885. Her childhood in St. Louis, Missouri, was not the comfortable middle-class idyll she portrays in her 1958 autobiography *Anatomy of Me*. There were many crises, medical, financial, and emotional. When she was four years old, her only sister died during a diphtheria epidemic. Her father had a hard time earning a living, changing businesses four times during her girlhood, never achieving much financial success, and failing in business at least once. The family had eleven addresses before she was sixteen. Hurst graduated from Washington University in 1909 with an A.B. Shortly thereafter she moved to New York City, where she lived and wrote for the rest of her life. In 1915 she secretly married Russian Jewish immigrant Jacques Danielson, a brilliant pianist who made a career as a teacher and accompanist. The marriage became public in 1920 and lasted until his death in 1952, from which she never fully recovered, despite her full public and literary life and despite being courted by a number of prominent men.

Although Hurst had a lifelong memory of herself as a fat child, pictures from her early years show a sturdily built, strong, healthy child. Her distorted body image deprived her of a good deal of self-esteem, intellectual and emotional energy, and pleasure. Her obsession with body size culminated in an episode of obsessive and angry fasting that resulted in dramatic and permanent weight loss in her mid-thirties. The struggle is recorded in her short autobiographical memoir *No Food with My Meals* (1935).

Fannie Hurst was the literary chronicler of the lower-class and lower-middle-class urban working woman from c. 1912 to c. 1935. She especially singled out and wrote stories dealing with the lives and struggles of women working in the "rag trade"—whether clerking in department stores, modeling in wholesale houses in the garment district, or designing clothes. These stories included "The Nth Commandment," "T. B.," "White Goods," "Oats for the Woman," and "Summer Resources." She also portrayed the circumstances of women clerking for small businesses, laboring in private homes and large office buildings as domestic workers, and other urban sex-segregated jobs.

Hurst's first novel, about an artist coming of age, *Star-dust: The Story of an American Girl* (1921), gives—according to literary critic Glynis Carr—a unique, antiromantic perspective on art and on work in Hurst's writing. Carr concludes that for Hurst all work in the arts is true labor that, as much as any other, ought to be fairly compensated and performed in healthy, safe circumstances and ought not to expose women to sexual harassment. Hurst helped working women recognize that these problems as well as inadequate benefits and age discrimination were problems of all working women and not just the problem of one woman here and there, at one or another place of employment. Her images of working women encouraged their real-life models to take pride in the heroism of their daily lives.

Social scientists found Hurst's portraits believable counterparts of the data they collected. The few autobiographies by working women of the period further validate Hurst's portrayals.

Hurst's advocacy for working women extended beyond her fiction; she was involved in a variety of organizations designed to improve their lot. Her first contact with her good friend Eleanor Roosevelt and her subsequent involvement with the women of the New Deal occurred, as Hurst remembers in her autobiography, when the two women came independently to the cause of domestic workers. Hurst's civic activities included the presidency and vice presidency of the Authors' Guild of America and chairing the Woman's National Housing Commission (both in 1936–1937). She was secretary of the New York World's Fair Commission, belonged to the National Committee of the Works Progress Administration (1940–1941), chaired the New York Committee on Workmen's Compensation, and belonged to the (New York City) Mayor's Advisory Committee on Unity from 1945 to 1947; she was a board member of the New York Urban League, an active supporter of the NAACP, and a United States delegate in 1952 to the World Health Organization. She served on the boards of trustees of the Heckscher Foundation and the Russell Sage Foundation. She worked tirelessly on bond drives during World War I and World War II and was a member of the War Writers Board. She campaigned for the relief of Eastern European Jews and supported the state of Israel. She helped raise funds for the Children's Welfare Fund, the Salvation Army, the YWCA, the American Cancer Society, the Federation of Jewish Philanthropies, Hadassah, and the Albert Einstein College of Medicine at Yeshiva University. She was a member of the Heterodoxy Club founded by Jenny Marie Howe and a great friend of Ruth Bryant Owen, Zona Gale, and many of the other writers, jurists, settlement house founders, journalists, performing artists, lawyers, and public health workers who also belonged to the club.

There is boundless testimony not only in the statistics about books printed and sold but in the sacks of letters she received that Fannie Hurst meant a great deal to many people; she provided her readers—who seem to have been mostly women, since she published most of her stories in women's magazines—with a means of examining and reflecting on their own lives. She is reputed to have been one of the most highly paid writers in the United States and to have published more than three hundred short stories during her career. Of these, sixty-three were collected from their original periodical publications and reprinted in eight books. She wrote eighteen novels, among them *Lummox* (1923), her personal favorite, *Back Street* (1931), and *Imitation of Life* (1933), all of which were translated into films. Between 1918 and 1961, twenty-nine films were made from Hurst fiction, including, besides the above, the classic ghetto films "Humoresque" and "The Younger Generation" made from her story "The Gold in Fish" which Patricia Erens, in *The Jew in American Cinema* (1984), discusses at length for their thematic importance and their cinematic value.

She appeared on many radio shows, traveled and lectured widely, and, during the early days of television, hosted her own show. During her lifetime, she was often compared to Eleanor Roosevelt. She died in New York City.

Her short stories are among the finest ever produced by an American writer. She knew how to tell a story; she created characters who breathed; she captured the reality of a segment of the American population with a rare seriousness and sympathy. An important American naturalist, she transferred the meticulous artistry of the nineteenth-century regionalists to urban workers of the early twentieth century. She was a great ironist, a great humorist, and as close to a great tragedian as we have seen in this century.

• The Harry Ransom Humanities Research Center at the University of Texas, Austin, houses the major collection of Hurst material, including original typescripts of many of her stories and novels, letters from readers, clippings, and correspondence relating to her many organizational activities. The Beinecke Library at Yale houses the correspondence between Hurst and her longtime close friend Carl Van Vechten. When she died, she willed her estate to be divided between Washington University in St. Louis and Brandeis University; hence, each has an important collection of Hurst materials. Cynthia Ann Brandimarte, "Fannie Hurst and Her Fiction: Prescriptions for America's Working Women" (Ph.D. diss., Univ. of Texas, 1980), is a valuable bibliographical resource, as is Brandimarte, "Fannie Hurst: A Missouri Girl Makes Good," *Missouri Historical Review* 81, no. 3 (Apr. 1987): 275–95. The most important recent examinations of her life and assessments of her work are collected in Susan Koppelman, ed., *Fannie Hurst: Essays on Her Life and Writing* (1995). Essays on Hurst by Blanche Colton Williams in *Our Short Story Writers* (1923), and Grant Overton in *The Women Who Make Our Novels* (1928), summarize Hurst's contemporaries' assessments of her writing. Zora Neale Hurston's autobiography, *Dust Tracks on a Road: An Autobiography*, ed. Robert E. Hemenway (2d ed., 1984), contains Hurston's memories of Hurst. An obituary is in the *New York Times*, 24 Feb. 1968.

SUSAN KOPPELMAN

HURSTON, Zora Neale (7 Jan. 1891?–28 Jan. 1960), writer and anthropologist, was born in Eatonville, Florida, the daughter of John Hurston, a Baptist minister and carpenter, and Lucy Ann Potts. John Hurston's family had been Alabama tenant farmers until he moved to Eatonville, the first African-American town incorporated in the United States. He served three terms as its mayor and is said to have written Eatonville's ordinances. Zora Neale Hurston studied at its Hungerford School, where followers of Booker T. Washington taught both elementary academic skills and self-reliance. Growing up in an exclusively black community gave her a unique background that informed and inspired much of her later work.

Much of the chronological detail of Hurston's early life is obscured by the fact that she later claimed birth dates that varied from 1898 to 1903. Most often she cited 1901 as her birth year, but the census of 1900 lists a Zora L. Hurston, born in 1891, as the daughter of John and Lucy Hurston. According to Zora Neale Hurston's later accounts, she was nine years old when her mother died, and, when her father remarried, she left Eatonville to be "passed around the family like a bad penny." At fourteen, she tells us, she joined a traveling Gilbert and Sullivan theater company as maid and wardrobe girl. After eighteen months on the road, she left the company in Baltimore, Maryland. There Hurston worked in menial positions and studied at Morgan Academy, the preparatory school operated by Morgan College.

After she graduated from Morgan Academy in 1918, Hurston moved to Washington, D.C. She worked in a variety of menial positions and was a part-time student at Howard University from 1919 to 1924. At Howard, Hurston studied with Alain Locke and Lorenzo Dow Turner, who encouraged her to write for publication. Accepted as a member of Stylus, the campus literary club, she published her first short story, "John Redding Goes to Sea," in its literary magazine, the *Stylus*, in May 1921. Three years later Charles S. Johnson's *Opportunity*, a major literary vehicle for writers of the Harlem Renaissance, published two of Hurston's stories, "Drenched in Light" and "Spunk." In these early stories she staked out a perspective characteristic of her later African-American folktales. They celebrate the lives of ordinary black people who had little interaction with or sense of oppression by a white community.

In 1925, after winning an award for "Spunk," Hurston moved to New York City, where she joined other writers and artists of the Harlem Renaissance. As secretary and chauffeur to novelist Fannie Hurst, Hurston also gained access to contemporary white literary circles. In September 1925 she began studying at Barnard College on a scholarship. Nine months later Hurston, Aaron Douglas, Langston Hughes, and Wallace Thurman launched a short-lived, avant-garde magazine, *Fire!* Against the claim of older African-American mentors, such as W. E. B. Du Bois and Alain Locke, that a black writer was obliged to express a racial consciousness in the face of white hostility, they held that the creative artist's obligation was to give voice to the vitality of an African-American culture that was more than simply a reaction to white oppression. Hurston's short story "Sweat" is the most important of her published essays and short stories in this period.

At Barnard, Hurston became a student of noted anthropologist Franz Boas. "Papa Franz," as she called him, encouraged Hurston's interest in the folklore of her people. Her first field research took Hurston to Alabama to interview a former slave, Cudjo Lewis, for Carter G. Woodson's Association for the Study of Negro Life and History. Her article "Cudjo's Own Story of the Last African Slaves," which appeared in the *Journal of Negro History* (1927), was marred, however, by plagiarism from Emma Langdon Roache's *Historic Sketches of the Old South*. When Hurston received a B.A. from Barnard in 1928, she was the first African

American known to have graduated from the institution.

In 1927 Hurston married Herbert Sheen, a medical student with whom she had begun a relationship in 1921 when they were both students at Howard University. Four months after their marriage, however, Hurston and Sheen parted company, and they were divorced in 1931.

Hurston's literary career illustrates the difficult struggle of an African-American female writer for support and control of her work. From 1927 to 1932 Hurston's field research was sponsored by a wealthy white patron, Charlotte Osgood Mason. With that support Hurston made her most important anthropological forays into the South, revisiting Alabama and Florida, breaking new ground in Louisiana, and journeying to the Bahamas. Working in rural labor camps and as an apprentice to voodoo priests, she collected an anthropologist's treasure of folklore, children's games, prayers, sermons, songs, and voodoo rites. Yet, the hand that sustained was also the hand that controlled. Mason insisted that Hurston sign a contract that acknowledged the white patron's ownership of and editorial control over the publication of Hurston's research.

In the spring of 1930, Hurston and Langston Hughes collaborated in writing a play, *Mule Bone*. Only its third act was published, but in 1931 Hughes and Hurston quarreled over its authorship. When she claimed that its material was hers, he accused her of trying to take full credit for the play. The two authors never resolved their differences in the matter, but it seems clear that Hurston's anthropological research supplied the material to which Hughes gave dramatic form.

By the mid-1930s Hurston had begun to reach her stride. Her first novel, *Jonah's Gourd Vine*, was published in 1934. Its protagonist, John Buddy "Jonah" Pearson, is a folk preacher whose sermons display Hurston's mastery of the idiom. Indeed, the folk material threatens to overshadow the novel's characters and plot. Like her other work, the novel was also criticized for ignoring the effects of racial oppression in the South. In 1934, after a semester of teaching at Bethune-Cookman College in Daytona Beach, Florida, Hurston received a Rosenwald Fellowship and enrolled for graduate work in anthropology at Columbia University. Briefly in 1935–1936 she was employed as a drama coach by the Works Progress Administration (WPA) in New York. Hurston never completed a graduate degree, but she received Guggenheim field research fellowships for the 1935–1936 and 1936–1937 academic years. Her first major anthropological work, *Mules and Men*, appeared in 1935. It mined the rich lode of her research in southern African-American folklore in the late 1920s and early 1930s. The Guggenheim Fellowships took Hurston to Jamaica and Haiti to study Caribbean folk culture. Those studies produced her second major anthropological work, *Tell My Horse*, in 1938.

Now at the peak of her productive years, Hurston published her second major novel, *Their Eyes Were Watching God*, in 1937. Written in eight weeks, during which Hurston was recovering from a passionate romantic relationship, *Their Eyes Were Watching God* is the most successful of her novels artistically. Its heroine, Janie Starks, is a free-spirited woman who pursues her dream of emotional and spiritual fulfillment. Janie and her third husband, Tea Cake, like most of Hurston's folk subjects, enjoy their laughter and their sensuality even in their poverty. In her own life, however, Hurston was less successful in love. In 1939, after a year as an editor for the Federal Writers' Project in Florida and a year of teaching at North Carolina College in Durham, Hurston married Albert Price III, a WPA playground director who was at least fifteen years her junior. After eight months they filed for a divorce. There were attempts at a reconciliation, but the divorce became final in 1943.

Hurston's subsequent fiction was less successful artistically. *Moses, Man of the Mountain*, published in 1939, depicted the leader of the biblical exodus and lawgiver as a twentieth-century African-American witch doctor. In 1942 Hurston published her autobiography, *Dust Tracks on the Road*. It was the most successful of her books commercially. As autobiography, however, it was an accurate portrait not of Hurston's life but of the persona she wanted the public to know: an ambitious, independent, even "outrageous" woman, with a zest for life unhindered by racial barriers. Yet her life became increasingly difficult. Arrested on a morals charge involving a retarded sixteen-year-old boy, Hurston was eventually cleared of the accusations. The African-American press gave graphic coverage to the sensational nature of the case, and the publicity had a devastating effect on her career. Hurston's efforts to win funding for a field trip for research in Central America were frustrated until she received an advance for a new novel. In 1947 Hurston left the United States for the British Honduras, where she did anthropological research in its black communities and completed *Seraph on the Suwanee*, her only novel whose characters are white. Published in 1948, *Seraph on the Suwanee's* portrait of Arvay Henson Meserve as a woman entrapped in marriage might have found a more receptive audience two decades earlier or two decades later.

By 1950 Hurston's failure to find a steady source of support for her work forced her to take a position in Miami as a domestic worker. There was a stir of publicity when her employer found an article in the *Saturday Evening Post* written by her maid. During the 1940s and 1950s, however, Hurston's essays were more likely to appear in right-wing venues, such as the *American Legion Magazine* or *American Mercury*, rather than the mainstream press. By then her celebration of African-American folk culture and her refusal to condemn the oppressive racial climate in which it was nurtured had allied Hurston with forces hostile to the civil rights movement. A 1950 article titled "Negro Votes Bought" seemed to oppose the enfranchisement of African Americans. Four years later, in a letter to the editor of a Florida newspaper, which was widely reprinted, Hurston attacked the U.S. Supreme Court's decision in *Brown v. Board of Education* on the grounds that it undervalued the capacity of African-American institutions to educate African-American people and of African-American people to learn apart from a white presence.

Throughout the 1950s Hurston worked intermittently as a substitute teacher, a domestic worker, and a contributor to a local newspaper, but she was ill and without a steady income. She spent much of her time writing and revising a biography of Herod the Great, but both the subject and the language of the manuscript lacked the vitality of her earlier work. Even after a stroke in 1959, Hurston refused to ask her relatives for help. She died in the county welfare home at Fort Pierce, Florida. After a public appeal for money to pay for her burial, Hurston was laid to rest in Fort Pierce's African-American cemetery. In 1973 writer Alice Walker placed a granite tombstone in the cemetery, somewhere near her unmarked grave.

• Material from Hurston's early career is scattered in collections at the American Philosophical Society Library, the Amistad Research Center at Tulane University, Fisk University's Special Collections, Howard University's Moorland-Spingarn Research Center, the Library of Congress, and Yale University's Beinecke Library. The Zora Neale Hurston Collection at the University of Florida includes letters and manuscripts from her later years. Hurston was "rediscovered" in Darwin T. Turner, *In a Minor Chord: Three Afro-American Writers and Their Search for Identity* (1971); Mary Helen Washington, "Zora Neale Hurston: The Black Woman's Search for Identity," *Black World*, Aug. 1972, pp. 68–75; Arthur P. Davis, *From the Dark Tower: Afro-American Writers, 1900–1960* (1974); Alice Walker, "In Search of Zora Neale Hurston," *Ms.*, Mar. 1975, pp. 74–79, 85–89; and Addison Gayle, *The Way of the New World: The Black Novel in America* (1975). The Hurston renaissance produced a standard biography, Robert E. Hemenway, *Zora Neale Hurston: A Literary Biography* (1977); a Hurston reader, edited by Alice Walker, with an introduction by Mary Helen Washington, *I Love Myself When I Am Laughing and Then Again When I Am Looking Mean and Impressive* (1979); and a guide to research, Adele S. Newson, *Zora Neale Hurston: A Reference Guide* (1987). Important subsequent work includes Eric J. Sundquist, *The Hammers of Creation: Folk Culture in Modern African-American Fiction* (1992); Henry Louis Gates, Jr., and K. A. Appiah, eds., *Zora Neale Hurston: Critical Perspectives Past and Present* (1993); John Lowe, *Jump at the Sun: Zora Neale Hurston's Cosmic Comedy* (1994); and Cheryl A. Wall, *Women of the Harlem Renaissance* (1995). An obituary is in the *New York Times*, 5 Feb. 1960.

RALPH E. LUKER

HURT, Mississippi John (3 July 1893?–2 Nov. 1966), blues singer and guitarist, was born John Smith Hurt in the hamlet of Teoc, Carroll County, Mississippi, the son of Isom Hurt and Mary Jan McLain, farmers. When he was two his family moved to Avalon, a town between Greenwood and Grenada, Mississippi, where he remained most of his life. He attended St. James School, dropping out after the fourth grade to help support the family. Inspired by a local guitarist, William Hilliard, who often stayed at Hurt's house, he picked up Hilliard's guitar one evening and began to make music when he was only eight years old.

Hurt's son John, Jr., claimed his father told him years later that his musical ability had come to him "in a dream . . . his mama sat up in bed, said, 'Oh, my son done started playing the guitar.'" Taking this as a sign of his talent, his mother bought him a secondhand guitar for a dollar and a half, and from around 1904 on he was playing local parties, picnics, and dances, as well as "serenading" local residents. He often worked with fiddlers, playing square dance music for both black and white audiences.

Along with his casual weekend music events, Hurt worked a variety of jobs: farming, maintaining river levees, and, for a brief period, lining track. Around 1923 he began to play dances with a gifted Carroll County fiddler. "There was a white dude called Willie Narmour," his son recalled. "He drew the bow on the fiddle and they played 'Carroll County Blues.' Man, you talking about fun. Then daddy, he never said a bad word, but he'd say, 'Hot dog, let's get down.'"

Hurt's association with Narmour led to his initial recording session. Through a fiddling contest, Narmour won the opportunity to record for OKeh Records. Recording director T. J. Rockwell, in Avalon to pick up Narmour, asked about other local musicians, and Narmour recommended Hurt. Supposedly they roused Hurt in the middle of the night, and after an impromptu audition Rockwell arranged to record Hurt in Memphis on 14 February 1928. Hurt cut eight sides, from which the ballad "Frankie" and the flip side "Nobody's Dirty Business" were released, and enjoyed moderate success.

Ten months later, at Rockwell's invitation, Hurt traveled to New York City by train and recorded twelve additional titles in two sessions on 21 and 28 December 1928. These included ballads, spirituals, and dance tunes as well as blues. Rockwell requested at least four "old-time tunes." Supposedly Hurt's first releases were listed as old-time music rather than as race records, demonstrating his ambivalent songster status and appeal to white listeners. Hurt recalled later that guitarist Lonnie Johnson served as producer and chaperone during the New York sessions.

Hurt returned to Avalon and to his wife, Jessie Lee Cole, whom he had married in 1927 and with whom he had fourteen children, and resumed the life of a farmer and laborer. Despite his interest in more recording, he would not record again for thirty-five years.

In the 1950s, when two of Hurt's 1928 recordings, "Frankie" and "Spike Driver Blues," were included in a Folkways Records anthology of American folk music, a new audience had a chance to hear his music. By the early 1960s record collectors and blues researchers were actively hunting for blues artists who had recorded in the 1920s and 1930s. Hurt's "rediscovery" by Washington, D.C., blues enthusiast Tom Hoskins was the result of one of a half-dozen fruitful searches.

Hurt could still play, his repertoire seemingly frozen in time. Hoskins persuaded Hurt to come to Washington, where he stayed with Richard K. Spottswood, an avid researcher and record producer. On 15 and 23 July 1963 Hurt recorded eighty-one songs and three folk tales in Coolidge Auditorium at the Library of Congress. Public interest in his rediscovery and his music led to stories in *Time, Newsweek,* and the *New York Times* and appearances at the Newport Folk Festival in 1963, 1964, and 1965. Hurt relocated his family to Washington, where he became the resident artist at a club, Ontario Place. His presence in Washington sparked a local "blues revival," according to one of his musical cronies, Maryland blues singer Archie Edwards, who recalled, "You'd see people coming out of music stores with guitars—you'd say, 'Uh oh, John has done spread an epidemic.'" Hurt signed with Dick Waterman's booking agency, Avalon Productions, which took its name from the town where Hurt grew up. Enjoying several years of fame, he appeared on NBC television's "Tonight Show," made festival appearances, and recorded for Piedmont and Vanguard. He preferred the country life, however, and as soon as he could afford it, returned to Avalon. He died in nearby Grenada.

One of the success stories of the 1960s, Hurt was lionized as the embodiment of what a folk artist should be: a friendly, gentle, deeply religious man who made countless friends and left a lasting impression on musicians and audiences alike. At heart he was a simple country person whose life was twice interrupted by celebrity, first as a rural musician who happened to be recorded in the late 1920s and then as a blues-revival hero in the 1960s. His complex three-finger guitar style, which he referred to as "cotton picking," seemed closer to East Coast tradition than that of Mississippi. Perhaps it represented an older, pre-Delta blues strain, or maybe it was simply idiosyncratic. Regardless, it was effective in supporting his varied songster repertoire, which spanned the nineteenth and twentieth centuries. His vocal approach was unforced, almost reserved, in contrast to the impassioned vocals of many Delta artists and was equally accessible to black and white audiences, whether at country dances in the 1920s or on the 1960s festival and coffeehouse circuit.

• For more biographical information on Hurt, see Sheldon Harris, *Blues Who's Who: A Biographical Dictionary of Blues Singers* (1979; repr. 1989). For a discussion of his finger-picking technique, see Happy Traum, *Finger-Picking Styles for Guitar* (1966). For an early reference, see Dick Spottswood, "Mississippi John Hurt," in *Nothing but the Blues,* ed. Mike Leadbitter (1971); for an account of his rediscovery, see Eddie Dean, "Skip James: Hard Time Killing Floor Blues," *Washington City Paper,* 25 Nov.–1 Dec. 1994, pp. 24–34. See also Peter Seeger, "An Interview with Mississippi John Hurt," *Broadside,* 10 May 1967, pp. 9–11, 24 May 1967, pp. 10–11, and 7 June 1967, p. 6. Tom Hoskins's interview is in Stefan Grossman, "'Scrapin' the Heart and Knockin' Them Back': A Classic Interview with the Legendary Mississippi John Hurt," *Sing Out* 39, no. 4 (Feb.–Mar.–Apr. 1995): 52–57. For discographical information, see Robert M. W.

Dixon and John Godrich, *Blues and Gospel Records: 1902–1943* (1982); Leadbitter and Neil Slaven, *Blues Records 1943–1966* (1968); and Paul Oliver, ed., *The Blackwell Guide to Blues Records* (1989). To hear his music, try *Mississippi John Hurt: The 1928 Sessions* (Yazoo 1065) and *Mississippi John Hurt Today* (Vanguard VSD 79220).

BILL MCCULLOCH
BARRY LEE PEARSON

HURTY, John Newell (21 Feb. 1852–27 Mar. 1925), pharmacist and sanitarian, was born in Lebanon, Ohio, the son of Josiah Hurty, a teacher and school superintendent, and Irene Walker. In 1869, while still in high school in Paris, Illinois, Eli Lilly, as Hurty was later to write, "beguiled" him into the "drug business," and he became an apprentice in Binford and Lilly's Red Front Drug Store. There he learned chemistry as well as pharmacy in 1871–1872, and, with the encouragement of Lilly, he studied at the Philadelphia College of Pharmacy. In 1873 Hurty followed Lilly to Indianapolis, where Lilly began to manufacture pharmaceuticals in partnership with Dr. John Johnston. Hurty was responsible for determining the purity of raw materials and assaying finished products. When the firm of Johnston and Lilly dissolved in 1879, Hurty, who had in 1877 married Johnston's daughter, Ethel (with whom he had two children), opened his own pharmacy in Indianapolis. He became a prominent pharmacist, a founding member in 1882 of the Indiana Pharmaceutical Association and its president in 1890. Attached to his shop he developed an analytical chemistry laboratory and devoted considerable time to the assaying of items such as water, coal, and wine and did some work in forensic toxicology. In 1891 Hurty was appointed chemist and toxicologist at the Indianapolis City Hospital. He remained active in his pharmacy and laboratory until he became secretary of the Indiana State Board of Health in 1896. He then turned over the management of the pharmacy to an assistant and in 1901 sold him his entire interest.

In 1881 Hurty had begun a career as a part-time teacher at the Central College of Physicians and Surgeons of Indianapolis; he remained in teaching for the rest of his life. He soon left the medical school to teach at the Indiana Dental School, where he was professor of chemistry and metallurgy and where he instructed in sanitation and hygiene as well. Associated with the dental school for the remainder of his life, he was a stockholder and secretary of the board of trustees of the school, and he became president of the board in 1896, although after 1914 he had little to say in the management of the school. In 1887 he was made an honorary member of the Indiana State Dental Association.

In 1884 Hurty was named professor and, nominally, dean, of the new program in pharmacy established at Purdue University. The program had come into existence as a result of a suggestion made by Hurty to James H. Smart, president of Purdue. Hurty traveled to Lafayette once a week to lecture on pharmacy but under pressure from his other activities discontinued doing so in 1886, although he did remain as an occasional special lecturer until 1888.

The 1887 catalog of the Medical College of Indiana listed Hurty as a lecturer in chemical philosophy and hygiene. He remained on the staff of the college through its various changes in name and affiliation. The membership list of the American Association for the Advancement of Science, of which he became a member in 1907 and a Fellow in 1909, designated him as a professor of hygiene and preventive medicine in the Medical Department of Indiana University. Hurty did not have a reputation as an effective teacher, especially later in his career.

In 1891 Hurty attained a doctor of medicine degree from the Medical College of Indiana. Although he was licensed to practice, Hurty never went into medical practice.

In 1896 the Indiana State Board of Health elected Hurty as secretary of the board and regularly reelected him to that post until he resigned in 1922. Every aspect of the sanitary movement engaged his interest and energy. His ardent activity in procuring public health legislation and his strident and aggressive enforcement often earned him characterizations such as "stormy petrel," "pertinacious," "crank," "publicity seeker," "sensationalist," and "traitor to the state." Hurty claimed when running for the legislature in 1922 that during his tenure, "with very few exceptions" he "wrote every law and rule or regulation dealing with the public health." But he had powerful supporters who backed him despite the antagonism he engendered among farmers and others, and especially among legislators. Hurty was brusque, given to plain language, and not above scare tactics.

Hurty neglected no aspect of the sanitary movement; several of his efforts gained him national attention. For example, as a result of his effective campaign for hygienic, well-ventilated, heated, and lighted schools, many teacher groups from all over the country invited him to speak. In his 1912 presidential address to the American Public Health Association and in an address to the International Congress of Hygiene and Demography several days later, both in Washington, D.C., he castigated farm hygiene, asserting that "the American farmer stinks." This brought down on him the wrath of the people of Indiana but gained him even more national attention.

An ardent Darwinist, Hurty was interested in the eugenics movement and became a zealous advocate of the sterilization of mental "defectives" and others. With his efforts and support Indiana became the first state in 1907 to adopt a sterilization law.

Recognition came to Hurty early in his career. A member of the Indiana State Medical Association in 1882, he became chairman of the association's committee on public health and hygiene in 1897 and 1898 and was its vice president in 1911. Also in 1897 he became secretary of the National Conference of State Boards of Health. In 1899 Hurty was elected vice president of the Conference of State and Provincial Boards of Health of North America, and in 1904 he was president of the conference. He also served as chairman of the section on preventive medicine and public health of the American Medical Association in 1910 and as chairman of the committee on state methods of public education in hygiene (as well as chairman of the AMA's committee on nominations) in 1911.

In 1910 Hurty served as a member of the International Commission of the American Veterinary Medical Association on the control of bovine tuberculosis, and in 1912 he was president of the American Public Health Association. The presentations of the Indiana Board of Health won a silver medal at the Paris International Exposition in 1900; both Hurty and the board received bronze medals for their contributions to the St. Louis Exposition of 1904, and he received a gold medal from the Jamestown Exposition in 1907.

Contributions from Hurty's pen were rather ephemeral pieces, first in pharmaceutical journals, next a few articles in dental journals dealing with hygiene, and then a series of newspaper columns on sanitation. His one book, *Life with Health: A Text-Book on Physiology, Hygiene, and Sanitation* (1906), written for schools, was "not well accepted." Much more important were the vast array of publications that issued from his office. The quarterly *Bulletin of the Indiana State Board of Health* soon became a monthly. Distributed free, it gained national attention, as did *The Indiana Mothers' Baby Book*, first issued in 1915. In addition, 200,000 copies of a circular on the prevention of tuberculosis were distributed to the people of Indiana.

Hurty left the board of health a highly organized and departmentalized institution with considerable power. After retirement in 1922, having unspecified difficulties with the board and feeling that it was time for "a man of another temperament to take over the work," he ran for the Indiana House of Representatives. Although he was elected without needing to campaign, his tenure proved frustrating. Every measure he proposed was rejected, and he was particularly distressed that his plans to reorganize the state board of health and to establish state and county full-time health officers failed.

Hurty was a member of several local clubs, the University Club, the Columbia Club, and the Contemporary Club. He was most active in the Literary Club, of which he was treasurer from 1887 to 1915 and president from 1915 to 1916. He presented a substantial number of papers before the Literary Club, essentially on chemical subjects at first but later on sanitation. Hurty died in Indianapolis.

• Files of newspaper clippings and scrapbooks pertaining to Hurty are in the archives of the Indiana State Department of Health in Indianapolis. A detailed biography, Thurman B. Rice, *The Hoosier Health Officer: A Biography of Dr. John N. Hurty* (1946), originally appeared serially in the *Bulletin of the Indiana State Board of Health* from Jan. 1939 to Dec. 1946. The *Indianapolis News*, 9 Sept. 1922, carried a lengthy account of Hurty's career.

DAVID L. COWEN

HUSBAND, Herman (3 Oct. 1724–June 1795), back-country planter and radical millennialist, was born in Cecil County, Maryland, the son of William Husband and Mary Kinkey, slaveholders and members of the local planter gentry. Husband's early education included tutoring by his grandfather, Herman Kinkey; he also read on his own. Religion played an important part in his youth. William Husband demanded that the family attend Anglican services. Herman Kinkey emphasized the need for personal salvation, and Mary Husband concurred, following a strict moral code of behavior that clashed with her husband's and son's gambling, dancing, and other pastimes.

In December 1739 the Husband family heard a sermon by George Whitefield, the most famous preacher of the Great Awakening. Herman Husband then struggled to attain salvation and underwent a series of religious experiences culminating in the New Birth. He formed a belief in the imminent millennium and looked for an earthly church that would lead in the redemption of society. He began attending a nearby Presbyterian church and followed a New Side (evangelical) faction when it broke away from the original congregation.

As the religious enthusiasm of the New Side Presbyterians waned, Husband made inquiries about the Society of Friends. He read the Dutch Friend William Sewell's *History of the Rise, Increase and Progress of the Christian People Called Quakers*, about their early sufferings, and Robert Barclay's *An Apology for the True Christian Divinity*, a treatise on Quaker beliefs. Around 1743 he secretly joined the Quakers.

When Husband turned twenty-one, he married Quaker Phoebe Cox and openly acknowledged his membership in the Society. Throughout the late 1740s and 1750s Husband was an active member in good standing and served in several posts in the hierarchy of Society meetings, enforcing rules of conduct known as the Discipline. In 1750 he wrote *Some Remarks on Religion* but did not publish these memoirs until 1761.

Husband also was a planter in Cecil and Baltimore counties, operated a pig iron works on his family lands, invested in a schooner, and traveled to Barbados in 1750 for curiosity and trade. He first visited North Carolina in 1751 and returned in 1754 as an agent for a group of Maryland investors, intent on speculating in land in the colony's Granville district. The enterprise was short-lived. In 1756 Husband wrote the earl of Granville warning that corruption in the district's land office, favoritism shown Anglican ministers by the colonial assembly, and the appearance of slavery were causing recent settlers to return north. Husband's partners never followed through with their purchases. Between 1755 and 1762, however, Husband purchased for himself about ten thousand acres in Orange and Rowan counties, setting up a grist mill and iron works.

Around this time, his first wife died, leaving three children. Husband returned to Maryland and in 1760 was part owner and manager of the Fountain Copper Works in Frederick County. In 1762, though, he re-settled his family on his North Carolina lands and married Mary Pugh, a Quaker, at the Cane Creek monthly meeting. They had one child before her death in 1764 or 1765.

During the 1760s Husband clashed with other Friends over the extent to which members could disagree with actions of a higher meeting. He favored free exercise of conscience and led a faction in the monthly meeting that opposed many provisions of the Discipline. The Cane Creek meeting disowned him in 1765. In 1766 he married Amy Allen; they had four children.

The Stamp Act protest inspired Husband to enter politics to redeem society and prepare the way for the millennium. Husband and neighbors along Sandy Creek formed an association in 1766 that demanded county officials be accountable to voters. County officers threatened retaliation, and the association collapsed. At this time, Husband read political reformer George Sims's *An Address to the People of Granville County*, which praised the English Constitution and asserted the right of voters to instruct elected officials, and English minister James Murray's *Sermon to Asses*, which called on countrymen to vote their own interests.

In 1768 farmers calling themselves Regulators began demanding numerous political and economic reforms. Husband did not join the Regulators but advised and encouraged them, helped draft their resolutions and petitions, and wrote two pamphlets in 1770, *An Impartial Relation of the First Rise and Cause of the Recent Differences in Publick Affairs* and *A Continuation of the Impartial Relation*. He led moderate Regulators, who elected him twice to the assembly, but officials, convinced he was their ringleader, jailed him twice. That spring Governor William Tryon led colonial militia into the backcountry to suppress the Regulators and on 16 May defeated a large, disorganized gathering of Regulators along the Alamance Creek. Husband tried to negotiate a truce but left the field before the battle and then fled the colony under the alias Toscape Death. Meanwhile, the two sides clashed: the militia defeated the Regulators and marched onto Husband's property and confiscated it.

Proclaimed a traitor by Governor Tryon, with a price on his head, Husband found refuge in Pennsylvania's mountainous Bedford County and began purchasing land, becoming one of the region's largest resident landowners. His family joined him in 1772. When the Revolution broke out, Husband supported it and in 1777–1778 served as county representative in the unicameral state assembly held at Lancaster, publishing a paper money scheme that advocated a fixed rate of depreciation.

For Husband, the Revolution did not go far enough to perfect government. While hiking in the Alleghenies in 1779, he later wrote, he beheld a vision of the New Jerusalem rising west of the mountains. This inspired him to interpret passages in the biblical book of Ezekiel as prophesying those constitutional reforms necessary to usher in the millennium. Over the next decade he expanded his ideas in a series of works, many of which were published.

In 1788 Husband opposed ratification of the new federal Constitution, proposing instead interlocking regional combinations of states, overseen by an executive council. He patterned his confederation after one published by English radical Richard Price for Europe. Husband believed that the millennium would begin in the capital of the western empire of his confederation.

While a delegate to the Pennsylvania legislature in Philadelphia in 1789–1790, Husband published a pamphlet again proposing his confederation as an amendment to the new federal Constitution. He opposed Hamiltonian assumption and funding of the revolutionary debt and welcomed the French Revolution as a rebirth of the spirit of liberty. In unpublished commentaries on the book of Daniel, he predicted that the millennium would begin in the American West between 1814 and 1844. He saw the Whiskey Rebellion as another opportunity to promote his plan. Although Husband was not a major leader of the excise opposition, neighbors elected him a representative to the meeting of rebels at Parkinson's Ferry in 1794. There he served with Albert Gallatin, H. H. Brackenridge, and David Bradford on a committee to draw up resolutions. The rebels approved resolutions calling for negotiations and appointed Husband to committees to meet with Pennsylvania and federal authorities.

In the fall of 1794 President George Washington led federal militia into western Pennsylvania to crush the insurrection. In October troops seized Husband; charged with treason, he was taken with other prisoners to Philadelphia. He remained in jail through the winter, but in May a grand jury failed to indict him for treason. He died outside of Philadelphia, awaiting the arrival of his wife.

Husband was one of the leading socially radical millennialists of eighteenth-century America, with a public career spanning five decades, from the Great Awakening to the early Federal period. He combined millennialism with radical agrarianism to produce a unique utopian vision of a confederation of states with a western New Jerusalem.

• A treatment of Husband's entire life and all of his known writings is Mark H. Jones, "Herman Husband: Millenarian, Carolina Regulator, and Whiskey Rebel" (Ph.D. diss., Northern Illinois Univ., 1983). Husband's *Some Remarks on Religion* and *An Impartial Relation* are in W. K. Boyd, ed., *Some Eighteenth Century Tracts concerning North Carolina* (1927). See also Archibald Henderson, "Herman Husband's Continuation of the Impartial Relation," *North Carolina Historical Review* 18 (1941): 48–55. The following tracts by Husband are found in photostat form in the Mary E. Lazenby Papers, 1933–1955, Darlington Memorial Library, University of Pittsburgh: *Proposals to Amend and Perfect the Policy of the Government of the United States of America* (1782), *A Sermon to the Bucks and Hinds of America* (1788), *Fourteen Sermons on the Characters of Jacob's Fourteen Sons* (1789), and *A Dialogue between an Assembly-Man and a Convention-Man* (1790). See the Lazenby papers for Husband's unpublished commentaries on the book of Daniel, written around 1793.

See A. Roger Ekirch, "'A New Government of Liberty': Hermon [*sic*] Husband's Vision of Backcountry North Carolina, 1755," *William and Mary Quarterly* 34 (Oct. 1977): 632–46, for his letter to the earl of Granville. In the same issue, see also James Penn Whittenberg, "'The Common Farmer (Number 2)': Herman Husband's Plan for Peace between the United States and the Indians, 1792," pp. 647–50.

MARK H. JONES

HUSE, Caleb (11 Feb. 1831–11 Mar. 1905), soldier and Confederate arms procurement agent in Europe, was born in Newburyport, Massachusetts, the son of Ralph Cross Huse and Caroline Evans, occupations unknown. In 1851 he graduated from the U.S. Military Academy, seventh in his class. A year later he married Harriet Pinckney, a union that produced thirteen children. From 1852 until 1859 Huse was assigned to West Point as an assistant professor of chemistry, mineralogy, and geology, serving under Superintendent Robert E. Lee, whom he greatly admired. A trip to Europe in 1859 and 1860 while on extended leave produced valuable foreign civilian and military contacts.

Having served less than a year as commandant of cadets at the University of Alabama at Tuscaloosa, First Lieutenant Huse resigned his commission in February 1861 rather than acquiesce in a War Department transfer to Washington, D.C. His decision to leave the army appears to have been influenced by his close association with many southerners, especially his in-laws. Early in April 1861 he was commissioned as a captain in the Confederate army and ordered to travel to Europe to purchase rifles, cannon, and other military supplies to be paid for with shipments of southern cotton smuggled through the Federal naval blockade of Confederate ports. Based in England, with occasional trips to Austria, Huse acquired huge quantities of military ordnance.

Major Edward C. Anderson, sent from Montgomery to investigate Huse's efficiency and fidelity to the Confederate cause, soon concluded that the New Englander was "a singular . . . man of considerable intelligence and indomitable perseverance; honest and very earnest in the discharge of his duties" but indiscreet and a poor judge of people. Huse's indiscretion consisted mainly of an apparent eagerness to impress acquaintances with the importance of his duties as a Confederate agent, which led to his constant shadowing by detectives employed by the U.S. government and probably diminished his effectiveness. However, his dedication to the cause of the South and his resourcefulness in locating and acquiring weapons of war for his government, frequently without immediate access to sufficient funds to pay for them, were remarkable.

In contracting for weapons in England, Huse had to rely on promises to pay from Fraser, Trenholm & Company of Liverpool, a bank with branches in New York and Charleston, South Carolina, whose officers were avidly pro-Confederate. Payment for Huse's early purchases was eventually made out of the receipts for cotton slipped on fast, shallow draft vessels through the northern blockaders to Bermuda, Nassau, and Havana, where it was transferred to large ships for the voyage to Liverpool. Huse's most significant shipment of arms, which included rifles, cannon, revolvers, gunpowder, and bayonets, arrived late in 1861 at Savannah, Georgia, in the *Fingal* in time to furnish Confederate forces defending Richmond with the equipment needed to stop Union general George McClellan's spring offensive against the southern capital.

Thereafter working on his own authority, since Major Anderson had returned home on the *Fingal*, Huse continued to enter into contracts not only for the Confederate War Department but also for the Navy Department. Four steamships, which he purchased in England, ran the blockade forty-four times during the year 1863 alone, delivering desperately needed supplies to the southern armies and repeatedly running cargoes of cotton out through the blockade to be used as collateral for large loans negotiated with European bankers, without which arms purchases could not have continued.

Approximately nine out of every ten small arms used by Confederate forces during the first two years of the Civil War were acquired in Europe. The best of these, more than 100,000 British Enfield rifles, were purchased by Huse. In Austria he obtained another 100,000 rifles, the highest quality small arms available on the European continent. There, too, he also acquired sixty rifled cannon, along with the ammunition, carriages, and other equipment needed to fulfill their lethal potential.

By the end of the Civil War, Huse had sent the Confederate War Department munitions with a value exceeding $10 million, at least $2 million of which remained unpaid to European creditors when the conflict terminated. His total acquisitions included more than 350,000 rifles, approximately 150 cannon, many thousands of revolvers, huge quantities of ammunition, as well as bayonets, swords, leather goods, blankets, and medical supplies.

The collapse of the Confederacy left Huse virtually destitute with a large family to support. Unable to establish himself in business in England, in 1868 he moved back to the United States, where economic deprivation appeared to follow him. Finally, in 1876 he established a military preparatory school at Sing Sing (now Ossining), New York, and thereafter prospered. For two decades his institution, moved in 1879 to Highland Falls, fed its graduates to the U.S. Military Academy at West Point, from which some rose to general officer rank in the U.S. Army.

Having in 1904 published a brief memoir in which he recounted his exploits during the Civil War, Huse died the following year at Highland Falls. "Without a doubt," wrote historian Richard Lester, Huse "was a key man in the Confederate military campaigns, and without him the South would have been beaten to her knees much sooner."

• Huse, who appears not to have left any personal papers to posterity, has escaped the attentions of biographers. An article, "Caleb Huse," by Peggy Robbins in *Civil War Times Illustrated* 17 (Aug. 1978): 30–40, is drawn mostly from the *Dictionary of American Biography* and from Huse's own pamphlet, *The Supplies for the Confederate Army* (1904), which adds little to *The War of the Rebellion: A Compilation of the Official Records of the Union and Confederate Armies* (128 vols., 1880–1901). Huse's activities in Europe are described most extensively in Samuel B. Thompson, *Confederate Purchasing Operations Abroad* (1935; repr. 1973), which may be supplemented by Richard I. Lester, *Confederate Finance and Purchasing in Great Britain* (1975), and Edward C. Anderson, *Confederate Foreign Agent: The European Diary of Maj. Edward C. Anderson*, ed. W. Stanley Hoole (1976). An obituary is in the *New York Times*, 12 Mar. 1905.

NORMAN B. FERRIS

HUSING, Ted (27 Nov. 1901–10 Aug. 1962), radio announcer, was born Edward Britt Husing in the Bronx, New York, the son of Henry Frederick Husing and Bertha Hecht. His father worked as a club steward and the family relocated several times during Husing's childhood, depending upon the father's job. As a teenager, he was quite active in sports but was kicked out of two high schools for poor grades. He had an equally difficult time finding steady work as an adult. He worked brief stints as an actor, a policeman, and a pilot, and as a real estate agent during the Florida land boom.

In 1924 Husing was working as a furniture salesman in New York City with the intention of marrying his girlfriend, Helen Gelderman. She insisted, however, on waiting until he had a better job. He spotted an ad in a newspaper for a radio announcer and sent in his résumé, adding a degree from Harvard. After competing against hundreds of other applicants, he was hired as an announcer for station WJZ. By that time he had married Helen, with whom he had one child. A lifelong sports fan, Husing was anxious to broadcast sporting events, but those duties belonged to another WJZ announcer, pioneering sportscaster J. Andrew White. Husing's big break came on Thanksgiving 1925. WJZ was broadcasting the Penn-Cornell football game, but White arrived at the stadium barely in time for the kickoff. A quick-thinking Husing took over the microphone in the interim and impressed WJZ so much that in 1926 he began covering sporting events on a regular basis.

In 1927 Husing was hired as one of the first employees of the fledgling CBS radio network. In *Ten Years before the Mike*, Husing wrote that "1929 was the year everything broke for Ted Husing." He broadcast two of the biggest sporting events of the year, the World Series and the Kentucky Derby. Relying on his extensive knowledge of sports, Husing won accolades for covering every type of sporting event, from tennis to boxing. Although he was primarily known for his sports broadcasting, Husing also covered many news events, including political conventions and presidential elections. He also served as announcer on a variety of radio programs, including those of Ethel Merman,

Eddie Cantor, and Burns and Allen. On 21 July 1931 Husing was master of ceremonies on a variety show that launched CBS's earliest venture into television on the experimental station W2XAB.

Husing's years as a broadcaster garnered him a modest amount of fame, but he received the greatest attention from the press following a 1931 broadcast of a Harvard-Dartmouth football game. After two ineffectual plays by the Harvard offense, Husing used the adjective "putrid" to describe the performance of the Harvard quarterback. This choice of words so enraged the Harvard supporters and administration that Husing was banned from broadcasting any Harvard football game for a year.

Husing's demanding broadcasting duties left little time for a family life, and in 1934 his marriage ended in divorce. In 1936 he was married for less than a year to actress Frances Sizen, known professionally as Ann St. George. He continued to cover sporting events for CBS and married Iris Lemerise in 1944; they had one child.

In 1946 he was hired by station WHN as a disc jockey, hosting "Ted Husing's Bandstand." Although in his autobiography he had disparaging words for announcers who played records, Husing's opinion was changed by the enormous salary. WHN offered him $250,000 a year to spin records, an amount that attracted national press attention. Husing's love of sports was too strong for him to completely give up sportscasting, and he moonlighted at station WCAP, broadcasting boxing matches and football games. In 1950 and 1951 Husing worked for CBS, broadcasting weekly boxing matches on television.

In 1954 a nonmalignant tumor was removed from Husing's brain. This operation destroyed most of his sight and left him virtually blind. He ended his broadcasting career and moved alone to Pasadena, California, to live with his mother. He received financial support from a group known as the Skeeters. Founded in 1950 by Husing, this group was composed of executives from the sports, restaurant, and theatrical fields. In 1958 he was hired on a $150-a-week trial basis by the CBS radio affiliate in Los Angeles, California. Although his vocal ability was fine, he was unable to read any scripts and was not hired permanently. That same year his third wife divorced him.

He published his second autobiography in 1959, *My Eyes Are in My Heart*, a book filled with regrets. In this book he wrote, "I raced through life with my foot pressed firmly against an imaginary accelerator that propelled me too fast and swept aside too many who innocently strayed into my egocentric path" (p. 7). This second autobiography tempers some of the claims made in his first autobiography. Where he had originally written about running away as a teenager, he subsequently described the experience as hitchhiking to an aunt's house in Missouri. He explained his brief second marriage as a mistake made while under the influence of alcohol.

Husing died in a Pasadena convalescent home. Although he did not achieve long-standing fame, he was one of the best-known radio announcers during the 1930s and 1940s.

• The best sources of information about Husing's life are his two autobiographies. In 1958 *Look* magazine ran a three-part series about Husing. The three articles, dated 7 and 21 Jan. and 4 Feb., are excellent sources of information and contain interviews with many of Husing's co-workers and fellow broadcasters. An obituary is in the *New York Times*, 11 Aug. 1962.

NOAH ARCENEAUX

HUSSEY, Curtis Grubb (11 Aug. 1802–25 Apr. 1893), copper and steel manufacturer, was born near York, Pennsylvania, the son of Christopher Hussey and Lydia Grubb, farmers of Quaker ancestry. Shortly after his birth, the family moved to Little Miami, Ohio. Hussey spent his early years on the family farm, attending school sporadically. In 1813 the family moved again, this time to a farm near Mount Pleasant, Ohio.

In 1820 Hussey began to study medicine in the office of a Mount Pleasant physician. In 1825 he moved to Morgan County, Indiana, to begin practice. A successful physician, Hussey within four years had accumulated sufficient capital to purchase a local general store. Over the next few years he bought interests in several other general stores in the region, exercising general supervision during his medical travels. In 1829 Hussey was elected to the Indiana House of Representatives; he declined reelection after serving only one term owing to the rapid growth of his businesses.

Because specie was scarce, Hussey frequently accepted in-kind payments, especially pigs, for medical services and in his general stores. Since there was little market for pigs locally, Hussey established a pork packing plant at Gosport, Indiana, and began shipping pork, first downriver to New Orleans and later upriver via Pittsburgh to the eastern states. Around 1835 Hussey abandoned his medical practice to devote all his energies to his mercantile ventures. In 1839 he married Rebecca Updegraff, a highly principled and intelligent woman from a prominent Mount Pleasant family. She served Hussey as confidante and adviser. The couple had five children.

Around 1840, the year following his marriage, Hussey moved to Pittsburgh to supervise his pork business more closely, for Pittsburgh was the main link in his pork shipments to the East. The business continued to prosper, but in the 1840s Hussey shifted his focus to a radically different field, copper.

In 1843 John Hays of Cleveland, a druggist and hunting and fishing companion, sought Hussey's financial assistance for a trip to Lake Superior to visit the area where large deposits of copper had been reported. Hussey agreed to pay half Hays's expenses and furnish funds for potential copper investments. Hays bought one-sixth interest in three claims for Hussey that year.

In the winter of 1843–1844, Hussey persuaded other Pittsburgh entrepreneurs to join him. This group, with additional capital from Boston investors, formed the Pittsburgh and Boston Mining Company and purchased the claims entirely. The company's first pits, sunk near Copper Harbor, Michigan, in 1844, were disappointing. In 1845 the company abandoned the site and moved operations a few miles southwest, near Eagle Harbor. In 1846 the new mine, called the Cliff, began producing large quantities of copper. In 1848 the Cliff paid its first dividend and became the first commercially successful Lake Superior copper mine. It stimulated the growth of one of America's most profitable and longest lived mining districts. Hussey was active in the early operations of the Cliff and served as president of the controlling company from 1858 to its disbandment in 1879.

Ironically, the huge masses of copper produced by the Cliff caused problems, which led Hussey to create one of America's first vertically integrated industrial empires, a forerunner of John D. Rockefeller's oil refining empire and Andrew Carnegie's iron and steel empire. Initially, eastern smelters could not easily handle the Cliff's large copper boulders, which had to be laboriously cut into small chunks for processing. High smelting charges ate up mining profits. Frustrated, Hussey sent Hays to England to inspect copper smelters, while simultaneously initiating experiments himself. Hussey eventually designed a reverberatory furnace with a movable top. The new furnace was more heat efficient than its predecessors, and its movable top allowed large copper masses to be lifted by crane and lowered into the furnace.

In 1849, with backing from his partners in the Cliff, Hussey formed C. G. Hussey & Co. to build and operate a smelting facility in Pittsburgh. He then added a rolling mill to fabricate sheet copper and brass, the first such facilities west of the Alleghenies. Finally, he erected a warehouse to market the finished products, displacing the New York commission house that had marketed all American copper products for years. By 1850 Hussey had control over all aspects of copper production from mining to consumer sales. Hussey was the leading figure in the American copper industry in the 1850s and early 1860s, and his firms remained profitable through the remainder of the century. In relative terms his position declined, however, in the late 1860s as the Cliff's output diminished and as other interests erected smelters in the Lake Superior copper district and in Detroit.

In the late 1850s, with his copper empire prospering, Hussey turned to "fine" (crucible) steel production. For decades Britain's Sheffield area had dominated the American market in high quality steels required for cutlery and for tools used to cut metals. Sheffield produced fine steels in two steps. First, steelmasters heated thin strips of wrought iron sandwiched in a mixture of powdered animal bone and charcoal for several weeks to produce "blister" steel. They then placed the blister steel, a material of uneven quality, in special clay crucibles and melted it, allowing impurities to be skimmed off and ensuring even quality. Between 1830 and 1860 American ironmasters, often with help from immigrant English artisans, made numerous attempts to duplicate British crucible steel and market it successfully. But they failed due to prejudice against American steels, irregularities in production quality, and British competition.

Around 1858 Hussey began to investigate crucible steel. A strong supporter of the new Republican party, he believed that if it came to power its strong protectionist policies could be directed against English tool steel imports and leave room for a major domestic producer. Hussey intended to be that producer. He dispatched an associate, Calvin Wells, to the eastern seaboard to learn about the crucible process and began experimentation. In 1859 Hussey organized Hussey, Wells & Co. and purchased the Pittsburgh plant of McKelvy & Blair, which had abandoned crucible steel production five years earlier. In 1860, after spending several hundred thousand dollars on experiments, Wells produced crucible steel using a new "direct" process that omitted the traditional blister steel stage. Despite continuing suspicion of American-produced fine steels and the direct process, Hussey's new enterprise succeeded, making Hussey, Wells & Co. the first firm in the United States to engage successfully in the manufacture of fine steels.

Hussey initiated no major new industrial ventures after crucible steel, although he remained active in his firms. In 1862 he was offered American rights to the Bessemer process but declined. Hussey's poor health and the high risk involved were the deciding factors, but the capital needed may have been another. Hussey's financial resources were somewhat limited because he never borrowed money, a practice unusual for the era, keeping large cash reserves in his concerns to avoid becoming dependent on outside interests.

By the 1860s Hussey had accumulated a large fortune and began to devote more time to philanthropy. In 1860 he purchased land near Pittsburgh for the Allegheny Observatory, which he largely equipped. Hussey was particularly interested in education for women. He was a founder of Pittsburgh's School of Design for Women. He contributed thousands to Wesleyan College for Women in Cincinnati and to the Hussey School for Girls in Matamoros, Mexico. In addition he gave to schools in Tennessee, North Carolina, and the Indian Territory, to Earlham College in Indiana, and to Western University (now the University of Pittsburgh), where he served as a trustee from 1864 until his death in Pittsburgh.

Despite his industrial prominence and widespread (but unostentatious) philanthropy, Hussey did not have an active social life. He was quiet, retiring, and modest, much preferring the company of his family to high society.

• It is likely that the major floods of 1907 and 1936, which swept through the factories of Hussey-founded firms in Pittsburgh, destroyed Hussey records. Few primary source materials exist. The most extended reviews of Hussey's life are "Curtis G. Hussey," *Magazine of Western History* 3 (Feb. 1886): 329–48; *History of Allegheny County, Pennsylvania*, vol. 2 (1889), pp. 254–58; and Bruce E. Seely, "Dr. Curtis Grubb Hussey," in *The Iron and Steel Industry in the Nine-*

teenth Century, ed. Paul F. Pascoff, *Encyclopedia of American Business History and Biography* (1989), pp. 181–85. Other accounts are in Erasmus Wilson, ed., *Standard History of Pittsburgh* (1898), pp. 1001–3; and John W. Jordan, *Encyclopedia of Pennsylvania Biography*, vol. 6 (1916), pp. 2215–19. Hussey's early involvement in copper mining and smelting is best described in Donald Chaput, *The Cliff: America's First Great Copper Mine* (1971). The context for Hussey's work in the smelting of copper is provided by James B. Cooper, "Historical Sketch of Smelting and Refining Lake Copper," Lake Superior Mining Institute, *Proceedings* 7 (1901): 44–49. Hussey's involvement in crucible steel is reviewed in Harrison Gilmer, "Birth of the American Crucible Steel Industry," *Western Pennsylvania Historical Magazine* 36 (Mar. 1953): 17–36. For a broader picture of the crucible steel industry as a context for Hussey's work see Geoffrey Tweedale, *Sheffield Steel and America: A Century of Commercial and Technological Interdependence, 1830–1930* (1987). An obituary is in the *Pittsburgh Dispatch*, 26 Apr. 1893.

TERRY S. REYNOLDS

HUSSEY, William Joseph (10 Aug. 1862–28 Oct. 1926), astronomer, was born in Mendon, Ohio, the son of John Milton Hussey and Mary Catherine Stevens. He worked his way through the University of Michigan, graduating with a B.S. in civil engineering in 1889. His first interest was in astronomy, and he was able to pursue it briefly at the U.S. Nautical Almanac Office and then at the University of Michigan, where he taught mathematics and astronomy for three years. During this period he also served as acting director of the Detroit observatory of the University of Michigan (1891–1892).

In 1892 he received an appointment as assistant professor of astronomy at Stanford University and was promoted to professor the following year. He married Ethel Fountain in 1895, and they had two children before her death in 1915. From his appointment at Stanford he worked as a volunteer at the newly opened Lick Observatory on nearby Mount Hamilton, and in 1896 he was appointed astronomer on the staff of Lick Observatory. While on the staff at Lick he investigated possible observatory sites in Southern California, Arizona, and Australia for the Carnegie Institution, recommending both Mount Wilson and Mount Palomar. His report contributed to the selection of Mount Wilson in Pasadena, California, and the construction of the solar observatory there. He served with Lick Observatory until 1905, when he led an expedition for that institution to Egypt.

In 1905 he accepted an appointment as professor of astronomy and director of the Detroit observatory at the University of Michigan. He continued his affiliation with the University of Michigan for the rest of his life.

Hussey's major contribution was in the discovery and measurement of double stars; he was credited eventually with the discovery of about 1,700 such doubles. He was also noteworthy for his ability to organize the management of astronomical observatories. He made some of the discoveries of double stars during his stay at the Lick Observatory, using the 36-inch and twelve-inch refractor telescopes. He published some of his first discoveries in the Lick Observatory papers as early as 1901. He also worked with planetary astronomy, publishing observations on the satellites of Saturn in 1905. He added to his discovery of double stars later at the University of La Plata in Argentina in 1912. He was a strong advocate of the expansion of observation in the Southern Hemisphere with up-to-date equipment, which could have the effect of nearly doubling the universe known to the professional astronomical community. He did some of his most important work in Argentina and in planning expansion of observation in South Africa.

While he was at Michigan, Hussey served as professor of astronomy at the University of La Plata and as director of the Argentine National Observatory there from 1911 to 1917. He published reports of his work in Argentina in *Science*, describing both his discoveries of double stars and his reorganization of the work of the Argentine facility. In 1912 he led an expedition from La Plata to Brazil to observe an eclipse of the sun. In 1917 he married Mary McNeal Reed.

At Michigan Hussey reorganized the Detroit observatory on an efficient basis and secured a new 37.5-inch reflector telescope with a spectrograph for astrophysical work. He also continued to organize observation expeditions. One such trip, in cooperation with Hobart College, to Geneva, New York, was planned in January 1925, involving a balloon ascent to observe a solar eclipse. A violent wind and snow storm destroyed the balloon and prevented any observation of the eclipse.

His discovery of double stars earned Hussey international recognition. The French Academy awarded him the Lalande Prize in 1906. He was a foreign associate of the Royal Astronomical Society of London, a member of the Astronomical Society of Mexico, and a member of the American Astronomical Society, the American Mathematical Society, and the Astronomical Society of the Pacific. He published several books and numerous short reports and articles, several in the reports of the Lick Observatory and in the publications of the observatory at the University of Michigan.

After a decade of planning and organization, Hussey received financial support from R. P. Lamont to establish in 1926 a new observatory in Bloomfontein, South Africa, as a station of the University of Michigan. Among the equipment was a 27-inch refractor telescope, primarily intended for new double-star observations. On the way to install the new observatory, Hussey stopped in London to address the Astronomical Club of London on 29 October 1926. He died suddenly that evening after delivering the talk. His untimely death shocked his colleagues and the astronomical community.

• A collection of Hussey's papers is at the Bentley Historical Library, University of Michigan. Hussey's publications include a double star catalog compiled from data published over the period from 1900 through 1915, on deposit at the University of Michigan library. He also published *Micromet-*

rical Observations of the Double Stars Discovered at Pulkowa (1901), *Report of the Committee on Southern and Solar Observatory Sites* (1903), *Logarithmic and other Mathematical Tables* (1891; 5th ed., 1907), and several publications in *Lick Observatory Bulletin* (1901–1907) and in *Publications of the Astronomical Observatory of the University of Michigan* (1912–1915). Obituaries are in *Popular Astronomy* 34 (1926) and *Monthly Notices of the Royal Astronomical Society* 87 (1927).

RODNEY P. CARLISLE

HUSTED, Marjorie Child (1892?–23 Dec. 1986), public relations consultant, was born in Minneapolis, Minnesota, the daughter of Sampson Reed Child, a lawyer, and Alice Alberta Webber. Her first experience as a businesswoman was at the state fair, where she sold incubators, an exhibit her father acquired from a client in lieu of cash. A fortune-teller told her that she would make money by her own efforts, but she thought the idea crazy since no women she knew did such a thing.

According to her West High School yearbook, Child possessed "a tender heart; a will inflexible." She was a Latin scholar, a member of Kappa Alpha Theta honor society, and active in dramatics. At the University of Minnesota she earned a bachelor of arts in German and a bachelor of education in home economics. She participated in athletics and remained fit throughout her life playing tennis and hiking. After graduating in 1914 Child worked with the Infant Welfare Society of Minneapolis and then joined the Red Cross when the United States entered World War I, directing the publicity bureau of the home service department. After the war she joined the staff of the Women's Cooperative Alliance, an organization working with parents' groups to prevent juvenile delinquency.

In 1923 Child was hired by the Creamette Company in Minneapolis to do promotional advertising; the next year she went into field service for Washburn-Crosby, predecessor to General Mills, a demanding job that took her to cooking schools and clubs in prairie towns and southern outposts in six states. She often lectured to standing-room-only crowds of women desperate to learn the rudiments of bread baking and other homemaking skills. In the meantime, General Mills was receiving growing numbers of cooking and baking inquiries by mail. Two other home economists, Janette Kelley and Agnes White, were assigned to test recipes and compose responses, but the correspondence was signed by male executives until Harry Bullis, company president, decided on the "personification" of the endeavor. Betty Crocker, imaginary homemaking expert, was conceived. As Betty, Blanche Ingersoll chatted on Twin Cities radio.

But it was not until the dynamic and articulate Marjorie Child introduced "Betty Crocker's Cooking School of the Air," the first women's service program to go national, that Betty had a soul. Child did not chat. She expanded the format to include cooking hints, music, information on new products, recipes, and menus—always pretested—and the dramatization of listeners' letters. An early theme was "Interviews

with Eligible Bachelors" who discussed their expectations in prospective brides. Presumably, it was at WCCO's studio in the Nicollet Hotel that Marjorie Child met broadcaster K. Wallace Husted, whom she liked to describe as a Clark Gable lookalike. The couple married in 1925; they had no children.

In the 1930s Marjorie Husted as Betty Crocker made public appearances, lectured, and traveled to Hollywood to interview movie stars such as Jean Harlow, Helen Hayes, Robert Young, Delores Del Rio, and Gable. She encouraged them to talk about their home life, and when idols such as Margaret Sullavan and Jean Harlow admitted they were "bread-eating" women who still maintained model's figures, executives at General Mills were ecstatic. Neysa McMein, an outstanding New York illustrator, was commissioned to do a portrait of Betty Crocker, which was subsequently reproduced in countless advertisements. The concept was to blend the features of several of the home service department women, but the blue-eyed, brown-haired image most resembled Husted herself. That portrait served for twenty years until McMein's bohemian lifestyle was revealed.

During World War II Husted used her radio program to advise on the use of rationed foods. In the "Design for Happiness" segment, women discussed for the first time on public airwaves the intense feelings they harbored about being alone, overworked, and unrecognized. At that time Husted herself was alone, as her husband was serving with the Red Cross in Europe.

Fortune magazine in 1945 described Husted's home service department at General Mills as a "blend of woman's club, tearoom, cooking school, and business office," a flattering but ominous critique, as it made obvious that the aims of Betty Crocker's masters and those of her human personification were bound to clash. While General Mills gloated about Crocker's numerous marriage proposals, Husted was confiding in speeches that the letters from women seeking advice often made her cry. The company wanted Betty Crocker to symbolize a friendly, dignified gentlewoman with a rather dull (and never mentioned) private life. Husted was anything but dull, exemplifying instead a warm, sophisticated intellectual who was delightfully combining marriage and career. Husted rose in General Mills only because none of her achievements was publicized under her own name. But that was soon to change.

In 1948 Husted's job description was expanded to that of consultant in advertising and public relations, equivalent to—but without the pay and prestige of—a vice presidency. She broke tradition when she moved her secretary along with her into the executive offices. Opening the annual newspaper food editors' conference at the Waldorf-Astoria in New York in 1948, Husted declared good housekeeping an art. During that same year she served as consultant to the U.S. Department of Agriculture on food conservation, and in October she wrote an article for the *Journal of Home Economics* titled "Would You Like More Recognition?" which outlined the bold plan to empower women in public relations adopted by the American Home Economics Association at their national convention.

Husted's glimpse of stardom began on 14 May 1949 when she received an award from the Women's National Press Club in Washington, D.C. It was the first award ever given to a businesswoman. Husted, Eleanor Roosevelt, Anna Mary "Grandma" Moses, and three other achievers accepted their plaques from guest of honor President Harry S. Truman. In June Husted claimed the Advertising Woman of the Year Award from the Advertising Federation of America, the first home economist to do so. Also during 1949 she was elected president of the Women's Advertising Club of Minneapolis and chair of the local Home Economists in Business. These prizes garnered considerable publicity. The Twin Cities celebrated Marjorie Child Husted Day; only Eleanor Roosevelt was more popular than Betty Crocker in the United States.

Meanwhile, Husted's supervisory work on *Betty Crocker's Picture Cookbook* (1950), begun in 1947, continued unabated. Her staff by then numbered about forty nutritionists, home economists, and technicians. The final product was a stylish compilation of no-fail recipes and inspiring cooking tips expressed in perfect layout, with irresistible color photographs. It was an immediate bestseller.

Husted retired from General Mills at the height of her career in 1950, to form her own consulting firm. There is no record of the circumstances surrounding her decision; but at that time her audiences were mixed, and she was challenging men with a "bias quiz" to reveal their "traditionalist" views. Soon after, General Mills initiated a campaign to obscure Husted as nucleus of the Betty Crocker legend with the connection of at least ten women's names as equally sharing the credit; attempts at reassigning Betty's personification failed. In November 1978 Husted gave a remarkably candid interview to reporter Carol Pine of *Twin Cities* magazine, recording for posterity evidence of the bias that contained her ambition. Calling herself a feminist, she told the story of how General Mills, when threatened by a lawsuit from a competitor, asked her to come forward to prove that Betty Crocker was a genuine person.

From 1950 to 1956 Husted was a member of the National Committee on the Status of Women. During the final three decades of her life she was active in the American Association of University Women, the National Committee on the Status of Women, the Minneapolis Historical Society, the Symphony Orchestra, and the Young Women's Christian Association.

Husted died in Minneapolis. She was as proficient in the boardroom as in the family room, and her own achievements were as groundbreaking for women in the workplace as were Betty Crocker's mythological deeds for women in the kitchen.

• No Husted papers have been located. Birth date research has been inconclusive. Newspaper articles and yearbooks are held at the Minneapolis Public Library. Publicity releases, public service bulletins, and articles in *Modern Mill Wheel* (1921–1950) about Husted were not easily obtained from General Mills; Mary Anna DuSablon, *America's Collectible Cookbooks: The History, the Politics, the Recipes* (1993), pp. 109–15, is an important record of this material. The entry in *Current Biography Yearbook 1949* was probably written by Husted and differs from subsequent General Mills–influenced material, including obituaries. Articles about Betty Crocker are listed under General Mills in the *Periodical Index*. Editions of the *Betty Crocker Cookbook* after 1959 do not reflect Husted's contribution. An obituary is in the *New York Times*, 28 Dec. 1986.

MARY ANNA DUSABLON

HUSTON, John (5 Aug. 1906–28 Aug. 1987), film director and screenwriter, was born in Nevada, Missouri, the son of Walter Huston, an actor, and Rhea Gore, a journalist. When Huston was three years old, his parents separated, divorcing three years later, and he was raised by his mother. He did not finish high school, although he later studied at the Art Students League in Los Angeles. In 1924 he went to live with his father, who was about to star in the first New York production of Eugene O'Neill's *Desire Under the Elms*. Attending the play's rehearsals and watching his father perform on stage turned Huston toward the idea of writing and acting. He briefly acted in New York during 1925, then turned to writing; he published his first short stories in 1929 in the *American Mercury*.

In 1931 Walter Huston was able to get his son a job writing dialogue at Universal Pictures, but seven years passed before Huston's major screenwriting credits began with the Warner Bros. production *Jezebel* (1938). Under contract to Warner Bros., he wrote *The Amazing Dr. Clitterhouse* (1938) and was one of several writers on the prestige biography *Juarez* (1939), although he was unhappy with changes that the film's star, Paul Muni, demanded. Two screenplays that Huston contributed to, *Dr. Ehrlich's Magic Bullet* (1940) and *Sergeant York* (1941), were nominated for Academy Awards in the original screenplay category. Huston's 1941 *High Sierra* is the most Hustonian of his writing-only credits, a tough adventure picture about an ex-convict who tries to organize one last heist but is killed because of his involvement with two women, one innocent and one not-so-innocent. Many of Huston's films have a misogynist element in them. His men are never saints, but his women in one form or another are nearly always trouble for the men.

In 1941 Huston persuaded Warner Bros. to let him direct for the first time. The studio had made two previous films of Dashiell Hammett's 1930 novel *The Maltese Falcon* in 1931 and 1936, but Huston's script was more faithful to the novel. The script kept Hammett's tough view of its characters and their behavior, and the dialogue that Huston had his perfect cast play quickly and sharply retained the feel of the original. Both camera placement (usually shooting at a medium distance from the actors) and movement were at the service of the story and the characters, a style typical of all of Huston's directorial work.

During World War II Huston made three documentaries for the U.S. Army. The first was a conventional propaganda film, but *The Battle of San Pietro* (1945) showed the horrors of combat so effectively that the army held up its release for a year. *Let There Be Light* (1946) showed treatments that army doctors had developed to cure soldiers of battlefield neurosis, or combat fatigue. While Huston felt the film was "the most hopeful and optimistic and even joyous thing I ever had a hand in," the army declined to release the film on grounds that it violated the soldiers' privacy, although film historians think the army was more upset at how vividly the film showed the psychological damages caused by war. The film was not made available for public showing until 1981.

When Huston returned to Warner Bros. after World War II he wrote and directed an adaptation of B. Traven's novel *The Treasure of the Sierra Madre* (1948). Huston dropped most of Traven's leftist political observations and focused on the story of three typical Huston characters, outsiders (here down-and-out Americans in Mexico in the twenties) who quest for riches (in this case gold). As is also typical of Huston's characters, they end up losing: bandits kill one prospector and scatter the gold dust to the wind, thinking it nothing but sand. Much of the film was made on location, although there are distracting studio sets in some scenes. Often Huston's camera sits at a middle distance and watches the characters "stew in their own juices," as he described it. While not a financial success, the film was a considerable artistic success and Huston won Academy Awards for both writing and directing, and his father, playing the older prospector, won an Oscar for best supporting actor.

In 1950 Huston moved to MGM where he cowrote with Ben Maddow and directed a striking adaptation of the W. R. Burnett novel *The Asphalt Jungle*. Again a collection of outsiders (professional crooks) go for a big score, in this case an ultimately unsuccessful robbery of a large jewelry store. Although the film was the first—of many that followed—to show in almost educational detail the planning and execution of a heist, Huston was as interested in the characters and their behavior. The respectable lawyer who finances the operation calls crime "only a left-handed form of human endeavor," a description that might serve for the acts of many of Huston's characters.

Huston next wrote and directed an adaptation of Stephen Crane's classic novel *The Red Badge of Courage* (1951). Huston's version of the film was cut by twenty minutes by MGM after disastrous sneak previews at which audiences laughed at what were intended to be serious scenes. Journalist Lillian Ross followed the production of the film and wrote a book about it called *Picture* (1952), which was serialized in four issues of the *New Yorker*. Along with an article by James Agee in *Life* in 1950, Ross's book established Huston as a colorful character who constantly fought against the studio establishments and who, like the people in his films, frequently lost. As Huston's films of the fifties and sixties were perceived as inferior to his previous work, Huston was seen by film critics such as Andrew Sarris as using his fights with the studios as excuses for his flawed films.

Agee and Huston collaborated on the 1951 adaptation of C. S. Forester's 1935 novel *The African Queen*. Although the script is credited solely to Agee, Huston worked on it, as he did on other films he directed, receiving writing credit for only some of them. The novel and the screenplay, about a trip down an African river by a woman missionary and a drunken riverboat captain, were originally intended seriously, but Huston discovered that when Katharine Hepburn and Humphrey Bogart acted together, they were funny. He encouraged them, and the comedy element was added, not in changed lines, but in the way the lines were read. As both writer and director, Huston was less concerned with the meaning of the moment than in making it come alive. He tended not to discuss the roles in depth with actors, but to give them simple, vivid ideas as a guide. The best-known example of this is Huston's instruction to Hepburn to play Rosie (in *The African Queen*) as if she were Eleanor Roosevelt, smiling awkwardly while visiting wounded soldiers.

Huston's 1952 *Moulin Rouge* told the story of the French painter Toulouse-Lautrec, and Huston and cinematographer Oswald Morris worked out a more subdued color palette for the film than had previously been seen in Technicolor films. Morris and Huston again experimented with color desaturation in *Moby Dick* (1956), and Huston also played with color in *Reflections in a Golden Eye* (1967). The two earlier films in particular led other filmmakers to experiment with less garish color.

Huston's 1954 film *Beat the Devil*, cowritten with Truman Capote, was seen by many as a parody of earlier Huston films such as the *The Maltese Falcon*, since it did not take its international thriller plot seriously. The film has since gained a reputation as a cult film, but it was not a commercial success at the time. Huston's films of the later fifties, *The Barbarian and the Geisha* and *The Roots of Heaven* (both 1958), were projects misconceived from the start, although a variation on *The African Queen* called *Heaven Knows, Mr. Allison* (1957) was successful enough to be nominated for an Academy Award for the screenplay by Huston and John Lee Mahin.

The Misfits (1961) was directed by Huston from a script by playwright Arthur Miller about a group of modern-day cowboys who capture wild mustangs. Miller's dialogue is overly literary for the characters, but Huston's direction effectively captures the vast spaces of the West the characters live in, particularly during the horse roundups. Huston's 1962 film *Freud* was something of a return to the prestige biography films of his Warner Bros. days. However, the film's treatment of Freud's work was limited by the censorship of the time.

In 1963 Huston began to act in films as well as direct. For director Otto Preminger he played a wily cardinal in the 1963 film *The Cardinal*, for which he received an Academy Award nomination. Huston appeared in many other pictures, his best performance being as the corrupt Noah Cross in *Chinatown* (1974).

Huston also appeared in his own films. In 1966 for producer Dino De Laurentiis he directed, narrated, read the voice of God, and played Noah in *The Bible*, a film based on the first twenty-two chapters of the Book of Genesis. The film is something of a narrative hodgepodge, but there are scenes of visual interest (the Noah's Ark sequence) and power (the story of Abraham and Isaac).

In 1972 Huston directed *Fat City* from Leonard Gardner's adaptation of his novel. The film lacks the narrative drive of earlier Huston films, but Huston uses the more flexible shooting abilities of the newer cameras and faster film to capture effectively the seedy atmosphere of small-town, semi-professional boxing.

In 1975 Huston returned to a project he had been thinking about for more than twenty years, an adaptation of Rudyard Kipling's adventure story *The Man Who Would Be King*. Sean Connery and Michael Caine played the disreputable ex-soldiers who go to an exotic land with the intent of stealing its riches. As with many of Huston's quests, this one goes wrong. The film's reviews were the best that Huston had received in many years.

After several minor films and two flawed but not uninteresting adaptations, *Wise Blood* (1979) and *Under the Volcano* (1984), Huston's final two films were two of his best. In 1985 he directed Richard Condon and Janet Roach's adaptation of Condon's dark comic novel *Prizzi's Honor*, about a Mafia hitman who falls in love with a freelance hitwoman who also has stolen money from the Prizzi family. Huston's daughter Anjelica received an Academy Award as best supporting actress for her role as the woman who, spurned by the hitman, in turn gets her revenge.

Anjelica gave another excellent performance in Huston's last film, *The Dead* (1987), an adaptation of the James Joyce story. The tone of the film is quiet, elegant, and supremely touching. The technique, especially the simplicity of Huston's directing, was as usual at the service of characters and story.

Huston married five times, divorced four times, and was widowed: Dorothy Jeane Harvey, 1926–1933; Lesley Black, 1937–1944; film actress Evelyn Keyes, 1946–1950, with whom he adopted a son; Erica "Ricki" Soma, 1950–1969 (killed in a car accident), with whom he had two children, Tony (a screenwriter) and Anjelica; Celeste "Cici" Shane, 1972–1977. He also had a son, Danny (a film director), from his liaison with Zoë Salis. Huston died in Newport, Rhode Island.

Huston's reputation varied greatly during his lifetime. His directorial debut in 1941 brought him attention, and his films of the late forties and early fifties led to his perhaps being overpraised. The criticism of his films of the late fifties and early sixties tended to undervalue his skills. Many critics and historians prefer directors with more flamboyant styles, but Huston's best work provides a balance between substance and style that few directors can match.

• Huston's papers, including his correspondence, scripts, and other writings, are in the Margaret Herrick Library of the Academy of Motion Pictures Arts and Sciences, Los Angeles. Lawrence Grobel, *The Hustons* (1989), is the most detailed biography of Huston, with as much about his flamboyant personal life as about his filmmaking. Huston's memoirs, *An Open Book* (1980), is not as open as the title would indicate, but it gives a good firsthand account of his life and work. Stuart Kaminsky, *John Huston: Maker of Magic* (1978), is particularly good on the changes from book to screen in the material that Huston adapted and his style as a director. Richard T. Jameson, "John Huston," *Film Comment*, May–June 1980, pp. 25–56, is an example of the reevaluation Huston received from film historians late in his career.

TOM STEMPEL

HUSTON, Walter (6 Apr. 1884–7 Apr. 1950), actor, was born Walter Houghston in Toronto, Canada, the son of Robert Moore Houghston, a cabinetmaker, and Elizabeth McGibbon. He changed the spelling of his name as a young man to simplify its pronunciation. Walter was the youngest of four children, all of whom were of school age when their father died. Walter's older brother Alec supported the family, enabling the other children to continue their schooling. Huston attended public school until age seventeen, when he took a job in a hardware store. He continued his education by taking drama classes at the Toronto College of Music, performing on stage for the first time at age eighteen. After accompanying a drama company on their tour through New York State, Huston settled in New York City. In 1905 he appeared in his first New York production in a minor part in *In Convict Stripes*; shortly thereafter he appeared in Richard Mansfield's production of *Julius Caesar*, in which he played a spear carrier. However, Huston was quickly fired from this part after forgetting his short speech. In 1905 he married Rhea Gore, a newspaperwoman; they had one child, John Marcellus Huston, who later won renown as a film director.

After getting married, Huston gave up acting for an engineering career. He moved to the small town of Nevada, Missouri, where he worked in a small local power plant. He did not remain in Nevada long, however: he was fired from his job for turning off the water supply during a fire, causing massive damage. Moving to Weatherford, Texas, and then to St. Louis, Missouri, Huston continued to work as an engineer, although he grew more and more dissatisfied with this career. In 1909 he met Bayonne Whipple, a singer and performer, and went back on stage with her in a song-and-dance routine, writing some of the music himself. Huston divorced his wife in 1913 and married Whipple the following year.

In 1924 Huston played two minor roles, the first in Brock Pemberton's production of *Mr. Pitt*, a play by Zona Gale, and the second in *The Easy Mark*. His first major role was the part of Ephraim Cabot in Eugene O'Neill's *Desire under the Elms* (1924). The *New York Times* lauded his performance, saying he was "everywhere trenchant, gaunt, fervid, harsh, as he should be" (12 Nov. 1924). For this performance he won the New York Drama Critics Circle Award in 1924. He continued acting on stage until 1929, scoring consistent minor successes.

Huston's first foray into motion pictures was a role in *Gentlemen of the Press* (1929), starring Charles Ruggles. He followed that with a role in *The Lady Lies* (1929), starring Claudette Colbert, and in the first talking film version of the popular novel *The Virginian* (1924), starring Gary Cooper. These roles launched his career, which continued to grow in subsequent years. Huston acted in as many as eight films per year, with his most notable performance being the starring role in *Abraham Lincoln* (1930), directed by D. W. Griffith. After his second wife divorced him for desertion, Huston married Ninnetta Eugenia Sunderland in 1931.

Huston returned to the stage, acting in the lead role of an adaptation of Sinclair Lewis's novel *Dodsworth* (1934). Critical and popular acclaim extended the stage run to more than 1,200 performances. Between performances of *Dodsworth*, Huston starred as the lead in *Othello* in Central City, Colorado; his brother-in-law Robert Edmund Jones produced the play. Before accompanying the *Dodsworth* cast on tour, Huston played the lead in the English film *Rhodes* (1935), directed by Berthold Viertel and based on the novel by Sarah Gertrude Millin. *Dodsworth* was made into a film in 1936, with Huston in the leading role. In 1937 the production of *Othello* in which Huston starred went briefly to Broadway but quickly closed, representing a rare failure for Huston. Regarding *Othello*, the *New York Times* wrote that Huston's "listless Moor shows [that] he has no experience in the acting of a heroic tragedy." He then appeared in the role of Governor Peter Stuyvesant in *Knickerbocker Holiday* (1938), garnering his usual good reviews. Huston's rendition of "September Song," a poignant ballad about love and old age, was unusual for being spoken more than sung. The song was quickly acclaimed as a major highlight of the musical.

Although he appeared with less frequency in the late 1930s and 1940s, Huston gave a notable performance in the film *All That Money Can Buy* (1941), an adaptation of *The Devil and Daniel Webster*, by Stephen Vincent Benét and Douglas Moore. During World War II he narrated a documentary on Russia and an army orientation film. He also appeared in many of the films directed by his son John, including a small role in *The Maltese Falcon* (1941) and as an old miner in *The Treasure of Sierra Madre* (1948), for which he won the Academy Award for best supporting actor. Huston died in Beverly Hills, California. Two minutes of silence were observed in his honor in all Hollywood studios on 11 April 1950.

Huston was known for his simple, natural acting style, which, combined with his height and rugged good looks, made him the epitome of the self-reliant American frontiersman. His most successful roles, including both Dodsworth and Ephraim Cabot in *Desire under the Elms*, were all a similar type: that of the si-

lent, sad loner. This type both defined and limited him as an actor, as when his failure in *Othello* revealed his inability to deviate from his trademark character.

• Newspaper clippings and scrapbooks with biographical information pertaining to Huston can be found in the Billy Rose Theatre Collection at the New York Public Library for the Performing Arts, Lincoln Center. An article by Huston about the failure of *Othello* is "In and out of the Bag," *Stage*, Mar. 1937. See also William Nolan, *John Huston: King Rebel* (1965), a biography of Huston's son that includes information on the older Huston's life; and John Huston, *An Open Book* (1980), a memoir. See also Lawrence Grobel, *The Hustons* (1989). An obituary is in the *New York Times*, 8 Apr. 1950.

ELIZABETH ZOE VICARY

HUTCHESON, Charles Sterling (23 July 1894–24 Oct. 1969), federal judge, was born on a farm near Baskerville in Mecklenburg County, Virginia, the son of Herbert Farrar Hutcheson, a farmer, and Mary Hutcheson Young. Twelve years later, the family moved to nearby Boydton, when the elder Hutcheson became clerk of the Mecklenburg circuit court, a post he held until his death in 1934. The younger Hutcheson later liked to tell how he was "raised in a courthouse" (*Richmond Times-Dispatch*, 10 Mar. 1944), for he spent much of his youth attending trials, copying legal documents, and serving as an errand boy. After attending the College of William and Mary (1913–1914), he worked with his father as deputy clerk of court (1915–1918). Then he served during World War I as a private in the U.S. Army and in 1919 studied law at the University of Virginia.

Hutcheson was admitted to the bar in Mecklenburg County in 1919 and practiced law in Boydton with his brother John Young Hutcheson (Hutcheson and Hutcheson). He married Betsy Wiggins Ballou in 1927 but had no children. In 1933, on the recommendation of Senators Carter Glass and Harry F. Byrd, President Franklin D. Roosevelt appointed Hutcheson as U.S. attorney for the Eastern District of Virginia. He held that position until Roosevelt nominated him in 1944 to replace Luther B. Way, who had died, as a judge in United States District Court for the Eastern District of Virginia. Confirmed by the Senate, he took the oath of office before his brother Nathaniel Goode Hutcheson, who had succeeded their father as clerk of the Mecklenburg circuit court. In 1956 the Richmond Bar Association endorsed him for a position on the Fourth Circuit Court of Appeals when Judge Armistead M. Dobie retired, but Hutcheson was not offered the nomination and remained a district judge until his retirement on 1 September 1959. He died ten years later at his farm home in Boydton.

Judge Sterling Hutcheson was often in the news as a consequence of his involvement in cases regarding "separate but equal" public schools. In the late 1940s his decisions were notable for his siding with Oliver W. Hill and other black National Association for the Advancement of Colored People lawyers when they insisted that teachers' pay and curricula in segregated schools be equalized. Examples are *Kelly v. School Board of Surry County* (1948) and *Ashley v. School Board of Gloucester County* (1948). But desegregation was another matter. He was one of the three judges who ruled against plaintiffs in the 1951 school desegregation case that came out of Prince Edward County. Appealed to the U.S. Supreme Court, the Prince Edward case was joined there with cases from South Carolina, Delaware, and Kansas, and the district court decision was overturned in *Brown v. Board of Education* (1954). After *Brown*, Hutcheson continued to oppose integration. He ruled against efforts to open Prince Edward County's white schools to black students in 1958. When he declined to set a date for desegregation of the county's schools, the Fourth Circuit Court of Appeals directed him to do so. He gave local authorities until 1965 to begin desegregating the schools, but the Fourth Circuit overruled him and directed that the schools be desegregated in September 1959. In response, Prince Edward authorities closed the public schools until, under court order, they reopened them in 1964.

Judge Hutcheson chose to retire when he could. Time had passed him by. He had appeared in the 1940s to be in advance of white public opinion regarding racial discrimination, but in the 1950s higher courts overruled him when he urged delay in school desegregation. Black lawyers such as Oliver Hill remembered him as a judge who consistently supported segregation but just as insistently, within segregation, mandated equalization. The judge had not changed; the nature of the questions before him had. He was prepared to accept what he saw as the full implications of *Plessy v. Ferguson* (1896). He regarded as impractical, and was unprepared to cooperate with, what he saw as precipitous efforts to implement that decision's reversal. As the *Richmond Times-Dispatch*, ever sympathetic to the positions Judge Hutcheson took in the 1950s, phrased it in an editorial (30 July 1959) on his announced retirement, "For an honorable, upright gentleman, such as he, resignation is preferable to following mandates from higher courts which are repugnant to his deeply-cherished beliefs."

Admired for his patience, fairness, and calm judicial temperament, Hutcheson was an Episcopalian and a vestryman of St. James Episcopal Church in Boydton. He enjoyed farming, hunting, and reading, and he published *A Brief History of Boydton, Virginia* in 1962. At his death he had been for many years a member of the executive committee of the Virginia Historical Society as well as a member of the board of the Virginia State Library. He served as a member of the board of visitors of the College of William and Mary in 1928–1933 and again in the 1960s and as rector from 1962 to 1964.

• The Charles Sterling Hutcheson Papers are at the Virginia State Library and Archives, Richmond. Hutcheson's career can be tracked through the *Richmond Times-Dispatch* of 10 Mar. 1944; 10 Feb. 1956; 24, 25 Jan. 1957; 5, 6 Aug. 1958; and 29, 30 July 1959; and the *Richmond News Leader*, 3 Nov. 1953, 14 Nov. 1956, 5 Aug. 1958, and 24 Oct. 1969. His role in the Prince Edward case is developed in Bob (Robert Collins) Smith, *They Closed Their Schools: Prince Edward County, Virginia, 1951–1964* (1965). Obituaries are in the Virginia State Bar Association *Proceedings* 81 (1970), the *Richmond Times-Dispatch*, 25 Oct. 1969, and the *Richmond News Leader*, 24 Oct. 1969.

PETER WALLENSTEIN

HUTCHESON, William Levi (7 Feb. 1874–20 Oct. 1953), labor leader, was born in Saginaw, Michigan, the son of Daniel Orrick Hutcheson, a carpenter, farmer, and seasonal migrant worker, and Elizabeth Culver. William grew up in Saginaw, where he attended school until the age of thirteen, when he became a carpenter's apprentice to his father.

Hutcheson entered his trade in a period marked by labor activism and protest. He developed an early interest in trade union and labor affairs. As a young man, he saw American Federation of Labor (AFL) president Samuel Gompers speak in Detroit and witnessed a successful regional strike led by the Knights of Labor. While he trained in carpentry, Hutcheson himself earned a reputation for fighting over labor issues with another apprentice. At the age of seventeen, he left Saginaw and worked on a dairy farm in Auburn, Michigan. There he met Bessie King, who became his first wife in 1893. Bessie and William had four children, including Maurice Hutcheson, born in 1897, who would succeed his father as the president of the United Brotherhood of Carpenters and Joiners. Bessie and William divorced in 1928, and that same year Hutcheson married Jessie Tufts Sharon. When Jesse died in 1948, he married Madelaine Wilson. He had no children from either marriage.

Before Hutcheson began his long career as a union leader, he worked a number of temporary and seasonal farming jobs. Initially thwarted by the depression of the 1890s in his search for work, Hutcheson traveled across the Northwest looking for employment. He witnessed several prominent labor disputes of the 1890s, including the suppression of a miners' strike in Coeur d'Alene, Idaho, by federal troops. He followed the trials of Eugene Debs and the Pullman strike with great interest. Both events nurtured in him a strong suspicion of government intervention in labor affairs, an attitude that persisted throughout his career. In 1902 Hutcheson took work as a carpenter at the Midland Chemical Company in Midland, Michigan. He helped organize a union in 1904, but Midland summarily broke the union and fired its leaders, including Hutcheson. He returned to Saginaw, took work in carpentry, and devoted himself to reorganizing Saginaw's two carpenters' union locals. In 1906 he became the locals' business agent, launching what was to become a lifelong career in leadership of the United Brotherhood of Carpenters and Joiners. Within three months of his election as second vice president of the international in 1913, the first vice president resigned, and Hutcheson moved into the second-highest office of the Brotherhood. When the Brotherhood president died of food poisoning in 1915, Hutcheson became the president of the United Brotherhood of Carpenters and Joiners, a position he would hold for thirty-seven years.

As president of the Brotherhood, Hutcheson centralized control of the Carpenters' union. Before he took office, the Brotherhood had been a loosely organized confederation of local unions that included strong pockets of autonomous leadership as well as radical and socialist sympathy. Hutcheson quickly established tight control over local unions. Between 1915 and 1917, he won a significant battle with the nearly autonomous New York City locals by breaking a strike, removing independent leadership, and reorganizing the local unions under men who supported him. After the New York affair, the international maintained a supreme authority in all local bargaining and strike situations that went virtually unchallenged for the rest of Hutcheson's career. By the late 1920s, he had also largely silenced or expelled left-wing political influence within the Brotherhood. A conservative advocate of "business unionism" over "ideological unionism," Hutcheson spearheaded early efforts within the American labor movement to oust communists. Speaking to the 1924 Brotherhood convention, he declared, "Our membership should remember there are only two 'isms' that should enter into our organization—that is unionism and Americanism, and that all other 'isms' or advocates of that sort of thing should be kicked out and kicked out quickly" (Galenson, p. 216).

Hutcheson significantly expanded the membership and power of the Brotherhood within the industry and the labor movement. His efforts, however, focused less on organizing than on winning members through jurisdictional struggles with other unions. As president, Hutcheson involved the Brotherhood in a series of near-constant struggles within the AFL to establish the carpenters' jurisdiction over any aspect of work that could be defined as carpentry. As a decisive leader in the building trades, president of the largest union in the AFL, and member of the AFL executive board, Hutcheson frequently won interunion battles by withdrawing or threatening to withdraw the Brotherhood from the AFL. In the mid 1930s, he vigorously opposed efforts by the new leaders of the Congress of Industrial Organizations (CIO) to establish industrywide unions because their bargaining units would have included carpenters. In a key 1935 AFL convention debate on industrial unionism and jurisdiction over rubber workers, United Mine Workers president John L. Lewis punched Hutcheson in the jaw, and the two fell into fisticuffs on the convention floor.

A lifelong Republican, Hutcheson also established himself as a prominent political figure. Although he opposed the no-strike pledge during World War I, Hutcheson was appointed a member of the National War Labor Board. He enjoyed close relationships with successive Republican presidential administrations in the 1920s. During the 1930s, even as the labor movement developed increasingly strong allegiances to the Democratic party, Hutcheson remained a stalwart Republican and an opponent of Franklin Roosevelt's New Deal. In 1936 he resigned from his position as vice president of the AFL to protest the federation's ties to Roosevelt.

Hutcheson's unceasing quest to enlarge his union through jurisdictional battles eventually led to an indictment of himself and the Brotherhood under the Sherman Antitrust Act. In *United States v. Hutcheson*, the Justice Department charged the union with illegal conspiracy in connection with a jurisdictional dispute over millwright work in the Anheuser-Busch brewery in St. Louis. The Brotherhood, claiming jurisdiction over work contracted to the Machinists, called a strike and instituted a boycott. In 1941 the case against Hutcheson and the Carpenters went to the Supreme Court, which upheld a dismissal of charges by a lower court.

Like his lifetime, the final years of Hutcheson's career were marked with controversy. In 1952 Hutcheson elevated his son to the position of the first vice presidency of the Brotherhood. The move was controversial, but, as usual, Hutcheson silenced all opposition to Maurice at a subsequent convention. Typical of conservative business-minded trade unionists who dominated the AFL in the early twentieth century, and contentious to the very end, William Hutcheson closed his career on the AFL Executive Board by opposing the federation's merger with the CIO, walking out, and removing the Brotherhood from the AFL. Characteristically, his final opposition stemmed from a jurisdictional issue, as the merger had proposed a no-raiding agreement between the labor federations. Hutcheson died in Indianapolis, Indiana, just one year after his resignation from the presidency in 1952. His influence over the Carpenters persisted long after his death in the person and politics of his son Maurice, who remained president until his own retirement in 1972.

• A biography of Hutcheson is Maxwell C. Raddock's *Portrait of an American Labor Leader: William L. Hutcheson* (1955), commissioned by the Brotherhood. Although Raddock is the only biographer who had access to Hutcheson's personal papers, the book's reputation has been severely tarnished by charges of plagiarism, factual errors, and deliberate inaccuracies exposed during the McClellan Committee Senate hearings in 1958. This controversy, as well as some of the major events of Hutcheson's career, are considered at length in Walter Galenson's *The United Brotherhood of Carpenters: The First Hundred Years* (1983), which was written with access to the Brotherhood files and papers. A thorough biographical account of Hutcheson's childhood and rise to power in the Brotherhood and the AFL in the 1920s appears in Irving Bernstein's *The Lean Years: A History of the American Worker, 1920–1933* (1960). Philip Taft, *The A.F. of L. from the Death of Gompers to the Merger* (1959), provides an account of Hutcheson's activities in AFL leadership. Robert A. Christie, *Empire in Wood: A History of the Carpenters' Union* (1956), and "Boss Carpenter," *Fortune Magazine*, Apr. 1946, provide interesting contemporary accounts of his career.

MICHELLE BRATTAIN

HUTCHINS, Grace (19 Aug. 1885–15 July 1969), labor researcher and social reformer, was born in Boston, Massachusetts, the daughter of Edward Webster Hutchins, a lawyer, and Susan Barnes Hurd. Descendants of early Massachusetts colonists, her parents held an elite position in Boston society, were members of the Trinity Episcopal Church, and were actively involved in the community. Her father helped form the Boston Bar Association and founded the Legal Aid Society. Her mother participated heavily in philanthropic work.

Privately educated, Hutchins toured the world with her parents from 1898 to 1899 and returned to further her education at Bryn Mawr College, where she excelled in athletic activities. A tennis champion, captain of the varsity basketball team, and a member of the varsity field hockey team, Hutchins was also active in the suffrage cause at college. After receiving a bachelor's degree in 1907, she traveled to China in 1912 as a missionary and served first as a teacher and later as a principal of an Episcopal school for Chinese girls. While in China she kept journals on the medical, educational, and social conditions of women.

Hutchins returned to Boston in 1916 because of illness and parental pressure and taught at a social training school in New York City. Her anti-interventionist stance led her to join the Socialist party and to protest as America entered combat during World War I. Her involvement with socialism nearly brought her dismissal from teaching. Between 1920 and 1921 she studied labor problems at the New York School of Social Work and continued her studies as a graduate student at the Teachers College at Columbia University (1922–1923). She learned firsthand about women's labor conditions when she worked ten-hour days in a cigar factory while continuing her schooling.

Throughout her life Hutchins was greatly influenced in both her career and her private life by Marxist economist and historian Anna Rochester, who had attended Bryn Mawr from 1897 to 1899. The friendship lasted forty years, and as co-workers and devoted friends they shared an apartment in Greenwich Village in Manhattan from 1924 until the end of their lives. Rochester wrote many books on capitalism and was able to transform statistical and complex data so that the general public could understand it.

Both Hutchins and Rochester were supporters of nonviolence. In the early 1920s Hutchins joined the Fellowship of Reconciliation (FOR), a Christian pacifist organization, and served as business executive from 1925 to 1926 and press secretary between 1924 and 1926. She became a contributing editor to the FOR's monthly paper, the *World Tomorrow*, from 1922 to 1924, and Rochester served as editor in chief on the same paper from 1922 to 1926. The two women traveled and lectured for the FOR and wrote a book together, *Jesus Christ and the World Today*, published in 1922. Their travels took them throughout Europe, India, and the Far East, where they visited social reform leaders. They went to factories and were appalled by what they saw. They wrote articles to American publications describing the terrible conditions of the factories. In 1927 Hutchins became a correspondent for the Federated Press.

Between 1926 and 1927 the pair traveled extensively throughout the Soviet Union from Moscow to the Caucasus. The country had a profound effect on Hutchins. Wherever she went, she was impressed to see Russian people working hard despite deprivation and felt they seemed to be overcoming their problems as a result of Communist rule. These viewpoints clashed with FOR policies, and when the two women returned to the United States they left the church and joined the Communist party in 1927. In August of the same year Hutchins was arrested during a Boston demonstration in support of Nicola Sacco and Bartolomeo Vanzetti. Although her father felt disgraced by her actions, he continued to give her a substantial allowance and provided for her in his will.

Hutchins became an investigator for the New York Department of Labor's Bureau of Women in Industry in 1927, but illness forced her to resign after five months. In the same year she, Rochester, and Robert W. Dunn formed the Labor Research Association (LRA), an organization that compiled a series of books, reports, and statistics for labor unions and publications. Hutchins remained with the LRA from 1929 to 1967, writing pamphlets on labor, children, and women's issues. She coedited seventeen volumes of their biennial reference series and edited the organization's *Railroad Notes* from 1937 to 1962. An active supporter of many strikes, Hutchins was present at textile strikes in New Jersey in 1924 and in Massachusetts in 1928. These experiences led to her book on industry conditions, *Labor and Silk* (1929). Women's working conditions prompted her writing of *Women Who Work*, which appeared in three editions in 1933, 1934, and 1952. In an article for *The Worker*, Hutchins told Betty Feldman that the Marxist movement "has explained the economic basis for the exploitation of women workers as no one ever did before."

Her activism in the Communist party brought Hutchins into politics. A treasurer for the Communist National Election Campaign Committee in 1936, she ran as party candidate for alderman in 1935, controller in 1936, and lieutenant governor in 1938; she was defeated each time. In 1948 Whittaker Chambers, key witness in the trial of Alger Hiss, accused Hutchins of threatening to kill him after he withdrew from the Communist party. Hutchins denied any involvement in death threats and refuted these claims in articles and interviews.

As trustee of the Communist party–backed Bail Bond Fund of the Civil Rights Congress that supported defendants in the Smith Act, Hutchins became involved in litigation concerning the fund's liquidation between 1951 and 1956. When Communist leader Elizabeth Gurley Flynn was indicted under the act in 1951, Hutchins posted a $10,000 bail for her friend. Although the Civil Rights Congress and the American Committee for Protection of Foreign Born received pressure for their radical sympathies, Hutchins continued to support them and remained a stockholder for the Communist newspaper *Daily Worker* from 1940 until 1956.

Hutchins died in New York City. She never married. Dedicating her life to the plight of workers and toward the improvement of their conditions, she used her time and talents to fight for women laborers through her writings, her political advocacy, and her continued belief in communism as a solution to the existing system.

• Manuscript sources include the Grace Hutchins, Anna Rochester, and Robert W. Dunn collections at the University of Oregon Library. Additional papers and documents can be found at the Swarthmore College Library Peace Collection and at Bryn Mawr College. Photographs of Hutchins and Rochester are at the University of Oregon Library. Hutchins's works include *Youth in Industry* (1931), *Children under Capitalism* (1933), *Women and War* (1933), *Japan's Drive for Conquest* (1935), *The Truth about the Liberty League* (1936), and *Japan Wars on the United States of America* (1941). A biographical sketch is in *American Reformers* (1985). The *World Tomorrow*, 1922–1926, gives a chronology of Hutchins's association with that publication. Other sources include Sidney Streat, "Grace Hutchins—Revolutionary," *Daily Worker*, 16 Sept. 1935; Betty Feldman, "Grace Hutchins Tells about 'Women Who Work,'" *The Worker*, 1 Mar. 1953, p. 12; Meyer A. Zeligs, *Friendship and Fratricide: An Analysis of Whittaker Chambers and Alger Hiss* (1967); U.S. Senate Committee on the Judiciary, Subcommittee to Investigate the Administration of the Internal Security Act and Other Internal Security Laws of the Committee on the Judiciary, *The Communist Party of the United States of America: What It Is, How It Works; A Handbook for Americans* (1955). Obituaries are in the *New York Times*, 16 July 1969, and the *Daily World*, 17 July 1969.

MARILYN ELIZABETH PERRY

HUTCHINS, Harry Burns (8 Apr. 1847–25 Jan. 1930), lawyer and educator, was born in Lisbon, New Hampshire, the son of Carlton B. Hutchins and Nancy Walker Merrill. His parents' occupations are unknown. After receiving his early education at seminaries in Tilton, New Hampshire, and Newbury, Vermont, he entered Wesleyan University in 1866 but had to drop out because of poor health. He spent the months following his unscheduled departure studying premedical subjects, dividing his time between the University of Vermont and Dartmouth College. Attracted to the University of Michigan by the presence on its faculty of several textbook authors whom he admired, Hutchins entered that university in the fall of 1867. Following a successful undergraduate career, including such honors as serving as class orator and commencement speaker, he graduated with a Ph.B. in 1871, becoming the first person to receive a degree from the university's first president, James B. Angell.

After serving for a year as superintendent of public schools in Owosso, Michigan, Hutchins returned to his alma mater as instructor in history and rhetoric in 1872. That same year he married Mary Louise Clemens, with whom he had one son. Promoted to assistant professor during the following year, Hutchins also

began the study of law. He remained at Michigan until 1876, when he resigned his faculty position to enter the practice of law in partnership with his father-in-law, Thomas M. Crocker. The firm of Crocker & Hutchins conducted business in both Mount Clemens and Detroit and soon argued cases before the highest courts in the state. Hutchins's success in the legal profession did not pass unnoticed by his alma mater, and following an abortive run for the position of university regent in 1883, he returned to the Ann Arbor campus in the following year as the Jay Professor of Law.

In 1887 Hutchins accepted an invitation from the trustees of Cornell University to move to that campus and help organize that institution's law school. During his eight years in Ithaca, Hutchins helped build the law school into one of the leading facilities of its kind in the country. Called yet again into the service of his alma mater, Hutchins returned to the Michigan campus for good in 1895. As dean of the Michigan law school, Hutchins provided his most notable contributions to pedagogy. The legal profession had only recently abandoned its former method of instructing neophytes, the time-honored method of apprenticing or "reading law" under the supervision of a practicing attorney, in favor of a more formal approach involving graduate-level academic instruction. Under Hutchins's direction, academic standards were raised, and the course work requirement was increased from two to three years. Most importantly, the Michigan law school assumed a leading role in decreasing the use of formal lectures in favor of the in-depth study of various legal cases that became the standard method of legal instruction.

Hutchins further demonstrated his administrative skills during the year 1897–1898, when he assumed the duties of acting president of the university while President Angell served as envoy extraordinary and minister plenipotentiary to Turkey. He served in a similar capacity in the year following President Angell's resignation (1909–1910) and was the unanimous choice to succeed Angell as president. Elected to the position on 28 June 1910, Hutchins initially agreed to serve for a maximum of five years.

The Hutchins administration proved to be a period of unprecedented growth for the university. Additional courses in areas as diverse as aeronautics, municipal administration, and public health were added to the curriculum. The engineering department grew to include specializations such as sanitary, automobile, and highway engineering, and programs were initiated in the fine arts and business administration. During Hutchins's administration, the Graduate School became a separate administrative unit. Student numbers increased from less than 5,000 to more than 9,000, faculty numbers increased from 427 to 618, and a student health service was instituted.

Hutchins's relations with the citizens of Michigan contributed to his long-lasting impact on the development of the university. To meet the educational needs of the people of the state, he initiated an extension program, and he crisscrossed the state on speaking tours on behalf of the school. He played a critical role in revitalizing and reorganizing the alumni association, and state legislative appropriations increased dramatically during his presidency. With the combined increases in both public and private support, he completed an extensive building program, including the university's first dormitory for women.

Professional demands left Hutchins with little time to pursue his own research interests, but he did publish an American edition of Joshua Williams's *Principles of the Law of Real Property* in 1894 (originally published in 1845) and his own *Cases on Equity Jurisprudence* in 1895. He also contributed a biography of Thomas M. Cooley to W. D. Lewis's *Great American Lawyers* in 1909 and wrote numerous articles that appeared in legal journals. He chaired the Committee on Legal Education of the American Bar Association and served as the U.S. representative on the United States–Uruguay Treaty Commission. Hutchins retired from the presidency on 1 July 1920 and spent his final years quietly contributing unofficial assistance to the university. He died in Ann Arbor.

Hutchins left a profound mark on his two professions. He was a leader in changing the methods of legal education, and his administration of the University of Michigan laid the groundwork for that institution's continued growth and development.

• Hutchins's papers are at the University of Michigan Archives in Ann Arbor. The best recent scholarship on his life and career is Shirley W. Smith, *Harry Burns Hutchins and the University of Michigan* (1951). Dated but still useful are Wilfred B. Shaw, ed., *The University of Michigan: An Encyclopedic Survey* (4 vols., 1942), and B. A. Hinsdale, *History of the University of Michigan* (1906). An obituary is in the *Detroit Free Press*, 26 Jan. 1930.

EDWARD L. LACH, JR.

HUTCHINS, Margaret (21 Sept. 1884–4 Jan. 1961), librarian and professor, was born in Lancaster, New Hampshire, the daughter of Frank D. Hutchins, a flourishing attorney and banker, and Elizabeth Carleton. Hutchins graduated from Lancaster High School and Academy in 1902 and enrolled in Smith College that fall. A double major in Greek and philosophy, Hutchins was a member of the Literary Society and the Philosophical Club and could also read French, German, and Latin. Upon her graduation with a bachelor of arts degree in June 1906, she was elected to Phi Beta Kappa.

Hutchins studied with Frances Simpson, to whom she later dedicated her 1944 textbook, in the library school of the University of Illinois. She graduated with a bachelor of library science with honors in June 1908. In evaluating her work there, Albert S. Wilson and Stella Bennett wrote: "Miss Hutchins has done good work showing care and thought. Does not write a very good library hand but does neat typing. Careful as to details." Invited to stay on at the University of Illinois as a lecturer in the library school, she also worked in the University of Illinois library as a reference assistant (1908–1912), a library assistant in the classics department (1912–1913), and a reference librarian (1913–1927). During World War I she selected military books, compiled bibliographies for the National Council of Defense, and entertained military personnel at Chanute Field. Writing about reference work in June 1923, she said, "One of the hardest things we have to do is to find out what a person wants." Her first book, *Guide to the Use of Libraries: A Manual for College and University Students*, was written with Alice S. Johnson and Margaret S. Williams and, published by H. W. Wilson, went through five editions from 1920 to 1935.

Hutchins taught at the 1926 and 1927 summer Chautauqua Institutes, which led to an offer of the position of first assistant in the Queens Borough (New York) Public Library. In asking to be released from her post at Illinois, she wrote the head librarian, Phineas L. Windsor, "It offers the opportunity to teach reference to the training class as well as build up their reference work." Without a doubt, Windsor thought highly of Hutchins, for he wrote: "Miss Margaret Hutchins is about as good a reference librarian as I have ever known, and I have seen some good ones. She has an unusually keen mind, broad interests, a splendid knowledge of what we call reference material, is quick at catching new points of view, has good common sense, good judgment, and is herself a hard worker." During her three-year stint in New York, she was promoted to superintendent of branch reference work and instructor. With the need for continuing her education in mind, Hutchins accepted a Carnegie Fellowship and started work on her master's in librarianship at Columbia University, studying under Isadore Mudge. During that time she was deeply influenced by the educational theories, especially the concept of the artist-teacher, of Dr. W. C. Bagley of Columbia Teachers College. Based on her firsthand observation of library practices in England and Ireland during the summer of 1930, Hutchins in her master's thesis covered the historical aspects and organization of interlibrary loans in Great Britain.

In 1931 Hutchins joined the faculty of the School of Library Service at Columbia University as an instructor. She was promoted to assistant professor in 1935 and associate professor in 1946. During a search for a new dean, she wrote her longtime friend and mentor Simpson: "They will try to make me take over the direction of the library school and I have never hankered to run a library school—it's too much work and responsibility. I had much rather just teach or run a reference department." Another telling insight into her thinking comes from this same letter, "Salary never had been so much in my mind as opportunity to try out my ideas."

In her 1937 article in *Library Quarterly*, Hutchins articulated, probably for the first time in print, how reference librarians use "the power to analyze a question or problem and connect it, first, with the proper type of book and, second, with the right individual book" in order to answer questions. In this same article she also anticipated the need, which was not fulfilled for over twenty years, for "an analysis of just what features of the commonest reference books a reference librarian uses and a tabulation of the reference books most used."

The landmark work of Hutchins's forty-four year career was the appearance of *Introduction to Reference Work* (American Library Association, 1944), which was reprinted at least six times. Not a revision of James I. Wyer's earlier textbook, *Reference Work* (American Library Association, 1927; repr. 1930), Hutchins intended hers to deal, as she said, "with the principles and methods of reference work in general." In addition, it contains a fascinating section titled "By Way of Introduction," which readers should not miss. Dedicated to Simpson and Mudge, her classic text emphasized method over materials or even detailed knowledge of the library user. In particular, she analyzed four types of reference questions: bibliographical, biographical, historical and geographical, and current information and statistics. In her classroom, she employed the problem-discussion approach.

Frances Cheney, one of her early students, wrote: "Margaret Hutchins was a fine, thorough teacher, and although she intimidated her students with difficult examinations, she was fair in her assignments, and her lectures were clearly organized. Without the flair of Isadore Gilbert Mudge . . . she nevertheless inspired her students with a desire to do careful reference work. She was withall [*sic*] quiet, modest, and pleasant in manner."

Following her retirement from Columbia in 1952, Hutchins spent much of each year May to Nov. at her Lancaster, New Hampshire, summer home, with its spectacular setting in the White Mountains, and wintered at the House of the Holy Nativity, an Episcopalian convent. She died in the Southside Hospital, Bay Shore, Long Island. Recognized as the "Hutchins heuristic," her reference method of classifying the question by type of source and then by specific title continues to serve American reference librarians as their foundational technique.

• Some of Hutchins's papers are extant in the archives at the University of Illinois and at Columbia University.

JOHN V. RICHARDSON JR.

HUTCHINS, Robert Maynard (17 Jan. 1899–14 May 1977), university administrator and philanthropic foundation executive, was born in Brooklyn, New York, the son of William James Hutchins, a Presbyterian minister, and Anna Laura Murch. Hutchins was introduced to progressive politics and Social Gospel reform in his earliest years in his father's parish in Brooklyn. His mother read Dickens to Robert and his two brothers, early requiring them to think about the cruelty of poverty and the effects of human foibles. Her irreverent humor and unfailing civility were balanced by their father's more temperate, gentle, and judicious personality. Between them, Hutchins's understanding of civic responsibility and his wise-cracking sense of humor were irrevocably shaped. In 1907 the

family moved to Oberlin, Ohio, where William Hutchins taught Bible and homiletics at Oberlin College and Theological Seminary. Hutchins attended family prayers every day, church twice on Sundays, and YMCA summer camps, where his father also preached.

In this environment, Hutchins acquired a strong sense of right and wrong, of duty, and of excellence. His father's scholarly accomplishments and oratorical skill were standards guiding his academic endeavors. Unusually bright and fun, he led his Oberlin College classmates in academic performance, in debates, and in playing pranks in and around Oberlin. After two years of college, he served in the U.S. Army Ambulance Corps in Italy until he was discharged in 1919, having won the Croce di Guerra for bravery under fire. Returning home, Hutchins transferred to Yale, where he finished his A.B. and studied law in his senior year. Like his father, he earned Phi Beta Kappa and won the DeForest Prize for the best oration of 1921. In addition to being a good sport, quick wit, and intelligent conversationalist, he was remarkably attractive. Tall, dark, and handsome, he possessed a deep voice resonant with conviction. His contemporaries at Yale included Thornton Wilder, Henry Luce, Walter Millis, and William Benton. His classmates voted him most likely to succeed, probably in politics.

Hutchins married Maude Phelps McVeigh, a painter and sculptor, in 1921. To support her, he taught at the Lake Placid School in upstate New York until 1923, when President James R. Angell of Yale appointed him secretary to the Yale Corporation. After receiving an LL.B. from Yale's law school in 1925, Hutchins assumed an assistant professorship there. His intellectual interest in the developing legal realist movement intrigued the faculty. As a result, Angell appointed Hutchins acting dean in 1927, then dean of the law school in 1928.

Hutchins worked with Charles E. Clark to introduce reforms into the law school. These included an honors program offering independent work and seminars linking social science research with studies of legal administration and procedure, faculty projects involving social scientists at Yale and elsewhere, and philanthropic foundation support for both endeavors. He was successful to a point. The honors program was instituted. He recruited William O. Douglas, Underhill Moore, and others interested in cross-disciplinary study and law. He pursued a research project examining exceptions to the law of evidence, sharing a Commonwealth Fund grant with Mortimer Adler and Jerome Michael, who were working on a related project at Columbia Law School. In 1929 Dean Milton Winternitz of the medical school, Hutchins, and Angell persuaded the Rockefeller Foundation to finance cross-disciplinary research in medicine, law, and the social sciences in the new Institute of Human Relations.

This experience at Yale's law school was both revealing of endemic flaws in Hutchins's leadership and useful to his later career as an administrator in education. He alienated some law alumni and older faculty members with his brash treatment of their concerns about reform. He inspired faculty support of interdisciplinary work but did not sustain it. His own research reflected a transient commitment to using social science to understand law. Nevertheless, when the University of Chicago was seeking a president to replace Max Mason in 1928, Hutchins was known as an administrator with terrific energy, an uncanny ability to attract financial support, and exceptional intelligence. Philanthropic foundation officials with long-standing relationships with the university strongly endorsed him. As is common in university searches, he was chosen because of this support and because he represented the most acceptable compromise in light of the university's internal politics.

Hutchins was inaugurated as the University of Chicago's fifth president less than a month after the stock market crash of October 1929. He faced numerous pressing problems in the early years of his presidency, not the least of which was to steer the institution through the worst economic depression ever to hit the country. Undergraduate education, never a central concern of the faculty at Chicago, had become increasingly important to alumni and trustees. It offered a source of income and students for the university's preeminent graduate and professional programs. Between 1892 and 1929, the undergraduate curriculum had been revised and survey courses introduced, but the graduate faculty, by and large, resisted efforts to divert funds and attention from the graduate programs. By immediately addressing the complicated financial structure of the institution as well as the issues raised in a curriculum committee report on undergraduate education, Hutchins established his reputation for administrative brilliance and recalcitrance.

He reorganized the university administration into four divisions of academic disciplines (social sciences; biological sciences, which included the medical school; physical sciences; and humanities) and the college. Each division had an equally powerful dean who oversaw departments, making budgetary and personnel recommendations to the president. Hutchins used this structure to redefine the mission of the university by carefully choosing the deans of each division and working closely with them on appointment and promotion decisions. He met with them weekly and sought their counsel for all the major changes he promoted. By contrast, his relationships with most faculty members were distant. Three factors played a role in Hutchins's ongoing contentious dealings with university faculty: his friendship with Mortimer Adler, his ideas about collegiate education and the mission of the university, and his deteriorating marriage to Maude Hutchins.

Adler, a self-appointed philosophical critic, had taken John Erskine's reading seminar in the great books at Columbia University. After reading Aristotle, Aquinas, and others, he became interested in the role of logic in the epistemological foundations of all the academic disciplines. When Hutchins met Adler, in 1927, he was working on the logical foundations of the law at Columbia. Hutchins and Adler formed a close and lasting friendship. Both men were smart, well read, and iconoclastic in their views of higher education. Shortly after Hutchins's appointment to the presidency, he consulted Adler about organizing undergraduate education at the University of Chicago to best meet the needs of students who planned to pursue graduate or professional degrees as well as those who did not. Adler suggested Erskine's great books seminar as a model for general education. When Hutchins recruited him to the philosophy faculty at Chicago, they decided to offer a freshman honors seminar using great books. Encountering philosophy department resistance to Adler's appointment, Hutchins pushed the faculty to accept him. After they did, and he tried to impose two of Adler's friends on the department, Hutchins faced his first faculty battle, only a year into his presidency. As a result, the trustees intervened. Hutchins backed down, and Adler was moved to the law school.

Hutchins again alarmed faculty when he began advocating a particular kind of program for the college. To replace the quarter-term electives of the old program in 1931, the college curriculum committee introduced required, yearlong courses into the undergraduate program. These courses corresponded broadly to fields covered in the divisions and used comprehensive examinations to measure student performance. After a year teaching the freshman seminar, Hutchins began arguing for the inclusion of great books in the college syllabi. He appointed Adler to the curriculum committee. Social sciences committee members, wary of Hutchins, resisted efforts to incorporate Adler's book lists into the courses. In the end, the college curriculum never offered the kind of wide and deep grounding in classic Western texts that Hutchins advocated. Over time, however, he lobbied for substantial changes in undergraduate education.

By making the college dean as powerful as any other dean, and by instituting a policy that granted the college greater independence from the divisions in curriculum and faculty decisions, Hutchins ensured the college's sovereignty. He appointed college deans who shared his vision of general education. The college began admitting some students after the sophomore year in high school, eventually instituting a four-year fully prescribed general education program for all students working toward a B.A. Such a transformation in the university's undergraduate program, which provoked lively universitywide debate, could not have occurred without Hutchins's stubborn and determined leadership.

In 1936 Hutchins published *The Higher Learning in America*. In it he suggested that universities were too concerned about pleasing donors and overemphasized research as opposed to teaching, failings that led to disciplinary isolation and fragmentation of knowledge. He offered as one solution the great books, or "permanent studies," as the finest possible college education, because such study engaged students in discussions of the deepest and most persistent problems of human existence, offered them a coherent understanding of the sources of modern thought, and prepared them to confront the problems of modern democracy and capitalism. Another solution was to use metaphysics to order and unify all the other academic disciplines and to determine which research problems were fundamental to the work of the modern university. This last recommendation in particular alarmed the Chicago faculty.

In the same year, Hutchins and Adler established at the university the Committee on the Liberal Arts, which faculty correctly perceived as an attempt to bring in appointments without departmental approval. It disbanded in 1937 when committee members went to St. John's College to develop a great books curriculum. But this attempt, and Hutchins's habitually slow response to some department chairs' recommendations about appointments and promotions, increased tension on campus. In 1937–1938, the Chicago chapter of the American Association of University Professors conducted an investigation of tenure and promotion practices at the university and recommended many changes that Hutchins and the trustees incorporated into university policy. Yet the faculty-president battles continued. In 1942 Hutchins proposed a complete reorganization of the university, granting the president greater control over educational policy, reducing the faculty senate, and providing the faculty power to impeach the president. In *Education for Freedom* (1943), Hutchins argued that the university's duty was to fight fascism and totalitarian governments by formulating and clarifying ideals to guide human conduct in a democracy. A year later he informed the faculty that the university should lead a moral, spiritual, and intellectual revolution to redefine the values animating human societies. Coupled with his other proposals and various changes in university policy, this latest claim moved a majority of the faculty to protest Hutchins's efforts to prescribe their institution's functions and goals. The trustees appointed Hutchins chancellor in 1945, to concentrate on educational policy in close coordination with various faculty bodies.

His contentious relationship with the faculty, compounded by a lack of much social contact with them over the first decade of his presidency, began to wear on Hutchins by the early 1940s. Maude Hutchins had made it clear in 1929 that she would not act as hostess for the entire university community. Fiercely dedicated to her own work and protective of the family's privacy (the marriage produced three children), she increasingly resented and interfered with Hutchins's professional obligations. He took a leave of absence in 1946 to serve as editor of *Encyclopaedia Britannica* (EB) and try to repair his failing marriage and spend more time with Maude. His editorial responsibilities continued until his death, but he and Maude were divorced, after a year's separation, in 1948. He married Vesta Sutton Orlick in 1949 and adopted her daughter.

Hutchins's national reputation grew in the 1930s. Considered for various New Deal posts under Franklin D. Roosevelt, he refused to participate in the necessary politicking. When his friend William O. Douglas left the Securities and Exchange Commission, Hutchins was offered and turned down the chairmanship. He served as public representative to the New York Stock Exchange but left when he suspected the board of inadequately investigating the Whitney case. He wanted a Supreme Court associate justiceship, but Roosevelt nominated Douglas instead.

In the 1940s, various activities enlarged his exposure and influence. William Benton acquired the EB for the university and appointed Hutchins as editor. Adler's great books discussion groups spread nationally under the auspices of the Great Books Foundation (1946), and Hutchins edited the fifty-four volume *Great Books of the Western World* (1952), published by EB, for the groups' use. Henry Luce persuaded Hutchins to lead an investigation of press freedom that Luce financed through the university. The Commission on the Freedom of the Press published seven volumes in 1946 and 1947; Hutchins was largely responsible for *A Free and Responsible Press*, the commission's summary statement. The university's involvement with the Manhattan Project during the Second World War inspired Hutchins, after atomic bombs were dropped on Hiroshima and Nagasaki, to sponsor the Atomic Scientists of Chicago, Inc., to ensure civilian control of atomic energy. Social scientists at the university, concerned about world peace, asked him to address the issue. He formed the Committee to Frame a World Constitution, which published its discussions in *Common Cause*, and issued a draft of a world constitution in 1947.

These activities offered Hutchins some relief from campus tensions. But not all of his relations with faculty were marked by discord. In fact, they shared a fundamental agreement about one of the most troublesome issues faced by American universities from the 1930s to the 1950s: academic freedom. One legacy of Hutchins's leadership was a firm stand on academic freedom. In 1935 the university was called before an Illinois senate investigating committee because the drugstore magnate Charles R. Walgreen had complained that the social sciences undergraduate course required students to read a work by Karl Marx. As Hutchins told the committee, the university also required students to read works by other economic, political, and social theorists. He rallied support from the trustees and community, and the investigation closed without finding subversive activity on campus. Walgreen, persuaded by Hutchins of the folly of his act, atoned by financing a foundation for the study of American institutions at the university with $500,000. The Walgreen investigation prepared the university for another, more difficult trial in 1949. In the early postwar period of the federal loyalty-security program, a number of colleges tried to suppress the activity of Communist clubs on campuses and fire faculty members suspected of having been members of the

Communist party. The Illinois Broyles Commission investigated the University of Chicago after students protested the passage of bills requiring loyalty oaths of public employees. Hutchins made the opening statement for the university, and it was one of the clearest and most cogent arguments for the preservation of academic freedom ever offered. He defended the right of students as citizens to protest legislation of which they disapproved, and he reminded the commission that the University of Chicago did not believe in guilt by association or in punishment of people for their beliefs or associations. He even offered positions at Chicago to any University of California professor fired for refusing to sign California's loyalty oath. His defense of academic freedom stands in stark contrast to the abdication of most university administrators to the hysteria of the McCarthy era.

Another legacy Hutchins left the university was interdisciplinary teaching and research. Under his presidency, numerous interdisciplinary committees and research institutes grew out of his divisional reorganization. They bridged departments with faculty collaboration and graduate studies. Hutchins established interdisciplinary institutes in nuclear sciences after World War II to develop peaceful uses of atomic energy and assure open access to research findings. These were remarkable accomplishments in an institution known for the power and autonomy of its departmental structure.

Hutchins left the University of Chicago in 1951. He took an associate directorship at the Ford Foundation, under Paul Hoffman. Hutchins developed three semi-independent funds: the Fund for the Advancement of Education, the Fund for Adult Education, and the Fund for the Republic. The first two, which were run by others, supported various kinds of projects, from liberal arts programs for future teachers to civic and race relations education to great books reading groups. After the foundation board decided that Hutchins's stands on First Amendment rights and on education projects were liabilities for the foundation during the McCarthy era, he was appointed director of the Fund for the Republic in 1954 as part of his severance settlement. Hutchins had been investigated by the Cox Committee in 1952 and would be by the House Un-American Activities Committee (HUAC) in 1956, primarily because of this fund's policies.

With a terminal grant from the foundation, the Fund for the Republic parted company with the Ford Foundation. The fund supported research in such controversial areas as the history of communism in the United States, federal loyalty-security investigations, and blacklisting in the entertainment industry, and it financed community-based education programs in race relations and civil liberties. Hutchins stubbornly defended these unpopular activities, putting the fund at risk of an IRS investigation, in addition to the HUAC threat, and alienating board members who were reluctant to endanger the fund and their own reputations. Hutchins fought to keep his job and decided to devote the fund's remaining assets to a continuing discussion of constitutional issues rather than to financing other projects. He reorganized the fund in 1959, moved it from New York City to Santa Barbara, California, and renamed it the Center for the Study of Democratic Institutions.

Hutchins possessed a powerful streak of idealism that had been forged in the moral imperatives of the Protestant enclave of Oberlin and invigorated in the cosmopolitan environment of the University of Chicago. It gave him great strength to face down state and federal investigating committees that threatened academic freedom and First Amendment rights. It also reinforced his dogged stands on great books and the mission of the university. In the Santa Barbara hills, his intellectual vision encountered little resistance. He hand picked his colleagues, who participated in dialogues about the nature of freedom and responsibility, about education in a democracy, about law, and about world peace. It was in this atmosphere that Hutchins formulated the central ideas of *Learning Society* (1968), in which he probed deeply into education in its practical, plural, and democratic contexts while holding onto his long-held and principled beliefs about what knowledge was of greatest worth.

In his last years, Hutchins struggled with dwindling funds, trying to bring in on a permanent basis the most able people to discuss these problems. During his lifetime he helped raise four daughters, survived his first, difficult, marriage, and found great contentment in his second. He published numerous books about education, and directed one of the foremost research institutions in the United States. He assisted the wealthiest philanthropic foundation in history spend almost $200 million on education. And he was among the very few who defended freedom of speech and association during the Cold War hysteria of the late 1940s and early 1950s. He died in Santa Barbara.

• Hutchins's papers are located in Special Collections, Joseph Regenstein Library, the University of Chicago. Papers of the Yale Law School are in Manuscripts and Archives, Sterling Memorial Library, Yale University. Papers of the Fund for the Republic are in Special Collections, Princeton University. Other useful material can be found in the Oberlin College Archives, Berea College Archives, the Rockefeller Archive Center, and the Ford Foundation Archives. Hutchins's additional major publications include *No Friendly Voice* (1936), *St. Thomas and the World State* (1949), *The Democratic Dilemma* (1951), *The Great Conversation: The Substance of a Liberal Education* (1952), *The University of Utopia* (1953), *The Conflict of Education in a Democratic Society* (1953), *Some Observations on American Education* (1956), and *Freedom, Education, and the Fund: Essays and Addresses, 1946–1956* (1956). Harry S. Ashmore, *Unseasonable Truths: The Life of Robert Maynard Hutchins* (1989), is a compendium of information about Hutchins and focuses on his activities after he left the University of Chicago, as does Frank K. Kelly, *Court of Reason: Robert M. Hutchins and the Fund for the Republic* (1981). Mary Ann Dzuback, *Robert M. Hutchins: Portrait of an Educator* (1991) analyzes his relationship to the modern university by examining his early life and later pursuits and by emphasizing his leadership of the University of Chicago. An obituary is in the *New York Times*, 16 May 1977.

MARY ANN DZUBACK

HUTCHINS, Thomas (1730?–28 Apr. 1789), cartographer and surveyor, was born on the New Jersey frontier. Orphaned before the age of sixteen, by the end of the French and Indian War, in 1756, he was an ensign with Pennsylvania troops. In 1760, after several years of frontier service, he took leave to become an Indian agent. His most publicized assignment was a diplomatic mission to tribes of the Northwest. Hutchins prepared well-written narratives of his travels and generally included maps with surveyed areas. In some instances he was the first person to attempt a map of a large region. His maps and reports led to an offer of a regular British army commission, without purchase fees. Hutchins accepted and gradually became North America's premier frontier surveyor and mapper. In 1764, 1766, and 1768 he accompanied parties exploring the vast region of the eastern Mississippi River Valley from Minnesota to New Orleans. Other assignments also contributed to his geographic expertise. In 1763, for example, he traveled through the southern colonies as an army recruiter.

Hutchins's skills as a woodsman, surveyor, and cartographer were recognized formally in 1766 by an army assignment to engineering duties. Initially he mapped the frontier but then became a quartermaster. In 1770, at Fort Chartres in present-day Illinois, he led an effort to have the post commandant court-martialed on charges of graft and general malfeasance. The commandant retired. Not sharing graft may have been his downfall. Hutchins returned to engineering duties. He was sent to Pensacola, on the Florida frontier, to strengthen military defenses, map the region, and gather data on Spanish fortifications. Having traveled widely in Spanish Territory, in 1773 he filed an intelligence report with a map that accurately located many natural features, such as the coastal lakes of what are now Mississippi and Louisiana. With this map, his report offered a detailed plan for the capture of New Orleans, if that should become desirable.

In 1784 Hutchins published a version of this report as a book, hoping for profit. It was part of a lifelong focus on money. He often billed the British army and other employers for overtime work. In Hutchins's era some officers gained income by using their influence to help merchants. No formal contract is known, but Hutchins seems to have helped the firm of Bayton, Wharton, & Morgan. He also speculated in real estate. When he mapped in the South he acquired 4,600 acres of prime land, mostly near Natchez and Baton Rouge. In 1776 his expanding estate required a will. A lifelong bachelor, he left his assets to three illegitimate children, each with a different mother. Little else is known of his personal life.

In 1776 a promotion to captain allowed Hutchins to avoid immediate involvement in the revolutionary war. Instead, he traveled to London to meet high-ranking officers. By submitting detailed plans for engineering projects, he hoped to become the senior British army engineer for the Gulf Coast. In 1778 he enhanced his reputation by publishing a commercial book on the natural history and terrain of the American northwestern frontier. By 1779 the last of his engineering plans was nearing approval. He also negotiated a 10,000-acre land grant that was tentatively approved. Just when success seemed assured, someone intercepted letters to Hutchins from Samuel Wharton, a long-time associate and an American merchant who was living in France. The letters led to seven weeks in prison. Falsely charged with treason, for sympathizing with American colonists, Hutchins was found innocent and released, but his career was in shambles.

After prison he went to Paris where Benjamin Franklin (1706–1790) administered an oath of loyalty to the United States. In May 1781 Congress employed Hutchins as a geographer to serve the army in the South. He was to get the same pay as Simeon De Witt, geographer to the rest of the army. At Hutchins's request, Congress designated both men as "Geographer of the United States."

Once appointed, Hutchins took leave to earn higher fees representing Virginia and other states in boundary disputes. Then he assumed his federal duties. By 1785 he was the only official geographer of the United States. In that year a new ordinance required a survey of the Northwest Territory. In mapping this region a corps of surveyors, under Hutchins, made the first use of the Township-Section-Range system, which is standard in modern surveys; Hutchins may have designed the system. In 1788 he produced a map and report on "The Seven Ranges," a block of land in Ohio that was to be opened for sale. This report brought Hutchins great acclaim, but his health was impaired, perhaps by the rigors of the frontier. He was also upset by poor federal funding for his field work and inadequate staffing.

In 1788 Hutchins secretly joined an effort to revitalize New Spain, the long-established Spanish colonial presence on the western frontier of the United States. He planned to renounce his American citizenship and become surveyor general to the King of Spain. Before this plan could be implemented, Hutchins died during a stay in Pittsburgh, his normal point of departure for the frontier. In death he was the prototypic American hero: a penniless, uneducated orphan who rose above his circumstances and did great things.

• Many of Hutchins's reports as a British Army officer and as an Indian agent are in the British Museum. The best single archive is the Thomas Hutchins Papers in the Pennsylvania Historical Society, Philadelphia. Fort Chartres, at Kidd, Ill., is much as it was in Hutchins's day, but there are no known portraits or personal artifacts there or elsewhere. Details of his life are hard to document from published sources. Even his participation in the New Spain conspiracy is not mentioned in old, but standard, reports such as Arthur P. Whitaker, "Spanish Intrigue in the Old Southwest: An Episode, 1788–1789," *Mississippi Valley Historical Review* 12 (1925): 155–76. The best biographical source is Anna Margaret Quattrocchi, "Thomas Hutchins, 1730–1789" (Ph.D. diss., Univ. of Pittsburgh, 1944). His books have been republished as Frederick C. Hicks, ed., *Thomas Hutchins, a Topographical Description of Virginia, Pennsylvania, Maryland, and North*

Carolina (1904), and Joseph C. Tregle, Jr., ed., *Thomas Hutchins, a Historical Narrative and Topographical Description of Louisiana and West Florida* (1968). There are dozens of articles about Hutchins. Two examples, published a century apart, are Charles Whittlesey, "Origin of the American System of Land Surveys: Justice to the Memory of Thomas Hutchins," *Journal of the Association of Engineering Societies* 3 (1884): 275–80, and Louis M. Waddell, "New Light on Boquet's Ohio Expedition: Nine Days of Thomas Hutchins' Journal, October 3 to October 11, 1764," *Western Pennsylvania Historical Magazine* 60 (1983): 271–9.

JAMES X. CORGAN

HUTCHINSON, Anne (1591?–1643), religious leader, was born in Alford, Lincolnshire, England, the daughter of Francis Marbury, minister of the Church of England, and Bridget Dryden. She learned scripture and theology from her father, who had been silenced and imprisoned for long periods of time by his bishop for complaining about the poor training of English clergymen.

In 1612 Anne married William Hutchinson, a successful merchant; they had fourteen children. As the Puritan controversy grew in England the Hutchinsons were persuaded of the rightness of the Puritan beliefs by one of the leading Puritan preachers, John Cotton. Archbishop William Laud's persecution of the dissenters spurred a migration to the colonies in the New World, and Cotton sailed there in 1633 to avoid arrest. The Hutchinson family sailed the following year and took their place among the leaders of the colony. Anne was skilled in herbal medicine, and her services were essential in a place where adequate medical facilities were lacking. Soon after her arrival, at the urging of Cotton, she began to hold weekly prayer meetings in her home. A controversy soon developed between Puritans who stressed the importance of human cooperation with divine grace and those who relied totally on God's grace, the Covenant of Grace. Cotton belonged to the latter group and preached total reliance on the goodness and grace of God rather than on personal good works. Convinced of the truth of this message, Anne Hutchinson became an articulate defender of the position at the meetings in her home. Attendance grew, and soon sixty people, including the newly elected governor, Sir Henry Vane, were in attendance.

The majority of ministers and magistrates in the colony saw this new movement as a threat. They named Hutchinson and her followers "Antinomian"—against customary law—as a term of derision. The relationships of state to Puritan congregations in the Massachusetts Bay Colony were threatened by the rejection of this polity by Hutchinson, an unusually articulate woman. Early colonial women, who had few opportunities for public social intercourse, were isolated from the mainstream of activity. Understandably Hutchinson's movement attracted many women frustrated by their exclusion from congregational decisions and hence restricted to a traditional social and gender role.

Pastor John Wilson and former governor John Winthrop, both, according to Hutchinson, staunch exponents of the Covenant of Works, began to stir up opposition to the Antinomians. The ministers called the first synod of the Congregational church in 1637 in order to denounce Hutchinson. Cotton at first defended her, but he yielded to the pressure of the majority and joined the others in her denunciation at the synod held in August 1637. There it was decided that the security of the colony required getting rid of the dissenters, especially their leader, Hutchinson. In November of the same year Hutchinson was brought to trial in Newtowne, a location chosen to separate her from her Boston followers. The trial record shows that chief among the accusations was that Hutchinson presumed to teach men who attended these meetings. She was also accused of failing to honor the ministers of the colony. Not content with defending herself, Hutchinson attempted to persuade her accusers of the error of their ways. When asked where she received the authorization to teach, she claimed the spirit of God. She compared herself to Abraham in following God's word by immediate revelation. This claim to immediate revelation, made by various radical Israelite and later Christian prophets throughout history, constituted for the court proof of Hutchinson's heresy. She and her family were banished from the colony, and at a subsequent trial she was excommunicated from the church. The exiles joined Roger Williams in Rhode Island. Williams, himself a dissenter, insisted on freedom of conscience.

The leadership of the Massachusetts Bay Colony was not content to be rid of Hutchinson and sent delegations to Rhode Island to prevent her continuing ministry. After Will Hutchinson died in 1642, Anne and the remainder of her family left for Dutch territory on Long Island to be free of persecution from Massachusetts Bay. The following year she and her entire family, with the exception of one daughter who escaped, were killed in an Indian massacre. Until recently, most scholars were convinced that the attack was an act of reprisal against whites for taking Indian territory. However, some current scholarship speculates that Puritan authorities incited the Indians to attack. The wealth of detail reported about the massacre suggests that English observers had been present. A pamphlet containing these details was written by Edward Johnson, a military leader in Massachusetts. It is certain that the leaders of the Bay Colony had been deeply concerned about Hutchinson's influence among the women in their midst. Her accusers at the trial complained that her actions were unseemly for one of her sex and that she encouraged women to rebellion. In an act of defiance, Hutchinson's closest friend, Mary Dyer, rose from the congregation to accompany Anne on the day that she was banished from the Boston church. Later Dyer visited England and while there was converted to the beliefs of the Society of Friends. Some scholars cite this link with Dyer, as well as Hutchinson's claim to immediate revelation, as evidence that Anne Hutchinson was a proto-Quaker. Whether Hutchinson can be regarded as an early Quaker or not, in refusing to admit that ministers were superior simply by reason of their ordination she struck a blow for the ministry of all believers as well as for the doctrine of immediate revelation.

Anne Hutchinson is one of the leading figures in the early history of Massachusetts. In an era when women were admonished to obedience, passivity, and meekness, Hutchinson defended her theological position and provided the women of the Massachusetts Bay Colony with a model of independence and resourcefulness. She is widely considered to be the earliest feminist in the New World. She continues to be a focus for feminist historical study because she was clearly a woman who embodied new possibilities for the leadership of women in a radically different vision of both religious and political life.

• David Hall, *The Antinomian Controversy 1636–1638* (1968), contains the records of both trials as well as John Winthrop, "A Short Story of the Rise, Reign, and Ruin of the Antinomians, Familists and Libertines," and John Cotton, "Way of the Congregational Churches Cleared." Other important sources are Thomas Hutchinson, *A Collection of Original Papers Relative to the History of the Colony of the Massachusetts Bay* (1865), *Anne Hutchinson and Other Papers* in the publications of the Westchester County Historical Society, ed. O. Hufeland (1929), and Thomas Hutchinson, *History of the Colony and Province of Massachusetts Bay* (1936). Elaine Huber, *Women and the Authority of Inspiration* (1985), places Hutchinson in the line of women prophets who challenge ecclesiastical authority. Lyle Koehler, "The Case of the American Jezebels: Anne Hutchinson and Female Agitation during the Years of Antinomian Turmoil 1636–1640," *William and Mary Quarterly* 31 (Jan. 1974): 55–78, and James Maclear, "The Heart of New England Rent," *Mississippi Valley Historical Review* 42 (Mar. 1956): 621–52, provide important background on the historical struggles. Ben Barker-Benfield, "Anne Hutchinson and the Puritan Attitude toward Women," *Feminist Studies* 1 (Fall 1972): 65–96, and Anne King, "Anne Hutchinson and Anne Bradstreet: Literature and Experience, Faith and Works in Massachusetts Bay Colony," *International Journal of Women's Studies* 1, no. 5 (Sept.–Oct. 1978): 445–67, present insights from current feminist scholarship. New information on Hutchinson's death is provided by M. J. Lewis in "Anne Hutchinson," in *Portraits of American Women*, ed. G. J. Barker-Benfield and Catherine Clinton (1991).

ELAINE C. HUBER

HUTCHINSON, Frank (20 Mar. 1897–9 Nov. 1945), singer and guitarist, was born in the mountainous area around Raleigh County, West Virginia. His parents' names are unknown. Hutchinson moved with his family to Logan County as a young boy. There he was reared by his mother and by his foster father, Bob Deskins. His interest in guitar music was born when, as a boy of seven or eight, he began listening to African-American section hands working on the railroad near his home. Like many young white Appalachian musicians, he was fascinated with the blues-style playing he heard from black musicians who had come into the mountains to work on railroads. In Hutchinson's case the mentor was Henry Vaughn, who played the guitar in unusual tunings and with a homemade slide to note the strings. Hutchinson earned enough to buy his own guitar and began teaching himself to play.

Soon he fashioned a wire rack and was able to hold and play a harmonica while he played guitar, prefiguring the techniques used later by Woody Guthrie and Bob Dylan.

In 1917 Hutchinson married a local woman, Minnie Garrett; began a family that would eventually include two daughters; and settled near the tiny town of Ethel, West Virginia. To maintain his family, he occasionally worked in the nearby coal mines, but for a decade (roughly 1925 to 1935) he was able to make a decent full-time living with his music. He did this by playing at area schoolhouses, motion picture theaters, coal camps, and similar venues. He also made a series of recordings—some thirty-eight between 1926 and 1929—for the nationally known OKeh label (General Phonograph Corp.). His first recording was "Worried Blues" backed by "The Train That Carried the Girl from Town" (OKeh 45114; 1926); both were popular sellers and helped define the genre of "white country blues." The latter piece, done with the guitar in an open D tuning, became a well-known standard for later country and bluegrass musicians in the area, including guitarist Doc Watson and Wade Mainer.

Other records soon followed. One was "Coney Isle" (OKeh 45083; 1927), a droll comedy song about a popular amusement park in Cincinnati. "The Miner's Blues" developed even further his use of blues lyrics and instrumental techniques, while "Johnny and Jane" and "The Last Scene of the Titanic" drew on much older folk traditions. In 1930 Hutchinson was popular enough with record buyers that the OKeh company included him in a six-part skit they released called the OKeh Medicine Show, starring most of their best-known entertainers.

For various reasons, one of which was the Great Depression, which seriously hurt record sales, Hutchinson quit music in the mid-1930s, convinced there was no future in it. Moving to Lake, West Virginia, he opened and operated a grocery store until it was destroyed by a fire in 1942. The family then moved to Dayton, Ohio, where Hutchinson died from liver cancer.

Though Hutchinson was largely forgotten by the commercial country music industry by the time he died, in the 1960s the folk revival movement attracted new interest in his recordings. Reissues of his recordings on new LPs followed, and a number of his songs were even transcribed in various songbooks. To many younger musicians who copied his songs and styles, Frank Hutchinson became a vibrant example of the "melting pot" theory of southern folk music, a theory that stated that most of the creative geniuses of southern music often mixed and merged both black and white and popular and traditional musics.

• For more on Hutchinson, see Mark Wilson, liner notes to *Frank Hutchinson: The Train That Carried My Girl from Town* (Rounder Records LP no. 1007), and Charles K. Wolfe, "A Lighter Shade of Blue: White Country Blues," in *Nothing but the Blues*, ed. Larry Cohn (1995).

CHARLES K. WOLFE

HUTCHINSON, James (29 Jan. 1752–6 Sept. 1793), physician and surgeon, was born in Makefield Township, Bucks County, Pennsylvania, the son of Randall Hutchinson, a farmer and stonemason, and Catherine Rickey. Both parents were plain country Friends (Quakers). Apprenticed at fifteen to the druggists Moses and Isaac Bartram, young Hutchinson in 1771 became the pupil of Cadwalader Evans, a Philadelphia physician. He served as apothecary of the Pennsylvania Hospital (1773–1775) and earned a bachelor of medicine degree from the College of Philadelphia in 1774. He spent a year (1775–1776) in London, where, encouraged by John Fothergill to prepare particularly for surgery, he became a pupil of Percivall Pott at St. Bartholomew's Hospital and attended the lectures and dissections of William Hunter and John Hunter. He returned home via France in March 1777, carrying dispatches from Benjamin Franklin to the Continental Congress. In May he was elected a physician at the Pennsylvania Hospital.

The outbreak of the War of Independence caused Hutchinson to question his Quaker pacifist principles. "I have too great an affection for my Country not to feel its distresses," he wrote in December 1775. He tended the wounded from the battle of Germantown in October 1777, and on December 1 he was named senior surgeon of the Flying Camp of the Middle Department of the Continental Army. At Valley Forge he and six aides inoculated more than 3,000 men against smallpox. In 1778 he was appointed surgeon of the Pennsylvania state navy. This quasi-military service led to his being disowned by the Society of Friends on 26 February 1779.

Hutchinson's professional career continued to advance. In 1779 he was reappointed to the staff of the Pennsylvania Hospital, where he made surgery and obstetrics his specialty. He was also named one of the port's quarantine physicians. In 1787 he was a founder of the College of Physicians of Philadelphia, serving first as secretary, then as a censor, responsible for upholding ethical standards and professional conduct. He was an original member of the Philadelphia Medical Society of 1792. As a trustee of the University of the State of Pennsylvania after 1779, he endeavored to revive medical instruction, and in 1789 he accepted election as professor of chemistry and materia medica in that institution. At the University of Pennsylvania, created in 1791 by the union of the old College and the new University of the State of Pennsylvania, he became professor of chemistry. He was elected a member of the American Philosophical Society in 1779.

Meanwhile Hutchinson, motivated by his sense of civic duty and desire for the Revolution to succeed in Pennsylvania, become increasingly active in politics. He served briefly in the state assembly in 1780 but decided that he was not interested in being an elected official. A supporter of Pennsylvania's radical constitution of 1776, he became an anti-Federalist after 1788; he was an ardent supporter of Jefferson and a founder of the Pennsylvania Democratic Society in 1793. He wrote squibs and letters to the newspapers, corre-sponded with fellow Democrats, and kept himself informed about Federalist schemes. He was one of a committee that received the French minister Edmond Charles Genêt, who was stirring up American public opinion to support the French revolutionary government and adopt an anti-British stance. Years later in a letter to Jefferson, John Adams, with typical exaggeration, declared that only Hutchinson's death prevented the fall of Washington's administration in the 1793 summer of pro-French agitation. In fact, Washington's firmness and popularity undercut the schemes of the French and their American allies, such as Hutchinson.

In the yellow fever epidemic of 1793, Hutchinson was seen moving among his patients with humanity and quiet courage. He was himself stricken on August 30 and died a week later in Philadelphia. Hutchinson's death increased public dismay—if the doctors could not save one of their own, what hope was there for others?—and helped to intensify the debate, led by Benjamin Rush, over the source and treatment of the disease.

Hutchinson was one of the very few American medical students before the Revolution who undertook to prepare himself for a career in surgery. Although he seems to have had a successful practice, he was soon deflected by political events from surgery to public life. In Pennsylvania and on the national scene, he was a tireless and effective advocate and operative for radical and republican causes.

Hutchinson was married twice, to Lydia Biddle in 1779 and to Sydney Howell in 1786. He and Howell had a daughter, who died in infancy, and two sons.

• A small collection of Hutchinson's papers is in American Philosophical Society. They were a source for Whitfield J. Bell, Jr., "James Hutchinson (1752–1793): A Physician in Politics," in *Medicine, Science and Culture: Historical Essays in Honor of Owsei Temkin*, ed. Lloyd G. Stevenson and Robert P. Multhauf (1968), pp. 265–83; several are quoted fully in Bell, "James Hutchinson (1752–1793): Letters from an American Student in London," College of Physicians of Philadelphia, *Transactions and Studies* 4th ser., 34 (1966): 20–23. On Hutchinson in the yellow fever epidemic, see John H. Powell, *Bring Out Your Dead* (1949). Details of the treatment Hutchinson received in his final illness are in W. S. W. Ruschenberger, *An Account of the Institution and Progress of the College of Physicians of Philadelphia . . . from January, 1787* (1887), pp. 62–65.

WHITFIELD J. BELL, JR.

HUTCHINSON, Thomas (9 Sept. 1711–3 June 1780), colonial historian, royal official, and Loyalist refugee, was born in Boston, Massachusetts, the son of Colonel Thomas Hutchinson and Sarah Foster, both children of Boston merchants. He grew up in one of the finest mansions in Boston, plain in style but filled with busts of classical and British figures and pictures of historic events such as the destruction of the Spanish Armada. Preferring reading history to playing with other children, Thomas became absorbed in the history of England and New England and admired Charles I. He attended North Grammar School and at the age of twelve entered Harvard, where his family's social standing entitled him to be ranked third in his class. In 1734 he married Margaret Sanford, daughter of a wealthy Rhode Island merchant and governor, and thereupon became linked by family ties and affection to Andrew Oliver (1706–1774) (Margaret's sister's husband) and to Andrew's brother, Peter Oliver. The brothers remained his lifelong political allies.

Elected to the Massachusetts House of Representatives in 1737, Hutchinson emerged in the 1740s as a member of the broad coalition that supported the administration of Governor William Shirley. For the next twelve years he fought to replace the province's depreciated money supply with hard currency. He led the fight to block a variety of money schemes based on silver and land reserves in the 1739–1740 session and was one of the hard money men rewarded by Shirley's predecessor, Jonathan Belcher, with an appointment as justice of the peace for Suffolk County. In the climax of the currency wars in 1748–1749, he persuaded the Massachusetts House to pledge the use of its reimbursement for its 1745 expedition against the French fortification at Louisbourg to stabilize its currency. As Speaker of the house of representatives from 1746 to 1748 he pushed through a vote of 40 to 37 to redeem the colony's silver coins at a ratio of eleven to one. As a result of the victory, Hutchinson was feared and hated by the "popular" opposition party. But it also secured his leadership of the court party of Massachusetts, which supported the royal prerogative as the basis for governing the colony.

Hutchinson did not seek his role as an ally of the Crown. Rather, he was a vigorous and conventional defender of Massachusetts interests. He opposed, for example, the impressment of Massachusetts inhabitants by British naval vessels. In 1742 he confronted Captain William Scott on the deck of H.M.S. *Astraea* and demanded the release of one seaman and the hostage wife of a man Scott was attempting to impress. Hutchinson persuaded Shirley to intervene in their behalf. In 1747 Speaker Hutchinson mediated between a violent anti-impressment mob and the provincial government; the Massachusetts House approved such a strong anti-impressment resolution that the mob dispersed.

Hutchinson's *History of Massachusetts-Bay* (2 vols., 1760, 1768) accurately recounted these events and contained sympathetic accounts of Puritanism; the Antinomian heresy of Hutchinson's ancestor, Anne Hutchinson; and Massachusetts opposition in the 1680s to the "tyrannical disposition" of the royalist governor, Sir Edmund Andros, and his administration's "harpies." Hutchinson's *History* acknowledged the multiplicity of jostling interest groups in Massachusetts and the duty of government to protect the public interest from the demands of self-interested groups like the advocates of an inflated money supply he had battled in the 1740s. Though Benjamin Franklin (1706–1790) got credit for the Albany Plan

of colonial union in 1754, Hutchinson played an equally important role in drafting the document.

As chief justice of Massachusetts from 1760 to 1771, Hutchinson drew on his historical knowledge and political experience—and on his conservative view that a contagion of violence and illegality jeopardized the safety of colonial society—in the best tradition of the knowledgeable, conscientious legal laymen who held judicial posts in the Bay Colony. In the writs of assistance case in 1762, he upheld the validity of new, tougher search warrants used by customs officers. An activist chief justice, Hutchinson lectured jurors on doing their duty to stem the tide of violence and refusing to be intimidated by the populace. John Adams (1735–1826) accused Hutchinson of "harangu[ing]" jurors with "party principles," but William Pencak, a modern scholar sharply critical of British colonial policy, places Hutchinson's speeches from the bench in the tradition of Mathew Hale and Edmund Burke. Hutchinson served as chief justice until 1771, though he stopped hearing cases in 1769.

When Hutchinson read a copy of the Stamp Act he composed a long letter to Massachusetts's colonial agent, Richard Jackson, refuting the ministerial claim that the colonists were virtually represented in Parliament, that they owed Britain the cost of their military defense, and indeed that they had been planted and nourished by British generosity. Hutchinson's letter almost certainly found its way into the hands of the pro-American member of Parliament, Isaac Barre, who closely followed Hutchinson's logic and historical evidence when he thundered during the debate over the wisdom of the Stamp Act, "Your oppressions planted them. . . . They grew by your neglect. . . . They have nobly taken up arms in your defense." Thus when a mob ransacked Hutchinson's fine town house in Boston, believing that he had conspired in the enactment of the Stamp Act, Hutchinson "must have reflected," in Edmund S. Morgan's words, "with some bitterness on the irony of his situation, . . . a traitor . . . in the eyes of his countrymen . . . while Barre . . . basked in a shower of fulsome tributes."

Hutchinson's most significant participation in the politics of the prerevolutionary period was private. His Stamp Act letter to Jackson was only the first of a series of private letters and memoranda searching for a solution to the imperial impasse. The most significant were his "Essay on Taxation" and "A Dialogue between an American and a European Englishman," both written in 1768, and two private letters in 1770 and 1772 applying lessons from Roman history to the imperial controversy.

The "Dialogue" involved a British and a colonial speaker debating the issues dividing the two sides in the dispassionate, respectful fashion that Hutchinson found so lacking among his contemporaries. The "Dialogue" also represented Hutchinson's response to John Dickinson's (1732–1808) *Letters of a Pennsylvania Farmer*. His choice of names for the two speakers, "American Englishman" and "European Englishman," expressed his belief that a common history and language ought to provide the basis for respectful, dispassionate, healing discussion. "American Englishman" started where Hutchinson left off in his Stamp Act letter to Jackson, claiming that all British taxes levied on the colonists violated the well-established precedent against taxation without representation. The "European Englishman" retorted that "this dispute . . . has been carried on with great zeal and warmth of temper. This temper must subside before there can be any hope for an accommodation." Zeal and warmth, continued the British voice, characterized those colonists who resisted the Townshend Acts because they violated colonial rights; the resisters were "submitting to just nothing" and in effect denying any link at all to the mother country. In order to demonstrate their loyalty, the colonists would have to make unqualified and sincere professions of submission. A self-righteous posture was delusive because British authority was, in its nature, hidden, potential, and slumbering and could never be defined with precision. The American voice in the dialogue tried to meet this objection by citing John Locke's compact theory; the British voice replied that Locke did not justify individuals in defying abusive authority but only the entire populace, acting almost in unison, in withdrawing their obedience.

In his discussion of the Roman historian Livy, Hutchinson cited the example of some recalcitrant Roman colonies that refused to pay requisitions during the Punic Wars. The Roman Senate serenely gave the rebellious colonies twenty years to pay the taxes and arrears, and ultimately prevailed. Here was a model for British authority that Hutchinson could admire unreservedly: calculating in its use of power and capable of responding to bluster with a lofty insistence on principle.

With increasing urgency and specificity, Hutchinson beseeched British officials in the early 1770s to act in just such a fashion. Shortly after becoming acting governor in 1769, he offered to resign to make room for a new governor with greater authority and capacity for severe measures. He suggested that all royal governors be British noblemen and serve for three-year terms, "as in New Spain." He recommended imposing oaths on colonial legislators that they would uphold British law, and outlawing organized opposition to the enforcement of British law in the colonies. In a letter that caused a sensation when it was leaked to the press in 1775, he said that colonial liberty might have to be curtailed in order to restore order and calm. His recommendation for a new royal council in Massachusetts appointed by the Crown later became the centerpiece of the Coercive Acts of 1774. His purpose in these grim recommendations was to allow the British to reassert their authority, to stun the Massachusetts populace into ending its turbulent, self-destructive conduct, and to then usher in a period of healing, negotiation, and finally reconciliation.

Three public disputes erupted during this period. The Boston Massacre in March 1770 prompted Hutchinson's most skillful leadership. He confronted the British officer responsible and demanded an explanation. Then he spoke to the outraged crowd and persuaded the people that the soldiers would be placed on trial. Finally, he managed to delay the trial for nearly six months, giving time for anger to subside and the soldiers' lawyer, John Adams, time to prepare a defense based on the soldiers' legitimate fear of death at the hands of the snowball- and stone-throwing crowd. A second revealing dispute involved Hutchinson's removal, on orders from the Crown, of the Massachusetts legislature from Boston to Cambridge from 1769 to 1772. Hutchinson defended the power of the Crown to discipline the assembly in this fashion and his own obligation to obey the removal order and disregard objections of both the lower and upper houses. Finally, when the Boston town meeting circulated a wholesale indictment of British policy to every other town in the province, Hutchinson retorted, in a lengthy exchange with the house and council, that "no line can be drawn between the supreme authority of Parliament and the total independence of the colonies," a statement his opponents misinterpreted as denying that the colonies had any rights instead of as the prudential warning against confrontational language that Hutchinson had intended to convey.

When the first ship bearing tea taxed under the Tea Act arrived in November 1773 and the Boston town meeting tried to pressure the captain to depart forthwith, Hutchinson enforced the acts of trade by refusing to let the ship leave Boston harbor until its cargo was unloaded and customs formalities were completed. After the destruction of the cargo in the Boston Tea Party, Hutchinson was called to London for consultations and was succeeded as governor by General Thomas Gage (1721–1787). In England he spoke at length with the king, Lord North, and with several members of North's ministry. In 1776 he was joined in exile by the rest of the Hutchinson and Oliver families. With Peter Oliver, his brother-in-law and successor as chief justice, he received an honorary doctorate of civil laws from Oxford. He then published a knowledgeable rebuttal to the accusations in the Declaration of Independence. His homesickness for his estate in Milton, Massachusetts, and the death of a daughter in 1777 and a son in 1780 devastated him. He died in London of apoplexy and was buried in a family crypt in Croydon.

"Nothing would have pleased him more," Carl L. Becker wrote in a classic portrait of Hutchinson, "than that New England should have shown its emancipation from provincialism by meriting the good will of the King. His irritation with America in general and Boston in particular was the irritation of a proud and possessive father with a beloved but wayward child who fails to do him credit in high places."

• Hutchinson's correspondence in the Massachusetts Archives and his family papers in the British Library are available in transcript and photocopy at the Massachusetts Historical Society. There is no modern biography of Hutchinson, but Bernard Bailyn, *The Ordeal of Thomas Hutchinson* (1974), is an intellectual and political study that spans his entire life while focusing on the prerevolutionary period. Malcolm Freiberg, "Thomas Hutchinson: The First Fifty Years (1711–1761)," *William and Mary Quarterly* 15, no. 1 (1958): 35–55, and Clifford K. Shipton, "Thomas Hutchinson," in *Sibley's Harvard Graduates*, vol. 8 (1951), provide other biographical details. Malcolm Freiberg, *Prelude to Purgatory: Thomas Hutchinson in Provincial Massachusetts Politics, 1760–1770* (1990), is the standard work on that decade. William Pencak, *America's Burke: The Mind of Thomas Hutchinson* (1982), discovered Hutchinson's role in anti-impressment riots. Edmund S. Morgan and Helen M. Morgan, *The Stamp Act Crisis* (1953), document his private opposition to the act. Robert M. Calhoon, *The Loyalists in Revolutionary America, 1760–1781* (1973) and *The Loyalist Perception and Other Essays* (1989), recounts his private reflection and role in the removal of the General Court from Boston. Carl Becker's sketch in the *Dictionary of American Biography* remains the most insightful short portrait (see Michael Kammen, ed., *What Is the Good of History?* [1973]).

ROBERT M. CALHOON

HUTCHINSON, Woods (3 Jan. 1862–26 Apr. 1930), physician and author, was born in Selby, Yorkshire, England, the son of Charles Hutchinson and Elizabeth Woods. In 1874 he immigrated with his parents to the United States and settled in Iowa, first in Oskaloosa and later in Des Moines, where his father became an investment banker. He received his A.B. and A.M. from Oskaloosa's Penn College in 1880 and 1883, respectively, and his M.D. from the University of Michigan in 1884. He spent the next two years studying medicine at the universities of London, Oxford, Vienna, and Berlin.

In 1886 Hutchinson returned to Des Moines and opened a medical practice. He also began teaching physiology and hygiene at Des Moines Medical College. In 1891 he accepted a position as professor of anatomy and hygiene at the State University of Iowa. He married Cornelia Maria Williams in 1893; they had one child. In 1896 Hutchinson closed his practice to become a professor of comparative pathology and embryology in the medical department of the University of Buffalo (N.Y.) and professor of methods of science teaching and anthropology in its pedagogy department. After leaving Buffalo in 1898, he spent a year lecturing on comparative pathology at the London Medical Graduates' College and the next year lecturing on biology at the University of London's extension department. In 1900 he settled in Portland, Oregon, where he established another medical practice, wrote the textbook *Studies in Human and Comparative Pathology* (1901), and in 1903 became the first secretary of the state board of health.

In 1905 Hutchinson retired from the active practice of medicine and moved to New York City. Although he taught clinical medicine at the New York Polyclinic from 1907 to 1909, he devoted most of his remaining years to writing about medicine and health. Realizing that a great number of Americans possessed little knowledge about the scientific principles of health and hygiene, he aimed to make such subjects more intelligible to the general public by discussing them in layman's terms. His articles and syndicated columns became standard fare in such popular periodicals as *American Magazine, Contemporary Review, Cosmopolitan, Harper's Monthly, McClure's Magazine, Saturday Evening Post, Success, Woman's Home Companion*, and the *New York Times*. His favorite topic was preventive medicine; on this subject he authored a number of textbooks and handbooks, many of which were published as part of "The Woods Hutchinson Health Series." His more popular titles included *Instinct and Health* (1908), *Health and Common Sense* (1909), *Preventable Diseases* (1909), *The Conquest of Consumption* (1910), *Exercise and Health* (1911; 2d ed., 1918), *Common Diseases* (1913), *Civilization and Health* (1914), *Community Hygiene* (1916; 2d ed., 1929), and *Building Strong Bodies* (1924). Their sales brought Hutchinson a considerable fortune.

By far the most influential of his works was *A Handbook of Health*. First published in 1911, it went through three editions (with some copies titled *Hutchinson's Handbook of Health*) and twenty printings by 1922, largely because its comprehensive content was presented in a highly readable style. The compact book presented in fewer than 400 pages of text a relatively simple but complete discussion of how the human body functions and how to take care of it. Organized around the central theme that the body operates along the same principles as a steam engine or automobile, the book intended "to enable a beginner to fuel it, run it, and make roadside repairs" (1911, p. v) by discussing what sorts of "food-fuel" ought to be supplied to the "body-engine," the importance of providing pure water and air to the "boiler" and "lung-bellows," how the "heart-pump" and its "pipe-lines" operate, and how its bones resemble "stiffening rods." It also likened the excretory system to "plumbing and sewering," the nervous system to a "telephone exchange and its cables," and the sensory organs to the "lookout department." In addition, the handbook discussed infections and how to avoid them, presented proper techniques for cooking and food preparation, addressed the importance of good personal hygiene and physical exercise, and outlined what to do in case of accidents and emergencies.

Hutchinson was particularly interested in the health and care of children and specifically addressed this topic in two books. *We and Our Children* (1911) advised parents on the care and feeding of young children and in particular urged fathers to restructure their business and social lives so that they could spend time each day with their children. *The Child's Day*, which first appeared in 1912 and went through two editions and fifteen printings by 1921, attempted to teach children how to care for their bodies properly by rephrasing the basic message and content of *A Handbook of Health* into language that could be read and understood by school-age children. To this end Hutchinson abandoned the engine analogy and instead discussed health and hygiene as they relate to the events of a child's typical day.

When the United States entered World War I, Hutchinson volunteered for the U.S. Army Medical Corps, but he was turned away because of his age. Instead, he went to Europe as an unofficial observer along the Western Front and reported in particular about the hardships endured by the peasants in occupied France. After the war he returned to New York and resumed his medical writing career. He toured Europe with his family from 1922 to 1924 and the Far East and Pacific from 1926 to 1928. In 1929 he retired to Brookline, Massachusetts, where he died.

Hutchinson served as president of the American Academy of Medicine from 1915 to 1916. He was editor of *Vis Medicatrix* from 1890 to 1891 and the *Polyclinic* from 1899 to 1900. His primary contribution to the advance of American society consisted of his ability to bring health and hygiene to the attention of the general public so that it understood and benefited from his message.

• An obituary is in the *New York Times*, 27 Apr. 1930.

CHARLES W. CAREY, JR.

HUTNER, Isaac (1906–27 Nov. 1980), rabbi, philosopher, and leader of Orthodox Judaism in the United States and Israel, was born in Warsaw, Russian Poland, into a family of prominent supporters of the Hasidic school of Kotzk. He received a traditional Jewish education. Having gained a reputation as a prodigy (*ilui*) in his Talmudic study, he pursued advanced rabbinical education in the yeshiva in Slobodka, Lithuania (1922–1925) and in the branch it had established in Hebron, Palestine (1925–1929). At Slobodka he was influenced by Rabbi Nathan Zvi Finkel, a leading heir of the *mussar* (morality) school of Lithuanian Judaism. While in Palestine he also came under the intellectual influence of Rabbi Abraham Isaac Kook, the chief rabbi of Palestine and one of the prominent mystics of twentieth-century Judaism. He pursued higher education for a time in 1929 at the University of Berlin. In 1935 he emigrated from Poland to the United States, where he taught at the Rabbi Jacob Joseph School. In 1936 he joined the faculty of Yeshiva Rabbi Chaim Berlin in New York, and in 1939 he became its head (*rosh yeshiva*). In 1950 he founded and headed Kolel Gur Aryeh for advanced rabbinic studies, affiliated with Chaim Berlin. He headed these institutions, as well as their sister institution in Jerusalem, commuting between the United States and Israel until he settled in Israel in the late 1970s.

Hutner was an extraordinarily influential figure in the history of American Orthodox Judaism. His acknowledged mastery in Talmudic scholarship earned him a place among the most influential heads of yeshivot at a point in which these rabbinical academies were beginning to exercise a decisive influence on the direction of Orthodoxy toward a more stringent interpretation of *halakha* (Judaic law) as well as a more confrontational approach to non-Orthodox society. Through this, American Orthodoxy, which hitherto had developed largely in the direction of accommodation with American secular society and non-Orthodox Jews, began rejecting the ultimate legitimacy of that society and its values. He thus engaged in a trenchant criticism of Zionism, which had become a unifying factor within American and world Jewry. Also, perhaps influenced by the events of the Holocaust, he severely criticized Christianity in its historical and ideological relationship to Judaism. Although he himself had studied at a university, he did not think it desirable that ordinary people combine Judaic and secular study. He did not forbid secular study per se; however, in contradistinction to the point of view espoused by the Orthodox leader, Rabbi Joseph Baer Soloveitchik, he maintained that primary emphasis had to be placed on strengthening students against the intellectual challenges inherent in secular humanistic learning. He was able, moreover, to exercise a great influence on his many students due to the strength of his personality, which evoked fierce loyalty.

Hutner's thought combined hasidic as well as *mitnagdic* (nonhasidic) influences, thus bridging the two most powerful intellectual currents of the Orthodox Jewish world. The basis of his extensive writings was his analysis of Judaic law. These writings, however, contain as well a complicated admixture of philosophical and mystical, or kabbalistic, ideas. In this synthesis, it is possible to recognize the sixteenth-century rabbi Judah Loewe (Maharal) of Prague as an important intellectual influence on his thought.

Hutner published extensively on Judaic subjects. He is most famous for his collected discourses, which were originally issued anonymously, in pamphlet form, starting in 1945. Beginning in 1951, they were issued in his name in book form. Collectively titled *Pahad Yizhak*, these essays have been issued in thirteen volumes. They reflect his intellectual odyssey in both the hasidic and *mitnagdic* traditions and have served to spread his influence within the Orthodox Jewish community by providing an intellectually compelling apologia for traditional Orthodox Judaism. His writings are particularly known for their adumbration of the ideology of the yeshiva as well as their approach to the apparent contradictions between Torah and positivist philosophy, which, for Orthodox Jews, constitutes a potentially dangerous challenge to their faith.

Hutner died in Jerusalem.

• Hutner's earliest publication, *Torat ha-Nazir* (1932) was a commentary on Maimonides' codification of the Talmudic laws of the Nazirite. He later published a partial edition of the thirteenth century Hillel of Verona's commentary on the Tannaitic midrash *Sifra* (1938). This edition was somewhat expanded in *Kovez ha'arot le-Rabbenu Hillel* (1961). An extensive biographical sketch by a source close to the family is provided in Yosef Buksboim, ed., *Sefer ha-Zikkaron le-Maran Ba'al ha-Pahad Yitshak* (1983–1984). A more critical attempt at a biographical sketch may be found in Hillel Goldberg, "Rabbi Isaac Hutner: a Synoptic, Interpretive Biography," *Tradition* 22, no. 4 (Winter 1987): 18–46, and in his *Between Berlin and Slobodka: Jewish Transition Figures from Eastern Europe* (1989): 63–87. See also Steven Schwarzschild, "An Introduction to the Thought of R. Isaac Hutner,"

Modern Judaism 5 (1985): 235–77, and Schwarzschild's "Isaac Hutner" in *Interpreters of Judaism in the Late Twentieth Century*, ed. Steven T. Katz (1993). An analysis of his intellectual contribution to an understanding of the Holocaust can be found in Lawrence Kaplan, "Rabbi Isaac Hutner's 'Daat Torah Perspective' on the Holocaust: a Critical Analysis," *Tradition* 18, no. 3 (Fall 1980): 235–48. English translations of some of his lectures can be found in Steven Schwarzschild, "Two Lectures of Rabbi Isaac Hutner," *Tradition* 14, no. 4 (Fall 1979): 90–109, and Shalom Carmy, "Rav Yitzhak Hutner's Lecture to a Teachers' Conference," *Tradition* 19, no. 3 (Fall 1981): 218–26. An obituary is in the *Jewish Observer* 15, no. 10 (Dec. 1981): 7–15.

IRA ROBINSON

HUTTO, J. B. (26 Apr. 1926–12 June 1983), blues singer and guitarist, was born Joseph Benjamin Hutto in Elko, South Carolina, the son of Calvin Hutto and Susie Johnson, farmers. He spent his first three years on a farm but grew up primarily in Augusta, Georgia, where his family moved in 1929. Raised in a religious family, he and his siblings developed an early interest in spirituals, forming a family gospel group known as the Golden Crowns, which sang in two Augusta churches.

The family moved to Chicago sometime in the 1940s, and Hutto began working as a painter and plumber. Not yet twenty-one, he also began sneaking into clubs, he recalled later, to see blues artists such as Big Bill Broonzy, Memphis Minnie, and Memphis Slim. With his gospel experience, Hutto was comfortable as a vocalist and was soon singing and playing drums in a band led by Johnny Ferguson, a guitarist who played in what musicians called "Sebastapol" tuning—to an open D or E chord. Given a chance to play Ferguson's guitar during breaks, Hutto began to develop his own open-tuned slide style.

In the late 1940s Hutto put together a four-piece band, the Hawks, and began playing at house parties, which he called "basement jumps," and West Side taverns such as the 1015 Club and the Globetrotter Lounge in Chicago. In the early 1950s he married Lulubelle Wade Black. Although they had no children of their own, he helped raise her two children from a previous marriage and stayed with her the rest of his life. After a stint with the military during the Korean War, Hutto returned to the West Side tavern scene in 1954, and the following year he signed with Chance Records, a small Chicago label. Hutto and the Hawks recorded nine sides, six of which were issued, including "Now She's Gone," "Lovin' You," and the aggressively erotic "Pet Cream Man." Although Chance folded soon after their release, these initial 78-rpm records gave strong indication that Hutto was coming into his own as an artist. By the late 1950s, however, he was out of the music business—disillusioned by too many ten-dollar-a-night club bookings and an incident in which a club patron supposedly broke his guitar by using it to assault her husband.

After working as an undertaker for a time, Hutto moved to the city's South Side, and by the mid-1960s he had returned to music. Playing three nights a week with a new incarnation of the Hawks at Turner's Blue Lounge, Hutto came to the attention of three documentary record producers: Sam Charters, Pete Welding, and Robert Koester. In December 1965 he recorded several songs for Charters—works that eventually made their way on to volume one of the historically significant *Chicago/The Blues/Today* series on Vanguard. In June 1966 he teamed up with harmonica virtuoso Walter Horton, guitarists Johnny Young and Lee Jackson, and drummer Fred Below to record for Welding's Testament label. Six months later he recorded for Koester's Delmark label. Because of sound problems and illnesses, the Delmark session took two years to finish, but the resulting album was a critical success, helping to spread Hutto's name beyond the city's tavern circuit.

By 1969 Hutto was living in Harvey, Illinois, after touring in California, and was becoming a regular on the U.S. festival circuit and in blues/rock venues across the country. He led his first European tour in 1972. In 1975, after fellow Chicago slide guitarist Hound Dog Taylor died, Hutto took over Taylor's band, the Houserockers. Two years later he moved to Boston and formed yet another version of the Hawks. Despite an ongoing battle with diabetes, Hutto continued to tour and record through the late 1970s, working more and more with young, white sidemen. At the same time, he began teaching two teenage nephews, James Young and Ed Williams, to carry on his music. Diagnosed with cancer in the early 1980s, he moved back to Harvey, where he later died. Two years later he was inducted into the Blues Foundation's Hall of Fame in Memphis.

Although he was in his twenties before he began playing guitar, Hutto developed a slashing slide attack that was partly his own and partly derived from his most important influence, Elmore James. He also became a capable songwriter. For those who saw him in the late 1960s and early 1970s, though, Hutto is best remembered for his energetic showmanship. A small, seemingly shy man off the bandstand, he was transformed during performances into what author Bruce Cook described as a "roaring, howling Mr. Hyde, bigmouthing his blues in memorably earthy style" (Cook, p. 142). In midsong, he would sometimes lead his band in a near-religious procession around a club, working and reworking every last nuance from a musical groove. While Hutto was not a stylistic influence in the manner of Muddy Waters or Elmore James, his music was carried on by his newphew's group, Lil' Ed (Williams) and the Blues Imperials.

• For different accounts of Hutto's life and music, see Bruce Cook, *Listen to the Blues* (1973); Dan Forte, "J. B. Hutto," in *Blues Guitar: The Men Who Made the Music*, ed. Jas Obrecht (1990); Dave Weld, "Living Blues Interview: J. B. Hutto," *Living Blues* 30 (Nov.–Dec. 1976): 14–24; and Sheldon Harris, *Blues Who's Who: A Biographical Dictionary of Blues Singers* (1979; repr. 1989). An extensive discography is provided in Mike Leadbitter and Neil Slaven, *Blues Records 1943–1966: A Selective Discography*, vol. 1, *A–K* (1987), and Paul Oliver, ed., *The Blackwell Guide to Blues Records* (1989). For a representative sampling of his music, try *Hawk Squat*, Delmark DD617; *Slidewinder*, Delmark DD636; and *Slideslinger*, Varrick 003. For an obituary, see Weld, "J. B. Hutto," *Living Blues* 57 (Autumn 1983): 12–13.

BILL MCCULLOCH
BARRY LEE PEARSON

HUTTON, Barbara Woolworth (14 Nov. 1912–11 May 1979), socialite, was born in New York City, the daughter of Franklyn Laws Hutton, a stockbroker, and Edna Woolworth, the daughter of Frank Winfield Woolworth, founder of the first "five-and-dime" stores. Hutton was four when her mother died of what was recorded as a cerebral thrombosis but believed to be a suicide. Hutton was sent to live with her maternal grandparents until her grandfather's death in 1919. She spent the remainder of her adolescence shuttling between relatives, friends, and boarding schools. She graduated from Miss Porter's School for Girls in Farmington, Connecticut, in 1930 and made her debut into society that same year.

Hutton received an inheritance of millions from the estates of her grandfather and mother. At the age of six her yearly allowance was $5,000 and was substantially increased each year. By her twenty-first birthday, her allowance was $300,000 a year. Wealth earned her the nickname of "Poor Little Rich Girl," and her name became associated with the "baby" in the song "I Found a Million-Dollar Baby (in a Five and Ten Cent Store)." An aunt attempted to change Hutton's image by having her sing and dance at a charity carnival in 1932. Although her performance won praise, negative publicity continued.

In 1933 Hutton married Russian prince Alexis Mdivani, a man ten years her senior. Newspapers criticized her when she presented her new husband with a gift of $2.25 million. Always generous to her friends as well as to charities, Hutton established the annual "Princess Barbara Christmas Dinner" and contributed a thousand Christmas baskets to the poor, but her good deeds were buried in bad press. The public heard little about her deliveries of food and clothing to the children in India's hospitals and medical clinics.

During the depression years adverse publicity increased, especially when film loosely based on Hutton's life, *The Richest Girl in the World* (1934), was released. Americans living at poverty level followed newspaper accounts of her extravagant spending. A crowd of Woolworth workers confronted Hutton as she returned to New York from Europe with placards reading, "Babs, we live on $15.60 a week—could you?" Throughout the 1930s and 1940s similar pickets greeted Hutton upon her return trips to the United States. Lonely and suffering from bouts of depression, she often wrote poetry as a child and continued to do so as an adult. Her sentimental poems were a form of escape, and she carried them everywhere in a suitcase. Upon a friend's suggestion she had the poems privately published in a limited volume titled *The Enchanted* (1934). She published a second volume, *The Wayfarer*, in 1957.

Hutton's first of seven marriages ended in divorce in 1935. None of her subsequent marriages would be to American-born men or last longer than six years. She married for a second time in 1935 to Danish count Kurt Haugwitz-Reventlow, with whom she had her only child. In the days after her son's birth, Hutton became ill and nearly died. Grateful to have survived, she donated thousands to a number of British hospitals. Upon the advice of her husband, Hutton adopted Danish citizenship.

Divorced from the count in 1941, Hutton married actor Cary Grant in 1942. A photograph taken of the couple was widely reproduced, and the press dubbed them "Cash and Cary." In 1945 Hutton bought a house in Tangier, where she believed she would find "the peace and dignity I have sought all my life." In Tangier, Hutton demonstrated her generosity by sending checks to dozens of charitable and philanthropic organizations in the area in amounts between $1,000 and $50,000 and repeated the process each year. She established a soup kitchen that fed more than a thousand people each day. She and Grant were divorced in 1945.

Suffering from intestinal problems because of dieting, alcohol, sedatives, and painkillers, Hutton had numerous hospitalizations and operations after her marriage to Lithuanian prince Igor Toubetzkoy in 1947. The two divorced in 1951, and in 1953 she married Porfirio Rubirosa from the Dominican Republic. The marriage lasted for seventy-two days. In 1955 she married German tennis star Baron Gottfried von Cramm. In 1964 she was wed (for the final time) to Prince Raymond Doan Vinh Na Champacak, a Vietnamese chemist. They separated in 1966.

In the 1960s Hutton embarked on a philanthropic endeavor that would give her great satisfaction when she started a fellowship program that enabled poor children to attend the American School in Tangier. She built a dormitory to house the children and provided their clothing and access to all books, learning materials, tutors, and teachers. The program included children from the first to the twelfth grade, with a college education given to those who showed academic promise.

Always viewed by others as the "Poor Little Rich Girl," a title she despised, Hutton generously shared her wealth with friends. Many of her donations were given anonymously, and few acknowledged her generosity. During World War II she gave financial aid to the French underground. She gave money to help with cancer research, the New York City Mission Society, the American Red Cross, the Musicians Emergency Fund, the New York Foundling Hospital, the Metropolitan Museum of Art, the San Francisco Opera Company, and the New York City Restoration Fund. She funded scholarships to Bryn Mawr and Vassar. She contributed to a list of other "private" charities that were dedicated to helping women without funds or family.

A woman who lived life in extremes, Hutton sought to find an elusive happiness that she claimed money never brought. Her life was shrouded by tragedy and worsened by her own problems with addiction and depression. Often she threatened and made attempts to commit suicide. After the death of her son in 1972, and in the years before her own death, she lived a nearly reclusive existence. Although American by birth, her wealth alienated her from the American people, who more often commented on what they perceived as her debauchery than on her philanthropy. "It didn't matter what she did," a friend stated. "Everybody was very quick to criticize her." Hutton died from heart failure in Los Angeles, California.

• For biographical information see Dean Jennings, *Barbara Hutton: A Candid Biography* (1968); Sheilah Graham, *How to Marry Super Rich; or, Love, Money and the Morning After* (1974); Philip Van Rensselaer, *Million Dollar Baby: An Intimate Portrait of Barbara Hutton* (1979); C. David Heymann, *Poor Little Rich Girl: The Life and Legend of Barbara Hutton* (1984); and Kit Konolige, *The Richest Women in the World* (1985). Other information on Hutton can be found in Eleanor Harris, "The Sad Story of Barbara Hutton," *Look*, 27 July 1954, and Louise Tanner, *Here Today* (1959). An obituary appears in the *New York Times*, 13 May 1979.

MARILYN ELIZABETH PERRY

HUTTON, E. F. (7 Sept. 1875–11 July 1962), stockbroker, businessman, and syndicated columnist, was born Edward Francis Hutton in New York City, the son of farmer James Laws Hutton, an Ohioan who moved to New York to seek work. His mother's name is not known.

Hutton grew up in New York City and attended the New York Latin School before transferring to Public School 69. At the age of fifteen he dropped out of school to take a job as a "grease monkey" in the Diamond Truck & Car Gear Factory. Two years later he became a mail boy for a Wall Street firm but was terminated after a year because he failed to report to work for an extended time. He next worked for the Manhattan Trust Company as a check writer but resigned after his poor penmanship drew criticism from President John I. Waterbury. Yet the criticism furthered his career. Waterbury told young Hutton to enroll in school and to improve his writing. Hutton did exactly that: he took night courses at Packer's Business College and at one time also attended Trinity Chapel School.

With partners, in 1895 Hutton organized Harris, Hutton and Company, a brokerage firm, and for $375 bought a seat on New York's Consolidated Stock Exchange, one that dealt in odd lots. After the firm was dissolved in 1901, Hutton negotiated with an uncle, William E. Hutton, who was a broker in Cincinnati, Ohio. The uncle opened a New York branch of his firm, and young Hutton became resident partner and a member of the New York Stock Exchange. Just three years later the young man founded his own firm, E. F. Hutton and Company.

The new company grew rapidly as did Hutton's wealth. He bought memberships on at least six other regional stock exchanges, including those in Boston, Salt Lake City, and New Orleans, and on eighteen different commodity exchanges. Hutton's firm was the first to establish a securities wire to California. He remained as senior partner in the firm until 1921 when he became a limited partner, a post he held until his death. Meanwhile, his personal and business life converged. His first wife Blanche Horton died in 1918, and their only son died in 1920. That year, he married Marjorie Merriweather Post Close, heir of Postum Cereal Company's founder Charles W. Post. The couple had a daughter who achieved motion picture stardom as Dina Merrill.

In 1921 Hutton joined the Postum Cereal Company, becoming its unsalaried board chair two years later. Earlier he had learned that the company was undergoing a decline in sales, and he helped reverse that trend. Working with Colby M. Chester, the company's treasurer turned president, Hutton not only saved the company but expanded its organization by merging fifteen food and grocery manufacturers. Postum had evolved into the General Foods Corporation by 1929. Six years later Hutton and his second wife divorced, and he resigned his chairmanship of General Foods. A year later he married Dorothy Metzger; they had no children.

Hutton attracted much note in the 1930s for becoming an outspoken opponent of President Franklin D. Roosevelt's New Deal. Like many rich businessmen, he had no sympathy with the less fortunate people of the land and refused to consider any government aid programs to help them. He believed that the hopeless masses had to just "grin and bear it" until supposed natural economic "laws" restored the country's economic health. As an archenemy of any government regulation that limited the power of businessmen, he publicly criticized Roosevelt's policies and urged the American business community to "gang up" against the president and his New Dealers. He also began what was to be a continuing hallmark—he frequently placed full-page advertisements to promote laissez-faire free enterprise and to espouse his brand of patriotism. In 1949 he founded the Freedoms Foundation, a conservative institution dedicated to free market capitalism and "constitutionalism." The foundation, headquartered at Valley Forge, Pennsylvania, gave medals and other awards to individuals and groups that promoted "patriotic ideals," as defined by E. F. Hutton, who received the Wall Street American Legion's Bill of Rights gold medal in 1949 for his outspoken "patriotism."

In the 1950s Hutton continued to speak out against any program, policy, or individual that regulated business. From 1953 to 1960 he wrote a syndicated column, "Think It Through," that appeared in more than sixty newspapers, including the *New York Herald Tribune*. The column, of course, allowed Hutton to continue to damn big government and its "meddling" in private business affairs.

Concurrently continuing to manage his own business affairs, Hutton at various times in his career served in many posts: as board chair of Zonite Products and as board director for the Manufacturers Hanover Trust Company, Chrysler Corporation, and Coca-Cola.

Hutton believed in living the good life, and one of his passions was sailing. He owned several crafts, including a four-masted Hussar yacht that was 322 feet long and required a crew of seventy. His winter home was in fashionable Palm Beach, Florida. He also held memberships in a variety of social and sports clubs.

Although the Wall Street firm he founded would eventually fail, the failure came many years after Hutton had retired from the firm. E. F. Hutton himself was an American success story. Rising from relative poverty, he became one of the country's best known and wealthiest businessmen. He died at his home in Westbury, Long Island, New York.

• A biographical and career profile appears in the *New Yorker*, 6 July 1958. A work that gives excellent coverage of Hutton and the growth of his financial empire is Mark Stevens, *Sudden Death: The Rise and Fall of E. F. Hutton* (1989). Also useful are Hurd Baruch, *Wall Street: Security Risk* (1971), and Robert Sobel, *The Big Board: A History of the New York Stock Market* (1965). Both have interesting sections on Hutton. *White Collar Crime* (1987), released by the U.S. Senate Committee on the Judiciary, documents the fall of Hutton's company. An obituary is in the *New York Times*, 12 July 1962.

JAMES M. SMALLWOOD

HUTTON, Ina Ray (13 Mar. 1916–19 Feb. 1984), bandleader, was born Odessa Cowan in Chicago, Illinois. Her parents' names and occupations are unknown. She began her career as a child tap dancer with the Gus Edwards revue at the Palace in New York City. In 1934 she moved to Broadway, where she performed as a dancer and chorus girl in Lew Leslie's *Clowns in Clover*, George White's *Melody*, and the *Ziegfeld Follies*. Recognizing the commercial potential of an all-woman swing band, producer Irving Mills chose Hutton that same year to lead musicians in a band that became known as Ina Rae Hutton and the Melodears (some sources spell her middle name Rae).

Hutton initially was not an accomplished musician, but she was chosen as the bandleader because of her glamorous appearance and sex appeal—characteristics that subsequently came to epitomize female bandleaders. In the early months of rehearsals, reed player Audrey Hall set the tempos for the group, and Hutton simply held the baton. According to *Variety*, however, Hutton "spelled box office forward and backward," and the Melodears were successful almost immediately. Hutton became known as the "Blonde Bombshell of Rhythm" and soon embodied the stereotype of the female bandleader of the 1930s.

The original Hutton band included trumpeters Kay Walsh, Estelle Slavin, and Elvirah Rohl; trombonists Ruth McMurray and Althea Heuman (also known as Althea Conley); reed players Ruth Bradley, Betty Sticht, Helen Ruth, and Hall; pianists Jerrine Hyde and Miriam Greenfield; guitarist Helen Baker; bassist Marie Lebz; and drummer Lil Singer. The acclaimed talents of the following women were added later: pianists Gladys Mosier, Betty Roudybush, Ruth Lowe (writer of the hit song "I'll Never Smile Again"), and Marguerite Rivers (who also plucked a string bass); guitarist Marian Gange; and reed players Evelyn Healm, Mildred Wilhelm, Betty Scittley, and Nadine Friedman. Also among the personnel were trombonist Alsye Wills, a former Chicago Women's Symphony member, who is documented as playing more than twenty instruments and touring with Tommy Dorsey; and Virginia Mayers, who played trumpet, drums, saxophone, guitar, and clarinet.

Pianist and composer Alex Hill did the arrangements for the Hutton band; he also was an arranger for Fats Waller, Andy Kirk, and Benny Carter. By 1936 the band reorganized and Eddie Durham became band manager and arranger. After three weeks of rehearsals under Durham's guidance, the band played first at the Paramount Theater in Newark, New Jersey, before opening at the Paramount in New York City. (It is documented that Durham often stood offstage giving tempos to the band until Hutton would make her usual grand entrance later in the program.) The band was a huge hit. Though the majority of female musicians of that period had few opportunities to record, the Hutton band, promoted by the Irving Mills agency, did considerable recording.

The Melodears comprised white women musicians perhaps with, some researchers believe, a few African-American women who were passed off as Asian or East Indian during these years of segregation. Following the success at the New York Paramount, the Melodears went on to enjoy other triumphs. They were featured in various films, including *The Big Broadcast of 1937* (1935; also known as *The Big Broadcast of 1936*), *Ever Since Venus* (1944), *Melodies and Models*, *Club Hutton*, and *Feminine Rhythm*. They also played in film shorts, which generally adhered to the formula of one instrumental number, followed by a "novelty" rendition, ending the set with another upbeat instrumental piece. These shorts include *Accent on Girls* (1936) and *Swing, Hutton, Swing* (1937).

During performances Hutton would wave her baton and tap dance her way around the stage. She became known for her six costume changes a night, and her stage wardrobe, which was reported to have included over four hundred gowns, became legendary. With her salary drawn from the Melodears, Hutton bought out Mills's share in the band in 1939. Without the band's association with the Mills agency, it was unable to survive financially. When it dissolved later in 1939, Hutton put together an "all-male" unit, with the press reporting that she was "tired" of female musicians. This band continued working until the end of World War II.

In 1949 Hutton returned to the all-woman format, organizing a more commercially oriented fourteen-piece band to fit into the relatively new medium of television. It was featured in its own weekly hour-long program on WKLA in Los Angeles. Meanwhile, she changed her "Blonde Bombshell" image by going from platinum to brunette. In 1955 she revived the "all-girl" film format with *Girl Time*. A year later she appeared with a fifteen-piece women's band on an NBC national television show that failed to become a regular series. Although in 1960 she began a five-piece male band, Hutton soon retired, moving to California as the wife of Randy Brooks, an industrial tool and electronics manufacturer. She died in Ventura, California.

When once asked about the role of women in jazz, Hutton replied, "For some reason, the formation of a girl band today is regarded by everyone as an unusual achievement. It is true that the formation of any kind of a successful band is quite a job, but I am very happy in the realization that I am a member of one group which has played its way into a state of popular approval. . . . Jazz is here and in swing, presents a formidable job for anyone to put over correctly. But putting it over is well within the capabilities of the fairer members of the human tribe, and wherever music goes when it develops away from swing, the girls will have little trouble accompanying it" (Placksin, p. 98).

• The New York Public Library for the Performing Arts, Lincoln Center, has a Hutton file. For additional biographical information see Charles Garrod, *Ina Ray and Her Orchestra* (1989). Useful secondary sources that focus on women musicians are Linda Dahl, *Stormy Weather: The Music and Lives of a Century of Jazzwomen* (1989), pp. 49–51, and Sally Placksin, *American Women in Jazz, 1900 to the Present* (1982), pp. 95–98. Other general sources include Walter Bruyninckx, *Sixty Years of Recorded Jazz, 1917–1977* (1980), pp. H851–52, and Barry Kernfeld, ed., *New Grove Dictionary of Jazz* (1988), pp. 549–50. See also "Ina Ray Hutton Comes Up the Hard Way from Queen of Burlesque to Sophisticate," *New York World Telegram*, 16 Sept. 1940.

NANETTE DE JONG

HUXLEY, Aldous (6 July 1894–22 Nov. 1963), author, was born Aldous Leonard Huxley near Godalming, Surrey, England, the son of Leonard Huxley, a schoolmaster and editor, and Julia Arnold, a schoolmistress. Grandson of Thomas Henry Huxley and grandnephew of Matthew Arnold, Huxley came from an intellectual class to whom critical thinking and education were of primary importance. He was educated at home and at Eton. In 1911, his last year at Eton, he was struck by an inflammation of the cornea and left almost entirely blind. This blindness destroyed his plans for being a scientist but paradoxically contributed to making him a writer.

Some sight gradually returned, and in 1913 Huxley entered Balliol College, Oxford. Using a magnifying glass, he read a great deal, wrote verse, and translated French poetry. His sight was poor the rest of his life, but he saw enough to read omnivorously and to build up an almost universal expertise. In 1916 he left Oxford with an honors degree in English literature.

Although, because of his blindness, Huxley could not serve, World War I led him to pacifism. That pacifism, philosophical and not religious, created political difficulties; it was, for instance, essentially the cause of his being refused American citizenship.

Huxley married Maria Nys, a Belgian war refugee, in 1919. They had one child. His wife was invaluable to him in that she could and did take care of practical matters. But by this time Huxley had succeeded in establishing himself as a writer. He was extraordinarily productive all his life, writing poetry, drama, essays, travel books, and defenses of eye exercises and of pacifism, as well as novels, history, biography, and works on mysticism—in part because he had to write in order to make a living.

In 1921 he published his first novel, *Crome Yellow*, which was followed by *Antic Hay* in 1923 and *Those Barren Leaves* in 1925. These novels satirize the emptiness of upper-class British life with a rather bitter wit. Huxley was recognized as one of the important new novelists, although he himself admitted that he was "one who is not congenitally a novelist" but was, rather, "some sort of an essayist sufficiently ingenious to get away with writing a very limited kind of fiction" (*Letters*, pp. 538, 525).

In 1928 he published *Point Counter Point*, considered by many critics to be his finest novel, although it too suffers from being more about ideas than about life. Certainly neither story nor character was ever very important to Huxley's fiction. In *Point* every one of the characters is a representative of an attitude toward existence. Philip Quarles is based on Huxley himself, an intellectual uncertain of what he believes in. But it is D. H. Lawrence, serving as the model for the artist Mark Rampion, with his rejection of bodiless intellect or one-sided commitment, who is central to the values presented by the novel. However, in the end, even this novel is negative, in that Rampion too is limited.

In *Do What You Will*, a collection of essays published in 1929, Huxley stated that "the purpose of life, outside the mere continuance of living (already a most noble and beautiful end), is the purpose we put into it; its meaning is whatever we may choose to call the meaning." But simply "giving meaning" is an act of will, a kind of relativism. During the 1920s he was regarded as a cynical observer of modern life; he later said that he had rejected meaning, but that this rejection was in a sense necessary in order to get rid of old beliefs.

Huxley published *Brave New World*, probably his best-known work, in 1932. This novel, with its dark vision of a future utopia-dystopia, is the expression of Huxley's disbelief that social engineering can cure human ills. More and more he emphasized that change and significance begin with the searching individual. "Good," he later proclaimed, "is a product of the ethical and spiritual artistry of individuals; it cannot be mass-produced" (*Collected Essays*, p. 247). He was politically a pacifist-anarchist, opposed to the overwhelming state but also to any coercive political movement, no matter what its aims.

During his early travels Huxley had visited the United States and had reacted disparagingly to its materialism. However, with war threatening in Europe and needing a climate warmer than England's, in 1937 he came to the United States on a lecture tour and remained, finally settling in southern California, where he stayed the rest of his life. He began writing for the movies as well as producing more books of essays and novels, among them *After Many a Summer Dies the Swan* (1939), which satirizes the longings for immortality on the part of the powerful.

More important, in California he became interested in the religious ideas of the East. Huxley was never a rigid follower of Eastern thought or religious practices, but he believed that such thought gave insights into the ultimate ground of being. In his later years he experimented with hallucinogenic drugs as a means of achieving mystical insight, suggesting they were a shorthand way of arriving at those insights. His works, such as *The Perennial Philosophy* (1945), which he defined as "the highest common factor of all the highest religions" (*Letters*, p. 514), began to reflect his apparently new attitudes, although long before he himself had denied the material world as the only object of knowledge. That same year he wrote that "it was through the aesthetic that I came to the spiritual—having begun by rejecting the spiritual in favour of the aesthetic" (*Letters*, p. 538).

Huxley also composed biographical and historical works, among them *Grey Eminence: A Study in Religion and Politics* (1941) and *The Devils of Loudun* (1952), both of which suggest that the search for power is the opposite of the true religious life. In 1962 he published *Island*, a novel that, though it ends in violence, is a response to his own *Brave New World*, for it suggests that humankind is capable of creating the ideal society.

After his first wife's death in 1954, Huxley married Laura Archera in 1956. They had no children. He died in Los Angeles.

Although Huxley's reputation sank after his death, the political insights of *Brave New World* kept his name alive. His writings on religious mysticism also have been continually popular.

• Because of a house fire in 1969, most of Huxley's personal papers were lost. Material on Huxley can be found in the British Library, the New York Public Library, the University of California at Los Angeles Library, and at the University of Texas. A good introduction to Huxley's essays is his *Collected Essays* (1959). His other novels include *Eyeless in Gaza* (1936), *Time Must Have a Stop* (1944), and *Ape and Essence* (1948), a cautionary tale on the dangers of the atomic age. The most complete biography is Sybille Bedford, *Aldous Huxley* (2 vols., 1973–1974). Useful is *Letters of Aldous Huxley*, ed. Grover Smith (1969). For Huxley's enormous bibliography, see Claire John Eschelbach and Joyce Lee Shober, *Aldous Huxley: A Bibliography, 1916–1959* (1961), and Thomas D. Clareson and Carolyn S. Andrews, "Aldous Huxley: A Bibliography, 1960–1964," *Extrapolation* 6, no. 1 (1964–1965): 2–21. An obituary is in the *New York Times*, 24 Nov. 1963.

L. L. LEE

HYATT, Alpheus (5 Apr. 1838–15 Jan. 1902), paleontologist and marine biologist, was born in Washington, D.C., the son of Alpheus Hyatt, a wealthy merchant, and Harriet Randolph King. He spent a year at Yale College and another year in Rome before completing his college education at Harvard (B.S., 1862, summa cum laude); there he began his study of marine fossils under the influence of Louis Agassiz. From 1862 until 1865 he served the 47th Massachusetts Volunteer Infantry during the Civil War. After the war he settled in Salem, Massachusetts, where in 1867 he was appointed curator of the Essex Institute, the first of his many administrative and leadership roles. That same year Hyatt married Ardella Beebe of Kinderhook, New York, who bore him four children. Also in 1867, Hyatt joined with his former classmates Alpheus S. Packard, Frederic W. Putnam, and Edward S. Morse to found both the Peabody Academy of Sciences, located in Salem, and the *American Naturalist*, the first and oldest biology journal in the United States; Hyatt served as its first editor (1867–1871).

In 1870 Hyatt moved to Boston, where he served the Boston Society of Natural History as one of its custodians from 1870 to 1881 and as its curator from 1881 to 1902. He also started and directed a program run by this society to educate schoolteachers in the sciences, for which he published a series of short educational pamphlets. He taught zoology and paleontology at the Massachusetts Institute of Technology (1870–1888) and at Boston University (1877–1902). During this time he conducted his research work at Harvard's Museum of Comparative Zoology, spending his summers collecting and studying marine animals along the New England coast. With the help of the Women's Educational Society of Boston, he founded a natural-history laboratory at Annisquam on Cape Ann in 1879. In 1888 this laboratory was moved to Woods Hole, Massachusetts, and incorporated as the Marine Biological Laboratory, with Hyatt as first president of its board of trustees.

At Harvard Hyatt was responsible for organizing the collection of fossil and recent mollusks, especially the cephalopods (squids and their relatives, including the extinct ammonoids). From 1889 on he also served as paleontologist to the U.S. Geological Survey. In recognition of his achievements, Hyatt was elected to membership in the American Academy of Arts and Sciences and the National Academy of Sciences. He continued his teaching and research activities until his death in Cambridge, Massachusetts.

Hyatt studied a variety of marine invertebrate groups, including the sponges, bryozoans, brachiopods, trilobites, echinoids, and mollusks, always from an evolutionary perspective. He is best known for his researches on cephalopods and for the evolutionary theories which grew out of his cephalopod studies. He insisted on studying large samples and on paying attention to individual variation and to the shell, which documented the earlier growth stages of each individual. Beginning with his earliest publication on cephalopods in 1866, Hyatt emphasized the parallelism between individual growth and the succession of species through the fossil record. This comparison between embryology and geological succession had already been noted by Louis Agassiz and Johann Meckel, and it later became the basis for Ernst Haeckel's theory of recapitulation, best known from the aphorism, "Ontogeny recapitulates phylogeny"—embryological development summarizes the previous history of the species. Hyatt took this idea to its logical extreme in his theory of racial senescence or "racial old age," in which he proposed that each evolving lineage has a period of youth marked by increased variation, a period of maturity marked by steady progress without further diversity, and a period of senescence ending in extinction.

Hyatt also theorized about the nature of evolutionary sequences, but he was unwilling to accept Darwin's concept of natural selection. Elaborating on the parallelism between embryological and geological sequences, Hyatt taught that evolution consisted of the addition of adult adaptations to the terminal stage of an existing embryological series, thus extending the series. In order for development to take place within a reasonable time, Hyatt argued in 1866, the earlier embryological stages must be compressed in time and thus speeded up. This "acceleration of growth" was a common theme shared by a number of Hyatt's contemporaries, particularly Edward D. Cope (who independently published similar ideas the same year Hyatt did) and Alpheus S. Packard.

Together, these three scientists were influential in editing and promoting the *American Naturalist* during its early years, and they formed the nucleus of an American school of neo-Lamarckism. As part of their explanation of the manner in which new adult adaptations would be inherited and incorporated into the developmental sequence, Hyatt and the others of this neo-Lamarckian school relied on the concept of use-inheritance, often called the "inheritance of acquired characteristics." In his famous studies on fossil cephalopods Hyatt described several "acquired characteristics" that first appeared in the shell structure of ammonoids as new or altered growth stages; he offered the evolution of these traits in support of neo-Lamarckian theory. Although he admitted that evolution was sometimes a branching process, Hyatt more often emphasized the unbranching linear sequences that formed the basis for the later theory of orthogenesis, which flourished briefly around the turn of the twentieth century. In common with these theories of orthogenesis, and in contrast to Lamarck's original theory, Hyatt came to support the possibility of nonadaptive evolutionary sequences. Indeed, he argued that his theory of racial senescence required that each lineage would ultimately degenerate into a "racial old age" marked by a loss of adult adaptations and a return to the simple appearance of its earlier embryonic stages. This extreme version of Hyatt's theory never attracted any significant following, but it was responsible for one of his rare speculations on human evolution. Late in his life Hyatt argued that any increase in similarity between men and women, in either behavior or morphology, would represent a type of degeneration foreshadowing racial senility and ultimately extinction.

• Harvard's Museum of Comparative Zoology and University Archives, Cambridge, Mass., has a large collection of Hyatt's works (including autograph copies) and his correspondence with other naturalists. Other papers are in the Special Collections Library, Syracuse University. Correspondence between Hyatt and Alfred Marshall Mayer is in Princeton University Library. Hyatt's correspondence with Charles Darwin is published in *More Letters of Charles Darwin*, vol. 1 (1903). Hyatt's contributions to evolutionary biology are summarized readably by Peter Bowler in two books, *The Eclipse of Darwinism* (1983) and *Evolution: The History of an Idea* (1984). Hyatt's theory of racial senescence is discussed in Stephen Jay Gould, *Ontogeny and Phylogeny* (1977). Contemporary memorials included Alpheus Packard, *American Academy of Arts and Sciences* (1903); W. K. Brooks, National Academy of Sciences, *Biographical Memoirs* 6 (1909): 311–25; and Robert T. Jackson, *American Naturalist* 47 (1913): 195–205.

Hyatt's voluminous writings include "On the Parallelism between the Different Stages of Life in the Individual and Those in the Entire Group of the Molluscous Order Tetrabranchiata," *Memoirs of the Boston Society of Natural History* 1 (1866): 193–209; "Sponges Considered as a Distinct Sub-Kingdom of Animals," *Proceedings of the Boston Society of Natural History* 19 (1876): 12–17; "The Genesis of the Tertiary Species of *Planorbis* at Steinheim," *Anniversary Memoir of the Boston Society of Natural History* (1880), pp. 1–114; "Evolution of the Cephalopods," *Science* 3 (1884): 122–27, 145–49; "Genesis of the Arietidae," *Memoirs of the Museum of Comparative Zoology* 16 (1889): 1–238; "Phylogeny of an Acquired Characteristic," *Proceedings of the American Philosophical Society* 32 (1893): 349–647; "Cycle in the Life of the Individual (Ontogeny) and in the Evolution of Its Own Group (Phylogeny)," *Proceedings of the American Academy of Arts and Sciences* 32 (1897): 209–24; and "The Influence of Woman in the Evolution of the Human Race," *Natural Science* 11 (1897): 89–93. Hyatt's last contribution, "The Triassic Cephalopod Genera of America," *U.S. Geological Survey Professional Paper*, no. 40, pp. 1–394 (with James P. Smith), appeared posthumously in 1905. An obituary is in the *New York Times*, 16 Jan. 1902.

ELI C. MINKOFF

HYATT, John Wesley (28 Nov. 1837–10 May 1920), inventor, was born in Starkey, New York, the son of John Wesley Hyatt, a blacksmith, and Anne Gleason. His education in ordinary schools was supplemented by one year at the Eddystone Seminary. At the age of sixteen Hyatt moved to Illinois, where he took up his first trade as a printer. It was perhaps in this work that he could begin to display some of his considerable abilities as a mechanic.

After working in Albany, New York, as a journeyman printer in the mid-1860s, Hyatt embarked on the inventive career that was to be his life's work. Attracted by the advertisement of a New York City billiards supplier offering $10,000 to the developer of an effective substitute for the increasingly expensive ivory used in billiard balls, Hyatt sought to devise a composition that could be molded into the hard, perfect spheres. The approaches he brought to this challenge were not especially novel, consisting largely of fillers like bone, wood, and ivory dust bound with shellac. The effort, however, directed his attention to the kinds of products that could be made from these materials and manipulated in presses initially not too unlike those of his chosen profession. The result was the establishment of the Embossing Company of Albany, in which he recruited the assistance of his two brothers. In 1869 he married Anna E. Taft; they had two children.

Continued experiments on billiard balls brought Hyatt into contact with collodion, a substance then in use for photography and medical dressings. Collodion was made of nitrated cotton (or some other vegetable fiber) dissolved in alcohol and ether, and in ordinary use a thin application would dry to a thin, transparent film. The flexibility and smoothness of the dried collodion led Hyatt to experiment with ways to turn it into a solid, plastic mass. Not the first to pursue this path to making a generally useful plastic, Hyatt ran into the same problems that had bedeviled experimenters such as Alexander Parkes as much as a decade earlier, especially the difficulty of ridding the collodion of its volatile solvents without leaving the resulting substance a shapeless, brittle mass.

Hyatt admitted in later patent litigation that he had encountered the use of camphor as a solvent of nitrocellulose in the literature, but he insisted that his approach for mixing the two materials to make a solid, plastic, and stable material was truly novel. By combining thorough mixtures of nitrocellulose and camphor under moderate heat and pressure, with just enough alcohol to soften the mixture, Hyatt was able to produce a material that was easily colored and molded, took desirable decorative effects (such as tortoiseshell, mother-of-pearl, or ivory), and maintained its form and surface with only a modicum of care. The most fundamental of Hyatt's patents on nitrocellulose plastics was issued on 12 July 1870 (U.S.P. 105,338).

While the new material made no better billiard balls than earlier substances had, this did not stop Hyatt and his elder brother, Isaiah Smith Hyatt, from attempting to exploit their invention for other uses. The elder Hyatt is credited with coining the name "celluloid," and the Celluloid Manufacturing Company was organized in Albany in early 1871. Substantial commercial operations did not begin, however, until late 1872, when the recruitment of significantly more capital (supplied by the new company president, Marshall Lefferts) allowed the construction of a factory in the Ironbound district of Newark, New Jersey. There the celluloid makers proceeded slowly to develop the promise of their new material, promoting such applications as knife handles, combs and brushes, and collars and cuffs.

John Wesley Hyatt's role in the company extended little beyond the technical. Between 1869 and 1891 he received over sixty patents related to celluloid's manufacturing and fabrication (eleven of them for collar and cuff making alone). His inventions were largely mechanical, not chemical, for both Hyatt's talents and the needs of the emerging industry were in the realm of machinery for pressing, extruding, molding, and otherwise shaping or decorating the new plastic. Hyatt, often with Isaiah by his side, pursued a variety of other interests in the following decades, tackling technical problems that seemed susceptible to the efforts of a persistent and ingenious mechanic and also held out the promise of genuine financial reward. Through much of the 1880s, the Hyatt brothers concerned themselves with developing techniques for water purification, developing processes that came to be applied both in urban water systems and in industry. Next came the development of new processes and machinery for sugar refining, which in turn led to the other key invention still associated with Hyatt's name, the flexible roller bearing.

While the idea of ball bearings had been around for several centuries, it was not until the vigorous growth of the bicycle industry, beginning in the 1870s, that bearing design came to be a subject of widespread mechanical interest. Hyatt's work in the 1880s with heavy machinery for crushing sugar cane directed his attention to the problem of reducing friction on rotating machinery. His solution to the problem was the flexible roller bearing, in which the rollers were made from flat spring steel wound into helices. The principle of such a design was to allow the bearing to bend and slip without breaking under stress or shock. His primary patents for the invention were U.S.P. 485,938 (1891) and 487,530 (1892).

The Hyatt Roller-Bearing Company was organized in Harrison, New Jersey, in 1892 and proceeded on a small scale to develop a specialized business, supplying the new bearings to makers of heavy industrial machinery, such as traveling cranes and paper mills. Hyatt remained general manager of the company until 1899, but the inability to secure larger markets for the product made the company's future less than bright. At this point, Hyatt stepped aside to make way for a young MIT electrical engineering graduate, Alfred P. Sloan. The 24-year-old Sloan targeted the new automobile industry as the outlet for the Hyatt bearing's future resulting in great commercial success for the company. By this time, Hyatt had moved on to other things, continuing his work as a professional inventor. He devised heavy-duty sewing machines for making machine belting, experimented with machinery for straightening steel shafting, and returned to improvements on sugar-milling equipment. Another problem to which he returned, and which seemed to hold a lifelong fascination for him, was billiard balls. In a Newark factory set up in 1908, he kept his hand in billiard ball manufacture until the end of his life, constantly seeking improvements both in materials and in machinery. At first relying on ground ivory mixed under pressure with celluloid, he enthusiastically adopted the new phenolic plastic, bakelite, when it first became available in 1909. The readiness with which the 71-year-old Hyatt could take up the novel material, at the expense of celluloid, the invention most closely associated with his life's work, was striking to contemporaries.

Extant portraits of Hyatt show an elderly man, balding, with full white beard and strikingly bright blue-gray eyes. He was animated in conversation and always ready to discuss new ideas. He strayed from the strict Methodism of his upbringing both in thought and habits, going so far as to adopt the practice of consuming a half-bottle of champagne for lunch every day, to ward off consumption, he claimed. He died in Short Hills, New Jersey.

• Only brief assessments of Hyatt have been written. The most useful of these are P. W. Bishop, "John Wesley Hyatt and the Discovery of Celluloid," *Plastics World*, Oct. 1968, pp. 30–38; Charles F. Chandler, "Presentation Address," *Journal of Industrial and Engineering Chemistry* 6 (Feb. 1914): 156–58; and Robert Friedel, *Pioneer Plastic: The Making and Selling of Celluloid* (1983). Further technical information about Hyatt's inventions can be found in Edward C. Worden, *Nitrocellulose Industry* (1911), and Hudson T. Morton, *Anti-Friction Bearings* (1954). Obituaries are in the *New York Times*, *Newark Evening News*, and *Newark Star-Eagle*, all 11 May 1920.

ROBERT FRIEDEL

HYDE, Edward (1661–1723). *See* Cornbury, Viscount.

HYDE, Edward (1667–8 Sept. 1712), proprietary governor of North Carolina, was the son of Robert Hyde and Phillis (or Felice) Sneyd, who lived at "Norbury Manor" and "Hyde Manor" in Cheshire County, England. The Hyde family had been landed gentry for centuries. Edward Hyde was orphaned by the age of three, and he and his two sisters were raised by their grandmother Anne Brooke Hyde. In 1683 Hyde entered Christ Church College, Oxford, but did not complete a degree. His youth was clouded by financial burdens resulting from heavy fines levied by Charles II on Hyde's grandfather, Edward Hyde, who had supported Oliver Cromwell during the Civil War. Hyde eventually had to sell Norbury Manor and other property around 1690 to settle his debts, and he never seemed able to regain economic security. In 1708 he feared "utter ruine" from the "very deplorable condition" of his finances. He married Catherine Rigby in 1692; they had four children.

Hyde's public career was propelled by his relationship to the Stuart monarchs Mary II and Anne through a common ancestor, Robert Hyde. The queens were the granddaughters of Edward Hyde, first earl of Clarendon, who was an original lord proprietor of Carolina and lord chancellor under Charles II. Possibly as a consequence of his financial insecurity, Edward Hyde of Hyde Manor sought royal patronage through his cousin Lawrence Hyde, first earl of Rochester, a leading Tory. An uncle of Queen Anne, the earl influenced her to appoint Hyde provost marshal of Jamaica in 1702. Hyde found that the position generated little income, primarily because the deputies in Jamaica would not release the fees. In 1708 the queen supported Hyde's petition to be named governor of Carolina. This position had been filled recently by Colonel Edward Tynte, but the deputy governorship of northern Carolina was open. Early in 1709 the proprietors authorized Tynte to appoint Hyde to this post.

The Hyde family and their servants arrived in Virginia in August 1710 and were greeted with ceremony at the capital in Williamsburg by Governor Alexander Spotswood. There Hyde learned to his dismay that Governor Tynte had died and that he could not be commissioned deputy governor. His position was further complicated by continuing political turmoil in northern Carolina. The colony was virtually split between Anglicans and dissenters, who were primarily Quakers. By 1708 Thomas Cary, who was supported by the dissenters, had forced his chief rival, William Glover, to flee to Virginia. Hyde was in a position to mediate the dispute, but his uncertain authority simply added to the confusion. Hyde's reputation based on his relationship to the queen, and the known intent of the proprietors to appoint him governor eventually led Cary to acquiesce to Hyde's becoming president of the council or acting governor until further instructions were received from the proprietors. The Hydes now entered Carolina, settling on the William Duckenfield plantation on Salmon Creek west of the Chowan River.

Hyde took office on 22 January 1711 in a potentially volatile setting. The bitterness of the division between his followers and Cary called for a skilled diplomatic hand, but Hyde did not possess the political acumen to curb the vengeance of his Anglican supporters. The new council and assembly soon voided previous acts and challenged the legality of Cary's former government. A strengthened vestry act also threatened the security of the dissenters by bolstering the Anglican establishment. Finally, the arrest and impeachment of Cary and John Porter, Sr., touched off an armed conflict now known as the Cary Rebellion. Cary gathered his supporters at a fortified plantation in Bath County. Discovering that Cary's position was too strong to take by available force, Hyde withdrew into the Albemarle Sound and withstood Cary's attack. On an appeal from Hyde, Governor Spotswood sent marines and a warship to his aid, and this show of royal force finished the rebellion. Cary was arrested in Virginia for treason, sent to England for protracted hearings, but finally was released for lack of evidence.

On the heels of the rebellion came the Tuscarora War, the most devastating Indian war in the history of the colony. Alarmed by settlers on the Neuse and Pamlico rivers near the heart of the Tuscarora Indian country, the Tuscarora took the opportunity provided by division among the English to eradicate the new settlements. On 22 September 1711, during a yellow fever epidemic and a prolonged summer drought, the Tuscarora and their allies attacked without warning, killing hundreds of colonists and ravaging Bath County. To meet the common enemy, Hyde appointed Thomas Pollock to command the militia and pushed for passage of a militia draft act and an act issuing £4000 of currency to meet the war expenses. His request for help from the neighboring colonies brought an expedition from South Carolina led by John Barnwell. In January 1712 Barnwell defeated the Tuscarora with some local support and negotiated a truce with their leader, King Hancock. When the North Carolina Assembly rejected the unauthorized truce and refused to pay Barnwell's expenses, Barnwell enslaved his captives and returned home. The outraged Tuscarora resumed the conflict.

To alleviate the confusion in Hyde's status as governor, the Lords Proprietors decided to eliminate the position of deputy governor; accordingly, on 24 January 1712 they appointed Hyde as the first governor of North Carolina. His commission arrived on 9 May 1712. The governor now sought to rally the colony to continue the war by taking personal command of the campaign. In the middle of preparations for a punitive expedition into Tuscarora country, Hyde succumbed to yellow fever at his home on Albemarle Sound. The war was concluded successfully by Thomas Pollock, who was named president of the council. Hyde was buried on his plantation, and Catherine Hyde returned to England the next year. She later lived in New York with her daughter Anne and son-in-law George Clarke, who was lieutenant governor and acting governor of that colony. A copy of a portrait of Governor Hyde is on display in the North Carolina Museum of History.

Edward Hyde's significance rests on his twenty months as governor of North Carolina. Considering that he was for the first sixteen months undermined by his ambiguous position as acting governor without proprietary authority, Hyde did quite well in successfully resolving two of the most significant crises of the proprietary period—the Cary Rebellion and the Tuscarora War. Although his uncertain position may explain his initial vacillation during the rebellion, he rallied support from within and without the colony to defeat Cary. His decisive intervention especially in the second phase of the Tuscarora War helped to bring the conflict to a close at the time of his death. Entering a colony torn by internal political strife, Hyde in less than two years established a government that would remain relatively stable for the remainder of the proprietary period and laid the groundwork for the colony's economic growth.

• Hyde's official papers are in Cecil Headlam, ed., *The Calendar of State Papers, Colonial Series, America and West Indies* (1922–1926); William S. Price, Jr., ed., *North Carolina Higher-Court Records, 1709–1723* (1974); and William L. Saunders, ed., *The Colonial Records of North Carolina, 1709–1723*, vols. 1 and 2 (1886). The most informative biographical study is Rebecca Swindell and Norman H. Turner, *Edward Hyde: Governor of North Carolina, 1710–1711* (1977). Also of value for background are George Ormerod, *The History of the County Palatine and City of Cheshire*, vol. 3 (1882); Thomas Parramore, "The Tuscarora Ascendency," *North Carolina Historical Review* 59 (Oct. 1982): 307–26; Steven J. White, "From the Vestry Act to Cary's Rebellion: North Carolina Quakers and Colonial Politics," *Southern Friend* 8 (Autumn 1986): 3–26; and Vincent H. Todd, ed., *Christoph von Graffenried's Account of the Founding of New Bern* (1920).

LINDLEY S. BUTLER

HYDE, Henry Baldwin (15 Feb. 1834–2 May 1899), insurance company founder and father of modern life insurance, was born in Catskill, New York, the son of Henry Hazen Hyde, a storekeeper, and Lucy Baldwin Beach. The boy quickly demonstrated unusual intellectual powers but, because his mother was sickly, often was lonely. In 1849 or 1850 his widowed father read a recruiting brochure for life insurance agents, moved his family to Pennsylvania, and became an agent for the Mutual Life Insurance Company, the most successful life insurer in the country. Hyde, only sixteen, soon traveled alone to New York City, where after a spell as a store clerk, he worked at Mutual Life as an office assistant and cashier (treasurer). He became intimately familiar with the actuarial, sales, and financial advances in the nascent and rapidly expanding American life insurance industry.

Hyde became convinced that Mutual Life and other insurers were mistaken in not marketing policies aggressively and not requiring policyholders to pay their premiums in cash rather than promissory notes. Encouraged by his father, by then a successful agent in Boston, Hyde in 1859 founded a new company, The Equitable Life Assurance Society of the United States, whose name he borrowed from Britain's most successful life insurer ("equitable" and "assurance" refer to fair, guaranteed payments of death benefits and dividends). To raise the $100,000 he needed in capital to qualify for a New York State charter, Hyde sold shares in the company to merchants and lawyers whom he met at Manhattan's Fifth Avenue Presbyterian Church. The investors were led by the family of the rector, James Waddell Alexander (1804–1859), son of the founder of Princeton Theological Seminary, Archibald Alexander.

Hyde insisted that the company be run on the mutual system, with policyholders participating in the company's profits through dividends. He succeeded in limiting shareholders' dividends to 7 percent, as against the 10 percent that many of them wanted, but his backers then passed him over for the position of president in favor of William C. Alexander, one of the rector's sons. Hyde still dominated Equitable from the beginning and formally became its chief executive at William Alexander's death in 1874. Over time, he also acquired a majority of the company's shares.

Hyde's chief concern was sales. "Hyde's genius for *thinking* his way through marketing problems produced the beginnings of merchandising in life insurance," wrote the best historian of life insurance sales, J. Owen Stalson (Stalson, pp. 600–1). Hyde's marketing innovations included a carefully thought-out advertising program to instill public trust in Equitable. He was sure that in a time of deep religious conviction, when clergymen attacked the purchase of a life policy as a denial of the promise of divine protection, life insurance must be promoted as a moral good. Therefore, Equitable's advertising characterized life insurance as a benevolent activity providing otherwise unavailable financial protection for widows and orphans. (Decades before Social Security and most corporate pensions, this claim was largely true.) Hyde successfully solicited endorsements from Henry Ward Beecher and other leading preachers, and he commissioned a corporate symbol—the first of any American company—that showed the Greek goddess Pallas Athena holding a shield over a mother and child. He put up over a dozen large Equitable office buildings to demonstrate the company's strength and reliability. Hyde also pioneered in consumerism: Equitable was the first American life company to give policyholders the benefit of the doubt in disputes and one of the first to offer policies to women.

Equitable had the largest, best compensated, and most aggressive sales force in the life insurance industry. "I want hustling agents to get business," he asserted (Rousmaniere, p. 25), and he stimulated that hustle with sales commissions that reached to over 100 percent of the first year's premiums on policies. The most popular Equitable policy, which Hyde introduced in 1868, was an annuity contract called the "tontine" (after its seventeenth-century originator, Lorenzo Tonti). In exchange for paying annual premiums, tontine policyholders received a small death benefit plus dividends that began to be paid after a contracted period of time, ranging from five to twenty years. As policyholders died off, dividends increased until the last survivor was awarded the entire tontine pool, less the amount reserved by Equitable. Sometimes called "deferred dividend" policies and taking several forms that offered unprecedented choice to the policyholders, the tontine at first was criticized by other life insurers and insurance regulators as a form of gambling that distracted consumers from traditional life insurance. Tontines, however, quickly became extremely popular. They were flexible, their projected interest rates were higher than those of the limited number of other savings instruments available at the time, and Hyde drove his agents to sell them aggressively. Owing largely to tontine sales, between 1869 and 1899 Equitable's insurance in force increased from $134 million to over $1 billion. Because dividend payments were deferred, Equitable had vast assets to invest at the high interest rates prevailing in 1870–1890. Hyde, whose chief concern was marketing, had little interest in the company's investments outside of constructing many Equitable-owned office buildings in the United States and abroad. Following the recommendations of advisers, Equitable invested the large bulk of its assets in long-term government bonds while also acquiring several banks and trust companies and making a few loans to American railroads. The company's capital base—already strong because of Hyde's policy of demanding premiums in cash—was the strongest of any insurance company, with more than $16 million in 1886. At the turn of the century Equitable, with assets of $280 million and capital of $61.1 million, was one of the largest financial institutions in the world along with the Bank of England, Mutual Life, and New York Life. This growth was helped by Equitable's expansion overseas. One of the first international corporations, Equitable placed agencies in ninety-one countries between 1860

and 1890. By 1893 almost one-fourth of Equitable's premium income was derived from foreign sales. Most of Hyde's competitors eventually set aside their criticisms and sold tontines. The success of these annuity policies turned U.S. life insurance into the world's largest financial services industry. By 1905 the face amount of tontine policies totaled $6 billion—two-thirds of all the business of U.S. life insurers and the equivalent of 7½ percent of U.S. total national wealth.

Hyde's weaknesses were the shadows of his strengths. Equitable's costly sales program left the company burdened with large overhead. When interest rates plummeted during the depression of the 1890s, Hyde closed down many foreign offices and imposed new disciplines. In addition, Hyde's authoritarian confidence led him to insist on an unwise act of nepotism. When he died in Bay Shore, Long Island, New York, in 1899, exhausted by forty years of overwork, he left his majority interest in Equitable to his 23-year-old son, James Hazen Hyde, who had no aptitude for the life insurance business. (In 1864 the father had married Annie Fitch, with whom he had had four children.) As vice president, the heir spent his time engaged in high-stakes, often chancy corporate finance. In 1905 a fight for control between young Hyde and President James W. Alexander (1839–1915, the nephew of the first president) almost wrecked Equitable's public credibility and stimulated the Armstrong committee investigation of the life insurance industry led by Charles Evans Hughes. The resulting legislation outlawed tontines, capped sales commissions, and restricted investments but otherwise left intact the framework that Henry Hyde had built at Equitable and that shaped American life insurance.

• The two collections of correspondence, memoranda, business records, advertisements, and other materials concerning Hyde and the first forty years of the Equitable Life Assurance Society are the Equitable Life Assurance Society Collection in the Baker Library at the Harvard University Graduate School of Business Administration, Boston, Mass., and the Equitable Archives in the company's headquarters in New York, N.Y. R. Carlyle Buley, *The Equitable Life Assurance Society of the United States, 1859–1964* (1967), and John Rousmaniere, *The Life and Times of The Equitable* (1995), are two histories of the company. Accounts of the early history of American life insurance offering perspectives on Hyde are J. Owen Stalson, *Marketing Life Insurance: Its History in America* (1942), and Morton Keller, *The Life Insurance Enterprise, 1885–1910: A Study in the Limits of Corporate Power* (1963). The Armstrong committee's investigation of the life insurance industry, which concerned Hyde because of his influence on the business, is covered in great detail by Keller. Transcripts of the committee's hearings are in *Joint Committee of the Senate and Assembly of New York to Investigate and Examine into the Business and Affairs of Life Insurance Companies Doing Business in the State of New York: Testimony*, 7 vols. (1906). An obituary is in the *New York Times*, 3 May 1899.

JOHN ROUSMANIERE

HYDE, Ida Henrietta (8 Sept. 1857–22 Aug. 1945), physiologist, was born in Davenport, Iowa, the daughter of Meyer H. Hyde, a merchant, and Babette

Loewenthal. Her father had changed his surname from Heidenheimer when he settled in the United States from Württemberg, Germany. He left the family when Ida was very young. The mother and children moved to Chicago, where Babette Hyde did mending and cleaning. Ida attended public schools and began work in a millinery in Chicago in 1873 when she was sixteen. She advanced to buyer and sales clerk. When she found and enjoyed reading a book by Alexander von Humboldt, Hyde decided to pursue her education. She took evening classes at the newly established Chicago Athenaeum, a school for working people.

In 1881 Hyde enrolled in the University of Illinois but in a year returned home to support the family when her brother became ill. For several years she taught elementary grades in the Chicago public schools, to which she introduced science programs. In 1888 she entered Cornell University, where she received an A.B. in 1891 in the biological sciences.

A person of great determination, Hyde began advanced studies in 1891 on a scholarship at Bryn Mawr College under physiologist Jacques Loeb and zoologist Thomas Hunt Morgan, serving as a student assistant and fellow in biology until 1893. The results of her research project on jellyfish were brought to the attention of Alexander Wilhelm Goette at the University of Strassburg (now Strasbourg), who was engaged in a dispute with Professor Klaus at Vienna on jellyfish embryonic development. Goette invited Hyde to pursue her research at his university, and with a fellowship from the Association of Collegiate Alumnae, she went to Strassburg in 1893.

Even though at that time no university in Germany accepted women as students, Goette assigned her laboratory space. She soon found that she "was regarded by the students, faculty members, and their wives as a curiosity" ("Before Women Were Human Beings"). Because of opposition by some of the faculty, it appeared impossible for her to be accepted to work for a Ph.D. at Strassburg. Therefore, while Hyde continued her research there, she also wrote to the University of Heidelberg to ask about obtaining a degree. The prolonged inquiry involved the Reichstag minister of education, the minister of education and justice in the duchy of Baden, the grand duke of Baden, and the dean of the faculty of natural sciences and mathematics. Because there was neither written stricture against women nor anything allowing them, a special petition became necessary. The faculty voted unanimously to allow women to be candidates for the doctor's degree. When the other agencies and the grand duke agreed, Hyde broke a barrier that had been presumed to exist for all women Ph.D. candidates.

At the University of Heidelberg she readily obtained permission to take courses from professors in the zoology and chemistry departments, but the medical school forbade women. There she was not allowed to attend lectures but was permitted to study notes taken by the assistants of professor of physiology Wilhelm Kühne. Supported by a fellowship for women to study abroad that had been established by philanthropist Phoebe Hearst (wife of businessman George Hearst of San Francisco), Hyde pursued her courses and was awarded a Ph.D. in 1896, with honors. She commented that the students at Heidelberg always treated her with the greatest courtesy.

Upon receiving her degree she was invited by Kühne to conduct research in the medical school, the first woman to do so. She also was awarded support by the University of Heidelberg to study at the Naples Zoological Station in 1896, where she conducted research on the salivary glands of the octopus. She then spent a few months at the University of Bern, Switzerland, by invitation, where she met Henry P. Bowditch of the Harvard Medical School. Bowditch recommended her to become the first woman to work in that facility, which she did from late 1896 to 1898 on a fellowship from Radcliffe College. Her research with physiologist William Townsend Porter focused on blood flow of the heart. She also taught at nearby preparatory schools.

In 1898 Hyde became assistant professor of zoology at the University of Kansas and associate professor of physiology the next year. In 1905 she advanced to professor in the newly created Department of Physiology and held an appointment in the university's medical school. In Kansas she established a program to provide health examinations for schoolchildren for communicable diseases, and she lectured widely on public health, including sexuality. She wrote the textbooks *Outlines of Experimental Physiology* in 1905 and *Laboratory Outlines of Physiology* in 1910 and was acknowledged as a stimulating teacher. During the summers from 1908 to 1912 she attended Rush Medical School in Chicago, and in many other summers she did research at the Marine Biological Laboratory in Woods Hole, Massachusetts. She taught at the University of Kansas until 1920. For the academic year 1922–1923 she studied the biological effects of radium at the University of Heidelberg.

Hyde's research projects in physiology were varied; she examined circulation, respiration, embryology, and sense organs. She studied the effects of the environment and nutrition on the nervous system, the reactions of various animals to drugs, alcohol, and stress, and the effects of caffeine on humans. She also developed a microelectrode that enabled her to stimulate and study a single cell. Her papers were noted by colleagues for their precision and originality.

Always concerned with the advancement of qualified women, Hyde founded an association to establish a research table for American women at the Naples Zoological Station. Such a "table" was actually an equipped laboratory, supported by a $500 annual donation from research agencies, who could select the researcher each year. The table continued to be funded until 1933. She also helped to arrange a research facility for women at the Marine Biological Laboratory, served on a board of accreditation for women students applying for study abroad, endowed scholarships for women students in science at the University of Kansas and at Cornell University, and established the Ida H.

Hyde Woman's International Fellowship of the American Association of University Women.

A member of several scientific societies, Hyde is especially noted as the first woman member of the American Physiological Society (1902). She never married. About 1925 she moved to California, first to San Diego and then to Berkeley, where she died.

• Some of Hyde's papers are in the Kenneth Spencer Archives of the University of Kansas; others, including diaries, are at the archives of the American Association of University Women in Washington, D.C. Hyde's own account, "Before Women Were Human Beings," *Journal of the American Association of University Women* (June 1938): 226–36, candidly recounts her admission and success at the University of Heidelberg. Information on the table at Naples is in Jan Butin Sloan, "The Founding of the Naples Table Association for Promoting Scientific Research by Women, 1897," *Signs: Journal of Women in Culture and Society* 4 (1978): 208–16. A significant biographical account is by Gail Susan Tucker, "Ida Henrietta Hyde: The First Woman Member of the Society," *The Physiologist* 24 (Dec. 1981): 1–9, with an annotated bibliography. Another account is by Tucker, "Reflections on the Life of Ida Henrietta Hyde, 1857–1945," *Creative Woman Quarterly* (Spring 1978): 4–8. An obituary is in the *Journal of the American Association of University Women* (Fall 1945).

ELIZABETH NOBLE SHOR

HYDE, James Nevins (21 June 1840–6 Sept. 1910), dermatologist and author, was born in Norwich, Connecticut, the son of Edward Goodrich Hyde, a merchant, and Hannah Huntington Thomas. Hyde attended Andover Academy and Yale, receiving his A.B. in 1861. He won prizes in his sophomore year for composition and poetry and wrote a "Parting Ode" for Presentation Day.

After a year at the College of Physicians and Surgeons in New York City, Hyde was sent by the U.S. Sanitary Commission with several physicians to transfer sick and wounded Civil War soldiers from Virginia to New York. The group then sailed on the *Spaulding* to Harrison's Landing and took many badly wounded soldiers to Washington, D.C. Hyde worked in Washington hospitals for ten months and was then appointed an acting assistant surgeon of volunteers in the navy in July 1863. After serving on the North Atlantic Blockading Squadron, he received a commission in the regular navy as an assistant surgeon. Hyde's next major assignment, for most of 1864, was on the *San Jacinto*, the flagship of the East Gulf Blockading Squadron. There he performed so well during an epidemic of yellow fever that he received a special letter of appreciation from the secretary of the navy. As a reward, Hyde was ordered to the *Ticonderoga* for Admiral Farragut's almost two-year tour of western Europe, the Mediterranean, Russia, and the west coast of Africa. Back in the United States, Hyde became a passed assistant surgeon on 23 December 1867 and was assigned to the Clare Naval Hospital in Washington, D.C. He resigned from the navy in February 1869.

In Philadelphia Hyde then took the required second course of medical lectures at the University of Pennsylvania, which gave him his M.D. in 1869. He moved to Chicago and began a private practice as a general physician. On 31 July 1872 he and Alice Louise Griswold of Chicago were married. Alice's sister, Clara, married Episcopalian bishop Charles Edward Cheney, and the two couples shared a house for almost forty years. The Hydes had one son.

Hyde's medical interests gradually shifted to dermatology. He established a large clinic for skin diseases at the Central Free Dispensary and used this as both a treatment and an educational facility. In 1876 he became one of the founders of the American Dermatological Society, serving as its president in 1881 and 1896. At each annual meeting he reported statistics on the cases he and his colleagues had seen during the previous year. Of even more interest was his annual exhibit of photographs and oil and watercolor paintings; many dermatologists looked on these exhibits as a high point of the conventions.

In 1901 Hyde was a founder and charter member of the Chicago Dermatological Society; he served as its first president and was reelected for 1908. Hyde presented many papers to his societies and served frequently on committees. At the 1878 annual meeting of the Illinois State Medical Society he presented a well-received clinic on skin and venereal diseases; he gave these regularly for many years. He was also a member of the American Medical Association and the Congress of American Physicians and Surgeons.

Michael Reese Hospital named Hyde its dermatologist in 1883, and Presbyterian Hospital did the same in 1884. He also had appointments to the Chicago Hospital for Women and Children and the Chicago Floating Hospital.

Hyde was soon recognized as an innovative, popular, and polished teacher. Rush Medical College appointed him lecturer on syphilis and dermatology in 1873, a position he held until 1876 when Northwestern's Chicago Medical College enticed him away as professor of dermatology. Rush won him back as professor of skin and venereal diseases in 1879, and Hyde remained there until his death. In 1898 his title lengthened to professor of skin, genito-urinary, and venereal diseases, and in 1905 he became head of the department. He also served as secretary of the college's council of administration from 1898, and as secretary of the faculty from 1899. From 1895 to 1898 he was a member of the board of trustees.

As an author, Hyde became best known for his immensely popular textbook, *A Practical Treatise on Diseases of the Skin, for the Use of Students and Practitioners* (1883). His office associate, Frank Hugh Montgomery, coauthored the fourth through eighth editions, ending with his accidental death. Oliver S. Ormsby, who became Hyde's associate in 1908, took over as coauthor until Hyde's death and then carried the book through eight more editions; for the last three, Frank Montgomery's son Hamilton was coauthor. The text was continuously in print for more than seventy years. In 1895 Hyde and Frank Hugh Montgomery produced *A Manual of Syphilis and Venereal*

Diseases (2d ed., 1900). Hyde's book *Early Medical Chicago* (1879) is still useful.

Hyde also wrote about one hundred medical articles. Among the more important were his reports on blastomycosis (among the first publications on this subject) and those on pellagra and sporotrichosis. Hyde described synovial lesions of the skin in 1883 and was the first to do so. He was also the first to draw attention to the influence of light on the production of skin cancer, in a 1906 article. Hyde named prurigo nodularis, a skin condition, although he was not the first to describe it; this is still known as "Hyde's disease." Through his writings and correspondence, Hyde became well known throughout the United States and in many foreign countries.

In addition, Hyde wrote literary and historical works in poetry and prose. In 1875 he became a member of the Chicago Literary Club and remained so until his death. During this time he presented nineteen papers before the club and served as its president (1889–1890). Hyde died suddenly from a heart condition while vacationing in Prout's Neck, Maine, overlooking his beloved ocean. He was a founder of dermatology in the United States, an innovative clinician and teacher, and an accomplished writer in both his chosen field and his avocation.

• Hyde's article on light and skin cancer is "On the Influence of Light in the Production of Cancer of the Skin," *American Journal of the Medical Sciences* 131 (1906): 1–22; the original report on prurigo nodularis, or Hyde's disease, appeared in the eighth edition of his *Treatise* (1909), pp. 174–75. Useful information is in William K. Beatty, "James Nevins Hyde: Pioneer Dermatologist and Staunch Navy Man," *Proceedings of the Institute of Medicine of Chicago* 35 (1982): 139–42. Contemporary accounts of his life and work are in the *Yale College Class of 1861. Class Reports*, 11th–12th (1912), pp. 80–87; James B. Herrick's obituary of him in *Rush Alumni Association Bulletin* 7, no. 5 (Oct. 1911): 3–10; and Oliver S. Ormsby's obituary in the same *Bulletin* 7, no. 1 (Oct. 1910): 8–9.

WILLIAM K. BEATTY

HYDE, William DeWitt (23 Sept. 1858–29 June 1917), minister, author, and college president, was born in Winchendon, Massachusetts, the son of Joel Hyde and Eliza DeWitt. The family, of English descent and Congregational religion, was prosperous, in a small way, from their business of manufacturing wooden ware such as buckets, scoops, and shovels. Hyde's mother died when he was an infant, and his father died when he was seven. Raised by a succession of relatives, his inheritance enabled him to attend Phillips Academy and Harvard, graduating in 1879. He attended Union Theological Seminary for a year, and then Andover, from which he graduated in 1882. He was ordained in September 1883 as a Congregational minister. In November of that same year he married Prudence Phillips. The couple had one child.

Hyde was briefly pastor of a church in Paterson, New Jersey. However, one of his Andover teachers was on the Board of Trustees of Bowdoin College and recommended him for the positions of professor of philosophy and president of the small men's college. The board agreed, and Hyde accepted in June 1885, remaining as Bowdoin's president until his death.

Hyde was one of those college presidents who helped invent the American non-university liberal arts college during the time that American universities were defining themselves in imitation of a German ideal. When he arrived at Bowdoin, the curriculum was almost entirely prescribed and heavily weighted toward the classics and classical history, with some modern languages. He enlarged the offerings in these areas and greatly increased attention to the social and natural sciences and, of course, philosophy, moving the curriculum partially toward an elective system. He reorganized the financial system of the college. He also added buildings, including a gymnasium and student union. The college was tiny when he arrived, with only 12 faculty and 119 students, but it grew steadily. At the beginning of World War I, in addition to a small medical school, there were 400 undergraduates and 29 faculty members.

Hyde became well known in the world of higher education as a young and successful college president. He was rumored to have been approached about becoming president of major universities, perhaps even Stanford. He chose, however, to remain "Hyde of Bowdoin." He became more known through his popular writings on religious topics and, for him, the religion-related issues of ethics and education. Science, or more generally, rationalism, was producing astounding and much celebrated benefits. Religious spokesmen felt that they had to try to fit the religion of their fathers into the now not-so-new world of technological rational progress. This was one of the main tasks that Hyde set for himself in his writing.

On neither this nor other subjects did Hyde break new ground. In simple and straightforward prose, he summed up the views and prejudices of a rather conventional, well-educated Christian of his era and background. Much of his writing had the tone of a gentle, reasonable sermon and in fact had often started out that way.

President Hyde also was professor of philosophy, and as such he kept up with his field, using books by William James and John Dewey almost as soon as they appeared. He rejected the idea of the human mind as a blank slate, and instead, following Kant and James, asserted the interactivity of mind and sensation. This mind, interacting with a natural and orderly world, could increasingly throughout history perceive the self-consistent, rational whole. The basis for such a rational whole was Absolute Thought, or God. But God was not merely a clock maker who set the whole thing in motion. God was transcendent.

This natural world was evolving—for Hyde accepted evolution—and similarly society was evolving toward a more and more moral order in increasing accordance with what Hyde called the Universal Will. This more moral order accepted the social nature of our being rather than assuming that individual self seeking is our essence. This evolution, too, is a manifestation of God and would lead mankind in the direction of Jesus, the son of God. It is vain and impoverishing, Hyde believed, to try to approach God other than through Christ.

In addition, Hyde wrote simple guides to ethics and education. In *Practical Ethics* (1892) he put together a series of rules against alcohol, drugs, tobacco, dishonesty, and so forth, and explained why each rule was good and what the penalty for breaking it would be. One such penalty was that "mental and moral deterioration is handed down to offsprings" (p. 51). He also had rather conventional views on the roles of the sexes. By 1906, some fourteen years before passage of the equal suffrage amendment, he wrote that women's rights had been secured, and the nation now had to explore the question of the appropriate roles for women. With some exceptions in all categories, men were naturally the producers, women the consumers. Women were better at such things as music and fiction writing, but in general their role was to provide a happy home for their families. Too much education might impinge on their "normal functions [and] habitual cheerfulness" (*The College Man and the College Woman* [1906], p. 204). Only rarely did questions of social, economic, or public policy engage Hyde. In 1904 he wrote in favor of maintaining segregation "in the interests of racial integrity," but he was in favor of the franchise for some particularly well-qualified "negroes." In 1912 he defined political and economic issues in a way that might be called moderately progressive, implicitly favoring either Woodrow Wilson or Theodore Roosevelt over the conservative William Howard Taft and the Socialist Eugene V. Debs.

Besides his twenty books and pamphlets, some widely reviewed, Hyde wrote scores of articles in magazines of broad general circulation, such as *Outlook*, *Forum*, *Review of Reviews*, and *Atlantic*, rather than specialized theological or academic journals. By the end of his life, his viewpoint and even many of the questions that he addressed were becoming a bit old fashioned. If the world of the nineteenth century ended with the First World War, it is fitting that Hyde died in the midst of it, in Brunswick, Maine.

• There is no collection of Hyde papers, but catalogs of Bowdoin during his presidency and other college publications are in the Bowdoin Library, Brunswick, Maine. His major works not already mentioned include *Outlines of Social Theology* (1895), *Practical Idealism* (1897), *God's Education of Man* (1899), *Jesus's Way* (1902), *The Five Great Philosophies of Life* (1904), *From Epicurus to Christ* (1906), *The Teacher's Philosophy in and out of School* (1910), *The Quest of the Best* (1913), *The Gospel of Good Will* (1913), and *The Best Man I Know* (1917). A biography is Charles T. Burnett, *Hyde of Bowdoin: A Biography of William DeWitt Hyde* (1931). See also Charles C. Calhoun, *A Small College in Maine: Two Hundred Years of Bowdoin* (1993). An obituary is in the *New York Times*, 30 June 1917.

DANIEL LEVINE

HYER, Tom (1 Jan. 1819–26 June 1864), boxer and politician, was born Thomas Hyer in New York City, the son of Jacob Hyer, a butcher and boxer, and Johanna (maiden name unknown). Little is known about Hyer's childhood. Like his father, he was apprenticed as a butcher, but he remained in the trade only a few years. More frequently he worked as a bartender and volunteer fireman.

By his teenage years, Hyer had developed an impressive and powerful physique, a "broad, formidable chest, and long muscular limbs," by one account. In his prime he was 6'1" and 180 pounds. His physical prowess was a considerable asset for a popular gang leader and intimidating street brawler. From 1836 until 1838 he served brief prison sentences after leading groups of "brothel bullies" in assaults on at least four houses of prostitution, attacking and gang raping the female residents.

Violent gangs such as Hyer's played a key role in the formation, establishment, and exercise of power of New York's political machine before the Civil War. The rise of competitive party politics from 1830 until 1860 created a new relationship between the municipality and youth gangs. Elected officeholders employed neighborhood toughs like Hyer to defend ballot boxes, keep adversaries away from the polls, and enforce political conformity. Members of other gangs like the "Bowery B'hoys" and the "Dead Rabbits" also worked for volunteer fire companies and saloons. At various times Hyer was associated with the Branch Hotel (36 Bowery), the Fountain House (28 Park Row), and other Broadway and Bowery drinking spots. These institutions, divorced from female and familial control, promoted a camaraderie that valued drinking, gambling, "whoring," and fighting.

Hyer's violent proclivities were eventually parlayed into organized pugilism. In 1848 the Irish immigrant James "Yankee" Sullivan (whose real name was Frank Ambrose) was a reigning boxing champion. After several years of insult and verbal bravado between him and Hyer, supporters organized the "Great $10,000 Fight." The winner-take-all contest not only revived national interest in boxing, but it generated unprecedented newspaper and telegraph coverage. It was one of the first sporting events promoted by national media. Gamblers wagered more money on the match than on any American sporting event up to that time, estimates going as high as $40,000 (probably equivalent to about $500,000 in the late twentieth century). Coming in the wake of massive Irish immigration and growing nativism in American cities, promoters played to ethnic and class tensions. The confrontation, one newspaper reporter wrote, attracted the attention of the well-born and the plebian, the rich and "the rowdies of the Bowery." The New York *Herald* estimated that public excitement nationally over the Hyer-Sullivan match approached that of the recent Mexican-American War.

The memorable fight occurred on 7 February 1849—but barely. At the last moment local officials near Poole's Island, Maryland, in the Chesapeake Bay tried to cancel it. Promoters quickly moved the bout to Still Pond Heights, Maryland. Fighting illegally in late afternoon on a frozen field, Hyer's heavier, brawnier, and taller advantage prevailed; in less than eighteen minutes he emerged victorious. The next day the victor was given a hero's welcome in Philadelphia whereupon he was arrested, then released when Maryland officials dropped the case. Hyer immediately returned to New York City and was declared "the Champion of America," one of the first times such a title was used.

The Hyer-Sullivan match marked the beginning of organized pugilism in the United States. The fight was one of the earliest contests to follow formal rules emphasizing not only safety and fairness but ritual. Boxers were banned from the common practices of choking, biting, kneeing, eye gouging, and hitting below the belt. The stylized actions, patterned behavior, and uniform procedures transformed boxing into a theater-like drama of larger social conflict. Hyer became one of the first national sports celebrities. His popularity made him a hero not only with native-born boxing fans but with actors, politicians, and theatrical producers. In 1849 he even tried show business, playing the lead in a production of *Tom and Jerry*. A half-century after the fight, lithographs of Hyer and Sullivan still graced the walls of working-class taverns.

Hyer never entered the prize ring again. His uncompromising demands for only the most expensive stakes discouraged opponents and left him unchallenged. More often he participated in barroom brawls and similar rough-and-tumble activities. Despite his well-publicized "whoring," Hyer married Emma Beke in the late 1840s; they had one child. During the 1850s Hyer operated several Bowery saloons and a Park Place gambling spot. These ventures ended in financial failure. In 1853 he accepted John Morrissey's challenge for a fight, but plans for the event fell apart when Morrissey failed to raise the necessary $10,000. Hyer even reconciled with his old antagonist Yankee Sullivan, bailing him out of a Lenox, Massachusetts, jail in 1853. Hyer's popularity remained strong throughout the 1850s, his admirers nicknaming him "the Chief" and "Young America" in reference to his dignified manners and nativist sympathies.

Hyer was a member of the Whig party from the 1840s until its eclipse with the slavery issue and the rise of the Republican party. Opportunistic in his politics, he allied himself at different times with nativist William Poole and his Mercer Street gang, the radical Democrat Mike Walsh and his Bowery B'hoys (although this was little more than a drinking relationship), and the Republican William Seward (whom he backed at the Republican convention in 1860). When Poole was killed in a barroom fight in 1855, Hyer served as a pallbearer. Bowery B'hoys sometimes donned "Tom Hyer hats" to prove their admiration. During Abraham Lincoln's New York visit in 1860, the former boxing champion met the future president at the Astor House.

Hyer was probably an alcoholic most of his adult life, consuming more than a dozen drinks per day by his own account. After 1860 his hard-drinking ways caught up with him as he physically broke down from a diseased liver and an enlarged spleen. Hyer succumbed to heart failure in New York City.

• Hyer left no known personal papers or manuscripts. Newspapers and pamphlets remain the best primary sources, including *American Fistiana* (1849), *National Police Gazette*, and *Spirit of the Times*. The Hyer-Sullivan fight is extensively covered in Ed James, *The Life and Battles of Tom Hyer* (1879) and *The Life and Battles of Yankee Sullivan* (1854). The most complete coverage of Hyer is Elliott J. Gorn, *The Manly Art: Bare-Knuckle Prize Fighting in America* (1986). Also see Timothy J. Gilfoyle, *City of Eros: New York City, Prostitution, and the Commercialization of Sex, 1790–1920* (1992); Alvin F. Harlow, *Old Bowery Days: The Chronicles of a Famous Street* (1931); Herbert Asbury, *The Gangs of New York: An Informal History of the Underworld* (1928); and Peter Gammie, "Pugilists and Politicians in Antebellum New York: The Life and Times of Tom Hyer," *New York History* 75 (July 1994): 265–96.

TIMOTHY J. GILFOYLE

HYMAN, John Adams (23 July 1840–14 Sept. 1891), North Carolina senator and U.S. congressman, was born a slave near Warrenton, Warren County, North Carolina. Nothing is known about his parents. In 1861 Hyman worked as a janitor for a jeweler who with his wife taught Hyman to read and write. When that was discovered, the jeweler and his wife were driven from Warrenton, and Hyman was sold and sent to Alabama. Having been at least eight times "bought and sold as a brute," as he described it, Hyman in 1865 returned to Warren County, where he was a farmer and store manager. Sometime between 1865 and 1867 he became a trustee of one of the first public schools in Warren County.

Hyman's formal political career began in September 1866, when at the age of twenty-six he was a delegate to the Freedmen's Convention of North Carolina. In that body he served on the Committee on Invitations, whose purpose was to ensure that influential public officials and private citizens were invited to participate in the convention. In 1867 Hyman was a delegate at the Republican State Convention and was appointed to the state executive committee. That year he served as a register for Warren County, organizing and assisting in black voter registration.

In 1868 Hyman was elected to the state constitutional convention. He also served as a state senator (1868–1874), representing the Twentieth Senatorial District in Warren County. He was a strong advocate for black civil rights throughout his term. He opposed Andrew Johnson's leniency toward ex-Confederates, particularly his unwillingness to require ratification of the Fourteenth Amendment before states could be readmitted to the Union. In 1872 he voted against the conviction of North Carolina governor William W. Holden, who was impeached for ordering the arrest of Ku Klux Klan members suspected of lynching and terrorizing blacks. Hyman, however, offered no opinion for his position. His senate career was tarnished by charges of fraud and corruption related to the selection of a penitentiary site in Warrenton and the Milton S. Littlefield–George Swepson railroad bond scandal between 1868 and 1871.

In 1872 Hyman ran for Congress but was defeated by Charles R. Thomas. In 1874 he successfully won the congressional seat for the gerrymandered Second District, which included Warren County, defeating G. W. Blount by 7,000 votes. As congressman from the district referred to as the "Black Second," Hyman was a strong advocate for black civil rights. He submitted at least "fourteen petitions to Congress," asking for continuing aid to agencies assisting the freedmen (Reid, p. 231). He also supported relief efforts for Cherokee Indians. Hyman's congressional career ended in 1876, when he failed to gain the Republican nomination.

Hyman left Washington in 1877, but that year President Rutherford B. Hayes appointed him special deputy collector of internal revenue for the Fourth Congressional District of North Carolina, a position he held from 2 July 1877 to 30 June 1878. By 1878 he had mortgaged or disposed of nearly all of his land to cover debts incurred while living in Washington. Hyman operated a liquor store in Warren County, joined the Colored Masons of North Carolina, and was a member of the Warrenton Negro Methodist Church, where he served as superintendent of the Sunday school. In 1879 the church leaders asked him to leave, accusing him of misappropriation of Sunday school funds and disapproving of his selling liquor.

Shortly afterward Hyman went to Washington, D.C., where he served as an assistant mail clerk until 1889. He then worked for the Agriculture Department in the seed dispensary. Hyman died of a stroke in Washington. His wife and four children survived him.

Hyman was one of five blacks elected to the North Carolina Senate in 1868 and the first black and only Republican to represent the state in the Forty-fourth Congress of 1874. Though he gave few speeches, his presence in the political arena reflected Republican hopes for the reconstructed South. He gained political notoriety during an era of unprecedented racial violence in the Tarheel State. His brief success may have offered hope to newly freed blacks, indicating that they could realize, even for a brief time, the freedoms the Constitution guaranteed all persons. Although marred by corruption, Hyman's political prominence did represent, to a degree, triumph for some Reconstruction efforts in North Carolina.

Hyman's life illuminates a different interpretation of Reconstruction that contradicts the view held immediately afterward and well into the twentieth century. His career reflects the struggles of many black political leaders during an era in which North and South failed to thoroughly support the efforts of ex-slaves to obtain full civil rights and unconditional economic participation. Given that Hyman had been a slave for twenty-five years, his success is significant in that he surmounted adverse odds and held a visible presence in North Carolina politics. His life is symbolic of black achievement even as they struggled to obtain complete citizenship as guaranteed in the U.S. Constitution.

• Hyman's life is traced through the Record of Deeds, books 34–36, Warren County Courthouse; *The North Carolina Biographical Dictionary* (1993); and Benjamin Perley Poore, comp., *The Political Register and Congressional Directory* (1878). Hyman's service in the N.C. Senate and the U.S. Congress is covered in the *North Carolina Senate Journal*, 1868–1872 (1865); *Congressional Record*, 44th Cong., 1875–1877; and *The Trial of William W. Holden before the Senate of North Carolina* (1871). Hyman is mentioned in context with other black congressmen in Eric Foner, *Reconstruction: America's Unfinished Revolution, 1863–1877* (1988), which cites a letter from Hyman to Charles Sumner dated 24 Jan. 1872. Hyman's public and private life is covered in George W. Reid, "Four in Black: North Carolina's Black Congressmen, 1874–1901," *Journal of Negro History* 64 (Summer 1979): 229–43; and Maggie L. Armstrong, "The Public Life of John Adams Hyman, 1840–1891" (M.A. thesis, North Carolina Central Univ., 1975). An obituary is in the *Washington Post*, 15 Sept. 1891.

DEBI HAMLIN

HYMAN, Libbie Henrietta (6 Dec. 1888–3 Aug. 1969), zoologist, was born in Des Moines, Iowa, the daughter of Joseph Hyman and Sabina Neumann. Hyman's father, a Polish/Russian Jew, adopted the surname when he immigrated to the United States as a youth. He successively owned clothing stores in Des Moines, in Sioux Falls, South Dakota, and in Fort Dodge, Iowa, but the family's resources were limited. Hyman attended public schools in Fort Dodge. At home she was required to do much of the housework. She enjoyed reading, especially books by Charles Dickens in her father's small library, and she took a strong interest in flowers, which she learned to classify with a copy of Asa Gray's *Elements of Botany*. She also collected butterflies and moths and later wrote, "I believe my interest in nature is primarily aesthetic."

Hyman graduated from high school in Fort Dodge in 1905 as the youngest member of her class and the valedictorian. Uncertain of her future, she began work in a local factory, pasting labels on cereal boxes. Her high school teacher of English and German persuaded her to attend the University of Chicago, which she entered in 1906 on a one-year scholarship. She continued at the university with further scholarships and nominal jobs. Turning away from botany because of an unpleasant laboratory assistant, she tried chemistry but did not like its quantitative procedures. She then took zoology and was encouraged in it by Professor Charles Manning Child. After receiving a B.S. in zoology in 1910, she accepted Child's advice to continue with graduate work at the University of Chicago. Supporting herself as laboratory assistant in various zoology courses, she concluded that they needed a better laboratory text. She received a Ph.D. in zoology in 1915, with a thesis on regeneration in certain annelid worms. Again unsure of her future, she accepted a position as research assistant in Child's laboratory, and she taught undergraduate courses in comparative anatomy.

After Hyman's father's death in 1907, her mother had moved to Chicago, bringing Hyman "back into the same unhappy circumstances which lasted until the death of my mother in 1929. I never received any encouragement from my family to continue my academic career; in fact my determination to attend the University met with derision. At home, scolding and fault-finding were my daily portion" (quoted in Hutchinson, p. 106).

At the request of the University of Chicago Press, Hyman wrote *A Laboratory Manual for Elementary Zoology* (1919), which promptly became widely used, to her astonishment. She followed this, again at the publisher's request, with *A Laboratory Manual for Comparative Vertebrate Anatomy* (1922), which also had great success. She was, however, much more interested in invertebrates. By 1925 she was considering how to prepare a laboratory guide in that field but "was persuaded by [unnamed] colleagues to write an advanced text" (quoted in Hutchinson, p. 107).

While at the University of Chicago, Hyman also wrote significant taxonomic papers on such invertebrates as the Turbellaria (flatworms) and North American species of the freshwater cnidarian *Hydra*. She published an enlarged edition of her first laboratory manual in 1929.

In 1931 Hyman concluded that she could live on the royalties of her published books. She also recognized that her mentor Child was about to retire, so Hyman resigned her position at Chicago. She toured western Europe for fifteen months and then returned to begin writing a treatise on the invertebrates. Settling in New York City in order to use the library of the American Museum of Natural History, she became in December 1936 an unpaid research associate of the museum, which provided her with an office for the rest of her life.

There Hyman created her six-volume treatise on invertebrates, *The Invertebrates*, drawing on her familiarity with several European languages and Russian, which she had learned from her father. Without any assistant, she compiled notes from books and scientific papers, including those in the many journals to which she subscribed, organized the notes on cards, and wrote an account of each invertebrate group. Colleagues said that she had a prodigious memory. She took art lessons in order to illustrate her work professionally. She also spent several summers studying specimens and drawing illustrations at Bermuda Biological Laboratory, Marine Biological Laboratory, Mt. Desert Island Biological Laboratory, and Puget Sound Biological Station.

Volume I (Protozoa through Ctenophora) of *The Invertebrates*, published in February 1940, was acknowledged as "comprehensive" and "authoritative," with "illustrations designed for clarity and simplicity." Volume 2 (Platyhelminthes and Rhynchocoela) and Volume 3 (Acanthocephala, Aschelminthes, and Entoprocta), both published in 1951, were followed by Volume 4 (Echinodermata) 1955, Volume 5 (Smaller Coelomate Groups) in 1959, and Volume 6 (Mollusca I) in 1967. Her biographer Horace Wesley Stunkard noted that *The Invertebrates* "incorporates incisive analysis, judicious evaluation and masterly integration of information." Declining health did not allow her to finish the entire subject. The completed volumes, which continue to be significant references in zoology, represent an astonishing accomplishment by an individual.

In addition to her major project, Hyman extensively revised *Comparative Vertebrate Anatomy* in 1942 into a textbook as well as laboratory manual; she referred to it as her "bread and butter" for its income. She wrote about 136 papers on physiology and systematics of the lower invertebrates and published technical papers on annelid and polyclad worms and on other invertebrates. She commented in a letter: "The polyclads of Bermuda were so pretty that I could not resist collecting them and figuring out Verrill's mistakes" (quoted in Schram, p. 126). Addison Emery Verrill had been an earlier expert in invertebrate classification.

Hyman served as editor of *Systematic Zoology* from 1959 to 1963. She was honored in 1961 with membership in the National Academy of Sciences, from which she had received the Daniel Giraud Elliot Medal in 1951. She also received the gold medal of the Linnean Society of London (1960), and a gold medal from the American Museum of Natural History (1969). She was described as independent, outspoken, and given to poignant epithets, and as warm and generous to her few close friends. Hyman never married. She died in New York City.

• Hyman did not keep her correspondence, according to Frederick R. Schram, who found some of her letters to Martin Burkenroad in the archives of the San Diego Natural History Museum (see Schram's "A Correspondence between Martin Burkenroad and Libbie Hyman; or, Whatever Did Happen to Libbie Hyman's Lingerie," *Crustacean Issues, History of Carcinology*, ed. F. Truesdale [1993], pp. 119–42). A tribute to Hyman is in Edna Yost, *American Women of Science* (1943), pp. 122–38. Memorials are by Richard E. Blackwelder in *Journal of Biological Psychology* 12 (1970): 1–15; by Horace W. Stunkard (unsigned) in *Nature* 225 (1970): 393–94, and in *Biology of the Turbellaria* (1974, "Libbie H. Hyman Memorial Volume"), pp. ix–xiii, with a bibliography; and by G. Evelyn Hutchinson in National Academy of Sciences, *Biographical Memoirs* 60 (1991): 103–14, which includes an autobiographical account by Hyman and a selected bibliography. An obituary is in the *New York Times*, 5 Aug. 1969.

ELIZABETH NOBLE SHOR

HYMAN, Stanley Edgar (11 June 1919–29 July 1970), literary critic, was born in New York City, the son of Moe Hyman, part-owner of a paper company, and Lulu Marshak. He attended public schools in the city and Syracuse University, from which he received a B.A. in English literature in 1940. At Syracuse he met Shirley Jackson, a fellow student who later became a well-known fiction writer, and they were married several months after graduation. The couple had four children.

After working briefly as an editorial assistant at the *New Republic*, Hyman began his professional career as a staff writer for the *New Yorker* in 1940, and that association continued until his death three decades later. During that time he wrote numerous book reviews for the magazine, most of them brief and without lasting critical impact. Hyman was also a frequent contributor of reviews and essays to the *New Leader*, where he served as literary critic from 1961 to 1965. From 1945 to 1946 he taught English at Bennington College in Vermont; he rejoined the faculty in 1952 and at his death held the rank of full professor. Hyman was a popular teacher, and his course on myth and ritual in literature was the most well attended of Bennington's offerings during his years there.

Hyman's critical approach to literature was grounded in modern studies of human behavior, specifically the disciplines of sociology, psychology, and cultural anthropology and their emphasis on the scientific method. His cultural heroes were Darwin, Freud, Marx, and Sir James Frazer, the author of *The Golden Bough*, and his admiration for them is reflected in most of his criticism.

Hyman's first book, *The Armed Vision: A Study in the Methods of Literary Criticism*, was published in 1948 and remains his best-known work. Devoting a chapter to each of twelve influential twentieth-century critics, including T. S. Eliot, Yvor Winters, I. A. Richards, William Empson, and Kenneth Burke, Hyman argued that the most effective and significant contemporary literary criticism owed its vitality to the influence of modern social science. Thus he dismissed "old-fashioned" critics like Eliot and Winters while reserving his highest praise for Empson, Richards, and Burke.

The Armed Vision was widely reviewed and discussed in academic circles. Although some critics liked the book, most criticized its arbitrary categorizations and what they believed were its extremely subjective analyses. Hyman blatantly proclaimed his biases: for example, he vigorously opposed any critical approach that took organized religion seriously (he often described himself as a "militant atheist"), and his dismissal of Eliot and Winters was based in part on their religious sympathies.

A revised edition of *The Armed Vision* was published in 1955. In his subsequent books, Hyman attempted to write the sort of criticism that he had praised in *The Armed Vision*. These included *Poetry and Criticism* (1961), *The Tangled Bank* (1962), and studies of Nathanael West and Flannery O'Connor. Hyman's *New Yorker* and *New Leader* essays were collected in two volumes: *The Promised End* (1963) and *Standards* (1966). In addition, he edited *The Critical Performance* (1956), an anthology of literary criticism; *Darwin for Today* (1963), extracts from the scientist's writings; and two volumes of essays by Kenneth Burke.

Following the death of Shirley Jackson in 1965, Hyman edited several collections of her novellas and short stories. In 1966 he married Phoebe Pettingell, with whom he had one son. Hyman died of a heart attack at his home in North Bennington. His final book, *Iago*, a study of Shakespeare's character, was published posthumously in 1970. A posthumous collection of Hyman's essays, *The Critic's Credentials*, was edited by his widow and published in 1978.

Most academicians consider Hyman an idiosyncratic critic whose writings and influence were ephemeral. This reluctance to give more weight to his work, however, may in part be owing to his lack of scholarly credentials: he had no academic training beyond his undergraduate work. Thus he was never taken as seriously as he might have been had he acquired a doctoral degree and published in scholarly journals. *The Armed Vision* did, however, accurately foreshadow the advent of a multidisciplinary approach to the study of literature.

• The Shirley Jackson Collection in the Library of Congress contains papers relevant to Hyman. Biographical information on Stanley Edgar Hyman can be found in *Who Was Who*, vol. 5 (1973), and *Contemporary Authors*, vols. 85–88 (1980), which includes a complete list of his book-length publications. Judy Oppenheimer's biography of Shirley Jackson, *Private Demons* (1988), also includes personal information about Hyman. For an evaluation of Hyman's importance as a critic, see "Hyman, Stanley Edgar" in *Contemporary Literary Critics* (1977), and Howard Nemerov, "A Survey of Criticism," in *Poetry and Fiction: Essays* (1963). An obituary appears in the *New York Times*, 31 July 1970.

ANN T. KEENE

HYNEK, J. Allen (1 May 1910–27 Apr. 1986), astronomer and unidentified flying object researcher, was born Josef Allen Hynek in Chicago, Illinois, the son of Josef Hynek, a cigar maker and seller, and Bertha Waska, a schoolteacher. From an early age Hynek was fascinated by things in the sky. After obtaining his doctorate in physics and astrophysics from the University of Chicago, he accepted a position as a professor of astronomy at Ohio State University in 1935. He married Miriam Curtis in 1942 and had five children. His steadily progressing astronomical career included a stint as codirector with Fred Whipple of the Smithsonian Institution's prestigious satellite tracking program from 1956 to 1960. During these years he served as visiting lecturer at Harvard University. In 1960 he became chairman of the Astronomy Department at Northwestern University in Evanston, Illinois, and director of the Dearborn Observatory.

While Hynek's career in astronomy was distinguished, his career in the field of research into the unidentified flying object (UFO) sighting phenomenon dominated the last twenty years of his life and became the area in which he achieved fame. In 1948, while at Ohio State University, Hynek was offered a contract by the U.S. Air Force to filter out astronomical sightings from the flying saucer reports that it had been receiving. He accepted the position thinking that the UFO phenomenon was a "silly season" fad. From 1948 until 1969 he served as the air force's chief scientist involved with UFO reports. In the early years of his career, he was a "debunker," assuming that the phenomenon had no objective reality. As he reviewed the data, however, he found many of the reports more difficult to dismiss than he had originally thought. As early as 1952 he said in a speech to the American Optical Society that the subject of UFOs warranted increased attention, but he did not become a public advocate for this position. For many years he kept these doubts to himself, still believing that the great bulk, if not all, of the phenomena could be conventionally explained. In 1953 he served as an associate member of the Central Intelligence Agency–sponsored Robertson Panel. This panel of prestigious scientists concluded that UFOs were not a threat to the national security but UFO reports were, because the Soviet Union could use flying saucer hysteria as a decoy to send bombers to the United States. They therefore advised the air force to downplay the UFO mystery. Although extremely uncomfortable with these recommendations, Hynek decided that he would not go public with his reservations. The public controversy was too great, and emotions were running too high.

By 1964 Hynek had become bolder. Investigating a case in New Mexico in which a police officer claimed to have seen a UFO on the ground with occupants standing around it, Hynek could find no evidence of deception and no conventional explanation. This case, plus the preponderance of the data that he had been investigating for the previous sixteen years, had slowly changed his mind to the belief that the phenomenon did indeed have an objective reality and that it probably was nonterrestrial. Rather than breaking with the air force, Hynek chose to stay on and work from within not only to try to change air force policy but to keep tabs on the reports received by Project Blue Book, the air force's UFO study group. By 1967 he had become a forceful advocate for the anomalous quality of the UFO phenomenon.

In 1969 the Committee for the Scientific Study of Unidentified Flying Objects, formed by the air force at the University of Colorado, issued a controversial report. Even though 33 percent of the UFO reports that it studied could not be identified, the conclusions written by project head Edward U. Condon suggested that the UFO phenomenon was unworthy of further attention. Unlike his actions after the Robertson Panel report, Hynek became a vocal and tireless critic of the committee's methodology and conclusions, embarking on a campaign to inform the public and the scientific community about the flaws in the study.

As a result of the Condon committee's conclusions, the air force closed Project Blue Book in 1969. Hynek had by this time become the best-known UFO researcher in the United States. Always an advocate of scientific conservatism and the scientific method, his cautious, careful methodology prevented his detractors from tarnishing his career or prestige, although he underwent the ridicule that all researchers in this field have suffered.

In 1972 Hynek published *The UFO Experience: A Scientific Inquiry*, which outlined his career in UFO research and became one of his greatest contributions. In it he devised a taxonomy for UFO sighting reports that provided a common language for UFO researchers around the world. The phrase "close encounters of the third kind"—UFO sightings in which witnesses reported occupants—was part of this classification system. This term became the title of a 1977 motion picture, in which Hynek had a walk-on role. In 1973 Hynek, with colleague Sherman Larsen, founded the Center for UFO Studies in Evanston, Illinois. Intended to be the first UFO research organization with a scientific stance, it helped confer legitimacy on UFO research. The center investigated cases, issued reports, and published monographs on the subject.

Hynek, with UFO researcher Jacques Vallee, published *The Edge of Reality* (1975), a conversation about

UFO research, and *The Hynek UFO Report* (1977), about the air force's study of UFOs and specific case histories from its files. He also contributed with Phil Imbrogno to *Night Siege: The Hudson Valley UFO Sightings* (1987). Hynek gained recognition as a serious scientist studying what the scientific community considered to be an "illegitimate" phenomenon. He traveled the world, meeting with UFO researchers in other countries, and he gave numerous papers and speeches at UFO conferences.

Although Hynek felt that UFOs were extraterrestrial in origin, he had great difficulties with the "nuts and bolts" extraterrestrial hypothesis—that beings get into ships and fly here from somewhere else. He felt that the distances were too great and the time to travel too long to justify the great numbers of sightings, their mysterious behavior, and the lack of formal contact. He theorized that UFOs might be interdimensional or that they arrived here in ways that were as yet unknown. This led him into speculations about what he deemed their possible origins in a parallel reality. However, he remained nondogmatic and entertained other ideas that fit the data.

When Hynek died in Scottsdale, Arizona, he was widely recognized as a sober, responsible scientist investigating a phenomenon steeped in ridicule and derision. He had bestowed a degree of legitimacy on UFO research that enabled other scientists and academics to study the UFO phenomenon. The Center for UFO Studies was renamed the J. Allen Hynek Center for UFO Studies in his honor.

• The J. Allen Hynek Papers are located at the J. Allen Hynek Center for UFO Studies, Chicago, Ill. In addition to Hyneck's works already mentioned, he edited a book of papers on astrophysics, *Astrophysics: A Topical Symposium* (1951), and coauthored a textbook in astronomy, *Astronomy One* (1972). He also wrote over forty articles and editorials on the UFO phenomenon that appeared mainly in the annual *MU-FON UFO Symposium Proceedings* and the *International UFO Reporter*, the publication of the Center for UFO Studies. Among the most important were "Unusual Aerial Phenomena," *Journal of the Optical Society of North America* 43 (1953): 311–14, and "Twenty-one Years of UFO Reports," in *UFOs: A Scientific Debate*, ed. Carl Sagan and Thornton Page (1972). David M. Jacobs, *The UFO Controversy in America* (1975), traces his UFO career, and Jacques Vallee, *Forbidden Science* (1993), talks in detail about Hynek's UFO studies in the mid-1960s. An obituary is in the *New York Times*, 1 May 1986.

DAVID M. JACOBS

HYSLOP, James Hervey (18 Aug. 1854–17 June 1920), psychologist and psychical researcher, was born in Xenia, Ohio, the son of Robert Hyslop and Martha Ann Boyle, farmers. Hyslop lived and worked on his family's farm through his college years. Although he held firmly to the strict doctrines and life of his parents' Associate Presbyterian church through his youth, he began to doubt some of his religious principles during his studies at Wooster University.

After earning his A.B. from Wooster in 1877, Hyslop taught school in Ohio for two years before moving on to teach at the college level. From 1880 to 1882 he taught at the Academy of Lake Forest University in Illinois. Hoping to further his study of philosophy, Hyslop traveled to England with the intention of eventually studying at the University of Edinburgh. While working in London his growing religious doubts moved him toward agnosticism. This changed the direction of his studies. From 1882 to 1884 he studied at the University of Leipzig, where he took courses with Wilhelm Wundt, who is considered to be the founder of experimental psychology. After his return to the United States in 1884, Hyslop taught for one year at Lake Forest University, then at Smith College from 1885 to 1886. He then won a scholarship competition that allowed him to earn his Ph.D. at Johns Hopkins University in 1887. Hyslop spent the next year (1888–1889) teaching at Bucknell University. He accepted a position in 1889 in philosophy, ethics, and psychology at Columbia University. In 1891 he married Mary Fry Hall; they had two children.

Psychology was still closely aligned with philosophy at most American universities in the late nineteenth century. Hyslop's first appointment to Columbia included explicit reference to psychology as well as philosophy, and he continued to teach introductory psychology courses even when promoted to instructor in ethics (1891–1895); he probably taught psychology as a professor of logic and ethics as well (1895–1902). In his book *Problems of Philosophy* (1905), Hyslop criticized the transcendentalist trends in philosophy and urged philosophers to make use of the discoveries of physical science, revising their questions along the lines indicated by empirical science. This did not, however, lead him to materialism. Hyslop considered psychology to be the study of consciousness; consequently, psychology was the "science of a *spiritual* as opposed to a *material* subject" (*Elements of Psychology* [1895], p. 7). Although he had studied with Wundt, Hyslop cited William James (a Wundt critic) more frequently than other authorities in the published syllabus for his introductory course on psychology. Rather than accepting Wundt's analytical approach to the elements of consciousness, Hyslop was clearly interested in extending the study of psychology into the subliminal or unconscious regions of the mind, and he believed that research into a wide variety of phenomena—including somnambulism, hypnotic trance, delusions, and automatisms—would enlarge the scientific understanding of psychology.

Hyslop's interest in psychological topics outside the range of normal consciousness appears to have led him toward psychical research and away from his earlier agnosticism. During the 1890s he attended seances, and in 1898 he joined Richard Hodgson, secretary of the American branch of the British Society for Psychical Research, in the study of the well-known medium, Leonore Piper. Hyslop's lengthy research notes and reports included what he considered compelling evidence for communication with the spirits of the dead. His decision to devote all of his time to psychical research coincided with his contracting tuberculosis, which forced him to leave his position at Columbia in 1902 for a period of recuperation spent in the Adirondacks. In 1906, as a consequence of disagreements with the Society for Psychical Research, he organized and became the secretary of the American Institute for Scientific Research. While Section A of the society, devoted to the study of abnormal psychology, was never realized, Section B—the American Society for Psychical Research—produced extensive research reports and proceedings under Hyslop's leadership and editorship.

Hyslop took seriously the need for scientific method and skepticism in the study of psychical phenomena, including apparitions, crystal gazing, telepathy, clairvoyance, premonitions, and "mediumistic phenomena." In *Life After Death: Problems of the Future Life and Its Nature* (1918), Hyslop expressed his belief that once one abandons the Cartesian psychology that views normal consciousness as the mind or self and recognizes that the self might include a range of activities "not defined by normal consciousness," then the spiritualistic explanation loses some of its force (p. 141). His own investigations showed that such physical manifestations of spiritual communication as materializations or rappings were probably either frauds or hallucinations. He admitted that gullibility and neurosis could account for some spiritualistic claims. Hyslop identified the strong personal desire for survival after death as the main weakness in the spiritualist argument in *Science and a Future Life* (1905). In *The Smead Case* (1918), Hyslop documented sessions with a medium whose automatic writing purported to be messages from beyond the grave and from Mars. He concluded that, while telepathy might have entered into the revelations, in general they could be explained as a case of secondary (multiple) personality and subliminal fabrication.

Nevertheless Hyslop argued against the exclusive claims of materialism and the closing of scientific thought to psychical evidence. His friend and assistant Walter F. Prince considered Hyslop "the most sagacious of all guides to the mazes of the phenomena of psychical research. . . . I saw that he viewed his subject-matter on all sides, weighed every hypothesis in a spirit of fairness, and preferred a conservative interpretation of every case when it could without violence be made to fit the facts" (Prince, p. 431).

He died in Upper Montclair, New Jersey.

• Hyslop's early writings included *Elements of Logic* (1892), *Elements of Ethics* (1895), *Democracy: A Study of Government* (1899), and his philosophy textbook, *Problems of Philosophy or Principles of Epistemology and Metaphysics* (1905). Hyslop published a series of works intended to bring psychical research to a broader reading audience and to consider the implications of psychical research. These works include *Enigmas of Psychical Research* (1906) and *Psychical Research and Survival* (1914). Memoirs and tributes to Hyslop are in *Journal of the American Society for Psychical Research* 14 (Sept. and Oct. 1920), particularly Walter F. Prince, "James Hervey Hyslop: Biographical Sketch and Impressions" (Sept. 1920): 425–32. An obituary is in the *New York Times*, 18 June 1920.

JOHN C. SPURLOCK

I

IAMS, Lucy Dorsey (13 Nov. 1855–26 Oct. 1924), welfare worker and reform legislator, was born Lucy Virgina Dorsey in Oakland, Maryland, the daughter of James Francis Dorsey, a doctor and Methodist minister, and Charlotte Hook. After the early death of her parents, Iams was raised by her maternal grandparents in Waynesburg, Pennsylvania. She received her B.A. from Waynesburg College in 1873, then taught in the public school system. In August 1877 she married lawyer Franklin Pierce Iams, who had also attended Waynesburg College. They had two children.

Iams moved to Pittsburgh in 1886 with her husband after he passed Pennsylvania's bar exam. She gained substantial knowledge of local and state legislation while assisting her husband for years as his legal secretary. She simultaneously maintained a successful career as court stenographer, which alerted her to the inadequacy with which the lower courts administered justice. In 1902, after repeatedly observing in the courtroom the number of deserted women and children penalized for truancy, Iams dedicated herself to legislative reform. She maintained her job as court stenographer and conducted the majority of her reform efforts through the Legislative Committee of the Civic Club of Allegheny County, for which she served as vice president from 1902 to 1924. The Civic Club informed members about needed changes in taxation, civil service, and social legislation. Under Iams's direction, it became one of the few welfare agencies in Pittsburgh to instigate reforms in health, housing, education, conservation, and penal institutions.

Iams believed that a direct correlation existed between poor housing conditions and the fate of the underprivileged. The Pittsburgh steel industry, which was the mainstay of the local economy, built its factories on the city's best land and polluted the small area that remained for residential development. Lax housing regulations resulted in overcrowding, unsanitary conditions, and insufficient lighting and plumbing. As chairperson of the Civic Club's tenement house committee, Iams was instrumental in drafting and enacting the state tenement house law of 1903. When the housing law failed to be effective, Iams supported in 1904 a citywide housing association to enforce housing codes. The same year she supported the construction of the Soho Public Baths and arranged for children to receive medical checkups in Pittsburgh public schools. In 1908 there were still 3,000 tenements in Pittsburgh, and 50 percent of old one-family houses were crowded with multiple families. In 1910 the Civic Club's housing committee (along with the Chamber of Commerce and the Civic Commission) held a conference to discuss the problems of housing and sanitation. In the meantime, Iams, as director of the Pennsylvania Housing and Town Planning Association, counseled Pittsburgh and other cities on how to enact efficient housing legislation. Her persistence paved the way for the establishment in 1928 of the Pittsburgh Housing Association, which rehabilitated old houses, secured adequate law enforcement for their upkeep, supported regional planning activities, and considered new housing projects for low-income families.

Iams also served on a number of child welfare agencies concerned with assistance to underprivileged children. She was director of the Children's Service Bureau of Pittsburgh and was an active member of the child welfare division of the Public Charities Association of Pennsylvania. Her efforts led to the creation of the Pennsylvania Children's Service Bureau in 1916, and following World War I she supported the establishment of a federal children's bureau. The federal bureau's purpose was to investigate child welfare cases, oversee the care of children in foster homes, and correct community conditions that interfered with the welfare of children. In 1921 Iams's efforts contributed to the founding of the Pennsylvania Public Welfare Department.

Iams proposed child labor laws as a response to the high rate of juvenile delinquency. Pennsylvania was behind other states in making fourteen the mandatory number of years a child had to remain in school (1907) and the minimum age at which a child could begin to work in factories and stores (1905). The labor law was difficult to enforce, however, because the parent's word was often accepted as sufficient to determine the child's age, and most magistrates were not strict in enforcing the laws that existed. Iams helped establish Pennsylvania's Department of Labor and Industry in 1913 to oversee the enforcement of these laws. She supported federal aid for vocational training and the organization of a federal department of education with a cabinet-level position to help improve public education.

Iams also advocated prison reform and took it upon herself to investigate the condition of, and methods practiced by, penal institutions. In 1909 she established the Allegheny County Industrial and Training School for Boys at Thornhill and in 1913 the State Reformatory for Women and Farm Colony at Laurelton. She found a platform to voice her concerns for prison reform as a member of the state prison board. In 1921 she was appointed by Governor Gifford Pinchot to serve three years as a trustee of the Western Penitentiary of Pennsylvania.

Iams paved the way for women in legislative reform. From 1903 to 1923 she was chairperson of the legislative committees of both the General Federation and the Pennsylvania State Federation of Women's Clubs. She successfully proposed legislation to allow women to use the notary public seal in Pennsylvania. She fought for the rights of wage-earning women and co-operated with the federal government in World War I to develop the Pittsburgh Employment Bureau. Following the war, she argued for fairness in dealing with immigrants, particularly those accused of entering the country illegally. She also acted on her conviction to preserve the environment by supporting legislation to protect the forests, national park preserves, and Niagara Falls. Iams died in Pittsburgh, Pennsylvania. She is best known for her success at reforming state legislation affecting women, children, housing conditions, and penal institutions in western Pennsylvania.

• See the Civic Club archives of Allegheny County, Pennsylvania, for documentation in its *Minutes* and *Annual Reports* of reform activities by Iams. See also the biographical entry on Iams in Gertrude B. Biddle and Sarah D. Lowrie, eds., *Notable Women of Pennsylvania* (1942). For information on social reform in Pittsburgh, particularly the organizations that Iams supported, see Paul Underwood Kellog, ed., *The Pittsburgh Survey* (6 vols., 1914), and Philip Klein, *A Social Study of Pittsburgh: Community Problems and Social Services of Allegheny County* (1938).

BARBARA L. CICCARELLI

IBERVILLE, Sieur d'. *See* Le Moyne, Pierre.

ICHHEISER, Gustav (25 Dec. 1897–Nov. 1969), psychologist, was born into a Jewish family in Cracow, Poland, then a city in the Austro-Hungarian Empire. He had one brother, but little else is known of his early life. During World War I he served in the Austrian army on the Russian and Italian fronts. After the war Ichheiser studied at the University of Vienna, first in the Faculty of Law and then in the Faculty of Philosophy. He completed his doctoral thesis in 1924 on the topic of aesthetics. His supervisor was Karl Bühler, a Gestalt psychologist of such merit as to have been offered the chair of psychology at Harvard University. In 1925 Ichheiser sojourned in Italy to study Machiavelli.

In 1926 Ichheiser began working for Vienna's Vocational Guidance Bureau, and by 1928 he was its chief psychologist. He also taught psychology and sociology in the University of Vienna's extension program and regularly visited the Institute for Social Problems in Warsaw. Ichheiser's closest friend was Gaston Roffenstein, a pioneer in the field of political psychology. His suicide in 1928 had a serious effect on Ichheiser and aggravated an already suspicious nature.

During this period Ichheiser developed his major theme: the split between appearances and reality in human affairs. His lifelong project was to describe and explain the normal cognitive processes by which we routinely misrepresent ourselves, misperceive each other, misinterpret motivations, and misunderstand the social forces that shape our thoughts and perceptions. Ichheiser was not part of the intellectual movements of psychoanalysis and logical positivism then centered in Vienna. Rather, he traced his thinking to phenomenology, sociology of science, and social theorists such as Duc François de la Rochefoucauld, Bernard de Mandeville, Karl Marx, and Vilfredo Pareto.

In 1938, when Nazi Germany took over Austria, Ichheiser escaped to Switzerland. He reached England but was classified as an enemy alien because of his Austrian citizenship. In 1940 he immigrated to the United States. His mother, brother, sister-in-law, and niece all perished in the Holocaust.

With a letter of introduction from sociologist Karl Mannheim, Ichheiser sought an academic position at the University of Chicago. He was unsuccessful, but he would persist in this effort for the rest of his life. He lost his first job at a Chicago publishing firm because he said at a public meeting that winning World War II would not result in permanent peace. In 1943 he was a staff psychologist at the state psychiatric hospital in Manteno, Illinois. However, after a brief marriage and a scandalous extramarital affair, he returned to Chicago. From 1944 to 1948 Ichheiser taught psychology and sociology at Talladega College in Alabama. In 1949 he was back in Chicago, taking temporary research jobs. In 1950, after several years' delay due to his divorce, Ichheiser obtained his U.S. citizenship. During this period he continued to be intellectually productive. He even applied for janitorial work in order to have a university affiliation for publication purposes. But continuing poverty and his friends' apparent indifference to his plight caused him to become increasingly suspicious.

In 1951 the welfare services committed Ichheiser to the state hospital in Peoria, Illinois, for "paranoid schizophrenia" and "inability to manage his own estate." He wrote numerous letters to people at the University of Chicago, pleading for help in getting released. In 1960, from the hospital, he published a letter in the *Bulletin of the Atomic Scientists* explaining that French nationalism was less dangerous than American nationalism because the French at least knew that they were nationalists. This letter led to a Rockefeller Foundation grant to write a book, and his first paycheck caused him to be released from psychiatric confinement. Ichheiser noted with irony that either he was not schizophrenic when committed or he was still schizophrenic when released; either way, paychecks cannot cure schizophrenia.

The Rockefeller grant was hosted at the University of Chicago's Foreign Policy Center. The final manuscript, "On Our Current Illusions Concerning the Basic Issues of Peace and War," was held back from publication by Hans Morgenthau. Ichheiser continued to take small research jobs and to publish his insightful articles. He had finished editing a collection of his English writings shortly before he died, alone in a Chicago hotel room. His body was found several days later by Eithel Knight, a volunteer with the Jewish Family and Community Service who delivered meals to him. There were suggestions of suicide; no obituary was ever written. The reprint volume was published in 1970 as *Appearances and Realities*.

Despite the many disruptions and difficulties in Ichheiser's life, he still published three books and more than seventy academic papers. Whether writing in German, Polish, or English, he had a rich and persuasive mastery of language and an abundance of original ideas. His life was a tragedy, especially considering the advanced state of his work in cognitive social psychology. For example, in the 1940s a standard theory was that stereotyping causes prejudice—as seen in German and American racism—and that if stereotyping were stopped, prejudice and racism would be cured. Ichheiser argued that stereotyping is natural and inevitable and that minority groups are partly responsible for their stereotyped images.

Another standard theory was that strict, punitive child rearing, as commonly practiced in Germany, causes an authoritarian personality that is prone to fascism. Ichheiser argued that the very idea of a unified and consistent personality is a misconception arising from the perceptual salience of the physical person and the relative invisibility of the social contexts and social roles in which the person is placed. A third commonly accepted theory was that frustration causes aggression. Ichheiser called this ideology parading as science because it blames those who are frustrated for any ensuing violence and thus makes those who cause the frustration appear to be the victims.

In most of these examples, Ichheiser's explanations have prevailed; their acceptance, however, came too late to positively affect his life. Reviewers of his 1970 reprint volume did not realize that his writings dated from the 1940s, and they therefore accused Ichheiser of taking ideas from books written in the 1960s without giving due credit. Clearly, Ichheiser is the one deserving of credit.

• Ichheiser was twice dispossessed of his personal papers and scholarly notes, in 1938 and 1951. However, some of his correspondence is at the University of Chicago, among the archived files of Sol Tax and Louis Wirth. Ichheiser's magnum opus, "Misunderstandings in Human Relations: A Study in False Social Perceptions," first appeared as a supplement to the *American Journal of Sociology* 55 (1949); it was published later that year as a book with the same title. Ichheiser's biography and bibliography appear in F. W. Rudmin et al., "Gustav Ichheiser in the History of Social Psychology: An Early Phenomenology of Social Attribution," *British Journal of Social Psychology* 26 (1987): 165–80.

F. W. RUDMIN

ICKES, Anna Wilmarth Thompson (27 Jan. 1873–31 Aug. 1935), Illinois state legislator and reformer, was born in Chicago, Illinois, the daughter of Henry Martin Wilmarth, a businessman and banker, and Mary Jane Hawes. Anna grew up comfortably in North Chicago, finishing high school and then attending Miss Hersey's School in Boston for two years.

After a year in Paris, Anna returned to Chicago in 1893 and became one of the first women students to enroll at the University of Chicago. She did not complete her degree but married a young history instructor named James Westfall Thompson in 1897. Thompson would later become a nationally recognized medieval historian at the University of Chicago.

With Thompson she had one son, Wilmarth, and later adopted a daughter, Frances. In 1909, however, they divorced. Two years later on 16 September 1911 Anna married Harold LeClair Ickes, a Chicago lawyer, whom she had known since her days at the University of Chicago. With Harold she had a son, Raymond Wilmarth, and adopted another, Robert.

Influenced by her mother, Ickes held a strong interest in local politics, and throughout her life she could be described as a progressive Republican. As a young woman she had joined her mother in supporting the Women's Trade Union League, and on more than one occasion she provided bail for young women arrested on the picket line. Her interest in reform led her and her new husband to actively press for the creation of the Progressive party in Illinois. Woodrow Wilson's subsequent victories in 1912 and 1916 kept the Progressive wing of the Republican party at bay, and both Anna and Harold Ickes returned to the Republican mainstream, though neither supported Warren Harding as the 1920 Republican standard bearer. In 1924 Illinois governor Len Small appointed Ickes to a vacancy on the University of Illinois board of trustees. Later that year she was reelected to her own four-year term and served until January 1929. Like her mother before her, she served as president of the Chicago Women's Club in 1925. Reflecting her interest in improving the welfare of the less fortunate, she also served on the boards of the Chicago Home for the Friendless and the Chicago Regional Planning Association.

In the early 1920s the Ickes family began spending part of each year in New Mexico to get away from the damp winters of Chicago, which had given Anna periodic attacks of asthma. Ickes quickly fell in love with the beauty of the desert and built a small adobe house in nearby Coolidge, New Mexico, on the edge of a Navajo Indian reservation. From this vantage point she began a sustained study of the Navajo and Hopi people, their land and culture. She became fluent in Navajo, and in 1933 she published *Mesa Land*, a work of history and amateur anthropology. Her interest in Native American affairs resulted in her appointment to the board of the Indian Rights Association of Chicago.

In 1928 Ickes ran for the state legislature as a representative from the Seventh Congressional District, which comprised the northern and western suburbs of Cook County. With her husband as her campaign manager, she won handily and was readily reelected in 1930 and 1932. Ickes enjoyed immensely her time in the legislature, and by 1933 she was sitting on seven committees, including those on civil service, education, charities and corrections, and industrial affairs. Her deep sense of noblesse oblige was satisfied through this challenging, yet rewarding, work in the public arena.

In the 1932 presidential election Harold Ickes supported Franklin D. Roosevelt and as a reward was appointed secretary of the interior in 1933. With her husband now in Washington, Ickes sought at first to divide her time between Springfield, Illinois, and the nation's capital, where she had duties as the spouse of a cabinet member. This rigorous schedule became too difficult and taxing on her energies, and although she would have most likely been reelected she did not seek a new term in 1934 but devoted herself to her cultural studies in New Mexico. While traveling in August 1935 to attend a Navajo ceremony, she was fatally injured in an automobile accident near Velarde, New Mexico, about forty miles north of Santa Fe.

Anna Wilmarth Ickes was a well-educated, handsome, and dignified woman who believed that those better off should assist the downtrodden wherever possible. Confident and strong-willed, she was an active proponent of the reformist ideals that characterized the Progressive Era of her youth.

• Correspondence relating to Anna Ickes can be found in the voluminous Harold L. Ickes Papers at the Library of Congress. Parts of Harold Ickes's published diary are pertinent, *The First Thousand Days, 1933–1936* (1953). Also useful is his *Autobiography of a Curmugeon* (1943). Two biographies of Harold Ickes contain numerous references to Anna: Tom H. Watkins, *Righteous Pilgrim: The Life and Times of Harold L. Ickes, 1874–1952* (1990), and Graham White and John Maze, *Harold Ickes of the New Deal: His Private Life and Public Career* (1985). Obituaries appear in the *New York Times* and the *Chicago Tribune*, both on 1 Sept. 1935.

EDWARD GOEDEKEN

ICKES, Harold LeClair (15 Mar. 1874–3 Feb. 1952), secretary of the interior under Franklin D. Roosevelt and (briefly) Harry S. Truman, was born in Hollidaysburg, Pennsylvania, the son of Jesse Boone Williams Ickes, a notions salesman and accountant, and Matilda "Mattie" McCune. Shortly after Harold's birth the family settled in nearby Altoona. When his mother died of pneumonia in 1890, Ickes and a sister were sent to live with an aunt and uncle in the Chicago suburb of Englewood.

It was a difficult, even dismal time for the young man. His father, footloose and alcoholic, gave him virtually no support. His uncle was demanding and parsimonious, offering little more than room and board, in exchange for which Ickes worked long hours in the family drugstore while attending high school. In spite of this, Ickes graduated as senior class president and valedictorian in 1892, demonstrating early on the furious determination to succeed and the nearly pathological dedication to work that would characterize his later public service.

Ickes worked his way through the University of Chicago, intermittently teaching English to immigrants at night in Chicago schools and taking any other job he could find. He graduated with a respectable record in 1896. Uncertain as to profession, he took a job as a newspaper reporter in Chicago, where he became exposed to the corrupt but exciting world of urban politics. More important, he was exposed to a reform movement led by Raymond Robins, head of the Northwestern University Settlement House; Robins's wife, Margaret Dreier Robins, a cofounder of the Na-

tional Womens' Trade Union League; Charles E. Merriam, a professor of political science at the University of Chicago; Jane Addams, the famous mistress of Hull House; and other stalwarts whose liberal principles and dedication to good government informed the rest of Ickes's political life.

In 1903 John Harlan hired Ickes to manage his campaign for the Republican nomination for mayor. Harlan lost, though not for want of prodigious labor on Ickes's part. In 1904 Ickes returned to the University of Chicago for a law degree, received it in 1907, passed the Illinois bar, hung out a shingle, and after several years on his own joined the firm of Donald Richberg, another young lawyer.

By then, the Chicago reformers had become part of the Progressive wing of the national Republican party. Ickes soon found himself in the company of such figures as former president Theodore Roosevelt (1858–1919); Roosevelt's chief forester (and later Pennsylvania governor), Gifford Pinchot; Herbert Croly, founding editor of the *New Republic*; William Allen White, editor and owner of the *Emporia* (Kansas) *Gazette*, the best-known small-town newspaper in the United States; and Hiram Johnson, governor of California.

In 1911 Ickes married Anna Wilmarth Thompson, a wealthy divorcée. It was a tempestuous and troubled marriage that produced one child. Ickes was unhappy much of the time and aggravated by chronic insomnia and bouts of pain from an old and badly healed mastoid operation—afflictions that haunted him all his life. Nevertheless, Ickes respected his wife's intelligence and political drive—he directed her successful campaigns for the Illinois General Assembly in 1928, 1930, and 1932—and her wealth removed the need for him to grub for a living.

Ickes swiftly rose to prominence as a political reformer and campaign manager in the steamy cauldron of Chicago politics. During Theodore Roosevelt's unsuccessful run at a third term in 1912 as the candidate of the Progressive (Bull Moose) party, Ickes was his Cook County campaign manager, delivering the city of Chicago and its environs to Roosevelt.

During World War I, Ickes served overseas with the YMCA. He returned to the political wars of Chicago undaunted by the apparent triumph of conservative Republicanism in the 1920s, both nationally and in Chicago, where crime and corruption reigned under Mayor William Hale "Big Bill" Thompson.

Early in 1932 Ickes was asked by Franklin Roosevelt's campaign organizers to head a Western Independent Republican Committee for Roosevelt. He did so, but only after promising his wife, who had an abiding interest in the plight of the Indian, that he would ask to become commissioner of Indian affairs if Roosevelt won. After Roosevelt's election in November, however, Ickes changed his mind: he decided to go after the job of secretary of the interior, on the theory, he explained in his *Autobiography of a Curmudgeon* (1943), that it "would be no more painful or fatal to be hung for a secretary than for a commissioner." After considerable lobbying by Ickes and typically enigmatic behavior by Roosevelt, the appointment came to pass. "I liked the cut of his jib," the president-elect told adviser Raymond Moley.

During the nearly thirteen years of his tenure as secretary of the interior, Ickes was assigned or appropriated more tasks, covered more bureaucratic territory, involved himself in more controversy, and arguably worked harder, longer, and better than any interior secretary in American history. What is certain is that he was one of the greatest public administrators of all time and a man whose dedication to liberal principles helped shape the character and quality of life in the depression and World War II years.

The inherited responsibilities of his agency included the supervision of more than 30,000 employees scattered over forty states and territories; the management of the National Park System, nearly 300 million acres of unappropriated public lands, and all the grass, timber, oil, natural gas, hydropower, coal, and other mineral resources they contained; the government of Hawaii, Alaska, Puerto Rico, the Virgin Islands, and other U.S. possessions (with the addition of the Philippines after 1934); and the administration of a plethora of agencies, institutions, and subbureaucracies, chief among them the Bureau of Reclamation, the Office of Education, the Geological Survey, and the corrupt and incompetent Bureau of Indian Affairs (a situation Ickes tried to reverse with the appointment of John Collier as commissioner of Indian affairs).

Quite enough to fill anyone's plate, but the famous "Hundred Days" that embodied Roosevelt's efforts to deal with the Great Depression gave Ickes even more to do. In March 1933, with Secretary of Agriculture Henry A. Wallace, Labor Secretary Frances Perkins, and Secretary of War George Dern, Ickes established the structure of the Civilian Conservation Corps (CCC). His department's Office of Education supervised the education of the young men in the CCC camps, while the National Park Service employed thousands to make improvements in the national parks.

In June 1933 Ickes was appointed to direct the Public Works Administration (PWA), which he had helped to form. Over the six-year life of this program, he supervised the expenditure of nearly $6 billion for the construction of dams, hospitals, tunnels, bridges, schools, highways, irrigation works, post offices, and the like all over the country. There were 19,000 projects in all, including 583 municipal water systems, 622 sewerage systems, 263 hospitals, 522 schools, 368 street and highway projects, as well as such well known items as Boulder (later Hoover) Dam on the Colorado River and many of the facilities of the Tennessee Valley Authority (TVA). What is more, it was all accomplished without any taint of corruption, a record that earned Ickes the nickname "Honest Harold."

Ickes may have been "a builder to rival Cheops," as one historian described him, but he was also a dedicated conservationist. Roosevelt was no mean conservationist himself, and as a result the national parks and public lands of the United States received more loving care than at any previous time. Creation of the Grazing Service in 1934, and the consequent protective withdrawal of 142 million acres, helped to bring erosion on public grazing lands under control. The Soil Erosion Service (later the Soil Conservation Service) was established to do the same for private farms. The Everglades, Great Smoky Mountains, and Shenandoah national parks, already established, were completed during Ickes's reign, and such major new parks as Olympic National Park in Washington, Kings Canyon National Park in California, and Jackson Hole National Monument in Wyoming were created, most in spite of powerful political opposition. Furthermore, in 1939 Ickes drafted legislation that would have established inviolate wilderness areas in the National Park System. Although the legislation failed, it presaged the revolutionary Wilderness Act of 1964.

Left to his own devices, Ickes would have taken on even more conservation work—namely, the National Forest System, which throughout his tenure he repeatedly (and fruitlessly) tried to persuade Roosevelt to transfer from the Department of Agriculture to Interior. These efforts did not endear him to Henry Wallace, and the New Deal years were enlivened by a nearly constant bureaucratic squabble between the two men.

Ickes had a similar relationship with Harry Hopkins, head of the Works Progress Administration (WPA), each man vying for dominance in the spending of public monies and for the favor of Roosevelt. These conflicts—together with Roosevelt's notorious vagueness with regard to administrative matters—led to numerous hot-tempered resignations on the part of Ickes, all rejected by the president.

Ickes's responsibilities continued to multiply in any case. In 1939 the Department of Interior took over the U.S. Biological Survey, which administered the National Wildlife Refuge System, and the Bureau of Fisheries, which controlled offshore fishing. In May 1941, as war drew near, Ickes was appointed the head of the Petroleum Administration for National Defense, an entity designed to assure the supply and distribution of oil and gasoline. After Pearl Harbor, the agency was renamed Petroleum Administration for War, and Ickes and his staff initiated the first gasoline rationing program (voluntary and largely unsuccessful) and constructed the famed "Big Inch" and "Little Inch" pipelines from Texas. He supervised the wartime distribution of oil, gasoline, and aviation fuel so brilliantly that the agency earned encomiums from General George C. Marshall, Jr. The agency attempted unsuccessfully to gain control over future oil supplies in Saudi Arabia, while Ickes also campaigned unsuccessfully for a coherent national oil policy.

The relationship between Ickes and Roosevelt was frequently troubled by arguments, most of them, it must be said, initiated by Ickes, who was as thin skinned as he was stubborn. Nevertheless, through it all Ickes remained the president's staunchest and most useful political ally in the cabinet. A tireless, colorful, and effective stump speaker, he was a major force in the reelection campaigns of 1936, 1940, and 1944 and, in fact, was the first administration figure to speak out in favor of Roosevelt's controversial third term of 1940. What is more, he was a prominent spokesman in a number of sensitive areas, constantly speechifying against fascism, the growing horror of the Nazi persecution of Jews, other right-wing movements, and isolationism. He also vigorously promoted the civil rights of African Americans. He had served as the Chicago director of the NAACP in 1923, and his reputation as a supporter of black causes led him to become, as historian Arthur M. Schlesinger, Jr., put it, "an informal Secretary of Negro Relations." His best-known accomplishments in this regard included the desegregation of the Interior Department, the appointment of William Hastie as the first African-American federal judge (in the U.S. Virgin Islands, an Interior responsibility), and helping Eleanor Roosevelt arrange Marian Anderson's famous Easter Sunday concert at the Lincoln Memorial in 1939 after the Daughters of the American Revolution refused Anderson the use of its Constitution Hall. Ickes himself introduced the singer at the concert.

After Roosevelt's death in April 1945, Ickes lasted less than a year before a conflict with Harry Truman over the appointment of oilman Edwin Pauley as undersecretary of the navy spurred one more resignation, this one promptly accepted on 13 February 1946. Ickes spent the remaining six years of his life commuting between his farm in Olney, Maryland, and an office in Washington, where he continued to add to the voluminous diary he had started the first day of his tenure as secretary of the interior. He worked as a columnist for the *New York Post* and the *New Republic*; dictated articles, including an eight-part memoir for the *Saturday Evening Post*; worked on a book; and supported a bevy of liberal causes.

His wife, Anna, was killed in an automobile accident in 1935, and in 1938 Ickes married Jane Dahlman, who was nearly forty years his junior. This was a happy marriage that produced two children. After Ickes's death in Washington, D.C., Jane Ickes edited the three volumes of his *Secret Diary*, one of the central documents of the age of Roosevelt.

For all his flaws and excesses, his curmudgeonly ways and sometimes irresponsible tongue, Ickes was driven by a strain of liberal optimism as old and as durable as the Republic. He believed that men and women could take hold of their government and shape it to great ends. It was a vision to which he held to the day of his death, and it remains his most enduring legacy.

• The bulk of the Harold L. Ickes Papers, including personal and public letters and documents, reside in the Library of Congress. The papers contain more than 150,000 items, among them the 4.8 million words of his diary and four separate unpublished autobiographical works. Additional Ickes papers are in the Franklin D. Roosevelt Memorial Library in Hyde Park, N.Y.; the Bancroft Library at the University of California at Berkeley; the Harry Slattery Papers in the William R. Perkins Library at Duke University; and several of the records offices of the National Archives, including those in Kansas City and Washington, D.C. About 800,000 words of the Ickes diaries were published as *The Secret Diaries of Harold L. Ickes: The First Thousand Days, 1933–1936* (1953); *The Inside Struggle, 1936–1939* (1954); and *The Lowering Clouds, 1939–1941* (1954). See also Linda Lear, *Harold L. Ickes: The Aggressive Progressive, 1874–1933* (1981), an excellent political study of his Chicago years; Graham White and John Maze, *Harold Ickes of the New Deal: His Private Life and Public Career* (1985), a "psychobiography" that in spite of its title does not cover his public career in much detail; T. H. Watkins, *Righteous Pilgrim: The Life and Times of Harold L. Ickes, 1874–1952* (1990), an attempt at a complete life; and Arthur M. Schlesinger, Jr., *The Coming of the New Deal* (1958) and *The Politics of Upheaval* (1959).

T. H. WATKINS

IDDINGS, Joseph Paxson (21 Jan. 1857–8 Sept. 1920), petrologist and educator, was born in Baltimore, Maryland, the son of William Penn Iddings, a merchant, and Almira Gillet. With the encouragement of his father, Iddings graduated in 1877 with a Ph.B. in civil engineering from the Sheffield Scientific School of Yale University. He spent the next year in graduate study of chemistry and mineralogy while assisting in courses in mechanical drawing and surveying. He continued his studies in geology and assaying during 1878–1879 at the Columbia School of Mines, mainly as a result of the influence of a lecture at Yale by Clarence King. During 1879–1880 Iddings studied microscopical petrography under K. H. F. Rosenbusch at Heidelberg, the principal experience that guided his career. As a result of his meeting Arnold Hague in London in the spring of 1880, Iddings returned to the United States to work at the U.S. Geological Survey.

He first worked as an assistant geologist to Hague in the Eureka, Nevada, mining district, sharing a tent with Charles D. Walcott, who eventually became director of the Geological Survey. He briefly spent some time with George F. Becker at the Virginia City, Nevada, ore deposits after a brief visit in April 1880 to the American Museum of Natural History, New York, primarily to study the collections of the Fortieth Parallel Survey on temporary deposit there until 1884. The first folio of the *Geologic Atlas of the United States*, the Livingstone, Montana, quadrangle, was produced by Iddings and Walter Harvey Weed in 1894. For seven field seasons (1883–1890) Iddings worked with Hague on the exploration and mapping of the geology of Yellowstone National Park. It was here that he developed most of his original, and often controversial, ideas that were to influence greatly future petrologic thinking. He concluded that the graduations of crystalline textures and mineral compositions were dependent on the physical conditions attending the consolidation of an igneous magma; phenocrysts (a term invented by Iddings in 1889 for prominent crystals in a porphyritic rock) resulted from rapid crystallization before final consolidation of a magma; volatile constituents served as mineralizing agents; and associated igneous rocks were related to a common magma. He challenged the view that granular rocks were produced only in large masses at depth. These fundamental concepts on the origin of igneous rocks were summarized in a long paper presented to the Philosophical Society of Washington in 1892. As a result of the elimination of his statutory position and reduction in funds at the Geological Survey in July 1892, Iddings resigned to accept, on 1 January 1893, at the request of Thomas C. Chamberlin at the University of Chicago, the first independent chair of petrology in the world. He had also been considered for positions at Yale, Stanford, and Johns Hopkins.

Teaching renewed his interest in the classification of igneous rocks that had arisen earlier when he translated and abridged Rosenbusch's "Mikroskopische Physiographie der Petrographisch wichtigen Mineralien" (1888). He consulted early in 1893 with C. Whitman Cross, Louis V. Pirsson, George H. Williams, and Henry S. Washington, and, after the death of Williams, they produced in 1902 the C. I. P. W. quantitative system for classifying igneous rocks from chemical analyses expressed as ideal or normative end-member minerals, a work that had a profound influence on both field and experimental petrology. Even with the aid of his new classification of igneous rocks, Iddings did not like to teach, and his students did not consider him an effective teacher. Only two Ph.D. theses were carried out under his supervision. In the spring of 1908 he appears, on the basis of several accounts, to have been informed of the death of an aunt and of a substantial inheritance. Iddings abruptly departed from the university, and although he was granted a year's leave of absence, he never returned. He settled at the family estate, "Riverside," at Brinklow, Maryland.

Now free to write, lecture, and travel, Iddings produced a two-volume work titled *Igneous Rocks* (vol. 1, 1909; vol. 2, 1913); a series of lectures at Yale, which was published as *The Problem of Volcanism* (1914); and revisions to his *Rock Minerals* (1911). He circled the globe twice, in each direction, collecting rocks, particularly in the South Pacific Islands. Iddings was active at the Cosmos Club in Washington, D.C. (1885–1920) and in the Petrologists Club (1910–1919), which met for many years in the home of his close friend C. Whitman Cross. He gradually retired from public life, unmarried, and rented the "Grove Hill Farm," near the family estate, in 1915 with his sister Lola LaMotte Iddings, a poet. He was a member of the Congregational church, although his grandfather, Caleb P. Iddings, was a Quaker who had been "disowned" on his marriage to a Calvinist. Iddings died at the Montgomery County, Maryland, hospital of chronic interstitial nephritis. Fittingly, his tombstone in the Woodside Cemetery of Brinklow, Maryland, is a large rock boulder.

Iddings has been described as a reserved, cultured gentleman who made lasting friendships wherever he went in the world. He was elected a foreign member of the Scientific Society of Christiania (1902) and the Geological Society of London (1904); a member of the National Academy of Sciences (1907) and the American Philosophical Society (1911); an honorary member of the Société francaise de Mineralogie (1914); and a fellow of the Geological Society of America (1889, serving as vice president in 1916). Yale University gave him an honorary doctor of science in 1907. The mineral iddingsite, described initially by Iddings (1892) and now believed to consist of several phases resulting from the alteration process of iddingsization, was named in his honor by Andrew C. Lawson in 1893. He was also honored by the name of an early Cambrian trilobite, *Olenellus iddingsi* Walcott (1884), that was later recognized as a new genus and called *Peachella iddingsi* Walcott (1910). A scholarship in his name was set up at Yale University by his sister Estelle Iddings Cleveland with the residua of his estate and supplementary funds.

• Letters written during Iddings's travels to the South Pacific during 1914, and correspondence with Charles Walcott, are in the Archives of the Smithsonian Institution. His correspondence with Arthur Day, director of the Geophysical Laboratory, from 1907 to 1920, is in the archives of that laboratory. Letters to Thomas C. Chamberlin are in the archives of the Department of Geophysical Sciences, University of Chicago. Iddings's unfinished autobiographical manuscript, "Recollections of a Petrologist," given to C. Whitman Cross before Iddings's death and referred to in the most extensive biography of Iddings—E. B. Mathews, "Memorial of Joseph Paxton [sic] Iddings," *Bulletin of the Geological Society of America* 44 (1933): 352–74—is not among the Cross papers retained by his namesake grandson. The Mathews biography contains a detailed bibliography of Iddings's publications. Some of the more important investigations include "On the Crystallization of Igneous Rocks," *Bulletin of the Philosophical Society of Washington* 11 (1889): 67–113; "The Eruptive Rocks of Electric Peak and Sepulchre Mountain, Yellowstone National Park," *U.S. Geological Survey, Annual Report* 12 (1891): 569–664; "The Origin of Igneous Rocks," *Bulletin of the Philosophical Society of Washington* 12 (1892): 89–213; *Microscopical Petrography of the Eruptive Rocks of the Eureka District, Nevada*, U.S. Geological Survey Monograph, no. 20 (1892), pp. 335–96; "Extrusive and Intrusive Igneous Rocks as Products of Magmatic Differentiation," *Quarterly Journal of the Geological Society of London* 52 (1896): 606–7; "On Rock Classification," *Journal of Geology* 6 (1898): 92–111; "The Igneous Rocks of the Absaroka Range and Two Ocean Plateau and of the Outlying Portions of the Yellowstone National Park," *U.S. Geological Survey Monograph* 32 (part 2, chap. 8; 1899): 269–325; "A Quantitative Chemico-mineralogical Classification and Nomenclature of Igneous Rocks" (with C. W. Cross, L. V. Pirsson, and H. S. Washington), *Journal of Geology* 10 (1902): 555–690; and *The Isomorphism and Thermal Properties of the Feldspars. Part II. Optical Study*, Carnegie Institution of Washington Publication no. 31 (1905), pp. 79–95.

H. S. YODER, JR.

IDE, John Jay (26 June 1892–12 Jan. 1962), aviation pioneer and advocate, was born at Narragansett Pier, Rhode Island, the son of George E. Ide, a rear admiral of the U.S. Navy, and Alexandra Bruen. Ide was the great-great-grandson of John Jay, early U.S. diplomat and first chief justice of the U.S. Supreme Court. Ide attended the Browning School in New York City, and upon graduation from Columbia University in 1913 he received a certificate in architecture. He then studied architecture at the École des Beaux-Arts in Paris for the next year before returning to New York to work as an architect. When the United States entered World War I in 1917, Ide enlisted in the Naval Reserve Flying Corps and rose to the rank of lieutenant. He also took the opportunity to court and marry Dora Browning Donner of Philadelphia, the daughter of philanthropist and steel financier William Henry Donner. They had no children.

It was during his service in the navy that Ide became interested in the course of aviation, especially its technological development. His language skills and familiarity with the culture of Europe and especially that of France helped him land an appointment in 1921 as the European representative for the National Advisory Committee for Aeronautics (NACA), a governmental organization created in 1915 to foster aeronautical technology. Spending much of that time also as the air attaché at the U.S. embassy in both Paris and London, Ide was well positioned to aid the NACA in maintaining currency in European aviation advances. From those posts Ide participated in several early international conferences in Europe, where he worked on laws and regulations for commercial aviation. Through his efforts, for the first time in 1928 the American aviation industry began to participate in European air shows and exhibitions.

Ide's greatest achievement for the NACA, however, came in the latter half of the 1930s, when he kept the agency and the U.S. government as a whole informed of aeronautical developments in Hitler's Germany. The NACA was a sleepy institution until the first part of 1936, when Ide fired off an alarming report on the state of aeronautical science in Europe. Ide, the part-time technology expert, part-time intelligence analyst, and part-time expatriate socialite, reported on greatly increased aeronautical research activities in Great Britain, France, Italy, and especially Germany. He observed that new and quite modern wind tunnels were being erected to aid in the development of higher-performance aircraft and suggested that the NACA review its own equipment to determine whether it met contemporary demands. Ide enlisted the assistance of Charles A. Lindbergh, an executive NACA committee member living in seclusion in England, to confirm his report. Because of this, the NACA's 1936 report commented on the arms race in Europe and concluded that

increased recognition abroad of the value and of the vital necessity of aeronautical research has led to recent tremendous expansion in research programs and to multiplication of research facilities by other progressive nations. Thus has the foundation been laid for a serious challenge to America's present leadership in the technical development of aircraft. (*Twenty-second Annual Report of the National Advisory Committee for Aeronautics* [1937], p. 3)

Because of these developments, in 1936 Ide arranged an invitation to Germany for several NACA leaders to tour its aeronautical research facilities. While there Ide and other NACA leaders toured several aeronautical facilities with Dr. Adolph Bäumker, the head of research and development for the German government, and was both impressed and disquieted by their activities. They learned that Luftwaffe chief and Hitler stalwart Hermann Göring was "intensely interested in research and development." With Göring's support Bäumker greatly expanded aeronautical research and development, decentralizing it at three major stations: one for research on new aircraft, one for fundamental research without application to specific aircraft designs, and one for the development of new propulsion systems. It was a powerful combination, especially when Reichmarks were flowing to fund accelerated experimentation. To maintain American primacy in aviation, Ide realized, the nation should immediately start the NACA's expansion. Accordingly, during the next five years the NACA built two new research laboratories and expanded its activities in other ways as a counter to German aviation development.

With war clouds gathering around the world, in 1940 the U.S. Navy recalled Ide to active duty, commissioning him as a lieutenant commander and placing him in command of the Foreign Intelligence Branch of the Bureau of Aeronautics in Washington. He served in that post until 1943, when the federal government appointed him a technical air intelligence officer in Europe. In this capacity Ide helped to survey the aeronautical capabilities of defeated Nazi Germany at the conclusion of the war in Europe.

Although mustered out of active military duty with the rank of navy captain in late 1945, Ide remained in Europe as representative for the NACA for the next five years. There he continued the work he had undertaken in 1921 as a representative for the organization and as a conduit for technical information about the development of aviation technology on the Continent. He retired from that position in 1950.

John Ide returned to the United States soon after retirement from the NACA, residing in New York City. He was socially prominent in that city, as well as in Washington, D.C., and Palm Beach, Florida. He served in a variety of honorary positions during this period: vice president of the International Aeronautic Federation, president of the International Sporting Commission, board member of the National Aeronautic Association, trustee of the Museum of the City of New York, manager of the American Bible Society, and vestryman of the St. Bartholomew's Protestant Episcopal Church in New York.

Ide returned to France in 1958 to present a plaque to commemorate the site in Paris where John Jay participated in the signing of the peace treaty between Britain and the United States in 1783 that ended the American Revolution. He died at his Park Avenue home in New York City.

• The best collection of John J. Ide Papers is in the National Air and Space Museum, Smithsonian Institution, Washington, D.C., but another collection is at the Library of Congress. Additional information about Ide can be found in Alex Roland, *Model Research: The National Advisory Committee for Aeronautics, 1915–1958* (1985), and in James R. Hansen, *Engineer in Charge: A History of the Langley Aeronautical Laboratory, 1917–1958* (1987). An obituary is in the *New York Times*, 13 Jan. 1962.

ROGER D. LAUNIUS

IGLESIAS, Santiago (22 Feb. 1872–5 Dec. 1939), labor organizer and Puerto Rico's territorial representative in Congress, was born in La Coruña, Spain, the son of Manuel Iglesias, a carpenter, and Josefa Pantín. At age twelve, when his father died, he became a carpenter's apprentice. When his employer denied workers permission to attend a Sunday meeting to protest sales taxes, he organized a walkout in 1884 that was broken up by soldiers who fired on the protesters.

Iglesias joined the Spanish Socialist party and emigrated to Cuba in 1887; there he got a job in a furniture factory and began to organize workers against the twelve-hour day. Spanish authorities suppressed his efforts and shadowed him after the Cuban war for independence broke out in 1895. To escape harassment, he fled to Puerto Rico in late 1896, but Spanish authorities there jailed him for his labor organizing activities.

After U.S. forces headed by General John R. Brooke occupied the island, Spanish officials tried unsuccessfully to deport Iglesias to Spain. Iglesias became a guide and interpreter for General Brooke and presided over the first convention of the Puerto Rican Federation of Labor on 20 October 1898. He soon went to Brooklyn, New York, where he worked as a carpenter and attended night classes at Cooper Union. He convinced American Federation of Labor (AFL) president Samuel Gompers to launch an organizing campaign in Puerto Rico and accompanied him to the White House to discuss with President Theodore Roosevelt (1858–1919) plans to return to the island as an AFL organizer.

When Iglesias returned to Puerto Rico in November 1901, insular authorities arrested him for failing to appear in court on charges related to an earlier arrest and conviction in the summer of 1900 for having violated an old Spanish law against conspiring to raise the price of labor. Gompers posted his bail and intervened with President Roosevelt. Authorities released Iglesias after he served seven months of a three-and-one-half-year jail term.

Iglesias married Justa Bocanegra of Puerto Rico in 1902; the marriage produced eleven children. He headed the AFL-affiliated Federación Libre de Trabajadores de Puerto Rico between 1900 and 1935, founded the Puerto Rican Socialist party in 1915, and served in the Puerto Rican senate from 1917 to 1933. Deep democratic convictions and a vague sense of social justice rather than a clear theoretical understanding of socialism informed his thought and actions. These tendencies, along with his pro-Americanism and pleasant personality, made him acceptable to the more conservative Gompers, who used him to extend AFL influence and promote favorable views of the United States in Latin America.

Iglesias urged Gompers to form the Pan American Federation of Labor (PAFL) to protect workers against the growing economic penetration of Latin America by American capital. Gompers had strategic objectives in mind, however, when he sent Iglesias, John Murray, and James Lord on a secret mission to Mexico in May 1918 to lay the groundwork for the first PAFL conference. The real purpose of their mission, funded covertly by the U.S. government, was to promote the Allied war effort among Mexican workers. Iglesias skillfully deflected criticism of the AFL's motives by pro-German newspapers and leftists in the Mexican labor movement. An AFL report praised his relations with Mexican workers, noting that "he is conversant with their history and wrongs, speaks their language, and succeeds in bringing the most radical to agree with him on programs and methods."

Iglesias was Puerto Rico's resident commissioner in Congress between 1933 and 1939. He suffered minor wounds when a nationalist unhappy over his pro-statehood activities in Congress tried to assassinate him in 1936. In late 1939 the AFL sent Iglesias on a mission to Mexico to resurrect the PAFL and combat growing radical challenges to its influence in Latin America. He died in Washington, D.C., shortly after contracting malaria in Mexico.

Iglesias served as secretary of the PAFL from 1925 to 1939. He played an important role in the AFL's efforts to shape the Mexican Revolution and promote business unionism in Latin America. He also helped to defeat more radical labor elements, explaining publicly that the PAFL was an expression of the AFL's determination to prevent the growth of a revolutionary labor movement "at its backdoor."

• Iglesias's papers are in the possession of Igualdad Iglesias de Pagán, Santurce, Puerto Rico. For his autobiography, see *Luchas Emancipadoras* (1929). Other books by him include *Quienes Somos* (1910) and *¿Gobierno Propio para Quién?* (1914). He edited *Ensayo Obrero*, 1897–1899; *Justicia*, 1914–1925; *Porvenir Social*, 1899–1900; and *Unión Obrera*, 1903–1906. Igualdad Iglesias de Pagán, *El obrerismo en Puerto Rico: Época de Santiago Iglesias (1896–1905)* (1973), highlights his role in the early Puerto Rican labor movement. For other secondary works that discuss his labor and political activities, see Gregg Andrews, *Shoulder to Shoulder?: The American Federation of Labor, the United States, and the Mexican Revolution, 1910–1924* (1991); *Biographical Dictionary of American Labor* (1984); Harvey Levenstein, *Labor Organizations in the United States and Mexico: A History of Their Relations* (1971); Sinclair Snow, *The Pan-American Federation of Labor* (1964); and William Whittaker, "The Santiago Iglesias Case, 1901–1902: Origins of American Trade Union Involvement in Puerto Rico," *Americas* 24 (Apr. 1968): 378–93. An obituary is in American Federation of Labor, *Report of Proceedings of the Sixtieth Annual Convention of the A.F.L.* (1940).

GREGG ANDREWS

II, John Papa (3 Aug. 1800–2 May 1870), native Hawaiian jurist and historian, was born at Waipio, Ewa, Oahu Island, Kingdom of Hawaii, the son of Malamaekeeke and Wanaoa, descendants of the chiefs of Hawaii Island. Ii's family were intimates and junior relatives of the ruling royal family, the Kamehameha dynasty. He was named Papa Ii (pronounced ēē) after an uncle who held a particularly high station in the Kamehameha court. He took the name John (Ioane) upon his conversion to Christianity. John Papa Ii was born into the aristocracy of ancient Hawaii and was a child of privilege. The family had been granted the rich lands at Waipio following the conquest of Oahu by King Kamehameha I during his unification of the islands in 1795.

Like his older relatives, around 1810 the younger Ii entered the service of the Kamehamehas, specifically to attend the young heir apparent, Liholiho. Court life in the early years of the Hawaiian kingdom was proscribed by elaborate ritual and *kapu* (taboo). While Ii held a favored position in the royal court, service to the king was hazardous duty, as a trivial error or breach of protocol could result in death. Ii's stepbrother, Maoloha, was put to death for such an infraction. In later life, Ii related an event in which he feared for his life for taboo transgressions: "Ii, who was carrying the young chief's [Liholiho's] spittoon in front of him, had a brush with death when somehow the cover slipped off, struck his knee, and bounced up again. He was able to catch it and so was saved from death, for had it dropped to his feet, his fate would have been that of Maoloha" (*Fragments*, p. 59).

Upon the arrival of the first American Congregationalist missionaries in 1820, Liholiho, now King Kamehameha II, became interested in learning to read and write. The king sent John Papa Ii to the schools of the Reverends Asa Thurston and Hiram Bingham to learn on the king's behalf. Ii was one of the first Hawaiians to have the opportunity of a Western education and was quick to learn. He soon began to assist Bingham in translating texts into Hawaiian and interpreting sermons to native Hawaiians. Bingham's *A Residence of Twenty-one Years in the Sandwich Islands* chronicles Ii's maturation as a Christian scholar and preacher, referring to him successively as an "engaging pupil," a "faithful assistant," and finally an "associate." Ii was baptized in 1827 and was a lifelong advocate of the gospel. At times Ii was literally called upon to defend the faith, and he inserted his tall, muscular frame between Bingham and belligerent European seamen on more than one occasion.

In the late 1820s Ii moved into his longtime home known as "Mililani" (literally, "Beloved place [of] chiefs") in downtown Honolulu in close proximity to both the royal palace and the missionary's compound. His home was a center of hospitality for the Hawaiian aristocracy and foreigners alike.

In addition to his youthful service to Kamehameha II, Ii had a long and honorable career in service to the government of Hawaii under Kamehamehas III, IV, and V. In 1841 Ii was the superintendent of schools on Oahu Island and authored the first compilation of the laws of the kingdom of Hawaii. He was appointed a member of the treasury board by Kamehameha III in 1842 and was instrumental in the establishment of systematic record keeping. Ii represented the interests of the aristocracy in the House of Nobles of the legislature from 1841 to 1854 and again from 1858 to 1868. In 1845 he was made a member of the Privy Council, where he was a trusted adviser of Kamehameha III. This king appointed Ii to the Board of Commissioners to Quiet Land Titles, and he was the only Hawaiian member to serve for the entire term of this board. In 1846 Ii was appointed acting governor of the island of Oahu. Ii began his judicial service in 1848 with his appointment as associate justice to the Superior Court of Law and Equity. He held this position until the court was abolished by the constitution of 1852. Ii served on a three-member commission that prepared a draft of the constitution of 1852. From 1852 to 1864 Ii served as an associate justice of the Supreme Court of Hawaii.

Perhaps the best surviving description of Judge Ii was penned by American businessman Gorham D. Gilman in his "1848, Honolulu As It Is: Notes for Amplification":

John Ii by his unbending and strict integrity . . . is the most important civilian in the nation and is wholly a self-made man. Having had a good education at the Mis: Sem: early embracg the Christn Relign and adorning to a high degree his profesn he has & does enjoy the fullest confidence of the King who looks to him for his advice & council in all times of doubt and need—and his council is eagerly sought tho' never forced upon his friends. One of the remarkable traits is his humility—and unostentatious appearance—and even on occasions wh call for some distinguishing badge—his is the most simple—and plain. He is kind and gentlemanly in his intercourse—of a quick mind—and a deep thinker . . . and an able orator—claiming & fixing deep attention by the clearness and force of his reasoning. . . . His influence is of much weight and always upon the side of law & order virtue & religion. . . . He is fearless—& unsparing in his denunciation of sin in all places. All in all—he is *the* man and his place can not be filled by any other native living—either in his social religious or political relations & influence. (*Hawaiian Journal of History* 4 [1970]: 127–28)

While Judge Ii's work on behalf of education, Christianity, and jurisprudence may have "aided in sowing the seeds of Americanism" in the Hawaiian Islands, he set himself resolutely against annexation to the United States when the issue was raised in 1854. He remained ever loyal to the Kamehameha dynasty.

Judge Ii was married at least twice, first in 1823 to the widow Sarai Hiwauli, who died in 1856. It appears that he then married a woman named Kamaka in 1857, but it is unknown when or how this marriage ended. In 1862 he married Maraea, who bore Ii's only surviving child. After a lifetime in service to the Hawaiian monarchy, Ii retired to his Waipio lands to preach the gospel until his death.

John Papa Ii is best known today for his historical writings, which originally appeared as a series of articles in the Hawaiian-language newspaper *Ku'oko'a* (The independent) between 1866 and 1870. Ii's writings are of particular import because they offer an authentic firsthand account of life under the *kapu* system that was swept away in the cultural revolution in 1819. He offers an insider's intimate view of the court life of Kamehameha the Great (Kamehameha I), members of the royal family, and their attendants, with a wealth of detail available in no other source. Ii's history is a rare and outstanding contribution to our knowledge of the culture of ancient Hawaii.

• Important collections of Ii's writings are at the Hawaii Mission Children's Society Library and the state archives in Honolulu. His historical writings were translated by noted Hawaiian scholar Mary Kawena Pukui, edited by Dorothy Barrere, and published by Bishop Museum Press, Honolulu, as *Fragments of Hawaiian History* in 1959. Thumbnail sketches of Ii are in George F. Nellist, ed., *The Story of Hawaii and Its Builders* (1925), and Ralph Simpson Kuykendall, *The Hawaiian Kingdom*, vol. 1, *1778–1854* (3 vols., 1938–1967).

DAVID W. SHIDELER

ILLINGTON, Margaret (23 July 1879–11 Mar. 1934), actress, was born Maude Light in Bloomington, Illinois, the daughter of Israel H. Light, a horse dealer, and Ellen Mary Chamberlain. Determined from childhood to become an actress, she attended Illinois Wesleyan University but completed her education with two years at Conway's Dramatic School in Chicago, where she won a medal for her work in Shakespearean parts. She left Illinois for New York in 1900 with strong letters of recommendation, youth, beauty, charm, and a nature that a critic later described as both "vivacious" and "temperamental." Also, she was frankly ambitious.

The first producer Illington went to, Daniel Frohman, admired her gifts, concocted her stage name of Illington from syllables of her home town and state, and hired her immediately to play a gypsy girl in *The Pride of Jennico* (1900). Although he was twenty-eight years her senior, Frohman also took a personal interest in the young woman that was instrumental in her rapid rise to leading roles. In the 1901–1902 season she became a member of Frohman's stock company at Daly's Theatre. In the summer of 1902 she played various roles with the Richmond (Va.) Stock Company. During a performance of *The Dancing Girl* there, she injured her back by flinging herself headlong down a stage staircase. Thus began a careerlong pattern of injuries and nervous collapses resulting from her unrestrained style of emotional acting, which she told Ada Patterson came more from "feelings" than "technique."

Later in 1902 Illington replaced the ailing Cecilia Loftus as E. H. Sothern's leading lady in *If I Were King*. In 1903, back at Daly's Theatre under Frohman's aegis, she achieved great success playing Yuki, a young woman who abandons her American love to follow the wishes of her Japanese family in *A Japanese Nightingale*. A few days after its opening she married Frohman, who had made her a star in three years. In 1904 Illington took on the role of Henriette in an "all-star" revival of *The Two Orphans*, among other pro-

ductions. In 1905 she gained more success in *Mrs. Leffingwell's Boots*, playing a married woman who seems to be morally compromised when her bedroom slippers, or "boots," are found in a young bachelor's apartment.

Illington took on a more demanding role in February 1906, when she played Shirley Rossmore, the young woman who confronts a multimillionaire with the harm he has done her father, in the Chicago production of one of the period's great hits, *The Lion and the Mouse*. A Chicago reviewer wrote that Illington brought Shirley alive with "her fresh, girlish beauty and . . . a charm of manner, a sincerity of expression, both facial and verbal, and an abundance of fine, subtle but suggestive byplay" (*Chicago Tribune*, 16 Feb. 1906). That May Illington opened in the London production of *The Lion and the Mouse*. Beginning in September she appeared opposite John Drew in *His House in Order*, playing a second wife who is browbeaten by her husband's domineering sister. She continued in the role on tour until she suffered a nervous collapse in April 1907. One month later, while horseback riding in Central Park, she was thrown from her horse and knocked unconscious.

Despite the year's mental and physical strains, Illington welcomed a challenging role in *The Thief* (1907), playing a woman who commits a crime and lets her lover take the blame. In the original French play the character was unsympathetic, cold and emotionless. Playing the role for sympathy, Illington evoked grand emotional displays, an interpretation that was a huge success. Even the New York critics, always skeptical of her swift rise to stardom, had to concede her triumph in the part: "For an actress who a few years ago was comparatively obscure, Miss Illington succeeds remarkably well" (*New York Times*, 10 Sept. 1907). Illington played the part for fourteen months in New York and on tour and then, in Boston, suffered her worst collapse yet. At that point she announced her retirement from the stage. (She was actually twenty-nine, though she had begun to claim 1881 as her birth year.) Using the florid language of her stage characters, she told the press, "I have worked for five long years, giving up all my pleasures to my ambition, and thinking no sacrifice too great. I have worked like a slave—but a willing one. . . . I have loved the life. But now it is over, and I must rest" (unidentified clipping, scrapbook #287, Robinson Locke Collection, New York Public Library).

By now emotional strain was affecting her private as well as her professional life. Sometime earlier Illington had met Edward J. Bowes, a wealthy land owner and developer from San Francisco and Tacoma. In January 1909 she went to a California sanitarium for some "rest." Bowes was a frequent visitor there. The next month Frohman told the press that he and his wife were considering a divorce. It was granted to Illington in Reno on 9 November 1909, and five days later she married Bowes. She had no children with either husband.

Illington soon came out of retirement. Now under the management of her new husband, she toured the country in various plays through 1910 and into 1911. None proved satisfactory until Bowes read a script called *Kindling*, by young newspaperman Charles Kenyon, and the couple decided to produce it. Illington starred as Maggie, a slum wife who steals to provide for the unborn child her husband says they cannot afford. When the play went to Chicago in 1911, it opened almost unnoticed and unattended, but then a group of nineteen writers began to talk it up, and before the play had been running for a week, Illington was the toast of Chicago. She returned to Broadway a bigger star than before and, according to one reviewer, "achieved greater heights of acting than her friends had ever seen" (*New York Times*, 6 Dec. 1911). The *New York American* reviewer, after admitting that he had not admired her work before, and that he thought she had done "bad things" in *The Thief*, wrote that Illington played the role of Maggie "with quite remarkable force and repressed effort" (7 Dec. 1911). She toured in *Kindling*, the culminating success of her acting career, through 1913.

By the spring of 1912, Illington had expressed an increasing attachment to private life with her husband. From 1913 on she no longer took on taxing roles, appearing instead in road tours and in limited-run revivals. She and Bowes built a country estate in Westchester County, New York, called "Dream Lake" after the lake they created by damming up a stream. In his memoir, producer Crosby Gaige, who lived nearby, called Illington "a natural social leader" and described the Boweses' home as "a magnet" for other theatrical greats. The only new play that Illington appeared in during these years was *Our Little Wife*, produced by Gaige in 1916. Gaige later attributed its failure to his having cast "a high-powered actress like Margaret Illington in . . . a light comedy," which, in retrospect, he realized was "comparable to using the Big Berthas then in the news for . . . sparrow shooting" (p.108).

In 1917 Illington made two movies, *Sacrifice* and *The Inner Shrine*, but was not a success in either. After another stage failure in 1919, *A Good Bad Woman*, she retired permanently. In the 1920s she began to suffer ill health, never specifically identified in the press, though she reportedly underwent a serious abdominal operation in 1925. She died nine years later in a Miami Beach hospital, Bowes at her bedside.

Illington's career was meteoric: a rapid rise propelled by talent and ambition plus a hint of shrewdness as suggested by her choice of a husband, followed by a period of stardom that lasted as long as she was able to sustain eight bravura performances a week, and ending in a rapid decline after the personal toll proved unbearable and an alternative life beckoned. One of Broadway's leading exponents of the romantic style of acting, Illington followed in the grand European tradition of Sarah Bernhardt but brought to it her own vibrant American personality.

• Materials on Illington's life and career, including numerous clippings and obituary articles, are in the Billy Rose Theatre Collection at the New York Public Library for the Performing Arts, Lincoln Center. A list of her stage roles is in *Who Was Who in the Theatre 1912–1976* (1978). Information on her two screen appearances is in the *American Film Institute Catalog, 1911–1920* (1988). Ada Patterson's interview, "A Chat with Margaret Illington," appeared in *Theatre Magazine*, May 1912. Personal reminiscences are in Crosby Gaige, *Footlights and Highlights* (1948). An evocative portrait photograph accompanies the Patterson interview in *Theatre Magazine*, and other portraits are listed in the *Cumulated Dramatic Index* (1965). Obituaries are in the *New York Times*, the *New York Herald Tribune*, and the *New York Sun*, all 12 Mar. 1934.

WILLIAM STEPHENSON

IMBER, Naphtali Herz (27 Dec. 1856–8 Oct. 1909), Hebrew poet, was born in Złoczów (Galicia), Poland, the son of Samuel Jacob and Hodel (maiden name unknown). Samuel Jacob Imber eked out a difficult living as a cider maker and saloonkeeper. The young Imber was reared in a strictly orthodox home and received a traditional Jewish education. He was orphaned at the age of fourteen, and he early began the travels that characterized his life.

On a visit to Brody (also in Galicia) he met the scholar Joshua Heschel Schorr, who encouraged him to write. In Lemberg (now Lwów) Imber made the acquaintance of Abraham Krochmal, who helped him publish his first poetry booklet, *Austria*, written in 1875 on the centenary of the annexation of Bukovina by Austria and dedicated to Emperor Franz Josef. From Lemberg Imber went to Vienna, where he submitted his poem and received a gift of money from the emperor. He proceeded to Budapest and traveled through Serbia, Bulgaria, and Romania. He remained in Romania for some time and supported himself by private tutoring. Following the Russo-Turkish War he went to Constantinople where in 1882 he met Lawrence Oliphant, the Christian Zionist and mystic, who invited Imber to accompany him and his wife Alice to Palestine.

In Palestine Imber served as Oliphant's secretary and was a frequent visitor to the new Jewish settlements. Many of the poems he wrote during this period were in praise of the pioneering efforts of the settlers. He also contributed to the Palestine Hebrew press in which he was often the subject of controversy regarding settlement affairs and other matters.

After spending more than four years in Palestine, Imber set out for Europe in 1887 and settled in London. Here he was befriended by Israel Zangwill, who used Imber as the prototype for the character Melchizedek Pinchas in his stories. It was in England that Imber began to write in English. He contributed to the *Jewish Standard* a series of articles on the Talmud as well as autobiographical sketches based largely on his Palestine experiences.

In 1891 Imber emigrated to the United States. He lived for a time in Boston, where in 1895 he issued just one number of *Uriel*, a magazine devoted to "Cabbalistic Science." He contributed widely to both English-Jewish and general publications, and many of his writings demonstrated a talent for wit and satire. In the course of his wanderings from coast to coast he made contact with theosophical groups and addressed audiences on Jewish mysticism. In 1899 he married Amanda Katie Davidson, but the following year the marriage ended in divorce. He endeavored to support himself by writing but often lived in abject poverty. Only in Judge Mayer Sulzberger of Philadelphia did he find a patron who provided him with a small stipend.

Imber's fame as a Hebrew bard rests largely on his role as the author of the Jewish national anthem "Hatikvah" ("The Hope"). It is generally thought to have been written in 1878 in Jassy, Romania, under the influence of the nationalist movements that were sweeping Europe. The poem reiterates the age-old hope of a return to the land of Israel and ends with the assertion that "Only with the end of the Jews will come the end of the hope." It became popular first in Palestine where, according to the most recent scholarly opinion, it was adapted to the music of a Romanian folk song by Samuel Cohen. It then became a staple of Zionist gatherings in Europe and elsewhere and serves today as the official anthem of the state of Israel.

The first version of "Hatikvah" appeared in Imber's collection *Barkai* (Morning Star) (Jerusalem, 1886). In addition, he published two other collections, *Barkai he-Hadash* (The New Barkai) (Złoczów, 1900) and *Barkai ha-Shelishi* (The Third Barkai) (New York, 1904). Imber also published a Hebrew translation of Edward FitzGerald's *Rubaiyat of Omar Khayyam*, entitled *Ha-Kos* (The Cup) (New York, 1905). This effort was indicative of his aim to eschew lamentation and to stress the spirit of love and joy in his poetry. He also wrote Yiddish poems and even tried his hand at English verse.

The poet's scattered English writings include two books dealing with folklore and legends, *Treasures of Ancient Jerusalem* (1898) and *Treasures of Two Worlds* (1910). He also produced a series of brochures, two of which bear a Populist stamp, as Imber tried to find a basis for the ideals of populism in biblical legislation. His brochure *The Fall of Jerusalem: Reflecting upon the Present Condition of America* (1894), for example, presents a critique of capitalism in the spirit of populism and sees in the Bible a parallel to the contemporary political movement. The other brochure, *History of Money; or, Sixteen to One of the Jewish Talmud* (1899), tries to demonstrate the viability according to the Bible and the Talmud of William Jennings Bryan's program for the free coinage of silver.

Imber spent the last years of his life on the East Side of New York, where he was a familiar figure at cafés and Zionist assemblies. As a colorful figure and a nonconformist, he was a favorite subject for memoirists, many of whom wrote of his addiction to drink. When he died in New York, thousands of admirers paid him homage for keeping the hope of Jewish national regeneration alive, a hope that served as the central theme of his poetry and his strivings. After the establishment of the state of Israel a movement arose for the transfer of his remains to Jerusalem, and he was reburied there in 1953.

• Hebrew letters from Imber are in the Manuscript Collection of the Jewish National and University Library in Jerusalem. A number of these are reproduced by Jacob Kabakoff in an appendix to his Hebrew monograph on the poet, *Naphtali Herz Imber, 'Baal Hatikvah'* (1991). Kabakoff has also edited Imber's selected English writings, together with an introduction and select bibliography, under the title *Master of Hope* (1985). See also *Kol Shire Naphtali Herz Imber* (1950), with a biography by Shemaryahu Imber and an introduction by Dov Sadan. An obituary is in the *New York Times*, 9 Oct. 1909.

JACOB KABAKOFF

IMBODEN, John Daniel (16 Feb. 1823–15 Aug. 1895), army officer and lawyer, was born near Staunton in Augusta County, Virginia, the son of George William Imboden and Isabella Wunderlich. Little is known of his parents except that his father fought in the War of 1812. He attended Washington College in 1841 and 1842. Later, in Staunton, he read law, was admitted to the bar, and practiced for some years. He served two terms in the state legislature. After the election of Abraham Lincoln, Imboden ran unsuccessfully for a seat in Virginia's secession convention. A friend of former Virginia governor and prominent secessionist Henry A. Wise, Imboden was also among those who advocated immediate secession from the Union.

When the Civil War broke out, Imboden raised and organized the Staunton Artillery and became its first captain. The newly organized battery was among the Virginia troops that occupied the abandoned Federal arsenal at Harpers Ferry on 19 April 1861. At the first battle of Bull Run (Manassas) on 21 July 1861, Imboden led his battery in action, supporting the brigade of General Barnard Bee in some of the thickest fighting to hold crucial Henry House Hill. Imboden's duties during the months after Bull Run remain unknown, but the next spring he appeared again, this time raising the First Partisan Rangers Regiment, later known as the Sixty-second Virginia Mounted Infantry, a formation of mounted troops intended to make guerrilla raids behind enemy lines. Nevertheless, he fought in "Stonewall" Jackson's forces at Cross Keys and Port Republic, 8 and 9 June 1862, in the Shenandoah Valley. The following winter Imboden was promoted to brigadier general on 28 January 1863. His command thereafter was the Northwestern Brigade of the Department of Northern Virginia.

In the spring of 1863 Imboden carried out his most significant exploit as a partisan ranger, leading a raid into West Virginia from 20 April to 14 May, fighting several skirmishes, cutting the Baltimore & Ohio Railroad, and bringing back thousands of horses and cattle desperately needed by the Army of Northern Virginia as it prepared for its summer 1863 invasion of the North. When Robert E. Lee did march north, Imboden's command screened the army's left flank. He did some good service but also disappointed Lee by halting his advance for several days without notifying him. Imboden's brigade was the last to reach the field of Gettysburg, arriving about noon on 3 July. As one of the freshest units at hand in an army all but used up by three days of hard fighting, Imboden's brigade was charged with covering the army's wagon train, including ambulances loaded with the thousands of wounded, during the subsequent retreat. At Williamsport, Maryland, the army was cut off by the flooded Potomac, and Imboden found his wagon train threatened by marauding Federal cavalry. He fought hard against heavy Federal pressure and succeeded in saving the trains.

The following October Imboden captured the Union garrison of Charleston, West Virginia. This feat, in contrast to his performance the previous summer, won Lee's commendation. Thereafter Imboden served in the Shenandoah Valley. During the winter and early spring months of 1864, with few Confederate forces stationed in the valley, he exercised overall command of the district. As the 1864 campaign heated up and larger formations were transferred there from the main armies, he came under the command of higher ranking officers, first General John C. Breckinridge and later General Jubal A. Early. He was at the Confederate defeat at Piedmont (5 May 1864), the victory at New Market (15 May 1864), and Early's advance toward Washington later in the summer. As Early was driven back down the Shenandoah Valley that fall, Imboden saw action at Third Winchester (19 Sept. 1864), Fisher's Hill (22 Sept. 1864), and Cedar Creek (19 Oct. 1864). Later that autumn he developed typhoid and was ill for some weeks. Some doubts already existed in the minds of high ranking Confederates, notably Lee, as to the efficiency and discipline of Imboden's command. When illness rendered Imboden unfit for service, authorities lost no time in relieving him from command. After his recovery he was transferred to duty at a prisoner of war camp in Aiken, South Carolina.

For a decade after the Civil War, Imboden made his home in Richmond, Virginia, and practiced law. In 1875 he moved to Washington County, Virginia, and founded a settlement known as Damascus. He was active in promoting outside investment in the development of Virginia's natural resources. Not long after the Civil War, he wrote three letters to the editor of the *New York Tribune* that were published in 1869 as a pamphlet entitled *Virginia, the Home of the Northern Farmer*. In 1872 he wrote and published a pamphlet titled "The Coal and Iron Resources of Virginia." From his home in the southwestern part of the state, he worked to promote the development of Virginia coal mines and railroads. In 1876 he was a commissioner to the Centennial Exhibition, and seventeen years later, in 1893, he had the same role at the Columbian Exposition. He died in Damascus.

During the course of his life, Imboden married five times. At the time of his death, five of his nine children were still living. The names of his wives were (in order of his marriage to them) Eliza McCue, Mary Wilson McPhail, Edna Porter, Anna Lockett, and Florence Crockett.

• Imboden wrote articles for *Battles and Leaders of the Civil War*, ed. Robert U. Johnson and Clarence C. Buel (1884–1887). His reports and those of others about him are included in *The War of the Rebellion: A Compilation of the Official Records of the Union and Confederate Armies* (128 vols., 1880–1901). A biography is Harold R. Woodward, Jr., *Defender of the Valley: Brigadier General John Daniel Imboden, C.S.A.* (1996). His Civil War career is treated in Edward Porter Alexander, *Military Memoirs of a Confederate* (1907), and Douglas Southall Freeman, *Lee's Lieutenants: A Study in Command* (1942). His place in the secession movement is mentioned in Henry T. Shanks, *The Secession Movement in Virginia, 1847–1861* (1934), and his postwar activities are discussed in Alan W. Moger, *Virginia: Bourbonism to Byrd, 1870–1925* (1968). An obituary is in the Staunton Vindicator, 23 Aug. 1895.

STEVEN E. WOODWORTH

IMES, Elmer Samuel (12 Oct. 1883–11 Sept. 1941), physicist, was born in Memphis, Tennessee, the son of Benjamin A. Imes, a minister, and Elizabeth Wallace. Imes attended school in Oberlin, Ohio, and at the Agricultural and Mechanical High School in Normal, Alabama. Imes then enrolled at Fisk University in Nashville, Tennessee, where he received his B.A. in science in 1903. Upon graduating, Imes accepted a position at Albany Normal Institute in Albany, Georgia, where he taught mathematics and physics. He returned to Fisk in 1910 and for the next five years worked toward an M.S. in science while serving as an instructor in science and mathematics. After receiving his master's degree in 1915, Imes entered the University of Michigan's doctoral physics program, where he worked closely with Harrison M. Randall, who had recently returned from Germany. Randall had studied the infrared region of the spectrum in Friedrich Paschen's spectroscopy laboratory at Tübingen University.

For the next three years, Imes investigated the infrared spectrum of three diatomic molecules: hydrogen chloride (HCl), hydrogen bromide (HBr), and hydrogen fluoride (HF). Experimental and theoretical work had already shown that the molecular vibrational spectrum is quantized. Imes and Randall were interested in obtaining definitive evidence that the rotational spectrum was also quantized. In 1918 Imes received his Ph.D. and published his dissertation in a long article in the *Astrophysical Journal* (50 [1919]: 251–276). This work had a major impact on atomic physics: "In 1919, Randall and Imes published a single work that opened an entirely new field of research: the study of molecular structure through the use of high resolution infrared spectroscopy. Their work revealed for the first time the detailed spectra of simple-molecule gases, leading to important verification of the emerging quantum theory and providing, for the first time, an accurate measurement of the distances between atoms in a molecule" (Krenz, p. 12). Another view of Imes's research was presented by Earle Plyler in a 1974 speech at Fisk: "Imes' work formed a turning point in the scientific thinking, making it clear that quantum theory was not just a novelty, useful in limited fields of physics, but of widespread and general application."

Imes's results were immediately recognized by quantum scientists in both North America and Europe. In the two decades after its publication the paper was extensively cited in research papers and reviews on the rotational-vibrational spectra of diatomic molecules. Within a very short time, discussions of his work and his precision spectrum of HCl was incorporated into the standard textbooks on modern physics. Imes's experimental results also provided the first evidence for the existence of nuclear isotopics. This was shown by examining the doublet structure in his absorption band structure of HCl at 1.76 microns. This feature was interpreted to mean that two isotopes of chlorine were present.

As a black scientist holding a doctorate degree, Imes found his employment opportunities essentially limited to teaching at a black southern college or to seeking a position within industry or the federal government. For the next decade, Imes lived in and around New York City, where he was employed as an engineer and applied physicist. Imes's applied research and engineering activities resulted in four patents, each in the general area of measuring the properties of magnetic materials and the construction of instruments to conduct such tests. In 1920 Imes married Nella Larsen; they had no children. His own scholarly and literary interests, as well as his marriage to Larsen, one of the better-known writers of the Harlem Renaissance, allowed him to associate with many members of the "Negro" intellectual and power elite, including W. E. B. Du Bois, Charles S. Johnson, Arna Bontemps, Langston Hughes, Aaron Douglas, Walter White, and Carl Van Vechten. Many of these people would reappear in Imes's life in the 1930s as members of the Fisk University faculty or through some other strong connection to the institution.

In 1930 Imes was appointed chair of and professor in the physics department at Fisk, a position he held until his death. Imes initially devoted much of his time to the reorganization of the undergraduate physics curriculum and made preliminary preparations for the initiation of a full-fledged graduate program centered on research in infrared spectroscopy. Both Imes and his students were involved in several research projects; they used both X-rays and magnetic procedures to characterize the properties of materials and in the study of the fine structure of the infrared rotational spectrum of acetylene. Imes spent at least one summer at New York University carrying out experiments on magnetic materials, and he returned to the University of Michigan several summers to continue his research in infrared spectroscopy. He was active in three professional societies: the American Physical Society, the American Society for Testing Materials, and the American Institute of Electrical Engineers. Because of segregationist laws in the southern states he would only attend national meetings of these organizations

when they were held in large northern cities or in Canada.

Imes felt that the students at Fisk, as well as his friends and colleagues, should be exposed to the general outline and themes of science. To this end he developed a course, "Cultural Physics," and wrote a rather large manuscript to be used for the course. In addition to his duties as chair, Imes did detailed work on the planning and design of a new science building, and he carried out extensive correspondence with other researchers, equipment designers, and equipment manufacturers. Imes was heavily involved in the general academic and social life of the university. He operated film equipment for various university clubs, participated in both the planning and execution of the Annual Spring Arts Festival, and served on various scholarship and disciplinary committees. One of his major concerns was the education and training of his students; several of them enrolled in graduate studies in physics at the University of Michigan.

Imes's marriage ended in 1933 when Larsen divorced him on the legal grounds of "cruelty." The couple had already been separated for a number of years, mainly because of her desire to pursue a writing career in New York. Imes died in New York City.

Throughout his career, Imes was held in high regard by his scientific colleagues. They immediately grasped the significance of the work he did at the University of Michigan showing that both the vibrational and rotational energy levels of molecules are quantized. His experiments also provided a precise set of data that could be used to make a critical test of the emerging quantum mechanics that was being formulated in Europe. Understood but never openly articulated during his lifetime was the fact that Imes's race had placed limitations on what he could achieve in science in America.

• A modest collection of Imes's papers is at the Fisk University Library, Special Collections. In addition to letters dealing with routine administrative work, there is extensive correspondence with the president of the university. Other Imes papers are located in the Carl Van Vechten Personal Collection at the New York Public Library and the James Weldon Johnson Collection, Beinecke Rare Book and Manuscript Library at Yale University. For an evaluation of Imes's scientific contributions, see Gary D. Krenz, "Physics at Michigan: From Classical Physics to Nuclear Research, 1888–1938," *LSA Magazine* 2 (Fall 1988): 10–16. An obituary is W. F. G. Swann, "Elmer Samuel Imes," *Science* 94 (1941): 600–601.

RONALD E. MICKENS

IMLAY, Gilbert (9 Feb. 1754–20 Nov. 1828), speculator and author, was born probably in Monmouth County, New Jersey, the son of Peter Imlay, a landowner. His mother's name is not known, and only segments of his life appear in the historical record. He served as a lieutenant and paymaster in a Continental regiment in 1777–1778, subsequently assuming the title of captain. In 1783 he began acquiring paper claims to tens of thousands of acres in Kentucky. In those dealings Imlay, who also became a deputy county surveyor, associated with notable inhabitants of the western country such as Daniel Boone and James Wilkinson. As early as 1784 he became the defendant in court actions seeking payment of bonds and notes given in the course of his speculations. He left Kentucky for the seaboard late the next year and probably never returned to the western country. Writs from Kentucky courts continued to seek him, in vain, for some years.

Imlay's whereabouts from 1786 to 1793 are unknown, although it is likely that by 1787 he had left America. In 1792 his first book, *A Topographical Description of the Western Territory of North America*, was published in London. The title page inflated his surveyor's position into that of "Commissioner for laying out Lands in the Back Settlements." The core of the book consists of a series of letters purportedly written in Kentucky. They form a promotional description that tends to lack intimacy of observation despite the pretense that the author had grown up in the back settlements. Footnotes by an anonymous "editor" often contribute more substantial information than that found in the text. The letters referred to other authors' accounts and may have drawn on still others without attribution. Second and third editions of the book in 1793 and 1797 appended lengthy tracts from John Filson, Thomas Hutchins, and other sources. Despite the limited amount of original material, the work was well known to those interested in the North American interior. Unfortunately nothing can be said of Imlay's motivation or method in creating it.

The same is true of Imlay's novel, *The Emigrants*, published in London in 1793. Through letters, it tells the stories of an English family transplanted to the Ohio Valley frontier and of family members and friends in England. Like the *Topographical Description*, the novel seeks to contrast "the simple manners and rational life" of backcountry Americans "with the distorted and unnatural habits of the Europeans" (*Topographical Description*, 3d ed., p. 1). It also, however, speaks out strongly against the oppression of women by English law and marriage custom. Imlay's background offers no source for such a distinctive stance, which raises the prospect that some role in writing the novel was played by Mary Wollstonecraft, English author of *A Vindication of the Rights of Woman* (1792), with whom Imlay was romantically involved by 1793. Certainly there are references in *The Emigrants* that find clear parallels in Wollstonecraft's life and work. Yet it has been impossible to establish that Imlay and Wollstonecraft had a relationship before the book was published. Wollstonecraft never laid claim to any part in writing the novel, and students of her work have shown scant inclination to claim a role for her. Yet if Imlay wrote it alone, he fortuitously anticipated opinions that appealed strongly to Wollstonecraft. In any event, reviewers criticized the novel's style, and it received little attention.

Imlay was in Paris by the spring of 1793, when mutual acquaintances first noted his relationship with Wollstonecraft. His views are not known, but she clearly desired a long-term union without formal marriage. She used his surname, and he certified her as his spouse to provide, in the disrupted state of affairs in revolutionary France, some protection by way of pretended U.S. citizenship. They were part of a circle of Britons and Americans that included Thomas Paine and Joseph Priestley. At some point he also became acquainted with Crèvecœur. Whatever took him to France, Imlay wrote memoranda in support of plans by the Girondist government to take control of Spanish possessions in the Mississippi Valley. He asserted that U.S. citizens in the region would participate in such a venture, but a change of government in Paris halted the schemes.

In the fall of 1793 Imlay went to Le Havre and engaged in commercial activities, some of which likely involved importation from Scandinavia. The next year he went to London. He and Wollstonecraft had talked of going to the United States once he put aside a sufficient sum from his business affairs to buy a farm. Yet Imlay embarked into what Wollstonecraft called a "wearisome labyrinth" of "visionary prospects of future advantage" (*Collected Letters*, pp. 271, 275). She followed him first to Le Havre, where their daughter Fanny Imlay was born in May 1794, then to London. Meanwhile Imlay had entered into a relationship with an actress from a roving theatrical company. In an incident about which little is known, Wollstonecraft either attempted or seriously threatened suicide and then traveled to Scandinavia to resolve some business for Imlay. He was the nominal recipient of letters she composed on the trip for later publication, which cast some light, if often oblique, on relations between them. At the end of her journey she confronted Imlay, who was unwilling to give up his new relationship. Wollstonecraft then nearly succeeded in an attempt to kill herself by drowning in the Thames.

After a chance meeting with Wollstonecraft in the spring of 1796, Imlay virtually drops from the historical record. Wollstonecraft had declared her intention to support herself and their daughter independently of him, and in 1797 she married William Godwin. She died soon after, and Godwin adopted Fanny. Imlay engaged in unidentified business activities in England. Sometime after 1801 he relocated to Jersey, in the Channel Islands, where he died.

Wollstonecraft once wrote to him that "it is your own maxim to 'live in the present moment'" (*Collected Letters*, p. 272). Imlay's significance derives from two of the unrelated vignettes that make up what is known of his life: the *Topographical Description*, which provided a compilation of information about Kentucky at an important time in the region's development, and his relationship with Wollstonecraft.

• A diligent effort to establish the facts of Imlay's life was provided by Joseph Lewis Fant III in "A Study of Gilbert Imlay (1754–1828): His Life and Works" (Ph.D. diss., Univ. of Pennsylvania, 1984); see also Ralph Leslie Rusk, "The Adventures of Gilbert Imlay," *Indiana University Studies* 10, study 57 (Mar. 1923), and Oliver Farrar Emerson, "Notes on Gilbert Imlay, Early American Writer," *Publications of the Modern Language Association* 39 (1924): 406–39. Much of what is known about his relationship with Wollstonecraft is documented in Ralph M. Wardle, ed., *Collected Letters of Mary Wollstonecraft* (1979), and William Godwin's *Memoirs of the Author of a Vindication of the Rights of Woman* (1798). Wollstonecraft's letters from Scandinavia appeared as one of her most fondly regarded books, *Letters Written during a Short Residence in Sweden, Norway, and Denmark* (1796). Robert R. Hare made the only concerted effort to ascribe authorship of *The Emigrants* to Wollstonecraft; see his introduction to the 1964 facsimile reprint of the novel.

JAMES P. MCCLURE

INCE, Thomas Harper (6 Nov. 1882–19 Nov. 1924), motion picture producer and director, was born in Newport, Rhode Island, the son of John E. Ince, a vaudeville comedian, and Emma B. (maiden name unknown), a traveling actress. He had two brothers, John and Ralph, who also became motion picture directors. Thomas made his stage debut at the age of six and toured in both vaudeville and legitimate theater. When he was fifteen he debuted on Broadway in *Shore Acres*. After barnstorming through Canada with the Beryl Hope Stock Company and performing as a song and dance man, Ince returned to the New York stage in *Hearts Courageous*, where he met William S. Hart, with whom he later shared an apartment. In 1905 Ince tried to promote his own stock company, but it failed. He finally landed a featured part in a musical comedy success, *For Love's Sweet Sake*, which ran for two years, and in 1907 he married another member of the cast, Elinor Kershaw. The couple had three children.

After several more years of intermittent stage work, in the fall of 1910 Ince auditioned as an actor for Independent Motion Picture Company (IMP), whose studios were located on Fifty-sixth Street in New York. Ince later recalled that the studios reminded him of the dreadful tank-town theaters he had played while on the road. At IMP he was hired for a bit part in a one-reeler that was being directed by an old vaudeville acquaintance; he was subsequently signed as a stock actor. A few weeks later Ince played a heavy in a Biograph film, *His New Lid* (1910), which starred his sister-in-law Lucille Lee Stewart. However, Ince wanted to direct movies rather than act in them, so he returned to IMP to replace the director of a one-reeler based on an old poem, "Little Nell's Tobacco"; he rewrote the script and shot it in record time. Based on his success, Carl Laemmle, the head of IMP, gave him a permanent position as a director. Laemmle, who operated motion picture theaters and a film exchange in Chicago, was being sued by the Motion Picture Patents Company and was scouting for new locations beyond the reach of the patent's trust. When he received discouraging reports about the suitability of California, Laemmle sent Ince to Cuba, where he was put in charge of films starring Mary Pickford, the Biograph star who had been wooed away by IMP. Although Pickford soon returned to the United States, Ince remained in Cuba and gained valuable technical experience while overseeing the shooting of several one-reel films there.

In October 1911 Ince left IMP to join Kessel and Bauman's New York Motion Picture Corporation and to take charge of their production company, Bison Life, located in Edendale, a suburb of Los Angeles. He immediately moved the production location north of Santa Monica and hired Miller Brothers' 101 Ranch Wild West Show, thereby acquiring a complete company of cowboys, Indians, longhorn cattle, buffalo, wagons, stagecoaches, and enough equipment to stage large-scale westerns. When he shot his first western for Bison, a two-reeler titled *War on the Plains* (1912), it had the look of authenticity. The movie received good reviews, and Ince was prompted to make several more. His most ambitious project of this period, *Custer's Last Raid* (1912), starred Francis Ford—John's brother and later a director for Ince—as Custer and used Sioux Indians for a realistic staging of the Battle of the Little Big Horn.

Ince survived the merger of Bison with Laemmle's film holding company and became a producer as well as a director for the new studio. In that year he supervised the production of some 150 films, which included westerns and stories about the Civil War and the American melting pot; he often delegated the directing to others. His movies became famous for their defined story line, clear photography, good characterization, and spectacular action. Ince was a meticulous craftsman who often supplied directions for even the tiniest details, including the facial expressions of his actors.

Ince did much to professionalize the early movie industry by pioneering the introduction of formal shooting scripts and carefully managed production schedules, which helped to systematize filmmaking. Ever mindful of the commercial nature of the new medium, Ince remained a stickler for applying production values that would enhance both the narrative and visual appeal of his movies. By better organizing the industry he was able to increase the profitability of its product.

The period from 1912 to 1914 was probably Ince's most creative, and he experimented with extended and more complex films, most of them five reels in length. His reputation as a filmmaker grew, and his sprawling movie lot in Santa Ynez canyon eventually became know as "Inceville." Unfortunately, most of the movies from these years no longer survive, including *The Battle of Gettysburg* (1913), which was perhaps the only feature length film Ince ever directed. However, many of its props, sets, and action scenes were used in a Mack Sennett short, *Cohen Saves the Flag*, and provide an idea of the look of the original. Another notable five-reeler from the period was *The Wrath of the Gods* (1914), which featured Sessue Hayakawa in his screen debut. Hayakawa was the first major star Ince discovered, but he soon departed to appear in films made at the Lasky (later Paramount) studios.

In order to restrict Adolph Zukor's growing monopoly on filmmaking, on 20 July 1915 Ince's backers formed the Triangle Film Corporation, which he was to operate jointly with Mack Sennett and D. W. Griffith. Triangle bought up stars and production talent, including the stage actor Douglas Fairbanks and

Ince's old friend, William S. Hart. Ince moved his studios to Culver City, where five large, glass-enclosed stages and supporting buildings were built. These structures later became part of MGM. It was here that Ince produced his most ambitious and successful film, *Civilization* (1916), which is about a monarch who plunges his subjects into war and is later redeemed by the appearance of Christ. Inspired by Woodrow Wilson's campaign slogan, "He kept us out of war," the film was credited at the time with helping to reelect the president.

However, Ince's relations with Triangle deteriorated, and in 1918 he left the company to negotiate a personal contract with Adolph Zukor, who hired him to direct a series of feature films of his own choosing and to produce a series of westerns starring William S. Hart. Although Ince was already a seasoned director and producer of westerns, it was in partnership with Hart, a former Shakespearean actor, that he made many of his most famous western movies. Hart and Ince made many films together, with the actor directing most of them himself and insisting on a certain authenticity of story and immediacy of locale. Critics have singled out the psychological accuracy of his performances and the extensive use of background incident as hallmarks of these films, yet they also bear the stamp of Ince's attention to cinematic values. The quality of the camera work and importance paid to the details of the production recall other Ince films.

Although the partnership between Ince and Hart proved enormously successful and elevated Hart as America's leading cowboy actor as well as an international star, the friendship between the actor and producer eventually deteriorated, and the two men terminated their business relationship. Even though Ince continued to turn out films at a phenomenal rate, when Hart formed his own production company, Zukor cancelled Ince's contract with Paramount-Artcraft.

In 1919 Ince and seven others formed Associated Producers, a distribution company that flourished until 1922 when once again Ince was squeezed out and forced to make films as an independent. During the 1920s Ince remained a powerful figure in the motion picture industry, but his best filmmaking was behind him, and he made fewer and fewer movies as the decade progressed. The last films he produced included *Lorna Doone* (1922); *Anna Christie* (1923); a Civil War drama, *Barbara Frietchie* (1924); and the posthumously released *Enticement* (1925), a romance set in the French Alps.

In late 1924 it was reported that Ince was on the verge of signing a lucrative contract with Cosmopolitan Pictures, a movie company financed by newspaper magnate William Randolph Hearst, to headline Hearst's lover, the actress/comedienne Marion Davies. But on Sunday night, 16 November 1924, Ince was taken seriously ill aboard Hearst's yacht *Oneida* while entertaining celebrity guests, which included Hearst, Davies, and gossip columnist Louella Parsons. He was rushed to his home in Beverly Hills, where he died in the early morning. Although the attending physician listed the cause of death as angina pectoris resulting from ptomaine poisoning or acute indigestion, there were confusing questions surrounding the diagnosis. No inquest was held, and the body was quickly cremated. One of Hearst's rival newspapers even suggested the possibility of foul play, implying that Hearst may have had Ince killed because of his jealousy over Ince's attentions to Davies. Ince's death remains one of the great unsolved mysteries of Hollywood.

Thomas Ince has not received the attention due his prominence in the early film industry, being often overshadowed by his rivals, D. W. Griffith and Cecil B. DeMille. But, along with Griffith, Charlie Chaplin, and Mack Sennett, he was one of the founders of modern Hollywood. In hundreds of films, most often as a producer but also as a screenwriter and director, he introduced innovative production techniques and quality standards that helped to mold the distinctive image of Hollywood cinema during the formative years of the industry. Ince remains one of the most influential figures in the history of American film.

• A full-length study written about Ince is Jean Mitry, *T. H. Ince: Maître du Cinéma* (1956), which is full of inaccuracies. "Thomas H. Ince: His Esthetic, His Films, His Legacy," *Cinema Journal* 22, no. 2 (1983): 2–25, is a translated excerpt from Mitry's book. The best overview of Ince's life and career in English is George Mitchell, "Thomas H. Ince," *Films in Review* 11 (1960): 464–84. Comprehensive listings of extant Ince films are appended to the Mitry article in the *Cinema Journal* and to Richard Dyer MacCann, *The First Film Makers* (1989), which also contains a chapter, "Ince and Hart," that collects a useful number of early articles on both Ince and William S. Hart. Hart wrote extensively about their relationship in his autobiography, *My Life East and West* (1959). A good essay on Ince's contribution to the history of the western appears in the chapter, "The Western at Inceville," from Jon Tuska, *Filming of the West* (1976). Both Dennis Lee Daggett, *The House That Ince Built* (1980), and Kalton C. Lahue, *Dreams for Sale: The Rise and Fall of the Triangle Film Corporation* (1971), examine Ince's importance in the building of the early film industry, as does Janet Staiger's "Dividing Labor for Production Control: Thomas Ince and the Rise of the Studio System," *Cinema Journal* 18, no. 2 (1979): 16–25.

CHARLES L. P. SILET

INGALLS, John James (29 Dec. 1833–16 Aug. 1900), journalist, lawyer, and U.S. senator, was born in Middletown, Massachusetts, the son of Elias Theodore Ingalls, a businessman, and Eliza Chase. His father operated a shoe factory in Lynn, a town one of his ancestors helped found in 1629. Ingalls attended public school in Haverhill until he was sixteen then studied Latin with a tutor before enrolling at Williams College in 1851. After graduation in 1855 he read law with John J. Marsh for two years and was admitted to the Essex County bar in 1857.

Possessing an adventurous spirit and hoping to make his fortune in the West, Ingalls moved to Kansas, settling in the boom town of Sumner. When it failed, he moved a few miles up the Missouri River to Atchison, where he kept his residence for the rest of his life. Unable to earn a living at first by practicing law, he turned to journalism and politics, writing for his hometown Haverhill *Gazette* and the New York *Evening Post*. A New Englander drawn into the Free State movement, in 1859 he represented his area at the Wyandotte Convention, serving as chairman of the Committee on Phraseology. He claimed to be the penman of the final version of the Kansas state constitution, its "language, expression and arrangement" (Williams, p. 32). This document was the last of four constitutions written for Kansas during its territorial period; it banned slavery from the area.

In 1860 Ingalls was a delegate to the Republican Territorial Convention in Lawrence, although he failed in his attempt to be selected as a delegate to the national convention. In addition to joining a law firm in Atchison, which earned him very little money, he served as engrossing clerk for the territorial council, 1860–1861. When Kansas entered the Union, he became secretary of the first state senate. He failed to win election to the state senate in November 1861 but a bit later was chosen by voters to fill the vacancy created when state senator John A. Martin resigned to enter the army. Ingalls also replaced Martin as editor of the *Atchison Champion* from 1863 to 1865. He lost bids to become lieutenant governor in 1862 and 1864. Late in the Civil War, at the time of Sterling Price's raid (Sept.–Oct. 1864), he was commissioned a major in the Kansas militia and served several weeks as judge advocate in General George W. Deitzler's command. In 1865 he married Anna Louisa Chesebrough; they had eleven children, seven of whom lived to maturity.

After the war Ingalls continued to practice law, involve himself in politics, and write, helping found the *Kansas Magazine*. His effort to replace Senator Samuel C. Pomeroy, known variously as "Old Subsidy" or "Old Beans," seemed hopeless until state senator Alexander M. York dramatically charged Pomeroy with bribery during balloting in January 1873 and produced $7,000, which he claimed was the bribe money. The scene and its main participants appear as "Senator Dilworthy" and "Mr. Noble" in Mark Twain and Charles Dudley Warner's *The Gilded Age*, which was published that same year. Although Ingalls was not as well known as many other Kansas Republicans, his satiric criticism of border ruffian Democrats in "Catfish Aristocracy" (*Kansas Magazine*, Feb. 1872), played an important role in his election to the U.S. Senate in 1873, as did the support of several important Atchison backers. When Ingalls stood for reelection in 1879, bribery charges were raised against him but were not proven by investigations in Kansas and in the U.S. Senate.

Ingalls spent eighteen years in the Senate, during which he introduced over 900 bills. He was chairman of the Committee on the District of Columbia and the Committee on Pensions and served on the Judiciary, Education and Labor, Indian Affairs, and Privileges and Elections committees. He was chosen president pro tempore of the Senate, defeating George F. Hoar in February 1887, according to the *New York Times*, "a mild honor" of "no importance" (24 Feb. 1887).

Ingalls supported many of the major reforms of his day—the Civil Rights Act of 1875, the Bland-Allison Act of 1878, the Interstate Commerce Act of 1887, and the Sherman Antitrust and Silver Purchase Acts of 1890. He opposed civil service reform and was absent when the Pendleton Act was voted on in 1883. He had voted for the resumption of specie payments in 1875 but was an advocate of free silver when that movement became popular with westerners in the late 1880s. He was a foe of woman suffrage, whose advocates he once described as "the long-haired men and the short-haired women—the unsexed of both sexes" (*New York Times*, 17 Aug. 1900). Although generally opposed to prohibition, on occasion he spoke against saloons and the liquor interests. Many found this in keeping with his usual approach to controversial matters. He supposedly was a "trimmer," a term used by opponents to describe him as indecisive and opportunist. His name was never linked directly with any legislation of enduring significance. His fame rested on his oratory.

Ingalls was a compelling speaker, who was at his best when berating and belittling opponents and the Democratic party. While he was not part of the "bloody shirt" faction in the Senate, he was an able "bloody shirt" orator. In 1886, during debate over removal of Republicans from office by President Grover Cleveland, who supposedly supported civil service, Ingalls charged the president with "misrepresentation, sophistry, and false pretense." He called the supporters of civil service men who "sing falsetto, and they are usually selected as the guardians of the seraglios of Oriental despots" (*Congressional Record* 17, pt. 3, pp. 2785–86). His criticisms of Cleveland were famous, no doubt prompting the president to assess Ingalls's senatorial defeat in 1890 as one that "ought to please Democrats and decent people" (*New York Times*, 25 Nov. 1890).

Easily reelected in 1885, Senator Ingalls ran afoul of economic hard times in Kansas during the late 1880s. Already opposed by prohibitionists and woman suffragists, he lost support among Kansas farmers. He tried to win them back by embracing many of the programs advanced by the Farmers' Alliance and the nascent People's party, but the effort was to no avail. Populist victories in legislative contests doomed him, and he was replaced by William A. Peffer in 1891.

Ingalls spent the remainder of his life as a public speaker and writer. He covered various types of political, social, and sporting events for magazines and newspapers and continued his literary efforts. His poem, "Opportunity," is sometimes printed in anthologies, as is his best essay, "Blue Grass." Yet he is remembered mainly for his speeches, especially the oft-quoted epigram that some feel captures the essence of late nineteenth-century politics: "The purification of politics is an iridescent dream. Government is force. Politics is a battle for supremacy. Parties are armies.

The Decalogue and Golden Rule have no place in a political campaign" (*New York World*, 13 Apr. 1890).

A warm and loving husband and father, Ingalls had no lasting friends and was considered cold. The *New York Times* said he was a man who would rather "fight than eat" (17 Aug. 1900). He was dogged, quick, and bitingly sarcastic in debate, but he adjusted his positions for political gain. Populist leader Mary Elizabeth Lease, who like others claimed he plagiarized speeches and literary efforts, rendered the harshest judgment of him, saying, "He is the most erratic, inconsistent, contradictory, pitiful and contemptible figure in Kansas history" (Topeka *State Journal*, 12 Sept. 1895). Ingalls died in Las Vegas, New Mexico, where he had gone for his health, and was buried in Atchison. In 1905 the Kansas legislature placed his statue in the U.S. Capitol's Statuary Hall.

• Letters and papers of Ingalls are located in collections at the Kansas State Historical Society in Topeka, the Kansas Collection at the University of Kansas Library in Lawrence, and the Williams College Library in Williamstown, Mass. The best and most recent biography is Burton J. Williams, *Senator John James Ingalls: Kansas' Iridescent Republican* (1972). William E. Connelley, *Ingalls of Kansas: A Character Study* (1909), is useful, despite including extensive excerpts from Ingalls's speeches and writings, as is Connelley, ed., *A Collection of the Writings of John James Ingalls: Essays, Addresses, and Orations* (1902). For an intimate view of Ingalls see Mrs. John J. Ingalls, *Our Yesterdays* (1915). A substantive obituary is in the *New York Times*, 17 Aug. 1900.

ROBERT S. LA FORTE

INGALLS, Marilla Baker (25 Nov. 1828–17 Dec. 1902), missionary, was born in Greenville, New York, the daughter of Selah Baker and Sarah Tremain. Remembered as an attractive, outgoing young woman, she early became interested in foreign missions. After her father's death, her mother remarried and the family moved to Eastport, Wisconsin, where her stepfather ministered to a Baptist congregation. There she met Lovell Ingalls, a missionary on leave from Burma, where his wife had died, leaving him with two small children. They were married on 23 December 1850; they had no children. On 10 July 1851 the Ingalls sailed for Burma, where Lovell Ingalls resumed his work, first at Akyab, then in Rangoon. Marilla Ingalls became a teacher, providing able leadership to the educational aspects of the mission and accompanying her husband on tours. After his death on 14 March 1856, she returned home to provide for her stepdaughter's education.

On the long voyage home Ingalls wrote a book for juveniles, *Ocean Sketches of Life in Burmah*. Published in 1857, it revealed her deep, emotional piety, her love for the people of Burma, and her determination to bring Christianity and western civilization to those whom she regarded as lost heathens unless they converted. She was appointed by the American Baptist Missionary Union as missionary to the Burmans and sailed on 26 November 1858, resolutely choosing to serve alone at a new station in the village of Thongze

(Thonze) in wild jungle country, a week's journey by boat up Hlaing Creek from Rangoon. Here, despite the opposition of roaming bands of robbers, probably responsible for fires that several times destroyed mission buildings, and of resistance from native religious leaders, she won many converts, including Buddhist priests, and founded several outstations. After taking a sick leave in the United States (1865–1867), she returned fully recovered and with characteristic buoyancy again headed her expanding mission, directing its school; selecting, teaching, and guiding women and men in understanding and communicating Christian faith; helping native churches appoint pastors; and organizing new churches. Her acceptance by the people grew when she obtained an audience with the queen of Burma in 1872, presenting a Bible signed by Queen Victoria.

The coming of the railroad to Thongze in 1877 opened new lines of communication for Ingalls as she organized tract distribution and opened reading rooms for railroad personnel at depots. She made a last trip to her homeland in 1889–1891, addressing many groups at a time when enthusiasm for the foreign missionary enterprise in Protestantism was very high. During her final period of service in Burma, she energetically applied her organizational skills to reach new areas, until weakened by diabetes; she died at Thongze after more than fifty years of missionary service. Her life illustrated something of the force of the missionary movement of her time, driven by persons of single-minded devotion to a cause in which they so deeply believed. Her labors forcefully demonstrated that women could indeed provide impressive leadership in foreign mission.

• A biographical file on the Ingalls family, including her personal papers and official correspondence, is at the American Baptist Board of International Ministries Library at Valley Forge, Pa. See chapters on her by Annie Ryder Gracey, *Eminent Missionary Women* (1898), and by Walter Sinclair Stewart, *Early Baptist Missionaries and Pioneers*, vol. 2 (1926). Obituaries are in *Baptist Missionary Magazine* 82 (Feb. 1903): 59–61, and (Mar. 1903): 101–2.

ROBERT T. HANDY

INGALLS, Melville Ezra (6 Sept. 1842–11 July 1914), railroad executive, was born at Harrison, Maine, the son of Ezra Thomas Ingalls and Louisa M. Mayberry, farmers. His early years spent on the family farm, he was educated at the district school and at Bridgton Academy. He attended Bowdoin College briefly but left for lack of funds. Back home Ingalls read law with a local attorney, A. A. Stront, and later he attended Harvard Law School for a year, graduating in 1863.

Ingalls started practicing law in Gray, Maine, but in 1864 he moved to Boston, entering the law firm of Judge Charles Levi Woodbury. In 1867 he married Abbie M. Stimson; the couple had six children. Ingalls served on the Boston City Council and in 1867 was elected from the sixth district to serve in the Massachusetts Senate. He declined renomination in 1869. Ingalls turned his back on a political career because he had a greater interest in corporation law, especially its application to railroads.

In 1870 Woodbury sent Ingalls to the headquarters in Cincinnati of the Indianapolis, Cincinnati & Lafayette Railroad to survey and investigate the company's finances because several of Woodbury's clients had major investments in the Indiana railroad. In 1870 the IC&L was a 179-mile line with 700 employees and larger debts than prospects. Henry Lord, the line's president, did not greet the 28-year-old newcomer from Boston with any great warmth. Ingalls soon found the finances of the road to be in worse shape than the investors had earlier believed. The eastern owners at once insisted that Ingalls take over the line as receiver. Ingalls worked to gain the confidence of the line's workers, and he also sought advice from shippers and business leaders in Cincinnati. When state legislators considered new regulation for Indiana lines, Ingalls warned that such action might injure the prosperity of Indiana.

During his first years with the IC&L, Ingalls walked over most of the track mileage of the line. He even managed to pay off some of the road's large debt. Even so the line remained in receivership much of the decade. In 1880 the railroad was finally reorganized as the Cincinnati, Indianapolis, St. Louis and Chicago Railway, with Ingalls as president. By 1882 the new company was operating a 343-mile system, had reduced its operating ratio (operating expenses as a percentage of total revenue) to a healthy 60 percent, and was paying modest dividends.

During the same years Cornelius Vanderbilt II, who presided over the New York Central line, had become interested in the railroads of Ohio. In 1882 the younger Vanderbilt controlled the Cleveland, Columbus, Cincinnati & Indianapolis Railroad, a 700-mile line that ran North and East from Indianapolis and Cincinnati to Sandusky and Cleveland and West to St. Louis. During the prosperous 1880s the Ingalls line in Indiana and the Vanderbilt line serving Ohio both grew and prospered. In 1889 the two roads merged to form the Cleveland, Cincinnati, Chicago & St. Louis Railway, with Ingalls as president. Although Indianapolis was the center and hub of the consolidated line, the city had lost its place in the corporate name. Known as the Big Four Route, the 1,800-mile line was controlled by the New York Central, but its headquarters was in Cincinnati, and Ingalls was its manager. The Big Four's mileage constituted a major portion of the New York Central's system south of Chicago and the Great Lakes.

Just before the creation of the Big Four, Ingalls had also been made the president of another line, the Chesapeake & Ohio Railway. During the 1870s the Chesapeake & Ohio had been extended westward 200 miles to Huntington, West Virginia, under the leadership of Collis P. Huntington. Throughout the 1880s the C&O was in financial difficulty, and in 1887 Huntington himself asked for the appointment of a receiver. Vanderbilt and J. P. Morgan investment interests worked out a reorganization in October 1888, with Ingalls replacing Huntington as president.

Ingalls found the C&O in very poor condition. In the next decade he improved the equipment, the track, and the roadbed. Heavier rail was laid to upgrade the main line and dozens of more powerful locomotives were acquired. By 1889 a new line from Ashland, Kentucky, to Covington-Cincinnati was completed, and a new bridge transversing the Ohio was opened to traffic. The C&O purchased by foreclosure sale the Richmond & Allegheny Railroad, a 230-mile road from Richmond via Lynchburg to Clifton Forge, Virginia. Service North to Washington, D.C., was opened with trackage rights over the Virginia Midland Railway. Coal traffic over the C&O increased nearly fourfold during the Ingalls years, climbing from approximately 1.4 million tons in 1888 to nearly 5 million tons in 1900. Ingalls's relations with C&O labor were generally good, and he avoided major strikes during the 1890s. In the late 1890s Ingalls, near the close of his career, was responsible for about 2,800 miles of road (Big Four plus the C&O) and nearly 15,000 railroad employees. Late in the decade J. P. Morgan planned to urge the New York Central and the Pennsylvania to acquire the Chesapeake & Ohio jointly. Ingalls viewed the Morgan plan as a mistake and abruptly resigned as president in 1899. He remained as chairman of the C&O until 1905.

Ingalls was a favorite Vanderbilt lieutenant during the 1890s and was given considerable freedom to control the Big Four from his Cincinnati office. Cornelius Vanderbilt II and Ingalls were nearly the same age, and the two men worked well together. However, poor health forced Vanderbilt to retire from active management in 1896, and control of the New York Central was passed on to his brother William. Because William had only a limited interest in railroad management, Morgan interests eventually achieved a controlling share of the New York Central. Ingalls disliked his changed status and gave up the Big Four presidency in 1900.

Melville Ingalls played an early and active role in the cultural, political, and business life of Cincinnati. He was one of the founders and longtime president of the Cincinnati Art Museum. He was also a life member of the Ohio Mechanics Institute and one of the founders of the Cincinnati Technical School. Ingalls was a trustee of the Cincinnati Music Hall and headed up the group that remodeled the hall in the mid-1890s. He believed in physical culture and advocated more recreational playgrounds and parks for Cincinnati. After retiring from active railroading, Ingalls and his associates purchased control of the Merchants National Bank of Cincinnati. In politics he was a "sound money Democrat," supporting McKinley in both 1896 and 1900. In 1903 he ran for mayor of Cincinnati as a Democrat but was defeated. In 1905 Ingalls was made president of the National Civic Federation.

A typical nineteenth-century railroad president, Ingalls was an intense, hard-driving executive who worked long hours and expected the same of his employees. His subordinates and colleagues found him affable and approachable, but he was a leader who always followed the rule book. Like most railroad officials of his day, he was opposed to any vigorous regulation of railroads. Ingalls died in Hot Springs, Virginia.

• There are no known depositories of Ingalls papers. For additional information, see Charles W. Turner et al., *Chessie's Road* (1956, rev. ed. 1986), which reviews Ingalls's years with the Chesapeake & Ohio. Alvin F. Harlow, *The Road of the Century* (1947) covers his presidency of the Big Four. The same years are reviewed in John Paul Jones, "The Big Man of the Big Four, M. E. Ingalls," *Railroad History* 130 (Spring 1974): 41–50. An obituary is in the *New York Times*, 12 July 1914.

JOHN F. STOVER

INGE, William (3 May 1913–10 June 1973), playwright, was born William Motter Inge in Independence, Kansas, the son of Luther C. Inge, a traveling salesman, and Maude Gibson. The youngest child, "Billy" was called a "mama's boy" because his mother pampered him in his father's frequent absence. His peers also called him a "sissy" because he recited for ladies' clubs and showed a performing flair that he was to display throughout his childhood and later at the University of Kansas, where he appeared in many dramas both on and off campus. He aspired to an acting career.

Upon earning his B.A. in 1935, however, Inge realized that he had neither the connections nor the nerve to try serious acting. Moreover, he felt the pressure of social taboos to conceal his homosexuality, which added to his bewildered uncertainty. He therefore turned first to graduate school at George Peabody College in Nashville, and then to teaching high school drama in Columbus, Kansas. After returning to finish his M.A. at Peabody in 1938, Inge began teaching English and drama at Stephens College in Columbia, Missouri, where for several years he taught with growing frustration and depression. Though he often traveled to St. Louis to ease his spirit with cultural and romantic possibilities, his despair about not following his acting ambition, coupled with his necessarily closeted life, fueled the solitary drinking that compounded his problems.

During St. Louis trips Inge befriended Reed Hynds, entertainment critic for the *Star-Times*, who was drafted for World War II. Inge left Stephens in 1943 to be Hynds's wartime replacement and began writing reviews of plays, films, musicals, records, and books. He often felt he could write better plays than those he was reviewing. In late 1944 Inge interviewed Tennessee Williams, who had come home to St. Louis to relax before *The Glass Menagerie* went into rehearsals. A powerful friendship resulted, and Inge told Williams of his own playwriting ambitions.

Encouraged by Williams, and sensing that his writing might finally make the change he sought for his life, Inge wrote *Farther Off from Heaven*, his first play. Like *The Glass Menagerie*, *Farther Off from Heaven* is a family memoir play, featuring a small-town midwestern family based on Inge's own. It was characteristic, for all of Inge's later plays drew upon his store of experience as a native of a small Kansas town. Williams liked the play and brought it to the attention of Audrey Wood, Williams's New York agent, and Margo Jones, a director who was organizing a regional theater in Dallas. Wood declined the play but encouraged Inge to keep writing. Jones agreed to produce it in Dallas in 1947, where it met with enough success that Inge was determined to continue playwriting, even though the regular critic's return had forced him to resume teaching, this time at St. Louis's Washington University.

In 1948 Inge's second play, *Front Porch*, was produced first in St. Louis and then in Galveston, Texas. Though both productions of this play about women in a small Kansas town were reasonably successful, Inge still could not interest Wood in a New York production. Again discouraged and fearing he would always have to teach and waste his creativity, Inge was hospitalized for nervous exhaustion. Similar episodes had occurred earlier in his life, but he now had the additional complications of alcoholism and suicidal tendency. Still, he managed a recovery and began attending Alcoholics Anonymous after his release from the hospital.

Inge's alcoholism and his intermittent success in keeping it controlled combined with ideas for a new play, *Come Back, Little Sheba*, written during the summer of 1948. *Sheba* features Doc Delaney, a deeply disappointed man who settled for chiropractic and booze when his dream of becoming an M.D. was lost because he had to marry Lola, his no-longer-beautiful wife. Doc and Lola now live despondent lives in a midwestern city, having lost their youth, dreams, child, and ability to have more children. Lola calls for her lost dog Sheba, symbol of her vanished youthful beauty, and Doc calls on the support of AA to maintain his fragile sobriety. Events compel a violent scene in which a drunken Doc threatens Lola's life, and the resolution brings them back together in the realization that they must make the best of their circumstances—a theme that dominates most of Inge's work.

Wood considered *Sheba* Inge's best play yet, and worth bringing to New York producers. Though it seemed to Inge to take far too long, preparations began in late 1949 for *Sheba*'s Broadway production. Eager to quit teaching, Inge resigned and moved to New York. Production delays soon exacerbated his anxiousness, and Inge again required treatment for his alcoholism and depression. He began psychoanalysis, finding it personally helpful and valuable to his playwriting. When *Sheba* finally premiered in 1950, Inge had again regained his tenuous equilibrium, but he would have to fight to maintain it for the rest of his life.

The New York Drama Critics' Circle voted Inge the "Most Promising Playwright" of the 1950 season and named *Sheba* the season's second-best new play. Sale of *Sheba* to Hollywood eased Inge's longtime financial worries, and the success of that film made Inge even more popular. Now he tackled new problems—what to write next and how to deal with his celebrity while resisting alcohol and keeping his sexuality a secret from the public. Inge's attitude about his homosexuality was fairly typical for someone of his background and generation; he felt great shame and, in fact, was never able to accept it. The success of his work, however, encouraged him, giving him a reason to continue writing and battling his problems.

Deciding what to write next proved easier than solving other problems. He reworked *Front Porch* into *Picnic*, a play about a handsome male drifter's effect upon a group of women in a small Kansas town resembling Inge's native Independence. Hal Carter, the drifter, disturbs the women's lives in various ways, most notably by bringing genuine romance to Madge Owens, the town beauty who feels suffocated by the worshipful way others regard her; and desperate self-knowledge to Rosemary Sydney, an aging schoolteacher. Such disturbance, of course, cannot be tolerated, and Hal is run out of town. In Inge's original script, Madge is left behind; however, the director, Joshua Logan, pressured Inge to please audiences by having Madge follow Hal. The play debuted in 1953 and became Inge's greatest success, winning a Pulitzer Prize and being sold to Columbia Pictures, who made it into a wide-screen commercial blockbuster. Inge's reputation as a can't-miss playwright whose work translated into film success was established.

Inge's third consecutive successful play, *Bus Stop*, premiered in 1955. A romantic comedy, *Bus Stop* is about a group of bus travelers stranded in a Kansas blizzard. Bo Decker, a rambunctious Montana cowboy, and Cherie, a second-rate singer, provide the focus of the play, which is the only Inge work that depicts a successful romantic relationship (he later rewrote *Picnic* as *Summer Brave*, with Madge staying behind). Sold to movies, *Bus Stop*, like its predecessors, became box office gold as audiences flocked to see Marilyn Monroe as Cherie. Though a romantic comedy, *Bus Stop* continued Inge's by now familiar small-town settings and themes of accepting life's ups and downs.

Inge brought his psychoanalysis to bear in his fourth and final successful play, the autobiographical *The Dark at the Top of the Stairs*, which began on Broadway in 1957. A reworking of *Farther Off from Heaven*, *Stairs* portrays the Flood family of an Oklahoma village, each of its four members fighting fears of inadequacy to meet life's demanding changes. The father, a traveling salesman, must learn to sell something new. The mother must accept her husband's need to travel and sell; moreover, she must forgive his past infidelity while overcoming her Oedipal bond with her young son. The son must outgrow his "sissy" image, and the daughter must vanquish her pathetic shyness. These problems are worked out in the course of the play, which also became a popular film.

By 1958 Inge was often called one of America's greatest postwar playwrights. But things quickly went bad for him. As theater and critical tastes began to change in the late 1950s, Inge's fifth play, *A Loss of Roses* (1959), featuring another small-town Oedipal relationship, met with harsh rejection. It was as though critics suddenly tired of Inge's family dramas and their hopeful resolutions. Stung by this rejection, which he took personally, Inge managed a brief rally in 1961 by writing an original screenplay, *Splendor in the Grass*, which again used his familiar Kansas village setting and which won him an Academy Award. He sought to regain critical favor in 1963 with a violent play set in urban Chicago, *Natural Affection*, but only drew sharp criticism for his attempts at sensationalism.

Feeling completely rejected in New York, Inge moved to Hollywood, only to learn that he commanded even less respect there. His original screenplay for the 1965 film *Bus Riley's Back in Town* was changed so drastically that he personally removed his name from the credits. In 1966 Inge made a last attempt on Broadway with *Where's Daddy?*, about a Manhattan couple who think they are too sophisticated for parenthood but discover that the primal bonds of family are much stronger than they realized. Though this play is interesting because Inge revealed much of himself through the character of an aging homosexual teacher, it also failed and was roundly criticized.

After 1966 Inge's health and spirit began to fail, mirroring the failure of his latest work. He continued to write, but little of his later writing was produced or published. His last publications were novels: *Good Luck, Miss Wyckoff* (1970), about a sexually repressed female teacher in a Kansas village; and the highly autobiographical *My Son Is a Splendid Driver* (1971), about the regrets of a writer who considers himself second-rate. Neither novel sold well. When a despondent Inge took his own life, he was unable to envision that he would come to be considered one of America's most important playwrights, his major works reflecting midwestern small-town America with a verisimilitude achieved by only the best realistic stage writers of the first half of the twentieth century.

• The largest gathering of Inge manuscripts, correspondence, papers, and other memorabilia is the William Inge Collection at Independence Community College in Independence, Kans. Other manuscripts and correspondence may be found in the Kansas Collection at the Spencer Research Library at the University of Kansas in Lawrence, the Harry Ransom Humanities Research Center at the University of Texas in Austin, and the Billy Rose Theatre Collection at the New York City Public Library at Lincoln Center. All of Inge's major plays were published separately by Random House after their New York debuts; the four successful plays were published in one volume by Random House in 1958. Random House also published *Summer Brave and Eleven Short Plays* (1962). Ralph F. Voss, *A Life of William Inge: The Strains of Triumph* (1989), is a full biography. Robert Baird Shuman, *William Inge* (rev. ed., 1989), a book-length critical study of the writings. For a thorough bibliography, see Arthur F. McClure and C. David Rice, eds., *A Bibliographical Guide to the Works of William Inge (1913–1973)* (1991). An obituary is in the *New York Times*, 11 June 1973.

RALPH F. VOSS

INGELFINGER, Franz Joseph (20 Aug. 1910–26 Mar. 1980), research physician and editor, was born in Dresden, Germany, the son of Joseph Ingelfinger, an assistant professor of bacteriology at the University of Göttingen, and Eleanor Holden, an American schoolteacher. In 1922 the family moved to Boston, Massachusetts, where Ingelfinger's parents encouraged him in literary pursuits, and he helped his mother tutor students in English. After attending Phillips Andover Academy in New Hampshire, Ingelfinger entered Yale University. There he majored in English, played on the football team, took premedical courses in his senior year, and received an A.B. in 1932. He became a U.S. citizen in 1931.

After graduation, Ingelfinger enrolled in the School of Medicine of Harvard University, which with the city of Boston had assembled in 1925 an enthusiastic group of doctors interested in research at the new Thorndike Memorial Laboratory, led by Francis Peabody. Ingelfinger was trained by such experts as Chester Scott Keefer, George Richards Minot, and William Bosworth Castle at Thorndike and at Boston City Hospital. He decided to become a gastroenterologist, because only two others in Boston were then specializing in diseases of the digestive system. After receiving an M.D. in 1936 he was appointed to Thorndike Laboratory. Through its auspices he went to the University of Pennsylvania in Philadelphia in 1939 to work with researchers T. Grier Miller and William Osler Abbott, who had devised a drainage tube for relief of distention in the small intestine.

In 1940 Ingelfinger was appointed instructor at Boston University's School of Medicine and chief of gastroenterology at Evans Memorial Hospital. He married Sarah Shurcliff in 1941; they had two children. A demanding, autocratic, and charismatic teacher and a perfectionist, he was highly regarded by the more than fifty medical students who trained with him, endured sharp criticism, enjoyed his humor, and called themselves "Fingerlings."

Ingelfinger's quest for ways to define and measure activities of the human digestive system involved human subjects because "he disliked studies in animals and felt that virtually all worthwhile experiments should be carried out in humans" (Levitt, p. 1064). His approach included experiments on himself that involved inserting tubes through his nose and mouth to the stomach and intestines. He measured the movement in the small intestine and its absorption and secretion. During the 1940s, in what he considered his most substantial research, he determined the sequence of events following surgical removal of the stomach and the consequent length of time for a deficiency of vitamin B-12 to develop and cause anemia. He developed treatment by acid-neutralizing substances for gastric-ulcer patients (1945) instead of prescribing the bland diet recommended by B. W. Sippy in 1915. With Stanley Bradley he developed a technique for measuring blood flow in the liver (1945), which led to further research by others on liver diseases. During the 1950s, with colleagues, he developed methods for measuring pressure in the esophagus, which helped to define abnormalities in it. Ingelfinger defined the normal movements of the esophagus and identified abnormal ones ("Diseases of the Esophagus," *Principles of Internal Medicine*, ed. Tinsley Randolph Harrison, 3d ed. [1958]). In the 1960s he and colleagues developed a method of measuring the absorption of sugars and other substances in the small bowel and the absorption of salt and water in the colon. These investigations established a sound basis for later researches on the intestine at many laboratories.

In 1961 Ingelfinger was appointed the first Conrad Wesselhoeft Professor of Medicine at Boston University and chief of the medical services at Boston City Hospital. In this role, he recruited additional faculty, improving the teaching facility. Although he had few patients himself, his colleague R. M. Donaldson, Jr., noted that "on the wards, he was an exemplary physician unsurpassably accurate in his diagnoses" (p. 1061).

From 1954 to 1969 Ingelfinger edited articles on the digestive system for the *Yearbook of Medicine*, and from 1963 to 1968 he was chairman of the editorial board of *Gastroenterology*. Continuing at Boston University, he in 1967 also became editor of the *New England Journal of Medicine*, for which he had demanded standards for content, accuracy, and word usage. During his editorship the circulation greatly increased, from 106,000 to 170,000. In a distinctive editorial policy, he encouraged debate on medical subjects and ethics in letters to the editor, and he "sought columns by philosophers and gadflies of every persuasion" (Hoffman, p. 410). Among these columns was one by Norman Cousins, editor of the *Saturday Review*, who maintained that he had conquered an inflammatory disease with large doses of vitamin C, laughter, and no doctors (1977); the piece was later expanded into Cousins's *Anatomy of an Illness* (1979). Ingelfinger established a rule that the journal would not print articles that included data previously released in a medical or general publication. He believed that research must be validated by peer review. Adopted by other journals, this rule has reduced the tendency of clinical researchers to announce findings to reporters.

Ingelfinger was president of the American Gastroenterological Association in 1961–1962 and of the Inter-American Association of Gastroenterology from 1964 to 1967.

Ingelfinger diagnosed his own final illness in 1975 as cancer of the esophagus, then usually fatal within a year. He endured drastic treatment, finally resigned as editor of the *New England Journal of Medicine* in 1977, and died in Boston. His researches had introduced quantitative measurements into studies of the human digestive system, and his views on the practice of medicine had gained a wide and receptive audience in the journal that he edited.

• Academic records of Ingelfinger are at Boston University School of Medicine. Biographical accounts are Claude E. Welch, "Franz Ingelfinger, Editor Emeritus," *New England*

Journal of Medicine 296 (1977): 1475–76; Nancy Yanes Hoffman, "Franz Ingelfinger, M.D.: A Redoubtable Character," *Journal of the American Medical Association* 243 (1980): 409–11, 414; Arnold S. Relman, "Franz J. Ingelfinger, 1910–1980," *New England Journal of Medicine* 302 (1980): 859–60; R. M. Donaldson, Jr., "Franz J. Ingelfinger: His Accomplishments," *Gastroenterology* 80 (1981): 1059–62; and Michael D. Levitt, "Franz J. Ingelfinger: The Man," *Gastroenterology* 80 (1981): 1062–66. An obituary is in the *New York Times*, 27 Mar. 1980.

ELIZABETH NOBLE SHOR

INGERSOLL, Charles Jared (3 Oct. 1782–14 May 1862), attorney, author, and congressman, was born in Philadelphia, Pennsylvania, the son of Jared Ingersoll, Jr., an attorney, judge, and colonial official, and Elizabeth Pettit. Ingersoll spent his childhood in Philadelphia, then entered Princeton University in 1796. He left Princeton in his third year and returned to Philadelphia, where he took up writing. Ingersoll published poetry and wrote a play, *Edwy and Elgiva*, which was produced at the New Theatre in Philadelphia in 1801. He then turned to studying law and was admitted to the bar in Pennsylvania in 1802. He spent the next year traveling in Europe. On his return to the United States in 1803, Ingersoll began practicing law. The following year he married Mary Wilcocks, with whom he had eight children, including Edward Ingersoll, who became a prominent author and attorney.

In 1808 Ingersoll published a pamphlet, *View of the Rights and Wrongs, Power and Policy, of the United States of America*, in which he championed American culture and criticized admirers of England. Two years later he produced another pamphlet, *Inchiquin, the Jesuit's Letters*, which defended American culture as both independent of and superior to English culture in several instances. Both pamphlets were widely read and have been credited with helping to create an American cultural nationalism in the early republic.

Ingersoll entered electoral politics in 1811, when he was nominated for a seat in the Pennsylvania assembly by the Jeffersonian Republican party. Ingersoll lost in the election for the assembly, but the following year he was elected to Congress after a campaign in which he strongly urged war against England. In Congress he gained the chairmanship of the Judiciary Committee and became a member of the Foreign Relations Committee. In part because of the military losses suffered by the United States in the War of 1812, the pro-war Ingersoll lost in his bid for reelection in 1814.

After leaving Congress, Ingersoll returned to practicing law in Philadelphia, and in 1815 he was appointed U.S. district attorney for the city, a position he held until his removal by President Andrew Jackson in 1829. Ingersoll remained active in politics in the 1820s, serving on various commissions as an advocate of railroads and protective tariffs. During that time he also continued writing fiction and essays, notably a scholarly paper entitled "The Influence of America on the Mind," which was published in several countries, and a play, *Julian: A Tragedy*, published in 1831.

Ingersoll returned to political office in 1830 when he served a term (1830–1831) in the Pennsylvania assembly. In 1830 the Pennsylvania legislature nominated him to fill the seat of departing U.S. senator William Marks, but Ingersoll was defeated in the legislature's election for the seat. In the early 1830s Ingersoll was particularly outspoken on the controversy surrounding the Bank of the United States, which was based in Philadelphia. Ingersoll initially supported rechartering the bank but withdrew his support after bank president Nicholas Biddle campaigned against President Jackson in the election of 1832. By switching allegiance from Biddle to Jackson, Ingersoll drew the wrath of many prominent Philadelphians. During the 1830s Ingersoll remained active in Pennsylvania politics as well. He helped revise the state constitution (1837) and lobbied unsuccessfully to limit the powers of corporations.

In part because of Ingersoll's opposition to the bank, the Democratic party in 1837 nominated him for a seat in Congress. He was defeated in the general election, but three years later he was renominated and won the seat, which represented parts of Philadelphia County. In Congress Ingersoll held the chairmanship of the Committee on Foreign Affairs. Partly as a result of his urging, in 1845 Congress adopted a joint resolution for the annexation of Texas. Ingersoll also took a leading position in the sectional debates that occupied many of the floor speeches in Congress in the late 1840s. He consistently attacked northern abolitionists as "extremists" and called for a mediated settlement between "the slave-holding southwest and the slave-hating northeast" (Meigs, p. 252).

In 1849, at the end of his fourth term in office, Ingersoll retired from Congress. In 1853 he was appointed U.S. judge for the district of Connecticut, but he spent much of the remainder of his life writing his memoirs and finishing a four-volume history of the War of 1812, which was published in 1849 and 1853. His memoirs, entitled *Recollections*, were published in two volumes in 1861. Ingersoll died in Philadelphia.

Though never a leading figure in either literature or statecraft, Ingersoll nonetheless exerted considerable influence as a contrarian pamphleteer and politician. His speeches and voluminous writings were characterized by a vigorously independent spirit that often placed him on the margins of mainstream political thought.

• Ingersoll's papers are held by the Historical Society of Pennsylvania in Philadelphia. His work on the War of 1812 was published as *Historical Sketch of the Second War Between the United States of America and Great Britain* (1849) and *History of the Second War Between the United States of America and Great Britain* (1853). William M. Meigs, *The Life of Charles Jared Ingersoll* (1897), is a sympathetic but thoughtful biography written by the subject's grandson. See also L. D. Avery, *A Genealogy of the Ingersoll Family in America* (1926).

THADDEUS RUSSELL

INGERSOLL, Jared (23 June 1722–25 Aug. 1781), lawyer and royal official, was born in Milford, Connecticut, the son of Jonathan Ingersoll, a joiner, and Sarah

Miles. Ingersoll went to Yale, graduating in 1742 but able to stay on at the college for another year of study, thanks to a Berkeley scholarship. He then prepared for the law and in 1743 married Hannah Whiting, the daughter of a prominent New Haven family.

During the 1740s Ingersoll moved surely and quickly into the inner circles of Connecticut's ruling group due to his ability, ambition, and a good marriage. His appointment as king's attorney for New Haven in 1749 was a token of his acceptance into the establishment. His law practice centered on financial and property matters, and his position on key issues of the day was consistently conservative. He thus became a pillar of support for the "Old Lights," the orthodox wing of the Congregational church, and firmly resisted the "New Light" evangelical doctrines emanating from the Great Awakening. He also supported the liberal administration at Yale and publicly opposed President Thomas Clap's efforts to impose strict discipline on the students and to turn the college into a New Light institution. He was equally opposed from the start to the efforts of the Susquehannah Company to claim for Connecticut some disputed lands in the Wyoming Valley of Pennsylvania. As long as conservative forces dominated Connecticut, through control of the governorship and the council, Ingersoll's political views and his eminence as a lawyer made him one of the most important figures in the colony.

Ingersoll's portrait reveals a rather heavyset man with a broad face and high forehead, dressed stylishly in the genteel fashions of the day. His letters reveal a paternalistic figure, solicitously involved in the lives of his wife and their two children, as well as a man capable of forming close, enduring friendships with colonial leaders such as William Livingstone of New York and William Samuel Johnson of Connecticut. A thread of sarcastic wit also runs through Ingersoll's letters, suggesting that he thoroughly enjoyed his privileged status and had little patience for those with lesser standing. Doubtless Ingersoll was respected and even feared throughout Connecticut for his zealousness in enforcing the law, but he did not command public affection or seek it.

In 1758 Ingersoll reached the summit of his career when he was appointed Connecticut's agent to London, charged with pressing the colony's claims against the British government for reimbursement of military expenses the colony had incurred during the French and Indian War and with urging the admiralty to use the Connecticut River as a shipping lane for the white pine mast logs being cut in western Massachusetts. This latter project was eventually blocked by New Hampshire's powerful Wentworth family, but in general Ingersoll's three years in London were a personal success. He formed friendships with Benjamin Franklin and several English colonial sympathizers, including Thomas Whately and Richard Jackson, saw the newly crowned King George III, and enjoyed the sights and conviviality of London. He returned to Connecticut in 1762 and then went back to England in 1764 to oversee the sale of a shipload of masts he had acquired. While there Ingersoll was asked to serve once again as Connecticut's agent on the recently passed Sugar Act and the proposed Stamp Act. Ingersoll pursued these duties vigorously. He informed London officials that the Sugar Act was financially ruinous to colonial merchants and denounced the new enforcement campaign against smuggling as "burning a barn to roast an egg" ("Papers," p. 306).

Ingersoll was more equivocal on the Stamp Act. He and Franklin had been chosen by the colonial agents in London to represent them at an interview with Secretary of State George Grenville. In the momentous conversation that ensued, the two men told Grenville of their fears regarding the colonial response to the proposed act. Ingersoll in particular pleaded the poverty of Connecticut after a long war. He further noted that the colony was extremely proud of the fact it had developed independently, without any support from the British government, and that it would probably oppose an exertion of parliamentary authority at this late date. Grenville heard both men out and then presented his arguments in favor of a stamp tax. He noted that Britain had born the financial brunt of the recent French and Indian War, that British taxpayers were already paying many times more taxes than Americans, that all monies gathered from the Stamp Act would be spent in America in support of British government and troops, and finally, that more permissive, voluntary methods of collecting monies in America had proved utterly inadequate.

Both Ingersoll and Franklin were impressed by Grenville's arguments and his obvious goodwill, which included the suggestion that the empire should be restructured to give the colonies a greater voice in policymaking. The agents retreated therefore from their opposition to the Stamp Act and began working with imperial officials on the details of the legislation. Ingersoll in particular was proud of his success in getting the duty on three sensitive items removed from the final bill. After the Stamp Act was passed in Parliament, Ingersoll at Franklin's urging accepted the office of stamp distributor for Connecticut.

Clearly Ingersoll was totally unprepared for the tidal wave of angry resistance that engulfed colonial America when passage of the Stamp Act became known. Massachusetts was the first scene of violent resistance, but Connecticut proved almost as adamant. Inevitably Ingersoll became the symbol of the hated act: his effigy was burned in four different towns and his motives in accepting the office of stamp distributor denounced in letters to the colony's newspapers. At first Ingersoll tried to mollify his countrymen by a public letter declaring he only wished to serve his colony and would never use force to make people pay the tax. When this proved insufficient, he set out for Hartford to bring his case before the general assembly. En route a troop of more than 500 men, including several uniformed veterans of the French and Indian War, detained Ingersoll for several hours and used an escalating series of threats to force him to resign his office. When Ingersoll later withdrew his resignation on the grounds that he had acted under coercion, the assaults on his public reputation by the newly formed Sons of Liberty continued, until he finally decided to quit the post forever for the sake of peace.

It was a crucial moment in the history of colonial Connecticut. Ingersoll and his allies were well aware that a host of issues in addition to the Stamp Act were at stake, including paper money, New Light versus Old Light control of religious policy, the Susquehannah claims, and the future of Yale. Indeed, defeat of the Stamp Act also signaled defeat of the Old Light faction in Connecticut. The New Lights elected their candidate for governor, William Pitkin, in 1766 and would control provincial politics for the rest of the colonial period.

These events also ended Ingersoll's public leadership. Although he made strenuous efforts to justify his actions, public confidence in his judgment was gone. His private practice continued to flourish, and he twice represented the merchant Benedict Arnold in lawsuits in the 1760s. In 1767 he accepted an appointment as judge of the vice admiralty court sitting in Philadelphia. It was a lucrative post and was specifically given to compensate Ingersoll for his losses during the Stamp Act protests. He exercised his duties conscientiously but quietly. Nonetheless, in 1774 he was again attacked in the newspapers for cracking down on smugglers. When war broke out he stayed in Philadelphia until he was expelled by the revolutionary government. A broken man, he was granted permission to return to New Haven on parole where he could observe his surviving son and his favorite nephew supporting the cause of American independence. After his father's death in New Haven, Jared Ingersoll, Jr., would go on to be a delegate to the Constitutional Convention in 1787 and the Federalist candidate for the vice presidency of the United States in 1812.

At the end of his life Ingersoll mournfully described himself as "like a Saint of old . . . having no abiding city" ("Papers," p. 456). In American annals the harsher comment of an old friend of his, President Ezra Stiles of Yale, has prevailed: "About noon died Jared Ingersoll Esq. . . . He has passed thro' a Variety in Life. By accepting the Office of Stamps 1765 he rendered himself obnoxious; he had formerly the confidence of his country & was sent over Agent by Connecticut to G. Britain. He was Judge of Admy. with £600 sterlg. saly. But all this made him unhappy" (*Stiles Diary*, vol. 2, p. 552).

• The primary printed source for Ingersoll's life is Franklin B. Dexter, ed., "A Selection from the Correspondence and Miscellaneous Papers of Jared Ingersoll," *Papers of the New Haven Colony Historical Society* 9 (1918): 201–472; his portrait is reproduced on p. 200. The published papers of three other men are also instructive: Leonard Labaree, ed., *The Papers of Benjamin Franklin*, vols. 9–16 (1959–1992); Dexter, ed., *The Literary Diary of Ezra Stiles* (3 vols., 1901); and *The Fitch Papers: Correspondence and Documents during Thomas Fitch's Governorship of the Colony of Connecticut, 1754–1766*, vol. 2, in Connecticut Historical Society, *Collections* 18 (1920). The classic biography is Lawrence Henry Gipson, *Jared Ingersoll: A Study of American Loyalism in Relation to British Colonial Government* (1920). A modern interpretation is in Edmund S. Morgan and Helen S. Morgan, "Jared Ingersoll," in their *The Stamp Act Crisis: A Prologue to Revolution* (1952). The British perspective is in P. D. G. Thomas, *British Politics and the Stamp Act Crisis: The First Phase of the American Revolution, 1763–1767* (1975). The role of the colonial agents in London is described in depth in Michael Kammen, *A Rope of Sand: Colonial Agents, British Policy, and the American Revolution* (1968).

An excellent account of the social tensions in Connecticut is in Richard Bushman, *From Puritan to Yankee: Character and Social Order in Connecticut, 1690–1765* (1967), which should be read in conjunction with Robert J. Taylor, *Colonial Connecticut: A History* (1979). Equally illuminating are two major biographies of Ingersoll's contemporaries: Edmund S. Morgan, *The Gentle Puritan: A Life of Ezra Stiles, 1727–1795* (1962), and Elizabeth P. McCaughey, *From Loyalist to Founding Father: The Political Odyssey of William Samuel Johnson* (1980). For the enforcement of British trade regulations, see Oliver M. Dickerson, *The Navigation Acts and the American Revolution* (1951), and Carl Ubbelohde, *The Vice Admiralty Courts and the American Revolution* (1960). To understand why Ingersoll's work as judge of the vice admiralty court was so unpopular, see David Lovejoy, "Rights Imply Equality: The Case against Admiralty Jurisdiction in America, 1764–1776," *William and Mary Quarterly*, 3d ser., 16 (1959): 459–84.

ANN GORMAN CONDON

INGERSOLL, Robert Green (11 Aug. 1833–21 July 1899), orator and lawyer, was born in Dresden, New York, the son of the Reverend John Ingersoll, a fiery Congregational orator and abolitionist, and Mary Livingston. When Robert was two years old his mother died. His father then moved the family through a dozen or more pastorates in New York, Ohio, Kentucky, Indiana, Michigan, and Illinois. Robert came to reject his father's gloomy Calvinism but embraced his oratorical style, abolitionism, and his assiduous reading habits. Although the itinerant status of the family limited his formal schooling, Ingersoll was well versed in the classics. He taught for two years at subscription schools in Mount Vernon and Metropolis, Illinois, and in Waverly, Tennessee. Both Robert and his brother Ebon Clark Ingersoll, a future congressman, were introduced to the law and politics when they read law for a few months in the office of Democratic congressman Willis Allen, in Marion, Illinois, where they were admitted to the bar in 1854. Robert served as a legal clerk in various federal, county, and circuit courts in southern Illinois. In late 1857 or early 1858 the brothers moved to Peoria, where they developed a thriving legal practice.

Robert Ingersoll professed to hate politics, which he described in a letter as "a low dirty scramble through misrepresentation, slander, falsehood, and filth." Yet, he confessed, "I find myself planning and scheming all the time, thinking what I will try for, and calculating the chances" (17 Mar. 1865). Although never elected to any public office, Ingersoll was the Democratic nominee for Congress in 1860 and aspired to be the Republican nominee for Illinois congressman-at-large in 1864 and 1866 and also for governor in 1868. He was more successful in applying his oratorical skills in support of other candidates for office. In 1862 he married Eva A. Parker; they had two children.

Ingersoll came into the Civil War as a Stephen A. Douglas Democrat and emerged as a supporter of Abraham Lincoln and the radical Republicans. The metamorphosis began when he raised and commanded the Eleventh Regiment of the Illinois Volunteer Cavalry. The regiment served at the battle of Shiloh on 6 and 7 April 1862, but Ingersoll was subsequently captured near Lexington, Tennessee, on 18 December. He was paroled a few days later, pending exchange. When exchange appeared unlikely, he resigned from the service on 30 June 1863 and returned to Peoria. His transformation into an antislavery Union Republican was complete upon the death of abolitionist congressman Owen Lovejoy, when the Republicans nominated and elected his brother Clark to the Fifth Illinois congressional seat in the special election of 7 May 1864. During the fall elections Ingersoll made dozens of speeches on behalf of Republicans.

Ingersoll held the South responsible for the assassination of President Lincoln and for "a greater crime," slavery. In the fight between President Andrew Johnson and the Radical Republican Congress over Reconstruction policy, Ingersoll favored the radicals. After Johnson vetoed a civil rights bill in 1866, Robert urged his brother to "Stand by principle, old boy. Let every office in the district go to pot" (Wakefield, pp. 138–39) if necessary to override the veto. When a London *Times* reporter asked Johnson why there was so much opposition to his reconstruction policy, the president replied that his policy was popular in the heartland and, showing a telegram he had received from his supporters in Peoria, stated, "Look at Peoria." Ingersoll took up the challenge and felt vindicated when his brother was reelected to Congress by a two-to-one margin. "Now look at Peoria," the Radical Republicans crowed, and an early version of "How does it play in Peoria?" was born (Plummer, pp. 31–35).

During the 1866 campaign, Ingersoll and Governor Richard Oglesby often spoke in tandem and were touted as the best stump speakers in the country. After the election, Oglesby appointed Ingersoll attorney general of Illinois, the only public office he ever held. In 1868 Ingersoll decided to enter the contest for the Republican nomination for governor, but he was defeated by Major General John M. Palmer (1817–1900). Years later the legend grew among Ingersoll admirers that Robert had lost because he refused to publicly renounce his atheism, but the popularity of General Palmer and Ingersoll's limited constituency were the determining factors.

Before his defeat in 1868, Ingersoll had veiled his religious skepticism in patriotism. In his 1868 Decoration Day address in Peoria, he declared: "Human Liberty is the shrine at which I worship. Progress is the religion in which I believe. . . . Liberty is the condition precedent to all progress" (*Peoria Daily Tran-*

script, 1 June 1868). In 1870 he broke ranks with many of his political supporters when he participated in a woman suffrage convention in Peoria whose featured speaker was Susan B. Anthony. He also befriended Frederick Douglass and supported universal suffrage. Ingersoll chose a Tom Paine celebration in nearby Fairbury, Illinois, in January 1872 for his first public assault on religion. He began his lecture, "The Gods," with, "An honest God is the noblest work of man" and proceeded to ridicule all gods, including the Christian God. In 1874 Ingersoll published *The Gods and Other Lectures*, which included the lectures "Humboldt," "Thomas Paine," "Individuality," and "Heretics and Heresies." In these discourses Ingersoll took perverse pleasure in characterizing himself as an "infidel" and a "heretic," while arguing that the Bible was the evil source that had inspired the burning of heretics, the building of dungeons, the Inquisition, and the trampling "upon the liberties of men."

By 1876 Ingersoll's oratorical skills had brought him national prominence as a lawyer. He gained a surprise acquittal of a whiskey ring member, Daniel W. Munn, by impeaching the government's chief witness. The *Chicago Post and Mail* parodied, "an honest Munn is the noblest work of Ingersoll." In 1876 presidential aspirant James G. Blaine asked Ingersoll to make his nomination speech at the Republican National Convention. Ingersoll characterized Blaine as "the Plumed Knight" in a crusade against the Democrats. Although Blaine failed to obtain the nomination, Ingersoll gained national prominence. He campaigned for the Republican nominee, Rutherford B. Hayes, and painted a picture of a treasonous Democratic party in his often quoted classic "bloody shirt" speech, "The Vision of War." To a veteran's group in Indianapolis he exclaimed: "Soldiers, every scar you have on your heroic bodies was given you by a Democrat. Every scar, every arm that is lacking, every limb that is gone, is a souvenir of a Democrat." Hayes won the disputed election of 1876 and was grateful to Ingersoll, but a move to appoint him to the diplomatic mission in Berlin collapsed under an avalanche of protests from religious groups.

Ingersoll's national political prominence increased the demand for his rationalist and biographical lectures. On tour in 1877, he delivered "Ghosts" and "The Liberty of Man, Woman, and Child." At the invitation of his beloved brother Ebon Clark, he moved in 1877 to Lafayette Square in Washington, D.C., where he continued his practice of law and often defended Republican officeholders, as in the "Star Route" cases of 1882–1883. When Clark Ingersoll died in 1879, Robert's eulogy included a faint hope for immortality: "From the voiceless lips of the unreplying dead there comes no word, but in the night of death hope sees a star and listening love can hear the rustle of a wing."

Ingersoll became the target of hundreds of fundamentalist preachers who took exception to his lectures, which included "What Must We Do to Be Saved?" and "Some Mistakes of Moses" (1880); "Some Reasons

Why" and "The Great Infidels" (1881); "Orthodoxy" and "Which Way?" (1884); and "Myth and Miracle" (1885). Both his detractors and his proponents seemed willing to pay to see Ingersoll display his wit and wisdom. His extended speaking tours attracted thousands of listeners, who loved to hate his message while they enjoyed his performance.

In 1885 Ingersoll moved to New York City, where he continued his remunerative legal career with an emphasis on corporation and probate litigation. Resuming his profitable lecture circuit with a mixture of biographies and agnostic pieces, he delivered "Shakespeare" and "Liberty in Literature" in 1891, "About the Holy Bible" and "Abraham Lincoln" in 1894, "Foundations of Faith" in 1895, "Why I Am an Agnostic" and "How to Reform Mankind" in 1896, "The Truth" and "A Thanksgiving Sermon" in 1897, "Superstition" in 1898, and "The Devil" and "What Is Religion?" in 1899. Some religious critics predicted that Ingersoll would recant as he neared death, but the family insisted that there was no recantation when he died of heart disease at Dobbs Ferry, New York. Ingersoll was cremated, and his ashes were buried in Arlington National Cemetery in 1932. A statue in his remembrance was erected at Glen Oak Park in Peoria in 1911.

• Significant collections of Ingersoll papers are found in the Library of Congress, the Illinois State Historical Library in Springfield, and in the New York Public Library. Ingersoll published most of his lectures in *The Works of Robert G. Ingersoll* (12 vols., 1903). *The Letters of Robert G. Ingersoll*, ed. Eva Ingersoll Wakefield (1951), contains the best collection of published letters available. An exhaustive bibliography of works by and about Ingersoll is Gordon Stein, *Robert G. Ingersoll: A Checklist* (1969). David D. Anderson, *Robert Ingersoll* (1972), is the best brief biography. See also C. H. Cramer, *Royal Bob: The Life of Robert G. Ingersoll* (1952), and Mark Plummer, *Robert G. Ingersoll: Peoria's Pagan Politician* (1984).

MARK A. PLUMMER

INGERSOLL, Royal Eason (30 June 1883–20 May 1976), naval officer, was born in Washington, D.C., the only son of Royal Rodney Ingersoll, a naval officer who later served as chief of staff of the "Great White Fleet" and attained the rank of rear admiral, and Cynthia Eason. Raised primarily in Annapolis and LaPorte, Indiana, his ancestral home, he accompanied his father on the gunboat *Annapolis*, of which his father was captain, on the midshipman summer cruise of 1899. Two years later he entered the Naval Academy, from which he graduated with distinction in gunnery near the top of the class of 1905. Short tours of duty aboard three separate vessels culminated with assignment to the commissioning crew of the battleship *Connecticut* (1906–1907, 1908–1911), including the latter portion of the global voyage of the Great White Fleet. He married Louise Van Harlingen in June 1910; they had one daughter and one son. The

latter, Lieutenant R. R. Ingersoll II, was killed on board the aircraft carrier *Hornet* as part of the ship's company at the battle of Midway in June 1942.

Ingersoll's quiet intellect, self-effacing manner, and administrative talents placed him in great demand for staff and shoreside assignments in addition to choice seagoing billets in the battleship navy. After teaching international law, seamanship, and English at the Naval Academy (1911–1913), he joined the armored cruiser *Saratoga* in the Asiatic Fleet, only to be reassigned as flag lieutenant (aide) successively to two of its commanders. Recalled to the Communications Office at the Navy Department in mid-1916, he brilliantly superintended its expansion for the navy's operations during World War I, bringing him promotion to the rank of commander. He was thereupon selected to establish the communications office in Paris for the Versailles peace conference in 1918–1919. He returned to the *Connecticut* as executive officer, transferring to the same post on the battleship *Arizona*, during 1920–1921. He served three years in the Office of Naval Intelligence and for two years in command of the survey gunboat *Nokomis*, employing aircraft for the first time to chart the coasts of Cuba and Haiti. After spending 1926–1927 as a senior student at the Naval War College, he transferred to the college staff in the rank of captain for a year.

Admiral William V. Pratt utilized Ingersoll's multifaceted abilities as his assistant chief of staff of the Battle Fleet (1928–1929), then of the U.S. Fleet (1929–1930) and finally as his director of fleet training while Pratt was chief of naval operations (CNO) (1930–1933). He successively commanded two heavy cruisers, briefly the *Augusta* before bringing the *San Francisco* into commission. Early in his three-year tenure as director of the war plans division he participated in the abortive London naval conference (1935–1936) as a technical assistant. He returned there in 1937 to initiate informal discussions with Britain over possible Anglo-American cooperation in any future war with Japan. Promoted rear admiral in May 1938, he commanded a heavy cruiser division in the Pacific until assigned as assistant to the CNO, Admiral Harold R. Stark, in 1940. A key figure in the preparation of the navy for war, Ingersoll was selected to command the Atlantic Fleet immediately after the Pearl Harbor attack, assuming the post in the rank of vice admiral on 1 January 1942. He was promoted to full admiral the following 1 July.

Quietly and unobtrusively, Ingersoll, headquartered at Norfolk, Virginia, concentrated his efforts on the Battle of the Atlantic against Germany's U-boats during World War II, also organizing the immense sealift and naval escort of the invasion force from the United States to the coast of North Africa in November 1942 and thereafter supporting Allied naval operations in the Mediterranean. With the creation of the Tenth Fleet under the direct control of the commander in chief of the U.S. Fleet, Admiral Ernest J. King, in May 1943, to mount counterattacks by hunter-killer task groups against the U-boats, Ingersoll provided the necessary escort carriers and destroyers from his Atlantic Fleet and ingeniously worked out the timetables for deploying them to maximum effect. Working closely with King, he issued the orders to the escort carrier groups that effectively neutralized the German submarine menace by the spring of 1944, enabling the Normandy landings to proceed that June. Ingersoll was clearly "one of the principal architects of Allied victory over the U-boat" (Morison, p. 25).

To facilitate the complex logistical planning for the projected invasion of Japan, Admiral King appointed Ingersoll to three "hats" in November 1944: Commander Western Sea Frontier, deputy commander in chief U.S. Fleet, and deputy CNO. Based at San Francisco, he had only begun to coordinate the redeployed naval forces from the Atlantic into the Pacific Fleet when the war ended. In October 1945 he relinquished his two deputy positions and his command of the Western Sea Frontier the following April; he retired in August. Ingersoll died in Washington, D.C.

• The Naval Historical Center has an outline biography and pertinent documents relating to Ingersoll and the Atlantic Fleet in World War II. *Current Biography, 1942* contains an essay on him. His part in the Battle of the Atlantic is treated in Samuel Eliot Morison, *The Atlantic Battle Won* (1956); the frontispiece, featuring Ingersoll, is taken from an oil painting. An obituary is in the *New York Times*, 22 May 1976.

CLARK G. REYNOLDS

INGERSOLL, Royal Rodney (4 Dec. 1847–21 Apr. 1931), naval officer, was born in Niles, Michigan, the son of Harmon Wadsworth Ingersoll, the superintendent of the Studebaker Wagon Works, and Rebecca A. Deniston. Ingersoll entered the U.S. Naval Academy on 23 July 1864 and graduated in 1868. He began sea duty as the U.S. Navy entered a period of deterioration following the Civil War. In 1873 he married Cynthia Eason. They had one child. Until 1874 Ingersoll served with the European Squadron aboard a series of obsolete steam sloops, which were wooden-hulled sailing ships with auxiliary steam power and smooth-bore cannon. Now a lieutenant, he spent the next two years on the Asiatic Station aboard the *Kearsarge*, the ship that sank the Confederate raider *Alabama* during the Civil War. From 1876 to the end of the decade he was an instructor in mathematics at the Naval Academy. He returned briefly to sea with the Pacific Squadron and then served ashore at the Naval Observatory until 1883.

Ingersoll was developing expertise in naval gunnery as the navy began its technological renaissance. In 1883, the year Congress funded the first steel cruisers for the U.S. Navy, he became an ordnance instructor at the Naval Academy. The next year he wrote his first book, *Textbook of Ordnance and Gunnery* (1884), in collaboration with Lieutenant J. F. Meigs. In 1887 Ingersoll rejoined the European Squadron for three years before becoming the head of the ordnance department at the Naval Academy in 1890. While at Annapolis, he wrote two more books on naval gunnery,

Exterior Ballistics (1891) and *The Elastic Strength of Guns* (1891). After his promotion to lieutenant commander in 1893, Ingersoll served as executive officer of the *Philadelphia*, flagship of the Asiatic Squadron, until 1897. During the Spanish-American War Ingersoll received his first command, the refrigerator ship *Supply*. After the war and his subsequent promotion to commander, Ingersoll returned to the Naval Academy as head of the ordnance department until 1901.

On 5 April 1901 Ingersoll took command of the gunboat *Helena* with the Asiatic Squadron. The commander in chief of the squadron, Rear Admiral Robley Evans, chose the *Helena* as his flagship on a cruise up the Yangtze River in 1902. On the cruise Ingersoll impressed the admiral with his knowledge of the river and his diplomatic skill in dealing with the Chinese. Later he worked to improve the gunnery of Evans's squadron. During his last year on the Asiatic Station, he received command of the protected cruiser *New Orleans*. For the next two years Ingersoll studied at the Naval War College and then served as a member of the General Board of the Navy. From 1905 to 1907 he commanded the new armored cruiser *Maryland*.

Ingersoll is best remembered for his prominent part in the world cruise of the "Great White Fleet." The commander in chief of the Atlantic Fleet was Evans, who chose Ingersoll as his chief of staff. Because of his Civil War wounds, Evans was too ill to command the fleet effectively. Shortly after leaving Hampton Roads, Evans's condition deteriorated to the point that he was able to go on deck only twice. Consequently, Ingersoll often acted as the admiral's proxy. During the voyage Ingersoll became a rear admiral. Evans's health did not improve, and he asked to be relieved of command when the fleet reached San Francisco. Ingersoll remained with Evans when he went ashore. Ingersoll was on the General Board until he retired from the navy on 4 December 1909. The Navy Department called him out of retirement during World War I to head a special naval ordnance board that advised the department on the quality of new gunnery inventions.

Ingersoll spent his retirement at La Porte, Indiana, where he died. His son, Admiral Royal Eason Ingersoll, became commander in chief of the Atlantic Fleet during World War II, and his grandson, Lieutenant Royal Rodney Ingersoll II, was killed aboard the carrier *Hornet* at the battle of Midway.

Ingersoll's naval career spanned the years when the U.S. Navy rose from the twelfth-ranked navy in the world to the third greatest navy, behind only Britain and Germany. As a naval ordnance expert, he participated in the technological revolution that transformed the U.S. fleet into a modern fighting force and the United States into a respected naval power.

• Ingersoll's papers, mostly official correspondence and memorabilia, are in the Navy Collection at the Manuscript Division, Library of Congress. For a genealogy of the Ingersolls, see L. D. Avery, *A Genealogy of the Ingersoll Family in America* (1926). Ingersoll's service record is outlined in L. R. Hamersly, *Records of Living Officers of the U.S. Navy and*

Marine Corps (1902). For Ingersoll's time in China with Evans, see Robley D. Evans, *An Admiral's Log* (1910). An account of Ingersoll's role during the world cruise is in James Reckner, *Teddy Roosevelt's Great White Fleet* (1988). An obituary is in the *New York Times*, 22 Apr. 1931.

JERRY W. JONES

INGHAM, Charles Cromwell (1796–10 Dec. 1863), painter, was born in Dublin, Ireland. Nothing is known of his family or education, but a contemporary account records that he was inspired to become an artist after sitting for his own portrait as a child. He attended drawing classes at the Royal Dublin Society and in 1810 became an apprentice to William Cuming, Dublin's leading painter of women's portraits. He studied with Cuming for at least four years, and the older artist undoubtedly inspired Ingham's specialization in portraits of women and children. Little else is known about Ingham's training. His mature style, which is characterized by vivid color, smooth surface, and fine detail, suggests that he studied the work of French neoclassical painters. Cuming may also have encouraged Ingham to paint subjects based on literary sources. Ingham's *The Death of Cleopatra* (date and location unknown) is said to have won a prize in Dublin. He must have been pleased with it, for he brought the painting with him when he moved to New York in 1816. That year he submitted the picture, along with a portrait of a gentleman, to the grand opening exhibition of the American Academy of the Fine Arts.

Over the next decade Ingham exhibited portraits of actors, such as *Edwin Forrest* (c. 1827, Pennsylvania Academy of the Fine Arts), statesmen, including *De Witt Clinton* (two versions, both 1824, New-York Historical Society and Century Association, N.Y.) and the *Marquis de Lafayette* (two versions, both 1825, New-York Historical Society and New York State Capitol, Albany), and other prominent citizens. By 1830 his highly finished and sophisticated technique, as seen in portraits such as *Amelia Palmer* (1830, Metropolitan Museum of Art, N.Y.), made him one of the city's most popular and respected artists. He also tried his hand at landscape painting; his *The Great Adirondack Pass, Painted on the Spot* (1837, Adirondack Museum, Blue Mountain Lake, N.Y.) is a rare extant example of his work in this genre. In addition, Ingham was esteemed by his colleagues. In 1825 he joined with other New York artists to establish the National Academy of Design and served on the council of directors and as vice president. He further supported the new institution by sending his best portraits to the annual exhibitions. In 1834 the author and painter William Dunlap, whose portrait Ingham painted in about 1830 (National Academy of Design), commented that Ingham "is among that large class of our present artists who are looked up to, and sought for, in the most enlightened society." Dunlap was also among those artists dazzled and impressed by Ingham's technique, which produced brilliant surface effects. He speculated that Ingham employed a "process of successive glazings" in order to achieve "a transparency, richness and harmony of colouring rarely seen in any country." The author of a Stuyvesant Institute exhibition catalog refuted Dunlap's assessment of Ingham's technique, explaining that "his practice is the use of colour without any glazings by repeated touches" (*Catalogue of the Exhibition of Select Paintings by Modern Artists* [1838], p. 8).

His meticulously painted and lushly colored portraits and fancy pictures of the 1840s, exemplified by *The Flower Girl* (1846, Metropolitan Museum of Art), attracted still more attention. The writer Charles Lanman, in his *Letters from a Landscape Painter* (1845), described Ingham as "the universal favorite among the ladies, and probably the most faultless painter in this country of those charming but incomprehensible creations of Heaven" (p. 252). Ingham continued painting successfully for many years and remained a valued member of the New York art world. A founding member of the Sketch Club in 1829, he was a leader in its reorganization to form the Century Association in 1847. He died in New York City; he is not known to have married. The self-portrait he painted in fulfillment of membership requirements at the National Academy remains in that collection.

• Ingham has not been the subject of a full-length monograph, and there is no known collection of his papers. For basic information on his life and work, see William Dunlap, *The History of the Rise and Progress of the Arts of Design in the United States*, vol. 2 (1834), pp. 271–74; Thomas Seir Cummings, *Historic Annals of the National Academy of Design* (1865), p. 353; Henry T. Tuckerman, *Book of the Artists* (1867), pp. 69–70; Albert Ten Eyck Gardner, "Ingham in Manhattan," *Metropolitan Museum of Art Bulletin* 10 (May 1952): 245–53; and John Caldwell and Oswaldo Rodriguez Roque, *American Paintings in the Metropolitan Museum of Art*, vol. 1, *A Catalogue of Works by Artists Born by 1815* (1994), pp. 396–404.

CARRIE REBORA

INGHAM, Mary Hall (24 Nov. 1866–1 Jan. 1937), suffragist and reform activist, was born in Philadelphia, Pennsylvania, the daughter of coal operator William Armstrong Ingham and Catherine Keppele Hall. Her paternal grandfather, Samuel Delucenna Ingham, was a congressman and former secretary of the Treasury under Andrew Jackson. Ingham grew up in Philadelphia and received her preparatory education at the Agnes Irwin School. Dissatisfied with the social life normally expected of daughters of prominent families such as her own, however, she returned to school at the age of thirty-one. She enrolled in the Woman's Medical College of Pennsylvania in 1898, and two years later transferred to Bryn Mawr College, where she completed an A.B. in 1903. After graduating, she taught art history as a private tutor and as an instructor at the Agnes Irwin School from 1903 to 1915. For most of these years Ingham, who never married, kept house for her father who, according to her biographers, was a congenial and supportive companion.

Like many of the female college graduates of her generation, Ingham became active in a number of civic, labor, and women's reform causes after graduation.

She joined the Philadelphia branch of the Association of Collegiate Alumnae and served as its president from 1906 to 1909. She served as the director of the Octavia Hill Association, a local group working for better tenement housing conditions, and served on the board of managers of the Day Nursery Association. In 1909 she became a founding member of the Equal Franchise Society of Philadelphia, an organization intended to build support for the cause of female suffrage among society women. Ingham was also active in working-class and labor causes. In 1910 she actively supported the Philadelphia garment workers' strike for shorter hours. When the Women's Trade Union League (WTUL) formed a Philadelphia branch in 1915, she became its vice president and a member of the advisory board.

Ingham's identification with progressive politics also led her into municipal reform and political organizing. She served as the director of the Bureau of Municipal Research in Philadelphia, an organization that sought progressive reforms such as the short ballot and the city manager plan. In 1911 she also organized support for reform candidates Rudolph Blackenburg for mayor of Philadelphia and Theodore Roosevelt for president. In 1912 she was the vice chair of the Women of Washington party, the Roosevelt organization in Pennsylvania. After Roosevelt's defeat, Ingham was instrumental in the formation of the Progressive League of Philadelphia, an organization of former Roosevelt supporters committed to nonpartisan civic reform. From 1915 to 1919 she also worked as the manager of the women's department of Bonbright and Company, a Philadelphia investment broker.

After 1917 Ingham dedicated her considerable political energies to the cause of woman suffrage. In that year she became the Pennsylvania state director of the National Woman's party (NWP), a suffrage organization led by feminist Alice Paul. Modeling its tactics on those of British suffragists, the NWP, in contrast to mainstream American woman suffrage organizations, staged dramatic protests at the White House and deliberately provoked arrests to publicize the cause of suffrage. Ingham played a key role in many of the NWP's protests, and she was arrested several times. In a demonstration emblematic of NWP tactics, Ingham staged a public burning of Woodrow Wilson's 4 July 1914 speech "in the name of the women of Pennsylvania who [were] demanding action of the President" to protest his failure to act on woman suffrage before going overseas (Irwin, p. 398). Most famously, she was one of sixteen NWP members arrested for picketing the White House gates on 14 July 1917 and later sentenced to thirty days in the Occoquan workhouse. Ingham and her comrades served three days before receiving a pardon from President Wilson. In 1919, as congressional passage of the suffrage amendment drew near, Ingham and other NWP members who had been arrested in the course of their protests publicized the cause by touring the country dressed in prison uniforms abroad a train car nicknamed the "Prison Special." After the Nineteenth Amendment was passed by Congress, Ingham coordinated NWP forces in Pennsylvania to ensure ratification. On 24 June 1919 Pennsylvania became the first state without a woman suffrage statute to ratify the amendment. After success in her home state, Ingham joined other NWP members in the broader ratification drive, picketing the 1920 Republican National Convention and lobbying presidential candidate Warren Harding in order to hasten ratification in Republican states.

After the amendment finally became law in 1920, Ingham briefly joined the NWP's campaign for an Equal Rights Amendment and lent her political support to the League of Nations. In the early 1920s she took graduate courses in government at Radcliffe College. Although she gradually dropped out of politics, she remained active in the pursuit of her personal interests until her final days. Well into her sixties, she continued mountain climbing, completing several difficult climbs in the European Alps. She died in Bryn Mawr, Pennsylvania.

• An article by Ingham from the *Philadelphia North American*, 8 July 1913, and a letter from her to Jane Addams, 16 Dec. 1912, are in Addams's papers at Swarthmore College. Brief biographical sketches of Ingham appear in Doris Stevens, *Jailed for Freedom* (1920), and the *Bryn Mawr College Register* (1920). Details on Ingham's suffrage activities are in Inez Haynes Irwin, *Uphill with Banners Flying* (1964, a reprint of Irwin's 1921 *Story of the Women's Party*); Caroline Katzenstein, *Lifting the Curtain: The State and National Woman Suffrage Campaigns in Pennsylvania as I Saw Them* (1955); and Henrietta L. Krone, "Dauntless Women: The Story of the Woman Suffrage Movement in Pennsylvania, 1910–1920" (Ph.D. diss., Univ. of Pennsylvania, 1946). On Ingham's other political activities, see the WTUL's *Life and Labor*, Mar. 1915. A helpful biographical sketch on Ingham, based on interviews with NWP president Alice Paul, WTUL member Pauline Newman, Pennsylvania suffrage activist Caroline Katzenstein, and other acquaintances of Ingham, appears in *Notable American Women*.

MICHELLE BRATTAIN

INGLE, Richard (1609–c. 1653), pirate and rebel, was born possibly in Redriff, Surrey, England, the son of unknown parents. Virtually nothing is known of his early life before he appeared in the colony of Maryland shortly after its 1634 founding. His first known occupation was that of ship captain and tobacco merchant, and his first definite appearance in the historical record was in March 1642, when he transported Captain Thomas Cornwallis, a member of the original colony council, from England on the ship *Eleanor*. He next appeared in Maryland in 1643, when he acted as attorney for a Mr. Penniston and his partners in suing the estate of a Mr. Cockshott. While Ingle was thus engaged, civil war was erupting between the forces of the king and those of Parliament in England. The ramifications of this conflict were soon felt in the colonies and served to shape the remainder of Ingle's career.

In early 1644 Ingle returned yet again to Maryland and was served with a warrant charging him with high treason (based on alleged statements made by Ingle) on 18 January of that year. On the basis of the testimony of a tailor, William Hardidge, acting governor Giles Brent issued the warrant that resulted in the capture of Ingle and the seizure of his vessel, the *Reformation*. In light of the civil war occurring in England at the time, Brent's actions unsettled many. The proprietary government of Maryland, while owing its continuing position to King Charles I, presided over a small, weak, and poorly defended set of settlements. Possibly to avoid antagonizing the adherents of Parliament for fear of their ultimate triumph in the struggle, the authorities (including Cornwallis and Sheriff Edward Parker) conspired to let Ingle escape. Given the confused state of affairs in the colony at the time, it was not surprising that various parties continued to seek indictments against Ingle on charges of either piracy or treasonous statements. After a number of failed attempts to gain jury acquiescence in an indictment, Ingle was charged on 20 January 1644 with assaulting the vessels, goods, and person of one Henry Bishop. Given consideration of damages that would result from his being delayed by a trial, Ingle was allowed to post a barrel of powder and 400 pounds of shot as a guarantee of his (or his attorney's) appearance in the following year. Ingle, for his part, resumed his trading activities and even acquired a small island off the Maryland coast and stocked it with hogs.

The government, perhaps seeking an official scapegoat for Ingle's escape, punished several of the men involved; Sheriff Parker was temporarily relieved of his duties, and Cornwallis received a stiff fine of 1,000 pounds of tobacco. While the fine was temporarily remitted, Cornwallis found conditions so distasteful that he shortly left Maryland and returned to England with Ingle. Ingle's departure did not end his troubles with the law; in his absence, it was discovered that he had failed to pay customs, and his goods were sequestered as a result.

Ingle's final visit to Maryland proved the most memorable. He returned to the colony in February 1645 in possession of letters of marque from the lord high admiral and professing his support of the parliamentary cause. Choosing to take the broadest possible interpretation of his newly acquired powers, he proposed to his crew a "man of war cruize" with a sixth of all plunder as the crew's reward. His proposal met with ready acceptance. After sailing to the mouth of St. Ignatius Creek, he captured a Dutch ship, the *Speagle* (or *Looking Glass*). Now in possession of two heavily armed ships, Ingle held the divided and poorly organized colony at his mercy. He shortly captured St. Thomas' Fort, after which he burned numerous houses, stole large quantities of tobacco, guns, and silverware, and kidnapped numerous slaves and indentured servants. Even Cornwallis, against whom Ingle now (for reasons that remain unclear) bore a deep hatred, did not escape Ingle's forces; his large home near Port Tobacco, Maryland, was ransacked. With Governor Leonard Calvert having fled into Virginia, the colony lay in chaos and remained so until December 1646, when Calvert regained control. Ingle shortly departed for England, taking with him as prisoners Giles Brent,

Thomas Copley, and John Lewger, all of whom had played a role in the original seizure of his ship.

Once back in England, Ingle sued to have the *Speagle* as a prize of war, but his original claim was rejected; there is no record of the appeal verdict. In the fall of 1646 he also began a long legal battle to disallow Lord Baltimore's legal title to Maryland. After a period of about five years, his claims and petitions were found to be "unprovided to prove his charges." Ingle also engaged in a long series of suits and countersuits with Cornwallis over the damages to Cornwallis's Port Tobacco home. The suits were ultimately settled about 1647 by Ingle's transference of both power of attorney and a set of bills and debts for collection to Cornwallis. In February 1650 Ingle informed the Council of State that two ships, the *Flower de Luce* and the *Thomas and John*, were about to sail for Virginia carrying Commonwealth enemies; for this and for his service in the keeping of a Captain Gardner (arrested for treason in the betrayal of Portland Castle), he received a reward of £30 sterling in April of the same year.

Ingle's final appearance in the historical record was in November 1653, when he wrote to Edward Marston seeking payment for two prizes (one of which he sought for his wife, whose name, date of marriage, and progeny remain unknown). Ingle's life and career was one of continuing controversy. While his devotion to the cause of Parliament remains debatable, there is no doubt that his presence in the early days of Maryland ultimately resulted in a period of turmoil in the colony that lasted nearly two years.

• There is no organized collection of Ingle's papers; however, his career can be traced through official records such as the *Calendar of State Papers, Domestic Series 1653–54* (1879) and the *Archives of Maryland*, vol. 4 (1887) and vol. 10 (1891). Secondary scholarship is limited. Although *Captain Richard Ingle: The Maryland "Pirate and Rebel," 1642–1653* (1884), by Edward Ingle, contains a wealth of information, it was written in an attempt to exonerate Ingle and should be used with caution. The best sources remain Bernard C. Steiner, *Maryland during the English Civil Wars* (1906–1907)—part of the *Johns Hopkins University Studies in History and Political Science*, series 24 and 25—and H. F. Thompson, "Richard Ingle in Maryland," *Maryland Historical Magazine* 1 (1906), pp. 125–40.

EDWARD L. LACH, JR.

INGLIS, Alexander James (24 Nov. 1879–12 Apr. 1924), professor, educational surveyor, and author, was born in Middletown, Connecticut, the son of William Grey Inglis and Susan Byers. While attending Wesleyan University in Middletown, Inglis earned distinction both as a scholar and athlete by taking all the school's Latin prizes, attaining membership in Phi Beta Kappa, excelling in track, and playing varsity football and baseball. After receiving an A.B. in 1902, he was awarded a one-year Wesleyan fellowship that allowed him to study at the American School of Classical Studies in Rome. This overseas study afforded opportunity for broadening his educational views and later influenced his educational opinions and philosophy.

Between 1903 and 1912 Inglis taught in secondary schools in Pennsylvania, New York City, and California. In New York, he taught Latin and served as acting principal at the Horace Mann School. While teaching, Inglis's attention turned to writing with his publication of three Latin texts, *First Book in Latin* (with Virgil Prettyman, 1906), *Exercise Book in Latin Composition* (1908), and *High School Course in Latin Composition* (with C. McC. Baker, 1909).

A man of unlimited energies, while gaining recognition as a Latin instructor and textbook writer Inglis continued his studies, graduating from Teachers College, Columbia University, with an A.M. in 1909 and a Ph.D. in 1911. While attending Columbia, he met Antoinette Clark of Cortland, New York, whom he married in 1911. The couple had no children.

Educational recognition for work outside the field of Latin came to Inglis after he published *The Rise of the High School in Massachusetts* (1911), which was a revision of his Columbia University dissertation. In that year he became headmaster of the Belmont School in California, a position he held for one year. After completing his doctorate, Inglis was appointed to serve on the Commission on the Reorganization of Secondary Education, a review committee designated by the National Education Association. The commission produced several landmark publications, including the *Cardinal Principles of Secondary Education*, a pamphlet to which Inglis contributed extensively, issued by the U.S. Bureau of Education in 1918. It provided greater insight into the reconstruction of secondary education curricula in the United States than any other work of the period.

Inglis's first higher education position came in 1912 when he was appointed professor of the science of education and head of the Department of Education at Rutgers College, where he also became director of the summer school and extension courses, retaining this position until spring 1914. That fall he accepted an assistant professorship in education at Harvard, where he initially prepared Harvard and Radcliffe students for teaching careers in secondary education and supervised practice teaching.

By 1915 Inglis had become involved in defining educational aims based on three types of meaningful social behavior. These included civic, vocational, and, as Inglis stated, individualistic or "those activities of life which cannot be considered directly and immediately civil or vocational." According to Inglis, even this latter behavior was to be monitored and controlled to prevent "social degeneracy."

Stressing the gradual and changeable development of adolescence, Inglis became convinced that secondary education should be expanded from four to six years to allow students to gradually enter the upper grades. This led him to become a leading advocate of the junior high school movement.

By 1918 Inglis had been given considerably more freedom in his course teaching. With a new emphasis on the broader issue of policy, Inglis concentrated his lectures on theory of education rather than the problems of initial secondary teaching. From these lectures he wrote *Principles of Secondary Education* (1918), which became his most extensive and constructive work. Inglis's *Principles* gave credence to ideas and concepts already existing in educational discussion. His work, based on his 1911 dissertation of the growth of the Massachusetts high school system, meticulously evaluated the immense literature of the social sciences in an attempt to provide insight into the implications of effectual discoveries of secondary education. Inglis showed through his research that as society evolves the secondary school environment becomes the chosen agent by which society prepares for changes.

In 1918 Inglis served on the organization committee on education and special training of the General Staff's War Plans Division. The next year he became director of the state education survey in Virginia. In this position, authorized by the state legislative committee, Inglis conducted a survey on the educational systems of Virginia schools. When published, this report, *Virginia Public Schools* (1919), with Inglis as nearly the sole contributor, became a model of survey literature. Surveys based on his work were subsequently conducted in Maine and Vermont. Inglis also served on survey staffs in Washington, South Dakota, and Indiana, publishing reports including *A Survey of the Educational Institutions of the State of Washington* (1916), *The Educational System of South Dakota* (1918), and *Public Education in Indiana* (1923). In 1921 he also authored *Intelligence Quotient Values*, which extended his theoretical and practical application of testing and survey methods.

On 10 May 1920, due in part to his publications, testing, and survey accomplishments, Inglis received a full professorship and became an eminent member of Harvard's educational faculty.

Besides Inglis's active and prominent service in the National Education Association, he was also an influential and supportive member of several other educational and scholarly societies, including the American Association for the Advancement of Science, National Society for the Scientific Study of Education, and Society of College Teachers of Education. Inglis also found time to edit a series of textbooks on *Theory and Practice of Education*.

Inglis died following abdominal surgery at Massachusetts General Hospital in Boston. At the time of his death he was working on a revised plan for developing vocational testing. A previous plan, which he had instituted, had proven exceptionally useful.

Inglis was dedicated to the field of secondary education. As a man of outstanding intellectual stamina and fortitude, Inglis's accomplishments, including his educational surveys, achievement testing in Latin, English, and other secondary subjects, Latin textbooks, and works on secondary education, afforded him the distinction of greatly influencing America's development and understanding of secondary education. As a theoretician of the socialization of secondary education, Inglis's analysis afforded teachers and administrators a broad base for evaluating educational aims, options, and practical applications.

• "Minutes on the Life and Services of Professor Alexander James Inglis" and other unpublished records, located at the Harvard Graduate School of Education, are important sources of information on Inglis's life, teaching career, and accomplishments. Arthur G. Powell, *The Uncertain Profession: Harvard and the Search for Educational Authority* (1980), is a significant source relating to Inglis's contributions to secondary education while teaching at Harvard. *In Memoriam—Alexander Inglis 1879–1924* (1925) is a volume composed of contributions from Inglis's colleagues and students. See also news clippings relating to his appointment to Harvard in the *Boston Herald*, 22 Oct. 1914 and 29 Jan. 1915. Obituaries include the *Harvard Alumni Bulletin* (1924), p. 823, *Wesleyan University Alumnus*, May 1924, pp. 38–39, *Harvard Graduates' Magazine*, June 1924, pp. 609–11, the *New York Times*, 13 Apr. 1924, and the *Boston Transcript*, 12 Apr. 1924.

C. E. LINDGREN

INGLIS, Charles (1734–24 Feb. 1816), Anglican minister, Loyalist, and first bishop of Nova Scotia, was born in Glencolumbkille, Donegal, Ireland, the son of the Reverend Archibald Inglis (mother's name unknown). For four generations his family supplied pastors for important Anglican parishes, but Charles, orphaned at eleven, grew up in a poor parish, where his Protestant family was outnumbered five to one by Roman Catholic neighbors. Charles had hoped to follow the family tradition of attending Trinity College, Dublin, but poverty blocked any college education. Because of his Irish origins, poverty, religious minority status, and lack of a university education, Inglis held a lifelong antipathy to dissenters and deeply craved respectability and social status.

Necessity forced Charles to accept the help of John Inglis, a relative living in Philadelphia. He immigrated to Pennsylvania about 1754, possibly as an indentured tutor to the Inglis boys. Then from 1755 to 1758 he served as assistant master at £25 a year at the Free School, a school for German immigrants in Lancaster, Pennsylvania. During these three years Inglis went through an intense period of spiritual self-examination and probably served as catechist at St. James. After ordination in London in 1758, Anglican officials sent him out as a missionary for the Society for the Propagation of the Gospel to Dover, Delaware, with a salary of £50 per year. A Quaker who heard missionary Inglis preach wrote that Inglis was "Frugal, Industrious, Meek and free from Pride and Ostentation." He also achieved fame as a "gospel preaching" minister who doubled the number of parishioners taking communion, preached to standing room only audiences, and was the only missionary in either Delaware or Pennsylvania who admitted African-American slaves to the communion table. In 1764 Inglis married Mary Vining, sister of the chief justice of Delaware, positioning him in one of the "first families" in Delaware. Tragi-

cally, after only eight months of marriage, Mary died in childbirth.

Primarily because of his reputation as a powerful pulpit preacher and his evangelical commitment, in 1765 Inglis became assistant rector at a salary of £200 to the Reverend Samuel Auchmuty at Trinity Church in New York City, the largest and most prestigious parish in colonial America. During his six years as a missionary at Dover, Inglis became so infatuated with the writings of the Christian mystic Jacob Boehme that he was identified as a "sound Whitefieldian," and in his first sermon at Trinity Church he stated, "I glory in being called a Methodist." However, this evangelical period was short-lived and like most Anglicans, Inglis rejected the Great Awakening's stress on an overwhelming emotional experience of a new birth.

Sensing his deficient education, while at Trinity Church Inglis launched into a program of self-education and learned Hebrew, Syriac, and Aramaic and polished up his Greek and Latin. At this time he also became an ardent promoter of education for the Mohawk Indians and as a high churchman urged England to appoint an American Anglican bishop. In 1768, for partisan political motives, William Livingston and his Presbyterian followers wrote sixty-four essays, under the title "American Whig," opposing an American episcopate. Inglis entered the fray by writing pro-episcopate newspaper articles under the pen name "Whip." In 1768 Inglis also published his only theological work, a 180-page scholarly essay defending the Anglican practice of infant baptism. Academic acceptance soon followed. King's College had awarded him an M.A. in 1767 and in 1771 appointed him to its board of governors; from 1771 to 1773 he was president of King's. Oxford University recognized his scholarship by granting him an M.A. in 1770 and a D.D. degree in 1778. Inglis had remarried in 1773 to Margaret Crooke, who was fourteen years his junior, and quickly they had four children.

During the American Revolution, Inglis turned his keen wit to authoring some thirty imprints. The most notable was *The True Interest of America Impartially Stated*, an essay answering Thomas Paine's *Common Sense*. His *Letters of Papinian* in 1779 was a scathing attack on the Congress, which he asserted followed Machiavellian techniques. Because of his published pamphlets and pro-British sermons, Inglis deserves the title "foremost propagandist for the Loyalist cause."

When New York City was occupied by the American army in February 1776, Inglis acted courageously. He still fervently prayed for the king, even when George Washington attended services at Trinity. On another Sunday the service was interrupted by 100 rebel soldiers entering the church with drums beating and bayonets fixed in place. They threatened to shoot him if he prayed for George III but did nothing when Inglis read the normal prayers for the king. In June 1776, when many Loyalists in his church were beaten and arrested, Inglis visited them in jail, even though it brought suspicion on his own character. From 1778 on he served as chaplain to the British army at New York and also as chaplain to the New Jersey Volunteers. In 1780 he wrote a pamphlet critical of George Washington for the "murder" of Major John André.

By the fall of 1776 Inglis was definitely a conspicuous Loyalist, with high ranking British officials praising him as "very solid and sensible," and New York patriots labeling him a "dangerous and insidious enemy." In 1777 Auchmuty died, and Inglis became rector of Trinity Church with an income of £459 (salary and fees), making him the senior clergyman in North America. In 1779 the state of New York attainted Inglis for high treason and legally confiscated all his property (worth £7,909). When the British evacuated New York City, Inglis petitioned to remain, but when the state rejected his request he left for England with his family.

In exile Inglis soon became the principal adviser on American affairs for the archbishop of Canterbury, John Moore. In August 1787 he was sent as first colonial bishop over all of Nova Scotia and in a second patent made bishop over Quebec, New Brunswick, and Newfoundland. Although Anglicans were a minority denomination in Nova Scotia, Inglis used St. Paul's in Halifax as his cathedral church, and during his episcopacy from 1787 to 1816 he and his assistants founded forty-four churches. He also founded in 1795 the oldest overseas British university—King's College at Windsor, Nova Scotia. An amateur architect, Inglis designed the plans for King's College and most of the forty-four churches, creating an indigenous maritime style.

Although suffering from gout and recurring bouts with malaria, Inglis energetically toured his geographically expansive diocese, issuing instructions to his clergy, confirming believers, and ruling on issues of church polity. A believer in Lockean natural religion and the efficacy of the sacraments for salvation, Inglis fought for the twenty-nine years of his episcopate against the twin evils of infidelity and religious enthusiasm (New Light and Methodist) and confirmed at least 4,300 individuals before dying at his summer home "Clermont," near the Parish Church of Aylesford. His youngest son John in 1825 carried on the family tradition and became the third bishop of Nova Scotia. Charles Inglis's memorial tablet summarized his fifty-eight years of pastoral ministry: "Sound Learning and Fervent Piety Directed by Zeal According To Knowledge And Supported by Fortitude, Unshaken Amidst Peculiar Trials."

• Inglis's papers are scattered, with the bulk in possession of his descendants; other papers are in the Anglican Diocesan Archives, Halifax, Nova Scotia; the Public Archives of Canada; the Archives of the Protestant Episcopal Church, Austin, Tex.; the Public Archives of Nova Scotia; and the Archives of the Society for the Propagation of the Gospel in Foreign Parts, Oxford, England. Many of his letters to the SPG appear in John Wydekker, *The Life and Letters of Charles Inglis* (1936). A short biography by his son-in-law is in William Sprague, *Annals of the American Pulpit* 5 (1969): 186–91. For his service at the parish of Trinity Church and extracts of sermons consult Morgan Dix, *A History of the Parish of Trinity Church in the City of New York* (1898). For full citations on his published sermons and pamphlets see "Eighteenth-Century Short Title Catalog" (1992), CD-ROM. For his Loyalist claim see American Loyalists Claims, Public Record Office, Audit Office 12/20/368ff; 12/109/176ff. There are a number of biographies on Inglis: a standard is Reginald V. Harris, *Charles Inglis: Missionary, Loyalist, Bishop (1734–1816)* (1937); but the best biography on Inglis is Brian Cuthbertson, *The First Bishop: A Biography of Charles Inglis* (1987).

DAVID E. MAAS

INGRAHAM, Joseph Holt (26 Jan. 1809–18 Dec. 1860), novelist and minister, was born in Portland, Maine, the son of James Milk Ingraham, a merchant, and Elizabeth Thurston. The second generation of a successful merchant and shipping family, the Ingrahams moved to Hallowell, Maine, in 1818. There Ingraham attended Hallowell Academy, studying languages and classics in preparation for college. His family's status offered him many opportunities, and at least once, at age seventeen, he traveled to South America aboard one of his grandfather's ships. In 1828 Ingraham entered Yale but remained for only one year before being dismissed for misconduct.

In 1830 Ingraham again sailed south, this time for Cuba and New Orleans, finally settling in Natchez, Mississippi. In nearby Washington, Mississippi, he became affiliated with Jefferson College, Possibly as an instructor in languages, and appropriated the title "Professor," under which he would publish works for the rest of his life. In 1832 he married Mary Elizabeth Brookes and settled at her family's plantation, "Rose Cottage." His writing career began in 1833 with his series of "Letters from Louisiana and Mississippi by a Yankee" in the *Natchez Courier*. Recounting both his travels from New England to the South and his stay in New Orleans and Natchez, the series ran for two years before being published in 1835 in book form as *The South-West, by a Yankee*. The book's sales and reviews were sufficient to steer him toward writing as a lifelong vocation.

Ingraham abandoned the travel genre for historical romances, and his success over the next seven years made him a rival of successful authors such as James Fenimore Cooper and William Gilmore Simms. Both a financial and critical success, his first novel, *Lafitte: The Pirate of the Gulf* (1836), chronicles its Byronic character's adventures in lush New Orleans. He followed this success with *Burton* (1838), the story of Aaron Burr's early life; *Captain Kyd* (1839), the first of many returns to the domain of pirates; and *The Quadroone* (1841). With these novels and many periodical pieces, Ingraham attained wide popularity, but his critical appraisal soon declined. As Edgar Allan Poe, his most frequent and harshest critic, observed, Ingraham was "one of our most *popular* novelists, if not one of our best. He appeals always to the taste of the ultraromanticists (as a matter, we believe, rather of pecuniary policy than of choice). . . . Still, he is capable of better things" (*Graham's Magazine*, Nov. 1841). As

Poe astutely perceived, Ingraham's aim in writing was more often financial than artistic. However, because he arranged one poor publishing agreement after another, he seldom prospered from his novels and continually struggled to support his family of five children, even declaring bankruptcy in 1842.

In the late 1830s and early 1840s, as the literary market adapted to economic and public demands, the long two-volume romances Ingraham had been writing were no longer in vogue. Displaying true adaptability, Ingraham quickly began to produce a more marketable product, shorter romances of only ten chapters; the first of these, *The Dancing Feather*, appeared in 1842. The success of this work initiated a new phase in Ingraham's career, as he began to churn out novel after novel at a phenomenal rate, eight books in 1843, nineteen in 1844, twenty-five in 1845, sixteen in 1846, and ten in 1847. He did manage to evade the narrative strictures of the shorter length and maintain the tone of his longer works by publishing subsequent books as sequels to earlier ones. For instance, *The Dancing Feather* is continued in *Morris Graeme* (1843), permitting a narrative longer than current fashion allowed. Although he became one of America's bestselling and most prolific authors (he is reportedly responsible for nearly 10 percent of the fiction titles published in the 1840s), Ingraham's literary reputation suffered because it was apparent that his novels were meant only as a means of sustenance. His contemporary Henry Wadsworth Longfellow, for example, remarked in 1846 that Ingraham "has written eighty novels, and of these twenty during the last year; till it has grown to be merely mechanical with him" (*Life of Henry Wadsworth Longfellow*, vol. 2 [1886], p. 35).

Despite his exhaustive work, Ingraham still found it impossible to support his family with his writing. In 1847 he abandoned his writing career and moved to Nashville, Tennessee, to study for the ministry in the Episcopal church. He became principal of the Vine Street Female Academy as well as an advocate of tax-supported public education and the education of prison inmates. After he was ordained a minister in 1852, a series of assignments followed, in Aberdeen, Mississippi; Mobile, Alabama; and Riverside, Tennessee. The family eventually settled in Holly Springs, Mississippi, in 1858.

Ingraham started writing again in 1850, publishing a series of "Letters from Adina," an epistolary account of a young Jewish girl's life during the time of Christ, in the Episcopalian periodical *Evergreen*. In 1855 these letters were published as the biblical novel *The Prince of the House of David* and became Ingraham's most successful and most enduring work. He followed this book's success with further biblical epics, *The Pillar of Fire* (1859) and *The Throne of David* (1860). After these novels, Ingraham finished only one other book, *The Sunny South* (1860), a response to *Uncle Tom's Cabin* composed of letters recording a northern governess's pleasant experiences in the South. While working on another religious novel, Ingraham died in Holly Springs from an apparently accidental self-inflicted gunshot wound.

Though Ingraham is a minor figure in American literature, his greatest achievement appears in his religious novels. These works, especially *The Prince of the House of David*, are considered some of the earliest successful fiction based on biblical sources. Their popularity fostered the development of this subgenre, setting the stage for more famous works, such as Lew Wallace's *Ben-Hur*. (Cecil B. DeMille consulted *The Pillar of Fire* for his 1956 film *The Ten Commandments*.) It was not as a popular romancer but as a writer of biblical fiction that Ingraham made his most lasting contribution to American culture.

• A comprehensive study of Ingraham's life and work is Robert W. Weathersby II, *J. H. Ingraham* (1980). Other useful sources include E. A. Alderman and Joel C. Harris, eds., *Library of Southern Literature*, vol. 6 (1907); Warren G. French, "A Sketch of the Life of Joseph Holt Ingraham," *Journal of Mississippi History* 11 (1949): 155–71, and "A Hundred Years of a Religious Best Seller," *Western Humanities Review* (1955–1956): 45–54; Jay B. Hubbell, *The South in American Literature, 1607–1900* (1954); and James B. Lloyd, ed., *Lives of Mississippi Authors, 1817–1967* (1981). An obituary is in the *Mississippi Free Trader*, 24 Dec. 1860.

PAUL CHRISTIAN JONES

INGRAHAM, Prentiss (28 Dec. 1843–16 Aug. 1904), writer and soldier, was born in Adams County, Mississippi, the son of Joseph Holt Ingraham, a minister and writer, and Mary Brooks, the daughter of a wealthy southern planter. Ingraham attended Jefferson College (Miss.) and Mobile Medical College until the Civil War ended his academic career. At the age of seventeen, Ingraham enlisted in Colonel William Temple Withers's Mississippi Regiment; he later served as a scout commander in a Texas cavalry brigade. At the siege of Port Hudson, Ingraham was wounded in the foot and captured, but he escaped while being transported to a northern prison.

For several years after the Civil War, Ingraham was a soldier of fortune in several locations around the globe. He served under Benito Juárez in Mexico and fought for Austria in its 1866 war with Prussia; he fought against the Turks in Crete and for the khedive in Egypt. In 1869 he returned to North America, where he aided the Cuban resistance in the Ten Years' War against Spanish rule, serving as an officer in both the Cuban navy and the Cuban army; he used his Cuban army title of colonel throughout his literary career. Ingraham purchased a ship, the *Hornet*, to run filibustering expeditions. He was captured by the Spanish and given a death sentence, but he once again escaped.

Though Ingraham had published several poems and articles during a brief stay in London in 1869, he began his literary career in earnest during the early 1870s after he moved to New York. By 1872 he was writing regularly for the publishing firm Beadle and Adams in its *Saturday Journal*; he soon became one of the most popular and productive writers for the successful dime novel publishers. He churned out stories of adventure and intrigue with exotic settings, some of which were drawn indirectly from his war experiences, for example, *The Cretan Rover; or, Zuleikah, the Beautiful* (1877) and *The Boy Bugler in Cuba* (1897). He also wrote in the emerging genre of the dime novel detective story; among other sleuths he created were *Darkie Dan, the Colored Detective* (1881) and *The Jew Detective* (1885). In addition, he adapted several of his father's novels for Beadle and Adams.

Many of Ingraham's dime novels were westerns. Though he invented several fictional western heroes, he was most noted for his stories employing actual western personages; he wrote several novels featuring Wild Bill Hickock and ghostwrote novels signed by John B. Omohundro ("Texas Jack") and Dr. Frank Powell. Ingraham is undoubtedly best known, however, for his 121 stories featuring William F. Cody, known as Buffalo Bill.

Ingraham began writing Buffalo Bill stories in 1876. He probably first met Cody in 1879, when he wrote the play *The Knight of the Plain; or, Buffalo Bill's Best Trail*. This meeting was propitious for both men's careers: Ingraham wrote Cody's next play, *Buffalo Bill at Bay; or, The Pearl of the Prairies*, and served as a press agent for the first few seasons of Buffalo Bill's Wild West show, begun in 1883. Ingraham is also thought to have ghostwritten a number of works for Cody. Though his Buffalo Bill dime novels did not overtly advertise the Wild West show, the success of the shows and the novels was mutually beneficial. After Cody singled out Buck Taylor as a star performer, Ingraham wrote several novels about the "King of the Cowboys," emphasizing the roping skills Taylor demonstrated in the shows.

Ingraham helped to develop the image of the western plainsman and cowboy from ungrammatical hick to well-spoken dandy. Unlike Ned Buntline's Buffalo Bill, Ingraham's Buffalo Bill is fond of rhetorical flourishes and is equipped with many of the trappings of the stereotypical medieval knight, including ornate garb and weaponry. Ingraham is one of the first writers to elevate the figure of the cowboy, which in the 1880s had a dubious public image; his chivalric treatment of Buck Taylor anticipates Owen Wister's gentlemanly Virginian.

Ingraham's association with Beadle and Adams concluded when the firm dissolved in the late 1890s. In 1901 he began to contribute to a Buffalo Bill series for the Street and Smith firm; the name "Colonel Prentiss Ingraham" had become so popularly associated with Buffalo Bill that stories written by other Street and Smith writers were frequently attributed to him.

Ingraham was remarkably prolific. Estimates of his total output vary considerably; some have credited him with almost a thousand novels, though he himself claimed to have written closer to six hundred. His bibliography is complicated by the numerous works he is suspected of having ghostwritten as well as the various pseudonyms he employed, many of which reflect his penchant for titles, including Major Dangerfield Burr,

Midshipman T. W. King, Major H. B. Stoddard, and Colonel Leon Lafitte. He reputedly wrote all his works in longhand at a rapid pace; he is said to have once written a 35,000-word novel in a day and a half and a 70,000-word novel in five days.

In addition to his dime novels for series and periodicals published by Beadle and Adams and Street and Smith, Ingraham wrote several plays and works of nonfiction, including *Saratoga* (1885) and *Land and Lore: Sketches of Romance and Reality on the Eastern Shore of the Chesapeake* (1898).

In 1875 Ingraham married Rosa Langley of New York, an author, artist, and composer. In 1897 the couple moved from New York to Easton, Maryland, and in 1902 to Chicago. Ingraham died at the Beauvoir Confederate Home in Biloxi, Mississippi. He was survived by his wife and three children.

At Ingraham's death, *The Bookman* noted that "the extraordinary side of his work is of a nature that appeals to the statistician rather than to the literary critic." Yet he helped shape late nineteenth-century American popular culture, playing a key role in the evolution of the dime novel western, particularly in its image of the cowboy, and in promoting the popular phenomenon of Buffalo Bill.

• A collection of Ingraham's manuscripts is at the New York Public Library; some additional material can be found at the University of Mississippi and Tulane University. Biographical information about Ingraham is scarce; the most extensive biographical and bibliographical information is in Albert Johannsen, *The House of Beadle and Adams and Its Dime and Nickel Novels*, vol. 2 (1950). Don Russell, *The Lives and Legends of Buffalo Bill* (1960), provides an examination of the relationship between Ingraham and William F. Cody. Useful discussions of Ingraham's contribution to the development of the dime novel western may be found in Daryl Jones, *The Dime Novel Western* (1978), and Henry Nash Smith, *Virgin Land: The American West as Symbol and Myth* (1950).

RANDALL C. DAVIS

INGRAM, Edgar Waldo (28 Dec. 1880–20 May 1966), founder of the White Castle hamburger chain and the originator of American fast food, was born in Leadville, Colorado, the son of Charles W. Ingram, a land agent, and Frances Amelia West. The Ingrams soon moved to the San Luis Valley in Colorado, then to Omaha, Nebraska, and later to St. Joseph, Missouri. Young Ingram, called "Billy," graduated from high school in St. Joseph in 1896 and the same year moved back to Omaha, where for a couple of years he was a reporter and editor for the *Omaha Bee*. After this short career as a journalist, Ingram worked in various business capacities, including as a traveling agent for R. G. Dun and Company (the predecessor of Dun & Bradstreet). R. G. Dun transferred him to its Wichita, Kansas, office, where he worked until 1907. After less than a year in Wichita, Ingram cofounded the insurance partnership of Ingram, Yankey and Company and devoted the next thirteen years to building a series of profitable insurance, oil, and real estate businesses. By 1921 Ingram was the managing partner in the successful insurance and real estate firm of Stone and Ingram and enjoyed a sound reputation in the Wichita community. In 1909 he had married Jesse Gibb, with whom he had one child. The couple divorced in 1934.

In the process of brokering a real estate deal in 1921, Ingram was asked by a client to cosign a lease. This client, Walter Anderson, owned three hamburger stands on street corners in downtown Wichita and was trying to lease space from a dentist to further expand his business. Because hamburger stands had a dubious reputation in that era, the property owner wanted additional guarantees. Ingram agreed to cosign the lease and soon after became a full partner in Anderson's business once he learned more about the growth potential of the hamburger industry. Although Anderson knew how to make popular hamburgers, he had little business acumen. Once Ingram entered the business he quickly realized how their operation and profits could be greatly expanded. The largest obstacle in his path was a negative popular perception about the purity of meat that was spawned a decade earlier by Upton Sinclair's *The Jungle* (1906). Meat in itself was suspect, and many consumers believed that it was only ground up to hide spoilage or other defects.

In an effort to dispel the public's deep bias against ground beef, Ingram began a massive campaign to promote and legitimize the hamburger sandwich. His first move was to repackage and market his company as the epitome of cleanliness and quality. Ingram chose White Castle System as the company name; "White" to signify purity and "Castle" to symbolize strength and permanence. He also chose an architectural style for his company restaurants in keeping with the new name: whitewashed stone-block buildings with crenelated roofs and turrets made to resemble medieval castles. Painted on the exterior of each of these new structures was "White Castle Hamburgers 5 Cents" and the company's new slogan, "Buy 'em by the Sack." The interior of each White Castle was standardized in exactly the same layout, with five stools, a counter, and a grill operated by two male employees, serving a streamlined menu of hamburgers, Coca-Cola, coffee, and pie. The hungry working-class consumers of Wichita showed their approval by buying many sacks of Ingram's new hamburgers, thus fueling the company's rapid growth.

The high degree of standardization that Ingram insisted on would soon become a norm for most other hamburger companies. The entire operation of the White Castle System, in fact, became the prototype for the entire fast-food industry that followed. Other entrepreneurs quickly took notice as Ingram's new company spread rapidly east of the Mississippi in the early 1920s. Imitators immediately began to appear, exactly copying White Castle's distinctive architecture, food products, and even the slogan. Even more extraordinary, these early imitators also closely copied White Castle's company name, operating under such derivatives as "White Tower," "Royal Castle," "White Palace," "White Turrets," and "Red Castles." By the end of the decade at least 100 hamburger chains bore

names similar to White Castle's, and virtually all hamburger restaurants in the 1920s and 1930s were small whitewashed buildings where hamburgers identical to White Castle's were sold.

White Castle's primacy in the fast-food hamburger industry was actually declared in federal court. One imitator, the White Tower System founded in 1926, brought suit against White Castle in 1929 when Ingram expanded his operation into the Detroit area. Because White Tower already had restaurants in Detroit, the company claimed that White Castle, using its originating architecture, foods, and slogan, was infringing on White Tower territory. The court held that White Tower's claim was invalid because White Tower's buildings, products, and "Take Home a Bagful" slogan were imitations of White Castle. Ingram countersued and forced White Tower to alter its exteriors. By this time, however, the White Castle image and foods were largely in the public domain. By 1930 the hamburger that Ingram had marketed so effectively was already entrenched as America's favorite food, and countless businesses were selling it. In 1933 he bought out Anderson for $350,000, and the next year the company moved from Wichita to Columbus, Ohio, to be at the center of its expanded territory. By the end of the 1930s (its peak under Ingram), White Castle had approximately 200 restaurants. Despite increasingly tough competition in the industry he almost singlehandedly founded, Ingram ran White Castle until his death in Columbus. His heirs have continued to wholly own and directly manage this relatively small, profitable chain.

Edgar Ingram brought to the American palate the hamburger and fast-food style of eating, just as Henry Ford made the automobile an American necessity. Both men changed American consumption patterns and behaviors and also provided their products at a price that common people could afford. In the course of less than a decade, Ingram's marketing efforts inexorably embedded the hamburger into American culture. Some theorists even suggest that Ingram's hamburger itself has become America's primary ethnic food and, hence, a delineator of American ethnicity. What is certain is that Ingram's lone efforts to legitimize and market his hamburger product resulted in a new style of eating in the United States and an undisputed favorite food.

• The only records and writings of Edgar W. Ingram exist in an incomplete collection of White Castle records dating from 1921 to the 1960s, held at the Ohio Historical Society in Columbus. This uncataloged collection contains numerous pieces of company correspondence, some personal records, a carefully preserved record of all newspaper coverage of Ingram, and a monthly company newsletter to which Ingram regularly contributed. The Newcomen Society also published Ingram's 1964 address to that organization titled "All This from a 5-cent Hamburger: The Story of the White Castle System," which provides his personal reflections on his achievements. Most volumes on food history or twentieth-century culture give brief mention to his contributions.

DAVID GERARD HOGAN

INGRAM, Jonas Howard (15 Oct. 1886–10 Sept. 1952), naval officer, was born in Jeffersonville, Indiana, the son of William Thomas Ingram, who ran a sand and gravel business, and Anna Howard. He was appointed to the U.S. Naval Academy in 1903. An avid athlete, Ingram played football, ran track, and captained the rowing crew. For his outstanding performance in football (he scored the winning touchdown in the army-navy game of 1906), the Naval Athletic Association presented him with its Sword for General Excellence in Athletics. However, Ingram graduated in the bottom quarter of his class in 1907.

Commissioned an ensign in 1909, Ingram was first assigned as a gunnery officer aboard the USS *Nebraska* during the cruise of the Great White Fleet. In 1910 Ingram reported to the *Hartford*, transferring the following year to the battleship *Iowa*. He subsequently served as turret officer aboard the battleship *Arkansas*, during which time the ship established naval gunning records with its twelve-inch guns. During the U.S. intervention at Veracruz, Mexico, in April 1914, Ingram led a battalion of bluejackets and marines ashore and, during the subsequent fighting, was responsible for the skillful employment of the battalion's artillery and machine guns. Several months afterward, Ingram married Jean Fletcher-Coffin; the couple had two children. The navy awarded him the Medal of Honor for his outstanding conduct at Veracruz.

Detached from the *Arkansas* in November 1914, Ingram had a quick succession of assignments aboard the *Wisconsin*, the *Kearsarge*, the *Kentucky*, and the *Alabama*. He returned to the Naval Academy in April 1915 to coach the football team. After the United States entered the First World War in April 1917, the navy assigned him to the staff of Admiral Hugh Rodman, commander, Division Three, Battle Force, Atlantic Fleet (later commander, U.S. Sixth Battle Squadron). Ingram served as Admiral Rodman's aide and flag lieutenant aboard the *New York* and was present when the German High Seas Fleet surrendered on 21 November 1918. For his wartime work, the navy awarded Ingram its cross for distinguished service.

Until May 1921 Ingram remained as aide and flag lieutenant to Rodman, who became commander in chief, U.S. Pacific Fleet. Ingram then became chief of staff to the commandant, Ninth Naval District, headquartered at the Great Lakes Naval Training Facility. He resumed sea duty from July 1924 to May 1926, commanding the destroyer *Stoddert* and serving as a division commander of destroyers attached to the U.S. Battle Fleet, Pacific. In June 1926 Ingram, now a captain, returned to the U.S. Naval Academy, where he served as director of football and athletics until February 1930. After the battleship *Pennsylvania*'s refitting, Ingram became that vessel's executive officer and temporarily served as its commanding officer when *Pennsylvania* became the flagship of the commander in chief, Pacific Fleet. In 1932 Captain Ingram was appointed officer in charge of public relations for the U.S. Navy in Washington, D.C. Three years later he became an aide to Secretary of the Navy Claude Swan-

son but quickly returned to sea duty as commander of Destroyer Squadron Six, Battle Force, with the *Litchfield* as his flagship. In July 1937 Ingram became captain of the yard at the Navy Yard, New York. Two years later he reported to the U.S. Naval War College in Newport, Rhode Island, where he completed the senior course in May 1940. Ingram then served as the commanding officer of the *Tennessee*.

Advanced in December 1940 to rear admiral, Ingram the next month assumed a major command, Cruiser Division Two, with the *Memphis* as his flagship. He initially policed the Caribbean. As the United States, even before formally entering the Second World War, expanded its efforts to protect Allied shipping, Ingram's force moved into the South Atlantic and, specifically, Brazilian waters, in order to guard seaborne commerce from Nazi ships and submarines. Two months after the attack on Pearl Harbor, Ingram's title changed to commander, Task Force Twenty-Three, and later to commander, Fourth Fleet. He was promoted to vice admiral in 1942.

Though Ingram seemed the very image of the old seadog and went so far as to complain that President Franklin Roosevelt was "making a third-rate diplomat out of a first-rate fighting man" (*Contemporary Biography 1947*, p. 329), he proved most skillful, indeed, in treating with Brazilian officials. His efforts helped solidify Brazilian allegiance to the Allied cause and allowed that nation to make a real contribution to the war in the South Atlantic. The Brazilians agreed to allow Ingram to build U.S. air, naval, and other facilities on their territory. He, in turn, oversaw much of the Brazilian military effort, seeing to it that its navy and air force were sufficiently fitted out and prepared for combat. Among his greatest accomplishments was the construction of one of the world's largest air bases on Ascension Island, in the Atlantic over a thousand miles off the Brazilian coast. From there Ingram could conduct aerial warfare, and not simply surface actions, against German U-boats. His planes sent eight of them to the bottom in the summer of 1943, and by the end of that year he was able to declare the Atlantic between Brazil and West Africa secured. The old coach and fullback insisted that he had employed football strategy to fight the Nazi submarines. Whatever the case, he subsequently won the Distinguished Service Medal and Gold Star for his achievements.

On 15 November 1944 Ingram became commander in chief, Atlantic Fleet, and advanced to the rank of full admiral. In this capacity, his main responsibilities involved the protection of shipping routes to and from the European theater of operations. Though he worried in public about U-boats attempting a rocket attack on New York City, Ingram had, instead, simply to confound the Germans' final efforts at more conventional submarine warfare. He remained commander in chief, Atlantic Fleet, until September 1946.

Transferring to the retired list in April 1947, Ingram resumed the other of his life's passions, serving as commissioner of the All-America Football Conference until 1949. During his tenure, he proved unable to persuade the National Football League to agree to an interleague championship game. Also a vice president of Reynolds Metal Company, Ingram spent his final years in San Diego, where he died. He had been an outstanding member of that generation of naval officers who distinguished themselves by their service at sea during both the First and Second World Wars, but especially through their mastery of airpower in the latter conflict.

• Some official papers and other materials related to Ingram's career are at the U.S. Naval Historical Center, U.S. Navy Yard, Washington, D.C. The U.S. Navy's Biographic Branch, Office of Information, published a useful sketch, *Admiral Jonas H. Ingram, U.S. Navy (Deceased)* (1958). A good source for Ingram's service during the Second World War is Samuel Eliot Morison, *History of United States Naval Operations in World War II*, particularly vol. 1: *The Battle of the Atlantic, September 1939–May 1943* (1947) and vol. 10: *The Atlantic Battle Won, May 1943–May 1945* (1956). See also Clark Reynolds, *Famous American Admirals* (1978); Karl Schuon, *U.S. Navy Biographical Dictionary* (1964); and *Current Biography 1947*, pp. 327–30.

LEO J. DAUGHERTY III

INKPADUTA (1800?–1879?), Wahpekute Dakota chief who achieved great notoriety for leading the "Spirit Lake Massacre" of 1857, was born in southern Minnesota, the son of chief Black Eagle (Wamdisapa). The name of his mother is not known. Inkpaduta's Anglicized name was Scarlet Point.

The Wahpekutes were the smallest tribal division of the Dakota confederation, having only about 550 people in the early 1800s. They generally camped at the head of the Cannon River (present-day Faribault, Minnesota) and hunted south into Iowa. In the 1820s His Cane (Tàsagya) became principal chief of the tribe, and his cousin, Black Eagle, became a band leader. This was a period of devastating warfare with the Sac and Fox, during which one of Black Eagle's wives was killed. The tribe was further diminished by smallpox in 1837. Explorer Joseph N. Nicollet met Black Eagle in 1838 and said that he had only ten lodges.

Inkpaduta was a tall, stoutly built man, with high cheekbones, sunken eyes, high nose, and large mouth and teeth. He was nearsighted, and his face was greatly pockmarked. He had two wives (names unknown), and among his dozen or more children were two sets of twin boys. Several traders who knew Inkpaduta attested to his good character and hunting ability. He was also said to have distinguished himself in warfare with the Sac and Fox, Omaha, and Potawatomi. He is supposed to have had a brother, Red All Over (Sintominiduta), or Two Fingers, who led a small group of mixed Wahpekutes and Sissetons.

In 1841 a tribal dispute resulted in the killing of His Cane. Black Eagle and Inkpaduta were generally blamed for the murder, though sources are not certain that either man was personally responsible. Inkpaduta fled to northwestern Iowa, while his father remained in the Traverse des Sioux region. About 1846 Black Eagle died, and his band followed Inkpaduta as their chief.

Red All Over, with Inkpaduta's support, resisted white intrusion into the territory west of the Des Moines River. In 1848 he ran out a group of surveyors and a white trader named Henry Lott. However, the embittered trader came back and murdered Red All Over and his family in January 1854. Inkpaduta took his brother's bones to Fort Dodge and demanded justice, but Lott fled the country. Inkpaduta was thought to have brooded over his loss and become increasingly angry with the whites. He was not involved in the Treaty of 1851, which ceded all of the Dakotas' land to the government and did not remove to the reservation on the upper Minnesota River.

During the winter of 1856–1857 he and his band were encamped near Smithland, Iowa. During a hunting dispute, a white settler beat up one of Inkpaduta's men, and (about 14 Feb. 1857) a posse disarmed Inkpaduta's band in spite of the chief's remonstrations. The starving group moved north and at Peterson, Iowa, forcefully took what guns they could and killed the settlers' cattle. When they reached Lake Okoboji, the band massacred thirty-two whites and took four women captive (8–9 March); they later killed more people at Jackson, Minnesota (26 March). An expedition under Captain Bernard Bee marched to the scene but failed to find Inkpaduta's camp at Heron Lake. The band then divided into two parties; Inkpaduta received shelter among the Yanktonai Dakotas. On 28 July an expedition of Dakotas under Little Crow killed several of Inkpaduta's band, including a son of the chief, but no other reprisals were successful.

While Inkpaduta remained among the Yanktonais, the Dakota War of 1862 broke out. Some observers felt that it had been caused in part by the failure of the U.S. military to punish Inkpaduta. They thought that if Inkpaduta had been summarily punished, the Dakotas would have been afraid of similar retribution for any attack on whites and therefore would not have started the war of 1862. When the war spread to the plains of North Dakota, Inkpaduta was enveloped in battles of Lakotas and Dakotas with U.S. soldiers at Whitestone Hill (3 Sept. 1863) and Killdeer Mountain (28 July 1864); some historians argue that Inkpaduta played a major leadership role in these engagements.

Inkpaduta eventually threw his fortunes in with the Hunkpapa Teton Lakotas under the rising leadership of Sitting Bull. On 25 June 1876 he was with the large Indian camp on the Little Bighorn when it was attacked by Lieutenant Colonel George A. Custer. It was thought that Inkpaduta's sons killed the last survivor of the Custer battalion and that one of them secured Custer's horse. Inkpaduta followed Sitting Bull into Canada in May 1877 and is thought to have died about two years later at Batoche.

Inkpaduta spent some two decades in open hostility against the whites. Turn-of-the-century white historians basically saw him as a villain. Doane Robinson, for example, wrote that Inkpaduta "was a postgraduate in savage deviltry" and a "conscienceless Ishmael, whose hand was against every man, white and Indian alike." On the other hand, he was considered to be an elderly patriot and distinguished veteran of the plains wars by the Teton Lakotas. Charles A. Eastman, too, felt that "according to the Indians' customs and usages, Inkpaduta commanded a very high respect from all of the tribes."

• Much of the literature on Inkpaduta is fraught with error and the negative bias of the authors. His most definitive short biography is in Mark Diedrich, *Famous Chiefs of the Eastern Sioux* (1987). Another revisionist look at the chief is Peggy R. Larson, "A New Look at the Elusive Inkpaduta," *Minnesota History* 48 (1982): 24–35. Literature before this time generally vilifies him. See the works of Doane Robinson, *A History of the Dakota or Sioux Indians* (1904); Thomas Teakle, *The Spirit Lake Massacre* (1918); and Abbie Gardner Sharp, *History of the Spirit Lake Massacre* (1885). Much research on the chief was conducted by Frank I. Herriot, whose papers are in Iowa State Department of History and Archives, Des Moines; see particularly his correspondence with Josephine F. Waggoner and Charles A. Eastman. Herriot also wrote several important articles, including "The Origins of the Indian Massacre between the Okobojis, March 8, 1857," *Annals of Iowa* 18 (1932): 323–82. A more sympathetic view of Inkpaduta is given in Joseph H. Taylor, "Inkpaduta and Sons," *North Dakota Historical Quarterly* 4 (1929–1930): 153–59.

MARK F. DIEDRICH

INMAN, Henry (20 Oct. 1801–17 Jan. 1846), artist, was born in Utica, New York, the son of William Inman, a land agent, and Sarah (maiden name unknown). As a child, Inman attended the school of Reverend Daniel R. Dixon, who encouraged Inman to exercise his artistic talents. He also received lessons from an itinerant drawing master. In 1814, two years after his family moved to New York City, Inman was taken by the portraitist John Wesley Jarvis as an apprentice. In Jarvis's studio, which was filled with commissions for New York City Hall and other important patrons, Inman was responsible for painting backgrounds and drapery in Jarvis's portraits. According to Dunlap, Inman's assistance made it possible for Jarvis to complete six portraits each week. Inman traveled extensively with Jarvis and learned miniature painting while in his employ. By Inman's own account, he began his professional career as a portraitist in 1820, but a portrait by him of his brother John dates from 1817.

Inman left Jarvis to establish his own studio in 1822, by which time he had an apprentice of his own, Thomas Seir Cummings, who became his partner in 1824. Inman and Cummings agreed to split their commissions—Inman to paint the oil portraits and Cummings the miniatures—although Inman continued to paint miniatures nonetheless.

Inman achieved prominence in New York's art community partially by virtue of his participation in the city's rival art organizations, the American Academy of the Fine Arts, where he was elected an academician in 1824, and the National Academy of Design, of which he was among the principal founders and the first vice president. Before the establishment of the National Academy in 1825–1826, the American Academy exhibited Inman's first narrative painting, *Rip Van Winkle Awakening from His Long Sleep* (unlocated). Inspired by the work of Washington Irving, whose writings provided subject matter for many American artists, the painting was not an isolated effort for Inman but the first in a series of works that reveal his desire to be known for more than just his portraits. The *Port-Folio* published Inman's illustrations of scenes from James Fenimore Cooper's novels in 1823 and 1824.

Portraiture, however, remained Inman's primary interest, and beginning in 1826 he sent many likenesses to the annual exhibitions of the National Academy. Following the exhibition of his full-length portrait of the popular actor William Charles Macready in the role of William Tell (unlocated) in 1827, his production of portraits increased in response to demand from other actors and patrons of great prominence, wealth, and notoriety. His group portrait of the six children of Henry Livingston (1827, Brooklyn Museum) is perhaps his most ambitious composition from this period; his likeness of the satirical poet Fitz-Greene Halleck (1828, New-York Historical Society) numbers among his most dignified works.

Inman's prominence among New York's artists was also marked by the promising painters who applied to him for training. William Sidney Mount apprenticed to Inman in the late spring of 1828, as did Charles Jarvis, the son of Inman's former teacher, and George Twibill. As acting president of the National Academy during Samuel F. B. Morse's sojourn abroad during 1830, Inman influenced countless fledgling portraitists with his respect for traditional artistic methods and his kindly manner.

Commissions for full-length portraits from New York's most prestigious organizations, including City Hall and the American Bible Society, crowned Inman's achievements in portraiture and made his decision to move to Philadelphia in 1831 difficult for his colleagues, competitors, and patrons to understand. There he formed a partnership with the influential engraver and lithographer Cephas G. Childs, who helped Inman obtain a commission from the Penn Society for a full-length portrait of William Penn (1832, Independence National Historical Park, Philadelphia). The firm of Childs and Inman produced prints of many of Inman's finest portraits from the early 1830s, including his likeness of Chief Justice John Marshall (1831, Philadelphia Bar Association). The association with Childs facilitated Inman's involvement in the most extensive project of his career, the publication of Thomas L. McKenney and James Hall's *History of the Indian Tribes of North America* (1836–1844), for which he painted engraver's copies of Charles Bird King's portraits of American Indians.

In order to devote himself entirely to painting, Inman dissolved his partnership with Childs in early 1832, almost as abruptly as he had entered into it the year before. He moved to Mount Holly, New Jersey, and made frequent trips to New York, Philadelphia, and Baltimore, where he painted the portrait of the noted art collector and connoisseur Robert Gilmor, Jr. (1833, Maryland Historical Society). He became known as a portraitist of clergymen, painting likenesses for such ministers as William Heathcote DeLancey of Philadelphia (c. 1831, St. James Episcopal Church, Philadelphia), Bishop Charles Pettit McIlvaine of Ohio (1833, private collection), and Bishop George Washington Doane of New Jersey (1834, Union College, N.J.), among many others.

In 1834 Inman moved back to New York, where he was welcomed with a commission to paint Mayor Gideon Lee and by the attention of young painters who flocked to him for advice and training. He proved his determination to reestablish his favor with local art patrons, which had not been much diminished by his absence, by exhibiting his accomplished and novel painting of the *Bride of Lammermoor* (1834, private collection) at the National Academy in 1835. (He had the painting engraved by Asher B. Durand the next year.) His decision to capitalize on his first history painting—actually a literary subject drawn from the writings of Sir Walter Scott—before sending it to the South Carolina art collector Hugh Swinton Ball, who had commissioned it, betrays his ambition to paint grand subjects, despite his continued pursuit of portrait commissions. His foray into history painting brought him a highly coveted commission to paint a scene depicting the emigration of Daniel Boone in the U.S. Capitol rotunda. In fact, Inman never completed the painting, but the commission alone brought him great recognition, and during the late 1830s his studio was filled with portraits of mayors, clergymen, and other public figures, including Vice President Martin Van Buren. Inman had painted a full-length portrait of Van Buren, then secretary of state, in 1830 for New York City Hall, and his bust-length likeness of 1835 (New-York Historical Society) was so well received that Inman produced numerous replicas, most with the assistance of his student Edward Mooney.

As Inman's production of portraits increased, his income rose proportionally. He is reported to have earned over $10,000 in 1837. Henry T. Tuckerman proposed that "no one of our artists has achieved greater prosperity by his labors in portraiture than Inman," a significant feat in a field governed by "the caprices of fashion and of fame" (p. 236).

Inman's fortunes as a portraitist fell during the early 1840s, although a few of his finest portraits, including his innovative and graceful portrait of Angelica Van Buren (1842, White House), date from this period. As his portrait commissions fell off, Inman increasingly turned his attention to narrative subjects. Paintings such as *The Newsboy* (1841, Addison Gallery of American Art), *Mumble the Peg* (1842, Pennsylvania Academy of the Fine Arts), and *Dismissal of School on an October Afternoon* (1845, Museum of Fine Arts, Boston), in which Inman offered rather moralizing visions of city and country children, are landmarks in the history of American genre painting.

Inman was also a talented landscape painter, as revealed in *Trout Fishing in Sullivan County, New York*

(c. 1841, Munson-Williams-Proctor Institute), but the infrequency of his work in either genre or landscape painting suggests that he felt compelled to remain a portraitist despite his longing to paint more challenging compositions. Inman once told the writer Charles Edwards Lester that "people are fond of their own portraits before they care a fig for a fine landscape, or a noble historical piece. . . . The time will come when the rage for portraits in America will give way to a higher and purer taste" (p. 43). In many of his last portraits, such as that of New York mayor William Henry Seward (1844, New York City Hall), who is shown standing in a manicured garden, Inman exercised his talents both as a portraitist and as a landscapist. When he combined his skills, as in this instance, Inman produced some of the finest works of his career.

In the spring of 1844 Inman traveled to England with commissions from various New York patrons to paint portraits of the poet William Wordworth, the historian Thomas Babington Macaulay, and the theologian Thomas Chalmers. While in London he received further commissions, socialized with some of the city's leading portraitists, and enjoyed renewed prosperity for a short time. When his health failed in early 1845, however, he forfeited plans to travel through Europe and returned to New York. He continued to work through the year, but succumbed to chronic asthma and heart problems in New York.

Inman was extensively eulogized in the New York press and at events connected to the memorial exhibition of his work that was mounted by his friends and colleagues at the American Art–Union. The *New York Spirit of the Times* reported that "next to his devotion to his friends and his art" came his interest in fishing, hunting, and shooting. The proceeds of the exhibition, the first retrospective exhibition of the works of one man ever held in America, went to support Inman's wife, Jane Riker O'Brien, whom he had married in 1832, and their five children.

• The most complete and recent source on Inman is the catalog for the National Portrait Gallery's retrospective exhibition, *The Art of Henry Inman* (1987), which includes a biographical essay by William H. Gerdts and catalog entries by Carrie Rebora on many of the artist's most important paintings. William H. Gerdts, "Henry Inman, Genre Painter," *American Art Journal* 9 (May 1977): 26–48, contains detailed information on his narrative pictures. Theodore Bolton, "Henry Inman, An Account of His Life and Work," *Art Quarterly* 3 (Autumn 1940): 353–75, is the first modern assessment of his art, with an annotated checklist of over two hundred paintings, miniatures, and drawings. See also biographical essays by authors personally acquainted with Inman: William Dunlap, *A History of the Rise and Progress of the Arts of Design in the United States* (1834); C. E. Lester, *Artists of America* (1846); and Henry T. Tuckerman, *Book of the Artists* (1867).

CARRIE REBORA

INMAN, John Hamilton (23 Oct. 1844–5 Nov. 1896), financier, was born in Danridge, Jefferson County, Tennessee, the son of Shadrach Walker Inman, a planter and banker, and Jane Martin Hamilton. Inman received his early education from experience on his father's plantation and general store and attending a local academy. After refusing his father's offer of a college education, he left at the age of fourteen for Ringgold, Georgia, to work in an uncle's bank, where he first displayed the financial ability that would eventually make him wealthy. Inman served in the Confederate army from 1862 to 1865 and, upon his discharge, returned to his family's home in East Tennessee. Because the war had bankrupted his father and owing to the area's Unionist sentiment, he traveled to New York City in 1865 to seek his fortune with only a small amount of money.

In New York Inman found a position in a cotton brokerage firm where his diligence and ability to master the intricacies of the cotton trade so impressed his employers that he was made a junior partner in 1867. In 1870 he joined his fellow Tennessean James Swann to form their own firm, Inman, Swann and Co. As a leading cotton trader, Inman helped organize the New York Cotton Exchange in which he remained active for the rest of his life. While still in the cotton trade, Inman branched out into banking and insurance, serving as director of the Home Insurance Co. and Fourth National Bank, both of New York, and the Royal Insurance Co. of England. By the age of thirty-five Inman was a multimillionaire, and, according to *Appleton's Cyclopedia of American Biography*, was known throughout the United States as "the Cotton King." In 1870 Inman married Margaret McKinney Coffin, with whom he had six children.

For the last fifteen years of his life Inman was a major investor in southern enterprises that extended beyond cotton into mining, manufacture, and railroads. His first southern venture was the purchase in 1881 of the Tennessee Coal Co., which was reorganized that year as the Tennessee Coal, Iron and Railroad Co. (TCI). TCI grew first by the purchase in 1882 of the Southern States Coal, Iron and Land Co., which operated iron furnaces in the environs of Chattanooga; in 1886 the company moved to Birmingham with the purchase of the Pratt Coal and Iron Co. With the purchase in 1892 of the Cahaba Coal Mining Co., TCI dominated the iron industry in Birmingham and became the largest industrial company in the South. During this period Inman was the leading investor in TCI as well as its Wall Street connection, though Inman took little interest in the daily management of TCI.

Inman also invested heavily in southern railroads, serving as either a director, officer, or investor in the following lines: Louisville & Nashville Railroad, Central Railroad & Banking Co. of Georgia, Richmond & Danville Railroad, and Richmond & West Point Terminal Railroad & Warehouse Co. As president of the last two railroads, Inman presided over a series of stock manipulations that included the Central of Georgia, which ended in receivership for all three and financial disaster for Inman. The financial panic of 1893 and ensuing depression further damaged Inman's for-

tune. In 1896 he attempted to regain his fortune through speculation in cotton, but his old skill abandoned him as every move seemed to be wrong. These misfortunes led to his physical collapse and possibly to his early death (perhaps by his own hand) in a sanatorium in New Canaan, Connecticut.

Though born in the antebellum era and a Confederate soldier in the Civil War, Inman turned his back on the "lost cause" of his youth and embraced the material goals of the Gilded Age. Of greatest historical importance was his belief in the potential of industry in the South. His claim to have directed $100 million of investment to the South may well have been an exaggeration, though he was easily the leading Wall Street investor in southern industry and transportation.

Inman's interest in the South, however, was more as a speculator than as a builder. Many of his speculations led to bankruptcy (as in the case of the Richmond Terminal Co., though its assets became the core of the Southern Railway, now the Norfolk & Southern) or near bankruptcy, as in the case of TCI, which was absorbed by U.S. Steel in 1907. Inman's life, like the capitalism of the robber baron era with which it was associated, was cyclical, offering him first great wealth and prestige, then collapse and ignominy—truly a life that reflected the age in which it was lived.

• There are no Inman papers. A brief biographical sketch of him appeared near the time of his death in Henry Hall, ed., *America's Successful Men of Affairs: An Encyclopedia of Contemporaneous Biography*, vol. 1 (2 vols., 1895–1896). Secondary historical literature captures much of Inman's business dealings. These works include the following for his investments in the iron/steel industry: Ethel Armes, *The Story of Coal and Iron in Alabama* (1910; repr. 1972); Justin Fuller, "History of the Tennessee Coal, Iron, and Railroad Company, 1852–1870" (Ph. D. diss., Univ. of North Carolina at Chapel Hill, 1966); and W. David Lewis, *Sloss Furnaces and the Rise of the Birmingham District: An Industrial Epic* (1994). For his railroad investments, see E. G. Campbell, *The Reorganization of the American Railroad System, 1893–1900* (1938; repr. 1968); John F. Stover, *The Railroads of the South, 1865–1900* (1955); Maury Klein, *The Great Richmond Terminal: A Study in Businessmen and Business Strategy* (1970); and Klein, *History of the Louisville & Nashville Railroad* (1972). He is also discussed briefly in Daniel E. Sutherland, *The Confederate Carpetbaggers* (1988). An obituary is in the *New York Times*, 6 Nov. 1896, as well as a notice of the settlement of his estate, 7 Mar. 1913.

STEPHEN GOLDFARB

INNES, James (1754–2 Aug. 1798), lawyer, military officer, and Virginia attorney general, was born in Caroline County, Virginia, the son of Robert Innes, a well-educated Scottish clergyman, and Catherine Richards. After receiving a classical education from his father, Innes attended the renowned school of Donald Robertson in King and Queen County, Virginia, with his older brother Harry. At age sixteen he entered the College of William and Mary, where he excelled in his studies. At the college he also cemented a lifelong friendship with fellow student St. George Tucker, later a prominent Virginia judge, author, and legal educator.

While a student, Innes authored a series of pseudonymous articles for the *Virginia Gazette* denouncing Great Britain's ill treatment of her American colonies. These essays enraged the royal governor, Lord Dunmore, and cost Innes his post as usher at the school. When war broke out, Innes joined the Williamsburg Volunteer Rifle Company and the following year (Nov. 1776) was commissioned an officer in the Continental Line. As lieutenant colonel of the Fifteenth Virginia Infantry Regiment, he fought in numerous actions, notably rallying his troops bravely during the battle of Germantown. He returned to the Old Dominion early in 1778 to recruit soldiers for General George Washington, served on the Virginia Navy Commission later that year and as president of the Board of War in 1779, and led militia forces called up to contest the invasion of Virginia by the British in 1781. After his return to Virginia in 1778, Innes married Elizabeth Cocke, the daughter of James Cocke of Williamsburg. The couple had two children.

Innes appears to have read law just before the Revolution, perhaps under the guidance of George Wythe, like his friend Tucker. While his natural abilities and classical education helped to propel him into the forefront of the Tidewater bar following the war, Innes detested the drudgery and routine of country practice. After several years riding the county court circuit, as well as a stint as notary public for Williamsburg in 1784, he garnered sufficient experience to join the distinguished bar practicing before the superior courts in Richmond. He quickly took a position of leadership among his colleagues. "Colonel Innes," declared the observant Benjamin Henry Latrobe, "ranks I think, first in genius, in force of thought, in power of expression, in effect of voice and manner. He is, at the same time a man of the most amiable and benevolent disposition, open, generous, and unreserved" (*The Virginia Journals of Benjamin Henry Latrobe*, vol. 1, p. 130).

Contemporaries almost universally characterized Innes as the foremost orator in Virginia. Some placed him above Patrick Henry in rhetorical skill and effectiveness. Indeed, Henry himself lavished praise on his colleague when the Federalists chose Innes to make the last impassioned plea for the federal Constitution before the vote on ratification in the Virginia convention of 1788. The anti-Federalist Henry labeled Innes's eloquent performance as "splendid, magnificent and sufficient to shake the human mind!" Unfortunately, little direct evidence of Innes's skill as an orator other than this convention speech survives in written or published form.

James Innes represented James City County in the Virginia General Assembly in the session of 1780–1781 and the city of Williamsburg in the sessions of 1781–1782 and 1785–1787. Unlike many of his contemporaries, however, he did not see the law as a steppingstone to political power. He made his reputation, as well as his greatest contributions to the legal culture

of his native state, as attorney general of Virginia (succeeding Edmund Randolph in 1786) and as defense cocounsel with John Marshall, Alexander Campbell, and Patrick Henry in the so-called British debt cases of *Jones v. Walker* and *Ware v. Hylton* before the Virginia Supreme Court of Appeals.

In later life Innes suffered from ill health, some of which no doubt resulted from his enormous size. Many contemporaries also alluded to a streak of indolence in the attorney. His poor health, coupled with lingering concern about his personal finances, forced Innes to refuse a number of political appointments, including the post of judge advocate of the Continental army. He also declined to run for Congress (despite Thomas Jefferson's urging of the "purity of your republicanism") and eventually resigned the office of Virginia attorney general in 1796. At the same time, Innes remained as active as possible in community affairs, belonging to both the Constitution Society (a political debating group) and the Amicable Society (a traveler's aid organization) in Richmond in the 1780s, as well as holding the post of rector at his alma mater, the College of William and Mary.

In 1794 Innes acceded to George Washington's request that he visit Kentucky to quell popular outrage over John Jay's supposed capitulation in negotiations with Spain over navigation rights on the Mississippi River. Two years later he again heeded Washington's call to serve as a high commissioner under Article 6 of Jay's treaty with Great Britain, which awarded damages to Loyalists for claims arising from the American Revolution. While in Philadelphia in the summer of 1798 engaged in commission work, Innes died suddenly of "dropsy of the abdomen."

• Scattered correspondence and documents of James Innes may be found in the Harry Innes Papers at the Library of Congress and in the Tucker-Coleman collection at the College of William and Mary. Official records of his service as attorney general are housed in the Virginia State Library and Archives, Richmond, most notably among the executive papers. The Virginia Historical Society in Richmond also holds material, including an autograph legal opinion and the papers of Hugh Blair Grigsby, an early historian of the Virginia Ratifying Convention of 1788, who collected data about convention delegates. Among published sources see Jane D. Carson, *James Innes and His Brothers of the F.H.C.* (1965); Edward C. Carter II, ed., *The Virginia Journals of Benjamin Henry Latrobe* (3 vols., 1980); Herbert A. Johnson et al., eds., *The Papers of John Marshall*, vols. 1, 2, and 5 (1974–); E. G. Swem, *Virginia Historical Index* (2 vols.; repr. 1965); and appropriate volumes of the *Journal of the House of Delegates of the Commonwealth of Virginia* (1780, 1782, 1785–1787). Synopses of Innes's arguments before Virginia's highest courts may be found in the first eight volumes of *Virginia Reports* (1798–1833). His speech before the ratifying convention, along with Henry's comments, appear in Jonathan Elliott, ed., *The Debates, Resolutions, and Other Proceedings in Convention on the Adoption of the Federal Constitution*, vol. 3 (1836), pp. 459–63, 472.

E. LEE SHEPARD

INNESS, George (1 May 1825–3 Aug. 1894), landscape painter, was born near Newburgh, New York, the son of John William Inness, a merchant, and Clarissa Baldwin. The family had left their home and business in New York City for a farm on the Hudson River in hopes that Inness's father would recover his health in the country. They returned to the city by 1828 but soon moved to another rural area near Newark, New Jersey, where Inness spent his youth. He suffered from poor health, including epilepsy, which impaired his schooling. He attended the Newark Academy until age fourteen or fifteen. His father then brought him into the grocery business, but Inness showed no more aptitude for commercial life than he had shown for scholastic work. The family finally agreed that he would be allowed to pursue his interest in art instead of continuing in the mercantile trade. He studied very briefly with a local painter named John Jesse Barker, an itinerant portraitist and landscapist.

In 1841 Inness's mother died. Around this same time he left home for New York City, where he found work with the engraving firm of Sherman & Smith; but it was a job he found "long winded" and "tiresome." He still wanted to become a professional artist. Régis François Gignoux, a French landscape painter living in New York, provided him with some practical lessons and guidance. Within a few years Inness's career as a painter was firmly established. He sent two paintings to the spring exhibition of the National Academy of Design in 1844; by the following year the Art-Union accepted two of his works for distribution. He would continue to exhibit at both places for many years. In 1847 Ogden Haggerty, a wealthy New York auctioneer, became Inness's first patron, and his work began to attract attention. The *Literary World*, for example, sharply criticized the artifice they saw in some of his paintings but considered him an artist of promise nevertheless.

Little is known about Inness's first wife, Delia Miller, except that she came from Newark and died less than a year after their marriage. In 1850 he met Elizabeth Hart. The Hart family disapproved of Inness's artistic profession, so the young couple courted in secret, sometimes at Candace Wheeler's Long Island farm, where many young artists congregated. They married within the year and had six children, five of whom survived to adulthood.

In late 1850 or early 1851 Inness embarked upon his first trip to Europe, financed by Haggerty. He and his wife sailed together to Italy; their first child was born in Florence, where he had his studio. Florence was then the site of a flourishing community of American artists, including William Page, who would become a great influence in Inness's life. Apparently Inness did not systematically study art or copy paintings during this sojourn, as most American artists did while abroad; instead, he devoted himself to producing finished paintings. In 1852 he and his family settled in Rome, where another vibrant community of American artists lived. Not long after his arrival, however, he had an altercation with some French officers in St. Pe-

ter's Square. He did not remove his hat during the papal blessing, and the officers took exception. A fight then ensued. Inness was arrested, and, following his release a short time later, he and his family sailed for New York.

At this point in his career, Inness found himself struggling financially. It became more difficult for Inness to earn his livelihood after the American Art-Union closed in 1851. But he did have other avenues through which to sell his work, and now he had European experiences, subjects, and credentials to add to his repertoire. Over the next couple of years he was able to reverse his fortunes and raise enough money to return to Europe. On this trip Inness spent most of his time in France, where he came under the influence of the Barbizon school. He lightened his tones and simplified his compositions, at first only experimenting but gradually breaking with both the tradition of Old Masters and with the Hudson River school. One of Inness's best-known paintings dates from this period: *The Lackawanna Valley* (c. 1855), commissioned for $75 by the first president of the Delaware, Lackawanna and Western Railroad. It presents an ambivalent view of the technological progress that so many American landscape artists unequivocally celebrated. While this is certainly the "civilized landscape" that Inness said he preferred to depict, the canvas also displays the price of that civilization in the profusion of tree stumps along the railroad's path—the stumps, as it were, of Thomas Cole's pristine American forests.

Inness continued to struggle up through the Civil War years to establish his reputation as an artist. Although he maintained close contact with New York, he found the Boston art market more congenial to his work, and in the summer of 1860 he moved to Medfield, Massachusetts. At last he attracted important new patrons, including the Reverend Henry Ward Beecher. He tried to enlist in the Union army but his poor health disqualified him from service; he then raised bounties and sent ten men to fight in his place. The Civil War inspired him to paint several allegorical canvases in his barn studio in Medfield, including *The Light Triumphant* (1860–1862) and *The Sign of Promise* (1863). As critics began to admire his work and call him a genius, Inness gained new confidence and expressed greater individuality in his work.

In 1864 Inness moved to "Eagleswood," an estate near Perth Amboy, New Jersey, owned by retired merchant Marcus Spring. Other artists also lived there, including the celebrated painter William Page. Inness's experiences at Eagleswood proved formative to his life as well as his art. He had always been deeply concerned with religious faith; when he joined the Baptist church in 1849 he had written his brother James that if his health had permitted, he would have devoted himself to metaphysical studies. At Eagleswood he encountered a religion he found even more personally meaningful: the Church of New Jerusalem, better known as Swedenborgianism. Page was a follower of the theology of Emmanuel Swedenborg and probably introduced the system to Inness. Much of Inness's subsequent work represents his efforts to develop a Swedenborgian art, especially by representing the spiritual world and the world of nature.

In 1867 Inness returned to New York, and the following year the National Academy elected him a full academician. (He had been an associate of the National Academy since 1853.) In 1870 he and his family sailed to Europe for the third time. They stopped in London and Paris, then went on to Rome, where they remained until 1874, spending summers in the city's outskirts. They then settled in Paris so that his son George might study drawing. Unlike Inness's previous trips abroad, this was essentially a commercial venture. According to his arrangement with Williams & Everett, the Boston picture dealers, whatever Inness could not sell in Europe, he agreed to send and exhibit with Williams & Everett. He clearly attempted to produce more easily marketable paintings during these years, with the greater detail and higher finish that American audiences preferred.

Inness sailed back to the United States in 1875 and set up a studio in Boston. He spent that summer in the White Mountains at North Conway, New Hampshire, working alongside his son (who was already attracting attention as an artist), his student John A. Monks, and his friend, the amateur artist George Waldo Hill. A new expressiveness and distinct use of color mark his work from this period. But his commercial arrangement with dealers Doll & Richards turned sour, and a dispute over ownership of *Pine Grove of the Barberini Villa* convinced Inness to return to New York. During this time he began to write a theoretical work on art, which was never completed and has not survived.

When Thomas B. Clarke began acting as his patron and agent, Inness's landscapes became fashionable among American art collectors. By the 1880s his art received almost universal adulation. The *Boston Transcript* pronounced his landscapes "the best painted in our time and country, in many instances the best painted in any time or country." Now finally financially secure, he settled permanently in Montclair, New Jersey, and began summering in Milton-on-the-Hudson, New York. He did not like large exhibitions and refused to participate in the 1889 Paris Exposition. But the U.S. committee borrowed his *Short Cut, Watchung Station* from an art gallery and sent it to Paris anyway. Inness's outrage turned to embarrassment when his painting won a gold medal there. The painting *October* (1886) is an excellent example of his late work. He depicts the scene naturally but at the same time paints it flat, using a formal composition, and unifies it with color. The resulting canvas is imbued with an atmosphere that seems to transcend physical reality and approach a portrait of mood, spirit, or mind.

Although his health was in decline Inness continued to travel. He first saw—and painted—Niagara Falls in 1883. He also went to England in 1887; Tarpon Springs, Florida, where he kept a house and studio, in 1890; and California and Mexico in 1891. In June 1894 he and his wife sailed to Europe. In Paris, Baden-Ba-

den, and Munich, he visited museums and galleries rather than attending exclusively to his own work as he had done on previous stays abroad. On the last part of the trip, the couple went to rest and relax in Scotland. Inness died there, in the town of Bridge-of-Allan. His body arrived back in New York City on the nineteenth of August and was laid in state at the National Academy of Design, only the third artist to receive this honor in the history of the institution.

By the time Inness died he was regarded as one of the finest painters in the world, certainly among the best landscape painters in the United States. Although this reputation faded in the early twentieth century, he has since been reclaimed as an innovative, individualistic artist with modernist sympathies. His earliest work reflected the influence of the Hudson River school, but Inness was soon attempting to translate the more painterly Barbizon style into a personal American idiom. The body of his work fits neither the Hudson River tradition, nor luminism, nor impressionism, which he flatly rejected. In late paintings such as *Home of the Heron* (1893), he approached realization of his ultimate goal: the representation of spirit through color and form. His great talent in unifying the literal and the figurative, fact and mysticism, objectivity and subjectivity in his art has earned him a significant place in the painting of nineteenth-century American landscape.

• Few of Inness's personal papers survive. Magazine articles provide the richest contemporary sources on his life. "American Artists: George Inness," *Harper's Weekly*, 13 July 1867, and "American Painters: George Inness," *Art Journal* 2 (1876), trace his biography. See also "A Painter on Painting," *Harper's New Monthly Magazine*, Feb. 1878; "Mr. Inness on Art-Matters," *Art Journal* (1879); and, most incisively, "George Inness" by Charles de Kay (writing as Henry Eckford) in *Century Magazine*, May 1882. Inness's interview with George William Sheldon, published in *Harper's Weekly*, 22 Apr. 1882, provides an interesting autobiographical perspective. Alfred Trumble, *George Inness, N.A., A Memorial of the Student, the Artist, and the Man* (1895), is one of many volumes of reminiscences of Inness by his friends and colleagues. In the early twentieth century Elliott Daingerfield wrote several works on Inness's art, including *Fifty Paintings by George Inness* (1913). The first book-length biography of Inness soon followed, written by his son, George Inness, Jr., *Life, Art, and Letters of George Inness* (1917). In the mid–twentieth century, scholars of art began to reassess the life and art of George Inness. Elizabeth McCausland, *George Inness: An American Landscape Painter, 1825–1894* (1946), was the first study in three decades. See also LeRoy Ireland, *The Works of George Inness: An Illustrated Catalog Raisonné* (1965), and Nicolai Cikovsky, Jr., *The Life and Work of George Inness* (1977) and *George Inness* (1971). Alfred Werner, *Inness Landscapes* (1973), asserts Inness's importance as a landscape painter. The catalogs of two exhibitions, George Inness at the Los Angeles County Museum of Art in 1985 and George Inness: Presence of the Unseen at the Montclair Art Museum in 1995, demonstrate his integral place in nineteenth-century American art.

LAURA PRIETO CHESTERTON

INSKIP, John Swanel (10 Aug. 1816–7 Mar. 1884), Methodist Episcopal clergyman and evangelist, was born in Huntingdon, England, the son of Edward Inskip, a businessman, and Martha Swanel. The family immigrated to the United States in 1820 and settled in Wilmington, Delaware. In 1832 the family moved to Chester County, Pennsylvania.

Although his father was skeptical about religion, Inskip's mother read the Bible to her children and taught them to pray when her husband was not present. While attending a Methodist meeting on 10 April 1832, Inskip was converted under the preaching of Levi Scott, who later became a bishop in the Methodist Episcopal church. After joining the Methodist congregation at Grove, Pennsylvania, he felt it his duty to exhort others to commit themselves to the Christian faith. He was licensed as a local preacher on 23 May 1835 and for the next year worked with the preachers assigned to the Springfield circuit in the Philadelphia Annual Conference. In the spring of 1836 he was admitted on trial to the Philadelphia Conference and was appointed to assist on the Cecil circuit. In November 1836 he married Martha Jane Foster, who occupied an important role in his entire ministry, supporting it with her singing, teaching, organizing, and fundraising. The couple had one child. In 1838 Inskip was ordained a deacon in Wilmington, Delaware. The following year he became assistant on the Nottingham circuit, which he served until 1839.

Inskip's first appointment as preacher in charge occurred in 1840 when he was sent to Easton, Pennsylvania. That same year he was ordained an elder in Philadelphia. From 1841 until 1845 he served churches in or near Philadelphia, each of the churches growing under his evangelistic preaching and pastoral leadership. In 1846 he transferred his membership to the Ohio Conference when he accepted appointment to the Ninth Street Church in Cincinnati, which had requested that he become their pastor. During the next six years he served Ohio Conference churches in Dayton, Urbana, Spingfield, and Troy.

While pastor in Dayton and Springfield, Inskip became involved in controversy when he instituted "family sittings" in the church, allowing men and women to sit together for worship, a practice considered by many contrary to the discipline of the denomination and a dangerous innovation. He made his views on the matter more widely known in 1851 when he published *Methodism Explained and Defended*, in which he argued that the church's rule on separate seating was not mandatory but merely advisory. When Inskip's position was considered by the Ohio Conference in 1851, it voted to "admonish him of his error." He appealed this decision to the 1852 General Conference, and after a brilliant self-defense, the ruling of his conference was reversed.

In 1852 Inskip transferred to the New York East Conference and became pastor of the Madison Street Church. Subsequently, he served pastorates at five churches in New York and Brooklyn. He favored the abolition of slavery but feared the "violence and blood-shed" it would entail. In 1861 he accepted the chaplaincy of the Fourteenth Brooklyn Regiment in the Union army and held this position until poor health forced him to resign fourteen months later.

In 1862 Inskip was appointed pastor to a church in Birmingham, Connecticut, and then to churches in New York City. In 1864 he claimed to experience "entire sanctification," in which he felt a fuller measure of God's presence and power. "I cannot tell," he said, "when I was ever more filled with the Spirit."

Inskip subsequently moved to the New York, Baltimore, and New York East Conferences, serving as pastor to various congregations between 1866 and 1871. Throughout this time he became an active leader in the "holiness movement," which emphasized an experience of the deeper work of God beyond personal conversion and living a very disciplined life. When the National Camp Meeting Association for the Promotion of Holiness was formed in 1867 in Vineland, New Jersey, to foster "entire sanctification," Inskip became its first president and served until his death. After 1871 his ministry was mostly that of a traveling evangelist preaching at camp meetings and revivals. One of his most successful preaching campaigns took place across the United States in 1871 including meetings in Missouri, Kansas, Iowa, Utah, and California. He conducted another noteworthy series of evangelistic meetings in England, India, and Australia in 1880–1881. He was also editor of the *Christian Standard*, a weekly periodical of the holiness movement published in Philadelphia from 1876 until his death. In October 1883 he suffered a paralyzing stroke from which he never completely recovered. He died in Ocean Grove, New Jersey.

Inskip was an outstanding and successful pastor in the Methodist Episcopal church, and he was especially skilled in preaching. Through his preaching, writing, and leadership of the National Camp Meeting Association he was one of the most important leaders in the development of the holiness movement in the United States after the Civil War.

• Microfilm of many of Inskip's handwritten sermon manuscripts is at Asbury Theological Seminary, Wilmore, Ky. Other significant papers and letters are at the Archives and History Center of the United Methodist Church, Madison, N.J. Important sources for his theological views, especially on holiness, are his editorials and articles in the *Christian Standard*. See also Eleuthera I. D. Pepper, *Memorial of Rev. John S. Inskip* (n.d.); William McDonald and John E. Searles, *The Life of Rev. John S. Inskip* (1885); *Minutes of the Annual Conferences of the M. E. Church* (1884); Lawrence E. Breeze, "The Inskips: Union in Holiness," *Methodist History* 13 (1975): 25–45; and Kenneth O. Brown, "'The World-Wide Evangelist'—The Life and Work of Martha Inskip," *Methodist History* 21 (1983): 179–91. An obituary is in the *New York Times*, 8 Mar. 1884.

CHARLES YRIGOYEN, JR.

INSULL, Samuel (11 Nov. 1859–16 July 1938), electric utilities executive and holding company entrepreneur, was born in London, England, the son of Samuel Insull, a clergyman, and Emma Short, sometime keeper of Insull's Temperance Hotel. Insull started work in a London auctioneering house for five shillings a week. In 1881 he left London for the United States, where he became the personal secretary of Thomas Edison, who was then developing his incandescent lighting system. Insull took part in the establishment of New York City's Pearl Street electric generating station, which provided power for the world's first incandescent lighting network. In 1889 he became an executive with the pioneer electrical equipment manufacturer, General Electric. Insull later wrote that Edison "grounded me in the fundamentals . . . no one could have had a more considerate and fascinating teacher" (Hughes, p. 203). In 1892 Insull gave up the vice presidency of a $50 million company (General Electric) to assume the presidency of an $885,000 corporation, the Chicago Edison Company (after 1907, Commonwealth Edison), which supplied power to a low-voltage, direct-current network of incandescent lights. When Insull joined Chicago Edison, the economic and technical requirements of large-scale electricity utilities were little understood.

From the first, Insull had a clear concept of the economics of power production: it was capital intensive. Electricity was a perishable commodity that could not (with minor exceptions) be stored, and the market demand varied throughout the day. Furthermore, steam generators could not be turned off or on at will. They required many hours to come on-line and had to be kept spinning at maximum capacity with ample reserves for peak consumption demand. During nonpeak periods, power sales often fell to 10 percent or less of production. By 1900 Insull had learned that his users seldom bought more than 25 percent of his generating capacity. The load factor was such that nearly 75 percent of the capital and an equal amount of the production costs were wasted. The existence of large amounts of unsold power caused Insull to search for ways to bring new users on-line, which led him to a strategy of lowering power charges.

Insull installed meters (instead of charging flat, fixed monthly rates for each Chicago Edison customer and then kept meticulous records of power consumption. This enabled him to discern demand patterns and thereby to discover that various users experienced their peak demand at different times: street railways peaked between 6:30 A.M. and 9:00 A.M. and between 4:00 P.M. and 6:30 P.M. Electric lights peaked in the evening between 5:00 and 9:00. Time zones also influenced peak power requirements.

By 1900 Insull's business strategy had become clear. He took advantage of the economies of scale by concentrating electricity production in ever-larger generating stations, and he closed small, inefficient generating plants. He increased his load partly by merging with more than twenty rival Chicago-area power producers, thereby adding their customers to his system. He took advantage of the load diversity that resulted when customers' consumption peaked at different times. Insull offered very low rates to industries that used power at nonpeak times. His production costs kept falling, and Chicago's power rates ranked among the world's lowest. Insull's concepts of power production were soon followed by most American utilities.

Insull faced many obstacles, both political and technological, in achieving his large-scale utility system. He battled with the corrupt Chicago City Council, whose members tried to extort money from utilities. Insull became an astute politician. His consistent efforts—he was not above bribing city councillors or elected state officials—resulted in the transfer of utilities regulation from local authorities to the state of Illinois. He advocated state regulation in order to soften criticism arising from his creation of a giant private power monopoly. Insull felt little threat from honest regulators because he knew that his policies would improve service and lower rates. He also worked to convince the electric utility lobby, the National Electric Light Association (NELA), to support state regulation and was active in the National Civic Federation, which by 1907 had subscribed to the NELA's views on state regulation. In that year the Civic Federation issued a report that became the basis for early utilities regulatory commissions founded in such states as Wisconsin and Massachusetts.

Technological imperatives drove Insull. The main problem in the 1890s was that technology made the formation of large systems difficult. Each major power user generated its own electricity. The Edison system used direct current (DC). The transmission of direct current at low voltages, especially 600 volts or fewer, required thick, expensive copper wires. Edison's system was not economical outside of densely populated cities. In contrast, Westinghouse developed alternating current (AC), which relied on high-voltage transmission (the higher the voltage the more efficient the transmission). Westinghouse's first commercial incandescent lights began in 1886 and used power transmitted at 1,000 volts, which was transformed at the point of consumption into a fifty-volt current. Alternating current's main advantage lay in cheap, long-distance transport of electricity; it was chosen by most suburban towns. Even within AC or DC systems there were many choices made to suit individual large customers. Traction used 600-volt DC, and various industries requested that power be delivered using different cycles, which ranged from 25-cycle currents up to 133⅓ cycles. In the early 1890s it was impossible to convert DC to AC, and changing frequencies and voltages was difficult.

Insull pioneered the commercial use of technological breakthroughs. In 1894, within two years of his arrival in Chicago, he built individual generators that each produced 2,400 kilowatts of direct current. The units were propelled by 1,250-horsepower condensing, reciprocating steam engines. In 1900 Insull placed the first order, by an American electric utility, for a 5,000-kilowatt steam turbine; 12,000-kilowatt steam turbines became standard by 1905. For a time, Chicago Edison had the largest steam turbine generators in the United States. Insull used technology to ensure that all of Chicago's electric-generating capacity could fall under one company. His new power-generation units supplied all kinds of power. By 1900 he used a rotary convertor (Chicago Edison was the first American utility to install one, although Boston Edison first experimented with this invention) to change direct current into alternating current and vice versa. Chicago Edison also mastered the use of transformers and frequency changers, which allowed power to be converted from one voltage to another and determined the number of cycles delivered. By 1910 Commonwealth Edison produced at its main central generating stations a three-phase alternating current of 9,000 volts and twenty-five cycles. For long-distance transmission, transformers converted this power into AC with 20,000 volts. Within the city itself, rotary converters and frequency changers converted power into the 110-volt DC 60-cycle current required by the incandescent lighting systems and the 600-volt DC needed by the city's streetcars and elevated trains.

The search for an increased load factor and diversity caused Insull to gain control of all the city and suburban power users, including the city's vast traction system which, in 1908, accounted for 65 percent of power consumption. Starting about 1910 Insull expanded his system into Indiana, Wisconsin, Ohio, and other midwestern states. This required vast amounts of capital, and Insull raised it through holding companies that bought control of operating companies. Insull created one of the most complex financial structures ever known in American business. Some of the most important holding companies were Insull Utilities Investments Incorporated, Corporation Securities of Chicago, and Middle West Utilities. Insull used the holding companies to purchase the controlling share of the many operating companies, such as Chicago's Commonwealth Edison, Wisconsin Power & Light, and Public Service Corporation of Indiana. Insull guaranteed his control by a simple strategy. He sold bonds in the holding companies to the general public and paid the interest on the holding company bonds from dividends received from the operating companies. Insull's bondholders had no vote in the holding companies, and through voting the common shares he elected the boards of directors who appointed managers who set policy for the operating firms.

The stock market crash of 1929 did not destroy Insull. The real damage came in 1931, when business activity fell drastically, reducing power consumption and traction riding. The operating companies could not pay enough dividends to meet interest payments on the holding company bonds. For example, Insull's Chicago, North Shore & Milwaukee Railway (the North Shore Line), an operating company, considered by many to be the best-run and most-modern interurban electric railway in the world, had in 1929 a gross income exceeding $8 million and profits of about $750,000. By 1931 gross revenues were only one-half of those in 1929. The line had a net loss of nearly $750,000. The North Shore's financial performance was actually better than that of most other American traction companies. Insull's electric utilities also suffered major earnings falls.

In 1931 Insull's holding companies faced an increasing cash squeeze. The Chicago utilities entrepreneur had numerous enemies, especially New York's powerful House of Morgan, which resented Insull's effort to avoid Wall Street by arranging his finances through local Chicago institutions. The end came in April 1932, when Owen D. Young, chairman of the board of General Electric, and a group of New York bankers pushed into bankruptcy several of Insull's holding companies, including the Corporations Securities Company of Chicago, Insull Utility Investments, and Middle West Utilities Company. The loss by the public was very large. In 1932 the public owned more than $2.6 billion of securities in Insull's holding and operating companies. When all claims had been settled, the public loss amounted to $638 million or 24.1 percent of their value.

Insull was condemned as a reckless financier who built holding companies out of thin air for huge profits. Frederick Lewis Allen, writing in 1935, argued that "because it was so easy to show profits, the stock could be watered and the magnates at the centre of things could make much money through financing operations. Because so much money could be made, the systems became more and more ambitious and tried to get hold of more and more operating companies. . . . It was an endless sequence; and it was enough to turn the head of any but the coolest of financiers" (Allen, pp. 276–77). Allen asserted that Insull's head had been turned thoroughly by 1926.

After the collapse Insull fled to Europe. He was taken into custody off the coast of Turkey from a Greek steamship and returned to the United States. Between 1934 and 1935 he was tried three times on separate charges of mail fraud, embezzlement, and violations of the bankruptcy act. He was acquitted each time. Afterward, Insull retired to Europe, where he died a few years later of heart failure in a Paris metro station. He had been married to Margaret Anna Bird, with whom he had had one child, a son; Samuel Insull, Jr., born in 1900, went into his father's utility business.

Since the 1960s the view of Insull has changed substantially. Thomas Hughes, a leading historian of the electric power industry, concluded in 1983 that "contrary to public opinion, the origins of developments of several leading electric utility holding companies [including Insull's] are to be found rooted more deeply in technology and management than in finance" (Hughes, p. 393). Arthur Taylor, writing in the Summer 1962 *Business History Review*, concluded that the public's "percentage of loss . . . [was] lower than that sustained by investors in some other significant areas of the economy" (p. 260). However, the losses hit the Insull empire unevenly. Of the total $638 million lost by the public, slightly more than $517 million had been invested in seven holding companies. The public lost nearly all of the monies it invested in these firms. The other major disaster area was traction, especially the four operating companies that accounted for $78 million of investor losses. There was comparatively little water in the traction shares; the street and interurban traffic suffered from a loss of business because of the automobile and the downturn in riding during the depression. Furthermore, Insull purchased control of traction not as a speculative venture but as a direct result of his successful attempt to create load diversity for his electric utility corporations. In contrast, most of the major operating utilities such as Commonwealth Edison, Wisconsin Power & Light, and dozens of smaller utilities avoided bankruptcy, paid all of the interest on their debts, and retired debt according to plan. Most kept up dividends, albeit at a reduced rate, during the depression's depth.

In 1929, at the height of his career, Insull was the most powerful man in Chicago and through his control of various holding companies, was responsible for between $2 to $3 billion invested in electric and other utilities, such as natural gas. His organization provided nearly 10 percent of the nation's electric power and served 5,000 communities in thirty-two states. Insull's financial collapse in 1932 was one of the largest in America's history and quickly turned him from a widely admired industrial statesman into a scapegoat for the financial excesses that allegedly caused the Great Depression of the 1930s.

• The early evaluation of Insull's career was generally unfavorable and is typified by Frederick Lewis Allen's *The Lords of Creation* (1935; repr. 1966). Forrest McDonald published his full-scale biography, *Insull*, in 1962. Insull's early technical career before 1900 can be traced in Harold C. Passer's excellent volume *The Electrical Manufacturers, 1875–1900* (1953). The best picture of Insull and the technological imperatives of power producing is in Thomas P. Hughes, *Networks of Power: Electrification in Western Society, 1880–1930* (1983). For Insull's role in traction see William D. Middleton, *North Shore: America's Fastest Interurban* (1964). A short biography of Insull is in John N. Ingham, *Biographical Dictionary of American Business Leaders* (1983). For an estimation of the public's losses in Insull's collapse see Arthur R. Taylor, "Losses to the Public in the Insull Collapse: 1932–1946," *Business History Review* 34 (Summer 1962): 188–204. An obituary is in the *New York Times*, 17 July 1938.

STEPHEN SALSBURY

IPATIEFF, Vladimir Nikolaevich (9 Nov. 1867–29 Nov. 1952), chemist and organizer of science, was born in Moscow, Russia, the son of Nikolai Aleksandrovich Ipatieff, a prominent architect, and Anna Dmitrievna Gliky. His mother came from a well-known intellectual family and took an active interest in the education of Vladimir. A mediocre student, Ipatieff graduated from the Mikhail Artillery Academy in 1892. That same year he married Varvara Dmitrievna Ermakova, whom he had known for ten years. They had four children.

Within a few years Ipatieff chose a scientific career, returning to teach at the academy in 1899. Research on catalytic high-pressure reactions was Ipatieff's most significant contribution to science and industry. However, his initial scientific achievement was the development in 1894, in collaboration with his scientific mentor A. Y. Favorsky, of a new method for synthesis of unsaturated hydrocarbons. This method yielded isoprene, the basic monomeric component of natural rubber. The fact that isoprene could be produced in a directed fashion from lighter hydrocarbons rather than by cracking heavier molecules of natural compounds made Ipatieff's work fundamental for future industrial developments in rubber and petroleum chemistry.

By the end of the century Ipatieff turned his attention to catalytic properties of alumina, and more generally, to heterogeneous catalysis. He later introduced high pressures into catalytic synthesis and in 1903 invented the autoclave, which is also known as the "Ipatieff bomb." This new device enabled him to synthesize the simplest organic compound, methane, from its two constituent elements, carbon and hydrogen. In 1912 he developed the use of multicomponent catalysts, which greatly enhanced petroleum refining and petrochemical synthesis. In 1913 he accomplished the polymerization of ethylene thus opening the way to the production of polyethylene, a major man-made material of the twentieth century used in the production of most varieties of plastic. Ipatieff considered the years 1900–1914 as the most productive of his scientific career.

In 1897 Ipatieff was appointed member of the Explosives Commission of the Chief Artillery Administration, a position that enabled him to reduce Russia's traditional dependence on Germany as the main supplier of chemicals for the production of explosives. In 1914 he was elected associate member, and two years later full member, of Russia's Academy of Sciences, which confirmed both his scientific fame and his active involvement with the government.

Ipatieff maintained a strong interest in industrial applications of chemistry throughout his life. In 1915 he was among the initiators of KEPS, the Commission for the Study of Natural Resources established at Russia's Academy of Sciences in response to the country's war effort. Later, in spite of his reservations with respect to the new Bolshevik regime, he maintained a strong commitment to the welfare of the country and became actively involved in several government agencies. In 1921 he was nominated to the Supreme Soviet of National Economy to head the newly formed General Chemical Administration, in which he played an active role for nearly a decade. Ipatieff came into contact with major figures in the Bolshevik government, including Lenin and Trotsky. Many developments in the Soviet chemical industry, which underwent impressive expansion in the course of the first five-year plans (1928–1938), were based on the research and development work he had done during the first decade of the Soviet regime. In 1927 he organized the State Institute for High Pressures in Moscow. In the course of the 1920s he also regularly consulted major chemical industries in Germany.

Several trials of engineers and scientists marked the consolidation of a totalitarian society by Stalin in the late 1920s and early 1930s. Ipatieff saw more and more of his colleagues and collaborators demoted and later arrested. In the face of imminent imprisonment Ipatieff left the Soviet Union in 1930 and would never see his homeland again. In 1931 he immigrated to the United States to join Universal Oil Products and there organized the Catalytic High Pressure Laboratory at Northwestern University, Evanston, Illinois. However, he considered his sojourn in the United States a temporary contingency and refused to buy a house and otherwise settle down. He lived in a hotel to the end of his days.

Upon arrival in the United States, Ipatieff was over sixty years old, a world-renowned chemist and industrial consultant, and author of approximately 200 scientific papers and several books. During his work at Universal Oil Products, he conducted a broad range of investigations into the nature of catalysis and catalysts. He went beyond the usual trial and error approaches to the study of catalysis and attempted, often successfully, to identify general properties and develop theoretical foundations of chemical catalysis. Applications of multifunction catalysis to reforming and cracking of petroleum enabled the United States to expand its oil refining capacity many times over during World War II. Following his immigration to the United States, he published several books, scores of scientific articles, drew dozens of patents, and pursued an active teaching career.

Ipatieff's many distinctions include the Butlerov Prize of the Russian Physical-chemical Society (1896), the Légion d'honneur (1916), the Lenin Prize (1927), the Berthelot Medal (1928), the Lavoisier Medal (1939), the Willard Gibbs Medal (1940), and the title of Modern Pioneer from the National Association of Manufacturers (1940). Although he lost his membership in the Soviet Academy of Sciences (1937), he was elected to the U.S. National Academy of Sciences (1939) and the Académie de la France (1939). The USSR Academy of Sciences expelled Ipatieff in 1936 and reinstated him, posthumously, in 1990. Ipatieff died in Chicago.

• Ipatieff's archives can be found at the Russian Academy of Sciences and at Northwestern University. His most important scientific book is *Catalytic Reactions at High Pressures and Temperatures* (1936). His autobiography, *The Life of a Chemist*, was published in 1946. Because his name was banned in the Soviet Union after 1936, a biography written by Vladimir I. Kuznetsov in 1967 for Ipatieff's centenary could not be published; see Vladimir I. Kuznetsov, "Vozrozhdenie pravdy ob akademike Ipatieve" (Rebirth of truth about academician Ipatiev), *Voprosy istorii estestvoznaniia i tekhniki* 4 (1991): 61–71. The book finally appeared in 1992 as V. I. Kuznetsov and A. M. Maksimenko, *Vladimir Nikolaevich Ipatiev, 1867–1952*.

YAKOV M. RABKIN

IREDELL, James (5 Oct. 1751–20 Oct. 1799), statesman and jurist, was born in Lewes, England, and raised in Bristol, the son of Francis Iredell, a merchant, and Margaret McCulloh. Little is known of Iredell's early education. The family's circumstances were modest, and when his father suffered a paralytic stroke in 1766, the Iredells were forced to appeal to their well-connected relatives for assistance. In February 1768 one of these relatives, Sir George Macartney, secured for James a position as comptroller of customs for Port Roanoke in Edenton, North Carolina. Aided by his friendly disposition and his family connection to Henry Eustace McCulloh, one of the largest landholders in the colony, Iredell soon entered into Edenton society. He took up the study of law with Samuel Johnston (1733–1816), Edenton's leading citizen, whose sister Hannah became Iredell's wife in 1773; they had three children.

Iredell obtained his license to practice law in the inferior North Carolina courts in 1770 and in its superior courts the following year. In 1774 his career in colonial government began to flourish: he was promoted to collector of customs for Port Roanoke and appointed a deputy king's attorney. Ironically, even as he advanced in the royal service he began to take up his pen in support of the revolutionary cause. In 1774 he issued an address, "To the Inhabitants of Great Britain," in which he contended that Parliament had no authority over the colonies because they originally had been the possession of the king. Rather than arguing for separation, Iredell envisioned a federation of independent legislatures united by a common monarch. In late 1775 or early 1776 Iredell made similar arguments in "The Principles of an American Whig," and in June 1776 he published a lengthy, untitled tract that recounted the events that had led the colonies to the brink of rebellion. On the eve of the Declaration of Independence he continued to hope for reconciliation, perhaps influenced by his family ties to England and by the knowledge that he stood to lose a large inheritance from an uncle if he sided with the rebels. Despite these considerations, he ultimately took the side of independence.

Although it is unclear how widely Iredell's writings were circulated, he soon gained a solid reputation. In 1776 the Provincial Congress appointed him to a committee charged with reviewing the statutes of North Carolina and suggesting revisions. In December 1777 the general assembly elected him one of three judges of the superior courts, the highest judicial authority in the state. Iredell accepted the post reluctantly, feeling himself unqualified and dreading the prospect of riding circuit. He resigned six months later. After a brief return to private practice, he accepted the post of attorney general in July 1779 and served in that post until the end of 1781.

Iredell aligned himself with what has generally been viewed as the conservative faction in North Carolina politics. He opposed the indiscriminate seizure of Loyalist property and was dismayed by the state's refusal to adhere to the Treaty of Paris (1783) and the Articles of Confederation. He was also an early and vigorous proponent of the principle of judicial review as a check on legislative excesses. As early as 1783, in his *Instructions to Chowan County Representatives*, Iredell argued in favor of judicial independence as "a point of the utmost moment in a Republic where the Law is superior to any or all the Individuals, and the Constitution superior even to the Legislature, and of which the Judges are the guardians and protectors." In 1787, as an attorney in the case of *Bayard v. Singleton*, he persuaded the North Carolina Superior Court to declare an act of the legislature unconstitutional.

In November 1787 the legislature appointed Iredell to revise and compile the laws of North Carolina, which resulted in the publication of *Laws of the State of North-Carolina* in 1791. In 1788 he was elected to the governor's council of state and served as a delegate to North Carolina's first ratifying convention. In January, under the pseudonym Marcus, Iredell published "Answers to Mr. Mason's Objections to the New Constitution"—a tract that brought him national recognition. He became the leader of the delegation that favored ratification and spoke eloquently during debate. Despite his efforts, North Carolina did not ratify the U.S. Constitution until a second convention was held in November 1789.

Iredell's efforts on behalf of ratification brought him to the attention of President George Washington. On 6 February 1790, after Robert H. Harrison, chief judge of the Maryland General Court and a former aide-de-camp to Washington, had declined an appointment to the U.S. Supreme Court, Washington noted in his diary that he had determined to appoint "Mr. Iredall of No. Carolina; because, in addition to the reputation he sustains for abilities, legal knowledge and respectability of character he is of a State of some importance in the Union that has given *No* character to a federal Office." Iredell was nominated for the post on 8 February and confirmed by the Senate two days later. At thirty-eight, Iredell became the youngest member of the Court. As an associate justice Iredell once again faced the arduous task of riding circuit, which had contributed to his decision to resign from the North Carolina Superior Court in 1778. Now, however, he was required to ride even longer distances. Although his frequent letters to his wife indicate that he enjoyed the hospitality that was extended to him in various parts of the country, he soon wearied of the dangers and difficulties of this aspect of his job. Nevertheless he faithfully delivered grand jury charges that served as instructive essays on the fledgling national government and admonished its citizens to support it.

Iredell's most famous Supreme Court opinion was his dissent in *Chisholm v. Georgia* in 1793, in which he alone adhered to the view that a state could not be sued by a citizen of another state in federal court. While it has been suggested that his reasons for this decision were primarily pragmatic and political, his opinion rested on narrow and technical grounds. He sought to avoid a constitutional holding and indeed would have rejected the suit on the grounds that Congress had authorized the federal courts to issue only writs that were "agreeable to the principles and usages of law" (which

Iredell interpreted to mean the common law of the several states). That common law, in his view, derived from the common law of England and incorporated the principle of sovereign immunity, that is, the principle that the sovereign power could not be sued without its consent. In dictum, Iredell added that even if the Constitution could be interpreted to allow Congress to authorize federal jurisdiction over suits brought by citizens against states, he believed that such a provision would be unwise as a matter of policy. Five years later, in 1798, the states ratified the Eleventh Amendment to the Constitution, overturning the result in *Chisholm* and vindicating Iredell's position.

Iredell died at his home in Edenton less than ten years after he joined the Court. Although his dissent in *Chisholm* has led some commentators to view him as an early champion of states' rights, in fact his primary efforts both before and after his appointment to the bench were directed at strengthening the union and ensuring its success.

• The bulk of Iredell's papers are in the Charles E. Johnson Collection at the North Carolina State Department of Archives and History, while others are deposited at Duke University. Griffith J. McRee, *Life and Correspondence of James Iredell* (1857), contains transcripts of a number of letters that have since been lost. A more modern, multivolume collection of Iredell's correspondence is Don Higginbotham, ed., *The Papers of James Iredell* (1976–). Many documents and letters relating to Iredell's tenure on the Supreme Court can be found in Maeva Marcus, ed., *The Documentary History of the Supreme Court, 1789–1800* (4 vols.; 1985, 1988, 1990, 1992). See also Fred L. Israel, "James Iredell," in *The Justices of the United States Supreme Court 1789–1960: Their Lives and Major Opinions*, ed. Leon Friedman and Fred L. Israel, vol. 1 (1969), pp. 121–32; Christopher Graebe, "The Federalism of James Iredell in Historical Context," *North Carolina Law Review* 69 (1990): 251–72; Jeff B. Fordham, "Iredell's Dissent in *Chisholm v. Georgia*," *The North Carolina Historical Review* 8 (1931): 155–67; H. G. Connor, "James Iredell: Lawyer, Statesman, Judge," *University of Pennsylvania Law Review* 60 (1912): 225–53; John Charles Waldrup, "James Iredell and the Practice of Law in Revolutionary Era North Carolina," (Ph.D. diss., Univ. of North Carolina–Chapel Hill, 1985).

NATALIE WEXLER

IRELAND, John (11 Sept. 1838–25 Sept. 1918), first Roman Catholic archbishop of St. Paul, Minnesota, was born in Burnchurch, County Kilkenny, Ireland, the son of Richard Ireland, a carpenter, and Judith Naughton. At the age of eleven he emigrated with his family first to Burlington, Vermont, then to Chicago, and finally, in 1852, to St. Paul, Minnesota Territory. The following year he was sent to France by the first bishop of St. Paul, Joseph Cretin, and enrolled in the preparatory seminary at Meximieux, near Lyons. Here he studied the classics until 1857 when he moved to the Marist seminary at Montbel, near Toulon, where he spent another four years studying philosophy and theology. Ireland's sojourn in France left him fluent in written and spoken French and a lifelong devotee of French culture and literature.

Ireland returned to St. Paul in the autumn of 1861 and, on 22 December, was ordained to the priesthood by Cretin's successor, Thomas Langdon Grace. After a few months' tenure as curate in the cathedral parish, the young priest was named chaplain of the Fifth Minnesota Regiment, Volunteer Infantry, a capacity he filled between June 1862, and April 1863. During that time he participated in the campaign that culminated in the second battle of Corinth, Mississippi (3–4 Oct. 1862), and in the early stages of the siege of Vicksburg. This direct if brief experience of the Civil War was a source of lasting satisfaction to Ireland, who always prided himself at having been "a soldier of Mr. Lincoln."

Back in St. Paul, Ireland served first as curate and then as rector of the cathedral parish until 1875 when he was appointed coadjutor to Bishop Grace. When that venerable prelate retired nine years later, Ireland automatically succeeded him as third bishop of St. Paul. Rapid population growth in the Upper Midwest induced the Vatican in 1888 to create several new dioceses and to establish a new ecclesiastical province embracing Minnesota and North and South Dakota, with St. Paul as the metropolitan see. From this date, therefore, Ireland enjoyed the rank of an archbishop and exercised direct jurisdiction over the Catholics living in the Twin Cities and in the rural areas west to the South Dakota border.

During these busy years the essential elements of Ireland's career assumed their permanent configuration. He ministered to an immigrant people whose numbers were constantly increasing, whose financial resources were meagre, and whose religion was viewed with suspicion by what was still a predominately Protestant society. Ireland concluded that the role of church leadership, and his role specifically, was to provide Catholics with a physical presence—churches, schools, and other functioning institutions in which to fulfill their religious obligations—but also to imbue them with the determination to become full participants in the mainstream of American life. This belief, enhanced by his own deep patriotic sentiments, was the lodestar of his ministry.

One instance of this preoccupation was Ireland's insistence that the Catholics in his charge take an active part in civic affairs. Nor did he hesitate to do so himself: he was a consistent promoter of Minnesota and the Twin Cities, as well as an active and voluble advocate of the Republican party. More important, however, was Ireland's recognition of damage done to his people, especially the Irish, by alcohol abuse. He became and remained a stout champion of Total Abstinence, and his temperance crusades were the occasions that first brought him into national prominence. The drunken Catholic immigrant, he proclaimed repeatedly, would never find a welcome in the sober and productive American commonwealth.

Another significant initiative that aimed at the same goal was the establishment of the Catholic Colonization Bureau of St. Paul. Between 1876 and 1881 Bishop Ireland, acting as agent for several railroad companies anxious to have customers along their rights-of-way, was able to allocate at advantageous terms upward of 350,000 acres of land to Catholic immigrants willing to settle in western Minnesota. This program, which resulted in the founding of ten viable agricultural communities, testified to Ireland's conviction that responsible landowners made better Americans and better Catholics.

Thanks to Grace's retirement, Ireland attended the Third Plenary Council of Baltimore (Nov. 1884) as a bishop in his own right. This landmark meeting of the American hierarchy afforded him national exposure—the speech he delivered there, "The Church, the Support of Just Government," received particular attention—and it also served as an occasion to discuss with his peers the future direction of the Catholic church in the United States. These discussions proved to be the prologue to the fierce controversies that would engage the Catholic community over the next fifteen years and that would culminate with the so-called Americanist crisis.

The quarrels, which involved strong personalities as well as contending policies, turned upon disagreement over the pace and the degree to which Catholic immigrants should be amalgamated into the larger American society. Ireland, leader of the liberal or Americanist faction, argued that the United States and its democratic institutions offered a unique opportunity to the Catholic church's apostolate and, at the same time, that the church and its doctrines could stand as a bulwark of virtue and good order for the Republic. Those who opposed him did so out of concern that the rapid absorption of Catholic immigrants into a society at once Protestant and highly materialistic could lead to the diminishing of their faith and religious practice. Particularly anxious on this score were the German Catholics, prelates and people alike, who contended that maintaining the customs and language of the old country was essential for the preservation of their religion in their new country. They found allies among diverse conservative groups, including the Society of Jesus and certain influential bishops, like Michael Augustine Corrigan of New York.

The battle was fought out on various fronts. Thus Ireland endeavored to make the Catholic University of America, of which he was a founder (1889), an intellectual center of Americanist opinion. He strongly resisted efforts to secure appointment of a quota of German-born or German-speaking bishops to American dioceses. He advocated indulgence with regard to Catholic membership in fraternal organizations, such as the Odd Fellows and the Knights of Pythias, on the ground that, contrary to conservative opinion, they were not anti-Catholic "secret societies" as were the Masonic sects common in Europe. Of special importance in this regard was the forceful backing Ireland gave to James Cardinal Gibbons, archbishop of Baltimore, in his campaign to avert condemnation as a secret society of the Knights of Labor, the only significant organization of workingmen at the time.

The greatest source of contention among American Catholics during these years was the disparity of opinion over general education. Ireland supported strongly the public system as an agency of Americanization, and moreover he realized that the maintenance of an alternative parochial system, mandated by the Third Plenary Council, was beyond the financial resources of a poor Catholic populace. By proposing the Faribault School Plan, named for the Minnesota town in which it was briefly applied, he attempted an accommodation that he hoped might become a national model. In this scheme the Catholic school building was leased to the local school board for a nominal sum, in return for which the board assumed payment of ordinary expenses, including compensation of the nuns who taught there. Religious instruction was restricted to the hour after the regular scholastic day. When after a year's trial the voters of Faribault rejected this arrangement, Ireland proceeded with his accustomed vigor to provide the people of his diocese with as many confessional schools as possible. Neither his relative success in this endeavor nor the fact that the Faribault plan became so soon a dead letter prevented Ireland's opponents among his co-religionists from accusing him of intending to undermine the parochial system.

Given the high degree of administrative centralization the Roman Catholic church had developed by the end of the nineteenth century, resolution of these and other related contentions had to be sought at the Vatican. Both American factions lobbied the Roman Curia relentlessly. Ireland traveled to Rome on many occasions during the 1890s, and he maintained an agent there. Thanks partially to his efforts, the Catholic University was awarded pontifical status. He won Pope Leo XIII's approval of the Faribault plan in the teeth of opposition from the overwhelming majority of his fellow bishops. He did not fare so well, however, in trying to win the Vatican's acceptance of the so-called secret societies. One of Ireland's Roman triumphs that went awry was the dispatch of the first apostolic delegate to the United States, an event orchestrated by the archbishop of St. Paul and calculated to win the pope's favor. But the appointment further alienated Ireland from the other bishops, most of whom opposed it. Then, to his chagrin, the delegate gradually allied himself with Corrigan and began to warn his superiors in Rome of the dangers of Americanism.

In January 1899 Leo XIII promulgated a pontifical letter, *Testem benevolentiae*, in which he deplored certain "opinions that some include under the head of Americanism." The pope was careful to distinguish the "Americanism" he condemned from "the characteristic qualities which reflect honor on the people of America." Indeed, he insisted that the censured opinions—for example, the preference of activism to contemplation, of natural virtues to supernatural—were often foreign misinterpretations of allegedly American principles. Nevertheless, the pope warned that it was wrong to "desire a church in America different from that which is in the rest of the world." Ireland, who had gone to Rome in hopes of heading off the issuance of such a document, immediately made public his adherence to it, but he also sharply asserted his "indignation that the word 'Americanism' should have designated errors and extravagances of this sort." This declaration went unchallenged by Leo, and the subsequent judgment that Americanism was a "phantom heresy" appears to have been just.

Ireland's commitment to the Republican party stemmed largely from his dedication to the causes of temperance and racial equality. His influence within the party was heightened by his support for William McKinley in the presidential election of 1896. Two years later, at the request of the Vatican, he lobbied the administration in Washington strenuously, but in vain, to resist pressure to declare war on Spain. In 1902 he was instrumental in the success of the negotiations between the Vatican and the Taft Commission to settle disputes over church property in the Philippines. Always fascinated by politics of any kind, Ireland maintained warm and cordial relations with William Howard Taft and Theodore Roosevelt (1858–1919).

At home in Minnesota, Ireland presided over the vast expansion of the Catholic community. Hundreds of churches, schools, and charitable institutions were built under his direction. His concern for higher education was reflected in the founding of a Catholic college for men, another for women, and a major seminary. He devoted his last years to the construction of a great cathedral in St. Paul and a hardly less magnificent procathedral in Minneapolis. He died in St. Paul.

In his ideals, his tastes, and his orotund speaking style, John Ireland was a man of America's Gilded Age. He believed firmly in the manifest destiny of his country and of his church. He gave courageous leadership to immigrant Catholics, and he lived long enough to have witnessed his people's coming of age as Americans. His contribution to the development of his city and state was as distinguished as that of any person of his generation. His bitter disappointment at not having achieved his church's ultimate accolade, a cardinal's hat, did not disillusion him. He was idolized by many, hated by some, and respected by all. The posthumous tribute of his friend Cardinal Gibbons might stand as his epitaph: John Ireland "contributed perhaps more than any other to demonstrate the harmony that exists between the constitution of the Church and the constitution of the United States."

• Ireland's personal and professional papers are preserved in the Archives of the Catholic Historical Society of St. Paul. They have been microfilmed (twenty-two rolls) by the Minnesota Historical Society. Other significant collections of correspondence are in the archives of the Archdiocese of Baltimore and of the Diocese of Richmond, as well as in the Secret Vatican Archives and the Archives of the Sacred Congregation for the Evangelization of Peoples in Rome. The most notable of Ireland's speeches have been published in *The Church and Modern Society* (2 vols., 1904). The two full-length biographies are James H. Moynihan, *The Life of Archbishop John Ireland* (1954), and Marvin R. O'Connell, *John Ireland and the American Catholic Church* (1988).

MARVIN R. O'CONNELL

IRELAND, Shadrach (baptized 16 Jan. 1718–11 Sept. 1778), craftsman and lay preacher, was born to Abraham Ireland and Abigail Greenland of Cambridge, Massachusetts. Little is known about Ireland's early life except that he settled in Charleston, Massachusetts, as a young man, married, and alternately assumed employment as a joiner, carver, and maker of pipes (for tobacco, by one account; see Nourse, p. 256). He and his wife, Martha, had six children.

Ireland's life changed dramatically after 1740, when British evangelist George Whitefield visited Boston on his second American tour. After experiencing a conversion, Ireland abandoned his home and family and for the next several years toured as an itinerant exhorter. In the 1750s, he evidently gained considerable popularity in Medfield, Sutton, and Uxbridge, Massachusetts, and the adjoining towns of Easton, Taunton, and Raynham. Meanwhile, he also scandalized opponents with unorthodox religious views and by living outside legal wedlock with a female companion, the widow Abigail Lougee. By 1753, claimed Separate-Baptist historian Isaac Backus, Ireland was in danger of "being punished by authority" (*History*, vol. 2, p. 462). Withdrawing from public scrutiny, Ireland finally settled in Harvard, Massachusetts, around 1760 with disciples who concealed him for the next two decades in a large house built especially for him.

Theologically, Ireland's followers distinguished themselves by claiming tangible progress toward moral perfection. Members also asserted their own eventual immortality on earth and believed in the imminent end of time as foretold in the book of Revelation. Ireland himself apparently assumed a messianic persona. So "blasphemous" was Ireland, wrote Backus, that he "set himself up as the head of the church, and assumed God's prerogatives" (*History*, vol. 2, p. 462). According to Backus, Ireland and his disciples rejected the legitimacy of civil marriage as well, insisting instead that the basis of matrimony should be spiritual in nature rather than sexual. Celibacy, however, was to cease with the attainment of perfection. For Ireland and his disciples to take "spiritual" spouses reflected movement toward "a state of perfection in this World so as to be free from all Sinckings And trouble" (Backus, *Diary*, vol. 1, p. 141).

Ireland's death proved as sensational as his life. One autumn evening, recalled former disciple Isaac Holden, Ireland calmly announced his own forthcoming demise and instructed followers not to bury him, "'for the Time is very Short,' he said. 'God is a Coming to take the Church.'" Afterward, Ireland knelt down and prayed "Very Extensively"; then he reclined on his bed and "Expired Instantly." For nearly a year Ireland's corpse supposedly remained indoors, housed in a long white box filled with lime. Finally, wrote Backus, "the body scented so much that it was carried out in the night and buried in a corn-field" (*History*, vol. 2, p. 462). The fates of Ireland's legal wife, Martha, his six children, and the widow Lougee are unknown.

Ireland's movement, an embodiment of recurring perfectionist themes in American thought, was one of many sects that blossomed in New England between the First Great Awakening and the era of the American Revolution. In its perfectionism and thinking on celibacy and the millennium the Irelandites resembled the Shakers, whose founder, Ann Lee, moved into Ireland's Harvard house in 1781 and gained the support of many former Ireland disciples.

• No writings by Ireland have survived. Scattered details about his early life, parents, legal and spiritual wives, and children can be found in Henry S. Nourse, *History of the Town of Harvard Massachusetts, 1732–1893* (1894), and Frederick Lewis Weis, *The Colonial Clergy and the Colonial Churches of New England* (1936; repr. 1961). Additional information can be found in "Notes," *New England Historic Genealogical Society Records* 65 (1911): 381. For Ireland's life as an itinerant preacher, see three unfriendly but generally reliable works: Isaac Backus, *A History of New England. With Particular Reference to the Denomination of Christians Called Baptists*, vol. 2, ed. David Weston, rev. ed. (1871); Ezra Stiles, *Extracts from the Itineraries and Other Miscellanies of Ezra Stiles, D.D., LL.D., 1755–1794*, ed. Franklin Bowditch Dexter (1916); and *The Diary of Isaac Backus*, 3 vols., ed. William G. McLoughlin (1979). In addition, the Backus Collection at the Andover Newton Theological School, Newton Centre, Mass., contains minutes of a church council at Easton, Mass., dated 27 June and 18 Sept. 1764, that inquired into the beliefs of Separate-Baptists involved with Ireland. A letter from Isaac Holden to Isaiah Parker, 18 May 1784, in the same collection, describes Ireland's death. For Ireland and the Shakers, see Edward Deming Andrews, *The People Called Shakers: A Search for the Perfect Society* (1953).

LEIGH JOHNSEN

IRISH, Ned (6 May 1905–21 Jan. 1982), basketball promoter and sports journalist, was born Edward Simmons Irish in Lake George, New York, the son of Clifford Irish, a concessionaire for a boat rental business, and Madeleine Lancaster, a practical nurse and dermatologist. After his father's early death, Irish and his mother moved to Brooklyn, where he worked his way through Erasmus Hall High School by waiting on cafeteria tables, coaching the swimming team, and covering high school sports for several local newspapers. He attended the University of Pennsylvania, regularly reporting on campus sports for New York and Philadelphia newspapers.

Graduating with a business degree in 1928, Irish joined the sports staff of the *New York World-Telegram*. In the early 1930s he married Katherine Bridgeman, with whom he had two children. For much of the decade he moonlighted simultaneously as publicity director for the New York Giants football club and the National Football League. His big break occurred in 1931 when he joined a committee of sportswriters promoting benefit basketball programs at Madison Square Garden for unemployment relief. Inspired by success, Irish offered Madison Square Garden president John Reed Kilpatrick a set fee for rental of the arena and a percentage of the profits once the guarantee was paid. That arrangement allowed Irish to schedule games, advertise, and sell tickets independently.

Irish's formula for success featured doubleheaders of local college teams hosting midwestern and western opponents. More than 16,000 spectators turned out in late December 1934 to see St. John's University lose to Westminster College, 37–33, and New York University defeat Notre Dame, 25–18. Shortly thereafter, he resigned from the *World-Telegram* to become the Garden's director of basketball programs. A year later he booked Stanford with its heralded forward, Hank Luisetti, to play Long Island University, winners of forty-three consecutive games. A large corps of journalists and 17,623 fans responded to Irish's hard sell that promised a new kind of game based on, not the layup or stationary set shot, but Luisetti's innovative, running, one-handed shot. Although Luisetti scored only 15 points in Stanford's 45–31 victory, his unorthodox style and an attentive New York press worked in tandem to revolutionize the game of basketball. Irish's entrepreneurial hand, in part, was behind that change.

Irish also contributed greatly to creating the National Invitational Tournament (NIT) in March 1938. His promotions having made the Garden the mecca of quality college basketball, New York's Metropolitan Basketball Writers Association selected the teams competing for a mythical national crown. Founded a year before the start of the National Collegiate Athletic Association tournament, the NIT reigned for more than a decade as college basketball's premier end-of-season championship event—until a major gambling scandal in 1951 seriously damaged the NIT's prestige and allowed the NCAA tourney to gain dominance.

Before that scandal, postwar Madison Square Garden basketball thrived under Irish's direction. In 1945–1946 he booked twenty-nine college programs (mostly doubleheaders, some tournaments) and averaged attendance of 98 percent of capacity. The following season the Garden was sold out for twenty of its twenty-one basketball events.

Yet Irish restlessly sought new areas for investment. In 1946 he led in creating an eleven-team professional league, the Basketball Association of America (BAA). For New York's entry, the Knickerbockers, he served as president. Three years later he helped negotiate a merger of the BAA with an older professional league, the National Basketball League, to form the National Basketball Association (NBA). As executive vice president of Madison Square Garden, which was larger than most arenas, he negotiated for each NBA home team to keep its own gate receipts.

Under Irish's presidency, the Knicks pioneered in the regular use of chartered planes for distant games, and the franchise led in the racial integration of professional basketball, signing a former Harlem Globetrotter, Nat "Sweetwater" Clifton, as one of a handful of blacks breaking into the NBA in 1950. Irish, though, was primarily a businessman, not a liberal reformer. To friends, he seemed honest and principled; to critics, he seemed aloof and conniving. He was elected to the Naismith Memorial Basketball Hall of Fame in 1964. He aggressively opposed giving up the reserve clause by which a player was bound to one team for

life. In the early 1970s he supported the merger of the NBA with the upstart American Basketball Association as a way to prevent competitive bidding and higher salaries for players.

Irish's wife, a loyal Knicks fan, died just before the Knicks won the NBA championship in 1970. With his second wife, Jacqueline (maiden name unknown), whom he married in 1971, he retired to Florida in 1974. He died in New York. He left basketball radically different from the game he found. Before him, the old YMCA spirit, amateur and low-key, still imbued the college sport; touring professionals mostly played in armories and dance halls. Irish tapped college basketball's commercial possibilities as a big-time spectator sport. "He helped lay the foundation upon which we all have built," observed Lawrence O'Brien, the NBA's commissioner in the early 1980s.

• Useful information is available in the Irish file at the Basketball Hall of Fame archives in Springfield, Mass., and in Albert Gammon Applin II, "From Muscular Christianity to the Marketplace: The History of Men's and Boys' Basketball in the United States, 1891–1957" (Ph.D. diss., Univ. of Massachusetts, 1982); "Peach-basket Soccer Goes on the Big Time," *News-Week*, 14 Dec. 1935, p. 26; and "Peach-baskets into Profits," *Literary Digest*, 28 Dec. 1935, p. 32. The Madison Square Garden context is in Joseph Durso, *Madison Square Garden: 100 Years of History* (1979); statistical data is in Zander Hollander, ed., *The Modern Encyclopedia of Basketball* (1979); and helpful reminiscences are in Red Holtzman and Harvey Frommer, *Red on Red* (1987). An obituary is in the *New York Times*, 22 Jan. 1982.

WILLIAM J. BAKER

IRONSIDE, Henry Allan (14 Oct. 1876–15 Jan. 1951), evangelist, was born in Toronto, Canada, the son of John Williams Ironside, a bank teller, and Sophia Stafford. It is said that Ironside was believed dead at birth; only after forty minutes did the nurse detect a heartbeat in the newborn child. This was taken as a miracle by his deeply religious parents. His father, a lay preacher of the Plymouth Brethren, was nicknamed the "Eternity Man" for his characteristic inquiry, "Where will you spend eternity?" He died when Henry was only two, leaving the family in destitute financial circumstances. His mother became a seamstress, working long hours but only barely able to support the family. In 1886 she moved her family to Los Angeles, California. Remaining deeply religious, she opened their house to itinerant clergy, and the house became a way station and gathering place for many in the religious community. By age twelve, Henry was attending the revival movements of Dwight L. Moody, the famous evangelist, and he was teaching his own Sunday school class. Two years later he decided to dedicate his life to the church. The realization of his call came while he meditated on a verse from Proverbs: "Because I have called, and ye refused; I have stretched out my hand, and no man regarded" (Prov. 1:24–32).

After finishing grammar school, Ironside joined the Salvation Army. Elevated to the rank of captain at age twenty-one, he was given responsibility for large areas of California. Although he became a fervent street preacher, after a time he grew doubtful of the authenticity of his religious conversion, which put him at odds with the Salvation Army's creed. He eventually left the Salvation Army to join the Plymouth Brethren, the religious group to which his father had belonged. In contrast to the rigid hierarchical structure of the Salvation Army, the Brethren had no religious rankings, and members referred to each other as "Christian" or "Brethren." Strongly opposed to any organization or authority that was not directly biblically based, the Brethren were noted for their strongly Protestant doctrine, which occasionally made them outspoken opponents of Catholicism, and their emphasis on the importance of the coming millennium. Their practice of baptism required immersing the head three times in running water. Having joined the group, Ironside continued his itinerant preaching, supporting himself from the donations of his listeners. In January 1898 he married Helen G. Schofield; they had two children. After his marriage, Ironside settled in Oakland, California. He continued his evangelical work, often targeting Jews and the Japanese population of California.

To compensate for his lack of formal education, Ironside undertook a rigorous program of self-education. He learned Greek and Chinese and read extensively in Christian doctrine. He began publishing texts of biblical commentary, starting with *Notes on Esther* (1900) and *Notes on Jeremiah* (1902). To facilitate their publication, Ironside founded the Western Book and Tract Company, a nonprofit publisher of Christian writings, in 1912. That same year he embarked on missionary work with Native-American tribes, a project that continued each summer for the next ten years. Ironside, who freelanced as a visiting preacher at many Bible conferences around the country, also held summer jobs with the Moody Bible Institute (1924–1930) and a visiting lectureship at the Dallas Theological Seminary (1925–1943).

For much of his life, Ironside worked as an itinerant preacher rather than as pastor of one church because of Brethren injunctions against religious organization. However, when the Moody Memorial Church in Chicago, perhaps the most influential and best-known fundamentalist church in the country, offered him its pastorship, Ironside accepted and began service there in 1930. Under his leadership, the church paid off the $319,999 debt remaining on its construction costs and expanded its missionary program. Although he faithfully appeared in Chicago every Sunday, Ironside's contract allowed him to preach elsewhere during the week, and his schedule of travel and appearances was impressive. His book, *Except Ye Repent* (1937), was awarded a $1,000 prize by the American Tract Society. A year after the death of his first wife in 1948, Ironside married Ann Hightower; they had no children. When he retired from the pulpit of the Moody Memorial Church in 1948, he continued to preach and write prolifically until his death. He died in Rotu Rua, near Cambridge, New Zealand, while on a preaching tour.

A fundamentalist, Ironside insisted on the Bible's literal truth and inerrancy; such events as the Virgin Birth and the Resurrection were viewed as actual historical occurrences. His simple, unpretentious preaching style made him popular with the mass audiences who heard his sermons every Sunday at the Moody Church or on radio. His sermons were most often verse-by-verse expositions rather than lectures on a general topic. Ironside seldom repeated himself, and by the end of his career he had preached more than 10,000 different sermons.

Ironside's success was part of the growth of Fundamentalism in the United States from the 1920s to the 1940s, a period when other denominations were experiencing a decline. The large personal following he acquired was characteristic of the major fundamentalist preachers of his time, including William B. Riley, J. Frank Norris, and later Billy Graham. Like them, his interests were focused on evangelism rather than social or political issues.

• Other works by Ironside include *Notes on the Minor Prophets* (1904); *Notes on Proverbs* (1906); *The Mass vs. the Lord's Supper* (1926); *Lectures to a Roman Catholic Priest* (1926); *Random Reminiscences from Fifty Years of Ministry* (1939); and *A Historical Sketch of the Brethren Movement* (1942). For biographical information, see E. Schuler English, *H. A. Ironside: Ordained of the Lord* (1946), and Donald E. Hoke, *Archbishop of Fundamentalism* (1944). An obituary is in the *New York Times*, 17 Jan. 1951.

ELIZABETH ZOE VICARY

IRVIN, Rea (26 Aug. 1881–28 May 1972), artist and cartoonist, was born in San Francisco, California, the son of George C. Irvin and Mary Jane Morse, who had made the journey west by covered wagon in the 1850s. Although Rea attended Hopkins Art Institute in San Francisco, he also entertained the idea of a career in acting, which he pursued briefly beginning in 1903. He served in the art departments of several newspapers, including the *Honolulu Advertiser*, but eventually he moved to New York, and by the 1920s he had achieved a good measure of success as a newspaper and magazine cartoonist, becoming art editor of the humor magazine *Life*. His thespian inclinations remained, however, finding expression in his theatrical manner of attire and in his demeanor, which radiated the stage presence of an accomplished actor. He was a familiar figure at both the Players Club and the Dutch Treat Club. In 1916 he married Dorothy Goodwin; they had two children.

When Harold Ross began planning the *New Yorker* magazine in about 1924, he enlisted Irvin to help with the art chores. Irvin, who had a flourishing freelance art agency, agreed to serve as "art consultant" (Ross eschewed formal titles) but stipulated that he could afford to give only one day a week to the task. Over the months of preparation, Irvin prepared the layout for the first issue, drew most of the department headings, and designed the distinctive typeface for the magazine (modifying a typeface developed by Carl Purington Rollins). But when the magazine debuted on 21 February 1925, Irvin's most-noted contribution was the puzzling cover drawing: it depicted a Beau Brummell–like dandy in top hat and high stock who was inspecting a butterfly through his monocle.

Writing of the magazine's founder's intention to establish a sophisticated urbane journal, Brendan Gill in *Here at the New Yorker* expressed astonishment at this "unexpected and inappropriate" picture of "a preposterous figure out of a dead and alien past. . . . One is baffled to see how an early-nineteenth century English fop, scrutinizing through a monocle, with a curiosity so mild that it amounts to disdain, a passing butterfly, could hope to represent the jazzy, new-rich, gangster-ridden, speakeasy-filled New York of the twenties, which Ross claimed to be ready to give an accurate rendering of " (p. 87). Irvin's supercilious boulevardier was merely an adaptation of his drawing for the magazine's leading department, the gossipy "Talk of the Town," to which the artist turned when Ross, desperate for something for the cover of his first issue, pleaded with him to produce something. According to Ross's wife at the time, Jane Grant, Ross thought the Irvin cover was "the only successful feature" of the first issue. And Ross was so pleased with it that he ran it every year on the anniversary issue of the magazine, published the last week in February. The character in the picture was eventually christened Eustace Tilley, but the name was borrowed from another dandy the magazine had invented several months later for promotional purposes.

Irvin's drawing style usually deployed a spare albeit supple line to make decorative but curiously flat and unelaborate pictures that Gill correctly saw as vaguely Chinese in appearance. But, as Gill observed, Irvin could draw in any style, and when the *New Yorker* produced a parody of the English humor magazine *Punch*, the artist filled its pages with drawings that imitated flawlessly the work of many celebrated British artists and cartoonists. For the old *Life*, Irvin produced several series of large, full-page tableaux in the prevailing fashion of the time. One such series appeared under the heading "The Phrase Testers." In one of these, Irvin showed a group of judges deliberating about the relative inebriated conditions of a well-dressed dignitary and a shabbily dressed bum as they determine "the point at which a man becomes 'drunk as a lord.'" In another, a man's mouth opens as the starting gun is fired and a judge with a stopwatch is determining "the celerity of saying 'Jack Robinson.'" And Irvin did similar work for the early *New Yorker* as well as producing a great number of the magazine's covers.

The day that Irvin gave to the magazine every week was the day he helped Ross select the cartoons for the next issue. Irvin's taste in art was expansive: he liked classic and modern art, he was sympathetic to anything new, and he knew good craftsmanship when he saw it. Moreover, he was articulate about art: he could tell artists specifically what to do to improve their work and make it acceptable to the magazine. When a drawing amused him during the art conference, he chuckled; and he often gave little lectures on art appreciation. James Thurber, assessing Irvin's contribution to the magazine in *The Years with Ross*, says unequivocally that Irvin "did more to develop the style and excellence of *New Yorker* drawings and covers than anyone else, and was the main and shining reason that the magazine's comic art in the first two years was far superior to its humorous prose" (p. 42). Because the *New Yorker* style of cartoon has set the pace for American magazine cartooning since the early 1930s, Irvin looms large in the history of the medium as a major influence.

Irvin continued to preside at these weekly meetings until Ross died in 1951; shortly after that, the artist feuded with the new management and stopped doing work regularly, although he retained his putative position until he retired because of ill health in 1955. He had lived in Newton, Connecticut, commuting to New York for most of his career. In 1966 he moved permanently to a home he had purchased in 1948 in Estate Le Grange near Fredicksted, the Virgin Islands, where he died after suffering several strokes.

• Virtually all of the substantial information on Rea Irvin is contained in *The World Encyclopedia of Cartoons* and in books about Harold Ross and the history of the *New Yorker*. See Jane Grant, *Ross, the New Yorker and Me* (1968), Dale Kramer, *Ross and the New Yorker* (1952), James Thurber, *The Years with Ross* (1959), and Brendan Gill, *Here at the New Yorker* (1975). The obituary in the *New York Times*, 29 May 1972, adds very little to what is rehearsed in these books.

ROBERT C. HARVEY

IRVINE, James (4 Aug. 1735–28 Apr. 1819), revolutionary war general and Pennsylvania state legislator, was born in Philadelphia, Pennsylvania, the son of George Irvine and Mary Rush. His father emigrated from Ireland, and his mother was a distant cousin of Benjamin Rush. James was not related to his contemporary, General William Irvine. He became a hatter in Philadelphia and held no local political office before 1775. Irvine obtained a commission in the Pennsylvania militia in 1760 and reached the rank of captain in 1763. He served on Colonel Henry Bouquet's expedition against Pontiac's uprising in 1764. Irvine became a delegate to the Pennsylvania Provincial Conference in 1775 but forsook that for military action.

He was commissioned a lieutenant colonel in the Continental army in November 1775 and saw action in Virginia and on the Canada expedition. Unhappy because he was not promoted to general, Irvine resigned his commission in June 1777 but was soon appointed brigadier general in the Pennsylvania militia. He commanded a brigade of militia under General John Armstrong at the battle of Germantown in October 1777. When George Washington sought his generals' advice in November and December 1777 about whether and where to go into winter quarters, Irvine replied that unless substantial militia support appeared, the army should take up winter quarters somewhere west of the Schuylkill River, twenty to thirty miles from Philadelphia, to threaten any British incursions. Nearly all other generals advised Washington to canton the army in buildings in separated, distant, or indefensible towns. Irvine argued that the army could build huts for shelter; the officers could also take the opportunity to drill and discipline the troops. It was Irvine's advice and that of William Alexander, Lord Stirling, that Washington followed in quartering at Valley Forge.

On 5 December 1777, when Sir William Howe led nearly his whole army out of Philadelphia to Chestnut Hill, hoping to lure Washington's inferior force to engage him, Washington sent Irvine and 600 of the Pennsylvania militia out as skirmishers. His militia detachment proved to be too weak to repel the British, and in heavy fighting, as the militia was forced back, Irvine was wounded and captured. Whether the militia ran away, leaving their general to his fate, is a debated point. As a prisoner, Irvine vainly sought exchange. Finally released in 1781, he received from the state in 1782 a disability pension of $62 specie per month. He had lost three left fingers and had suffered a neck injury in the Chestnut Hill skirmish.

Irvine entered politics in October 1781 when he ran as a Constitutionalist for election from Philadelphia to the assembly, but he was defeated. The next year he won a three-year term on the Supreme Executive Council and in 1784 became its vice president under President John Dickinson. After his term expired in 1785 he won an assembly seat for a one-year term. The Constitutionalists lost support in 1786, and Irvine's political career was over. He was commissioned a Pennsylvania major general in 1782, a post he held until 1793.

• For biographical information, see scattered references in the *Pennsylvania Magazine of History and Biography* 1 (1877): 44–54; 3 (1879): 197; 5 (1881): 269–70; 6 (1882): 98, 125; 10 (1886): 160; 14 (1890): 275; 17 (1893): 161, 325–35, 421; 18 (1894): 340–42; 19 (1895): 75; 24 (1900): 232–33, 392; 26 (1902): 107; 27 (1903): 121; 39 (1915): 379; 42 (1918): 276; 56 (1932): 246; and 60 (1936): 42. For Irvine's reports to Washington, see Worthington C. Ford, "Defenses of Philadelphia in 1777," *Pennsylvania Magazine of History and Biography* 20 (1896): 106–7, 402–3; 21 (1897): 68, 82. For other military details, see Christopher Ward, *The War of the Revolution*, vol. 1 (1952); John S. Pancake, *1777: The Year of the Hangman* (1977); James T. Flexner, *George Washington*, vol. 2 (1968); and Douglas S. Freeman, *George Washington*, vol. 4 (1951). For political details, see Robert L. Brunhouse, *The Counter-Revolution in Pennsylvania, 1776–1790* (1942), and Jackson T. Main, *Political Parties before the Constitution* (1973).

BENJAMIN H. NEWCOMB

IRVINE, William (3 Nov. 1741–29 July 1804), revolutionary war officer and congressman, was born near Enniskillen, Fermanagh County, northern Ireland. The names of his parents are unknown. His ancestors emigrated from Scotland. Irvine attended grammar school at Enniskillen and is believed to have enrolled in Trinity College, Dublin, but his name was not entered into the Dublin University catalog of graduates. Irvine was commissioned a cornet of dragoons in the British army, but, quarreling with his colonel, he soon resigned. Irvine then studied medicine and surgery at Dublin University. He served as a surgeon in the Royal Navy during part of the Seven Years' War.

In 1763 Irvine came to America, soon followed by two brothers, one of whom was also a surgeon. The next year he settled in Carlisle, Pennsylvania, where he practiced medicine. Irvine married Anne Callender, daughter of Captain Robert Callender of Carlisle. They had ten children—five sons and five daughters; three sons became army officers.

Irvine was a delegate to the Pennsylvania Convention at Philadelphia in July 1774; this body expressed opposition to the Boston Port Act and called for an intercolonial congress. Irvine entered the Continental army, as colonel of the Sixth (later Seventh) Pennsylvania Regiment; Congress issued him his commission on 9 January 1776. He and his regiment joined the Canadian expedition commanded by General John Thomas and then by General John Sullivan. Irvine was captured during a surprise attack against a much superior British force at Three Rivers (Trois Rivières), on the north bank of the St. Lawrence River, on 8 June 1776. As a prisoner of war at Quebec he was paroled on 3 August 1776 but not exchanged until 6 May 1778.

Irvine resumed active military duty as George Washington prepared to leave Valley Forge. He fought at the battle of Monmouth on 28 June 1778 and was a member of the court-martial that convicted General Charles Lee for dereliction of duty at that engagement. Molly Pitcher (Mary Ludwig Hays), the heroine of Monmouth, whose husband was in Irvine's unit, was also a domestic servant to the Irvines in Carlisle. During 1778–1779 Irvine commanded a line of outposts in New Jersey, and on 12 May 1779 he was promoted to brigadier general. He participated in General Lord Stirling's unsuccessful attack on the British on Staten Island, 14–15 January 1779, and in General Anthony Wayne's futile attempt to seize the British blockhouse at Bull's Ferry, New Jersey, 21–22 July 1780.

On Washington's recommendation, on 24 September 1781 Congress appointed Irvine commander of the western military department, with headquarters at Fort Pitt. He assumed this new position in November 1781. Irvine fairly but severely exacted discipline from among the nearly mutinous troops at Fort Pitt. He was more sympathetic toward the rough pioneer settlers and hunters around the fort than were his predecessors. On 3 December 1781 he wrote to the president of the Pennsylvania executive council, "I had no reason to complain of the people for the refractory, ungovernable, loose manners generally ascribed to them. I assure you, sir, my pity for their situation is rather excited than wrath or indignation kindled." Not having enough troops himself, Irvine approved volunteer militia expeditions against the Indians in the upper Ohio country, which resulted in the massacre of innocent Moravian Indians at Gnaddenhutten on 8 March 1782 and then the defeat by the Indians of a force under Colonel William Crawford. In revenge for the massacre, the Indians tortured and killed Crawford. Irvine displayed little compassion for the Indians. In reference to the Gnaddenhutten massacre, he wrote, "Many children were killed in their wretched Mother's arms. Whether this was right or wrong I do not pretend to determine." However, with an eye toward public opinion, he cautioned his wife not to "express my sentiment for or against these deeds."

Irvine left his Pittsburgh command on 1 October 1783 and resigned from the army on 3 November 1783. From 1783 to 1784 he was a member of the Pennsylvania council of censors, the group that could recommend changes in the state constitution and could call a constitutional convention. On 26 March 1785 he was appointed to examine and select donation lands promised to Pennsylvania soldiers. He recommended that the state acquire the "Triangle" area fronting Lake Erie. Congress, by concluding a treaty with the Iroquois and settling claims of other states, eventually allowed Pennsylvania to purchase the 202,287-acre Triangle tract for seventy-five cents an acre. In 1786 Irvine was appointed one of the commissioners to settle accounts between the states and the Confederation government. He served in the Confederation Congress, 1786–1788, in which he supported internal improvements. In 1790 Irvine was a delegate to the Pennsylvania convention that brought forth a new state constitution. His other state service included that of commissioner to establish the boundary between Huntington and Mifflin counties in 1791 and to lay out the towns of Erie, Waterford, Warren, and Franklin, Pennsylvania in 1794. Elected on his second try, Irvine served in the third U.S. Congress, 1793–1795.

Irvine declined a federal appointment to lead military expeditions against the western Indians. During the Whisky Rebellion of 1794 in western Pennsylvania, however, he accepted a commission as senior major general of Pennsylvania troops under Governor Thomas Mifflin. Irvine, beforehand, had served as one of two commissioners appointed by the governor in an attempt to arbitrate a peaceable settlement between the whiskey insurgents and the federal government and had favored having President Washington suspend the collection of the whiskey excise tax until Congress was back in session, which the president refused to do. In 1798, during the Quasi-War with France, Irvine accepted command of 800 Pennsylvania troops ordered out by Congress; the crisis soon ended, and the new army quickly dissolved.

Irvine did not seek a second congressional term but, nevertheless, became an important operative in the gubernatorial and presidential campaigns in Pennsylvania, forming a close friendship and alliance with the state's Democratic-Republican party manager, John Beckley. As a presidential elector in 1796 he voted for Thomas Jefferson and Aaron Burr.

In 1800 Irvine moved from Carlisle to Philadelphia. President Jefferson, in March 1801, appointed him one of four intendants of military stores under the War Department. Irvine served as president of the Pennsylvania chapter of the Society of the Cincinnati from 1801 until his death.

Irvine died of cholera morbus in Philadelphia. Though never fully tested in the field, Irvine was regarded as a very competent, if stern, officer. In civic affairs he had a high sense of the public trust. An obituary in *Poulson's American Daily Advertiser* (1 Aug. 1804) said of Irvine, "In him neither disguise nor chicanery, superseded the honest integrity of the heart; sincere in his friendships and as sincere in his dislikes—he respected none but those he deemed worthy, and those he despised he shunned in silence."

• The Historical Society of Pennsylvania has substantial holdings of Irvine's correspondence and records: the Irvine Family Papers, the Irvine-Newbold Family Papers, and miscellaneous military records and orderly books. The Washington papers, Library of Congress, include Washington-Irvine letters. *Washington Correspondence . . . 1781 to 1783*, ed. C. W. Butterfield (1882), contains many letters between Irvine and military officers other than Washington. Small published collections include "Letters of Gen. Irvine to His Family," *Historical Magazine* 7 (1863): 81–83; "Letters of Gen. Joseph Reed to Gen. Irvine," *Historical Magazine* 8 (1864): 129–38; and "Extracts from the Papers of General William Irvine," *Pennsylvania Magazine of History and Biography* 5 (1881): 259–75. Among brief sketches of Irvine, see Charles W. Heathcote, "General William Irvine—A Trusted Pennsylvania Officer and Friend of Washington," *Picket Post* 67 (Feb. 1960): 6–14. For accounts of Irvine's western command, also see Butterfield, *An Historical Account of the Expedition against Sandusky under Col. William Crawford in 1782* (1873), and Edward G. Williams, *Fort Pitt and the Revolution on the Western Frontier* (1978). For Irvine and politics, see Kenneth R. Rossman, *Thomas Mifflin and the Politics of the American Revolution* (1952), and Edmund Berkeley and Dorothy S. Berkeley, *John Beckley: Zealous Partisan in a Nation Divided* (1973). Lucinda Boyd, *The Irvines and Their Kin* (1908), has information on the numerous branches of the Irvine family but does not establish the names of Irvine's parents.

HARRY M. WARD

IRVING, John Duer (18 Aug. 1874–20 July 1918), geologist, was born in Madison, Wisconsin, the son of Roland Duer Irving, a professor of geology and metallurgy at the University of Wisconsin, and Abby Louis McCulloh. During Irving's formative years, his father, a notable petrographer, was engaged in preparing the first comprehensive monograph on the iron and copper deposits of the Lake Superior region. When his father died, Irving, at age fourteen, decided to continue in his father's line of work. He enrolled in Columbia University in 1892 and received a bachelor's degree in 1896, a master's degree in 1898, and a doctorate in 1899. The petrographer J. F. Kemp supervised his doctoral research. His summer vacations were spent in geological work with vertebrate paleontologist Henry Fairfield Osborne in Utah in 1895, with Kemp in northern New York in 1896, and with Whitman Cross, a prominent petrographer in the U.S. Geological Survey, in the San Juan Mountains of Colorado. He also spent four months in the Black Hills of South Dakota on field work for his dissertation.

Irving joined the U.S. Geological Survey as a geologic aide in 1899, was promoted to assistant geologist in 1900, and to geologist in 1906. From 1903 through 1907 he worked for the survey only during the summer field seasons. In addition to his field work, Irving was on staff at the University of Wyoming from 1902 to 1903 as an acting professor of mining and geology. He left Wyoming in 1903 for an assistant professorship of geology at Lehigh University and was promoted to professor three years later.

Early in his career, Irving came under the direction and influence of Samuel Francis Emmons, the first person to introduce precise geologic study to the search for and exploitation of ore deposits. Irving met Emmons through his survey work, and the two men established a lifelong close professional association. They jointly published studies, including "Ore Deposits of the Northern Black Hills" (U.S. Geological Survey Professional Paper 26 [1904]: 43–222), which was one of Irving's most significant works on major mining districts. In this study, Irving completed the first published comprehensive geologic map and description and geologic interpretation of the Homestate Mine at Lead, South Dakota, one of the largest gold mines in the world. Another article written with Emmons was "The Downtown District of Leadville, Colorado" (U.S. Geological Survey, Bulletin 320 [1907]), a detailed preview of part of Emmons's second, definitive monograph on one of the most productive silver-lead deposits of North America. Emmons died before this work could be published.

In addition to his work with Emmons, Irving published many shorter articles on a number of mining districts in the Black Hills, southwestern Colorado, and Cuba. His theoretical work is limited to single studies on the origin of replacement deposits and localization of ore "shoots" in mineral veins. Not only did he write numerous articles, but Irving also edited *Economic Geology*, a journal established at the instigation of geologist Waldemar Lindgren. In 1905 the applied geologists of the United States, mostly mineral deposit specialists, felt the need for a journal, neither governmental nor academic, devoted to their special field. Irving was a natural choice as editor because of his direct experience in the field. Serving in this capacity for thirteen years, he was instrumental in setting the tone of what became the leading American journal devoted to mineral deposit geology.

Despite his involvement with the journal and his responsibilities as a college professor, Irving continued to work on summer surveys. In 1907 he was a geologist for the Alaska Syndicate run by N. Guggenheim Sons and J. P. Morgan and Company, the mining entrepreneurs most famous for developing the Kennecot copper mine. That same year Irving was appointed professor of economic geology in the Sheffield Scientific School of Yale University. Volunteering for the U.S. Army in 1916, he sailed for France in July 1917 as a captain in the Eleventh Regiment of Engineers. There, involved in the construction of railways, he came under fire. Later he was an instructor in mining at the Army Engineers' School, developing and teaching dugout construction. While on duty in Flanders, Belgium, Irving contracted "Spanish" influenza, which progressed to pneumonia and resulted in his death there.

Before he died, Irving was engaged in preparing Emmons's second monograph for publication. With the death of both Irving and Emmons, G. F. Laughlin finally published the work as "Geology and Ore Deposits of the Leadville District, Colorado" (U.S. Geological Survey Professional Paper 148 [1927]).

Irving, who never married, probably would have been a major contributor to mineral deposits geology. In his fourteen-year career, he contributed substantially to two monographic studies and set the principal journal in his field on its course. He was a fellow of the American Association for the Advancement of Science and of the New York Academy of Science and was a member of the Society of Mining Engineers and the Washington Geological Society.

• Biographical materials are limited to memorials, including J. F. Kemp, "John Duer Irving," *Science*, n.s., 48 (1918): 255–56; Kemp, "Memorial of John Duer Irving," *Bulletin of the Geological Society of America* 30 (1919): 37–42; and Waldemar Lindgren, "John Duer Irving: To His Memory," *Economic Geology* 13 (1918): 413–18. Obituaries are in the *New York Times*, 2 Aug. 1918; *Engineering and Mineral Journal* 106 (1918): 260–63; and *Bulletin of the American Institution of Mining Engineers* 141 (1918): 1–7.

RALPH L. LANGENHEIM, JR.

IRVING, Peter (30 Oct. 1772–27 June 1838), writer, was born in New York City, the son of William Irving, a merchant, and Sarah Sanders. Irving grew up in an austere environment colored by his father's strict Presbyterian principles, which had little lasting effect on him. In October 1785 he entered Columbia College but dropped out after three years without taking a degree. Although inclined toward the law, under pressure from his father he returned to Columbia, completed his M.D. in 1794, and opened an office in the same building as his brother William's business. After a short time he abandoned the healing arts for social and literary activities that were more to his liking. He became active in Masonry and held various offices in the order. He also participated in the activities of the Calliopean Society, a literary club devoted to the study of literature and the promotion of friendship.

In 1802 Irving was asked to edit the *Morning Chronicle*, a newspaper that supported the liberal principles of Aaron Burr, Thomas Jefferson's vice president, in opposition to the Hamiltonian Federalism of the *Evening Post*. When Burr ran for governor of New York in 1804, Irving started a short-lived paper, the *Corrector*, and with the help of his brother Washington, turned out abuse, invective, and satire against the Federalists and the Clinton Democrats. Caught up in the partisan political enthusiasm, Peter Irving ran unsuccessfully as a Burrite for the New York State Assembly. After Burr's duel with Hamilton, Irving continued to edit the *Morning Chronicle*, suffering the insulting personal attacks of rival newspaper editors like James Cheetham of the *American Citizen* and William Coleman of the *Evening Post*. Finally in December 1805 Irving was replaced, and he turned his attention to more decorous activities, such as the secretaryship of the American Academy of Arts and joining Washington Irving and George Caines in a translation of François de Pons, *Voyage à la partie orientale de la terre-ferme*.

In January 1807, after leaving behind aborted careers in medicine and political journalism, Irving sailed for France in the company of William Paulding, the future mayor of New York, to follow roughly the route taken by his brother Washington from 1804 to 1806. As Peter Irving observed, "I anticipate both pleasure & improvement from this excursion and flatter myself the time it occupies will be usefully as well as agreeably employed" (letter to Col. Richard Dodge, 7 Jan. 1806 [Yale]). As he traveled through southern France, Italy, northern France, and England, he dutifully recorded in his journals his reactions to the geography, people, and culture of these regions and showed his relief and pleasure at escaping the political turmoil at home.

On his return to New York early in 1808 Irving was greeted by *Salmagundi*, the satiric pamphlet series produced by his brothers Washington and William and by William's brother-in-law James Kirke Paulding. After its demise Peter and Washington began to plan a burlesque history of the city as an attack on the social pretensions and pomposities of its Dutch segment. Before the project was completed, Peter, as a partner in P. and E[benezer] Irving and Company, dealers in "whitehead, glassware, Epaulets, Sword Knots, Sashes, Hardware, Etc." (*New York Gazette*, 1 Mar. 1811), was sent to Liverpool by his brothers to look after the overseas aspects of the faltering family business. From his office in Liverpool he arranged for the purchase of English cutlery through the agency of his brother-in-law Henry Van Wart in Birmingham and for its shipment to New York. Owing to the political and economic tensions between England and the United States at the time and to Peter Irving's impracticality and misjudgment, the English operation was in desperate straits by 1815, when Washington Irving, a silent partner in the enterprise, was sent to Liverpool to assist his brother, who was suffering from arthritis and erysipelas. But Washington, inexperienced in business, was unable to rescue the firm, and in the spring of 1818 it was declared bankrupt.

Following the bankruptcy Peter Irving divided his time between Liverpool and his sister's home in Birmingham, nursing his ailments and whiling away his time in reading and socializing. Seeing his brother's success with *The Sketch Book*, he wrote *Giovanni Sbogarro: A Venetian Tale* (1820), adapted from a French story by Charles Nodier. Earlier he had used his knowledge of French to help his brother Washington with some translations, and later he would assist him with his researches in Paris and Madrid.

In August 1820 Peter Irving accompanied Washington to France. They stopped briefly in Le Havre to visit Reuben Beasley, an old New York friend who was now U.S. consul. Beasley, who was involved in a Seine River steamboat venture, encouraged the Irvings to invest in the project, which turned out disastrously for them, especially for Peter, who had borrowed money from Washington and his brothers in New York.

During his subsequent residence in Paris, Irving mingled with American and English visitors, coped with his increasingly severe headaches, and spent much time in desultory reading. As Washington Irving observed, "The kind of life he at present leads, is just suited to his taste & habits. Surrounded by books, with excellent libraries at hand, and the varied resources of a refined & elegant place like Paris to resort to when disposed to go abroad for amusement. He, however, is very domestic, and I think keeps too much at home" (*Letters*, vol. 2, p. 76). After remaining in Paris while Washington traveled to England and Germany, Peter was ready to accompany him to Bordeaux in the fall of 1825 to observe the wine-making process and to go with him to Madrid a few months later. There he assisted in the research for Washington's biography of Columbus by checking facts in the Spanish archives and in Obadiah Rich's library. After spending two years in Spain and suffering from incessant headaches, Peter returned to the hospitable environs of France. His needs were provided for by Washington, who directed his brother Ebenezer to set up a trust fund to provide him with a dependable annual income.

Peter Irving returned to the United States in 1836 and settled in with relatives in New York City until his death there two years later. His nephew John Treat Irving, Jr., acknowledged his interest and encouragement by dedicating *The Hawk Chief: A Tale of Indian Country* (1837) to him. As a bachelor Peter Irving had few obligations or commitments, so during his last twenty years, despite his physical pain, he lived a leisurely, uncomplicated life that suited his tastes and inclinations. In the eyes of some he was a failure, but in the eyes of Washington he was a reliable companion and trusted confidant who encouraged and supported him in times of trial and crisis.

• Few of Irving's writings survive. A collection of his letters is in Columbia University Library, with a few others scattered in repositories chiefly on the East Coast. Copies of his novel, *Giovanni Sbogarro: A Venetian Tale* (1820), are in the Boston Public Library and the University of Illinois Library. His surviving journals were edited by Leonard B. Beach et al. and published in 1943 as *Peter Irving's Journals, Edited from Manuscripts . . . .* Biographical information is in Washington Irving's *Journals and Notebooks* (5 vols.) and *Letters* (4 vols.) in the Twayne Edition, in Pierre M. Irving's *Life and Letters of Washington Irving* (4 vols., 1863), and in Stanley T. Williams's *The Life of Washington Irving* (2 vols., 1935). A useful study of Irving's source for his novel is Francis Smith, "Peter Irving, Translator of *Jean Sbogar*," *Franco-American Review/Revue Franco-Américaine* 1 (1937): 342–46.

RALPH M. ADERMAN

IRVING, Washington (3 Apr. 1783–28 Nov. 1859), author, was born in New York City, the son of William Irving, a Scottish merchant, and his English wife, Sarah Sanders, who had emigrated to America in 1763. A middle-class family of very modest means, the Irvings gradually prospered in the economic expansion that followed the American Revolution. In time the father's business, heavily dependent on imports from England and France, became the family business, in which his five sons were involved in varying degrees at various times. Irving was the youngest child, and his mother and three sisters lavished affection and attention on him in his early years. The father, however, a Presbyterian deacon and elder, dominated the family until his death in 1807, imposing on the household a strict religious discipline, which his youngest son strongly resisted. Although Irving was interested in literature from an early age, authorship in the United States was generally seen as at best an avocation. Thus in 1799 he began an apprenticeship with a lawyer, partly as an escape from the family business. But literary pursuits, a troublesome lung condition, and social distractions delayed his qualifying for the bar for several years.

He owed his start as a published writer to his brother Peter Irving, who, though nominally a physician, dabbled in literature, journalism, and politics. In 1802–1803 Peter's small newspaper, the *Morning Chronicle*, carried a series of essays written by Washington under the pseudonym "Jonathan Oldstyle," several of which satirized performances and audiences at the city's chief theater. Peter also edited the intensely partisan, though short-lived, *Corrector*, aligned politically with Aaron Burr (1756–1836), for which in 1804 Washington wrote numerous brief, unsigned, scurrilous but clever attacks on opposition candidates. In May 1804 he embarked at family expense on a two-year grand tour of France, Italy, Switzerland, the Low Countries, and England. His poor health partly prompted the excursion, but his brothers also recognized that his artistic talents (he could draw as well as write) warranted nurturing. Although he proved a somewhat casual tourist, too often content merely to socialize in polished circles, he did absorb enough European high culture that, when he got home, he passed or posed in New York as something of a cosmopolite.

Finally admitted to the bar late in 1806, he began, without enthusiasm, to practice law with his brother John. He also occasionally acted as agent or representative for the family in business affairs, his personal charm obviously an advantage as the Irvings' commercial contacts with older New York families multiplied. But he found plenty of time in 1807 to collaborate with his brother William Irving and another New York writer, James Kirke Paulding, in composing and editing the breezy pseudonymous *Salmagundi* (1807–1808). In this burlesque periodical the young writers unsparingly parodied periodical-essay conventions derived from Joseph Addison and Sir Richard Steele while also mocking the taste, manners, institutions, and politics of their readers'—and their own—narrow,

self-satisfied, pseudosophisticated world. They caricatured New Yorkers as furiously engaged in the momentous pursuit of keeping up with the latest fashions, and their scathing satire reduced the young American republic to a "logocracy" or government of words. There was no love lost for President Thomas Jefferson in *Salmagundi*.

It had scarcely ceased publication before Irving, this time with Peter, began planning what became slightly less than two years later the *History of New York from the Beginning of the World to the End of the Dutch Dynasty*, written purportedly by one Diedrich Knickerbocker. Peter went abroad before the book advanced very far, leaving Irving to write most of it. In the meantime, however, he suffered through the most painful ordeal of his life. He had fallen in love with Matilda Hoffman, the daughter of Judge Josiah Ogden Hoffman, an erstwhile legal mentor, who treated him almost like a member of the family. Matilda being only seventeen, her father would not consent to a marriage before his prospective son-in-law proved that he could support her. This meant becoming the judge's full-time law partner. Threatened with the curtailment of his literary life, Irving accepted the conditions, only to see Matilda overwhelmed suddenly by consumption. She died within a few weeks in April 1809. Irving was never to marry.

For solace he threw himself into completing *Knickerbocker's History*, which appeared in December. A monument of mock-erudition, it is perhaps his greatest book. As history, it is mostly exaggeration and invention, spurious by design. As humorous fiction, it is an odd coupling of sense and nonsense held together by the inspired contrivance of Knickerbocker, the rattlebrained scholar whose "history," left behind in a New York rooming house, is the text with which the reader must contend. Knickerbocker is vehemently opinionated and irrational—unless his self-contradictions are read as facetious. Blessed with Irving's verbal gifts, he expatiates wildly and interminably on almost anything and everything, especially the writing of history, but he cannot sustain a simple, straightforward narrative. His presentation of political controversies in Dutch New York doubles as satire on factional politics in the era of Jefferson, and his straining to wrest historic grandeur from the obscure exploits of his seventeenth-century Dutch ancestors casts an odd light on the new republic's urgent need to mythologize its origins. The burlesque creates an image of history as unending war and oppression, perpetrated by powerful leaders for glory's sake. Through it all Knickerbocker staggers vaingloriously to the end, finishing his book, as foolish—or canny—as ever, eulogizing Peter Stuyvesant as "a valiant soldier—a loyal subject—an upright governor, and an honest Dutchman—who wanted only a few empires to desolate, to have been immortalized as a hero!"

Although Irving earned literary recognition and a substantial sum of money from the book, he was still not ready to risk his future on writing alone. He accepted a silent partnership in his brothers' business, acting occasionally as its agent or lobbyist. He edited the *Analectic Magazine* for two years and served briefly as a noncombatant in the War of 1812. In 1815 he sailed on another European tour, but at Liverpool, his first stop, he found the branch of the family importing firm there in grave difficulties and Peter Irving, its manager, in poor health. For the next two years he worked as a bona fide businessman to stave off bankruptcy—but to no avail. It was the "soul-killing" drudgery of this experience that at last drove him to try professional writing. He proceeded, however, in a very businesslike way, canvassing the literary market and taking advantage of acquaintances with Walter Scott, Francis Jeffrey, the publisher John Murray, and other literary people. In response to new tastes, he shifted to a less caustic, at times wistful, humor and to a more direct kind of storytelling, aiming now to ingratiate himself with his readers rather than disconcert them.

The result, brought out in several installments, was *The Sketch Book of Geoffrey Crayon, Gent.*, a mildly romantic assortment of essays, sketches, and short fiction, diversely offering gothic excitement, sentimentality, humor (at times satirical), and musings on English history, literature, scenery, customs, and traditions. The whole gathering more or less reflected the personality, attitudes, and feelings of Geoffrey Crayon, an aging American bachelor rather like Irving, at times lonely, pensive, and bookish, charmed by England but seldom completely at home there. Applauded on both sides of the Atlantic, the book seemed to fulfill longings of Americans of English descent to know more about the old country, while English critics hailed Irving as America's first genuinely talented author, the first to write classic English prose. Furthermore he had, with the help of brothers and friends, circumvented the wholesale piracy of the work in either the United States or England by publishing and copyrighting it almost simultaneously in both countries. Suddenly he had a name that would sell books for the rest of his life.

From a literary point of view, *The Sketch Book* is most notable for "Rip Van Winkle" and "The Legend of Sleepy Hollow," often cited as the earliest examples of the genre now termed the short story—as distinguished from "tales" or "legends" largely dependent for interest on plot, mystery, and suspense. Both stories owe something to Irving's reading, at Scott's behest, in German folklore and romantic fiction. But they also stand as early examples of American local color writing, fondly evoking Hudson Valley landscapes, customs, and character types. Their "gothic" effects are only half-serious. In the end Irving's humor shrugs off both the twenty-year sleep of Rip Van Winkle and the "ghost" that terrorizes Ichabod Crane in Sleepy Hollow.

Commercially also *The Sketch Book* had far-reaching effects, catering, as it did, to the interests and desires of a rapidly expanding middle-class readership in the United States and Britain, the larger portion of which was female. Dignified but not pompous, alternately humorous and serious without being intellectually demanding, the book reinforced rather than challenged conventional notions. It seemed to belong to the home, soon to be idealized in America as "woman's sphere," the realm of love, nurture, and moral decency as opposed to the stressful male world of enterprise, the marketplace, and hard bargaining. Readers especially liked the Christmas sketches, in which a homesick Crayon finds refuge for the holidays at the ancestral hall of the amusingly toryish Squire Bracebridge, who keeps up seasonal rituals—eating, drinking, singing, dancing, and game playing—in the hearty old English way. This sequence helped touch off a popular revival of Christmas, later encouraged in England by such writers as Charles Dickens and William Makepeace Thackeray. In the United States ornate, lavishly illustrated Christmas gift-books targeted for the middle-class home appeared as early as 1825. Not unlike *The Sketch Book* itself, these annual miscellanies contained short pieces of poetry and prose appropriate for the season, many of them written by well-known American authors, including Irving.

His new style, at its best leisurely, unpretentious, wry, and half-ironic, was influential in America for several decades, as both *The Sketch Book* and Geoffrey Crayon were widely imitated. Irving himself eventually wrote four more miscellanies by Geoffrey Crayon or "the author of *The Sketch Book*." The first, *Bracebridge Hall* (1822), loosely structured as Crayon's extended stay at the hall for the wedding of the squire's son, seems unsure of its intentions. "The Stout Gentleman" is one of Irving's best stories. But, as though contemplating a manor-house novel, he added numerous characters drawn less from life than from English literature. No major action develops, and somewhat surprisingly, politics intrudes. Crayon, the American republican, voices regret at the growing social irresponsibility of the English landed gentry. A village "radical" who reads William Cobbett denounces May Day celebrations as inappropriate at a time when Englishmen are starving. Portrayed less sympathetically than in *The Sketch Book*, the squire's traditionalism comes to seem a vain beckoning toward the feudal past in the face of the commercial and industrial future against which he rails impotently.

Although Irving enjoyed being accepted in patrician society, his politicoeconomic position was less aristocratic than bourgeois. True, he often satirized the vulgar ostentation and spoilsport puritanical earnestness of upwardly mobile businessmen like Mr. Faddy in *Bracebridge Hall*. But two of the book's characters, both of middling rank, stand out as more substantial figures than either the squire or Faddy. The first, Ready-Money Jack, is a yeoman farmer in the neighborhood; the second is the title character of "Dolph Heyliger," a rambling peripheral narrative set in America, a ghost-adventure-success story. Both men are enterprising, self-determined individuals, by and large generous-spirited, and affable and informal in their dealings with others. Together they hint at Irving's politics of moderation and his somewhat unstable affiliation at various times with Burrite Democratic-Republicans, Federalists, Jacksonian Democrats, and Whigs.

His next major effort was a dismal disappointment. He had spent more than a year in Germany in 1822–1823, supposedly preparing a German "sketch book." But in *Tales of a Traveller* (1824) Crayon never gets to Germany, and to many readers his "tales" seemed at best weak imitations of German romantic fiction. Much of the book, like the one item that is now genuinely admired, "Adventure of the German Student," actually satirizes gothic conventions. But on the whole the humor went unappreciated, while bawdy innuendos in a few of the tales provoked charges that Irving had betrayed the trust of readers who revered him as a family author.

Deeply distressed by the reviews and uncertain about his future, he accepted a suggestion that he go to Madrid early in 1826 to translate a recently published collection of documents pertaining to the voyages of Christopher Columbus. He saw, however, that a good biography of the explorer, especially in English, was urgently needed and would be far more lucrative. Changing plans, he researched and wrote *The History of the Life and Voyages of Christopher Columbus* in less than two years—a remarkable performance by the onetime mock-historian. Based on an abundance of documents available in Madrid, the biography was authoritative enough that it remained useful to scholars throughout the nineteenth century. Its understanding of history is not profound, but it offers a protagonist of heroic proportions, whose short-lived triumph turned to tragedy and who was both acclaimed and vilified for exploits that changed the course of history. Irving did not suppress Columbus's failure as a colonial viceroy or his role in the ultimately genocidal subjugation of the Indians. His Columbus is still half medieval, as much quixotic visionary as protomodern enlightened realist, a servant of God as well as master of the Ocean Sea, bent on redeeming pagan souls and discovering the earthly paradise. Ironically this book projects more romantic intensity than any of Irving's purely fictional texts.

From then on he was to be less a writer of fiction than a historian, although the two genres tend to merge in his work. His stay in Spain lasted three and one-half years. There he completed *Chronicle of the Conquest of Granada* (1829) and parts of both *The Alhambra* (1832) and the inconsequential *Voyages of the Companions of Columbus* (1831). *Granada* is a literary curiosity, history conceived almost entirely as romantic coloring and fascination with late medieval chivalry and the exoticism of things Moorish or more generally oriental. It virtually reduces historical causation to preordained fate, on the model of Spanish and Moorish legends and ballads quoted in the text. While accurate enough as a minimal outline of a complicated sequence of events, it is quaintly presented as based on an ancient chronicle by a fictitious and fiercely bigoted monk, Fray Antonio Agapida.

The Alhambra, the best of the Crayonesque miscellanies after the original *Sketch Book*, partly fictionalizes Irving's few-weeks' residence in 1829 in the deserted ancient palace of the Moors overlooking Granada. He explores mysterious chambers and courtyards, strolls about the surrounding hills meditating on historic landmarks, and tells tales of Arabian enchantment and buried treasure. Living in an imagined past, the Crayon/Irving persona seems so serenely at home that his farewell to the Alhambra at the end becomes an exile from paradise, like that of Boabdil el Chico, the last Moorish king of Granada, driven from the palace—and Spain—at the end of *The Conquest*.

The reality that Irving left for was the post of secretary of the American legation in London, an appointment engineered by the New York politician Martin Van Buren, with much prodding from the Irving family. Capitalizing on his large number of English acquaintances, Irving proved surprisingly effective as a diplomat. Together with the success of *Columbus*, his service for the government quieted complaints at home that he had largely de-Americanized both himself and his writing. In 1832, after seventeen years abroad, he returned to the United States something of a national hero, only to rush off soon afterward on an extensive tour of the Mississippi valley and regions to the west.

Aware of the growing American interest in the frontier, Irving published in rapid succession "A Tour of the Prairies" (a volume in *The Crayon Miscellany* [1835]), *Astoria* (1836), and *Adventures of Captain Bonneville* (1837). The first is a colorful, amusing, and thoughtful account of his trek in 1832 into Pawnee territory in what is now Oklahoma, where his party encountered Indians, hunted buffalo, and traveled with frontiersmen and mounted rangers. The second is an account of the ill-fated effort (1810–1812) of John Jacob Astor (1763–1848) to establish a fur-trading post at the mouth of the Columbia River by sending out two expeditions, one by sea, the other across the Rocky Mountains. It is based primarily on voluminous documents put at Irving's disposal by Astor himself. *Bonneville* derives from a similar windfall, Benjamin L. E. de Bonneville's journal of his fur-trading activities and explorations in the Rockies, turned over to Irving after the two men met in Astor's office. Fundamentally factual, these books, especially *Bonneville*, romanticize the wilderness, highlighting heroic enterprise, for instance, and adding local color in the form of trappers' stories and Indian lore. All three of the western books were widely read. They solidified Irving's reputation as an "American" writer, even though his attitude toward western expansion and commercial exploitation of the frontier was by no means that of a shrill proponent of Manifest Destiny.

In 1836 he had established a home for himself and five nieces, whom he supported, in a picturesque old Dutch house that he called "Sunnyside" overlooking the Hudson River near Sleepy Hollow. Not yet entirely at ease in the new, aggressively democratic America, however, he accepted an appointment as minister to Spain and served with distinction from 1842 to 1846. Back in the United States in 1846, he resumed his literary career. *Oliver Goldsmith* (1849), *Mahomet and His Successors* (1849–1850), and *Wolfert's Roost* (1855), a collection of fugitive pieces, are among his weaker books. But in 1848 he began revising his earlier writings for an edition of his collected works, to include eventually texts he had not then completed. Published by G. P. Putnam, this venture, a landmark for an American author, proved highly profitable.

His final project, long contemplated, was a five-volume *Life of George Washington* (1855–1859), elaborately researched and agonizingly completed as his health failed. He lived long enough to see the last volume published, dying soon afterward at Sunnyside. The book was designed—incongruously, given its length—for both scholars and average American readers. It tended to reaffirm standard conceptions of the nation's most revered patriot, who, for Irving, was a nearly perfect hero. A country gentleman, a soldier, and a republican, motivated by civic virtue as well as a sense of noblesse oblige, he had served his country disinterestedly, carefully mediating, for instance, while president, between Jeffersonian and Hamiltonian extremes. Irving went to great lengths to make him a less remote, less glacial figure. Ironically, however, most Americans probably read the book, if at all, in abridged versions.

That Irving was the first American to earn a comfortable living by his writing is more than a historical oddity. He had grown up in a young republic rapidly becoming more democratic and commercial. With literary patronage virtually unknown, aspiring American writers who lacked independent means had to reckon with the marketplace. Irving showed other authors how to take advantage of consumer demands, but living in some uncertainty as to whether he belonged to literature or to what is now called popular culture, he strained to produce books rapidly while trying to satisfy simultaneously readers of various levels of sophistication. His talent had revealed itself early. *Salmagundi* and *Knickerbocker* fairly bristle with the spontaneity and exuberance of young writers not overly anxious about pleasing an audience. Of his later writings only a few stories and sketches now seem indisputably first-rate. But he wrote a number of salable books informed by the intriguing style and personality of one who had seen a good deal of the world yet was not exactly worldly. In spite of appearances, Irving remained a rather innocent American. He did not presume to know what the great world was all about, although first and last he had a lot to say about it in one form or another. He said it in admiration, amazement, amusement, mockery, sadness, disdain, and disgust—usually also with tolerance, sympathy, and good humor. Holding his own amid the vicissitudes of the book trade, he won at last a considerable measure of esteem for the profession of letters in the United States.

• Substantial collections of Irving's papers are housed at the New York Public Library, Yale University, and the University of Virginia. The reader interested in locating specific Irving documents is advised to consult appropriate sections of *The Complete Works of Washington Irving* (which includes his letters, journals, and notebooks), published in twenty-nine volumes under the general editorship of Henry A. Pochmann, Herbert L. Kleinfield, and Richard D. Rust (1969–1988). *Washington Irving: A Reference Guide* (1976), compiled by Haskell Springer, is an annotated bibliography of materials about the author that were published between 1807 and 1974. The principal biography is Stanley T. Williams, *The Life of Washington Irving* (1935). Edward Wagenknecht, *Washington Irving: Moderation Displayed* (1962), and Mary Weatherspoon Bowden, *Washington Irving* (1981), are briefer and more recent biographies. *Adrift in the Old World: The Psychological Pilgrimage of Washington Irving* by Jeffrey Rubin-Dorsky (1988) is a critical biography of the author in the crucial period 1815–1829. *The World of Washington Irving* by Van Wyck Brooks (1944) describes American intellectual and artistic life in the antebellum period. Pochmann's introduction to *Washington Irving: Representative Selections* (1934) provides detailed information on the literary and historical background of Irving's career. A special study is Walter Reichart, *Washington Irving and Germany* (1957). *A Century of Commentary on the Works of Washington Irving*, ed. Andrew B. Myers (1976), is a useful collection. Major critical studies are William L. Hedges, *Washington Irving: An American Study, 1802–1832* (1965); Martin Roth, *Comedy and America: The Lost World of Washington Irving* (1976); and Peter Antelyes, *Tales of Adventurous Enterprise: Washington Irving and the Poetics of Western Expansion* (1990).

WILLIAM L. HEDGES

IRVING, William (15 Aug. 1766–9 Nov. 1821), merchant, politician, and author, was born in New York City, the son of William Irving, Sr., a merchant and a deacon of the Presbyterian church, and Sarah Sanders. Their youngest child was the future author Washington Irving. Irving's father, from the Orkney Islands north of Scotland, and mother, from Falmouth, England, married in 1761 and immigrated two years later to New York City. The elder Irving read from the Bible to his family nightly and took them to three sermons every Sunday. When he was seventeen, young William Irving joined his father at the office; soon thereafter, he was a fur trader along the Mohawk River from 1787 to 1791. In New York City, he was active in the Calliopean Society, a literary club that met to debate, read papers, and develop friendships. In 1790 the group held a debate on the advisability of requiring men once they turned twenty-eight to marry or be heavily taxed for the public good. Irving took the negative side and lost. In 1792 he was elected the Calliopean's second vice president.

In 1793 Irving, by this time a leader among merchants on New York's East River dealing with foreign trade, married Julia Paulding, the sister of the future writer James Kirke Paulding, who while a teenager (in 1796 or 1797) lived for a time in their home and later became one of Irving's closest friends. (Paulding at one time described Irving as "a man of great wit, genius, and originality.") Irving and his wife had six children, one of whom, Pierre Monro Irving, was later of immense help to Washington Irving, his favorite uncle. Earlier, William Irving and his brother Ebenezer, a business associate, grew worried that Washington was consumptive and financed a grand, 22-month European tour for him (1804–1806). William Irving, however, required frequent written reports of his brother's activities and saw fit, on occasion, to criticize him for inefficient dilly-dallying.

In 1806 Irving helped establish a literary and social club called variously "The Ancient and Honorable Order," "The Ancient Club of New-York," "The Lads of Kilkenny," and "The Nine Worthies." The group included, in addition to William Irving, Washington Irving, their brother Peter, earlier the founder and editor of the *Morning Chronicle* (1802–1805), and William Irving's business associate. The membership was rounded out by Henry Brevoort, Peter Kemble and his brother Gouverneur Kemble, David Longworth, Richard McCall, Henry Ogden, Paulding, Frederick Philipse, and David Porter—obviously totaling well over nine in number. Many of these "lads" were or quickly became distinguished in society, business, publishing, diplomacy, and the navy. In town, they met at Dyde's Tavern on Park Row or in a porterhouse at John and Nassau streets. Out of town, they convened in Newark or—more enjoyably—at "Mount Pleasant," a Kemble country estate along the Passaic River just north of Newark. A rollicking publication resulting from these meetings was *Salmagundi; or, the Whim-whams and Opinions of Launcelot Langstaff, Esq. & Others*. William and Washington Irving and Paulding, probably the instigator, met in William's house to plan it. Coauthored by the three, it was published as a fortnightly serial from 24 January 1807 to 25 January 1808. Its announced purposes were to instruct the young, reform the old, correct the town, and castigate the age. *Salmagundi* combined witty characterizations, racy gossip, poetry, social commentary, and theater criticism, all in a style imitative of witty eighteenth-century British satirists. It featured three personae: in addition to the bachelor Launcelot Langstaff, Esq., Anthony Evergreen, Gent., was the fashion commentator, and William Wizard, Esq., was the literary critic. It is impossible to determine for certain which of the three men wrote each of the twenty numbers. But it is now thought that William Irving wrote all of the poetry and the Mustapha letters in number 5 and number 14 and probably the Mustapha letters in number 7 and number 9—Mustapha Rub-a-dub Keli Khan being a puzzled observer from Tripoli visiting New York. Mount Pleasant was the model of "Cockloft Hall," which figures as a locale in *Salmagundi*. Washington Irving dubbed William "Pindar Cockloft"; his club nickname was "the Membrane."

Irving supported the War of 1812 as an ardent patriot. In 1812 he helped prepare an important naval dinner; in 1813 he spoke effectively at the Democratic assembly, and when President James Madison and the Congress, short of money because of the war, authorized a $16 million loan to the United States, Irving and his partners subscribed $70,000; and in 1814, at a public dinner, he praised and toasted Commodore Oliver Hazard Perry and Captain Jesse Duncan Elliott for their Lake Erie victory over the British navy some months before. At the same time, however, Irving, as a jeopardized New York merchant, objected to the Nonimportation Act and lobbied for modification of its ruinous terms. In 1813 he defeated John Jay's son Peter Augustus Jay and was elected to the U.S. House of Representatives, where he served, rather timidly, until 1819. By 1814 he was also a partner in the firm of his brothers Ebenezer and Peter, was a leading member of the auctioneering firm of Irving and Smith, and was a director of the City Bank in New York. In 1816 his brother Peter, who had foolishly invested in shipping and mining companies, misread the domestic market and carelessly overpurchased British goods for import to the United States and resale; soon the Irvings were all in dire financial straits. In 1818 the Liverpool branch of their business went bankrupt, after which Peter remained in Europe and turned to literary pursuits there. In 1820 William Irving's property for tax purposes was assessed at only $8,000. He died in New York City of tuberculosis the following year.

William Irving, whose name is mainly associated with that of his famous brother Washington Irving, was a talented though minor writer, a loyal politician, and a canny, respected merchant of old New York.

• The bulk of Irving's papers are at the New-York Historical Society in New York City. Accounts of commerce during the War of 1812 are included in Walter Barrett (Joseph Alfred Scoville), *The Old Merchants of New York City* (1872); Rocellus Sheridan Guernsey, *New York City and Vicinity during the War of 1812–15 . . .* (2 vols., 1889–1895); Glenn Tucker, *Poltroons and Patriots: A Popular Account of the War of 1812* (2 vols., 1954); and John K. Mahon, *The War of 1812* (1972). Washington Irving's journals, notebooks, and letters shed light on William Irving, especially *Journals and Notebooks*, vol. *1: 1803–1806*, ed. Nathalia Wright (1969); and *Letters*, vol. *1: 1802–1823*, ed. Ralph M. Aderman et al. (1978). Marcel Heiman, "Rip Van Winkle: A Psychoanalytic Note on the Story and Its Author," *American Imago* 16 (Spring 1959): 3–47, sees William Irving as a surrogate father for Washington Irving after his father's death in 1807. In their introduction, Bruce I. Granger and Martha Hartzog, eds., *Letters of Jonathan Oldstyle, Gent.; Salmagundi: or, The Whim-whams and Opinions of Launcelot Langstaff, Esq. & Others* (1977), include discussion of William Irving's part in *Salmagundi*. Wayne R. Kime, *Pierre M. Irving and Washington Irving: A Collaboration in Life and Letters* (1977), concerns the relationship of William Irving's son Pierre and Washington Irving. An obituary is in the *New York Daily Advertiser*, 10 Nov. 1821.

ROBERT L. GALE

IRWIN, Agnes (30 Dec. 1841–5 Dec. 1914), educator and college dean, was born in Washington, D.C., the daughter of William Wallace Irwin, U.S. congressman and minister to Denmark, and Sophia Arabella Dallas Bache, great-granddaughter of Benjamin Franklin (1706–1790). She was educated privately. Irwin went with her family to New York in 1862 when the capital became unsafe because of the war and began teaching at Mrs. Ogden Hoffman's school. Summers were spent in a Philadelphia summer colony on Mount Desert, Maine.

Irwin was asked by S. Weir Mitchell in 1869 to take over the West Penn Square Seminary for Young Ladies and for twenty-five years remained "owner, chairman of the board of directors, headmistress, and the outstanding member of the faculty." The school, which was renamed Miss Irwin's School of Philadelphia in 1875, soon trebled in size and moved twice. Irwin brought academic rigor to the school curriculum and although not a scholar, was a brilliant teacher whose pedagogical obiter dicta were later published by her friend Agnes Repplier.

In 1894 Irwin was invited to become the first dean of Radcliffe College, a suggestion warmly endorsed by Harvard president Charles W. Eliot, her summer neighbor in Maine. Her acceptance led Radcliffe president Elizabeth Cary Agassiz to note in her diary "an immense relief" that she had persuaded such a seasoned educator to join the college. Agnes Irwin arrived at a critical period: Radcliffe had been recently incorporated as a degree-giving college, affiliated with Harvard, but was lacking a formal operating structure. Irwin brought to the deanship her long experience in the education of young women, exceptional culture, brilliance of mind, executive ability, and an assured presence. As dean she took charge of students, served on the academic board and board of trustees, and deftly steered academic policy without alienating the crucial support of Harvard. Irwin's role grew as President Agassiz's age and status as "honorary president" (1899–1903) led her to withdraw from college affairs. But Irwin's expectations of becoming Radcliffe's second president were disappointed when LeBaron Russell Briggs, dean of the Harvard faculty, was elected in 1903. However, the collaboration and mutual respect of dean and president continued as before.

Noting in 1897 that "the days of small things are over," Agnes Irwin established new priorities for Radcliffe. Her deanship (1894–1909) saw the growth of the endowment, the expansion of the student body from 255 to 457 students, the completion of the Radcliffe Yard, the purchase of a site for dormitories and playing fields in North Cambridge (1900), and the acquisition of the Greenleaf estate (1905). The Yard was reshaped by Arthur Shurcliff (Arthur Shurtleff) and a trio of neo-Georgian buildings was constructed: the gymnasium (1898), Agassiz House (1904), and the library (1907). Bertram Hall (1901) and Eliot Hall (1907) offered new amenities and opportunities for residential living that made it possible to attract more than local students.

Known for her conservative demeanor, Irwin was not popular with the undergraduates. She frowned on their robust athleticism, censored their reading and their plays, required correct attire, and forbade the wearing of trousers in dramatic productions, insisting on bloomers and herself measuring with a ruler the amount of leg visible. Her wit and conversation, however, won the admiration of many advanced students who came to know her better. Her objectives remained consistent: "The pride of Radcliffe has always been the instruction offered by [Harvard] college; to other colleges for women beautiful surroundings, splendid buildings, college life, . . . to Radcliffe large and liberal opportunities to learn and to teach." Irwin's valedictory report (1909) further refined this goal: "the destiny of Radcliffe is to be a college offering the best opportunities for advanced study to competent students, to be in short a graduate school of the highest type." Arrangements for graduate study were particularly favorable since graduates could enroll in most Harvard graduate courses, and their scholarship was published in the Radcliffe Monograph Series, considered, wrote Irwin, "the high water mark of scholarship in the colleges for women in the United States." The school awarded the A.M. degree from 1894 but delayed conferring the Ph.D. in anticipation that Harvard would grant its own degree to women. The Harvard faculty's vote (1898) not to do so, and concern that the absence of the Ph.D. would harm the careers of graduates, convinced Irwin and the Radcliffe board to award the Ph.D. in 1902.

Irwin contributed greatly to the community, serving as president of the Woman's Education Association of Boston (1901–1907), member of the Cambridge branch of the Woman's Auxiliary of the Civil Service Reform Association, and on a commission to investigate the condition of the adult blind in the Commonwealth of Massachusetts. Although without a formal college degree, she received three honorary degrees: from Western University of Pennsylvania, now the University of Pittsburgh (1895); the University of Pennsylvania (1898); and St. Andrew's University, Scotland (1906).

At her retirement in 1909, Irwin returned to Philadelphia. She did not renew her involvement in her school but traveled abroad extensively, served as president of the Head Mistresses' Association of Private Schools, and at the time of her death in Philadelphia, was engaged in raising funds for war relief.

Irwin was one of the most prominent women educators of her day. She had founded, and served as principal of, an eminent girls' school in Philadelphia. She had come to Radcliffe as dean when the college was still at an experimental stage and its relationship with Harvard unclear, and she left it on a firm foundation. President Briggs believed that no small part of Radcliffe's success was due to her, and the *Boston Herald* (28 May 1894) succinctly commented that "no man could have been so good and no woman better."

• There is a dearth of primary material in the Radcliffe College Archives and in the Agnes Irwin School, Rosemont, Pa. However, Irwin's letters are found in the papers of Elizabeth Cary Agassiz (Radcliffe College Archives); Charles W. Eliot (Harvard Archives); L. B. R. Briggs (in both the Harvard Archives and Radcliffe College Archives); M. Carey Thomas (Bryn Mawr College and on microfilm); and in many collections in the Schlesinger Library of Radcliffe College. Irwin's opinions about education and her policy at Radcliffe can be deduced from the dean's annual reports and her commencement addresses in *Harvard Graduates Magazine* 4, no. 13 (1895): 96–98 and in the *Radcliffe Bulletin*, no. 15 (Aug. 1909): 1–4. There are two brief addresses in the *Publications of the Association of Collegiate Alumnae*, 3d ser., no. 13 (Feb. 1906): 50, and no. 17 (Feb. 1908): 63–64. With Sarah Butler Wister, Irwin wrote an anonymous novel, *Brisée*, and edited a collection of brief lives entitled *Worthy Women of Our First Century* (1877), which was commissioned for the Centennial Exposition in Philadelphia.

The only book-length biography is Agnes Repplier, *Agnes Irwin, a Biography* (1934). The Radcliffe College Archives has a folder of clippings, and there are articles about her in the *Radcliffe Bulletin*, no. 14 (May 1909): 1–5; *Radcliffe Magazine*, Feb. 1915, pp. 57–59; and *Radcliffe Quarterly*, Apr. 1927, pp. 25–27. Joanne Loewe Neel, *Miss Irwins's of Philadelphia* (1969), describes the early history of the Agnes Irwin School. Several books contribute insightfully to an understanding of Agnes Irwin's role in the development of Radcliffe College: Lucy Allen Paton, *Elizabeth Cary Agassiz* (1919); Louise Hall Tharp, *Adventurous Alliance* (1959); and Helen Horowitz, *Alma Mater* (1984).

JANE S. KNOWLES

IRWIN, Elisabeth Antoinette (29 Aug. 1880–16 Oct. 1942), educator and psychologist, was born in Brooklyn, New York, the daughter of William Henry Irwin and Josephina Augusta Easton. Her father, a cotton merchant, provided a comfortable living, sending Irwin to Packer Collegiate Institute in Brooklyn and to Smith College (A.B., 1903). As with many Smith students of the day, Irwin became interested in the settlement house movement and in a career in social work. During the summer after graduation, she took classes at the New York School of Philanthropy (later the New York School of Social Work). That fall she began work supervising a playground (1903–1904) and then became a resident at the College Settlement on New York's Lower East Side. She also worked for a time as a freelance journalist.

Irwin's life's work, however, was in education, a field that she entered under the auspices of the Public Education Association (PEA). In 1911 she joined the PEA and became affiliated with its Committee on Special Children as a visiting teacher/psychologist. Strongly influenced by the views of Henry H. Goddard, adapter of the Binet intelligence scale, the committee sought to alert public educators to the needs of children deemed "defective." Irwin's work for that committee resulted in one of her early publications, "A Study of the Feeble-Minded in a West Side School in New York City" (*PEA Bulletin*, no. 21, 8 Dec. 1913).

Irwin's work took her into public schools, where she experimented with the new IQ tests in conjunction with the Board of Education's Department of Ungraded Classes. In 1916 she began an experiment at P.S. 64 in Manhattan to identify "superior children" and to help provide for their education. By 1921 the testing program had been extended to all children in the school, grouping them in homogeneous classes based on group-administered IQ tests. In the winter of 1921 the PEA began a small curriculum experiment in an annex to P.S. 61, in a building owned by the Children's Aid Society. Under Irwin's leadership over the next ten years, the site of this experiment was moved several times, from the annex to P.S. 61 proper and finally to P.S. 41, but it would always be called The Little Red School House. The number of students involved in the experiment was small, with a maximum of 267 students at P.S. 41, which had a total enrollment at the time of more than 2,500. During this period, Irwin studied psychology at Teachers College, Columbia University, and received the M.A. in 1923.

In 1932, facing opposition from educationally conservative segments of the Greenwich Village community, where P.S. 41 was located, the school's students' achievement levels were tested by the New York City Board of Education. Irwin had decided not to push reading and other basic skills in the early grades but rather to wait until the curiosity of the child was stimulated naturally by the curriculum. The test results were interpreted by many as demonstrating a slower rate of progress among The Little Red School House students, and the experiment was thus deemed a failure. Fueled by these results and the loss of support from the PEA because of the controversy and the economic limits imposed by the depression, the school was threatened with closing. Indeed, the public phase of The Little Red School House came to an end. A group of enthusiastic parents would not let the experiment end, however, and the independent phase of The Little Red School House began in the fall of 1932. Parents raised the money to pay rent and teachers' salaries, and tuition fees were instituted. Irwin remained its head until her death. The Little Red School House continues to thrive to the present. A high school division was opened in 1941 and was renamed Elisabeth Irwin High School after Irwin's death. It, too, continues to operate.

Throughout Irwin's work, two critical positions characterized her efforts. First, she had an early and abiding faith in the improvements scientific psychology would offer education. In particular, she argued that accurate measurement of the "mental capacity" of students was essential to better "fit the school to the child." In *Fitting the School to the Child* (1924), Irwin and her coauthor Louis A. Marks asserted that if "carried through early, the psychological classification has the value of a preventive measure. It makes it possible to keep bright children from marking time and to save dull ones from useless failure and discouragement" (p. 312). Yet they were also aware of their limitations: "All that these measuring devices can tell us is whether any individual is below, equal to, or above the statistical norm for his [*sic*] age or class. The scientific classification cannot pretend to do more than this" (p. 313). They warned against inappropriate use of the tests but indicated that the tests could provide essential data for the proper individualization of education. Second, Irwin was a staunch critic of pedagogy as it was then practiced. She thought it emphasized memorization rather than experience, abstraction and symbols rather than the realities of the child's life, and that it disregarded the interests and capacities of children by forcing subject matter on them before they were mature enough to appreciate it. Irwin and Marks conclude, "In short, . . . [it] has been built up to follow the development of a logical sequence from the point of view of the adult mind rather than to follow the development of spontaneous interests of the child" (p. 118).

In Irwin's school no direct academic instruction was introduced until the second half of the second grade. Before then, the curriculum was organized around direct experiences, projects, group work, and field trips that were aimed at keeping and developing childrens' interests and facilitating the development of their social relations. No one was left behind; all children experienced the same educational experiences and teaching methods. The development of the child's personality, of sound habits of thinking and acting, and of emotional security were seen as primary early education goals that, once properly established, would provide a firm basis on which to build.

During the 1930s and onward, The Little Red School House became widely known as a site of progressive education and was visited yearly by thousands of educators, parents, journalists, and others. Irwin, herself, was widely known in New York City and beyond through her writings and her work with the PEA. In a tribute in *Progressive Education* (20 [Feb. 1943]: 65), written at the time of Irwin's death by Lucy Sprague Mitchell, Irwin is eulogized as tough, resourceful, and vigorous, without a trace of pettiness. Even today her writing is contemporary, realistic, and practical.

The experiments Irwin undertook, although resulting in the establishment of a private school, came from a commitment to reform public education. In *The Little Red School House* (1942, foreword by John Dewey), Agnes De Lima, an educational writer who was associated with Irwin and her school and was also director of public relations at the New School for Social Research, asserted: "Our primary aim . . . has been to demonstrate how the type of education which we believe in can be applied to public schools. Therefore, we accept the ordinary public-school conditions. We have classes of thirty to thirty-five children to a teacher and we get along on a budget no larger per capita than that provided by the city" (p. 7).

Irwin was one of a number of New York women active in educational reform in the city, including Mitchell (founder of what became the Bank Street College of Education), Caroline Pratt (founder of City and Country School), and Helen Parkhurst (founder of Dalton School). These women had somewhat different views about education but all frequently worked together for progressive reform. With John Dewey and his daughter Evelyn, Lilian Wald, founder of the Henry Street Settlement, and others, they constituted an important force for reform of the city's schools during the first half of the twentieth century. For a time, Irwin chaired the Associated Experimental Schools, a group composed of Walden, City and Country, Hessian Hills, Manumet, Cooperative School for Teachers,

Harriet Johnson Nursery School, and The Little Red School House.

Through her own work Irwin was an influential leader in progressive education. With others, she had an impact on New York City education, though over time progressive education and her particular version of it lost support among the larger public. Support for the school she founded, however, remains strong.

From the 1920s to the 1940s Irwin was an active member of the Heterodox Club, a group self-identified as radical feminists. Located in Greenwich Village, the club was bohemian and experimental in nature, and its members included women engaged in many feminist and reform groups. Irwin and her long-time companion, Katharine Anthony, a widely published biographer of well-known women, were prominent members. Irwin and Anthony apparently adopted two (perhaps more) children, including at least one legally.

• No book-length biography has yet been published of Irwin's life nor is it known whether her papers have been saved. Good material about her is located in the files of the Public Education Association's *Bulletin* (later renamed *The Public and the Schools*). Irwin's work with the PEA is described in Sol Cohen, *Progressives and Urban School Reform: The Public Education Association of New York City, 1895–1954* (1964). She is also frequently mentioned in Joyce Antler, *Lucy Sprague Mitchell: The Making of A Modern Woman* (1987). Her personal life and relationship with Katharine Anthony receive some attention in Judith Schwartz's *Radical Feminists of Heterodoxy: Greenwich Village, 1912–1940* (1982; rev. ed., 1986). Obituaries appear in the *New York Herald Tribune* and the *New York Times*, both 17 Oct. 1942.

FLOYD M. HAMMACK

IRWIN, George Le Roy (26 Apr. 1868–19 Feb. 1931), army officer, was born at the old army post in Fort Wayne, Michigan, the son of Bernard John Dowling Irwin, a brigadier general in the U.S. Army, and Antionette Elizabeth Stahl. General Irwin was a veteran of the Civil War and Indian wars and a recipient of the Medal of Honor. Irwin attended private schools and supplemented his schooling through a trip to Europe that apparently increased an already existing knowledge of French and Spanish. In 1885 he received an appointment to the U.S. Military Academy.

Irwin graduated from West Point in 1889, ranking in the middle of a class that produced a dozen general officers during World War I. He was commissioned a second lieutenant in the artillery with assignments in the Fifth and Third Field Artillery Regiments during the first three years of his career. In 1892 he married Maria Elizabeth Barker; they had three children. Two years later he graduated from the artillery school at Fort Monroe, Virginia, and served as an artillery officer at various posts in the United States.

During the Philippine insurrection, 1899–1901, Irwin temporarily served as assistant quartermaster of volunteers, then chief quartermaster for the First and Fourth Districts of southern Luzon. Almost two months of his service in the Philippines were spent in an army hospital in Manila because of illness. When the United States sent an expeditionary force to Cuba in 1906 to quell disturbances between two opposing government forces, Irwin was ordered to command a battery of the Second Field Artillery Regiment in what was known as the Army of Cuban Pacification.

From 1909 to 1910 Irwin attended the Army War College in Washington, D.C., then served as its assistant director for a year. Although he served for a time in the Quartermaster Department, he distinguished himself as a field artillery specialist. His expertise in this area led to his participation in the expedition at Veracruz, Mexico. His exceptional service in that campaign earned him promotion to the rank of colonel on 1 July 1916 and the command of the post of Corozal, Canal Zone. He stayed there until late 1916.

The United States entered World War I in 1917, and in preparation for the American Expeditionary Force's movement to France, Irwin was assigned to command posts and artillery units at Jefferson Barracks, Missouri, Camp Grant, Illinois, and Camp Mills, New York, before assuming command of the Forty-first Division on 10 December 1917. Two days later he sailed for France with the Forty-first Division, which upon landing was made a replacement unit. His initial assignment in France involved training artillery units at La Courtine, Camp de Souge, and Le Valdchon. In May 1918 he was designated to command the Fifty-seventh Field Artillery Brigade and remained with that unit until a few days before the armistice.

As a brigade commander, Irwin performed brilliantly on the battlefield. Beginning at Alsace and Verdun, he actively took part in all of the major offensives. During the second battle of the Marne, Irwin supported the Eighty-second Division in the capture of Juvigny and Terny Sorny and later in the assault on Côte Dame Marie and the Kremhilda Stellung. His brigade was withdrawn from the front lines after an exceptionally long phase under German fire. Irwin was placed in charge of the artillery school at Saumur until January 1919, then commanded the Fifty-seventh Field Artillery Brigade for the remainder of his overseas tour of duty.

Irwin returned home in May 1919 with a number of honors, including the Legion of Honor and the croix de guerre from the French government. The United States awarded him the Distinguished Service Medal for "the success of the division whose advance he supported, was due in large part to his technical skill and ability as an artillerist." After World War I he served four years as assistant to the inspector general of the army. On 2 March 1923 he was appointed a brigadier general and commanded the Sixteenth Infantry Brigade at Fort Howard, Maryland. The following June he was placed in charge of the field artillery school at Fort Sill, Oklahoma, serving there until 1928, when he was promoted to major general and assigned to head the Panama Canal Division.

Irwin traveled to Europe in 1930 to renew his health, which had been weakened by amoebic dysentery contracted nineteen years before in the Philippines. While on his leave of absence, he learned that he was reassigned to command the First Division at Fort Hamilton, New York. Returning to Panama on the Italian steamer *Virgilio*, he died off the Port of Spain, Trinidad.

• No known personal papers of Irwin survive. The principle primary sources for his military service are his War Department files in the custody of the National Archives in Washington, D.C., including a personnel file, 1889–1917, in the Records of the Adjutant General's Office (RG 94) and general correspondence relating to his assignments with the War College Division in the Records of the War Department General and Special Staffs (RG 165). Personnel information for Irwin's service in World War I and until the time of his death is in his military personnel record, Military Personnel Records Center, St. Louis, Mo. Additional information on his military career is George W. Cullum, *Biographical Register of the Officers and Graduates of the U.S. Military Academy* (1901); Francis B. Heitman, *Historical Register and Dictionary of the U.S. Army* (1903); and the *Official Army Register* (1899–1931). Information on his life outside the military can be obtained from obituaries in the *New York Times*, 20 Feb. 1931; the *Sixty-second Annual Report of the Association of Graduates of the United States Military Academy at West Point, New York, June 10, 1931*; and the *Field Artillery Journal*, May–June 1931.

MITCHELL YOCKELSON

IRWIN, Inez Leonore Haynes Gillmore (2 Mar. 1873–25 Sept. 1970), writer and feminist, was born in Rio de Janeiro, Brazil, the daughter of Gideon Haynes, a prison warden and social reformer, and Emma Jane Hopkins, a Lowell Mills girl (factory mill worker) before her marriage. After two years in Brazil the family returned to Boston, where Irwin grew up, genteely poor, with thirteen brothers and sisters. "As I look back on my life," she wrote in an article for the *Nation* (1 Dec. 1926), "it seems to be bound by the Boston *Transcript*, the Boston Public Library, the Boston Symphony, and the *Atlantic Monthly*." She graduated as valedictorian from Bowdoin Grammar School in 1887 and from Girl's High School in 1890. Her determination to go to college was postponed by her father's death and her mother's suicide one year later. Irwin taught elementary school in Charlestown, Massachusetts, until she saved enough money to enter Radcliffe College in 1896. She earned a two-year degree in English and graduated with honors in 1898. Two pivotal events occurred there: Irwin began a lifelong friendship with Maud Wood Park, who later was the first president of the National League of Women Voters, and she became a suffrage activist.

The woman suffrage movement shaped Irwin's life for more than twenty years. Introduced to women's rights by her father and two independent aunts, she wrote her first feminist essay, "Should Women Vote," in the eighth grade. As college students, when Radcliffe sponsored an antisuffrage speaker, Irwin and Park retaliated by secretly inviting suffragist Alice Stone Blackwell to address their fellow students. In 1900 the two "friends in feminism" cofounded the College Equal Suffrage League (CESL), the first American woman suffrage organization for college-educated women. They believed women owed their hard-won privilege to education to the pioneers in women's rights; taking the suffrage torch from that aging generation would repay their debt. The CESL quickly grew from a small, Boston-based organization into a national one. By 1908 the state branches merged to form the National CESL; with Bryn Mawr president M. Carey Thomas at the helm, the organization affiliated with the National American Woman Suffrage Association until 1917, when the league disbanded. When Alice Paul began the Congressional Union/National Woman's Party (NWP) in 1913—which used radical tactics to fight for a national suffrage amendment—Inez Irwin's militant spirit inspired her to join immediately. Her husband Will Irwin credited her with giving NWP president Alice Paul the idea of picketing the White House, labor union style, for woman suffrage. Inez Irwin later wrote *The Story of the Woman's Party* (1921), the official history of the organization's suffrage campaign; was associate editor of *Equal Rights*; and served on the NWP's National Council for decades. In her unpublished autobiography, "Adventures of Yesterday" (1950), Irwin described what the movement had meant to her. "This struggle, which engaged all my youth and much of my maturity, is a part of my life on which I look back with a sense of satisfaction, so soul-warming that I find no adjective to describe it. What women I met! What fights I joined! How many speeches I made! How many words I wrote! But best of all—what women I met! How I pity any generation of women who cannot know that satisfaction!"

Irwin's life embraced many social movements of the modern era. The first fiction editor of Max Eastman's radical periodical the *Masses*, she was part of the creative community of artists, writers, and leftists living in Greenwich Village in the 1910s. Her travels in prewar Europe led her to meet Gertrude Stein and other American expatriates, French impressionist artists, and Russian revolutionaries. From 1916 to 1918 she served as a correspondent in World War I, reporting from the French and Italian fronts for American magazines. Irwin was one of the earliest members of Heterodoxy, the renowned club for "unorthodox women" founded in 1912 by Marie Jenney Howe, and of Query, a luncheon club whose members included many leading women writers of the day. In 1931 she became the first woman president of the Authors' League of America; she also served as president of the Authors' Guild (1925–1928). From 1935 to its demise in 1940, Irwin chaired the Board of Directors of the World Center for Women's Archives, an organization begun by historian Mary Beard to collect and preserve women's historical documents.

A prolific writer, Irwin wrote forty-two books, including thirteen novels, five short-story collections, seventeen children's books, five murder mysteries, three nonfiction books, and numerous articles. She also authored a second women's history book, *Angels and Amazons*, published in 1933. Although not always critically acclaimed, she was an immensely popular writer who took pride in the economic independence her profession gave her. She published her first novel, *June Jeopardy*, in 1908 and wrote steadily through the next four decades. Her writings included children's books: the *Maida* series for independent-minded girls and the *Phoebe and Earnest* books for adolescents. "The Spring Flight" (1924) won the O. Henry Memorial Prize for best short story of the year. Several of Irwin's best novels address feminist themes. *Angel Island* (1914) is a feminist allegory about winged women whose all-female utopia is shattered by the coming of men, who marry them and clip their wings. *The Lady of Kingdoms* (1917) is a study of modern women in the radical circles of New York. In *Gertrude Haviland's Divorce* (1925) Irwin considers the financial vulnerability of wives; *Gideon* (1927) also deals with divorce.

Irwin herself was ambivalent about marriage. Observing her mother's burdens, she vowed to have a career and never to become trapped in domesticity and motherhood. "Marriages seemed to me," she recalled in "The Making of a Militant" (1926), "at least so far as women were concerned, the cruelest of traps." But she did marry, twice: journalist Rufus Gillmore in 1897 (they were divorced in 1913) and journalist William Henry Irwin in 1916. As Inez Haynes Gillmore she published two searching articles in *Harper's Bazar* in 1912, "Confessions of an Alien" and "The Life of an Average Woman," in which she described her feelings of alienation as a professional woman in a culture that relegated most married, white, middle-class women to the home. The world of the average woman was, she wrote, "a world which holds out to her no hope of real independence, personal freedom, or spiritual privacy; a world in which she lives in the chill of economy . . . a world . . . so silent that it is as though her sex were dumb." Never content with a limited sphere for herself, Irwin remained childless by choice (although she was a stepmother to one son through her second marriage) and paid for domestic services that freed her to devote much of her time to writing. Her marriage to Will Irwin, himself a self-proclaimed feminist and well-respected writer, was egalitarian and immensely happy. The Irwins lived in a century-old house in Greenwich Village for thirty years and summered at the coast in Scituate, Massachusetts. Their marriage ended with his death in 1948.

Adventurous, generous, and militant in spirit, Inez Irwin had a life rich in friends, creativity, and social conscience. She died in a Norwell, Massachusetts, nursing home. An energetic publicist of feminist ideas and movements, and a loyal NWP leader and activist, Inez Haynes Irwin represents the radical wing of the suffrage movement in its final decade, and the modern woman of the early twentieth century.

• Irwin's papers, including her unpublished autobiography, are in the Inez Haynes Irwin Collection at the Schlesinger Library, Radcliffe College. Some of her letters are in the Marjorie White Papers, also at the Schlesinger Library, and the National Woman's Party Papers and the National American Woman Suffrage Association Papers, both available on microfilm. Her essay about her family, "The Making of a Militant," originally published in the *Nation*, 1 Dec. 1926, was reprinted in Elaine Showalter, ed., *These Modern Women: Autobiographical Essays from the Twenties* (1978), pp. 33–40. Her own books and numerous articles in periodicals such as *Harper's Bazar*, *Collier's*, *Woman's Home Companion*, *Century*, and *Good Housekeeping* are also excellent resources on her thought and life. See also Mary K. Trigg, "Four American Feminists, 1910–1940: Inez Haynes Irwin, Mary Ritter Beard, Doris Stevens, and Lorine Pruette" (Ph.D. diss., Brown Univ., 1989). An obituary is in the *New York Times*, 1 Oct. 1970.

MARY K. TRIGG

IRWIN, May (27 June 1862–22 Oct. 1938), comedienne, was born Georgia Campbell in Whitby, Ontario, Canada, the daughter of Robert E. Campbell, a businessman, and Jane Draper. Georgia and her older sister Ada sang in the local Episcopal church choir and frequently performed duets for the entertainment of family friends. They attended school at St. Cecilia Convent in Port Hope, Ontario, until 1875, when their father failed in business and their mother, seeking to support the family, put them on the stage. The sisters made their debut at the Theatre Comique in Rochester, New York, on 8 February 1875, billed by manager Daniel Shelby as "May and Flo, the Irwin Sisters." They continued touring for two years, performing African-American dialect songs like "Don't You Hear Dem Bells?" Jane Campbell all but ran her daughters' careers for some years. "I never make a move without consulting her," May said at age thirty-four, "and if she doesn't like a song, that settles it" (*Dramatic Mirror*, 27 Feb. 1897).

May and Flo Irwin made their later celebrated debut at Tony Pastor's Broadway Theatre on 8 October 1877. They became fixtures at the theater, the popularity of the rather buxom May surpassing that of her sister, due especially to May's work in Pastor's burlesques of light opera.

The Irwin Sisters split in the fall of 1883, when May, who had married Frederick W. Keller five years earlier, was engaged for Augustin Daly's company. (She and Keller would have two sons together.) Daly's was the most celebrated American theater organization of the day, performing in London, Glasgow, Edinburgh, Hamburg, Berlin, Paris, Liverpool, and Dublin, in addition to the major U.S. cities. Its members included John Drew, Ada Rehan, Otis Skinner, Edith Kingdon, David Belasco, William Gillette, and James Lewis, among others. May became well known for her comic servant roles, notably as Lucy in *The Recruiting Officer* and Susan in *A Night Off*. She left the company (which had held her back to some extent due to Daly's rigid adherence to the stock system) following the death of her husband in 1886 and spent the next two years playing variety.

Irwin was a member of the Howard Athenaeum Company in Boston before going under the management of Charles Frohman, appearing with James T. Powers in *A Straight Tip* (1889) and with Henry Miller in *The Junior Partner* and *His Wedding Day*. Irwin

scored a major hit in *The Poet and the Puppets*, a travesty of *Lady Windermere's Fan*, in which she introduced Charles K. Harris's song "After the Ball." She subsequently appeared with Peter Dailey in *A Country Sport* (1893).

Irwin's first starring role was as Beatrice Byke in *The Widow Jones* in 1895. It was the kissing scene from this play that was filmed by the Edison Company and became known as *The Kiss*. Irwin is shown primping herself and looking quite embarrassed as she and her leading man, John Rice, embrace and kiss three times.

Irwin introduced or prominently featured many of the most popular songs of her era, including "Mister Johnson, Turn Me Loose," "A Hot Time in the Old Town Tonight," "The Bully Song," "The Frog Song," "I Couldn't Stand to See My Baby Lose," and "You've Been a Good Old Wagon but You Done Broke Down." "Songwriters used to come around to my dressing room after the show or up to my house or almost anywhere there was a piano, and they would play their songs for me," Irwin told interviewer Lincoln Barnett in January 1936. "I always listened. I never turned them away. And if I liked their stuff I would buy it, and the songs would be in my show the next night. They used to call me 'Do-it-now May Irwin.' I never liked to wait. If I wanted a song, I wanted it quickly. Sometimes, I would rehearse them right in front of the audience. I would just step down to the footlights and say, 'Here's a new song I just found. Now, if you don't mind, we'll try it out right now.'"

May Irwin's great flair for comedy, big voice, and cheerful personality made her one of the most popular and loved performers on the American popular stage. In 1899 Lewis C. Strang called her "the personification of humor and careless mirth, a female Falstaff, as it were, whose sixteenth century grossness and ribaldry has been refined and recast in a nineteenth century mould."

Irwin also starred in *Courted into Court* (1896), *The Swell Miss Fitzwell* (1897), *Kate Kip, Buyer* (1898), *Sister Mary* (1899), *The Belle of Bridgeport* (1900), *Madge Smith, Attorney* (1900), *Mrs. Black Is Back* (1904), and *Mrs. Wilson, That's All* (1906). She had put on weight by the time she married her manager, Kurt Eisfeldt, in May 1907, and when she began playing vaudeville in the fall of that year, *Variety* said that at her entrance at the Orpheum Theatre in New York in November she looked like a sister team.

Irwin alternated vaudeville with appearances in "legitimate" productions like *Mrs. Peckham's Carouse* (1908), *Getting a Polish* (1910), and *Widow by Proxy* (1913). She starred in a film version of *Mrs. Black Is Back* for the Famous Players Film Company in 1914, the exteriors of which were shot at Irwin's summer home in New York's Thousand Islands. In 1916, after President Woodrow Wilson and most of his cabinet had attended a performance of Irwin in *No. 13 Washington Square*, Irwin visited the White House, where the president named her his unofficial "Secretary of Laughter."

Irwin was also a good businesswoman who co-wrote and produced some of her many stage successes and invested wisely in New York real estate. (She once owned several blocks along Lexington Avenue.) She retired to her farm at Clayton, in New York's Thousand Islands in the St. Lawrence River, following her last Broadway appearance in *The 49ers* in 1922, but she returned to vaudeville briefly for "Old Timers' Week" at the Palace in 1925. Her farm served as a retreat for many stars, including her sister Flo.

Irwin agreed to come out of retirement for a three-night run of *Mrs. Peckham's Carouse* at the Clayton Civic Theatre in Watertown, New York, in August 1934. However, she withdrew at the last moment because of emotional strain due to the deaths of several close friends, including Maggie Cline, Marie Dressler, and Brand Whitlock.

May Irwin spent her last years raising trotters and pacers on her farm from April through November, traveling to the West Indies and to Central and South America, and attending plays in New York City. She died in her apartment at the Park Crescent in New York City.

May Irwin's career was fairly typical of the top stars of her day—the young debut, trouping, a successful debut in New York, further apprenticeship in a prestigious company, growing popularity, elevation to stardom under a top manager, and, finally, stardom under her own management. The growth of film study has tended to dismiss all stars of whom there is scant motion picture record, Irwin among them. However, the success of her contemporary Marie Dressler in sound films bears testament to the genius of comediennes of Irwin's generation. She was one of the most universally popular performers on the American stage for more than twenty years, when the theater was the popular medium of the day, and performers who could communicate the essence of a song, story, or character in the most endearing or interesting manner were those who attained success.

• "The Business of the Stage as a Career," an article in the Apr. 1900 issue of *Cosmopolitan*, was apparently produced after an interview with Irwin. Though of little value biographically, it nonetheless throws light upon the development of the American theater in the late nineteenth century, showing Irwin as intelligent, insightful, and remarkably objective—qualities that helped her as a businesswoman. Lincoln Barnett's interview with Irwin entitled "The Music Used to Go Roun' and Roun' When May Irwin Sang Forty Years Ago," in the *New York Tribune*, 26 Jan. 1936, shows her as unpretentious, a loving mother, and possessed, as might be expected, of keen humor. Janet Juhnke's article in *Notable Women in the American Theatre: A Biographical Dictionary* (1989) is well researched and covers the key elements in Irwin's life and long theater career. Anthony Slide, *The Vaudevillians* (1981), gives the impression that Irwin was primarily a vaudevillian; after 1888 her appearances in that medium were probably less frequent than those of Ethel Barrymore. The *New York Times* reviewed all of Irwin's New York appearances in the legitimate theater, and the *Times Index to the The-*

atre (1870–1919) is extremely helpful in compiling a chronologically accurate log of her stage work. Obituaries of Irwin were numerous and frequently quite lengthy.

HERBERT G. GOLDMAN

IRWIN, Robert Benjamin (2 June 1883–12 Dec. 1951), educator and long-time executive director of the American Foundation for the Blind, was born in Rockford, Iowa, one of twelve children of Robert Payne Irwin, a pharmacist, and Hattie Edith Chappell. When Irwin was three, the family moved to Vaughn, Washington, where his father opened a small drugstore that also served as the town's post office. Although his father supplemented their income by working in lumber camps, the family lived close to poverty.

Irwin was born with normal vision, but at age five he contracted inflammatory rheumatism, which infected his eyes. His vision had been damaged beyond repair by the time he received medical attention. Within a year of the infection he had become "dark blind," unable to distinguish light and form. In 1890 he entered the State School for Defective Youth (later the Washington State School for the Blind) in Vancouver; he was the school's first blind graduate in 1901. He continued his education at the University of Washington in Seattle, graduating in 1906. Irwin developed a variety of enterprises to support himself in Seattle, including selling stereoscopic equipment, operating a cigar store, and renting a house and subletting rooms. His experience as a boarding student in Vancouver and as an enterprising undergraduate in Seattle had profound effects on his later beliefs and programs. He believed, for example, that disabled students should be helped in their home environments rather than segregated in specialized institutions and that blind people could function well on their own in the sighted world.

With a scholarship from the University Club of Seattle, Irwin entered Harvard to study for a master's degree in history, which he earned in 1907. While there he decided on a career in education for the blind and spent the next two years studying education and working on a thesis, "The Administration of Schools for the Blind." He left Harvard in 1909 for Cleveland, where the board of education had decided to follow the example of John B. Curtis in Chicago to establish classes for the blind in the public schools.

Irwin served as supervisor of classes for the blind in the Cleveland public schools from 1909 until 1923. He organized classes in Braille, assigned readers and tutors to blind students and placed them in regular classes for sighted students for as much of their work as was practical, and made other innovations in educating the blind. To aid students who suffered only from impaired vision, Irwin established sight-saving classes using large-type books and specially lighted classrooms. He successfully lobbied the state legislature for subsidies for public school classes for blind and partially sighted students, and by 1913 he was traveling throughout Ohio establishing educational programs similar to the one he had begun in Cleveland. To provide sufficient materials for visually handicapped students, Irwin established the Howe Publishing Society for the Blind (1911–1931) to produce Braille materials and in 1920 set up the Clear Type Publishing Company to publish large-type books.

In working to help the blind, Irwin wrote in 1941 that "the primary objective should be the restoration of the blind to social and economic independence . . . either by the improvement of vision through proper medical care or . . . through vocational training, employment, and the instruction of the adult blind in their homes." Irwin endeavored to provide Cleveland's blind public school students with some experience and training in independent living through residential training cottages. "The pupils lived [in these cottages] three or four days out of every week for a year or more," Irwin explained in his autobiography, "so that they might receive training in table manners and other social niceties" as well as practical, gender-specific chores, such as shoveling snow and tending the furnace for boys and cooking, sweeping, and making the beds for girls. Instruction in these residential cottages was later deemed too costly.

Irwin's work in Cleveland introduced him to Mary Janet Blanchard, a sighted social worker and visiting teacher for the Cleveland Society for the Blind. They were married in 1917 and had one child, who died in infancy. His wife died in 1949.

Irwin soon gained a national reputation for his work in educating the blind. He spent the summer of 1914 helping psychologist Henry H. Goddard of the Vineland (N.J.) Training School for the Feeble Minded adapt the Benet intelligence tests for use with blind children, but their efforts were later discarded as unreliable. In 1918 the American Red Cross commissioned Irwin to survey existing state pension laws for the blind, resulting in *Blind Relief Laws, Their Theory and Practice* (1919; rev. in 1929). He also published *Sight-Saving Classes in the Public Schools* (1920).

In 1923 Irwin left Cleveland to assume two new posts. He was elected president of the American Association of Workers for the Blind, a position he held until 1927; more importantly, he became director of the bureau of research at the newly created American Foundation for the Blind in New York City. From 1929 until his retirement in 1949 he served as executive director of the foundation and was involved, as either a protagonist or a lobbyist, in all major public policy issues affecting the blind during the 1930s and 1940s.

As director of the foundation's bureau of research, Irwin undertook an investigation of Braille printing methods and promoted double-sided Braille publishing with interpointing to reduce the cost and bulk of Braille publications. With support from the Carnegie Corporation, the foundation developed the machinery for publishing in this fashion, reducing both the bulk and cost of Braille publishing by 40 percent. At the behest of the American Library Association, the foundation also studied library services for the blind. Finding these services inadequate, Irwin and his colleagues proposed that the federal government fund the distribution of books through select libraries across the country. The resulting Pratt-Smoot legislation adopted in 1931 appropriated funds to the Library of Congress for the publication and distribution of Braille books. Irwin also served as chairman of the American Uniform Type Committee and had a role in the London conference that established a uniform Braille system for use in the English-speaking world in 1932.

While these efforts made publishing in Braille less costly and increased the availability of such books, they did not help those blind persons who could not read Braille, and Irwin turned to the phonographic recording as a means of making books available to those who found Braille slow, difficult, or impossible to read. Again with assistance from the Carnegie Corporation, in 1932 the foundation developed the Talking Book, a long-playing spoken record, and successfully amended the Pratt-Smoot Act to include its production and distribution.

In addition to making literature more accessible for the blind, Irwin's legislative efforts also sought to improve their social welfare. In 1927 he successfully lobbied for interstate commerce legislation to permit a blind person and a guide to travel for a single fare on trains and buses. He had less success, however, with the provisions he sought to include for the blind in the Social Security legislation; the act that Congress finally approved established a separate relief category for the blind, but it failed to include many of the services Irwin proposed. In 1938 Irwin lobbied successfully for the Wagner-O'Day Act that steered federal business toward workshops for the blind, and that same year he was among the founding officers of the National Industries for the Blind. Irwin also was involved in planning for the care and rehabilitation of servicemen blinded during World War II, serving on committees set up for this purpose by the American Association of Workers for the Blind (1941), the U.S. Army (1945), and the Veterans Administration (1946).

Irwin's work on behalf of the blind was not limited to the United States. In 1931 he organized the first World Conference on Work for the Blind in New York City, and in 1949 he chaired the conference that laid the groundwork for establishment of the World Council for the Welfare of the Blind in 1951. In 1946 Irwin became executive director of the American Foundation for Overseas Blind, and he was awarded membership in the Legion of Honor by the French government in 1947 for his work with the blinded members of the Resistance.

"Always dignified and sometimes rigidly formal," according to one biographer, Irwin operated with a "high-principled indifference to popularity" and a "driving perfectionism." Proudly independent, he traveled alone on routine trips, using only a walking cane. In 1950 he moved back to the Puget Sound area of his childhood. He died in Port Orchard, Washington.

• The Archives of the American Foundation for the Blind in New York City contain materials documenting Irwin's work for that organization. His posthumously published autobiography, *As I Saw It* (1955), consists of the ten chapters he had begun for a history of the work for the blind and deals little with his personal life. Entries on Irwin are included in several of the standard biographical reference books, but the most useful overview of his life and career is found in Frances A. Koestler, *The Unseen Minority: A Social History of Blindness in the United States* (1976). An obituary is in the *New York Times*, 13 Dec. 1951.

KENNETH ROSE

IRWIN, William Henry (14 Sept. 1873–24 Feb. 1948), writer, was born in Oneida, New York, the son of David Smith Irwin, a bookkeeper and entrepreneur, and Edith Greene. Moving from the Finger Lakes country of upper New York in the late 1870s, the Irwin family joined the silver rush to Leadville, Colorado. Irwin's father tried lumber, hotel, and dairy businesses with little success, and in 1889 the Irwins moved to Denver.

In high school Irwin excelled in writing and graduated in three years. Diagnosed with incipient pulmonary tuberculosis, he was given the customary prescription of several months of roughing it, and he worked as a cowboy on cattle drives and as an actor in touring melodramas.

With the financial panic of 1893, it looked as if Irwin would be unable to attend college, but one of his high school English teachers loaned him money. He worked his way through Stanford University from 1894 until 1898, when he withdrew under the threat of expulsion for rowdiness. In 1898 he also secretly married another student, Harriet Sophia Hyde. The next year he was allowed to complete his studies and to receive a bachelor of arts in English. He was trying to decide whether to pursue a career in theater or one in journalism when a job as a writer and subeditor at the *San Francisco Wave* opened up. While working for the literary weekly, he freelanced for other publications and collaborated on a book of short stories, *Stanford Stories* (1900), with Charles K. Field.

When the *Wave* closed in 1900, Irwin became a reporter on the daily *San Francisco Chronicle*. In 1901 he and "Hallie" were married publicly, and in 1903 their only child, William Hyde, was born. Promoted, Irwin edited special editions and sections and was named Sunday editor in 1902. But desk work did not satisfy his desire for experience or for the publishing mecca of New York City. Neither did publishing two novels, contributing stories and articles to national magazines, and writing a play for the Bohemian Club. So in 1904 he ventured east without his family to join his brother Wallace, a journalist and humor writer, on the staff of the *New York Sun*. On general assignment, Bill became a star reporter. His most notable achievements included coverage of the 1906 San Francisco earthquake and fire in a marathon session at a desk in the New York newsroom and writing a moving obituary-tribute to San Francisco, "The City That Was." Irwin gained instant fame in the newspaper business.

Bored with daily reporting and wanting to try something that was more literary, in 1906 Irwin accepted the managing editorship of the premier muckraking magazine, *McClure's*. He soon became its editor, but he could not get along with the publisher, S. S. McClure, and in 1907 he resigned. He returned to freelancing for magazines and continued to write fiction and nonfiction books.

In the years before World War I, Irwin was divorced (1908) and saw the publication of eight books, including two biographies and two mysteries. He became best known as a muckraker for his fictional and factual exposés in the *Saturday Evening Post* and *Collier's*. His fifteen-part muckraking and historical series for *Collier's* in 1911, "The American Newspaper," set standards for newspaper criticism for decades.

In 1914 Irwin began covering the war in Europe for the *Saturday Evening Post*, the *New York Tribune*, and other publications. In 1916 he married writer Inez Haynes Gillmore; they had no children. Two years later he left reporting for six months to serve as chairman of the Division of Foreign Service of the Committee on Public Information. Three collections of his war correspondence were published, *Men, Women and War* (1915), *The Latin at War* (1917), and *A Reporter at Armageddon* (1918).

After the war Irwin lectured on the Lyceum and Chautauqua circuits. Opposition to war was his favorite topic in lectures, articles, and books, including *The Next War* (1921) and *Christ or Mars?* (1923). In 1925 he finished what is probably his best novel, *Youth Rides West*, a western set in his childhood Leadville.

Irwin's friendship with Herbert Hoover, which had begun during their undergraduate days at Stanford, led to two notable books, one a campaign biography, *Herbert Hoover* (1928), the other a history of propaganda and an attack on Hoover's detractors, *Propaganda and the News* (1936).

In 1942 Irwin completed his autobiography, *The Making of a Reporter*, which was criticized for not revealing enough of himself. During World War II he continued to write, though at a slower pace, and was dismayed to find that his expertise as a war correspondent was unwanted. The year 1946 brought a crowning achievement to his long career when his musical *Lute Song*, coauthored with Sidney Howard, opened on Broadway with Mary Martin and Yul Brynner in the starring roles. The musical was based on an ancient Chinese play (*Pi-Pa-Ki*) Irwin had seen in San Francisco about forty years before. An English-language version (without music) written by Irwin had been first staged in 1930.

After his death in New York City, Irwin's relatives and friends remembered him as a genial conversationalist, quick with a quip and always ready to join a convivial gathering, but his sense of humor rarely surfaced in his writing. In the media he was remembered as a friend of Hoover and as the author of more than thirty-five books and plays but most of all as a journalist with far-ranging interests.

• The main depository of Irwin papers, including his and Inez's diaries and letters, is in the Collection of American Literature of the Beinecke Rare Book and Manuscript Library at Yale University. Irwin's novels include two mysteries with the same female protagonist, *The House of Mystery* (1910) and *The Red Button* (1912), as well as *The Readjustment* (1910), *Where the Heart Is* (1912), and *Columbine Time* (1921). His nonfiction books include *Pictures of Old Chinatown*, with photographer Arnold Genthe (1908), *The Confessions of a Con Man* (1909), *Beating Back* (1914), *How Red Is America?* (1927), *Highlights of Manhattan* (1927), *The House that Shadows Built* (1928), and *Spy and Counterspy* (1940). His *Collier's* series is available in a facsimile edition as *The American Newspaper*, ed. C. F. Weigle and D. G. Clark (1969). A recollection by a friend of Irwin's is William Rose Benét, "The Phoenix Nest," *Saturday Review of Literature*, 12 June 1948, p. 36. For his biography see Robert V. Hudson, *The Writing Game* (1982). An obituary is in the *New York Times*, 25 Feb. 1948.

ROBERT V. HUDSON

ISAACS, Edith Juliet Rich (27 Mar. 1878–10 Jan. 1956), editor and theatre critic, was born in Milwaukee, Wisconsin, the daughter of Adolph Walter Rich and Rosa Sidenberg. Her father, a Hungarian immigrant, owned a shoe factory. Isaacs graduated from Milwaukee-Downer College (now a part of Lawrence University) in 1897, with a bachelor of arts in English composition. She was literary editor for the *Milwaukee Sentinel* in 1903. Following her marriage to New York lawyer and composer Lewis Montefiore Isaacs in 1904, and the birth of two of her three children in 1906 and 1908, Isaacs became drama critic for *Ainslee's Magazine* in 1913. She also wrote freelance articles for a variety of magazines, including theater reviews for *Theatre Arts* magazine. For her articles in women's magazines like the *Ladies' Home Journal*, she often used the penname "Mrs. Pelham."

After the birth of her third child in 1915, Isaacs served as chief of the Women's Publicity Department of the Liberty Loan Campaign from 1917 to 1918. She became an editor of *Theatre Arts* in 1918, at the invitation of the magazine's editor in chief, Sheldon Cheney. In 1922 Isaacs became editor in chief herself. She changed the magazine from a quarterly to a monthly in 1924 and made it in part a forum for the work of new artists, including playwrights Eugene O'Neill and Thornton Wilder, and dancer Martha Graham. She also expanded the magazine's coverage to include dance, mime, music, and art. Under her editorship, *Theatre Arts* was credited with upholding the "intellectual and artistic dignity of the theatre" (*History of the American Theatre*, p. 374). Isaacs's power as editor was augmented by her investments in the magazine, which made her its chief stockholder. In 1946, Isaacs retired, having become bedridden with severe arthritis. Two years later, *Theatre Arts* was sold, then combined with the *Stage* under the editorship of Charles MacArthur. The magazine was discontinued in 1964.

Isaacs's writing championed American theater. In her introduction to the 1927 collection *Theatre: Essays on the Arts of the Theatre*, which she edited, Isaacs said:

"Whatever else the theatre is in America today, it is alive. . . . The American theatre is more alive today than the theatre of any other country in the world." Placing theater in historical context and predicting its rise in industrial America, she continued, "The theatre, to a people who stand all day at attention before the mass and the machine, is bound to be an increasingly welcome release from the self." Isaacs edited two other essay collections: *Architecture for the New Theatre* (1935), for the National Theatre Conference; and *The Negro in the American Theatre* (1947). With *Plays of American Life and Fantasy* (1929), which featured eighteen plays that had previously appeared in *Theatre Arts*, Isaacs sought to make the essence of the theater more widely available. "In a country, like this great America of ours," she wrote, "where there are so few cities with living theatres, the man who wants to find a way to set himself free for an hour from every day's necessities can do no better than learn to read plays, or rather to see plays, reading them."

Along with her writing and editing, Isaacs carried out many other projects on behalf of the theater. Rosamond Gilder, who succeeded Isaacs as editor of *Theatre Arts*, praised her for her "unique and beneficial influence on the American theatre," with her understanding of its "economic as well as . . . aesthetic problems," and noted Isaacs's personal influence on a number of artists (*Oxford Companion to the Theatre*, p. 480). Isaacs helped create the National Theatre Conference in 1925 and was its head from 1932 to 1936. She also lobbied for the creation of the American National Theatre and Academy, which was chartered in 1935; she served as its first vice president. Her belief in the importance of the Little Theatre movement led to her involvement with the Works Progress Administration Federal Theatre Project in the 1930s. Her interest in black culture was evidenced by her cosponsoring, with Alain Locke, the New York exhibition of the Blondiau–Theatre Arts Collection of Primitive African Art and by the special issue of *Theatre Arts* on "The Negro in American Theatre," which she later expanded to an essay collection.

Isaacs's husband, Lewis, died in 1944. In 1951, she moved to a nursing home in White Plains, New York, where she died a few years later. A Theatre Arts Project for East Harlem was dedicated to her memory in 1958.

• Edith Isaacs's papers, including correspondence and other materials regarding both her personal and professional life, are at the Wisconsin Center for Theatre Research in Madison. The Billy Rose Theatre Collection at the New York Public Library houses Isaacs's Liberty Loan Campaign scrapbooks and a clippings file. In addition to editing the essay collections mentioned above, Isaacs wrote *The American Theatre in Social and Educational Life: A Survey of Its Needs and Opportunities* (1932). An obituary is in the *New York Times*, 11 Jan. 1956.

KATHY D. HADLEY

ISAACS, Samuel Myer (4 Jan. 1804–19 May 1878), rabbi and journalist, was born in Leeuwarden, Holland, the son of Myer Samuel Isaacs, a banker and teacher (mother's name unknown). Isaacs and his family moved to London when he was young during Napoleon's occupation of the Netherlands. He received his elementary and secondary school education in London and served for a brief period as principal of an orphan asylum.

Isaacs's talent as a teacher and administrator led New York City's largest Ashkenazic congregation, B'nai Jeshurun, to invite him to become their cantor and preacher in 1839. He served in this capacity for six years, until 1845, when a group of B'nai Jeshurun members decided to form a new congregation in New York City called Shaaray Tefila. Isaacs agreed to become their rabbi, a position he maintained until his death.

Like most Jewish immigrant clergy, Isaacs did not have rabbinical ordination. He was, however, unique among American rabbis of the time in his command of the English language, and he was one of the first Jewish congregational leaders to preach regularly in English, a talent that, in a community eager to Americanize, earned him respect and influence.

As the Jewish population of the United States grew, particularly during the 1850s, Isaacs emerged as a major figure in the communal leadership of New York City Jewry. He was one of the founders of Jews' Hospital (1852), which later became Mount Sinai Hospital. His philanthropic endeavors included assisting in the formation of the Hebrew Orphan Asylum, the Jewish Home for the Aged, and the United Hebrew Charities, all located in New York City.

Isaacs's concern with Jewish communal issues was not limited to matters pertaining to New York City Jewry but extended to Jewish issues throughout the United States. He was one of the organizers of the Board of Delegates of American Israelites (1859) and supported the first religious seminary for Jews, Maimonides College, established in Philadelphia in 1867. He also was active in the nationwide debate over Reform Judaism. During the 1850s, Reform congregations began emerging in the United States under the leadership of an articulate group of rabbis and lay leaders. Reform Judaism not only challenged what Isaacs considered to be the theological integrity of Judaism but also, from Isaacs's perspective, threatened the public institutions of Jewish life, which hitherto had conformed to Orthodox tradition. Isaacs became a vocal opponent of theological and ritual change, and, to this end, he established a national newspaper, *The Jewish Messenger* (1857), in which he advocated a traditional perspective regarding matters of Jewish law and custom. Nevertheless, although *The Jewish Messenger* advocated traditional Orthodox Jewish values in a religious environment that was becoming increasingly Reform, Isaacs always encouraged unity in the political and religious life of American Jewry.

Like most Jewish clergy of the northeastern United States, Isaacs opposed slavery in the South and supported the Union during the Civil War. Commenting on the death of Abraham Lincoln, Isaacs praised his commitment to freedom, unity, and peace: "Even when his most ardent friends assured him that the wicked should be pursued with evil, that the blood of thousands slain on the battle field, the cry of untold widows and orphans demanded vengeance, his answer was . . . let slavery be abolished, let our land be one of true freedom, and then we will have peace."

Isaacs died in New York City and was eulogized by the prominent Philadelphia Jewish minister, Sabato Morais.

• A few of Isaacs's personal letters may be found in the American Jewish Archives, Cincinnati, Ohio. He contributed several articles to the Jewish periodicals *The Asmonean* and *The Occident* during the years 1850–1856. His tribute to Lincoln is "The President's Death," in *Abraham Lincoln: The Tribute of the Synagogue*, ed. Emanuel Hertz (1927). For brief accounts of Isaacs's career, see Abram Isaacs, "Reverend Samuel M. Isaacs," *Magazine of American History* 25, no. 3 (1891): 210–14; *Jewish Messenger*, suppl., 6 Jan. 1882; Henry Morais, *Eminent Israelites of the Nineteenth Century* (1880); and Shmuel Singer, "Teacher of New York City Jews," in *The Torah Personality*, ed. Nisson Wolpin (1980). For a thesis on Isaacs, see E. Yechiel Simon, *Samuel Myer Isaacs: A Nineteenth Century Jewish Minister in New York City* (Thesis, Yeshiva Univ., 1974). Isaacs's achievements are discussed in Simon Cohen, *Shaaray Tefila: A History of Its One Hundred Years, 1845–1945* (1945); Moshe Davis, *The Emergence of Conservative Judaism* (1963); Alexander Dushkin, *Jewish Education in New York City* (1918); Israel Goldstein, *A Century of Judaism in New York* (1930); Hyman Grinstein, *The Rise of the Jewish Community of New York* (1945); and James A. Patten, *Lives of the Clergy of New York and Brooklyn* (1874). Obituaries are in the *New York Times*, 20, 21, and 23 May 1878.

MOSHE D. SHERMAN

ISELIN, Columbus O'Donnell, II (25 Sept. 1904–5 Jan. 1971), physical oceanographer, was born in New Rochelle, New York, the son of Lewis Iselin, a banker, and Marie de Neufville. Iselin expected to join the family's banking business and entered Harvard College intending to major in mathematics. Marine biologist Henry Bryant Bigelow turned his attention to oceanography. From childhood Iselin had enjoyed sailing, encouraged by a great-uncle.

During summers in his college years Iselin took long sailing trips in the Atlantic Ocean with boyhood friend Terrence Keogh. In his senior year he designed a 78-foot schooner, *Chance*, and had it built in Nova Scotia. For the next two summers, with college friends and Keogh, Iselin sailed to northern Labrador and to Bermuda, using equipment provided by Bigelow to make observations of the Labrador Current and the Gulf Stream. He received an A.B. at Harvard in 1926 and an A.M. in 1928. That year he had a 98-foot schooner built in Nova Scotia, which he and Keogh sailed across the Atlantic and back, again making observations. In 1929 Iselin married Keogh's cousin, Eleanor Emmet Lapsley. They had five children.

Woods Hole Oceanographic Institution (WHOI) was established in Massachusetts in 1930. Bigelow was its director, and he appointed Iselin his general assistant. His first assignment was to design a research ship. WHOI had the 142-foot auxiliary ketch built in Copenhagen, Denmark, in 1930–1931 and christened it *Atlantis*. Iselin accepted the ship there and was in charge of its maiden voyage to home base. That vessel served as a research ship for WHOI until 1966.

Iselin was appointed physical oceanographer at the institution in 1932 and, after Bigelow's retirement in 1940, became its director, a position he held until 1950. He continued to serve WHOI as senior physical oceanographer, was again director from 1956 to 1958, and then held an endowed appointment until his death. Simultaneously, at Harvard University he was assistant professor from 1936 to 1939, associate professor from 1939 to 1960, and professor from 1960 until his death. He was also a professor at Massachusetts Institute of Technology from 1959 until his death.

According to his colleague Roger Revelle, Iselin "never thought of himself as a professional scientist. . . . He loved the sea, in all its complexity, unpredictability, and wild grandeur, and he loved to study the ocean. . . .[He was] one of the creators of the modern multidisciplinary oceanographic institution, which takes the world ocean as its object of study." As director of WHOI, Iselin appointed enthusiastic amateurs and technicians to his research staff as well as trained scientists. A tall man, Iselin was considered shy and reserved by his colleagues but was also a leader and easily approached for advice.

Iselin's researches were primarily on currents of the Atlantic Ocean, including their distribution, physical nature, and chemistry. He directed a series of trips on *Atlantis* to carry out systematic exploration of the Gulf Stream in all seasons. The dramatic effect of this strong current had been described by Benjamin Franklin in 1768 and later from observations by American whalers. Iselin's trips measured temperature and salinity down to more than 4,000 meters, which provided many cross-sections in the northwestern Atlantic Ocean. Iselin's publications defined the Gulf Stream as a narrow, deep boundary between warmer waters of the Sargasso Sea and colder waters of the continental slope. He noted that, as a result of the earth's rotation, water in the boundary zone near the surface moves northeast with velocities to nine kilometers per hour in a narrow band. Iselin estimated the enormous volume of water transported in the northwest Atlantic, and he theorized on the relative importance of vertical and lateral mixing in water masses. His analyses of vertical distribution of water density proved useful to the U.S. Coast Guard in predicting the movements of icebergs in the north Atlantic.

As an administrator Iselin attempted to keep *Atlantis* at sea steadily, so he encouraged scientists from other institutions to use it. Maurice Ewing of Lehigh University carried out pioneering studies of the sea-floor sediments and underwater photography on *Atlantis* from 1935 onward. With support from the National Defense Research Council, Woods Hole Oceanographic Institution became a year-round facility for ocean studies from 1940 through World War II. Ewing's research group transferred to it, as did others.

An early project of Iselin and Ewing in the Caribbean was to determine why underwater sound waves seemed to diminish in the afternoon. Such sonar waves were just coming into use to detect submarines. With Athelstan F. Spilhaus, inventor of the bathythermograph, Iselin had first looked into this problem for the U.S. Navy in 1938. He and Ewing determined that the heating of surface water bent the sound rays downward and created an acoustic shadow zone.

Major projects on the transmission of sound in seawater, on fouling organisms, on underwater explosives, as well as on the development of undersea instruments were all directed by Iselin under wartime secrecy, and with his own participation in some of them. The scientists produced reports of great value to the navy, which led to a dramatic increase in its postwar support of oceanography.

Iselin became a dedicated member of the Committee on Undersea Warfare of the National Academy of Sciences (1946–1970) and of the NAS Committee on Oceanography (1957–1964). With Francis Minot shortly after World War II he founded the Ocean Resources Institute to focus on the problems of fishermen. Beginning in the late 1950s he took considerable interest in international problems related to the use of ocean resources.

Iselin received the Agassiz Medal of the National Academy of Sciences in 1943; he was elected to the academy in 1951. He was awarded the U.S. Medal of Merit in 1948, and from WHOI he received the Henry Bryant Bigelow Medal in 1966. With his wife, Iselin operated a dairy farm on Martha's Vineyard. Daily he sailed the nine miles to his office in a forty-foot launch named *Risk*. He died in Falmouth, Massachusetts.

• Iselin's papers are at Woods Hole Oceanographic Institution. His most important publications are "The Influence of Vertical and Lateral Turbulence on the Characteristics of the Waters at Mid-depths," *Transactions of the American Geophysical Union* 20 (1939): 414–19, and "Preliminary Report on Long-period Variations in the Transport of the Gulf Stream System," *Papers in Physical Oceanography and Meteorology* 8 (1940): 1–40. A biographical account is in *Oceanus* 16 (June 1971); the entire issue, with articles by many colleagues, is devoted to Iselin and lists all of his publications. See also Roger Revelle, "Columbus O'Donnell Iselin II," *Yearbook of the American Philosophical Society* (1977), pp. 61–71.

ELIZABETH NOBLE SHOR

ISHAM, Ralph Heyward (2 July 1890–13 June 1955), literary collector, was born in New York City, the son of Henry Heyward Isham, a banker and financier, and Juliet Calhoun Marsh. Isham attended Cornell and Yale Universities, where his interest in eighteenth-century literature was first aroused. He then pursued a variety of activities, ranging from journalism to big-game shooting in Malaya and Mexico. He also began his collection of antiquarian books.

In 1914 Isham married Marion Gaynor of New York City, daughter of Mayor William J. Gaynor;

they had one child. After a year the couple separated and were divorced in 1920. In 1915 he enlisted in the British army and was later commissioned second lieutenant. He rose to the rank of lieutenant colonel, serving on the staffs of Field Marshalls Sir William Robertson and Earl Haig. He did valuable work after the armistice restoring morale among disaffected troops, in recognition of which he was made a Commander of the Order of the British Empire (CBE).

After the war he returned to a business career in America, and in 1924 he married his second wife, Margaret Dorothy Hurt; they had two children. In 1925 he heard from his book-collecting friend A. Edward Newton that the bulk of Boswell's private papers, which were generally thought to have perished, had in fact survived. They were at Malahide Castle, near Dublin, seat of the sixth Lord Talbot de Malahide, Boswell's great-great-grandson. They had been seen by Chauncey B. Tinker of Yale, and A. S. W. Rosenbach, the New York book dealer, had tried unsuccessfully to buy them.

Isham was fired by the idea of acquiring the papers and making them available to the world. Rosenbach had been rebuffed because of the commerciality of his approach. Isham's strategy was more subtle. He had the advantage that, despite his American birth, his bearing and manner of speech were British, and he had a wide circle of distinguished British friends. He was strikingly handsome with great charm of manner and formidable powers of persuasion. Newton called him "a fascinating devil."

Isham, armed with an impeccable letter of introduction, managed to get himself invited to Malahide to see what was there. He was amazed by the richness and bulk of the material and determined to try to acquire it. After eighteen months of delicate negotiation he succeeded in purchasing all the Boswell papers, including the journal, then known to exist at Malahide for a price in excess of £35,000.

Isham then proceeded with his scheme of publishing the papers at his expense in a sumptuous private edition designed by Bruce Rogers and printed by W. E. Rudge, which eventually comprised eighteen volumes plus a catalog and an index. The cost was enormous, but Isham hoped that a profitable trade edition would follow that would repair the damage to his fortune.

For his editor, Isham approached first Professor Tinker, who declined, and then his friend T. E. Lawrence (Lawrence of Arabia), who also declined. Finally he chose Geoffrey Scott (author of *Portrait of Zélide*) on Newton's recommendation.

These were heady days for Isham, but problems lay ahead. In August 1929 Geoffrey Scott died suddenly, and Frederick A. Pottle of Yale was appointed his successor. In October 1929 the Wall Street market crashed. Subscribers for the private edition fell away, and Isham found himself in serious financial difficulty. Then, in 1930 Lady Talbot wrote to report the discovery of a mass of additional papers in an old croquet box at Malahide, including the original manuscript of

the *Tour to the Hebrides*. Isham was obliged to purchase this further find for £4,000 for the sake of completeness and to include it in the private edition at no additional cost to the subscribers. It was not until 1936 that the private edition and index were complete. Meanwhile, Isham's second marriage had ended in divorce in 1933 because of his "infatuation with non-income bearing manuscripts"; his home on Long Island and the cream of his book collection had to be sold; and to raise money he undertook an arduous schedule of lectures and a weekly series of radio broadcasts, "The Romance of Literature." However, he could now look forward to the profits from commercial publication.

Almost immediately his hopes were dashed by news of the discovery of a further mass of Boswell papers at Fettercairn House in Scotland. They included the London journal of 1762–1763 and more than 1,300 letters. These papers had been taken to Fettercairn by a descendant of Sir William Forbes, Boswell's literary executor. The question of legal ownership was referred to the Scottish courts. Isham claimed ownership as Lord Talbot's assignee in a lawsuit that dragged on for thirteen years. The papers were awarded in equal shares to Isham and the Cumberland Infirmary, who laid claim to them as residuary legatee of Boswell's great-granddaughter Mrs. Mounsey. Isham had to buy out the interest of the infirmary and meet the entire cost of the litigation before he could reunite the Fettercairn papers with the main collection from Malahide. Meanwhile, there had been two further important finds at Malahide, the first in 1937 by Isham himself when visiting Malahide and the second in 1940 in an old grain loft. The first of these finds was given to Isham by the Talbots without payment, but he had to find substantial funds to purchase the second.

By 1949 Isham was in dire financial straits, and it was clear that his collection, substantially complete at last, would have to be sold. Negotiations were concluded with Yale, who purchased the papers in July 1949 for $450,000, apart from a residue still at Malahide, which Isham helped to acquire for Yale in 1950.

Bereft of the papers, Isham lost much of his zest for life. His third marriage in 1937 to Christine, Viscountess Churchill, had ended in divorce in 1938. In 1949 he married as his fourth wife Sarah Lummus McAdoo. Her devotion and the success of his sons Heyward and Jonathan (by his second wife) were his chief consolation in his last few years of declining health. His last two marriages produced no children. He died at his home in New York City; but his great work of literary salvage had been accomplished, and the world of scholarship will be forever in his debt.

Isham's great achievement was to recover and reunite the private papers of James Boswell, biographer of Dr. Samuel Johnson. It was a task that obsessed him for most of the last thirty years of his life. It led to the breakdown of his second marriage and the depletion of his personal fortune to the point of impoverishment; but, as he himself remarked, when he first became interested in the Boswell papers he "grasped a bear by the tail and couldn't let go." The papers comprise a huge and important collection of eighteenth-century literary and historical materials that were hopelessly scattered after Boswell's death. But for Isham, they would never have been retrieved and publishable as a single collection.

• Isham's private papers, including those of Trumbull Securities Corporation, of which he was president, were given by his family to the Beinecke Library at Yale University. They include correspondence, topical files, business and financial documents, photographs, and printed material covering, inter alia, his British army service and his collecting and publishing of the Boswell papers. For published biographical information, see David Buchanan, *The Treasure of Auchinleck* (1974), F. A. Pottle, *Pride and Negligence* (1982), Herman W. Liebert, "Ralph Heyward Isham 1890–1955," in *Grolier 75*, ed. Alexander Davidson, Jr., et al. (1959), pp. 233–36, and Mary Hyde Eccles, "The Pursuit of Boswell's Papers," *Yale University Library Gazette*, Apr. 1992, pp. 141–49.

Isham arranged and paid for the editing and private printing of *The Private Papers of James Boswell from Malahide Castle in the Collection of Lt.-Colonel Ralph Heyward Isham*, ed. Geoffrey Scott and F. A. Pottle (18 vols., 1928–1934), together with a catalog of the collection by F. A. Pottle and M. S. Pottle (1931) and an index by F. A. Pottle and others (1937). He contributed a highly regarded article on Lawrence for *T. E. Lawrence by His Friends*, ed. Arnold Lawrence (1937). Obituaries are in the *New York Times*, 15 June 1955, and in *Newsweek* and *Time*, both 27 June 1955.

E. DAVID BUCHANAN

ISHERWOOD, Benjamin Franklin (6 Oct. 1822–19 June 1915), marine engineer, was born in New York City, the son of Benjamin Isherwood, a physician, and Eliza Hicks. His father died soon after the boy was born, and his mother married a civil engineer, John Green, in 1824. In 1831 Isherwood enrolled in Albany Academy, an exacting preparatory school that emphasized "mechanical pursuits" (Sloan, p. 6). At age fourteen, in his final school year, Isherwood was expelled for unspecified "serious misconduct."

Capable in mathematics and engineering, Isherwood soon found work. As a draftsman in the locomotive shop of the Utica and Schenectady Railroad for more than two years, he learned the characteristics of steam boilers and engines, as well as road and bridge construction. When that railroad was completed, he went to work for his stepfather, who was building the Croton Aqueduct to supply water to New York City. After its completion Isherwood worked for the New York and Erie Railroad under division engineer Charles B. Stuart, later superintendent of the Erie Canal. In 1842 Isherwood coauthored a pamphlet, *Description and Illustration of Spaulding and Isherwood's Plan of Cast Iron Rail and Superstructure for Railroads*, which was praised by Stuart and others. He next worked for the Lighthouse Bureau of the Treasury Department, for which he designed a lighthouse on Nantucket Island, Massachusetts; he also went to France to oversee the manufacture of lighthouse lenses of his own design.

As the shift began from sail to steam, the Engineer Corps of the U.S. Navy was established in 1842, and it interested Isherwood as a new career. To gain the required experience on marine engines he worked for two years for the engine- and ship-building firm of Novelty Iron Works in New York City. In 1844 he received an appointment as first assistant engineer in the U.S. Navy. After a year at the navy yard at Pensacola, Florida, however, he was demoted to second assistant engineer after oral examination by the newly-established board of chief engineers. In 1846, during the Mexican War, he served in bombarding and blockading the Mexican coastline and once joined a landing party that had a brief battle with Mexican soldiers. In 1847 he regained the rank of first assistant engineer. Isherwood married Anna Hansine Munster Ragsdale in 1848; they had several children. That year he again was sent to Europe for duty associated with lighthouses; he also gathered information there on the effective use of steam in engines. His promotion to chief engineer in 1849 finally made him a commissioned officer.

Charles B. Stuart, appointed civilian engineer in chief of the navy in 1850, promptly assigned Isherwood as his assistant in Washington, D.C. In a new design for the steamer *Allegheny*, Isherwood replaced the paddlewheels with a screw propeller and set the engines crosswise to the ship, with horizontal connecting rods from the pistons to the propeller shaft. The sea trials in 1853 were a failure because of inadequate bracing against the hull, which convinced Isherwood to design stronger framing in later work, but the system was considered a success. Known as the "Isherwood engine," it was much used during the Civil War. For the *Water Witch* he devised a new type of paddlewheel, the "Isherwood wheel," in which the paddles remained vertical for greater effectiveness and speed. This was the first use of the technique by the U.S. Navy. From 1854 to 1858 Isherwood served as chief engineer on the *San Jacinto* in the Far East.

Few engineers or mechanics had described the practical use of steam for power. Isherwood conducted carefully measured experiments on engines and summarized them in the *Journal of the Franklin Institute* during the 1850s. In 1859 he published the two-volume *Engineering Precedents for Steam Machinery*, which consisted of reports on ship machinery, comparisons with foreign ships, experiments on types of coal, and costs per unit of power. In the second volume he took issue with the unquestioning use of Mariotte's (or Boyle's) law for a perfect gas in the design of steam engines. This law stated that volume was proportional to pressure and that temperature was a constant. Using this assumption, builders of steam engines, for fuel economy, cut off steam injection early in the piston stroke so that expanding vapor would complete the stroke. Isherwood argued that enough steam was lost by condensation, leakage, and transfer of heat through the cylinder walls that efficiency was reduced.

As head of a board of engineers in 1860, Isherwood tested a range of values for the cutoff of piston stroke on the engine of the *Michigan*, operated for a month at constant speed with carefully measured coal and water. This established that the use of early cutoff of the steam injection distinctly lowered efficiency. The results of this first test on engine performance were praised by British physicist W. J. Macquorn Rankine and became accepted by engineers.

In March 1861 Isherwood was appointed engineer in chief of the U.S. Navy, just before the Civil War began. When ordered to remove the *Merrimack* from Gosport Navy Yard at Norfolk, Virginia, as that state threatened secession, Isherwood supervised the ship repairs at top speed. Then the commodore of the yard refused to let the ship sail, and after Isherwood's departure he scuttled all the ships. Confederate forces salvaged the *Merrimack* and built an ironclad vessel on its hull which faced the Union's *Monitor* in March 1862.

The daunting task of the Union navy in 1861 was to provide enough ships to blockade supply routes to the Confederacy along 3,000 miles of coast. Its fleet consisted of forty-two ships, many of them in distant ports. Needed were small gunboats for nearshore use, sidewheel double-ended vessels that would not have to turn around during river operations, medium-sized ships, and large ones. In a reorganization in 1863 Isherwood became the first chief of the Bureau of Steam Engineering, which was separated from the Bureau of Construction and Repair. Between 1861 and 1865 he designed machinery for forty-six paddlewheel vessels and seventy-nine screw steamers, with detailed specifications. His goal was to provide reliable and durable engines that could be operated by inexperienced personnel. He visited many engine-builders to determine their ability to produce satisfactory equipment. In 1862 he advocated building some large, fast, heavily armed, and armored ships, which he called "commerce destroyers," intended to prevail against the British and the French navies.

Isherwood also arranged for controlled experiments on engine equipment. In 1863 he published *Experimental Researches in Steam Engineering*, "crammed with statistics and spiced with a forthright statement of engineering philosophy" (Sloan, p. 93). Its second volume appeared in 1865, and both were later translated into six languages.

During the war civilian engineer John Ericsson, who had designed the ironclad *Monitor*, urged that the navy build more vessels of this type for coastal defense. Some members of Congress were enthusiastic about the design, but Isherwood was not. An engineer-turned-lawyer, Edward Nicoll Dickerson, obtained a contract for machinery of his own design for large gunboats. His ship *Algonquin* failed dismally in 1866 in trials against the *Winooski*, powered by Isherwood's machinery. Ericsson and Dickerson became bitter enemies of Isherwood.

The supercruisers Isherwood wanted were in construction from 1863 until after the Civil War. Isherwood and ship designer B. F. Delano designed one around the required engine space, in a square section,

and eliminated the ship's typical overhanging bow. The boilers and large engines, geared to the propeller shaft, were designed by Isherwood. As completion of the *Wampanoag*, the first of these, approached, the *Army and Navy Journal* attacked all new aspects of the design as "fit only for the scrap heap" (29 Dec. 1866) and viciously referred to Isherwood's "professional incapacity" (2 Nov. 1867). In sea trials in February 1868 the *Wampanoag* sailed well, ran economically on fuel, and reached the previously unobtainable speed of seventeen and three-quarters knots. It was the fastest ship in the world, not exceeded for fifteen years, and a forerunner in shape to modern vessels.

Criticism of Isherwood continued—from civilian engineers, from members of Congress, and from line officers who contended that large steam engines reduced space for sleeping quarters and that funnels interfered with sails. Isherwood was ousted as chief of the Bureau of Steam Engineering in 1869. He continued in the navy until his retirement in 1884, serving from 1869 to 1870 at Mare Island Navy Yard in California, where he conducted useful experiments on ship propellers. He then moved back to New York City, where he served on many engineering boards of investigation, and took a long tour in Europe. After retirement he received the rank of rear admiral. Isherwood died in New York City.

Isherwood's achievements were the controlled tests of steam equipment and the rapid design and construction of a steam-powered fleet for the Civil War. To do this he bypassed the usual procurement procedures, purchasing the tools for the navy to build its own engines, and incurred criticism. Eventually, however, many of his ideas became widely accepted. In 1904 the Naval Academy named for him its building of marine engineering and naval construction.

• A model of the *Wampanoag* was chosen by the Navy Department in the 1930s as one of six historic vessels representing stages in the development of ships to be exhibited at the David W. Taylor Model Basin. In addition to his books, Isherwood wrote about 150 articles on marine engineering. A biography that concentrates on Isherwood's years from 1861 to 1869 is Edward William Sloan III, *Benjamin Franklin Isherwood: Naval Engineer* (1965). See also a tribute, George W. Dyson, "Benjamin Franklin Isherwood," *U.S. Naval Institute Proceedings* 67, pt. 2 (1941): 1138–46. Obituaries are in *Transactions of the American Society of Mechanical Engineers* 37 (1915): 1510–11, and in the *New York Times*, 20 June 1915.

ELIZABETH NOBLE SHOR

ISHERWOOD, Christopher (26 Aug. 1904–4 Jan. 1986), writer, was born in High Lane, Cheshire, England, the son of Francis Edward Isherwood, a military officer, and Kathleen Machell-Smith. After a year (1924–1925) at Cambridge University, Isherwood went to London, where he was secretary to the violinist André Mangeot and his Music Society String Quartet, and he also worked as a private tutor. He enrolled as a medical student at Kings College, University of London, in 1928, the same year his first novel, *All the*

Conspirators, was published. In 1929 he left England to visit W. H. Auden in Germany and remained there, teaching English from 1930 to 1933.

The two books that derived from Isherwood's German experience, *The Last of Mr. Norris* (1935, published in England the same year as *Mr. Norris Changes Trains*) and *Goodbye to Berlin* (1939), were the foundation of his literary reputation and, more generally, of his public persona. The 1946 collection, *The Berlin Stories*, which brings together both of these books and *Sally Bowles* (1937), was adapted early in 1951 by John van Druten, who used Isherwood's own phrase, "I am a camera," for the title of the play he made from these texts. The 1966 stage musical and 1972 film versions, both known as *Cabaret*, adapted this material still further.

As Carolyn Heilbrun has noted, Isherwood's first two novels, *All the Conspirators* and *The Memorial: Portrait of a Family* (1932), share the misogyny of many of his contemporaries, who blamed women and particularly mothers for the smugness, jingoism, and oppressive familism that characterized British culture. Living in Germany in the years when Nazism was gathering strength taught Isherwood to analyze the institutional aspects of the social phenomena he despised, rather than blaming individuals, who were, in any case, likely to be the victims as often as they were perpetrators or beneficiaries.

By having two narrators with whom he is strongly identified use the same phrase, "I am a camera," Isherwood creates a metaphor for his own impersonal, disinterested approach. The phrase also suggests his interest in the act of the eye as both recorder and narrator. Queried about his avocational interests, he replied, "I was a born film fan," and he first came to the United States in 1939 as a screenwriter. (He became a naturalized citizen in 1946.) His screen credits include one British film, *Little Friend* (1934), as well as *A Woman's Face* (1941), *Rage in Heaven* (1941), *Forever and a Day* (1943), *The Great Sinner* (1949), *Diane* (1955), *The Loved One* (1965), *The Sailor from Gibraltar* (1967), and *Frankenstein: The True Story* (1973).

Isherwood's collaborator on the last of these projects was Don Bachardy, who was his lover from 1954 until Isherwood's death more than thirty years later. Isherwood's writing for the stage was also collaborative. With Auden, he wrote *The Dog beneath the Skin; or, Where Is Francis?* (1936), *The Ascent of F6* (1937), and *A Melodrama in Three Acts: On the Frontier* (1938), as well as adapting several other works; he and Bachardy also collaborated on the 1972 stage adaptation of Isherwood's novel *A Meeting by the River* (1967).

Much of Isherwood's most important work involved translating the events of his own life into fiction, as in *A Single Man* (1964), or into nonfiction, as in his early autobiography, *Lions and Shadows: An Education in the Twenties* (1938), *Kathleen and Frank* (1971), which combines selections from his mother's diaries with his own recorded memories, and *Christopher and His Kind* (1976), a memoir of the 1930s centering on his homosexuality. In his life as well as his writing, Isherwood rejected the militaristic, nationalistic, and Christian assumptions of his class and family background. His autobiographical writing is that of a pacifist, an internationalist, and a Vedantist (who was also affiliated with the Quakers).

It is also openly the work of a homosexual for whom the experience and politics of erotic relationships between men are central. The theme is present in his earliest novels, where the protagonists are "weak, lost" young men, and the effect is one of sad alienation. In later writing, from Berlin on, Isherwood mastered a range of tones for approaching homosexuality and other issues, becoming what he himself called "a serious comic writer." It was in this vein that, long before it became a modish catchphrase, he introduced the theory of "high camp" into his 1954 novel *The World in the Evening*. And it was in this spirit that he fought for gay rights long before there was an organized movement dedicated to that cause.

As a resident student of the Vedanta Society of Southern California from 1943 to 1945, Isherwood co-edited the society's magazine, *Vedanta and the West*; his coeditor was Swami Prabhavananda, with whom he also collaborated on several translations of key Hindu texts: *The Song of God: Bhagavad-Gītā* (1944), *Shankara's Crest-Jewel of Discrimination* (1947), and *How to Know God: The Yoga Aphorisms of Patanjali* (1953). Isherwood also elaborated on his spiritual views in *An Approach to Vedanta* (1963), the biography *Ramakrishna and His Disciples* (1965), *Essentials of Vedanta* (1969), the autobiographical *My Guru and His Disciple* (1980), and *The Wishing Tree: Christopher Isherwood on Mystical Religion* (1987), edited by Robert Adjemian; he also edited several volumes intended to introduce the modern western reader to Vedantic thought. According to Heilbrun, in Vedanta, Isherwood "chose a religion which did not claim to identify 'sin' or to judge him, a homosexual, differently from others. . . . [He] was drawn to Vedanta when his 'guru' declared that lust was ill-advised, but no form of lust especially damned."

Isherwood's work was honored by the Brandeis University Creative Arts Award (1974–1975), the PEN Body of Work Award (1983), and the Common Wealth Award for distinguished service in literature (1984). He died in Santa Monica, California. At the time of his death, he was working on a second volume of *Christopher and His Kind*.

• In addition to the works mentioned above, Isherwood published Bertolt Brecht, *A Penny for the Poor* (trans. 1937); *Journey to War*, with W. H. Auden (1939); *Prater Violet* (1945); *Vedanta for the Western World* (ed. 1945); Charles Baudelaire, *Intimate Journals* (trans. 1947); *The Condor and the Cows: A South American Travel Diary* (1949); *Vedanta for Modern Man* (ed. 1951); Bertolt Brecht, *Threepenny Novel* (trans. verse sections, 1956); *Great English Short Stories* (ed. 1957); *Down There on a Visit* (1962); *Exhumations: Stories, Articles, Verses* (1966); and *People One Ought to Know*, with Sylvain Mangeot (1982). In addition, Isherwood wrote an autobiographical record of a single month in his life, *October* (1980), illustrated by Don Bachardy. Biographies include

Brian Finney, *Christopher Isherwood: A Critical Biography* (1979), Jonathan Fryer, *Isherwood: A Biography of Christopher Isherwood* (1977), and John Lehmann, *Christopher Isherwood: A Personal Memoir* (1987). Articles on specific aspects of his life include J. Bloom, "A Stranger in Paradise," *American Film* 12 (Oct. 1986): 53–57, D. Robb, "Brahmins from Abroad: English Expatriates and Spiritual Consciousness in Modern America," *American Studies* 26 (Fall 1985): 45–60, and Stephen Spender, "Issyvoo's Conversion," *New York Review of Books*, 14 Aug. 1980, pp. 18–21. Spender's letters to Isherwood are published as *Letters to Christopher* (1980). An obituary by Carolyn Heilbrun is in the *Dictionary of Literary Biography Yearbook 1986*, ed. J. M. Brook (1986), pp. 230–34.

LILLIAN S. ROBINSON

ISHI (1862?–25 Mar. 1916), the last "Stone Age" Indian in California and, probably, in the entire United States, was a member of the Yahi people of northeastern California. He was encountered in a slaughterhouse corral in Oroville, California, on 29 August 1911, thirty-eight years after the last major Indian conflict in the state. When taken into custody by Sheriff J. B. Webber of Butte County, Ishi was naked save for a scrap of old wagon canvas, worn like a cape, and very weak from exposure and near starvation. Communication with him, other than in sign language, was impossible, although English, Spanish, and several Indian tongues—such as Maidu and Wintun—were tried.

When the story of the "Wild Man of Oroville" broke in San Francisco, University of California professors Alfred Kroeber and T. T. Waterman were immediately interested. They remembered the 1908 rumor of "untamed" Indians scattering before a surveying party in the Mount Lassen foothills. Waterman had subsequently tried to find the mysterious natives but had failed. Kroeber telegraphed the sheriff: "Hold Indian till arrival professor State University who will take charge and be responsible for him. Matter important account aboriginal history."

Waterman escorted the Neolithic Californian to San Francisco, where it became obvious that this "missing link" was a lone survivor of a primitive, and presumed extinct, subtribe of the Yana band, or tribe, the Yahi. California's first ethnographer, Stephen Powers, as early as 1874 had remarked on the Yana's determination to resist civilization "to the last man, squaw and papoose." The Yana and Yahi were then virtually exterminated by settlers avenging thefts of property and livestock and a few murders by the so-called Mill Creek Indians.

Kroeber and Waterman gave their charge a sanctuary in the university's Museum of Anthropology. The Yahi's rescue gave the budding science of anthropology a wealth of information. The Yahi had a name, but no one ever learned it. It was a quasi-religious custom of the tribe not to reveal one's name. So the professors dubbed him Ishi, meaning "man" in Yahi. Kroeber and Waterman picked up his language quickly, but Ishi, intelligent enough, was reluctant to learn more than pidgin English.

The story of Ishi's life was shocking. His doomed people had been hunted down like deer by whites. He had seen his people reduced by guns and disease from about 300 to 400 souls to just five individuals in 1908. When surprised by the surveyors, they had scattered, and Ishi never saw or heard of his fellow tribe members again. They simply disappeared. Apparently the sole survivor of his people and of Neolithic Native American life, Ishi was driven to the white settlements—and into the twentieth century—by hunger as game grew scarce in the chaparral of the volcanic canyons of Mill and Deer creeks. Thus ended what Ishi's biographer, Theodora Kroeber, called the Long Concealment.

In San Francisco, Ishi came to enjoy riding on ferryboats and streetcars and loved to shop and to roam the city, once he overcame his initial fear of crowds. When taken to a theater, he showed more interest in the audience than in the actors performing on the stage. But some aspects of civilization distressed him. He would never enter the Old Bone Room of the museum. He was frightened by the hospital's anesthesia because he believed that one's soul left the body during an unconscious state. And he was horrified by the dissection of cadavers in the medical school.

The University of California faculty protected Ishi from those who would have exploited him as a sideshow savage. He was found to be anything but savage and was quite the reverse of the dirty, miserable Digger Indian of white stereotyping. He was so concerned with cleanliness that he was put on the museum payroll as an assistant janitor. Gentle, kind, and warmhearted, he was more reserved than shy and welcomed (well-behaved) visitors. He patiently submitted to their photographs and even early motion pictures. He was particularly interested in visiting Chinese and those Caucasians who wore any sort of uniform. Ishi had few friends, but they were all very close: Waterman; Kroeber; Saxton Pope of the medical school; assistant curator Edward Gifford; the janitorial staff, museum guards, and preparators; and a Papago Indian, Juan Dolores, who liked to visit him.

Ishi was much better at showing than telling. He demonstrated his accuracy with bow and arrows, his skill at making fire with a drill, and his proficiency in napping (flaking) razor-sharp arrowheads from obsidian, flint, and even beer-bottle glass. He taught archery so well to Pope that the doctor later hunted lions in Africa with a bow and arrows. Ishi guided his new friends to his old hunting grounds in 1914 and there practically reenacted his life in a sort of extended pantomime. Kroeber scheduled special trips with him for an annual acorn harvest and a salmon run, extremely important events in aboriginal life. But World War I forced a postponement that became indefinite as Ishi's health declined.

A common cold brought on pneumonia that led to tuberculosis. Ishi was given the very best medical care but died. He was cheerful and content, stoically awaiting death without self-pity. The professors were devastated by Ishi's death. Waterman wrote to Kroeber, away in New York, "He was the best friend I had in the world." Kroeber ordered his colleagues to give their friend the last rites of his religion and to prevent any autopsy. "As to the disposal of the body, yield nothing, at all, under any circumstance. If there is any talk about the interests of science, say for me that science can go to hell! We propose to stand by our friends."

But Kroeber's allies could not prevent the ultimate indignity of a postmortem. However, after the autopsy, the anthropologists did their best to make amends to Ishi's spirit. They placed with his body a bow and five arrows, some acorn meal and tobacco, shell beads, and obsidian chips for his last journey. They then cremated the last Stone Age man in America in accordance with Yahi custom. As a last gesture of friendship, they spurned the standard urn of Mount Olivet Cemetery and placed his ashes in a black pottery jar of Pueblo design.

• For the original story on Ishi see the *Oroville Register*, 29 Aug. 1911. There are two excellent books on Ishi and his people: Theodora Kroeber, *Ishi in Two Worlds* (1961), and Kroeber and Robert Heizer, *Ishi, the Last Yahi: A Documentary History* (1979). The best semi-documentary movie is *Ishi, the Last Yahi*, directed by Jed Riffe and Pamela A. Roberts (1993). Obituaries are in the *Chico Record*, 28 Mar. 1916, and the *San Mateo Labor Index*, 30 Mar. 1916.

RICHARD H. DILLON

ISOM, Mary Frances (27 Feb. 1865–15 April 1920), librarian, was born in Nashville, Tennessee, the daughter of Frances A. Walter and John Franklin Isom, a prominent Union army surgeon from Cleveland, Ohio. Isom attended Cleveland public schools, and in 1883 she attended Wellesley College but left after one year because of poor health. Her mother died in 1891, and Isom took over managing the house for her father.

When her father died in 1899, Isom entered the Pratt Institute Library School in Brooklyn, New York, at the urging of her friend Josephine Rathbone, who was on the faculty. She graduated in 1901 and accepted the position of cataloger for the recently acquired Wilson collection at the Library Association of Portland, Oregon, a private subscription library. John Wilson, a local businessman and state legislator, had left close to 8,000 books to the Library Association with the stipulation that it become a public lending library. When the move was begun from subscription library to public library, the librarian gave notice and left. In 1902 the board named Isom librarian, and under her administration the Library Association changed from a private subscription library to a public library. In 1903 the library became a county library serving all of Multnomah County.

When Isom began the public library in 1902, she started with 40,000 volumes of books, which grew to 294,000 books by 1919. During her tenure as librarian she established a children's area in the library, library branches in Multnomah County, school libraries, hospital libraries, study clubs, a technical library, and a municipal reference library. In 1903 there were three

branches and the 40,000 books had a circulation of 140,329, of which 68.3 percent was fiction. The expense of operating the library, including purchase of new books, was $20,340.90. In 1919 there were 211 agencies, including 146 schools; the circulation was ten times as great; and the expenditures grew to $188,946.55. The percentage of fiction circulation decreased from 68.3 to 41.2.

Isom's philosophy of the library explained why the library system she began and maintained was so successful. She believed that the "public library is the people's library, it is maintained by the people for the people, it is the most democratic of our democratic institutions; therefore to be of service to all the people of the community to meet their needs and to contribute to their pleasure is its simple duty" (Library Association, *Monthly Bulletin* [May 1920]: 5). Isom argued that a library was for self-education and that it needed to contain not only classics but the best in modern thought as well as works on engineering, agriculture, housekeeping, and all trades.

Isom thought that libraries should benefit everyone, especially children, and she set up a close working relationship between the public schools and the library. She asked the school board to make an annual appropriation of $10,000 to purchase books for the children in the schools under the supervision of the library. Under this plan the school department of the library was organized and a school librarian appointed. Besides hiring children's librarians, she arranged library classes where pupils were instructed in the use of books, branch libraries were placed in the eight secondary schools of the city with a librarian, and sub-branch libraries were installed in some of the grade school buildings. Classes for teachers concerning literature for children were held on Saturday mornings.

In 1904 Isom organized the Oregon Library Association. In 1905 she, along with wealthy lumberman Winslow B. Ayer, helped establish a state library commission. At this time there were no public libraries in Oregon except for small associations in Salem and Eugene. In 1909 she was a leader in the organization of the Pacific Northwest Library Association and served as its second president in 1910–1911. She also served as second vice president of the American Library Association (ALA) in 1912–1913.

Isom believed that it was important to make available professional training for those who wished to become librarians. Because there was no library school in Portland, Isom instituted systematic training for her assistants, and she early established a regular training class that came to be recognized as one of the best maintained by any library in the country.

Under Isom's supervision, the central library building was designed and built in 1913. Isom and architect Albert E. Doyle made a cross-country trip to visit and talk to librarians and architects in Denver, New York, and Boston. In the Central Multnomah Library there are five reading rooms of 4,600 square feet each and no corridors. This building is still considered a model for librarians throughout the country from the standpoint of efficiency of operation and architectural beauty. Isom was also instrumental in obtaining Carnegie grants for seven large permanent branches in 1911–1913.

Isom's religious affiliation was Episcopalian. She was by conviction a person of liberal democratic views and was deeply depressed by World War I. She supported the Liberty Fund drives and personally organized hospital and camp libraries in Oregon and Washington. During the war her assistant librarian, an avowed pacifist, refused to buy bonds. Isom defended the woman's right to her opinion against angry public attacks.

Although already ill with cancer, Isom volunteered for service in France in the ALA unit under the Red Cross. In April 1919 she went to France and worked to set up libraries in hospitals in Mesves, Mars, Savenay, Nantes, Bordeaux, Chaumont, and Bar-sur-Aube. According to Burton E. Stevenson, the director of the ALA War Service in France, Isom "was a good Soldier—and, in the A.E.F. at least, there is no higher tribute." When Isom returned from Europe, she was very ill, but she continued working in her library part-time and finally from her Portland home until she died. A resolution adopted by the board of directors of the Library Association upon Isom's death states that "her genius lay in discovering new and better ways of attracting people to the library, in developing its system to fill wider needs and in making it a necessary part of public and private life" (Library Association, *Monthly Bulletin* [May 1920]: 12, 16).

• The Multnomah Library in Portland, Oreg., has a small book in its special collection of unpublished letters sent by Isom to friends during her sojourn in France during World War I. The Library Association of Portland has a 25-page memorial tribute to Isom that covers her career with tributes from friends and colleagues. See also Bernard Van Horne, "Mary Frances Isom: Creative Pioneer in Library Work in the Northwest," *Wilson Library Bulletin* 33, no. 6 (1959): 409–16. An obituary is in the *Portland Telegraph*, 16 Apr. 1920.

PAMELYN NANCE DANE

ITO, Michio (13 Apr. 1892–6 Nov. 1961), choreographer, performer, and teacher, was born in Tokyo, the son of Tamekichi Ito, an architect, friend of Frank Lloyd Wright, and the first Japanese to graduate from the University of California, and Kimiye Iijima, the daughter of a zoologist. As a youth in Japan Michio had a close association with Noh, the traditional, stylized lyric drama of Japan, and also received training in the popular theatrical form, kabuki. In 1911 he traveled to Paris and Berlin where he saw Isadora Duncan and the Diaghilev Ballets Russes and became interested in dance. Starting in 1912–1913 he was a student at the Dalcroze School in Hellerau, Germany, where he pursued interests in music and rhythmic movement, but at the outbreak of World War I he left Germany and stayed in England for two years. There he began developing his abilities as a solo dance performer/choreographer, appearing along with other acts for a two-

week engagement in 1915 at the Coliseum and at private parties and theater benefits. It was in London at the same time that he met and worked with William Butler Yeats and Ezra Pound and helped Yeats to produce his play *At the Hawk's Well*, based on Noh drama. For Ito the production in spring 1916 was integral to his search for ways of combining Eastern theater techniques, which emphasized symbolic illusion, with what he had learned in the West about movement, music, lighting, costuming, and choreography.

Ito was offered a contract to appear in a New York theater and arrived in fall 1916. Although the initial contract was not to his liking and was canceled almost immediately, Ito was to spend thirteen years in New York, involved in numerous dance and theater activities as a performer, teacher, choreographer, and director. Among the highlights of his varied activities, he was choreographer and scenic designer for *Bushido* with the Washington Square Players (1916); created two works for Adolph Bolm's Ballets-Intime and toured with that company (1917); produced and directed *At the Hawk's Well* (1918); directed and created two productions of *Tamura*, with Noh translation by Ernest Fenollosa and Ezra Pound (1917, 1921); and produced and directed three musical reviews— *Greenwich Village Follies* (1919), *What's in a Name* (1920), and *Michio Itow's Pinwheel Revel* (1922). In 1928 he choreographed for the experimental Neighborhood Playhouse group, using fellow dance artists Martha Graham and Benjamin Zemach; the group performed at the Manhattan Opera House and the Neighborhood Playhouse.

Although versatile and able to work in a variety of capacities in the performing arts, Ito was mainly interested in dance. Here his emphasis was on distillation of emotion, inner concentration, and symbolic use of gesture and space, which were influential directions for others to explore in the ferment of artistic experimentation that was going on during the years 1916 through 1929 in New York. Pauline Koner, who went on to become a major dance artist, studied and performed with Ito in 1928–1929 and noted in her autobiography, *Solitary Song*, that "Ito's premise was the blending of Eastern and Western cultures . . . a style that could express emotions motivated by the kernel of an idea. Most of his works demanded absolute concentration and a filtering of all naturalism from an emotion. . . . It had the purity and the clarity of a single brush stroke in a Japanese painting and at the same time it was like a modern painting influenced by the Japanese style." The dance critic John Martin wrote in 1936, "Of all the foreign artists who have been active here in recent times, none has had so direct an effect upon dance as Michio Ito" (*America Dancing*, p. 170).

It was in New York that Ito began developing a teaching methodology that emphasized training the body for economy of movement, conciseness of statement, and mysteriousness of mood. His technique was based on ten arm gestures, used with numerous variations of context, rhythm, space, and energy, which he combined in many ways. He felt that the upper body and movements of the arms and head were the important communicating mechanisms; movements of the lower body were auxiliary and would follow the direction and intent of upper-body gestures. Ito wanted to train dancers who would have the ability to express their own feelings and ideas; he wrote in a program note, "When the technique of any art form is mastered, it is possible to express the inner life. Everyone has his own individual feeling and mode of expression, therefore the dance should be a creation not an imitation."

In 1928 Ito put together a small concert group of six dancers who had studied with him, in preparation for a performance in New York, followed by a national tour. Ito's wife, American-born Hazel Wright (they married in 1924 and divorced in 1936), was one of the dancers and brought along their two children. Among the cities on the tour were Detroit, Chicago, Kansas City, El Paso, San Francisco, Seattle, and Los Angeles, where Ito decided to stay after disbanding the company in March 1929 for lack of funds. He made his Los Angeles debut in a performance on 28 April 1929 at the Figueroa Playhouse, and then began teaching. Among his first students was Lester Horton, soon to become one of the foremost choreographers in Los Angeles and chosen by Ito to play the lead in his production that summer of *At the Hawk's Well*. It was also in 1929 that Ito did choreography for a sequence in the movie *No, No, Nanette* (released 1930). He later worked on two other movies: *Madame Butterfly* (1933) and *Booloo* (1938).

In Los Angeles Ito's work took on a new dimension. His choreography in the city was characterized by large group dances accompanied by live orchestra, which he called "symphonic choreographies." The first was presented on 20 September 1929 in the Pasadena Rose Bowl, with 180 dancers, symphony orchestra, and a chorus, followed by appearances in 1930 at the Hollywood Bowl and in 1936 at the Redlands Bowl. The most important took place at the Hollywood Bowl on 19 August 1937 when he presented a large group work to Johann Strauss's "Blue Danube Waltz" and *Etenraku*, based on Japanese forms but using Western ideas of use of space and forms of movement. For *Etenraku* Ito took a stanza from a sixteenth-century Noh play as a basis for the dance; the Japanese conductor Viscount Hidemaro Konoye led the musicians in his contemporary orchestration of eighth-century Gagaku music.

In 1940 Ito married a woman by the name of Tsuyako. He lived in Los Angeles until 1941, when he was evacuated from the West Coast after Pearl Harbor along with the rest of the Japanese community. In 1943 he was allowed to return to Japan, where he was active in theater and dance and resumed teaching. He occasionally returned to the United States, the last time in 1959, and died in Tokyo.

Ryuko Maki, one of Ito's students, kept alive his repertory and training methods, passing them on to Satoru Shimazaki, a Japanese contemporary choreographer/performer. When Shimazaki came to New York to study in the 1970s he began presenting Ito's work in concert, and did so through the 1980s. In 1977 Helen Caldwell, a Los Angeles student of Ito's, published a biography and in 1987 Naima Prevots published *Dancing in the Sun*, which includes a chapter on Ito.

The documentation and live performances reinforced Ito's importance as an original artist who influenced modern dance in America. He brought to this country from his Japanese heritage the concept of evoking an emotional quality through suggestive gesture and understated movement. In his teaching and choreography he emphasized the value of abstracting the essence of an image or feeling through intensive use of torso, hands, and strongly defined body shape. For Ito, each movement carried its own weight and significance and the poetry of dance consisted in clarity of the individual minute components. He regarded time as a companion in his journey for expression, an element that was to be savored and caressed allowing for contemplative exchange of images between audience and performer.

• Helen Caldwell, *Michio Ito, the Dancer and His Dances* (1977), remains the only full biography although Pauline Koner in *Solitary Song* (1989) devotes a chapter to her experiences of working with Ito and Janet Soares in *Louis Horst: Musician in a Dancer's World* (1992) discusses Horst's training with him. The summary of a lecture-demonstration on Ito exists in the *Proceedings of the Twelfth Annual Conference of the Society of Dance History Scholars* (1989), pp. 155–56: "East and West in the Work of Michio Ito," by Satoru Shimazaki and Mary-Jean Cowell.

NAIMA PREVOTS

ITURBI, José (28 Nov. 1895–28 June 1980), pianist and conductor, was born in Valencia, Spain, the son of Ricardo Iturbi, a gas company employee who supplemented his income tuning pianos, and Teresa Baguena, an opera singer. His musical talent became apparent at an early age. Iturbi entered the Escuela de Musica de Maria Jordan when he was five and by age seven was earning money by giving lessons himself and performing in silent movie theaters, at balls, and at recitals. He entered the Conservatorio de Musica in Valencia and also studied privately under Joaquin Malats. Citizens of his hometown raised donations to send the young Iturbi to the Conservatoire de Musique in Paris to complete his studies, where he worked under the tutelage of Staub. After graduating with first honors, Iturbi moved to Zurich and earned money playing in a fashionable café. There he attracted the notice of the director of the Geneva Conservatory, who immediately hired Iturbi to be head of the conservatory's piano department. In June 1916 Iturbi was married to Maria Giner, who died soon after the birth of their daughter, Maria.

From 1919 to 1921 Iturbi immersed himself in his teaching responsibilities. In 1921 he began to give concerts again, and two years later he quit his teaching post entirely to devote himself to performance. Iturbi made his London debut in 1923 on tour with Igor Stravinsky, performing the composer's new chamber piece, *L'Histoire du soldat*. After successful tours in Europe, Iturbi made his American debut in October 1929 with the Philadelphia Philharmonic Orchestra, playing Beethoven's G Major Concerto no. 4, under the direction of Leopold Stokowski. Two months later Iturbi debuted in New York playing Mozart's D Minor Concerto, K. 466, and Liszt's *Hungarian Fantasia* with the New York Philharmonic.

Iturbi's much-acclaimed conducting debut occurred in Mexico City, at the Teatro Hidalgo. Its success prompted his engagement for eleven more performances and, later, an invitation to conduct two concerts in New York City. He began to work frequently with the Philadelphia and Detroit Orchestras and was appointed permanent conductor of the Rochester Philharmonic Orchestra in 1936. He appeared as guest conductor with most of the major American orchestras. Even when Iturbi's status as a conductor grew, he did not give up appearing as a performing pianist. His 1942 recital at Town Hall in New York was acclaimed by a *New York Times* critic as "an evening of almost supersmooth piano playing."

The feat for which Iturbi is best remembered is his simultaneous performances as conductor and piano soloist. These displays garnered enthusiastic critical and popular reaction. Of his February 1941 performance at Carnegie Hall, a *New York Times* critic wrote "Jose Iturbi['s] . . . stunt . . . brought down the house. . . . when he added to his piano duties a vivid job of leading his band he had the audience at his mercy. Mr. Iturbi did not miss a cue. If his hands were occupied he beat time with his head. If one hand was playing a fragment of music the other hand beat time or gave a cue" (26 Feb. 1941).

In addition to conducting and playing piano, Iturbi appeared in several films, generally playing himself. He played piano in a variety of musical styles and conducted a military band in his first film, *Thousands Cheer* (1943), which starred Kathryn Grayson and Gene Kelly. His most significant appearances were a starring role with Jeanette MacDonald in *Three Daring Daughters* (1948) and an on-screen appearance in *A Song to Remember* (1945), for which he recorded Frédéric Chopin's Polonaise in A Flat, a record that would sell over a million copies. He also acted in the films *Music for Millions* (1944), *Two Sisters and a Sailor* (1944), *Anchors Aweigh* (1945), *Holiday in Mexico* (1946), and *That Midnight Kiss* (1949). Iturbi also composed music, primarily works for piano with a Spanish flavor, the best known of which is *Pequeña danza española*.

Iturbi was awarded a number of honors, including the Order of St. George by the Greek government and the Order of the Légion d'Honneur from France. He died in Los Angeles, California.

José Iturbi was one of the leading American conductors of his time. Although sometimes criticized for a showiness that detracted from the artistic depth of his performances, he earned much critical and popular praise. In films Iturbi typically played a placid, wise,

supportive master musician, but off-screen he was a controversial and temperamental figure, prone to prima donna behavior. His provocative assertion in an interview that women were "temperamentally limited" and unable to attain the same standards of musical performance as men drew public outrage. The sexism of this opinion was at odds with Iturbi's actual behavior; he frequently toured with his sister, Amparo Iturbi, who was also an exceptionally talented pianist. Further comment was caused by Iturbi's last-minute withdrawal from a concert in which Benny Goodman was performing as a soloist; Iturbi claimed to object to the combination of jazz and classical music. He later protested during a concert in Cleveland because members of the audience were eating hot dogs too loudly.

• Articles on Iturbi appear in David Ewen, *Dictators of the Baton* (1943); Ewen, ed., *Living Musicians* (1940); and the *International Cyclopedia of Music and Musicians*, ed. Oscar Thompson (1985). An obituary is in the *New York Times*, 29 June 1980.

ELIZABETH ZOE VICARY

IVES, Burl (14 June 1909–14 Apr. 1995), folk singer and actor, was born Burl Icle Ivanhoe Ives in Hunt City Township, Illinois, the son of Frank Ives, a tenant farmer and highway culvert builder, and Cordella White. A bird, singing on an oak branch outside his mother's window, ushered in Ives's birth, and his brothers made him a cornstalk fiddle when he was just a toddler, but it was his pipe-smoking grandmother Kate White who made him a singer. She knew hundreds of folksongs and would fix her bright, black-button eyes on him and sing. Ives was age four when, at an old soldiers' reunion, he first performed in public. Although he had just eaten two hot dogs that he purchased on credit, he sang well, received one dollar, paid his debt, and spent the remainder on merry-go-round rides. At age twelve he sang and played his banjo at a local camp meeting and was asked while still in the sixth grade to be part of a high school theater group that performed in neighboring towns. He spent his junior and senior years in a consolidated high school in nearby Newton and played football as a fullback and as an all-conference guard.

Thinking he would become a high school football coach, Ives attended Eastern Illinois State Teachers College (1927–1930). One day in his third year the U.S. map on the classroom wall grew "more luminous" while the teacher's voice, discussing *Beowulf*, "grew dimmer," and Ives "headed for the door" and kept on moving. He toured forty-six of the then forty-eight states, singing and learning the songs of the people while admiring "the mighty mountains, silver rivers, and wide sweeping plains, magnificent cities" (*Wayfaring Stranger*, p. 108). When he could not hitch rides on highways, he hopped freight trains, and once a railroad guard cut his right middle finger to the bone with a "billy stick" when he knocked Ives from the ladder of a moving boxcar.

After returning to his family in 1931, Ives briefly attended Indiana State Teachers College in Terre Haute. While there he secured a job singing tenor in the town's only paid church choir on the condition that he train with a voice coach, Clara Bloomfield Lyon. She encouraged him to study music, interested him in reading great literature, and suggested that he move to New York City to secure further training. There, at International House, he cleared tables for his meals and sometimes sang his folksongs to fifty or sixty people near Grant's Tomb in Riverside Park, and he convinced his voice teacher, Ella Toedt, that "the minstrels of old must have sung that way" (*Burl Ives Song Book* [1953], p. 303).

It took Ives a half decade to get a start in New York. Although he won a contest held by bandleader George Olsen to find new singing talent, he did not appear with Olsen's band since he did not like the songs that he would be required to sing. It was not until 1938 that he secured his first professional acting job, with the Rockridge Stock Company in Carmel, New York. In a three-week engagement he played bit parts and later that same year, back in New York City, went to an audition for *The Boys from Syracuse* but found that all the parts had been assigned. The stage manager, however, spotted his guitar and asked George Abbott, Richard Rodgers, Lorenz Hart, Ezra Stone, and Jerry White to remain a minute to see and hear Ives. Impressed by his dramatic singing and playing, they created a special part, the Tailor's Apprentice, for him. He earned $40 a week in this small, nonsinging role for thirty-five weeks and, on Abbott's recommendation, studied acting with Benno Schneider and found that what he was learning helped his singing as well. In the fall of 1939 he was with the road company of *I Married an Angel*, which he accompanied back to New York.

With folksongs often dismissed as hillbilly music in the 1930s, Ives searched for an audience. Like other folk singers of that era, he found it primarily through unions and "so-called progressive organizations" that were later labeled Communist fronts. In the spring of 1944 he went to a few open meetings of the Communist Political Association and to its music group and art club. His attendance at these gatherings, which he later estimated to be six or seven times, documented his flirtation with the Communist party. Intensely patriotic, very independent, and never one to propagandize, he soon felt uncomfortable among these associates. Insisting that his mission was to peddle American ballads and folksongs, he moved away from the Far Left, becoming what R. Serge Denisoff called an "integrated folk entrepreneur," an individual "who composes and performs songs in the folk idiom in order to exploit a market outside of the original folk group" (p. 16). Sickened by the rampant anti-Americanism of Communist parades he witnessed while on a European tour, he voluntarily testified in 1952 before a U.S. Senate committee on Communist infiltration in the entertainment industry.

In 1940, when offered his own radio program by the National Broadcasting Company, Ives decided to become "a distinct personality" with whom listeners could identify. Influenced by Thomas Wolfe's question "Which of us is not forever a stranger and alone?" he took as his theme song "I'm Just a Poor, Wayfarin' Stranger" and grew a beard to fit the part (*Wayfaring Stranger*, pp. 244, 245). Although the beginning of his first broadcast was interrupted with a news flash that France had capitulated to Hitler, and Ives was drafted into the army in 1942, his radio program, which moved to the Columbia Broadcasting System, made his reputation. He was discharged for medical reasons after a year in the army but, having appeared in Irving Berlin's *This Is the Army*, stayed on to entertain the troops. Ives became closely identified with the song "Rodger Young," which Frank Loesser wrote in 1945 as a tribute to U.S. infantrymen.

Ives had the first of his many folksong concerts at New York City's Town Hall in 1945. That same year he married Helen Peck Ehrlich. They had one child and were divorced in 1971. Later that year he married Dorothy Koster. The more folksongs Ives collected and the more lyrics he knew—they would eventually top 500—the more respect he had for the songs themselves. "Through me, like a current, emotion and words and story flowed," he proudly noted. "Between the audience and me, I lifted poetry and music as one would hold up a fine and rare jewel for all to behold." When he found that Samuel Pepys had mentioned the song "Barbara Allen" in his seventeenth-century diary, it occurred to Ives that "any singer is only a moment in the life of such a great song." Despite his respect for these songs, he did not hesitate to change their words or tunes when he knew he "had better ones" (*Wayfaring Stranger*, pp. 186, 194, 253).

Admired also for his acting and with a gigantic body made for the part, Ives was Big Daddy in Tennessee Williams's *Cat on a Hot Tin Roof* both in the 1955 Broadway production and the 1958 movie version. He portrayed Gregory Peck's business rival in the 1958 film *The Big Country*, which won him an Academy Award for the best performance in a supporting role. In all, he was in more than thirty movies and half that many Broadway productions. He also starred in numerous radio, television, and summer stock performances, soloed in hundreds of concerts all over the world, and cut more than 100 record albums.

"An American sentimentalist in the tradition of Carl Sandburg and Norman Rockwell," Ives, through his songs, made "American history and legend shine like stars." With his "pure, keening tenor" voice and his "quietly authoritative stage manner," he remained a much-loved, remarkably unchanged folk-music institution who especially left his stamp on "The Blue Tail Fly" and "Big Rock Candy Mountain" (*New York Times*, 6 Dec. 1982, and 28 Feb. 1988; *Burl Ives Song Book*, p. 303). He died at his home in Anacortes, Washington.

• The Burl Ives Papers are in the Billy Rose Theatre Collection at the New York Public Library for the Performing Arts, Lincoln Center. Among them is a large collection of clippings. Though it fails to give dates, Ives's early autobiography, *Wayfaring Stranger* (1948), is very useful. Also helpful is his review of his early career and his listings of many of his numerous appearances, activities, and concerts, often with dates, in U.S. Congress, Senate Committee on the Judiciary, "Testimony of Burl Icle Ives, 20 May 1952," *Subversive Infiltration of Radio, Television, and the Entertainment Industry*, 82d Cong., 2d sess., pt. 2, pp. 205–28. His numerous books include *Tales of America* (1954) and a children's book, *Sailing on a Very Fine Day* (1955). Informative articles in the *New York Times* are Stephen Holden, "Folk Song: Burl Ives As Ever," 6 Dec. 1982, and "The Cream of Folk, Reunited for a Cause," 19 May 1993, and John Rockwell, "What the Child Hears Sounds Right to the Man," 28 Feb. 1988. For the social and political context of American folk music in the depression decade and after, see R. Serge Denisoff, *Sing a Song of Significance* (1972). An obituary is in the *New York Times*, 15 Apr. 1995.

OLIVE HOOGENBOOM

IVES, Charles (20 Oct. 1874–19 May 1954), composer, was born Charles Edward Ives in Danbury, Connecticut, the son of George Edward Ives and Mary Elizabeth "Mollie" Parmelle. The Iveses were a leading business family in a town noted for hatmaking. George Ives, however, was the exception: he took up music in his youth, led a Union band during the Civil War, and returned home to pursue the unusual trade (for the Ives family) of bandmaster and music teacher. He combined considerable gifts as a conventional musician with an experimental bent; for instance, he tinkered with ideas such as quarter-tones, having his children sing a melody in one key while accompanying in another, and marching two bands past one another playing different tunes.

George Ives trained his precocious son Charlie in several instruments and in the fundamentals of music; the boy grew up in a stimulating atmosphere of performance and experimentation. At age fourteen he became the youngest church organist in Connecticut. His first compositions include marches, songs for church services, and similar functional music. From his father he also learned to respect vernacular music and the amateurs who performed it. Moreover, he was allowed latitude to develop his father's scattered experiments into real compositional devices. Ives's organ piece *Variations on "America,"* written at age seventeen, includes some interludes combining keys, perhaps the first use of polytonality in music. From imitating drums and church bells on piano, Ives early discovered the complex sonorities that would mark his mature music.

In Danbury Ives also absorbed an indelible feeling for how music functions in a community. His childhood was filled with church services, gigantic hymn-sings, parades, holidays, band concerts in the park, and polite parlor musicales. All these occasions and the human joys and aspirations that went into them were contained, for Ives, in the music that accompanied them. Years later he would write to his wife, "Music is life." In his mature work he would remake the everyday music of his childhood into a transcendent representation of human experience, spirituality, and community.

At the same time that he was developing in music, Ives also acquired a passion for sports. Inevitably, he felt divided in his loyalties; he would later write in his *Memos*, "As a boy [I was] partially ashamed of [music]. . . . When other boys . . . were out driving grocery carts, or doing chores, or playing ball, I felt all wrong to stay in and play piano." He felt both attracted to and threatened by Danbury's female-dominated world of "cultivated" classical music. His love of "manly" sports—and of the unpretentious life of bandsmen—left him in adulthood with an unusual sensibility for a composer writing for the concert hall. While he had grown up a prodigy in a musical family, he was primarily a church musician with relatively little experience of urban concert life, and he became highly critical of that life and of professional music making.

Ives matriculated at Yale in 1894, where he soon received the news that his father had died. This tragedy marked him; he developed a fanatical reverence for the memory of his prime mentor in life and music.

Ives sought new mentors at Yale, with imperfect success. He studied organ with leading teachers and composition with then-celebrated Horatio Parker. Parker was a conservative teacher who laughed off the experimental pieces George Ives had encouraged, among them the elegantly polytonal *Psalm 67*, but he did impart to his student a strong sense of motivic development and large-scale musical form. As homework, Ives wrote the European-style First Symphony, a work of considerable individuality and effectiveness for a young composer writing in a borrowed idiom. The First String Quartet (1890), based on familiar gospel tunes, is more adventuresome but still essentially traditional.

As the organist of Center Church in New Haven, Ives worked under a sophisticated and open-minded choirmaster, John Cornelius Griggs, who occasionally let him try out an experimental piece in services, among them the polytonal *Thanksgiving Prelude* for organ. Meanwhile Ives barely passed his courses, avidly played intramural sports, and wrote a number of light pieces for fraternity shows and such. He became conversant with the new African-American craze called ragtime, which would be an important component of his music.

Except for the social aspect, from which he would retreat after his marriage, Ives lived at Yale as he would for his entire active career, pursuing a busy external life and composing a steady stream of music both conservative and experimental. Besides the folk music, hymns, patriotic tunes, marches, ragtime, and other vernacular-tradition genres that he would write as such and also integrate into concert pieces, he established a thread of logic that would unify his whole creative evolution. A steadily increasing independence of line in a composition, evident even in his early work, went further with the addition of polytonality and polyrhythm and finished logically in his late works with more or less complete pieces superimposed on one another like a collage. Given that much of his basic material is quoted, this led naturally to a collage of styles as well. In many ways this musical technique, which reached its most highly developed state in the Fourth Symphony (1909–1923), reflected his mature political ideas. He saw society as a loose collection of individuals, held together by common principles rather than by leaders, and progressing toward an ever more democratic and universal social order.

At some point before he died, George Ives had advised his son not to try to make a living in music. Charles had become determined to explore new musical materials, but he did not want, as he put it, to "starve on dissonances." Accordingly, upon graduation from Yale in 1898, he went to New York and took a job with the Mutual Life insurance company. He would pursue that trade for the rest of his career, ending up a partner in Ives & Myrick, one of the most successful agencies of its time.

During his first decade in New York, Ives lived with a collection of young career men in a series of apartments they dubbed "Poverty Flat." With his customary energy he worked full time at the office, pitched on company baseball teams, took law courses, served as a church organist and choirmaster, and composed prolifically. Works of the years before 1906 include conventional music for his church jobs (much of it now lost), relatively conservative large works such as the second and third symphonies and the beginnings of his violin sonatas, a steady output of songs, and pathbreaking works such as the *Four Ragtime Pieces* of 1902 and the *Country Band March* of 1903. The latter represents the foibles of small-town bandsmen with fractured rhythms and quasi-accidental counterpoint. In two seminal works of 1906 he made important discoveries: *The Unanswered Question* juxtaposes three groups—strings, four winds, and a solo trumpet— each playing in its own style, the coordination left somewhat to chance. In a song called "The Cage" he used quartal harmonies in free, unmetered, but still systematic rhythmic patterns.

In 1902 Ives resigned from the last of his church jobs. He would not perform in public again until the 1920s. Occasionally he hired players to run through pieces; sometimes he approached well-known musicians. The repeated humiliations he experienced in this process had much to do with his later lambasting of professional musical life, which he considered overly commercial, conservative, and feminized.

By 1906 he had begun courting Harmony Twichell, a settlement-house nurse. Some of the courtship involved Ives setting Harmony's poetry, notably in the song "Autumn." They were married in Hartford in 1908. They adopted one daughter. Through many sorrows—including her near-death the next year and Ives's later debility—they were very close. Ives wrote in his *Memos*, "*She* gave me not only help but a confidence that no one else since father had given me." His musical maturity can be dated from the year of their marriage.

That maturity is seen in the string of extraordinarily imaginative and innovative works he produced mostly between 1908 and 1916: the symphony *Holidays*, *Three Places in New England*, the Second Orchestral Set, the *Robert Browning Overture*, the Second String Quartet, the Third Violin Sonata, the *Concord* Sonata, songs, including "General William Booth Enters into Heaven," and the Fourth Symphony. All were written during nights, weekends, and holidays away from his insurance agency, which in those years also became one of the most innovative and profitable in the country. Most of this music is founded on earlier pieces; for example, *Putnam's Camp*, the second of the *Three Places*, was based on the old *Country Band March* and the overture *1776*. All these works are programmatic, largely arising from the experiences, feelings, and everyday music of his New England childhood. In these mature pieces we find the essential Ivesian personality: his unprecedented blend of traditional and radical, old and new, naive and sophisticated, "high" and "low." More than any other composer, Ives succeeded in unifying the ideals and genres of the European classical tradition with the musical vernacular of the American people.

After 1916 Ives's productivity fell, due mainly to the stresses of the war; he also added volunteer work to his already hectic schedule. That led to a severe heart attack in 1918, from which point both his creativity and his health declined. His last completed work, the song "Sunrise," dates from 1926. From then on he would only tinker with old pieces, to the despair of his later editors. In 1919–1920 he had the *Concord* Sonata and *114 Songs* engraved and sent them out to hundreds of musicians, and likewise the *Essays before a Sonata*. In the guise of essays on Ralph Waldo Emerson, Nathaniel Hawthorne, Louisa May Alcott, and Henry David Thoreau (the movements of the *Concord*), Ives lays out his sense of music and its relationship to life. Though his printings elicited some ridicule and much indifference, a few musicians were intrigued and began to perform his pieces, often to enthusiastic critical response. By 1930 Ives was known to avant-garde circles and had acquired champions, notably the composer and promoter Henry Cowell.

Also by 1930, Ives had retired from business due to heart trouble and diabetes; from then on he was only occasionally able to promote his own work and fight his own battles. Partly for that reason, and partly because the avant-garde was eclipsed by the conservative "Americana" composers of the next decades, Ives's music made slow headway. There were some important performances, including Nicolas Slonimsky's of *Three Places in New England* in the early 1930s and John Kirkpatrick's triumphant premiere of the *Concord* Sonata in 1939. Critic Lawrence Gilman hailed the latter as "the greatest music composed by an American." Meanwhile Ives dispatched a good deal of his fortune in support of composers and new musical activities all over the country.

Ives's rising reputation was confirmed with the 1946 Pulitzer Prize for the relatively tame Third Symphony. The real explosion of interest followed a decade after his death with Leopold Stokowski's 1965 premiere of the Fourth Symphony. The work was greeted internationally as a masterpiece.

Despite many predictions of decline from still-resistant critics, Ives's music has persisted in the public ear, though it has not and may never reach standard-repertoire status. One suspects that this situation would please its creator. Certainly his enormous output is uneven; many of his lesser works are not really finished. The pieces he cared most about, however, he worked out painstakingly in draft after draft. His status as a prophet of musical modernism—the first to explore polytonality, polyrhythm, atonality, dissonant harmony, and many other unconventional techniques—has receded as modernism itself has receded, and as the deeper values of his music have been better understood. That, too, would certainly have pleased Ives. He created a singular and compelling world in sound, and he believed passionately in the spiritual worth of individuals. His art is a powerful symbol of the human community, of life as it is lived, and for that it is irreplaceable. He died in New York City.

• The composer's papers and manuscripts are in the Ives collection at Yale University. In *Essays before a Sonata, and Other Writings* (1962), one finds most of Ives's public writings, ranging from the visionary to the blustery, the obscure to the delightful. Vivian Perlis's interviews with those who knew Ives, collected in *Charles Ives Remembered: An Oral History* (1974), are informative and readable. The *Memos* (1972), assembled by John Kirkpatrick, contain much valuable material and some of Ives's private blowing off of steam. The first book-length study, and still a valuable one, is Henry Cowell and Sidney Cowell, *Charles Ives and His Music* (1954; 2d ed., 1969). See also Frank R. Rossiter, *Charles Ives and His America* (1975), a pathbreaking study of the cultural influences on the composer; H. Wiley Hitchcock, *Ives: A Survey of the Music* (1977), an excellent introduction for musicians; Stuart Feder, *Charles Ives, "My Father's Song": A Psychoanalytic Biography* (1992); J. Peter Burkholder, *All Made of Tunes: Charles Ives and the Uses of Musical Borrowing* (1995); Jan Swafford, *Charles Ives: A Life with Music* (1996); Burkholder, ed., *Charles Ives and His World* (1996); and Geoffrey Block and Burkholder, eds., *Charles Ives and the Classical Tradition* (1996). Recordings are highly variable. For the orchestral music, see recordings by Stokowski, Bernstein, and Thomas; otherwise, refer to reviews in such sources as *Gramophone, Stereo Review*, and the *Penguin Guide* to compact discs, cassettes, and LPs (1980).

JAN SWAFFORD

IVES, Chauncey Bradley (14 Dec. 1810–2 Aug. 1894), sculptor, was born near Mount Carmel, Hamden Township, Connecticut, the son of Jared Ives and Sylvia Bradley, farmers. After a childhood spent on the family farm he was apprenticed around 1825 to Rodolphus E. Northrop, a New Haven woodcarver who taught him the rudiments of decorative carving and modeling. Within two years Ives had decided on a career as a professional sculptor, a decision that his family did not fully support.

Ives sought the advice and instruction of Hezekiah Augur, New Haven's best-known sculptor. Ives probably modeled his first works in New Haven in the early 1830s, and by 1838 he was producing portrait busts of citizens of that city and of Hartford, Connecticut, including those of Edward E. Salisbury (1838, unlocated), Benjamin Silliman (1839, New-York Historical Society), Noah Webster (1839, Yale University Art Gallery), and Ithiel Towne (1840, Yale University Art Gallery). In search of further commissions, Ives went to Boston, probably several times, during the late 1830s. There he modeled the busts of some of Boston's famous inhabitants, including Edward Everett (1838, unlocated), but competition for artistic patronage was very stiff in that city. By the autumn of 1840 Ives had moved on to New York City, where he placed several of his busts on informal exhibition in his rooms. After receiving favorable notice in the local press, he began to show his works in the more public venues of the annual exhibitions of the Apollo Association and the National Academy of Design in New York, the Pennsylvania Academy of the Fine Arts in Philadelphia, and the Boston Athenaeum.

On the advice of his doctor, who was treating him for consumption, and some of his more supportive clients, Ives decided to go to Europe. In 1844 he departed the United States for Italy, where he made his home for the rest of his life. Ives first settled in Florence to seek portrait commissions, mostly from visiting Americans. He also put into marble the plaster busts that he had modeled at home. In a very short time he was able to repay his debts and to establish himself in comfortable quarters.

Like most sculptors of the period, however, Ives was interested in creating works that showed more imagination than simple portraiture could. He soon executed a number of ideal works with mythological, religious, or literary themes. The first of these to achieve some popularity was his bust *Flora*, created in 1846, of which he eventually made three marble replicas for American clients. Busts of the Old Testament heroine *Ruth* (1849, Chrysler Museum, Norfolk, Va.) and of a classical *Bacchante* (1848, private collection) soon followed.

For much of his career Ives kept a written record of the titles of his works and where they were modeled. This studio list indicates that he made several brief visits to the United States during the late 1840s. On returning to Italy in 1850 from a trip to New York, he decided to settle in Rome. By that time more American artists were choosing to live in Rome rather than Florence. For Ives, the change was evidently an inspirational one, for soon after his arrival in that city he began work on his first major ideal work and first major female nude, *Pandora* (1851, Virginia Museum of Fine Arts, Richmond). The sculpture was undoubtedly influenced by Hiram Powers's famous *The Greek Slave*, which had only recently toured Europe and America to great acclaim. Three marble replicas of *Pandora* were produced and eventually sold to clients of some renown, including Major Philip Kearny and

John H. B. Latrobe. A revised version, completed in 1863, proved to be even more popular; it was replicated at least nineteen times in various sizes (versions at Brooklyn Museum; National Museum of American Art; St. Johnsbury [Vt.] Athenaeum).

Meanwhile, Ives continued to investigate the ideal. In 1852 he created another full-length ideal, *Flora* (private collection), and a bust of *Ariadne* (one version at Chrysler Museum). The latter proved to be one of the sculptor's more popular works, with thirteen replicas made over a number of years, but it was surpassed by his *Rebecca at the Well* (1854, Metropolitan Museum of Art), a life-size figure that was reproduced in twenty-five examples. In 1859 his next major ideal piece appeared, *Undine Receiving Her Soul* (Yale University Art Gallery), with its subject taken from a popular romance that was published in 1823 by Baron de la Motte-Fouqué.

During the 1850s Ives continued to fill the usual portrait commissions and also modeled several genre figures, including *The Piper* (1854) and *Cupid Fishing* (1853), both of which were based on portraits of children. His last major work before the Civil War was *Shepherd Boy and Kid* (High Museum, Atlanta, Ga.), which he modeled in Rome in 1859 and which was replicated four times. In the fall of 1860 Ives returned to the United States for a visit, and there, on 4 October 1860, he married Maria L. Davis of Brooklyn, New York. Over the next two decades the couple had seven children, all but one of whom were born in Italy.

Ives received commissions for few portrait busts during the American Civil War, but he did produce an important historical work during these years, a group sculpture known as *The Willing Captive* (1862–1868), which proved to be his most complicated work, both thematically and compositionally. Taking his subject from Bancroft's *History of the United States*, he began modeling the sculpture in Rome in 1862. His hopes for obtaining a commission for the conception were not realized until 1886, when he reworked the original model, had it cast in bronze, and exhibited it in the United States. In the early 1890s Jonathan Ackerman Coles of Newark, New Jersey, purchased it and donated it to his native city for erection in a public park, where it remains (another cast is in the Chrysler Museum). Following the war Ives received commissions for two other public sculptures: portrait statues of Jonathan Trumbull and Roger Sherman that were ordered by the state of Connecticut to be presented to Statuary Hall in the U.S. Capitol building in Washington, D.C., where they were unveiled in 1872.

Ives remained productive during the 1870s, although by that time interest in the neoclassical style in which he worked was waning. Notable among his sculptures of this period are the genre pieces *The Truant* (1871, Chrysler Museum) and *The Pets*; the biblical *Jephthah's Daughter* (1874, Buffalo and Erie County [N.Y.] Historical Society); and the classicizing *Ino and Bacchus* (1873) and *Egeria* (1876, Virginia Museum of Fine Arts). His output slowed during the 1880s, and by 1890 he had more or less retired from the field.

Among his last ideal works were the life-size allegorical figures *Evening* (1886) and *America* (1889). The sculptor's final years were spent in Rome, where he died. He was buried in Rome's Protestant Cemetery.

Of the many American neoclassical sculptors who worked between 1825 and 1875, Chauncey Ives was certainly one of the most prolific. His output in the realm of the ideal is especially impressive. He conceived and executed more than thirty-five ideal works during his lifetime, while even the better-known Hiram Powers created only about twenty ideal conceptions during his long career.

• A small collection of papers related to Ives is at the Archives of American Art, Smithsonian Institution. The best published source remains William H. Gerdts, "Chauncey Bradley Ives: American Sculptor," *Antiques* 94 (Nov. 1968): 714–18. Also see William Todd, "Chauncey B. Ives," *Publications of the Hamden Historical Society* 1 (1938): 52–57; Wayne Craven, *Sculpture in America* (1968); Gerdts, *American Neo-Classic Sculpture: The Marble Resurrection* (1973); George Heard Hamilton, "New Haven Sculptors," *Bulletin of the Associates in Fine Arts at Yale University* 8 (June 1938): 70–71; and Margaret Farrand Thorp, *The Literary Sculptors* (1965).

DAVID B. DEARINGER

IVES, Frederic Eugene (17 Feb. 1856–27 May 1937), inventor, was born in Litchfield, Connecticut, the son of Hubert Leverit Ives and Ellen Amelia Beach. He attended public schools in Litchfield, Norfolk, and Newtown, Connecticut, but left school at the age of eleven when his father died. He became a clerk in a country store, then an apprentice for three years in the *Litchfield Inquirer* printing office. During his apprenticeship he gained expertise as a job compositor and pressman. He also edited and published an amateur paper, learned wood engraving, and developed an interest in photography. When his apprenticeship ended in 1873, he took a job in an Ithaca, New York, printing office. He quit this job after six months to take up photography. He learned the trade by working for his cousin and then opened his own studio in Ithaca in 1874.

Ives's pursuit of photography led to a position in 1874 at Cornell University, where he supervised the photographic laboratory until 1878. Taking advantage of access to university resources, he established a pattern of experimentation and invention, especially in the areas of photoengraving and color photography, that continued throughout his career. He conducted experiments to attack the problem of type-press reproduction of photographs from nature, seeking a process for using purely photographic means for producing engraved printing plates. He developed a method that he used to illustrate college papers at Cornell as well as publications at other institutions. In 1878 he invented the first commercially successful process of halftone engraving. The process was based on the trichromatic principle, namely that human color vision involves three types of retinal sensory receptors. His three-color printing process allowed typographic presses to print photographic images in natural color.

In 1878 Ives moved to Baltimore, Maryland, to set up a photoengraving plant for an illustrated newspaper. The following year, he started another photoengraving plant for Crosscup and West Engraving Company of Philadelphia, Pennsylvania. This facility began to manufacture his halftone plates commercially in 1881, first for the June issue of the *Philadelphia Photographer*. Production continued until fire destroyed the plant in 1885. Ives's relationship with Crosscup and West continued until 1890. During this period, he continued to experiment with the halftone process, aiming to improve and simplify it. In 1886 he succeeded at developing a wholly photographic process of halftone photoengraving, one that used a ruled and sealed cross-line or pinhole glass screen to fix a photographic image to film.

Because Crosscup and West advised him against seeking patents for his work, Ives received no royalties from his halftone process. In 1890 he severed his relationship with that company and worked on developing three-color printing and color photography. In 1885 he demonstrated the use of three halftone plates to photomechanically reproduce a colored image. He also developed the photochromoscope, or Kromskop, a three-negative system of color photography. This invention, which produced very high fidelity colored views, garnered Ives medals and honors from photographic and scientific societies. It was not, however, a commercial success. The photochromoscope resembled a stereoscope in that an optical instrument was used to display photographs made by special cameras that took a triple photograph at one exposure on a single plate. Through the viewing instrument, the image appeared in realistic three-dimension. This system enjoyed some success in Philadelphia and in England. Ives lived in London for several years promoting it. However, consumers continued to prefer color photography on paper, and Ives ceased to manufacture these devices in 1911.

Most, though not all, of Ives's other inventions related to color photography. In 1912 he devised the Tri-pak color camera. In addition to his three-color printing process, he also developed quick-transferring dyes and created a successful process for rendering moving pictures in natural color. In the late 1920s he introduced Polychrome, a two-color process. He invented many devices, including the parallax stereogram in 1903, a photographic transparency that threw an image into perfect stereoscopic relief by positioning it optimally in front of the viewer. He also designed inexpensive but effective glass-sealed diffraction gratings for use in spectroscopes. Both these instruments became well known in college and university physics and chemistry laboratories. Other inventions included a novel binocular microscope (1904), a sensitive tint photometer (1908–1909), and a "universal colorimeter" (1908–1909). The latter measured a color and gave it numerical expression in three digits. These could be sent by mail, telegraph, or cable to any person with a colorimeter, who could set the instrument to show exactly the original color.

Ives married Mary Elizabeth Olmstead in 1879. They had two sons, of whom one, Herbert Eugene, became an experimental physicist and engineer specializing in physical problems associated with producing, measuring and using light, especially with respect to color photography and television. After his wife died in 1904, Ives married Margaret Campbell Cutting in 1913.

Throughout his career, Ives earned seventy U.S. patents for the devices and processes he invented. He received more than eighteen medals from scientific and photographic societies. These included the Elliot Cresson gold medal and the Scott Legacy medal (for the parallax stereogram) from the Franklin Institute; a special gold medal from the Photographic Society of Philadelphia; the Progress medal and the Science medal from the Royal Photographical Society; and the Rumford medal from the American Academy of Arts and Sciences for inventions in color photography and photoengraving. In 1911 the International Photo-Engravers Association presented him with a testimonial and gold watch for his contributions to the industry. Active in many scientific and technical institutions, Ives was a fellow of the Royal Photographic Society and the Royal Microscopic Society; an honorary member of the Philadelphia Photographic Society and the New York Camera Club; and a member of the Physical Society, Franklin Institute, and American Microscopical Society. He died at his home in Philadelphia.

A pioneer in the fields of photoengraving and color photography, Ives parlayed his understanding of scientific principles into technical solutions to problems that had baffled other investigators. He invented instruments and processes that found wide application; many continue in use.

• The papers of Ives and his son Herbert Eugene Ives are held at the Library of Congress, Manuscript Division. Ives wrote and published privately his life story, *The Autobiography of an Amateur Inventor* (1928). Louis Walton Sipley wrote several books about Ives and the development of color photography, including the biography *Frederic E. Ives: Photo-Graphic-Arts Inventor* (1956) and *Photography's Great Inventors* (1965). Obituaries are in the *New York Herald Tribune*, 28 May 1937, *Camera*, July 1937, *American Philosophical Society Year Book*, 1937, and *Journal of Applied Physics*, Apr. 1938.

HELEN M. ROZWADOWSKI

IVES, George (3 Aug. 1845–4 Nov. 1894), bandmaster and choral director, was born in Danbury, Connecticut, the son of George White Ives, a prominent local businessperson, and Sarah Hotchkiss Wilcox, a schoolteacher. Ives showed a gift for music at an early age and received a thorough, conventional education in classical music. He received lessons on the cornet, his primary instrument, and attended the Philharmonic concerts in New York. At various times, he also learned to play the violin, piano, and organ, and possibly the flute. He pursued formal studies with Charles A. Foeppl, a teacher in New York City, from August 1860 until May 1862.

Ives entered the Union army as bandmaster of the First Connecticut Volunteer Heavy Artillery and was sworn in on 16 June 1863. He was responsible for recruiting the members of his band. The youngest bandmaster in the Union army, George's rank as "principal musician . . . was the equivalent of second lieutenant of infantry" (Feder, pp. 37–38). An article in the *Danbury Evening Times*, "Col. Wildman Reminisces" (2 Aug. 1932), reports the following conversation between President Abraham Lincoln and General Ulysses S. Grant, discussing "the relative merits of the various sections of the army":

"That's a good band," President Lincoln remarked, indicating the First Connecticut Heavy Artillery band under Mr. Ives's leadership. Mr. Ives was then but a boy of 16 years [by then 19].

"It's the best band in the army they tell me," General Grant replied. "But you couldn't prove it by me. I know only two tunes. One is *Yankee Doodle* and the other isn't" (*Memos*, fn. 5, p. 45)

Ives was court-martialed on 3 July 1864 for refusing to fulfill his responsibilities as bandmaster; we have no concrete information about the reason or about any subsequent conviction. However, we know that he did receive an honorable discharge with his regiment on 25 September 1865. Ives's only extant commentary on his army experience is found in a music notebook: "A space of Three years servitude as Leader . . . & one year sick."

Music lessons were resumed with Foeppl from December 1866 through 1868. In 1874 Ives married Mary Elizabeth Parmelee. They had two children, one of whom was the composer Charles Edward Ives. George Ives's career in music included working as a cornet soloist in concert performances, as a director of several bands (some of which included brass and/or strings, indicating a highly varied repertory), as a choir director, and as a theory teacher. He supplemented his income by working in various capacities in different family businesses. He is known to have toured with Lou Fenn's Alabama Minstrels, Fortescue's Burlesque, and the Swedish Ladies' Vocal Quartet between 1876 and 1878. Ives had a predilection for musical invention and experimentation, was a devoted music educator, and was abreast of contemporary European music and music theory pedagogy, developing a highly critical sense of the latter.

His critical acumen in regard to theory and pedagogy is evident in an essay he started within weeks of his death. The essay is particularly significant because it provides objective criteria by which to assess his contribution to his son's musical education and a context for the innovative nature of Charles Ives's music. In the period of crisis in music theory at the end of the nineteenth century, when theory, pedagogy, and analytical practice could not explain the innovations that had appeared in musical compositions, George Ives's ideas were in the vanguard of musico-theoretical thinking. He addressed some of the anomalies created by contemporary music that violated or were inexpli-

cable in existing theory, such as those created by a lack of appropriate notation and terminology. He took a pragmatic approach based on how things sound. "His comprehension of the problem was rooted in his understanding of modern music (particularly Wagner's), in his experience as a practical musician (for example, as a choral director), and his experimental bent, which may well have been stimulated by Helmholtz's discussions of culturally determined systems" in *Lehre von den Tonempfindungen* (Baron [1992], p. 246). His subtle approach led to a realistic historical evaluation of tuning systems (whereby pure intonation was appropriate for simple traditional music, but equal temperament was needed for modern music), a profound understanding of the relation of notation to musical systems, and the imagination to envision new approaches to musical composition. Ives died in Danbury of a stroke.

In addition to his musical accomplishments, Ives developed independent ideas that were frequently out of step with those prevailing in his Danbury, Connecticut, community. For example, he sided with the labor movement against exploitative management. He also aligned himself with proponents of professionalism, education, and science against the aspirations of the pretentious, half-educated "genteel" society in the cultural politics of the developing democracy that existed from the 1870s through the 1890s in the United States.

Based on the foregoing, the breadth of Ives's self-education, originality, musical insights, and intellectual achievements can be reassessed. Earlier evaluations of George Ives maintained that what we know about him is an idealized "fictional persona created by his son" (Maynard Solomon, "Charles Ives: Some Questions of Veracity," *Journal of the American Musicological Society* 40 [1987]: 450), and Stuart Feder characterized him as essentially an oddball and the failed member of a distinguished business family, thus misinterpreting his character and intelligence.

George Ives has been known principally as the father of the composer Charles Ives and is remembered mainly for nurturing the gifts of his son. However, the father's own accomplishments are noteworthy on their own merits within the historical context of music theory and American cultural developments. What he accomplished was done essentially in isolation, aside from the interaction between him and his son. George Ives's critical insights in music theory explain "how Charles Ives's . . . innovations could predate comparable radical developments in the music of European composers: George Ives provided fecund suggestions that stimulated and even set directions for the languages . . . Charles would develop" (Baron [1992], p. 253).

• The extant portions of both the manuscript and the typed versions of George Ives's essay are housed in the Charles Ives Collection in the John Herrick Jackson Music Library, New Haven, where his student notebooks can also be found. The essay is discussed most thoroughly in Carol K. Baron, "George Ives's Essay in Music Theory: An Introduction and

Annotated Edition," *American Music* 10 (Fall 1992): 239–88, and discussed in a historical context in Baron, "At the Cutting Edge: Three American Theorists at the End of the Nineteenth Century," *International Journal of Musicology* 2 (1993): 193–247. An earlier, positive discussion of the essay is David Eiseman, "George Ives as Theorist: Some Unpublished Documents," *Perspectives of New Music* 75 (1975): 139–47. Knowledge of his musical activities is derived mainly from newspaper reports and from Charles Ives's autobiographical reminiscences of his father in his *Memos*, ed. John Kirkpatrick (1972), which contains biographical material about the family, assembled by Kirkpatrick, in appendices. The fullest source of biographical material on George Ives is found in Stuart Feder's psychobiography, *Charles Ives: My Father's Song* (1992), although Ives's image is based on earlier misleading historiographical evaluations of the material; see the review by Carol K. Baron in *Musical Quarterly* 78 (Spring 1994): 206–19.

CAROL K. BARON

IVES, Herbert Eugene (31 July 1882–13 Nov. 1953), physicist and inventor, was born in Philadelphia, Pennsylvania, the son of Frederic Eugene Ives, a photographer and inventor, and Mary Elizabeth Olmstead. He attended public school in Philadelphia as well as the University College School in London, England, in 1892 and the Lawrence Sheriff School in Rugby, England, from 1897 to 1898. In 1898 he joined his father's business, the Ives Kromskop Company, and spent the next three years designing and building various pieces of equipment for producing three-color negative photographs. He also attended the Franklin Institute Night School of Mathematics for a year before matriculating at the University of Pennsylvania in 1901. After receiving a B.S. from Pennsylvania in 1905, he accepted a teaching fellowship in physics at Johns Hopkins University, where he experimented with different methods for producing photographs in color. His work with the diffraction process, whereby lightwaves are bent around the close, equidistant, parallel lines of a diffraction grating and dispersed into the various colors of the visible spectrum, gained him the Franklin Institute's Longstreth Medal in 1906 and a Ph.D. in physics in 1908.

After graduation Ives married Mabel Agnes Lorenz, with whom he had three children. He also went to work as an assistant physicist for the Bureau of Standards in Washington, D.C., and developed legal definitions for standards of light. In 1909 he moved to Cleveland, Ohio, where he joined the National Electric Lamp Association Research Laboratory as a physicist. In this capacity he developed a photometer that rated the efficiency of incandescent light bulbs by measuring watts per candle and invented a device for measuring human visual acuity and defects. In 1912 he returned to Philadelphia to accept a position as research physicist with the United Gas Improvement Company, where he experimented with the production, measurement, and use of light. He was particularly interested in the measurement of color and in 1912 was largely responsible for introducing into the United States tristimulus colorimetry, whereby the dominant wavelength and luminance of a color are determined by visually matching it against the three primary colors. However, his principal contribution to science while at United Gas involved the invention of artificial daylight (1913). By artificially illuminating a variable neutral-tint screen of his own design, he was able to create light equivalent in every respect to direct sunlight. Artificial daylight proved to be useful in color matching and earned for him a second Longstreth Medal in 1915. He won a third Longstreth Medal three years later for his efforts to improve the performance of the Welsbach mantle, a chemically treated hood for a gas jet that gave off incandescent light when heated.

In 1918 Ives joined the U.S. Army Signal Corps as a captain in the Aviation Section. His duties included developing methods and equipment for taking aerial photographs under extreme vibration and weather conditions. His pioneering work in this regard, the results of which were published in *Airplane Photography* (1920), contributed significantly to the U.S. war effort.

Because United Gas was forced to close its laboratory during World War I for lack of manpower, Ives could not return to his old job after being discharged from the army in 1919. After a six-month period of unemployment, he moved to New York City to become affiliated with Bell Telephone Laboratories (BTL) as a member of the technical staff. His initial assignment involved working with electrical contacts and resulted in improved performance and reduced operating costs of telephone switching equipment.

In the early 1920s Ives began experimenting with photoelectric cells, light-sensitive devices that open or close electrical circuits depending on the amount of light they detect, in the hope that they could be used to transmit pictures over telephone lines by translating light-intensity into electric current. He was placed in charge of BTL's efforts in this area, and in 1924 he supervised the successful electric transmission of photographs taken at the Democratic and Republican national conventions. Shortly thereafter a group of researchers under his direction developed an apparatus consisting of two Nipkow disks, spirally apertured rotating disks that analyze the light intensity of an image, controlled by Ives-designed photoelectric cells. In 1927 this device was used to transmit sequentially by telephone line a moving image from Washington, D.C., to neon lamp receivers in New York City, thereby producing the first long-distance television broadcast. That same year Ives's researchers transmitted pictures by radio from Whippany, New Jersey, to New York and in 1929 transmitted moving images in color from Washington, D.C., to New York.

In the 1930s Ives undertook an investigation of the applicability of the Doppler effect, whereby a sound decreases in frequency as its source moves away from the listener, to the measurement of the relative speed of light sources. By projecting a stream of hydrogen ions into a special tube capable of producing extremely narrow spectral lines, he and G. R. Stilwell demonstrated that the Doppler effect applies to electromagnetic radiation as well as to sound.

Ives served as contributing editor of *Lighting Journal* from 1913 to 1915 and associate editor of *Journal of the Optical Society of America*. He served as president of the Physics Club of Philadelphia from 1917 to 1918, president of the Optical Society of America from 1924 to 1925, and vice president of the American Association for the Advancement of Science's Section B in 1938. He served as a member of the National Defense Research Committee from 1941 to 1946, for which he was awarded the Medal of Merit. He was an avid collector of coins, specializing in English nobles, Venetian ducats, and Florentine florins, and was president of the American Numismatic Society from 1942 to 1947. He received the City of Philadelphia's John Scott Medal in 1927, the Optical Society of America's Frederic Ives Medal in 1937, and the American Academy of Arts and Sciences' Rumford Medal in 1951. He was elected to the National Academy of Sciences in 1933. He retired from BTL in 1947 and died in New York City.

Ives held some 100 patents, the bulk of them related to electro-optical image transmission. Although he considered his work with photoelectricity to be his most important contribution to physics, his work with photometry and colorimetry also made significant contributions to science and technology.

• Ives's papers are in the Library of Congress, Manuscript Division. A biography, including a bibliography and a list of patents, is Oliver E. Buckley and Karl K. Darrow, "Herbert Eugene Ives," National Academy of Sciences, *Biographical Memoirs* 29 (1953): 145–89. Obituaries are in the *New York Times*, 15 Nov. 1953; *Time* and *Newsweek*, 23 Nov. 1953; and *Nature*, 16 Jan. 1954.

CHARLES W. CAREY, JR.

IVES, Irving McNeil (24 Jan. 1896–24 Feb. 1962), U.S. senator, was born in Bainbridge, New York, the son of George Albert Ives, the owner of a feed and grain store, and Lucy Keeler. His education at Hamilton College was interrupted in 1917 when he enlisted in the army infantry. During World War I he served in the Argonne-Meuse and St.-Mihiel offensives, rising to the rank of first lieutenant before being discharged in 1919. In 1920 he received his A.B. from Hamilton College, having been elected to Phi Beta Kappa. In the same year, he married his childhood sweetheart, Elizabeth Minette Skinner; they had one child.

After spending three years as a bank clerk for Guaranty Trust Company in New York City, Ives moved to Norwich, in upstate New York, to accept a position as manager of a new business division of Manufacturers Trust Company. He held this position until 1930, when, with the support of a reform faction in the Chenango County Republican party, he was elected to the first of eight terms in the New York State Assembly. Continuing to align himself in the assembly with the reform wing of his party, he rose to the position of minority leader in 1935 and Speaker in 1936. Ousted from the Speakership a year later by a party revolt, he was demoted to majority leader, a position he held until he left the assembly after the 1946 session.

During his tenure in the state legislature, Ives established a reputation as a moderate liberal, a careful legislative craftsman, and a conciliatory leader respectful of the opposition. Through his leadership of key social and labor measures in the late 1930s and the war years, he helped to erase the obstructionist label that Old Guard Republicans had burdened the party with during the Great Depression. His reputation benefited greatly from his achievements as chair of the Joint Legislative Committee on Industrial and Labor Conditions (including securing amendments to the state's labor relations laws that provided additional safeguards for unions, an increase in state unemployment and workmen's compensation benefits, and establishment of the New York State School of Industrial and Labor Relations at Cornell University) and especially from his authorship of the Ives-Quinn Law (1945), which established the nation's first state-level Fair Employment Practices Commission to protect against job discrimination on racial, religious, or ethnic grounds.

After his hopes for the 1944 Republican nomination for the U.S. Senate were thwarted by Governor Thomas E. Dewey (who preferred to have a Catholic nominated in order to balance the state ticket), Ives accepted the deanship of the new Industrial and Labor Relations School at Cornell in 1945 and announced his intention to retire from the legislature. The next year, however, Dewey was persuaded by leading state Republicans that Ives should be nominated for New York's other Senate seat. With Dewey's full support, Ives gained the nomination and handily defeated the popular former governor Herbert Lehman in the general election, inflicting on Lehman the only electoral loss of the latter's career and becoming the first Republican senator from New York since 1927. Following his election, Ives resigned his position as dean, from which he had taken leave to campaign. In 1947 his wife Elizabeth died; in July of the following year, Ives married Marion Mead Crain, who had served as his secretary since his early days in the New York State Assembly.

In the Senate, Ives was generally considered a liberal Republican, though his record was somewhat less predictable than that label suggested, and, in fact, he preferred such adjectives as "realistic" or "progressive." A committed internationalist from his days in Europe during World War I, he supported the major legislative underpinnings of containment, including the Marshall Plan and the North Atlantic Treaty Organization (NATO) and most other foreign policy measures proposed by the Truman administration. On the other hand, it was he who in late 1950 successfully urged his fellow Republican senators to adopt a resolution demanding the resignation of Secretary of State Dean Acheson over the issue of Asian policy. On labor-management issues, Ives was considered an expert and was clearly more liberal than most congressional Republicans. In 1947, though a freshman senator at the time, he waged a strong and partially successful fight against powerful senator Robert A. Taft to modify several provisions of what became the Taft-Hartley Act. In particular, Ives persuaded Taft to eliminate wording that would have sharply restricted industry-wide collective bargaining. Though not fully comfortable with the final bill, Ives voted for both its passage and the override of Harry S. Truman's veto. Ives's generally liberal stance was also reflected in the fact that he was one of the seven GOP senators to sign a "Declaration of Conscience" protesting the Communist-baiting tactics of Joseph R. McCarthy in 1950.

Reelected to the Senate in 1952 with a comfortable 55.2 percent of the vote, in his second term Ives was a strong supporter of Dwight D. Eisenhower's internationalist policies and the civil rights legislation of the mid-1950s. He again played a major role in the area of labor legislation, teaming up with Senator John F. Kennedy in 1958 to construct a mild labor-reform bill that was eventually passed in harsher form as the Landrum-Griffin Act in 1959.

Closely identified with Governor Dewey from his first days in the Senate and prominent among the early backers of General Eisenhower for the Republican presidential nomination in 1952, Ives was by many measures a quintessential "middle-of-the-road" Republican of the period. Though not a great orator, he was an effective and productive legislator who clearly enjoyed his responsibilities and who was highly regarded for his expertise on labor and social issues, his integrity, and his skills in committee and at the conference table. The only significant political misstep in his career occurred in 1954, when he succumbed to Dewey's urging to accept (reluctantly, as he later admitted) the Republican nomination for governor of New York. After a troubled campaign, in which he never led, he suffered the only electoral defeat of his career—an 11,000-vote loss to Democrat Averell Harriman.

Ives finished out his second Senate term after his defeat in the gubernatorial election but was forced by ill health not to seek reelection for a third. In January 1959 he retired to Norwich, where he died.

• Ives's papers, useful mostly for his Senate career, are available at Cornell University, Ithaca, N.Y. He also contributed an oral history to the Columbia University Oral History Project. There is no biography of Ives; nor did he publish memoirs. A good assessment of his early career and personality is Warren Moscow, "Freshman Senator Makes His Mark," *New York Times Magazine*, 25 May 1947. The most extensive obituary is in the *New York Times*, 25 Feb. 1962.

GARY W. REICHARD

IVES, James Merritt (5 Mar. 1824–3 Jan. 1895), lithographer and partner in the firm of Currier & Ives, was born in New York City, where his father was superintendent of Bellevue Hospital (his parents' names are unknown). Ives ended his formal education and began working when he was twelve. He had a strong interest in art, however, and continued to educate himself informally by visiting galleries, libraries, and exhibitions. In 1852 Ives married Caroline Clark of Keese-ville, New York. They had six children. Also in 1852 he was hired by Nathaniel Currier as a bookkeeper for his lithography firm, N. Currier, and in 1857 he was made a partner in the company, which was then renamed Currier & Ives. Ives not only served as general business manager for the firm but also contributed some drawings, oversaw print production, supervised the staff artists, and helped select subjects. The extremely successful partnership between Currier and Ives created the major print publishing company in the United States in the nineteenth century. The company slogan, "publishers of cheap and popular pictures," indicates the elements that made the firm successful. Prices of prints were low, ranging at retail from fifteen cents to three dollars. The company made use of the relatively new process of lithography, producing prints from a design drawn on stone. The simplicity of the process made it possible to produce pictures by a kind of assembly line, which included artists who drew the designs, lithographers who prepared the stones, printers who operated the hand presses, and colorists who hand-tinted the prints.

The popularity of the pictures resulted from the partners' exceptional ability to choose subjects of wide appeal. The firm first achieved success by commissioning artists to depict current news events: shipwrecks, fires, parades, and sporting events. They expanded the subject areas to include landscapes, sentimental domestic scenes, portraits, vignettes of rural life, sports, and contemporary national experiences such as the Civil War, the growth of railroads, and the settlement of the West. The firm published more than 7,000 prints in the course of its history. These were widely marketed through direct sales at the New York store, by pushcart peddlers throughout the city, through dealers across the United States and in Europe, and by mail order. In a period when the public had little access to pictures of contemporary life, Currier & Ives filled a large need, both for information and for affordable decorative art.

Outside of his business activities, Ives was active in politics and civil welfare work. During the Civil War he organized and served as captain of F Company, Twenty-third Regiment of Brooklyn, a unit that saw active service at Carlisle, Pennsylvania, in 1863. In 1865 he moved his family from Brooklyn to Westchester County, finally settling in Rye, New York.

After Currier retired in 1880, Ives remained active in the company in partnership with Currier's son, Edward West Currier. Ives died in Rye, New York, leaving his interest in the company to his son Chauncey Ives. The Currier & Ives firm remained in business until 1907. By that time the advent of the newer techniques of photography, photoengraving, chromolithography, and the appearance of illustrated newspapers and weeklies were all providing the public with pictures that had once been available primarily in the firm's hand-colored lithographs.

In its prime, Currier & Ives greatly appealed to American popular taste and informed the public. The work the firm left behind forms an important pictorial record of nineteenth-century American life and tastes. Currier & Ives prints are still widely collected and admired for their picturesque portrayal of the culture of their time.

• The authoritative work on the history of Currier & Ives and the biographies of the two partners is Harry T. Peters, *Currier & Ives: Printmakers to the American People* (1942). Walton Rawls, *The Great Book of Currier & Ives' America* (1979), and Russel Crouse, *Mr. Currier and Mr. Ives* (1930), both give overviews of the historic context of the firm's work. A list of all known Currier & Ives prints appears in *Currier & Ives: A Catalogue Raisonné*, ed. C. Carter Smith and Cathy Coshion (1984).

LINDA S. CHASE

IVES, Joseph Christmas (25 Dec. 1828–12 Nov. 1868), soldier, engineer, and explorer, was born in New York City, the son of Ansel Wilmot Ives and Laura (maiden name unknown), occupations unknown. Little is known of his early years. Apparently, he was raised in a boardinghouse in New Haven, Connecticut. He attended Yale College and graduated fifth in his class at West Point in 1852. Commissioned as a brevet second lieutenant of ordnance, Ives served at the Watervliet, New York, arsenal (1852–1853) and was transferred to the topographical engineers in 1853. He was an assistant topographical engineer on the Pacific Railroad Survey (1853–1854) and in the Pacific Railroad Office in Washington, D.C. (1854–1857). In 1855 he married Cora Semmes, who came from a prominent southern family; they eventually had three children, all sons, two of whom would serve in the U.S. military. In 1857 Ives was promoted to first lieutenant and was named to lead an expedition up the Colorado River in order to develop potential routes of supply in the event of a war between the national government and the Mormon settlements in Deseret (Utah).

Ives's expedition included John Strong Newberry as naturalist, the Prussian Heinrich Balduin Möllhausen as artist and unofficial diarist, and F. W. Egloffstein as topographer. Ives purchased a steamboat in Philadelphia. The vessel was taken apart and shipped via the Isthmus of Panama to California and thence to the mouth of the Colorado River, where Ives and the members of his expedition rendezvoused late in 1857.

Ives and his men reassembled the steamboat and christened it the *Explorer*. They launched the ship on 31 December 1857 and set out on their journey of reconnaissance. They progressed northward for two months, passing through Mojave Canyon and Bill Williams's Fork, before the ship hit a rock on 5 March 1858. Following this setback, Ives divided his men into two parties, one to return with the boat, the other to return by land. Ives led the latter group, which consisted of Newberry, Egloffstein, Möllhausen, Peacock, three laborers, the Mexican packers, and twenty soldiers commanded by Lieutenant John Tipton. The groups parted company on 23 March 1858, and Ives's group soon entered the most rewarding part of their travels. On 3 April they had their first sight of what Ives called the "Big Cañon" (what today is called the

Grand Canyon). Ives recorded his reactions, "a splendid panorama burst suddenly into view . . . vast plateaus, towering one above the other thousands of feet in the air, the long horizontal bands broken at intervals by wide and profound abysses, and extending a hundred miles to the north, till the deep azure blue faded into a light cerulean tint that blended with the dome of the heavens." Ives and his men descended as far as they could that day, and the next morning (4 Apr. 1858) they stood on the floor of the Grand Canyon. Spanish explorers had sighted the Grand Canyon in 1540, and trappers probably had seen it, but Ives and his party appear to have been the first white men to visit the floor of this great natural wonder.

Ives's party pushed on and visited Cataract Canyon on 12 April. On 2 May Ives divided his party again and led a small group to the villages of the Moqui. He and his men then pushed eastward and reached Fort Defiance on 23 May 1858, concluding their journey there. Their expedition had been productive in many particulars, but Ives made a strange prediction in his report, "It seems intended by nature that the Colorado River, along the greater portion of its lone and majestic way, shall be forever unvisited and undisturbed." The next century would prove quite the opposite to be the case.

Ives was the engineer and architect of the Washington Monument (1859–1860). In 1861 he declined the offer of a captaincy in the Union army and chose instead to serve as a captain of engineers with the Confederate forces. Three factors appear to have influenced Ives in this matter: his marriage to a southern woman, his admiration of Robert E. Lee, who had been his commandant at West Point, and his friendship with Jefferson Davis, whom he had known in Washington, D.C. Ives rose to the rank of colonel in the Confederate forces and also became aide-de-camp to President Davis. In addition, the Ives home in Richmond, Virginia, became one of the focal points of high society during the Civil War. The Iveses were known as superb hosts, and the performance of the comedy *The Rivals* at their home in February 1864 was the best-remembered event of Richmond society. After the Civil War ended, Ives moved his family to New York City, where he died a few years later after a short illness.

Ives led a life that appeared to embody heroic and romantic purposes. Starting from what was probably an impoverished youth, he became a member of a small and elite group, the U.S. Topographical Engineers, and was influential in the society of Washington, D.C., before the Civil War and in Richmond society during the war. He has the distinction of being the leader of the first group of white men to visit the floor of the Grand Canyon, where his party made significant geological observations. Ives's explorations have seldom been celebrated in U.S. history, perhaps because he joined the Confederacy and died at an early age, and he has seldom received his full due as an explorer. However, as Lewis R. Freeman wrote, "Ives' delightfully-told story of the day-to-day doings of his party set a mark for descriptive writing that has rarely been equalled in a Government report. . . . Ives' untimely death was a real loss to both science and literature" (p. 170).

• Ives's record of exploration, *Report upon the Colorado River of the West*, 36th Cong., 1st sess., 1861, is a masterpiece of factual description combined with a discoverer's euphoria. The document has been made accessible for younger readers by Alexander L. Crosby, ed., *Steamboat up the Colorado* (1965). A full-length biography has yet to be published, but information on Ives can be found in William H. Goetzmann, *Army Exploration in the American West* (1959) and *Exploration and Empire* (1966); Lewis R. Freeman, *The Colorado River Yesterday, To-Day, and To-Morrow* (1923); David H. Miller, "The Ives Expedition Revisited: A Prussian's Impressions," *Journal of Arizona History* 13 (Spring 1972): 1–25; Herman J. Viola, *Exploring the West* (1987); and Wallace Stegner, *Beyond the Hundredth Meridian* (1953). Ives's career with the Confederacy is discussed briefly in Hudson Strode, *Jefferson Davis, Confederate President* (1959), and Thomas Cooper De Leon, *Belles, Beaux and Brains of the 60s* (1909).

SAMUEL WILLARD CROMPTON

IVES, Levi Silliman (16 Sept. 1797–13 Oct. 1867), Episcopal bishop, was born in Meriden, Connecticut, the son of Levi Ives and Fanny Silliman, farmers. He served in the War of 1812 and in 1816 entered Hamilton College, Clinton, New York, to prepare for the Presbyterian ministry but did not graduate because of ill health. Ives then took charge of an academy in Pottsdam, New York, where he led Sunday services and preached for the Presbyterians who had no resident pastor. In 1819 Ives joined the Episcopal church and stated his reason for so doing in a letter to Bishop John Henry Hobart of New York: "And that the present Ep. Ch. is the true church I think is evident from the *uninterrupted succession* of her ministry and the primitive form of her worship" (Malone [1970], p. 6). The importance of the liturgy of the Episcopal church and the apostolic succession of Episcopal bishops would shape Ives's theology and churchmanship.

Ives studied theology under Hobart and at the General Theological Seminary, when it moved from New Haven, Connecticut, to New York City. Hobart ordained him deacon on 4 August 1822 at St. John's Church, New York. His first assignment as a deacon was at St. James' Church, Batavia, New York. In June 1823 Ives became the rector of Trinity Church, Philadelphia, and on 14 December 1823 was ordained priest at Trinity Church by Bishop William White of Pennsylvania. In 1825 Ives married Rebecca Smith Hobart, the bishop's daughter; they had two children, both of whom died in childhood. After three years at Trinity Church Ives became co-rector of St. James' Church, Lancaster, Pennsylvania, in 1826, replacing William Augustus Muhlenberg. After only a year, he moved in September 1827 to New York City to become assistant minister at Christ Church. This move brought him back to proximity with the Hobart family. Having had enough of assistantships, Ives accepted

a new position as rector of St. Luke's Church, New York City, in March 1828.

It is unclear how Ives's name came before the clergy of the diocese of North Carolina, but on 21 May 1831 he was elected the second bishop of that diocese to succeed the influential and prominent high churchman John Stark Ravenscroft. Ives was ordained and consecrated bishop on 22 September 1831 at Trinity Church, Philadelphia. One of Ives's major concerns as bishop was missionary and educational work among the slaves of North Carolina. He urged Episcopal slave owners to have their slaves baptized and catechized. Ives also supported educational efforts for boys and girls in the diocese. The Episcopal School of North Carolina opened at Raleigh on 2 June 1834 to instruct Episcopal boys in "the doctrine, discipline, and worship of the Church" and to prepare students for the ministry who were unable to attend the General Theological Seminary. Ives also supported the founding of St. Mary's School for girls at Raleigh, which opened on 12 May 1842.

Bishop Ives first began to take steps toward the establishment of a mountain mission in Watauga County at a place he named Valle Crucis (Valley of the Cross) in 1844. This mission was to extend the gospel throughout a territory inhabited by a religiously destitute people and to give instruction to the poor children of the immediate vicinity. It was to train young men of talent from the surrounding country on the condition that they would serve as teachers and catechists for a certain time after graduation and to give theological training to candidates for holy orders. This mission was also to have an agricultural school and to maintain a model farm to instruct the surrounding population in improved agriculture. In October 1847 five men made their profession to the religious life before Bishop Ives at St. Luke's Church, New York, thus founding the Order of the Holy Cross. Some of them went to Valle Crucis, and by "1849 the mission at Valle Crucis had begun to drift away from the teachings of the Church, and was fast becoming a feeble and undignified imitation of the monastic institutions of the Church of Rome" (Haywood, p. 112). Many believed that Ives was a part of the Oxford Movement, which emphasized monasticism, auricular confession, the real presence of Christ in the Eucharist, the reservation and adoration of the sacrament, prayers to the saints, and other Roman Catholic practices.

After numerous controversies within his diocese and a hearing at the diocesan convention in 1848 on his heterodox views, Ives on 27 September 1852 informed the standing committee of the diocese that on account of the ill health of his wife and himself he wanted a leave of absence for six months beginning on 1 October, with an advance of $1,000 of his salary, so that they could travel. This was granted, and they left for Europe. By this time Ives, like John Henry Newman, had become convinced that the Roman Catholic church was the one true church. On 22 December 1852 Ives wrote to the diocese of North Carolina and stated, "I hereby *resign* into your hands my office as

Bishop of North Carolina; and further, that I am determined to make my submission to the Catholic Church." He made his formal submission to Pope Pius IX on Christmas Day. The House of Bishops of the Episcopal church deposed him on 14 October 1853. He told the story of his conversion to Roman Catholicism in *The Trials of a Mind in Its Progress to Catholicism: A Letter to His Old Friends* (1854).

Ives returned to New York City in 1854 as a Catholic layman. He became a lecturer in rhetoric at St. Joseph's Seminary and St. John's College, and he lectured at the convents of the Sacred Heart and the Sisters of Charity. His main career was in Catholic charities—he was president of New York's Superior Council, and in 1863 he organized the New York Catholic Protectory and became its first president. He died at Manhattanville, New York, the only Episcopal bishop to abandon the Episcopal church over the Oxford Movement controversy.

• Some of Ives's letters and papers are in the Archives of the Episcopal Church, Austin, Tex., and in the Southern Historical Collection, University of North Carolina, Chapel Hill. Some of his major publications are *Humility, a Ministerial Qualification* (1840), *The Apostles' Doctrine and Fellowship* (1844), and *The Obedience of Faith* (1849). Several of his sermons and episcopal charges to the diocese also were published. The major and most sympathetic study of Ives is Michael T. Malone, "Levi Silliman Ives: Priest, Bishop, Tractarian, and Roman Catholic" (Ph.D. diss., Duke Univ., 1970). A study from the Catholic perspective is John O'Grady, *Levi Silliman Ives: Pioneer Leader in Catholic Charities* (1933). Marshall D. Haywood, *Lives of the Bishops of North Carolina: From the Establishment of the Episcopate in That State Down to the Division of the Diocese* (1910), has a lengthy treatment of Ives with a number of primary sources. Ives is treated in the context of the history of the diocese of North Carolina in Blackwell P. Robinson, "The Episcopate of Levi Silliman Ives," in *The Episcopal Church in North Carolina, 1701–1959*, ed. Lawrence F. London and Sarah McCulloh Lemmon (1987). Two helpful articles are Malone, "The Gentle Ives and the Unruly Prescott: Changes in the Church," *Anglican Theological Review* 69 (1987): 363–74, and Richard Rankin, "Bishop Levi S. Ives and High Church Reform in North Carolina: Tractarianism as an Instrument to Elevate Clerical and Lay Piety," *Anglican and Episcopal History* 57 (1988): 298–319.

DONALD S. ARMENTROUT

IVINS, Anthony Woodward (16 Sept. 1852–23 Sept. 1934), businessman, rancher, and church leader, was born in Toms River, New Jersey, the son of Israel Ivins, a pioneer physician and farmer, and Anna Lowrie. Shortly after Ivins's birth, his family converted to the Church of Jesus Christ of Latter-day Saints (Mormon). They moved west to the Salt Lake Valley, and in 1861 Israel Ivins was assigned by Brigham Young to help in the settlement of southern Utah. The Ivins family settled in the area of St. George, where Anthony spent his childhood. He attended public schools but was mostly self-taught, including his legal education.

In 1875 Ivins was assigned by leaders of the Mormon church to assist in exploring Arizona, New Mexico, and northern Mexico, where future colonies of Mormon immigrants would be settled. After returning to St. George in 1877, he was appointed the constable of the growing city. A short time later, in 1878, he was assigned a proselytizing mission to the Indians and Mexicans in New Mexico. He retained a special interest in these two groups his whole life. In 1878 he married Elizabeth Ashby Snow; they had nine children, eight of whom survived childhood. Ivins never entered into plural marriages.

By 1882 Ivins was elected prosecuting attorney for Washington County in southern Utah and was an active member of the St. George City Council (1882, 1886–1888). He also served in various leadership positions within the Mormon church. In April 1882 he was assigned another preaching mission, this time to Mexico City, where he labored as president of the Mexican mission until 1884 and learned Spanish. Returning to St. George in 1884, Ivins again became involved in the business and church affairs of southern Utah. He was the manager of the Mohave Land and Cattle Company and an owner of the Kaibab Cattle Company, which were the two largest owners of cattle in southern Utah and northern Arizona. In 1888 he was one of the organizers of the "Sagebrush Democrats," arguing that Utah's prior political parties, organized as they were into Mormon and non-Mormon groups, would not serve well Utah's pending application for statehood. Thus he became a strong voice encouraging Utah voters to align themselves more fully with the national political parties. He remained a Democrat throughout his life, even as other church leaders moved into the Republican party. During this time he was also mayor of St. George (1890–1894), county assessor and collector of Mohave County, Arizona Territory (1884–1890), and special agent for the Shivwits Indians (1891–1893). He was elected to two terms in the Utah territorial legislature (1894–1895) and in 1894 was chosen as a representative to the Utah State Constitutional Convention. His growing popularity suggested to many that he was a prime candidate to be the first governor of the new state.

In 1895 Ivins's life moved in another direction when he was asked by Mormon church president Wilford Woodruff to return to Mexico to assist in establishing Mormon colonies there. Ivins spent the next thirteen years in Mexico, establishing his headquarters in Colonia Juárez, Chihuahua. Officially he was the president of the Juárez Latter-day Saints (LDS) Stake (comparable to a diocese) and vice president and general manager of the Mexican Colonization and Agricultural Company, the organization under which the Mormon colonies in Mexico were founded and operated. A total of eight colonies in the Mexican states of Chihuahua and Sonora looked to Ivins for leadership. His responsibility for the settlements continued even after he was called back to Utah to be a member of the Quorum of Twelve Apostles in October 1907. He was actively involved with the evacuation of the Mormon colonies when church members were forced to flee Mexico in response to the upheavals of 1912 and 1913.

After Ivins left Mexico in 1907, his involvement in various business and church activities increased. He was president of the Utah Savings and Trust Company; president of the board of trustees of Utah State Agricultural College; president of Utah State National Bank; on the board of directors of Zion's Savings Bank and Trust Company; vice president of Zion's Cooperative Mercantile Institution and Beneficial Life Insurance Company; a member of the National Boy Scout Committee; a director of the Deseret Savings Bank and the U.S. Fuel Company; and the owner of the Ivins Investment Company in Salt Lake City, which held a large ranch in Enterprise, Utah. An active leader in Mormon church youth organizations, he served as a member of the General Board of the Young Men's Mutual Improvement Association from 1909 to 1929 and general superintendent from 1919 to 1921. He was vice president of the Genealogical Society of Utah from 1921 to 1925 and president from 1925 to 1934. This society was the foundation of what has become one of the largest genealogical and family history libraries in the world. Remaining active in ranching throughout his life, Ivins is credited with introducing purebred cattle into southern Utah. For his extensive involvement in the ranching and cattle industries, he was voted into the National Cowboy Hall of Fame in 1970.

In 1921 Ivins was chosen to be second counselor to Heber J. Grant in the First Presidency, the highest governing body in the LDS church. Ivins's call to service in this important body was a testament to his life of service and to the high esteem in which he was held by his peers. In 1925 he was named first counselor, a position he held until his death in Salt Lake City. In 1924 he was given full membership in the Paiute Indian tribe for his work in acquiring land in southern Utah for the Paiutes. In 1932 the tribe sent him a leather vest expressing the sentiment "Tony Ivins, he no cheat," and upon his death the Paiutes held a ceremony in his honor.

• The majority of Ivins's personal papers and journals are in the Utah State Historical Society, Salt Lake City, Utah. These include sixty diaries (1875–1932), twenty-two notebooks, correspondence files, and some business records. A detailed register to the collection is available. An Anthony W. Ivins Collection, which includes an autobiography, is in the Historical Department, Church of Jesus Christ of Latter-day Saints, Salt Lake City, Utah. See also H. Grant Ivins, "Polygamy in Mexico as Practiced by the Mormon Church, 1895–1905," an unpublished manuscript in Archives and Manuscripts, Lee Library, Brigham Young University, Provo, Utah. His official addresses were published in the semiannual *Conference Reports*. His only published book is *The Relationship of "Mormonism" and Free-Masonry* (1934). Secondary works include a biographical series by his son Stanley S. Ivins, "Anthony W. Ivins," *The Instructor* 78 and 79 (Nov. 1943–June 1944). William R. Palmer, "Anthony W. Ivins," *The Instructor* 79 (July 1944): 311–14, discusses the high regard Native Americans had for Ivins. Other biographical sketches are David Dryden, *Biographical Essays on Three General Authorities of the Early Twentieth Century: Anthony W. Ivins, George F. Richards, and Stephen L. Richards*, Task Papers in LDS History no. 11 (1976); and Andrew Jenson, *Latter-day Saint Biographical Encyclopedia*, vols. 1, 3 (4 vols., 1901–1936). Additional information on Ivins and his career is in B. Carmon Hardy, "The Mormon Colonies in Northern Mexico: A History, 1885–1912" (Ph.D. diss., Wayne State Univ., 1963); and F. Lamond Tullis, *Mormons in Mexico: The Dynamics of Faith and Culture* (1987). Ivins remained monogamous his whole life, but information on the larger context of Mormon marriage practices, including those marriages Ivins performed in Mexico, is in Hardy, *Solemn Covenant: The Mormon Polygamous Passage* (1992). Obituaries are in the *Deseret News*, 24 and 27 Sept. 1934, and *Salt Lake Tribune*, 24 Sept. 1934.

DAVID J. WHITTAKER

IVINS, William Mills (22 Apr. 1851–23 July 1915), lawyer and municipal reformer, was born in Freehold, New Jersey, the son of Augustus Ivins, a prominent street railway builder, and Sarah Mills, a noted charity worker. Ivins attended Adelphi Academy and then secured employment with local publisher D. Appleton & Company. He soon entered Columbia Law School, graduating and gaining admission to the bar in 1873. In 1879 he married Emma Laura Yard of Freehold, New Jersey.

In Brooklyn during the 1870s, Ivins began law practice and his lifelong municipal reform activities. He joined the movement against "Brooklyn Ring" boss Hugh McLaughlin and aided in prosecuting corrupt Brooklyn aldermen. In 1881 Ivins moved to Manhattan, where he became New York mayor William R. Grace's private secretary. After a Democrat-Tammany alliance defeated Grace in the 1882 mayoral election, Ivins left the Democratic party and joined Grace as a business partner. Upon being reelected in 1884, Grace appointed Ivins to the post of city chamberlain, a job he retained until 1889. Ivins also served as a New York City school commissioner from 1883 to 1885 and as New York State judge advocate-general from 1886 to 1888. From this experience Ivins acquired a deep hatred of Tammany politics, a hostility that the *New York Times* later said "seemed born into him."

In April 1889 Ivins resigned as city chamberlain to conduct business in Brazil for W. R. Grace & Company, a large merchant firm specializing in South American trade. At the time, Brazil was undergoing a revolution, and U.S. businesses were expanding investments there. Sent to investigate a failing Amazon rubber company, Ivins cultivated business and political connections that he pursued long after retiring from Grace in September 1889. In 1892, as president of the United States and Brazil Mail Steamship Company, he regularly visited South American ports. In 1893 Brazil hired him as counsel in the boundary dispute with Argentina that was resolved by President Grover Cleveland. In 1897 he traveled to St. Petersburg for an American firm to sell battleships to Russia's government. Shortly before the Spanish-American War, he declared support for the Cuban Revolution and successfully defended rebel leader Calixto Garcia against charges of running munitions to Cuba. In 1904 he became president of the General Rubber Company, an importer of crude rubber from South America. In 1910 he filed an amicus curiae brief for the American Tobacco Company's antitrust case before the U.S. Supreme Court. Through these long years of business, Ivins amassed a sizable fortune.

Despite his business dealings, contemporaries knew Ivins best for his municipal reform work. One of many urban middle-class professionals of his time who supported structural reform of city government to eliminate machine politics, he earned renown by promoting ballot reform, public utility regulation, and New York City charter revision. As city chamberlain during the 1880s, Ivins became very familiar with urban administration and politics. His 1887 Commonwealth Club speech, published as "Machine Politics and Money in Elections in New York City," denounced the patronage system and advocated election law reform. Consequently in 1890 the state senate made him counsel to its committee investigating corruption in city government. This work contributed in 1895 to New York State's adoption of the Australian "secret" ballot, a popular electoral reform of the day that challenged machine control over local politics.

After 1900 Ivins affiliated with Republican reformers led by Charles Evans Hughes. In 1905 Ivins ran a distant third as the anti-Tammany Republican candidate for New York mayor against Tammany Hall's George B. McClellan (1865–1940) and newspaper publisher William Randolph Hearst. With fraud suspected in McClellan's election, Ivins represented Hearst in an unsuccessful recount. Four years later, he managed Hearst's mayoral campaign.

When Hughes became governor of New York in 1907, Ivins joined progressive reform circles as an adviser to the governor. Focusing on public utility reform, he promoted enactment of New York's 1907 Public Service Commissions Act, which subjected financially unstable gas, electricity, and street railway companies to public oversight. As special counsel to the state's new Public Service Commission, Ivins became an authority on public utilities law. His *Control of Public Utilities* (published with Herbert Mason in 1908) was the definitive contemporary legal treatise on the subject, and his 1909 *Century Magazine* article forcefully defended public utilities law as an essential administrative tool for controlling utilities' financial abuses. In 1907 Ivins also headed the commission that developed a modern New York City charter. The proposed charter would have shifted city functions from the mayor and aldermen to administrative bureaus, but party chieftains prevented its adoption by the legislature.

Ivins was a family man with wide-ranging personal interests. He had four children, one of them William Mills Ivins, Jr., noted print historian and museum curator. Ivins himself cultivated many avocations—learning five foreign languages, collecting Napoleonic war relics, practicing botany, and leaving unpublished manuscripts on diplomacy and the rubber trade as well as unpublished translations of works by Henri Bergson and Friedrich Nietzsche. Friends remembered him as witty, well traveled, and "many-sided," with a zeal for public service.

Ivins ended his days laboring on new public endeavors. During 1914 and 1915, as senior member of New York City law firm Ivins, Wolff & Hoguet, a partnership established in 1905, Ivins represented former New York State Republican party leader William Barnes in a widely publicized libel suit against ex-president Theodore Roosevelt (1858–1919). At the trial, Ivins grilled the former president in more than forty hours of cross-examination, but the jury decided in Roosevelt's favor. Despite that deep disappointment, Ivins went immediately after the trial to a state convention drafting a new judiciary article for New York's constitution. He was working on the judiciary article at his New York City home when he collapsed and died.

• Ivins's papers are contained in the William Mills Ivins, Jr., Papers at the Archives of American Art, Smithsonian Institution, Washington, D.C. His published speeches, reports, and legal briefs are held in scattered libraries. His municipal reform work is briefly discussed in Martin J. Schiesl, *The Politics of Efficiency: Municipal Administration and Reform in America, 1800–1920* (1977), while his 1905 New York City mayoral race receives coverage in Richard L. McCormick, *From Realignment to Reform: Political Change in New York State, 1893–1910* (1981), and in Irwin Yellowitz, *Labor and the Progressive Movement in New York State, 1897–1916* (1965). The *New York Times Index* will yield dozens of entries about his activities over the years. An obituary and editorial on his life are in the *New York Times*, 24 July 1915. Memorials are in the *New York County Lawyers' Association Yearbook* (1916): 249–56; the *New York State Bar Association Proceedings* 39 (1916): 502–6; and the *Association of the Bar of the City of New York Yearbook* (1918): 188–93.

DONALD W. ROGERS

IVY, Andrew Conway (25 Feb. 1893–7 Feb. 1978), medical scientist, was born in Farmington, Missouri, the son of Henry McPherson Ivy, a chemistry professor, and Cynthia Smith, a biology teacher. Shortly after Andrew's birth, the family moved to Cape Girardeau, Missouri, where Ivy's father taught at the State Normal School, and his mother taught at a local high school. When Ivy was five years old, he seized on the idea of becoming a physician, inspired by a local doctor who traveled about the Mississippi River town with a horse and buggy. In 1907 Ivy's father was killed in a horse-riding accident. Ivy paid his own way at the Normal School in Cape Girardeau by teaching part time at a local high school. While juggling the responsibilities of both student and teacher, he played second base on the baseball team (he was offered a contract by a St. Louis Cardinals farm team), starred as quarterback and defensive end on the football team, and achieved other successes as a basketball player, tennis player, gymnast, wrestler, boxer, musician, and debater.

After receiving an A.B. and a B.Pd. in 1913, Ivy did not have sufficient funds to proceed directly to medical school. Instead, he accepted a position as principal and athletic coach at a high school in Clarksdale, Mississippi. After two years Ivy had saved enough money to enroll at the University of Chicago, where he quickly came under the influence of the renowned physiologist Anton J. "Ajax" Carlson. Mentored by Carlson, Ivy earned three degrees at Chicago in quick succession: B.S. (1916), M.S. (1917), and Ph.D. (1918). Carlson directed Ivy to research in gastrointestinal physiology, which became the subject of Ivy's doctoral dissertation and the focus of much of his most significant later scientific work.

After completing his Ph.D. Ivy entered Rush Medical School and received an M.D. in 1922. Again, Ivy functioned as both pupil and professor: while finishing his doctorate and working toward his medical degree, he was an instructor in physiology at the University of Chicago (1917–1919) and associate professor of physiology at Loyola University School of Medicine (1919–1923). After his stint at Loyola, Ivy returned to the University of Chicago, where he served as an associate professor for two years (1923–1925). Northwestern University then lured Ivy to become chair of its Department of Physiology and Pharmacology. Ivy held this position for more than twenty years. In 1946 he accepted an offer to become vice president of the University of Illinois, with responsibility for the Chicago professional schools (medicine, dentistry, and pharmacy). Simultaneously, he served as head of the medical school's Department of Clinical Science.

Between 1919 and 1955 Ivy published with various co-workers more than 1,500 papers, averaging more than forty every year for thirty-five years. At his peak, he was producing one publication every week. During this same period he supervised more than 300 physiology graduate students (at the height of his activity, as many as forty graduate students worked under him at once). Ivy also taught physiology to roughly 6,000 medical students during his career. Indeed, he considered his students his greatest contribution to the world of science. But Ivy's peers also recognized him for the excellence of his research. In 1938 the American Medical Association (AMA) presented Ivy with a Gold Medal for Research, recognizing his work on the experimental production of intersexuality. Three years later Ivy won another AMA Gold Medal in recognition of his investigation of bile formation. Ivy received an AMA Silver Medal for Research in 1944 for work that he had done on the effect of caffeine on the stomach. In 1950 Ivy filled out his collection of AMA medals with a bronze award for his use of flicker photometry in the investigation of cardiovascular disease. He served as president of the American Physiological Society in 1939 and of the American Gastroenterological Association in 1940–1941. During World War II Ivy carried out investigations in several areas of vital military significance, including work on sea water desalination that was put to use in Allied life rafts. Ivy also led important wartime research in the field of aviation medicine, contributing to the development of oxygen masks for pilots and the general understanding of the physiological challenges associated with high-altitude flight. From 1942 through 1943 Ivy commuted regularly to Bethesda, Maryland, where he served as director of the Naval Medical Research Institute. In 1948 Ivy received a Presidential Certificate of Merit for "outstanding fidelity and meritorious conduct in World War II."

Ivy also came to be recognized by newspaper reporters as an accessible expert who could be relied on to explain complex medical developments in a simple, pithy fashion. As a result, according to a story on Ivy in *Life* magazine (9 Oct. 1964), "Ivy's name became a household byword" in the middle decades of the twentieth century. Recognizing Ivy's deep knowledge of medical science, his commitment to high-quality research, and his ability to communicate well with nonexperts, the AMA chose Ivy when prosecutors preparing for the postwar Nuremberg Medical Trial approached the organization looking for an expert medical consultant. In this trial, Ivy offered behind-the-scenes advice and courtroom testimony on matters of medical science and medical ethics. A *Time* magazine article describing Ivy's role in the trial identified him as both "the conscience of U.S. science" and as "one of the nation's top physiologists" (13 Jan. 1947, p. 47). In his testimony, Ivy argued that widely recognized, but unwritten, standards for the proper conduct of human experiments existed, which the Nazi defendants had clearly violated in horrific experiments on concentration camp inmates. Ivy asserted that all medical scientists working with human subjects understood the moral necessity of obtaining consent from their subjects and the obligation to conduct humane, well-planned experiments. The members of the Nuremberg Tribunal drew heavily on Ivy's testimony when they crafted these previously unwritten standards into a ten-point statement on research ethics. This decalogue first appeared in the final judgment of the Nuremberg Medical Trial, handed down in August 1947, and it continues to stand as an influential milestone in medical ethics.

In the spring of 1949 Ivy received a visit from Stevan Durovic, a physician who had fled to Argentina from his native Yugoslavia during World War II. During his sojourn in Argentina, Durovic had supposedly developed an anti-cancer drug after extensive research, which had been funded primarily by Durovic's wealthy brother Marco (the two had left Yugoslavia together). During his initial meeting with Ivy, Durovic showed slides that seemed to demonstrate the effectiveness of his new drug, which he had dubbed "Krebiozen." Durovic was unwilling, however, to share with Ivy the techniques for developing Krebiozen, claiming that he needed to hold the process in secret to protect his brother's investment. Ivy, who had long been interested in cancer research, was intrigued by Durovic's initial presentation and, for reasons that remain unclear, soon became fixated on Krebiozen as a genuine cure for cancer.

Ivy's personal enthusiasm for Krebiozen and his reputation as one of the nation's leading medical scientists quickly combined to bring this cancer "cure" national attention. Unfortunately, Durovic continued to evade queries about Krebiozen's chemical composition and precise therapeutic action. Virtually all members of the medical community soon dismissed Durovic as a quack and Krebiozen as medically useless. Ivy nevertheless maintained his commitment to the potential of Krebiozen as a treatment for cancer through tumultuous controversy, at great cost to his career.

Perhaps most significantly, Krebiozen brought an end to Ivy's tenure as vice president of the University of Illinois in 1953, when he resigned from this position under pressure. After giving up his administrative post, Ivy maintained his faculty appointment at the university until 1961. Then, he moved to a much less prestigious institution in Chicago, Roosevelt University, where he was a professor of biochemistry from 1961 to 1966. Ivy spent the last active decade of his life working in the laboratories of the privately funded Ivy Cancer Research Foundation in Chicago. He died in Chicago.

Ivy had an able domestic and intellectual partner through his years of scientific fame and infamy: in 1919 he had married Emma Anna Kohman, who had also received a Ph.D. in physiology at the University of Chicago. Occasionally, she assisted Ivy in his laboratory work, but most of her energy was consumed in raising their five sons.

In an almost classic version of the American rags-to-riches story, Ivy rose above the challenges of his early life to achieve not wealth but scientific prominence. Likewise, his fall during his final two decades approached mythic dimensions. Even after Ivy's personal reputation plummeted as a result of his obsession with Krebiozen, however, medical scientists continued to make use of the important work that Ivy had done before—and immediately after—his fateful meeting with Durovic in 1949. Indeed, a fellow physiologist claimed, based on a review of *Science Citation Index*, that as late as "the period from 1964 to 1971 Ivy's articles were cited more often than any other scientist in the world" (Grossman, p. 11).

• Ivy's personal papers do not seem to have been preserved. The transcript of an interview conducted by James David Boyle with Ivy on 4 Nov. 1968 as part of a formal oral history project organized by the American Gastroenterological Association can be found at the National Library of Medicine, Bethesda, Md. A copy of Ivy's lengthy personal bibliography is attached to the interview transcript. Perhaps the best recounting of Ivy's involvement with Krebiozen is in Patricia Spain Ward, "'Who Will Bell the Cat?' Andrew C. Ivy and Krebiozen," *Bulletin of the History of Medicine* 58 (1984): 28–52. George D. Stoddard, who was president of the University of Illinois during the early 1950s (and who was forced to resign from this post by pro-Ivy forces on the university's board of trustees), published a book-length analysis of the Krebiozen scandal, *Krebiozen: The Great Cancer Mystery* (1955). Stoddard also gave the protracted story more attention in his autobiography, *The Pursuit of Education: An Autobiography* (1981). Another particularly rich source on Ivy's career in general and Krebiozen in particular is Warren R. Young, "Whatever Happened to Dr. Ivy? A Famous Scien-

tist's Strange Obsession with a Cancer 'Cure,'" *Life*, 9 Oct. 1964, pp. 110–24. Significant biographical notices published after Ivy's death include Morton I. Grossman, "Andrew Conway Ivy (1893–1978)," *Physiologist* (Apr. 1978):11–12, and D. B. Dill, "A. C. Ivy—Reminiscences," *Physiologist* (Oct. 1979): 21–22. An obituary is in the *New York Times*, 10 Feb. 1978.

JON M. HARKNESS

IZARD, George (21 Oct. 1776–22 Nov. 1828), army officer and territorial governor of Arkansas, was born in the Richmond district of London, England, the son of Ralph Izard, a planter and diplomat, and Alice DeLancey. His parents were members of influential families in both South Carolina and New York. Izard spent his early years abroad, received his initial education at the Collège de Navarre in Paris, and accompanied his mother back to Charleston in 1783. When his father was elected senator in 1789, the family relocated to New York City. There Izard attended King's College (now Columbia University) and graduated in 1792 at the age of fifteen. He then accompanied Minister to Great Britain Thomas Pinckney on a European tour to complete his education. Izard attended military academies in England, Scotland, and Germany and in 1795 was admitted to the prestigious *École du Génie* in Metz, France, under the auspices of James Monroe, then minister to that country. While in attendance he also received a second lieutenant's commission dated 2 June 1794. Returning to South Carolina three years later, Izard served as engineer at Castle Pinckney, Charleston harbor, and acquitted himself well. Considering the lack of professionalism in the American army of his day, Izard's training and abilities were regarded as exceptional.

The impending quasi-war with France advanced Izard's military career, and on 12 July 1799 he became captain of engineers. He also briefly served as aide to Alexander Hamilton, the senior general officer of the provisional army. Once the prospect of war dissipated, Izard took leave of the military to become secretary to the chargé d'affaires at Lisbon, Portugal, until January 1801. He then returned to the United States, assumed command of Fort Mifflin, Pennsylvania, and resigned his commission on 1 June 1803. That year he also married Elizabeth Carter Shippen of Bucks County, Pennsylvania, settled in Philadelphia, and raised three sons. Intellectually inclined, Izard became an active member of both the American Philosophical Society and the U.S. Military Philosophical Society. It is not known what profession he followed during this time.

Izard resumed active duty on 12 March 1812, when he became colonel of the Second Artillery Regiment in anticipation of war with England. He was initially stationed at Philadelphia but subsequently transferred to Military District Three with headquarters in New York City. Izard functioned effectively, was promoted brigadier general on 12 March 1813, and took a post with the Right Division at Plattsburgh, New York. He then accompanied Major General Wade Hampton's offensive against Montreal, fought well at the 26 October 1813 battle of Châteauguay, and skillfully directed the American rearguard. When Hampton resigned in disgrace, Izard was promoted major general to succeed him on 24 January 1814. He thus nominally outranked noted contemporaries Jacob Brown and Andrew Jackson by two months and, at the age of thirty-eight, had become the army's senior general officer.

In May 1814 Izard repaired to Plattsburgh to assume control of the Right Division, which he found unpaid, untrained, and lacking supplies and equipment. Izard labored throughout the summer to completely overhaul his charge by recruiting, clothing, and disciplining a force of 5,000 regular soldiers. It was an impressive achievement by the standards of the time and eclipses the smaller but more famous efforts of Winfield Scott at Buffalo. Izard felt confident in repelling any offensive the British could undertake against northern New York when remarkable orders were sent by the War Department. Secretary of War John Armstrong, discounting reports of a British buildup at Montreal, ordered the Right Division to march 400 miles west to Niagara and assist American forces there. Izard pleaded with the secretary to relent, for Governor General Sir George Prevost had massed 10,000 Napoleonic veterans on the border. When no change of orders was forthcoming, Izard dutifully marched west with 4,000 men. This move precluded his participation in the decisive American victory of Plattsburgh, 11 September 1814.

Izard arrived at Niagara after a fatiguing march of twenty-nine days and succeeded Major General Jacob Jennings Brown of the Left Division as theater commander. Their combined strength was 6,000 men, twice as many as British forces commanded by Lieutenant General Sir Gordon Drummond, whose capture was anticipated. However, these two strong-willed and capable leaders were at cross purposes. The aggressive Brown wanted to storm Drummond's position behind the Chippewa River in Canada while Izard sought to lure him into the open first. Izard ordered several demonstrations in front of Drummond's line, but when he refused to fight Brown grew disillusioned and marched his division east to Sackets Harbor, New York.

Izard, meanwhile, refused to commit his troops to costly frontal assaults and sought to turn the British right by dispatching Brigadier General Daniel Bissell's brigade to attack Cook's Mills. On 28 October 1814 Bissell drove off a British force and burned a large quantity of grain, after which he was recalled. Izard, mindful of approaching winter and learning that the British had regained control of Lake Ontario on his flank, felt it prudent to suspend operations. Amidst howls of protest he abandoned Fort Erie, Ontario, and withdrew the Right Division to Buffalo, New York. News of peace arrived shortly after, but the general was so embarrassed by his lack of success that he tendered his resignation. James Monroe, now acting secretary of war in place of Armstrong, sensibly refused his old friend's request and permitted him to be honorably discharged on 13 June 1815. Considering Iz-

ard's talent and training and the resources involved, the prevailing public opinion of his performance was one of disappointment.

After the war, Izard opted for a life of seclusion in Philadelphia and resumed his interest in the American Philosophical Society. He also maintained close ties with Monroe, who, as president, appointed him governor of the Arkansas territory on 4 March 1825. His tenure in that capacity was much like his military career, effective but controversial. Izard was successful in carrying out Indian policy and relocated the Quapaw and Choctaw tribes to reservations without incident. The scholarly governor had less success with his unruly frontier legislature, however, and they passed several resolutions condemning his dictatorial manner toward them. He also contributed to the development of factionalism by arguing with territorial secretary Robert Crittenden over what was considered Crittenden's unauthorized absences from the territory. Before these issues could be resolved, Izard died at Little Rock of an illness caused by gout. Izard County, Arkansas, was posthumously named in his honor.

Despite his senior rank, Izard remains an enigmatic and rather maligned figure. He was the best-educated officer of his grade throughout the War of 1812 and, on balance, performed well. As an organizer and disciplinarian he fully equaled his great contemporary, Winfield Scott, but his contributions are overlooked. Historians and contemporaries alike charged him with timidity for not storming Drummond's entrenchments at Chippewa, but Izard, lacking supplies, naval support, and heavy artillery and operating in winter, was determined to preserve the integrity of his division. Professionalism, not timidity, characterized Izard's behavior, whether in resurrecting the Right Division at Plattsburgh, marching it to Niagara intact, or refusing to launch costly frontal assaults at Brown's behest. Scholarly and aloof, he was constantly transferred from one sector to another and never given an opportunity to distinguish himself. Prudence, restraint, and foresight, however, establish Izard as one of the most capable commanders of the War of 1812.

• Early Izard correspondence appears in the Ralph Izard Papers, Caroliniana Library, University of South Carolina. Official War of 1812 materials are in RG 94, Records of the Adjutant General, and RG 107, Records of the Secretary of War, National Archives. For personal correspondence consult the Jonathan Williams Papers, Lilly Library, Indiana University; the Thomas A. Smith Papers, State Historical Society of Missouri, Columbia; the Perkins Library, Duke University; the Clements Library, University of Michigan; the Historical Society of Pennsylvania; and the James Monroe Papers in the Manuscript Division, Library of Congress and in the New York Public Library. For a defense of his military career see George Izard, *Official Correspondence with the Department of War* (1816). Other printed sources include John C. Fredriksen, ed., "General George Izard's Journal of the Chateauguay Campaign," *New York History* 71 (Apr. 1995): 173–200; Harold W. Ryan, ed., "Diary of a Journal by General George Izard," *South Carolina Historical Magazine* 53 (Apr.-Oct. 1952): 67–76, 155–60, 223–29; Charlton DeSaussure, ed., "Memoir of General George Izard," *South

Carolina Historical Society 78 (Jan. 1977): 43–55; and Clarence E. Carter, ed. *Territorial Papers of the United States*, vols. 19 & 20 (1950). For favorable biographical treatment consult two articles by George Manigault, "Military Career of General George Izard," *Magazine of American* 20 (June 1888): 465–72, and "General George Izard's Military Career; A Reply to Henry Adams," *Magazine of American History* 26 (Dec. 1891): 457–62. His political affairs are covered in Richard Robertson, "General George Izard: Governor of Territorial Arkansas," *Pulaski County Historical Review* 27 (Winter 1979): 107–11. A recent overall interpretation is John C. Fredriksen, "Niagara, 1814: The United States Army Quest for Tactical Parity in the War of 1812 and Its Legacy" (Ph.D., Providence College, 1993).

JOHN C. FREDRIKSEN

IZARD, Ralph (23 Jan. 1742–30 May 1804), planter and politician, was born near Charleston, South Carolina, the son of Henry Izard, a planter, and Margaret Johnson. His great-grandfather (also Ralph Izard) had emigrated from England in 1682, acquired land, and gained prominence in provincial politics. By the mid-eighteenth century, when the family properties in Berkeley County, South Carolina, descended to Izard's parents, the family had maintained a strong position in the Carolina house of assembly and in the Anglican vestry.

Izard was born at the family seat, the "Elms," and was the oldest of four surviving siblings. From the age of twelve he was educated in England, first at a school in Hackney and then at Trinity Hall, Cambridge University, where he matriculated in 1761. He returned to South Carolina in 1764 and began to manage the family's plantations and slaves. He also visited other colonies, especially New York, where he met and in 1767 married Alice Delancey, daughter of Peter Delancey and niece of former New York chief justice and lieutenant-governor James Delancey. Alice Izard was also the granddaughter of noted naturalist (and New York lieutenant-governor) Cadwallader Colden and evidently typified a standard of female learning new to the colonial elite; she was therefore a suitable match for Izard, who had considerable interest in the learning and arts that were lingua franca for wealthy colonists.

Because of these interests Izard had little desire to pursue his family's activities in provincial politics. Instead, the Izards evidently visited the European continent two years after their marriage, in 1769. They probably had the intention, common among the richest Carolina rice planters, to live abroad on their American income and to participate in European cultural life. They went to England in 1771 (their first child and heir, Henry, was born at sea in that year, the first of fourteen children born to the couple) and bought a London house, but revisited the European continent in 1774. During his Old World travels, Izard collected art; he was the first patron in Europe of American painter John Singleton Copley. In Rome in 1774 Copley painted a double portrait of the Izards with the couple posed among classical antiquities.

The Izards returned to London in 1775, just as tensions between America and Britain reached the breaking point. When the conflict peaked in 1776, the family moved to neutral Paris but regained little peace and stability. At this time Izard entered the career in public affairs he had heretofore avoided. In May 1777 the Continental Congress appointed him its commissioner to Tuscany. Unable to travel to Italy (the grand duke of Florence did not wish to receive agents from Britain's rebellious colonies), Izard instead corresponded from Paris with Tuscan officials.

Izard also helped Alexander Gillon to gain funds for American warships and assisted Arthur Lee in negotiating a treaty with the French. Because of his suspicions of the French and by allying with Lee, Izard distanced himself from Benjamin Franklin and Silas Deane. Izard disagreed especially with a "molasses article" in the Franco-American treaty that favored French interests, and he thought the French had designs on British Florida. Izard's strained relations with Franklin and Deane and his inability to reach Tuscany led to his recall in 1779, though his explanations for his difficulties were later accepted by Congress (which also disapproved of the "molasses article") and that body removed any opprobrium attached to Izard's recall. But stresses on the Izard family pressed in from all sides. They had attracted patriot scrutiny because Alice Izard's New York family was Loyalist; the Izards also learned that their South Carolina estates had been confiscated when the British invaded the state.

Izard returned alone to America and joined George Washington's headquarters at Philadelphia in August 1780; he helped procure General Nathanael Greene's appointment as commander over the Continental army in the southern states, where the war was in its final, crucial stages. Izard then served as a South Carolina delegate to Congress from 1782 until the peace in 1783, when his family joined him from Paris. The Izards returned to South Carolina, and Izard undertook the task of repairing his properties, which had been neglected after their confiscation. Slavery seemed not to trouble Izard's conscience—an attitude common among wealthy whites in the lower South. He felt no need to apologize for the persistence of slavery in the southern states and was angered by external criticism of the institution; he predicted that because of antislavery "enthusiasm" the "property in Negroes will be rendered of no value."

Izard's political career continued after the war. He declined to stand as candidate for state governor but served in the legislature. He was instrumental, as anonymous author of the 22 November 1788 broadside *Another Elector for Charleston District*, in scotching David Ramsay's bid for election to the federal House of Representatives. Izard accused Ramsay of harboring antislavery sentiments that would undermine South Carolina's interests. After the ratification of the federal Constitution, Izard served as one of his state's first two senators during the First through Third Congresses (1789–1795). In the Senate Izard served on committees to establish federal judicial courts and compose the presidential oath and was president pro tempore in the Third Congress. He also opposed ratification of the Bill of Rights and argued that the Senate should refuse to consider antislavery petitions.

Izard retired from political service in 1795 and devoted himself to agricultural innovations. His health failing after a stroke in 1797, he transferred care of his properties to his children and refocused his energies on literature—an interest that he had presumably neglected since 1776. He read the newest works, but his lifelong (and perhaps simplistic) admiration for John Milton was not altered by new acquaintance with authors such as Mary Wollstonecraft. Izard died in Charleston. After his death Izard's wife, who had never liked living with slavery and among slaves, moved to Philadelphia, where she died in 1832.

• The bulk of Izard's papers is in the Library of Congress and in the South Caroliniana Library, University of South Carolina, Columbia; some records of his affairs are in the Manigault papers in the South Caroliniana Library and in the letterbook of Peter Manigault, South Carolina Historical Society, Charleston. The National Archives holds his correspondence relating to the Continental Congress. Published portions of his writings appear in *The Correspondence of Mr. Ralph Izard*, ed. Anne Izard Deas (1844), and Francis Wharton, *The Revolutionary Diplomatic Correspondence of the United States* (6 vols., 1889). Records relating to his later political career appear in the *Journals of the Continental Congress* (1904–1937); Merrill Jensen and Robert A. Becker, eds., *The Documentary History of the First Federal Elections, 1788–1790*, vol. 1 (1976); and Linda Grant De Pauw, ed., *Documentary History of the First Federal Congress of the United States of America*, vols. 1 and 2 (1972, 1974).

JOYCE E. CHAPLIN

J

JACK, Captain. *See* Captain Jack.

JACKSON, Andrew (15 Mar. 1767–8 June 1845), soldier and seventh president of the United States, was born in the Waxhaw Settlement, South Carolina, the son of Andrew Jackson and Elizabeth Hutchinson, farmers. Like many other Scotch-Irish at the time, Andrew and Elizabeth Jackson migrated to this country from the port of Carrickfergus in Northern Ireland in 1765, landing most probably in Philadelphia and then journeying southward to join relatives living in the Waxhaw Settlement along the northwestern boundary separating North and South Carolina. They settled with their two sons, Hugh and Robert, on a stretch of land on the south side of Twelve Mile Creek, a branch of the Catawba River, and for two years tried to scratch a living from this acid soil. Then, early in March 1767, Andrew died suddenly. Approximately two weeks later, on 15 March, Elizabeth gave birth to her third son and named him after her deceased husband. Later a dispute arose over the exact location of the birthplace of the future president—whether he was born in North or South Carolina—but Jackson himself always believed and repeatedly stated that he was born in South Carolina.

Elizabeth moved into the home of her invalid sister, Jane Crawford, the wife of James Crawford, where for the next ten or twelve years she acted as housekeeper and nurse. Here she raised her three sons, sending them to local schools. But because she hoped that her third son would become a Presbyterian minister, she placed him in an academy run by Dr. William Humphries. Later she enrolled him in another school conducted by James White Stephenson, a Presbyterian minister. Although Andrew formally joined the Presbyterian church late in life, he never had any interest in the ministry and received a rather meager education.

With the outbreak of the American Revolution, Andrew quit school and, at the age of thirteen, joined the regiment of Colonel William Richardson Davie. He participated in the battle of Hanging Rock on 1 August 1780, probably as a courier. A year later he and his brother Robert were captured by the British. When he refused to obey an officer's command to clean his boots, the officer struck him with his sword, leaving marks on Andrew's head and fingers that he carried through life. He was imprisoned in Camden, where he contracted smallpox. His mother won the release of her two sons by assisting in arranging an exchange of prisoners. Robert died during the difficult journey home. After Andrew's recovery, Elizabeth went to Charleston to nurse prisoners of war being held in prison ships and shortly after her arrival died from cholera, making Andrew an orphan at the age of fourteen.

Andrew resided with relatives for the next few years, drifting from one job to another. With the conclusion of the war and the establishment of a new nation under the Articles of Confederation, he decided in 1784 to move to Salisbury, North Carolina, to study law. He entered the law office of Spruce McCay, a distinguished trial lawyer, where for the next two years he copied legal documents, ran errands, cleaned the office, read law books, and performed a number of other menial tasks. At night he let off steam by leading a group of law students in a wild and unbridled display of practical jokes, drunken sprees, and other high jinks. He soon earned the reputation of being the "most roaring, rollicking, game-cocking, horse-racing, card-playing, mischievous fellow that ever lived in Salisbury."

Jackson completed his law training in the office of Colonel John Stokes. He spent six months in Stokes's office and on 26 September 1787 appeared for examination before two justices of the Superior Court of Law and Equity of North Carolina. The judges pronounced him a man of "unblemished moral character" and knowledgeable of the law and authorized him to practice as an attorney in the several courts of pleas and quarter sessions within the state.

For the next year Jackson drifted around North Carolina before deciding that his future lay in the West. He was offered the position of public prosecutor for the western district of the state in what is now Tennessee. In the spring of 1788, together with several friends and companions and following the Wilderness Trace, he journeyed across the mountains to Jonesborough, the principal town of East Tennessee. Here Jackson fought his first duel, with a man named Waightstill Avery, on 12 August 1788. Avery allegedly questioned Jackson's legal ability, and in a typical outburst of temper Jackson tore a leaf from a law book, scribbled a few words on it, and flung it at Avery. The next day he wrote a formal challenge. Fortunately, neither man was injured in the ensuing duel.

A few months later Jackson and his party left Jonesborough and, journeying through dangerous frontier country, arrived in Nashville on 26 October 1788. Jackson took lodging with the widow of John Donelson and over the next seven years became a successful public prosecutor and lawyer in western Tennessee. Most of his cases involved land titles, debts, and assault and required him to travel regularly between Nashville and Jonesborough through hostile Indian territory. During these years Jackson, like most frontiersmen, frequently participated in armed engagements against Indians.

While living in the home of the widow Donelson, he fell in love with her daughter, Rachel. At the time Rachel was already married to Lewis Robards but had separated from him and had returned home. Jackson's courtship of Rachel provoked Robards into seeking a divorce on the grounds of his wife's desertion and adultery with another man. In the spring of 1791 a rumor circulated in Nashville that the divorce had been granted and, according to a statement later written by the Nashville Central Committee during the presidential election of 1828, Rachel and Andrew married in Spanish Natchez in the summer of 1791. No evidence of this marriage has ever been found, however.

In fact, no divorce had been granted in 1791, and not until 27 September 1793 did Lewis Robards actually receive a decree of divorce, when a jury found Rachel guilty of desertion and "adultery with another man." On 17 January 1794 Rachel and Andrew exchanged vows before the local justice of the peace. Fifteen years later they adopted a son, Andrew Jackson, Jr.

The strange, controversial and unfortunate circumstances of Jackson's marriage, which have never been adequately explained or documented, hounded him for the next thirty years and played an important role during the campaign of 1828 when he was elected president of the United States.

Jackson was twenty-six at the time of his marriage. Standing over six feet tall, rail-thin in frame (he never weighed more than 145 pounds), his face long and accentuated by a sharp and jutting jaw, he always radiated an air of authority and command. He carried himself at all times with military stiffness, even when later plagued by chronic dysentery and the effects of wounds from gunfights. His hair was a light sandy color and stood almost as erect as he did. His bright, intensely blue eyes frequently registered his mood, particularly when agitated or angered. He had a mean, vicious temper and could hate with biblical fury. But he frequently feigned anger just to frighten his victims into doing his bidding. Anyone who disobeyed him, whether soldier, slave, or politician, felt the brunt of his wrath. He could be gentle and generous to those he loved or acknowledged as friends. But if he would go to infinite lengths to assist a loved one or a friend, he also went to infinite lengths to punish an enemy. Those who opposed him in politics he treated as enemies, not only his enemies but the enemies of the American people.

Having married into one of the first families of the future state of Tennessee, Jackson quickly achieved a position of social prominence in the region. When he entered politics he rose rapidly within the political hierarchy because of the strong support he received from William Blount, the former territorial governor and leader of the ruling clique. Jackson was also helped by his own excellent record as a prosecutor and attorney as well as by his attractive and commanding personality. On 19 December 1795 he was elected a delegate to the constitutional convention that drew up Tennessee's first constitution preceding its admission as a

state in the Union. Jackson contributed little to the debates in the convention, but his participation indicated his growing political importance in western Tennessee. This was confirmed when he was elected as Tennessee's sole representative in the U.S. House of Representatives upon Tennessee's admission as the sixteenth state on 1 June 1796.

Jackson did not particularly distinguish himself in the House, except that he was one of a very few men who voted against paying tribute to President George Washington on the occasion of his farewell from office. He believed that the Jay Treaty concluded by the Washington administration stained the honor of the Republic. Elected in 1797 to the U.S. Senate, Jackson established an even worse legislative record there. He felt uncomfortable and out of place in the august Senate chamber and abruptly resigned his post the following year. His decision to resign was further prompted by his desire for a seat on the state superior court, Tennessee's highest tribunal. He was elected to the court without opposition and served for the next six years. Few of his decisions as a judge survive, but James Parton, an early biographer, claimed that his opinions were "short, untechnical, unlearned, sometimes ungrammatical, and generally right."

Virtually from the moment of his arrival in Tennessee, and throughout his congressional and judicial careers, Jackson engaged in extensive land speculation, that being the quickest and surest road to financial success. On 4 August 1804 he purchased the "Hermitage" property on which he later built his imposing mansion befitting a planter of substance and social position. However, his involvement in land speculation with David Allison in 1795 almost landed him in debtors' prison with Allison. As a consequence, he developed a lifelong aversion to debt, and as president he took great pride in achieving the elimination of the national debt.

Jackson also developed an extensive business in commercial trade, extending as far east as Philadelphia and as far south and west as Natchez and New Orleans. He traded in cured meats, tobacco, salt, furs and pelts, barrel staves, lime, tallow, lumber, and swan skins. By 1802 he was sending horses, slaves, and cotton down the Mississippi River to both Natchez and New Orleans. At various times he formed partnerships with Samuel Donelson, John Overton, Thomas Watson, John Hutchings, and John Coffee.

Jackson spent several years trying to win election as major general in the Tennessee militia, a position decided by the vote of the field officers of the three divisions within the state and a position of the highest importance after governor. John Sevier, a revolutionary war hero and a very popular governor, could not constitutionally succeed himself as governor and therefore decided to seek the post of major general in 1802. The election ended in a tie vote that was broken in Jackson's favor by the new governor, Archibald Roane, whom Jackson had supported for the governorship. The rivalry between Sevier and Jackson intensified over the following months and resulted in a ludicrous duel with drawn pistols and sword canes in which neither man was injured. Three years later, on 30 May 1806, in a quarrel over a horse race wager, Jackson killed Charles Dickinson, reputedly the "best shot in Tennessee." In the duel Jackson himself took a bullet in the chest; he lived with the bullet for the rest of his life, suffering as a result periodic hemorrhaging that was misdiagnosed as tuberculosis. Jackson was also wounded in the shoulder in a gunfight on 4 September 1813 with Thomas Hart Benton (1782–1858) and his brother, Jesse. That bullet was surgically removed during Jackson's presidency.

When former vice president of the United States Aaron Burr (1756–1836) arrived in Nashville in May 1805, he elected to reside in Jackson's home for his five-day visit. He discussed with Jackson his plans for an "adventure" down the Mississippi River, presumably to assault the Spanish in Florida and the Southwest, and Jackson agreed to build boats for the expedition. When President Thomas Jefferson denounced the expedition as a conspiracy against the United States, Jackson refused to believe it and steadfastly insisted on Burr's innocence. His involvement was subsequently used as a political issue in the presidential election of 1828.

With the outbreak of war against Great Britain in 1812, Governor Blount of Tennessee dispatched Jackson with his militia against the Creek Indians, who used the war as an opportunity to attack the southern frontier. Although lacking in military training or experience, Jackson soon developed into an excellent general. His outstanding leadership qualities and a superhuman, indeed demonic, determination to defeat the enemy account for his incredible military victories. His soldiers accorded him the nickname "Old Hickory" as a sign of their affection and respect. In a series of successful engagements, and suffering tremendous hardships, Jackson crushed the Creeks at the battle of Horseshoe Bend and imposed a draconian treaty that stripped the Indians of some twenty-three million acres of land, or roughly three-fifths of the present state of Alabama and one-fifth of Georgia. He was rewarded with a commission as major general in the U.S. Army.

Jackson then hurried to New Orleans to check a British invasion. Gathering a force of regular soldiers, militiamen from Louisiana, Tennessee, and Kentucky, Mississippi dragoons, Indians, pirates, and a battalion of free blacks, he strung them out behind a rampart he built on the edge of an old millrace, a ditch four feet deep and ten feet wide that ran from the eastern bank of the Mississippi River to a cypress swamp about three-quarters of a mile inland. Jackson placed 4,000 men along this line and held 1,000 more in reserve behind them. For the British to seize New Orleans as planned, they had to smash through this line. They were squeezed into a narrow plain between a broad river and a dense swamp. Against this impenetrable line the British commander, Lieutenant General Sir Edward Michael Pakenham, hurled 2,200 men, who marched forward in near-perfect military order,

only to be struck by grape, musketry, rifle-fire, and buckshot from the Americans crouched behind their ditch. Some 2,000 British soldiers were killed, wounded, and captured or declared missing during the assault; Jackson suffered hardly more than a dozen casualties.

It was a tremendous victory and instantly made Jackson a national celebrity. He had proved to the nation and the world that the American people had the will and ability to successfully defend their freedom, even against the greatest power in the world. Although peace between the United States and Great Britain had already been signed on Christmas Eve in Ghent, Belgium, the British could have, and most probably would have, repudiated the treaty, since it had not yet been ratified, had they won the battle of New Orleans.

For the remainder of his life Andrew Jackson was the most popular man in America—more popular than George Washington, Thomas Jefferson, Benjamin Franklin (1706–1790), or anyone else, living or dead. At the age of forty-eight, Jackson captured the loyalty and devotion of the American people, and he never lost it during his lifetime. That devotion and pride swelled when he was sent against and defeated the Seminole Indians in Spanish Florida who periodically raided the Alabama-Georgia frontier. Requesting permission to seize Florida from Spain, and later convinced that he had that permission, he stormed across the Florida border on 15 March 1818, captured St. Marks and Pensacola, and executed two British subjects, Robert Ambrister and Alexander Arbuthnot, both of whom were accused of aiding the Indians in their attacks upon the American frontier. The invasion and executions might have triggered a confrontation with both Spain and Great Britain, and indeed President James Monroe and a majority of his cabinet seemed prepared to disavow Jackson's actions and censure him, but the secretary of state, John Quincy Adams, successfully defended Jackson and then convinced Spain to relinquish Florida for $5 million in assumed claims against Spain by American citizens. In addition, Spain agreed to a western boundary of the Louisiana Territory that extended to the Pacific Ocean, thus transforming the United States into a transcontinental power.

Upon the ratification of the treaty of acquisition, which took several years to accomplish, Monroe appointed Jackson governor of the new territory and authorized him to formally receive Florida from Spain. Jackson resigned his army commission on 1 June 1821 and set off for Florida. On 17 July, after an unseemly dispute with Spanish officials over protocol, he received the territory and proceeded to set up an efficient and energetic government that greatly facilitated the transfer of what was essentially a foreign land with alien customs and an unfamiliar language into the American political system. He also appointed to office men whose abilities proved to be most important in Florida's future development. At times high-handed, arbitrary, and quarrelsome, and invariably impatient with Spanish temperament, Jackson nonetheless achieved a remarkable success as territorial governor. But the effort wore him down, and on 13 November 1821 he resigned the governorship and returned to the Hermitage.

Despite Jackson's lack of adequate credentials as a public official, many Americans had begun to think of him as a presidential contender. He was so beloved that the electorate could deny him nothing, not even the presidency, an attitude soon observed by a number of sharp-eyed politicians. Although he feigned disinterest and lack of ability to hold the office, Jackson decided to run for the presidency, and with the aid of his Tennessee friends—John H. Eaton, John Overton, William B. Lewis, Felix Grundy, and others—he unanimously won nomination for the presidency from the Tennessee legislature on 20 July 1822. Then, to enhance his candidacy, among other reasons, his friends had him elected to the U.S. Senate on 1 October 1823. It was the last thing Jackson wanted, "but . . . I am compelled to accept," he said.

Thus, for the second time, Jackson assumed a seat in the Senate. He met a number of important senators at this time who would be important to him later on, most especially Martin Van Buren of New York. He also resolved his old dispute with Thomas Hart Benton of Missouri and in all respects conducted himself with dignity and a bearing that many observers, even partisans of other candidates, called presidential.

The other candidates in the presidential election of 1824 were John Quincy Adams, Henry Clay and William Harris Crawford. Jackson won a plurality of popular and electoral votes in the fall election, but he did not have the constitutionally mandated majority of electoral votes, and so the election went to the House of Representatives. Under the Twelfth Amendment to the Constitution the House selects the president from the top three contenders. Henry Clay was low man and thus disqualified from consideration, but because of his position as Speaker of the House he had enormous influence with the other representatives. Clay threw his support to Adams and was subsequently appointed by Adams as secretary of state. Jackson resigned his Senate seat and returned home, convinced that Adams and Clay had contracted a "corrupt bargain" to deprive him of the presidency. He and his friends immediately began a campaign to win the presidency in 1828 and were joined by Martin Van Buren, John C. Calhoun, and Thomas Hart Benton, among others. Together they assembled an organization that subsequently called itself the Democratic party. Van Buren was the actual genius behind this organizational revamping of Jefferson's old Republican party. Van Buren brought Crawford and many states' rights stalwarts with him into the new party. After a particularly vicious and sordid campaign in which Jackson's marriage, his several duels, his involvement in the Burr conspiracy, his gambling, his cock-fighting, and his all-around lack of presidential qualifications were paraded repeatedly before the electorate, Old Hickory won a stunning popular and electoral victory over Adams. A month later, on 23 December 1829, his wife Rachel died suddenly of a heart attack.

Jackson served two terms as president (1829–1837) during a period of enormous economic, political, social, and cultural change. The market revolution embodying the industrial and transportation revolutions that developed immediately after the War of 1812, and the communications revolution that followed, inaugurated the emergence of an industrial society in America. State constitutions were changed providing universal white male suffrage that greatly assisted the development of democracy. In the minds of many Americans Andrew Jackson symbolized this transition. He himself was regarded as a "self-made man," a term coined at this time. His name was later associated with a brand of democracy that advocated equality of opportunity for all. His public statements resonated with his devotion and commitment to democracy. "The people are sovereign," he wrote, "their will is absolute." In his first message to Congress he announced his firm belief that in the United States the "majority is to govern." He also advocated the direct election of presidents, senators, and judges. He even argued the right of voters to instruct their representatives on important issues.

Upon taking office, Jackson had a general sense of what he wished to accomplish as president and labeled it a program of "reform retrenchment and economy." Specifically, he set out to open government employment to all, practice the strictest economy in governmental expenditures in order to pay off the national debt, distribute surplus funds to the states for internal improvements and education once the debt had been paid, and obtain a revision of the tariff. He also had in mind an alteration of the operations of the Second National Bank along with the removal of the southern Indian tribes to an area beyond the Mississippi River. And much of this program he accomplished.

In initiating a "rotation" policy to make government employment more accessible to average Americans, Jackson contended that government office was not the prerogative of an elitist class. Most duties of public offices are "so plain and simple," he wrote, "that men of intelligence may readily qualify" to fill them. His opponents called the policy a "spoils system," but rotation was really intended to democratize American institutions at every level.

Because he advocated government and fiscal restraint, Jackson opposed federal funding of internal improvements, particularly where his opponents would benefit from such projects. Consequently he vetoed a number of public works, most notably the Maysville Road bill, which proposed to build an extension of the National Road in Kentucky from Maysville to Lexington. Jackson said that the Constitution did not authorize something that was "of purely local character." He stopped short of denying federal power over internal improvements, particularly those works of national character. But he stated that the "friends of liberty" had a right to expect that "expedience" would not be made the "rule of construction in interpreting the Constitution."

Jackson's sustained policy of fiscal restraint resulted in the accomplishment of one of his most cherished objectives: payment of the national debt. When he took office the debt stood at approximately $60 million. By 1835—after he had annulled the Washington Turnpike bill, as well as legislation for building lighthouses and beacons, dredging harbors, and promoting similar public works, and thanks to a huge revenue from the tariff and the sale of public land—the debt was completely extinguished. It was the only time in American history when the nation was free of debt. It was one of Jackson's proudest accomplishments.

Jackson wielded the veto power rather extensively for his time. He vetoed more than all his predecessors combined; he used the pocket veto for the first time; and he was the first president to veto legislation for other than constitutional reasons. He believed that as president he had the right to annul what he deemed harmful to the public interest. By his creative and imaginative use of the veto he vastly expanded presidential power.

Not only did he prove to be an aggressive president, ready to implement his constitutional authority and force issues when his more timid friends like Van Buren urged caution, but he also assumed complete control of the Democratic party and dictated the choice of his successor. It had been supposed that John C. Calhoun, his vice president, would succeed him. But the two men broke over Calhoun's insistence that the states retain the right to nullify federal legislation and over the revelation that Calhoun had urged Jackson's censure in the Monroe cabinet for the seizure of Florida. Jackson was an intense nationalist who rejected both nullification and secession. No state could leave the Union, he said, and no state could nullify federal law. At a celebration to honor the birthday of Thomas Jefferson, Jackson faced down the nullifiers in Congress by proposing the toast: "Our Union, it must be preserved!" When South Carolina adopted Calhoun's theory of interposition and nullified the tariffs of 1828 and 1832 as a violation of its interests and rights, Jackson threatened to use force to compel compliance. Fortunately, the compromise tariff of 1833 was worked out in Congress, and South Carolina backed off. Calhoun was shunted aside as successor to Jackson, however, in favor of Martin Van Buren, who was duly nominated for vice president by the Democratic party at its first national nominating convention in time for the election of 1832.

The campaign for Jackson's reelection to the presidency centered on his veto of a bill initiated by Henry Clay and the National Republican party to extend the charter of the Second National Bank of the United States another twenty years. Jackson regarded the bank as a "hydra-headed monster." He accused it of using its money to influence political elections and buy the votes of congressmen. In his mind it constituted a threat to liberty. In his ringing veto message of 10 July 1832 he charged the institution with using its government-granted privileges to benefit the moneyed elite. "It is to be regretted," he wrote in the message, "that the rich and powerful too often bend the acts of government to their selfish purposes." When the laws undertake "to make the rich richer and the potent more powerful, the humble members of society—the farmers, mechanics, and laborers . . . have a right to complain of the injustice of their Government."

Henry Clay ran against Jackson on the National Republican ticket but was soundly defeated. The president followed up his victory by removing the government's funds from the bank and placing them in selected state banks, called "pet banks" by the opposition. Clay responded in the Senate by winning passage of two motions censuring the president and the secretary of the treasury for the removal. Jackson responded in a "protest" message in which he proclaimed himself the representative of all the people and, as such, responsible to them. In effect, he publicly declared himself the head of the government. Clay, Calhoun, and Daniel Webster, the so-called Great Triumvirate of the Senate, denounced Jackson's interpretation of his presidential role as a "revolutionary" departure from the intentions of the Founders. The president's specie circular of 11 July 1836, which required gold and silver for the purchase of public lands, reinforced Jackson's conceptions of his executive authority and prerogatives.

In killing the Second Bank of the United States, Jackson drove home the point that when corporate wealth is used to buy influence and power from public officials the liberty of the nation is placed in danger. Jackson feared not only a strong central government— "the world is governed too much," was the motto of the Washington *Globe*, the Democratic party's mouthpiece in Washington—but also the influence of money in the operation of government. Both threatened liberty. The only antidote to these dangers, in Jackson's mind, was the free exercise of the suffrage. "Our government," he wrote, "is founded upon the intelligence of the people. . . . I have great confidence in the virtue of the great majority of the people." Jacksonian democracy, as it developed during the antebellum era, in addition to preaching equality, freedom, and rule by the majority, advocated limited government, fiscal restraint, laissez-faire economics, and support of the states in their proper spheres of activity.

Unfortunately, Jackson's support of the states in one area had devastating consequences for Native Americans. Indeed, the first major legislation of the Jackson administration was the Indian Removal Act, which set up a territory—now the state of Oklahoma— to which the Five Civilized Tribes of Creeks, Cherokees, Choctaws, Chickasaws, and Seminoles were to be removed. Several states, lusting after Indian land, demanded removal, Georgia especially, and Jackson agreed with their argument. But he himself was motivated by two considerations: national security and the preservation of the tribes. The present location of southern tribes, said Jackson, constituted a danger to the safety of the nation. He remembered the Creek

War of 1813 that almost coincided with the British invasion of New Orleans. Had it occurred simultaneously with the invasion, the outcome of the battle of New Orleans might have been disastrous for the United States. In addition, Jackson believed that if the Indians were not removed they faced inevitable annihilation. They will "disappear and be forgotten," he told them. Unfortunately, the implementation of removal was a monstrous act of unmitigated horror and forever stained the honor and reputation of the nation.

In foreign affairs Jackson pursued a vigorous, sometimes aggressive, policy, as might be expected. He demanded respect by other nations for the sovereignty of this democracy, insisting that they act honestly and honorably toward the United States: "To ask nothing that is not clearly right, and to submit to nothing that is wrong," was the way he put it to Congress in an annual message. In Jackson's mind that translated into foreign nations paying the United States what they owed on account of spoliation claims by American citizens for seizure of ships and cargoes during the Napoleonic Wars. He nearly provoked a war with France over the issue but ultimately received 25 million francs in settlement. He also settled American claims against Denmark and the Kingdom of Naples. In 1833 the United States' first treaty with an Asian nation was signed with Siam, providing for trade on a "most favored nation" basis. And Jackson successfully terminated the dispute with Great Britain over trade with the West Indies, so that the ports of the United States and the West Indies were opened on terms of full reciprocity.

Jackson was a much beloved and much hated figure during most of his adult life, and that reaction to him continues to the present day. During many reform periods in American history he has been seen as a hero, and Jacksonian democracy has been extolled as one of the most important advances in the development of popular government. But in the final decades of the twentieth century there has been a dramatic reversal of attitudes. Jacksonians have been tagged as "men on the make," out for their own economic and political advantage, beguiling the electorate with populist "claptrap." Jackson himself has been denounced as a fraud and opportunist who nearly wrecked the credit and currency facilities of this nation, a right-wing reactionary, a defender of slavery, and a vengeful murderer of Native Americans. While some or all of these negative opinions can be argued from a twentieth-century point of view, nevertheless Jackson remains one of the most important spokesmen for majoritarian rule in this country, a president who worried over the abuse of power by the central government and urged greater democracy through direct election for all government officers, and a president who brought into sharp focus the never-ending efforts of privileged elites who seek to use the government for their particular and selfish purposes and in the process endanger liberty and betray American democracy. No doubt his legacy and his reputation will always invite reinterpretation and controversy.

With Van Buren's election to the presidency in 1836, Jackson retired to the Hermitage, from which he continued to influence and direct national politics for the remainder of his life. He died there at the age of seventy-eight, probably of a heart attack, and was buried in the garden alongside his beloved Rachel.

• The largest collection of Jackson's papers can be found in the Library of Congress. An index to this collection by John McDonough, *Index to the Andrew Jackson Papers* (1967), is a useful guide. A microfilm edition, *Andrew Jackson Papers*, was published in 1967 as part of the Presidents' Papers Series by the Library of Congress; additional material was published in 1987 in a microfilm supplement, *The Papers of Andrew Jackson, 1770–1845*, with a *Guide and Index to the Microfilm Editions*, ed. Harold D. Moser et al. The largest collections of manuscript sources outside the Library of Congress can be found in the National Archives, the Archivo General de Indias in Seville, Spain, the Tennessee Historical Society in Nashville, the Ladies' Hermitage Association at the Hermitage, the Chicago Historical Society, and the New York Public Library. The Jackson Papers project at the University of Tennessee, Knoxville, has acquired copies of all Jackson materials available and has begun publishing the most important of the papers in a series entitled *The Papers of Andrew Jackson*. The only extended publication of Jackson materials in print is John Spencer Bassett, ed., *The Correspondence of Andrew Jackson* (6 vols., 1926–1935). Many of Jackson's most important state papers are available in J. D. Richardson, *A Compilation of the Messages and Papers of the Presidents*, vol. 2 (1896).

A recent bibliography of works by and about Jackson is Robert V. Remini and Robert O. Rupp, *Andrew Jackson: A Bibliography* (1991). A modern, scholarly biography of Jackson is the three-volume *Andrew Jackson and the Course of American Empire, 1767–1821* (1977), *Andrew Jackson and the Course of American Freedom, 1821–1832* (1981), and *Andrew Jackson and the Course of American Democracy, 1833–1845* (1984) by Robert V. Remini. A one-volume abridgement of this work is entitled *The Life of Andrew Jackson* (1988). See also Remini, *The Legacy of Andrew Jackson: Essays on Democracy, Indian Removal and Slavery* (1988). James Parton, *The Life of Andrew Jackson* (3 vols., 1859–1860), remains one of the most successful and interesting studies and is absolutely essential to an understanding of Jackson's early life. John Reid and John Henry Eaton, *The Life of Andrew Jackson* (1817; repr. 1974), has important information on Jackson's military career and is one of the earliest campaign biographies. See also W. G. Sumner, *Andrew Jackson* (1882; repr. 1980); John Spencer Bassett, *The Life of Andrew Jackson* (2 vols., 1911); and Marquis James, *The Life of Andrew Jackson* (2 vols., 1933, 1937). Arthur M. Schlesinger, Jr., *The Age of Jackson* (1946), is a landmark study and a major reinterpretation of the Jacksonian era, as are Richard Hofstadter, "Andrew Jackson and the Rise of Liberal Capitalism," in *American Political Tradition and the Men Who Made It* (1948), and Lee Benson, *The Concept of Jacksonian Democracy: New York as a Test Case* (1961). For Jackson's foreign policy, see John M. Belohlavek, *Let the Eagle Soar! The Foreign Policy of Andrew Jackson* (1985).

ROBERT V. REMINI

JACKSON, Charles Loring (4 Apr. 1847–31 Oct. 1935), chemist, was born in Boston, Massachusetts, the son of Patrick Tracy Jackson II, a cotton manufacturer and businessman, and Susan Mary Loring. As a young man, Jackson was encouraged by both his parents to pursue his interest in science. Entering Harvard with the class of 1867, Jackson took courses in chemistry and biology, although he did not excel academically because of his frail health, which would plague him all his life. He did, however, impress Josiah Parsons Cooke, Jr., Erving Professor of Chemistry and Mineralogy, who asked Jackson to become one of his lecture assistants after graduating. Cooke introduced student laboratory instruction and fought for proper accommodations and recognition of the importance of laboratory instruction in chemistry. Cooke has been credited with being one of the most important Americans in raising the standards of chemical education in the nineteenth century. Cooke was a major influence on Jackson, who would ensure the goals set by his mentor were fulfilled.

From 1868 to 1873 Jackson served as Cooke's assistant and filled in many gaps in his chemical knowledge. Jackson, who was never in good health from childhood, suffered an attack of rheumatic fever in 1873, and Cooke advised him to go for a year to Germany, which was the center for the study of chemistry in Europe. In Heidelberg Jackson entered the laboratory of Robert Bunsen, one of the most renowned inorganic chemists of the nineteenth century. Jackson wrote of his six-month stay in Heidelberg, "I was well satisfied with this first half-year. I had sufficiently mastered quantitative and gas analysis, had got some idea of inorganic preparation, and had greatly increased my knowledge of inorganic chemistry from Bunsen's lectures and my own reading."

For the next six months Jackson was to study organic chemistry with August Von Hofmann in Berlin; however, this turned out to be almost two years. As Jackson recalled, "As soon as I fairly tasted blood in organic chemistry that plan went by the board and I lost my heart to organic and have been faithful to my love ever since." A student of Liebig, Hofmann had spent twenty years in London as head of the Royal College of Chemistry and its successors. During this time he did some of the most important fundamental work in aromatic chemistry, particularly the amines and their application to the dye industry. In 1865 Hofmann was called to the most prestigious post in Germany, the professor of organic chemistry at the University of Berlin. He was responsible for the founding of the German Chemical Society and its journal *Berichte*. Whereas Bunsen's laboratory instruction was very mechanical, Hofmann encouraged his students to use their analytical abilities. In this atmosphere Jackson thrived. As he recalled later in life, "He encouraged you to think for yourself and received new ideas proposed by you most kindly, advising you to try them instead of saying, Poo! That will not work." Jackson stayed on in Hofmann's laboratory continuing his research at a frantic pace, but he did not take time for the formalities of obtaining his Ph.D. After two years this work resulted in eight papers in leading German chemical journals.

Jackson returned to Harvard in 1875 and spent the rest of his active career there. His professional advancement was rapid: he was made a professor in 1881, an Erving Professor in 1897, and a professor emeritus in 1912. In addition he was elected to the National Academy of Sciences in 1883 and the American Academy of Arts and Sciences.

Jackson had the distinction of preparing the first new organic chemical at Harvard, parabromobenzylbromide (1877). The development of organic chemistry at Harvard, which would produce several Nobel Prize winners in the twentieth century, can be traced to these pioneering experiments performed by Jackson. The study of aromatic halogen compounds was to be a recurring theme in Jackson's research. He made the observation that the placement of electronegative groups para to a halogen would convert these normally unreactive aromatic compounds into very reactive ones towards substitution. He also was able to isolate stable salts (1903) that were the addition products of the reaction of a nucleophile and an aromatic halide. These complexes were simultaneously discovered by the German chemist Jacob Meisenheimer and are known as Meisenheimer-Jackson complexes. These observations were to be explained later by the addition-elimination mechanism of nucleophilic aromatic substitution. The other major field of investigation pursued by Jackson was the reactions of halogen with quinones and their subsequent replacement reactions. In all Jackson published approximately 150 papers in American and German journals. Two of his most distinguished students, Frank C. Whitmore and Roger Adams, became two of the leading academic organic chemists of the first half of the twentieth century. Another outstanding student, Elmer K. Bolton, became director of research at DuPont and developed the commercial process for nylon manufacture.

Jackson's most outstanding achievements were in the development of chemical education in the United States. The popularity of introductory chemistry at Harvard was because of his unique presentation of the chemistry of the elements, as well as the individualistic laboratory instruction. Students in the second half of the course were assigned various projects involving both separation and preparation of various inorganic compounds. Jackson challenged his students by the use of the Socratic method both in lecture and particularly in the laboratory. The skills in inductive reasoning were honed early in his course, which he viewed as a preparation for future research work. Jackson introduced chemistry as part of the processes of nature and revealed its contributions to the development of civilization to students over the course of forty years. No doubt his approach was responsible for many students choosing to continue their study of chemistry.

Jackson never married and died in Boston, Massachusetts.

• There is no known repository of Jackson's papers. A biographical sketch of Jackson by George Shannon Forbes and a complete list of all publications by Jackson may be found in National Academy of Sciences, *Biographical Memoirs* 37 (1966).

MARTIN D. SALTZMAN

JACKSON, Charles Thomas (21 June 1805–28 Aug. 1880), chemist and geologist, was born in Plymouth, Massachusetts, the son of Charles Jackson, a merchant and shipbuilder, and Lucy Cotton. Both of Jackson's parents died when he was thirteen. In his teens Jackson showed an interest in chemistry and, with his friend the young mineralogist Francis Alger, made two excursions, in the summers of 1827 and 1829, to Nova Scotia, where he carried out mineralogical and geological studies. The result was Jackson's first publication (with Alger), "A Description of the Mineralogy and Geology of a Portion of Nova Scotia" (*American Journal of Science* 14 [1828] and 15 [1829]).

In 1829 Jackson received an M.D. from Harvard Medical School and in the fall went to Europe, where he remained for three years. While abroad, he studied medicine at the University of Paris and geology and mineralogy at the École Royale des Mines, where he attended geological lectures by Jean B. Elie de Beaumont. He made a walking tour of southern Europe and participated in Vienna in autopsies on some 200 victims of cholera.

On his return voyage in 1832, Jackson's fellow passenger was Samuel F. B. Morse. There was shipboard conversation about electricity and its possible uses in communication, and Jackson later claimed to have planted with Morse the idea of the electric telegraph, which was later developed by and credited to Morse. Back in Boston, Jackson entered medical practice, and in 1834 he married Susan Bridge. (At his death there were five surviving children.) In 1836 Jackson abandoned medicine and established a commercial chemistry laboratory in Boston, where he engaged in chemical, mineralogical, and geological analysis for mining and other interests. It was one of the earliest such American establishments to take in students.

From 1837 to 1839 Jackson was state geologist of Maine, where he carried out field studies that included lands that were owned by the state of Massachusetts. His annual reports appeared in 1837, 1838, and 1839. During the years 1839–1840, Jackson also conducted a survey of Rhode Island, and from 1839 to 1843 he was New Hampshire state geologist. As the first geologist for three of the New England states, he put much effort into this work and gathered and published considerable factual information. Jackson's geological work emphasized his chemical and mineralogical interests and the practical and economic inclinations that were his own and those of his government sponsors.

In 1844 and 1845 Jackson carried out geological studies in Michigan for the Lake Superior Copper Company and in 1847 was appointed U.S. geologist to conduct a survey of the Lake Superior area before the sale of public lands. Opposition to the survey arose among the citizenry in Michigan, where Douglass Houghton had already carried out a state survey. During the course of the survey differences developed between Jackson and his two assistants, Josiah Dwight Whitney and John W. Foster, who accused Jackson, among other charges, of neglect of duty and conflict of interest with his other consulting work. After an investigation in Washington, D.C., Jackson was dismissed from the survey in spring 1849. His report, largely an undigested compilation, was published in December 1849. Only recently has Jackson been credited with significantly contributing to an understanding of the geology of the lake region by contradicting the then conventional wisdom in mining that native (i.e., naturally separated) copper deposits predicted only low yields in mining (see Krause).

The German-Swiss chemist C. F. Schonbein announced his discovery of the explosive known as guncotton in 1846, and Jackson followed his pattern and claimed priority in this development. This contention and the Lake Superior survey controversy were overshadowed, however, by the larger and more enduring conflict over credit for the introduction of sulphuric ether inhalation as surgical anesthetic.

In 1842 Jackson had experimented on himself in the use of ether to counteract the effects of accidental inhalation of chlorine and had devised what he considered a safe means of administration. In 1844 William T. G. Morton became his student and boarder and Jackson passed on to Morton some of what he had learned about ether. After Morton successfully administered ether during surgery at the Massachusetts General Hospital on 16 October 1846, Jackson claimed priority. The ensuing and largely unresolved controversy cast a shadow over the remainder of Jackson's life and his historic reputation. He continued his work as a consultant in chemistry, mineralogy, and mining but lost no opportunity to press his claim for credit for the discovery of ether.

Jackson had a compelling drive toward fame. His years of study in Europe were formative for him and contributed to a desire for a scientific reputation that extended beyond his native country. In late 1846 he wrote to Elie de Beaumont of his discoveries in the administration of ether, and the next year Beaumont presented his case to the Academie des Sciences. Later, Jackson published *A Manual of Etherization* (1861), ostensibly for the benefit of surgeons and sailors but in effect to present his own case. There he stated that it had been his intention to divulge his 1842 work on the use of ether to the European community but that his geological commitments at the time had prevented a foreign visit. Although in the case both of the telegraph and the ether discovery Jackson had a degree of claim as a participant, the more enterprising Morse and Morton had taken the available knowledge, derived in part from Jackson, and turned it to practical purposes.

In 1837 Jackson had become a member of the American Academy of Arts and Sciences, scene of a bitter confrontation at the time of his Lake Superior survey troubles when he unsuccessfully tried to block the election to membership of J. D. Whitney. As a counterweight, Jackson was a mainstay for the Boston Society of Natural History, where he was an active meeting participant, and he served as its vice president from 1843 until 1873. In 1845–1846 he was chair of the Association of American Geologists and Naturalists. In addition to his government geological reports, Jackson published a number of journal articles on chemical analyses of mineralogical and other materials as well as geological studies that related to a variety of locations, which appeared especially in the *American Journal of Science* and the *Proceedings of the Boston Society of Natural History*.

The controversies in which Jackson's life became entangled bear witness to a personal dysfunction on his part that ended in a mental breakdown. In 1873 he entered the McLean Hospital for the mentally ill in Somerville, Massachusetts, where he remained until his death. Jackson's life had been one of both accomplishment and torment. His failure to achieve a higher level of fame should not overshadow his substantial contributions through his geological surveys and the identification of mineralogical resources. His not wholly unfounded, though much exaggerated, claims to credit for the invention of the telegraph and the anesthetic uses of ether are themselves evidence of his insightful study of topics of considerable value and interest among his contemporaries.

• No major collection of Jackson's papers is known. Small collections are in the Library of Congress and the Massachusetts Historical Society. Papers are also found in other collections, including the R. W. Emerson Papers in the Houghton Library, Harvard University. Jackson's publications include *Report on the Geological and Agricultural Survey of the State of Rhode Island* (1840), *Final Report on the Geology and Mineralogy of the State of New Hampshire, with Contributions Towards the Improvement of Agriculture and Metallurgy* (1844), and *Report on the Geological and Mineralogical Survey of the Mineral Lands of the United States in the State of Michigan* (1849). The fullest biographical study (stressing geology) is J. B. Woodworth, "Charles Thomas Jackson," *American Geologist* 20 (1897): 69–110, which includes the most complete bibliography of his writings. Albert H. Miller, "Two Notable Controversies: Over the Invention of the Electric Telegraph and the Discovery of Surgical Anesthesia," *Annals of Medical History*, n.s., 6 (1934): 110–23, includes Morse's portrait of him and a bibliography that includes references to contemporary publications relating to the telegraph and ether controversies. There is no overall and unbiased account of the ether controversy; Barbara M. Duncum, *The Development of Inhalation Anaesthesia, with Special Reference to the Years 1846–1900* (1947), presents a number of the relevant facts. For Jackson's work in the Lake Superior region see David J. Krause, *The Making of a Mining District: Keweenaw Native Copper, 1500–1870* (1992). Robert V. Bruce, *The Launching of Modern American Science, 1846–1876* (1987), helps to place Jackson and his work in the general scientific context of his time. Family background is found in Delores Bird Carpenter, ed., *The Selected Letters of Lidian Jackson Emerson* (1987), a work about Jackson's sister.

CLARK A. ELLIOTT

JACKSON, Claiborne Fox (4 Apr. 1806–6 Dec. 1862), governor of Missouri, was born in Flemingsburg, Fleming County, Kentucky, the son of Dempsey Jackson and Mary Pickett, farmers. He received a common school education. Sometime in the 1820s he moved to Old Franklin, Missouri, where he clerked in a mercantile business, of which he eventually became a partner. When Old Franklin was washed away by a Missouri River flood around 1830, he moved to Arrow Rock in Saline County, where he continued in the mercantile business. There he became associated with Dr. John Sappington, whose three daughters he married: Jane Breathitt Sappington in February 1831, who lived but a few months after their marriage; Louisa Catherine Sappington in September 1833, who died in May 1838 and with whom he had three children; and Eliza W. Sappington Pearson in November 1838, with whom he also had three children.

During the Black Hawk War in 1832, Jackson organized a company of volunteers and served as its captain. He was elected as a Democrat to the Missouri legislature from Saline County in 1836 for one term while serving also as the Arrow Rock postmaster. A strong supporter of hard money throughout his career, Jackson strongly opposed the chartering of the Bank of Missouri but accepted the position of cashier at its branch in Fayette, Howard County, following its establishment. Jackson became an influential member of the so-called "Central Clique," which dominated Missouri politics in the 1840s. In 1842 he returned to the lower house of the Missouri General Assembly from Howard County, serving until 1848, when he was elevated to the state senate. He was elected Speaker of the Missouri house in 1844 and 1846. He also played a significant role in the state constitutional convention of 1845, serving as chair of the Committee on Banks and Corporations. There he attempted unsuccessfully to abolish the state bank, having to settle for stringent regulation of note issues and the several liability of stockholders in corporations.

In 1848 Jackson sought the Democratic nomination for governor but was beaten by Austin A. King, who had the backing of Senator Thomas Hart Benton (1782–1858). Although he had supported Benton earlier, Jackson now turned against him because of Benton's stand against the expansion of slavery into the territories and the enmity growing out of the 1848 state Democratic convention. Always a strong proslavery man, Jackson pushed through the legislature a series of resolutions bearing his name that placed Missouri squarely behind slavery expansion and instructed the state's congressmen and senators to abide by them. Benton refused to do so, disrupting the Missouri Democratic party and costing the senator the seat he had held for thirty years.

Jackson returned to the Missouri house in 1852 but failed in bids for a congressional seat in 1854 and 1856 because of the split in the Democratic party. After the death of Sappington in 1856, Jackson returned to Arrow Rock. The following year he was appointed state bank commissioner and continued in that post until 1860, when he finally received the Democratic nomination for governor. In the tumultuous campaign that followed the Democratic division at the national level,

Jackson, although sympathetic with the Breckinridge wing, openly supported Stephen A. Douglas for president as the best means of holding the Missouri party together. Even so, the Breckinridge men nominated their own candidate for governor; but the party stalwarts, led by Senator James S. Green, supported Jackson, who secured election over three rival candidates.

In the aftermath of Abraham Lincoln's election, Jackson made it clear at his own inauguration that he strongly supported the southern states in their quarrel with the Union. While not calling for secession, Jackson advocated the convening of a state convention to resolve that issue. He also asked the legislature to provide for the reorganization of the militia to put the state on a war footing. The legislature agreed with the former proposal but stalled on the militia issue. When the convention met, it voted against secession, but Jackson still favored a prosouthern neutrality. When Lincoln called on him for volunteers after the firing on Fort Sumter, Jackson refused to furnish them, denouncing the request as "illegal, unconstitutional, and revolutionary." He secretly sought arms from the Confederacy while providing for militia encampments throughout the state, including one at St. Louis. The latter encampment, known as Camp Jackson, was surrounded by Union troops under General Nathaniel Lyon on 10 May on the grounds that it was pro-Confederate and forced to surrender.

The legislature now approved militia reorganization, giving the governor virtually unlimited military powers. Jackson called for 50,000 volunteers to defend the state, which seemed on the verge of open conflict. A truce was temporarily worked out but subsequently voided by Union leaders in St. Louis, whereupon Jackson evacuated his capital at Jefferson City and became the leader of a government in exile. Defeated by Lyon at the battle of Boonville on 17 June, Jackson and the remnants of his newly organized Missouri State Guard retreated into the southwest corner of Missouri. There the governor left his forces under the command of General Sterling Price and traveled to Richmond to secure support from the Confederate government. This done, he returned to Missouri and called the remnants of the state legislature into session at Neosho, where it passed an ordinance of secession on 28 October. In the meantime, the state convention had met and deposed the Jackson government, replacing it with a provisional one that would control Missouri throughout the war. Thereafter Jackson continued a shadow government in various locations in Arkansas, cooperating with Confederate authorities, until his death from cancer in Little Rock.

• No body of Jackson papers has been preserved. Jackson's official papers as governor are in *Messages and Proclamations of the Governors of Missouri*, vol. 3, ed. Buel Leopard and Floyd C. Shoemaker (1922), which also contains a biographical sketch by Jonas Viles. Jackson's wartime career is detailed in William E. Parrish, "Missouri," in *The Confederate Governors*, ed. W. Buck Yearns (1985). The best view by a contemporary is Thomas L. Snead, *The Fight for Missouri* (1886).

WILLIAM E. PARRISH

JACKSON, Dunham (24 July 1888–6 Nov. 1946), mathematician, was born in Bridgewater, Massachusetts, the son of William Dunham Jackson, a professor of science and mathematics at the Normal School in Bridgewater, and Mary Vose Morse. Jackson received an A.B. in 1908 and an A.M. in 1909, both in mathematics, from Harvard University, along with a number of honors for academic achievement. Having obtained a fellowship from Harvard to pursue doctoral studies abroad, he left for Göttingen University in the fall of 1909. Göttingen, the home of such mathematical luminaries as Felix Klein, David Hilbert, Edmund Landau, and Ernst Zermelo, had served as a popular destination for American students studying mathematics since the late nineteenth century. Jackson's professor and mathematical mentor at Harvard, Maxime Bôcher, had received his Ph.D. under Felix Klein, and Bôcher's reputation among the Göttingen mathematicians may have helped pave the way there for Jackson.

With Landau as his adviser, Jackson earned his doctoral degree in 1911 for his work on the approximation of continuous functions by trigonometric sums. His dissertation appeared only in pamphlet form, published by Göttingen University, but Jackson later published refined versions of the results in some of his articles. Indeed, much of his research program throughout his life focused on the use of trigonometric sums and polynomials in approximations and dealt with the properties of certain systems of such functions.

Jackson left Germany and returned in 1911 to Harvard, where he continued his research and taught, supervising the work of two Ph.D. students. In 1918 he married Harriet Spratt Hulley, with whom he had two children, and was commissioned as a captain in the U.S. Army's Ordnance Department. More than 200 American mathematicians were involved in national service during World War I, including a large group who analyzed ordnance tests for the army. For a year Jackson worked in Washington, D.C., with a team of eight mathematicians headed by the mathematical astronomer Forest R. Moulton of the University of Chicago. Jackson's contributions focused on numerical methods of solving differential equations used in computing trajectories in ballistics.

The University of Minnesota offered Jackson a professorship in 1919. When he began his work there in the fall, more than 8,000 students had enrolled—2,000 more than in any year before the war. At the time, little graduate work was being done in the mathematics department, but the university anticipated increased demand for advanced mathematics. Jackson thus had the opportunity to play an important role in shaping the department at all levels of instruction.

In addition to teaching graduate courses and functioning as the dissertation adviser for nineteen students, Jackson enjoyed teaching undergraduate mathematics courses. Commenting on his popularity and effectiveness as a teacher, one colleague recalls that a question from a student "was treated [by Jackson] as if it were an indication of special understanding and commendable intellectual honesty. This attitude of Jackson in disseminating mathematical knowledge was one of his most valuable characteristics as a teacher" (Hart, *Biographical Memoirs*, pp. 158–59).

Some of Jackson's publications reflect his desire to provide mathematical education to students who were not pursuing the subject in its most theoretical form. For example, he wrote a number of articles of general interest to mathematics teachers at the secondary and college levels. In 1941 the Mathematical Association of America published his *Fourier Series and Orthogonal Polynomials* as one of its Carus Mathematical Monographs. With this series, the MAA sought to provide expositions not only for specialists in mathematics but also for scientists in other fields. Jackson saw value in both the pure and applied research of his fellow mathematicians, maintaining that "[c]ollectively and in the long run we are finding out things that the world wants to know, however ephemeral most of our individual contributions may be" ("The Human Significance of Mathematics," p. 410).

As an outgrowth of his desire to promote the uses of mathematics, Jackson played a significant role in developing the study of statistics at the University of Minnesota. In the mid-1920s, when few American universities offered opportunities to do mathematical research in statistics, Jackson introduced a course at the elementary graduate level called "The Mathematical Theory of Statistics." He published several articles of an expository nature on statistics, including the text of an invited address delivered to the American Mathematical Society on the theory of small samples. As Jackson's interest in the subject emerged, applied statistics was becoming more prominent at the university. In particular, the Department of Botany added a division of biostatistics, and the School of Business Administration introduced an undergraduate major in statistics.

Jackson remained at the University of Minnesota for the rest of his career. He suffered a heart attack at the age of fifty-two, and his health began to deteriorate rapidly a few years later. He died in Minneapolis.

Jackson's contributions to mathematics extended beyond his many research publications and his teaching activities. Throughout his career he served on a number of committees of the AMS, as well as on its governing council. He was the society's vice president in 1921 and served as the managing editor of its *Transactions* from 1926 to 1931. An invited speaker at several national and sectional meetings of the AMS, he gave a series of Colloquium Lectures at the society's summer meeting in 1925. The colloquia, instituted by the AMS in 1896, served to provide a general mathematical audience with fairly extensive exposure to a current topic of research. In addition to his activities in the AMS, Jackson was a charter member of the MAA and served as its vice president and president in the mid-1920s. He was vice president of the American Association for the Advancement of Science in 1927 and a member of the National Academy of Sciences. Jackson's commitment to teaching and his talent for conveying mathematical ideas drew students into mathematics. His active participation in research extended knowledge in his subject, and his contributions to the administrative work of various organizations helped to strengthen the American mathematics community.

• Jackson's "The Human Significance of Mathematics," *American Mathematical Monthly* 35 (1928): 406–11, was his address as the retiring president of the MAA; his Colloquium Lectures were published in 1930 as *The Theory of Approximation*. Jackson's colleague and friend has written the most complete biographies: William L. Hart, "Dunham Jackson, July 24, 1888–November 6, 1946," National Academy of Sciences, *Biographical Memoirs* 33 (1959): 142–79, and "Dunham Jackson, 1888–1946," *Bulletin of the American Mathematical Society* 54 (1948): 847–60. The former contains a complete list of Jackson's publications, as well as a list of his twenty-one Ph.D. students, while the latter includes a more detailed discussion of his research.

PATTI WILGER HUNTER

JACKSON, Edith Banfield (2 Jan. 1895–5 June 1977), pediatrician and psychoanalyst, was born in Colorado Springs, Colorado, the daughter of William Sharpless Jackson, a railroad executive, mining entrepreneur and banker, and Helen Fiske Banfield, an 1879 graduate of Vassar College. Jackson graduated with Phi Beta Kappa honors from Vassar College in 1916 and from the Johns Hopkins University School of Medicine in 1921. She held an internship at University of Iowa Hospital in 1921–1922 and a pediatric internship at Bellevue Hospital in 1922–1923. After four years on a rickets research project at the Yale School of Medicine, Jackson began a residency in psychiatry at St. Elizabeth's Hospital in Washington, D.C. in 1928. Between 1930 and 1936 she completed a training analysis with Sigmund Freud and participated in seminars at the Vienna Psychoanalytic Institute. Upon leaving Vienna, Jackson provided Anna Freud with the seed money to establish the world's first day-care center for infants from impoverished families. The "Edith Jackson Krippe" became the prototype for the Hampstead Nurseries for refugee children that Anna Freud directed in England during World War II.

Jackson was clinical professor of pediatrics and psychiatry at the Yale School of Medicine from 1936 to 1959. From 1946 to 1953 she directed the Yale Rooming-In Research Project, which she designed to test her hypothesis that the long-term psychological well-being of infants and their families would be enhanced if hospitals replaced their clock-bound, impersonal postpartum regimes with practices that had been commonplace when childbirth occurred at home. Arguing that parturition had become "hospital-centered in the first place and patient-centered in the second," Jackson organized two four-bed rooming-in units at Grace-New Haven Community Hospital in which newborns roomed with their mothers instead of in the hospital nursery, mothers fed their infants at will rather than on the hospital's four-hour schedule, and fathers could visit and hold their babies whenever they wished instead of merely viewing them at visiting hours through the nursery window.

The Rooming-In Project established Jackson as a pioneer in "family-centered" maternity and infant care and in "preventive pediatrics." First, rooming-in, contemporaneous with the Grantly Dick-Read "natural childbirth" movement and the Spock revolution, downplayed medical expertise and emphasized, in Jackson's words, "*parents'* participation in, . . . and . . . knowledge about processes which affect them and their infants" (1953, p. 492). Second, rooming-in procedures repudiated the widely accepted claim of child development experts like Dr. L. Emmett Holt that babies would be "spoiled" if they were played with or comforted and instead implemented Jackson's view that a "child's freedom to learn, and his capacity for self-discipline" were "rooted in his infantile and early childhood *satisfactions*" (1947, p. 588). Third, rooming-in promoted parent-infant "bonding" decades before that concept became modish in the 1970s. Jackson insisted that "*essential* psychological needs of both mother and child [had] been disregarded" in the American hospital setting, and she believed that hospitals, "without losing the protection of modern institutional medicine," could help "parents achieve . . . warm parent-child relationships" (1953, p. 484). The *International Medical Digest* agreed, calling rooming-in "the most progressive step in mental hygiene in the first half of the twentieth century" (54 [1949]: 183).

About forty other hospitals in the United States also instituted rooming-in between 1946 and 1950. While their goals were exclusively clinical—aiming, for instance, to prevent nursery infections, promote breast feeding, or facilitate ad-lib infant feeding—Jackson's project had educational and research components as well. It alone had a full-time medical director, director of research, and nursing and pediatric fellows to plan, oversee, document, and analyze its work. The American Psychiatric Association acknowledged Jackson's pathbreaking contributions to preventive psychiatry in 1964 when it named her the first recipient of the Agnes McGavin Award, and in 1968 she received the prestigious C. Anderson Aldrich Award in child development from the American Academy of Pediatrics. (Subsequent winners have included Benjamin Spock, Erik Erikson, Anna Freud, and T. Berry Brazelton.)

After retiring to Denver in 1960, Jackson continued to pioneer on behalf of the psychological well-being of children and families. She designed a rooming-in unit for the Colorado General Hospital and counseled unwed mothers who had made the decision, which was radical in the 1960s, to keep their "illegitimate" babies instead of putting them up for adoption. She also helped launch what became the Denver-based national center for the prevention and treatment of child abuse. In her own home she hosted planning meetings and kept records for the Colorado Association for the Study of Abortion, whose work spearheaded the passage, by the Colorado legislature in 1967, of the first liberalized abortion law in the United States.

Jackson never married, but she had devoted siblings, nieces, and nephews in Colorado and numerous close friends. Among the latter were Grover F. Powers, Yale Pediatrics Department chairman from 1927 to 1951 and one of the most honored pediatricians in the nation; Marian C. "Molly" Putnam, a Hopkins Medical School classmate and psychoanalyst; Anna Freud; and the families of her Rooming-In Fellows, who were devoted to her and with whom she remained in close contact throughout her life. She died at her home in Denver.

In the 1940s, when scientific hospital-centered medicine was widely acclaimed in the United States, Jackson was a respected member of the small vanguard of psychologically oriented, hospital-based academic pediatricians, obstetricians, and child psychiatrists who argued that a patient's psychological well-being was as important as her somatic status. Jackson's efforts produced mixed results. Rooming-in, although enthusiastically endorsed by the parents, physicians, nurses, and hospital administrators familiar with it, did not become normative in American hospitals after the Rooming-In Project ended. Jackson herself observed in 1966 that "the shortness of the maternity patients' stay seems . . . to be working against strong interest in the mother-infant relationship" because pediatric residents "do not find it worthwhile to involve themselves with" maternity patients who are discharged so soon after admission.

On the other hand, Jackson and her colleagues articulated in the 1940s a broad-based agenda to humanize medical care, which American medicine resisted but finally could not ignore. Consequently, lying-in procedures at American hospitals in the late twentieth century, while not precisely duplicating Jackson's model, are notably more flexible and "family-centered" than in Jackson's day; and programs to instruct medical students about their patients' fears and feelings, as well as about their diseases, are increasingly commonplace in American schools of medicine. "Things are not where they should be," Morris Wessel, a former Rooming-In Fellow observed in 1988, but "we are further along [in the direction of humanizing the practice of medicine in the United States] because of Edie's insistence on what she believed" (personal communication, 24 Apr. 1988).

• The largest collection of Jackson's papers is in the Schlesinger Library, Radcliffe College, Cambridge, Mass. There are also Jackson papers in the Yale University Library. Letters from Jackson to her siblings are in the William S. Jackson, Jr., Papers at the Denver Public Library. Between 1933 and 1956 Jackson authored or coauthored thirty articles. Among the more notable are: "Treatment of the Young Child in the Hospital, *American Journal of Orthopsychiatry* 12 (1942): 56–67; "Clinical Sidelights on Learning and Discipline," *The American Journal of Orthopsychiatry* 17 (1947): 580–89; "Pediatric and Psychiatric Aspects of the Yale Rooming-In Project," *The Connecticut State Medical Journal* 14 (1950): 616–23; "The Development of Rooming-In at Yale," *Yale Journal of Biology and Medicine* 25 (1953): 484–94; and, with Ethelyn H. Klatskin, "Methodology of the Yale Rooming-In Project on Parent-Child Relationship," *The American Journal of Orthopsychiatry* 25 (1955): 81–108, 373–97.

Articles about Jackson's career include Sara Lee Silberman, "Pioneering in Family-Centered Maternity and Infant Care: Edith B. Jackson and the Yale Rooming-In Research Project," *Bulletin of the History of Medicine* 64 (1990): 262–87, and "The Curious Pattern of a Distinguished Medical Career: A Psychoanalytic Portrait of Edith B. Jackson," *Biography* 17 (summer 1994); and Morris A. Wessel, "Caring for Families: Edith Jackson Taught the Ways," *Yale Alumni Magazine*, Dec. 1980, pp. 14–17. Obituaries are in the *New York Times*, 10 June 1977, and *Pediatrics* 61 (1978): 801–2.

SARA LEE SILBERMAN

JACKSON, Gardner (10 Sept. 1897–17 Apr. 1965), newspaperman, public official, and liberal gadfly also known as "Pat," was born in Colorado Springs, Colorado, the son of William Sharpless Jackson, a wealthy banker and railroad magnate, and Helen Banfield. In the Jackson family, affluence mingled with sympathy for the oppressed: Jackson's father was a Quaker, and his mother was the niece of his father's late and revered second wife, Helen Hunt Jackson, whose books *A Century of Dishonor* (1881) and *Ramona* (1884) had stirred the nation's conscience about the maltreatment of the American Indians.

In 1914 Pat Jackson went east to Amherst College, where he combined undergraduate high spirits with concern for Polish farmhands in the tobacco and onion fields of the Connecticut valley. His intellectual curiosity, exuberance, and charm won him the friendship of both Alexander Meiklejohn, the reform-minded president of Amherst, and Meiklejohn's enemy Robert Frost, the crusty poet. Frost eventually told his young protégé that college was a waste of his time, and Jackson entered the army in 1917. After World War I he briefly attended the Columbia School of Journalism. In 1920 he married Dorothy Sachs, with whom he had four children.

As a reporter on the *Boston Globe*, Jackson grew interested in the case of Nicola Sacco and Bartolomeo Vanzetti. Convinced that the two Italian anarchists had been condemned for their political beliefs, he became executive secretary of the Sacco-Vanzetti Defense Committee in 1926 and played a leading and fervent role in organizing protests against their execution the next year. Later with Marion Frankfurter, the wife of Felix Frankfurter, he edited *The Letters of Sacco and Vanzetti* (1928).

In 1930 he left Boston to become Washington correspondent for the *Montreal Star*. The election of Franklin D. Roosevelt in 1932 soon filled Washington with kindred reform spirits, and Jackson, with his talent for friendship, his ties to Felix Frankfurter and to Justice Louis D. Brandeis, and his passion for the underdog, formed warm friendships with leading New Dealers from the president and Eleanor Roosevelt down. Appointed assistant consumer's counsel in the Agricultural Adjustment Administration in 1933, he worked with AAA lawyers—Jerome Frank, Lee Pressman, Alger Hiss, and others—to get a better break for southern tenant farmers. Chester Davis, the AAA

chief, prevailed on the reluctant Secretary of Agriculture Henry A. Wallace to "purge" Frank, Pressman, and Jackson in 1935.

Jackson now threw himself into the cause of the sharecroppers, giving time, money, and energy to the Southern Tenant Farmers' Union, organized in Arkansas in 1934 in the interests of sharecroppers and tenant farmers. In 1936 he persuaded Senator Robert M. La Follette, Jr. (1895–1953), to set up the Civil Liberties Committee to investigate violations of labor's right to organize. He also promoted the movement to establish the Farm Security Administration, an agency set up in 1937 to help poor farmers. John L. Lewis and the new Congress of Industrial Organizations hoped to organize farm workers, and Jackson, who was active in the CIO's Labor's Non-Partisan League during the 1936 election, soon became a Lewis confidante.

The friendship with Lewis came to an abrupt end in 1940 with Lewis's isolationism and his decision to support Wendell L. Willkie in the presidential election. Jackson also ended his relationship with Lee Pressman, a Communist who had greatly influenced him and who was the CIO's general counsel. Pressman's cynical defense of Stalinist methods and the Communist switch to isolationism after the Soviet-Nazi pact of 1939 made Jackson thereafter a vocal and vigorous anti-Communist.

Jackson now became labor reporter for the new liberal New York newspaper *PM*, where he was prominent in the internal struggle between liberals and Stalinists. He returned briefly to the Department of Agriculture in 1943, but his concern for subsistence farmers once again led to his dismissal. His militant anti-Stalinism brought about in 1944 a physical assault by members of the Communist-controlled National Maritime Union, blinding him in one eye. After World War II Jackson joined the staff of the National Farmers Union, but his success in leading a floor fight for an anti-Communist resolution in the 1946 convention provoked James G. Patton, the union's president, to fire him. In 1947 he was one of the founders of the anti-Communist liberal organization Americans for Democratic Action.

In the postwar years Jackson pursued his manifold reform interests. He restored his relations with the Farmers Union when Patton purged the party-liners after the outbreak of the Korean War. He was active in the cause of the American Indians and of Mexican migrant farm workers. In 1952 Congressman John F. Kennedy enlisted Jackson in Kennedy's campaign for the Senate in Massachusetts. Jackson's determination to make Senator Joseph McCarthy an issue caused an angry showdown with Joseph P. Kennedy, the candidate's father. Jackson and the younger Kennedy remained on good terms, however, and during Kennedy's presidency Jackson served as a consultant for George McGovern, the director of the Food for Peace program. Jackson died in Washington, D.C.

Jackson's was a humane and irrepressible liberal faith, generous and disorderly, passionate without self-righteousness. Not devoid of human frailties, in particular a weakness for drink, he always distinguished between the sin and the sinner. People mattered to him more than dogma. His courage and persistence in reform efforts, as the *Washington Post* obituary put it, "cost him several jobs, his inherited wealth and the sight of one eye." "The underdog has him on a leash," one friend said, and he was known as the "champion of lost causes." A minor character in the New Deal drama, he embodied many salient characteristics of the period.

• Most of Jackson's papers are at the Franklin D. Roosevelt Library, Hyde Park, N.Y. Papers having to do with the Sacco-Vanzetti case and other matters are in the Gardner Jackson Room at the Brandeis University Library and in the papers of Aldino Felicani at the Boston Public Library. Subject to the usual discounts of oral history, "The Reminiscences of Gardner Jackson" (1959) in the Columbia Oral History Collection conveys Jackson's spirit and his comments on personalities and issues. Chapter 3, "The Dry Bones: Gardner Jackson and Lee Pressman," in Murray Kempton, *Part of Our Time: Some Monuments and Ruins of the Thirties* (1955), is an illuminating portrait. There are informative obituaries by Willard Clopton in the *Washington Post*, 18 Apr. 1965 (and an editorial on 22 Apr.); by James A. Wechsler in the *New York Post*, 19 Apr. 1965; by Arthur M. Schlesinger, Jr., in the *New Republic*, 1 May 1965; and by William V. Shannon in *Commonweal*, 4 June 1965. Jackson appears in biographies and/or journals and letters of Robert Frost, Louis D. Brandeis, Henry A. Wallace, Felix Frankfurter, John L. Lewis, Edmund Wilson, and John Dos Passos. He is also discussed in Joseph P. Lash, *Dealers and Dreamers: A New Look at the New Deal* (1988).

ARTHUR M. SCHLESINGER, JR.

JACKSON, Hall (11 Nov. 1739–28 Sep. 1797), physician, was born in Hampton, New Hampshire, to Clement Jackson, a physician, and Sarah Hall. After studying medicine with his father and his uncle, Dr. Anthony Emery, Jackson spent a year in London hospitals before going into practice at Portsmouth, New Hampshire, in 1763. In 1765 he married Mary Dalling Wentworth, widow of a navy officer, and they had three children.

Although most of his professional contemporaries were generalists in their practices, Jackson was known for his expertise in several areas. One was inoculation for smallpox, the preventive technique first popularized in Boston in 1721 by Dr. Zabdiel Boylston and Rev. Cotton Mather. Jackson headed inoculation hospitals at Charlestown (1764) and Marblehead, Massachusetts (1773–1774, 1777), and Portsmouth (1766, 1778, 1782, and 1797). He was also skilled in obstetrics. In February 1775 his reputation prompted John Wentworth, the royal governor of New Hampshire, to employ Jackson to deliver his wife's baby, despite the doctor's well-known reputation as a patriot. Jackson was most famous, however, for his unusually wide repertory of surgical skills. Newspapers described several of his operations, especially his amputations of injured or frostbitten limbs and his cataract operations. He was credited with devising a new form of bullet extractor while in London in 1762 and with

introducing to the colonies the relatively new French technique for total removal of cataracts. Although it is not clear why most of Jackson's surgery patients even in wartime did not die of the overwhelming infections that killed many others, he may simply have been intuitively more attentive to cleanliness than most surgeons of the time.

As a member of the Portsmouth Committee of Safety, Jackson made several trips as a volunteer regimental surgeon to the New Hampshire men at the siege of Boston in 1775. There he came into conflict with Dr. Benjamin Church (1734–1778?), the newly appointed director general of the Continental army hospital service, who was trying to replace the regimental hospitals favored by General John Sullivan's New Hampshire troops and their surgeons with a general hospital for the entire army. To make matters worse, Congress disregarded Sullivan's recommendation of an appointment for Jackson, which diluted his commitment to the patriot cause. In October 1775, when Church was unmasked as the new country's first documented traitor, Jackson felt that the director general's undisguised attempts to compromise several of his own professional actions could be explained by Church's treasonable attempts to disrupt the army as a whole.

After leaving Boston in October 1775, Jackson became chief surgeon to the New Hampshire troops stationed around Portsmouth. When the Continental Congress finally did offer him a senior medical post in 1777, he refused it on the ostensible grounds that he was too busy inoculating at Marblehead; by then, he felt it was too little too late. His last military assignment was as a regimental surgeon with Sullivan's forces at the siege of Newport, Rhode Island, in the fall of 1778. At home he continued to drill the militia supported by the Portsmouth selectmen and to study his favorite military specialty, artillery.

His fame continued to grow after the war. In 1786 he anonymously published a small book on diphtheria, *Observations and Remarks on the Putrid Malignant Sore-Throat*, chiefly for use in the home. That he understood the physiology of the cardiovascular system better than many of his colleagues is clear in his report of the autopsy he performed on the body of General William Whipple of Portsmouth in 1785.

The following year Jackson wrote to one of England's most eminent physicians, Dr. William Withering of Birmingham, to ask for seeds of the purple foxglove (*Digitalis purpurea*), which Withering had shown in his pioneering *Account of the Foxglove* (1785) to be the first dependably effective diuretic remedy for dropsy (now known as congestive heart failure). Jackson later sent foxglove seeds to prominent physicians in other states, recommending that they try digitalis for their own dropsy patients. Although Dr. Edward Augustus Holyoke, president of the Massachusetts Medical Society, could not be persuaded to have Jackson's account of his successful treatments with the drug read at a regular meeting of the society, word of the drug spread among that state's physicians anyway.

Jackson was one of the small but astonishing group of men who, collectively, comprised the first generation of medical scientists in America. His surgical skills earned him honorary fellowship in the Massachusetts Medical Society in 1783, and they and his promotion of digitalis prompted his honorary M.D. from Harvard ten years later. Active in civic and professional affairs, he became the second grand master of the Grand Masonic Lodge of New Hampshire in 1790, and in 1791 he was among the founders of the New Hampshire Medical Society.

Jackson died at home following a carriage accident. The predictably complimentary funeral eulogies emphasized Jackson's care for his patients, his devotion to scientific medicine, and his sparkling conversation. Yet he was also known for his hedonism and for his "not always admirable" frankness; Rev. Timothy Alden once described Jackson as one who might "adopt the [Epicurean] maxim, *dum vivimus vivamus*."

• See J. Worth Estes, *Hall Jackson and the Purple Foxglove: Medical Practice and Research in Revolutionary America 1760–1820* (1979).

J. WORTH ESTES

JACKSON, Hartley Harrad Thompson (19 May 1881–20 Sept. 1976), mammalogist and government official, was born in Milton, Wisconsin, the son of Harrad Jackson and Mary Thompson, English immigrants who settled in that state, and the only one of their eight children who was born in the United States. Educated in the local schools, he developed an interest in birds and later in mammals, the latter of which would become the focus of his lifelong research. He soon began a personal collection of study skins. At the age of fourteen he met Ludwig Kumlien, a prominent Wisconsin naturalist and Arctic explorer, who gave Jackson useful guidance in his natural history pursuits. His first article, on screech owls, was published in *The Nidiologist* in 1897, when he was sixteen.

While attending Milton College, Jackson published the first of his many titles on mammals, this one having to do with Wisconsin meadow mice. He received his B.S. degree in 1904, and over the next four years he taught school in Carthage, Missouri; Juda, Wisconsin; and Waukegan, Illinois. He returned to his studies in 1908, completed his M.S. at the University of Wisconsin in 1909, and began his professional career in 1910 as staff member in charge of the United States Biological Survey's mammal collection in Washington, D.C. He continued his studies, earning his Ph.D. from George Washington University in 1914.

A good part of Jackson's early career with the Biological Survey was spent on a cooperative project involving the Biological Survey with the Wisconsin Geological and Natural History Survey. Jackson began working on a study of the state's faunal resources in 1912, and he and others spent some time making field observations in Wisconsin every year until 1922, when the project was discontinued. In 1940, soon after the Biological Survey had been combined with the U.S. Fish Commission in the Interior Department and reconstituted as the U.S. Fish and Wildlife Service, the effort was revived. Despite Jackson's then very heavy administrative responsibilities, a series of eleven short pieces dealing with the "Summer Birds of Northwestern Wisconsin" were published in *Passenger Pigeon* (1941–1943). Not until 1949, however, when Jackson had been appointed senior biologist and others had succeeded to his administrative tasks, was he able to return to Wisconsin. Focusing this time on the state's mammals, he published *Mammals of Wisconsin* in 1961, which soon became one of the leading studies of a state's mammal fauna in the United States.

Jackson was one of a minority of biologists who defended the "life zone" concept of Clinton Hart Merriam, founding chief of the Biological Survey, which had largely fallen into disrepute by the 1930s. Jackson employed this approach to biogeographical distribution in categorizing Wisconsin mammals and plants into three life zones. In the course of his other early field work with the Biological Survey, Jackson completed "A Review of the American Moles" (no. 38 in the *North American Fauna Series* [1915]) and later "A Taxonomic Review of the American Long-Tailed Shrews (Genera Sorex and Microsorex)" (*North American Fauna* 51 [1928]). With a few minor changes, the classification of these animals which he set forth in this work has remained the standard. In 1951 Jackson and Stanley P. Young collaborated on *The Clever Coyote*, with Jackson contributing the section on coyote classification.

Jackson's initial interest in small mammals, particularly shrews and moles, changed in the 1930s with his growing administrative responsibilities for furbearing species. He was made chief of the Division of Biological Investigations from 1924 to 1926, and he was in charge of mammal research for the Survey between 1927 and 1936. He was in charge of the Section of Wildlife Surveys from 1936 to 1940, and, following the reorganization of that year, in charge of the section of Biological Surveys for the Fish and Wildlife Service from 1940 to 1951. Between 1937 and 1946, after creating some standard estimating techniques, he devised methods of counting larger mammals in the United States and published an annual compilation of "big game surveys." Trappers, forest rangers, game wardens, Native Americans, and citizens generally were encouraged to assist with this censusing project, which provided an important basis for wildlife legislation, including hunting regulations. Airplanes were employed as an observation and counting tool, an important innovation in the late 1930s. In this effort Jackson was assisted by Ira Gabrielson, a colleague who shortly became the last chief of the Biological Survey and the first director of the Fish and Wildlife Service.

During World War II Jackson prepared lists of rodents in East Asia, the Pacific, and Australia for the Rodent Control Subcommittee of the National Research Council, and he provided geographic information on Alaska for the Office of Strategic Services. He was senior biologist for the Fish and Wildlife Service from 1949 to 1951, when he formally retired. He was consulting mammalogist at the Smithsonian Institution from 1951 to 1966, during which he worked on a history of the Biological Survey that remained incomplete at his death. In 1916 Jackson and several colleagues discussed the need for a national association of mammalogists, and in large part through his efforts, the American Society of Mammalogists was established in 1919. Jackson served on the society's board of directors from 1919 until his death. He was corresponding secretary (1919–1925), vice president (1937), and president (1938–1940), and became an honorary member in 1952. In addition he edited the *Journal of Mammalogy* from 1925 to 1929.

Jackson married Anna Marcia Adams in 1910; they had no children, and she died in 1968. In 1970, he married Stephanie Hall, whom he had known since his boyhood in Wisconsin. Her first husband had been associated with Jackson on the biological reconaissance of Wisconsin as a graduate student at the University of Wisconsin in 1917, and her father had been president of Jackson's alma mater, Milton College. Following his second marriage, Jackson sold his home in Chevy Chase, Maryland, and moved to Durham, North Carolina, where he died.

• The archival records of the American Society of Mammalogists are in the Smithsonian Institution Archives, Washington, D.C. There is a biographical sketch of Jackson by John W. Aldrich in the *Journal of Mammalogy* 58 (1977); a shorter biographical outline is in Elmer C. Birney and Jerry R. Choate, eds., *Seventy-Five Years of Mammalogy (1919–1994)*, Special Publication no. 10, American Society of Mammalogists (1994). This same volume contains a detailed discussion of Jackson's role in the founding of the American Society of Mammalogists by Donald Hoffmeister. See also Hoffmeister, "A History of the American Society of Mammalogists," *Program of the 50th Anniversary Celebration of the American Society of Mammalogists* (1969). Jackson's role in the large mammal surveys of the late 1930s and early 1940s is discussed in Richard L. Neuberger, "Great American Snout Count," *Saturday Evening Post*, 22 June 1946.

KEIR B. STERLING

JACKSON, Helen Hunt (14 Oct. 1830–12 Aug. 1885), writer and reformer, was born Helen Maria Fiske in Amherst, Massachusetts, the daughter of Nathan Welby Fiske, a professor of languages at Amherst College, and Deborah Vinal. Her mother, recognizing Helen's inclination toward independent thought and behavior, described her as "quite inclined to question everything; the Bible she says does not feel as if it were true" (Banning, p. 11). Despite a sporadic education at a series of boarding schools, she was better educated than most women of her time, having exposure to mathematics, science, and philosophy as well as the usual "finishing school" subjects.

In 1852 Helen Fiske married Edward Bissell Hunt, a mechanical engineer in the U.S. Army. His frequent changes of station gave her the opportunity to live at the artists' colony of Newport, Rhode Island, and in Washington, D.C., where she met a number of the leading writers and publishers of her day. The Hunts had two sons; one died in infancy and the other in childhood. In 1863 Major Hunt was killed in a military accident, and Helen Hunt turned to writing as a form of solace as well as a possible source of income.

Using her literary contacts, Helen Hunt began her career in 1865 with two poems published in the *New York Evening Post*. Her first poetry collection, *Verses*, appeared in 1870, followed by a prose collection, *Bits of Travel*, in 1873. Under the tutelage of Thomas Wentworth Higginson, whom she had met at Newport, Hunt emulated other female writers who had successfully met the requirements of publishers catering to female readers. Carefully adhering to the woman's sphere of domesticity, she stressed in lyrics, essays, and travel sketches the moral and emotional qualities a woman was expected to possess in her role as exemplar to husband and children. She was able to bring a sprightly air to plodding subjects and to subdue fashionable melodramatic excesses without losing dramatic effect. Her rapid success can also be attributed to her astute cultivation of literary contacts as well as the size of the female readers' market. Her popularity established, she added short stories, children's stories, and novels, published under several pseudonyms but most often simply "H.H."

Through her acquaintance with Higginson, Hunt came into contact with her childhood friend Emily Dickinson. They began a correspondence that lasted until Hunt's death. In her characteristic way, Dickinson occasionally enclosed a poem. Though sometimes admitting that the lines puzzled her, Hunt was aware she was in touch with talent that far surpassed her own. Consistently she pleaded that Dickinson allow her to help with publication. She chided Dickinson for not giving her "day & generation" the privilege of reading her poems. Like no other of Dickinson's known correspondents, Hunt unhesitatingly expressed her conviction that her friend was a great poet.

Hunt's early travel sketches were about her excursions into quaint New England and European byways; then in 1872 a trip by transcontinental railroad from New York City to San Francisco gave her material for essays collected in *Bits of Travel at Home* (1878). When in 1873, after a period of ill health, Hunt returned to the West to try its restorative powers, she went to the new town of Colorado Springs, where in 1875 she married William Sharpless Jackson, a banker and railroad executive. For the rest of her life she called Colorado Springs home but made many trips back east to maintain contact with publishers and other authors, and regular journeys to California, which attracted her for its history as well as its beauty.

In 1879, while visiting in Boston, she attended a reception for representatives of the Ponca and Omaha Indian tribes who were touring the East in an attempt to arouse public indignation over the confiscation of their tribal lands by the U.S. government. Jackson had never shown any interest in reform movements, nor had her experiences in the West sparked any concern for Indian rights, but suddenly she was transformed. She wrote a friend that she had become what she had previously considered "the most odious thing in the world, 'a woman with a hobby'" (Banning, p. 149). Her dedication to the cause of justice for Indian tribes resulted in a well-researched exposé of Indian mistreatment published in 1881 as *A Century of Dishonor*; the government-commissioned *Report on the Conditions and Needs of the Mission Indians*, with Abbot Kinney (1883); *Ramona* (1884), one of the most popular novels of its day; and a series of essays on the California Mission Indians, collected in *Glimpses of California and the Missions* (1902).

When her nonfiction writings did not initiate the reforms that Jackson sought, she said of *Ramona*, "I am going to write a novel, in which will be set forth some Indian experiences in a way to move people's hearts. . . . People will read a novel when they will not read serious books" (Banning, p. 200). Critics and readers responded positively, but Jackson was dismayed by the focus of the reviews: "Not one word for the Indians; I put my heart and soul in the book for them. It is a dead failure" (Banning, p. 216). Instead of recognizing Jackson's intent, readers were captivated by the charm of the southern California setting and the romance between a half-breed girl raised by an aristocratic Spanish family and an Indian forced off his tribal lands by white encroachers.

In little more than a year following the publication of *Ramona*, Jackson died of cancer in San Francisco. She was eulogized in newspapers from coast to coast. Publishers rushed to produce reprints and new collections. *Ramona* became the impetus for the romanticization of southern California history. For a time a body of literature about "Ramona Country" flourished, and various sites from the book became tourist attractions. It has gone through over 300 printings and transformation into stage plays, movies, and pageants.

Of all her work, Jackson believed only *Ramona* and *A Century of Dishonor* would survive. She was close to being right; however, her travel sketches and essays, especially those about the West, also deserve a continuing readership. One of the few cultivated women to travel to the West and write about the journey, and then to marry and establish a home there, her responses to these experiences are unique among nineteenth-century travelogues. Although she was disappointed that her dedication to the cause of justice for the American Indians did not have more immediate results, her writings inspired other reformers to continue their efforts. *A Century of Dishonor* and *Report on the Conditions and Needs of the Mission Indians* were frequently used as resources in the speeches and writings of such organizations as the Indian Rights Association and the Women's National Indian Association. Especially in her exposure of the treatment of the Mission Indians of California, Jackson influenced reform legislation.

• Major collectors of Jackson's papers and letters are the Huntington Library in San Marino, Calif., and the Tutt Library of Colorado College in Colorado Springs. A comprehensive bibliography appears in Valerie Sherer Mathes, *Helen Hunt Jackson and Her Indian Reform Legacy* (1990). Two biographies are Ruth Odell, *Helen Hunt Jackson* (1939), and Evelyn I. Banning, *Helen Hunt Jackson* (1973). See also the Jackson chapter in Susan Coultrap-McQuin, *Doing Literary Business: American Women Writers in the Nineteenth Century* (1990).

ROSEMARY WHITAKER

JACKSON, Henry Martin (31 May 1912–1 Sept. 1983), politician, was born in Everett, Washington, the son of Norwegian immigrants Peter (Gresseth) Jackson, a plasterer, and Marine Anderson. He was known all his life by the nickname "Scoop." After earning his undergraduate and law degrees from the University of Washington, Jackson, a Democrat, was elected Snohomish County prosecuting attorney in 1938 and to the U.S. Congress in 1940. He was an isolationist before the Japanese attack on Pearl Harbor but afterward became a fervent believer in the assumption of world responsibilities by the United States. In 1952 he was elected to the U.S. Senate and was never seriously challenged for reelection. He aspired to the presidency in 1972 and 1976 but gained minimal popular support in the primaries.

Jackson's only interests were politics and public policy. He never sought personal wealth, nor was he accused of impropriety. Although sometimes called "the Senator from Boeing," referring to the huge defense contractor in his home state, Jackson became the Senate's leading authority on national security policy out of patriotic conviction. Beginning in 1959 he chaired important hearings on the conduct of foreign and defense policy. In the 1960s he became an articulate critic of nuclear arms control proposals lest they sacrifice American advantage over the Soviet Union. He reluctantly supported the Nuclear Test Ban Treaty of 1963 but anticipated that the vital interests of the United States might require withdrawal. He found the 1972 Strategic Arms Limitation Treaties (SALT I) biased in favor of the Soviet Union and won approval for an amendment declaring that all future agreements must provide for numerical equality between American and Soviet nuclear weapons.

Jackson was a strong supporter of the state of Israel and a critic of human rights violations in the Soviet Union, especially the restrictions placed on the right of Jews to emigrate. In 1974 he was the driving force behind the passage of the Jackson-Vanik amendment, which made favorable trade relations between the United States and the Soviet Union conditional on liberalization of Soviet emigration policy.

Jackson's greatest influence came during the presidency of Jimmy Carter, when he directed a barrage of detailed criticism against the 1979 Strategic Arms Limitation Treaty (SALT II). If Carter had not withdrawn the treaty from Senate consideration because of the Soviet invasion of Afghanistan, the treaty almost certainly would have been defeated, largely because of Jackson's efforts.

Jackson's political power derived from his seniority, mastery of issues, skill in persuading colleagues and building coalitions, trustworthiness, and talent for recruiting outstanding personal staff. On the arcane details of arms control, for example, his assistant was Richard Perle, who later became a hardline Defense Department official in the administration of President Ronald Reagan. Jackson was noted for long, very detailed, analytically powerful speeches setting forth his positions. The speeches were often reprinted and widely circulated.

In the 1960s and 1970s Jackson's Cold War militancy separated him from liberals in the Democratic party while bringing him great admiration from Republicans and neoconservative intellectuals. He agreed with President Reagan that the influence of communism and the Soviet Union in Central America constituted a strategic threat of dire dimensions and staunchly upheld the policy of supporting the armed opposition to the Sandinista regime in Nicaragua. The bipartisan commission on Central America, called the Kissinger commission, was established by President Reagan on Jackson's recommendation. Senator Jackson worked for close ties between the United States and the People's Republic of China. As early as 1966 he concluded that China was not an enemy and that it was in American interests to establish a dialogue and search for areas of mutual interest. President Richard Nixon achieved what Jackson had long advocated. Senator Jackson died suddenly in Everett just after returning from a trip to Beijing.

Jackson was a liberal Cold War Democrat with unsurpassed influence on defense issues in the U.S. Senate for forty years. He stood for big military budgets, a confrontational stand toward the Soviet Union, opposition to most arms control proposals, and anti-Communist activism in the Third World. He supported the Vietnam War. In domestic affairs, Senator Jackson was for the nuclear power industry, conservation of natural resources, organized labor, civil rights, racial equality, and the need for the federal government to assist the poor and disadvantaged.

• Jackson's papers are in the University of Washington Library. He edited three studies based on his hearings into the conduct of foreign and defense policy, *The Secretary of State and the Ambassador* (1964), *The National Security Council* (1965), and *The Atlantic Alliance* (1967). Dorothy Fosdick, ed., *Henry M. Jackson and World Affairs: Selected Speeches, 1953–1983* (1990), is usefully annotated. Fosdick, ed., *Staying the Course: Henry M. Jackson and National Security* (1987), is a collection of essays by people who worked closely with Jackson. Peter J. Ognibene, *Scoop: The Life and Politics of Henry M. Jackson* (1975), is informative, critical, and journalistic. Paula Stern, *Water's Edge: Domestic Politics and the Making of American Foreign Policy* (1979), is a case study of the Jackson-Vanik amendment.

GADDIS SMITH

JACKSON, Howell Edmunds (8 Apr. 1832–8 Aug. 1895), associate justice of the U.S. Supreme Court, was born in Paris, Tennessee, the son of Alexander Jackson, a physician, and Mary W. Hurt. After graduating from West Tennessee College in 1849, Jackson completed two years of study at the University of Virginia. He was then tutored in the law by Judge A. W. O. Totten of the Tennessee Supreme Court and in 1856 received a law degree with first honors from Cumberland University at Lebanon, Tennessee.

Jackson began his law practice in Jackson, Tennessee, but moved to Memphis in 1858, where he formed a partnership with David M. Currin, a former member of Congress. In 1859 Jackson married Sophia Malloy. The marriage produced four children before Sophia's death in 1873. Jackson's law partnership with Currin was short lived due to Tennessee's secession from the Union in 1861. Although Jackson, a Whig, was personally opposed to secession, he nevertheless accepted an official position with the Confederate government as receiver of confiscated Union property. After hostilities ended, Jackson returned to Memphis and resumed the practice of law in partnership with B. M. Estes. The practice, which involved litigation in both state and federal courts, proved to be highly successful and lucrative. During this period Jackson established a reputation as one of the state's ablest appellate lawyers.

In April 1874 Jackson married his second wife, Mary Harding of Nashville; they had three children. Through this marriage Jackson came into possession of "West Meade," a magnificent horse farm on the western outskirts of Nashville. The adjoining estate, known as "Belle Meade," passed to Jackson's younger brother William, who also had married into the Harding family.

Like many southern Whigs, Jackson joined the Democratic party shortly after the Civil War ended. But he did not share the hostility toward the Union and the federal government that typified southern Democrats of his era. It would be fair to describe Jackson's political views as moderate.

In 1875 Jackson was appointed to the provisional Court of Arbitration for West Tennessee. When this tribunal was abolished two years later, Jackson sought a position on the Tennessee Supreme Court, but by a single vote failed to win the Democratic nomination. In 1880, after a bitter campaign, he was elected to the state house of representatives. Within a matter of months the state legislature chose Jackson to fill the U.S. Senate seat being vacated by James E. Bailey.

In Washington, D.C., Jackson developed friendships with President Grover Cleveland and with Republican Senate colleague Benjamin Harrison, who would succeed Cleveland as president in 1889. In 1887 Jackson left the Senate to take a position on the U.S. Sixth Circuit Court at the request of President Cleveland. Jackson had not actively sought the position; indeed, he had suggested the name of another Tennessee Democrat to fill the vacancy created by the death of Judge John Baxter. But Cleveland insisted that Jackson accept the nomination. After some protest and a little embarrassment, Jackson finally accepted the nomination to the federal bench. He was confirmed by a unanimous Senate vote.

As a circuit judge, Jackson decided some ninety cases. Only two were reversed by the Supreme Court, and Jackson earned a reputation as a careful and conservative jurist who religiously followed precedent. In 1891, when the Sixth Circuit Court of Appeals was established at Cincinnati, Jackson became the new court's first presiding judge.

Jackson's decisions on the circuit court both impressed and pleased President Harrison, who would ultimately select Jackson for the Supreme Court. In one noteworthy case, *United States v. Patrick* (1893), Jackson upheld the prosecution of three Tennesseans under the Civil Rights Act of 1870. The defendants had been indicted for conspiring to interfere with the civil rights of federal officers. The district court dismissed the case, holding that any conspiracy that existed had been directed against the agents in their official capacities rather than as "citizens of the United States." Jackson reversed the district court ruling and allowed the prosecution to go forward. A number of southern commentators blasted Jackson for what they perceived as an unwarranted expansion of a despised Reconstruction statute, but to Harrison, Jackson's decision indicated his sympathy toward the Union.

When Justice Lucius Q. C. Lamar of Mississippi died on 23 January 1893, Harrison, by then a lame duck, took the opportunity to elevate Jackson to the Supreme Court. As is usually the case with Supreme Court appointments, political considerations loomed large in the nomination. The Democrats controlled the Senate, so it was not likely that a lame-duck Republican president would win confirmation of a Republican nominee. Howell Jackson fit the bill perfectly. He was a southern Democrat with impeccable credentials, strong ties to the Senate, and, above all, he held views of the federal system similar to Harrison's. Jackson's appointment was immediately confirmed by the Senate without opposition.

Jackson took his seat on the Supreme Court on 4 March 1893. Owing to failing health caused by tuberculosis, however, his tenure on the Court was only two and a half years. Moreover, illness prevented Jackson from participating in most of the important decisions rendered by the Court during his brief tenure. The most important case in which Jackson did cast a vote was *Pollock v. Farmer's Loan and Trust Company* (1895), in which the Court, divided 5 to 4, struck down a federal income tax law in spite of Jackson's formidable dissent. To Jackson, the decision of the Supreme Court in *Pollock* was "the most disastrous blow ever struck at the constitutional power of Congress" (p. 704). When the Sixteenth Amendment was ratified in 1913, Congress recovered its power to assess an income tax.

When the Supreme Court finished its term in late spring 1895, a feeble Justice Jackson returned to his home at West Meade, where he died.

• Justice Jackson's papers are part of the Southern Historical Collection housed at the University of North Carolina at Chapel Hill. The literature on Jackson is rather sparse. The most complete treatment is Irving Schiffman, "Howell E. Jackson," in *Justices of the United States Supreme Court 1789–1969: Their Lives and Major Opinions*, ed. Leon Friedman and Fred L. Israel, vol. 2 (1969), pp. 1603–15. Another biographical sketch is "Two United States Circuit Judges," *Tennessee Law Review* 18 (1944): 311–22. The U.S. Supreme Court's proceedings commemorating Jackson may be found at 159 U.S. 703 (1895).

JOHN M. SCHEB II

JACKSON, James (21 Sept. 1757–19 Mar. 1806), congressman, U.S. senator, and governor of Georgia, was born in Moreton Hampstead, Devonshire, England, the son of James Jackson, Sr., and Mary Webber, about whom nothing is known. At age fifteen he immigrated alone to Savannah, Georgia, where lawyer John Wereat took him in. Young Jackson received no formal education, but within the next few years the American Revolution transformed and gave focus to his life. In 1777 he was a delegate to the Georgia Constitutional Convention. More notably, he served in the state militia, fought in numerous engagements, including Cowpens in 1781, and became a major general in 1792. For his leadership of the patriot forces that repossessed Savannah after the British departure in July 1782, the assembly awarded him a house and lot in the town. In 1785 he married Mary Charlotte Young; they had five sons. By 1796 Jackson's estate had grown to include several thousand acres of rice and cotton producing lands, including 4,594 acres from grants made to him by Georgia governors in recognition of war service. Showing little interest in selling this domain, he apparently was immune from the land speculation fever of his day. After studying with George Walton, he began a lucrative law practice in Savannah that added more than 3,000 pounds annually to the profits from his plantations. More important to his career than wealth, however, was the central lesson he drew from English political history and from his own revolutionary experience: that concentrations of power—economic or otherwise—in the hands of scheming men presented an immediate threat to liberty.

After Jackson served several terms in the Georgia Assembly (1781–1787, 1789), his fellow legislators elected him governor in 1788, but he declined, partly because he thought himself too young for the job. Instead, the Georgia Tidewater voters sent him, at age thirty-two, to the First Congress in 1789. Within months he joined Elbridge Gerry of Massachusetts and John Page of Virginia in opposing the dominant Hamiltonian clique, whose approach to issues of vital importance—executive influence, public debt, and the power of the federal government—violated Jackson's conception of republican principle. An erect 5'7" and broad-shouldered, he gained a reputation for hot-spirited candor, a brawling style, and a voice that one member compared to a "furnace bellows." Few were quicker to voice current antifederalist fears of monarchy, monied aristocracy, and ministerial intrigue in the national government. The creation of the executive departments, especially the Treasury, triggered Jackson's suspicion that a "high game of corruption" was afoot, threatening to subvert the independence of the legislative branch. "This thirst of power," he declared, "will introduce a Treasury bench into the House."

On payment of the federal debt, Jackson, along with James Madison, advocated a plan that would favor the original holders of government securities over speculators who bought shares for a fraction of their face value. Jackson was so opposed to furthering speculators' interests that he preferred heavy direct taxation to the funded federal debt that Treasury Secretary Alexander Hamilton proposed. Passing the burden of payment to unborn generations, with future taxes on "the honest, hard-working part of the community," he warned, would "promote the ease and luxury of men of wealth." For similar reasons, he protested the Bank of the United States, and he thought Hamilton's 1790 proposal of federal assumption of state debts discriminated against the southern states, unfairly increasing their tax burden and eroding their freedom from central authority.

In 1791 Jackson lost his House seat to Anthony Wayne, who later was found to have benefited in Georgia's eastern district from various election rule violations and vote tampering on the part of Judge Henry Osborne. Afterward Jackson returned to the Georgia legislature, where he served three more times (1791, 1796, 1797). Allies in that body sent him in 1793 to the U.S. Senate, where he briefly chaired the Military Affairs Committee. Jackson left only two years into his term, when the Yazoo controversy at home stirred up a hornet's nest of public contempt for some of the state's most prominent men.

The fraudulent Yazoo land deal began in the mid-1790s, when four well-financed land companies, backed in part by Jackson's archrival in Georgia, the Federalist senator James Gunn, descended on the state capital, offering blandishments galore. In January 1795 the legislature passed a bill conveying 35 million acres—two-thirds of Georgia's western land claims—to the four companies for a mere $500,000 in specie. Only one of the assemblymen who voted for the bill refused to be bribed. After revelation of this betrayal, Georgia voters demanded repeal of the offending statute. Jackson, elected again to the legislature in late 1795, spearheaded the movement that produced the 1796 Georgia Repeal Act, which the John Marshall Court in *Fletcher v. Peck* (1810) declared an unconstitutional violation of the contract clause. Jackson was also a conspicuous member of the Georgia convention of 1798 that produced a new state constitution with specific anti-Yazoo provisions. He was elected governor of Georgia, and serving from 1798 to 1801, he continued to hound leading planters, like former state treasurer John Berrian, for involvement in the Yazoo fraud. His annual message in January 1799 advocated cession of the lands west of the Chattahoochee to the United States for a "moderate compensation"—the solution finally adopted in 1802.

Jackson's hasty Senate resignation looked like a personal sacrifice for the anti-Yazoo cause and its republican values, but his true motives were more complicated. He honestly deplored corrupt influence peddling and saw the Revolution as mandating a loftier ideal of public behavior, but he also used the issue to unite up-country yeomen and Tidewater elements who opposed a would-be aristocracy of well-connected speculator interests. The resulting Jackson organization was, in essence, the Jeffersonian party in Georgia. Two of Jackson's machine protégés, William H. Crawford and George M. Troup, carried the party's influence well into the 1820s.

Elected to Gunn's Senate seat in 1801, Jackson favored a wholesale dismissal of Federalists from government office and backed the Thomas Jefferson administration on most policy questions, especially repeal of the Judiciary Act of 1801 and the Louisiana Purchase in 1803. He championed sectional interest as well as party, urging repeal of the Hamiltonian excise duties and promoting a federally funded road from Kentucky to Augusta, Georgia.

Jackson was as volatile in private life as he was impassioned in public. Hypersensitive to insult, he practiced the "code duello" and eventually was dubbed the "prince of Savannah duelists." In 1780 he killed the acting governor of Georgia, George Wells, after himself receiving a bullet through both knees. Jackson died in Washington, D.C., from dropsy apparently related to wounds he suffered in his last trip to the dueling field.

• The largest collections of Jackson's papers are gathered in the Georgia Historical Society Library, Savannah, and in the Georgia Department of Archives and History, Atlanta. Gales and Seaton, comps., *Annals of Congress, 1789–1824* (42 vols., 1834–1856), is the best primary source on his career in the House of Representatives and the Senate. On his contribution to the First Congress, Lance Banning, *The Jeffersonian Persuasion: Evolution of a Party Ideology* (1978), is especially helpful. The finest work on the Yazoo episode and on Jackson's role in it is C. Peter Magrath, *Yazoo: Law and Politics in the New Republic* (1966). For a full-scale biography of Jackson, see William O. Foster, Sr., *James Jackson: Duelist and Militant Statesman, 1757–1806* (1960). An obituary is in the *National Intelligencer and Washington Advertiser*, 21 Mar. 1806.

JOHN R. VAN ATTA

JACKSON, James (3 Oct. 1777–27 Aug. 1867), physician and medical educator, was born in Newburyport, Massachusetts, the son of Jonathan Jackson, a banker and merchant, and Hannah Tracy. Jackson, whose family's prosperity was undercut during the Revolution, nevertheless received the A.B. degree from Harvard College in 1796. He worked for more than a year following graduation, mainly for his father as a clerk, then began studying medicine by attending lectures at Harvard and becoming an apprentice to the eminent Salem (Mass.) physician Edward Augustus Holyoke.

He received the A.M. degree from Harvard in 1799, and in October of that year he obtained free passage to London on a ship commanded by his brother Henry.

During a year in London, which was then the favored destination for New Englanders seeking advanced medical training abroad, Jackson attended lectures at the United Hospitals of Guy's and St. Thomas's, studied anatomy with Astley Cooper, and served as a surgical dresser at St. Thomas's. He also paid for instruction from William Woodville, at St. Pancras Smallpox and Inoculation Hospital; there he learned the new technique of vaccinating patients with cowpox matter against smallpox as a safer alternative to inoculation with smallpox matter itself.

In October 1800, immediately after his return to Boston and $3,000 in debt from his education, Jackson opened his medical practice. His special knowledge of the then-novel practice of vaccination, combined with the supply of cowpox matter he had brought with him from England, helped him quickly win both public attention and a lucrative practice. Though still working his way out of debt, in October 1801 he married Elizabeth Cabot, with whom he had nine children. He received the M.B. degree from Harvard in 1802 and also was appointed as a physician to the Boston Almshouse.

The Boston surgeon John Collins Warren, a friend of Jackson at Harvard College and in London, returned from England in 1801, and the two began a series of professional collaborations that helped make Boston a leading medical center of the early republic. Together they organized the Medical Improvement Society around 1803; promoted the reorganization of the Massachusetts Medical Society, transforming it from an aristocratic clique to a more inclusive organization for all physicians; and in 1808 led a committee of the medical society to prepare a new pharmacopoeia. In 1809 Jackson received the M.D. degree from Harvard, having written as his thesis "Remarks on the Brunonian System," an assault on speculative system-building in medicine that targeted in particular the influential theories and practices of the Edinburgh physician John Brown.

In 1810 Jackson was appointed to the newly created professorship of clinical medicine at Harvard and began giving clinical instruction at the Boston Almshouse. Two years later he succeeded Benjamin Waterhouse as Hersey Professor of the Theory and Practice of Physic. In 1810 Jackson and Warren jointly published a circular letter announcing plans to create the Massachusetts General Hospital and soliciting support for the new charitable institution; they continued to work in behalf of the new institution throughout the 1810s, and Jackson would serve as attending physician when its wards finally opened in 1821.

From the 1810s through the 1820s, Jackson's work at Harvard established him as one of the most prominent medical teachers in the United States. The surviving lecture notebooks kept by his students depict a physician wary of the dogmatic theoretical systems of pathology and therapeutics that still held considerable sway over American medicine. They also indicate that he was open but cautious to technical and conceptual innovations, such as those emanating from the ascendant Paris Clinical School. He urged a notably modest assessment of the physician's ability to actively cure disease and, though he recommended all the mainstays of heroic therapy, stressed the importance of the healing power of nature. His teachings both reflected and helped shape a characteristically New England therapeutic reliance on nature's healing powers. Jackson regularly contributed reports on his medical observations to Massachusetts medical periodicals, including the first description of what later was identified as alcoholic neuritis. What drew the largest contemporary notice among his clinical publications, however, was the preface and appendix he wrote for his son-in-law C. G. Putnam's translation of the French clinician Pierre Louis's *Researches on the Effects of Bloodletting in Some Inflammatory Diseases* (1836), which was varyingly seen as a challenge or confirmation to the value of therapeutic bleeding.

Jackson's wife died in 1817, and shortly thereafter he married her sister, Sarah Cabot, with whom he had no children. The family loss that would most profoundly change Jackson's life, though, was the death of his eldest son and namesake, also a physician, in 1834. The next year he published *A Memoir of James Jackson, Jr.*, which included extracts from the correspondence between them, and the poignant volume drew widespread attention from American physicians. Jackson resigned his post at Harvard in 1836 and at the Massachusetts General Hospital in 1837.

Over the next three decades Jackson continued his private medical practice but was no longer an active professional leader. The two significant publications of his later years, *Letters to a Young Physician* (1855) and *Another Letter to a Young Physician* (1861), were in no small measure further memorials, written to his lost son. Jackson died in Boston.

• Francis A. Countway Library of Medicine, Boston, holds the largest collection of Jackson's professional and personal correspondence, medical case books, and lecture notes, in addition to student notes taken from his lectures. The Massachusetts Historical Society, Boston, holds a substantial collection of letters to Jackson in the James Jackson Papers, as well as material in the Putnam, Jackson, and Lowell papers. Additional correspondence from Jackson is in the Isaac Hays Papers and Caspar W. Pennock Papers, American Philosophical Society, Library, Philadelphia; the William W. Gerhard Papers, College of Physicians of Philadelphia, Library; the Parsons Family Papers, Special Collections, John Hay Library, Brown University, Providence, R.I.; and the Bartlett (Elisha) Family Papers, Rush Rees Library, University of Rochester, N.Y. James Jackson Putnam, *A Memoir of Dr. James Jackson* (1905), is the fullest biographical source; it also contains ample extracts from Jackson's correspondence and from some of his writings and a partial bibliography of his medical publications.

JOHN HARLEY WARNER

JACKSON, James Caleb (28 Mar. 1811–11 July 1895), abolitionist and physician, was born in Onondaga County, New York, the son of James Jackson, a physician, and Mary Ann Elderkin. Jackson studied at Manlius Academy, a preparatory school, until the death of his father in 1828. He then gave up plans for a college education and took up farming. Jackson married Lucretia E. Brewster in 1830; they had one child.

Jackson displayed an early interest in religion and reform, which in his view were intimately connected, and was attracted to the evangelical antislavery movement as early as 1831. Originally active in the nonresistance wing of the movement associated with William Lloyd Garrison, Jackson moved into the camp of the political abolitionists in 1838. In that year in a letter to abolitionist Gerrit Smith he stated his belief that the established parties were corrupt and quoted Scripture to support the formation of a distinct antislavery party: "Come out from among them and *be ye separate* and touch not the unclean thing and I will receive you."

Jackson lectured for the Massachusetts Anti-Slavery Society and in 1840 became secretary of the American Anti-Slavery Society. Over the next six years he was involved in the affairs of the Liberty party, a radical reform party organized to push Democrats and Whigs in the direction of antislavery by drawing off support from them in an era of delicate political balance. As editor of the *National Anti-Slavery Standard* (1840), the *Madison County Abolitionist* (1841), the *Liberty Press* (1842–1843), and the *Albany Patriot* (1844–1846), he was also steeped in antislavery journalism. In 1847 Jackson was one of the sponsors of the Liberty League, a group that split with the Liberty party to form a universal reform party intended as a permanent political organization. Poor health, however, forced Jackson to give up journalism and activist politics for a time.

After being under the hydrotherapeutic care of doctors for several months, he joined in partnership with them in 1848, opening a hygienic institute known as the Glen Haven Water Cure. In 1858 Jackson founded Our Home Hygienic Institute in Dansville, New York, where patients were treated with the water cure (frequent baths and the consumption of large quantities of water) instead of traditional medicine. His interest in hydropathy and his battle against drug medication, which he considered the "popular delusion of the nineteenth century," became his favorite reforms. For many years, he helped edit *The Laws of Life*, a periodical devoted mainly to the principles of hydropathy and the promotion of his institute, which became one of the largest of its kind in the world. In 1880 Jackson turned the management of the institute over to his son.

Jackson continued to support other causes, such as dress reform, woman suffrage, temperance, and antislavery. He published eight books between 1861 and 1882, including *American Womanhood: Its Peculiarities and Its Necessities* and *How to Treat the Sick without Medicine*, and was a regular contributor to political, religious, and agricultural journals until his death, which, evidently, occurred in Dansville, New York.

• Letters from Jackson are in the Gerrit Smith Miller Papers at Syracuse University. Important material about Jackson's life can be found in D. W. Elderkin, *Genealogy of the Elderkin Family* (1888); W. P. Garrison and F. J. Garrison, *William Lloyd Garrison* (4 vols., 1885–1889); J. H. Smith, *History of Livingston County, N.Y.* (1881); and Gerald Sorin, *New York Abolitionists* (1971). An obituary is in the *Buffalo Courier*, 12 July 1895.

GERALD SORIN

JACKSON, James, Jr. (15 Jan. 1810–27 Mar. 1834), physician, was born in Boston, Massachusetts, the son of James Jackson, a physician, and Elizabeth Cabot. As eldest son of James Jackson—Harvard medical professor and founder of the Massachusetts General Hospital—Jackson, Jr., grew up assuming that both duty and opportunity pointed him toward the medical profession. After graduating from Harvard College in 1828, he studied medicine with his father, attended medical lectures at Harvard, and witnessed practice at the Massachusetts General Hospital.

In April 1831 Jackson sailed to Europe, where he studied during the next two years chiefly in the hospitals of Paris. Such professional finishing was becoming common for ambitious young American physicians from affluent families, though most had received an M.D. degree before leaving the United States. In Paris, Jackson joined a community of several dozen young American physicians that would include his Harvard classmates Oliver Wendell Holmes, Sr., Jonathan Mason Warren, and Henry Ingersoll Bowditch. During his time abroad Jackson wrote detailed letters fortnightly to his father, reporting on the Parisian medical world and the progress of his studies.

Jackson's uncle, the physician Charles Thomas Jackson, was already in Paris when the young man arrived and advised him on the vast array of public and private courses that afforded free access to the bodies of French patients at bedside and on the dissecting table. He "held out to me a bill of fare, which I may say almost crazed me," James wrote to his father (Jackson papers, 30 May 1831). What Jackson wanted in Paris was practical experience, and while he deplored the therapeutic passivity he witnessed in the French clinic, he eagerly embraced opportunities to study pathology and clinical diagnosis, particularly using the stethoscope. He followed clinical instruction at the Hôpital des Enfants Malades and at the St. Louis, but most especially that of Gabriel Andral and Pierre Charles Alexandre Louis at La Pitié.

By early 1832 Jackson had come to deeply admire Louis's approach to investigating the natural history of disease, particularly his "numerical method" of analyzing large numbers of clinical and postmortem observations to establish fixed pathological laws. Jackson also had begun to see as his objective not just gaining practical experience but advancing medical knowledge. In February Louis agreed (for a fee) to give private lessons on stethoscopic examination to Jackson and Philadelphians William Wood Gerhard and Caspar Wistar Pennock; Jackson began to write of Louis as "my master" and second medical father (18 Mar. 1832). Along with fourteen other students of Louis, Jackson established the Société d'observation médicale to foster "the exact study of disease" (18 Mar. 1832). At meetings presided over by Louis, members in turn would report their clinical observations for discussion and criticism.

The coming of Asiatic cholera to Paris in late March 1832 was a turning point for Jackson. He saw the disease, new to the West, as a splendid opportunity to put into practice the research ideals he was embracing. Although he promised his father he would leave Paris for the relative safety of London, he disobeyed. He had become fully preoccupied with the prospect of contributing something new to medical knowledge and thereby vindicating French medical ways in the eyes of physicians in America. He systematically recorded detailed notes on cholera patients he observed at La Pitié and of the autopsies of those who died. "Never had I or shall I again have a similar opportunity," he told his father (3 Apr. 1832). Finally on his way to London at the end of April, he wrote his father of his discipleship to Louis—"I blush with shame and yet with joy and pride as I write his name"—and the Louisian program for medicine (25 Apr. 1832). The ensuing six months spent in Britain strengthened this commitment; he pined for Paris and reported disdainfully on English medical science. Jackson spent much of his time in London preparing for publication his *Cases of Cholera Collected at Paris, in the Month of April, 1832, in the Wards of MM. Andral and Louis, at the Hospital La Pitié*, which his father had printed that year in Boston.

Even before the cholera epidemics, Jackson had begun to embrace a Parisian ideal of pure medical research, an ideal his father worried was seducing the young man away from practical medicine. In October Jackson returned to Paris and to Louis's wards, "living, breathing, studying, investigating the morbid phenomena themselves" (29 Apr. 1833). He had taken up a new image of his identity and his future as one who would "seek & find *truth*, pathological & therapeutic" (22 Feb. 1833). Yet he was expected to return to practice in America, where a career in pure research was not an option. Louis had written the elder Jackson proposing that the young man devote five years to investigation in Paris before starting practice, but the father vetoed this plan. Louis then urged that James return to Boston but postpone practice for several years in favor of studying disease. The father deferred a final decision but insisted his son return home. He was deeply proud of James's professional ardor and industry but feared that in American society excessive devotion to science would taint the young man's reputation as a practical healer.

The elder Jackson's will prevailed. James left Paris in July 1833. He was afflicted with gastrointestinal illness almost immediately after returning but nonetheless received his M.D. degree from Harvard in February 1834 and made medical observations at the Massachusetts General Hospital. Unable to devote himself entirely to scientific investigation, however, he

began plans to start a private medical practice and on 5 March announced in the newspaper the scheduled opening of his office. That same day he was stricken by what he diagnosed as "typhus fever," grew seriously ill, and, at the age of twenty-four, died in Boston. He had never married. As a memorial to his son, in 1835 the elder Jackson published and distributed widely a carefully edited selection of the letters his son had written from Paris as *A Memoir of James Jackson, Jr., M.D., with Extracts from His Letters to His Father; and Medical Cases, Collected by Him*. Although the father continued to practice and teach medicine, his son's death virtually ended his creative medical career.

Jackson, Jr., called attention to the importance of the prolonged expiratory sound in the diagnosis of incipient pulmonary tuberculosis and is credited with discovering a familial tendency in emphysema. But it was his ardent consecration to the pursuit of medical truth at a time when a career fully spent in medical research was not possible in the United States that distinguished his short life. Through the remainder of the nineteenth century, to the American disciples of French medicine and to later professional leaders such as William Osler, Jackson's life emblemized a professional ideal of scientific devotion in American medicine.

• Jackson's correspondence with his father and contemporaries, his medical notebooks, and letters of condolence to the father are deposited in the Jackson papers, Holmes Hall, Francis A. Countway Library of Medicine, Boston. Correspondence to Jackson is at the Massachusetts Historical Society, Boston. The fullest review of his life is in the *Memoir* by his father. See also James Jackson Putnam, *A Memoir of Dr. James Jackson* (1905); Russell M. Jones, "An American Medical Student in Paris, 1831–1833," *Harvard Library Bulletin* 15 (1967): 59–81; Ronald J. Knudson, "Familial Emphysema Discovered by James Jackson, Jr.," *New England Journal of Medicine* 300 (1979): 374; and Margaret Warner, "Letters from a Young Physician: James Jackson Jr. and His Two Medical Fathers," *Harvard Medical Alumni Bulletin* 60, no. 1 (1986): 40–45. For the wider meaning of his work in Paris for American medicine and his memorialization, see Russell M. Jones, "American Doctors and the Parisian Medical World, 1830–1840," *Bulletin of the History of Medicine* 47 (1973): 40–65, and John Harley Warner, "Remembering Paris: Memory and the American Disciples of French Medicine in the Nineteenth Century," *Bulletin of the History of Medicine* 65 (1991): 301–25.

JOHN HARLEY WARNER

JACKSON, Joe (1880?–14 May 1942), pantomimist, was born Josef Francis Jiranek in Vienna, Austria, the son of a grocer. His parents' names are unknown. As a boy he was an avid cyclist and became a champion racer and virtuoso rider in his country. As a teenager he joined a bicycle polo team that toured Europe. Around the turn of the century, Jackson's team met with financial difficulties in London and disbanded. Jackson then landed a job in a circus as a dashing trick rider, but his "straight" act was not particularly popular. The circus was booked into London's Crystal Palace when one of the clowns suggested that Jackson enliven his act by adding makeup. He painted Jackson as a clown, and that was the genesis of Jackson's persona as a bicycle tramp. Jackson was not an immediate favorite, however. Publicity stories have it that Jackson's comic material was introduced by accident one night when the handlebars came off his bike and he waved them in wild despair at the audience, creating a roar of laughter. On closer examination, however, it appears that Jackson, an expert trick rider with a brain for inventions and later several patents to his credit, was more calculating than that. Evidence suggests that he slowly began testing and accruing comic elements in his act, until his mere appearance made the audience convulse, and he became one of the most renowned figures on the vaudeville circuit worldwide.

In 1915 Jackson appeared as a tramp in a Shubert revue, *Maid in America*, at the Winter Garden Theatre in New York and was a complete success. During this time, he also played midnight performances at the roof garden theater of the Coconut Grove to the smart set of New York. After his stint at the Winter Garden, he moved directly to Dillingham's revue *The Big Show* at the New York Hippodrome. A notice in a newspaper reported that "Jackson never works alike from one show to another. He is continually up to some mischief or other" (25 Jan. 1915), indicating that Jackson was still tinkering with, revising, and updating his act. Whatever the variations were, though, he enjoyed rave reviews such as the one that appeared in the *New York Star* when he played Keith's:

Joe Jackson doesn't say a word the whole time he is on the stage, but a dictionary adequately used could not bring forth the rounds of laughter which greeted the efforts of the pantomimist. In a most trampy costume and with the very worst looking bicycle, Mr. Jackson really "convulses" his spectators with merriment, aided and abetted with a cuff which won't stay put, and a ridiculously flexible mouth.

In 1916 Jackson made his movie debut in the feature film *A Modern Enoch Arden*, supported by Betty Marsh and Mack Swain, at the Keystone studios. It was so well received that the director, Mack Sennett, quickly cast him in a second comedy-thriller, *Gypsy Joe* (1916). In 1917 Jackson married Maria Rialto; they had one child, Joe Jackson, Jr. However, within a few years, the couple divorced.

Jackson continued to play vaudeville and wow audiences wherever he traveled. It appears that by the early 1920s Jackson basically had perfected his act. Concurrently, many performers tried to duplicate his routine, and, according to one undated, unattributed newspaper clipping, "his imitators outnumbered those of Geo. M. Cohan, Eddie Foy and other celebrities for awhile." To stop the theft of his material, Jackson took out a series of advertisements in *Variety* naming his imitators, such as Downey and Claridge and Sam Barton. In the case of Downey, according to Jackson's obituary in *Variety* (20 May 1942), one night he visited the theater where Downey was playing, the Rialto on Forty-second Street, seized Downey's bicycle, per-

formed his own act for the audience, smashed the bike, and "administered a physical beating to Downey himself out in the alley." Jackson was also in and out of court, suing a personality referred to as Reno (twice) and others. He ultimately made a film of his act, which was reportedly deposited in Washington, D.C. (probably the Library of Congress), and with his attorney Nathan Burkman in New York.

Jackson continued to headline vaudeville bills, here and abroad, with what drama critic Brooks Atkinson fondly called his "knockabout fooling," for the rest of his career. By about 1937 he had taught his son his entire act down to the minutest detail, and one day he had Jackson, Jr., substitute for him at Radio City Music Hall. No one, including the management and stage crew, perceived the difference. Jackson, Jr., went on to perform in his own right and did the bike act on ice in the Ice Capades.

In the late 1930s Jackson bought considerable property in Greenwood Lake, New York, where he cultivated a frog farm and had a shop in which he invented gadgets that he patented. He continued to perform, however, and one of his most notable appearances at the time was in "American Jubilee" at the 1939 New York World's Fair. During a backstage interview by Atkinson, between two of the four shows a day he played, Jackson spoke enthusiastically about his farm and his plans to open a dance hall and restaurant with his son on his acreage.

On 14 May 1942, shortly before the opening of his long-awaited restaurant, Jackson completed his act at the Roxy, took five curtain calls, and then collapsed and died backstage. The crowd of 3,500, composed of old and young alike, some of whom were probably seeing Jackson for the first time, was still cheering. Jackson, according to all accounts, remarked that the audience was still applauding. He then clutched the sleeve of Otto Legel (his longtime friend who had quit the stage years earlier to become the comic's constant companion) and fell unconscious. A few minutes later an ambulance doctor pronounced Jackson dead of natural causes. According to the *New York Times* obituary (15 May 1942), Legel said of Jackson's death, "Joe had his wish fulfilled, he always wanted to die in harness."

Jackson's costume was described in the *New York Herald Tribune*: "A huge red nose adorned his white-smeared clown's face, and gigantic shoes flapped up and down" (15 May 1942). In addition, a description of his act appeared in the *Variety* obituary:

Jackson's entrance on a stage was always the same. A jolly tramp whose furtive efforts to steal a bicycle, usually parked in front of a rich residence, got the audience laughing. He would shush to audience, and, finally mount the bicycle for a joy ride. The horn came off and Jackson would step on it, fearfully looking around to see if he had alarmed the bike's owner; then the handlebars would come off; then one of the pedals; then the seat, and it was always a big laugh when Jackson sat down where the seat was supposed to be. And when the clown went into his trick riding finish his nonsense had usually completely captivated his audience.

In some ways, Jackson was a typical vaudevillian. He created a costume, a character, and an act that he performed with slight variations for decades. His career was unique, however, because of the degree of success he enjoyed and the inspired originality of his comedy. He never spoke a word on stage but was a poet of pantomime. He redefined comedy. Referring to Jackson, one critic admonished, "If you have ever believed you knew what comedy was, go to the Grand this week, and see if you haven't made a mistake. If you have ever said to yourself that this or that man was the last word in the comedian line [*sic*], watch the act of Joe Jackson before you publish your opinion. It is probable that you may change some of your ideas" (*Atlanta Constitution*, 5 Aug. 1912).

• Clippings files on Joe Jackson, Sr., and Joe Jackson, Jr., are at the New York Public Library for the Performing Arts, Lincoln Center. A film of his act is at the Library of Congress.

TINA MARGOLIS

JACKSON, Joe (c. 1887–1951). *See* Jackson, Shoeless Joe.

JACKSON, John George (22 Sept. 1777–28 Mar. 1825), congressman and federal judge, was born near Buckhannon, Virginia (now W. Va.), the son of George Jackson, congressman and farmer, and Elizabeth Brake. Details of his formal education are obscure, but he read avidly in the classics and practical subjects, gained proficiency in Latin and Greek, and associated intellectually with the learned men of Clarksburg, where he lived most of his life.

Jackson represented Harrison County in the Virginia House of Delegates from 1798 to 1801 and in 1811–1812. A staunch Jeffersonian Republican and states' rights advocate, he was also a forceful spokesman for western interests, including internal improvements and banking. He supported constitutional reform to liberalize voting and representation in Virginia and was one of the chief promoters of the Staunton Convention of 1816.

As congressman from the First District of Virginia from 1803 to 1810 and from 1813 to 1817, Jackson was widely regarded as a spokesman for James Madison, his brother-in-law. He frequently crossed verbal swords with other congressmen, especially John Randolph (1773–1833), in fiery defenses of the president. One exchange led to a duel with Congressman Joseph Pearson of North Carolina, in which Jackson received wounds that later led to his resignation from Congress which he attributed to ill health. Had he retained his seat, he almost certainly would have been one of the most ardent and vocal of the War Hawks. Although he was appointed a brigadier general in the Virginia militia in the War of 1812, he resigned his post because of conflicts with regular officers. Returning to Congress in 1813, he championed nationalistic tendencies, including a protective tariff, a national bank, and federally funded internal improvements. In 1819 President James Monroe appointed him judge of the newly created District of Virginia West of the Allegheny Mountains, a position he retained until his death.

Along with his legal practice and extensive landholdings, Jackson was one of the foremost entrepreneurs of the upper Monongahela Valley, with grist mills, a woolen and cotton factory, iron works, and salt distilleries. He was also the chief promoter of the Virginia Saline Bank at Clarksburg and the principal stockholder and officer of the Monongalia Navigation Company, formed in 1817 to build locks and dams in the West Fork of the Monongahela River. Interested in scientific agriculture, he introduced to the region merino sheep and fuller's teasel, which was derived from Old World plants and used to produce napped surfaces on fabrics.

In 1800 or 1801 Jackson married Mary Payne, a sister of Dolley Madison, and they had four children, of whom only a daughter, Mary, survived her mother, who died in 1808. Also in 1800 Jackson became the father of an illegitimate son, John J. Jackson, later a prominent Clarksburg attorney. In 1810 Jackson married Mary Sophia Meigs; they had eight children. Following a rapid decline in his health, Jackson died of a stroke at his home in Clarksburg.

• The most extensive collections of Jackson's papers are at the Lilly Library, Indiana University, Bloomington; the Meigs-Jackson papers, Blennerhassett Historical Park Commission, Parkersburg, W. Va.; the Meigs-Jackson papers, Ohio Historical Society, Campus Martius Museum, Marietta; and the Jackson family papers, Virginia Historical Society, Richmond. Documents of the Monongalia Navigation Company in the Records of the Virginia Board of Public Works, Richmond, and Records of the United States District Court of the District of Virginia West of the Allegheny Mountains in Record Group 21, National Archives Records Center, Suitland, Md., are highly pertinent to Jackson's career and activities. Two full-length biographies are Stephen W. Brown, *Voice of the New West: John G. Jackson, His Life and Times* (1985), best for an assessment of Jackson's public career, and Dorothy Davis, *John George Jackson* (1976), useful for Jackson's family and personal affairs. More specific accounts are Stephen W. Brown, "Satisfaction at Bladensburg: The Pearson-Jackson Duel of 1809," *North Carolina Historical Review* 58 (1981): 23–43 and "Congressman John George Jackson and Republican Nationalism, 1813–1817," *West Virginia History* 38 (1977): 93–125.

STEPHEN W. BROWN

JACKSON, Laurence. *See* Baby Laurence.

JACKSON, Luther Porter (11 July 1892–20 Apr. 1950), historian and activist, was born in Lexington, Kentucky, the son of Edward William Jackson, a dairy farmer, and Delilah Culverson, a schoolteacher. He was the ninth of twelve children of parents who had been slaves. Jackson attended Fisk University in Nashville, Tennessee, completing his A.B. in 1914 and his M.A. in 1916. Meanwhile, he began teaching in 1915 at

Voorhees Industrial School in Denmark, South Carolina, where he was also director of the academic department. In 1918 he left South Carolina to become instructor of history and music at the Topeka Industrial Institute in Topeka, Kansas.

Jackson moved to New York in 1920, hoping to do graduate study at Columbia University, but Columbia would not accept his Fisk degrees as being up to Columbia's standards. Undaunted, he enrolled for a year at the City College of New York, where he studied history and education. He then spent a year at Columbia, receiving his second master's degree in 1922 from Columbia Teachers College.

That fall he joined the faculty of Virginia Normal and Industrial Institute (later Virginia State College and now Virginia State University) in Petersburg. Also in 1922 he married Johnella Frazer, a former classmate at Fisk, who had been employed at the institute since 1916 as instructor of music. Both spent the remainder of their careers on the Virginia State College faculty. The Jacksons had four children, a daughter and three sons.

From 1922 to 1928 Jackson served as director of the college's High School department. From 1930 to 1950 he was chairman of the Department of History. He started as assistant professor of history, rose to associate professor in 1925, and to professor of history in 1929. Meanwhile, he enrolled at Columbia University in the summer of 1923 but then transferred to the University of Chicago in 1928. On leave from Virginia State, he fulfilled the residence requirement at Chicago during 1928–1929 and 1932–1933. He received his Ph.D. in history from the University of Chicago in 1937.

Jackson became an authority on African-American history, especially in Virginia. He wrote five books, four ranging from 46 to 112 pages, one longer. The first of his five books, about a black teachers group, was *The History of the Virginia State Teachers Association* (1937). Jackson's second book, *A Short History of the Gillfield Baptist Church of Petersburg Virginia* (1941), documented 144 years of one of the nation's oldest black churches. His doctoral dissertation was selected for publication by the American Historical Association, in conjunction with the American Council of Learned Societies; it was titled *Free Negro Labor and Property Holding in Virginia, 1830–1860* (1942). Jackson traveled throughout the state visiting courthouses and unearthing birth and marriage records, estate records, property lists, tax records, and wills. He also used census findings. His other books include *Virginia Negro Soldiers and Seamen in the Revolutionary War* (1944) and *Negro Office Holders in Virginia, 1865–1895* (1945). His five scholarly books remain the standard accounts in each of these areas.

Jackson was more than an ivory tower historian. He loved to interact with people off campus. Hence he became a social activist throwing himself wholeheartedly into crusades. He was both a scholar and a man of the people. Jackson loved music, was very proficient at it, taught it at times, and played the cornet well. He

formed a 100-voice community choir and conducted annual concerts of this Petersburg Community Chorus from 1933 to 1941.

His major reform activity was a crusade for voting rights during the 1930s and 1940s when Virginia barred most of his race from voting. In 1934 he organized the Petersburg League of Negro Voters, which became the Virginia Voters League, directing it until his death. Every year he compiled data on "The Voting Status of Negroes in Virginia." He preached to his students and to the masses that a voteless people is a hopeless people. He traveled throughout the state carrying this message. The Southern Regional Council asked Jackson in 1947 to conduct a study of black voting in the South. The study, "Race and Suffrage in the South since 1940," was published in a special issue of *New South* (June–July 1948).

Another area of his community service was fundraising for two causes dear to his heart: the Association for the Study of Negro Life and History (ASNLH) and the National Association for the Advancement of Colored People (NAACP). Carter Woodson's ASNLH had branches all over the nation. Dr. Woodson worked closely with Jackson and asked him to lead fundraising efforts. Under Jackson's tutelage the Virginia chapter became one of the most productive of all state chapters. He did the same for W. E. B. Du Bois's NAACP. Jackson spoke at rallies all over Virginia, promoting the NAACP and voting rights. The state conference of the NAACP honored him for his devoted work on behalf of voting rights. Jackson also formed the Petersburg Negro Business Association in 1937, expanding this in 1941 into the Virginia Trade Association. Furthermore, he wrote a column, "Rights and Duties in a Democracy," for the weekly *Norfolk Journal and Guide* from 1942 to 1948. He also served on many boards such as the Virginia World War II History Commission, the Southern Regional Council, and the Virginia Association of Elks.

To keep up with all these activities, he drove himself relentlessly, rising very early, walking to his office from his home on campus, taking a brief nap at midday, and returning to his office after dinner to work until midnight. He developed a heart condition, concealed it from his wife, and continued his frantic pace. He had a heart attack and died in Ettrick, Virginia. Jackson was a hearty, cheerful, enthusiastic man with a great zest for life. He was well loved on campus and in the community.

• Jackson's papers are in the archives at the James Hugo Johnston Memorial Library on the campus of Virginia State University. These papers were arranged and described by the university archivist, Lucious Edwards, Jr. Bibliophile Dorothy Porter compiled the most thorough bibliography of Jackson's writings, listing sixty-one articles, books, brochures, newspaper columns, and pamphlets in *The Negro in the United States: A Selected Bibliography* (1970). A brief account of Jackson's life and work is in August Meier and Elliott Rudwick, *Black History and the Historical Profession, 1915–1980* (1986).

EDGAR ALLAN TOPPIN

JACKSON, Mahalia (26 Oct. 1911–27 Jan. 1972), gospel singer, was born in New Orleans, the daughter of John Jackson, a dockworker, barber, and preacher, and Charity Clark, a maid. Her mother died when Jackson was five, and she moved in with her mother's sister, Mahalia Paul, also known as Aunt Duke. She worked both for her aunt and for a local white family from an early age, and during the eighth grade (the last grade she attended before quitting school), she also worked as a laundress for five hours after school. She began to sing as a young child, particularly at the Mount Moriah Baptist Church, but she was also profoundly influenced by the Bessie Smith recordings her more worldly cousin Fred owned. However, Jackson was most powerfully shaped by her experiences with the Sanctified Church that was next door to her house. As she later noted, the church had no organ or choir. Members played drums, cymbals, and tambourines, and "everybody in there sang and they clapped and stomped their feet and sang with their whole bodies. They had a beat, a powerful beat, a rhythm we held on to from slavery days, and their music was so strong and expressive it used to bring the tears to my eyes" (Jackson, pp. 32–33).

In 1928 Jackson moved to Chicago, where her Aunts Hannah and Alice already lived. For a decade she supported herself by doing laundry for white families and working as a hotel maid. She joined the choir of the Greater Salem Baptist Church, which became her second home, and cofounded the "Johnson Gospel Singers" with another woman and three of the minister's sons. The group sang in churches for $1.50 a night, often traveling throughout Indiana and Illinois. Jackson herself sang in churches as far away as Buffalo, New York, and at revivals, homes, and hospitals, already employing the down-home, deeply emotive style that created a powerful tie with her audience and accentuated a sense of community. The larger black churches wanted nothing to do with this style at first, so she sang most often for storefront and basement congregations.

In 1935 Jackson met Isaac Hockenhull, a college-trained chemist who worked as a mail carrier. The two married in 1938; they had no children. For a time she traveled around the region selling cosmetics made from Hockenhull's own formulas, but by 1939 she had earned enough money from her singing to leave this and her other jobs and open an enterprise she named Mahalia's Beauty Salon. The business thrived, and she soon attached a flower shop, generating business for the latter at the many funerals at which she was invited to sing. While her commitment to religious singing grew, her husband wanted her to take voice lessons and become a concert singer; he urged her to pursue a role in an all-black production of *The Mikado*, but she refused. The two grew apart and divorced in 1943, although they remained lifelong friends.

In 1937 Jackson began to work with gospel composer Thomas A. Dorsey, and she made her recording debut that year with "God's Gonna Separate the Wheat from the Tares," a song already punctuated with her trademark moans and growls. Dorsey became her champion, and she traveled widely, singing his songs at churches; he wrote "Peace in the Valley" for her in 1937 and served as her accompanist from 1937 to 1946. Realizing the uniqueness of her style, Dorsey encouraged Jackson to open her songs at a more tempered level, and to gradually build the excitement until the audience was ready for her uniquely celebratory climax: "In her deeply individualistic manner—running and skipping down the church and concert hall aisles, her eyes closed, hands tightly clasped, with feet tapping and body throbbing, all the while her voice soaring as if there were no walls to confine its spiritual journey—she was utterly possessed and possessing" (Schwerin, p. 62).

Jackson was a "stretch-out" singer who changed melody and meter as the spirit moved her. Her style borrowed from the "Baptist lining style," "a slow, languorous manner, without a regular pulse . . . that allowed the singer to execute each syllable by adding several extra tones, bending these added tones in myriad directions, and reshaping the melody into a personal testimony" (Boyer, p. 11). Thus her voice was at its most resonant and beautiful in slow hymns like "Just As I Am," sung with precise control and intense feeling. Her work with Dorsey also made Jackson a powerful presence in the city and raised the position of church singer to a new status; politicians frequently hired her to sing at funerals, an unprecedented "professionalization" of a sacred calling.

In 1945 Chicago broadcaster Studs Terkel brought new attention to Jackson when he played one of her recordings, "I'm Goin' to Tell God All about It One of These Days," over and over again on the air. Deeply impressed, Bess Berman signed her to a contract with Apollo Records in 1946, guaranteeing her $10,000 a year. Her first four sides sold poorly, but her 1947 recording of "Move On Up a Little Higher" brought her royalties of $300,000 in the first year alone, earning her the title of "Gospel Queen." From 1946 to 1954 she recorded seventy songs for Apollo, and she commanded fees of $1,000 a night for appearances in New York and Chicago. Stung by dishonest promoters earlier in her career, she always insisted on being paid in cash on the day of her performance.

In 1950 the jazz historian and critic Marshall Stearns invited Jackson to perform at the Music Inn, near Tanglewood in Massachusetts, at a symposium on the history of jazz. Her appearance transformed her into an overnight national celebrity; she received dozens of offers to perform, appeared on "The Ed Sullivan Show," and was appointed the official soloist for the National Baptist Convention. She also sang at the first of a series of Carnegie Hall concerts that broke all house records. Her 1952 recording of "I Can Put My Trust in Jesus" was awarded a prize by the French Academy of Music and led to her first European tour, with stops in England, Holland, Belgium, Denmark, and France. Although she collapsed in Paris six weeks after starting the tour, she received acclaim almost everywhere she sang, and her recording of "Silent Night" became a bestseller in Norway.

Courted by John Hammond, who was impressed by her rejection of the commercialization of gospel music, Jackson signed a lucrative contract with Columbia Records in 1953. She had her own radio show on a CBS station in Chicago in 1954, later converted to a half-hour television show. Although the reviews were excellent and the audience large, the network turned her down when she asked about taking the show national; they argued that they would never be able to get sponsors for the southern audience. And though she was often invited to appear on Chicago television, she found the experience frustrating, with arrangers trying to tone down her style and telling her how to sing her own songs. Even at Columbia, for which she recorded more than a dozen albums, producers filled her repertoire with "pop-gospel" songs like "A Rusty Old Halo," a "cute" crossover song, and burdened her with orchestras and choirs that only dampened the powerful impact of her impassioned voice. But Jackson enjoyed the popularity and the money, even as she complained that commercialization was compromising the music. And the results were not always disappointing; witness her 1955 recording of "Joshua Fit the Battle of Jericho," which clearly incorporates the battle against slavery into its meaning.

Jackson also toured widely during the 1950s, generally with her regular accompanist, Mildred Falls, and her cousin John Stevens. The three experienced the segregation that continued to curse the South, even while Jackson was enjoying huge commercial successes in the national white music market, and she soon immersed herself in the civil rights struggle. She appeared in Montgomery, Alabama, in 1956, for instance, when Rev. Ralph Abernathy asked her to sing at a ceremony honoring Rosa Parks. And she personally experienced the racial hypocrisy of the North in 1957, when she bought a house on Chicago's South Side in a white neighborhood. Someone fired air rifle pellets into her living-room windows, and once again she found herself a national figure. The journalist Edward R. Murrow interviewed her on his "Person-to-Person" television show at her house, and for days crowds of people gathered outside in sympathy. She developed a close relationship with Martin Luther King, Jr. In May 1957, at the Lincoln Memorial, she sang "I Been 'Buked and I Been Scorned" as part of a Southern Christian Leadership Conference Prayer Pilgrimage for Freedom. In 1959 she recorded "Great Gettin' Up Morning," highlighting the song's implicit attack on slavery. She was most proud of her participation in the August 1963 March on Washington, where she again sang "I Been 'Buked and I Been Scorned," beginning soft and gentle, then shouting for joy and leading the crowd in singing and clapping.

Jackson's involvement in the civil rights movement enhanced her career. After the Murrow interview she appeared on "The Dinah Shore Show," the two singing a duet of the antiwar gospel song "Down by the Riverside." She appeared as guest star on most of the popular television variety shows of the decade, including those hosted by Bing Crosby, Perry Como, Steve Allen, Red Skelton, and Ed Sullivan. She even made a movie appearance in 1958 (albeit a somewhat embarrassing one) as a happy "colored" servant in the film *Imitation of Life*; racist typecasting was all too typical of Hollywood in the 1950s. And, of course, her singing continued to garner approval. Duke Ellington featured her on his 1958 recording of the "Black, Brown, and Beige" suite; for the studio version of "Come Sunday," Ellington had the lights turned out while Jackson sang by herself in the dark. Her national reputation was enshrined when she sang "The Star-Spangled Banner" at President John F. Kennedy's inauguration eve gala. In 1961 she enjoyed huge popular success on a European tour and made one of her very greatest recordings, "Elijah Rock," at a concert in Stockholm, Sweden, accompanied only by Falls on the piano.

Jackson's health began to deteriorate in 1963, and she was periodically hospitalized over the last years of her life for exhaustion and heart problems. Yet in 1964 she embarked on a hugely successful European tour that ended with a private papal audience in Rome and a longed-for visit to Jerusalem. That same year she married Sigmund Galloway in 1964; they had no children and divorced in 1967. That year she starred at the first-ever gospel concert at Lincoln Center. She appeared at the Newport Jazz Festival in 1970 and began another European tour in 1971, cut short by her last illness. She sang "Take My Hand, Precious Lord," at King's funeral, and sang at Robert F. Kennedy's funeral. She also expanded her business operations, establishing the "Mahalia Jackson Chicken System," eventually a chain of 135 stores, and continued to pursue her little-publicized charitable efforts through the Mahalia Jackson Scholarship Foundation, using her own money to send students to college. Jackson died in Evergreen Park, a Chicago suburb. She was buried in New Orleans and was commemorated at funerals both there and in Chicago, the latter attended by scores of dignitaries and marked by Aretha Franklin singing "Precious Lord."

By the end of her life, Jackson had immersed herself in business and real estate deals, and she seemed to spend more and more of her time meeting with accountants and lawyers. Her appearance fees were far beyond the reach of even prosperous churches to pay. But though purists attacked her commercial concessions, she remained a regal, matriarchal presence in gospel and in American music in general. As the writer Anthony Heilbut noted, "All by herself, Mahalia was the vocal, physical, spiritual symbol of gospel music" (Heilbut, p. 57). Jazz, blues, and gospel enthusiasts found a common bond in her rhythmic energy and spiritual intensity. She was the first to carry gospel music beyond the black community, and she affected lives in an unparalleled personal way. Ellington noted that his encounter with Jackson "had a strong influence on me and my sacred music, and also made me a much handsomer kid in the Right Light" (Ellington, p. 256). As Jackson herself stated in her autobiography, "There's something about music that is so penetrating that your soul gets the message. No matter what trouble comes to a person, music can help him face it" (Jackson, p. 184).

• Jackson's most important recordings include her early sessions for Apollo Records. On Columbia the listener should begin with the 1991 compilation *Gospels, Spirituals, and Hymns*; also recommended are *Newport 1958* (1958) and *How I Got Over* (1976). Jackson's autobiography, written with Evan McLeod Wylie, is *Movin' On Up* (1966). Laurraine Goreau, *Just Mahalia, Baby* (1975), remains valuable for the vast amount of information it contains, but it lacks scholarly focus and documentation. Also essential is Jules Schwerin, *Got to Tell It: Mahalia Jackson, Queen of Gospel* (1992). There are some useful comments in Duke Ellington, *Music Is My Mistress* (1973), and excellent lengthier analyses are in Michael W. Harris, *The Rise of the Gospel Blues: The Music of Thomas Andrew Dorsey in the Urban Church* (1992); Anthony Heilbut, *The Gospel Sound: Good News and Bad Times*, rev. ed. (1992); and Horace Clarence Boyer, commentary in the booklet accompanying *Gospels, Hymns, and Spirituals* (Columbia Records, 1991). Finally, the 1976 Schwerin film *Got to Tell It*, narrated by Studs Terkel, is valuable viewing. An obituary is in the *New York Times*, 28 Jan. 1972.

RONALD P. DUFOUR

JACKSON, Patrick Tracy (14 Aug. 1780–12 Sept. 1847), merchant and industrial manufacturer, was born in Newburyport, Massachusetts, the son of Captain Jonathan Jackson, a merchant, and Hannah Tracy, a merchant's daughter. He enjoyed more schooling than most young men of the post-Revolutionary period, attending Newburyport public schools and Dummer Academy. Growing up in a commercial family, however, he was anxious to prove his business acumen. From 1795 he served as an apprentice clerk to the wealthy merchant William Bartlett, as captain's clerk to his brother Henry and as shipmaster on his own account. Jackson impressed experienced merchants and sea masters with his initiative and knowledge of navigation and maritime commerce. Four trading voyages abroad between 1800 and 1807 enabled him to gain both experience in the Eastern trade and a respectable capital base. He returned to the United States in the latter year and established his place as an East India merchant in Boston, where opportunities were greater than in Newburyport. Jackson established himself, as well, as a sound businessman with a reputation for sobriety, reliability, and dependability. In 1810 he married Lydia Cabot in Boston; the couple had nine children.

Jackson's transition from commerce to manufacturing was gradual and fortuitous. His brother-in-law and fellow Boston merchant, Francis Cabot Lowell, conceived the idea that would propel Jackson into the upper ranks of industrialists during the years of the early republic. Economic instability occasioned by the Napoleonic Wars—particularly the Jefferson administration's 1806 Non-Importation Act and 1807 Embargo—battered American merchants. Those who remained solvent shifted operations to New York or retired. The revival of the Non-Importation Act in 1811 nudged Lowell to consider fresh opportunities. From 1810 through 1812 he toured Britain with an eye to bringing the emergent textile technologies and organizations of the first Industrial Revolution to the young republic.

Meanwhile, Jackson weighed his own doubts about continuing opportunities as a Boston merchant. Through 1812 he gradually withdrew from the trade. "He was consequently in a receptive mood when Francis Cabot Lowell . . . returned from England," as historian Kenneth Porter notes. When Lowell solicited Jackson's support, they pooled their finances toward building a mill. In 1813 they bought a water-powered paper mill on the Charles River in Waltham, procured a charter for incorporation of the Boston Manufacturing Company, and invited trusted fellow merchants—the future Boston Associates—to invest in the enterprise. By 1814 Lowell, working with the brilliant mechanic Paul Moody, developed a viable power loom, and operations commenced. The original plan was to build a weaving mill; however, they soon realized the economic advantages of spinning the yarn, as well. So emerged the nation's first fully integrated factory—not only a technological marvel but also an enterprise that demanded a strong managerial hand.

As company agent, Jackson's organizational strategies anticipated a fundamental transformation in American business—from owners actively involved in daily operations to general managers as salaried employees. As early as 1813 letters show him ordering timber and machines, finding workmen, discussing wages, and virtually living at Waltham, apart from his family. After Lowell's death in 1817 Jackson emerged as a visionary leader, early on recognizing the limitations of the Waltham facility and the enormous latent demand for cotton cloth. Along with Nathan Appleton and other Boston Associates, he piloted the strategy of the Boston Manufacturing Company in the post–Cabot Lowell period. In their famous "perambulation" of November 1821, Jackson, Appleton, and other directors scanned the Merrimack River's Pawtucket Falls. By 1826 they had constructed a network of canals that monopolized the power of the Merrimack River. In so doing, they laid the foundations for America's first industrial park. The property they covertly bought up about the river housed a new company, the Merrimack Manufacturing Co., and inaugurated the nation's first industrial city—Lowell.

For early manufacturers such as Jackson, the expectation that demand would meet production was tested by the primitive roads of the early republic. Jackson was one who saw the answer in European innovations in transportation, particularly in the first experiments in harnessing steam to coaches. Following the successful trials of the Stephenson's steam locomotive in 1829, Jackson began a project to pioneer the first railroad in New England. This affair he approached in his typically methodical fashion, and he fastidiously took the time to study what worked and what did not. As superintendent for construction of the Boston & Lowell railroad from 1830, only he had the confidence of the business community to carry the enterprise through to completion in 1835.

Jackson's widespread responsibilities demonstrate the difficulties of learning how to manage the emergent business systems of the era. Overlapping interests in manufacturing and transportation led the usually provident Jackson into risky real estate speculation—a misadventure—and he lost much of his estate, for at least the second time in his life, in the depression of 1836–1837. Thus, his need to recover his finances at an advanced age (fifty-seven) kept his hand in business. As president of the Concord Railroad Corporation (1836), agent of the Merrimack Locks and Canals Corporation (1838–1845), and agent and treasurer for the Great Falls Manufacturing Co. (1840), he continued to demonstrate his business prowess. These efforts took their toll, however. Overextended responsibilities and unrelenting strain kept him susceptible to the diseases of the age. The New England business community was shaken to learn Jackson had died at a seaside resort in Beverly, Massachusetts.

Jackson was a representative business figure of his age, exemplifying the significant transition from the general merchant of the colonial period to the industrial manufacturer in the early republic. Although a lesser-known figure, Jackson pioneered some of the most important innovations in the management of the new manufacturing and transportation enterprises, and, so, personified the managerial revolution of the 1840s and after.

• Primary and related materials include the letterbooks and invoice books of Jackson & Bromfield in the Henry Lee Shattuck Collections of the Massachusetts Historical Society and materials in the Patrick Tracy Jackson, Jr., Collection in Boothbay Harbor, Maine. Scant attention has been devoted to the life of Patrick Tracy Jackson, who remains one of the lesser figures of the first Industrial Revolution in the United States. The chief treatment can be found in Kenneth W. Porter, *The Jacksons and the Lees: Two Generations of Massachusetts Merchants, 1765–1844* (2 vols., 1937). Freeman Hunt's apotheosized *Lives of American Merchants*, vol. 1 (1856), includes a glowing essay on Jackson. Benjamin W. Labaree traces the rise and decline of Newburyport in *Patriots and Partisans: The Merchants of Newburyport, 1764–1815* (1962). An obituary is in the *Boston Courier*, 14 Sept. 1847.

DANE MORRISON

JACKSON, Peter (3 July 1861–13 July 1901), boxer, was born in Frederiksted on the island of St. Croix, Virgin Islands, the son of a fisherman and a homemaker whose names are unknown. His father became weary of fishing the waters of the Caribbean and, seeking better opportunities in the South Pacific, moved the family to Australia in 1873. Three years later, however, Jackson's parents tired of life in Australia and returned to the Virgin Islands. An adventurous youth, Jackson stayed behind and became a boatman and sailor in the area around Sydney. He never saw his parents again.

A natural athlete, Jackson developed a marvelous physique competing in sculling matches and became an excellent swimmer. Jackson got his start in boxing while working as a sailor for a shipping firm owned by Clay Callahan. A successful American businessman and local boxer, Callahan saw in Jackson a quiet, polite young man who had the athletic skills and heart to become a first-rate boxer. He introduced Jackson to Larry Foley, a prominent boxing instructor and former pugilist. Foley took Jackson on as a pupil and brought him along slowly at his White Horse Saloon in Sydney. At a little over six feet tall and close to 200 pounds, Jackson appeared to Foley as a promising candidate to contend for the world heavyweight championship.

For two years Jackson trained under Foley's supervision in the gymnasium in the basement of the saloon. During this period Jackson sparred with outstanding boxers such as future heavyweight champion Bob Fitzsimmons, Frank Slavin, and Jim Hall, all of whom were also training with Foley. Beginning in 1882 Foley arranged a series of fights for Jackson. After earning a string of victories in these fights, Jackson was knocked out by Bill Farnan in 1884 and managed only a draw in a rematch later that year. Disappointed by his lack of success against Farnan, Jackson continued to develop his techniques at Foley's saloon. As a result he became heavyweight champion of Australia on 25 September 1886, when he defeated Tom Lees from Victoria in a 30-round fight in Foley's saloon.

As Australia's first black heavyweight champion, Jackson quickly found it difficult to fight worthy opponents, both because he outclassed most competitors and because some boxers, such as Jack Burke, simply would not fight against black opponents. In 1888 Jackson set sail for San Francisco in search of profitable matches and perhaps an opportunity to fight the world heavyweight champion, John L. Sullivan. He soon became associated with the California Athletic Club where he was appointed as a professor of boxing. In the United States Jackson again found it difficult to schedule matches because of racial prejudice. By the end of the nineteenth century segregation, either legal or informal, was becoming more common in American sports. While there was no categorical racial barrier in boxing, certain white boxers observed the color line. Jackson did defeat African-American boxer George Godfrey in 1888 to claim the "colored heavyweight championship of the world" and followed that victory with a knockout of Joe McAuliffe, considered the best heavyweight on the West Coast.

Jackson left California in 1889 and headed for New York, where he hoped to engage in more lucrative bouts, but quickly moved on to London when a chance came to fight the former heavyweight champion of England, Jem Smith. Jackson soundly defeated Smith in two rounds in November 1889, and the sporting public began to clamor for a match between Jackson and Sullivan. Despite receiving several attractive offers, Sullivan refused to fight Jackson because he was black. Jackson's extreme disappointment and frustration at Sullivan's stance made him melancholy and adversely affected his performance in the ring during 1890. His spirits were revived in 1891 when he was able to arrange a match with James J. Corbett in San Francisco. In a rather slow moving bout the two boxers fought to a 61-round draw. The match improved Corbett's chance for a title bout with Sullivan and convinced many boxing authorities that Jackson had reached the end of his career.

In early 1892 Jackson returned to England, where he was embraced by the sporting public and polite society, to fight against an old rival, fellow Australian Frank Slavin. Jackson knocked out Slavin in the tenth round in one of the most exciting fights ever held in England. He returned to the United States in late 1892 in hopes of getting another match with Corbett, who recently had won the heavyweight championship from Sullivan. For the next two years Jackson and his manager "Parson" Davies attempted unsuccessfully to arrange a title match with Corbett. The two boxers could not agree on terms and exchanged insults with one another. In the end Jackson's pride prevented him from accepting a match with Corbett under unfavorable conditions. Discouraged, in 1894 he returned to England, where his health deteriorated partly because of excessive drinking. Jackson fought his last boxing match in San Francisco in 1898 against the future heavyweight champion, Jim Jeffries. Badly out of condition, Jackson lost the contest by a technical knockout when he failed to answer the bell for the fourth round. After suffering a near-fatal case of viral pneumonia, Jackson returned to Australia in 1900. He died of tuberculosis in Roma, Australia. One of the most noted athletes of his time, Jackson enjoyed a following among sports enthusiasts, both black and white.

• Biographies include Tom Langley, *The Life of Peter Jackson: Champion of Australia* (1974), and A. G. Hales, *Black Prince Peter: The Romantic Career of Peter Jackson* (1931). An excellent interpretive essay on Jackson's career is David K. Wiggins, "Peter Jackson and the Elusive Heavyweight Championship: A Black Athlete's Struggle against the Late Nineteenth Century Color-Line," *Journal of Sport History* 12 (Summer 1985): 143–68. Also see Nathaniel S. Fleischer, *Black Dynamite: The Story of the Negro in the Prize Ring from 1782 to 1938* (3 vols., 1938), and Michael T. Isenberg, *John L. Sullivan and His America* (1988). An obituary is in the *Cleveland Gazette*, 24 Aug. 1901.

JOHN M. CARROLL

JACKSON, Rachel Donelson Robards (15 June 1767–22 Dec. 1828), wife of President Andrew Jackson, was born on the frontier near Pittsylvania County, Virginia, the daughter of John Donelson, a surveyor, and Rachel Stockley. When Rachel was born, the Donelsons were one of the leading families in the county. Though she later loathed politics, the petite, dark-eyed girl visited Washington and Jefferson with her father, a Virginia aristocrat. Often described as illiterate, Rachel in fact received an exemplary education by frontier standards; she could read, write, and was skilled at the harpsichord and household arts.

When Rachel was twelve, her father entered into a partnership to settle the area on the banks of the Cum-

berland River in Tennessee. Finding their first settlement too dangerous, the Donelsons later moved to Kentucky, where at the age of seventeen Rachel met Lewis Robards, a member of a prominent family in Mercer County. Robards and Rachel Donelson were married on 1 Mar. 1785. The marriage was not a happy one. Robards had fits of jealous rage, accusing Rachel of infidelity with boarders, while he pursued other women. They separated for the first time in 1788.

After a year, Rachel agreed to the first of three attempted reconciliations, but Robards grew increasingly violent. In July 1790, fearing for her daughter's safety, Rachel's mother asked a young lawyer who boarded in her home, Andrew Jackson, to escort Rachel back to Tennessee. Distraught, yet convinced that her marriage was over, Rachel resolved to move as far away as possible and joined a trading party en route to Natchez, Mississippi, to live with relatives. At her family's request, Jackson, who was by then in love with Rachel, agreed to go on the hazardous journey to ensure her safety.

Infuriated, Lewis Robards petitioned and was granted permission by the Virginia legislature to sue for divorce on the grounds of desertion in December 1790. Divorce was very uncommon, and Rachel was concerned for her reputation, yet she agreed to marry Andrew Jackson in the hope of achieving some happiness. Jackson assumed that the action of the legislature in 1790 granted the divorce because that was procedure in North Carolina where he had studied law. No record of the couple's marriage in Natchez exists. As Protestants in a Roman Catholic county Rachel and Andrew were probably married by a government official in secrecy. Recent scholarship suggests that the ceremony was conducted sometime in February or March 1791, the earliest time after the divorce that Jackson could fulfill his commitments and return to Natchez. In April 1791 the couple returned to Tennessee to make their home.

Unknown to either of the Jacksons, Robards did not pursue a final divorce until over a year after filing his petition. Exactly why Robards chose this course of action is unclear, but he could have chosen to delay either to lay claim to a portion of Rachel's father's estate or to ensure that she and Jackson were living together to sue for divorce on the grounds of adultery. The final divorce decree was not granted in Kentucky until 27 September 1793. The shock and shame Rachel experienced on learning that she was not legally married to Andrew Jackson remained with her always. Jackson attempted to make amends and defended Rachel's honor for the rest of his life, even to the extent of killing a man in a duel on one occasion. The couple eventually went through a second marriage ceremony on 18 January 1794 in Nashville.

In 1804 the Jacksons built the Hermitage plantation, Rachel's home for the rest of her life. While concerned for his wife's welfare, Andrew Jackson did little to curb his own ambitions in order to give her the family life she craved. His military and political career led to frequent separations, sometimes over a year in duration. As her husband's career accelerated, Rachel grew increasingly disheartened, imploring him to return home. She fought her loneliness by devoting her energies to managing their growing household. She gave advice and loaned tools to new settlers, visited the sick, and looked after orphaned children and slaves. Although the Jacksons had no children of their own, the Hermitage was always full; "Aunt Rachel" raised at least thirteen children, including a nephew adopted at birth and an Indian orphan.

Another major source of solace for Rachel was her religion. By 1816 she was converted to a strict form of Presbyterianism under the guidance of Gideon Blackburn, her "father in the Gospel." Not surprisingly, her religious zeal made the stout woman who smoked a pipe and cared little for the latest fashions even less suitable for public life. After her husband secured the governorship of Florida, newspapers openly ridiculed her, calling her a "fat dumpling" when she danced. Her pressure on her husband to institute stricter Sabbath laws in Florida brought further ridicule. Though officials close to the Jacksons praised Rachel's abilities as a hostess as well as her generosity, the criticism against her intensified when her husband ran for the presidency unsuccessfully in 1824. His opposition made much of the irregularity of their marriage, depicting them both as illiterate and immoral. The fierce personal attacks escalated during the 1828 campaign and caused Rachel to slip into melancholy. She grew obese, and her health deteriorated. "For Mr. Jackson's sake I am glad," she said when informed that he had won the election. "For my own part, I never wished it" (Parton, vol. 3, p. 153).

After the election of 1828, Rachel remained in Tennessee. "I would rather be a door-keeper in the house of God than to live in that palace in Washington," she said (Parton, vol. 3, p. 170). Several months before her husband was sworn in, she died at the Hermitage after a heart attack. Many believed that her death had been hastened by the grief that gossip and slander had caused her. She was buried at the Hermitage in her inaugural gown. Andrew Jackson never recovered from his wife's death, nor from his feeling of bitterness over her treatment at the hands of his political enemies.

Rachel Jackson's significance lies both in her private role as a frontier woman who managed a large household on her own and in her public role as a woman victimized because she deviated from expected societal norms.

• Most of Rachel Jackson's papers were destroyed in the Hermitage fire in 1834. The Tennessee State Library and Archives, Nashville, has materials related to Rachel Jackson in at least fifteen different collections. The Andrew Jackson Papers in the Library of Congress also include relevant material on Rachel Jackson. The marriage license for Rachel Donelson Robards and Andrew Jackson dated 18 January 1794 is in the Autograph Collection, Harvard University Library. See also published correspondence containing letters of Rachel Jackson, including James Parton, *The Life of Andrew Jackson*

(3 vols., 1860), and John S. Bassett, *Correspondence of Andrew Jackson*, vols. 1–3 (1926–1928).

The most complete biography of Rachel Jackson is the flattering *General Jackson's Lady* (1936), by Mary French Caldwell. See also Marquis Jones, *Andrew Jackson: The Border Captain* (1933) and *Andrew Jackson: Portrait of a President* (1937), and Carl S. Anthony, *First Ladies: The Saga of the Presidents' Wives and Their Power, 1789–1961* (1990). For the marriage of Rachel and Andrew Jackson, see Arthur LaSalle, *The Marriage of Andrew Jackson at Springfield Plantation* (1987); Peggy Robbins, "Andrew and Rachel Jackson," *American History Illustrated* 11 (Winter 1976): 337–50, and 12 (Aug. 1977): 22–28; and Helen C. Owsley, "The Marriage of Rachel Donelson," *Tennessee Historical Quarterly* 37 (Winter 1977): 479–92. For Rachel's religious sentiments, see Joseph G. Smoot, "A Presbyterian Minister Calls on Presidential Candidate Andrew Jackson," *Tennessee Historical Quarterly* 21 (1962): 287–90.

SHERYL A. KUJAWA

JACKSON, Rebecca Cox (15 Feb. 1795–24 May 1871), itinerant preacher, religious writer, and Shaker eldress, was born a free African American in Horntown, Pennsylvania. According to sketchy autobiographical information, she was the daughter of Jane (maiden name unknown) Cox. No reference is made in her writings to her father, who probably died shortly after her birth. Rebecca Cox lived with her grandmother (never named) until she was between three and four years old, but by age six she was again living with her mother, who had remarried and was now called Jane Wisson or Wilson. Her stepfather, a sailor, died at sea the next year. At age ten, she was in Philadelphia with her mother and a younger sister and infant brother, the offspring, it seems, of a third marriage of her mother. Responsibility for caring for her younger siblings seems to have deprived Rebecca of the schooling her mother was somehow able to provide for the other children. Her mother died when she was thirteen, whereupon she probably moved into the household of her older brother Joseph Cox (1778?–1843), a tanner and clergyman eighteen years her senior.

The exact date of Rebecca Cox's marriage to Samuel S. Jackson is unknown, but it must have occurred before 1830, the year of her spiritual awakening and the year her autobiographical narrative begins. Apparently childless, she and her husband were living with Joseph Cox. She cared for her brother's four children and also worked as a seamstress, a relatively highly skilled and respected occupation for African-American women at that time. Jackson had been brought up as a Methodist, presumably in the African Methodist Episcopal (AME) church. Her brother Joseph was an influential preacher at the Bethel AME Church in Philadelphia but Rebecca and her husband apparently were not active church members prior to her spiritual awakening, which occurred during a violent thunderstorm. Her career as an independent preacher began shortly thereafter.

Carried on the waves of a religious revival, she soon moved from leading a small praying band to public preaching. She stirred up controversy within AME circles not only as a woman preacher, but also because she had come to believe that celibacy was a necessary precondition of a holy life. She insisted that she be guided entirely by the dictates of an inner voice, which she identified as the authentic voice of God. In her incomplete spiritual autobiography, which she began to write in the 1840s, perhaps using earlier journal entries as a source, Jackson recorded a wide variety of visionary experiences, dreams, and supernatural gifts, including a remarkable "gift of reading," or literacy, in direct response to prayer in 1831. This "gift" gave her independent access to the divine word and allowed Jackson to free herself from what she believed was censorship in the letters she dictated to her clergyman brother. She also recorded instances of healing, the gift of foresight, and the more mysterious "gifts of power," spiritual means of protecting herself from threats, both natural and human.

By the late 1830s Jackson had separated from her husband, broken with the AME church, and successfully launched a career of itinerant preaching that took her throughout Pennsylvania, northern Delaware, New Jersey, southern New England, and New York State. Her first experience with religious communal life occurred during this period, when she became involved with a group of religious Perfectionists organized near Albany, New York, by a man named Allen Pierce in 1837. This group valued visions and revelations and acknowledged Jackson's gifts in this realm. In 1843, when the community dissolved, sixteen of them joined the nearby Shaker community at Watervliet.

Jackson visited the Shakers (the United Society of Believers in Christ's Second Coming) at this time and was attracted by their religious celibacy, their emphasis on spiritualistic experience, and their dual-gender concept of deity. In 1835 she had had a vision, which she believed was a "revelation of the mother spirit," and clearly was impressed by the sect's acknowledgment of the Holy Mother Wisdom as a "co-eternal" partner with the Almighty Father. With her younger disciple and lifelong companion, Rebecca Perot, Jackson lived in the Watervliet Shaker community from June 1847 until July 1851. The two women then returned to Philadelphia on an unauthorized mission to bring the truths of Shakerism to the African-American community. In Philadelphia they experimented with seance spiritualism. In 1857 they returned to Watervliet, and after a brief second residence Jackson won the right to found and head a new Shaker "outfamily" in Philadelphia.

Little is known of the small Philadelphia Shaker family during the remainder of Jackson's life. Over the next twenty-five years, the family varied in size and was located at several different Philadelphia sites. There was always a core group of African-American women, some living together in a single house. They supported themselves by daywork as laundresses and seamstresses and held religious meetings at night. In 1878 the Shaker historian Alonzo G. Hollister visited with his copy of the collected writings of Rebecca

Jackson—based on manuscripts entrusted to the Shakers by Perot after Jackson's death—and at that time, the core group comprised about a dozen women, including at least one Jewish sister. A smaller number of men, including one or two white spiritualists, also were associated with the community. Perot and several other aging Philadelphia sisters retired to the Watervliet community by 1896, but Shaker records indicate that the community still existed in some form as late as 1908.

Jackson was one of a surprisingly large number of African-American women preachers in the nineteenth century who mounted significant challenges to the exclusionary practices of established churches, using their claim to extraordinary, direct experience of the divine to carve out careers as religious leaders despite the patriarchal biases of their churches. More theologically radical than most, Jackson sought a perfectionist religion that would acknowledge a "mother divinity," at first using only her own religious experience as her guide but later incorporating the dual-gender godhead theology developed by Shakerism. Her permanent legacy, however, was not a new religious sect, but a remarkable body of visionary writing that writer Alice Walker has said "tells us much more about the spirituality of human beings, especially of the interior spiritual resources of our mothers, and, because of this, makes an invaluable contribution to what we know of ourselves" (p. 78).

• Jackson's manuscript writings are in the Shaker collections of the Western Reserve Historical Society in Cleveland, Ohio, the Library of Congress, and the Berkshire Athenaeum at the Public Library in Pittsfield, Mass. Her complete autobiographical writings were published by Jean McMahon Humez as *Gifts of Power: The Writings of Rebecca Jackson, Black Visionary, Shaker Eldress* (1981). Critical discussions of her writing are found in Joanne Braxton, *Black Women Writing Autobiography* (1989); Diane Sasson, *The Shaker Spiritual Narrative* (1983); and Alice Walker, *In Search of Our Mothers' Gardens* (1983).

JEAN MCMAHON HUMEZ

JACKSON, Robert Houghwout (13 Feb. 1892–9 Oct. 1954), lawyer and U.S. Supreme Court justice, was born in Spring Creek, Pennsylvania, the son of William Eldred Jackson, a farmer and small businessman, and Angelina Houghwout. When Jackson was five, the family moved to Frewsburg in western New York state near Jamestown. Jackson began his legal career at the age of eighteen, immediately after high school, as a clerk to his cousin Frank H. Mott, a prominent Jamestown lawyer active in the Democratic party. Although he did attend the Albany Law School for a year, Jackson described himself as "a vestigial remnant of the system which permitted one to come to the bar by way of apprenticeship in a law office." He was the last member of the Supreme Court of the United States to become a lawyer in that fashion.

After being admitted to the bar in 1913, Jackson pursued a successful career for two decades as one of the leading trial lawyers in western New York. In 1916 he married Irene Gerhardt, with whom he had a son and a daughter. Apart from a few months in 1917 and 1918 in Buffalo, which he abandoned because he found it too large a city, Jackson practiced law in Jamestown. Throughout his career he kept in his office a framed sketch of a young man studying by lamplight over a caption quoting Rudyard Kipling: "He travels fastest who travels alone." Jackson styled himself a "country lawyer" and especially valued the independence and lack of administrative entanglements that small-town legal practice permitted.

In addition to pursuing a satisfying and successful law practice in Jamestown, Jackson was active in bar association affairs and to some degree in Democratic politics. He became an adviser to Franklin D. Roosevelt after Roosevelt's election as governor of New York in 1928. Somewhat reluctantly, Jackson left Jamestown to join Roosevelt's national administration in February 1934 as general counsel in the Treasury Department's Bureau of Internal Revenue. While the principal work of the general counsel was to head a litigation staff in the day-to-day business of collecting taxes, Jackson also led the government's civil prosecution of former Treasury secretary Andrew Mellon, which established that Mellon owed some half million dollars of tax.

Jackson moved to the Department of Justice in March 1936 as assistant attorney general in charge of the Tax Division. Just two months later he was named assistant attorney general in charge of the Antitrust Division. His work, however, was not limited to the concerns of his designated divisions; of the ten cases he argued in the Supreme Court while assistant attorney general, only one actually dealt with antitrust issues.

When Stanley Reed was elevated to the Supreme Court in March 1938, Jackson was appointed to replace him as solicitor general of the United States. Jackson's skill as the chief appellate advocate for the government in the Supreme Court led Justice Louis D. Brandeis to observe that Jackson should be appointed solicitor general for life. As a senior Justice Department official, Jackson testified before Congress in 1937 in support of President Roosevelt's bill to enlarge the Supreme Court. That unsuccessful legislation, widely criticized as a threat to the separation of powers and judicial independence, was designed to break down impediments to Roosevelt's New Deal program erected by conservative members of the Supreme Court. As solicitor general, Jackson shaped legal strategies to relax judicial review of New Deal economic and social initiatives. His book *The Struggle for Judicial Supremacy* (1941) detailed the transformation of the Supreme Court during the New Deal into a more restrained judicial body.

Jackson was identified as a potential candidate for three Supreme Court vacancies that arose during his tenure as solicitor general. But Roosevelt, who valued Jackson's role in his administration, appointed Felix Frankfurter, then William O. Douglas, and finally Attorney General Frank Murphy to those seats. With Murphy's elevation to the Supreme Court, Roosevelt made Jackson attorney general in January 1940. As attorney general, Jackson also functioned as a close political adviser to the president and fashioned the legal opinion on which Roosevelt based his exchange of American destroyers to Great Britain for military bases in Bermuda, Labrador, and other British possessions. When the resignation of Chief Justice Charles Evans Hughes gave Roosevelt an additional vacancy to fill in the spring of 1941, the president had conversations with Jackson that led Jackson to believe he would be next in line for a future chief justiceship. At that point, however, Roosevelt chose to elevate Associate Justice Harlan Fiske Stone to chief justice and appoint Jackson as an associate justice.

Jackson immediately established himself as a strong supporter of a nationalist conception of the Constitution and as a skillful draftsman of judicial opinions. In one of his first Supreme Court opinions, he concurred in a decision striking down as unconstitutional a California law that sought to limit the right of entry into the state by those without visible means of support. Jackson wrote that unless U.S. citizenship meant at least the right to enter each of the several states, "then our heritage of constitutional privileges and immunities is only a promise to the ear to be broken to the hope, a teasing illusion like a munificent bequest in a pauper's will" (*Edwards v. California* [1941]).

Grounding his nationalist conception in economic affairs on the Commerce Clause of the U.S. Constitution, Jackson afforded the federal government broad authority to regulate the economy even when the controls were exercised over seemingly local transactions. Writing for a unanimous court in *Wickard v. Filburn* (1942), a case involving penalties against a dairy farmer who planted wheat to feed his own livestock and make flour for home consumption, Jackson upheld the Second Agricultural Adjustment Act, which imposed quotas on wheat production and other commodities in order to support prices. As Jackson later wrote in another case, when "it is interstate commerce that feels the pinch, it does not matter how local the operation which applies the squeeze" (*United States v. Women's Sportswear Mfg. Ass'n.* [1949]).

Jackson was an eloquent defender of civil liberties, at least in cases where he did not view competing dangers as clear and present. His majority opinion in *West Virginia State Board of Education v. Barnette* (1943), declaring unconstitutional a state statute requiring schoolchildren to salute the flag, is one of the most powerful statements of the purposes of the First Amendment to the Constitution. Jackson concluded his opinion with a stirring peroration: "If there is any fixed star in our constitutional constellation, it is that no official, high or petty, can prescribe what shall be orthodox in politics, nationalism, religion, or other matters of opinion or force citizens to confess by word or act their faith therein."

During World War II Jackson dissented from the Court's decision in *Korematsu v. United States* (1944), which upheld the conviction of an American-born citizen of Japanese descent for failing to report to a relocation center. He contended the conviction provided judicial sanction for "the principle of racial discrimination in criminal procedure and of transplanting American citizens." However, Jackson at the same time acknowledged that the military had the force to arrest citizens in what the military deemed a wartime emergency and said he was unwilling to contend "the courts should have attempted to interfere with the Army in carrying out its task." Rather he maintained that civilian courts "cannot be made to enforce an order that violates constitutional limitations even if it is a reasonable exercise of military authority."

When he perceived immediate dangers posed by the expression of political opinions, Jackson was prepared to grant broad power to government authorities to intervene. In *Terminiello v. Chicago* (1949), he dissented from a decision overturning the breach of the peace conviction of a quondam priest whose inflammatory pro-Fascist and anti-Semitic speech "provoked a hostile mob and incited a friendly one, and threatened violence between the two." Contending that the majority of the court had fixed "its eyes on a conception of freedom of speech so rigid as to tolerate no concession to society's need for public order," Jackson warned that "if the Court does not temper its doctrinaire logic with a little practical wisdom, it will convert the constitutional Bill of Rights into a suicide pact."

In the years immediately following his appointment to the Court, Jackson was somewhat frustrated in his work. The Court moved out of the mainstream of the nation's larger concerns during World War II, and he found himself in some personal conflict with other justices, principally Hugo Black. The conflict roiled beneath the surface during the spring of 1945 when Jackson privately suggested that Black had engaged in judicial impropriety when Black failed to disqualify himself in a case argued before the Court by Black's former law partner. Consequently, Jackson more than welcomed the opportunity to take a sabbatical from the Court by accepting President Harry S. Truman's appointment in April 1945 as chief counsel for the United States in the prosecution of senior Nazi officials at Nuremberg. Jackson later described his work on the Nuremberg trials "as infinitely more important than my work on the Supreme Court."

Jackson was instrumental in shaping the structure of the Nuremberg tribunal's proceedings in negotiations with Great Britain, France, and the Soviet Union. At the trial he took an active role as principal prosecution counsel. His opening statement and closing argument captured the purposes and conclusions of the proceeding. In his opening in November 1945, he declared that the "wrongs which we seek to condemn and punish have been so calculated, so malignant and so devastating, that civilization cannot tolerate their being ignored because it cannot survive their being repeated. That four great nations, flushed with victory and stung with injury stay the hand of vengeance and voluntarily submit their captive enemies to the judgment of the law is one of the most significant tributes

that Power ever has paid to Reason." In his closing in July 1946, he said that if "you were to say of these men that they are not guilty, it would be as true to say there has been no war, there are no slain, there has been no crime." Lord Elwyn-Jones, a British prosecutor at Nuremberg and later lord chancellor of England, said that Jackson's "two main Nuremberg speeches are amongst the finest ever pronounced in any Court for the great beauty of their language and the passionate conviction they expressed."

Jackson's handling of witnesses, particularly his cross-examination of Hermann Göring, commander in chief of the German air force, chief of War Economy, and Hitler's designee as his successor, was not as well regarded. Göring, a clever and resourceful figure, eluded control on cross-examination and managed to use the occasion for extended and self-serving speeches and banter with Jackson. Moreover, Jackson's inattention to and disinterest in the administration of his 150-lawyer team caused difficulties in the prosecution camp. Nor was Jackson's extended absence from the Court fully accepted by his colleagues. Chief Justice Stone privately expressed the view, shared by others, that the War Crimes Tribunal was simply an elaborate pretext for victors' justice or, as he pungently put it on one occasion, "Jackson is away conducting his high-grade lynching party in Nuremberg."

The Nuremberg trials nevertheless firmly established the proposition that individuals can be held responsible for war crimes and punished under international law. As an immediate result of the Nuremberg trial of the Nazi leaders prosecuted by Jackson, twelve of the defendants were sentenced to death by hanging, three to life imprisonment, and four to imprisonment for terms ranging from 10 to 20 years; three of the defendants were acquitted.

When Stone died on 22 April 1946, newspaper reports appeared that Jackson, still in Nuremberg, believed to have been instigated by his antagonist, Justice Black. The reports publicized conflict among members of the Court and alluded to Black's opposition to appointing Jackson as chief justice. President Truman—who had not been a party to any conversations between Roosevelt and Jackson about Jackson's future prospects for the chief justiceship—sidestepped the controversy and chose his own secretary of the Treasury, Fred M. Vinson, to succeed Stone. Jackson thereupon delivered a forceful statement to the press publicly resurrecting his concerns over the propriety of Black's deciding a case involving his former law partner. The controversy reflected poorly on both Jackson and Black. Yet when Jackson returned to the Court for the October term of 1946, he took up his judicial work without further controversy, and his interactions with Black were distant but polite and professional.

Influenced by his experience with the results of totalitarianism in Nuremberg, Jackson upheld measures to control Communist party activists and voted to affirm the conviction of officers of the Communist party for conspiring to teach and advocate the overthrow of the government in *Dennis v. United States* (1951). Even when upholding inquiry into actual membership in the Communist party, however, Jackson was unwilling to endorse government efforts to inquire about private views, such as the requirement that union officers swear an oath of nonbelief in the purposes of the party. "The priceless heritage of our society is the unrestricted constitutional right of each member to think as he will. Thought control is a copyright of totalitarianism, and we have no claim to it," Jackson wrote (*American Communications Ass'n. v. Douds* [1950]).

Jackson's extensive legal and political experience provided a firm foundation for thoughtful, informed, and practical opinions on the proper relationships among governmental institutions. His most important opinion in this area was his concurrence in *Youngstown Sheet & Tube Co. v. Sawyer* (1952), the Steel Seizure case, in which the Court invalidated Truman's takeover of private steel mills to prevent a strike during the Korean War. In it Jackson provided a structure for addressing separation of powers issues. Jackson maintained that the president's constitutional powers vary in relation to whether Congress has spoken on the issue. Jackson's opinion explained that when Congress has authorized executive action, the president's powers are broadest; when Congress has prohibited executive action, the president's powers are most limited; and when Congress is silent, the extent of executive power is uncertain. Because Congress had taken no action to authorize the takeover of the steel mills, Jackson concluded that the president lacked the constitutional power to do so. William H. Rehnquist, his law clerk that term, observed, when he himself became chief justice, that Jackson's Steel Seizure case opinion "has yet to be surpassed in its statesmanlike and lawyerlike analysis of the executive branch of the federal government."

Throughout his career on the bench, Jackson was concerned with the need to respect the limitations on judicial power and with the correlative need for responsible exercise of power by the other branches of government. He expressed himself with pointed yet disarming candor on these issues. Jackson once deprecated the Supreme Court's omniscience in judicial review by observing "we are not final because we are infallible, but we are infallible only because we are final" (*Brown v. Allen* [1953]). His fundamental concern, shared by his colleague Justice Felix Frankfurter, with whom he was frequently aligned, was that the courts exercise their powers of decision in a restrained manner so as not to displace the elected branches of government. In the Godkin Lectures he delivered at Harvard in 1954, posthumously published in his book *The Supreme Court in the American System of Government* (1955), Jackson warned against relying on the Court to shape "the constitutional practice of the future" and that doing so constitutes "a doctrine wholly incompatible with faith in democracy, and in so far as it encourages a belief that the judges may be left to correct the result of public indifference to issues of liberty in choosing Presidents, Senators, and Representatives, it is a vicious teaching." Jackson acknowledged in sounding his warning that "I may be biased against this attitude because it is so contrary to the doctrines of critics of the Court, of whom I was one, at the time of the Roosevelt proposal to reorganize the judiciary."

Jackson's sense of the scope and limits of the duties of judicial office were placed in graphic relief when confronting the school desegregation cases during his last full term. In an unpublished memorandum he prepared while the cases were under advisement, Jackson found little in the legislative or judicial history of responses to the problem that would provide a foundation for banning segregated schools. He concluded that the only way the Court could, "with intellectual honesty," strike down public school segregation would be to recognize candidly that the meaning of constitutional provisions may vary over time. Ultimately, Jackson's impulse toward preparing a separate opinion of unvarnished candor was subordinated to his own sense of the larger institutional imperatives for the Supreme Court. In *Brown v. Board of Education* (1954), the new Chief Justice, Earl Warren, persuaded Jackson that a visible show of unity by all members of the Court would best serve those institutional imperatives and encourage respect for the development of the law in this highly charged area. Jackson therefore left the hospital bed where he was recuperating from a heart attack to be on the bench when Warren read the Court's decision on 17 May 1954. Jackson died in McLean, Virginia, less than five months later of a second heart attack suffered after returning to the Court, against his doctor's warnings.

As a prose stylist, Jackson ranks with the very finest of American legal writers. He wrote, as Solicitor General Simon Sobeloff said during a memorial service for him at the Supreme Court, "with a trenchant, concrete, Saxon style of great beauty and vigor, nurtured chiefly on the King James version of the Bible and on Shakespeare." As a consequence, he remains among the most frequently quoted American judges. Jackson's nationalist view of American economic life and solicitous protection of the right of free thought are deeply and firmly embedded in the ground of American constitutional law in no small part because of his compelling opinions.

• Jackson's papers are in the Library of Congress, and he provided a lengthy interview for the Columbia University Oral History Project, (1952). The oral history is quoted extensively in a biographical article by Philip B. Kurland, "Robert H. Jackson," in *The Justices of the United States Supreme Court*, ed. Leon Friedman and Fred L. Israel (1969). An exhaustive bibliography of Jackson's judicial opinions and his extrajudicial publications, including many of his speeches, is gathered in *Stanford Law Review* 8 (1955): 60–76. An annotated selection of his judicial writings is found in Glendon Shubert, ed., *Dispassionate Justice: A Synthesis of the Judicial Opinions of Robert H. Jackson* (1969). An uncritical book-length biography of Jackson is Eugene C. Gerhardt, *America's Advocate, Robert H. Jackson* (1958). Jackson's work as Nuremberg prosecutor is discussed in a clear-eyed fashion by his aide in the prosecution, Telford Taylor, *The Anatomy of the Nuremberg Trials* (1992). G. Edward White places Jackson in context in chap. 11 of *The American Judicial Tradition* (1988). Several lengthy essays have captured aspects of Jackson's career, including Paul A. Freund, "Individual and Commonwealth in the Thought of Mr. Justice Jackson," in Freund, *On Law and Justice* (1968); Charles S. Desmond, Paul A. Freund, Potter Stewart, and Lord Shawcross, *Mr. Justice Jackson: Four Lectures in His Honor* (1969); Edwin M. Yoder, Jr., "Black v. Jackson: A Study in Judicial Enmity," in Yoder, *The Unmaking of a Whig* (1990); E. Barrett Prettyman, Jr., "Robert H. Jackson: 'Solicitor General for Life,'" *Journal of Supreme Court History* (1992): 75–85; and Bernard Schwartz, "Chief Justice Rehnquist, Justice Jackson, and the *Brown* Case," *Supreme Court Review* (1988): 245–67. Memorial tributes with substantial analytical pieces by Warner W. Gardner, Charles Fairman, and Telford Taylor are in *Columbia Law Review* 55, no. 4 (Apr. 1955), and by Louis L. Jaffe in *Harvard Law Review* 68, no. 6. A memorial proceeding in the Supreme Court is in *U.S. Reports*, vol. 319. An obituary is in the *New York Times*, 10 Oct. 1954.

DOUGLAS P. WOODLOCK

JACKSON, Robert R. (1 Sept. 1870–12 June 1942), politician, was born in Malta, Illinois, the son of William Jackson and Sarah Cooper. He spent most of his childhood in Chicago. At age nine he began selling newspapers and shining shoes in Chicago's central business district; he left school in the eighth grade to work full time. By age eighteen he had garnered an appointment as a clerk in the post office, a position coveted by African Americans in this era because of its security relative to most other occupations open to them. He left the postal service as an assistant superintendent in 1909 to devote himself full time to his printing and publishing business, the Fraternal Press. In partnership with Beauregard F. Mosely in 1910 he cofounded the Leland Giants, Chicago's first African-American baseball team. In 1912 Jackson won election as a Republican to the state legislature. From there he moved to the Chicago City Council, where he served as an alderman from 1918 through 1939. After leaving politics, Jackson returned to baseball, where he served a two-year stint as commissioner of the Negro American League.

Jackson built both his printing business and his political success on a remarkable level of participation in fraternal organizations, apparently bounded only by racial exclusion. A 1923 city directory described him a "a member of nearly all the Fraternal orders in Chicago." These included the American Wood, Appomattox Club, Dramatic Order of Knights of Omar, Elks, Knights of Pythias, Masons, Odd Fellows, and Royal Arch. He also participated actively in the establishment of the first cooperative grocery in black Chicago, joined the Musicians Union, and volunteered with the Boy Scouts and the Young Men's Christian Association. Estimates of his membership in voluntary organizations have run as high as twenty-five, a political asset that assured him continued visibility in the community.

Jackson's military career represents one particularly important aspect of his role as a joiner and a leader.

Rising from a drummer to a major in what came to be known in black America as the "Famous Eighth Illinois" infantry (notable for having an African-American commanding officer, and ceaselessly promoted by the *Chicago Defender*), Jackson took advantage of his National Guard career by identifying himself as "Major" R. R. Jackson whenever he ran for office. His most notable service came during the Spanish-American War when the unit, then known as the Eighth Regiment of Illinois Volunteers, fought in Cuba. Characteristically, while in Cuba he organized the Mañana Club, dedicated to improving relations between Cubans and African-American officers.

Jackson ranked among the foremost African-American politicians of his generation. At a time when no African Americans could win election to federal office, and extremely few to state legislatures, his career epitomized the limitations imposed by racial discrimination. His route through business and fraternal organizations was one of the few paths to office for black politicians. As a state legislator he was most vocal on issues related to racial discrimination, most notably opposing an attempt to prohibit intermarriage and helping to block legislation that would have reduced African-American employment on railroads. His most significant accomplishment was his role in securing state funding for Chicago's Emancipation Golden Jubilee in 1913. He exercised little influence on issues unconnected to race relations.

In the Chicago City Council, Jackson's nonconfrontational style endeared him to white power brokers, helping him to secure for his constituents such major capital projects as a large park, a library, and a playground, in addition to minor improvements and standard services. As a loyal member of a Republican organization dominated by Mayor William Hale Thompson (1915–1923, 1927–1931), however, Jackson compiled a record that did not endear him to reformers opposed to Thompson's renowned tolerance of vice and corruption. He sponsored little major legislation other than an ordinance providing for a system of milk inspection.

Along with Edward H. Wright and Oscar DePriest, Jackson helped to establish the foundation of an approach to African-American political leadership that would remain influential in Chicago until the 1950s. This approach was characterized by loyalty to a white-dominated organization in return for recognition, patronage, and occasional (though highly visible) public works projects. It was made possible by the residential segregation—and therefore political consolidation—of a black population that increased dramatically during and immediately after World War I. These newcomers from the South identified Democrats with southern politics and Republicans with Abraham Lincoln, providing a base that not only elected first DePriest and then Jackson and others to the city council but also provided the margin of victory for Thompson in both primary and general elections.

As African-American voters began moving into the Democratic party in the 1930s, in many cases followed by their elected officials, Jackson remained a Republican. During his last eight years as alderman, a Democratic mayor and city council pushed him to the margins; his influence already diminished, he finally lost his seat to a Democrat in 1939. The emerging alliance between African-American Democrats and the "Kelly-Nash" Democratic machine, however, was characterized by the familiar exchange of votes for recognition and power within the ghetto. Like Jackson and his peers, William Dawson, the dominating figure in Chicago black politics in the 1940s and 1950s, exercised little power on issues unrelated to race. Eventually he came to symbolize what African-American activists in the 1960s would call "plantation politics."

Jackson, his colleagues, and their successors had only minimal impact on public policy at the city or state level. They did, however, mobilize African Americans into a political force capable of electing black candidates and demanding recognition as legitimate participants in the urban polity. Jackson, in particular, stands out not only for his honesty amid a Chicago City Council notorious for corruption but also for his skill as a legislator who worked the system successfully within the considerable limits imposed by the exclusion of African Americans from the corridors of power. He died in Chicago, survived by his wife, Hattie Ball Lewis, and a son.

• No known collection of Jackson's papers exists. Biographical data on Jackson and his peers are available in Harold Gosnell, *Negro Politicians: The Rise of Negro Politics in Chicago* (1935). On Chicago's black community during Jackson's career, see Allan H. Spear, *Black Chicago: The Making of a Negro Ghetto, 1890–1920* (1967), and James R. Grossman, *Land of Hope: Chicago, Black Southerners, and the Great Migration* (1989). The classic sociological study remains St. Clair Drake and Horace Cayton, *Black Metropolis: A Study of Negro Life in a Northern City* (1945). The most comprehensive study of Chicago's black politicians is Charles R. Branham, "The Transformation of Black Political Leadership in Chicago, 1864–1942" (Ph.D. diss., Univ. of Chicago, 1981). Obituaries are in the *Chicago Defender*, 20 June 1942, and the *Chicago Sun*, 14 June 1942.

JAMES R. GROSSMAN

JACKSON, Samuel (22 Mar. 1787–4 Apr. 1872), physician and medical educator, was born in Philadelphia, Pennsylvania, the son of David Jackson, a pharmacist, and Susan (or Susanna) Kemper. In 1801 Jackson's father died, leaving the family's pharmacy business to Jackson's older brother. Jackson studied medicine initially under James Hutchinson, Jr., who died shortly thereafter, and then under Casper Wistar. In 1808 Jackson received an M.D. from the University of Pennsylvania. He dedicated his thesis, "Suspended Animation," to his teacher Wistar, who became professor of anatomy at Philadelphia the same year. At the death of his older brother in 1809, Jackson was left to salvage a failing pharmacy business.

During the War of 1812, Jackson joined the First Troop of City Cavalry in Philadelphia and was deployed in operations along the Chesapeake Bay. After the war, he sold the family's pharmacy business and opened a medical practice in Philadelphia. Jackson succeeded in private practice and established himself in the medical community. On 20 March 1820 the city elected Jackson president of the board of health, and he was instrumental in resisting the yellow fever epidemic during that year. Jackson promoted the local-origin theory of the disease, that is, the idea that the fever arose locally as a result of the squalor in the community. His position brought him into conflict with David Hosack, professor of surgery and midwifery at the College of Physicians and Surgeons of New York, who advocated a contagion theory.

In 1821 Jackson helped found the Philadelphia College of Pharmacy, as chair of the committee responsible for planning the institution. That year the college elected him a trustee, and from 1821 to 1827 he served as professor of materia medica and pharmacy. In 1822 the Philadelphia Almshouse appointed Jackson attending physician, where he was one of the first physicians in the United States to promote the use of auscultation, a technique of listening to bodily sounds with a stethoscope, introduced by René Laënnec in 1819, for the diagnosis of disease. Jackson was also an instructor of medical chemistry and then materia medica at the Medical Institute of Philadelphia. In 1817 Nathaniel Chapman had organized the institute, which included a number of prominent members of the profession, including William Dewees, and William Horner. Jackson taught at the institute until 1844. In 1827 he became an assistant to Chapman at the University of Pennsylvania and was responsible for teaching the physiology section of Chapman's course. In 1835, with Chapman's health declining, the university promoted Jackson to the chair of the institutes of medicine, a post he held until his retirement in 1863. From 1842 to 1845 Jackson also taught on the wards of the Philadelphia Hospital.

In 1830 Jackson served as one of the vice presidents for the Medical Society of Philadelphia. At public meetings of the society, Jackson debated Daniel Drake—then professor of the institutes and practice of medicine at the rival Jefferson Medical College—over medical issues such as Brunonianism. Jackson was an early advocate of John Brown's doctrine of excitability, the property of living organisms responsible for physiological and pathological processes. At the beginning of the nineteenth century, the notion of vitalism was a disputed issue in the medical literature. In an 1826 article on vitality and vital forces, Jackson framed his philosophy of medicine on the doctrine of irritability, as defined by Francis Glisson, Albrecht von Haller, and others. For Jackson, however, irritability was a proximate, not an ultimate, cause of life.

In 1832 Jackson published *The Principles of Medicine Founded on the Structure and Functions of the Animal Organism*. He dedicated the textbook to his colleague Chapman. In the *Principles of Medicine*, Jackson restricted his system to no particular authority but relied on the writings of "Haller, Bichat, Beclard, Broussais, Adelon, Gendrin, Andral, Meckel, Bell,

Wedemeyer, Begin, Bourdon, Tiedemann [all influential physicians] and the different journals of the day" (p. xx). He also depended on current advancements in anatomy and physiology. The textbook received a favorable review by Eli Geddings in a journal founded by Chapman but received a critical review by an anonymous reviewer—believed to be Charles Caldwell—in the *Transylvania Journal of Medicine and the Associate Sciences* and was not reissued in another edition.

Jackson continued to develop the notion of vitality throughout his career. In an 1851 introductory lecture to the institutes of medicine class, he summarized the changes in his understanding of the notion. In his lecture, Jackson noted his first correlation of vital forces with physical and chemical forces was in an 1837 introductory lecture. As the conception of physical and chemical forces continued to change during the first half of the 1800s, he adapted these changes to medicine in order to secure a scientific basis for his profession. Finally, in an 1856 introductory lecture near the end of his career, Jackson argued the "fundamental laws" of living organisms were analogous to those of "rational mechanics."

In 1832 the Sanitary Board of Councils for Philadelphia sent Jackson, Richard Harrison, and Charles D. Meigs to investigate the outbreak of Asiatic cholera in Montreal, Canada. To the board, they reported the disease was "malignant" (life-threatening). While in Canada, Jackson married the daughter of a British officer, whose surname was Christie. Jackson returned to Philadelphia, and when cholera struck that city in the same year the city appointed him physician in chief of Cholera Hospital No. Five. He published his practical experience with the disease, just as he had with yellow fever. Along with twelve other physicians and surgeons, Jackson received a silver pitcher from the city's board of health for his work during the cholera epidemic. Throughout his career Jackson also wrote several papers on various topics, including pulmonary disease, James's Fever Powder, Swaim's Panacea, amnesia, tetanus, the pulse and circulation, starch and the liver, and inflammation.

Jackson was a member of various professional and scholarly societies, including the College of Physicians of Philadelphia and the American Philosophical Society. As a popular teacher and dedicated physician, who recognized the significance of European advances in anatomy and physiology for medical training in the United States, Jackson played an important role during the nineteenth century in the development of American medicine, pharmacy, and medical education.

• The Jackson Collection is housed at the College of Physicians of Philadelphia. A comprehensive biographical account that includes an extensive list of Jackson's writings is Joseph Carson, *A Discourse Commemorative of the Life and Character of Samuel Jackson, M.D.* (1872). For shorter accounts, see Cato (pseud.), "Sketches of Eminent Living Physicians; No. XIV, Samuel Jackson, M.D.," *Boston Medical and Surgical Journal* 41 (1850): 319–22; Frederick P. Henry, ed., *Standard History of the Medical Profession of Philadelphia* (1897);

and William S. Middleton, "Samuel Jackson," *Annals of Medical History* 7 (1935): 538–49. For the role of Jackson in the founding of the Philadelphia College of Pharmacy, see Joseph W. England, ed., *The First Century of the Philadelphia College of Pharmacy, 1821–1921* (1922). For an analysis of Jackson's position on vitalism, see Edward C. Atwater, "'Squeezing Mother Nature': Experimental Physiology in the United States before 1870," *Bulletin of the History of Medicine* 52 (1978): 313–35.

JAMES A. MARCUM

JACKSON, Samuel Macauley (19 June 1851–2 Aug. 1912), church historian and philanthropist, was born in New York City, the son of George T. Jackson, a businessman, and Letitia Jane Aiken Macauley. Born into a socially prominent and financially comfortable family, Jackson embodied the intellectual tastes and public mindedness often found among members of that class. In 1870 he graduated from the College of the City of New York and for the next year studied divinity at Princeton Theological Seminary. In 1871 he transferred to Union Theological Seminary in New York City, graduating with a B.D. degree in 1873. For two years thereafter he toured Europe and took advanced courses at the universities in Leipzig and Berlin. Upon his return to the United States, he earned an A.M. degree from the College of the City of New York in 1876 and was ordained as a Presbyterian minister. For four years he served as pastor of a church in Norwood, New Jersey.

It seems that Jackson found the scholar's cloister more appealing than the varied demands of parish life, and by 1880 he moved from clerical duties to academic pursuits. He never married, and a generous inheritance made it possible for him to follow diverse interests without worrying about employment or salary. Those interests often touched on social problems, and there Jackson evinced a moral earnestness that characterized him throughout his life. He genuinely wanted to do some good in society and benefit those around him. He was, for example, for almost three decades a member of the Charity Organization Society in New York, serving as its vice president from 1903 until his death. In that capacity he sought to understand the relationship between poverty and crime in order to help Christian groups accomplish charity work more effectively. He also maintained a perennial interest in foreign missions, particularly those in China. Jackson served as president of the Board of Trustees of Canton Christian College from 1905 to 1912. He made frequent gifts to the Chinese institution, donated funds to build a residence for its president, and provided liberally for it in his will.

There was a more distinctive aspect to Jackson's philanthropic activities, one that blended perceptibly with his scholarly inclinations. Most of the gifts he made to organizations from his personal estate came in the form of books. Clearly he thought that leaders of society had a moral responsibility to seek the common welfare, but this solemn duty was best met, in his view, after careful study of problems and all their ramifications. In that vein Jackson collected hundreds of works on penology for the Prison Association of the State of New York. In his concern to further the cause of missions, he compiled a comprehensive list of missionary publications and made it available through several evangelical centenaries and reports. He acted on the principle that full and correct information facilitated proper and effective performance, which rescued his many activities from dilettantism and gave them cogency.

From the day he first met Philip Schaff at Union Seminary, Jackson was that professor's disciple. For two decades he worked modestly in the background and facilitated publication of his mentor's many projects. In 1880 he helped complete Schaff's *Dictionary of the Bible*. In 1889 he managed to issue a three-volume reference work on history and theology, expanding it later to the thirteen-volume *The New Schaff-Herzog Encyclopedia of Religious Knowledge* (1908–1914). He labored to bring out an *Encyclopedia of Living Divines* in 1887 and served with customary humility as secretary to the American Society of Church History, becoming president of that professional association in 1912. Between 1893 and 1897 he was joint editor of the American Church History Series, a thirteen-volume study of denominations in this country that inaugurated modern historical scholarship regarding American churches. As a final tribute to his hero, Jackson endowed the Philip Schaff Chair of Church History at New York University and occupied it without salary from 1895 to 1912.

As was the case with many church historians of his day, Jackson concentrated heavily on the Protestant Reformation. He was particularly interested in the Swiss reformer, Huldreich Zwingli, producing over time a biography as well as modern editions of selected works. Jackson also ranged over most centuries of Christian history, displaying his greatest strength as a bibliographer. Before church history reached maturity as a discipline in American universities, he aided its development by synthesizing titles for study. His lists were painstakingly accurate and valuable to later generations because of the attention he paid to minute details. He also contributed countless articles, essays, and entries to encyclopedias and dictionaries for the furtherance of knowledge about the Christian past. After he died in Washington, Connecticut, many of his books and papers were donated to Union Seminary. His life was characterized by strong emphases on moral stewardship and social responsibility, these sustained by a pursuit of learning.

• Many of Jackson's contributions to scholarship are obscured due to his willingness to let them appear in works bearing someone else's name. Several encyclopedias, dictionaries, and bibliographies contain his entries without giving him due credit. Titles for which he was exclusively responsible include *Concise Dictionary of Religious Knowledge Bibliographical, Doctrinal, Historical, and Practical* (1889); *Bibliography of Foreign Missions* (1891); *Biographical Sketches of the Principal Christian Writers from the Sixth to the Twelfth Centuries, with an Analysis of Their Writings* (1892); *Huldreich*

Zwingli, the Reformer of German Switzerland (1901); *Selected Works of Huldreich Zwingli* (1901); and *The Latin Works and the Correspondence of Huldreich Zwingli Together with Selections from His German Works* (1912). There is no biography of Jackson, only sketches in memorial addresses. A short obituary is in the *New York Times*, 4 Aug. 1912.

HENRY WARNER BOWDEN

JACKSON, Sheldon (18 May 1834–2 May 1909), Presbyterian missionary, was born at Minaville, New York, the son of Samuel Clinton Jackson, a prosperous farmer, and Delia Sheldon. He graduated from Union College in Schenectady, New York, in 1855, and Princeton Theological Seminary in 1858. He was ordained by the presbytery of Albany on 5 May 1858, and a few days later married Mary Voorhees; they had five children, two of whom survived to maturity. He had applied to the Presbyterian Board of Foreign Missions for an overseas assignment, but because of concerns about his health he was appointed instead to teach at Spencer Academy, a school for Choctaw boys in Indian Territory, where he arrived in October 1858. He contracted malaria and departed the following spring, accepting a commission from the Board of Domestic Missions to "the Churches of La Crescent, Hokah, and vicinity Minnesota." Churches were not yet organized there, but Jackson, taking seriously his assignment to the "vicinity," not only established a church at La Crescent but traveled throughout the entire border region of Minnesota and Wisconsin. In 1863 he moved to nearby Rochester, Minnesota, having served two months as a chaplain with the Union army. During the 1860s he helped organize twenty-seven area churches, and recruited ministers and financial support for most of them.

In 1869 three presbyteries in the synod of Iowa invited Jackson, at his urging, to serve as a "district missionary" to evangelize the West. With the passage of the Homestead Act seven years earlier, and the construction of the transcontinental railroad, they wanted to assure that churches would follow the flood of settlers moving across the Missouri River. Jackson accepted the assignment, although no provision was made for salary and expenses, to serve as "superintendent of missions for Western Iowa, Nebraska, Dakota, Idaho, Montana, Wyoming, and Utah or as far as our jurisdiction extends" (Stewart, p. 101). In his first year alone he traveled 29,000 miles and organized twenty-two churches. The Board of Home Missions later provided its authorization and some financial support and added missions among Indians, especially in Arizona, to his assignment. In 1872 he staffed the *Rocky Mountain Presbyterian*, sent free to Presbyterian ministers, to promote the cause of domestic missions. He pushed for the development of a Women's Executive Committee of Home Missions, established in 1878 (later the Women's Board of Home Missions), especially to support mission teachers and schools. In general, he spent a dozen years promoting Presbyterian home missions west of the Missouri River.

In 1882 Jackson moved to New York City as editor and business manager of the *Presbyterian Home Missionary*, successor of the *Rocky Mountain Presbyterian*. Yet he continued to travel and raise money for mission projects, and his new focus was Alaska. He first visited there in 1877, ten years after the United States purchased Alaska from Russia, and returned repeatedly. He lobbied churches, the federal government, and the general public to help establish churches, schools, and civil government for the "district," which had not yet attained status as a territory and for which Congress had not yet made provisions for governmental structures. He helped establish a mission school there on his first Alaskan trip in 1877 (under the direction of Amanda McFarland), was present at the organization of the first Alaskan Presbyterian church in 1879 (Fort Wrangell), and recruited missionaries and funds. The U.S. Commissioner of Education's report for 1883 recognized Jackson's efforts, indicating that Jackson had presented approximately 900 addresses promoting Alaska and its welfare.

In 1883 Alaskan Presbyterian missionaries asked the Home Mission board to name Jackson as superintendent of missions in Alaska. The board declined, but a year later it appointed him as missionary to Sitka, the seat of federal authority in Alaska. John Eaton, the commissioner of education who had praised Jackson, appointed him general agent of education in Alaska in 1885; he served as Alaska's superintendent of public instruction until his retirement. He also continued to receive some financial support from the Presbyterians as a missionary, which eventually became a matter of controversy. Under his supervision, Alaskan government schools often were established in relationship with church missions, of various denominations, in what was seen as an efficient way to fill great needs with limited funds.

Jackson is also known for his introduction of reindeer into Alaska. Concerned about Eskimo (or Inuit) starvation because of their declining traditional food sources, he tried to persuade the federal government to purchase reindeer from Siberia to establish domestic herds, to provide a stable supply of food and hides, and to allow native people to remain on their traditional lands. When the government resisted, he raised private funds to import the first small numbers in 1891 and 1892. Federal assistance began in 1893, and over 1,200 reindeer were eventually imported before Siberia halted further purchases in 1902. Between 1891 and 1900 Jackson made thirty-three trips to Siberia for this purpose. In 1897 he also assisted in transplanting a small colony of Laplanders and their reindeer to Alaska. Forty years after their first arrival, Alaskan herds included more than half a million reindeer, about 70 percent native owned.

In the midst of these efforts for Alaskan schools, missions, and reindeer, Jackson also helped establish the Alaskan Society of Natural History and Ethnology at Sitka (1887), edited the *North Star* (1887–1897), and was elected moderator of the Presbyterian General Assembly, the national church's highest honor (1897). In 1896 he participated in the founding of Westminster College in Salt Lake City, Utah, in the region of his former mission work.

Jackson was a tireless missionary entrepreneur whose tendency to forge ahead even without official approval led at times to friction with mission agencies and government officials. He became embroiled in Alaskan politics, where his dynamism, personal influence, and sometimes unyielding positions created strong supporters and detractors, around issues such as the allocation of educational resources among natives and whites, local autonomy and federal control, and competing visions of Alaska's future.

Jackson lived in Washington, D.C., in his final years, continuing to oversee Alaska's educational affairs from the nation's capital until ill health forced his retirement in 1907. In 1909 he traveled to North Carolina to make yet another address about Alaska, after which he was hospitalized in Asheville for an operation from which he did not recover.

• Manuscript materials relating to Jackson can be found in the Presbyterian Historical Society, Philadelphia, and in Speer Library, Princeton Theological Seminary. In addition to Jackson's articles in the periodical he edited, the *Rocky Mountain Presbyterian*, Jackson also published *Alaska, and Missions on the North Pacific Coast* (1880), *The Presbyterian Church in Alaska, an Official Sketch of Its Rise and Progress, 1877–1884* (1886), and many annual reports for the government on Alaskan education and on the introduction of reindeer. The most frequently cited biography of Jackson was written by his friend, Robert Laird Stewart, whose account was published the year before Jackson's death, *Sheldon Jackson* (1908). Other biographies include John Thomson Faris, *The Alaskan Pathfinder* (1926); Winifred Hulbert, *The Bishop of All Beyond* (1948); J. Arthur Lazell, *Alaskan Apostle: The Life Story of Sheldon Jackson* (1960); and Norman J. Bender, *Winning the West for Christ: Sheldon Jackson and Presbyterianism on the Rocky Mountain Frontier, 1869–1880* (1996). See also Alvin K. Bailey, "Sheldon Jackson, Planter of Churches," *Journal of the Presbyterian Historical Society* 26, no. 3 (Sept. 1948): 129–48, 26, no. 4 (Dec. 1948): 193–214, and 27, no. 1 (Mar. 1949): 21–40; Theodore C. Hinckley, "Sheldon Jackson, Presbyterian Lobbyist," *Journal of Presbyterian History* 40, no. 1 (Mar. 1962): 3–23; and Hermann N. Morse, "Sheldon Jackson (1834–1909): Christ's Fool and Seward's Folly," in *Sons of the Prophets: Leaders in Protestantism from Princeton Seminary*, ed. Hugh Kerr (1963).

BRUCE DAVID FORBES

JACKSON, Shirley (14 Dec. 1916–8 Aug. 1965), author, was born Shirley Hardie Jackson in San Francisco, California, the daughter of Leslie Hardie Jackson, a lithograph company executive, and Geraldine Bugbee. When she was in high school, the family moved to Rochester, New York. From 1934 to 1936 she attended the University of Rochester, but she withdrew with low grades and spent a year at home, writing daily. In 1937 she enrolled at Syracuse University. A collection from her creative writing class included Jackson's first publication, "Janice," a story about a student who has attempted to commit suicide. With Stanley Edgar Hyman, she founded and edited the *Spectre*, an unconventional campus magazine that published her poetry and fiction as well as editorials written with Hyman that championed civil rights and freedom of the press.

After graduating from Syracuse University with a bachelor's degree in English in 1940, Jackson moved to New York and married Hyman. The next year, the *New Republic* printed the humorous story "My Life with R. H. Macy," her earliest work in a major periodical. "After You, My Dear Alphonse" (1943), an implicit critique of racism, was Jackson's first story for the *New Yorker*. When Hyman joined the faculty of Bennington College in 1945, they moved to Vermont with their son, the first of four children. Jackson wrote *The Road through the Wall* (1948), whose California setting is unusual for her fiction. Like Nathanael West's *The Day of the Locust* (1939), Jackson's novel exposes the selfishness and loneliness of a group of West Coast Americans in the decade before World War II. Both authors develop a theme of lost innocence that culminates in acts of violence. Experimental in narrative technique, *The Road through the Wall* shifts rapidly from one Pepper Street household to another, centering on the children. The increasing tension, the sense of ceremony in the neighborhood games, and especially a girl's death by stoning have parallels in "The Lottery," the contemporaneous story that established Jackson's fame.

First published in the 26 June 1948 *New Yorker*, "The Lottery" dispassionately describes an annual drawing whose winner becomes the village scapegoat. The townspeople's genial conversation about tractors and taxes as they gather for the lottery on a beautiful June day is incongruous with their communal attack against the reluctant victim at the end of the story: "'It isn't fair, it isn't right,' Mrs. Hutchinson screamed, and then they were upon her." Jackson told a Syracuse University instructor that the story originated in his folklore class. An influence closer to home was Hyman, whose national reputation as a literary critic owed much to his study of myth and ritual. Jackson quotes from the letters of shocked readers in "Biography of a Story," a speech on "The Lottery" that Hyman published after her death in *Come Along with Me: Part of a Novel, Sixteen Stories, and Three Lectures* (1968). Although she was reluctant to interpret the tale allegorically, Hyman said she was "always proud that the Union of South Africa banned 'The Lottery,' and she felt that *they* at least understood the story."

In 1949 Jackson collected several of her early stories in a volume entitled *The Lottery or, the Adventures of James Harris*. In this context the lottery becomes a symbol of vulnerability, especially woman's vulnerability. Imposing a loose unity on the twenty-five stories, Jackson revised several of her previously published works to emphasize the mythic "daemon lover" motif of a mysteriously threatening man, epitomized by the legendary James Harris of her subtitle. In the story "The Daemon Lover," the naive female protagonist is deserted by Jamie Harris on the morning they were to marry, and in "The Tooth" a dowdy housewife

loses her identity, along with her painful tooth, and runs off with an enigmatic "Jim." Most stories in the *Lottery* collection convey a sense of menace, though not always in the form of a seductive male. Even the kindergartner's mother in "Charles," one of the few stories with a consistently light tone, follows a pattern of initial uneasiness, rising anxiety, and final unpleasant epiphany.

Jackson's third book, *Hangsaman* (1951), is a female bildungsroman, or a novel about the growth and development of a young character. Published in the same year as J. D. Salinger's *The Catcher in the Rye*, *Hangsaman* too portrays a sensitive teenager who becomes disillusioned with adult society. Despite her humorous satire of academia, however, Jackson's mood is bleaker than Salinger's, and Natalie Waite—her seventeen-year-old protagonist—experiences traumas that may include rape and a lesbian relationship. The exact nature of Natalie's encounters with an older man at a cocktail party and with Tony, a fellow student at her women's college, is obscured by a limited, and sometimes surreal, third-person point of view. Unexpectedly, Natalie emerges from a confusing late-night episode in a remote wooded area with a new sense of independence. Whether the woods is meant to symbolize a moral wilderness or a path to self-discovery, in leaving the manipulative Tony under the dark trees and in moving toward the lighted streets of town, Natalie turns her back on her childhood. "As she had never been before, she was now alone, and grown-up, and powerful, and not at all afraid," the novel concludes.

In contrast to Jackson's first three books, the semiautobiographical *Life among the Savages* (1953) is a domestic comedy. Like its sequel, *Raising Demons* (1957), this family chronicle incorporates into a continuous narrative many stories about her children that Jackson had published in *Good Housekeeping, Ladies' Home Journal*, and other magazines. Although some critics have detected notes of resentment in the voice of the unnamed housewife-narrator (ostensibly Jackson herself), James Egan argues that both memoirs record the "vision of a nurturing domestic world." Babysitters and baseball games, pajama parties and broken furnaces present sudden challenges, but, like the television heroines of the 1950s situation comedies, the cheerful mother survives each episode with no scars on her psyche.

Most of the protagonists in Jackson's novels, though, are seriously scarred. Twenty-three year old Elizabeth Richmond of *The Bird's Nest* (1954) suffers a four-way personality split that seems to have sources in construction problems at the museum where she works, the death of her mother several years earlier, and, some time before that, a possible sexual assault by her widowed mother's boyfriend. Jackson researched schizophrenia extensively and based the novel on a real case history. An unusual aspect of the narrative is Jackson's alternation of third-person viewpoint with first-person chapters related by the psychiatrist Dr. Victor Wright, a Thackeray fan who appends occasional footnotes to his rambling summary of Elizabeth's case. *The Bird's Nest* ends happily when the progressively more violent split is resolved after two years of treatment.

The plots of the novels that followed—*The Sundial* (1958), *The Haunting of Hill House* (1959), and *We Have Always Lived in the Castle* (1962)—reach grimmer conclusions. Prominent in all three are such Gothic features as remote country mansions and hints of the supernatural or, at least, the bizarre. *The Sundial* is an apocalyptic novel whose Chaucerian and Elizabethan allusions contribute to the emphasis on mortality imaged in the sundial of the title. With a blackly humorous blend of skepticism, dread, and hope, several members and friends of the unpleasant Halloran family board up the house in the closing pages to await the end of this world and the start of a new one. Several characters also gather in *The Haunting of Hill House*, but their aim is to study psychic phenomena under the direction of Dr. John Montague, an anthropologist who reads himself to sleep with the fiction of Samuel Richardson. When the desperately unhappy Eleanor Vance seems to awaken evil forces in the old building, the rest of the group forces her to leave. She drives her car straight into a tree by the driveway, but it is unclear whether she commits suicide or whether "Hill House itself, not sane" has murdered her. This most eerie of Jackson's works was effectively adapted for film as *The Haunting* (1963), produced by Robert Wise.

Critics have described Mary Katherine Blackwood, the eighteen-year-old narrator of the bestselling *We Have Always Lived in the Castle*, as a "murderous psychotic" because she poisoned most of her family at dinner when she was twelve. Yet the dead Blackwoods were cruel, and Merricat's older sister Constance protectively destroyed the incriminating evidence. Jackson's last novel, like all its predecessors, focuses on extreme psychological states. Merricat's drastic step almost makes sense in a world where her greedy cousin Charles tries to marry Constance for the family fortune and the fire department maliciously lets the sisters' house burn. In some of her short stories too, Jackson implies that a woman may need to break the law to secure her freedom and preserve her identity. Still, the narrator's final line—"'Oh, Constance,' I said, 'we are so happy'"—is spoken in a ruined home whose doors are barricaded against the kind townspeople as well as the heartless ones.

When Jackson died in North Bennington, Vermont, of a heart attack, she had begun a seventh novel, *Come Along with Me*, a comic first-person narrative about a middle-aged widow with a talent for séances. Obituaries stressed Jackson's Gothic fiction and the much-anthologized "The Lottery," but Hyman said her work was "very little understood." In the preface to his *Magic of Shirley Jackson* collection (1966), he added that her "fierce visions" are "a sensitive and faithful anatomy of our times, fitting symbols for our distressing world of the concentration camp and the Bomb." Hyman also underscored the craftsmanship and the variety of Jackson's writing. Her favorite authors included Richardson, Fanny Burney, Jane Austen, Katherine Anne Porter, and Elizabeth Bowen, but she has most frequently been compared with Edgar Allan Poe, Kafka, and H. P. Lovecraft. Although several of her stories were chosen for the annual series *Best American Short Stories* and she won two Edgar Allan Poe Awards, Hyman believed she was underrated and predicted that "the future will find her powerful visions of suffering and inhumanity increasingly significant and meaningful."

• The Shirley Jackson Papers at the Library of Congress contain forty-one boxes of manuscripts, correspondence, early diaries, scrapbooks, and other material, including about fifty early unpublished stories. The Shirley Jackson file at the George Arents Research Library, Syracuse University, includes newspaper clippings, a few short story manuscripts, and material from her college years; also available at the Arents Research Library are the *Spectre* and the *Syracusan*, literary magazines in which some of her earliest stories were published. A partial list of works by Jackson not mentioned in the text includes the following children's books: *The Witchcraft of Salem Village* (1956), *The Bad Children: A Musical in One Act for Bad Children* (1959), *9 Magic Wishes* (1963), and *Famous Sally* (1966). For primary bibliographies, see Robert S. Phillips, "Shirley Jackson: A Checklist," *Papers of the Bibliographical Society of America* 56, no. 1 (1962): 110–13, and "Shirley Jackson: A Chronology and a Supplementary Checklist," *Papers of the Bibliographical Society of America* 60, no. 2 (1966): 203–13. The only book-length biography is Judy Oppenheimer, *Private Demons: The Life of Shirley Jackson* (1988). For a comprehensive study of Jackson's works, see Lenemaja Friedman, *Shirley Jackson* (1975). The collected and uncollected short stories are the focus of Joan Wylie Hall, *Shirley Jackson: A Study of the Short Fiction* (1993). James Egan discusses the familial motif of several stories and books in "Sanctuary: Shirley Jackson's Domestic and Fantastic Parables," *Studies in Weird Fiction* 6 (1989): 15–24. Representative studies of "The Lottery" are Helen E. Nebeker, "'The Lottery': Symbolic Tour de Force," *American Literature* 46 (1974): 100–107, and Gayle Whittier, "'The Lottery' as Misogynist Parable," *Women's Studies* 18 (1991): 353–66. Essays on specific novels include Lynette Carpenter, "The Establishment and Preservation of Female Power in Shirley Jackson's *We Have Always Lived in the Castle*," *Frontiers* 8 (1984): 32–38, and Tricia Lootens, "'Whose Hand Was I Holding?': Familial and Sexual Politics in Shirley Jackson's *The Haunting of Hill House*," in *Haunting the House of Fiction: Feminist Perspectives on Ghost Stories by American Women*, ed. Lynette Carpenter and Wendy K. Kolmar (1991). Obituaries are in the *New York Times* and the New York *Herald Tribune*, both 10 Aug. 1965.

JOAN WYLIE HALL

JACKSON, Shoeless Joe (16 July 1887 or 1888–5 Dec. 1951), baseball player, was born Joseph Jefferson Jackson in Dickens County, South Carolina, the son of George Jackson and Martha (maiden name unknown). During Jackson's early childhood, the family moved from rural Dickens County to Greenville, the location of newly opened cotton mills. While still a child, Jackson went to work in the mills and missed having even a rudimentary education. In his youth, Jackson excelled as a player on mill baseball teams. A left-handed batter, strong, sinewy, 6'1", young Jackson signed to play professionally as an outfielder for Greenville of the Carolina Association in 1908. The following year he played for Savannah in the South Atlantic League and in 1910 for New Orleans in the Southern League. He led each league in batting average. After being bothered once by sore feet, he played in his socks, earning the nickname "Shoeless Joe." The sobriquet stuck, ridiculing Jackson's country mannerisms. On 19 July 1908 he married his Greenville sweetheart, Kathryn Wynn. She gradually helped him overcome his awkwardness and advised him on business affairs.

Jackson's play interested Connie Mack, manager of the Philadelphia Athletics. He played Jackson briefly with the Athletics late in the 1908 and 1909 seasons. Jackson found the transition to major league baseball difficult. All franchises were located in the North, and eight or nine of every ten players were from outside the South. Jackson's teammates aimed jokes and pranks at him, reminding him of his poor white origins. Mack offered to hire a tutor to overcome Jackson's illiteracy, but Jackson was too embarrassed to accept. Initially reluctant to venture north, he left the Athletics three times, preferring to play in Savannah or New Orleans. In contrast to his play in the southern cities, he did poorly in Philadelphia. Even the patient Mack grew irritated at his departures, dispatching him to Cleveland for a journeyman player.

On his third try as a major leaguer late in the 1910 season, a more mature Jackson found himself. He became acclimated to Cleveland, and he and his wife began to enjoy northern urban life. He handled relations with his teammates better than he had in Philadelphia. Rival players, fans, and sportswriters continued to dwell on the "Shoeless Joe" caricature, reminding him of his Philadelphia defections, and impugning his courage, but his batting feats belied the criticism. In 1911 he batted .408, one of only eight players in this century to date to hit over .400. In other years he three times led the league in triples, twice in total bases, and once each in hits, doubles, and slugging average. His lifetime batting average of .356 in a truncated career trails only Ty Cobb and Rogers Hornsby. Further, Jackson was a good defensive outfielder with a strong throwing arm. These accomplishments earned him a large following in Cleveland and later in Chicago. His salary, business investments, and postseason vaudeville appearances provided a handsome income. To rise to be a much admired sports star was an outstanding achievement for the one-time South Carolina mill hand.

In August 1915 the financially squeezed Indians traded Jackson to the Chicago White Sox for three players and $15,000. In Chicago he continued to star, helping the White Sox win pennants in 1917 and 1919. The clubhouse environment, however, revived his uneasiness. Owner Charles A. Comiskey was extremely parsimonious. The team was faction-ridden. In 1918, Jackson's public standing tumbled. When he became eligible for the military draft, his response was to accept a draft-exempt job at a shipbuilding factory where he mostly played company baseball. This act led many to criticize him; Comiskey publicly denounced him for his lack of patriotism.

In the first postwar season, the White Sox won the pennant, but Jackson became involved with several players in his team's deliberate loss of the World Series. During the season he had again demonstrated his remarkable batting skill, causing fans to forget his 1918 exemption and to acclaim him anew. But beneath the surface, there was team unrest. Most White Sox players were seriously underpaid, and their protests to the owner went unheeded. Jackson's 1919 salary amounted to $6,000, while Ty Cobb, Walter Johnson, and the new star Babe Ruth made, respectively, $20,000, $15,000, and $10,000. Other top players also made much more. The strain between the team's factions grew. One group gravitated around second baseman Eddie Collins, a well-educated northerner who was paid the club's only high salary. The other faction comprised at least two knockabout players, who were underpaid and undereducated, and their friends. Incompatible with the first group, Jackson associated with the second. Chick Gandil, one of the players in the socially marginal faction, initiated the contacts with professional gamblers that culminated in the White Sox World Series loss to the Cincinnati Reds. Gandil induced six or seven other players, including Jackson, to participate in the scheme. No one from the Collins group was approached.

The scandal broke near the close of the 1920 season when several players admitted their involvement. When Jackson emerged from the Chicago courthouse after testifying, several newspapers reported that a crowd of boys said, "It isn't true, is it, Joe?" Jackson later denied any such incident, but the phrase, rendered as "Say it ain't so, Joe," became part of the nation's folklore.

Jackson's exact role in the scandal is difficult to assess because the evidence is incomplete and ambiguous. Easily influenced, he may have participated halfheartedly because of peer pressure. It is clear that he accepted $5,000, but only reluctantly. He had expected $20,000. His .375 batting average for the Series could not have been more commendable. However, doubts exist about his defensive performance. Immediately after the fourth game—not a year later, when speculation was easy and rife—a *Chicago Daily News* reporter criticized White Sox outfielders (not naming but clearly meaning Jackson and fellow participant Happy Felsch) for positioning themselves too shallow for Cincinnati hitters. Several possibly catchable long flies did fall safely for damaging hits. The same duo also made two or three costly wayward throws. As a result of the scandal, baseball's moguls installed the flamboyant Judge Kenesaw Mountain Landis in the powerful new office of commissioner. Landis made no distinctions about degrees of participation in the scheme, declaring all those involved as ineligible to play organized major or minor league professional baseball for the rest of their lives.

For years, Jackson and other Black Sox played ball sporadically for unsanctioned teams. At times, his income from this source exceeded his major league salary. Subsequently, he operated a dry-cleaning business with his wife, managed semiprofessional mill teams, and owned a liquor store. Occasional sympathetic newspaper reports suggested that the Jacksons verged on destitution, but they lived a comfortable, middle-class existence. Of course, they remained unhappy over Jackson's continued exclusion from organized baseball. In these years, he repeatedly denied that he had let up in his play during the fateful World Series. Several efforts were made to secure his reinstatement, but Judge Landis and his successors maintained the disqualification.

Jackson's rags-to-riches story and figurative return to his original condition has made him a legendary sports figure. Sympathy for his humble origins, admiration of his great natural ability, and dismay at his eventual exclusion from baseball's Hall of Fame caused many sports fans to identify with his name and career. This nearly mythic figure of Joe Jackson haunted two popular novels, Bernard Malamud's *The Natural* (1952) and W. P. Kinsella's *Shoeless Joe* (1982); Hollywood adaptations made these works into the movies *The Natural* (1984) and *Field of Dreams* (1989). Eliot Asinof's *Eight Men Out* (1963), the history of the Black Sox scandal, was the basis and namesake of John Sayles's film (1988). In the early 1990s Jackson's name surfaced again in connection with Pete Rose's ineligibility for the Hall of Fame. As an inadvertent popular antihero, Jackson has remained a memorable figure in American history.

• Jackson's testimony before the Chicago grand jury appears in the *Chicago Tribune* and other Chicago newspapers, 29 Sept. 1920, and the *New York Times*, 29 and 30 Sept. 1920. The official transcript was stolen and is not part of the court record. Testimony in the Black Sox trial for conspiracy appears in the *Chicago Tribune* and the *New York Times*, 8–31 July 1921. For day-by-day accounts of the games, see the Chicago and Cincinnati newspapers and the *New York Times* 2–10 Oct. 1919. Consult also Harold Seymour, *Baseball, The Golden Age* (1971), a valuable history of the sport in the early twentieth century, and Harvey Frommer, *Shoeless Joe and Ragtime Baseball* (1992). Marjorie A. Potivin, *Cotton Mill People of the Piedmont* (1927), conveys a sense of Jackson's social background. The definitive study of the 1919 World Series continues to be Asinof's, *Eight Men Out*. A first-rate, sympathetic biography of Jackson is Donald Gropman, *Say It Ain't So, Joe!* (1979).

LOWELL L. BLAISDELL

JACKSON, Stonewall. *See* Jackson, Thomas Jonathan.

JACKSON, Thomas Jonathan (21 Jan. 1824–10 May 1863), Confederate general, known as "Stonewall," was born in Clarksburg, Virginia (now West Virginia), the son of Jonathan Jackson, an attorney, and Julia Beckwith Neale. He had an empty, often unhappy childhood. Orphaned at the age of six, the lad spent ten formative years of his life with an uncle who owned lumber and grist mills in Lewis County south of Clarksburg. Although Jackson would later say, "Uncle was like a father to me," parental affection was sadly lacking in his life. He grew up shy, introverted, and awkward.

In 1842 Jackson gained admission to the U.S. Military Academy. His preparatory credentials were poor; his social graces were practically nonexistent. Jackson sought few friends and made few. His first two years at West Point were literally a day-and-night struggle with his studies. Extraordinary patience and perseverance won out in the end. From near the bottom of his class in 1842, Jackson improved his ranking to seventeenth of fifty-nine cadets in his 1846 graduating class, which included many future generals, including George B. McClellan and George E. Pickett.

Lieutenant Jackson went immediately into the Mexican War as a member of the First U.S. Artillery. Gallant conduct in the battles of Vera Cruz, Contreras, and Chapultepec earned him promotions to the rank of brevet major. No West Point classmate achieved as much in the Mexican conflict.

Following a year's duty with the army of occupation in Mexico, two years at Fort Hamilton, New York, and six months at Fort Meade, Florida, Jackson in 1851 resigned from the army to accept a professorship of optics and artillery tactics at the Virginia Military Institute in Lexington. He spent the next ten years—a fourth of his life—at VMI. There the Jackson of fact and legend emerged.

He was a large man for that time, standing just under six feet tall and weighing 170 pounds. He had dark blue eyes, a large pointed nose, a high forehead, brown hair, and thin lips that were usually pressed together. He walked with long, ungraceful strides, enormous feet adding to the spectacle, and he sat a horse as if leaning into a strong wind. His reticence made people uncomfortable.

Convinced that none of his organs functioned properly, Jackson became a regular patron of hydrotherapy and annually visited spas from Virginia to New England. While many of his ailments were probably imaginary, weak eyesight and poor hearing were real impairments.

Jackson was one of VMI's poorest instructors. He was too rigid, too inflexible in his presentations, too demanding of his students. Cadets quickly made him the butt of jokes and pranks. They referred to him as "Tom Fool," "Hell and Thunder," and "crazy as damnation."

The Lexington years, however, brought Jackson happiness in other ways. After but three months in the community, he ended a long search for a religious denomination by joining the Presbyterian church and becoming a devoted Calvinist. Religion became the overriding element of his being. Until the day he died, Jackson's life and labors belonged to God.

In 1853 he married Eleanor Junkin, the daughter of a Presbyterian minister and president of Washington College, who died in childbirth fourteen months later. In the summer of 1857 Jackson wed Mary Anna Morrison, also the daughter of a Presbyterian cleric. This union produced one surviving daughter.

The war clouds forming in 1860–1861 disturbed Jackson. He was a strong Unionist, but at the same time, he believed strongly in states' rights and the sovereignty of Virginia. When Old Dominion left the Union in mid-April, Jackson offered his sword to his beloved state. On 21 April he led a contingent of VMI cadets to Richmond to serve as drillmasters for the hundreds of recruits gathering daily at the capital.

Jackson swept into war with cool professionalism and grim determination. He viewed the Civil War as a test of America by the Almighty: bloodshed would be terrible, but victory would come to the more devout side. Hence, Jackson carried into the conflict the faith of the New Testament and the ferocity of the Old Testament.

Following his appointment as colonel of infantry in April 1861, Jackson took charge of volunteers and militia defending the important outpost of Harpers Ferry. On 17 June he was promoted to brigadier general and assigned to lead a brigade of five regiments from western Virginia. The most famous nickname in the Civil War came to the general and his men a month later in the first major battle of the war (First Manassas). Federals were driving southern troops back in confusion when South Carolina general Barnard E. Bee sought to rally his broken lines. Pointing to the top of a hill that was the key to the battlefield, Bee shouted something to the effect of: "Look, men! There stands Jackson like a stone wall! Rally behind the Virginians!" Jackson's subsequent attack helped turn the tide and bring victory to the Confederates as well as fame and the sobriquet of "Stonewall" to himself.

That autumn he received a major general's commission and command of the Shenandoah Valley district. From the beginning, Jackson's responsibilities in the Valley were twofold: to protect the Valley from Union invasion and to prevent Federal troops from leaving the area to reinforce the huge northern army then advancing on Richmond. Jackson had no more than 6,000 soldiers at the outset. Confronting him were 38,000 Federals. Nevertheless, Jackson went on the offensive.

Repulsed at Kernstown on 23 March 1862, he retreated southward up the Valley. On 8 May Jackson suddenly struck a second Federal force at McDowell and drove it off, thereby saving the key town of Staunton. Jackson then led his "foot cavalry" on a rapid sweep down the Valley. He picked up reinforcements en route, overpowered an enemy garrison at Front Royal on 23 May, and two days later sent the main Union army reeling from Winchester in defeat.

Three northern forces totaling 64,000 soldiers then converged on Jackson's little band of 17,000 men. Jackson avoided a trap near Winchester through hard marching and moved southward again through the Valley. On 8–9 June he turned and inflicted twin defeats on his pursuers at Cross Keys and Port Republic. These engagements ended the 1862 Valley Campaign. Jackson had inflicted 7,000 casualties at one-third the cost to his own army; he had captured tons of badly needed weapons, ammunition, medical stores, and military supplies; he had completely disrupted Federal operations throughout Virginia; and he had brought optimism to a young nation then in despair. In June 1862, Stonewall Jackson was the most famous soldier in the Civil War.

Giving God the credit for his successes, Jackson then joined General Robert E. Lee for the Seven Days' counteroffensive east of Richmond. A combination of extreme fatigue, unfamiliarity with the terrain of the peninsula, and a lack of up-to-date communications from Lee were principal factors in Jackson's less than sterling performance in the Seven Days' campaign. Lee and Jackson, however, quickly developed into a nearly perfect military team. In mid-July Lee dispatched Jackson to northern Virginia to blunt an advance by General John Pope's Union forces. Jackson carried out his task on 9 August at Cedar Mountain. Once Lee arrived with the rest of the southern army, Jackson executed a secret, 56-mile flank march around Pope's army. The destruction of the Union supply base at Manassas Junction was the first inkling the Federals had of Jackson's whereabouts. Jackson held off Pope's assaults at the battle of Second Manassas until Lee arrived with the rest of the army and won a smashing victory.

Jackson was equally conspicuous in the September invasion of Maryland. His forces seized a large Union garrison at Harpers Ferry and then rushed northward to reunite with Lee's army. In the battle of Antietam on 17 September—the bloodiest day in American history—Jackson's men comprised Lee's left. For three hours they withstood heavy assaults, reinforcing Jackson's right to be called Stonewall.

Lee reorganized his Army of Northern Virginia in the autumn of 1862. To the surprise of no one, Jackson moved up to lieutenant general and took command of the newly formed Second Corps. He now led half of the South's principal army. Jackson demonstrated his ability for such high command in the one-sided Confederate triumph at the battle of Fredericksburg in December.

In the spring the Federal army struck southward again toward Richmond. On 2 May Jackson performed his most spectacular flanking movement by leading 28,000 soldiers on an all-day, twelve-mile march on wagon paths coursing through dense woodland known as the Wilderness. Late in the afternoon Jackson's massed columns delivered a devastating flank attack that knocked a third of the Union army back some two miles toward the crossroads called Chancellorsville. Jackson sought to press the attack even after sundown. In the confusion of darkness, battle, and dense woods, he was accidentally shot by his own men. The injuries necessitated the amputation of his left arm, which led to pneumonia, and he died on 10 May after murmuring, "Let us cross over the river and rest under the shade of the trees." He is buried in Stonewall Jackson Cemetery in Lexington, Virginia.

His death was the greatest personal loss suffered by the Confederacy. Combining hard marches, knowledge of terrain, unexpected tactics, concentrated attacks, relentless pursuit, and unalterable faith that God was with him, Jackson brought victory and hope to his people—as he bequeathed brilliant tactics to generations of future military commanders.

• Jackson papers abound in dozens of collections at depositories throughout the United States. The Jedediah Hotchkiss Collection at the Library of Congress and the Charles W. Dabney Papers at the University of North Carolina at Chapel Hill contain the largest accumulations of Jackson material. Jackson biographies seem to appear in approximately three-year cycles. However, the last scholarly studies of the general are Frank E. Vandiver, *Mighty Stonewall* (1957), and Lenoir Chambers, *Stonewall Jackson* (1959). For a study of Jackson's troops, see James I. Robertson, Jr., *The Stonewall Brigade* (1963).

JAMES I. ROBERTSON, JR.

JACKSON, William (9 Mar. 1759–18 Dec. 1828), revolutionary war officer and secretary of the Constitutional Convention, was born in Cumberland County, England, the son of an English father and a Scotch mother (their names have not been identified). Orphaned as a child and having come into some inheritance, Jackson was sent to Charleston, South Carolina, where he was placed under the guardianship of Owen Roberts, a prominent patriot leader. He studied "under private tuition." In 1775 he joined a Charleston militia regiment and in May 1776 received a commission as second lieutenant in the First Regiment of South Carolina infantry; the next year he was promoted to lieutenant.

Jackson served in General Robert Howe's 1778 expedition into Florida. Disease, shortage of supplies and munitions, and the arrival of enemy reinforcements caused the invasion to proceed no further than the capture of Fort Tonyn on the St. Mary's River. Jackson fought in the battles at Tulifinny Hill, 3 May 1779; Stono Ferry, 20 June 1779; and Savannah, 9 October 1779. He was promoted to captain on 9 October 1779 and subsequently became an aide-de-camp to General Benjamin Lincoln, commander of the Southern army. In his staff position Jackson carried the rank of major. At the British siege of Charleston, Jackson led a sortie against one of the enemy's positions. Made a prisoner of war upon the fall of the city, 12 May 1780, Jackson gained his freedom by exchange on 9 November 1780.

On 9 February Jackson set sail for Europe, as secretary to John Laurens, who was special envoy to France to assist Benjamin Franklin in allocating funds donated by the French government for the American cause. Laurens was to purchase military stores and to bring the balance in specie to the United States. Laurens stayed a short while and left Jackson behind to complete the purchasing and shipping arrangements. Jackson bought supplies from an Amsterdam firm. He purchased goods in excess of funds available, drawing on moneys that Franklin had set aside to cover unpaid

bills. Jackson returned to the United States in February 1782.

With his friend and former commander Benjamin Lincoln at the head of the new Department of War, a reporting agency established by Congress to maintain liaison with the armies, Jackson accepted the post of assistant secretary of war at $1,250 a year. Jackson helped to quiet a mutiny of Pennsylvania troops from Lancaster who marched on Congress in June 1783. Congress took the added precaution of fleeing to Princeton, New Jersey. Jackson resigned from the war office in October 1783 to act as a business agent for Robert Morris in England.

Returning from England in 1784, Jackson studied law with William Lewis in Philadelphia. On 9 June 1788 he was admitted to the Pennsylvania bar to practice before the inferior courts but, according to law, had to wait out a two-year probationary period before being admitted to practice before the state's supreme court.

Nominated by Alexander Hamilton, Jackson was elected by the Constitutional Convention on 25 May 1787 as its secretary. For four months' work he was paid $866.60. Jackson had the honor of delivering the U.S. Constitution to Congress, which was then sitting in New York City. Adhering to the secrecy pledge of the convention, Jackson destroyed the records of the proceedings, except for a journal, a few loose sheets, and a tally of the yeas and nays. Jackson's journal and notations of the votes have been combined with written observations of other delegates, chiefly James Madison, to form a published "record" of the Constitutional Convention.

In 1788 Jackson was an unpaid volunteer in the Second Troop of Philadelphia Light Horse. Financially burdened, he went job seeking in 1789. He was an unsuccessful candidate for secretary of the U.S. Senate. Jackson applied to President George Washington, on 19 April 1789, for a position, pointing out that he was financially strapped because of expenses incurred while an army officer, and business involvement was not "congenial to my temper." He was still in the probationary period before being permitted to practice law before Pennsylvania's highest court.

Washington appointed Jackson as one of his five secretaries, or "writing aides," at a salary of $600 a year. In public appearances and in the tours of New England and the South, 1789–1791, Jackson wore the full-dress uniform of a major. He resigned in 1791 to resume law practice and to become part of a business venture. In 1792 Jackson declined an offer from Washington to be adjutant general of the army.

Jackson served as agent for William Bingham for the sale of several million acres of land in Maine. Henry Knox and William Duer had originally formed a partnership for the land speculation, but Duer went bankrupt, and Knox brought in Bingham who provided the needed capital; Bingham would receive two-thirds of the profits, and Knox, one-third. Jackson represented the partnership in France and England, receiving a commission on sales. Jackson arrived in

France in December 1793. Although failing to interest the French Committee on Public Safety as a buyer, Jackson wrote a glowing report on the stability of the French government. He was more successful in selling land in England and returned to the United States about 1 June 1795.

Jackson married Elizabeth Willing, daughter of a prosperous merchant, in November 1795; Washington, Thomas Jefferson, and other dignitaries attended the church wedding in Philadelphia. The couple had one son and three daughters.

On 14 January 1796 the Senate approved Washington's nomination of Jackson as surveyor and inspector of the revenue in Philadelphia. Jackson lost this office in 1801 when President Jefferson conducted a clean sweep of Federalists. A reason given for Jackson's dismissal was that he had too politicized his office. On 22 February 1800 at Christ Church, Philadelphia, Jackson delivered an oration, "Eulogium on the Character of General Washington" (published 1800). His only other published speech was *An Oration to Commemorate the Independence of the United States* (1786). From 1801 to 1815 Jackson edited a daily Federalist newspaper in Philadelphia, the *Political and Commercial Register*.

Jackson succeeded Henry Knox as secretary general of the Society of the Cincinnati in 1799 and held that office until his death. In 1816 a group of surviving Continental army officers appointed Jackson as their lobbyist in Congress to secure a pension of half of their army pay for life. He did not succeed, but in 1826 Congress granted full pay for life to all officers who were still around to collect it. Jackson published *Documents Relative to the Claim of Surviving Officers of the Revolutionary Army for an Equitable Settlement of the Half Pay for Life* (1818). Jackson's last public act was to welcome General Lafayette to Philadelphia in 1824. Jackson died at his home in Philadelphia.

Raised in the grandee society of South Carolina, married into great wealth, a protégé of George Washington, and possessing great charm, Jackson easily consorted with the great figures of his time. John Adams's daughter remarked that "my papa calls him the Sir Charles Grandison of this age"—the perfect eighteenth-century gentleman, in reference to the title character of Samuel Richardson's 1753 novel. His own talents never fully measured, Jackson seemed most fitted for service behind the scenes of great persons and events.

• Major collections of Jackson's papers are the Henry Knox and the Benjamin Lincoln Papers at the Massachusetts Historical Society; the William Bingham Papers, Historical Society of Pennsylvania; the Papers of the Continental Congress, National Archives; and the George Washington Papers, Library of Congress. Published collections containing Jackson letters include *The Papers of George Washington, Presidential Series*, ed. W. W. Abbot, vols. 1–4 (1987–1993), and *The Papers of Robert Morris*, ed. E. James Ferguson, vols. 4–8 (1978–1995). Francis Wharton, ed., *The Revolutionary Diplomatic Correspondence of the United States*, vol. 4 (1889), has a few letters, and Frederick S. Allis, Jr., *William Bingham's Maine Lands, 1790–1820*, vol. 1 (1954), pp. 280–385, has letters and discussion of his activities in relation to Bingham. Jackson's journal of the Constitutional Convention is in Max Farrand, ed., *The Records of the Federal Convention of 1787*, vols. 1–3 (1911), vol. 4 (1937). The long letter on the conditions in revolutionary France to Thomas Pinckney, Apr. 1794, is in *American Historical Review* 9 (1903–1904): 525–32. Douglas S. Freeman, *George Washington*, vol. 6 (1954), notes Jackson's role as Washington's secretary, and Harry M. Ward, *The Department of War, 1781–1795* (1962), comments on the war office experience. Charles W. Littell, "Major William Jackson, Secretary of the Federal Convention," *Pennsylvania Magazine of History and Biography* 2 (1878): 353–69, has details of his early life, derived from a letter from his eldest daughter, Ann Willing Jackson. A great amount of information on Jackson is found in Robert C. Alberts, *The Golden Voyage: The Life and Times of William Bingham, 1752–1804* (1969). An obituary is in the *United States Gazette*, 23 Dec. 1828.

HARRY M. WARD

JACKSON, William Alexander (25 July 1905–18 Oct. 1964), librarian and bibliographer, was born in Bellows Falls, Vermont, the son of Charles Wilfred Jackson, a Baptist clergyman, and Alice Mary Fleming. The family moved to Canada and then to South Pasadena, California, where Jackson had his schooling, graduating from the local high school in 1922. At an early age, inspired by writings of the bibliophile A. Edward Newton, and stimulated by proximity to the newly founded (1919) Huntington Library (its first librarian, George Watson Cole, was a neighbor), Jackson determined to devote his life to books. He chose to attend Williams College because it had just received from Alfred Clark Chapin a collection of 12,000 volumes, mainly of English literature. While still a student, Jackson obtained a job in the library and so fully demonstrated his capacities to carry out the detailed bibliographical plan of his own devising that Chapin paid him to produce a descriptive catalog of the collection. Although Jackson essentially completed Chapin's catalog by early 1930, Chapin decided that he could not afford to publish it.

Even when an undergraduate Jackson visited the major collections of early books in this country to make bibliographical comparisons between the copies of corresponding titles in their collections. He spent the summer of 1926 in the United Kingdom, where he made the acquaintance of the major figures of the rare book world. During that summer appeared A. W. Pollard and G. R. Redgrave's *Short-Title Catalogue of Books Printed in England, Scotland, & Ireland and of English Books Printed Abroad 1475–1640* (STC). Jackson immediately interleaved a copy and began to annotate it. In addition to his bibliographical work, Jackson strove, as he wrote to his parents in May or June of 1926, "to become familiar with the literatures of all nations and all times."

In 1929 Jackson married Dorothy Judd, with whom he had one son. The following year Jackson went to New York, where he undertook a descriptive catalog for Carl H. Pforzheimer, Sr., resulting in the three-volume *Carl H. Pforzheimer Library: English Litera-ture, 1475–1900*, which appeared in 1940. He further broadened his background while there by becoming a member of the country's premier collecting club, the Grolier Club, and in 1935 he delivered his first paper to the club.

Jackson was thus extraordinarily well qualified to be in charge of the Treasure Room in Harvard's Widener Library and to be professor of bibliography, a position he accepted in 1938, the year he received his A.M. from Williams College. His accomplishments were correspondingly great. In 1942 the Houghton Library opened, and it set a new standard for the physical housing of books and manuscripts. Jackson brought together an exceptionally able and dedicated staff, which included Philip Hofer, Jackson's virtual part-ner, albeit in a junior role; Hofer established the De-partment of Printing and Graphic Arts in the Hough-ton Library and went on to become perhaps the greatest benefactor in the history of the Harvard Li-brary.

Jackson's major accomplishment was in collecting. The earlier library policy of avoiding manuscripts was overturned, and Jackson brought into Houghton the personal papers—and sometimes the libraries—of im-portant literary figures, thus helping to establish a pat-tern that other libraries emulated. Although Jackson emphasized New England authors in collecting manu-script materials, in printed books he ranged through-out western culture. As he wrote in his annual report for 1955–1956, "If the book is intrinsically important, however unusual its nature, it is from the point of view of this library a desirable book." His accomplishment benefited Harvard most directly, but the benefits went far beyond, for, as Jackson frequently emphasized, many of the books were the only copies known and many more the only ones recorded in this country. Harvard awarded Jackson the honorary L.H.D. in 1962; the citation termed him Harvard's "grand ac-quisitor."

Despite involvement in all aspects of the Houghton Library, Jackson continued his work on Pollard and Redgrave's STC, the most fundamental project that a bibliographer in the Anglo-American world could un-dertake. Most days, including Saturdays and Sundays, he did some work on it, and it served as the basis for the revised STC that was published in three volumes from 1976 to 1991. Jackson meanwhile produced a steady stream of published works; a bibliography of his own works contains 126 items.

A member of the Massachusetts Historical Society, the American Antiquarian Society, and the American Academy of Arts and Sciences, Jackson also served as president of the Bibliographical Society of America. Jackson belonged to the Athenaeum in London, the Century Association and Grolier Club in New York, the Club of Odd Volumes and the Tavern Club in Bos-ton, and the Walpole Society, and he was a fellow of the Society of Antiquaries. In 1964 the Roxburghe Club, the senior book collectors' club of the English-speaking world, elected him to membership. Jackson

was awarded the Litt.D. from Oxford in 1964. The Stationers' Company of London honored Jackson with its medal in 1958, and the Bibliographical Society, London, awarded him posthumously its gold medal (1965). He died in Cambridge, Massachusetts.

The honors bestowed on Jackson reflect the wide-spread recognition of his learning, which was based fundamentally on a critical and sophisticated examina-tion of copy after copy of books. Other scholars were more theoretical or emphasized more fully the rela-tionship of bibliography to textual studies, but no one had a wider knowledge of the early books of the Eng-lish-speaking world. And he acquired this knowledge directing a library and enriching significantly the re-sources available to American scholars. Jackson's suc-cess as a librarian helped to make the collecting of rare books and manuscripts an integral part of libraries in higher education, not simply an activity of independ-ent research libraries.

• Jackson's office files are in the Houghton Library. William H. Bond's introduction to *Records of a Bibliographer* (1967) is a 29-page biographical sketch of Jackson by a close colleague who had access to papers in the possession of the family; it vividly recreates the personality of the man and the spirit of the Houghton Library during Jackson's era. A bibliography of Jackson's published writings follows Bond's essay. Wil-liam Bentinck-Smith, "Prince of the Eye: Philip Hofer and the Harvard Library," *Harvard Library Bulletin* 22 (1984): 317–47, recounts the circumstances behind what is now the Houghton Library. For a detailed record of Jackson's collect-ing, see the series of annual reports titled *The Houghton Li-brary Report of Accessions* that began in 1942. Obituaries are in the *New York Times*, 19 Oct. 1964, and the *Harvard Uni-versity Gazette* 60, no. 25 (13 Mar. 1965).

KENNETH E. CARPENTER

JACKSON, William Henry (4 Apr. 1843–30 June 1942), photographer and painter, was born in Keeseville, New York, the son of George Hallock Jackson, a blacksmith and carriage builder, and Harriet Maria Allen, an amateur watercolorist. Having done most of his early schooling in Peru, Jackson's academic educa-tion ended when he was about sixteen. His mother taught him to draw and paint in watercolor. She pre-sented him with a copy of J. G. Chapman's American Drawing Book, of which Jackson wrote, "No single thing in my life, before or since, has ever been so im-portant to me." Jackson's father experimented with the daguerreotype photography process, and though he did not pursue photography himself, he kept the camera and gave parts of it to Jackson as a toy.

In 1858 Jackson began his career as a photographic retouching artist in C. C. Schoonmaker's studio in Troy, New York. In 1860 he went to work in Frank Mowrey's studio in Rutland, Vermont. It was here that Jackson gained a knowledge of photographic and business practices. He served in the Union army be-tween 1862 and 1863, part of the time acting as staff artist and map maker. Upon finishing his military service, he returned to Frank Mowrey's studio. He worked in several different Vermont studios until

1866, when he had a falling out with his fiancée and as a result moved out west. He opened his first photographic studio in 1867 in Omaha, Nebraska, with his younger brother Edward. In 1869 Jackson married Mary "Mollie" Greer. She died in childbirth in 1872.

Jackson's move west signaled the beginning of his career as a landscape photographer. The construction of the railroad, and the territory it crossed, were subjects of intense interest. Knowing this, Jackson lobbied the Union Pacific Railroad and received a commission to photograph 10,000 views along the train's route. To carry out the commission, Jackson and his assistant, Arundel C. Hull, received passes to ride on the Union Pacific Railroad. He soon discovered that his work in the studio was far different from photography on the move. The technical challenges that Jackson faced, outfitting a portable darkroom, for example, proved later to be invaluable field experience. These images, reviewed by Ferdinand Vandeveer Hayden, director of the U.S. Geological Survey of the territories, led to Hayden's invitation to Jackson to join the survey team. Jackson did so from 1870 to 1879.

The team's first season was spent on the Lodge Pole, Chugwater, Platte, and Sweetwater rivers. The 1871 season, which included Jackson and painter Thomas Moran, was spent surveying Utah, Nevada, and the territory that would later become Yellowstone. Jackson and Moran's friendship influenced their respective representations of the landscape. Jackson submitted his photographs for an exhibition show in the capitol building in Washington, D.C., and members of Congress were so affected by the stunning beauty of the landscape that they moved in March of 1872 to make Yellowstone the nation's first national park.

Jackson launched his second season with the survey group with an exploration of Yellowstone, Grand Tetons, and mining operations in the Montana territory. In 1973 Jackson married Emilie Painter, whom he had met on an Omaha reservation while her father was an Indian agent. The couple had three children. She died in 1918 and Jackson did not remarry. From 1873 through 1879 the survey focused on Colorado and the four corners region. Jackson discovered and photographed the Mountain of the Holy Cross (1873) and the Mancos Canyon Ruins (1874–1875, Mesa Verde, Colo.).

His photographs, a familiar sight in both scientific and mainstream journals, helped support his family with a weekly photograph for *Harper's Weekly* when he was away surveying. In 1875 Jackson developed an exhibition of the survey findings for the Centennial Exposition in Philadelphia. This exhibit included Jackson's photographs, artifacts, and a diorama of the Mancos Canyon Ruins. In 1877 an unsuccessful attempt to use a dry plate process resulted in a loss of the season's work.

In 1879 Jackson established a studio in Denver and returned to life as a commercial photographer. He focused on landscape images for popular reproduction and his partner, Albert E. Rinehardt, created portraits. Their partnership lasted until 1894. Despite Jackson's success in Denver, he continued to travel extensively, photographing the routes of the Santa Fe and B. & O. Railroads (1892); the World's Colombian Exposition in Chicago (1893), on a commission by Daniel Burnham; and the World's Transportation Company (1894–1896). Jackson moved to Detroit in 1898 to join the Detroit Photographic Company, later the Detroit Publishing Company, a firm specializing in national and international views. He remained with the firm until 1924, when it went bankrupt.

Jackson spent the years between 1924 and the end of his life painting. He was commissioned by the Oregon Trail Memorial Association in New York to make watercolors and oils based on events and people along the trail. In addition, in 1936 Jackson was hired by the Works Progress Administration to paint murals based on the survey. In 1937 he obtained a position painting for the National Park Service. Jackson died in New York and was buried in Arlington National Cemetery.

During his prolific and productive career, Jackson photographed numerous views of the West between Nebraska and California, from cliff dwellings to industrial urban centers. His photographs embodied the transformation of the West and educated the East with the greater vision of the United States as a country. His significance lay in his ability to demonstrate through a camera the astounding beauty of an area of the country barely discovered.

• Various collections of Jackson's photographs are in the Library of Congress, the Smithsonian Institution, the National Archives, the Colorado State Historical Society, the International Museum of Photography, the National Park Service, and the United States Geological Service. Jackson was involved in two publications about his life, his autobiography, *Time Exposure* (1940), and a second book written with Howard R. Driggs, editor of the Pioneer Life Series for boys, called *The Pioneer Photographer* (1934). Jackson's diaries covering 1866–1874 were published in 1959 as *The Diaries of William Henry Jackson, Frontier Photographer*, ed. LeRoy R. Hafen and Ann W. Hafen (volume 10 in the Far West and the Rockies Historical Series). Jackson's landscape photography is the subject of Peter B. Hale's monograph, *William Henry Jackson and the Transformation of the American Landscape* (1988); and his paintings are presented with a foreword by his son, Clarence Seymour Jackson, in *The Veritable Art of William Henry Jackson* (1959). Jackson's photography is discussed in the context of the American West in Weston Naef and James Wood, *Era of Exploration: The Rise Of Landscape Photography in the American West, 1860–1885* (1975).

KATHLEEN BUTLER

JACKSON, William Hicks (1 Oct. 1835–30 Mar. 1903), army officer and horse breeder, was born in Paris, Tennessee, the son of Alexander Jackson, a doctor, and Mary W. Hurt. William grew up in Jackson, Tennessee, to which his parents had moved while he was still young, and went on to attend West Tennessee College. Prior to graduation there, however, he accepted an appointment to the U.S. Military Academy at West Point, entering in 1852 and graduating four years later. Commissioned a second lieutenant, Jackson was stationed with a regiment of mounted rifles in Texas, and served in operations against the American Indians in New Mexico.

On 16 May 1861 Jackson resigned his commission and subsequently entered the service of the Confederacy as captain of Company D, First Tennessee Light Artillery. His first action came 7 November 1861 at the battle of Belmont, Missouri. Stationed with his battery on the east bank of the Mississippi opposite Belmont as part of the Confederate main body, Jackson received orders to cross the river to reinforce the southern troops there, who were retreating before Federal forces led by Ulysses S. Grant. Unable to land his guns on the steep western bank of the river, Jackson went in person to the field, attached himself to the staff of General Gideon J. Pillow, and led an infantry charge that was part of the general Confederate counterattack. Severely wounded, he was out of action for some weeks.

Upon his recovery Jackson was promoted to colonel and in April 1862 given command of the First Tennessee Cavalry (the regiment's designation was later changed to the Seventh Tennessee Cavalry). On 20 December 1862 he was part of the calvary force under Major General Earl Van Dorn that raided and destroyed Grant's supply base at Holly Springs, Mississippi, forcing the Union general to abandon his overland campaign against Vicksburg. For his part in the affair, Jackson was promoted to brigadier general, dated 29 December 1862.

Called "Red" Jackson by his men, he gained a reputation as a bold and aggressive leader of mounted troops. During 1863 he led a division of cavalry in operations in West Tennessee and Mississippi, first under the command of Van Dorn and later, after that officer's death in May, under General Joseph E. Johnston. Jackson took part in some of the peripheral combat of the Vicksburg campaign, skirmishing with Federal forces at Jackson, Mississippi. Under the command of Lieutenant General Leonidas Polk (1806–1864), he took part in the resistance to William T. Sherman's February 1864 advance on Meridian, Mississippi.

In May 1864 Jackson and his division were part of the sizable Confederate force that Polk took with him in his transfer from Mississippi to Georgia. There Jackson participated in the Atlanta campaign. After the fall of Atlanta, he was part of John B. Hood's disastrous foray into Middle Tennessee and, though still a brigadier general, was made commander of all of the Tennessee cavalry operating in Lieutenant General Nathan Bedford Forrest's Department of Alabama, Mississippi, and East Louisiana. Thus he led one of Forrest's two cavalry divisions. His chief action in this capacity was the attempt to resist the advance of Union general James H. Wilson's large cavalry force into central Alabama during the closing weeks of the war. On 4 May 1865 Jackson and his men were included in the surrender agreement worked out between Confederate lieutenant general Richard Taylor (1826–1879) and Union major general E. R. S. Canby at Citronelle, Alabama.

After the war Jackson operated his father's extensive cotton plantations. In December 1868 he married Selene Harding, daughter of General William G. Harding. They had three children. General Harding owned "Belle Meade," a large horse farm near Nashville, and there Jackson joined him and devoted himself to horse breeding. The horses of Belle Meade gained an excellent reputation throughout the South. Jackson himself was highly regarded, serving for a number of years as president of the National Agricultural Congress and the Tennessee Bureau of Agriculture. He died at Belle Meade and was buried in Mount Olivet Cemetery in Nashville.

• Sources on Jackson are not abundant. W. W. Clayton, *History of Davidson County, Tennessee* (1880), and John Woolridge, ed., *History of Nashville, Tennessee* (1970), may be consulted for his pre- and postwar life. The best information on the war years is to be gleaned from *The War of the Rebellion: A Compilation of the Official Records of the Union and Confederate Armies* (128 vols., 1880–1901) published by the U.S. War Department.

STEVEN E. WOODWORTH

JACOBI, Abraham (6 May 1830–10 July 1919), physician, pediatrician, and medical educator, was born in Hartum, Westphalia, Prussia, the son of Eliezer Jacobi, a poor Jewish shopkeeper, and Julia Abel. Following Gymnasium in Mindin, he attended the Universities of Greifswald (1847–1848), Göttingen (1848–1849), and Bonn (1849–1851), from which he received his medical degree. In Berlin to take his state medical examinations in 1851, he was arrested for his part in the German revolution of 1848 and imprisoned for nearly two years. A close friend and fellow revolutionary, Carl Schurz, said of Jacobi, "Thus to have served a term in prison was with him a mark of fidelity to his conception of his duty as a citizen" (*Proceedings*, 1900). Fleeing Germany to avoid rearrest, he went in 1853 to Manchester, England, where he failed in an attempt to establish a medical practice. A few months later he left for Boston, where he again was unsuccessful. In New York City later in 1853 he successfully established himself at 20 Howard Street, beginning what would become a lucrative practice. In his introduction to the *Collectanea Jacobi* (1909), he recalled: "The first of my professional successes was the fact that it took my first patient only a fortnight . . . to call on me with his twenty-five cent fee. I think I must have gathered many more such fees, for after less than four years I was one of the founders of the German dispensary, in which treatment was strictly gratuitous." His professional success was always tempered by social commitment. Ending an address to a group of physicians in New York, he said, " . . . you cannot be good doctors unless you are good citizens." Russell Viner, in England, discovered evidence that Jacobi was "active in socialist labor politics as a correspondent of Marx into the 1860s—and although he moderated somewhat later in life, his socialism was clearly very important for his medicine" (personal communication). In 1856 he married his childhood sweetheart, Fanny Meyer. Within a year she died in childbirth; their son lived only one day. Several years later he married a former patient, Kate Rosalie Rabbe. She had three stillbirths and one premature infant who died.

Although he practiced general medicine, surgery, and obstetrics, as did most physicians of his day, Jacobi's major contributions all concern children and the evolution of pediatrics into a specialty in the United States. His fame as a "pediatrist" developed early as a result of his contributions to the *New York Medical Journal*, initially abstracts from German periodicals and later original works. In 1857, less than four years after his arrival in New York, Jacobi delivered his first formal lecture on a pediatric subject, the diseases of the young larynx and laryngismus stridulus, at the College of Physicians and Surgeons, where both he and J. Lewis Smith, had been appointed lecturers on the pathology of infancy and childhood. In 1860 he was appointed professor of infantile pathology and therapeutics at New York Medical College (no connection with the modern medical school by the same name), the first chair in pediatrics in the United States. This landmark appointment marks the beginning of pediatrics as a medical and academic discipline in the United States; it established Abraham Jacobi as the "father of American pediatrics." During the 1860–1861 academic year at New York Medical College, Jacobi initiated bedside clinical teaching of pediatrics for medical students and established the first free clinic for diseases of children. Bedside clinical teaching had never been done before anywhere in medical education; this innovation marks the beginning of the modern era of clinical education. In 1865 Jacobi was appointed clinical professor of diseases of children at New York University Medical College. In 1870 he was appointed clinical professor of diseases of children at the College of Physicians and Surgeons (Columbia University), a position he held until 1902, when he became professor emeritus.

In 1872 Abraham Jacobi met Mary Corinna Putnam, when he presided at her induction into the New York County Medical Society; they were married the following year. Their first child died within hours; two survived into childhood. In 1883, just short of his eighth birthday, and three years after the publication of Jacobi's book on diphtheria, their older child died of that very disease. The marriage was irreparably harmed. Jacobi's grandchildren recalled how on each anniversary of the lost child's birth Jacobi would become deeply morose. Mary Putnam Jacobi and Abraham Jacobi shared common interests in child welfare, improved public policy for the needy, and many areas of medical science and practice, including pediatrics. Both were leaders and innovators in American medicine.

Although he had been involved with nearly every hospital in New York City, Jacobi's major affiliation was with the Jews Hospital (later Mount Sinai Hospital), where he established the first "outdoor" (ambula-tory) pediatric service in 1874 and the first department of pediatrics in a general hospital in the United States in 1878. He was particularly proud of the fact that during his lifetime every medical school in the United States had opened a department of pediatrics. Invited to become chair of pediatrics at Berlin to succeed Henoch in 1894, he declined, citing his devotion to his adopted country. In 1903 he again was invited to take the chair in Berlin but again declined.

Jacobi was both a prolific writer of articles and books, nearly 200 in all, and an effective leader of American medicine. His major scholarly contributions were in infant nutrition, especially breastfeeding and the preparation of safe breastmilk substitutes, diphtheria, gastrointestinal diseases, dental disorders, and pediatric therapeutics. He invented but never patented the first laryngoscope. A medical history scholar, he wrote about pediatrics before and after 1800, as well as histories of meningitis, diphtheria, tracheotomy, and nursing.

Jacobi played a major leadership role in American medicine, locally and nationally. In New York he was president of the New York Obstetrical Society (1864), the New York Pathological Society (1864), the New York County Medical Society (1870–1872), which he helped to found, the New York State Medical Society (1882), and the New York Academy of Medicine (1885–1889). Organized pediatrics in the United States began with Jacobi's establishment of the Pediatric Section of the American Medical Association in 1880 (three years before the creation of the German Pediatric Society) and the Pediatric Section of the New York Academy of Medicine in 1885. With J. Lewis Smith and others, he was instrumental in creating the American Pediatric Society in 1888, the first independent medical specialty society in the United States. He was elected its first president. His election as president of the American Medical Association in 1912 recognized his broad prominence in American medicine.

During the summer of 1918, with his autobiography nearly completed, Jacobi went to sleep on the second floor of his house in Lake George, New York. Some hours later the sound of fire awakened him. Alone in the house, he escaped through a window and dropped to the ground ten feet below. Unhurt but stunned, he watched the fire consume the only copy of his autobiography and all of his personal papers, letters, and notes. He died the following summer in the house he had built for his dear friend, Carl Schurz, adjacent to where his own home had stood.

The great social activist Lillian Wald summarized the life of Abraham Jacobi: "We owe him a debt that no bestowal of honors could ever pay for, because of his insistence on the social implications of medical work for children" ("Abraham Jacobi, 1830–1919," *Survey*, 19 July 1919, p. 595).

• Jacobi's primary fields of expertise were documented in six major books: *Contributions to Midwifery, and the Disease of Women and Children*, with E. Noeggerath (1859), *Dentition and Its Derangements* (1862), *Infant Diet*, ed. Mary Putnam

Jacobi (1872, 1875, 1885), *A Treatise on Diphtheria* (1880), *The Intestinal Disease of Infancy and Childhood* (1887), which opens with a lengthy discussion of breastfeeding and its importance to infant health, as well as preparation of breastmilk substitutes, and his major general pediatric textbook, *Therapeutics of Infancy and Childhood* (1895, 1898, 1903). The most complete source for his published articles, speeches, and previously unpublished letters is the eight-volume *Collectanea Jacobi* (1909). Abraham Jacobi's three-part "History of Pediatrics in New York," *Archives of Pediatrics* (1917), provides much detail about his role in the development of pediatrics and medical education. The most comprehensive biographical report is Victor Robinson, "The Life of A. Jacobi," *Medical Life* 35 (1928). The most personal and often lighthearted comments on his life and achievements are in the *Proceedings and Addresses at the Complimentary Dinner Tendered to Dr. A. Jacobi on the Occasion of the Seventieth Anniversary of His Birthday, May Five, Nineteen Hundred* (1900), which includes tributes by William Osler, Seth Low, and Carl Schurz. A fictionalized biography of Abraham and Mary Putnam Jacobi by Rhoda Truax, *The Doctors Jacobi* (1952), provides a colorful interpretation of their lives. Comprehensive obituaries are in the *New York Times* and *New York Sun*, 12 July 1919.

LAWRENCE M. GARTNER

JACOBI, Mary Corinna Putnam (31 Aug. 1842–10 June 1906), physician, medical educator, and writer, was born in London, England, the daughter of George Palmer Putnam, a publisher, and Victorine Haven. George Putnam was in London to establish a British office for his firm. The family returned to New York in 1847 when Putnam's partnership ended, and he started his own company. First of eleven children, Jacobi was a precocious child who determined early that she would be a physician, even though few women physicians existed. Her early education was primarily at home, although two years at the new school for girls on Twelfth Street, from which she graduated in 1859, stimulated her writing. Already an accomplished writer at seventeen, she had a story, "Found and Lost," published in the *Atlantic Monthly* in 1860, with another appearing a year later. After graduating she began studying Greek and science privately, as well as medicine with Elizabeth Blackwell and other physicians. Although George Putnam considered medicine a "repulsive" profession, he ultimately supported his daughter's unusual goal of becoming a physician. In 1861, however, he asked her to suspend medical studies for two years in order to stay at home and help her mother. She delayed leaving New York to go to medical school but continued private study and courses at the College of Pharmacy of the City of New York, where she completed the two-year course in 1863, the school's first woman graduate. She also attended some medical school lectures in New York as a non-matriculant—no women were admitted.

In June 1863 Jacobi traveled alone to wartime New Orleans, Louisiana, to nurse her soldier brother, ill with malaria. Finding him convalescent, she stayed on in New Orleans, earning money by writing newspaper articles. That fall she entered the Female Medical College of Pennsylvania, the first medical school for wom-

en. Despite the objections of the dean, she received her medical degree in April 1864, after only one term of lectures.

A brief internship at the New England Hospital for Women and Children convinced Jacobi that she knew too little to practice medicine. She studied chemistry privately and determined to pursue her medical and scientific education in Paris. Her persistent efforts to enter the medical school of the University of Paris, repeatedly rebuffed, are vividly described in her letters home. She studied with physicians at hospitals, won entrance into certain courses, and finally, with the help of the minister of education, was the first woman to enter the school in 1868. She supplemented the modest funds her family could afford by selling stories and articles to American magazines and newspapers. Despite the interruptions of the Franco-Prussian War and the siege of Paris, during which Jacobi volunteered to replace an intern at war, she passed all examinations with high honors, won a medal for her thesis, and received a degree in the spring of 1871. The prestigious *Archives de Médicine* commended her thesis for both style and content.

Jacobi returned to New York City in 1871 to begin the practice of medicine and to teach therapeutics and materia medica (pharmacology) at the Women's Medical College of the New York Infirmary, founded by Elizabeth and Emily Blackwell. She worked continually to strengthen courses and programs and to raise money for the school. Throughout her career she was attending physician at the New York Infirmary and other hospitals. Jacobi was in charge of Mount Sinai Hospital's first outpatient department, in pediatrics, which opened in 1874. When postgraduate medical education began, she was appointed professor of the diseases of children at New York Postgraduate Medical School (1882), the first woman to teach in a regular male medical school.

Although Jacobi was the first woman to enter several medical associations, joining the Medical Society of the County of New York, which already had a woman member, had the most profound effect on her life. She married Abraham Jacobi, the president who inducted her, in 1873. She had ended two previous engagements, first to her chemistry professor, Ferdinand Mayer, who she realized was too weak, then to a Paris medical student. Writing earlier from Paris (1867), she had reassured her mother, "If at home I should ever come across a physician, intelligent, refined, more enthusiastic for his science than me, but who would like me . . . I think I would marry such a person if he asked me and would leave me full liberty to exercise my profession." She commented later with typical mordant wit, "It is desirable that every woman remain as inferior to her own husband as may be feasible and convenient; it is for that purpose she marries him, or should do so. But, the generalization of this relative inferiority to the comparative capacities of all men and all women . . . is a most injurious absurdity" ("Shall Women Practice Medicine?" 1882). The Jacobis' first child died soon after birth. The second died of diphtheria shortly before his eighth birthday, a loss that further strained a difficult marriage and shattered the parents' well-being. Only the third, a daughter, survived.

Mary Jacobi's clinical work and medical publications spanned many areas, focusing first on pathology and later on neurology. She did not consider herself a pediatrician and advised against specialization. Along with her clinical and teaching responsibilities, she pursued laboratory work at the New York Infirmary and then at home when she left the school in 1888. Jacobi wrote wryly to the antivivisectionist Elizabeth Blackwell in 1888 that she was "tolerably confident" that she herself was the only woman in the country experimenting on animals. Sir William Osler stated at a 1907 memorial meeting that Jacobi "compelled recognition by the character of work accomplished in the science and in the art of medicine," but he regretted that "the conditions here were not such as to allow her to follow a scientific career," a recognition she herself made earlier when she chose clinical over scientific medicine.

Jacobi published nearly 150 medical articles, chapters, and books. She adapted Abraham Jacobi's *Infant Diet* into a popular book for mothers (1874). Her article on infantile paralysis (1874) was the first definitive description of poliomyelitis. In 1877 she published *The Question of Rest for Women during Menstruation*, an erudite study using extensive survey data. The work had won Harvard's prestigious Boylston Prize in 1876—the first time it was awarded to a woman. Only in women, Jacobi argued, had normal functions been considered pathological. So capable is the human intellect of overcoming physical limitations, she wrote, "that the discovery of limits usually proves hopeless in only one case, namely, when they are perceived to apply to a different race, class, or sex, from that to which the investigator himself belongs."

Jacobi's nine books also included a philosophical work on positivism and one on primary education. She stopped writing fiction in 1871—she believed it took too much from her—but she continued presenting conference papers and contributing articles to popular magazines and social science journals.

Jacobi worked to improve conditions for working women and actively participated in the suffrage movement. When it failed, she conceived and helped found the League for Political Education to lay the groundwork for later efforts. Her book *"Common Sense" Applied to Woman Suffrage* (1894) was reprinted during the final successful effort to win the vote. Jacobi's lifelong cause was improving educational and vocational opportunities for women, especially in medicine. She founded and worked in associations, mentored individuals, and wrote hard-hitting articles. When efforts to open Harvard's medical school to women failed, she was active in the successful campaign to open the new Johns Hopkins School of Medicine to qualified women. Always ruthlessly realistic and farsighted, she saw that women would not have real equality until they were accepted into every area of medicine and evaluated on the same basis as men. Results, she forecast accurately, would not come until a century after women had truly equal opportunities, including admission to "privileged work in addition to the drudgeries imposed by necessity" ("Women in Medicine," in *The National Exposition Souvenir*, ed. L. H. Farmer [1893]).

In 1896 Jacobi suffered the first symptoms of a disease that made her an invalid for her last few years. Consultations with experts brought no diagnosis. In 1903 she described the course of her disease in a letter; published after her death, "Description of the Early Symptoms of the Meningeal Tumor Compressing the Cerebellum, from Which the Author Died. Written by Herself" (Jacobi, *A Pathfinder in Medicine, with Selections from Her Writings and a Complete Bibliography*, ed. Women's Medical Association of New York City [1925], pp. 501–4) has been called a classic of medical writing. She died in New York City.

At her core, Jacobi was a writer who believed that when one discovered or learned something, one had to contribute to society by sharing it. Dedication to her profession, women, education, and social improvement never diminished her devotion to what society saw as feminine obligations to family, which for her included her many siblings. Emily Blackwell called her "an unsparing and outspoken critic of shallow knowledge, slip-shod methods, and hollow pretense in any shape," noting that "these qualities did not always add to her popularity" (1907). Brilliant, loyal, and principled, she demanded the most of herself. At her death, contemporaries saw her as an eminent physician, not an eminent woman physician, and emphasized her influence on her time; writers since have concurred.

• The Schlesinger Library, Radcliffe College, has a collection of Jacobi's papers. Letters and other materials are in various collections, including the Herbert Putnam Papers (Library of Congress) and the Blackwell papers (Library of Congress and Columbia Univ.). Her major published works, in addition to those mentioned in the text, are *The Value of Life: A Reply to Mr. Mallock's Essay, "Is Life Worth Living?"* (1879), expressing a positivist philosophy; *On the Use of the Cold Pack Followed by Massage in the Treatment of Anaemia*, with V. A. White (1880); *Essays on Hysteria, Brain-Tumor, and Some Other Cases of Nervous Disease* (1888); *Physiological Notes on Primary Education and the Study of Language* (1889); *Uffelman's Manual of the Domestic Hygiene of the Child*, ed. Jacobi (1891); *From Massachusetts to Turkey* (1896), on women's issues; and *Stories and Sketches* (1907), a collection of magazine stories and articles. Ruth Putnam, *Life and Letters of Mary Putnam Jacobi* (1925), is the major published source. Rhoda Truax, *The Doctors Jacobi* (1952), a fictionalized biography of Mary Putnam and Abraham Jacobi, emphasizes her life and is valuable because of Truax's use of primary sources, family papers, and extensive discussions with their daughter, Marjorie Jacobi McAneny. *In Memory of Mary Putnam Jacobi* (1907) is a collection of tributes from a memorial meeting. Every major work on women in medicine discusses Jacobi; Regina Morantz-Sanchez, *Sympathy and Science: Women Physicians in American Medicine* (1985), contains the most extensive treatment. See also Joy Harvey, "Medicine and Politics: Dr. Mary Putnam Jacobi and the Paris Commune," *Dialectical Anthropology* 15 (1990): 107–17, and her "La Visite:

Mary Putnam Jacobi and the Paris Medical Clinics," in *French Medical Culture in the Nineteenth Century*, ed. Ann La Berge and Mordechai Feingold (1994). Among her obituaries are those in the *Boston Medical and Surgical Journal* 154 (1906): 690, the *British Medical Journal* (30 June 1906), the *New York Times*, 12 June 1906, and the *Journal of the American Medical Association* (23 June 1906).

CAROL B. GARTNER

JACOBS, Frances Wisebart (29 Mar. 1843–3 Nov. 1892), welfare worker and charity organizer, was born in Harrodsburg, Kentucky, the daughter of Leon Henry Wisebart, a cutter (probably a tailor) and an officer in the B'nai B'rith Jewish service organization, and Rosetta Marx. When Frances was a young child, the family moved to Cincinnati, Ohio, where German Jews had established their own press and a theological school. Raised in a traditional Jewish home, Frances received her education in the city's public school system and went on to become a teacher at a school in Cincinnati.

Married to Abraham Jacobs in 1863, Frances left Ohio with her new husband in 1864 to live in Colorado, where they had three children, one of whom died in childhood. Of German birth, Abraham Jacobs had lived in Cincinnati at one time but had left in 1859 to join the throng of approximately 50,000 people in the Pikes Peak Gold Rush. He had settled in the frontier mining town of Central City, Colorado, and in 1861 opened a mining outfitters' store with Frances's brother. In 1865 they opened a clothing store in Denver. Frances and Abraham Jacobs moved to Denver permanently following an 1874 fire that destroyed Central City and their store.

Frances Jacobs arrived in Denver following the gold boom, when the population had burgeoned and the problems associated with rapid growth had emerged. Combating respiratory ailments turned into the largest difficulty for this society, as fortune seekers to the West arrived with tuberculosis that they had contracted back East. As the situation worsened, sectarian groups formed, and the Jewish community banded together to help their own. When Frances Jacobs came to Denver, she responded to these needs by joining the newly formed Hebrew Benevolent Ladies Aid Society, founded in 1872; shortly thereafter she won election as its president. In 1874 she became the first vice president of a new agency, the Ladies' Relief Society. The society distributed food and clothing, established clinics and nurseries, and found homes for women, children, and the aged.

Jacobs realized that the problems of the city transcended class and religious lines and could not be dealt with simply by individual organizations. Thus, her attempts to create a cohesive atmosphere among all the groups in Denver began in earnest. In 1881 she helped to organize the first charity ball held in the city; this intensified efforts to unite charity organizations that focused on a range of issues. Jacobs, together with two Protestant ministers, two Catholic priests, and another man, worked toward a cooperative charity organization that resulted in the founding of the Charity Organization Society (COS) in 1887. COS combined the efforts of many existing groups, and funds were solicited by COS workers through private citizens and businessmen. The Hebrew Ladies Benevolent Society became one of the charter members of the COS, and Jacobs served as secretary of the COS until her death. She also was a regular representative to the National Conference of Charities and Correction.

Fund drives enabled COS to survive and later to become Denver's Community Chest. Jacobs worked tirelessly for the new organization but continued as president of the Ladies' Relief Society as well. The Jewish community was especially hard hit, as there was continual growth with the exodus of Jews from Russia seeking safe haven in the United States. Jacobs stressed their needs and gave special attention to homeless and working women. She encouraged women to come together and fight for fair wages and an eight-hour workday, a battle the men had already won. Seeing that small children had kindergarten facilities in other areas, Jacobs helped form a kindergarten association in 1891. She promoted the Newsboys' Home and was secretary of the Board of Control of the House of the Good Shepherd.

In 1883 Jacobs had a dream of building a community hospital, and so she sponsored a benefit to that effect. The dream, which was not realized until the erecting of the Jewish Hospital in 1892, was short-lived for Frances Jacobs, who died that year at the age of forty-nine. A woman who had dedicated long hours to those less fortunate than herself and had considered the health of others more important than her own died of peritonitis after she caught a cold. Her funeral services were multidenominational, attended by three Christian clergymen and a rabbi. As a lasting tribute to her memory, in 1900 Jacobs became the only woman and one of sixteen pioneers given a memorial tribute, a stained-glass portrait in the Capitol rotunda. The hospital she had worked so hard to finance was renamed the Frances Jacobs Hospital.

Said to be a woman "freed from all bondage of prejudice," Jacobs was referred to as Colorado's "Mother of the Charities." She was drawn to those in need, and even in the face of criticism, she involved herself personally in the lives of the needy. Optimistically facing the future, Jacobs injected spirit into all her endeavors, whether officiating at a meeting or wading through mud to get to the home of someone in need. Although a member of Denver's higher social stratum, she remained an active participant in aiding the poor and was not above collecting newspapers and clothes, making home visits as many as fifteen times in a day, and sometimes paying for a doctor's services for the needy.

• Information on Frances Wisebart Jacobs can be found in *Memoir of Mrs. Frances Jacobs* (1892), a collection of tributes; Ida Libert Uchill, *Pioneers, Peddlers, and Tsadikim* (1957); John H. Monnett and Michael McCarthy, *Colorado Profiles: Men and Women Who Shaped the Centennial State* (1987); files of the *Denver Republican*, *Rocky Mountain News*, *Colorado Sun*, and *Colorado Times*; John C. Fleming, "Golden Anniversary," in the fiftieth anniversary program of the Denver Community Chest (1937); and Joseph Emerson Smith, "Jewish Builders of Colorado," *Intermountain Jewish News*, 15 Sept. 1939. Denver's charity system is described in Frank Dekker Watson, *The Charity Organization Movement in the United States* (1971).

MARILYN ELIZABETH PERRY

JACOBS, Harriet (c. 1813–7 Mar. 1897), autobiographer and reformer, was born into slavery in Edenton, North Carolina, the daughter of Elijah, a skilled slave carpenter, and Delilah, a house slave. In her slave narrative *Incidents in the Life of a Slave Girl: Written by Herself* (1861), published under the pseudonym Linda Brent, Jacobs explained that although it was illegal, she learned to read and to spell at six, when, after her mother's death, she was taken in by her mistress. When Jacobs reached puberty this mistress died, and she was willed to the woman's niece and sent into that child's home, where her new mistress's father subjected her to unrelenting sexual harassment. To save herself from concubinage, at sixteen she began a sexual liaison with a young white neighbor. (In *Incidents* called Mr. Sands, he was Samuel Tredwell Sawyer, later a member of Congress.) This union produced a son and daughter. When she was twenty-one, her young mistress's father again threatened her with concubinage and, after she defied him, vowed to make her children plantation slaves. In June 1835 she ran away, hoping that instead of raising the children he would sell them and that their father would buy and free them. Her hopes were partially realized: the children were bought by their father, who permitted them to live with her grandmother, now a freedwoman, but he did not free them.

As a fugitive slave in the South, Jacobs hid for almost seven years in a tiny space under the roof of her grandmother's home. In June 1842 she escaped to Philadelphia. She was eventually reunited with her children in the North. In 1849 she joined an abolitionist circle in Rochester, New York. Jacobs wrote that after passage of the 1850 Fugitive Slave Law, she was sought by her North Carolina mistress but rejected an offer to buy her freedom: "The more my mind had become enlightened, the more difficult it was for me to consider myself an article of property; and to pay money to those who had so grievously oppressed me seemed like taking from my sufferings the glory of triumph" (*Incidents*, p. 199).

Despite her protest, in 1853 Jacobs was purchased from Mary Matilda Norcom Messmore by her New York employer, Cornelia Grinnell Willis, and she and her children were free from the threat of reenslavement. Persuaded to tell her story by Amy Post, a Rochester abolitionist and feminist friend, and after a futile attempt to enlist bestselling author Harriet Beecher Stowe as her amanuensis, Jacobs spent years writing her book. When she finished, the black writer and activist William C. Nell introduced her to the white antislavery writer and activist Lydia Maria Child, who edited the manuscript and helped obtain financial backing from Boston abolitionists.

With the publication of *Incidents* in January 1861, Jacobs entered public life as "Linda, the slave girl." Praised in the black and reform press for its vivid dramatic power, her book appeared the following year in two London editions, one pirated. Renamed *The Deeper Wrong: Incidents in the Life of a Slave Girl, Written by Herself*, Jacobs's book won excellent reviews in mainstream newspapers such as the *Morning Star and Dial* (London), which heralded it as "the first personal narrative in which one of that sex upon whom chattel servitude falls with the deepest and darkest shadow described her own bitter experience" (10 Mar. 1862).

Had the Civil War not broken out, Jacobs might have followed other slave narrators onto the lecture platform. Instead, throughout the war and early postwar years she aided the "contraband," black refugees crowding behind the Union lines, by using her celebrity to raise money and supplies from northern sympathizers and to publish a series of newspaper reports on the condition of the refugees. In 1862 she did relief work in Washington, D.C.; the following year she and her daughter Louisa moved to Alexandria, Virginia, where with the help of the New England Freedman's Aid Society they established the Jacobs Free School.

Jacobs's philanthropic and reform efforts were acknowledged in 1864, when she was named to the executive committee of the Women's Loyal National League, headed by Elizabeth Cady Stanton and Susan B. Anthony. Jacobs and Louisa later continued their philanthropic work in Savannah, Georgia. In 1868 she sailed to London to raise money for an orphanage and old people's home. Welcomed by British reformers familiar with her *Deeper Wrong* and her newspaper reports from the South, Jacobs was successful at fundraising. Nevertheless, she recommended to her Quaker sponsors that the asylum not be built in Georgia, where the Ku Klux Klan was riding and burning.

When Jacobs returned to the United States with her daughter later in 1868 she retreated from public life. She moved first to Massachusetts and in 1877 to Washington, D.C., where, her health failing, she privately continued her work for the freed women and children.

Jacobs died of nephritis at her Washington home. She was eulogized by her longtime friend, Rev. Francis J. Grimke, as "no reed shaken by the wind, vacillating, easily moved from a position. She did her own thinking; had opinions of her own, and held to them with great tenacity."

Incidents in the Life of a Slave Girl is the most important antebellum autobiography written by an African-American woman. Although nineteenth-century readers recognized Harriet Jacobs as the pseudonymous "Linda," before the Harvard edition appeared in 1897 many twentieth-century scholars thought the book was white-authored fiction. Since then, it has been recognized as black-authored autobiography. Jacobs's pseudonymous slave narrative, which centers on her struggle against sexual oppression in slavery and on her efforts to win freedom, defied nineteenth-century taboos against women discussing their sexual experiences. Jacobs's public letters, published during the Civil War and Reconstruction, present a unique first-person account of the black war refugees and the freed people in the South.

• Jacobs's papers are scattered in several collections. The most important are the Isaac and Amy Post Family Papers, University of Rochester, and the Dr. J. Norcom Papers, North Carolina State Archives. Other sources include the Lydia Maria Child Papers (on microfilm); the Rochester Ladies' Anti-Slavery Society Papers, Clements Memorial Library, the University of Michigan; and the Julia Wilbur Papers, Haverford College.

The standard edition of *Incidents in the Life of a Slave Girl*, ed. Jean Fagan Yellin (1987), includes a scholarly introduction, annotates the text, and presents selections of Jacobs's correspondence. Documentary materials are also included in Dorothy Sterling, ed., *We Are Your Sisters: Black Women in the Nineteeth Century* (1984). Discussions of Jacobs's narrative include William C. Andrews, *To Tell a Free Story: The First Century of Afro-American Autobiography* (1986); Joanne Braxton, *Black Women Writing Autobiography: A Tradition within a Tradition* (1989); Hazel Carby, *Reconstructing Womanhood: The Emergence of the Afro-American Woman Novelist* (1987); Frances Smith Foster, *Written by Herself: Literary Production of African-American Women, 1746–1892* (1993); Bell Hooks, *Feminist Theory: From Margin to Center* (1984); Carla L. Peterson, *"Doers of the Word"* (1995); Valerie Smith, *Narrative Authority in Modern Afro-American Fiction* (1979); Mary Helen Washington, *Invented Lives: Narratives of Black Women, 1860–1960* (1987); and Yellin, *Women and Sisters* (1989). A collection of literary essays is Deborah M. Garfield and Rafia Zafar, eds., *Harriet Jacobs and Incidents in the Life of a Slave Girl* (1996).

JEAN FAGAN YELLIN

JACOBS, Henry Eyster (10 Nov. 1844–7 July 1932), historian, theologian, and churchman, was born in Gettysburg, Pennsylvania, the son of the Reverend Michael Jacobs, a college professor, and Julianna Matilda Eyster. Michael Jacobs taught natural science at the Lutheran Pennsylvania (now Gettysburg) College. As a consequence, from the outset Henry Jacobs lived in the contexts of education and church. In his youth Jacobs's world view was also profoundly influenced by witnessing at close range the battle of Gettysburg, fought when he was nineteen, and by hearing Abraham Lincoln deliver the Gettysburg Address. His response to the latter is found in his *Lincoln's Gettysburg World-Message* (1919).

Jacobs obtained his formal education in Gettysburg; he graduated from Pennsylvania College in 1862 and from Gettysburg Seminary three years later. His career began with an appointment as tutor at his college alma mater. He completed a thesis in which he rejected Lutheran observation of the Sabbath in accord with Puritan standards of rigor and abstention as inconsistent with Christian freedom and then served as pastor of a congregation in Pittsburgh, Pennsylvania, from 1867 to 1868. His work there came to an abrupt end

after he refused to make an open invitation to the Lord's Supper, then a common practice.

From this juncture on Jacobs worked in educational institutions while also publishing for scholarly and general audiences and participating in church governance. Following faculty appointments at Thiel College (1868–1870) and at Pennsylvania College (1870–1883), he went to the Lutheran Theological Seminary in Philadelphia as professor of systematic theology in 1883. There he filled the position vacated by C. Porterfield Krauth, a member of the original faculty. In 1894 Jacobs was made dean; in 1920 president. Although he retired from administration in 1927, he continued to teach throughout the remainder of his life.

Jacobs was married to Laura H. Downing in 1872. Of their five children, three survived him. Charles Michael Jacobs entered the same work as his father and succeeded him as president of the Lutheran Theological Seminary.

Henry Jacobs's contributions to American religious life, in particular to American Lutheranism, were in three areas: as a teacher of pastors and professors; as an author, translator and editor; and as a participant in church governance. Among the approximately 1,000 young men who sat in his classes were many who followed him into the professorate and extended his influence into the South and Midwest by their own teaching.

From early on Jacobs demonstrated his ability as a historian and theologian. Like Krauth, he supported the confessional stance of the General Council, the more moderate of the two general Lutheran bodies. In his thesis on Sabbath observance he used classic Lutheran authorities to argue against the common practice, a position that turned his childhood friends against him. The same sort of study grounded his defense of closing communion to all except Lutherans. Concern that contemporary controversies be informed by the best historical wisdom was a consistent theme in his work and was evident both in his translations (e.g., of *The Book of Concord* and of Lutheran orthodox theologian Heinrich Schmid) and in his original scholarship concerning the history of Lutheranism in England and the United States. In addition to his specialized publications, he was a prolific writer for popular audiences, as in the *Lutheran*, whose editor he was from 1888 to 1895.

However, concern that current decisions be informed by the past did not prejudice Jacobs's integrity as a historian or cause him to reject modern methods of study. Rather, he was an advocate as well as practitioner of the emerging scientific standards in historical work. He was a member of the newly formed American Historical Association, the Pennsylvania German Society (president 1910–1911), the American Society of Church History (president 1907–1909), and the Pennsylvania Bible Society.

Jacobs's involvement in American Lutheranism extended into various committees and projects. His participation included serving as president of the General Council's Board of Foreign Missions, presiding at general conferences in 1899, 1902, and 1904, and chairing the United Lutheran church commission of adjudication. In particular, his historical knowledge contributed to the development of the Common Service (1887), a liturgical order based on sixteenth-century German and some English models, and he participated in the formation of the United Lutheran Church in America in 1918. His most original volume, *Lutheran Movement in England during the Reigns of Henry VIII and Edward VI and Its Literary Monuments* (1894), provided solid historical background for American Lutherans' efforts to devise an English-language liturgy.

Jacobs served repeatedly as the official representative of the General Council at meetings of other bodies. On those occasions his personal generosity and integrity contributed much to the cause of reunifying the strands of colonial Lutheranism. At the same time he was eager that Lutheranism respond to the needs of the time. He expressed these dual expectations: "The United Lutheran Church should be historical in its temper, cherishing every truth confessed in the past as a precious possession, and at the same time progressive; observant of precedents and yet not mechanically bound by them; full of the freedom of the Reformation period, because its foundations are sure and its truth many sided, and its capabilities of development are exhaustless" (cited by Henry E. Horn, *Memoirs of Henry Eyster Jacobs*, vol. 1, p. xiv).

Although Jacobs's scholarly works are no longer the standards in their fields, his significance as a historian, theologian, and churchman can be measured in his influence on the development of American Lutheranism at a critical time. His careful study and personal presence encouraged both confessional integrity and engagement with the larger culture. He died in Philadelphia.

• Jacobs's papers are held by the archives at Lutheran Theological Seminary in Philadelphia. His memoirs, edited and annotated by Henry E. Horn, were privately published in 1974. His significant works include *A History of the Evangelical Lutheran Church in the United States* (1893) and *The German Immigration to America, 1709–1740* (1898). A comprehensive listing of his publications is found in the *Lutheran Church Quarterly* 6, no. 2; the preceding number contains assessments of his contributions by several of his contemporaries. More recent views include Paul A. Baglyos, "Lutheran Stories and American Context: Three Histories of American Lutheranism from the Late Nineteenth Century," *Concordia Historical Institute Quarterly* 64 (1991): 154–75; C. George Fry, "Henry Eyster Jacobs: Confessional Pennsylvania-German Lutheran," *Concordia Historical Institute Quarterly* 55 (1982): 158–62; and Abdel R. Wentz, "Henry Eyster Jacobs as Church Historian," *Lutheran Historical Conference* 4 (1972): 78–84.

L. DeAne Lagerquist

JACOBS, Hirsch (8 Apr. 1904–13 Feb. 1970), Thoroughbred horse trainer and owner-breeder, was born in New York City, the son of an immigrant tailor. Jacobs graduated from public school in 1917 and worked as a steamfitter before joining Charlie Ferraro, his fi-

nancial backer and the brother of Jacobs's boss, in 1921 to train pigeons. Jacobs won most of the major Atlantic seaboard sweepstakes in pigeon racing, and in 1923 he served as racing secretary for the Brooklyn, East New York, and Queensborough Concourse clubs. In 1924 Ferraro expanded the partnership into horse racing by purchasing the horse Demijohn in a claiming race (a race in which an eligible trainer can place a "claim" to purchase an entered horse by depositing a preestablished amount before the running) and asking Jacobs to be the trainer. For Ferraro, Jacobs won twenty-eight races worth $27,515 in 1926 and fifty-nine races worth $51,580 in 1927. Jacobs then trained for Johnny Mascia and Louie Sylvestri before meeting his lifetime partner in horse racing and financial backer, Isidor Bieber, in 1928.

Not relying solely on workouts, as was customary, Jacobs raced horses into shape. He claimed his first Thoroughbred, Reveillon, for $1,500 in 1926 and raced him sixteen times in the next thirty-eight days, a virtually unprecedented frequency. Reveillon started winning in his thirteenth race. In 1933 Jacobs married Ethel Dushock, with whom he had three children.

Jacobs developed his first big stakes winner in 1936 with Action, a failed steeplechase horse, which won the Aqueduct, Edgemere, and Manhattan handicaps and a total of eleven races in thirteen starts. Later for $1,500, Jacobs claimed Stymie, which won thirty-five races and became the leading money earner ($918,485) and 1945 handicap champion. These winnings enabled Jacobs and Bieber to buy Stymie Manor near Monkton, Maryland, their new breeding headquarters. Jacobs next purchased Searching; by experimenting with different horseshoes to protect her thin hoof walls, he enabled her to win twenty-five races and $327,381. (She was elected to the Official National Thoroughbred Racing Hall of Fame in 1978.) Searching and her offspring, Affectionately, Admiring, and Priceless Gem, earned the partnership more than $2 million. Jacobs saddled a record forty-nine stakes winners, including Hail to Reason (1960 Two-Year-Old Champion), Affectionately (1966 Sprint Champion), Regal Gleam (1966 Two-Year-Old Filly Champion), Straight Deal (1967 Champion Handicap Mare), and Personality (1970 Three-Year-Old Champion).

Jacobs had a prodigious memory concerning horses and an eye for fine detail, especially in noticing small indicators of a horse's condition and emotional state. He was known for making winners of horses that failed for others. "You just got to use common sense and know when a horse *feels* like running." He also used innovative training methods, in at least one instance having his horses swim in the surf for their workout. Interested in veterinary practices, Jacobs seemed to enjoy some success in devising topical medicines.

Jacobs involved his family in the horse business. His father was his stable foreman, three of his brothers trained horses, and a fourth brother managed Stymie Manor. From 1963 through 1969 his son John was his principal assistant trainer and won fifty-four races and $1,043,122. Jacobs often listed as owner of the horses he raced either Bieber or, beginning in 1936, his wife. (Ethel Jacobs led American owners in races won in 1936, 1937, and 1943.) In 1959 he began to record his daughter, Patrice, as the owner of some of the racehorses.

After a stroke in 1966, Jacobs sold two-thirds of his stable. During a Hialeah racing meeting, he died in Miami, Florida.

As trainer, Jacobs saddled a record 3,596 winners, earned $15,340,354, and led U.S. trainers in wins eleven times and in earnings three times. As breeders, he and Bieber led all other stables in earnings from 1964 through 1967 and won 3,513 races and $18,311,412. As owners, Jacobs, Bieber, and Jacobs's family won 2,947 races and earned $15,800,545. The National Turf Writers of America elected Jacobs to the Official National Thoroughbred Racing Hall of Fame in 1958. Pimlico racetrack instituted the Hirsch Jacobs Stakes in 1975.

• Biographical sketches of Hirsch Jacobs include Arnold Kirkpatrick, "Hirsch Jacobs," in *Hoofprints of the Century*, ed. William Robertson and Dan Farley (1976), and G. F. T. Ryall, "Profiles: Pigeon Man's Progress," *New Yorker*, 5 Aug. 1939. See also "Hirsch Jacobs Stakes," *Blood-Horse* 101 (27 Jan. 1975): 506; Stu Camen, "Personality Takes Wood, Silent Screen Second," *Lexington* (Ky.) *Leader*, 19 Apr. 1970; "Hirsch Jacobs Posts 3,500th Victory of His 41-Year Career," *Daily Racing Form*, 28 July 1966; "153 Horses of Bieber-Jacobs Stable Stable Thus Far for $3,074,600 Total," *Daily Racing Form*, 21 Nov. 1966; "Jacobs Honored by Turf Group," *Lexington Leader*, 8 Feb. 1966; "Jacobs Entry Runs 1-2-3 at Aqueduct," *Miami Herald*, 15 Apr. 1965; Betty Moore, "Hirsch Jacobs Was 'Greatest Horseman,'" *Morning Telegraph*, 10 Aug. 1970; Tom O'Reilly, "Hirsch Jacobs," *Chronicle of the Horse*, 13 May 1960, p. 30; and O'Reilly, "Hirsch Jacobs 'Winningest' Trainer," *Daily Racing Form*, 2 May 1959, p. 22D. Obituaries are in the *Blood-Horse* 96 (21 Feb. 1970): 652–58; the *Bloodstock Breeders' Annual Review* 59 (1970): 212; and the *New York Times* and the *Lexington Leader*, both 14 Feb. 1970.

STEVEN P. SAVAGE

JACOBS, Joseph (29 Aug. 1854–30 Jan. 1916), literary critic, folklorist, and Jewish historian, was born in Sydney, New South Wales, Australia, the son of John Jacobs and Sarah (maiden name unknown). He received a B.A. from St. John's College, Cambridge, England, in 1876, and the following year he went to Berlin to study with the famous Jewish scholars Moritz Lazarus and Moritz Steinschneider. Upon returning to England, he studied anthropology with Sir Francis Galton. He married Georgina Horne (date unknown); they had three children.

Jacobs was an active literary critic and student of folklore who often integrated Jewish and general themes. His first published essay, "Mordecai," appeared in *Macmillan's Magazine* (England) in June 1877; it was a study of George Eliot's *Daniel Deronda*. He became an active contributor to the *Athenaeum* magazine and wrote introductions to reprints of well-known works such as Jane Austen's *Emma* and the *Arabian Nights*. In 1895 Jacobs published a volume of criticism, *Literary Studies*, followed by *Wonder Voyages* (1896) and *Story of Geographical Discovery* (1898).

As a folklorist, Jacobs's specialty was tracing the development of folktales from one culture to another. In 1888 he published *The Earliest English Version of the Fables of Bidpai*, followed by an edition of Caxton's *Fables of Aesop* the following year. In 1890 Jacobs published *English Fairy Tales*, beginning a series that was to ensure his scholarly reputation while reaching a broad popular audience as well, delighting generations of children with his charming renditions of the traditional stories. In 1891 he published *Celtic Fairy Tales*, followed by *Indian Fairy Tales* (1892), *More English Fairy Tales* (1893), and *More Celtic Fairy Tales* (1894). In 1899 he issued an English volume of Boccaccio's *Tales*, and in 1916 his last folklore work, *Europa's Fairy Book*, appeared. In England Jacobs edited *Folklore* magazine and was named honorary secretary of the International Folk-lore Council.

Jacobs's Jewish scholarship was equally varied and multifaceted. In England he was regarded as one of the Jewish community's intellectual leaders. With men such as Solomon Schechter, Israel Zangwill, Lucien Wolf, Asher Myers, Moses Gaster, and Israel Abrahams, Jacobs was part of an informal elite group known as the "Wanderers" that met to discuss Jewish issues. In January 1882 Jacobs published two articles in *The Times* (London) dealing with the persecution of the Jews in Czarist Russia, and it was these writings that aroused British public opinion and led to the establishment of the Mansion House Committee and Fund, which sought to help Russian Jewry. Jacobs served as secretary of this committee from 1882 to 1900. In connection with his work for Russian Jewry, Jacobs became interested in a statistical analysis of the Jewish people and published several articles that were reprinted as *Studies in Jewish Statistics* (1890).

In 1887 Jacobs took an active part in organizing the Anglo-Jewish Historical Exhibition; and, along with Lucien Wolf, he edited the exhibition's catalog. An ardent student of English Jewish history, Jacobs published *The Jews of Angevin England* in 1893. One of the founders of the Jewish Historical Society of England, he served as its president in 1898–1899. Jacobs was also interested in Iberian Jewish history: a trip to Spain in 1888 enabled him to copy some 1,700 documents from Spanish archives, resulting in *An Inquiry into the Sources of the History of the Jews in Spain* (1894). Subsequently, the Royal Academy of History in Madrid elected him a corresponding member. Turning to biblical studies, Jacobs published *Studies in Biblical Archaeology* in 1894, and the following year he published a novel about the life of Jesus from a Jewish perspective, *As Others Saw Him*.

A frequent contributor to London's *Jewish Chronicle*, Jacobs also inaugurated the publication of the *Jewish Year Book* in 1896, editing it until 1899. Also in 1896 a collection of his essays on Jewish history and philosophy appeared as *Jewish Ideals*. That same year he visited the United States to lecture at Gratz College in Philadelphia on the topic of the "Philosophy of Jewish History," and the lecture was subsequently repeated before the National Council of Jewish Women in Philadelphia, New York City, and Chicago.

In the spring of 1900 Jacobs went to New York City to serve as the revising editor of the *Jewish Encyclopedia* (1901–1905), a work that was to fully occupy him for six years. Jacobs led the research in the areas of the Jews of England and anthropology, he helped collect many of the illustrations used in the work, and he personally contributed more than 400 articles to the encyclopedia. That a scholar of Jacobs's prominence would transfer his activities to the United States was a sign of the growing intellectual maturity of the American Jewish community. In 1906 Jacobs published a companion volume to the larger work, *The Jewish Encyclopedia: A Guide to Its Contents, an Aid to Its Use*.

Upon completing his work on the encyclopedia, Jacobs served for six years as a professor of English and rhetoric and as the registrar at the Jewish Theological Seminary of America in New York City, which was headed by his close friend Solomon Schechter. In 1908 Jacobs was named to the Jewish Publication Society's board of editors, which was responsible for a new translation of the Hebrew Bible. In 1913 Jacobs left the seminary to assume full-time employment as the editor of the New York weekly the *American Hebrew*, at which he remained until his death. He also served as the head of the Bureau of Statistical Research of the American Jewish Committee. He edited the *American Jewish Year Book* for the Jewish Publication Society in 1915, and his last literary work, *Jewish Contributions to Civilization*, appeared posthumously in 1919.

A lighthearted, almost playful man, Jacobs was known for his keen intellect and fine sense of humor, which won him a large circle of friends in both England and the United States. Intellectually he was an outstanding representative of the school of thought that was called *Wissenschaft des Judentums* in Germany and that sought to apply the methods of scientific critical study to Jewish scholarship. He died at his residence in New Rochelle, New York.

• For further biographical details on Jacobs see the *Jewish Encyclopedia*, vol. 7 (1912) and Mayer Sulzberger's article "Joseph Jacobs," in the *American Jewish Year Book 5677* (1916). A description of Jacobs's personality and intellectual interests is found in Norman Bentwich, *Solomon Schechter: A Biography* (1948). For an assessment of Jacobs's work as a Jewish scholar, see the memorial addresses by Lucien Wolf, Israel Zangwill, and Israel Abrahams in *Transactions of the Jewish Historical Society of England* 8 (1918), which includes a bibliography; and Alexander Marx, "The Jewish Scholarship of Joseph Jacobs," in his *Essays in Jewish Biography* (1947). A thorough assessment of Jacobs's work on the *Jewish Encyclopedia* is found in Shuly Rubin Schwartz, *The Emergence of Jewish Scholarship in America: The Publication of the "Jewish Encyclopedia"* (1991). An obituary is in the *New York Times*, 1 Feb. 1916.

ROBERT E. FIERSTIEN

JACOBS, Little Walter (1 May 1930–15 Feb. 1968), blues singer and instrumentalist, was born Marion Walter Jacobs in Marksville, Louisiana, the son of Adam Jacobs and Beatrice Leviege, sharecroppers. Soon after Walter's birth, the family moved to Alexandria, where he grew up, and at age eight he began playing the harmonica, absorbing the sounds of white harmonica-player Lonnie Glosson and Cajun music. At age eleven or twelve he ran away from home, his destination New Orleans, where he played on the streets and perhaps in some clubs in 1942 and at the Liberty Inn Club in Monroe in 1943. By 1944 he was in Helena, Arkansas, learning a few pointers from Rice Miller and appearing in radio on "King Biscuit Time" and "Mother's Best Flour Hour" in 1945–1946. Jacobs married Pearl Lee around 1945; they moved to East St. Louis and St. Louis before arriving in Chicago by 1946.

Although Jacobs had played in clubs in St. Louis, in Chicago he faced the tough Maxwell Street Market area, where hustling musicians battled for spare change on street corners. Maxwell Street became his home base, although he may have played some club dates in 1946 with established Chicago artists such as Bill Broonzy, Tampa Red, and Memphis Slim. Most important, he met his idol and major influence, John Lee "Sonny Boy" Williamson, whom Jacobs rated as the best blues harmonica-player he had ever heard. In 1947 Bernard Abrams, owner of a Maxwell Street radio store, recorded Jacobs for his Ora Nelle label, cutting two takes each of "I Just Keep Loving Her" (with Jacobs singing and playing the harmonica and Othum Brown on guitar), "Ora Nelle Blues" (with Brown taking over the vocals), and a reworking of Sleepy John Estes's "Liquor Store Blues" retitled "Little Store Blues" (with Jimmy Rogers on vocals and guitar). Sales were limited, but the recordings revealed a brash, raucous sound that clearly pushed the limits of Williamson's Bluebird label sound and foretold the new wave of tough Chicago blues to come.

Williamson's influence was further revealed in Jacobs's recording as part of a group for the Tempotone label in 1948, with Sunnyland Slim on piano as well. But the most important feature of this session was the presence of guitarist Muddy Waters—his and Jacobs's first of many studio collaborations; together they forged the emergent Chicago blues sound. Waters began experiencing success with his recordings on the Aristocrat (later Chess) label, and Jacobs joined his band, touring extensively through the South but not yet appearing on Waters's recordings for Aristocrat. However, Monroe Passis signed Jacobs, Waters, and Baby Face Leroy for trio sessions in January 1950 for the Parkway label that yielded eight sides, four with lead vocals by Jacobs and all featuring his developing harmonica work or expressive guitar, with the interplay between Waters's slide guitar, Jacobs's harmonica, and moaning group vocals being particularly ferocious on "Rollin' and Tumblin' (part 2)."

Jacobs and Waters finally recorded together for Chess in August 1950, establishing a record-label relationship that would last the rest of Jacobs's life. In addition, he was Waters's harmonica-player on other recording sessions for the next decade. He also recorded accompaniments for Jimmy Rogers, Johnny Shines, Floyd Jones, John Brim, the Coronets, and Bo Diddley, but it was his recordings as leader of his own group that best established his reputation. At an 11 July 1951 session Jacobs finally played amplified harmonica on record, accompanying Waters on "Country Boy." Other harmonica-players had experimented with amplification previously, among them Williamson, Miller, and Snooky Pryor, but Jacobs forged a sound that explored the possibilities of amplification most successfully.

A 12 May 1952 session designed to provide Jacobs with his Chess label debut as a leader featured Waters's band and introduced Jacobs's mature style—a unique hybrid of Williamson, Louis Jordan, and Earl Bostic, often awash in distortion and reverberation, and riding over tight, intricate, swinging band arrangements. His jazzy, melodic, and powerful yet controlled playing, often heavily amplified, demonstrated his imaginative flair and set the standard for amplified harmonica-players. The band's first recording, "Juke," had been its signature tune, but when released under the name "Little Walter and His Night Cats" it went to number one on the rhythm and blues (R&B) charts, prompting Jacobs to leave Waters's band and trade places with Junior Wells. Wells joined Waters, and Jacobs took over Wells's band, the Aces, which was renamed the Jukes.

Over the next eleven years Jacobs recorded more than eighty songs as a leader for Chess, from the moody ("Blue Midnight") to the sensitive ("Everybody Needs Somebody") and the desperate ("Blue and Lonesome"), from lightly swinging ("Off the Wall") to pounding boogie ("Back Track"), and from the traditional ("Key to the Highway") to the startlingly new ("Roller Coaster"). On both diatonic and chromatic harmonicas he fashioned an approach that was unique and influential. He was an expressive, but never flashy, vocalist whose tunes, both instrumental and vocal, found favor with a wide audience. Fifteen of Jacobs's recordings, including "Juke," "Sad Hours," "Tell Me Mama," "Off the Wall," "You're So Fine," "Oh Baby," and "My Babe," were R&B chart hits between 1952 and 1959. Disagreements about money caused a falling out between Jacobs and his band members in 1954, but the replacements, particularly Robert Lockwood and Luther Tucker on guitars, helped create an even more unique, jazzy sound unlike any other in the blues genre.

Behind his chart successes Jacobs played not only in Chicago but toured widely all over the country, performing at the Apollo in New York City (1952 and 1953), at the Hippodrome Ballroom in Memphis (1954), with Alan Freed's Diddley Daddy Package Show in Boston (1955), and at the Regal Theatre in Chicago (c. 1957). In addition to more than 150 recordings on which he appeared while at Chess, Jacobs also accompanied Otis Rush for the Cobra label in 1957. In 1959 Jacobs recorded the blues classic "Everything's Going to Be Alright," and though he continued to record a number of other exciting songs, it

was his last R&B hit to reach the "Top 25" list. However, the blues revival in England and Europe provided Jacobs with another venue, and he was greeted as a star and genius when he arrived in Britain in September 1964 and began touring as a single or with the Rolling Stones. His final recording session as a leader for Chess in 1966 revealed a man who was literally sick and tired. His supersession recording with Waters and Diddley in 1967 was little better. However, back in England and Europe with the American Folk Blues Festival Tour in 1967, Jacobs recaptured his earlier successes. Always a volatile personality, he got into a street fight with a gang of drunks in Chicago, and the resultant injuries caused his death there.

Speaking of Jacobs, Waters told researcher Paul Guralnick, "I'll tell you, I had the best harmonica player in the business, man." It was a sentiment echoed over and over by musicians and fans alike. Little Walter Jacobs had helped establish the harmonica, often thought of as a mere toy, as a legitimate instrument, one capable of infinite expressiveness, and he himself became the major proponent and standard-setter in the blues and rock idioms. His use of amplification and effects was distinctive and lustrous, but it was his ideas, his ability to improvise imaginatively and seemingly endlessly and to astonish and to move that made him a major voice. And even as he spoke through his instrument, his singing also moved his audiences. John Lee Hooker called Jacobs his "favorite singer" (Leadbetter, p. 123). Singer, harmonica-player, composer, Jacobs was a consummate blues artist, pivotal for his imagination, daring, and honest and heartfelt delivery, and for his ability to so reshape the playing of the harmonica that virtually no harmonica-player after him in blues or rock could deny his influence.

• Biographical information on Little Walter Jacobs can be found in Sheldon Harris, *Blues Who's Who* (1979); an interview with Bill Lindeman in *Living Blues*, Winter 1971, pp. 17–25; and an interview with Muddy Waters in Peter Guralnick, *Feel Like Going Home* (1971). See also booklet notes for the indispensable and exhaustive CD reissues, *Little Walter: The Chess Years 1952–1963*, Charly CD Red Box 5, and *The Complete Muddy Waters 1947–1967*, Charly CD Red Box 3. *The Essential Little Walter*, MCA Chess CHD2-9342, presents a sterling overview of Jacobs's Chess years. His Ora Nelle recordings are available on *Chicago Boogie*, P-Vine PCD-1888, and his Parkway sessions are available on *The Blues World of Little Walter*, Delmark DD-648. John Lee Hooker on Jacobs is quoted in Mike Leadbetter, *Nothing but the Blues* (1971).

STEVEN C. TRACY

JACOBS, Mike (10 Mar. 1880–24 Jan. 1953), sports promoter, was born Michael Strauss Jacobs in New York City, the son of Isaac Jacobs, a tailor, and Rachel Strauss, Polish-Jewish immigrants. Raised on the Lower West Side of Manhattan near the Battery, Jacobs left school after the sixth grade to work as a paperboy and sell refreshments on excursion boats. As a teenager, he obtained the concession rights on the boats, chartered others, and scalped tickets for theatrical, operatic, and sporting events, amassing $1,000 by age sixteen.

By the time he was twenty-four, Jacobs was making money organizing charity balls and fashion shows. He financed bicycle races at the old Madison Square Garden (Madison Avenue at 26th Street), and in return he got to scalp the best seats. He opened a ticket brokerage office in the heart of the theater district in the Hotel Normandie, reselling admissions purchased from season ticket holders. As he became more successful, Jacobs began advancing money for theatrical shows, purchasing entire orchestra sections, or buying out the houses of longer-running productions. He became an excellent judge of show potential, and he was considered an accurate barometer for the ticket brokerage trade. "I make those attractions possible with my financial backing . . . ," he said. "I take the big chances. I should make some profit. How I get my first class tickets is nobody's business." Jacobs also promoted wrestling, basketball, the circus, and tours of such artists as opera tenor Enrico Caruso. In 1911, Jacobs reputedly cleared $100,000 scalping tickets for the World Series.

Jacobs first got involved in boxing after attending the Terry McGovern-George Dixon featherweight championship bout at the Broadway Athletic Club in 1900; he purchased $5 tickets for $7 apiece and resold them for $30 each. In 1915 he helped finance Tex Rickard's promotion of the heavyweight championship fight between titlist Jess Willard and contender, Frank Moran at Madison Square Garden, and he interceded with local politicians who threatened to interfere with the fight. Rickard recognized Jacobs's judgment and flair for ticket-selling, and they became partners. In 1916 Jacobs married Josie Polo; they adopted one child. His first major promotion with Rickard was the 1921 Jack Dempsey-Georges Carpentier heavyweight championship fight in Jersey City, New Jersey, which was advertised as a match between a slacker and a war hero. The promoters raised capital through heavy advance sales, including $200,000 in tickets to New York scalpers. The bout drew a record 80,000 spectators and a $1,789,238 gate, the first to surpass $1 million.

Jacobs helped finance the third Madison Square Garden, built in 1924 at 49th Street and Broadway, a site he had recommended to Rickard because the theater district was moving in that direction. Jacobs was paid $117,000 for getting the bankrupted Manhattan Railway to sell their site for $2.5 million. The block along 49th Street between Eighth Avenue and Broadway became known as "Jacobs' Beach," a popular thoroughfare for the sporting crowd.

When Rickard died in 1929, Jacobs wanted to succeed him as the Garden's boxing promoter, but James J. Johnston was selected instead. In 1933 Jacobs formed the Twentieth Century Sporting Club, with Hearst sports editors Bill Farnsworth of the *New York Journal*, Ed Frayne of the *New York American*, and columnist Damon Runyon, to promote major bouts

for Phoebe Apperson Hearst's Milk Fund at the Bronx Coliseum and the Hippodrome in mid-Manhattan. By 1935 Jacobs was the club's sole owner. One of the club's main innovations was securing sponsored radio broadcasts of its fights.

Early in 1935 Jacobs took a huge step toward becoming the nation's preeminent boxing promoter by signing an exclusive contract with the talented but unpolished heavyweight Joe Louis. He convinced Louis's managers, John Roxborough and Julian Black, that he could help make their fighter champion. Because of the color line, no African-American heavyweight since Jack Johnson had gotten a title shot. Jacobs brought Louis to New York to fight important bouts, beginning with ex-champion Primo Carnera at Yankee Stadium. In 1937 Jacobs got Louis a title match against champion Jimmy Braddock, who was scheduled to fight former champion Max Schmeling. Jacobs persuaded Joe Gould, the champion's manager, to cancel the Schmeling bout by guaranteeing Braddock 10 percent of his share of Louis's purses through 1947. Louis knocked out Braddock on 22 June at Chicago's Comiskey Park.

By the fall of 1937, Jacobs's control over many top fighters and his access to New York's baseball parks for major contests convinced Madison Square Garden officials that they needed him to enhance their boxing business. They rented him space for one year, and in 1938 Jacobs became the Garden's boxing promoter and a full partner.

Louis held the heavyweight title for twelve years. His twenty-three defenses were all promoted by Jacobs. The most memorable were the Schmeling fight in 1938, for which Jacobs was vilified by various Jewish organizations for promoting a fighter whom the public identified with Hitler and Nazi oppression, and the first Billy Conn defense in 1941. Jacobs's most profitable promotion was the Louis-Conn rematch in 1945, attended by 45,266 at Yankee Stadium, with a ringside top of $100, that grossed $1,925,584, second only to the $2.65 million for the 1927 Dempsey-Gene Tunney rematch. Jacobs reportedly made nearly $10 million from all twenty-six of Louis's fights.

From 1937 until 1947 Jacobs promoted sixty-one world championship matches and more than 1,500 fights. His 320 boxing shows at Madison Square Garden, which were attended by 4 million fans, grossed $15 million. Jacobs virtually monopolized boxing championships in New York by signing up contenders to exclusive contracts, giving substantial advances, paying more than his competition, cooperating with the underworld, and controlling boxing at metropolitan arenas and baseball parks.

Critics like Damon Runyon felt Jacobs curtailed opportunities for new managers and fighters, while boxing journalist Nat Fleischer, who recognized Jacobs's integrity in dealing with fighters, felt he lacked honor in his private affairs because he did not pay Fleischer a commission on a radio deal. Supporters claimed he stabilized the anarchic sport, never reneged on a promise, and held honest bouts. Jacobs was an excellent businessman whose promotions were usually paid for in advance. He used radio extensively and planned for paid, limited-access television. He was the most important promoter of the 1930s and 1940s. After suffering a stroke in December 1946, he became less involved in his business, which was sold for $110,000 in May 1949 to the newly organized International Boxing Club. He died in Miami Beach, Florida. Jacobs was elected to the Boxing Hall of Fame in 1982.

• For a biography of Jacobs, see Dan Daniel, *The Mike Jacobs Story* (1950). His work with the Twentieth Century Sporting Club is critically evaluated by his former public relations associate, John V. Grombach, in *The Saga of the Fist: The 9,000 Year Story of Boxing in Text and Pictures* (1977). Highly informative on his career in boxing are Frank Graham, Jr., *Farewell to Heroes* (1981); Barney Nagler, *James Norris and the Decline of Boxing* (1964); Budd Schulberg, "Champions for Sale: The Mike Jacobs Story," *Collier's*, 15, 22, 29 Apr., 6, 13 May 1950; and Francis Albertanti, "Mike Jacobs, Successor to Tex Rickard," *Ring*, July 1936, pp. 6–7. See also John Field and Earl Brown, "The Boxing Racket," *Life*, 17 June 1946. For a personal view of Jacobs, see Nat Fleischer, *50 Years at Ringside* (1960). An obituary is in the *New York Times*, 25 Jan. 1953.

STEVEN A. RIESS

JACOBS, Pattie Ruffner (2 Oct. 1875–22 Dec. 1935), suffragist and social reformer, was born in Malden, West Virginia, the daughter of Lewis Ruffner, a wholesale merchant, and Virginia Louise West. When she was a child, Ruffner's family moved to Nashville, Tennessee, where they enjoyed social and economic prominence. Ruffner attended the Ward Seminary in Nashville and the Birmingham (Ala.) Training School for Teachers before focusing on an education in the arts. From 1894 to 1896 she received one year of voice lessons in Paris and two years of art classes in New York City. Upon returning to Alabama, she married Solon Harold Jacobs, a wealthy railroad businessman, and raised two daughters. In a diary kept before her marriage, Ruffner confided that she longed to "break away and do something really unconventional and new." The early twentieth-century women's movement provided her the opportunity to fulfill her goal.

With the financial and moral support of her husband, Jacobs quickly became involved in social reform and the woman suffrage movement. Women's activism through women's clubs and other associations grew rapidly at the turn of the century. Many women saw their involvement in social reform as an extension of their housekeeping and child care duties and thus, for example, worked to reform education, health, and sanitation, and to establish libraries and reformatories. Like other reformers, Jacobs became a suffragist because of the frustration she experienced in her powerless efforts to pass reform bills. In March 1911 she heard Jean Gordon and Belle Bennett, two nationally known southern suffragists and reformers, speak in Birmingham on the necessity of gaining the vote for women in order to pass child labor laws. Jacobs, provoked by her own inability to persuade the mayor of

Birmingham to act on her plans for sewage disposal, enthusiastically took up the cause. She became the first president of the newly formed Birmingham Equal Suffrage Association. Throughout her work as a suffragist, she argued that woman suffrage was necessary for women to be able to protect themselves, their children, and their communities.

Jacobs quickly gained prominence in the Alabama woman suffrage movement. She was the president of the Alabama Equal Suffrage Association from its formation in 1912 through the passage of the Nineteenth Amendment in 1920, vacating her post only from 1916 to 1918 while she served as auditor of the National American Woman Suffrage Association (NAWSA). She traveled throughout the state, giving speeches, lobbying representatives, and encouraging press coverage. Jacobs led the unsuccessful attempts to win a state woman suffrage amendment in 1915 and to pass the federal amendment in 1919, for which she gained pledges from representatives who then did not vote as promised.

Jacobs's significance to the woman suffrage movement extends beyond her influence in Alabama because she represented southern suffragists to the nation. For example, in 1913 Jacobs spoke at the NAWSA convention, where she declared herself a "living refutation" of the assumption that southern women did not want the vote, attracting press coverage throughout the nation. In 1915 she testified in front of the U.S. Senate on behalf of working women, arguing that, despite the tradition of chivalry in the South, such women needed the vote in order to enact legislation to protect themselves. Because of her intensive involvement on the state, regional, and national levels, she was bitterly disappointed when the NAWSA classified Alabama as a "hopeless" state during the final push for ratification of the Nineteenth Amendment. The refusal of Alabama, and indeed most southern states, to pass the amendment diminished her rejoicing at the passage of woman suffrage. At the 1920 NAWSA convention, she spoke for suffragists from the South. She complained that the "tyranny of tradition" in the South, which resisted new gender roles, restrained southern women and prevented them from gaining a voice in governing their community.

Jacobs is notable for her strong support of the federal amendment in the South, where many women and men argued against it under the guise of states' rights. She allied herself with NAWSA and staunchly opposed Kate Gordon and the Southern States Woman Suffrage Conference, an organization so dedicated to gaining suffrage through state amendments that it preferred no enfranchisement to a federal amendment. Gordon and her organization, like the antisuffragists in the South, argued against the federal amendment because they feared it would enfranchise African-American women. Although Jacobs generally stayed away from virulently racist tactics, in testimony to the U.S. Senate and in a subsequent letter to the *Birmingham News*, she did attempt to appease southern congressmen by reminding them that even with a federal amendment states could still prevent black women from voting by using the same tactics with which they had disfranchised black men, including poll taxes and literacy requirements.

True to her original motivation for joining the woman suffrage movement, Jacobs remained interested in other social reform activities after passage of the Nineteenth Amendment. She was an important figure in the fight against child labor and against the convict lease system. She also became involved in the League of Women Voters and party politics as the Alabama Democrats' first national committeewoman. Through her friendship with Eleanor Roosevelt, she served two appointments under Franklin Roosevelt as head of the Women's Division of the Consumer Advisory Board of the National Recovery Administration in 1933 and subsequently as head of public relations for the Tennessee Valley Authority in Alabama. She died in Birmingham while serving as a TVA official.

Jacobs played a key role in the woman suffrage movement not only because of her leadership in Alabama and in the national organization but also because she was responsible for alerting the nation to southern women's desire for the vote. Despite her pride in southern tradition, she broke with the states' rights argument and supported the federal amendment. As a woman suffragist and a social reformer, Jacobs helped ease the transition from tradition to progress, claiming a place for the New Woman in the early twentieth-century South.

• The Pattie Ruffner Jacobs Papers are located in the Department of Archives and Manuscripts, Birmingham Public Library. Additional information on her suffrage activities is in the minutes and correspondence of the Birmingham Equal Suffrage Association and the Alabama Equal Suffrage Association collections, both at the Alabama Department of Archives and History, Montgomery. Excerpts from Jacobs's speeches can be found in Ida Husted Harper, ed. *History of Woman Suffrage*, vol. 5 (1922), and in the *Woman's Journal*, 6 Dec. 1913. Jacobs's significance to the Alabama woman suffrage movement is analyzed by Mary Martha Thomas in *The New Woman in Alabama* (1992) and her role in the southern movement by Marjorie Spruill Wheeler in *New Women of the New South* (1993). An older but comprehensive biography of Jacobs is Lee N. Allen, "The Woman Suffrage Movement in Alabama, 1910–1920" (master's thesis, Auburn Univ., 1949). Obituaries are in the *Birmingham News* and the *Birmingham Age-Herald*, both 23 Dec. 1935.

JOAN MARIE JOHNSON

JACOBS, Walter L. (15 July 1896–6 Feb. 1985), rental car industry pioneer, was born in Chicago, Illinois, the son of Leon Jacobs and Anna (maiden name unknown). In 1916 Jacobs became a salesman for the Ford Motor Company in Chicago, and he opened his own Ford dealership the following year. In 1918 he married Jeanette Rothschild; they had one son who was killed in action during World War II. In 1918 Jacobs encountered a slump in automobile sales and found himself with a fleet of Model T Fords that he could not sell. As a result, he founded a car rental business with a dozen Model T Fords that he main-

tained himself. Jacobs, who had traveled with his father on a rented horse and buggy, believed that consumers would rent and return cars in the same way that they did with horses and buggies. He named his new venture Rent-a-Ford and added four cars to his fleet the next year. The enterprise grew rapidly. By 1923 Jacobs's fleet comprised more than 500 vehicles and the company boasted annual revenues of about $1 million. During that year Chicago entrepreneur John Hertz, president of the Yellow Cab and Yellow Truck and Coach Manufacturing Company, bought the company from Jacobs, hoping to use as rental vehicles the cab that his company manufactured. The rental business was renamed the Hertz Drive-Ur-Self System, and Jacobs remained as the company's top executive.

In 1926 Hertz sold both the rental business and his Yellow Cab and Yellow Truck Coach Manufacturing Company to General Motors (GM). Once again, Jacobs remained as head of the Hertz Drive-Ur-Self operation. In 1953, when GM attempted to sell its Hertz subsidiary, Jacobs attempted to buy it but was outbid by the Omnibus Corporation, which bought the company for $10.8 million. Although he was bitter that ownership of the company that he had founded had eluded him, he remained with the company, which officially became the Hertz Corporation after Omnibus dropped its own name in favor of the Hertz name. Jacobs served as the first president and chief operating officer of the Hertz Corporation.

Under its new board of directors, the Hertz Corporation began an ambitious program of expansion, acquiring local car-rental companies in various regions of the country and engaging in international operations. Jacobs, a cautious business leader by nature, opposed the expansion program but reluctantly agreed to accept it. Ultimately, Hertz's new acquisitions proved lucrative and established the corporation as the nation's dominant car-rental concern.

In 1958 Jacobs, who still made most of the major company decisions himself, made a critical error when, in an effort to upgrade the corporation's image, he tried to replace 80 percent of Hertz's entire car and truck fleet at once. When the company attempted to sell its old cars, it found the used-car market stagnant and was forced to take heavy losses. The corporation's profits sagged, and as a result of this fiasco, a major overhaul of management took place. In 1960 Jacobs retired as president and chief executive officer of Hertz, but he remained a director of the corporation until 1968. His first wife died in 1964, and later that year he married Mildred Michele (last name unknown). They had one son.

During the 1930s Jacobs was a champion tournament bridge player, winning the U.S. Open Pair Championship in 1936 and the Team-of-Four Championship in 1938. The cautious, conservative management style that he espoused in running the Hertz Corporation was analogous to the careful circumspection needed to win bridge games. Although this leadership style led Jacobs to oppose Hertz's expansion, he still succeeded in guiding the corporation during a period that spanned more than four decades, surviving different transitions and owners. Moreover, as the original founder of Hertz, Jacobs is often recognized as the father of the car-rental business. He died in Miami.

• The Hertz Corporation of Park Ridge, N.J., maintains articles and public relations material on the life of Jacobs. Obituaries are in the *Miami Herald*, 7 Feb. 1985, and the *New York Times*, 6 Feb. 1985.

YANEK MIECZKOWSKI

JACOBSON, John Christian (8 Apr. 1795–24 Nov. 1870), Moravian church educator and administrator, was born Christian Jacobsen in Burkal, Denmark, the son of Jens Jacobsen and Anna Maria (maiden name unknown), home missionaries of the Moravian church. Jacobson was educated at the Moravian school in Christiansfeld, Denmark, where he developed musical interests that would remain an avocational pursuit throughout his life. He studied for the ministry at the Moravian school in Niesky, Germany. There he received an education stressing the classical languages and theology. In 1816 he emigrated to the United States. Immigration authorities gave him, upon his arrival in New York City, an additional first name and changed the spelling of his family name.

After completing his studies, Jacobson accepted appointment as a teacher at Nazareth Hall, a church boarding school for boys in Nazareth, Pennsylvania. In 1820 he became an instructor at Moravian Theological Seminary, also located in Nazareth. In addition to teaching theological subjects, he taught physics, arithmetic, and drawing. In 1826 he married Ann Lisette Schnall, a Canadian. They had seven children.

In 1826 Jacobson was ordained deacon in Salem (now Winston-Salem), North Carolina, and was called to serve the Moravian congregation in nearby Bethania. From 1827 to 1831 he also served as pastor of the Bethabara Moravian Church. In 1834 Jacobson moved to Salem where, for the next ten years, he was inspector (principal) of the Moravian Girls Boarding School (now Salem Academy) and co-pastor of the congregation. As inspector, he increased the school's enrollment and constructed additional educational facilities. In 1838 he was ordained a presbyter in the Moravian ministry, and in 1841 he was appointed to the Provincial Helpers' Conference (executive board) of the Moravian church in North Carolina.

Jacobson returned to Nazareth in 1844 to begin a four-year period as principal of Nazareth Hall. During these years he presided over a general strengthening of the school's program. In 1844 he also became a member of the Provincial Helpers' Conference for the northern district of the Moravian church.

Jacobson was active in denominational affairs crucial to the development of the Moravian church in America. Final authority in administrative matters rested with a governing board located in Herrnhut, Germany, and American Moravians were increasingly dissatisfied with this arrangement. In 1848 Jacobson was one of the American delegates at an international general synod, held in Germany, that approved a gradual restructuring of the Moravian church, granting the Americans control over their own internal affairs. In the following year Jacobson was elected by the newly created Northern Provincial Synod as president of the Provincial Elders' Conference, as the executive board was now called. He resigned his duties at Nazareth Hall and moved to Bethlehem, Pennsylvania, site of the provincial headquarters. In 1852 he made official visits to Moravian congregations and missions in the midwestern United States and eastern Ontario, Canada. In 1854 he was consecrated a bishop.

Final plans for restructuring of the denomination were developed by a Northern Provincial Synod in 1855. Jacobson was reelected president of the Provincial Elders' Conference, a position to which he would continue to be returned until his retirement in 1867. He led the church through the years when it developed its institutional life as an American denomination. This involved the care of existing congregations and oversight of work in new congregations being established among German and Scandinavian immigrants in areas he had visited earlier. He also participated in the reordering of educational institutions, including the establishment of Moravian College for Men and Moravian Theological Seminary as separate from Nazareth Hall. Jacobson's contemporaries remarked upon his broad, nonsectarian theological views, his joyful spirit, and his abiding interest in young people and their education.

Following his retirement he lived in Bethlehem, where he died.

• Materials by and about Jacobson are in Eugene M. Johnson and Ruth Mewaldt Johnson, eds., *John Christian Jacobson: Letters and Drawings* (1989); in the Reeves Library, Moravian College and Theological Seminary, Bethlehem, Pa.; and in the collections of the Moravian Archives (Northern Province), Bethlehem, Pa., and the Moravian Archives (Southern Province), Winston-Salem, N.C. For the North Carolina years, see John H. Clewell, *History of Wachovia in North Carolina* (1902), and Frances Griffin, *Less Time for Meddling* (1979). For Jacobson's educational work, see H. H. Hacker, *Nazareth Hall* (1910), and W. N. Schwarze, *History of the Moravian College and Theological Seminary* (1910). See also J. T. Hamilton and K. G. Hamilton, *History of the Moravian Church* (1967). An obituary is in the *Moravian*, 1 Dec. 1870.

DAVID A. SCHATTSCHNEIDER

JACOBY, Ludwig Sigismund (21 Oct. 1813–21 June 1874), founder of Methodism in Germany, was born in Alt-Sterlitz, Mecklenburg, Germany, the son of Samuel Jacoby and Henriette Hirsch, who were pious Jews. He was apprenticed at fifteen to a merchant in Hamburg and became a traveling salesman at twenty-three for a Leipzig company. He was converted to Christianity in 1835 and was baptized into the Evangelical Lutheran church in Germany, although he doubted much of what he read in the Bible and had, he later claimed, "no idea of true Christianity" (Miller, p. 125).

In 1839 Jacoby immigrated to America, where he taught German among the growing German population of Cincinnati, Ohio, and published a German grammar for English readers. His first encounter with a German congregation of the Methodist Episcopal church came when some of his friends suggested they attend a service to make fun of the preachers. Instead he found himself impressed by what he heard. The following Sunday he returned to hear the preaching of Wilhelm Nast, the dominant figure in German-language American Methodism, and was struck when Nast proclaimed, "There may be a Saul among us, whom God will convert into a Paul" (Miller, p. 126). Attending prayer meetings during the week and visiting Nast at his home, he joined the church on the Monday before Christmas in 1839 and had a conversion experience during the watch-night service on New Year's Eve.

Embracing his new life, he wrote ten days later a short article about his experience among the Methodists in *Der Christliche Apologete* (Jan. 1840), the widely read German-American Methodist newspaper, and spent three months in prayer and study. After receiving a license to preach, he began a ministry among the canal laborers of the city. In September 1840 he married Amalie Theresa Nuelson, a former Roman Catholic and recent Methodist convert; they had eight children.

Bishop Thomas Asbury Morris asked Jacoby to begin a mission among the Germans in St. Louis, Missouri. Arriving on 1 August 1841, he observed St. Louis to be a "wicked place" in which "the Germans distinguished themselves especially by profaning the Sabbath" and, in Jacoby's opinion, knew nothing of "practical Christianity" (Miller, p. 131). He rented a small church, distributed tracts, and advertised a preaching service that eventually filled with the curious when he rang the church's bell. His evangelistic doctrines and marketplace preaching earned him denunciations in the local German Catholic press, and his moral militancy against alcohol and Sabbath breaking earned him enemies among saloon keepers. Threatened by mobs, he was protected by a group of "watchmen" authorized by the mayor; undoubted, he expanded his work, preaching in the market on the city's southside. A Methodist Episcopal congregation was formally organized on 22 November 1841 with twenty-two members, and by the next August they had dedicated a new building. He also founded the first day school in St. Louis and put it under the direction of Heinrich Nuelsen, his brother-in-law. His work in south St. Louis resulted in the formation of a second congregation in September 1843.

When the 1844 General Conference of the Methodist Episcopal church authorized the creation of German-speaking districts, Jacoby became the superintendent of the St. Louis district, which included churches in Missouri, Illinois, Iowa, and later Wisconsin. The demanding work and extensive travel took a toll on his health, and in 1849 he nearly died of pneumonia. During his illness he found comfort in reading accounts of the faithful deaths of other Christians and much later published a collection of these stories as *Letzte Stunden* (Last Hours, 1874).

In May 1849 Morris and the Methodist Mission Society asked Jacoby to found a mission to Germany in Bremen, the principal point of departure for immigrants to America. Despite his need for rest and his wife's resistance to returning to Germany, they left New York on his thirty-sixth birthday with a few tracts and Bibles. Arriving in Bremerhaven on 7 November 1849, he wrote in his journal, "Here is the place where I must and can work. But am I the man for the job? That is the question. I have neither the health nor the strength for that. Yet the Lord will help" (Mann, p. 41).

His work in Bremen followed much the same pattern as that in St. Louis. He rented a hall at the *Amthaus* (a public building) and advertised preaching meetings. As the crowds grew he found it necessary to move his meetings to a larger adjoining space, even preaching in a rented dance hall in the Bremen suburbs. A class of twenty-one formed on Easter 1850, and the congregation held its first quarterly conference on 21 May 1850.

Responding to his requests for help, the Mission Board sent him sorely needed funds; Jacoby introduced a biweekly magazine, *Der Evangelist*, first published on 25 May 1850. The board also made him superintendent of the German Mission and sent two new missionaries, Carl H. Döring and Ludwig Nippert, who arrived in June 1850. With the additional help, Jacoby was able to open the first Sunday school in Germany on 16 June 1850 in Bremen. It was so effective that its pattern was soon adopted by the *Landeskirche* (state church) and spread throughout Germany.

With the arrival of several more missionaries and the emergence of local leaders, Jacoby was able to expand the mission work farther south. In 1855 Methodism began in Switzerland when he appointed missionaries to Lausanne and Zurich. In 1856 he returned to America to attend the General Conference in Indianapolis during which the growing German-Swiss nation became its own Mission Conference. Back in Germany, he helped form a theological seminary in Bremen to train preachers and directed its work for ten years. By 1868 the German Mission Conference was accorded the full rights of an annual conference, at which time Jacoby gave up his position of the superintendency of the entire work and became superintendent of the Oldenburg district.

In 1871 Jacoby and his family returned to America so that he could reassume the pastorate of the church in south St. Louis that he had founded in 1843. Despite his health problems he was again appointed the superintendent of the St. Louis district. He died in St. Louis. Shortly thereafter, the almost 9,000 Methodists in Germany marked the twenty-fifth anniversary of their beginnings under him.

• In 1855 Jacoby published *Handbuch des Methodismus* (Handbook of Methodism) and *Kurzer Inbegriff der Christli-*

chen Glaubenslehre (Brief Summary of the Christian Faith). He also wrote *Christliche Geschichten* (Christian Stories, 1957), *Predigt-Entwürfe über freie Texte* (Sermon—Sketches on Free Texts, 1858), and *Geschichte des Methodismus* (History of Methodism, 1870). His account of his conversion and early work is told in Adam Miller, *Experience of German Methodist Preachers* (1859). Heinrich Mann, *Ludwig S. Jacoby* (1892), has the most complete bibliography. William G. Chrystal, "'Hope Does Not Disappoint Us': Ludwig S. Jacoby and German Methodism," *Perkins Journal of Theology* 32 (Summer 1979): 31–43, is a more contemporary treatment in English. Paul Douglass includes important information in his *The Story of German Methodism* (1939). An obituary is in the *St. Louis Daily Globe*, 21 June 1874.

CLIFTON F. GUTHRIE

JACOBY, Oswald (8 Dec. 1902–27 June 1984), bridge champion and actuary, was born in Brooklyn, New York, the son of Oswald Nathaniel Jacoby, a prosperous attorney, and Edith Sondheim. From them, at the age of ten, he learned the card game that was to make him famous.

Jacoby had two months of army service in World War I, apparently concealing from authorities that he was only fifteen. He then studied at Columbia University, where he was remembered for objecting to the blackboard solution of a ballistics problem; the instructor later admitted that Jacoby's rapid mental solution was correct. He left college in his junior year and qualified as an actuary at twenty-one, the youngest ever at that time and an achievement not challenged until 1980. He worked four years for Metropolitan Life before going into actuarial business for himself, a venture that ended with the 1929 stock market crash. He continued practice as a consulting actuary for the rest of his life.

In 1929 Jacoby won the American Whist League's National Team Championship. This was auction bridge, a development from whist, but a form of the game already declining. Its replacement, contract bridge, which required players to bid the full value of their hands, had been codified by Harold Stirling Vanderbilt in 1925 and was sweeping North America. Jacoby became one of its earliest experts by winning the 1929 Goldman Pairs, the first important contest in the new form of the game. He was to remain at the top for fifty-five years.

Jacoby became front-page news in December 1931 when Sidney Lenz chose him to be his partner in the "Bridge Battle of the Century." Lenz, then fifty-eight, was the leader of the bridge establishment, a group of authorities who had made their reputations in the days of auction. Lenz had accepted a challenge from Ely Culbertson, the most famous personality in contract bridge. The American public had adopted the Culbertson System, with its emphasis on slow development of the bidding and honor-trick valuation, to the annoyance of his professional rivals. The match was to consist of 150 rubbers and was played at the Chatham Hotel in New York City. Jacoby and Lenz played together for 103 rubbers, at which point disagreements between them became explosive. Jacoby stalked away from the table and announced to the press: "Our differences are of ideas and methods of treating bridge . . . I have now become convinced that it would be unfair to him [Lenz] for me to reenter the match." This was a diplomatic exit, since, instead of apologizing for his own numerous errors, Lenz had criticized Jacoby's imaginative bidding tactics. Lenz continued with another partner, and Culbertson won the match, but Jacoby was now a household name.

Jacoby was familiarly known to the public as "Ozzie," and his activities were widely reported. He built a reputation for disruptive, psychological warfare at the bridge table; a "Jacoby" became synonymous with any bid made on practically nothing. Critics wondered why a man with a logical, mathematical mind should revel in such tactics.

From 1931 to 1933 Jacoby won a series of titles with David Burnstine, P. Hal Sims, and Willard Karn. They called themselves the "Four Horsemen"—a name that suited Jacoby, who had played polo at Columbia. He and Burnstine then joined with Howard Schenken and Michael Gottlieb to form the "Four Aces," the most famous team in bridge's early years.

In 1932 Jacoby married Mary Zita McHale, a Texan, and she persuaded him to move from New York City to Dallas two years later.

The Four Aces dominated tournament play in the thirties and won the first world championship in a match played against a French team in Madison Square Garden in 1935. However, Culbertson still held the public's attention and regularly outmaneuvered the Aces. His many books sold in great numbers, and their one book did not sell at all. In 1937 it was the Culbertson team that went to Budapest for the second world championship, while the Four Aces, who had qualified for the trip by winning a selection tournament, stayed home. Culbertson, as head of the U.S. Bridge Association, provocatively announced that the Aces would be representing the Culbertson System, and they indignantly withdrew. Instead, they challenged him to a match, but he refused.

In 1936 the American Bridge League named ten Life Masters on the basis of tournament success, and Jacoby was Life Master #2. The ABL was the rival to Culbertson's organization, and the two merged a year later.

Over the next five years Jacoby's successes earned him more master-points—the tournament currency—than anyone else. But when Pearl Harbor was attacked in 1941, he promptly left a tournament and joined the navy, in which he rose to the rank of lieutenant commander before his discharge. He returned to service during the Korean War, served as a commander in intelligence, and was an original staff member at the Panmunjom armistice conference.

A decade of limited play had left Jacoby far behind in the master-point standings, but the fifties brought him a string of successes. In 1962 he overtook Charles Goren as the player with most career master-points, and in 1963 he became the first player to win more than a thousand points in a calendar year. From 1959 to 1963 he was a four-time winner of the McKenney Trophy, awarded to the player accumulating the most master-points in a single year. In 1960 he played in the first World Team Olympiad in Turin, Italy, on a team that finished fifth.

In 1950 Jacoby had become daily bridge columnist for the Newspaper Enterprise Association, and by 1982 he had written more than 10,000 columns. In his late years he shared the writing with one of his two sons, James. In 1970 and 1971 the family helped the United States win world team titles, with Oswald as nonplaying captain and James as a player.

In 1973, at the age of seventy, Jacoby won the world championship of backgammon. He was skilled at many other card games and at chess. He wrote books on mathematics, gambling, poker, and backgammon as well as four books on bridge and two best-selling books on canasta.

His earliest contribution to the theory of bridge was the weak jump overcall, an attempt to crowd opposing bidding, which is now standard practice. Later in life he introduced the Jacoby Transfer bid, a bid of a suit below the one held in order to make the opening no-trump bidder the declarer, and the Jacoby Two No-trump response, showing slam interest and a fit for the partner's major suit. Both are widely used by modern tournament players.

Jacoby won the two most prestigious American championships, the Vanderbilt Knockout and the Spingold Knockout, seven times each. The last of his twenty-four national victories was remarkable—the Reisinger Board-a-Match Teams in November 1983, when he was eighty years old and fighting the cancer that claimed his life in Dallas seven months later.

• An account of Jacoby's early bridge career appears under the title "Irrepressible Ozzie" in *Championship Bridge as Played by the Experts* (1949), by J. Patrick Dunne and Albert A. Ostrow. See also *The Bridge Immortals* (1967), by Victor Mollo, and the *Official Encyclopedia of Bridge*, 4th ed. (1984). An obituary is in the *New York Times*, 28 June 1984.

ALAN TRUSCOTT

JACUZZI, Aldo Joseph (26 Apr. 1921–21 Feb. 1989), pump manufacturing executive, was born in Berkeley, California, the son of Giuseppe Jacuzzi and Rena Beggio. Jacuzzi's father was one of five brothers who started a family machine shop making airplane propellers in Berkeley in 1915. The business was incorporated in 1920. When one brother, Giocondo, was killed in an experimental plane crash in 1921, his death caused the other brothers to decide to get out of the airplane business. Seeking a new product, they settled on crop defrosters. Later, water pumps for irrigation became the firm's main products. In 1937, upon the death of the oldest brother, Rachele, Giuseppe became president of the company.

After graduation from high school in 1939, Jacuzzi went to work at Jacuzzi Brothers, Inc., primarily installing water pumps in the field, while he continued his studies part time at Armstrong Business College in Berkeley and at the University of California in San Francisco. On his twenty-first birthday, he married his high school sweetheart, Granuccia Maria Amadei, who was a native of Lucca, Italy, and who had emigrated to the United States when she was seven. They had three children.

Jacuzzi's college studies were permanently interrupted when he was drafted during the same week in 1944 that twelve other first cousins in the family business also received their draft notices. He entered the U.S. Navy as a machinist apprentice at San Diego and left with an honorable discharge as a machinist mate, third class, in 1946. He then returned to Jacuzzi Brothers, Inc., as a purchasing agent. From 1951 to 1954, he served as a director on a special corporate board within the company, overseeing an expansion project into Canada. Later he became a director on the executive boards of both Jacuzzi Mexico S.A. and Jacuzzi Domestic-International Sales Corp.

In 1954 the work of Jacuzzi Brothers, Inc., underwent another important change when it began to shift from manufacturing primarily agricultural irrigation equipment to manufacturing whirlpool baths for spa and home use, a change Aldo Jacuzzi supported. After a few years, the firm achieved multimillion dollar, multinational status. Jacuzzi relocated his family to Little Rock, Arkansas, when the firm moved its international headquarters there in 1963. Upon the death of his father in 1965, Jacuzzi was promoted to his first position of prominence in the company, as vice president for purchasing. He served in that office until 1970, when he became board chairman.

Although he was not an inventor himself, Jacuzzi actively promoted and expanded sales of the patented inventions of the nine family members who were granted U.S. patents, particularly those developed by his uncle Candido. As chairman, Jacuzzi made a distinctive contribution to the firm by smoothly completing the international expansion of the business. He made several trips to Jacuzzi plants abroad and to offices of major licensees in South America, sometimes with his wife serving as a translator, to carry out important public relations work for the firm.

Jacuzzi steered a corporate course that rode the wave of social changes, such as increased leisure time and a focus on health issues, and rising affluence that marked his tenure during the entire 1970s. Not only did he understand the ongoing social changes as they were taking place, but also he helped to create them by the skillful use of marketing tools. Thus, the company was not surprised by changes in the marketplace during this transitional period. Consequently, he was able to take financial advantage of these marketplace changes as they occurred. Jacuzzi also had a great compassion for his workers and they, in turn, felt that they could go directly to him as chairman to discuss any issue that concerned them.

In 1979 Jacuzzi engineered the sale of the company to Kidde, Inc., headquartered in Saddle Brook, New Jersey, and stepped down as chairman in 1980. He and his wife then started Aldo Jacuzzi Investments, while Kidde, Inc., retained him as a consultant, a position in which he remained active for three years. As a private citizen, he was active in a number of organizations, particularly the Little Rock Chamber of Commerce, the Leonardo da Vinci Cultural Society, and the Sons of Italy. He served on the local boards of the Salvation Army and the United Way. He also financially supported the Boy Scouts and the Girl Scouts. He was a lifelong Roman Catholic. In his personal life, he was an accomplished accordionist, as was his wife, with whom he sometimes performed publicly. He was also a singer, sculptor, painter, and woodworker. Similarly, he was a serious amateur gemologist and philatelist.

In 1986 Jacuzzi developed a form of spinal paralysis called amyotrophic lateral sclerosis (ALS), better known as Lou Gehrig's disease. His wife cared for him at home for almost three years up to a few days before he died at St. Vincent's Infirmary in Little Rock.

• Personal information about Jacuzzi was obtained from his wife during a series of telephone interviews conducted with the author in 1992. Condensed biographies are in *Who's Who in America*, 42d ed. (1982–1983), p. 1656; *Standard & Poor's Register of Directors and Executives*, vol. 2 (1984), p. 651, which contains information on his executive positions not in other references; and *Who Was Who in America*, vol. 9 (1985–1989), p. 181. Obituaries are in the *New York Times*, 23 Feb. 1989, and the *Washington Post*, 25 Feb. 1989.

JOSEPH SCAFETTA, JR.

JACUZZI, Candido (24 Feb. 1903–7 Oct. 1986), inventor and pump manufacturing executive, was born in Casarsa della Delizia in the Friuli region of northeastern Italy, the son of Giovanni Jacuzzi and Teresa Arman, farmers. Because of his family's poverty, Jacuzzi left elementary school after five years to help his parents and siblings on the farm. In March 1920 he arrived with his two oldest sisters to join five of his six older brothers already in the United States. His parents and other siblings emigrated in 1921. They settled in Berkeley, California, where the brothers operated a machine shop. Jacuzzi started work as an apprentice machinist as soon as he arrived at the Jacuzzi Bros. Co. In 1925 he married Inez Ranieri; they had four children. He was promoted from master machinist to sales manager in 1933. After applying for his first two U.S. patents relating to agricultural well pumps, which formed the heart of the family business at that time, Jacuzzi was promoted from sales manager to general manager in 1940.

Jacuzzi's youngest son, born in 1941, developed rheumatoid arthritis as a toddler, and when the boy was about seven his doctor recommended hydrotherapy. Unfortunately, facilities for such treatment were located only in distant spas and in communal tubs in large hospitals, neither of which was accessible or particularly appropriate for a small boy with severe arthritis. Jacuzzi, already an experienced inventor with four U.S. patents related to pumps credited to him, attacked the problem, and in 1949 he developed a unique type of pump that created a swirling whirlpool in a bathtub. When his son's suffering was temporarily relieved by the treatment, Jacuzzi patented this invention and assigned it to the family business, which, in turn, assigned one percent of the royalties to Candido's son in order to provide for his well-being. After Jacuzzi further modified the invention to make it suitable for mass production and to meet state safety requirements, which had delayed its introduction, the company began commercial marketing of the finished product in the early 1950s as a hydromassage unit for bathtubs of conventional sizes. Jacuzzi later developed the product into a whirlpool pump system for spas and incorporated it into specially designed large baths, which became known as hot tubs.

Between 1933 and 1971, Jacuzzi acquired thirty-one U.S. patents in his own name. Meanwhile, twenty other U.S. patents were issued to eight different Jacuzzi family members, principally for improvements in water-pumping systems for agricultural and domestic devices in the company's other lines of business. As general manager, Jacuzzi maintained a strong hand in all operations and stayed in this position for twenty-five years. When the company headquarters were moved to Little Rock, Arkansas, in 1963 to centralize production and distribution throughout the United States, he relocated his family there. Upon the death of his brother Giuseppe in 1965, Candido became president of the firm and continued the international expansion of the business begun in the 1950s during Giuseppe's tenure. Even before becoming president, Candido had been the prime moving force behind the overseas drive. He accelerated the expansion, not only because he believed in the global sales opportunities awaiting the company, but also because he wanted to create enough management positions for the second and future generations of the Jacuzzis. In that regard, concern for his large, extended family was often his stated reason for either taking or not taking any business action.

Primarily because of his series of inventions that related to submersible pumps and whirlpool baths, the company continued to expand in the late 1960s and the early 1970s. Jacuzzi established manufacturing facilities in Mexico, Canada, Italy, Brazil, and Chile, to meet a growing demand abroad. International sales grew steadily until they leveled off at about 50 percent of the firm's $300 million dollar volume. While he was president, Candido returned to northern Italy to set up a factory there for sales throughout Europe. As a sideline, he familiarized himself with viniculture and produced an Italian wine called Piccolit. It was made from a rare white grape. He did not market the wine commercially but, rather, personally distributed it to his family members, friends, and business associates in Europe. In 1968 he created a soft, metal-framed bathing suit, which was open at the sides. Jacuzzi dubbed it the "Coquillini." Highly popular when it was introduced on the Italian and French rivieras, this seashell-like outfit won first prize from the *Marie Claire* magazine at a swimwear trade show held in Nice, France, in 1969.

During his tenure as president, the company's sales emphasis for Jacuzzi whirlpool baths changed from solely health treatment to recreational use, both indoors and outdoors, at public spas and in private residences. In the consumer-oriented business world that expanded rapidly after World War II, in which many people were financially able to pay for luxurious and sensational products, Jacuzzi foresaw the potential enthusiasm for the hot tub, if it were marketed properly. Moreover, he was able to react more quickly than his competitors to the evolving demand for whirlpool baths because he was its principal developer and stayed technologically ahead of the others. The baths became so popular that the family name became the generic term for the hot tub. "Jacuzzi" now appears in most English dictionaries.

Jacuzzi remained president until 1971, at which time he retired and moved from Little Rock. Nevertheless, he remained active on the board of directors until he became paralyzed in 1975. Resigning from the board, he died a decade later at his home in Scottsdale, Arizona.

• A brief biography was written by Nathan Aaseng in *The Problem Solvers* (1989). Information about his U.S. patents is available in the assignment records in the Public Search Room of the U.S. Patent and Trademark Office, Arlington, Virginia. Information about his personal life was obtained from Kenneth A. Jacuzzi, Candido's youngest son, during a series of telephone interviews conducted with the author in 1992. Obituaries are in the *London Times*, *New York Times*, and *Washington Post*, 10 Oct. 1986; *Newsweek*, 20 Oct. 1986; *People Weekly*, 27 Oct. 1986; and *Contemporary Newsmakers* (1988).

JOSEPH SCAFETTA, JR.

JACUZZI, Rachele (11 Nov. 1886–24 Aug. 1937), inventor, was born in Casarsa della Delizia in northeastern Italy, the son of Giovanni Jacuzzi and Teresa Arman, farmers. After only three years of schooling, he began selling newspapers in the local train station where his father worked part-time as a porter. At age fourteen he began working during the summers at a brick-making factory near Wiesbaden, Germany. At nineteen he was employed full-time as a telegraph operator but soon enlisted in the Italian army. He attended the communications training school in Florence before being assigned to Asmara, the capital of Eritrea, an Italian colony in northeastern Africa. After his discharge in 1909, he sold his gold watch and bought a ticket to the United States, where he joined his brothers Valeriano and Francesco picking oranges in Los Angeles in 1910.

Shortly thereafter, Jacuzzi got a job repairing airplanes and building propellers for a firm in Los Angeles. By 1915 he had saved enough money to travel to the Panama-Pacific International Exposition being held in San Francisco. There he took another job as an aircraft mechanic and invented a laminated wooden, metal-tipped propeller that he dubbed "the toothpick." It was so successful that he rented a small machine shop in nearby Oakland and began to man-

ufacture it. In 1916 he married Olimpia Calugi. Four brothers moved into their home, and a new Jacuzzi homestead was established in California. The couple adopted one child.

After the United States entered World War I in March 1917, Jacuzzi obtained a government contract for the toothpick propeller. To satisfy the demand for thousands of them he moved the firm to a larger facility in Berkeley.

After the war Jacuzzi brought the rest of his family to California and incorporated the business in 1920. He and his brothers had great enthusiasm for aviation and soon constructed a small monoplane using a rebuilt Ford Model T auto engine. When the aircraft was successfully flown, they dubbed it "the Mosquito" and decided to build a larger version. The result was a high-winged monoplane powered by a 200-horsepower L-6 Hall-Scott engine. Because the plane carried a pilot and six passengers, it was nicknamed the J-7. Since the plane was the first to have a large, fully enclosed cabin, the Air Mail Service agreed to a test flight in April 1921. It was flown from San Francisco, over the Sierra Nevada Mountains, 187 miles to Reno, Nevada, in about two hours. Unfortunately, during the last test flight on 14 July 1921, the engine exploded and four men were killed, including 26-year-old Giocondo Jacuzzi. The six surviving brothers then agreed to get out of the aircraft business.

Jacuzzi's practical knowledge of fluid dynamics led him next to develop a crop defroster, which was sold under the "Frostifugo" trademark. This "frost machine" blew hot air over California fruit orchards via a large propeller driven by a powerful engine. Although some sales sustained the Jacuzzi brothers' company during the early and mid-1920s, the machine was not a great success.

In 1925 Jacuzzi began research on a small steam jet. In the process he realized that the steam injection principle could be applied to water. Later in 1926 he built his first water jet injection pump for moving water from below ground in a deep agricultural well. Patent no. 1,758,400 was issued to him on 13 May 1930. This invention revolutionized the agricultural industry first in California and later throughout the United States because it allowed farmers to expand and cultivate land that, lacking nearby surface water sources, had to rely on deep underground water pumped to the surface. Later in 1930 he exhibited his radical jet pump at the California State Fair in Sacramento, where the California Agricultural Society awarded the company a gold medal for "Meritorious Invention." A 1933 patent covered an improvement that used centrifugal force in a single-stage pump to discharge water from a deep well at particularly high pressures. Although the Great Depression adversely affected general business conditions Jacuzzi expanded the line of pumps manufactured by his company by developing a turbine pump, a high-pressure car-wash pump, a filter for a wine pump, a multistage pump, and a slow speed pump.

In 1936 he published two booklets: "Creation" and "Wind, Solar, and Geologic Power." Despite his lack of formal education, he liked to discuss his theories, particularly about atomic energy, with professors at the University of California. Because of the controversial nature of some of his ideas, he published the booklets pseudonymously. Many of his ideas were extremely insightful. For example, in "Creation," which appeared under the pen name R. J. Veltro, he predicted that "any attempt to remove atomic energy will probably give us the annihilation of matter," thus presaging by nine years the destructive power of the atomic bomb. Further, he predicted that "everything would collapse into a cold, small body of tremendous density," thus predicting the destruction of the solar system by being sucked into a black hole not yet discovered in outer space. Likewise, in "Wind, Solar and Geologic Power," written under the nom de plume of J. V. Raquelote, he predicted by twenty-two years the Soviet Sputnik satellite with the statement that "Some day we will probably be able to build an asteroid that will fly around the earth from west to east." Jacuzzi died in Berkeley from a coronary thrombosis.

• There is no known standard reference work that includes a biography of Rachele Jacuzzi. However, some trade publications and company magazines include brief biographies about some or all aspects of Jacuzzi's life. The best-known accounts are the following: Ted Palmer, "A Story of the Jacuzzi Brothers," *Westward Magazine* (Kaiser Steel Corp.), May 1952; "The Jacuzzi Brothers: Rachele," *The Injector* (Jacuzzi Bros. Inc.), Dec. 1958; "Pioneer of Flight," *The Injector* (Jacuzzi Bros. Inc.), Summer 1967; and "Jacuzzi: A Name for Quality since 1915" (Kidde, Inc.), 1980. Additional personal information about Rachele Jacuzzi was obtained from his last secretary, Lola Jacuzzi Fenolio, during a series of telephone interviews conducted in 1992.

JOSEPH SCAFETTA, JR.

JADWIN, Edgar (7 Aug. 1865–2 Mar. 1931), soldier and engineer, was born in Honesdale, Pennsylvania, the son of Cornelius Comegys Jadwin, a druggist, and Charlotte Ellen Wood. He attended Lafayette College for two years and then in 1886 received an appointment to the U.S. Military Academy at West Point, from which he graduated first in his class four years later. Jadwin was commissioned a second lieutenant in the Army Corps of Engineers and assigned as senior inspector on the project to enlarge the immigration station at Ellis Island, New York. In February 1891 he reported to the Engineer School of Application at Willet's Point, New York, where he took the postgraduate course; he remained as quartermaster of the battalion of engineers until 1895, when he became the assistant to the district engineer in Wilmington, North Carolina, working on various river and harbor improvements. In October 1897 he became an assistant in the Fortification Section in the Office of the Chief of Engineers in Washington, D.C.

During the Spanish-American War, Jadwin was promoted to major and then lieutenant colonel, Third U.S. Volunteer Engineers, and enlisted recruits for the regiment in New Mexico, Arkansas, and Texas. In December 1898 he went to Cuba and commanded a battalion at Matanzas until the end of February 1899. During this time he oversaw many municipal projects, including the construction of roads, water supply systems, camps, and a dock, and he considerably improved sanitary conditions. Promoted to the regular rank of captain in 1900, Jadwin subsequently served as Los Angeles district engineer from March 1902 to June 1903 and as Galveston district engineer from June 1903 to January 1904. In the latter position he supervised the extension of the seawall at Fort Crockett, part of the plan to protect Galveston against a recurrence of the enormous loss of life and property the island had suffered during the 1900 hurricane.

In July 1907, then Major Jadwin began serving as division engineer of the Chagres Division in the Panama Canal. A year later he became resident engineer of the Atlantic Division, Harbor and Channel Section, during which time he supervised the construction of the Colon breakwater, the operation of harbor dredges, and the transport of material for lock and dam construction. He continued his work in Panama until August 1911, when he returned to the United States. After a few months as district engineer in Nashville, Tennessee, Jadwin organized a new Miscellaneous Civil Section in the Office of the Chief of Engineers. The section regulated the building of structures in and over navigable waters. In October 1913 Jadwin was promoted to lieutenant colonel. He served as Pittsburgh District Engineer from June 1916 to May 1917.

During World War I Jadwin organized railway troop regiments and commanded one of the regiments, the Fifth Reserve Engineers (name later changed to Fifteenth Engineers, Railway). In France the regiment constructed supply depots, storehouses, and railway tracks. In December 1917 Jadwin was promoted to the rank of brigadier general in the National Army. Three months later he was transferred to Langres to be chief engineer of the Advance Lines of Communication. From March to May 1918 he was director of light railways and roads. Then he was assigned to the Headquarters of the Service of Supply as director of construction and forestry. He supervised the construction of docks, railroads, roads, barracks, hospitals, and various storage facilities. At the height of this activity he commanded 160,000 engineer troops.

In 1919 Jadwin went to Poland as part of the American Mission, and later he traveled as an observer to the Ukraine. Assuming his regular rank of colonel, he returned to the United States in November 1919 and was assigned as Engineer of the Eighth Corps Area at Fort Sam Houston, Texas. In July 1922 Jadwin became the Charleston, South Carolina, district engineer and supervised construction of various parts of the Intracoastal Waterway and of harbors stretching from North Carolina to Florida. He became assistant chief of engineers in June 1924, with the rank of brigadier general. Concurrently he served on several engineer boards, including an international Joint Board of Engineers on the St. Lawrence River.

Jadwin became chief of engineers in June 1926, with the rank of major general. Upon retirement from that position in August 1929, he was elevated to the rank of lieutenant general, a promotion resulting from a 1915 congressional act that recognized the services of military officers who had contributed to the construction of the Panama Canal. In the winter and spring of 1927, a major flood disaster hit the lower Mississippi River, forcing the Corps of Engineers to re-examine its reliance on levees. Jadwin ordered a complete investigation. The result was the so-called "Jadwin Plan," submitted to Congress in December 1927. It emphasized the importance of complementing levees with dredging, controlled outlets, and revetment work. The plan proposed three different floodways (the principal one was through the Atchafalaya Basin in Louisiana) to shorten the distance to the Gulf and lessen flows past New Orleans and Baton Rouge and one spillway to connect the Mississippi River with Lake Pontchartrain. Though controversial and modified on many occasions, the plan became the basis for all subsequent flood control work on the lower Mississippi River.

After retirement Jadwin served as a delegate to the World Engineering Congress and consulted on a number of engineering projects. He declined President Herbert Hoover's offer to make him chairman of the Federal Power Commission but later became chairman of the Interoceanic Canal Board, which investigated the possibility of a sea-level canal through Nicaragua or, alternatively, increasing the capacity of the Panama Canal. He died in Panama after suffering a cerebral hemorrhage.

Jadwin married Jean Laubach in 1891; the couple had two children. A man of high intelligence but somewhat frail constitution, he struggled with poor eyesight his entire life. Conscientious about examining a question thoroughly, he became impatient when obstacles prevented execution after a decision was reached. Political delays, especially ones that seemingly brought into question the competence of the Corps of Engineers, annoyed him. His defense of the Corps occasionally alienated him from members of Congress and from civilian engineers. For instance, when a member of Congress asked him in a hearing whether Congress should accept his plan for the Mississippi River simply because he, as chief of engineers, presented it, Jadwin replied, "I think you would do a whole lot better to take our engineering than your own." Pressed further, Jadwin testily noted, "You have force of engineers, a competent force of engineers authorized for this purpose." Challenged to answer the question directly, Jadwin finally admitted, "Yes, I think you ought to do it."

• There is no adequate biography of Jadwin, and no collection of his personal papers exists. The Office of History, Headquarters, U.S. Army Corps of Engineers, has a biographical file on Jadwin containing information on his career.

See also Herbert Deakyne's memoir of Jadwin published in the *Transactions of the American Society of Civil Engineers* 96 (1932): 1498–1503.

MARTIN REUSS

JAEGER, Werner Wilhelm (30 July 1888–19 Oct. 1961), classical scholar and humanist, was born at Lobberich, a small German town in the lower Rhineland, the only child of Lutheran parents, Karl August Jaeger, a textile merchant, and Helene Birschel. One of the giants of twentieth-century classical scholarship, Jaeger, after one semester of study at the University of Marburg (1907), transferred to the University of Berlin at the age of nineteen. At Berlin he studied under some of the most famous classicists of the time, including Hermann Diels and Ulrich von Wilamowitz-Moellendorff. Jaeger's dissertation on Aristotle was published in two parts, *Emendationum Aristotelearum Specimen* (1911) and *Studien zur Entstehungsgeschichte der Metaphysik des Aristoteles* (1912). These studies already contain the kernel of what is perhaps Jaeger's greatest work, his book on Aristotle published in 1923; he had reached his main conclusions when he was hardly more than twenty-one. After a year's stay in Rome to study Greek manuscripts, he published his *Nemesios von Emesa* in 1914. In this same year he was invited to assume the chair of Greek at the University of Basel, the same chair that Friedrich Nietzsche had once held. Jaeger accepted; he was twenty-six. The next year he went to Kiel as professor ordinarius; then in 1921 he was called to Berlin to be Wilamowitz's successor. Jaeger was thirty-three. In the same year appeared the first two volumes of what was to be a lifelong project for Jaeger, the first truly critical edition of the works of the fourth-century church father and mystical theologian Gregory of Nyssa.

In 1923 Jaeger published his masterpiece, *Aristoteles: Grundlegung einer Geschichte seiner Entwicklung*. The book literally caused a revolution. For centuries Aristotle had been regarded as a profound but dogmatic thinker whose philosophy was a closed system. Jaeger's thesis was that Aristotle had in fact begun his philosophical journey—for such it was—as a Platonist but that he gradually moved away from his master's views and, while never completely abandoning certain Platonic tendencies, developed an original, and hardly static, philosophy of his own. This reconstruction of Aristotle's thought and development involved enormous problems, philological as well as philosophical, which Jaeger handled in a masterly manner. The result was, for the first time, a picture of Aristotle as a real person of flesh and blood, not some vague abstraction. No work on Aristotle in the twentieth century has generated so much discussion.

Jaeger was always interested in the ancient Greeks as educators who had something to teach modern man. The great monument to this side of his thought is his famous three-volume work *Paideia: The Ideals of Greek Culture*. The first volume, written in German, was published in 1934 (English translation by Gilbert Highet in 1939); the second and third volumes appeared first in Gilbert Highet's English translation in 1943 and 1944 and in German in 1944 and 1947.

Between the appearance of the first and second volumes of *Paideia*, the alarming tendencies of Hitler and the Third Reich had become ever clearer. In 1934 Jaeger went to the University of California as the Sather Professor of Greek. His expanded lectures resulting from this appointment appeared as *Demosthenes: The Origin and Growth of His Policy* (1938). However, the Sather was a visiting professorship only, and in 1935 Jaeger returned to Germany. In 1936, when the University of Chicago offered him a professorship, Jaeger determined to give up his Berlin chair and his homeland. In the same year he gave the Gifford Lectures at the University of St. Andrews in Scotland (published in 1947 as *The Theology of the Early Greek Philosophers*).

Jaeger's first marriage (1914–1931), to Theodora Dammholz, produced three children but ended in divorce. In 1931 Jaeger married Ruth Heinitz, with whom he had one child. The second Mrs. Jaeger and children from both marriages accompanied Jaeger to the United States. After three years at the University of Chicago, Jaeger was invited in 1939 to come to Harvard as one of the new university professors who were entitled to teach in any area of their interest and were exempted from routine departmental or administrative responsibilities. He accepted and taught at Harvard until his retirement in 1959.

The years at Harvard were productive. Here Jaeger completed *Paideia*. Here too he continued his edition of Gregory of Nyssa with the help of various collaborators. The authorities at Harvard, upon his arrival, had established for him the Harvard Institute for Classical Studies, which facilitated this research. After Jaeger's death, the project continued. Jaeger never lost his interest in Aristotle, and in 1956 he published his edition of Aristotle's *Metaphysics*, a work upon which he had been engaged since his student days. Jaeger had from the start intended to write a fourth volume of *Paideia* dealing with the reception of Greek culture in the early Christian world. No longer confident that age would permit the completion of this large project, he published as a "down payment" on the subject *Early Christianity and Greek Paideia* (1961). It was to be his last book; he saw an advance copy only days before his death in Boston.

Jaeger's writings brought him wide recognition and many accolades, including honorary degrees from Athens, Cambridge, Kenyon College, Manchester, Salonica, and, most notably, Harvard, his adoptive university, on the occasion of its tercentenary celebration. As a teacher, Jaeger exerted great influence in Germany, and many of his German students went on to become renowned scholars in their own right—for example, Wolfgang Schadewalt, Friedrich Solmsen, and Richard Walzer. At Harvard he was a beloved figure, and students considered a class with him an experience not to be missed. Most striking, indeed unique, was his gentle and patient manner with all who came to see him; this man who achieved so much quite literally never hurried.

• Jaeger's papers are preserved at the Houghton Library, Harvard University. His personal library is now part of the collection at the Center for Hellenic Studies in Washington, D.C. His autobiographical *Entwürfe zu Lebenserinnerung (Anfang)*, a fascinating but fragmentary sketch, is printed, with English translation, in *Werner Jaeger: Five Essays*, trans. Adele M. Fiske, R.S.C.J., with a bibliography of Werner Jaeger prepared by Herbert Bloch (1966). His introduction to *Scripta Minora* (2 vols., 1960) also contains autobiographical material. Other important books by Jaeger not mentioned in the text include *Humanistische Reden und Vorträge* 2d ed. (1963), *Diokles von Karystos: Die Griechische Medizin und die Schule des Aristoteles* (1938), and *Two Rediscovered Works of Ancient Christian Literature: Gregory of Nyssa and Macarius* (1954). There is no biography of Jaeger. Wolfgang Schadewalt published an important remembrance, "Gedenkrede auf Werner Jaeger, 1888–1961," in *Schweizer Monatshefte* 42 (1962), reprinted separately in 1963 and also in Schadewalt's *Hellas und Hesperien* (1970); this also contains the fullest bibliography of Jaeger's works. Ruth Jaeger published a brief but rich memoir of her husband in *Germans in Boston* (1981). See also Friedrich Solmsen, "Classical Scholarship in Berlin between the Wars," *Greek, Roman, and Byzantine Studies* 30 (1989): 117–40, for Jaeger's Berlin years. William M. Calder III has written much on Jaeger; see especially his chapter in *Classical Scholarship: A Biographical Encyclopedia*, ed. Ward W. Briggs and William M. Calder III (1990). An international conference, Werner Jaeger: The Man and His Work, was held at the University of Illinois at Urbana-Champaign, 26–28 Apr. 1990; the conference papers have been published as William M. Calder III, ed., "Werner Jaeger Reconsidered," *Illinois Classical Studies*, supp. vol. 3 (1992). Obituaries are in the *New York Times*, 20 Oct. 1961, and in the classical periodical *Gnomon* 34 (Mar. 1962): 101–5.

ROBERT RENEHAN

JAFFE, Sam (8 Mar. 1891–24 Mar. 1984), stage, screen, and television character actor, was born Shalom Jaffe in New York City, the son of Bernard Barch Jaffe, a jeweler, and Ada Steinberg, a stage actress. As a young man Jaffe emphasized scholarly pursuits and never planned to become an actor. He received a B.S. in engineering from the City College of New York in 1912 and then began a master's degree program at the Columbia School of Engineering. He also studied philosophy, painting, and language, was an accomplished pianist and composer, and served as dean of mathematics at the Bronx Cultural Institute, a college preparatory school. But his mother, a popular actress in the thriving Yiddish theater, apparently swayed him to turn his back on academia and begin a stage career.

Jaffe joined the Washington Square Players in 1915 and then toured with Kearns Sommes Shakespearean Company. He also performed in vaudeville and the Yiddish theater. In 1921 he made his first appearance on Broadway with Jacob Ben-Ami, a leading Yiddish actor, in *The Idle Inn*. In 1925 he appeared in *Ruint* with John Huston (who would become a close friend and later direct him in three films). During the run of this play he married his first wife, Lillian Taiz, who died in 1941; they had no children.

His stage career accelerated in 1925 when he played Yudelson in *The Jazz Singer* with George Jessel. The critical acclaim he received helped secure the play's three-year run, a run that ended only when Warner Bros.'s film version premiered. In 1930 Jaffe scored his biggest theatrical success in *Grand Hotel*. He played Kringelein, a dying clerk who makes a final attempt at happiness. The strength of this performance led to a screen test for MGM's adaptation of the play. He lost the role to a major Hollywood star, Lionel Barrymore, but his film career bloomed. Jaffe "commuted" between stage and screen for the rest of his professional life.

In his film debut in Joseph von Sternberg's *The Scarlet Empress* (1934), he played Grand Duke Peter III opposite Marlene Dietrich's Catherine the Great. His performance as a wild-eyed madman began a period of being typecast as an exotic eccentric. His next role as the High Lama in Frank Capra's *Lost Horizon* (1937) perpetuated this image but also introduced another, and eventually more dominant kind of typecasting as a quiet, elderly sage. Even though both roles were minor, he created vivid and indelible characterizations. Jaffe's impressive skill in developing two opposing kinds of stereotypes earned him praise as a consummate character actor.

His ultimate role as an exotic eccentric was Gunga Din in George Stevens's *Gunga Din* (1939). In this film he played a Hindu water boy opposite three major stars, Cary Grant, Victor McLaglen, and Douglas Fairbanks, Jr. Even with this competition, Jaffe created the most memorable character. Bosley Crowther said in his *New York Times* review, "As Sam Jaffe plays him, Gunga Din is not only a better man than any in the cast; he should be a serious contender for the best performance of the year" (27 Jan. 1939). As a character actor Jaffe specialized in the part of the highly educated elder in such roles as Dr. Romley in *The Accused* (1949), Professor Lieberman in *Gentleman's Agreement* (1947), Dr. Barnhardt in *The Day the Earth Stood Still* (1951), and others.

Typecasting never limited Jaffe's stage roles. Besides his work in *The Jazz Singer* and *Grand Hotel*, he played important roles in productions as varied as Max Reinhardt's *The Eternal Road* (1937), Jed Harris's *A Doll's House* (1937), the Group Theatre's *The Gentle People* (1939), and Anton Chekhov's *The Sea Gull* (1954). He played characters as diverse as Shylock in *The Merchant of Venice* (1939), the title roles in *King Lear* (1940) and *Tartuffe* (1956), Hymie (a wise-cracking busboy) in *Cafe Crown* (1942), and Mr. Zero in a revival of Elmer Rice's *The Adding Machine* (1956).

In Hollywood, he continued to work with such top directors as Frank Borzage (*Stage Door Canteen*, 1943), Elia Kazan (*Gentleman's Agreement*, 1947) William Dieterle (*The Accused*, 1948), William Wyler (*Ben-Hur*, 1959), and Robert Wise (*The Day the Earth Stood Still*, 1951). He even appeared in *Les Espions* (1957) by Henri-Georges Clouzot, one of France's most successful directors. This impressive list reflects Jaffe's seriousness as an actor. "I only want to do a part

that means something," he commented. Perhaps his best role was as Dr. Riedenschneider in John Huston's *The Asphalt Jungle* (1950). His performance as a criminal mastermind won him an Oscar nomination as best supporting actor, the Best Actor Award at the Venice Film Festival, and the Cannes Award for Best Performance of the Year.

His involvement with the New York City theater community was not limited to acting. In 1943 he cofounded the Equity Library Theatre with George Freedley, curator of the Theatre Collection of the New York Public Library. The enterprise gave an opportunity to a great number of actors and directors to demonstrate their talent. As a council member of Actors Equity, he proved instrumental in securing rehearsal pay for Equity actors. For his association with Actors Equity and political activism (and to some extent for appearing in the anti–Cold War *The Day the Earth Stood Still*), Jaffe found himself blacklisted in Hollywood. Unable to work in film between 1951 and 1957, he devoted his talents to the stage. His lifelong friend John Huston finally broke that blacklist in 1958 when he cast Jaffe in *The Barbarian and the Geisha*.

In 1961 he turned his attention to television. For four years he played Dr. Zorba on Ben Casey (which also featured his second wife, Bettye Ackerman, whom he married in 1956; they had no children). He earned an Emmy nomination in 1961 for this character, which reinforced his Hollywood image as a wise elder. Jaffe now juggled TV work with film and stage performances. He appeared on "Playhouse 90," "Alfred Hitchcock Presents," "The Streets of San Francisco," "Kojak," and "Love Boat" (in a "May-September" episode written especially for him and his second wife, who was thirty-seven years younger). He also appeared in a number of well-received TV films: *Night Gallery* (1969), *The Old Man Who Cried Wolf* (1970), *QB VII* (1974), and *Gideon's Trumpet* (1980).

Jaffe's last stage role was as a Gandhi-like seer in a 1979 Broadway production of Christopher Isherwood's *A Meeting by the River*. His final film was *West of Hester Street* (1983), an award-winning documentary about Texas Jews that he narrated. Reportedly, John Huston planned to cast him as the don of the Prizzi family in *Prizzi's Honor* (1985), but Jaffe died in Beverly Hills before shooting began.

Even though best remembered as a Hollywood character actor, Jaffe had a career that went beyond the label. His stage performances demonstrated skills never fully utilized in Hollywood or on TV: physical agility, assertiveness, and wit. He continued working until his death, ironically fulfilling the prophecy of a comment he had made during one of his last interviews: "When you stop working, you're dead." An actor's actor, Jaffe left a highly respected legacy of precise and sharply drawn characters in three media.

• A complete biography and filmography of Sam Jaffe is in Jordan Young's *Reel Characters* (1986). A critical evaluation of his career and filmography is in *The International Dictionary of Films and Filmmakers*, vol. 3 (1992). Another biographical sketch is in N. U. Vaybrama's *John Huston: An Open Book* (1980). Reviews of his important films can be found in the *New York Times*: *Lost Horizon* (4 Mar. 1937), *Gunga Din* (27 Jan. 1939), *Gentleman's Agreement* (12 Nov. 1947), *The Accused* (13 Jan. 1949), *The Asphalt Jungle* (9 June 1950), and *The Day the Earth Stood Still* (19 Sept. 1951). Reviews of his important plays can also be found in the *New York Times*: *The Jazz Singer* (15 Sept. 1925), *Grand Hotel* (14 Nov. 1930), *The Eternal Road* (8 Jan. 1937), *Cafe Crown* (24 Jan. 1942), and *The Adding Machine* (10 Feb. 1956). Obituaries are in the *New York Times* and the *Los Angeles Times*, both 25 Mar. 1984; *Variety*, 28 Mar. 1984; and *Revue du Cinema*, July/Aug. 1984.

GREG S. FALLER

JAFFEE, Irving W. (15 Sept. 1906–20 May 1981), speed skater, was born in New York City; little is known of his parents, other than that they were Russian immigrants. He attended De Witt Clinton High School, where he pursued his first dream to play major league baseball; this changed, however, when he failed to make the school team. Jaffee began his illustrious speed skating career, oddly enough, as a newspaper carrier during his teenage years; he had chosen to wear roller skates in order to quicken his route. He first took to the ice at the Roseland Ballroom off Broadway in New York City, and he received first pair of ice skates, which were three sizes too large, from his sister. As a result, he had to wear nine pairs of socks so he could skate, despite which he frequently fell. Nevertheless, Jaffee had found his calling, and at the age of fifteen he dropped out of school to pursue speed skating as a career.

At the outset Jaffee was unsuccessful, failing in twenty-two consecutive competitions. This changed in 1926 with his first victory in the Silver Skates two-mile event. The following year Jaffee set a world record and several U.S. records in the five-mile event in Lake Placid, New York. A member of the national team for the 1928 Winter Olympics in St. Moritz, Switzerland, he set a one-mile time of 2:30.2, establishing a new world record.

Jaffee began his first Olympics with high hopes, placing fourth in the 5,000-meter race, just 0.2 seconds off the bronze medal time. However, the 10,000-meter race was his specialty. After defeating reigning world champion Bernt Evensen in a preliminary heat of the 10,000-meter race, Jaffee was heavily favored to capture the gold medal. Unfortunately, warm temperatures caused the outdoor ice rink to soften and melt such that officials eventually canceled the event. Protests were then lodged by Evensen and other competitors calling for Jaffee to be awarded the gold medal. The executive committee of the International Olympic Committee agreed; however, a day later the International Skating Federation rescinded the order. Jaffee was declared the unofficial champion but no medal for the event would be awarded.

Jaffee hoped to prove his mettle in the 1932 Winter Olympics held at Lake Placid. However, he experienced personal problems in 1931 when his mother fell ill. Having foresaken his training in order to be with his mother, he still managed to make the 1932 U.S. speed skating team, albeit barely. Jaffee then stepped up his training, resolving to win the gold medal. The races at Lake Placid proved to be no contest for him, as he emerged victorious in both the 5,000- and 10,000-meter events. The 10,000-meter final became one of the more storied races of the Lake Placid Games. Going into the final turn, Jaffee was side by side with his Norwegian foe before he shot off with a display of unparalleled sprinting ability, sprawling across the finish line in triumph. In his first competition in a distance race of over 10,000 meters, he covered twenty-five miles in 1:26.00.1, setting another world record. His courage and competitive spirit gained him international respect and admiration.

During the hard times of the Great Depression, in one of the stranger tales of Olympic history, Jaffee sold his Olympic medals and 400 other medals to a Harlem pawnshop for $2,000 to help his financial situation at home. When he had enough money he went back to the pawnbroker to repurchase his treasures, but the pawnbroker had gone out of business and the medals were gone.

Little is known about the remainder of Jaffee's life. He served for a time as the winter sports director at the Grossinger Resort in New York, where he coached several U.S. Olympic speed skaters, and he was a promoter of competitive events in the Catskill Mountains. He died in San Diego, California.

• There are no known archival sources. Jaffee's Olympic achievements are described in Bill Mallon and Ian Buchanan, *Quest for Gold, The Encyclopedia of American Olympians* (1984); and David L. Porter, ed., *Biographical Dictionary of American Sports: Outdoor Sports* (1988).

SHARON KAY STOLL
KURT R. ZIMMERMAN

JAGGAR, Thomas Augustus, Jr. (24 Jan. 1871–17 Jan. 1953), geologist and volcanologist, was born in Philadelphia, Pennsylvania, the son of Thomas Augustus Jaggar, a bishop of the Protestant Episcopal church, and Anita Louisa Lawrence. From an early age Jaggar participated in hiking and other outdoor activities, an interest he learned from his father. They took hiking trips to the backwoods of Maine and eastern Canada, and a trip to Europe in 1875 spurred Jaggar's commitment to the earth sciences when it included a climb of Mt. Vesuvius. He graduated from Harvard University with a B.A. in 1893 and an M.A. in 1894, both in geology. For nearly two years he studied mineralogy and petrography at the Universities of Munich and Heidelberg in Germany and then returned to Harvard, where he obtained his Ph.D. in geology in 1897.

In 1895, while still a graduate student, Jaggar was appointed instructor in geology at Harvard University and in 1903 was promoted to assistant professor. During the summers he was also a member of the United States Geological Survey, working in the Black Hills of South Dakota, Yellowstone National Park, Wyoming, and in Arizona. This work resulted in his first major publication, *The Laccoliths of the Black Hills* (1901).

Even then Jaggar was most interested in dynamic geologic processes, and he set about applying experimental laboratory methods of physics and chemistry to geology. Several of his early publications reflect this interest. However, he quickly became much more interested in applying these methods to measuring and analyzing dynamic geologic processes in operation under actual field conditions. Two of the most dynamic phenomena of geology are earthquakes and volcanoes, and to Jaggar their study was irresistible. He first realized this ambition when in 1902 he was one of the scientists sent by the U.S. government to the Antilles to investigate the catastrophic volcanic eruptions of Soufriere and Mount Pelee, which killed some 30,000 persons. This expedition strongly influenced Jaggar to pursue the field study of active volcanoes and earthquakes with a strong emphasis on the effects of both on human beings. Shortly after returning to Harvard, on 15 April 1903, Jaggar married Helen Kline. This union did not last, however; after two children were born, the marriage ended in divorce, apparently when Helen Jaggar refused to leave Boston and move with her husband to the Hawaiian Islands.

In 1906 Jaggar, already a much-published and highly respected geologist, writer, and lecturer, became head of the geology department at the Massachusetts Institute of Technology (MIT). Over the next several years he undertook a series of expeditions to study active volcanoes and earthquakes in Italy, Japan, the Aleutians, Hawaii, and Central America. As a result of these investigations, Jaggar became increasingly disturbed over how little scientists of his day knew about volcanism and earthquakes and other earth processes that bring about great natural disasters and how little effort was being expended to learn more. Only at the Vesuvius Observatory in Italy and a few small stations in Japan were actual field observations of these phenomena being undertaken. He believed the time had come to direct more studies toward the prediction of volcanic eruptions and earthquakes and the development of engineering techniques and types of construction to lessen their disastrous consequences. He was convinced also that the traditional method of making brief expeditions to affected areas was inadequate and that permanent observatories needed to operate in areas of recurring volcanic and seismic activity.

Jaggar's dream of establishing a permanent volcanological monitoring station was realized in July 1909 when the Whitney Estate gave $25,000 to MIT for geophysical research that would aid in the protection of human lives and property. At Jaggar's urging these funds were applied to the establishment of an observatory at the summit of Kilauea volcano in Hawaii. Kilauea was chosen because of the constancy and moderation of its volcanic activity, which allowed investigators to work with active lava at close range. Thus Jaggar embarked on his true life's work—the development and operation of the Hawaiian Volcano Ob-

servatory (HVO), formally established in 1911. Much to his disappointment, however, Jaggar was unable to participate in the first project conducted at the new Hawaiian observatory, as he was not allowed to take leave from his teaching duties at MIT until the following year. Instead, during the summer of 1911 E. S. Shepard, a chemist from the Geophysical Laboratory of the Carnegie Institute of Washington, and F. A. Perrett, a volcanologist from the Volcanic Research Society of Springfield, Massachusetts, conducted the initial scientific work at HVO by making temperature measurements in the Halemaumau lava lake at Kilauea summit.

In the spring of 1912 Jaggar left MIT and moved to Hawaii as the first director of the HVO. Funds from the Whitney Estate were augmented by the enthusiastic financial support of the people of Hawaii who, led by Jaggar and Lorrin A. Thurston, editor of the *Honolulu Advertiser*, then the principal Honolulu newspaper, formed the Hawaiian Volcano Research Association, which provided an additional $5,000 a year to operate the HVO. In addition, the people of Hilo contributed the money for construction of the first HVO building. During his early years in Hawaii, Jaggar met Isabel Maydwell, a co-worker and lifelong colleague who shared his love for geology and the study of active volcanoes; they were married in 1917.

Jaggar's initial years at HVO were scientifically exhilarating as he established fundamental techniques and pioneered many new monitoring instruments. From the beginning, however, finances were inadequate. At times, Jaggar served wholly without a regular salary, and once he had to partially finance the observatory's operations with money he made raising pigs. Perhaps one of Jaggar's greatest contributions was his determination and singleness of purpose, which allowed him, even in the most discouraging of times, to somehow keep the program going. Financial stability was finally assured in 1919, when the U.S. government took over fiscal responsibility for the HVO, first putting it under the auspices of the Weather Bureau and then, in 1924, assigning it to the U.S. Geological Survey. In 1926 the Geological Survey established a Section of Volcanology, and Jaggar was named as its first chief.

Under Jaggar's direction, work at the observatory was extremely diverse. In addition to routine seismic observations and the continuous monitoring of volcanic activity of Kilauea and Mauna Loa, HVO scientists recorded the levels, temperature, depth, and viscosity of the molten lava lake in Halemaumau, collected and analyzed volcanic gases, performed detailed studies of Kilauea's crater floor, studied the different types of lavas and how they formed, and conducted petrologic studies of the rocks as well as a special study of tsunamis, the destructive ocean waves that sometimes are generated by submarine earthquakes.

After establishing the HVO, Jaggar continued to study volcanoes and earthquakes, visiting more than sixty of the world's approximately 450 active volcanoes. In 1927–1928 he headed an expedition organized by the National Geographic Society to study Aleutian volcanoes. To facilitate exploring inaccessible Aleutian beaches he invented an amphibious vehicle that was later developed for use as a landing craft in World War II. For this, in 1945, he was awarded the National Geographic Society's Franklin L. Burr Prize.

Jaggar believed that the wonders of the great Hawaiian volcanoes should belong to the American people, and from his first days in Hawaii he strongly advocated the creation of a national park to include Kilauea and Mauna Loa. His vision was realized in 1916 with the establishment of the Hawaii Volcanoes National Park. In 1935 the operation of HVO was temporarily transferred to the National Park Service, and from then until his retirement in 1940, Jaggar worked for the national park he had helped to establish. After his retirement he became a research associate in geophysics at the University of Hawaii, a position he retained until his death in Honolulu.

Many of Jaggar's methods and techniques for studying active volcanoes have become standard the world over. In addition to his contributions to volcanology, he will be long remembered for his efforts to protect humanity and its property from lava flows. He was the first to use aerial bombing in an attempt to deflect or stop a lava flow, and he developed detailed plans for the use of barriers to deflect flows away from the city of Hilo. In January 1987 the Thomas A. Jaggar Museum, situated on Kilauea's summit overlooking Halemaumau Crater, adjacent to the Hawaiian Volcano Observatory, was dedicated in his honor.

• The most complete collection of Jaggar's published works is in the Thomas A. Jaggar Collection at Sinclair Library, the University of Hawaii at Manoa. Jaggar was a prolific writer. His most important works include the *Hawaiian Volcano Observatory Bulletin*, vols. 1–15 (1912–1927), and the *Volcano Letter*, nos. 1–469 (1925–1940), the first systematic publications of a volcanic observatory; *Origin and Development of Craters* (1947); *Steam Blast Volcanic Eruptions* (1949); and the autobiographical *My Experiments with Volcanoes* (1956). For additional information see G. A. Macdonald and Thomas August Jaggar, *Volcano Letter* no. 519 (1953); G. A. Macdonald, *Volcanoes* (1972); F. M. Bullard, *Volcanoes, in History, in Theory, in Eruption* (1962); and *Volcanism in Hawaii*, vol. 2, U.S. Geological Survey Professional Paper 1350 (1987).

FRANK L. PETERSON

JAKOBSON, Roman Osipovich (11 Oct. 1896–18 July 1982), linguist, literary historian, and theorist, was born in Moscow, Russia, the son of Jewish parents, Osip Jakobson, a chemical engineer and industrialist, and Anna Volpert. Jakobson's high school education was at the Lazarev Institute of Oriental Languages in Moscow, where he obtained his diploma with silver medal in 1914. During this period he started to collect and study Russian folklore, legends, and choral and ritual songs. In 1915, together with six other students, Jakobson founded the Moscow Linguistic Circle, the purpose of which was to elucidate linguistic problems of poetics, folklore, and ethnology. He served as president until 1920. In 1917 he spent a semester at Petersburg University, studying Sanskrit. In 1918 he received his master's degree and was appointed research associate at Moscow University, a position he held until 1920.

Poetry was Jakobson's first passion. In *Dialogues* (1983), a book of recollections, introspection, and exploration of his entire career, he states, "My very first attempts at writing verse were closely tied for me to the investigation of verbal art. I recall with some astonishment that at the age of nine or ten I was trying to represent the verses that I read, as well as my own feeble efforts at poetry, through peculiar metrical schemes that I would invent on the spot for the purpose" (p. 2). When he was still in Moscow, Jakobson became associated with the group of Russian futurist poets led by Vladimir Mayakowsky and Velemir Khlebnikov, whose doctrine considered that the meaning of a word is intimately related to its sound. Jakobson published a series of futurist poems under the pseudonym Alyagrov. His first book of literary criticism, *Contemporary Russian Poetry* (1921), focused on the futurist movement. Jakobson perceived the blossoming of modern Russian poetry as a natural consequence of the development of modern painting, influenced by French postimpressionism and cubism, in which everything is based on relationships and interdependences among various elements and features.

The concepts of space, color, contour, and texture in painting intersect the concepts of nature and significance of the elements of verbal meaning and poetic language. The interaction among parts and wholes, between the representation and the represented, between the two parts of the sign, the *signans* and the *signatum*, were considered by Jakobson as a binary opposition. His later studies reflect and amplify the relationship between the external, phonic side of language and its internal component, the various facets and connotations of meaning, manifested particularly in poetic language.

In 1920 Jakobson went as a translator for the USSR Red Cross Mission to Czechoslovakia. After leaving the mission he remained in Czechoslovakia to continue his doctoral studies at Prague University. He received his Ph.D. in 1930. In 1926, together with other Czech and Russian scholars, he founded the Prague Linguistic Circle. The activity of the circle became public at the first international conference of Slavic linguists, held in Prague in 1929. Jakobson's research on the phonological evolution of Russian and other Slavic languages led him to the conclusion that a correlation existed between the description of sound systems and the explanation of their evolution. He identified the phoneme as the minimal unit of language capable of discriminating word meanings and viewed the phoneme as an indivisible atom. These advances constituted the starting point of a new approach in linguistics and phonology, according to which each language is distinguished from all others by its phonemic system, that is, by the inclusion or omission of particular phonemes from the set of all phonemes available to human speech.

In 1931 Jakobson started teaching at T. G. Masaryk University in Brno, where in 1937 he assumed a chair of Russian philology and old Czech literature. In 1935 he married Svatava Pirkova, a professor of Slavic languages. In 1939 the Nazi occupation of Czechoslovakia forced him to flee to Denmark, then to Norway, and after the German invasion of Norway, he escaped to Sweden in 1940. He held visiting lecturer positions in each of these countries, at the Universities of Copenhagen, Oslo, and Uppsala. The most important accomplishment of this period was his research on the linguistic study of aphasia. Jakobson's book *Kindersprache, Aphasie and allgemeine Lautgesetze* (Child language, aphasia, and phonological universals, 1941) represents one of the earliest linguistic studies of language pathology and laid the fundamentals for neurolinguistics.

In June 1941 Jakobson came to the United States; he was naturalized in 1952. American structural linguistics at that time was dominated by Edward Sapir and Leonard Bloomfield. Their empiricist approach contrasted with Jakobson's theory of language, which was based on the reassessment of the doctrine of Ferdinand de Saussure and focused on the opposition between synchrony, which considers the language as a static system, and diachrony, which reflects the dynamic development of the language. Language was seen as a system, a whole that interacts with each of its component parts. Jakobson emphasized the semiotic character of language as a system of signs and analyzed the place of language in culture.

He also studied the differences between various forms of art, particularly between the pictorial sign as an element of painting and the verbal sign as an element of language. Jakobson's American period was marked by his linguistic interpretation of metaphor based on associations and similarities and of metonymy based on contiguities. He studied the characteristics of cinematographic art, which he considered metonymic in essence, and related them to Boris Pasternak's poetry and poetic prose.

He taught at the École Libre des Hautes Études in New York from 1942 to 1946. In 1943 he was appointed T. G. Masaryk Professor of Czechoslovak Studies at Columbia University, and in 1949 he became Samuel Cross Professor of Slavic Languages and Literatures at Harvard University, where he taught until his retirement in 1967. From 1957 on he held a concurrent position as institute professor at Massachusetts Institute of Technology. Most of the linguists and Slavic scholars who studied in the United States were Jakobson's students. When Jakobson moved from Columbia to Harvard, an impressive number of graduate students followed him. "What attracted students to him was not only his extraordinary knowledge, scientific imagination and his dramatic lecture style; much more important were the close personal relationships into which he involved almost every one of his many students," states Morris Halle in the biographical sketch on Jakobson in the *International Encyclopedia of the Social Sciences* (vol. 18 [1979], p. 339).

In 1942 he was among the founders of the Linguistic Circle of New York. He was president of the Linguistic Society of America in 1956. Inspired by the concept of information and the communication theory developed by Claude E. Shannon and Warren Weaver, as well as by the discoveries of semiotician Charles Sanders Peirce, Jakobson explored language as a means of communication and developed his theory on the interrelation between the speech event and the functions of language. In his turn, Jakobson influenced the work of Morris Halle and Noam Chomsky, the founders of generative linguistics. His approach of literary theory, semiotics, and structural anthropology inspired Claude Lévi-Strauss's interpretation of communication. In 1962 Jakobson married Krystyna Pomorska. He had no children with either of his wives. Jakobson died in Boston, Massachusetts.

Jakobson's work had a significant impact on almost every field of study pertaining to communications, from the humanities (ethnography, folklore, mythology, poetics, literary criticism, semiotics, and structural anthropology) to the sciences (information theory, cybernetics, neurolinguistics, and sociolinguistics). He was fluent in six languages—Russian, French, Polish, German, Czech, and English—and knew enough Norwegian and Finnish to be able to lecture. He also learned to read twenty-five other languages. His sixtieth, seventieth, and eightieth birthdays were marked by extensive Festschriften published in individual volumes. He was the recipient of numerous honors, including the title of chevalier of the Légion d'Honneur, the Antonio Feltrinelli International Prize for Philology and Linguistics, and the Hegel Prize.

• Jakobson was extremely prolific, and the work *Roman Jakobson 1896–1982: A Complete Bibliography of His Writings*, comp. Stephen Rudy (1990) lists 666 entries, some of which are revisions or reprints of earlier publications. Some of Jakobson's works were published in eight volumes of *Selected Writings* between 1962 and 1988. His complex personality and activity constituted the subject of numerous articles published in periodicals, as well as monographs, including R. Bradford, *Roman Jakobson: Life, Language, Art* (1994); M. Halle, ed., *Roman Jakobson: What He Taught Us* (1983); D. Armstrong and C. H. Van Schooneveld, eds., *Roman Jakobson: Echoes of His Scholarship* (1977); E. Holenstein, *Roman Jakobson's Approach to Language* (1976); L. R. Waugh, *Roman Jakobson's Science of Language* (1976); G. Steiner, *Extraterritorial: Papers on Literature and the Language of Revolution* (1972); and N. Berberova, *The Italics Are Mine* (1969).

HERMINA G. B. ANGHELESCU

JAMES, Alice (7 Aug. 1848–6 Mar. 1892), diarist, was born in New York City, the daughter of Henry James, Sr., and Mary Walsh. Supported by money inherited from his own father who had come to America from Ireland and become a successful merchant, Henry, Sr., was a theologian, philosopher, author of several books, and utopian dreamer whose friends included such important artists and intellectuals of his day as Ralph Waldo Emerson and Thomas Carlyle. Alice's mother was the more practical of her parents and managed the family home. Alice, the fifth and youngest child, was the only daughter. Her two oldest brothers, Henry James the author and William James the psychologist and philosopher, achieved very high regard and enduring fame in their respective fields. Alice James attained a posthumous literary reputation through a diary she kept during the last few years of her life, which, except for four privately printed copies, was not published until more than forty years after her death.

James's brothers were educated by private tutors and governesses, sometimes at private schools, and by travel abroad in Europe, but James received somewhat less of this education as she was kept home at times while her brothers were sent to experimental schools. She recalled of her youth that the family tended to move about too much for her taste, and when older she advised her brother William not to impose on his own children the kind of unsettling "hotel" childhood they had endured themselves. Although she grew up feeling the target of excessive teasing from her brothers, it appears that James was able to assert and defend herself by "sassing" all of the men in her family including her father.

By the time James reached the age of fifteen her education was further interrupted periodically by health problems she developed for which doctors were unable to discover any physical cause. By the end of the Civil War, James's health was even worse. If a conversation were to become intensely emotional, for example, she was prone to faint. At night she suffered from panic attacks while trying to fall asleep. James and her brothers Henry and William all suffered breakdowns during the 1860s, but the most serious that afflicted Alice struck in 1878. During this time her father wrote that she was much of the time nearly insane. At one point James asked her father if he thought it a sin to commit suicide. He tried a bit of reverse psychology, telling her that he did not believe it a sin if one sincerely needed relief from suffering and that she might do so whenever she felt she must. Her father's permission paradoxically made her less prone to suicidal thoughts. Unfortunately, after her recovery she had no change in the routines of her life, and a renewal of her problems eventually followed.

Doctors applied a variety of diagnoses to her problems, such as neuralgia, spinal neurosis, rheumatic gout, and nervous hyperaesthesia, but still no clear physical source for James's problems was found. A number of treatments were attempted—blistering baths, electric and ice therapy, massages, admissions to an asylum—but none was successful. On 30 January 1882 James's mother died, and she managed to muster up the strength to serve as nurse to her father as his health declined. He died in December of that year, leaving James a good income that was supplemented by her brother Henry, whose earnings from his writing were so substantial that he turned over to her some of his rental property income.

A few years before the deaths of her mother and father, James had met and become close friends with Katharine Peabody Loring, who was one year younger than James. In 1884 Katharine decided to take her ailing sister to Europe to improve her health. James was apparently unwilling to be apart from her good friend for so long and joined the sisters for this trip. She would never return to the United States. The ocean crossing, though in reality a relatively calm one, left James in such a bad state that upon her arrival in England she had to be carried off the ship. The prospect of another sea crossing was so dreadful she preferred to remain in England. She lived most of the time with Katharine, at times in London and some of the time in Leamington.

James began keeping a commonplace book in December 1886, and for the next couple of years she recorded quotations collected from a rich variety of writings, including works by George Sand, Leo Tolstoy, Guy de Maupassant, George Eliot, and Gustave Flaubert. A passage from *War and Peace* is in French because she read the novel in that language, a reminder of how intellectually motivated she was in spite of her informal and unconventional education. On 31 May 1889 James began a diary entry by writing, "I think that if I get into the habit of writing a bit about what happens, or rather doesn't happen, I may lose a little of the sense of loneliness and desolation which abides with me." For the rest of her life she maintained this personal record, and even when her health became too impaired during the final months of her life, she dictated entries.

In the year before her death James finally acquired a diagnosis arising from a tangible physical problem. Although the discovery that she had breast cancer was grim news, curiously enough James was relieved. She wrote in her diary, "Ever since I have been ill, I have longed and longed for some palpable disease, no matter how conventionally dreadful a label it might have." It is a measure of how important the literary outlet of her diary was to James that the day before she died she dictated an entry, and during her last day even asked to have a sentence revised. Her brother Henry and Katharine Loring attended her last hours at Kensington during which James said she had a dream about some of her dead friends who rode on rough seas in a boat while signaling her to join them as the boat disappeared into darkness. After her death, her ashes were carried by Katharine to Cambridge, Massachusetts, and buried with her parents.

In spite of her poor health and isolation, James's diary reveals a personality that is in many ways a strong and courageous one. She was opposed to all tyranny, whether political, social, or psychological, and she wrote frequent criticism in her diary of flaws she perceived in English society. She was especially indignant at the arrogance of the upper classes, and the unhappy conditions to which the majority of the population passively acquiesced. She was unable to get out much, and she confessed to the "poverty of my outside experience," so she relied on newspaper articles, some of which she pasted in her diary, and on stories told her by her brother Henry, as the bases for her commentary. In places she also reveals how repressed she felt by the requirements of her day for women of her class. She wrote on one occasion, for example, "how sick one gets of being 'good,' how much I should respect myself if I could burst out and make every one wretched for 24 hours." And at another time she wrote: "It is an immense loss to have all robust and sustaining expletives refined away from one!"

The last year of James's diary is also the record of her struggle with her fatal illness. Though she faced her approaching death and the physical pain heroically, there were times when she recorded the boring and agonizing aspects of the experience. On one day she says, "This long slow dying is no doubt instructive, but it is disappointingly free from excitements." The day before the end she wrote: "I am being ground slowly on the grim grindstone of physical pain, and on two nights I had almost asked for K.'s lethal dose, but one steps hesitantly along such unaccustomed ways and endures from second to second."

After James's death Katharine Loring took the two diaries written by her friend, made a few deletions and revisions, added a few footnotes, and had four copies printed, one each for James's three brothers still alive and one for herself, hoping that the brothers would approve further publication. Henry James, however, strongly urged her not to publish, arguing that the diaries contained too many details about people he knew that might embarrass them. He even destroyed his own copy. Loring honored Henry's wishes, but some forty years after James's death she gave a copy of the diary to Mary James Vaux, daughter of James's brother Robertson, and Vaux published it as part of a book devoted to the less-well-known siblings of Henry and William James, entitled *Alice James: Her Brothers— Her Journal* (1934). Even more changes were made this time than had been made by Katharine, and it was not until 1964, more than seventy years after James's death, that Leon Edel, biographer of Henry James, published an edition faithful to the original.

In spite of his objections to the diary, Henry James nevertheless praised it in a letter written in 1894 to his brother William saying that the diary "is heroic in its individuality, its independence—its face-to-face with the universe for and by herself—and the beauty and eloquence with which she often expresses this, let alone the rich irony and humor, constitute . . . a new claim for the family renown. This last element—her style, her power to write—are indeed to me a delight." In 1964 Edel wrote in his introduction to *The Diary of Alice James* that although there is much gossip and exaggeration in its pages, it is "not the pages, but the spirit residing in them, [that] gives the diary its unique place in literature and testifies to its continuing appeal." Today James's diary is considered a moving human record of the life and character of another gifted member of her family and a significant contribution to the genre of diary writing.

• A number of Alice James's letters and the copy of her diary privately printed by Katharine Peabody Loring that she presented to William James are located at the Houghton Library at Harvard University. *The Diary of Alice James*, ed. Leon Edel (1964), restores material deleted in both Loring's printed version and in that published by James's niece Mary James Vaux, in 1934, and it includes a biographical portrait of James. Edel also discusses James's relationship with her brother Henry in his five-volume biography *Henry James* (1953–1972) in various parts of vol. 2, *The Conquest of London, 1870–1881*, and vol. 3, *The Middle Years, 1881–1895*. F. O. Matthiessen, ed., *The James Family* (1947), mentions James numerous times and devotes a specific chapter to her. Other sources include *The Death and Letters of Alice James*, ed. Ruth Bernard Yeazell (1981), with a biographical essay, and Jean Strouse's *Alice James: A Biography* (1980).

ALAN KELLY

JAMES, Daniel, Jr. (11 Feb. 1920–25 Feb. 1978), U.S. Air Force officer, was born in Pensacola, Florida, the son of Daniel James, a migrant laborer and handy man, and Lillie Anna Brown, who operated a private elementary and junior high school. Nicknamed "Chappie," James was the youngest of seventeen children. After completing high school in Pensacola, he attended Tuskegee Institute, an all-black college in Alabama. While at Tuskegee, he learned to fly in a government-sponsored program. He graduated with a degree in physical education in 1942. In November of that year he married Dorothy Watkins; they had three children.

James entered the U.S. Army Air Corps as a cadet in January 1943 and was mostly an instructor pilot for black pilot-trainees throughout World War II. Following the war, he was posted to Ohio and the Philippines. During the Korean War, he flew 101 combat missions as a fighter pilot against North Korean forces. A member of the 12th Fighter-Bomber Squadron, he initially flew P-51 Mustang aircraft in 1950 and 1951, mostly on ground support missions. He also flew the highly vulnerable T-6 spotter aircraft in hazardous forward air controller missions. Later, he flew the F-80 Shooting Star, jet fighter, and was shot down and rescued in one such mission. He was promoted to captain in October 1950.

Following his tour in Korea, James was assigned to Clark Air Force Base in the Philippines. From 1953 until 1956 he was the commander of the 437th and, subsequently, the 60th Fighter Interceptor Squadrons at Otis Air Force Base in Massachusetts. During his assignment at Otis, James was promoted to major. He received his first Pentagon tour in 1957 after graduating from the Air Command and Staff College at Maxwell Air Force Base in Alabama. From 1960 until 1964 he was stationed in England, when he returned to the United States. He was stationed in Arizona until 1966.

In 1966 James was sent to Southeast Asia. Based in Thailand, he flew F-4C Phantom jets. His seventy-eight combat missions mostly involved flights over North Vietnam. He was one of the flight leaders of the famed 2 January 1967 Operation Bolo. Conceived, planned, and led by Colonel Robin Olds, this operation was a bait-and-trap ploy in which seven MIG 21s were destroyed without the loss of a single American aircraft. That year he was promoted to colonel. On his return to the United States, he was assigned to Eglin Air Force Base, Florida, serving as vice commander of the 33rd Tactical Fighter Wing.

In 1969 James was appointed commander of Wheelus Air Force Base in Libya. On 1 September of that year, Muammar Khadafy seized control of the Libyan government in a military coup and indicated his intention to revoke the 1954 U.S.-Libyan agreement on base rights. Heading the delicate negotiations with the Libyans on what would be left at the base and what would be taken back under U.S. control, James earned the respect and gratitude of senior Nixon administration officials, especially Secretary of Defense Melvin Laird. Under Colonel James's control, transfer of the base to the Libyan government began in January 1970. In March 1970 James became deputy assistant to the secretary of defense for public affairs. He was promoted to brigadier general in July 1970 and later to major general.

In September 1974 James, now a lieutenant general, became the vice commander of the Military Airlift Command at Scott Air Force Base in Illinois. On 1 September 1975 he became the first African American to hold the rank of four-star general. On his promotion to that rank, he was named commander of the North American Air Defense Command with operational command of all U.S. and Canadian air defense forces. Suffering heart problems, he retired from the Air Force in early February 1978 and died of a heart attack later that month.

When James entered the U.S. Army Air Corps, the armed forces were segregated. He firmly believed that racial integration must be based on merit, and his military career is a testament to that belief.

• James's life is detailed in two biographies, J. Alfred Phelps, *Chappie: America's First Black Four-Star General: The Life and Times of Daniel James, Jr.* (1991), and an earlier work, James R. McGovern, *Black Eagle: General Daniel "Chappie" James, Jr.* (1985). A scholarly treatment of the racial integration of the United States Air Force is contained in Alan L. Gropman, *The Air Force Integrates: 1945–1964*, (1978). The World War II experience of blacks in the Army Air Force is detailed in Alan M. Osur, *Blacks in the Army Air Forces during World War II* (1977). An obituary is in the *New York Times*, 26 Feb. 1978.

ROD PASCHALL

JAMES, Daniel Willis (15 Apr. 1832–13 Sept. 1907), merchant and philanthropist, was born in Liverpool, England, the eldest son of Daniel James, a merchant, and Elizabeth Woodbridge Phelps, the eldest daughter of Anson G. Phelps, the head of Phelps, Dodge & Company, a major New York metal firm. James's father was the resident partner in England of Phelps, Dodge & Company. After attending school in Edinburgh, Scotland, from age thirteen to seventeen, James was sent to New York to enter in the world of work preparatory to joining the family business.

Founded in 1834, by the mid-nineteenth century Phelps, Dodge & Company had become an important importer and manufacturer of metal: tinplate, sheet iron, zinc, copper nails, rivets, lead, and solder. Anson Phelps died in 1853 after which the partnership was reformed. Daniel Willis James received a 5 percent share in the family firm according to the 1854 partnership agreement, increased to 12 percent in 1859, and 18 percent in 1873. He remained a partner until his death, by 1878 becoming one of the two dominant partners and eventually the senior partner.

Under James's guidance, Phelps, Dodge gradually shifted from being a mercantile house to becoming a producer of metal. During this era, the American economy changed from a colonial economy with a heavy reliance on foreign trade to a domestic economy in which foreign commerce played a decreasing role. This process, otherwise known as the transportation revolution, began with the opening of the Erie Canal in 1825 and accelerated with the coming of the railroad, outstanding as a low-cost carrier of high bulk– low value primary products anywhere and everywhere all year around. Thus in 1881 Phelps, Dodge invested in an Arizona copper mine and by 1906 ceased trading in metals to focus on copper mining and manufacture. Following in the wake of William E. Dodge, his uncle, and others associated with Phelps, Dodge, James made a fortune in iron and steel both by selling it and by investing in capital-intensive manufacturers to support the enormous expansion of the railroad network. For example, the variously named Lackawanna Iron & Coal Company prospered owing to the capital and mercantile services furnished by Dodge, James, and their allies.

James frequently invested in southern and western developmental railroads not only for their intrinsic merits as investments but also to profit by supplying their construction needs for railroad-related iron and steel products. During the 1860s and early 1870s James was a notable stockholder in the Dubuque & Sioux City, an Iowa railroad, together with outstanding New York railroad commission merchants and private bankers such as Morris Ketchum Jesup and John Stewart Kennedy. In 1873 James became a director of this line, later absorbed by the Illinois Central Railroad.

Because he knew Kennedy, James became an early investor in the St. Paul, Minneapolis & Manitoba Railway. Hitching his wagon to James J. Hill, the empire builder, James joined the Manitoba board in 1882 and resigned in 1889, having played a significant role as a finance expert. During his service, the Manitoba grew westward from St. Paul, Minnesota, to Montana; soon thereafter the Manitoba changed its name to the Great Northern Railway and expanded to the Pacific Northwest. James also served as a director and vice president of the Northern Securities Company, a holding company formed in 1901 to control the Hill railroads following the Northern Pacific Railroad panic and the climactic struggle with Edward H. Harriman. In 1904 the Supreme Court ruled (5–4) that the Northern Securities Company had violated the Sherman Antitrust Act.

James was a Scots Presbyterian who felt accountable as a steward for his wealth to both God and humanity. Two of his philanthropies illustrate his concern for those less fortunate than he as well as for the importance of organized religion. He was a trustee of the Children's Aid Society of New York (1863–1907) and its president (1892–1901). Founded in 1853 by Charles Loring Brace with a Phelps as a founding trustee, this charity used the placing-out system for orphans and other needy juveniles as an alternative to institutionalization. Vitally interested in religious education, James in 1867 became a director of the Union Theological Seminary in New York. Organized in 1836 by William E. Dodge, among others, the seminary was supported, in the family tradition, by James and other moneyed Presbyterians. When he was vice president of the seminary, James urged it to become nondenominational. In 1905 he offered $1 million for a new site in furtherance of that aim and later added more than $300,000. His handsome gift largely made possible its relocation to Morningside Heights adjacent to Columbia University. He was also a trustee and benefactor of Amherst College.

In 1854 James married Ellen Stebbins Curtiss. Their one son, Arthur Curtiss James, entered the family business, becoming a partner in 1892. Daniel Willis James died at the Mount Washington Hotel, Bretton Woods, New Hampshire. His estate of about $40 million included millions in securities of mining companies and of the Great Northern and Northern Pacific railroads. He served as a director of the Northern Pacific and of the First National Bank as well as a trustee of the United States Trust Company of New York. Significant as a supplier and investor in the railroad age, James epitomized the transition from merchant to industrial capitalist.

• No personal papers of James are available. Robert Glass Cleland, *A History of Phelps Dodge 1834–1950* (1952), although lacking both footnotes and a bibliography, remains the standard study of this company. Robert T. Handy, *A History of Union Theological Seminary in New York* (1987), deals with James's philanthropy. Ralph W. Hidy et al., *The Great Northern Railway: A History* (1988), is the definitive work on this railroad in which James invested so heavily in money and time. Richard Lowitt, *A Merchant Prince of the Nineteenth Century* (1954), provides a definitive treatment of William E. Dodge, one of the founders of Phelps, Dodge. Albro Martin, *James J. Hill and the Opening of the Northwest* (1976), is an outstanding biography of a businessman associated with James for almost thirty years. An obituary is in the *New York Times*, 14 Sept. 1907.

SAUL ENGELBOURG

JAMES, Edmund Janes (21 May 1855–17 June 1925), political economist and university president, was born in Jacksonville, Illinois, the son of Colin Dew James, a Methodist minister and presiding elder, and Amanda Keziah Casad. In 1863 the family removed to Normal, Illinois. James entered the classical department of Northwestern University in 1873, remaining two terms, then spent six months with a survey crew on the Great Lakes, after which he continued with the classics at Harvard College for a year. Discontent with his collegiate fare, he left in 1875 for Germany, where he studied historical economics under Johannes Conrad at the University of Halle.

Returning to Illinois in 1877 with a doctorate and a strong reverence for German institutions, James served successively as principal of high schools in Evanston and at Illinois State University in Normal, and in 1879 he married Anna Margarethe Lange of Halle. Two years later he and Charles De Garmo became proprietors of the *Illinois School Journal* and transformed it into a crusading magazine. James wrote on national educational issues in this "bold and breezy" monthly and gained a national audience by contributing to John J. Lalor's encyclopedia of politics, economics, and history (3 vols., 1881–1884). His article on the history of political economy first brought the German school of historical economics to American readers.

In 1883 James became professor of public finance and administration at the University of Pennsylvania, where he also directed the Wharton School of Finance and Economy, the nation's first business school. James was a pioneer in the revolt against laissez-faire economic thought in the United States. In May 1885 he and Simon Patten formed the Society for the Study of National Economy and called on the state to take an active role in promoting public welfare. Their bold proposal stimulated the formation of the American Economic Association that September. James chaired the committee on organization and aspired to head the new group, but others eclipsed him in the leadership.

Envisioning an agency to coordinate all the social sciences, James formed the American Academy of Political and Social Science in December 1889. He served as president and as editor of its quarterly, the *Annals of the American Academy of Political and Social Science*. In these years James also gained a national reputation as an authority on municipal administration. He fought the private interests that attempted to lease the Philadelphia gas works, and his 1886 study of municipal gas launched a campaign for municipal ownership or control of utilities that soon reached nationwide proportions. James was instrumental in organizing the Philadelphia Municipal League in 1891.

James actively promoted higher commercial education. In 1883 he went to Europe for the American Banker's Association to study commercial education; the report he later published laid the foundations for commercial education in the United States. The training of businessmen was essential in the struggle for national mercantile supremacy, he insisted, and businessmen needed exposure to university influences to check the materialism bred by commercial life. James valued university extension as a forum for civic enlightenment, and in 1891, a year after the American Society for the Extension of University Teaching was organized in Philadelphia, he became its president.

James gave many public addresses, often published his remarks, and also wrote prolifically. His writings drew heavily on German sources and summarized the existing literature while advancing progressive views. Because he thrived on controversy, he made enemies, and in 1894 a new president at the University of Pennsylvania fired James on the grounds that he lacked confidence in him.

Leaving Philadelphia in 1895, James went to the University of Chicago as professor of public administration and head of university extension. In January 1902 he accepted the presidency of Northwestern University, a Methodist institution comprising a college and several professional schools. James wished to transform a fundamentally liberal arts college into a university, but his vision was premature, so in August 1904 he accepted his election as the fourth president of the University of Illinois in Urbana-Champaign.

James was determined to make Illinois a world-class university. He inspired new enthusiasm for scholarship, insisted on high standards, and emphasized advanced degrees. Thus he made the graduate college a separate unit, recruited outstanding scholars, and created a splendid library to support research. He completed the acquisition of a medical school in Chicago. James stimulated the ideals of culture as well as of scholarship. He actively encouraged art and music, valued athletics as a unifier of the campus, and sought to free undergraduates from excessive paternalism. A devoted Methodist, he encouraged the planting of religious foundations near the campus to serve the spiritual needs of students of all faiths.

James dreamed big dreams and had a special talent for promotion and publicity. He pressed relentlessly for larger appropriations, organizing statewide lobbying to win support for his plans in Springfield. By 1910 no Illinois politician dared be openly hostile to the university.

An admirer of German culture with a German wife (she died in 1914, leaving two sons and a daughter), James was nevertheless a zealous advocate of preparedness as the United States became entangled in the European war. In a celebrated case of the alleged disloyalty of certain faculty members in 1917, however, James did not actively defend their academic freedom.

James nourished large personal ambitions, and he cooperated with an influential friend who boosted him for the Republican party's presidential nomination in 1916. When this effort fizzled, a faction of the divided Illinois Republican party urged him to run for governor. James later declared that he would run only as a unity candidate and ultimately withdrew on the grounds that he was indispensable to the university.

James was eager to go overseas for the Red Cross or another American agency late in the war, and on 28 October 1918 he received notice that President Woodrow Wilson had appointed him as a cultural ambassador to the universities of the Allied powers on the Continent. After the armistice soon ended these plans, James returned to his presidential duties, but his health began to fail. He asked to resign in June 1919, but the trustees persuaded him to take a year's leave of absence, regain his health, and return to service. In May 1920 his resignation was accepted, and thereafter he lived mostly in California, dying at a sister's home in Covina.

Vain and masterful, James was highly visible in American public life for forty years. He pioneered in criticizing laissez-faire economics and in advocating that the state should take an active part in advancing human welfare. He was a leading exponent of higher business education. A recognized authority on municipal affairs, he gave impetus to the national movement for municipal ownership or control of utilities. He strongly endorsed federal aid to education at all levels and tirelessly promoted the establishment of a national university. James brought "the kindling capacity of a great creative leader" (*Memorial*, p. 14) to a number of educational institutions. He gave the University of Illinois a "permanent bias toward excellence and distinction" (*Memorial*, p. 15) and was instrumental in transforming it into one of the leading universities in the United States.

• Some James papers are in the University of Pennsylvania and the Northwestern University archives, but the bulk of them are in the University of Illinois Archives. Subject-finding aids are available. James published monographs on a wide range of topics. They include *Outline of a Proposed School of Political and Social Science* (1885), *The Relation of the Modern Municipality to the Gas Supply* (1886), *Needed Improvements in Our Transportation Systems* (1890), *Schools of Finance and Economy* (1891), *The Education of Business Men in Europe* (1893), *A Plea for the Establishment of Commercial High Schools* (1893), *The Elements of a Model Charter for American Cities* (1895), *The Place of the Political and Social Sciences in Modern Education* (1898), *Commercial Education* (1899), *Municipal Administration in Germany* (1901), *Some Features of American Higher Education* (1902), and *The Origin of the Land Grant Act of 1862* (1910), which argues the untenable thesis that Illinois leaders were primarily responsible for securing the Morrill Act. James's inaugural address, "The Function of the State University," *Science*, n.s., 22 (1905): 609–28, reveals his obsessive reverence for "science." The *Installation of Edmund Janes James . . . as President of the University of Illinois* (1906) illustrates James's love of pomp and ceremony and reports on conferences dealing with college trustees, commercial education, and religious education. *Sixteen Years at the University of Illinois* (1920) provides useful information on his presidency. A *Memorial of the Funeral Services for Edmund Janes James* (1925) contains valuable tributes.

James B. Childs, comp., "A Bibliography of the Published Writings and Addresses of Edmund Janes James" (1920), is available in the Rare Book and Special Collections Library at the University of Illinois at Urbana-Champaign. James's articles in Lalor's *Cyclopaedia* are listed in volume three of that work. James's own *Relation of Our Colleges and Universities to Higher Commercial Education* (1901) lists sixteen of his writings on the subject.

The best comprehensive biography is Richard A. Swanson, "Edmund Janes James, 1855–1925: A 'Conservative Progressive' in American Higher Education" (Ph.D. diss., Univ. of Illinois, 1966). Jerome L. Rodnitzky, "A History of Public Relations at the University of Illinois, 1904–1930" (Ph.D. diss., Univ. of Illinois, 1967), discusses James's promotional activities. An obituary is in the *New York Times*, 20 June 1925.

WINTON U. SOLBERG

JAMES, Edwin (27 Aug. 1797–28 Oct. 1861), botanist and physician, was born in Weybridge, Vermont, the son of Daniel James, a farmer, and Mary Emmes. He entered Middlebury College, Middlebury, Vermont, in 1812, graduating with a bachelor's degree in 1816. During the next three years he studied medicine in Albany with his physician brothers Daniel and James; the New York State Medical Society granted his official license to practice medicine in 1822. James also attended lectures given by Amos Eaton and often corresponded with the eminent botanist and geologist, who in turn introduced him to John Torrey, one year James's senior and also beginning a distinguished botanical career.

In 1820 Torrey recommended James to fill the position of physician and botanist for the second year of Major Stephen H. Long's western scientific expedition ordered to explore the Platte, Arkansas, and Red rivers and to make detailed observations on the topography, natural history, botany, and geology of the country. Appointed also to assume the duties of geologist, James with the rest of the party left Engineer Cantonment near Council Bluffs, where Long's 1819 expedition had wintered, on 6 June 1820. Proceeding along the Platte and the South Platte rivers, the men arrived in July at the "Grand Peak" that explorer Zebulon Pike had sighted (but neither climbed nor named) in 1806. With two companions, on 14 July James reached the 14,110-foot summit, which Long subsequently called "James Peak" on the expedition maps. The honor, however, did not last; by the 1859 gold rush "Pikes Peak" had emerged the clear winner. Today Edwin James is commemorated in the Colorado Rockies by another James Peak (13,294 feet) to the north.

Departing from the mountains, the party separated into two groups and reunited at Forth Smith, Arkansas, before returning east. James traveled to Philadelphia, where in late 1821 he began compiling the expedition report. Published in 1822–1823 in Philadelphia and London, *Account of an Expedition from Pittsburgh to the Rocky Mountains* contained a wealth of descriptive and statistical information. It also characterized the plains as the "Great American Desert," dry, desolate, and unfit for cultivation. This controversial assessment—myth or reality?—both helped to retard westward expansion until after the Civil War and obscured the expedition's noteworthy scientific contributions.

After completing the report, in early 1823 James was appointed an assistant surgeon in the U.S. Army and ordered temporarily to Fort Bellefontaine near St. Louis. Meanwhile, Long named James botanist, geologist, and physician for his 1823 expedition to the upper Mississippi River area and Canada, but his instructions did not reach James en route. Others took over the duties he would have fulfilled, while a "disappointed and chagrined" James stayed for a short time at Bellefontaine before going on to Fort Crawford at Prairie du Chien, Wisconsin.

James remained at Fort Crawford until that post was briefly closed in the fall of 1826. He then spent the winter months in the East, visiting family and friends. In April 1827 in Philadelphia he married Clarissa "Clara" Rogers, with whom he had one son. Shortly after his marriage, James was stationed at Fort Mackinac, Michigan, before new orders took him to Fort Brady, Sault Ste. Marie, Michigan, where he served until the spring of 1832.

During his years in Wisconsin and Michigan James spent much time studying the native peoples and their languages. While at Fort Mackinac he met interpreter John Tanner, taken as a child by Shawnee Indians from his Kentucky border home. His story, which James "prepared for the press" as *A Narrative of the Captivity and Adventures of John Tanner*, was published in New York in 1830; it was issued also in British (1830), French (1835), and German (1840) editions. James's work with Indian dialects resulted in the publication of the first complete Ojibwa translation of the New Testament (1833), *Chippewa First Lessons in Spelling and Reading* (1832), and three Ojibwa spellers (1833, 1835, and 1846).

After leaving Michigan, James was assigned to posts near Annapolis and Albany before the surgeon general called for his resignation in 1833. Some in Albany thought that "anti-temperance influences" were responsible, since James had been working with the New York State Temperance Society. James continued as the society's editor and corresponding secretary until late 1836; shortly thereafter he abruptly left Albany to go west—family accounts cite a "row with the City Fathers." He settled on a farm near Burlington, Iowa, where he remained, except for brief interludes, until his death.

During one such period, James served as an Indian subagent at the Old Council Bluffs subagency near Bellevue, Nebraska. Assuming his duties in mid-June 1837, he worked primarily with Potawatomi being resettled from lands in Missouri. Transferred to the Osage subagency in west-central Missouri in early 1838, he resigned before taking up that position.

James returned then to his Iowa farm, leaving periodically in the early 1840s to undertake surveying contracts in Illinois and Missouri. During the 1850s he devoted much of his energy to helping fugitive slaves, and his home became a noted stop on the Underground Railroad. He also continued his interest in botany, remarking to one friend that he could "walk one hundred miles to see a new plant, but would like to take the steamboat back." To the end he remained a man of pronounced (many thought eccentric) ideas. In an obituary in the *American Journal of Science and Arts* in 1862, the botanist C. C. Parry wrote, "With him to espouse a cause, was to carry it to the farthest possible extreme, often erroneous and it is to be feared at times positively wrong."

In 1854 James told John Torrey that "it was not for me to 'make my mark upon the age.'" Yet make it he did. When he climbed present Pikes Peak, he became the first scientist to collect alpine flora above timberline in North America. That feat also marked the first recorded ascent of a 14,000-foot North American peak. As a botanist, James is remembered especially for his 1820 discoveries of the blue-and-white columbine (*Aquilegia coerulea*), now Colorado's state flower, and the hydrangia *Jamesia americana*. Despite all that he did in the four decades following the Long expedition, nothing surpassed his accomplishments during those brief summer months of 1820.

• Although James's housekeeper reportedly was ordered to destroy his papers after the death of Clara James in 1854, significant documentary material has nonetheless survived. A small manuscript collection is in the Archibald Church Library, Northwestern University Medical School, Chicago, and a diary (1820–1827) is in the Special Collections, Butler Library, Columbia University. Especially important are ninety letters (1819–1825) from Edwin James to John James, apparently saved by family members and acquired by Yale University in 1983. The first work based on these letters is Carlo Rotella, "Travels in a Subjective West: The Letters of Edwin James and Major Stephen Long's Scientific Expedition of 1819–1820," *Montana* 41 (Autumn 1991): 20–35. An earlier account, L. H. Pammel, "Dr. Edwin James," *Annals of Iowa*, 3d ser., 8 (Oct. 1907): 161–85 and (Jan. 1908): 276–95, includes extracts of letters written by Edwin James between 1827 and 1859. Because James served the government in several capacities, records in the National Archives are of prime importance. *Account of an Expedition from Pittsburgh to the Rocky Mountains* was issued in 1905 as volumes 14–17 of the Early Western Travels Series. Annotated by Reuben Gold Thwaites, this version represents the best scholarly text. One-volume abridged editions include those prepared by Howard Lamar (1972) and Maxine Benson (1988). For modern assessments of Long and the expedition, see Roger Nichols and Patrick Halley, *Stephen Long and American Frontier Exploration* (1980), and Richard G. Beidleman, "The 1820 Long Expedition," *American Zoologist* 26 (1986): 307–13. The most comprehensive biography of James is Maxine Benson, "Edwin James: Scientist, Linguist, Humanitarian" (Ph.D. diss., Univ. of Colorado, 1968). Good brief accounts are Joseph Ewan, "Edwin James," in *Rocky Mountain Naturalists* (1950), and Richard G. Beidleman, "Edwin James, Pioneer Naturalist," *Horticulture* 44 (Dec. 1966): 32–34.

MAXINE BENSON

JAMES, Elmore (27 Jan. 1918–24 May 1963), blues singer and guitarist, was born in rural Holmes County, Mississippi, the son of Leola Brooks, a fifteen-year-old farm worker. Born Elmore Brooks, he later took the surname of his stepfather, Joe Willie James. He showed an early interest in music, constructing such homemade instruments as a one-string guitar, or "diddley bow," before graduating to a regular guitar and performing locally while still in his teens.

In 1937 James's musical world broadened when his parents moved to the Turner Brothers Plantation in the Delta town of Belzoni. There he purchased a better guitar, entered a brief marriage to Josephine Harris, and met two musicians, guitarist Robert Johnson and harmonica wizard Aleck Miller (later known as Sonny Boy Williamson II), who would change his life. James was so impressed by Johnson's slide guitar technique that he added Johnson's "I Believe I'll Dust My Broom" to his repertoire. It became his signature song. Johnson and Miller eventually moved on (Johnson was murdered the next year), but James and Miller kept in touch and remained close for the rest of their lives.

Working with Miller and later with a combo that included saxophone, trumpet, and drums, James stayed relatively close to home for the next few years, alternating his music with seasonal farm work. Despite lifelong heart troubles, he entered the navy in 1943, serving on Guam. Discharged in 1945, he put together an electric band in Memphis, performing with a cousin, guitarist Homesick James Williamson, or with guitarist Eddie Taylor. In 1947 he married Georgianna Crump and resumed performing around Belzoni. Periodically he visited his former partner Miller, who had become the South's foremost blues radio personality. The two of them teamed up briefly in 1947 to do a radio show pitching Talaho, an alcohol-based tonic made by a local drugstore. The show, broadcast across the heart of the Delta, brought new notoriety to James, allowing him to meet and work with other musicians, including Greenville pianist Willie Love and guitarist Arthur "Big Boy" Crudup.

In 1951 James traveled with Miller to Jackson, Mississippi, where Miller, by now performing as Sonny Boy Williamson, had a date to record for the Trumpet label. James was willing to play backup for Williamson but was reluctant to record his own tune, "Dust My Broom." According to legend, a surreptitious recording of the tune was made during a rehearsal in August 1951. With another artist on the flip side of the record, "Dust My Broom" was released in early 1952 and broke onto the rhythm and blues charts that April. The unexpected success drew interest from Trumpet's competitors, particularly Joe Bihari, who owned several West Coast labels in partnership with his two brothers. James was still under contract to Trumpet, however—even though he never recorded another song for the label—so Bihari was leery of releasing any James material.

Finally, in 1952, Bihari lured James to Chicago to record; the resulting sides came out on Bihari's Meteor label. Other sessions for Bihari followed, as did an apparently illegal session for Checker. Over an eleven-year recording career, James had releases on Chess and Mel London's Chief label, both based in Chicago, and on Bobby Robinson's New York–based Fire label and its subsidiaries. The backup group on many of these sides was tabbed the Broomdusters—Johnny Jones on piano, Odie Payne, drums, J. T. Brown, tenor sax, and, at times, Homesick James, second guitar.

James returned South in 1958, working briefly as a radio disk jockey in Jackson, but soon returned to steady club dates in Chicago, where he often worked with Big Bill Hill, a club owner, promoter, and disc jockey. By 1961 James was again touring with his own band, but after trouble with the musicians union he returned to Jackson. Despite failing health he continued to perform close to home for the next two years. In 1963 Big Bill Hill resolved the union problem and brought James to Chicago for a comeback. Before his appearance at Hill's Copacabana club, however, James suffered a fatal heart attack at the home of Homesick James. His body was returned South and buried in Durant, Mississippi. He was inducted into the Blues Foundation Hall of Fame in 1980 and the Rock and Roll Hall of Fame in 1992.

One could argue that Elmore James, like his mentor Robert Johnson, became more famous in death than he ever was in life. As one of the first artists to take Delta blues and electrify it, he was a clear link between down-home blues and world rock. His sound was emulated by rock artists Eric Clapton, Johnny Winter, George Thorogood, and the Allman Brothers, to name a few. Possibly because of his failure to work with a single powerful record label or perhaps because of his down-home sound, James never achieved the stature of Muddy Waters or Howling Wolf. Still, his music was popular with audiences in rural juke joints and big-city clubs alike.

Although the body of his work has at times been judged repetitive—often the mark of a traditional artist who achieves a signature sound—his best works were transcendent. On such songs as "Dust My Broom," "The Sky Is Crying," "Rollin' and Tumblin'," and "My Bleeding Heart," the combined force of his searing, driving slide technique and his hoarse, impassioned vocals could be breathtaking. Big Bill Hill put it this way: "No one touched me more than this man . . . I mean blues-wise, because he did it from [his heart]. No imitation—originality. . . . An old timer, he played the blues because he felt the blues and he lived them." Fellow Delta blues artist Big Joe Williams echoed Hill: "Elmore, he had a way of playing and singing, nobody could get close to it. It come from his heart. And like he sung, he lived . . . he sung it real hard."

• For discographical information, see Mike Leadbitter and Neil Slaven, *Blues Records 1943–1966* (1968). For more details about his life, see Ron Weinstock, "Elmore James: A BRQ Profile," *Blues Revue Quarterly* 12 (Spring 1994): 24–33; Sheldon Harris, *Blues Who's Who: A Biographical Dictionary of Blues Singers* (1979; repr. 1989); Mike Rowe, *Chicago Blues: The City and the Music* (1973; U.S. ed., 1975); and Gayle Dean Wardlow and Leadbitter, "Canton Mis'sippi Breakdown," *Blues Unlimited* 91 (May 1972): 5–10. For a sample of his music, try *Elmore James: King of the Slide Guitar—The Fire/Fury/Enjoy Recordings*, Capricorn Records, 9 42006-2; *Elmore James and His Broomdusters: The Classic Early Recordings, 1951–1956*, Flair, 725383963126.

BARRY LEE PEARSON
BILL MCCULLOCH

JAMES, Harry (15 Mar. 1916–5 July 1983), trumpeter and bandleader, was born in a show business hotel in Albany, Georgia, the son of Everette Robert James, director of and trumpet soloist in the touring Mighty Haag circus, and Maybelle Stewart, a circus aerialist. His middle name was Haag. James's father taught him drums around age seven and trumpet by age ten. Within a few years James was leading the second band

in the Christy Brothers Circus. In 1931 the family settled in Beaumont, Texas, where he attended high school and where his father eventually headed a music school.

James began working in dance bands, touring as far as New Orleans, but mainly performing in Texas. He was discovered in Dallas by Ben Pollack, in whose dance band he played in 1935–1936 and made his first recordings, including "Jimtown Blues." In January 1937 he became a part of the Benny Goodman orchestra's acclaimed trumpet section with Ziggy Elman and Chris Griffin, who are featured together on James's arrangements "Peckin'" and "*Life* Goes to a Party," recorded that same year. James displayed a firecracker improvisatory style and a concomitant enthusiasm which, in combination with Gene Krupa's flamboyant drumming, made this band, for many, the most fondly remembered of Goodman's orchestras. James also demonstrated a considerable feeling for blues playing, a testimony to his Texas roots. He was a prominent soloist on many of the band's recordings, including versions of "Sing, Sing, Sing" (1937–1938), "One O'Clock Jump" (1938), and a jam session on "Honeysuckle Rose" from Goodman's concert at Carnegie Hall in 1938. He also recorded with Goodman's sidemen Teddy Wilson ("Just a Mood," 1937) and Lionel Hampton ("Shoe Shiner's Drag," 1938). His studio career as a leader began at a session with Goodman's pianist Jess Stacy and members of Count Basie's band. Away from work, James's hobby was baseball, which he played with passion on teams organized from Goodman's bandsmen and later from his own.

Under the management of Goodman's agent Willard Alexander and with Goodman's blessing and financial support, James quit late in 1938 to start a big band, which he led from 25 January 1939 until his death. He showed an ear for talent when he hired the then unknown Frank Sinatra, who later regretted his shaky contribution to one of James's recorded versions of "Ciribiribin" (November 1939), the band's theme song. James was struggling for steady, profitable work, and when the opportunity came for Sinatra to join Tommy Dorsey's big band in 1940, in which he rose to stardom, James supported the move. Dick Haymes replaced Sinatra.

The following year James added to the conventional big band of brass, reeds, and rhythm instruments, a string section, which he expanded and continued to use into the 1950s. He had some success with novelty versions of the classic etudes "Flight of the Bumble Bee" and "Carnival of Venice" (both February 1941), and then a huge hit record with "You Made Me Love You" (May 1941), featuring his trumpet in an instrumental translation of Judy Garland's singing "played with warm emotion and a vibrato so broad that at times it seemed almost comic," said jazz critic John S. Wilson. With singer Helen Forrest providing a vocal complement to the leader's trumpet, and with an emphasis on lyrics expressing wartime sentiments—"I Don't Want to Walk Without You" (1941), "I Cried for You" (1942)—this sort of schmaltzy pop music made James for a few years the most popular band-leader of the swing era, surpassing even Glenn Miller. Interspersed among these titles were swing numbers, including "The Mole" (recorded in 1941 and one of the finest examples of a string section incorporated into the context of swing), "I'm Beginning to See the Light" (1944, with singer Kitty Kallen having replaced Forrest), and "Friar Rock" (1945). Two other major hits during this period were "I'll Get By" (1941, with Haymes) and "It's Been a Long, Long Time" (1945, with Kallen). James began to be heard on radio five times each week with his own program (September 1942–March 1944) and on Jack Benny's show; he also played a sensationally popular engagement at the Paramount in New York, April–May 1943.

James first married Goodman's singer Louise Tobin in May 1935; they had two children. Following a divorce in June 1943, his second marriage was to movie star Betty Grable on 5 July 1943, at the height of his fame; they had two children. This was a highly publicized romance, James's band at the time being based in Hollywood and appearing in several movies, including *Springtime in the Rockies* (with Grable, 1942), *Best Foot Forward* (1943), *Two Girls and a Sailor, Bathing Beauty* (both 1944), and *Do You Love Me?* (1946). With his newfound wealth, James intensified an ongoing hobby by acquiring his own stable of racehorses. Later, he served as technical adviser for the movie *Young Man with a Horn*, for which he played the trumpet parts for actor Kirk Douglas (1950). He hosted a television series in 1952 and acted in *The Benny Goodman Story* (1955). In 1957 his band toured Europe.

One critic has observed that James's career reversed the norm. A fine teenage jazz musician, he rapidly achieved huge commercial success and then turned increasingly back toward jazz. His big band from the mid-1940s to the early 1980s was never innovative or historically significant, but it preserved the swing tradition, and it provided an outlet for such sidemen as valve trombonist Juan Tizol (1944–1951, 1954–1957), alto saxophonist Willie Smith (1944–1951, 1954–1963), and drummers Louie Bellson (intermittently 1950s and 1960s), Buddy Rich (intermittently 1950s, regularly 1962–1966), and Sonny Payne (1966–1973), as well as for many leading arrangers, most notably Neal Hefti and Ernie Wilkins.

Around 1963, James moved his base of operations from Hollywood to Las Vegas, where the band played shows while maintaining a dance repertory for long-standing engagements at Disneyland and extensive tours, including periodic reunions with Sinatra and trips to Europe (1970 and 1971) and Argentina (1981). In 1979, James was featured in a nostalgic and highly successful Broadway revue, *The Big Broadcast of 1944*.

James was divorced from Grable in 1965. He then married Joan Boyd; they had one child. From April 1983, James suffered from lymphatic cancer. Soon after giving his last performance in Los Angeles, he died in Las Vegas.

During his time with the Goodman orchestra James was, after Goodman himself, the finest jazz soloist in the band, but his improvising was nonetheless somewhat shallower in content than that of the best jazz trumpeters of his era. Thus, despite his long-standing involvement in jazz, his greater significance lies in popular music, where his sentimental playing remains one of the dominant sounds heard on nostalgic big band radio shows.

• A bibliography of early periodical sources on James follows a wonderfully humorous account in *Current Biography, 1943*. Frank Stacy published an early biography, *Harry James Pin-up Life Story* (1944). Surveys and interviews are by Charles Emge, "James Still Fronts Crack Band," *Down Beat*, 23 Feb. 1951, pp. 3, 18, which includes a list of jazz-oriented recorded titles; John Tynan, "The Horn Still Blows," *Down Beat*, 23 Jan. 1958, pp. 17, 34–35; Les Tomkins, "The Harry James Story," *Crescendo*, Nov. 1970, pp. 20–23, reprinted incomplete as "The Classic Interview: Harry James," *Crescendo International*, July 1987, pp. 12–14; and George T. Simon, *The Big Bands*, 4th ed. (1981), pp. 262–76, 534–37. Detailed assessments from a jazz perspective are Albert McCarthy, *Big Band Jazz* (1984), and Gunther Schuller, *The Swing Era: The Development of Jazz, 1930–1945* (1989). For a chronology of his years with Goodman, see D. Russell Connor, *Benny Goodman: Listen to His Legacy* (1988); an appreciation of his contributions is in James Lincoln Collier, *Benny Goodman and the Swing Era* (1989), pp. 230–46. An exhaustive list of his recordings as a leader is by Charles Garrod and Peter Johnston, *Harry James and His Orchestra* vol. 1, *1937–1950* (1975), vol. 2, *1951–1975* (1975), and vol. 3, *1955–1982* (1985). An obituary by John S. Wilson appeared in the *New York Times*, 6 July 1983.

BARRY KERNFELD

JAMES, Henry (3 June 1811–18 Dec. 1882), author, was born in Albany, New York, the son of William James, a prosperous merchant and investor, and Catharine Barber. The critical event of James's childhood was a serious burn and the subsequent loss of his right leg above the knee. He was apparently confined to his bed for years and suffered at least two amputations, performed without anesthetic; the final operation took place when he was sixteen. James had little to say about this traumatic experience, which seems to have fostered a certain morbid guilt and extremism.

Although his teachers in Albany included the physicist Joseph Henry, James came to regard his formal education as ill conceived and irrelevant. He attended Union College and after five rather mediocre terms was allowed to graduate in 1830. Afterward, in obedience to his father's demands, he made a feint at studying the law but soon abandoned this career and took to drinking and gambling, a pattern followed by some of his younger brothers, one of whom (John Barber James) lost large amounts of money at faro in the 1850s and committed suicide.

At the age of twenty-three James underwent a powerful conversion, joined his parents' Presbyterian church, and entered Princeton Theological Seminary with the aim of becoming a minister. After about two years at this seminary, then staunchly Calvinist, James became convinced that modern Protestant denomination had deviated from gospel purity. He left Princeton and edited Robert Sandeman's *Letters on Theron and Aspasio* (1757), a fierce attack on the institution of the clergy. He also wrote a pamphlet, *The Gospel Good News to Sinners*, that sought to correct the errors of his Presbyterian teachers by setting forth a strict construction of sin, regeneration, and justification by faith. In 1840, following the practice of Sandeman's British followers, James was married in a civil ceremony to Mary Robertson Walsh.

Spending his early married years chiefly in New York and Albany, James seems to have devoted his time to private study. His literal approach to Scripture and his essentially Calvinist beliefs were not compatible with the Transcendentalist modes of thought then coming into vogue, and he was soon involved in a major new religious and intellectual crisis, stimulated in part by Ralph Waldo Emerson's 1842 lecture series in New York. Emerson put James in touch with Henry David Thoreau and Margaret Fuller and in other ways introduced him to a wider and less parochial world of thought. James regarded Emerson as the first candid truth-seeker he had known, and Emerson pronounced James "the best apple on the tree."

In the spring of 1843 James tried to articulate his new nonliteral religious ideas in a series of lectures entitled "Inward Reason of Christianity." But he lost his audience and had trouble turning the lectures into a book, and when his health became unsteady, he decided to sell his home in New York and go abroad for a year. In London he became acquainted with Thomas Carlyle and John Sterling. Midway through the year, he was incapacitated by a psychic collapse. He apparently sought treatment at Sudbrook Park, a recently established hydropathic institution just east of London, but the baths and showers did little to alleviate his distress. A lady living in the vicinity, Mrs. Sophia Chichester, advised him that he was undergoing what Emanuel Swedenborg called a vastation—a laying waste, a making void. Convinced that his breakdown was part of a necessarily painful regenerative process, James appropriated some of Swedenborg's ideas in order to reconstruct his earlier Calvinism. He fixed on an allegorical method of biblical interpretation and worked out a universalized conception of the spiritual life.

James's first two children, William James and Henry James (1843–1916), had been born shortly before his trip to England. The last three—Garth Wilkinson, Robertson, and Alice James—were born after his return. Recovering from his breakdown and residing chiefly in New York, James decided to pursue a career as writer, lecturer, and public philosopher. Simultaneously, he was drawn to the thought of Charles Fourier, whose American followers were then starting up numerous communes or "phalansteries." In the fall of 1847 James became associated with the leading Fourierist magazine in America, the *Harbinger*, to which he contributed articles and reviews on an almost weekly basis. He also translated a French pamphlet, *Love in the Phalanstery*, which set forth the various alternatives to marriage that Fourier had advocated. Conser-

vative opinion saw this pamphlet as an attack on the family. In the ensuing controversy James expressed views that anticipated the free-love movement of the 1850s: "If society left its subject free to follow the divine afflatus of his passion whithersoever it carried him, we should never hear of such a thing as sexual promiscuity or fornication."

The lectures James delivered in New York City from 1849 to 1851 proved to be the most daring, attention getting, and vigorous of his career. Brought out as books—*Moralism and Christianity* (1850) and *Lectures and Miscellanies* (1852)—they show James at his most assertive and outspoken. "Nature and society," he insisted, "should have no power to identify me with a particular potato-patch and a particular family of mankind all my days." Free self-expression, the imminent perfection of society, and the plastic nature of reality were among his major themes.

In 1852 James began to qualify his revolutionary and romantic assertions. Instead of anticipating new and relaxed forms of marriage, he pronounced monogamy a necessary discipline in the life of man. Opposed to the early feminist movement, he declared woman to be an intellectually limited being who humbly served man even as she enabled him to transmute his selfish brutality into more social uses. James's next few books tended to address narrow readerships rather than the cultivated general public. *The Church of Christ Not an Ecclesiasticism* (1854) insisted that Swedenborg did not intend to found a new denomination. *The Nature of Evil* (1855), a lengthy rejoinder to a book by Rev. Edward Beecher, developed the idea that man's sense of individual agency was his one great sin. *Christianity the Logic of Creation* (1857) argued that the Bible was a sort of hieroglyphic of the founding principles of human selfhood.

In 1850 James became an occasional contributor to the *New York Tribune*. His essays pushing for more liberal divorce laws led to his involvement in a controversial exchange on marriage and free love that saw print under the title *Love, Marriage, and Divorce* (1853). His contributions often focused on topics of the day—spirit-rapping, alcoholism, theological controversies, and various contemporary scandals and crimes. In 1855 he wrote some hard-hitting editorials supporting the suppression of New York's gambling establishments. He also sent the *Tribune* a long series of letters on affairs in Switzerland, France, and England. However, Horace Greeley, the *Tribune*'s owner and editor, felt that James was too impractical and paradoxical, and a dispute between the two men brought James's contributions to an end in 1859.

Between 1855 and 1860, James and his family resided in Europe for two extended periods. His chief purpose in going abroad was to provide his children, William in particular, with a better education than seemed available in the United States. The children attended schools in Geneva, London, Paris, Boulogne, and Bonn, had English and French tutors and governesses, and learned French and German. James himself made no significant new contacts and lost touch with political and intellectual currents in the United States. His closest friends and correspondents tended to be former radicals who had settled into lives of comfortable alienation. He became more genial, relaxed, and home loving.

Although James had not been an abolitionist, he strongly supported the Union side when the Civil War broke out. He saw the war as heralding an apocalyptic transformation of human life, and in an 1861 Fourth of July oration that may well be his most widely known work, "The Social Significance of Our Institutions," he contrasted the United States with Europe and celebrated the sentiment of human equality in American history. But equality was less a political than a spiritual concept for James, and at war's end he confided to an old friend, Parke Godwin, that "democracy is the crowning invention of human stupidity."

Moving to Boston in 1864 and then, two years later, to Cambridge, where he bought a house bordering Harvard Yard, James became a sort of brilliant excrescence of Brahmin New England. He belonged to the Saturday Club, frequented and sometimes addressed the Radical Club, spoke to the New England Women's Clubs, and occasionally attended the Examiner Club, which had a strong Unitarian presence. He was an occasional contributor to the *Atlantic Monthly*, the *North American Review*, and the *Nation*. In 1874 a confidential letter of his on marriage and divorce was published in a radical free-love periodical, *Woodhull & Claflin's Weekly*, and he became embroiled in an embarrassing public exchange. Perhaps his most successful productions were his lively reminiscences of Carlyle and Emerson.

James's last three books were *Substance and Shadow* (1863), *The Secret of Swedenborg* (1869), and *Society the Redeemed Form of Man* (1879). In these works James restated and re-argued his fundamental idea, which he called creation—the tortuous process by which absolute spiritual reality replicates itself. In defending his system, James often abused other philosophers, saying of Immanuel Kant: "I for my part do not hesitate to profess my hearty conviction that he was consummately wrong, wrong from top to bottom, wrong through and through, in short all wrong." James's son William is said to have designed a humorous frontispiece for *Substance and Shadow* that showed a man beating a dead horse. Asked for his opinion of *The Secret of Swedenborg*, William Dean Howells is supposed to have declared that James "kept it."

Those who knew James were impressed by his intellectual energy, his unrestrained and often intemperate manner, his explosive humor, and his evident self-contradictions. Many objected to his high-handed absolutism; some considered him remarkably humble. Most saw him as both obscure and doctrinaire. He did not force his system on his children, but they absorbed its leading features—the aversion to respectable "moralism," the conviction that mundane or despised things had a deep significance. Perhaps James's greatest achievement was to energize his children's minds, exposing them to a wide range of experience and at the same time persuading them to refuse standard categorizations, allegiances, assessments. Yet if William, Henry, and Alice's relative freedom from the shibboleths and maxims of their time may be attributed to their father, it is also the case that his extraordinary ambiguities led these children to leave certain aspects of their own lives unfaced and unexamined. For good and bad, James was the creative force responsible for one of the most brilliant and productive families in American life. He died in Boston.

• Most of James's papers are in the Houghton Library at Harvard University. There are also holdings at Amherst College, Union College, and Colby College. His heavily marked Swedenborg books are in Newton, Mass., at the Swedenborg School of Religion. The only known copy of *The Gospel Good News to Sinners* is at the New-York Historical Society. His correspondence with Joseph Henry has been published in *The Papers of Joseph Henry*, ed. Nathan Reingold (1972–). There are two biographies: Austin Warren, *The Elder Henry James* (1934), and Alfred Habegger, *The Father: A Life of Henry James, Sr.* (1994). Jean Strouse, *Alice James* (1980), and Howard M. Feinstein, *Becoming William James* (1984), offer helpful biographical interpretations of James in relation to two of his children. Chapter 6 of Henry James, Jr.'s memoir, *Notes of a Son and Brothers* (1914), gives a vivid evocation of James.

Frederick Harold Young has written a sympathetic interpretation of James's thought in *The Philosophy of Henry James* (1951). Shorter but well-informed interpretations are in Julia A. Kellogg, *Philosophy of Henry James* (1883); William James's introduction to his edited volume, *The Literary Remains of the Late Henry James* (1885); Ralph Barton Perry, *The Thought and Character of William James*, vol. 1 (1935); and Quentin Anderson, *The American Henry James* (1957). Raymond H. Deck, Jr., discusses James's relation to Swedenborgian thought in "The 'Vastation' of Henry James, Sr.," *Bulletin of Research in the Humanities* 83 (Summer 1980): 216–47, and Alfred Habegger treats his relation to Calvinist thought in "Henry James, Sr., in the late 1830s," *New England Quarterly* 64 (Mar. 1991): 46–81, and his teachings on women and sexuality in *Henry James and the "Woman Business"* (1989).

ALFRED HABEGGER

JAMES, Henry (15 Apr. 1843–28 Feb. 1916), writer, was born in New York City, the son of Henry James, a religious philosopher, and Mary Robertson Walsh. His brother was philosopher William James. His grandfather William James, an Irish immigrant, landed in America in 1789; a bold, shrewd, and far-sighted entrepreneur who benefited from intelligent involvement in New York politics, he prospered in Albany and Syracuse in shipping, extensive real estate speculation, and the very lucrative development of salt refining and died one of the wealthiest men in the country, leaving his heirs "leisured for life," as his son Henry put it. James's knowledge of Europe began early and was regularly refreshed by his father's constant transatlantic journeys in the belief that European experience was essential. By the time James was eighteen, he had spent about one-third of his life abroad. He attended a variety of schools and studied with tutors in both Europe and the United States. James was a precocious "devourer of libraries," but in the spirit of Ralph Waldo Emerson, Father James wanted the children to see for themselves. The lad was early introduced to the spirit of the age that was still freshly taken with experiment, empiricism, self-reliance, and independent-mindedness. The religious atmosphere of the James home was broadly that of Protestant Christianity; the tradition of John Milton, William Blake, Nathaniel Hawthorne (like Emerson, a family friend), and the Swedenborgianism of James senior. Young Henry's painting lessons with William Morris Hunt and his friendship with John LaFarge sharpened his visual sense; LaFarge (at Newport, R.I.) in 1860 opened his eyes to the *Revue des deux mondes* and the fiction of Honoré de Balzac. In 1862 Henry followed William to Harvard. The youths did not participate in the Civil War, although their younger brothers Garth Wilkinson and Robertson served and were wounded. Henry remained for a year, ostensibly studying law but in fact writing stories. In 1864 he achieved his first two publications, a tale called "A Tragedy of Error" and a critical piece ("Essays on Fiction") mainly on Sir Walter Scott. He went abroad alone for the first time early in 1869; a planned rendezvous for the next spring in Italy with his cousin Mary "Minny" Temple was frustrated by her death. Minny was the love of his life. Her death marked the end of his youth (James wrote years later), but her memory continued to haunt him—and his fiction.

James's early fiction was in the style of Hawthornesque romance and so continued on into the 1870s. Writing for the *North American Review*, he was associated with its coeditor Charles Eliot Norton, who introduced him to English literati, including John Ruskin, Charles Darwin, and Dante Gabriel Rosetti, during his year abroad alone, when he also met George Eliot. In 1875 publication of his first novel, *Roderick Hudson* (*Watch and Ward* had prior serialization, but the work was not published as a book until 1878), inaugurated his major "international" fiction in combination with major depiction of the artist as hero. That year saw publication of his first book of travel literature, *Transatlantic Sketches*, and his first collection of tales, *A Passionate Pilgrim and Other Tales*. In the title story the hero, Clement Searle, exemplifies "the latent preparedness of the American mind" to be delighted by England, a sympathy that is "fatal and sacred." This is also the theme of the novel James was working on at his death.

James began his own expatriation by moving to Paris in November 1875. He met the Gustave Flaubert group of writers (Émile Zola, Alphonse Daudet, Edmond de Goncourt, Guy de Maupassant, and Russian expatriate Ivan Turgenev), whom he called "the grandsons of Balzac." He then moved to London and entered society, something he had been unable to do when among the French, and he met William Ewart Gladstone, Herbert Spencer, Thomas Henry Huxley, and Robert Browning. He was elected to the Reform Club and to the Athenaeum. A pair of international novels, *The American* (1877) and *The Europeans*

(1878), the latter reversing the usual transatlantic visit, was accompanied by his first book of critical essays, *French Poets and Novelists* (1878), and his first bestseller, *Daisy Miller* (1878). Then appeared his first critical biography, the portentous *Nathaniel Hawthorne* (1879): after a suitable tribute James faults his earliest mentor for being insufficiently realistic. James's novel of 1880, *Washington Square*, continued his new focus on heroines, which was joined to his international theme in *The Portrait of a Lady* (1881). Isabel Archer is a healthier-minded Daisy Miller but not less independent-minded. The innocent American in Europe is attracted to the nicely mannered Europeanized American Gilbert Osmond and marries him to share her newly won inheritance; Gilbert seems poor and deserving. Her recognition of evil at the center of her marriage is aided by the generous and loving Ralph (who got her the inheritance without her knowing its source). At his death Isabel's discovery of his generosity accompanies the realization of her maturity and courage, the achievement of a Blakean "higher innocence." She decides to refuse the various escapes open to her and to remain faithful to her discovered mature self: she returns to Rome to face Gilbert. James acknowledged (to Grace Norton) that *The Portrait* owed something to Minny Temple, but he did not point out that it is Ralph rather than Isabel who derives from Minny; Ralph is to Isabel as the dying Minny was to Henry James.

He interrupted his expatriation to return to the United States in October 1881 and was held there by the death of both parents during 1882 (although he was back in England between the two sad events). He was named executor of his father's estate and so stayed on until August 1883. He had immediately added his share of the inheritance to that of his sister, Alice (then thirty-four), who would soon need complete care. He was particularly attentive to her (with the help of Katherine Loring) from 1884, when she came to England, until her death in 1892. Macmillan published his first *Collective Edition* in November 1883, by "Henry James"—no longer "Junior."

In 1884 James returned to Paris. Later that year he published an essay, "The Art of Fiction," stressing the importance of "solidity of specification" in rendering "the look of things, the look that conveys their meaning." In those last six words lies the important qualification. He praises treatment of "psychological reasons," and he distinguishes between what is moral and what is mere moralizing. Finally the essay demands meaningful artistic structure, expressive form. James had recognized by this time that the phenomenon of American tourists in Europe provided him with the metaphor of his international theme. For his fictions are not merely studies in cultural contrasts (the look of things) but, via that surface presentation, comments on the human condition (the meaning that their look conveys). His three novels of the later 1880s, *The Bostonians* (1886), *The Princess Casamassima* (1886), and *The Tragic Muse* (1890), exemplify the precepts of "The Art of Fiction" and intentionally follow the lead of his French contemporaries; they are his own version of Zola's "experimental novel," realistic (or naturalistic) portrayal of the influence of heredity and environment. The basic distinction between James and his French confrères is his psychological emphasis, the focus on what his characters *believe* about their hereditary makeup rather than the makeup itself. The characters' "point of view" is really the determining factor.

In December 1888 actor-manager Edward Compton invited James to turn *The American* into a play for his company and thus opened a new phase in James's career. James had published four plays but none had been produced. He knew the theater, especially the French theater, very well, and the dramatic mode appealed to him because of its immediate contact with its audience. He accepted Compton's offer and wrote to his friend Robert Louis Stevenson that *The Tragic Muse* would be his last long novel. He would write plays and "short lengths." *The Tragic Muse* dealt with the sacrifices demanded by art. Actress Miriam Rooth gives up an advantageous marriage to an English diplomat in order to pursue her art, and Nick Dormer disappoints the political ambitions of his family and potential (and wealthy) bride in order to pursue a career as a painter. The novel embodied art in conflict with the world.

Protracted visits to the Continent kept him in touch with his friends there, especially in Florence, Venice, and Rome, and in particular with the grandniece of James Fenimore Cooper, Constance Fenimore Woolson, the nearest to a true romance in his adult life. In May 1889 he met with a small group that included French critic Hippolyte Taine. James had written half a dozen pieces on Taine from 1868 onward. Taine's importance, he felt, rested on an attitude to fiction that resembled Balzac's and contributed to Zola's notion of the *roman expérimental*. Taine postulated the important influence of race, environment, and historical moment as determining the nature of a writer. What most touched James was that part of Taine's attitude that closely resembled his own notion of the importance of the psychological aspect. That is visible in Taine's introduction to his *Histoire de la littérature anglaise*: The "external man" is only a manifestation of the hidden, "internal man." After the luncheon James set down in his notebook something worth remembering: "Taine used the expression, very happily, that Turgenieff so perfectly cut the umbilical cord that bound the story to himself." James was then trying to learn to make a similar cut.

In 1891 *The American* succeeded in the provinces but was not well received in London. James had made it melodramatic and also provided a happy ending (which his friend and editor William Dean Howells had wanted for the novel). He had promised to give himself until 1895 to complete his experiment in the theater, and he wrote another six plays, only one of which was produced. Four of the others he published in 1894 as *Theatricals* and *Theatricals Second Series*. In December of that year he wrote prophetically to a

friend, "I may be meant for the Drama—God knows!—but I wasn't meant for the Theatre." The theater was a horror for him: painful cuts in his scenarios, tiresome rewriting, long and onerous rehearsals, time limits imposed on productions, and the dull, insensitive audiences. Opening night of his next play, *Guy Domville*, on 5 January 1895 was a fiasco. The nervous James had gone to see another of Oscar Wilde's successes, *An Ideal Husband*, playing nearby. He returned to his own at curtain-fall and was then presented to a disturbed audience that hissed and booed. Several perceptive reviewers such as George Bernard Shaw, A. B. Walkley, and H. G. Wells praised the play, but it survived for only four weeks. James was shaken.

During the years of the theatrical experiment, James had published a series of tales of artists variously in conflict with the world, a continuation of his theme in *The Tragic Muse*. The series included "The Private Life" (1892); "The Real Thing" (1892), an instructive complement to "The Art of Fiction"; "The Middle Years" (1893); "The Death of the Lion" (1894); "The Coxon Fund" (1894); "The Figure in the Carpet" (1896); and perhaps most pertinent, "The Next Time" (1895), developed from the first entry in his notebooks after the theatrical fiasco. It tells the story of a respected but unpopular writer who tries to bend his artistic talent to the production of potboilers but always "fails." James had complained that writing for the British stage was like trying to make a sow's ear out of a silk purse; that is the theme of "The Next Time." The theatrical experiment was not a complete loss, James felt. He realized abundant compensation in the lesson "*of the singular value for a narrative plan too* of the . . . divine principle of the Scenario . . . a key that, working in the same *general* way fits the complicated chambers of *both* the dramatic and the narrative lock." He later called his discovery "the sacred mystery of structure."

The "divine principle" accounts for the techniques of most of his subsequent fiction, dramatic fiction free of the omniscient author. That role is often taken over by a character whose point of view ("angle of vision" rather than "opinion") controls the presentation; that feature is often accompanied by "reflexive characterization," which James had used as early as "A Bundle of Letters" (1878). In that tale the correspondents inadvertently expose themselves in letters they believe are recounting the news of the day. Reflexive characterization is illustrated in two major tales of 1898: "In the Cage," where the heroine exposes her own soul in the vicarious life she creates out of the materials of the telegrams she handles in her "cage," and "The Turn of the Screw," where the fascinating associations of two children with ghosts of two servants returned to win them to evil are almost entirely the projections of the rather disturbed psyche of the children's governess. *The Sacred Fount* (1899), James's only novel to rely on first-person narration, is a similar case of such projection. The technique achieves its culmination in *The Ambassadors* (1903). Novels of the period were planned out as though intended to be plays. Substantial notes for *The Spoils of Poynton* (1896) and for *The Awkward Age* (1899) show James's thinking in terms of acts and scenes. A bonus was the ease with which he could then revise a piece of fiction for the stage, or a play into a novel or tale.

Immediately after the failure of *Guy Domville* Ellen Terry asked James to write a play for her. In August 1895 he sent her the one-act *Summersoft*, which pleased her but which she never used. Three years later he recovered it and turned it into the tale "Covering End," and in 1909 it became the three-act play *The High Bid*. In 1893 James planned a new play for Edward Compton. It did not get beyond the note stage, but in 1896 he developed the note into the novel *The Other House*, which became a three-act play in 1909.

James was at Torquay in the fall of 1895 while his Kensington flat was being redecorated and having electricity laid on, yet he was already yearning for a house outside London. He spent the summer of 1896 in the home of Reginald Blomfield at Point Hill, Playden, on the north edge of Rye, Sussex. In August he moved into Rye proper ("The Vicarage") and discovered the old Georgian house with a generous garden called "Lamb House." He signed a 21-year lease the following year and in June 1898 took possession. It was his country house for the rest of his life. When his Kensington flat was sold, he was able to secure rooms in the Reform Club as his London "perch." He kept the Smith couple, who had served him in the flat, and added a houseboy, Burgess Noakes, and a maid, and gladly retained the services of George Gammon, the prize-winning gardener. Just five steps east of the house and inside the garden wall was a small structure called the Garden Room, where James worked in good weather; in winter he used the Green Room, on the second floor of Lamb House.

Following the fiasco of January 1895 James had embarked upon a series of stories that featured children and young adults as though to reinforce his sense of starting over again; actually this was an intensification of an earlier trend. "The Pupil" (1891) tells of the precocious Morgan Moreen and his pretentious but impoverished family, who unload the boy onto his reluctant tutor. "Owen Wingrave" (1892) features dire family pressure—its military tradition resembles the political tradition of Nick Dormer's family in *The Tragic Muse*—which cannot accept young Owen's artistic and pacifist sentiments. *What Maisie Knew* appeared in the year James moved into Lamb House. It is the story of a little girl's efforts to comprehend the various combinations of parents and surrogates and their complex liaisons. "The Turn of the Screw" features the two children, Miles and Flora, thought by the governess to be pursued by evil spirits. Both "Owen" and "Miles" are names that mean "soldier" and similarly underline the adversarial situation in which they find themselves—and the similar ends they meet. *The Awkward Age* looks at two young women who are not quite ready to enter adult society but no longer young enough to be kept with the children. The

novel develops its Blakean (Miltonic and Hawthornesque) theme of the importance of leaving Innocence, confronting the world of Experience bravely, and defining Evil clearly to oppose it and so achieve human maturity, as Isabel Archer had done in *The Portrait of a Lady*.

This series of fictions about the vulnerability of the young to the nefarious threats of the wide world matches closely the series published in the same period about similarly vulnerable and victimized writers. If James was working out his own sense of vulnerability via those two related series, then a sense of triumph over the threats emerges from *The Awkward Age*. The book's "happy ending," such as it is, brings together the young protagonist and a mature benefactor.

While working on *What Maisie Knew*, James suffered a severe attack of writer's cramp. Early in 1897 he hired William MacAlpine to take dictation in shorthand and transcribe it on a typewriter. He soon began dictating directly to MacAlpine as a typist. Henceforth James dictated much of his fiction and correspondence, having bought a Remington, the "music" of which he definitely preferred. Reliance on the typewriter somewhat curtailed his travel; "portable" machines were still in the future. That reliance may also have contributed to what some readers feel is James's prolixity and a tendency toward the baroque. Thus, while he did visit the channel coast in the summer of 1897, he did not get back to the Continent until early 1899. In February a serious fire in Lamb House gave him an urgent excuse to depart, and he traveled in Europe for several months.

On his return to England in July 1899, James learned that Lamb House was now for sale. He bought it for $10,000 and put up the Kensington flat (where his friend Jonathan Sturges had been living while James was on the Continent) for sale at once. He engaged James B. Pinker as his literary agent, and with the beginning of the new century he was set to create the three great novels of his Major Phase—*The Wings of the Dove* (1902), *The Ambassadors* (1903), and *The Golden Bowl* (1904)—and with them his second venture into biography, *William Wetmore Story and His Friends* (1903). His younger colleagues began to call him Master.

In the years clustered around the turn of the century James found himself at Lamb House in the center of a group of writers, mostly younger than he, who lived in the surrounding area: Joseph Conrad, Stephen Crane, Ford Madox Ford, Rudyard Kipling, and Wells. James could be a genial companion but was a severe critic. He told Mrs. Humphry Ward, "I'm a wretched person to *read* a novel—I begin so quickly and concomitantly, *for myself*, to write it rather—even before I know clearly what it's about!" Yet he was ready, especially in his later years, to give attention and encouragement to young writers whom he found promising. Among those were, most prominently, Wells, Hugh Walpole, and Edith Wharton. Another young writer, of modest success, deserves mention—Jonathan Sturges, often a guest at James's home. In 1889 Harper published his translation of thirteen tales by Maupassant, for which James had provided an introduction. In October 1895 Sturges went to Torquay to visit James and told him an anecdote about meeting Howells in Paris and being given by him some urgent advice: "Oh, you are young. . . . Be glad of it and *live*. Live all you can; it's a mistake not to." James made a note of it and thought there might be a story there but worried about the American-in-Paris cliché—"so obvious, so usual to make Paris the vision that opens his eyes." That is what he did, however, resuming after twenty years his old international theme in *The Ambassadors*. It is not *The American* retold. A comparison of Christopher Newman and Lambert Strether indicates the immense distance James's art had traveled in the interim.

Strether comes to Paris as an avuncular ambassador to recover his young compatriot Chad Newsome from the "great grey Babylon." He has been gone too long, is needed at home to manage the family business, and must have fallen into the snare of a femme fatale. Strether finds, instead of the callow youth he expected, a smoothly finished gentleman. When he meets and is impressed by the charming Madame Marie de Vionnet, evidently Chad's friend and cultural benefactress, he can but conclude that the only female involvement here for Chad is with Jeanne, her daughter. Besides, Bilham, Chad's friend, has assured Strether that the relationship between the mother and Chad is "a virtuous attachment." Bilham knew that Strether would understand the adjective in the Puritan New England sense, but he trusted that Strether was the man of good will he and other of Chad's friends (including Madame de Vionnet) believed him to be and would finally recognize that the attachment was indeed virtuous in the sense Bilham understood it to be. Strether is at last confronted with inescapable evidence that he and the folks back home in Woollett were "right" about what was keeping Chad in Paris, but he cannot conclude that Madame de Vionnet is a "bad woman," for he knows her to be the "lady" he has always taken her for. He has changed sides; he now insists Chad remain in Paris. He also realizes that the finished Chad has been selfishly using Madame de Vionnet, that she loves him, and that he has no intention of requiting that love or recognizing his indebtedness. The innocent Strether, despite his age, has managed to identify the evil at the core of his experience and to rise to that condition of maturity (of higher innocence) that the theme usually requires. Strether has at last learned to *live*, perhaps not quite according to Howells's exhortation to Sturges, but according to the equation set up by Bilham's misremembering Strether's advice to him as "*see* all you can." Strether has learned to see, clearly.

The Ambassadors is a third-person narrative, but the controlling point of view is always Strether's, although that might not be obvious until the reader has gone some distance into the novel. Strether is an "unreliable" focus. The story is both literally and figuratively the demonstration of Strether's steadily improving vision, and its implication is that only with clear-eyed self-reliance can one truly live.

A reprise of *The Americana* (as James early called *The Portrait of a Lady*) may perhaps be found, however, in the subsequent *The Wings of the Dove*. It was published in August 1902, while *The Ambassadors* began its serialization in January 1903. Yet the 20,000-word Project of the latter was sent to Harper on 1 September 1900, and James actually completed the novel before *The Wings of the Dove*. This is the story of Milly Theale, a wealthy American girl, "potential heiress of all the ages," though suffering ill health. An innocent, like Isabel Archer, and a long step away from the aggressively naive Daisy Miller, she is plunged into the gamey world of experience, where everyone seems bent on gaining her wealth. The dove experiences the evil of the world and defines it for herself. It is, specifically, manipulation of human beings by their fellows, use of people as though they were things. Milly looks at the famous Bronzino portrait she is said by all to resemble, finds it is "dead, dead, dead," and comments, "I shall never be better than this"—never better for them than a picture.

The title of *The Wings of the Dove* comes from Psalms 55:6 and 68:13, and its theme derives from Blake's poetry (especially *Songs of Innocence* and *Songs of Experience*), with some reinforcement from Hawthorne's *The Marble Faun*. The third novel of the Major Phase, *The Golden Bowl*, is sometimes thought to have taken its title from Ecclesiastes 12:6–7; a likelier source is Blake's epigraph to "The Book of Thel":

> Does the Eagle know what is in the pit,
> Or wilt thou go ask the Mole?
> Can Wisdom be put in a silver rod?
> Or Love in a golden bowl?

Furthermore, the behavior of Blake's Thel, a frantic flight from confrontation with the fallen world, is a negative counter to the behavior of Maggie Verver. The American Maggie and her father come to Europe to find what it has to offer that they may purchase. Adam Verver is a more sophisticated Christopher Newman, and wealthier. They find Prince Amerigo, an attractive and somewhat impoverished Italian nobleman with a long pedigree. He and Maggie marry, but because she clings to her father, Amerigo seeks companionship with his former mistress, Charlotte Stant (also American and the Serena Merle of the novel). Amerigo and Charlotte go shopping to find a suitable wedding gift for her to give her friend Maggie (who is ignorant of their association); Charlotte wants to get a golden bowl, but Amerigo disagrees when he perceives that the bowl has a crack and is merely gilded crystal. Maggie later purchases the very bowl; the shopkeeper tells her of the pair who had nearly bought it. From his description Maggie recognizes the pair and the implied closeness of their relationship. The bowl comes to represent the adultery she now must deal with—the evil in her fallen world. The innocent Maggie has the choice either to confront the evidence and all it indicates or to turn her back on the evil and flee (like Blake's Thel) to the protection of her father. Her knowing friend Fanny Assingham seeks to solve Maggie's dilemma by smashing the evidence; the richly symbolic bowl breaks into three pieces. But Maggie *sees* that she herself has contributed to the creation of the evil to be faced; she also *sees* that mere destruction of the bowl and all it represents (including her love of and marriage to Amerigo) will solve nothing. Successful completion of the Blakean theme comes with Maggie's responsibly gathering up the pieces of the bowl into her own hands, where Love *can* be held. That mature and charitable gesture (she explains to Fanny that she is doing it "for love") represents her saving of the marriage, just as their son, the Principino (the only baby born in James's fiction who is allowed to live), becomes a gauge for their future. The final novel of James's Major Phase is thus provided with a happy ending. He told his publisher, Scribner, that *The Golden Bowl* was "the most *done* of my productions—the most composed and constructed and completed."

While still working on *The Golden Bowl*, James had decided to make a trip to America, where he would undertake a lecture tour and travel the country as never before; he arranged with Scribner in New York to prepare a selective edition of his novels and tales to be called the New York Edition. James sailed in August 1904 to see the scenes of his childhood after an absence of more than twenty years. His tour took him down the Atlantic seaboard; across to the southwestern tip of the country, Coronado Beach; up through the Midwest; and even into Canada. His lecture was "The Lesson of Balzac," an extensive and hearty tribute to the writer he called "the father of us all"; for his return engagement at Bryn Mawr he wrote a second lecture, "The Question of Our Speech." He also visited old friends and members of his extended family whom he barely remembered.

One new friend he was pleased to renew acquaintance with was Edith Wharton at "The Mount," her country place in Lenox, Massachusetts. Their friendship blossomed. James offered her literary advice and stood by her during her affair with his friend William Morton Fullerton and again during the strife of her divorce from poor mismatched Edward "Teddy" Wharton. Her opportunity for returning kindness to James arose as he grew older. His connection with Wharton was not romantic, except perhaps vicariously. They shared a delight in the saltiness of the life of George Sand and of her friend Hortense Allart de Méritens, and James was hopefully inquisitive about the romantic "progress" of her young gentlemen friends Robert Norton and John Hugh Smith, after the departure of Fullerton and Teddy. The nearest to a romantic involvement for James was his extended association with Constance Fenimore Woolson from 1880 onward. Her evident suicide in January 1894 may well have resulted from her frustration at James's inability to respond more fully to her overtures, or so he seems to have thought. Although he and Wharton had begun correspondence late in 1900, they did not meet until December 1903. In February 1903 James had published

one of his greatest tales, "The Beast in the Jungle," the earliest preparatory note for which he set down in February 1895, a year after Woolson's death and a month after the opening-night horror of *Guy Domville*: "the idea of *Too late* . . . the wasting of life. And the wasting of life is the implication of death."

The story of the egoistic John Marcher waiting for the extraordinary event he is convinced will happen to him and the gentle May Bartram, who knows his secret and agrees to wait and watch with him (but only, Marcher requires, as a friend), displays the unlived life and unrecognized love that are Marcher's lot. May's selfless love and devotion to him is the extraordinary event. One might see in this tale rehearsal of James's remorse over his failure to grasp (as Marcher ought to have done) the love generously offered to him, and further, maybe, a prophetic exhortation to himself not to miss such an opportunity if offered again—awakened by Wharton's attention. (Wharton had sent him good wishes for the opening night of *Guy Domville*.) But 1903 also saw publication of *The Wings of the Dove*, Minny Temple's novel. "The Beast in the Jungle" presents the selfless love of May, almost sacrificial, as *Wings* presents that of Milly Theale; but in neither case is the benevolence directed toward an artist, like James, whose faithfulness to his muse (*mon bon*) restricts other devotion. The phrase "the wasting of life" in James's note for 5 February 1895 might as usefully be read as a warning to himself not to waste his dramatic talent further in the ungrateful theater. From early in his young manhood James apparently recognized that passionate human intercourse was not to be his, that he was not made to participate in what he called "the great relation of men and women, the constant world renewal." For him the world was full of *persons*, none of whom were "sex objects." A friend of his in the American Legation in London, Ehrman Syme Nadal, observed of James in 1875, "He seemed to look at women rather as women looked at them. Women look at women as persons; men look at them as women. The quality of sex in women, which is the first and chief attraction to most men, was not their chief attraction to James" (quoted in Leon Edel, *Henry James, the Conquest of London: 1870–1881*, vol. two of Edel's *Henry James* [1953–1972], p. 359). The same might be said of the younger men he befriended and encouraged in his later years: "The quality of sex . . . was not their chief attraction"—he looked at them, too, as persons.

James returned to Lamb House at the beginning of August 1905. An immediate task was to create out of the extensive notes of his amazed impressions of America the articles (one already published) that would make up *The American Scene* (1907). It was not an agreeable task, for his impressions of his "old home" were largely unpleasant. His comment in a letter of March 1906 gives a summary: "an immense impression of material and political power; but almost cruelly charmless." "The Jolly Corner" (1908) develops that impression in the story of a man who returns to his native America after years of expatriation and is confronted by his ghostly alter ego, the person he might have been had he remained at home. That figure is maimed: two fingers of its right hand are missing, as if they had been "shot away." Would James have been maimed, in his right, his writing, hand if he had remained in America? he seems to be asking in this tale.

James soon began the pleasanter if no less demanding task of rereading his earliest fiction and revising much of it, in some cases (*The American* and *The Portrait of a Lady*) extensively. The revised *Portrait of a Lady* merits a place beside the three great novels of the Major Phase. A complementary undertaking was the creation of eighteen prefaces for the edition; together they constitute a magnificent statement on the art of fiction and belong with his essay of that title. The New York Edition in twenty-four volumes appeared between December 1907 and the end of July 1909. Much of the revision for the edition and all of the prefaces he had dictated to his new amanuensis, Theodora Bosanquet, who came to him in October 1907. MacAlpine had departed at Easter 1901 when *The Ambassadors* was nearly complete; he was replaced by Mary Weld. She aided James with that and other work until he left for America and she married. He took an extended holiday beginning in March 1907 when he spent two weeks in Paris with Wharton, who then took him for a three-week tour of the country as recorded in her *A Motor-Flight through France* (1908). The visit concluded with another fortnight in Paris; then he turned south for three weeks in Italy. Bosanquet, who was about to begin a literary career of her own, suited James admirably. Her service to him extended well beyond his death.

Bosanquet took James's dictation for a new foray into the theatrical arena. Johnston Forbes-Robertson's request for a script derived from the tale "Covering End" led to *The High Bid* and its modest run of five matinees in London. Herbert Trench's repertory plan encouraged James to turn the grim novel *The Other House* into a play, but the plan folded. Finally, as 1909 came to a close, James finished *The Outcry* for Charles Frohman's repertory group. Illness prevented James from attending rehearsals, and he would not let them go ahead without him. The death of Edward VII in May 1910 ended Frohman's plans. Illness, indeed, plagued James throughout the rest of his life.

In the spring of 1909 he repeated his visit of the preceding year to the Continent. Wharton introduced him to Faubourg St. Germain society, and he continued south to bid his adieux to his beloved Italy. Back in England James resumed his regime of writing and visiting, though he was plagued by what he feared was heart trouble. Ford Madox Ford's short-lived *English Review* brought out four of James's tales that year. James's earnings from the New York Edition, from which he had hoped for so much, were minuscule, however, and he was depressed. At Lamb House in October he emptied drawers and files of letters and other personal papers and destroyed them in a huge bonfire. At the beginning of 1910 he dictated some last

notes for *The Ivory Tower* and gave Bosanquet a leave. Digestive ills further complicated his life. His brother William, on his way to Bad Nauheim to take the waters, arrived in April with his wife. Henry and his sister-in-law joined him in May, and in August Henry accompanied his seriously ill brother back to America. William died just two weeks after reaching home. Henry stayed on for almost a year. He dined in New York with Wharton, Fullerton, and Walter Berry; spent two weeks in 1911 with Mary Cadwalader Jones (Wharton's former sister-in-law); kept a series of medical appointments; and sat for his portrait to William's son Billy James and to Cecilia Beaux. In June he stopped at Lenox with the Whartons and went to Harvard to accept an honorary degree. Having said his last farewell to what had been his homeland, he left for England in July.

The solitude of Rye made him uneasy. He escaped in travel: two weeks at the Charles Hunters' "Hill Hall" in Epping Forest, four days at Frederick Macmillan's "Overstrand," five days in Scotland, and a couple of days with Howard Sturgis (banker Russell's son) at "Queen's Acre" in Windsor. The Reform Club was still his base and he wanted to get back to work, but he was not allowed to have Bosanquet there. She soon found him rooms adjoining her flat in Chelsea, where he could resume his dictating. He began there what was intended to be a biographical tribute to William but quickly became James's autobiography: *A Small Boy and Others* (1913), *Notes of a Son and Brother* (1914), and a volume left unfinished, *The Middle Years* (1917). Billy James had just married; as a wedding present James gave him tenancy of Lamb House beginning in February and continuing for several months. In February James sat to John Singer Sargent for a portrait commissioned by Edith Wharton (the first sitting was on 24 January, and there would be two more in March). He read his Browning tribute, "The Novel in *The Ring and the Book*," in May and accepted an honorary degree from Oxford in June. At the end of July Wharton came to Lamb House and then took James on a round of visits to Sturgis's Queen's Acre, to Lady St. Helier's at Newbury, with Sturgis to Ascot to see the English Ranee of Sarawak (Margaret Brooke), and finally to Waldorf and Nancy Astor's "Cliveden" on the Thames. At Cliveden, James suffered a heart attack on 1 August. Wharton's motor carried him to Lamb House, and Wharton returned a week later to see him. Early in September he found, with Bosanquet's help, a handsome five-bedroom flat in Chelsea on the north bank of the Thames. At the end of the month he suffered an attack of shingles.

Wharton was worried (needlessly) about James's financial status, so she arranged with Scribner during the last three months of 1912 to offer James an advance on a new American novel; $8,000 was to be drawn secretly from her royalties to fund it—$4,000 on signing the contract and $4,000 on delivery. She had worked diligently through 1911 with the help of Edmund Gosse and Howells to get the Nobel Prize for James, unsuccessfully. James was delighted at the encouragement of the Scribner advance and planned to resume work on *The Ivory Tower* as soon as possible. He moved into his Chelsea flat during the first week of January, still plagued with shingles and his heart condition. Plans were afoot to honor James on his seventieth birthday. In England, Gosse, Percy Lubbock, and Hugh Walpole gathered modest donations (£50 maximum) from friends and admirers of James to present him with a silver gilt porringer (a "golden bowl") and a portrait by Sargent. The painter would accept no fee (the portrait hangs in the National Portrait Gallery and an exact replica in Lamb House), so it was instead given to the young sculptor Derwent Wood for a bust of the Master (it is in Lamb House). Wharton had begun a similar plan in America, asking for contributions of $5,000 (she hoped for enough for him to buy an automobile); James got wind of it and stopped proceedings at once. He added her name and Walter Berry's, however, to the list of subscribers to the English plan in his gracious public letter of gratitude (21 Apr.). James dined at 10 Downing Street on his birthday and continued work on the second volume of his autobiography.

February 1914 began six weeks of extensive dental work for James. He managed to prepare a two-part essay for the *Times Literary Supplement* (19 Mar., 2 Apr.) on "The Younger Generation" of novelists. It is a flawed critical performance, kind to his young friends Walpole, Compton Mackenzie, and Wharton; condemning the "money-opportunism" of Wells and Enoch Arnold Bennett; and baffled by D. H. Lawrence. The acclaim that greeted the publication of *Notes of a Son and Brother* in March pleased him.

On 4 August World War I broke out. The ailing James threw himself at once into war work. Here was an opportunity to compensate for what he had missed in his other war. On 2 September he wrote to Helena Gilder, "During the first days I felt in the air the recall of our Civil War shocks and anxieties, and hurryings and doings, of 1861, etc., the pressure in question has already become a much nearer and bigger thing, and a more formidable and tragic one." In September, enemy bombing of Rheims and damage to its magnificent cathedral provoked a passionate letter from James to Wharton; the first two-thirds of it were immediately translated and read to the Académie Française on 9 October. Following the battle of Ypres, Belgian refugees streamed into England. James donated his Watchbell Street studio (adjoining the southwest corner of Lamb House garden) to house those who came to Rye, and he was also active in supporting those in Chelsea. He wrote of these experiences in "Refugees in England" (Oct. 1915, called "Refugees in Chelsea" in *Within the Rim* [1919]). He also served as chairman in England of the American Volunteer Motor-Ambulance Corps in France; his twelve-page pamphlet describing its activities was published in November. Wounded soldiers in St. Bartholomew's Hospital in London welcomed his visits, which he recorded in his "The Long Wards." That essay was included in Wharton's *The Book of the Homeless* (1916). For another volume produced to raise funds for war relief, *The Book of France* (1915), James contributed his essay "France" and his translation of an essay by Maurice Barrès, "The Saints of France." Many of James's young friends had enlisted: his valet Burgess Noakes, Rupert Brooke, Philip Gosse, Jocelyn Persse, Desmond MacCarthy (Red Cross), and Hugh Walpole (war correspondent). A visit in January 1915 to Walmer Castle just up the coast from Dover brought him closer to the action; it was a stronghold used by Prime Minister Herbert Asquith for cabinet meetings, and on this occasion Winston Churchill, first lord of the admiralty, was also present.

In the midst of all this flutter James put together *Notes on Novelists with Some Other Notes*, a collection of pieces written between 1894 and his recent "Younger Generation," for publication in October 1914. That month he dispatched Bosanquet to Rye to recover his unfinished fantasy *The Sense of the Past*, the story of an American who goes to England and literally walks into 1820, the past of his English ancestors, and changes places with a figure in a portrait. It is a reprise of his early tale "A Passionate Pilgrim" and related to the theme of "The Jolly Corner" (mentioned in the notes Bosanquet fetched). The attempt to complete it was his last work as a novelist. His grief over the failure of the United States to enter the war at the side of the Allies led to his decision to renounce American citizenship; he became a British subject on 26 July 1915. That month H. G. Wells left for James at the Reform Club a copy of *Boon*, which contained Wells's cruel satire and parody of his erstwhile friend. James was deeply hurt, but his controlled response is a valiant defense of the art of fiction as he practiced it and a firm rejection of what Wells espoused. In October, his depression aggravated, he went down to Rye for a second bonfire of his remaining papers. His last piece of work was an introduction to Rupert Brooke's *Letters from America*, the final editing of which fell to Bosanquet.

His physical decline continued. A series of strokes in early December forecast the end. James rallied sufficiently in January 1916 to accept from King George's envoy Lord Bryce the highest award his sovereign could bestow on a British civilian, the Order of Merit.

James died in his Chelsea flat with his sister-in-law and his niece Peggy at his bedside. Funeral services were held nearby at Chelsea Old Church; his ashes were buried in the family plot in Cambridge, Massachusetts. A commemorative tablet honoring Henry James was placed in the Poets' Corner of Westminster Abbey in 1976.

James's career offers in itself a brief history of fiction from the Romanticism of Sir Walter Scott and Hawthorne to the height of modernism. His experiments and achievements in the art of fiction—elimination of the intrusive omniscient author, the emphasis on "dramatic" presentation, his insistent concern with the importance of expressive form and structure, and his realistic portrayal of psychological motivation—helped create an atmosphere that fostered the work of Marcel Proust, Dorothy Richardson, Ford Madox Ford,

James Joyce, William Faulkner, and James Baldwin. And with that, his continuation of the moral tradition of Milton and Blake also realized his idea that "there is one point at which the moral sense and the artistic sense lie very near together; that is in the light of the very obvious truth that the deepest quality of a work of art will always be the quality of the mind of the producer" ("The Art of Fiction"). The development of the important school of New Criticism in the first half of the twentieth century depended heavily on James's substantial critical theory and extensive practice. Such eminent modern writers as Gertrude Stein, Ezra Pound, and T. S. Eliot have been significantly influenced by him; Eliot observed that James taught us that poetry could be as well written as prose. And in spite of James's failure in the theater during his lifetime, his compensatory lesson about "the divine principle of the Scenario" stood his fiction in such good stead that an impressive number of theatrical and cinematographic productions based on his fictions—such as *The Heiress* (based on *Washington Square*), *The Europeans*, *The Portrait of a Lady*, *The Turn of the Screw*, *The Ambassadors*, and *The Golden Bowl*—have been successfully staged since his death. His travel literature is a major contribution to a fading art as well. His comment on Maupassant may aptly be applied to himself: "He is a lion in our path."

• The Houghton Library in Harvard University has the principal deposit of James papers, including his notebooks and private diaries. The surprising paucity of James manuscripts, given his creative abundance, is due to the fact that he burned most of his documents in two separate bonfires. *The Novels and Tales of Henry James*, the New York Edition, was augmented by the addition in 1917 of the unfinished novels *The Ivory Tower* and *The Sense of the Past* as vols. 25 and 26. A reprint of the completed edition was issued in 1961. *The Complete Tales of Henry James*, ed. Leon Edel (12 vols., 1962–1964), delivers what the title promises; *The Complete Plays of Henry James*, ed. Edel (rev. ed., 1990), does the same. *The Complete Notebooks of Henry James*, ed. Edel and Lyall H. Powers (1987), contains all that survives of James's private notes and diaries. New editions of his volumes of travel essays and of his literary criticism include *Portraits of Places* (1883), ed. George Alvin Finch (1948); *A Little Tour in France* (1884), ed. Edel (1983); *English Hours* (1905), ed. Edel (1981); *Italian Hours* (1909), ed. John Auchard (1992); *French Poets and Novelists* (1878), ed. Edel (1964); and *Partial Portraits* (1888), ed. Edel (1970). For a full listing of James's publications, see *A Bibliography of Henry James*, ed. Edel and Dan H. Laurence assisted by James Rambeau (1982). The largest gathering of letters is *Henry James Letters*, ed. Edel (4 vols., 1974–1984). Light on an important aspect of James's life is offered by Ignas K. Skrupskelis and Elizabeth M. Berkeley, eds., *The Correspondence of William James*, vols. 1–3 (1992–1994). Leon Edel's biography *Henry James* (5 vols., 1953–1972) has been acclaimed for its scholarship and artistry; in 1977 he published a 2-vol. revised and enlarged version, *The Life of Henry James*; and his 1-vol. *Henry James: A Life* (1985) is a digest of the 5-vol. biography yet contains new material. Supplementary biographical information is provided by *The Diary of Alice James*, ed. Edel (1964), and Jean Strouse, *Alice James: A Biography* (1980), and by studies of the three brothers: H. M. Feinstein, *Becoming William James* (1984), and Jane Maher, *A Biography of Broken Fortunes: Wilkie and Bob, Brothers of William, Henry, and Alice James* (1986). Austin Warren, *The Elder Henry James* (1934), has been superseded in many ways but remains useful as a sensitive and sympathetic approach to its subject, and Alfred Habegger, *The Father: A Life of Henry James, Sr.* (1994), is a thoroughly detailed and responsible biography that further illuminates the life of Henry, Jr. R. W. B. Lewis, *The Jameses* (1991), the most recent biography of the family, should be used in concert with the biographies mentioned above. The literary milieu in which James began is depicted in William Veeder, *Henry James: The Lessons of the Master: Popular Fiction and Personal Style in the Nineteenth Century* (1975). In *The French Side of Henry James* (1990), Edwin Sill Fussell illustrates what the deep experience of France and its writers meant to James's career. Special mention must be made of Adeline R. Tintner's unique and brilliant series of books that show how James made use of aspects of his cultural background and contemporary environment: on the visual arts, *The Museum World of Henry James* (1986); on the literary classics, *The Book World of Henry James* (1987); on popular thrillers, fairy tales, public scandals, science fiction, etc., *The Pop World of Henry James* (1989); on cosmopolitan literature by English, French, Italian, and German contemporaries, *The Cosmopolitan World of Henry James* (1991); and on thirteen European artists, *Henry James and the Lust of the Eyes* (1993). Information on the commercial aspect of James's career is set out in Marcia Jacobson, *Henry James and the Mass Market* (1983), and Michael Anesko, *"Friction with the Market": Henry James and the Profession of Authorship* (1986). James's work has been the subject of countless critical appreciations and explications. One of the earliest and soundest is Dorothea Krook, *The Ordeal of Consciousness in Henry James* (1962); the title accurately indicates its important focus. Another solid and responsible general treatment is Laurence Holland, *The Expense of Vision: Essays on the Craft of Henry James* (1964; rev. ed., 1982). Henry wrote to brother William on publication of the latter's *Pragmatism* (1907) to express his "wonder of the extent to which all my life I have . . . unconsciously pragmatised"; Richard A. Hocks examines fully the implications of that remark in his *Henry James and Pragmatistic Thought: A Study in the Relationship between the Philosophy of William James and the Literary Art of Henry James* (1974). Paul Armstrong, *The Phenomenology of Henry James* (1983), offers a most satisfactory reading of James's work on the basis of philosophical approach. John Carlos Rowe in his challenging *The Theoretical Dimensions of Henry James* (1984) proves the efficacy of various critical theories for elucidating James's fiction.

LYALL H. POWERS

JAMES, Janet Wilson (23 Dec. 1918–10 June 1987), historian, was born in New York City, the daughter of Willard Oliver Wilson, an automobile executive, and Helen Augusta Peters. The family moved several times in and around New York before relocating to Dallas, Texas, in 1928. These early upheavals and a traumatic relationship with her mother shadowed her childhood; she found sustenance in a close and protective relationship with her much younger sister, Lucy. After completing her secondary education at the Hockaday School in 1935, Janet joined her parents in New York, where Willard Wilson, who had lost his job due to the depression, found employment with the Chrysler corporation.

That fall she entered Smith College, her mother's alma mater. Inspired by Dean Marjorie Hope Nicolson, an outstanding literary scholar, Wilson early resolved to become a college teacher. A senior thesis on revolutionary war leaders in the postwar years, deemed "brilliantly written" by her mentor Ray A. Billington, capped her undergraduate career; she received the Vera Lee Brown Prize for "excellence in history" and graduated cum laude in 1939. She went on to study history at Bryn Mawr College (M.A. 1940), returned to Smith for two years as a teaching fellow, and in 1942 began doctoral work at Radcliffe College with Harvard Professor Arthur M. Schlesinger, Sr., an eminent historian who had helped define the field of social history. She served as a tutor and teaching fellow in the History and Literature Program (1943–1944), one of the first two women tutors in this concentration, and as a teaching assistant in the history department (1944–1946).

For her dissertation, Wilson took up Schlesinger's 1922 call for serious scrutiny of women's past. Despite doubts—the subject was "out of the mainstream, not one a man would have chosen, and therefore second-class," she later observed—she warmed to the project, which reminded her of the narratives of polar explorers she had "consumed" as a preteen. "Changing Ideas about Women in the United States, 1776–1825" was a pathbreaking study of the origins of the cult of domesticity, anticipating the scholarship that launched women's history nearly two decades later.

In 1945 Wilson married Edward T. James, a fellow Schlesinger student then serving in the navy. She spent the next several years working on her dissertation. The Jameses taught at Mills College in Oakland, California, from 1950 to 1953, he on a regular appointment in history and government, she on a pickup basis in history and English. They returned to Cambridge and completed their dissertations in 1954. After a promising start—she published two articles and several authoritative book reviews as a graduate student—Janet James encountered obstacles that often sidelined women who tried to combine a career with marriage and motherhood. In 1954 she became an instructor at Wellesley College and gave birth to a son, Ned; her husband's appointment in New York as an editor of the *Dictionary of American Biography* made theirs a commuting marriage. After a year, Janet James resigned from Wellesley with great regret, moved to New York, and devoted herself to full-time motherhood; a daughter, Lucy, was born in 1957.

The following year the family moved back to the Cambridge area, where Edward James assumed the editorship of *Notable American Women*, a biographical dictionary undertaken by Radcliffe at Schlesinger's instigation. Janet James returned to work part time in 1961 as assistant, later associate, editor of the project, beginning a ten-year collaboration with her husband. To this task she brought concentrated energy, humor, and a firm editorial hand. From 1965 to 1969 she also served as director of Radcliffe's Arthur and Elizabeth Schlesinger Library on the History of Women in America. Coinciding with the emergence of the modern women's movement and women's history as an intellectual field, publication of *Notable American Women, 1607–1950* (3 vols., 1971) was a landmark event. Janet James's searching introduction highlighted women's community-building activities, a theme later documented by others.

That same year she achieved her long-deferred goal. Boston College hired her as an instructor soon after the Jesuit institution admitted women; she became a full professor in 1981 and taught there until shortly before her death in Boston. During these years she came into her own as a teacher, scholar, and influential member of the profession. An inspiring teacher, she introduced courses on U.S. social, women's, and health-care history and conveyed to students her exacting standards, as she did to the many scholars who sought her advice. Her formidable knowledge, dedication, and respectability enabled her to advance women's studies and the careers of younger female colleagues. Nationally, she helped set the research and publishing agenda for women's history. As the historical profession acknowledged the presence of women, she was in demand as a consultant and committee member, activities to which she gave herself generously.

James's publications were exhaustively researched, beautifully crafted, and free of sentiment. Going beyond her middle-class WASP background and the limits of her training, she developed a vision of women's history that encompassed Catholics and Jews, African Americans and ethnic minorities. Her declaration, in the introduction to her otherwise unrevised dissertation, published in 1981, that she had "joined the new generation" was characteristic of her ability to reassess any situation in the light of new circumstances. She modestly proclaimed her much cited, classic work "a connecting link in the historiography of the field." *Women in American Religion* (1980), an edited volume, included an introduction that synthesized a burgeoning field and advanced it by posing new questions.

James's main scholarly contribution in her later years was to the history of nursing, which she helped establish as a research specialty. Once again she served as a "connecting link," this time between nurses and social historians, both of whom she encouraged to write nursing history. An influential article published in 1979 on Isabel Hampton, first director of the Johns Hopkins Hospital Training School for Nurses, and her unflinching review, "Writing and Rewriting Nursing History" (*Bulletin of the History of Medicine* 58 [1984]: 568–84), combine unimpeachable professionalism with a feminist outlook. *A Lavinia Dock Reader* (1985) is the most revealing work on the militant feminist nurse and historian whose biography James had hoped to write.

James brought an incisive intelligence and seemingly inexhaustible capacity for wonder to everything she did. Her warmth and forthrightness, extending even to the treatment she underwent for cancer, belied an initial impression of propriety. Ahead of her time, yet grounded in an exceptional knowledge of the past, James is remembered not only for her role as a pioneer in writing women's history, but for her living of it.

• Letters documenting James's work at the Schlesinger Library and for *Notable American Women* are at the Schlesinger Library, Radcliffe College. Information about her academic career comes from the college archives at Smith, Bryn Mawr, Radcliffe, and Wellesley; the Smith College registrar; the *Smith Alumnae Quarterly*; and the Mills College Library. The best starting point for understanding James's intellectual development is "Recollections of a Veteran in Women's History," the introduction to her published dissertation. Her publications include her master's essay, "The Bank of North America and Pennsylvania Politics: 1781–1787," *Pennsylvania Magazine of History and Biography* 66 (Jan. 1942): 3–28; "The Early Anti-Slavery Propaganda," *More Books: The Bulletin of the Boston Public Library* 19 (1944): 343–60, 393–405, and 20 (1945): 51–67; "History and Women at Harvard: The Schlesinger Library," *Harvard Library Bulletin* 16 (Oct. 1968): 385–99; "Isabel Hampton and the Professionalization of Nursing in the 1890s," in *The Therapeutic Revolution*, ed. Morris J. Vogel and Charles E. Rosenberg (1979); and *Women at Work: A Massachusetts Historical Society Picture Book* (1983). Memorial tributes are published in *Janet Wilson James, 1918–1987* (Schlesinger Library, n.d.). Obituaries are in the *Boston Globe*, 11 June 1987; *Proceedings of the* Massachusetts Historical Society 99 (1988): 174–77; and *Perspectives* (the newsletter of the American Historical Association), Apr. 1988, p. 15. Interviews with Edward T. James, Lucy Wilson Benson, Kay Pinneo Adamson, Paul Boyer, Barbara Miller Solomon, Anne Firor Scott, Susan Reverby, Ann J. Lane and Judy Smith, among others, helped to elucidate James's life and work.

BARBARA SICHERMAN

JAMES, Jesse (5 Sept. 1847–3 Apr. 1882), outlaw, was born Jesse Woodson James in Clay County, Missouri, the son of Robert James, a Baptist minister who cofounded William Jewell college, and Zerelda Cole. His father died of cholera in 1850; his mother, after marrying and divorcing a second husband, married Reuben Samuel, a doctor, in 1855.

Raised in a rural Missouri county by slave-owning parents, Jesse James grew up experiencing at close hand the violent conflicts between antislavery elements in nearby Kansas and proslavery groups in Missouri before the outbreak of the Civil War. The Civil War intensified these conflicts, as the region experienced numerous atrocities carried out by rival guerrilla bands. After his parents were abused by Union soldiers and his mother imprisoned, James at seventeen joined his brother Frank James and several future criminal associates in "Bloody Bill" Anderson's Confederate guerrilla outfit and participated in several battles, earning a reputation for courage and skill.

What happened to Jesse James immediately following the war is uncertain. Widely accepted is the story that he was shot and left for dead when he surrendered to Union troops, giving rise to the belief that he became an outlaw because he was not granted amnesty. Many Confederate guerrillas, some more infamous at the time than James, did make the postwar transition to law-abiding citizen, making the tale seem more a convenient fiction than a historical fact.

James's first ventures into bank robbery probably began in 1866. It was not until December 1869, however, that he and his brother were publicly identified as suspects following a bank robbery in Gallatin, Missouri. Popular feeling ran strongly against the James brothers, with a local newspaper reporting that, if captured, they "would be shot down in their tracks, so great is the excitement among citizens" (*Liberty [Mo.] Tribune*, 17 Dec. 1869).

Unlike most bandits, however, Jesse James recognized the power of public opinion and worked to shape it. An open letter published in the *Liberty Tribune* (24 June 1870) by the outlaw proclaimed his innocence and suggested he was the victim of political persecution by Radical Republicans in Missouri for his wartime service to the Confederacy. This was the first of several letters James published in local newspapers sympathetic to the Confederate cause, politicizing his criminality.

For the next ten years James and other ex-Confederates were glorified by the press and politicians of the Confederate wing of Missouri's Democratic party. Prominent editor John Newman Edwards was the prime force in shaping a "Robin Hood" image for James through numerous editorials and in his book *Noted Guerrillas* (1877). In one essay Edwards describes James and his band as "men who might have sat with Arthur at the Round Table, ridden in tourney with Sir Lancelot, or won the colors of Guinevere" (*Kansas City Times*, 29 Sept. 1872). James was cast as a righteous avenger who robbed from the wealthy railroads and banks victimizing the common folk. He was also presented, rather inconsistently, as an innocent victim of those who used the law illegitimately.

Edwards served as an able "campaign manager" for the James gang, but these outlaws also had a shrewd sense of how to construct a good public image. Beside writing letters to newspapers claiming innocence and condemning the Republicans holding office, the bandits dramatized their robberies in meaningful ways. At an 1874 train robbery a written version of the event was given to passengers to distribute among the media, exaggerating the height of the outlaws. Accounts of the robbery also indicated that the hands of passengers were examined so that working men would not be robbed. During a stagecoach robbery the valuables of a Confederate war veteran were returned. Through such actions, the gang fostered a Robin Hood image tinged with postwar politics.

In June 1874 the *St. Louis Dispatch* broke the news that the celebrated Jesse James had been snared at last, "his captor a woman, young, accomplished beautiful." James granted interviews and announced that he had married Zerelda "Zee" Mimms on 24 April "for love, and that there cannot be any . . . doubt about our marriage being a happy one." Papers throughout the land praised the outlaw for his style; with the appearance of the modern Maid Marian, and later two children, the portrayal of James as Robin Hood was easier to believe.

The event that generated popular sympathy more than any other was a raid on the James family home by Pinkerton detectives on 26 January 1875. An illuminating device tossed through a window exploded, killing James's nine-year-old half brother and shattering his mother's arm so badly that it required amputation. Receiving national attention, the incident was almost uniformly condemned. It was used by the Confederate wing of the Democratic party in Missouri as an excuse to propose an amnesty resolution before the Missouri House of Representatives describing James and his band as men who were driven into crime by Missouri Republicans and characterizing them as "men too brave to be mean, too generous to be revengeful, and too gallant and honorable to betray a friend or break a promise." The resolution also stated that "most if not all the offenses with which they are charged have been committed by others, and perhaps by those pretending to hunt them." Supported by every ex-Confederate in the legislature, the resolution narrowly missed the two-thirds majority needed to pass.

During the next year the Democratic and Republican presses warred. Republicans blamed Democrats for supporting outlawry; Democrats condemned Republicans for slandering the James brothers and attempted to revive the amnesty resolution. Jesse James, in a note to the *Kansas City Times* (23 Aug. 1876), charged the son of a prominent railroad official with engineering a phony robbery, denounced detectives, and asked for amnesty: "If we have a wise Congress this winter . . . they will grant us a full pardon. I will not say pardon for we have done nothing to be pardoned for. . . . If the express companies want to do a good act they can take all the money they are letting those thieving detectives beat them out of and give it to the poor." Outlawry remained a volatile political topic for several years because the Republican press and party persistently made Democratic support of the outlaws a political issue. Even out-of-state papers from regions competing with Missouri for trade and immigration increased the notoriety of Missouri's bandits.

Attempts to revive the resolution were dashed by the attempted robbery of the Northfield, Minnesota, bank on 7 September 1876. Things went badly: three robbers were killed, and three Younger brothers, known associates of the James brothers, were wounded and captured. Only two of the outlaws escaped, presumably Frank and Jesse James. The most important implication of the Northfield disaster was that it destroyed years of carefully worded denials of guilt by the James gang and its backers, a fact eagerly seized upon by the region's Republican newspapers.

With the virtual destruction of their criminal gang at Northfield, Frank and Jesse James turned to men with less skill and reliability in carrying on their trade. The robberies became more violent, and there began a cycle of betrayal and murder within the band, culminating in the assassination of Jesse James by Robert Ford and Charles Ford on 3 April 1882 in St. Joseph, Mis-

souri. Even in death James's criminality continued to be politicized. Democratic governor Thomas Crittenden of Missouri, backed by railroad interests, publicly announced his role in the assassination plot and thus unwittingly implicated himself as an accessory to murder. Portions of the Democratic press, especially Edwards, led the condemnation. Six months later Crittenden accepted the surrender of Frank James and through a series of political maneuvers ensured that he would never be found guilty of any crime in a court of law in Missouri or elsewhere.

Jesse James is probably the most noted criminal in American history. On his death, the *New York Daily Graphic* 11 Apr. 1882) proclaimed him "the most renowned murderer and robber of his age." Unlike most habitual offenders, James received widespread adulation both in his own lifetime and in following generations. His notoriety resulted from several factors. First, he was supported through the media and in other ways by powerful friends in the Missouri political establishment. Second, he was helped by his identity as an ex-Confederate soldier from a respectable Missouri family. Other ex-Confederates from similar backgrounds also were glorified at the time, including Arthur McCoy, the Younger brothers, and Frank James. These social origins made it easier for segments of the population to identify with these brigands, and it also provided a network of support. Outlaws like Jesse James were undoubtedly protected by numerous otherwise lawful citizens in communities scattered throughout Missouri. As the editor of the *Sedalia (Mo.) Democrat* (14 Oct. 1882) observed, "Was it wrong for the Confederates of this state—when the war had closed—to look with some degree of gratitude upon men whose vigilance saved hundreds of rebel homes . . . from unmilitary desecration? . . . With their history as defenders of the faith, how natural it was for a generous people to extenuate the crimes that for seventeen perilous years have been charged to these men." It was the assassination of Jesse James, however, by the Missouri political establishment that established him as the most noted of Confederate guerrillas who turned to outlawry. Third, the social context of the 1870s made extralegal symbols of justice marketable to a broad audience. In addition to the political turmoil of Reconstruction politics in Missouri, there was an economic depression in the 1870s throughout the West that was widely blamed on banks, railroads, and land monopolies—the victims of outlaws of the time such as the James-Younger gang, Billy the Kid, and Sam Bass. Hundreds of books and articles have been written about Jesse James. He has been the feature of several popular Hollywood movies, and new ballads continue to praise and glorify him. He remains the archetypal American Robin Hood, a heroic criminal who in legend symbolized a form of "higher" justice than that represented by law.

• The definitive biography of Jesse James is William Settle, Jr., *Jesse James Was His Name* (1966), which includes a twenty-page chapter analyzing works related to the outlaw and a twenty-page comprehensive bibliography listing relevant public documents and manuscript and newspaper collections as well as articles and books related to the outlaw's career. The State Historical Society of Missouri (Columbia) and the Kansas State Historical Society are major sources for manuscripts, letters, and newspaper clippings. Other books of note include Eric Hobsbawm, *Bandits* (1981), and Paul Kooistra, *Criminals as Heroes: Structure, Power, and Identity* (1989), an explanation of how certain mass murderers and habitual criminals, like Jesse James, came to be glorified rather than uniformly condemned. Also useful are Robertus Love, *The Rise and Fall of Jesse James* (1926); Kent Steckmesser, *The Western Hero in History and Legend* (1965); and Frank Triplett, *The Life, Times, and Treacherous Death of Jesse James* (1882).

PAUL G. KOOISTRA

JAMES, Leon (27 Apr. 1913–30 July 1970), and **Albert Minns** (1 Jan. 1920–24 Apr. 1985), dancers, were born in New York City and Newport News, Virginia, respectively. James was the son of West Indian parents. He lived in New Jersey from about 1924 to about 1929, when he moved to New York City and began dancing socially in Harlem at the dances for teenagers at the Alhambra Ballroom above the Alhambra Theatre. Around 1933 he began to dance at the Savoy Ballroom on Lenox Avenue, the citadel of Lindy Hopping in New York City. There he became a member of a social club called the Jolly Fellows, which included first-generation Lindy Hoppers Shorty Snowden and Herbert "Whitey" White. When the latter began organizing a team of youngsters to perform the Lindy Hop in local clubs, theaters, and talent contests, James was among the first and most agile.

In the fall of 1935 James won the first Harvest Moon Ball, a dance contest sponsored by the *New York Daily News* that served to spread the popularity of the Lindy throughout the city. A few weeks later James and his partner Edith Mathews, along with fellow Lindy Hoppers Norma Miller and Billy Hill, joined a show making a tour of Europe, the first time a professional team of Lindy Hoppers appeared abroad. The two couples returned in the summer of 1936 to find that the Lindy had evolved significantly during their absence; it had become smoother and faster and now involved "air steps," in which one partner flipped the other. James never quite made the transition to the new style of dancing, although he continued to dance with Whitey's Lindy Hoppers. In the fall of 1936 he toured the country with a team behind Ethel Waters, partnered with Norma Miller. An assistant producer with Paramount Pictures spotted the act, and the dancers wound up with a ninety-second segment in the Marx Brothers' movie *A Day at the Races* (1937). Whitey's Lindy Hoppers broke up during World War II, and James was one of the only male members of the team not to be drafted (he was 4F because of health problems). But he continued to dance at the Savoy, and in 1943 *Life* magazine did a cover story on the Lindy ("A True National Folk Dance") that included pictures of James and Willamae Ricker photographed by Gjon Mili.

Albert Minns was the son of a laborer who played guitar at house parties thrown by the wealthy of Newport News, and by the age of five Albert was dancing as part of the act. Shortly thereafter Minns was brought to Harlem by his mother. He first began dancing at the Savoy with Whitey's team in 1938, and he won the Harvest Moon Ball that year with Mildred Pollard (Sandra Gibson). In 1939 he appeared in a film clip of the Lindy Hoppers doing the Big Apple, a popular circle dance of the day, in a black-cast film made in New York (*Keep Punchin'*, 1939, Film Arts Studio, frequently excerpted and repackaged in other formats). Minns's shows include *Knickerbocker Holiday*, *Hellzapoppin*, *Hot Mikado*, *Blackbirds of 1938*, and the show at the Savoy Pavilion at the 1939–1940 New York World's Fair. At the end of 1941, he was among eight of Whitey's dancers to travel to California for the filming of the Universal Studios movie *Hellzapoppin* (Minns's partner was Willamae Ricker) and the soundie (a short film played on jukebox-like machines called Panorams) *Hot Chocolate*, with music by Duke Ellington. A few days after filming was completed, Minns left on a tour of Brazil with five other Lindy Hoppers; the planned six-week trip turned into an eight-month stay when the Japanese attack on Pearl Harbor occurred the day after they landed. On his return to the United States Minns was drafted.

After the war, both Minns and James thought their days as dancers were over, but their careers took a peculiar twist. In 1947 an expatriate Russian modern dancer, Mura Dehn, who had met James and Minns at the Savoy before the war, sought them out and found them working in factories. She arranged for the two to give dance performances, the first one at a Manhattan art gallery. Dehn also filmed them extensively for a montage of dancing called *The Spirit Moves* (1950). Minns and James also appear in a twenty-minute short by Roger Tilton entitled *Jazz Dance*, filmed at the Central Plaza on Second Avenue in Manhattan and issued in 1954. In 1952 Hunter College English professor Marshall Stearns founded his Institute of Jazz Studies, and he began to feature them in a series of exhibitions and lecture-demonstrations for which Stearns himself served as commentator. In 1955, for instance, they performed with the Coleman Hawkins Quartet. To present jazz vernacular dance outside the nightclub or ballroom in a historical context as a significant dance form was utterly unfamiliar and groundbreaking, and it took them a few years to discover how to do so effectively. In 1957 Stearns made a short-lived attempt to create a professional dance group, the American Jazz Dancers, featuring James and Minns; they performed a concert at the Ninety-second Street Young Men's and Young Women's Hebrew Association in New York City that October.

Their big break came the following year, when Stearns took the two dancers to the Newport Jazz Festival, where they did a survey of the history of jazz dance, including the Cakewalk, Shake Dance, Camel Walk, Eagle Rock, Shimmy, Charleston variations, Lindy Hop, Truckin', Suzy-Q, Shorty George, and

Big Apple. Though one of the least publicized acts, it all but stole the show; *Variety* hailed it as "the best of the festival." The act was expanded and turned into a one-hour presentation that Stearns staged again in December 1958 at the Ninety-second Street Y. The act returned to Newport for many years thereafter; in 1960 James and Minns were introduced by Langston Hughes during an afternoon devoted to the blues.

Meanwhile, Stearns took James and Minns on numerous tours across the country and on television. Television shows included "David Garroway," "Ed Sullivan," "Playboy's Penthouse," "Milton Berle," and "American Musical Theatre." With his wife Jean, Stearns began a book on jazz dance (*Jazz Dance*, published posthumously in 1968), which for its three chapters on the Lindy relies heavily on James and Minns as informants; unfortunately, they were not always trustworthy. He had them perform at a series of sold-out concerts at Town Hall.

In their performances, James and Minns embodied quite different styles. James was precise, tall, comic, and almost never without an element of satire and mockery; in *A Day at the Races*, he is the one who clownishly rolls his eyes skyward, Sambo-style, awkwardly recalling an old racist stereotype. His signature step, which can also be seen in that movie, involved a way of wiggling his legs known as "legomania." Minns, by contrast, was smooth, serious, and fluid in the Snake Hips Tucker style. He danced gracefully and elegantly with his whole body, with a warm, boyish grin.

When Stearns died in December 1966, the careers of James and Minns all but ground to a halt. James went on welfare and worked for a time with the Neighborhood Youth Corps, while Minns worked in a factory in Farmingdale, New York. James, who had had heart problems throughout the late 1960s, died in New York City, leaving behind ten children. He had had two wives. Minns stopped dancing entirely for a dozen years; then his career took yet another turn. In June 1982 he danced in a performance at the Riverside Dance Festival, partnered with Ruth "Sugar" Sullivan, winner of the 1956 Harvest Moon Ball. That same month, he began to teach at the Sandra Cameron Dance Center in Manhatttan, where he continued to teach intermittently over the next two years. He soon acquired students from outside New York City and even abroad. In September 1984 he traveled to Stockholm to teach members of the Swedish Swing Society, and by the time of his return in November a group of his students and admirers had formed the New York Swing Dance Society. In February 1985 he became delirious and was hospitalized, and an inoperable tumor was found in his esophagus. He died in New York City, leaving behind five children with three mothers.

Although James and Minns never lived to see the resurgence of interest in Lindy Hop that took place in the late 1980s, they played an invaluable role in originating, preserving, and passing on one of the few dance forms that is entirely of U.S. origin.

• The Dance Collection at the New York Public Library for the Performing Arts, Lincoln Center, has a clipping file on James and Minns, as well as several film clips. Another valuable source on the early Lindy Hop, including remarks about James and Minns, is Frankie Manning, "Jazz Oral History Interview," Interviewer Robert P. Crease, at the Smithsonian Institution. The most important source on the early history of the Lindy Hop is Marshall Stearns and Jean Stearns, *Jazz Dance* (1968; repr. 1994), pt. 10. This account, however, is marred by the authors' overreliance on the stories of James and Minns, which resulted in a number of errors (including James being misidentified in a photo). Still, the Stearnses were diligent in tracking down and interviewing other informants, and the notes from these interviews are available at the Institute for Jazz Studies at Rutgers University. See also Robert P. Crease, "Divine Frivolity: Hollywood Representations of the Lindy Hop, 1937–1942," in *Representing Jazz*, ed. Krin Gabbard (1995).

ROBERT P. CREASE

JAMES, Louis (3 Oct. 1842–5 Mar. 1910), actor, was born in Tremont, Illinois, the son of Benjamin F. James, a jurist, and Almira H. Flagler. In his early twenties, after a short stint in the Union army, he made his acting debut at the Macauley Theatre in Louisville, Kentucky. His first role there was supernumerary, as a peasant, but he was soon regularly playing supporting roles. Although he never remained with one company for more than about five years and did not star in New York until the age of forty-four, James's career was nearly uninterrupted until his death, thanks to great success at several character types, mostly comic, and many tours.

James worked continuously after he left Kentucky, beginning at the Arch Street Theatre in Philadelphia, then managed by Louisa Lane Drew. One of his best-known roles there was as Joseph Surface in *School for Scandal*. Drew continued James's training, and he acquired at her theater "an ease of manner and a distinction of style that went well with his fine figure and deep, sonorous voice." He remained there for six years. Beginning in 1871 he worked in two of Augustin Daly's companies in New York, both before and after the fire that destroyed the Fifth Avenue Theatre. It was at Daly's that he expanded his range of roles to include many different parts in the area of light comedy. Because of his success at Daly's, James was able to perform several impressive leading roles in tours that followed the season of 1874–1875, including Othello, with Edwin Booth as Iago, and Macbeth, with Mary Anderson as Lady Macbeth.

James first starred on the New York stage in *Virginius* in 1886 (he had appeared at the Chicago Theatre in 1875 as a leading man, although without success). Also in 1886 he began a starring tour with his wife, Marie Wainwright, that lasted until 1889. Together they performed such classics as *Othello*, *As You Like It*, *Much Ado about Nothing*, *Romeo and Juliet*, and *School for Scandal*. He often participated in benefits for other actors or causes, including those for the Actor's Fund and the Academy of Music's benefit for the poor of New York.

From 1889 to 1892 James performed on tour in various cities, costarring with famous actors such as Joseph Jefferson. In 1892 he formed a combination company (a touring company that included both popular stars and entire accompanying productions, relieving the stars from the stress of playing with local companies) with Frederick Warde. James toured with this company up until his death just before going on stage in Helena, Montana. Interestingly, in the last two decades of his life he changed roles slightly and performed many heroic as well as classic comic roles.

James was married three times. He married Lillian Scanlon of Philadelphia in 1871; she died in 1876. His second marriage, to Marie Wainwright, ended in divorce. James's third wife, Aphie Hendricks of Philadelphia, whom he married in 1892, survived him. From his first marriage he had one daughter, Millie James, who later became an actress.

James was a very popular actor during the height of his career, but he was always much more appreciated on his tours than in New York. His comic roles in traditional classic plays earned him great respect throughout the country. Although he was never a great star and is not responsible for any significant innovations in American acting, James was privileged to work with many of the greatest actors and managers of his day. Drew and especially Daly made major contributions to American theater in the mid- and late 1800s, as did James's costars Booth and Jefferson. James's combination company of the 1890s was an excellent example of this form of touring, which dominated American theater for forty years.

• Articles on James appear in the *New York Dramatic Mirror*, 5 Oct. 1895, and in John B. Clapp and Edwin F. Edgett, *Players of the Present* (1899). There is an entry on James in the 1908–1909 edition of *Who's Who in America*. See also T. Allston Brown, *A History of the New York Stage* (3 vols., 1903). Extensive obituaries appear in the *New York Dramatic Mirror*, 12 Mar. 1910, and the *New York Times*, 6 Mar. 1910.

SUSAN KATTWINKEL

JAMES, Marquis (29 Aug. 1891–19 Nov. 1955), historian and biographer, was born in Springfield, Missouri, the son of Houston James and Rachel Marquis. His father's law practice and his mother's interest in reading and history were communicated early to James, whose future writings would often revolve around themes of past action and frontier glory. At the age of three, James moved with his parents to a prairie homestead in the Cherokee Strip near Enid, Oklahoma, then located on the leading edge of white settlement in the region. One year later, Rachel began teaching her son to read, typically with a history book as her text.

In adult life James liked to embellish tales of his frontier childhood, which was nowhere near as rustic as he claimed. He often called himself a "fifth or sixth cousin of Jesse James." His attraction for the breakers of tradition may have sprung in part from deficiencies in his formal education, and from his determined effort to compensate through an intense self-study of history and writing. The early death of his father forced him to seek work, but he managed to graduate from high school in 1909. After only a few months at Oklahoma Christian University, reasoning that the life of a newspaperman would be "a lot more fun than college," James quit to become a reporter for the *Enid Eagle*.

James's journalistic reach was broadened both geographically and stylistically by the itinerancy common to journalists of that time and by the opportunities for freelance pulp writing that came to the journeyman. During the first half of his twenties, while writing for the *Chicago Evening Journal*, the *Kansas City Journal*, the *St. Louis Globe-Democrat* and *New Orleans Item*, James moonlighted as a fiction writer, turning out purple prose for the tabloids. He married fellow *Item* reporter Bessie Williams Rowland in 1914; they had one daughter.

The United States' entry into the First World War occurred in the midst of James's two-year stint with the *New York Tribune*; he enlisted in the army in 1917 and served out the war as an infantry captain. In the years immediately after the war, he ghosted articles for the American Legion, chronicling its history while serving as its national director of publicity. While helping launch the *American Legion Monthly*, James contributed articles to the new journal designed to promote a historical literature at once colorful and dramatic in style and unassailable in research and documentation. Magazine editors warmed to his approach (he was hired by the *New Yorker* to contribute historical accounts), but scholars remained unimpressed. Perhaps nettled by a perceived slight, James left the *New Yorker* in 1926 and devoted the following four years to a "serious" biography of his boyhood hero, the founder and president of Texas, Sam Houston.

James won his first Pulitzer Prize for the Houston biography, *The Raven* (1930). Well received both financially and critically (100,000 copies were sold in its first decade), the book inspired James to turn his efforts to the life of an even more colorful character, U.S. president Andrew Jackson. James's philosophy of history was displayed in sharpest relief in the writing of this two-volume history, the work for which he became best known. Uncritical of a character with whom he strongly identified, James painted Jackson in brightly colored brushstrokes and Jackson's enemies in darkly somber tones. To get close to Jackson spiritually, James spent one summer during the seven years he devoted to the project writing from a cabin in the Great Smoky Mountains of East Tennessee. Writing that "the public's preference for novels . . . [was] a reflection on the biographers," James worked hard to incorporate in the biographical form the novel's tendency, as he perceived it, toward "dependable representations of life and character."

The resulting volumes, *The Border Captain* (1933) and *Portrait of a President* (1937), were the product of meticulous research and the examination of more than 40,000 documents. Concerned almost exclusively with action and epic sweep, the biography devoted little attention to the complex military, political, and economic issues of Jackson's time. Although some historians in the 1930s were calling for a new kind of social history, James adopted instead the moralistic tone set by such nineteenth-century historians as James Parton and John Spencer Bassett, writers whom James would later credit as his models. He never lost his fascination for men involved in the rough and tumble of the climb to the top, whether in politics or the business world. Thus it seems fitting that his other independent biographies would be written about such characters as John Nance Garner (1939) and Alfred I. du Pont (1941).

In the 1940s James found lucrative work writing business histories for corporations willing to offer "an acceptable sum of money." James refused his initial assignment, from the Insurance Company of North America in 1940, until he had received assurances of academic freedom. Later, perhaps to avoid the reputation of being a historian for hire, he would remember finding and publishing unflattering information about this and other businesses. Nevertheless, most of these histories were kind enough in their appraisals to elicit contracts from other businesses, leading James to write *The Metropolitan Life: A Study in Business Growth* (1947); a study of the Texaco Oil Company, *The Texaco Story* (1953); and a book about the Bank of America, coauthored in 1954 with his now former wife, Bessie, from whom he had been divorced in 1952. In 1954 he married Jacqueline Mary Parsons; they had no children.

One of James's corporate histories, completed in 1948, was not published until 1993, *Merchant Adventurer: The Story of W. R. Grace.* As he had with several of the other business histories, James devoted most of his attention to the writing of the book and left nearly all of the research to Bessie. The result was a sense that the author never fully understood his subject. The historian who discovered and published the manuscript, Lawrence A. Clayton, attributed the Grace Company's refusal to publish the work not to the attitude of the author toward its subject (which was laudatory) but to internal business decisions unrelated to the thesis or writer.

Two projects of James's later years reflected his personal interests: an account of his youth and a projected "history of race relations in the United States" told through a biography of Booker T. Washington. The first project culminated in *The Cherokee Strip: A Tale of an Oklahoma Boyhood* (1945). James labored on the second for ten years, devoting full time to it only in 1952. Describing this project, which he never completed, as "quite the largest undertaking I have tackled to date," James was still at work on it when he suffered a cerebral hemorrhage on 1 August 1955. He died of a similar such attack three months later, while convalescing at his home in Rye, New York.

• James describes his methodology and philosophy as a writer in the acknowledgments to his *Portrait of a President* (1938). James's titles not already mentioned in the text are

Biography of a Business, 1791–1942: A History of the Insurance Company of North America (1942) and *Biography of a Bank: The Story of Bank of America* (1954), written with Bessie R. James. The most authoritative accounts of James's life are in Lawrence A. Clayton's introduction to James's *Merchant Adventurer: The Story of W. R. Grace* (1993), and Stanley J. Kunitz and Howard Haycraft, eds., *Twentieth Century Authors: A Biographical Dictionary of Modern Literature* (1942). Kunitz and Vineta Colby, eds., *Twentieth-Century Authors: A Biographical Dictionary of Modern Literature*, 1st supp. (1955), brings the story to the end of James's life. Brief but useful biographical sketches are in *Saturday Review of Literature*, 20 Oct. 1945, and *Time*, 24 Sept. 1945. An obituary is in the *New York Times*, 20 Nov. 1955.

RICHARD A. REIMAN

JAMES, Ollie Murray (27 July 1871–28 Aug. 1918), U.S. senator, was born Orlando Murray James near Marion, Crittenden County, Kentucky, the son of Lemuel H. James, a lawyer, and Eliza Jane Brailey. The location of his birth and his parentage indelibly marked James's life. His father had served in the Union army during the Civil War, but his mother's four brothers had fought for the Confederacy. Crittenden County, small in population and agrarian in character, was then a Republican enclave in the midst of a region dominated by the other party. A lifelong Democrat, James repeatedly noted that the circumstances of his youth supplied him with tolerance and the ability to move with ease through the variegated politics of his native state.

James spent several years at the Marion Academy, an institution of uncertain quality. A key moment in his life occurred at age sixteen, when his father secured his appointment as a page for the Kentucky General Assembly. The following year, 1888, he worked as the cloakroom keeper for the Kentucky Senate. These experiences set the course for his later career.

When James returned to Marion, he clerked for his father and studied law. Admitted to the bar in 1891, he became a partner in his father's firm. Two reasons account for his quick development into a successful lawyer. He became an apt student of forensics, and his height, six and a half feet, garnered the attention of any audience. Coupling meticulous arguments with old-fashioned phrasing, he emerged as a powerhouse orator. Inevitably, contemporaries compared him with another Kentucky native, Abraham Lincoln.

Political debates served as an important diversion for many rural Americans of this period, and James became an entertainer for residents in the First Congressional District of western Kentucky. He made his political debut while still a teenager, arguing at a Fourth of July celebration at Crittenden Springs in 1889 against the views of a Republican opponent, who supported the high rates in the proposed McKinley Tariff. Over the next several years, James created a speaking circuit and established Ollie James Days, at which he spoke or debated in support of the Democratic party. Largely because of this, the party selected him to be a Kentucky delegate to the 1896 Democratic National Convention in Chicago.

During the convention, the oration of William Jennings Bryan dazzled James. At the end of Bryan's "Cross of Gold" speech, the Kentuckian led the so-called "march of states" demonstration, guaranteeing Bryan the nomination for president. For years afterward, James followed Bryan as both friend and disciple, accepting the full range of Bryan's populist proposals, from the free coinage of silver to the strict regulation of railroads. James thoroughly canvassed Kentucky's First Congressional District for Bryan in 1896 and again in 1900. Despite the losing cause, James won plaudits for his vigorous defense of the party and its candidates.

In 1902 James decided to take advantage of his popularity in the region by running for office. He easily won the First District seat in the U.S. House of Representatives and served five successive terms, from 4 March 1903 to 3 March 1913. In a Republican-dominated Congress, he did not have his pick of assignments. Eventually, however, he became a standard fixture on the Elections and the Banking and Currency committees. In 1903 he married Ruth Thomas.

Even though James advocated populist causes and the Democratic party, his pleasant personality and vibrant oratory forced his Republican opponents to acknowledge his ability. Kentucky Democrats asked him to chair the Commonwealth's delegation to the Democratic National Conventions in 1904 and 1908. During the latter, he served as floor manager for Bryan and delivered a rousing seconding speech that helped secure the nomination for his mentor. State Democrats rewarded James for his years of partisan labor in 1912, when the state legislature elected him to serve in the U.S. Senate.

Senator-elect James chaired the 1912 Democratic National Convention in Baltimore. Though he was friendly to Champ Clark's candidacy, James treated all sides fairly in a protracted nominating contest. Once Woodrow Wilson won on the forty-sixth ballot, James gave the future president his full support. Indeed, contemporaries came to consider the Kentuckian a principal spokesperson for the New Freedom program. James became so identified with Wilson that he chaired the 1916 Democratic National Convention and delivered the keynote address that outlined Wilson's accomplishments. Later he campaigned nationwide in the successful bid to reelect the president. James continued to champion Wilson's cause in Congress until struck by kidney disease in 1918. He died in Baltimore. James was one of the last representatives of the great nineteenth-century tradition of political oratory.

• Collateral manuscript collections of contemporary political figures contain letters and other materials pertaining to James, including the Woodrow Wilson Papers, Library of Congress. Many of the orator's speeches are published in the *Congressional Record* (1903–1918). The most thorough source of information on James is Forrest C. Pogue, Jr., "The Life and Work of Senator Ollie Murray James" (M.A. thesis, Univ. of Kentucky, 1932). A more recent summary of his career is in John E. Kleber, ed., *The Kentucky Encyclopedia* (1992). Obituaries are in the *New York Times*, the *Louisville Courier-Journal*, the *Lexington Herald*, and the *Lexington Leader*, 29 Aug. 1918.

JAMES K. LIBBEY

JAMES, Skip (?21 June 1902–3 Oct. 1969), blues artist, was born Nehemiah James in Yazoo County, outside Bentonia, Mississippi, the son of Eddie James and Phyllis Jones. His father, reputed to be a musician and a bootlegger, moved north to Sidon, near Greenwood, to evade the law, leaving Skip with his mother on the Woodbine plantation, where she worked as a cook. After an attempt to reunite the family in Sidon, James and his mother returned to Bentonia, where he attended St. Paul School and Yazoo High School. At the age of eight or nine, inspired by local musicians, particularly guitarist Henry Stuckey, young James persuaded his mother to buy him a guitar. At the age of twelve he took one piano lesson from a cousin. Unable to pay for more lessons, he continued learning on an organ owned by an aunt.

After dropping out of high school at about age fifteen, James went to work at a sawmill near Marked Tree, Arkansas, just west of Memphis, Tennessee, where he met pianist Will Crabtree, who became a teacher and role model. Crabtree introduced James to public performance, and from 1921 on James worked house parties and juke joints with his guitar mentor, Stuckey. Through the 1920s James led the life of an itinerant musician, bootlegger, and hustler, roaming throughout the South. In the late 1920s he married sixteen-year-old Oscella Robinson. The couple organized their own house parties, with James providing music and whiskey. After a move to Dallas, Texas, they separated. James returned to Bentonia, working the barrelhouse circuit from Mississippi to Memphis. In 1931 he settled in Jackson, Mississippi, where he played the streets as a solo, worked parties with a protégé, Johnny Temple, and taught guitar in an informal music school.

In early 1931 he auditioned for H. C. Speir, a Paramount Records scout, and signed a two-year contract with Paramount, then located in Grafton, Wisconsin. A February 1931 recording session yielded eighteen sides, though James claimed he recorded twenty-six selections—in either case, a remarkable number of sides for an untried artist during the Great Depression. The musicianship on these sides guaranteed James's reputation as a singular artist, but the records were not commercially successful as the ravages of the depression and the looming demise of Paramount hampered sales. There are conflicting reports over just what James was paid—several hundred dollars, eight dollars in expense money, forty to sixty dollars in royalties. Whatever the amount, the failure of the records to sell so embittered the artist that he quit recording for more than three decades.

At the urging of his father, who had long since left the sporting life to become a well-known Baptist minister, James embraced the church and by 1932 was working with the Dallas Texas Jubilee Singers, a gospel group that traveled with his father. After religious study, James was ordained in both the Methodist and Baptist churches, and his religious activity continued through the 1940s. In the late 1940s he married Mabel (maiden name unknown), and by 1951 he was back in Mississippi, working in jobs unrelated to either music or the church.

Spurred by the blues revival, in which several artists who had recorded in the 1920s and 1930s were "rediscovered," blues researchers John Fahey, Bill Barth, and Henry Vestine tracked James to a Mississippi hospital in the summer of 1964. Although James had undergone surgery for cancer, a disease he attributed to a hoodoo jinx, he was soon performing at the July 1964 Newport Folk Festival—a living legend launching a second career as a professional blues artist.

Following his dramatic Newport appearance, James began recording and touring once again. In contrast to fellow blues rediscoveries Son House and John Hurt, however, James never caught on as a popular revival performer. The dark quality of his music made him inaccessible to mainstream audiences, and his aloof, egotistical personality made him difficult to work with. Despite moments of brilliance, his performances were erratic. Moreover, continuing health problems hampered his comeback. In 1965 he underwent more surgery for cancer in Washington, D.C.

Also in the mid-1960s he left his wife Mabel and began a common-law relationship with John Hurt's stepniece Lorenzo Meeks. Relocating in Philadelphia, he continued to try to make a living as a musician. He made several recordings for Vanguard, went to Europe in 1967, and attended the American Folklife Festival in 1968. In 1969 he entered the University of Pennsylvania Hospital in Philadelphia, where he died.

To a greater extent than most, James embodied the stereotype of the blues artist as outsider, loner, even misfit. Despite assertions that he was part of a broader, though lesser-known, regional Bentonia blues style shared by artists such as Henry Stuckey and Jack Owens, James's relation to tradition was more adversarial than accommodating. Whatever he chose to play bore his own idiosyncratic stamp: his piano style showed little affiliation with any other artist; he played guitar in open D minor tuning; his vocal style made use of a striking falsetto; his lyrics were often dark and brooding.

A well-spoken, complex man, James was regarded as a genius by many of his blues-revival fans. Yet he failed to make a satisfactory living from either of his dual callings—the blues or the church—and spent much of his life earning his keep in secular, nonmusical jobs, from bootlegger to miner to logger to overseer. Except for his single, remarkable recording session for Paramount in 1931, his niche in blues history might have amounted to little more than a footnote. Skilled on guitar or piano, he left some outstanding songs later reprised by artists ranging from Eric Clapton—who sang "I'm So Glad" in the band Cream—to John Cephas.

James was inducted to the Blues Foundation Hall of Fame in 1992.

• For discographical information, see Robert M. W. Dixon and John Godrich, *Blues and Gospel Records: 1902–1943* (1982); Mike Leadbitter and Neil Slaven, *Blues Records 1943–1970: A Selective Discography* (1987); and Paul Oliver, ed., *The Blackwell Guide to Blues Records* (1989). For a more detailed account of his life, see Stephen Calt, *I'd Rather Be the Devil: Skip James and the Blues* (1994). There is an interview and essay in Peter Guralnick, *Feel Like Going Home: Portraits in Blues and Rock and Roll* (1971), and a discussion of the Bentonia style in Ted Olson, "Bentonia Blues," *Living Blues*, no. 103 (May–June 1992). For representative recordings, try *Skip James: The Complete 1931 Session* (Yazoo 2009) and *Skip James Today* (Vanguard VSD 79219). An obituary is in the *New York Times*, 4 Oct. 1969.

BILL MCCULLOCH
BARRY PEARSON

JAMES, Thomas (4 Nov. 1782–17 Dec. 1847), fur trader and Mexican trade merchant, was born in Maryland, the son of Joseph Austin James and Elizabeth Hosten. In 1803 James traveled west with the rest of his family, first to Kentucky and then to the Illinois country, entering Missouri Territory in 1807. The family settled near the village of Ste. Ferdinand (San Fernando), later known as Florissant. James heard of the adventures of Lewis and Clark's successful expedition after their return to St. Louis in 1806. He determined to sign up with the Missouri Fur Company for a trading trip to the reaches of the upper Missouri River. After conflicts with his employers, he returned from the Missouri country in August 1810.

Soon after, James traveled to Pennsylvania, where he lived for two years and married. His wife's name, the year of their marriage, and the number of their children (if any) are unknown. In 1813 he bought a keelboat and traveled up and down the Ohio and Mississippi Rivers, freighting goods from Pittsburgh to St. Louis. In 1815 he opened a store in Harrisonville, Illinois. Three years later he traveled to Baltimore, Ohio, purchased a large amount of merchandise, and transferred the lot to St. Louis. During the depression years of 1819–1820 he could not sell the stock even for cost and faced bankruptcy. During this period he met Santa Fe trader John McKnight of the firm of McKnight and Brady; in 1810 John McKnight's brother Robert McKnight and others had been imprisoned in Santa Fe by the Spanish government for illegal trading. In 1821, probably in an attempt to extricate himself from debt and in an attempt to assist John McKnight in the freeing of his brother, James organized a trading expedition to Santa Fe. He left St. Louis on 10 May 1821, carrying a Spanish passport signed by the Spanish Ambassador Don Onis and Secretary of State John Quincy Adams. Traveling with eleven men, James went by way of the Mississippi south to the Arkansas River, then to Fort Smith, and from there across the plains to Santa Fe. During their travels, Mexican troops found them in an altercation with Comanches in the area known today as the Texas panhandle. James's party was informed of the successful Mexican revolution and escorted to Santa Fe, where they arrived on 1 December 1821.

James traded for a while in Santa Fe, but his attempts to move his business from Santa Fe to Sonora proved unsuccessful because of a lack of cooperation from Mexican authorities. He sold his goods at cost to local merchants, and when Robert McKnight had been freed, James left Santa Fe on 1 June 1822 and returned to Missouri and Illinois by way of Taos. He arrived at his home in Monroe County in July 1822, with, according to his testimony, only $2,500 from his original stock of $10,000 or $12,000. James continued to attempt to extricate himself from debt, embarking on yet another trading expedition to the Comanches in the fall of 1822, returning in 1824 with much the same results as in his two previous ventures. In Illinois he bought a mill at the village of New Design, later known both as James' Mill and Monroe City. His fellow citizens elected him a general in the Illinois militia in 1825 and also to the Illinois legislature, where he served from 1825–1828. He served as postmaster at James' Mill in 1827 and as a major in the Black Hawk War of 1832. According to James, he paid off his debts over the next twenty years.

James's relationship with the proprietors of the Missouri Fur Company, especially with Pierre Chouteau and Manuel Lisa and with the Mexican trader Hugh Glenn, proved particularly difficult. His career in the fur and Mexican, or Santa Fe, trade, unlike the careers of many of his contemporaries, was dissatisfying and calamitous, at least by his own accounts. According to his statements, he realized no profits from any of his adventures. The publication of his memoirs in the *Waterloo (Ill.) War Eagle* in 1846 during the Mexican War (oddly enough, a profitable period of the overland trade between Mexico and the United States) may represent an attempt to explain his failures in light of others' successes. He dictated his candid account to Nathanial Niles, a New York attorney who had moved to Belleville, Illinois, about 1839. On publication, the book received such unfavorable reviews and accusations of slander that Niles sought to obtain and destroy all copies soon after it came off the press. James's published account is valuable in that it represents the reminiscences of a participant in one of the early American trading ventures to Mexico. Although highly opinionated, James's account provides an articulate view of the fur and Mexican trades, picturing them not as a saga of riotous nationalistic success, but instead as the little-told American western story of struggle and defeat. James died at Monroe City, Illinois.

• Material on James is in the collections of the Missouri Historical Society: the Thomas James Papers, 1844–1904, include deeds, notes, bills, and a few business papers from James's descendants; the Richard Graham Papers include a list of horses and mules stolen from McKnight and James (31 Mar. 1822); the Santa Fe Trade Collection includes a letter from James to Andrew Jackson (21 Feb. 1834), photostat; the Fur Trade Collection includes a summons to John A. Graham in the case of *Thomas James v. the Saint Louis Missouri Fur Company*; the John F. Snyder Collection, 1915–1916, has two letters that refer to James; and the society collection includes two of James's account books (14 Feb. 1820, 21 Aug. 1821). James's memoirs, *Three Years among the Indians and Mexicans* (1916), have been republished and are in editions by Milton Quaife, ed. (1953), A. P. Nasatir, ed. (1962), and Walter B. Douglas, ed. (1962). See also Louise Barry, *The Beginning of the West: Annals of the Kansas Gate Way to the American West, 1540–1854* (1972), and Jacob Fowler, *Journal of Jacob Fowler Narrating an Adventure from Arkansas through the Indian Territory, Oklahoma, Kansas, Colorado, and New Mexico to the Sources of the Rio Grande del Norte, 1821–1822*, ed. Elliot Coues (1898).

PAT O'BRIEN

JAMES, Thomas Chalkley (31 Aug. 1766–5 July 1835), physician and teacher, was born in Philadelphia, Pennsylvania, the son of Abel James, a merchant, and Rebecca Chalkley. The son of devout Quaker parents, James was named after his maternal grandfather, Thomas Chalkley, an eminent Quaker writer and minister. His father, one of Philadelphia's leading merchants, was a member of the Provincial Assembly, a friend of Benjamin Franklin, and a member of the American Philosophical Society. James attended the Friends' School at Fourth and Walnut streets, where he obtained a classical education under the historian Robert Proud and developed a love of books and literature.

James decided to study medicine and was apprenticed to Adam Kuhn, professor of materia medica at the University of Pennsylvania. He entered the medical department of the university and received a bachelor of medicine degree in 1787. When his father's business failed, James could not afford to go abroad to continue his medical education; with the help of friends, however, he secured a commission as a surgeon on the *Sampson*, a merchant ship bound for the Cape of Good Hope and Canton, China. Thereby acquiring the financial means to continue his medical studies, James traveled to England in the fall of 1790. After a time as a house student in the Story Street Lying-in Hospital in London, James attended lectures in the medical school of the University of Edinburgh during 1792 and 1793, but he did not receive a medical degree.

James returned to Philadelphia in the summer of 1793, just as a deadly yellow fever epidemic broke out in the city. James joined the efforts of the city's medical professionals to fight the epidemic but, finding confrontation and conflict distasteful, he avoided the bitter debates over the disease's origin and treatment.

James gradually developed a large private practice, concentrating on obstetrical cases. In 1802 he commenced a private course of lectures in midwifery at the lying-in ward of the Philadelphia Almshouse, which he helped establish. The course was offered for a number of years and was very successful. Through his extensive medical practice and private course, James became a leading figure in Philadelphia obstetrics. He was appointed physician to the Pennsylvania Hospital in 1807, and in 1810 he was elected professor of midwifery at the University of Pennsylvania, defeating a strong challenge from another prominent candidate for the chair, William Potts Dewees. The amiable James was a popular teacher despite his lack of eloquence in the lecture hall. According to Samuel D. Gross, who as a medical student at Jefferson Medical College heard James's lectures, James seldom raised his eyes from his manuscript when lecturing and tended to blush when describing the female sexual organs, evincing an embarrassment "often painful to witness."

Reflecting the conservative nature of the Philadelphia medical profession at the time, James was neither a believer in untested contemporary medical theories and systems nor a pioneer in medical science. His medical philosophy was based solely on experience and observation. He was, however, one of the country's earliest supporters of English biologist Edward Jenner and the subsequent campaign for vaccination.

James's views on obstetrics were based mainly on the writings of such English authorities as Smellie, Denman, and Burns. He used in his course Burns's text, *Principles of Midwifery*, which Nathaniel Chapman (James's assistant at the University of Pennsylvania) edited for an 1810 American edition. James himself edited the 1813 American edition of Burns's work, which went on to be used in many American medical schools. He also edited the first American version of Samuel Merriman's *Synopsis of the Various Kinds of Difficult Parturition* (1816). James was a founder and editor of the *Eclectic Repertory and Analytical Review*, which was published in Philadelphia from 1811 to 1820. Aside from these publications, however, James published little. One of his papers, published in the *Eclectic Repertory* (1811), describes the first successful case of premature labor artificially induced—by himself—at the end of the seventh month of pregnancy because of a contracted pelvis.

For twenty-five years James was a member of the staff of the Pennsylvania Hospital. A bibliophile, he worked diligently to improve the hospital's library. He was a consulting physician to the Society of the Sons of Saint George, a charitable organization, and an attending physician to the Philadelphia Dispensary. He was also an active member of the Welsh Society and served as physician to the society's infirmary for Welsh immigrants. James was elected a member of the Philadelphia Medical Society, the College of Physicians of Philadelphia, and, like his father, the American Philosophical Society. He served the College of Physicians as librarian, vice president, and president. Intensely interested in state and local history, he was in 1824 one of the founders of the Historical Society of Pennsylvania and remained active in its affairs. He contributed an article on the discovery of anthracite coal to the society's *Memoirs* (1827).

In keeping with his Quaker principles James opposed slavery and was a member of the Pennsylvania Society for the Abolition of Slavery, but to the chagrin of many fellow Quakers, he supported gradual rather than immediate abolition. Active in the Colonization Society of Pennsylvania, which espoused creating a free black community on the west coast of Africa, James eventually was forced to resign from the society in the face of heavy Quaker pressure. He was also involved with other Philadelphia charitable organizations, including the Humane Society and the Union Benevolent Association, of which he was a founder and president.

Surprisingly shy, retiring, and lacking confidence in his abilities, James shrank from public speaking (except when teaching), writing, and scientific debate. A nervous disorder later in life forced him to retire from teaching and withdraw from social gatherings. Little is known of James's private life except that he married Hannah Morris in 1802, and that they had at least four children. Choosing the solitude of his library over the swirl of society, James spent many of his private moments reading and writing literature. Early in his career he wrote poetry under the pseudonym "P. D." and published it in *Port Folio* magazine. The modest James kept his literary pursuits secret to all but a few close friends. Fluent in several languages, James read the Bible in French, German, Greek, Hebrew, and Latin translations.

At his death, in Philadelphia, James was one of the country's more prominent figures in obstetrics, owing to his affiliation with the prestigious medical department of the University of Pennsylvania and the great number of students he had taught. James was neither a leader nor an innovator in the profession, however. In the words of Hugh L. Hodge, professor of obstetrics at the University of Pennsylvania from 1835 to 1863, James "was not one of the pioneers of the profession—not one who was remarkable for the novelty of his views, the importance of his discoveries, or the boldness of his practice—but he was numbered among the most respectable and useful class . . . who profited by the discoveries of others."

• It appears that James's personal papers have not survived. A few scattered manuscripts relating to his career are at the College of Physicians of Philadelphia. The archives of the College of Physicians of Philadelphia and the Historical Society of Pennsylvania also contain materials that document James's activities in these organizations. Useful contemporary accounts of James's career include Job R. Tyson, *Memoir of Thomas C. James, M.D.* (1836); Hugh L. Hodge, "Biography of Thomas C. James, M.D.," *American Journal of the Medical Sciences*, n.s., 6 (1843): 91–106; Caspar Morris, "Thomas C. James. 1766–1835," in *Lives of Eminent American Physicians and Surgeons of the Nineteenth Century*, ed. Samuel D. Gross (1861); and Gross, *Autobiography of Samuel D. Gross* (1887).

THOMAS A. HORROCKS

JAMES, Thomas Potts (1 Sept. 1803–22 Feb. 1882), botanist, was born in Radnor, Pennsylvania, the son of Isaac James, a medical doctor, and Henrietta Potts. When he was nine years old the family moved to an area near Trenton, New Jersey, where better educational opportunities existed for the children. Because of financial reverses, Isaac James was unable to send his sons to Princeton as he had planned. Both Thomas and his older brother John studied pharmacy, and in 1831 they started a wholesale drug business in Philadelphia that provided their livelihood. Thomas also studied medicine, but there is no record of his graduation. For a number of years he was a professor and examiner at the Philadelphia College of Pharmacy and an active member of several local scientific societies. It was probably while studying materia medica that he developed a serious interest in botany, and he soon became familiar with the local flora. James realized that an opportunity for original study lay in the field of cryptogamic botany, especially mosses and liverworts.

In December 1851 James married Isabella Batchelder in Christ Church, Cambridge, Massachusetts. She was a friend of botanist Asa Gray, and James met her during the period in which William Darlington was editing the correspondence of noted botanist John Bartram. She had provided valuable advice on the illustrations for that publication. As James's wife, she provided constant support for her husband's avocation. They had four children, and during his business career the family lived in the Philadelphia area. After thirty-five years as a drug wholesaler, James sold his interest in the organization and moved his entire family to Cambridge, where they resided with her father. He was thereafter free to devote the remainder of his life to the study of mosses.

Sometime before 1850 James became a correspondent of William S. Sullivant, who was at that time the foremost student of North American mosses. Sullivant helped James and other aspiring bryologists by identifying specimens and offering advice and publications.

Among James's earlier publications were two on the locale near his home: a list of mosses and liverworts for the third edition of Darlington's *Flora Cestrica* (1853) and the section on cryptogams in the flora of Delaware County, Pennsylvania, in the history of that county by George Smith, *History of Delaware County, Pennsylvania, . . . with . . . Catalogues of the Minerals, Plants, Quadrupeds and Birds* (1862). With the help of Sullivant his knowledge of mosses expanded. He published "An Enumeration of the Mosses Detected in the Northern United States, Which Are Not Comprised in the Manual of Asa Gray, M.D." in *Proceedings of the Academy of Natural Sciences of Philadelphia* (7 [1856]), and his account of the mosses is included in "Sketch of the Flora of Alaska" by J. T. Rothrock (Smithsonian Institution *Report* for 1867). For the *Report of the Geological Exploration of the Fortieth Parallel* (5 [1871]) and the *Report of the United States Geographical Surveys West of the One Hundredth Meridian in Charge of Lt. George M. Wheeler* (6 [1878]), he supplied catalogs of western mosses. These papers confirm his ability as a bryologist.

In addition to his continuing association with Sullivant, James began, early in his career as a bryologist, a correspondence with Charles Leo Lesquereux, the Swiss-born paleobotanist and bryologist who had immigrated to the United States and was then working with Sullivant in Columbus, Ohio, as a research assistant. Lesquereux and James may have met for the first time during a collecting trip in 1857; if not, the meeting was shortly thereafter.

After James moved to Cambridge there were occasions when he and Lesquereux met and discussed their mutual interests and work on mosses as Lesquereux had often consulted Louis Agassiz at Harvard regarding his paleobotanical and geological activities. Upon the death of Sullivant in April 1873, Sullivant's library, manuscript notes, and bryological specimens were sent to the Harvard University Herbarium as he had requested. One project that Sullivant left unfinished was his proposed manual of the mosses of North America. Gray persuaded James and Lesquereux to utilize Sullivant's materials and publish the much-needed volume. Because Lesquereux was at the time occupied with paleobotany and also suffered from vision problems, the microscopic examination of the specimens and the preparation of drawings based on the slides to be used in writing the descriptions became James's responsibility. In 1878 his physician suggested a period of rest for his health, and James took the opportunity to travel to Europe, where he could consult European botanists about the project. In 1879 he and Lesquereux published "Description of Some New Species of North American Mosses" in the February issue of the *Proceedings of the American Academy of Arts and Sciences*. When James died unexpectedly in Cambridge, his contribution to the manual was almost finished. Lesquereux completed the descriptions, but since he was unable to visit Cambridge because of his health he entrusted the bibliographic and editorial details to Sereno Watson, then at Harvard. In 1884 Lesquereux and James's *Manual of the Mosses of North America* was published. It included descriptions of about 900 species. This volume was a milestone in the history of North American bryology and was a final recognition that James was one of the foremost bryologists of his era.

• James's correspondence is partly at the Farlow Herbarium Library and partly at the Gray Herbarium Library, both at Harvard University. His herbarium and types are at the Farlow Herbarium and the Philadelphia Academy of Arts and Sciences. Mary Isabella James Gozzaldi, "Thomas Potts James," *Bryologist* 6 (Sept. 1903): 71–75, is an account of James by his eldest daughter. Although not a botanist, she gives her personal account of his life and study habits. John William Harshberger, *The Botanists of Philadelphia and Their Work* (1899), is an account of James's life in the city where he lived the greater part of his life. Memorials include those by Asa Gray in *Proceedings of the American Academy of Arts and Sciences* 17 (1881–1882): 405–6, and Joseph Trimble Rothrock in *Proceedings of the American Philosophical Society* 20 (1883): 293–97. An obituary is in the *Boston Transcript*, 27 Feb. 1882.

ANNA M. M. REID

JAMES, William (11 Jan. 1842–26 Aug. 1910), philosopher and psychologist, was born in New York City, the son of Henry James (1811–1882), a philosopher and religious writer, and Mary Robertson Walsh. His grandfather, William James of Albany, a penniless immigrant from Ireland, became one of the richest men in New York State by exploiting a new method of extracting salt and speculating in land along the Erie Canal. His son Henry James used his inheritance to lead a life of the mind, devoting himself to metaphysics in the grand style and publishing a number of books and essays on the relations between God and man, influenced by the Swedish seer, Emanuel Swedenborg. Henry James suffered extensive financial losses, and his five children, although heirs to some commercial property in Syracuse, New York, had to concern themselves with making a living. Besides William, there were the novelist Henry James (1843–1916); Civil War veteran Garth Wilkinson (1845–1883); the gifted but unfortunate Robertson (1846–1910), also a veteran of the Civil War; and Alice James, whose published letters and diary have led some to believe her a victim of domineering males.

William James's early life has been described as a life of "zigzag voyages." In October 1843 the Jameses departed for Europe, returning to America early in 1845 after stays in London and Paris. Until the autumn of 1847, the family maintained no fixed residence, spending most of their time in Albany with James's grandparents. In 1847 the family moved to New York City. Several months later they bought a house on West Fourteenth Street and lived there until June 1855. James's early schooling was erratic. Sometimes he had private tutors; at other times he was sent to private schools. With his younger brothers and friends, James roamed the streets of the city and frequented various theatrical performances, ranging from Shakespeare to vaudeville and circus acts. Home life was chaotic and noisy, with the children teasing each other and arguing.

From June 1855 to June 1858 the Jameses were again in Europe, spending their time in Geneva, London, Paris, and Boulogne. A number of letters from James to his friend Edgar Beach Van Winkle provide considerable information about his state of mind during this period. Writing from Boulogne on 1 March 1858, James set out to prove that the "choice of a profession" would not torment people in a well-ordered society in which everyone was assured of food, clothing, and shelter. Everyone would "follow out his own tastes" and "excel as much as possible in the particular line for which he was created." James professed his faith in the "innate good of mankind" and claimed that evil comes from "the law and the priests and the sooner these two things are abolished the better." In his letter of 26 May 1858, James thought that he had benefited from his stay abroad since he had learned to read and write French perfectly. On the other hand he had lost by not going through the "general routine" and was deficient especially in mathematics. James expressed his desire to enter Union College to study civil engineering and asked Van Winkle's advice as to how best to prepare for the entrance examination in mathematics.

James's hopes were never realized because his father thought that colleges were "hot beds of corruption" in which it was impossible to learn anything. The Jameses returned to America in 1858 and lived in Newport, where James studied drawing with William Morris Hunt. They returned to Europe in October 1859, and James spent the academic year at the academy in Geneva.

After returning to Newport in the fall of 1860, James studied painting in the studio of William Morris Hunt. One of his fellow students, John La Farge, a respected painter, believed that James had the talent to become one as well. The reasons why James abandoned art have become a matter of controversy. Some hold that he realized that he lacked talent, while others argue that he succumbed to paternal pressures. There is some indirect evidence that James's father threatened to commit suicide should James persist in pursuing a career in art.

James did not take part in the Civil War, the great event of his generation. While a number of letters from this period survive, they cast no light upon his reasons for not joining his younger brothers, some cousins, and many friends in fighting for a cause in which he believed. The death in battle of William James Temple, a cousin, for example, evokes normal expressions of sympathy, but nothing revealing James's own state of mind. Again, some suspect paternal influence. There is no evidence that James himself wanted to enlist.

In 1861 he entered the Lawrence Scientific School of Harvard University—a high school diploma was not required for admission—where he studied chemistry under Charles William Eliot, later president of Harvard, and attended lectures by Louis Agassiz, the leading geologist and zoologist in the United States and a prominent critic of Charles Darwin. James later changed his studies to comparative anatomy under Jeffries Wyman but left the school without a degree. In 1864 he entered Harvard Medical School and in 1865 published reviews of Thomas Henry Huxley, *Lectures on the Elements of Comparative Anatomy*, and of Alfred Russel Wallace, "The Origin of the Human Races." In these, his first publications, he committed himself to the evolutionism propagated by Darwin and Wallace. In April 1865 he went to Brazil, a member of a scientific expedition led by Louis Agassiz, collected specimens in the Amazon basin, and returned home in February 1866. In April 1867 he sailed for Europe, where he remained until November 1868. Besides taking the water cure at Teplice, Bohemia, he learned German, visited art museums in Dresden, and in Berlin attended lectures on physiology. In 1869 he received his M.D. from Harvard Medical School, his only earned degree.

He viewed himself as in poor health. In Brazil he had smallpox, which affected his vision and for some years rendered him unable to read for more than a few hours at a time. In 1867 he suffered back pains; his trip to Germany was in part a search for a cure. In 1870 he suffered a mental breakdown, the causes and nature of which remain unclear. He himself viewed it as part of a vocational crisis: although he felt the strong pull of philosophy, he thought it unhealthy to devote his life to abstract speculation. At the same time, he was troubled by the problem of free will. According to his diary, his recovery began on 29 April 1870 when, influenced by the French philosopher Charles Renouvier, he decided that his "first act of free will shall be to believe in free will." However, throughout this period of crisis, he continued to read extensively in physiology and philosophy and to write reviews for the *Nation*, the *Atlantic Monthly*, and the *North American Review*.

Brought up in a household dominated by religious and moral concerns, he had difficulty reconciling these with the naturalistic conception of man made prominent by the biological sciences. There is evidence that several years later, to further his Harvard career, he presented himself as occupying a middle ground, as a man fully versed in the new sciences but with strong sympathies for religious values. He retained an interest in religion all of his life, although he never joined any religious body and resisted attempts to convert him to some form of Christianity. It is a curious fact that Charles Sanders Peirce on one occasion argued with James as with a hard-hearted atheist, urging him to allow his feelings to have their play and thereby reach belief in God.

James was troubled by obscure ailments for most of his life. There are reports that some time later he was hospitalized in a mental institution, but because medical records remain confidential nothing definite is known about this episode. The obscurity of his ailments gives some grounds for believing that to an extent he engaged in medical politics, using his complaints to justify delaying the start of a career and remaining dependent upon the paternal purse. Apparently, in 1867, before fleeing to Germany, he resigned from a position with Massachusetts General Hospital.

Harvard University, where James spent his entire teaching career, was then in the forefront of educational reform under the leadership of Charles William Eliot, whose election in 1869 as president led to the transformation of Harvard from a small college into a modern university. James was one of many young men appointed by Eliot to assist in this work. On 3 August 1872 the Harvard authorities voted to offer him an instructorship in physiology to teach one course for half a year for $300. He began teaching in January 1873. After declining an offer to teach anatomy and physiology in 1873–1874, James went to Europe. In the fall of 1874 he began to teach at Harvard on a permanent basis. In 1875 James offered his first course in psychology, a graduate course on the relations between physiology and psychology. It is generally agreed that this course marks the beginning of the teaching of modern psychology in the United States. The following year he was made assistant professor of physiology, and he offered an undergraduate psychology course with emphasis on Herbert Spencer. In spite of the fact that James was sharply critical of Spencer's views, his proposal to teach the course encountered opposition from Francis Bowen, a critic of evolutionism and the best-known philosopher at Harvard at the time. In 1879–

1880, now assistant professor of philosophy, James taught his first philosophy courses: on the philosophy of evolution and on Charles Renouvier. In 1885 he was promoted to professor of philosophy. His title was changed to professor of psychology in 1889 and to professor of philosophy in 1897. In July 1898, while hiking in the Adirondack Mountains, perhaps because of overexertion, James experienced an irregular heartbeat and chest pains. He further aggravated his heart condition in June 1899 during another Adirondack hike. As a result, he did not teach from the fall of 1899 to the spring of 1901 but traveled in Europe in search of a cure, for extended periods taking baths and exercising at Bad Nauheim in Germany. After his return to Harvard he taught a reduced load until his retirement in 1907. He taught his last class on 22 January. His highest salary at Harvard was $5,000 per year. Throughout his career, he was a popular teacher, erratic but brilliant and without professorial pomp. Students found him approachable and he established strong friendships.

The year 1878 was pivotal. On 10 July he married Alice Howe Gibbens (1849–1922). The marriage was stormy but strong, and there is little reason to question the profound bond that existed between them. There is an oral tradition that James on at least one occasion was unfaithful. However, the documentary record does not support this tradition and at some points contradicts it. Nevertheless, it must be added that James enjoyed the companionship of women and that the record is a heavily edited one. It is demonstrable that his wife, Alice, destroyed much information she did not want posterity to have. Of their five children who survived beyond infancy, three achieved prominence: Henry, a lawyer and biographer; William, an artist associated with the Boston Museum of Fine Arts; and Alexander Robertson (initially named Francis Tweedy), a painter.

In 1878 James emerged as a thinker with his own point of view. Somewhat uncertain of his status at Harvard, he was flirting with the newly founded Johns Hopkins University and in 1878, to make himself known to the Hopkins authorities, gave a course of lectures in Baltimore. Later that same year, he lectured before the Lowell Institute in Boston. Finding himself in the position of having to publish or perish, he published that year his first signed essays, "Remarks on Spencer's Definition of Mind as Correspondence" and "Brute and Human Intellect." In these lectures and essays James rejected the then-popular view that consciousness was merely the reflection of physiological processes taking place in the brain, arguing that consciousness could in its own turn exert influence upon the brain. Consciousness is selective and by focusing attention on some stimuli and ignoring others, helps human beings to respond appropriately. James maintained that had consciousness not been useful, it would not have evolved. Also in 1878 he signed a contract with Henry Holt and Company for *The Principles of Psychology*, a book to which he devoted the next twelve years. Many of his numerous early papers were incorporated into *Principles*.

In 1880 he published "Great Men, Great Thoughts, and the Environment," defending the view that great men make a difference in history. In 1882 he published "The Sense of Dizziness in Deaf-Mutes," his only contribution to physiology. James showed that the semicircular canals of the ear are organs of balance.

James spent 1882–1883 in Europe, making valuable philosophical and scientific friends. On the Continent he met Ernst Mach, established a lifelong friendship with the psychologist Carl Stumpf, and attended lectures by the physiologist Ewald Hering, whose nativistic account of the perception of space James came to defend in *The Principles of Psychology*. In Britain he met Edmund Gurney, one of the organizers of the Society for Psychical Research, the philosophers Henry Sidgwick, Leslie Stephen, and Shadworth Hollway Hodgson, and the psychologist James Sully. In 1886 he acquired a farm in Chocorua, New Hampshire, which he converted into a summer home. In the fall of 1889 James and his family moved into their newly completed house at 95 Irving Street, Cambridge. Most of the 1880s were occupied with work on *The Principles of Psychology*. When finally published in 1890, this sprawling work became the main textbook of psychology in the United States and in Europe and provided the Jameses with a substantial income.

In *Principles* James sought to develop psychology as a natural science, without metaphysics. He argued that psychology could not be done without physiology and devoted an introductory chapter to the controversy concerning the localization of functions of the brain. Some physiologists maintained that every function of the brain is performed by the whole brain, while others tried to show by means of experiments that specific tasks are performed by distinct parts. After surveying the literature on the subject, James decided in favor of a modified localizationism, arguing that while each mental task is connected with its own neural region, in cases of damage by disease or injury other regions of the brain can learn to perform the functions of the damaged region.

Psychology, according to James, was still in its infancy, a mass of descriptive details and not a genuine explanatory science. Ultimately, all psychological explanations had to be physiological, correlating mental states with brain states, and this was impossible given the condition of knowledge. Tentatively he offered the view that neural currents "wear out" paths in the brain and that such paths are correlated with all organized mental functions. On the psychological side, he developed the view that consciousness is a stream, in opposition to the mental atomism of the British empiricists. He denied that in consciousness we find mental atoms, simple ideas that cannot be further analyzed. On the contrary, consciousness is an ever-changing succession of fields. Within a field, it is possible to distinguish between focus and margin, but no field can be analyzed into simple ideas. Again in opposition to the empiricists, James claimed that relations also are sensory in origin, that corresponding to such words as *and*, *or*, and other relational terms, there are distinct sensations just as there are distinct sensations corresponding to the words *white* and *sweet*, a claim central to his later radical empiricism. James described consciousness as an organ of selection, whose function is to ignore much of the buzzing confusion that surrounds us and thereby bring about an orderly world in which we can act effectively.

Principles contains an extended analysis of the self, a theory of habit, a theory of emotion, a theory of association, an extended and highly technical discussion of the perception of space, and much more. Where space is concerned, he defended a view known as nativism, arguing that there is a sensation of voluminousness that is the source of the idea of the third dimension. In respect of emotion, he expounded what has come to be known as the James-Lange theory according to which emotion is not the cause but the consequence of physical changes. This theory has given rise to numerous empirical investigations.

Principles is best viewed as a work in the tradition of John Locke's *An Essay concerning Human Understanding*, an effort to rethink many of the problems of empiricism in the light of the new biological sciences. It thus firmly belongs to the history of philosophy. John Dewey and others have claimed that it contains much of James's later thinking. The publication of *Principles* marks the beginning of the end of James's active involvement with experimental psychology. It is suggestive that while he was urged to revise the book and received offers of assistance, he never did so.

In 1899 he published his *Talks to Teachers on Psychology and to Students on Some of Life's Ideals*, an attempt to apply his psychology to problems of education. His pedagogy remains on the level of sound common sense and does not suggest the need for a radical transformation of education of the kind eventually urged by John Dewey.

After 1890 James's psychological interests became dominated by abnormal psychology, of which psychical research was a part. In 1884 he was one of the organizers of the American Society for Psychical Research and remained its leading intellectual light and organizer until 1907, when the group moved to New York. He discovered Leonora Piper, a trance medium, who became one of the mainstays of the American group and its parent society in England. In 1895 he published an encyclopedia article entitled "Telepathy," in which he claimed that the British psychical researchers had proved that one person can transmit ideas to another without any physical intermediaries. But within a few years much of the experimental work cited as evidence was shown to be fraudulent. James never retracted his article, perhaps because he believed that talk of fraud would prevent people from pursuing what in his view still remained a promising line of investigation. His final statement on the subject, "The Confidences of a 'Psychical Researcher'" (1908), was noncommittal. It remains unclear why he devoted so much time to investigations that he often found tiresome. He probably did not share his British colleagues' desire to find proofs of immortality. More likely, he hoped that psychical research would lead the sciences to a view of nature more in line with his own. Psychical facts did not fit any of the established theories and belonged to the "unclassified residuum," while scientific progress can be made only by attending to such exceptional phenomena. Psychical research held the promise of shaking up the "completed system of truth" that science pretended to be.

In 1890 he published "The Hidden Self," primarily a review of the work of Pierre Janet on hysteria and multiple personality. In 1896, before the Brooklyn Institute of Arts and Sciences and the Lowell Institute in Boston, he lectured on exceptional mental states, discussing hysteria, multiple personality, possession, trance mediumship, and related topics but remaining largely on the level of description. His interest in abnormal psychology culminated in his Gifford lectures at the University of Edinburgh in 1901 and 1902, published as *The Varieties of Religious Experience* (1902). This work initiated the psychological study of religion and became his most popular work, readily accessible to lay audiences. In his view, formal creeds and philosophical theology in general were not the primary data for the study of religion. He chose to emphasize the experiences of individual believers, paying special attention to religious conversion and regeneration. Religion, he claimed, consists essentially of a feeling that the natural world stands related to something more, by reference to which it is saved and regenerated.

In the mid-1890s James came to realize that he had not as yet presented a developed philosophical position to the public. He devoted most of his remaining years to working out a philosophy that he called radical empiricism, consisting of a postulate, a hypothesis, and several distinct claims about reality. James postulated that philosophers can discuss things only in terms drawn from experience, developed the hypothesis of pure experience, argued that reality is pluralistic, that relations are as real as the terms which they relate, and that consciousness is not an entity but a function. The earliest attempts to work out radical empiricism are found in the fragmentary notes of his psychology seminar of 1895–1896. He announced his adherence to radical empiricism in the preface to *The Will to Believe* (1897), a collection of popular essays illustrating the attitude of radical empiricism.

James proposed that our experience as such is neutral, neither mental nor physical, neither inner nor outer. Given experience is pure in the sense that it is neither a thing nor a thought but becomes one or the other by association with other experiences. The same felt quality becomes a mental event by being placed in some person's inner world. It becomes part of a thing by association with experiences viewed as outer. James claimed that the notion of pure experience allows philosophy to state the facts of experience without the paradoxes and contradictions into which other assumptions lead, but he never developed this side of radical empiricism in detail.

Prominent in his writings is the claim that radical empiricism is pluralistic. In the preface to *The Will to Believe*, he claimed that the difference between "monism and pluralism is perhaps the most pregnant of all the differences in philosophy." For monists, the absolute idealists of his time, there is a point of view from which the totality of what exists is intelligible. Absolute idealists solve the problem of evil by claiming that evils are only fragments of a universe that when viewed as a whole is harmonious and absolutely good. Radical empiricism abandons as hopeless the search for such a comprehensive point of view. Some aspects of reality will always remain crude and uncomprehended facts. The universe contains "real catastrophes," "real evils" that cannot be interpreted as aspects of a perfect harmony. James's most extensive statement of his pluralism is found in *A Pluralistic Universe* (1909). There he developed his distinctive conception of God as a finite being struggling against evil, facing the possibility of failure, and in need of human help. According to James, this is the common-sense conception of God.

James published *The Will to Believe* with the expectation that eventually he would give his radical empiricism technical shape. In late 1902, with *Varieties* out of the way, he began to write what he hoped would be his great work, "The Many and the One." He thought that philosophy had reached a critical stage and was ripe for a radical restatement of its basic problems. His own work was to bring various converging tendencies to a focus and shift philosophy decisively in the direction of radical empiricism. By 1904, when he abandoned the project, he had composed only thirty-two manuscript pages, but his efforts led to a series of essays published posthumously as *Essays in Radical Empiricism* (1912). In these essays, he was especially concerned to explain how for radical empiricism different minds can know the same thing. This became a matter of special difficulty, because for radical empiricism only experience is real, and experience exists only for consciousness; since according to *Principles* experience is always personal and the same experience cannot always be found in two fields, no two minds can have the same experience. It thus seems impossible for two minds to know the same thing: radical empiricism seems to imply solipsism.

The basic difficulty concerns the compatibility between radical empiricism and some of the most characteristic teaching of *The Principles of Psychology*. James's wrestlings with this difficulty are recorded in what have come to be known as the Miller-Bode notebooks. In *A Pluralistic Universe*, he devoted much of the chapter titled "The Compounding of Consciousness" to a survey of how his view of the problem had changed. To find a solution, he was forced to abandon what he called the logic of identity, made bold to do so by his reading of Henri Bergson. James conceded that much of this remains on the level of "dark sayings." He died before he could formulate his position clearly and in detail.

In the history of philosophy James remains primarily identified with pragmatism. According to James, pragmatism was first propounded by Charles Sanders Peirce in the early 1870s and lay dormant until it was brought to public notice by James in his lecture "Philosophical Conceptions and Practical Results" (1898). In *Pragmatism* (1907), which incorporates much of the earlier lecture, James claimed that pragmatism is first a method of settling metaphysical disputes by tracing the "concrete" consequences of abstract concepts: "whenever a dispute is serious, we ought to be able to show some practical difference that must follow from one side or the other's being right." He applied this method especially to the controversy between monism and pluralism, showing that the claim that reality is one can be understood in various ways, some of them having no consequences either for our conduct or our knowledge. Thus the universe is one in the sense that it can be referred to by one word, but this is a trivial unity providing merely "abstract comfort." By contrast, it is important to know the extent of causal interaction between things. However, this is a matter that cannot be decided by metaphysics and must be left to the sciences.

In the second case, pragmatism offers a theory of truth, identifying the truth of propositions with their successful working in experience. According to what has become his best-known formula, truths have "only this quality in common, that they pay." The pragmatic theory of truth became a matter of philosophic and public controversy.

Interpretations of James's theory were much influenced by the association between James and his essay "The Will to Believe" (1896). In this, his most famous essay, James argued that our "passional nature" may commit us to beliefs when we cannot postpone action and when there is not enough evidence to decide the question on intellectual grounds. He intended the paper as an investigation of a problem in the ethics of belief and recognized that the will to believe is as much a defense of atheistic beliefs as of theistic ones. But the paper was and often still is regarded as an apology for religion, a justification for believing anything no matter how absurd when belief promises emotional comfort. Such misreadings, combined with James's characteristic attacks on intellectualism, led many critics to conclude that his pragmatism was merely an apology for loose and wishful thinking.

Against such critics James emphasized the view he had maintained in his early paper "The Function of Cognition" (1885), that the relation between knowledge and its object is a concrete relation, consisting of a series of experiences that can be traversed. The assertion, for example, that there are tigers in India is related to actual tigers by paths of experiences that if traversed successfully would place the knower in the presence of tigers. For James, in the case of assertions of fact, the claim that truth "pays" is to be understood with reference to his description of the cognitive relation. The truth of scientific theories and of metaphysical and religious overbeliefs involves much more than simple matters of fact. Because of this, in science, metaphysics, and religion, factual evidence alone cannot decide all controversies, and practical and emotional considerations must be given a role.

James collected his polemical papers on the subject of truth in *The Meaning of Truth* (1909). His major allies in the pragmatism wars were the English philosopher Ferdinand Canning Scott Schiller, who preferred the term humanism, and John Dewey, who preferred instrumentalism.

The term pragmatism is sometimes used in a broader sense as a name for those philosophical theories that regard mind as a function of the biological and social organism. James is a pragmatist in this broader sense but did not use the term in this way.

From the middle 1890s, James began to take various stands on public issues. In 1876 he opposed President Grover Cleveland's willingness to intervene in the Venezuela crisis and, later, American imperialism in Cuba and the Philippines. He wrote a series of public letters protesting the "epidemic" of lynching. In 1909 he commented on the disagreements between Booker T. Washington and W. E. B. Du Bois, one of his former students, concerning the direction American blacks should take. James claimed that blacks need both industrial training, as advocated by Washington, and political action, as advocated by Du Bois. In his last years he became a major moral and financial supporter of the movement to reform mental hospitals initiated by Clifford W. Beers. William James died at his summer home in Chocorua, New Hampshire. His ashes are buried in the Cambridge Cemetery, Cambridge, Massachusetts.

The history of philosophy still treats him in a one-sided way. He is known for popularizing a certain theory of truth, but for little else. Philosophy was revolutionized, but not in the Jamesian direction. No one has tried to develop a philosophy along the lines of his radical empiricism, and the fruitfulness of his work for philosophy is still largely untested. Should James's call for a complete rethinking of empiricism be taken up and lead to important results, he could emerge as a major philosopher. But failing that, he will continue to be seen as a philosopher who has made definite but limited contributions. Where psychology is concerned, James's broad and reflective psychology was replaced by the very narrow Watsonian behaviorism that merely ignored him. This decades-long silence is ending with the recent revival of interest in philosophical psychology under the title of cognitive science. In the meantime, there is general agreement that James was a forceful and lively personality and that his place in American culture is more a function of character than of doctrine. One of the major figures of America's intellectual golden age, he has attracted more attention from biographers and historians than he has from philosophers.

• Most of James's papers, including numerous annotated books, are in the Houghton Library of Harvard University. All of his published writings appear in *The Works of William*

James, ed. Fredson Bowers and Ignas K. Skrupskelis (1974–1988), a critical edition with Frederick Burkhardt as general editor; also included are James's manuscript remains, but not his marginalia, diaries, and autobiographical fragments. In addition to the works mentioned in the text above, James was the author of *Psychology* (1982), *Human Immortality* (1898), and *Some Problems of Philosophy* (1911). Among his more important essays not discussed above are "The Teaching of Philosophy in Our Colleges" (1876), "The Dilemma of Determinism" (1884), "What the Will Effects" (1888), "The Moral Philosopher and the Moral Life" (1891), "Is Life Worth Living?" (1895), "The True Harvard" (1903), "Humanism and Truth" (1904), "The Energies of Men" (1907), "Confidences of a Psychical Researcher" (1909), and "The Moral Equivalent of War" (1910). His extensive correspondence is being published as *The Correspondence of William James* (1993–), ed. Ignas K. Skrupskelis and Elizabeth Berkeley, with John Mcdermott as general editor.

Henry James described his brother William's childhood in *A Small Boy and Others* (1913) and his later life in *Notes of a Son and Brother* (1914). Still valuable as a general study of his life and thought is Ralph Barton Perry, *The Thought and Character of William James* (1935); Perry was James's student and literary heir. A more recent general study is Gerald E. Myers, *William James: His Life and Thought* (1986). Gay Wilson Allen, *William James: A Biography* (1967), is a useful general biography. Howard M. Feinstein, *Becoming William James* (1984), is a controversial study of James's youth, focusing on father and son conflicts. George Cotkin, *William James: Public Philosopher* (1990), argues that James's doubts concerning his vocation were typical of those of his generation who did not fight in the Civil War. Jacques Barzun, *A Stroll with William James* (1983), offers a general appreciation of James's character, R. W. B. Lewis, *The Jameses: A Family Narrative* (1991), provides a chronicle of the Jameses through more than five generations. Basic to an understanding of family relations are Jean Strouse, *Alice James: A Biography* (1980), and Leon Edel, *The Life of Henry James* (5 vols., 1953–1972). Ignas K. Skrupskelis, comp., *William James: A Reference Guide* (1977), lists writings on James. Andrew J. Reck, *Introduction to William James* (1967), and Graham Bird, *William James* (1986), provide general surveys of his thought. Bruce Wilshire, *William James and Phenomenology* (1968), studies the relations between James's *Principles of Psychology* and European philosophy. James C. S. Wernham, *James's Will-to-Believe-Doctrine* (1987), provides a detailed analysis of one of James's most controversial essays. Charlene Haddock Seigfried, *William James's Radical Reconstruction of Philosophy* (1990), offers a distinctive interpretation of James's basic philosophical position. The standard study of the American pragmatists is H. S. Thayer, *Meaning and Action* (1968).

IGNAS K. SKRUPSKELIS

JAMES, Will Roderick (6 June 1892–3 Sept. 1942), western author and artist, was born Joseph Ernest Nephtali Dufault in St. Nazaire de Acton, Quebec, Canada, the son of Jean Dufault and Josephine (maiden name unknown). When the Dufault family moved to Montreal, he attended a Catholic school and his father ran a hotel, in which the boy heard stories of trappers that he later used to fabricate parts of his *Lone Cowboy: My Life Story*. According to it, his parents were William and Bonnie James and he was born near Great Falls, Montana. He also claimed that his father was a cattle drover from West Texas and his mother

was a Spanish, Scotch-Irish Californian. He even said that his middle name derived from Rodriguez, his mother's maiden name. He added that after his father was killed by a steer in 1895, he was adopted by a French trapper named Jean Beaupré, with whom he worked along Canadian rivers until the old man disappeared in 1906 and was thought to have drowned.

In reality, James remained in Montreal until 1907, became a cowboy in Saskatchewan and Alberta provinces (1907–1910), may have been arrested in connection with a murderous brawl, and then called himself C. W. Jackson, W. R. James, and finally Will R. James. He left Canada for Montana and then Idaho, where he gathered wild horses (1911–1912), moved into Nevada, served time in the state prison there for cattle rustling (1915–1916), went to Los Angeles and acted as a stunt man in western movies, and served in the U.S. Army in California (1918–1919). James had long shown a talent for drawing. He sketched on any surface available, including flour sacks, bed tarpaulins, and canvas wagon sheets, and he once earned fifty cents for drawing a picture on a saloon mirror with a bar of soap. He had an uncanny ability to sketch horses at rest and in movement. In 1919 he studied in the California School of Fine Arts in San Francisco, but he soon grew bored and moved into the artists' colony at Sausalito for a time. Bored again, he decided to avoid further professional associations and developed a unique, untutored style instead. He enjoyed such quick success, with the acceptance of several of his drawings by the *Sunset Magazine*, beginning in January 1920, that he returned to Nevada and married a fellow broncobuster's sister, Alice Conradt, that July. They had no children. He sketched even as he held cowhand jobs in Arizona and New Mexico. He accepted a scholarship at the Yale Art School in 1921 but soon quit, lived in New York briefly, and then returned to Nevada in 1922.

James drifted into remarkable success. He wrote essays and illustrated them, beginning with "Bucking Horses and Bucking-Horse Riders" (*Scribner's Magazine*, Mar. 1923) and continuing with similar semifictional pieces in the *Saturday Evening Post*, *Sunset Magazine*, and *Redbook*. He also sold drawings to pulp magazines and companies publishing calendars. He invested his royalties in land in Frankton, Nevada, on which his in-laws built a cabin for him and for his wife. Maxwell Perkins, the genius of Scribner's editorial staff, helped shape into publishable form James's *Cowboys North and South* (1924), *The Drifting Cowboy* (1925), *Smoky, the Cowhorse* (1926, the John Newbery Medal winner as the best children's book of the year), and *Cow Country* (1927). The books' substantial earnings prompted James to sell his Nevada holdings in 1927, take up some 8,000 acres outside Pryor, Montana, and establish his Rocking R Ranch there. He soon began dividing his time between the ranch in the summer and San Francisco and Hollywood in the winter and spun out book after book, all illustrated with his own animated drawings. *Lone Cowboy*, his partly faked autobiography, hoodwinked the vast American buying public, and even his wife, and was a 1930 selection of the Book-of-the-Month Club. (Its dishonesty was not exposed until 1967.)

Although he wrote eighteen more books, James slowly lost his self-assurance, sense of well-being, and artistic inspiration. He constantly feared being found out as a prevaricating autobiographer. He also fell into the habit of repeating some of his previously successful formulas. He turned to alcohol for stimulation and escape, which only made his decline more certain. In 1934 he was committed to a sanitarium in La Crescenta, California, for acute alcoholism. A year later his wife obtained a legal separation from him. His death, which occurred in a Hollywood hospital, was listed as caused by "alcoholic complications." His ashes were scattered over his Rocking R Ranch.

James's novels are *The Three Mustangeers* (1933), *Home Ranch* (1935), *Flint Spears, Cowboy Rodeo Contestant* (1938), and *The American Cowboy* (1942). Typical is the "mustangeers" yarn, involving the escapades of good-hearted outlaws and narrated most ungrammatically. The books James wrote for juvenile readers are *Smoky, Sand* (1929), *Big Enough* (1931), *Sun Up: Tales of the Cow Camps* (1931), *Uncle Bill: A Tale of Two Kinds of Cowboy* (1932)—*In the Saddle with Uncle Bill* (1935) and *Look-See with Uncle Bill* (1938) were continuations—*Young Cowboy* (1935), *Scorpion, a Good Bad Horse* (1936), *The Dark Horse* (1939), *My First Horse* (1940), and *Horses I've Known* (1940). *Smoky*, one of the finest horse stories ever written, tells how the mouse-colored Smoky is gentled, loved, and trained as a peppy cowpony by a ranch hand named Clint. James's adult nonfictional books are *Cowboys North and South, The Drifting Cowboy, Cow Country, Lone Cowboy, All in a Day's Riding* (1933), *Cowboy in the Making* (1937), and *The Will James Cowboy Book* (1938). Representative is *The Drifting Cowboy*, which describes bronco wrestling in rodeos, stunt men's actions in movies, range riding, and turning greenhorns into veterans—all in convincingly salty language. *Book of Cowboy Stories* (1951) is a posthumous collection of his short fiction.

James's two best books are *Smoky* and *Lone Cowboy*. Both were made into movies, as *Smoky* (1933) and *Shoot Out* (1971), respectively. Ironically, his two most popular books are *Smoky*, which was written for children, and *Lone Cowboy*, which is partly spurious. These two facts call into question the validity of much of his literary work. Most critics have been uniform in their preference for his startlingly vivid drawings over his increasingly hackneyed prose. Ultimately irksome is cowpuncher lingo such as "Uncle Bill would of liked to went along" and even "I figgers." Still and all, James at his best is fresh, natural, and pungent, and his word pictures are now pure nostalgia.

• Hundreds of letters to and from James, as well as four manuscripts and many galley and page proofs, are in the Princeton University Library. Other James papers, far fewer in number, are widely scattered in university libraries in Calif., Mass., Nebr., Nev., N.Y., Okla., Pa., Tex., and Va. Alice

Payne Hackett in *60 Years of Best Sellers 1895–1955* (1956) lists James's *Lone Cowboy* as a moderate bestseller. The most reliable biography of James is Anthony Amaral, *Will James: The Gilt Edged Cowboy* (1967; rev. ed., *Will James: The Last Cowboy Legend* [1980]). An excellent short discussion of James's writings by James K. Folsom is in *Twentieth Century Western Writers*, ed. James Vinson (1982), pp. 425–27. James's obituary in the *New York Times*, 4 Sept. 1942, repeats as fact several falsities appearing in James's autobiography.

ROBERT L. GALE

JAMESON, Horatio Gates (1778–24 Aug. 1855), anatomist and surgeon, was born in York, Pennsylvania, the son of David Jameson, a physician, and Elizabeth Davis. Jameson began his medical studies at age fifteen with his father and practiced with him from 1795, as the family moved first to West Virginia and then to Pennsylvania. In 1797, at the age of nineteen, he married Catherine Shevell of Somerset County, Pennsylvania; they had nine children. After marriage, he resided successively in Somerset County, Pennsylvania; Wheeling, West Virginia; and Adamstown and Gettysburg, Pennsylvania. In 1810 Jameson and his family moved to Baltimore. Shortly thereafter, he began to attend lectures at the University of Maryland at Baltimore, obtaining his medical degree in 1813. In addition to maintaining his medical practice he operated an apothecary.

During the War of 1812, Jameson was surgeon to the U.S. troops at Baltimore. Following the war, he continued his medical practice and wrote several papers on fevers and a popular book, *American Domestick Medicine or Medical Admonisher* (1817; rev. ed., 1818). He served as physician to the Baltimore City Jail, was surgeon to the Baltimore Hospital from 1814 to 1835, and was consulting physician to the Baltimore Board of Health from 1821 to 1835.

According to biographer Otto Juettner, Jameson "aspired to a position on the staff of the University of Maryland where he would have an opportunity to display his talents as a surgeon and teacher. Some of the men connected with the University were jealous of his rapidly gained reputation and prevented his appointment" (Juettner, p. 194). This professional snub led Jameson, along with others, to form the rival Washington Medical College in 1827. A long and bitter feud arose between the two schools resulting in both overt and covert attacks on each other. Ultimately the feud led Jameson to bring a suit in Baltimore City Court against one of his detractors, Dr. Frederick E. B. Hinze (or Hintze), for defamation of character; Hinze was found guilty and was fined. At the time, it was one of the most sensational episodes in medical annals. About the case, which was documented in the *American Medical Recorder* (Jan. 1829), the journal's editors state, "We present it without comment, not doubting that every reader will observe the nature of the *volunteer evidence*, and be pleased to see that Dr. Jameson has triumphed over the efforts of a *combination* to injure and destroy his professional reputation" (p. 209).

Jameson was founder in 1829 of the *Maryland Medical Recorder* and became one of the most influential medical editors in the United States during its years of publication (1829–1832). The conclusion of the defamation case, which was widely reported, as well as his editorial and clinical skills and his brilliance as a teacher, enhanced Jameson's reputation both nationally and abroad. In 1830 he was invited to address the medical section of the Society of German Naturalists and Physicians, which met that year in Hamburg. He was the first American to be so honored. He delivered the paper "The Non-contagiousness of Yellow Fever," which was well received, and returned to Baltimore after a two-month tour of Europe to continue his clinical and teaching activities.

In 1835 Jameson was invited by Daniel Drake, one of the most illustrious physicians of his time, to come to Cincinnati, Ohio. Drake had founded the Medical College of Ohio (the second medical school to be opened west of the Alleghenies) in 1819. Following a falling out with the faculty in 1822, Drake left the college he had founded but continued to wage an unrelenting war against the school. In 1835, under the charter of the Cincinnati College, Drake opened a rival medical school. At Drake's invitation, Jameson became president of the college and the chair of surgery at this new institution, the Medical Department of Cincinnati College. According to Juettner, it "was the crowning glory of Drake's career as a teacher." Others on the faculty with Jameson included Samuel D. Gross, who shared the chair with Drake in pathological anatomy (Gross became a revered faculty member of Jefferson Medical College in Philadelphia and at the time of his death in 1884 was generally recognized as the greatest figure in American surgery); Joseph Nash McDowell, professor of anatomy (later founder of the Missouri Medical College in St. Louis, a predecessor of the School of Medicine of Washington University); and James B. Rogers, chair in chemistry (later, a distinguished professor of chemistry at the University of Pennsylvania and one of the founders of the American Medical Association). After just one term, Jameson resigned his post in Cincinnati and returned to Baltimore in 1836 because of the failing health of his wife. She died in the following year. Jameson in 1851 married a widow, Hannah J. D. Ely; they had no children.

Jameson is described by biographer Eugene F. Cordell as a man who was

about five feet ten inches in height, well built, erect and muscular but not corpulent; his head was covered with a sufficiency of snow-white hair; his face was always cleanshaven, his complexion florid and healthy, his eyes dark brown and piercing and surmounted by bushy eyebrows, his face remarkably smooth and free from wrinkles. He retained his strength and power of endurance to the last. He wore heavy—remarkably heavy—gold spectacles. He dressed in black with a black tie, and was very careful and neat in his appearance—no one ever saw him look untidy. (Cordell, p. 786)

Among Jameson's many publications in the *Maryland Medical Recorder* and the *American Medical Recorder* were papers on the anatomy of the neck, traumatic hemorrhage, and anatomy of the parts concerned in lithotomy; extirpation of the upper jaw with ligation of the carotid artery, the first time in medical annals that this operation was performed (performed 11 November 1820, reported in the *American Medical Reporter* in 1821); ligation of the external iliac artery for an aneurism (1821); a successful tracheotomy for removal of a watermelon seed (1822); stricture of the urethra and its treatment through dilatation (1824); surgical anatomy of the neck (1824); the earliest recorded case of amputation of the cervix uteri in America in 1824 (the procedure was first done in Europe by Osiander in 1801); stricture of the esophagus with illustrations of the probes used in the treatment (1828); and a variety of other surgical reports.

Jameson was the first surgeon to conduct animal experiments to prove the superiority of animal ligatures, first introduced by Dr. Philip Syng Physick of Philadelphia, in 1814. Jameson's prize-winning research essay, "Observations upon Traumatic Hemmorrhage, Illustrated by Experiments upon Living Animals," was published in the *American Medical Recorder* in 1827. In 1854 he published a new method for treating extensive fistulae in the *American Journal of the Medical Sciences*. *A Treatise on Epidemic Cholera* was published in Philadelphia in 1854.

In 1854 Jameson returned to his birthplace in York, Pennsylvania, in the hope of obtaining the family homestead and estate. When fire destroyed the property, he moved to a residence in Philadelphia. In August 1855, while visiting New York City on matters related to his book on cholera, he was suddenly taken ill and died. Jameson is remembered for his role in establishing the Washington Medical College in Baltimore, as founder and editor of the *Maryland Medical Recorder*, and as the first surgeon to use animal experimentation to prove the value of animal ligatures.

• A significant collection of material related to Jameson can be found in the historical section of the Health Sciences Library of the University of Maryland at Baltimore. The most complete, authoritative biography is in Eugene Fauntleroy Cordell, *The Medical Annals of Maryland: 1799–1899* (1903). A shorter version by Cordell appears in *A Cyclopedia of American Medical Biography*, ed. Howard A. Kelly (1912). Otto Juettner, *Daniel Drake and His Followers: Historical and Biographical Sketches* (1909), includes a section on the Medical Department of Cincinnati College and a sketch and photograph of Jameson. Obituaries are reported to be in the *New York Evening Post* and the *Baltimore Sun*, 28 Aug. 1855.

STANLEY L. BLOCK

JAMESON, John Franklin (19 Sept. 1859–28 Sept. 1937), history professor and journal editor, was born in Somerville, Massachusetts, the son of John Jameson, a schoolteacher, lawyer, and postmaster, and Mariette Thompson. Jameson attended public schools and later the Roxbury Latin School. He was admitted to Harvard University but moved with his family to attend

Amherst College in 1875. He lived at home all four years and graduated in 1879 as class valedictorian. At Amherst, political science professor John W. Burgess and history professor Anson W. Morse made a deep impression on Jameson's intellectual development, but an equally significant influence was exerted by Herbert Baxter Adams, an Amherst alumnus who was building a department of history and political science at the Johns Hopkins University in Baltimore. Jameson received his A.B. from Amherst in 1879. Unable to pursue immediately his goal of study in Germany, he then spent an unhappy term as an instructor of Latin and history in the Worcester, Massachusetts, high school, resigning his position before he could be fired. Within the year, Adams had recruited him as a graduate student at Johns Hopkins.

Jameson spent eight years at Johns Hopkins and received the first doctorate in history given by the new school in 1882. He won a fellowship in his second year at the university and became an instructor in the fall of 1882. He was promoted to the rank of associate in 1883. His first-year thesis on the municipal history of New York City became the basis for the doctoral dissertation he completed in 1882. Publishing his dissertation, "The Origin and Development of the Municipal Government of New York City," as a two-part article in the *Magazine of American History* in 1882, another article drawing on the dissertation the following year in the same journal, and then a biography of the Dutch entrepreneur and explorer Willem Usselinx in 1887, Jameson began to establish a reputation as a scholar in institutional history and the Middle States. He also developed a strong interest in social history, which his patrician instincts prevented him from pursuing personally. Consequently, he mapped out a career as a student of historiography and an academic entrepreneur, by which means he could encourage other historians to pursue social history within a tightly controlled institutional framework.

Jameson gave a series of lectures on historiography and historical criticism at Johns Hopkins in the fall of 1886 that were published as *The History of Historical Writing in America* in 1891. His family's fragile finances collapsed when his father failed to be reappointed postmaster of Amherst following the election of 1884 and Johns Hopkins president Daniel C. Gilman made it clear that Jameson would not receive a permanent appointment at the university. In the spring of 1888, however, Brown University president Ezekiel G. Robinson invited Jameson to accept the professorship of history there, and Jameson eagerly returned to New England.

Jameson's aloof personality and dislike of Brown's genteel atmosphere made his initial experience at the university somewhat unhappy, but the arrival of former Brown professor E. Benjamin Andrews as president in the fall of 1889 and Jameson's marriage to Sara Elizabeth Elwell, a schoolteacher, in April 1893, transformed his outlook. The couple had two children.

Jameson worked to improve the instructional resources at Brown, raising money for history books and serving as the secretary of the library committee. He created a modest replica of the Johns Hopkins seminary for history undergraduates and published the best papers as a book in 1894. Seeing an opportunity in the centennial celebration of the adoption of the Constitution, Jameson enlisted past and present members of the Johns Hopkins seminary to contribute to a volume titled *Essays in the Constitutional History of the United States*, which he edited and published in 1889. He attempted to chart the early political and constitutional history of the United States, lecturing on the origin of political parties in the United States at Brown in 1889, and on the political and constitutional history of the South at Johns Hopkins in the spring of 1891. These lectures remained unpublished in his lifetime, and the lectures he delivered at Barnard College in 1895 on the American Revolution as a social movement were not published until 1926. His most substantial scholarly production at Brown was an edition of the papers of John C. Calhoun, published in the annual report of the American Historical Association (AHA) for 1899.

It was the AHA, which Jameson helped to establish in 1884, that supplied him with the proper outlet for his talents and ambition. He was named the first chair of its Historical Manuscripts Commission in 1895. Leaders of the AHA gave him his opportunity for permanent distinction the same year by appointing him the first managing editor of the *American Historical Review* (*AHR*), a post he held till 1928, with the exception of the years 1901 to 1905. Elected second vice president of the AHA in 1905, Jameson became the first professional historian to gain its presidency in 1907. These activities kept him from writing a major historical work.

Jameson left Brown in the spring of 1901 to accept the chair of the history department at the University of Chicago. There he reinvigorated a stagnating department and added both new professors and new courses in American social history. Yet another opportunity soon emerged, however, when philanthropist Andrew Carnegie decided in January 1902 to establish a $10 million endowment for an institute of scientific research in Washington, D.C. This made realistic Jameson's plans for a school of historical studies in the nation's capital. An AHA committee that Jameson chaired won the approval of the Carnegie Institution of Washington for a Bureau of Historical Research. Jameson's close associate, Andrew C. McLaughlin, became the first director of the bureau in 1903, but his resignation two years later gave Jameson the opportunity to abandon university teaching and come to Washington as director of the renamed Department of Historical Research.

At the Carnegie Institution, Jameson saw himself building a scientifically rigorous and intellectually autonomous historical profession, but the difficulty of accomplishing this task soon became apparent. Jameson's training as a scientific historian told him that the discovery of documents was primary, and his most substantial achievement during his first decade at the Carnegie Institution was the publication of a series of guides to foreign archives for significant documents in American history as well as a guide to archives useful for religious history in the United States. Still, the physical scientists who controlled the Carnegie Institution expressed skepticism at Jameson's claim that as a scientific historian, he could discover facts but draw no conclusions, and they sharply limited the scope of his activities. He raised money to produce *Writings on American History*, an annual bibliography, but found few individuals and libraries willing to subscribe to it. A congressional charter granted to the AHA in 1889 enabled it to publish its annual report, containing historical articles and documents, at public expense through the Smithsonian Institution. The Smithsonian excluded material it deemed politically sensitive, however, tarnishing Jameson's reputation as acting AHA secretary. Jameson generated considerable public support in 1906 for a national archives building and a national historical publications commission, but he could not persuade Congress to appropriate funds for these objectives.

Jameson returned in 1906 as managing editor of the *AHR* after a four-year hiatus. Although he proceeded to raise the journal to a new standard of excellence, his authoritarian attitude angered many historians outside the northeastern United States, who found their work slighted. Between 1913 and 1915, insurgent historians charged Jameson and his colleagues in the AHA leadership with being both dictatorial and malfeasant. The AHA membership dismissed these charges at its 1915 annual meeting but voted changes in the AHA charter that made its procedures more democratic.

The entry of the United States into World War I in April 1917 gave Jameson an opportunity to enhance his claim to leadership by sponsoring the creation of the National Board for Historical Service at the Carnegie Institution. Jameson wrote and edited historical material to be presented to soldiers in their training camps, and he encouraged the publication of articles in the *AHR* that supported the Allies. In 1918 he and Samuel N. Harper, a professor of political science at the University of Chicago, were recruited by George Creel, the director of the government's Committee on Public Information, to authenticate documents obtained by American businessman George Sisson that purported to demonstrate a German-Bolshevik conspiracy. The "Sisson documents" were denounced in the press as a hoax, and Jameson's professional reputation once more came under attack.

In the postwar years Jameson attempted to lower his profile within the AHA but maintained an intense level of activity in a wide range of projects. With the archival guides largely completed, he focused attention on the creation of documentary editions of the letters of delegates to the Continental Congress, the slave trade, slave law cases, and the papers of Andrew Jackson. Jameson personally edited a volume of documents on privateering and piracy in 1923. He directed the preparation of an atlas of American history. Jameson involved himself in the restoration of historical scholarship in Europe, incorporated the American Council of Learned Societies in 1919, and used the ACLS as a platform to secure $500,000 from Adolph S. Ochs, the publisher of the *New York Times*, for the creation of the multivolume *Dictionary of American Biography*, beginning in 1927. In 1926 Jameson achieved permanent scholarly distinction through the publication of his *The American Revolution Considered as a Social Movement*, a revised version of the Barnard lectures that he had presented the previous year as the Vanuxem Lecturer at Princeton University. When Congress appropriated funds in 1926 as part of the Omnibus Public Buildings Act for a national archives building, Jameson served on an intergovernmental committee that oversaw the construction of the building, finally completed in 1934. He played a key role in writing legislation that created the National Archives as a federal agency in 1934, and successfully promoted the candidacy of Robert D. W. Conner, a history professor at the University of North Carolina, as the first archivist of the United States.

John C. Merriam, a paleontologist who became the president of the Carnegie Institution in 1920, decided in 1927 that both the department of historical research and its director had outlived their usefulness. Jameson was informed that he would not be permitted to remain in his position beyond age seventy, the mandatory retirement age, in 1929. On his departure, the institution's department of historical research redirected its attention to historical archaeology in Mexico under the supervision of A. V. Kidder, and Jameson also resigned his editorship of the *AHR*.

As his career at the Carnegie Institution ended, Jameson received an offer from Herbert Putnam, the librarian of Congress, to take direction of the Division of Manuscripts at the Library of Congress and to occupy a newly endowed chair in American history. Jameson assumed his new responsibilities in the fall of 1928 and remained in charge of the Division of Manuscripts until his death. He distinguished himself and enhanced the reputation of the Library of Congress by acquiring the papers of Alexander Stephens, Andrew Carnegie, Joseph Pulitzer, Admiral John Dahlgren, and other significant figures in American history. In good health most of his life, Jameson suffered a heart attack in April 1932 and was forced to curtail much of his activity. After being struck by a car and suffering a broken leg in March 1937, he returned to his work at the Library of Congress shortly after Labor Day. On 21 September he left the library early complaining of chest pains and died a week later in his Washington, D.C., home from heart disease and pneumonia.

Jameson intended to provide a unifying explanation for American history. Instead, he stimulated a dialogue about that history among scholars, as well as between scholars and the general public, that continued through the remainder of the twentieth century.

• Jameson's papers are housed in the Library of Congress, as are the records of the American Historical Association, the American Council of Learned Societies, and the National Board for Historical Service. A collection of Jameson's correspondence, *An Historian's World: Selections from the Correspondence of John Franklin Jameson*, ed. Elizabeth Donnan and Leo F. Stock (1956), includes an informative biographical sketch. Ruth Anna Fisher and William Fox, eds., *J. Franklin Jameson: A Tribute* (1965), contains personal recollections and an annotated bibliography. The first volume of Morey Rothberg and Jacqueline Goggin, eds., *John Franklin Jameson and the Development of Humanistic Scholarship in America* (3 vols., 1993–1999), contains a biographical overview and comprehensive bibliography of writings by and about Jameson. See also Morey Rothberg, "Servant to History: A Study of John Franklin Jameson, 1859–1937" (Ph.D. diss., Brown Univ., 1982), and Fred Shelley, "The Interest of J. Franklin Jameson in the National Archives, 1908–1934," *American Archivist* (Apr. 1949). An obituary appeared in the *New York Times*, 29 Sept. 1937.

MOREY ROTHBERG

JAMISON, Cecilia Viets (1837?–11 Apr. 1909), painter and writer, was born in Yarmouth, Nova Scotia, Canada, the daughter of Viets Dakin and Elizabeth Bruce. Her Tory family had left the United States during the American Revolution. They resettled in Nova Scotia, where her paternal relatives had lived, including her great-grandfather, the Reverend Roger Viets, who was vicar general of Canada. When she was a teenager, she and her family moved back to the United States, settling in Boston. There and in New York she attended private schools, where she studied to be an artist.

Around 1860 Jamison married George Hamilton, a Boston artist in whose studio she worked. Little is known of their divorce and less of their marriage. Sometime after her marriage she traveled to Europe, settling in Rome for three years to follow her vocation as an artist. She also pursued writing and mingled with a circle that included Henry Wadsworth Longfellow. He read and corrected her draft of *Woven in Many Threads*, and his remarks encouraged the publication in 1872 of this first novel, which the public received well.

Jamison kept studios in New York City and Boston and continued to work as an artist even as her writing career began its arc. She completed portraits, the best known being of the naturalist Louis Agassiz and Longfellow. She published *Something To Do: A Novel* (1871), *A Crown from the Spear* (1872), *Ropes of Sand, and Other Stories* (1873), and *My Bonnie Lass* (1877), as well as shorter works of fiction and nonfiction for periodicals. On 28 October 1878 she married Samuel Jamison, a man eleven years her junior (which may be one reason she preferred to give her birth date as 1848). Her husband kept a law office in New York City although he was a Louisiana native. The newly married couple returned to his farm, "Live Oak Plantation" (near Thibodeaux).

In 1887 the Jamisons moved to New Orleans, where Jamison wrote her most successful novels: *The Story of an Enthusiast* (1888), *Lady Jane* (1891), *Toinnette's*

Philip (1894), *Seraph, the Little Violiniste* (1896), *Thistledown* (1903), and *The Penhallow Family* (1905). Though childless, she developed an ability to write about and for children through her juvenilia. For example, in "Part Fifth: A Strange Legacy" of *A Crown from the Spear*, Jamison describes the child Aimée, found by a priest: "She is so ugly one can never love her, and she is so wicked one can scarcely pity her." The narrator continues the description: "When he thought she was a strange looking object, he thought correctly; for a more impish, weird-looking little creature, with folded hands and ridiculously grave face, never disturbed the peace of a celibate." The child transfigures those around her before the hortatory novel ends.

In an 1894 profile for *St. Nicholas*, a children's magazine, Olive Otis remarked on two of Jamison's books, *The Story of an Enthusiast* and *Lady Jane*: "Both are stories of child-life showing a profound study of that tender and imaginative age when impressions are so vivid, sufferings so keen and when startling events leave indelible traces on the pliable mind and unformed character of the child." Otis also compared Jamison's *Lady Jane* with Frances Hodgson Burnett's *Little Lord Fauntleroy* and referred to them as "companion" pieces (neither read seriously 100 years after their composing). *Lady Jane* was translated into Norwegian, French, and German and set in Braille.

Jamison lived in a "pretty cottage" on St. Charles Avenue in New Orleans and, preferring quiet to society, she filled her world with books and flowers and her work. A portrait reproduced in Otis's article shows Jamison in 1880, her face averted from the artist and dignity defining her carriage. The Jamisons wintered in Louisiana, where the novelist invested in the social welfare of New Orleans, and summered in Nahant, Massachusetts, where Cecilia Jamison's sister kept a summer home. She returned to Nahant when her husband died in 1902, and she died in Roxbury, Massachusetts.

Jamison published short stories in such periodicals as *Scribner's*, *Appleton's Journal*, and *Harper's*. Her novels sometimes first appeared as serials in these publications; for example, Otis's profile of Jamison in *St. Nicholas* followed the final installment of *Toinnette's Philip*. Jamison gained a reputation as a writer of "local color" and has been labeled a "regionalist." Her notable art work included portraits of Longfellow and of Louis Agassiz, the naturalist.

• Biographical information about Jamison is in Olive Otis, "Mrs. Cecile Viets Jamison," *St. Nicholas*, Apr. 1894. Obituaries appear in the *Boston Transcript* and the *New Orleans Daily Picayune*, both 13 Apr. 1909.

MARTHA K. BAKER

JAMISON, David (1660–26 July 1739), colonial lawyer and provincial official, was born in Scotland and probably went to college there. Nothing is known for certain regarding his parentage or early life. His coming to New York in 1685 was hardly auspicious. Jamison was expelled from his native country and transported to America because of his association with religious zealots known as the "Sweet Singers." Their defiance of both Anglican orthodoxy and the restored Stuart monarchy landed them in jail, from whence they were deported. However, his arrest in Scotland, transportation to New York, and subsequent servitude apparently wrought a change in Jamison's attitude. Far from remaining the religious and political outcast, he diligently sought acceptance.

To pay for his voyage to New York, Jamison was bound out for four years to George Lockhart of Woodbridge, New Jersey, but he shortly passed into the hands of the Reverend Josiah Clarke, Anglican chaplain of the British troops at Fort James. Some of the principal men in New York City purchased his time from Clarke and set up the well-educated young Scot as master of a Latin school, one of the earliest in New York City. Sometime over the next few years he also became a clerk to Matthew Clarkson, provincial secretary. It is not clear how long he continued the Latin school, but in 1691 Jamison was made deputy provincial secretary and clerk of the council. He subsequently farmed the secretaryship from Clarkson and began to study law, though whether he studied on his own or in someone's office is not known. In 1692 Jamison married Mary Hardenbrook; they had two children.

As clerk of the council, Jamison kept the minutes of the notorious court that condemned Jacob Leisler and Jacob Milborne to death in late 1691. Thereafter Jamison was identified with the Anti-Leislerians, who dominated the provincial government under Governor Benjamin Fletcher (1692–1698). His education and growing knowledge of the law made him especially useful to Governor Fletcher, who turned New York City into a haven for pirates and parceled out most of the available land in the province to his friends and associates. As clerk of the council, Jamison recorded documents turning millions of acres of New York's best lands to Fletcher's cronies. Jamison garnered extensive acres, including part of the Great Nine Partners Patent in Duchess County and lands in Westchester County held in partnership with Caleb Heathcote. However, because of his close association with the Fletcher regime, Jamison incurred the wrath of the Earl of Bellomont, who became governor in 1698 and removed Jamison as deputy secretary and clerk of the council.

Lord Bellomont, allying himself with the Leislerians, was determined to rid New York of its pirates and land grabbers. He described Jamison as a "violent enemy of the government," one "condemned to be hanged in Scotland for burning the Bible and for blasphemy" (O'Callahan and Fernow, vol. 4, p. 429). According to Bellomont, Jamison and most of the other New York lawyers were "all under such a scandalous character, that it would grieve a man to see our noble English laws so miserably mangled and profaned" (O'Callaghan and Fernow, vol. 4, p. 442). Finally, the new governor denounced Jamison, the former religious zealot, as a hypocritical bigamist who had left a wife and child in Scotland and had married another woman in New York. The charge was false, but it resonated well among the New York Leislerians.

The Anti-Leislerians fought back against Bellomont, with Jamison coordinating their efforts in New York City. When Bellomont's zeal to expel the pirates led in 1698 to the rigorous enforcement of the Navigation Acts in New York, Jamison joined with other city merchants in complaining to King William that the governor had ruined commerce in the province. When Bellomont tried in May 1699 to take back the Manhattan property known as the King's Farm, whose rents Governor Fletcher had turned over to Trinity Church, Jamison joined with other leading Anglicans in protesting to the bishop of London. After Bellomont died in 1701, his successor, Lieutenant Governor John Nanfan, continued his policies, much to the chagrin of Jamison and other Anti-Leislerians.

The next royal governor, Lord Cornbury, was, unlike Bellomont, a Tory. Cornbury favored the Anti-Leislerians, propagated the Anglican faith, granted land to his friends, and pocketed lucrative fees for doing so. A staunch Anglican who served periodically as church warden and vestryman of Trinity Church, Jamison appreciated Cornbury's patronage of the Anglican faith, especially his transferring ownership of the Queen's Farm (formerly the King's Farm) to Trinity Church. Cornbury also strengthened the charter of Trinity Church and prevailed upon the Anglican Society for the Propagation of the Gospel in Foreign Parts to subsidize missionaries in New York. However, in 1707, when Cornbury arrested the Presbyterian Francis Makemie for preaching without a license, Jamison believed the governor was threatening religious freedom and served as one of the attorneys who defended Makemie.

Although an Anti-Leislerian partisan and a dedicated Anglican, Jamison recognized the benefits of both political compromise and religious toleration. As early as 1701, the year he reentered provincial government as surveyor general, he advocated moderation toward the Leislerians. "We desire none of them hurt," he wrote to Livingston regarding the Leislerians. Similarly, his defense of Makemie relied heavily on the necessity of toleration, given New York's religiously diverse population.

Jamison's commonsense attitude toward both religion and politics was much appreciated by Governor Robert Hunter (1710–1719), under whose enlightened leadership New York society finally transcended the factious political legacy of Leisler. Economic issues, especially commercial regulations and land policy, were coming to dominate politics, and Jamison possessed considerable influence among the merchants of New York City and the Hudson Valley landlords. In matters of both church and state, Governor Hunter sought his advice and praised his legal abilities "as inferior to none on this side" of the Atlantic. Contrary to Bellomont's portrayal, Hunter defended Jamison as "ye greatest man I ever knew; and I think of the most unblemished life and conversation of any of his rank in these parts." As for the charge of having a wife and child in Scotland, Hunter admitted that a woman had come to New York who claimed to have had a child by Jamison "in his wild days." Jamison never married the woman in question. His first wife having died, in 1703 he married Johanna Meech.

Hunter rewarded Jamison handsomely. The governor in 1711 appointed Jamison chief justice of New Jersey and in 1712 recorder of the city of New York and attorney general of New York. In 1716 Jamison was perhaps the leading attorney in New York City and was known to have "acquired a considerable estate." On several occasions Hunter recommended Jamison for membership on the councils of both New York and New Jersey, though the Board of Trade, still influenced perhaps by Bellomont's earlier accusations, never did approve the recommendation. Early in the tenure of Governor William Burnet (1720–1728), Jamison's political influence began to wane, and he lost the offices of attorney general of New York in 1721, chief justice of New Jersey in 1723, and recorder of the city of New York in 1724.

Jamison died in New York City. Although he began as an indentured servant, he had the education and possessed the drive to become a member of the economic and political elite. His greatest contribution was to New York politics, building coalitions among various factions and moderating the vindictiveness of the Leisler era.

• Jamison's correspondence is widely scattered in the collected papers of others, especially the Robert Livingston Manuscripts in the Livingston-Redmond papers at the Franklin D. Roosevelt Library, Hyde Park, N.Y. Jamison's career and comments about him by Bellomont and Hunter are traced in Edmund B. O'Callaghan and Berthold Fernow, eds., *Documents Relative to the Colonial History of the State of New York*, vols. 4–5 (15 vols., 1856–1887). Jamison's relationship with the Anglican church in New York is in Edward T. Corwin and Hugh Hastings, eds., *Ecclesiastical Records of the State of New York*, vol. 3 (7 vols., 1901–1916). His involvement in the Makemie controversy is noted in William Smith, Jr., *The History of the Province of New York*, ed. Michael Kammen (1972). His career is summarized by O'Callaghan, "David Jamison, Attorney-General of the Province of New York, 1710," *Magazine of American History* 1, no. 1 (Jan. 1877): 19–24. Jamison's political involvement is discussed in Lawrence Leder, *Robert Livingston, 1654–1728, and the Politics of Colonial New York* (1961), and Mary Lou Lustig, *Robert Hunter, 1666–1734: New York's Augustan Statesman* (1983). Jamison's genealogy is discussed briefly in the *New York Genealogical and Biographical Record* (Oct. 1874).

RONALD W. HOWARD

JANAUSCHEK, Fanny (20 July 1830–28 Nov. 1904), actress, was born Franziska Romana Magdalena Janauschek in Prague, Bohemia, the daughter of a tailor and a theater laundress (names unknown). Given the family's modest economic circumstances, the nine Janauschek offspring were sent to work from childhood. Fanny danced in a children's corps de ballet and later studied piano under Herr Stegmeyer; however, a serious cut to her hand at age thirteen prevented her planned debut that year. Fanny, a mezzo-soprano, entered the Prague Conservatory in her early teens to train for the operatic stage. She remained there until an actor named Baudius detected her dramatic talent and began coaching her for a career in theater.

Janauschek made her stage debut in 1846 at the age of sixteen at the Royal Theatre of Prague in a comedy, *Ich Bleibe Ledig* (*I'm Still Single*). She went on to win recognition in the German theater, appearing with companies in Kemnitz, Heilbron, and Leipzig. In 1848 an engagement at Cologne's Stadttheater brought Janauschek to the attention of Julius Benedix, who further trained her and that same year made her his leading actress in the Stadttheater of Frankfurt am Main. While engaged there (1849–1861) and at the Hoftheater in Dresden (1861–1863), Janauschek earned renown on tours to Russia, as well as throughout Germany and Austria. The king of Bavaria fêted her during a four-month guest engagement in Munich. As an actress of classic tragic roles in the grand declamatory manner, she earned the sobriquet "the German Rachel" after the great French actress Rachel (Elisabeth Félix), who revived neoclassicism at the Comédie-Française when Romanticism was at its peak.

Producer Jacob Grau brought Janauschek to the United States in 1867, and she made her American debut in the title role of Franz Grillparzer's *Medea* on 9 October 1867 at the New York Academy of Music under the management of Max Maretzek. She performed in German in a repertoire that included *Mary Stuart*, *Deborah*, and *Brunhilde*. Following her New York engagement, Janauschek performed in Chicago and other cities with large German populations. In Boston on 7 November 1868 Janauschek played Lady Macbeth in German to actor Edwin Booth's Macbeth in English. Encouraged by her success with American audiences and at the urging of producer Augustin Daly, she began studying English. Two years later she was ready to make her English-language debut. Under Daly's management Janauschek opened with *Deborah* at the New York Academy of Music on 9 October 1870. Her English was found surprisingly accurate, and her acting, though employing "melodramatic effects," demonstrated "the vital fire of genius" (*New York Daily Tribune*, 10 Oct. 1870). That season she also performed in English her other roles from the German repertoire, as well as Lady Macbeth.

During Janauschek's 1874 engagement at Booth's Theatre, the *New York Times* declared her Mary Stuart to be her "most powerful character" (4 Mar. 1874). Her Medea brought

the revelation of the most superlatively original and unmistakable histrionic genius we have ever seen. . . . The first act served chiefly as an exhibition of Janauschek's marvelous declamatory powers. . . . The second act afforded Janauschek her grandest opportunities. Here every passion by which *Medea* is shaken was brought into view. One succeeded the other with extraordinary rapidity. . . . [In the third act] sorrow and despair contended with pride, jealousy, and hatred, and the pathos of the scene, as Janauschek played it, was a pathos too deep for tears. The whole of this act was a marvel not of art, but of genius. (7 Mar. 1874)

Her Lady Macbeth "brought forth a number of original readings, which, while never given for the mere sake of effect, evidenced, in the strongest possible light, the originality and strength of this actress's peculiar genius" (8 Mar. 1874). As Queen Katharine in *King Henry VIII*, "Mme. Janauschek displayed those powers of intensely fervent acting which she undoubtedly possesses, coupled with the womanly pride and queenly dignity" (13 Mar. 1874). After spending several years in Europe (1874–1880) Janauschek returned to Booth's Theatre for a March 1881 engagement, repeating her previous roles and others to similar acclaim. The only major roles she added to her repertoire were Hortense and Lady Dedlock in *Bleak House* and Meg Merrilies, the old gypsy woman in *Guy Mannering*.

Janauschek continued touring until the 1890s, but by then her grand manner had been deemed old-fashioned. Hoping to revitalize her career, she turned to melodrama and, briefly, vaudeville. As Mother Mandelbaum in *The Great Diamond Robbery* during the 1895–1896 season, Janauschek deployed her larger-than-life passions, but the material embarrassed her. Paralyzed by a stroke in 1900, she lived out her last years in poverty and blindness; she died in Amityville, Long Island.

She may have married Frederick J. Pillot in 1854, but both denied it. Pillot, a self-styled baron, seems to have made some financial claims on her before he died of drink in 1884.

Janauschek's American stage career was distinguished by her tragic power in the classic plays of the nineteenth century. At the end of her career she was regarded as the last of the great international actresses in the grand tradition.

• Materials on Janauschek are held in the Harvard Theatre Collection and the Billy Rose Collection at Lincoln Center. The *New York Dramatic Mirror* published an interview with Janauschek on 4 Aug. 1894. In addition to entries in the standard biographical sources, see those in John Bouvé Clapp and Edwin Francis Edgett, *Players of the Present* (1899), and Frederic Edward McKay and Charles E. L. Wingate, eds., *Famous American Actors of To-Day* (1896). She is also included in William C. Young, *Famous Actors and Actresses of the American Stage*, vol. 1 (1975). An obituary is in the *New York Dramatic Mirror*, 10 Dec. 1904.

FELICIA HARDISON LONDRÉ

JANEWAY, Charles Alderson (26 May 1909–28 May 1981), medical researcher, was born in New York City, the son of Theodore Caldwell Janeway and Eleanor C. Alderson. Janeway's father and his grandfather, Edward G. Janeway, were both eminent physicians and professors of medicine. In the spring of 1914 William Henry Welch lured Charles's father from his position as a professor of medicine at Columbia to a similar post at Johns Hopkins School of Medicine in Baltimore.

Theodore Janeway died, however, a few years after the arrival of the family in Baltimore, his health broken by his frenetic dual service to Hopkins and to the surgeon general's office during the early months of U.S. entry into World War I. At the age of eight, Charles was left without a father but with a legacy of achievement in medicine. He attended several private schools, including the Milton Academy in Massachusetts. In 1930 he graduated with a B.A. from Yale University. He then gained admission to Cornell University Medical College in New York City, where he studied for two years before transferring to Johns Hopkins School of Medicine. Janeway married Elizabeth Bradley in 1932; they had four children. In 1934 he received an M.D. from Johns Hopkins.

After hospital internships in Boston and Baltimore, Janeway was called in 1937 to join the staff of Harvard University Medical School, where he would spend the remainder of his long, illustrious career. During World War II he worked under Harvard physical chemist Edwin J. Cohn as a member of a large research team investigating the chemical components of human blood. Janeway supervised many of the clinical tests associated with this important wartime research, which was funded at a high level by the federal government because of the military urgency of developing and maintaining a massive medical supply of blood products.

Largely on the basis of his accomplishments with Cohn's group during the war, Janeway rapidly rose through the ranks at Harvard. In 1937 he had begun as a research fellow in bacteriology and immunology, and less than ten years later (1946) he was named Thomas Morgan Rotch Professor of Pediatrics. In the same year he was granted this endowed chair, he was also named physician in chief at Boston's Children's Hospital Medical Center. Janeway was thus able to exercise a powerful influence on the development of pediatrics at Harvard. Under his leadership the Department of Pediatrics at Harvard also grew to become a center for the training of leading pediatric practitioners who came from and returned to many nations.

Janeway believed in the value of research and was himself a highly productive medical scientist, publishing more than 200 papers in scientific journals during his career. Much of his most important work dealt with the therapeutic uses of gamma globulin. As department chair, he encouraged those under him to follow his investigative example, and he played a major role in providing the facilities necessary for many types of pediatric research at Harvard. But Janeway's vision of medicine was not a restricted, technical one. On the contrary, he believed strongly in the necessity of a connection between academic and community medicine. This belief was best demonstrated by his successful effort to establish Harvard's Family Health Care Program in 1954. This venture provided an organized approach to the education of medical students and residents in the delivery of primary patient care to families in the community surrounding Harvard Medical School. In this work Janeway was a pioneer in a trend that took hold more firmly three or four decades later: the emphasis in American medical schools on the training of family physicians rather than the preparation of narrow specialists.

Janeway also assumed many important responsibilities outside Harvard. From 1945 through 1950 he served the American Red Cross as chair of the committee on blood and blood derivatives. He was chair of a similarly named committee for the National Research Council from 1948 through 1951. He chaired the medical advisory board of the National Foundation for Muscular Dystrophy from the mid-1950s to the late 1960s. He maintained active membership in a number of professional associations, serving as president of the Society of Pediatric Research (1955) and the American Pediatric Society (1971).

Janeway died in Weston, Massachusetts. He had lived up to and even exceeded the medical success that his grandfather and father had found before him.

• The work and reputations of Janeway's father and grandfather are addressed in Simon Flexner and James Thomas Flexner, *William Henry Welch and the Heroic Age of Medicine* (1941), pp. 121–22, 325–26; and Saul Benison, *Tom Rivers: Reflections on a Life in Medicine and Science* (1967), pp. 25–27, 39–42. Biographical information is in Henry Beecher and Mark Altschule, *Medicine at Harvard: The First Three Hundred Years* (1977), pp. 352–53. The blood research in which Janeway participated during World War II is addressed in Edwin J. Cohn, "The History of Plasma Fractionation," pp. 365–66, and Charles A. Janeway and J. L. Oncley, "Blood Substitutes," pp. 450–54, both in *Advances in Military Medicine*, ed. E. C. Andrus (1948); and Douglas Starr, "Again and Again in World War II, Blood Made the Difference," *Smithsonian* 25 (Mar. 1995): 125–38. An obituary is in the *New York Times*, 31 May 1981.

JON M. HARKNESS

JANEWAY, Edward Gamaliel (31 Aug. 1841–10 Feb. 1911), physician and professor of medicine, was born in New Brunswick, New Jersey, the son of George Jacob Janeway, a physician, and Matilda Smith. Janeway attended Rutgers College, from which he graduated in 1860, and then entered the College of Physicians and Surgeons in New York. His study of medicine was interrupted for a year by service at the U.S. Army Hospital in Newark (1862–1863), which significantly augmented his clinical experience. He received his medical degree in 1864 and joined the house staff of Bellevue Hospital. In 1866 Janeway became curator of Bellevue. In this position, with his colleagues Francis Delafield and J. W. Southack, he improved the hospital's record keeping and autopsy service and published methodical case reports of the autopsies performed. This extensive experience with dissection formed the basis for his thorough knowledge of pathological anatomy and his remarkable diagnostic acumen. During this period, he also served as visiting physician (1868–1871) and chief of staff (1870–1871) at Charity Hospital in New York City, as visiting physician at the Hospital for Epileptics and Paralyzed (1870–1874), and as professor of physiological and pathological anatomy at the University of the City of New York (1871–1872). He married Frances Strong Rogers in 1871; they had four children, including Theodore Caldwell Janeway, who also became a noted physician.

In 1872 Janeway became professor of pathological anatomy at Bellevue, a position that he held for nine years. In addition to giving anatomy lectures, he at various times conducted anatomy demonstrations for medical students, taught courses in physical diagnosis, and lectured on materia medica, therapeutics, and clinical medicine. In 1876 he was appointed to professorships in histology, clinical medicine, and the nervous system. From 1875 to 1881 he also served as health commissioner of New York City. As a public health official, Janeway worked to improve disease surveillance, the uniformity of vital statistics, and city sanitation, and he strongly advocated the use of autopsies as a valuable public health tool. In 1881 he was named professor of diseases of the mind and nervous system and associate professor of medicine at Bellevue and in 1886 succeeded Austin Flint as professor of the principles and practice of medicine and clinical medicine. He was then at the height of his career and widely sought after as a consultant. He prided himself on his availability to physicians and patients, maintaining a reasonable fee schedule and traveling willingly throughout the city and suburbs to see cases.

Janeway's reputation was built on his superior diagnostic skills and his knowledge and interest in many different areas of medicine. Differential diagnosis, the systematic comparison and contrasting of clinical findings to determine the correct diagnosis among those possible for a given patient, particularly interested him and inspired several papers. He cautioned against overreliance on any one specific symptom or "sign," and promoted the use of the new laboratory and microscopic diagnostic tools. Rudolf Virchow's work on cellular pathology and Jean-Martin Charcot and Edward Seguin's on neurological disease interested Janeway, and he incorporated these ideas into his own teaching. He also wrote and lectured on cancer, liver disease, and tuberculosis. Among other contributions, he is credited with the first American description of leukemia (1876) and with the differential diagnosis of chronic (tertiary) syphilitic fever and tuberculosis (1898).

Janeway always disdained self-promotion and the machinations of medical politics. In 1892, unable to resolve a policy dispute with his Bellevue colleagues, he was forced to resign his chair. He then devoted most of his time to his consultation practice and to clinical teaching. From 1898 to 1905 he served as professor of medicine and dean of the faculty of the merged medical schools of New York University and Bellevue. He was elected president of the New York Academy of Medicine (1897–1898) and of the Association of American Physicians (1900). He returned to public health as an advisor to the New York City Chamber of Commerce during the threatened cholera outbreak of 1892 and advised Hermann Biggs, director of laboratories of the New York City Health Department, on establishing an effective program of tuberculosis surveillance. Janeway served as visiting physician to Mt. Sinai Hospital from 1883 to 1897 and as consulting physician to many of the city's major hospitals until his death. In his last decade he was very active in the antituberculosis movement; he attended several international congresses and advocated improved surveillance, the establishment of sanitoria, and an end to the stigmatization of tuberculosis victims. He became president of the National Association for the Study and Prevention of Tuberculosis in 1910. After some months of illness, he died at his country home in Summit, New Jersey.

• Janeway published little in comparison with other physicians of his stature, but several of his papers are of interest. In particular see "Danger of Error in Diagnosis between Chronic Syphilitic Fever and Tuberculosis," *American Journal of the Medical Sciences* 116 (1898): 251–55; "Limitations of Pathognomonic Signs and Symptoms," *Journal of the American Medical Association* 3 (1884): 116–20; and "The Progress of Medicine," *Transactions of the New York Academy of Medicine* 12 (1895): 449–79. No biography exists, but there is James Bayard Clark, *Some Personal Recollections of Dr. Janeway* (1917), as well as some short articles by persons who knew Janeway: Theodore C. Janeway, "Edward Gamaliel Janeway," in *Dictionary of American Medical Biography*, ed. Howard A. Kelly and Walter L. Burrage (1928), pp. 649–52; and S. Adolphus Knopf, "Dr. Edward G. Janeway," *New York Medical Journal* 95 (1912): 105–107, which examines in particular Janeway's antituberculosis work.

DANIEL M. FOX
MARCIA L. MELDRUM

JANIS, Elsie (16 Mar. 1889–26 Feb. 1956), variety artist and writer, was born Elsie Jane Bierbower in Marion, Ohio, the daughter of John Eleazer Bierbower, a railway worker, and Jane Elizabeth Cockrell, a real estate agent. At the age of four she was a natural mimic, adept at picking up the mannerisms and idiosyncrasies of visitors to her parents' home. Though she was considered a dreadful child by the proper ladies of Marion, "Little Elsie" soon became a popular addition at church gatherings, dinner parties, and club affairs. Her formal career began with a local stock company, where she made her debut as Cain in *The Charity Ball* on 24 December 1897. Elsie's father was set against her theatrical pursuits, whereupon Jenny Bierbower sued for divorce, secured custody of her two children, and thereafter devoted her life to directing her daughter's career. Elsie later recounted these early years in her autobiography: "I was a strange little puppet. She pulled the strings, or turned me on and off at will, like a music box. She even made up my face until I was past thirteen!"

"Little Elsie" made her New York debut in 1900 at E. E. Rice's Casino Theatre Roof Garden, imitating well-known stars of the day—Edna May, May Irwin, Eddie Foy, Weber and Fields, Lillian Russell, and Dan Daly. Her impersonations were so accurate that her mother had her imitate performers who had recently played in the same theater, allowing the audience to compare the original with the imitation. It was often said that Elsie did not resemble any of the men and women she impersonated. She used only her body and voice, with her hair as the main prop. She kept a small comb concealed in one hand, and after quickly twisting, pulling, or patting her hair into a certain configuration, she would jam the comb into place and proceed with the imitation. Despite her popularity, Elsie was forced to leave New York by the Gerry Society (whose goal was to prohibit children under sixteen from singing and dancing on the public stage), and for the next several years she successfully toured the Keith-Albee and Orpheum circuits with her program of impersonations.

"Little Elsie" adopted the stage name of Elsie Janis when a theatrical photographer lopped off Bierbower and modified her middle name. In 1904 she joined a musical stock company and continued her specialties in *Jack in the Beanstalk*, *The Belle of New York*, *The Fortune Teller*, and *The Little Duchess*. Her first substantial "hit" was at the New York Wistaria Grove in a vaudeville show entitled *When We Are Forty-One* (1905). In that production she earned up to $1,000 a week, making her the highest-paid sixteen-year-old in the country. For the next five years she starred in several Broadway musicals, written as vehicles for her imitations: *The Vanderbilt Cup* (1906), *The Hoyden* (1907), *The Fair Co-Ed* (1908), and *The Slim Princess* (1910). She made her British musical hall debut at the Palace Theatre in London in a revue entitled *The Passing Show of 1914*, scoring one of the greatest successes ever achieved by an American entertainer. The following year she was hired by a Hollywood producer to write and star in four unsuccessful silent films: *The Caprices of Kitty*, *Betty in Search of a Thrill*, *Nearly a Lady*, and *'Twas Ever Thus*. She reappeared at the Palace Theatre in a 1915 edition of *The Passing Show* and subsequently returned to the United States to star in three new musical comedies and once again tour the vaudeville circuit.

In 1918, nine months after the United States entered World War I, Elsie Janis embarked on what she described as "the eight most glorious months of my life." She became the first American entertainer to perform for the American Expeditionary Forces in France—singing, dancing, telling jokes, handing out cigarettes, and earning the title "Sweetheart of the A.E.F." Alexander Woollcott, drama critic for the *New York Times*, declared Elsie Janis "as essential to the success of this Army as a charge of powder is essential to the success of a shell" (17 June 1918). After the war she put together a series of successful soldier revues called *Elsie Janis and Her Gang*, which featured both professional entertainers and former servicemen.

Throughout the 1920s Janis continued to appear in her own musical revues. In *Puzzles of 1925*, she hit upon a gimmick that would revolutionize her work. She began to imitate personalities performing unlikely material, such as George M. Cohan as Romeo or John Barrymore as Hamlet singing the popular song, "Yes, We Have No Bananas." She also performed concert tours throughout Europe, contributed to a comic strip, and wrote poems, short stories, and feature-length articles for various magazines. In 1926 Janis starred in an early "talking picture," *Behind the Lines*, recreating the role she played on the front with the allied armies. Two years later she settled in Beverly Hills to work on projects for Paramount Studios and became the first woman to produce a "talkie," supervising the production of her revue *Paramount on Parade!* in 1929. In 1928 she began her "farewell" vaudeville appearances, retiring from the stage shortly after the death of her mother in July 1930. On 31 December 1931 she married Gilbert Wilson, a bond salesman hoping to make a career in motion pictures. The marriage lasted a short time and the two eventually separated. In 1935 medical expenses for an injury sustained in an automobile accident forced her to auction off most of her belongings, including "Philipse Manor," her historic estate in Tarrytown, New York. After a failed attempt at a comeback in 1939 and a brief appearance in the film *Women in War* (1940), Janis spent her remaining years in virtual seclusion at her home in Beverly Hills, California.

Through talent and the unbridled determination of her mother, Elsie Janis created and sustained a 33-year career that spanned enormous changes in popular entertainment. As one biographer noted: "She was born during the infancy of vaudeville and retired as vaudeville lay dying. She began her musical comedy career in a show by Victor Herbert and ended with a show by George and Ira Gershwin. She made her first films in film's first years and went on to become the first woman to produce a Hollywood 'talkie' . . . and by following her throughout her career, we see the "career" of American popular entertainment" (Morrow, p. 313).

• Janis's own version of her life is her autobiography, *So Far, So Good!* (1933), and *The Big Show: My Six Months with the American Expeditionary Forces* (1919), both of which tend to amplify her successes and gloss over her failures. Her other published works include *Love Letters of an Actress* (1913) and *If I Know What I Mean* (1925). The most comprehensive biography is Lee Alan Morrow, "Elsie Janis: A Compensatory Biography" (Ph.D. diss., Northwestern Univ., 1988), which contains a list of her songs and revues as well as an extensive bibliography of reviews and critical accounts by other performers in the entertainment industry. Other works of interest include Diana Serra Cary, *Hollywood's Children: An Inside Account of the Child Star Era* (1978), and Jacques Charles, *De Gaby Deslys à Mistinguett* (1932). An obituary is in the *New York Times*, 28 Feb. 1956.

LORIEN A. CORBELLETTI

JANIS, Sidney (8 July 1896–23 Nov. 1989), art dealer and collector, was born in Buffalo, New York, the son of Isaac Janis, a clothing salesman and champion roller skater, and Celia Cohn. After attending elementary and vocational school in Buffalo, Janis performed on the Gus Sun Time vaudeville circuit. Working as a ballroom dancer, he demonstrated new dances such as the hesitation waltz, the one step, and others. In 1917 he joined the U.S. Naval Air Force and was sent to the Aeronautical College at the Great Lakes Naval Training Station in Waukegan, Illinois, to study mechanics.

After being discharged from the navy in 1919, Janis returned to Buffalo to work for his brother's chain of shoe stores. While traveling to New York City on business trips, he visited art galleries. In 1925 he married Harriet "Hansi" Grossman and moved to New York City. The couple had three children. In 1926 Janis purchased his first work of art, a small Whistler etching which he later traded for a Matisse. The Matisse was in turn traded a few years later for Picasso's *Painter and Model* (1928, Museum of Modern Art). In 1928, with the aid of his wife, Janis founded the M'Lord shirt manufacturing company. M'Lord's sole product was a shirt with two breast pockets. The shirt was a huge success, particularly in the South, and soon Janis was able to spend more time expanding his art collection.

Visiting Europe for the first time in 1928, Janis met Fernand Léger and other leading artists of the modern movement. Throughout the 1920s and 1930s he made several trips to Europe, collecting the works of artists such as Piet Mondrian, Picasso, Paul Klee, Juan Gris, and others. Recognition of Janis as a leading collector of modern art came in 1934 when he was appointed to the advisory committee of the Museum of Modern Art in New York City. The following year, the Janis Collection was shown at the Arts Club of Chicago and the University of Minnesota Gallery in Minneapolis. It was also shown, anonymously, to the Museum of Modern Art.

Janis's acquisition of Henri Rousseau's *The Dream* (Museum of Modern Art) in 1934 excited his interest in primitive and folk art. When not traveling to Europe, Janis was scouring America for the work of naive artists. Among those he collected were Patrick J. Sullivan, William Doriani, Morris Hirshfield, and Grandma Moses (Mary Anne Robertson).

Retiring on the profits from M'Lord in 1939, Janis committed himself to writing and lecturing on art. He organized the exhibition, "Contemporary Unknown American Painters" at the Museum of Modern Art in 1939. Three years later, he published *They Taught Themselves: American Primitive Painters of the 20th Century* (1942), an extension of the earlier exhibition. His exhibition of the work of primitive painter Morris Hirshfield at the Museum of Modern Art in 1943 was lambasted in the art press. Undaunted, Janis rebutted his critics in a letter to *Art Digest* (1 Aug. 1943) in which he defended Hirshfield and other "self-taught painters." Other critical works published by Janis in the 1940s include *Abstract and Surrealist Art in America* (1944) and *Picasso: The Recent Years, 1939–1946* (1946), coauthored with his wife. Sharing an interest in dancing and boogie-woogie jazz, he established a friendship with Mondrian. This friendship deepened when the artist moved to New York in 1940 and lasted until the artist's death in 1944.

In 1948, short of money, Janis opened his own commercial gallery; the inaugural exhibition was a selection of recent works by Léger. Among the artists exhibited in the first years of the gallery were, in their first American exhibitions, Jean Arp, Robert Delaunay, and Henri Rousseau. Janis also presented exhibitions on futurism (1954), cubism (1956), and dada (1953, organized by Marcel Duchamp).

Although the first seasons at the gallery were devoted primarily to European artists, Janis soon turned his attention to contemporary American artists. In 1950 he presented a group exhibition of works by Arshile Gorky, Willem de Kooning, Franz Kline, Jackson Pollock, and Mark Rothko. His association with these and other artists who would form the Abstract Expressionists was further enhanced when he became the dealer for Pollock, Gorky, de Kooning, Rothko, Philip Guston, and Robert Motherwell. Janis's championing of the so-called New York School led critic Clement Greenberg to remark: "His policy not only implied, it declared, that Pollock, de Kooning, Kline, Guston, Rothko, and Motherwell were to be judged by the same standards as Matisse, and Picasso, without condescension, without making allowances" ("Introduction to an Exhibition in Tribute to Sidney Janis" in *Clement Greenberg: The Collected Essays and Criticism*, ed. John O'Brian, vol. 4 [1985], pp. 52–54).

Janis presented one of the first gallery exhibitions of the new Pop Art movement with "The New Realists" in 1961. Although his promotion of the Pop Artists put him at odds with some of his older artists such as Mark Rothko, it brought into his stable such artists as Claes Oldenburg, George Segal, Jim Dine, and Tom Wesselmann.

Janis donated his private collection to the Museum of Modern Art in 1967. Containing works by Picasso, Mondrian, Klee, Boccioni, and many others, it was valued at over $2 million at the time of its donation and well over $100 million at the time of Janis's death. At the time, Alfred H. Barr, Jr., director of the museum, stated: "In its size, breadth of taste, considered balance, and immediate availability, the Sidney and Harriet Janis Collection of some hundred paintings and sculptures, is one of the great gifts of works of art received by The Museum of Modern Art" (*The Sidney and Harriet Janis Collection: A Gift to the Museum of Modern Art*, 1968).

Janis turned over management of the Sidney Janis Gallery to his sons and grandson in 1986 but continued to live an active life. Even in retirement, Janis's role as "one of the most important tastemakers and deal-cutters in the New York art world through four decades" remained unchallenged (James, p. 85). He continued to encourage avant-garde art, supporting exhibitions of the work of graffiti artists such as TOXIC. The always dapper Janis was an avid tennis player well into his eighties and gave a tango demonstration at the Museum of Modern Art's celebration of his ninetieth birthday. He died in New York City.

• Extensive taped interviews with Janis as well as the typescript of Janis's memoirs, "Keeping in Step with Art: Memoirs of an Art Dealer," are at the Archives of American Art,

Smithsonian Institution. Additional archival material is held by the Sidney Janis Gallery, New York City. Biographical details are in *Three Generations of Twentieth-Century Art: The Sidney and Harriet Janis Collection of the Museum of Modern Art* (1972), *The Sidney and Harriet Janis Collection: A Gift to the Museum of Modern Art* (1968), and the exhibition catalog from the John and Mable Ringling Museum of Art, *The Sidney Janis Painters: Albers, Baziotes, Gorky, Gottlieb, Guston, Kline, De Kooning, Motherwell, Pollock, Rothko* (1961). See also John Brooks, "Why Fight It?" *New Yorker*, 12 Oct. 1960; Judd Tully, "Sidney Janis' Gift of the New," *Washington Post*, 20 July 1987; Jamie James, "Sidney Janis Waiting a Year for the Blue," *ArtNews* 86 (Dec. 1987): 85–86; and Kate Linker, "Post-Graffiti, Sidney Janis Gallery," *Artforum* 22 (Mar. 1984): 92–93. Obituaries are in the *New York Times* and the *Los Angeles Times*, both 24 Nov. 1989, and *Art in America* (Jan. 1990).

MARTIN R. KALFATOVIC

JANNEY, Russell Dixon (14 Apr. 1885–14 July 1963), writer, press agent, and theatrical producer, was born in Wilmington, Ohio, the son of Reynold Janney, a mechanic and builder of bicycles, and Ella Dixon. Soon after his birth his family moved to Chillicothe, Ohio, where his father served as principal of the high school. In 1894 Janney's father gave up his career in education and moved his family again, this time to Keene, New Hampshire, where he set up in business as a mechanic. Keene was at this time often a stopover town for theater companies traveling between Boston and Montreal, and Janney developed an interest in working in the theater. He enrolled at Yale University, where he wrote and produced several plays for his fraternity, Beta Theta Pi. After he graduated in 1906 he settled briefly in New York, but the following year he departed for London to pursue a career as a press agent and freelance writer. He achieved modest success abroad, counting among his employers several leading figures in the British theater, including Sir Herbert Beerbohm Tree and George Edwardes, for whom he created publicity.

Returning to the United States in 1910, Janney comanaged stock companies in Indianapolis and Milwaukee and served as advance man for George Arliss and for a popular farce, *Parlor, Bedroom and Bath* (1917). He contributed to such popular magazines as *Smart Set*, created sketches for the *Ziegfeld Follies*, and represented Stuart Walker's Portmanteau Theatre in New York and on tour. Janney also served as press agent for Fox Films, creating the publicity for Theda Bara, the first of the great film vamps. His first successful production in New York was a stage adaptation of Booth Tarkington's *Seventeen* (1918), but Janney did not really begin to make his mark as a producer until 1925, when he coauthored and produced (with Professor Brian Hooker of Yale) *The Vagabond King*, based on the life of the colorful French poet François Villon. The popular composer Rudolf Friml provided the music for this major success, which had 511 performances on Broadway and was later performed across the country by seven road companies simultaneously. Other well-known productions by Janney include *June Love* (1921), a musical about an attractive widow and an amateur golf champion by Otto Harbach and W. H. Post with music by Friml and lyrics by Brian Hooker; Hugo Felix and Catherine Cushing's *Marjolaine* (1922), a romantic musical comedy based on Louis N. Parker's *Pomander Walk*; *Sancho Panza* (1923), based on the island Barataria sequence in *Don Quixote* by Melchoir Lengyel, with music by Felix; Hooker and Post's *White Eagle* (1927), a musical based on Edwin Royle's *The Squaw Man*; and a historical operetta, *The O'Flynn* (1934), based on Justin McCarthy's novel and play, with book by Janney and Hooker and music by Franklin Hauser. He also served as manager for Otis Skinner and as play doctor for many New York productions.

Although Janney remained a familiar figure in the New York theater scene, reviving the popular *Vagabond King* in 1943, he essentially suspended his stage activities to write his first novel, *The Miracle of the Bells* (1946). The novel is a highly romanticized and somewhat autobiographical story of a cynical, big-city press agent and the religious events he witnesses in a small, Polish-American Catholic town, where he is involved in the funeral of a beautiful young actress. The work aroused little enthusiasm from reviewers. A critic for *Time* magazine wrote, "As a novel, *The Miracle of the Bells* is one of the worst ever published; as a business proposition it has cornered the schmaltz market and provides a role for every star in Hollywood" (16 Sept. 1946, p. 110). The work was, however, a great popular success and the basis for a much-loved film of the same name.

The popularity of *The Miracle of the Bells*, along with its sentimental advocacy of such themes as religious tolerance, the redemptive power of faith, and the pleasures of smoking, earned Janney the attention and support of the National Conference of Christians and Jews, who organized and sponsored a nationwide lecture tour, and of major tobacco companies, who provided extensive advertising. Janney's pleas for religious tolerance often included condemnations of communism, seen by him as a serious threat to tolerance and a source of civic divisiveness. When he was selected in 1949 as a juror in the New York trial of Communist leaders accused of threatening the United States, his public statements against communism were recalled, and a bitter controversy, led by the leftist newspaper *The Worker*, surrounded his appointment. The judge nevertheless refused to remove Janney from the jury or to declare a mistrial. When at last a verdict was returned, finding Gus Hall and others guilty of conspiracy to bring about the violent overthrow of the U.S. government, Janney was seen by many as the manifestation of a compromised judicial process.

The highly publicized trial cast a shadow over Janney's final years, and, clearly suffering from the attacks on his character and motives, he largely withdrew from the public eye. He did make two attempts to further his career, with the publication of a verse drama, *The Vision of Red O'Shea*, in 1949 and a second novel, *So Long as Love Remembers*, in 1953. Neither work, however, enjoyed much success, and Janney became increasingly solitary in the years before his death in New York. Despite Janney's long and productive career in theatrical production and his close association with many important figures of his time, it is for his one highly successful novel, *The Miracle of the Bells*, that Janney is most remembered.

• Other than entries in standard reference works, very little published information on Janney is available. An obituary is in the *New York Times*, 15 July 1963.

MARVIN CARLSON

JANSEN, Reinier (Apr. 1648?–c. Feb. 1706), Quaker and printer, was born probably in Harlingen, Friesland, the Netherlands, the son of Jan Reiners Jansen and Jancke Keimpes. Little is known about Jansen's early life and even less can be documented. J. G. Riewald, a Dutch scholar who did research on both sides of the Atlantic, published a biography in 1970 in which he corrected many errors made by earlier writers and pieced together as much as he could verify along with surmises and tentative conclusions. While Riewald found that Jansen was married with two children by 1670, he did not discover the wife's name nor the dates of their marriage or her death. Court records indicate he married Sjoucken Jans in 1676, but she must have died not long after, for a Harlingen deed dated 17 November 1678 lists his wife at that time as Trijntje Hedserts. Jansen had at least seven children in his three marriages.

As a young man Jansen rejected his boyhood religion and sought a new faith, first with the Flemish mystic Antoinette Bourignon and then with the Dutch Quakers. In writing to Bourignon in 1670, Jansen referred to a deep religious upheaval three years earlier. From 1670 until 1673 he followed this Flemish mystic and for a time worked at a clandestine printing press that she maintained. Because he had been trained as a lace maker he was able to take up printing, but he never became really proficient in this craft. In 1672 Jansen and a number of others from Friesland moved to Nordstrand, in Schleswig-Holstein, to join the select group living with Bourignon in her community called the Light of the World. By the end of the year he was disillusioned with the community, and he and his family moved to Friedrichstadt early in 1673.

Jansen then turned to the Friends, or Quakers, after he moved back to Harlingen. He appeared in Quaker records in 1675 when he and several Friends in Amsterdam and Harlingen went to Emden to visit imprisoned Quakers and were themselves jailed. Jansen remained a Friend for the remainder of his life, though he was sometimes disciplined for his behavior. In 1679 at Harlingen, using an unnamed printer, he published two Quaker tracts in Dutch, one by George Fox, called "the Younger," to differentiate him from the founder of Quakerism, and the other by Marmaduke Stephenson, the New England martyr. By 1690 Jansen had moved from Harlingen to a community in Northern Holland, probably Sneek or Alkmaar, and lived in the latter town until he and his family emigrated to Philadelphia.

Like other Dutch Friends, Jansen became interested in the new Quaker province in America, Pennsylvania, when promotional pamphlets translated into Dutch began to circulate on the continent. Jansen became acquainted with William Penn in 1677 when the English Quaker spent some weeks in religious visitation among Dutch Friends and traveled in the western German states. After Jansen read Penn's *Some Account of the Province of Pennsylvania* in 1681, he purchased land in the new province and corresponded with persons from Friesland who had migrated to Germantown and elsewhere. In 1698 Jansen, his wife Trijntje Hedserts, and six children crossed the Atlantic to Philadelphia and settled in Germantown, ten miles north of the provincial capital.

Pennsylvania had been without a printer for five years, and Jansen was soon pressed into service. William Bradford (1663–1752), the first printer, had come from London in 1685. Son-in-law of the experienced Quaker publisher Andrew Sowle, he brought his press with him and served the province for eight years. Bradford was not happy in his post, however, for he found that the Quaker leaders wished to control what he printed and sharply criticized him for supporting the schismatic Quaker leader George Keith and publishing tracts for him. In 1693 Bradford moved to New York and took his press with him. By 1697 the Pennsylvania Friends realized they needed a printer. They decided to purchase a press and other equipment and employ a person who would follow their orders, for Bradford always maintained his independence. Jansen, recently arrived from Holland, was named as the printer. He moved from Germantown into Philadelphia, where he set up business in a shop provided by the Friends. Not long after the family moved into Philadelphia, a yellow fever epidemic swept the town in 1699, killing Jansen's wife and two of his children.

In the following seven years Jansen published forty-three titles, more than half of which were religious works, largely written by Friends. Riewald, who assembled a catalog of his imprints, reported that six of the other titles were political documents and another six were almanacs. His most famous book, and his first publication, was *God's Protecting Providence . . .* (1699), a journal kept by Jonathan Dickinson when shipwrecked off the coast of Florida, captured by the Indians, and eventually allowed to walk more than 200 miles to St. Augustine. Two other publications in 1699 included a broadside against pirates written by Penn after he returned to Pennsylvania for his second visit.

The ten items printed in 1700 included two Swedish hymnals and the first of seven titles against Keith and his followers by Caleb Pusey and others, *Satan's Harbinger Encountered . . . .* Keith, a Scottish minister, had denounced his fellow Quakers in Philadelphia for their political activity and their acceptance of slavery, as well as some of their religious tenets. His followers, who withdrew from the main body, called themselves Christian Quakers.

The ten titles issued in 1701 included *An Abstract or Abridgement of the Laws . . .* (of Pennsylvania), a reprint of Fox's essay exhorting Friends to deal humanely with their African-American slaves and servants, *Gospel Family Order . . .* , and several tracts directed toward Quaker youth, including *Good Advice to Youth*, by William Shewen.

Only four titles appeared in 1702, including a reprint of *Instructions for Right-Spelling . . . Reading and Writing*, a primer prepared by Fox and Ellis Hookes. Jansen and his two sons, Tiberius Johnson and Joseph Reyners, who had joined him in his work, published the second of six almanacs for Jacob Taylor that year. While Jansen was allowed to use the press to print material for individuals and the provincial government, the volume of work decreased after 1701. He and his sons only issued sixteen items in the last four years of his life. Fortunately, he was allowed to operate a store on the property provided by the Quakers, where he sold books from Europe, stationery supplies, and all sorts of other items ranging from hardware to spices.

Jansen served Friends and the province for seven years until his death in Philadelphia. He is remembered as one of the early printers in the American colonies, the second in Pennsylvania, and the first employed by Friends. The press issued important Quaker publications and was especially useful in responding to Keith, who returned to the Delaware valley in 1702 as an Anglican priest to attack the Friends. The quality of Jansen's printing was criticized by individuals and by the yearly meeting. While there was some justification for the dissatisfaction, he came to the work without adequate training, was using an unfamiliar language, and suffered from a shortage of type, poor ink, uneven paper, and a poor press. Even so, the scholar Lawrence C. Wroth believed that Jansen's work was not measurably inferior to other colonial printers of his time.

• There is no collection of Jansen papers, and most of the biographical references to him published in the past contain errors. J. G. Riewald, *Reynier Jansen of Philadelphia, Early American Printer* (1970), is as yet the only authoritative source of information about this early printer. Riewald evaluated the writings of others in chapter four of his book, pp. 42–44, and concluded that only one scholar was useful: William I. Hull, *William Penn and the Dutch Quaker Migration to Pennsylvania* (1935).

EDWIN B. BRONNER

JANSKY, Karl Guthe (22 Oct. 1905–14 Feb. 1950), electrical engineer and discoverer of radio emissions originating in the Milky Way galaxy, was born in Norman, Oklahoma, the son of Cyril Methodius Jansky and Nellie Moreau. His father, after 1908 a professor of electrical engineering at the University of Wisconsin, stimulated his intellectual growth through chess and bridge and family discussions that resembled critical debates. Jansky's lifelong interest in electronics began when as a child he built a crystal radio and continued into his senior thesis on vacuum tubes at the University of Wisconsin. He was elected to Phi Beta

Kappa and received a B.S. in physics in 1927. He was awarded an M.S. in physics by the same institution in 1936.

After a year as a graduate student, and instructor, Jansky sought employment at the Bell Telephone Laboratories. A pre-employment physical examination revealed that his kidneys had been damaged by Bright's disease. Intercession by his brother C. Moreau Jansky, a former Bell Labs employee who knew the corporate doctors, overcame their objections, and Jansky joined Bell Labs in August 1928. He married Alice La Rue Knapp in 1929; they had two children.

Assigned to the reception branch of the Bell Labs Radio Research Division at Cliffwood, New Jersey, Jansky worked in a small research group supervised by Harald Friis. His first project was to identify the sources of static that regularly interfered with transoceanic radiotelephone communications and specifically to determine the angle and direction from which the radio noise arrived at an antenna. To attack this problem Jansky designed a large antenna that rotated around its short central axis in the horizontal plane once every twenty minutes. The project was delayed by relocation of the laboratory to Holmdel, but by August 1931 Jansky recognized that his 24-hour recordings exhibited a regular maximum of steady, hiss static in addition to episodic peaks correlated with local or distant storms. Initially Jansky associated the daily maximum with the sun, but it soon became apparent that the noise maximum was moving away from the sun. Within six months he was certain that the hiss static maximum was extraterrestrial in origin. In April 1932 Friis agreed and directed Jansky to prepare a report of his results. Published later that same year in *Proceedings of the Institute of Radio Engineers* (*PIRE*), the paper carried an ultraconservative title that, following Friis's directions, obscured the revolutionary nature of Jansky's findings: "Directional Studies of Atmospherics at High Frequencies."

As laboratory staffing shrank because of the depression, Jansky was assigned other research projects. By December 1932, however, with a few additional observations and tutoring from his Bell Labs colleague A. M. Skellett, Jansky became certain that the steady hisslike static originated at a fixed point in space that apparently moved across the sky each day because of the earth's rotation. With some difficulty he developed approximate celestial coordinates for that point. Then, in two *PIRE* papers published in 1933, he described the basic astronomy involved; in language again conservatively guided by Friis, he articulated his revolutionary claim that the hiss static seemed to have its origin in our Milky Way galaxy, with a maximum in a direction that pointed close to the galactic center. Other work priorities soon displaced research on this galactic radio noise, and after 1936 Jansky made no more observations.

Astronomers were not completely unresponsive to Jansky's discovery, although his only direct effort to stimulate their interest was with one 1933 paper in *Popular Astronomy*. The following year Harlan True Stetson discussed Jansky's discovery in his book on radio waves and their interaction with the earth. Fred Whipple, his student Jessie Greenstein at Harvard University, and others hypothesized that the radio energy detected by Jansky originated in interstellar dust. Greenstein in particular seems to have been convinced of the importance of Jansky's observations. Still, Friis was correct in noting in his retrospective assessment that there had been no encouragement to Jansky from the astronomical community, despite nationwide publicity surrounding his initial discovery.

After 1936 Jansky's work continued to involve improvements in radiotelephony, including projects on siting receivers for transatlantic radio communications and on manmade sources of radio noise. He received a citation for his research on radio direction finding during World War II. Jansky's health was never secure and declined rapidly after 1945. Progressive failure of his kidneys led to hypertensive cardiovascular disease, the underlying cause of his death from a cerebral thrombosis in Red Bank, New Jersey.

Jansky's observation of extraterrestrial radio waves and his identification of their origin in the direction of the galactic center were among the most important fundamental astronomical discoveries of the twentieth century. As a result of his observations and those of later experimenters, astronomers broadened their focus from visible light, for millennia the sole medium of astronomical observation, to include radiation at both higher and lower frequencies, a shift that transformed astronomy and greatly enlarged the understanding of the universe. Although Jansky was unable to pursue this interest and was never honored for his discovery during his lifetime, his work was taken up by others. In 1944 Grote Reber published the first crude radio map of the sky, based on observations with a homemade parabolic reflector in Wheaton, Illinois. After World War II British and Australian engineers, working with surplus radio and radar equipment, refined Reber's map and identified discrete radio sources, many of which were soon correlated with optical counterparts. Thereafter radio astronomy grew in importance during the last half of the twentieth century. In recognition of his contribution the basic unit of measurement for flux density (for any wavelength of radiation) is named the jansky.

• Jansky's working notebooks and papers are in the Bell Telephone Laboratories Archives. Some of his letters to family members are in the C. M. Jansky Papers in the University of Wisconsin Archives. Jansky's articles in the *Proceedings of the Institute of Radio Engineers* in 1932 (pp. 1920–32), 1933 (pp. 1158–63, 1517–30), and 1935 (pp. 1517–30), are well illustrated. See also his articles in *Nature* 132 (8 July 1933): 66, and *Popular Astronomy* 44, no. 10 (Dec. 1933): 548–55. C. Moreau Jansky reminisced about his brother in a talk published in *American Scientist* 45 (Jan. 1957): 5–12. A biographical essay is W. T. Sullivan III, "Karl Jansky and the Discovery of Extraterrestrial Radio Waves," in his *The Early Years of Radio Astronomy* (1984). Sullivan reviews a controversy that arose after Jansky's death, centering on Friis's conservative approach to the announcement of Jansky's discovery, as well as allegations that Jansky's desire to continue working on his discovery was thwarted by Friis. The debate was prompted by Jansky's later supervisor, George C. Southworth, in "Early History of Radio Astronomy," *Scientific Monthly* 82 (Feb. 1956): 55–66, and it was possibly encouraged by C. Moreau Jansky, "The Discovery and Identification by Karl Guthe Jansky of Electromagnetic Radiation of Extraterrestrial Origin in the Radio Spectrum," *Proceeding of the Institute of Radio Engineers* 46 (1958): 13–15. Friis published an account in his own defense, "Karl Jansky: His Career at Bell Telephone Laboratories," *Science* 149 (1965): 841–42.

THOMAS R. WILLIAMS

JANSON, Horst Woldemar (4 Oct. 1913–30 Sept. 1982), art historian, was born in St. Petersburg, Russia, the son of Friedrich Janson, a German merchant, and Helene Porsch. The Russian Revolution forced the family, which by then included a second son, Halmar, to flee to Hamburg, Germany, via Finland. After the revolution, his father continued to trade with the Russians until his death in 1926. To avoid the limits placed on the earnings of foreigners in Germany, his mother became a German citizen. After graduating from the Wilhelm Gymnasium, Janson enrolled in 1932 at the University of Hamburg, where Erwin Panofsky had been appointed to the first professorship in art history. Janson subsequently moved into the boardinghouse run by the mother of his fellow student, William Heckscher, with whom he divided study assignments; together they formed a triumvirate with Liselotte Müller (later curator at the Museum für Kunst und Gewerbe, Hamburg) that resulted in lifelong friendship. After Panofsky was forced by the Nazis to flee to the United States in 1933, Janson and Heckscher decided to join the small group of Aryans that left Germany voluntarily. Janson convinced the Nazis that he was trustworthy, and so he won a government scholarship to study in the United States, which was actually awarded as a Charles Holtzer fellowship by Harvard University, where he went to study in 1935. Heckscher arranged to have his fare paid by the Warburg bank, which agreed to help him because of his staunch anti-Nazism.

When Janson arrived in the United States, he quickly acquired an American identity, which he cherished. In 1936, after a brief final visit to his mother in Hamburg, he was granted landed immigrant status and continued his studies at Harvard under Chandler Post and Arthur Sachs. There he formed an enduring friendship with Sydney J. Freedberg, with whom he later shared an apartment, and met Dora Jane Heineberg, a Radcliffe undergraduate whom he married in 1941. The couple had four children. He helped to support himself as a teaching assistant and by lecturing at the Worcester Art Museum in 1936. While teaching at Iowa State University he received his M.A. in 1938 and his doctorate in 1942 upon acceptance of his dissertation on the Italian Renaissance sculptor Michelozzo.

Although he was able to keep his position at Iowa after he ran afoul of Grant Wood for taking a group of students to see the Picasso exhibition in Chicago, Janson moved to Washington University in St. Louis. He attracted the first of what was later to become a legion of devoted followers, including Irving Lavin and Marilyn Aronson Lavin. He was also instrumental in updating the university art museum's collections by deaccessioning a large group of paintings in 1945 and using the funds to acquire important examples of twentieth-century art by the leading figures of modernism. He contributed to the war effort by teaching Russian and physics to U.S. soldiers.

In 1948 two important events took place: he was reunited with his mother, who survived the war under the most harrowing conditions, and he received a year's fellowship to Harvard. By that time he had already assumed a leading position among the younger generation of art historians. The following year he was appointed chair of the fine arts department at Washington Square College, New York University. During his twenty-five years as chair, he was able to build one of the strongest undergraduate departments of art history in the country by hiring some of the brightest young scholars in the field. An inspiring teacher, he attracted numerous pupils, including graduate students at the Institute of Fine Arts, where he was adjunct professor, although his relations with the department were sometimes strained. He was dedicated to his students, whom he helped with unfailing generosity.

In 1952 Janson published two books that changed his career: *Apes and Ape Lore in the Middle Ages and the Renaissance*, for which he received the Charles Rufus Morey Prize from the College Art Association, and *The Story of Painting for Young People, from Cave Painting to Modern Times*, written in collaboration with his wife and published by Harry N. Abrams, which demonstrated an uncommon ability to write for a lay audience. The association with Abrams, suggested by Meyer Shapiro, led him to write his classic *History of Art* (1962), which became the leading textbook of its generation in the field and helped to make him the most famous American art historian of his time. In the meantime he won a second Morey prize in 1957 for his monograph on Donatello. (The only other art historian to gain the award twice was his mentor, Panofsky.) These were, however, only the most notable among a very long list of publications that occupy eight pages in his festschrift titled *Art the Ape of Nature*, which appeared in 1982. His final book, on nineteenth-century sculpture, was completed shortly before his death.

Janson's mind was notable for its breadth and discipline among a generation of scholars in whom such attributes were common. He possessed an unquenchable appetite for life and endless curiosity, which made him a voracious reader in many disciplines. These qualities were bound to a forceful personality and overpowering intellect, which was marked by insistent rationality and rigorous methodology. Less well known but no less essential were a playful sense of humor and lively imagination, which, though not intuitive, led him to rethink subjects and investigate new ones with often startling originality. His wife, an accomplished art historian in her own right, played an important role in stimulating his interests.

Janson was also a masterful politician who used his considerable prestige to benefit the field of art history. His numerous contributions included serving as book review editor and later editor of the *Art Bulletin*, as well as president of the College Art Association in 1970–1972.

• Besides the works mentioned in the text, Janson wrote several other important histories of art: *The Sculpture of Donatello* (1957), *Sixteen Studies* (1973), and *Nineteenth-century Sculpture* (1985). He and Robert Rosenblum collaborated on *Nineteenth-century Art* (1984).

ANTHONY JANSON

JANSSEN, Werner Alexander (1 June 1899–19 Sept. 1990), composer and conductor, was born in New York City, the son of August Janssen, a well-known restaurateur, and Alice Boeckman. Because his father was opposed to his son's career in music, Janssen was responsible for supporting his own education at Dartmouth College by playing the piano in theaters and dance halls as well as attempting to sell popular songs he had written. His principal instructors in composition were Philip Greeley Clapp at Dartmouth and Frederick Converse and George Chadwick at the New England Conservatory. He studied piano, probably in New York, with Arthur Friedheim, a Liszt pupil. After serving in the infantry during World War I, Janssen returned to Dartmouth, where he received his bachelor of music degree in 1921. His college achievements included the composition of two musical comedies that were performed by the Dartmouth Dramatic Association: *Heave To* (1918) and *Oh Doctor!* (1919). Janssen's first recordings, as piano soloist on two of his own popular songs, "My Java Belle" and "Ragamuffin," were made in New York City for Pathé in 1920 with the credited Hub Dance Orchestra.

Composing popular songs, shows, and material for the Ziegfeld *Follies* of 1925 and 1926 helped Janssen finance his conducting studies with Felix Weingartner in Basel, Switzerland (1920–1921), and Hermann Scherchen in Strasbourg, France (1921–1925). He also conducted theater orchestras, and beginning in late 1929 he spent four months in Cleveland composing and conducting program music for station WTAM, a local NBC affiliate. This engagement ended in April 1930 when he received a fellowship from the American Academy in Rome, awarded in part for his composition *New Year's Eve in New York*, a symphonic poem for orchestra and jazz band introduced by Howard Hanson and the Rochester Philharmonic on 8 May 1929 and recorded the same year by Nathaniel Shilkret and the Victor Symphony Orchestra.

Janssen spent the next three years studying in Rome, where Respighi was his mentor. Compositions begun or developed there included the *Louisiana Suite* for orchestra (1931–1932), from which a fugue on "Dixie" was later extracted as a separate work, and the

string quartet, *American Kaleidoscope*, first performed in 1930 by the Quartetto di Roma. Janssen also spent a great deal of time composing an opera, *Manhattan Transfer*, based on the novel by John Dos Passos, who contributed the libretto, but after two years of work, the manuscript disappeared from his apartment in Rome under mysterious circumstances and the project was abandoned. He was more fortunate in his conducting activities: appearances with the Royal Symphony Orchestra of Rome were followed by engagements in Berlin, Turin, Milan, Budapest, and Riga, as well as in Helsinki, where he led the Helsinki Municipal Orchestra in a program of Sibelius's music on 9 February 1934. The unqualified praise that the concert received in Finland, which included the composer's endorsement of both the performance and the young conductor's interpretations, was undoubtedly a factor in Janssen's subsequent appointment as an associate conductor of the New York Philharmonic-Symphony Orchestra for the 1934–1935 season.

Hailed as the first native-born New Yorker to conduct the Philharmonic, Janssen embarked upon a series of ambitious programs that included contemporary American works as well as standard repertory. Reviews of Janssen's concerts, in particular his choice of repertory, were encouraging, although his inexperience and the unevenness of his interpretations did not escape notice. After his season with the Philharmonic, he received numerous invitations to conduct in the United States and Europe, and he soon held a new position as leader of the Baltimore Symphony (1937–1939). His conducting earned him Finland's Order of the White Rose, awarded in 1936 for his continued efforts on behalf of Sibelius's music.

In the midst of widely scattered conducting engagements, Janssen began composing film music. His first score, written for Paramount's *The General Died at Dawn* (1936) and massive at 600 pages, was nominated for an Academy Award. While in Hollywood he met actress Ann Harding and married her in London in January 1937; the marriage, which produced no children, ended in divorce in 1963. From 1938 to 1942 Janssen was the musical director for Walter Wanger Productions, composing and conducting scores for five feature films. He later scored several films for United Artists, including Jean Renoir's *The Southerner* (1945), and composed music for documentary films and for television. In the late 1940s Janssen was producer and vice president of Musicolor, Inc. ("David L. Loew Musicolor Shorts"), which produced one-reel, color short subjects on classical compositions, many of which he conducted.

In 1940 Janssen formed the Janssen Symphony of Los Angeles, a virtuoso ensemble that provided a forum for contemporary music until 1952. Seen as something of a threat by the vulnerable Los Angeles Philharmonic, the smaller orchestra was occasionally financed by Janssen himself when sponsors and performers were lured away by the Philharmonic's management. The first seasons of the Janssen Symphony included numerous premieres, children's concerts, and radio appearances on NBC's "Standard Hour" during the summer months from 1941 through 1943. The orchestra first recorded for RCA Victor in 1942, performing a diverse repertory that eventually included film music (Max Steiner's *Symphonie Moderne* from the 1939 film *Four Wives*), musical theater (Jerome Kern's 1941 *Scenario for Orchestra* based on themes from *Showboat*), and contemporary works such as Barber's Overture to the *School for Scandal*. In the late 1940s the orchestra—sometimes identified as the "Symphony of Los Angeles"—appeared on the Artist label. Among these performances, issued between 1947 and 1950, were the first recorded excerpts from Berg's *Wozzeck*, with soprano Charlotte Boerner; the *Genesis Suite* for orchestra and narrator, with movements contributed by Schoenberg, Milhaud, Stravinsky, and others, commissioned by Nathaniel Shilkret and first performed by the Janssen Symphony in 1945; and a compilation of works by Copland, Ives, Cowell, and Henry Gilbert, titled *Four American Landscapes*. Long-playing releases by the Janssen Symphony included Hindemith's Symphony in E-flat and Virgil Thomson's orchestral suite from *The Mother of Us All* for Columbia (both 1951) and Berg's *Der Wein*, again with Charlotte Boerner, for Capitol (1951). Other notable recordings presented orchestral and chamber works of Villa-Lobos—selections from the *Bachianas Brasileiras* and *Chôros* for Capitol (1951) and the *Missa São Sebastião* for Columbia (1952).

In the 1950s Janssen's conducting posts moved away from the West Coast, where he had led the Utah Symphony Orchestra in its first professional season (1946–1947), the Portland Symphony (1947–1949), and the San Diego Philharmonic (1952–54), to positions in New York, Canada, and Europe: the NBC Symphony Orchestra ("Symphony of the Air") in 1956, the Toronto Symphony in 1956–1957, and the Vienna State Opera Orchestra (1959–1961) and Vienna Volksoper. Recordings with the latter two organizations include Karl Blomdahl's opera, *Aniara*, subtitled *An Epic of Space Flight in 2038 A.D.*, and Prokofiev's *War and Peace*. By the early 1970s Janssen had returned to the United States to live on Long Island with his second wife, Christina Heintzmann, and their three children. He died in Stony Brook, New York.

In spite of a tendency toward dissonant harmonies and unusual instrumental combinations, Janssen was a relatively conservative composer. His works, once described as "orchestral news-writing," rely extensively on popular songs, folk themes, and programmatic techniques. They range in style from the cleverly scored medley, *Foster Suite* (1937), to the more sophisticated and highly effective *New Year's Eve in New York*, an outstanding example of "symphonic jazz." His tastes as a conductor were more adventurous, and this devotion to new and untried music undoubtedly contributed to his nomadic career among the lesser American orchestras and encouraged the formation of his own ensemble. Contemporary composers had a most worthy advocate in Janssen. Sympathetic in mat-

ters of style and uncompromising in their high standards of performance, his recordings remain milestones in the recorded history of contemporary music.

• A collection of Janssen's papers is at Dartmouth College's Baker Memorial Library and includes concert programs, scrapbooks, sheet music, scores, and other materials related to Janssen's career through the early 1950s, as well as his correspondence for the years 1934–1972. Alva Johnston's two-part profile, "American Maestro," *New Yorker*, 20 Oct. 1934, pp. 22–26 and 27 Oct. 1934, pp. 23–26, provides a detailed if somewhat anecdotal account of Janssen's activities up to that year. An obituary is in the *New York Times*, 21 Sept. 1990.

SUSAN NELSON

JANSSENS, Francis (17 Oct. 1843–10 June 1897), Catholic archbishop, was born in Tilburg, Netherlands, the son of Cornelis Janssens, a wealthy woolen merchant, and Josephina Anna Dams. Aspiring to the priesthood from his youth, Janssens attended the local diocesan minor seminary at Beekvliet (1855–1862) and the major seminary at Haaren (1862–1866), where in 1866 he responded to the appeal of visiting bishop John McGill to become a priest of his diocese of Richmond, Virginia. Janssens then completed his studies at the American College, Louvain, Belgium, before ordination to priesthood in 1867. His arrival in Richmond in September 1868 inaugurated his career as a missionary priest of independent means serving in the South, where Catholic activities depended heavily on outside personnel and funding. McGill at once appointed him rector of Richmond's St. Peter Cathedral and diocesan chancellor. After McGill's death in 1872, Janssens served as the Richmond diocese's vicar general under Bishop James Gibbons, the future archbishop of Baltimore and cardinal, and Bishop John Keane.

In 1881 Janssens became bishop of the diocese of Natchez, a jurisdiction encompassing the state of Mississippi. There he continued his predecessors' practice of recruiting priests and raising funds in Europe. He opened schools for African Americans and a mission for Choctaw Indians. His article in the nationally circulating *Catholic World* (May 1887) in support of developing a black Catholic clergy for ministry to blacks reflected his growing concern for African Americans. He was the first American bishop to advocate openly the ordination of black priests.

In 1888 Janssens was appointed archbishop of New Orleans, a difficult position because the largely French-born Louisiana clergy were displeased that the tradition of French archbishops had ended. Janssens dealt with the heavy debt the archdiocese had contracted during institutional expansion after the Civil War. In cooperation with leading laity and after negotiation with creditors in Paris, he devised a plan for debt liquidation. Aiming to end his archdiocese's dependence on clergy recruited from abroad, Janssens secured the services of Benedictine monks from St. Meinrad Abbey in Indiana to open in 1891 a seminary at Gessen, Louisiana, where local youth could be trained for the diocesan priesthood. He began forming parishes for the exclusive use of African Americans so that they would not suffer the segregation then practiced within Catholic churches. For the growing number of Italian immigrants in New Orleans, Janssens invited Mother Frances Xavier Cabrini and her Missionary Sisters of the Sacred Heart to staff a school. He strongly exhorted Catholics to support parish schools.

Janssens's promotion in the hierarchy is credited to the influence of the American Catholic church's foremost leader, Cardinal James Gibbons. But Janssens was not thereby drawn into national Catholic movements and causes of the period. Instead, with hardworking and exact habits, he was devoted to the internal development of the dioceses in which he served and for which he gave generously from his personal fortune. In 1897 he embarked for Europe to visit his family and to make payments on the archdiocesan debt in Paris. While sailing to New York on a coastal steamer, he died unexpectedly.

• Janssens's papers are held in the Archives of the Archdiocese of New Orleans and the Archives of the Diocese of Jackson, Miss. (formerly the diocese of Natchez). The archives of the Archdioceses of Baltimore and Cincinnati, whose archbishops were in frequent correspondence with Janssens, also hold letters. Anne Marie Kasteel, *Francis Janssens, 1843–1897: A Dutch-American Prelate* (1992), is the first scholarly biography of Janssens. For Janssens's role in diocesan histories, see Roger Baudier, *The Catholic Church in Louisiana* (1939), and Richard Oliver Gerow, *Catholicity in Mississippi* (1939).

JOSEPH M. WHITE

JANSSON, Eric (19 Dec. 1808–13 May 1850), founder of the Janssonist religious sect and Bishop Hill utopian community, was born in Biskopskulla, Sweden, the son of Johannes Mattson, a landowner, and Sara Ersdotter. Jansson was born into and raised as a member of the Swedish Lutheran church. At age twenty-two, however, Jansson felt a personal call from God and was miraculously relieved of recurring bouts of rheumatism. Because his healing had occurred without the benefit of clergy, Jansson indicted the state church. "It dawned on me," he noted, "that I had been deceived in the faith which I had received from the so-called evangelical Lutheran teaching," and he concluded that "all the preachers and teachers were blind leaders" (quoted in Elmen, p. 3). These ideas festered within Jansson over the next decade as he became a *läsare*, a morally strict lay preacher, but it was not until thirteen years after his calling that he began to break away from the state church. In 1835 he married Maria Kristina Larsdotter (called "Maja Stina"). The union caused a rift with members of his well-to-do family, who felt it was beneath his station to marry the pregnant, twenty-year-old servant girl.

In 1843 Jansson made his first trip to the northern region of Sweden, which had a history of accepting radical religion. Ostensibly traveling to sell wheat flour, he sought out the *läsare* of each village and attempted to convince each one that he needed reform too. A typical response to Jansson's message was the one given by the minister who proclaimed to his flock, "I confess before God . . . that I have taught you to walk along a way on which the Lord is not to be found. . . . He that despises Eric Jansson does not despise a man, but God and his Holy Spirit!" (Elmen, p. 20). Just as typical of a Jansson-motivated conversion, however, was this same pastor's eventual opposition to the itinerant pastor when the perfectionist and separatist implications of his message became clear.

Jansson taught not only that the clergy were leading the people to a comfortable destruction, but that Christians could and should take literally Christ's command to be perfect. "I am perfect as God is perfect," proclaimed one of Jansson's hymns. "The Father's life is mine as well" (Elmen, p. 40). The earthly model for this perfection was Jansson himself, who included in his catechism the belief that "Christ's coming is revealed in its full height by Eric Jansson's obedience before God," leading one follower to reply to an interviewer, "Eric Jansson is as good as God" (Elmen, pp. 40, 41).

The doctrine of Jansson's perfection was not spoiled even by accusations of sexual impropriety, which came to a head on his third trip to the North. In 1845 six Lutheran church members, including one of his own followers, charged that Jansson had tried to seduce a 27-year-old known as Bos-Karin with the offer to "give you a little baby." Jansson told at least three versions of his defense over the years, initially claiming that he was testing her and eventually, in his memoirs, blaming her completely. "I knew that in fourteen years I had not felt any sexual temptation," he recalled confidently, "and so I had reason to think that whatever was happening between us was her fault. To find out whether this was true, I deliberately made myself guilty . . . .Bos-Karin, like Potiphar's wife, was frustrated in her lust for me and then she said it was my fault" (Elmen, p. 30). Such acts apparently did not disillusion his followers. As one stated plainly, "Even though Eric Jansson did this and that, his heart was nevertheless righteous before God, no matter what his body does" (Elmen, p. 31).

In tandem with perfectionism, Jansson proclaimed a virulent anticlerical message, which culminated in an 1844 vision that commanded him to burn every book but the Bible because "the idols from which the heart must be purified are first of all the idolatrous books and leaders" (Elmen, p. 64). Public book burnings focused governmental attention on Jansson's attacks on the state church and led to a series of imprisonments and daring escapes. While living as a fugitive, he and his leading followers, Jonas and Olaf Olsson, concluded that their only escape was to the United States. Having obtained blanket permission from King Oscar I for all Janssonists to emigrate, the sect crossed the Atlantic, starting with Jansson and his family in June 1846. Between 800 and 1,200 followers eventually left Sweden, many enabled by their fellow believers, who contributed the profits from selling their possessions to a common purse. After arriving in America, the immigrants first passed through New York City and then traveled overland to Bishop Hill, an Illinois settlement named for Jansson's birthplace.

Jansson organized Bishop Hill as a commune, with the faithful living in dank dwellings shaped from dirt and sod. The colony initially did very well, selling excess wheat in 1848 at markets in Chicago and Peoria. In 1849, however, as many as 200 residents, including Jansson's wife, died in a cholera epidemic that cost the colony thousands of dollars in doctor's fees. Many who survived the plague defected as their confidence in Jansson's doctrines and his business sense waned.

The following year brought a new and more personal crisis that eventually cost Jansson his life. In March, a Swedish immigrant named John Root, who had lived for a time at Bishop Hill, tried to kidnap his wife, Jansson's cousin Charlotte Lovisa, because she had refused to leave the colony. Jansson and his followers prevented the abduction and then retrieved her after Root took her a few weeks later. When Root gathered a mob of the colony's American neighbors, Jansson fled with his cousin and his new bride, the former Anna Sophia Gabrielsson, to St. Louis, where they remained for three weeks. Upon his return to Illinois, Jansson appeared in court at Cambridge on 13 May 1850 to speak for the colony. Between sessions, Root confronted Jansson in the courtroom and shot and killed him with a pistol. Jansson was buried when it became apparent to his followers that he was not going to rise from the dead, as many had believed. Jonas Olsson took control of Bishop Hill, which prospered for several more years before finally declining in dissension. Many from Bishop Hill, including Olsson, eventually became Seventh Day Adventists.

Although Eric Jansson and his followers converted no Americans to their faith, his preaching inspired many Swedes to emigrate to America, where his sect lived in a utopian community for more than a decade.

• The most accessible biography of Jansson is Paul Elmen, *Wheat Flour Messiah: Eric Jansson of Bishop Hill* (1976), which includes many quotes from Jansson's untranslated and unfinished autobiography. Most other works dealing with Jansson's life in the United States focus on the Bishop Hill colony, including Michael Mikkelsen, *The Bishop Hill Colony: A Religious Communistic Settlement in Henry County, Illinois* (1892; repr. 1972); Olov Isaksson and Soren Hallgren, *Bishop Hill: A Utopia on the Prairie* (1969); Emma Shogren Farman, "A Plymouth of Swedish America: The Town of Bishop Hill and Its Founder, Eric Janson," *The American Scandinavian Review* 2 (Sept. 1914): 30–36; and Sivert Erdahl, "Eric Jansson and the Bishop Hill Colony," *Journal of the Illinois State Historical Society* 17 (Oct. 1924): 503–74. For a detailed chronology of the Janssonist emigration, see Erik Wiken, "New Light on the Erik Janssonists' Emigration, 1845–1854," *Swedish-American Historical Quarterly* 45 (July 1984): 221–38. For a reprint of documents dealing with Jansson's assassination, see Henry Pratt, "The Murder of Eric Janson, Leader of the Bishop Hill Colony," *Journal of the Illinois State Historical Society* 45 (Spring 1952): 55–69. To set the colony in the context of other utopian enterprises, see Brian Berry, *America's Utopian Experiments* (1992), and Everett Webber, *Escape to Utopia: The Communal Movement in America* (1959). Finally, for a sociological comparison between Jansson and 1970s cult leader Jim Jones, see "Jonestown and Bishop Hill: Continuities and Disjunctures in Religious Conflict," in *New Religious Movements, Mass Suicide and People's Temple*, ed. Rebecca Moore and Fielding McGehee III (1989).

D. SCOTT CORMODE

JANVIER, Margaret Thomson (Feb. 1844–Feb. 1913), author, was born in New Orleans, Louisiana, the daughter of Francis de Haes Janvier, an author of prose and poetry, and Emma Newbold, an author of children's stories. Janvier was educated at home and in New Orleans public schools. She began to write at an early age, probably inspired by her parents. She never married.

Using the pseudonym "Margaret Vandegrift," she published mostly poetry and juvenile literature. Some of her works were published in leading magazines, including *St. Nicholas*, *Harper's Young People*, the *Youth's Companion*, *Wide Awake*, the *Century*, and the *Atlantic*. "To Lie in the Lew" (leeward of a hedge—the South Country ideal of peace) was one of Janvier's more popular poems and was published in *Scribner's Magazine*, April 1913. In the poem, the anonymous narrator (a soldier) reflects on life and war while lying in the lew. Because of an injury, he "fell out of line long before they took the city to which" they all were marching:

And should a thankful heart be singing lauds and
  praises
That the chance to fight is gone, that there's nothing left
  to do?
Tell me, oh million hearts that this dreadful life amazes,
With all its unfulfilments, its doubts and fears and
  crazes—
For my heart is very cold, and it is not singing praises
  As I lie in the lew.

The narrator remains in the lew, where "the sounds are the voices of a peaceful summer meadow."

"The Sandman," one of Janvier's poems for juveniles, traces the Sandman's journey:

The rosy clouds float overhead,
  The sun is going down;
And now the sandman's gentle tread
  Comes stealing through the town.
"White sand, white sand," he softly cries,
  And as he shakes his hand,
Straightway there lies on babies' eyes
  His gift of shining sand.
Blue eyes, gray eyes, black eyes, and brown,
As shuts the rose, they softly close, when he goes
  through the town.

At the break of day, he gathers sand from "sunny beaches far away—yes, in another land . . . his little boat alone may float within that lovely bay." The Sandman knows each child well, and if a baby cries, he "takes dull gray sand to close the wakeful eyes." The poem ends with the request that children lie quietly until "he strews the shining sands" by their beds.

One of Janvier's best-known books, *Clover Beach* (1880), deals with the Cheston family members and their activities at the Clover Beach summer resort. The family consists of Mr. and Mrs. Cheston and their eight children: Lina and Charlie (the twins and the oldest—fourteen years old), Dick, Nora, Kitty, Rob, Polly, and Tom (the youngest—three years old). Each year the Chestons go to Clover Beach in June then leave when the weather becomes "too cold for comfort there" and return to the city. This summer, however, is a little different from the others, for Mr. Cheston's "business had failed to yield the usual income." Hence, Mr. Cheston asks that the family members go "as poor travellers" since he cannot afford to buy them new clothes for the vacation, a condition to which they eagerly agree. The children also consent, after discussions with Mrs. Cheston, "not to worry poor papa" during the trip. In spite of Mr. Cheston's financial concerns, the vacation is pleasant, and the children recover from the minor misunderstandings and minor incidents that they experience. The novel ends with the assertion that the Cheston children, who are just beginning the "battle of life," "will not be gloomy or grave because they have enlisted under the flag of that great Leader who asks their allegiance that he may give them His protection, 'strengthened with all might, according to His glorious power, unto all patience and long-suffering, *with joyfulness*.'"

Little Helpers (1889), another book for younger readers, chronicles moral lessons (such as being independent, listening to parents, and following God's laws) that the children of the Leslie family learn. Janvier's juvenile literature provides valuable insight into nineteenth-century American culture and values. She died in Moorestown, New Jersey. Margaret Thomson Janvier's work, taken as a whole, is a notable part of American literary history. Further, she made numerous contributions to juvenile literature.

• Other works by Janvier include *Under the Dog Star* (1881), *The Queen's Body Guard* (1883), *Doris and Theodora* (1884), *Little Bell and Other Stories* (1884), *The Absent-Minded Fairy* (1884), *Rose Raymond's Wards* (1885), and *The Dead Doll and Other Verses* (1889). Burton Egbert Stevenson, *The Home Book of Verse American and English* (1953), contains Janvier's two poems "Little Wild Baby" and "The Sandman."

SANDRA M. GRAYSON

JARAMILLO, Cleofas Martínez (6 Dec. 1878–30 Nov. 1956), folklorist, writer, and businesswoman, was born in the northern New Mexican village of Arroyo Hondo, the daughter of Julian Antonio Martínez, a landholder who raised sheep and cattle, farmed, and engaged in the mercantile trade, and Marina Lucero de Martínez. Both parents were descended from Spanish pioneers who settled the territory for New Spain in the late sixteenth century. One of seven children, Jaramillo spent her early years amidst the pleasures and hard work of a prosperous, upper-class, large country household. At age nine she entered the Loretto Convent School in Taos, New Mexico, and later attended the Loretto Academy in Santa Fe. There she was courted by her cousin, Colonel Venceslao Jaramillo, whom she married in Taos in 1898. After a wedding trip to California, they settled in El Rito.

The Jaramillos were among the elite of Spanish New Mexican culture. Venceslao served on the staff of territorial governor Miguel Antonio Otero, who attended their wedding. His income-producing occupations included the traditional family inheritances of store ownership, farming, and sheep ranching. He also owned rental property in Denver, Colorado. At the same time he became increasingly involved in territorial politics, serving as state senator from Rio Arriba County and joining the 1912 constitutional convention to draft laws for the new state of New Mexico. The couple maintained an active social life, entertaining at home and traveling broadly from New York to Mexico City. Of their three children, two died in infancy.

The death of Venceslao on 27 May 1920 after a debilitating illness left Jaramillo in the position of having to enter a world of financial affairs previously managed by her husband. She did so, finding that what had been a prosperous life was to a large extent dwindling under increasing debt, bad investments, and bank failures. With the help of family and friends, she took charge of her husband's properties and businesses and did what she could to discharge the debt and maintain a reduced, though still comfortable, standard of living for herself and her daughter. She succeeded but was struck again by tragedy in 1931 when her daughter, asleep at night in her front bedroom, was murdered by an intruder.

These events are recorded in Jaramillo's autobiography, *Romance of a Little Village Girl* (1955), a text written toward the end of her life in which she wove the circumstances of her childhood, marriage, motherhood, and widowed survival with the evocation of Spanish folk culture subject to rapidly changing times. Her interest in preserving a record of cultural customs began several years after her daughter's death, when she read an article about Spanish cooking in *Holland Magazine* that showed little expertise. As she commented in *Romance*, "These smart Americans make money with their writing, and we who know the correct way sit back and listen." Another article, about the Natchez pilgrimage, an annual event celebrating the customs of antebellum society, gave her the idea of organizing a Spanish-speaking contingent for the Santa Fe fiesta, thereby promoting the underrepresented Spanish origins of the city. This first effort at reconstructing the past involved wearing old-fashioned gowns in the fiesta parade, forming a religious procession escorted by mounted and costumed caballeros, serving a Spanish barbecued supper, and presenting a program of Spanish songs during a *merienda*, or tea. Flush with the event's success and recalling J. Frank Dobie's earlier invitation that she join the Texas Folklore Society, she decided to start an organization in New Mexico. La Sociedad Folklórica was founded in 1935 according to rules drafted by Jaramillo, which, she states in *Romance*, included the injunction that members "must be of Spanish descent, and that the meetings must be conducted in the Spanish language, with the aim of preserving our language, customs and traditions."

She subsequently wrote several books, all of which documented the habits and customs of a Spanish New Mexico fast disappearing under the modernizing influence of Anglo culture. All were self-published through small regional presses, a consequence of Jaramillo's resistance to the mining of her culture by prominent Anglo outsiders with better access to larger institutional venues. *Cuentos del Hogar* (Spanish fairy stories), a collection of tales passed to her primarily from her mother that are highly reminiscent of Iberian culture, was published in 1939. *Sombras del Pasado* (Shadows of the past), portions of which reoccur in *Romance*, appeared in 1941, followed quickly by *The Genuine New Mexico Tasty Recipes* (1942). Throughout, she continued her work with La Sociedad Folklórica, sponsoring social functions and promoting yearly religious and cultural festivities in the effort to recall the Spanish population to its traditional past. She died in El Paso, Texas, not long after the publication of her autobiography.

The importance of Jaramillo's work lies in the unique combination of personal narrative, detailed vignettes of cultural practice, and a nostalgia for an older culture that reveals much about a declining aristocracy little known in the broad context of American history. Jaramillo, along with her peers Nina Otero Warren and Fabiola Cabeza de Baca, pioneered in the realm of Hispanic women's literary production. Characteristic of her work is the evocation of a past Edenic world, its natural beauty enhanced by the graceful habits of a Spanish settlement quite distinct from the perceived lesser qualities of indigenous and Anglo cultures. Toward the end of *Romance* she wrote, "The glamour and beauty which appeals to the senses of the artists and the writers who have come into our country, should appeal more forcefully to us, the heirs of the artistic culture and of the poetry and the religious traditions which our Spanish ancestors left to crystallize on the crests of our New Mexico mountains." Making use of her own familial resources, Jaramillo initiated in her region a method of preservation that embraced the personal and collective remembrances of those native to New Mexican Spanish culture.

• Discussions of Jaramillo's work and her position among other Hispanic women writers of her period can be found in Genaro M. Padilla, "Recovering Mexican-American Autobiography," in *Recovering the U.S. Hispanic Literary Heritage*, ed. Ramón Gutiérrez and Genaro Padilla (1993), and Tey Diana Rebolledo, "Narrative Strategies of Resistance in Hispana Writing," *Journal of Narrative Technique* 20, no. 2 (1990): 134–46. See also Rebolledo, "Las Escritoras," in *Pasó por Aquí*, ed. Erlinda Gonzales-Berry (1989). An obituary is in the *Santa Fe New Mexican*, 3 Dec. 1956.

JANE CREIGHTON

JARDINE, William Marion (16 Jan. 1879–17 Jan. 1955), secretary of agriculture and college president, was born in Oneida County, Idaho, the son of William Jardine and Rebecca (maiden name unknown), farmers. Jardine learned ranching and farming from his father, who had homesteaded the family land in the 1860s. At the age of sixteen, Jardine left Idaho and worked several years as a lumberjack and dairy helper in Montana. When he was twenty years old, he persuaded the Agricultural College of Utah in Logan to admit him even though he lacked a high school diploma. He graduated in 1904 with a degree in agronomy and accepted an offer to teach that subject at the college.

In 1905 Jardine married Effie Nebecker; they had three children. He left the college in 1907 to join the Department of Agriculture in Washington, D.C., where he investigated dryland farming as related to grain production. As an assistant cerealist, Jardine traveled extensively and gained firsthand knowledge about farming practices in various sections of the United States. In 1910 he resigned to join the faculty at Kansas State Agricultural College. A nationally recognized expert in agronomy, he became dean of agriculture in 1913. At about the same time, he purchased land near Manhattan, Kansas, where he practiced scientific agriculture to show farmers how to increase crop yields. During World War I, he planned agricultural production for the state of Kansas.

In 1918 Jardine was appointed president of Kansas State Agricultural College. A competent administrator, he launched a building program and approved curricula changes. In 1921 Kansas State offered a course in rural commerce that eventually became the business administration program. Other changes included the addition of chemical engineering, landscape architecture, and architectural engineering programs. The conservative side of the president emerged in November 1919, during a strike of coal workers in the southeast corner of Kansas, when Jardine suggested that male students from the college go work in the mines.

Jardine remained at Kansas State College until 1925, when President Calvin Coolidge asked him to join the cabinet as secretary of agriculture. In that position, Jardine reduced the number of administrators in the department, sent more agents into the field, and stressed the business or marketing side as opposed to the production phase of farming. As an innovator, Jardine made use of the radio to keep those in rural areas informed of new ideas and changes in agriculture. During his tenure as secretary, he was an outspoken critic of the McNary-Haugen Bill, which was designed to help farmers by maintaining the prices of farm products during times of surpluses. Under the proposed legislation, a federal farm board would buy the surplus commodities, which would then be kept in reserve or sold abroad at the existing price. To help alleviate the problems farmers faced, Jardine instead stressed the cooperative, with which he believed farmers would have more political and economic clout and farming would be more efficient and less expensive. He also argued that the cooperative could relieve some of the financial problems for farmers with the organization of a credit corporation. The solution for farmers' problems with overproduction, according to Jardine, was greater efficiency and better management. He concluded that if the McNary-Haugen Bill became law, farmers would produce more and create an even greater surplus of agricultural goods. He also faulted the bill because he opposed direct government intervention to help farmers in principle. As an alternative, Jardine proposed what eventually became the Cooperative Marketing Act, which Congress passed in 1926.

After Herbert Hoover became president in 1929, he appointed Jardine minister to Egypt. It was a unique opportunity for Jardine to observe firsthand Egyptian farming practices and to broaden his governmental experience. When he returned to the United States in 1933, he served for one year as state treasurer of Kansas during the administration of Governor Alf M. Landon.

In 1934 Jardine accepted the position of president of the Municipal University of Wichita (now Wichita State University). One of his goals was to reduce friction between the community and the faculty by recognizing and supporting the youthful enthusiasm and potential of the city. When three professors failed to support his plan, Jardine removed them. That action prompted an investigation by the American Association of University Professors (AAUP), which did not agree with Jardine but at the same time did not impose sanctions. His tenure at Wichita did include more positive actions. In particular, he encouraged growth and improvements with a building campaign and higher salaries for faculty. A new library and an enlarged science department sparked an increase in enrollments. The university constructed Veterans' Field in 1948 to honor those students who had served in World War II. Jardine also supported the establishment of the Institute for Logopedics, which enjoyed a worldwide reputation for research and treatment of handicapped children. He resigned in 1949 and retired with his wife to San Antonio, Texas, where he died.

Jardine devoted a large portion of his life to public service. Although he grew up in rural areas, he adjusted to the nation's urbanization. He recognized that the United States was undergoing changes that created conflict between industrialization and agriculture. His efforts concentrated on securing for farmers a share in the prosperity of the times. Jardine was successful in his endeavors in part because of his engaging personality. As an administrator, he was noted for his ability to make decisions that reflected careful analysis. He was an outspoken, energetic leader who stood firm in his beliefs.

• Jardine's papers are in the Special Collections Department, Ablah Library, Wichita State University, which also houses a manuscript study of his tenure as president, John Rydjord, "University of Wichita History." Additional Jardine papers are in the Library of Congress, and the U.S. Department of Agriculture records for 1925–1929 in the National Archives are useful. C. Fred Williams addresses Jardine's experiences as secretary of agriculture in "William M. Jardine: The Far-

mers and McNary-Haugenism" (M.A. thesis, Wichita State Univ., 1966). For a detailed study of Jardine when he was president of the University of Wichita, see Craig Miner, *Uncloistered Halls: The Centennial History of Wichita State University* (1995). See Donald R. McCoy, *Landon of Kansas* (1996), for Jardine's role as state treasurer, and Julius T. Willard, *History of Kansas State College of Agriculture and Applied Science* (1940), for a discussion of Jardine's tenure as president there. An obituary is in the *New York Times*, 18 Jan. 1955.

JUDITH R. JOHNSON

JARMAN, W. Maxey (10 May 1904–9 Sept. 1980), corporate executive and philanthropist, was born Walton Maxey Jarman in Nashville, Tennessee, the son of James Franklin Jarman, part-owner of a shoe company, and Eugenia Maxey. In his youth Jarman liked working with cars and radios and attended a local public high school specializing in engineering and other technical subjects. He also had a hand in starting WSM, Nashville's first radio station. He enrolled at Massachusetts Institute of Technology as an electrical engineering major, but quit during his junior year in 1924 to join his father in starting a new shoe factory. The firm, known at first as Jarman Shoe Company, began with capital of $130,000. It reached $1,000,000 in sales and turned a profit the first year and established the pattern of doubling sales and profits every six years. Jarman married Sarah McFerrin Anderson of Gallatin, Tennessee, in 1928. She had studied math at Randolph-Macon Woman's College and was an accomplished diver, noted for her jumps from cliffs into the Cumberland River. The couple raised three children.

Jarman's father brought him into the shoe company as a clerk, then kept moving him around. He had jobs as a correspondent and buyer and thereafter in sales, credit, advertising, finance, and administration. When his father's health began to fail Jarman, then age twenty-eight, became president. He was later made chairman.

As the business grew, the name was changed to General Shoe Corporation. With the addition of lines of clothing and the acquisition of numerous retail outlets it became Genesco Inc. Among the 1,750 stores it operated by 1968 were such legendary Fifth Avenue establishments as Tiffany, Bonwit Teller, Henri Bendel, and I. Miller. Sales that year topped $1 million, and with 65,000 employees the company was described as the world's largest apparel conglomerate. Following policy disputes with officers who succeeded him—including his son, Franklin—Jarman left the Genesco board at the end of 1974.

Jarman's introduction to philanthropic activities also came courtesy of his father, who placed newspaper ads offering a free Bible to all who would promise to read a chapter a day for a month. As a boy, Jarman had the responsibility of wrapping and mailing Bibles to those who responded. The chore helped to develop his intense lifelong fascination with the Bible.

In a starkly lucid book, something of an autobiography written a few years before his retirement, Jarman, a Southern Baptist, recalled his being brought up to attend church each Sunday and to contribute to it regularly from his allowance. "My life," he wrote, "was carefully restricted as to amusements and worldly activities. As a family we read from the Bible at breakfast every morning and I was often exposed to conversation about it. . . . When I was eleven I had a conversion experience and became a member of our church." Thereafter he read the Bible through each year.

His book *A Businessman Looks at the Bible* (1965) describes Jarman's days at MIT as "a rough experience" in which he felt misgivings about things that he had previously been sure of. He noticed, however, that the skeptics who were pelting him with questions did not know much about the Bible themselves and were simply parroting the opinions of others. So he made it a personal credo in both religion and business to avoid assumptions before making authentically objective investigations.

Soon after, Jarman also concluded that although he was an avid reader of many kinds of literature, the best way to make judgments about the Bible's worth was to try to live by it and that the best way to understand it was to try to teach it. His first attempt at the latter was a class of 14-year-old boys at the First Baptist Church of Nashville, wherein he remembers learning something about people as well. One of his students became president of the Southern Baptist Convention, the largest Protestant denomination in America.

Jarman's evangelical views, coupled with his generosity, got him involved with a host of Christian institutions, including the American Bible Society, where he served a term as vice president. His tenure as a trustee of Moody Bible Institute stretched across nearly forty years. In addition, he was closely associated with Billy Graham's organization and was an original board member of Christianity Today, Inc., a publishing operation founded by the evangelist to promote Biblical theology. Through a foundation begun by his father, Jarman gave large sums to build churches around the world.

Jarman also served as a trustee of the National Jewish Hospital in Denver, and his company sent employees to Israel to help the new nation build and operate a shoe manufacturing facility there.

So wide was his range of interests that Jarman came across as an extraordinarily complex individual. Many saw a shy manner in him. Others knew him as tough but fair, daring but analytical. An ardent Republican, he was nonetheless an admirer of Robert Kennedy. Jarman kept in close touch with his party, but only tried to gain office once. He lost a bid to become the state GOP gubernatorial nominee in 1970.

Over the years Jarman collected abstract paintings. He eventually took art classes and tried his own hand at it. Jarman died in Nashville.

Jarman's ambitious management style ignited an apparel industry revolution that extended into the latter years of the twentieth century. The revolution, driven initially by Jarman's quest for major new synergies, eventually emerged with worldwide consumer demand for designer labels as its centerpiece. Simultaneously, Jarman's avocational interests propelled him into behind-the-scenes leadership roles in the aggressive promotion of evangelical Christianity.

• A few documents relating to Jarman are retained by the Moody Bible Institute in Chicago and the Jarman Foundation in Nashville. A small file of published materials about him is in the custody of the Historical Commission of the Southern Baptist Convention in Nashville. In addition to *A Businessman Looks at the Bible*, Jarman also compiled an anthology of Bible passages designed for daily devotional reading, *O Taste and See* (1957). *The Genesco Formula for Growth*, published by the Newcomen Society in North America in 1969, featured an address by Jarman. The most comprehensive account of his life is found in Richard Hammer, "The Cold-Blooded Dreamer of Nashville and Seventh Avenue," *Fortune*, Feb. 1961. Brief descriptive tributes following his death appear in *Christianity Today*, 10 Oct. 1980, and an obituary is in the *New York Times*, 10 Sept. 1980.

DAVID E. KUCHARSKY

JARRATT, Devereux (17 Jan. 1733–29 Jan. 1801), Anglican, later Episcopal, minister, was born in New Kent County, Virginia, the son of Robert Jarratt, a middling carpenter-farmer, and Sarah Bradley. According to his autobiography, published posthumously in 1806, the family was comfortable but hardly affluent, and Jarratt himself noted major differences between the simplicity of his own existence and the gentle circumstances of the class-conscious Virginia aristocrats. When Robert Jarratt died, his oldest son, also named Robert and also a carpenter, inherited the family plantation and became guardian of his younger brother, who was then between six and seven years old. Devereux attended a local English school until age eleven or twelve, then led the life of a typical eighteenth-century farm lad for a half-dozen years. Nominally Anglican, Jarratt reported in his autobiography that religion played only a small role in his life during that time. However, he continued to study secular subjects on his own and by age nineteen had acquired such renown as a self-taught scholar that Jacob Moon, an overseer in Albemarle County, invited him one hundred miles west to take up a position as schoolmaster.

While lodging with the Moon family Jarratt first became aware of George Whitefield, through reading some of the great evangelist's published sermons that a visitor had left at the farm. By Jarratt's own admission, Whitefield's sermons made no great impact on him, but after two lean years as a schoolmaster, he became a tutor in the household of Albemarle County planter John Cannon, whose wife started the young teacher on the New Light path. Jarratt stayed with the Cannon family for the next five or six years, devoting an increasing amount of time to introspection and to the study of religious texts. At about age twenty-five he moved to Cumberland County to open a school. Instead, Jarratt himself became a student for a year, studying with Alexander Martin, a Princeton graduate and future North Carolina governor and senator, who had come to Virginia as a tutor. When Martin returned to New Jersey after a year, Jarratt again took up the role of tutor, in Cumberland County.

To that point, most of the positive forces in Jarratt's religious life had been Presbyterian. It must have been something of a shock to the many friends who had urged him to become a Presbyterian minister when he traveled to England for ordination as an Anglican priest in 1763. Jarratt returned to Virginia the following year to become rector of Bath Parish in Dinwiddie County, where he preached at the Butterwood, Hatcher's Run, and Saponey churches. Upon establishing himself in Bath Parish, Jarratt married Martha Claiborne, the daughter of a prominent Dinwiddie County planter, Burnell Claiborne. Jarratt thus acquired connections to a politically powerful family as well as considerable wealth. It is not known whether the Jarratts had any children. Although he denied the charge when Methodist critics attacked him for owning slaves, Dinwiddie County tax rolls between 1782 and 1800 show that as many as twenty-four slaves worked the Jarratt plantation.

Jarratt took up his duties in Bath Parish as the Great Awakening began to shake the religious, social, and political foundations of the Old Dominion. He emerged as the Anglican clergyman most identified with the revivalist cause. Preaching tirelessly to large audiences throughout the Virginia Southside region and also in North Carolina, on the eve of the American revolution, Jarratt adopted the emotional style associated with evangelical Presbyterian, Baptist, and Methodist ministers, though his theology never truly strayed very far from Calvinism.

Jarratt succeeded as an evangelist, but he suffered censure within the traditionally oriented Anglican establishment. In those ecclesiastical battles he clearly landed as many blows as he received, to the extent that modern historians have often accepted uncritically Jarratt's derogatory comments on the character of fellow Anglican clergymen. Initially friendly to Methodist preachers, he later chastised them for abandoning the Anglican Church, thereby opening a breech that never healed. A somewhat reluctant Whig during the struggle for independence, Jarratt remained at his post as rector of Bath Parish after the disestablishment of the Anglican Church, but his then-Episcopal congregation dwindled to a mere shadow of its size during the late colonial era. About 1794 Jarratt contracted cancer and, after struggling with the disease for some seven years, he died in Bath Parish.

• While there is no collection of Jarratt's personal papers, there is *The Life of the Reverend Devereux Jarratt, Rector of Bath Parish, Dinwiddie County, Virginia. Written by Himself, in a Series of Letters Addressed to the Rev. John Coleman, One of the Ministers of the Protestant Episcopal Church, in Maryland* (1806), most of which is reprinted in Douglass Adair, ed., "The Autobiography of the Reverend Devereux Jarratt, 1723–1763," *William and Mary Quarterly*, 3d ser., 9 (July 1952): 346–93. All modern historians of the Great Awakening in Virginia have relied extensively on this memoir, often taking Jarratt's questionable assertions at face value. See, for example, William Warren Sweet, *Religion in Colonial America* (1942), and Rhys Isaac, *The Transformation of Virginia, 1740–1790* (1982). Of particular note on this point, see David L. Holmes's insightful foreword to the 1995 reprinting of Jarratt's *Life*.

JAMES P. WHITTENBURG

JARRELL, Helen Ira (27 July 1896–27 Aug. 1973), teacher and school administrator, was born in Meriwether County, Georgia, the daughter of William Henry Jarrell and Emma Hutchison, farmers. Jarrell's father moved the family to Atlanta in 1901 because of bad economic times for farmers. Ira, as she was called, attended Atlanta public schools, where she began to pursue her goal of becoming a teacher. She graduated from Atlanta's Girls' High School and then entered the Atlanta Normal School to prepare for teaching. She earned both a bachelor's (1928) and a master's degree (1931) from Oglethorpe University, north of Atlanta. She began teaching in an Atlanta elementary school in 1916. In 1930 she was promoted to the position of senior teacher, and in 1934 she became an elementary school principal.

Just before her promotions Jarrell had become active in the Atlanta Public School Teachers' Association (APSTA), Local 89 of the American Federation of Teachers (AFT). She moved up quickly in the association hierarchy, eventually becoming president of the APSTA in 1936. She was an effective union officer, navigating well in the waters of city and state politics. The APSTA, in addition to being an AFT local, was also affiliated with the Atlanta Federation of Trades, the city's central labor body. Jarrell and the trades federation worked together in 1937 to elect a board of education attuned to the interests of the teacher organization. As a teacher unionist, Jarrell led the majority faction of the APSTA. Her approach to teacher unionism was careful and conservative, though she was not afraid to pursue teachers' economic interests vigorously. In turn, she and her members respected the system's central administration and the role and responsibility of school principals. The minority faction, which sought social and political change as well as economic improvement, proved impotent in the face of its small numbers and Jarrell's considerable political abilities.

In 1944 Jarrell was appointed by the board of education to the position of superintendent of the Atlanta public schools. She remained in that position until 1960. During her administration, the number of schools in the Atlanta system doubled, the enrollment more than doubled as did the number of teachers, and nearly $40 million was spent on the construction of new buildings. In 1947 she began a reorganization of Atlanta's high schools that replaced the five citywide high schools—including the long-established and much revered Boys', Girls', and Tech High Schools—with ten coeducational high schools. Her ability to accomplish this reorganization, in the face of powerful political opposition from the alumni of the existing high schools, further testified to the political power that she had accumulated in her position. Other priorities of her superintendency included improving teacher salaries, a longstanding commitment of the APSTA. She also made strides in the provision of special educational opportunities for the city's handicapped children. Finally, she pioneered the establishment of a planetarium and a radio station as part of the city school system.

Jarrell's relations with the city's black community, its schools, and its teachers, were not harmonious. In the early 1940s she helped the APSTA successfully fend off the legal challenge of the city's black teachers for equal pay with whites. To accomplish this, the APSTA acquiesced in the formal disbanding of the teachers' salary scale, thereby reversing a reform that it had long advocated. The issue of racial equity within the scale thus became moot. After the 1954 *Brown v. Board of Education* school desegregation decision, she made no effort to deflect, let alone contravene, the forces of "massive resistance" to the decision that were unleashed in Atlanta and elsewhere in the South. As the Atlanta public schools moved toward formal compliance with *Brown* in 1959, in response to a suit filed by the city's black citizens, the superintendent was notably reluctant to participate. In 1960 she resigned from the superintendency, leaving to her successor the task of desegregation.

After her resignation, Jarrell worked briefly for the state department of education. Poor health caused her to resign from that position after a few years. She soon left the city to live with her brother in Arkansas, where she died. Jarrell was one of the first women to become a school superintendent. Although she did not promote the interests of women or minorities in that office, her successful career as superintendent testified to the reality that women could function as mainstream leaders of school systems and not necessarily as reformers.

• No collection of Jarrell's papers is available. The archives of the Atlanta public schools contain a wide variety of primary source material relevant to her career in Atlanta. The most comprehensive secondary account of Jarrell and her educational work is in Melvin Ecke, *From Ivy Street to Kennedy Center: A Centennial History of the Atlanta Public School System* (1972). A more interpretive account of Jarrell's career is in Joseph W. Newman, "A History of the Atlanta Public School Teachers' Association, Local 89 of the Atlanta Federation of Teachers, 1919–1956" (Ph.D. diss., Georgia State Univ., 1978). An obituary is in the *Atlanta Constitution*, 28 Aug. 1973.

WAYNE J. URBAN

JARRELL, Randall (6 May 1914–14 Oct. 1965), poet and critic, was born in Nashville, Tennessee, the son of Owen Jarrell and Anna Campbell. Owen's working-class family was from Shelbyville, Tennessee; Anna Jarrell came from a prosperous Nashville business family. During the first year or so of Jarrell's life, the family moved several times. In 1915 they settled on a 45-acre farm outside Los Angeles, not far from Owen Jarrell's parents and grandmother. Jarrell's father and mother separated, and she returned to Nashville with Jarrell and his younger brother. It was during this time that Jarrell served as a model for Ganymede in the bas-relief sculpture on Nashville's replica of the Parthenon. According to an often cited story, the sculptors were so taken with young Jarrell, who entertained them with stories of mythology, that they told his mother they would like to adopt him. Jarrell's mother did not tell him of the offer, for fear that he would want to go with the sculptors. When Jarrell finally heard of the story much later, he answered, "She was right. I'd have gone with them like *that*."

While Jarrell's parents were divorcing, he was sent back to California to live with his paternal grandparents and great-grandmother. His memories of that time in 1926, when he experienced the wonders of the movie industry and the closeness of his family, are related in his three-part poem *The Lost World*. By the time Jarrell graduated from high school in Nashville, his mother had remarried. Her wealthy brother, Howell Campbell, declined to give his sister a gift for her second wedding and offered instead to be responsible for Jarrell's education. As a result of his uncle's generosity, Jarrell went to Vanderbilt University, where he majored in psychology and took creative writing from John Crowe Ransom. Jarrell earned his B.A. in psychology in 1935 and then switched to English for his M.A. Ransom left Vanderbilt for Kenyon College in Ohio, and Jarrell soon followed, teaching at Kenyon while continuing to work on his dissertation with Donald Davidson back at Vanderbilt. During his years at Vanderbilt and Kenyon, Jarrell met Ransom, Robert Penn Warren, Peter Taylor, Alan Tate, and Robert Lowell, all literary figures who became his lifelong friends. After earning his M.A., Jarrell was hired by the University of Texas in Austin, where he taught from 1939 to 1942. In 1940 he married Mackie Langham, who was also a member of the English faculty. They had no children, but they had a long-haired black cat named Kitten, whom Jarrell loved and kept until 1956, when the cat was struck by a car.

Jarrell began to acquire a reputation as a fine young poet. His first publication was five poems in a poetry supplement edited by Alan Tate for the May 1934 issue of the *American Review*. With the help of Warren at the *Southern Review* and Ransom at the *Kenyon Review*, Jarrell experienced no trouble getting published. Jarrell's work made its first appearance in the prestigious *Poetry* magazine in the July 1939 issue. In 1940 his collection of twenty poems was featured in *Five Young American Poets*, and in 1942 his first volume of verse, *Blood for a Stranger*, was published.

Jarrell enlisted in the U.S. Army Air Force in October 1942 and served until February 1946, spending most of his time at Davis-Monthan Field in Tucson, Arizona, as an instructor in celestial navigation. Although Jarrell never saw combat, he wrote many war poems during his military service, and it is for these that he is best known by the general public. The most familiar is perhaps "The Death of the Ball Turret Gunner," a five-line poem that ends with "When I died they washed me out of the turret with a hose." *Little Friend, Little Friend*, published in 1945, contains many of the poems that draw upon Jarrell's military service.

Jarrell taught briefly at Sarah Lawrence College while filling in for a year as literary editor of *The Nation*. In 1947 he was hired as assistant professor at Women's College, University of North Carolina at Greensboro. Except for the two years when he was a consultant in poetry at the Library of Congress (1956–1958), Jarrell remained on the faculty the rest of his life.

In July 1951 Jarrell taught at the Rocky Mountain Writers' Conference in Boulder, Colorado. There he met and fell in love with Mary von Schrader, who was recently divorced and the mother of two daughters. He soon separated from Mackie, and the divorce was final in October 1952. Jarrell and von Schrader were married on 8 November. They remained married until he was struck and killed by an automobile while walking down a road one evening in Chapel Hill, North Carolina. Although the medical examiner ruled the death an accident, some speculate that his death was suicide. Jarrell had slashed his wrist several months earlier in a suicide attempt and was under treatment for emotional problems. Further, the occupants of the car reported that he had seemed to lunge into the path of the car. Mary Jarrell denied the possibility of suicide, pointing out in *Randall Jarrell's Letters* that the nature of his injuries and the fact that he was in good spirits indicate his death was an accident.

Jarrell was best known for his poetry. In addition to his war poetry, he wrote haunting poems about the loneliness of childhood, frequently using the motif of the lost sibling, evocative of a sister who died before his birth. Jarrell, who never wanted children of his own, wrote several acclaimed children's books, including *The Bat-Poet*, illustrated by Maurice Sendak. He also wrote one novel, *Pictures from an Institution* (1954). Among academics he was known as an insightful, if often harsh, critic of poetry. His other accomplishments include translations of *Faust* and the works of Rilke and Grimm.

• Jarrell's papers are at the library of the University of North Carolina at Greensboro and in the Berg Collection at the New York Public Library. William H. Pritchard, *Randall Jarrell: A Literary Life* (1990), is essential reading. Drawing on published and unpublished correspondence, interviews with those who knew Jarrell, and various public documents, the book discusses the events of Jarrell's life and also his works. It includes ten pages of photographs of Jarrell, from childhood to 1963. Bernetta Quinn, *Randall Jarrell* (1981), is a more concise discussion of Jarrell's life and works, and is noteworthy for the remembrances of Jarrell by his students. *Randall Jarrell's Letters*, ed. Mary Jarrell (1985), contains not only many letters from Jarrell, but also explanatory notes by his widow.

Richard Flynn, *Randall Jarrell and the Lost World of Childhood* (1990), discusses the effect of Jarrell's childhood on his work; the bibliography of secondary sources is comprehensive. Suzanne Ferguson, ed., *Critical Essays on Randall Jarrell* (1983), and Robert Lowell, ed., *Randall Jarrell 1914–1965* (1967), both reveal how Jarrell was regarded by his colleagues. For insightful critiques of Jarrell's poetry, see J. A. Bryant, *Understanding Randall Jarrell* (1986), and M. L. Rosenthal, *Randall Jarrell* (1972). The most complete listing of Jarrell's works is Stuart Wright, *Randall Jarrell: A Descriptive Bibliography, 1929–1983* (1985).

CLAUDIA MILSTEAD

JARRELL, Tommy (1 Mar. 1901–28 Jan. 1985), banjo player and fiddler, was born Thomas Jefferson Jarrell in Round Peak, North Carolina, the son of Ben Jarrell, a well-known local fiddler who made pioneering string-band recordings with an organization called Da Costa Woltz's Southern Broadcasters in 1927, and Susan (maiden name unknown). Strangely, his father did not encourage him much in his music, and young Jarrell learned the old-style clawhammer banjo style from Baugie Cockerham, a family hired hand. By 1911 Jarrell had also started playing the fiddle, emulating his father's style as well as the unorthodox tunings used by area fiddlers, some of whom were veterans of the Civil War.

After Ben Jarrell left his family to try his luck in Oregon in 1918, Tommy Jarrell found himself working from dawn to dusk to eke out a living farming; by 1920 he had taken up another of his father's traditions, making moonshine liquor. (North Carolina had voted in Prohibition in 1909.) He and his brother Fred led a rough, sometimes violent, life during these days, and at one point they had to flee across the state line into Virginia to escape an assault warrant sworn out by their uncle. There, in Lambsburg, Jarrell met his future wife, Nina (maiden name unknown); they married in 1923 and eventually raised a family of three children.

Though he continued to develop his music, Jarrell spent much of his later life running a grader for the North Carolina Department of Transportation. One of his projects was to work on the building of the Blue Ridge Parkway. Though he was recognized as a superb musician by fans in his native Surry County, he was reluctant to record and to enter contests, and it was only after he retired in 1966 that the outside world began to hear of him. His son mentioned him to Alan Jabbour, later the director of the American Folklife Center, and Jabbour recorded him; this led to commercial recordings on the County label, as well as a series of invitations to folk festivals.

By the 1970s Jarrell was constantly being sought by younger musicians who marveled at his technical skill and who were impressed by the fact that he played in an archaic style that dated from deep in the Appalachian tradition. He attended the Smithsonian Institution's Festival of American Folklife numerous times, and in 1982 he won a National Heritage Fellowship Award from the National Endowment for the Arts, which recognized him as a "master traditional musician." He died in Mount Airy, North Carolina.

• Little has been written about Jarrell. For more information see Cecelia Conway, "Thomas Jefferson Jarrell," *North Carolina Folklore Journal* 30, no. 1 (1982): 3. See also the liner notes booklet to the compact disc *Tommy and Fred* (Tommy Jarrell and Fred Cockerham), County CD 2702 (1992).

CHARLES K. WOLFE

JARRETT, Mary Cromwell (21 June 1877–4 Aug. 1961), social work educator, was born in Baltimore, Maryland, the daughter of Caroline Watkins and Frank Asbury Jarrett, a bookkeeper, partner in a tailoring business, and reporter. Almost nothing is known of her early life. She graduated from the Woman's College of Baltimore (later Goucher College) in 1900, taught for a short time, and did some volunteer work for the Baltimore Charity Society. From this typical female activity of the period, she moved to a paid position and the beginning of a lifetime career in social work and social work education.

In 1903 Jarrett took a position as a welfare worker with the Boston Children's Aid Society, where she was trained on the job in the emerging social work casework method. By the time she left a decade later, she was the head of the casework department. For the next four years (1913–1917) Jarrett worked at the Boston Psychiatric Hospital, where its influential director, Dr. E. E. Southard, invited her to organize and head a social service department. Her collaboration with Southard was a turning point for her because together they developed the clinical team approach to patients with psychiatric disorders, which they named "psychiatric social work." The clinical team, which included, at a minimum, a psychiatrist and a social worker, incorporated the most recent knowledge of psychology and psychiatry to develop new counseling and rehabilitation techniques for workers and others with emotional problems. They developed this method of working with patients in all social classes and rejected the prevailing notion of social work as an activity directed to the poor and the powerless.

In 1918, with Southard's encouragement, Jarrett developed an intensive summer training program for psychiatric social workers who would work with soldiers suffering from war-induced emotional injuries. At the end of the war the rationale for the program shifted. Jarrett and Southard spearheaded a movement to begin a graduate program in psychiatric social work that would place personality development at the center of the curriculum. They justified women's entrance into this field by downplaying, as Southard indicated, the "somewhat strong food of modern psychiatry and psychopathology" and emphasizing the links to traditional notions of female service.

Jarrett moved to Northampton, Massachusetts, in 1919 to become the associate director of the new psychiatric social work graduate program at Smith College. Although she had outstanding experience, she did not have the appropriate credentials to become the director. That position went to F. Stuart Chapin, a professor of sociology at Smith College who brought a Ph.D. to the office. Jarrett was a leading force at the school in developing a curriculum and institutionalizing a professional training program. She wrote, lectured, and actively lobbied for the development of a career for women that combined knowledge of psychiatry with the more traditional social work tasks of working with the families of patients in the hope of manipulating the social environment. With Southard she wrote *The Kingdom of Evils: 100 Case Histories* (1922), which became an important early text in the field. Jarrett also gave the field organizational permanence. In 1920 she organized the National Psychiatric Social Workers' Club, which in 1922 developed into the Section on Psychiatric Social Work of the American Association of Hospital Social Workers. Four years later the members voted to become the American Association of Psychiatric Social Workers, an independent organization.

The growth of psychiatric social work caused some disagreement in the mental health community. While Jarrett and her associates saw the mental hygiene movement (as it was also called) creating new opportunities for women, others in the field, particularly Mary Richmond, feared that patients' social problems would be ignored as the focus shifted to personality disorders. Some of Jarrett's major adversaries were alumnae of Smith College.

Jarrett resigned her position at Smith at what seemed to be the height of her career. Her mentor, Southard, had died, and the first director, Chapin, had been replaced by Everett Kimball, a professor of history and government at Smith College. Kimball had a Ph.D. from Harvard but had not been trained in social work. Jarrett's and Kimball's personalities clashed, and she resigned in 1923. There were several reasons for her ouster. In addition to the personality conflict, she suffered from lack of support from influential Smith graduates. Southard's death deprived her of a powerful ally just at the time when his initial ideas about psychiatry were being replaced by the introduction of Freudian psychology. She personally attributed the problems to the fact that Kimball was "jealous and resented any attention I received."

Whatever the combination of reasons for losing her position at Smith, Jarrett did leave the field of psychiatric social work education. In the late 1920s she moved with her lifetime companion, Katrine Collins, to New York City, where she spent the rest of her career developing programs for the elderly and the chronically ill.

In 1927 Jarrett became associated with the Welfare Council of New York City, working first as a member of the Research Bureau (1927–1933), then as secretary to the Committee on Chronic Illness (1933–1943), and finally as secretary of the Health Division (1941–1943). She wrote *Chronic Illness in New York City* (1933), the first comprehensive investigation into the problem of chronic illness in the United States. The study adopted a forward-looking approach to chronic illness and its management, emphasizing the need for comprehensive mental health and medical services, research, and the development of preventive programs.

Under Jarrett's direction, the Welfare Council also did various studies demonstrating the need for more and better nursing homes. She was also a leader in recommending the development of a community program that would meet the needs of the chronically ill, provide prevention and treatment services for the elderly, and integrate mental health services with medical care for those with physical disabilities. She died in New York City.

• Jarrett's papers are in the Sophia Smith Collection at Smith College and in the files of the Alumnae Association of the Smith College School for Social Work. An unpublished oral memoir of Jarrett by Maida Herman Solomon is in the William E. Wiener Oral History Library of the American Jewish Committee, New York, and a copy is also in the Schlesinger Library, Radcliffe College. Jarrett wrote many articles and books, including "Combating Chronic Illness," *Public Welfare*, June 1945; and, with Michael M. Davis, *A Health Inventory: A Study of Health Services in New York City* (1929). A discussion of her Smith College years can be found in Penina M. Glazer and Miriam Slater, *Unequal Colleagues: The Entrance of Women into the Professions, 1890–1930* (1987). An obituary is in the *New York Times*, 5 Aug. 1961.

PENINA MIGDAL GLAZER

JARVES, James Jackson (20 Aug. 1818–28 June 1888), journalist, diplomat, and art connoisseur, was born in Boston, Massachusetts, the son of Deming Jarves, the inventor of Sandwich glass, and Anna Smith Stutson. Jarves received some formal education at Chauncy Hall School in Boston and enhanced his knowledge by extensive reading. At fifteen he was bedridden by what was diagnosed as a "rush of blood to the head" that left him temporarily blind and unable to continue at school. Gradually he improved but when the doctors recommended that he live in a milder climate than New England he had to forgo a Harvard education.

In March 1837 Jarves headed toward the Pacific, stopping in South America and reaching Hawaii in late July. His first visit to Hawaii was short. In December he sailed for home and marriage, in October 1838, to Elizabeth Russell Swain of New Bedford, Massachusetts. The couple, who would eventually have three children, immediately returned to the Hawaiian islands, reaching there in April 1839.

James Jarves initially received a comfortable income from his father, although it did not continue indefinitely and throughout his life he was in and out of financial quagmires. Upon his return to the islands, he considered careers in journalism and business. One of his first articles for the *Hawaiian Spectator*, a quarterly review, so infuriated certain members of the public that in its aftermath Jarves had to move to the island of Kauai, where he tried to grow silkworms. The silkworm plantation did not prosper, and Jarves returned to journalism in Honolulu. In 1840 he published the first edition of the *Polynesian*, an English-language newspaper. It proved to be lively in content but a financial failure, closing after eighteen months. Jarves and his wife returned to Boston, where he settled down to some serious writing.

His first two books reflect his youthful travels but demonstrate his acquisitive mind. In 1843 he published *History of the Hawaiian or Sandwich Islands* and *Scenes and Scenery in the Sandwich Islands, and a Trip Through Central America*. Both volumes were well received by the public, and the first is still referred to by historians of Hawaii, though they make allowances for its promissionary bias. In 1886 King Kalakaua would give Jarves the order of Kamehameha I (knight commander) for his writing on Hawaiian history and his services to the kingdom.

Jarves's thoughts turned once again to Hawaii, returning there in April 1844 and bringing with him presses and other equipment needed to reestablish the *Polynesian*. Its first issue appeared on 18 May 1844; two months later it was purchased by the Hawaiian government as its "official journal." Jackson was retained as editor, with the title director of government printing. Jarves also tried his hand in a variety of mercantile and agricultural enterprises but without outstanding success. Elizabeth Jarves did not accompany her husband to the islands, preferring to remain in New England for the birth of their second child. It was two years before the family rejoined Jarves in Hawaii. From then on their marriage was marked by frequent separations and dissension.

In January 1848 Jarves resigned from the editorship of the *Polynesian* and sailed for Boston, his family home. He continued to be interested in the affairs of the Hawaiian kingdom. In October he had an unofficial yet fruitful meeting with Secretary of State James Buchanan during which he explained the desire of the Hawaiian government to enter into a treaty with the United States designed to respect the independence of the Kingdom of Hawaii and to foster mutual trade. He transmitted an account of that interview to the Hawaiian government, and in April 1849 Jarves was appointed by King Kamehameha III as his special commissioner to negotiate a treaty with the government of the United States and to obtain, from Great Britain and France, certain concessions in their treaties with the Hawaiian government.

By the time his commission reached Jarves in Boston, John M. Clayton was the new secretary of state, but he shared his predecessor's views favoring Hawaiian sovereignty and trade reciprocity. The Clayton-Jarves treaty was signed on 6 December 1849. Meanwhile, a similar treaty had been negotiated in San Francisco by the newly appointed U.S. commissioner to Hawaii, Charles Eames, and Dr. Gerrit P. Judd, a member of the Hawaiian government who was bound for Washington and Europe on diplomatic business for the kingdom. Judd confidently left the problem of the dual treaties to Jarves, who successfully negotiated an amalgam of the two treaties, which were signed on 20 December 1849. When duly ratified by both governments, they were the basis of relations between the United States and Hawaii until the islands were annexed to the United States at the end of the century.

Although Jarves never conducted business for the Hawaiian government in Europe, he did go there in

1851 and became so intrigued with the continent that he never returned to Hawaii and seldom to the United States. While in Paris he wrote *Parisian Sights and French Principles, Seen Through American Spectacles* (1852) before finding a more permanent home in Florence. Jarves's first wife died there in 1861, and he married Isabella Kast Heyden in 1862; they had three children.

In Florence, Jarves finished *Art-Hints, Architecture, Sculpture and Painting* (1855) and *Italian Sights and Papal Principles* (1856). He allowed himself one short reversion to his Hawaiian days in a romantic novel, *Kiana: A Tradition of Hawaii* (1857), and then turned to an introspective work, *Why and What Am I? The Confessions of an Inquirer* (1857), before returning to his new writing interest with *Art Studies: The "Old Masters" of Italy; Painting* (1861), *The Art-Idea: Part Second of Confessions of an Inquirer* (1864), and *Art Thoughts, the Experiences and Observations of an American Amateur in Europe* (1870).

His ability to write about art was so encompassing that in 1876 he produced *A Glimpse of the Art of Japan*, which was well received although he wrote it without ever visiting that country. His final works were *Italian Rambles, Studies of Life and Manners in New and Old Italy* (1883) and his posthumously published *Pepero, the Boy-Artist*. His *A Brief Memoir of James Jackson Jarves, Jr.* (1891) was a tribute to his talented son, who died at the age of fifteen. During his lifetime Jarves also contributed articles to *Harper's New Monthly Magazine* and other publications and wrote or contributed to numerous art catalogs.

In conjunction with his writing, Jarves began to collect art in Europe, concentrating on early Italian masters. He did so not only for his own pleasure but to accumulate a collection that would be a potential resource for American art students. He hoped to have the collection purchased intact, but that was not feasible. Yale University bought 119; a second collection of 52 paintings was sold in 1884 to Liberty E. Holden and given to the Cleveland Art Museum; a collection of Venetian glass was given to the Metropolitan Museum of Art in New York City; and a collection of textiles was sold to the Farnsworth Museum at Wellesley College in Massachusetts. Despite his valiant efforts to enthuse the American public with the grandeur of early Italian art, the catalogs he produced, and the lectures he gave, the American art world remained largely indifferent to Jarves's collections.

While in Italy Jarves served for two years as U.S. vice consul in Florence, from September 1880 to December 1882, and in 1887 he was decorated by the king of Italy with the order of Cavaliere della Corona d'Italia in recognition of his services to Italy at the Boston exhibition. Jarves died while vacationing in Switzerland, shortly after the death of his second wife.

The life of Jarves is divided into two unequal parts. During his Hawaiian days he worked as a journalist and merchant, but he is best remembered there for his history of the Hawaiian islands and for completing the treaty between Hawaii and the United States that bears his name and lasted more than forty years. His European days were devoted to collecting and recording the great art of Italy, but perhaps his most important contribution was his organization or interpretation of his collections so that they could be of greatest use to future generations of art students.

• For the life of Jarves see Francis Steegmuller's biography, *The Two Lives of James Jackson Jarves* (1951), which includes a full list of books, articles, and catalogs by Jarves; Theodore Sizer, "James Jackson Jarves, A Forgotten New Englander," *New England Quarterly* (June 1933): 328–52; and Riley H. Allen, "Hawaii's Pioneers in Journalism," *Hawaiian Historical Society Report* 37 (1928): 69–103. In *The Hawaiian Kingdom*, vol. 1 (1968), pp. 377–80, Ralph S. Kuykendall gives a detailed explanation of U.S.–Hawaiian treaty negotiations in 1849.

RHODA E. A. HACKLER

JARVIS, DeForest Clinton (15 Mar. 1881–18 Aug. 1966), physician and author, was born in Plattsburgh, New York, the son of George Delaker Clinton Jarvis and Abbie Gena Vincent. After attending public schools in Burlington, Vermont, Jarvis received his M.D. in 1904 from the University of Vermont. He took residency training at a Burlington hospital and in 1909 began to practice otolaryngology in Barre, Vermont, which he continued until early in 1966. In 1908 Jarvis married Pearl Maeferd Macomber; they had one child.

Jarvis participated actively in medical and cultural affairs. He served as president of the American Laryngology, Rhinology and Otology Society, fellow of the American Medical Association, consultant to the Public Health Service, director of the Vermont Tuberculosis Association, and rural medicine editor of *Medical World*. A musician who could play many instruments, he founded and directed a junior symphony orchestra in Barre.

A fifth-generation native of Vermont on his mother's side, Jarvis developed an intense interest in the state's folk medicine. He learned its lore from conversations with old-timers and sought to test its verity by simple experiments on his daughter and other children and with animals, including chickens, mink, goats, cats, dogs, horses, and especially dairy cattle. He exchanged ideas about his growing convictions by developing a national correspondence network of physicians.

Jarvis became persuaded that "Nature [had] opened the first drugstore" and that Vermont folk medicine was concerned with "three R's—Resistance, Repair, and Recovery," with the priority being the prevention of illness. Health could best be maintained by a natural diet that was high in carbohydrates (corn not wheat) and sour drinks like cranberry juice, low in protein, and devoid of milk, citrus fruits, white flour, white sugar, and processed foods. According to Jarvis, people should rely on a regimen of four preventive remedies: two teaspoonfuls each of apple cider vinegar and honey in a glass of water, kelp tablets, and Lugol's solution of iodine, which would help the body maintain and restore its healthy acidity, necessary to resist pathogenic microorganisms and to withstand taxing weather changes. Kelp provided needed minerals, and iodine ensured the body's ability to relieve nervous tension and to promote clear thinking.

Serendipitous circumstances got Jarvis's theories into print. He had heard of an outbreak of mastitis among cattle that were owned by the Murchison family in Texas, and he sent the suggestion that vinegar should be added to the rations. The cattle recovered, and a family member who was a director of Henry Holt and Company suggested to the publisher that Jarvis put his ideas into a book. His *Folk Medicine: A Vermont Doctor's Guide to Good Health* (1958) was folksy in language, didactic in tone; it explained disease in simple terms and revived for a new day of discontented civilization the ideal of the simple natural life. Promising a cure for virtually all diseases and assuring a long and healthy life, the book became a major commercial success. When Jarvis published a sequel in 1960, *Folk Medicine* had been on the *New York Times* bestseller list for seventy-five weeks. *Arthritis and Folk Medicine* repeated the basic pattern of the first book, with special focus on the disease that its title featured. Sales reached the millions.

Scientists took Jarvis to task for his errors and oversimplifications, arguing that the acid/alkaline balance of the body as an explanation for most disease was baseless and unsafe for self-regulation. While vinegar and honey posed no danger, neither did they offer the universal curative competence that Jarvis promised. Not all of the various ailments that fell under the name arthritis were identical or amenable to Jarvis's simple treatments. They found his experimental techniques fatally flawed. Fredrick J. Stare, M.D., professor and founder of Harvard's department of nutrition, charged: "This claptrap is strictly for those gullible birds stung by the honeybee. The book . . . is good entertainment, but it properly belongs on the fiction list." "Much of the theory concerning disease and its treatment expressed in this book," wrote R. W. Lamont-Havers of the Arthritis Foundation, "stems from fallacious reasoning." When presented with such condemnations, the "white-thatched, square-jawed" author "with piercing eyes" replied: "Folks can criticize all they like. Some day scientific medicine will catch up."

Jarvis's claims for the therapeutic prowess of his recommended medications were challenged in other ways. When the publisher cited them in advertising *Folk Medicine*, the Federal Trade Commission ordered Holt to cease and desist. The book's regimens, the commission held, did not constitute "an adequate, effective or reliable treatment for the common cold, arthritis, kidney trouble, digestive disorders, high blood pressure, overweight and obesity, chronic fatigue, headaches including migraine, hay fever, asthma, dizziness, run down feelings, lack of energy, lack of fertility, sinus infections, or other nagging ills and chronic ailments, or diseases which defy conventional medical diagnosis and treatment" (*FTC Decisions* 57 [1960]:

1192). When commercial firms vended mixtures of apple cider vinegar and honey in proximity to copies of Jarvis's first book or with citations from the book in printed labeling, the Food and Drug Administration brought misbranding charges and seized the mixtures—one was named "Honegar"—which forced the practice to stop (FDA, *Notices of Judgment under the Federal Food, Drug, and Cosmetic Act*, nos. 6237, 6484, 6729, 7116, issued between Mar. 1961 and Aug. 1963). Jarvis was not personally involved in these cases, although he had mentioned commercial brand names in his books.

Jarvis's death in South Barre, Vermont, did not halt the sale of his books or the considerable reliance upon vinegar and honey in the popular culture. In 1992 the Arthritis Foundation was still answering letters of inquiry by stating that no evidence existed to show that honey and vinegar had any effect on a person's arthritis. Jarvis was a major figure in the midcentury upsurge in the United States of distorted doctrines of nutrition that made books and products relating to food pseudoscience the largest single component of a burgeoning health quackery.

• Information on Jarvis and his books appears in the *New York Post*, 22 Oct. 1959 and 15 Apr. 1974; *Life*, 21 Dec. 1959, pp. 74, 76; *Reader's Digest*, Mar. 1960, pp. 42–44; and Ronald M. Deutsch, *The Nuts among the Berries* (1961). Reviews of the Jarvis books include *New York Times*, 18 Sept. 1960; *Library Journal* 83 (1958): 596, and 85 (1960): 3094; *Vermont History* 27 (1959): 76–77, and 29 (1961): 56–57. Critique of Jarvis's ideas is found in the Arthritis Foundation archives in Atlanta, and material on the Food and Drug Administration cases is in the FDA archives, Record Group 88, Washington National Records Center, Suitland, Md. Nutritional quackery is a theme in James Harvey Young, *American Health Quackery* (1992). An obituary is in the *New York Times*, 19 Aug. 1966.

JAMES HARVEY YOUNG

JARVIS, Edward (9 Jan. 1803–31 Oct. 1884), psychiatrist and statistician, was born Asa Jarvis in Concord, Massachusetts, the son of Francis Jarvis, a baker and farmer, and Millicent Hosmer. In 1821 he changed his name to Edward Asa Jarvis, and shortly thereafter he stopped using his middle name. Raised in a patriarchal household, Jarvis imbibed the Unitarian faith in an orderly and moral world. He entered Harvard College in 1822 and graduated four years later. After successive apprenticeships with Drs. George C. Shattuck and Benjamin Lincoln, he received an M.D. from the Harvard Medical School in 1830. In 1834 he married Almira Hunt; they had no children. The two collaborated in treating mentally ill patients in their home as well as in professional work. Between 1830 and 1837 he practiced successively in Concord and Northfield, Massachusetts, and then moved to Louisville, Kentucky, where he remained until 1842. His ventures in private practice, however, proved disappointing because relatively few patients returned for visits. In 1842 he returned to Massachusetts and settled in

Dorchester. He quickly made the practice of psychiatry his specialty, which included caring for a small number of private mentally ill patients in his home.

Jarvis's success in psychiatric practice gave him the time to explore a variety of social and medical problems that confronted his native state and the nation. As a Unitarian who was trained in Scottish Common Sense philosophy, committed to a Baconian (that is, inductive) interpretation of science, and influenced by rising doubts about the efficacy of traditional therapeutics, he became part of a group that sought to synthesize medicine, morality, and social activism. Much of his adult career was devoted to developing an explanatory framework that would serve as a guide to individual and social improvement. His faith in the existence of a lawful and orderly universe led him to emphasize the importance of knowledge and education. In 1847 he published *Practical Physiology*, a text on human physiology and health for families and students. In his eyes, disease was the product of the willful violation of the natural laws that governed human behavior and thus was indissolubly linked to filth, immorality, ignorance, and improper living conditions. Within this intellectual framework medicine occupied a crucial role. By emphasizing fundamental principles, developing a universally valid nomenclature of diseases, and gathering statistical data, medicine could illuminate the laws that governed health and disease, and thus help to alter individual and social behavior.

Jarvis's first venture into statistical inquiry came with the publication of the federal census of 1840, which seemed to show a disproportionately high incidence of insanity among free northern African Americans. Jarvis published several pieces that pointed out errors in the census and then unsuccessfully sought to have the data corrected when southern defenders of slavery used the census to demonstrate that African Americans were not suited to freedom. Fascination with statistical inquiry led him to take an active and important role in improving federal censuses. He assisted in the preparation of the census of 1850, prepared the mortality volume for the census of 1860, and assisted in the preparatory work of designing the census of 1870. His preoccupation with the census was but a reflection of his belief that statistical data could illuminate social reality and inform the social policy-making process.

Like other nineteenth-century sanitarians, Jarvis contributed to the growing awareness of the importance of morbidity and mortality patterns and their relationships to the social and physical environment. In this sense he anticipated the emergence of twentieth-century social science and epidemiology. Consequently, he was active in the fight to improve registration systems to collect vital statistics and served as president of the American Statistical Association from 1852 to 1883. His most famous studies dealt with insanity and social policy. He was one of the first to point out that there was a relationship between community residents' distance from a mental hospital and the extent to which they used it. In a lengthy paper of 1850 he

emphasized that differential rates of insanity among males and females were but a function of their differing social roles. In 1854 he undertook for the Massachusetts legislature a comprehensive demographic and statistical study of mental illnesses. The *Report on Insanity and Idiocy in Massachusetts* (1855) related insanity to a variety of social, ethnic, and class factors and was clearly the most important nineteenth-century statistical analysis of insanity. Jarvis was also active in the Association of Medical Superintendents of American Institutions for the Insane (later the American Psychiatric Association), which was founded in 1844. He worked for the Sanitary Commission during the Civil War and took part in a number of public health debates between the 1850s and 1870s that dealt with the importance of the sanitary environment. During the last decade of his life he authored an unpublished autobiography and a long manuscript history of Concord. He and his wife died in Concord within two days of each other.

Jarvis's importance lay precisely in his efforts to unify medicine, science, and religion; he insisted that disease could never be understood apart from individual behavior or the state of society. From this followed his statistical researches on the social basis of insanity and his efforts to modernize the federal census. In many ways he anticipated the emergence of the social and behavioral sciences and the belief that morbidity and mortality patterns were but a reflection of the social and physical environment.

• The bulk of the Jarvis papers are at the Countway Library of Medicine, Harvard Medical School, and the Concord Free Public Library. His manuscript autobiography at the Houghton Library of Harvard University has been edited by Rosalba Davico, *The Autobiography of Edward Jarvis* (*Medical History*, suppl. no. 12 [1992]). Most of Jarvis's writings appeared in medical, psychiatric, and religious journals. His books included *Practical Physiology* (1847) and *Primary Physiology* (1848). For his career see Gerald N. Grob, *Edward Jarvis and the Medical World of Nineteenth-Century America* (1978), which also contains a complete bibliography of his writings.

GERALD N. GROB

JARVIS, Gregory B. *See* Challenger Shuttle Crew.

JARVIS, John Wesley (1781–14 Jan. 1840), portrait painter, was born in South Shields, England, the son of American-born parents John Jarvis and Ann Lambert. Jarvis's father, a scrivener and an active Methodist, probably had returned to England during the Revolution because of his Loyalist beliefs. Some time after Jarvis was born his father returned to America, settling ultimately in New York. Jarvis remained in England with his mother and his siblings. For at least some of this time they lodged in the household of his mother's great-great-uncle, Methodism's founder John Wesley (earlier biographical directories have claimed a closer relationship between Jarvis and his namesake), until they immigrated to New York City around 1785. The Jarvises eventually settled in Philadelphia in the early 1790s. In 1793 Ann Jarvis was listed in the Philadelphia city directory as a midwife.

Jarvis became an artist by following the typical American trajectory of beginning as an artisan and moving into painting. As a youth he became entranced with Philadelphia's street culture and joined a group of sign painters and artists, including Jeremiah Paul and Matthew Pratt. Determined to make a career in the arts, Jarvis first decided to become an engraver, perhaps because it suited his mechanical abilities and, given the burgeoning market for reproductions, provided a steady income. In 1796 he apprenticed with the artist Edward Savage, with whom he not only learned the trade but also began experimenting in other media, including drawing and oil painting, especially with his fellow worker in Savage's shop, David Edwin.

Savage moved his shop and employees to New York City in 1800, and when Jarvis ended his apprenticeship later that year he remained in that city to start his own career as an engraver, but he quickly moved away from a concentration on engraving and branched out into other areas of portraiture. By 1803 he was working in partnership with Joseph Wood primarily as a miniaturist but also painting portraits and taking portrait-profiles using a physionotrace, which traced an exact likeness of the subject's features. That the physionotrace was used by other colonial painters, such as the Peales, indicates that early American artists were committed to the primacy of a likeness and to an aesthetic of empiricism. Jarvis and Wood made a profitable living, but their partnership dissolved by 1810, possibly for personal reasons.

From 1810 to 1813 Jarvis lived in Baltimore, where he painted such local notables as Mr. and Mrs. Soloman Etting (Maryland Historical Society) and art patron Robert Gilmor, Jr. (Pennsylvania Academy of the Fine Arts), as well as Supreme Court justice Samuel Chase (private collection). Jarvis returned to New York City in 1813 and undertook the commission that cemented his reputation as a portraitist: a series of six full-length portraits of heroes of the War of 1812 for New York City Hall. Jarvis actually was only the city's third choice, but after Gilbert Stuart and Thomas Sully hesitated, he willingly accepted the commission. Jarvis's eagerness to put himself forward earned him the disdain of Stuart, who dismissed him as a careerist. The commission was begun in 1815 and completed in 1817; Jarvis painted a likeness of himself as a boatman in the portrait of Commodore Oliver Hazard Perry. In addition to Perry, the city hall portraits were of William Bainbridge, Jacob Jennings Brown, Isaac Hull, Thomas MacDonough, and Joseph Gardner Swift.

The city hall portraits provided Jarvis with the cachet to attract sitters and to make him a nationally preeminent portraitist. By the 1820s he was making frequent trips to the Upper South as well as to New Orleans, which proved a profitable market for his paintings; Jarvis boasted of grossing more than $6,000 per season. In 1814 he hired Henry Inman as an assistant and, later, John Quidor. Working extremely quickly and from brief sittings, Jarvis turned out six portraits a week from his studio. Relying on his assistants, Jarvis created a production line of portraits. Although an accurate count has never been made, Jarvis probably produced between 750 and 1,000 portraits during his career. As one of the most popular artists of his time, Jarvis catered to and depended on the consumer market created by the rising American middle classes for portraits done expeditiously, producing a straightforward likeness of the sitter that fulfilled and confirmed the self-image of respectable America in the early nineteenth century.

Jarvis married his first wife, Betsy Burtis of Long Island, in 1809. She, with whom he had two children, including the artist Charles Wesley Jarvis, died in 1813. He married Lydia Liscome in 1819. Their marriage broke up in part because of Jarvis's drinking and profligacy in money matters. He entered into a dispute with his estranged wife over the custody of their two daughters. Jarvis lost the suit, and the public airing of his private behavior lost him the clientele of respectable New Yorkers on whom he depended. Jarvis suffered a stroke in 1834 and lived with a sister until his death in New York.

• Jarvis left no papers, and Harold E. Dickson did a heroic job of piecing together Jarvis's career in *John Wesley Jarvis: American Painter, 1780–1840: With a Checklist of His Works* (1949). William Dunlap, *A History of the Rise and Progress of the Arts of Design in the United States* (1834; repr. 1969), contains a wealth of anecdotes about Jarvis by a friend. John Caldwell et al., *American Paintings in the Metropolitan Museum of Art*, vol. 1 (1994), pp. 295–305, assesses his career. A self-portrait is owned by the Walters Art Gallery in Baltimore; a contemporary copy by Bass Otis is owned by the National Portrait Gallery in Washington, D.C.; and a much later (c. 1880) copy by George Reynolds (formerly attributed to Otis) is owned by the New-York Historical Society. A portrait of Jarvis by Henry Inman is owned by the Fogg Art Museum, Harvard University; and a miniature by Inman is owned by the National Museum of American Art in Washington, D.C.

DAVID C. WARD

JARVIS, Thomas Jordan (18 Jan. 1836–17 June 1915), governor of North Carolina and U.S. senator, was born in Jarvisburg, Currituck County, North Carolina, the first child of Bannister Hardy Jarvis, a farmer and Methodist minister, and Elizabeth Daley. Although his father owned five slaves and some land, Jarvis began at age nineteen to put himself through Randolph-Macon College. By borrowing money and teaching school in the summers, he was able to graduate with honors in 1860 and earn a master of arts degree in 1861. Jarvis was teaching school when North Carolina joined the Confederacy. Enlisting in the Seventeenth North Carolina Regiment, Jarvis soon became first lieutenant of Company B, Eighth North Carolina Regiment. Serving throughout the war, he saw considerable action from Virginia to Georgia, was imprisoned briefly in 1862, rose to the rank of captain, and suffered a crippling wound to his right arm at the battle of Drewry's Bluff in 1864.

Returning to Jarvisburg in 1865, Jarvis operated a general store and then studied law, obtaining his license to practice in 1867. In 1865 Currituck County voters sent him to the constitutional convention required by President Andrew Johnson, where Jarvis bitterly opposed Reconstruction. He objected to the writing of a new constitution and supported only the minimum revisions necessary to comply with federal policy. In 1868 voters in Tyrrell County elected him as a Conservative (or Democrat) to a seat in the state house of representatives, where he stubbornly fought the Republican majority. Jarvis's opposition to Republican aid to railroads, new taxes, and an expanded suffrage that included black voters helped him become Speaker of the House when Conservatives gained a majority in 1870. In that office he played a leading role in impeaching Republican governor William W. Holden and in fighting the Republican party's Reconstruction program.

In 1872 Jarvis was a Democratic elector-at-large for presidential candidate Horace Greeley, and in 1874 he accepted the Democratic nomination for a judgeship but was defeated. Despite these electoral reverses Jarvis remained prominent among Democrats. In 1874 he married Mary Woodson; they had no children. After moving to Greenville and opening a law practice, Jarvis thoroughly organized Pitt County's Democrats and won election to the state constitutional convention of 1875. Again he played a leading role, writing a key amendment that allowed the legislature to abrogate elected local governments. This was a major goal of Democrats from the eastern part of the state, who objected to the political power of the large numbers of black voters who lived in their area. By means of Jarvis's amendment, the Democratic-controlled legislature removed many Republican and black officeholders in the eastern part of the state after 1876. On the strength of his stalwart service to the Democratic party, Jarvis narrowly won its nomination for lieutenant governor in 1876. In the ensuing campaign, which featured the oratorical talents of running mate Zebulon B. Vance and strident appeals to white supremacy, Jarvis worked energetically, and the Democratic party prevailed.

In 1879, when Governor Vance left office to become U.S. senator, Jarvis assumed the duties of chief executive of the state and in 1880 sought a full term. The Republican party was far from moribund in North Carolina, and Jarvis lacked the magnetic personality that distinguished Vance. As a result, the election was close, but Jarvis won. During his six years in office he pursued conservative, but not completely hidebound, policies. He gave consistently strong support to state asylums and to both the extension of railroads and their regulation by a state commission. A staunch advocate of the use of convict labor, Jarvis delivered hundreds of convicts to railroad construction projects but also sent commissions to investigate their health and living conditions. Jarvis insisted upon economy in government but made sure that the state was represented at commercial expositions in Atlanta, Boston, and elsewhere. When the legislature declined to appropriate money for this purpose, Jarvis used employees of the state's Department of Agriculture to prepare an exhibit. At the exposition in Boston he gave a well-publicized speech on the industrial promise of the New South.

By the end of Jarvis's term it was apparent that he was more willing than the General Assembly to spend money on education and social improvements. He suggested substantial tax increases to support education, but the legislature largely ignored these proposals. Under his administration, improvements in public education included more rigor in certifying teachers, state recommendations on textbooks, better support for eight normal schools, permission for towns to vote special taxes for graded schools, and small annual appropriations to the University of North Carolina.

In 1885 President Grover Cleveland rewarded Jarvis's service to the Democratic party by appointing him United States minister to Brazil. Jarvis had hoped for a seat in the cabinet, but he accepted the post and studied Portuguese and other languages during his three years in Brazil. His hopes of winning renomination for governor ended in disappointment, largely because he was not on the scene to advance his interests.

Returning to North Carolina, Jarvis resumed the practice of law and active support of the Democratic party. When Vance died in April 1894, Jarvis was appointed to fill the vacancy, but his service was short; rather than seek election to Vance's unfinished term, Jarvis unsuccessfully tried to wrest his party's nomination for a full term from Matt W. Ransom. Some Democrats thought Jarvis was too close to the Populists, and Ransom was the incumbent. With their opponents, the Republicans and Populists, cooperating effectively, most Democrats chose to avoid a costly intraparty competition. Through the decade of the 1890s Jarvis consulted and worked with Democratic party leaders, who faced a strong Populist challenge. In this context Jarvis stood out as a comparatively liberal, reform-minded Democrat. He criticized corporate power, urged attention to the problems of farmers, and advocated free silver. But he remained loyal to the party throughout and worked with his personal foe, Furnifold Simmons, to raise large sums from corporations for the 1898 white supremacy campaign. Jarvis was active in community affairs in Greenville, helping in 1907 to establish the teachers' training school that became East Carolina University. He died in Greenville.

• Jarvis's papers are in the North Carolina Division of Archives and History in Raleigh. One volume of these has been published as *The Papers of Thomas Jordan Jarvis*, ed. W. Buck Yearns (1969) and contains the most thorough biographical sketch of Jarvis. Additional letters can be found in the papers of Samuel A'Court Ashe and other prominent North Carolina Democrats. See also June Dunn Parker, "Thomas Jordan Jarvis," in *Dictionary of North Carolina Biography*, ed. William S. Powell, vol. 3 (1988), and Paul D.

Escott, *Many Excellent People* (1985). Obituaries are in the *Charlotte Daily Observer* and the *News and Observer* (Raleigh), 18 June 1915.

PAUL D. ESCOTT

JARVIS, William Chapman (13 May 1855–30 July 1895), laryngologist, was born in Fortress Monroe, Virginia, the son of Nathan Sturges Jarvis, an army physician, and Jane B. Mumford. After his father died from disease in 1862, Jarvis and his mother relocated to Baltimore, Maryland. As a boy he developed a fascination for mechanical objects and exhibited considerable ability in drawing and tinkering with them. After completing his secondary education in a private school in Baltimore, he matriculated at the University of Maryland, where he decided to become a physician. He received an M.D. there in 1875 and spent the next two years at Johns Hopkins University doing postgraduate work in biology and chemistry.

In 1877 Jarvis moved to New York City, where he opened a general medical practice. Later that year he became affiliated with Bellevue Hospital's Nose and Throat Service, an outpatient department, as the assistant to Francke Huntington Bosworth. One of the first American laryngologists, Bosworth is also generally acknowledged as the founder of rhinology, the scientific study of the nose and its diseases, as a separate medical specialty. Although Jarvis continued to treat patients privately for a wide variety of medical conditions, his close association with Bosworth probably induced him to become a charter member of the American Laryngological Association, co-founded by Bosworth in 1879, and definitely led him to specialize in the various diseases of the nose and throat.

Jarvis subsequently developed several innovations for their diagnosis and treatment, the most important one being the Jarvis snare (1881). This surgical instrument consisted of a slender hollow shaft with a finger grip on one end and a curved loop of silver wire on the other that could be inserted deep into a patient's nose. After being looped around a tumorous growth in the nasal cavity, the wire was gradually tightened around the base of the growth by means of the finger grip until it snipped it off. Quite possibly Jarvis modeled the snare after a similar but much larger device that had been used for at least fifty years to remove tonsils. In any event, his invention greatly simplified the excision of intranasal tumors and reduced the danger of hemorrhage that often resulted from traditional procedures of nasal surgery.

Jarvis's published description of the Jarvis snare brought him to the attention of the University of the City of New York (now New York University), and in 1881 he accepted a position as lecturer in laryngology. In addition to teaching, he continued to innovate in matters concerning surgery of the nose and throat. In 1884, two years before he was promoted to professor, he modified the mignon lamp, essentially a tiny light bulb that had just been developed by the eminent inventor Thomas A. Edison, so that it could be used to illuminate the larynx's deeper reaches. In 1887, three

years after it was first used during eye surgery by the Viennese surgeon Carl Koller, Jarvis became the first operator to administer cocaine as a local anesthetic during surgery within the nasal cavity. In 1890 he pioneered the technique of straightening a deviated nasal septum, the bony partition that separates the nasal passages, by using an electric drill. He invented an applicator for burning away chemically the ulcerous sores resulting in the larynx from tuberculosis as well as a mirror that made it possible to observe the nasal cavity's interior during surgery. He also developed the Jarvis operation, a procedure by which part of a nasal concha, one of the horizontal bony projections of the nasal cavity wall, is removed; though it was once a commonly performed operation, modern procedures have rendered it obsolete.

These and other developments Jarvis shared with the medical community via his authorship of thirty-one articles, whose style reveals much about his methodic nature and unassuming character. His longest publication is a chapter on intranasal surgery in Charles Henry Burnett's *System of Diseases of the Ear, Nose and Throat* (1893). All the others are short, to the point, and completely devoid of self-promotion; for example, the article outlining his pioneering use of cocaine in intranasal surgery, which appeared in the *New York Medical Record* 26 (1887), consists of only two pages.

Jarvis never married, choosing instead to devote his full energy to his profession. In the early 1890s the years of overwork apparently resulted in an obscure and untreatable abdominal condition that forced him to retire in 1893. He died while visiting his brother in Willet's Point, New York.

Jarvis was one of the foremost American medical experts on the nose and throat of his day. He contributed to the advance of medicine by inventing and developing a number of apparatuses and procedures that greatly facilitated laryngeal and rhinological surgery.

• Jarvis's papers have not been located. A biography is "Biography and Bibliography of William Chapman Jarvis," an anonymous and unpublished manuscript in the New York Academy of Medicine library. An obituary is in the *New York Times*, 1 Aug. 1895.

CHARLES W. CAREY, JR.

JASPER, John (4 July 1812–30 Mar. 1901), Baptist preacher and orator, was born in Fluvanna County, Virginia, the son of slave parents, Philip Jasper, a slave preacher, and Nina, head servant of the Peachy family. (His father served as a preacher at slave funerals.) John worked as a cart boy accompanying the plantation ox cart and on errands around the Peachy "great house." In 1825 his master hired him out to Peter McHenry, for whom he worked one year in Richmond before returning to the Peachy plantation. He later labored in the coal mines of Chesterfield County. Jasper's master sent him to Richmond a third time to work at Samuel Hargrove's tobacco warehouse. Jasper led a life he later confessed to have been irreligious and riotous. A fellow slave taught him to read and spell.

Jasper experienced conversion about mid-August 1837 while working in Hargrove's tobacco warehouse. Of his conversion, Jasper said, "I was as light as a feather; my feet was on de mount'n; salvation rol'd like a flood thru my soul, an' I felt as if I could 'nock off de fact'ry roof wid my shouts." Jasper began preaching in 1840 shortly after giving evidence of his conversion to members of the First African Baptist Church of Richmond, a large and stable organization. He quickly earned a reputation as an outstanding orator.

A man of imposing physical presence, Jasper impressed audiences, black and white alike, with his vivid imagery, command of the Bible (much of which he could recite from memory), and insight into human nature. Jasper made preaching funeral sermons his specialty, and white planters frequently called on his services as a preacher to their slaves. Two Sundays a month Jasper was allowed to go to Petersburg, Virginia, where the Third Baptist Church, a small black congregation, called him as pastor. During his travels he met and married Elvy Weaden, a slave woman of Williamsburg, Virginia. They had no children and separated when Jasper had to return to Richmond. Elvy later married another man, and Jasper, lacking formal divorce papers, went to the members of Richmond's African church to receive permission to remarry. He married his second wife, Candus Jordan, in 1844. They had nine children before they divorced. In 1863 he married Mary Anne Cole, who died in 1874. He married a fourth time, but his last wife's name is unknown.

Whites who attended his services, either out of curiosity or concern that he might be stirring black discontent, came away deeply impressed with his preaching abilities. His sermons focused on spiritual themes, and his style was part of the tradition later called "ol' time preaching." Jasper received even more public notoriety in the Richmond area when he began to preach his famous "The Sun Do Move" sermon. A contemporary estimated that Jasper delivered this sermon at least 250 times over a period of twenty years. Jasper interpreted Joshua 10: 12–13 literally. He argued that the sun, which he believed rotated around the earth, stood still so that the Israelites could defeat the Canaanite confederacies. Jasper used this story to demonstrate the omnipotence of God, but many of his hearers were struck more by his antiquated cosmology, including his notion of a flat earth.

During the Civil War Jasper worked as a factory hand in Richmond. He preached to the sick and wounded in the city's Confederate hospitals. After the fall of Richmond in 1865, Jasper joined the ranks of the freedmen and took charge of the Third Baptist Church of Petersburg. He also helped organize a black church at Weldon, North Carolina. In December 1866 Jasper gave up his ministry in Petersburg and returned to Richmond, where he did general missionary work. In 1867 he and nine other blacks organized a Baptist church that was housed in a wooden shanty opposite Richmond on Brown's Island in the James River. The congregation next rented a carpenter's shop at Fourth and Cary. Jasper's members eventually purchased an old brick church from the Presbyterians. The church was located at Duval and St. John's streets in the northwestern part of Richmond known as "Africa" and was called Sixth Mount Zion Baptist.

Sixth Mount Zion, which became an important Richmond landmark, was housed by 1887 in a large Norman-Gothic structure, and reached a membership of 2,000 during Jasper's lifetime. William Hatcher, a member of Richmond's First Baptist Church, was a frequent visitor to Jasper's church and wrote *John Jasper: The Unmatched Negro Philosopher and Preacher.* Hatcher wrote of Jasper: "In the circle of Jasper's gifts his imagination was preeminent. It was the mammoth lamp in the tower of his being. A matchless painter was he." Jasper was known as "Father Abraham" among the black population of Richmond.

Jasper's style of preaching drew many of the curious to Richmond's First African Baptist Church. Some came to be amused by his shouting style and harsh words for what he called the "eddicated" preachers. Others sought him out because of his unique oratorical gifts and advocacy of a geocentric universe. Jasper was a Richmond sensation. Visitors to Richmond were taken to hear him, and a syndicate of investors sent him on a tour of the North. Jasper preached in Baltimore, Philadelphia, and Washington, D.C. French newspapers published his "The Sun Do Move" sermon, and his flat earth and geocentric views were discussed in England. Jasper's literal interpretation of the Bible and the relentlessness of his advocacy of an outdated cosmology earned him considerable notoriety among whites who were amused by his views but drew opposition from several of Richmond's black clergy.

In the latter part of his life Jasper was known as something of a hermit. He lived alone in a small house at 1112 North St. James, contenting himself with reading the Bible and smoking a pipe. He continued to pastor Sixth Mount Zion until the end of his life. He supported missionary work in Africa and condemned the practice of "hoodooism," or conjuring, among his members. He could often be seen walking the streets of Richmond with a top hat and cane or sitting on a bench in the Capitol Green gardens. Fifty years a slave, he had perhaps no more than six months of formal education, but he was a fluent speaker. At age eighty-nine he preached his last sermon. On his death in Richmond, the *Richmond Dispatch* described Jasper as a local institution. The *Dispatch* also commented, "Some people have the impression that John Jasper was famous simply because he flew in the face of the scientists and declared that the sun moved. In one sense, that is true, but it is also true that his fame was due, in great measure, to a strong personality, to a deep earnest conviction, as well as to a devout Christian character." Whatever Jasper's personal convictions or understanding of his role, many whites viewed him as a caricature of the slave exhorters from the days of plantation slavery when black preachers had to veil their hopes of a better life in the religious imagery of the Bible.

• Promoters of Jasper's lecture tours published a fifteen-page pamphlet under his name titled *"The Sun Do Move!" The Celebrated Theory of the Sun's Rotation around the Earth, as Preached by Rev. John Jasper of Richmond, Virginia. With a Memoir of His Life* (1882). The earliest books about Jasper primarily treat him as a Richmond celebrity and must be used with care. Perhaps the most useful is Edwin A. Randolph, *The Life of Rev. John Jasper, Pastor of Sixth Mt. Zion Baptist Church, Richmond, Va.; From His Birth to the Present Time, with His Theory on the Rotation of the Sun* (1884). The following two sources are not biographies of Jasper in the strict sense but offer some factual material on his life: William E. Hatcher, *John Jasper: The Unmatched Negro Philosopher and Preacher* (1908), is based on firsthand knowledge of Jasper; Howard Harlin relies heavily on Hatcher as the basis for *John Jasper—A Case History in Leadership* (1936). See also H. H. Smith, "John Jasper: 'The Unmatched Negro Philosopher and Preacher,'" *Methodist Quarterly Review (South)* 72 (July 1923): 466–80, and Richard Ellsworth Day, *Rhapsody in Black: The Life Story of John Jasper* (1953). More reliable yet is Mary Jo Bratton, "John Jasper of Richmond: From Slave Preacher to Community Leader," *Virginia Cavalcade* 29 (1979): 32–39. An obituary is in the *New York Times*, 31 Mar. 1901.

MILTON C. SERNETT

JASTROW, Joseph (30 Jan. 1863–8 Jan. 1944), psychologist, was born in Warsaw, Poland, the son of Marcus Jastrow, a rabbi, and Bertha Wolfsohn. His father was an internationally eminent Talmudic scholar, and his brother Morris was a distinguished Semitic scholar of the University of Pennsylvania. In the 1860s his father moved the family from Germany to Poland when he accepted a call to lead a congregation in Warsaw. There Rabbi Jastrow became involved in the Polish rebellion against Russian rule, which resulted in his exile from Poland and which later created political pressure in Germany that compelled him in 1866 to move his family to the United States. In Philadelphia, at the Congregation Rodeph Shalom, Rabbi Jastrow became a prominent leader of Conservative Judaism in America.

Thus Joseph Jastrow grew up in an articulate, multilingual, and international environment. He was an accelerated student, receiving his B.A. with honors from the University of Pennsylvania in 1884 and his doctorate in 1886 from Johns Hopkins, where he studied with G. Stanley Hall and Charles S. Peirce. Jastrow's doctoral degree has been occasionally cited as the first formally recognized Ph.D. in psychology in the United States, although there is disagreement on how that priority should be determined. His dissertation—still noted in today's scientific literature—reported experimental studies of perceptual judgment and concluded that subliminal factors could influence such judgments.

Jastrow had difficulty obtaining a university position even though American universities were then rapidly expanding. Two reasons for his difficulty were that individuals with European degrees were preferred and that anti-Semitism was a significant professional barrier in American academia at that time. In 1888 Jastrow accepted a newly created position as professor of experimental and comparative psychology at the University of Wisconsin. In that same year he married Rachel Szold, daughter of a prominent Baltimore rabbi in whose home he had lived while attending Johns Hopkins.

As soon as he arrived at Wisconsin, Jastrow created a laboratory for experimental psychology. Only two others in the United States were in existence, at Indiana and Johns Hopkins. Those latter two laboratories, however, were soon closed when their directors left for other positions. Jastrow's laboratory was the first continuously operating psychology laboratory in the United States.

When active as an experimentalist, Jastrow developed apparatus to assess differences between voluntary and involuntary movement—a sort of scientific Ouija board that would record patterns of involuntary hand movements. His work on illusions was well known, particularly work with ambiguous figures; his drawing of the ambiguous rabbit-duck figure is still frequently reproduced. His study of the dreams of the blind is still often cited ("Dreams of the Blind," *New Princeton Revue* [1888]: 41–53). In that investigation he discovered that people who lose vision before approximately ages five to seven will have no visual dream imagery, whereas people blinded later will experience visual dream imagery.

At the 1893 World's Columbian Exposition in Chicago Jastrow organized the first large exhibition of the new experimental psychology that attracted leading psychologists and samples of their apparatus from the United States and Europe. An adjacent part of that psychology pavilion also contained exhibits on the study of child development. Using the apparatus contained in that exhibit Jastrow collected thousands of measurements of the perceptual and reaction-time abilities of people who visited there. He never published the results of that work.

As a result of the administration of the world's fair exhibit and because of a ruinous exhaustion of his resources from the building of an exotic palatial home on the edge of the Wisconsin campus, Jastrow fell into a serious depression in 1894, which kept him away from teaching and under medical care for a year. He was plagued by recurring depressions for the rest of his life. By the end of the century, however, he was in full health and was elected president of the American Psychological Association in 1900.

The university president at Wisconsin continuously refused salary increases to Jastrow, who remained at a low salary during his entire time there. Several possible reasons for this include Jastrow's failure as a productive experimentalist, his appearance as a popularizer (however, that activity may have been forced as a way to supplement his low salary), anti-Semitism, recurring bouts of depression (which may have been an effect rather than cause of this lack of advancement), and Jastrow's vocal opposition to the then-emerging new type of American university president.

In the course of Jastrow's career he witnessed a change in the style of the college and university president, from scholar-presidents, chosen from the faculty, to businessman-booster presidents responsible to and hired by interests external to the university and community of scholars. This change was brought about, according to Jastrow, by the sudden expansion of land-grant colleges and other institutions of higher education at the beginning of the twentieth century. Jastrow believed that the new presidents assumed bold new power and sought to reconceptualize the university in business corporation terms. With that model in mind, Jastrow said, they then decreed that the university would offer more public services and entertainments. At that time the major competitive sports and the Greek-letter, socially oriented fraternities were introduced, replacing earlier academically oriented organizations. Jastrow joined forces with others who publicly condemned these changes, becoming one of the most vocal and controversial critics.

Although Jastrow began as an experimental psychologist, he soon found he lacked the temperament for it. He took greater pleasure in his activities as a writer and public speaker. Nevertheless, he began the experimental study of hypnosis at Wisconsin in the 1890s and initiated a tradition of hypnosis research there that was continued by Jastrow's best-known student, Clark Hull, and by Milton Ericksen. In general, Jastrow's interests in psychology always concerned acts of judgment, rationality, and self-control and the susceptibility to subconscious forces that undermine those acts. All his life he wrote diatribes against tricksters, faith-healers, propagandists, and others who attempt to manipulate judgment and self-control. In fact during his earliest days at Wisconsin, if not earlier, he had become fascinated with the critical study and exposé of magicians, mediums, and other types of spiritualists. It was an interest that held a prominent position in his writings and thoughts for the rest of his life. For that reason he was frequently embroiled in public debates with mystics, spiritualists, cultists, and various religious groups. This likely played a part in his abandonment of Judaism. These interests stand out in his widely read early book, *Fact and Fable in Psychology* (1901), and they continue throughout his writings in the next four decades.

Jastrow retired early from Wisconsin in 1927, having been increasingly inactive in his last few years there. He moved to New York City and for the rest of his life was professionally and financially successful as a popular writer and a radio personality. He was a lecturer at the New School for Social Research (1927–1933), and he lectured periodically at Columbia. He was in demand as a speaker for clubs and other groups. The most frequent theme of his later popular writings and lectures was always the health of one's rational mental skills and the avoidance of deception and undisciplined thinking.

Jastrow was an early supporter of both the Behaviorist and the Freudian movements but later turned against them when he perceived them as evolving into cults too narrow in their theoretical orientations and as demanding a religious type of adherence by their followers. Thereafter Jastrow was a vocal polemicist against both movements.

What Jastrow lacked as an experimentalist he made up for as a prolific and florid writer. He was America's greatest early popularizer of the then new scientific psychology, which he preferred to describe as "naturalistic" psychology rather than behavioral psychology. He was a frequent contributor to many of the popular magazines of the day, including *The Nation*, *Popular Science Monthly*, *Outlook*, *Scribners*, *The Dial*, and *Saturday Review of Literature*. He also traveled across the country lecturing to popular audiences. From 1935 to 1938 he had his own radio program on the NBC network, "Keeping Mentally Fit," the same title that headed his syndicated newspaper column, which appeared in papers across the country.

The Jastrows had no children but had adopted a son, Benno, who was killed during World War II. Rachel died in 1926. Jastrow died while under treatment for depression at the Austen Riggs Foundation in Stockbridge, Massachusetts.

• Numerous letters, newspaper clippings, unpublished writings, and other personal materials concerning Jastrow are in the Rare Manuscripts Department of the Duke University Library. A review of the lifestyle of the Jastrows in their early years at Wisconsin, with their many involvements in local social and cultural events, is in Alexandra L. Levin, "The Jastrows in Madison: A Chronicle of University Life (1888–1900)," *Wisconsin Magazine of History*, Summer 1963, pp. 243–56. A description of Jastrow's early psychology laboratory at Wisconsin is available in French in M. Henry de Varigny, "Le laboratoire de psychologie experimental de l'universite de Madison," *Revue Scientifique* 1 (19 May 1894): 624–29. His most extensive writing on the problem of the university presidency is in James M. Cattell, ed., *University Control* (1913), pp. 315–48. An extensive listing of Jastrow's more academic writings can be found in Carl Murchison, ed., *The Psychological Register*, vol. 3 (1932): 116–18. Jastrow's chapter-length autobiography is in Murchison, ed., *A History of Psychology in Autobiography*, vol. 1 (1930). Clark Hull, a supreme experimentalist of a different temperament from Jastrow and thus not sympathetic to him, wrote an obituary for the *American Journal of Psychology* 57 (Oct. 1944): 581–85. Another prominent obituary by Walter B. Pillsbury is in the *Psychological Review* 51 (Sept. 1944): 261–65.

ARTHUR L. BLUMENTHAL

JASTROW, Marcus Mordecai (5 June 1829–13 Oct. 1903), rabbi, was born in Rogasen, province of Posen, Prussian Poland, the son of Abraham Jastrow, a businessman, and Yetta Rolle. After study in German Gymnasia in Rogasen and Posen and at the University of Berlin, Jastrow earned his doctorate from the University of Halle in 1855, writing a thesis on the philosophy of medieval biblical scholar Abraham Ibn Ezra. Rabbi Moses Feilchenfeld had ordained Jastrow in Berlin in 1853; Rabbi Wolf Landau from Dresden confirmed the ordination in 1857. Jastrow was also taught by Michael Sachs, an adherent of *Wissenschaft des Judentums*, the scientific study of Judaism, and a theological straddler between German orthodoxy and reform. Jastrow taught in Sachs's school in Berlin until 1858. Jastrow married Bertha Wolfsohn in 1858, and they had seven children.

Recommended by German Jewish historian Heinrich Graetz, Jastrow became rabbi of the progressive German congregation in Warsaw in 1858. Serving during a period of Polish unrest under Russian oppression, Jastrow was deported in February 1862 to Germany after having spent three months in jail for preaching anti-Russian sermons. He then served a brief tenure in the Mannheim pulpit in 1862, before returning to Warsaw upon the revocation of his banishment in November 1862. When Poland erupted in revolution in 1864 Jastrow moved to Worms, Germany, to preach. He remained there until 1866, when he moved to Philadelphia, Pennsylvania, to assume the pulpit of Rodeph Shalom congregation.

Opposing both orthodoxy and the anti-*halakhic* orientation (rejection of the concept that rabbinic law governed contemporary Jewish practice) of Isaac Mayer Wise, the founder of the liberal Union of American Hebrew Congregations (UAHC) and Hebrew Union College (HUC), Jastrow attempted to balance tradition and innovation as Rodeph Shalom's rabbi and became a leader in the movement that evolved into Conservative Judaism. For example, he assented to the congregation's requests for occasional English sermons in place of the customary German and for a shortened Sabbath service, and he introduced late Friday services. Rodeph Shalom's new synagogue building, a response to increased membership that followed Jastrow's arrival, was built in 1871 and contained an organ and an area for a choir. Main-floor seating for both men and women replaced the traditional balcony seating for women. Allied theologically with Benjamin Szold, the rabbi of the Oheb Shalom congregation in Baltimore, Maryland, Jastrow helped to revise Szold's and Henry Hochheimer's prayerbook *Abodat Yisrael* (1871), which contains significant theological departures from traditional Judaism.

Jastrow's reforms invited further liberalizations, but he drew the line in the 1880s when tense relations with Wise, dating back to his arrival in the United States, grew into antagonistic theological debates over Jewish dietary laws, the nature of Sabbath observance, and the place of Hebrew in religious services. Jastrow attended—but walked out of—the Treifa Banquet in 1883, so named because the caterer for the dinner honoring the first graduating class of Wise's Hebrew Union College served nonkosher food. Disputes over observance of the Jewish dietary laws contributed to Jastrow's decision to withdraw his congregation from the UAHC in 1884 and to object to the Pittsburgh Platform of 1885, formulated by a conference of liberal rabbis, which rejected all Jewish laws, save moral laws, and instead called for a universalistic Judaism based on the teachings of the prophets.

In 1886 Jastrow's son Morris, who had received a European rabbinical and university education designed to groom him to succeed his father and who had spent a year as Rodeph Shalom's assistant rabbi, resigned his position and committed himself to an academic career. Rodeph Shalom retired Jastrow in 1892; his farewell sermon criticized congregants for their materialism and their failure to observe Jewish law. HUC graduate Henry Berkowitz, who replaced Jastrow, brought the congregation back into the UAHC in 1894 and substituted the *Union Prayer Book*, published by the Central Conference of American Rabbis, the association of liberal rabbis, for *Avodat Yisrael*. Jastrow's published criticisms of these changes led the directors of the congregation to request that he cease publication of newspaper articles that stirred up controversy within the congregation.

Jastrow's multifarious community activities included helping to found the Young Men's Hebrew Association and the United Jewish Charities and collaborating with the Alliance Israélite Universelle, which defended Jewish interests and cared for Jewish migrants. He also worked for the creation of Talmud Torah schools associated with synagogues. Illness forced him to reduce his commitments after 1876, but his commitment to Zionism led to his election as vice president of the Federation of American Zionists in 1897.

Ill health prompted Jastrow's turn to scholarship. His magnum opus, the Aramaic-English *Dictionary of the Targumim, the Talmud Babli and Yerushalmi, and the Midrashic Literature* (1886–1903), built on the work of German rabbi and Talmudic lexicographer Jacob Levy, was the first large-scale English-language dictionary of the Talmud.

In 1867 Jastrow had helped to establish Maimonides College in Philadelphia. There he taught Talmud, religious philosophy, Jewish history, and Biblical exegesis, and he served as provost after the death of founder Isaac Leeser, from 1868 to 1873. Maimonides closed in 1873 for lack of support and students, but Jastrow and other Philadelphia rabbis continued to offer informal instruction. Students and teachers in this group helped to found the Jewish Theological Seminary of America in New York City in 1886 as a more traditional alternative to the liberalism of Hebrew Union College.

Jastrow's objections to the appropriation of scholarly projects by seminary and university professors—especially the exclusion of rabbis from the governance of the Jewish Publication Society (founded 1888) and the American Jewish Historical Society (founded 1892)—led to the symbolic inclusion of rabbis. He fostered scholarly cooperation between Jewish factions during his tenure from 1895 to 1903 as chair of the editorial board of *The Holy Scriptures*, the Bible project sponsored by the Jewish Publication Society. Translators included traditional and liberal rabbis, as well as professors. The board's cumbersome procedures precluded success under his leadership, and the project was twice reorganized after his death. Jastrow headed the

Talmud department of the *Jewish Encyclopedia* (1901–1905), another ambitious, cooperative venture.

Jastrow died in Germantown, Pennsylvania, only days after attending the opening of the new building for the Jewish Theological Seminary and only hours after receiving final proofs of his magnum opus. His influential polemics and his prayer book revision persuaded some congregations to remain out of the liberal camp and encouraged others to disaffiliate. These congregations provided important support to the nascent Jewish Theological Seminary. But few American rabbis could have devoted the time necessary to produce scholarly contributions as significant as Jastrow's Talmudic dictionary, and Jewish scholarship in the United States increasingly became the province of the laity.

• Jastrow published political tracts while in Poland, including *Kazania Polskie* (1863). His *Vier Jahrunderte aus der Geschichte der Juden* (Four centuries of Jewish history covering the period from the destruction of the first temple to the consecration of the temple by the Maccabees) (1865), emphasizes Jewish institutions. *Abodat Yisrael*, sometimes known as *Minhag Jastrow*, was reissued as *A Prayer Book for the Services of the Year at the Synagogue* (1940). Jastrow's valedictory sermon appears in his *A Warning Voice* (1892). On Jastrow, see Edward Davis, *The History of Rodeph Shalom Congregation, Philadelphia, 1802–1926* (1926); articles in *American Hebrew*, 16 Oct. 1903, 23 Oct. 1903, and 6 Nov. 1903; and Henry Samuel Morais, *The Jews of Philadelphia: Their History from the Earliest Settlements to the Present Time* (1894). Moshe Davis, *The Emergence of Conservative Judaism* (1963), chronicles the liberalizations at Rodeph Shalom, analyzes Jastrow's theology and his prayer book, and includes a biographical sketch. See also Henrietta Szold, "Marcus Jastrow," *Publications of the American Jewish Historical Society* 12 (1904): 181–83. Obituaries are in the following Philadelphia newspapers: the *Jewish Exponent*, 13 Oct. 1903, the *Public Ledger*, 14 Oct. 1903, and the *Public Press*, 14 Oct. 1903.

HAROLD S. WECHSLER

JASTROW, Morris (13 Aug. 1861–22 June 1921), Semitist, was born in Warsaw, Poland, the son of Rabbi Marcus Jastrow and Bertha Wolfsohn. Morris came to Philadelphia in 1866 when his father acceded to the pulpit of the Rodeph Shalom congregation in that city. After attending private schools in Philadelphia, he studied in the arts department of the University of Pennsylvania, his future employer, graduating in 1881.

Groomed to succeed his father in the Rodeph Shalom pulpit, Jastrow taught at the synagogue school beginning in 1879, and in 1881 began rabbinical studies at the Jewish Theological Seminary at Breslau. He also studied Oriental languages at the universities of Breslau, Leipzig, Strasbourg, and Paris, receiving his Ph.D. from Leipzig in 1884. His thesis translated a partial text by Judah Ben Davud Hayyuj, a tenth-century Hebrew grammarian.

In Europe Jastrow became critical of the materialism he perceived in American Jewry and feared that he lacked the temperament to oppose the reformism of Isaac Mayer Wise, who directed Hebrew Union College, America's only Jewish seminary. Jastrow's doubts about the rabbinate increased each year, as did the seriousness with which he considered the academic calling. He remained in Europe for a year of advanced studies in Semitics to continue the weighing process. His early correspondence did not extol the attractions of Semitics, but scholarship was an attractive alternative if his doubts prevailed.

Jastrow worked during 1885–1886 at Rodeph Shalom as assistant rabbi and congregational school teacher and at the University of Pennsylvania, where he taught Arabic and Hebrew. He opted for an academic career after closely observing American Jewry—"The pulpit exercises but little influence today"—and American Judaism, conceived by Reform so widely "as to be vague and indeterminate." His parting sermon at Rodeph Shalom in December 1886 called for agreement on fundamentals between minister and congregation. A rabbi, he noted, "must not be expected to do anything merely for the sake of appearances, and, if expected, must refuse."

At the University of Pennsylvania, Jastrow considered himself a specialist in Arabic, Assyrian, and rabbinical literature in connection with biblical exegesis. He aspired to a contemplated professorship of Assyrian, which went to Herman V. Hilprecht, his rival at Pennsylvania for the next quarter-century. Instead, the university appointed Jastrow to a professorship in Arabic and rabbinics. In 1891 the university changed his title to professor of Semitics. Jastrow added Assyriology to his course offerings and soon began to publish monographs on Babylonian and Assyrian religion.

While in Europe as a graduate student, Jastrow had studied the history and philosophy of religions with Cornelius Petrus Tiele of the University of Leiden. Jastrow argued that a "scientific" understanding of religion required study of "religions which are more naïve, which are less the result of conscious effort, in which speculation plays a minor part, which, in a word, are *direct* manifestations of man's emotional or religious nature," that is, "the religion of savages and of people living in a primitive condition of culture." He offered courses on the history of religion in 1894–1895—one of the earliest listings in an American university. Because of a lack of student interest, however, Jastrow did not teach the course again until 1908. In 1910–1911 the university recognized the history of religions as one of twenty graduate programs, but the field attracted few students anywhere in the United States before World War II—Pennsylvania awarded only four doctorates between 1889 and 1927.

The rivalry between Hilprecht and Jastrow culminated in the "Peters-Hilprecht" controversy, during which Jastrow and former Pennsylvania Hebrew professor John P. Peters disputed Hilprecht's claims about his role in and the discoveries made during four University of Pennsylvania–sponsored archaeological expeditions to Nippur, a significant commercial and religious center in ancient Babylonia. The Pennsylvania trustees exonerated Hilprecht from wrongdoing after a 1905 hearing. But university authorities surprised Hilprecht in 1910 by accepting his resignation, submitted to protest Jastrow's entrance into his office to investigate the possible deterioration of university-owned antiquities. Jastrow produced his magnum opus, *Aspects of Religious Belief and Practice in Babylonia and Assyria* (1911), during this controversy.

As university librarian (1898–1919), Jastrow supported the growth of many new academic subjects. He represented the United States at numerous European academic conferences and helped to plan an American archaeological school in Baghdad. Jastrow edited a Semitics series with Richard Gottheil of Columbia University and edited sections of and contributed articles to general and religious encyclopedias. In 1893 Jastrow married Helen Bachman. She edited and translated *Selected Essays of James Darmesteter* (1895), to which Morris contributed a memoir of the French Orientalist. Jastrow died in Jenkintown, Pennsylvania.

Comparing Jastrow to French Orientalist Ernest Renan, in an address at a meeting in memory of Jastrow Ethical Culture Society leader Felix Adler noted, "Both had discovered their inability to expound the teachings of the religion in which they were raised." He continued, "Both, being religious-minded men, were mastered by the desire to understand that mighty force in human nature called Religion, which had exercised its spell over so many generations and to which they, too, confessed." Forsaking the rabbinate, Jastrow instead established at the University of Pennsylvania a major American center for Oriental studies and for the academic study of religion and contributed to the contemporary debate on the ancient Near East.

• Jastrow's final sermon at Rodeph Shalom was published as *Jews and Judaism: An Address by Morris Jastrow Jr., Ph.D., before the Congregation Rodef Shalom, December 9, 1886* (1886). Assyriological treatises include *The Religion of Babylonia and Assyria* (1898) and *The Civilization of Babylonia and Assyria: Its Remains, Language, History, Religion, Commerce, Law, Art, and Literature* (1915). Representative writings on the history of religion include "The Historical Study of Religions in Universities and Colleges," *Journal of the American Oriental Society* 20 (July–Dec. 1899): 317–25, and *The Study of Religion* (1901). He published several analyses of contemporary conditions in the Middle East, including *Zionism and the Future of Palestine: The Fallacies and Dangers of Political Zionism* (1919), an anti-Zionist tract. His final publications included several biblical commentaries, including *A Gentle Cynic: Being a Translation of the Book of Koheleth, Commonly Known as Ecclesiastes, Stripped of Later Additions, Also Its Origin, Growth, and Interpretation* (1919).

Biographical articles by contemporaries include J. A. Montgomery, "Morris Jastrow, Jr.," *American Journal of Semitic Languages and Literatures* 38 (1921–1922): 1–11; memorial essays and a bibliography in the *Journal of the American Oriental Society* 41 (Dec. 1921): 322–44; and A. T. Clay's tribute in *Proceedings of the American Philosophical Society* 40 (1921): x–xviii. On Jastrow's decision to abandon a rabbinical career, see Harold S. Wechsler, "Pulpit or Professoriate: The Case of Morris Jastrow," *American Jewish History* 74 (June 1985): 538–55. On his tenure at the University of Pennsylvania, see Cyrus Gordon, *The Pennsylvania Tradition of Semitics* (1986); C. Wade Meade, *Road to Babylon: Development of U.S. Assyriology* (1974); Paul Ritterband and Wechsler, "A Message to Lushtamar: The Hilprecht Controversy and Semitic Scholarship in America," *History of Higher Education Annual* 1 (1981): 5–41; and Paul Ritterband and Wechsler, *Jewish Learning in American Universities: The First Century* (1994). On Jastrow's contributions to the history of religions, see Robert S. Shepard, *God's People in the Ivory Tower: Religion in the Early American University* (1991), pp. 33–39. Obituaries are in the *Philadelphia Public Ledger*, 23 June 1921, and the *New York Times*, 23 June 1921.

HAROLD S. WECHSLER

JAVITS, Jacob Koppel (18 May 1904–7 Mar. 1986), senator, was born in New York City, the son of Morris Javits, a janitor, and Ida Littman. He grew up in a teeming Lower East Side tenement, and when not in school he helped his mother hawk dry goods from a pushcart in the street. Javits graduated in 1920 from George Washington High School, where he was president of his class. He worked part-time at various jobs while attending night school at Columbia University, then in 1923 he enrolled in the New York University Law School, from which he earned his J.D. in 1926. Javits was admitted to the New York State bar in June 1927 and joined his brother Benjamin Javits, who was nearly ten years older, as partner to form the Javits and Javits law firm. The Javits brothers specialized in bankruptcy and minority stockholder suits and became quite successful. In 1933 Javits married Marjorie Joan Ringling; they had no children and divorced in 1936. In 1947 he married Marian Ann Boris, with whom he had three children.

In his youth Javits had watched his father work as a ward heeler for Tammany Hall and experienced first-hand the corruption and graft associated with that notorious political machine. Tammany's operations repulsed Javits so much that, despite his Jewish heritage, he forever rejected the city's Democratic party and in the early 1930s joined the Republican-Fusion party, which was supporting the mayoral campaigns of Fiorello H. La Guardia. Deemed too old for regular military service when World War II began, Javits was commissioned in early 1942 as an officer in the army's Chemical Warfare Department, where he served throughout the war, reaching the rank of lieutenant colonel. After the war he became the chief researcher for Jonah Goldstein's unsuccessful 1945 bid for mayor on the Republican-Liberal-Fusion ticket. Javits's hard work in the Goldstein campaign showed his potential in the political arena and encouraged the small Manhattan Republican party to nominate him as their candidate for the Upper West Side's Twenty-first Congressional District seat in 1946. Although the Republicans had not held the seat since 1923, Javits campaigned energetically and won.

Throughout his career in Congress—in the House and later in the Senate—Javits was part of a small group of liberal Republicans who were often isolated ideologically from their mainstream Republican colleagues. Although he frequently differed with the more conservative members of his party, Javits always maintained that a healthy political party should tolerate diverse opinions among its members. He rejected the idea that either party should reflect only one point of view. Javits liked to think of himself as a political descendant of Theodore Roosevelt's Progressive Republicanism. He was strongly committed to social issues, believing that the federal government should have a role in improving the lives of Americans. Yet as a lawyer who had for years represented business clients, Javits also advocated a mixed economy in which business and government would cooperate to further the national welfare.

During his first two terms in the House, Javits often sided with the Harry Truman administration. For example, in 1947 he supported Truman's veto of the Taft-Hartley Bill, which he declared was antiunion. A strong opponent of discrimination, Javits also endorsed anti–poll tax legislation in 1947 and 1949, and in 1954 he unsuccessfully sought to have enacted a bill banning segregation in federally funded housing projects. Unhappy with the witch hunt atmosphere in Washington during the Cold War, he publicly opposed continuing appropriations for the House Un-American Activities Committee in 1948. Always a staunch supporter of Israel as a Jewish homeland, Javits served on the House Foreign Affairs Committee during all four of his terms and supported congressional funding for the Marshall Plan and all components of the Truman Doctrine.

In 1954 Javits left the House to run for New York State attorney general against a well-known and well-funded opponent, Franklin D. Roosevelt, Jr. Javits's vote-getting abilities carried the day, and he was the only Republican to win a statewide office that year. As attorney general, Javits continued to promote his liberal agenda, supporting such measures as antibias employment legislation and a health insurance program for state employees.

In 1956 Javits interrupted his service as attorney general to seek the Senate seat vacated by the retiring Herbert Lehman. His Democratic opponent was the popular mayor of New York, Robert F. Wagner, Jr. In the early stages of that campaign Javits vigorously and successfully denied charges that he had once sought support from members of the American Communist party during his 1946 race for Congress. He went on to defeat Wagner by nearly half a million votes. Upon taking office, Javits resumed his role as the most outspoken Republican liberal in Congress. For the next twenty-four years the Senate was Javits's home. His wife had no interest in living in Washington, D.C., a town she considered a boring backwater, so for over two decades Javits commuted between New York and Washington nearly every week to visit his "other" family and conduct local political business. During his first term he supported the limited 1957 Civil Rights Act, which was bitterly opposed by many of his southern colleagues. In foreign affairs he backed the Eisenhower Doctrine for the Middle East and also pressed for more foreign military and economic assistance.

Reelected easily in 1962, Javits actively supported Lyndon Johnson's civil rights measures and generally endorsed the Great Society programs. To promote his views on social legislation, he served on the Senate Labor and Human Resources Committee for twenty years, most of that time as the second-ranking minority member. Javits initially backed Johnson during the early years of America's involvement in the Vietnam War, supporting, for example, the Gulf of Tonkin Resolution in 1964. By the end of 1967, however, he was becoming disenchanted with the war's progress and joined twenty-two other senators in calling for a peaceful solution to the conflict. By 1970 his rising opposition to the war led him to support the Cooper-Church Amendment, which barred funds for U.S. troops in Cambodia, and he also voted to repeal the Gulf of Tonkin Resolution. Increasingly concerned about the erosion of congressional authority in foreign affairs, Javits sponsored the 1973 War Powers Act, which limited to sixty days a president's ability to send American armed forces into combat without congressional approval. Despite his unhappiness with President Richard Nixon over the Vietnam War, Javits was slow to join the anti-Nixon forces during the Watergate scandal of 1973–1974. Until almost the very end of the affair, Javits's position reflected his legal training: Nixon was innocent until proven guilty, and the best way to determine guilt or innocence was by legal due process. Javits's position was not popular among his constituency, and his reelection in 1974 over Ramsey Clark was by fewer than 400,000 votes, a third of his 1968 margin of victory. During his last term Javits shifted his interests more and more to world affairs, especially the crises in the Middle East. Working with President Jimmy Carter, he journeyed to Israel and Egypt to facilitate discussions that led to the 1978 Camp David Agreement.

In 1980, though Javits was still vigorous mentally, his physical health began to suffer the early ravages of a motor neuron disease. Nevertheless, he believed he could readily serve a fifth term. He was then the longest-serving senator in New York State history. With the strong possibility that Ronald Reagan could win the presidency and the Republicans would become the majority party in the Senate, Javits's long-held dream of chairing the Senate Foreign Relations Committee would become a reality. Unfortunately his liberal Republicanism had become old-fashioned, and as the party continued the rightward shift it had begun with Barry Goldwater, Javits became vulnerable to conservative opposition from within the state party. Alfonse D'Amato won the nod from the Republicans, forcing Javits to run on the Liberal party ticket. He lost by a wide margin, and his defeat was an ironic disaster for political liberalism in New York State, because Javits refused to leave the race after his primary loss, thereby splitting the liberal vote and guaranteeing D'Amato's victory. His last years were spent in retirement, giving speeches and writing articles. He died in Palm Beach, Florida.

Throughout his years in Congress, Javits seldom enjoyed favor with his party's inner circle. His liberalism was a vestige of a Republican party of an earlier era, and though he hung tenaciously to his liberal precepts, his influence was more subtle than obvious. Few pieces of legislation bear his name, yet he was especially proud of his work in creating the National Endowment for the Arts, of his sponsorship of the Erisa Act, which guaranteed private pensions, and of his leadership in the passage of the 1973 War Powers Act. He was widely regarded by friends and foes as one of the brightest and hardest-working members of the Senate. Though he often labored in vain for his cherished principles, his industrious and ceaseless efforts on behalf of those whom he believed the government was obligated to assist made him a champion for the average American.

• Javits's papers are housed at the State University of New York at Stony Brook. A major published source is his autobiography, *Javits: The Autobiography of a Public Man* (1981), which he wrote with Rafael Steinberg. Other books authored by Javits include *Discrimination* (1960); *Order of Battle* (1964; rev. ed., 1966); *Who Makes War: The President versus Congress*, written with Don Kellermann (1973); and *The Defense Sector and the American Economy*, coauthored by Charles J. Hitch and Arthur F. Burns (1968). Also valuable for anecdotal information is Frank Cummings and Daniel Szabo, eds., *Senator Javits and His Staff: Collected Remembrances from the Staff of U.S. Senator Jacob K. Javits* (1985). Javits's obituary is in the *New York Times*, 8 Mar. 1986.

EDWARD A. GOEDEKEN

JAWORSKI, Leon (19 Sept. 1905–9 Dec. 1982), attorney and Watergate prosecutor, was born Leonidas Jaworski in Waco, Texas, the son of Joseph Jaworski, an Evangelical clergyman, and Marie Mira. Jaworski received a law degree from Baylor University at the age of nineteen and became the youngest person ever admitted to the Texas bar. After receiving a master of law degree from George Washington University in 1926, he practiced law for three years in Waco. His early practice involved a wide variety of civil and criminal matters and included the defense of many persons charged with the illegal sale of alcohol. Despite the opposition of clients and friends, he also undertook the unsuccessful defense of an indigent African American who was accused of murdering a white couple.

Two years after moving to Houston in 1929, Jaworski joined the firm of Fulbright, Crooker, Freeman & Bates, with which he remained associated for most of the remainder of his life, as a litigator of complex commercial cases. In 1931 he married Jeannette Adam; they had three children.

Jaworski served as a trial lawyer in the army's judge advocate general's corps during the Second World War. In 1945 he was prosecutor of two of the most significant of the many war crimes trials in Germany that preceded the Nuremberg trials of Nazi leaders. In those trials, he obtained the convictions of German civilians who had killed American prisoners of war and of sanatorium employees who had murdered Russian and Polish slave laborers. Jaworski also supervised an investigation of the Dachau concentration camp prior to the prosecution of the camp's officials.

Returning to private practice after the war, Jaworski handled a number of significant cases, including litigation that enabled Lyndon B. Johnson to run for reelection to the Senate in 1960 even though he was also the Democratic vice presidential nominee. Active in professional affairs, Jaworski was president of the Texas Bar Association in 1962–1963 and president of the American Bar Association in 1971–1972.

During the early 1960s, Jaworski served as special prosecutor in the federal government's action against Mississippi governor Ross Barnett for defying a federal court order for the racial integration of the University of Mississippi. In 1964 he was one of four Texans who served as special counsel to the Warren Commission, which investigated the assassination of President John F. Kennedy. On the basis of their investigations in Texas, Jaworski and his co-counsel prepared a supplemental report that supported the conclusion of the commission's report that there was no conspiracy.

Jaworski's most prominent public role was as director of the Watergate Special Prosecution Force, which investigated the Nixon administration's participation in an attempted burglary at Democratic party headquarters at Washington's Watergate Hotel in 1972. Jaworski became special prosecutor in November 1973, at a time of public turmoil caused by President Richard M. Nixon's dismissal of Jaworski's predecessor, Archibald Cox, who had unsuccessfully urged Nixon to comply with a court order to produce tape recordings of White House conversations. Acting quickly to maintain public confidence in the independence and determination of the prosecution force, Jaworski continued its vigorous investigation into the administration's involvement in the Watergate burglary.

Although Jaworski originally believed that illegal activity was limited to Nixon's subordinates, several tapes released by Nixon late in 1973 convinced him that Nixon had personally attempted to interfere with investigations of the burglary. In an effort to gather more evidence, he served a subpoena for additional tapes. Nixon's refusal to comply with Jaworski's subpoena led to litigation in which Jaworski disputed Nixon's claim that the doctrine of executive privilege excused Nixon from producing the tapes. In *United States v. Nixon*, a landmark decision on 24 July 1974, the U.S. Supreme Court unanimously endorsed most of Jaworski's arguments, holding that the president's "presumptive privilege" was outweighed by the need to protect the integrity of the criminal justice system. A few days later, Nixon produced the tapes, which contained conversations in which Nixon ordered his staff to use the Central Intelligence Agency to obstruct the investigation of the Watergate burglary. Facing impeachment, Nixon officially resigned on 9 August 1974.

Even though Jaworski believed that his investigation had provided an ample basis for Nixon's indictment on charges of obstructing justice, he did not seek an indictment because he believed that Nixon could not obtain a fair trial. Jaworski later refused to challenge the legality of President Gerald R. Ford's pardon of Nixon because he concluded that the pardon was constitutionally permissible. Both decisions were highly controversial and subjected Jaworski to criticism among persons who otherwise admired his zeal and fairness as special prosecutor.

As special prosecutor, Jaworski obtained indictments of former attorney general John Mitchell and several Nixon aides, who subsequently were convicted and served time in prison for obstructing justice. Jaworski's investigations also led to the prosecution and conviction of numerous other persons in connection with illegal Nixon campaign contributions and other illegal activities related to the Nixon administration. He resigned as special prosecutor in October 1974, after the prosecution force had completed its most significant work.

During his final years, Jaworski continued to practice law, although he increasingly devoted time to writing, lecturing, and working on his Texas ranch. He returned to public life briefly in 1977–1978, when he served as special counsel to the House of Representatives Ethics Committee that investigated the alleged receipt of illegal payments by members of Congress from an agent of the South Korean government. He died while working on his ranch near Wimberley, Texas.

Even though Jaworski never held public office, he was one of the more significant public servants of his generation. Jaworski used his legal talents to assist many public causes, but his vigorous investigation and prosecution of the Watergate crimes are his most memorable and enduring legacy. As Jaworski explained in his memoir *The Right and the Power*, Watergate provided a reminder that "our Constitution works," and reaffirmed that "no one—absolutely no one—is above the law."

• Jaworski's papers are at Baylor University and include taped oral memoirs. He also published four autobiographies: *After Fifteen Years* (1961), an account of his work as a war crimes prosecutor; *The Right and the Power: The Prosecution of Watergate* (1976); *Confession and Avoidance*, with Mickey Herskowitz (1979), essays about prominent matters on which he had worked; and *Crossroads*, with Dick Schneider (1981), reflections on how his religious convictions influenced his career. His other writings include "Our High Prerogative: The Attorney's Responsibilities to the Law," *University of Dayton Law Review* 6 (Winter 1981): 1–10, and "The Lawyer in Society," *Baylor Law Review* 33 (Winter 1981): 1–49. Jaworski's experience as a war crimes prosecutor is studied in Mark Daniel Long, "Leon Jaworski and the Nazi War Crimes Trials" (master's thesis, Baylor Univ., 1992). For a bibliographical source on Watergate see Myron J. Smith, Jr., *Watergate: An Annotated Bibliography of Sources in English, 1972–1982* (1983). Memorial tributes are found in *Baylor Law Review* 34 (Fall 1982): v–xvii. Obituaries are in the *New York Times* and the *Los Angeles Times*, 10 Dec. 1982, and in the *Washington Post*, 14 Dec. 1982.

WILLIAM G. ROSS

JAY, Allen (11 Oct. 1831–8 May 1910), Quaker minister and educator, was born in Miami County, Ohio, the son of Isaac Jay, a farmer and Quaker minister, and Rhoda Cooper. The Jays were a large and prominent Quaker family, and Allen Jay spent his early life in a Quaker community surrounded by relatives. He received his early education in Quaker schools in Miami and Montgomery counties, Ohio. In 1850 his family moved to Grant County, Indiana. Jay subsequently attended the Friends Boarding School (now Earlham College) at Richmond, Indiana, the Farmers Institute Academy near Lafayette, Indiana, and Antioch College (Yellow Springs, Ohio). On 20 September 1854 he was married at Farmers Institute to Martha Ann Sleeper; they had five children.

After their marriage, Allen and Martha Jay settled on a farm near Farmers Institute. In 1864 he was recorded a Quaker minister, after having preached for five years in Indiana. His perceived call to preach was a challenge because Jay suffered from a cleft palate, which gave him, in the words of a contemporary, "a speech like nothing ever heard before." During the Civil War, although a firm Unionist and abolitionist, Jay remained true to Quaker pacifism and refused to enlist or even pay an exemption tax, despite threats of fines and seizure of property.

Jay first emerged as a national Quaker figure when he moved to North Carolina in 1868 to superintend the work of the Baltimore Association. The Civil War had left the scattered Quaker communities in North Carolina dispirited and impoverished, with many Friends convinced that only migration west was the solution to their problems. Well-to-do Baltimore Quakers had established the Baltimore Association to rebuild Quakerism in the state. Beginning with basic charitable relief, the association moved on to emphasize establishing schools and improving farming methods. The effort was successful not only in rebuilding North Carolina Quakerism, but also in permanently improving the quality of education in the state.

Jay's work in North Carolina coincided with the beginning of dramatic change in American Quakerism. Between 1870 and 1895 a wave of revivalism swept through Quaker congregations from New England to Oregon. Most Friends gave up conventional ways of plainness and silent worship and moved very close to the practices of other Protestant denominations. In this period, Jay was a powerful voice of moderation, often participating in Quaker evangelistic work but with sensitivity to older and more conservative Friends. He refused to preach what he called "the terrors of the law" or second-experience sanctification, subjects dear to most Quaker revivalists but an anathema to traditional, more introspective Friends.

In 1877 Jay left North Carolina to become treasurer of a Quaker institution in Providence, Rhode Island, that was later known as the Moses Brown School. He remained there four years before accepting the same position at Earlham College. For the next thirty years, until his death, Jay was connected with Earlham as an administrator or trustee. He had a particular talent for raising money. He solicited most of the funds for the erection of five new buildings and for an endowment for the college. As a result, by 1910 enrollment had increased tenfold. He performed similar duties for other Quaker colleges in North Carolina, Iowa, Nebraska, Oregon, and California.

Jay continued to play a leading role in American Quaker affairs after he returned to Indiana. In the 1870s he had traveled in Great Britain and Europe, forming important ties with Friends there. In the 1880s he was a prominent opponent of David B. Updegraff, the Ohio Quaker minister who advocated water baptism. In the 1890s, as Indiana Quakers moved toward a pastoral system of ministry, Jay oversaw its beginnings as pastoral superintendent of Indiana Yearly Meeting. In 1899 Martha Jay died, and in 1900 Jay married Naomi (Morgan) Harrison; they had no children together.

Jay's final battles involved the beginning of modernism among American Friends. Modernist Friends emphasized a scientific rather than literal study of the Bible and were skeptical of revivalism, emphasizing instead a return to what they saw as traditional Quaker emphasis on individual religious experience and social concern. By 1900 a small group of Quaker scholars, including Rufus Jones and Elbert Russell, had begun to introduce modernist methods of biblical study into Quaker schools, such as Earlham. They met with fierce opposition from holiness Friends, who were committed to biblical literalism and who saw modernism as infidelity. Jay allied himself to the modernist cause, or at least to tolerance of it, although his own views of religion changed little. His support for the beleaguered liberal Friends was critical, winning them a hearing in circles that otherwise would have been closed to them. Jay died in Richmond, Indiana.

Jay was one of the most influential figures in American Quakerism between 1860 and 1910. Probably more than any other person, he was responsible for the survival of Quakerism in North Carolina. During a period of dramatic change among American Friends, he was a vital moderate influence. His fundraising work was critical for a half dozen Quaker schools in their infancy. And, Jay helped nurture modernist Quakerism at a time when its survival was far from certain in many parts of the United States.

• Jay's papers are in the Friends Collection at Earlham College. His only published work is the main source for his life: *Autobiography* (1910). A sympathetic brief biography appears in *Quaker Biographies*, ser. 2, vol. 3. For Jay's place in Quaker affairs, see Thomas D. Hamm, *The Transformation of American Quakerism: Orthodox Friends, 1880–1907* (1988).

THOMAS HAMM

JAY, John (12 Dec. 1745–17 May 1829), diplomat and first chief justice of the U.S. Supreme Court, was born in New York City, the son of Peter Jay, a prosperous merchant, and Mary Van Cortlandt, a member of one of the great Dutch patroon landed families of the Hudson Valley. On 28 April 1774 John Jay joined another powerful landlord clan by marrying Sarah Livingston, daughter of a future governor of New Jersey; the couple had seven children.

Jay's family connections had a profound influence on him. His grandfather was a French Huguenot who had escaped imprisonment in the fortress at St. Malo and was taken by ship to America. As a consequence, Jay was a pious Protestant who distrusted both the Catholic church and the French nation that had persecuted his forebears. The wealth, power, and politics of his family connections also affected him. The Jay, Van Cortlandt, and Livingston families were among the minority of New York aristocrats who sided with the Whigs during the revolutionary crisis.

Jay was a latecomer to New York politics and the patriot cause. He graduated from King's College (later Columbia University) in 1764, clerked in the offices of a prominent Tory lawyer, was admitted to the bar in 1768, and embarked on a legal career in which he represented Whig and Tory clients with equal energy. He concentrated on his law career until 1774, when he was elected to the Committee of Correspondence in New York City. Shortly afterward he was named one of New York's five delegates to the First Continental Congress.

In both the Committee of Correspondence and the congress, Jay opposed radical moves toward resistance and war. Nevertheless, after militant members succeeded in passing resolutions that called Parliament's acts unconstitutional, advised the arming of local militias, and recommended trade sanctions, Jay drafted the congress's *Address to the People of Great Britain*, justifying their actions. In it he denounced Parliament for claiming the right to tax the colonists without their consent and proclaimed that Americans would "never consent to be hewers of wood or drawers of water." In accommodating himself to the majority, Jay evinced a characteristic that made him invaluable to the conservative cause throughout his career—a willingness to compromise and cooperate with opponents.

As a delegate to the Second Continental Congress in 1775, Jay continued on his moderate course. Despite his wish to avoid all-out measures against Great Britain following the outbreak of war at Lexington and Concord, he again took up his pen to appeal to Canadians to join in the rebellion. "The fate of the Protestant and Catholic colonies" was linked, he said, despite his Huguenot background and anti-Catholic sentiments.

But Jay continued to resist the attempts of John Adams and other militants to declare outright independence. Jay was back in New York as a member of the colonial legislature when the Continental Congress finally voted for a declaration of independence. But he would surely have voted against independence because he was instrumental in instructing New York's representatives in Philadelphia to oppose the measure.

Once the congress declared independence and the British simultaneously launched a major invasion of New York, however, Jay abandoned all reluctance and threw himself headlong into the war. He helped deliver cannon to George Washington's troops defending New York, headed a council to root out spies and traitors in the colony, and organized an espionage ring that James Fenimore Cooper later immortalized in his novel *The Spy* (1821).

Jay also accepted the invitation of the New York Convention to help draft a constitution for the state. In it he again showed his ability to compromise and reconcile opposing views. On the one hand, for instance, the constitution reduced the property requirements to vote for the lower house of the legislature. On the other, it raised the requirements to vote for governor and the upper house. The delicately balanced constitution was readily accepted by all factions in the state and lasted many years, something of which Jay was pardonably proud.

One incident at the New York Constitutional Convention, however, showed a different side of Jay. He proposed a clause that denied civil rights to anyone who would not forswear allegiance to priest, pope, or other foreign power. When that was defeated he offered one variant after another until finally he settled for a mere warning against using freedom of conscience to encourage "licentiousness."

Jay could be stubborn and prickly. At times this took the form of an admirable refusal to compromise basic principles, as when he accepted suspension from college rather than inform on fellow students who had broken a table, even though he readily admitted his own guilt. At other times, however, Jay's concern for his reputation could turn to pettiness, pride, and arrogance. He proclaimed to one minor offender that he "had rather reject the friendship of the world than purchase it by patience under indignities offered by any man in it." He came close to a duel with a man whom he blackballed from a private club because of the man's social status. Jay defended his personal dignity with a cold, formal, and taciturn public persona. Privately he could be much warmer, but still his wife, with whom he had a loving relationship, always referred to him as "Mr. Jay."

Jay's adversaries often believed that his excessive self-regard and concern for his own dignity was a weak characteristic of which they could take advantage. As one knowledgeable Briton reported, Jay could "bear any opposition to what he advocates provided regard is shown to his ability . . . Mr. Jay's weak side is *Mr. Jay.*"

When the New York Constitution was adopted in 1777, the convention elected Jay chief justice of the state supreme court. He spent two years judging mostly criminal trials, after which the legislature took advantage of the provision in the constitution that permitted the chief justice to serve simultaneously as a delegate to the Continental Congress, and it returned him to Philadelphia. Congress quickly elected Jay president, just in time for him to preside over a messy foreign policy debate about how closely the United States should cooperate with its ally France and on what terms it should offer to make peace with Great Britain.

Members of Congress, many influenced by the French representative in the United States, mistakenly counted Jay as a person who would favor French inter-

ests; that was one of the reasons they had elected him president to replace the more obstreperous Henry Laurens. It was also one reason why, nine months later, they selected Jay as U.S. representative to Spain and to serve concurrently with Adams and Benjamin Franklin as a commissioner to make peace with Britain whenever negotiations should become possible.

Jay's sojourn in Spain was an unhappy one. Even though Spain had entered the war against Britain as an ally of France, it refused to ally with the United States or formally accept Jay as America's representative. The Spanish were willing to supply some aid to the Americans, but they wanted no public connection with revolutionaries who denounced monarchy and threatened Spanish colonial claims to the Mississippi region. Even when Congress instructed Jay to give up American demands for navigation of the Mississippi to win other concessions from Spain, the Spanish refused. Although personally relieved that Spain had not accepted the Mississippi proposal, Jay considered Spanish conduct insulting to both himself and his country. When Franklin called him to Paris to join the peace negotiations with the British, Jay was seething at France as well as Spain for France's refusal to do more to help him in Madrid.

By the time Jay arrived in Paris he was ready to defy Congress's instructions that the commissioners keep the French allies fully informed on America's negotiations with Great Britain and abide by French advice. When the French foreign minister, the comte de Vergennes, advised Jay and Franklin to open formal negotiations with the British envoy despite the fact that his credentials were addressed to the American colonies rather than to the independent United States, Jay refused. In forcing Franklin to join him in demanding new credentials for the British delegate that would recognize American independence prior to the conclusion of any formal treaty, Jay caused a major delay in the negotiations that Franklin had already informally begun. Meanwhile, Jay took another step toward negotiating peace independent of the French ally. When he heard that Vergennes's secretary had left Paris on a secret mission to London, Jay immediately suspected that the French were negotiating separately to the detriment of American interests. Without informing Franklin, Jay sent his own messenger to ask the British to reject any proposals by the French that would adversely affect the United States.

When Adams arrived in Paris, he supported Jay against Franklin. Franklin loyally put aside his doubts and joined them in reopening negotiations without informing the French. In the end, Jay, Franklin, and Adams secured a treaty that recognized American independence and extended the nation's borders to the Mississippi River. Vergennes was chagrined at the commissioners' independent agreement, but he was also impressed by the terms and grateful that the agreement gave him an excuse to push Spain toward peace without delivering on the French promise to continue fighting until Spain regained Gibraltar. In 1783 the French, Spanish, Americans, and British all signed the Treaty of Paris that incorporated America's preliminary peace agreement.

Historians have long debated whether the United States could have had an even more favorable northern boundary with Canada if Jay had not delayed negotiations until the British had improved their bargaining position by beating off the Franco-Spanish assault on Gibraltar. But Jay and Adams insisted throughout their lives that their refusal to accept the guidance of the French had been essential to the success of their mission. The terms they achieved were sufficient to muzzle congressional critics tempted to argue against their treaty or their treatment of France.

Jay returned from the peace negotiations to a hero's welcome and found himself appointed secretary for foreign affairs under the recently adopted Articles of Confederation. As foreign secretary he received reports from Adams and Thomas Jefferson, America's representatives to Britain and France, respectively, that the European powers were treating the United States with contempt. Consequently, Jay chafed at the inability to retaliate under the weak confederation government. After Alexander Hamilton and James Madison had failed to gain the unanimous congressional vote necessary to impose a tariff on foreign commerce, Jay despaired of gaining the revenue and trade leverage needed to secure American goals by independent action. He decided that he would have to trade away some goals to win others. Thus in 1786 he agreed with Spanish minister Diego de Gardoqui that the United States would give up the right to navigate the Mississippi for thirty years in exchange for a Spanish trade treaty and a mutual guarantee of each other's territory in the Western Hemisphere. Such a commercial treaty would lock in the beneficial terms on which the United States was already conducting its trade with Spain while the mutual guarantee of territory might exert pressure against British occupation of several Great Lakes posts on American territory. When Jay broached the possibility of this treaty to Congress, southerners were so outraged at Jay's willingness to abandon the Mississippi that they blocked any further negotiations. Many southerners and westerners distrusted Jay ever after.

The Constitutional Convention of 1787 created a stronger federal government. Although Jay was not a member of the convention, he helped secure ratification of the Constitution by joining Madison and Hamilton in writing the classic defense of the new system, *The Federalist Papers*. Once the states had ratified the Constitution, President George Washington appointed Jay to become chief justice of the U.S. Supreme Court.

As chief justice Jay continued his attempts to strengthen the federal government. In 1793 he delivered the majority opinion in *Ware v. Hylton*, in which the Court reinforced the sanctity of federal treaty obligations. That same year, in *Chisholm v. Georgia*, Jay led the majority in deciding that individuals could sue a state in federal court. This challenge to state sovereignty raised an immediate outcry. The state of Geor-

gia decreed a penalty of hanging for any person who assisted the federal courts in carrying out the decision. By 1798 the states had ratified the Eleventh Amendment to the Constitution, which denied that federal judicial power extended to suits against states by citizens of other states or subjects of foreign nations.

In 1792 Jay accepted the nomination for governor of New York. He won a narrow majority of the vote but was defeated when a partisan election commission ruled invalid the returns of three counties. It was a mark of his character that he accepted the decision, discouraged his backers from the extralegal challenges some had planned, and continued his work on the Supreme Court.

Throughout this period, Washington often consulted Jay on matters outside the purview of the Supreme Court, particularly on foreign affairs. Jay wrote the first draft of Washington's famous Neutrality Proclamation after war broke out between Great Britain and revolutionary France in 1793. When British violations of American neutral rights during that conflict brought the United States itself to the brink of war, Jay, still a justice of the Court, accepted Washington's invitation to go as special envoy to London to negotiate a settlement. In doing so he stepped into a maelstrom of partisan combat.

Former secretary of state Jefferson and House leader Madison, along with many of their friends in Congress who were coming to be known as Republicans, had long advocated commercial retaliation against Great Britain. They supported trade restrictions not only to force the British to respect American neutral rights but also to make them abandon the occupied forts on the Great Lakes and open their West Indies to American shipping on terms similar to those that had existed when America had been part of the British Empire. Secretary of the Treasury Hamilton and his so-called Federalist advocates, including Jay, wanted desperately to avoid a conflict with Great Britain that could interrupt the flow of British imports and the tariff revenue the federal government derived from them. The tariff supported the financial system that Hamilton was using to strengthen the federal government.

Jay immediately sided with Hamilton in advising Congress against the commercial retaliation that Jefferson and Madison proposed. Instead, he favored a conciliatory manner and a compromising stance. The threat that war would inevitably occur if no agreement could be found was implicit. The Jay Treaty that he negotiated was only a partial success. The British did agree to evacuate the Great Lakes posts. They also promised to open their West Indies to American ships, although on terms so onerous that the Senate ultimately rejected that article. The British also promised to compensate American shipowners for some of the most egregious of British seizures. But Jay could not get British recognition of America's claims to neutral rights. Moreover, by agreeing not to interfere with British trade for ten years, Jay gave away the right of commercial retaliation, the one lever with which the Republicans thought they could extort a proper respect for neutral rights and other concessions from the British.

Republicans roundly attacked Jay and his treaty. They accused him of purposely selling out American interests to protect Hamilton's financial system and to support monarchical Britain against democratic France. They held mass meetings and submitted petitions to Washington to get him to refuse ratification of the treaty. When that failed they sent massive petitions to urge Congress to refuse the monetary appropriations necessary to implement the treaty.

The Federalists at first defended Jay and his treaty only tepidly, saying that at least he had prevented a ruinous war. But as they saw the challenge the Republicans were mounting, they turned to similar meetings and petitions to defend the treaty and themselves, eventually securing Senate consent to the treaty and defeating an attack on the implementation of the treaty in the House. Thus did Jay and his treaty act as a catalyst to help transform the Federalists and Republicans from mere factions in Congress to organized grassroots parties.

Jay detested the hurly-burly of partisan politics, but he found on his return from England in 1795 that he had already been elected governor of New York. He accepted and served two terms. His most notable contribution as governor was to reject a scheme Hamilton urged on him to change the method by which New York selected its presidential electors so as to deprive Jefferson of victory in the election of 1800. Jay's integrity on this occasion was a fitting climax to his public career.

In November 1800 Jay refused Adams's offer to reappoint him chief justice on the ironic grounds that the federal court system was too weak to support the national government properly. Thus he opened the way for John Marshall to prove him wrong. Jay then retired with his wife to a small estate in Bedford, New York, a two days' ride from New York City. His wife died shortly thereafter in 1802 and left him to live out his lengthy retirement without her. He died twenty-seven years later at his home in Bedford.

Despite John Jay's contributions to revolutionary America, he has been overshadowed by his more illustrious compatriots. He was eclipsed by Adams as a revolutionary legislator, by Jefferson as an author of revolutionary justifications, by Franklin as a diplomat, by Madison as a constitution-maker, by Washington as an executive, by Hamilton as a party leader, and by Marshall as a chief justice. Nevertheless, Jay contributed significantly in all of these areas, and he bore a great responsibility for the creation and survival of the United States. Above all, his qualities of intelligence, integrity, and cooperativeness at critical times of great emotional conflict helped institute the civility and compromise necessary for a democratic culture.

• Columbia University holds the largest collection of Jay's manuscript papers. Some of those papers appear in a collection edited by Henry P. Johnston, *Correspondence and Public Papers of John Jay* (4 vols., 1890–1893). Richard B. Morris

capped a lifetime study of Jay by publishing a supplement of papers not included in Johnston's collection, *John Jay: The Making of a Revolutionary: Unpublished Papers, 1745–1780* (1975) and *John Jay: The Winning of the Peace: Unpublished Papers, 1780–1784* (1980). Morris never did write a complete biography of Jay; for that one must rely on Frank Monaghan, *John Jay: Defender of Liberty* (1935). But Morris contributed several important books on various aspects of Jay's career, including *The Peacemakers: The Great Powers and American Independence* (1965), *Witnesses at the Creation: Hamilton, Madison, Jay, and the Constitution* (1985), and *John Jay, the Nation, and the Court* (1965). Alfred F. Young places Jay in the context of New York politics and society in an outstanding book, *The Democratic Republicans of New York* (1967). On Jay's most important contribution, the Jay Treaty of 1794, see Samuel Flagg Bemis, *Jay's Treaty: A Study in Commerce and Diplomacy* (1923; rev., 1962), and Jerald A. Combs, *The Jay Treaty: Political Battleground of the Founding Fathers* (1970).

JERALD A. COMBS

JAY, William (1792 or 1793–17 Apr. 1837), architect, was born in Bath, England, the son of the Reverend William Jay, a well-known clergyman, and Ann Davis, an author of children's stories. Jay, who is best known for the introduction of regency-style architecture to the developing Georgia and South Carolina colonies, was raised in the English resort community of Bath, where his father was a minister in an Independent Presbyterian (Congregational) chapel. His father's position and relative fame, achieved through many published texts and sermons, brought Jay into contact with a number of influential people, many of whom would later have an impact on his career. His father had also trained as a stoneworker, which influenced Jay's choice of career.

Educated primarily in Bath, the young William Jay was apprenticed at around the age of fourteen to the London architect and surveyor David Ridal Roper. Roper had been involved in the rebuilding of Regent Street and was noted for his designs for the Church of St. Mary Lambeth and for the Haberdashers' Almshouse, Hoxton, both executed in the Greek revival style then popular in Great Britain. Jay worked as a draftsman but by 1809 was exhibiting designs of his own in the Royal Academy exhibitions. His submissions included projects for a public library (1809), a boathouse (1810), and a "prospect room" (1815). In 1816 he was independently responsible for the design of the Albion Chapel in Moorgate, a severe rectangular block surmounted by a low dome and embellished by a pedimented entry with recessed Ionic columns.

Jay departed for Savannah in 1817, having that year already exhibited a drawing of a proposed Independent Presbyterian church at the Royal Academy. Although he was unsuccessful in his bid to design the proposed building, Jay drew upon his nonconformist connections and his family ties to secure work in the rapidly developing southern coastal city. Among his earliest clients was Richard Richardson, whose wife Frances was related to Jay's brother-in-law Robert Boltin, a successful cotton merchant. Jay designed a house for Richardson (1817–1819) and later designed a building for the Savannah branch of the Bank of the U.S. (1820–1821), of which Richardson was the first president. He soon designed other houses for well-to-do merchants and bankers, including William Scarbrough (1818), Archibald Bulloch (1818), Robert Habersham (1819), and Alexander Telfair (1820). Other public and commercial buildings in Savannah attributed to Jay include the Savannah Theater (1818) and possibly the City Hotel (1821–1822).

Jay's architectural work extended to Charleston, where he maintained a separate office from as early as 1818. Serving as the first architect for the Charleston Board of Public Works, Jay had an influence on the overall urban character of the city as well as designing a number of private houses and public buildings. His domestic work in Charleston included the Patrick Duncan house (Ashley Hall) on Rutledge Avenue (1818–1819) and the William Mason Smith house on Meeting Street (1820). A number of other Charleston houses were probably also designed by Jay, who is often referred in building records or other notices as simply "an English architect." His proposal for a fireproof public records office anticipated and clearly influenced the later (1822) design by the Charleston architect Robert Mills, now considered a pioneering example of fire-resistant construction. Jay also designed several South Carolina courthouses and at least one jail, all of which were completed by Mills.

Jay returned to England in 1822 because of economic reversals in the cotton business that adversely affected the building trade. After a short time in Bath, he reestablished himself at Henley-on-Thames, where he continued to design nonconformist chapels and private houses, including an impressive resort row of terrace houses in Cheltenham. In 1827 he married Louisa Coulson of Henley, with whom he had three children. Ultimately unsuccessful in his business dealings and architectural work, in 1836 Jay accepted a poorly paid post as a government architect in the British colony of Mauritius, in the Indian Ocean. He died there the following year (of an unidentified tropical fever) shortly after the death of his six-year-old son.

Jay was one of several English activists who contributed to the arts of America during the early years of the republic. His influence was not immediately significant, probably because his stay in America was so short. His buildings nonetheless had a great impact, especially on Savannah and Charleston, where he introduced newer architectural ideas based on both the picturesque and classical principles of better-known regency-period architects such as John Soane and John Nash.

Jay's buildings were generally square or rectangular in mass and were characterized by strong horizontal divisions, austere classical porticoes or pediments, and, particularly at the rear, projecting octagonal or semicircular bays. Smooth, almost monolithic-looking stuccoed surfaces were embellished with often highly individualized Greek and other classical motifs. Windows were typically recessed with arched openings; entrance halls were often lit by skylights and half-circular thermal windows. Innovations included the use of cast-iron elements that became more or less a hallmark of Jay's urban designs. Noted for his amiable disposition and his easy way with friends and clients, Jay introduced a new level of architectural sophistication to the former English colonies.

• Records relating to Jay's buildings are found in the papers of various clients, including the Scarbroughs (Taylor papers, Georgia Department of Archives and History, Atlanta) and Telfairs (Few papers, Georgia Department of Archives and History, Atlanta), as well as in the minutes of the Savannah City Council and in Chatham County records. His Charleston and South Carolina work is documented in various papers held by the South Carolina Department of Archives and History. Background on the Jay family can be found in George Redford and John Angell James, *The Autobiography of the Reverend William Jay* (1854), and Cyrus Jay, *Recollections of William Jay of Bath* (1859). His earliest work and that of his contemporaries is described in James Elmes, *Metropolitan Improvements, or London in the Nineteenth Century* (1827). An overview of his life is found in Thomas Gamble, "Romance of William Jay, Savannah Architect: His Genius is Reflected in Buildings Here," *Savannah Morning News*, 8 May 1932. Architectural studies touching on his work include Frederic Doveton Nichols, *The Early Architecture of Georgia* (1957); Alice R. Huger Smith and P. E. Huger Smith, *The Dwelling Houses of Charleston* (1917); Mills Lane, *Architecture of the Old South: Georgia* (1986) and *Architecture of the Old South: South Carolina* (1984); and John Linley, *Georgia Catalogue: Historic American Buildings Survey* (1982). More specific architectural and biographical studies include G. L. M. Goodfellow, "William Jay and the Albion Chapel," *Journal of the Society of Architectural Historians* 22 (1963): 225–27; James Vernon McDonough, "William Jay: Regency Architect in Georgia and South Carolina" (Ph.D. diss., Princeton Univ., 1950); and Hanna Hryniewiecka Lerski, *William Jay: Itinerant English Architect, 1792–1837* (1983).

WILLIAM R. CHAPMAN

JEAN, Sally Lucas (18 June 1878–5 July 1971), health educator and nurse, was born in Towson, Maryland, the daughter of George Jean, a teacher, and Emilie Watkins Selby. Her mother was a devout Episcopalian from the South, while her father, who had fought for the northern troops during the Civil War, had been raised in a Presbyterian family. Jean, the youngest of their three children, had two experiences early in life that led her to dream of a nursing career. A close friend died of diphtheria, and shortly after that Jean played Florence Nightingale in a school play. Learning of Nightingale's life-saving heroics, Jean resolved to follow in her footsteps. When Jean was fifteen her father died and she told her family of her desire to become a nurse. They urged her to become a teacher instead like her father. Obligingly she entered the Maryland State Normal School, from which she graduated in 1896.

Jean's interest in nursing did not abate. During the summer vacation of her first year in school, she interned at the local homeopathic hospital and soon thereafter entered the Maryland Homeopathic Training School for Nurses. After graduating from this school in 1898, she took a job as an army nurse. When the Spanish-American War came to a close, Jean returned to Baltimore as an operating room nurse. The hospital setting did not appeal to her, so she switched to private duty nursing.

At the age of thirty-two Jean accepted a job as a school nurse within the Baltimore Department of Health and found her métier. Assigned to a poor neighborhood of immigrants, she concentrated on teaching her young charges the basics of proper hygiene. Among the seemingly simple but ingenious ideas that she implemented were mounting health exhibits, opening a public bathing facility for children, and instituting a program to loan children who arrived at school with wet feet dry shoes and socks. In 1914 the state appointed her organizer and director of their Social Health Service, a post she held for three years.

Jean lectured frequently, hoping to share with others the successful measures she implemented in her hometown. In the audience at one of these lectures sat the director of the People's Institute, based in New York. So impressed was he with Jean's performance that he offered her a job as the organizer of the institute's Department of Health Service. At first she demurred, agreeing to take on the job only for the summer, after which she would return to Baltimore. But the job proved more exciting than she had expected, and Jean stayed in New York, where she entered a national circle of public health educators.

At the end of World War I Jean served as secretary of the New York Academy of Medicine's Committee of Wartime Problems of Childhood under the direction of L. Emmett Holt. When the war came to a close, the group decided to continue their efforts for children's health and founded the Child Health Organization (CHO). Jean was named the organization's first director in 1918. Five years later the CHO merged with the American Child Hygiene Association to become the American Child Health Association. Herbert Hoover was named to the presidency of the new hybrid organization, with Holt as its vice president and Jean as its director of health education.

Although this amalgamation seemed promising at first, within a year of the association's birth Jean found herself embroiled in office politics. When the division funds were cut from the budget, she opted to resign rather than continue her work with a shoestring staff. With her ever-growing reputation, extensive contacts in the field, and indisputable knack for health education, she did not stay unemployed for long. Within three months after she resigned, she had started an active business as a health consultant, securing contracts early on with the Metropolitan Life Insurance Company and the National Dairy Council and later with companies such as Quaker Oats and the Cleanliness Institute. Charging $50 per an eight-hour day of work, Jean carved out a more lucrative career for herself than she ever would have had as a teacher or a nurse.

Jean maintained an interest in child hygiene in other countries and cultures. In 1932 she co-wrote with Grace T. Hallock a children's book, *Spending the Day in China, Japan and the Philippines*, which chronicled life in those three countries in an attempt to persuade young readers that even those who have "ways that seem strange" share many of the same concerns. Soon after the publication of that book, she had an opportunity to test her cultural relativism closer to home when a former colleague of hers from the People's Institute became commissioner of Indian Affairs and appointed her supervisor of health education for the Indian Service. In the year that she spent in the post, Jean started a program to eradicate trachoma on Indian reservations and started a health institute for Indian girls with high school degrees to teach them how to be better mothers, nurse's aides, and health aides.

Continuing to consult, Jean threw herself into professional public health associations. From 1937 to 1940 she served as president of the Association of Women in Public Health. She also held the executive posts on the public health education section of the American Public Health Association and from 1941 to 1942 chaired the section. Her next long-term assignment came in 1943 at the age of sixty-six for the National Foundation for Infantile Paralysis. Essential to the public health campaign about polio, Jean was eventually promoted to director of education service, a post from which she stepped down in 1951.

One of the more prolific public health professionals of the century, Jean was at the forefront of many of the most memorable public health ventures and originated a number of programs. Although Jean never married or had children—she lived with her secretary, Dorothy Goodwin, who was also a close friend—her work imparted hygienic habits to children around the world. When she died in New York City, the *New York Times* called her a pioneer in health education.

• Marguerite Vollmer's dissertation, "Sally Lucas Jean: Her Contribution to Health Education" (Columbia Univ., 1968), is probably the most complete account of Jean's life and includes interviews with her. Norman Gevitz has written a pared-down account of her life for the *Dictionary of American Medical Biography*, ed. Martin Kaufman et al. (1984). An extensive obituary is in the *New York Times*, 7 July 1971.

SHARI RUDAVSKY

JEANES, Anna Thomas (7 Apr. 1822–24 Sept. 1907), philanthropist, was born in Philadelphia, Pennsylvania, the daughter of Isaac Jeanes, a merchant, and Anna Thomas. The youngest of ten children, she was raised by her sister Mary after their mother's death in 1826. Her family were members of the Society of Friends, and she was active in the liberal Hicksite meetings in Philadelphia. Jeanes never married, and as an adult she lived with family members, including three brothers, Samuel and Joshua, who prospered as merchants, and Joseph, whose wealth derived from his holdings of Pennsylvania coalfields.

Jeanes's education did not continue past the secondary level. However, she sustained her various intellectual interests through wide and deep reading on the world's religions, especially Buddhism, and on China,

Japan, India, and Egypt, and through memberships in the Philadelphia Academy of Natural Sciences, the Philadelphia Zoological Society, and the Philadelphia Academy of Fine Arts. In 1886 she published a book, *The Sacrificer and the Non-Sacrificer*, which examined the concepts of the formal priesthood (the sacrificers) and the "natural" community of believers (the non-sacrificers) within Buddhism, Judaism, Hinduism, and Christianity. A later book of poetry, *Fancy's Flight* (1899), similarly explored religious beliefs.

Jeanes developed the habit of giving annually to various Philadelphia charities, including the Society of Friends. After the deaths of Joseph and Samuel in 1894, the family fortunes went to her as the only surviving sibling. In the last twelve years of her life, she gave her accumulated inheritance, totaling approximately $5 million, to various causes. One of her first large gifts, $200,000 earmarked for educational purposes, went to the Philadelphia Yearly Meeting in 1895 and helped publish the Quakers' *Friends' Intelligencer*. In addition to donating $100,000 to refurbish Quaker meetinghouses, in 1896 she gave $200,000 to build homes for Pennsylvania's elderly Quakers in Kennett Square, Moorestown, Norristown, Newtown, Trenton, West Chester, Woodstown, and Philadelphia, and another $200,000 to erect the Friends' Boarding Home in Germantown, which she herself designed and where she lived from 1904 until the end of her life.

Jeanes's interest in the welfare of African Americans may have been inspired generally by Quaker antislavery activism and specifically by her sister Mary's founding of Philadelphia's Home for Destitute Colored Children in 1855. Jeanes gave periodically to support education for African Americans in rural areas, a project she undertook with help from Hampton Institute principal Hollis B. Frissell and Tuskegee Institute principal Booker T. Washington and which eventually led to her donation of $200,000 to the General Education Board. A few months before her death she established a $1 million endowment, later called the Negro Rural School Fund, Anna T. Jeanes Foundation (the Jeanes Fund), the income from which underwrote the cost of countywide outreach services throughout the South that included master teachers traveling to local schools to establish and improve vocational and industrial training classes. Although she wrote the provision of the endowment fund into her will, stressing that it "be devoted solely to the assistance of Rural, Community, or Country Schools for Southern Negros . . . for the purpose of rudimentary education and to encourage moral influence and social refinement which shall promote peace in the land, and good will among men," she released the money early, in April 1907. Among the trustees of the fund were Washington, steel baron and philanthropist Andrew Carnegie, Hampton Institute's Robert Moton, and Tulane University's James Dillard. The best-known Jeanes supervisor was Virginia Estelle Randolph, whose work in the state of Virginia served as a model for improving education for African Americans throughout the rural South. The Jeanes Fund was combined with other similar endowments in 1937 to become known as the Southern Education Foundation.

In her will, Jeanes distributed her remaining estate, estimated at $3 million, to various organizations in Philadelphia, including $5,000 each for the Home for Aged and Infirm Colored Persons and the Home for Destitute Colored Children, and $20,000 to support Friends' Freedmans' schools. She left money to the Fireman's Pension Fund, the Pennsylvania Working Home for Blind Men, and the Penn Asylum for Widows and Single Women. Her attempt to leave her brother's coal interests to Swarthmore College failed when the college declined the gift because it required withdrawal from all intercollegiate sports. In addition to giving a bequest to the Women's Hospital of Philadelphia, Jeanes also left instructions to found a cancer hospital on the grounds of "Stapeley Farm" at Fox Chase, Pennsylvania, an estate her brothers had acquired in 1845.

Jeanes died in Germantown at the Friends' Boarding Home, and her body was cremated and the ashes buried in the family plot at the Fair Hill Burying Ground, to which she left $20,000 to encourage the practice of cremation and $5,000 to maintain the premises. Although she led a quiet life in keeping with nineteenth-century expectations of women, her writing, her architectural design, and especially her detailed instructions regarding the disposition of her estate all reveal the workings of an independent mind intent on translating beliefs into action.

• Scattered original sources are housed in the Friends Historical Library of Swarthmore College, including "The Last Will and Codicils of Anna T. Jeanes, Deceased" and a Jeanes family history. Brief biographical sketches are in James H. Dillard, "Fourteen Years of the Jeanes Fund," *South Atlantic Quarterly* 22, no. 3 (July 1923): 193–201; Arthur D. Wright, *The Negro Rural School Fund, Inc. (Anna T. Jeanes Foundation), 1907–1933* (1933); and Friends General Conference, *Quaker Torch Bearers* (1943). A description and assessment of the Negro Rural School Fund's teachers are in Lance G. E. Jones, *The Jeanes Teacher in the United States, 1908–1933: An Account of Twenty-five Years' Experience in the Supervision of Negro Rural Schools* (1937); Quaker women are described in Margaret Hope Bacon, *Mothers of Feminism: The Story of Quaker Women in America* (1986), and Elisabeth Potts Brown and Susan Mosher Stuard, eds., *Witnesses for Change: Quaker Women over Three Centuries* (1989).

CHERYL KNOTT MALONE

JEFFERS, Robinson (10 Jan. 1887–20 Jan. 1962), poet, was born John Robinson Jeffers in Pittsburgh, Pennsylvania, the son of the Reverend Dr. William Hamilton Jeffers and Annie Robinson Tuttle. A professor of Old Testament literature and exegesis and a reserved, reclusive person, Dr. Jeffers initiated his son's education at home by tutoring him in Greek, Latin, and Presbyterian doctrine. The Jeffers family traveled frequently to Europe, where Robinson attended boarding schools in Leipzig, Vevey, Lausanne, Geneva, and Zurich. In 1902 Robinson Jeffers entered the University of Western Pennsylvania (now the University of Pittsburgh) as a sophomore, with a mastery of French, German, Greek, and Latin. When the family moved to Los Angeles the next year, Jeffers matriculated as a junior at Occidental College, from which he was graduated in 1905. Jeffers immediately entered graduate school as a student of literature at the University of Southern California. In the spring of 1906 he was back in Switzerland at the University of Zurich, taking courses in philosophy and literature. Returning to USC in September 1907, he was admitted to the medical school, but in 1910, without completing his academic program at USC, Jeffers entered the University of Washington to study forestry for a year.

Jeffers met Una Call Kuster in 1906; she was three years older than he and married to a prominent Los Angeles attorney. In each other, Jeffers and Kuster found intellectual and emotional stimulation and compatibility that drew them powerfully together. At length, Kuster obtained a divorce and married Jeffers in August 1913. A year later the couple moved to Carmel, where, except for occasional trips to Europe and New Mexico, they spent the rest of their lives. In 1916 they became the parents of twin sons (a daughter born earlier did not survive infancy), and Jeffers began to build a stone cottage for his family. Later he added the famous forty-foot stone tower, the emblem of "Tor House" (as they called their home). Both structures—the house and the tower overlooking Carmel Bay and facing Point Lobos—figured significantly in Jeffers's life and poetry.

As an undergraduate and graduate student Jeffers had regularly contributed poems to various student publications. By 1911 he had written a number of generic love poems to Kuster and other women, and in 1912 he privately published some of these and other works in *Flagons and Apples*, to be followed by another collection, the commercially published *Californians* (1916). With the publication of *Tamar and Other Poems* (1924), however, Jeffers turned from the derivative versifying of his first volumes to themes and presentation that quickly won him an enthusiastic audience. The intensity of the long narratives he then began to write contrasted strikingly not only with his earlier work, but also with the works of other poets. In the introduction he wrote for Random House's reissue (1935) of *Roan Stallion, Tamar and Other Poems*, Jeffers described briefly his misgivings about the direction and advance of the poetry of the 1920s. Without originality, he said, a poet was "only a verse-writer." Some of his contemporaries were pursuing originality by "going farther and farther along the way that perhaps Mallarmé's aging dream had shown them, divorcing poetry from reason and ideas, bringing it nearer to music." But, he demurred, "It seemed to me that Mallarmé and his followers, renouncing intelligibility in order to concentrate on the music of poetry, had turned off the road into a narrowing lane. . . . ideas had gone, now meter had gone, imagery would have to go; then recognizable emotions would have to go." To make an advance, to contribute to poetry, Jeffers af-

firmed, would require "emotions or ideas, or a point of view, or even mere rhythms, that had not occurred to [his contemporaries]." To this plan to be "original"—which also meant, it should be noted, to recover the former vigor of poetry and to keep poetry related to reality—Jeffers brought enormous learning in literature, religion, philosophy, languages, myth, and the sciences.

Initially, *Tamar and Other Poems* received no acclaim, but when East Coast reviewers discovered the work and began to compare Jeffers to Greek tragedians, Boni & Liveright reissued an expanded edition as *Roan Stallion, Tamar and Other Poems* (1925). In these works, Jeffers began to articulate themes that contributed to what he later identified as Inhumanism. Mankind was too self-centered, he complained, and too indifferent to the "astonishing beauty of things." The metaphors of incest in "Tamar" and in subsequent poems symbolized mankind's inability to "uncenter" itself. "Humanity is the mold to break out of" announces the narrator of "Roan Stallion." However, California, the heroine of this poem, discovers that she cannot achieve the intimate identification with the deity of nature she yearns for. Jeffers's longest and most ambitious narrative, *The Women at Point Sur* (1927), startled many of his readers. Heavily loaded with Nietzschean philosophy and other ideological cargo, it nearly capsized, but Jeffers was surprised that many readers of the poem insisted on focusing on what they perceived to be its sensational elements, instead of on the philosophical statement he meant to be of greater significance. Nevertheless, the balance of the 1920s and the early 1930s were especially productive for Jeffers, and his reputation was secure. In *Cawdor and Other Poems* (1928), *Dear Judas and Other Poems* (1929), *Descent to the Dead, Poems Written in Ireland and Great Britain* (1931), *Thurso's Landing* (1932), and *Give Your Heart to the Hawks* (1933), Jeffers continued to explore the questions of how human beings could find their proper relationship (free of human egocentrism) with the divinity of the beauty of things. These poems, set in the Big Sur region (except *Dear Judas* and *Descent to the Dead*), enabled Jeffers to pursue his belief that the natural splendor of the area demanded tragedy: the greater the beauty, the greater the demand. Several of the poems are, indeed, tragedies, a few of them having evident Euripidean antecedents. As Euripides had, Jeffers began to focus more on his own characters' psychologies and on social realities than on the mythic. The human dilemmas of Phaedra, Hippolytus, and Medea fascinated Jeffers, as is clearly evident in his works.

If the narratives in *Solstice and Other Poems* (1935), *Such Counsels You Gave to Me and Other Poems* (1937), and *Be Angry at the Sun* (1941) sounded fatigued and strident, most of the lyrical poems sustained the fine elevation of their predecessors. Random House's *The Selected Poetry of Robinson Jeffers* (1938), however, was warmly received and remained the central Jeffers text until after the Robinson Jeffers Centennial (1987), when the Stanford University Press began to publish the multivolume scholarly edition of *The Collected Poetry of Robinson Jeffers*. Jeffers's adaptation of Euripides' *Medea* (1946), written for Dame Judith Anderson, was a great success when it was produced in New York in 1947. Two of Jeffers's most interesting and problematic narratives—"The Love and the Hate" and "The Inhumanist"—were at the center of *The Double Axe and Other Poems* (1948), which appeared with a disclaimer from the publisher. Many of Jeffers's references to current events and political figures (for example, Pearl Harbor, Teheran, Adolf Hitler, Joseph Stalin, Franklin D. Roosevelt) highlighted his isolationism and raised questions about his patriotism. In the preface to *The Double Axe*, Jeffers explicitly described "a philosophical attitude" he named Inhumanism, which had been implicit in his work since "Tamar"—certainly since "Roan Stallion." Inhumanism called for

a shifting of emphasis and significance from man to notman; the rejection of human solipsism and recognition of the transhuman magnificence. . . . This manner of thought and feeling is neither misanthropic nor pessimist. . . . It offers a reasonable detachment as rule of conduct, instead of love, hate and envy. . . . it provides magnificence for the religious instinct, and satisfies our need to admire greatness and rejoice in beauty.

Soon thereafter, Jeffers's beloved Una fell ill with cancer and died in 1950. She had played many roles for him: lover, wife, muse, protectress, and his ears and eyes to the social world he shunned. Jeffers's last volume, *Hungerfield and Other Poems* (1954), contains a moving eulogy to Una, who, for him, may have come closest to embodying Inhumanism. Jeffers died in Carmel; a posthumous collection, *The Beginning and the End and Other Poems*, appeared in 1963.

By the time of his death, Jeffers had lost most of his popular audience, and within two decades his works had virtually disappeared from anthologies and his name from classrooms, even as his works were being translated for avid readers in Eastern European countries. However, burgeoning projects by Jeffers scholars and the revising, in the late 1980s, of the canon of American literature reestablished Jeffers as an important figure in American literature and Modernism, who sought, like Ezra Pound, T. S. Eliot, and Wallace Stevens, to redefine the role of poetry in the human experience and to identify the authentic relationship of the human experience to the world at large and to God but, perhaps unlike them (Jeffers would affirm), also to preserve the reality beyond the poem.

• The largest collections of Jeffers manuscripts and materials are in the Humanities Research Center at the University of Texas and in the libraries at Occidental College, the University of California, and Yale University. One should also consult *The Selected Letters of Robinson Jeffers, 1887–1962* (1968).

Other books of criticism and poetry by Jeffers are *Poetry, Gongorism and a Thousand Years* (1949), *Themes in My Poems* (1956), *Robinson Jeffers: Selected Poems* (1965), *The Alpine Christ and Other Poems* (1974), *"What Odd Expedients" and Other Poems* (1981), and *Rock and Hawk: A Selection of Shorter Poems by Robinson Jeffers* (1987).

Sydney S. Alberts, *A Bibliography of the Works of Robinson Jeffers* (1933), is informative but incomplete. One should also consult William Nolte, *The Merrill Checklist of Robinson Jeffers* (1970); Jeanetta Boswell, *Robinson Jeffers and the Critics, 1912–1983* (1986); and Alex A. Vardamis, *The Critical Reputation of Robinson Jeffers: A Bibliographical Study* (1972), which remains most useful for the scholar.

Biographical studies include George Sterling, *Robinson Jeffers: The Man and the Artist* (1926); Louis Adamic, *Robinson Jeffers* (1929); Melba Bennett, *Robinson Jeffers and the Sea* (1936) and *The Stone Mason of Tor House* (1966); Edith Greenan, *Of Una Jeffers* (1939); Mabel Dodge Luhan, *Una and Robin* (1976; written in 1933); Ward Ritchie, *Jeffers: Some Recollections of Robinson Jeffers* (1977); and James Karman, *Robinson Jeffers: Poet of California* (1987), which is the most authoritative of the group.

Books about Jeffers's career include L. C. Powell, *Robinson Jeffers: The Man and His Work* (1940; repr. 1973); Radcliffe Squires, *The Loyalties of Robinson Jeffers* (1956); Frederic I. Carpenter, *Robinson Jeffers* (1962); William Everson, *Robinson Jeffers: Fragments of an Older Fury* (1968); Arthur B. Coffin, *Robinson Jeffers: Poet of Inhumanism* (1971); Robert Brophy, *Robinson Jeffers: Myth, Ritual and Symbol in His Narrative Poems* (1973); Bill Hotchkiss, *Jeffers: The Sivaistic Vision* (1975); William H. Nolte, *Rock and Hawk: Robinson Jeffers and the Romantic Agony* (1978); Robert Zaller, *The Cliffs of Solitude: A Reading of Robinson Jeffers* (1983); William Everson, *The Excesses of God: Robinson Jeffers as a Religious Figure* (1988); Robert Brophy, ed., *The Robinson Jeffers Newsletter: A Jubilee Gathering, 1962–1988* (1988); James Karman, ed., *Critical Essays on Robinson Jeffers* (1990); and Robert Zaller, ed., *Centennial Essays for Robinson Jeffers* (1991). The *Robinson Jeffers Newsletter*, ed. Robert Brophy, is a valuable scholarly resource.

An obituary is in the *New York Times*, 22 Jan. 1962.

ARTHUR B. COFFIN

JEFFERS, William Nicholson (16 Oct. 1824–23 July 1883), naval officer and author, was born in Swedesboro, New Jersey, the son of John Ellis Jeffers, a lawyer, and Ruth Westcott. William was early devoted to service in the U.S. Navy, probably influenced by his maternal uncles who were members of that service. At age fifteen he joined the navy as a midshipman aboard the USS *United States* and sailed on a Pacific Ocean cruise. In 1844–1845 he performed midshipman duties aboard the *Congress* in Brazilian waters. Not yet a passed midshipman, Jeffers was required to finish his training at the new U.S. Naval Academy established in Annapolis, Maryland, in 1845. On 11 July 1846 he graduated fourth in a class of forty-seven.

Early in his naval career, Jeffers exhibited a flair for writing technical and official or quasi-official naval books and pamphlets. Soon after his graduation, he published *The Armament of Our Ships of War*. During the war with Mexico, he saw action against Mexican shore defenses aboard the *Vixen*. Following that conflict, Jeffers returned to the United States and was assigned to the Naval Academy as an instructor and acting master. While there he published two more books, *Nautical Routine and Stowage with Short Rules in Navigation*, written with J. M. Murphy (1849), and *A Con-*

cise Treatise on the Theory and Practice of Naval Gunnery (1850). In 1850 he married Lucy LeGrand Smith, daughter of army surgeon S. B. Smith. The couple had a son and a daughter.

During most of the 1850s, Jeffers was involved in survey activities in Latin America. In 1852–1853 he performed cartographic work in Honduras in conjunction with a proposed project to build a transisthmus railway across that country to link the Atlantic to the Pacific. He returned to this duty in 1857. During 1859–1860 he was assigned to hydrographer duties in a potential Chiriqui canal route.

Between these transisthmus projects, Jeffers was involved in an action that created a foreign policy problem between the United States and Paraguay. During 1855–1856 he was the skipper of the *Water Witch*, performing survey duties on the Paraná River and the River Plata. The Paraguayans fired on the *Water Witch*, leading to the U.S. Navy's reprisal on Paraguay in 1857. Jeffers was promoted to lieutenant on 30 January 1855.

The navy used Jeffers's technical and tactical expertise during the Civil War. At the outset of the war, in April–May 1861, he commanded the steamer *Philadelphia* in the Potomac River. Following this duty, he was skipper of the *Roanoke* with blockade duties. During January–February 1862 he received accolades from the navy for "zeal and intelligence" while commanding the *Underwriter* and conducting operations off the coast of North Carolina. On 13 March 1862 he became the skipper of the ironclad *Monitor* after its 9 March clash with the Confederate ironclad *Virginia*, during which the *Monitor*'s skipper, Lieutenant John L. Worden, was wounded. On 15 May the *Monitor* and other Federal warships bombarded the Confederate works protecting the river approach to the Confederate capital, Richmond, at Drury's Bluff. In that unsatisfactory encounter for the northerners, the *Monitor* was unable to raise its guns sufficiently to engage the southerners' riverside positions. Jeffers wrote a detailed report on the *Monitor* and made appropriate recommendations for improvement of this new design.

On 16 July 1862 Jeffers was promoted to lieutenant commander and assigned to shore duty in Philadelphia and then in Washington, D.C., for the rest of the war. He was charged with improving ordnance, and in Washington he held the position of inspector of experimentation. These duties were briefly interrupted in late 1864, when he assisted in preparing the ex-Confederate blockade-runner *Louisiana* for an attack on the southern-held fortress of Fort Fisher. On the night of 24 December the *Louisiana*, crammed with 200 tons of gunpowder, was run close to the fort and exploded by a time fuse. The fort was relatively unharmed, and the planned Federal assault was abandoned. During the Civil War Jeffers edited *Inspection and Proof of Cannon*, published in its revised form in 1864.

Following the war, Jeffers commanded a number of ships, continued his work in naval ordnance, and resumed his writing career. His chief ordnance contributions were made during 1873–1881, when he was

the chief of ordnance. In some quarters, Jeffers was regarded as too slow to take advantage of known technology in improving the U.S. Navy's guns. He was also criticized for the time-consuming practice of awaiting European trials of naval guns before making adjustments or changes in U.S. weaponry. However, he modified many of the navy's obsolete, eleven-inch, bottle-shaped Dahlgren smoothbore cannons into harder hitting, eight-inch rifled cannon. Similarly, he transformed 100-pound Parrott guns into modern breechloaders. In addition, he produced a systematic plan to convert all calibers of naval deck ordnance up to twelve-inch into breechloading weapons. Thus Jeffers was instrumental in modernizing, however slowly, much of America's naval firepower prior to the Spanish-American War.

Jeffers's post–Civil War publications included two revisions of *Ordnance Instructions of the U.S. Navy*. He wrote *Nautical Surveying* (1871) and *Care and Preservation of Ammunition* (1874). He died in Washington, D.C.

Despite occasional criticism for being too slow and cautious, Jeffers was a well-known, popular figure in the U.S. Navy. His contribution to the United States undoubtedly lies in his modernization of U.S. naval ordnance prior to its use in the Spanish-American War.

• Jeffers's career highlights are in L. R. Hamersly, *The Records of Living Officers of the U.S. Navy and Marine Corps*, 3d ed. (1870), and Hamersly, *A Naval Encyclopaedia* (1881). His 1854 experience in Paraguay is summarized in Robert W. Love, Jr., *History of the U.S. Navy* (1992). His Civil War service is in *The Official Records of the Union and Confederate Navies in the War of the Rebellion* (30 vols., 1894–1922). Obituaries are in the *Army and Naval Journal* (28 July 1883) and the *Washington Post*, 24 July 1883.

ROD PASCHALL

JEFFERSON, Blind Lemon (July 1897?–Dec. 1929), blues singer-guitarist, was born on a small farm near Wortham, Texas, the son of Alec Jefferson and Classie Banks, farmers. Because Jefferson was a poor, rural African American, few official documents exist to verify biographical details. Some researchers speculate that Jefferson, one of seven children, was born as early as 1880 (based on a studio portrait c. 1926 that reveals graying hair) and question the legend that he was blind from birth (printed in 1927 in *The Paramount Book of Blues*). Indeed, he may never have been totally blind, given stories about his ability to travel independently and to identify the denomination of paper money by its "feel." One account dates his performing career from around 1912, at parties and picnics and on the streets in Wortham, but he had moved to the streets, barrelhouses, and brothels of Waco and of the "Deep Ellum" area of Dallas by 1917. Around this time he may have worked as a wrestler and likely met singer-guitarist Huddie Ledbetter before Leadbelly went to prison in 1918. From that time into the 1920s, Jefferson remained the itinerant blues singer, hopping freights and traveling extensively, especially in many southern states, and playing at various social functions and, eventually, at house rent parties in Chicago. Around 1922 Jefferson married a woman named Roberta (last name unknown), later fathering a son, Miles, who also became a musician.

Jefferson's big career break came in 1925 when either Dallas dealer R. J. Ashford or pianist Sammy Price alerted J. Mayo Williams, manager of the "Race Artist Series" for Paramount Records, to Jefferson's talent. The peak years of the female vaudeville-blues artists were coming to an end by then. Paramount, seeking a followup to their success marketing male blues artist Papa Charlie Jackson, reaching the rural audience through their strong mail-order business, recorded Jefferson in Chicago in 1925. Though Jefferson was known as a blues performer, his first two recordings were spirituals, "Pure Religion" and "I Want to Be Like Jesus in My Heart." These were not issued until Jefferson had had four releases, and then under the thinly disguised pseudonym L. J. Bates. The name was also used for the 1928 release of his other two recorded religious songs, presumably because of Christians' antipathy to singers of what they sometimes termed Devil's music, the blues. Jefferson's second session, circa March 1926, yielded his first two Paramount releases, the second of which, "Got the Blues"/"Long Lonesome Blues," garnered six-figure sales. Altogether Jefferson had eight Paramount releases in 1926, recording every few months for the next four years, and was the company's premier blues artist for the rest of the decade. During those years Jefferson's ninety-four released sides (seven were unissued) on forty-three records reportedly sold in excess of one million copies. In 1927 his records were released at the rate of about one a month, and a special yellow and black label and photograph graced Paramount 12650, captioned "Blind Lemon's Birthday Record."

Jefferson's records enjoyed continuing popularity until and beyond the time of his death, despite his narrowing vocal range and repetition of basic instrumental arrangements on many of his final recordings. Jefferson was officially listed as a porter living at Forty-fifth and State streets in Chicago in 1928–1929, despite his continued popularity recording and performing. For example, he sang with a medicine show and with performer Rubin Lacy in Mississippi, where Jefferson reportedly refused $20 to play a blues song because it was Sunday.

Jefferson died in Chicago under mysterious circumstances sometime in December 1929, possibly of a heart attack or exposure, or both, perhaps abandoned by his chauffeur. There are various accounts left by various blues musicians. One story has an unknown woman cleaning out Jefferson's bank account and shipping his body to Mexia, Texas, while another has pianist Will Ezell accompanying his body to Dallas for burial in the Wortham Negro Cemetery on New Year's Day 1930. A grave marker was finally placed in and dedicated on 15 October 1967.

Jefferson is indisputably one of the most influential American musicians of the twentieth century. Primary catalyst for the recording of male blues performers, Jefferson provided a vocal and instrumental model for generations of blues, country, jazz, rhythm and blues, and rock performers. Emerging from the same milieu as Texas Alexander and Henry Thomas, two probably older performers who reflected the field holler and folk song traditions of Texas, Jefferson melded traditional songs and themes with a highly original, idiosyncratic style that galvanized his listeners. He combined high vocals with a percussive and complex polyrhythmic guitar style consisting of interspersed bass runs and single-string treble riffs and arpeggios. His vast knowledge of traditional lyrics, increasingly modified by an original, poetic turn of mind, was so widely disseminated through recordings and appearances that his influence turns up in the work of blues performers of all styles and eras. So great was Jefferson's popularity that many performers claim it a badge of honor to have seen, played with, or led him around on the streets. One who apparently did lead him, T-Bone Walker, adapted Jefferson's guitar style to an urbanized, large band format that made Walker a seminal blues figure in the 1940s and shaped the guitar playing of B. B. King. King recorded Jefferson's "Bad Luck Blues" and in turn became a major blues figure who influenced countless musicians. One of Jefferson's compositions, "Match Box Blues," has been recorded by blues artists, country performer Larry Hensely (1934), rockabilly's Carl Perkins (1955), and the Beatles (1964), among many others.

Immediately upon his death, Jefferson became a figure of mythical status. Rev. Emmet Dickinson's 1930 tribute compared him to Christ, while Walter Taylor and John Byrd's flip-side tribute also lamented his death, albeit in less grandiose terms. Roark Bradford's 1931 novel *John Henry* employed Jefferson as the archetypical blues singer/sage. But behind the mythologizing is the reality of his greatness—his originality, virtuosity, and intensity—recognized by literary artists such as Langston Hughes and Sterling Brown, critics, and fans. He has entered the American consciousness to the extent that his face appeared on T-shirts, sweatshirts, and matchbox covers. Jefferson is a member of the Blues Hall of Fame.

Blues performer Tom Shaw stated it simply: "He was the King."

• All but four of Jefferson's released recordings are collected on *Complete Recorded Works in Chronological Order* (vols. 1–4, Document DOCD 5017–5020). The most complete discussion of Jefferson is Bob Groom's *Blind Lemon Jefferson* (1970). See also the section on Jefferson by Alan Govenar in *Bluesland: Portraits of Twelve Major American Blues Masters*, ed. Pete Welding and Toby Byron (1991); Stephen Calt's liner notes to *King of Country Blues* (Yazoo CD 1069); Sheldon Harris, *Blues Who's Who* (1979); and Sam Charters, *The Bluesmen* (1967). David Evans, *Big Road Blues* (1982), discusses the changing nature of Jefferson's lyrics throughout his career. Max E. Vreede, *The Paramount 12000/13000 series*

(1971), explores the Paramount blues series, and R. M. W. Dixon and John Godrich, *Blues and Gospel Records 1902–1942* (1982), offers complete discographical details.

STEVEN C. TRACY

JEFFERSON, Eddie (3 Aug. 1918–9 May 1979), jazz singer, lyricist, and tap dancer, was born Edgar Jefferson in Pittsburgh, Pennsylvania. Information about his parents is unknown. It is known that he started dancing around age eight. He also played tuba in a school band and taught himself guitar and drums, experiences that later gave his singing a firm musical foundation. In Pittsburgh he was accompanied by pianist Art Blakey, before Blakey took up drums, and he danced and sang with the Zephyrs at the Chicago World's Fair in 1933. In 1937 Jefferson danced in the Knockouts, a trio that included Dave Tate and Irv Taylor (Little Irv), and he worked in a dance team called Billy and Eddie in 1939. Around 1940 he performed with Coleman Hawkins's big band at Dave's in Chicago. While in the army he was in charge of a drum and bugle corps (c. 1942).

Jefferson and Taylor are credited with the innovation of setting lyrics to recorded instrumental jazz improvisations, thus creating what has come to be known as vocalese. This term describes a practice standing in opposition to the similarly sounding French term *vocalise*, which applies to wordless singing (a high-brow cousin of jazz scat-singing). Jefferson initially put the idea to work with melodies from big band recordings, such as tenor saxophonist Lester Young's solos on Count Basie's "Panassié Stomp" and "Taxi War Dance." In the late 1940s he set lyrics to Hawkins's famous solo from 1939, "Body and Soul." He had not intended these adaptations to be commercial projects: "It was just something for my wife [Tiny Brown, a singer] and I to do around the house" (Silsbee, p. 11). But in 1951, while Jefferson was working with bassist Jack McDuff (later better known as an organist) at the Cotton Club in Cincinnati, King Pleasure (Clarence Beeks) heard Jefferson sing his vocalese "Moody's Mood for Love," a setting of tenor saxophonist James Moody's recorded improvisation on "I'm in the Mood for Love." In February 1952 King Pleasure recorded the tune for the Prestige label, and it became a hit. Prestige's Bob Weinstock asked Pleasure for more such pieces, and he replied that this was not his work, but Jefferson's.

Thus in July, Jefferson recorded four titles. Three were further examples of vocalese: "The Birdland Story," an outstanding tribute to Moody's bebop soloing when Jefferson heard the tenor saxophonist performing with alto saxophonist Charlie Parker, trumpeter Dizzy Gillespie, pianist Bud Powell, an unnamed bassist, and drummer Shadow Wilson at Birdland in New York; "I Got the Blues," based on Young's solo on "Lester Leaps In"; and "Body and Soul," not from Hawkins's 1939 version, but from a less distinguished improvised melody, again by Moody. The fourth title, "Honeysuckle Rose," showed Jefferson in another vein, delivering a swinging paraphrase of Fats Waller

and Andy Razaf's theme and then moving into a gritty-voiced adaptation of Ella Fitzgerald's scat-singing style.

Jefferson continued dancing into 1953, when he met Moody after a performance with Taylor at the Apollo Theater in New York. Moody, having fallen out with his singer Babs Gonzales, initially hired Jefferson for a week. He stayed for sixteen years as Moody's singer and manager. During his first tenure, from 1953 to 1962, Jefferson recorded "Disappointed" on Moody's album *Hi-Fi Party*, "I Got the Blues" on *Moody's Moods* (both from 1955), and "I'm in the Mood for Love," on *Moody's Mood for Love* (1956). Jefferson also worked with King Pleasure at the Zebra Lounge in Los Angeles in 1957, and he sang with Miles Davis for two weeks in 1958 at Cafe Bohemia in New York while Moody was in the hospital. After Moody's mid-1960s membership in Dizzy Gillespie's group, during at least a portion of which Jefferson worked once again as a tap dancer, he rejoined Moody from 1968 to late 1973 and under his own name recorded the album *Body and Soul*, including the title track and a version of Miles Davis's "So What" (1968).

Jefferson joined drummer Roy Brooks's band the Artistic Truth from 1974 to 1975. The next year he formed a partnership with alto saxophonist Richie Cole that lasted until Jefferson's death. His albums from this period include *Things Are Getting Better* (1974), with versions of Davis's "Bitches Brew," Eddie Harris's "Freedom Jazz Dance," and Parker's "Billie's Bounce," and *The Live-Liest* (1976), including "Parker's Mood." Jefferson's popularity was growing. He performed on the PBS television show *Sound Stage* with singers Jon Hendricks, Annie Ross, and Leon Thomas. He sang in concert with Sarah Vaughan and Betty Carter at Carnegie Hall on 23 March 1979, and he made a film, *Eddie Jefferson: Live at the Showcase*, in May. But two days later he was murdered by a shotgun blast when he stepped out of the door at the end of an opening night's engagement at Baker's Keyboard Lounge in Detroit. He had been presented the key to the city by Mayor Coleman Young the previous February.

Jazz is often said to tell a story. With Jefferson it literally did. A number of his lyrics presented typical fare about love life. A few offered social commentary. His discussion of street violence, "Zap! Carnivorous," on his 1976 album *Still on the Planet*, was particularly ironic given his murder three years later. His most distinctive lyrics were the direct tributes to jazz musicians whose melodies Jefferson celebrated in vocalese. Although in some instances these settings have become badly dated (their mid-century hipsterisms sounding corny to a later generation), Jefferson's finest reworkings of Moody, Hawkins, and Parker testified to his unusual and timeless feeling for jazz melody and his talent for transforming it into text.

• Interviews are by Carol Crawford, "Woodshed: Eddie Jefferson, Vocalese Giant," *Jazz Magazine* [U.S.] 3, no. 1 (1978): 46–51, including a notated musical example of "Moody's Mood for Love"; Bob Rusch, "A Talk with Eddie Jefferson," *Cadence* 2 (Nov. 1978): 6–8; Kirk Silsbee, "An Interview with Eddie Jefferson," *Coda* 174 (Aug. 1980): 10–11; and George Victor Johnson, Jr., "Eddie Jefferson the Innovator," *Jazz Spotlite News* 2, no. 3 (1981): 46–50. Obituaries are in the *New York Times*, 10 May 1979, and *Down Beat*, 46 (21 June 1979): 15.

BARRY KERNFELD

JEFFERSON, Isaac (Dec. 1775–c. 1850), enslaved blacksmith, was born at "Monticello" in Virginia, the son of George, a foreman and overseer, and Ursula, a pastrycook and laundress. In 1773 Thomas Jefferson purchased Isaac's parents from two different owners in Powhatan County. George rose from foreman of labor to become, in 1797, overseer of Monticello—the only slave to reach that position. Ursula, who had been a "favorite house woman" of Martha Jefferson's, was given charge of many of the domestic operations of the plantation.

The slave couple's third son, Isaac spent his childhood at Monticello near his mother. From an early age he performed simple tasks for the Jefferson household—lighting fires, carrying water and fuel, and opening gates. When Thomas Jefferson became governor of Virginia during the American Revolution, Isaac and his family accompanied their master to Williamsburg and Richmond. During Benedict Arnold's raid on Richmond in 1781, Isaac and other Jefferson slaves were captured by the British and taken to an internment camp near Yorktown, where they apparently remained until after the surrender. These experiences made a deep impression on the five-year-old slave. In 1847 author and teacher Charles Campbell recorded Isaac Jefferson's vivid memories of plundering soldiers and terrified slaves and the sights and sounds of battle. "Seemed like heaven and earth was come together," Isaac remembered almost seventy years later.

Isaac Jefferson also recalled that his father "got his freedom" for saving Governor Jefferson's silver from Arnold's troops. Although there is no documentary evidence of such a release from servitude, there are indications of a special status for Isaac's parents. Jefferson's farm book reveals that George and Ursula received larger food rations than did other Monticello slaves. As overseer, George was paid a wage equivalent to almost half that of free white Monticello overseers. Whatever the status of his parents, Isaac Jefferson and his brothers remained slaves.

About 1790 Isaac began his training in the metalworking trades. Jefferson took him to Philadelphia, where he was apprenticed for several years to a Quaker tinsmith. Isaac's recollections provide the only evidence of this apprenticeship and the unprofitable two-year tinsmithing operation that was established at Monticello. Isaac Jefferson also trained as a blacksmith under his brother George and, after the opening of a nail factory in 1794, became a nailer as well, dividing his time between nailmaking and smith work. Jefferson's records indicate that Isaac was the most productive and efficient of his nailers, and that he was

paid a three-penny premium for each pair of plow chains he made.

In 1797 Jefferson gave Isaac, his wife Iris, and their sons Squire and Joyce to his daughter Maria on her marriage to John Wayles Eppes. Jefferson's other son-in-law, Thomas Mann Randolph, then hired Isaac from the Eppeses, evidently purchasing him at a later date (Isaac and Iris's third child, Maria, was sold by Randolph to Monticello overseer Edmund Bacon). Isaac continued to live and work at or near Monticello until a few years before Jefferson's death in 1826. When Campbell met Isaac Jefferson in Petersburg, Virginia, in 1847, he was apparently a free man, still practicing blacksmithing at age seventy-one. He "bore a good character," said Campbell.

Thomas Jefferson, rather than Isaac Jefferson, is the central figure in Isaac's memoirs, as recorded by Campbell. "Nary man in this town walked so straight as my old master," the blacksmith recalled, and his observations of his master's domestic activities—reading, hunting, gardening, or lockmaking—are rare and authentic pieces of evidence. The recollections fail to mention, however, some of the most significant events of Isaac Jefferson's own life. There is no reference to his wife and children, to the sudden deaths in 1799 and 1800 of his parents and brother, or to how he became free or acquired the Jefferson surname. Childhood memories preponderate in his recollections, and it is mainly a child's view of slavery that he shared with Campbell. He spoke of the kindness of both his masters, and tempered an account of the whippings doled out by Archibald Cary, a frequent Monticello visitor, with a grateful recollection of his handsome tips. According to Jefferson's memorandum book, an Isaac belonging to Randolph tried to run away in 1812. If this was Isaac Jefferson, he chose neither to mention the event nor to recall the feelings that provoked it.

Isaac Jefferson's account of life at Monticello has been a rich source for writers and scholars since its publication in 1951. Providing a rare perspective on historic events and a historic figure, it continues to inspire interpreters of the past with its vivid expressions and authentic testimony. Its immediacy is enhanced by a striking daguerrotype of Isaac Jefferson in his blacksmith's apron in 1847. His image and memories have helped to give voice and substance to thousands of enslaved men, women, and children who were unable to leave records of their lives.

• Isaac Jefferson's own account of his life, as taken down by Charles Campbell in 1847, is the only source for many of the details of his biography. Prepared for publication by Campbell in 1871, it did not appear in print until 1951, as *Memoirs of a Monticello Slave*, ed. Rayford W. Logan; it was simultaneously published in the *William and Mary Quarterly*, 3d ser., 8 (1951): 561–82. A more extensively annotated edition appeared in 1967, edited by James A. Bear, Jr., as part of *Jefferson at Monticello*. Further biographical details appear in the facsimile pages of *Thomas Jefferson's Farm Book* (1953), ed. Edmund Morris Betts. The nailery account book, 1796–1800, is in the Clark Memorial Library at UCLA. The daguerrotype of Isaac Jefferson and the most complete version of Campbell's manuscript are in the University of Virginia Library.

LUCIA C. STANTON

JEFFERSON, Joseph, I (1774–4 Aug. 1832), actor, was born in Plymouth, England, the son of Thomas Jefferson and his wife, whose maiden name was May, both actors. Jefferson grew up around the stage, learning the trade from his parents at the theater in Plymouth, which was managed by his father. Having acted in London with David Garrick at the Drury Lane Theatre, the elder Jefferson was, if not a major star, a respected member of the profession. Career aspirations, republican sentiment, and disapproval of his father's second marriage motivated the younger Jefferson's emigration to the United States in 1795. Arriving first in Boston, he made quick acquaintance with visiting members of the American Company, our nation's most famous early troupe of professional actors, and moved quickly to join them at their regular home at New York's John Street Theatre. In 1798 he moved with the company to the newly built Park Theatre. Among Jefferson's early roles, the rustic Verges from *Much Ado About Nothing*, despite its small size, was best remembered by manager and theater historian William Dunlap: "He was then a youth, but even then an artist. Of small and light figure, well-formed, with singular physiognomy, a nose perfectly Grecian, and blue eyes full of laughter, he had the faculty of exciting mirth to as great a degree by power of feature, although handsome, as any ugly-featured low comedian ever seen" (*History of the American Theatre*, vol. 1, p. 281). Jefferson played many types of roles, but he established his reputation as a "low comedian" and player of old men. "Low comedy" refers to broad, physical humor, as opposed to intellectually-based wit. Though there are many famous "low" characters—kinsmen to Shakespeare's Falstaff and Dogberry—it was a talent that Jefferson might inject into any role, including his old men. Montrose Moses reported that "long before the years had begun to leave their trace upon him the actor was dubbed 'Old Jefferson' by those who had seen him, a tribute to his inimitable art" (*Famous Actor Families*, p. 65).

He married Euphemia Fortune (the date is unknown); they had eight children. In 1803 the Jeffersons left New York City and, after playing a summer season in Albany, New York, joined the company at the Chestnut Street Theatre in Philadelphia. Here they enjoyed many prosperous years while also making excursions to Washington and Baltimore (regular venues for the players from Philadelphia) and to other towns. Many of the roles Jefferson portrayed, though popular in his time, are in plays that have long since been forgotten. William Winter lists 198 roles Jefferson undertook, and even that number he admitted to being incomplete. Winter wrote of these years:

Jefferson—conscientious and thorough, and at the same time brilliant—ranged from Mercutio [*Romeo and Juli-et*] to Dominie Sampson [*Guy Mannering*], from Touchstone [*As You Like It*] to Dogberry [*Much Ado*], and from Farmer Ashfield [a bucolic character in *Speed the Plow*, a comic melodrama which featured a race between the recently mechanized implements] to Maw Worm [the false religious man in *The Hypocrite*, adapted from *Tartuffe*], and was a consummate artist in all. (Winter, p. 66)

A critic analyzing his Farmer Ashfield for the *Mirror of Taste* captured Jefferson's style:

In the rustic deportment and dialect, in the artless effusions of benignity and undisguised truth, and in those masterly strokes of pathos and simplicity . . . , Jefferson showed uniform excellence; and as in the humourous parts his comic powers produced their customary effect, so, in the serious overflowings of the farmer's honest nature—the mellow, deep impressive tones of the actor's voice, vibrated to the heart, and excited the most intense and exquisite sensations.

Many Chestnut Street Theatre casts also included Jefferson's wife and one or more of the Jefferson children and their spouses. Occasionally, Jefferson also contributed scenic effects to these productions.

As Jefferson grew older, he became increasingly susceptible to the debilitating symptoms of gout. Though he was active to the end of his days, his drawing power declined in comparison to touring stars and younger company members. In the later 1820s benefit performances at Chestnut Street failed to yield respectable returns. The Jefferson family left Philadelphia in 1829 and took to the road under the management of son Joseph, playing in the smaller theater towns of Pennsylvania, Maryland, Virginia, and Washington, D.C. Professional decline was complicated by personal misfortune. In 1824 his son Thomas suffered an accident during a performance that led to his death. Son John, regarded as the "most brilliant of this family" (Winter, p. 94), died suddenly in 1831. This tragedy was compounded by the deaths of Jefferson's wife, his daughter Euphemia (married to actor William Anderson), and his seventeen-year-old daughter Jane (who did not act), later that year. Jefferson was acting in Harrisburg, Pennsylvania, when he died.

For many years associated with America's premiere theater company at the Chestnut Street Theatre in Philadelphia, Jefferson provided a direct link between the acting traditions of England and the United States. His surviving son, Joseph Jefferson II, was a well-liked and persistent actor, manager, and scenic artist who succeeded in a modest fashion to make a life in the theater. Grandson Joseph Jefferson III, who originated the stage version of Rip Van Winkle, became one of America's most popular and respected comic actors of all time. Montrose Moses's genealogical table of the Jeffersons and related families beginning with Joseph Jefferson's father, Thomas Jefferson, identifies fifty actors from this great actor family.

• Material on Jefferson can most readily be found with material concerning his grandson, Joseph III, or the entire family. The Harvard University Theater Collection contains assorted material on Jefferson as well. One of the most complete treatments of Jefferson is in William Winter, *The Jeffersons* (1881). This work also refers to relatively scarce original sources, mostly memoirs of other performers and managers. Briefer overviews of both the subject and these sources can be found in Montrose J. Moses, *Famous Actor Families in America* (1906), and in William C. Young, *Famous Actors and Actresses on the American Stage*, vol. 1 (1975). An analytical review of Jefferson's career and his professional practices and talents is in James C. Burge, *Lines of Business: Casting Practice and Policy in the American Theatre, 1752–1899* (1986), pp. 243–56.

MAARTEN REILINGH

JEFFERSON, Joseph, III (20 Feb. 1829–23 Apr. 1905), actor, was born in Philadelphia, Pennsylvania, the son of Joseph Jefferson II and Cornelia Frances Thomas Burke, both actors. Jefferson grew up in one of America's most distinguished theatrical families. His grandfather, Joseph Jefferson I, came to the United States from England in 1795 and established himself as a leading comedian. Jefferson's father, though less renowned than either his father or his son, was a complete man of the theater: actor, manager, scene painter, and carpenter. From a previous marriage, Cornelia Jefferson had had one son, Charles Burke, a beloved half brother to Joseph, who authored an early dramatic script for *Rip Van Winkle* (which Joseph later adapted) and whose own promising theatrical career was cut short by death.

That young Joseph III (always known as Joe) would likewise go on the stage seemed a foregone conclusion. At age four, in blackface, he was carried onstage by the father of minstrelsy, Thomas D. Rice, to "dance Jim Crow." In his early years Jefferson's family performed in cities along the Atlantic seaboard. But in 1837, seeking a "dramatic El Dorado in the West," they headed to Chicago and from there began a long barnstorming tour of the Mississippi valley and the South. The experience of frontier theater, sometimes performed in barns or warehouses, is vividly described in Jefferson's autobiography. He had had virtually no formal schooling, and this was professional education nonpareil. But at Mobile, Alabama, in 1842 Jefferson's father died of yellow fever. Jefferson, his mother, and his younger sister Cordelia continued touring the South, heading west to Texas and then following the U.S. army into Mexico in 1846 as theatrical camp followers, performing for the troops and—when their company disbanded—opening a coffee shop.

Returning north in late 1846, the family briefly revisited New Orleans, where Jefferson found new inspiration for theatrical greatness from the comedian John E. Owens. He then returned to the East alone, meeting his half brother in Philadelphia and joining the Arch Street Theatre stock company. Like so many other actors, Jefferson found the stock company experience to be a mixed blessing. Its constant mix of plays provided an excellent dramatic apprenticeship. But

the petty tyranny of many managers (in Jefferson's case William E. Burton) demeaned actors' sense of professionalism.

Jefferson first caught the attention of New York audiences in 1849 as Jack Rackbottle in *Jonathan Bradford*. Over the next few years Jefferson performed with several stock companies—most notably Chanfrau's National Theater and William Mitchell's Olympic—and had the chance to perform alongside the leading performers of midcentury. In 1850 he married Margaret Clements Lockyer, with whom he had four children who survived to adulthood. Tugged by the allure of stardom and the unknown adventures of the road, Jefferson and his partner, John Ellsler, set out on tour in the early 1850s, beginning in Baltimore and traveling a circuit of southern cities. Following this adventure, Jefferson joined Philadelphia's Chestnut Street Theatre stock company as first comedian, and then he tried his hand at stage manager at the Baltimore Museum in 1853 and then at John Ford's Richmond theater the following year. In 1856 Jefferson journeyed to Europe to learn from the stars of the English and French stages.

Returning to the United States that summer, Jefferson joined Laura Keene's company in New York. He was only twenty-seven years of age, but already he possessed an unusual richness of stage experience. Yet nothing in his early career foretold the success that would soon overtake him. In the fall of 1857, portraying the socially striving scholar Dr. Pangloss in George Colman's comedy *The Heir at Law*, Jefferson triumphed. The next year, as Asa Trenchard in the original production of Tom Taylor's *Our American Cousin*, Jefferson won wide acclaim for the "rustic grace, simple manliness, unconscious drollery, and unaffected pathos" of his part. Keene's production of the play continued for 140 nights, a long run by the day's standards.

Jefferson's career never lagged after these achievements. Personal differences with the strong-willed Keene led him to decamp for Dion Boucicault's company at the Winter Garden in 1859. Here Jefferson added two more significant roles to his repertoire: Caleb Plummer in Boucicault's adaptation of Charles Dickens's *The Cricket on the Hearth*, and the good-natured plantation overseer Salem Scudder in Boucicault's own *The Octoroon*. But Jefferson's professional success was pierced by the death of his wife in 1861. Grief-stricken and ailing, Jefferson escaped to the West Coast and subsequently to Australia. Three and a half years of highly successful performances there (including ventures to Tasmania and New Zealand) restored his health and good spirits. His emotional recovery included a liaison with an actress in his company. This encounter produced a son, Thomas Joseph Sefton, who never saw Jefferson but who in the late 1880s struck up an epistolary relationship with him and was remembered in Jefferson's will. He sailed to South America in April 1865 and then on to England.

Reunited with Boucicault in London, Jefferson presented the celebrated dramatist with his idea for resurrecting a stage version of Washington Irving's *Rip Van Winkle*. Although several versions of the story had been staged in preceding decades with indifferent success, Jefferson says in his autobiography that not until 1859 did he seriously envision himself in the role of Rip. He had tried out the play in Australia but did not know how to correct its dramatic inadequacies. He hired Boucicault to craft a new version, including some alterations Jefferson suggested. This joint endeavor produced the most dramatically satisfactory *Rip Van Winkle* ever staged, first seen at London's Adelphi Theatre in the fall of 1865. Jefferson had an immediate triumph, "the most important dramatic event of my life," he would recall. In the comedy he found a vehicle that would carry him to stardom, where he remained for the remainder of his career.

Jefferson brought *Rip* to the United States in September 1866 at New York's Olympic Theater and found an equally enthusiastic public. His "kindly, simple *insouciant* face," noted a writer for the *Atlantic Monthly*, "the lounging, careless grace of the figure; the low, musical voice . . . all combine to produce an effect which is rare in its simplicity and excellence, and altogether satisfying." A star in a role that Americans took to their hearts, Jefferson played Rip almost exclusively for the next decade and a half (interspersing it occasionally with a few other popular roles). A pioneer in one of the theater's most consequential changes, the combination system, Jefferson toured the country extensively with the play. The subsequent decline of the stock system, widely decried by theater traditionalists, failed to disturb Jefferson, who not only benefited from the new system but who also by temperament considered such changes to be a part of a beneficent, inevitable progress.

The annual tours of *Rip Van Winkle* made Jefferson an American institution. "Fifty years from now," critic William Winter wrote in 1892, "the historian of the American stage, if he should be asked the name of the actor of this period who was most beloved by the people of this generation, will answer that it was Joseph Jefferson." Like James O'Neill's Count of Monte Cristo or Frank Mayo's Davy Crockett, Jefferson's Rip became his professional persona. But Jefferson's popularity and his art surpassed other "one-part" actors. He also escaped the sense of role entrapment that O'Neill, particularly, felt.

Several important events in Jefferson's personal life occurred in the later 1860s and 1870s. In December of 1867 he was married for a second time, to Sarah Warren, the niece of another notable Philadelphia comedian, William Warren, and herself a distant cousin of Jefferson. Their marriage, which produced three children, was a fulfilling one that lasted until her death in 1894. In 1872 successful eye surgery helped Jefferson escape a career-threatening bout of glaucoma. Three years later, Jefferson and his family embarked on a 2½-year stay in England. For about ten months of that time Jefferson performed several roles at London's Princess and Haymarket theaters. Returning to New York in the fall of 1877, Jefferson again donned the tattered costume of Rip in the familiar environs of Booth's theater.

Though he could have comfortably settled into *Rip Van Winkle* for the remainder of his career (demand for it never seemed to slacken), Jefferson tackled the role of Bob Acres in Richard Brinsley Sheridan's *The Rivals* in 1880. Jefferson had briefly performed the role early in his career and had long been intrigued by Sheridan's eighteenth-century comedy, sensing its potential appeal to contemporary audiences that preferred a more visually oriented and less oratorically stilted drama. As with *Rip Van Winkle*, Jefferson freely emended *The Rivals*, transforming Bob Acres into a very different, and more appealing, character than Sheridan had created. Brilliantly cast with Mrs. John Drew as Mrs. Malaprop, the play was revived at Philadelphia's Arch Street Theatre in September 1880 and became a part of Jefferson's repertoire.

Few nineteenth-century actors prospered from the theater more than Jefferson. With a large summer residence at Buzzards Bay, Massachusetts, ample winter homes at Palm Beach, Florida, and an estate near New Iberia, Louisiana, Jefferson enjoyed a patrician lifestyle. Beginning in the 1880s he toured only twelve weeks in the fall and six in the spring, retreating at other times to one of his homes, where, like Rip, he was surrounded by children. Jefferson's fame also allowed him to move easily among the artistic and public-affairs elite of the late nineteenth century. Grover Cleveland, for example, was a neighbor and fishing companion. Jefferson clearly relished the good fortune he had known. The brooding introspection and sturm-und-drang life of some actors were simply not a part of his personal makeup.

Jefferson, like his father and grandfather before him, possessed artistic gifts that extended beyond the stage. He was a respected painter of landscapes and a connoisseur of European art. He authored what remains the classic autobiography of the American theater, a work that conveys with unflagging energy the texture of nineteenth-century theater. He was also an astute student of his craft, in high demand as a lecturer during the last two decades of his life. In 1892 and 1895 respectively Yale and Harvard universities bestowed honorary degrees on him.

Above all, however, Jefferson remained a man of the theater. His esteem among his peers had few equals. In turn, Jefferson displayed great loyalty to the other members of his profession and was ready to donate his talents to theatrical benefits. Jefferson had a number of close friendships among actors, including Edwin Booth, America's reigning tragedian. Fittingly, in 1893 when Booth stepped down from the presidency of The Players (the theatrical club he had founded), Jefferson assumed the title.

A high point of Jefferson's later career came in an 1896 all-star tour of *The Rivals*, where he was reunited with Mrs. Drew and joined by Julia Marlowe, Otis Skinner, and the comedians William Crane and Francis Wilson. Jefferson gave up the stage only begrudgingly, with his last performance, culminating a career spanning seventy-one years, coming on 7 May 1904. The next winter he became ill and died in Palm Beach, Florida, on Shakespeare's birthday.

Jefferson's close public identification with Rip Van Winkle belies a career that included at least five other major roles he originated or reprised frequently and over one hundred roles he assumed in all. But he will always be remembered as Irving's amiable ne'er-do-well. Often asked if he tired of the role, Jefferson invariably replied that he continually found new facets to the part that kept it a fresh challenge. Indeed, critics detected no hint of staleness in his portrayal even after many years. A melodramatic vehicle of no particular distinction, *Rip Van Winkle* has not survived Jefferson's death as part of the standard dramatic repertory. Rather, its popularity sprang from one of those rare and magical confluences of role and personality.

Although he appeared primarily in the standard melodramatic fare of his age, where subtlety in acting was rarely a virtue, Jefferson is widely credited with introducing "a fresher and truer naturalism than our stage—perhaps any stage—had seen" (Watson, p. 421). He creatively combined sentimental romance, pathos, and ethnic comedy, and his characterization of Rip brought to fruition the comic techniques he had been refining in his first thirty years on the stage. Jefferson had the physical traits for comedy: a flexible body and a malleable face, with eyes that seemed to jump out of his head in either delight or pathos. Dignified, generous, reflective, and beloved, Joseph Jefferson epitomized the best of the American theater.

• There is no central repository of Jefferson papers. Letters, photographs, prompt books, and clippings files on Jefferson's career are variously located at the Billy Rose Theatre Collection of the New York Public Library for the Performing Arts, Princeton University, Yale University, the Harvard Theatre Collection, and the Hoblitzelle Theatre Arts Library at the University of Texas at Austin, among other places. Jefferson's *Autobiography* (1890) is the finest source on his life. Helpful biographies by two men who knew Jefferson well include dramatic critic William Winter, *Life and Art of Joseph Jefferson* (1893), and comedian Francis Wilson, *Joseph Jefferson: Reminiscences of a Fellow Player* (1906). Eugenie Paul Jefferson, *Intimate Recollections of Joseph Jefferson* (1909), provides some personal details related by his daughter-in-law. Montrose Moses, *Famous Actor-Families in America* (1906), contains a chapter on the Jeffersons. Ernest Bradlee Watson, "Joseph Jefferson," *Theatre Arts* 13 (1929): 420–30, is an incisive appreciation. Additionally, Alan Downer's introduction to the John Harvard Library edition of the *Autobiography* (1964) is very perceptive. Also excellent is Douglas McKenzie's unpublished dissertation, "The Acting of Joseph Jefferson III" (Univ. of Oregon, 1973). Gladys Malvern, *Good Troupers All: The Story of Joseph Jefferson* (1945), is a fictionalized treatment of limited usefulness.

BENJAMIN MCARTHUR

JEFFERSON, Mark Sylvester William (1 Mar. 1863–8 Aug. 1949), geographer, was born in Melrose, Massachusetts, the son of Daniel Jefferson, a literary editor, and Mary Mantz. The wooded areas in and around Melrose afforded Jefferson his earliest contacts with nature, while his father's work instilled in him a love of learning. Jefferson entered Boston University in 1880 but left after three years and moved to Argentina. There he used his mathematical skills as an assistant at the National Observatory in Córdoba from 1883 to 1886, then for an equal amount of time as the superintendent of a sugar estate at Tucumán. The experiences and insights he absorbed living in these two locales on Argentina's western reaches later were woven into several works he completed on southern South America after World War I.

Jefferson returned to Massachusetts in 1889, completed his Boston University baccalaureate degree that year, and spent the next dozen years living in a number of communities in his native state variously employed as a public-school teacher, principal, and superintendent. In 1891 he married Theodora Augusta Bohnstedt, with whom he had five children. She died in 1913. Three other children were born to him and his second wife, Clara Hopkins, whom he married in 1915. Concurrently, he furthered his education at Harvard, where he earned a second bachelor's degree in 1897 and a master's degree the following year. At Harvard his interest shifted to geography under the mentorship of physical geographer William Morris Davis, then the leading academic geographer in the country.

In 1901 Jefferson removed himself from Massachusetts and his public-school teaching to accept a professorship of geography at Michigan State Normal College (now Eastern Michigan University) in Ypsilanti. As was typical in such schools at the time, Jefferson taught many courses and thousands of students over the next thirty-eight years. Atypical of most teachers' college faculty, however, Jefferson published steadily, a practice he began in 1897 and sustained until 1941.

Over his professional lifetime, Jefferson single-handedly wrote more than 300 works, using a coauthor in only one instance. He wrote textbooks, articles, research notes, and reviews that appeared in outlets that reached both the geography and the education communities. The first decade of his writing focused on subjects in physical geography, reflecting the training he received under his mentor Davis. But increasingly Jefferson grew dissatisfied with "geography without man" and by World War I he had redressed that imbalance in his writings (without abandoning entirely topics in physical geography), so that over his long career he wrote many pieces on other topics, especially on population and settlement (both rural and urban) and on maps, with Latin America and Europe the most favored areas of his regionally focused research.

Maps were always a central feature of Jefferson's research and teaching. It was for these reasons along with personal knowledge of the man that his student Isaiah Bowman appointed him in 1918 chief cartographer of the Inquiry, which was headquartered at the American Geographical Society of New York. Bowman was the society's director and the guiding force behind the Inquiry, an interdisciplinary group of scholars on leave from academia to aid the war effort by preparing maps and research documents that would be used at the Paris Peace Conference in 1919 to determine how the boundaries of postwar Europe would be configured. Jefferson also went to Paris as chief cartographer of the American Peace Commission, an appointment arranged by Bowman.

Notwithstanding Jefferson's considerable research productivity, however, his legacy rests on his role as a teacher. Though his research brought him offers over the years to move to more prestigious colleges and universities, he declined them all and remained in Ypsilanti, where he left a considerable pedagogical mark. Jefferson was a demanding but highly effective teacher who was widely read and who invested much time in preparing up-to-date materials for his classes. As much as possible, Jefferson based his classes on experiments and fieldwork. "He had no taste for the subjective and personal. His choice was concrete material that one could build into the permanent structure of science," remarked Bowman in the *Geographical Review* (40 [1950]: 135–36). He was outspoken as well and did not suffer fools gladly, nor did he endear himself to colleagues when he contemptuously criticized educational "methods." His plain speaking about matters educational and otherwise perhaps explains why the presidency of the National Council of Geography Teachers (now the National Council for Geographic Education), the nation's leading organization of geography teachers, eluded him, though he did receive its Distinguished Service Award in 1939, the year he entered forced retirement at the age of seventy-six from Eastern Michigan University. He harbored much bitterness and resentment in the last decade of his life because he was not thanked for his nearly forty years of service to the institution and emeritus status was not conferred on him. In addition his less-than-promised retirement salary cast a cloud of financial worry over his final years. He died in Ypsilanti, Michigan.

Jefferson's contribution as a teacher is distinctive in the annals of American academic geography. The geography department at Ypsilanti has been aptly called the "nursery of American geography" because of the notable number of its students who went on to leadership positions in the discipline, including three who became president of the Association of American Geographers, the highest elected honor that geographers can bestow on their peers. In achieving that accolade, undoubtedly they were inspired by their teacher Mark Jefferson, who was its president in 1916.

• The library at Eastern Michigan University contains the single largest collection on Jefferson, including several thousand letters, his lectures, field notes, diaries, slides, and photographs, and some of his personal library. Of Jefferson's many writings, only two are cited occasionally in geographical literature: "The Civilizing Rails," *Economic Geography* 4 (1928): 217–31, and "The Law of the Primate City," *Geographical Review* 29 (1939): 226–32. The standard biography is Geoffrey J. Martin, *Mark Jefferson: Geographer* (1968).

ALLEN D. BUSHONG

JEFFERSON, Martha Wayles Skelton (19 Oct. 1748–6 Sept. 1782), wife of Thomas Jefferson, was born in Virginia, the daughter of John Wayles, a lawyer and planter, and Martha Eppes. England-born John Wayles worked as Virginia agent to a British merchant, bought land, and established the plantation in Charles City County where Martha Jefferson was most likely born. Her mother died soon after, leaving land and slaves to Martha, her only child, who then spent her early years in the care of a stepmother with whom John Wayles had three more daughters. After this stepmother's death, Wayles married and lost a third wife within a year, leaving thirteen-year-old Martha once again motherless. At eighteen, Martha Wayles was married to Bathurst Skelton, a planter, and their son John Skelton was born the following year. Less than a year later, Bathurst Skelton was dead, and his widow had returned with her baby to her father's home.

Thomas Jefferson met Martha Skelton in the society of nearby Williamsburg and began courting her the next year. Tradition has it that rival suitors for the wealthy young widow's hand, hearing Martha and Thomas happily making music together, gave up and went home. As the couple made plans in 1771 to marry, Jefferson also prepared to become the guardian of John Skelton, but the child died at three years old that summer. If this loss shadowed the wedding plans, it did not alter Thomas Jefferson's vision of married life, shared with a friend at the time: "In every scheme of happiness she is placed in the foreground of the picture, as the principal figure." Nor did Martha's recent loss prevent the same friend, who was also her brother-in-law, from describing her as possessing "the greatest fund of good nature" and "that sprightliness and sensibility which promises to ensure the greatest happiness." On New Year's Day 1772 Martha Skelton and Thomas Jefferson were married at her father's home and traveled to "Monticello," the home that would be under incessant construction, renovation, and reconstruction through their married life.

In the ten years that followed, while Thomas Jefferson's public life eventfully proceeded, family life at Monticello was marked by birth, illness, and personal loss. One daughter died in September 1775, just as Thomas Jefferson departed for the Continental Congress in Philadelphia. Fearing for his wife's health (as well as for the future of the Commonwealth of Virginia), he spent the first five months of 1776 back at Monticello and again, distracted with worry, rushed home after the momentous Philadelphia summer of 1776. That fall, for family reasons, he declined a post in Paris (he would accept such a post only in 1782, just after Martha's death).

When Thomas Jefferson accepted the governorship of Virginia, Martha and the family accompanied him to Williamsburg, where a daughter was born and died. Altogether, Martha gave birth to five Jefferson daughters and one son, losing three of them at less than two years old. For Thomas Jefferson, family tragedies were deeply felt but arguably contained by his public concerns; for him, the tragedies would be balanced, in memory, at least, by domestic happiness. How this equation of loss and domestic happiness worked out for Martha Jefferson, we do not know. Nor do we know whether Martha shared her husband's pleasure at the addition of Jefferson's widowed sister and six orphaned children to the Monticello family. Meanwhile, when John Wayles had died in 1773, his daughter inherited more than 11,000 acres of land and 135 slaves. Trying to clear himself of his father-in-law's debts, Jefferson immediately sold half the land, and soon, consolidating his holdings, he sold and exchanged much of the remainder, including land left to his wife by her first husband. The transactions were complex, but the immediate effect was simple: the ease of his own circumstances, Jefferson would later recall, was doubled by his wife's inheritance.

The family at Monticello, over which Thomas and Martha Jefferson presided, consisted in the mid-1770s of 117 souls, including sixteen free male employees and their families and eighty-three slaves. These last included the Hemings family, who, like the majority of Jefferson's slaves, had come to him as part of his wife's inheritance. Some of the six children of Betty Hemings were said to have been sired by Martha Jefferson's own father, John Wayles. It is often assumed that for slaveholding women the presence of slaves of "bright" complexion who are likely one's own kin was a source of stress, but there is no evidence to suggest that Martha Jefferson agonized over the Hemings family or that she was troubled by slavery as such. Many of the slaves at Monticello were people with whom she had lived all of her life.

In May 1782, after giving birth to a daughter, Lucy, named after the child who had died the year before, Martha Jefferson entered what was to be her final illness. The Jeffersons' eldest daughter later remembered that her mother "lingered" four months, nursed by Thomas Jefferson and her half-sisters and sister-in-law. It was presumably sometime during these last months that Martha and Thomas Jefferson together created the only document that survives to show their interaction. Martha started the page by writing out some lines taken from Laurence Sterne's *Tristram Shandy*: "Time wastes too fast: every letter I trace tells me with what rapidity life follows my pen. The days and hours of it are flying over our heads like clouds of windy day never to return." From the same passage of Sterne, Thomas Jefferson added these lines: "And every time I kiss thy hand to bid adieu, every absence which follows it, are preludes to that eternal separation which we are shortly to make!" Not quite thirty-four years old, Martha Jefferson died. The baby Lucy died two years later; daughters Martha Jefferson (Randolph) and Mary Jefferson (Eppes) lived to adulthood.

Martha Jefferson was probably not an extraordinary woman. Her pleasures and tragedies, and even the personal charms that her family treasured, were typical enough of Chesapeake women of her time and status. Her achievement was to provide an interlude of simple private happiness to one of the most complicat-

ed public figures of American history. Although he preserved more than 25,000 letters from others and kept copies of 18,000 of his own, Thomas Jefferson destroyed Martha Jefferson's correspondence, even going so far as to collect her letters from friends for the purpose. As his biographer Dumas Malone succinctly put it: "His wife did not belong to posterity; she belonged to him" (p. 397).

• The main facts about Martha Jefferson's life are in Dumas Malone's *Jefferson and His Time*, vol. 1: *Jefferson the Virginian* (1948). These same scant facts, along with the few surviving contemporary mentions and personal reminiscences of Martha Jefferson, are presented deftly by Elizabeth Coles Langhorne in *Monticello: A Family Story* (1987) and provokingly by Fawn Brodie in *Thomas Jefferson: An Intimate History* (1974). Surviving documents in Martha Jefferson's hand—a single letter written in her capacity as the wife of the governor of Virginia and the poignant transcription mentioned above—are in *The Papers of Thomas Jefferson*, ed. Julian P. Boyd, vols. 5 and 6 (1951–1952).

MARION NELSON WINSHIP

JEFFERSON, Thomas (13 Apr. 1743–4 July 1826), philosopher, author of the Declaration of Independence, and president of the United States, was born at Shadwell, in what became Albemarle County, Virginia, the son of Peter Jefferson, a pioneer farmer and surveyor, and Jane Randolph. He always valued the enterprising example of his father, who set him in the path of education; he became "a hard student," indeed remained one throughout his life. Peter Jefferson died in 1757, leaving to his son a fair estate—5,000 acres and the slaves to work them. Less than three years later, Jefferson, already a proficient classical scholar, enrolled at the College of William and Mary in Williamsburg.

In the brief autobiography Jefferson wrote near the end of his life, he recalled in particular the influence of a trio of philosophers who admitted him, a tall, lanky, red-haired lad, to their circle. The first of these, Dr. William Small of Scotland, the only nonclergyman on the faculty of the Anglican college, became his constant teacher. From him, Jefferson said, "I got my first views of the expansion of science & of the system of things in which we are placed," and this "probably fixed the destinies of my life" (*Jefferson Writings*, p. 4). George Wythe, a leader of the provincial bar, and a man of exemplary learning and character, would become Jefferson's mentor in the law, his chosen career. The circle was completed by the urbane royal governor, Francis Faquier, who set before the youth an example of cultivated manners, taste, and sensibility. The spirited conversation of this circle lingered in Jefferson's memory for mingling more wit, learning, and philosophy than he encountered in all his life besides.

Admitted to the bar after prolonged study in 1767, Jefferson entered upon a successful practice. It was overtaken seven years later, however, by the onrush of the American Revolution, and he never resumed the profession. His political career fairly commenced in 1769, when the freeholders of Albemarle elected him to the House of Burgesses. Here during the next seven years he learned the craft of a legislator and became a leader in the movement for American independence. At each successive crisis Jefferson stood with the radicals around Patrick Henry in opposition to Parliament's persistent attempts to impose its will upon the colonies.

In 1774, after passage of the Coercive Acts, Jefferson drafted resolutions adopted by the Albemarle freeholders that were unique, first, in declaring Parliament void of lawful authority not alone to tax but to legislate in any manner for the colonies and, second, for introducing the language of "natural rights" into an argument heretofore conducted in terms of legal and constitutional rights. Jefferson then developed his position in a paper of some 7,000 words, which he proposed for adoption by the convention of "the late members of the House of Burgesses"—an incipient revolutionary body—called to meet at Williamsburg on 1 August. Falling ill on the road, he forwarded this work intended as instructions to the Virginia delegates elected to the expected continental congress. But the leap he proposed was thought too bold; the convention held to the old ground that conceded Parliament's authority to regulate the trade of the empire even if revenue was incident to the regulation. Jefferson's friends at Williamsburg saw to publication of his paper without ascription of authorship, and without his consent, under the title *A Summary View of the Rights of British America*. His first published work, it was at once reprinted in Philadelphia and soon in England. Although he drew his argument from the venerable tradition of the English constitution, Jefferson reached the radical conclusion that the Americans possessed the natural right to govern themselves. This mingling of legalism and rationalism was thoroughly characteristic of the young revolutionary. The logic of the argument pointed to independence. Neither Jefferson nor anyone else was yet ready for that leap, however, and having repudiated Parliament's authority he left allegiance to a common king the only bond of empire. The *Summary View* thus opened the final chapter in the polemics of the Revolution.

Meanwhile, Jefferson learned the craft of an architect by building his home, "Monticello," on a densely wooded summit adjoining Shadwell. He learned architecture as he learned most things from books, and he early discovered his master in the Renaissance Italian Andrea Palladio, who had turned to Roman antiquity for his models. Monticello was a modified Palladian villa, and all of Jefferson's later architectural masterpieces—the Virginia Capitol, "Poplar Forest," the University of Virginia—were in the Palladian manner. Early in 1772, long before the mansion was finished, he brought his bride, a young widow from the low country, Martha Wayles Skelton, to Monticello. The first of their six children was born there in September.

The death of Martha's father the following year doubled Jefferson's estate. Two valuable plantations, "Elk Hill," on the James River, and "Poplar Forest," in Bedford County, came to him. The management of so large an estate—over 10,000 acres and about 180 slaves—was a heavy responsibility. As the Revolution advanced, and public responsibilities crowded upon him, Jefferson found less and less time for it. Unfortunately, too, the Wayles estate came to him burdened with debts to English merchants. Jefferson waged a losing battle all his life to get free of them.

In June 1775 Jefferson assumed a seat in the Second Continental Congress at Philadelphia. His reputation had gone before him. He brought into Congress, John Adams said, "a reputation for literature, science, and a happy talent for composition" (Malone, vol. 1, p. 204). He was at once set to work drafting revolutionary state papers. In June 1776, as last hopes of reconciliation with Britain faded, Jefferson found himself appointed the head of a five-man committee to draft a united declaration of independence. Although two of the committee members, Benjamin Franklin and Adams, were decidedly senior and better known, the task of drafting the document fell to him for political reasons and because he possessed that "peculiar felicity of expression" wanted in a work of this kind. He showed a preliminary draft to Franklin and Adams, who suggested only minor changes, revised it to his own satisfaction, and reported it to the committee. From there it went unaltered to Congress. After adopting the Virginia resolution for independence on 2 July, Congress debated the proposed declaration line by line for two and one-half days. The author squirmed under this ordeal. The philosophical preamble was speedily approved, but the delegates made many changes in the body of the work, the long indictment of George III. Jefferson thought the declaration lost more than it gained in the process, and some modern interpreters have sharply differentiated "Jefferson's Declaration of Independence" from the document adopted by Congress.

Be that as it may, the Declaration of Independence bore unmistakably the stamp of Jefferson's genius. Its language was bold yet elevated, plain and direct yet touched with philosophy, as befitted a solemn appeal to the reason of mankind. Its argument, though founded in English law, suppressed the recondite legalism of tradition to the revolutionary principles born of the Enlightenment. Jefferson encapsulated a cosmology, a political philosophy, and a national creed—for so it would become—in the celebrated second paragraph.

The truths there declared to be "self-evident" were not new; indeed, as Jefferson later said, his purpose was "not to find out new principles, or new arguments . . . , but to place before mankind the common sense of the subject" (*Jefferson Writings*, p. 1501). For the first time in history these truths were laid at the foundation of a nation. Human equality, the natural rights of man, the sovereignty of the people—these principles endowed the American Revolution with high moral purpose and heralded the democratic future not only in America but in the world. Some years passed before Jefferson's authorship was generally known, but in due time the Declaration of Independence became his first title to fame.

Returning to Virginia in the fall, Jefferson immediately entered the newly constituted House of Delegates with plans to reform the old order there. While he was in Philadelphia a constitution had been adopted for the new commonwealth, but it was not at all to Jefferson's liking. It left the old elite entrenched in power, excluded one-half of the white male citizenry from the political process, and was silent on feudal land tenures, the religious establishment, and other aristocratic abuses. Moreover, the constitution had been adopted without the "consent of the governed," laid down as a first principle in the Declaration, and without provision for periodic adjustment and revision. Jefferson had drafted a more democratic instrument and sent it to Williamsburg, but it was said to have arrived too late for consideration. Now he postponed the objective of a new constitution for the duration of the war and, from his seat in the House of Delegates, sought far-reaching reforms by ordinary legislation. Repeatedly in years to come Jefferson mounted his charger to overturn the first Virginia constitution, always without success.

Most of Jefferson's reforms were part of a comprehensive revision of the laws, reported in 1779, of which he was the principal author. The rational aim of a revised code miscarried, but the general assembly eventually adopted or rejected 126 bills of the revisal one by one. The abolition of entail and primogeniture—vestiges of feudalism—worked in the direction, already manifest, of a uniformly individualistic system of land tenure. Jefferson took special pride in the Statute of Religious Freedom, drafted in 1777 and finally enacted in 1786. Religious freedom, being wholly a matter of private conscience in Jefferson's philosophy, admitted neither protection nor support from the state. The celebrated statute became a powerful directive for the unique relationship of church and state in America and, by its bold assertion that the opinions of men are beyond the reach of civil authority, one of the great charters of the free mind as well.

But the Virginia oligarchs defeated his other major reforms. His Bill for the More General Diffusion of Knowledge (1778) offered a complete plan of public education from elementary schools through to a state university, with a state library and museum as well. Jefferson's "quixotism" on the subject of education was rooted in political principles. Education being essential to the making of republican citizens, it became a paramount responsibility of government. The opposition's objections rang down the years. It was "impractical." It was "godless." It unfairly taxed the rich to educate the poor. By creating new units of local government called "wards" it undercut the authority of the oligarchical county courts. The plan was defeated in 1785. Jefferson, then in France, was crushed by the news. "I think by far the most important bill in our whole code is that for the diffusion of knowledge among the people," he wrote to Wythe. "Let our countrymen know . . . that the tax which will be paid for this purpose is not more than the thousandth part of what will be paid to kings, priests, and nobles who will

rise up among us if we leave the people in ignorance" (*Jefferson Writings*, pp. 859–60).

Slavery, like ignorance, was another obstacle to the hopes of republicanism. In retrospect, the fact that Jefferson was a Virginia slaveholder all his adult life has placed him at odds with his moral and political principles. Yet there can be no question of his genuine hatred of slavery or, indeed, of the efforts he made to curb and eliminate it. In his draft of the Declaration of Independence he denounced the African slave trade imposed by Britain as a "cruel war against human nature itself," but Congress struck this passage. Partly through his efforts, Virginia became the first state to close its doors to this infernal traffic. A plan of gradual emancipation was part of Jefferson's reform system, but it was held back on the plea of expediency. His draft of a new Virginia constitution in 1783 mandated gradual emancipation of the slaves by declaring all persons born after the year 1800 free. The plan of emancipation to which he adhered all his life included provision for colonization of freed blacks in Africa or elsewhere, for he assumed this was a necessary condition for the citizenry's adoption of emancipation and because Jefferson himself had no faith in the feasibility of an equal biracial society. Of course, no convention materialized in 1783, and Jefferson became convinced that, at least in Virginia and the other southern states, emancipation was a political impossibility. Unwilling to martyr himself uselessly, he looked to the younger generation to turn the fate of this question.

On 1 June 1779 Jefferson was elected governor of Virginia. The republican convictions, benevolent temperament, and philosophical turn of mind that had given him eminence in the legislative forums of the Revolution proved less serviceable to executive leadership in a situation pregnant with disaster. The executive office was weak, and Jefferson, with his aversion to anything bordering on arbitrary rule, was not the governor to strengthen it. As the British attempted to defeat the rebellion from the southward, Virginia became a battleground. Early in January 1781, the traitor-general Benedict Arnold invaded the state from the coast, sped through the low country to Richmond, now the capital, and scattered government. Jefferson met the crisis bravely, though not without censure, and upon his return to the capital acted with greater vigor, still to no avail. When General Charles Cornwallis marched his southern army into Virginia in the spring, the government moved to safer quarters in Charlottesville, near Jefferson's home. The redcoats followed, and on 4 June, after his term of office had expired but before a successor could be elected, he was chased from Monticello. At this crescendo of humiliation and defeat, the House of Delegates voted an inquiry into the conduct of the executive during Arnold's invasion. In December, several months after the British surrender at Yorktown, Jefferson attended the legislature on this business; but no inquiry was held, and the assembly instead voted him a resolution of thanks for his services, which if not a vindication lifted the cloud of censure.

Exhausted by his ordeal, stung by criticism, and disgusted that his exertions had been of so little account, Jefferson resolved to quit the public stage. Every effort to draw him back, by Congress, by the general assembly, by his Albemarle constituents, was rebuffed. A series of personal misfortunes, culminating in his wife's death in September 1782, plunged him into darkest gloom. Yet it was Martha Jefferson's death that finally led him back into the path of destiny. "Before that event my scheme in life had been determined," he wrote to a friend in November. "I had folded myself into the arms of retirement, and rested all prospects of future happiness on domestic and literary objects. A single event wiped away all my plans and left me a blank which I had not the spirit to fill up" (*Jefferson Writings*, p. 780). Fortunately, Congress threw him a lifeline, renewal of the commission, earlier declined, to negotiate peace in Paris. Peace came before he could sail, however, and Jefferson wound up in Congress instead.

During his retirement Jefferson wrote, in large part, his only book, *Notes on the State of Virginia*. Actually it did not begin as a book or with any view to publication, but as a response to a series of questions about Virginia posed by the secretary of the French legation in Philadelphia. Becoming fascinated with the questions, Jefferson converted the task—one of instructing America's revolutionary ally—into an intellectual self-discovery of his native land, the greater Virginia of that day. The manuscript grew as he worked at it, and he was finally induced to publish it, originally in a private edition, in Paris in 1785. A digest of information and opinion on many subjects, *Notes on Virginia* is uniquely interesting as a guide to Jefferson's mind as well as to his country. It exhibits his insatiable curiosity, his manifold interests, painstaking detail, and speculative bent. It reveals the man of science disciplined to empirical fact and eager to possess nature for the mind, yet also the man of almost romantic sensibility enraptured by the wonders of the American continent even as he quested for useful knowledge. Of special importance was Jefferson's vindication of American nature against current European theories of biological impotence and decay in the New World. The book was a virtual manual of Jefferson's political opinions, and some of its passages—on slavery, on the virtues of husbandry, on religious freedom, on the errors of the Virginia constitution—became so well known that they were said to be "stereotyped in the public voice." The book whetted the appetite of the tiny community of American philosophers and won Jefferson a scientific and literary reputation on both sides of the Atlantic.

Jefferson's service in Congress, while brief, from November 1783 to the following May, was highly productive. Legislation he proposed laid the foundations of national policy in important areas, for instance the decimal system of coinage on the dollar unit. (Later, as secretary of state, he also proposed a decimal system of weights and measures, but without success.) After Virginia, with several other states, ceded to Congress its claims to western lands, Jefferson authored the first plan of government for the vast trans-Appalachian domain. The Ordinance of 1784 established the principle of creating new, free and equal self-governing states as Americans moved west. To Jefferson's great regret his provision to bar slavery from the West was defeated, though Congress later rectified the error, in part, in the Northwest Ordinance. The Land Ordinance of 1785 embodied Jefferson's rectilinear plan of survey and revealed, once again, his passion for rational order and precision. Throughout his life he showed remarkable vision toward the West. As early as 1780 he spoke of the American experiment as an "empire of liberty" (*Jefferson Papers*, vol. 4, p. 237). Unlike Old World empires, he believed it rested not on colonial subservience to a supreme power but on the expansion of liberty and self-government over a continent.

In May Congress appointed Jefferson to a commission, whose other members were Franklin and Adams, to negotiate treaties of commerce with European states. The commission, which met in Paris, experienced indifferent success, but Jefferson continued his efforts in commercial diplomacy when, ten months later, he succeeded Franklin as minister to France. So often portrayed as a narrow "agrarian" in his economic outlook, he was, in fact, an ardent commercial expansionist. He believed that if the country was to remain agricultural, thereby avoiding the vices of cities and manufactures, it had to find foreign markets for its surpluses. The conditions for the development of a large "home market" did not then exist. Cut adrift from the British trading empire, anxious to secure economic as well as political independence from the mother country, the United States was obliged to widen its foreign markets along the avenues of free trade. Jefferson regarded France, already an ally and Britain's habitual rival, as the key to the free commercial system so important to the country's future. In negotiations at Versailles, where he was assisted by the marquis de Lafayette, Jefferson won valuable concessions for American commerce and navigation, yet he could not shake British hegemony. Without abandoning the aim of throwing American commerce into a new orbit, he looked increasingly to the progress of reform in Europe and a stronger national government in the United States to attain it.

Jefferson was probably never happier than during his five-year residence in France. Paris showered him with the infinitely varied pleasures of the mind and spirit. He read French like a native and soon became proficient in speaking the language. He haunted the bookstores. He frequented the fashionable salons. He indulged his appetite for art and music and theater. He was excited by ingenious inventions—phosphorous matches, the copying press, the screw propeller—smitten by the architecture, and captivated by the cuisine. For one brief season he was swept up in winsome romance with an English visitor, Maria Cosway, the talented wife of an English painter and the bemused recipient after her departure of Jefferson's "Dialogue between My Head and My Heart." He toured in the south of France, briefly in Italy, in England, the Netherlands, and the Rhineland, not alone for business or pleasure but to learn things useful to his own country. He interpreted the New World to the Old and presided over the intercourse of the arts and sciences. Some of this had profound effects, as in his design for the Virginia Capitol, which inaugurated the Roman style in American civic architecture, and in his transmission of American republicanism to the French.

Toward France, and Europe generally, Jefferson expressed ambivalent feelings. All he coveted—enlightenment, civility, artistic splendor—was offset by luxury and debauchery, ignorance and oppression. On balance, the more he saw of Europe the dearer his own country became. "My God!" he exclaimed. "How little do my own country men know what precious blessings they are in possession of, and which no other people on earth enjoy. I confess I had no idea of it myself" (*Jefferson Writings*, p. 808).

Despite the restraints of his official position, Jefferson was an open friend of the French Revolution of 1789. He advocated liberal reform of the Bourbon monarchy, including the establishment of representative assemblies, guarantees of individual liberties, and abolition of feudal privileges. He doubted the French people were ready for democratic revolution on the American plan and cautioned his friends in Paris against pushing things too fast and too far lest they provoke a counterrevolution. Nevertheless, as the movement grew more radical so, too, did Jefferson. He went with the Revolution, and at each critical juncture realigned his thinking with a swiftness that would put a closet philosopher to shame. By the time he returned to the United States in the fall of 1789, he could look upon the French Revolution as an extension of the American, and he was convinced that his own country had a vital stake in its future. "Here," he declared, "is but the first chapter in the history of European liberty" (*Jefferson Writings*, p. 956).

Jefferson went home on leave, fully expecting to return to Paris, but President George Washington prevailed upon him to become secretary of state in the new government under the Constitution. The United States had undergone a kind of revolution of its own. Jefferson was cordial to the new experiment. He had, after all, seen the feeble confederation kicked and scoffed abroad and had gone begging to Dutch bankers to keep it afloat. Still, pondering the new frame of government in Paris, where tyranny not anarchy was the problem, he felt the "demigods" at Philadelphia had been too much influenced by disorders like Shays's Rebellion and disenchantment with the democracy released in 1776. He objected, in particular, to perpetual reeligibility of the chief executive, fearing that the office would degenerate into a corrupt monarchy, and to the omission of a bill of rights. While he set aside the former, he pressed the latter; and his influence, especially as it fell upon his friend James Madison, contributed to the addition of the Bill of Rights to the Constitution.

The tall, soft-spoken, and accomplished Virginian took up his duties in New York, the temporary capital,

on 21 March 1790. He brought impressive qualifications to the conduct of the nation's foreign affairs, the chief business of the State Department. His main objectives during a tenure of almost four years were, first, settlement of Anglo-American issues left over from the treaty of peace and regularization of relations with Britain; second, the further expansion of American commerce, which he associated with a strengthened French alliance; third, the redemption of the West from European colonialism, the Spanish to the south, the British to the north, along with pacification of the Indians; finally, the manipulation of American neutrality in any European war to advance American national interests. In each case the problems proved intractable. Jefferson succeeded in bringing Britain to the bargaining table in 1791. Removal of His Majesty's troops from below the Great Lakes and resolution of other nagging issues was a prerequisite to improved relations. In diplomacy with Britain Jefferson believed the United States had a potent yet pacific weapon at its disposal, commercial discrimination. Britain could be made to pay for its virtual monopoly of the American market; and if this was not enough to force concessions, then Britain's dependence in war on American provisions, both at home and in the West Indies, would be. But in negotiations with Britain Jefferson was thwarted by the secretary of the treasury, Alexander Hamilton, whose fiscal system turned on British trade, credit, and power. Jefferson's system, on the other hand, looked to commercial liberation, alliance with France, and progress of democratic revolution in Europe. His commitment to the French Revolution was more than philosophical. He believed its success was "necessary to stay up our own [revolution], and to prevent it from falling back into that kind of Half-way house, the English constitution" (*Jefferson Writings*, pp. 971–72).

But the conflict between Jefferson and Hamilton—the archetypal conflict of American politics—transcended foreign policy. In Jefferson's opinion, the New Yorker's measures to fund the debt, establish a national bank, and subsidize infant manufactures was a system of privilege. It enriched the few at the expense of the many, excited speculation and fraud, corrupted the Congress, and broke down the restraints of the Constitution. It went hand in hand with the counterrevolutionary opinions the Virginian heard from Hamilton and his friends and even from Vice President Adams. To combat these tendencies, which he labeled "Anglican" and "monarchial," Jefferson cooperated with the emerging opposition in Congress led by Madison. As the party division between Federalists and Republicans deepened, becoming a conflict in public opinion and in the newspapers, Jefferson was denounced by Hamilton and his followers as the "generalissimo" of the Republicans and the real enemy of the administration he pretended to serve. His role was not an easy one, but he endeavored to separate loyalty to President Washington from opposition to the ruling party.

When war erupted between France and Britain in 1793, the contrary disposition of the parties toward the belligerents threatened American peace. Jefferson acquiesced in the neutrality declared by the president, yet attempted to employ it to lever concessions from Britain and sustain the French alliance. Again checked by Hamilton, he was embarrassed by the firebrand minister of the new French Republic, Edmond Genet, whose warlike antics spoiled everything. To preserve peace, and to preserve the Republican party from the threatened explosion, Jefferson was forced to get rid of Genet. The operation was successful. Indeed, Jefferson deftly restored Britain as the principal enemy of American peace and prosperity before he left office at the year's end.

Return to the orange-red highlands of his native Albemarle—"the Eden of the United States"—was a return to the paradise of Jefferson's soul. From his little mountain he portrayed himself as a plain farmer, a patriarch among his children, reading not a single newspaper, and while still capable of ejaculations against the enemies of liberty, "preferring infinitely to contemplate the tranquil growth of my lucerne and potatoes" (*Jefferson Writings*, p. 1014). He made agricultural improvements, such as his mouldboard of least resistance for the plow. In practical farming, however, he showed more science than skill. He engaged in simple manufactures, a nailery for instance. He rebuilt Monticello—no small expense for the next fifteen years—the better to accommodate his family and the better to express his personal ideal.

As before, the pastoral idyll he imagined at Monticello eluded his grasp, and in 1796 he yielded to pressures drawing him back into the politics he professed to hate. "Wasn't it wonderful," John Adams cynically remarked, "how political plants grew in the shade!" (letter to Abigail Adams, 14 Jan. 1797, Adams Papers Microfilm, Letterbooks). The Republicans made Jefferson their presidential candidate against Adams, who prevailed in a close contest. Jefferson succeeded his old friend as vice president, the post he preferred at this critical juncture in the nation's affairs. Jay's Treaty with Britain, signed in 1794, had inflamed partisan passions as never before and angered America's foreign ally. Adams's administration revolved around peace or war with France. Things came to a head in the XYZ affair of 1798. This clumsy attempt by French agents to extort concessions from American envoys sent to negotiate peace drove the administration toward war. In the enveloping hysteria, Jefferson clung to the hope of peace and rallied the battered Republicans against the Federalist "war system." Enactment of the repressive Alien and Sedition laws convinced him that the Federalists aimed, under the smokescreen of war, to destroy the Republican party. Because the Federalists controlled all branches of the national government, Jefferson chose to invoke the authority of the state governments to arouse opposition to these laws. Thus he secretly drafted the Kentucky Resolutions of 1798. Madison, meanwhile, drew up similar, if milder, resolutions for the Virginia legislature. Jefferson's resolutions pronounced these laws unconstitutional usurpations and set forth the remedy of "nullification" to defeat them. The Virginia and Kentucky resolutions would later be mixed up with the constitutional issue upon which the Civil War was fought, but they originated in a struggle for political survival and addressed the fundamental issue of freedom and self-government descending from the American Revolution.

In 1800 Jefferson was elected president over Adams after a bitter contest in which he was vilified as a Jacobin incendiary, infidel, visionary, demagogue, and enemy of Washington, the Constitution, and the Union. Actually, he was not finally elected until 17 February 1801, and not by the people or their electors but by the House of Representatives. A tie between Jefferson and Aaron Burr, his running mate, threw the choice to that body where the Federalists, defiant to the end, supported Burr. (Before another election the Twelfth Amendment of the Constitution corrected the problem that produced the tie.)

Inaugurated in Washington, the infant capital on the Potomac River he had himself helped to plan, Jefferson was anxious to quiet the political storms of the past decade and to introduce into government that serene and noiseless course that, in his opinion, was the mark of society going forward in happiness. His inaugural address—a political touchstone for a century to come—contained a lofty appeal for the restoration of harmony and affection. "We have called by different names brethren of the same principle. We are all republicans—we are all federalists." Conciliation did not exclude reform, however. He offered a brilliant summation of the Republican creed. He pledged to preserve "the whole constitutional vigor" of government, yet at the same time, in a memorable passage, called for "a wise and frugal government, which shall restrain men from injuring one another, which shall leave them otherwise free to regulate their own pursuits of industry and improvement, and shall not take from the mouth of labor the bread it has earned" (*Jefferson Writings*, p. 494). In retrospect, Jefferson called the Republican ascendancy "the revolution of 1800" (*Jefferson Writings*, p. 1425), for through the processes of democratic election it accomplished as real a revolution in the principles of government as that of 1776 had in its form.

Jefferson dominated his administration more completely than had either of his predecessors. To the authority of his office he added the authority of party leader. His eminence as a philosopher-statesman was unchallenged; and by some personal magnetism he drew men to him, persuaded them to follow, and inspired their loyalty. His style of leadership was averse to dissension and confrontation. The harmony and stability of his cabinet, composed of moderate Republicans like Madison and Albert Gallatin, was unprecedented. With a painstaking capacity for detail, Jefferson was a good administrator. He also provided effective leadership of Congress. In Republican theory, got from the Whig tradition, Congress was superior to the president and he should not interfere in its business. Jefferson bowed to the theory but in practice employed the arts of persuasion together with the network of party leadership outside constitutional channels to control Congress. This system, so successful during Jefferson's first term, began to break down during his second as the Republicans quarreled among themselves and Federalist intransigence hardened.

Jefferson had hoped to appease the Federalists, in part, by a fair and equitable policy toward officeholders. In 1801 the offices from judges to postmasters were monopolized by Federalists; Republicans craved them, of course, but Jefferson was repelled by the politics of spoils and proscription. He preferred to convert the incumbents to Republicanism and to achieve a proper balance gradually. In the end, however, he was compelled to introduce the partisan standard. By 1804 he had appointed Republicans to one-half of the major offices. In doing so he broadened the heretofore elitist base of the civil establishment, taking in more westerners and more men of talent without wealth or privilege.

Growing Republican domination embittered the shrinking Federalist remnant. Thomas Paine's return to the United States at the president's invitation in 1802 inflamed the old slanders of Jacobinism and infidelity. At the same time Jefferson faced a new slander got up by the grubstreet journalist and disappointed officeseeker James T. Callender, and adopted by the rancorous Federalists, that he had for many years kept an African concubine, Sally Hemings, at Monticello and fathered several slave children by her. Thus began the prolific career of a tale that, although it had no foundation in the historical record, would on occasion figure prominently in the history of myth and legend about Jefferson. He never replied to the libel, doubtless on the theory that any reply would stimulate rather than arrest it. Moreover, he was committed to what he called his "experiment" in unfettered freedom of the press; and although he twice acquiesced in prosecutions for libel, he did no injury to that experiment.

Reform was bottomed on fiscal policy. Hamilton's system had rested on a large funded debt, taxes to service it, and a national bank, all anathema to the Republicans. Jefferson proposed a plan devised by Secretary of the Treasury Gallatin to extinguish the debt in sixteen years yet, amazingly, abolish the hated internal taxes at the same time. The plan required a reduction of the army and navy and some other services, and it assumed peace and rising revenues from foreign trade. After seven years, before the interruption of foreign commerce, the debt was actually reduced about 40 percent. The president agonized a good deal over Hamilton's fiscal system. "We can pay off his debt in fifteen years," he wrote in 1802, "but we can never get rid of his financial system. It mortifies me to be strengthening principles which I deem radically vicious, but the vice is entailed on us by the first error. . . . What is practicable must often control pure theory" (*Jefferson Writings*, p. 1101). A case in point was the Bank of the United States. Its charter ran to

1811; moreover, Gallatin found the institution serviceable, and in a thriving economy a banking interest grew up in the Republican party.

The Federalist judiciary became the principal political battleground of Jefferson's first term. The opening battle of the so-called war on the judiciary was fought over the partisan Judiciary Act of 1801. The eleventh-hour act of a dying administration, it created a whole new tier of courts and judgeships and in other ways augmented the power of a judiciary monopolized by Federalists. In Jefferson's view, the defeated party had retired to the judiciary as a stronghold. The Repeal Act of 1802 returned the judiciary to its prior footing. Another conflict centered on the case of *Marbury v. Madison* (1803). Marbury and others sued the secretary of state for the execution of commissions—"midnight appointments" of the outgoing administration—as justices of the peace in the District of Columbia. In a landmark decision Chief Justice John Marshall ruled for the plaintiffs. He avoided a showdown with Jefferson, however, by declaring unconstitutional the authority of the court to issue writs of mandamus to enforce valid contracts, as given by the Judiciary Act of 1789. The decision laid the basis for what became the imposing edifice of judicial review. But in 1803 Jefferson opposed the decision less because of theoretical claims to a judicial power he distrusted than because the chief justice traveled outside the case, pretending to a jurisdiction he then disclaimed, in order to take a gratuitous stab at the president. Another phase of the Republican campaign was the impeachment of federal judges who had violated the public trust. Its high point was the trial of Supreme Court justice Samuel Chase. After his acquittal by the Senate in 1805, Jefferson turned away from impeachment in disgust. Yet he remained anxious about the unchecked power of the judiciary. He would face other encounters with Marshall, as in the acquittal of Burr on the charge of treason in 1807; but the "war on the judiciary" ended without serious disturbance to the foundations of judicial power.

The president's greatest triumph, and greatest defeat, came in foreign affairs. In 1801 peace was on the horizon in Europe, and Jefferson dared to hope that the United States, securely anchored on its Atlantic shore, "a chosen country," as he said in his inaugural address, "with room enough for our descendants to the thousandth and thousandth generation" (*Jefferson Writings*, p. 494), need no longer meddle in European politics. The French Revolution was dead, assassinated by "the beast" Napoleon, and so was the old alliance. Jefferson looked to a foreign policy characterized by peace and commerce only. Immediately, however, he faced a burgeoning crisis on the Mississippi River. Spain's retrocession of Louisiana with the great port of New Orleans to France threatened American peace and the future prosperity of the American West. For two years Jefferson and Madison skillfully negotiated the crisis. The president waved the thunderbolt of "marry[ing] ourselves to the British fleet and nation," if necessary, to secure American interests on the Mississippi (*Jefferson Writings*, p. 1105). But the crisis was resolved when the American ministers in Paris signed a treaty to purchase Louisiana on 2 April 1803. It included more than Jefferson had sought: the whole of Louisiana with New Orleans, some 800,000 square miles, westward to the Rocky Mountains and beyond, doubling the size of the American union, for a price of under $15 million. The acquisition undergirded Jefferson's vision of an expanding agricultural nation for decades to come.

For several months Jefferson had been planning a voyage of discovery across the continent. Now, by happy coincidence, the Lewis and Clark expedition became a reconnaissance of the distant domain. Unfortunately, the luster of the Louisiana Purchase was dimmed for Jefferson by the conviction it breached the limits of the Constitution. He drafted an amendment to sanction the acquisition retroactively. When it found no support in Congress, he buried his fears of making the Constitution "a blank paper by construction" (*Jefferson Writings*, p. 1140) and proceeded with the treaty. Jefferson also proposed to confine settlement for an uncertain term to lower Louisiana, locking up the rest and turning it into a vast Indian reserve to which eastern tribes, pressed for their lands, might remove. This policy met with indifferent success.

Flush with the triumph of the Louisiana Purchase the president easily won reelection in 1804. Yet Jefferson's second term proved to be an ordeal. His method of working with Congress lost its charms, especially after it became known he would not seek a third term. His relentless pursuit of the Floridas vitiated his diplomacy abroad and exposed him to attack at home. The Burr conspiracy in the southwest angered Jefferson, and he almost turned the ensuing trial at Richmond into a personal vendetta against Burr and the presiding judge, Marshall. With the formation of the Third Coalition against Napoleonic France in 1805, all Europe was ablaze. The United States became the last neutral of consequence. The neutral trade was highly profitable. Unfortunately, of the chief belligerents, the French and the British, each demanded that trade on its own terms, and neither feared war with the country whose president declared peace his passion.

Britain loomed as the chief aggressor in Jefferson's eyes. It impressed thousands of American seamen into its service, thereby assaulting the very existence of American nationality. British ships infested American waters and plundered American carriers. Diplomatic initiatives to settle these issues of neutral trade and seamen's rights failed. The inflammatory *Chesapeake-Leopard* affair followed. The brutality of HMS *Leopard*'s attack on the U.S. frigate aroused the whole country against Great Britain. War awaited only the president's signal. But he cooled the crisis and attempted to make it a lever in further negotiations, alas without success.

The upshot of these events—the denouement of Jefferson's administration—was the embargo of American commerce and navigation from the oceans, enacted by Congress on the president's recommendation on 22 December 1807. More than an alternative to war, or preparation for it, the Embargo Act was an experiment to test the effectiveness of "peaceable coercion" in international disputes. The United States possessed in its commerce, Jefferson had long believed, "another umpire than arms" (*Jefferson Writings*, p. 1007) to secure justice from European powers together with its own peace. To enforce the embargo, he and Gallatin stretched the capacities of government to the limit—in time beyond the constitutional limits Jefferson advocated. Although not without mounting effect abroad, the embargo produced more compelling privations and discontents at home. Finally, in the waning hours of the administration, it was repealed. The sequel three years later was the War of 1812. Jefferson always believed that this inglorious outcome might have been avoided had the nation shown the unity and the courage to persevere with the embargo. He probably erred in this judgment; if so, it was because he had become the captive of his own idealism.

Jefferson's popularity, though shaken, remained high when he retired to Monticello in 1809. Monticello was more than a home; it was already a monument and a shrine. Visitors, the great and the ordinary, came from far and near to see the Sage of Monticello. His daughter Martha managed a household filled with adoring grandchildren. One of them described him as in excellent health, light complexioned, with hazel eyes, his reddish hair now turned sandy, six feet two and one-half inches tall, carriage erect, step firm and elastic, with a temper strong but under perfect control. "My mornings are devoted to correspondence," Jefferson wrote to a friend in 1810. "From breakfast to dinner [midafternoon], I am in my shops, my garden, or on horseback among my farms; from dinner to dark, I give to society and recreation with neighbors and friends; and from candle light to early bed-time, I read" (Peterson, *Jefferson and the New Nation*, p. 927). His favorite reading was in the ancient classics. But his intellectual pursuits spanned a wide front. For eighteen years, until 1815, he was president of the American Philosophical Society, the nation's premier scientific institution. He sold his great library of some 6,000 volumes to Congress in 1815, and it became the nucleus of the Library of Congress. He carried on a large correspondence, ranging over such subjects as Indian languages, constitutions, Plato and the Bible, horizontal plowing, conveyor belts and hopper-boys. Its best fruit was the correspondence with John Adams, the revolutionary comrade with whom he was reunited in friendship in 1812.

Although Jefferson wrote no books in retirement, he penned a memoir of his life before 1790, translated two works from the French, collected documents, compiled political notes and memoranda, essayed brief characterizations or lives of contemporaries, and in other ways contributed to the writing of American history. Some years before his death he completed a task begun in 1803 that is now known as the Jefferson Bible. Through a rough sort of New Testament criticism, he attempted to identify the real teachings of Jesus amid the Platonizing corruptions of priests and theologians. In his youth he had gone to the ancients for moral instruction; he still did, but now, in the ripeness of years, he concluded that the plain, unsophisticated teachings of Jesus made the best of all moral systems. He called his bible distilled from the four gospels "The Life and Morals of Jesus of Nazareth" and thought it proof that he whom the priests and pharisees called infidel was "a true Christian" in the only sense that mattered, the love of man taught by Jesus. Of course, believing religion wholly a matter of the private conscience, Jefferson disdained public profession. Even his family knew nothing of the red morocco-bound volume. And it had to be rediscovered some seventy years after his death. Clearly Jefferson was on the track of a unifying religion of humanity, enlightened, morally earnest but stripped of supernaturalism, of which he saw anticipations in Unitarianism.

The "holy cause" to which Jefferson gave himself in old age was public education. In 1814 he revived his plan for a state system. Again the legislature rejected it. However, shamed, cajoled, and outwitted by Jefferson and a little band of "Monticello men" in the assembly, it approved one part of the plan, the state university. Jefferson wondered at the folly of raising the apex of the pyramid without laying the foundations in primary and secondary schools. He rejoiced in the university, nonetheless. Chartered by the state in 1819, located in Charlottesville, he could legitimately call himself its father. His architectural design of an "academical village" was strikingly original, perfectly attuned to his purpose, and cleanly executed in brick and mortar and wood under his watchful eye. He sent abroad for a faculty, formed the curriculum, acquired the library, and attended to countless details. Secular and modern in conception, raised against massive obstacles—legislative parsimony, sectarian fanaticism, and public indifference—the University of Virginia opened its doors to students only sixteen months before Jefferson's death.

Jefferson's last years were etched with sadness and disappointment. His health began to fail in 1818. At the same time, his personal fortune was doomed. Years of embargo, nonintercourse, and war had injured all Virginia agriculture, and recovery had only begun when the panic of 1819 struck. New debts piled upon old, some descending from the Revolution, and sank Jefferson into bankruptcy. In the end not even Monticello could be saved from the wreckage. He was deeply troubled, too, by the course of national affairs. The Missouri Compromise "fanaticized" politics on a sectional line dividing free and slave states; the Supreme Court, fulfilling his worst fears, became "a subtle corps of sappers and miners" of the Constitution (*Jefferson Writings*, p. 1446); and the drift toward consolidation in the national head threatened both individual liberty and the federal balance upon which the Union depended. Under these blows Jefferson retreated to the safety of old Republican dogmas and gave aid

and comfort to the revival of states' rights politics in Virginia.

Through all this Jefferson preserved his serene faith in freedom, enlightenment, and the progress of humanity. He died at Monticello on the fiftieth anniversary of American independence. A methodical man to the end, he penned his own epitaph—designed his tombstone as well—in which he chose to be remembered as the author of the Declaration of Independence and the Virginia Statute for Religious Freedom, and as Father of the University of Virginia. In a celebrated last letter he wrote an inspiring testament to posterity: "All eyes are opened, or opening, to the rights of man. The general spread of the light of science has already laid open to every view the palpable truth, that the mass of mankind has not been born with saddles on their back, nor a favored few booted and spurred, ready to ride them legitimately, by the grace of God" (*Jefferson Writings*, p. 1547). It almost seemed that he had appointed the hour of his death to embellish his legend. The reported last words of John Adams, who also died on that day of jubilee, were "Thomas Jefferson still survives." The course of American democracy testified to the truth of the utterance.

• The major collection of Jefferson's papers is in the Library of Congress; other important collections are in the Massachusetts Historical Society and the University of Virginia. The definitive edition, far from completion, is *The Papers of Thomas Jefferson*, ed. Julian P. Boyd et al. (25 vols. to date, 1950–1992). Of older editions of Jefferson's writings only, the most useful are *The Writings of Thomas Jefferson*, ed. Paul L. Ford (10 vols., 1892–1899), and *The Writings of Thomas Jefferson*, ed. A. A. Lipscomb and A. E. Bergh (20 vols., 1903). *Thomas Jefferson Writings*, ed. Merrill D. Peterson (1984), is a comprehensive one-volume edition. Of many collections on particular subjects, *Thomas Jefferson's Garden Book, 1766–1824*, ed. Edwin M. Betts (1944), is especially notable.

Dumas Malone, *Jefferson and His Time* (6 vols., 1948–1981), is the authoritative biography. Among biographies in one volume are Peterson, *Thomas Jefferson and the New Nation: A Biography* (1970), and Noble E. Cunningham, Jr., *In Pursuit of Reason: The Life of Thomas Jefferson* (1987). Peterson is the editor of the composite *Thomas Jefferson: A Reference Biography* (1987). Peter S. Onuf, ed., *Jeffersonian Legacies* (1993), is a contemporary reassessment by sixteen scholars. The best guide to the literature is Frank Shuffelton, *Thomas Jefferson: A Comprehensive, Annotated Bibliography of Writings about Him, 1826–1980* (1983), with a supplement (1992).

Specialized studies may be conveniently divided between political and cultural, the latter encompassing "the renaissance man." For political thought, see Carl Becker, *The Declaration of Independence: A Study in the History of Political Ideas* (1922), a classic; Garry Wills, *The Inventing of America: Jefferson's Declaration of Independence* (1978); and Garrett Sheldon, *The Political Philosophy of Thomas Jefferson* (1991). Adrienne Koch, *Jefferson and Madison: The Great Collaboration* (1951), and Peterson, *Adams and Jefferson: A Revolutionary Dialogue* (1976), are studies of associates. See also John Chester Miller, *The Wolf by the Ears: Thomas Jefferson and Slavery* (1977); Leonard W. Levy, *Jefferson and Civil Liberties: The Darker Side* (1963); and Robert W. Tucker and David C. Hendrickson, *Empire of Liberty: The Statecraft of Thomas Jefferson* (1990), which focuses on foreign affairs. For the presidency, the first half of Henry Adams, *History of the United States during the Administrations of Jefferson and Madison* (9 vols., 1891–1893), is still important. See also Forrest McDonald, *The Presidency of Thomas Jefferson* (1976); Robert Johnstone, Jr., *Jefferson and the Presidency: Leadership in the Young Republic* (1978); and Cunningham, *The Process of Government under Jefferson* (1978).

Daniel J. Boorstin, *The Lost World of Thomas Jefferson* (1948), and Karl Lehman, *Thomas Jefferson, American Humanist* (1947), offer contrasting views of Jefferson's intellectual outlook. See also Charles A. Miller, *Jefferson and Nature: An Interpretation* (1988). Special studies include Silvio A. Bedini, *Thomas Jefferson, Statesman of Science* (1990); Roy J. Honeywell, *The Educational Work of Thomas Jefferson* (1931); and Bernard Sheehan, *Seeds of Extinction: Jeffersonian Philanthropy and the American Indian* (1973). Fiske Kimball, *Thomas Jefferson, Architect* (1916), is fundamental. See also William Howard Adams, ed., *The Eye of Thomas Jefferson* (1976); Jack McLaughlin, *Jefferson and Monticello: The Biography of a Builder* (1989); and Susan R. Stein, *The Worlds of Thomas Jefferson at Monticello* (1993). Merrill D. Peterson and Robert C. Vaughan, eds., *The Virginia Statute for Religious Freedom: Its Evolution and Consequences in American History* (1988), collects conference papers. Peterson, *The Jefferson Image in the American Mind* (1960), pursues the Jefferson theme and symbol in American thought and imagination.

MERRILL D. PETERSON

JEFFORDS, Thomas Jonathan (1 Jan. 1832–19 Feb. 1914), frontiersman and Indian agent, was born in Chautauqua County, New York, the son of Eber Jeffords and Almira Wood, occupations unknown. Although a man of some education, Jeffords was reticent about his earlier career. He served as a sailor on the Great Lakes, for which he was later called "Captain," and went west in 1858, laying out the road from Leavenworth, Kansas, to Denver, Colorado. After prospecting in New Mexico, he carried army dispatches from Mesilla to Tucson, Arizona, in 1862 and is believed to have then accompanied James H. Carleton's California Column from Tucson to Fort Thorn, New Mexico. Further prospecting followed, but in 1868–1869 Jeffords supervised part of the Southern Overland U.S. Mail and Express Line Company's run between Socorro, New Mexico, and Tucson. On 20 December 1869 he was appointed a trader to the Mimbres Apaches at Cañada Alamosa (now Monticello, N.M.) but had his license revoked the following April after a disagreement with the reservation Indian agent.

During ensuing years Jeffords demonstrated a remarkable influence with the Chokonen, Mimbres, and Nednhi bands of Chiricahua Apaches, then involved in intermittent warfare against Mexico and the United States or being settled on reservations. "I have seen no man who has so complete control over his Indians," wrote a superior. "If the Apaches can be taught to work, Jeffords is the man who can teach them." The origin of his friendship with the Chokonen chief Cochise is obscure. Some contemporaries regarded Jeffords as "a bad egg" who sold liquor and ammunition to hostile Indians. In 1914 Jeffords told historian

Thomas Edwin Farish that while he was running the mail, he tired of attacks on his riders and rode alone into one of Cochise's camps to establish a private truce with him. This story is supported by his claim, made in 1869 when applying for a trading license, that he was already "well acquainted" with the Indians. However, Jeffords apparently also said that he did not meet Cochise until after becoming an Indian trader, in which case he would have become acquainted with the chief at Cañada Alamosa in October 1870.

Whichever, Jeffords proved invaluable in ending the war between the Chokonens and the United States. Three times in 1871 and 1872 Jeffords helped persuade Cochise to meet U.S. officials for peace talks. On the last occasion Jeffords guided Brigadier General Oliver Otis Howard, a peace commissioner sent by Washington, to Cochise's stronghold in the Dragoon Mountains of Arizona, where in October 1872 the Chokonens agreed to cease hostilities against the United States in return for a reservation in their own country. With this agreement the main phase of warfare between the Americans and the Apaches came to an end.

Jeffords was installed as agent on the new reservation, more than 4,000 square miles in southeastern Arizona, in January 1873. His ability to manage the Apaches was widely acknowledged: "I do not believe any other man living could now manage them, wild as they are," wrote Governor Anson P. Safford of Arizona. Jeffords respected Indian culture, often sharing the Apache viewpoint and, rather than establishing a police force on the reservation, worked through Cochise and other chiefs, seeking their trust and cooperation. Not surprisingly, he made little progress in imposing the alien economic practices encouraged by the American government. Despite the problem of securing sufficient supplies from a parsimonious Indian service, however, he maintained control, and Apache atrocities in that part of Arizona and New Mexico virtually ceased. But Cochise insisted that he had not made peace with Mexico, which shared a boundary with the reservation, and his Indians continued to raid Mexican settlements. With some justification, critics of the reservation, including the Mexican government, the Tucson press, and General George Crook, claimed that it was a haven for warriors raiding Mexico or those bolting from other American reservations.

Jeffords vigorously defended his policy of rationing visiting Indians, maintaining that by doing so he reduced their need to raid. But in April 1876, two years after Cochise's death, the murder of some whites on the reservation was made the pretext for closing it, and in May Jeffords was suspended. The following month John P. Clum mustered only 325 Indians for transfer to the San Carlos Reservation, many having fled to resume the hostilities Cochise, Jeffords, and Howard had ended four years before.

In his later years Jeffords occasionally assisted the army. In 1879 he helped locate Juh, Geronimo, and others in the Guadalupe Mountains and facilitated their willing surrender. He served as a scout against the Apaches in General Nelson Miles's campaign of

1886. More often he prospected and mined. In 1879 he sold a mine near Tombstone, Arizona, where he briefly also was employed as a deputy sheriff in 1882. Jeffords transferred his activities to the Tucson area in 1892 and built a house close to his mine workings north of the town, at the Owls Heads buttes. Rarely seen in Tucson itself, he was a charter member of the Arizona Pioneers Historical Society.

Tom Jeffords never married and had few close friends. A modest man who enjoyed his own company, he had little ambition or interest in material possessions. He was, nevertheless, intelligent, efficient, and courageous and had none of the anti-Indian bigotry so common on the frontier. Howard described him as "a tall, spare man with reddish hair and whiskers of considerable length." Jeffords died at his home at Owls Head, Pinal County.

• Jeffords's reports as agent for the Chiricahua reservation, filed in records of the Bureau of Indian Affairs (RG 75 of the National Archives, Washington, D.C.), represent the only extended collection of writings. For Jeffords's own account of his relationship with Cochise, see vol. 2 of Thomas Edwin Farish, *History of Arizona* (1915–1918). Oliver Otis Howard, *My Life and Experiences among Our Hostile Indians* (1907), contains useful recollections of Jeffords in 1872. The traditional interpretation of Jeffords's career, introduced by Farish and developed by Frank C. Lockwood, *The Apache Indians* (1938), reached its apotheosis in Elliott Arnold's novel *Blood Brother* (1947) and the consequent trail-breaking motion picture *Broken Arrow* (1950). Recent research has considerably modified this view. Valuable biographical studies have been written by Harry G. Cramer, "Tom Jeffords, Indian Agent," *Journal of Arizona History* 17 (1976): 265–300; C. L. Sonnichsen, "Who Was Tom Jeffords?" *Journal of Arizona History* 23 (1982): 381–406; and Dan L. Thrapp, *Encyclopedia of Frontier Biography* (1988), pp. 723–24. Essential contextual material is supplied by Thrapp, *Victorio and the Mimbres Apaches* (1974), and Edwin R. Sweeney, *Cochise, Chiricahua Apache Chief* (1991). D. C. Cole, *The Chiricahua Apache, 1846–1876* (1988), based on a dissertation treating the reservation of 1872–1876, is strong on that subject. Dan L. Thrapp kindly furnished some additional details for the present sketch. An obituary is in the *Tucson Daily Citizen*, 20 Feb. 1914.

JOHN SUGDEN

JEFFRIES, Edward John, Jr. (3 Apr. 1900–2 Apr. 1950), politician, was born in Detroit, Michigan, the son of Edward John Jeffries, an attorney, and Minnie J. Stotts. Raised in a comfortable middle-class home, he graduated from the University of Michigan with a B.A. in 1920 and an LL.B. in 1923. He studied Roman and British common law at Lincoln's Inn in London, England, in 1823 and visited much of postwar Europe before returning one year later to open a Detroit practice with his college roommate Paul E. Krause. In 1929 Jeffries became general counsel for the Maccabees, an influential fraternal insurance society. He held that position for the duration of his life, enabling him to pursue a political career. The following year he married Florence O. Bell, and, after a decade of marriage, they adopted a young son.

Within a year of his wedding, Jeffries began a nonpartisan political career that lasted until his death. In 1931 he won his first election to the Common Council, benefiting from his father's reputation as a liberal recorder's court judge and the reform movement in municipal government launched by the elder Jeffries and fellow judges (including future mayor Frank Murphy). Thereafter, Jeffries served several terms on the council and became its president for 1938–1940.

As a council member during the Great Depression, Jeffries supported most Murphy-led efforts to keep the municipality afloat by budget cuts, including reductions in the pay of city employees, and additional borrowing. He also endorsed the mayor's conflict with bankers, who insisted on full interest payments for municipal debts while Detroit struggled for economic survival. Realizing that New Deal programs alone could save the city, he ascertained both the need for federal aid and the outside threat that it, as well as private moneylenders, posed for local governance.

In 1939 Jeffries defeated incumbent Richard W. Reading to become mayor. He won overwhelmingly against the backdrop of labor strife in the recovering automobile industry and charges of scandal in the police department, which led to more than 100 indictments and several prison sentences, including that of Reading. He called himself "mayor of all the people" and drew votes across race, ethnic, and class lines as a reform candidate promising civic leadership. He genuinely viewed himself as a public servant, embracing his father's nonpartisanship and honesty. However, he shied from the elder Jeffries's crusading style and singular support for the working class, identifying more with the middle class from which he sprang. His belief in orderly, efficient government was reinforced by John C. Lodge, the politically moderate and personally dignified former mayor, fellow councilman, and elder statesman. Progressive and pragmatic, Jeffries believed himself capable of resolving labor-management conflict and reestablishing fiscal responsibility.

In fact, with the aid of a recovering economy, Jeffries revived Detroit. He replaced the police commissioner, city comptroller, and corporation counselor with respected individuals, while also appointing blacks and ethnics to positions of authority and seeing that many more received municipal jobs. His sincere efforts to resolve racial and labor conflict impressed voters, who reelected him over recorder's court judge Joseph A. Gillis in 1941. Nevertheless, Jeffries's first administration hinted at the racial tension that intensified in the face of wartime migration and inadequate housing, recreation, and transportation facilities.

Over the next year and a half, Jeffries proved ineffective when dealing with worsening animosities. Near full employment in a burgeoning defense economy notwithstanding, the races contested job promotions, experienced overcrowded, delapidated, and scarce housing and a congested transportation system, and turned on each other in a series of bloodletting incidents that culminated in the worst urban riot of World War II: 34 dead, 765 injured, $2 million in damage, and 1 million hours of lost production. Stunned by the violence of 20–22 June 1943 and by the criticism of the police department's and his handling of the upheaval, Jeffries turned to the right for political survival. From the August primary until the November election, he engaged in race baiting and scare tactics to defeat Frank Fitzgerald, who was supported by the Congress of Industrial Organizations (CIO) and was guilty of similar innuendos. Rank-and-file unionists defying their leaders and conservatives fearing labor control of city hall supported Jeffries over the circuit court commissioner.

Thereafter, Jeffries suppressed racial violence by enforcing a segregated housing policy, which the federal government endorsed, and by supporting an Interracial Committee, which focused on defusing tension rather than resolving socioeconomic inequities such as lack of black housing and job promotions. In 1945 he conducted another sensational campaign to defeat United Automobile Workers (UAW) officer Richard Frankensteen. The next year, surprisingly and unsuccessfully, Jeffries sought the gubernatorial candidacy of the Republican party. For the first time, he ran as a partisan politician from the largely Democratic city, which doubtlessly contributed to his loss of the mayoralty in 1947 to the well-respected, moderate councilman Eugene I. Van Antwerp. In part, Jeffries lost a record fifth mayoral term because of the uncertainty of the postwar future in a rapidly changing society that sought a complete break with its past. He returned to chambers as a councilman in 1949, having received the second highest number of votes among eighteen candidates.

Despite his expedient political campaigns, Jeffries was a historically significant wartime mayor. He created one of the first permanent interracial committees and presided over the nation's most significant matériel-producing industrial center—the Arsenal of Democracy—as it contributed to the Allied victory. He also established a money-saving city insurance reserve and expanded municipal revenues, rallying other Michigan mayors to pressure the state for a portion of its sales tax. He adopted a citywide zoning code and set aside financing for postwar slum clearance, recreation facilities, and expressways, while also advancing the Detroit Plan for an airport, civic center, and medical center. Although he remained skeptical of big government, he was enthused over Detroit's future. Struggling with war-induced socioeconomic developments that strained the urbanization process, Jeffries accelerated Detroit's shift from city building to suburbanization and hastened, as did the war, its immediate recovery. He supported the Municipal League, endeavoring to address urban problems nationwide. In the long run, however, his efforts, like those in other industrial centers, proved insufficient to stem urban decline. Long before that devolution became apparent, he died of a heart attack while on vacation in Miami Beach, Florida.

• Jeffries's papers are in the Burton Historical Collection of the Detroit Public Library. Robert Conot, *American Odyssey* (1974), is a massive, sometimes episodic overview of Detroit history, and Alan Clive, *State of War* (1979), provides an analysis of the city within the context of World War II; both authors make reference to Jeffries. See August Meier and Elliott Rudwick, *Black Detroit and the Rise of the UAW* (1979), for Jeffries's role in that important subject and Dominic J. Capeci, Jr., and Martha Wilkerson, *Layered Violence* (1991), for his response to the Detroit riot of 1943. Capeci, *Race Relations in Wartime Detroit* (1984), contains the fullest interpretation of Jeffries's background, political philosophy, and earliest mayoral terms. Every local daily carries an obituary of substance, as does the *New York Times*, 3 Apr. 1950.

DOMINIC J. CAPECI, JR.

JEFFRIES, James Jackson (15 Apr. 1875–3 Mar. 1953), professional boxer, was born in Carroll, Ohio, the son of Alexis C. Jeffries, a lay Free Methodist evangelist, and Rebecca Boyer. The family moved in 1882 to a farm in East Los Angeles, California. By the age of fifteen, Jeffries was the best wrestler in a crowd of his rough friends. At age sixteen, he began work as a boilermaker for the Lacey Manufacturing Company of Los Angeles. According to legend, he engaged in his first professional fight in 1893 when he accepted the challenge of an African American named Hank Griffin, a fellow worker who bet a fistful of gold coins that he could defeat anyone in the factory. Jeffries knocked him out in the fourteenth round.

In 1896 Jeffries, who was 6′1½″ and 220 pounds, turned professional. That year he defeated Dan Long for a $1,000 purse in Denver by breaking Long's nose in the second round. He knocked out Eddie Baker in San Francisco in the ninth round. After Johnny Brink, a Los Angeles businessman-boxer, hurt him with a fierce body blow while they were sparring together, Jeffries began to develop his famous crouch in order to protect his stomach and his jaw. He learned other ring techniques as James J. Corbett's sparring partner in Carson City, Nevada. Jeffries later also fared well with Joe Choynski, a tough prize fighter who was to act as his trainer.

In 1899 Jeffries knocked out the world heavyweight champion Robert Fitzsimmons at Coney Island, New York, in the eleventh round, and he retained the title until 1905. Later in 1899 Jeffries fought Tom Sharkey, broke several of Sharkey's ribs, and won a 25-round decision.

Jeffries won one of his most momentous fights in 1900 against Corbett. For nineteen rounds, Corbett outboxed Jeffries. However, Jeffries had more stamina, took advantage of Corbett's fatigue and his carelessness when the crowd roared for blood, and knocked him out in the twenty-third round. In 1901 he knocked out Gus Ruhlin in the fifth round. The following year, in a rematch with Fitzsimmons, Jeffries sustained a broken nose in the eighth round, but knocked Fitzsimmons out one round later. In 1903 he again defeated Corbett and a year later knocked out Jack Munroe in the second round. In 1904 he married a woman from New York known now only as Frieda, a year later retired undefeated, and bought a cattle ranch outside Burbank, California. He relaxed, traveled abroad, and enjoyed the adulation of crowds of visitors from near and far.

Jeffries is best known, however, for coming out of retirement to fight Jack Johnson, America's first black heavyweight champion. Johnson was disliked by most white people in the United States—and elsewhere—and even by many of his fellow blacks, because in addition to defeating all white opponents, he had a white wife and otherwise openly violated aspects of the rampant racial segregation of the times. As a result, a search was conducted for a "Great White Hope" who would vindicate current notions of white supremacy. Jeffries resisted at first, through unwillingness to fight any black; but he avidly answered the call upon being told by boxing promoter George Lewis "Tex" Rickard that the prize money would be $101,000, with 60 percent going to the winner. Before that, Jeffries had rarely earned as much as $5,000 per fight.

The 15-round Johnson-Jeffries championship fight took place on 4 July 1910 in Reno, Nevada, then a frontier village of 10,000. Originally, the event was to be held in San Francisco; but when the governor of California banned the fight, Rickard moved it to Nevada, the only state in which boxing was then legal. Rickard publicized the contest as pitting a slugger (Jeffries) against a boxer (Johnson), and a revered white against a despised black. It has been said that the Johnson-Jeffries fight was the most electrifying purely American event between the San Francisco earthquake of 1906 and Charles Lindbergh's transatlantic flight of 1927. In addition to the 18,000 ticket holders, 2,000 other persons rushed through the fence, paid five dollars each, and caused considerable delay. The 6'3", 200-pound Johnson entered the ring first, boldly flashing his famous gold-toothed smile at the hostile crowd. Then came the 35-year-old Jeffries, soft from too much food and drink, but back down from 300 to 230 pounds, and overly confident.

Accounts of the Johnson-Jeffries fight were telegraphed nationwide and to such locations as the Caribbean, London, Berlin, and South America. The first round was mostly preliminary sparring. But in the second round, Johnson with a left hook paralyzed the right side of Jeffries' face and blurred his vision. Thereafter, it was no contest; Jeffries raged like a bull, goaded by the volubly contemptuous Johnson. By the end of the twelfth round, Johnson was so dazzling that some members of the crowd applauded his efforts, and Jeffries was so bloody that one of his friends at ringside left the scene in tears. Questions remain as to whether Johnson prolonged the torture to create a longer movie or to punish yet another white challenger. In the fifteenth round, the bewildered, helpless Jeffries was floored three times and forced to quit. In retaining the title, Johnson earned $190,000, including film royalties; Jeffries received $117,000. Johnson himself was not victimized by hostile whites in the days following the fight. However, race riots in Arkansas, Delaware, Illinois, Georgia, Kentucky, Louisiana, Missouri, Ne-

braska, New York, Pennsylvania, South Carolina, West Virginia, and elsewhere cost many lives. Congress quickly passed a law making it a federal crime to show the fight films. All the same, the Johnson-Jeffries fight, especially its film rights, did much to show talented black athletes a road to riches and to elevate boxing events from illegal brawls to big business.

Jeffries's professional record was 18 wins (15 by knockout), two draws, and one loss. Jeffries, affectionately known as "Big Jim" and "The Boilermaker," never fought again after his loss to Johnson. He was an occasional promoter and an amateur referee, and he continued profitable alfalfa farming in Burbank. He lost heavily in the 1929 stock market crash but recovered well by shrewd real-estate speculation. His wife was killed in an automobile accident in 1941. Jeffries died in Burbank after an automobile accident. He was elected to *The Ring* magazine's Boxing Hall of Fame in 1954.

• William Inglis, in *Champions Off Guard* (1932), has a chapter on Jeffries, whom he knew personally. The following authorities discuss Jeffries briefly: Harold Rice, *Within the Ropes: Champions in Action* (1946); Nathaniel S. Fleischer, *Heavyweight Championship* (1949); John Duran, *Heavyweight Champions* (1971); Henry Cooper, *The Great Heavyweights* (1978); Randy Roberts, *Papa Jack: Jack Johnson and the Era of White Hopes* (1983); and Jeffrey T. Sammons, *Beyond the Ring: The Role of Boxing in American Society* (1988). Al-Tony Gilmore, *Bad Nigger! The National Impact of Jack Johnson* (1975), discusses racial overtones and exploitation of the Johnson-Jeffries fight, which Sal Fradella, *Jack Johnson* (1990), describes blow by blow. An informative essay is Jerone Bennett, Jr., "Jack Johnson and the Great White Hope," *Ebony*, Apr. 1994, pp. 86, 88, 90, 92, 94, 96. A long obituary, which begins on the front page, is in the *New York Times*, 4 Mar. 1953.

ROBERT L. GALE

JEFFRIES, John (5 Feb. 1745–16 Sept. 1819), physician, surgeon, and the first American to fly, was born in Boston, Massachusetts, the son of David Jeffries, Boston's treasurer for more than thirty years, and Sarah Jaffrey. Jeffries was named for a wealthy uncle who arranged for his early education. He entered Harvard College in 1759, receiving his master of arts with honors in 1763. He studied medicine with James Lloyd, a leading Boston physician. Assigned to attend patients at the Smallpox Hospital, Castle Island, he pioneered a new treatment for the disease that emphasized the reduction of fever.

Jeffries joined the ranks of the best-trained American physicians of his generation when he sailed for Great Britain in May 1768. He enrolled at Marischal College, Aberdeen University, where he was awarded the degree of docter of physic on 1 June 1769. While in Great Britain he supplemented classroom training with practical experience, working as a surgical dresser at Guy's Hospital, London.

Jeffries returned to Boston in 1769 and married Sarah Rhoads the following year. The couple had three children. On 6 March 1770 Jeffries treated the dying

Patrick Carr, who had been wounded in the fighting with British troops the evening before. Called as a witness for the defense at the trial of the officer commanding the troops at the Boston Massacre, Jeffries testified that Carr had remarked that "he really thought that [the British troops] did fire to defend themselves; that he did not blame the man, whoever he was, that shot him" (L. K. Wroth and H. B. Zobel, eds., *Legal Papers of John Adams*, vol. 3 [1965], p. 213n).

Jeffries, the son of a patriot leader and himself an associate of the Sons of Liberty, now began to align himself with the royal government. In 1771 he accepted a post as assistant surgeon attached to a shore-based British naval hospital. As tensions mounted in Boston, Jeffries's friend, Dr. Joseph Warren, urged him to return to the patriot fold. After the battle at Breed's Hill on 17 June 1775, Jeffries is said to have identified Warren's body for General Sir William Howe.

Along with other Loyalists, Jeffries and his family sailed for Halifax, Nova Scotia, in 1775, when the British garrison evacuated Boston. Appointed a surgeon on the staff of the military hospital at Halifax on 24 May 1776, he was promoted to the rank of purveyor general to the hospitals (21 Aug. 1778) and apothecary general (Dec. 1778). In an effort to obtain confirmation of his appointments, Jeffries and his family sailed for England in the spring of 1779. Arriving in London on 2 April, he made the acquaintance of Benjamin Thompson, a Massachusetts Loyalist serving as an American expert on the staff of Lord George Germain, the secretary of state for the colonies.

Thompson embroiled Jeffries in a series of personal and political intrigues. He presented to King George III a set of letters embarrassing to leading American revolutionaries, including Benjamin Franklin, which Jeffries had obtained from his father. Finally, in July 1779, Jeffries was examined by the great English surgeon John Hunter, who approved him for a commission as a surgeon major with the Royal Navy.

Jeffries sailed for North America aboard the HMS *Raleigh* on 4 October 1779. After a lengthy stay in Cork, Ireland, the vessel finally reached Savannah, Georgia, in February 1780. Jeffries served as a fleet medical officer aboard vessels based at Savannah and Charleston, South Carolina, through the summer of 1780, when he received word from Thompson that Jeffries's wife had died suddenly in September. After considerable difficulty, Jeffries was allowed to travel to the fleet headquarters at New York, where he requested permission to return to England to arrange for the care of his children. He served on the fleet medical staff while awaiting a decision and made the acquaintance of Benedict Arnold and other high-ranking officers of the Royal Navy and Army. Refused permission to leave New York, Jeffries sold his medical commission to Joshua Loring, a nonphysician, and sailed for England, arriving on 26 December 1780.

Having installed his children in boarding schools, Jeffries attempted to obtain another government appointment. Accused of having abandoned his post in New York, however, this proved impossible. Instead, he established a private medical practice. Specializing in what would become known as obstetrics and gynecology, he also served the medical needs of the large American Loyalist community in London. He became a familiar figure in the theaters, pleasure gardens, art galleries, and coffeehouses of the city.

Jeffries also pursued amateur scientific interests. On 15 September 1784 he attended a balloon ascension made by Vincenzo Lunardi, secretary to the Neopolitan ambassador, from the artillery ground at Moorfields. A month later he witnessed a flight by the French aeronaut Jean-Pierre-François Blanchard. Determined to make a flight himself, Jeffries approached Blanchard and offered to fund an ascent on which he would fly as a passenger. The two men ascended from the London Rhedarium on 30 November 1784.

His appetite whetted, Jeffries now offered to fund Blanchard's plan for the first aerial voyage across the English Channel. The pair launched from Dover at 1:07 P.M. on 7 January 1785. They returned safely to earth near Ardres, France, almost three hours later, having been forced to jettison all excess weight, including most of their clothing, in an effort to keep the balloon aloft. Blanchard and Jeffries became instant celebrities.

Jeffries had carried a letter across the Channel from his friend and fellow Loyalist William Franklin, residing in London, to Franklin's estranged father, Benjamin Franklin, who headed the American embassy in Paris. Franklin arranged for Jeffries to meet John Paul Jones, the marquis de Lafayette, and John Adams and Abigail Adams and their daughter Abigail, whose first child he would deliver some years later when the family was residing in London. Returning to England, Jeffries was given a pension and honored with membership in the Royal Society.

The relationship between Jeffries and Blanchard could not stand the strain of success. Blanchard charged that Jeffries had attempted to steal the credit for their achievement and remarked that the doctor's account of their flights, *A Narrative of Two Aerial Voyages* (1786), was "filled with lies." After an interview with Blanchard, one London newspaper reported that "the Doctor was incapable of making any [scientific observations], which his companion ascribes to his ignorance, to his being petrified with fear, and to his frequent recourse to the brandy bottle during the voyage" (*Loyd's Evening Post*, 28–30 June 1786). When Blanchard repeated his charges during a visit to Philadelphia in 1793, Jeffries sued his old companion for libel and won.

Jeffries married Hannah Hunt in 1787. The couple would eventually have eleven children. Returning to Boston for a visit after the death of his father in 1789, Jeffries discovered that his Loyalist sympathies had been forgiven, if not completely forgotten. He moved his growing family back to Massachusetts in 1790 but refused to apply for American citizenship. During the War of 1812, Elbridge Gerry, governor of Massachusetts, is said to have remarked that, in the event of a British invasion, he intended to take refuge with John

Jeffries. English troops would surely never burn the home of a loyal subject of the Crown.

After his return to America, Jeffries resumed his role as one of the leading physicians of Boston and emerged as a pioneer in the training of American surgeons. Jeffries, the first American to fly and the physician whom Oliver Wendell Holmes identified as "a leader of medical opinion in America," died at his home in Boston.

• The diaries, letters, and papers of Jeffries are preserved at the Houghton Library, Harvard University. The Massachusetts Historical Society holds an extensive collection of Jeffries family materials. Useful biographical accounts include *New England Journal of Medicine and Surgery*, Jan. 1820, pp. 63–72; *Medical Dissertations of the Massachusetts Medical Society*, vol. 3 (1822), pp. 415–17; *Columbian Centinel* (Boston), 22 Sept. 1819; J. T. L. Jeffries, *The Jeffries of Massachusetts, 1658–1914* (n.d.); and E. A. Jones, *The Loyalists of Massachusetts* (1930). Secondary studies containing accounts of Jeffries's career include Mary Beth Norton, *The British Americans: The Loyalist Exiles in England, 1774–1789* (1972); Phillip Young, *Revolutionary Ladies* (1977); and Tom. D. Crouch, *Eagle Aloft: Two Centuries of the Balloon in America* (1983).

TOM D. CROUCH

JEFFRIES, Zay (22 Apr. 1888–21 May 1965), metallurgist, was born in Willow Lake, Dakota Territory, the son of Johnston Jeffries and Florence Sutton, farmers. In 1890 he moved with his family to Fort Pierre, South Dakota. He received his B.S. in mining engineering from the South Dakota School of Mines in 1910. He worked briefly as an ore analyzer and mine superintendent before accepting a position as an instructor of metallurgy and ore dressing at the Case School of Applied Science in Cleveland, Ohio, in 1911. That same year he married Frances Schrader, with whom he had two children.

At the time metallurgists knew practically nothing about grain structure, the arrangement of the small, randomly-distributed crystals of varying sizes from which solid metals are composed, but they suspected that many cases of metal failure were related to grain structure. Jeffries explored this phenomenon by using X-ray diffraction analysis, a technique European scientists had developed to examine the atoms of salt crystals. Over the next five years he developed the "Jeffries' method" for measuring grain size and demonstrated that variations in the size of individual grains and the manner in which they interface determine the physical properties of solid metals. These findings, published in "Grain Size Measurements in Metals and Importance of Such Information" (*Transactions of the Faraday Society* 12, pt. 1 [1916]), contributed significantly to the scientific study of metallurgy and earned Jeffries a promotion to assistant professor that same year.

In 1914 Jeffries began consulting for several Cleveland manufacturers, including the General Electric (GE) Company's Cleveland Wire Works, which retained him to solve problems in the manufacture of tungsten wire for use in electric light-bulb filaments. By developing new techniques for forming and hardening the wire, thereby decreasing its susceptibility to breaking, he contributed to a significant increase in filament production. In 1915 he solved a major problem involving the manufacture of fuse body castings for the Russian army by the Aluminum Castings Company (ACC); he became ACC's director of research the next year.

In 1917 Jeffries resigned from Case to consult full time for GE and ACC and to complete his formal education. He received a D.Sc. degree from Harvard University in 1918, after satisfying all the requirements except for a one-year residency while teaching and working in Cleveland. That same year GE asked him to find a way to prevent the filament's tungsten molecules from migrating to the glass bulb, thereby darkening the glass, which dimmed the light, and thinning the filament, which reduced the bulb's life. He soon discovered that the heat of electrical current alters the grain structure of tungsten and that foreign elements trapped within tungsten's molecular structure partly determine its strength. These findings, published in "The Metallography of Tungsten" (*Transactions of the American Institute of Mining and Metallurgical Engineers* 60 [1919]: 588–656), resulted in major improvements in the way filaments were produced and the adoption of tungsten as the standard filament material for light bulbs.

In 1920 Jeffries became consulting metallurgist for the Aluminum Company of America (Alcoa) when it acquired ACC's assets. In 1921 he and Robert S. Archer, his assistant at Alcoa, developed the slip interference theory of metal-hardening. They postulated that slip planes within individual crystals permanently harden the edges of adjacent planes when shearing forces cause them to slide against one another. This theory contributed to a better understanding of metal strength and hardness and stimulated further discoveries in that area. Between 1923 and 1926 the partners were awarded patents for seven different aluminum alloys and coauthored *The Science of Metals* (1924), the first American textbook of broad metallurgical importance.

In 1925 Jeffries became the technical director of GE's Incandescent Lamp Department (ILD) at its National Lamp Works in Cleveland. In 1932 he also became president of the Carboloy Company, a GE subsidiary that manufactured cutting tools tipped with an alloy composed of cobalt and tungsten carbide. In addition to being able to machine steel much faster than conventional cutting tools, Carboloy's tools were the only ones capable of machining the new aluminum alloys. In 1936 Jeffries terminated his relationship with Alcoa to devote himself to ILD and Carboloy; his work on product development and improvement at the latter company resulted in cutting tools of such exceptional value to the Allies during World War II that the U.S. government awarded him its Medal for Merit in 1948.

Jeffries further contributed to the Allied war effort by participating in the Manhattan Project as a member of the Metallurgical Laboratory's advisory board. In 1944 he headed a "Met Lab" committee that wrote "Prospectus on Nucleonics," also known as the "Jeffries Report." This report coined the term "nucleon," meaning protons and neutrons collectively, and addressed the future of "nucleonics," its term for scientific and industrial endeavors of a nuclear nature. The report also offered one of the first assessments of the potential effect of atomic energy on international relations.

In 1945 Jeffries moved to Pittsfield, Massachusetts, to become vice president and general manager of GE's new chemistry department. He oversaw GE's nonelectrical manufacturing facilities and its contract to produce plutonium at the Atomic Energy Commission's (AEC) Hanford Works in Washington State until he retired in 1950. He then consulted on a part-time basis, served as director-general of the World Metallurgical Congresses in 1951 and 1957, and chaired the Department of Defense's Technical Advisory Panel on Materials from 1954 to 1959. He died in Pittsfield.

Jeffries received the James Douglas Medal of the American Institute of Mining and Metallurgical Engineers (1927), the Albert Sauveur Achievement Award of the American Society of Metals (1935) and its Gold Medal (1943), the first Powder Metallurgy Medal of the Stevens Institute of Technology and the Francis J. Clamer Silver Medal of the Franklin Institute (1945), and the John Fritz Gold Medal in 1946. He was elected president of the American Society of Metals in 1929 and a fellow of the National Academy of Sciences in 1936.

Jeffries's slip interference theory and his studies of grain structure and tungsten were important theoretical contributions to American metallurgy. His work with aluminum alloys, tungsten filaments, and tungsten carbide cutting tools made important practical contributions to American manufacturing. His work for the Metallurgical Laboratory and the AEC was useful in the development of nuclear energy.

• Jeffries's papers are located in the archives of the American Philosophical Society in Philadelphia, Pa. A brief autobiography is "Autobiographical Notes of a Metallurgist," in *The Sorby Centennial Symposium on the History of Metallurgy*, ed. Cyril Stanley Smith (1965), pp. 109–20. His biography, including a complete bibliography of his work, is William D. Mogerman, *Zay Jeffries* (1973). Obituaries are in the *New York Times*, 22 May 1965, and the *Journal of Metals* 17 (Sept. 1965).

CHARLES W. CAREY, JR.

JELLIFF, John (30 July 1813–2 July 1893), furniture designer and manufacturer, was born in Saugatuck, Connecticut, the son of Hezekiah Jelliff and Nancy Bennett, farmers. In 1828 Jelliff was apprenticed by his parents to Alonzo W. Anderson, a wood-carver in New York City. Two years later his apprenticeship was transferred to cabinetmakers Lemuel M. and Daniel B. Crane in Newark, New Jersey. Jelliff was made a freeman in Newark in 1835. He married Mary Marsh of Elizabeth, New Jersey, in 1836; they had ten children, three of whom died in childhood.

Jelliff started his own furniture-making firm in 1836, in partnership with Thomas L. Vantilburg. The firm advertised in the earliest Newark city directories as being "Manufacturers and dealers in Cabinet Furniture, Mahogany Chairs, Sofas, Mattresses, etc." This was not the ideal time to start a business in Newark. A great fire ravaged the city in 1836, followed by the national financial panic of 1837, which further strained the economic partnership of Jelliff & Vantilburg. The firm struggled along until 1843, when the partnership was dissolved, and Jelliff opened his own business on Newark's Broad Street. He described himself in 1844, after the hard early years, as "where I began in the world—penniless, but out of debt" (Dietz, "Edwin Van Antwerp's Jelliff Furniture," p. 913, note 6). In the R. G. Dun & Co. credit ledgers of 1845 Jelliff was given a similar assessment, "good character, industrious, embarrassed but improved; done a good business the last year." From this point forward the firm grew and prospered without faltering.

Newark was incorporated as a city in 1836, having been founded by Puritans from Connecticut in 1666. Once it got back on its feet after the fire and depression of the late 1830s, the city became a Victorian boomtown. Beer brewing, silversmithing, jewelry making, and leather tanning were among the major industries. Only nine miles from New York City, Newark prospered and grew, becoming one of the richest and most diversified manufacturing centers of nineteenth-century America. In the aftermath of the panic of 1837, Jelliff found himself to be the leading player in the city's small furniture industry. His success and reputation grew with the city's prosperity.

Throughout the 1840s and 1850s Jelliff & Co. designed and produced rosewood, mahogany, and walnut furniture in the prevailing fashion of the time: neorococo, Elizabethan, gothic, and other romantic styles. In 1854 Jelliff took on a business partner, Henry H. Miller. During this period the firm's clientele was probably local, owing to the city's growth and industrialization and to the consequent increase in demand for fine household furniture. Old-guard Protestant Dutch and English families were refitting their homes with new business-based wealth, and Newark's fast-growing population of prosperous Germans (Catholic, Lutheran, and Jewish) and Irish Catholics created a growing market for fine-quality locally made goods. New Jersey's first synagogue and Catholic cathedral were both built around 1850, and Jelliff's firm was undoubtedly involved in furnishing them both. (The original bishop's cathedra from St. Patrick's Pro-Cathedral is still in place; the synagogue is no longer extant.) By 1852 the Dun credit ledgers were giving Jelliff glowing reports, describing him as "industrious and economical, has gradually gained an excellent reputation for taste and workmanship and has accumulated considerable property" (vol. 20, p. 65). By the end of the 1850s John Jelliff & Co. had become the leading furniture manufacturer in Newark, a position it maintained until its demise in 1890.

Jelliff & Co.'s furniture probably began to gain a reputation outside the Newark area after the Civil War, when eastern products were shipped west and south by railroad in ever-increasing quantities. The position of the major New York City railroad terminus near Newark in Jersey City placed Jelliff's products comfortably at the gateway between Manhattan and the rest of the United States. New York, having the most direct access to European fashion, was the style setter for the nation throughout the century. As cities and towns grew up in the Midwest and West, there was a growing demand for "New York" furniture. Jelliff appears to have taken advantage of this demand by using New York City furniture wholesalers, such as M. & H. Schrenkeisen, and their nationwide distribution system. While furniture in Jelliff's earlier romantic styles has remained largely in the Northeast, his rosewood parlor suites in the neo-Grec style newly fashionable in the late 1860s have turned up in every corner of the country. These parlor sets were purchased for high-style townhouses and villas in northeastern cities like New York and Meriden, Connecticut, and in cities as far west as Chicago and Evansville, Indiana. Parlor sets consisting of—at minimum—a sofa, two armchairs, and four side chairs, feature elaborate quasi-architectural crests in solid carved rosewood or walnut, ornamented with inset plaques of mother-of-pearl, bronze, marquetry, and even painted porcelain. Most distinctive are the Roman-profiled female heads and bearded warriors that form the armrests for his seating furniture. It is unlikely that Jelliff invented this design feature, which probably owes its origins to French designers of the 1850s. Other manufacturers in New York and the Midwest also produced these caryatid-armed parlor sets, but the style has come to be associated with the Jelliff factory's output. Today nearly every sofa and armchair featuring any sort of classical head as carved decoration is referred to as "Jelliff type."

In his *Industrial Interests of Newark, N.J.* (1874), William Ford reports that "fully one half of the sales [of Jelliff & Co.] are made outside of Newark, and largely to citizens of New York City. . . . In addition, sales are made in Washington, Richmond and farther South" (quoted in Johnson, pp. 257, 260). By 1874 the Jelliff factory in Newark had grown threefold from its 1860 status, encompassing 40,000 square feet, employing forty-five men, and doing an annual business of $100,000. The company was known for "parlor, library, dining room, and chamber furniture of all descriptions, from medium grades to the most expensive and highly finished products of the art" (Johnson, p. 260). In all probability the parlor sets of Jelliff & Co. that made their way into southern and midwestern parlors were purchased as "New York" furniture. In Jelliff's own lifetime his furniture may have been well known all over the country, but outside the industry and his home town, his company's name was not.

Jelliff began to withdraw from active furniture making in the 1860s, owing to a stomach disorder. He did not retire completely until 1868, and he then remained active with the firm as an adviser until 1890. With Jelliff's retirement, his longtime business partner changed the name to Henry H. Miller, successor to John Jelliff & Co. In 1886 Jelliff was honored at a dinner celebrating his fiftieth anniversary in the furniture industry, an event written up in the furniture trade periodical the *Trade Bureau*. Jelliff died at his Italianate villa on Johnson Avenue in Newark.

Scholarly interest in Jelliff began in the mid-1920s, when the first pieces associated with the firm came to the collections of the Newark Museum from descendants of the original owners. As interest in Victorian design grew in the 1960s, culminating in the Metropolitan Museum's exhibition *Nineteenth-Century America* in 1970, Jelliff's name became as synonymous with the neo-Grec style as John Belter's was with the neorococo style. Subsequent research and publication over the years have expanded understanding of Jelliff as an entrepreneur and designer. Growing understanding of industrial practices in the American furniture trade have placed him in the context of the larger American furniture industry.

One of the most celebrated figures in the decorative arts of Victorian America, Jelliff rose from obscure apprenticeship to leadership in the nineteenth-century American furniture industry, though Jelliff himself remains something of a mystery. His firm was the most important furniture manufacturer in New Jersey in its day. It produced fashionable, high-quality furniture that earned Jelliff a strong reputation in his lifetime and even today links his name with the style of America's post–Civil War years. Surviving examples of Jelliff & Co.'s output and growing interest in the Victorian past have brought his firm historical celebrity in the twentieth century.

• The Newark Museum houses the largest single grouping of Jelliff's furniture, ranging from the 1850s to the 1880s, as well as one of two known labeled pieces by his apprenticeship masters Lemuel and Daniel Crane. A large collection of pencil sketches and drawings in Jelliff's hand survive in the museum archives, demonstrating both his direct influence in the design of his company's furniture and the range of styles the firm produced in this period. Also in the museum is a pencil illustration of Jelliff's Newark home drawn by one of his grandsons, along with a silhouette of Jelliff and family. For information on Jelliff, see the R. G. Dun and Company Collection, N.J., vols. 20 and 21, housed at the Baker Library, Harvard University Graduate School of Business Administration, Cambridge, Mass. Also useful are Ulysses G. Dietz, "A Major New Piece in the Jelliff Puzzle," *Antiques*, May 1986, pp. 1096–99; Dietz, "Edwin Van Antwerp's Jelliff Furniture," *Antiques*, Apr. 1990, pp. 906–13; and G. Stewart Johnson, "John Jelliff, Cabinetmaker," *Antiques*, Aug. 1972, pp. 256–61.

ULYSSES G. DIETZ

JELLIFFE, Smith Ely (27 Oct. 1886–25 Sept. 1945), neurologist, psychoanalyst, and medical editor, was born in New York City, the son of William Munson

Jelliffe and Susan Emma Kitchell, both teachers. Jelliffe entered the civil engineering program at Brooklyn Polytechnic Institute and left without graduating in 1886 to enroll in the College of Physicians and Surgeons in New York City. He received his M.D. with honors in 1889 and interned for a year at St. Mary's Hospital, Brooklyn, after which he traveled to Europe for a year. There he studied medicine and botany and visited cultural and historical sites. On his return in 1891, Jelliffe opened a general practice in his parents' home in Brooklyn. To pay off his debts he did part-time clinical and pathological work in a hospital. His botanical studies in Europe had also qualified him to be a sanitary inspector for the Brooklyn Board of Health and to teach materia medica and botany at the Brooklyn College of Pharmacy at night. In 1894 Jelliffe married his longtime fiancée, Helena Dewey Leeming. The couple moved to New York City where they had five children. A year after his wife's sudden death in 1916, he married Belinda Dobson; they had no children.

In 1895 Jelliffe set up a practice in New York City and joined the staff of the Vanderbilt Neurological Clinic. Aided by his wife, Helena, he wrote anonymous editorial material and book reviews for various medical journals until about 1899. He was also named an instructor in pharmacognosy and materia medica at the New York College of Pharmacy in 1895. To advance his position there Jelliffe returned to Brooklyn Polytechnic to complete his A.B. in general studies in 1896; in 1899 he received a Ph.D. in botany from Columbia University with a thesis on the flora of Long Island. Jelliffe's early publications dealt with botany and pharmacology, and from 1897 to 1901 he edited the *Journal of Pharmacology*, which was published by the New York College of Pharmacy. During the summer of 1896, when his practice was almost at a standstill, and he had no teaching obligations, Jelliffe worked at the Binghamton (N.Y.) State Hospital, where he became increasingly interested in psychiatry. The following two summers were also spent at state institutions. In 1899 he began editorial work on the *Journal of Nervous and Mental Diseases*, a leading monthly in neurology and psychiatry and the official organ of the American Neurological Association. In 1902 he became its owner and managing editor. Recognized for his neurological knowledge and increasing psychiatric skills, Jelliffe often acted as a medical expert on insanity in court cases until the 1930s.

Continuing to expand his psychiatric knowledge, Jelliffe studied with Emil Kraepelin, a pioneer in psychiatric classification, for three months in Munich, Germany, in 1906 and again in 1907. In 1908 he spent a full year abroad, working with Georg Ziehen, one of Germany's leading neurologists, in Berlin for six months and with Jules Déjerine, the preeminent French neurologist, in Paris for six months. When he returned home Jelliffe adapted his neurological practice to include psychiatry and later psychoanalysis. In 1907 Jelliffe gave up teaching pharmacology, and until 1913 he served as clinical professor of mental disease at

Fordham College's medical school. In 1912 he also set up a special series of lectures on neurology and psychiatry, to which he invited many foreign speakers, including Carl G. Jung. Jung's presence at the series is credited with precipitating the break between Jung and Sigmund Freud. Freud viewed Jung's first major step on his own as abrogating his responsibilities to the psychoanalytic movement.

Jelliffe belonged to a large number of professional societies and was often invited to address them. He earned an international reputation as a specialist in nervous and mental diseases and was honored by foreign society memberships. He was, however, repeatedly passed over for leadership positions until 1929–1930, when he was elected president of the American Neurological Association. His writings on psychoanalysis and psychosomatic medicine had put him outside the circle of conventional neurologists and psychiatrists. As one of the first American gentiles to become a psychoanalyst he stood apart, and within psychoanalytic circles he was a nonconformist who continued to use lay analysts, under his supervision, well into the 1920s. This contradicted the position of most American analysts, who were trying to force the psychoanalytic movement to operate within strictly medical channels. Jelliffe also honored variant analysts such as Alfred Adler, Constantin von Monakow, Sándor Ferenczi, and Jung when they were no longer acceptable to the local psychoanalytic society. Once he became interested in psychoanalysis, Jelliffe sought to discover the psychic determinants of organic pathology. This effort to weld Freudian psychic mechanisms to organic disease processes earned him the title of the "Father of Psychosomatic Medicine." This too set him apart from the profession at large.

By his own account, Jelliffe had no talent for teaching, and produced no protégés to carry on his message. While his publications and lectures sometimes inspired, they were often too turgid and unsystematic in form. His influence lay in conveying the ideas of others, for example, by translating Paul Dubois's *The Psychic Treatment of Nervous Disorders* in 1905, which gave impetus to the psychotherapy movement in American medicine. Jelliffe made his greatest contribution to the medical profession as a medical editor. From 1900 to 1906 he served as editor of the weekly *Medical News* and as coeditor of its successor, the *New York Medical Journal*, from 1906 to 1908. From 1902 to 1917 Jelliffe shared the editorship of the *Journal of Nervous and Mental Diseases* with William Spiller, an organic neurologist, who edited the original articles while Jelliffe took charge of the book reviews. When Spiller left, Jelliffe handled all the editorial duties until 1945. Aware that the vast majority of neurologists and psychiatrists were disturbed by the inclusion of psychoanalytic articles in the journal, Jelliffe and William Alanson White founded and coedited the *Psychoanalytic Review* in 1913 for the publication of this material, making it the first English language psychoanalytic periodical. Despite his intentions to the contrary, Jelliffe soon reverted to carrying some psychoanalytic material in the *Journal*. In reaction, the American Neurological Association made the new *Archives of Neurology and Psychiatry* its official organ in 1919.

In 1907 Jelliffe founded the Nervous and Mental Disease Publishing Company, which published the *Journal*, the *Psychoanalytic Review*, and the *Nervous and Mental Disease Monograph Series*. The latter issued sixty-nine volumes between 1907 and 1943, mostly translations of obscure but important neurological works and new psychoanalytic literature. Jelliffe had become a recognized authority in America for his unparalleled knowledge of neurological literature. He also influenced American medical practice through his textbook, *Diseases of the Nervous System*, coauthored with White, the first major textbook to integrate neurological and psychiatric thought. Six editions appeared between 1915 and 1935. Although he enjoyed a vigorous and energetic life, Jelliffe suffered in his later years from Paget's disease. He died at his summer home in Huletts Landing, New York, on Lake George.

• The bulk of Jelliffe's correspondance can be found in the Manuscript Division of the Library of Congress, and several hundred letters written from Europe in 1890–1891 are in the New York Academy of Science. Useful autobiographical accounts of Jelliffe include "Psychotherapy in Modern Medicine," *Long Island Medical Journal* 24 (1930): 152–61; "Glimpses of a Freudian Odyssey," *Psychoanalytic Quarterly* 2 (1933): 318–29; and "The Editor Himself and His Adopted Child," *Journal of Nervous and Mental Diseases* 89 (1939): 545–74. Bibliographies of Jelliffe's work are in Nolan D. C. Lewis, "Smith Ely Jelliffe: The Man and Scientist," *Journal of Nervous and Mental Diseases* 106 (1947): 234–53, and Alexander Grinstein, *The Index of Psychoanalytic Writings*, vol. 2 (1957). Major secondary accounts include John C. Burnham, *Jelliffe. American Psychoanalyst and Physician*, published with William McGuire, ed., *His Correspondance with Sigmund Freud and C. G. Jung* (1983); Lewis, "Smith Ely Jelliffe. 1866–1945. Psychosomatic Medicine in America," in *Psychoanalytic Pioneers*, ed. Franz Alexander, Samuel Eisenstein, and Martin Grotjahn (1966), pp. 142–59; David Krasner, *Smith Ely Jelliffe and the Development of American Psychosomatic Medicine* (1984); and Karl Menninger and George Devereaux, "Smith Ely Jelliffe—Father of Psychosomatic Medicine in America," in *Psychoanalysis in America*, ed. Murray Herbert Sherman (1966), pp. 31–46. For background see Clarence Paul Oberndorf, *A History of Psychoanalysis in America* (1953); Burnham, *Psychoanalysis and American Medicine, 1894–1918* (1967); Frederick Tilney and Smith Ely Jelliffe, eds., *Semi Centennial Anniversary Volume of the American Neurological Association* (1924); and William Alanson White, *The Autobiography of a Purpose* (1938). Obituaries include Clarence Charles Burlingame, *American Journal of Psychiatry* 102 (1945): 430–31; Abraham Arden Brill, *Journal of Nervous and Mental Diseases* 106 (1947): 228–32; Menninger, *Bulletin of the Menninger Clinic* 9 (1945): 177–78; Oberndorf, *International Journal of Psychoanalysis* 26 (1945): 181–82; and Gregory Zilboorg, *Psychoanalytic Quarterly* 15 (1946): 1–5.

DAVID KRASNER

JEMISON, Alice Mae Lee (9 Oct. 1901–6 Mar. 1964), American Indian political activist and journalist, was born at Silver Creek, New York, near the Cattaraugus Reservation of the Seneca, one of the Six Nations of the Iroquois. She was the daughter of Daniel A. Lee, a cabinetmaker of Cherokee descent, and Elnora E. Seneca, a member of a prominent Seneca family. Lee's uncle, Cornelius Seneca, was one of the most prominent and respected Seneca leaders of the twentieth century. The tradition among the matrilineal Seneca of women exercising significant, if not formal, political influence undoubtedly shaped Lee's character and career.

Lee's youthful ambition to become an attorney was frustrated by her family's poverty. Her formal education ended with her graduation in 1919 from Silver Creek High School, where she had studied debating and journalism. That same year she married Le Verne Leonard Jemison, a local Seneca steelworker. They were separated nine years later, and Alice Jemison thereafter had to support her mother and her two children. Living on the Cattaraugus Reservation through the 1920s, she struggled to provide for her family, working in a factory and as a clerk, peddler, dressmaker, practical nurse, stone and gravel hauler, and as a legal researcher for a Buffalo attorney. In 1929 she became the secretary to, and researcher for, Ray Jimerson, then president of the Seneca Nation. The next year Jemison worked for the U.S. Bureau of the Census, gathering information on the reservation.

A turning point in Jemison's life came with the Marchand murder case of 1930, the most notorious event in Buffalo's history since the 1901 assassination of President William McKinley. Two American Indian women were accused of killing a white woman, Clothilde Marchand, the wife of noted artist and museum designer Jules Henri Marchand. Jemison moved to Buffalo to work with Iroquois leaders who were seeking federal intervention in the case and challenging disparaging portrayals of Indians. Jemison wrote letters to public figures and began writing for the *Buffalo Evening News*. The two women were convicted, but after serving time in prison they were freed because of legal questions involving the fairness of their trial. The experience Jemison gained in lobbying and publicity and the contacts she made in the journalistic world became her springboard for a new career. By 1932 her articles were being syndicated by the North American Newspaper Alliance and were reaching a wide audience.

In 1934 Jemison moved to Washington, D.C., and began writing for the *Washington Star*. She also served as a lobbyist for the Seneca Nation and monitored congressional activities on Indian affairs. As both a staunch defender of Iroquois treaty rights and a political conservative, she was suspicious of Indian policies emanating from the federal government. Influenced by the thinking of Carlos Montezuma, the noted Yavapai physician and pan-Indian leader, Jemison argued for the abolition of the Bureau of Indian Affairs (BIA), a frequently mismanaged federal agency. Objecting to the agency's bureaucratic administration and paternalism, she declared that Indians "consider that we are in a better position than anyone else to know what we need."

In addition to her objection on principle to the BIA, Jemison criticized the reformist policies proposed by Franklin Roosevelt's commissioner of Indian affairs, John Collier. Jemison viewed the far-reaching Indian Reorganization Act of 1934—which, among other things, ended the allotment system and provided for the organization, under federal auspices, of tribal governments through formal elections and constitutions—as simply adding new levels of bureaucracy to Indian life and as intruding on tribal sovereignty. The Indian Reorganization Act, she complained, "provides only one form of government for the Indian and that is communal or cooperative form of living." Collier, she asserted, should "give us the right to continue to live under our old tribal customs if we wanted to."

Jemison's criticisms found receptive audiences, particularly among her own Iroquois people, many of whom regarded the provisions of the law as unsuited to their circumstances. Many Indians, too, objected to the provisions for tribal plebiscites, required with the acceptance of the terms of the act. They believed the act undermined boycott strategies by requiring a majority of adult Indians actually to vote against the Indian Reorganization Act to keep it from going into effect. Jemison furthermore accused the BIA of manipulating congressional hearings on the legislation by looking more favorably on requests for travel funds from the act's supporters than from its opponents.

Throughout the debate over the "Indian New Deal" Jemison served as spokeswoman for the American Indian Federation, a national organization headed by Joseph Bruner, a Creek Indian from Oklahoma. She edited the federation's newspaper, *First American*, and served as the organization's major lobbyist on Capitol Hill. From 1934 until her resignation from the federation in 1939, Jemison appeared at more congressional hearings on Indian affairs than any other Native American. She constantly urged representatives to dispense with the Indian Reorganization Act, remove Collier from office, abolish the BIA, and end federal intervention in tribal affairs. Among other things, she attacked Collier's implementation of a herd-reduction program among the Navajo as authoritarian and opposed the building of the Blue Ridge Parkway through Cherokee land in North Carolina.

Jemison sometimes went to extremes in her attacks, labeling her adversaries within the federal government as communists and atheists. She was in turn embraced by right-wing critics of the New Deal, including the Daughters of the American Revolution and the Silver Shirts, an American fascist organization that admired Hitler and Mussolini. She appeared before the House Committee on Un-American Activities in 1938 and 1940 together with self-styled fascists and, because she was impoverished through much of this period, even accepted financial support from one such source. Placed under FBI observation as early as 1938, Jemison was branded as an Indian fascist by Interior Department officials. In spite of her opposition to the drafting of American Indians under the Selective Service Act of 1940, she was able to satisfy federal authorities regarding her loyalty well enough to secure government employment in the Bureau of the Census during the Second World War.

After the war, Jemison remained in Washington and continued to call for the BIA's abolition while opposing the transfer of criminal jurisdiction over Indians in New York from federal to state government. In 1953 she revived the *First American*, which she edited and published until 1955, once more covering Indian policy on Capitol Hill. She died in Washington, leaving her militance as a legacy to the Red Power Movement of the 1970s. Jemison was buried in the United Mission Cemetery on the Cattaraugus Reservation.

• Jemison's correspondence can be found in BIA Central Classified Files, 1907–1939, and in the Office File of Commissioner John Collier, RG 75, National Archives. Some documents relating to her, including a résumé, are located in the Indian Collection, Buffalo and Erie County Historical Society. Her career is discussed in detail in Laurence M. Hauptman, *The Iroquois and the New Deal* (1981) and *The Iroquois Struggle for Survival: World War II to Red Power* (1986). For a revisionist view of her organization, see Hauptman, "The American Indian Federation and the Indian New Deal: A Reinterpretation," *Pacific Historical Review* 52 (Nov. 1983): 378–402. Jemison's FBI file was obtained through the Freedom of Information and Privacy Act; a death certificate was furnished by the District of Columbia Department of Public Health. For a different view of Jemison and the American Indian Federation, see Kenneth Philp, *John Collier's Crusade for Indian Reform, 1920–1954* (1977), and Alison Bernstein, *American Indians and World War II* (1991). An obituary is in the *Buffalo Evening News*, 10 Mar. 1964.

LAURENCE M. HAUPTMAN

JEMISON, Mary (1743?–1833), captive, was born on a ship en route to colonial Pennsylvania from Ireland, the daughter of Thomas Jemison and Jane Erwin, a Protestant couple of Scotch-Irish background. The family settled on a farm in Franklin Township, Adams County, in south central Pennsylvania about ten miles northwest of present-day Gettysburg.

On 5 April 1758, when Mary was about fifteen, the Jemison family and visiting friends were attacked by Shawnee and French forces during the French and Indian War. By the second day of her capture her parents, two brothers, a sister, and the visitors were killed. Only she and the friends' young boy were spared. Two other brothers escaped. On 12 April, the eighth day of her captivity, the Shawnees had marched her to Fort Duquesne (soon to be Fort Pitt, later Pittsburgh) at the junction of the Monongahela and Allegheny rivers. There she was given to two Seneca women. The women continued with her down the Ohio River to a Seneca camp near the Sciota (Scioto) River. There she became their sister by means of a ritual adoption.

In 1760, with the urging of her new sisters, she married Sheninjee, a Delaware. Later in life when she told her story to James E. Seaver, she spoke of her husband as "a noble man; large in stature; elegant in appearance; generous in his conduct; courageous in war; a friend to peace, and a great lover of justice. . . . [He] soon gained my affection; and strange as it may seem, I loved him!" In 1761 she gave birth to a child who died shortly thereafter. In 1762 their second child was born.

Her sisters wanted to return to Genishau, a large Seneca town on the Genesee River in New York, and so they began, with the help of their brothers, a 600-mile trek through Ohio and Pennsylvania and into west central New York. Sheninjee began the trip and was to rejoin the party, but he died that year. The small Seneca entourage including Jemison and her baby arrived in western New York, where they moved in with Jemison's new mother. Within a year (c. 1762–1763) she remarried, this time to a man of her own choosing, Hiokatoo, a Seneca warrior many years her senior. With him she had six children.

When the American Revolution came to the country of the Six Nations Iroquois, two of those tribes sided with the rebelling colonies, but the Senecas and three other tribes cast their lot with their then traditional ally, Great Britain. Jemison saw the war for independence from the Seneca side of the frontier. She recollects pounding samp for Colonel John Butler and Joseph Brandt (Thayendanehea), Mohawk commander. Her account of the war and its aftermath is one of the few "Indian" sources of the impact of the Revolution on native people. It depicts the fury of the expedition of John Sullivan as it came through Iroquois country and burned cornfields and towns in reprisal for British and Iroquois raids along the Pennsylvania and New York frontiers.

In the Treaty of Big Tree (Geneseo, 15 Sept. 1797) following the Revolution all the land west of the Genesee River was sold. With some few exceptions Senecas were moved onto reservations, which developed into what one historian has called "slums in the wilderness." Through negotiations and with the help of her brother Kau-jises-tau-ge-au (Black Coals), Jemison was given the Gardow tract, 17,927 acres of prime river property along the Genesee near present-day Castile. On 9 April 1817 the legislature of the state of New York passed an act naturalizing Mary Jemison and giving her title to the land.

Although Jemison and her family owned land, the loss of a spiritual, economic, and moral base in the native community led to an increase in alcoholism. In 1811 and 1812 two of Jemison's sons were killed in alcohol-related deaths. Jemison lived on her land on the Gardow flats with her family until she sold or lost it to white settlers and finally moved with her daughters to the Indian community at Buffalo Creek in the mid-1820s, where she died.

Jemison's story became one of the most popular captivity narratives in U.S. history, going into over twenty editions in its first hundred years. The work was first published by James E. Seaver as *A Narrative of the Life of Mrs. Mary Jemison* (1824). Seaver met with Jemison for three days in November 1823. Although the book that resulted is hardly a word-for-word rendering of Jemison and includes additions and florid language that are hardly in the style of a bilingual frontier woman, it is, however, the best account we have of Jemison's life.

After Seaver became sick and died in 1827, the narrative was subsequently republished in increasingly supplemented and ornate editions, first by his brother William Seaver, then by small printers and larger publishers on both sides of the Atlantic, then by businessman and philanthropist William Prior Letchworth, and in many editions by Charles Delamater Vail for the New York Scenic and Historic Preservation Society. *Indian Captive: The Story of Mary Jemison* (1941) became a popular and prize-winning children's version of Jemison's story written by Lois Lenski.

The compelling story was prized as an exotic tale of the New York frontier, a historical and ethnographic window into the past, and a dramatic story of a remarkable woman's life. In many ways, however, the adoption of Jemison by Senecas was a common custom among Iroquoian and other Native Americans of the Northeast. It was carried out on enemy women and children as part of a longtime practice of "mourning war" used on all enemies, regardless of race or culture, and predating European contact. Jemison was one of a number of captives who chose not to return to white society following both the French and Indian War and the American Revolution.

Mary Jemison is still both a heroine and a legend in upstate New York. A sculpture of her and her baby on their trek to New York commissioned by Letchworth from sculptor Henry K. Bush-Brown, cast in bronze and dedicated in 1910, stands in Castile at New York's Letchworth State Park. Just as earlier white pioneers claimed Jemison as "the White Woman of the Genesee," today Seneca and Iroquois people claim her as their own, know her story, and see her life as a testament to the enduring power of Seneca life, Seneca women's lives, and Iroquois survival in times of change.

• There are few manuscript materials for Mary Jemison and no known original draft copy of Seaver's narrative. However, there are collections of newspaper articles and antiquarian pieces in the William Prior Letchworth Museum in Castile, N.Y. The Reverend Charles Delamater Vail's edition of James E. Seaver, *A Narrative of the Life of Mary Jemison: The White Woman of the Genesee*, 22d ed. (1925), has abundant notes on many details of New York history and Jemison's life. A complete bibliography of Jemison pieces and associated primary and secondary literature may be found, along with an introductory essay on Jemison and the Seaver narrative, in June Namias, ed., *A Narrative of the Life of Mrs. Mary Jemison* (1992).

An extended essay on Jemison is chap. 5, "Mary Jemison: The Evolution of One Captive's Story," in Namias, *White Captives: Gender and Ethnicity on the American Frontier* (1993). Other writings on Jemison include Susan Walsh, "'With Them Was My Home': Native American Autobiography," and "A Narrative of the Life of Mrs. Mary Jemison," *American Literature* 64, no. 1 (Mar. 1992): 49–70; extended commentary in Annette Kolodny, *The Land before Her: Fantasy and Experience of the American Frontiers, 1630–1860*

(1984); Dawn Lander Gherman, "From Parlour to Tepee: The White Squaw on the American Frontier" (Ph.D. diss., Univ. of Massachusetts, 1975); and Richard Slotkin, *Regeneration through Violence: The Mythology of the American Frontier, 1600–1860* (1973).

For a history of the Iroquois and the meaning of captivity and adoption, see Daniel K. Richter, *The Ordeal of the Longhouse: The Peoples of the Iroquois League in the Era of European Colonization* (1992). For a focus on the years of the Senecas in the time of Mary Jemison, see Anthony F. C. Wallace, *The Death and Rebirth of the Seneca* (1972). For another analysis of white captivity, see James Axtell, "The White Indians of Colonial America" and "The Scholastic Philosophy of the Wilderness," in *The European and the Indian: Essays in the Ethnohistory of Colonial North America* (1981).

JUNE NAMIAS

JENCKES, Thomas Allen (2 Nov. 1818–4 Nov. 1875), lawyer and congressman, was born in Cumberland, Rhode Island, the son of Thomas Bowen Jenckes, a cotton manufacturer, and Abigail W. Allen. An only child whose father died before he was a year old, Jenckes, after preparatory work in the public schools and with a minister, graduated in 1838 from Brown University, where he distinguished himself in literature, mathematics, and the physical sciences. After studying law with Samuel Y. Atwell in Chepachet, Rhode Island, he gained admission to the bar in 1840, formed a partnership with Edward H. Hazard, and began practicing in Providence. A voracious reader with intense powers of concentration and an amazing memory, he became an outstanding lawyer. Coming from a distinguished New England family, Jenckes, despite an austere, aloof manner and a tendency to ignore public opinion, entered politics immediately, when the Rhode Island House of Representatives elected him reading clerk in 1840. In the Dorr Rebellion he sided with the conservatives, who initially upheld but then abandoned the property requirement of the 1663 charter/constitution, which prevented more than half of the adult males from voting. Jenckes served as secretary of the Freeholders' Constitutional Convention (1841–1842), whose proposed constitution was rejected, and of the more successful "Algerine" Constitutional Convention (1842), whose constitution went into effect in 1843. The excitement of the Dorr Rebellion did not deter Jenckes from marrying Mary Jane Fuller in 1842; they had seven children.

In 1842, under the old charter, Jenckes was named secretary of the governor's council and under the new constitution served as clerk of the state senate until 1844. For approximately ten years, beginning in 1845, he was Rhode Island's adjutant general, and from 1854 to 1857 he served in the state house of representatives, where he was a member of the Committee to Revise the State Statutes. Jenckes was also chief counsel for Rhode Island in its boundary dispute with Massachusetts, which he argued before the U.S. Supreme Court (1857–1861).

Jenckes's ability and interest in science and mechanics led him to specialize in patent law. He became involved in many important cases, including the struggle between Frederick E. Sickels and George H. Corliss over improvements to the steam engine, and much of his practice was in New York City, where he maintained a second office. Some of Jenckes's patent cases served as a springboard to his numerous business enterprises. Representing Horace H. Day in his controversy with Charles Goodyear (1800–1860) led Jenckes into the infant rubber industry. His Rubber Sole Shoe Company made spittoons as well as shoes, which the U.S. government declined to purchase during the Civil War because of their poor quality. Another Jenckes business interest, the American Wood Paper Company, controlled the manufacture of paper from wood pulp through the patents it held.

Serving in Congress as a Republican from 1863 to 1871, Jenckes supported Abraham Lincoln during the war and after it backed Radical Reconstruction. He wrote an article of Andrew Johnson's impeachment and narrowly missed election as a House of Representatives manager at the impeachment trial. Jenckes's impact in Congress was primarily institutional; the reports he drafted and the laws he crafted facilitated the functioning of the economy and the government but did little to boost his party. As head of a Special Committee on the Ventilation of the Halls of Congress, his grasp of the mechanics involved astonished his colleagues and impressed experts. He served on the Patent and Judiciary committees, where he revised patent laws, shepherded bankruptcy legislation through Congress, and sponsored civil service reform legislation. National bankruptcy acts in 1800 and 1841 proved unsatisfactory and were quickly repealed, but business failures following the panic of 1857 and the repudiation of debts by southerners in 1861 when war began, in addition to the clamor to collect those debts after the war, again provoked Congress to action. The Bankruptcy Act of 1867, which passed by narrow margins, was largely Jenckes's creation, but to secure its approval, compromises were made that jeopardized its effectiveness. In debate, those representing debtors secured concessions that exempted more property from distribution among creditors and also removed the penalty against those who, realizing they were about to fail, wasted their remaining assets. On the other hand, laborers and farmers objected to the provision that a single creditor could petition a defaulter into involuntary bankruptcy. With many forced needlessly into bankruptcy, creditors also suffered (usually receiving only ten cents on a dollar), as assets disappeared in fees to lawyers and administrators. The product of a Radical Republican Congress, the act prevented unrepentant rebels from filing for bankruptcy, since petitions had to be accompanied with an oath of allegiance to the United States. After several amendments furthered debtor interests, the Bankruptcy Act became so unpopular that in 1878 it was repealed, primarily at the behest of creditors.

Jenckes is not remembered for patent or bankruptcy legislation but as the father of civil service reform. The growth of mass-based political parties in the decades before the Civil War was facilitated by the rise of the spoils system, which rewarded party workers with civil service jobs and assessed their salaries to finance electioneering. Their frequent rotation in and out of office resulted in an inefficient and nonprofessional bureaucracy, whose weakness was accentuated by the abnormal demands of the Civil War. Upon his arrival in Washington, Jenckes, who was "struck at once at the great difference" between the military and the civil service, studied the systems of other countries and was impressed by the "wise and practical system" of appointments in the British civil service (*Congressional Globe*, 39th Cong., 2d sess., 6 Feb. 1867, p. 1034). Jenckes patterned his civil service reform bill, which he introduced in December 1865, after the British system. It was designed not only to achieve efficiency but also to neutralize the civil service politically and to prevent President Johnson from mobilizing it in support of his lenient treatment of former Confederate states. Under Jenckes's bill, only those scoring high on open competitive examinations could receive most federal civil service appointments, vacancies above the lowest grade were to be filled by promotion or by special examination, and the system was to be administered by a civil service commission. In its general outline, this original Jenckes Bill furnished a model for the 1883 Pendleton Civil Service Reform Act.

Initially, Jenckes's proposal received support only in the *Nation* and the *New York Times*. He persisted, and his speech on 29 January 1867 backing a modified bill (exempting postmasters from its application) attracted wide support among businesspeople and intellectuals and enunciated the arguments civil service reformers would reiterate over the next sixteen years. By eliminating the spoils system, his proposal would eliminate disreputable employees, who gave the civil service a low social status, and by promoting efficiency, his proposal would shrink the bureaucracy and reduce taxation. Fearing the effect of the bill on political organizations, Jenckes's opponents defeated his bill in a close bipartisan vote. They claimed his bill was "antidemocratic," suited for class-conscious, aristocratic monarchies, "where the masses are mere machines; but in free America," they insisted, "it will never work" (*Congressional Globe*, 39th Cong., 2d sess., 6 Feb. 1867, pp. 1034–36). Subsequent tinkering with his bill and speeches on its behalf failed to win its passage before Jenckes was defeated for reelection in the spring of 1870, but support for reform grew outside Congress. Following his retirement from Congress, Jenckes was a counsel for the Poland Committee (1872–1873), which inquired into the corruption of congressmen by the Crédit Mobilier, but ill health (accentuated by the death of his wife on 11 Jan. 1872) deprived him of a leading role in that capacity. Although he was denied his hope to hear the "death-knell sounded" for the spoils system (*Congressional Globe*, 41st Cong., 2d sess., 5 May 1870, p. 3261), seven years after Jenckes died in Cumberland, Rhode Island, his principles triumphed in the Pendleton Act.

• The Jenckes papers are in the Library of Congress. See also *In Memoriam: Thomas Allen Jenckes, Born November 2, 1818. Died November 4, 1875* (1876), which reprints obituaries from the *Providence Journal*, 5 Nov. 1875, and the *Providence Evening Press*, 5 Nov. 1875; William B. Browne, *Genealogy of the Jenks Family of America* (1952); George M. Dennison, *The Dorr War: Republicanism on Trial, 1831–1861* (1976); Charles Warren, *Bankruptcy in United States History* (1935); Peter J. Coleman, *Debtors and Creditors in America: Insolvency, Imprisonment for Debt, and Bankruptcy, 1607–1900* (1974); Martin A. Frey et al., *An Introduction to Bankruptcy Law* (1990); and Ari Hoogenboom, *Outlawing the Spoils: A History of the Civil Service Reform Movement, 1865–1883* (1961). An additional obituary is in the *New York Times*, 5 Nov. 1875.

ARI HOOGENBOOM

JENIFER, Daniel of St. Thomas (1723–16 Nov. 1790), planter, merchant, and political leader of the American revolutionary era, was born in Charles County, Maryland, the son of Daniel Jenifer, a chirurgeon, and Elizabeth Mason. A fourth-generation native known to his contemporaries as "the Major," Jenifer inherited 504 acres of land in Charles County on his father's death circa 1729, and by 1766 he had purchased at least 2,000 acres more. He resided at "Retreat," his Charles County home near Port Tobacco, for many years, but by 1766 he was living in Maryland's capital, Annapolis. During the next two decades he purchased more than 3,000 acres in Anne Arundel County, including "Stepney," an 800-acre plantation near South River, just outside Annapolis, where he lived from about 1784 until his death. In addition to his activities as a planter, Jenifer was a partner in the mercantile firm of Jenifer and Hooe and owner of the ship *Jenifer*. He also purchased part of a share in the Baltimore Company iron works in 1784. At his death he owned some 11,000 acres of land in Charles, Anne Arundel, and Baltimore counties and at least fifteen slaves, and left an estate worth nearly £1,500. Although Jenifer never publicly criticized slavery during his lifetime and sold slaves during the 1760s and 1770s, his will provided for the manumission of all his bondspeople in 1796, six years after his death. Never married, Jenifer died without progeny.

Jenifer's prerevolutionary political career included service as a justice for Charles County (1749–1764), Anne Arundel County (1766–1770), and of the provincial court (1766–1773), as a delegate to the lower house of the Maryland Assembly for Charles County (1756–1757), as rent roll keeper of the Western Shore (1768), and as a member in 1760 of the commission to resolve Maryland's boundary dispute with Pennsylvania and Delaware, which produced the Mason-Dixon line settlement. In 1771 he gained his first important positions from Maryland's proprietor, becoming chief agent escheater and receiver general of rents and a member of the governor's council. He retained his seat on the council until the revolution.

His newly acquired status in the proprietary establishment, proximity to the governor, and generally conservative nature made Jenifer reluctant to support those who advocated independence from the mother country during the early days of the imperial dispute, and at first he ignored the overtures of Maryland's patriot or "popular" party. Accused by Governor Robert Eden in 1774 of having "intimate" connections with the popular party because of his correspondence with some of its leaders, Jenifer rapidly made the transition from courtier to rebel and in August 1775 assumed the presidency of the newly formed revolutionary executive body, the council of safety, a position he held until 1777. Notwithstanding this shift, Jenifer, like other politically ambitious popular party members, hoped it would be possible to oust proprietary placemen and secure positions of power within the government without separating from Great Britain, because he feared the military conflict required to secure independence would bring internal dissension and disorder to Maryland. Accordingly, Jenifer arranged a meeting between Governor Eden and the patriot leaders early in 1776, in a private, unsuccessful effort to preserve peace. Although he ultimately came to accept the inevitability of independence, Jenifer retained his cautious attitude and somber expectations regarding the war's outcome, writing in 1778 that "I still think that all our money must go to support the war and if our liberty be established (which I doubt) and we can keep our lands and Negroes we shall be well off—no people ever yet procured their liberty so as to be benefitted themselves. To do it for posterity to reap the advantage is what has ever been aimed at."

Despite his pessimistic attitude Jenifer nevertheless continued to serve the cause he had chosen, both as a member of the Maryland Senate in 1776–1781 and as a delegate to Congress in 1779–1781. As a senator he supported two radical fiscal measures designed to quell widespread civil disorder within Maryland and to win popular support and legitimacy for the new government created by the state's conservative constitution, a document that guaranteed power to wealthy men by establishing high property qualifications for holding office. As a member of the slaveholding, landed, creditor class, Jenifer suffered financially from laws the Maryland legislature enacted in 1777 that shifted the basis of taxation from polls to land and slaves and made paper money legal tender for the payment of debts. Acknowledging that "the tender bill will be hard upon monied men," he nevertheless recognized that its popularity with the people meant that it must be endured, and he observed philosophically in March 1778, "it matters little whether the Money we have be sterling or Currency, as it must all go to support the present Contest." As a delegate to Congress, Jenifer urged a policy of fiscal restraint, strongly supported the alliance with France, and upheld Maryland's refusal to ratify the Articles of Confederation until Virginia ceded its claims to western land in January 1781.

During the Confederation period, Jenifer continued his political service to the new nation, filling two important political offices, both of which helped shape the nationalist position he would later assume with regard to the federal constitution. In 1785 he served on a joint Maryland-Virginia commission that drafted the Mount Vernon Compact, an agreement on the use and navigation of the Chesapeake Bay and the Potomac and Pocomoke rivers. The commission's proceedings led indirectly to the calling of the Annapolis Convention in 1786 and ultimately to the Federal Convention of 1787. Between 1782 and 1788, Jenifer exercised his nationalist convictions within Maryland as intendant of revenue, an office created by the legislature to bring fiscal stability to the state and to deal with the problems posed by enormous war debts, inadequate tax revenues, and inflation. Charged with overseeing the collection of taxes and obligations owed to the state, the sale of confiscated British property, and the payment of the state's creditors, the intendant inevitably became embroiled in controversy as conflicting demands strained limited resources. Undeterred by the enormity of the challenge he faced, Jenifer throughout his tenure sought to implement fiscal policies that would retire the national debt as quickly as possible, and he did not hesitate to privilege the demands of Congress over those of Maryland's local creditors.

Jenifer rendered his final public service as a delegate to the Constitutional Convention in 1787. Arriving in Philadelphia on 2 June, he remained at the convention the entire summer—the only Maryland delegate to do so—but he did not play a major part in the convention's proceedings. Generally siding with the nationalists on such issues as a strong central government and giving Congress broad financial powers, like the ability to tax, independent of the states, he often split Maryland's vote with Antifederalist Luther Martin. Jenifer signed and supported the finished Constitution but took no active role in promoting its ratification in Maryland. Praised at his death in Annapolis for his "benevolence, disinterestedness, patriotism, and attachment to the rights of man," he left most of his property to his brother's son, Dr. Daniel Jenifer, but he also made many bequests to other nephews, nieces, and friends, the most notable among the last being James Madison, to whom he devised all the French books in his library.

• No major collection of Jenifer's papers exists, but documents relating to his term as intendant of the revenue are located in the Records and Papers of the Intendant, Maryland State Archives, Annapolis, and the Maryland Historical Society has a small collection of manuscripts pertaining to him, 1782–1785, MS 1326. The Carroll papers, MS 206, located at the Maryland Historical Society, contain primary materials about Jenifer, including correspondence between him and members of the Carroll family. Edward C. Papenfuse et al., eds., *The Era of the American Revolution, 1775–1789, an Inventory of Maryland State Papers*, vol. 1 (1977), indexes loose papers relating to him. The Papers of the Continental Congress, Library of Congress, Washington, D.C., are also useful. Printed sources include Paul H. Smith et al., eds., *Letters of Delegates to Congress, 1774–1789* (1976–); Worthington C. Ford, et al., eds., *Journals of the Continental Congress* (1904–1937); and Max Farrand, ed., *The Records of the Federal Convention of 1787*, rev. ed. (4 vols., 1937). Ronald Hoffman, *A Spirit of Dissension: Economics, Politics, and the Revolution in Maryland* (1973), discusses his role in the revolutionary leadership coalition, and Papenfuse, "The Legislative Response to a Costly War: Fiscal Policy and Factional Politics in Maryland, 1777–1789," in *Sovereign States in an Age of Uncertainty*, ed. Ronald Hoffman and Peter J. Albert (1981), examines his career as intendant of revenue. Papenfuse et al., eds., *A Biographical Dictionary of the Maryland Legislature, 1635–1789*, vol. 2 (1985) is also helpful. For Jenifer's obituary see the *Annapolis Maryland Gazette*, 18 Nov. 1790.

RONALD HOFFMAN

JENISON, Nancy Blanche (8 July 1876–7 Nov. 1960), physician, was born in Republic, Ohio, the daughter of Edward Spencer Jenison, a Chicago architect and civil engineer, and Caroline M. Spooner. In 1898 she earned an A.B. from Wells College, a women's college in Aurora, New York. She taught high school for several years before deciding to become a medical doctor. Her career spanned the period when women physicians, characteristically drawn from middle-class families, enjoyed high visibility in America's reform movements that emphasized civic responsibility and social duty.

Jenison's late decision was typical for women entering medicine, for the career required a woman to be strong in character and her opportunities had to be weighed realistically. Jenison concluded that she could help many more children as a physician than as a teacher or mother. Eradicating suffering appealed to her lifelong inclination to ethics. Financial independence may have motivated her as well, for the average income of a woman doctor in 1881 was three times that of a male white-collar worker; normally, women made two-thirds less than men. Women physicians could pursue a career and reform society without overstepping too far the bounds of accepted propriety. Jenison's maternal uncle was a medical doctor. Furthermore, the admission of females to an elite medical school in 1890 was an unprecedented victory for women.

The Women's Fund Committee, founded by four wealthy and capable Baltimore women, endowed $500,000 to the financially strapped Johns Hopkins University on the condition that women be admitted to its School of Medicine on the same terms as men from the day it opened in 1893. To prepare for its high entrance requirements, Jenison took additional classes at the University of Chicago. In 1907 she was admitted to Johns Hopkins, a first-rate coeducational medical school that emphasized research in the basic sciences. She was one of seven women in the 1911 class of ninety graduates and about the sixty-seventh woman to graduate from Johns Hopkins as an M.D.

In 1900 only 7,000 of America's doctors were women, yet this was a significant advance (5.6 percent) over England's 258 and France's ninety-five. Opportunities did not improve for American women, however. In the year Jenison matriculated, the Johns Hopkins School of Medicine had only 6.76 percent women, compared to the 15.66 percent when the school first opened. By the time she graduated, the opening of medicine to women during the 1890s had

clearly reversed; their numbers continued to drop, except for wartime, until 1970. Middle-class women entered other occupations.

At age thirty-five Jenison was licensed by the state of New York. Women physicians often gravitated to what became "feminine" medical specialties, and Jenison likewise chose pediatrics. By concentrating on children's health, women physicians hoped to raise the moral tone of society through the improvement of family life. Jenison herself remained single all her life; the successful combination of career and family was difficult and she clearly liked her freedom. More and more educated women rejected marriage in favor of the pursuit of meaningful work.

Jenison succeeded in establishing her practice in New York City; urban sites were favored by most women doctors. She joined the New York County Medical Society and the American Medical Society. She enjoyed the cultural events that a large city had to offer. Her sister Madge C. Jenison also lived in New York City.

Jenison's medical practice (she was affectionately addressed as "Dr. Nancy") flourished for two decades. A disproportionately large percentage of patients were female, and women often preferred a woman doctor. Jenison kept correspondence with many of her patients after they had moved away and received photographs of the children she had treated as they grew up. In 1931 she retired from practice to live in the countryside in Bound Brook, New Jersey.

At the age of sixty-six Jenison studied for a year in Mexico City at the National School of Anthropology. While researching her family history, she learned that her great-great-grandfather had owned slaves in Maryland. Jenison moved to Washington, D.C., to work on improving race relations. (She was as convinced that African Americans had equal rights with other citizens as she was of women's rights.)

Jenison likely met George E. Beauchamp, the leader of the Washington Ethical Society, at civil rights events. She agreed with the society's social message and loved Beauchamp and his wife. He was personally devoted to racial justice in the nation's capital, and his ethical beliefs matched hers. She became a member of the society in 1950, and the Beauchamps became "family" to her.

No longer practicing medicine except to give emergency assistance or to help poor children in a clinic downtown, Jenison served poor neighborhoods in Washington and the Ethical Society. Knowledgeable about plant nurture, she took charge of the front lawn of the society's building, worked regularly on its monthly newsletter, served as a member of the Hospitality Committee, sold souvenirs from her travels to Mexico, South America, and Scandinavia at the society's fairs, and sold plants after the Sunday services.

A few years after the Beauchamps retired to Florida, Jenison returned to New York City to care for her ailing sister. She died there soon after her sister's death. Edward L. Ericson, then the leader of the Washington Ethical Society, conducted a memorial service for her in Washington. Only after the service was it discovered that Jenison, despite appearances, had been wealthy. Her will established a scholarship fund at the Johns Hopkins University for deserving women medical students; the rest of her estate ($75,000) was left to "the Ethical Society where George and Catherine Beauchamp are members" (Beauchamp, p. 162). Her bequest enabled the construction of a new and larger Washington Ethical Society building in 1966.

Catherine Beauchamp described Jenison as "a lovely, gentle person with ideas and strong convictions" (Beauchamp, p. 151). A freethinker devoted to laws fair to women as well as men and to black people as well as white, she found a kindred spirit in Ethical Culture, a movement that had been founded in the United States in the year of her birth. Her independence and determination, which had enabled her to become one of the nation's few female physicians, served her to the end. While some thought it sad that she was childless, old, and solitary with her gardening, sketching, and bird watching, she lived exactly as she chose. Her hobbies fit her scientific training and her frugality permitted the growth of the Washington Ethical Society—thereby enabling her to return the favor that the Baltimore Women's Fund Committee had afforded her. She invested in the humanistic religion that encouraged members to be ethical catalysts in the community at large.

• Jenison's remaining photos, letters, drawings, and mementos are at the Washington Ethical Society. Jenison is discussed in Catherine Weaver Beauchamp, *Family Ties and Tales* (1989); Alan M. Chesney and William H. Howell, *The Johns Hopkins Hospital and the Johns Hopkins University School of Medicine: A Chronicle*, vols. 1–3 (1943–1963); and L. D. MacIntyre, *The Washington Ethical Society, 1943–1944—1963–1964: A Story of Its Beginnings and Its Development* (1964). General historic context for women physicians is analyzed in John Duffy, *From Humors to Medical Science: A History of American Medicine* (1993); Regina Markell Morantz-Sanchez, *Sympathy and Science: Women Physicians in American Medicine* (1985); Paul Starr, *The Social Transformation of American Medicine* (1982); and Mary Roth Walsh, *"Doctors Wanted: No Women Need Apply": Sexual Barriers in the Medical Profession, 1835–1977* (1977). Obituaries are in the *Johns Hopkins Magazine*, Mar. 1961, and the *Washington Post*, 12 Nov. 1960.

MIRIAM CLAUDE MEIJER

JENKINS, Albert Gallatin (10 Nov. 1830–21 May 1864), congressman and Confederate general, was born at "Greenbottom," Cabell County, Virginia (now West Virginia), the son of William A. Jenkins, businessman and planter, and Jeannette Grigsby McNutt. Before settling in western Virginia along the Ohio River on his Greenbottom plantation, William A. Jenkins had prospered as the owner of a shipping business that exported tobacco and cotton to South America in exchange for coffee. Albert received preparatory schooling at the Marshall Academy in nearby Huntington. In 1846 he and his two brothers enrolled at Jefferson College in Canonsburg, Pennsylvania, graduating two years later. From 1848 to 1850 Jenkins attended Harvard Law School, earning his LL.B. degree in July 1850. Returning to his native state, he was admitted to the bar and began his legal practice in Charleston. In 1858 he married Virginia Southard Bowlin. The couple had three children who lived to adulthood and, according to family history, a fourth who died in infancy.

A gifted orator and debater, Jenkins fashioned a successful career as an attorney and immersed himself in politics. He served as a delegate to the Democratic National Convention in 1856 and was elected to the U.S. House of Representatives the following spring. Reelected two years later, he served a second term until Congress adjourned in March 1861. During his four years in Washington, Jenkins supported an activist foreign policy and spoke vigorously for the southern position on tariffs and slavery. Jenkins was nominated for a third time, but Virginia's secession on 17 April ended his candidacy. At the time, Jenkins told his supporters: "I shall carry with me an undying devotion to those principles of States' Rights Democracy, whose success I have ever believed to be necessary to preserve the rights and liberties of the people."

Within days of Virginia's withdrawal from the Union, Jenkins, with the rank of captain, organized the Border Rangers, establishing their camp at his family's Greenbottom plantation. Western Virginia was bitterly divided over the state's secession, and Jenkins's initial forays were against Union sympathizers in the Kanawha River Valley. The Border Rangers' first combat occurred in July 1861, at Barboursville, in a skirmish with five companies of the Second Kentucky. In August the Eighth Virginia Cavalry was organized, with Jenkins elected colonel. On 24 September the Confederate war department commissioned Jenkins a lieutenant colonel.

The Eighth Virginia Cavalry operated in mountainous western Virginia throughout the autumn of 1861 and the winter of 1862. In February 1862 Jenkins was elected as the representative of the Fourteenth Virginia Congressional District in the First Confederate Congress. Resigning his commission on 20 February, he journeyed to Richmond, where he remained for the next six months. On 5 August he was commissioned a brigadier general of cavalry and assigned to command of the Eighth and Fourteenth Virginia Cavalry regiments. Within a fortnight Jenkins reported to his command in western Virginia.

On 20 August Jenkins and about 550 cavalrymen left on a raid down the Kanawha Valley to the Ohio River. At Buckhannon they routed one Union force before marching westward. A week later Jenkins led his raiders across the Ohio River into southern Ohio. He captured a small Union garrison at Racine and seized numerous arms and supplies. By mid-September, Jenkins's command had rejoined the army. In one month they had covered 500 miles, inflicting over 1,000 casualties and destroying an estimated 5,000 small arms.

Jenkins and his small brigade remained in the region until the summer of 1863. In March 1863 he conducted another raid down the Kanawha River, capturing the town of Point Pleasant and firing on steamboats on the Ohio River. By June the brigade, comprising three regiments and two battalions, was stationed in the Shenandoah Valley. When Robert E. Lee's Army of Northern Virginia marched northward in its invasion of Pennsylvania, Lee attached Jenkins's brigade to the cavalry corps of the army.

Jenkins's 1,300-man brigade rode in the van of the invading army, entering Pennsylvania on 15 June 1863. While Lee's infantry corps marched toward Pennsylvania, Jenkins's troopers roamed throughout the commonwealth's southern tier, gathering livestock and commissary stores. The raiders penetrated as far north as Mercersburg, collecting approximately 3,000 head of cattle and horses. On 29 June Jenkins's brigade advanced on Mechanicsburg, across the Susquehanna River from the state capital at Harrisburg, and skirmished with Pennsylvania militia.

On 1 July the brigade reached Gettysburg and guarded prisoners from the first day's battle. On 2 July, while reconnoitering Federal lines, Jenkins was struck in the head by a piece of shell and seriously wounded. He returned to duty in the fall and was stationed with the brigade in southwestern Virginia. The command wintered there, plagued by sickness and inadequate supplies.

In May 1864 a Union army advanced against the Virginia & Tennessee Railroad. On 9 May two Confederate brigades under Jenkins met the Federals at Cloyd's Mountain. In the vicious engagement, Union troops crushed the Confederate line, achieving a victory. While rallying his troops, Jenkins fell wounded, his left arm shattered by a musket ball. Union surgeons amputated his limb on 13 May. The brigadier rallied, but early on the morning of 21 May, he died from a hemorrhage.

Jenkins forged a reputation as a raider, not as a combat officer. A tall, slender man with a long face and beard, he was popular with his troops but was neither a firm disciplinarian nor an able tactician. Raiding suited his abilities, and he served the Confederacy well in that capacity. After the Gettysburg campaign, he tendered his resignation so that he could care for his ill wife, but it was not accepted by the authorities. At the time, Robert E. Lee described Jenkins as "a gallant officer, [who] has organized a large brigade of brave men who only require instruction. I know of no one now with whom to replace him." It was a fair assessment of the brigadier.

• There is no collection of Albert G. Jenkins's papers. The only biography of Jenkins is Jack L. Dickinson, *Jenkins of Greenbottom: A Civil War Saga* (1988). Additional information is contained in Douglas Southall Freeman, *Lee's Lieutenants: A Study in Command* (3 vols., 1942–1944), and Wilbur Sturtevant Nye, *Here Come The Rebels!* (1965).

JEFFRY D. WERT

JENKINS, Andrew (26 Nov. 1885–1956), folk composer and gospel singer, was born in Jenkinsburg, near Atlanta, Georgia. His parents' names are unknown.

Jenkins was partially blinded as an infant when the wrong medication was put into his eyes. By the time he was nine he had joined the Methodist church and was climbing up on tree stumps to preach sermons to his family and friends. He preached his first formal sermon in a church in 1909, when he was twenty-four. Among his influences were two Atlanta residents who had gained nationwide reputations in the field of religion, composer Charlie Tillman (who had written the song "Life's Railway to Heaven") and evangelist Sam P. Jones (who published many gospel songbooks and traveled around the South doing tent revivals). To supplement his income, Jenkins sold newspapers on the streets of Atlanta and soon acquired a reputation as a folk preacher.

Jenkins's other dominating passion was music. A prodigy of sorts, he seemed able to play almost any instrument he encountered; he also found he was adept at writing songs and at once began to use this talent in his growing ministry. His first songs were gospel pieces written in the seven-shape note system popular in the South; these efforts were published by the Morris-Henson Company, a successful Atlanta publisher of gospel songbooks. Among these gospel compositions was "God Put a Rainbow in the Clouds," which remained in gospel and bluegrass repertoires throughout the rest of the century. By 1920 Jenkins had written enough songs that Morris-Henson published an entire book of them.

Jenkins had married Mattie Chandler early in his career, but in 1919 he remarried, this time to an Atlanta widow named Francis Jane Walden Eskew. Eskew had three children from a former marriage, including a married daughter, Irene Spain. All three were musically inclined; Spain especially was skilled in reading, writing, and transcribing music. With this family, Jenkins formed a gospel group and began to appear on Atlanta's new radio station WSB in August 1922. Response was favorable, and soon the Atlanta newspaper was trumpeting a headline that read, "Radio World Applauds Gospel Melodies of Dr. Jenkins' Program." Fan mail came in from Canada to Mexico. Soon Jenkins began to supplement his singing with readings from his own poems on various subjects.

Through the efforts of Atlanta furniture-store owner Polk Brockman, Jenkins began making commercial phonograph records to feed the growing demand for "southern" and "old time" tunes. In August 1924, accompanied by stepdaughters Irene Spain and Mary Lee Spain, he recorded a number of songs for the OKeh label under the name the Jenkins Family. These included several very influential records, such as "If I Could Hear My Mother Pray Again" (OKeh 40214), "The Church in the Wildwood" (with its familiar "Come, come, come" refrain, OKeh 40214), and "Sail On" (OKeh 40249). A few months later the family made even more records, creating additional popular hits such as "Will There Be Any Stars in My Crown?" "Shout and Shine for Jesus," and two special twelve-inch discs on which the group tried to recreate in sound a typical old-time tent revival meeting. These records, and later ones, were among the first efforts to capture on commercial disc the rich tapestry of southern grassroots gospel music.

Though the Jenkins Family, sometimes called the Jenkins Sacred Singers, continued to record through 1934, Andrew Jenkins also began to record more secular music as a soloist. In April 1925 he recorded a topical song that he had written about local outlaw Frank DuPree and saw the OKeh disc released under the name "Blind Andy." More dramatic, though, was a similar ballad Jenkins had written a few months earlier. In January 1925 Floyd Collins, a Kentucky spelunker, was trapped in a cave, and efforts to rescue him attracted national attention. Polk Brockman asked Jenkins if he could write a song about Collins, and in four hours Jenkins dashed off "The Death of Floyd Collins." Sent to New York, the song was at once recorded by studio singer Vernon Dahlhart and became one of the decade's biggest sellers. In fact, it began a fad in early country music for "event songs"—songs about recent tragedies, murders, or disasters. Jenkins became a master of this genre, and soon New York publishers were asking him to write more.

Jenkins obliged, eventually creating pieces like "Little Marian Parker," "Ben Dewberry's Final Run," "Kinnie Wagner," and "Billy the Kid." Many of these new songs were so successful at imitating the folk idiom that some entered folk tradition and for generations after were collected by unsuspecting folk song collectors. The composer Aaron Copland even used the melody of "Billy the Kid" in his ballet of the same name, believing it was a traditional American melody. Jenkins's total song output eventually surpassed 800 titles; his daughter recalled, "Daddy made songs similarly to the mill grinding out wheat." Unfortunately, Jenkins often sold the rights of his songs outright for a flat fee and reaped little of the long-term rewards from their popularity.

Jenkins continued to record prolifically, sometimes under pseudonyms such as Blind Andy, Gooby Jenkins, and with other composers like Carson Robison and W. C. Childers. Most of these were done for OKeh throughout the 1920s, though he recorded one session for Bluebird in 1934. In later years Jenkins continued to make an occasional record for minor labels but earned most of his income from evangelism. He was killed in an auto accident some ten years before folklorists began to understand and appreciate his role in the development of country music and vernacular songwriting.

• Copies of Irene Spain's papers and scrapbooks are in the Southern Folklife Collection at the University of North Carolina. Little has been written about Jenkins, and most information available on him is based on personal interviews conducted by Charles K. Wolfe. See Wolfe, "Frank Smith, Andrew Jenkins, and Early Commercial Gospel Music," *American Music* 1, no. 1 (Spring 1983): 49–60.

CHARLES K. WOLFE

JENKINS, Charles Jones (6 Jan. 1805–14 June 1883), judge and governor of Georgia, was born in Beaufort, South Carolina, the only child of Charles J. Jenkins, a planter and the ordinary of the district. His mother's name is unknown. In 1816 the family moved to Jefferson County, Georgia. Jenkins attended the famous school of Moses Waddel in the Abbeville district in South Carolina and then Franklin College, later the University of Georgia, of which Waddel had become president. He completed his schooling at Union College in Schenectady, New York, from which he graduated in 1824.

After studying law with J. M. Berrien, a leading Georgia lawyer and politician, Jenkins practiced in Sandersville and then in Augusta, becoming a well-known figure among the political lawyers in Georgia's northern circuit. In 1830 he ran successfully for the state legislature, which elected him attorney general a year later. Resigning this position in 1834 to run again for the legislature, he was initially unsuccessful but, in 1836, was elected to the first of six successive one-year terms. Then, after a defeat in 1842, he served without a break until 1850. In the terms beginning in 1840, 1843, 1845, and 1847, Jenkins was also Speaker of the house.

In 1832, Jenkins married Sarah Jones of Burke County, Georgia; they had three children. Sarah died in 1847, and in 1854 he married Emily Barnes.

As a leader of Georgia's Whig party, Jenkins was a prominent opponent of disunion during the crisis of 1850–1852 in the South. Indeed, he was the author of the famous "Georgia Platform" endorsed by the special state convention that was called to respond to the admission of California as a free state. Abiding by the Compromise of 1850 "as a permanent adjustment," though not approving it, the platform set out the conditions for Georgia's remaining in the Union, among them "faithful execution" of the Fugitive Slave Law and maintenance of the interstate slave trade and of slavery in the District of Columbia. While it satisfied the Southern Rights extremists, it also embodied the position on the sectional question of the Constitutional Union party that was to control the state's politics for the next few years.

By 1852 Jenkins's stature among Georgia's Union Whigs was such that they nominated him for vice president on the bolting Whig ticket headed by Daniel Webster. A year later, he was the party's candidate for governor, though he lost to Democrat Herschel V. Johnson by only 510 votes—47,638 to 47,128. Deploring the South's drift toward secession, he affiliated reluctantly with the Know Nothings and served in the state senate in 1856. In 1860 he was invited to attend the state's secession convention as a distinguished political figure, along with Governor Joseph E. Brown and Howell Cobb. Later that year, Governor Brown appointed him a judge of the Georgia Supreme Court, a post he held throughout the war.

During Reconstruction, Jenkins assumed a pivotal role in the politics of his state. He was elected to the constitutional convention of 1865, where he chaired the important committee on business that set the agenda of the convention, whose presidency he had earlier declined. As chair he refused to report out the ordinance to repudiate Georgia's war debt. A few months later, when Georgia was to elect its governor, Jenkins was put forward, after Alexander H. Stephens and Joseph Brown had decided not to run, and was elected unopposed. As governor at a time when Georgia's postwar status was still undetermined, Jenkins's responsibilities were considerable. He raised loans to pay for the costs of government and for rations and relief for its citizens, while in his inaugural address he advocated legal rights for the freedmen, though adding that "the necessity of subordination and dependence should be riveted on their convictions."

In dealing with the federal authorities, however, Governor Jenkins was perhaps the most confrontational chief executive in the Reconstruction South. First, he urged the legislature in the fall of 1866 to reject the proposed Fourteenth Amendment which constituted Congress's initial set of terms for southern readmission requiring leading Confederates to be disqualified from officeholding. Then, he sought an injunction from the U.S. Supreme Court to prevent the secretary of war, Edwin M. Stanton, from implementing the 1867 Reconstruction Act in Georgia. When *Georgia v. Stanton* proved unsuccessful, the governor advised Georgia voters to thwart the Reconstruction elections by refusing even to register. When Jenkins later declined to pay the costs of the constitutional convention of 1867, he and the state treasurer were removed from office by General George G. Meade, commander of the Third Military District.

Jenkins fled the state, taking with him the executive seal, the records of his administration, and $40,000 in state funds that he then deposited in a New York bank. After living for a time in Baltimore and in Halifax, Nova Scotia, he returned to Georgia in 1870 to continue his law practice. When the Democrats returned to power in 1872, he was lionized as custodian of the symbols and resources of the state during the four years of Republican rule. He was president of the board of trustees of the University of Georgia, 1876–1883, as well as of the Merchants and Planters Bank and the Augusta Cotton Factory. In 1877 he was elected to, and then was chosen to preside over, Georgia's constitutional convention, which renounced most of the priorities of the Republicans during Reconstruction.

In 1881, a few years before Jenkins's death, I. W. Avery, the celebrated chronicler of Georgia's history, wrote that "no man in the state has enjoyed a larger measure of respect than Mr. Jenkins." Jenkins died in Summerville, near Augusta. Although less well known than his more flamboyant contemporaries in Georgia politics, the conservative and legalistic Jenkins was nevertheless a leading Whig who promoted economic development in his state and opposed disunion and later, as probably the South's most defiant governor, Reconstruction.

• Jenkins's official gubernatorial papers, although thin, are at the Georgia Department of Archives and History in Atlanta. Also see Ulrich B. Phillips, "The Correspondence of Robert Toombs, Alexander H. Stephens, and Howell Cobb," in *Annual Report of the American Historical Association for 1911*, vol. 2 (1913), and Thomas E. Schott, *Alexander H. Stephens of Georgia* (1988), for letters from Jenkins and references to him. Jenkins's career can be traced in C. C. Jones, *The Life and Services of Ex-Governor C. J. Jenkins* (1884); W. J. Northern, *Men of Mark in Georgia*, vol. 3 (1910); the biographical sketch by Olive H. Shadgett in *Georgians in Profile*, ed. Horace Montgomery (1958); and Shadgett, "The Public Life of Charles J. Jenkins, 1830–1865" (master's thesis, Univ. of Georgia, 1952). His role in the 1850 crisis is discussed in Richard H. Shryock, *Georgia and the Union in 1850* (1926), and Royce McCrary, "The Authorship of the Georgia Platform of 1850: A Letter by Charles J. Jenkins," *Georgia Historical Quarterly* 54 (1970): 211–27. On Reconstruction, see Alan Conway, *The Reconstruction of Georgia* (1966); Elizabeth S. Nathans, *Losing the Peace: Georgia Republicans and Reconstruction* (1968); and Michael Perman, *Reunion Without Compromise: The South and Reconstruction, 1865–1868* (1973). An obituary is in the *Atlanta Constitution*, 16 June 1883.

MICHAEL PERMAN

JENKINS, David (1811–5 Sept. 1877), editor and abolitionist, was born in Lynchburg, Virginia, the son of William Jenkins. It is not known whether his father was a white slaveholder or a free black, and his mother's name is unknown. Jenkins received a sound education at the hands of a private tutor hired by his father. In 1837 he took up residence in Columbus, Ohio, employing himself as a house painter and glazier. Jenkins's business acumen led to real estate investment and capital accumulation. The 1850 census for Franklin County, Ohio, records that Jenkins owned real estate valued at $1,500. The census also shows that he was married to Lucy Ann (maiden name unknown), a native of Virginia, and that they had one child.

On 27 December 1843 Jenkins founded and edited the *Palladium of Liberty*, an antislavery weekly newspaper also dedicated to the advancement of the African American in the United States. Inspiration for the establishment of the newspaper evolved from the Ohio State Convention of Colored People held in August 1843. While primarily antislavery, the *Palladium* also provided editorial support for the education of African-American children, temperance, moral reform, and suffrage. The paper drew readers from Ohio and the northeastern United States. Among its local and traveling subscription agents were Charles Langston, Henry Highland Garnet, William Wells Brown, William P. Newman, and James Sharp. The *Palladium* ceased publication in the winter of 1844 because of limited financial resources; nevertheless, Jenkins continued his journalistic pursuits with contributions to Frederick Douglass's *North Star*.

Jenkins advocated tireless agitation against slavery. From the time of his move to Columbus until the end of the Civil War, he aggressively pursued this position with numerous speeches and writings. He played a key role in the African-American convention movement on both the national and state levels. He attended the 1843 National Convention of Colored Citizens in Buffalo, the 1848 National Convention of Colored Freemen in Cleveland, and the 1853 Colored National Convention in Rochester. At the 1848 national convention he coauthored with Douglass, Henry Bibb, and William H. Day "An Address to the Colored People of the United States," which urged blacks "to act with white anti-slavery societies wherever they could and where they could not set up societies for themselves without exclusiveness." During the 1850s Jenkins frequently participated in Ohio African-American conventions; over the decade his services included the presidency in 1851 and membership on the state central committee. He contributed to the founding of the Ohio Anti–Slavery Society in 1858 at the State Convention of Colored Men. Associates at these meetings included African Americans of national prominence such as Charles H. and John M. Langston of Oberlin and Peter H. Clark of Cincinnati.

Throughout the 1840s and 1850s, Jenkins corresponded with both white and African-American abolitionists, including Cassius Clay, Martin Delany, Frederick Douglass, Horace Mann, Joshua Giddings, John Quincy Adams, and Benjamin F. Wade. He also regularly attended sessions of the Ohio General Assembly, presenting petitions and memorials on behalf of African-American rights. These appearances in the legislative chambers earned Jenkins the nickname "Member at Large." He carried on his person a supply of handbills with blank spaces that could be filled in as needed to advertise meetings denouncing slavery.

Jenkins's abolitionist activities moved beyond his speeches and writings and included direct involvement with the Underground Railroad in central Ohio counties. He also joined the Masonic order, serving as worshipful master of St. Marks Lodge No. 7 in Cincinnati from 1858 to 1860 and in a variety of other posts throughout the 1860s and 1870s.

During the Civil War Jenkins, a Union supporter, encouraged the enlistment of African-American volunteers. In 1863 he presided over a statewide committee appealing for funds to assist African-American troops and the Union cause. Two years later, just prior to the termination of the war, Jenkins was selected vice president of the Ohio State Auxiliary Equal Rights League.

Following the war Jenkins was involved with local Republican party activities, but was thwarted in his efforts to gain political office and appointment. Frustrated, in 1873 he moved from Columbus to Canton, Mississippi, to teach for the Freedman's Bureau. Two years later Jenkins was elected to the Mississippi legislature and served a single two-year term, dying two years later in Canton. Jenkins's role in the antislavery movement was a critical one, especially in Ohio. His indefatigable energy on behalf of African-American rights nationwide over four decades was matched by only a handful of African-American leaders of his era.

• The most complete biographical sketch of David Jenkins is in William H. Parham and Jeremiah A. Brown, *An Official History of the Most Worshipful Grand Lodge Free and Accepted Masons for the State of Ohio* (1906). The files of the *Palladium*, at the Ohio Historical Society, capture Jenkins's views on slavery and related issues of the day. His correspondence is contained in the microfilm edition (1981) of the *Black Abolitionist Papers*, ed. C. Peter Ripley and George C. Carter. His involvement with the various African-American conventions is recounted in Howard H. Bell, ed., *Minutes of the Proceedings of the National Negro Conventions, 1830–1865* (1969), and in Philip S. Foner and George E. Walker, ed., *Proceedings of the Black State Conventions, 1840–1865*, vol. 1 (1979). Scattered throughout copies of the Ohio house and senate journals are references to Jenkins's presence at legislative sessions.

FRANK R. LEVSTIK

JENKINS, Edmund Thornton (9 Apr. 1894–12 Sept. 1926), clarinetist, composer, and conductor, was born in Charleston, South Carolina, the son of Daniel Jenkins, a former slave, minister, and founder-director of the Jenkins Orphanage Band, and Lena James. Jenkins attended the Avery Institute in Charleston. As a child, he learned to play violin, clarinet, and piano. His first music teachers were his father and other instructors at the orphanage, which was founded in December 1891 and formally incorporated as the Orphan Aid Society in July 1892. By the time he was fourteen years old, Jenkins had learned to play all the instruments of his father's brass band. In 1908 he entered Atlanta Baptist College (now Morehouse College) where he studied violin with Kemper Harreld. Jenkins participated in the symphony orchestra, glee club, and other musical activities. During vacations he performed, directed, and toured with the orphanage band. Jenkins left college during the summer of 1914 to travel with the band to London for the Anglo-American Exposition, organized by the Hungarian Imre Kiralfy. The band's original ten-week engagement was cut short by the outbreak of World War I in early August. The Exposition closed on 11 August, and the band returned to the United States at the end of October.

Jenkins remained in London to study music. In September 1914 he entered the Royal Academy of Music to study composition with Frederick Corder. He studied clarinet with Edward J. Augarde, and in his fourth year he studied organ with H. W. Richards. He also studied piano. While at the Academy, he won several prizes, including a bronze medal in singing (spring 1915); the Oliviera Prescott Prize in composition; the Charles Lucas Prize for merit (July 1918); the Battison Haynes Prize for composition (Dec. 1918); and the Ross Scholarship (Sept. 1919). Entering into the extracurricular life of the school, he edited the academy's student publication, the *Academite*, during the lenten and midsummer terms of 1919. He also organized musical groups and performed as clarinetist, organist, and conductor.

In 1918 Jenkins became involved in black politics in Britain. He and a group of friends organized the African Progress Union, established to promote racial understanding. In March or April 1919 Jenkins organized the Coterie of Friends, a social club for young men of color residing permanently or temporarily in Great Britain, including African-American soldiers stationed in London during World War I. He also participated in the Pan-African Congress held in London in 1921. That same year Jenkins completed his studies at the Royal Academy of Music and received a distinguished honor: he was elected an associate of the Academy, a promotion from his previous position as a subprofessor of clarinet.

Jenkins was studying in England just as jazz spread to Europe. In April 1919 the Original Dixieland Jass [*sic*] Band toured Britain, and on 4 July Will Marion Cook's Southern Syncopated Orchestra (with which he played briefly) appeared at London's Philharmonic Hall. Black musicians were hired by London hotels and cafes, restaurants, theaters, music halls, and dances to take the place of German musicians. Jenkins began to play regularly at Madame Henry's Dance Hall on Regent Street. In October 1920 Jenkins and Herbert Henry converted the rooftop chamber music hall of Queen's Hall in Langham Place into a nightclub run by their company, the QSH Syndicate, Limited. Jenkins led four other men in a small band. In May 1921 the band made its first recordings in Hayes, Middlesex, on His Master's Voice, the British associate of Victor. Jenkins gained further experience as a dance-band musician in Paris in early 1922, working as a saxophonist and clarinetist (and later conductor) in Art Hickman's Orchestra. A white band, Hickman's Orchestra was one of the leading dance orchestras of America, ranked with those of Vincent Lopez and Paul Whiteman. They played at the Ermitage de Longes Champs in the Bois de Boulogne, a chic Paris tea and night dancing place. Jenkins's contract expired in February 1923, and in the fall he returned to London where he worked briefly with James P. Johnson.

In 1923 Jenkins went to the United States hoping to organize a symphony orchestra of black musicians, establish a music academy, and found a music publishing company with Will Vodery and Robert Young. He vainly tried to find financial backing in New York, Washington, D.C., Boston, Charleston, Chicago, and Baltimore. Only with the financial assistance of his father was he able to found the Anglo-Continental-American Music Press (the elder Jenkins had founded *The Charleston Messenger*, which began circulation in October 1894). Based in Paris, Jenkins's firm published art music compositions as well as popular songs and dance music. Jenkins conducted Will Marion Cook's 21-piece orchestra in a series of concerts at the Shubert Theatres in New York, beginning an engagement Sunday night, 27 January 1924. By October 1924 he had returned to Paris, and by the following spring he was directing a band of black musicians, the International Seven. He continued to compose and published some of his own works. He also traveled throughout Europe, often to hear performances of his works or to conduct his dance band. Admitted to the Hôpital Tenon in Paris on 15 July 1926, Jenkins died following an operation for appendicitis. He was never married.

Jenkins ranks among the first generation of twentieth-century African-American art music composers. Inspired by African-American musical idioms, in 1919 he completed *Folk Rhapsody*. In 1925 his works *African War Dance* for full orchestra and Sonata in A minor for violoncello won Holstein Prizes in New York. Recognized internationally, his *Charlestoniana* was premiered by François Rasse in the Jursaal, Ostend, Belgium, in September 1925. His second *Rhapsody* was presented posthumously during the 1926 season by the Pasdeloup Concert Orchestra with Rhene Baton conducting. All but forgotten in favor of his contemporary Sidney Bechet, Jenkins was also important as a transmitter of an early style of jazz to Europe. His 1921 recordings are in a style current in the United States prior to 1914.

Jenkins composed nearly fifty works in various genres, large and small, for both instrumental and vocal ensembles. Among his other well known and successful works were *Afram*, an opera in three acts (1924); *Rapsodie spirituelle*, for orchestra (1923); and *Rêverie phantasie*, for violin and piano (1919). He won the Holstein Prizes for his Cello Sonata in A minor in 1925 and for his *African War Dance* for orchestra in 1926. Jenkins made a total of twenty-one recordings, including "Idol of Mine" (B-1237), "Turque" (B-1236), "The Wind in the Trees" (B-1237), and "I'm Wondering if It's Love" (B-1236) in 1921 on His Master's Voice. The arrangements of the items recorded in 1921 were similar to those of Paul Whiteman.

• The main biographical work on Jenkins is Jeffrey P. Greene, *Edmund Thornton Jenkins: The Life and Times of an American Black Composer, 1894–1926* (1982). A brief entry on Jenkins is also included in Maud Cuney Hare, *Negro Musicians and Their Music* (1936). The context in which Jenkins pursued his studies and early career is discussed in Howard Rye and Jeffrey Green, "Black Music Internationalism in England in the 1920s," *Black Music Research Journal* 15 (1995): 93–107. A study of the Jenkins Orphanage Band is John Chilton, *A Jazz Nursery: The Story of the Jenkins' Orphanage Bands* (1980). Jenkins's activities were reported in the contemporary African-American press; see, for example, "Edmund T. Jenkins: Musician," *Opportunity*, Nov. 1925; Benjamin Brawley, "Edmund T. Jenkins: An Appreciation," *Opportunity*, Dec. 1926; Edward Silvera, "On the Death of a Young Friend," *Opportunity*, Dec. 1926; "Will Marion Cook to Give Concerts at Shubert Theatre," *New York Age*, 12 Jan. 1924; Lucien H. White, "In the Realm of Music: Edmund T. Jenkins Dies in Paris," *New York Age*, 2 Oct. 1926; and White, "In the Realm of Music: Brilliant Musician and Composer Lost to Race in Untimely Death in Paris of Edmund Thornton Jenkins, Sept. 12," *New York Age*, 23 Oct. 1926; and various issues of *The Crisis*. An important inventory concerning the location and rediscovery of many of his manuscripts was made by Betty Hillmon, "In Retrospect: Edmund Thornton Jenkins: American Composer: At Home Abroad," *Black Perspective in Music* 14 (1986): 143–80.

GAYLE MURCHISON

JENKINS, Edward Hopkins (31 May 1850–6 Nov. 1931), agricultural chemist, was born in Falmouth, Massachusetts, the son of John Jenkins and Chloe

Thompson. Jenkins studied at Phillips Academy in Andover, Massachusetts, and Yale University, where in addition to his studies of chemistry he was a member of Psi Upsilon fraternity and stroke oar on the varsity crew team. Jenkins received his A.B. in 1872 and then continued graduate work in chemistry at Yale. In 1875–1876 he went to Germany, where he studied at the University of Leipzig and then at the Forest School in Tharandt, Saxony. He then returned to the United States and received his Ph.D. in chemistry from Yale in 1879.

In 1877 Jenkins joined the new Connecticut Agricultural Experiment Station at New Haven, the first such station in the United States, under the direction of Professor W. O. Atwater of Wesleyan University. Jenkins began as a botanist and chemist and remained associated with the station throughout his career. He was made vice director in 1884 and was director from 1900 and treasurer from 1901 to 1923, when he became director emeritus until his death. He was also director of the agricultural experiment station at Storrs from 1912 until 1923. In 1883 Jenkins was also made an officer of the state board of agriculture; in 1899 he became a member of the board of trustees of the Connecticut State Agricultural College.

Jenkins remained professionally active throughout his long life. He was a founding member of the Association of Official Agricultural Chemists and served as its president in 1887; he was a member of its Committee on Uniform Fertilizer Laws in 1888 and the Committee on Food Standards for many years, beginning in 1897. He also was very active in the Association of American Agricultural Colleges and Experiment Stations, serving on committees on nomenclature, uniform fertilizer laws, and seed testing, and served as president of the association (1912–1913). Jenkins was also chair of the Connecticut State Sewerage Commission (1897–1903), a member of the Connecticut Forestry Association and the Society for the Promotion of Agricultural Science, and a fellow of the American Association for the Advancement of Science.

Jenkins's earliest work at the experiment station focused on chemical analysis of commercial fertilizers sold in Connecticut. His findings revealed wide differences among products, and in response the legislature passed in 1882 a requirement that all fertilizer sold in the state deposit a sample at the station and be labeled with its chemical composition. The success of this research led in the mid-1880s to the chemical analysis of insecticides and feeds. Jenkins also reported on diverse experiments such as the effect of plant spacing on corn quality and yield and the value of ashes as fertilizer. Responding to requests from the state dairy commission and private companies, Jenkins undertook chemical analyses of dairy products, molasses, and vinegar and regularly testified to his findings in court. In 1885 he married Elizabeth Elliot Foote; they had no children.

In the early 1890s Jenkins and other researchers at the station began to focus increasingly on the problems of tobacco culture. In 1892, in cooperation with the private Connecticut Tobacco Experiment Company, Jenkins directed field experiments on tobacco fertilizer. At about the same time the station hired a mycologist to study tobacco diseases, such as fire blight, and the possibilities of using heat curing to prevent "pole sweat." Studies of tobacco curing also led to the development of bulk fermentation methods.

In 1900, under Jenkins's direction and in cooperation with the U.S. Department of Agriculture's Bureau of Soils, the station began to experiment with shade-grown Sumatran tobacco, which the bureau's analysis showed had been successfully grown on similar soils in Florida. The experiments proved highly successful, and the new methods spread rapidly, inducing a boom in the value of good tobacco land. In 1905 Jenkins hired geneticist Edward Murray East and later published his *Inheritance in Maize* (1911), which became a classic in the early literature of genetics.

Jenkins was the author of *A History of Connecticut Agriculture* (1925). With A. L. Winton he published *A Compilation of Analyses of American Feeding Stuffs* (USDA Experiment Station, *Bulletin* 11 [1892]), which reviewed and compared all previous studies of the chemical composition of animal fodder. He prepared the definitions of chemical terms for the *Century Dictionary* and presented a number of papers to professional societies, but his most important publications were contained in the numerous reports and bulletins of the experiment station; the most notable were "Can Wrapper Leaf Tobacco of the Sumatra Type Be Raised at a Profit in Connecticut?" (Connecticut Agricultural Experiment Station, *Bulletin* 137 [1902]) and "Studies on the Tobacco Crop of Connecticut" (Connecticut Agricultural Experiment Station, *Bulletin* 180 [1914]).

As both a scholar and administrator, Jenkins was an important contributor to the growth and professionalization of agricultural chemistry and extension work, and his career reflects the increasing importance of science to American agriculture. Thanks to Jenkins and his coworkers, the experiment station expanded its scope to include entomology, forestry, botany, economic botany, plant breeding, and soil science. Jenkins and other station workers both taught and provided field trials for insecticide use, developed more accurate methods to measure butterfat in milk, improved plant breeding, and established an experimental forest. He died in New Haven.

• A small collection of Jenkins's correspondence is at the University of Connecticut, Storrs. Basic details of Jenkins's life appear in *American Men of Science*, 4th ed. (1927), and *Biographical Record of the Class of 1872, Yale College* (1913). His career and the rise of agricultural research may be traced in the Connecticut Agricultural Experiment Station's *Reports* and *Bulletins*. See also the Association of Official Agricultural Chemists' Annual Convention, *Proceedings*, beginning in 1884, and those of the Association of American Agricultural Colleges and Experiment Stations, beginning in 1887. The *Handbook of Experiment Station Work*, USDA Experiment Station, *Bulletin* 11 (1893) briefly describes the context and history of experiment stations, as does Clarence Smith, *The Agricultural Extension System of the United States* (1930). Margaret Rossiter, *The Emergence of Agricultural Science: Justus Liebig and the Americans, 1840–1880* (1975), provides scientific background. Also useful for context is Elizabeth Ramsey, *The History of Tobacco Production in the Connecticut Valley* (1930), a volume in the Smith College Studies in History series.

MARK ALDRICH

JENKINS, Gordon (12 May 1910–1 May 1984), music arranger, composer, and conductor, was born in Webster Groves, Missouri. His parents' names are unknown. At ten Jenkins filled in as relief organist for his father, a church organist, at a Chicago movie theater. During the depression Jenkins played piano in a St. Louis speakeasy after dropping out of high school. After a time he sang and played the organ, piano, and accordion in the early morning hours on a St. Louis radio station. In 1925 Jenkins won an amateur contest in St. Louis, playing the ukelele in a competition judged by Cliff "Ukelele Ike" Edwards.

Jenkins left St. Louis as a musician with Henry Santry's orchestra in 1930. When he became ill with influenza, he returned home and worked at the Fox Theatre in Webster Groves, accompanying the films and writing original material for the various acts that played the theater. In 1936 Jenkins was hired by orchestra leader Isham Jones as a pianist and an arranger. When Jones broke up his band later that year, Jenkins went to work as an arranger for Woody Herman, who had also been in Jones's employ. In this era Jenkins also began contributing arrangements to the orchestras led by Paul Whiteman, Benny Goodman, Lenny Hayton, Vincent Lopez, and Andre Kostelanetz. Jenkins wrote "Goodbye," which Goodman used as the closing theme of his performances, and "Blue Prelude," which Herman used as his theme in the 1930s. Jenkins married his high school sweetheart, Nancy Harkey, in 1931, and they had three sons and a daughter.

Jenkins took a job as conductor for the Broadway revue *The Show Is On* (1936), starring Beatrice Lillie, but he soon grew tired of conducting the same score night after night. His only other significant connection with Broadway was his score for the musical *Along Fifth Avenue* (1940), which starred Jackie Gleason. In 1938 Jenkins began a five-year stint in California as musical director for NBC and also worked with Dick Haymes on the singer's radio show in the early 1940s.

In 1945 Jenkins composed the popular suite "Manhattan Tower," which consisted of a four-part musical tribute to New York City. Some of Jenkins's other songs included "P.S., I Love You," "San Fernando Valley," "This Is All I Ask," and "When a Woman Loves a Man." Also in 1945 Jenkins signed on as a conductor, and later musical director, for Decca Records. At Decca, he accompanied a diverse array of the outstanding performers of the era, including Al Jolson, Louis Armstrong, Martha Tilton, Peggy Lee, and the Weavers (who recorded "Good Night, Irene" with

Jenkins's orchestra, a recording that spent thirteen weeks as the number one song in 1950 and ultimately sold more than two million copies). He also had some significant success with his own recordings as a conductor and arranger, including three records that hit the Top Ten list simultaneously in 1950: "I Wanna Be Loved," "Bewitched," and "My Foolish Heart." *Time* magazine noted that all of these were "tricked out with sobbing, throbbing violins and choruses of female voices." Between 1942 and 1953 Gordon Jenkins and His Orchestra had no fewer than twenty recordings that made it to the top of the charts. He became particularly known for his lush arrangements that most critics applauded. However, music critic Will Friedwald's view is more mixed. In *Sinatra! The Song Is You*, he wrote that Jenkins "simultaneously put the anal in banal but also the taste in tasteful."

Jenkins only made a few forays into composing for the movies. His scores for motion pictures include *San Fernando Valley* (1944), *Bwana Devil* (1952), which was the first 3-D feature film, and *The First Deadly Sin* (1980), which starred Frank Sinatra, with whom Jenkins maintained a long and fruitful relationship. Although most of Sinatra's finest work was done with the arrangements of Nelson Riddle, Jenkins also contributed significantly to Sinatra's legend. He arranged and conducted Sinatra's 1973 "comeback" special on television and won a Grammy Award for his arrangement for Sinatra's recording of "It Was a Very Good Year" that same year. In 1980 Jenkins composed the "Future" song cycle for Sinatra's "Trilogy, Part Three: The Future." Other greats of popular music for whom Jenkins arranged and/or conducted were Nat King Cole, Billie Holiday, Ella Fitzgerald, and Judy Garland, for whom he composed *The Letter*, a concept album that included what critic Friedwald calls "one of the composer's most moving arias, 'That's All There Is.'" Jenkins was conductor for Garland's 1957 London concert appearance, and he collaborated in this same period with Tom Adair and Johnny Mercer.

Jenkins's second wife, Beverly Mahr, had been the "Miss" in the singing group Six Hits and a Miss and had worked with Jenkins on numerous occasions from the 1940s on, including as a soloist on his "Manhattan Tower" recording; they did not have children. Jenkins died in Malibu, California. At the time of Jenkins's death, Sinatra called him "one of the modern geniuses of good pop music."

• For information on Jenkins, see Will Friedwald, *Jazz Singing: America's Great Voices from Bessie Smith to Bebop and Beyond* (1990); Friedwald, *Sinatra! The Song Is You: A Singer's Art* (1995); Robert Lissauer, *Lissauer's Encyclopedia of Popular Music in America* (1991); and Joel Whitburn, *Pop Memories 1890–1954* (1986). Obituaries are in the *New York Times*, 3 May 1984, and the *Los Angeles Times*, 2 May 1984.

JAMES FISHER

JENKINS, Helen Hartley (16 Aug. 1860–24 Apr. 1934), philanthropist, was born in New York City, the daughter of Marcellus Hartley, a manufacturer of munitions and firearms, and Frances Chester White. Helen's inclination toward charity work followed the examples set by her grandfather, founder of the Association for Improving the Condition of the Poor, and her father, organizer of the New York social settlement of Hartley House in 1897. Hartley House provided young girls with training in domestic skills as well as social and educational development for unskilled women. A Presbyterian, Helen attended private schools in New York.

Helen Hartley married George Walker Jenkins, a lawyer and businessman, in 1892. The pair had two daughters and later separated. When her father died in 1902, Helen Jenkins became the beneficiary of a great deal of money, which she used to continue charitable works that she had begun in her youth. A supporter of education, she and her nephew donated Hartley Hall, a dormitory, to Columbia University in 1903. Jenkins also contributed $350,000 to have a Philosophy Hall at Columbia and endowed and equipped the Marcellus Hartley Laboratories for the purpose of research.

An advocate of specialized education, Jenkins took the position of trustee of Teachers College, Columbia University, holding that post from 1907 to 1934. When approached to provide monies, she gave generously, which enabled nurses who had already completed schooling in hospitals to further their education to rise in position as heads of nursing schools, nursing teachers, and public health nurses. Financial support for other institutions and organizations furthered her desire to promote education, to improve medical training, and to aid in relief work. A principal donor of the New York Polyclinic Hospital building and endower of the Marcellus Hartley Chair of Materia Medica at New York University Medical School, Jenkins served on the governing boards of a number of hospitals. The School of Nursing at Memorial Hospital, Morristown, New Jersey, was named for her.

Maintaining Hartley House remained a constant in Jenkins's life, and she served as president of its board of trustees from 1926 to 1934. Branching into other areas concerning the poor, Jenkins moved into tenement-house reform along with her daughter Helen. In 1913 she opened the Hartley Open Stair Tenement, which housed a health center and a lunchroom and provided residents with a model of correct sanitation and comfortable living. She renovated other tenements and had one-family and two-family houses built outside New York City. In Towaco, New Jersey, Hartley Farms served as a summer place for underprivileged girls and women.

Jenkins held strongly to the ideals of Americanization and worked hard to aid in the adjustment of Slavic immigrants. In 1909 she opened the Slavonic Immigrant Home in New York City to offer Croats, Czechs, Slovaks, Lithuanians, and Serbians coming into the United States lodging and food and to provide a meeting place for the Serbian Federation. Jenkins established a separate house for the federation's Educational and Benevolent Fund when conditions became too crowded. In keeping with her belief in education she founded the Serbo-American Ecclesiastical Fund to help Serbian schools and churches in the United States. A Presbyterian herself, she donated money to New York's Jan Hus Bohemian Presbyterian Church. During World War I she sought donations to equip a mobile hospital for the Serbian army. Her efforts merited her a gold medal from the National Institute of Social Sciences as well as a medal from the National Slavonic Society and decorations from the Order of St. Sava and the Serbian Red Cross. She became president of the institute in 1923.

Deeply involved in various philanthropic concerns, Jenkins helped to found the Mutual Welfare League of Sing Sing Prison, served on the executive committee of the New York State Prison Council, and was appointed to the Prison Survey Committee, which investigated New York State's prison system. She endowed two professorships in nursing at Columbia University, one in 1910 and one in 1923. In 1921 a bill introduced on her behalf allowed millions of dollars to be dispersed through the Hartley Trust Corporation, which allotted monies to charitable, welfare, and educational facilities. Jenkins died in Morristown, New Jersey.

Helen Hartley Jenkins never gave her money indiscriminately but carefully considered and weighed the choices she made for donations, giving to those whose need she felt was the greatest. She opened her home so that the various organizations she affiliated with, such as the "fusion" movement consisting of bipartisan reformers seeking good government, could meet there. Tactful, organized, and visionary, Jenkins saw to the needs of those less fortunate. She attributed her caring spirit to the generations of Hartleys who Jenkins said believed in their "obligation to do for others and to try at least to live unselfish lives."

• Jenkins appears in numerous *New York Times* articles, including 28 Dec. 1913, 22 Jan. and 12 Aug. 1916, and 29 Jan. and 11 Nov. 1921. See also Lavinia L. Dock, *A Short History of Nursing* (1925); Lawrence A. Cremin et al., *A History of Teachers College, Columbia University* (1954); and W. Morgan Hartshorn, *History of the New York Polyclinic Medical School and Hospital* (1942). Information on Hartley House can be found in Robert A. Woods and Albert J. Kennedy, *Handbook of Settlement* (1911). Obituaries are in the *New York Times* and the *New York Herald Tribune*, 25 Apr. 1934.

MARILYN ELIZABETH PERRY

JENKINS, Micah (1 Dec. 1835–6 May 1864), Confederate general, was born on Edisto Island, South Carolina, the son of John Jenkins, a wealthy planter, and Elizabeth Clark. Educated at the South Carolina Military Academy, he graduated in 1854 at the head of his class. Despite his youth, in 1855 he helped establish the King's Mountain Military School at Yorkville, South Carolina, where he remained until the outbreak of the Civil War. He married Caroline Jamison in 1856; they had four children.

Jenkin's father-in-law, D. F. Jamison, was president of the South Carolina secession convention. This factor, in addition to Jenkins's own high social position, probably assisted his election as colonel of the

Fifth South Carolina Infantry, which he had helped organize. After participating in the first battle of Manassas, he recruited and led the "Palmetto Sharpshooters." At the battle of Seven Pines in May 1862, he commanded a brigade, and his service during the Seven Days' campaign (25 June–1 July 1862) won him promotion to brigadier general in July 1862. Jenkins fought well at the battle of Second Manassas in August 1862, but the story given in John F. Thomas's biography that Robert E. Lee predicted his rise to the rank of lieutenant general is not credible. At Second Manassas Lee was still in temporary command of the Army of Northern Virginia and had no reason to believe his assignment to it would last long enough for Jenkins to rise to high command; also, the rank of lieutenant general had yet to be created by the Confederate Congress. Wounded at Second Manassas, Jenkins missed the battle of Antietam but fought at Fredericksburg in December 1862.

During the winter and spring of 1863, Lee detached James Longstreet to operate in southeastern Virginia. Longstreet, who had made Jenkins his protégé in 1861 following the First Manassas campaign, selected Jenkins's brigade to accompany him and sought opportunities for Jenkins to win higher command. Jenkins directed his men skillfully, but the unsuccessful operations against Suffolk, Virginia, brought him neither glory nor advancement. Moreover, when Longstreet rejoined Lee for the Gettysburg campaign, the War Department (over Lee's protests) held Jenkins's men at Petersburg, Virginia, to forestall an enemy advance, which turned out to be a diversion.

Jenkins's brigade joined John Bell Hood's division (as part of the reinforcements Longstreet brought to Braxton Bragg's army in Georgia) in time for the battle of Chickamauga in September 1863. As the senior brigadier, Jenkins assumed temporary command of the division when Hood fell wounded, producing such intense competition between Jenkins and Brigadier General Evander McIvor Law that the division's effectiveness was severely compromised. Longstreet's open favoritism toward Jenkins exacerbated the tension considerably. As a result, Jenkins unfairly blamed Law for allowing the Federals to gain a foothold near the base of Lookout Mountain during the subsequent Confederate siege of Chattanooga, Tennessee. By the time Longstreet's force was detached from Bragg's to operate against Knoxville, Tennessee, Jenkins and Law were open enemies. Bitter, complex relations continued until the War Department finally named an outsider, Charles W. Field, to command Hood's division.

Jenkins's brigade returned with Longstreet's corps to Virginia in the spring of 1864. During the battle of the Wilderness on 6 May 1864, Jenkins was wounded when he and Longstreet were struck down by a misdirected volley from the Twelfth Virginia. Longstreet recovered, but Jenkins died later that day. He was buried in Charleston, South Carolina. His accidental death deprived the Confederacy of an aggressive combat commander of great promise.

• Jenkins's papers are at Duke University, and many of his reports are printed in *The War of the Rebellion; A Compilation of the Official Records of the Union and Confederate Armies*, (128 vols., 1880–1901). He is the subject of an outdated biography: John F. Thomas, *Career and Character of General Micah Jenkins, C.S.A.* (1905). The fullest modern assessment of his contribution is found in passing in Douglas Southall Freeman, *Lee's Lieutenants: A Study in Command* (3 vols., 1942–1944). Jenkins is praised highly in James Longstreet, *From Manassas to Appomattox* (1896), and G. Moxley Sorrel, *Recollections of a Confederate Staff Officer* (1905). He also receives significant favorable attention in Donald Bridgman Sanger and Thomas R. Hay, *James Longstreet* (1952). But he is severely criticized in Guy R. Swanson and Timothy D. Johnson, "Conflict in East Tennessee: Generals Law, Jenkins, and Longstreet," *Civil War History* 31 (June 1985): 101–10.

WILLIAM GARRETT PISTON

JENKINS, Thornton Alexander (11 Dec. 1811–9 Aug. 1893), naval officer and author, was born in Orange County, Virginia. His parentage is unknown. Preparing for a college education, Jenkins was forced to work as a clerk under the supervision of a merchant. With the help of friends, including Dolley Madison, he joined the U.S. Navy as a midshipman on 1 November 1828. His first tour of duty was in the West Indies fighting pirates from 1828 until 1833. Returning to shore duty, he took an examination for promotion to lieutenant in 1834. Throughout his career Jenkins established a reputation for academic excellence. Accordingly, he passed the examination first in a field of eighty-two examinees and was promoted to lieutenant in 1839.

Jenkins was assigned to coastal surveys, working from 1834 to 1842 in Latin American waters and in the Mediterranean during 1842–1845. From 1845 to 1846 he studied lighthouses in Europe and filed a report with the navy in 1846.

Jenkins initially participated in the war against Mexico as an executive officer aboard the USS *Germantown*, commanding the landing parties at Tuxpan and Tabasco. Later he took command of the *Relief*, a hospital ship used during the conflict, and subsequently commanded the supply station at Salmadena Island.

After the Mexican War, Jenkins resumed his lighthouse and survey work, initially making observations of the Gulf Stream as a part of the 1848–1852 Coast Survey. In 1850–1852 he was secretary of the country's first temporary Lighthouse Board and drafted the law creating the U.S. Lighthouse Service. From 1852 to 1858 he was secretary of the permanent Lighthouse Board established by that law. During the U.S. expedition to Paraguay in 1858–1859, Jenkins was the skipper of the *Preble*, then he returned to the secretaryship of the Lighthouse Board in 1861–1862. In 1861 he published the *Code of Flotilla and Boat Squadron Signals for the United States Navy*.

Jenkins began a distinguished record in the American Civil War by leading the successful expedition to preserve the fortifications at Key West and Dry Tortugas in early 1861. While serving as the skipper of the

Wachusett in the James River from June to September 1862, he was promoted to captain in July. Participating in the Peninsula campaign with the *Wachusett*, he saw action at both City Point and Coggin's Point. In November of that year he drew blockade duty as the captain of the *Oneida* near Mobile, Alabama, serving from 12 November until 28 December as the senior Union naval officer off Mobile.

Jenkins took command of the USS *Mississippi* in February 1863, serving as Admiral David G. Farragut's flag captain. In March of that year Jenkins was the skipper of the *Hartford* when it ran the guns of the Confederate bastions of Port Hudson and Grand Gulf. Later he transferred to the command of the *Richmond* and was in charge of U.S. naval forces below Port Hudson until that fort's surrender in July. He received a slight wound aboard the *Monongahela* on 7 July, the day before Port Hudson's surrender.

Jenkins had a short reprieve from battle during the fall of 1863, when he sailed the *Richmond* to New York for refitting and repair. In December he sailed south, returning to the blockade of Mobile Bay, a mission he performed until February 1865. He commanded the Second Division under Farragut at the battle of Mobile Bay in 1864. Admiral Farragut's August 1864 report on the battle lauded Jenkins's abilities, persistence, and performance of duty. Jenkins finished the war not far from where he had been in September 1862, in the James River, supporting General Ulysses S. Grant's forces besieging Richmond.

After the Civil War, Jenkins was chosen as the navy's chief of the Bureau of Navigation. He resumed his writing career, publishing *Instructions for Hydrographic Surveyors* in 1868. The next year he published three key maritime texts, *The Rule of the Road at Sea and in Inland Waters*, *The Barometer, Thermometer, Hygrometer and Atmospheric Appearances at Sea and on Land as Aids in Foretelling Weather*, and *Ship's Compasses*. He served as Navigation Bureau chief until 1869, earning praise from Secretary of the Navy Gideon Welles, who called Jenkins one of the best-informed officers in the navy. On 13 July 1870 Jenkins was made a rear admiral, and he was placed in command of the Asiatic Squadron in 1872. He retired on 11 December 1873.

Little is known of Jenkins's home life. He was initially married to a woman named Powers and then to a daughter of Navy Paymaster Thornton. He and his second wife had three daughters and two sons. He died in Washington, D.C. Jenkins provided the country with competent leadership at sea and outstanding performance in battle. In addition, he advanced the maritime knowledge and expertise of the United States.

• A biographical sketch of Jenkins is in L. G. Tyler, *Encyclopedia of Virginia Biography* (1915). Jenkins's career highlights are in L. R. Hamersly, *The Records of Living Officers of the U.S. Navy and Marine Corps*, 4th ed. (1890). His Civil War service is in *The Official Records of the Union and Confederate*

Navies in the War of the Rebellion (30 vols., 1894–1922). Obituaries are in the *Army and Naval Journal*, 12 Aug. 1893, and the *Washington Post*, 10 Aug. 1893.

ROD PASCHALL

JENKS, Jeremiah Whipple (2 Sept. 1856–24 Aug. 1929), political economist, was born in St. Clair, Michigan, the son of Benjamin Lane Jenks and Amanda Messer. Jenks's early education was in the St. Clair public school system. In 1878 he received his B.A. degree in classics from the University of Michigan. Following graduation, he began a lengthy academic career.

Jenks's first teaching post was at Mount Morris College in Mount Morris, Illinois (1879–1880 and 1881–1883), where he taught classical languages and German. In addition to his teaching responsibilities, Jenks earned an M.A. from Michigan in 1879 and studied law as well. In 1881 he was admitted to the Michigan bar.

During his stay at Mount Morris, Jenks became interested in the rapidly developing discipline of political economy. This interest led him to the second major career change of his adult life (the study of law being his first). Jenks left his teaching position at Mount Morris to pursue doctoral studies in political economy in Germany. In 1885 he received his Ph.D. in political economy from the University of Halle. His dissertation, entitled *Henry C. Carey als Nationalokonom* (Henry C. Carey as National Economist), was published the same year. Jenks was married in 1884 to Georgia Bixler; they had three children.

Jenks returned to the United States in 1886, accepting a position teaching both English literature and political science at Knox College in Galesburg, Illinois. In 1889 he moved to Indiana University where he taught both political economy and social science (1889–1891). In 1891 Jenks became professor of political economy at Cornell University. He remained at Cornell for twelve years, during which time he also actively consulted for the federal government in economic matters (mainly involving industrial combinations, currency regulation, and immigration). While at Cornell, Jenks's intellectual attitude grew less abstract and more pragmatic. He refocused his research on the application of economic theories to politics. Jenks's practical approach to understanding and resolving political problems—anticipating, in many ways, modern public-choice scholarship—garnered much praise and enabled him to become the first American economist to devote a major portion of his career to service on government commissions and panels.

Jenks's first position with the federal government (1899–1901) was as an expert agent for the U.S. Industrial Commission. The commission at the time investigated the effects of industrial combinations on the economics of the United States and Europe. Jenks conducted a major empirical investigation of industrial trusts in both locations. Jenks authored the main essay, "Industrial Combinations and Prices," which appeared in the first volume of the commission's report,

Preliminary Report on Trusts and Industrial Combinations (1900). He also wrote volume eighteen, *Industrial Combinations in Europe* (1901). Out of this research, he wrote *The Trust Problem* (1900). (A revised version of this work, written with W. E. Clark, appeared in 1917.)

In 1901–1902 Jenks served as a special expert on questions of currency, labor, taxation and policy in the Orient; in this capacity he traveled to the Philippines, where he familiarized himself with the approach taken to these subjects in the Far East. Research conducted there led to the publication of *Economic Questions on the English and Dutch Colonies in the Orient* (1902). With this work Jenks secured his reputation as an international currency expert. He was thus appointed in 1903 by the Mexican government as a consultant on currency reform.

Also in 1903 Jenks accepted an appointment from President Theodore Roosevelt to serve, along with Charles A. Conant and Hugh H. Hanna, on the temporary Commission on International Exchange. This commission was created to study international monetary exchange in North America, Europe, and Asia. As a commissioner, Jenks returned in 1903 to Asia, again studying the Philippines and for the first time studying China. The commission's research and recommendations were published in a two-volume set (1903, 1904). It recommended that countries on the silver standard adopt instead the gold standard. Doing so, the commissioners argued, would stabilize international exchange rates and, hence, reduce unnecessary financial uncertainty afflicting foreign trade. American exports would thus be promoted.

Jenks pursued many interests. Between 1889 and 1909 he published five books related neither to trusts nor to currency-exchange problems: *Road Legislation for the American State* (1889), *Citizenship and the Schools* (1909), *Great Fortunes* (1906), *The Political and Social Significance of the Life and Teachings of Jesus* (1906), and *The Principles of Politics* (1909). Jenks served as president of the American Economic Association from 1906 to 1907.

That Jenks possessed a multifaceted intellect is apparent not only in his diverse publications but also in a review of the various government positions he held. In 1907 he accepted an appointment as a member of the U.S. Immigration Commission. As with his earlier studies, Jenks's labors for this commission were largely empirical, providing him with data for new research. In 1913 he coauthored *The Immigration Problem*, with W. Jett Lauck, which became a popular collegiate textbook. During his tenure on the immigration commission, Jenks persuaded the U.S. Congress to enact legislation condemning the white slave trade. Jenks resigned in 1912 from Cornell and moved to New York City, where he taught government and public administration at New York University. There, Jenks became president of the Alexander Hamilton Institute (1913–1921).

Jenks took a hiatus from government work during the Taft administration, only to return in 1917 as the U.S. High Commissioner for Nicaragua. Jenks's connection to Nicaragua also extended to the private sector; he served as director of the Pacific Railroad of Nicaragua from 1918 until his death. His work in Nicaragua included helping the country to revise its banking laws in 1925. In the postwar period Jenks was also called on by the German Weimar government for his expertise on currency issues.

In his academic work Jenks maintained generally conservative positions. But, although not a progressive, Jenks possessed great faith that scientific methods could usefully be brought to bear on public policy questions. His cautious approach to policy reform is evidenced by the final sentence in *The Trust Problem*, where he assessed the wisdom of taxing monopoly profits for purposes of wealth redistribution: "That result, however, desirable as it is, and one upon which our eyes should be fixed as the ultimate goal, is one which can be secured by legislation without great harm to our delicate industrial machinery only through the knowledge that comes from wider and longer experience."

Jenks died in New York City and was buried in St. Clair, Michigan.

• Jenks's Works not cited in the text include "Land Transfer Reform," in *The Annals of the American Academy of Political and Social Science*, vol. 2 (1892), *Economic Legislation* (1893), "The Social Basis of Proportional Representation," in *The Annals of the American Academy of Political and Social Science*, vol. 6 (1895), "English Colonial Fiscal Systems in the Far East," in *American Economic Association Publications*, n.s., vol. 3 (1900), "The Modern Standard of Business Honor," in *American Economic Association Publications*, 3d ser., vol. 8 (1907), *Government Action for Social Welfare* (1910), *Twelve Studies in the Making of a Nation: The Beginnings of Israel's History*, with Charles Foster Kent (1912), *The Character and Influence of Recent Immigration* (1913), *The Trend toward Government Management of Business* (1915), *Business and the Government* (1917), "A World Centre of Communication: Economic Advantages," in *Creation of a World Centre of Communication*, ed. Hendrik C. Andersen and Olivia C. Andersen, vol. 2 (Paris, 1918), *The Soul of Business* (1919), *Great American Issues*, with John Hays Hammond (1921), *International Exchange*, with E. L. S. Patterson (1924), *America: Our Government, Our History, Our Work*, with Joseph French Johnson, Rufus Daniel Smith, and Albert Bushnell Hart (1925), *We and Our Government*, with Rufus Daniel Smith (1927), *The Science of Business* (1927), "Industrial Combinations," in *A Century of Industrial Progress*, ed. Frederic W. Wile (1928), "The Philippines Under American Government," in *Colonies of the World*, ed. Edward J. Payne (1939), and "Late Events and Present Conditions," in *China*, ed. Robert K. Douglas (1939). Obituaries are in the *New York Times*, 25 Aug. 1929, and the *American Economic Review* 19 (Dec. 1929): 745.

DONALD J. BOUDREAUX

JENKS, Joseph (c. 1599–Mar. 1683), ironworker and inventor, was born in London, England, the son of John Jenks, a cutler, and Sarah Fulwater, the daughter of an immigrant German cutler. Having also learned the cutler's trade, Jenks married Jone Hearne in Buckinghamshire in 1627; they had two children.

In the 1630s Jenks worked under German supervision in Benjamin Stone's water-powered sword factory at Hounslow in the earl of Northumberland's estate in Middlesex, southwest of London. Charles I had imported German ironworkers to train English journeymen and apprentices at Stone's factory, established in 1629, whence survives a broadsword inscribed "IENCKES IOSEPH ME FECIT HOUNSLOW". In 1639 the earl of Northumberland granted Jenks a plot of ground downriver from Stone's factory to set up a "New invented Engine or Blade Mille" at Woorton Bridge, but, by late 1641, Jenks had emigrated to Maine. There he worked as blacksmith at Agamenticus (now York).

On a trip to Maine in the winter of 1643–1644, John Winthrop, Jr., probably informed Jenks about plans to establish an ironworks in New England. Jenks joined in plans for a bog-iron "plantation" at Nashaway (now Lancaster) in Massachusetts, but they were aborted. In mid-1646 the General Court of Massachusetts approved Jenks's petition for an exclusive privilege, or fourteen-year patent, to set up mills for making scythes and other edge tools and a "new Invented Saw Mill." Instead of a sawmill, in early 1648 Jenks established an edge-tool mill at the Hammersmith ironworks, which had recently been built by Richard Leader, Winthrop's successor in ironmaking, on the Saugus River at Lynn, Massachusetts.

Water from the tailrace of the Hammersmith blast furnace ran three waterwheels at his mill, presumably to power the bellows, hammers, and grindstones he used in making scythes, axes, saws, and other edge tools.

The Saugus works gave Jenks bar and cast iron for constructing his waterpower system and sold bar iron to him thereafter. He in turn sold his products to the ironworks and to others. Richard Leader built a sawmill on the Piscataqua River in Maine in 1650, which probably used Jenks-made saws.

Jenks's wife had died in 1635, and around 1650 he married a woman named Elizabeth (maiden name unknown); they had five children. His sons, including his son from his first marriage, followed him into the ironworking trade.

Jenks acquired a reputation for energy and inventiveness. The Boston selectmen were authorized in 1654 to ask him to make "Ingins to Carry water in Case of fire," and the next year the General Court granted him a seven-year monopoly to manufacture an "engine . . . for the more speedy cutting of grasse." In 1667 the General Court rejected Jenks's petition for a subsidy in order to start a wire-drawing operation and instead offered a two-pound encouragement for the manufacture of pins and wool cards from wire. Numerous pins excavated from the site of Jenks's forge suggest that he produced them. The General Court rejected Jenks's offer in 1672 "for making of money"; instead, silver coins of pine tree design were minted in Boston by John Hull. Like later "ingenious Yankees," Jenks gathered credit posthumously for more inventions and "firsts" than recent scholarship has substantiated, such

as sawmills, fire engines, lawn mowers, American-style scythes, and coinage.

Outliving his second wife, Jenks continued to work into his old age and died in Lynn (now Saugus), Massachusetts. His son Samuel carried on his father's blacksmith shop from 1679, probably with his brother John's help, until his death in 1738. The youngest son, Daniel, joined Jenks's oldest son, Joseph Jenks, Jr., at the forge that he had set up in Pawtucket in 1672. At both places the Jenkses trained apprentices who in turn established ironworking shops elsewhere, thereby continuing and adapting the skilled tradition Jenks had learned from Germans in England, to supply American sawmills with mill saws, lumbermen with axes, and farmers with scythes. The proliferation of skills in using water power to make edge tools was an important precondition for the subsequent growth of New England's machine-making and -using industries in the late eighteenth and nineteenth centuries.

• Historical files at Saugus Iron Works National Historic Site, Saugus, Mass., contain copies of documents on Jenks's life in England and New England and unpublished papers about him. A booklet by Stephen P. Carlson, *Joseph Jenks, Colonial Toolmaker and Inventor* (1973; repr. 1981), gives a brief account of his life, stripped of the legends that derive from Alonzo Lewis, *The History of Lynn, Essex County, Massachusetts* (1829), and are repeated in William Bradford Browne, comp., *Genealogy of the Jenks Family in America* (1952). Meredith Bright Colket, Jr., *The Jenks Family in England* (1956), also provides genealogical information. Edward Neal Hartley, *Ironworks on the Saugus: The Lynn and Braintree Ventures of the Company of Undertakers of the Ironworks in New England* (1957), tells the story of the ironworks, which underwent archaeological excavation in the late 1940s and early 1950s. Reconstructed without Jenks's forge, it is operated by the U.S. National Park Service.

CAROLYN C. COOPER

JENNEWEIN, C. Paul (2 Dec. 1890–23 Feb. 1978), sculptor, was born Carl Paul Jennewein in Stuttgart, Germany, the son of Louis Jennewein, a die engraver, and Emilia Weber. At age thirteen he became an apprentice technician at the Stuttgart Museum, where he learned painting and sculptural techniques. After immigrating to the United States in 1907, he settled in New York City. Through his father's associations he obtained a two-year apprenticeship at the firm of Buhler and Lauter, commercial modelers and sculptors who worked extensively for the architectural firm of McKim, Mead and White. In the evenings Jennewein began studying drawing with George Bridgman at the Art Students' League; in 1910 he also studied with the painter DeWitt Clinton Peters. At the beginning of his career he worked both as a painter and ornamental sculptor, creating decorations for the elegant New York homes of John D. Rockefeller, Jr., and Archer Huntington, murals for the Woolworth Building and Columbia University Chapel (both in New York City), the Church of the Holy Spirit in Kingston, New York, and a design for a decorative gate at Harvard University. In 1912 he traveled through France, Germany, Italy, and Egypt to expand his education.

In 1916 Jennewein won the prestigious Prix de Rome for sculpture. His residence at the American Academy in Rome determined his future as a leading exponent of the academy. He remained in Italy until 1920, his studies interrupted for a year (1918–1919) when he worked for the American Red Cross. While there in 1918 Jennewein married an Italian painter, Gina Pirra; they had five children. Jennewein immersed himself in drawing and studying ancient Greek, Roman, and Italian Renaissance art. Usually mythological in subject matter, his early figurative work demonstrated a delicate sense of line and proportion. His young children often served as inspiration, although he always avoided sentimentality. *Cupid and Gazelle* (1919) became the first of his works to enter a public institution when the Metropolitan Museum of Art purchased it in 1922.

Upon his return to the United States Jennewein devoted most of his time to executing a series of important commissions for fountains, including Darlington Memorial Fountain, in Washington, D.C. (1920–1923), and Pilgrims Memorial Fountain, in Plymouth, Massachusetts (1921). He also completed several memorials, including the Soldiers' and Sailors' Memorial, in Barre, Vermont (1921–1924); the Soldiers and Sailors Memorial, in Providence, Rhode Island (1927–1929; and the Tours War Memorial, in France (1928–1931). But his work for the new Philadelphia Museum of Art established his reputation as one of the country's premier architectural sculptors. In 1924 Jennewein, along with John Gregory, began to plan the overall concept for a sculptural ensemble that would be in accord with the archaeologically accurate neoclassical building that Charles Borie of the Philadelphia firm of Borie, Trumbauer, Zantzinger, Associated Architects had designed. Borie hired Jennewein because he considered the sculptor's academy training compatible with the aesthetics of the building and knew of his interest in polychromy. Jennewein accompanied him to Greece to examine the vestiges of color on Greek statuary. Later, with the advice of Leon Solon, an authority on polychromy, he was able to follow the ancient Greek custom of coloring statuary. The completed sculptures were cast in glazed terracotta by Atlantic Terra Cotta Company, Perth Amboy, New Jersey, to insure the vividness of their hues. Such use of polychrome was revolutionary for early twentieth-century sculpture.

During these years Jennewein also won awards and critical praise for a number of smaller figurative bronze sculptures created for private consumption. The most famous, *Greek Dance* (1926, Los Angeles County Museum of Art), was his most stylized treatment of the human figure: in pose and outline the classical nude echoes the angular movements of a Ballet Russe dancer. No doubt inspired by his work for the Philadelphia Museum, Jennewein experimented with a variety of different color patinas, even creating several polychrome versions of *Greek Dance* (San Diego Museum of Art). His use of a monochromatic black patina would become typical of neoclassical sculpture of the period. His most popular independent sculpture, *Greek Dance* was cast twenty-five times; along with Paul Manship's *Salome*, it came to epitomize American art deco sculpture.

Jennewein's reputation was firmly established by the time of the completion of the Philadelphia Museum sculptures in 1933. Grand Central Galleries in New York accorded him a solo exhibition in 1927, followed by a second in 1935 that included his superb academic drawings and recent work in porcelain and aluminum. In 1924 he had built a large studio in the Bronx, and during the 1930s he hired several artists to assist him. The decade was successful, despite the depression, for Jennewein continued to receive some of the most desirable commissions of the period. He was one of many artists chosen to decorate the new Rockefeller Center in New York City, his nine symbolic bronze figures designed for the entrance of the British Empire Building. Charles Borie gave him the commission for the sculpture of the new Department of Justice Building on the Federal Triangle in Washington, D.C., some fifty sculptures in a variety of materials and sizes. His ability as a decorative artist was tested with the gold-leaf sculpted pylons at the Brooklyn Public Library. Although the figure remained his major motif, Jennewein departed from it for his Spanish War Memorial (Rochester, N.Y.), a powerfully simple, symbolic composition of an eagle on the prow of a ship.

Although his art was aesthetically eclipsed by the dominance of modernism after World War II, Jennewein continued to receive commissions until the early 1960s. His most significant late project was the Ardennes Memorial in Neuville-en-Condroz, Belgium. Thereafter he devoted most of his energy to designing commemorative plaques and medals. An ardent proponent of academic art throughout his life, Jennewein served as president of the National Sculpture Society from 1960 to 1963. In 1980, two years after his death in Larchmont, New York, the Tampa Museum, having become the repository of most of his estate, accorded Jennewein a retrospective exhibition.

• The artist's papers (personal and business correspondence, catalogs, sketchbooks, biographical material, and photographs) and the transcript of a 1978 interview by George Gurney, are at the Archives of American Art, Smithsonian Institution. Other papers (studio ledger, account books, and transcript of a 1971 interview) are at the Tampa Museum, Tampa, Fla. The artist's reminiscence about the Philadelphia Museum project is in "Sculpture and the Challenge of Color," *National Sculpture Review* 9 (Winter 1960–1961): 5. See also Kineton Parkes, "Plastic Form and Colour: The Work of Paul Jennewein," *Apollo* 17 (Apr. 1933): 130–34, and John J. Cunningham, ed., *C. Paul Jennewein* (1950). The most comprehensive monograph is Shirley Reiff Howarth, *C. Paul Jennewein, Sculptor* (1980), an exhibition catalog with extensive chronology and a bibliography. See also a chapter on the artist in Janis Conner and Joel Rosenkranz, *Rediscoveries in*

American Sculpture: Studio Works, 1893–1939 (1989), pp. 79–86. Steven Eric Bronson discusses the Philadelphia project in "John Gregory: The Philadelphia Museum of Art Pediment" (M.A. thesis, Univ. of Delaware, 1977), and George Gurney describes the Department of Justice Building in *Sculpture and the Federal Triangle* (1985).

ILENE SUSAN FORT

JENNEY, William Le Baron (25 Sept. 1832–15 June 1907), engineer and architect, was born in Fairhaven, Massachusetts, the son of William Proctor Jenney, a prosperous whaling ship owner, and Eliza Le Baron Gibbs. Jenney received his early education at Phillips Academy in Andover, Massachusetts, and other New England schools. After visiting the California gold fields and touring the islands of the South Pacific (1850–1851), including the Philippines, he decided to become a civil engineer. He enrolled in the Lawrence Scientific School of Harvard University but, finding it inadequate, transferred to the École Centrale des Arts et Manufactures in Paris in 1853. He graduated in 1856 and became one of the few professionally trained engineers in the United States. The École Centrale intended that its graduates work in private industry, as opposed to the École Polytechnique, whose graduates entered the military or civil service. The École Centrale, which gave a course in architecture as part of its curriculum, introduced Jenney to a philosophy of classical functionalism based on the architectural program of Polytechnique established by J. N. L. Durand.

After leaving Centrale Jenney worked in Mexico for a year building a railroad on the Isthmus of Tehuantepec. In 1859 he again traveled to France for the Berdon Bakery Company to design a "mechanical bakery" for the French army. He socialized with American expatriates such as the artist James Abbott McNeill Whistler and decided at this time to become an architect.

With the outbreak of the Civil War, Jenney entered the army as an engineering officer and served with distinction on the staffs of Generals Ulysses S. Grant and William T. Sherman. He left the army in 1866 as a brevet major and began architectural practice in Chicago within a year. In 1867 he married Elizabeth Hannah Cobb of Cleveland, Ohio; they had two sons. He laid out the West Chicago Park System and, with Frederick Law Olmsted, Sr., the garden suburb of Riverside, Illinois, in 1869–1870.

Jenney designed numerous homes in Chicago and throughout the Midwest. Invariably he planned them in an open and commodious manner, employing every possible modern convenience. He worked in almost every style but preferred a modern Gothic.

Jenney's fame derives primarily from his Chicago office buildings. He tried to make each functional and bright. Using a system of iron columns similar to French grain warehouses, he braced the exterior masonry walls of the first Leiter Building (1879) and thereby created a wall in which glass predominated. He did not fireproof it, however. This he accomplished in the Home Insurance Building (1884–1885).

Using contemporary technologies of hollow tile arches on iron beams and interior iron columns sheathed with terra cotta in combination with his own innovation of exterior iron columns enclosed in brickwork, Jenney came close to creating a skeletal building in which a metal frame supported the masonry envelope.

The Home Insurance was only nine and a half stories high, hardly a "skyscraper." Jenney achieved a breakthrough in the Manhattan Building (1890), possibly the first sixteen-story commercial structure supported entirely by an iron frame. Most critics consider his second Leiter Building (1891—later Sears, Roebuck) his greatest aesthetic success. Using iron columns and steel lintels, he opened the walls to an unprecedented degree. Its severe classicism and minimal decoration embodied the principles that Jenney learned at the École Centrale, yet it anticipated the functionalist design of the International School by over a generation. He also designed the Horticultural Building of the World's Columbian Exposition (1893).

Jenney was well read in the theory and history of architecture. He conveyed his knowledge through writing, lecturing, and teaching. Because so many, such as Louis Sullivan and Daniel Burnham, who passed through his atelier later attained renown, it can be said that he founded the Chicago School of architecture. Jenney died in Los Angeles.

• Letters and other documents relating to Jenney are in the Ryerson-Burnham Library of the Chicago Art Institute, the University of Michigan Historical Collection, and the Archives of the École Centrale des Arts et Manufactures. Jenney wrote *Principles and Practice of Architecture* (1869) and contributed many articles to the *Inland Architect*. References to him are also in *The War of the Rebellion: A Compilation of the Official Records of the Union and Confederate Armies* (128 vols., 1880–1901). See also Carl W. Condit, *The Chicago School of Architecture* (1964); Frank A. Randall, *History of the Development of Building Construction in Chicago* (1949); and Theodore Turak, *William Le Baron Jenney: Pioneer of Modern Architecture* (1986).

THEODORE TURAK

JENNINGS, Herbert Spencer (8 Apr. 1868–14 Apr. 1947), biologist, was born in Tonica, Illinois, the son of George Nelson Jennings, a physician, and Olive Taft Jenks. Jennings's father accumulated an extensive home library, and the boy learned to read very young. The family lived from 1874 to 1879 in various places in California, then returned to Tonica, where Jennings attended public high school. He then taught in country schools for a short time.

Jennings attended Illinois State Normal School, near Bloomington, in 1887–1888. The next year he was assistant professor of botany and horticulture at Texas A & M College. In 1890 he enrolled at the University of Michigan and there became interested in zoology through a course offered by Jacob Reighard. He also enjoyed the philosophy courses of John Dewey. During college summers he worked for the Michigan Fish Commission on a survey of lakes. For it, at the urging of Reighard, he concentrated on the microscopic animal group of rotifers (invertebrates with anterior cilia common in fresh water and the ocean). He received a B.S. in zoology in 1893 and remained for a year at the University of Michigan as a graduate assistant. He then undertook graduate studies at Harvard University, where he received an M.A. in zoology in 1895. That summer he did research at the Agassiz Laboratory in Newport, Rhode Island, an experience he found stimulating. He received a Ph.D. in zoology in 1896, with a thesis on the early embryology of a rotifer. During his graduate years he was especially influenced by Charles Benedict Davenport, then an instructor at Harvard, who turned Jennings's interests from descriptive to experimental biology.

Through a Parker Travelling Fellowship Jennings spent 1896–1897 in Europe, where he studied physiology and psychology under Max Verworn at Jena, Germany. His researches were on the behavior and responses to stimuli of the protozoan *Paramecium*. He then went to the Naples Zoological Laboratory, where he became acquainted with many European biologists.

On his return to the United States, Jennings served as professor of botany at Montana State Agricultural and Mechanical College (1897–1898); instructor in zoology at Dartmouth (1898–1899), to replace a professor on leave; and instructor (1899–1901) and assistant professor (1901–1903) in zoology at the University of Michigan. He married artist Mary Louise Burridge in 1898; they had one son. Jennings was coauthor with Reighard of the textbook *Anatomy of the Cat* (1901), and in summers he continued as an assistant with the Michigan lake surveys under Reighard and in 1902 was director of the program for the U.S. Fish Commission Biological Survey of the Great Lakes.

From 1896, at the various locations, Jennings pursued experimental studies on primitive animals and their reactions. His many published papers were mostly in biological journals, but one was in *American Journal of Psychology* ("The Psychology of a Protozoan," 10 [1899]: 503–15). He had become much interested in the complexity of behavior of these organisms, which he credited to their entire structure. This theme drew the attention of biologist Jacques Loeb, who maintained that actions of living forms can be explained solely as physical and chemical reactions. Loeb and colleagues attacked Jennings's work severely in print. At a scientific meeting in 1900, however, Jennings demonstrated his experiments and obtained agreement from Loeb of their validity.

In 1903 Jennings was appointed assistant professor of zoology at the University of Pennsylvania, with permission for a year's leave of absence at the Naples Zoological Laboratory through a grant from the Carnegie Institution of Washington. Jennings published the results of his researches at Naples as *Contributions to the Study of the Behavior of Lower Organisms* (1904). His next book was *Behavior of Lower Organisms* (1906), which, according to his biographer Tracy Morton Sonneborn, "became a classic in the history of experimental biology and behaviorist psychology."

In 1906 Jennings went to Johns Hopkins University as associate professor and the next year became professor of experimental zoology. He was provided with laboratory facilities and a light teaching program. His title from 1910 was Henry Walters Professor, and he served as director of the zoological laboratory from 1910 until his retirement in 1938.

The field of biology had been stimulated by the rediscovery in 1900 of the earlier work of Gregor Mendel on inheritance in certain plants. Jennings was among those attracted to the field. At Johns Hopkins he began studies of the genetics and evolution of the unicellular organisms *Paramecium* and *Difflugia*. His efforts were aimed at determining the origin of hereditary variations in a biological entity in which reproduction is primarily asexual. He established that the asexual progeny of an individual protozoan were identical with the original source, and, through studies by some of his graduate students, he recognized that the same was true in multicellular organisms that have asexual reproduction.

As a result of his appointment to director of the zoological laboratory and his increasing university commitments, Jennings had less time for his own researches but continued to supervise graduate students. His participation in national and international programs included service to the Food Administration during World War I, five years of committee service on the National Research Council (1920–1925), considerable outside lecturing, and the publication of several popular books, including *Life and Death: Heredity and Evolution in Unicellular Organisms* (1920), *Prometheus; or, Biology and the Advancement of Man* (1925), *The Biological Basis of Human Nature* (1930), and *The Universe and Life* (1933). His more technical books were *Genetics of the Protozoa* (1929) and his textbook *Genetics* (1935).

Shortly after his retirement from Johns Hopkins in 1938, Jennings's wife died, and the next spring he accepted an invitation as visiting professor at the University of California, Los Angeles. He continued there as a research associate and resumed his researches of *Paramecium*, on which he published several significant papers. In 1939 he married Lulu Plant Jennings, the widow of his brother. They had no children.

Jennings's work was of interest to biologists and philosophers. According to Sonneborn, "Finally, he synthesized this approach to the two fields of behavior and genetics into a beautiful, integrated view of science, philosophy, and the practice of human living. . . . In the lower and higher organisms, and in man, behavior was viewed as determined, though at increasing levels of complexity, by the properties of organismic structure and its responses to previous experience."

Jennings received several honorary degrees and was elected to the National Academy of Sciences in 1914. He died in Santa Monica, California.

• Many records of Jennings, including diaries and letters, are in the library of the American Philosophical Society in Philadelphia. The primary biographical articles are by Tracy Morton Sonneborn in *Genetics* 33 (1948): 1–4, and National Academy of Sciences, *Biographical Memoirs* 47 (1975): 142–223, with bibliography. The introduction by Donald D. Jensen to the 1962 edition of Jennings's book *Behavior of the Lower Organisms* includes an analysis of his scientific work. Another account of his scientific work is Carl Pontius Swanson, "A History of Biology at the Johns Hopkins University," *Bios* 22 (1951): 223–62.

ELIZABETH NOBLE SHOR

JENNINGS, Hugh Ambrose (2 Apr. 1871–1 Feb. 1928), baseball player and manager, was born in Pittston, Pennsylvania, the son of James Jennings, a coal miner. (His mother's name is unknown.) Like his Irish immigrant father, Hughie, as everyone called him, went to work in the mines, starting at 90 cents a day. While still in school, however, he found that he could make five dollars a game playing baseball on Sundays, and he soon left the mines permanently. He was a good enough player that in 1890 he signed with Allentown of the Eastern Interstate League. Within a year he was promoted to Louisville of the American Association, and from 1893 to 1899 he starred for the famous Baltimore Orioles.

Jennings, who threw and batted right-handed, played shortstop on a team that included John McGraw, Willie Keeler, Joe Kelley, and Wilbert Robinson, all future Hall of Famers. During Jennings's years in Baltimore, the Orioles won three consecutive National League pennants. They played hard, tough baseball, stressing base stealing and the hit-and-run play. Jennings fit easily into the mold. The Orioles were broken up by a league realignment after the 1899 season, and he and some of his teammates went briefly to Brooklyn and Philadelphia.

Jennings spent most of 1899 with Brooklyn, but he hurt his arm and played less than half the season. In 1900 he played 115 games at first base for Brooklyn, his last full season as a player. He played part time for Philadelphia and Brooklyn from 1901 until 1903. In 1900 major league baseball went through one of its periodic readjustments. Baltimore was one of the cities losing its franchise, emerging in 1904 as a minor league team in the Eastern League. Jennings was selected as its manager, and in the next four years he directed Baltimore to three first division finishes, while playing only on occasion.

His close friend, McGraw, wrote that he persuaded Jennings to finish school while they were still young players. The two attended St. Bonaventure College together, then Jennings matriculated at Cornell University school of law in 1901–1902. He finished law school in 1904 and was admitted to the Pennsylvania state bar in 1907. He continued to play major league ball during his college days, and he paid his tuition by coaching the collegians.

Jennings's performance as manager earned him a promotion back to the major leagues. From 1907 through 1920 he managed the Detroit Tigers, then finished his baseball career as a coach for McGraw's New York Giants, occasionally managing during McGraw's frequent illnesses. Jennings retired after the team's 1925 tour of Japan.

Jennings's record as a player included a .311 batting average in 1,285 games. His average of .401 in 1896 was his best, and it was the highest achieved by a National League shortstop. Three times he led the league in fielding until a sore arm forced his move to first base. He was also an accomplished base stealer, stealing 53, 70, and 60 bases in three straight seasons. But perhaps his most unusual record was for being hit by pitched balls. Although weighing only 165 pounds, he refused to yield the inside of the plate to pitchers; he was hit three times in one game and forty-nine times in one season. One wild pitch struck him in the head, inflicting a concussion, which was made more dangerous because of an earlier skull fracture suffered in a diving accident.

To fans of a later generation, Jennings was best known for his managerial skills and style. When he took over the Detroit Tigers in 1907 he inherited a second-division team that rarely kept a manager for more than a year. In Jennings's first season the team batting average improved by about twenty points, and it generally remained there during his long tenure. He relied on his own outstanding playing reputation, his ability to coach young players, and his fiery will to win in leading the Tigers. His managerial skills especially affected Sam Crawford and the young Ty Cobb, both of whom raised their batting averages dramatically in Jennings's first few years. Cobb would probably have been Cobb under any circumstances, but Jennings encouraged his fierce playing style. In Jennings's first three years the Tigers won the American League pennant three times, but in each case their inferior pitching cost them the World Series. Although in his fourteen years at Detroit the team finished in the first division ten times, the Tigers never won the pennant under him again. Eventually, Jennings's sarcasm and drive to win irritated his players, and his last few years with Detroit were often bitter. His overall record as a manager, including a few games with the New York Giants, was 1,163 wins and 984 losses. Jennings coached with the Giants from 1921 through 1925, after which he retired.

Most players who remembered Jennings commented on his fiery coaching style at third base, where he stood on one leg and screamed something that sounded like "Eee-yah" at opponents. He claimed (confirmed by one umpire) to have invented "Attaboy," a corruption of "That's the boy."

Jennings's abrasive reputation on the playing field did not carry over into his business career. He developed a thriving law practice off-season, served as a bank director and an officer of country clubs, and he avidly participated in charitable activities. In 1925 he suffered what was described as a "nervous breakdown," and he was never normally active again. One writer, Richard Bak, declared that Jennings's judgment had been crippled by alcoholism, but he also was badly hurt when his car overturned shortly before he contracted meningitis, the apparent cause of his death in Scranton, Pennsylvania.

Jennings was selected by the Veterans Committee of the Baseball Writers of America to the National Baseball Hall of Fame in 1945. He was married twice and had one child. His second wife's name was Nora, but further information about his marriages is unavailable.

• A file at the National Baseball Hall of Fame and Museum includes some family information. Cornell University provided academic material. Most of the statistical information on Jennings comes from John Thorn and Pete Palmer, eds., *Total Baseball*, 3d ed. (1993). *Baseball* (1987), ed. David L. Porter, has a thorough sketch by Charles C. Alexander. Many personal sidelights are to be found in John McGraw, *My Thirty Years in Baseball* (1923). For Jennings's years with the Tigers, see Alexander, *Ty Cobb* (1984), and Richard Bak, *Cobb Would Have Caught It* (1991). An obituary is in the *New York Times*, 2 Feb. 1928.

THOMAS L. KARNES

JENNINGS, Jonathan (1784?–26 July 1834), politician and governor, was the son of the Reverend Jacob Jennings, a physician and Presbyterian minister, and Mary Kennedy. His family moved from New Jersey to western Virginia in 1784, and both the date and place of Jennings's birth are unknown. From the age of eight he was raised in the frontier country of southwestern Pennsylvania. He was educated in the classical tradition at Canonsburg Academy in Canonsburg, Pennsylvania, which became Jefferson College during his attendance, but he left before completing his degree.

In January 1806 Jennings traveled to Steubenville, Ohio, his trip financed by his brother-in-law Dr. David Mitchell. After a few months studying law with his older brother Obadiah, Jennings moved to Vincennes, in the Indiana Territory. Although he was admitted to the bar in April 1807, Jennings apparently never practiced law. He served for about a year as clerk of the federal land office but failed in his effort to become clerk of the territorial house of representatives, narrowly avoiding a duel with the successful candidate. Suffering from poor health and caught up in political controversies, including a hostile investigation of his conduct as clerk of the trustees of Vincennes University, Jennings moved to Charlestown, in southern Indiana, late in 1808.

After failing in brief speculations in land and trade, Jennings soon found success as the political spokesman for the small landholders of southeastern Indiana. He campaigned vigorously to become the territory's delegate in Congress, attacking Governor William Henry Harrison and his "Virginia aristocrats" for their efforts to establish slavery in Indiana. Jennings was young and popular, and as he campaigned he would stop to help a pioneer repair his cabin or split rails. In May 1809 he narrowly defeated Thomas Randolph, the territorial attorney general, and became the territorial delegate. He survived a complex legal challenge to the validity of his election.

In Washington, Jennings favored the interests of the ordinary pioneer and maneuvered to undermine the governor's position, prompting Harrison to describe him as "the poor animal who represents us." With the elimination of property requirements for voting, Jennings was easily reelected by the anti-Harrison faction in 1811. He presented a statehood petition from the territorial legislature in January 1812, but the war with Britain delayed full consideration for four years.

With peace there was a westward rush of settlers, and early statehood was certain. Jennings's achievement was in arranging the details in 1816: Indiana's boundary was shifted ten miles northward, giving the new state a shoreline on Lake Michigan, and the early election for the constitutional convention allowed Jennings's friends to dominate the meeting. He presided over the convention and then became the state's first governor, handily defeating Thomas Posey, the incumbent territorial governor.

Governor Jennings proposed educational and transportation improvements, but the state's financial condition prevented effective action. The only significant political disturbance came in 1818 when he negotiated a land purchase treaty with the Indians on behalf of the federal government. Lieutenant Governor Christopher Harrison claimed that Jennings had forfeited office by accepting a federal appointment. Jennings angrily tossed his federal commission into the fire and dared anyone to prove it had ever existed. He was in plain violation of the state constitution but escaped censure and won easy reelection in 1819 over his accuser.

Indiana was virtually insolvent as a result of the panic of 1819, but Jennings urged education and road projects as well as banking reform. His administration was also troubled by Kentuckians attempting to seize their escaped slaves within Indiana, another issue impossible for the state to resolve. Ineligible for reelection as governor, Jennings offered himself as a candidate for Congress in 1822. The campaign was vigorous and bad tempered, fought entirely on a personal basis without organized political parties on either side. Jennings prevailed with a sound majority and resigned three months before the end of his term as governor in order to take his seat in Congress.

Jennings's interests in Washington were strictly local. He vigorously supported federal appropriations for road and canal construction, particularly to extend the National Road westward by way of Indianapolis. His successful campaign for reelection in 1824 was untouched by the emerging Jacksonian political organization. Although he personally favored John Quincy Adams, Jennings understood clearly the will of his constituents and voted for Andrew Jackson when the presidential election was thrown into the House of Representatives.

In 1826 Jennings was returned to the House without opposition, despite widespread rumors of his drunkenness. He appeared twice with his former enemy William Henry Harrison to advance the anti-Jackson cause in Indiana as well as his own frustrated hopes for a Senate seat. Despite his now open opposition to Jackson, he was overwhelmingly reelected in 1828.

Although only in his mid-forties, Jennings's poor health and notoriously heavy drinking virtually incapacitated him as a member of Congress. In 1831 he came in a dismal fourth among six candidates in an election dominated by the Jacksonian Democrats. He retired to his small farm in Clark County, where he also kept a whiskey still. He participated occasionally in political arguments. Jennings's farm was sold for unpaid taxes, and he survived on the charity of his friends. He died near Charlestown, leaving extensive debts, and was buried in an unmarked grave.

His letters show that Jennings relied greatly on his sister Ann and her husband David Mitchell for emotional support. He married Ann Gilmore Hay in 1811, but none of their letters survives. Little more than a year after her death in 1826 he married Clarissa Barbee. There were no children from either marriage. Politics was his only interest, and the loss of his congressional seat left Jennings impoverished and desolate. He is notable solely as the first governor of Indiana.

• Jennings's scattered letters can be located in Eric Pumroy, ed., *Guide to the Manuscript Collections of the Indiana Historical Society and the Indiana State Library* (1986), and in the William H. English Collection, the University of Chicago. Jennings's public papers appear in Logan Esarey, ed., *Indiana Historical Collections*, vol. 12 (1924), pp. 1–269, and selected family and political correspondence is in Indiana Historical Society, *Publications* 10 (1932): 149–278. For a full-length study of Jennings see Brent E. Smith, "Jonathan Jennings: Indiana's First State Governor" (Ph.D. diss., Ball State Univ., 1987). An older published account is Dorothy Riker, "Jonathan Jennings," *Indiana Magazine of History* 28 (1932): 223–29.

PATRICK J. FURLONG

JENNINGS, May Elizabeth Mann (25 Apr. 1872–24 Apr. 1963), civic leader and social activist, was born in Centerville, New Jersey, the daughter of Austin Shuey Mann and Rachel Kline. In 1873 the Mann family moved to Hernando County, Florida, where Austin Mann pursued business and political interests, serving three terms as a state senator and as a leader of the national Farmer's Alliance. After the death of her mother in 1882, May was enrolled as a year-round boarder at St. Joseph's Academy in St. Augustine. She graduated as valedictorian of her class in 1889 and spent the next two years managing her father's offices in Brooksville and Tallahassee.

In 1891 May Mann married William Sherman Jennings, a cousin of William Jennings Bryan. A Hernando County judge, William Jennings served in the state legislature and one term as governor (1901–1904); the couple had one child. In 1905 they moved to Springfield, a suburb of Jacksonville, where they made their primary home. They also owned a farm at Middleburg and a vacation home near Miami. From 1905 May Jennings expended considerable political acumen and energy on behalf of various civic and social causes. She chaired the Jacksonville Woman's Club's civic and public health committees, served as chair of the Daughters of the American Revolution's state old trail and roads committee, served as president of the Springfield Improvement Association, and chaired committees that aided Jacksonville's Children's Home Society, Daniel Memorial Orphanage, St. Luke's Hospital, and Young Women's Christian Association.

From 1914 to 1917 Jennings served as president of the Florida Federation of Women's Clubs, the state's largest women's organization with more than ten thousand members. As leader she promoted the establishment of local libraries, parks, and public sanitation and beautification projects, and she led the fight to modernize the state's reform schools and to create a humane juvenile justice system. In addition the federation lobbied to secure compulsory education, child labor, and food and drug laws and to obtain the franchise for women.

But May Jennings is remembered primarily for her lifelong promotion of conservation and the role she played in the struggle to save the state's flora, fauna, and environment from developers. Under her leadership the federation acquired land near Homestead, where it established Royal Palm Park (1916), the state's first privately funded and operated public park. Royal Palm became the forerunner and nucleus of Everglades National Park (1947). From 1917 to 1936 while Jennings chaired the federation's conservation committee, few projects or causes relating to the environment escaped her involvement. In 1919 she cofounded the Florida Forestry Association, and from the 1920s until her death she worked to save Turtle Mound and other state historic and wildlife sites. As a founding member of the Florida Audubon Society she was a lifelong advocate of the state's pelicans and other shore birds. From 1927 to 1961 she chaired the Florida Chamber of Commerce's statewide beautification committee and during those same years she headed the Duval County Highway Beautification Association.

A staunch supporter of the Democratic party, May Jennings was a cofounder of the state League of Women Voters, the Democratic Women's Clubs of Jacksonville, and the Florida Legislative Council, and from 1933 to 1962 she served as president of Duval County Democratic Women, Inc.

During her long public career May Jennings received numerous state and national awards, including a Citation of Merit from the National Park Service (1947). A state highway marker near Yulee stands in her honor. She died in Jacksonville.

• May Jennings's papers, including correspondence president of the Florida Federation of Women's Clubs, are in the P. K. Yonge Library of Florida History, University of Florida, Gainesville. A short sketch of Jennings's accomplishments as a clubwoman is in Lucy Worthington Blackman, *The Women of Florida*, vol. 2 (1940). The most important source is the biography by Linda D. Vance, *May Mann Jennings, Florida's Genteel Activist* (1985).

LINDA D. VANCE

JENNYS, Richard (1734?–1809), and his son William Jennys (1774–1858), itinerant portraitists, were born probably in Boston, Massachusetts, though Richard might have been born in England. He was the son of Richard Jennys, a notary public, and Ann (maiden name unknown); Richard's wife and William's mother was Sarah Ireland. The single known fact about Richard's early life, his acceptance in the class of 1744 at the Boston Latin School, would seem to indicate that the family had attained a certain position in the community. One of his classmates was Nathaniel Smibert, son of John Smibert, Boston's leading portraitist of the period, and through this contact Jennys might have gained entrée to the wider world of art.

There is no record of such, but it seems certain that Richard had some formal training as an artist, for from the very beginning of his career he exhibited a sure hand as a draftsman, a skill most likely learned as an apprentice. He may have been influenced also by Peter Pelham, John Singleton Copley's stepfather. In about 1766 Richard scraped a mezzotint of the Reverend Jonathan Mayhew that in many ways appears to have been influenced by Pelham's earlier print of the famous Boston minister. This print also reinforces the known contact between Jennys and Paul Revere; the silversmith's books for 1764 record the sale of artist's materials to Richard; then, in what is regarded as the highest form of flattery, Revere later made an inept line engraving of Mayhew that was clearly based on Richard's version.

For some reason Jennys failed to gain any further success in his chosen profession. The probable cause was the rising star of John Singleton Copley, who before the Revolution came to dominate the field of portraiture in Boston. In one way or another thwarted, in 1768 Richard took his first step toward a career as a dry-goods merchant, a vocation he would follow for the next fifteen years with only occasional forays into painting.

In 1783, apparently having left his wife and five children behind, Richard appeared in Charleston, South Carolina, which was his home for two years followed by an eight-year stay in Savannah, Georgia. In both cities he ran a number of advertisements seeking commissions as a portraitist, yet no examples of his work from this period have been found. It is surmised that his failure in the South was due to overwhelming competition, in this case from Henry Benbridge. A popular portraitist in Charleston before the Revolution, Benbridge returned to the city just months after Richard's arrival and quickly regained his favored position, subsequently attracting commissions from Savannah as well.

Richard returned north, to New Haven, Connecticut, where in 1792 he advertised as a portraitist in the local paper and announced his intention to start a school for young artists. A reasonable case can be made that William, now age eighteen, was one of his pupils, an assumption strengthened by the 1793 newspaper advertisement that William ran seeking patrons in nearby New London. That year also marked the start of a sixteen-year odyssey through most of New England, during which father and son created more than 250 portraits. For the most part they traveled separately, but on at least five occasions they were together, four times signing and dating portraits on which they had collaborated. In the smaller towns that they visited their patrons were not the landed gentry but rather merchants, successful farmers, doctors, lawyers, and ministers, locally prominent persons whose influence seldom extended farther than their own communities.

Those who sat for the Jennyses apparently were comfortable with the stiffly uniform and uncompromising style of the artists. Unadorned simplicity and the Calvinist absence of pretense were their hallmarks. With but a few exceptions their figures were portrayed waist-length, turned three-quarters of the way toward the viewer. The focus was on the face. Arms and hands, when shown, were for the most part crudely drawn and little emphasized. The backgrounds were plain greenish-brown; William often used dark spandrels (triangular shapes) in the corners to form an oval. At the start of their travels William's style of painting very much resembled his father's, and this makes it difficult to distinguish the authorship of some of their early portraits. In 1797, however, William ventured alone to New York City. There, over the course of two years, a stylistic difference emerged. The maturing artist adopted a freer brush stroke and somewhat brighter colors and began to draw the faces of his sitters in a more sculptural manner.

Returning to New England, William first concentrated his efforts in Connecticut. Toward the turn of the century, again with his father, he roamed central and western Massachusetts with extended forays into Vermont and New Hampshire. During the next phase of his career, 1804 to 1809, William settled in Newburyport, Massachusetts; he was followed there by his father, who died a few years later (exact site unknown). In 1806 William married Polly George. Sometime after her death (date unknown), he married her sister, Laura Columbia George.

Of the more than 200 works created by William Jennys, the thirty portraits done in Newburyport are among his most accomplished works. While there he also began to involve himself in real-estate transactions, and his success in this realm probably led him toward other business pursuits. Over the next fifty years William was to become, successively, a merchant in the Bahamas, a comb maker and florist in New York City (where his two children were born, presumably to his second wife), a dry-goods peddler, a farmer and taverner in northern New Hampshire, and again a florist in New York City, where he died. Over the last half-century of his life there is no record of his ever having worked again as an artist.

The artistic achievement of Richard and William Jennys, and the sitters they portrayed, reflect a then-emerging phenomenon in American life after the revolutionary war. The hope of those who commissioned paintings was that they would serve as lasting family remembrances, but the owners were not unaware of the effect that the portraits had on their neighbors and how they indicated a heightened social position. So it may be said these commissions represented the aspirations of the emerging middle class, now recovered from the hardships of the Revolution and anxious to participate in the prosperity of the Federal period. Yet what sets Richard and William Jennys apart from their contemporaries and raises their portraiture to a distinctive art is the particular way in which they portrayed their subjects. The artists painted penetrating psychological studies that were very different from most of the portraits created by other contemporary artists and that remain arresting likenesses two centuries after their appearance.

• The initial assessment of Richard Jennys was made by Frederic Fairchild Sherman in *Richard Jennys: New England Portrait Painter* (1945). The lives and works of both artists are addressed in two articles by William Lamson Warren in the bulletin of the Connecticut Historical Society (CHS), "The Jennys Portraits," *CHS Bulletin* 20 (1955): 97–128, and "A Checklist of Jennys Portraits," *CHS Bulletin* 21 (1956): 33–64; and by William Bright Jones in "The Portraits of Richard and William Jennys and the Story of Their Wayfaring Lives," a chapter in *Painting and Portrait Making in the American Northeast* (1996), which was published in connection with the Dublin Seminar in New England Folklife held in 1994.

WILLIAM BRIGHT JONES

JENSEN, Jens (30 Sept. 1860–1 Oct. 1951), landscape architect, was born in Dybbol, Denmark, son of Christian Jensen and Magdalen (Maria) Sophia Petersen, affluent farmers. Although he became a German national as a consequence of the Danish-Prussian war of 1864, he was educated in the folk high schools of Denmark. After serving in the German army, Jensen came to the United States in 1884 with his wife, the former Anne Marie Hansen. Following brief periods in Florida and Iowa, he found a job with the West Park System in Chicago, rising to the position of superintendent of Humboldt Park, a position he held from 1894 to 1900. In that year he left the park system to establish his own practice as a landscape designer, only to return in 1906 as landscape architect and superintendent of the West Park System. He served in these capacities until 1909 and continued in a consulting relationship until 1920, when he resigned from the park service. Thereafter he enjoyed a large practice designing private estates throughout the Midwest and occasionally in other sections of the country. Among his clients were the Rosenwalds, the Kuppenheimers, the Florsheims, and, most important of all, Henry Ford and Edsel Ford. In 1935 he retired to found a school, "The Clearing" at Ellison Bay, Wisconsin, which continued to operate following his death there.

Jensen was unquestionably one of the greatest American landscape designers of his time. In style he belonged to the grand informal tradition. His work may be compared with that of the Englishman Humphrey Repton, the German Hermann Püchler-Mus-

kau, and Frederick Law Olmsted (1822–1903). Intellectually he had much in common with the Chicago architects of his day, especially those belonging to the Prairie School. Like Louis Henry Sullivan and Frank Lloyd Wright, he rejected formalism in all his work and turned to nature for inspiration. Throughout his career he insisted on the use of plantings native to the Midwest and sought purity of expression. His favorite materials were rocks, water, shrubs, and trees, and with this limited palette he realized impressive spatial effects. In the public sector his finest works are Columbus Park (Chicago, Ill., 1915) and the Lincoln Gardens (Springfield, Ill., 1935). In the private field his estates for Henry Ford (Dearborn, Mich., 1916–1924) and Edsel Ford (Grosse Pointe, Mich., 1924–1928) were especially noteworthy. The large resources of the Fords enabled Jensen to create genuine spatial magnificence; these places are important works of American art.

Jensen's influence is difficult to assess. In his own time he was a controversial figure, and he may well have been more esteemed in Europe than in the United States. He espoused a naturalistic style in American landscape design at a time when formal gardens derived from Renaissance precedent were extremely popular. In Chicago, because of his insistence on honesty in the administration of the West Parks, he was known as the "Graft-Fighting Dane," and until his retirement he was a major figure in the cultural life of the city. Vachel Lindsay and Frank Lloyd Wright were close friends, as was Professor Henry Cowles of the University of Chicago. On the other hand, his difficult relations with the American Society of Landscape Architects paralleled those of Frank Lloyd Wright with the American Institute of Architects. Like Wright, he was never loath to tell his colleagues of the error of their ways, and he spoke with great eloquence.

In many ways he was a paradoxical figure. Not much published in the United States during his lifetime, he was well known in Europe, especially in Germany. He was also a close friend of the English architect and planner Sir Raymond Unwin. Not greatly interested in theories of town planning, Jensen was primarily concerned with parks and park systems, up to and including such large land holdings as the Cook County Forest Preserves and the Indiana Dunes. He was an impressive public speaker, and he fought hard for these public reservations all his life. Often compared with the elder Olmsted, he was probably less effective in the public arena because he was not as able a writer. His only publication, *Siftings* (1939), is a series of meditations on the meaning of nature; it is only partially successful. Writing was difficult for Jensen, and often his prose did not adequately carry his message. Jensen's true legacy is in his work, which, even today, has not been fully explored and assessed.

• The most important collection of Jensen's plans is in the library of the College of Architecture and Urban Planning of the University of Michigan. Additional manuscript material is at the Michigan Historical Collections, also in Ann Arbor, and the Morton Arboretum, Lisle, Ill. Leonard K. Eaton, *Landscape Artist in America: The Life and Work of Jens Jensen* (1964), contains a bibliographical essay giving periodical citations on the artist up to the date of publication. A survey of the more recent literature is included in "Jens Jensen Reconsidered," in Leonard K. Eaton, *Gateway Cities and Other Essays* (1990), pp. 129–41. Robert Grese, *Jens Jensen: Maker of Natural Parks and Gardens* (1992), is an important recent addition to the literature.

LEONARD K. EATON

JEPSON, Willis Linn (19 Aug. 1867–7 Nov. 1946), botanist, was born on the Little Oak Ranch, Vacaville, California, the son of William Jepson and Martha Potts, pioneer California ranchers originally from New England. Growing up on the family ranch in the Vaca Valley of Solano County (to the northeast of the San Francisco Bay), Jepson identified closely with the California terrain and especially its native plants, which he learned to identify early by using Volney Rattan's keys to local floras. On meeting physician Albert Kellogg at the California Academy of Sciences as a young man, he decided that he would devote the rest of his life to the study of California flora.

Jepson's lifelong association with the University of California, Berkeley, began when, as an undergraduate there, he fell under the influence of pioneering western systematic botanist Edward Lee Greene. Jepson obtained a bachelor's degree in 1889 and a Ph.D. in 1899, with a major in systematic botany and a minor in plant physiology and paleobotany. From 1895 to 1898 Jepson served as instructor in botany at Berkeley and trained with Greene, William Albert Setchell, and J. C. Merriam. He also studied with G. F. Atkinson and W. W. Rowlee at Cornell University (in 1895) and with Benjamin L. Robinson at Harvard University (in 1896–1897). In 1899 he became assistant professor at Berkeley; in 1911, associate professor; in 1918, professor; and in 1937, professor emeritus. During these years, he distinguished himself by becoming the leading taxonomic expert on the flora of California.

Jepson produced several works, some of which went through two or more editions, including *Trees of California* (1909), *The Silva of California* (1910), *A Flora of the Western Middle California* (based on his Ph.D. thesis and published in 1901), and *High School Flora of California* (1935). He became best known, however, for his *Manual of the Flowering Plants of California* (1925). Covering 4,019 species, "Jepson's Manual"—as it came to be known—was the first handbook on the California flora. It became the West Coast analog of the celebrated "Gray's Manual" for eastern North America.

Jepson distinguished himself as a scientist by his massive *Flora of California*, which took thirty-five years of effort beginning with the appearance of the first of two parts in 1909 and the twelfth part in 1943. Although Jepson had been a student of Greene (who held to the fixity of species), he chose to follow the British systematic tradition associated with John Torrey and Asa Gray in the United States. The completed flora was a monograph-length study that included extensive field observations, accurate and numerous illustrations that described the ranges and distribution of the California plants, full bibliographic references, and detailed citations of collections and manuals. It became not only the authoritative work on California botany, but also what Berkeley botanist Lincoln Constance in 1947 viewed as "perhaps the outstanding work of a regional flora thus far produced in this country" (*Science* 105: 614).

From many accounts, Jepson appears to have pursued his botanical interests with a passionate intensity. Never marrying, he devoted nearly all of this time to his scientific pursuits. Although he went on botanical explorations to Alaska in 1899 and Palestine and Syria in 1926, his primary interest remained the botanical exploration of California. When not locked away in his laboratory, Jepson explored the diverse habitats of California plants. He appears to have crossed the Sierras at every pass, explored California's deserts, and made detailed observations and collections from little-known regions, which he meticulously recorded in heavily indexed notebooks. In addition to his vast field notes, Jepson also amassed an extensive private collection and library, possibly the finest collection of such botanical material on the West Coast.

In addition to scientific pursuits, Jepson devoted time to editorial and administrative work. From 1893 to 1900 he served as editor of *Erythea*, which he took over from Greene. In the mid-1910s Jepson founded the California Botanical Society and its journal, *Madroño*, of which he served as guiding force and editor from 1916 until 1934. He also edited issues of *Nemophila*, the field guide of the California Botanical Society. He was active in conservation work, serving in the Save-the-Redwoods League and the Point Lobos Association. Additional interests included the history of botany, and throughout his career he contributed a series published in *Madroño* on "Botanical Explorers of California." He also collected extensive memorabilia on California botanists, including Greene and John Gill Lemmon.

Jepson's honors included the Berkeley Faculty Research Lectureship in 1934. He twice served as president of the California Botanical Society, from 1913 to 1915 and 1918 to 1929; he was fellow of the California Academy of Sciences, American Academy of Arts and Sciences (Boston), Royal Society of Arts (London), and American Geographical Society and belonged to numerous other societies, including Sigma XI and Phi Beta Kappa. In 1906 he was selected as one of the leading 100 botanists in the United States by J. McKeen Cattell for his first survey leading to his *American Men of Science*. Jepson also received one of the greatest honors given to botanists: a genus of saxifragaceous plant was named after him as *Jepsonia* (this is in addition to his name being given to numerous specific epithets).

Resulting in part from what appears to have been an obsessive pursuit of California botany, Jepson became an isolated figure, developing a neurotic personality bordering on what historian Joseph Ewan termed a "martyr-complex." While his co-workers agreed that he had a "stormy" personality and was suspicious of others, they also agreed that he could be a charming, witty, and congenial host, frequently amusing friends with his knowledge of literature (he was especially fond of Rudyard Kipling). Berkeley colleague Herbert Mason also noted that Jepson's work suffered as a result of these personal problems: "His countless hours spent in brooding over fancied wrongs cost him dearly in time and in energy and robbed him of the vitality that he needed to complete his life work" ("Willis Linn Jepson," *Madroño* 9 [1947]: 62). At the time of Jepson's death, his monumental *Flora* was only three-fourths completed and published. Although some of these personal problems carried over to his relationships with the few graduate students who worked with him (they frequently complained of his tendency to have one-way relationships), Jepson also appears to have inspired numerous other students with his enthusiasm and his fostering of independent thinking. Beginning early in his career as teacher of introductory freshman botany, Jepson later taught only upper-class and graduate students taxonomic botany.

Jepson died in Berkeley, California. His will provided for $320,000 to be endowed to the Department of Botany at Berkeley and stipulated that it be used for the maintenance and care of the Jepson Herbarium (then numbering some 40,000 specimens) and the furtherance of studies on the flowering plants of California and adjacent areas. His work on the flora of California became the foundation for subsequent work in the California botany.

• The correspondence of Jepson between 1887 and 1946, bound in sixty-two volumes, is at the Jepson Herbarium Archives at the University of California, Berkeley. His scientific writings between 1891 and 1942 are listed in Lawrence R. Heckard et al., "The Scientific Writings of Willis Linn Jepson," *Madroño* 19 (1967): 97–108, which also includes an extensive list of obituaries and tributes. By far the best assessment of Jepson's work is by David Keck, "The Place of Willis Linn Jepson in California Botany," *Madroño* 9 (1948): 223–28. For a history of botany and Berkeley, see Lincoln Constance, *Botany at Berkeley: The First Hundred Years* (1978), and the earlier obituary by Constance in *Science* 105 (1947): 614. For an overview of Jepson and his role in American botany, see Joseph Ewan, ed., *A Short History of Botany in the United States* (1969).

VASSILIKI BETTY SMOCOVITIS